The Broadview Anthology of

BRITISH LITERATURE

Concise Edition
Volume B
Third Edition

The Broadview Anthology of British Literature: Concise Edition

The Age of Romanticism
The Victorian Era
The Twentieth Century and Beyond

The Broadview Anthology of

BRITISH LITERATURE

Concise Edition
Volume B
Third Edition

GENERAL EDITORS

Joseph Black, University of Massachusetts
Leonard Conolly, Trent University
Kate Flint, University of Southern California
Isobel Grundy, University of Alberta
Don LePan, Broadview Press
Roy Liuzza, University of Tennessee
Jerome J. McGann, University of Virginia
Anne Lake Prescott, Barnard College
Barry V. Qualls, Rutgers University
Claire Waters, University of California, Davis

broadview press

BROADVIEW PRESS — www.broadviewpress.com
Peterborough, Ontario, Canada

Founded in 1985, Broadview Press remains a wholly independent publishing house. Broadview's focus is on academic publishing; our titles are accessible to university and college students as well as scholars and general readers. With over 600 titles in print, Broadview has become a leading international publisher in the humanities, with world-wide distribution. Broadview is committed to environmentally responsible publishing and fair business practices.

LIBRARY AND ARCHIVES CANADA CATALOGUING IN PUBLICATION

Title: The Broadview anthology of British literature / general editors, Joseph Black, University of Massachusetts, Leonard Conolly, Trent University, Kate Flint, University of Southern California, Isobel Grundy, University of Alberta, Don LePan, Broadview Press, Roy Liuzza, University of Tennessee, Jerome J. McGann, University of Virginia, Anne Lake Prescott, Barnard College, Barry V. Qualls, Rutgers University, Claire Waters, University of California, Davis.

Other titles: British literature | Anthology of British literature

Names: Black, Joseph Laurence, 1962- editor.

Series: Broadview anthology of British literature (Series)

Description: Concise edition, Third edition. | Series statement: Broadview anthology of British literature | Includes bibliographical references and indexes. | Contents: Volume B.

Identifiers: Canadiana 20169069621 | ISBN 9781554814374 (Volume B; softcover)

Subjects: LCSH: English literature.

Classification: LCC PR1109 .B772 2017 | DDC 820.8—dc23

Broadview Press handles its own distribution in North America:
PO Box 1243, Peterborough, Ontario K9J 7H5, Canada
555 Riverwalk Parkway, Tonawanda, NY 14150, USA
Tel: (705) 743-8990; Fax: (705) 743-8353
email: customerservice@broadviewpress.com

Distribution is handled by Eurospan Group in the UK, Europe, Central Asia, Middle East, Africa, India, Southeast Asia, Central America, South America, and the Caribbean. Distribution is handled by Footprint Books in Australia and New Zealand.

Canada

Broadview Press acknowledges the financial support of the Government of Canada for our publishing activities.

Typeset by Kathryn Brownsey
Cover design by Lisa Brawn

PRINTED IN CANADA

Contributing Editors and Writers

Managing Editor	Laura Buzzard
Developmental Editor	Jennifer McCue
General Academic and Textual Editors	Laura Cardiff, Joe Davies, Colleen Franklin, Don LePan, Bethany Qualls, Nora Ruddock
Design Coordinator	Kathryn Brownsey

Contributing Editors

Katherine O. Acheson
Suzy Anger
Melissa Bachynski
Robert Barrett
Gisele Baxter
Donald Beecher
Sandra Bell
Emily Bernhard Jackson
Joseph Black
Carol Blessing
Robert Boenig
Sarika Bose
Matthieu Boyd
Andrew Bretz
Benjamin Bruch
Laura Buzzard
Michael Calabrese
Laura Cardiff
Lisa Celovsky
Noel Chevalier
Mita Choudhury
Youngjin Chung
Massimo Ciavolella
Anna Clark
Elisha Cohn
Thomas J. Collins
Leonard Conolly
Matthew Davis
Darryl Domingo
Annmarie Drury
Dianne Dugaw
Siân Echard
Rose Eckert-Jantzie
Warren Edminster
Rachel Eisendrath
Garrett Epp
Michael Faletra
Emily Farrell
Christina Fawcett
Christina Fitzgerald
Adrienne Fitzpatrick
Andrew Fleck
Melissa Free
Maura Giles Watson
Stephen Glosecki
Amanda Goldrick-Jones
Katie Gramich
Erik Gray
John Greenwood
Melissa Gregory
Isobel Grundy
Stephen Guy-Bray
Douglas Hayes
Peter C. Herman
Heather Hill-Vasquez
John Holmes
Diane Jakacki
Eleanor Johnson
Ian Johnston
Essaka Joshua
Susan Kattwinkel
Michael Keefer
Amy King
David Klausner
Scott Kleinman
Chris Koenig-Woodyard
Gary Kuchar
Roger P. Kuin
Lydia K. Lake
Wendy Lee
Don LePan
Ruth Lexton
Roy Liuzza
Kirsten Lodge
Marie Loughlin
D.L. Macdonald
Hugh Magennis
Anne McWhir
Tobias Menely
Britt Mize
Alexander Mueller
Ian Munro
Sarah Neville
Meghan Nieman
David Oakleaf
Maureen Okun
Philip S. Palmer
Pam Perkins
Virginia Philipson
Jude Polsky
Kristen Pond
Anne Lake Prescott
Joyce Rappaport
Andrew Reszitnyk
Joseph Rezek
Shelby Richardson
Terry Robinson
Herbert Rosengarten
Nora Ruddock
Jason Rudy
Janice Schroeder
Chester Scoville
John T. Sebastian
Helena Snopek
Kelly Stage
Emily Steiner
Ashley Streeter
Martha Stoddard-Holmes
Julie Sutherland
David Swain
Carol Symes
Andrew Taylor
Peggy Thompson
Jane Tolmie
Rebecca Totaro
David Townsend
Yevgeniya Traps

Melissa Valiska Gregory
Martine van Elk
Fred Waage
Andrea Walkden
Craig Walker
Claire Waters
David Watt
William Weaver
Vivienne Westbrook
Dan White
David Williams
Adrienne Williams Boyarin
James Winny

Contributing Writers

Victoria Abboud
Jane Beal
Jennifer Beauvais
Rachel Bennett
Emily Bernhard Jackson
Rebecca Blasco
Matthieu Boyd
Julie Brennan
Andrew Bretz
Laura Buzzard
Laura Cardiff
Emily Cargan
Adrienne Eastwood
Wendy Eberle-Sinatra
Zachary Edwards
Peter Enman
Emily Farrell
Christina Fawcett
Joanne Findon
John Geddert
Jane Grove
Camille Isaacs
Erik Isford
Shoshannah Jones Square
Stephanie King
Chris Koenig-Woodyard
Gabrielle L'Archeveque
Don LePan
Anna Lepine
John McIntyre
Carrie Nartkler
Byron Nelson
Robin Norris
Kenna Olsen
Kendra O'Neal Smith
Laura Pellerine
Virginia Philipson
Jude Polsky
Nora Ruddock
Jason Rudy
Anne Salo
Janice Schroeder
Carrie Shanafelt
Nicole Shukin
Helena Snopek
James Soderholm
Anne Sorbie
Jenna Stook
Ashley Streeter
Alexandria Stuart
Candace Taylor
Yevgeniya Traps
David Van Belle
Sarah Vickers
Deirdra Wadden
Shari Watling
Matthew Williams
Bj Wray
Nicole Zylstra

Layout and Typesetting

Kathryn Brownsey

Illustration Formatting and Assistance

Cheryl Baldwin
Lisa Brawn
Eileen Eckert

Production Coordinators

Tara Lowes
Tara Trueman

Permissions Coordinators

Merilee Atos
Chris Griffin
Emily Cargan
Amy Nimegeer
Jennifer Elsayed

Proofreaders

Jennifer Bingham
Joe Davies
Lynn Fraser
Lynn Neufeld
Martin Boyne
Judith Earnshaw
Anne Hodgetts
Bethany Qualls
Lucy Conolly
Rose Eckert-Jantzie
Amy Neufeld

Editorial Advisors

Rachel Ablow, University at Buffalo, SUNY
Phanuel Antwi, University of British Columbia
Dabney Bankert, James Madison University
Stephen C. Behrendt, University of Nebraska
Sumangala Bhattacharya, Pitzer College
Kim Blank, University of Victoria
Rita Bode, Trent University
Andrew Bretz, Wilfred Laurier University
David Brewer, Ohio State University
Susan Brown, University of Guelph
Daniel Burgoyne, Vancouver Island University
Catherine Burroughs, Wells College
Elizabeth Campbell, Oregon State University
William Christmas, San Francisco State University
Nancy Cirillo, University of Illinois, Chicago
Joanne Cordón, University of Connecticut
David Cowart, University of South Carolina
Alex Dick, University of British Columbia
Len Diepeveen, Dalhousie University
Daniel Fischlin, University of Guelph
Robert Forman, St. John's University
Peter Francev, Victor Valley College
Mark Fulk, Buffalo State College, SUNY
Julia Garrett, University of Wisconsin
Barbara Gates, University of Delaware
Dawn Goode, James Madison University
Chris Gordon-Craig, University of Alberta
Bruce Graver, Providence College
Natalie Grinnell, Wofford College
Jennifer Gustar, University of British Columbia, Okanagan
Stephen Guy-Bray, University of British Columbia
Tassie Gwilliam, University of Miami
Elizabeth Hodgson, University of British Columbia
John Holmes, University of Reading
Romana Huk, University of Notre Dame
Heidi Kaufman, University of Oregon
Michael Keefer, University of Guelph
Gordon Kipling, University of California, Los Angeles
Emily Kugler, University of California, San Diego
Sara Landreth, University of Ottawa
William Liston, Ball State University
Paula Loscocco, Lehman College
Kathleen Lundeen, Western Washington University
Peter Mallios, University of Maryland
Carl G. Martin, Norwich University
Martin McKinsey, University of New Hampshire
Rod Michell, Thompson Rivers University
Peter Murphy, Thompson Rivers University
Julie Nash, University of Massachusetts, Lowell
Byron Nelson, West Virginia University
Robin Norris, Carleton College
Michael North, University of California, Los Angeles
Nick Pawliuk, Thompson Rivers University
Lesley Peterson, University of North Alabama
John Pollock, San Jose State University
Joseph Rezek, Boston University
Jason Rudy, University of Maryland
Andrew Scheil, University of Minnesota
Carol Senf, Georgia Tech
Ken Simpson, Thompson Rivers University
Sharon Smulders, Mount Royal University
Goran Stanivukovic, St. Mary's University
Marni Stanley, Vancouver Island University
Tim Stretton, St. Mary's University
Nanora Sweet, University of Missouri-St. Louis
Nicholas Watson, Harvard University
Kevin Whetter, Acadia University
Julian Yates, University of Delaware

Contents

[Note to Instructors: *Frankenstein* is among over 400 available editions from Broadview, any one of which may be packaged together with this anthology volume at no extra cost to students.]

THE VICTORIAN ERA

THE TWENTIETH CENTURY AND BEYOND

[Note to Instructors in Canada, UK, and Australia: *Mrs. Dalloway* is among over 400 available editions from Broadview, any one of which may be packaged together with the anthology volume at no extra cost to the student. (For copyright reasons, Broadview is unable to make its edition of *Mrs. Dalloway* available for sale in the United States until 2021.)]

Preface

A Fresh Approach

The publication of the first edition of this anthology in 2006 was widely hailed as an exciting achievement, with many academics concluding that its comprehensiveness, its consistency, its visual appeal, and its fresh approach made the Broadview the "new standard" in anthologies of British literature. We have also been taking a fresh approach in issuing new editions of the anthology's volumes. Rather than publishing new editions of each of the six volumes simultaneously, we are publishing new editions of the individual volumes at the rate of approximately one per year. Each volume thus appears in a new edition roughly every six years. We recognize that our main competitors have in recent years made it a practice to issue new editions much more frequently than that, but our feeling is that it is better to allow several years to elapse between editions—not least of all, as a new edition may represent a considerable inconvenience to academics teaching from the anthology. (The approach also has real practical advantages for a smaller publisher such as Broadview; rather than gearing up for a massive process of revision every few years and then gearing down again in the wake of publication, we can proceed at a steady pace with the work of updating and revising.)

The third edition features a great deal of new material. Many authors previously available on the anthology's website component—among them Dorothy Wordsworth, John Clare, Emily Brontë, Walter Pater, Isaac Rosenberg, and Jeanette Winterson—are now included in this bound book volume. The bound book also features two new longer works: Robert Louis Stevenson's *Strange Case of Dr. Jekyll and Mr. Hyde* and Samuel Beckett's *Endgame*. New shorter works include Elizabeth Gaskell's short story "The Manchester Marriage," Charles Dickens's performance fiction based upon his novel *David Copperfield*, two new short stories by Angela Carter, and numerous updates to the omnibus section that concludes the volume's coverage of the twentieth and twenty-first centuries. We have also added selections from Shelley's *Frankenstein*, from Barrett Browning's *Aurora Leigh*, from Tennyson's *In Memoriam*, from Eliot's *Middlemarch*, and from Joyce's *Ulysses*. (For instructors who prefer to teach these works in their entirety, most of these—and hundreds of other texts—remain available in stand-alone editions, any one of which can be packaged with the anthology at no extra cost to the student.)

Even more than previous editions, this new edition includes writers who should not be understood as British but whose work is grounded in national histories heavily impacted by British imperialism; these new writers include Chimamanda Ngozi Adichie (Nigerian), Tomson Highway (Cree Canadian), Derek Walcott (Saint Lucian), and Kamau Brathwaite (Barbadian). With the anthology's third edition we are also striving to offer improved representation of Irish, Welsh, and Scottish literature, especially as its traditions differ from the English traditions that too often dominate literary studies of the British Isles. To that end, we have included a substantial new section titled "Ireland, Scotland, and Wales: Literary Currents in the Long Nineteenth Century"; we have also added new material by twentieth- and twenty-first-century poets such as Sorley MacLean, Gillian Clarke, and Paul Muldoon.

Significant changes have also been made to the anthology's contextual materials and apparatus. We have strengthened our coverage of important generic developments, with "Contexts" sections representing developments in Gothic literature of the Romantic period and the development of Modernism in the twentieth century. The "Contexts" section on "Slavery and Its Abolition" now includes material showing connections between the Haitian Revolution and Britain's abolitionist movement; the "Contexts" section on the French

Revolution has been revised as well, with the addition of writings by Edmund Burke, Mary Wollstonecraft, and William Godwin. Also new to the Concise anthology is a selection of contextual materials addressing World War II. Throughout the volume, introductions have been revised to reflect recent developments in scholarship and to bring greater balance to the anthology's treatment of gender, sexual orientation, and race, as well as to more accurately represent the relationships among England, Scotland, Ireland, and Wales.

Cuts, of course, have been necessary to make room for this new material. A few authors whom we have found to be taught infrequently—among them Augusta Webster, Bernard Shaw, A.E. Housman, Hugh MacDiarmid, Sylvia Townsend Warner, and Ian McEwan—are no longer represented by individual sections in the bound book. Also omitted from this edition of the bound book are some contextual materials, including those on "Reading, Writing, Publishing," "The Place of Humans and Non-Human Animals in Nature," and "Work and Working-Class Life." In most cases, however, this material remains available as part of the volume's online component. The website also features material new to the Concise anthology that could not be accommodated in the bound book; these additions include Byron's long poem *Manfred*, Janice Galloway's short story "Jellyfish," and a selection of contextual materials addressing the history of Ireland in the long nineteenth century, with particular emphasis on the Great Irish Famine.

As we have from the start with *The Broadview Anthology of British Literature*, we have enlisted the help of a substantial number of people in the preparation of this book's contents. Rather than dividing up the vast amount of work entailed in preparing such a large anthology among a relatively small number of academics, and asking each of them to handle on their own the work of choosing, annotating, and preparing introductions to texts in their own areas of specialization, we chose to involve a large number of contributors in the process (as the pages following the title page to this volume attest), and to encourage a high degree of collaboration at every level. First and foremost are the distinguished academics who serve as our General Editors for the project, but in all there have literally been hundreds of people involved at various stages in researching, drafting headnotes or annotations, reviewing material, editing material, and carrying out the work of designing and typesetting the texts and other materials. That approach allowed us to draw on a diverse range of talent, and to prepare the first edition of a large anthology with extraordinary efficiency. It has also facilitated the maintenance of a high degree of consistency. Material has been reviewed and revised in-house at Broadview, by outside editors, by a variety of academics with an extraordinarily diverse range of backgrounds and academic specialities, and by our team of General Editors for the project as a whole. The aim has been not only to ensure accuracy but also to make sure that the same standards are applied throughout the anthology to matters such as coverage provided in introductions, level of annotation, tone of writing, and student accessibility.

As with the first and second editions, several core principles have guided the selection of texts for this volume. We have endeavored to provide a selection that is broadly representative, while also being mindful of the importance of choosing texts that have the capacity to engage readers' interest today. We have for the most part made it a policy to include long works in their entirety or not at all; readers will find complete in *The Broadview Anthology* works such as *Utopia*, "Beachy Head," *The History of Mary Prince*, and *In Memoriam* that are often excerpted in (or omitted from) other anthologies. In our Concise and Compact anthologies, space constraints have in some cases (such as *In Memoriam* and *Confessions of an English Opium-Eater*) led us to make excerpts available in the bound book while offering full texts on the anthology website. Where editions of works are available separately in our acclaimed Broadview Editions series, we have often decided to omit them from the anthology, on the grounds that those wishing to teach one or more such works may easily do so in a combination package with the anthology.

Any discussion of what is distinctive about *The Broadview Anthology of British Literature* must focus above all on the contents. In every volume of the anthology there is material that is distinctive and fresh—including not only selections by lesser-known writers but also less familiar selections from canonical writers. The anthology takes a fresh approach too to a great many canonical texts. The first volume of the anthology includes not only Roy Liuzza's translation of *Beowulf* (widely acclaimed as the most engaging and reliable translation available), but also new translations by Liuzza of many other works of Old English poetry and prose. Unique to the first volume of this anthology are a new verse translation of *Judith* by Stephen Glosecki and new translations by Claire Waters of several of the *Lais* of Marie de France. And so on through all six volumes.

In a number of these cases the distinctive form of the anthology facilitates the presentation of content in an engaging and practical fashion. Notably, the adoption of a two-column format allows for some translations (the Marie de France *Lais*, the James Winny translation of *Sir Gawain and the Green Knight*, poetry in Old Irish and other Celtic languages) to be presented in parallel column format alongside the original texts, allowing readers to experience something of the flavor of the original, while providing convenient access to an accessible translation. Similarly, passages from four translations of the Bible are laid out parallel to each other for ready comparison.

The large trim-size, two-column format also allows for greater flexibility in the presentation of visual materials. Throughout our intent is to make this an anthology that is fully alive to the connections between literary and visual culture, from the discussion of the CHI-RHO page of the Lindisfarne Gospels in the first volume of the anthology (and the accompanying color illustration) to the inclusion in Volume 6 of a number of selections (including Graham Greene's "The Basement Room," Tom Stoppard's "Professional Foul," and several skits from "Monty Python's Flying Circus") that may be discussed in connection with film or television versions. Along the way appear several full-page illustrations from the Ellesmere manuscript of Chaucer's *Canterbury Tales* and illustrations to a wide variety of other works, from *Robinson Crusoe* and *Gulliver's Travels* to *The Adventure of the Speckled Band* and *The Road to Wigan Pier*.

CONTEXTUAL MATERIALS

Visual materials are also included in the background materials that form an important part of the anthology. These materials are presented in two ways. Several "Contexts" sections on particular topics or themes appear in each volume of the anthology, presented independent of any particular text or author. These include broadly based groupings of material on such topics as "Religion and Spiritual Life," "Print Culture," "India and the Orient," "Slavery and Its Abolition," "The New Art of Photography," and "The End of Empire." The groups of "In Context" materials each relate to a particular text or author. They range from the genealogical tables provided as a supplement to *Beowulf*, to materials on "The Eighteenth-Century Sexual Imagination" (presented in conjunction with Haywood's *Fantomina*); to a selection of materials relating to the Peterloo massacre (presented in conjunction with Percy Shelley's "The Mask of Anarchy"); to materials on "'The Vilest Scramble for Loot' in Central Africa" (presented in conjunction with Conrad's "An Outpost of Progress"). For the most part these contextual materials are, as the word suggests, included with a view to setting texts in their broader literary, historical, and cultural contexts; in some cases, however, the materials included in "Contexts" sections are themselves literary works of a high order. The autobiographical account by Eliza M. of nineteenth-century life in Cape Town, for example (included in the section in Volume 5 on "Britain, Empire, and a Wider World"), is as remarkable for its literary qualities as it is for the light it sheds on the realities of colonial life. In the inclusion of texts such as these, as well as in other ways, the anthology aims to encourage readers to explore the boundaries of the literary and the non-literary, and the issue of what constitutes a "literary text."

Texts by Women Writers

A central element of the broadening of the canon of British literature in recent generations has of course been a great increase in the attention paid to texts by women writers. As one might expect from a publisher that has played an important role in making neglected works by women writers widely available, this anthology reflects the broadening of the canon quantitatively, by including a substantially larger number of women writers than have earlier anthologies of British literature. But it also reflects this broadening in other ways. In many anthologies of literature (anthologies of British literature, to be sure, but also anthologies of literature of a variety of other sorts) women writers are still too often set somewhat apart, referenced in introductions and headnotes only in relation to issues of gender, and treated as important only for the fact of their being women writers. *The Broadview Anthology* strenuously resists such segregation; while women writers are of course discussed in relation to gender issues, their texts are also presented and discussed alongside those by men in a wide variety of other contexts, including seventeenth-century religious and political controversies, the abolitionist movement, and World War I pacifism. Texts by women writers are front and center in the discussion of the development of realism in nineteenth-century fiction. And when it comes to the twentieth century, both Virginia Woolf and Dorothy Richardson are included alongside James Joyce as practitioners of groundbreaking modernist narrative techniques.

"British," "English," "Irish," "Scottish," "Welsh," "Other"

The broadening of English Studies, in conjunction with the expansion and subsequent contraction of British power and influence around the world, has considerably complicated the issue of exactly how inclusive anthologies should be. In several respects this anthology (like its two main competitors) is significantly more inclusive than its title suggests, including a number of non-British writers whose works connect in important ways with the traditions of British literature. We endeavor to portray the fluid and multilingual reality of the medieval period through the inclusion not only of works in Old and Middle English but also of works in Latin, in French, in Irish, in Welsh, and in Scots. We have extended this approach throughout the anthology with the inclusion of Celtic-language works from the early modern era, the long nineteenth century, and the twentieth century.

In later periods the word "British" becomes deeply problematic in different respects, but on balance we have preferred it to the only obvious alternative, "English." There are several objections to the latter in this context. Perhaps most obviously, "English" excludes authors or texts not only from Ireland but also from Scotland and from Wales, both of which retain to this day cultures quite distinct from that of the English. "English literature," of course, may also be taken to mean "literature written in English," but since the anthology does not cover *all* literature written in English (most obviously in excluding American literature), the ambiguity would not in this case be helpful.

The inclusion of Irish writers presents a related but even more tangled set of issues. At the beginning of the period covered by the six volumes of this anthology we find works, such as the *Book of Kells*, that may have been created in what is now England, in what is now Scotland, in what is now Ireland—or in some combination of these. Through most of the seventeenth, eighteenth, and nineteenth centuries almost the whole of Ireland was under British control—but for the most part unwillingly. In the period covered in the last of the six volumes Ireland was partitioned, with Northern Ireland becoming a part of the United Kingdom and the Republic of Ireland declared independent of Britain on 6 December 1921. Less than two months earlier, James Joyce had completed *Ulysses*, which was first published as a complete work the following year (in Paris, not in Britain). It would be obviously absurd to regard Joyce as a British writer up to just before the publication of *Ulysses*, and an Irish writer thereafter. And arguably he and other Irish writers should never be regarded as British, whatever the politics of the day. If on no other grounds than their overwhelming influence on and connection to the body of literature written in the British Isles, however, we have included Irish writers—among them Swift, Sheridan, Edgeworth, Wilde, Shaw, Beckett, Bowen, Muldoon, and Heaney as well as Joyce—throughout this anthology. We have also endeavored to give a real sense in the introductions to the six volumes of the anthology, in the headnotes to individual authors, and in the annotations to the texts themselves, of the ways in which the histories and the cultures of England, Ireland, Scotland, and Wales, much as they interact with one another, are also distinct.

Also included in this anthology are texts by writers from areas that are far removed geographically from the British Isles but that are or have been British possessions. Writers such as Mary Rowlandson, Olaudah Equiano, and Phillis Wheatley are included, as they spent all or most of their lives living in what were then British colonial possessions. Writers who came of age in an independent United States, on the other hand, are not included, unless (like T.S. Eliot) they subsequently put down roots in Britain and became important British literary figures. Substantial gray areas, of course, surround such issues. One might well argue, for example, that Henry James merits inclusion in an anthology of British literature, or that W.H. Auden and Thom Gunn are more American poets than British ones. But the chosen subject matter of James's work has traditionally been considered to mark him as having remained an American writer, despite having spent almost two-thirds of his life in England. And both Auden and Gunn so clearly made a mark in Britain before crossing the Atlantic that it would seem odd to exclude them from these pages on the grounds of their having lived the greater part of their adult lives in America. One of our competitors includes Sylvia Plath in their anthology of British literature; Plath lived in England for only five of her thirty years, though, and her poetry is generally agreed to have more in common with the traditions of Lowell, Merwin, and Sexton than with the currents of British poetry in the 1950s and '60s.

As a broad principle, we have been open to the inclusion of twentieth and twenty-first century work in English not only by writers from the British Isles but also by writers from British possessions overseas, and by writers from countries that were once British possessions and have remained a part of the British Commonwealth. In such cases we have often chosen selections that relate in one way or another to the tradition of British literature and the British colonial legacy. The Margaret Atwood selections in the anthology include work imagining the experience of British emigrants to Canada in the nineteenth century, while the selection by Tomson Highway addresses ongoing colonization in the twentieth; the Chinua Achebe story in the anthology concerns the divide between British colonial culture and traditional Nigerian culture; and so on.

THE HISTORY OF LANGUAGE, AND OF PRINT CULTURE

Among the liveliest discussions we had at meetings of our General Editors were those concerning the issue of whether or not to bring spelling and punctuation into accord with present-day practice. We finally decided that, in the interests of making the anthology accessible to the introductory student, we should *in most cases* bring spelling and punctuation in line with present-day practice. An important exception has been made for works in which modernizing spelling and punctuation would alter the meaning or the aural and metrical qualities. In practice this means that works before the late sixteenth century tend to be presented either in their original form or in translation, whereas later texts tend to have spelling and punctuation modernized. But where spelling and punctuation choices in later texts are known (or believed on reliable authority) to represent conscious choice on the part of the author rather than simply the common practice of the time, we have in those cases, too, made an exception and retained the original spelling and punctuation. (Among these are texts by Edmund Spenser; by William Cowper; by William Blake, John Clare, and several other poets of the Romantic era; by George Bernard Shaw; and by contemporary figures such as Linton Kwesi Johnson.)

Beyond this, we all agreed that we should provide for readers a real sense of the development of the language and of print culture. To that end we have included in each volume examples of texts in their original form—in some cases through the use of pages shown in facsimile, in others by providing short passages in which spelling and punctuation have not been modernized. A list of these appears near the beginning of each volume of the anthology.

We have also included a section of the history of the language as part of the introduction to each volume. And throughout the anthology we include materials—visual as well as textual—relating to the history of print culture.

A Dynamic and Flexible Anthology

Almost all major book publishing projects nowadays are accompanied by an adjunct website, and most large-scale anthologies are accompanied by websites that provide additional materials in electronic form. Since this anthology's inception, we have viewed its website component as precisely that—a *component* of the anthology itself. The notion of a website of this sort grew organically out of the process of trying to winnow down the contents of the first edition of the anthology to a manageable level—the point at which all the material to be included would fit within the covers of bound books that would not be overwhelmingly heavy. And we simply could not do it. After we had made a very substantial round of cuts we were still faced with a table of contents in which each volume was at least 200 or 300 pages longer than our agreed-upon maximum. Our solution was not to try to cut anything more, but rather to select a range of material to be made available in a website component of the anthology. This material is in every way produced according to the same high standards of the material in the bound books; the editorial standards, the procedures for annotation, the author introductions, and the page design and layout—all are the same. The texts on the web, in short, are not "extra" materials; they are an integral part of the full anthology. In accordance with that principle, we have been careful to include a wide range of texts by lesser-known writers within the bound books, and a number of texts by canonical writers within the web component of the anthology.

The latter may be used in a variety of ways. Most obviously, readings from the web component are available to any purchaser of the book. Instructors who adopt *The Broadview Anthology of British Literature* as a course text are also granted permission to reproduce any web material for which Broadview holds copyright in a supplementary coursepack. An alternative for instructors who want to "create their own" anthology is to visit the "Custom Texts" page on the Broadview website or contact the publisher directly; Broadview can make available to students through their university bookstore a custom-made coursepack with precisely the desired materials included. Other options are available too. Volumes of the anthology itself may of course be shrink-wrapped together at special prices in any desired combination. They may also be combined in a shrink-wrapped package with one of the over 400 volumes in the Broadview Editions series, at no additional cost to the student (or with more than one edition for a modest additional charge).

We anticipate that over the years the web-based component of the anthology will continue to grow—every year there will be a greater choice of web-based texts in the anthology. But we do not foresee a day when the web will be the only option; we expect physical books always to remain central to Broadview's approach to publishing.

The Broadview List

One of the reasons we were able to bring a project of this sort to fruition in such a relatively short time was that we were able to draw on the resources of the full Broadview list: the many titles in the Broadview Editions series, and also the considerable range of other Broadview anthologies. As the contributors' pages and the permissions acknowledgments pages indicate, a number of Broadview authors have acted as contributing editors to this volume, providing material from other volumes that has been adapted to suit the needs of the present anthology; we gratefully acknowledge their contribution.

As it has turned out, the number of cases where we have been able to draw on the resources of the Broadview list in the full sense, using in these pages texts and annotations in very much the same form in which they appear elsewhere, has been relatively small; whether because of an issue such as the level of textual modernization or one of style of annotation, we have more often than not ended up deciding that the requirements of this anthology were such that we could not use material from another Broadview source as-is. But even in these cases we often owe a debt of gratitude to the many academics who have edited outstanding editions and anthologies for Broadview. For even where we have not drawn directly from them, we have often been inspired by them—inspired to think of a wider range of texts as possibilities than we might otherwise have done, inspired to think of contextual materials in places where we might otherwise not have looked, inspired by the freshness of approach that so many of these titles exemplify.

Editorial Procedures and Conventions, Apparatus

The in-house set of editorial guidelines for *The Broadview Anthology of British Literature* runs to over 40 pages, covering everything from conventions for the spacing of marginal notes, to the use of small caps for the abbreviations CE and BCE, to the approach we have adopted to references in author headnotes to name changes. Perhaps the most important core principle in the introductions to the various volumes, in the headnotes for each author, in the introductions in "Contexts" sections, and in annotations throughout the anthology, is to endeavor to provide a sufficient amount of information to enable students to read and interpret these texts, but without making evaluative judgments or imposing particular interpretations. In practice that is all a good deal more challenging than it sounds; it is often extremely difficult to describe why a particular author is considered to be important without using language that verges on the interpretive or the evaluative. But it is a fine line that we have all agreed is worth trying to walk; we hope that readers will find that the anthology achieves an appropriate balance.

ANNOTATION: It is also often difficult to make judgments as to where it is appropriate to provide an explanatory annotation for a word or phrase. Our policy has been to annotate where we feel it likely that most first- or second-year students are likely to have difficulty understanding the denotative meaning. (We have made it a practice not to provide notes discussing connotative meanings.) But in practice the vocabularies and levels of verbal facility of first- and second-year students may vary enormously, both from institution to institution and within any given college or university class. On the whole, we provide somewhat more annotation than our competitors, and somewhat less interpretation. Again, we hope that readers will find that the anthology has struck an appropriate balance.

THE ETHICS AND POLITICS OF ANNOTATION: On one issue regarding annotation we have felt that principles are involved that go beyond the pedagogical. Most anthologies of British literature allow many words or phrases of a racist, sexist, anti-Semitic, or homophobic nature either to pass entirely without comment, or to be glossed with apologist comments that leave the impression that such comments were excusable in the past, and may even be unobjectionable in the present. Where derogatory comments about Jewish people and money-lending are concerned, for example, anthologies often leave the impression that money-lending was a pretty unsavory practice that Jewish people entered by choice; it has been all too rare to provide readers with any sense of the degree to which English society consistently discriminated against Jews, expelling them entirely for several centuries, requiring them to wear physical marks identifying their Jewish status, prohibiting them from entering most professions, and so on. *The Broadview*

Anthology endeavors in such cases, first of all, not to allow such words and phrases to pass without comment; and second, to gloss without glossing over.

DATES: We make it a practice to include the date when a work was first made public, whether publication in print or, in the case of dramatic works, made public through the first performance of the play. Where that date is known to differ substantially from the date of composition, a note to this effect is included in parentheses. With medieval works, where there is no equivalent to the "publication" of later eras, where texts often vary greatly from one manuscript copy to another, and where knowledge as to date of original composition is usually imprecise, the date that appears at the end of each work is an estimate of the date of the work's origin in the written form included in the anthology. Earlier oral or written versions are of course in some cases real possibilities.

TEXTS: Where translations appear in this anthology, a note at the bottom of the first page indicates what translation is being used. Similar notes also address overall textual issues where choice of copy text is particularly significant. Reliable editions of most works are listed in the bibliography for the anthology, which is included as part of the website component rather than in the bound books, to facilitate ready revision. (In addition to information as to reliable editions, the bibliography provides for each author and for each of the six periods select lists of important or useful historical and critical works.) Copyright information for texts not in the public domain, however, is provided within the bound books in a section listing Permissions Acknowledgments.

INTRODUCTIONS: In addition to the introductory headnotes for each author included in the anthology, each "Contexts" section includes a substantial introduction, and each volume includes an introduction to the period as a whole. These introductions to the six volumes of the anthology endeavor to provide a sense not only of the broad picture of literary developments in the period, but also of the historical, social, and political background, and of the cultural climate. Readers should be cautioned that, while there is inevitably some overlap between information presented here and information presented in the author headnotes, an effort has been made to avoid such repetition as much as possible; the general introduction to each period should thus be read in conjunction with the author headnotes. The general introductions aim not only to provide an overview of ways in which texts and authors included in these pages may connect with one another, but also to give readers a sense of connection with a range of other writers and texts of the period.

READING POETRY: For much of the glossary and for the "Reading Poetry" section that appears as part of the appendices to each volume we have drawn on the superb material prepared by Herbert Rosengarten and Amanda Goldrick-Jones for *The Broadview Anthology of Poetry*; this section provides a concise but comprehensive introduction to the study of poetry. It includes discussions of diction, imagery, poetic figures, and various poetic forms, as well as offering an introduction to prosody.

MAPS: Also appearing within each of the bound books are maps especially prepared for this anthology, including, for each volume, a map of Britain showing towns and features of relevance during the pertinent period; a map showing the counties of Britain and of Ireland; maps both of the London area and of the inner city; and world maps indicating the locations of some of the significant places referenced in the anthology, and for later volumes showing the extent of Britain's overseas territories.

GLOSSARY: Some other anthologies of British literature include both glossaries of terms and essays introducing students to various political and religious categories in British history. Similar information is included in *The Broadview Anthology of British Literature*, but we have adopted a more integrated approach, including political and religious terms along with literary ones in a convenient general glossary. While we recognize that looking online for information of this sort is often the student's first resort (and we recognize too the value of searching the web for the wealth of background reference information available there), we also recognize that information culled from the Internet is often far from reliable; it is our intent, through this glossary, through our introductions and headnotes, and through the wealth of accessible annotation in the anthology, to provide as part of the anthology a reliable core of information in the most convenient and accessible form possible.

OTHER MATERIALS: A chart of Monarchs and Prime Ministers is also provided within these pages. A range of other adjunct materials may be accessed through *The Broadview Anthology of British Literature* website. "Texts and Contexts" charts for each volume provide a convenient parallel reference guide to the dates of literary texts and historical developments. "Money in Britain" provides a thumbnail sketch of the world of pounds, shillings, and pence, together with a handy guide to estimating the current equivalents of monetary values from earlier eras. And the website offers, too, a variety of aids for the student and the instructor. An up-to-date list of these appears on the site.

Acknowledgments

The names of those on the Editorial Board that shaped this anthology appear on the title page, and those of the many who contributed directly to the writing, editing, and production of the project on the following two pages. Special acknowledgment for this new edition should go to Developmental Editor Jennifer McCue, who has been instrumental in tying together all the vast threads of this project and in making it a reality; to General Academic and Textual Editor Nora Ruddock, and Contributing Writer Helena Snopek, who have played a key role in drafting introductory materials and annotations for the new material, and done so with great skill and unfailing grace; to Kathryn Brownsey, who has been responsible for design and typesetting, and has continued to do an outstanding job and to maintain her good spirits even when faced with near-impossible demands; to Joe Davies and Bethany Qualls for the range of their general knowledge as well as for their keen eyes as our primary proofreaders for the entire project; and to Merilee Atos, who has done superb work on the vast job of clearing permissions for the anthology.

The academic general editors and all of us in-house at Broadview owe an enormous debt of gratitude to the hundreds of academics who have offered assistance at various stages of this project. In particular we would like to express our appreciation and our thanks to the following:

Rachel Ablow, University of Rochester
Katherine Acheson, University of Waterloo
Kenet Adamson, Southwestern Community College
Bryan Alexander, Middlebury College
Sharon Alker, Whitman College
James Allard, Brock University
Ella Allen, St. Thomas University
Rosemary Allen, Georgetown College
Laurel Amtower, San Diego State University
Robert Anderson, Oakland University
Christopher Armitage, University of North Carolina, Chapel Hill
Clinton Atchley, Henderson State University
Gerry Baillargeon, University of Victoria
John Baird, University of Toronto
William Baker, Northern Illinois University
Karen Bamford, Mount Allison University
John Batchelor, University of Newcastle
Lynn Batten, University of California, Los Angeles
Stephen Behrendt, University of Nebraska
Alexandra Bennett, Northern Illinois University
John Beynon, California State University, Fresno
Daniel Bivona, Arizona State University
Robert E. Bjork, Arizona State University
John Black, Moravian College
Scott Black, Villanova University
Rita Bode, Trent University
Robert Boenig, Texas A&M University
Matthew Borushko, Stonehill College
Rick Bowers, University of Alberta
Patricia Brace, Columbus State University
David Brewer, Ohio State University
William Brewer, Appalachian State University
Glen Brewster, Westfield State University
Susan Brown, University of Guelph
Sylvia Brown, University of Alberta
Sheila Burgar, University of Victoria
Catherine Burroughs, Wells College
Rebecca Bushnell, University of Pennsylvania
Michael Calabrese, California State University

Elizabeth Campbell, Oregon State University
Katey Castellano, James Madison University
Gregory Castle, Arizona State University
Cynthia Caywood, University of San Diego
Jane Chance, Rice University
Ranita Chatterjee, California State University, Northridge
William Christmas, San Francisco State University
Nancy Cirillo, University of Illinois, Chicago
Eric Clarke, University of Pittsburgh
Jeanne Clegg, University of Aquila, Italy
Thomas J. Collins, University of Western Ontario
Thomas L. Cooksey, Armstrong Atlantic State University
Kevin Cope, Louisiana State University
David Cowart, University of South Carolina
Catherine Craft-Fairchild, University of St. Thomas
Jenny Crisp, Dalton State College
Laura Dabundo, Kennesaw State University
Roger Davis, Red Deer College
Carol Davison, University of Windsor
JoEllen DeLucia, Central Michigan University
Alexander Dick, University of British Columbia
Len Diepeveen, Dalhousie University
Mary Dockray-Miller, Lesley College
James Doelman, Brescia University College, University of Western Ontario
Frank Donoghue, Ohio State University
Chris Downs, Saint James School
Alfred Drake, Chapman University
Ian Duncan, University of California, Berkeley
Julie Early, University of Alabama, Huntsville
Roxanne Eberle, University of Georgia
Siân Echard, University of British Columbia
Garrett Epp, University of Alberta
Joshua Eyler, Columbus State University
Ruth Feingold, St. Mary's College, Maryland
Dino Franco Felluga, Perdue University
Joanne Findon, Trent University
Larry Fink, Hardin Simmons University
Daniel Fischlin, University of Guelph
Christina Fitzgerald, University of Toledo
Verlyn Flieger, University of Maryland
Robert Forman, St. John's University
Allyson Foster, Hunter College
Lorcan Fox, University of British Columbia
Peter Francev, Victor Valley College
Roberta Frank, Yale University
Jeff Franklin, University of Colorado, Denver
Maria Frawley, George Washington University
Mark Fulk, Buffalo State College
Christine Gallant, Georgia State University
Andrew Galloway, Cornell University
Michael Gamer, University of Pennsylvania
Barbara Gates, University of Delaware
Laura George, Eastern Michigan University
Denise Gigante, Stanford University
Jonathan C. Glance, Mercer University
Susan Patterson Glover, Laurentian University
Jennifer Golightly, University of Denver
Daniel Gonzalez, University of New Orleans
Jan Gorak, University of Denver
Chris Gordon-Craig, University of Alberta
Evan Gottlieb, Oregon State University
Ann-Barbara Graff, Georgia Tech University
Bruce Graver, Providence College
Mary Griffin, Kwantlen University College
Michael Griffin, formerly of Southern Illinois University
George C. Grinnell, University of British Columbia, Okanagan
Jonathan Gross, DePaul University
Elisabeth Gruner, University of Richmond
Bonnie Gunzenhauser, Roosevelt University
Kevin Gustafson, University of Texas at Arlington
Stephen Guy-Bray, University of British Columbia
Ruth Haber, Worcester State College
Dorothy Hadfield, University of Guelph
Margaret Hadley, University of Calgary
Robert Hampson, Royal Holloway University of London
Carol Hanes, Howard College
Michael Hanly, Washington State University
Lila Harper, Central Washington State University
Joseph Harris, Harvard University
Katherine Harris, San Jose State University
Anthony Harrison, North Carolina State University
John Hart, Motlow State Community College

Douglas Hayes, Lakehead University
Jennifer Hellwarth, Allegheny University
David Herman, Ohio State University
Peter Herman, San Diego State University
Jillian Hess, Bronx Community College, CUNY
Kathy Hickock, Iowa State University
John Hill, US Naval Academy
Thomas Hill, Cornell University
Elizabeth Hodgson, University of British Columbia
Jim Hood, Guilford College
Joseph Hornsby, University of Alabama
Scott Howard, University of Denver
Jennifer Hughes, Averett University
Sylvia Hunt, Georgian College
Tara Hyland-Russell, St. Mary's College
Catherine Innes-Parker, University of Prince Edward Island
Jacqueline Jenkins, University of Calgary
John Johansen, University of Alberta
Gordon Johnston, Trent University
Essaka Joshua, University of Notre Dame
Richard Juang, Susquehanna University
Michael Keefer, University of Guelph
Sarah Keefer, Trent University
Lloyd Kermode, California State University, Long Beach
Brandon Kershner, University of Florida
Jon Kertzer, University of Calgary
Waqas Khwaja, Agnes State College
Helen Killoran, Ohio University
Gordon Kipling, University of California, Los Angeles
Anne Klinck, University of New Brunswick
Elizabeth Kraft, University of Georgia
Mary Kramer, University of Massachusetts, Lowell
Scott Krawczyk, United States Military Academy
Wai-Leung Kwok, San Francisco State University
Marilyn Lantz, East Mississippi Community College
Kate Lawson, University of Waterloo
Nathanial Leach, Cape Breton University
Linda Leeds, Bellevue Community College
Mary Elizabeth Leighton, University of Victoria
Eric Lindstrom, University of Vermont
Harriet Linkin, New Mexico State University
William Liston, Ball State University
Sharon Locy, Loyola Marymount University
Ross MacKay, Malaspina University-College
Peter Mallios, University of Maryland
Arnold Markley, Penn State University
Louis Markos, Houston Baptist University
Nick Mason, Brigham Young University
Pamela McCallum, University of Calgary
Patricia McCormack, Itawamba Community College
Kristen McDermott, Central Michigan University
John McGowan, University of North Carolina
Brian McHale, Ohio State University
Jim McKeown, McLennan Community College
Thomas McLean, University of Otago, New Zealand
Susan McNeill-Bindon, University of Alberta
Jodie Medd, Carleton University
Rod Michell, Thompson Rivers University
David Miller, Mississippi College
Kitty Millett, San Francisco State University
Britt Mize, Texas A&M University
Richard Moll, University of Western Ontario
Amy L. Montz, Texas A&M University
Monique Morgan, McGill University
John Morillo, North Carolina State University
Lucy Morrison, Salisbury University
Lorri Nandrea, University of Wisconsin-Steven's Point
Mara Narain, Texas Christian University
Byron Nelson, West Virginia University
Carolyn Nelson, West Virginia University
Claudia Nelson, Southwest Texas State University
Holly Faith Nelson, Trinity Western University
John Niles, University of Wisconsin, Madison
Michael North, University of California, Los Angeles
Mary Anne Nunn, Central Connecticut State University
David Oakleaf, University of Calgary
Tamara O'Callaghan, Northern Kentucky University
Karen Odden, Assistant Editor for *Victorian Literature and Culture* (formerly of University of Wisconsin, Milwaukee)
Erika Olbricht, Pepperdine University
Patrick O'Malley, Georgetown University
Patricia O'Neill, Hamilton College
Delilah Orr, Fort Lewis College

John Pagano, Barnard College
Kirsten Parkinson, Hiram College
Diana Patterson, Mount Royal College
Cynthia Patton, Emporia State University
Russell Perkin, St. Mary's University
Marjorie G. Perloff, Stanford University
Jim Persoon, Grand Valley State University
John Peters, University of North Texas
Todd Pettigrew, Cape Breton University
Alexander Pettit, University of North Texas
Jennifer Phegley, The University of Missouri, Kansas City
John Pollock, San Jose State University
Mary Poovey, New York University
Gautam Premnath, University of Massachusetts, Boston
Regina Psaki, University of Oregon
Laura Quinney, Brandeis University
Katherine Quinsey, University of Windsor
Tilottama Rajan, University of Western Ontario
Geoff Rector, University of Ottawa
Walter Reed, Emory University
Margaret Reeves, Atkinson College, York University
Cedric Reverand, University of Wyoming
Gerry Richman, Suffolk University
John Rickard, Bucknell University
Michelle Risdon, Lake Tahoe Community College
David Robinson, University of Arizona
Solveig C. Robinson, Pacific Lutheran University
Laura Rotunno, Pennsylvania State University, Altoona
Brian Rourke, New Mexico State University
Christopher Rovee, Louisiana State University
Nicholas Ruddick, University of Regina
Jason Rudy, University of Maryland
Shannon Russell, John Cabot University
Donelle Ruwe, Northern Arizona University
Jon Saklofske, Acadia University
Michelle Sauer, Minot State University
John Savarese, University of Waterloo
SueAnn Schatz, Lock Haven University of Pennsylvania
Dan Schierenbeck, Central Missouri State University
Norbert Schürer, California State University, Long Beach
Debora B. Schwartz, California Polytechnic University
Janelle A. Schwartz, Loyola University
John T. Sebastian, Loyola University
David Seed, University of Liverpool
Karen Selesky, University College of the Fraser Valley
Carol Senf, Georgia Tech University
Sharon Setzer, North Carolina State University
Lynn Shakinovsky, Wilfred Laurier University
John Sider, Westmont College
Judith Slagle, East Tennessee State University
Johanna Smith, University of Texas at Arlington
Sharon Smulders, Mount Royal College
Jason Snart, College of DuPage
Malinda Snow, Georgia State University
Yasmin Solomonescu, University of Georgia
Goran Stanivukovic, St. Mary's University
Thomas Steffler, Carleton University
Richard Stein, University of Oregon
Eric Sterling, Auburn University Montgomery
James Stokes, University of Wisconsin, Stevens Point
Mary-Ann Stouck, Simon Fraser University
Nathaniel Strout, Hamilton College
Brad Sullivan, Western New England College
Lisa Surridge, University of Victoria
Joyce A. Sutphen, Gustavus Adolphus College
Beth Sutton-Ramspeck, Ohio State University
Nanora Sweet, University of Missouri, St. Louis
Dana Symons, Simon Fraser University
Andrew Taylor, University of Ottawa
Elizabeth Teare, University of Dayton
Doug Thorpe, University of Saskatchewan
Jane Toswell, University of Western Ontario
Kim Trainor, University of British Columbia
Herbert Tucker, University of Virginia
John Tucker, University of Victoria
Mark Turner, King's College, University of London
Eleanor Ty, Wilfrid Laurier University
Deborah Tyler-Bennett, Loughborough University
Kirsten Uszkalo, University of Alberta
Lisa Vargo, University of Saskatchewan
Gina Luria Walker, The New School, New York City
Kim Walker, Victoria University of Wellington
Miriam Wallace, New College of Florida

Orrin Wang, University of Maryland
Hayden Ward, West Virginia State University
David Watt, University of Manitoba
Ruth Wehlau, Queen's University
Lynn Wells, University of Regina
Dan White, University of Toronto at Mississauga
Patricia Whiting, Carleton University
Thomas Willard, University of Arizona
Tara Williams, Oregon State University
Chris Willis, Birkbeck University of London
Lisa Wilson, SUNY College at Potsdam
Ed Wiltse, Nazareth College
Anne Windholz, Augustana College
Rosemary Winslow, The Catholic University of America
Susan Wolfson, Princeton University
Kenneth Womack, Pennsylvania State University
Gillen Wood, University of Illinois, Urbana-Champaign
Carolyn Woodward, University of New Mexico
Julia Wright, Wilfrid Laurier University
Julian Yates, University of Delaware
Arlene Young, University of Manitoba
Lisa Zeitz, University of Western Ontario

The Age of Romanticism

Perhaps the spirit and ethos of the Romantic era and its creative output are nowhere better captured than in the evolution of clothing during the period. When the artistic, literary, and political changes that are usually associated with Romanticism began in the 1780s, the heavy and elaborate costumes of the eighteenth century still prevailed, constricting their wearers into a rigid formality and mirroring contemporaneous social and aesthetic structures. In the heady years surrounding the French Revolution, when the possibility of greater freedom seemed within reach, these stiff garments gave way to loose, flowing dresses for women, clothes cut from muslins and patterned cottons that had been rendered relatively inexpensive by increasing British imperial control in the East and by technological advances in weaving in Britain itself. During the same period, local militiamen, sporting magnificent military uniforms, demonstrated Britain's growing national pride, all the while masking persistent fear of French invasion. By the time the Romantic period drew to a close in the mid-1830s, these looser fashions and glittering uniforms had themselves been superseded by the tightly laced corsets, salt-and-pepper trousers, and bell skirts heavily supported by hoops and petticoats that are now inextricably associated with English Victorianism.

Morning dress, c. 1800.

Ball dress, c. 1800.

Richard Dighton, *George "Beau" Brummell*, 1805. Brummell, the leading "dandy" of the age, brought into fashion a new style of dress coat, pantaloons, and black evening dress for men. Brummell was fastidious about cleanliness as well as clothing, but denounced perfume for men and any form of showy display.

As the combination of freedom and militarism expressed by Romantic fashions suggests, the fifty years between the French Revolution and the reign of Queen Victoria were neither historically simple nor culturally straightforward. Despite its seeming cohesiveness and unity, the Romantic period was a complex nexus of revolution and conservatism, of bold iconoclasm and hidebound conventionality. Revolutions played a central role in shaping the Romantic period—and continue to shape our perceptions of it. The form and structure of the British Romantic era, as well as the very concept of "Romanticism," have changed radically in recent decades. What in the mid-twentieth century was seen as a literary period centered on five or six major poets—all male—and a select number of prose writers—also all male—has gradually come to be seen as an era made up of writers and thinkers of different genders, beliefs, and social backgrounds. Whereas familiarity with British Romantic poetry once meant having read only William Blake, William Wordsworth, Samuel Taylor Coleridge, Lord Byron, Percy Bysshe Shelley, and John Keats (collectively known as "The Big Six"), today, the voices of Mary Robinson, Anna Laetitia Barbauld, Felicia Hemans, and Letitia Landon—all respected and popular in their day but largely unstudied for much of the twentieth century—are seen as integral to a proper understanding of the period's verse. So too with Romantic non-fiction, which was once seen as consisting of the prose of Coleridge, Charles Lamb, and William Hazlitt, but now encompasses the proto-feminist writing of Mary Wollstonecraft, the didactic prose of Hannah More and Maria Edgeworth, and the natural sketches and observations of Dorothy Wordsworth. The prose fiction of the period (aside from a nod or two acknowledging Jane Austen and Sir Walter Scott) was once given short shrift; the drama was, generally, neglected. At this moment, Mary Shelley's novels—particularly *Frankenstein* (1818) and *The Last Man* (1826)—receive at least as much critical attention as do the works of her husband Percy Shelley, with *Frankenstein* probably being read more widely than any other single work of the Romantic period; Austen's works are now seen to hold a central position in the history of the novel; and the work of other writers of fiction—from William Godwin to Mary Hays, Amelia Opie, Mary Robinson, and Charlotte Smith—has been much more fully and more favorably assessed. In the study of drama, a similar, if less marked, shift has occurred, with the importance of the work of Hannah Cowley, Elizabeth Inchbald, and Joanna Baillie, as well as that of Percy Shelley and of Byron, being broadly recognized.

If the past several decades have brought a substantial shift in the emphasis placed on various authors in the study of the Romantic period, they have also brought a shift in the way the period as a whole is perceived. Whereas Romantic literature in English was once discussed far more with reference to nature and to the imagination than it was with reference to politics or to ideology, a broader perspective is now almost universally acknowledged as essential to a more comprehensive sense of the period. Not everything has changed however; it is still almost universally accepted that the Romantic mindset and the literary works it produced were shaped, above all, by the French Revolution and the Industrial Revolution.

For Romanticism, the French Revolution was epochmaking. When the Bastille fell on 14 July 1789 and the French National Constituent Assembly issued its democratic, anti-monarchical *Declaration of the Rights of Man and Citizen* on 27 August of the same year, it seemed to the people of Great Britain, a mere 12 miles across the Channel, that a new dawn was on the horizon. For liberals and for many authors, artists, and intellectuals this dawn was a rosy one, promising not only greater equality and better government in France itself, but also the beginning of a thoroughgoing transformation of the world. Mary Robinson's "Ainsi Va Le Monde" (1791) provides a vivid sense of the degree to which a fervent faith in and enthusiasm for freedom knew no bounds in the breasts of many writers of the time:

> Hark! "Freedom" echoes thro' the vaulted skies.
> The goddess speaks! O mark the blest decree,—
> Tyrants Shall Fall—Triumphant Man Be Free!

Wordsworth, present in France during the early days of the Revolution, famously wrote of it later, "Bliss was it in that dawn to be alive!" while his friend and fellow poet Robert Southey recalled that "a visionary world seemed to open … [N]othing was dreamt of but regeneration of the human race." Mary Wollstonecraft, who had recently published *A Vindication of the Rights of Woman*, moved to Paris in 1792, inspired by revolutionary idealism. The Revolution became a central Romantic metaphor, as well as a central psychological influence on the first generation of Romantic writers.

The younger generation too, particularly Byron and Percy Shelley, were stirred by revolutionary fervor. What these poets hoped for, however, was a continuation of the *spirit* of the French Revolution. For, in actuality, Wordsworth's new dawn soon darkened into a terrible thunderstorm and a rain of blood. In August of 1792, the leaders of the Revolution overthrew the French monarchy, and, a month later, a Parisian mob massacred more than a thousand prisoners whom they believed to be Royalist conspirators. Extremist Jacobins[1] now prevailed over more moderate Girondins,[2] and the Revolution turned into the Reign of Terror (1793–94). In January 1793, King Louis XVI went to the guillotine; Marie Antoinette followed him in October. France declared war on Britain in 1793, and Britain quickly reciprocated the declaration. As the Terror progressed under the guidance of Maximilien Robespierre, thousands of aristocrats, clergy, and alleged opponents of the Revolution were guillotined including, eventually, Robespierre himself. In 1794, France offered to support any and all revolutions abroad, and proceeded to invade its neighbors. In 1799, Napoleon had himself named First Consul for life, and, in 1804, he crowned himself Emperor. When he invaded the Iberian Peninsula in 1807, Britain intervened to aid the Spanish and Portuguese. The Napoleonic Wars, as these military conflicts came to be known, did not end until Napoleon was thoroughly routed at the Battle of Waterloo in 1815.

What had begun as a movement for democracy, then, had become a military dictatorship. Looking back from a distance of 24 years, Byron wrote, in *Childe Harold's Pilgrimage* (1812–18), that the French made themselves a fearful monument:

> The wreck of old opinions …
> … the veil they rent
> And what behind it lay all earth shall view.

[1] The term "Jacobin" was used throughout the Romantic period to denote those in sympathy with the radical, revolutionary ideals associated with the French Revolution. Those opposing the Revolution were termed "anti-Jacobins." The ideological differences between the radical Jacobins and the conservative anti-Jacobins were often played out in the novels of the late eighteenth and early nineteenth centuries.

[2] A loosely affiliated coalition of moderate republicans, the Girondins controlled the French Legislative Assembly from late 1791 to late 1792, when they were ousted by more radical politicians. Many Girondin leaders were summarily executed during the Reign of Terror.

William Heath, *The Battle of Waterloo* (detail), 1815. British infantrymen to the right are firing into the ranks of the French cavalry. The full battle involved approximately 75,000 French troops under Napoleon; the Duke of Wellington commanded an allied force of well over 100,000. The casualties totaled over 50,000—60 per cent of them French.

But good with ill they also overthrew,
Leaving but ruins, wherewith to rebuild
Upon the same foundation, and renew
Dungeons and thrones ... (*Childe Harold* 3.82)

The Revolution's promise of freedom died in a frenzy of oppression, destruction, violence, and imperialism, and many of Britain's intellectuals watched in horror, gradually turning from bold liberalism to a cautious conservatism they saw as both pragmatic and necessary. To use the political terminology that first developed out of the seating arrangements in the French National Constituent Assembly in 1789, they moved from the left of center to the right of center; Wordsworth, Coleridge, and Southey, all radical thinkers in their youth, were firm conservatives by the end of their lives. Others—such as Barbauld—remained politically on the left but became disillusioned, both by the course that revolution had taken in France and by the failure of the British to embrace the principles of freedom. Barbauld surveyed what seemed to her a decadent and oppressive England in "Eighteen Hundred and Eleven" (1812)—"The worm is in thy core, thy glories pass away"—and Percy Shelley despaired in "England in 1819" (composed in 1819, but not published until 1839) at "Rulers who neither see nor feel nor know, / But leechlike to their fainting country cling."

The British government's response to the developments in France had been swift and repressive. In 1794, the right of habeas corpus—which required the state to show legitimate cause for imprisonment and to carry out trials in a timely manner—was suspended. As a result, those accused of crimes could be held for an indefinite period. In 1795, Parliament passed the Treasonable Practices Act, which made criticism of the government a crime; in the same year, it passed an act that limited the size of public meetings and the places in which they could be held. The Combination Acts of 1799 and

1800 forbade workers to associate for the purposes of collective bargaining. To enforce all these restrictive measures, the government set loose a herd of spies, many of whom acted as *agents provocateurs*, infiltrating liberal and radical groups and prompting them to commit criminal acts they otherwise might not have committed. In at least one important case, that of the Cato Street Conspiracy of 1820—a scheme to murder cabinet ministers and stage a government coup—these government agents first urged on and then exposed conspirators who were punished with hanging or with transportation to Australia. (In Scotland and Ireland, authoritarianism could be even more severe.)

If the French Revolution and the 22 years of war with France that followed produced ruinous government authoritarianism, they also acted to create for the first time a widespread sense—among the English, at least—that England, Wales, Scotland and, to a lesser extent, Ireland, formed one cohesive nation: Great Britain. Scotland had been linked to England by the Union of 1707, while union with Ireland, which had been firmly under English control since the time of Cromwell, was made official with the Acts of Union in 1800. (This sense of England, Scotland, Wales, and Ireland forming a cohesive whole was rarely if ever to be found in many areas of Scotland, Wales, or Ireland—of which more will be said below.) The wars with France allowed the populace to see themselves as leading a larger body defending liberty and freedom (even if that liberty and freedom were now, ironically, defined by a conservative authoritarian mind-set). At the same time, the wars raised very real threats of invasion—there were scares in 1778, 1796–98, and 1803, and Wales was actually invaded in a very modest fashion in 1797 (though the drama of that episode quickly dissolved into farce).

The threats from without acted to foster cohesion within. Foreign travel was out of the question for all but the very rich or the very brave; interest among the English in all things British rose. Sir Walter Scott's collection of folk-songs and ballads, *Minstrelsy of the Scottish Border* (1802–03); Thomas Moore's *Irish Melodies* (1807–34); and Felicia Hemans's *Welsh Melodies* (1822) gave their readers a sense of a rich past, while simultaneously celebrating the blend of cultures that went into making up Great Britain. Poets such as Robert Burns and John Clare gave proud voice to local

T.W. Huffram, *Theobald Wolfe Tone*, date unknown. Tone is shown in French uniform.

James Gillray, *United Irishmen in Training*, 1798. The famous English caricaturist here portrays the Irish as cruel buffoons; they are assaulting a British uniform stuffed with straw.

Thomas Girtin, *Westminster from Lambeth*, c. 1800. Girtin's watercolor was one of a series of sketches for a panorama of London (now lost).

cultures, so that the individual nations which made up the one great nation were simultaneously celebrated for their respective traditions and recognized as within the British fold. Long poetical works such as John Thelwall's *The Hope of Albion; or Edwin of Northumbria* (1801) expanded the sense of an epic British mythology, while collections such as Hemans's *Tales and Historic Scenes* (1819), a celebration of military valor, fostered a sense of pride in present-day accomplishments.

The history of the very words *English* and *British* offers another indication of the change. Until 1780 the word *English* appeared in English books at least three times as often as did the word *British*; by 1800 that ratio had slipped to 2:1, and by 1840 it had slipped to 1.5:1. (Not until just after the Second World War did the two terms begin to be used with roughly the same frequency.)

The sense of a larger Britain with England at its center further strengthened the English belief that England itself was particularly, even divinely, favored. Such notions were perhaps given their most memorable, if also most ambivalent, expression in the opening to William Blake's "Preface" to *Milton* (1804), in which ancient England is linked with Christ:

And did those feet in ancient time
Walk upon England's mountain's green?
And was the Holy Lamb of God
On England's pleasant pastures seen?
And did the countenance divine
Shine forth upon our clouded hills?[1]

Although Blake leaves it up to his reader to determine whether the answers to these rhetorical questions are yes or no, the stanza that follows explicitly figures England as a land worthy of being the new Jerusalem (if only sometime in the future):

[1] The opening two stanzas of this poem (a total of 16 lines) were set to music by Charles H.H. Parry in 1916; under the title "Jerusalem," these verses have become an unofficial national anthem for the English.

I will not cease from mental fight,
Nor shall my sword sleep in my hand,
Till we have built Jerusalem
In England's green and pleasant land.

Between these invocations of the divine in England, however, Blake inserts an insidious question, one that began to plague English writers and citizens more and more as the Romantic period progressed: "was Jerusalem builded here / Among these dark Satanic mills?" The phrase "dark Satanic mills" has become the most famous description of the force at the center of the Industrial Revolution. Even as the French Revolution changed the consciousness of the British people, this other revolution in their own country had as much impact on them as did any conflagration abroad.

In the sixteenth and seventeenth centuries, the British Isles, and England in particular, had begun to undergo extensive changes in economic structure. The pace of change increased dramatically as the eighteenth century progressed. From being a largely rural nation with a largely agricultural economy, Britain became an urban nation with an economy based in manufacturing. James Watt's refinement of the steam engine and James Hargreaves's invention of the Spinning Jenny (a machine that allowed cotton to be spun on several spindles simultaneously) were only the most famous of a host of changes that produced a boom in industrialization. Factories sprang up in what had once been countryside, and the populations of towns and cities, particularly those associated with manufacture, swelled. At the beginning of the 1770s, about a quarter of England's population lived in urban centers, but by 1801 that proportion had risen to one-third, and by the 1840s half of the English population resided in cities. In 1750, the total English population was roughly 5.5 million; by the time of the first census in 1800, it had grown to 8 million, while the population of Scotland and Ireland totaled more than 6.5 million. By 1831, the total population of Great Britain was thus approximately 14 million. This increase fueled the Industrial Revolution from both ends, supplying more consumers eager to acquire goods and more bodies to work in factories that produced those goods.

Illustration of an early locomotive engine, 1808.

Industrialization also contributed to an important shift in the country's social structure. The paradigm of classes and ranks that placed the nobility at the top with everyone else keeping to their places beneath had begun to change as early as the seventeenth century, with those involved in business and commerce growing wealthy enough to exert power of their own. The process was greatly accelerated in the late eighteenth and early nineteenth centuries as more and more industrialists and business owners—the majority of whom were men, and a disproportionate number of whom were non-conformist[1]—amassed larger and larger fortunes. Still, the road that led from newly acquired wealth to social acceptance remained a long and circuitous one. An inherited

[1] The term *non-conformist* was applied to Methodists, Baptists, Quakers, and others whose religious beliefs did not accord with the doctrines of the established church—the Church of England.

George and I.R. Cruikshank, *Sporting a Toe at Almacks*, 1821. Many clubs were restricted to men; Almack's was an exclusive London club controlled by a group of society women. During "the season" a fashionable ball was held at Almack's every week.

fortune stemming from longstanding ownership of large amounts of land—and the rents thereby produced—remained the most respectable form of wealth. To possess a good deal of money as a result not of belonging to the "landed gentry" but rather of having amassed it through commercial activity was considered more than faintly disreputable. It might take two or three generations before the taint of anyone in the family having been "in trade" (a term applied to industrialists as much as to tradespeople) was removed, and the source of the family fortune forgotten. The social nuances involved in such transitions were vividly captured in the novels of Jane Austen; here, for example, is her description of the Bingley sisters in *Pride and Prejudice* (1813):

> They were rather handsome, had been educated in one of the first private seminaries in town, had a fortune of twenty thousand pounds, were in the habit of spending more than they ought, and of associating with people of rank; and were therefore in every respect entitled to think well of themselves, and meanly of others. They were of a respectable family in the north of England; a circumstance more deeply impressed on their memories than that their brother's fortune and their own had been acquired by trade.

Fine gradations of respectability were attached to every occupation, with social position often at odds with financial circumstances. Members of the clergy and their families, for instance, though sometimes impecunious, were generally respected; whether members of the gentry or born into the working class, they often moved in elevated social circles. Physicians, defined as those medical men who had a degree from a university, could sometimes move in the "best circles" in a community, although apothecaries and surgeons, who gained their knowledge through apprenticeship, could not.

The Romantic literary world reflected the increased social mobility possible during the period. John Keats, for example, was the son of a stable keeper who had increased his financial standing by marrying the daughter of the stable owner. Keats trained as a surgeon-apothecary (a job that combined the duties of a present-day pharmacist, general practitioner, and surgeon), but, at the age of 18, he came into an inheritance and was able to devote himself entirely to literature. He wrote to a friend that he thought he would "be among the English poets" after his death, and, as it turned out, no social barriers could prevent that from occurring. Similarly, Samuel Taylor Coleridge, a parson's son who attended a London charity school as a child, ended his life lauded and respected as "The Sage of Highgate."

The Industrial Revolution may have increased social mobility; it certainly allowed goods to be produced more efficiently. But it also devastated large portions of England's underclasses, the agricultural laborers and peasants who had benefited, however slightly, from the land-based economy that was passing away. In Wordsworth's "Tintern Abbey" (1798), the reference to "vagrant dwellers in the houseless woods" describes a very real phenomenon. In the late eighteenth and early nineteenth centuries, a series of Enclosure Acts resulted in the continued conversion of formerly common land into large, privately held farms.[1] To be fair, enclosures did often result in an increase in agricultural production, but they also often spelled ruin for thousands of small farmers. Large landholders benefited from their enlarged acreage, but many of those who had heretofore been able to eke out a living from a tiny patch of land and sell their modest surpluses now lost all ability to support themselves. These smallholders and their families were forced either to labor for others for meager wages, to migrate to the city and enter the manufacturing workforce, or to turn to begging or thievery. Poor harvests in 1794–95, 1799–1800, and 1810–11 worsened the plight of the rural poor even further. The proliferation of vandals, vagrants, and beggars in the writing of this era thus reflected a growing social reality.

The leading literary figures of the day were, for the most part, sympathetic to the plight of the poor in a time of growing inequity, but, beyond that, they held widely divergent attitudes concerning these developments, and concerning the commoners themselves. Anna Laetitia Barbauld was one writer who sought to ameliorate the inequities that had become so characteristic of English life; she condemned the power relations involved, harshly criticizing the privileged, and took a view of commoners that saw them as prey to vice as a result of the circumstances in which they had been placed through economic hardship and lack of education. As she wrote in *Thoughts on the Inequality of Conditions* (1800),

> Power enables the indolent and the useless not only to retain, but to add to their possessions, by taking from the industrious the natural reward of their labour, and applying it to their own use.... It is not sufficiently considered how many virtues depend upon comfort, and cleanliness, and decent apparel. Destroy dirt and misery, and you will destroy at once a great many vices.

It is the approach of William Wordsworth, however, that has more often been taken to characterize British Romanticism. That approach posits nature as central to human experience—nature in its simpler or wilder forms, not distorted by human artifice. Wordsworth was interested not only in "the beautiful and permanent forms of nature" but also in the ways in which human passions are excited by these forms; he describes "the mind" (rather than nature) as "My haunt, and the main region of my song." He was vitally interested, too, in the minds of those whom he saw as most closely connected to the natural world. If Barbauld's focus was very largely on the struggle to ameliorate conditions for the poor, Wordsworth's was more on the worth inherent in the hearts and minds of rural common folk—and on the associated poetic value. In the same year as Barbauld wrote her *Thoughts on the Inequality of Conditions*,

[1] The process of enclosure was not new; it had been occurring since the late Middle Ages, in response to population pressures and as Britain was transformed first into a largely mercantile economy and then into an industrial society.

Wordsworth expressed his ideals in the 1800 "Preface" to *Lyrical Ballads*:

> The principal object, then, proposed in these Poems was to choose incidents and situations from common life.... Humble and rustic life was generally chosen, because, in that condition, the essential passions of the heart find a better soil in which they can attain their maturity, are less under restraint, and speak a plainer and more emphatic language; because in that condition of life our elementary feelings coexist in a state of greater simplicity, and, consequently, may be more accurately contemplated, and more forcibly communicated; because the manners of rural life germinate from those elementary feelings, and, from the necessary character of rural occupations, are more easily comprehended, and are more durable; and, lastly, because in that condition the passions of men are incorporated with the beautiful and permanent forms of nature.

Poems in *Lyrical Ballads*, such as "Michael," "The Ruined Cottage," "The Idiot Boy," and "Resolution and Independence," represent Wordsworth's attempt to put those ideals into practice. In "Resolution and Independence," the poet encounters an old, poor, itinerant leech-gatherer, ending the poem by admiring "In that decrepit Man so firm a mind." Whereas Barbauld regarded theft as a justifiable response to the oppression of extreme poverty in an iniquitous social system, Wordsworth pays homage to the old leech-gatherer for earning an "honest maintenance" despite the "many hardships" he must endure.

If the rural working-poor fared badly during these years, life for the workers in the cities and the unemployed-poor was just as bad. In 1815, at the instigation of large land holders, who stood to benefit from high prices for grain, the government passed the Corn Laws to institute a substantial tariff on imports of grain from foreign countries, making such imports much more expensive.[1] The tariff was effective in protecting British grain producers; at the same time, it inflated the price of bread and other foodstuffs for the consumer. The poor in the cities suffered particularly, and, from 1815 until the Corn Laws were finally repealed in 1845, they remained a lightning rod for political dissent.

Had conditions for the urban poor been better in other respects, the Corn Laws might have had less impact. The British government, however, assured by Adam Smith's highly influential work of economic philosophy, *The Wealth of Nations* (1777), that the best way to encourage national economic success was to leave businesses free to grow without hindrance, for the most part adopted a laissez-faire[2] approach to regulating treatment of employees and working conditions during this period. In practice, "laissez-faire" ultimately meant shifts of as much as 15 hours at a stretch, often for very young children. Wages were kept as low as manufacturers could manage and injuries were common; children were the preferred workers for clearing jams in mechanized looms, for example, and the frequent result was the loss of the tiny fingers and hands that made them ideal for the job. Workers' health was often ruined by unsanitary working and living conditions—employers often owned not only the factories, but the slums in which their workers lived—and by unfettered pollution.

It is often assumed that the worst extremes of the Industrial Revolution in Britain occurred during the Victorian era, but, by the time Victoria came to the throne, Parliament had already been pressed to take a succession of measures to restrict the abuse of children: the largely ineffectual Health and Morals of Apprentices Act (1802), the Regulation of Cotton Mills and Factories Act (1819), and the Act to Regulate the Labour of Children and Young Persons in the Mills and Factories of the United Kingdom (1833). Even after the passage of this last, children as young as nine could be forced to work nine-hour days, and thirteen-year-olds to work twelve-hour days; still, this represented a degree of improvement from the late eighteenth and early nineteenth centuries. Robert Blincoe, for example, an orphan raised in a London workhouse and transported in 1799, at the age of seven, to work in the Lowdham Mill near Nottingham, described his life at the mill to John Brown in 1822:

[1] In Britain, corn denotes grain, most commonly wheat; what North Americans call corn is referred to in Britain as maize.

[2] French: allow to do.

> Blincoe heard the burring sound [of the machinery] before he reached the portals and smelt the fumes of the oil with which the axles of twenty-thousand wheels and spindles were bathed the moment he entered the doors. The noise appalled him, and the stench seemed intolerable. It was the custom at Lowdham Mills, as it is in most water mills, to make the apprentices work up lost time [i.e., time when the machines had been unable to run during regular working hours], by working over hours. … When children of seven years of age had to work fourteen hours every day in the week, Sundays excepted, any addition was severely felt. … Almost from the first hour [Blincoe] entered the Mill, till he arrived at a state of manhood, it was one continual round of cruel and arbitrary punishment. … I asked him if he could state the average number of times in which he might safely say he had suffered corporal punishment in a week. His answer invariably was, that his punishments were so various and so frequent, it was impossible to state with anything approaching to accuracy. … Supper consisted of milk-porridge, of a very blue complexion [together with] bread partly made of rye—very black, and so soft they could scarcely swallow it, as it stuck like bird-lime to their teeth.

If the government addressed such outrages only with reluctance—sometimes Parliamentary committees looking into allegations would not hear any direct testimony from the workers—many citizens found them harder to ignore. Demonstrations of popular dissatisfaction were frequent and took various forms. Luddites, followers of the imaginary "General Ned Ludd," attacked and broke machinery during the years 1811–16, sometimes to force concessions from their employers but sometimes simply to express their dissatisfaction with creeping mechanization. After the bad harvests and the passage of the Corn Laws in 1815, food riots occurred across the country. Coercion Acts were passed in 1817 to try to stifle dissent, but they provoked strong antagonism, and both in London and in parts of Scotland some republican groups advocated revolution. Throughout the 1820s, farm workers staged violent protests, culminating in mass barn-burnings in 1830. Perhaps the most famous popular uprising was the 1819 gathering of roughly 80,000 mill workers at St. Peter's Field, near Manchester. A peaceful demonstration that ended with an address to the crowd by Henry Hunt,[1] this gathering so alarmed the local gentry that they sent drunken, armed militiamen to break it up and arrest Hunt. The militiamen attacked the crowd with their sabers when it jeered them, and the ensuing melee left 11 dead—including one trampled child—and more than 400 injured, many from saber wounds.

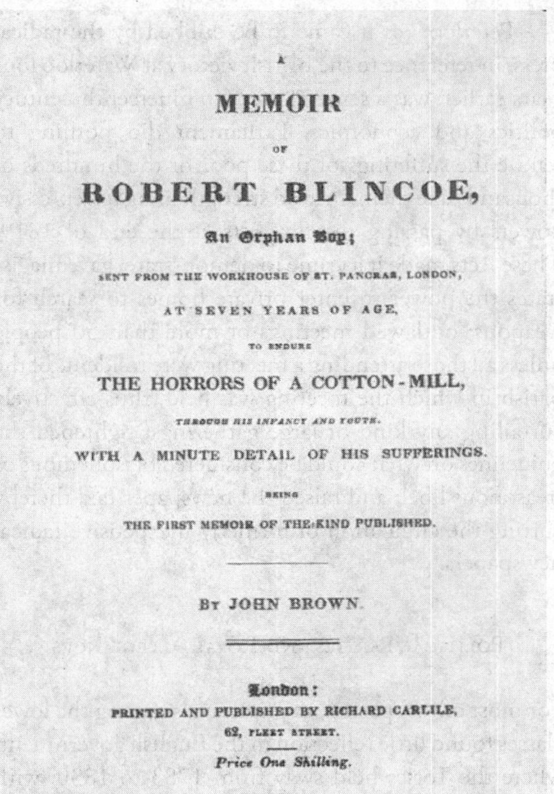

A

MEMOIR

OF

ROBERT BLINCOE,

An Orphan Boy;

SENT FROM THE WORKHOUSE OF ST. PANCRAS, LONDON,

AT SEVEN YEARS OF AGE,

TO ENDURE

THE HORRORS OF A COTTON-MILL,

THROUGH HIS INFANCY AND YOUTH,

WITH A MINUTE DETAIL OF HIS SUFFERINGS.

BEING

THE FIRST MEMOIR OF THE KIND PUBLISHED.

BY JOHN BROWN.

London:

PRINTED AND PUBLISHED BY RICHARD CARLILE,

62, FLEET STREET.

Price One Shilling.

Title page, *A Memoir of Robert Blincoe*, first published in 1828, re-issued in 1832. Demonstrations in 1832 and 1833 for factory reform frequently cited the evidence of factory conditions that he had provided, and Blincoe testified before the Royal Commission that investigated the issue of child labor in 1833.

[1] Known as the "Orator," Hunt (1773–1835) was a radical speaker and agitator, renowned for his advocacy of Parliamentary reform and the abolition of the Corn Laws.

"Peterloo," as it came to be dubbed by the radical press, in reference to the British victory at Waterloo four years earlier, was a seminal event in nineteenth-century politics and economics. Parliament did nothing to relieve the sufferings of these poor or the hundreds of thousands like them, instead strengthening its repressive powers by passing the Six Acts at the end of 1819. These Acts made it a crime to demonstrate; gave magistrates the power to enter private homes to search for weapons; outlawed meetings of more than 50 people unless all those attending a meeting were residents of the parish in which the meeting was held, thus effectively curtailing any kind of large gatherings; tightened the guidelines on what could be considered blasphemous or treasonous libel; and raised the newspaper tax, thereby cutting the circulation of formerly inexpensive radical newspapers.[1]

POLITICAL PARTIES AND ROYAL ALLEGIANCES

For most of this period, the upheavals among the lower classes found little reflection in the English government, where the Tories held sway from 1783 to 1830, with only one short interruption. The Tories were the conservative party: they saw themselves as upholders of law and tradition, determined to preserve the prevailing political and social order. From 1793 to 1801, and again from 1804 to 1806, the Tories—and the country—were led by Prime Minister William Pitt, whose fiscal restraint and willingness to suppress political protest (sometimes with open brutality) made him a hero to some and a villain to many others. After Pitt died in office in 1806, certainly of overwork and probably of alcoholism—his last words were, depending on the source, either, "Oh, my country! how I leave my country!" or "I think I could eat one of Bellamy's veal pies"—the Tories continued in power, on their own or in coalition, until 1830.

The Whigs, who remained the party of opposition during this time, presented themselves against the Tories as advocates of greater civil and religious liberty. In reality, neither party would have been called "Liberals" or "Democrats" by today's standards, but the Whigs did advocate the abolition of the slave trade, Catholic emancipation (which would allow greater political participation to Catholics, heretofore barred from a role in government), and Parliamentary reform. From 1782 to 1806, the leader of the Whigs was the charismatic Charles James Fox, gambler, gourmand, and political colossus, whose political machinations made him as many enemies as friends. Not until 1806, a year after Fox's death, would the Whigs participate in government—and then for only a relatively short period, as part of a coalition. They would not gain power in their own right until 1830. They were then at last able to pass the Reform Act of 1832 (also known as the Great Reform Act), which extended voting rights to a broader spectrum of propertied males,[2] redistributed Parliamentary seats, and brought significantly fairer political representation.

While the politicians plotted and schemed, the British royal family suffered its own difficulties. George III, who had ascended the throne in 1760, embodied Toryism both politically and personally; traditionalist, ponderous, and domestic, he produced a large family, embraced conservative politics, and allegedly liked to wander the countryside incognito, chatting with farmers. In 1788, however, he suffered a bout of mental illness that lasted until early 1789. This illness, now believed to be the result of the hereditary blood disease porphyria, reappeared in 1810, leaving him permanently insane. In 1811, when it became apparent that the king would not recover, his eldest son was declared regent.

Monarchs of the House of Hanover traditionally clashed with their eldest sons, and George III and the prince who would become George IV were no different. The regent was a stark contrast to his thrifty father; in 1787, when he was 25, his debts totaled more than

[1] The Six Acts ultimately proved repugnant to certain members of the liberal Whig party—who subsequently became politically powerful—and led to the liberal Reform Act of 1832. Thus, the long-term result of the massacre was modest relief from the extraordinarily repressive measures it had spawned.

[2] The changes are estimated to have altered the composition of the electorate to approximately one in seven males from fewer than one in ten.

Sir Thomas Lawrence, *The Prince Regent in Profile*, c. 1814. The prince knighted Lawrence, the leading English portraitist of the day, in 1815, saying that he was "proud in conferring a mark of his favour on one who had raised the character of British art in the estimation of all Europe."

Sir Thomas Lawrence, *Caroline Amelia Elizabeth of Brunswick*, 1804 (detail).

£160,000 (equivalent to about £8,000,000 today). He lived with a Roman Catholic mistress whom he later married, secretly and unconstitutionally, before abandoning her for a series of other mistresses. Later, to secure relief from debts, he married his cousin Caroline of Brunswick, a woman he found so instantly and completely loathsome that his first words upon seeing her were "I am not well; pray get me a glass of brandy." Although they did manage to produce one daughter, Charlotte, who later died in childbirth, the prince and his wife never lived together, and his attempt to divorce her after his accession in 1820 was one of the great scandals of the period.

George IV was not without redeeming virtues; notably, he was a keen patron of the arts, particularly architecture. In addition to a magnificent pavilion in Brighton, he and his architects built Trafalgar Square, modified and improved Buckingham House into Buckingham Palace, and created parks, streets, and crescents throughout London. He was an enthusiastic reader and promoter of literature, as well as a generous patron of the sciences, establishing several fellowships and prizes. Nonetheless, the prince became a figure of increasing public contempt. Leigh Hunt described him as "a libertine head over heels in debt and disgrace, a despiser of domestic ties"; Percy Shelley called him, in prose, an "overgrown bantling [infant]," and, in poetry, "the dregs of [his] dull race." When he died in 1830, *The Times* wrote, "There never was an individual less regretted by his fellow creatures than this dead King."

IMPERIAL EXPANSION

Even as Britain was experiencing its own internal power struggles and upheavals, the nation was expanding its presence around the globe. Throughout the first half of the nineteenth century, Britain was well on its way to forging the empire that would reach full flower in the Victorian period. The East India Company, founded by a group of London merchants in 1600, controlled most of eastern India by 1765, and thereafter continued to extend its administrative and governmental control over the sub-continent. British interest in China began in the late eighteenth century, when Britain began to import the tea that would soon become a staple of the British table, and that interest rose throughout the 1800s. Increased contact with—and domination of—various parts of the Far East led to increased fascination with its cultures, a fascination widely reflected in literature. "Eastern" influence pervades the prose and poetry of this period, from William Beckford's novel *The History of the Caliph Vathek* (1786), to Byron's *Eastern Tales* (1813–14), to Percy Shelley's *Alastor* (1816), where the protagonist makes his way

> through Arabie
> And Persia, and the wild Carmanian waste,
> And o'er the aerial mountains which pour down
> Indus and Oxus from their icy caves,
> In joy and exultation [he] held his icy way,
> Till in the vale of Cashmire …
> he stretched
> His languid limbs.

Wearing her India cotton frock, sipping her tea from Canton, coffee from Yemen, or chocolate from Mexico, the English consumer of the Romantic period felt the influence of imperial expansion everywhere, from the commodities she purchased to the pages she turned.

But if the British Empire brought rewards to the nation's citizens, it all too often entailed exploitation and horror in the colonies themselves. Chief amongst these was the slavery that fueled the economy of the British West Indies. The mass of sugar required to sweeten Britain's tea, coffee, and chocolate was cultivated, cut, and processed on these islands by enslaved people who worked under inhuman conditions until they literally wore out—at which point their white masters simply purchased fresh replacements. Over the course of the eighteenth century, British slavers transported some three million enslaved people to the West Indies and other agricultural colonies; the economic success of the port towns Bristol and Liverpool was based in large part on the important part they played in the English slave trade—and the trade in sugar from plantations that relied on the labor of enslaved people.[1]

Arguably the strongest resistance to slavery in the West Indies came from the enslaved people themselves. The British invaded the formerly French island of Saint-Dominique in 1793 in order to aid in the suppression of an uprising of enslaved people led by Toussaint Louverture, but they withdrew five years later, having sent more troops to the West Indies over that period than they had sent to America during the War of Independence. When a subsequent effort by Napoleon also failed, the formerly enslaved people founded the Republic of Haiti in 1804, sending the message that emancipation was inevitable.

Emancipation was also spurred by a widespread and effective protest movement within Britain. Between 1787, when protests first began, and 1791, abolitionists gathered 500 petitions against slavery from across Britain. In all some 400,000 signatures were collected; this was Britain's first large-scale petition campaign. The abolitionist movement attracted support from Evangelicals, from Whig politicians, and from radicals, and has been described as the first British political movement in the modern sense. The leading figures in the movement were abolitionists Thomas Clarkson, Granville Sharp, and William Wilberforce, but it also drew considerable support from the poets of the day, among them William Cowper, Hannah More, William Blake, Mary Robinson, Anna Laetitia Barbauld, and Ann Yearsley (whose *A Poem on the Inhumanity of the Slave Trade* [1788] inveighed against the very business that supported her home town of Bristol).

[1] At the start of the American Revolution, British imports from the largest sugar plantation center, Jamaica, were worth five times more than British imports from the Thirteen Colonies.

James Gillray, *Fashionable Contrasts, or the Duchess' Little Shoe Yielding to the Magnitude of the Duke's Foot*, 1792. At the time this print was published, the press had been fawning over Princess Frederica Charlotte Ulrica Catherina, who had just married Frederick Augustus, Duke of York; the daintiness of her feet had been particularly praised.

James Gillray, *The Plum Pudding in Danger*, 1805. Napoleon and British Prime Minister William Pitt are shown carving up the globe, with Napoleon skewering Europe and Pitt helping himself to the ocean. (1805 saw both the Battle of Trafalgar, at which the British under Lord Nelson established dominance at sea, and the Battle of Austerlitz, at which Napoleon defeated Russian and Austrian armies to cement his

Sir Charles D'Oyly, *The Emporium of Taylor & Co. in Calcutta*, c. 1825–28.

Central to the literature of the abolitionist movement were books written by formerly enslaved people, such as Olaudah Equiano and Mary Prince, which laid out plainly the horrors of enslavement and openly sought sympathy and fellow-feeling from readers. In his autobiography, *The Interesting Narrative of the Life of Olaudah Equiano* (1786), Equiano described conditions both in the West Indies and in America. As he observed with telling effect, the system bred degradation for "free negroes" as well as for enslaved people:

> I have often seen slaves, particularly those who were meagre, in different islands, put into scales and weighed; and then sold from three pence to six pence to nine pence a pound. My master, however, whose humanity was shocked at this mode, used to sell by the lump. And at or after a sale it was not uncommon to see negroes taken from their wives, wives taken from their husbands, and children from their parents, and sent off to other islands, and wherever else their merciless lords chose, and probably never more during life to see each other! …
>
> [Free negroes] live in constant alarm for their liberty; and even this is but nominal, for they are universally insulted and plundered without the possibility of redress; for such is the equity of West Indian laws, that no free negro's evidence will be admitted in their courts of justice.

Such accounts, coupled with a determined and prolonged campaign and with the effects of the growth of the Asian sugar trade, led to the abolition of the slave trade in 1806–07, and (following another uprising, this time in Jamaica in 1831–32) to an act in 1833 that provided for the full abolition of slavery. The persecution of blacks by whites, however, continued both in the West Indies and throughout the British Empire.

Several of the leading names of English Romantic poetry are noticeably absent from the list of writers who wrote frequently and explicitly in favor of abolition. Wordsworth,[1] Coleridge, Byron, Percy Shelley, and Keats were in general all sympathetic to the aims of the abolitionist movement, and Coleridge in particular spoke out strongly both against slavery itself and against the maintenance of the slave trade, memorably writing that "a slave is a person perverted into a thing," and enslavement not so much "a deviation from justice as an absolute subversion of all morality." (Coleridge's views regarding enslavement became significantly more conservative, however, later in his life.) It has been plausibly suggested that some major works of Romantic poetry (notably Coleridge's "The Rime of the Ancient Mariner" [1798] and Keats's "Lamia" [1819]) may usefully be read in relation to the slave trade. But directly pressing for the abolition of enslavement through verse in the manner of Cowper, Robinson, and Yearsley was never a significant part of these poets' agendas.

Scotland, Ireland, Wales

The Jacobite Rising of 1745 and the 1746 Battle of Culloden that put an end to it cast a shadow over Scotland well into the nineteenth century. The defeat of the Scottish rebels by the English (led with brutal efficiency by the Duke of Cumberland) initiated a long period of repression and of social and economic upheaval. Thousands who had been active in the Jacobite uprising were killed either during the battle or shortly thereafter (those who lay wounded on the battlefield were bayonetted to death rather than taken prisoner); many more died in prison, and many others were transported to colonies overseas to work as servants. Various new laws placed restrictions on "highland dress," on the carrying of arms, and on public gatherings, and the use of Gaelic was discouraged even more thoroughly than it had been previously. Some of these cultural restrictions were repealed in the 1780s, but the structural changes to the legal and economic systems that were introduced following the crushing of the rebellion were permanent. The powers of the Highland chieftains were drastically curtailed, and the clan system itself severely undermined—as was the old system of tenant farming. That system had been a largely cooperative one under which strips of farming land were rotated from one tenant to another (so as to ensure fairness), and tenants had shared access to grazing land; multiple tenants worked under the management of supervisors known as tucksmen. Under the new system the tucksmen were gradually eliminated—and so too were many of the tenants; evictions became common, and farms became larger (and fewer in number), with much of the land cleared not for common use but for the grazing of herds under single ownership. Those tenants who remained became crofters holding small individual plots; many others left for the cities—or for North America. English interventions created tremendous poverty among those displaced by "the clearances"; more broadly, the traditions of Highland Scotland that had formed the guiding principles of economic and social life were reduced by the English to little more than cultural trappings.

The great irony here is that (as touched on above), at the very point at which the English had succeeded in destroying much of the Gaelic culture of Highland Scotland, the English began to display an unprecedented interest in Scottish traditional culture. They embraced with tremendous enthusiasm the sort of romanticized portrayal of Highland culture generally (and of the doomed rebellion of '45 in particular) that Sir Walter Scott presented. In his postscript to *Waverley* (1817), Scott described "the present people of Scotland" as "a class of beings as different from their grandfathers as the existing English are from those of Queen Elizabeth's time." Glossing over the extent of British oppression, he described the changes time had wrought as "steadily and rapidly progressive" while yet lamenting the fading away of those

[1] In *The Prelude*, Wordsworth admits that in the 1790s "this particular strife had wanted power / To rivet my affections." He did write two sonnets (one to Clarkson, one to Toussaint Louverture) in 1807, the year in which abolition of the slave trade was accomplished.

> who still cherished a lingering, though hopeless, attachment to the house of Stewart. This race has almost entirely vanished from the land, and with it … many living examples of … attachment to the principles of loyalty which they received from their fathers, and of old Scottish faith, hospitality, worth, and honour.
>
> It was my accidental lot, though not born a Highlander (which may be an apology for much bad Gaelic) to reside, during my childhood and youth, among persons of the above description; and now, for the purpose of preserving some of the ancient manners of which I have witnessed the almost total extinction, I have embodied in imaginary scenes, and ascribed to fictitious characters, a part of the incidents which I then received from those who were actors in them. Indeed, the most romantic parts of the narrative are precisely those which have a foundation in fact.

The culture romanticized by Scott and so many others was primarily that of Gaelic-speaking Highland Scotland, just as the socio-economic system that had been largely destroyed by the English was that of Highland Scotland. Scots-speaking and English-speaking Lowland Scotland was a different story—far less romanticized, far more connected to English social, intellectual, and economic life, and far less oppressed.

Economically, Scottish inventors and engineers (most prominent among them James Watt, famous for his steam engine) made highly significant contributions to the industrialization of Britain. Scottish cities became world leaders in industries such as ship-building and engine-making. Politically too, Scots were often highly influential. Most notably, Henry Brougham played a key role in reforming the British legal system and in securing passage of the Reform Bill of 1832.

Intellectually, authors from the Scottish Lowlands—first Robert Burns, writing both in Scots and in English, and later Walter Scott—had arguably as great an impact on the English literary world as they did on that of Scotland. So too did two Scottish-based journals. The *Edinburgh Review,* revived by Francis Jeffrey and others in 1802, quickly became the most interesting and most influential literary, cultural, and political journal of its era. The *Edinburgh Review*'s political leanings were always towards the progressive side; as a counter, conservative book publisher William Blackwood in 1817 founded a rival journal (originally the *Edinburgh Monthly Magazine*, later *Blackwood's Edinburgh Magazine*). Though less "highbrow" than *The Edinburgh Review*, *Blackwood's* too became a significant force in the cultural and political life of England as well as Scotland.

If English oppression, rebellion, and displacement of the local populace from lands occupied for centuries are central threads of the history of Scotland in this period, they are if anything even more central to the history of Ireland. In the wake of Cromwell's seventeenth-century campaign of conquest, a great many Catholic landowners had been forced to forfeit their land so that it could be given to English Protestants. Further restrictions had followed; a series of early eighteenth-century laws made it illegal for Catholics to inherit or to purchase land—or to lease land for any period longer than 31 years. The laws had the desired effect: by 1778 no more than 7 per cent of Ireland was still owned by Catholics. In some cases those Catholics with the means to do so went abroad; more commonly those who had been displaced were effectively forced to become tenant farmers on lands now held by Protestant English or Anglo-Irish landowners—or else to face desperate poverty, even starvation.

Even for those who did become established as tenant farmers, starvation remained a real possibility through most of the eighteenth and nineteenth centuries. The import and export restrictions that enforced Irish economic dependence on England helped to keep prices high, and absentee landlords often failed to maintain their properties, increasing the level of hardship suffered by tenant farmers.

Throughout this period, then, the Protestant, English-speaking Anglo-Irish class dominated and exploited the much larger native Irish population, which spoke Irish Gaelic (often referred to simply as *Irish*) and was predominantly Catholic. Confiscation of land and severe economic hardship for the Irish Catholic majority were only the most visible manifestations of deprivation at the hands of Protestant English and Anglo-Irish rule; a wide range of Penal Laws discriminated against

Catholics in myriad ways. By the 1790s some of the more extreme of the Penal Laws imposed in the seventeenth and eighteenth centuries had been weakened or repealed, but the weight of the system was still overwhelmingly oppressive for the Catholic majority. In such circumstances it can hardly be surprising that the possibility of rebellion was continually mooted.

The figure who became the leading voice for sweeping change was a Protestant rather than a Catholic; the young lawyer Wolfe Tone's idealistic vision was of an Ireland freed from the yoke of English control—an Ireland in which Catholic and Protestant (including not only Anglicans but also Presbyterians, who had, like the Catholics, been disenfranchised) could live side by side on an equal footing, and at peace. In 1791 Tone became one of the founders of the Society of United Irishmen, a group devoted to bringing those ideals to fruition. Within a few years the group—which by 1797 numbered over 300,000—began to contemplate seriously the possibility of an armed insurrection, and major rebellions were planned both in 1796 and 1798. The first of these foundered when bad weather threw off a planned invasion by a large French fleet; the second did indeed become a major rebellion, but the French provided far less support than the rebels had hoped for, and the uprising was suppressed in short order by government forces. Most of the leaders were captured and executed (Tone slit his own throat in prison before he could be hanged), but the spirit of rebellion was not extinguished; guerrilla attacks occurred periodically, and another rebellion briefly broke out in 1803.

Though Ireland had long been effectively under English control, the Irish had always been allowed a separate parliament—and a new Irish constitution in 1782 had granted that parliament a greater degree of autonomy than it had previously possessed. (Here it is important to remember that the "Irish" parliament was in fact open only to the Anglo-Irish; the native Irish population was entirely excluded from political life.) Even before the rebellion of 1798 many in England felt that the Anglo-Irish were doing a poor job of running Ireland, and that English as well as Anglo-Irish interests would be better served by uniting Ireland with England—thereby bringing Ireland under the direct control of the English. The rebellion strengthened those feelings, and in 1800 Acts of Union were introduced in both the English and Irish Parliaments.

Whether or not to support the Acts was an issue that to some extent cut across established lines. Many in England who were essentially anti-Irish felt that "the Irish" had to be brought under tighter control, and that this was the way to do it. But supporters of the Acts of Union were also to be found among those who believed that a fair deal for Catholics in Ireland would come sooner from an English Parliament than an Anglo-Irish one, and that union would put an end to many of the trade restrictions and other forms of economic discrimination that had held back the Irish economy. In Ireland, these arguments were not as well received; the remnants of the United Irishmen were of course against greater English control—but so was the conservative Anglo-Irish aristocracy that the United Irishmen had so bitterly opposed in the rebellion. The idea was so unpopular among the Anglo-Irish elite that the English resorted to outright bribery in order to ensure that an Act of Union was passed by the Irish parliament.

The union continued throughout the century to be highly unpopular in Ireland, and periodic attempts were made over the succeeding decades to have it repealed and a "Kingdom of Ireland" restored, such that Ireland would retain some control over its domestic affairs, with England continuing to act on its behalf in foreign affairs. (By 1840 the cause of bringing a measure of independence to Ireland had come to be known as "Home Rule.") Increasingly, however, such efforts were led not by Anglo-Irish leaders but by Catholic ones—most notably Daniel O'Connell. O'Connell achieved a partial success with the passage in 1829 of the Roman Catholic Relief Act, which repealed the last of the Penal Laws, allowing Catholics to be elected to parliament and to be accorded the same civil rights as Protestants. There was, however, a catch: in conjunction with the Roman Catholic Relief Act, Parliament also passed the Parliamentary Elections (Ireland) Act, which effectively disenfranchised most of the Catholic population by quintupling the financial qualification required to qualify as a voter. (Prior to 1829 the vote was available to men owning or renting land worth two pounds; with the 1829 act the amount was increased to ten pounds.)

A success so qualified was still an enormous step forward; not for nothing did O'Connell come to be referred to as "The Liberator" and "The Emancipator." O'Connell was known too for the power of his rhetoric; aesthetically as well as politically, Ireland was for O'Connell (and for most other Irish people) a nation unto itself:

> Among the nations of the earth, Ireland stands number one in the physical strength of her sons and in the beauty and purity of her daughters. Ireland, land of my forefathers, how my mind expands, and my spirit walks abroad in something of majesty, when I contemplate the high qualities, inestimable virtues, and true purity and piety and religious fidelity of the inhabitants of your green fields.... Nature herself has written her character with the finest beauty in the verdant plains that surround us. Let any man run around the horizon with his eye, and tell me if created nature ever produced anything so green and so lovely, so undulating, so teeming with production.

Pride in Ireland may have remained strong through this era, but the Irish language was in steady decline. In 1800 a majority of the Irish peasantry were able to speak English, but most spoke Irish too; in western counties such as Kerry and Donegal many spoke only Irish. By 1850, it is estimated that those able to speak Irish were in the minority, and almost no one was a unilingual Irish-speaker.

Given the degree to which Irish was discouraged, it is hardly surprising that the Irish literature of the era is almost entirely in English. The novels of Maria Edgeworth and of Gerald Griffin; the novels, plays, and poems of John Banim (most notably the short fiction collected in the three volumes of *Tales of the O'Hara Family*); and the poems of Thomas Moore—all these were written in English. So too was *Pizarro*, the last work of Richard Brinsley Sheridan, an author usually associated with the literature of the previous era. The five-act play, first performed in 1799, became one of the most popular dramatic works of the entire nineteenth century. Set during the Spanish Conquest of Peru, *Pizarro* dramatizes English fears of invasion by Revolutionary France, but also engages critically with Britain's colonial exploits abroad.

Though the history and culture of Wales are arguably as distinct from that of England as are the histories and cultures of Scotland and Ireland, Wales experienced a period of relative calm through the late eighteenth and early nineteenth centuries. English control of Wales assumed softer forms in this era, without brutal oppression or violent rebellion. A majority appear to have been fluent in Welsh (education in Welsh was not prohibited), but as in Scotland and Ireland, published literature was almost exclusively written in English; indeed, the most significant Welsh writer of the period—Felicia Hemans[1]—became known in the later nineteenth and early twentieth centuries above all for her patriotic poems "Casabianca" and "The Homes of England." Other notable writers of the period include the poet Jane Cave and the poet and hymn-writer Ann Griffiths.

The greatest conflicts in Wales during the period were religious in nature. Methodism and Calvinism had grown in Wales throughout much of the eighteenth and early nineteenth centuries, and in 1811 the Welsh branch of the Church of England seceded from the larger body. By 1823 the Presbyterian Church of Wales had been formed—and various other forms of non-conforming Protestantism had also developed deep roots.

Like Scotland, Wales was far more affected by the Industrial Revolution in the late eighteenth and early nineteenth centuries than was Ireland. Mining—and in particular the coal mining industry—drove economic growth, especially in the cities of Cardiff and Swansea. Overall, the population of Wales increased from little more than a half million in the late eighteenth century to more than a million by 1840.

[1] Though Hemans was born in Liverpool and is sometimes treated as an English poet, she considered herself Welsh and spent most of her life in Wales.

The Romantic Mind and Its Literary Productions

It is not surprising that in a world overwhelmingly concerned with change, revolution, and freedom the makers of literature should be similarly preoccupied; as has already been discussed, the French Revolution and its aftermath lent vital force to the Romantic impulse. That force, though, was not exerted on all the literary minds in the Romantic era with equal force or in quite the same direction. For several of the leading figures of English Romanticism, the freedom that animated the poetic imagination was only tangentially related to the collectivist enterprise that the revolution in France had represented. Instead, it was very much an *individual* freedom; the freeing of the individual mind and the individual soul took pride of place. Subjective experience and the role that it played in the individual's response to and experience of reality are dominant themes in the works of the Romantics. Wordsworth's "Ode: Intimations of Immortality" (1807) surveys what becomes of the "heaven-born freedom" with which every individual who enters the world is born. Percy Shelley's *Mont Blanc* (1817) is an extended exploration of power and creativity, and Keats's various odes continually express their author's fascination with the connection between physical experience and the individual human imagination. In Byron's work, subjectivity, creativity, and epistemological questing all find expression in a series of heroes for whom the power of the will is a central concern. The question of what it means to be an individual looms large in the works of all these authors.

Nature became a fulcrum in the balancing of subjective and objective in the Romantic construction of reality, and most of the period's leading writers were particularly preoccupied with the relationship between the natural world and the individual mind. Percy Shelley appealed to the wind, "Make me thy lyre, even as the forest is," and, in "Tintern Abbey," Wordsworth recognized nature as

> The anchor of my purest thoughts, the nurse,
> The guide, the guardian of my heart, and soul
> Of all my moral being.

This commingling of self and nature was, at least in part, an expression of the late eighteenth- and early nineteenth-century tendency to see the natural world in opposition to the human world. In the same poem, for example, Wordsworth describes himself as coming to nature

> more like a man
> Flying from something that he dreads than one
> Who sought the thing he loved.

Less frequently did poets of the Romantic period comment on the relationship between humans and nature as an objective reality. The focus was much more often on what non-human nature had to offer to the individual human soul than on how humans in aggregate were reshaping the natural world. Barbauld was unusual in observing and commenting on the latter clearly; in her grim survey of England in "Eighteen Hundred and Eleven," she described how

> Science and Art urge on the useful toil,
> New mould a climate and create the soil, …
> On yielding Nature urge their new demands,
> And ask not gifts but tribute at her hands.

Such clear-eyed observations of human manipulation of nature were few and far between.

The importance of the subjective sense of reality to the Romantic imagination also comes out clearly in the widespread fascination with the visions experienced in dreams, in nightmares, and other altered states. The question Keats poses at the end of "Ode to a Nightingale" (1819)—"Was it a vision, or a waking dream?"—is of a sort that occurs frequently in the literature of Romanticism. Among the many works of the period that touch on this theme are Coleridge's fragment "Kubla Khan" (which he claimed came to him during a drug-induced sleep); Keats's visionary *The Fall of Hyperion: A Dream*; Mary Shelley's *Frankenstein* (the story of which she claimed came to her in a "waking dream," and in which Victor Frankenstein acquires the habit of taking "every night a small quantity of laudanum" in order to "gain the rest necessary for the preservation of life"); and De Quincey's *Confessions of an English Opium-Eater*.

J.M.W. Turner, *Melrose Abbey*, 1822. Courtesy of the Clark Art Institute, Williamstown, MA. The lines in the lower left corner are (slightly misquoted) from Canto 2 of Sir Walter Scott's long poem *The Lay of the Last Minstrel* (1805): "If thou would'st view fair Melrose aright, / Go visit it by the pale moonlight."

In the work of female writers of the period, interest in the individual and the mind often took different forms from those that engaged the interest of male writers. Many were concerned with education: Hannah More produced a series of Cheap Repository Tracts designed to enlighten the poor, while Maria Edgeworth gained fame as a children's writer and educationalist. Mary Wollstonecraft authored not only her famous *Vindication of the Rights of Woman*, but also *Thoughts on the Education of Daughters* (1787) and *The Female Reader* (1789). The Romantic period abounded in outspoken female writers who engaged with the issues of their day and sought to make a difference in their world. While Wollstonecraft would eventually be condemned for supposed sexual immorality, another more conservative group of educated women were derided as "Bluestockings," unnatural women who revealed their prudishness through their interest in intellectual pursuits. In their own day, the writings of these authors made little, if any, difference to the social, legal, and economic position of women, who remained little more than property in the eyes of the law for many more years. But over the longer term their impact was considerable; Wollstonecraft and the Bluestockings laid the intellectual foundations for the social and political progress of women that would slowly be achieved over the next 200 years and more.

It would be a mistake to think of the female writers of the Romantic period as solely concerned with women's rights and with the stereotypical "female arenas" of education and religion, however. Much of the writing by women in this period is as broadly engaged in the issues of the time as anything produced by their male counterparts, and many women writers exerted a significant shaping effect on the style and substance of Romantic literature. Mary Robinson, for example—famous first as an actress and mistress of the Prince of Wales, then as a successful poet and novelist—earned the admiration of both Wordsworth and Coleridge (who called her "an undoubted genius") and preceded them in the writing of poetry concerned with the poor and disenfranchised. In her influential *Elegiac Sonnets* (1784), Charlotte Smith modeled an approach to emotional intensity and incisive self-examination that has come to be associated with the male Romantics—and did so more than a decade before the publication of *Lyrical Ballads*. Poet Felicia Hemans rivaled (indeed, perhaps surpassed) Byron in popularity. Playwright Joanna Baillie, famous for producing works that, as she put it, "delineate the progress of the higher passions in the human breast," was considered by Walter Scott to be "the best dramatic writer since the days of Shakespeare."

One area of common ground for almost all Romantic writers, male and female, was a strong interest in the "Imagination," the creative power by which an individual took the raw material of the physical world and transformed it into art. Although "Imagination" was recognized as being distinct from religious inspiration, descriptions of imaginative or poetic power often took on strong religious overtones, as in Blake's assertion that "One Power alone makes a Poet: Imagination, the Divine Vision." Coleridge, Blake, and Wordsworth were all deeply invested in the notion of the poet as *vates*, or prophet. And the imagination was seen as invested with moral as well as prophetic power, as the Romantics saw the realms of the aesthetic and the moral as being closely bound up with each other. Earlier ages, too, had linked the aesthetic and the moral, but had tended to see literature as expressing truths emanating from elsewhere and the ethical element of literature as inhering in its ability to illustrate virtues and vices and point out moral lessons. In contrast, leading Romantics tended to locate the moral aspects of literature—and life itself—largely in the imagination, and tended to see the imagination as embodying truth as well as morality. "The great instrument of moral good," wrote Percy Shelley in his *Defence of Poetry* (1821), "is the imagination," while Keats proclaimed that "what the imagination seizes as beauty must be the truth."[1] More broadly, a belief took root among poets—the most prominent male Romantic poets in particular—that the aesthetic and imaginative

[1] Keats's notion of the value of "negative capability—that is, when a man is capable of being in uncertainties, mysteries, doubts, without any irritable reaching after fact and reason"—destabilizes in interesting ways the connections that he and other Romantics drew between morality and the imagination and between the imagination and truth.

truths of poetry were possessed of a transcendent status, a status that placed such insights above the historical or scientific truths of the ordinary world.

Another opposition that animates the literature of the Romantic period is that between sense and sensibility—a tension with parallels to that between reason and emotion in the intellectual landscape of any age, but also one possessing elements particular to the late eighteenth and early nineteenth centuries. In this era, the terms "sentiment," "sentimentality," "sentimentalism," and "sensibility" were all widely used (and to some extent overlapped in meaning), but none was more used than "sensibility." The concept of "sensibility" entailed strong emotional responsiveness, with life and literary work animated by powerful feeling. Indeed, "sensibility" was frequently associated with emotional excess: when Jane Austen describes Marianne's "excess of sensibility" in *Sense and Sensibility* (1811), she is using the notion of sensibility in ways that would have been familiar to any late eighteenth- or early nineteenth-century reader:

> She was sensible and clever; but eager in every thing; her sorrows, her joys, could have no moderation. She was generous, amiable, interesting: she was every thing but prudent. The resemblance between her and her mother was strikingly great. Elinor saw, with concern, the excess of her sister's sensibility; but by Mrs. Dashwood it was valued and cherished.

It may well be that most educated Britons of the period privileged sense over sensibility in very much the way that Austen appears to do. But it is also true that the feelings associated with Romantic sensibility—above all, as they were expressed in poetry—became the defining passions of the age. And the poetry of sensibility carried ideological as well as aesthetic force; for a considerable period it stood in the vanguard of the movement for social and political change.

That is not to say that the distinction separating poets of sensibility from the rest was entirely clear; far from it. Rather in the way that competing factions today will sometimes each accuse the other of being controlled by their emotions rather than their reason, many in the late eighteenth century tried to situate sensibility in a natural alliance with political views they opposed. Anti-Jacobins suggested there was a natural affinity between the supposed excesses of sensibility and those of political radicalism, while radicals often portrayed sensibility as associated with reactionary political views. In truth, the language of sensibility was used by both sides.

Also among the oppositions that occur throughout the literature of the Romantic period is that between the natural and the artificial, which was sometimes linked to the opposition between the original and the imitative. If "artificial" is taken simply to mean "human-made," of course, the distinction between the natural and the artificial is purely a matter of physical process. But "artificial" and "natural" as matters of taste and of style have more fluid meanings. As the culture of sentiment and of sensibility grew over the course of the eighteenth century, "artificial" came to be used less and less frequently to mean "displaying special art or skill" and more and more frequently to mean "contrived, shaped in a way not spontaneous or natural," or even "not expressive of reality." The divide between natural and artificial was felt to connect with that between "novelty" of thought and expression—"originality," as we would call it—and the "servility" of the stale or overly imitative. Whereas the Neoclassical poets had proudly imitated classical models, often devoting themselves to translating Classical works into English poetry, Romantic writers—and the leading Romantic poets in particular—had little interest in seeing the work of earlier eras as models to be imitated. They might admire the poets of earlier eras, they might be inspired by them—by Shakespeare and by Milton above all—and they might aspire to similar glory, but they had no interest in taking the same path to glory. If not entirely for the first time, then certainly to an unprecedented degree, originality came in the Romantic period to be seen as a criterion of poetic achievement.

Even at the beginning of the period we find originality embraced as an aesthetic value. A 1791 assessment of a volume of Robinson's poetry, for example, praises originality, even as it sets up an opposition between the original and the natural—two qualities often assumed to normally accompany each other:

Henry Fuseli, *The Nightmare*, 1790–91. The Swiss-born artist Fuseli (1741–1825) moved to England in 1779, and soon became one of the leading artistic figures of the day. Beginning in 1781, Fuseli painted several different versions of *The Nightmare*, for which he became famous; it remains an iconic image of the Gothic sensibility, and of Romantic interest in what we now term "the unconscious."

Fuseli moved in London's artistic and intellectual circles through the 1790s, and was briefly involved romantically with Mary Wollstonecraft before her marriage to William Godwin.

Anne-Louis Girodet de Roussy-Trioson, *Sommeil d'Endymion* (*The Sleep of Endymion*), 1791. According to Greek myth, the mortal man Endymion was so beautiful that he attracted the love of the goddess Diana (associated with chastity and the moon). Zeus placed Endymion in an eternal sleep, but also gave him eternal youth to preserve his appearance. Girodet's painting depicts the slumbering Endymion, visited by Diana in the form of a moonbeam, as Amor (Cupid) watches disguised as Zephyr (the west wind). Girodet, a student of the important Neoclassical artist Jacques-Louis David (1748–1825), signaled his independence from David and established his reputation with this work, which played an influential role in the development of early Romantic painting.

Jacques-Louis David, *Bonaparte*, 1798.

Artist unknown, *A Stoppage to a Stride over the Globe*, 1803.

William Blake, "The Sun Standing at His Eastern Gate," illustration to John Milton's "L'Allegro," c. 1816–20.

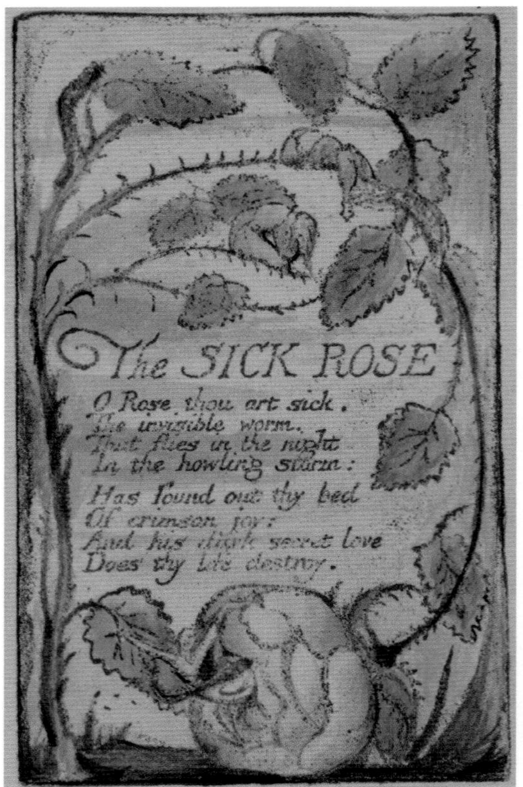

William Blake, "The Sick Rose," from *Songs of Experience*, 1794.

Philip James de Loutherbourg, *Coalbrookdale by Night*, 1801. The small Shropshire town of Coalbrookdale has been sometimes described as the birthplace of the Industrial Revolution. Located in a gorge on the River Severn, it was the site of the first ironworks that used the modern method of smelting with coke rather than charcoal (an innovation of Joseph Darby in 1709). Together with the adjacent towns of Madeley, Ironbridge, Jackfield, and Coalport, Coalbrookdale was part of an early industrial powerhouse; at the end of the eighteenth century it had a greater concentration of furnaces and forges than anywhere else in the world. Darby's son Abraham also constructed the world's first iron bridge nearby in 1779; the bridge and much of the old ironworks remain today, and the Ironbridge Gorge has been declared a World Heritage Site.

Thomas Phillips, *George Gordon, Lord Byron*, 1813. Byron is wearing clothing of a sort native to the region of Epirus (then part of Albania, now part of northern Greece); he had bought this outfit while traveling through the area in 1809.

John Martin, *The Bard*, 1817. According to legend, when Edward I conquered Wales for England in the late thirteenth century, he ordered the killing of all the Welsh bards—professional poet-musicians and keepers of Welsh history and tradition. The story of "the massacre of the bards" inspired a number of writers and artists of the eighteenth and nineteenth centuries, including John Martin, whose painting above depicts a survivor of the massacre; the English army is also visible in the lower foreground. Martin, born in poverty in rural Northumberland, achieved enormous popular success during his lifetime with his large-scale paintings, many of which depict biblical scenes.

Elizabeth Leveson-Gower, *Mountain Landscape*, c. 1830. Leveson-Gower published two volumes based on her watercolor images of Scottish landscapes, the first a collection of etchings, *Views of Orkney and the North-Eastern Coast of Scotland* (1807), and the second a volume of twenty aquatints, *Views on the Northern and Western Coasts of Sutherland* (1833). The artist intended that various of the wide Sutherland images be joined together to form 360 degree scenic panoramas.

Louis Édouard Fournier, *The Funeral of Shelley*, 1889. To the left stand Shelley's friends Edward Trelawny, Leigh Hunt, and George Gordon, Lord Byron. According to Trelawny's account, Shelley's heart "would not take the flame." It was said to have been given initially to Leigh Hunt and then to Mary Shelley; Shelley's other remains were buried in Rome.

Shelley's funeral occurred on 16 August 1822. We know that this much later image is in some respects inaccurate; Leigh Hunt, for example, remained in the carriage throughout the ceremony. (National Museums, Liverpool)

John Orlando Parry, *A London Street Scene*, 1835. This watercolor shows the posters in extraordinary detail, and shows, too, a number of small details of human life in the activities of the figures—among them a pickpocket, a guard, a chimney sweep, and a woman selling roasted chestnuts.

J.M.W. Turner, *The Burning of the Houses of Parliament*, 1835. In the 1830s it became Turner's practice to send unfinished work (often with only rough underpainting completed) to the Royal Academy in advance of its annual exhibition. During the period devoted (in the case of other artists) to the varnishing of already-completed work, Turner would complete the painting itself, often watched by a sizeable crowd. An eyewitness, E.V. Rippingille, described Turner completing *The Burning of the Houses of Parliament* in 1835:

> For [the] three hours I was there ... he never ceased to work, or even once looked or turned from the wall in which his picture was hung. A small box of colors, a few very small brushes, and a vial or two, were at his feet ... In one part of the mysterious proceedings Turner, who worked almost entirely with his palette knife, was observed to be rolling and spreading a half-transparent stuff over his picture, the size of a finger in length and thickness. As Callcott was looking on I ventured to say ... "What is that he is plastering his picture with?" to which enquiry it was replied, "should be sorry to be the man to ask him" ... Presently the work was finished: Turner gathered his tools together, put them into and shut the box, and then with his face still turned to the wall, and at the same distance from it, went sidelong off, without speaking a word to anybody ... Maclise, who stood near, remarked, "There, that's masterly, he does not stop to look at his work; he knows it is done, and he is off!"

J.M.W. Turner, *Slavers Throwing Overboard the Dead and Dying—Typhoon Coming On*, 1840. Turner's painting depicts a 1781 incident in which Captain Luke Collingwood of the slave ship *Zong*, with his ship running short of water and other supplies when it had been blown off-course during a severe storm, ordered that all sick and dying slaves be thrown overboard; 133 were killed as a result. Insurance was a factor in Collingwood's decision; compensation could be claimed for property lost or jettisoned in storms, but not for slaves killed by disease or other natural causes. The incident became widely publicized and spurred support for the abolitionist movement. In the ensuing legal case the court upheld the insurance company's financial liability; no criminal charges were brought against the captain. In the twentieth century the incident became the basis for several literary works, including a long poem by David Dabydeen and a novel by Fred D'Aguiar.

> The attempt at originality is in all pursuits laudable. Invention is a noble attribute of the mind. But the danger is, lest, by pursuing it too intensely, we deviate so far from ease and nature, that the real object of Poetry, that of touching the heart, be lost.

A more familiar set of oppositions involving the natural and the artificial, the "original" and the imitative, is put forward by William Hazlitt in his *The Spirit of the Age* (1825), as he assesses at the end of the Romantic period the place of Wordsworth in the poetry and the intellectual life of the age:

> His popular, inartificial style gets rid (at a blow) of all the trappings of verse, of all the high places of poetry: "the cloud-capt towers, the solemn temples, the gorgeous palaces," are swept to the ground.... All the traditions of learning, all the superstitions of age, are obliterated and effaced. We begin *de novo* on a *tabula rasa* of poetry.... He chooses to have his subject a foil to his invention, to owe nothing but to himself.... Taught by political opinions to say to the vain pomp and glory of the world, "I hate ye," seeing the path of classical and artificial poetry blocked up by the cumbrous ornaments of style and turgid common-places, so that nothing more could be achieved in that direction but by the most ridiculous bombast or the tamest servility, he has ... struck into the sequestered vale of humble life, sought out the muse among sheep-cotes and hamlets, and the peasant's mountain-haunts, has discarded all the tinsel pageantry of verse, and endeavored (not in vain) to ... add the charm of novelty to the familiar.

In passages such as this one, we may see the paradigms according to which the literature of the Romantic period is still largely seen being articulated even before the period had ended. On the one side are the natural, the spontaneous, the original, fresh and new; on the other, the artificial, the studied, the imitative, the tired, and traditional. On the one side, imagination and sensibility; on the other, excessive rationalism. On the one side, a passion for freedom, especially, aesthetic freedom and freedom of the spirit; on the other, restraint, reaction, oppression. On the one side, in short, the Romantic; on the other, the classical, the Neoclassical, the conservative.

If these sets of oppositions often bear some correspondence to reality, it is important to recognize that the correspondences are just as often loose and unreliable. Romantic literature—the Romantic period itself—is filled with unexpected parallels, with surprising evolutions, with unexpected paradoxes, with outright contradictions. The Della Cruscans[1] and their followers, for example, have often been taken to task for the supposed artificiality of their verse. Wordsworth, usually seen as the great poet of a natural world set apart from the oppressive workings of the human-made world of cities and factories, wrote, in 1833, that "Steamboats, Viaducts, and Railways ... Nature doth embrace / Her lawful offspring in Man's art." Coleridge, who in the early 1790s felt strongly the attractions of sensibility and planned to establish a community in Pennsylvania founded on revolutionary democratic ideals, became in later life as dismissive of sensibility as he was of revolutionary fervor. Byron, the paradigmatic Romantic figure, professed to reject many of the impulses at the core of the Romantic movement; in "To Romance" (1807), he vows to leave the realms of romance "for those of truth":

> Romance! disgusted with deceit,
> Far from thy motley court I fly,
> Where Affectation holds her seat,
> And sickly Sensibility ...

Keats, for his part, is perhaps at his most enthusiastic when he exclaims not over nature or freedom but over the experience of classical literature ("On First Looking into Chapman's Homer" [1816]) and classical art ("On Seeing the Elgin Marbles" [1817], "Ode on a Grecian Urn" [1819]). The distinctions made in the attempt to define the essence of the Romantic, in short, often become elusive or indistinct when it comes to particulars; indeed, such divisions can be downright misleading. Throughout most of the nineteenth and twentieth

[1] The Della Cruscans were poets of sensibility who, in the late 1780s and early 1790s, took the lead in exuberantly embracing revolutionary freedom in the wake of the French Revolution.

centuries, literary critics and theorists tended to accept very much at face value the Romantics' self-representations of the nature and importance of their work; more recently, these self-representations have been frequently problematized and widely challenged.

There have been few challenges, however, to the view that this was a period of revolutionary developments—or to the notion that at the center of those developments (so far as English literature is concerned) was an extraordinary body of verse. Looking back, in 1832, Letitia Landon was among those who identified poetry as a particular locus of change:

> Already there is a wide gulf between the last century and the present. In religion, in philosophy, in politics, in manners, there has passed a great change; but in none has been worked a greater change than in poetry, whether as regards the art itself, or the general feeling towards it.

Poetic ambition was in itself central to the spirit of Romanticism. When they spoke of the confident outpouring of Romantic verse, Romantic poets did not hesitate to compare their own work to that of the great poets of the past—and to feel themselves capable of such greatness. "I would sooner fail than not be among the greatest," wrote Keats.

The tendencies of our own age, when poetry is usually taken in small doses and the lyric mode predominates, sometimes lead modern readers to place far less emphasis than did the Romantics themselves on their longer works. The shorter poems of the Romantic canon are justly celebrated—among them Smith's *Elegiac Sonnets* (1784–97), Blake's *Songs of Innocence and of Experience* (1794), several of the sonnets in Robinson's *Sappho and Phaon* sequence (1796), Wordsworth's "The World Is Too Much with Us" and "I Wandered Lonely as a Cloud" (both 1807), Coleridge's "Dejection: An Ode" (1802), Byron's "She Walks in Beauty" (1814), Percy Shelley's "To a Skylark" (1820), Barbauld's "The Caterpillar" (1825), and Keats's odes and sonnets. Wordsworth and Coleridge's *Lyrical Ballads* is rightly seen as the era's most significant single volume of literature. But even as these works retain pride of place, it is important to give full notice to the vast range of the ambitions of the Romantic poets—ambitions that found their fullest expression in extended poetic work. Blake's long prophetic poems charted new territory for English verse, both in the poetry itself and in his unique marriage of the verbal and the visual. Robinson's more substantial works include the series of longer poems on related themes that were eventually published as the sequence *The Progress of Liberty* (1806). Landon was arguably best known in her lifetime for long works such as "The Improvisatrice" (1824), a series of love narratives linked by a larger narrative frame. Over the course of some 50 years, Wordsworth reworked his poetic autobiography, *The Prelude*, into an 8,000-line epic. Coleridge's narrative poems "The Rime of the Ancient Mariner" and "Christabel" (1800) are works of modest extent by comparison with these—but still long by modern standards. Byron gave extraordinary new life to the epic romance with *Childe Harold*, broke new ground poetically with what he termed the "epic satire" of *Don Juan* (1824), and wrote seven full-length poetic dramas. Mary Tighe published little other than her long poem *Psyche* (1805), but that poem alone was enough to establish her as a significant poet. Percy Shelley's long works encompass not only the complex allegorical drama *Prometheus Unbound* (1820) but also the poems "The Mask of Anarchy" (1819) and "Adonais"[1] (1821) and the poetic drama *The Cenci* (1819). Keats's *Endymion* (1818) is another memorable work of epic proportions. And, though Keats abandoned both the original epic-length version of his *Hyperion* (1819) and the later *The Fall of Hyperion: A Dream* (1821), what remains of both also constitutes a very substantial poetic achievement. Charlotte Smith's monumental poem of history, nature, and the self, "Beachy Head" (1807), is a landmark in early nineteenth-century poetry, while George Crabbe's *The Borough* (1810) memorialized village life in meticulous detail. Felicia Hemans's most significant works are the poetic drama *The Siege of Valencia* (1823) and the 19 poems that together comprise *Records of Woman* (1828).

[1] Subtitled "An Elegy on the Death of John Keats," the poem is a pastoral elegy, written by Shelley upon hearing of Keats's death.

The ambitions of the Romantic poets extended, too, to poetic theory and criticism; to a heretofore unprecedented degree, the leading writers of the time were also the leading critics and theorists. Wordsworth's "Preface" to the *Lyrical Ballads*, in its various versions; Shelley's *A Defence of Poetry*; Coleridge's enormously influential body of literary theory and criticism; Baillie's "Introductory Discourse" to her *Plays on the Passions* (1798); Barbauld's extensive body of critical commentary on the novel; Landon's reviews for *The Critical Gazette*; and Keats's critically insightful letters have all long been regarded as central documents in the literature of Romanticism.

The novel, dramatic writing, and the essay all flourished alongside poetry in the Romantic period, even if these genres were not accorded the same degree of respect as poetry. Barbauld commented wryly on the situation of the novel in 1810:

> A collection of novels has a better chance of giving pleasure than of commanding respect. Books of this description are condemned to the grave and despised by the fastidious; but their leaves are seldom found unopened, and they occupy the parlour and the dressing-room while productions of higher name are often gathering dust upon the shelf.

Though such laments reflected the perception of the novel fairly accurately, the novel nonetheless became increasingly popular, and the changes and innovations to the form arising during the Romantic period continue to reverberate and resonate to this day.

The Romantic era saw the decline of that mainstay of eighteenth-century prose, the epistolary novel, and the development and proliferation of other forms of fiction. James Hogg produced one of the great masterpieces of psychological literature, *The Private Memoirs and Confessions of a Justified Sinner* (1824). This period also saw the development and increasing popularity of historical novels. Maria Edgeworth's widely read *Castle Rackrent* (1800), a work considered by many to be the first in the genre, displays attributes of the comedy of manners alongside qualities of the nascent historical novel; in the Irish dialect of its quirky unreliable narrator, *Castle Rackrent* recounts the moral and financial failures of the Anglo-Irish Rackrent family. Edgeworth's novel was followed by works such as Sydney Owenson's *The Wild Irish Girl* (1806) and Jane Porter's *Scottish Chiefs* (1810), which similarly celebrated specific nationhood within Britain. Inspired by Edgeworth's work in particular, Sir Walter Scott developed the historical novel into the genre we now recognize, reshaping notions not just of "the historical novel" but of the novel itself. After beginning his career as a highly successful poet, he switched to long fiction in 1814 and produced a succession of extraordinarily popular novels, including *Waverley* (1814), *Rob Roy* (1817), and *Ivanhoe* (1819), the first modern bestsellers. Using his works to explore the ongoing political struggles of the time—the clash between traditionalism and progress, the tempting attractions of an idealized past that is really a cover for abuse and exploitation, the struggles and missteps that characterize the creation of a just society—Scott at the same time created vivid, entirely engrossing characters. Indeed, one hallmark of his writing is his ability to use these fully realized individuals to give human expression to broad social and political issues.

Scott produced more than twenty-five full length novels, as well as a number of other works. His use of dialect (following Edgeworth) and his decision to set his works almost exclusively in Scotland validated the language and folklore of regional and marginalized people at a time when "British" was increasingly equated with "English." His use of editorial personae, interlocutors, mediated (sometimes twice-mediated) story presentation, and complexly constructed authorial selves raise questions about the natures of authority and authorship, the difficulty of interpretation, and the concept of truth itself. Scott not only largely created the now well-known version of "Scotland" as a land of kilts and clans, with fierce rivalries fought out against a backdrop of misty mountains and purple heather, filled with eccentric but kind-hearted peasants, he also anticipated or pioneered many of the devices associated with modern and post-modern literature.

Many novels of the period, including Scott's, had roots in an earlier form of long prose fiction, the romance. Whereas "romance novel" today usually denotes a form of pulp fiction focused on romantic love as wish-fulfillment, the tradition of romance literature has its roots in medieval tales of the supernatural, of chivalry, and of courtly love, in which a sense of the extraordinary or the fantastic continually colors the narrative. The genre of romance made its influence felt in several different sorts of literary work in the Romantic era, but none more so than the Gothic. Gothic works of the late eighteenth and early nineteenth centuries—novels, but also poems, short stories, and plays—typically investigate human responses to real or apparent supernatural occurrences, or those things thought to be "impossible," thanks to the advances of science and natural history. These works tend to feature stereotypical characters and to take place in worlds temporally or geographically distant from England. The surrounding landscape is often highly symbolic, reflecting the psychological world of the characters, and the heroine's plight—and the protagonist was almost without fail a heroine—is usually rendered in highly expressive rhetoric, full of rhapsodic feeling. The structure of Gothic literary work frequently corresponds to the political and social tensions that result from the integration of long-ago, remotely historical time—preserved in ancient castles or abbeys—into an otherwise modern world. The Gothic setting of Charlotte Smith's *Emmeline, the Orphan of the Castle* (1788), for example, allows for the exploration of social concerns such as English laws of primogeniture[1] and women's social status and identity within the frame of a courtship novel. Her novel illustrates the ways in which the frightening, distorted world of the Gothic could also serve as a forum for social commentary—as it also does in William Godwin's *Caleb Williams* (1794) and in Eliza Fenwick's *Secresy* (1795). Gothic novels such as Matthew Lewis's *The Monk* (1796), Charlotte Dacre's *Zofloya, or The Moor* (1806), Charles Maturin's *Melmoth the Wanderer* (1820), and Ann Radcliffe's series of highly successful Gothic novels, including *The Romance of the Forest* (1791) and *The Mysteries of Udolpho* (1794), welcomed their readers into a world marked by sexual perversity, threatened female virtue, and grotesque sights and experiences. Concerned with revealing what lay repressed or hidden behind the mask of middle-class conformity, the Gothic also often veered into savagery and melodrama, tendencies captured perfectly in the following exchange from *The Vampyre* (1819), by John Polidori, in which a mysterious villain extracts a promise from his traveling companion:

> "Swear!" cried the dying man raising himself with exultant violence. "Swear by all your soul reveres, by all your nature fears, swear that for a year and a day you will not impart your knowledge of my crimes or death to any living being in any way, whatever may happen, or whatever you may see."—His eyes seemed bursting from their sockets; "I swear!" said Aubrey; he sunk laughing upon his pillow, and breathed no more.

If the heightened atmosphere of the Gothic novel often tends toward imaginative excess, it can also foster literary art of the highest order—as *Frankenstein*, Mary Shelley's famous first novel, amply demonstrates. The story of a "monster" who turns against his creator Victor Frankenstein, *Frankenstein* is, on one level, a gripping tale of adventure, written with apparent simplicity. But it is also a text that brings together virtually all the great themes of the era: freedom and oppression; science and nature; society and the individual; knowledge and power; gender and sexuality; dream and reality; creation and destruction; self-deception and self-discovery; death and life; God and the universe.

If one strand of the tradition of romance literature runs through the evolution of the Gothic novel, a strand also runs through the development of the courtship novel in the Romantic period. From Frances Burney's *Camilla* (1796) to Elizabeth Susan Ferrier's *The Inheritance* (1824), the pages of Romantic fiction are filled with young people who are misguided, thwarted, and, ultimately, united in marriage. It seems no exaggeration to say that no author of the period was as successful with the courtship genre as was Jane Austen. Between 1811 and 1817, her six major novels were published, all of them warmly engaging yet sharply observant and often satirical, telling of courtship, social class, and domestic

[1] Primogeniture refers to the common law right of the first-born son to inherit the entire estate, to the exclusion of female and younger male siblings.

life. Much as her novels do not engage directly or obviously with the large issues of her age, Austen reveals a shrewd awareness of both politics and economics, particularly as they concern women; her novels emphasize the limited possibilities open to women during the period in which she wrote. Within this frame, Austen provides a vividly three-dimensional picture of the shaping of character, of the inner world of the emotions as much as the outer world of social behavior. Austen's heroines are preoccupied with wooing, marriage, and the minutiae of income, entailment,[1] and other details of domestic and marital economy, precisely because these dominated and defined the lives of middle- and upper-class women of the period, while her concentration on "3 or 4 Families in a country village" (as she famously remarked to her niece) draws attention to the geographical and physical constraints imposed on such women during this time. Even the happy endings that have delighted generations of Austenites are undercut by the obvious and acknowledged fictionality of the novels—emphasized through authorial asides, direct appeals to the reader, and other devices—by means of which Austen suggests that all happy endings may be mere fictions.

Austen was a skilled stylist, as well as a keen-eyed social critic, bringing to her novels an unprecedented range of novelistic technique. With *Lady Susan* (an early novella, written around 1794 but not published until 1871), she proved herself adept at epistolary narrative; with *Sense and Sensibility*, *Pride and Prejudice*, and *Emma* (1815), she brought new flexibility to the use of the third person narrative voice, demonstrating perfect pitch in a variety of ironic tones, and pioneering the technique now known as free indirect discourse. In this mode of narration, the apparently independent third-person narrative voice temporarily assumes the viewpoint of one or more of the characters—or indeed of an entire social class, as is the case with the famous opening to *Pride and Prejudice*: "It is a truth universally acknowledged, that a single man in possession of a good fortune, must be in want of a wife." In her tone, Austen is at a great remove from the leading poets of the Romantic period, but in the importance she places on the exercise of moral imagination—both by her characters and through her own narrative style—she is very much at one with the age.

Other Romantic novels sought to reflect social and political concerns in fiction more directly than did either most Gothic novels or most courtship novels; a number of writers used the novel as a means of challenging prevailing beliefs and mores. Maria Edgeworth's series of Irish novels—*Castle Rackrent* (1800), *Ennui* (1809), *The Absentee* (1812), and *Ormond* (1817)—explored the colonial relationship between England and Ireland. William Godwin's *Caleb Williams* (1794) sought to reveal, in the author's words, the "perfidiousness exercised by the powerful members of the community against those who are more privileged than themselves." Hogg's *Private Memoirs* was a powerful indictment of the smug superiority that could be engendered by religious zeal. And Mary Hays's *The Victim of Prejudice* (1799), a passionate tale of a young woman who dares to resist the pressure put upon her to marry the man who has raped her, was among those novels that spoke powerfully of injustice in a male-dominated society. Conservative voices also spoke out loudly through the medium of prose fiction; important anti-Jacobin novels of the period include Jane West's *A Tale of the Times* (1799), Elizabeth Hamilton's *Memoirs of Modern Philosophers* (1800), and Charles Lucas's *The Infernal Quixote* (1801). And a number of novelists used the novel as a means of making politically pointed connections with other parts of the world, whether to cast a critical eye on the course of European imperialism—as in Sydney Owenson's *The Missionary* (1811)—or to criticize aspects of British society by presenting them through the view of an outsider—as in Hamilton's *Translations of the Letters of a Hindoo Rajah* (1796).

While the novel prospered and evolved, so too did the genre of non-fiction prose. With the rise of the periodical (see "The Business of Literature" section below) came the rise of first critical and then more general essays, designed to engage, enlighten, and entertain the reader. William Hazlitt, originally intended

[1] Entailment refers to a common law placing restrictions on how a property was to be used and who could inherit it; in practice, entailment was most frequently used to keep property in the hands of male heirs.

for the Church and later an aspiring painter and philosopher, turned his hand to writing and became the most trenchant cultural critic of his time. His works include dramatic, literary, and art criticism, as well as political journalism, general essays, and his famous work *The Spirit of the Age* (1824), a collection of pieces on important figures of the eighteenth century and the Romantic period. His friend Charles Lamb rivaled Hazlitt's renown as an essayist, although his style was very different. Where Hazlitt used plain language and popular modes of construction to express his points cleanly and carefully, Lamb cultivated a more genteel style, rich in allusions and puns, with the resulting prose emerging as both thoughtful and rhetorically complex. Together, the two played a central role in the development of the essay during the Romantic period, but they were far from the only practitioners of the art. From Francis Jeffrey, whose pieces in the *Edinburgh Review* made literary criticism an exercise in stylish perspicacity, to Thomas De Quincey, whose psychological probing anticipates Freud, and Mary Wollstonecraft, whose work anticipates twentieth-century feminism as well as displaying "robust and unwavering" aesthetic judgment, Romantic essay writers worked with a vast range of styles and subjects.

In the field of drama, the Romantic period is traditionally seen as an era of great "closet dramas."[1] In contrast to the drama of the Restoration and early eighteenth century—or that of the later nineteenth and twentieth centuries—serious dramatic writing in the Romantic period was very largely in verse. The period produced Byron's powerful verse drama, *Manfred* (1816–17); his iconoclastic meditation on sin and damnation, *Cain* (1822); and Percy Shelley's mythographic masterpiece, *Prometheus Unbound*; its reputation as a breeding ground for rich, multi-layered poetic theatricals is well deserved. Other serious plays failed on the stage but were widely read and highly praised as literature. Chief among these was Joanna Baillie's series of tragedies, collectively entitled *Plays on the Passions* (1798–1812); depicting the passions "in their rise and progress in the heart" was Baillie's intent, and she believed that such drama could have a moral purpose, though she made no transcendent claims for the moral value of the imagination. Drama, in her view, "improves us by the knowledge we acquire of our own minds, from the natural desire we have to look into the thoughts, and observe the behaviour of others." Baillie's explorations in psychology harked back to Enlightenment concepts, but her plays also engaged powerfully with the issues of her own day, including the question of women's rights.

In Byron's view, the distaste many serious writers felt for the public theater in this period was entirely justified:

> When I first entered upon theatrical affairs, I had some idea of writing for the [play]house myself, but soon became a convert to Pope's opinion of that subject. Who would condescend to the drudgery of the stage, and enslave himself to the humours, the caprices, the taste or tastelessness, of the age? Besides, one must write for particular actors, have them continually in one's eye, sacrifice character to the personating of it, cringe to some favourite of the public, neither give him too many nor too few lines to spout. …

Baillie was rather more charitable, attributing the low tolerance of audiences for serious drama to an escapism born of a desire to find refuge from the "commercial hurricane" of the age—and locating a good deal of the problem in the poor acoustics and lighting of the theaters of the day:

> The Public have now to choose between what we shall suppose are well-written and well-acted plays, the words of which are not heard, or heard but imperfectly by two-thirds of the audience, while the finer and more pleasing traits of the acting are by a still greater proportion lost altogether; and splendid pantomime, or pieces whose chief object is to produce striking scenic effect, which can be seen and comprehended by the whole.

As both Byron's and Baillie's comments indicate, the theater in this period was, in some sense at least, thriving. People thronged to the theaters, where they saw work by such popular and prolific career playwrights as

[1] Closet dramas are plays written not for the stage but for private performance—in a private room or "closet"—or to be read.

Thomas Rowlandson, *Dr. Syntax and a Bookseller*, 1812.

Hannah Cowley and Elizabeth Inchbald. Writers perhaps better known for other genres also wrote successful plays, such as Samuel Taylor Coleridge's *Remorse* (1812) and Charles Maturin's *Bertram* (1816). The Stage Licensing Act of 1737 meant that, in London, only a few theaters—Covent Garden and Drury Lane, and, in the summer, the Haymarket—were permitted to present "legitimate" drama, but this in no way limited theatrical production. Stage entertainments of all sorts were held in venues from pubs to tents. In cities and provinces outside London, theaters sprang up to meet the demands of an increasing audience: a survey completed in 1804 counted 280 playhouses throughout the nation. The Licensing Act also required the texts of plays to be submitted to the Lord Chamberlain for censorship before performance. As a result, many works intended for the stage were forced into the closet; perhaps the most famous example is Percy Shelley's *The Cenci*, a verse drama that features not only father-daughter incest but also parricide. Many new plays, however, were permitted, and a roll call of drama produced between 1780 and 1834 includes everything from light comedy to melodramatic tragedy and from pantomimes to operas, as well as spectacles that featured impressive special effects.

The Business of Literature

The thriving literary scene of the period is intimately tied to developments in the worlds of book publishing, bookselling, and book marketing. The most influential of these was the rise of the periodical. By the 1760s, there were more than 30 periodicals in London alone, including monthly journals, quarterly magazines, and collections of reviews and essays, all designed to inform and stimulate their readers. This boom in the periodical press meant increased employment for those who sought to establish themselves as writers; the demand for articles often outweighed the supply. For readers and publishers, it meant an ever-growing number of publications in which reviews of the latest books might appear. Bound volumes of new books were expensive—a three-volume novel could cost a total of between nine and sixteen shillings—equivalent to $100 or more today.[1] Reviews often printed long extracts, and thus readers who could not afford to buy a book could to some extent experience it through the review. But new books re-

[1] Given that working- and middle-class people in Britain tended to have far less purchasing power than they do now, this price put book-buying out of the reach of most people; if considered relative to the wages of an average British worker, spending nine shillings would be akin to spending several hundred or even several thousand dollars today.

J. Bluck, after Augustus Charles Pugin, *Ackermann's Art Library* (detail), c. 1812–15. Rudolf Ackermann (1764–1834) moved to London from his native Germany and opened a print shop in London on the Strand in 1795, selling books and artist supplies as well as prints, and exhibiting paintings. He later also began to publish color-plate books, the most notable of which was *The Microcosm of London*, a three-volume set with 104 hand-colored aquatint plates by various artists (including Thomas Rowlandson and Augustus Pugin), published between 1808 and 1811.

mained expensive throughout the period; that a great growth in reading and in book buying nevertheless occurred from 1774 (when the old "perpetual copyright" regime ended) onwards is attributable very largely to the publication of cheap octavo editions of works no longer protected by copyright—what literary historian William St. Clair has termed "the old canon" of works by seventeenth- and eighteenth-century authors no longer living.

At the same time as the number of books and of periodicals increased, so did ways of obtaining them. Between 1740 and 1790, the number of outlets nearly doubled. Most obviously, books could be bought: well-established bookshops flourished in cities all over the nation. In provincial towns and villages, where bookselling was not profitable on its own, literature was often sold side by side with stationery, patent medicines, and even groceries. Because the cost of books put them outside the means of many readers, however, some booksellers began to lend volumes to customers for a small fee, thus initiating the circulating library. Payment of a yearly fee enabled patrons to borrow books as they pleased.

Although both circulating and subscription libraries offered a good value, they still lay outside the financial resources of those below the lower middle classes. For these readers, there were other alternatives. Peddlers[1]

[1] Peddlers are travelers who make their living by selling small items they carry with them in a pack.

and hawkers sold street literature that included ballads, sermons, and tracts. Those who could not afford library subscriptions but who wished to read something more than broadsheet ballads or pamphlets often formed book clubs in which a number of people contributed money to buy a single copy of a new book, which they would then share. After all had read the book, it might well be sold to a local bookseller, with the proceeds put toward the price of a new one. Slightly more formally, in numerous towns and villages, the local male elite came together to select and discuss books and pamphlets, usually on a controversial topic of the day. This literature, too, was sold on, often by means of an auction among members at the end of the year.

Perhaps as a result of these efforts in group reading, or perhaps simply because people enjoyed it, reading aloud remained a feature of the Romantic era. The fiction and the non-fiction of the period abounds in scenes of communal reading, and the visions that come down to us range from Countess Granville's admission that when her husband read *Don Juan* to her "I roared till I could neither hear nor see" to Henry Austen's description of his sister Jane as one who "read aloud with very great taste and effect. Her own works, probably, were never heard to such advantage as from her own mouth." Writers of the Romantic period were not very far removed from a time when illiteracy was more common than literacy, a time when literature was still an oral art. It is worth bearing in mind that many of them wrote texts intended to be read aloud, and many of their works gain luster from being heard.

"Romantic"

Of the six periods into which the history of British literature has long been conventionally divided, the era of Romanticism is by far the briefest, extending over less than 40 years. Arguably it is also the most intense, particularly during the years 1789 to 1815: the era not only of the French Revolution and the Napoleonic Wars but also of the most tumultuous literary developments—and an extraordinary number of lasting literary achievements.

This was unquestionably an age of contradiction. It was a period in which political consciousness spread through society in unprecedented ways, with a great growth in collective awareness not only among those whose hearts resonated with revolutionary developments on the continent but also amongst workers, the disenfranchised poor, women, and anti-slavery activists. It was also a time of unprecedented growth in awareness of humans as individuals, of a rights-based political individualism, and of the individualism of the soul.

Applying a broad title to any literary or historical period is always risky. As much as any group of authors and thinkers may at first appear to have in common, deeper examination tends to reveal complexities and complications. Literature, like history, does not occur in isolation. One idea bleeds into another: revolutions are often old ideas returning under new names; factions develop, and their members deny that they are in any way related to the members of other factions. In its own time, Romanticism—a label never used by any of its writers, but rather first applied by the Victorians looking back on the period—was very frequently a house divided. "Lakers"[1] such as Wordsworth and Southey denounced the "Satanic School"[2] of Percy Shelley and Byron, who in turn produced vicious satires of these elders. "The Cockney School"[3] of Londoners Leigh Hunt and John Keats was derided by critics of the day, while writers who were later ignored, such as Hannah More, Samuel Rogers, and Thomas Moore, were lauded for their skill and rewarded with tremendous popularity. The Romantic era gains richness and interest if we view it not as a perfect stream but rather more accurately as a thick murmuring torrent of powerful voices that

[1] The Lake Poets were so known because they resided in the Lake District of northwest England; the three most famous Lake Poets were Wordsworth, Coleridge, and Southey. The name "the Lake School of Poetry" was first used—derisively—in the *Edinburgh Review*.

[2] The name "Satanic School" was first used by Southey in *A Vision of Judgment* (1821), as a condemnation of writers, Byron and Shelley foremost among them, whose literary output was "characterized by a Satanic spirit of pride and audacious impiety."

[3] The term "Cockney School" first appeared in negative reviews of Hunt's poetry in *Blackwood's Magazine* in 1817. John Scott, the editor of *The Statesman*, a literary journal founded by Hunt, died in a duel fought over the contemptuous "Cockney" designation.

chorused and clashed, that simultaneously sought and struggled. These mingled tones together make up the voice of a movement that changed English literature.

A Changing Language

Of all the places in which the political clashes of the Romantic period made themselves felt, perhaps the most surprising was in the arena of linguistics. Concern with questions of nationalism and political loyalties affected the very language of Britain. From 1750 onward, the book market was flooded with pronunciation guides, a deluge inspired by the belief that standardized pronunciation would foster a sense of national unity. In this case, "standard" pronunciation meant the speech of educated urban dwellers. Even as many adhered to the essentially Tory belief that this supposedly standard speech was superior, there grew up a precisely opposite point of view, largely expressed by radical publishers and writers, that in the everyday speech of the common people one might find all that was best and most true about England: honesty, frankness, and English liberty given verbal form. In his *Classical Dictionary of the Vulgar Tongue* (1785), Francis Grose transcribed and celebrated the speech of commoners in their many regional variations, and, in 1818, the radical William Cobbett published his *Grammar of the English Language*, a book which explicitly treated language as a political matter. Cobbett took issue with the "false grammar" that he saw as having been put forward by eighteenth-century "authorities" such as Samuel Johnson, and attacked the grammatical slips as well as the privileged position of kings and nobles in a chapter entitled "Errors and Nonsense in a King's Speech." He addressed his work to the less privileged classes, who he believed should be enabled to participate in political discussions—"to assert with effect the rights and liberties of [their] country." As Cobbett saw it, "tyranny has no enemy so formidable as the pen."

Evidence of the Romantic celebration of "common language" can be found throughout the literature of the period. It accounts in part for the huge popularity of Robert Burns—a poet whose greatest effects come from his mixing of standard English dialect with his native Scots dialect. But it finds its most famous expression in the "Preface" to the 1800 edition of *Lyrical Ballads*. There, Wordsworth writes that

> "men" in "low and rustic life" hourly communicate with the best objects from which the best part of language is originally derived; and because, from their rank in society and the sameness and narrow circle of intercourse, being less under the influence of social vanity they convey their feelings and notions in simple and unelaborated expressions. Accordingly, such language, rising out of repeated experience and regular feelings, is a more permanent, and a far more philosophical language[.] …

Still, it is important to note that Wordsworth's opinions on this point represented a minority view, and the Romantic belief in the "philosophical language" of "low and rustic life" was altogether short-lived, becoming less and less widely held. Fifteen years later, one finds Wordsworth's collaborator on *Lyrical Ballads*, Coleridge, writing that

> The best part of human language, properly so called, is derived from reflection on the acts of the mind itself. It is formed by a voluntary appropriation of fixed symbols to internal acts, to processes and results of imagination, the greater part of which have no place in the consciousness of the uneducated man. …

As the Romantic period slid into the Victorian and the vogue for rustic or uneducated authors passed away, so the point of view represented in Coleridge's remark came to dominate, and "standard" educated English became more and more widely accepted as an ideal to which all should aspire. However, even as the varieties of English were to some extent dissolving into the form of standard English over the course of this period, many regional variations persisted, and the form of standard English itself was far from unchanging.

In pronunciation, the most significant change in "standard British English" was the disappearance of the / r / sound before many consonants, and before a pause, so that in words such as "harm" or "person," for example, the "r" has since the late eighteenth century been flattened into the smooth "hahm" or "pehson" associated with modern "standard English" pronunciation. Interesting geographical variations have developed over this change, however. In Scotland and in Ireland, as in Canada and most of the United States, the "r" has continued to be sounded in such contexts; these varieties of English are referred to by linguists as "rhotic." In Australia, New Zealand, and South Africa, on the other hand, as well as in some parts of the United States, for instance in Massachusetts and some other parts of New England, non-rhotic forms have come to predominate in much the same way as they have in England.

As the rhymes of English poetry reveal, there were also changes in the sounding of some vowels in the late eighteenth century. In the early eighteenth century, for example, Alexander Pope rhymed "tea" with "obey"; other rhymes suggest that "sea" was pronounced in a manner closer to "say" than to "see." By 1797, however, Coleridge could rhyme "sea" with "free"; and by the end of the Romantic period the older pronunciations of such words had almost certainly died out.

Eighteenth-century habits of capitalization and punctuation were also largely abandoned during this period. Capitalization and typography had generally been considered the business of the compositor rather than that of the author, and the tendency in the early and mid-eighteenth century had been to capitalize (or sometimes italicize) a wide range of nouns. By the end of the century, patterns of usage were coming to approximate the conventions of modern English.

Paragraphing remained less strongly conventionalized than it is now—many writers tended to start new paragraphs very infrequently—and the conventions for writing direct speech were still unstable, with the practice of using double quotation marks surrounding the exact words spoken starting to become common at the end of the eighteenth century. The practice of using single rather than double quotation marks did not become common in Britain until later in the nineteenth century and did not become entirely standardized as British usage until the twentieth century.

HISTORY OF THE LANGUAGE AND OF PRINT CULTURE

In an effort to provide for readers a direct sense of the development of the language and of print culture, examples of texts in their original form (and of illustrations) have been provided in each volume of this anthology. A list of material relevant to the language and print culture of the Romantic period within the present volume appears below. Overviews of "The Business of Literature," and of developments in the history of language during this period appear on pages 31 to 35, and a "Contexts" section on various aspects of "Reading, Writing, Publishing" appears on the website component of this anthology (sites.broadviewpress.com/bablonline).

John Brown, title page for *A Memoir of Robert Blincoe*, 1832, p. 11.

Thomas Rowlandson, *Dr. Syntax and a Bookseller*, 1812, p. 31.

J. Bluck, *Ackermann's Art Library*, c.1812–15, p. 32.

Charlotte Smith, all poems (1784–1807) in original spelling and punctuation, pp. 50–52.

James Gillray, *THE RIGHTS OF MAN*, 1791, p. 66.

Thomas Rowlandson (after a drawing by Lord George Murray), *The Contrast*, 1792, p. 67.

William Blake, all poems (1789–95) in original spelling and punctuation, pp. 77–102.

William Blake, *Songs of Innocence and of Experience*, 1789–94, title page for the full work, p. 77; "The Little Black Boy," p. 79; title page for *Songs of Experience*, p. 82; frontispiece, *Songs of Experience*, p. 82; "The Tyger," p. 85. See also the color insert pages.

William Blake, *The Marriage of Heaven and Hell*, 1793, illustrated plates, pp. 96–100.

Mary Robinson, all poems (1795–1804) in original spelling and punctuation. (sites.broadviewpress.com/bablonline)

Robert Burns, all poems (1783–96) in original spelling and punctuation, pp. 142–47.

Illustration from *The Mysteries of Udolpho*, 1803, p. 160.

Frontispiece and title page from *The True and Affecting History of the Duchess of C*****, 1803, p. 164.

Frontispiece from *The Midnight Assassin*, 1802, p. 165.

William Wordsworth, "I wandered lonely as a Cloud," 1807, facsimile of page from *Poems in Two Volumes* with manuscript additions, p. 211.

Samuel Taylor Coleridge, all poems (1795–1828) in original spelling and punctuation, pp. 313–44.

William Blake, illustrations for John Stedman, *Narrative of Five Years' Expedition against the Revolted Negroes of Surinam*, 1796, p. 417.

John Clare, all material (written 1821–48) in original spelling and punctuation, pp. 507–12.

John Keats, all poems (1816–98) in original spelling and punctuation, pp. 515–39.

Theodor von Holst, frontispiece for *Frankenstein; or, the Modern Prometheus*, 1831, p. 579.

Anna Laetitia Barbauld

1743 – 1825

William Blake admired Anna Laetitia Barbauld's poetry, as did Samuel Taylor Coleridge, who walked forty miles to meet her, and William Wordsworth, who said about the Barbauld poem "Life": "I am not in the habit of grudging people their good things, but I wish I had written those [final] lines." Although born in the provinces, Barbauld was a leading figure in London literary life, as well as a prominent educator and a committed political and social activist. She composed innovative and influential poetry, hymns, children's literature, political pamphlets, essays, and works of literary criticism.

Anna Laetitia Aikin was born in Leicestershire to Jane Jennings and John Aikin, a nonconformist Presbyterian minister and schoolteacher at the Warrington Dissenting Academy in Yorkshire. Schooled by her father, she was a precocious child who studied the classics early in life. In her late teens she became acquainted with the influential educator and scientist Joseph Priestley and developed a lasting friendship with him and his wife. He was impressed by her poetry and eventually encouraged her to publish her first volume, *Poems* (1773). This collection of lyrics, hymns, epistles, and mock-heroic poems, published under her birth name, went through five editions in four years and received considerable critical acclaim, *The Monthly Review* calling it a "great accession to the literary world." That same year Barbauld printed *Miscellaneous Pieces in Prose* with her brother, John Aikin (later the editor of a radical journal, *Monthly Magazine*).

Living at Warrington Academy prepared Barbauld to run her own boys' boarding school, which she started with her husband, the dissenting clergy member Rochemont Barbauld, whom she married in 1774. During this period she wrote her popular and influential *Lessons for Children* (1787–88) and *Hymns in Prose for Children* (1787), designed for the very young. Both went through many printings and continued to be widely-read in the United States and England for more than a century. During the school breaks Barbauld and her husband often stayed in London; she became acquainted with important writers such as Joanna Baillie, Hannah More, and, in later years, Maria Edgeworth (who was briefly her pupil, and who became a friend), Walter Scott, and William Wordsworth. She associated with a variety of religious dissenters and was herself broadly speaking Unitarian in her views, though she seems to have been more concerned with the influence of religion on human sympathies than she was with theological issues. By 1785 her husband's mental instability required them to close the school (he eventually became violent and later committed suicide), and from this point on, Barbauld committed herself solely to literary work.

In her political pamphlets and essays of the 1790s, Barbauld addressed ethics, education, and political economy, and argued for freedom of religion and conscience—a cause dear to the hearts of Dissenters. She also argued strongly for the abolition of slavery (at a moment when the movement had suffered a setback) in her verse *Epistle to William Wilberforce* (1791); and in the essay *Sins of*

Government, Sins of Nation (1793) she derided the British government for its involvement in the war against France. Barbauld then turned to editorial work, producing the first collection of *The Correspondence of Samuel Richardson* (1804), which includes her biography of the author. She also published *The British Novelists* (1810), a fifty-volume collection featuring the work of 28 novelists, along with Barbauld's biographical and critical prefaces. In her general introduction to *On the Origin and Progress of Novel-Writing*, she argued for the value of novels for both education and enjoyment. This was pioneering in its recognition of the novel as a serious genre.

In 1812 Barbauld published the prophetic poem *Eighteen Hundred and Eleven*. Written in a pessimistic tone, the poem traces the cyclical rise and fall of national empires, indicts Britain for its involvement in the war with France, and predicts the fall of the British Empire. At the end of the poem, "Genius" leaves for America, the nation Barbauld suggests will replace Britain as the new empire. The poem elicited widespread criticism for what was deemed its "anti-patriotism." John Wilson Croker's abusive attack in the *Quarterly Review* used to be credited with effectively ending Barbauld's publishing career, but this is not accurate: she continued writing into the 1820s. After her death in 1825 her niece published two collections of her works.

⌘⌘⌘

The Mouse's Petition

Oh! Hear a pensive prisoner's prayer,
Forbhu liberty that sighs;
And never let thine heart be shut
Against the wretch's cries.

For here forlorn and sad I sit
Within the wiry grate;
And tremble at th'approaching morn,
Which brings impending fate.

If e'er thy breast with freedom glowed
And spurned a tyrant's chain,
Let not thy strong oppressive force
A free-born mouse detain.[1]

Oh! do not stain with guiltless blood
Thy hospitable hearth;
Nor triumph that thy wiles betrayed
A prize so little worth.

The scattered gleanings of a feast
My frugal meals supply;
But if thine unrelenting heart
That slender boon deny,

The chearful light, the vital air,
Are blessings widely given;
Let nature's commoners enjoy
The common gifts of heaven.

The well-taught philosophic mind
To all compassion gives;
Casts round the world an equal eye,
And feels for all that lives.

If mind, as ancient sages taught,
A never dying flame,
Still shifts through matter's varying forms,
In every form the same.

---

[1] *If e'er ... detain* Barbauld may well be alluding here to political positions Priestley had taken in support of freedom. In 1769, Priestley (who eventually emigrated to the United States) had taken issue with the British government's "enslaving" of the American colonies, and had argued for "a just idea of natural and civil rights."

Beware, lest in the worm you crush,
A brother's soul you find;
And tremble lest thy luckless hand
Dislodge a kindred mind.

Or, if this transient gleam of day
Be *all* of life we share,
Let pity plead within thy breast
That little *all* to spare.

So may thy hospitable board
With health and peace be crowned;
And every charm of heartfelt ease
Beneath thy roof be found.

So, when destruction lurks unseen,
Which men, like mice, may share,
May some kind angel clear thy path,
And break the hidden snare.
—1773

Washing Day

… and their voice,
Turning again towards childish treble, pipes
And whistles in its sound.[1]

The Muses[2] are turned gossips; they have lost
The buskined step,[3] and clear high-sounding
phrase,
Language of gods. Come, then, domestic Muse,
In slipshod measure loosely prattling on
Of farm or orchard, pleasant curds and cream,
Or drowning flies, or shoe lost in the mire
By little whimpering boy, with rueful face;
Come, Muse, and sing the dreaded Washing-Day.
Ye who beneath the yoke of wedlock bend,
With bowed soul, full well ye ken° the day *know*
Which week, smooth sliding after week, brings on
Too soon; for to that day nor peace belongs
Nor comfort; ere the first grey streak of dawn,
The red-armed washers come and chase repose.
Nor pleasant smile, nor quaint device of mirth,
E'er visited that day; the very cat,
From the wet kitchen scared, and reeking hearth,
Visits the parlour, an unwonted° guest. *infrequent*
The silent breakfast meal is soon dispatched
Uninterrupted, save by anxious looks
Cast at the lowering sky, if sky should lower.
From that last evil, O preserve us, heavens!
For should the skies pour down, adieu to all
Remains of quiet; then expect to hear
Of sad disasters—dirt and gravel stains
Hard to efface, and loaded lines at once
Snapped short—and linen-horse° by dog *clotheshorse*
thrown down,
And all the petty miseries of life.
Saints have been calm while stretched upon the rack,
And Guatimozin[4] smiled on burning coals;
But never yet did housewife notable
Greet with a smile a rainy washing-day.
But grant the welkin° fair, require not thou *sky*
Who call'st thyself perchance the master there,
Or study swept, or nicely dusted coat,
Or usual 'tendance; ask not, indiscreet,
Thy stockings mended, though the yawning rents
Gape wide as Erebus,[5] nor hope to find
Some snug recess impervious; should'st thou try
The 'customed garden walks, thine eye shall rue
The budding fragrance of thy tender shrubs,
Myrtle or rose, all crushed beneath the weight

---

[1] *and their voice … sound* Cf. Shakespeare's *As You Like It* 2.7.161–63: "and his big manly voice, / Turning again toward childish treble, pipes / And whistles in his sound."

[2] *Muses* In classical mythology, nine goddesses who presided over learning and the arts.

[3] *buskined step* I.e., tragic mode. Actors in Athenian tragedy wore buskins, or high, thick-soled boots.

[4] *Guatimozin* Cuauhtémoc, the last Aztec emperor (c. 1495–1522), was captured and tortured by Cortés's Spanish conquistadors when they invaded the Aztec capital (now Mexico City).

[5] *Erebus* In Greek mythology, a place below the earth that the dead pass through on their way to Hades, or the underworld.

Of coarse checked apron, with impatient hand
Twitched off when showers impend: or crossing lines
Shall mar thy musings, as the wet cold sheet
Flaps in thy face abrupt. Woe to the friend
Whose evil stars have urged him forth to claim
On such a day the hospitable rites;
Looks, blank at best, and stinted courtesy,
Shall he receive. Vainly he feeds his hopes
With dinner of roast chicken, savoury pie,
Or tart or pudding:—pudding he nor tart
That day shall eat; nor, though the husband try,
Mending what can't be helped, to kindle mirth
From cheer deficient, shall his consort's brow
Clear up propitious; the unlucky guest
In silence dines, and early slinks away.
I well remember, when a child, the awe
This day struck into me; for then the maids,
I scarce knew why, looked cross, and drove me from
them;
Nor soft caress could I obtain, nor hope
Usual indulgencies; jelly or creams,
Relic of costly suppers, and set by
For me their petted one; or buttered toast,
When butter was forbid; or thrilling tale
Of ghost, or witch, or murder—so I went
And sheltered me beside the parlour fire:
There my dear grandmother, eldest of forms,
Tended the little ones, and watched from harm,
Anxiously fond, though oft her spectacles
With elfin cunning hid, and oft the pins
Drawn from her ravelled stocking, might have soured
One less indulgent.—
At intervals my mother's voice was heard,
Urging dispatch; briskly the work went on,
All hands employed to wash, to rinse, to wring,
To fold, and starch, and clap, and iron, and plait.[1]
Then would I sit me down, and ponder much
Why washings were. Sometimes through hollow
bole° *bowl*
Of pipe amused we blew, and sent aloft
The floating bubbles, little dreaming then
To see, Mongolfier,[2] thy silken ball
Ride buoyant through the clouds—so near approach
The sports of children and the toils of men.
Earth, air, and sky, and ocean, hath its bubbles,[3]
And verse is one of them—this most of all.
—1797

[1] *clap* Smooth; *plait* Fold.

Eighteen Hundred and Eleven,[4] A Poem

Still the loud death drum, thundering from afar,
O'er the vext nations pours the storm of war:
To the stern call still Britain bends her ear,
Feeds the fierce strife, the alternate hope and fear;
Bravely, though vainly, dares to strive with fate,
And seeks by turns to prop each sinking state.
Colossal Power[5] with overwhelming force
Bears down each fort of freedom in its course;
Prostrate she lies beneath the despot's sway,
While the hushed nations curse him—and obey.
Bounteous in vain, with frantic man at strife,
Glad Nature pours the means—the joys of life;
In vain with orange blossoms scents the gale,
The hills with olives clothes, with corn the vale;
Man calls to Famine,[6] nor invokes in vain,
Disease and Rapine° follow in her train; *plunder*
The tramp of marching hosts disturbs the plough,

[2] *Mongolfier* Montgolfier brothers, from Annonay, France, who invented and launched the first hot-air balloon in 1783.

[3] *Earth … bubbles* Cf. Shakespeare's *Macbeth* 1.3.83: "The earth hath bubbles, as the water has."

[4] *Eighteen Hundred and Eleven* Britain's war with France, begun in 1793, would not end until the Battle of Waterloo in 1815. By 1811, Russia, Austria, and Spain, Britain's allies, had already capitulated to the strength of Napoleon's army; Britain was in financial distress; and King George III had been declared insane.

[5] *Colossal Power* Napoleon Bonaparte (1769–1821), emperor of France.

[6] *Famine* In 1811 there was widespread hunger in Britain and much of Europe due to crop failures in the preceding years, as well as the necessity of providing food for soldiers.

The sword, not sickle, reaps the harvest now,[1]
And where the soldier gleans the scant supply,
The helpless peasant but retires to die;
No laws his hut from licensed outrage shield,
And war's least horror is the ensanguined° field. *blood-stained*
Fruitful in vain, the matron counts with pride
The blooming youths that grace her honoured side;
No son returns to press her widowed hand,
Her fallen blossoms strew a foreign strand.
—Fruitful in vain, she boasts her virgin race,
Whom cultured arts adorn and gentlest grace;
Defrauded of its homage, Beauty mourns,
And the rose withers on its virgin thorns.
Frequent, some stream obscure, some uncouth name
By deeds of blood is lifted into fame;
Oft o'er the daily page some soft one bends
To learn the fate of husband, brothers, friends,
Or the spread map with anxious eye explores,
Its dotted boundaries and penciled shores,
Asks where the spot that wrecked her bliss is found,
And learns its name but to detest the sound.
And think'st thou, Britain, still to sit at ease,
An island queen amidst thy subject seas,
While the vext billows, in their distant roar,
But soothe thy slumbers, and but kiss thy shore?
To sport in wars, while danger keeps aloof,
Thy grassy turf unbruised by hostile hoof?
So sing thy flatterers; but, Britain, know,
Thou who hast shared the guilt must share the woe.
Nor distant is the hour; low murmurs spread,
And whispered fears, creating what they dread;
Ruin, as with an earthquake shock, is here,
There, the heart-witherings of unuttered fear,
And that sad death, whence most affection bleeds,
Which sickness, only of the soul, precedes.
Thy baseless wealth dissolves in air away,[2]
Like mists that melt before the morning ray:
No more on crowded mart or busy street
Friends, meeting friends, with cheerful hurry greet;
Sad, on the ground thy princely merchants bend
Their altered looks, and evil days portend,
And fold their arms, and watch with anxious breast
The tempest blackening in the distant West.[3]
Yes, thou must droop; thy Midas dream is o'er;
The golden tide of Commerce leaves thy shore,
Leaves thee to prove the alternate ills that haunt
Enfeebling Luxury and ghastly Want;
Leaves thee, perhaps, to visit distant lands,
And deal the gifts of Heaven with equal hands.
Yet, O my country, name beloved, revered,
By every tie that binds the soul endeared,
Whose image to my infant senses came
Mixt with Religion's light and Freedom's holy flame!
If prayers may not avert, if 'tis thy fate
To rank amongst the names that once were great,
Not like the dim cold crescent[4] shalt thou fade,
Thy debt to Science and the Muse unpaid;
Thine are the laws surrounding states revere,
Thine the full harvest of the mental year,
Thine the bright stars in Glory's sky that shine,
And arts that make it life to live are thine.
If westward streams the light that leaves thy shores,
Still from thy lamp the streaming radiance pours.
Wide spreads thy race from Ganges[5] to the pole,
O'er half the western world thy accents roll:
Nations beyond the Appalachian hills[6]
Thy hand has planted and thy spirit fills:
Soon as their gradual progress shall impart
The finer sense of morals and of art,
Thy stores of knowledge the new states shall know,
And think thy thoughts, and with thy fancy glow;

[1] *The sword … now* Napoleon sent his soldiers out unencumbered with provisions; consequently, most of them were starving and were forced to steal food.

[2] *Thy baseless wealth … away* 1810 saw the failure of many British businesses, and in 1811, the country itself was threatened with financial collapse.

[3] *The tempest … West* Relations had been strained between England and the United States since the French Revolution; Barbauld here foresees the beginning of the War of 1812.

[4] *crescent* Symbol of the Ottoman Empire, which had been in decline throughout the eighteenth and into the nineteenth century.

[5] *Ganges* Sacred river of India.

[6] *Appalachian hills* Mountain range in the eastern United States.

Thy Lockes, thy Paleys[1] shall instruct their youth,
Thy leading star direct their search for truth;
Beneath the spreading platan's[2] tent-like shade,
Or by Missouri's rushing waters laid,
"Old father Thames" shall be the poet's theme,
Of Hagley's woods[3] the enamoured virgin dream,
And Milton's tones the raptured ear enthrall,
Mixt with the roar of Niagara's fall;
In Thomson's glass[4] the ingenuous youth shall learn
A fairer face of Nature to discern;
Nor of the bards that swept the British lyre
Shall fade one laurel, or one note expire.
Then, loved Joanna,[5] to admiring eyes
Thy storied groups in scenic pomp shall rise;
Their high souled strains and Shakespeare's noble rage
Shall with alternate passion shake the stage.
Some youthful Basil[6] from thy moral lay
With stricter hand his fond desires shall sway;
Some Ethwald,[7] as the fleeting shadows pass,
Start at his likeness in the mystic glass;
The tragic Muse resume her just control,
With pity and with terror purge the soul,
While wide o'er transatlantic realms thy name
Shall live in light, and gather all its fame.
  Where wanders Fancy down the lapse of years
Shedding o'er imaged woes untimely tears?
Fond moody Power! as hopes—as fears prevail,
She longs, or dreads, to lift the awful veil,
On visions of delight now loves to dwell,
Now hears the shriek of woe or Freedom's knell:
Perhaps, she says, long ages past away,
And set in western waves our closing day,
Night, Gothic night, again may shade the plains
Where Power is seated, and where Science reigns;
England, the seat of arts, be only known
By the gray ruin and the mouldering stone;
That time may tear the garland from her brow,
And Europe sit in dust, as Asia now.
  Yet then the ingenuous youth whom Fancy fires
With pictured glories of illustrious sires,
With duteous zeal their pilgrimage shall take
From the Blue Mountains,° or Ontario's lake, *in Pennsylvania*
With fond adoring steps to press the sod
By statesmen, sages, poets, heroes trod;
On Isis' banks[8] to draw inspiring air,
From Runnymede[9] to send the patriot's prayer;
In pensive thought, where Cam's[10] slow waters wind,
To meet those shades that ruled the realms of mind;
In silent halls to sculptured marbles bow,
And hang fresh wreaths round Newton's[11] awful brow.
Oft shall they seek some peasant's homely shed,
Who toils, unconscious of the mighty dead,
To ask where Avon's[12] winding waters stray,
And thence a knot of wild flowers bear away;
Anxious enquire where Clarkson,[13] friend of man,
Or all-accomplished Jones[14] his race began;
If of the modest mansion aught remains
Where Heaven and Nature prompted Cowper's[15] strains;
Where Roscoe, to whose patriot breast belong

---

[1] *Lockes ... Paleys* Men as eminent as John Locke and William Paley. John Locke (1632–1704), English philosopher who wrote about political, intellectual, and religious freedom and William Paley (1743–1805), English theologian and moral philosopher, who defended Christianity in many of his texts.

[2] *platan* Plane tree.

[3] *Hagley's woods* Cf. *The Seasons*, "Spring," in which James Thomson writes about Lord Lyttleton's lush estate in Worcestershire.

[4] *glass* Mirror; i.e., nature as reflected in Thomson's *The Seasons*.

[5] *Joanna* Scottish playwright Joanna Baillie (1762–1851), who was often compared with Shakespeare.

[6] *Basil* Character in Baillie's tragedy *Count Basil* (1798).

[7] *Ethwald* Character in Baillie's tragedy *Ethwald* (1802).

[8] *Isis' banks* The River Thames at Oxford was known as the Isis.

[9] *Runnymede* Site where King John signed the Magna Carta (1215).

[10] *Cam* River at Cambridge.

[11] *Newton* Sir Isaac Newton (1642–1727), mathematician, physicist, and professor at Cambridge University.

[12] *Avon* River that runs through Stratford, where Shakespeare was born.

[13] *Clarkson* Thomas Clarkson (1760–1846), abolitionist, whose work helped to end the British slave trade in 1807.

[14] *Jones* Sir William Jones (1746–94), judge and scholar, who promoted Asian and Sanskrit studies.

[15] *Cowper* William Cowper (1731–1800), English poet.

The Roman virtue and the Tuscan song,
Led Ceres to the black and barren moor
Where Ceres never gained a wreath before:[1]
With curious search their pilgrim steps shall rove
By many a ruined tower and proud alcove,
Shall listen for those strains that soothed of yore
Thy rock, stern Skiddaw, and thy fall, Lodore;[2]
Feast with Dun Edin's° classic brow their sight, *Edinburgh's*
And visit "Melrose by the pale moonlight."[3]
    But who their mingled feelings shall pursue
When London's faded glories rise to view?
The mighty city, which by every road,
In floods of people poured itself abroad;
Ungirt by walls, irregularly great,
No jealous drawbridge, and no closing gate;
Whose merchants (such the state which commerce brings)
Sent forth their mandates to dependant kings;
Streets, where the turbaned Moslem, bearded Jew,
And woolly Afric, met the brown Hindu;
Where through each vein spontaneous plenty flowed,
Where Wealth enjoyed, and Charity bestowed.
Pensive and thoughtful shall the wanderers greet
Each splendid square, and still, untrodden street;
Or of some crumbling turret, mined by time,
The broken stairs with perilous step shall climb,
Thence stretch their view the wide horizon round,
By scattered hamlets trace its ancient bound,
And, choked no more with fleets, fair Thames survey
Through reeds and sedge pursue his idle way.
    With throbbing bosoms shall the wanderers tread
The hallowed mansions of the silent dead,
Shall enter the long isle and vaulted dome
Where Genius and where Valour find a home;[4]
Awestruck, midst chill sepulchral marbles breathe,
Where all above is still, as all beneath;
Bend at each antique shrine, and frequent turn
To clasp with fond delight some sculptured urn,
The ponderous mass of Johnson's[5] form to greet,
Or breathe the prayer at Howard's[6] sainted feet.
    Perhaps some Briton, in whose musing mind
Those ages live which Time has cast behind,
To every spot shall lead his wondering guests
On whose known site the beam of glory rests:
Here Chatham's eloquence in thunder broke,
Here Fox persuaded, or here Garrick[7] spoke;
Shall boast how Nelson, fame and death in view,
To wonted victory led his ardent crew,
In England's name enforced, with loftiest tone,
Their duty—and too well fulfilled his own:[8]
How gallant Moore,[9] as ebbing life dissolved,
But hoped his country had his fame absolved.[10]
Or call up sages whose capacious mind
Left in its course a track of light behind;
Point where mute crowds on Davy's[11] lips reposed,
And Nature's coyest secrets were disclosed;

---

[1] *Roscoe … before* William Roscoe (1753–1831), historian and MP, who promoted the use of the moors for agriculture; *Ceres* Roman goddess of agriculture.

[2] *Skiddaw … Lodore* Mountain and waterfall in the Lake District, England.

[3] *Melrose … moonlight* Site of the beautiful Melrose Abbey ruins in the Scottish Borderlands; cf. Sir Walter Scott's *The Lay of the Last Minstrel* 2.1: "If thou woud'st view fair Melrose aright, / Go visit it by the pale moonlight."

[4] *vaulted dome … home* St. Paul's Cathedral, home to statues of eminent British men and women.

[5] *Johnson* Samuel Johnson (1709–84), scholar and author.

[6] *Howard* John Howard (1726–90), prison reformer and philanthropist.

[7] *Chatham* William Pitt, 1st Earl of Chatham (1708–78), prime minister and famous patriot and orator; *Fox* Charles James Fox (1749–1806), parliamentarian and orator; *Garrick* David Garrick (1717–79), famous English actor and dramatist.

[8] *Nelson … his own* Admiral Horatio Nelson, English war hero, spoke these famous words before he died at the Battle of Trafalgar in 1805: "England expects that every man will do his duty."

[9] *Moore* Sir John Moore (1761–1809), general who led a retreat during the Napoleonic Wars; he saved his troops, but died in the process.

[10] [Barbauld's note] "I hope England will be satisfied," were the last words of General Moore.

[11] *Davy* Sir Humphrey Davy (1778–1829), physicist and chemist, whose lectures were renowned.

Join with their Franklin, Priestley's[1] injured name,
Whom, then, each continent shall proudly claim.
Oft shall the strangers turn their eager feet
The rich remains of ancient art to greet,
The pictured walls with critic eye explore,
And Reynolds be what Raphael[2] was before.
On spoils from every clime their eyes shall gaze,
Egyptian granites and the Etruscan vase;
And when midst fallen London, they survey
The stone where Alexander's ashes lay,[3]
Shall own with humbled pride the lesson just
By Time's slow finger written in the dust.
There walks a Spirit o'er the peopled earth,
Secret his progress is, unknown his birth;
Moody and viewless° as the changing wind, *invisible*
No force arrests his foot, no chains can bind;
Where'er he turns, the human brute awakes,
And, roused to better life, his sordid hut forsakes:
He thinks, he reasons, glows with purer fires,
Feels finer wants, and burns with new desires:
Obedient Nature follows where he leads;
The steaming marsh is changed to fruitful meads;
The beasts retire from man's asserted reign,
And prove his kingdom was not given in vain.
Then from its bed is drawn the ponderous ore,
Then Commerce pours her gifts on every shore.
Then Babel's towers[4] and terraced gardens rise,
And pointed obelisks invade the skies;
The prince commands, in Tyrian purple drest,
And Egypt's virgins weave the linen vest.
Then spans the graceful arch the roaring tide,
And stricter bounds the cultured fields divide.
Then kindles Fancy, then expands the heart,
Then blow° the flowers of Genius and of Art; *blossom*
Saints, Heroes, Sages, who the land adorn,
Seem rather to descend than to be born;
Whilst History, midst the rolls consigned to fame,
With pen of adamant inscribes their name.
The Genius now forsakes the favoured shore,
And hates, capricious, what he loved before;
Then empires fall to dust, then arts decay,
And wasted realms enfeebled despots sway;
Even Nature's changed; without his fostering smile
Ophir[5] no gold, no plenty yields the Nile;
The thirsty sand absorbs the useless rill,° *stream*
And spotted plagues from putrid fens distill.
In desert solitudes then Tadmor[6] sleeps,
Stern Marius then o'er fallen Carthage weeps;[7]
Then with enthusiast love the pilgrim roves
To seek his footsteps in forsaken groves,
Explores the fractured arch, the ruined tower,
Those limbs disjointed of gigantic power;
Still at each step he dreads the adder's sting,
The Arab's javelin, or the tiger's spring;
With doubtful caution treads the echoing ground,
And asks where Troy or Babylon[8] is found.
And now the vagrant Power no more detains
The vale of Tempe, or Ausonian plains;[9]
Northward he throws the animating ray,
O'er Celtic nations bursts the mental day:

[1] *Franklin* Benjamin Franklin (1706–90), American scientist, inventor, and politician; *Priestley* Joseph Priestley (1733–1804), English scientist and theologian, whose correspondence with Franklin led to Priestley's experimentation with and discoveries regarding electricity; Priestley was persecuted for his support of the French and American Revolutions, which led to his emigration from England to America.

[2] *Reynolds … Raphael* Sir Joshua Reynolds (1723–92), eminent English portrait artist, and Raphael (1483–1520), famous Italian Renaissance painter and architect.

[3] *stone … lay* The British Museum mistakenly believed it had purchased the tomb of Alexander the Great.

[4] *Babel's towers* Cf. Genesis 11.3–9. The Babylonians attempted to create a tower that would reach heaven; God punished them by giving them different languages and scattering them around the earth.

[5] *Ophir* Cf. 1 Kings 9.28: "And they came to Ophir, and fetched from thence gold."

[6] *Tadmor* Biblical land in ancient Syria.

[7] *Marius … weeps* Gaius Marius (157–86 BCE), Roman Consul and general who was once called the "savior of Rome"; upon aging and falling from power, he was said to have wept among the ruins of Carthage.

[8] *Troy* Ancient city in Asia Minor, subject of the Trojan War in Homer's *Iliad*; *Babylon* Ancient Mesopotamian city known for its wealth and beauty, destroyed in 689 BCE.

[9] *vale of Tempe* Valley in Greece celebrated by ancient poets for its beauty; *Ausonian plains* Virgil called Italy "Ausonia."

And, as some playful child the mirror turns,
Now here now there the moving lustre burns;
Now o'er his changeful fancy more prevail
Batavia's dykes than Arno's[1] purple vale,
And stinted suns, and rivers bound with frost,
Than Enna's plains or Baia's[2] viny coast;
Venice the Adriatic weds in vain,
And Death sits brooding o'er Campania's[3] plain;
O'er Baltic shores and through Hercynian groves,[4]
Stirring the soul, the mighty impulse moves;
Art plies his tools, and Commerce spreads her sail,
And wealth is wafted in each shifting gale.
The sons of Odin[5] tread on Persian looms,
And Odin's daughters breathe distilled perfumes;
Loud minstrel bards, in Gothic halls, rehearse
The Runic rhyme, and "build the lofty verse:"[6]
The Muse, whose liquid notes were wont to swell
To the soft breathings of the Aeolian shell,[7]
Submits, reluctant, to the harsher tone,
And scarce believes the altered voice her own.
And now, where Caesar saw with proud disdain
The wattled hut and skin of azure stain,[8]
Corinthian columns rear their graceful forms,
And light verandas brave the wintry storms,
While British tongues the fading fame prolong
Of Tully's eloquence and Maro's[9] song.
Where once Bonduca whirled the scythed car,
And the fierce matrons raised the shriek of war,[10]
Light forms beneath transparent muslins float,
And tutored voices swell the artful note.
Light-leaved acacias and the shady plane
And spreading cedar grace the woodland reign;
While crystal walls the tenderer plants confine,
The fragrant orange and the nectared pine;
The Syrian grape there hangs her rich festoons,
Nor asks for purer air, or brighter noons:
Science and Art urge on the useful toil,
New mold a climate and create the soil,
Subdue the rigour of the northern Bear,[11]
O'er polar climes shed aromatic air,
On yielding Nature urge their new demands,
And ask not gifts but tribute at her hands.
London exults:—on London Art bestows
Her summer ices and her winter rose;
Gems of the East her mural crown adorn,
And Plenty at her feet pours forth her horn;[12]
While even the exiles her just laws disclaim,
People a continent, and build a name:
August she sits, and with extended hands
Holds forth the book of life to distant lands.
But fairest flowers expand but to decay;
The worm is in thy core, thy glories pass away;
Arts, arms and wealth destroy the fruits they bring;
Commerce, like beauty, knows no second spring.
Crime walks thy streets, Fraud earns her unblest bread,
O'er want and woe thy gorgeous robe is spread,
And angel charities in vain oppose:
With grandeur's growth the mass of misery grows.
For see,—to other climes the Genius soars,
He turns from Europe's desolated shores;
And lo, even now, midst mountains wrapt in storm,
On Andes' heights he shrouds his awful form;

---

[1] *Batavia* Republic, now the Netherlands; *Arno* River in Italy.

[2] *Enna* Sicilian valley; *Baia* Italian village on the Bay of Naples, celebrated for its spas in Roman times.

[3] *Campania* Italian province whose plains were marshy and malarial.

[4] *Hercynian groves* Black Forest in Germany.

[5] *Odin* Supreme Norse god.

[6] *build the lofty verse* From Milton's *Lycidas* (10–11): "He knew / Himself to sing, and build the lofty rhyme."

[7] *Aeolian shell* Aeolian harp, a musical instrument that produces sound when the wind passes over its strings.

[8] *Caesar … stain* Cf. Julius Caesar's *The Gallic Wars* 5.14: "All the Britains, indeed, dye themselves with wood, which occasions a bluish color, and thereby have a more terrible appearance in fight."

[9] *Tully* Marcus Tullius Cicero (106–43 BCE), Roman orator, philosopher, and politician; *Maro* Publius Vergilius Maro, or Virgil (70–19 BCE), Roman poet, author of the *Aeneid*.

[10] *Bonduca … war* Queen of the ancient Iceni Celts, Boadicea (sometimes written as "Bonduca" or "Boudicca") led a massive rebellion against the Romans in about 60 CE; she committed suicide upon the failure of the mission.

[11] *northern Bear* The constellation Ursa Major (Latin: Great Bear).

[12] *horn* Horn of plenty, or cornucopia, contains an abundance of the essentials and luxuries of life.

On Chimborazo's[1] summits treads sublime,
Measuring in lofty thought the march of Time;
Sudden he calls:—"'Tis now the hour!" he cries,
Spreads his broad hand, and bids the nations rise.
La Plata[2] hears amidst her torrents' roar,
Potosi[3] hears it, as she digs the ore:
Ardent, the Genius fans the noble strife,
And pours through feeble souls a higher life,
Shouts to the mingled tribes from sea to sea,
And swears—Thy world, Columbus, shall be free.
—1812

On the Death of the Princess Charlotte[4]

Yes, Britain mourns, as with electric touch
For youth, for love, for happiness destroyed,
Her universal population melts
In grief spontaneous, and hard hearts are moved,
And rough unpolished natures learn to feel
For those they envied, leveled in the dust
By Fate's impartial stroke; and pulpits sound
With vanity and woe to earthly goods,
And urge and dry the tear. Yet one there is
Who midst this general burst of grief remains
In strange tranquility;[5] whom not the stir
And long drawn murmurs of the gathering crowd,
That by his very windows trail the pomp
Of hearse,[6] and blazoned arms, and long array
Of sad funereal rites, nor the loud groans
And deep-felt anguish of a husband's[7] heart,
Can move to mingle with this flood one tear.
In careless apathy, perhaps in mirth
He wears the day. Yet is he near in blood,
The very stem on which this blossom grew,
And at his knees she fondled, in the charm
And grace spontaneous which alone belongs
To untaught infancy. Yet oh forbear!
Nor deem him hard of heart; for awful, struck
By heaven's severest visitation, sad,
Like a scathed oak amidst the forest trees,
Lonely he stands—leaves bud, and shoot, and fall;
He holds no sympathy with living nature
Or time's incessant change. Then, in this hour,
While pensive thought is busy with the woes
And restless cares of poor humanity,
Think then, oh think of him, and breathe one prayer,
From the full tide of sorrow spare one tear
For him who does not weep!
—1819

The Rights of Woman[8]

Yes, injured Woman! rise, assert thy right!
Woman! too long degraded, scorned, opprest;
O born to rule in partial° Law's despite, *biased*
Resume thy native empire o'er the breast!

Go forth arrayed in panoply[9] divine;
That angel pureness which admits no stain;
Go, bid proud Man his boasted rule resign,
And kiss the golden sceptre of thy reign.

Go, gird thyself with grace; collect thy store
Of bright artillery glancing from afar;

---

[1] *Chimborazo* Volcanic mountain in Ecuador.

[2] *La Plata* City in Argentina.

[3] *Potosi* City in Bolivia. All three countries were home to movements resistant to colonial rule. The region was famous for its gold and silver deposits.

[4] *Death … Charlotte* The popular Princess Charlotte Augusta (1796–1817), daughter of the Prince of Wales, the future King George IV, died at the age of 21 of complications from childbirth.

[5] *one there is … tranquility* Charlotte's father is said to have openly expressed his disdain of his daughter, linked, no doubt, to his feud with her mother.

[6] *by his … hearse* The Prince of Wales did not attend his daughter's funeral.

[7] *husband* Leopold of Saxe-Coburg, whom Charlotte married in 1816.

[8] *The Rights of Woman* Cf. Mary Wollstonecraft's *A Vindication of the Rights of Woman* (1792).

[9] *panoply* Lavish ceremonial attire.

Soft melting tones thy thundering cannon's roar,
Blushes and fears thy magazine° of war. *storehouse*

Thy rights are empire: urge no meaner claim,—
Felt, not defined, and if debated, lost;
Like sacred mysteries, which withheld from fame,
Shunning discussion, are revered the most.

Try all that wit and art suggest to bend
Of thy imperial foe the stubborn knee;
Make treacherous Man thy subject, not thy friend;
Thou mayst command, but never canst be free.

Awe the licentious, and restrain the rude;
Soften the sullen, clear the cloudy brow:
Be, more than princes' gifts, thy favours sued;—
She hazards all, who will the least allow.

But hope not, courted idol of mankind,
On this proud eminence secure to stay;
Subduing and subdued, thou soon shalt find
Thy coldness soften, and thy pride give way.

Then, then, abandon each ambitious thought,
Conquest or rule thy heart shall feebly move,
In Nature's school, by her soft maxims taught,
That separate rights are lost in mutual love.
—1825

The Caterpillar

No, helpless thing, I cannot harm thee now;
Depart in peace, thy little life is safe,
For I have scanned thy form with curious eye,
Noted the silver line that streaks thy back,
The azure and the orange that divide
Thy velvet sides; thee, houseless wanderer,
My garment has enfolded, and my arm
Felt the light pressure of thy hairy feet;
Thou hast curled round my finger; from its tip,
Precipitous descent! with stretched out neck,
Bending thy head in airy vacancy,
This way and that, inquiring, thou hast seemed
To ask protection; now, I cannot kill thee.
Yet I have sworn perdition to thy race,
And recent from the slaughter am I come
Of tribes and embryo nations: I have sought
With sharpened eye and persecuting zeal,
Where, folded in their silken webs they lay
Thriving and happy; swept them from the tree
And crushed whole families beneath my foot;
Or, sudden, poured on their devoted heads
The vials of destruction.[1]—This I've done,
Nor felt the touch of pity: but when thou—
A single wretch, escaped the general doom,
Making me feel and clearly recognise
Thine individual existence, life,
And fellowship of sense with all that breathes—
Present'st thyself before me, I relent,
And cannot hurt thy weakness.—So the storm
Of horrid war, o'erwhelming cities, fields,
And peaceful villages, rolls dreadful on:
The victor shouts triumphant; he enjoys
The roar of cannon and the clang of arms,
And urges, by no soft relentings stopped,
The work of death and carnage. Yet should one,
A single sufferer from the field escaped,
Panting and pale, and bleeding at his feet,
Lift his imploring eyes—the hero weeps;
He is grown human, and capricious Pity,
Which would not stir for thousands, melts for one
With sympathy spontaneous: 'Tis not Virtue,
Yet 'tis the weakness of a virtuous mind.
—1825

[1] *vials of destruction* I.e., pesticides.

Charlotte Smith

1749 – 1806

Charlotte Smith was, as Wordsworth wrote, "a lady to whom English is under greater obligations than are likely to be acknowledged or remembered." As a poet, she initiated a revival of the sonnet by demonstrating its potential to capture quintessentially Romantic emotional experiences. As a novelist, she contributed significantly to debates surrounding the French Revolution and other issues of importance to liberals of her time. Her work was enormously popular in her own day and exerted a strong influence on other Romantic poets. By the middle of the nineteenth-century, however, her poems and novels had fallen out of fashion, and it was not until the late twentieth century that they once again received substantial critical attention and more extensive readership.

Smith (née Turner) was born into the landed gentry in 1749 in London; her father was a country gentleman in Sussex, to which county Smith remained devoted throughout her life. Charlotte was the second of three children and her mother died giving birth to her brother when Charlotte was three years old. Her education was typical for someone of her gender and social class; she attended a fashionable boarding school between the ages of eight and twelve, at which point she left school and entered "society." Her father remarried in 1764, and it was arranged that Charlotte would marry the following year, at the age of 15. Her husband, Benjamin Smith, was the son of a West Indian merchant and was living beyond his means. Her father-in-law died in 1776, leaving a will that attempted to prevent his legacy from being wasted by his wayward son. The document was so complicated, however, that Smith was to spend the rest of her life going to the courts to fight for her children's inheritance. (Her case became well known in London, and it is probably the basis for the unending, impoverishing, and misery-inducing law case in Dickens's *Bleak House*.) Benjamin Smith continued his spendthrift ways and was imprisoned for debt in 1783. For a time, Smith and their growing family lived with him in prison.

In 1784, when Smith first turned to writing professionally, she was 35 years old and had nine living children. Desperate for money while her husband was still in prison, she composed *Elegiac Sonnets*. These remarkable sonnets, famous for their melancholy, pessimism, and pathos, represent an important stylistic achievement in their ability to convey a highly personal effect through an understated and impersonal style. This volume was extremely popular, and she later repeatedly rearranged and enlarged the collection. Among the additions were many poems supposedly written by characters in the novels she wrote later. By 1851 her sonnets had gone through 11 editions. Both Wordsworth and Coleridge learned from her, admiring her more in their youth than they were later willing to admit. Both used Smith's work as a model for working out their new style of Romantic self-expression.

More money troubles were to follow for Smith. When her husband was released from prison in 1785, he fled to France to escape his creditors and Smith followed with the family. While in France, she discovered Antoine-François Prevost's controversial novel *Manon Lescaut* and translated it into English.

In 1785 Smith returned to England with her children; she separated from her husband one year later. From this point onward, she was the sole supporter of her family, a position made more difficult by the fact that at this date everything earned by a wife legally belonged to her husband. In 1788 her first novel, *Emmeline*, was published; from then on she published almost a novel a year. Smith drew on the circumstances of her own life for her fiction: she often portrayed women married to cruel or dissolute husbands, and still more often grasping or incompetent lawyers, while scenes from her stay in debtor's prison appear both in *Ethelinde* and in *Marchmont*. If her own life figured frequently in her work, however, so did many of the great public issues of the day; her fiction is sharply critical of empire, the slave trade, the class system, and marriage laws. She was a strong early supporter of the French Revolution, but was also sensitive to the plight of French emigrés in England after the Terror; in 1793 she published the 800-line blank-verse poem *The Emigrants*.

Although she came to be known primarily as a novelist and, in the later part of her life, as a children's author, Smith continued to write poetry. *Beachy Head*, one of her finest poems, was published the year after her death, in 1807.

⌘⌘⌘

from *Elegiac Sonnets*

1

The partial Muse,[1] has from my earliest hours
Smil'd on the rugged path I'm doom'd to tread,
And still with sportive° hand has snatch'd wild flowers, *playful*
To weave fantastic garlands for my head:
But far, far happier is the lot of those
Who never learn'd her dear delusive art,
Which while it decks the head with many a rose,
Reserves the thorn, to fester in the heart.
For still she bids° soft Pity's melting eye *commands*
Stream o'er the ills she knows not to remove,
Points° every pang, and deepens every sigh *sharpens*
Of mourning friendship, or unhappy love.
Ah! then, how dear° the Muse's favors cost, *expensive*
If those paint sorrow best—who feel it most![2]

[1] *partial* Favorable, prejudiced; *Muse* Goddess of poetic inspiration, the invocation of which is a tradition going back to Classical antiquity.

[2] [Smith's note] "The well-sung woes shall soothe my pensive ghost; / He best can paint them who shall feel them most." Pope's "Eloisa to Abelard." 366th line.

2

Written at the Close of Spring

The garlands fade that Spring so lately wove,
Each simple flower which she had nursed in dew,
Anemonies,[3] that spangled every grove,
The primrose wan, and hare-bell[4] mildly blue.
No more shall violets linger in the dell,° *wooded valley*
Or purple orchis variegate[5] the plain,
Till Spring again shall call forth every bell,° *flowering plant*
And dress° with humid hands her wreaths again.— *prepare*
Ah! poor Humanity! so frail, so fair,
Are the fond visions of thy early day,
Till tyrant Passion,° and corrosive Care, *suffering*
Bid° all thy fairy colours fade away! *orders*
Another May new buds and flowers shall bring;
Ah! why has happiness—no second Spring?

[3] [Smith's note] Anemonies. *Anemony Nemeroso*. The wood Anemony. [Flowering plant having brilliant blossoms, common to Great Britain.]

[4] *primrose* Wild flowering plant noted for its yellow blossoms; *hare-bell* Wild hyacinth, blue-bell.

[5] *orchis* Orchids; *variegate* Make varied.

11
To Sleep

Come, balmy Sleep! tired Nature's soft resort![1]
On these sad temples all thy poppies[2] shed;
And bid gay dreams, from Morpheus'[3] airy court,
Float in light vision round my aching head![4]
Secure of all thy blessings, partial° Power! *favorable, prejudiced*
On his hard bed the peasant throws him down;
And the poor sea-boy, in the rudest° hour, *most harsh*
Enjoys thee more than he who wears a crown.[5]
Clasp'd in her faithful shepherd's guardian arms,
Well may the village-girl sweet slumbers prove;
And they, O gentle Sleep! still taste thy charms,
Who wake to labour, liberty, and love.
But still thy opiate aid dost thou deny
To calm the anxious breast, to close the streaming eye.

39
To Night

I love thee, mournful, sober-suited° *darkly clothed*
Night!
When the faint moon, yet lingering in her wane,
And veil'd in clouds, with pale uncertain light
Hangs o'er the waters of the restless main.° *sea*
In deep depression sunk, the enfeebled mind
Will to the deaf cold elements complain,
And tell the embosom'd grief, however vain,
To sullen[6] surges and the viewless wind.
Tho' no repose on thy dark breast I find,
I still enjoy thee—cheerless as thou art;
For in thy quiet gloom the exhausted heart
Is calm, tho' wretched; hopeless, yet resign'd.
While to the winds and waves its sorrows given,
May reach—tho' lost on earth—the ear of Heaven!

44
Written in the Church-yard at Middleton in Sussex

Press'd by the Moon, mute arbitress° of *female judge*
tides,
While the loud equinox[7] its power combines,
The sea no more its swelling surge confines,
But o'er the shrinking land sublimely rides.
The wild blast, rising from the Western cave,
Drives the huge billows from their heaving bed;
Tears from their grassy tombs the village dead,[8]
And breaks the silent sabbath of the grave!
With shells and sea-weed mingled, on the shore
Lo! their bones whiten in the frequent wave;
But vain to them the winds and waters rave;
They hear the warring elements no more:
While I am doom'd—by life's long storm opprest,
To gaze with envy, on their gloomy rest.

59
Written September 1791, during a remarkable thunder storm, in which the moon was perfectly clear, while the tempest gathered in various directions near the earth

What awful pageants° crowd the *majestic displays*
evening sky!
The low horizon gathering vapours shroud;
Sudden, from many a deep-embattled cloud
Terrific thunders burst, and lightnings fly—

---

[1] *balmy* Soothing; *resort* Escape.

[2] *poppies* Opium, which induces sleep, is made from poppies.

[3] *Morpheus* God of sleep and dreams.

[4] [Smith's note] "Float in light vision round the poet's head." Mason. [Cf. line 12 of William Mason's "Elegy V. On the Death of a Lady" (1760).]

[5] [Smith's note] "Wilt thou upon the high and giddy mast / Seal up the ship boy's eyes, and rock his brains / In cradle of the rude impetuous surge?" Shakespeare's *Henry IV*. [Cf. *2 Henry IV*, 3.1.18–20. Smith here substitutes "impetuous," for the original "imperious."]

[6] *sullen* Make sluggish or slow.

[7] *equinox* Time of year at which the sun crosses the equator, rendering day and night of equal length.

[8] [Smith's note] Middleton is a village on the margin of the sea, in Sussex, containing only two or three houses. There were formerly several acres of ground between its small church and the sea, which now, by its continual encroachments, approaches within a few feet of this half-ruined and humble edifice. The wall, which once surrounded the church-yard, is entirely swept away, many of the graves broken up, and the remains of bodies interred washed into the sea; whence human bones are found among the sand and shingles on the shore.

While in serenest azure,° beaming high, *intense blue*
Night's regent,° of her calm pavilion proud, *moon*
Gilds the dark shadows that beneath her lie,
Unvex'd by all their conflicts fierce and loud.
—So, in unsullied dignity elate,
A spirit conscious of superior worth,
In placid elevation firmly great,
Scorns the vain cares that give Contention birth;
And blest with peace above the shocks of Fate,
Smiles at the tumult of the troubled earth.

70
On being cautioned against walking on an headland overlooking the sea, because it was frequented by a lunatic

Is there a solitary wretch who hies° *hastens*
To the tall cliff, with starting° pace or slow, *fitful*
And, measuring, views with wild and hollow eyes
Its distance from the waves that chide° below; *scold*
Who, as the sea-born gale with frequent sighs
Chills his cold bed upon the mountain turf,
With hoarse, half-utter'd lamentation, lies
Murmuring responses to the dashing surf?
In moody sadness, on the giddy° brink, *dizzying*
I see him more with envy than with fear;
He has no *nice felicities*° that shrink[1] *good fortunes*
From giant horrors; wildly wandering here,
He seems (uncursed with reason) not to know
The depth or the duration of his woe.

74
The Winter Night

"Sleep, that knits up the ravell'd sleeve of care,"[2]
Forsakes me, while the chill and sullen blast,
As my sad soul recalls its sorrows past,
Seems like a summons, bidding me prepare
For the last sleep of death.—Murmuring I hear
The hollow wind around the ancient towers,[3]
While night and silence reign; and cold and drear
The darkest gloom of Middle Winter lours;° *scowls*
But wherefore° fear existence such as mine, *why*
To change for long and undisturb'd repose?
Ah! when this suffering being I resign,
And o'er my miseries the tomb shall close,
By her,[4] whose loss in anguish I deplore,
I shall be laid, and feel that loss no more!

84
To the Muse[5]

Wilt thou forsake me who in life's bright May
Lent warmer lustre to the radiant morn;
And even o'er Summer scenes by tempests torn,
Shed with illusive light the dewy ray
Of pensive pleasure?—Wilt thou, while the day
Of saddening Autumn closes, as I mourn
In languid, hopeless sorrow, far away
Bend° thy soft step, and never more return?— *aim*
Crush'd to the earth, by bitterest anguish pressed,
From my faint eyes thy graceful form recedes;
Thou canst not heal an heart like mine that bleeds;
But, when in quiet earth that heart shall rest,
Haply° may'st thou one sorrowing vigil keep, *by chance*
Where Pity and Remembrance bend° and weep![6] *kneel*
—1784–97

---

[1] [Smith's note] "This delicate felicity that shrinks / When rocking winds are loud." Walpole. [Horace Walpole (1717–97); these lines are untraced.]

[2] [Smith's note] Shakespeare. [Cf. *Macbeth* 2.2.36.]

[3] [Smith's note] These lines were written in a residence among ancient public buildings.

[4] *her* Smith's daughter, Anna Augusta (d. 1795). Cf. Smith's "Sonnet 65," not included in this anthology.

[5] *Muse* Goddess of poetic inspiration, the invocation of whom is a tradition going back to Classical antiquity.

[6] [Smith's note] "Where melancholy friendship bends and weeps." Thomas Gray. [Cf. "Epitaph on Sir William Williams," line 12, by Thomas Gray (1716–71).]

The French Revolution

CONTEXTS

Debate about the French Revolution, which was to open English eyes to the possibility of political change in their own country, began shortly after the 14 July 1789 storming of the Bastille (during which a Parisian crowd swarmed the prison in search of ammunition, freeing seven prisoners and killing the governor in the process). The Revolution forced English men and women to re-examine their most basic societal tenets: their system of government and their handling of issues such as individual civil rights and liberties, rights of inheritance, and sufferance. Discussion of the Revolution triggered a massive increase in the production of written materials. On the pages of novels, periodicals, sermons, chapbooks, handbills, song sheets, and poetry, English writers debated their new relationship with France and its implications for issues of social and political reform at home.

On 4 November 1789, moral philosopher, mathematician, and dissenting preacher Richard Price delivered a sermon venerating the French Revolution and equating it with England's Glorious Revolution of 1688–89, the bloodless revolution in which James II was replaced by William III and Mary II—a key moment in the evolution of constitutional monarchy in Britain. "Struggle no longer against increasing light and liberality," he warned. "Restore to mankind their rights; and consent to the correction of abuses, before they and you are destroyed together." Such views became more and more widespread over the course of the next few months. On 14 July 1790, Parisians gathered near the ruins of the Bastille to celebrate the Revolution's first anniversary, and there was celebrating in Britain too; according to the London *Times*, the anniversary gathering represented "a magnificent association of FREE MEN, emancipated from the shackles of despotism within so short a space of time." The newspaper declared the Revolution "a Phenomenon on which surrounding empires look with admiration." Such feelings ran counter to age-old habit; since 1688, the English had tended to think of themselves as progressive guardians of liberty and the French as intolerant and slavish in their Catholicism. To many in Britain, however, English attitudes did not seem to have changed. Rather, the French Revolution merely represented their long-overdue and much-needed Glorious Revolution.

To be sure, English support for the ideals of the French Revolution was far from being universal. The most important expression of early opposition to those ideals was that of politician and writer Edmund Burke, whose *Reflections on the Revolution in France* was published on 1 November 1790. Burke had strongly supported the American Revolution fifteen years earlier as representing an ordered and constitutionally-based response to tyranny, and he surprised many with his vigorous condemnation of the French Revolution as undermining the foundations of constitutional monarchy. In Burke's view, the suggestion of Price and others that a monarch owes his lawful authority solely "to the choice of the people" was either "nonsense, and therefore neither true nor false, or it affirms a most unfounded, dangerous, illegal and unconstitutional position."

Burke's long essay came to be regarded as a classic statement of conservative principles, and one of the works written in answer to it, Thomas Paine's *Rights of Man*, as a classic expression of Enlightenment principles of human liberty. The voice of Paine, an expatriate from England who had moved to America in 1774, was joined in Britain by voices such as those of William Godwin, Mary Wollstonecraft, and other prominent reformers who were later labeled "Jacobins." Condemning

Burke's allegiance to "canonized forefathers," Wollstonecraft accused him of clinging to an ideology of inherited rights: "any personal present convenience should prevent a struggle for the most estimable advantages. This is sound reasoning," she quipped, "in the mouth of the rich and short-sighted."

In 1792, a Republic was declared in France, and the Revolution's violence escalated. In May, the English government, fearing rebellion on its own soil, vowed to eradicate "wicked and seditious writings"; shortly thereafter, it banned Paine's *Rights of Man (Part II)*. In August, Louis XVI and Marie Antoinette were marched out of the Palace of the Tuileries and placed under house arrest—and an increasing number of English began to feel alienated from their French neighbors. Within the conservative English imagination, the French were becoming savages, choosing anarchy over liberty. Even some reformers began to reconsider their view of the Revolution, although they continued to lobby in England for expanded suffrage, electoral reform, and the natural rights of citizens. British attitudes toward the concept of revolution were further complicated by the similarly violent events of the Haitian Revolution (1791–1804), in which black slaves rose up against the island's French colonizers and eventually created an independent state.[1]

In late 1792, Maximilien Robespierre and his Committee for Public Safety took control of Paris and brutally demonstrated their intolerance for any enemy of the republic. The Committee put Louis XVI on trial, and the King and Queen soon joined the list of beheaded aristocrats, clergy, and counter-revolutionary suspects. The English anti-Jacobin movement gathered momentum as citizens expressed horror at these "un-English" acts. By this time other European nations had been considering intervention in France for more than two years. In April 1792, France declared war on Austria; after the execution of the King in early 1793, other countries (Britain included) joined to form the "First Coalition" against France. Over the next several years, the French government remained in a state of turmoil, but French forces held their own against their various enemies, with a young general named Napoleon Bonaparte playing an increasingly important military role. In 1799, Bonaparte seized power, and, for the next fifteen years, the powerful Corsican dominated the European stage.

For some in England, the French by that time had lost their way. In William Wordsworth's view, the oppressed had, in a few short years, "become Oppressors in their turn," and had "changed a war of self-defence / For one of conquest, losing sight of all / Which they had struggled for." Yet, as Godwin noted, all "the great points embraced by the revolution remain entire: hereditary government is gone; hereditary nobility is extinguished; the hierarchy of the Gallican church is no more; the feudal rights, the oppressive immunities of a mighty aristocracy, are banished never to return."

⌘⌘⌘

[1] See "The Haitian Revolution" in "Contexts: Slavery and Its Abolition," elsewhere in this volume.

from Richard Price, *A Discourse on the Love of Our Country, Delivered on Nov. 4, 1789, at the Meeting-House in the Old Jewry, to the Society for Commemorating the Revolution in Great Britain*

Richard Price (1723–91) was a well-known dissenting preacher, mathematician, and political thinker. This sermon initiated England's debate about the French Revolution by likening it to England's Glorious Revolution of 1688.

The love of our country has in all times been a subject of warm commendations; and it is certainly a noble passion; but, like all other passions, it requires regulation and direction. There are mistakes and prejudices by which, in this instance, we are in particular danger of being misled. I will briefly mention some of these to you, and observe,

First, That by our country is meant, in this case, not the soil or the spot of earth on which we happen to have been born; not the forests and fields, but that community of which we are members; or that body of companions and friends and kindred who are associated with us under the same constitution of government, protected by the same laws, and bound together by the same civil polity.

Secondly, It is proper to observe, that even in this sense of our country, that love of it which is our duty, does not imply any conviction of the superior value of it to other countries, or any particular preference of its laws and constitution of government. … All our attachments should be accompanied, as far as possible, with right opinions.—We are too apt to confine wisdom and virtue within the circle of our own acquaintance and party. Our friends, our country, and in short every thing related to us, we are disposed to overvalue. A wise man will guard himself against this delusion. He will study to think of all things as they are, and not suffer any partial affections to blind his understanding. …

Thirdly, It is proper I should desire you particularly to distinguish between the love of our country and that spirit of rivalship and ambition which has been common among nations.—What has the love of their country hitherto been among mankind? What has it been but a love of domination; a desire of conquest, and a thirst for grandeur and glory, by extending territory, and enslaving surrounding countries? What has it been but a blind and narrow principle, producing in every country a contempt of other countries, and forming men into combinations and factions against their common rights and liberties? … As most of the evils which have taken place in private life, and among individuals, have been occasioned by the desire of private interest overcoming the public affections; so most of the evils which have taken place among bodies of men have been occasioned by the desire of their own interest overcoming the principle of universal benevolence: and leading them to attack one another's territories, to encroach on one another's rights, and to endeavour to build their own advancement on the degradation of all within the reach of their power. …

… I have just observed, that there is a submission due to the executive officers of government, which is our duty; but you must not forget what I have also observed, that it must not be a blind and slavish submission. … [T]he tendency of every government is to despotism; and in this the best constituted governments must end, if the people are not vigilant, ready to take alarms, and determined to resist abuses as soon as they begin. … This vigilance, therefore, it is our duty to maintain. Whenever it is withdrawn, and a people cease to reason about their rights and to be awake to encroachments, they are in danger of being enslaved, and their *servants* will soon become their *masters*.

… We have, therefore, on this occasion, peculiar reasons for thanksgiving—But let us remember that we ought not to satisfy ourselves with thanksgivings. … Let us, in particular, take care not to forget the principles of the Revolution.[1] …

First; The right to liberty of conscience in religious matters.

[1] *Revolution* England's Glorious Revolution of 1688, which ended the reign of King James II and limited the monarch's power under a constitutional monarchy.

Secondly; The right to resist power when abused. And,

Thirdly; The right to choose our own governors; to cashier them for misconduct; and to frame a government for ourselves....

I would farther direct you to remember, that though the Revolution was a great work, it was by no means a perfect work; and that all was not then gained which was necessary to put the kingdom in the secure and complete possession of the blessings of liberty....

But the most important instance of the imperfect state in which the Revolution left our constitution, is the INEQUALITY OF OUR REPRESENTATION.... When the representation is partial, a kingdom possesses liberty only partially ... but if not only extremely partial, but corruptly chosen, and under corrupt influence after being chosen, it becomes a *nuisance,* and produces the worst of all forms of government—a government by corruption. ... We are, at present, I hope, at a great distance from it. But it cannot be pretended that there are no advances towards it, or that there is no reason for apprehension and alarm.

The inadequateness of our representation has long been a subject of complaint. But all attention to it seems now lost, and the probability is, that this inattention will continue, and that nothing will be done towards gaining for us this essential blessing, till some great calamity again alarms our fears, or till some great abuse of power again provokes our resentment; or, perhaps, till the acquisition of a pure and equal representation by other countries ... kindles our shame....

What an eventful period is this! I am thankful that I have lived to it. ... I have lived to see a diffusion of knowledge, which has undermined superstition and error—I have lived to see the rights of men better understood than ever; and nations panting for liberty, which seemed to have lost the idea of it. I have lived to see THIRTY MILLIONS of people, indignant and resolute, spurning at slavery, and demanding liberty with an irresistible voice; their king led in triumph, and an arbitrary monarch surrendering himself to his subjects. —After sharing in the benefits of one Revolution, I have been spared to be a witness to two other Revolutions, both glorious.[1]—And now, methinks, I see the ardour for liberty catching and spreading; a general amendment beginning in human affairs; the dominion of kings changed for the dominion of laws, and the dominion of priests giving way to the dominion of reason and conscience.

Be encouraged, all ye friends of freedom, and writers in its defence! ... Behold kingdoms, admonished by you, starting from sleep, breaking their fetters, and claiming justice from their oppressors! Behold, the light you have struck out, after setting AMERICA free, reflected to FRANCE, and there kindled into a blaze that lays despotism in ashes, and warms and illuminates EUROPE!

Tremble all ye oppressors of the world! Take warning all ye supporters of slavish governments, and slavish hierarchies! Call no more (absurdly and wickedly) REFORMATION, innovation. You cannot now hold the world in darkness. Struggle no longer against increasing light and liberality. Restore to mankind their rights; and consent to the correction of abuses, before they and you are destroyed together.

from Edmund Burke, *Reflections on the Revolution in France* (1790)

A political writer and politician, Edmund Burke (1730–97) wrote the *Reflections* as a rebuttal to Price's *Discourse on the Love of Our Country.* Burke's conservative critique of the revolution was published two years before Louis XVI was executed, and it set the tone for the loyalist side of England's revolution debate.

... When I see the spirit of liberty in action, I see a strong principle at work; and this, for a while, is all I can possibly know of it. The wild *gas,* the fixed air, is plainly broke loose: but we ought to suspend our judgment until the first effervescence is a little subsided, till the liquor is cleared, and until we see something deeper than the agitation of a troubled and frothy surface. I must be

[1] *After sharing ... both glorious* Price refers first to the Glorious Revolution, then to the American and French revolutions.

tolerably sure, before I venture publicly to congratulate men upon a blessing, that they have really received one. Flattery corrupts both the receiver and the giver; and adulation is not of more service to the people than to kings. I should therefore suspend my congratulations on the new liberty of France, until I was informed how it had been combined with government; with public force; with the discipline and obedience of armies; with the collection of an effective and well-distributed revenue; with morality and religion; with the solidity of property; with peace and order; with civil and social manners. All these (in their way) are good things too; and, without them, liberty is not a benefit whilst it lasts, and is not likely to continue long. The effect of liberty to individuals is that they may do what they please: we ought to see what it will please them to do, before we risk congratulations, which may be soon turned into complaints. Prudence would dictate this in the case of separate, insulated, private men; but liberty, when men act in bodies, is *power*. Considerate people, before they declare themselves, will observe the use which is made of *power*; and particularly of so trying a thing as *new* power in *new* persons, of whose principles, tempers, and dispositions they have little or no experience. …

It appears to me as if I were in [the midst of] a great crisis, not of the affairs of France alone, but of all Europe, perhaps of more than Europe. All circumstances taken together, the French Revolution is the most astonishing that has hitherto happened in the world. The most wonderful[1] things are brought about in many instances by means the most absurd and ridiculous; in the most ridiculous modes; and, apparently, by the most contemptible instruments. Everything seems out of nature in this strange chaos of levity and ferocity, and of all sorts of crimes jumbled together with all sorts of follies. In viewing this monstrous tragi-comic scene, the most opposite passions necessarily succeed, and sometimes mix with each other in the mind; alternate contempt and indignation; alternate laughter and tears; alternate scorn and horror. …

[1] *wonderful* Remarkable, extraordinary (not necessarily with any positive connotation).

Whatever may be the success of evasion in explaining away the gross error of fact, which supposes that his Majesty (though he holds it in concurrence with the wishes) owes his crown to the choice of his people, yet nothing can evade their full, explicit declaration concerning the principle of a right in the people to choose—which right is directly maintained, and tenaciously adhered to. … The political divine proceeds dogmatically to assert that, by the principles of the Revolution,[2] the people of England have acquired three fundamental rights …: that we have acquired a right

1. "To choose our own governors."
2. "To cashier[3] them for misconduct."
3. "To frame a government for ourselves."

This new, and hitherto unheard-of bill of rights, though made in the name of the whole people, belongs to those gentlemen and their faction[4] only. The body of the people of England have no share in it. They utterly disclaim it. They will resist the practical assertion of it with their lives and fortunes. They are bound to do so by the laws of their country, made at the time of that very Revolution which is appealed to in favour of the fictitious rights claimed by the society which abuses its name. …

The people of England will not ape the fashions they have never tried, nor go back to those which they have found mischievous on trial.[5] They look upon the legal hereditary succession of their crown as among their rights, not as among their wrongs; as a benefit, not as a grievance; as a security for their liberty, not as a badge of

[2] *the Revolution* The English Revolution of 1688, known as the Glorious Revolution. This revolution led to the passing of the Bill of Rights in 1689, limiting the authority of the monarch and laying out rights for English citizens and Parliament. Richard Price believed the Glorious Revolution to have paved the way for the French Revolution, which he supported.

[3] *cashier* Depose.

[4] *those gentlemen and their faction* I.e., Richard Price and those thinkers who agree with him.

[5] *which they have found mischievous on trial* Which they have, after having tried them, found to be productive of bad results.

servitude. They look on the frame of their commonwealth,[1] such as it stands, to be of inestimable value, and they conceive the undisturbed succession of the crown[2] to be a pledge of the stability and perpetuity of all the other members of our constitution.[3] …

You will observe, that from Magna Charta to the Declaration of Right,[4] it has been the uniform policy of our constitution to claim and assert our liberties, as an *entailed*[5] *inheritance* derived to us from our forefathers, and to be transmitted to our posterity; as an estate specially belonging to the people of this kingdom, without any reference whatever to any other more general or prior right. By this means our constitution preserves a unity in so great a diversity of its parts. We have an inheritable crown; an inheritable peerage;[6] and a House of Commons[7] and a people inheriting privileges, franchises, and liberties, from a long line of ancestors.

This policy appears to me to be the result of profound reflection; or rather the happy effect of following nature, which is wisdom without reflection, and above it. A spirit of innovation is generally the result of a selfish temper, and confined views. People will not look forward to posterity, who never look backward to their ancestors. Besides, the people of England well know, that the idea of inheritance furnishes a sure principle of conservation, and a sure principle of transmission; without at all excluding a principle of improvement. It leaves acquisition free; but it secures what it acquires. Whatever advantages are obtained by a state proceeding on these maxims, are locked fast as in a sort of family settlement; grasped as in a kind of mortmain[8] for ever. By a constitutional policy, working after the pattern of nature, we receive, we hold, we transmit our government and our privileges, in the same manner in which we enjoy and transmit our property and our lives. The institutions of policy, the goods of fortune, the gifts of providence, are handed down to us, and from us, in the same course and order. Our political system is placed in a just correspondence and symmetry with the order of the world, and with the mode of existence decreed to a permanent body composed of transitory parts; wherein, by the disposition of a stupendous wisdom, moulding together the great mysterious incorporation of the human race, the whole, at one time, is never old, or middle-aged, or young, but, in a condition of unchangeable constancy, moves on through the varied tenor of perpetual decay, fall, renovation, and progression. Thus, by preserving the method of nature in the conduct of the state, in what we improve, we are never wholly new; in what we retain, we are never wholly obsolete. By adhering in this manner and on those principles to our forefathers, we are guided not by the superstition of antiquarians, but by the spirit of philosophic analogy. In this choice of inheritance we have given to our frame of polity the image of a relation in blood; binding up the constitution of our country with our dearest domestic ties; adopting our fundamental laws into the bosom of our family affections; keeping inseparable, and cherishing with the warmth of all their combined and mutually reflected charities, our state, our hearths, our sepulchres, and our altars.

Through the same plan of a conformity to nature in our artificial institutions, and by calling in the aid of her unerring and powerful instincts, to fortify the fallible and feeble contrivances of our reason, we have derived several other, and those no small benefits, from considering our liberties in the light of an inheritance. Always acting as if in the presence of canonized forefathers, the

[1] *frame of their commonwealth* Political structure of their kingdom.

[2] *undisturbed succession of the crown* Uninterrupted hereditary succession of monarchs.

[3] *perpetuity* Permanence; *members of our constitution* Various documents, such as the Magna Carta, comprising the body politic of England, which has no single codified constitution.

[4] *Magna Charta* England's Great Charter of 1215 was a precedent-setting document that limited the power of King John; *Declaration of Right* Brought about by the Glorious Revolution, this bill increased the power of Parliament and is fundamental to English constitutional law.

[5] *entailed* Alludes to the legal concept of the entail, a form of inheritance in which property is inherited according to a pre-existing rule of succession, from which one may not legally deviate.

[6] *peerage* Nobility.

[7] *House of Commons* Lower house of Parliament, to which representatives from various districts are elected.

[8] *mortmain* Legal term for the perpetual tenure of land by a corporation (often ecclesiastical).

spirit of freedom, leading in itself to misrule and excess, is tempered with an awful[1] gravity. This idea of a liberal descent inspires us with a sense of habitual native dignity, which prevents that upstart insolence almost inevitably adhering to and disgracing those who are the first acquirers of any distinction. By this means our liberty becomes a noble freedom. It carries an imposing and majestic aspect. It has a pedigree and illustrating ancestors. It has its bearings and its ensigns armorial. It has its gallery of portraits; its monumental inscriptions; its records, evidences, and titles. We procure reverence to our civil institutions on the principle upon which nature teaches us to revere individual men; on account of their age, and on account of those from whom they are descended. All your sophisters[2] cannot produce anything better adapted to preserve a rational and manly freedom than the course that we have pursued, who have chosen our nature rather than our speculations, our breasts rather than our inventions, for the great conservatories and magazines[3] of our rights and privileges. …

History will record, that on the morning of the 6th of October, 1789, the king and queen of France, after a day of confusion, alarm, dismay, and slaughter, lay down, under the pledged security of public faith, to indulge nature in a few hours of respite, and troubled, melancholy repose. From this sleep the queen was first startled by the voice of the sentinel at her door, who cried out her to save herself by flight—that this was the last proof of fidelity he could give—that they were upon him, and he was dead. Instantly he was cut down. A band of cruel ruffians and assassins, reeking with his blood, rushed into the chamber of the queen, and pierced with a hundred strokes of bayonets and poniards the bed, from whence this persecuted woman had but just time to fly almost naked, and, through ways unknown to the murderers, had escaped to seek refuge at the feet of a king and husband, not secure of his own life for a moment.

This king, to say no more of him, and this queen, and their infant children, (who once would have been the pride and hope of a great and generous people,) were then forced to abandon the sanctuary of the most splendid palace in the world, which they left swimming in blood, polluted by massacre, and strewed with scattered limbs and mutilated carcasses. Thence they were conducted into the capital of their kingdom. Two had been selected from the unprovoked, unresisted, promiscuous slaughter, which was made of the gentlemen of birth and family who composed the king's body guard. These two gentlemen, with all the parade of an execution of justice, were cruelly and publicly dragged to the block, and beheaded in the great court of the palace. Their heads were stuck upon spears, and led the procession; whilst the royal captives who followed in the train were slowly moved along, amidst the horrid yells, and shrilling screams, and frantic dances, and infamous contumelies,[4] and all the unutterable abominations of the furies of hell, in the abused shape of the vilest of women. After they had been made to taste, drop by drop, more than the bitterness of death, in the slow torture of a journey of twelve miles, protracted to six hours, they were, under a guard, composed of those very soldiers who had thus conducted them through this famous triumph, lodged in one of the old palaces of Paris, now converted into a Bastile[5] for kings.

Is this a triumph to be consecrated at altars? to be commemorated with grateful thanksgiving? to be offered to the divine humanity with fervent prayer and enthusiastic ejaculation? …

It is now sixteen or seventeen years since I saw the queen of France, then the dauphiness, at Versailles; and surely never lighted on this orb,[6] which she hardly seemed to touch, a more delightful vision. I saw her just above the horizon, decorating and cheering the elevated sphere she just began to move in,—glittering like the morning-star, full of life, and splendour, and joy. Oh!

[1] *awful* Inspiring awe or reverence (not necessarily with a negative connotation).

[2] *sophisters* People who make skillfully persuasive but fallacious arguments.

[3] *magazines* Warehouses.

[4] *contumelies* Humiliations, abuses.

[5] *Bastile* Name of the major political prison in France.

[6] *then the dauphiness* Marie Antoinette was Dauphine of France from April 1770 until May 1774, as the wife of Louis-Auguste, Dauphin of France, prior to his ascension to the throne; *this orb* The earth.

what a revolution! and what a heart must I have to contemplate without emotion that elevation and that fall! Little did I dream when she added titles of veneration to those of enthusiastic, distant, respectful love, that she should ever be obliged to carry the sharp antidote against disgrace concealed in that bosom; little did I dream that I should have lived to see such disasters fallen upon her in a nation of gallant men, in a nation of men of honour, and of cavaliers. I thought ten thousand swords must have leaped from their scabbards to avenge even a look that threatened her with insult. But the age of chivalry is gone. That of sophisters, economists, and calculators, has succeeded; and the glory of Europe is extinguished for ever. Never, never more shall we behold that generous loyalty to rank and sex,[1] that proud submission, that dignified obedience, that subordination of the heart, which kept alive, even in servitude itself, the spirit of an exalted freedom. The unbought grace of life, the cheap defence of nations, the nurse[2] of manly sentiment and heroic enterprise, is gone! It is gone, that sensibility of principle, that charity of honour, which felt a stain like a wound, which inspired courage whilst it mitigated ferocity, which ennobled whatever it touched, and under which vice itself lost half its evil, by losing all its grossness.

This mixed system of opinion and sentiment had its origin in the ancient chivalry; and the principle, though varied in its appearance by the varying state of human affairs, subsisted and influenced through a long succession of generations, even to the time we live in. If it should ever be totally extinguished, the loss I fear will be great. It is this [system] which has given its character to modern Europe. It is this which has distinguished it under all its forms of government, and distinguished it to its advantage, from the states of Asia, and possibly from those states which flourished in the most brilliant periods of the antique world. It was this, which, without confounding ranks, had produced a noble equality, and handed it down through all the gradations of social life. It was this opinion which mitigated kings into companions, and raised private men to be fellows with kings. Without force or opposition, it subdued the fierceness of pride and power; it obliged sovereigns to submit to the soft collar of social esteem. …

But now all is to be changed. All the pleasing illusions, which made power gentle and obedience liberal, which harmonized the different shades of life, and which, by a bland[3] assimilation, incorporated into politics the sentiments which beautify and soften private society, are to be dissolved by this new conquering empire of light and reason. All the decent drapery of life is to be rudely torn off. All the superadded ideas, furnished from the wardrobe of a moral imagination, which the heart owns, and the understanding ratifies, as necessary to cover the defects of our naked, shivering nature, and to raise it to dignity in our own estimation, are to be exploded as a ridiculous, absurd, and antiquated fashion.

On this scheme of things, a king is but a man, a queen is but a woman; a woman is but an animal, and an animal not of the highest order. All homage paid to the sex in general as such,[4] …, is to be regarded as romance and folly. Regicide, and parricide, and sacrilege,[5] are but fictions of superstition, corrupting jurisprudence by destroying its simplicity. The murder of a king, or a queen, or a bishop, or a father, are only common homicide; and if the people are by any chance, or in any way, gainers by it, a sort of homicide much the most pardonable, and into which we ought not to make too severe a scrutiny.

On the scheme of this barbarous philosophy, which is the offspring of cold hearts and muddy understandings, and which is as void of solid wisdom as it is destitute of all taste and elegance, laws are to be supported only by their own terrors, and by the concern

[1] *generous loyalty to rank and sex* I.e., chivalric reverence due to those of the upper classes and of the female sex; *generous* Noble, magnanimous.

[2] *cheap defence of nations* Often erroneously quoted as "Education is the cheap defence of nations"; *cheap* Unbought, costing nothing; *nurse* That which nurtures.

[3] *bland* Pleasant, soothing.

[4] *to the sex … as such* To women, inherently because of their womanhood.

[5] *Regicide, and parricide, and sacrilege* Killing of one's king, killing of one's father, and violation of the sacred.

which each individual may find in them from his own private speculations, or can spare to them from his own private interests. In the groves of their academy, at the end of every vista, you see nothing but the gallows. Nothing is left which engages the affections on the part of the commonwealth. On the principles of this mechanic philosophy, our institutions can never be embodied, if I may use the expression, in persons; so as to create in us love, veneration, admiration, or attachment. But that sort of reason which banishes the affections is incapable of filling their place. These public affections, combined with manners, are required sometimes as supplements, sometimes as correctives, always as aids to law. The precept given by a wise man, as well as a great critic, for the construction of poems, is equally true as to states:—*Non satis est pulchra esse poemata, dulcia sunto*.[1] There ought to be a system of manners in every nation, which a well-formed mind would be disposed to relish. To make us love our country, our country ought to be lovely.

But power, of some kind or other, will survive the shock in which manners and opinions perish; and it will find other and worse means for its support. The usurpation which, in order to subvert ancient institutions, has destroyed ancient principles, will hold power by arts similar to those by which it has acquired it. When the old feudal and chivalrous spirit of fealty, which, by freeing kings from fear, freed both kings and subjects from the precautions of tyranny,[2] shall be extinct in the minds of men, plots and assassinations will be anticipated by preventive murder and preventive confiscation, and that long roll of grim and bloody maxims, which form the political code of all power, not standing on its own honour, and the honour of those who are to obey it. Kings will be tyrants from policy, when subjects are rebels from principle.

When ancient opinions and rules of life are taken away, the loss cannot possibly be estimated. From that moment we have no compass to govern us; nor can we know distinctly to what port we steer. Europe, undoubtedly, taken in a mass, was in a flourishing condition the day on which your revolution was completed. How much of that prosperous state was owing to the spirit of our old manners and opinions is not easy to say; but as such causes cannot be indifferent in their operation, we must presume, that, on the whole, their operation was beneficial.

We are but too apt to consider things in the state in which we find them, without sufficiently adverting to[3] the causes by which they have been produced, and possibly may be upheld. Nothing is more certain, than that our manners, our civilization, and all the good things which are connected with manners and with civilization, have, in this European world of ours, depended for ages upon two principles; and were indeed the result of both combined; I mean the spirit of a gentleman, and the spirit of religion. The nobility and the clergy, the one by profession, the other by patronage, kept learning in existence, even in the midst of arms and confusions, and whilst governments were rather in their causes than formed. Learning paid back what it received to nobility and to priesthood, and paid it with usury,[4] by enlarging their ideas, and by furnishing their minds. Happy if they had all continued to know their indissoluble union, and their proper place! Happy if learning, not debauched by ambition, had been satisfied to continue the instructor, and not aspired to be the master! Along with its natural protectors and guardians, learning will be cast into the mire, and trodden down under the hoofs of a swinish multitude.[5] …

We know, and what is better, we feel inwardly, that religion is the basis of civil society, and the source of all good and of all comfort. In England we are so convinced of this, that there is no rust of superstition, with

[1] *Non satis … dulcia sunto* Latin: It is insufficient for poems to be beautiful; they should also be sweetly pleasing (quoted from Horace's *Ars Poetica* or *The Poetic Arts*).

[2] *precautions of tyranny* Anticipatory acts (such as are mentioned a few words on—preventive murder, etc.).

[3] *adverting to* Taking note of; paying attention to.

[4] *usury* Interest, especially at an exorbitantly high rate.

[5] *swinish multitude* This became one of Burke's most infamous and frequently-cited comments. Though Burke is probably here referring to a particular faction of extremists, and not to average citizens, many reformers took this comment as proof of arrogance on the part of Burke and the conservative faction.

which the accumulated absurdity of the human mind might have crusted it over in the course of ages, that ninety-nine in a hundred of the people of England would not prefer to impiety. …

If our religious tenets should ever want a further elucidation, we shall not call on atheism to explain them. We shall not light up our temple from that unhallowed fire. It will be illuminated with other lights. It will be perfumed with other incense, than the infectious stuff which is imported by the smugglers of adulterated metaphysics. If our ecclesiastical establishment should want a revision, it is not avarice or rapacity, public or private, that we shall employ for the audit, or receipt, or application of its consecrated revenue. Violently condemning neither the Greek nor the Armenian, nor, since heats are subsided, the Roman system of religion,[1] we prefer the Protestant; not because we think it has less of the Christian religion in it, but because, in our judgment, it has more. We are Protestants, not from indifference, but from zeal.

We know, and it is our pride to know, that man is by his constitution a religious animal; that atheism is against, not only our reason, but our instincts; and that it cannot prevail long. But if, in the moment of riot, and in a drunken delirium from the hot spirit drawn out of the alembic[2] of hell, which in France is now so furiously boiling, we should uncover our nakedness, by throwing off that Christian religion which has hitherto been our boast and comfort, and one great source of civilization amongst us, and amongst many other nations, we are apprehensive (being well aware that the mind will not endure a void) that some uncouth, pernicious, and degrading superstition might take place of it. …

When the people have emptied themselves of all the lust of selfish will, which without religion it is utterly impossible they ever should, when they are conscious that they exercise, and exercise perhaps in a higher link of the order of delegation, the power, which to be legitimate must be according to that eternal, immutable law, in which will and reason are the same, they will be more careful how they place power in base[3] and incapable hands. In their nomination to office they will not appoint to the exercise of authority, as to a pitiful job, but as to a holy function; not according to their sordid, selfish interest, nor to their wanton caprice, nor to their arbitrary will; but they will confer that power (which any man may well tremble to give or to receive) on those only, in whom they may discern that predominant proportion of active virtue and wisdom, taken together and fitted to the charge, such, as in the great and inevitable mixed mass of human imperfections and infirmities, is to be found.

To avoid therefore the evils of inconstancy and versatility,[4] ten thousand times worse than those of obstinacy and the blindest prejudice, we have consecrated the state, that no man should approach to look into its defects or corruptions but with due caution; that he should never dream of beginning its reformation by its subversion; that he should approach to the faults of the state as to the wounds of a father, with pious awe and trembling solicitude. By this wise prejudice we are taught to look with horror on those children of their country, who are prompt rashly to hack that aged parent in pieces, and put him into the kettle of magicians, in hopes that by their poisonous weeds, and wild incantations, they may regenerate the paternal constitution, and renovate their father's life.

Society is indeed a contract. Subordinate contracts for objects of mere occasional interest may be dissolved at pleasure—but the state ought not to be considered as nothing better than a partnership agreement in a trade of pepper and coffee, calico or tobacco, or some other such low concern, to be taken up for a little temporary interest, and to be dissolved by the fancy of the parties. It is to be looked on with other reverence; because it is not a partnership in things subservient only to the gross[5] animal existence of a temporary and perishable nature.

[1] *neither the Greek … religion* Neither the Greek and Eastern Orthodox churches, nor Roman Catholicism; i.e., the two primary branches of Christianity other than Protestantism, which was the official religion of England.

[2] *alembic* Alchemical device which distills substances via a long tube.

[3] *base* Common, not of noble rank.

[4] *versatility* I.e., in the sense of being changeable or fickle.

[5] *gross* Coarse, material.

It is a partnership in all science; a partnership in all art; a partnership in every virtue, and in all perfection. As the ends of such a partnership cannot be obtained in many generations, it becomes a partnership not only between those who are living, but between those who are living, those who are dead, and those who are to be born. Each contract of each particular state is but a clause in the great primeval contract of eternal society, linking the lower with the higher natures, connecting the visible and invisible world, according to a fixed compact sanctioned by the inviolable oath which holds all physical and all moral natures, each in their appointed place. …

But am I so unreasonable as to see nothing at all that deserves commendation in the indefatigable labours of this Assembly?[1] I do not deny that, among an infinite number of acts of violence and folly, some good may have been done. They who destroy everything certainly will remove some grievance. They who make everything new, have a chance that they may establish something beneficial. To give them credit for what they have done in virtue of the authority they have usurped, or which can excuse them in the crimes by which that authority has been acquired, it must appear, that the same things could not have been accomplished without producing such a revolution. Most assuredly they might. … The improvements of the National Assembly are superficial, their errors fundamental.

Whatever they are, I wish my countrymen rather to recommend to our neighbours the example of the British constitution, than to take models from them for the improvement of our own. In the former they have got an invaluable treasure. They are not, I think, without some causes of apprehension and complaint; but these they do not owe to their constitution, but to their own conduct. I think our happy situation owing to our constitution; but owing to the whole of it, and not to any part singly; owing in a great measure to what we have left standing in our several reviews and reformations, as well as to what we have altered or superadded. Our people will find employment enough for a truly patriotic, free, and independent spirit, in guarding what they possess from violation. …

I have little to recommend my opinions but long observation and much impartiality. They come from one who has been no tool of power, no flatterer of greatness; and who in his last acts does not wish to belie the tenor of his life. They come from one, almost the whole of whose public exertion has been a struggle for the liberty of others; from one in whose breast no anger durable or vehement has ever been kindled, but by what he considered as tyranny. …

[1] *this Assembly* I.e., the French National Assembly.

from Mary Wollstonecraft, *A Vindication of the Rights of Men, in a Letter to the Right Honourable Edmund Burke; Occasioned by His* Reflections on the Revolution in France (1790)

The primary purpose of this pamphlet by Mary Wollstonecraft (1759–97) was the defense of Richard Price, whom Edmund Burke described as a radical in his *Reflections on the Revolution in France* (1790). Price, like Wollstonecraft, advocated republicanism in opposition to Burke's championing of constitutional monarchy. In the following excerpts, Wollstonecraft challenges Burke's conservative attachment to tradition and his enshrinement of hereditary private property as essential to civilized life.

Sir,

… I perceive, from the whole tenor of your Reflections, that you have a mortal antipathy to reason; but, if there is any thing like argument, or first principles, in your wild declamation, behold the result: that we are to reverence the rust of antiquity, and term the unnatural customs, which ignorance and mistaken self-interest have consolidated, the sage fruit of experience: nay, that, if we do discover some errors, our *feelings* should lead us to excuse, with blind love, or unprincipled filial affection, the venerable vestiges of ancient days. These are gothic notions of beauty—the ivy is beautiful, but, when it insidiously destroys the trunk from which it receives support, who would not grub it up?[2]

[2] *grub it up* Tear it out.

Further, that we ought cautiously to remain for ever in frozen inactivity, because a thaw, whilst it nourishes the soil, spreads a temporary inundation; and the fear of risking any personal present convenience should prevent a struggle for the most estimable advantages. This is sound reasoning, I grant, in the mouth of the rich and short-sighted.

Yes, Sir, the strong gained riches, the few have sacrificed the many to their vices; and, to be able to pamper their appetites, and supinely exist without exercising mind or body, they have ceased to be men. Lost to the relish of true pleasure, such beings would, indeed, deserve compassion, if injustice was not softened by the tyrant's plea—necessity; if prescription was not raised as an immortal boundary against innovation. Their minds, in fact, instead of being cultivated, have been so warped by education, that it may require some ages to bring them back to nature, and enable them to see their true interest, with that degree of conviction which is necessary to influence their conduct.

The civilization which has taken place in Europe has been very partial,[1] and, like every custom that an arbitrary point of honour has established, refines the manners at the expense of morals, by making sentiments and opinions current in conversation that have no root in the heart, or weight in the cooler resolves of the mind. And what has stopped its progress?—hereditary property—hereditary honours. …

And what is this mighty revolution in property?[2] The present incumbents only are injured, or the hierarchy of the clergy, an ideal part of the constitution, which you have personified, to render your affection more tender. How has posterity been injured by a distribution of the property snatched, perhaps, from innocent hands, but accumulated by the most abominable violation of every sentiment of justice and piety? Was the monument of former ignorance and iniquity to be held sacred, to enable the present possessors of enormous benefices[3] to *dissolve* in indolent pleasures? Was not their convenience, for they have not been turned adrift on the world, to give place to a just partition of the land belonging to the state? And did not the respect due to the natural equality of man require this triumph over Monkish rapacity?[4] Were those monsters to be reverenced on account of their antiquity, and their unjust claims perpetuated to their ideal children, the clergy, merely to preserve the sacred majesty of Property inviolate, and to enable the Church to retain her pristine splendor? Can posterity be injured by individuals losing the chance of obtaining great wealth, without meriting it, by its being diverted from a narrow channel, and disembogued[5] into the sea that affords clouds to water all the land? Besides, the clergy not brought up with the expectation of great revenues will not feel the loss; and if bishops should happen to be chosen on account of their personal merit, religion may be benefited by the vulgar nomination.[6] …

But, among all your plausible arguments, and witty illustrations, your contempt for the poor always appears conspicuous, and rouses my indignation. The following paragraph in particular struck me, as breathing the most tyrannic spirit, and displaying the most factitious feelings. "Good order is the foundation of all good things. To be enabled to acquire, the people, without being servile, must be tractable and obedient. The magistrate must have his reverence, the laws their authority. The body of the people must not find the principles of natural subordination by art rooted out of their minds. *They must respect that property of which they cannot partake. They must labour to obtain what by labour can be obtained; and when they find, as they commonly do, the success disproportioned to the endeavour, they must be*

[1] *partial* Incomplete.

[2] *mighty revolution in property* Speaking of the French Revolution, Burke wrote in his *Reflections* that "few barbarous conquerors have ever made so terrible a revolution in property."

[3] *enormous benefices* Rich livings (of property and money) given to the clergy of the Catholic church. During the French Revolution, church lands were confiscated and made over to the state; in 1790, the Civil Constitution of the Clergy was passed, which officially subordinated the Church to the French state, and which mandated that bishops and priests be elected by the people.

[4] *Monkish rapacity* Clerical greed.

[5] *disembogued* Emptied out (from a river mouth).

[6] *vulgar nomination* Popular vote.

taught their consolation in the final proportions of eternal justice. Of this consolation, whoever deprives them, deadens their industry, and strikes at the root of all acquisition as of all conservation. He that does this, is the cruel oppressor, the merciless enemy, of the poor and wretched; at the same time that, by his wicked speculations, he exposes the fruits of successful industry, and the accumulations of fortune," (ah! there's the rub)[1] "to the plunder of the negligent, the disappointed, and the unprosperous."

This is contemptible hard-hearted sophistry, in the specious form of humility, and submission to the will of Heaven. It is, Sir, *possible* to render the poor happier in this world, without depriving them of the consolation which you gratuitously grant them in the next. They have a right to more comfort than they at present enjoy; and more comfort might be afforded them, without encroaching on the pleasures of the rich: not now waiting to enquire whether the rich have any right to exclusive pleasures. What do I say?—encroaching! No; if an intercourse were established between them, it would impart the only true pleasure that can be snatched in this land of shadows, this hard school of moral discipline. …

Your real or artificial affection for the English constitution seems to me to resemble the brutal affection of some weak characters. They think it a duty to love their relations with a blind, indolent tenderness, that *will not* see the faults it might assist to correct, if their affection had been built on rational grounds. They love they know not why, and they will love to the end of the chapter.

Is it absolute blasphemy to doubt of the omnipotence of the law, or to suppose that religion might be more pure if there were fewer baits for hypocrites in the church? But our manners, you tell us, are drawn from the French, though you had before celebrated our native plainness. If they were, it is time we broke loose from Dependence—Time that Englishmen drew water from their own springs; for, if manners are not a painted substitute for morals, we have only to cultivate our reason, and we shall not feel the want of an arbitrary model. Nature will suffice; but I forget myself: Nature and Reason, according to your system, are all to give place to authority; and the gods, as Shakespeare makes a frantic wretch exclaim, seem to kill us for their sport, as men do flies.[2] …

from Thomas Paine, *Rights of Man* (1791 and 1792)

Thomas Paine (1737–1809) was indicted for treason because of his unflinching reformist reply to Burke's *Reflections on the Revolution in France.* After fleeing to France, he was imprisoned for not supporting Louis XVI's execution. He was spared the guillotine, and spent the rest of his years in America.

There is scarcely an epithet of abuse to be found in the English language, with which Mr. Burke has not loaded the French Nation and the National Assembly. Every thing which rancour, prejudice, ignorance, or knowledge, could suggest, are poured forth in the copious fury of near four hundred pages. In the strain, and on the plan Mr. Burke was writing, he might have written on to as many thousands. When the tongue or the pen is let loose in a frenzy of passion, it is the man, and not the subject, that becomes exhausted. …

As Mr. Burke occasionally applies the poison drawn from his horrid principles, not only to the English nation, but to the French Revolution and the National Assembly, and charges that august, illuminated and illuminating body of men with the epithet of *usurpers,* I shall, *sans ceremonie,* place another system of principles in opposition to his.

The English Parliament of 1688 did a certain thing, which, for themselves and their constituents, they had a right to do, and which it appeared right should be done: But, in addition to this right, which they possessed by delegation, *they set up another right by assumption,* that of binding and controlling posterity to the end of time. The case, therefore, divides itself into two parts;

[1] *there's the rub* Therein lies the difficulty. Cf. *Hamlet* 3.1.65.

[2] *the gods … as men do flies* Cf. *King Lear* 4.1.36–37.

"THE RIGHTS OF MAN;—or—TOMMY PAINE, the little American Taylor, taking the Measure of the CROWN, for a new Pair of Revolution-Breeches." Humbly dedicated to the Jacobine Clubs of France & England!!! by Common Sense, 1791. This anti-Jacobin caricature suggests that Thomas Paine, who was once a tailor, is no match for the enormous legacy of the English monarchy.

the right which they possessed by delegation, and the right which they set up by assumption. The first is admitted; but, with respect to the second, I reply—

There never did, there never will, and there never can exist a parliament, or any description of men, or any generation of men, in any country, possessed of the right or the power of binding and controlling posterity to the "*end of time*," or of commanding forever how the world shall be governed, or who shall govern it; and therefore, all such clauses, acts, or declarations, by which the makers of them attempt to do what they have neither the right nor the power to do, nor the power to execute, are in themselves null and void. Every age and generation must be as free to act for itself, *in all cases*, as the ages and generations which preceded it. The vanity and presumption of governing beyond the grave, is the most ridiculous and insolent of all tyrannies. … It is the living, and not the dead, that are to be accommodated. When man ceases to be, his power and his wants cease with him; and having no longer any participation in the concerns of this world, he has no longer any authority in directing who shall be its governors, or how its government shall be organized, or how administered. …

While I am writing this, there are accidentally before me some proposals for a declaration of rights by the Marquis de la Fayette[1] (I ask his pardon for using his former address, and do it only for distinction's sake) to the National Assembly, on the 11th of July 1789, three days before the taking of the Bastile; and I cannot but remark with astonishment how opposite the sources are from which that Gentleman and Mr. Burke draw their principles. Instead of referring to musty records and mouldy parchments to prove that the rights of the living are lost, "renounced and abdicated forever," by those who are now no more, as Mr. Burke has done, M. de la Fayette applies to the living world, and emphatically says, "Call to mind the sentiments which Nature has engraved in the heart of every citizen, and which take a new force when they are solemnly recognized by all:—For a nation to love liberty, it is sufficient that she knows it; and to be free, it is sufficient that she wills it." …

It was not against Louis the XVIth, but against the despotic principles of the government, that the nation revolted. These principles had not their origin in him, but in the original establishment, many centuries back[.] … Perhaps no man, bred up in the stile of an absolute King, ever possessed a heart so little disposed to the exercise of that species of power as the present King of France. But the principles of the government itself still remained the same. The Monarch and the Monarchy

[1] *Marquis de la Fayette* Vice president of the National Assembly. La Fayette composed the initial draft of the *Declaration of the Rights of Man and of the Citizen*.

The Contrast, by Thomas Rowlandson, after a drawing by Lord George Murray, 1792.

were distinct and separate things; and it was against the established despotism of the latter, and not against the person or principles of the former, that the revolt commenced, and the revolution has been carried.

… When despotism has established itself for ages in a country, as in France, it is not in the person of the King only that it resides. It has the appearance of being so in show, and in nominal authority; but it is not so in practice, and in fact. It has its standard every-where. Every office and department has its despotism, founded upon custom and usage. Every place has its Bastile, and every Bastile its despot. The original hereditary despotism, resident in the person of the King, divides and subdivides itself into a thousand shapes and forms, till at last the whole of it is acted by deputation. This was the case in France; and against this species of despotism, proceeding on through an endless labyrinth of office, till the source of it is scarcely perceptible, there is no mode of redress. It strengthens itself by assuming the appearance of duty, and tyrannises under the pretense of obeying. …

As to the tragic paintings, by which Mr. Burke has outraged his own imagination, and seeks to work upon that of his readers, they are very well calculated for theatrical representation, where facts are manufactured for the sake of show, and accommodated to produce, through the weakness of sympathy, a weeping effect. But Mr. Burke should recollect that he is writing history, and not *plays*; and that his readers will expect truth, and not the spouting rant of high-toned exclamation. …

Not one glance of compassion, not one commiserating reflection, that I can find throughout his whole book, has he bestowed on those who lingered out the most wretched of lives, a life without hope, in the most miserable of prisons. … His hero or his heroine must be a tragedy-victim expiring in show, and not the real prisoner of misery, sliding into death in the silence of a dungeon.

As Mr. Burke has passed over the whole transaction of the Bastile (and his silence is nothing in his favour), and has entertained his readers with reflections on supposed facts distorted into real falsehoods, I will give, since he has not, some account of the circumstances which preceded that transaction. They will serve to show, that less mischief could scarcely have accompanied such an event, when considered with the treacherous and hostile aggravations of the enemies of the Revolution. …

The mind can hardly picture to itself a more tremendous scene than what the city of Paris exhibited at the time of taking the Bastile, and for two days before and after, nor conceive the possibility of its quieting so soon. At a distance, this transaction has appeared only as an act of heroism, standing on itself; and the close political connection it had with the Revolution is lost in the brilliancy of the achievement. But we are to consider it as the strength of the parties, brought man to man, and contending for the issue. The Bastile was to be either the prize or the prison of the assailants. The downfall of it included the idea of the downfall of Despotism. …

That the Bastile was attacked with an enthusiasm of heroism, such only as the highest animation of liberty could inspire, and carried in the space of a few hours, is an event which the world is fully possessed of. I am not undertaking a detail of the attack; but bringing into view the conspiracy against the nation which provoked it, and which fell with the Bastile. The prison to which the new ministry were dooming the National Assembly, in addition to its being the high altar and castle of despotism, became the proper object to begin with. This enterprise broke up the new ministry, who began now to fly from the ruin they had prepared for others. …

During the latter part of the time in which this confusion was acting, the King and Queen were in public at the balcony, and neither of them concealed for safety's sake, as Mr. Burke insinuates. Matters being thus appeased, and tranquillity restored, a general acclamation broke forth, of *Le Roi à Paris—Le Roi à Paris*—The King to Paris. It was the shout of peace, and immediately accepted on the part of the King. By this measure, the King and his family reached Paris in the evening, and were congratulated on their arrival by Mr. Bailley, the Mayor of Paris, in the name of the citizens. …

The French constitution says, *There shall be no titles*; and, of consequence, all that class of equivocal generation, which in some countries is called "*aristocracy*" and in others "*nobility*" is done away, and the *peer*[1] is exalted into MAN. …

It is, properly, from the elevated mind of France that the folly of titles has fallen. It has outgrown the baby-clothes of *Count* and *Duke*, and breeched itself in manhood. France has not levelled; it has exalted. It has put down the dwarf, to set up the man. The puny-ism of a senseless word like *Duke*, or *Count*, or *Earl*, has ceased to please. Even those who possessed them have disowned the gibberish; and, as they outgrew the rickets, have despised the rattle. The genuine mind of man, thirsting for its native home, society, contemns the gewgaws[2] that separate him from it. Titles are like circles drawn by the magician's wand, to contract the sphere of man's felicity. He lived immured within the Bastile of a word, and surveys at a distance the envied life of man. …

[1] *peer* Member of the hereditary nobility.

[2] *gewgaws* Gaudy baubles.

The patriots of France have discovered, in good time, that rank and dignity in society must take a new ground. The old one has fallen through. It must now take the substantial ground of character, instead of the chimerical ground of titles; and they have brought their titles to the altar, and made of them a burnt-offering to Reason.

If no mischief had annexed itself to the folly of titles, they would not have been worth a serious and formal destruction, such as the National Assembly have decreed them; and this makes it necessary to enquire farther into the nature and character of aristocracy. …

Nothing can appear more contradictory, than the principle on which the old governments began, and the condition to which society, civilization, and commerce, are capable of carrying mankind. Government, on the old system, is an assumption of power, for the aggrandisement of itself; on the new, a delegation of power, for the common benefit of society. The former supports itself by keeping up a system of war; the latter promotes a system of peace, as the true means of enriching a nation. The one encourages national prejudices; the other promotes universal society, as the means of universal commerce. The one measures its prosperity, by the quantity of revenue it extorts; the other proves its excellence, by the small quantity of taxes it requires. …

Never did so great an opportunity offer itself to England, and to all Europe, as is produced by the two Revolutions of America and France. By the former, freedom has a national champion in the Western world; and by the latter, in Europe. When another nation shall join France, despotism and bad government will scarcely dare to appear. To use a trite expression, the iron is becoming hot all over Europe. The insulted German and the enslaved Spaniard, the Russ and the Pole, are beginning to think. The present age will hereafter merit to be called the Age of Reason, and the present generation will appear to the future as the Adam of a new world.

from William Godwin, *An Enquiry Concerning Political Justice and Its Influence on General Virtue and Happiness* (1793)

Political philosopher, novelist, and anarchist William Godwin (1756–1836) was a leading figure in radical circles in London. In *Enquiry Concerning Political Justice*, he sought to give philosophical grounding to the ideas of Paine and Rousseau, and to oppose the arguments in Burke's conservative *Reflections on the Revolution in France* (1790). In the following selections, Godwin considers the responsibilities of the citizen in society, as well as the best mode of effecting revolutionary change, particularly such fundamental change as the abolishment of private property.

from BOOK 4: MISCELLANEOUS PRINCIPLES

from CHAPTER 2: OF REVOLUTIONS

SECTION 1: DUTIES OF A CITIZEN

No question can be more important than that which respects the best mode of effecting revolutions. Before we enter upon it however, it may be proper to remove a difficulty which has suggested itself to the minds of some men, how far we ought generally speaking to be the friends of revolution; or, in other words, whether it be justifiable in a man to be the enemy of the constitution of his country.

"We live," it will be said, "under the protection of this constitution; and protection, being a benefit conferred, obliges us to a reciprocation of support in return."

To this it may be answered, first, that this protection is a very equivocal thing; and, till it can be shown that the vices, from the effects of which it protects us, are not for the most part the produce of that constitution, we shall never sufficiently understand the quantity of benefit it includes.

Secondly, gratitude, as has already been proved,[1] is a vice and not a virtue. Every man and every collection of men ought to be treated by us in a manner founded upon their intrinsic qualities and capacities, and not according to a rule which has existence only in relation to ourselves.

Add to this, thirdly, that no motive can be more equivocal than the gratitude here recommended. Gratitude to the constitution, an abstract idea, an imaginary existence, is altogether unintelligible. Affection to my countrymen will be much better proved, by my exertions to procure them a substantial benefit, than by my supporting a system which I believe to be fraught with injurious consequences.

He who calls upon me to support the constitution must found his requisition[2] upon one or two principles. It has a claim upon my support either because it is good, or because it is British.

Against the requisition in the first sense there is nothing to object. All that is necessary is to prove the goodness which is ascribed to it. But perhaps it will be said, "that, though not absolutely good, more mischief will result from an attempt to overturn it, than from maintaining it with its mixed character of partly right and partly wrong." If this can be made evident, undoubtedly I ought to submit. Of this mischief however I can be no judge but in consequence of enquiry. To some the evils attendant on a revolution will appear greater, and to others less. Some will imagine that the vices with which the English constitution is pregnant are considerable, and some that it is nearly innocent. Before I can decide between these opposite opinions and balance the existing and the possible evils, I must examine for myself. But examination in its nature implies uncertainty of result. Were I to determine before I sat down on which side the decision should be, I could not strictly speaking be said to examine at all. He that desires a revolution for its own sake is to be regarded as a madman. He that desires it from a thorough conviction of its usefulness and necessity has a claim upon us for candour and respect.

As to the demand upon me for support to the English constitution, because it is English, there is little plausibility in this argument. It is of the same nature as the demand upon me to be a Christian, because I am a Briton, or a Mahometan,[3] because I am a native of Turkey. Instead of being an expression of respect, it argues contempt of all government, religion and virtue, and every thing that is sacred among men. If there be such a thing as truth, it must be better than error. If there be such a faculty as reason, it ought to be exerted. But this demand makes truth a matter of absolute indifference, and forbids us the exercise of our reason. If men reason and reflect, it must necessarily happen that either the Englishman or the Turk will find his government to be odious and his religion false. For what purpose employ his reason, if he must for ever conceal the conclusions to which it leads him? How would man have arrived at his present attainments, if he had always been contented with the state of society in which he happened to be born? In a word, either reason is the curse of our species, and human nature is to be regarded with horror; or it becomes us to employ our understanding and to act upon it, and to follow truth wherever it may lead us. It cannot lead us to mischief, since utility, as it regards percipient beings,[4] is the only basis of moral and political truth.

SECTION 2: MODE OF EFFECTING REVOLUTION

To return to the enquiry respecting the mode of effecting revolutions. If no question can be more important, there is fortunately no question perhaps that admits of a more complete and satisfactory general answer. The revolutions of states, which a philanthropist would desire to witness, or in which he would willingly co-

[1] *has already been proved* See Book 2.2, "On Justice": "Gratitude ... a principle which has so often been the theme of the moralist and the poet, is no part either of justice or virtue. By gratitude I understand a sentiment, which would lead me to prefer one man to another, from some other consideration than that of his superior usefulness or worth: that is, which would make something true to me ... which cannot be true to another man, and is not true in itself."

[2] *requisition* Request.

[3] *Mahometan* Muslim.

[4] *percipient beings* Conscious and perceptive beings.

operate, consist principally in a change of sentiments and dispositions in the members of those states. The true instruments for changing the opinions of men are argument and persuasion. The best security for an advantageous issue[1] is free and unrestricted discussion. In that field truth must always prove the successful champion. If then we would improve the social institutions of mankind, we must write, we must argue, we must converse. To this business there is no close; in this pursuit there should be no pause. Every method should be employed, not so much positively to allure the attention of mankind, or persuasively to invite them to the adoption of our opinions, as to remove every restraint upon thought, and to throw open the temple of science and the field of enquiry to all the world.

Those instruments will always be regarded by the discerning mind as suspicious, which may be employed with equal prospect of success on both sides of every question. This consideration should make us look with aversion upon all resources of violence. When we descend into the listed field,[2] we of course desert the vantage ground of truth, and commit the decision to uncertainty and caprice. The phalanx[3] of reason is invulnerable; it advances with deliberate and determined pace; and nothing is able to resist it. But when we lay down our arguments, and take up our swords, the case is altered. Amidst the barbarous pomp of war and the clamorous din of civil brawls, who can tell whether the event[4] shall be prosperous or miserable?

We must therefore carefully distinguish between informing the people and inflaming them. Indignation, resentment and fury are to be deprecated; and all we should ask is sober thought, clear discernment and intrepid discussion. Why were the revolutions of America and France a general concert of all orders and descriptions of men, without so much (if we bear in mind the multitudes concerned) as almost a dissenting voice; while the resistance against our Charles the first divided the nation into two equal parts?[5] Because the latter was the affair of the seventeenth century, and the former happened in the close of the eighteenth. Because in the case of America and France philosophy had already developed some of the great principles of political truth, and Sydney and Locke and Montesquieu and Rousseau[6] had convinced a majority of reflecting and powerful minds of the evils of usurpation. If these revolutions had happened still later, not one drop of the blood of one citizen would have been shed by the hands of another, nor would the event have been marked so much perhaps as with one solitary instance of violence and confiscation.

There are two principles therefore which the man who desires the regeneration of his species ought ever to bear in mind, to regard the improvement of every hour as essential in the discovery and dissemination of truth, and willingly to suffer the lapse of years before he urges the reducing his theory into actual execution. With all his caution it is possible that the impetuous multitude will run before the still and quiet progress of reason; nor will he sternly pass sentence upon every revolution that shall by a few years have anticipated the term that wisdom would have prescribed. But, if his caution be firmly exerted, there is no doubt that he will supersede many abortive attempts, and considerably prolong the general tranquility. …

[1] *issue* Outcome.

[2] *listed field* Ground enclosed for jousting or dueling (i.e., a place for settling disagreement with physical force).

[3] *phalanx* Group of soldiers arranged in a classical military formation.

[4] *event* Outcome.

[5] *two equal parts* The English Civil War (1642–51) was a series of armed conflicts between Royalists (loyal to Charles I) and Parliamentarians (who fought for a constitutional monarchy rather than an absolute monarchy). The Parliamentarians conquered the armies of Charles I in the end, leading to the execution of the king in 1649.

[6] *Sydney … Rousseau* Eighteenth-century philosophers whose ideals of reason, liberty, and equality were influential in shaping the American and French Revolutions.

from BOOK 8: OF PROPERTY
from CHAPTER 8: OF THE MEANS OF INTRODUCING THE GENUINE SYSTEM OF PROPERTY[1]

… No idea has excited greater horror in the minds of a multitude of persons, than that of the mischiefs that are to ensue from the dissemination of what they call levelling principles.[2] They believe "that these principles will inevitably ferment in the minds of the vulgar, and that the attempt to carry them into execution will be attended with every species of calamity."[3] They represent to themselves "the uninformed and uncivilized part of mankind, as let loose from all restraint, and hurried into every kind of excess. Knowledge and taste, the improvements of intellect, the discoveries of sages, the beauties of poetry and art, are trampled under foot and extinguished by barbarians. It is another inundation of Goths and Vandals,[4] with this bitter aggravation, that the viper that stings us to death was warmed in our own bosoms."

They conceive of the scene as "beginning in massacre." They suppose "all that is great, preeminent and illustrious as ranking among the first victims. Such as are distinguished by peculiar elegance of manners or energy of diction and composition, will be the inevitable objects of envy and jealousy. Such as intrepidly exert themselves to succour the persecuted, or to declare to the public those truths which they are least inclined, but which are most necessary for them to hear, will be marked out for assassination."

Let us not, from any partiality to the system of equality delineated in this book, shrink from the picture here exhibited. Massacre is the too possible attendant upon revolution, and massacre is perhaps the most hateful scene, allowing for its momentary duration, that any imagination can suggest. The fearful, hopeless expectation of the defeated, and the bloodhound fury of their conquerors, is a complication of mischief that all which has been told of infernal regions[5] cannot surpass. The cold-blooded massacres that are perpetrated under the name of criminal justice fall short of these in their most frightful aggravations. The ministers and instruments of law have by custom reconciled their minds to the dreadful task they perform, and bear their respective parts in the most shocking enormities, without being sensible to the passions allied to those enormities. But the instruments of massacre are actuated with all the sentiments of fiends. Their eyes emit flashes of cruelty and rage. They pursue their victims from street to street and from house to house. They tear them from the arms of their fathers and their wives. They glut themselves with barbarity and insult, and utter shouts of horrid joy at the spectacle of their tortures.

We have now contemplated the tremendous picture; what is the conclusion it behooves us to draw? Must we shrink from reason, from virtue and happiness? Suppose that the inevitable consequence of communicating truth were the temporary introduction of such a scene as has just been described, must we on that account refuse to communicate it? The crimes that were perpetrated would in no just estimate appear to be the result of truth, but of the error which had previously been infused. The impartial enquirer would behold them as the last struggles of expiring despotism, which, if it had survived, would have produced mischiefs, scarcely less atrocious in the hour of their commission, and infinitely more calamitous by the length of their duration. If we would judge truly, even admitting the unfavourable supposition above stated, we must contrast a moment of horror and distress with ages of felicity. No imagination can sufficiently conceive the mental improvement and the tranquil virtue that would succeed, were property once permitted to rest upon its genuine basis. …

[1] *GENUINE SYSTEM OF PROPERTY* For Godwin, this means a system of property based on just principles (i.e., an egalitarian society in which property is abolished).

[2] *levelling principles* Ideas that promote social equality.

[3] *that these … of calamity* The sources of this and the following two quotations are unknown; they may be real quotations, or they may be invented statements summarizing positions held by conservative politicians.

[4] *Goths and Vandals* Germanic tribes that fought against the Roman Empire; the Vandals conquered Rome in 455. These tribes were long thought of as barbarians seeking to destroy Roman culture.

[5] *infernal regions* Hell.

It being then sufficiently evident that truth must be told at whatever expense, let us proceed to consider the precise amount of that expense, to enquire how much of confusion and violence is inseparable from the transit which mind has to accomplish. And here it plainly appears that mischief is by no means inseparable from the progress. In the mere circumstances of our acquiring knowledge and accumulating one truth after another there is no direct tendency to disorder. Evil can only spring from the clash of mind with mind, from one body of men in the community outstripping another in their ideas of improvement, and becoming impatient of the opposition they have to encounter. …

No maxim can be more pernicious than that which would teach us to consult the temper of the times, and to tell only so much as we imagine our contemporaries will be able to bear. This practise is at present almost universal, and it is the mark of a very painful degree of depravity. We retail[1] and mangle truth. We impart it to our fellows, not with the liberal measure with which we have received it, but with such parsimony as our own miserable prudence may chance to prescribe. We pretend that truths fit to be practised in one country, nay, truths which we confess to be eternally right, are not fit to be practised in another. That we may deceive others with a tranquil conscience, we begin deceiving ourselves. We put shackles on our minds, and dare not trust ourselves at large in the pursuit of truth. This practise took its commencement from the machinations of party,[2] and the desire of one wise and adventurous leader to carry a troop of weak, timid and selfish supporters in his train. There is no reason why I should not declare in any assembly upon the face of the earth that I am a republican. There is no more reason why, being a republican under a monarchial government, I should enter into a desperate faction to invade the public tranquillity, than if I were monarchial under a republic. Every community of men, as well as every individual, must govern itself according to its ideas of justice. What I should desire is, not by violence to change its institutions, but by reason to change its ideas. I have no business with factions or intrigue; but simply to promulgate the truth, and to wait the tranquil progress of conviction. …

[1] *retail* Parcel out, sell.

[2] *party* Political party.

William Blake

1757 – 1827

"I labor upwards into futurity," etched William Blake onto the back of one of the copper plates that constituted the "tablets" of his visionary art. A poet and artist whose work was sorely undervalued during his own lifetime, Blake recognized that his was a genius before its time. The mysterious and powerful poetry that he crafted to convey his vision would eventually come to be appreciated for its revolutionary significance; for the past century or more Blake has been widely considered to be among the greatest poets of the Romantic era.

Blake was born one November evening in 1757 above his parents' hosiery shop in the Soho district of London. James and Catherine Blake, religious Dissenters whose non-compromising beliefs were those of a growing number of tradespeople, allowed their son to pursue a program of self study that saved him from being schooled under the institutional authorities he instinctively abhorred. Although his parents were generally indulgent, there are hints that Blake balked even under their natural expressions of authority. He received a thrashing for declaring he had seen the face of God, and was accused of lying when he reported passing a tree bespangled with angels. Since his family could not afford the expense of artistic training, he was apprenticed at fourteen to a highly respected engraver, with whom he lived for seven years while learning the trade which would thereafter earn him his living.

During the period of his apprenticeship, Blake began writing the poems that were eventually collected in *Poetical Sketches* (1783)—the only volume of his verse originally printed by letterpress rather than by the "illuminated" methods he later originated. Of his parents and three siblings, Blake retained lasting affection only for his younger brother, Robert. Blake claimed to communicate daily with the spirit of Robert after his early death from tuberculosis. Indeed, the unique style of relief etching or "Illuminated Printing" which Blake later devised was imparted, he claimed, by Robert in a visitation. Etching words backwards into copper plates so that they would reverse to normal upon printing, Blake in 1788 produced his first illuminated texts with "All Religions Are One" and "There Is No Natural Religion." It was a defining moment for him, one in which words and images converged into prophetic expression. He soon applied his new method of printing to a larger project, the poetic and pictorial depiction of a young soul descending into the realm of matter, recounted in *The Book of Thel.*

Blake's words and designs "interanimate each other," in the words of one critic; a master of color, he achieved unearthly effects in his hand-tinted books, of which no two copies were exactly the same. Rather than reflecting the tones of the natural world, Blake's color—and indeed the vividness of his verse—aim toward the supernatural. Similarly, what separates his poetry from that of contemporaries, such as Wordsworth and Coleridge, is his lack of interest in "painting Nature." For Blake, the true aim of art was to tune the senses and the imaginative faculties to the higher pitch of a spiritual reality, not to the natural world. For this reason, Blake detested what he called the "muddy" colors, nuanced shade work, and secular sensibilities of an artist such as Rembrandt, while revering the determined outlines, bright colors, and unequivocal contrasts of light and dark achieved by High Renaissance painters such as Michelangelo and Raphael.

The bold, declarative, and (to some modern eyes) exaggerated style that Blake admired in painting is paralleled in many of his literary preferences. His work has close associations with the declamatory traditions of prophecy, aphorism, political writing, and proverb. *The Marriage of Heaven and Hell* (1790) contains some of his most chiseled epigrams, such as "The cut worm forgives the plow" and "The tigers of wrath are wiser than the horses of instruction." The Bible was a tremendous imaginative reserve upon which he drew all of his life. He admired Dante, Milton, Spenser, and Shakespeare, supplied commissioned designs for editions of Milton's *L'Allegro*, *Il Penseroso*, *Paradise Lost*, and *Paradise Regained*, and left behind an unfinished series of watercolors illustrating Dante's work. He was also influenced by the architecture and sepulchral art of Westminster Abbey and by the literary gothic of Edward Young's *Night Thoughts* and Robert Blair's *The Grave*, versions of which he illustrated. If he was in many respects an outsider to his own culture, Blake was fully a man of the times in his love of the popular "forgeries" of James Macpherson (author of the "Ossian" poems) and Thomas Chatterton, as well as in his enjoyment of works of Gothic fiction such as Ann Radcliffe's *The Mysteries of Udolpho* (1794).

On at least two occasions Blake struck out to earn a reputation as an artist in his own right. The first occasion came at the end of his apprenticeship, when he submitted a portfolio to the Royal Academy of Arts (under the presidency of Sir Joshua Reynolds) and was accepted into the Academy. Yet he failed to emerge out of obscurity, and was forced to set up an engraver's shop. For twenty years, Blake would resign himself to the grueling schedule of a copy engraver, recognized only by a few of his friends as a formidably original artist, and almost wholly overlooked as a poet. In 1809, energized by a gallery showing of works by Dürer, Michelangelo, Giulio Romano, and others, Blake renewed his association with the Royal Academy to launch a solo exhibition of his own work. With the exception of a caustic review or two, the public remained unmoved by the idiosyncratic light Blake cast upon subjects such as "The Body of Abel found by Adam and Eve."

Blake found his soul mate in Catherine Boucher, the illiterate daughter of a market gardener. He taught her to read and trained her in the preparation of copper plates, the hand coloring of prints, and the stitching of pages into bound copies. Catherine was evidently a submissive, devoted wife, and some have denigrated Blake's traditional and even misogynist approach to marriage, citing his pronouncement that "the female … lives from the light of the male." At the same time, however, Blake approved of the arguments for sexual equality made by Mary Wollstonecraft in *A Vindication of the Rights of Woman* (1793). He also radically proposed that carnal pleasure was a portal to the divine. In *Visions of the Daughters of Albion* (1793), Blake abjures sexual domination and celebrates "the moment of desire!" in a manner highly unconventional at the time. Visitors to the Blake home reported coming across the couple reading naked in a garden house in their back yard, enjoying the innocence of their private Eden and rejecting the narratives of shame and the Fall.

The rewriting of the biblical drama of the Creation and Fall that underlies nearly all of Blake's work was influenced by radical Dissenters who celebrated nudity as a symbol of unfallen humanity. Blake was also influenced by the mystical systems of Emanuel Swedenborg and Jacob Boehme, and he tapped into veins of esoteric knowledge related to the cabbalistic teachings of the Freemasons, the Rosicrucians, and Paracelsus. He also had associations with decidedly non-mystical political movements that were bravely calling for democratic reforms at a time when the English monarchy was intent on quashing sympathizers with the American War of Independence and the French Revolution.

Blake, however, never fully participated in an organized movement of any kind, be it religious or political. His was "a voice crying in the wilderness," urging men and women to realize their "human form divine." Unwilling to conform to any system not of his own creation, Blake's language grew increasingly esoteric and opaque in later major prophecies such as *The Four Zoas*, *Milton* (1804), and *Jerusalem* (1804–20).

One vision that Blake explores over and over again is that of an earthly Eden triumphing over forces of repression. This is the common theme of *The French Revolution* (1791), *America: A Prophecy* (1793), *Europe: A Prophecy* (1794), and *The Book of Urizen* (1794). When Blake summons Albion, figure of the human form divine in *Jerusalem*, to "Awake!" he is calling for a spiritual revolution in which humanity awakens to the knowledge that the republic of heaven is immanent.

Blake imagined the spiritual dimensions of the geography of London in particularly vivid detail. That the material double of his holy city was corrupt lends a sharp edge to Blake's vision. As one Blake biographer writes, "it was a time when mobs and rioters often controlled large areas of the city; there were riots by sailors, silk-weavers, coal-heavers, hatters, glass-grinders … and bloody demonstrations over the price of bread." The biting simplicity of "The Chimney Sweeper" and "The Little Black Boy" in Blake's *Songs of Innocence and of Experience* (1789–94) are testimony to his acute sensitivity to the realities of poverty and exploitation that accompanied the "dark satanic mills" of the Industrial Revolution.

In this London, Blake admitted to living in fear that his artistic vision and eccentric tendency to converse with angels and ghosts would land him in trouble with the authorities—a fear horribly realized in 1803. The Blakes had been generously invited by William Hayley, an eminent poet and wealthy patron of the arts, to live in a country cottage at Felpham. One day a private in the Royal Dragoons, John Scofield, while drunk fell into a heated argument with Blake at his garden gate. Blake physically evicted the abusive soldier from the premises. Scofield subsequently accused Blake of making seditious remarks against the Crown, an offense punishable by death. Hayley generously paid for his friend's bail and his defense, and Blake was eventually acquitted, to the thunderous approval of the court. However, the incident stamped itself upon his sensitive mind; he raised it to mythological proportions in the convoluted poetic symbology of *Jerusalem*, where the Law is figured as the nauseous region of "Bowlahoola," while Scofield and his cohorts appear as "ministers of evil."

As the culture around him placed increasing faith in the physical laws of natural science, Blake's insistence on the incorruptible coordinates of imaginative truth cast him as an increasing oddity. Many of Blake's contemporaries considered him insane. London was shifting to a secular orientation under the rise of industrial culture. Against the grain of the times, Blake continued producing labor-intensive printings of illuminated books, none of which proved to be a commercial success. Only twenty-eight copies of *Songs of Innocence and of Experience* are known to exist, sixteen of *The Book of Thel*, nine of *The Marriage of Heaven and Hell*, and five of *Jerusalem*.

In his last years, just as he had reconciled himself to poverty and obscurity, Blake attracted the first following he had ever enjoyed, a small group of painters called "the Ancients." Charles Lamb and a few other writers of the period also expressed admiration, but the glimmerings of a full-fledged "Blake industry" did not appear until years after his death, when his art and poetry were discovered by Dante Gabriel Rossetti and the Pre-Raphaelites. Rossetti and, later, William Butler Yeats edited volumes of Blake's poems, and appreciation grew of his powerful poetic as well as painterly achievements. By the middle of the twentieth century, academics around the world were devoting themselves to the scholarly study of Blake's work, which was also exerting a profound influence on the literary and popular culture of the time. Blake was an inspiration to the generation of Beat poets clustered around Allen Ginsberg and to many in the 1960s' counterculture who took up his call to open the "doors of perception" (words straight from *The Marriage of Heaven and Hell*), trying everything from the hallucinogenic drugs proposed by Aldous Huxley, to communal living and free love to approximate his visionary universe. The future had finally caught up with William Blake.

⌘⌘⌘

from *Songs of Innocence and of Experience Showing the Two Contrary States of the Human Soul*[1]

from *Songs of Innocence*

Title page, *Songs of Innocence and of Experience.*

[1] *Songs of Innocence … Soul* The usual practice of this anthology regarding modernization of spelling and punctuation has not been followed in the case of Blake; his idiosyncrasies have been retained.

Introduction

Piping down the valleys wild
Piping songs of pleasant glee
On a cloud I saw a child,
And he laughing said to me,

"Pipe a song about a Lamb":
So I piped with merry chear.
"Piper pipe that song again"
So I piped, he wept to hear.

"Drop thy pipe thy happy pipe
Sing thy songs of happy chear."
So I sung the same again,
While he wept with joy to hear

"Piper sit thee down and write
In a book that all may read—"
So he vanish'd from my sight
And I pluck'd a hollow reed,

And I made a rural pen,
And I stain'd the water clear,
And I wrote my happy songs,
Every child may joy to hear.

The Shepherd

How sweet is the Shepherd's sweet lot!
From the morn to the evening he strays:
He shall follow his sheep all the day
And his tongue shall be filled with praise.

For he hears the lamb's innocent call,
And he hears the ewe's tender reply.
He is watchful while they are in peace,
For they know when their Shepherd is nigh.

The Ecchoing Green

The Sun does arise,
And make happy the skies.
The merry bells ring
To welcome the Spring.
The sky-lark and thrush,
The birds of the bush,
Sing louder around,
To the bells' chearful sound.
While our sports shall be seen
On the Ecchoing Green.

Old John with white hair
Does laugh away care,
Sitting under the oak,
Among the old folk.
They laugh at our play,
And soon they all say,
"Such such were the joys,
When we all girls & boys,
In our youth-time were seen,
On the Ecchoing Green."

Till the little ones weary
No more can be merry
The sun does descend,
And our sports have an end:
Round the laps of their mothers.
Many sisters and brothers,
Like birds in their nest,
Are ready for rest:
And sport no more seen,
On the darkening Green.

The Lamb[1]

Little Lamb who made thee
Dost thou know who made thee
Gave thee life & bid thee feed,
By the stream & o'er the mead;
Gave thee clothing of delight,
Softest clothing wooly bright;
Gave thee such a tender voice,
Making all the vales rejoice:
Little Lamb who made thee
Dost thou know who made thee

Little Lamb I'll tell thee,
Little Lamb I'll tell thee:
He is called by thy name,
For he calls himself a Lamb:
He is meek & he is mild,[2]
He became a little child:
I a child & thou a lamb,
We are called by his name.
Little Lamb God bless thee:
Little Lamb God bless thee.

The Little Black Boy

My mother bore me in the southern wild,
And I am black, but O! my soul is white.
White as an angel is the English child:
But I am black as if bereav'd of light.

My mother taught me underneath a tree
And sitting down before the heat of day.
She took me on her lap and kissed me.
And pointing to the east began to say.

"Look on the rising sun! there God does live
And gives his light and gives his heat away.
And flowers and trees and beasts and men receive
Comfort in morning joy in the noon day.

"And we are put on earth a little space,
That we may learn to bear the beams of love,

[1] *The Lamb* The question-and-answer form of this poem recalls the Church of England's catechism for children.

[2] *He ... mild* Cf. Charles Wesley's hymn, "Gentle Jesus, Meek and Mild" (1742).

"The Little Black Boy."

And these black bodies and this sun-burnt face
Is but a cloud, and like a shady grove.

"For when our souls have learn'd the heat to bear
The cloud will vanish we shall hear his voice.
Saying: 'come out from the grove my love & care,
And round my golden tent like lambs rejoice.'"

Thus did my mother say and kissed me.
And thus I say to little English boy,
When I from black and he from white cloud free,
And round the tent of God like lambs we joy:

I'll shade him from the heat till he can bear.
To lean in joy upon our father's knee
And then I'll stand and stroke his silver hair,
And be like him and he will then love me.

The Chimney Sweeper [1]

When my mother died I was very young,
And my father sold me while yet my tongue,
Could scarcely cry "weep weep weep weep."[2]
So your chimneys I sweep & in soot I sleep.[3]

There's little Tom Dacre who cried when his head
That curl'd like a lamb's back, was shav'd. so I said,
"Hush Tom never mind it, for when your head's bare,
You know that the soot cannot spoil your white hair."

And so he was quiet, & that very night,
As Tom was a sleeping he had such a sight,
That thousands of sweepers Dick, Joe Ned & Jack
Were all of them lock'd up in coffins of black,

And by came an Angel who had a bright key,
And he open'd the coffins & set them all free.
Then down a green plain leaping laughing they run
And wash in a river and shine in the Sun.[4]

Then naked & white, all their bags left behind,
They rise upon clouds, and sport in the wind.
And the Angel told Tom if he'd be a good boy,
He'd have God for his father & never want joy.

And so Tom awoke and we rose in the dark
And got with our bags & our brushes to work.
Tho' the morning was cold, Tom was happy & warm.
So if all do their duty, they need not fear harm.

---

[1] *The Chimney Sweeper* Children were often forced to climb up chimneys to clean them—a filthy, dangerous, and unhealthy job. A law ameliorating their working conditions was passed in 1788, but it was rarely enforced.

[2] *weep ... weep* The child is attempting to say "sweep," the chimney-sweeper's street cry. The act of 1788 should have prevented the apprenticing of children younger than eight.

[3] *in soot I sleep* The sweeps used their bags of soot as blankets.

[4] *And wash ... Sun* The act of 1788 called for weekly washings for sweeps.

The Little Boy Lost

"Father father where are you going
O do not walk so fast.
Speak father speak to your little boy
Or else I shall be lost."

The night was dark no father was there
The child was wet with dew.
The mire was deep & the child did weep
And away the vapour flew.

The Little Boy Found

The little boy lost in the lonely fen,
Led by the wand'ring light,
Began to cry, but God ever nigh
Appear'd like his father in white.

He kissed the child & by the hand led
And to his mother brought,
Who in sorrow pale thro the lonely dale
Her little boy weeping sought.

The Divine Image

To Mercy Pity Peace and Love,
All pray in their distress:
And to these virtues of delight
Return their thankfulness.

For Mercy Pity Peace and Love,
Is God our father dear:
And Mercy Pity Peace and Love,
Is Man his child and care.

For Mercy has a human heart
Pity a human face:
And Love, the human form divine.
And Peace, the human dress.

Then every man of every clime,
That prays in his distress,
Prays to the human form divine
Love Mercy Pity Peace.

And all must love the human form,
In heathen, turk or jew.
Where Mercy, Love & Pity dwell,
There God is dwelling too.

Holy Thursday [1]

'Twas on a Holy Thursday their innocent faces clean
The children walking two & two in red & blue & green[2]
Grey headed beadles[3] walkd before with wands as white as snow
Till into the high dome of Paul's they like Thames' waters flow.

O what a multitude they seemd these flowers of London town
Seated in companies they sit with radiance all their own.
The hum of multitudes was there but multitudes of lambs,
Thousands of little boys & girls raising their innocent hands.

Now like a mighty wind they raise to heaven the voice of song
Or like harmonious thunderings the seats of heaven among.
Beneath them sit the aged men wise guardians of the poor,
Then cherish pity, lest you drive an angel from your door.[4]

---

[1] *Holy Thursday* Beginning in 1782, the thousands of children in London's charity schools were brought to St. Paul's Cathedral on Ascension Day for an annual service of Thanksgiving; these services always occurred on a Thursday ("Holy Thursday"), usually in May.

[2] *in … green* The school uniforms.

[3] *beadles* Church officials.

[4] *cherish … door* Cf. Hebrews 13.2: "Be not forgetful to entertain strangers; for thereby some have entertained angels unawares."

Nurse's Song

When the voices of children are heard on the green
And laughing is heard on the hill,
My heart is at rest within my breast
And every thing else is still

"Then come home my children, the sun is gone down
And the dews of night arise
Come come leave off play and let us away,
Till the morning appears in the skies."

"No no let us play, for it is yet day
And we cannot go to sleep
Besides in the sky, the little birds fly
And the hills are all coverd with sheep"

"Well well go & play till the light fades away
And then go home to bed."
The little ones leaped & shouted & laugh'd
And all the hills ecchoed.

Infant Joy

"I have no name
I am but two days old."
What shall I call thee?
"I happy am
Joy is my name."
Sweet joy befall thee!

Pretty joy!
Sweet joy but two days old.
Sweet joy I call thee;
Thou dost smile,
I sing the while
Sweet joy befall thee.

A Dream

Once a dream did weave a shade,
O'er my Angel-guarded bed,
That an Emmet° lost its way *ant*
Where on grass methought I lay.

Troubled wilderd° and folorn *bewildered*
Dark benighted travel-worn,
Over many a tangled spray° *branch*
All heart-broke I heard her say:

"O my children! do they cry
Do they hear their father sigh.
Now they look abroad to see,
Now return and weep for me."

Pitying I drop'd a tear,
But I saw a glow-worm near:
Who replied, "What wailing wight° *creature*
Calls the watchman of the night.

"I am set to light the ground,
While the beetle goes his round:
Follow now the beetles' hum,
Little wanderer hie thee home."
—1789

from *Songs of Experience*

Introduction

Hear the voice of the Bard!
Who Present, Past, & Future sees
Whose ears have heard,
The Holy Word,
That walk'd among the ancient trees.[1]

[1] *Holy Word … trees* Cf. Genesis 3.8: "And they heard the voice of the Lord God walking in the garden in the cool of the day: and Adam and his wife hid themselves from the presence of the Lord God amongst the trees of the garden."

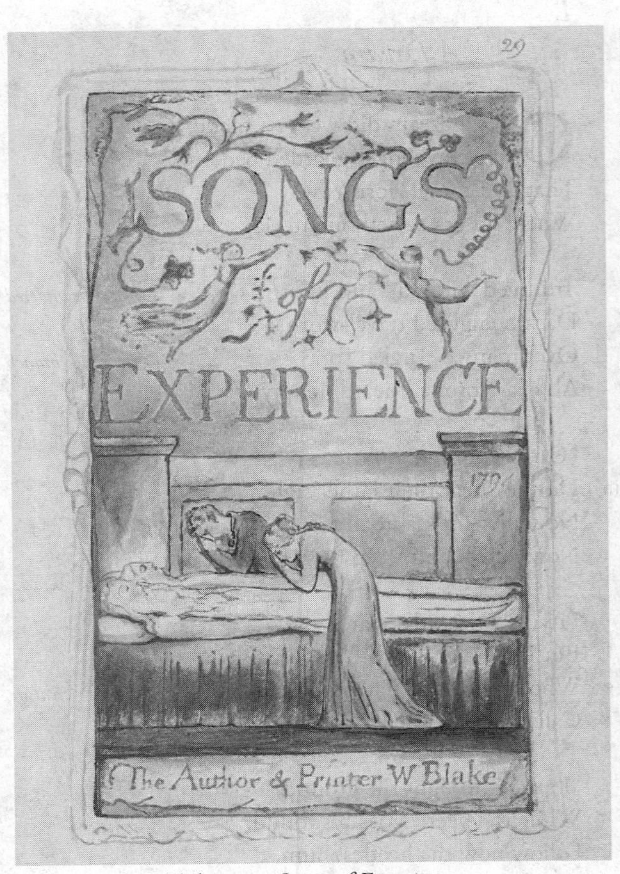

Title page, *Songs of Experience.*

Frontispiece, *Songs of Experience.*

Calling[1] the lapsed Soul
And weeping in the evening dew:
That[2] might controll
The starry pole:
And fallen fallen light renew!

"O Earth, O Earth return!
Arise from out the dewy grass:
Night is worn,
And the morn
Rises from the slumberous mass.

"Turn away no more:
Why wilt thou turn away
The starry floor[3]
The watry shore
Is giv'n thee till the break of day."

The Clod & the Pebble

"Love seeketh not Itself to please.
Nor for itself hath any care;
But for another gives its ease,
And builds a Heaven in Hell's despair."

So sang a little Clod of Clay,
Trodden with the cattle's feet;
But a Pebble of the brook,
Warbled out these metres meet.

"Love seeketh only Self to please,
To bind another to Its delight;
Joys in another's loss of ease,
And builds a Hell in Heaven's despite."[4]

[1] *Calling* The subject here is ambiguous, and could either be the bard or the Holy Word.

[2] *That* Most likely the referent here is the lapsed soul, but it may also be the Holy Word.

[3] *starry floor* The sky, the floor of heaven.

[4] *builds … despite* In Milton's *Paradise Lost* (1.254–55), Satan declares, "The mind is its own place, and in itself / Can make a Heaven of Hell, a Hell of Heaven."

Holy Thursday

Is this a holy thing to see,
In a rich and fruitful land,
Babes reducd to misery,
Fed with cold and usurous hand?[5]

Is that trembling cry a song?
Can it be a song of joy?
And so many children poor?
It is a land of poverty!

And their sun does never shine.
And their fields are bleak & bare.
And their ways are fill'd with thorns.
It is eternal winter there.

For where-e'er the sun does shine,
And where-e'er the rain does fall:
Babe can never hunger there,
Nor poverty the mind appall.

The Chimney Sweeper

A little black thing among the snow:
Crying "weep, weep," in notes of woe!
"Where are thy father & mother? say?"
"They are both gone up to the church to pray.

"Because I was happy upon the heath.
And smil'd among the winters snow:
They clothed me in the clothes of death,
And taught me to sing the notes of woe.

"And because I am happy & dance & sing,
They think they have done me no injury:
And are gone to praise God & his Priest & King
Who make up a heaven of our misery."

[5] *usurous hand* I.e., the hand of someone engaged in lending money at interest.

The Sick Rose

O Rose thou art sick.
The invisible worm,
That flies in the night
In the howling storm:

Has found out thy bed
Of crimson joy:
And his dark secret love
Does thy life destroy.

The Fly

Little Fly
Thy summer's play,
My thoughtless hand
Has brush'd away.

Am not I
A fly like thee?[1]
Or art not thou
A man like me?

For I dance
And drink & sing:
Till some blind hand
Shall brush my wing.

If thought is life
And strength & breath:
And the want
Of thought is death;[2]

Then am I
A happy fly,
If I live,
Or if I die.

The Tyger

Tyger Tyger, burning bright,
In the forests of the night;
What immortal hand or eye,
Could frame thy fearful symmetry?

In what distant deeps or skies,
Burnt the fire of thine eyes?
On what wings dare he aspire?[3]
What the hand, dare seize the fire?[4]

And what shoulder, & what art,
Could twist the sinews of thy heart?
And when thy heart began to beat,
What dread hand? & what dread feet?

What the hammer? what the chain,
In what furnace was thy brain?
What the anvil? what dread grasp,
Dare its deadly terrors clasp!

When the stars threw down their spears[5]
And water'd heaven with their tears:
Did he smile his work to see?
Did he who made the Lamb make thee?

Tyger Tyger burning bright,
In the forests of the night:
What immortal hand or eye,
Dare frame thy fearful symmetry?

[1] *Am … thee* Cf. Shakespeare, *King Lear* 4.1.36–37: "As flies to wanton boys, are we to the gods, / They kill us for their sport."

[2] *If thought … death* Cf. René Descartes's statement "Cogito, ergo sum" ("I think, therefore I am").

[3] *what … aspire* In Greek mythology, Icarus attempted to fly using wings fashioned from wax and feathers; these melted when he flew too close to the sun.

[4] *What … fire* Prometheus stole fire from heaven to give to humans.

[5] *threw down their spears* Either in surrender or as an act of rebellion—it is uncertain which.

Ah! Sun-Flower

Ah Sun-flower! weary of time,
Who countest the steps of the Sun:
Seeking after that sweet golden clime
Where the traveller's journey is done.

Where the Youth pined away with desire,
And the pale Virgin shrouded in snow:
Arise from their graves and aspire,
Where my Sun-flower wishes to go.

The Garden of Love

I went to the Garden of Love,
And saw what I never had seen:
A Chapel was built in the midst,
Where I used to play on the green.

And the gates of this Chapel were shut,
And "Thou shalt not"[1] writ over the door;
So I turn'd to the Garden of Love,
That so many sweet flowers bore.

And I saw it was filled with graves,
And tomb-stones where flowers should be:
And Priests in black gowns were walking their rounds,
And binding with briars,[2] my joys & desires.

London

I wander thro' each charter'd[3] street,
Near where the charter'd Thames does flow,
And mark in every face I meet
Marks of weakness, marks of woe.

In every cry of every Man,
In every Infants cry of fear,
In every voice; in every ban.
The mind-forg'd manacles I hear

How the Chimney-sweepers cry
Every blackning Church appalls,
And the hapless Soldier's sigh
Runs in blood down Palace walls.

---

[1] *Thou shalt not* The phrase that introduces most of the Ten Commandments (Exodus 20.3–17).

[2] *binding with briars* Prior to the nineteenth century, binding graves with briars was a common practice.

[3] *charter'd* Subject to a charter, a document granting rights to a group of people (either to all the people of a state or to a privileged class) or a document certifying the ownership of a property. "Chartered" could also mean "mapped" or "hired out."

But most thro' midnight streets I hear
How the youthful Harlot's curse[1]
Blasts the new born Infant's tear[2]
And blights with plagues the Marriage hearse.

The Human Abstract

Pity would be no more,
If we did not make somebody Poor:
And Mercy no more could be,
If all were as happy as we;

And mutual fear brings peace;
Till the selfish loves increase.
Then Cruelty knits a snare,
And spreads his baits with care.

He sits down with holy fears,
And waters the ground with tears:
Then Humility takes its root
Underneath his foot.

Soon spreads the dismal shade
Of Mystery over his head;
And the Catterpiller and Fly,
Feed on the Mystery.

And it bears the fruit of Deceit,
Ruddy and sweet to eat;
And the Raven his nest has made
In its thickest shade.

The Gods of the earth and sea,
Sought thro' Nature to find this Tree
But their search was all in vain:
There grows one in the Human Brain.

[1] *Harlot's curse* Referring both to the oaths she utters and the venereal diseases she spreads.

[2] *Blasts … tear* A reference to the blindness caused in infants if they contract certain venereal diseases (such as gonorrhea) from the mother.

Infant Sorrow

My mother groand! my father wept.
Into the dangerous world I leapt:
Helpless, naked, piping loud;
Like a fiend hid in a cloud.

Struggling in my father's hands:
Striving against my swadling bands:
Bound and weary I thought best
To sulk upon my mother's breast.

A Poison Tree[3]

I was angry with my friend:
I told my wrath, my wrath did end.
I was angry with my foe:
I told it not, my wrath did grow.

And I waterd it in fears,
Night & morning with my tears:
And I sunned it with smiles,
And with soft deceitful wiles.

And it grew both day and night,
Till it bore an apple bright.
And my foe beheld it shine,
And he knew that it was mine.

And into my garden stole,
When the night had veild the pole;
In the morning glad I see.
My foe outstretched beneath the tree.

[3] *A Poison Tree* A manuscript version of this poem is entitled "Christian Forbearance."

A Little Boy Lost

"Nought loves another as itself,
Nor venerates another so.
Nor is it possible to Thought
A greater than itself to know:

"And Father, how can I love you,
Or any of my brothers more?
I love you like the little bird
That picks up crumbs around the door."

The Priest sat by and heard the child,
In trembling zeal he seiz'd his hair:
He led him by his little coat:
And all admir'd the Priestly care.

And standing on the altar high,
"Lo what a fiend is here!" said he:
"One who sets reason up for judge
Of our most holy Mystery."

The weeping child could not be heard,
The weeping parents wept in vain:
They strip'd him to his little shirt,
And bound him in an iron chain.

And burn'd him in a holy place,
Where many had been burn'd before:
The weeping parents wept in vain.
Are such things done on Albion's° shore. *England's*

A Little Girl Lost

Children of the future Age,
Reading this indignant page:
Know that in a former time,
Love! sweet Love! was thought a crime.

In the Age of Gold,
Free from winter's cold:
Youth and maiden bright,
In the holy light,
Naked in the sunny beams' delight.

Once a youthful pair
Fill'd with softest care,
Met in garden bright,
Where the holy light,
Had just remov'd the curtains of the night.

There in rising day,
On the grass they play:
Parents were afar:
Strangers came not near:
And the maiden soon forgot her fear.

Tired with kisses sweet
They agree to meet,
When the silent sleep
Waves o'er heaven's deep:
And the weary tired wanderers weep.

To her father white
Came the maiden bright:
But his loving look,
Like the holy book,
All her tender limbs with terror shook.

"Ona![1] pale and weak!
To thy father speak:
O the trembling fear!

[1] *Ona* In Blake's mythology, Ona is one of the daughters of Urizen, an elderly figure embodying conventional reason and law.

O the dismal care!
That shakes the blossoms of my hoary° hair!" *grey*
—1794

A Divine Image[1]

Cruelty has a Human Heart
And Jealousy a Human Face
Terror, the Human Form Divine
And Secrecy, the Human Dress

The Human Dress is forged Iron
The Human Form, a fiery Forge
The Human Face, a Furnace seal'd
The Human Heart, its hungry Gorge.
—1795

[Plate 1][2]

The Marriage of Heaven and Hell[3]

[Plate 2]

The Argument[4]

Rintrah[5] roars & shakes his fires in the burdend air;
Hungry clouds swag[6] on the deep

Once meek, and in a perilous path,
The just man kept his course along
The vale of death.
Roses are planted where thorns grow,
And on the barren heath
Sing the honey bees.

Then the perilous path was planted:
And a river, and a spring
On every cliff and tomb;
And on the bleached bones[7]
Red clay[8] brought forth.

Till the villain left the paths of ease,
To walk in perilous paths, and drive
The just man into barren climes.

Now the sneaking serpent walks
In mild humility.
And the just man rages in the wilds
Where lions roam.

Rintrah roars & shakes his fires in the burdend air;
Hungry clouds swag on the deep.

[Plate 3]

As a new heaven is begun, and it is now thirty-three years since its advent: the Eternal Hell revives.[9] And lo! Swedenborg is the Angel sitting at the tomb; his writings are the linen clothes folded up. Now is the dominion of Edom,[10] & the return of Adam into Paradise; see Isaiah XXXIV & XXXV[11] chap.

---

[1] *A Divine Image* This poem was included in one copy of the combined *Songs of Innocence and of Experience* (copy BB, printed in 1795). In all other copies, the poem was omitted.

[2] *[Plate 1]* The illustrated plates are reproduced below on pp. 96–100.

[3] *The Marriage … Hell* The usual practice of this anthology regarding modernization of spelling and punctuation has not been followed in the case of Blake; his idiosyncrasies have been retained. Blake combines the titles of two works by the Swedish visionary Emanuel Swedenborg (1688–1772), *A Treatise Concerning Heaven and Hell, and of the Wonderful Things Therein, as Heard and Seen by Emanuel Swedenborg* (1758, trans. 1784) and *Conjugial Love* (1768, trans. 1790).

[4] *The Argument* For the imagery of "The Argument," cf. Isaiah 5.1–7, 7.23–25, 35.1–10.

[5] *Rintrah* The character of Rintrah, a prophet and herald, reappears in Blake's *Europe a Prophecy* (1794) as well as in his *Milton*.

[6] *swag* Sag, hang heavily.

[7] *bleached bones* Cf. Ezekiel 37.1–11, in which Ezekiel sees life resurrected from a valley of bones.

[8] *Red clay* Since God created Adam from "the dust of the ground" (Genesis 2.8), "Adam" is sometimes said to mean "red clay" in Hebrew.

[9] *As a … revives* Swedenborg had predicted that the Last Judgment would occur in 1757, coincidentally the year of Blake's birth. In 1790, the "now" of the poem, Blake is 33, Christ's age when he was crucified and rose again.

[10] *Edom* Cf. Genesis 27.40, in which "Edom" is another name for "Esau," whose brother Jacob stole his inheritance. Like "Adam," "Edom" suggests redness.

[11] *Isaiah XXXIV & XXXV* Prophecies of divine vengeance and restoration, respectively.

Without Contraries is no progression. Attraction and Repulsion, Reason and Energy, Love and Hate, are necessary to Human existence.

From these contraries spring what the religious call Good & Evil. Good is the passive that obeys Reason Evil is the active springing from Energy.

Good is Heaven. Evil is Hell.

[Plate 4]

The Voice of the Devil

All Bibles or sacred codes have been the causes of the following errors.

1. That Man has two real existing principles Viz: a Body & a Soul.

2. That Energy. calld Evil. is alone from the Body. & that Reason. calld Good. is alone from the soul.

3. That God will torment Man in Eternity for following his Energies.

But the following Contraries to these are True

1. Man has no Body distinct from his soul for that calld Body is a portion of soul discernd by the five Senses, the chief inlets of Soul in this age

2. Energy is the only life and is from the Body and Reason is the bound or outward circumference of Energy.

3. Energy is Eternal Delight

[Plate 5]

Those who restrain desire, do so because theirs is weak enough to be restrained; and the restrainer or reason usurps its place & governs the unwilling.

And being restrained it by degrees becomes passive till it is only the shadow of desire.

The history of this is written in *Paradise Lost*.[1] & the Governor or Reason is call'd Messiah.

And the original Archangel or possessor of the command of the heavenly host, is calld the Devil or Satan and his children are call'd Sin & Death[2]

But in the Book of Job Miltons Messiah is call'd Satan.

For this history has been adopted by both parties

It indeed appear'd to Reason as if Desire was cast out, but the Devils account is, that the Messiah [Plate 6] fell. & formed a heaven of what he stole from the Abyss[3]

This is shewn in the Gospel, where he prays to the Father to send the comforter[4] or Desire that Reason may have Ideas to build on, the Jehovah of the Bible being no other than he who dwells in flaming fire Know that after Christs death, he became Jehovah.

But in Milton; the Father is Destiny, the Son, a Ratio[5] of the five senses. & the Holy Ghost, Vacuum!

Note. The reason Milton wrote in fetters when he wrote of Angels & God, and at liberty when of Devils & Hell, is because he was a true Poet and of the Devils party without knowing it.

A Memorable Fancy[6]

As I was walking among the fires of hell, delighted with the enjoyments of Genius; which to Angels look like torment and insanity. I collected some of their Proverbs: thinking that as the sayings used in a nation. mark its character, so the Proverbs of Hell, shew the nature of Infernal wisdom better than any description of buildings or garments

When I came home; on the abyss of the five senses. where a flat sided steep frowns over the present world. I saw a mighty Devil folded in black clouds, hovering on

[1] *Paradise Lost* The rest of this section contains an unconventional reading of Milton's epic.

[2] *Sin & Death* Cf. *Paradise Lost* 2.746–814, in which the birth of Satan's daughter, Sin, and the son of their incestuous union, Death, are described.

[3] *It … Abyss* *Paradise Lost* 6.824ff. describes God's defeat of Satan, originally the Archangel Lucifer, and Satan's expulsion from heaven, along with his rebel faction.

[4] *he prays … comforter* In John 14.16–17, Christ says he will pray to the Father to give humankind another comforter, the Holy Ghost.

[5] *Ratio* Sum.

[6] *Memorable Fancy* Blake's "Memorable Fancies" are modeled on the "Memorable Relations" in which Swedenborg recounts his visionary experiences.

the sides of the rock, with corroding [Plate 7] fires[1] he wrote the following sentence now percieved by the minds of men, & read by them on earth.

How do you know but ev'ry Bird that cuts the airy way,
Is an immense world of delight, clos'd by your senses five?[2]

Proverbs of Hell[3]

In seed time learn, in harvest teach, in winter enjoy.
Drive your cart and your plow over the bones of the dead.
The road of excess leads to the palace of wisdom.
Prudence is a rich ugly old maid courted by Incapacity.
He who desires but acts not, breeds pestilence.
The cut worm forgives the plow.
Dip him in the river who loves water.
A fool sees not the same tree that a wise man sees.
He whose face gives no light, shall never become a star.
Eternity is in love with the productions of time.
The busy bee has no time for sorrow.
The hours of folly are measur'd by the clock, but of wisdom: no clock can measure.
All wholsom food is caught without a net or a trap.
Bring out number weight, & measure in a year of dearth
No bird soars too high. if he soars with his own wings.
A dead body. revenges not injuries.
The most sublime act is to set another before you.
If the fool would persist in his folly he would become wise
Folly is the cloke of knavery.
Shame is Prides cloke.

[Plate 8]

Prisons are built with stones of Law, Brothels with bricks of Religion.
The pride of the peacock is the glory of God.
The lust of the goat is the bounty of God.
The wrath of the lion is the wisdom of God.
The nakedness of woman is the work of God.
Excess of sorrow laughs. Excess of joy weeps.
The roaring of lions, the howling of wolves, the raging of the stormy sea, and the destructive sword. are portions of eternity too great for the eye of man.
The fox condemns the trap, not himself.
Joys impregnate. Sorrows bring forth.
Let man wear the fell of the lion. woman the fleece of the sheep.
The bird a nest. the spider a web. man friendship.
The selfish smiling fool & the sullen frowning fool. shall be both thought wise. that they may be a rod.
What is now proved was once only imagin'd.
The rat, the mouse, the fox, the rabbet; watch the roots, the lion. the tyger. the horse. the elephant. watch the fruits.
The cistern contains: the fountain overflows
One thought. fills immensity.
Always be ready to speak your mind, and a base man will avoid you.
Every thing possible to be believ'd is an image of truth.
The eagle never lost so much time as when he submitted to learn of the crow.

[Plate 9]

The fox provides for himself. but God provides for the lion.
Think in the morning. Act in the noon, Eat in the evening, Sleep in the night,
He who has sufferd you to impose on him knows you.
As the plow follows words, so God rewards prayers.
Thy tygers of wrath are wiser than the horses of instruction
Expect poison. from the standing water.
You never know what is enough unless you know what is more than enough.

[1] *corroding fires* A reference to Blake's use of acids to etch the copper plates from which he printed his poems. More extended accounts of the printing process occur on plates 14 and 15.

[2] *How do … five* Cf. Thomas Chatterton, *Bristowe Tragedie, or the Dethe of Syr Charles Bawdin* (1768): "How dydd I know that ev'ry darte / That cutte the airie waie / Myghte nott find passage toe my harte / And close myne eyes for aie?" (133–36).

[3] *Proverbs of Hell* A diabolical version of the Old Testament's Book of Proverbs.

Listen to the fools reproach! it is a kingly title!
The eyes of fire, the nostrils of air, the mouth of water, the beard of earth.
The weak in courage is strong in cunning.
The apple tree never asks the beech how he shall grow, nor the lion the horse, how he shall take his prey.
The thankful reciever bears a plentiful harvest.
If others had not been foolish, we should be so.
The soul of sweet delight, can never be defil'd,
When thou seest an Eagle. thou seest a portion of Genius. lift up thy head!
As the caterpiller chooses the fairest leaves to lay her eggs on. so the priest lays his curse on the fairest joys.
To create a little flower is the labour of ages.
Damn. braces. Bless relaxes.
The best wine is the oldest. the best water the newest.
Prayers plow not! Praises reap not!
Joys laugh not! Sorrows weep not!

[Plate 10]

The head Sublime, the heart Pathos, the genitals Beauty. the hands & feet Proportion.
As the air to a bird or the sea to a fish, so is contempt to the contemptible.
The crow wish'd every thing was black, the owl, that every thing was white.
Exuberance is Beauty.
If the lion was advised by the fox. he would be cunning.
Improvement makes strait roads, but the crooked roads without Improvement. are roads of Genius.
Sooner murder an infant in its cradle than nurse unacted desires
Where man is not nature is barren.
Truth can never be told so as to be understood. and not be believ'd.

Enough! or Too much

[Plate 11]

The ancient Poets animated all sensible objects with Gods or Geniuses, calling them by the names and adorning them with the properties of woods, rivers, mountains, lakes, cities, nations, and whatever their enlarged & numerous senses could perceive.

And particularly they studied the genius of each city & country. placing it under its mental deity.

Till a system was formed, which some took advantage of & enslav'd the vulgar by attempting to realize or abstract the mental deities from their objects: thus began Priesthood.

Choosing forms of worship from poetic tales.

And at length they pronounced that the Gods had ordered such things.

Thus men forgot that All deities reside in the human breast.

[Plate 12]

A Memorable Fancy

The Prophets Isaiah and Ezekiel dined with me, and I asked them how they dared so roundly to assert. that God spoke to them; and whether they did not think at the time, that they would be misunderstood, & so be the cause of imposition.

Isaiah answer'd. "I saw no God. nor heard any, in a finite organical perception; but my senses discover'd the infinite in every thing, and as I was then perswaded. & remain confirm'd; that the voice of honest indignation is the voice of God, I cared not for consequences but wrote"

Then I asked: "does a firm perswasion that a thing is so, make it so?"

He replied, "All poets believe that it does. & in ages of imagination this firm perswasion removed mountains; but many are not capable of a firm perswasion of any thing"

Then Ezekiel said. The philosophy of the east taught the first principles of human perception some nations held one principle for the origin & some another, we of Israel taught that the Poetic Genius (as you now call it) was the first principle and all the others merely derivative, which was the cause of our despising the Priests & Philosophers of other countries, and prophecying that all Gods [Plate 13] would at last be proved to originate in ours & to be the tributaries of the Poetic Genius, it was this. that our great poet King David desired so fervently & invokes so patheticly, saying by this he conquers enemies & governs kingdoms; and we so loved our God. that we cursed in his name all the deities of surrounding nations, and asserted that they had rebelled; from these opinions the vulgar came to think that all nations would at last be subject to the jews.

"This" said he, "like all firm perswasions, is come to pass, for all nations believe the jews code and worship the jews god, and what greater subjection can be"

I heard this with some wonder, & must confess my own conviction. After dinner I ask'd Isaiah to favour the world with his lost works, he said none of equal value was lost. Ezekiel said the same of his.

I also asked Isaiah what made him go naked and barefoot three years? he answered, "the same that made our friend Diogenes the Grecian."[1]

I then asked Ezekiel. why he eat dung, & lay so long on his right & left side?[2] he answered. "the desire of raising other men into a perception of the infinite this the North American tribes practise, & is he honest who resists his genius or conscience. only for the sake of present ease or gratification?"

[Plate 14]

The ancient tradition that the world will be consumed in fire at the end of six thousand years[3] is true. as I have heard from Hell.

For the cherub with his flaming sword is hereby commanded to leave his guard at tree of life, and when he does, the whole creation will be consumed, and appear infinite. and holy whereas it now appears finite & corrupt.

This will come to pass by an improvement of sensual enjoyment.

But first the notion that man has a body distinct from his soul, is to be expunged; this I shall do, by printing in the infernal method, by corrosives, which in Hell are salutary and medicinal, melting apparent surfaces away, and displaying the infinite which was hid.[4]

If the doors of perception were cleansed every thing would appear to man as it is, infinite.

For man has closed himself up, till he sees all things thro' narrow chinks of his cavern.[5]

[Plate 15]

A Memorable Fancy

I was in a Printing House in Hell & saw the method in which knowledge is transmitted from generation to generation

In the first chamber was a Dragon-Man. clearing away the rubbish from a caves mouth; within, a number of Dragons were hollowing the cave,

In the second chamber was a Viper folding round the rock & the cave, and others adorning it with gold silver and precious stones

In the third chamber was an Eagle with wings and feathers of air, he caused the inside of the cave to be infinite, around were numbers of Eagle like men, who built palaces in the immense cliffs.

In the fourth chamber were Lions of flaming fire raging around & melting the metals into living fluids.

In the fifth chamber were Unnam'd forms, which cast the metals into the expanse.

There they were reciev'd by Men who occupied the sixth chamber, and took the forms of books & were arranged in libraries.

[1] *Diogenes the Grecian* Founder of the Cynic school of philosophers, who advocated and practiced a lifestyle of extreme simplicity. In Isaiah 20.2–3, Isaiah is commanded by the Lord to walk "naked and barefoot" for three years.

[2] *why ... side* As he was instructed by the Lord in Ezekiel 4.4–6.

[3] *The ancient ... years* In Genesis 8.21, just after the Flood, God promises not to destroy the world again. The New Testament, however, contains several prophecies that it will be destroyed, this time by fire (Luke 12.49, 2 Peter 3.5–7). The traditional figure of six thousand years seems to have been obtained by combining the six days it took to make the world (Genesis 1) and the idea "that one day is with the Lord as a thousand years" (2 Peter 3.8).

[4] *this I ... hid* In conventional etching, only the lines of the design are burned away by the acid, the rest of the plate being protected by an acid-proof substance such as wax. In Blake's relief etching process, however, almost the whole surface of the plate is burned away, leaving the lines in relief.

[5] *chinks ... cavern* Cf. the allegory of the cave in Plato, *Republic*, and the image of the camera obscura in John Locke (1632–1704), *An Essay Concerning Human Understanding*.

[Plate 16]

The Giants who formed this world into its sensual existence and now seem to live in it in chains, are in truth. the causes of its life & the sources of all activity, but the chains are, the cunning of weak and tame minds. which have power to resist energy. according to the proverb, the weak in courage is strong in cunning.

Thus one portion of being, is the Prolific. the other, the Devouring; to the devourer it seems as if the producer was in his chains, but it is not so, he only takes portions of existence and fancies that the whole.

But the Prolific would cease to be Prolific unless the Devourer as a sea received the excess of his delights.

Some will say, "Is not God alone the Prolific?" I answer, "God only Acts & Is. in existing beings or Men."

These two classes of men are always upon earth. & they should be enemies; whoever tries [Plate 17] to reconcile them seeks to destroy existence.

Religion is an endeavour to reconcile the two.

Note. Jesus Christ did not wish to unite but to seperate them, as in the Parable of sheep and goats![1] & he says "I came not to send Peace but a Sword."[2]

Messiah or Satan or Tempter was formerly thought to be one of the Antediluvians[3] who are our Energies.

A Memorable Fancy

An Angel came to me and said. "O pitiable foolish young man! O horrible! O dreadful state! consider the hot burning dungeon thou art preparing for thyself to all eternity, to which thou art going in such career."

I said. "perhaps you will be willing to shew me my eternal lot & we will contemplate together upon it and see whether your lot or mine is most desirable."

So he took me thro' a stable & thro a church & down into the church vault at the end of which was a mill; thro' the mill; we went. and came to a cave. down the winding cavern we groped our tedious way till a void boundless as a nether sky appeard beneath us & we held by the roots of trees and hung over this immensity, but I said, "if you please we will commit ourselves to this void, and see whether providence is here also, if you will not I will?" but he answerd. "do not presume O young-man but as we here remain behold thy lot which will soon appear when the darkness passes away."

So I remaind with him sitting in the twisted [Plate 18] root of an oak. he was suspended in a fungus which hung with the head downward into the deep;

By degrees we beheld the infinite Abyss, fiery as the smoke of a burning city; beneath us at an immense distance was the sun, black but shining round it were fiery tracks on which revolv'd vast spiders. crawling after their prey; which flew or rather swum in the infinite deep, in the most terrific shapes of animals sprung from corruption. & the air was full of them, & seemd composed of them; these are Devils. and are called Powers of the air, I now asked my companion which was my eternal lot? he said, "between the black & white spiders."

But now, from between the black & white spiders a cloud and fire burst and rolled thro' the deep blackning all beneath, so that the nether deep grew black as a sea & rolled with a terrible noise: beneath us was nothing now to be seen but a black tempest, till looking east between the clouds & the waves. we saw a cataract of blood mixed with fire and not many stones throw from us appeard and sunk again the scaly fold of a monstrous serpent at last to the east, distant about three degrees[4] appeard a fiery crest above the waves slowly it reared like a ridge of golden rocks till we discoverd two globes of crimson fire. from which the sea fled away in clouds of smoke, and now we saw, it was the head of Leviathan,[5] his forehead was divided into streaks of green & purple like those on a tygers forehead: soon we saw his mouth & red gills hang just above the raging foam tinging the

[1] *Parable … goats* Cf. Matthew 25.32–46. God divides the nations "as a shepherd divideth his sheep from his goats," placing the sheep, who are to be saved, on his right hand, and the goats, who are damned, on his left.

[2] *I … Sword* From Matthew 10.34.

[3] *Antediluvians* Those who existed before the Flood.

[4] *three degrees* Paris is three degrees east of London.

[5] *Leviathan* The beast Leviathan is described in Job 4.1; Psalms 104.26; Isaiah 27.1; Revelation 11.7, 12.9, 13.2, 20.1–3. Blake may also be thinking of Thomas Hobbes's *Leviathan; or, The Matter, Form, and Power of a Commonwealth, Ecclesiastical and Civil.*

black deep with beams of blood, advancing toward [Plate 19] us with all the fury of a spiritual existence.

My friend the Angel climb'd up from his station into the mill; I remain'd alone, & then this appearance was no more, but I found myself sitting on a pleasant bank beside a river by moon light hearing a harper who sung to the harp. & his theme was, "The man who never alters his opinion is like standing water, & breeds reptiles of the mind."

But I arose. and sought for the mill, & there I found my Angel, who surprised asked me, how I escaped?

I answerd. "All that we saw was owing to your metaphysics: for when you ran away, I found myself on a bank by moonlight hearing a harper, But now we have seen my eternal lot, shall I shew you yours?" he laughd at my proposal; but I by force suddenly caught him in my arms, & flew westerly thro' the night, till we were elevated above the earths shadow: then I flung myself with him directly into the body of the sun, here I clothed myself in white,[1] & taking in my hand Swedenborgs volumes sunk from the glorious clime, and passed all the planets till we came to saturn, here I staid to rest & then leap'd into the void. between saturn & the fixed stars.[2]

"Here" said I! "is your lot, in this space, if space it may be calld," Soon we saw the stable and the church, & I took him to the altar and open'd the Bible, and lo! it was a deep pit, into which I descended driving the Angel before me, soon we saw seven houses of brick,[3] one we entred; in it were a [Plate 20] number of monkeys. baboons, & all of that species chaind by the middle, grinning and snatching at one another. but witheld by the shortness of their chains; however I saw that they sometimes grew numerous, and then the weak were caught by the strong and with a grinning aspect, first coupled with & then devourd, by plucking off first one limb and then another till the body was left a helpless trunk. this after grinning & kissing it with seeming fondness they devourd too; and here & there I saw one savourily picking the flesh off his own tail; as the stench terribly annoyd us both we went into the mill, & I in my hand brought the skeleton of a body, which in the mill was Aristotles Analytics.[4]

So the Angel said: "thy phantasy has imposed upon me & thou oughtest to be ashamed."

I answered: "we impose on one another, & it is but lost time to converse with you whose works are only Analytics."

Opposition is True Friendship

[Plate 21]

I have always found that Angels have the vanity to speak of themselves as the only wise; this they do with a confident insolence sprouting from systematic reasoning;

Thus Swedenborg boasts that what he writes is new; tho' it is only the Contents or Index of already publish'd books.

A man carried a monkey about for a shew. & because he was a little wiser than the monkey, grew vain. and conceiv'd himself as much wiser than seven men. It is so with Swedenborg; he shews the folly of churches & exposes hypocrites, till he imagines that all are religious. & himself the single [Plate 22] one on earth that ever broke a net.

Now hear a plain fact: Swedenborg has not written one new truth: Now hear another: he has written all the old falshoods.

And now hear the reason. He conversed with Angels who are all religious. & conversed not with Devils who all hate religion, for he was incapable thro' his conceited notions.

Thus Swedenborgs writings are a recapitulation of all superficial opinions, and an analysis of the more sublime. but no further.

[1] *clothed ... white* Cf. Revelation 7.9, in which those who have been redeemed are clothed in white when they appear before Christ's throne.

[2] *void ... stars* In the Ptolemaic world system, Saturn was the outermost planet, and bordered on the sphere of the fixed stars.

[3] *seven ... brick* John addresses the book of Revelation to the "seven churches which are in Asia" (Revelation 1.4).

[4] *Analytics* Aristotle's two treatises on logic.

Have now another plain fact: Any man of mechanical talents may from the writings of Paracelsus or Jacob Behmen,[1] produce ten thousand volumes of equal value with Swedenborg's. and from those of Dante or Shakespear. an infinite number.

But when he has done this, let him not say that he knows better than his master, for he only holds a candle in sunshine.

A Memorable Fancy

Once I saw a Devil in a flame of fire. who arose before an Angel that sat on a cloud. and the Devil uttered these words.

"The worship of God is. Honouring his gifts in other men, each according to his genius. and loving the [Plate 23] greatest men best, those who envy or calumniate great men hate God, for there is no other God."

The Angel hearing this became almost blue but mastering himself he grew yellow, & at last white pink & smiling, and then replied,

"Thou Idolater, is not God One? & is not he visible in Jesus Christ? and has not Jesus Christ given his sanction to the law of ten commandments and are not all other men fools. sinners, & nothings?"

The Devil answer'd; "bray a fool in a morter with wheat. yet shall not his folly be beaten out of him:[2] if Jesus Christ is the greatest man. you ought to love him in the greatest degree; now hear how he has given his sanction to the law of ten commandments: did he not mock at the sabbath,[3] and so mock the sabbaths God? murder those who were murderd because of him?[4] turn away the law from the woman taken in adultery?[5] steal the labor of others to support him?[6] bear false witness when he omitted making a defence before Pilate?[7] covet when he pray'd for his disciples, and when he bid them shake off the dust of their feet against such as refused to lodge them?[8] I tell you, no virtue can exist without breaking these ten commandments: Jesus was all virtue, and acted from impulse. [Plate 24] not from rules."

When he had so spoken: I beheld the Angel who stretched out his arms embracing the flame of fire & he was consumed and arose as Elijah.[9]

Note. This Angel, who is now become a Devil, is my particular friend: we often read the Bible together in its infernal or diabolical sense which the world shall have if they behave well

I have also: The Bible of Hell:[10] which the world shall have whether they will or no.

One Law for the Lion & Ox is Oppression

—1793

[1] *Paracelsus* Philippus Aureolus, Theophrastus Bombastus von Hohenheim (1493–1541), Swiss physician and alchemist; *Behmen* Jakob Boehme (1575–1624), German mystic.

[2] *bray ... him* Proverbs 27.22. This devil can quote scripture to his purpose; *bray* Crush.

[3] *mock ... sabbath* In Exodus 20.8–11; Matthew 12.8–12; Mark 2.27, 3.2–4; Luke 14.3–5; John 5.16.

[4] *murder ... him* In Exodus 20.13; see the martyrdom of Stephen (Acts 7.58–60).

[5] *turn ... adultery* In Exodus 20.14; John 8.3–11.

[6] *steal ... him* Cf. Exodus 20.15; Matthew 26.6–13.

[7] *bear ... Pilate* Cf. Exodus 20.16; Matthew 27.11–14; Mark 15.2–5.

[8] *covet ... them* Cf. Exodus 20.17; Matthew 10.14; Luke 9.5.

[9] *who ... Elijah* Cf. 2 Kings 2.11: "There appeared a chariot of fire, and ... Elijah went up by a whirlwind into heaven."

[10] *Bible of Hell* A reference to Blake's own work. In addition to the Proverbs of Hell (plates 7–10), this bible is sometimes said to include such later works as *The [First] Book of Urizen*, *The Book of Ahania*, and *The Book of Los* (1794–95).

THE MARRIAGE of HEAVEN and HELL

1

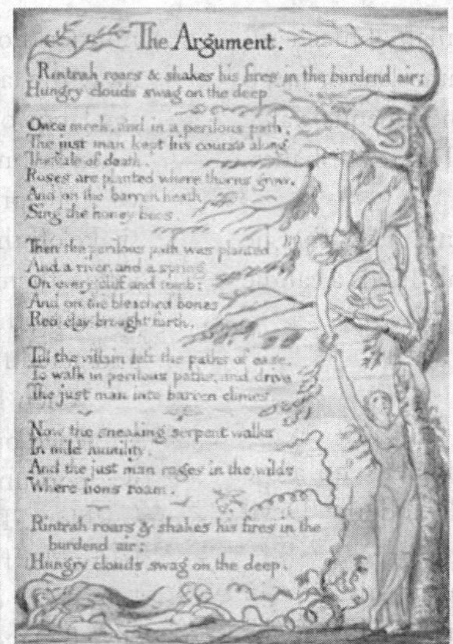
The Argument.

Rintrah roars & shakes his fires in the burdend air;
Hungry clouds swag on the deep

Once meek, and in a perilous path,
The just man kept his course along
The vale of death.
Roses are planted where thorns grow,
And on the barren heath
Sing the honey bees.

Then the perilous path was planted:
And a river, and a spring
On every cliff and tomb;
And on the bleached bones
Red clay brought forth.

Till the villain left the paths of ease,
To walk in perilous paths, and drive
The just man into barren climes.

Now the sneaking serpent walks
In mild humility.
And the just man rages in the wilds
Where lions roam.

Rintrah roars & shakes his fires in the burdend air;
Hungry clouds swag on the deep.

2

As a new heaven is begun, and it is now thirty-three years since its advent: the Eternal Hell revives. And lo! Swedenborg is the Angel sitting at the tomb; his writings are the linen clothes folded up. Now is the dominion of Edom, & the return of Adam into Paradise; see Isaiah XXXIV & XXXV Chap:

Without Contraries is no progression. Attraction and Repulsion, Reason and Energy, Love and Hate, are necessary to Human existence.

From these contraries spring what the religious call Good & Evil. Good is the passive that obeys Reason. Evil is the active springing from Energy.

Good is Heaven. Evil is Hell.

3

Devil

All Bibles or sacred codes, have been the causes of the following Errors.

1. That Man has two real existing principles Viz: a Body & a Soul.

2. That Energy, calld Evil, is alone from the Body, & that Reason, calld Good, is alone from the Soul.

3. That God will torment Man in Eternity for following his Energies.

But the following Contraries to these are True

1. Man has no Body distinct from his Soul for that calld Body is a portion of Soul discernd by the five Senses, the chief inlets of Soul in this age.

2. Energy is the only life and is from the Body and Reason is the bound or outward circumference of Energy.

3. Energy is Eternal Delight

4

Those who restrain desire, do so because theirs is weak enough to be restrained; and the restrainer or Reason usurps its place & governs the unwilling.

And being restraind it by degrees becomes passive till it is only the shadow of desire.

The history of this is written in Paradise Lost, & the Governor or Reason is calld Messiah.

And the original Archangel or possessor of the command of the heavenly host, is calld the Devil or Satan and his children are calld Sin & Death.

But in the Book of Job Miltons Messiah is calld Satan.

For this history has been adopted by both parties

It indeed appeard to Reason as if Desire was cast out. but the Devils account is that the Messi

5

ah fell, & formed a heaven of what he stole from the Abyss

This is shewn in the Gospel, where he prays to the Father to send the comforter or Desire that Reason may have Ideas to build on, the Jehovah of the Bible being no other than he who dwells in flaming fire.

Know that after Christs death, he became Jehovah.

But in Milton; the Father is Destiny, the Son, a Ratio of the five senses, & the Holy-ghost, Vacuum!

Note. The reason Milton wrote in fetters when he wrote of Angels & God, and at liberty when of Devils & Hell, is because he was a true Poet and of the Devils party without knowing it

A Memorable Fancy

As I was walking among the fires of hell, delighted with the enjoyments of Genius; which to Angels look like torment and insanity. I collected some of their Proverbs: thinking that as the sayings used in a nation, mark its character, so the Proverbs of Hell, shew the nature of Infernal wisdom better than any description of buildings or garments.

When I came home; on the abyss of the five senses, where a flat sided steep frowns over the present world. I saw a mighty Devil folded in black clouds, hovering on the sides of the rock, with cor ro-

6

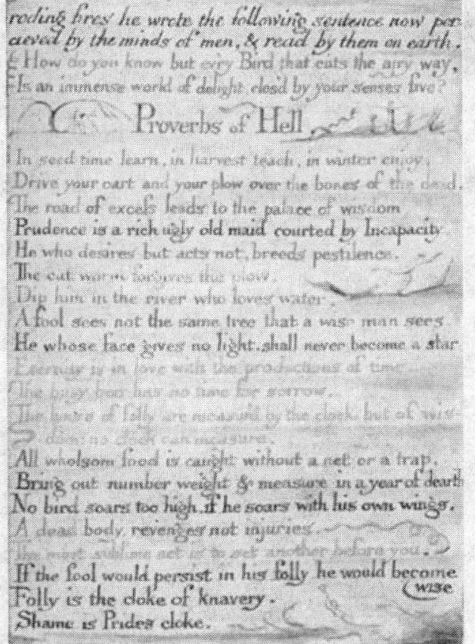

roding fires he wrote the following sentence now perceived by the minds of men, & read by them on earth.

How do you know but evry Bird that cuts the airy way,
Is an immense world of delight, clos'd by your senses five?

Proverbs of Hell

In seed time learn, in harvest teach, in winter enjoy.
Drive your cart and your plow over the bones of the dead.
The road of excess leads to the palace of wisdom
Prudence is a rich ugly old maid courted by Incapacity.
He who desires but acts not, breeds pestilence.
The cut worm forgives the plow.
Dip him in the river who loves water.
A fool sees not the same tree that a wise man sees.
He whose face gives no light, shall never become a star.
Eternity is in love with the productions of time.
The busy bee has no time for sorrow.
The hours of folly are measur'd by the clock, but of wisdom: no clock can measure.
All wholsom food is caught without a net or a trap.
Bring out number weight & measure in a year of dearth.
No bird soars too high, if he soars with his own wings.
A dead body, revenges not injuries.
The most sublime act is to set another before you.
If the fool would persist in his folly he would become wise
Folly is the cloke of knavery.
Shame is Prides cloke.

7

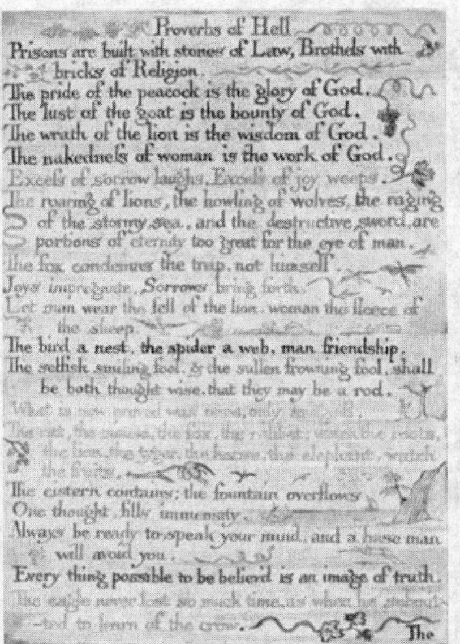

Proverbs of Hell

Prisons are built with stones of Law, Brothels with bricks of Religion.
The pride of the peacock is the glory of God.
The lust of the goat is the bounty of God.
The wrath of the lion is the wisdom of God.
The nakedness of woman is the work of God.
Excess of sorrow laughs. Excess of joy weeps.
The roaring of lions, the howling of wolves, the raging of the stormy sea, and the destructive sword, are portions of eternity too great for the eye of man.
The fox condemns the trap, not himself.
Joys impregnate. Sorrows bring forth.
Let man wear the fell of the lion, woman the fleece of the sheep.
The bird a nest, the spider a web, man friendship.
The selfish smiling fool, & the sullen frowning fool, shall be both thought wise, that they may be a rod.
What is now proved was once, only imagin'd.
The rat, the mouse, the fox, the rabbet: watch the roots, the lion, the tyger, the horse, the elephant, watch the fruits.
The cistern contains: the fountain overflows
One thought, fills immensity.
Always be ready to speak your mind, and a base man will avoid you.
Every thing possible to be believ'd is an image of truth.
The eagle never lost so much time, as when he submitted to learn of the crow.
The

8

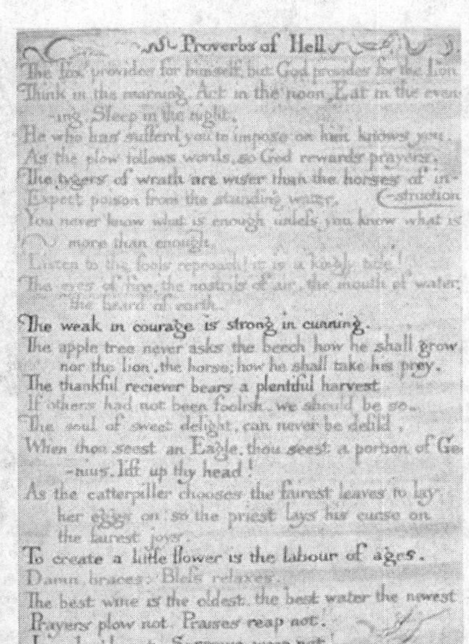

Proverbs of Hell

The fox provides for himself, but God provides for the lion.
Think in the morning, Act in the noon, Eat in the evening, Sleep in the night.
He who has sufferd you to impose on him knows you.
As the plow follows words, so God rewards prayers.
The tygers of wrath are wiser than the horses of instruction
Expect poison from the standing water.
You never know what is enough unless you know what is more than enough.
Listen to the fools reproach! it is a kingly title!
The eyes of fire, the nostrils of air, the mouth of water, the beard of earth.
The weak in courage is strong in cunning.
The apple tree never asks the beech how he shall grow, nor the lion, the horse; how he shall take his prey.
The thankful reciever bears a plentiful harvest.
If others had not been foolish, we should be so.
The soul of sweet delight, can never be defil'd.
When thou seest an Eagle, thou seest a portion of Genius. lift up thy head!
As the catterpiller chooses the fairest leaves to lay her eggs on, so the priest lays his curse on the fairest joys.
To create a little flower is the labour of ages.
Damn, braces: Bless relaxes.
The best wine is the oldest, the best water the newest.
Prayers plow not! Praises reap not!
Joys laugh not! Sorrows weep not!

9

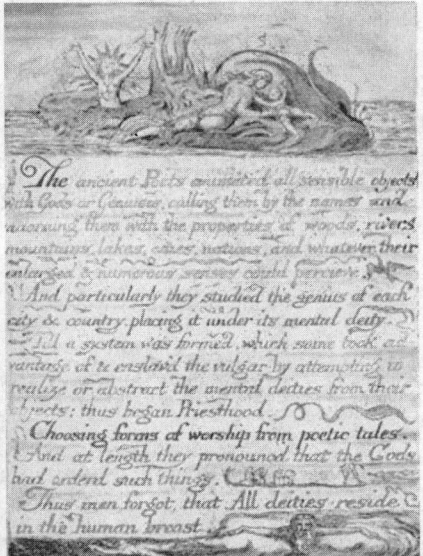

Proverbs of Hell

The head Sublime, the heart Pathos, the genitals Beauty, the hands & feet Proportion.
As the air to a bird or the sea to a fish, so is contempt to the contemptible.
The crow wish'd every thing was black, the owl, that every thing was white.
Exuberance is Beauty.
If the lion was advised by the fox, he would be cunning.
Improvent makes strait roads, but the crooked roads without Improvement, are roads of Genius.
Sooner murder an infant in its cradle than nurse unacted desires
Where man is not nature is barren.
Truth can never be told so as to be understood, and not be believ'd.
Enough! or Too much

10

The ancient Poets animated all sensible objects with Gods or Geniuses, calling them by the names and adorning them with the properties of woods, rivers, mountains, lakes, cities, nations, and whatever their enlarged & numerous senses could percieve.

And particularly they studied the genius of each city & country, placing it under its mental deity.

Till a system was formed, which some took advantage of & enslav'd the vulgar by attempting to realize or abstract the mental deities from their objects: thus began Priesthood.

Choosing forms of worship from poetic tales.

And at length they pronounc'd that the Gods had orderd such things.

Thus men forgot that All deities reside in the human breast.

11

A Memorable Fancy.

The Prophets Isaiah and Ezekiel dined with me, and I asked them how they dared so roundly to assert. that God spoke to them; and whether they did not think at the time, that they would be misunderstood, & so be the cause of imposition.

Isaiah answer'd. I saw no God, nor heard any, in a finite organical perception; but my senses discover'd the infinite in every thing, and as I was then perswaded, & remain confirm'd; that the voice of honest indignation is the voice of God. I cared not for consequences but wrote.

Then I asked: does a firm perswasion that a thing is so, make it so?

He replied. All poets believe that it does, & in ages of imagination this firm perswasion removed mountains; but many are not capable of a firm perswasion of any thing.

Then Ezekiel said. The philosophy of the east taught the first principles of human perception some nations held one principle for the origin & some another, we of Israel taught that the Poetic Genius (as you now call it) was the first principle and all the others merely derivative, which was the cause of our despising the Priests & Philosophers of other countries, and prophecying that all Gods would

12

would at last be proved, to originate in ours & to be the tributaries of the Poetic Genius; it was this. that our great poet King David desired so fervently & invokes so patheticly, saying by this he conquers enemies & governs kingdoms; and we so loved our God, that we cursed in his name all the deities of surrounding nations, and asserted that they had rebelled; from these opinions the vulgar came to think that all nations would at last be subject to the jews.

This said he, like all firm perswasions, is come to pass, for all nations believe the jews code and worship the jews god, and what greater subjection can be

I heard this with some wonder, & must confess my own conviction. After dinner I askd Isaiah to favour the world with his lost works, he said none of equal value was lost. Ezekiel said the same of his.

I also asked Isaiah what made him go naked and barefoot three years? he answerd, the same that made our friend Diogenes the Grecian.

I then asked Ezekiel, why he eat dung, & lay so long on his right & left side? he answerd, the desire of raising other men into a perception of the infinite this the North American tribes practise, & is he honest who resists his genius or conscience, only for the sake of present ease or gratification?

13

The ancient tradition that the world will be consumed in fire at the end of six thousand years is true, as I have heard from Hell.

For the cherub with his flaming sword is hereby commanded to leave his guard at tree of life, and when he does, the whole creation will be consumed and appear infinite. and holy whereas it now appears finite & corrupt.

This will come to pass by an improvement of sensual enjoyment.

But first the notion that man has a body distinct from his soul, is to be expunged; this I shall do by printing in the infernal method by corrosives, which in Hell are salutary and medicinal, melting apparent surfaces away, and displaying the infinite which was hid.

If the doors of perception were cleansed every thing would appear to man as it is: Infinite.

For man has closed himself up, till he sees all things thro' narrow chinks of his cavern.

14

A Memorable Fancy

I was in a Printing house in Hell & saw the method in which knowledge is transmitted from generation to generation.

In the first chamber was a Dragon-Man, clearing away the rubbish from a caves mouth; within, a number of Dragons were hollowing the cave.

In the second chamber was a Viper folding round the rock & the cave, and others adorning it with gold silver and precious stones.

In the third chamber was an Eagle with wings and feathers of air, he caused the inside of the cave to be infinite, around were numbers of Eagle like men, who built palaces in the immense cliffs.

In the fourth chamber were Lions of flaming fire raging around & melting the metals into living fluids.

In the fifth chamber were Unnam'd forms, which cast the metals into the expanse.

There they were reciev'd by Men who occupied the sixth chamber, and took the forms of books & were arranged in libraries.

15

The Giants who formed this world into its sensual existence and now seem to live in it in chains; are in truth. the causes of its life & the sources of all activity, but the chains are, the cunning of weak and tame minds. which have power to resist energy. according to the proverb, the weak in courage is strong in cunning.

Thus one portion of being, is the Prolific. the other, the Devouring: to the devourer it seems as if the producer was in his chains, but it is not so, he only takes portions of existence and fancies that the whole.

But the Prolific would cease to be Prolific unless the Devourer as a sea recieved the excess of his delights.

Some will say, Is not God alone the Prolific? I answer, God only Acts & Is, in existing beings or Men.

These two classes of men are always upon earth, & they should be enemies; whoever tries to

16

to reconcile them seeks to destroy existence.

Religion is an endeavour to reconcile the two.

Note. Jesus Christ did not wish to unite but to seperate them, as in the Parable of sheep and goats! & he says I came not to send Peace but a Sword.

Messiah or Satan or Tempter was formerly thought to be one of the Antediluvians who are our Energies.

A Memorable Fancy

An Angel came to me and said. O pitiable foolish young man! O horrible! O dreadful state! consider the hot burning dungeon thou art preparing for thyself to all eternity, to which thou art going in such career.

I said. perhaps you will be willing to shew me my eternal lot & we will contemplate together upon it and see whether your lot or mine is most desirable

So he took me thro' a stable & thro' a church & down into the church vault at the end of which was a mill: thro' the mill we went, and came to a cave. down the winding cavern we groped our tedious way till a void boundless as a nether sky appeard beneath us & we held by the roots of trees and hung over this immensity; but I said, if you please we will commit ourselves to this void, and see whether providence is here also, if you will not I will? but he answerd, do not presume O young-man but as we here remain behold thy lot which will soon appear when the darkness passes away

So I remaind with him sitting in the twisted

17

root of an oak. he was suspended in a fungus which hung with the head downward into the deep:

By degrees we beheld the infinite Abyss, fiery as the smoke of a burning city; beneath us at an immense distance was the sun, black but shining round it were fiery tracks on which revolv'd vast spiders, crawling after their prey; which flew or rather swum in the infinite deep, in the most terrific shapes of animals sprung from corruption. & the air was full of them, & seemd composed of them; these are Devils. and are called Powers of the air. I now asked my companion which was my eternal lot? he said, between the black & white spiders

But now, from between the black & white spiders a cloud and fire burst and rolled thro the deep blackning all beneath, so that the nether deep grew black as a sea & rolled with a terrible noise: beneath us was nothing now to be seen but a black tempest, till looking east between the clouds & the waves, we saw a cataract of blood mixed with fire and not many stones throw from us appeard and sunk again the scaly fold of a monstrous serpent. at last to the east, distant about three degrees appeard a fiery crest above the waves slowly it reared like a ridge of golden rocks till we discoverd two globes of crimson fire. from which the sea fled away in clouds of smoke, and now we saw, it was the head of Leviathan. his forehead was divided into streaks of green & purple like those on a tygers forehead: soon we saw his mouth & red gills hang just above the raging foam tinging the black deep with beams of blood, advancing toward us

18

us with all the fury of a spiritual existence.

My friend the Angel climb'd up from his station into the mill; I remain'd alone, & then this appearance was no more, but I found myself sitting on a pleasant bank beside a river by moon light hearing a harper who sung to the harp. & his theme was, The man who never alters his opinion is like standing water, & breeds reptiles of the mind.

But I arose, and sought for the mill, & there I found my Angel, who surprised asked me, how I escaped?

I answerd, All that we saw was owing to your metaphysics: for when you ran away, I found myself on a bank by moonlight hearing a harper, But now we have seen my eternal lot, shall I shew you yours? he laughd at my proposal; but I by force suddenly caught him in my arms, & flew westerly thro' the night, till we were elevated above the earths shadow: then I flung myself with him directly into the body of the sun, here I clothed myself in white, & taking in my hand Swedenborgs volumes sunk from the glorious clime, and passed all the planets till we came to saturn, here I staid to rest & then leap'd into the void, between saturn & the fixed stars.

Here said I! is your lot, in this space, if space it may be calld. Soon we saw the stable and the church, & I took him to the altar and open'd the Bible, and lo! it was a deep pit, into which I descended driving the Angel before me, soon we saw seven houses of brick, one we enterd; in it were a num

19

number of monkeys, baboons, & all of that species chaind by the middle, grinning and snatching at one another, but witheld by the shortness of their chains: however I saw that they sometimes grew numerous, and then the weak were caught by the strong and with a grinning aspect, first coupled with & then devourd, by plucking off first one limb and then another till the body was left a helpless trunk. this after grinning & kissing it with seeming fondness they devourd too; and here & there I saw one savourily picking the flesh off of his own tail; as the stench terribly annoyd us both we went into the mill, & I in my hand brought the skeleton of a body, which in the mill was Aristotles Analytics.

So the Angel said: thy phantasy has imposed upon me & thou oughtest to be ashamed.

I answerd: we impose on one another, & it is but lost time to converse with you whose works are only Analytics.

20

I have always found that Angels have the vanity to speak of themselves as the only wise; this they do with a confident insolence sprouting from systematic reasoning;

Thus Swedenborg boasts that what he writes is new; tho' it is only the Contents or Index of already publish'd books.

A man carried a monkey about for a shew, & because he was a little wiser than the monkey, grew vain, and concieve'd himself as much wiser than seven men. It is so with Swedenborg; he shews the folly of churches & exposes hypocrites, till he imagines that all are religious, & himself the single one

21

one on earth that ever broke a net.

Now hear a plain fact: Swedenborg has not written one new truth: Now hear another: he has written all the old falshoods.

And now hear the reason. He conversed with Angels who are all religious, & conversed not with Devils who all hate religion, for he was incapable thro' his conceited notions.

Thus Swedenborgs writings are a recapitulation of all superficial opinions, and an analysis of the more sublime, but no further.

Have now another plain fact: Any man of mechanical talents may from the writings of Paracelsus or Jacob Behmen, produce ten thousand volumes of equal value with Swedenborgs, and from those of Dante or Shakespear, an infinite number.

But when he has done this, let him not say that he knows better than his master, for he only holds a candle in sunshine.

A Memorable Fancy

Once I saw a Devil in a flame of fire, who arose before an Angel that sat on a cloud, and the Devil utterd these words.

The worship of God is, Honouring his gifts in other men each according to his genius, and loving the great

22

greatest men best, those who envy or calumniate great men hate God, for there is no other God.

The Angel hearing this became almost blue but mastering himself he grew yellow, & at last white pink & smiling, and then replied,

Thou Idolater, is not God One? & is not he visible in Jesus Christ? and has not Jesus Christ given his sanction to the law of ten commandments and are not all other men fools, sinners, & nothings?

The Devil answer'd: bray a fool in a morter with wheat, yet shall not his folly be beaten out of him: if Jesus Christ is the greatest man, you ought to love him in the greatest degree; now hear how he has given his sanction to the law of ten commandments: did he not mock at the sabbath, and so mock the sabbaths God? murder those who were murderd because of him? turn away the law from the woman taken in adultery? steal the labor of others to support him? bear false witness when he omitted making a defence before Pilate? covet when he pray'd for his disciples, and when he bid them shake off the dust of their feet against such as refused to lodge them? I tell you, no virtue can exist without breaking these ten commandments: Jesus was all virtue, and acted from impulse:

23

pulse: not from rules.

When he had so spoken: I beheld the Angel who stretched out his arms embracing the flame of fire & he was consumed and arose as Elijah.

Note. This Angel, who is now become a Devil, is my particular friend: we often read the Bible together in its infernal or diabolical sense which the world shall have if they behave well.

I have also: The Bible of Hell: which the world shall have whether they will or no.

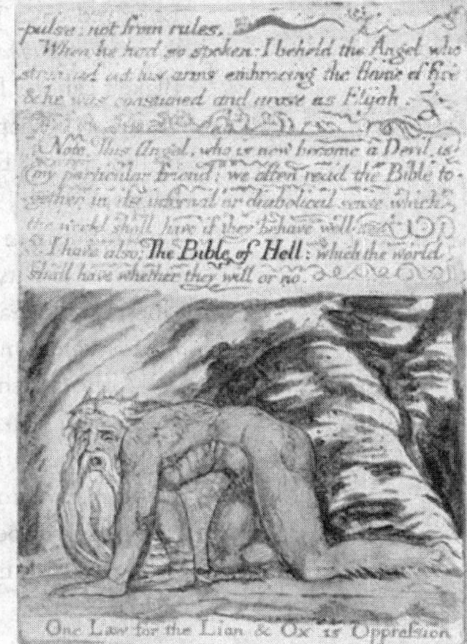

One Law for the Lion & Ox is Oppression

24

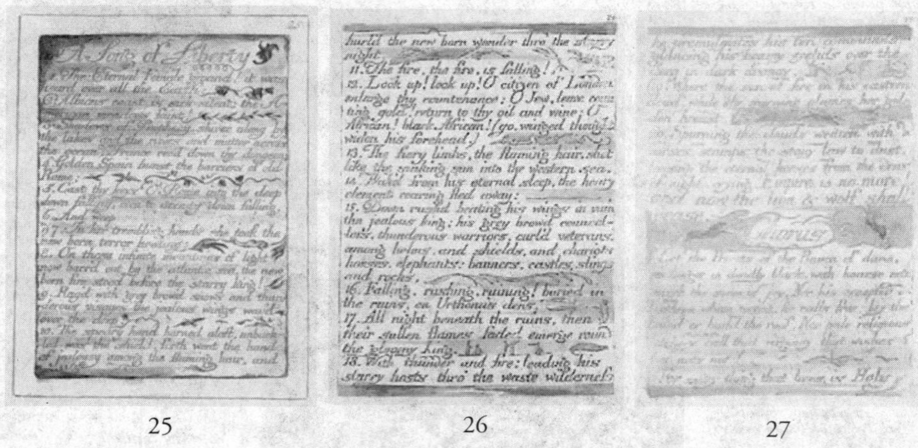

25 26 27

A Song of Liberty

Engraved circa 1792 and appended as the conclusion (plates 25, 26, and 27) to *The Marriage of Heaven and Hell* (1790–93), "A Song of Liberty" is an important part of Blake's canon. The poem reiterates and anticipates a number of themes significant to the artist; perhaps most prominent among these are the myth of revolution announced in the cry of "Empire is no more!"—and the prophetic belief in salvation through religious faith. The song can be seen as a key founding document of British Romanticism in its celebration of freedom, its rejection of reason as the focus of human existence, and its insistence on equality. Blake's engravings of vegetative motifs—looped vines, various leaves, branches, flame-like foliage—and two soaring birds to accompany the textual manuscript further contribute to the Romantic vision of the text.

Although the "Song" invariably appears as the last verse in all extant manuscript copies of *The Marriage of Heaven and Hell*, recent criticism suggests that the poem may not have been intended originally to serve as part of the longer work; some scholars have noted the sometimes striking differences in style and content between "A Song of Liberty" and the preceding plates, while others have suggested that the "Song" was to have been published as a separate pamphlet.

⌘⌘⌘

A Song of Liberty[1]

1. The Eternal Female[2] groand! it was heard over all the Earth:
2. Albions[3] coast is sick silent; the American meadows faint!
3. Shadows of Prophecy shiver along by the lakes and the rivers and mutter across the ocean? France rend down thy dungeon
4. Golden Spain burst the barriers of old Rome;[4]
5. Cast thy keys O Rome into the deep down falling, even to eternity down falling,
6. And weep[5]
7. In her trembling hands she took the new born terror howling:
8. On those infinite mountains of light now barr'd out by the atlantic sea, the new born fire stood before the starry king!
9. Flag'd with grey browd snows and thunderous visages the jealous wings wav'd over the deep.
10. The speary hand burned aloft, unbuckled was the shield, forth went the hand of jealousy among the flaming hair. and[6] hurl'd the new born wonder thro' the starry night.
11. The fire, the fire, is falling!
12. Look up! look up! O citizen of London enlarge thy countenance; O Jew, leave counting gold![7] return to thy oil and wine; O African! black African! (go, winged thought, widen his forehead.)
13. The fiery limbs, the flaming hair, shot like the sinking sun into the western sea.
14. Wak'd from his eternal sleep, the hoary element roaring fled away;
15. Down rushd beating his wings in vain the jealous king; his grey brow'd councellors, thunderous warriors, curl'd veterans, among helms, and shields, and chariots, horses, elephants: banners, castles, slings, and rocks,
16. Falling, rushing, ruining! buried in the ruins, on Urthona's[8] dens;
17. All night beneath the ruins, then their sullen flames faded emerge round the gloomy king.
18. With thunder and fire: leading his starry hosts thro' the waste wilderness[9] he promulgates his ten commands,[10] glancing his beamy eyelids over the deep in dark dismay,

---

[1] *A Song of Liberty* The poem appears as the last three plates (25–27) of *The Marriage of Heaven and Hell* (1790–93), Blake's long prophetic poem, composed in the period following the French Revolution.

[2] *Eternal Female* The Eternal Female appears in a variety of guises in Blake's poetry; cf. "Earth" and "Earth's Answer" in the opening poems of the *Songs of Experience* (1789), and the "nameless shadowy female" in the Preludium to *Europe* (1794). Here, it seems to birth the revolutionary spirit itself.

[3] *Albion* Ancient name for the island of Great Britain. Loosely influenced by Greek myth and British folklore, Blake developed his own mythological vision of the figure of Albion as an ancient man who is the father of all humankind.

[4] *old Rome* The center of religious authority for Catholics.

[5] *weep* "and bow thy reverend locks!" was deleted from the copper plate following "weep." These five words are absent in all extant manuscript copies except Copy L (now in the collection of Robert N. Essick) and Copy M (in the collection of E.B. Bentley and G.E. Bentley, Jr.); these two manuscripts consist of plates 25–27 only, with plate 25 in its first state.

[6] *and* This marks the end of Plate 25 in manuscripts of *The Marriage of Heaven and Hell*.

[7] *Jew … counting gold* Since the middle ages European Christian society has condemned Jews for the practice of money-lending, which was in most European countries one of the few professions that Jews were allowed to follow. Blake's anti-Semitic image reflects a stereotypical association, commonly held in England at the time, of Jews with greed.

[8] *Urthona* In later works such as *The Four Zoas* and *Milton a Poem* (1804), Blake develops Urthona as one of the four "Zoas," divisions that result from the fall of Albion; he is linked to the imagination, inspiration, and creativity. Urthona's female counterpart is "Enitharmon," and his fallen form is "Los," usually depicted as a blacksmith. The three other Zoas are "Urizen" (incarnation of law and reason), "Tharmas" (nature, instinct, and unity), and "Luvah" (passion and love).

[9] *wilderness* This marks the end of Plate 26.

[10] *ten commands* Blake repeatedly rejects the Ten Commandments throughout *The Marriage of Heaven and Hell*, a stance consistent with his antinomian position, which discards social law and morality in favor of individual faith, associated for Blake with energy and joy.

19. Where the son of fire in his eastern cloud, while the morning plumes her golden breast.
20. Spurning the clouds written with curses. stamps the stony law to dust. loosing the eternal horses from the dens of night, crying Empire is no more! and now the lion & wolf shall cease.[1]

Chorus

Let the Priests of the Raven[2] of dawn. no longer in deadly black, with hoarse note curse the sons of joy. Nor his accepted brethren whom tyrant, he calls free: lay the bound or build the roof: Nor pale religions letchery call that virginity that wishes but acts not!

For everything that lives is Holy[3]
—1792–93

[1] *Empire is no more! … shall cease* Cf. Plate 6 of Blake's *America* (1793): "For Empire is no more, and now the Lion & Wolf shall cease" (15).

[2] *Priests of the Raven* The Raven represents the fear of death; in its association here with the "priests," the Raven is connected to orthodoxy and its emphasis on such fear.

[3] *For everything that lives is Holy* Cf. Plate 8 of Blake's *America*: "For every thing that lives is holy, life delights in life" (13).

Mary Wollstonecraft

1759 – 1797

"Independence," Mary Wollstonecraft said, "I have long considered as the grand blessing of life." A key founder of feminist thought, Wollstonecraft was an unwavering advocate for political reform, for reducing the "unnatural distinctions" of class, and for educating women so they could achieve greater independence. When she died in 1797, she was a literary celebrity; her husband William Godwin wrote that she was "the firmest champion … her sex ever had to boast." Wollstonecraft has long been acknowledged as an important late eighteenth-century philosopher and writer, and *A Vindication of the Rights of Woman*, in particular, is widely read as a core text in the Western liberal tradition.

Wollstonecraft was born in London on 27 April 1759 to Elizabeth Dixon and Edward Wollstonecraft; she was the eldest daughter among seven children. The Wollstonecrafts were a middle-class, modestly prosperous family whose fortunes went into a gradual decline. Edward attempted to transform himself into a gentleman farmer, moving the family to Epping, to Barking, and finally to Beverley in Yorkshire. These moves exacerbated the family's financial difficulties. Wollstonecraft's father was also a violent man. As a child, Wollstonecraft frequently intervened in her father's outbursts in order to try to protect her mother. For solace and respite, she turned to her close friend Jane Arden. Arden's father, John, was a teacher and philosopher who encouraged Wollstonecraft's self-education and provided her with access to his library.

When Wollstonecraft was 15 the family moved to Hoxton, on the outskirts of London. Here, Wollstonecraft was befriended by her next-door neighbors, the Reverend and Mrs. Clare. They became her surrogate family and were responsible for introducing her to Fanny Blood, with whom she would develop an intensely passionate and possibly romantic friendship. Years later, Wollstonecraft described her connection to Blood as "a friendship so fervent, as for years to have constituted the ruling passion of my mind." Blood became the model for Ann in Wollstonecraft's autobiographical novel, *Mary, A Fiction*.

In 1778, Wollstonecraft made the decision to leave home and earn her own living. Now 19, she took a job as a paid companion to a Mrs. Dawson, a widow in Bath. When her mother became ill in 1781, however, Wollstonecraft returned to London to nurse her. After months of pain, Elizabeth Wollstonecraft died, and Mary took up residence with the Bloods. Shortly afterwards Wollstonecraft's sister Eliza married Meredith Bishop, a well-to-do shipwright. After Eliza gave birth to a daughter in 1783, she fell into a deep postpartum depression that Wollstonecraft attributed to Bishop's cruelty. Wanting to rescue her sister, Wollstonecraft convinced Eliza to run away from her husband and child. (At the time, children legally belonged to the father.) Bishop eventually gave up his attempts to bring his wife back, and their daughter died just days before her first birthday.

Wollstonecraft soon realized that she and Eliza would need to find their own source of financial support. In 1784, together with Fanny Blood, they opened a school at Newington Green, north of

London. Here, Wollstonecraft met Richard Price, a preacher and a leader of the Dissenters. His congregation was a Unitarian-like group whose political positions on freedom and equality influenced Wollstonecraft's developing ideas. In 1785, Fanny Blood left Newington Green to marry her longtime suitor, Hugh Skeys, in Lisbon. Wollstonecraft joined them several months later when she heard that Fanny was having trouble with her first pregnancy, but despite her efforts both Fanny and her child died a few days after the birth. Wollstonecraft returned to London where her school's financial problems had worsened during her absence. To raise money, she wrote her first book, *Thoughts on the Education of Daughters*. Joseph Johnson, a leading radical bookseller and a fellow Dissenter, published the book in 1787. The book's modest success was not enough to save the school, but it did establish Wollstonecraft in the debate on women's education.

Following the collapse of the school, Wollstonecraft became a governess to the Kingsborough family in Ireland, but it was not a happy development; she was doubtless drawing on experience when she later wrote that governesses "are not always treated in a manner calculated to render them respectable in the eyes of their pupils." She did, however, exert an apparently life-long influence on one of her pupils, who grew up to be a public champion of women's rights. Wollstonecraft soon fell into a depression that was diagnosed as nervous fever. She continued writing, though, beginning work on *Mary, A Fiction*. When she was dismissed from her position as governess, still within the year 1787, she returned to London and convinced Johnson to publish *Mary*. He also hired her as a reviewer for the *Analytical Review*, a monthly progressive periodical. Through her reviews she became an influential voice in the decade of ferment that was coming. Through Johnson, Wollstonecraft met Henry Fuseli, an artist and self-described genius. Although Fuseli was married, Wollstonecraft felt he was her soulmate, and they soon began an affair.

Wollstonecraft embraced the start of the French Revolution with excitement. When Edmund Burke published his *Reflections on the Revolution in France* (1790), a treatise that attacked revolutionary ideas, Johnson urged Wollstonecraft to write a reply. She quickly crafted *A Vindication of the Rights of Men*, published anonymously less than a month after the appearance of Burke's book. A few weeks later, a second edition was published under her name, and this solidified her reputation as a radical. In early 1792, she became famous throughout Europe when her new book, *A Vindication of the Rights of Woman*, was published. Written in only six weeks, *A Vindication* presented the case for universal rights, social equality, and women's economic independence. As Wollstonecraft pointed out, the refusal of those who had espoused revolutionary principles of equality to extend rights to women represented a betrayal of those supposedly universal principles.

Eager to obtain first-hand knowledge about the Revolution, and just as eager to escape her deteriorating affair with Fuseli, Wollstonecraft traveled to France in December 1792. There she met Gilbert Imlay, an American and a fellow radical whose lover she soon became. When she discovered she was pregnant, Imlay registered her at the American Embassy as his wife, even though they were not married, so that she could claim the protection of American citizenship. In May 1794, she gave birth to a daughter whom she called Fanny, and two months later Imlay returned to England, leaving mother and child alone. Wollstonecraft's *An Historical and Moral View of the French Revolution* was published in London later that year.

Wollstonecraft's relationship with Imlay was strained, and when she returned to London in April 1795 she discovered he had been unfaithful. Distraught, she attempted suicide but was prevented by him. As a way of distancing himself from her, as well as tracking some bothersome financial losses, Imlay sent her (with Fanny) to Scandinavia on a business trip. She returned to England in September to find him living with another woman. Outraged and increasingly depressed, Wollstonecraft attempted suicide a second time by jumping off Putney Bridge into the Thames. This time, fishers pulled her out of the water.

In January 1796, Wollstonecraft published *Letters Written during a Short Residence in Sweden, Norway, and Denmark*. The book was highly successful, and the praise she received on its publication helped to restore her sense of purpose and mental health. In March, she met Imlay for the final time, and in April she began to write her next novel, *Maria, or The Wrongs of Woman*. In that month she also began a relationship with William Godwin, a leading radical writer and political philosopher to whom she had been introduced by Johnson a few years earlier. They planned a serious mutual commitment without the form of a marriage service, but when Wollstonecraft became pregnant they decided to marry for the sake of the baby. On 30 August 1797, she gave birth to a daughter, Mary, later to become the wife of Percy Shelley and the author of *Frankenstein*. Only 38 years old, Wollstonecraft died on 10 September from complications resulting from childbirth.

Godwin soon began to work on a biography to honor Wollstonecraft's life and legacy, which he published as *Memoirs of the Author of a Vindication of the Rights of Woman* in 1798. Adhering to his own values of honesty and sincerity, he included controversial details of her sexual and emotional history, which shocked many of her admirers and affected her reputation for generations. The women's rights movement in the second half of the nineteenth century brought her work back into prominence, and the women's movement of the 1970s elevated her to the status of feminist icon.

⌘⌘⌘

from *A Vindication of the Rights of Woman*

Introduction

After considering the historic page, and viewing the living world with anxious solicitude,[1] the most melancholy emotions of sorrowful indignation have depressed my spirits, and I have sighed when obliged to confess that either nature has made a great difference between man and man, or that the civilization which has hitherto taken place in the world has been very partial.[2] I have turned over various books written on the subject of education, and patiently observed the conduct of parents and the management of schools; but what has been the result? A profound conviction that the neglected education of my fellow-creatures is the grand source of the misery I deplore; and that women, in particular, are rendered weak and wretched by a variety of concurring[3] causes, originating from one hasty conclusion. The conduct and manners of women, in fact, evidently prove that their minds are not in a healthy state; for, like the flowers which are planted in too rich a soil, strength and usefulness are sacrificed to beauty; and the flaunting leaves, after having pleased a fastidious eye, fade, disregarded on the stalk, long before the season when they ought to have arrived at maturity. One cause of this barren blooming I attribute to a false system of education, gathered from the books written on this subject by men who, considering females rather as women than human creatures, have been more anxious to make them alluring mistresses than affectionate wives and rational mothers; and the understanding of the sex has been so bubbled[4] by this specious[5] homage that the civilized women of the present century, with a few exceptions, are only anxious to inspire love, when they ought to cherish a nobler ambition, and by their abilities and virtues exact respect.

In a treatise, therefore, on female rights and manners, the works which have been particularly written for their improvement must not be overlooked; especially when it

[1] *solicitude* Concern.

[2] *partial* Biased.

[3] *concurring* Occurring together.

[4] *bubbled* Deluded, fooled.

[5] *specious* Superficially plausible yet misleading.

is asserted, in direct terms, that the minds of women are enfeebled by false refinement; that the books of instruction, written by men of genius, have had the same tendency as more frivolous productions; and that, in the true style of Mahometanism,[1] they are treated as a kind of subordinate beings, and not as a part of the human species, when improvable reason is allowed to be the dignified distinction which raises men above the brute creation, and puts a natural sceptre in a feeble hand.

Yet, because I am a woman, I would not lead my readers to suppose that I mean violently to agitate the contested question respecting the equality or inferiority of the sex; but as the subject lies in my way, and I cannot pass it over without subjecting the main tendency of my reasoning to misconstruction, I shall stop a moment to deliver, in a few words, my opinion. In the government of the physical world it is observable that the female in point of strength is, in general, inferior to the male. This is the law of nature; and it does not appear to be suspended or abrogated[2] in favour of woman. A degree of physical superiority cannot, therefore, be denied—and it is a noble prerogative! But not content with this natural pre-eminence, men endeavour to sink us still lower, merely to render us alluring objects for a moment; and women, intoxicated by the adoration which men, under the influence of their senses, pay them, do not seek to obtain a durable interest in their hearts, or to become the friends of the fellow creatures who find amusement in their society.

I am aware of an obvious inference—from every quarter have I heard exclamations against masculine women; but where are they to be found? If by this appellation men mean to inveigh[3] against their ardour in hunting, shooting, and gaming,[4] I shall most cordially join in the cry; but if it be against the imitation of manly virtues, or, more properly speaking, the attainment of those talents and virtues, the exercise of which ennobles the human character, and which raise females in the scale of animal being when they are comprehensively termed mankind—all those who view them with a philosophic eye must, I should think, wish with me that they may every day grow more and more masculine.

This discussion naturally divides the subject. I shall first consider women in the grand light of human creatures who, in common with men, are placed on this earth to unfold their faculties; and afterwards I shall more particularly point out their peculiar designation.

I wish also to steer clear of an error which many respectable writers have fallen into; for the instruction which has hitherto been addressed to women has rather been applicable to ladies, if the little indirect advice that is scattered through Sandford and Merton[5] be excepted; but, addressing my sex in a firmer tone, I pay particular attention to those in the middle class because they appear to be in the most natural state. Perhaps the seeds of false-refinement, immorality, and vanity have ever been shed by the great. Weak, artificial beings, raised above the common wants and affections of their race in a premature unnatural manner, undermine the very foundation of virtue, and spread corruption through the whole mass of society! As a class of mankind they have the strongest claim to pity; the education of the rich tends to render them vain and helpless, and the unfolding mind is not strengthened by the practice of those duties that dignify the human character. They only live to amuse themselves, and by the same law that in nature invariably produces certain effects, they soon only afford barren amusement.

But as I purpose taking a separate view of the different ranks of society, and of the moral character of women in each, this hint is, for the present, sufficient; and I have only alluded to the subject because it appears

[1] *Mahometanism* Archaic term for Islam.

[2] *abrogated* Repealed, abolished.

[3] *inveigh* Denounce.

[4] *gaming* Gambling.

[5] *Sandford and Merton* Thomas Day (1748–89), English poet, philanthropist, political essayist, and author of *The History of Sandford and Merton* (1783), a children's novel that gives expression to Day's educational theories, which are based on the work of Jean-Jacques Rousseau. Highly didactic, the novel contrasts the corrupt, conventional education of spoiled Tommy Merton, son of a Jamaican plantation owner, with the natural education of virtuous Harry Sandford, son of an honest farmer.

to me to be the very essence of an introduction to give a cursory account of the contents of the work it introduces.

My own sex, I hope, will excuse me if I treat them like rational creatures, instead of flattering their fascinating graces and viewing them as if they were in a state of perpetual childhood, unable to stand alone. I earnestly wish to point out in what true dignity and human happiness consists: I wish to persuade women to endeavour to acquire strength, both of mind and body, and to convince them that the soft phrases, susceptibility of heart, delicacy of sentiment, and refinement of taste are almost synonymous with epithets of weakness, and that those beings who are only the objects of pity and that kind of love, which has been termed its sister, will soon become objects of contempt.

Dismissing then those pretty feminine phrases, which the men condescendingly use to soften our slavish dependence, and despising that weak elegancy of mind, exquisite sensibility, and sweet docility of manners supposed to be the sexual characteristics of the weaker vessel, I wish to show that elegance is inferior to virtue; that the first object of laudable ambition is to obtain a character as a human being, regardless of the distinction of sex; and that secondary views should be brought to this simple touchstone.

This is a rough sketch of my plan; and should I express my conviction with the energetic emotions that I feel whenever I think of the subject, the dictates of experience and reflection will be felt by some of my readers. Animated by this important object, I shall disdain to cull[1] my phrases or polish my style: I aim at being useful, and sincerity will render me unaffected; for, wishing rather to persuade by the force of my arguments than dazzle by the elegance of my language, I shall not waste my time in rounding periods,[2] or in fabricating the turgid bombast of artificial feelings, which, coming from the head, never reach the heart. I shall be employed about things, not words—and, anxious to render my sex more respectable members of society, I shall try to avoid that flowery diction which has slid from essays into novels, and from novels into familiar letters and conversation.

These pretty superlatives, dropping glibly from the tongue, vitiate[3] the taste and create a kind of sickly delicacy that turns away from simple unadorned truth; and a deluge of false sentiments and over-stretched feelings, stifling the natural emotions of the heart, render the domestic pleasures insipid that ought to sweeten the exercise of those severe duties that educate a rational and immortal being for a nobler field of action.

The education of women has, of late, been more attended to than formerly; yet they are still reckoned a frivolous sex, and ridiculed or pitied by the writers who endeavour by satire or instruction to improve them. It is acknowledged that they spend many of the first years of their lives in acquiring a smattering of accomplishments; meanwhile strength of body and mind are sacrificed to libertine[4] notions of beauty, to the desire of establishing themselves—the only way women can rise in the world—by marriage. And this desire making mere animals of them, when they marry they act as such children may be expected to act: they dress, they paint,[5] and nickname God's creatures.[6] Surely these weak beings are only fit for a seraglio![7] Can they be expected to govern a family with judgment, or take care of the poor babes whom they bring into the world?

If then it can be fairly deduced from the present conduct of the sex, from the prevalent fondness for pleasure—which takes place of ambition and those nobler passions that open and enlarge the soul—that the instruction which women have hitherto received has

---

[1] *cull* Choose carefully.

[2] *rounding periods* Crafting graceful sentences.

[3] *vitiate* Render impure, corrupt.

[4] *libertine* Licentious.

[5] *paint* I.e., wear make-up.

[6] *they dress ... God's creatures* From Shakespeare's *Hamlet* 3.1.142–46: "I have heard of your paintings, well enough. God hath given you one face, and you make yourselves another. You jig and amble, and you lisp, you nickname God's creatures and make your wantonness your ignorance."

[7] *seraglio* Harem.

only tended, with the constitution of civil society, to render them insignificant objects of desire—mere propagators of fools! If it can be proved that in aiming to accomplish them without cultivating their understandings they are taken out of their sphere of duties, and made ridiculous and useless when the short-lived bloom of beauty is over,[1] I presume that rational men will excuse me for endeavouring to persuade them to become more masculine and respectable.

Indeed the word masculine is only a bugbear:[2] there is little reason to fear that women will acquire too much courage or fortitude, for their apparent inferiority with respect to bodily strength must render them, in some degree, dependent on men in the various relations of life; but why should it be increased by prejudices that give a sex to virtue and confound simple truths with sensual reveries?

Women are, in fact, so much degraded by mistaken notions of female excellence that I do not mean to add a paradox when I assert that this artificial weakness produces a propensity to tyrannize, and gives birth to cunning, the natural opponent of strength, which leads them to play off those contemptible infantine airs that undermine esteem even whilst they excite desire. Let men become more chaste and modest, and if women do not grow wiser in the same ratio, it will be clear that they have weaker understandings. It seems scarcely necessary to say that I now speak of the sex in general. Many individuals have more sense than their male relatives; and as nothing preponderates[3] where there is a constant struggle for an equilibrium without[4] it has naturally more gravity, some women govern their husbands without degrading themselves because intellect will always govern.

[1] [Wollstonecraft's note] A lively writer, I cannot recollect his name, asks what business women turned of forty have to do in the world? [Wollstonecraft is perhaps referring to a remark made by a libertine character in Frances Burney's *Evelina*, Lord Merton.]

[2] *bugbear* Imaginary creature invoked to cause fear.

[3] *preponderates* Weighs more, predominates.

[4] *without* Unless.

Chapter 2
The Prevailing Opinion of a Sexual Character Discussed

To account for, and excuse, the tyranny of man, many ingenious arguments have been brought forward to prove that the two sexes, in the acquirement of virtue, ought to aim at attaining a very different character: or, to speak explicitly, women are not allowed to have sufficient strength of mind to acquire what really deserves the name of virtue. Yet it should seem, allowing them to have souls, that there is but one way appointed by Providence to lead mankind to either virtue or happiness.

If then women are not a swarm of ephemeron[5] triflers, why should they be kept in ignorance under the specious name of innocence? Men complain, and with reason, of the follies and caprices[6] of our sex, when they do not keenly satirize our headstrong passions and grovelling vices. Behold, I should answer, the natural effect of ignorance! The mind will ever be unstable that has only prejudices to rest on, and the current will run with destructive fury when there are no barriers to break its force. Women are told from their infancy, and taught by the example of their mothers, that a little knowledge of human weakness, justly termed cunning, softness of temper, outward obedience, and a scrupulous attention to a puerile kind of propriety, will obtain for them the protection of man; and should they be beautiful, every thing else is needless for, at least, twenty years of their lives.

Thus Milton describes our first frail mother; though when he tells us that women are formed for softness and sweet attractive grace,[7] I cannot comprehend his meaning; unless, in the true Mahometan strain, he meant to deprive us of souls and insinuate that we were beings only designed by sweet attractive grace, and docile blind

[5] *ephemeron* Short-lived.

[6] *caprices* Whims, fancies.

[7] *Milton … grace* John Milton contrasts Adam and Eve, the first man and woman, in *Paradise Lost* (1667): "For contemplation he and valour formed, / For softness she and sweet attractive grace" (4.297–98).

obedience, to gratify the senses of man when he can no longer soar on the wing of contemplation.

How grossly do they insult us who thus advise us only to render ourselves gentle, domestic brutes! For instance, the winning softness so warmly, and frequently, recommended that governs by obeying. What childish expressions, and how insignificant is the being—can it be an immortal one?—who will condescend to govern by such sinister methods! "Certainly," says Lord Bacon, "man is of kin to the beasts by his body; and if he be not of kin to God by his spirit, he is a base and ignoble creature!"[1] Men, indeed, appear to me to act in a very unphilosophical manner when they try to secure the good conduct of women by attempting to keep them always in a state of childhood. Rousseau[2] was more consistent when he wished to stop the progress of reason in both sexes, for if men eat of the tree of knowledge,[3] women will come in for a taste; but, from the imperfect cultivation which their understandings now receive, they only attain a knowledge of evil.

Children, I grant, should be innocent; but when the epithet is applied to men, or women, it is but a civil term for weakness. For if it be allowed that women were destined by Providence to acquire human virtues and, by the exercise of their understandings, that stability of character which is the firmest ground to rest our future hopes upon, they must be permitted to turn to the fountain of light, and not forced to shape their course by the twinkling of a mere satellite.[4] Milton, I grant, was of a very different opinion; for he only bends to the indefeasible[5] right of beauty, though it would be difficult to render two passages, which I now mean to contrast, consistent. But into similar inconsistencies are great men often led by their senses.

> To whom thus Eve with *perfect beauty* adorn'd.
> My Author and Disposer, what thou bidst
> *Unargued* I obey; so God ordains;
> God *is thy law, thou mine*: to know no more
> Is Woman's *happiest* knowledge and her *praise*.[6]

These are exactly the arguments that I have used to children; but I have added, "Your reason is now gaining strength, and, until it arrives at some degree of maturity, you must look up to me for advice—then you ought to think and only rely on God."

Yet in the following lines Milton seems to coincide with me when he makes Adam thus expostulate[7] with his Maker.

> Hast thou not made me here thy substitute,
> And these inferior far beneath me set?
> Among *unequals* what society
> Can sort, what harmony or true delight?
> Which must be mutual, in proportion due
> Giv'n and receiv'd; but in *disparity*
> The one intense, the other still remiss
> Cannot well suit with either, but soon prove
> Tedious alike: of *fellowship* I speak
> Such as I seek, fit to participate
> All rational delight[8]—

In treating, therefore, of the manners of women, let us, disregarding sensual arguments, trace what we should endeavour to make them in order to co-operate, if the expression be not too bold, with the supreme Being.

By individual education, I mean—for the sense of the word is not precisely defined—such an attention to a child as will slowly sharpen the senses, form the temper, regulate the passions as they begin to ferment,

[1] *Certainly … creature* Francis Bacon (1561–1626), English philosopher, jurist, and political figure, author of *Essays or Counsels Civil and Moral* (1625). The quotation is from Essay 16, "Of Atheism."

[2] *Rousseau* Jean-Jacques Rousseau (1712–78), Geneva born philosopher, composer, and essayist.

[3] *tree of knowledge* In Genesis 2.17, God forbids Adam and Eve to eat of the tree of the knowledge of good and evil; tempted by the serpent, Eve disobeys and Adam follows suit.

[4] *satellite* Subordinate, secondary planet orbiting round a larger one.

[5] *indefeasible* Incapable of being defeated.

[6] *To whom … praise* Milton, *Paradise Lost*, 4.634–38. [Wollstonecraft's italics.]

[7] *expostulate* Remonstrate, argue.

[8] *Hast … delight* Milton, *Paradise Lost*, 8.381–91. [Wollstonecraft's italics.]

and set the understanding to work before the body arrives at maturity; so that the man may only have to proceed, not to begin, the important task of learning to think and reason.

To prevent any misconstruction, I must add that I do not believe that a private education can work the wonders which some sanguine[1] writers have attributed to it. Men and women must be educated, in a great degree, by the opinions and manners of the society they live in. In every age there has been a stream of popular opinion that has carried all before it, and given a family character, as it were, to the century. It may then fairly be inferred that until society be differently constituted, much cannot be expected from education. It is, however, sufficient for my present purpose to assert that whatever effect circumstances have on the abilities, every being may become virtuous by the exercise of its own reason; for if but one being was created with vicious inclinations that is positively bad, what can save us from atheism? Or, if we worship a God, is not that God a devil?

Consequently, the most perfect education, in my opinion, is such an exercise of the understanding as is best calculated to strengthen the body and form the heart. Or, in other words, to enable the individual to attain such habits of virtue as will render it independent. In fact, it is a farce to call any being virtuous whose virtues do not result from the exercise of its own reason. This was Rousseau's opinion respecting men:[2] I extend it to women, and confidently assert that they have been drawn out of their sphere by false refinement and not by an endeavour to acquire masculine qualities. Still the regal homage which they receive is so intoxicating that until the manners of the times are changed and formed on more reasonable principles, it may be impossible to convince them that the illegitimate power, which they obtain by degrading themselves, is a curse, and that they must return to nature and equality if they wish to secure the placid satisfaction that unsophisticated affections impart. But for this epoch we must wait—wait, perhaps, until kings and nobles, enlightened by reason, and preferring the real dignity of man to childish state, throw off their gaudy hereditary trappings: and if then women do not resign the arbitrary power of beauty, they will prove that they have less mind than man.

I may be accused of arrogance; still I must declare what I firmly believe: that all the writers who have written on the subject of female education and manners from Rousseau to Dr. Gregory[3] have contributed to render women more artificial, weak characters than they would otherwise have been; and, consequently, more useless members of society. I might have expressed this conviction in a lower key, but I am afraid it would have been the whine of affectation and not the faithful expression of my feelings, of the clear result which experience and reflection have led me to draw. When I come to that division of the subject, I shall advert[4] to the passages that I more particularly disapprove of in the works of the authors I have just alluded to; but it is first necessary to observe that my objection extends to the whole purport[5] of those books, which tend, in my opinion, to degrade one half of the human species and render women pleasing at the expense of every solid virtue.

Though, to reason on Rousseau's ground, if man did attain a degree of perfection of mind when his body arrived at maturity, it might be proper, in order to make a man and his wife one, that she should rely entirely on his understanding; and the graceful ivy, clasping the oak that supported it, would form a whole in which strength and beauty would be equally conspicuous. But, alas! Husbands, as well as their helpmates, are often only overgrown children; nay, thanks to early debauchery, scarcely men in their outward form—and if the blind

[1] *sanguine* Cheerfully optimistic.

[2] *Rousseau's … men* Jean-Jacques Rousseau, *Émile* (1762), Book One.

[3] *Dr. Gregory* John Gregory (1724–73), Scottish physician, author of *A Father's Legacy to His Daughters* (1774), an influential conduct book for young women.

[4] *advert* Take notice.

[5] *purport* Intention.

lead the blind,[1] one need not come from heaven to tell us the consequence.

Many are the causes that, in the present corrupt state of society, contribute to enslave women by cramping their understandings and sharpening their senses. One, perhaps, that silently does more mischief than all the rest is their disregard of order.

To do every thing in an orderly manner is a most important precept which women, who generally speaking receive only a disorderly kind of education, seldom attend to with that degree of exactness that men, who from their infancy are broken into method, observe. This negligent kind of guess-work—for what other epithet can be used to point out the random exertions of a sort of instinctive common sense, never brought to the test of reason?—prevents their generalizing matters of fact: so they do today what they did yesterday, merely because they did it yesterday.

This contempt of the understanding in early life has more baneful[2] consequences than is commonly supposed; for the little knowledge which women of strong minds attain is, from various circumstances, of a more desultory[3] kind than the knowledge of men, and it is acquired more by sheer observations on real life than from comparing what has been individually observed with the results of experience generalized by speculation. Led by their dependent situation and domestic employments more into society, what they learn is rather by snatches; and as learning is with them, in general, only a secondary thing, they do not pursue any one branch with that persevering ardour necessary to give vigour to the faculties and clearness to the judgment. In the present state of society, a little learning is required to support the character of a gentleman; and boys are obliged to submit to a few years of discipline. But in the education of women, the cultivation of the understanding is always subordinate to the acquirement of some corporeal accomplishment; even while enervated[4] by confinement and false notions of modesty, the body is prevented from attaining that grace and beauty which relaxed half-formed limbs never exhibit. Besides, in youth their faculties are not brought forward by emulation; and having no serious scientific study, if they have natural sagacity it is turned too soon on life and manners. They dwell on effects, and modifications, without tracing them back to causes; and complicated rules to adjust behaviour are a weak substitute for simple principles.

As a proof that education gives this appearance of weakness to females, we may instance the example of military men who are, like them, sent into the world before their minds have been stored with knowledge or fortified by principles. The consequences are similar; soldiers acquire a little superficial knowledge, snatched from the muddy current of conversation, and, from continually mixing with society, they gain what is termed a knowledge of the world; and this acquaintance with manners and customs has frequently been confounded[5] with a knowledge of the human heart. But can the crude fruit of casual observation, never brought to the test of judgment, formed by comparing speculation and experience, deserve such a distinction? Soldiers, as well as women, practice the minor virtues with punctilious[6] politeness. Where is then the sexual difference when the education has been the same? All the difference that I can discern arises from the superior advantage of liberty, which enables the former to see more of life.

It is wandering from my present subject, perhaps, to make a political remark; but, as it was produced naturally by the train of my reflections, I shall not pass it silently over.

Standing armies can never consist of resolute, robust men; they may be well-disciplined machines, but they will seldom contain men under the influence of strong

[1] *blind lead the blind* Matthew 15.14: "And if the blind lead the blind, both shall fall into the ditch."

[2] *baneful* Destructive, poisonous.

[3] *desultory* Irregular, unmethodical.

[4] *enervated* Mentally weakened.

[5] *confounded* Disordered, confused.

[6] *punctilious* Carefully polite.

passions or with very vigorous faculties. And as for any depth of understanding, I will venture to affirm that it is as rarely to be found in the army as amongst women; and the cause, I maintain, is the same. It may be further observed that officers are also particularly attentive to their persons, fond of dancing, crowded rooms, adventures, and ridicule.[1] Like the fair sex, the business of their lives is gallantry. They were taught to please, and they only live to please. Yet they do not lose their rank in the distinction of sexes, for they are still reckoned superior to women, though in what their superiority consists, beyond what I have just mentioned, it is difficult to discover.

The great misfortune is this: that they both acquire manners before morals, and a knowledge of life before they have, from reflection, any acquaintance with the grand ideal outline of human nature. The consequence is natural; satisfied with common nature, they become a prey to prejudices, and taking all their opinions on credit, they blindly submit to authority. So that, if they have any sense, it is a kind of instinctive glance that catches proportions and decides with respect to manners, but fails when arguments are to be pursued below the surface, or opinions analyzed.

May not the same remark be applied to women? Nay, the argument may be carried still further, for they are both thrown out of a useful station by the unnatural distinctions established in civilized life. Riches and hereditary honours have made ciphers[2] of women to give consequence to the numerical figure; and idleness has produced a mixture of gallantry and despotism into society which leads the very men who are the slaves of their mistresses to tyrannize over their sisters, wives, and daughters. This is only keeping them in rank and file, it is true. Strengthen the female mind by enlarging it and there will be an end to blind obedience; but, as blind obedience is ever sought for by power, tyrants and sensualists are in the right when they endeavour to keep women in the dark, because the former only want slaves, and the latter a play-thing. The sensualist, indeed, has been the most dangerous of tyrants, and women have been duped by their lovers, as princes by their ministers, whilst dreaming that they reigned over them.

I now principally allude to Rousseau, for his character of Sophia[3] is, undoubtedly, a captivating one, though it appears to me grossly unnatural; however, it is not the superstructure but the foundation of her character, the principles on which her education was built, that I mean to attack; nay, warmly as I admire the genius of that able writer, whose opinions I shall often have occasion to cite, indignation always takes place of admiration, and the rigid frown of insulted virtue effaces the smile of complacency, which his eloquent periods are wont to raise when I read his voluptuous reveries. Is this the man who, in his ardour for virtue, would banish all the soft arts of peace and almost carry us back to Spartan discipline?[4] Is this the man who delights to paint the useful struggles of passion, the triumphs of good dispositions, and the heroic flights which carry the glowing soul out of itself? How are these mighty sentiments lowered when he describes the pretty foot and enticing airs of his little favourite! But, for the present, I wave the subject, and, instead of severely reprehending[5] the transient effusions of overweening[6] sensibility, I shall only observe that whoever has cast a benevolent eye on society must often have been gratified by the sight of humble mutual love, not dignified by sentiment, or strengthened by a union in intellectual pursuits. The domestic trifles of the day have afforded matters for cheerful converse, and innocent caresses have softened toils which did not require great exercise of mind or

[1] [Wollstonecraft's note] Why should women be censured with petulant acrimony, because they seem to have a passion for a scarlet coat? Has not education placed them more on a level with soldiers than any other class of men? [See Jonathan Swift's "The Furniture of a Woman's Mind."]

[2] *ciphers* Neutral symbols which can change the value of other numbers depending on their position.

[3] *Sophia* Character in Jean-Jacques Rousseau, *Émile*, Book Five.

[4] *Spartan discipline* The militaristic Greek city-state of Sparta was infamous for its harsh laws, outlined in Plutarch's account of Lycurgus (*Lives*), which controlled nearly every aspect of the lives of its citizens.

[5] *reprehending* Finding fault with.

[6] *overweening* Arrogant.

stretch of thought: yet, has not the sight of this moderate felicity excited more tenderness than respect? An emotion similar to what we feel when children are playing, or animals sporting,[1] whilst the contemplation of the noble struggles of suffering merit has raised admiration and carried our thoughts to that world where sensation will give place to reason.

Women are, therefore, to be considered either as moral beings, or so weak that they must be entirely subjected to the superior faculties of men.

Let us examine this question. Rousseau declares that a woman should never, for a moment, feel herself independent, that she should be governed by fear to exercise her natural cunning, and made a coquettish slave in order to render her a more alluring object of desire, a sweeter companion to man whenever he chooses to relax himself.[2] He carries the arguments, which he pretends to draw from the indications of nature, still further and insinuates that truth and fortitude, the corner stones of all human virtue, should be cultivated with certain restrictions, because, with respect to the female character, obedience is the grand lesson which ought to be impressed with unrelenting rigour.

What nonsense! When will a great man arise with sufficient strength of mind to puff away the fumes which pride and sensuality have thus spread over the subject! If women are by nature inferior to men, their virtues must be the same in quality, if not in degree, or virtue is a relative idea; consequently, their conduct should be founded on the same principles and have the same aim.

Connected with man as daughters, wives, and mothers, their moral character may be estimated by their manner of fulfilling those simple duties; but the end, the grand end of their exertions should be to unfold their own faculties and acquire the dignity of conscious virtue. They may try to render their road pleasant, but ought never to forget, in common with man, that life yields not the felicity which can satisfy an immortal soul. I do not mean to insinuate that either sex should be so lost in abstract reflections or distant views as to forget the affections and duties that lie before them, and are, in truth, the means appointed to produce the fruit of life; on the contrary, I would warmly recommend them, even while I assert that they afford most satisfaction when they are considered in their true, sober light.

Probably the prevailing opinion, that woman was created for man,[3] may have taken its rise from Moses's poetical story;[4] yet, as very few, it is presumed, who have bestowed any serious thought on the subject ever supposed that Eve was, literally speaking, one of Adam's ribs,[5] the deduction must be allowed to fall to the ground; or, only be so far admitted as it proves that man, from the remotest antiquity, found it convenient to exert his strength to subjugate his companion, and his invention to show that she ought to have her neck bent under the yoke because the whole creation was only created for his convenience or pleasure.

Let it not be concluded that I wish to invert the order of things; I have already granted that, from the constitution of their bodies, men seem to be designed by Providence to attain a greater degree of virtue. I speak collectively of the whole sex; but I see not the shadow of

[1] [Wollstonecraft's note] Similar feelings has Milton's pleasing picture of paradisiacal happiness ever raised in my mind; yet, instead of envying the lovely pair, I have, with conscious dignity, or Satanic pride, turned to hell for sublimer objects. In the same style, when viewing some noble monument of human art, I have traced the emanation of the Deity in the order I admired, till, descending from that giddy height, I have caught myself contemplating the grandest of all human sights;—for fancy quickly placed, in some solitary recess, an outcast of fortune, rising superior to passion and discontent.

[2] *Rousseau ... himself* See Jean-Jacques Rousseau, *Émile*, Book Five.

[3] *woman ... man* "And the Lord God said, It is not good that the man should be alone; I will make him an helpmeet for him" (Genesis 2.18–25).

[4] *Moses's ... story* I.e., Genesis. Moses was believed to be the author of the Pentateuch, the first five books of the Bible: Genesis, Exodus, Leviticus, Numbers, and Deuteronomy.

[5] *Adam's ribs* "And the Lord God caused a deep sleep to fall upon Adam, and he slept: and he took one of his ribs, and closed up the flesh instead thereof; And the rib, which the Lord God had taken from man, made he a woman, and brought her unto the man" (Genesis 2.22–23).

a reason to conclude that their virtues should differ in respect to their nature. In fact, how can they, if virtue has only one eternal standard? I must, therefore, if I reason consequentially, as strenuously maintain that they have the same simple direction as that there is a God.

It follows then that cunning should not be opposed to wisdom, little cares to great exertions, or insipid softness, varnished over with the name of gentleness, to that fortitude which grand views alone can inspire.

I shall be told that woman would then lose many of her peculiar graces, and the opinion of a well-known poet might be quoted to refute my unqualified assertion. For Pope[1] has said, in the name of the whole male sex:

> Yet ne'er so sure our passion to create,
> As when she touch'd the brink of all we hate.[2]

In what light this sally[3] places men and women, I shall leave to the judicious to determine; meanwhile I shall content myself with observing that I cannot discover why, unless they are mortal, females should always be degraded by being made subservient to love or lust.

To speak disrespectfully of love is, I know, high treason against sentiment and fine feelings; but I wish to speak the simple language of truth, and rather to address the head than the heart. To endeavour to reason love out of the world would be to out Quixote Cervantes[4] and equally offend against common sense; but an endeavour to restrain this tumultuous passion, and to prove that it should not be allowed to dethrone superior powers, or to usurp the sceptre which the understanding should ever coolly wield, appears less wild.

Youth is the season for love in both sexes; but in those days of thoughtless enjoyment, provision should be made for the more important years of life when reflection takes place of sensation. But Rousseau, and most of the male writers who have followed his steps, have warmly inculcated[5] that the whole tendency of female education ought to be directed to one point: to render them pleasing.

Let me reason with the supporters of this opinion who have any knowledge of human nature: do they imagine that marriage can eradicate the habitude of life? The woman who has only been taught to please will soon find that her charms are oblique sunbeams, and that they cannot have much effect on her husband's heart when they are seen every day, when the summer is passed and gone. Will she then have sufficient native energy to look into herself for comfort and cultivate her dormant faculties? Or, is it not more rational to expect that she will try to please other men; and, in the emotions raised by the expectation of new conquests, endeavour to forget the mortification her love or pride has received? When the husband ceases to be a lover—and the time will inevitably come—her desire of pleasing will then grow languid, or become a spring of bitterness; and love, perhaps, the most evanescent of all passions, gives place to jealousy or vanity.

I now speak of women who are restrained by principle or prejudice; such women, though they would shrink from an intrigue with real abhorrence, yet, nevertheless, wish to be convinced by the homage of gallantry that they are cruelly neglected by their husbands; or, days and weeks are spent in dreaming of the happiness enjoyed by congenial souls until their health is undermined and their spirits broken by discontent. How then can the great art of pleasing be such a necessary study? It is only useful to a mistress; the chaste wife, and serious mother, should only consider her power to please as the polish of her virtues, and the affection of her husband as one of the comforts that render her task less difficult and her life happier. But, whether she be loved or neglected, her first wish should be to make herself respectable, and not to rely for all her happiness

[1] *Pope* Alexander Pope (1688–1744), English poet and satirist.

[2] *Yet … hate* Alexander Pope, "Epistle II: To a Lady (Of the Characters of Women)," from "Epistles to Several Persons," *Works*, lines 51–52 (1735).

[3] *sally* Sudden attack on an enemy.

[4] *out Quixote Cervantes* I.e., even more than the hero of Cervantes's picaresque novel, *Don Quixote*, be determined to carry out a lofty albeit impossible goal.

[5] *inculcated* Taught through force or persistence.

on a being subject to like infirmities with herself.

The worthy Dr. Gregory fell into a similar error. I respect his heart, but entirely disapprove of his celebrated *Legacy to his Daughters*.

He advises them to cultivate a fondness for dress,[1] because a fondness for dress, he asserts, is natural to them. I am unable to comprehend what either he or Rousseau mean when they frequently use this indefinite term. If they told us that in a pre-existent state the soul was fond of dress, and brought this inclination with it into a new body, I should listen to them with a half smile, as I often do when I hear a rant about innate elegance. But if he only meant to say that the exercise of the faculties will produce this fondness—I deny it. It is not natural; but arises, like false ambition in men, from a love of power.

Dr. Gregory goes much further; he actually recommends dissimulation,[2] and advises an innocent girl to give the lie to her feelings, and not dance with spirit, when gaiety of heart would make her feel eloquent without making her gestures immodest. In the name of truth and common sense, why should not one woman acknowledge that she can take more exercise than another? Or, in other words, that she has a sound constitution; and why, to damp innocent vivacity, is she darkly to be told that men will draw conclusions which she little thinks of? Let the libertine draw what inference he pleases; but I hope that no sensible mother will restrain the natural frankness of youth by instilling such indecent cautions. Out of the abundance of the heart the mouth speaketh;[3] and a wiser than Solomon[4] hath said that the heart should be made clean, and not trivial ceremonies observed,[5] which it is not very difficult to fulfil with scrupulous exactness when vice reigns in the heart.

Women ought to endeavour to purify their heart; but can they do so when their uncultivated understandings make them entirely dependent on their senses for employment and amusement, when no noble pursuit sets them above the little vanities of the day, or enables them to curb the wild emotions that agitate a reed over which every passing breeze has power? To gain the affections of a virtuous man is affectation necessary? Nature has given woman a weaker frame than man; but, to ensure her husband's affections, must a wife—who, by the exercise of her mind and body whilst she was discharging the duties of a daughter, wife, and mother, has allowed her constitution to retain its natural strength, and her nerves a healthy tone—is she, I say, to condescend to use art and feign a sickly delicacy in order to secure her husband's affection? Weakness may excite tenderness and gratify the arrogant pride of man; but the lordly caresses of a protector will not gratify a noble mind that pants for and deserves to be respected. Fondness is a poor substitute for friendship!

In a seraglio, I grant that all these arts are necessary; the epicure[6] must have his palate tickled or he will sink into apathy; but have women so little ambition as to be satisfied with such a condition? Can they supinely[7] dream life away in the lap of pleasure, or the languor of weariness, rather than assert their claim to pursue reasonable pleasures and render themselves conspicuous by practising the virtues which dignify mankind? Surely she has not an immortal soul who can loiter life away, merely employed to adorn her person, that she may amuse the languid hours, and soften the cares of a fellow-creature who is willing to be enlivened by her smiles and tricks when the serious business of life is over.

---

[1] *fondness for dress* Gregory, *A Father's Legacy to His Daughters*, lines 55–57.

[2] *dissimulation* Concealment, feigning; Gregory, *A Father's Legacy to His Daughters*, lines 57–58.

[3] *Out of … speaketh* "O generation of vipers, how can ye, being evil, speak good things? For out of the abundance of the heart the mouth speaketh" (Matthew 12.34).

[4] *a wiser than Solomon* I.e., Jesus; see Luke 11.31.

[5] *the heart … observed* "Woe unto you, scribes and Pharisees, hypocrites! For ye make clean the outside of the cup and of the platter, but within they are full of extortion and excess" (Matthew 23.25).

[6] *epicure* One devoted to physical pleasures.

[7] *supinely* Indolently, literally on one's back.

Besides, the woman who strengthens her body and exercises her mind will, by managing her family and practising various virtues, become the friend and not the humble dependent of her husband; and if she, by possessing such substantial qualities, merit his regard, she will not find it necessary to conceal her affection, nor to pretend to an unnatural coldness of constitution to excite her husband's passions. In fact, if we revert to history, we shall find that the women who have distinguished themselves have neither been the most beautiful nor the most gentle of their sex.

Nature, or, to speak with strict propriety, God, has made all things right; but man has sought him out many inventions to mar the work. I now allude to that part of Dr. Gregory's treatise where he advises a wife never to let her husband know the extent of her sensibility or affection.[1] Voluptuous precaution, and as ineffectual as absurd. Love, from its very nature, must be transitory. To seek for a secret that would render it constant would be as wild a search as for the philosopher's stone, or the grand panacea:[2] and the discovery would be equally useless, or rather pernicious, to mankind. The most holy band of society is friendship. It has been well said, by a shrewd satirist, "that rare as true love is, true friendship is still rarer."[3]

This is an obvious truth, and the cause, not lying deep, will not elude a slight glance of inquiry.

Love, the common passion in which chance and sensation take place of choice and reason, is, in some degree, felt by the mass of mankind; for it is not necessary to speak, at present, of the emotions that rise above or sink below love. This passion, naturally increased by suspense and difficulties, draws the mind out of its accustomed state and exalts the affections; but the security of marriage, allowing the fever of love to subside, a healthy temperature is thought insipid only by those who have not sufficient intellect to substitute the calm tenderness of friendship, the confidence of respect, instead of blind admiration and the sensual emotions of fondness.

This is, must be, the course of nature—friendship or indifference inevitably succeeds love—and this constitution seems perfectly to harmonize with the system of government which prevails in the moral world. Passions are spurs to action and open the mind; but they sink into mere appetites, become a personal and momentary gratification, when the object is gained and the satisfied mind rests in enjoyment. The man who had some virtue whilst he was struggling for a crown often becomes a voluptuous tyrant when it graces his brow; and, when the lover is not lost in the husband, the dotard,[4] a prey to childish caprices and fond jealousies, neglects the serious duties of life, and the caresses which should excite confidence in his children are lavished on the overgrown child, his wife.

In order to fulfil the duties of life, and to be able to pursue with vigour the various employments which form the moral character, a master and mistress of a family ought not to continue to love each other with passion. I mean to say that they ought not to indulge those emotions which disturb the order of society and engross the thoughts that should be otherwise employed. The mind that has never been engrossed by one object wants vigour—if it can long be so, it is weak.

A mistaken education, a narrow, uncultivated mind, and many sexual prejudices tend to make women more constant than men; but, for the present, I shall not touch on this branch of the subject. I will go still further and advance, without dreaming of a paradox, that an unhappy marriage is often very advantageous to a family, and that the neglected wife is, in general, the best mother. And this would almost always be the consequence if the female mind were more enlarged: for

[1] *never to let … affection* Gregory, *A Father's Legacy to His Daughters*, lines 87–88.

[2] *wild a search … panacea* Alchemists believed in the existence of a philosopher's stone, a substance which could turn base metals into gold, as well as a grand panacea, a medicine that could cure all illnesses.

[3] *that rare … rarer* François de La Rochefoucauld (1613–80), French essayist, author of *Réflexions; ou Sentences et maximes morales* (1665).

[4] *dotard* Senile person.

it seems to be the common dispensation[1] of Providence that what we gain in present enjoyment should be deducted from the treasure of life—experience; and that when we are gathering the flowers of the day and revelling in pleasure, the solid fruit of toil and wisdom should not be caught at the same time. The way lies before us, we must turn to the right or left; and he who will pass life away in bounding from one pleasure to another must not complain if he acquire neither wisdom nor respectability of character.

Supposing, for a moment, that the soul is not immortal, and that man was only created for the present scene; I think we should have reason to complain that love, infantine fondness, ever grew insipid and palled upon the sense. Let us eat, drink, and love, for to-morrow we die,[2] would be, in fact, the language of reason, the morality of life; and who but a fool would part with a reality for a fleeting shadow? But, if awed by observing the improbable powers of the mind, we disdain to confine our wishes or thoughts to such a comparatively mean field of action that only appears grand and important, as it is connected with a boundless prospect and sublime hopes, what necessity is there for falsehood in conduct, and why must the sacred majesty of truth be violated to detain a deceitful good that saps the very foundation of virtue? Why must the female mind be tainted by coquettish arts to gratify the sensualist and prevent love from subsiding into friendship, or compassionate tenderness, when there are not qualities on which friendship can be built? Let the honest heart show itself, and reason teach passion to submit to necessity; or, let the dignified pursuit of virtue and knowledge raise the mind above those emotions which rather embitter than sweeten the cup of life when they are not restrained within due bounds.

I do not mean to allude to the romantic passion which is the concomitant[3] of genius. Who can clip its wing? But that grand passion not proportioned to the puny enjoyments of life is only true to the sentiment and feeds on itself. The passions which have been celebrated for their durability have always been unfortunate. They have acquired strength by absence and constitutional melancholy—the fancy has hovered round a form of beauty dimly seen—but familiarity might have turned admiration into disgust; or, at least, into indifference, and allowed the imagination leisure to start fresh game. With perfect propriety, according to this view of things, does Rousseau make the mistress of his soul, Eloisa, love St. Preux[4] when life was fading before her; but this is no proof of the immortality of the passion.

Of the same complexion is Dr. Gregory's advice respecting delicacy of sentiment,[5] which he advises a woman not to acquire if she have determined to marry. This determination, however, perfectly consistent with his former advice, he calls indelicate, and earnestly persuades his daughters to conceal it, though it may govern their conduct—as if it were indelicate to have the common appetites of human nature.

Noble morality!, and consistent with the cautious prudence of a little soul that cannot extend its views beyond the present minute division of existence. If all the faculties of woman's mind are only to be cultivated as they respect her dependence on man; if, when a husband be obtained, she have arrived at her goal and, meanly proud, rests satisfied with such a paltry crown, let her grovel contentedly, scarcely raised by her employments above the animal kingdom; but if, struggling for the prize of her high calling, she look beyond the present scene, let her cultivate her understanding without stopping to consider what character the husband may have whom she is destined to marry. Let her only determine, without being too anxious about present happiness, to acquire the qualities that ennoble

[1] *dispensation* Divine ordering of the world.

[2] *Let us … die* Isaiah 22.13.

[3] *concomitant* Accompaniment.

[4] *Eloisa … St. Preux* Eloisa/Julie is the heroine of Rousseau's epistolary novel *Julie, ou, La Nouvelle Héloïse* (1761). Julie falls in love with her tutor, St. Preux, but is forced to marry her father's friend, Wolmar. St. Preux and Julie meet again many years later, and Julie ultimately admits on her deathbed that she has never stopped loving him.

[5] *advice … sentiment* Gregory, *A Father's Legacy to His Daughters*, lines 116–19.

a rational being, and a rough inelegant husband may shock her taste without destroying her peace of mind. She will not model her soul to suit the frailties of her companion, but to bear with them: his character may be a trial, but not an impediment to virtue.

If Dr. Gregory confined his remark to romantic expectations of constant love and congenial feelings, he should have recollected that experience will banish what advice can never make us cease to wish for, when the imagination is kept alive at the expense of reason.

I own it frequently happens that women who have fostered a romantic, unnatural delicacy of feeling waste their lives in imagining how happy they should have been with a husband who could love them with a fervid increasing affection every day, and all day. But they might as well pine married as single—and would not be a jot more unhappy with a bad husband than longing for a good one. That a proper education or, to speak with more precision, a well stored mind would enable a woman to support a single life with dignity, I grant; but that she should avoid cultivating her taste lest her husband should occasionally shock it, is quitting a substance for a shadow. To say the truth, I do not know of what use is an improved taste if the individual be not rendered more independent of the casualties of life; if new sources of enjoyment, only dependent on the solitary operations of the mind, are not opened. People of taste, married or single, without distinction, will ever be disgusted by various things that touch not less observing minds. On this conclusion the argument must not be allowed to hinge; but in the whole sum of enjoyment is taste to be denominated a blessing?

The question is whether it procures most pain or pleasure? The answer will decide the propriety of Dr. Gregory's advice, and show how absurd and tyrannical it is thus to lay down a system of slavery; or to attempt to educate moral beings by any other rules than those deduced from pure reason, which apply to the whole species.

Gentleness of manners, forbearance, and long-suffering[1] are such amiable Godlike qualities that in sublime poetic strains the Deity has been invested with them; and, perhaps, no representation of his goodness so strongly fastens on the human affections as those that represent him abundant in mercy and willing to pardon.[2] Gentleness, considered in this point of view, bears on its front all the characteristics of grandeur combined with the winning graces of condescension;[3] but what a different aspect it assumes when it is the submissive demeanour of dependence, the support of weakness that loves, because it wants protection, and is forbearing, because it must silently endure injuries, smiling under the lash at which it dare not snarl. Abject as this picture appears, it is the portrait of an accomplished woman, according to the received opinion of female excellence, separated by specious reasoners from human excellence. Or, they kindly restore the rib and make one moral being of a man and woman—not forgetting to give her all the "submissive charms."

How women are to exist in that state where there is to be neither marrying nor giving in marriage,[4] we are not told. For though moralists have agreed that the tenor[5] of life seems to prove that man is prepared by various circumstances for a future state, they constantly concur in advising woman only to provide for the present. Gentleness, docility, and a spaniel-like affection are, on this ground, consistently recommended as the cardinal virtues of the sex; and, disregarding the arbitrary economy of nature, one writer has declared that it is masculine for a woman to be melancholy. She was

[1] *Gentleness ... long-suffering* "But the fruit of the Spirit is love, joy, peace, longsuffering, gentleness, goodness, faith, meekness, temperance: against such there is no law" (Galatians 5.22–23).

[2] *abundant ... pardon* "Let the wicked forsake his way, and the unrighteous man his thoughts: and let him return unto the Lord, and he will have mercy upon him; and to our God, for he will abundantly pardon" (Isaiah 55.7).

[3] *condescension* Gracious behavior shown to a social inferior.

[4] *neither ... marriage* "For in the resurrection they neither marry, nor are given in marriage, but are as the angels of God in heaven" (Matthew 22.30).

[5] *tenor* Continuous meaning.

created to be the toy of man, his rattle, and it must jingle in his ears whenever, dismissing reason, he chooses to be amused.

To recommend gentleness, indeed, on a broad basis is strictly philosophical. A frail being should labour to be gentle. But when forbearance confounds right and wrong, it ceases to be a virtue; and, however convenient it may be found in a companion, that companion will ever be considered as an inferior and only inspire a vapid tenderness, which easily degenerates into contempt. Still, if advice could really make a being gentle, whose natural disposition admitted not of such a fine polish, something towards the advancement of order would be attained; but if, as might quickly be demonstrated, only affectation be produced by this indiscriminate counsel, which throws a stumbling-block in the way of gradual improvement and true melioration[1] of temper, the sex is not much benefited by sacrificing solid virtues to the attainment of superficial graces, though for a few years they may procure the individuals regal sway.

As a philosopher, I read with indignation the plausible epithets which men use to soften their insults; and, as a moralist, I ask what is meant by such heterogeneous associations as fair defects, amiable weaknesses, &c.? If there be but one criterion of morals, but one archetype for man, women appear to be suspended by destiny, according to the vulgar tale of Mahomet's coffin;[2] they have neither the unerring instinct of brutes, nor are allowed to fix the eye of reason on a perfect model. They were made to be loved, and must not aim at respect, lest they should be hunted out of society as masculine.

But to view the subject in another point of view. Do passive, indolent women make the best wives? Confining our discussion to the present moment of existence, let us see how such weak creatures perform their part. Do the women who, by the attainment of a few superficial accomplishments, have strengthened the prevailing prejudice merely contribute to the happiness of their husbands? Do they display their charms merely to amuse them? And have women, who have early imbibed notions of passive obedience, sufficient character to manage a family or educate children? So far from it that, after surveying the history of woman, I cannot help agreeing with the severest satirist, considering the sex as the weakest as well as the most oppressed half of the species. What does history disclose but marks of inferiority, and how few women have emancipated themselves from the galling yoke of sovereign man? So few that the exceptions remind me of an ingenious conjecture respecting Newton: that he was probably a being of a superior order accidentally caged in a human body.[3] Following the same train of thinking, I have been led to imagine that the few extraordinary women who have rushed in eccentrical directions out of the orbit prescribed to their sex were male spirits, confined by mistake in female frames. But if it be not philosophical to think of sex when the soul is mentioned, the inferiority must depend on the organs; or the heavenly fire, which is to ferment the clay, is not given in equal portions.

But avoiding, as I have hitherto done, any direct comparison of the two sexes collectively, or frankly acknowledging the inferiority of woman, according to the present appearance of things, I shall only insist that men have increased that inferiority until women are almost sunk below the standard of rational creatures. Let their faculties have room to unfold, and their virtues to gain strength, and then determine where the whole sex must stand in the intellectual scale. Yet let it be remembered that for a small number of distinguished women I do not ask a place.

It is difficult for us purblind[4] mortals to say to what height human discoveries and improvements may arrive when the gloom of despotism subsides, which makes us stumble at every step; but, when morality shall be settled on a more solid basis, then, without being gifted with a prophetic spirit, I will venture to predict that woman

---

1 *melioration* Betterment.

2 *Mahomet's coffin* It was believed that Mohammed's coffin was suspended in mid-air at his tomb in Medina, Saudi Arabia.

3 *Newton … body* Newton and his scientific discoveries were held in extremely high regard during the eighteenth century; consider, for example, Pope's *Epitaph. Intended for Sir Isaac Newton, in Westminster-Abbey* (1730): "Nature and nature's laws lay hid in night; / God said 'Let Newton be' and all was light."

4 *purblind* Imperfectly sighted.

will be either the friend or slave of man. We shall not, as at present, doubt whether she is a moral agent or the link which unites man with brutes. But, should it then appear that, like the brutes, they were principally created for the use of man, he will let them patiently bite the bridle and not mock them with empty praise; or, should their rationality be proved, he will not impede their improvement merely to gratify his sensual appetites. He will not, with all the graces of rhetoric, advise them to submit implicitly their understanding to the guidance of man. He will not, when he treats of[1] the education of women, assert that they ought never to have the free use of reason, nor would he recommend cunning and dissimulation to beings who are acquiring, in like manner as himself, the virtues of humanity.

Surely there can be but one rule of right, if morality has an eternal foundation; and whoever sacrifices virtue, strictly so called, to present convenience, or whose duty it is to act in such a manner,[2] lives only for the passing day and cannot be an accountable creature.

The poet then should have dropped his sneer when he says:

> If weak women go astray,
> The stars are more in fault than they.[3]

For that they are bound by the adamantine[4] chain of destiny is most certain, if it be proved that they are never to exercise their own reason, never to be independent, never to rise above opinion, or to feel the dignity of a rational will that only bows to God—and often forgets that the universe contains any being but itself and the model of perfection to which its ardent gaze is turned— to adore attributes that, softened into virtues, may be imitated in kind, though the degree overwhelms the enraptured mind.

If, I say, for I would not impress by declamation when Reason offers her sober light, if they be really capable of acting like rational creatures, let them not be treated like slaves, or like the brutes who are dependent on the reason of man when they associate with him; but cultivate their minds, give them the salutary, sublime curb of principle, and let them attain conscious dignity by feeling themselves only dependent on God. Teach them, in common with man, to submit to necessity, instead of giving, to render them more pleasing, a sex to morals.

Further, should experience prove that they cannot attain the same degree of strength of mind, perseverance, and fortitude, let their virtues be the same in kind, though they may vainly struggle for the same degree; and the superiority of man will be equally clear, if not clearer; and truth, as it is a simple principle, which admits of no modification, would be common to both. Nay, the order of society as it is at present regulated would not be inverted, for woman would then only have the rank that reason assigned her, and arts could not be practised to bring the balance even, much less to turn it.

These may be termed Utopian dreams—thanks to that Being who impressed them on my soul and gave me sufficient strength of mind to dare to exert my own reason until, becoming dependent only on him for the support of my virtue, I view, with indignation, the mistaken notions that enslave my sex.

I love man as my fellow; but his sceptre, real or usurped, extends not to me, unless the reason of an individual demands my homage; and even then the submission is to reason, and not to man. In fact, the conduct of an accountable being must be regulated by the operations of its own reason, or on what foundation rests the throne of God?

It appears to me necessary to dwell on these obvious truths because females have been insulated, as it were; and, while they have been stripped of the virtues that should clothe humanity, they have been decked with artificial graces that enable them to exercise a short-lived tyranny. Love, in their bosoms, takes the place of every nobler passion; their sole ambition is to be fair, to raise emotion instead of inspiring respect; and this ignoble desire, like the servility in absolute monarchies, destroys all strength of character. Liberty is the mother of virtue, and if women be, by their very constitution, slaves, and

[1] *treats of* Discourses on.

[2] *to act in such a manner* I.e., to sacrifice duty to convenience.

[3] *If weak … they* "Hans Carvel" (1700) by Matthew Prior.

[4] *adamantine* Unbreakable.

not allowed to breathe the sharp invigorating air of freedom, they must ever languish like exotics, and be reckoned beautiful flaws in nature.

As to the argument respecting the subjection in which the sex has ever been held, it retorts on[1] man. The many have always been enthralled by the few; and monsters, who scarcely have shown any discernment of human excellence, have tyrannized over thousands of their fellow-creatures. Why have men of superior endowments submitted to such degradation? For is it not universally acknowledged that kings, viewed collectively, have ever been inferior, in abilities and virtue, to the same number of men taken from the common mass of mankind—yet have they not, and are they not still treated with a degree of reverence that is an insult to reason? China is not the only country where a living man has been made a God.[2] Men have submitted to superior strength to enjoy with impunity[3] the pleasure of the moment; women have only done the same, and therefore until it is proved that the courtier, who servilely resigns the birthright of a man, is not a moral agent, it cannot be demonstrated that woman is essentially inferior to man because she has always been subjugated.

Brutal force has hitherto governed the world; and that the science of politics is in its infancy is evident from philosophers scrupling to give the knowledge most useful to man that determinate distinction.

I shall not pursue this argument any further than to establish an obvious inference: that as sound politics diffuse liberty, mankind, including woman, will become more wise and virtuous.

from CHAPTER 3
THE SAME SUBJECT CONTINUED

... I wish to sum up what I have said in a few words, for I here throw down my gauntlet and deny the existence of sexual virtues, not excepting modesty. For man and woman, truth—if I understand the meaning of the word—must be the same; yet for the fanciful female character, so prettily drawn by poets and novelists demanding the sacrifice of truth and sincerity, virtue becomes a relative idea, having no other foundation than utility, and of that utility men pretend arbitrarily to judge, shaping it to their own convenience.

Women, I allow, may have different duties to fulfil; but they are human duties, and the principles that should regulate the discharge of them, I sturdily maintain, must be the same.

To become respectable, the exercise of their understanding is necessary; there is no other foundation for independence of character. I mean explicitly to say that they must only bow to the authority of reason instead of being the modest slaves of opinion.

In the superior ranks of life how seldom do we meet with a man of superior abilities, or even common acquirements? The reason appears to me clear: the state they are born in was an unnatural one. The human character has ever been formed by the employments that the individual, or class, pursues; and if the faculties are not sharpened by necessity, they must remain obtuse. The argument may fairly be extended to women; for, seldom occupied by serious business, the pursuit of pleasure gives that insignificancy to their character which renders the society of the great so insipid. The same want of firmness, produced by a similar cause, forces them both to fly from themselves to noisy pleasures, and artificial passions, until vanity takes place of every social affection, and the characteristics of humanity can scarcely be discerned. Such are the blessings of civil governments, as they are at present organized, that wealth and female softness equally tend to debase mankind and are produced by the same cause; but allowing women to be rational creatures, they should be incited to acquire virtues which they may call their own, for how can a rational being be ennobled by any thing that is not obtained by its own exertions?

—1792

[1] *retorts on* Answers back.

[2] *China ... God* See *A Discourse on the Love of Our Country* (1789) by Richard Price (1723–91), English philosopher and writer.

[3] *impunity* Safety from punishment.

In Context

Contemporary Reviews of *A Vindication of the Rights of Woman*

Early reviews of *A Vindication of the Rights of Woman* divided largely along party lines. Reviewers from *The Analytical Review* and *The Monthly Review*, for example, praised the work while more conservative papers such as *The Critical Review*, *The General Magazine*, and *The Gentleman's Magazine* attacked it. Excerpts from *The Analytical Review* and *The Critical Review* are reprinted below.

from *The Analytical Review* (1792)

... It is with some reluctance that for the present we take our leave of this singular, and, on the whole, excellent production. The subjects which it investigates, are of the utmost importance to human nature, and we should be wanting in our engagements, and in our duty, if we passed it over too slightly. This circumstance makes it necessary to defer the further analysis to a future Review, when we shall proceed to the remaining topics of this volume.

It might have been supposed that Mrs. W. had taken advantage of the popular topic of the "Rights of Man" in calling her work "A Vindication of the Rights of Woman," had she not already published a work, one of the first answers that appeared to Mr. Burke, under the title of "A Vindication of the Rights of Man." But in reality the present work is an elaborate *treatise* of *female education*. The lesser wits will probably affect to make themselves merry at the title and apparent object of this publication; but we have no doubt if even her contemporaries should fail to do her justice, posterity will compensate the defect; and have no hesitation in declaring, that if the bulk of the great truths which this publication contains were reduced to practice, the nation would be better, wiser and happier, than it is upon the wretched, trifling, useless and absurd system of education which is now prevalent.

from *The Critical Review* (1792)

One of the strictest proofs in mathematical demonstrations, is the reducing the questions to an absurdity; by allowing, for instance, that the proposition is not true, and then showing that this would lead to the most obvious inconsistencies. Miss Wollstonecraft has converted this method of proceeding with the same success: reasoning on the boasted principles of the Rights of Man, she finds they lead very clearly to the object of her work, a Vindication of the Rights of Woman; and, by the absurdity of many of her conclusions, shows, while we admit the reasoning, that the premises must be, in some respects, fallacious.

> Dismissing then those pretty feminine phrases, which the men condescendingly use to soften our slavish dependence, and despising that weak elegancy of mind, exquisite sensibility, and sweet docility of manners, supposed to be the sexual characteristics of the weaker vessel, I wish to shew that elegance is inferior to virtue, that the first object of laudable ambition is to

> obtain a character as a human being, regardless of the distinction of sex; and that secondary views should be brought to this simple touchstone.

This is the outline of her plan; but before she proceeds to show that this change would be suitable, useful, advantageous, it will be first necessary to prove that there is no sexual distinction of character; that the female mind is equally fitted for the more arduous mental operations; that women are equally able to pursue the toilsome road of minute, laborious, investigation; that their judgments are equally sound, their resolution equally strong. After this is done, the benefit derived must be considered; and, when all are strong, to whom must the weaker operations belong? The female Plato will find it unsuitable to "the dignity of her virtue" to dress the child, and descend to the disgusting offices of a nurse: the new Archimedes will measure the shirts by means of the altitude taken by a quadrant; and the young lady, instead of studying the softer and more amiable arts of pleasing, must contend with her lover for superiority of mind, for greater dignity of virtue; and before she condescends to become his wife, must prove herself his equal or superior.—It may be fancy, prejudice, or obstinacy, we contend not for a name, but we are infinitely better pleased with the present system; and, in truth, dear young lady, for by the appellation sometimes prefixed to your name we must suppose you to be young, endeavour to attain "the weak elegancy of mind," the "sweet docility of manners," "the exquisite sensibility," the former ornaments of your sex; we are certain you will be more pleasing, and we dare pronounce that you will be infinitely happier. Mental superiority is not an object worth contending for, if happiness be the aim. But, as this is the first female combatant in the new field of the Rights of Woman, if we smile only, we shall be accused of wishing to decline the contest; if we content ourselves with paying a compliment to her talents, it will be styled inconsistent with "true dignity," and as showing that we want to continue the "slavish dependence."—We must contend then with this new Atalanta; and who knows whether, in this modern instance, we may not gain two victories by the contest? There is more than one bachelor in our corps; and, if we should succeed, Miss Wollstonecraft may take her choice.

This work is dedicated to M. Talleyrand-Perigord, late bishop of Autun, who, in his treatise on National Education, does not seem to be perfectly convinced that the rights of man extend to woman; yet in France the diffusion of knowledge, our author asserts, is greater than in any other European nation, on account of the more unreserved communication between the sexes, though what the ladies have gained in knowledge they seem confessedly to have lost in delicacy. The following passage we must transcribe, for we confess we do not fully understand it.

> Contending for the rights of woman, my main argument is built on this simple principle, that if she be not prepared by education to become the companion of man, she will stop the progress of knowledge, for truth must be common to all, or it will be inefficacious with respect to its influence on general practice. And how can woman be expected to co-operate unless she know why she ought to be virtuous! unless freedom strengthen her reason till she comprehend her duty, and see in what manner it is connected with her real good? If children are to be educated to understand the true principle of patriotism, their mother must be a patriot; and the love of mankind, from which an orderly train of virtues spring, can only be produced by considering the moral and civil interest of mankind; but the education and situation of woman, at present, shuts her out from such investigations.
>
> In this work I have produced many arguments, which to me were conclusive, to prove that the prevailing notion respecting a sexual character was subversive of morality, and I have contended, that to render the human body and mind more perfect, chastity must more

> universally prevail, and that chastity will never be respected in the male world till the person of a woman is not, as it were, idolized, when little virtue or sense embellish it with the grand traces of mental beauty, or the interesting simplicity of affection.

The first sentence is erroneous in fact and in reasoning: it is contradicted by the experience of ages, the practice of different nations. The second sentence is a curious one—How can she be supposed to co-operate (we *suppose* in the progress of knowledge) unless she know why she ought to be *virtuous?* Virtuous! Here must be some mistake: what has virtue to do with the progress of knowledge? As to freedom, strengthening the reason, &c. we see no occasion for metaphysical investigation on this subject: that virtue is connected with prosperity and happiness, and vice with misfortune and misery, she might learn, not from Locke, but the New Testament. The concluding sentence of the first paragraph is still more strange. Patriotism may be very properly instilled by a *father,* and we must beg leave to differ in opinion from this lady in another point: we are confident, from frequent and extensive observation, no arguments can confute the opinion that we have formed, and we must still persist in thinking, that the education and situation of women, *at present,* really and effectually *inspire* the *love* of *mankind.* We do believe with Miss Wollstonecraft, that chastity will be respected more, when the person of a woman ceases to be idolized, and the grand traces of mental beauty are principally conspicuous....

Women and Society

CONTEXTS

In the later eighteenth century, women's education and social status became a topic of heated debate among philanthropists, political and educational theorists, and many middle- and upper-class parents. As the first excerpt in this section, from William Blackstone's *Commentaries on the Laws of England*, shows, women's identity in marriage was subsumed under that of their husbands—as it was subsumed under that of their fathers before marriage. Women could not conduct business, own property (unless widowed), reject their fathers' choice of husbands for them, or choose to divorce their husbands. Without legal status they had no representation in Parliament; the idea of female suffrage was one entertained by only the most radical thinkers.

A common concern voiced by educational theorists at the time was that the fashion of educating women in "accomplishments" would help them to attract a husband but would not equip them to fulfill their roles as capable wives or mothers. Instead, many began to stress moral, religious, and domestic training. While more radical feminists, such as Mary Wollstonecraft, insisted that changes in gender roles and assumptions about female nature were essential to improving the status of women, these ideas were not generally accepted. Nevertheless, many of those who supported traditional notions of female roles and behavior advocated education reform along similar lines—insisting that practical education for women would benefit society as a whole. The excerpts printed here from Catharine Macaulay's *Letters on Education*, a series of letters to a fictional friend, Hortensia, criticize the idea that women's education "should be of an opposite kind to that of males." The weaknesses that were typically considered natural in women were a result of education and situation only, she argues, and women should not accept this assumption of inferiority. She proposes one standard of rational conduct by which both sexes should be judged and attacks traditional gender ideologies and the often-praised female art of "coquetry," by which women attempt to manipulate men. These ideas align Macaulay with Wollstonecraft, who was deeply influenced by the work, and later praised Macaulay in her *Vindication of the Rights of Woman* (1792). Others were less sympathetic, however; upon publication, Macaulay's *Letters* made her the subject of many personal attacks. In general, the work was more influential in France than in England.

The next excerpt is taken from French novelist and playwright Olympe de Gouges's *The Rights of Woman*, a piece with many similarities to Wollstonecraft's work of the following year. De Gouges's pamphlet also emphasizes the importance of female education and professional opportunities to the betterment of society and compares women's situation with that of slaves, demonstrating the corrupting effect on men of such arbitrary power over both groups. De Gouges's political agitation extended far beyond women's rights, and during the French Revolution she published writings that criticized the violent actions of the revolutionaries and were viewed as sympathetic towards the monarchy. When her expression of these opinions led to her arrest and execution, the newspaper of the Committee of Public Safety declared, "She wanted to be a statesman, and it seems the law has punished this conspiratress for having forgotten the virtues befitting her sex."

Like de Gouges, Wollstonecraft saw that to espouse revolutionary principles of equality but refuse to extend rights to women represented a betrayal of those supposedly universal principles. Her

Vindication of the Rights of Woman presents the case for women's social equality and economic independence, and argues that education should prepare women to lead rational, virtuous lives. Written in only six weeks, *A Vindication* made Wollstonecraft famous throughout Europe.

A more conservative approach to female education is exemplified in novelist Maria Edgeworth and her father Richard Lovell Edgeworth's *Practical Education*, excerpted here, which emphasizes moral education (as opposed to the acquisition of accomplishments). Conservative thinkers such as the Edgeworths tended to advocate women's training in "traditional female virtues" of modesty, piety, and obedience; such an education consisted of instruction in domestic duties and Christian principles. Quaker philanthropist Priscilla Wakefield's *Reflections on the Present Condition of the Female Sex* proceeds along similar lines, positing that women will be better able to fulfill their roles as wives and mothers if given opportunities for education and professional advancement. She also helps to bring to public attention the plight of many genteel women faced with social and economic difficulties while lacking the skills or opportunities that would enable them to help themselves.

Reverend Richard Polwhele's poem "The Unsexed Females" was part of the backlash against thinkers such as Macaulay and Wollstonecraft that occurred at the turn of the century, following a decade of debate initiated by those two women's works. While Polwhele's poem celebrates women he sees as modestly virtuous, it depicts Wollstonecraft and her followers as unnatural, anti-Christian women driven by a godless "Reason." His poem contains numerous footnotes (most of which are included here) that extend and amplify his arguments.

Hannah More's *Strictures on the Modern System of Female Education*, excerpted here, advocates separate spheres for men and women and emphasizes the education of young women in Christian virtue, morality, and rational education in practical matters. Like most conservative thinkers, More believed that social divisions of class and gender were ordained by God and should not be challenged. Though her ideas for the education of women are, practically speaking, similar to Wollstonecraft's, More insisted on female subordination to men.

The final piece excerpted here, William Thompson and Anna Wheeler's *Appeal of One Half the Human Race*, challenges those utilitarians who overlooked women in their search for universal happiness, as did many of Thompson and Wheeler's fellow reformers. It also argues for female suffrage and takes issue with the misogynist belief that women's interests are best represented by those of their husbands. Written primarily by Thompson but with key passages by Wheeler, the *Appeal* extends many of the ideas developed by Wollstonecraft in her *Vindication*. It examines the faults in the economic system that help to create the social iniquities Wollstonecraft examines, and extends Wollstonecraft's comparison of women to slaves, comparing the status of plantation laborers in the New World and of Turkish harem-slaves with that of Englishwomen.

⌘⌘⌘

from William Blackstone, *Commentaries on the Laws of England* (1765)

from Book 1, Chapter 15: Of Husband and Wife

By marriage, the husband and wife are one person in law: that is, the very being or legal existence of the woman is suspended during the marriage, or at least is incorporated and consolidated into that of the husband, under whose wing, protection, and *cover* she performs everything; and is therefore called in our law-French[1] a

[1] *law-French* Corrupt dialect of Norman French used in English law books until the reign of Edward III (1327–77).

feme-covert; is said to be a *covert-baron*, or under the protection and influence of her husband, her *baron*, or lord; and her condition during her marriage is called her *coverture*. Upon this principle, of a union of person in husband and wife, depend almost all the legal rights, duties, and disabilities that either of them acquire by the marriage. I speak not at present of the rights of property, but of such as are merely *personal*. For this reason, a man cannot grant anything to his wife, or enter into covenant with her; for the grant would be to suppose her separate existence, and to covenant with her would be only to covenant with himself. And therefore it is also generally true that all compacts made between husband and wife when single are voided by the intermarriage. A woman indeed may be attorney for her husband; for that implies no separation from, but is rather a representation of, her lord. And a husband may also bequeath anything to his wife by will; for that cannot take effect till the coverture is determined[1] by his death. The husband is bound to provide his wife with necessaries by law, as much as himself; and if he contracts debts for them, he is obliged to pay them: but for anything besides necessaries he is not chargeable. Also, if a wife elopes, and lives with another man, the husband is not chargeable even for necessaries—at least if the person who furnishes them is sufficiently apprized of her elopement. If the wife be indebted before marriage, the husband is bound afterwards to pay the debt; for he has adopted her and her circumstances together. If the wife be injured in her person or her property, she can bring no action for redress without her husband's concurrence, and in his name as well as her own; neither can she be sued without making the husband a defendant. …

These are the chief legal effects of marriage during the coverture, upon which we may observe that even the disabilities which the wife lies under are for the most part intended for her protection and benefit. So great a favourite is the female sex of the laws of England.[2]

from Catharine Macaulay, *Letters on Education* (1790)

from LETTER 21: MORALS MUST BE TAUGHT ON IMMUTABLE PRINCIPLES

… In order to take from public sentiment a reproach which leaves a deep stain on the human character, and to correct many irregularities, and even enormities, which arise from incorrect systems of ethics, it ought to be the first care of education to teach virtue on immutable principles, and to avoid that confusion which must arise from confounding the laws and customs of society with those obligations which are founded on correct principles of equity. But as you have had patience to go through my whole plan of education, from infancy to manhood, it is but fair that I should attend to your objections, and examine whether my plan is founded on error, or on the principles of reason and truth. Know then, good Hortensia, that I have given similar rules for male and female education, on the following grounds of reasoning.

First, that there is but one rule of right for the conduct of all rational beings; consequently that true virtue in one sex must be equally so in the other, whenever a proper opportunity calls for its exertion, and, *vice versa*, what is vice in one sex cannot have a different property when found in the other.

Secondly, that true wisdom, which is never found at variance with rectitude, is as useful to women as to men, because it is necessary to the highest degree of happiness, which can never exist with ignorance.

Lastly, that as on our first entrance into another world our state of happiness may possibly depend on the degree of perfection we have attained in this, we cannot justly lessen, in one sex or the other, the means by which perfection, that is another word for wisdom, is acquired.

It would be paying you a bad compliment, Hortensia, were I to answer all the frivolous objections which prejudice has framed against the giving a learned education to women; for I know of no learning worth having

[1] *determined* Terminated.

[2] *So great … England* Not until 1870, with the Married Woman's Property Act, did women gain the right to retain their earnings. In 1882, amendments to this Act allowed them to keep personal property that they brought to or acquired during a marriage. They also finally gained a legal identity separate from their husbands', and could then enter into legal contracts and seek restitution in courts.

that does not tend to free the mind from error and enlarge our stock of useful knowledge. Thus much it may be proper to observe, that those hours which are spent in studious retirement by learned women will not in all probability intrude so much on the time for useful avocation as the wild and spreading dissipations of the present day; that levity and ignorance will always be found in opposition to what is useful and graceful in life; and that the contrary may be expected from a truly enlightened understanding. However, Hortensia, to throw some illustration on what I have advanced on this subject, it may be necessary to show you that all those vices and imperfections which have been generally regarded as inseparable from the female character do not in any manner proceed from sexual causes, but are entirely the effects of situation and education. But these observations must be left to further discussion.

from LETTER 22: NO CHARACTERISTIC DIFFERENCE IN SEX

... It must be confessed that the virtues of the males among the human species, though mixed and blended with a variety of vices and errors, have displayed a bolder and a more consistent picture of excellence than female nature has hitherto done. It is on these reasons that when we compliment the appearance of a more than ordinary energy in the female mind, we call it masculine; and hence it is that Pope has elegantly said "a perfect woman's but a softer man."[1] And if we take in the consideration that there can be but one rule of moral excellence for beings made of the same materials, organized after the same manner, and subjected to similar laws of nature, we must either agree with Mr. Pope, or we must reverse the proposition, and say that "a perfect man is a woman formed after a coarser mold." The difference that actually does subsist between the sexes is too flattering for men to be willingly imputed to accident; for what accident occasions, wisdom might correct, and it is better, says Pride, to give up the advantages we might derive from the perfection of our fellow associates than to own that nature has been just in the equal distribution of her favours. These are the sentiments of the men; but mark how readily they are yielded to by the women—not from humility, I assure you, but merely to preserve with character those fond vanities on which they set their hearts. No; suffer them to idolize their persons, to throw away their life in the pursuit of trifles, and to indulge in the gratification of the meaner passions, and they will heartily join in the sentence of their degradation.

Among the most strenuous asserters of a sexual difference in character, Rousseau[2] is the most conspicuous, both on account of that warmth of sentiment which distinguishes all his writings, and the eloquence of his compositions: but never did enthusiasm and the love of paradox, those enemies to philosophical disquisition, appear in more strong opposition to plain sense than in Rousseau's definition of this difference. He sets out with a supposition that Nature intended the subjection of the one sex to the other; that consequently there must be an inferiority of intellect in the subjected party; but as man is a very imperfect being, and apt to play the capricious tyrant, Nature, to bring things nearer to an equality, bestowed on the woman such attractive graces, and such an insinuating address, as to turn the balance on the other scale. Thus Nature, in a giddy mood, recedes from her purposes, and subjects prerogative to an influence which must produce confusion and disorder in the system of human affairs. Rousseau saw this objection, and in order to obviate it he has made up a moral person of the union of the two sexes, which, for contradiction and absurdity, outdoes every metaphysical riddle that was ever formed in the schools. In short, it is not reason, it is not wit; it is pride and sensuality that speak in Rousseau, and, in this instance, has lowered the man of genius to the licentious pedant.

---

[1] *a perfect ... man* Reference to Alexander Pope, "Epistle 2: To a Lady, on the Characters of Women" (1735), lines 271–72: "Heaven, when it strives to polish all it can / Its last best work, but forms a softer man."

[2] *Rousseau* In his *Émile* (1762), French philosopher Jean-Jacques Rousseau argues that female children should be educated, but should be taught to remain subordinate and submissive to men.

But whatever might be the wise purpose intended by Providence in such a disposition of things, certain it is that some degree of inferiority, in point of corporal strength, seems always to have existed between the two sexes; and this advantage, in the barbarous ages of mankind, was abused to such a degree as to destroy all the natural rights of the female species and reduce them to a state of abject slavery. What accidents have contributed in Europe to better their condition would not be to my purpose to relate, for I do not intend to give you a history of women; I mean only to trace the sources of their peculiar foibles and vices, and these I firmly believe to originate in situation and education only: for so little did a wise and just Providence intend to make the condition of slavery an unalterable law of female nature, that in the same proportion as the male sex have consulted the interest of their own happiness, they have relaxed in their tyranny over women; and such is their use in the system of mundane creation, and such their natural influence over the male mind, that were these advantages properly exerted, they might carry every point of any importance to their honour and happiness. However, till that period arrives in which women will act wisely, we will amuse ourselves in talking of their follies.

The situation and education of women, Hortensia, is precisely that which must necessarily tend to corrupt and debilitate both the powers of mind and body. From a false notion of beauty and delicacy, their system of nerves is depraved before they come out of their nursery; and this kind of depravity has more influence over the mind, and consequently over morals, than is commonly apprehended. But it would be well if such causes only acted towards the debasement of the sex; their moral education is, if possible, more absurd than their physical. The principles and nature of virtue, which is never properly explained to boys, is kept quite a mystery to girls. They are told, indeed, that they must abstain from those vices which are contrary to their personal happiness, or they will be regarded as criminals, both by God and man; but all the higher parts of rectitude, everything that ennobles our being, and that renders us both innoxious and useful, is either not taught, or is taught in such a manner as to leave no proper impression on the mind. This is so obvious a truth that the defects of female education have ever been a fruitful topic of declamation for the moralist; but not one of this class of writers have laid down any judicious rules for amendment. Whilst we still retain the absurd notion of a sexual excellence, it will militate against the perfecting a plan of education for either sex. The judicious Addison animadverts on the absurdity of bringing a young lady up with no higher idea of the end of education than to make her agreeable to a husband, and confining the necessary excellence for this happy acquisition to the mere graces of person.[1]

Every parent and tutor may not express himself in the same manner as is marked out by Addison; yet certain it is that the admiration of the other sex is held out to women as the highest honour they can attain; and whilst this is considered as their *summum bonum*,[2] and the beauty of their persons the chief *desideratum*[3] of men, Vanity and its companion Envy must taint, in their characters, every native and every acquired excellence. Nor can you, Hortensia, deny that these qualities, when united to ignorance, are fully equal to the engendering and rivetting all those vices and foibles which are peculiar to the female sex—vices and foibles which have caused them to be considered, in ancient times, as beneath cultivation, and in modern days have subjected them to the censure and ridicule of writers of all descriptions, from the deep thinking philosopher to the man of ton and gallantry, who, by the by,[4] sometimes distinguishes himself by qualities which are not greatly superior to those he despises in women. …

---

[1] *judicious Addison … person* Reference to an article in *Spectator* No. 66 (16 May 1711) actually written by Richard Steele; *animadverts* Comments critically.

[2] *summum bonum* Latin: greatest good.

[3] *desideratum* Latin: thing desired.

[4] *by the by* Incidentally; as a side issue.

from Olympe de Gouges, *The Rights of Woman*[1] (1791)

Man, are you able to be just? It is a woman who asks you the question; you will not take that right, at least, away from her. Tell me: what has given you the sovereign power to oppress my sex? your strength? your talents? Observe the Creator in His wisdom; survey nature in all its grandeur, to which you seem to want to compare yourself, and give me, if you dare, an example of this tyrannical power. Go back to the animals, consult the elements, study the vegetables, cast a glance, finally, over all the modifications of organized matter; and submit to the evidence when I give you the means to; search, excavate, and distinguish the sexes, if you can, in the government of nature. Everywhere you will find them mingled, everywhere they cooperate as a harmonious consort in this immortal masterpiece.

Man alone has dressed up this exception as a principle. Bizarre, blind, bloated with sciences and degenerated, in this age of enlightenment and wisdom, into the crassest ignorance, he wants to rule like a despot over a sex which has received all the intellectual faculties; he pretends to rejoice in the revolution, and to claim his rights to equality, in order to say no more about it.

DECLARATION OF THE RIGHTS OF WOMAN AND OF THE FEMALE CITIZEN

To be decreed by the National Assembly in its last sessions or in that of the next legislature.

PREAMBLE

The mothers, daughters, sisters, representatives of the nation, demand to be formed into a national assembly. Considering that ignorance, neglect, or contempt of the rights of woman are the sole causes of public misfortunes and the corruption of governments, have resolved to set forth in a solemn declaration the natural, inalienable, and sacred rights of woman, that this declaration, being constantly present to all the members of the body social, may ever remind them of their rights and their duties; that the acts of the power of women, and those of the power of men, being capable of being every moment compared with the end of all political institutions, may be more respected; that the claims of the female citizens, founded hereafter on simple and incontestable principles, may always tend to the maintenance of the constitution and of good morals, and to the general happiness.

Accordingly, the sex that is as superior in beauty as in courage, in the sufferings of maternity, recognizes and declares, in the presence and under the auspices of the Supreme Being, the following Rights of Woman and of the Female citizen.

FIRST ARTICLE

Woman is born free and remains equal to man in rights. Social distinctions can only be founded on common utility.

2

The end of all political association is the preservation of the natural and imprescriptible[2] rights of woman and of man: these rights are liberty, property, security, and above all resistance to oppression.

3

The principle of all sovereignty resides essentially in the Nation, which is nothing more than the union of woman and man: no body, no individual, can exercise an authority which does not emanate expressly from it.

[1] *The Rights of Woman* Translated from the French by D.L. Macdonald.

[2] *imprescriptible* That cannot legally be taken away.

4

Liberty and justice consist in rendering to others all that belongs to them; thus the exercise of the natural rights of woman has no other limits than the perpetual tyranny that man opposes to it; these limits should be reformed by the laws of nature and of reason.

5

The laws of nature and of reason prohibit all actions hurtful to society: nothing that is not prohibited by these laws, wise and divine, may be hindered, nor may anyone be compelled to do what they do not enjoin.

6

The law should be the expression of the general will; all the female and male citizens should concur personally, or by their representatives, in its formation; it should be the same for all: all the female and all the male citizens, being equal in its eyes, should be equally admissible to all honours, positions, and public employments, according to their capacities, and without any other distinctions than those of their virtues and their talents.

7

No woman is exempt; she is accused, arrested, and detained in cases determined by the law. Women, like men, obey this rigorous law.

8

The law should impose only those penalties which are strictly and evidently necessary, and no one can be punished except by virtue of a law established and promulgated previously to the offense and legally applied to women.

9

Whenever a woman is declared guilty, all rigour is exercised by the law.

10

No one should be molested for their opinions, even fundamental ones; woman has the right to mount the scaffold; she should equally have the right to mount the tribune,[1] provided that her actions do not disturb the public order established by the law.

11

The free communication of thoughts and opinions is one of the most precious rights of woman, since this liberty ensures that fathers acknowledge their children. Every female citizen may therefore say freely, I am the mother of a child who belongs to you, without a barbarous prejudice to force her to conceal the truth, provided she is held responsible for the abuse of this liberty in the cases determined by the law.

12

The good of the majority is necessary in order to secure the rights of woman and the female citizen; this security should be instituted for the advantage of all, and not for the particular good of those women to whom it is entrusted.

13

For the maintenance of the public force, and for the expenses of government, the contributions of woman and man are equal; she takes part in all the drudgery, in all the laborious tasks; she should therefore take the same part in the distribution of positions, of employments, of commissions, of honours, and of business.

14

The female and male citizens have the right to determine, by themselves or by their representatives, the necessity of public contributions. The female citizens cannot enjoy this right except by being allowed an equal

[1] *tribune* Raised platform or dais for addressing an assembly.

share, not only in wealth, but also in public administration, and by being allowed to determine the amount, the basis, the collection, and the duration of taxation.

15

The mass of women, united for the purposes of taxation with that of men, has the right to demand of all its public agents an account of their administration.

16

Every society in which the security of rights is not assured, and the separation of powers is not determined, has no constitution; the constitution is null and void if the majority of the individuals who make up the nation has not cooperated in drawing it up.

17

Property belongs to both sexes, individually or collectively; it is everyone's inviolable and sacred right; as it is a true patrimony of nature, no one may be deprived of it, except when public necessity, legally ascertained, evidently demands it, and on condition of a previously established and just indemnity.

from Maria Edgeworth and Richard Lovell Edgeworth, *Practical Education* (1798)

from PRUDENCE AND ECONOMY

In the education of girls we must teach them much more caution than is necessary to boys: their prudence must be more the result of reasoning than of experiment; they *must* trust to the experience of others; they cannot always have recourse to what *ought to be*, they must adapt themselves to what is. They cannot rectify the material mistakes in their conduct. Timidity, a certain tardiness of decision, and reluctance to act in public situations are not considered as defects in a woman's character; her pausing prudence does not to a man of discernment denote imbecility, but appears to him the graceful auspicious characteristic of female virtue. There is always more probability that women should endanger their own happiness by precipitation than by forbearance.

Promptitude of choice is seldom expected from the female sex; they should avail themselves of the leisure that is permitted to them for reflection. "Begin nothing of which you have not well considered the end," was the piece of advice for which the Eastern Sultan paid a purse of gold, the price set upon it by a sage. The monarch did not repent of his purchase. This maxim should be engraved upon the memory of our female pupils by the repeated lessons of education. We should even in trifles avoid every circumstance which can tend to make girls venturesome, which can encourage them to trust to their good fortune, instead of relying on their own prudence.…

In the choice of friends, and on all matters of taste, young women should be excited to reason about their own feelings. "There is no reasoning about taste," is a pernicious maxim; if there was more reasoning, there would be disputation upon this subject. If women questioned their own minds, or allowed their friends to question them concerning the reasons of their "preferences and aversions," there would not probably be so many love matches, and so few love marriages. It is in vain to expect that young women should begin to reason miraculously, at the very moment that reason is wanted in the guidance of their conduct. We should also observe that women are called upon for the exertion of their prudence at an age when young men are scarcely supposed to possess that virtue; therefore women should be more early, and more carefully educated for the purpose. The important decisions of a woman's life are often made before she is twenty; a man does not come upon the theatre of public life, where most of his prudence is shown, till he is much older.

from Priscilla Wakefield, *Reflections on the Present Condition of the Female Sex; With Suggestions for Its Improvement* (1798)

from Chapter 3

The Necessity of Women Being Educated for the Exercise of Lucrative Employments Shown, and the Absurdity of a Woman Honourably Earning a Support Being Excluded from Society, Exposed

In the education of females, the same view actuates every rank: an advantageous settlement on marriage is the universal prize, for which parents of all classes enter their daughters upon the lists; and partiality or self-complacency assures to every competitor the most flattering prospect of success. To this one point tends the principal part of female instruction; for the promotion of this design, their best years for improvement are sacrificed to the attainment of attractive qualities, showy superficial accomplishments, polished manners, and, in one word, the whole science of pleasing, which is cultivated with unceasing assiduity as an object of the most essential importance.

The end is laudable, and deserving of every effort that can be exerted to secure it; a happy marriage may be estimated among the rarest felicities of human life, but it may be doubted whether the means used to accomplish it are adequate to the purpose, as the making a first impression is by no means effectual to determine the preference of a wise man. It is not then sufficient that a girl be qualified to excite admiration; her own happiness, and that of the man to whom she devotes the remainder of her days, depend upon her possession of those virtues, which alone can preserve lasting esteem and confidence.

The offices of a wife are very different from those of the mere pageant of a ballroom; and as their nature is more exalted, the talents they require are of a more noble kind: something far beyond the elegant trifler is wanted in a companion for life. A young woman is very ill-adapted to enter into the most solemn of social contracts who is not prepared, by her education, to become the participator of her husband's cares, the consoler of his sorrows, his stimulator to every praiseworthy undertaking, his partner in the labours and vicissitudes of life, the faithful and economical manager of his affairs, the judicious superintendant of his family, the wife and affectionate mother of his children, the preserver of his honour, his chief counsellor, and, to sum up all, the chosen friend of his bosom. If a modern female education be not calculated to produce these effects, as few surely will judge it to be, who reflect upon its tendency, it is incompetent to that very purpose, which is confessedly its main object, and must therefore be deemed imperfect, and require reformation. …

from Chapter 6

Lucrative Employments for the First and Second Classes Suggested … With Strictures on a Theatrical Life

Transitions in private life from affluence to poverty, like the sable pageantry of death, from their frequency produce no lasting impressions on the beholders. Unexpected misfortunes befall an acquaintance who has been caressed in the days of prosperity: the change is lamented, and she is consoled by the visits of her friends, in the first moments of affliction; she sinks gradually into wretchedness; she becomes obscure, and is forgotten. … A few remarks upon the nature of those employments which are best adapted to the higher classes of the sex, when reduced to necessitous circumstances, may, perhaps, afford useful hints to those who are languishing under the pressure of misfortune, and induce abler pens to treat a subject hitherto greatly neglected.

The most renowned actress of the day was Sarah Siddons (1755–1831), born into the theatrical family of Roger Kemble. Siddons's most famous role was that of Lady Macbeth, which she first played in 1785. Above left is a detail from a painting (c. 1790) of her playing the role opposite her brother; at right is George Henry Harlow's *Sarah Siddons in the Scene of Lady Macbeth Sleepwalking*, 1814. Siddons's farewell stage performance had been as Lady Macbeth in 1812.

Numerous difficulties arise in the choice of occupations for the purpose. They must be such as are neither laborious nor servile, and they must of course be productive, without requiring a capital.

For these reasons, pursuits which require the exercise of intellectual rather than bodily powers are generally the most eligible.

Literature affords a respectable and pleasing employment for those who possess talents and an adequate degree of mental cultivation. For although the emolument is precarious, and seldom equal to a maintenance, yet if the attempt be tolerably successful, it may yield a comfortable assistance in narrow circumstances and beguile many hours, which might otherwise be passed in solitude or unavailing regret. The fine arts offer a mode of subsistence congenial to the delicacy of the most refined minds, and they are peculiarly adapted, by their elegance, to the gratification of taste. The perfection of every species of painting is attainable by women, from the representation of historic facts to the minute execution of the miniature portrait, if they will bestow sufficient time and application for the acquisition of the principles of the art, in the study of those models which have been the means of transmitting the names and character of so many men to the admiration of posterity. The successful exercise of this imitative art requires invention, taste, and judgment: in the two first, the sex are allowed to excel, and the last may be obtained by a perseverance in examining, comparing, and reflecting upon the works of those masters who have copied nature in her most graceful forms. …

The stage is a profession to which many women of refined manners and a literary turn of mind have had recourse. Since it has been customary for females to assume dramatic characters, there appears to have been full as great a proportion of women who have attained celebrity among those who have devoted themselves to a theatrical life, as of the other sex—a fact which argues that there is no inequality of genius in the sexes for the imitative arts. The observation may operate as a stimulant to women to those pursuits which are less objectionable than the stage, which is not mentioned for the purpose of recommending it, but of proving that the abilities of the female sex are equal to nobler labours than are usually undertaken by women. The profession of an actress is indeed most unsuitable to the sex in every point of view, whether it be considered with respect to the courage requisite to face an audience, or the variety of situations incident to it, which expose moral virtue to the most severe trials. Let the daughters of a happier destiny, whilst they lament the evils to unpropitious circumstances that have cast them into a line of life in which it is scarcely possible to preserve that purity of sentiment and conduct which characterizes female excellence. When their errors are discussed, let the harsh voice of censure be restrained by the reflection that she who has made the greatest advances towards perfection might have fallen, had she been surrounded by the same influences.

That species of agriculture which depends upon skill in the management of the nursery ground, in rearing the various kinds of shrubs and flowers for the supply of gentlemen's gardens and pleasure grounds, would supply an elegant means of support to those women who are able to raise a capital for carrying on a work of that magnitude. Ornamental gardening, and the laying out of pleasure grounds and parks with the improvement of natural landscape, one of the refinements of modern times, may likewise afford an eligible maintenance to some of those females who, in the days of their prosperity, displayed their taste in the embellishment of their own domains.

The presiding over seminaries for female education is likewise a suitable employment for those whose minds have been enlarged by liberal cultivation, whilst the under parts of that profession may be more suitably filled by persons whose early views have been contracted within narrower limits. After all that can be suggested by general remarks, the different circumstances of individuals must decide the profession most convenient to them. But it is a consolatory reflection that amidst the daily vicissitudes of human life, from which no rank is exempt, there are resources from which aid may be drawn, without derogating from the true dignity of a rational being.

from Richard Polwhele, "The Unsexed Females: A Poem, Addressed to the Author of *The Pursuits of Literature*"[1] (1798)

Survey with me, what ne'er our fathers saw,
A female band despising Nature's law,[2]
As "proud defiance"[3] flashes from their arms,
And vengeance smothers all their softer charms.
I shudder at the new unpictured scene,
Where unsexed woman vaunts the imperious mien;° *bearing*
Where girls, affecting to dismiss the heart,
Invoke the Proteus of petrific[4] art;
With equal ease, in body or in mind,
To Gallic freaks or Gallic faith resigned,
The crane-like neck, as Fashion bids, lay bare,
Or frizzle,[5] bold in front, their borrowed hair;
Scarce by a gossamery film carest,
Sport,[6] in full view, the meretricious° breast;[7] *whorish*
Loose the chaste cincture,[8] where the graces shone,
And languished all the Loves, the ambrosial zone;
As lordly domes inspire dramatic rage,
Court prurient Fancy to the private stage;
With bliss botanic[9] as their bosoms heave,
Still pluck forbidden fruit, with mother Eve,
For puberty in sighing florets pant,
Or point the prostitution of a plant;
Dissect[10] its organ of unhallowed lust,
And fondly gaze the titillating dust;
With liberty's sublimer views expand,

[1] *the Author ... Literature* Thomas James Mathias, whose extremely popular satirical poem *The Pursuits of Literature* (1794–97) reacted against radical politics, particularly against feminists such as Mary Wollstonecraft. Polwhele draws on Mathias's comment in the poem's preface that "our *unsexed* female writers now instruct, or confuse, us and themselves, in the labyrinth of politics, or turn us wild with Gallic frenzy" (i.e., ideas inspired by the French Revolution).

[2] [Polwhele's note] Nature is the grand basis of all laws human and divine: and the woman who has no regard to nature, either in decoration of her person or the culture of her mind, will soon "walk after the flesh in the lust of uncleanness, and despise government." [Polwhele quotes from 2 Peter 2.10.]

[3] [From Polwhele's note] "A troop came next, who crowns and armour wore / And proud defiance in their looks they bore" Pope. The Amazonian band—the female Quixotes of the new philosophy are here too justly characterised.... [Polwhele quotes Alexander Pope's "The Temple of Fame" (1711), lines 342–43. *Amazons* Members of a legendary race of warrior women from Scythia; *Quixotes* Idealists, dreamers. "Female Quixotes" refers more specifically to Charlotte Lennox's famous novel of 1752, *The Female Quixote*.]

[4] *Proteus* God who could change shape at will; *petrific* Able to turn to stone, or to turn something else to stone.

[5] *frizzle* Curl in small curls.

[6] [Polwhele's note] To "sport a face" is a cant phrase in one of our universities, by which is meant an impudent obtrusion of a man's person in company. It is not applicable, perhaps, to the open bosom—a fashion which we have never invited or sanctioned.

[7] [From Polwhele's note] The fashions of France, which have been always imitated by the English, were, heretofore, unexceptionable in a moral point of view; since, however ridiculous or absurd, they were innocent. But they have now their source among prostitutes—among women of the most abandoned character. ...

[8] *cincture* Girdle for the waist, sometimes surrounding the breasts as well.

[9] [Polwhele's note] Botany has lately become a fashionable amusement with the ladies. But how the study of the sexual system can accord with female modesty, I am not able to comprehend. I had at first, written, "More eager for illicit knowledge pant, / With lustful boys anatomise a plant; / The virtues of its dust prolific speak, / Or point its pistil with unblushing cheek." I have, several times, seen boys and girls botanizing together.

[10] [Polwhele's note] Miss Wollstonecraft does not blush to say, in an introduction to a book designed for the use of young ladies, that, "in order to lay the axe at the root of corruption, it would be proper to familiarize the sexes to an unreserved discussion of those topics which are generally avoided in conversation from a principle of false delicacy; and that it would be right to speak of the organs of generation as freely as we mention our eyes or our hands." To such language our botanizing girls are doubtless familiarized; and they are in a fair way of becoming worthy disciples of Miss W. If they do not take heed to their ways, they will soon exchange the blush of modesty for the bronze of impudence. [Polwhele refers to Mary Wollstonecraft's "Introductory Address to Parents," from her *Elements of Morality, for the Use of Children* (1792), but he misrepresents her argument, which is that children can be discouraged from masturbating by being taught about the sexual organs and by having explained to them "the noble use which they were designed for." In her *Vindication of the Rights of Woman* (1792) she also argues that the study of botany can be consistent with female modesty.]

And o'er the wreck of kingdoms[1] sternly stand;
And, frantic, midst the democratic storm,
Pursue, Philosophy! thy phantom-form.[2]
Far other is the female shape and mind,
By modest luxury heightened and refined;
Those limbs, that figure, though by Fashion[3] graced,
By Beauty polished, and adorned by Taste;
That soul, whose harmony perennial flows,
In Music trembles, and in Color glows;
Which bids sweet Poesy reclaim the praise
With faery light to gild fastidious days,
From sullen clouds relieve domestic care,
And melt in smiles the withering frown of war.
Ah! once the female Muse,[4] to *Nature* true,
The unvalued store from *Fancy*, *Feeling* drew;
Won, from the grasp of woe, the roseate hours,
Cheered life's dim vale, and strewed the grave with flowers.
But lo! where, pale amidst the wild,[5] she draws
Each precept cold from sceptic Reason's[6] vase;
Pours with rash arm the turbid stream along,
And in the foaming torrent whelms the throng.[7] ...
See Wollstonecraft, whom no decorum checks,
Arise, the intrepid champion of her sex;
O'er humbled man assert the sovereign claim,
And slight the timid blush[8] of virgin fame.

from Hannah More, *Strictures on the Modern System of Female Education, With a View of the Principles and Conduct Prevalent among Women of Rank and Fortune* (1799)

from Volume 1, Chapter 4: Comparison of the Mode of Female Education in the Last Age with the Present Age

A young lady may excel in speaking French and Italian, may repeat a few passages from a volume of extracts; play like a professor, and sing like a siren;[9] have her dressing-room decorated with her own drawings, tables, stands, screens, and cabinets; nay, she may dance like Sempronia[10] herself, and yet may have been

[1] [Polwhele's note] The female advocates of democracy in this country, though they have had no opportunity of imitating the French ladies in their acts of atrocious cruelty, have yet assumed a stern serenity in the contemplation of those savage excesses. "To express their abhorrence of royalty, they (the French ladies) threw away the character of their sex, and bit the amputated limbs of their murdered countrymen. I say this on the authority of a young gentleman who saw it. I am sorry to add that the relation, accompanied with looks of horror and disgust, only provoked a contemptuous smile from an illuminated British fair-one." See Robison—p.219. [John Robison's *Proofs of a Conspiracy Against All the Religions and Governments of Europe* (1797).]

[2] [From Polwhele's note] Philosophism, the false image of philosophy. ...

[3] [Polwhele's note] I admit that we are quickly reconciled to the fashion of the day, and often consider it as graceful, if it offends not against delicacy.

[4] *Muse* One of nine daughters of Zeus and Mnemosyne, each of whom presided over and provided inspiration for an aspect of arts and sciences.

[5] [Polwhele's note] "A wild, where flowers and weeds promiscuous shoot; / A garden tempting with forbidden fruit" Pope. [From Alexander Pope's *Essay on Man* (1733) 1.7–8.]

[6] [Polwhele's note] A troubled stream only can proceed from the vase of skepticism; if it be not "the broken cistern that will hold no water" [from Jeremiah 2.13].

[7] [Polwhele's note] "Raging waves, foaming out their own shame"—St. Jude. Such were those infamous publications of Paine and others, which, like the torrents of December, threatened to sweep all before them—to overwhelm the multitude. [Polwhele quotes from Jude 1.13 and refers to Thomas Paine's *The Rights of Man* (1791–92), his reply to an attack on the French Revolutionaries by Edmund Burke.]

[8] [Polwhele's note] That Miss Wollstonecraft was a sworn enemy to the blushes, I need not remark. But many of my readers, perhaps, will be astonished to hear that at several of our boarding schools for young ladies, a blush incurs a penalty.

[9] *siren* Mythical creature, part woman and part bird, whose enchanted songs were said to lure sailors to their destruction.

[10] *Sempronia* Infamous woman of ancient Rome, known for her loose morals, who was said to have taken part in Cataline's conspiracy to overthrow the government in 63 BCE. According to Roman historian Sallust, Sempronia "had greater skill in lyre playing and dancing than there is any need for a respectable woman to acquire. There was nothing that she set a smaller value on than seemliness and chastity."

very badly educated. I am far from meaning to set no value whatever on any or all of these qualifications; they are all of them elegant, and many of them properly tend to the perfecting of a polite education. These things, in their measure and degree, may be done, but there are others which should not be left undone. Many things are becoming, but "one thing is needful." Besides, as the world seems to be fully apprized of the value of whatever tends to embellish life, there is less occasion here to insist on its importance.

But, though a well bred young lady may lawfully learn most of the fashionable arts, yet it does not seem to be the true end of education to make women of fashion dancers, singers, players, painters, actresses, sculptors, gilders, varnishers, engravers, and embroiderers. Most men are commonly destined to some profession, and their minds are consequently turned each to its respective object. Would it not be strange if they were called out to exercise their profession, or to set up their trade, with only a little general knowledge of the trades of all other men, and without any previous definite application to their own peculiar calling? The profession of ladies, to which the bent of their instruction should be turned, is that of daughters, wives, mothers, and mistresses of families. They should be therefore trained with a view to these several conditions, and be furnished with a stock of ideas and principles, and qualifications ready to be applied and appropriated, as occasion may demand, to each of these respective situations: for though the arts which merely embellish life must claim admiration, yet when a man of sense comes to marry, it is a companion whom he wants, and not an artist. It is not merely a creature who can paint, and play, and dress, and dance; it is a being who can comfort and counsel him; one who can reason and reflect, and feel, and judge, and discourse, and discriminate; one who can assist him in his affairs, lighten his cares, soothe his sorrows, strengthen his principles, and educate his children.

from VOLUME 1, CHAPTER 6: ON THE EARLY FORMING OF HABITS. ON THE NECESSITY OF FORMING THE JUDGMENT TO DIRECT THOSE HABITS

An early habitual restraint is peculiarly important to the future character and happiness of women. They should when very young be inured to contradiction. Instead of hearing their bon-mots[1] treasured up and repeated to the guests till they begin to think it dull when they themselves are not the little heroine of the theme, they should be accustomed to receive but little praise for their vivacity or their wit, though they should receive just commendation for their patience, their industry, their humility, and other qualities which have more worth than splendour. They should be led to distrust their own judgment; they should learn not to murmur at expostulation, but should be accustomed to expect and to endure opposition. It is a lesson with which the world will not fail to furnish them, and they will not practice it the worse for having learnt it the sooner. It is of the last importance to their happiness in life that they should early acquire a submissive temper and a forbearing spirit. They must even endure to be thought wrong sometimes when they cannot but feel they are right. And while they should be anxiously aspiring to do well, they must not expect always to obtain the praise of having done so. But while a gentle demeanor is inculcated, let them not be instructed to practise gentleness merely on the low ground of its being decorous and feminine, and pleasing, and calculated to attract human favour; but let them be carefully taught to cultivate it on the high principle of obedience to Christ.

[1] *bon-mots* French: witticisms.

from William Thompson and Anna Wheeler, *Appeal of One Half the Human Race, Women, Against the Pretensions of the Other Half, Men, to Retain Them in Political, and Thence in Civil and Domestic Slavery* (1825)

from INTRODUCTORY LETTER TO MRS. WHEELER

With you I would equally elevate both sexes. Really enlightened women, disdaining equally the submissive tricks of the slave and the caprices of the despot, breathing freely only in the air of the esteem of equals, and of mutual, *unbought*, *uncommanded* affection, would find it difficult to meet with associates worthy of them in men as now formed, full of ignorance and vanity, priding themselves on a *sexual* superiority, entirely independent of any merit, any superior qualities, or pretensions to them, claiming respect from the strength of their arm and the lordly faculty of producing beards attached by nature to their chins! No: unworthy of, as incapable of appreciating, the delight of the society of such women, are the great majority of the existing race of men. The pleasures of mere animal appetite, the pleasures of commanding (the prettier and more helpless the slave, the greater these pleasures of the brute) are the only pleasures which the majority of men seek for from women, are the only pleasures which their education and the hypocritical system of morals with which they have been necessarily imbued, permit them to expect. …

Even under the present arrangements of society, founded as they all are on the basis of individual competition, nothing could be more easy than to put the *rights* of women, political and civil, on a perfect equality with those of men. It is only to abolish all prohibitory and exclusive laws—statute or what are called "common"—the remnants of the barbarous customs of our ignorant ancestors; particularly the horrible and odious inequality and indissolubility of that disgrace of civilization, the present marriage code. Women then might exert in a free career with men their faculties of mind and body, to whatever degree developed, in pursuit of happiness by means of exertion, as men do. But this would not raise women to an equality of happiness with men: their rights might be equal, but not their happiness, because unequal powers under free competition must produce unequal effects.

In truth, the system of the most enlightened of the school of those reformers called political economists is still founded on exclusions. Its basis is too narrow for human happiness. A more comprehensive system, founded on equal benevolence, on the true development of the principle of Utility, is wanting.[1] Let the *competitive* political economists be satisfied with the praise of causing the removal of some of the rubbish of ignorant restrictions, under the name of laws, impeding the development of human exertion in the production of wealth. To build up a new fabric of social happiness, comprehending equally the interests of all existing human beings, has never been contemplated by them, and is altogether beyond the scope of their little theories; aiming at the utmost at increasing the number of what they style the happy middling orders, but leaving the great bulk of human beings to eternal ignorance and toil, requited by the mere means of prolonging from day to day an unhealthy and precarious existence. To a new science, the *social science*, or the science of promoting human happiness, that of political economy, or the mere science of producing wealth by individual competition, must give way.

from PART 2

As soon as adult daughters become wives, their civil rights disappear; they fall back again, and remain all their lives—should their owners and directors live so long—into the state of children or idiots, the passive property of their owners; protected by the law in some few respects only, like other slaves, from the excessive abuse of despotic power.

Woman is then compelled, in marriage, by the possession of superior strength on the part of men, by the want of knowledge, skill, and wealth, by the posi-

---

[1] *principle of Utility* Central principle of utilitarianism, an ethical theory developed by Jeremy Bentham and others; *wanting* Lacking.

tive, cruel, partial, and cowardly enactments of law, by the terrors of superstition, by the mockery of a pretended vow of obedience, and to crown all, and as the result of all, by the force of an unrelenting, unreasoning, unfeeling public opinion, to be the literal unequivocal *slave* of the man who may be styled her husband. I say emphatically the slave; for a slave is a person whose actions and earnings, instead of being under his own control, liable only to equal laws, to public opinion, and to his own calculations, under these, of his own interest, are under the arbitrary control of any other human being, by whatever name called. This is the essence of slavery, and what distinguishes it from freedom. A domestic, a civil, a political slave, in the plain unsophisticated sense of the word—in no metaphorical sense—is every married woman. No matter with what wealth she may be surrounded, with what dainties she may be fed, with what splendor of trappings adorned, with what voluptuousness her corporeal, mental, or moral sweets may be gathered; that high prerogative of human nature, the faculty of self-government, the basis of intellectual development, without which no moral conduct can exist, is to her wanting. … Till laws afford married women the same protection against the restraints and violence of the men to whom they are married, that they affect to afford them against all other individuals; till they afford them the same protection against the restraints and violence of their husbands, that their husbands enjoy against their caprices and violence, the social condition of the civilized wife will remain more completely slavish than that of the female slave of the West Indies. …

Be consistent, men! Ye stronger half of the race, be at length rational! Three or four thousand years have worn threadbare your vile cloak of hypocrisy. Even women, your poor, weak, contented slaves, at whose impotence of penetration, the result of your vile exclusions, you have been accustomed to laugh, begin to see through it and to shudder at the loathsomeness beneath. Cast aside this tattered cloak before it leaves you naked and exposed. Clothe yourselves with the new garments of sincerity. Be rational human beings, not mere male sexual creatures. Cast aside the ferocious brute of your nature: give up the pleasures of the brute, those of mere lust and command, for the pleasures of the rational being. So shall you enjoy the love of your *equals*, enlightened, benevolent, graceful, like yourselves, founded on an appreciation of your real merits: so shall you be happy. For the intercourse of the *bought* prostitute, or of the *commanded* household slave, you shall have full and equal participation in the compounded and associated pleasures of sense, intellect, and benevolence. To the highest enjoyments of which your nature is susceptible, there is no shorter road than the simple road of equal justice. …

Women of England! women, in whatever country ye breathe—wherever ye breathe, degraded—awake! Awake to the contemplation of the happiness that awaits you when all your faculties of mind and body shall be fully cultivated and developed; when every path in which ye can exercise those improved faculties shall be laid open and rendered delightful to you, even as to them who now ignorantly enslave and degrade you. …

Robert Burns

1759 – 1796

There is a riddle among certain linguists: "What is the difference between a language and a dialect?" Answer: "A language is a dialect that has an army and a navy." The point is well taken, and the prevalence of the British language across the planet no doubt is connected to the huge successes of the British navy in the last two and a half centuries. But when we sing Robert Burns's "Auld Lang Syne" on New Year's Eve we repeat a dialect piece that made good without the backing of an army or a navy. No doubt the distinctive resonance of Burns's Ayrshire dialect has helped to make the words of "Auld Lang Syne" memorable, but its popularity also rests on the degree to which it speaks the language of the heart, conveying a strong sense of mortality and of the blessings of memory itself.

Burns was born in Ayrshire, a county in southwestern Scotland, and spent his early years laboring with his father, a tenant-farmer who died in 1784. Intending to accept a position on a plantation in Jamaica, Burns gave up on this scheme when his first volume of poems, *Poems, Chiefly in the Scottish Dialect* (1786), brought him instant acclaim and the means to a more comfortable life. The Scottish dialect in which he wrote was descended from the Northumbrian dialect of Old English and had been known originally as "Inglis." In the eighteenth century it came to be called "Scots." Burns owes his reputation as "Heaven-taught plowman" to his ear for his Scots dialect, but he also knew how to write using English diction.

In some of his best poems, broad Scots and formal English alternate—indeed, nearly overlap. Burns's most famous narrative poem, the mock-heroic "Tam O'Shanter," is one in which we may see and hear the double-fluency of the poet, his broad Scots dialect giving way to "pure English." Many readers not fluent in Scots, both in Burns's time and in our own, have felt some relief when the poetry gives us a brief shower of more familiar language. But by not forsaking the richness of his dialect, Burns was helping to ensure his future status as Scotland's national poet—and dealing a blow to the class prejudice against him that was always present, despite the Edinburgh aristocracy's celebration of him when *Poems* first appeared.

Burns's *Poems* became known as the "Kilmarnock edition," after the place in which the book was published. At twenty-seven, Burns had already written his most famous poems, and he spent much of the rest of his short life helping to formalize an oral tradition in Scotland, contributing many of the works collected in James Johnson's *The Scots Musical Museum* and in George Thomson's *Select Collection of Original Scottish Airs*. Although never a wealthy man, Burns refused any money for his contribution to this work.

Burns's reputation as a lover for a time rivaled his fame as a poet. Having fathered several illegitimate children, he finally settled down in 1788 with a former lover, Jean Armour, in the town of Dumfries, where he received a commission as an excise (tax) officer. Thereafter he seems to have enjoyed relative prosperity in the last years of his life. Burns's love songs often express both his love of women and his feeling for his craft, as in "Green Grow the Rashes": "Auld nature swears, the lovely dears / Her noblest work she classes, O: / Her prentice han' she tries on man, / An' then she made the lasses, O." Burns also collected all the bawdy songs he inherited and invented in *The Merry Muses of Caledonia*, published shortly after his death (and subjected to expurgation and suppression even today).

A rebel in religion (he chafed against his strict Calvinist upbringing, although he attended church his entire life) and a sympathizer with the revolutions in America and France, Burns often wrote politically charged poems. In "Robert Bruce's March to Bannockburn" (popularly known as "Scots, wha hae"), for example, we hear a war-cry for emancipation: "Lay the proud usurpers low! / Tyrants fall in every foe! / Liberty's in every blow! / Let us do, or die!" Burns could also see the world from the lowliest, humblest places, even to the point of reckoning the mischief and malice of plowing up a field mouse from its home and seeing the calamity from the mouse's point of view ("To a Mouse").

Burns drew heavily on oral tradition, using the ballad form to produce what many consider his masterpiece: "Love and Liberty: A Cantata," commonly known as "The Jolly Beggars" (published posthumously in 1799). The cantata is a series of songs sung by a group of vagabonds, who recall past events in their lives. Burns was strongly influenced by his literary predecessors—perhaps most notably the Scottish Chaucerians of the fifteenth and sixteenth centuries (Gavin Douglas, William Dunbar), and the eighteenth-century Scottish poets Allan Ramsay and Robert Fergusson, whose work supplied him with materials and forms for his comprehensive refashioning of the lyric tradition in Scotland.

Burns was only thirty-seven when he died from an attack of rheumatic fever in 1796, on the day that his wife gave birth to the couple's ninth child. He was buried in St. Michael's Churchyard, Dumfries, Scotland, but his remains were later moved to a mausoleum. Scottish people around the world continue to celebrate Burns's birthday each year on 25 January.

⌘⌘⌘

To a Mouse, On Turning Her Up in Her Nest with the Plough

Wee, sleekit, cowrin, tim'rous beastie,
O, what a panic's in thy breastie!
Thou need na start awa sae hasty,
Wi' bickerin' brattle![1]
I wad be laith° to rin an' chase thee, *loathe*
Wi' murd'ring pattle!° *plough spade*

I'm truly sorry man's dominion
Has broken nature's social union,
An' justifies that ill opinion,
Which makes thee startle,
At me, thy poor, earth-born companion,
An' fellow mortal!

I doubt na, whyles,° but thou may thieve; *at times*
What then? poor beastie, thou maun° live! *must*
A daimen icker in a thrave[2]
'S a sma' request;
I'll get a blessin wi' the lave,° *rest*
An' never miss't!

Thy wee-bit housie, too, in ruin!
It's silly wa's° the win's are strewin! *walls*
An' naething, now, to big° a new ane, *build*
O' foggage° green! *moss*

[1] *bickerin' brattle* Hurrying scurry.

[2] *A daimen icker in a thrave* The odd ear in twenty-four sheaves of corn.

An' bleak December's winds ensuin,
Baith snell° an' keen! *bitter*

Thou saw the fields laid bare an' waste,
An's weary winter comin fast,
An' cozie here, beneath the blast,
Thou thought to dwell,
Till crash! the cruel coulter° past *plow blade*
Out thro' thy cell.

That wee-bit heap o' leaves an' stibble,
Has cost thee monie a weary nibble!
Now thou's turn'd out, for a' thy trouble,
But° house or hald,° *without / belongings*
To thole° the winter's sleety dribble, *bear*
An' cranreuch° cauld! *hoar frost*

But, Mousie, thou art no thy lane,[1]
In proving foresight may be vain:
The best-laid schemes o' mice an' men
Gang aft agley,[2]
An' lea'e us nought but grief an' pain,
For promis'd joy!

Still thou art blest, compar'd wi' me!
The present only toucheth thee:
But, Och! I backward cast my e'e
On prospects drear!
An' forward, tho' I canna see,
I guess an' fear!
—1785

The Fornicator

Ye jovial boys who love the joys,
The blissful joys of lovers;
Yet dare avow with dauntless brow,
When th'bony lass discovers;
I pray draw near and lend an ear,
And welcome in a frater,° *brother*
For I've lately been on quarantine,
A proven Fornicator.

Before the congregation wide
I pass'd the muster fairly,
My handsome Betsey by my side,
We gat our ditty° rarely; *sermon*
But my downcast eye by chance did spy
What made my lips to water,
Those limbs so clean where I, between
Commenc'd a Fornicator.

With rueful face and signs of grace
I pay'd the buttock-hire,[3]
The night was dark and thro the park
I could not but convoy her;
A parting kiss, what could I less,
My vows began to scatter,
My Betsey fell—lal de dal lal lal,
I am a Fornicator.

But for her sake this vow I make,
And solemnly I swear it,
That while I own a single crown,
She's welcome for to share it;
And my roguish boy his mother's joy,
And the darling of his pater,° *father*
For him I boast my pains and cost,
Although a Fornicator.

Ye wenching blades whose hireling jades° *prostitutes*
Have tipt ye off blue-joram,[4]
I tell ye plain, I do disdain
To rank ye in the quorum;
But a bony lass upon the grass
To teach her esse mater,[5]
And no reward but for regard,
O that's a Fornicator.

[1] *no thy lane* Not alone.

[2] *Gang aft agley* Go oft awry.

[3] *buttock-hire* Church fine charged to fornicators.

[4] *tipt ye off blue-joram* Given you the pox.

[5] *esse mater* Latin: to be a mother.

Your warlike kings and heroes bold,
Great captains and commanders;
Your mighty Caesars fam'd of old,
And conquering Alexanders;
In fields they fought and laurels[1] bought
And bulwarks strong did batter,
But still they grac'd our noble list
And ranked Fornicator!!!
—1785

Flow gently, sweet Afton[2]

Flow gently, sweet Afton, among thy green braes!° *banks*
Flow gently, I'll sing thee a song in thy praise!
My Mary's asleep by thy murmuring stream—
Flow gently, sweet Afton, disturb not her dream!

Thou stock-dove whose echo resounds thro' the glen,
Ye wild whistling blackbirds in yon thorny den,
Thou green-crested lapwing, thy screaming forbear—
I charge you, disturb not my slumbering fair!

How lofty, sweet Afton, thy neighbouring hills,
Far mark'd with the courses of clear, winding rills!° *brooks*
There daily I wander, as noon rises high,
My flocks and my Mary's sweet cot° in my eye. *cottage*

How pleasant thy banks and green valleys below,
Where wild in the woodlands the primroses blow;
There oft, as mild ev'ning weeps over the lea,
The sweet-scented birk° shades my Mary and me. *birch*

Thy crystal stream, Afton, how lovely it glides,
And winds by the cot where my Mary resides!
How wanton thy waters her snowy feet lave,° *wash*
As, gathering sweet flowerets, she stems thy clear wave.

Flow gently, sweet Afton, among thy green braes!
Flow gently, sweet river, the theme of my lays!° *song*
My Mary's asleep by thy murmuring stream—
Flow gently, sweet Afton, disturb not her dream!
—1792

Ae Fond Kiss[3]

Ae° fond kiss, and then we sever; *one*
Ae fareweel, alas, forever!
Deep in heart-wrung tears I'll pledge thee,
Warring sighs and groans I'll wage thee.
Who shall say that Fortune grieves him,
While the star of hope she leaves him?
Me, nae cheerful twinkle lights me;
Dark despair around benights me.

I'll ne'er blame my partial fancy,
Naething could resist my Nancy:
But to see her was to love her;
Love but her, and love forever.
Had we never lov'd sae kindly,
Had we never lov'd sae blindly,
Never met—or never parted,
We had ne'er been brokenhearted.

Fare-thee-weel, thou first and fairest!
Fare-thee-weel, thou best and dearest!
Thine be ilka° joy and treasure, *every*
Peace, Enjoyment, Love and Pleasure!
Ae fond kiss, and then we sever!
Ae fareweel, alas, forever!
Deep in heart-wrung tears I'll pledge thee,
Warring sighs and groans I'll wage thee.
—1792

[1] *laurels* Leaves of the bay laurel tree were once a symbol of victory in battle.

[2] *Afton* River that runs through southwestern Scotland.

[3] *Ae Fond Kiss* Burns wrote this love song for Nancy McLehose (the two called each other "Sylvander" and "Clarinda"), when she left England to reunite with her husband in Jamaica.

Robert Bruce's March to Bannockburn[1]

Scots, wha hae° wi' Wallace[2] bled, *who have*
Scots, wham° Bruce has aften led, *whom*
Welcome to your gory bed,
Or to victorie!

Now's the day, and now's the hour;
See the front o' battle lour;° *threaten*
See approach proud Edward's power—
Chains and slaverie!

Wha will be a traitor knave?
Wha can fill a coward's grave?
Wha sae base as be a slave?
Let him turn and flee!

Wha, for Scotland's King and Law,
Freedom's sword will strongly draw,
Free-man stand, or Free-man fa',
Let him on wi' me!

By Oppression's woes and pains!
By your Sons in servile chains!
We will drain our dearest veins,
But they shall be free!

Lay the proud usurpers low!
Tyrants fall in every foe!
Liberty's in every blow!—
Let us Do or Die!

—1795

A Man's a Man for A' That

Is there for honest poverty
That hings° his head, an' a'° that; *hangs / all*
The coward slave—we pass him by,
We dare be poor for a' that!
For a' that, an' a' that.
Our toils obscure an' a' that,
The rank is but the guinea's stamp,
The Man's the gowd° for a' that. *gold*

What though on hamely° fare we dine, *simple*
Wear hoddin grey,[3] an' a that;
Gie° fools their silks, and knaves their wine; *give*
A Man's a Man for a' that:
For a' that, and a' that,
Their tinsel show, an' a' that;
The honest man, tho' e'er sae° poor, *so*
Is king o' men for a' that.

Ye see yon birkie,[4] ca'd° "a lord," *called*
Wha struts, an' stares, an' a' that;
Tho' hundreds worship at his word,
He's but a coof° for a' that: *fool*
For a' that, an' a' that,
His ribband,° star,[5] an' a' that: *ribbon*
The man o' independent mind
He looks an' laughs at a' that.

A prince can mak a belted knight,
A marquis, duke, an' a' that;
But an honest man's aboon° his might, *above*
Gude faith, he mauna fa' that![6]
For a' that, an' a' that,
Their dignities an' a' that;
The pith° o' sense, an' pride o' worth, *importance*
Are higher rank than a' that.

Then let us pray that come it may,
As come it will for a' that,
That sense and worth, o'er a' the earth,

---

[1] *Robert Bruce … Bannockburn* In 1314, Robert the Bruce, King of the Scots, fought successfully for a free Scotland in a battle against the English under Edward II at Bannockburn.

[2] *Wallace* Sir William Wallace led numerous battles against the English under King Edward I.

[3] *hoddin grey* Coarse, woolen peasant cloth.

[4] *birkie* Conceited, swaggering fellow.

[5] *ribband, star* Emblems of nobility.

[6] *mauna fa' that* Musn't have that befall him.

Shall bear the gree,[1] an' a' that.
For a' that, an' a' that,
It's coming yet for a' that,
That Man to Man, the world o'er,
Shall brithers be for a' that.
—1795

Comin' thro' the Rye

Chorus

O, Jenny's a' weet,[2] poor body,
Jenny's seldom dry;
She draigl't[3] a' her petticoatie
Comin thro' the rye!

Comin thro' the rye, poor body,
Comin thro' the rye,
She draigl't a' her petticoatie,
Comin thro' the rye!

Gin° a body meet a body *suppose*
Comin thro' the rye,
Gin a body kiss a body,
Need a body cry?

Gin a body meet a body
Comin thro' the glen,
Gin a body kiss a body,
Need the warld ken?° *know*

Chorus

O, Jenny's a' weet, poor body,
Jenny's seldom dry;
She draigl't a' her petticoatie
Comin thro' the rye!
—1796

[1] *bear the gree* Have the victory.

[2] *a' weet* All wet.

[3] *draigl't* Draggled; dragged through the mud.

A Red, Red Rose

O, my luve's like a red, red rose,
That's newly sprung in June;
O, my luve's like the melodie,
That's sweetly play'd in tune.

As fair art thou, my bonie lass,
So deep in luve am I;
And I will luve thee still, my dear,
Till a' the seas gang° dry. *go*

Till a' the seas gang dry, my dear,
And the rocks melt wi' the sun;
And I will luve thee still, my dear,
While the sands o' life shall run.

And fare thee weel, my only luve!
And fare thee weel, a while!
And I will come again, my luve,
Tho' 'twere ten thousand mile!
—1796

Auld Lang Syne[4]

Should auld acquaintance be forgot,
And never brought to mind?
Should auld acquaintance be forgot,
And auld lang syne!

Chorus

For auld lang syne, my dear,
For auld lang syne.
We'll tak a cup o' kindness yet,
For auld lang syne.

And surely ye'll be° your pint stowp![5] *raise*
And surely I'll be mine!

[4] *Auld Lang Syne* Times long since passed.

[5] *stowp* Drinking glass.

And we'll tak a cup o' kindness yet,
For auld lang syne.

Chorus

We twa° hae run about the braes,° *two / hills*
And pou'd° the gowans° fine; *pulled / daisies*
But we've wander'd mony a weary fit,° *foot*
Sin'° auld lang syne. *since*

Chorus

We twa hae paidl'd in the burn,° *stream*
Frae morning sun till dine;
But seas between us braid° hae roar'd *broad*
Sin' auld lang syne.

Chorus

And there's a hand, my trusty fiere!° *friend*
And gie's° a hand o' thine! *give us*
And we'll tak a right gude willie-waught,[1]
For auld lang syne.

Chorus

—1796

[1] *gude willie-waught* Hearty glass of draught beer.

Gothic Literature, 1764–1830

CONTEXTS

An ancient castle full of mysteries; a blood-soaked specter; a beautiful woman pursued through an underground passage; a nefarious monk; an atmosphere of fear and suspense: many of the ingredients that make up what we now call Gothic literature solidified into a recognizable formula during the Romantic era. For readers, the Gothic at its best offered an imaginative escape and, through fear, a sublime encounter with the limits of rational understanding. For critics, the Gothic at its worst represented the degradation of public taste and morality.

The Gothic as a literary genre—with its castles, monasteries, dungeons, and graveyards—stemmed in part from what is known as the Gothic Revival, a faux medieval trend in architecture and interior decoration that became the dominant style of church architecture in the nineteenth century. One particularly influential early example is Strawberry Hill House (1749–76), an ordinary house that, under the direction of its owner, Horace Walpole, was transformed through a decades-long series of renovations into a fantastically ornate imitation Gothic castle. Not coincidentally, Walpole was living at Strawberry Hill when he wrote what is widely considered the first Gothic novel, *The Castle of Otranto* (1764). This novel established many of the conventions that came to be associated with the genre—supernatural occurrences, a heightened sense of the dramatic, atmospheric castles with secret passages, young heroines persecuted by villainous men.

Much as present-day readers may trace the history of "the Gothic novel" back to *Otranto*, writers and readers at the time did not use this term. To be sure, Walpole subtitled his book "A Gothic Story," but by *Gothic* he meant *medieval*, and, by extension, *irrational* and *uncivilized*, without many of the associations that came to be regarded as characteristic of the genre. And he would have been less likely to describe his work as a "novel" than as a "romance," a term used in reference to long narratives that could include elements of the fantastic. In his preface to the second edition of *Otranto*, Walpole described it as "an attempt to blend the two kinds of romance, the ancient and the modern. In the former, all was imagination and improbability: in the latter, nature is always intended to be, and sometimes has been, copied with success." The supernatural elements of "ancient" romances and the realism of "modern" novels proved to be a compelling combination, and *The Castle of Otranto* has never been out of print since its first publication. Walpole followed it with *The Mysterious Mother* (1768), an incest tragedy too shocking to be staged at the time; it is usually described as the first Gothic drama.

A few works inspired by Walpole were published in the decades immediately following *Otranto*, but the real vogue for Gothic fiction did not emerge until the enormously influential successes of Ann Radcliffe in the 1790s. Foreboding castles and persecuted heroines still figure prominently in Radcliffe's fiction, but her work also emphasizes sublime landscapes, and gives what was then a new twist to stories of the supernatural: a logical conclusion. In most of Radcliffe's novels, seemingly supernatural events are eventually revealed to have rational causes, and to be much less frightening than they had first appeared to be. The success of this approach—and especially of her fourth novel, *The Mysteries of Udolpho* (1794)—made Radcliffe the highest-earning writer of the decade. It also inspired a remarkable number of followers, often described as the "Radcliffe school."

Radcliffe herself was viewed with some degree of critical respect, though many critics were disappointed by her tendency to rationalize the supernatural out of existence; one anonymous reviewer (probably Mary Wollstonecraft) complained that "[a]fter being awakened to wonder by the rumbling of a mountain, the reader has an unpleasant sensation of being tricked ... when he perceives only a mouse creep out." Far greater critical ire, however, was reserved for the "crowd of copyists," as Walter Scott described them, "who came forward in imitation of Mrs. Radcliffe, and assumed her magic wand, without having the power of wielding it with effect."

While Radcliffe's closest emulators followed her in writing stories of the "explained supernatural," other writers of the period took the frightening aspects of the Gothic in an opposite direction, leaving fantastical events unexplained and amplifying their horrific qualities. The "horror" stream of Gothic fiction is best exemplified by Matthew Lewis's *The Monk: A Romance* (1796), a staggeringly popular success. That book's evocative descriptions of sexual content and of graphic violence, together with its unflattering depiction of religion, caused Coleridge to condemn it as "a poison for youth, and a provocative for the debauchee." In her posthumously published essay "On the Supernatural in Poetry" (1826), Radcliffe too disparaged such works of "horror," arguing that their explicit evocation of objects of fear "nearly annihilates" the faculties, while works of "terror," presumably such as her own, "expan[d] the soul" with material more suggestive of the sublime.

Lewis and writers like him were often inspired by their reading in German literature—and in part for that reason were sometimes referred to as members of the "German school." However, the importance of German literary influence was often overstated by critics who felt that the graphic and subversive content of their works was opposed to British values. Such content was undeniably attractive to many readers, though; for that reason, numerous British writers falsely subtitled their original work as having been translated or adapted "from the German." (In fairness, it should be noted that members of the much larger "Radcliffe school" were also sometimes associated with foreign degeneracy—an association created by their stories being set on the European Continent.)

Gothic novels were generally multi-volume affairs, but Gothic fiction was also available to those without the time, money, or literacy skills to enjoy a full-length novel. Any novel with a degree of popularity was likely to be pirated into a "chapbook" or "bluebook" abridgment—a short, cheap, pamphlet-style narrative that could be purchased on the street. Periodicals and collections might feature even shorter Gothic "tales," as well as "fragments," brief pieces of great dramatic intensity that commenced in the middle of the narrative action and ended before the plot was resolved.

The Gothic also appeared in a range of genres far beyond prose fiction. The work of Matthew Lewis illustrates the spread of the Gothic across genres: Lewis was also an influential writer of supernatural ballads, some of which were incorporated into *The Monk*, and he authored an extremely popular play, *The Castle Spectre* (1797), which thrilled audiences with the appearance of a ghost in a blood-stained white dress.

The Castle Spectre, along with theatrical adaptations of Radcliffe's works, contributed to a fashion for Gothic drama that paralleled that for the Gothic novel. Many of the most successful or important plays of the era—Joanna Baillie's *De Monfort* (1800), Coleridge's *Remorse* (1813), and Charles Maturin's *Bertram* (1816) among them—can be considered part of the genre. As with the novel, Gothic drama was not defined as such at the time, but it incorporated the same recognizable set of conventional elements, from gloomy foreign castles to persecuted heroines. It too was sometimes disparaged as an un-British reflection of the degraded tastes of the masses. Wordsworth, for example, quipped that *The Castle Spectre* "fitted the taste of the audience like a glove," and a critic in the *Monthly Review* expressed a commonplace complaint with his remark that "German spectres have almost driven Shakespeare and [the early-eighteenth-century English playwright William] Congreve from the stage." (Shakespeare, however, was also claimed by defenders of the Gothic, who pointed to his use of the supernatural in *Macbeth* as a model.)

The case against Gothic fiction and drama was in part based on the sheer number of works in the Gothic mode. As Clara Reeve, herself an author of Gothic novels, complained, "[e]very work of merit produced a swarm of imitators, till they became a public evil, and the institution of circulating libraries, conveyed them in the cheapest manner to every bodies hand." Circulating libraries, where books could be borrowed for a small fee, were commonplace by the close of the eighteenth century. This development meant that readers could read more books, and might choose them less discriminately, than if they had to buy them outright. Even if the phrase "Gothic novel" was not yet common, borrowers at circulating libraries knew that a book title referencing a castle, a monk, or a mystery promised a certain set of enjoyments. It is no accident that William Lane, the proprietor of a major circulating library, was also the owner of Minerva Press, a prolific publisher of Gothic novels. The disdain many felt for such novels is reflected in an unsubstantiated rumor widely repeated at the time that Minerva Press would pay £5 for any writer's manuscript, regardless of quality, so long as the story adhered to a certain set of conventions.

Concern regarding the proliferation of Gothic writing was compounded by the assumption, suggested by many reviewers, that the audience of the Gothic was primarily impressionable young women (who were assumed to be particularly sensitive to the Gothic's corrupting and frivolous qualities). Yet when Henry Tilney in Jane Austen's *Northanger Abbey* (1817) declares his liking for *The Mysteries of Udolpho*, he asserts that young men read "nearly as many" novels as women; he himself has read "hundreds and hundreds." The records of circulating libraries suggest that Henry's habits resembled those of many real male readers: borrowing practices appear to have been close to equal between the sexes. To be sure, many of the *writers* of Gothic novels, chapbooks, tales, and dramas were women—though, again, perhaps not as high a percentage as the critics suggested.

Critical condemnation of the Gothic as a corrupted and feminine form of low culture was increasingly complicated from the late 1790s onwards by the degree to which its influence permeated more "highbrow" literature. Coleridge, Wordsworth, Byron, Keats, and Baillie, for example, all wrote Gothic works, and Mary Robinson, Charlotte Smith, and Percy Shelley were Gothic novelists as well as poets.[1] Interestingly, strong Gothic influences in a writer's own work sometimes did little to mitigate that author's critical stance towards other writers more strongly associated with the Gothic. Byron was one of the few Romantic poets to openly express admiration for Walpole and other Gothic writers; Coleridge wrote scornful reviews of works by both Radcliffe and Lewis, while Wordsworth was likely thinking of the Gothic when he condemned contemporary readers for their "degrading thirst after outrageous stimulation." More than a decade later, Keats disparaged the failure of "[d]arkness, and worms, and shrouds, and sepulchres" to "lift the thoughts of man."

Though Gothic elements abound in Romantic poetry more broadly, the poems most strongly associated with the Gothic during the period were those written in the 1790s as part of a medieval and folk ballad revival movement. As Walter Scott later reflected in his "Essay on Imitations of the Ancient Ballad" (1830), contributors to the ballad revival tended to attempt one of two things. What

[1] The following is an incomplete list of Romantic-era works with Gothic elements appearing elsewhere in this anthology: Charlotte Smith, *Elegiac Sonnets* 39, 44, 70, and 74; Mary Robinson, "The Haunted Beach"; Robert Burns, "Halloween"; William Taylor, "Ellenore"; William Wordsworth, "The Thorn"; Sir Walter Scott, "The Eve of St. John," and "Glenfinlas"; Samuel Taylor Coleridge, *The Rime of the Ancient Mariner* and "Christabel"; George Gordon, Lord Byron, "Darkness"; Percy Shelley, *Alastor*; John Keats, "The Eve of St. Agnes," "La Belle Dame sans Merci," "La Belle Dame sans Mercy," "Lamia," and "This Living Hand"; John William Polidori, *The Vampyre*; Mary Shelley, from *Frankenstein* and "The Mortal Immortal." (Some of these selections may be found in the anthology's online component; many appear in the bound book.)

Scott called "real imitation[s] of the old ballads" aimed to replicate what their authors saw as the appealing simplicity of ballads of the past. What he called "legendary poems," on the other hand, appropriated aspects of the old ballads and attempted "to engraft modern refinement upon" them. This movement built on the work of slightly earlier poets and collectors, such as Robert Burns (1759–96) and Thomas Percy (1729–1811), but it was at its most overtly Gothic in the very late eighteenth and very early nineteenth centuries. The role of the Gothic in ballad writing intensified in 1796, when a flurry of interest developed surrounding Gottfried August Bürger's poem "Lenore" (1774), a German supernatural ballad that was published in five different English translations that year.[1] Another key event in 1796 was the publication of Matthew Lewis's poem "Alonzo the Brave and Fair Imogine," which was praised for bringing modern metric sophistication to the old ballad style. Building on this success, Lewis published a collection of ballads, *Tales of Wonder* (1800), that included translations and adaptations of older ballads alongside "original" works by himself and such ballad revival poets as Scott and Robert Southey. *Tales of Wonder* was a resounding critical failure, and it marked a change in direction for the poets involved; Scott, for example, abandoned his "German-mad" writings and began to focus more exclusively on Scottish history, while Southey went so far as to have his ballads removed from the second edition of *Tales*.

The popularity of the Gothic began to wane as the nineteenth century progressed, though this by no means signalled an end to the creation of important Gothic works. Some of the most widely acclaimed Gothic novels—including Mary Shelley's *Frankenstein* (1818), Charles Maturin's *Melmoth the Wanderer* (1820), and James Hogg's *The Private Memoirs and Confessions of a Justified Sinner* (1824)—were written long after enthusiasm for the Radcliffe school and the medieval-style ballad had dimmed. And many of the Gothic tropes established in the late eighteenth century would provide creative fodder for centuries to come—for Victorian classics such as *Strange Case of Dr Jekyll and Mr Hyde* (1886) and *Dracula* (1897), and for the "horror" films and novels of the twentieth and twenty-first centuries.

⌘⌘⌘

[1] William Taylor's translation, arguably the most influential, is reprinted in the online component of this anthology.

from Horace Walpole, *The Castle of Otranto*[1] (1764)

English antiquarian, writer, and politician Horace Walpole (1717–97) is best known as the author of *The Castle of Otranto*; among his other literary accomplishments are books on such subjects as history, gardening, and his own Gothic Revival home, Strawberry Hill.

In its first printing, Walpole published *The Castle of Otranto* under a pseudonym and presented it as a translation of a sixteenth-century southern Italian manuscript "found in the library of an ancient Catholic family in the north of England." After the popular success of the first edition, he confessed to being the author. *Otranto* provoked highly disparate critical responses—including in one case from the same reviewer, who praised it as a translation but condemned its "preposterous phenomena" upon learning it was an original work.

from CHAPTER 1

Manfred, Prince of Otranto, had one son and one daughter. The latter, a most beautiful virgin, aged eighteen, was called Matilda. Conrad, the son, was three years younger, a homely youth, sickly, and of no promising disposition; yet he was the darling of his father, who never showed any symptoms of affection to Matilda. Manfred had contracted a marriage for his son with the Marquis of Vicenza's daughter, Isabella, and she had already been delivered by her guardians into the hands of Manfred, that he might celebrate the wedding as soon as Conrad's infirm state of health would permit. Manfred's impatience for this ceremonial was remarked by his family and neighbours. The former, indeed, apprehending the severity of their prince's disposition, did not dare to utter their surmises on this precipitation. Hippolita, his wife, an amiable lady, did sometimes venture to represent the danger of marrying their only son so early, considering his great youth and greater infirmities, but she never received any other answer than reflections on her own sterility, who had given him but one heir. His tenants and subjects were less cautious in their discourses: they attributed this hasty wedding to the prince's dread of seeing accomplished an ancient prophecy, which was said to have pronounced that *the castle and lordship of Otranto should pass from the present family, whenever the real owner should be grown too large to inhabit it.* It was difficult to make any sense of this prophecy; and still less easy to conceive what it had to do with the marriage in question. Yet these mysteries, or contradictions, did not make the populace adhere the less to their opinion.

Young Conrad's birthday was fixed for his espousals. The company was assembled in the chapel of the castle, and everything ready for beginning the divine office, when Conrad himself was missing. Manfred, impatient of the least delay, and who had not observed his son retire, dispatched one of his attendants to summon the young prince. The servant, who had not stayed long enough to have crossed the court to Conrad's apartment, came running back breathless, in a frantic manner, his eyes staring, and foaming at the mouth. He said nothing, but pointed to the court. The company were struck with terror and amazement. The princess Hippolita, without knowing what was the matter, but anxious for her son, swooned away. Manfred, less apprehensive than enraged at the procrastination of the nuptials and at the folly of his domestic, asked imperiously what was the matter. The fellow made no answer, but continued pointing towards the courtyard; and at last, after repeated questions put to him, cried out,

"Oh! the helmet! the helmet!"

In the meantime, some of the company had run into the court, from whence was heard a confused noise of shrieks, horror, and surprise. Manfred, who began to be alarmed at not seeing his son, went himself to get information of what occasioned this strange confusion. Matilda remained, endeavouring to assist her mother, and Isabella stayed for the same purpose, and to avoid showing any impatience for the bridegroom, for whom, in truth, she had conceived little affection.

[1] *The Castle of Otranto* Please note that the complete text of *The Castle of Otranto* is available in the online component of this anthology (see the online materials listed for Volume 3).

The first thing that struck Manfred's eyes was a group of his servants endeavouring to raise something that appeared to him a mountain of sable plumes. He gazed without believing his sight. "What are ye doing?" cried Manfred wrathfully, "where is my son?"

A volley of voices replied, "Oh, my Lord! the prince! the prince! the helmet! the helmet!"

Shocked with these lamentable sounds and dreading he knew not what, he advanced hastily—but what a sight for a father's eyes! He beheld his child dashed to pieces and almost buried under an enormous helmet, an hundred times more large than any casque[1] ever made for human being, and shaded with a proportionable quantity of black feathers.

The horror of the spectacle, the ignorance of all around how this misfortune had happened, and, above all, the tremendous phenomenon before him, took away the prince's speech. Yet his silence lasted longer than even grief could occasion. He fixed his eyes on what he wished in vain to believe a vision, and seemed less attentive to his loss than buried in meditation on the stupendous object that had occasioned it. He touched, he examined the fatal casque; nor could even the bleeding mangled remains of the young prince divert the eyes of Manfred from the portent before him. All who had known his partial[2] fondness for young Conrad were as much surprised at their prince's insensibility as thunderstruck themselves at the miracle of the helmet. …

[Later the same day, Manfred requests that Isabella, his son's intended bride, be brought to him.]

"I sent for you, Lady," said he, and then stopped under great appearance of confusion.

"My Lord!"

"Yes, I sent for you on a matter of great moment," resumed he. "Dry your tears, young Lady. You have lost your bridegroom—yes, cruel fate, and I have lost the hopes of my race!—but Conrad was not worthy of your beauty."

"How, my Lord!" said Isabella. "Sure you do not suspect me of not feeling the concern I ought? My duty and affection would have always—"

"Think no more of him," interrupted Manfred. "He was a sickly, puny child, and Heaven has perhaps taken him away that I might not trust the honours of my house on so frail a foundation. The line of Manfred calls for numerous supports. My foolish fondness for that boy blinded the eyes of my prudence—but it is better as it is. I hope, in a few years, to have reason to rejoice at the death of Conrad."

Words cannot paint the astonishment of Isabella. At first she apprehended that grief had disordered Manfred's understanding. Her next thought suggested that this strange discourse was designed to ensnare her: she feared that Manfred had perceived her indifference for his son, and in consequence of that idea she replied, "Good my Lord, do not doubt my tenderness; my heart would have accompanied my hand. Conrad would have engrossed all my care, and wherever fate shall dispose of me, I shall always cherish his memory and regard your highness and the virtuous Hippolita as my parents."

"Curse on Hippolita!" cried Manfred. "Forget her from this moment, as I do. In short, Lady, you have missed a husband undeserving of your charms; they shall now be better disposed of. Instead of a sickly boy, you shall have a husband in the prime of his age who will know how to value your beauties, and who may expect a numerous offspring."

"Alas, my Lord," said Isabella, "my mind is too sadly engrossed by the recent catastrophe in your family to think of another marriage. If ever my father returns and it shall be his pleasure, I shall obey, as I did when I consented to give my hand to your son. But until his return permit me to remain under your hospitable roof, and employ the melancholy hours in assuaging yours, Hippolita's, and the fair Matilda's affliction."

"I desired you once before," said Manfred angrily, "not to name that woman; from this hour she must be a stranger to you, as she must be to me. In short, Isabella, since I cannot give you my son, I offer you myself."

"Heavens!" cried Isabella, waking from her delusion. "What do I hear! You, my Lord! You! My father-in-law!

[1] *casque* Military helmet.
[2] *partial* Preferential.

the father of Conrad! the husband of the virtuous and tender Hippolita!—"

"I tell you," said Manfred imperiously, "Hippolita is no longer my wife; I divorce her from this hour. Too long has she cursed me by her unfruitfulness. My fate depends on having sons, and this night I trust will give a new date to my hopes."

At those words he seized the cold hand of Isabella, who was half-dead with fright and horror. She shrieked and started from him. Manfred rose to pursue her, when the moon, which was now up and gleamed in at the opposite casement, presented to his sight the plumes of the fatal helmet, which rose to the height of the windows, waving backwards and forwards in a tempestuous manner, and accompanied with a hollow and rustling sound.

Isabella, who gathered courage from her situation, and who dreaded nothing so much as Manfred's pursuit of his declaration, cried, "Look, my Lord! see, Heaven itself declares against your impious intentions!"

"Heaven nor hell shall impede my designs," said Manfred, advancing again to seize the princess. At that instant the portrait of his grandfather, which hung over the bench where they had been sitting, uttered a deep sigh and heaved its breast.

Isabella, whose back was turned to the picture, saw not the motion, nor knew whence the sound came, but started and said, "Hark, my Lord! What sound was that?" and at the same time made towards the door. Manfred, distracted between the flight of Isabella, who had now reached the stairs, and yet unable to keep his eyes from the picture, which began to move, had however advanced some steps after her, still looking backwards on the portrait, when he saw it quit its panel and descend on the floor with a grave and melancholy air.

"Do I dream?" cried Manfred, returning, "or are the devils themselves in league against me? Speak, infernal spectre! Or, if thou art my grandsire, why dost thou too conspire against thy wretched descendant, who too dearly pays for—" Ere he could finish the sentence the vision sighed again, and made a sign to Manfred to follow him.

"Lead on!" cried Manfred. "I will follow thee to the gulf of perdition." The spectre marched sedately, but dejected, to the end of the gallery, and turned into a chamber on the right hand. Manfred accompanied him at a little distance, full of anxiety and horror, but resolved. As he would have entered the chamber, the door was clapped-to with violence by an invisible hand. The prince, collecting courage from this delay, would have forcibly burst open the door with his foot, but found that it resisted his utmost efforts.

"Since hell will not satisfy my curiosity," said Manfred, "I will use the human means in my power for preserving my race. Isabella shall not escape me."

The lady, whose resolution had given way to terror the moment she had quitted Manfred, continued her flight to the bottom of the principal staircase. There she stopped, not knowing whither to direct her steps, nor how to escape from the impetuosity of the prince. The gates of the castle she knew were locked, and guards placed in the court. Should she, as her heart prompted her, go and prepare Hippolita for the cruel destiny that awaited her, she did not doubt but Manfred would seek her there, and that his violence would incite him to double the injury he meditated, without leaving room for them to avoid the impetuosity of his passions. Delay might give him time to reflect on the horrid measures he had conceived, or produce some circumstance in her favour, if she could, for that night, at least, avoid his odious purpose. Yet where conceal herself? How avoid the pursuit he would infallibly make throughout the castle? As these thoughts passed rapidly through her mind, she recollected a subterraneous passage which led from the vaults of the castle to the church of St. Nicholas. Could she reach the altar before she was overtaken, she knew even Manfred's violence would not dare to profane the sacredness of the place; and she determined, if no other means of deliverance offered, to shut herself up for ever among the holy virgins, whose convent was contiguous to the cathedral. In this resolution, she seized a lamp that burned at the foot of the staircase, and hurried towards the secret passage.

The lower part of the castle was hollowed into several intricate cloisters, and it was not easy for one under so much anxiety to find the door that opened into the cavern. An awful silence reigned throughout those subterraneous regions, except now and then some blasts of wind that shook the doors she had passed, and which, grating on the rusty hinges, were re-echoed through that long labyrinth of darkness. Every murmur struck her with new terror, yet more she dreaded to hear the wrathful voice of Manfred urging his domestics to pursue her. …

Strawberry Hill and Fonthill Abbey

Horace Walpole's Strawberry Hill House (1749–76) is an early example of Gothic Revival architecture. A modest and ordinary building when he purchased it, Strawberry Hill became a decades-long project for Walpole, who enjoyed, as he wrote, the "satisfaction of imprinting the gloomth of abbeys and cathedrals on one's house." Strawberry Hill House was in no way an authentic Gothic building; even most of the stone used was artificial.

In a letter to a friend, Walpole wrote explicitly of the connections between Strawberry Hill and *The Castle of Otranto*: "You will even have found some traits [in the novel] to put you in mind of this place. When you read of the picture quitting its panel, did you recollect the portrait of Lord Falkland all in white in my gallery?"

Fonthill Abbey (1796–1807), a later and even more extravagant Gothic Revival home, was the creation of the architect James Wyatt and the art collector, writer, and politician William Beckford. Fonthill took Gothic artificiality to impractical extremes, featuring a cavernous dining room that could not be effectively heated and a tower so tall that it collapsed and had to be rebuilt multiple times. Beckford was also, like Walpole, an early participant in Gothic literature; his best-known work is the Orientalist Gothic novel *Vathek*, excerpted in the online component of this anthology.

Paul Sandby, *Strawberry Hill from the Southeast*, c. late eighteenth century.

J. Godfrey, "Library at Strawberry Hill," illustration from Horace Walpole, *Description of the Villa of Mr. Horace Walpole, Youngest Son of Sir Robert Walpole Earl of Orford, at Strawberry-Hill near Twickenham, Middlesex, with an Inventory of the Furniture, Pictures, Curiosities, &c.*, 1784.

Edward Edwards and James Newton, "Staircase at Strawberry Hill," illustration from *Description of the Villa of Mr. Horace Walpole.*

L. Martin and T. Higham, "Fonthill Abbey. View of the West & North Fronts," illustration from John Rutter, *Delineations of Fonthill and Its Abbey*, 1823.

G. Cattermole and M. Dubourg, "Fonthill Abbey, S. End of St. Michael's Gallery," illustration from *Delineations of Fonthill and Its Abbey.*

G. Cattermole and J.C. Varrall, "Fonthill Abbey. Interior of the Great Western Hall," illustration from *Delineations of Fonthill and Its Abbey*.

from Ann Radcliffe, *The Mysteries of Udolpho, a Romance* (1794)

The works of Ann Radcliffe (1764–1823) were tremendously popular, and inaugurated a period of proliferation of novels of "terror." None was more successful than *The Mysteries of Udolpho*, for which Radcliffe was paid a copyright fee of £500, about fifty times the price of an average manuscript. Radcliffe received even more for her next novel, *The Italian* (1797), after which she retired from writing—a decision that prompted unfounded but persistent rumors that she had been driven mad by her own work. Her last novel, *Gaston de Blondeville* (1826), was published posthumously.

The plot of *The Mysteries of Udolpho* concerns Emily St. Aubert, a young woman whose prospects for marriage and fortune are manipulated by her aunt and her aunt's new husband, the sinister Montoni. All of the following excerpts relate to a mysteriously veiled object at Udolpho, Montoni's castle; they begin as Emily is examining paintings in the castle with her aunt's maid, Annette.

from VOLUME 2
from CHAPTER 5

… Passing the light hastily over several other pictures, she came to one concealed by a veil of black silk. The singularity of the circumstance struck her, and she stopped before it, wishing to remove the veil, and examine what could thus carefully be concealed, but somewhat wanting courage. "Holy Virgin! what can this mean?" exclaimed Annette. "This is surely the picture they told me of at Venice."

"What picture?" said Emily. "Why a picture—a picture," replied Annette, hesitatingly—"but I never could make out exactly what it was about, either."

"Remove the veil, Annette."

"What! I, ma'amselle!—I! not for the world!" Emily, turning round, saw Annette's countenance grow pale. "And pray, what have you heard of this picture, to terrify you so, my good girl?" said she. "Nothing, ma'amselle: I have heard nothing, only let us find our way out."

"Certainly: but I wish first to examine the picture; take the light, Annette, while I lift the veil." Annette took the light, and immediately walked away with it, disregarding Emily's call to stay, who, not choosing to be left alone in the dark chamber, at length followed her. "What is the reason of this, Annette?" said Emily, when she overtook her, "what have you heard concerning that picture, which makes you so unwilling to stay when I bid you?"

"I don't know what is the reason, ma'amselle," replied Annette, "nor any thing about the picture, only I have heard there is something very dreadful belonging to it—and that it has been covered up in black EVER SINCE—and that nobody has looked at it for a great many years—and it somehow has to do with the owner of this castle before Signor Montoni came to the possession of it—and—"

"Well, Annette," said Emily, smiling, "I perceive it is as you say—that you know nothing about the picture."

"No, nothing, indeed, ma'amselle, for they made me promise never to tell:—but—"

"Well," rejoined Emily, who observed that she was struggling between her inclination to reveal a secret, and her apprehension for the consequence, "I will inquire no further—"

"No, pray, ma'am, do not."

"Lest you should tell all," interrupted Emily. …

from CHAPTER 6

… To withdraw her thoughts … from the subject of her misfortunes, she attempted to read, but her attention wandered from the page, and, at length, she threw aside the book, and determined to explore the adjoining chambers of the castle. Her imagination was pleased with the view of ancient grandeur, and an emotion of melancholy awe awakened all its powers, as she walked through rooms, obscure and desolate, where no footsteps had passed probably for many years, and remembered the strange history of the former possessor of the edifice. This brought to her recollection the veiled picture, which had attracted her curiosity, on the preceding night, and she resolved to examine it. As she passed through the chambers, that led to this, she found herself somewhat agitated; its connection with the late lady of the castle, and the conversation of Annette, together with the circumstance of the veil, throwing a mystery over the subject, that excited a faint degree of terror. But a terror of this nature, as it occupies and expands the mind, and elevates it to high expectation, is purely sublime, and leads us, by a kind of fascination, to seek even the object, from which we appear to shrink.

Emily passed on with faltering steps, and having paused a moment at the door, before she attempted to open it, she then hastily entered the chamber, and went towards the picture, which appeared to be enclosed in a frame of uncommon size, that hung in a dark part of the room. She paused again, and then, with a timid hand, lifted the veil; but instantly let it fall—perceiving that what it had concealed was no picture, and, before she could leave the chamber, she dropped senseless on the floor.

When she recovered her recollection, the remembrance of what she had seen had nearly deprived her of it a second time. …

from Volume 3
from Chapter 1

[Emily is locked into a room at Udolpho, and is afraid for the well-being of her aunt, as well as her own safety.]

… When her spirits had overcome the first shock of her situation, she held up the lamp to examine, if the chamber afforded a possibility of an escape. It was a spacious room, whose walls, wainscoted with rough oak, shewed no casement but the grated one, which Emily had left, and no other door than that, by which she had entered. The feeble rays of the lamp, however, did not allow her to see at once its full extent; she perceived no furniture, except, indeed, an iron chair, fastened in the centre of the chamber, immediately over which, depending on a chain from the ceiling, hung an iron ring. Having gazed upon these, for some time, with wonder and horror, she next observed iron bars below, made for the purpose of confining the feet, and on the arms of the chair were rings of the same metal. As she continued to survey them, she concluded, that they were instruments of torture, and it struck her, that some poor wretch had once been fastened in this chair, and had there been starved to death. She was chilled by the thought; but, what was her agony, when, in the next moment, it occurred to her, that her aunt might have been one of these victims, and that she herself might be the next! An acute pain seized her head, she was scarcely able to hold the lamp, and, looking round for support, was seating herself, unconsciously, in the iron chair itself; but suddenly perceiving where she was, she started from it in horror, and sprung towards a remote end of the room. Here again she looked round for a seat to sustain her, and perceived only a dark curtain, which, descending from the ceiling to the floor, was drawn along the whole side of the chamber. Ill as she was, the appearance of this curtain struck her, and she paused to gaze upon it, in wonder and apprehension.

It seemed to conceal a recess of the chamber; she wished, yet dreaded, to lift it, and to discover what it veiled: twice she was withheld by a recollection of the terrible spectacle her daring hand had formerly unveiled in an apartment of the castle, till, suddenly conjecturing, that it concealed the body of her murdered aunt, she seized it, in a fit of desperation, and drew it aside. Beyond, appeared a corpse, stretched on a kind of low couch, which was crimsoned with human blood, as was the floor beneath. The features, deformed by death, were ghastly and horrible, and more than one livid wound appeared in the face. Emily, bending over the body, gazed, for a moment, with an eager, frenzied eye; but, in the next, the lamp dropped from her hand, and she fell senseless at the foot of the couch. …

from Chapter 17

… It may be remembered, that, in a chamber of Udolpho, hung a black veil, whose singular situation had excited Emily's curiosity, and which afterwards disclosed an object, that had overwhelmed her with horror; for, on lifting it, there appeared, instead of the

Illustration from *The Mysteries of Udolpho*, 1803 edition. This illustration, from the fifth edition of Radcliffe's novel, depicts the scene from Volume 3, Chapter 1 reprinted above.

picture she had expected, within a recess of the wall, a human figure of ghastly paleness, stretched at its length, and dressed in the habiliments of the grave. What added to the horror of the spectacle, was, that the face appeared partly decayed and disfigured by worms, which were visible on the features and hands. On such an object, it will be readily believed, that no person could endure to look twice. Emily, it may be recollected, had, after the first glance, let the veil drop, and her terror had prevented her from ever after provoking a renewal of such suffering, as she had then experienced. Had she dared to look again, her delusion and her fears would have vanished together, and she would have perceived, that the figure before her was not human, but formed of wax. The history of it is somewhat extraordinary, though not without example in the records of that fierce severity, which monkish superstition has sometimes inflicted on mankind. A member of the house of Udolpho, having committed some offence against the prerogative of the church, had been condemned to the penance of contemplating, during certain hours of the day, a waxen image, made to resemble a human body in the state, to which it is reduced after death. This penance, serving as a memento of the condition at which he must himself arrive, had been designed to reprove the pride of the Marquis of Udolpho, which had formerly so much exasperated that of the Romish[1] church; and he had not only superstitiously observed this penance himself, which, he had believed, was to obtain a pardon for all his sins, but had made it a condition in his will, that his descendants should preserve the image, on pain of forfeiting to the church a certain part of his domain, that they also might profit by the humiliating moral it conveyed. The figure, therefore, had been suffered to retain its station in the wall of the chamber, but his descendants excused themselves from observing the penance, to which he had been enjoined.

This image was so horribly natural, that it is not surprising Emily should have mistaken it for the object it resembled. …

from Matthew Gregory Lewis, *The Monk: A Romance* (1796)

When *The Monk* was first published, anonymously, there was little indication that it would become one of the most notorious novels of its period; it was well received by critics as well as by general readers. Critical opinion, however, changed drastically later that year after Matthew Lewis (1775–1818) chose to publish the second edition under his own name—"M.G. Lewis, Esq., M.P."—and reviewers learned that the author of the novel was a person of significant stature. Coleridge, who condemned the book

[1] *Romish* I.e., Roman Catholic.

in the *Critical Review*, noted that "the author of the Monk signs himself a LEGISLATOR! We stare and tremble." Lewis would likely have faced criminal charges for obscene or blasphemous libel if he had not published a fourth edition of *The Monk* in which, as he wrote, he "expunged every syllable on which could be grounded the slightest construction of immorality." None of this seems to have diminished *The Monk*'s popularity; the novel appeared in several editions, as well as in numerous pirated chapbook abridgments and dramatic adaptations, in the years following its publication.

The following selections commence with a conversation between the nobleman Don Raymond (also called Alphonso) and Agnes, a noblewoman whose family wants to force her to become a nun.

from Volume 2
from Chapter 1

"... But can you possibly have lived at Lindenberg for three whole months without hearing of the bleeding nun?"

"You are the first who ever mentioned the name to me. Pray, who may the lady be?"

"That is more than I can pretend to tell you. All my knowledge of her history comes from an old tradition in this family, which has been handed down from father to son, and is firmly credited throughout the baron's domains. Nay, the baron believes it himself; and as for my aunt who has a natural turn for the marvellous, she would sooner doubt the veracity of the Bible than of the bleeding nun. Shall I tell you this history?"

I answered that she would oblige me much by relating it: she resumed her drawing, and then proceeded as follows in a tone of burlesqued gravity:[1]

"It is surprising that in all the chronicles of past times this remarkable personage is never once mentioned. Fain would I recount to you her life; but unluckily till after her death she was never known to have existed. Then first did she think it necessary to make some noise in the world, and with that intention she made bold to seize upon the Castle of Lindenberg. Having a good taste, she took up her abode in the best room of the house; and once established there, she began to amuse herself by knocking about the tables and chairs in the middle of the night. Perhaps she was a bad sleeper, but this I have never been able to ascertain. According to the tradition, this entertainment commenced about a century ago. It was accompanied with shrieking, howling, groaning, swearing, and many other agreeable noises of the same kind. But though one particular room was more especially honoured with her visits, she did not entirely confine herself to it. She occasionally ventured into the old galleries, paced up and down the spacious halls; or, sometimes stopping at the doors of the chambers, she wept and wailed there to the universal terror of the inhabitants. In these nocturnal excursions she was seen by different people, who all describe her appearance as you behold it here traced by the hand of her unworthy historian."[2]

The singularity of this account insensibly engaged my attention.

"Did she never speak to those who met her?" said I.

"Not she. The specimens indeed, which she gave nightly of her talents for conversation, were by no means inviting. Sometimes the castle rung with oaths and execrations: a moment after she repeated her paternoster:[3] now she howled out the most horrible blasphemies, and then chaunted De profundis,[4] as orderly as if still in the choir. In short she seemed a mighty capricious being: but whether she prayed or cursed, whether she was impious or devout, she always contrived to terrify her auditors[5] out of their senses. The castle became scarcely habitable; and its lord was so frightened by these midnight revels, that one fine morning he was found dead in his bed. This success seemed to please the nun mightily, for now she made more noise than ever. But the next baron proved too

[1] *burlesqued gravity* Seriousness exaggerated for comic effect.

[2] *as you behold ... historian* Raymond is looking at Agnes's drawing of the bleeding nun.

[3] *paternoster* Latin for "our father," a well-known Christian prayer.

[4] *chaunted* Intoned, especially in the style of traditional liturgical music; *De profundis* Conventional Latin title of Psalm 130, which in English begins "Out of the depths have I cried unto thee, O Lord."

[5] *auditors* Hearers.

cunning for her. He made his appearance with a celebrated exorciser in his hand, who feared not to shut himself up for a night in the haunted chamber. There it seems that he had a hard battle with the ghost before she would promise to be quiet. She was obstinate, but he was more so, and at length she consented to let the inhabitants of the castle take a good night's rest. For some time after no news was heard of her. But at the end of five years the exorciser died, and then the nun ventured to peep abroad again. However, she was now grown much more tractable and well-behaved. She walked about in silence, and never made her appearance above once in five years. This custom, if you will believe the baron, she still continues. He is fully persuaded, that on the fifth of May of every fifth year, as soon as the clock strikes one, the door of the haunted chamber opens. (Observe, that this room has been shut up for near a century.) Then out walks the ghostly nun with her lamp and dagger: she descends the staircase of the eastern tower; and crosses the great hall. On that night the porter always leaves the gates of the castle open, out of respect to the apparition: not that this is thought by any means necessary, since she could easily whip through the keyhole if she chose it; but merely out of politeness, and to prevent her from making her exit in a way so derogatory to the dignity of her ghostship."

"And whither does she go on quitting the castle?"

"To heaven, I hope; but if she does, the place certainly is not to her taste, for she always returns after an hour's absence. The lady then retires to her chamber, and is quiet for another five years."

"And you believe this, Agnes?"

"How can you ask such a question? No, no, Alphonso! I have too much reason to lament superstition's influence to be its victim myself. …"

> [Raymond and Agnes confess their love for each other. Agnes decides to disguise herself as the bleeding nun so as to escape her family and elope with Raymond:]

… She was habited exactly as she had described the spectre. A chaplet of beads hung upon her arm; her head was enveloped in a long white veil; her nun's dress was stained with blood; and she had taken care to provide herself with a lamp and dagger. She advanced towards the spot where I stood. I flew to meet her, and clasped her in my arms.

"Agnes!" said I, while I pressed her to my bosom,

> Agnes! Agnes! thou art mine!
> Agnes! Agnes! I am thine!
> In my veins while blood shall roll,
> Thou art mine!
> I am thine!
> Thine my body! thine my soul!

Terrified and breathless, she was unable to speak: She dropped her lamp and dagger, and sank upon my bosom in silence. I raised her in my arms, and conveyed her to the carriage. …

> [The lovers' carriage crashes, and Raymond is knocked unconscious; when he comes to his senses, Agnes is gone. He is assisted by some peasants, who take him to an inn to recover.]

… According to the physician's order, I swallowed a composing medicine; and as soon as the night shut in, my attendants withdrew, and left me to repose.

That repose I wooed in vain. The agitation of my bosom chased away sleep. Restless in my mind, in spite of the fatigue of my body, I continued to toss about from side to side, till the clock in a neighbouring steeple struck "one." As I listened to the mournful hollow sound, and heard it die away in the wind, I felt a sudden chillness spread itself over my body. I shuddered without knowing wherefore; cold dews poured down my forehead, and my hair stood bristling with alarm. Suddenly I heard slow and heavy steps ascending the staircase. By an involuntary movement I started up in my bed, and drew back the curtain. A single rush-light, which glimmered upon the hearth, shed a faint gleam through the apartment, which was hung with tapestry. The door was thrown open with violence. A figure entered, and drew near my bed with solemn measured steps. With trembling apprehension I examined this midnight visitor. God Almighty! It was the bleeding nun! It was my lost companion! Her face was still veiled, but she no longer held her lamp and dagger. She lifted up her veil slowly. What a sight presented itself to my startled eyes! I beheld before me an animated corse.[1] Her countenance was long and haggard; her cheeks and lips were bloodless; the paleness of death was spread over her features; and her eye-balls, fixed steadfastly upon me, were lustreless and hollow.

I gazed upon the spectre with horror too great to be described. My blood was frozen in my veins. I would have called for aid, but the sound expired ere it could pass my lips. My nerves were bound up in impotence, and I remained in the same attitude inanimate as a statue.

The visionary nun looked upon me for some minutes in silence: there was something petrifying in her regard. At length, in a low sepulchral voice, she pronounced the following words:

> Raymond! Raymond! Thou art mine!
> Raymond! Raymond! I am thine!
> In thy veins while blood shall roll,
> I am thine!
> Thou art mine!
> Mine thy body! Mine thy soul!——

Breathless with fear, I listened while she repeated my own expressions. The apparition seated herself opposite to me at the foot of the bed, and was silent. Her eyes were fixed earnestly upon mine: they seemed endowed with the property of the rattlesnake's, for I strove in vain to look off her. My eyes were fascinated, and I had not the power of withdrawing them from the spectre's.

In this attitude she remained for a whole long hour without speaking or moving; nor was I able to do either. At length the clock struck two. The apparition rose from her seat, and approached the side of the bed. She grasped with her icy fingers my hand which hung lifeless upon the coverture, and pressing her cold lips to mine, again repeated,

> Raymond! Raymond! Thou art mine!
> Raymond! Raymond!
> I am thine! &c.—

She then dropped my hand, quitted the chamber with slow steps, and the door closed after her. …

Gothic Chapbooks and Bluebooks

As much as critics condemned the proliferation of Gothic novels, they condemned even more vehemently a related form of fiction that became popular around the same time: short Gothic tales printed individually and sold cheaply. Initially, these tales were part of a more general trade in chapbooks—pamphlets or short books made available for purchase on the street—but they developed into a more specific subgenre known as "bluebooks" for the bright blue covers that identified them. Often authored by hack writers, bluebooks typically sold for sixpence or a shilling; they were cheaply produced, with the expectation that they would fall apart after reading. Many were unapologetically pirated condensations of longer, popular Gothic works (there are, for example, five surviving bluebook versions of *The Monk*), while others offered original stories that made use of the same plot conventions found in the full-length novels. The length of a bluebook—usually between twenty and seventy-five pages—encouraged a focus on action at the expense of description and character. Such publications often had very long titles, making it clear to readers exactly what thrills the book promised.

---

[1] *corse* Corpse.

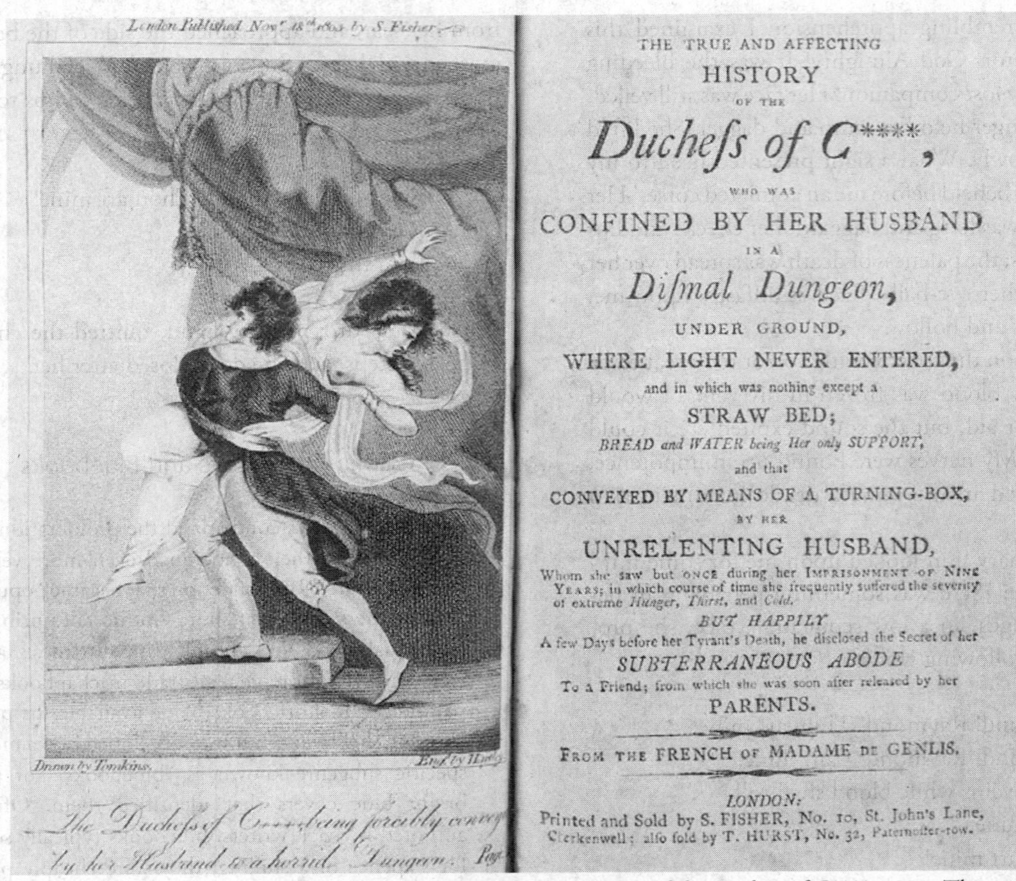

THE TRUE AND AFFECTING
HISTORY
OF THE
*Duchefs of C****,*
WHO WAS
CONFINED BY HER HUSBAND
IN A
Difmal Dungeon,
UNDER GROUND,
WHERE LIGHT NEVER ENTERED,
and in which was nothing except a
STRAW BED;
BREAD and WATER being Her only SUPPORT,
and that
CONVEYED BY MEANS OF A TURNING-BOX,
BY HER
UNRELENTING HUSBAND,
Whom she saw but ONCE during her IMPRISONMENT OF NINE YEARS; in which course of time she frequently suffered the severity of extreme *Hunger, Thirst,* and *Cold.*
BUT HAPPILY
A few Days before her Tyrant's Death, he disclosed the Secret of her
SUBTERRANEOUS ABODE
To a Friend; from which she was soon after released by her
PARENTS.

FROM THE FRENCH OF MADAME DE GENLIS.

LONDON:
Printed and Sold by S. FISHER, No. 10, St. John's Lane, Clerkenwell; alfo fold by T. HURST, No. 32, Paternofter-row.

Frontispiece and title page from *The True and Affecting History of the Duchess of C*****, 1803. This is one of several English retellings of the French novelist Stéphanie de Félicité's *Histoire de le duchesse de C**** (1782). The description on the title page reads as follows: "The true and affecting history of the Duchess of C****, who was confined by her husband in a dismal dungeon, under ground, where light never entered, and in which was nothing except a straw bed; bread and water being her only support, and that conveyed by means of a turning-box, by her unrelenting husband, whom she saw but once during her imprisonment of nine years; in which course of time she frequently suffered the severity of extreme hunger, thirst, and cold. But happily a few days before her tyrant's death, he disclosed the secret of her subterraneous abode to a friend; from which she was soon after released by her parents."

Frontispiece from *The Midnight Assassin: or, The Confessions of the Monk Rinaldi, Containing a Complete History of His Diabolical Machinations and Unparalleled Ferocity. Together with a Circumstantial Account of that Scourge of Mankind the Inquisition, with the Manner of Bringing to Trial Those Unfortunate Beings Who Are at Its Disposal*, 1802. This frontispiece, from a condensation of Radcliffe's *The Italian, or the Confessional of the Black Penitents* (1797), depicts the moment at which the villainous Catholic priest Schedoni is about to stab the virtuous orphan Ellena. He forbears when he sees that she is wearing a locket containing his picture and concludes that she must be his daughter.

from Anonymous, "Terrorist Novel Writing," *The Spirit of the Public Journals* (1797)

The following anonymous piece advances points that were commonly raised by critics of the burgeoning genre of "terror" fiction. A footnote attached to the title explained that "the satire of this letter is particularly levelled at a literary lady of considerable talents"—that is, Ann Radcliffe—and claimed that "[t]he *system of terror* which she has adopted is not the only reproach to which she is liable. Besides the tedious monotony of her descriptions, she affects in the most disgusting manner a knowledge of languages, countries, customs, and objects of art, of which she is lamentably ignorant. ... This shows how well a lady understands the wants of her sex [i.e., what is lacking in her gender.]"

I never complain of fashion, when it is confined to externals; to the form of a cap, or the cut of a lapel; to the colour of a wig, or the tune of a ballad; but when I perceive that there is such a thing as fashion, even in composing books, it is, perhaps, full time that some attempt should be made to recall writers to the old boundaries of common sense.

I allude, Sir, principally to the great quantity of novels with which our circulating libraries are filled, and our parlour tables covered, in which it has been the fashion to make *terror* the *order of the day*, by confining the heroes and heroines in old gloomy castles, full of spectres, apparitions, ghosts, and dead men's bones. This is now so common that a novelist blushes to bring about a marriage by ordinary means, but conducts the happy pair through long and dangerous galleries, where the light burns blue,[1] the thunder rattles, and the great window at the end presents the hideous visage of a *murdered* man, *uttering* piercing groans, and developing shocking mysteries. If a curtain is withdrawn, there is a bleeding body behind it; if a chest is opened, it contains a skeleton; if a noise is heard, somebody is receiving a deadly blow; and if a candle goes out, its place is sure to

[1] *light burns blue* According to tradition, blue flame is a sign of ghosts.

be supplied by a flash of lightning. Cold hands grasp us in the dark, statues are seen to move, and suits of armour walk off their pegs, while the wind whistles louder than one of Handel's choruses, and the still air is more melancholy than the dead march in Saul.[1]

Such are the dresses and decorations of a modern novel, which, as Bayes says, is calculated to "elevate and surprise"; but in doing so, carries the young reader's imagination into such a confusion of terrors as must be hurtful. It is to no great purpose, indeed, that we have forbidden our servants from telling the children stories of ghosts and hobgoblins, if we cannot put a novel into their hands which is not filled with monsters of the imagination, more frightful than are to be found in Glanvil,[2] the famous *bug-a-boo* of our forefathers.

A novel, if at all useful, ought to be a representation of human life and manners, with a view to direct the conduct in the important duties of life, and to correct its follies. But what instruction is to be reaped from the distorted ideas of lunatics, I am at a loss to conceive. Are we come to such a pass that the only commandment necessary to be repeated is, "Thou shalt do no murder"? Are the duties of life so changed that all the instruction necessary for a young person is to learn to walk at night upon the battlements of an old castle, to creep hands and feet along a narrow passage, and meet the devil at the end of it? Is the corporeal frame of the female sex so masculine and hardy that it must be softened down by the touch of dead bodies, clay-cold hands, and damp sweats? Can our young ladies be taught nothing more necessary in life than to sleep in a dungeon with venomous reptiles, walk through a ward with assassins, and carry bloody daggers in their pockets, instead of pincushions and needle-books?

Every absurdity has an end; and as I observe that almost all novels are of the terrific cast, I hope the insipid repetition of the same bugbears will at length work a cure. In the mean time, should any of your female readers be desirous of catching the season of terrors, she may compose two or three very pretty volumes from the following recipe:

Take—

An old castle, half of it ruinous.
A long gallery, with a great many doors, some secret ones.
Three murdered bodies, quite fresh.
As many skeletons, in chests and presses.
An old woman hanging by the neck, with her throat cut.
Assassins and desperadoes, *quant. suff.*[3]
Noises, whispers, and groans, threescore at least.

Mix them together, in the form of three volumes, to be taken at any of the watering-places before going to bed.

PROBATUM EST.[4]

from Jane Austen, *Northanger Abbey* (1817)

Northanger Abbey was largely written in 1798, but was kept out of print for many years as a result of a contractual dispute with the prospective publisher. Austen's brother, Henry Austen, finally purchased the rights back from that publisher in 1816, and Austen revised the manuscript that same year. She died in July of 1817, and the novel was published posthumously under Henry's oversight.

The work incorporates elements of many genres, from sentimental novel to parody; some of its most memorable scenes mock the works of Radcliffe and her imitators. The titular abbey is the family home of "a very gentlemanlike young man" named Henry Tilney, where the novel's protagonist, a young woman named Catherine, is invited to visit. A voracious reader of Gothic novels, she comes to act—with Henry's sly encouragement—as though she is a heroine in one.

[1] *Handel* George Frideric Handel (1685–1759), German-born British composer known for such works as the "Hallelujah" chorus; *the dead march in Saul* The "Dead March" from Handel's oratorio *Saul* (1739) is a sorrowful piece of music frequently played at important funerals.

[2] *Glanvil* Joseph Glanvill's *Saducismus Triumphatus* (1681) compiled descriptions of the deeds of witches and argued that they had real supernatural abilities.

[3] *quant. suff.* Abbreviation for the Latin "quantum sufficit," meaning "of sufficient quantity."

[4] *PROBATUM EST* Latin phrase placed at the conclusion of a recipe to indicate that the recipe has been tested and shown to work.

from Chapter 6

The following conversation, which took place between the two friends [Catherine and Isabella] in the pump-room[1] one morning, after an acquaintance of eight or nine days, is given as a specimen of their very warm attachment, and of the delicacy, discretion, originality of thought, and literary taste which marked the reasonableness of that attachment. …

"… But, my dearest Catherine, what have you been doing with yourself all this morning? Have you gone on with Udolpho?"

"Yes, I have been reading it ever since I woke; and I am got to the black veil."[2]

"Are you, indeed? How delightful! Oh! I would not tell you what is behind the black veil for the world! Are not you wild to know?"

"Oh! Yes, quite; what can it be? But do not tell me—I would not be told upon any account. I know it must be a skeleton, I am sure it is Laurentina's skeleton. Oh! I am delighted with the book! I should like to spend my whole life in reading it. I assure you, if it had not been to meet you, I would not have come away from it for all the world."

"Dear creature! How much I am obliged to you; and when you have finished Udolpho, we will read the Italian[3] together; and I have made out a list of ten or twelve more of the same kind for you."

"Have you, indeed! How glad I am! What are they all?"

"I will read you their names directly; here they are, in my pocketbook. Castle of Wolfenbach, Clermont, Mysterious Warnings, Necromancer of the Black Forest, Midnight Bell, Orphan of the Rhine, and Horrid Mysteries.[4] Those will last us some time."

"Yes, pretty well; but are they all horrid, are you sure they are all horrid?"

"Yes, quite sure; for a particular friend of mine, a Miss Andrews, a sweet girl, one of the sweetest creatures in the world, has read every one of them. …"

from Chapter 21

[Catherine is a guest at Northanger Abbey. In the previous chapter, Henry teasingly predicts that she will gain entry to "a small vaulted room" in which she will find "a large, old-fashioned cabinet of ebony and gold" containing a manuscript, but will be unable to read it before her lamp extinguishes itself.]

… The fire … died away, and Catherine, having spent the best part of an hour in her arrangements, was beginning to think of stepping into bed, when, on giving a parting glance round the room, she was struck by the appearance of a high, old-fashioned black cabinet, which, though in a situation conspicuous enough, had never caught her notice before. Henry's words, his description of the ebony cabinet which was to escape her observation at first, immediately rushed across her; and though there could be nothing really in it, there was something whimsical, it was certainly a very remarkable coincidence! She took her candle and looked closely at the cabinet. It was not absolutely ebony and gold; but it was Japan,[5] black and yellow Japan of the handsomest kind; and as she held her candle, the yellow had very much the effect of gold. The key was in the door, and she had a strange fancy to look into it; not, however, with the smallest expectation of finding any thing, but it was so very odd, after what Henry had said. In short, she could not sleep till she had examined it. So, placing the candle with great caution on a chair, she seized the key with a very tremulous hand and tried to turn it; but it resisted her utmost strength. Alarmed, but not discouraged, she tried it another way; a bolt flew, and she believed herself successful; but how strangely mysteri-

[1] *pump-room* Fashionable establishment in Bath where waters from the hot springs were distributed for drinking.

[2] *Udolpho … black veil* In Ann Radcliffe's novel *The Mysteries of Udolpho* (excerpted above), the protagonist lifts a black veil to discover what she comes to believe is the corpse of the murdered Signora Laurentini. It is later revealed that she saw only a "waxen image" of a dead body.

[3] *the Italian* Another Radcliffe novel, published in 1797.

[4] *Castle of … Mysteries* Titles of Gothic novels published between 1793 and 1798.

[5] *Japan* Wood lacquered in a Japanese style.

ous!—the door was still immovable. She paused a moment in breathless wonder. The wind roared down the chimney, the rain beat in torrents against the windows, and every thing seemed to speak the awfulness of her situation. To retire to bed, however, unsatisfied on such a point, would be vain, since sleep must be impossible with the consciousness of a cabinet so mysteriously closed in her immediate vicinity. Again, therefore, she applied herself to the key, and after moving it in every possible way for some instants with the determined celerity of hope's last effort, the door suddenly yielded to her hand: her heart leaped with exultation at such a victory, and having thrown open each folding door, the second being secured only by bolts of less wonderful construction than the lock, though in that her eye could not discern any thing unusual, a double range of small drawers appeared in view, with some larger drawers above and below them; and in the centre, a small door, closed also with a lock and key, secured in all probability a cavity of importance.

Catherine's heart beat quick, but her courage did not fail her. With a cheek flushed by hope, and an eye straining with curiosity, her fingers grasped the handle of a drawer and drew it forth. It was entirely empty. With less alarm and greater eagerness she seized a second, a third, a fourth; each was equally empty. Not one was left unsearched, and in not one was any thing found. Well read in the art of concealing a treasure, the possibility of false linings to the drawers did not escape her, and she felt round each with anxious acuteness in vain. The place in the middle alone remained now unexplored; and though she had "never from the first had the smallest idea of finding any thing in any part of the cabinet, and was not in the least disappointed at her ill success thus far, it would be foolish not to examine it thoroughly while she was about it." It was some time however before she could unfasten the door, the same difficulty occurring in the management of this inner lock as of the outer; but at length it did open; and not vain, as hitherto, was her search; her quick eyes directly fell on a roll of paper pushed back into the further part of the cavity, apparently for concealment, and her feelings at that moment were indescribable. Her heart fluttered, her knees trembled, and her cheeks grew pale. She seized, with an unsteady hand, the precious manuscript, for half a glance sufficed to ascertain written characters; and while she acknowledged with awful sensations this striking exemplification of what Henry had foretold, resolved instantly to peruse every line before she attempted to rest.

The dimness of the light her candle emitted made her turn to it with alarm; but there was no danger of its sudden extinction; it had yet some hours to burn; and that she might not have any greater difficulty in distinguishing the writing than what its ancient date might occasion, she hastily snuffed it.[1] Alas! it was snuffed and extinguished in one. A lamp could not have expired with more awful effect. Catherine, for a few moments, was motionless with horror. It was done completely; not a remnant of light in the wick could give hope to the rekindling breath. Darkness impenetrable and immovable filled the room. A violent gust of wind, rising with sudden fury, added fresh horror to the moment. Catherine trembled from head to foot. In the pause which succeeded, a sound like receding footsteps and the closing of a distant door struck on her affrighted ear. Human nature could support no more. A cold sweat stood on her forehead, the manuscript fell from her hand, and groping her way to the bed, she jumped hastily in, and sought some suspension of agony by creeping far underneath the clothes. To close her eyes in sleep that night, she felt must be entirely out of the question. With a curiosity so justly awakened, and feelings in every way so agitated, repose must be absolutely impossible. The storm too abroad so dreadful!—She had not been used to feel alarm from wind, but now every blast seemed fraught with awful intelligence. The manuscript so wonderfully found, so wonderfully accomplishing the morning's prediction, how was it to be accounted for?—What could it contain?—to whom could it relate?—by what means could it have been so long concealed?—and how singularly strange that it should fall to her lot to discover it! Till

[1] *snuffed it* Remove the burnt portion of the candle wick (so as to allow the flame to burn more brightly).

she had made herself mistress of its contents, however, she could have neither repose nor comfort; and with the sun's first rays she was determined to peruse it. But many were the tedious hours which must yet intervene. She shuddered, tossed about in her bed, and envied every quiet sleeper. The storm still raged, and various were the noises, more terrific even than the wind, which struck at intervals on her startled ear. The very curtains of her bed seemed at one moment in motion, and at another the lock of her door was agitated, as if by the attempt of somebody to enter. Hollow murmurs seemed to creep along the gallery, and more than once her blood was chilled by the sound of distant moans. Hour after hour passed away, and the wearied Catherine had heard three proclaimed by all the clocks in the house before the tempest subsided or she unknowingly fell fast asleep.

Chapter 22

The housemaid's folding back her window-shutters at eight o'clock the next day was the sound which first roused Catherine; and she opened her eyes, wondering that they could ever have been closed, on objects of cheerfulness; her fire was already burning, and a bright morning had succeeded the tempest of the night. Instantaneously, with the consciousness of existence, returned her recollection of the manuscript; and springing from the bed in the very moment of the maid's going away, she eagerly collected every scattered sheet which had burst from the roll on its falling to the ground, and flew back to enjoy the luxury of their perusal on her pillow. She now plainly saw that she must not expect a manuscript of equal length with the generality of what she had shuddered over in books, for the roll, seeming to consist entirely of small disjointed sheets, was altogether but of trifling size, and much less than she had supposed it to be at first.

Her greedy eye glanced rapidly over a page. She started at its import. Could it be possible, or did not her senses play her false?—An inventory of linen, in coarse and modern characters, seemed all that was before her! If the evidence of sight might be trusted, she held a washing-bill in her hand. She seized another sheet, and saw the same articles with little variation; a third, a fourth, and a fifth presented nothing new. Shirts, stockings, cravats, and waistcoats faced her in each. Two others, penned by the same hand, marked an expenditure scarcely more interesting, in letters, hair-powder, shoe-string, and breeches-ball.[1] And the larger sheet, which had enclosed the rest, seemed by its first cramp line, "To poultice chestnut mare"—a farrier's bill! Such was the collection of papers (left perhaps, as she could then suppose, by the negligence of a servant in the place whence she had taken them) which had filled her with expectation and alarm, and robbed her of half her night's rest! She felt humbled to the dust. Could not the adventure of the chest have taught her wisdom? A corner of it, catching her eye as she lay, seemed to rise up in judgment against her. Nothing could now be clearer than the absurdity of her recent fancies. To suppose that a manuscript of many generations back could have remained undiscovered in a room such as that, so modern, so habitable!—or that she should be the first to possess the skill of unlocking a cabinet, the key of which was open to all!

from George Gordon, Lord Byron, *Don Juan*, Canto 16 (1824)

Published in stages between 1819 and 1824, Byron's comic poem *Don Juan* details the adventures of its title character as he travels from his native Spain to Greece, Turkey, Russia, and eventually England. As the narrative unfolds, Byron satirizes everything from English politics and moral hypocrisy to—in the stanzas excerpted below—the genre of Gothic terror.

Canto 16, from which the following selection is taken, was the last Canto Byron finished. Don Juan is staying with the Lord and Lady Amundeville at Norman Abbey, their country estate; also present are Aurora Raby, with whom Juan is smitten, and the Duchess Grace Fitz-Fulke.

[1] *breeches-ball* Ball of colored substance used to cover stains on breeches.

Canto 16

15

Juan felt somewhat pensive, and disposed
For contemplation rather than his pillow:
The Gothic chamber, where he was enclosed,
Let in the rippling sound of the lake's billow,° *wave*
With all the mystery by midnight caused;
Below his window waved (of course) a willow;
And he stood gazing out on the cascade
That flashed and after darkened in the shade.

16

Upon his table or his toilet,°—which *dressing table*
Of these is not exactly ascertained—
(I state this, for I am cautious to a pitch
Of nicety, where a fact is to be gained)
A lamp burned high, while he leant from a niche,
Where many a Gothic ornament remained,
In chiselled stone and painted glass, and all
That time has left our fathers of their Hall.

17

Then, as the night was clear though cold, he threw
His chamber door wide open—and went forth
Into a gallery, of a sombre hue,
Long, furnished with old pictures of great worth,
Of knights and dames heroic and chaste too,
As doubtless should be people of high birth.
But by dim lights the portraits of the dead
Have something ghastly, desolate, and dread.

18

The forms of the grim knight and pictured saint
Look living in the moon; and as you turn
Backward and forward to the echoes faint
Of your own footsteps—voices from the urn
Appear to wake, and shadows wild and quaint
Start from the frames which fence their aspects stern,
As if to ask how you can dare to keep
A vigil there, where all but death should sleep.

19

And the pale smile of beauties in the grave,
The charms of other days, in starlight gleams,
Glimmer on high; their buried locks still wave
Along the canvas; their eyes glance like dreams
On ours, or spars within some dusky cave,
But death is imaged in their shadowy beams.
A picture is the past; even ere its frame
Be gilt, who sate hath ceased to be the same.

20

As Juan mused on mutability,
Or on his mistress—terms synonymous—
No sound except the echo of his sigh
Or step ran sadly through that antique house,
When suddenly he heard, or thought so, nigh,
A supernatural agent—or a mouse,
Whose little nibbling rustle will embarrass
Most people as it plays along the arras.[1]

21

It was no mouse, but lo! a monk, arrayed
In cowl and beads and dusky garb, appeared,
Now in the moonlight, and now lapsed in shade,
With steps that trod as heavy, yet unheard;
His garments only a slight murmur made;
He moved as shadowy as the sisters weird,[2]
But slowly; and as he passed Juan by,
Glanced, without pausing, on him a bright eye.

22

Juan was petrified; he had heard a hint
Of such a spirit in these halls of old,
But thought, like most men, there was nothing in't
Beyond the rumour which such spots unfold,
Coined from surviving superstition's mint,
Which passes ghosts in currency like gold,
But rarely seen, like gold compared with paper.
And *did* he see this? or was it a vapour?

---

[1] *arras* Tapestry hung around a room, usually with a gap between the fabric and the walls.

[2] *sisters weird* Name given to the three witches who appear in *Macbeth*.

23

Once, twice, thrice passed, repassed—the thing of air,
Or earth beneath, or heaven, or t'other place;
And Juan gazed upon it with a stare,
Yet could not speak or move; but, on its base
As stands a statue, stood: he felt his hair
Twine like a knot of snakes around his face;
He taxed his tongue for words, which were not granted,
To ask the reverend person what he wanted.

24

The third time, after a still longer pause,
The shadow passed away—but where? the hall
Was long, and thus far there was no great cause
To think his vanishing unnatural:
Doors there were many, through which, by the laws
Of physics, bodies whether short or tall
Might come or go; but Juan could not state
Through which the spectre seemed to evaporate.

25

He stood—how long he knew not, but it seemed
An age,—expectant, powerless, with his eyes
Strained on the spot where first the figure gleamed;
Then by degrees recalled his energies,
And would have passed the whole off as a dream,
But could not wake; he was, he did surmise,
Waking already, and returned at length
Back to his chamber, shorn of half his strength.

26

All there was as he left it: still his taper
Burnt, and not *blue*, as modest tapers use,[1]
Receiving sprites with sympathetic vapour;
He rubbed his eyes, and they did not refuse
Their office; he took up an old newspaper;
The paper was right easy to peruse;
He read an article the king attacking,
And a long eulogy of "patent blacking."[2]

27

This savoured of this world; but his hand shook—
He shut his door, and after having read
A paragraph, I think about Horne Tooke,[3]
Undrest, and rather slowly went to bed.
There, couched all snugly on his pillow's nook,
With what he had seen his phantasy he fed;
And though it was no opiate, slumber crept
Upon him by degrees, and so he slept.

28

He woke betimes;° and, as may be supposed, *early*
Pondered upon his visitant or vision,
And whether it ought not to be disclosed,
At risk of being quizzed for superstition.
The more he thought, the more his mind was posed:
In the mean time, his valet, whose precision
Was great, because his master brooked no less,
Knocked to inform him it was time to dress.

29

He dressed; and like young people, he was wont
To take some trouble with his toilet,[4] but
This morning rather spent less time upon't;
Aside his very mirror soon was put;
His curls fell negligently o'er his front,
His clothes were not curbed to their usual cut,
His very neckcloth's Gordian knot[5] was tied
Almost an hair's breadth too much on one side.

...

111

The night was as before: he was undrest,
Saving his night gown, which is an undress;
Completely "sans culotte,"[6] and without vest;
In short, he hardly could be clothed with less:
But apprehensive of his spectral guest,

---

[1] *Burnt, and not blue* According to tradition, blue flame is a sign of ghosts; *use* Usually do.

[2] *a long eulogy ... blacking* I.e., an extensive advertisement for a brand of shoe polish.

[3] *Horne Tooke* John Horne Tooke (1736–1812), English political reformer.

[4] *toilet* I.e., personal grooming.

[5] *Gordian knot* According to legend, the Gordian knot was so complex it was impossible to untie.

[6] *sans culotte* Literally, without breeches; usually, the expression refers to an impoverished person or to a French revolutionary.

He sate, with feelings awkward to express,
(By those who have not had such visitations)
Expectant of the ghost's fresh operations.

112

And not in vain he listened—Hush! what's that?
I see—I see—Ah, no!—'tis not—yet 'tis—
Ye powers! it is the—the—the—Pooh! the cat!
The devil may take that stealthy pace of his!
So like a spiritual pit-a-pat,
Or tiptoe of an amatory Miss,
Gliding the first time to a rendezvous,
And dreading the chaste echoes of her shoe.

113

Again—what is't? The wind? No, no,—this time
It is the sable Friar as before,
With awful footsteps regular as rhyme,
Or (as rhymes may be in these days) much more.
Again, through shadows of the night sublime,
When deep sleep fell on men, and the world wore
The starry darkness round her like a girdle
Spangled with gems—the monk made his blood curdle.

114

A noise like to wet fingers drawn on glass,
Which sets the teeth on edge; and a slight clatter
Like showers which on the midnight gusts will pass,
Sounding like very supernatural water,
Came over Juan's ear, which throbbed, alas!
For immaterialism's a serious matter;
So that even those whose faith is the most great
In souls immortal, shun them *tête-à-tête*.

115

Were his eyes open?—Yes! and his mouth too.
Surprise has this effect—to make one dumb,
Yet leave the gate which Eloquence slips through
As wide as if a long speech were to come.
Nigh and more nigh the awful echoes drew,
Tremendous to a mortal tympanum:
His eyes were open, and (as was before
Stated) his mouth. What opened next?—the door.

116

It opened with a most infernal creak,
Like that of hell. "Lasciate ogni speranza
Voi che entrate!"[1] The hinge seemed to speak,
Dreadful as Dante's rhima,[2] or this stanza;
Or—but all words upon such themes are weak;
A single shade's sufficient to entrance a
Hero—for what is substance to a Spirit?
Or how is't *matter* trembles to come near it?

117

The door flew wide, not swiftly—but, as fly
The sea-gulls, with a steady, sober flight—
And then swung back; nor close—but stood awry,
Half letting in long shadows on the light,
Which still in Juan's candlesticks burned high,
For he had two, both tolerably bright,
And in the door-way, darkening Darkness, stood
The sable Friar in his solemn hood.

…

120

Juan put forth one arm—Eternal Powers!
It touched no soul, nor body, but the wall,
On which the moonbeams fell in silvery showers
Checkered with all the tracery of the hall;
He shuddered, as no doubt the bravest cowers
When he can't tell what 'tis that doth appal.
How odd, a single hobgoblin's non-entity
Should cause more fear than a whole host's identity!

121

But still the shade remained; the blue eyes glared,
And rather variably for stony death;
Yet one thing rather good the grave had spared,
The ghost had a remarkably sweet breath.
A straggling curl showed he had been fair-haired;
A red lip, with two rows of pearls beneath
Gleamed forth, as through the casement's° ivy shroud *window*
The moon peeped, just escaped from a grey cloud.

[1] *Lasciate … entrate* Italian: Abandon all hope / You who enter here" (Dante, *Inferno* 3.9).

[2] *rhima* Reference to *terza rima*, the stanza form of Dante's *Inferno*.

122

And Juan, puzzled, but still curious, thrust
His other arm forth—Wonder upon wonder!
It pressed upon a hard but glowing bust,
Which beat as if there was a warm heart under.
He found, as people on most trials must,
That he had made at first a silly blunder,
And that in his confusion he had caught
Only the wall, instead of what he sought.

123

The ghost, if ghost it were, seemed a sweet soul
As ever lurked beneath a holy hood:
A dimpled chin, a neck of ivory, stole
Forth into something much like flesh and blood;
Back fell the sable frock and dreary cowl,
And they revealed—alas! that ere they should!
In full, voluptuous, but *not o'er*grown bulk,
The phantom of her frolic Grace—Fitz-Fulke!

from Ann Radcliffe, "On the Supernatural in Poetry" (1826)

A few years after Radcliffe died, the following essay was published in *The New Monthly*. Taking the form of a conversation between characters named W—— and S——, the essay draws most of its examples from depictions of the supernatural in Shakespeare's tragedies; the following excerpt contrasts the depictions of ghosts in *Macbeth* and *Hamlet*. In making this contrast, Radcliffe draws her famous distinction between "horror" and "terror."

… [W——:] "… Who ever suffered for the ghost of Banquo,[1] the gloomy and sublime kind of terror, which that of *Hamlet*[2] calls forth? … There, though deep pity mingles with our surprise and horror, we experience a far less degree of interest, and that interest too of an inferior kind. The union of grandeur and obscurity, which Mr. Burke[3] describes as a sort of tranquillity tinged with terror, and which causes the sublime, is to be found only in *Hamlet*; or in scenes where circumstances of the same kind prevail."

"That may be," said Mr. S——, "and I perceive you are not one of those who contend that obscurity does not make any part of the sublime."

"They must be men of very cold imaginations," said W——, "with whom certainty is more terrible than surmise. Terror and horror are so far opposite, that the first expands the soul, and awakens the faculties to a high degree of life; the other contracts, freezes, and nearly annihilates them. I apprehend that neither Shakespeare nor Milton by their fictions, nor Mr. Burke by his reasoning, anywhere looked to positive horror as a source of the sublime, though they all agree that terror is a very high one; and where lies the great difference between horror and terror, but in the uncertainty and obscurity, that accompany the first, respecting the dreaded evil?" …

---

[1] *Banquo* Character in *Macbeth* whose ghost appears in Act 3, Scene 4.

[2] *Hamlet* Hamlet's father's ghost appears in *Hamlet* 1.1, 1.4–5, and 3.4.

[3] *Mr. Burke* See Edmund Burke, *A Philosophical Enquiry into the Origin of Our Ideas of the Sublime and Beautiful* (1757), especially the excerpts from Part 2 included elsewhere in this anthology.

WILLIAM WORDSWORTH

1770 – 1850

Since about 1815, William Wordsworth has been acknowledged as a central figure in the English Romantic Movement. *Lyrical Ballads*, produced in conjunction with Samuel Taylor Coleridge though largely Wordsworth's project, marks a decisive break with the formalism and neo-classicism of eighteenth-century literature. It became the touchstone of a new literary sensibility that gave its faith to the benevolence of feeling, and of the vehicle it associated most with feeling: a poetry of sincerity. And it established the idea of Nature as the measure by which to judge whether a poem's expression of feeling was genuine or not. Wordworth's poems respond powerfully to the major developments of his day—including the French Revolution, war, and industrialization. That response, however, was marked by many tensions and contradictions.

Wordsworth was born in the Lake District of England, in West Cumberland, and spent his boyhood absorbing the natural beauty around him. The death of his mother when he was eight, and of his father only five years later, unsettled the lives of William and his four siblings. Their situation was worsened by the fact that the only substantial legacy their father left was a sum owed to him by his employer, Lord Lonsdale, who withheld the money until his own death in 1802. Along with his three brothers, William was sent to school at Hawkshead. His sister, Dorothy—later his confidante and source of inspiration, in addition to being a fellow writer whose work would influence his—found herself shifting among various relatives.

At Hawkshead Wordsworth and his brothers boarded at the home of Ann Tyson, who became a surrogate mother to Wordsworth, encouraging his love of nature and tolerating his habit of roaming the countryside. Wordsworth paid close attention to and frequently conversed with the town's working people. His observations would inform the representation of many of the humble rural characters who appear in his poetry. Leaving the Lake District for the first time in 1787, he entered St. John's College, Cambridge. During this period he made two walking tours with his friend Robert Jones, first through France and the Alps during a crucial period of the French Revolution, and later through Wales (excursions described in Books Six and Fourteen respectively of the 1850 *Prelude*).

These adventures quickened Wordsworth's belief in the healing powers of nature and of his own responsive imagination, and they also awakened radical sentiments. While traveling in France in 1791–92 he was swept up in the heady excitement that followed the French Revolution (1789). Young Wordsworth also fell in love with Annette Vallon, whose politics (Royalist) and religion (Catholic) he did not share, and they produced a daughter, Caroline, out of wedlock. Too poor to remain in France, which was now at war with England, Wordsworth returned to his country a divided man, his disillusionment growing as France fell into the Reign of Terror.

Financial concerns fed Wordsworth's doubts about his political convictions and his choice of vocation. In 1795, however, Wordsworth received a legacy of £900 from a friend, Raisley Calvert, whom he had nursed through his final illness. When, in 1797, other friends offered a rent-free cottage in Alfoxden, this sum enabled Wordsworth and his sister Dorothy to set up housekeeping there, with his friend Coleridge not far away at Nether Stowey. (Describing his relationship with Coleridge in an 1832 letter to a friend, Wordsworth declared, "He and my beloved sister are the two beings to whom my intellect is most indebted.") Long walks and talks with Coleridge resulted in an extraordinary literary collaboration, *Lyrical Ballads, with a Few Other Poems* (1798), a slender, anonymously published volume that opens with Coleridge's literary ballad "The Rime of the Ancient Mariner" and closes with Wordsworth's blank-verse meditation "Lines, Composed a Few Miles above Tintern Abbey." The volume sought to combat what the authors saw as the increasingly marginal position of the poet in society, and the overly artificial language on which poetry relied.

As Coleridge and Wordsworth had expected, critics attacked the tone and subject matter of the volume. In the Preface to the Second Edition (1800)—perhaps the most famous poetic manifesto in the language—Wordsworth explained and defended the decision he made "to choose incidents and situations from common life, and to relate or describe them, throughout, as far as was possible, in a selection of language really used by men." In poems such as "Michael" and "The Brothers" (added to the 1800 edition of *Lyrical Ballads*), Wordsworth depicts the Lake District's inhabitants as strong and dignified in the face of hardship, living in harmony with the natural world, removed from the taint of urban superficiality. Wordsworth was thus in an important sense what he is often taken to be, a "poet of nature." But his main object was not to depict directly "the beautiful and permanent forms of nature" but rather to explore how "the passions of men are incorporated with" such forms, and to depict the "ennobling interchange" between the natural world and the mental world. It is the mind, ultimately, that was Wordsworth's "haunt, and the main region of my song."

After a brief, inhospitable stay in Germany in 1798–99, during which Wordsworth wrote the "Lucy" poems (the identity of "Lucy" is unknown) and Coleridge assimilated German philosophy, Wordsworth and his sister returned to England and took up residence at Dove Cottage in Grasmere. Here Dorothy kept journals that have since become famous in their own right, and Wordsworth composed some of his finest lyrics, including "Resolution and Independence," "The Solitary Reaper" (a memorial of his walking tour through Scotland), and "Ode: Intimations of Immortality from Recollections of Early Childhood," all of which were later published in his *Poems, in Two Volumes* (1807).

In 1802, Wordsworth married a childhood friend, Mary Hutchinson, and began a period of relative tranquility and poetic fruitfulness, although these years were not without grief and disappointment. By 1812, two of his five children were dead, his brother John had been lost at sea, his friendship with Coleridge (whose health was deteriorating as his opium addiction deepened) had become strained, and *Poems, in Two Volumes* had suffered damaging reviews.

Then in 1814 Wordsworth published *The Excursion*, a long blank-verse meditation that was a forecast and first installment of his planned epic, *The Recluse*. The book was poorly reviewed, even ridiculed. Nevertheless, Wordsworth by this time had gained a growing audience of devoted admirers, and his reputation from this low point began to establish itself firmly.

Like *The Excursion*, *The Prelude*, which Wordsworth had begun in 1799, was intended as a subsidiary piece that would be incorporated into *The Recluse*. He completed a two-book version of *The Prelude* in 1799 and a much expanded thirteen-book poem in 1805. He then continued to revise the poem for the rest of his life. This epic in blank verse—which Coleridge, upon hearing it, declared a "prophetic Lay"—describes the growth of the poet's mind from earliest memories to adulthood. By the end of his journey in the poem, Wordsworth reaffirms both providential design and the revolutionary potential of the imagination. *The Prelude* is a great, long lesson showing "how the mind of Man becomes / A thousand times more beautiful than the earth / On which he dwells."

In 1813, the Wordsworth household left Grasmere for the more expansive environs of Rydal Mount. There the poet, his beloved sister, and his wife lived out their days. The move was made possible by Wordsworth's improved financial situation, the result of a literary patronage granted by Lord Lonsdale and a position as Stamp Distributor for Westmorland. In the eyes of the younger generation (including Percy Shelley, Lord Byron, and Robert Browning), the patronage and the government position seemed to transform the once radical poet into a hypocritical and complacent hireling. As they saw it, Wordsworth had abandoned his early commitment to be the voice of the disenfranchised and the poor. Increasingly skeptical of external revolutions and political agitation, Wordsworth saw himself not as having abandoned his ideals but rather as having internalized—or spiritualized—his commitment to truth and liberty.

During his middle and old age Wordsworth wrote numerous sonnets, including *Ecclesiastical Sketches* (1822), which takes England's religious history as a primary subject. Having begun as a poetic and political revolutionary, he ended his life an iconic figure of the early Victorian era. Queen Victoria crowned him her Poet Laureate in 1843, and admirers flocked to the Lake District to seek him out in his home. The influence of his poetic style remained strong until well into the twentieth century, and Victorian writers of prose and poetry alike—including Tennyson, Charles Dickens, George Eliot, and Elizabeth Gaskell—acknowledged their debt to the life he had breathed into ways of thinking about nature, poetic feeling, and the human imagination.

⌘⌘⌘

from *Lyrical Ballads, 1798*

Advertisement

It is the honourable characteristic of Poetry that its materials are to be found in every subject which can interest the human mind. The evidence of this fact is to be sought, not in the writings of Critics, but in those of Poets themselves.

The majority of the following poems are to be considered as experiments. They were written chiefly with a view to ascertain how far the language of conversation in the middle and lower classes of society is adapted to the purposes of poetic pleasure. Readers accustomed to the gaudiness and inane phraseology of many modern writers, if they persist in reading this book to its conclusion, will perhaps frequently have to struggle with feelings of strangeness and awkwardness: they will look round for poetry, and will be induced to enquire by what species of courtesy these attempts can be permitted to assume that title. It is desirable that such readers, for their own sakes, should not suffer the solitary word Poetry, a word of very disputed meaning, to stand in the way of their gratification; but that, while they are perusing this book, they should ask themselves if it contains a natural delineation of human passions, human characters, and human incidents; and if the answer be favourable to the author's wishes, that they should consent to be pleased in spite of that most dreadful enemy to our pleasures, our own pre-established codes of decision.

Readers of superior judgment may disapprove of the style in which many of these pieces are executed. It must be expected that many lines and phrases will not exactly suit their taste. It will perhaps appear to them that, wishing to avoid the prevalent fault of the day, the author has sometimes descended too low, and that many of his expressions are too familiar, and not of sufficient dignity. It is apprehended that the more conversant the reader is with our elder writers, and with those in modern times who have been the most successful in painting manners and passions, the fewer complaints of this kind will he have to make.

An accurate taste in poetry, and in all the other arts, Sir Joshua Reynolds[1] has observed, is an acquired talent, which can only be produced by severe thought, and a long continued intercourse with the best models of composition. This is mentioned not with so ridiculous a purpose as to prevent the most inexperienced reader from judging for himself; but merely to temper the rashness of decision, and to suggest that if poetry be a subject on which much time has not been bestowed, the judgment may be erroneous, and that in many cases it necessarily will be so.

The tale of Goody Blake and Harry Gill is founded on a well-authenticated fact which happened in Warwickshire. Of the other poems in the collection, it may be proper to say that they are either absolute inventions of the author, or facts which took place within his personal observation or that of his friends. The poem of the Thorn, as the reader will soon discover, is not supposed to be spoken in the author's own person: the character of the loquacious narrator will sufficiently show itself in the course of the story. The Rime of the Ancyent Marinere was professedly written in imitation of the style, as well as of the spirit of the elder poets; but with a few exceptions, the Author believes that the language adopted in it has been equally intelligible for these three last centuries. The lines entitled Expostulation and Reply, and those which follow, arose out of conversation with a friend who was somewhat unreasonably attached to modern books of moral philosophy.

[1] *Sir Joshua Reynolds* Renowned portrait and history painter, and first president of the Royal Academy (1723–92).

We Are Seven

A simple child, dear brother Jim,
That lightly draws its breath,
And feels its life in every limb,
What should it know of death?

I met a little cottage girl,
She was eight years old, she said;
Her hair was thick with many a curl
That cluster'd round her head.

She had a rustic, woodland air,
And she was wildly clad;
Her eyes were fair, and very fair
—Her beauty made me glad.

"Sisters and brothers, little maid,
How many may you be?"
"How many? seven in all," she said,
And wondering looked at me.

"And where are they, I pray you tell?"
She answered, "Seven are we,
And two of us at Conway[2] dwell,
And two are gone to sea.

"Two of us in the church-yard lie,
My sister and my brother,
And in the church-yard cottage, I
Dwell near them with my mother."

"You say that two at Conway dwell,
And two are gone to sea,
Yet you are seven; I pray you tell
Sweet Maid, how this may be?"

Then did the little Maid reply,
"Seven boys and girls are we;

[2] *Conway* Seaport of northern Wales.

Two of us in the church-yard lie,
Beneath the church-yard tree."

"You run about, my little maid,
Your limbs they are alive;
If two are in the church-yard laid,
Then ye are only five."

"Their graves are green, they may be seen,"
The little Maid replied,
"Twelve steps or more from my mother's door,
And they are side by side.

"My stockings there I often knit,
My 'kerchief there I hem;
And there upon the ground I sit—
I sit and sing to them.

"And often after sunset, Sir,
When it is light and fair,
I take my little porringer,[1]
And eat my supper there.

"The first that died was little Jane;
In bed she moaning lay,
Till God released her of her pain,
And then she went away.

"So in the church-yard she was laid,
And all the summer dry,
Together round her grave we played,
My brother John and I.

"And when the ground was white with snow,
And I could run and slide,
My brother John was forced to go,
And he lies by her side."

"How many are you then," said I,
"If they two are in Heaven?"
The little Maiden did reply,
"O Master! we are seven."

"But they are dead; those two are dead!
Their spirits are in heaven!"
'Twas throwing words away; for still
The little Maid would have her will,
And said, "Nay, we are seven!"

[1] *porringer* Small metal or earthenware basin from which broth or porridge is eaten.

Lines Written in Early Spring

I heard a thousand blended notes,
While in a grove I sat reclined,
In that sweet mood when pleasant thoughts
Bring sad thoughts to the mind.

To her fair works did nature link
The human soul that through me ran;
And much it griev'd my heart to think
What man has made of man.

Through primrose-tufts, in that sweet bower,
The periwinkle trail'd its wreathes;
And 'tis my faith that every flower
Enjoys the air it breathes.

The birds around me hopp'd and play'd:
Their thoughts I cannot measure,
But the least motion which they made,
It seem'd a thrill of pleasure.

The budding twigs spread out their fan,
To catch the breezy air;
And I must think, do all I can,
That there was pleasure there.

If I these thoughts may not prevent,
If such be of my creed the plan,
Have I not reason to lament
What man has made of man?

The Thorn[1]

1

There is a thorn;° it looks so old, *thorn bush*
In truth you'd find it hard to say,
How it could ever have been young,
It looks so old and grey.
Not higher than a two-years' child,
It stands erect this aged thorn;
No leaves it has, no thorny points;
It is a mass of knotted joints,
A wretched thing forlorn.
It stands erect, and like a stone
With lichens it is overgrown.

2

Like rock or stone, it is o'ergrown
With lichens to the very top,
And hung with heavy tufts of moss,
A melancholy crop:
Up from the earth these mosses creep,
And this poor thorn they clasp it round
So close, you'd say that they were bent
With plain and manifest intent,
To drag it to the ground;
And all had joined in one endeavour
To bury this poor thorn for ever.

3

High on a mountain's highest ridge,
Where oft the stormy winter gale
Cuts like a scythe, while through the clouds
It sweeps from vale to vale;
Not five yards from the mountain-path,
This thorn you on your left espy;
And to the left, three yards beyond,
You see a little muddy pond
Of water, never dry;
I've measured it from side to side:
'Tis three feet long, and two feet wide.

4

And close beside this aged thorn,
There is a fresh and lovely sight,
A beauteous heap, a hill of moss,
Just half a foot in height.
All lovely colours there you see,
All colours that were ever seen,
And mossy network too is there,
As if by hand of lady fair
The work had woven been,
And cups,° the darlings of the eye, *blossoms*
So deep is their vermilion° dye. *red*

5

Ah me! what lovely tints are there!
Of olive-green and scarlet bright,
In spikes, in branches, and in stars,
Green, red, and pearly white.
This heap of earth o'ergrown with moss,
Which close beside the thorn you see,
So fresh in all its beauteous dyes,
Is like an infant's grave in size
As like as like can be:
But never, never any where,
An infant's grave was half so fair.

6

Now would you see this aged thorn,
This pond and beauteous hill of moss,
You must take care and choose your time
The mountain when to cross.
For oft there sits, between the heap
That's like an infant's grave in size,
And that same pond of which I spoke,
A woman in a scarlet cloak,
And to herself she cries,
"Oh misery! oh misery!
Oh woe is me! oh misery!"

[1] [Wordsworth's note] Arose from my observing, on the ridge of Quantock Hill, on a stormy day a thorn which I had often passed in calm and bright weather without noticing it. I said to myself, "Cannot I by some invention do as much to make this Thorn permanently an impressive object as the storm has made it to my eyes at this moment?"

7

At all times of the day and night
This wretched woman thither goes,
And she is known to every star,
And every wind that blows;
And there beside the thorn she sits
When the blue day-light's in the skies,
And when the whirlwind's on the hill,
Or frosty air is keen and still,
And to herself she cries,
"Oh misery! oh misery!
Oh woe is me! oh misery!"

8

"Now wherefore thus, by day and night,
In rain, in tempest, and in snow,
Thus to the dreary mountain-top
Does this poor woman go?
And why sits she beside the thorn
When the blue day-light's in the sky,
Or when the whirlwind's on the hill,
Or frosty air is keen and still,
And wherefore does she cry?
Oh wherefore? wherefore? tell me why
Does she repeat that doleful cry?"

9

I cannot tell; I wish I could;
For the true reason no one knows,
But if you'd gladly view the spot,
The spot to which she goes;
The heap that's like an infant's grave,
The pond—and thorn, so old and grey;
Pass by her door—'tis seldom shut—
And if you see her in her hut,
Then to the spot away!
I never heard of such as dare
Approach the spot when she is there.

10

"But wherefore to the mountain-top
Can this unhappy woman go,
Whatever star is in the skies,
Whatever wind may blow?"
Nay rack your brain—'tis all in vain,
I'll tell you every thing I know;
But to the thorn, and to the pond
Which is a little step beyond,
I wish that you would go:
Perhaps when you are at the place
You something of her tale may trace.

11

I'll give you the best help I can:
Before you up the mountain go,
Up to the dreary mountain-top,
I'll tell you all I know.
'Tis now some two and twenty years,
Since she (her name is Martha Ray)
Gave with a maiden's true good will
Her company to Stephen Hill;
And she was blithe and gay,
And she was happy, happy still
Whene'er she thought of Stephen Hill.

12

And they had fix'd the wedding-day,
The morning that must wed them both;
But Stephen to another maid
Had sworn another oath;
And with this other maid to church
Unthinking Stephen went—
Poor Martha! on that woeful day
A cruel, cruel fire, they say,
Into her bones was sent:
It dried her body like a cinder,
And almost turn'd her brain to tinder.[1]

13

They say, full six months after this,
While yet the summer leaves were green,
She to the mountain-top would go,
And there was often seen.
'Tis said, a child was in her womb,

[1] *tinder* Dry, flammable substance that will take fire from a spark.

As now to any eye was plain;
She was with child, and she was mad,
Yet often she was sober sad
From her exceeding pain.
Oh me! ten thousand times I'd rather
That he had died, that cruel father!

14

Sad case for such a brain to hold
Communion with a stirring child!
Sad case, as you may think, for one
Who had a brain so wild!
Last Christmas when we talked of this,
Old Farmer Simpson did maintain,
That in her womb the infant wrought
About its mother's heart, and brought
Her senses back again:
And when at last her time drew near,
Her looks were calm, her senses clear.

15

No more I know, I wish I did,
And I would tell it all to you;
For what became of this poor child
There's none that ever knew:
And if a child was born or no,
There's no one that could ever tell;
And if 'twas born alive or dead,
There's no one knows, as I have said,
But some remember well,
That Martha Ray about this time
Would up the mountain often climb.

16

And all that winter, when at night
The wind blew from the mountain-peak,
'Twas worth your while, though in the dark,
The church-yard path to seek:
For many a time and oft were heard
Cries coming from the mountain-head,
Some plainly living voices were,
And others, I've heard many swear,
Were voices of the dead:
I cannot think, whate'er they say,
They had to do with Martha Ray.

17

But that she goes to this old thorn,
The thorn which I've described to you,
And there sits in a scarlet cloak,
I will be sworn is true.
For one day with my telescope,
To view the ocean wide and bright,
When to this country first I came,
Ere I had heard of Martha's name,
I climbed the mountain's height:
A storm came on, and I could see
No object higher than my knee.

18

'Twas mist and rain, and storm and rain,
No screen, no fence could I discover,
And then the wind! in faith, it was
A wind full ten times over.
I looked around, I thought I saw
A jutting crag, and off I ran,
Head-foremost, through the driving rain,
The shelter of the crag to gain,
And, as I am a man,
Instead of jutting crag, I found
A woman seated on the ground.

19

I did not speak—I saw her face,
Her face it was enough for me;
I turned about and heard her cry,
"O misery! O misery!"
And there she sits, until the moon
Through half the clear blue sky will go,
And when the little breezes make
The waters of the pond to shake,
As all the country know,
She shudders and you hear her cry,
"Oh misery! oh misery!"

20

"But what's the thorn? and what's the pond?
And what's the hill of moss to her?
And what's the creeping breeze that comes
The little pond to stir?"
I cannot tell; but some will say
She hanged her baby on the tree,
Some say she drowned it in the pond,
Which is a little step beyond,
But all and each agree,
The little babe was buried there,
Beneath that hill of moss so fair.

21

I've heard the scarlet moss is red
With drops of that poor infant's blood;
But kill a new-born infant thus!
I do not think she could.
Some say, if to the pond you go,
And fix on it a steady view,
The shadow of a babe you trace,
A baby and a baby's face,
And that it looks at you;
Whene'er you look on it, 'tis plain
The baby looks at you again.

22

And some had sworn an oath that she
Should be to public justice brought;
And for the little infant's bones
With spades they would have sought.
But then the beauteous hill of moss
Before their eyes began to stir;
And for full fifty yards around,
The grass it shook upon the ground;
But all do still aver
The little babe is buried there,
Beneath that hill of moss so fair.

23

I cannot tell how this may be,
But plain it is, the thorn is bound
With heavy tufts of moss, that strive
To drag it to the ground.
And this I know, full many a time,
When she was on the mountain high,
By day, and in the silent night,
When all the stars shone clear and bright,
That I have heard her cry,
"Oh misery! oh misery!
Oh woe is me! oh misery!"

Expostulation and Reply[1]

"Why William, on that old grey stone,
Thus for the length of half a day,
Why William, sit you thus alone,
And dream your time away?

"Where are your books? that light bequeath'd
To beings else forlorn and blind!
Up! Up! and drink the spirit breath'd
From dead men to their kind.

"You look round on your mother earth,
As if she for no purpose bore you;
As if you were her first-born birth,
And none had lived before you!"

One morning thus, by Esthwaite lake,[2]
When life was sweet I knew not why,
To me my good friend Matthew spake,
And thus I made reply.

"The eye it cannot choose but see,
We cannot bid the ear be still;
Our bodies feel, where'er they be,
Against, or with our will.

[1] *Expostulation and Reply* As Wordsworth suggests in the advertisement to *Lyrical Ballads*, this poem is based on a conversation he had with the writer and critic William Hazlitt (1778–1830).

[2] *Esthwaite lake* Located at Hawkshead (in England's Lake District), where Wordsworth attended grammar school. The real conversation that inspired the poem took place not at Hawkshead but at Alfoxden.

"Nor less I deem that there are powers,
Which of themselves our minds impress,
That we can feed this mind of ours,
In a wise passiveness.

"Think you, mid all this mighty sum
Of things for ever speaking,
That nothing of itself will come,
But we must still be seeking?

"—Then ask not wherefore, here, alone,
Conversing as I may,
I sit upon this old grey stone,
And dream my time away."

The Tables Turned

An Evening Scene on the Same Subject

Up! up! my friend, and clear your looks,
Why all this toil and trouble?
Up! up! my friend, and quit your books,
Or surely you'll grow double.[1]

The sun above the mountain's head,
A freshening lustre mellow,
Through all the long green fields has spread,
His first sweet evening yellow.

Books! 'tis a dull and endless strife,
Come, hear the woodland linnet,
How sweet his music; on my life
There's more of wisdom in it.

And hark! how blithe the throstle° sings! *thrush*
And he is no mean preacher;
Come forth into the light of things,
Let Nature be your teacher.

She has a world of ready wealth,
Our minds and hearts to bless—
Spontaneous wisdom breathed by health,
Truth breathed by cheerfulness.

One impulse from a vernal wood
May teach you more of man;
Of moral evil and of good,
Than all the sages can.

Sweet is the lore which nature brings;
Our meddling intellect
Mishapes the beauteous forms of things
—We murder to dissect.

Enough of science and of art;
Close up these barren leaves;
Come forth, and bring with you a heart
That watches and receives.

Lines Written a Few Miles above Tintern Abbey

On Revisiting the Banks of the Wye during a Tour, July 13, 1798[2]

Five years have passed; five summers, with the length
Of five long winters! and again I hear
These waters, rolling from their mountain-springs
With a sweet inland murmur.[3] Once again
Do I behold these steep and lofty cliffs,
Which on a wild secluded scene impress
Thoughts of more deep seclusion; and connect

[1] *double* Doubled over.

[2] *Lines … 1798* In a later commentary on this poem, Wordsworth writes that "No poem of mine was composed under circumstances more pleasant for me to remember than this. I began it upon leaving Tintern, after crossing the Wye, and concluded it just as I was entering Bristol in the evening, after a ramble of 4 or 5 days, with my sister. Not a line of it was altered, and not any part of it was written down till I reached Bristol."

[3] [Wordsworth's note] The river is not affected by the tides a few miles above Tintern.

The landscape with the quiet of the sky.
The day is come when I again repose
Here, under this dark sycamore, and view
These plots of cottage-ground, these orchard-tufts,
Which, at this season, with their unripe fruits,
Among the woods and copses lose themselves,
Nor, with their green and simple hue, disturb
The wild green landscape. Once again I see
These hedge-rows, hardly hedge-rows, little lines
Of sportive wood run wild; these pastoral farms
Green to the very door; and wreaths of smoke
Sent up, in silence, from among the trees,
With some uncertain notice, as might seem,
Of vagrant dwellers in the houseless woods,
Or of some hermit's cave, where by his fire
The hermit sits alone.
Though absent long,
These forms of beauty have not been to me
As is a landscape to a blind man's eye:
But oft, in lonely rooms, and 'mid the din
Of towns and cities, I have owed to them,
In hours of weariness, sensations sweet,
Felt in the blood, and felt along the heart,
And passing even into my purer mind
With tranquil restoration—feelings too
Of unremembered pleasure; such, perhaps,
As may have had no trivial influence
On that best portion of a good man's life;
His little, nameless, unremembered acts
Of kindness and of love. Nor less, I trust,
To them I may have owed another gift,
Of aspect more sublime; that blessed mood,
In which the burthen of the mystery,
In which the heavy and the weary weight
Of all this unintelligible world
Is lightened—that serene and blessed mood,
In which the affections gently lead us on,
Until, the breath of this corporeal frame,[1]
And even the motion of our human blood
Almost suspended, we are laid asleep
In body, and become a living soul:
While with an eye made quiet by the power
Of harmony, and the deep power of joy,
We see into the life of things.
If this
Be but a vain belief, yet, oh! how oft,
In darkness, and amid the many shapes
Of joyless daylight; when the fretful stir
Unprofitable, and the fever of the world,
Have hung upon the beatings of my heart,
How oft, in spirit, have I turned to thee
O sylvan Wye! Thou wanderer through the woods,
How often has my spirit turned to thee!

And now, with gleams of half-extinguished thought,
With many recognitions dim and faint,
And somewhat of a sad perplexity,
The picture of the mind revives again:
While here I stand, not only with the sense
Of present pleasure, but with pleasing thoughts
That in this moment there is life and food
For future years. And so I dare to hope
Though changed, no doubt, from what I was, when first
I came among these hills; when like a roe° *deer*
I bounded o'er the mountains, by the sides
Of the deep rivers, and the lonely streams,
Wherever nature led; more like a man
Flying from something that he dreads, than one
Who sought the thing he loved. For nature then
(The coarser pleasures of my boyish days,
And their glad animal movements all gone by)
To me was all in all.—I cannot paint
What then I was. The sounding cataract
Haunted me like a passion: the tall rock,
The mountain, and the deep and gloomy wood,
Their colours and their forms, were then to me
An appetite: a feeling and a love,
That had no need of a remoter charm,
By thought supplied, or any interest
Unborrowed from the eye. That time is past,
And all its aching joys are now no more,
And all its dizzy raptures. Not for this

[1] *corporeal frame* Physical body.

Faint[1] I, nor mourn nor murmur: other gifts
Have followed, for such loss, I would believe,
Abundant recompence. For I have learned
To look on nature, not as in the hour
Of thoughtless youth, but hearing oftentimes
The still, sad music of humanity,
Not harsh nor grating, though of ample power
To chasten and subdue. And I have felt
A presence that disturbs me with the joy
Of elevated thoughts; a sense sublime
Of something far more deeply interfused,
Whose dwelling is the light of setting suns,
And the round ocean, and the living air,
And the blue sky, and in the mind of man,
A motion and a spirit, that impels
All thinking things, all objects of all thought,
And rolls through all things. Therefore am I still
A lover of the meadows and the woods
And mountains; and of all that we behold
From this green earth; of all the mighty world
Of eye and ear, both what they half create,
And what perceive; well pleased to recognize
In nature and the language of the sense,[2]
The anchor of my purest thoughts, the nurse,
The guide, the guardian of my heart, and soul
Of all my moral being.
Nor, perchance,
If I were not thus taught, should I the more
Suffer my genial° spirits to decay: *creative*
For thou art with me, here, upon the banks
Of this fair river; thou, my dearest Friend,[3]
My dear, dear Friend, and in thy voice I catch
The language of my former heart, and read
My former pleasures in the shooting lights
Of thy wild eyes. Oh! yet a little while
May I behold in thee what I was once,
My dear, dear Sister! And this prayer I make,
Knowing that Nature never did betray
The heart that loved her; 'tis her privilege,
Through all the years of this our life, to lead
From joy to joy: for she can so inform
The mind that is within us, so impress
With quietness and beauty, and so feed
With lofty thoughts, that neither evil tongues,
Rash judgments, nor the sneers of selfish men,
Nor greetings where no kindness is, nor all
The dreary intercourse of daily life,
Shall e'er prevail against us, or disturb
Our cheerful faith that all which we behold
Is full of blessings. Therefore let the moon
Shine on thee in thy solitary walk;
And let the misty mountain winds be free
To blow against thee: and in after years,
When these wild ecstasies shall be matured
Into a sober pleasure, when thy mind
Shall be a mansion for all lovely forms,
Thy memory be as a dwelling-place
For all sweet sounds and harmonies; Oh! then,
If solitude, or fear, or pain, or grief,
Should be thy portion,[4] with what healing thoughts
Of tender joy wilt thou remember me,
And these my exhortations! Nor, perchance,
If I should be, where I no more can hear
Thy voice, nor catch from thy wild eyes these gleams
Of past existence, wilt thou then forget
That on the banks of this delightful stream
We stood together; and that I, so long
A worshipper of Nature, hither came,
Unwearied in that service: rather say
With warmer love, oh! with far deeper zeal
Of holier love. Nor wilt thou then forget,
That after many wanderings, many years
Of absence, these steep woods and lofty cliffs,
And this green pastoral landscape, were to me
More dear, both for themselves, and for thy sake.
—1798

[1] *Faint* Lose heart; grow weak.

[2] *the language of the sense* What the senses tell us.

[3] *my dearest Friend* I.e., Dorothy Wordsworth, Wordsworth's sister.

[4] *portion* Alloted fate.

from *Lyrical Ballads, 1800, 1802*

from Preface[1]

The first Volume of these Poems has already been submitted to general perusal. It was published as an experiment, which, I hoped, might be of some use to ascertain how far, by fitting to metrical arrangement a selection of the real language of men in a state of vivid sensation, that sort of pleasure and that quantity of pleasure may be imparted, which a Poet may rationally endeavour to impart.

I had formed no very inaccurate estimate of the probable effect of those Poems: I flattered myself that they who should be pleased with them would read them with more than common pleasure: and, on the other hand, I was well aware that by those who should dislike them they would be read with more than common dislike. The result has differed from my expectation in this only, that I have pleased a greater number than I ventured to hope I should please.

For the sake of variety, and from a consciousness of my own weakness, I was induced to request the assistance of a Friend,[2] who furnished me with the Poems of the *Ancient Mariner*, the *Foster-Mother's Tale*, the *Nightingale*, and the Poem entitled *Love*. I should not, however, have requested this assistance, had I not believed that the Poems of my Friend would in a great measure have the same tendency as my own, and that, though there would be found a difference, there would be found no discordance in the colours of our style; as our opinions on the subject of poetry do almost entirely coincide.

Several of my Friends are anxious for the success of these Poems from a belief that, if the views with which they were composed were indeed realized, a class of Poetry would be produced, well adapted to interest mankind permanently, and not unimportant in the multiplicity, and in the quality of its moral relations: and on this account they have advised me to prefix a systematic defence of the theory upon which the poems were written. But I was unwilling to undertake the task, because I knew that on this occasion the Reader would look coldly upon my arguments, since I might be suspected of having been principally influenced by the selfish and foolish hope of *reasoning* him into an approbation of these particular Poems: and I was still more unwilling to undertake the task, because, adequately to display my opinions, and fully to enforce my arguments, would require a space wholly disproportionate to the nature of a preface. For to treat the subject with the clearness and coherence of which I believe it susceptible, it would be necessary to give a full account of the present state of the public taste in this country, and to determine how far this taste is healthy or depraved; which, again, could not be determined without pointing out in what manner language and the human mind act and re-act on each other, and without retracing the revolutions, not of literature alone, but likewise of society itself. I have therefore altogether declined to enter regularly upon this defence; yet I am sensible that there would be some impropriety in abruptly obtruding upon the Public, without a few words of introduction, Poems so materially different from those upon which general approbation is at present bestowed.

It is supposed, that by the act of writing in verse an Author makes a formal engagement that he will gratify certain known habits of association; that he not only thus apprizes the Reader that certain classes of ideas and expressions will be found in his book, but that others will be carefully excluded. This exponent or symbol held forth by metrical language must in different areas of literature have excited very different expectations: for example, in the age of Catullus, Terence, and Lucretius and that of Statius or Claudian;[3] and in our own country, in the age of Shakespeare and Beaumont and Fletcher, and that of Donne and Cowley, or Dryden, or

[1] *Preface* This preface first appeared in the 1800 edition of *Lyrical Ballads*, and was revised for the 1802 edition.

[2] *Friend* Samuel Taylor Coleridge (1772–1834). Coleridge gives his account of their plan in his *Biographia Literaria*, Chapter 14.

[3] *Catullus, Terence, and Lucretius* Roman poets of the first and second centuries BCE; *Statius or Claudian* Roman epic poets of the first and fourth centuries CE, respectively.

Pope.[1] I will not take upon me to determine the exact import of the promise which by the act of writing in verse an Author, in the present day, makes to his Reader; but, I am certain, it will appear to many persons that I have not fulfilled the terms of an engagement thus voluntarily contracted. They who have been accustomed to the gaudiness and inane phraseology of many modern writers, if they persist in reading this book to its conclusion, will, no doubt, frequently have to struggle with feelings of strangeness and awkwardness: they will look round for poetry, and will be induced to inquire by what species of courtesy these attempts can be permitted to assume that title. I hope therefore the Reader will not censure me if I attempt to state what I have proposed to myself to perform; and also (as far as the limits of a preface will permit) to explain some of the chief reasons which have determined me in the choice of my purpose: that at least he may be spared any unpleasant feeling of disappointment, and that I myself may be protected from the most dishonorable accusation which can be brought against an Author, namely, that of an indolence which prevents him from endeavouring to ascertain what is his duty, or, when his duty is ascertained, prevents him from performing it.

The principal object, then, which I proposed to myself in these Poems was to choose incidents and situations from common life, and to relate or describe them, throughout, as far as was possible, in a selection of language really used by men; and, at the same time, to throw over them a certain colouring of imagination, whereby ordinary things should be presented to the mind in an unusual way; and, further, and above all, to make these incidents and situations interesting by tracing in them, truly though not ostentatiously, the primary laws of our nature: chiefly as far as regards the manner in which we associate ideas in a state of excitement. Low and rustic life was generally chosen because, in that condition, the essential passions of the heart find a better soil in which they can attain their maturity, are less under restraint, and speak a plainer and more emphatic language; because in that condition of life our elementary feelings co-exist in a state of greater simplicity, and, consequently, may be more accurately contemplated, and more forcibly communicated; because the manners of rural life germinate from those elementary feelings; and, from the necessary character of rural occupations, are more easily comprehended, and are more durable; and lastly, because in that condition the passions of men are incorporated with the beautiful and permanent forms of nature. The language, too, of these men is adopted (purified indeed from what appear to be its real defects, from all lasting and rational causes of dislike or disgust) because such men hourly communicate with the best objects from which the best part of language is originally derived; and because, from their rank in society and the sameness and narrow circle of their intercourse, being less under the influence of social vanity they convey their feelings and notions in simple and unelaborated expressions. Accordingly, such a language, arising out of repeated experience and regular feelings, is a more permanent, and a far more philosophical language, than that which is frequently substituted for it by Poets, who think that they are conferring honour upon themselves and their art, in proportion as they separate themselves from the sympathies of men, and indulge in arbitrary and capricious habits of expression, in order to furnish food for fickle tastes, and fickle appetites, of their own creation.[2]

I cannot, however, be insensible of the present outcry against the triviality and meanness both of thought and language, which some of my contemporaries have occasionally introduced into their metrical compositions; and I acknowledge that this defect, where it exists, is more dishonorable to the Writer's own character than false refinement or arbitrary innovation,

---

1 *Shakespeare and Beaumont and Fletcher* The age of Renaissance drama, during which Shakespeare, Francis Beaumont, and John Fletcher wrote; *Donne and Cowley* John Donne and Abraham Cowley, poets of the seventeenth century; *Dryden* John Dryden, Poet Laureate from 1668 to 1688; *Pope* Alexander Pope, a major poet of the eighteenth century.

2 [Wordsworth's note] It is worth while here to observe that the affecting parts of Chaucer are almost always expressed in language pure and universally intelligible even to this day.

though I should contend at the same time that it is far less pernicious in the sum of its consequences. From such verses the Poems in these volumes will be found distinguished at least by one mark of difference, that each of them has a worthy *purpose*. Not that I mean to say that I always began to write with a distinct purpose formally conceived; but I believe that my habits of meditation have so formed my feelings, as that my descriptions of such objects as strongly excite those feelings will be found to carry along with them a *purpose*. If in this opinion I am mistaken, I can have little right to the name of a Poet. For all good poetry is the spontaneous overflow of powerful feelings: but though this be true, Poems to which any value can be attached, were never produced on any variety of subjects but by a man who, being possessed of more than usual organic sensibility, had also thought long and deeply. For our continued influxes of feeling are modified and directed by our thoughts, which are indeed the representatives of all our past feelings; and, as by contemplating the relation of these general representatives to each other we discover what is really important to men, so, by the repetition and continuance of this act, our feelings will be connected with important subjects, till at length, if we be originally possessed of much sensibility, such habits of mind will be produced, that, by obeying blindly and mechanically the impulses of those habits, we shall describe objects, and utter sentiments, of such a nature and in such connection with each other, that the understanding of the being to whom we address ourselves, if he be in a healthful state of association, must necessarily be in some degree enlightened, and his affections ameliorated.

I have said that each of these poems has a purpose. I have also informed my Reader what this purpose will be found principally to be: namely to illustrate the manner in which our feelings and ideas are associated in a state of excitement. But, speaking in language somewhat more appropriate, it is to follow the fluxes and refluxes of the mind when agitated by the great and simple affections of our nature. This object I have endeavoured in these short essays to attain by various means; by tracing the maternal passion through many of its more subtle windings, as in the poems of the *Idiot Boy* and the *Mad Mother*; by accompanying the last struggles of a human being, at the approach of death, cleaving in solitude to life and society, as in the Poem of the *Forsaken Indian*; by showing, as in the Stanzas entitled *We Are Seven*, the perplexity and obscurity which in childhood attend our notion of death, or rather our utter inability to admit that notion; or by displaying the strength of fraternal, or to speak more philosophically, of moral attachment when early associated with the great and beautiful objects of nature, as in *The Brothers*; or, as in the *Incident of Simon Lee*, by placing my Reader in the way of receiving from ordinary moral sensations another and more salutary impression than we are accustomed to receive from them. It has also been part of my general purpose to attempt to sketch characters under the influence of less impassioned feelings, as in the *Two April Mornings*, *The Fountain*, *The Old Man Travelling*, *The Two Thieves*, &c., characters of which the elements are simple, belonging rather to nature than to manners, such as exist now, and will probably always exist, and which from their constitution may be distinctly and profitably contemplated. I will not abuse the indulgence of my Reader by dwelling longer upon this subject; but it is proper that I should mention one other circumstance which distinguishes these Poems from the popular Poetry of the day; it is this, that the feeling therein developed gives importance to the action and situation, and not the action and situation to the feeling. My meaning will be rendered perfectly intelligible by referring my Reader to the Poems entitled *Poor Susan* and the *Childless Father*, particularly to the last Stanza of the latter Poem.

I will not suffer a sense of false modesty to prevent me from asserting that I point my Reader's attention to this mark of distinction, far less for the sake of these particular Poems than from the general importance of the subject. The subject is indeed important! For the human mind is capable of being excited without the application of gross and violent stimulants; and he must have a very faint perception of its beauty and dignity who does not know this, and who does not further know that one being is elevated above another, in proportion as he possesses this capability. It has therefore appeared to me that to endeavour to produce or enlarge this capability is one of the best services in which, at any period, a Writer can be engaged; but this service, excellent at all times, is especially so at the present day. For a multitude of causes, unknown to former times, are now acting with a combined force to blunt the discriminating powers of the mind, and unfitting it for all voluntary exertion to reduce it to a state of almost savage torpor. The most effective of these causes are the great national events which are daily taking place,[1] and the increasing accumulation of men in cities, where the uniformity of their occupations produces a craving for extraordinary incident, which the rapid communication of intelligence hourly gratifies. To this tendency of life and manners the literature and theatrical exhibitions of the country have conformed themselves. The invaluable works of our elder writers, I had almost said the works of Shakespeare and Milton, are driven into neglect by frantic novels, sickly and stupid German Tragedies, and deluges of idle and extravagant stories in verse.[2] When I think upon this degrading thirst after outrageous stimulation, I am almost ashamed to have spoken of the feeble effort with which I have endeavoured to counteract it; and, reflecting upon the magnitude of the general evil, I should be oppressed with no dishonorable melancholy, had I not a deep impression of certain inherent and indestructible qualities of the human mind, and likewise of certain powers in the great and permanent objects that act upon it which are equally inherent and indestructible; and did I not further add to this impression a belief that the time is approaching when the evil will be systematically opposed, by men of greater powers, and with far more distinguished success.

Having dwelt thus long on the subjects and aim of these Poems, I shall request the Reader's permission to apprize him of a few circumstances relating to their *style*, in order, among other reasons, that I may not be censured for not having performed what I never attempted. The Reader will find that personifications of abstract ideas rarely occur in these volumes; and, I hope, are utterly rejected as an ordinary device to elevate the style, and raise it above prose. I have proposed to myself to imitate, and, as far as is possible, to adopt, the very language of men; and assuredly such personifications do not make any natural or regular part of that language. They are, indeed, a figure of speech occasionally prompted by passion, and I have made use of them as such; but I have endeavoured utterly to reject them as a mechanical device of style, or as a family language which Writers in metre seem to lay claim to by prescription. I have wished to keep my Reader in the company of flesh and blood, persuaded that by so doing I shall interest him. I am, however, well aware that others who pursue a different track may interest him likewise; I do not interfere with their claim, I only wish to prefer a different claim of my own. There will also be found in these volumes little of what is usually called poetic diction; I have taken as much pains to avoid it as others ordinarily take to produce it; this I have done for the reason already alleged, to bring my language near to the language of men, and further, because the pleasure which I have proposed to myself to impart is of a kind very different from that which is supposed by many persons to be the proper object of poetry. I do not know how without being culpably particular I can give my Reader a more exact notion of the style in which I wished these poems to be written than by informing him that I have at all times endeavoured to look steadily at my subject; consequently, I hope that there is in these Poems little falsehood of description, and that my ideas are expressed in language fitted to their respective importance. Something I must have gained by this practice, as it is friendly to one property of all good poetry, namely, good sense; but it has necessarily cut me off from a large portion of phrases and figures of speech which from father to son have long been regarded as the common inheritance of

---

[1] *great national … place* I.e., the wars against France and the Irish Rebellion.

[2] *frantic novels … verse* References to popular Gothic novels of the time, such as Matthew Gregory Lewis's *The Monk* (1796) and the novels of Ann Radcliffe, and to the German sentimental melodramas translated and staged during the 1780s.

Poets. I have also thought it expedient to restrict myself still further, having abstained from the use of many expressions, in themselves proper and beautiful, but which have been foolishly repeated by bad Poets, till such feelings of disgust are connected with them as it is scarcely possible by any art of association to overpower.

If in a Poem there should be found a series of lines, or even a single line, in which the language, though naturally arranged and according to the strict laws of metre, does not differ from that of prose, there is a numerous class of critics, who, when they stumble upon these prosaisms, as they call them, imagine that they have made a notable discovery, and exult over the Poet as over a man ignorant of his own profession. Now these men would establish a canon of criticism which the Reader will conclude he must utterly reject, if he wishes to be pleased with these volumes. And it would be a most easy task to prove to him that not only the language of a large portion of every good poem, even of the most elevated character, must necessarily, except with reference to the metre, in no respect differ from that of good prose, but likewise that some of the most interesting parts of the best poems will be found to be strictly the language of prose, when prose is well written. The truth of this assertion might be demonstrated by innumerable passages from almost all the poetical writings, even of Milton himself. I have not space for much quotation; but, to illustrate the subject in a general manner, I will here adduce a short composition of Gray,[1] who was at the head of those who by their reasonings have attempted to widen the space of separation betwixt Prose and Metrical composition, and was more than any other man curiously elaborate in the structure of his own poetic diction.

In vain to me the smiling mornings shine,
And reddening Phoebus[2] lifts his golden fire:
The birds in vain their amorous descant join,
Or cheerful fields resume their green attire:
These ears alas! for other notes repine;
A different object do these eyes require;
My lonely anguish melts no heart but mine;
And in my breast the imperfect joys expire;
Yet Morning smiles the busy race to cheer,
And new-born pleasure brings to happier men;
The fields to all their wonted tribute bear;
To warm their little loves the birds complain.
I fruitless mourn to him that cannot hear
And weep the more because I weep in vain.

It will easily be perceived that the only part of this Sonnet which is of any value is the lines printed in Italics: it is equally obvious that, except in the rhyme, and in the use of the single word "fruitless" for fruitlessly, which is so far a defect, the language of these lines does in no respect differ from that of prose.

By the foregoing quotation I have shown that the language of Prose may yet be well adapted to Poetry; and I have previously asserted that a large portion of the language of every good poem can in no respect differ from that of good Prose. I will go further. I do not doubt that it may be safely affirmed that there neither is, nor can be, any essential difference between the language of prose and metrical composition. …

I ask what is meant by the word Poet? What is a Poet? To whom does he address himself? And what language is to be expected from him? He is a man speaking to men: a man, it is true, endued with more lively sensibility, more enthusiasm and tenderness, who has a greater knowledge of human nature, and a more comprehensive soul, than are supposed to be common among mankind; a man pleased with his own passions and volitions, and who rejoices more than other men in the spirit of life that is in him; delighting to contemplate similar volitions and passions as manifested in the goings-on of the Universe, and habitually impelled to create them where he does not find them. To these qualities he has added a disposition to be affected more than other men by absent things as if they were present; an ability of conjuring up in himself passions, which are indeed far from being the same as those produced by real events, yet (especially in those parts of the general sympathy which are pleasing and delightful) do more

[1] *Gray* Thomas Gray (1716–71). Wordsworth quotes his *Sonnet on the Death of Richard West.*

[2] *Phoebus* Apollo, god of the sun and of poetry.

nearly resemble the passions produced by real events than any thing which, from the motions of their own minds merely, other men are accustomed to feel in themselves; whence, and from practice, he has acquired a greater readiness and power in expressing what he thinks and feels, and especially those thoughts and feelings which, by his own choice, or from the structure of his own mind, arise in him without immediate external excitement.

But, whatever portion of this faculty we may suppose even the greatest Poet to possess, there cannot be a doubt but that the language which it will suggest to him must, in liveliness and truth, fall far short of that which is uttered by men in real life, under the actual pressure of those passions, certain shadows of which the Poet thus produces, or feels to be produced, in himself. However exalted a notion we would wish to cherish of the character of a Poet, it is obvious that, while he describes and imitates passions, his situation is altogether slavish and mechanical, compared with the freedom and power of real and substantial action and suffering. So that it will be the wish of the Poet to bring his feelings near to those of the persons whose feelings he describes—nay, for short spaces of time, perhaps, to let himself slip into an entire delusion, and even confound and identify his own feelings with theirs; modifying only the language which is thus suggested to him, by a consideration that he describes for a particular purpose, that of giving pleasure. Here, then, he will apply the principle on which I have so much insisted, namely, that of selection; on this he will depend for removing what would otherwise be painful or disgusting in the passion; he will feel that there is no necessity to trick out or to elevate nature: and, the more industriously he applies this principle, the deeper will be his faith that no words which his fancy or imagination can suggest will be to be compared with those which are the emanations of reality and truth. …

It is not, then, in the dramatic parts of composition that we look for this distinction of language; but still it may be proper and necessary where the Poet speaks to us in his own person and character. To this I answer by referring my Reader to the description which I have before given of a Poet. Among the qualities which I have enumerated as principally conducting to form a Poet, is implied nothing differing in kind from other men, but only in degree. The sum of what I have there said is that the Poet is chiefly distinguished from other men by a greater promptness to think and feel without immediate external excitement, and a greater power in expressing such thoughts and feelings as are produced in him in that manner. But these passions and thoughts and feelings are the general passions and thoughts and feelings of men. And with what are they connected? Undoubtedly with our moral sentiments and animal sensations, and with the causes which excite these; with the operations of the elements and the appearances of the visible universe; with storm and sunshine, with the revolutions of the seasons, with cold and heat, with loss of friends and kindred, with injuries and resentments, gratitude and hope, with fear and sorrow. These, and the like, are the sensations and objects which the Poet describes, as they are the sensations of other men, and the objects which interest them. The Poet thinks and feels in the spirit of the passions of men. How, then, can his language differ in any material degree from that of all other men who feel vividly and see clearly? It might be *proved* that it is impossible. But supposing that this were not the case, the Poet might then be allowed to use a peculiar language when expressing his feelings for his own gratification, or that of men like himself. But Poets do not write for Poets alone, but for men. Unless therefore we are advocates for that admiration which depends upon ignorance, and that pleasure which arises from hearing what we do not understand, the Poet must descend from this supposed height, and, in order to excite rational sympathy, he must express himself as other men express themselves. To this it may be added, that while he is only selecting from the real language of men, or, which amounts to the same thing, composing accurately in the spirit of such selection, he is treading upon safe ground, and we know what we are to expect from him. Our feelings are the same with respect to metre; for, as it may be proper to remind the Reader, the distinction of metre is regular and uniform, and not like that which is produced by what is usually called poetic diction, arbitrary, and subject to infinite caprices upon which no calculation whatever can be made. In the one case, the Reader is utterly at the mercy of the Poet respecting what imagery or diction he may choose to connect with the passion, whereas, in the other, the metre obeys certain laws, to which the Poet and Reader both willingly submit because they are certain, and because no interference is made by them with the passion but such as the concurring testimony of ages has shown to heighten and improve the pleasure which co-exists with it.

It will now be proper to answer an obvious question, namely, why, professing these opinions, have I written in verse? To this, in addition to such answer as is included in what I have already said, I reply in the first place, because, however I may have restricted myself, there is still left open to me what confessedly constitutes the most valuable object of all writing whether in prose or verse, the great and universal passions of men, the most general and interesting of their occupations, and the entire world of nature, from which I am at liberty to supply myself with endless combinations of forms and imagery. Now, supposing for a moment that whatever is interesting in these objects may be as vividly described in prose, why am I to be condemned, if to such description I have endeavoured to superadd the charm which, by the consent of all nations, is acknowledged to exist in metrical language? To this, by such as are unconvinced by what I have already said, it may be answered that a very small part of the pleasure given by Poetry depends upon the metre, and that it is injudicious to write in metre, unless it be accompanied with the other artificial distinctions of style with which metre is usually accompanied, and that by such deviation more will be lost from the shock which will be thereby given to the Reader's associations than will be counterbalanced by any pleasure which he can derive from the general power of numbers. In answer to those who still contend for the necessity of accompanying metre with certain appropriate colours of style in order to the accomplishment of its appropriate end, and who also, in my opinion, greatly under-rate the power of metre in itself, it might perhaps, as far as relates to these Poems, have been almost sufficient to observe that poems are extant, written upon more humble subjects, and in a more naked and simple style than I have aimed at, which poems have continued to give pleasure from generation to generation. Now, if nakedness and simplicity be a defect, the fact here mentioned affords a strong presumption that poems somewhat less naked and simple are capable of affording pleasure at the present day; and, what I wished *chiefly* to attempt, at present, was to justify myself for having written under the impression of this belief.

But I might point out various causes why, when the style is manly, and the subject of some importance, words metrically arranged will long continue to impart such a pleasure to mankind as he who is sensible of the extent of that pleasure will be desirous to impart. The end of Poetry is to produce excitement in co-existence with an overbalance of pleasure. Now, by the supposition, excitement is an unusual and irregular state of the mind; ideas and feelings do not in that state succeed each other in accustomed order. But, if the words by which this excitement is produced are in themselves powerful, or the images and feelings have an undue proportion of pain connected with them, there is some danger that the excitement may be carried beyond its proper bounds. Now the co-presence of something regular, something to which the mind has been accustomed in various moods and in a less excited state, cannot but have great efficacy in tempering and restraining the passion by an intertexture of ordinary feeling, and of feeling not strictly and necessarily connected with the passion. This is unquestionably true, and hence, though the opinion will at first appear paradoxical, from the tendency of metre to divest language in a certain degree of its reality, and thus to throw a sort of half consciousness of unsubstantial existence over the whole composition, there can be little doubt but that more pathetic situations and sentiments—that is, those which have a greater proportion of pain connected with them—may be endured in metrical composition, especially in rhyme, than in prose. The metre of the old Ballads is very artless; yet they contain many passages which would illustrate this opinion, and, I hope, if the following Poems be attentively perused, similar instances will be found in them. …

I have said that Poetry is the spontaneous overflow of powerful feelings: it takes its origin from emotion recollected in tranquillity: the emotion is contemplated till by a species of reaction the tranquillity gradually disappears, and an emotion, kindred to that which was before the subject of contemplation, is gradually produced, and does itself actually exist in the mind. In this mood successful composition generally begins, and in a mood similar to this it is carried on; but the emotion, of whatever kind and in whatever degree, from various causes is qualified by various pleasures, so that in describing any passions whatsoever, which are voluntarily described, the mind will upon the whole be in a state of enjoyment. Now, if Nature be thus cautious in preserving in a state of enjoyment a being thus employed, the Poet ought to profit by the lesson thus held forth to him, and ought especially to take care that whatever passions he communicates to his Reader, those passions, if his Reader's mind be sound and vigorous, should always be accompanied with an overbalance of pleasure. Now the music of harmonious metrical language, the sense of difficulty overcome, and the blind association of pleasure which has been previously received from works of rhyme or metre of the same or similar construction, an indistinct perception perpetually renewed of language closely resembling that of real life, and yet, in the circumstance of metre, differing from it so widely, all these imperceptibly make up a complex feeling of delight, which is of the most important use in tempering the painful feeling which will always be found intermingled with powerful descriptions of the deeper passions. This effect is always produced in pathetic and impassioned poetry; while, in lighter compositions, the ease and gracefulness with which the Poet manages his numbers[1] are themselves confessedly a principal source of the gratification of the Reader. I might perhaps include all which it is *necessary* to say upon this subject by affirming what few persons will deny, that, of two descriptions, either of passions, manners, or characters, each of them equally well executed, the one in prose and the other in verse, the verse will be read a hundred times where the prose is read once. We see that Pope, by the power of verse alone, has contrived to render the plainest common sense interesting, and even frequently to invest it with the appearance of passion. …

I know that nothing would have so effectually contributed to further the end which I have in view as to have shown of what kind the pleasure is, and how that pleasure is produced, which is confessedly produced by metrical composition essentially different from that which I have here endeavoured to recommend: for the Reader will say that he has been pleased by such composition; and what can I do more for him? The power of any art is limited; and he will suspect that, if I propose to furnish him with new friends, it is only upon condition of his abandoning his old friends. Besides, as I have said, the Reader is himself conscious of the pleasure which he has received from such composition, composition to which he has peculiarly attached the endearing name of Poetry; and all men feel an habitual gratitude, and something of an honorable bigotry for the objects which have long continued to please them: we not only wish to be pleased, but to be pleased in that particular way in which we have been accustomed to be pleased. There is a host of arguments in these feelings; and I should be the less able to combat them successfully, as I am willing to allow that, in order entirely to enjoy the Poetry which I am recommending, it would be necessary to give up much of what is ordinarily enjoyed. But, would my limits have permitted me to point out how this pleasure is produced, I might have removed many obstacles, and assisted my Reader in perceiving that the powers of language are not so limited as he may suppose; and that it is possible that poetry may give other enjoyments, of a purer, more lasting, and more exquisite nature. This part of my subject I have not altogether neglected; but it has been less my present aim to prove that the interest excited by some other kinds of poetry is less vivid, and less worthy of the nobler powers of the mind, than to offer reasons for presuming that, if the object which I have proposed to myself were adequately attained, a species of poetry would be produced which

[1] *numbers* Meter.

is genuine poetry; in its nature well adapted to interest mankind permanently, and likewise important in the multiplicity and quality of its moral relations.

From what has been said, and from a perusal of the Poems, the Reader will be able clearly to perceive the object which I have proposed to myself: he will determine how far I have attained this object; and, what is a much more important question, whether it be worth attaining; and upon the decision of these two questions will rest my claim to the approbation of the public.

[*There was a Boy*]

There was a Boy, ye knew him well, ye Cliffs
And Islands of Winander![1] many a time,
At evening, when the stars began
To move along the edges of the hills,
Rising or setting, would he stand alone,
Beneath the trees, or by the glimmering lake,
And there, with fingers interwoven, both hands
Press'd closely palm to palm and to his mouth
Uplifted, he, as through an instrument,
Blew mimic hootings to the silent owls
That they might answer him. And they would shout
Across the wat'ry vale and shout again
Responsive to his call, with quivering peals,
And long halloos, and screams, and echoes loud
Redoubled and redoubled, a wild scene
Of mirth and jocund din. And, when it chanced
That pauses of deep silence mock'd his skill,
Then, sometimes, in that silence, while he hung
Listening, a gentle shock of mild surprise
Has carried far into his heart the voice
Of mountain torrents, or the visible scene
Would enter unawares into his mind
With all its solemn imagery, its rocks,
Its woods, and that uncertain heaven, receiv'd
Into the bosom of the steady lake.

Fair are the woods, and beauteous is the spot,
The vale where he was born: the Church-yard hangs
Upon a slope above the village school,[2]
And there along that bank when I have pass'd
At evening, I believe, that near his grave
A full half-hour together I have stood,
Mute—for he died when he was ten years old.

[*Strange fits of passion I have known*][3]

Strange fits of passion I have known,
And I will dare to tell,
But in the Lover's ear alone,
What once to me befell.

When she I lov'd, was strong and gay
And like a rose in June,
I to her cottage bent my way,
Beneath the evening moon.

Upon the moon I fix'd my eye,
All over the wide lea;° *meadow*
My horse trudg'd on, and we drew nigh
Those paths so dear to me.

And now we reach'd the orchard plot,
And, as we climb'd the hill,
Towards the roof of Lucy's cot° *cottage*
The moon descended still.

In one of those sweet dreams I slept,
Kind Nature's gentlest boon!
And, all the while, my eyes I kept
On the descending moon.

---

[1] *Winander* Windermere, the largest lake in England's Lake District.

[2] *the village school* Hawkshead Grammar School in Esthwaite.

[3] *Strange … known* This and the following two lyrics are part of a group of five lyrics now commonly called the "Lucy poems," all of which were composed during the winter of 1798–99, when Wordsworth and his sister were in Germany. The identity of Lucy is unknown (if she existed at all); she is not the Lucy of Wordsworth's poem *Lucy Gray* (1800). Some critics believe that in these poems Wordsworth attempts to express his feelings for his sister.

My horse mov'd on; hoof after hoof
He rais'd and never stopp'd:
When down behind the cottage roof
At once the planet dropp'd.

What fond and wayward thoughts will slide
Into a Lover's head—
"O mercy!" to myself I cried,
"If Lucy should be dead!"[1]

Song [*She dwelt among th'untrodden ways*]

She dwelt among th'untrodden ways
Beside the springs of Dove,[2]
A Maid whom there were none to praise
And very few to love.

A violet by a mossy stone
Half-hidden from the Eye!
—Fair, as a star when only one
Is shining in the sky.

She *liv'd* unknown, and few could know
When Lucy ceas'd to be;
But she is in her Grave, and Oh!
The difference to me.

[*A slumber did my spirit seal*][3]

A slumber did my spirit seal,
I had no human fears:
She seem'd a thing that could not feel
The touch of earthly years.

No motion has she now, no force
She neither hears nor sees
Roll'd round in earth's diurnal° course *daily*
With rocks and stones and trees!

Lucy Gray[4]

Oft I had heard of Lucy Gray,
And when I cross'd the Wild,
I chanc'd to see at break of day
The solitary child.

No Mate, no comrade Lucy knew;
She dwelt on a wide Moor,
The sweetest Thing that ever grew
Beside a human door!

You yet may spy the Fawn at play,
The Hare upon the Green;
But the sweet face of Lucy Gray
Will never more be seen.

"To-night will be a stormy night,
You to the Town must go,
And take a lantern, Child, to light
Your Mother thro' the snow."

[1] *If ... dead* In an earlier manuscript version, another stanza followed: "I told her this: her laughter light / Is ringing in my ears; / And when I think upon that night / My eyes are dim with tears."

[2] *Dove* Name of numerous rivers in England, one of which is in the Lake District.

[3] *A slumber ... seal* Of this poem, Coleridge wrote to a friend in April 1799: "Some months ago Wordsworth transmitted to me a most sublime epitaph. ... Whether it had any reality, I cannot say. Most probably, in some gloomier moment he had fancied the moment in which his sister might die."

[4] *Lucy Gray* Based on an account of a drowned girl told to Wordsworth by his sister. In his note, Wordsworth says that after the girl had become lost in a snowstorm, "her footsteps were traced by her parents to the middle of the lock of a canal, and no other vestige of her, backward or forward, could be traced. The body, however, was found in the canal. The way in which the incident was treated and the spiritualizing of the character might furnish hints for consulting the imaginative influences which I have endeavoured to throw over common life with Crabbe's matter of fact style of treating subjects of the same kind." (Wordsworth refers to the poet George Crabbe [1754–1832].)

"That, Father! will I gladly do;
'Tis scarcely afternoon—
The Minster°-clock has just struck two, *church*
And yonder is the Moon!"

At this the Father rais'd his hook,
And snapp'd a faggot-band;[1]
He plied his work, and Lucy took
The lantern in her hand.

Not blither° is the mountain roe, *more merry*
With many a wanton° stroke *frolicsome*
Her feet disperse the powd'ry snow,
That rises up like smoke.

The storm came on before its time,
She wander'd up and down,
And many a hill did Lucy climb:
But never reach'd the Town.

The wretched Parents all that night
Went shouting far and wide;
But there was neither sound nor sight
To serve them for a guide.

At day-break on a hill they stood
That overlook'd the Moor;
And thence they saw the Bridge of Wood,
A furlong[2] from their door.

And now they homeward turn'd, and cry'd
"In Heaven we all shall meet!"
When in the snow the Mother spied
The print of Lucy's feet.

Then downward from the steep hill's edge
They track'd the footmarks small;
And through the broken hawthorn-hedge,
And by the long stone-wall;

And then an open field they cross'd,
The marks were still the same;
They track'd them on, nor ever lost,
And to the Bridge they came.

They follow'd from the snowy bank
Those footmarks, one by one,
Into the middle of the plank,
And further there were none.

Yet some maintain that to this day
She is a living Child,
That you may see sweet Lucy Gray
Upon the lonesome Wild.

O'er rough and smooth she trips along,
And never looks behind;
And sings a solitary song
That whistles in the wind.

Nutting

It seems a day,
(I speak of one from many singled out)
One of those heavenly days which cannot die,
When forth I sallied from our cottage-door,
And with a wallet° o'er my shoulder slung, *knapsack*
A nutting crook[3] in hand, I turn'd my steps
Towards the distant woods, a Figure quaint,
Trick'd out in proud disguise of Beggar's weeds° *garments*
Put on for the occasion, by advice
And exhortation of my frugal Dame.[4]
Motley accoutrements! of power to smile
At thorns, and brakes,° and brambles, and, *thickets*
in truth,
More ragged than need was. Among the woods,

---

[1] *faggot-band* Cord for binding a bundle of firewood.

[2] *furlong* Measurement equal to 220 yards, or one-eighth of a mile.

[3] *nutting crook* Hooked instrument for gathering nuts.

[4] *my frugal Dame* Ann Tyson, at whose house Wordsworth boarded during his school years.

And o'er the pathless rocks, I forc'd my way
Until, at length, I came to one dear nook
Unvisited, where not a broken bough
Droop'd with its wither'd leaves, ungracious sign
Of devastation, but the hazels rose
Tall and erect, with milk-white clusters hung,
A virgin scene!—A little while I stood,
Breathing with such suppression of the heart
As joy delights in; and with wise restraint
Voluptuous, fearless of a rival, eyed
The banquet, or beneath the trees I sat
Among the flowers, and with the flowers I play'd;
A temper known to those, who, after long
And weary expectation, have been bless'd
With sudden happiness beyond all hope.
—Perhaps it was a bower beneath whose leaves
The violets of five seasons re-appear
And fade, unseen by any human eye,
Where fairy water-breaks[1] do murmur on
For ever, and I saw the sparkling foam,
And with my cheek on one of those green stones
That, fleec'd with moss, beneath the shady trees,
Lay round me scatter'd like a flock of sheep,
I heard the murmur and the murmuring sound,
In that sweet mood when pleasure loves to pay
Tribute to ease, and, of its joy secure
The heart luxuriates with indifferent things,
Wasting its kindliness on stocks° and stones, *stumps*
And on the vacant air. Then up I rose,
And dragg'd to earth both branch and bough, with crash
And merciless ravage; and the shady nook
Of hazels, and the green and mossy bower
Deform'd and sullied, patiently gave up
Their quiet being: and unless I now
Confound my present feelings with the past,
Even then, when from the bower I turn'd away,
Exulting, rich beyond the wealth of kings
I felt a sense of pain when I beheld
The silent trees and the intruding sky.
Then, dearest Maiden![2] move along these shades
In gentleness of heart with gentle hand
Touch—for there is a Spirit in the woods.

Michael

Wordsworth said this pastoral poem is founded on two real incidents, one of "the son of an old couple having become dissolute, and run away from his parents" and the other of "an old shepherd having been seven years in building up a sheepfold in a solitary valley." In combining these tales, he said in a letter to Thomas Poole, "I have attempted to give a picture of a man of strong mind and lively sensibility, agitated by two of the most powerful affections of the human heart—parental affection and the love of property, landed property, including the feelings of inheritance, home, and personal and family independence." As in his poem "Brothers," Wordsworth writes "with a view to show that men who do not wear fine clothes can feel deeply" and attempts "to draw a picture of the domestic affections, as I know they exist among a class of men who are now almost confined to the north of England. They are small independent proprietors of land, here called 'states-men,' men of respectable education, who daily labor on their own little properties. The domestic affections will always be strong amongst men who live in a country not crowded with population, if these men are placed above poverty. ... Their little tract of land serves as a kind of permanent rallying point for their domestic feelings, as a tablet on which they are written, which makes them objects of memory in a thousand instances, when they would otherwise be forgotten."

[1] *water-breaks* Places where the water flow is broken by underlying rocks.

[2] *Maiden* In a longer manuscript draft of the poem, a passage originally intended to lead up to "Nutting" describes a maiden named Lucy ravaging a bower.

Michael

A Pastoral Poem

If from the public way you turn your steps
Up the tumultuous brook of Green-head Gill,[1]
You will suppose that with an upright path
Your feet must struggle; in such bold ascent
The pastoral Mountains front you, face to face.
But, courage! for beside that boisterous Brook
The mountains have all open'd out themselves,
And made a hidden valley of their own.
No habitation can be seen; but such
As journey thither find themselves alone
With a few sheep, with rocks and stones, and kites[2]
That overhead are sailing in the sky.

It is in truth an utter solitude,
Nor should I have made mention of this Dell
But for one object which you might pass by,
Might see and notice not. Beside the brook
There is a straggling heap of unhewn stones!
And to that place a story appertains,
Which, though it be ungarnish'd with events,
Is not unfit, I deem, for the fire-side,
Or for the summer shade. It was the first,
The earliest of those tales that spake to me
Of Shepherds, dwellers in the valleys, men
Whom I already lov'd, not verily
For their own sakes, but for the fields and hills
Where was their occupation and abode.
And hence this Tale, while I was yet a boy
Careless of books, yet having felt the power
Of Nature, by the gentle agency
Of natural objects led me on to feel
For passions that were not my own, and think
At random and imperfectly indeed
On man; the heart of man and human life.
Therefore, although it be a history
Homely and rude, I will relate the same
For the delight of a few natural hearts,
And with yet fonder feeling, for the sake
Of youthful Poets, who among these Hills
Will be my second self when I am gone.

Upon the Forest-side in Grasmere Vale
There dwelt a Shepherd, Michael was his name,
An old man, stout of heart, and strong of limb.
His bodily frame had been from youth to age
Of an unusual strength: his mind was keen
Intense and frugal, apt for all affairs,
And in his Shepherd's calling he was prompt
And watchful more than ordinary men.
Hence he had learn'd the meaning of all winds,
Of blasts of every tone, and often-times
When others heeded not, He heard the South[3]
Make subterraneous music, like the noise
Of Bagpipers on distant Highland hills;
The Shepherd, at such warning, of his flock
Bethought him, and he to himself would say
The winds are now devising work for me!
And truly at all times the storm, that drives
The Traveller to a shelter, summon'd him
Up to the mountains: he had been alone
Amid the heart of many thousand mists
That came to him and left him on the heights.
So liv'd he till his eightieth year was pass'd.

And grossly that man errs, who should suppose
That the green Valleys, and the Streams and Rocks
Were things indifferent to the Shepherd's thoughts.
Fields, where with cheerful spirits he had breath'd
The common air; the hills, which he so oft
Had climb'd with vigorous steps; which had impress'd
So many incidents upon his mind
Of hardship, skill or courage, joy or fear;
Which like a book preserv'd the memory
Of the dumb animals, whom he had sav'd,
Had fed or shelter'd, linking to such acts,

---

[1] *Gill* Steep, narrow valley with a stream running through it. Green-head Gill is near Wordsworth's cottage at Grasmere.

[2] *kites* Small falcon-like birds of prey.

[3] *South* South wind.

So grateful in themselves, the certainty
Of honorable gains; these fields, these hills
Which were his living Being, even more
Than his own Blood—what could they less? had laid
Strong hold on his affections, were to him
A pleasurable feeling of blind love,
The pleasure which there is in life itself.

He had not passed his days in singleness.
He had a Wife, a comely Matron, old
Though younger than himself full twenty years.
She was a woman of a stirring life
Whose heart was in her house: two wheels she had
Of antique form, this large for spinning wool,
That small for flax, and if one wheel had rest,
It was because the other was at work.
The Pair had but one Inmate in their house,
An only Child, who had been born to them
When Michael telling° o'er his years began *counting*
To deem that he was old, in Shepherd's phrase,
With one foot in the grave. This only son,
With two brave sheep dogs tried in many a storm,
The one of an inestimable worth,
Made all their Household. I may truly say,
That they were as a proverb in the vale
For endless industry. When day was gone,
And from their occupations out of doors
The Son and Father were come home, even then
Their labour did not cease, unless when all
Turn'd to their cleanly supper-board,[1] and there
Each with a mess of pottage[2] and skimm'd milk,
Sat round their basket pil'd with oaten cakes,
And their plain home-made cheese. Yet when their meal
Was ended, LUKE (for so the Son was nam'd)
And his old Father, both betook themselves
To such convenient work, as might employ
Their hands by the fire-side; perhaps to card[3]
Wool for the House-wife's spindle, or repair
Some injury done to sickle, flail,[4] or scythe,
Or other implement of house or field.
Down from the ceiling by the chimney's edge,
Which in our ancient uncouth country style
Did with a huge projection overbrow° *overhang*
Large space beneath, as duly as the light
Of day grew dim, the House-wife hung a lamp;
An aged utensil, which had perform'd
Service beyond all others of its kind.
Early at evening did it burn and late,
Surviving Comrade of uncounted Hours
Which going by from year to year had found
And left the Couple neither gay perhaps
Nor cheerful, yet with objects and with hopes
Living a life of eager industry.
And now, when LUKE was in his eighteenth year,
There by the light of this old lamp they sat,
Father and Son, while late into the night
The House-wife plied her own peculiar work,
Making the cottage thro' the silent hours
Murmur as with the sound of summer flies.
Not with a waste of words, but for the sake
Of pleasure, which I know that I shall give
To many living now, I of this Lamp
Speak thus minutely: for there are no few
Whose memories will bear witness to my tale.
The Light was famous in its neighbourhood,
And was a public Symbol of the life,
The thrifty Pair had liv'd. For, as it chanc'd,
Their Cottage on a plot of rising ground
Stood single, with large prospect North and South,
High into Easedale, up to Dunmal-Raise,
And Westward to the village near the Lake.
And from this constant light so regular
And so far seen, the House itself by all
Who dwelt within the limits of the vale,
Both old and young, was nam'd The Evening Star.

Thus living on through such a length of years,
The Shepherd, if he lov'd himself, must needs
Have lov'd his Help-mate; but to Michael's heart

[1] *supper-board* Table.

[2] *pottage* Stew of vegetables, and sometimes meat, boiled in water.

[3] *card* Comb out impurities.

[4] *flail* Tool for threshing corn.

This Son of his old age was yet more dear—
Effect which might perhaps have been produc'd
By that instinctive tenderness, the same
Blind Spirit, which is in the blood of all,
Or that a child, more than all other gifts,
Brings hope with it, and forward-looking thoughts,
And stirrings of inquietude, when they
By tendency of nature needs must fail.
From such, and other causes, to the thoughts
Of the old Man his only Son was now
The dearest object that he knew on earth.
Exceeding was the love he bare to him,
His Heart and his Heart's joy! For oftentimes
Old Michael, while he was a babe in arms,
Had done him female service, not alone
For dalliance and delight, as is the use
Of Fathers, but with patient mind enforc'd
To acts of tenderness; and he had rock'd
His cradle with a woman's gentle hand.

And in a later time, ere yet the Boy
Had put on Boy's attire, did Michael love,
Albeit of a stern unbending mind,
To have the young one in his sight, when he
Had work by his own door, or when he sat
With sheep before him on his Shepherd's stool,
Beneath that large old Oak, which near their door
Stood, and from its enormous breadth of shade
Chosen for the Shearer's covert from the sun,
Thence in our rustic dialect was call'd
The CLIPPING° TREE, a name which yet it bears. *shearing*
There, while they two were sitting in the shade,
With others round them, earnest all and blithe,
Would Michael exercise his heart with looks
Of fond correction and reproof bestow'd
Upon the child, if he disturb'd the sheep
By catching at their legs, or with his shouts
Scar'd them, while they lay still beneath the shears.
And when by Heaven's good grace the Boy grew up
A healthy Lad, and carried in his cheek
Two steady roses that were five years old,
Then Michael from a winter coppice[1] cut
With his own hand a sapling, which he hoop'd
With iron, making it throughout in all
Due requisites a perfect Shepherd's Staff,
And gave it to the Boy; wherewith equipp'd
He as a Watchman oftentimes was plac'd
At gate or gap, to stem or turn the flock,
And to his office prematurely call'd
There stood the urchin, as you will divine,
Something between a hindrance and a help,
And for this cause not always, I believe,
Receiving from his Father hire of praise.
Though nought was left undone which staff, or voice,
Or looks, or threatening gestures, could perform.
But soon as Luke, full ten years old, could stand
Against the mountain blasts, and to the heights,
Not fearing toil, nor length of weary ways,
He with his Father daily went, and they
Were as companions, why should I relate
That objects which the Shepherd loved before
Were dearer now? that from the Boy there came
Feelings and emanations, things which were
Light to the sun and music to the wind;
And that the Old Man's heart seemed born again?
Thus in his Father's sight the Boy grew up:
And now when he had reached his eighteenth year,
He was his comfort and his daily hope.

While this good household thus were living on
From day to day, to Michael's ear there came
Distressful tidings. Long before the time
Of which I speak, the Shepherd had been bound
In surety for his Brother's Son, a man
Of an industrious life, and ample means,
But unforeseen misfortunes suddenly
Had press'd upon him, and old Michael now
Was summon'd to discharge the forfeiture,
A grievous penalty, but little less
Than half his substance. This un-look'd for claim
At the first hearing, for a moment took

[1] *coppice* Thicket of small trees.

More hope out of his life than he supposed
That any old man ever could have lost.
As soon as he had gather'd so much strength
That he could look his trouble in the face,
It seem'd that his sole refuge was to sell
A portion of his patrimonial fields.
Such was his first resolve; he thought again,
And his heart fail'd him. "Isabel," said he,
Two evenings after he had heard the news,
"I have been toiling more than seventy years,
And in the open sunshine of God's love
Have we all liv'd, yet if these fields of ours
Should pass into a Stranger's hand, I think
That I could not lie quiet in my grave.
Our lot is a hard lot; the Sun itself
Has scarcely been more diligent than I,
And I have liv'd to be a fool at last
To my own family. An evil Man
That was, and made an evil choice, if he
Were false to us; and if he were not false,
There are ten thousand to whom loss like this
Had been no sorrow. I forgive him—but
'Twere better to be dumb than to talk thus.
When I began, my purpose was to speak
Of remedies and of a cheerful hope.
Our Luke shall leave us, Isabel; the land
Shall not go from us, and it shall be free,[1]
He shall possess it, free as is the wind
That passes over it. We have, thou knowest,
Another Kinsman, he will be our friend
In this distress. He is a prosperous man,
Thriving in trade, and Luke to him shall go,
And with his Kinsman's help and his own thrift,
He quickly will repair this loss, and then
May come again to us. If here he stay,
What can be done? Where every one is poor
What can be gain'd?" At this, the old man paus'd,
And Isabel sat silent, for her mind
Was busy, looking back into past times.
There's Richard Bateman, thought she to herself,[2]
He was a parish-boy[3]—at the church-door
They made a gathering for him, shillings, pence,
And halfpennies, wherewith the Neighbours bought
A Basket, which they fill'd with Pedlar's wares,
And with this Basket on his arm, the Lad
Went up to London, found a Master there,
Who out of many chose the trusty Boy
To go and overlook his merchandise
Beyond the seas, where he grew wond'rous rich,
And left estates and monies to the poor,
And at his birth-place built a Chapel, floor'd
With Marble, which he sent from foreign lands.
These thoughts, and many others of like sort,
Pass'd quickly thro' the mind of Isabel,
And her face brighten'd. The Old Man was glad,
And thus resum'd. "Well! Isabel, this scheme
These two days has been meat and drink to me.
Far more than we have lost is left us yet.
—We have enough—I wish indeed that I
Were younger, but this hope is a good hope.
—Make ready Luke's best garments, of the best
Buy for him more, and let us send him forth
To-morrow, or the next day, or to-night:
—If he could go, the Boy should go to-night."

Here Michael ceas'd, and to the fields went forth
With a light heart. The House-wife for five days
Was restless morn and night, and all day long
Wrought on with her best fingers to prepare
Things needful for the journey of her Son.
But Isabel was glad when Sunday came
To stop her in her work; for, when she lay
By Michael's side, she for the last two nights
Heard him, how he was troubled in his sleep:
And when they rose at morning she could see
That all his hopes were gone. That day at noon
She said to Luke, while they two by themselves

[1] *free* I.e., not mortgaged.

[2] [Wordsworth's note] The story alluded to here is well known in the country. The chapel is called Ings Chapel and is on the road leading from Kendal to Ambleside.

[3] *parish-boy* Youth cared for and supported by the parish.

Were sitting at the door, "Thou must not go,
We have no other Child but thee to lose,
None to remember—do not go away,
For if thou leave thy Father he will die."
The Lad made answer with a jocund voice,
And Isabel, when she had told her fears,
Recover'd heart. That evening her best fare
Did she bring forth, and all together sat
Like happy people round a Christmas fire.
Next morning Isabel resum'd her work,
And all the ensuing week the house appear'd
As cheerful as a grove in Spring: at length
The expected letter from their Kinsman came,
With kind assurances that he would do
His utmost for the welfare of the Boy,
To which requests were added that forthwith
He might be sent to him. Ten times or more
The letter was read over; Isabel
Went forth to shew it to the neighbours round:
Nor was there at that time on English land
A prouder heart than Luke's. When Isabel
Had to her house return'd, the Old Man said,
"He shall depart to-morrow." To this word
The House-wife answered, talking much of things
Which, if at such short notice he should go,
Would surely be forgotten. But at length
She gave consent, and Michael was at ease.

Near the tumultuous brook of Green-head Gill,
In that deep Valley, Michael had design'd
To build a Sheep-fold,[1] and, before he heard
The tidings of his melancholy loss,
For this same purpose he had gathered up
A heap of stones, which close to the brook side
Lay thrown together, ready for the work.
With Luke that evening thitherward he walk'd;
And soon as they had reach'd the place he stopp'd,
And thus the Old Man spake to him. "My Son,
To-morrow thou wilt leave me; with full heart
I look upon thee, for thou art the same
That wert a promise to me ere thy birth,
And all thy life hast been my daily joy.
I will relate to thee some little part
Of our two histories; 'twill do thee good
When thou art from me, even if I should speak
Of things thou canst not know of.——After thou
First cam'st into the world, as it befalls
To new-born infants, thou didst sleep away
Two days, and blessings from thy Father's tongue
Then fell upon thee. Day by day pass'd on,
And still I lov'd thee with encreasing love.
Never to living ear came sweeter sounds
Than when I heard thee by our own fire-side
First uttering without words a natural tune,
When thou, a feeding babe, didst in thy joy
Sing at thy Mother's breast. Month follow'd month,
And in the open fields my life was pass'd
And in the mountains, else I think that thou
Hadst been brought up upon thy father's knees.
—But we were playmates, Luke; among these hills,
As well thou know'st, in us the old and young
Have play'd together, nor with me didst thou
Lack any pleasure which a boy can know."

Luke had a manly heart; but at these words
He sobb'd aloud; the Old Man grasp'd his hand,
And said, "Nay, do not take it so—I see
That these are things of which I need not speak.
—Even to the utmost I have been to thee
A kind and a good Father: and herein
I but repay a gift which I myself
Receiv'd at others hands, for, though now old
Beyond the common life of man, I still
Remember them who lov'd me in my youth.
Both of them sleep together: here they liv'd
As all their Forefathers had done, and when
At length their time was come, they were not loth
To give their bodies to the family mold.
I wish'd that thou should'st live the life they liv'd.
But 'tis a long time to look back, my Son,
And see so little gain from sixty years.
These fields were burthen'd° when they came to me; *mortgaged*

[1] *Sheep-fold* Stone-walled pen for sheep.

'Till I was forty years of age, not more
Than half of my inheritance was mine.
I toil'd and toil'd; God bless'd me in my work,
And 'till these three weeks past the land was free.
—It looks as if it never could endure
Another Master. Heaven forgive me, Luke,
If I judge ill for thee, but it seems good
That thou should'st go." At this the Old Man paus'd,
Then, pointing to the Stones near which they stood,
Thus, after a short silence, he resum'd:
"This was a work for us, and now, my Son,
It is a work for me. But, lay one Stone—
Here, lay it for me, Luke, with thine own hands.
Nay, Boy, be of good hope: we both may live
To see a better day. At eighty-four
I still am strong and stout; do thou thy part,
I will do mine. I will begin again
With many tasks that were resign'd to thee;
Up to the heights, and in among the storms,
Will I without thee go again, and do
All works which I was wont to do alone,
Before I knew thy face. Heaven bless thee, Boy!
Thy heart these two weeks has been beating fast
With many hopes—it should be so—yes—yes—
I knew that thou could'st never have a wish
To leave me, Luke, thou hast been bound to me
Only by links of love, when thou art gone
What will be left to us! But, I forget
My purposes. Lay now the corner-stone,
As I requested, and hereafter, Luke,
When thou art gone away, should evil men
Be thy companions, let this Sheep-fold be
Thy anchor and thy shield; amid all fear
And all temptation, let it be to thee
An emblem of the life thy Fathers liv'd,
Who, being innocent, did for that cause
Bestir them in good deeds. Now, fare thee well—
When thou return'st, thou in this place wilt see
A work which is not here, a covenant
'Twill be between us——but whatever fate
Befall thee, I shall love thee to the last,
And bear thy memory with me to the grave."

The Shepherd ended here; and Luke stoop'd down,
And as his Father had requested, laid
The first stone of the Sheep-fold; at the sight
The Old Man's grief broke from him, to his heart
He press'd his Son, he kissed him and wept;
And to the House together they return'd.
Next morning, as had been resolv'd, the Boy
Began his journey, and when he had reach'd
The public Way, he put on a bold face;
And all the Neighbours as he pass'd their doors
Came forth, with wishes and with farewell pray'rs,
That follow'd him 'till he was out of sight.
A good report did from their Kinsman come,
Of Luke and his well-doing; and the Boy
Wrote loving letters, full of wond'rous news,
Which, as the House-wife phrased it, were throughout
The prettiest letters that were ever seen.
Both parents read them with rejoicing hearts.
So, many months pass'd on: and once again
The Shepherd went about his daily work
With confident and cheerful thoughts; and now
Sometimes when he could find a leisure hour
He to that valley took his way, and there
Wrought at the Sheep-fold. Meantime Luke began
To slacken in his duty, and at length
He in the dissolute city gave himself
To evil courses: ignominy and shame
Fell on him, so that he was driven at last
To seek a hiding-place beyond the seas.

There is a comfort in the strength of love;
'Twill make a thing endurable, which else
Would break the heart: Old Michael found it so.
I have convers'd with more than one who well
Remember the Old Man, and what he was
Years after he had heard this heavy news.
His bodily frame had been from youth to age
Of an unusual strength. Among the rocks
He went, and still look'd up upon the sun,
And listen'd to the wind; and as before
Perform'd all kinds of labour for his Sheep,
And for the land his small inheritance.
And to that hollow Dell from time to time

Did he repair, to build the Fold of which
His flock had need. 'Tis not forgotten yet
The pity which was then in every heart
For the Old Man—and 'tis believ'd by all
That many and many a day he thither went,
And never lifted up a single stone.

There, by the Sheep-fold, sometimes was he seen
Sitting alone, with that his faithful Dog,
Then old, beside him, lying at his feet.
The length of full seven years from time to time
He at the building of this Sheep-fold wrought,
And left the work unfinished when he died.

Three years, or little more, did Isabel,
Survive her Husband: at her death the estate
Was sold, and went into a Stranger's hand.
The Cottage which was nam'd The Evening Star
Is gone, the ploughshare has been through the ground
On which it stood; great changes have been wrought
In all the neighbourhood, yet the Oak is left
That grew beside their Door; and the remains
Of the unfinished Sheep-fold may be seen
Beside the boisterous brook of Green-head Gill.
—1800 (PREFACE REVISED 1802)

[*I griev'd for Buonaparté*][1]

I griev'd for Buonaparté, with a vain
And an unthinking grief! the vital blood
Of that Man's mind what can it be? What food
Fed his first hopes? What knowledge could *He* gain?
'Tis not in battles that from youth we train
The Governor who must be wise and good,
And temper with the sternness of the brain
Thoughts motherly, and meek as womanhood.
Wisdom doth live with children round her knees:
Books, leisure, perfect freedom, and the talk
Man holds with week-day man in the hourly walk
Of the mind's business: these are the degrees
By which true Sway doth mount; this is the stalk
True Power doth grow on; and her rights are these.
—1802

[*My heart leaps up*]

My heart leaps up when I behold
A Rainbow in the sky:
So was it when my life began;
So is it now I am a Man;
So be it when I shall grow old,
Or let me die!
The Child is Father of the Man;
And I could wish my days to be
Bound each to each by natural piety.
—1804

Ode to Duty

Stern Daughter of the Voice of God![2]
O Duty! if that name thou love
Who art a Light to guide, a Rod
To check the erring, and reprove;
Thou, who art victory and law
When empty terrors overawe;
From vain temptations dost set free;
From strife and from despair; a glorious ministry.

There are who ask not if thine eye
Be on them; who, in love and truth,
Where no misgiving is, rely
Upon the genial° sense° of youth: *natural / vitality*
Glad Hearts! without reproach or blot;
Who do thy work, and know it not:

[1] *I ... Buonaparté* According to Dorothy Wordsworth, this sonnet was composed in 1802, the year that Napoleon Bonaparte declared himself First Consul of France for life.

[2] *Stern ... God* Cf. Milton, *Paradise Lost* 9.652–54: "God so commanded, and left that Command / Sole Daughter of His voice; the rest, we live / Law to ourselves, our Reason is our Law."

May joy be theirs while life shall last!
And Thou, if they should totter, teach them to stand
fast!

Serene will be our days and bright,
And happy will our nature be,
When love is an unerring light,
And joy its own security.
And bless'd are they who in the main
This faith, even now, do entertain:
Live in the spirit of this creed;
Yet find that other strength, according to their need.

I, loving freedom, and untried;
No sport of every random gust,
Yet being to myself a guide,
Too blindly have reposed my trust:
Resolved that nothing e'er should press
Upon my present happiness,
I shoved unwelcome tasks away;
But thee I now would serve more strictly, if I may.

Through no disturbance of my soul,
Or strong compunction in me wrought,
I supplicate for thy control;
But in the quietness of thought:
Me this uncharter'd freedom tires;
I feel the weight of chance desires:
My hopes no more must change their name,
I long for a repose that ever is the same.

Yet not the less would I throughout
Still act according to the voice
Of my own wish; and feel past doubt
That my submissiveness was choice:
Not seeking in the school of pride
For "precepts over dignified,"
Denial and restraint I prize
No farther than they breed a second Will more wise.

Stern Lawgiver! yet thou dost wear
The Godhead's most benignant grace;
Nor know we anything so fair
As is the smile upon thy face:
Flowers laugh before thee on their beds;
And Fragrance in thy footing treads;
Thou dost preserve the Stars from wrong;
And the most ancient Heavens, through Thee are fresh
and strong.

To humbler functions, awful Power!
I call thee: I myself commend
Unto thy guidance from this hour;
Oh! let my weakness have an end!
Give unto me, made lowly wise,
The spirit of self-sacrifice;
The confidence of reason give;
And in the light of truth thy Bondman let me live!
—1807

Resolution and Independence

There was a roaring in the wind all night;
The rain came heavily and fell in floods;
But now the sun is rising calm and bright;
The birds are singing in the distant woods;
Over his own sweet voice the Stock-dove° *wild pigeon*
broods;
The Jay makes answer as the Magpie chatters;
And all the air is fill'd with pleasant noise of waters.

All things that love the sun are out of doors;
The sky rejoices in the morning's birth;
The grass is bright with rain-drops; on the moors
The Hare is running races in her mirth;
And with her feet she from the plashy[1] earth
Raises a mist; which, glittering in the sun,
Runs with her all the way, wherever she doth run.

I was a Traveller then upon the moor;
I saw the Hare that rac'd about with joy;
I heard the woods, and distant waters, roar;

[1] *plashy* Having many puddles or pools of water; wet.

Or heard them not, as happy as a Boy:
The pleasant season did my heart employ:
My old remembrances went from me wholly;
And all the ways of men, so vain and melancholy.

But, as it sometimes chanceth, from the might
Of joy in minds that can no farther go,
As high as we have mounted in delight
In our dejection do we sink as low,
To me that morning did it happen so;
And fears, and fancies, thick upon me came;
Dim sadness, and blind thoughts I knew not nor could
 name.

I heard the Sky-lark singing in the sky;
And I bethought me of the playful Hare:
Even such a happy Child of earth am I;
Even as these blissful Creatures do I fare;
Far from the world I walk, and from all care;
But there may come another day to me,
Solitude, pain of heart, distress, and poverty.

My whole life I have liv'd in pleasant thought,
As if life's business were a summer mood;
As if all needful things would come unsought
To genial faith, still rich in genial good;
But how can He expect that others should
Build for him, sow for him, and at his call
Love him, who for himself will take no heed at all?

I thought of Chatterton,[1] the marvellous Boy,
The sleepless Soul that perish'd in its pride;
Of Him who walk'd in glory and in joy
Behind his plough, upon the mountain-side:[2]
By our own spirits are we deified;
We Poets in our youth begin in gladness;
But thereof comes in the end despondency and
 madness.

Now, whether it were by peculiar grace,
A leading from above, a something given,
Yet it befel, that, in this lonely place,
When up and down my fancy thus was driven,
And I with these untoward thoughts had striven,
I saw a Man before me unawares:
The oldest man he seem'd that ever wore grey hairs.

My course I stopped as soon as I espied
The Old Man in that naked wilderness:
Close by a Pond, upon the further side,
He stood alone: a minute's space I guess
I watch'd him, he continuing motionless:
To the Pool's further margin then I drew;
He being all the while before me full in view.

As a huge Stone is sometimes seen to lie
Couch'd on the bald top of an eminence;
Wonder to all who do the same espy
By what means it could thither come, and whence;
So that it seems a thing endued with sense:
Like a Sea-beast crawl'd forth, which on a shelf
Of rock or sand reposeth, there to sun itself.

Such seem'd this Man, not all alive nor dead,
Nor all asleep; in his extreme old age:
His body was bent double, feet and head
Coming together in their pilgrimage;
As if some dire constraint of pain, or rage
Of sickness felt by him in times long past,
A more than human weight upon his frame had cast.

Himself he propp'd, his body, limbs, and face,
Upon a long grey Staff of shaven wood:
And, still as I drew near with gentle pace,
Beside the little pond or moorish flood
Motionless as a Cloud the Old Man stood;
That heareth not the loud winds when they call;
And moveth altogether, if it move at all.

---

[1] *Chatterton* Poet Thomas Chatterton (1752–70), who, after failing to make a living as a poet in London, poisoned himself at the age of seventeen.

[2] *Of Him … mountain-side* Scottish poet Robert Burns (1759–96), known as "the Ploughman Poet" because of his farming background.

At length, himself unsettling, he the Pond
Stirred with his Staff, and fixedly did look
Upon the muddy water, which he conn'd,° *studied*
As if he had been reading in a book:
And now such freedom as I could I took;
And, drawing to his side, to him did say,
"This morning gives us promise of a glorious day."

A gentle answer did the Old Man make,
In courteous speech which forth he slowly drew:
And him with further words I thus bespake,
"What kind of work is that which you pursue?
This is a lonesome place for one like you."
He answer'd me with pleasure and surprise;
And there was, while he spake, a fire about his eyes.

His words came feebly, from a feeble chest,
Yet each in solemn order follow'd each,
With something of a lofty utterance drest;
Choice word, and measured phrase; above the reach
Of ordinary men; a stately speech!
Such as grave Livers[1] do in Scotland use,
Religious men, who give to God and Man their dues.

He told me that he to this pond had come
To gather Leeches,[2] being old and poor:
Employment hazardous and wearisome!
And he had many hardships to endure:
From Pond to Pond he roam'd, from moor to moor,
Housing, with God's good help, by choice or chance:
And in this way he gain'd an honest maintenance.

The old Man still stood talking by my side;
But now his voice to me was like a stream
Scarce heard; nor word from word could I divide;
And the whole Body of the man did seem
Like one whom I had met with in a dream;
Or like a Man from some far region sent;
To give me human strength, and strong admonishment.

My former thoughts return'd: the fear that kills;
The hope that is unwilling to be fed;
Cold, pain, and labour, and all fleshly ills;
And mighty Poets in their misery dead.
And now, not knowing what the Old Man had said,
My question eagerly did I renew,
"How is it that you live, and what is it you do?"

He with a smile did then his words repeat;
And said that, gathering Leeches, far and wide
He travelled; stirring thus about his feet
The waters of the Ponds where they abide.
"Once I could meet with them on every side;
But they have dwindled long by slow decay;
Yet still I persevere, and find them where I may."

While he was talking thus, the lonely place,
The Old Man's shape, and speech, all troubled me:
In my mind's eye I seem'd to see him pace
About the weary moors continually,
Wandering about alone and silently.
While I these thoughts within myself pursued,
He, having made a pause, the same discourse renewed.

And soon with this he other matter blended,
Cheerfully uttered, with demeanour kind,
But stately in the main; and, when he ended,
I could have laugh'd myself to scorn, to find
In that decrepit Man so firm a mind.
"God," said I, "be my help and stay° secure; *support*
I'll think of the Leech-gatherer on the lonely moor."
—1807

[1] *grave Livers* I.e., those who live seriously.

[2] *Leeches* Used at this time by doctors for drawing the blood of patients. A leech gatherer would find leeches by standing in shallow water and allowing them to attach themselves to his legs.

Composed upon Westminster Bridge
Sept. 3, 1803[1]

Earth has not any thing to show more fair:
Dull would he be of soul who could pass by
A sight so touching in its majesty:
This City now doth like a garment wear
This beauty of the morning; silent, bare,
Ships, towers, domes, theatres, and temples lie
Open unto the fields, and to the sky;
All bright and glittering in the smokeless air.
Never did sun more beautifully steep
In his first splendor valley, rock, or hill;
Ne'er saw I, never felt, a calm so deep!
The river glideth at his own sweet will:
Dear God! the very houses seem asleep;
And all that mighty heart is lying still!
—1807

[*The world is too much with us*]

The world is too much with us; late and soon,
Getting and spending, we lay waste our powers:
Little we see in nature that is ours;
We have given our hearts away, a sordid boon!
The Sea that bares her bosom to the moon;
The Winds that will be howling at all hours
And are up-gathered now like sleeping flowers;
For this, for every thing, we are out of tune;
It moves us not. Great God! I'd rather be
A Pagan suckled in a creed outworn;
So might I, standing on this pleasant lea,
Have glimpses that would make me less forlorn;
Have sight of Proteus coming from the sea;
Or hear old Triton blow his wreathed horn.[2]
—1807

[*It is a beauteous Evening*]

It is a beauteous Evening, calm and free;
The holy time is quiet as a Nun
Breathless with adoration; the broad sun
Is sinking down in its tranquillity;
The gentleness of heaven is on the Sea:
Listen! the mighty Being is awake
And doth with his eternal motion make
A sound like thunder—everlastingly.
Dear Child! dear Girl![3] that walkest with me here,
If thou appear'st untouch'd by solemn thought,
Thy nature is not therefore less divine:
Thou liest in Abraham's bosom[4] all the year;
And worshipp'st at the Temple's inner shrine,
God being with thee when we know it not.
—1807

London
1802[5]

Milton! thou should'st be living at this hour:
England hath need of thee: she is a fen
Of stagnant waters: altar, sword, and pen,
Fireside, the heroic wealth of hall and bower,
Have forfeited their ancient English dower

---

[1] *Composed … 1803* Wordsworth misremembered the date of composition, which was actually (according to Dorothy Wordsworth's *Grasmere Journals*) 1802, when Wordsworth took a brief trip to France, where his former lover Annette Vallon lived with their daughter, Caroline.

[2] *Proteus* Shape-changing sea god; *Triton … horn* Sea god with the head and torso of a man and the tail of a fish. He was usually depicted blowing on a conch shell.

[3] *Dear … Girl* Wordsworth's daughter Caroline.

[4] *Abraham's bosom* The resting place for souls bound for heaven. See Luke 16.22: "And it came to pass, that the beggar died, and was carried by the angels into Abraham's bosom."

[5] *London 1802* Written immediately after Wordsworth's return from France, when he was struck by the differences between his native country and France after the Revolution. Milton died in 1674.

Of inward happiness. We are selfish men;
Oh! raise us up, return to us again;
And give us manners, virtue, freedom, power.
Thy soul was like a Star and dwelt apart:
Thou hadst a voice whose sound was like the sea;
Pure as the naked heavens, majestic, free,
So didst thou travel on life's common way,
In cheerful godliness; and yet thy heart
The lowliest duties on itself did lay.
—1807

The Solitary Reaper[1]

Behold her, single in the field,
Yon solitary Highland Lass!
Reaping and singing by herself;
Stop here, or gently pass!
Alone she cuts, and binds the grain,
And sings a melancholy strain;
O listen! for the Vale profound
Is overflowing with the sound.

No Nightingale did ever chaunt
So sweetly to reposing bands
Of Travellers in some shady haunt,
Among Arabian Sands:
No sweeter voice was ever heard
In spring-time from the Cuckoo-bird,
Breaking the silence of the seas
Among the farthest Hebrides.

Will no one tell me what she sings?
Perhaps the plaintive numbers° flow *verses*
For old, unhappy, far-off things,
And battles long ago:
Or is it some more humble lay,
Familiar matter of today?
Some natural sorrow, loss, or pain,
That has been, and may be again!

Whate'er the theme, the Maiden sang
As if her song could have no ending;
I saw her singing at her work,
And o'er the sickle bending;
I listen'd till I had my fill:
And, as I mounted up the hill,
The music in my heart I bore,
Long after it was heard no more.
—1807

[1] *The Solitary Reaper* Suggested by the following passage in Thomas Wilkinson's *Tours to the British Mountains* (1824): "Passed a female who was reaping alone: she sung in Erse [a Gaelic language] as she bended over her sickle; the sweetest human voice I ever heard: her strains were tenderly melancholy, and felt delicious, long after they were heard no more."

IN CONTEXT

"I wandered lonely as a Cloud": Stages in the Life of a Poem

The earliest version of this poem was composed in 1804 and first published in 1807. It was evidently inspired by an entry in Dorothy Wordsworth's journal from two years earlier, describing a scene at Glencoyne Bay, Ullswater, observed by Dorothy and William on their way back to Grasmere after a long ramble. Appearing below are the scene as described by Dorothy in the journal; William's first version of the poem; a facsimile of the page in the copy of *Poems, in Two Volumes* in which William began to compose an additional stanza to the poem; a transcription of his handwritten jottings; and William's revised version, with the added stanza and some other changes (which was not published until 1815).

from Dorothy Wordsworth, *Grasmere Journal* (Thursday, 15 April 1802)

When we were in the woods beyond Gowbarrow park we saw a few daffodils close to the water side. We fancied that the lake had floated the seeds ashore and that the little colony had so sprung up. But as we went along there were more and yet more and at last under the boughs of the trees, we saw that there was a long belt of them along the shore, about the breadth of a country turnpike road. I never saw daffodils so beautiful. They grew among the mossy stones about and about them, some rested their heads upon these stones as on a pillow for weariness and the rest tossed and reeled and danced and seemed as if they verily laughed with the wind that blew upon them over the lake, they looked so gay ever glancing ever changing. This wind blew directly over the lake to them. There was here and there a little knot and a few stragglers a few yards higher up but they were so few as not to disturb the simplicity and unity and life of that one busy highway.

[*I wandered lonely as a Cloud*]

I wandered lonely as a Cloud
That floats on high o'er Vales and Hills,
When all at once I saw a crowd
A host of dancing Daffodils;
Along the Lake, beneath the trees,
Ten thousand dancing in the breeze.

The waves beside them danced, but they
Outdid the sparkling waves in glee—
A Poet could not but be gay
In such a laughing company:
I gazed—and gaz'd—but little thought
What wealth the show to me had brought:

For oft when on my couch I lie
In vacant or in pensive mood,
They flash upon that inward eye
Which is the bliss of solitude,
And then my heart with pleasure fills,
And dances with the Daffodils.
—1807

I wandered lonely as a Cloud
That floats on high o'er Vales and Hills,
When all at once I saw a crowd
A host of dancing Daffodills;
Along the Lake, beneath the trees,
Ten thousand dancing in the breeze.

The waves beside them danced, but they
Outdid the sparkling waves in glee:—
A Poet could not but be gay
In such a laughing company:
I gaz'd—and gaz'd—but little thought
What wealth the shew to me had brought:

VOL. II. B

I wandered lonely as a cloud[1]

l
A host of golden Daffodi ls
Beside
~~Along~~ the Lake beneath the trees
vernal
All dancing ~~dancing~~ in the breeze
Continuous
{ed
~~Close crowd{ing, [?like]~~
~~As numerous~~ ^ as the stars that shine
and twinkle
on}
At midnight, in} the milky way
{a}
They stretch'd {in} never ending line
Along the margin of a bay
Ten thousand saw I at a glance
Tossing their heads in spritely dance

[1] *I wandered … cloud* Transcription of Wordsworth's manuscript (see previous page for facsimile).

[*I wandered lonely as a cloud*]

I wandered lonely as a cloud
That floats on high o'er vales and hills,
When all at once I saw a crowd,
A host, of golden daffodils;
Beside the lake, beneath the trees,
Fluttering and dancing in the breeze.

Continuous as the stars that shine
And twinkle on the milky way,
They stretched in never-ending line
Along the margin of a bay:
Ten thousand saw I at a glance,
Tossing their heads in sprightly dance.

The waves beside them danced, but they
Outdid the sparkling waves in glee:
A poet could not but be gay,
In such a jocund company;
I gazed—and gazed—but little thought
What wealth the show to me had brought:

For oft, when on my couch I lie
In vacant or in pensive mood,
They flash upon that inward eye
Which is the bliss of solitude;
And then my heart with pleasure fills,
And dances with the daffodils.

—1815

Elegiac Stanzas

Suggested by a Picture of Peele Castle, in a Storm, painted by Sir George Beaumont[1]

I was thy Neighbour once, thou rugged Pile!° [castle]
Four summer weeks I dwelt in sight of thee:
I saw thee every day; and all the while
Thy Form was sleeping on a glassy sea.

So pure the sky, so quiet was the air!
So like, so very like, was day to day!
Whene'er I look'd, thy Image still was there;
It trembled, but it never pass'd away.

How perfect was the calm! it seem'd no sleep;
No mood, which season takes away, or brings:
I could have fancied that the mighty Deep
Was even the gentlest of all gentle Things.

Ah! THEN, if mine had been the Painter's hand,
To express what then I saw; and add the gleam,
The light that never was, on sea or land,
The consecration, and the Poet's dream;

I would have planted thee, thou hoary Pile!
Amid a world how different from this!
Beside a sea that could not cease to smile;
On tranquil land, beneath a sky of bliss:

Thou shouldst have seem'd a treasure-house, a mine
Of peaceful years; a chronicle of heaven—
Of all the sunbeams that did ever shine
The very sweetest had to thee been given.

A Picture had it been of lasting ease,
Elysian[2] quiet, without toil or strife;
No motion but the moving tide, a breeze,
Or merely silent Nature's breathing life.

Such, in the fond delusion of my heart,
Such Picture would I at that time have made:
And seen the soul of truth in every part;
A faith, a trust, that could not be betray'd.

So once it would have been—'tis so no more;
I have submitted to a new control:
A power is gone, which nothing can restore;
A deep distress hath humaniz'd my Soul.

Not for a moment could I now behold
A smiling sea and be what I have been:
The feeling of my loss will ne'er be old;
This, which I know, I speak with mind serene.

Then, Beaumont, Friend! who would have been the Friend,
If he had lived, of Him whom I deplore,° [mourn]
This Work of thine I blame not, but commend;
This sea in anger, and that dismal shore.

Oh 'tis a passionate Work!—yet wise and well;
Well chosen is the spirit that is here;
That Hulk which labours in the deadly swell,
This rueful sky, this pageantry of fear!

And this huge Castle, standing here sublime,
I love to see the look with which it braves,
Cased in the unfeeling armour of old time,
The light'ning, the fierce wind, and trampling waves.

Farewell, farewell the Heart that lives alone,
Hous'd in a dream, at distance from the Kind![3]
Such happiness, wherever it be known,
Is to be pitied; for 'tis surely blind.

[1] *Suggested by … Beaumont* In 1794, Wordsworth spent a month in Rampside, Lancashire, which is located across the Morecambe Bay from the Furness Peninsula, where the ruins of Peele Castle stand. In 1806 he saw the two pictures of this castle that had been painted by Sir George Beaumont, a landscape painter who was Wordsworth's friend and patron. Wordsworth's youngest brother, a captain with the East India Company, drowned when his ship sank off the Bill of Portland in February 1805.

[2] *Elysian* Blissful. Referring to Elysium, where, according to classical mythology, the blessed, virtuous, or heroic reside after death.

[3] *Kind* Human race.

But welcome fortitude, and patient cheer,
And frequent sights of what is to be born!
Such sights, or worse, as are before me here.
Not without hope we suffer and we mourn.
—1807

Ode
[*Intimations of Immortality*]

In an 1843 letter to Isabella Fenwick, Wordsworth explained the experiences from his own life on which this ode is based, saying, "Nothing was more difficult for me in childhood than to admit the notion of death as a state applicable to my own being. … I used to brood over the stories of Enoch and Elijah, and almost to persuade myself that, whatever might become of others, I should be translated, in something of the same way, to heaven. With a feeling congenial to this, I was often unable to think of external things as having external existence, and I communed with all that I saw as something not apart from, but inherent in, my own immaterial nature. Many times while going to school have I grasped at a wall or tree to recall myself from this abyss of idealism to the reality. At that time I was afraid of such processes. In later periods of life I have deplored, as we have all reason to do, a subjugation of an opposite character, and have rejoiced over the remembrances, as is expressed in the lines—

> Obstinate questionings
> Of sense and outward things,
> Fallings from us, vanishings; etc."[1]

Wordsworth wrote the first four stanzas of the poem in 1802, and two years elapsed before he completed the poem in 1804. In 1815 he changed the title to "Ode: Intimations of Immortality from Recollections of Early Childhood," its more common title today. He also replaced the Latin epigram from Virgil with the last three lines from "My heart leaps up": "The Child is Father to the Man: / And I could wish my days to be / Bound each to each by natural piety."

[1] *Obstinate … etc.* Lines 144–46.

Ode
[*Intimations of Immortality from Recollections of Early Childhood*]

Paulo majora canamus.[2]

There was a time when meadow, grove, and stream,
The earth, and every common sight,
To me did seem
Apparelled in celestial light,
The glory and the freshness of a dream.
It is not now as it has been of yore;—
Turn wheresoe'er I may,
By night or day,
The things which I have seen I now can see no more.

The Rainbow comes and goes,
And lovely is the Rose,
The Moon doth with delight
Look round her when the heavens are bare;
Waters on a starry night
Are beautiful and fair;
The sunshine is a glorious birth;
But yet I know, where'er I go,
That there hath passed away a glory from the earth.

Now, while the Birds thus sing a joyous song,
And while the young Lambs bound
As to the tabor's[3] sound,
To me alone there came a thought of grief:
A timely utterance gave that thought relief,
And I again am strong.
The Cataracts blow their trumpets from the steep,
No more shall grief of mine the season wrong;
I hear the Echoes through the mountains throng,
The Winds come to me from the fields of sleep,

[2] *Paulo majora canamus* Latin: Let us sing of loftier things. From Virgil's Fourth Eclogue.

[3] *tabor* Small drum.

And all the earth is gay,
Land and sea
Give themselves up to jollity,
And with the heart of May
Doth every Beast keep holiday,
Thou Child of Joy
Shout round me, let me hear thy shouts, thou happy
Shepherd Boy!

Ye blessed Creatures, I have heard the call
Ye to each other make; I see
The heavens laugh with you in your jubilee;
My heart is at your festival,
My head hath it's coronal,° *wreath*
The fullness of your bliss, I feel—I feel it all.
Oh evil day! if I were sullen
While Earth herself is adorning,
This sweet May-morning,
And the Children are pulling,
On every side,
In a thousand valleys far and wide,
Fresh flowers; while the sun shines warm,
And the Babe leaps up on his mother's arm:—
I hear, I hear, with joy I hear!
—But there's a Tree, of many one,
A single Field which I have looked upon,
Both of them speak of something that is gone:
The Pansy at my feet
Doth the same tale repeat:
Whither is fled the visionary gleam?
Where is it now, the glory and the dream?

Our birth is but a sleep and a forgetting:
The Soul that rises with us, our life's Star,
Hath had elsewhere it's setting,
And cometh from afar:
Not in entire forgetfulness,
And not in utter nakedness,
But trailing clouds of glory do we come
From God, Who is our home:
Heaven lies about us in our infancy!
Shades of the prison-house begin to close
Upon the growing Boy,
But he beholds the light, and whence it flows,
He sees it in his joy;
The Youth, who daily farther from the East
Must travel, still is Nature's Priest,
And by the vision splendid
Is on his way attended;
At length the Man perceives it die away,
And fade into the light of common day.

Earth fills her lap with pleasures of her own;
Yearnings she hath in her own natural kind,
And, even with something of a Mother's mind,
And no unworthy aim,
The homely° Nurse doth all she can *simple*
To make her Foster-child, her Inmate Man,
Forget the glories he hath known,
And that imperial palace whence he came.
Behold the Child among his new-born blisses,
A four year's Darling of a pigmy size!
See, where 'mid work of his own hand he lies,
Fretted by sallies of his Mother's kisses,
With light upon him from his Father's eyes!
See, at his feet, some little plan or chart,
Some fragment from his dream of human life,
Shaped by himself with newly-learned art;
A wedding or a festival,
A mourning or a funeral;
And this hath now his heart,
And unto this he frames his song:
Then will he fit his tongue
To dialogues of business, love, or strife;
But it will not be long
Ere this be thrown aside,
And with new joy and pride
The little Actor cons another part,
Filling from time to time his "humourous stage"[1]
With all the Persons, down to palsied Age,
That Life brings with her in her Equipage;
As if his whole vocation
Were endless imitation.

---

[1] *humourous stage* From Elizabethan poet Samuel Daniel's *Musophilus* (1599), in reference to the different character types (defined by their dominant temperaments, or "humors") depicted in Renaissance drama.

Thou, whose exterior semblance doth belie
Thy Soul's immensity;
Thou best Philosopher, who yet dost keep
Thy heritage, thou Eye among the blind,
That, deaf and silent, read'st the eternal deep,
Haunted for ever by the eternal mind—
Mighty Prophet! Seer blest!
On whom those truths do rest,
Which we are toiling all our lives to find;
Thou, over whom thy Immortality
Broods like the Day, a Master o'er a Slave,
A Presence which is not to be put by;
To whom the grave
Is but a lonely bed without the sense or sight
Of day or the warm light,
A place of thought where we in waiting lie;
Thou little Child, yet glorious in the might
Of untamed pleasures, on thy Being's height,
Why with such earnest pains dost thou provoke
The Years to bring the inevitable yoke,
Thus blindly with thy blessedness at strife?
Full soon thy Soul shall have her earthly freight,
And custom lie upon thee with a weight,
Heavy as frost, and deep almost as life!

O joy! that in our embers
Is something that doth live,
That nature yet remembers
What was so fugitive!
The thought of our past years in me doth breed
Perpetual benedictions: not indeed
For that which is most worthy to be blest;
Delight and liberty, the simple creed
Of Childhood, whether fluttering or at rest,
With new-born hope for ever in his breast:—
Not for these I raise
The song of thanks and praise;
But for those obstinate questionings
Of sense and outward things,
Fallings from us, vanishings;
Blank misgivings of a Creature
Moving about in worlds not realized,[1]
High instincts, before which our mortal Nature
Did tremble like a guilty Thing surprised:
But for those first affections,
Those shadowy recollections,
Which, be they what they may,
Are yet the fountain light of all our day,
Are yet a master light of all our seeing;
Uphold us, cherish us, and make
Our noisy years seem moments in the being
Of the eternal Silence: truths that wake,
To perish never;
Which neither listlessness, nor mad endeavour,
Nor Man nor Boy,
Nor all that is at enmity with joy,
Can utterly abolish or destroy!
Hence, in a season of calm weather,
Though inland far we be,
Our Souls have sight of that immortal sea
Which brought us hither,
Can in a moment travel thither,
And see the Children sport upon the shore,
And hear the mighty waters rolling evermore.

Then, sing ye Birds, sing, sing a joyous song!
And let the young Lambs bound
As to the tabor's sound!
We in thought will join your throng,
Ye that pipe and ye that play,
Ye that through your hearts to day
Feel the gladness of the May!
What though the radiance which was once so bright
Be now for ever taken from my sight,
Though nothing can bring back the hour
Of splendour in the grass, of glory in the flower;
We will grieve not, rather find
Strength in what remains behind,
In the primal sympathy
Which having been must ever be,
In the soothing thoughts that spring
Out of human suffering,

[1] *realized* Seeming real.

In the faith that looks through death,
In years that bring the philosophic mind.

And oh ye Fountains, Meadows, Hills, and Groves,
Think not of any severing of our loves!
Yet in my heart of hearts I feel your might;
I only have relinquished one delight
To live beneath your more habitual sway.
I love the Brooks which down their channels fret,
Even more than when I tripped lightly as they;
The innocent brightness of a new-born Day
Is lovely yet;
The Clouds that gather round the setting sun
Do take a sober colouring from an eye
That hath kept watch o'er man's mortality;
Another race hath been, and other palms[1] are won.
Thanks to the human heart by which we live,
Thanks to its tenderness, its joys, and fears,
To me the meanest flower that blows can give
Thoughts that do often lie too deep for tears.
—1807

Surprised by Joy

Surprised by joy—impatient as the Wind
I turned to share the transport—Oh! with whom
But Thee,[2] deep buried in the silent tomb,
That spot which no vicissitude can find?
Love, faithful love, recalled thee to my mind—
But how could I forget thee? Through what power,
Even for the least division of an hour,
Have I been so beguiled as to be blind
To my most grievous loss?—That thought's return
Was the worst pang that sorrow ever bore,
Save one, one only, when I stood forlorn,
Knowing my heart's best treasure was no more;
That neither present time, nor years unborn
Could to my sight that heavenly face restore.
—1815

Mutability[3]

From low to high doth dissolution climb,
And sink from high to low, along a scale
Of awful° notes, whose concord shall not fail; *awe-inspiring*
A musical but melancholy chime,
Which they can hear who meddle not with crime,
Nor avarice, nor over-anxious care.
Truth fails not; but her outward forms that bear
The longest date do melt like frosty rime,
That in the morning whitened hill and plain
And is no more; drop like the tower sublime
Of yesterday, which royally did wear
His crown of weeds, but could not even sustain
Some casual shout that broke the silent air,
Or the unimaginable touch of Time.
—1822

Steamboats, Viaducts, and Railways

Motions and Means, on land and sea at war
With old poetic feeling, not for this,
Shall ye, by Poets even, be judged amiss!
Nor shall your presence, howsoe'er it mar
The loveliness of Nature, prove a bar
To the Mind's gaining that prophetic sense
Of future change, that point of vision whence
May be discovered what in soul ye are.
In spite of all that beauty may disown
In your harsh features, Nature doth embrace
Her lawful offspring in Man's art; and Time,
Pleased with your triumphs o'er his brother Space,
Accepts from your bold hands the proffered crown
Of hope, and smiles on you with cheer sublime.
—1835

[1] *palms* Prizes. In ancient Greece, palm branches or wreaths were often awarded to the winners of foot races.

[2] *Thee* Catherine, the Wordsworths' daughter, who died in June 1812 at the age of three.

[3] *Mutability* From *Ecclesiastical Sonnets*, a sequence of poems dealing with the history of the Church of England.

The Prelude

Wordsworth first began this blank-verse epic poem—generally regarded as his crowning achievement—in 1798, as a preface to his projected masterpiece, *The Recluse*, a philosophical poem that was never completed. Throughout his life Wordsworth referred to *The Prelude* simply as "the poem on my life," "the poem on the growth of my mind," or "the poem to Coleridge." It was his wife, Mary, who, publishing the piece a few months after his death, gave it the title by which it is now known.

The history of *The Prelude* is a long and complex one, spanning over forty years of revisions that saw several preliminary versions before the final, fourteen-book poem was completed in 1839. Wordsworth began *The Prelude* in 1798, during a lonely, cold winter in Germany, during which he and his sister Dorothy struggled with homesickness. This first part, which deals with Wordsworth's early childhood, and a second part describing his adolescence (composed after Wordsworth's return to England in 1799) formed the two books of the 1799 *Prelude*.

Wordsworth returned to *The Prelude* again in 1804, expanding the piece to five books that covered his life through his residence at Cambridge. Around this time, he began to envision the project as a poem of epic proportions that would re-examine his life and convictions. In the expanded version of thirteen books, Wordsworth revisits France of the 1790s in his imagination, reliving those painful years and showing how, in the face of disappointment at the failure of the French Revolution and the growth of tyranny in Europe, he was restored through his ties with nature. This version, completed in May of 1805, begins with echoes of Milton's *Paradise Lost* as Wordsworth describes his vision of the fallen world in which he began his quest to develop his poetic imagination. Still spanning Wordsworth's childhood and maturity, the work no longer proceeds chronologically, but instead moves continuously between past and present as the poet recollects events and then examines their effects on his development. By the poem's end, he emerges from these events transformed and with his poetic sensibilities fully developed.

Wordsworth continued to revise *The Prelude* until 1839, when Dora Wordsworth (the poet's daughter) prepared a beautiful copy of the poem in its fourteen-book version. When *The Prelude* was first released in 1850, critics were often puzzled as to how it should be classified. In part, the poem is a familiar verse epistle to Coleridge and a testament to the power of friendship. At the same time, it is a personal narrative of spiritual journey. Yet the prophetic narrator and the deliberate parallels with other epics elevate the work above the merely personal and provide a representative story of a naive English adolescent who, maturing during the aftermath of a failed revolution, learns to celebrate his heritage.

It was not until the twentieth century that the earlier 1799 and 1805 versions of *The Prelude* were discovered. Both of these have since received much independent critical attention and have been seen by some critics as superior to the final version.

The Two-Part *Prelude* (1799)

FIRST PART

Was it for this
That one, the fairest of all rivers, loved
To blend his murmurs with my Nurse's song,
And from his alder[1] shades, and rocky falls,
And from his fords and shallows, sent a voice
That flowed along my dreams? For this didst thou
O Derwent, travelling over the green plains
Near my "sweet birth-place,"[2] didst thou beauteous Stream
Make ceaseless music through the night and day,
Which with its steady cadence tempering
Our human waywardness, composed my thoughts
To more than infant softness, giving me,
Among the fretful dwellings of mankind,
A knowledge, a dim earnest of the calm
Which Nature breathes among the fields and groves?
Beloved Derwent! fairest of all Streams!
Was it for this that I, a four year's child,
A naked Boy, among thy silent pools
Made one long bathing of a summer's day?
Basked in the sun, or plunged into thy streams,
Alternate, all a summer's day, or coursed
Over the sandy fields, and dashed the flowers
Of yellow grunsel,[3] or when crag and hill,
The woods and distant Skiddaw's[4] lofty height
Were bronzed with a deep radiance, stood alone,
A naked Savage in the thunder shower?
And afterwards, 'twas in a later day
Though early, when upon the mountain-slope
The frost and breath of frosty wind had snapped
The last autumnal crocus, 'twas my joy
To wander half the night among the cliffs

John "Warwick" Smith, *Ulls-water in Paterdale*, 1792–95.

[1] *alder* Tree resembling a birch and usually found in wet places.

[2] *sweet birth-place* From Coleridge's *Frost at Midnight* (1798). Wordsworth's childhood home was in Cockermouth, Cumberland, through which the Derwent River flows.

[3] *grunsel* Groundsel, a common weed.

[4] *Skiddaw* Mountain in Cumberland.

And the smooth hollows, where the woodcocks ran
Along the moonlight turf. In thought and wish,
That time, my shoulder all with springes° hung, *snares*
I was a fell destroyer. Gentle Powers!
Who give us happiness and call it peace!
When scudding on from snare to snare I plied
My anxious visitation, hurrying on,
Still hurrying hurrying onward, how my heart
Panted; among the scattered yew-trees, and the crags
That looked upon me, how my bosom beat
With expectation. Sometimes strong desire,
Resistless, overpowered me, and the bird
Which was the captive of another's toils[1]
Became my prey; and when the deed was done
I heard among the solitary hills
Low breathings coming after me, and sounds
Of undistinguishable motion, steps
Almost as silent as the turf they trod.
Nor less, in spring-time, when on southern banks
The shining sun had from his knot of leaves
Decoyed the primrose-flower, and when the vales
And woods were warm, was I a rover then
In the high places, on the lonesome peaks,
Among the mountains and the winds. Though mean
And though inglorious were my views, the end° *result*
Was not ignoble. Oh, when I have hung
Above the raven's nest, by knots of grass,
Or half-inch fissures in the slipp'ry rock,
But ill sustained, and almost, as it seemed,
Suspended by the blast which blew amain,° *violently*
Shouldering the naked crag, oh at that time,
While on the perilous ridge I hung alone,
With what strange utterance did the loud dry wind
Blow through my ears! the sky seemed not a sky
Of earth, and with what motion moved the clouds!
The mind of man is fashioned and built up
Even as a strain of music: I believe
That there are spirits, which, when they would form
A favoured being, from his very dawn
Of infancy do open out the clouds
As at the touch of lightning, seeking him
With gentle visitation; quiet Powers!
Retired and seldom recognized, yet kind,
And to the very meanest not unknown;
With me, though rarely, in my early days
They communed: others too there are who use,
Yet haply aiming at the self-same end,
Severer interventions, ministry
More palpable, and of their school was I.
They guided me: one evening, led by them,
I went alone into a Shepherd's boat,
A skiff that to a willow-tree was tied
Within a rocky cave, its usual home;
The moon was up, the lake was shining clear
Among the hoary mountains: from the shore
I pushed, and struck the oars, and struck again
In cadence, and my little Boat moved on
Just like a man who walks with stately step
Though bent on speed. It was an act of stealth
And troubled pleasure; not without the voice
Of mountain-echoes did my boat move on,
Leaving behind her still on either side
Small circles glittering idly in the moon
Until they melted all into one track
Of sparkling light. A rocky steep uprose
Above the cavern of the willow tree,
And now, as suited one who proudly rowed
With his best skill, I fixed a steady view
Upon the top of that same craggy ridge,
The bound of the horizon, for behind
Was nothing—but the stars and the grey sky.
—She was an elfin pinnace;[2] twenty times
I dipped my oars into the silent lake,
And, as I rose upon the stroke, my Boat
Went heaving through the water, like a swan—
When from behind that rocky steep, till then
The bound of the horizon, a huge Cliff,
As if with voluntary power instinct,° *imbued*
Upreared its head: I struck, and struck again,
And, growing still in stature, the huge cliff

[1] *toils* Meaning both "snares" and "labor."

[2] *pinnace* Small boat typically used to service larger vessels.

Rose up between me and the stars, and still
With measured motion, like a living thing,
Strode after me. With trembling hands I turned,
And through the silent water stole my way
Back to the cavern of the willow-tree.
There, in her mooring-place I left my bark,° *boat*
And through the meadows homeward went with grave
And serious thoughts: and after I had seen
That spectacle, for many days my brain
Worked with a dim and undetermined sense
Of unknown modes of being: in my thoughts
There was a darkness, call it solitude
Or blank desertion; no familiar shapes
Of hourly objects, images of trees,
Of sea or sky, no colours of green fields:
But huge and mighty forms, that do not live
Like living men, moved slowly through my mind
By day, and were the trouble of my dreams.
    Ah! not in vain ye Beings of the hills!
And ye that walk the woods and open heaths
By moon or star-light, thus from my first dawn
Of childhood did ye love to intertwine
The passions that build up our human soul,
Not with the mean and vulgar° works of man, *ordinary*
But with high objects, with eternal things,
With life and nature, purifying thus
The elements of feeling and of thought,
And sanctifying by such discipline
Both pain and fear, until we recognise
A grandeur in the beatings of the heart.
    Nor was this fellowship vouchsafed to me
With stinted kindness. In November days,
When vapours, rolling down the valleys, made
A lonely scene more lonesome, among woods
At noon, and 'mid the calm of summer nights
When by the margin of the trembling lake
Beneath the gloomy hills I homeward went
In solitude, such intercourse was mine.
    And in the frosty season when the sun
Was set, and, visible for many a mile,
The cottage windows through the twilight blazed,
I heeded not the summons: clear and loud
The village clock tolled six; I wheeled about
Proud and exulting like an untired horse
That cares not for its home.—All shod with steel
We hissed along the polished ice, in games
Confederate, imitative of the chase
And woodland pleasures, the resounding horn,
The pack loud bellowing, and the hunted hare.
So through the darkness and the cold we flew,
And not a voice was idle: with the din,
Meanwhile, the precipices rang aloud,
The leafless trees and every icy crag
Tinkled like iron, while the distant hills
Into the tumult sent an alien sound
Of melancholy not unnoticed while the stars,
Eastward, were sparkling clear, and in the west
The orange sky of evening died away.
    Not seldom from the uproar I retired
Into a silent bay, or sportively
Glanced sideway leaving the tumultuous throng
To cut across the shadow° of a star *reflection*
That gleamed upon the ice: and oftentimes
When we had given our bodies to the wind
And all the shadowy banks on either side
Came sweeping through the darkness, spinning still
The rapid line of motion, then at once
Have I, reclining back upon my heels,
Stopped short; yet still the solitary cliffs
Wheeled by me, even as if the earth had rolled
With visible motion her diurnal° round; *daily*
Behind me did they stretch in solemn train
Feebler and feebler, and I stood and watched
Till all was tranquil as a summer sea.
    Ye Powers of earth! ye Genii of the springs!
And ye that have your voices in the clouds
And ye that are Familiars of the lakes
And of the standing pools, I may not think
A vulgar hope was yours when ye employed
Such ministry, when ye through many a year
Thus by the agency of boyish sports
On caves and trees, upon the woods and hills,
Impressed upon all forms the characters° *signs*
Of danger or desire, and thus did make
The surface of the universal earth
With meanings of delight, of hope and fear,

Work° like a sea. *seethe*
Not uselessly employed
I might pursue this theme through every change
Of exercise and sport to which the year
Did summon us in its delightful round.
We were a noisy crew: the sun in heaven
Beheld not vales more beautiful than ours
Nor saw a race in happiness and joy
More worthy of the fields where they were sown.
I would record with no reluctant voice
Our home amusements by the warm peat fire
At evening, when with pencil, and with slate
In square divisions parcelled out, and all
With crosses and with cyphers scribbled o'er,[1]
We schemed and puzzled, head opposed to head
In strife too humble to be named in verse,
Or round the naked table, snow-white deal,° *pine*
Cherry or maple, sat in close array
And to the combat—Lu or Whist—led on
A thick-ribbed army,[2] not as in the world
Discarded and ungratefully thrown by
Even for the very service they had wrought,
But husbanded through many a long campaign.
Oh with what echoes on the board they fell—
Ironic diamonds, hearts of sable hue,
Queens gleaming through their splendour's last decay,
Knaves wrapt in one assimilating gloom,
And Kings indignant at the shame incurr'd
By royal visages. Meanwhile abroad
The heavy rain was falling, or the frost
Raged bitterly with keen and silent tooth,
And interrupting the impassioned game
Oft from the neighbouring lake the splitting ice
While it sank down towards the water sent
Among the meadows and the hills its long
And frequent yellings, imitative some
Of wolves that howl along the Bothnic main.[3]
Nor with less willing heart would I rehearse
The woods of autumn and their hidden bowers
With milk-white clusters hung; the rod and line,
True symbol of the foolishness of hope,
Which with its strong enchantment led me on
By rocks and pools where never summer-star
Impressed its shadow, to forlorn cascades
Among the windings of the mountain-brooks;
The kite, in sultry calms from some high hill
Sent up, ascending thence till it was lost
Among the fleecy clouds, in gusty days
Launched from the lower grounds, and suddenly
Dash'd headlong—and rejected by the storm.
All these and more with rival claims demand
Grateful acknowledgement. It were a song
Venial,° and such as if I rightly judge *pardonable*
I might protract unblamed; but I perceive
That much is overlooked, and we should ill
Attain our object if from delicate fears
Of breaking in upon the unity
Of this my argument I should omit
To speak of such effects as cannot here
Be regularly classed, yet tend no less
To the same point, the growth of mental power
And love of Nature's works.
Ere I had seen
Eight summers (and 'twas in the very week
When I was first transplanted to thy vale,
Beloved Hawkshead![4] when thy paths, thy shores
And brooks were like a dream of novelty
To my half-infant mind) I chanced to cross
One of those open fields which, shaped like ears,
Make green peninsulas on Esthwaite's lake.
Twilight was coming on, yet through the gloom
I saw distinctly on the opposite shore
Beneath a tree and close by the lake side
A heap of garments, as if left by one
Who there was bathing: half an hour I watched

[1] *With crosses … o'er* See Milton's *Paradise Lost* 8.83: "With centric and eccentric scribbled o'er." Here Wordsworth uses this heroic diction to describe a game of tick-tack-toe.

[2] *Lu or Whist* Popular card games; *thick-ribbed army* Pack of cards made of thick cardboard.

[3] *Bothnic main* Gulf of Bothnia, between Sweden and Finland.

[4] *Hawkshead* Where Wordsworth attended grammar school.

And no one owned them: meanwhile the calm lake
Grew dark with all the shadows on its breast,
And now and then a leaping fish disturbed
The breathless stillness. The succeeding day
There came a company, and in their boat
Sounded with iron hooks and with long poles.
At length the dead man 'mid that beauteous scene
Of trees, and hills, and water, bolt upright
Rose with his ghastly face.[1] I might advert
To numerous accidents in flood or field,
Quarry or moor, or 'mid the winter snows,
Distresses and disasters, tragic facts
Of rural history that impressed my mind
With images, to which in following years
Far other feelings were attached, with forms
That yet exist with independent life
And, like their archetypes, know no decay.
  There are in our existence spots of time
Which with distinct pre-eminence retain
A fructifying virtue,[2] whence, depressed
By trivial occupations and the round
Of ordinary intercourse, our minds
(Especially the imaginative power)
Are nourished, and invisibly repaired.
Such moments chiefly seem to have their date
In our first childhood. I remember well
('Tis of an early season that I speak,
The twilight of rememberable life)
While I was yet an urchin, one who scarce
Could hold a bridle, with ambitious hopes
I mounted, and we rode towards the hills;
We were a pair of horsemen: honest James[3]
Was with me, my encourager and guide.
We had not travelled long ere some mischance
Disjoined me from my comrade, and through fear
Dismounting, down the rough and stony moor
I led my horse and, stumbling on, at length
Came to a bottom where in former times
A man, the murderer of his wife, was hung
In irons; moulderedº was the gibbet[4] mast, *decayed*
The bones were gone, the iron and the wood,
Only a long green ridge of turf remained
Whose shape was like a grave. I left the spot,
And, reascending the bare slope, I saw
A naked pool that lay beneath the hills,
The beacon on the summit, and more near
A girl who bore a pitcher on her head
And seemed with difficult steps to force her way
Against the blowing wind. It was in truth
An ordinary sight but I should need
Colours and words that are unknown to man
To paint the visionary dreariness
Which, while I looked all round for my lost guide,
Did, at that time, invest the naked pool,
The beacon on the lonely eminence,
The woman and her garments vexed and tossed
By the strong wind. Nor less I recollect
(Long after, though my childhood had not ceased)
Another scene which left a kindred power
Implanted in my mind.
                One Christmas time,
The day before the holidays began,
Feverish, and tired and restless, I went forth
Into the fields, impatient for the sight
Of those three horses which should bear us home,
My Brothers and myself. There was a crag,
An eminence which from the meeting point
Of two highways ascending overlooked
At least a long half-mile of those two roads,
By each of which the expected steeds might come,
The choice uncertain. Thither I repaired
Up to the highest summit; 'twas a day
Stormy, and rough, and wild, and on the grass
I sat, half-sheltered by a naked wall;
Upon my right hand was a single sheep,
A whistling hawthorn on my left, and there,
Those two companions at my side, I watched

[1] *At length ... face* In June 1779, shortly after Wordsworth arrived at Hawkshead, a schoolmaster from a neighboring village drowned while swimming in Esthwaite Water.

[2] *fructifying virtue* I.e., power to make fruitful.

[3] *honest James* Most likely the family's servant.

[4] *gibbet* Structure similar to a gallows from which the bodies of people sentenced to execution are suspended, often inside a metal cage.

With eyes intensely straining as the mist
Gave intermitting prospects of the wood
And plain beneath. Ere I to school returned
That dreary time, ere I had been ten days
A dweller in my Father's house, he died,[1]
And I and my two Brothers, orphans then,
Followed his body to the grave. The event
With all the sorrow which it brought appeared
A chastisement, and when I called to mind
That day so lately passed when from the crag
I looked in such anxiety of hope,
With trite reflections of morality
Yet with the deepest passion I bowed low
To God, who thus corrected my desires;
And afterwards the wind, and sleety rain,
And all the business of the elements,
The single sheep, and the one blasted tree,
And the bleak music of that old stone wall,
The noise of wood and water, and the mist
Which on the line of each of those two roads
Advanced in such indisputable shapes,
All these were spectacles and sounds to which
I often would repair, and thence would drink
As at a fountain, and I do not doubt
That in this later time when storm and rain
Beat on my roof at midnight, or by day
When I am in the woods, unknown to me
The workings of my spirit thence are brought.
 Nor sedulous° as I have been to trace *diligent*
How Nature by collateral° interest *indirect*
And by extrinsic passion peopled first
My mind with forms, or beautiful or grand,
And made me love them, may I well forget
How other pleasures have been mine, and joys
Of subtler origin, how I have felt
Not seldom, even in that tempestuous time,
Those hallowed and pure motions of the sense
Which seem in their simplicity to own
An intellectual charm, that calm delight
Which, if I err not, surely must belong
To those first-born affinities that fit
Our new existence to existing things
And in our dawn of being constitute
The bond of union betwixt life and joy.
 Yes, I remember when the changeful earth
And twice five seasons on my mind had stamped
The faces of the moving year, even then,
A Child, I held unconscious intercourse
With the eternal Beauty, drinking in
A pure organic pleasure from the lines
Of curling mist or from the level plain
Of waters coloured by the steady clouds.
 The sands of Westmoreland, the creeks and bays
Of Cumbria's[2] rocky limits, they can tell
How when the sea threw off his evening shade
And to the Shepherd's hut beneath the crags
Did send sweet notice of the rising moon,
How I have stood to images like these
A stranger, linking with the spectacle
No body of associated forms
And bringing with me no peculiar sense
Of quietness or peace, yet I have stood
Even while my eye has moved o'er three long leagues
Of shining water, gathering, as it seemed,
Through the wide surface of that field of light
New pleasure, like a bee among the flowers.
 Thus often in those fits of vulgar joy
Which through all seasons on a child's pursuits
Are prompt attendants, 'mid that giddy bliss
Which like a tempest works along the blood
And is forgotten, even then I felt
Gleams like the flashing of a shield; the earth
And common face of Nature spake to me
Rememberable things: sometimes, 'tis true,
By quaint associations, yet not vain
Nor profitless if haply° they impressed *by chance*
Collateral[3] objects and appearances,
Albeit lifeless then, and doomed to sleep

[1] *ere I ... died* Wordsworth's father died on 30 December 1783. His mother had died five years earlier.

[2] *Westmoreland ... Cumbria* Westmorland and Cumbria (usually called "Cumberland") were counties in the Lake District.

[3] *Collateral* I.e., indirect, lying aside from the main interests of the poet.

Until maturer seasons called them forth
To impregnate and to elevate the mind.
——And if the vulgar joy by its own weight
Wearied itself out of the memory,
The scenes which were a witness of that joy
Remained, in their substantial lineaments
Depicted on the brain, and to the eye
Were visible, a daily sight: and thus
By the impressive agency of fear,
By pleasure and repeated happiness,
So frequently repeated, and by force
Of obscure feelings representative
Of joys that were forgotten, these same scenes
So beauteous and majestic in themselves,
Though yet the day was distant, did at length
Become habitually dear, and all
Their hues and forms were by invisible links
Allied to the affections.
I began
My story early, feeling, as I fear,
The weakness of a human love for days
Disowned by memory, ere the birth of spring
Planting my snow-drops among winter snows.
Nor will it seem to thee, my Friend,[1] so prompt
In sympathy, that I have lengthened out
With fond and feeble tongue a tedious tale.
Meanwhile my hope has been that I might fetch
Reproaches from my former years, whose power
May spur me on, in manhood now mature,
To honourable toil. Yet, should it be
That this is but an impotent desire,
That I by such inquiry am not taught
To understand myself, nor thou to know
With better knowledge how the heart was framed
Of him thou lovest, need I dread from thee
Harsh judgements if I am so loath to quit
Those recollected hours that have the charm
Of visionary things,[2] and lovely forms
And sweet sensations that throw back our life
And make our infancy a visible scene
On which the sun is shining?

SECOND PART

Thus far my Friend, have we retraced the way
Through which I travelled when I first began
To love the woods and fields: the passion yet
Was in its birth, sustained as might befall
By nourishment that came unsought, for still
From week to week, from month to month, we lived
A round of tumult: duly° were our games *fittingly*
Prolonged in summer till the day-light failed;
No chair remained before the doors, the bench
And threshold steps were empty, fast asleep
The labourer and the old man who had sat
A later lingerer, yet the revelry
Continued and the loud uproar: at last
When all the ground was dark, and the huge clouds
Were edged with twinkling stars, to bed we went
With weary joints and with a beating mind.
Ah! is there one who ever has been young
And needs a monitory voice to tame
The pride of virtue and of intellect,
And is there one, the wisest and the best
Of all mankind, who does not sometimes wish
For things which cannot be, who would not give,
If so he might, to duty and to truth
The eagerness of infantine desire?
A tranquillizing spirit presses now
On my corporeal frame, so wide appears
The vacancy between me and those days
Which yet have such self-presence in my heart
That sometimes when I think of them I seem
Two consciousnesses, conscious of myself
And of some other being. A grey stone
Of native rock, left midway in the square
Of our small market-village, was the home
And centre of these joys, and when, returned
After long absence, thither I repaired,
I found that it was split and gone to build
A smart assembly-room that perked and flared

[1] *my Friend* Coleridge.

[2] *visionary things* Things seen in the imagination.

With wash and rough-cast,[1] elbowing the ground
Which had been ours. But let the fiddle scream
And be ye happy! yet I know, my Friends,
That more than one of you will think with me
Of those soft starry nights and that old dame
From whom the stone was named, who there had sat
And watched her table with its huckster's wares,
Assiduous, for the length of sixty years.
—We ran a boisterous race, the year span round
With giddy motion. But the time approached
That brought with it a regular desire
For calmer pleasures, when the beauteous scenes
Of nature were collaterally attached
To every scheme of holiday delight
And every boyish sport, less grateful° else *pleasing*
And languidly pursued.
When summer came
It was the pastime of our afternoons
To beat along the plain of Windermere
With rival oars; and the selected bourn° *goal*
Was now an island musical with birds
That sang for ever, now a sister isle
Beneath the oak's umbrageous° covert sown *shady*
With lilies of the valley like a field,
And now a third small island[2] where remained
An old stone table and one mouldered cave,
A hermit's history. In such a race,
So ended, disappointment could be none,
Uneasiness, or pain, or jealousy;
We rested in the shade all pleased alike,
Conquered and conqueror. Thus our selfishness
Was mellowed down, and thus the pride of strength
And the vain-glory of superior skill
Were interfused with objects which subdued
And tempered them, and gradually produced
A quiet independence of the heart.
And to my Friend who knows me I may add,
Unapprehensive of reproof, that hence
Ensued a diffidence and modesty,
And I was taught to feel, perhaps too much,
The self-sufficing power of solitude.
No delicate viands sapped our bodily strength;
More than we wished we knew the blessing then
Of vigorous hunger, for our daily meals
Were frugal, Sabine fare![3] and then exclude
A little weekly stipend, and we lived
Through three divisions of the quartered year
In penniless poverty. But now to school
Returned from the half-yearly holidays,
We came with purses more profusely filled,
Allowance which abundantly sufficed
To gratify the palate with repasts
More costly than the Dame of whom I spake,
That ancient woman, and her board° supplied, *table*
Hence inroads into distant vales, and long
Excursions far away among the hills;
Hence rustic dinners on the cool green ground
Or in the woods or by a river-side
Or fountain,° festive banquets that provoked *spring*
The languid action° of a natural scene *effect*
By pleasure of corporeal appetite.
Nor is my aim neglected if I tell
How twice in the long length of those half-years
We from our funds perhaps with bolder hand
Drew largely, anxious for one day at least
To feel the motion of the galloping steed;
And with the good old Innkeeper in truth
I needs must say that sometimes we have used
Sly subterfuge, for the intended bound
Of the day's journey was too distant far
For any cautious man, a Structure famed
Beyond its neighbourhood, the antique walls
Of a large Abbey[4] with its fractured arch,
Belfry, and images, and living trees,

---

[1] *smart assembly-room* Hawkshead Town Hall, built in 1790; *wash* Whitewash; *rough-cast* Plaster made of lime and gravel.

[2] *third small island* Island of Lady Holm, where a chapel dedicated to the Virgin Mary was formerly located.

[3] *Sabine fare* The Sabines were an ancient Italian mountain tribe known for their austere living habits. "Sabine fare" may also refer to the sort of rustic food that would have been prepared at the Roman poet Horace's country estate, often called the "Sabine farm."

[4] *a large Abbey* Furness Abbey, a ruined abbey located approximately 25 miles south of Hawkshead.

A holy scene! Along the smooth green turf
Our horses grazed: in more than inland peace
Left by the winds that overpass the vale
In that sequestered ruin trees and towers
Both silent, and both motionless alike,
Hear all day long the murmuring sea that beats
Incessantly upon a craggy shore.
Our steeds remounted, and the summons given,
With whip and spur we by the Chantry[1] flew
In uncouth race, and left the cross-legged Knight
And the stone Abbot, and that single wren
Which one day sang so sweetly in the nave
Of the old church that, though from recent showers
The earth was comfortless, and touched by faint
Internal breezes from the roofless walls
The shuddering ivy dripped large drops, yet still
So sweetly 'mid the gloom the invisible bird
Sang to itself that there I could have made
My dwelling-place, and lived for ever there
To hear such music. Through the walls we flew
And down the valley, and, a circuit made
In wantonness of heart, through rough and smooth
We scampered homeward. O ye rocks and streams
And that still spirit of the evening air,
Even in this joyous time I sometimes felt
Your presence, when with slackened step we breathed[2]
Along the sides of the steep hills, or when,
Lightened by gleams of moonlight from the sea,
We beat with thundering hoofs the level sand.
There was a row of ancient trees, since fallen,
That on the margin of a jutting land
Stood near the lake of Coniston and made
With its long boughs above the water stretched
A gloom through which a boat might sail along
As in a cloister. An old Hall[3] was near,
Grotesque and beautiful, its gavel° end *gable*
And huge round chimneys to the top o'ergrown
With fields of ivy. Thither we repaired,
'Twas even a custom with us, to the shore
And to that cool piazza. They who dwelt
In the neglected mansion-house supplied
Fresh butter, tea-kettle, and earthen-ware,
And chafing-dish with smoking coals, and so
Beneath the trees we sat in our small boat
And in the covert eat° our delicate meal *ate*
Upon the calm smooth lake. It was a joy
Worthy the heart of one who is full grown
To rest beneath those horizontal boughs
And mark the radiance of the setting sun,
Himself unseen, reposing on the top
Of the high eastern hills. And there I said,
That beauteous sight before me, there I said
(Then first beginning in my thoughts to mark
That sense of dim similitude which links
Our moral feelings with external forms)
That in whatever region I should close
My mortal life I would remember you,
Fair scenes! that dying I would think on you,
My soul would send a longing look to you:
Even as that setting sun while all the vale
Could nowhere catch one faint memorial gleam
Yet with the last remains of his last light
Still lingered, and a farewell lustre threw
On the dear mountain-tops where first he rose.
'Twas then my fourteenth summer, and these words
Were uttered in a casual access
Of sentiment, a momentary trance
That far outran the habit of my mind.
Upon the eastern shore of Windermere,
Above the crescent of a pleasant bay,
There was an Inn,[4] no homely-featured shed,
Brother of the surrounding cottages,
But 'twas a splendid place, the door beset
With chaises, grooms, and liveries, and within
Decanters, glasses, and the blood-red wine.
In ancient times, or ere the Hall[5] was built
On the large island, had the dwelling been

[1] *Chantry* Altar or chapel which has been endowed for daily masses to be sung for the donor.

[2] *breathed* I.e., let the horses catch their breath.

[3] *old Hall* Coniston Hall, built in 1580.

[4] *an Inn* The White Lion Inn, which was located in Bowness Village.

[5] *the Hall* Built on Belle Isle in Lake Windermere in the early 1780s.

More worthy of a poet's love, a hut
Proud of its one bright fire and sycamore shade.
But though the rhymes were gone which once inscribed
The threshold, and large golden characters
On the blue-frosted sign-board had usurped
The place of the old Lion in contempt
And mockery of the rustic painter's hand,
Yet to this hour the spot to me is dear
With all its foolish pomp. The garden lay
Upon a slope surmounted by the plain
Of a small bowling-green; beneath us stood
A grove, with gleams of water through the trees
And over the tree-tops; nor did we want
Refreshment, strawberries and mellow cream,
And there through half an afternoon we played
On the smooth platform, and the shouts we sent
Made all the mountains ring. But ere the fall
Of night, when in our pinnace we returned
Over the dusky lake, and to the beach
Of some small island steered our course with one,
The minstrel of our troop, and left him there
And rowed off gently while he blew his flute
Alone upon the rock—oh then the calm
And dead still water lay upon my mind
Even with a weight of pleasure, and the sky,
Never before so beautiful, sank down
Into my heart and held me like a dream.
    Thus day by day my sympathies increased
And thus the common range of visible things
Grew dear to me: already I began
To love the sun, a Boy I loved the sun
Not, as I since have loved him, as a pledge
And surety of my earthly life, a light
Which while I view I feel I am alive,
But for this cause, that I had seen him lay
His beauty on the morning hills, had seen
The western mountain touch his setting orb
In many a thoughtless hour, when from excess
Of happiness my blood appeared to flow
With its own pleasure and I breathed with joy.
And from like feelings, humble though intense,
To patriotic and domestic love
Analogous, the moon to me was dear,
For I would dream away my purposes
Standing to look upon her while she hung
Midway between the hills as if she knew
No other region but belonged to thee,
Yea, appertained by a peculiar right
To thee and thy grey huts,[1] my native vale.
    Those incidental charms which first attached
My heart to rural objects day by day
Grew weaker, and I hasten on to tell
How nature, intervenient° till this time *extraneous*
And secondary, now at length was sought
For her own sake. But who shall parcel out
His intellect by geometric rules,
Split like a province into round and square;
Who knows the individual hour in which
His habits were first sown, even as a seed;
Who that shall point as with a wand and say,
This portion of the river of my mind
Came from yon fountain? Thou, my Friend, art one
More deeply read in thy own thoughts, no slave
Of that false secondary power by which
In weakness we create distinctions, then
Believe our puny boundaries are things
Which we perceive and not which we have made.
To thee, unblinded by these outward shows,
The unity of all has been revealed,
And thou wilt doubt with me, less aptly skilled
Than many are to class the cabinet
Of their sensations and in voluble phrase
Run through the history and birth of each
As of a single independent thing.
Hard task to analyse a soul in which
Not only general habits and desires
But each most obvious and particular thought,
Not in a mystical and idle sense
But in the words of reason deeply weighed,
Hath no beginning.
                Bless'd the infant Babe
(For with my best conjectures I would trace
The progress of our being) blest the Babe

[1] *grey huts* Gray stone cottages.

Nursed in his Mother's arms, the Babe who sleeps
Upon his Mother's breast, who when his soul
Claims manifest kindred with an earthly soul
Doth gather passion from his Mother's eye!
Such feelings pass into his torpid life
Like an awakening breeze, and hence his mind
Even in the first trial of its powers
Is prompt and watchful, eager to combine
In one appearance all the elements
And parts of the same object, else detached
And loath to coalesce. Thus day by day
Subjected to the discipline of love
His organs and recipient faculties
Are quickened, are more vigorous, his mind spreads
Tenacious of the forms which it receives.
In one beloved presence, nay, and more,
In that most apprehensive habitude[1]
And those sensations which have been derived
From this beloved presence, there exists
A virtue which irradiates and exalts
All objects through all intercourse of sense.
No outcast he, bewildered and depressed:
Along his infant veins are interfused
The gravitation and the filial bond
Of nature that connect him with the world.
Emphatically such a being lives
An inmate of this *active* universe;
From nature largely he receives, nor so
Is satisfied but largely gives again,
For feeling has to him imparted strength,
And powerful in all sentiments of grief,
Of exultation, fear and joy, his mind,
Even as an agent of the one great mind,
Creates, creator and receiver both,
Working but in alliance with the works
Which it beholds. Such verily is the first
Poetic spirit of our human life,
By uniform control of after years
In most abated and suppressed, in some
Through every change of growth or of decay
Preeminent till death.
From early days,
Beginning not long after that first time
In which, a Babe, by intercourse of touch
I held mute dialogues with my Mother's heart,
I have endeavoured to display the means
Whereby this infant sensibility,
Great birth-right of our being, was in me
Augmented and sustained. Yet is a path
More difficult before me, and I fear
That in its broken windings we shall need
The Chamois'[2] sinews and the Eagle's wing:
For now a trouble came into my mind
From obscure causes. I was left alone
Seeking this visible world, nor knowing why:
The props of my affections were removed[3]
And yet the building stood as if sustained
By its own spirit. All that I beheld
Was dear to me, and from this cause it came
That now to Nature's finer influxes° *influences*
My mind lay open, to that more exact
And intimate communion which our hearts
Maintain with the minuter properties
Of objects which already are beloved,
And of those only. Many are the joys
Of youth, but oh! what happiness to live
When every hour brings palpable access
Of knowledge, when all knowledge is delight,
And sorrow is not there. The seasons came
And every season brought a countless store
Of modes and temporary qualities
Which but for this most watchful power of love
Had been neglected, left a register
Of permanent relations, else unknown:
Hence life, and change, and beauty, solitude
More active even than "best society,"[4]

---

[1] *apprehensive habitude* Disposition most suited to learning.

[2] *Chamois* Agile goat-antelope found primarily in the mountains of Europe.

[3] *The props ... removed* Wordsworth's mother died just before his eighth birthday.

[4] *best society* See Milton's *Paradise Lost* 9.249: "For solitude sometimes is the best society."

Society made sweet as solitude
By silent inobtrusive sympathies
And gentle agitations of the mind
From manifold distinctions, difference
Perceived in things where to the common eye
No difference is: and hence from the same source
Sublimer joy; for I would walk alone
In storm and tempest or in starlight nights
Beneath the quiet heavens, and at that time
Would feel whate'er there is of power in sound
To breathe an elevated mood by form
Or image unprofaned: and I would stand
Beneath some rock listening to sounds that are
The ghostly language of the ancient earth
Or make their dim abode in distant winds.
Thence did I drink the visionary power.
I deem not profitless these fleeting moods
Of shadowy exaltation, not for this,
That they are kindred to our purer mind
And intellectual life, but that the soul
Remembering how she felt, but what she felt
Remembering not, retains an obscure sense
Of possible sublimity to which
With growing faculties she doth aspire,
With faculties still growing, feeling still
That whatsoever point they gain, they still
Have something to pursue.

And not alone
In grandeur and in tumult, but no less
In tranquil scenes, that universal power
And fitness in the latent qualities
And essences of things, by which the mind
Is moved with feelings of delight, to me
Came strengthened with a superadded soul,
A virtue not its own. My morning walks
Were early; oft before the hours of school
I travelled round our little lake, five miles
Of pleasant wandering, happy time more dear
For this, that one was by my side, a Friend
Then passionately loved;[1] with heart how full
Will he peruse these lines, this page, perhaps
A blank to other men, for many years
Have since flowed in between us, and, our minds
Both silent to each other, at this time
We live as if those hours had never been.
Nor seldom did I lift our cottage latch
Far earlier, and before the vernal° thrush *spring-time*
Was audible, among the hills I sat
Alone upon some jutting eminence
At the first hour of morning when the vale
Lay quiet in an utter solitude.
How shall I trace the history, where seek
The origin of what I then have felt?
Oft in those moments such a holy calm
Did overspread my soul that I forgot
The agency of sight, and what I saw
Appeared like something in myself—a dream,
A prospect° in my mind. 'Twere long to tell *view*
What spring and autumn, what the winter-snows
And what the summer-shade, what day and night,
The evening and the morning, what my dreams
And what my waking thoughts supplied, to nurse
That spirit of religious love in which
I walked with nature. But let this at least
Be not forgotten, that I still retained
My first creative sensibility,
That by the regular action of the world
My soul was unsubdued. A plastic° power *formative*
Abode with me, a forming hand, at times
Rebellious, acting in a devious mood,
A local spirit of its own, at war
With general tendency, but for the most
Subservient strictly to the external things
With which it communed. An auxiliar light
Came from my mind which on the setting sun
Bestowed new splendour, the melodious birds,
The gentle breezes, fountains that ran on
Murmuring so sweetly in themselves, obeyed
A like dominion, and the midnight storm
Grew darker in the presence of my eye.
Hence my obeisance, my devotion hence,
And *hence* my transport.° *exaltation*

Nor should this perchance

---

[1] *Friend … passionately loved* John Fleming, Wordsworth's friend at Hawkshead.

Pass unrecorded, that I still° had loved *always*
The exercise and produce of a toil
Than analytic industry to me
More pleasing, and whose character, I deem,
Is more poetic, as resembling more
Creative agency: I mean to speak
Of that interminable building reared
By observation of affinities
In objects where no brotherhood exists
To common minds. My seventeenth year was come,
And whether from this habit rooted now
So deeply in my mind, or from excess
Of the great social principle of life
Coercing all things into sympathy,
To unorganic natures I transferred
My own enjoyments, or, the power of truth
Coming in revelation, I conversed
With things that really are. I at this time
Saw blessings spread around me like a sea.
Thus did my days pass on, and now at length
From Nature and her overflowing soul
I had received so much that all my thoughts
Were steeped in feeling; I was only then
Contented when with bliss ineffable
I felt the sentiment of being spread
O'er all that moves, and all that seemeth still,
O'er all that, lost beyond the reach of thought
And human knowledge, to the human eye
Invisible, yet liveth to the heart,
O'er all that leaps, and runs, and shouts and sings
Or beats the gladsome air, o'er all that glides
Beneath the wave, yea, in the wave itself
And mighty depth of waters: wonder not
If such my transports were, for in all things
I saw one life and felt that it was joy.
One song they sang, and it was audible,
Most audible then when the fleshly ear,
O'ercome by grosser prelude of that strain,
Forgot its functions, and slept undisturbed.
If this be error, and another faith
Find easier access to the pious mind,
Yet were I grossly destitute of all
Those human sentiments which make this earth
So dear, if I should fail with grateful voice
To speak of you, ye mountains! and ye lakes
And sounding cataracts! ye mists and winds
That dwell among the hills where I was born.
If, in my youth, I have been pure in heart,
If, mingling with the world, I am content
With my own modest pleasures, and have lived
With God and Nature communing, removed
From little enmities and low desires,
The gift is yours: if in these times[1] of fear,
This melancholy waste° of hopes o'erthrown, *wasteland*
If, 'mid indifference and apathy
And wicked exultation, when good men
On every side fall off we know not how
To selfishness disguised in gentle names
Of peace, and quiet, and domestic love,
Yet mingled, not unwillingly, with sneers
On visionary minds, if in this time
Of dereliction and dismay I yet
Despair not of our nature, but retain
A more than Roman confidence, a faith
That fails not, in all sorrow my support,
The blessing of my life, the gift is yours,
Ye Mountains! thine, O Nature! thou hast fed
My lofty speculations, and in thee
For this uneasy heart of ours I find
A never-failing principle of joy
And purest passion.
Thou, my Friend, wast reared
In the great city 'mid far other scenes,[2]
But we, by different roads, at length have gained
The self-same bourne. And from this cause to thee

[1] *in these times* I.e., following the failure of the French Revolution, by which time many radicals were recanting. In a 1799 letter to Wordsworth, Coleridge asks him to write something about those who "have thrown up all hopes of the amelioration of mankind, and are sinking into an almost epicurean selfishness, disguising the same under the soft titles of domestic attachment and contempt for visionary *philosophes*."

[2] *Thou … other scenes* See Coleridge's "Frost at Midnight" 50–52, in which the speaker addresses his child: "thou shalt learn far other lore, / And in far other scenes! For I was reared / In the great city, pent 'mid cloisters dim."

I speak unapprehensive of contempt,
The insinuated scoff of coward tongues,
And all that silent language which so oft
In conversation betwixt man and man
Blots from the human countenance all trace
Of beauty and of love. For thou hast sought
The truth in solitude, and thou art one,
The most intense of Nature's worshippers,
In many things my brother, chiefly here
In this my deep devotion.
Fare thee well!
Health and the quiet of a healthful mind
Attend thee! seeking oft the haunts of men
But yet more often living with thyself
And for thyself, so haply shall thy days
Be many and a blessing to mankind.
—1799

from The Fourteen-Book *Prelude* (1850)

Book First
Introduction, Childhood, and School-time

O there is blessing in this gentle breeze,
A visitant that while he fans my cheek
Doth seem half-conscious of the joy it brings
From the green fields, and from yon azure sky.
Whate'er its mission, the soft breeze can come
To none more grateful than to me; escaped
From the vast city,[1] where I long had pined
A discontented sojourner: now free,
Free as a bird to settle where I will.
What dwelling shall receive me? in what vale
Shall be my harbour? underneath what grove
Shall I take up my home? and what clear stream
Shall with its murmur lull me into rest?
The earth is all before me.[2] With a heart
Joyous, nor scared at its own liberty,
I look about; and should the chosen guide
Be nothing better than a wandering cloud,
I cannot miss my way. I breathe again!
Trances of thought and mountings of the mind
Come fast upon me: it is shaken off,
That burthen of my own unnatural self,
The heavy weight of many a weary day
Not mine, and such as were not made for me.
Long months of peace (if such bold word accord
With any promises of human life),
Long months of ease and undisturbed delight
Are mine in prospect; whither shall I turn
By road or pathway, or through trackless field,
Up hill or down, or shall some floating thing
Upon the river point me out my course?

Dear Liberty! Yet what would it avail
But for a gift that consecrates the joy?
For I, methought, while the sweet breath of heaven
Was blowing on my body, felt within
A correspondent breeze, that gently moved
With quickening virtue, but is now become
A tempest, a redundant° energy, *abounding*
Vexing its own creation. Thanks to both,
And their congenial powers, that, while they join
In breaking up a long-continued frost,
Bring with them vernal° promises, the hope *spring-time*
Of active days urged on by flying hours—
Days of sweet leisure, taxed with patient thought
Abstruse, nor wanting° punctual[3] service high, *lacking*
Matins and vespers,[4] of harmonious verse!

Thus far, O Friend![5] did I, not used to make
A present joy the matter of a song,
Pour forth that day my soul in measured strains
That would not be forgotten, and are here

[1] *the vast city* I.e., London.

[2] *The earth ... me* See Milton's *Paradise Lost* 12.646. Milton writes that following the expulsion of Adam and Eve from Eden, "The world was all before them."

[3] *punctual* Appropriately timed.

[4] *Matins and vespers* Morning and evening prayer services, respectively.

[5] *O Friend* The addressee is Samuel Taylor Coleridge.

Recorded: to the open fields I told
A prophecy: poetic numbers° came *verses*
Spontaneously to clothe in priestly robe
A renovated spirit singled out,
Such hope was mine, for holy services.
My own voice cheered me, and, far more, the mind's
Internal echo of the imperfect sound;
To both I listened, drawing from them both
A cheerful confidence in things to come.

Content, and not unwilling now to give
A respite to this passion, I paced on
With brisk and eager steps; and came at length,
To a green shady place, where down I sat
Beneath a tree, slackening my thoughts by choice,
And settling into gentler happiness.
'Twas autumn, and a clear and placid day,
With warmth, as much as needed, from a sun
Two hours declined towards the west; a day
With silver clouds, and sunshine on the grass,
And in the sheltered and the sheltering grove
A perfect stillness. Many were the thoughts
Encouraged and dismissed, till choice was made
Of a known Vale,[1] whither my feet should turn,
Nor rest till they had reached the very door
Of the one cottage which methought I saw.
No picture of mere memory ever looked
So fair; and while upon the fancied scene
I gazed with growing love, a higher power
Than Fancy gave assurance of some work
Of glory there forthwith to be begun,
Perhaps too there performed.[2] Thus long I mused,
Nor e'er lost sight of what I mused upon,
Save when, amid the stately grove of oaks,
Now here, now there, an acorn, from its cup
Dislodged, through sere leaves rustled, or at once
To the bare earth dropped with a startling sound.
From that soft couch I rose not, till the sun
Had almost touched the horizon; casting then
A backward glance upon the curling cloud
Of city smoke, by distance ruralized;
Keen as a Truant or a Fugitive,
But as a Pilgrim resolute, I took,
Even with the chance equipment of that hour
The road that pointed toward the chosen Vale.
It was a splendid evening, and my Soul
Once more made trial of her strength, nor lacked
Æolian visitations;[3] but the harp
Was soon defrauded, and the banded host
Of harmony dispersed in straggling sounds,
And lastly utter silence! "Be it so;
Why think of any thing but present good?"
So, like a home-bound labourer I pursued
My way beneath the mellowing sun, that shed
Mild influence;[4] nor left in me one wish
Again to bend the Sabbath[5] of that time
To a servile yoke. What need of many words?
A pleasant loitering journey, through three days
Continued, brought me to my hermitage.
I spare to tell of what ensued, the life
In common things—the endless store of things,
Rare, or at least so seeming every day
Found all about me in one neighbourhood—
The self-congratulation,[6] and, from morn
To night, unbroken cheerfulness serene.
But speedily an earnest longing rose
To brace myself to some determined aim,
Reading or thinking; either to lay up
New stores, or rescue from decay the old
By timely interference: and therewith
Came hopes still higher, that with outward life
I might endue some airy phantasies
That had been floating loose about for years,

[1] *a known Vale* Grasmere, where Wordsworth and his sister moved in 1799.

[2] *some work ... performed* A planned poem, *The Recluse*, which was intended to be Wordsworth's major work. *The Prelude* was intended to be the first third of *The Recluse*; most of the rest was never written.

[3] *Æolian visitations* Influences that act on the poet's soul as winds act on an Aeolian harp, which makes music when touched by a breeze.

[4] *influence* Reference to astrological influence, exerted by the stars over human life.

[5] *Sabbath* Time of rest, especially one of religious significance.

[6] *self-congratulation* Self-rejoicing.

And to such beings temperately deal forth
The many feelings that oppressed my heart.
That hope hath been discouraged; welcome light
Dawns from the East, but dawns to disappear
And mock me with a sky that ripens not
Into a steady morning: if my mind,
Remembering the bold promise of the past,
Would gladly grapple with some noble theme,
Vain is her wish: where'er she turns she finds
Impediments from day to day renewed.

And now it would content me to yield up
Those lofty hopes awhile, for present gifts
Of humbler industry. But, oh, dear Friend!
The Poet, gentle creature as he is,
Hath, like the Lover, his unruly times;
His fits when he is neither sick nor well,
Though no distress be near him but his own
Unmanageable thoughts: his mind, best pleased
While she, as duteous as the mother dove,
Sits brooding,[1] lives not always to that end,
But, like the innocent bird, hath goadings on
That drive her as in trouble through the groves;
With me is now such passion, to be blamed
No otherwise than as it lasts too long.

When, as becomes a Man who would prepare
For such an arduous work, I through myself
Make rigorous inquisition, the report
Is often cheering; for I neither seem
To lack that first great gift, the vital soul,
Nor general Truths, which are themselves a sort
Of Elements and Agents, Under-powers,
Subordinate helpers of the living mind:
Nor am I naked of external things,
Forms, images, nor numerous other aids
Of less regard, though won perhaps with toil
And needful to build up a Poet's praise.
Time, place, and manners° do I seek, and these *habits*
Are found in plenteous store, but nowhere such
As may be singled out with steady choice;
No little band of yet remembered names
Whom I, in perfect confidence, might hope
To summon back from lonesome banishment,
And make them dwellers in the hearts of men
Now living, or to live in future years.
Sometimes the ambitious Power of choice, mistaking
Proud spring-tide swellings for a regular sea,
Will settle on some British theme, some old
Romantic tale by Milton left unsung;[2]
More often turning to some gentle place
Within the groves of Chivalry, I pipe
To shepherd swains,° or seated, harp in hand, *lovers*
Amid reposing knights by a river side
Or fountain, listen to the grave reports
Of dire enchantments faced and overcome
By the strong mind, and tales of warlike feats,
Where spear encountered spear, and sword with sword
Fought, as if conscious of the blazonry
That the shield bore, so glorious was the strife;
Whence inspiration for a song that winds
Through ever changing scenes of votive quest[3]
Wrongs to redress, harmonious tribute paid
To patient courage and unblemished truth,
To firm devotion, zeal unquenchable,
And Christian meekness hallowing faithful loves.[4]
Sometimes, more sternly moved, I would relate
How vanquished Mithridates northward passed,
And, hidden in the cloud of years, became
Odin, the Father of a race by whom
Perished the Roman Empire:[5] how the friends

[1] *While she ... brooding* See Milton's *Paradise Lost* 1.21–22, in which the narrator invokes the Holy Spirit, who, at the time of Creation, "Dovelike satst brooding on the vast Abyss / And madst it pregnant."

[2] *some old ... unsung* In *Paradise Lost* 9.24–41, Milton writes that he chose to compose a biblical rather than a romantic epic.

[3] *votive quest* Quest undertaken as the result of a vow.

[4] *And Christian ... loves* Reference to Spenser's *Faerie Queene* 1.1.9: "Fierce warres and faithful loves shall moralize my song."

[5] *How vanquished ... Empire* Mithridates was a king of Pontus (in present-day Turkey) who was defeated by the Romans in 66 BCE. In *Decline and Fall of the Roman Empire* (1776–88), Edward Gibbon associates the story of King Mithridates's downfall with the unsubstantiated tale of Odin, a chieftain who led his tribe out of Asia to establish the first European settlement of Goths. In the early fifth century CE,

And followers of Sertorius,[1] out of Spain
Flying, found shelter in the Fortunate Isles;
And left their usages, their arts and laws,
To disappear by a slow gradual death,
To dwindle and to perish one by one,
Starved in those narrow bounds: but not the soul
Of Liberty, which fifteen hundred years
Survived, and, when the European came
With skill and power that might not be withstood,
Did, like a pestilence, maintain its hold
And wasted down by glorious death that race
Of natural heroes: or I would record
How, in tyrannic times, some high-souled man,
Unnamed among the chronicles of kings,
Suffered in silence for Truth's sake: or tell
How that one Frenchman,[2] through continued force
Of meditation on the inhuman deeds
Of those who conquered first the Indian Isles,
Went single in his ministry across
The Ocean; not to comfort the oppressed,
But, like a thirsty wind, to roam about,
Withering the Oppressor: how Gustavus sought
Help at his need in Dalecarlia's mines:[3]
How Wallace[4] fought for Scotland; left the name
Of Wallace to be found, like a wild flower,
All over his dear Country; left the deeds
Of Wallace, like a family of Ghosts,
To people the steep rocks and river banks,
Her natural sanctuaries, with a local soul
Of independence and stern liberty.
Sometimes it suits me better to invent
A tale from my own heart, more near akin
To my own passions, and habitual thoughts;
Some variegated story, in the main
Lofty, but the unsubstantial structure melts
Before the very sun that brightens it,
Mist into air dissolving! Then a wish,
My best and favourite aspiration, mounts
With yearning toward some philosophic song
Of Truth that cherishes our daily life;
With meditations passionate from deep
Recesses in man's heart, immortal verse
Thoughtfully fitted to the Orphean lyre;[5]
But from this awful° burthen I full soon *awe-inspiring*
Take refuge and beguile myself with trust
That mellower years will bring a riper mind
And clearer insight. Thus my days are passed
In contradiction; with no skill to part
Vague longing, haply° bred by want of power, *by chance*
From paramount impulse not to be withstood,
A timorous capacity from prudence,
From circumspection, infinite delay.
Humility and modest awe themselves
Betray me, serving often for a cloak
To a more subtle selfishness; that now
Locks every function up in blank° reserve, *°total / inaction*
Now dupes me, trusting to an anxious eye
That with intrusive restlessness beats off
Simplicity and self-presented truth.
Ah! better far than this, to stray about
Voluptuously,° through fields and rural walks, *luxuriously*
And ask no record of the hours, resigned
To vacant musing, unreproved neglect
Of all things, and deliberate holiday.
Far better never to have heard the name
Of zeal and just ambition, than to live
Baffled and plagued by a mind that every hour
Turns recreant to her task; takes heart again,

Goths played a major role in the fall of the Roman Empire.

[1] *Sertorius* Roman general and ally of Mithridates who conquered much of Spain but was assassinated in 72 BCE. His followers were said to have emigrated to the Canary Islands (the "Fortunate Isles") to escape the Romans, and to have survived there until the fifteenth century, when they were defeated by the invading Spaniards.

[2] [Wordsworth's note] Dominique de Gourges, a French gentleman who went in 1569 to Florida to avenge the massacre of the French by the Spaniards there.

[3] *Gustavus … mines* Gustav Vasa (1496–1560) became King of Sweden after leading a successful revolt in Sweden against the ruling Danes. He found support for the revolt in the mining town of Dalecarlia.

[4] *Wallace* William Wallace (c. 1270–1305), Scottish hero who fought for the freedom of his country but was executed by Edward I in 1305.

[5] *Orphean lyre* Lyre of Orpheus, the poet of Greek myth who could charm all living things with his music.

Then feels immediately some hollow thought
Hang like an interdict° upon her hopes. *prohibition*
This is my lot; for either still I find
Some imperfection in the chosen theme,
Or see of absolute accomplishment
Much wanting, so much wanting, in myself,
That I recoil and droop, and seek repose
In listlessness from vain perplexity,
Unprofitably travelling toward the grave,
Like a false steward who hath much received,
And renders nothing back.[1]
                                        Was it for this[2]
That one, the fairest of all rivers, loved
To blend his murmurs with my nurse's song,
And, from his alder[3] shades and rocky falls,
And from his fords and shallows, sent a voice
That flowed along my dreams? For this, didst thou,
O Derwent![4] winding among grassy holms[5]
Where I was looking on, a babe in arms,
Make ceaseless music that composed my thoughts
To more than infant softness, giving me
Amid the fretful dwellings of mankind
A foretaste, a dim earnest, of the calm
That Nature breathes among the hills and groves?
When he had left the mountains and received
On his smooth breast the shadow of those towers
That yet survive, a shattered monument
Of feudal sway, the bright blue river passed
Along the margin of our terrace walk;
A tempting playmate whom we dearly loved.
Oh, many a time have I, a five years' child,
In a small mill-race[6] severed from his stream,
Made one long bathing of a summer's day;
Basked in the sun, and plunged and basked again
Alternate, all a summer's day, or scoured
The sandy fields, leaping through flowery groves
Of yellow ragwort; or when rock and hill,
The woods, and distant Skiddaw's[7] lofty height,
Were bronzed with deepest radiance, stood alone
Beneath the sky, as if I had been born
On Indian plains, and from my mother's hut
Had run abroad in wantonness, to sport
A naked savage, in the thunder shower.

Fair seed-time[8] had my soul, and I grew up
Fostered alike by beauty and by fear:
Much favoured in my birth-place, and no less
In that beloved Vale[9] to which erelong
We were transplanted—there were we let loose
For sports of wider range. Ere I had told
Ten birth-days, when among the mountain slopes
Frost, and the breath of frosty wind, had snapped
The last autumnal crocus, 'twas my joy
With store of springes[10] o'er my shoulder hung
To range the open heights where woodcocks° run *game birds*
Along the smooth green turf. Through half the night,
Scudding[11] away from snare to snare, I plied
That anxious visitation; moon and stars
Were shining o'er my head. I was alone,
And seemed to be a trouble to the peace
That dwelt among them. Sometimes it befell
In these night wanderings, that a strong desire
O'erpowered my better reason, and the bird
Which was the captive of another's toil[12]

---

[1] *false steward ... back* Reference to the biblical parable of the false steward, who wastes what his lord gives him (see Matthew 25.14–30).

[2] *Was it for this* For lines 269–498, cf. *The Two-Part Prelude of 1799* 1.1–247.

[3] *alder* Tree resembling a birch and usually found in wet places.

[4] *Derwent* Wordsworth was born and spent some childhood years in a house overlooking this river in Cockermouth, Cumberland, on the edge of the English Lake District.

[5] *holms* Areas of flat ground beside a river.

[6] *mill-race* Channel or stream that feeds a mill wheel.

[7] *Skiddaw* Mountain in Cumberland.

[8] *seed-time* Sowing season.

[9] *Vale* Probably Hawkshead, in the English Lake District. Wordsworth attended Hawkshead Grammar School after his mother's death in 1778.

[10] *springes* Snares. (The word was pronounced with two syllables: *sprin-jez.*)

[11] *Scudding* Moving quickly and smoothly.

[12] *toil* A pun, meaning both "snare" and "labor."

Became my prey; and when the deed was done
I heard among the solitary hills
Low breathings coming after me, and sounds
Of undistinguishable motion, steps
Almost as silent as the turf they trod.

Nor less when spring had warmed the cultured Vale,
Moved we as plunderers where the mother-bird
Had in high places built her lodge; though mean
Our object and inglorious, yet the end° *result*
Was not ignoble. Oh! when I have hung
Above the raven's nest, by knots of grass
And half-inch fissures in the slippery rock
But ill sustained, and almost (so it seemed)
Suspended by the blast that blew amain,° *with full force*
Shouldering the naked crag, oh, at that time
While on the perilous ridge I hung alone,
With what strange utterance did the loud dry wind
Blow through my ear! the sky seemed not a sky
Of earth—and with what motion moved the clouds!

Dust as we are, the immortal spirit grows
Like harmony in music; there is a dark
Inscrutable workmanship that reconciles
Discordant elements, makes them cling together
In one society. How strange that all
The terrors, pains, and early miseries,
Regrets, vexations, lassitudes° interfused *exhaustions*
Within my mind, should e'er have borne a part,
And that a needful part, in making up
The calm existence that is mine when I
Am worthy of myself! Praise to the end!
Thanks to the means which Nature deigned to employ;
Whether her fearless visitings, or those
That came with soft alarm, like hurtless light
Opening the peaceful clouds; or she may use
Severer interventions, ministry
More palpable, as best might suit her aim.

One summer evening (led by her) I found
A little boat tied to a willow tree
Within a rocky cave, its usual home.
Straight I unloosed her chain, and stepping in
Pushed from the shore. It was an act of stealth
And troubled pleasure, nor without the voice
Of mountain-echoes did my boat move on;
Leaving behind her still, on either side,
Small circles glittering idly in the moon,
Until they melted all into one track
Of sparkling light. But now, like one who rows,
Proud of his skill, to reach a chosen point
With an unswerving line, I fixed my view
Upon the summit of a craggy ridge,
The horizon's utmost boundary; far above
Was nothing but the stars and the grey sky.
She was an elfin pinnace;[1] lustily
I dipped my oars into the silent lake,
And, as I rose upon the stroke, my boat
Went heaving through the water like a swan;
When, from behind that craggy steep till then
The horizon's bound, a huge peak, black and huge,
As if with voluntary power instinct° *imbued*
Upreared its head. I struck and struck again,
And growing still in stature the grim shape
Towered up between me and the stars, and still,
For so it seemed, with purpose of its own
And measured motion like a living thing,
Strode after me. With trembling oars I turned,
And through the silent water stole my way
Back to the covert° of the willow tree; *shelter*
There in her mooring-place I left my bark,° *boat*
And through the meadows homeward went, in grave
And serious mood; but after I had seen
That spectacle, for many days, my brain
Worked with a dim and undetermined sense
Of unknown modes of being; o'er my thoughts
There hung a darkness, call it solitude
Or blank desertion. No familiar shapes
Remained, no pleasant images of trees,
Of sea or sky, no colours of green fields;
But huge and mighty forms, that do not live
Like living men, moved slowly through the mind
By day, and were a trouble to my dreams.

---

[1] *pinnace* Small boat typically used to service larger vessels.

Wisdom and Spirit of the universe!
Thou Soul that art the eternity of thought,
That givest to forms and images a breath
And everlasting motion, not in vain
By day or star-light thus from my first dawn
Of childhood didst thou intertwine for me
The passions that build up our human soul;
Not with the mean and vulgar works of man,
But with high objects, with enduring things—
With life and nature, purifying thus
The elements of feeling and of thought,
And sanctifying, by such discipline,
Both pain and fear, until we recognise
A grandeur in the beatings of the heart.
Nor was this fellowship vouchsafed to me
With stinted kindness. In November days,
When vapours rolling down the valley made
A lonely scene more lonesome, among woods
At noon, and 'mid the calm of summer nights,
When, by the margin of the trembling lake,
Beneath the gloomy hills homeward I went
In solitude, such intercourse was mine;
Mine was it in the fields both day and night,
And by the waters, all the summer long.

And in the frosty season, when the sun
Was set, and visible for many a mile
The cottage windows blazed through twilight gloom,
I heeded not their summons: happy time
It was indeed for all of us—for me
It was a time of rapture! Clear and loud
The village clock tolled six—I wheeled about,
Proud and exulting like an untired horse
That cares not for his home. All shod with steel,[1]
We hissed along the polished ice in games
Confederate,° imitative of the chase *united*
And woodland pleasures—the resounding horn,
The pack loud chiming, and the hunted hare.
So through the darkness and the cold we flew,
And not a voice was idle; with the din
Smitten,° the precipices rang aloud; *struck*
The leafless trees and every icy crag
Tinkled like iron; while far distant hills
Into the tumult sent an alien sound
Of melancholy not unnoticed, while the stars
Eastward were sparkling clear, and in the west
The orange sky of evening died away.
Not seldom from the uproar I retired
Into a silent bay, or sportively
Glanced sideway, leaving the tumultuous throng,
To cut across the reflex° of a star *reflection*
That fled, and, flying still before me, gleamed
Upon the glassy plain; and oftentimes,
When we had given our bodies to the wind,
And all the shadowy banks on either side
Came sweeping through the darkness, spinning still
The rapid line of motion, then at once
Have I, reclining back upon my heels,
Stopped short; yet still the solitary cliffs
Wheeled by me—even as if the earth had rolled
With visible motion her diurnal° round! *daily*
Behind me did they stretch in solemn train,
Feebler and feebler, and I stood and watched
Till all was tranquil as a dreamless sleep.

Ye Presences of Nature in the sky
And on the earth! Ye Visions of the hills!
And Souls of lonely places! can I think
A vulgar hope was yours when ye employed
Such ministry, when ye through many a year
Haunting me thus among my boyish sports,
On caves and trees, upon the woods and hills,
Impressed upon all forms the characters
Of danger or desire; and thus did make
The surface of the universal earth
With triumph and delight, with hope and fear,
Work° like a sea? *move restlessly*
Not uselessly employed,
Might I pursue this theme through every change
Of exercise and play, to which the year
Did summon us in his delightful round.

[1] *All shod with steel* I.e., wearing ice skates.

We were a noisy crew; the sun in heaven
Beheld not vales more beautiful than ours;
Nor saw a band in happiness and joy
Richer, or worthier of the ground they trod.
I could record with no reluctant voice
The woods of autumn, and their hazel bowers
With milk-white clusters hung; the rod° and line, *fishing rod*
True symbol of hope's foolishness, whose strong
And unreproved enchantment led us on
By rocks and pools shut out from every star,
All the green summer, to forlorn cascades
Among the windings hid of mountain brooks.
—Unfading recollections! at this hour
The heart is almost mine with which I felt,
From some hill-top on sunny afternoons,
The paper kite high among fleecy clouds
Pull at her rein like an impetuous courser;° *horse*
Or, from the meadows sent on gusty days,
Beheld her breast[1] the wind, then suddenly
Dashed headlong, and rejected by the storm.

Ye lowly cottages wherein we dwelt,
A ministration of your own was yours;
Can I forget you, being as you were
So beautiful among the pleasant fields
In which ye stood? or can I here forget
The plain and seemly countenance with which
Ye dealt out your plain comforts? Yet had ye
Delights and exultations of your own.
Eager and never weary we pursued
Our home-amusements by the warm peat-fire
At evening, when with pencil, and smooth slate
In square divisions parcelled out and all
With crosses and with cyphers scribbled o'er,[2]
We schemed and puzzled, head opposed to head
In strife too humble to be named in verse:
Or round the naked table, snow-white deal,° *pine*
Cherry or maple, sat in close array,
And to the combat, Loo or Whist, led on
A thick-ribbed army;[3] not, as in the world,
Neglected and ungratefully thrown by
Even for the very service they had wrought,
But husbanded through many a long campaign.
Uncouth assemblage was it, where no few
Had changed their functions; some, plebeian cards[4]
Which Fate, beyond the promise of their birth,
Had dignified, and called to represent
The persons of departed potentates.
Oh, with what echoes on the board they fell!
Ironic diamonds—clubs, hearts, diamonds, spades,
A congregation piteously akin!
Cheap matter offered they to boyish wit,
Those sooty knaves, precipitated down
With scoffs and taunts, like Vulcan out of heaven:[5]
The paramount ace, a moon in her eclipse,
Queens gleaming through their splendour's last decay,
And monarchs surly at the wrongs sustained
By royal visages. Meanwhile abroad
Incessant rain was falling, or the frost
Raged bitterly, with keen and silent tooth;
And, interrupting oft that eager game,
From under Esthwaite's splitting fields of ice
The pent-up air, struggling to free itself,
Gave out to meadow grounds and hills a loud
Protracted yelling,[6] like the noise of wolves
Howling in troops along the Bothnic Main.[7]

---

1 *breast* Reach the highest point of, as when climbing a mountain.

2 *With crosses … o'er* See Milton's *Paradise Lost* 8.83: "With centric and eccentric scribbled o'er." Here Wordsworth uses this heroic diction to describe a game of tick-tack-toe.

3 *Loo or Whist* Popular card games; *thick-ribbed army* Pack of cards made of thick cardboard.

4 *plebeian cards* I.e., numbered cards, not face cards such as a queen, king, or jack. Also cf. Alexander Pope's *The Rape of the Lock* (1712, 1717): "Gained but one Trump and one Plebian Card" (3.54).

5 *Vulcan out of heaven* Reference to the classical myth wherein the god Vulcan is thrown off Mount Olympus. In most versions of the story, he is cast out at birth by his mother, Juno, who is repulsed by his ugliness.

6 *From under … Protracted yelling* These lines describe the loud noises made by the ice as it breaks up in warming weather; *Esthwaite* Esthwaite Water, a lake near Hawkshead.

7 *Bothnic Main* The Gulf of Bothnia, between Sweden and Finland.

Nor, sedulous° as I have been to trace[1] *careful*
How Nature by extrinsic passion first
Peopled the mind with forms sublime or fair,
And made me love them, may I here omit
How other pleasures have been mine, and joys
Of subtler origin; how I have felt,
Not seldom even in that tempestuous time,
Those hallowed and pure motions of the sense
Which seem, in their simplicity, to own
An intellectual charm; that calm delight
Which, if I err not, surely must belong
To those first-born affinities that fit
Our new existence to existing things,
And, in our dawn of being, constitute
The bond of union between life and joy.

Yes, I remember when the changeful earth,
And twice five summers on my mind had stamped
The faces of the moving year, even then
I held unconscious intercourse with beauty
Old as creation, drinking in a pure
Organic pleasure from the silver wreaths
Of curling mist, or from the level plain
Of waters coloured by impending clouds.

The sands of Westmoreland, the creeks and bays
Of Cumbria's[2] rocky limits, they can tell
How, when the Sea threw off his evening shade,
And to the shepherd's hut on distant hills
Sent welcome notice of the rising moon,
How I have stood, to fancies such as these
A stranger, linking with the spectacle
No conscious memory of a kindred sight,
And bringing with me no peculiar sense
Of quietness or peace; yet have I stood,
Even while mine eye hath moved o'er many a league
Of shining water, gathering as it seemed
Through every hair-breadth in that field of light
New pleasure like a bee among the flowers.

Thus oft amid those fits of vulgar° joy *everyday*
Which, through all seasons, on a child's pursuits
Are prompt attendants, 'mid that giddy bliss
Which, like a tempest, works along the blood
And is forgotten; even then I felt
Gleams like the flashing of a shield—the earth
And common face of Nature spake to me
Rememberable° things; sometimes, 'tis true. *memorable*
By chance collisions and quaint accidents
(Like those ill-sorted unions, work supposed
Of evil-minded fairies), yet not vain
Nor profitless, if haply they impressed
Collateral° objects and appearances, *indirect*
Albeit lifeless then, and doomed to sleep
Until maturer seasons called them forth
To impregnate and to elevate the mind.
—And if the vulgar joy by its own weight
Wearied itself out of the memory,
The scenes which were a witness of that joy
Remained in their substantial° lineaments *material*
Depicted on the brain, and to the eye
Were visible, a daily sight; and thus
By the impressive[3] discipline of fear,
By pleasure and repeated happiness,
So frequently repeated, and by force
Of obscure feelings representative
Of things forgotten, these same scenes so bright,
So beautiful, so majestic in themselves,
Though yet the day was distant, did become
Habitually dear, and all their forms
And changeful colours by invisible links
Were fastened to the affections.

I began
My story early—not misled, I trust,
By an infirmity of love for days
Disowned by memory—ere the breath of spring
Planting my snowdrops among winter snows:

[1] *Nor, sedulous … to trace* For lines 544–635, cf. *The Two-Part Prelude of 1799* 1.378–468.

[2] *Westmoreland … Cumbria* Westmorland and Cumbria (usually called "Cumberland") were counties in the Lake District.

[3] *impressive* Capable of making an impression.

Nor will it seem to thee, O Friend! so prompt
In sympathy, that I have lengthened out
With fond and feeble tongue a tedious tale.
Meanwhile, my hope has been, that I might fetch
Invigorating thoughts from former years;
Might fix the wavering balance° of my mind, *scale*
And haply meet reproaches too, whose power
May spur me on, in manhood now mature,
To honourable toil. Yet should these hopes
Prove vain, and thus should neither I be taught
To understand myself, nor thou to know
With better knowledge how the heart was
framed° *constructed*
Of him thou lovest; need I dread from thee
Harsh judgments, if the song be loth to quit
Those recollected hours that have the charm
Of visionary things, those lovely forms
And sweet sensations that throw back our life,
And almost make remotest infancy
A visible scene, on which the sun is shining?

One end at least hath been attained; my mind
Hath been revived, and if this genial mood
Desert me not, forthwith shall be brought down
Through later years the story of my life.
The road lies plain before me; 'tis a theme
Single and of determined bounds;[1] and hence
I choose it rather at this time, than work
Of ampler or more varied argument,° *subject matter*
Where I might be discomfited and lost:
And certain hopes are with me, that to thee
This labour will be welcome, honoured Friend!

from BOOK FIFTH
BOOKS

When Contemplation, like the night-calm felt
Through earth and sky, spreads widely, and sends deep
Into the soul its tranquillising power,
Even then I sometimes grieve for thee, O Man,
Earth's paramount Creature! not so much for woes
That thou endurest; heavy though that weight be,
Cloud-like it mounts, or touched with light divine
Doth melt away; but for those palms achieved,
Through length of time, by patient exercise
Of study and hard thought; there, there, it is
That sadness finds its fuel. Hitherto,
In progress through this Verse, my mind hath looked
Upon the speaking face of earth and heaven
As her prime Teacher, intercourse with man
Established by the sovereign Intellect,
Who through that bodily Image hath diffused,
As might appear to the eye of fleeting time,
A deathless spirit. Thou also, man! hast wrought,
For commerce of thy nature with herself,
Things that aspire to unconquerable life;
And yet we feel—we cannot choose but feel—
That they must perish. Tremblings of the heart
It gives, to think that our immortal being
No more shall need such garments; and yet man,
As long as he shall be the child of earth,
Might almost "weep to have"[2] what he may lose,
Nor be himself extinguished, but survive
Abject, depressed, forlorn, disconsolate.
A thought is with me sometimes, and I say—
Should the whole frame of earth by inward throes
Be wrenched, or fire come down from far to scorch
Her pleasant habitations, and dry up
Old Ocean in his bed, left singed and bare,
Yet would the living Presence still subsist
Victorious, and composure would ensue,
And kindlings like the morning—presage sure
Of day returning, and of life revived.
But all the meditations of mankind,
Yea, all the adamantine° holds° *indestructible / fortresses*
of truth
By reason built, or passion, which itself
Is highest reason in a soul sublime;
The consecrated works of Bard and Sage,

[1] *determined bounds* Fixed boundaries.

[2] *weep to have* See Shakespeare's Sonnet 64, lines 13–14: "This thought [of the destruction caused by time] is as a death, which cannot choose / But weep to have that which it fears to lose."

Sensuous or intellectual, wrought by men,
Twin labourers, and heirs of the same hopes;
Where would they be? Oh! why hath not the Mind
Some element to stamp her image on
In nature somewhat nearer to her own?
Why, gifted with such powers to send abroad
Her spirit, must it lodge in shrines so frail?

One day, when from my lips a like complaint
Had fallen in presence of a studious friend,
He with a smile made answer, that in truth
'Twas going far to seek disquietude
But on the front of his reproof, confessed
That he himself had oftentimes given way
To kindred hauntings. Whereupon I told,
That once in the stillness of a summer's noon,
While I was seated in a rocky cave,
By the sea-side, perusing, so it chanced,
The famous history of the errant knight
Recorded by Cervantes,[1] these same thoughts
Beset me, and to height unusual rose,
While listlessly I sat, and, having closed
The book, had turned my eyes toward the wide sea.
On poetry, and geometric truth,
And their high privilege of lasting life,
From all internal injury exempt,
I mused upon these chiefly: and, at length,
My senses yielding to the sultry air,
Sleep seized me, and I passed into a dream.
I saw before me stretched a boundless plain
Of sandy wilderness, all blank and void;
And as I looked around, distress and fear
Came creeping over me, when at my side,
Close at my side, an uncouth shape appeared
Upon a dromedary, mounted high.
He seemed an Arab of the Bedouin tribes:
A lance he bore, and underneath one arm
A stone; and, in the opposite hand, a shell
Of a surpassing brightness. At the sight
Much I rejoiced, not doubting but a Guide
Was present, one who with unerring skill
Would through the desert lead me; and while yet
I looked, and looked, self-questioned what this freight
Which the New-comer carried through the waste
Could mean, the Arab told me that the stone
(To give it in the language of the dream)
Was "Euclid's Elements";[2] and "This," said he,
"Is something of more worth"; and at the word
Stretched forth the shell, so beautiful in shape,
In color so resplendent, with command
That I should hold it to my ear. I did so,
And heard that instant in an unknown tongue,
Which yet I understood, articulate sounds,
A loud prophetic blast of harmony;
An Ode, in passion uttered, which foretold
Destruction to the children of the earth,
By deluge, now at hand. No sooner ceased
The song than the Arab with calm look declared
That all would come to pass of which the voice
Had given forewarning, and that he himself
Was going then to bury those two books:
The one that held acquaintance with the stars,
And wedded soul to soul in purest bond
Of reason, undisturbed by space or time;
The other, that was a god, yea many gods,
Had voices more than all the winds, with power
To exhilarate the spirit, and to soothe,
Through every clime, the heart of human kind.
While this was uttering, strange as it may seem,
I wondered not, although I plainly saw
The one to be a stone, the other a shell,
Nor doubted once but that they both were books;
Having a perfect faith in all that passed.
Far stronger now grew the desire I felt
To cleave unto this man; but when I prayed
To share his enterprise, he hurried on
Reckless° of me: I followed, not unseen, *heedless*
For oftentimes he cast a backward look,
Grasping his twofold treasure. Lance in rest,

[1] *famous history … Cervantes* Miguel de Cervantes's *Don Quixote* (1605), in which the title character attempts to live as though he were a knight in a chivalric romance.

[2] *Euclid's Elements* Foundational geometry textbook by Euclid, a Greek mathematician of the third century BCE.

He rode, I keeping pace with him; and now
He, to my fancy, had become the knight
Whose tale Cervantes tells; yet not the Knight,
But was an Arab of the desert, too;
Of these was neither, and was both at once.
His countenance, meanwhile, grew more disturbed;
And looking backwards when he looked, mine eyes
Saw, over half the wilderness diffused,
A bed of glittering light: I asked the cause:
"It is," said he, "the waters of the deep
Gathering upon us"; quickening then the pace
Of the unwieldy creature he bestrode,
He left me: I called after him aloud;
He heeded not; but with his twofold charge
Still in his grasp, before me, full in view,
Went hurrying o'er the illimitable waste
With the fleet waters of a drowning world
In chase of him; whereat I waked in terror,
And saw the sea before me, and the book,
In which I had been reading, at my side.

Full often, taking from the world of sleep
This Arab phantom, which I thus beheld,
This semi-Quixote, I to him have given
A substance, fancied him a living man,
A gentle dweller in the desert, crazed
By love and feeling, and internal thought
Protracted among endless solitudes;
Have shaped him wandering upon this quest!
Nor have I pitied him; but rather felt
Reverence was due to a being thus employed;
And thought that, in the blind and awful° lair *awe-inspiring*
Of such a madness, reason did lie couched.
Enow° there are on earth to take in charge *enough*
Their wives, their children, and their virgin loves,
Or whatsoever else the heart holds dear;
Enow to stir for these; yea, will I say,
Contemplating in soberness the approach
Of an event so dire, by signs in earth
Or heaven made manifest, that I could share
That maniac's fond anxiety, and go
Upon like errand. Oftentimes, at least
Me hath such strong entrancement overcome,
When I have held a volume in my hand,
Poor earthly casket of immortal verse,
Shakespeare, or Milton, labourers divine!

Great and benign, indeed, must be the power
Of living nature, which could thus so long
Detain me from the best of other guides
And dearest helpers, left unthanked, unpraised,
Even in the time of lisping infancy;
And later down, in prattling childhood even,
While I was travelling back among those days,
How could I ever play an ingrate's part?
Once more should I have made those bowers resound,
By intermingling strains of thankfulness
With their own thoughtless melodies; at least
It might have well beseemed me to repeat
Some simply fashioned tale, to tell again,
In slender accents of sweet verse, some tale
That did bewitch me then, and soothes me now.
O Friend! O Poet! brother of my soul,
Think not that I could pass along untouched
By these remembrances. Yet wherefore speak?
Why call upon a few weak words to say
What is already written in the hearts
Of all that breathe?—what in the path of all
Drops daily from the tongue of every child,
Wherever man is found? The trickling tear
Upon the cheek of listening Infancy
Proclaims it, and the insuperable look
That drinks as if it never could be full.

That portion of my story I shall leave
There registered: whatever else of power
Or pleasure sown, or fostered thus, may be
Peculiar to myself, let that remain
Where still it works, though hidden from all search
Among the depths of time. Yet is it just
That here, in memory of all books which lay
Their sure foundations in the heart of man,

Whether by native prose, or numerous verse,[1]
That in the name of all inspirèd souls,
From Homer the great Thunderer, from the voice
That roars along the bed of Jewish song,
And that more varied and elaborate,
Those trumpet-tones of harmony that shake
Our shores in England—from those loftiest notes
Down to the low and wren-like warblings, made
For cottagers and spinners at the wheel,
And sun-burnt travellers resting their tired limbs,
Stretched under wayside hedge-rows, ballad tunes,
Food for the hungry ears of little ones,
And of old men who have survived their joys:
'Tis just that in behalf of these, the works,
And of the men that framed them, whether known,
Or sleeping nameless in their scattered graves,
That I should here assert their rights, attest
Their honours, and should, once for all, pronounce
Their benediction; speak of them as Powers
For ever to be hallowed; only less,
For what we are and what we may become,
Than Nature's self, which is the breath of God,
Or His pure Word by miracle revealed.

Rarely and with reluctance would I stoop
To transitory themes; yet I rejoice,
And, by these thoughts admonished, will pour out
Thanks with uplifted heart, that I was reared
Safe from an evil which these days have laid
Upon the children of the land, a pest
That might have dried me up, body and soul.
This verse is dedicate to Nature's self,
And things that teach as Nature teaches: then,
Oh! where had been the Man, the Poet where,
Where had we been, we two, beloved Friend!
If in the season of unperilous choice,
In lieu of wandering, as we did, through vales
Rich with indigenous produce, open ground
Of Fancy, happy pastures ranged at will,
We had been followed, hourly watched, and noosed,
Each in his several° melancholy walk *separate*
Stringed like a poor man's heifer at its feed,
Led through the lanes in forlorn servitude;
Or rather like a stallèd ox debarred
From touch of growing grass, that may not taste
A flower till it have yielded up its sweets
A prelibation to the mower's scythe.

Behold the parent hen amid her brood,
Though fledged and feathered, and well pleased to part
And straggle from her presence, still a brood,
And she herself from the maternal bond
Still undischarged; yet doth she little more
Than move with them in tenderness and love,
A centre to the circle which they make;
And now and then, alike from need of theirs
And call of her own natural appetites,
She scratches, ransacks up the earth for food,
Which they partake at pleasure. Early died
My honoured Mother, she who was the heart
And hinge of all our learnings and our loves:
She left us destitute, and, as we might,
Trooping together. Little suits it me
To break upon the sabbath of her rest
With any thought that looks at others' blame;
Nor would I praise her but in perfect love.
Hence am I checked: but let me boldly say,
In gratitude, and for the sake of truth,
Unheard by her, that she, not falsely taught,
Fetching her goodness rather from times past,
Than shaping novelties for times to come,
Had no presumption, no such jealousy,
Nor did by habit of her thoughts mistrust
Our nature, but had virtual faith that He
Who fills the mother's breast with innocent milk,
Doth also for our nobler part provide,
Under His great correction and control,
As innocent instincts, and as innocent food;
Or draws for minds that are left free to trust
In the simplicities of opening life
Sweet honey out of spurned or dreaded weeds.
This was her creed, and therefore she was pure
From anxious fear of error or mishap,

[1] *numerous verse* I.e., metrical verse (in which syllables are counted).

And evil, overweeningly° so called; *arrogantly*
Was not puffed up by false unnatural hopes,
Nor selfish with unnecessary cares,
Nor with impatience from the season asked
More than its timely produce; rather loved
The hours for what they are, than from regard
Glanced on their promises in restless pride.
Such was she—not from faculties more strong
Than others have, but from the times, perhaps,
And spot in which she lived, and through a grace
Of modest meekness, simple-mindedness,
A heart that found benignity and hope,
Being itself benign. …

There was a Boy: ye knew him well, ye cliffs[1]
And islands of Winander!—many a time
At evening, when the earliest stars began
To move along the edges of the hills,
Rising or setting, would he stand alone
Beneath the trees or by the glimmering lake,
And there, with fingers interwoven, both hands
Pressed closely palm to palm, and to his mouth
Uplifted, he, as through an instrument,
Blew mimic hootings to the silent owls,
That they might answer him; and they would shout
Across the watery vale, and shout again,
Responsive to his call, with quivering peals,
And long halloos and screams, and echoes loud,
Redoubled and redoubled, concourse° wild *assembly*
Of jocund° din; and, when a lengthened pause *cheery*
Of silence came and baffled his best skill,
Then sometimes, in that silence while he hung
Listening, a gentle shock of mild surprise
Has carried far into his heart the voice
Of mountain torrents; or the visible scene
Would enter unawares into his mind,
With all its solemn imagery, its rocks,
Its woods, and that uncertain heaven, received
Into the bosom of the steady lake.

This Boy was taken from his mates, and died
In childhood, ere he was full twelve years old.
Fair is the spot, most beautiful the vale
Where he was born; the grassy churchyard hangs
Upon a slope above the village school,
And through that churchyard when my way has led
On summer evenings, I believe that there
A long half hour together I have stood
Mute, looking at the grave in which he lies!
Even now appears before the mind's clear eye
That self-same village church; I see her sit
(The thronèd Lady whom erewhile we hailed)
On her green hill, forgetful of this Boy
Who slumbers at her feet—forgetful, too,
Of all her silent neighbourhood of graves,
And listening only to the gladsome sounds
That, from the rural school ascending, play
Beneath her and about her. May she long
Behold a race of young ones like to those
With whom I herded! (easily, indeed,
We might have fed upon a fatter soil
Of arts and letters—but be that forgiven)
A race of real children; not too wise,
Too learned, or too good; but wanton, fresh,
And bandied up and down by love and hate;
Not unresentful where self-justified;
Fierce, moody, patient, venturous, modest, shy;
Mad at their sports like withered leaves in winds;
Though doing wrong and suffering, and full oft
Bending beneath our life's mysterious weight
Of pain, and doubt, and fear, yet yielding not
In happiness to the happiest upon earth.
Simplicity in habit, truth in speech,
Be these the daily strengtheners of their minds;
May books and Nature be their early joy!
And knowledge, rightly honoured with that name—
Knowledge not purchased by the loss of power!

Well do I call to mind the very week
When I was first intrusted to the care
Of that sweet Valley; when its paths, its shores,
And brooks were like a dream of novelty
To my half-infant thoughts; that very week,

[1] *There was … ye cliffs* For lines 364–397, cf. "[There was a Boy]" (1800), included in this anthology.

While I was roving up and down alone,
Seeking I knew not what, I chanced to cross
One of those open fields, which, shaped like ears,
Make green peninsulas on Esthwaite's Lake:
Twilight was coming on, yet through the gloom
Appeared distinctly on the opposite shore
A heap of garments, as if left by one
Who might have there been bathing. Long I watched,
But no one owned them; meanwhile the calm lake
Grew dark with all the shadows on its breast,
And, now and then, a fish up-leaping snapped
The breathless stillness. The succeeding day,
Those unclaimed garments telling a plain tale
Drew to the spot an anxious crowd; some looked
In passive expectation from the shore,
While from a boat others hung o'er the deep,
Sounding with grappling irons and long poles.
At last, the dead man, 'mid that beauteous scene
Of trees and hills and water, bolt upright
Rose, with his ghastly face, a spectre shape
Of terror; yet no soul-debasing fear,
Young as I was, a child not nine years old,
Possessed me, for my inner eye had seen
Such sights before, among the shining streams
Of faëry land, the forest of romance.
Their spirit hallowed the sad spectacle
With decoration of ideal grace;
A dignity, a smoothness, like the works
Of Grecian art, and purest poesy. …

Here must we pause; this only let me add,
From heart-experience, and in humblest sense
Of modesty, that he, who in his youth
A daily wanderer among woods and fields
With living Nature hath been intimate,
Not only in that raw unpractised time
Is stirred to ecstasy, as others are,
By glittering verse; but further, doth receive,
In measure only dealt out to himself,
Knowledge and increase of enduring joy
From the great Nature that exists in works
Of mighty Poets. Visionary power
Attends the motions of the viewless° winds, *invisible*
Embodied in the mystery of words:
There, darkness makes abode, and all the host
Of shadowy things work endless changes—there,
As in a mansion like their proper home,
Even forms and substances are circumfused
By that transparent veil with light divine,
And, through the turnings intricate of verse,
Present themselves as objects recognized,
In flashes, and with glory not their own.

from Book Sixth
Cambridge and the Alps

The leaves were fading when to Esthwaite's banks
And the simplicities of cottage life
I bade farewell; and, one among the youth
Who, summoned by that season, reunite
As scattered birds troop to the fowler's lure,
Went back to Granta's[1] cloisters, not so prompt
Or eager, though as gay and undepressed
In mind, as when I thence had taken flight
A few short months before. I turned my face
Without repining from the coves and heights
Clothed in the sunshine of the withering fern;
Quitted, not both, the mild magnificence
Of calmer lakes and louder streams; and you,
Frank-hearted maids of rocky Cumberland,
You and your not unwelcome days of mirth,
Relinquished, and your nights of revelry,
And in my own unlovely cell sate down
In lightsome mood—such privilege has youth
That cannot take long leave of pleasant thoughts.

The bonds of indolent society
Relaxing in their hold, henceforth I lived
More to myself. Two winters may be passed
Without a separate notice: many books
Were skimmed, devoured, or studiously perused,
But with no settled plan. I was detached

[1] *Granta* Another name for the River Cam.

Internally from academic cares;
Yet independent study seemed a course
Of hardy disobedience towards friends
And kindred, proud rebellion and unkind.
This spurious° virtue, rather let it bear *so-called*
A name it now deserves, this cowardice,
Gave treacherous sanction to that over-love
Of freedom which encouraged me to turn
From regulations even of my own
As from restraints and bonds. Yet who can tell—
Who knows what thus may have been gained, both then
And at a later season, or preserved;
What love of nature, what original strength
Of contemplation, what intuitive truths,
The deepest and the best, what keen research,
Unbiassed, unbewildered, and unawed?

The Poet's soul was with me at that time;
Sweet meditations, the still overflow
Of present happiness, while future years
Lacked not anticipations, tender dreams,
No few of which have since been realised;
And some remain, hopes for my future life.
Four years and thirty, told this very week,[1]
Have I been now a sojourner on earth,
By sorrow not unsmitten; yet for me
Life's morning radiance hath not left the hills,
Her dew is on the flowers. Those were the days
Which also first emboldened me to trust
With firmness, hitherto but lightly touched
By such a daring thought, that I might leave
Some monument behind me which pure hearts
Should reverence. The instinctive humbleness,
Maintained even by the very name and thought
Of printed books and authorship, began
To melt away; and further, the dread awe
Of mighty names was softened down and seemed
Approachable, admitting fellowship
Of modest sympathy. Such aspect now,
Though not familiarly, my mind put on,
Content to observe, to achieve, and to enjoy.

All winter long, whenever free to choose,
Did I by night frequent the College groves
And tributary walks; the last, and oft
The only one, who had been lingering there
Through hours of silence, till the porter's bell,
A punctual follower on the stroke of nine,
Rang with its blunt unceremonious voice,
Inexorable summons! Lofty elms,
Inviting shades of opportune recess,
Bestowed composure on a neighbourhood
Unpeaceful in itself. A single tree
With sinuous trunk, boughs exquisitely wreathed,
Grew there; an ash which Winter for herself
Decked as in pride, and with outlandish grace:
Up from the ground, and almost to the top,
The trunk and every master branch were green
With clustering ivy, and the lightsome twigs
And outer spray profusely tipped with seeds
That hung in yellow tassels, while the air
Stirred them, not voiceless. Often have I stood
Foot-bound uplooking at this lovely tree
Beneath a frosty moon. The hemisphere
Of magic fiction, verse of mine perchance
May never tread; but scarcely Spenser's[2] self
Could have more tranquil visions in his youth,
Or could more bright appearances create
Of human forms with superhuman powers,
Than I beheld loitering on calm clear nights
Alone, beneath this fairy work of earth.

On the vague reading of a truant youth
'Twere idle to descant.[3] My inner judgment
Not seldom differed from my taste in books,
As if it appertained to another mind,
And yet the books which then I valued most
Are dearest to me *now*; for, having scanned,
Not heedlessly, the laws, and watched the forms
Of Nature, in that knowledge I possessed
A standard, often usefully applied. …

[1] *this very week* The week of 7 April 1804.

[2] *Spenser* English poet Edmund Spenser (c. 1522–99), author of *The Faerie Queene.*

[3] *descant* Discuss in detail.

When the third summer freed us from restraint,
A youthful friend, he too a mountaineer,
Not slow to share my wishes, took his staff,
And sallying forth, we journeyed side by side,
Bound to the distant Alps.[1] A hardy slight
Did this unprecedented course imply
Of college studies and their set rewards;
Nor had, in truth, the scheme been formed by me
Without uneasy forethought of the pain,
The censures, and ill-omening of those
To whom my worldly interests were dear.
But Nature then was sovereign in my mind,
And mighty forms, seizing a youthful fancy,
Had given a charter to irregular hopes.
In any age of uneventful calm
Among the nations, surely would my heart
Have been possessed by similar desire;
But Europe at that time was thrilled with joy,
France standing on the top of golden hours,[2]
And human nature seeming born again. …

'Tis not my present purpose to retrace
That variegated journey step by step.
A march it was of military speed,
And earth did change her images and forms
Before us, fast as clouds are changed in heaven.
Day after day, up early and down late,
From hill to vale we dropped, from vale to hill
Mounted—from province on to province swept,
Keen hunters in a chase of fourteen weeks,
Eager as birds of prey, or as a ship
Upon the stretch, when winds are blowing fair:
Sweet coverts did we cross of pastoral life,
Enticing valleys, greeted them and left
Too soon, while yet the very flash and gleam
Of salutation were not passed away.
Oh! sorrow for the youth who could have seen
Unchastened, unsubdued, unawed, unraised
To patriarchal dignity of mind,
And pure simplicity of wish and will,
Those sanctified abodes of peaceful man;
Pleased (though to hardship born, and compassed round
With danger, varying as the seasons change),
Pleased with his daily tasks, or, if not pleased,
Contented, from the moment that the dawn
(Ah! surely not without attendant gleams
Of soul-illumination) calls him forth
To industry, by glistenings flung on rocks,
Whose evening shadows lead him to repose.

Well might a stranger look with bounding heart
Down on a green recess, the first I saw
Of those deep haunts, an aboriginal vale,
Quiet and lorded over and possessed
By naked huts, wood-built, and sown like tents,
Or Indian cabins over the fresh lawns
And by the river side.
That very day,
From a bare ridge we also first beheld
Unveiled the summit of Mont Blanc,[3] and grieved
To have a soulless image on the eye
That had usurped upon a living thought
That never more could be. The wondrous Vale
Of Chamouny[4] stretched far below, and soon
With its dumb° cataracts and streams of ice, *unheard*
A motionless array of mighty waves,
Five rivers broad and vast, made rich amends,
And reconciled us to realities:
There small birds warble from the leafy trees,
The eagle soars high in the element,
There doth the reaper bind the yellow sheaf,
The maiden spread the haycock[5] in the sun,
While Winter like a well-tamed lion walks,

---

[1] *When … Alps* In 1790 Wordsworth traveled with Robert Jones, a friend from Cambridge, to the French, Italian, and Swiss Alps.

[2] *France … hours* In 1790 many English intellectuals were optimistic about the French Revolution, though most would change their views as the events of the Revolutionary period unfolded.

[3] *Mont Blanc* The highest mountain in the Alps.

[4] *Vale / Of Chamouny* Valley located at the foot of Mont Blanc. (The modern spelling is Chamonix.)

[5] *haycock* Conical pile of hay.

Descending from the Mountain to make sport
Among the Cottages by beds of flowers.

Whate'er in this wide circuit we beheld,
Or heard, was fitted to our unripe state
Of intellect and heart. With such a book
Before our eyes, we could not choose but read
Lessons of genuine brotherhood, the plain
And universal reason of mankind,
The truths of young and old. Nor, side by side
Pacing, two social pilgrims, or alone
Each with his humour,° could we fail to abound *disposition*
In dreams and fictions, pensively composed,
Dejection taken up for pleasure's sake,
And gilded sympathies, the willow[1] wreath,
And sober posies° of funereal flowers *bouquets*
Gathered among those solitudes sublime
From formal gardens of the lady Sorrow,
Did sweeten many a meditative hour.

Yet still in me with those soft luxuries
Mixed something of stern mood, an under-thirst
Of vigor seldom utterly allayed.
And from that source how different a sadness
Would issue, let one incident make known.
When from the Vallais[2] we had turned, and clomb
Along the Simplon's[3] steep and rugged road,
Following a band of Muleteers,° we reached *mule drivers*
A halting-place, where all together took
Their noon-tide meal. Hastily rose our guide,
Leaving us at the board; awhile we lingered,
Then paced the beaten downward way that led
Right to a rough stream's edge, and there broke off;
The only track now visible was one
That from the torrent's further brink held forth
Conspicuous invitation to ascend
A loft mountain. After brief delay
Crossing the unbridged stream, that road we took,
And clomb with eagerness, till anxious fears
Intruded, for we failed to overtake
Our comrades gone before. By fortunate chance,
While every moment added doubt to doubt,
A peasant met us, from whose mouth we learned
That to the spot which had perplexed us first
We must descend, and there should find the road,
Which in the stony channel of the stream
Lay a few steps, and then along its banks;
And that our future course, all plain to sight,
Was downwards, with the current of that stream.
Loth to believe what we so grieved to hear,
For still we had hopes that pointed to the clouds,
We questioned him again, and yet again;
But every word that from the peasant's lips
Came in reply, translated by our feelings,
Ended in this—*that we had crossed the Alps.*

Imagination—here the Power so called
Through sad incompetence of human speech,
That awful° Power rose from the *awe-inspiring*
mind's abyss
Like an unfathered vapour that enwraps,
At once, some lonely traveller. I was lost;
Halted without an effort to break through;
But to my conscious soul I now can say—
"I recognise thy glory:" in such strength
Of usurpation, when the light of sense
Goes out, but with a flash that has revealed
The invisible world, doth greatness make abode,
There harbours; whether we be young or old,
Our destiny, our being's heart and home,
Is with infinitude, and only there;
With hope it is, hope that can never die,
Effort, and expectation, and desire,
And something evermore about to be.
Under such banners militant, the soul
Seeks for no trophies, struggles for no spoils
That may attest her prowess, blest in thoughts
That are their own perfection and reward,
Strong in herself and in beatitude
That hides her, like the mighty flood of Nile

---

[1] *willow* Symbol of sadness.

[2] *Vallais* Canton in southern Switzerland, located in a valley between ranges of the Alps.

[3] *Simplon* Mountain pass connecting the Valais with Piedmont, Italy.

Poured from his fount of Abyssinian clouds
To fertilise the whole Egyptian plain.

The melancholy slackening that ensued
Upon those tidings by the peasant given
Was soon dislodged. Downwards we hurried fast,
And, with the half-shaped road which we had missed,
Entered a narrow chasm. The brook and road
Were fellow-travellers in this gloomy strait,
And with them did we journey several hours
At a slow pace. The immeasurable height
Of woods decaying, never to be decayed,
The stationary blasts of waterfalls,
And in the narrow rent° at every turn *steep gorge*
Winds thwarting winds, bewildered and forlorn,
The torrents shooting from the clear blue sky,
The rocks that muttered close upon our ears,
Black drizzling crags that spake by the way-side
As if a voice were in them, the sick sight
And giddy prospect of the raving stream,
The unfettered clouds and region of the Heavens,
Tumult and peace, the darkness and the light—
Were all like workings of one mind, the features
Of the same face, blossoms upon one tree;
Characters of the great Apocalypse,
The types and symbols of Eternity,
Of first, and last, and midst, and without end. …

Oh, most belovèd Friend! a glorious time,
A happy time that was; triumphant looks
Were then the common language of all eyes;
As if awaked from sleep, the Nations hailed
Their great expectancy: the fife of war
Was then a spirit-stirring sound indeed,
A black-bird's whistle in a budding grove.
We left the Swiss exulting in the fate
Of their near neighbours;[1] and, when shortening fast
Our pilgrimage, nor distant far from home,
We crossed the Brabant armies[2] on the fret
For battle in the cause of Liberty.
A stripling, scarcely of the household then
Of social life, I looked upon these things
As from a distance; heard, and saw, and felt,
Was touched, but with no intimate concern;
I seemed to move along them, as a bird
Moves through the air, or as a fish pursues
Its sport, or feeds in its proper element;
I wanted not that joy, I did not need
Such help; the ever-living universe,
Turn where I might, was opening out its glories,
And the independent spirit of pure youth
Called forth, at every season, new delights
Spread round my steps like sunshine o'er green fields.

from Book Thirteenth
Imagination and Taste, How Impaired and Restored (Concluded)

From Nature doth emotion come, and moods
Of calmness equally are Nature's gift:
This is her glory; these two attributes
Are sister horns that constitute her strength.
Hence Genius, born to thrive by interchange
Of peace and excitation,° finds in her *stimulus*
His best and purest friend, from her receives
That energy by which he seeks the truth,
From her that happy stillness of the mind
Which fits him to receive it, when unsought.

Such benefit the humblest intellects
Partake of, each in their degree: 'tis mine
To speak, what I myself have known and felt;
Smooth task! for words find easy way, inspired
By gratitude, and confidence in truth.
Long time in search of knowledge did I range
The field of human life, in heart and mind

[1] *their near neighbours* I.e., the French.

[2] *Brabant armies* Armies of the Brabant Revolution (1789–90), in which the people of what is now Belgium, but was then part of the Holy Roman Empire, revolted and briefly established a republic.

Benighted; but, the dawn beginning now
To re-appear, 'twas proved that not in vain
I had been taught to reverence a Power
That is the visible quality and shape
And image of right reason; that matures
Her processes by steadfast laws; gives birth
To no impatient or fallacious hopes,
No heat of passion or excessive zeal,
No vain conceits, provokes to no quick turns
Of self-applauding intellect; but trains
To meekness, and exalts by humble faith;
Holds up before the mind intoxicate
With present objects, and the busy dance
Of things that pass away, a temperate show
Of objects that endure; and by this course
Disposes her, when over-fondly set
On throwing off incumbrances, to seek
In man, and in the frame of social life,
Whate'er there is desireable and good
Of kindred permanence, unchanged in form
And function, or, through strict vicissitude
Of life and death, revolving. Above all
Were re-established now those watchful thoughts
Which, seeing little worthy or sublime
In what the Historian's pen so much delights
To blazon—power and energy detached
From moral purpose—early tutored me
To look with feelings of fraternal love
Upon the unassuming things that hold
A silent station in this beauteous world.

Thus moderated, thus composed, I found
Once more in Man an object of delight,
Of pure imagination, and of love;
And, as the horizon of my mind enlarged,
Again I took the intellectual° eye *inner, spiritual*
For my instructor, studious more to see
Great truths, than touch and handle little ones.
Knowledge was given accordingly; my trust
Became more firm in feelings that had stood
The test of such a trial; clearer far
My sense of excellence—of right and wrong:
The promise of the present time retired
Into its true proportion; sanguine° schemes, *confident*
Ambitious projects, pleased me less; I sought
For present good in life's familiar face,
And built thereon my hopes of good to come.

With settling judgments now of what would last
And what must disappear, prepared to find
Presumption, folly, madness, in the men
Who thrust themselves upon the passive world
As Rulers of the world; to see in these,
Even when the public welfare is their aim,
Plans without thought, or built on theories
Vague and unsound; and having brought the books
Of modern statists° to their proper test, *political theorists*
Life, human life, with all its sacred claims
Of sex and age, and heaven-descended rights,
Mortal, or those beyond the reach of death;
And having thus discerned how dire a thing
Is worshipped in that idol proudly named
"The Wealth of Nations,"[1] *where* alone that wealth
Is lodged, and how encreased; and having gained
A more judicious knowledge of the worth
And dignity of individual man,
No composition of the brain, but man
Of whom we read, the man whom we behold
With our own eyes—I could not but enquire—
Not with less interest than heretofore,
But greater, though in spirit more subdued,
Why is this glorious creature to be found
One only in ten thousand? What one is,
Why may not millions be? What bars are thrown
By Nature in the way of such a hope?
Our animal appetites and daily wants,
Are these obstructions insurmountable?
If not, then others vanish into air.
"Inspect the basis of the social pile:
Inquire," said I, "how much of mental Power
And genuine virtue they possess who live
By bodily toil, labour exceeding far
Their due proportion, under all the weight

[1] *The ... Nations* Reference to Adam Smith's *Inquiry into the Nature and Cause of the Wealth of Nations* (1776).

Of that injustice which upon ourselves
Ourselves entail." Such estimate to frame
I chiefly looked (what need to look beyond?)
Among the natural abodes of men,
Fields with their rural works, recalled to mind
My earliest notices,° with these compared *observations*
The observations made in later youth,
And to that day continued. For, the time
Had never been when throes of mighty Nations
And the world's tumult unto me could yield,
How far soe'er transported and possessed,
Full measure of content; but still I craved
An intermingling of distinct regards° *sights*
And truths of individual sympathy
Nearer ourselves. Such often might be gleaned
From the great City, else it must have proved
To me a heart-depressing wilderness;
But much was wanting; therefore did I turn
To you, ye pathways, and ye lonely roads;
Sought you enriched with every thing I prized,
With human kindness and simple joys. …

Here, calling up to mind what then I saw,
A youthful traveller, and see daily now
In the familiar circuit of my home,
Here might I pause, and bend in reverence
To Nature, and the power of human minds,
To men as they are men within themselves.
How oft high service is performed within,
When all the external man is rude in show—
Not like a temple rich with pomp and gold,
But a mere mountain chapel, that protects
Its simple worshippers from sun and shower.
Of these, said I, shall be my song; of these,
If future years mature me for the task,
Will I record the praises, making verse
Deal boldly with substantial things; in truth
And sanctity of passion, speak of these,
That justice may be done, obeisance paid
Where it is due: thus haply° shall I teach, *by chance*
Inspire, through unadulterated ears
Pour rapture, tenderness, and hope—my theme
No other than the very heart of man,
As found among the best of those who live,
Not unexalted by religious faith,
Nor uninformed by books, good books, though few,
In Nature's presence: thence may I select
Sorrow, that is not sorrow, but delight;
And miserable love, that is not pain
To hear of, for the glory that redounds
Therefrom to human kind, and what we are.
Be mine to follow with no timid step
Where knowledge leads me: it shall be my pride
That I have dared to tread this holy ground,
Speaking no dream, but things oracular;° *prophetic*
Matter not lightly to be heard by those
Who to the letter of the outward promise
Do read the invisible soul;[1] by men adroit
In speech, and for communion with the world
Accomplished; minds whose faculties are then
Most active when they are most eloquent,
And elevated most when most admired.
Men may be found of other mould than these,
Who are their own upholders, to themselves
Encouragement, and energy, and will,
Expressing liveliest thoughts in lively words
As native passion dictates. Others, too,
There are among the walks of homely life
Still higher, men for contemplation framed,
Shy, and unpractised in the strife of phrase;
Meek men, whose very souls perhaps would sink
Beneath them, summoned to such intercourse:
Theirs is the language of the heavens, the power,
The thought, the image, and the silent joy:
Words are but under-agents in their souls;
When they are grasping with their greatest strength,
They do not breathe among them:[2] this I speak
In gratitude to God, Who feeds our hearts
For His own service; knoweth, loveth us,
When we are unregarded by the world.

---

[1] *to the letter … soul* Form their opinion of the soul from the external qualities.

[2] *They do … them* I.e., such people do not exist ("breathe") in the realm of words.

Also, about this time did I receive
Convictions still more strong than heretofore,
Not only that the inner frame is good,
And graciously composed, but that, no less,
Nature for all conditions wants° not power *lacks*
To consecrate, if we have eyes to see,
The outside of her creatures, and to breathe
Grandeur upon the very humblest face
Of human life. I felt that the array
Of act and circumstance, and visible form,
Is mainly to the pleasure of the mind
What passion makes them; that meanwhile the forms
Of Nature have a passion in themselves,
That intermingles with those works of man
To which she summons him; although the works
Be mean, have nothing lofty of their own;
And that the Genius of the Poet hence
May boldly take his way among mankind
Wherever Nature leads; that he hath stood
By Nature's side among the men of old,
And so shall stand for ever. Dearest Friend!
If thou partake the animating faith
That Poets, even as Prophets, each with each
Connected in a mighty scheme of truth,
Have each his own peculiar° faculty, *specific*
Heaven's gift, a sense that fits him to perceive
Objects unseen before, thou wilt not blame
The humblest of this band who dares to hope
That unto him hath also been vouchsafed
An insight that in some sort he possesses,
A privilege whereby a work of his,
Proceeding from a source of untaught things,
Creative and enduring, may become
A power like one of Nature's. To a hope
Not less ambitious once among the wilds
Of Sarum's Plain,[1] my youthful spirit was raised;
There, as I ranged at will the pastoral downs[2]
Trackless and smooth, or paced the bare white roads
Lengthening in solitude their dreary line,
Time with his retinue of ages fled
Backwards, nor checked his flight until I saw
Our dim ancestral Past in vision clear;
Saw multitudes of men, and, here and there,
A single Briton clothed in wolf-skin vest,
With shield and stone-axe, stride across the
wold;° *countryside*
The voice of spears was heard, the rattling spear
Shaken by arms of mighty bone, in strength,
Long mouldered, of barbaric majesty.
I called on Darkness—but before the word
Was uttered, midnight darkness seemed to take
All objects from my sight; and lo! again
The Desert[3] visible by dismal flames;
It is the sacrificial altar, fed
With living men[4]—how deep the groans! the voice
Of those that crowd the giant wicker thrills
The monumental hillocks,[5] and the pomp
Is for both worlds, the living and the dead.
At other moments (for through that wide waste
Three summer days I roamed) where'er the Plain
Was figured o'er with circles, lines, or mounds,[6]
That yet survive, a work, as some divine,° *conjecture*
Shaped by the Druids, so to represent
Their knowledge of the heavens, and image forth
The constellations; gently was I charmed
Into a waking dream, a reverie
That, with believing eyes, where'er I turned,
Beheld long-bearded teachers, with white wands

[1] *Sarum's Plain* Salisbury Plain, the site of Stonehenge and other Neolithic archeological features. Wordsworth's 1793 walk across the plain was an apparently profound experience that he referenced in his poem *Salisbury Plain* (written 1793–94, but later revised, expanded, and retitled to produce several other versions).

[2] *downs* Chalky hills spanning much of southern England, including Salisbury Plain.

[3] *Desert* Expanse of wilderness.

[4] *sacrificial … living men* Druids were thought to have performed human sacrifices by placing the victims inside a giant wicker statue and setting it on fire.

[5] *monumental hillocks* I.e., burial mounds.

[6] *circles … mounds* Marks on the plain, which are the results of prehistoric construction, burial mounds, field enclosures, and other archaeological remains.

Uplifted, pointing to the starry sky,
Alternately, and plain below, while breath
Of music swayed their motions, and the waste
Rejoiced with them and me in those sweet sounds.

This for the past, and things that may be viewed
Or fancied in the obscurity of years
From monumental hints: and thou, O Friend!
Pleased with some unpremeditated strains
That served those wanderings to beguile,[1] hast said
That then and there my mind had exercised
Upon the vulgar forms of present things,
The actual world of our familiar days,
Yet higher power; had caught from them a tone,
An image, and a character, by books
Not hitherto reflected. Call we this
A partial judgment—and yet why? for *then*
We were as strangers; and I may not speak
Thus wrongfully of verse, however rude,
Which on thy young imagination, trained
In the great City, broke like light from far.
Moreover, each man's Mind is to herself
Witness and judge; and I remember well
That in life's every-day appearances
I seemed about this time to gain clear sight
Of a new world—a world, too, that was fit
To be transmitted, and to other eyes
Made visible; as ruled by those fixed laws
Whence spiritual dignity originates,
Which do both give it being and maintain
A balance, an ennobling interchange
Of action from without and from within;
The excellence, pure function, and best power
Both of the object seen, and eye that sees.

[1] *some unpremeditated ... beguile* Some verse that Wordsworth wrote to pass the time during his walk across the plain. In 1796, less than a year after the poets had first met, Wordsworth sent Coleridge a copy of his *Adventures on Salisbury Plain* (1795), a revised and expanded version of his 1793–94 poem.

Book Fourteenth
Conclusion

In one of those excursions (may they ne'er
Fade from remembrance!) through the Northern tracts
Of Cambria ranging with a youthful friend,[2]
I left Bethgelert's huts at couching-time,° *bedtime*
And westward took my way, to see the sun
Rise from the top of Snowdon. To the door
Of a rude cottage at the mountain's base
We came, and roused the shepherd who attends
The adventurous stranger's steps, a trusty guide;
Then, cheered by short refreshment, sallied forth.

It was a close, warm, breezeless summer night,
Wan, dull, and glaring,° with a dripping fog *rainy*
Low-hung and thick, that covered all the sky;
But, undiscouraged, we began to climb
The mountain-side. The mist soon girt us round,
And, after ordinary travellers' talk
With our conductor, pensively we sank
Each into commerce with his private thoughts:
Thus did we breast the ascent, and by myself
Was nothing either seen or heard that checked
Those musings or diverted, save that once
The shepherd's lurcher,[3] who, among the crags,
Had to his joy unearthed a hedgehog, teased
His coiled-up prey with barkings turbulent.
This small adventure, for even such it seemed
In that wild place and at the dead of night,
Being over and forgotten, on we wound
In silence as before. With forehead bent
Earthward, as if in opposition set
Against an enemy, I panted up
With eager pace, and no less eager thoughts.
Thus might we wear a midnight hour away,

[2] *In one ... friend* The trip referred to was a 1791 walking tour through North Wales (Cambria) with Robert Jones, the same friend with whom Wordsworth crossed the Alps. In this passage, they ascend Mount Snowdon, the highest peak in Wales, from the village of Bethgellert.

[3] *lurcher* Rabbit-hunting dog.

Ascending at loose distance each from each,
And I, as chanced, the foremost of the band:
When at my feet the ground appeared to brighten,
And with a step or two seemed brighter still;
Nor was time given to ask or learn the cause,
For instantly a light upon the turf
Fell like a flash, and lo! as I looked up,
The Moon hung naked in a firmament
Of azure without cloud, and at my feet
Rested a silent sea of hoary° mist. *white*
A hundred hills their dusky backs upheaved
All over this still ocean; and beyond,
Far, far beyond, the solid vapours stretched,
In headlands, tongues, and promontory shapes,
Into the main Atlantic, that appeared
To dwindle, and give up his majesty,
Usurped upon far as the sight could reach.
Not so the ethereal vault; encroachment none
Was there, nor loss; only the inferior stars
Had disappeared, or shed a fainter light
In the clear presence of the full-orbed Moon,
Who, from her sovereign elevation, gazed
Upon the billowy ocean, as it lay
All meek and silent, save that through a rift—
Not distant from the shore whereon we stood,
A fixed, abysmal, gloomy breathing-place—
Mounted the roar of waters, torrents, streams
Innumerable, roaring with one voice!
Heard over earth and sea, and in that hour,
For so it seemed, felt by the starry heavens.

When into air had partially dissolved
That vision, given to spirits of the night,
And three chance human wanderers, in calm thought
Reflected, it appeared to me the type
Of a majestic intellect, its acts
And its possessions, what it has and craves,
What in itself it is, and would become.
There I beheld the emblem of a mind
That feeds upon infinity, that broods
Over the dark abyss, intent to hear
Its voices issuing forth to silent light
In one continuous stream; a mind sustained
By recognitions of transcendent power,
In sense, conducting to ideal form,
In soul of more than mortal privilege.
One function, above all, of such a mind
Had Nature shadowed there, by putting forth,
'Mid circumstances awful and sublime,
That mutual domination which she loves
To exert upon the face of outward things,
So moulded, joined, abstracted, so endowed
With interchangeable supremacy,
That men least sensitive see, hear, perceive,
And cannot choose but feel. The power, which all
Acknowledge when thus moved, which Nature thus
To bodily sense exhibits, is the express
Resemblance of that glorious faculty[1]
That higher minds bear with them as their own.
This is the very spirit in which they deal
With the whole compass of the universe:
They, from their native° selves, can send abroad *natural*
Kindred mutations; for themselves create
A like existence, and whene'er it dawns
Created for them, catch it, or are caught
By its inevitable mastery,
Like angels stopped upon the wing by sound
Of harmony from heaven's remotest spheres.[2]
Them the enduring and the transient both
Serve to exalt; they build up greatest things
From least suggestions; ever on the watch,
Willing to work and to be wrought upon,
They need not extraordinary calls
To rouse them, in a world of life they live,
By sensible impressions not enthralled,
But by their quickening impulse made more prompt
To hold fit converse with the spiritual world,
And with the generations of mankind
Spread over time, past, present, and to come,
Age after age, till Time shall be no more.
Such minds are truly from the Deity,

---

[1] *that glorious faculty* I.e., imagination.

[2] *angels … spheres* Reference to the concept of the "music of the spheres," a literal or figurative music produced by the movements of the planets and other objects in space; it is audible only to angels.

For they are powers; and hence the highest bliss
That flesh can know is theirs—the consciousness
Of Whom they are, habitually infused
Through every image, and through every thought,
And all affections by communion raised
From earth to heaven, from human to divine;
Hence endless occupation for the Soul,
Whether discursive or intuitive;[1]
Hence cheerfulness for acts of daily life,
Emotions which best foresight need not fear,
Most worthy then of trust when most intense.
Hence, amid ills that vex, and wrongs that crush
Our hearts—if here the words of Holy Writ[2]
May with fit reverence be applied—that peace
Which passeth understanding,[3] that repose
In moral judgements which from this pure source
Must come, or will by Man be sought in vain.

Oh! who is he that hath his whole life long
Preserved, enlarged, this freedom in himself?
For this alone is genuine liberty:
Where is the favoured being who hath held
That course unchecked, unerring, and untired,
In one perpetual progress smooth and bright?—
A humbler destiny have we retraced,
And told of lapse and hesitating choice,
And backward wanderings along thorny ways:
Yet—compassed round by mountain solitudes,
Within whose solemn temple I received
My earliest visitations, careless then
Of what was given me; and which now I range,
A meditative, oft a suffering man—
Do I declare—in accents which, from truth
Deriving cheerful confidence, shall blend
Their modulation with these vocal streams—
That, whatsoever falls my better mind,
Revolving with the accidents of life,
May have sustained, that, howsoe'er misled,
Never did I, in quest of right and wrong,
Tamper with conscience from a private aim;
Nor was in any public hope the dupe
Of selfish passions; nor did ever yield
Wilfully to mean cares or low pursuits,
But shrunk with apprehensive jealousy° *dedication, watchfulness*
From every combination which might aid
The tendency, too potent in itself,
Of use° and custom to bow down the soul *habit*
Under a growing weight of vulgar sense,
And substitute a universe of death[4]
For that which moves with light and life informed,
Actual, divine, and true. To fear and love,
To love as prime and chief, for there fear ends,
Be this ascribed; to early intercourse,
In presence of sublime or beautiful forms,
With the adverse principles of pain and joy—
Evil, as one is rashly named by men
Who know not what they speak. By love subsists
All lasting grandeur, by pervading love;
That gone, we are as dust. Behold the fields
In balmy spring-time full of rising flowers
And joyous creatures; see that pair, the lamb
And the lamb's mother, and their tender ways
Shall touch thee to the heart; thou callest this love,
And not inaptly so, for love it is,
Far as it carries thee. In some green bower
Rest, and be not alone, but have thou there
The One who is thy choice of all the world:
There linger, listening, gazing, with delight
Impassioned, but delight how pitiable!
Unless this love by a still higher love
Be hallowed, love that breathes not without awe;
Love that adores, but on the knees of prayer,

---

[1] *discursive or intuitive* In *Paradise Lost,* Milton distinguishes between "discursive" reason, normally held by humans, and "intuitive" reason, belonging to the angels; the two are "differing in degree, of kind the same" (5.490).

[2] *Holy Writ* Scripture.

[3] *that peace … understanding* Cf. Philippians 4.7: "That peace of God, which passeth all understanding."

[4] *a universe of death* Cf. the description of hell in Milton's *Paradise Lost* 2.620–23: "many a Frozen, many a fiery Alp, / Rocks, Caves, Lakes, Fens, Bogs, Dens, and shades of death, / A Universe of death, which God by curse / Created evil."

By heaven inspired; that frees from chains the soul,
Lifted, in union with the purest, best,
Of earth-born passions, on the wings of praise
Bearing a tribute to the Almighty's Throne.

This spiritual Love acts not nor can exist
Without Imagination, which, in truth,
Is but another name for absolute power
And clearest insight, amplitude of mind,
And Reason in her most exalted mood.
This faculty hath been the feeding source
Of our long labour: we have traced the stream
From the blind cavern whence is faintly heard
Its natal murmur; followed it to light
And open day; accompanied its course
Among the ways of Nature, for a time
Lost sight of it bewildered and engulfed:
Then given it greeting as it rose once more
In strength, reflecting from its placid breast
The works of man and face of human life;
And lastly, from its progress have we drawn
Faith in life endless, the sustaining thought
Of human Being, Eternity, and God.

Imagination having been our theme,
So also hath that intellectual° Love, *inner, spiritual*
For they are each in each, and cannot stand
Dividually.° Here must thou be, O Man! *divided*
Power to thyself; no Helper hast thou here;
Here keepest thou in singleness thy state:
No other can divide with thee this work:
No secondary hand can intervene
To fashion this ability; 'tis thine,
The prime and vital principle is thine
In the recesses of thy nature, far
From any reach of outward fellowship,
Else is not thine at all. But joy to him,
Oh, joy to him who here hath sown, hath laid
Here, the foundation of his future years!
For all that friendship, all that love can do,
All that a darling countenance can look
Or dear voice utter, to complete the man,
Perfect him, made imperfect in himself,
All shall be his: and he whose soul hath risen
Up to the height of feeling intellect
Shall want no humbler tenderness; his heart
Be tender as a nursing mother's heart;
Of female softness shall his life be full,
Of humble cares and delicate desires,
Mild interests and gentlest sympathies.

Child of my parents! Sister of my soul![1]
Thanks in sincerest verse have been elsewhere
Poured out for all the early tenderness
Which I from thee imbibed: and 'tis most true
That later seasons owed to thee no less;
For, spite of thy sweet influence and the touch
Of kindred hands that opened out the springs
Of genial thought in childhood, and in spite
Of all that unassisted I had marked
In life or nature of those charms minute
That win their way into the heart by stealth
(Still to the very going-out of youth),
I too exclusively esteemed *that* love,
And sought *that* beauty, which, as Milton sings,
Hath terror in it.[2] Thou didst soften down
This over-sternness; but for thee, dear Friend!
My soul, too reckless of[3] mild grace, had stood
In her original self too confident,
Retained too long a countenance severe;
A rock with torrents roaring, with the clouds
Familiar, and a favourite of the stars:
But thou didst plant its crevices with flowers,
Hang it with shrubs that twinkle in the breeze,
And teach the little birds to build their nests
And warble in its chambers. At a time
When Nature, destined to remain so long
Foremost in my affections, had fallen back
Into a second place, pleased to become
A handmaid to a nobler than herself,

[1] *Child of … my soul!* I.e., the poet's sister Dorothy.

[2] *that beauty … it* Cf. Satan's description of Eve in Milton's *Paradise Lost* 9.490–92: "She fair, divinely fair, fit Love for Gods, / Not terrible, though terror be in Love / And beauty."

[3] *reckless of* Inattentive to.

When every day brought with it some new sense
Of exquisite regard for common things,
And all the earth was budding with these gifts
Of more refined humanity, thy breath,
Dear Sister! was a kind of gentler spring
That went before my steps. Thereafter came
One whom with thee friendship had early paired;[1]
She came, no more a phantom to adorn
A moment, but an inmate of the heart,
And yet a spirit, there for me enshrined
To penetrate the lofty and the low;
Even as one essence of pervading light
Shines, in the brightest of ten thousand stars,
And the meek worm° that feeds her lonely lamp *glowworm*
Couched in the dewy grass.
With such a theme,
Coleridge! with this my argument, of thee
Shall I be silent? O capacious Soul!
Placed on this earth to love and understand,
And from thy presence shed the light of love,
Shall I be mute, ere thou be spoken of?
Thy kindred influence to my heart of hearts
Did also find its way. Thus fear relaxed
Her overweening° grasp; thus thoughts and things *presumptuous*
In the self-haunting spirit learned to take
More rational proportions; mystery,
The incumbent mystery of sense and soul,
Of life and death, time and eternity,
Admitted more habitually a mild
Interposition[2]—a serene delight
In closelier gathering cares, such as become
A human creature, howsoe'er endowed,
Poet, or destined for a humbler name;
And so the deep enthusiastic joy,
The rapture of the hallelujah sent
From all that breathes and is, was chastened, stemmed,
And balanced by pathetic° truth, by trust *emotional*
In hopeful reason, leaning on the stay
Of Providence; and in reverence for duty,
Here, if need be, struggling with storms, and there
Strewing in peace life's humblest ground with herbs,
At every season green, sweet at all hours.

And now, O Friend! this history is brought
To its appointed close: the discipline
And consummation of a Poet's mind,
In every thing that stood most prominent,
Have faithfully been pictured; we have reached
The time (our guiding object from the first)
When we may, not presumptuously, I hope,
Suppose my powers so far confirmed, and such
My knowledge, as to make me capable
Of building up a Work that shall endure.
Yet much hath been omitted, as need was;
Of books how much! and even of the other wealth
That is collected among woods and fields,
Far more: for Nature's secondary grace
Hath hitherto been barely touched upon,
The charm more superficial that attends
Her works, as they present to Fancy's choice
Apt illustrations of the moral world,
Caught at a glance, or traced with curious pains.

Finally, and above all, O Friend! (I speak
With due regret) how much is overlooked
In human nature and her subtle ways,
As studied first in our own hearts, and then
In life among the passions of mankind,
Varying their composition and their hue,
Where'er we move, under the diverse shapes
That individual character presents
To an attentive eye. For progress meet,
Along this intricate and difficult path,
Whate'er was wanting, something had I gained,
As one of many schoolfellows compelled,
In hardy independence, to stand up
Amid conflicting interests, and the shock
Of various tempers; to endure and note
What was not understood, though known to be;

[1] *One whom … paired* Mary Hutchinson, the poet's wife, who was already a close friend of Dorothy's when the couple married.

[2] *Admitted … Interposition* I.e., began to suffuse the poet's usual thoughts in a gentle, moderate way.

Among the mysteries of love and hate,
Honour and shame, looking to right and left,
Unchecked by innocence too delicate,
And moral notions too intolerant,
Sympathies too contracted.° Hence, *limited*
when called
To take a station among men, the step
Was easier, the transition more secure,
More profitable also; for, the mind
Learns from such timely exercise to keep
In wholesome separation the two natures,
The one that feels, the other that observes.

Yet one word more of personal concern—
Since I withdrew unwillingly from France,[1]
I led an undomestic wanderer's life,
In London chiefly harboured, whence I roamed,
Tarrying at will in many a pleasant spot
Of rural England's cultivated vales
Or Cambrian° solitudes. A youth (he bore *Welsh*
The name of Calvert[2]—it shall live, if words
Of mine can give it life) in firm belief
That by endowments not from me withheld
Good might be furthered—in his last decay
By a bequest sufficient for my needs
Enabled me to pause for choice, and walk
At large and unrestrained, nor damped too soon
By mortal cares. Himself no Poet, yet
Far less a common follower of the world,
He deemed that my pursuits and labours lay
Apart from all that leads to wealth, or even
A necessary maintenance insures,
Without some hazard to the finer sense;
He cleared a passage for me, and the stream
Flowed in the bent of Nature.

Having now
Told what best merits mention, further pains
Our present purpose seems not to require,
And I have other tasks. Recall to mind
The mood in which this labour was begun,
O Friend! The termination of my course
Is nearer now, much nearer; yet even then,
In that distraction and intense desire,
I said unto the life which I had lived,
Where art thou? Hear I not a voice from thee
Which 'tis reproach to hear? Anon° I rose *then*
As if on wings, and saw beneath me stretched
Vast prospect of the world which I had been
And was; and hence this Song, which like a lark
I have protracted,° in the unwearied heavens *extended*
Singing, and often with more plaintive voice
To earth attempered° and her deep-drawn sighs, *adapted*
Yet centring all in love, and in the end
All gratulant,° if rightly understood. *joyful*

Whether to me shall be allotted life,
And, with life, power to accomplish aught of worth,
That will be deemed no insufficient plea
For having given the story of myself,[3]
Is all uncertain: but, beloved Friend!
When, looking back, thou seest, in clearer view
Than any liveliest sight of yesterday,
That summer, under whose indulgent skies,
Upon smooth Quantock's[4] airy ridge we roved
Unchecked, or loitered 'mid her sylvan° *wooded*
combs,° *valleys*
Thou in bewitching words, with happy heart,
Didst chaunt the vision of that Ancient Man,
The bright-eyed Mariner, and rueful woes

---

[1] *I withdrew … France* In 1792 financial pressures forced Wordsworth to return to England from France, leaving behind his lover, Annette Vallon, who gave birth to their daughter in the same year.

[2] *Calvert* Raisley Calvert, Wordsworth's friend, who died young of tuberculosis. He left Wordsworth £900, enough for him to set up house with his sister at Racedown Lodge and devote himself to his poetry.

[3] *Whether to … myself* Whether my life, abilities, and accomplishments will be considered to justify my writing about myself.

[4] *Quantock* Hills above Alfoxden House, in Somerset, where the Wordsworths moved for larger accommodations and to be closer to Coleridge. That summer while visiting them, Coleridge recited "The Rime of the Ancient Mariner" and "Christabel," both of which he had recently finished, and Wordsworth wrote "The Idiot Boy" and "The Thorn." Wordsworth and Coleridge published *Lyrical Ballads* the following year.

Didst utter of the Lady Christabel;
And I, associate with such labour, steeped
In soft forgetfulness the livelong hours,
Murmuring of him who, joyous hap,° *chance*
  was found,
After the perils of his moonlight ride,
Near the loud waterfall;[1] or her who sat
In misery near the miserable Thorn;[2]
When thou dost to that summer turn thy thoughts,
And hast before thee all which then we were,
To thee, in memory of that happiness,
It will be known, by thee at least, my Friend!
Felt, that the history of a Poet's mind
Is labour not unworthy of regard:
To thee the work shall justify itself.

  The last and later portions of this gift
Have been prepared, not with the buoyant spirits
That were our daily portion when we first
Together wantoned in wild Poesy,
But, under pressure of a private grief,[3]
Keen and enduring, which the mind and heart,
That in this meditative history
Have been laid open, needs must make me feel
More deeply, yet enable me to bear
More firmly; and a comfort now hath risen
From hope that thou art near, and wilt be soon
Restored to us in renovated health;
When, after the first mingling of our tears,
'Mong other consolations, we may draw
Some pleasure from this offering of my love.

  Oh! yet a few short years of useful life,
And all will be complete, thy race be run,
Thy monument of glory will be raised;
Then, though (too weak to tread the ways of truth)
This age fall back to old idolatry,
Though men return to servitude as fast
As the tide ebbs, to ignominy and shame
By nations sink together, we shall still
Find solace—knowing what we have learnt to know,
Rich in true happiness if allowed to be
Faithful alike in forwarding a day
Of firmer trust, joint labourers in the work
(Should Providence such grace to us vouchsafe)
Of their deliverance, surely yet to come.
Prophets of Nature, we to them will speak
A lasting inspiration, sanctified
By reason, blest by faith: what we have loved,
Others will love, and we will teach them how;
Instruct them how the mind of man becomes
A thousand times more beautiful than the earth
On which he dwells, above this frame of things
(Which 'mid all revolutions in the hopes
And fears of men doth still remain unchanged)
In beauty exalted, as it is itself
Of quality and fabric more divine.
—1850

[1] *Murmuring … waterfall* In "The Idiot Boy," a boy with disabilities is sent to fetch a doctor and does not return; his mother finds him atop his horse near a waterfall.

[2] *In misery … Thorn* A refrain in the poem "The Thorn" is "'Oh misery! oh misery! / Oh woe is me! oh misery!'"

[3] *a private grief* Wordsworth's brother John died in a shipwreck in 1805.

Benjamin Robert Haydon, *Wordsworth on Helvellyn*, 1842.

Dorothy Wordsworth

1771 – 1855

For Virginia Woolf, an ardent admirer of Dorothy Wordsworth's work, her journals have in them "the suggestive power which is the gift of the poet rather than of the naturalist, the power which, taking only the simplest facts, so orders them that the whole scene comes before us, heightened and composed, the lake in its quiet, the hills in their splendour." Wordsworth's exquisite observations on nature, her keen eye and ear for the details of the appearance and speech-patterns of the local populace—and her incisive sense of their harsh economic conditions and ingenious survival strategies—make her an important figure of Romanticism despite the fact that she published only a few poems during her lifetime. Her writing is of interest not only in its own right but also for the influence she exerted on her more famous brother William, who consulted her journals for inspiration for many of his poems.

Dorothy Wordsworth was born on Christmas Day of 1771 to John Wordsworth, an attorney, and Ann (née Cookson), in Cockermouth, Cumberland, in the Lake District of England. Her mother died when Wordsworth was only six, and her father sent her to Yorkshire to live with relatives. She rarely saw her father again up to the day he, too, suffered an untimely death. Her childhood was spent happily among aunts and cousins, but at age fifteen she was sent to live with her stern grandparents; in the nine years she lived there she longed for the company of her four brothers. Her dream of living with William was realized when in 1795 he was bequeathed a legacy by a college friend, allowing the two siblings to secure a home together in Dorset in southwestern England. They were never again parted until William's death 55 years later.

The two made the acquaintance of Samuel Taylor Coleridge while in Somerset, and soon after that they moved to Alfoxden House to be nearer him. The bond the triad created was powerful, "three persons with one soul," according to Coleridge. This friendship marked the beginning of an intensely creative time for Coleridge and for William Wordsworth, culminating in their "*annus mirabilis*" that yielded the *Lyrical Ballads*. This alliance was productive for Dorothy Wordsworth, as well. She began her Alfoxden journal (the earliest of her journals that has survived) in 1798, chiefly for the enjoyment of her brother, who took great delight in reading it (and sometimes writing his own poems in it). Her sensitive descriptions of farm workers, beggars, leech gatherers, and a myriad of other characters, as well her vivid images of rural scenes, were also an invaluable resource for William, who would use them to spark his memory when he later "recollected in tranquility" an event the two had experienced. According to Woolf, "Dorothy stored the mood in prose, and later William came and bathed in it and made it into poetry." When the Wordsworths moved to Dove Cottage in the Lake District, Dorothy wrote in her Grasmere journal (1800–03): "I never saw daffodils so beautiful they grew among the mossy stones about and about them, some rested their heads upon these stones as on a pillow for weariness and the rest tossed and reeled and danced and seemed as if they verily laughed with the wind …, they looked so gay ever glancing ever changing." These words became the inspiration for William's description of daffodils in his poem "I Wandered Lonely as a Cloud."

Wordsworth remained with her brother in Grasmere even after his marriage in 1802. The two continued to take many excursions together, which she recorded in various travel journals. Her writing was curtailed in 1829, when she suffered the first of a series of ailments that eventually debilitated her both physically and mentally. By June of 1835 she was an invalid from dementia said to be caused by arteriosclerosis. She remained so, albeit with brief periods of lucidity, for the following two decades, but she was cared for lovingly by those whom she had once tended. She died in 1855, outliving her beloved William by five years.

Wordsworth's poems, letters, journals, and travelogues were published long after her death. Once valued mainly as a resource for their insights into the work of the other poets in her circle, they are valued today for their descriptive power. Their author, according to Coleridge, possessed an "eye watchful in minutest observation of nature—and her taste a perfect electrometer—it bends, protrudes, and draws in at subtlest beauties and most recondite faults."

⌘⌘⌘

from *The Grasmere Journal*

May *14 1800* *Wm.* & John[1] set off into Yorkshire after dinner at ½ past 2 o'clock—cold pork in their pockets. I left them at the turning of the Low Wood bay[2] under the trees. My heart was so full that I could hardly speak to W. when I gave him a farewell kiss. I sat a long time upon a stone at the margin of the lake, and after a flood of tears my heart was easier. The lake looked to me I knew not why dull and melancholy, the weltering[3] on the shores seemed a heavy sound. I walked as long as I could amongst the stones of the shore. The wood rich in flowers. A beautiful yellow, palish yellow flower, that looked thick round and double, and smelt very sweet—I supposed it was a ranunculus—crowfoot, the grassy-leaved rabbit-toothed white flower, strawberries, geranium—scentless violet, anemones two kinds, orchises, primroses. The heckberry very beautiful as a low shrub. The crab coming out. Met a blind man driving a very large beautiful bull and a cow—he walked with two sticks. Came home by Clappersgate. The valley very green, many sweet views up to Rydale head when I could juggle away the fine houses, but they disturbed me even more than when I have been happier—one beautiful view of the bridge, without Sir Michael's.[4] Sat down very often, though it was cold. I resolved to write a journal of the time till W. and J. return, and I set about keeping my resolve because I will not quarrel with myself, and because I shall give Wm. pleasure by it when he comes home again. At Rydale a woman of the village, stout and well-dressed, begged a halfpenny—she had never she said done it before—but these hard times! Arrived at home with a bad headache, set some slips of privet.[5] The evening cold had a fire—my face now flame-coloured. It is nine o'clock—I shall soon go to bed. A young woman begged at the door—she had come from Manchester on Sunday morn with two shillings and a slip of paper which she supposed a bank note—it was a cheat. She had buried her husband and three children within a year and a half—all in one grave—burying very dear—paupers all put in one place—20 shillings paid for as much ground as will bury a man—a grave stone to be put over it or the right will be lost—11/6[6] each time the ground is opened. Oh! that I had a letter from William!

[1] *Wm. & John* Dorothy Wordsworth's brothers, William (often written as "Wm." or "W.") and John.

[2] *Low Wood bay* In the Lake District, where Dorothy and William Wordsworth lived.

[3] *weltering* Tumbling (of waves).

[4] *bridge, without Sir Michael's* Pelter Bridge, beyond Sir Michael le Fleming's castle.

[5] *privet* Common hedge plant.

[6] *11/6* Eleven shillings and sixpence.

Friday 3rd October. Very rainy all the morning—little Sally[1] learning to mark. Wm. walked to Ambleside after dinner. I went with him part of the way—he talked much about the object of his essay for the second volume of LB.[2] I returned expecting the Simpsons —they did not come. I should have met Wm. but my teeth ached and it was showery and late—he returned after 10. Amos Cottle's[3] death in the morning Post. Wrote to S. Lowthian.[4]

N.B.[5] When Wm. and I returned from accompanying Jones we met an old man almost double—he had on a coat thrown over his shoulders above his waistcoat and coat. Under this he carried a bundle and had an apron on and a night cap. His face was interesting. He had dark eyes and a long nose—John who afterwards met him at Wythburn took him for a Jew. He was of Scotch parents but had been born in the army. He had had a wife "and a good woman and it pleased God to bless us with ten children"—all these were dead but one of whom he had not heard for many years, a sailor—his trade was to gather leeches but now leeches are scarce and he had not strength for it—he lived by begging and was making his way to Carlisle where he should buy a few godly books to sell. He said leeches were very scarce partly owing to this dry season, but many years they have been scarce—he supposed it owing to their being much sought after, that they did not breed fast, and were of slow growth. Leeches were formerly 2/6 100; they are now 30/. He had been hurt in driving a cart his leg broke his body driven over his skull fractured—he felt no pain till he recovered from his first insensibility. It was then late in the evening—when the light was just going away.

[1] *little Sally* Sally Ashburner, daughter of the Wordsworths' neighbor.

[2] *LB* *Lyrical Ballads*, written with Samuel Taylor Coleridge (1798); William Wordsworth wrote a lengthy preface to the second edition, published in 1800.

[3] *Amos Cottle* Cottle was a poet, translator of Norse myths who had social connections to W. Wordsworth, Coleridge, and Southey; his brother, Joseph Cottle, was a poet and the publisher of Coleridge and W. Wordsworth's *Lyrical Ballads*.

[4] *S. Lowthian* Sally, one of Wordsworth's father's domestic staff.

[5] *N.B.* *Nota bene*: Note well (Latin); i.e., important note.

Saturday 11th A fine October morning—sat in the house working all the morning. Wm. composing—Sally Ashburner learning to mark. After dinner we walked up Greenhead Gill in search of a sheepfold. We went by Mr. Ollif's and through his woods. It was a delightful day and the views looked excessively cheerful and beautiful chiefly that from Mr. Oliff's field where our house is to be built. The colours of the mountains soft and rich, with orange fern. The cattle pasturing upon the hilltops kites[6] sailing as in the sky above our heads—sheep bleating and in lines and chains and patterns scattered over the mountains. They come down and feed on the little green islands in the beds of the torrents and so may be swept away. The sheepfold is falling away it is built nearly in the form of a heart unequally divided. Look down the brook and see the drops rise upwards and sparkle in the air, at the little falls, the higher sparkles the tallest. We walked along the turf of the mountain till we came to a cattle track—made by the cattle which come upon the hills. We drank tea at Mr. Simpson's returned at about nine—a fine mild night.

[November, 1801]

Tuesday 24th A rainy morning. We all were well except that my head ached a little and I took my breakfast in bed. I read a little of Chaucer, prepared the goose for dinner, and then we all walked out—I was obliged to return for my fur tippet and spenser[7] it was so cold. We had intended going to Easedale but we shaped our course to Mr. Gell's[8] cottage. It was very windy and we heard the wind everywhere about us as we went along the lane but the walls sheltered us—John Green's house looked pretty under Silver How[9]—as we were going along we were stopped at once, at the distance perhaps of 50 yards from our favorite birch tree. It was yielding to the gusty wind with all its tender twigs, the sun shone upon it and it glanced in the wind like a flying sunshiny shower—it was a tree in shape with stem and branches

[6] *kites* Birds (of prey).

[7] *tippet and spenser* Shawl and jacket.

[8] *Mr. Gell* Anthropologist Sir William Gell.

[9] *Silver How* Hill near Grasmere.

but it was like a spirit of water. The sun went in and it resumed its purplish appearance the twigs still yielding to the wind but not so visibly to us. The other birch trees that were near it looked bright and cheerful—but it was a creature by its own self among them. We could not get into Mr. Gell's grounds—the old tree fallen from its undue exaltation above the gate. A shower came on when we were at Benson's. We went through the wood—it became fair, there was a rainbow which spanned the lake from the island house to the foot of Bainriggs. The village looked populous and beautiful. Catkins[1] are coming out palm trees budding—the alder with its plum coloured buds. We came home over the stepping stones—the lake was foamy with white waves. I saw a solitary butter flower[2] in the wood. *I* found it not easy to get over the stepping stones—reached home at dinner time. Sent Peggy Ashburner some goose. She sent me some honey—with a thousand thanks—"alas the gratitude of men has &c."[3] I went in to set her right about this and sat a while with her. She talked about Thomas's having sold his land—"Ay" says she, "I said many a time he's not come fra London to buy our land however." Then she told me with what pains and industry they had made up their taxes interest &c. &c. —how they all got up at 5 o'clock in the morning to spin and Thomas carded,[4] and that they had paid off a hundred pound of the interest. She said she used to take such pleasure in the cattle and sheep—"Oh how pleased I used to be when they fetched them down, and when I had been a bit poorly I would gang[5] out upon a hill and look ower t' fields and see them and it used to do me so much good you cannot think"—Molly said to me when I came in "poor body! She's very ill but one does not know how long she may last. Many a fair face may gang before her." We sat by the fire without work for some time then Mary[6] read a poem of Daniel[7] upon learning. After tea Wm. read Spenser now and then a little aloud to us. We were making his waistcoat. We had a note from Mrs. C.[8] with bad news from poor C. very ill. William walked to John's grove—I went to meet him—moonlight but it rained. I met him before I had got as far as John Batys—he had been surprized and terrified by a sudden rushing of winds which seemed to bring earth sky and lake together, as if the whole were going to enclose him in—he was glad that he was in a high road.

In speaking of our walk on Sunday evening the 22nd November I forgot to notice one most impressive sight—it was the moon and the moonlight seen through hurrying driving clouds immediately behind the stone man upon the top of the hill on the forest side. Every tooth and every edge of rock was visible, and the man stood like a giant watching from the roof of a lofty castle. The hill seemed perpendicular from the darkness below it. It was a sight that I could call to mind at any time it was so distinct.

Friday 27th Snow upon the ground thinly scattered. It snowed after we got up and then the sun shone and it was very warm though frosty—now the sun shines sweetly. A woman came who was travelling with her husband—he had been wounded and was going with her to live at Whitehaven. She had been at Ambleside the night before, offered 4d at the Cock for a bed—they sent her to one Harrison's where she and her husband had slept upon the hearth and bought a pennyworth of chips for a fire. Her husband was gone before very lame. "Aye" says she, "I was once an officer's wife I, as you see me now. My first husband married me at Appleby. I had 18£ a year for teaching a school and because I had no fortune his father turned him out of doors. I have been in the West Indies—I lost the use of this finger. Just before he died he came to me and said he must bid farewell to his dear children and me—I had a muslin

[1] *Catkins* Cylindrical buds on birch and willow trees.

[2] *butter flower* Buttercup.

[3] *"alas … &c."* From William Wordsworth's "Simon Lee" 95–96: "I've heard of hearts unkind, kind deeds / With coldness still returning; / Alas! the gratitude of men / Hath oftener left me mourning."

[4] *carded* Combed the wool.

[5] *gang* Go.

[6] *Mary* Mary Hutchinson, Wordsworth's friend and William's future wife; Wordsworth often refers to her as MH in the journals.

[7] *Daniel* Samuel Daniel (1562–1619).

[8] *Mrs. C.* Mrs. Coleridge.

gown on like yours—I seized hold of his coat as he went from me and slipped the joint of my finger—he was shot directly. I came to London and married this man. He was clerk to Judge Chambray, that man that's going on the road now. If he, Judge Chambray, had been at Kendal he would given us a guinea or two and made nought of it, for he is very generous."

Before dinner we set forward to walk intending to return to dinner. But as we had got as far as Rydale Wm. thought he would go on to Mr. Luffs. We accompanied him under Loughrigg, and parted near the stepping stones—it was very cold. Mary and I walked quick home. There was a fine gleam of sunshine upon the eastern side of Ambleside vale. We came up the old road and turning round we were struck with the appearance. Mary wrote to her aunt. We expected the Simpsons. I was sleepy and weary and went to bed—before tea. It came on wet in the evening and was very cold. We expected letters from C. and Sara[1]—Sara's came by the boy. But none from C.—a sad disappointment. We did not go to meet Wm. as we had intended—Mary was at work at Wm's warm waistcoat.

[December]

Tuesday 22nd Still thaw. I washed my head. Wm. and I went to Rydale for letters—the road was covered with dirty snow, rough and rather slippery. We had a melancholy letter from C. for he had been very ill, though he was better when he wrote. We walked home almost without speaking—Wm. composed a few lines of the Pedlar.[2] We talked about Lamb's tragedy[3] as we went down the White Moss. We stopped a long time in going to watch a little bird with a salmon coloured breast—a white cross or T upon its wings, and a brownish back with faint stripes. It was pecking the scattered dung upon the road—it began to peck at the distance of 4 yards from us and advanced nearer and nearer till it came within the length of Wm's stick without any apparent fear of us. As we came up the White Moss we met an old man, who I saw was a beggar by his two bags hanging over his shoulder, but from a half laziness, half indifference and a wanting to *try* him if he would speak I let him pass. He said nothing, and my heart smote me. I turned back and said You are begging? "Ay" says he—I gave him a halfpenny. William, judging from his appearance joined in I suppose you were a Sailor? "Ay" he replied, "I have been fifty-seven years at sea, twelve of them on board a man-of-war[4] under Sir Hugh Palmer." Why have you not a pension? "I have no pension, but I could have got into Greenwich hospital[5] but all my officers are dead." He was seventy-five years of age, had a freshish colour in his cheeks, grey hair, a decent hat with a binding round the edge, the hat worn brown and glossy, his shoes were small thin shoes low in the quarters, pretty good—they had belonged to a gentleman. His coat was blue, frock shaped coming over his thighs, it had been joined up at the seams behind with paler blue to let it out, and there were three bell-shaped patches of darker blue behind where the buttons had been. His breeches were either of fustian[6] or grey cloth, with strings hanging down, whole and tight and he had a checked shirt on, and a small coloured handkerchief tied round his neck. His bags were hung over each shoulder and lay on each side of him, below his breast. One was brownish and of coarse stuff, the other was white with meal[7] on the outside, and his blue waistcoat was whitened with meal. In the coarse bag I guessed he put his scraps of meat &c. He walked with a slender stick decently stout, but his legs bowed outwards. We overtook old Fleming at Rydale, leading his little Dutchman-like grandchild along the slippery road. The same pace seemed to be natural to them both, the old man and the little child, and they went hand in hand, the grandfather cautious, yet looking proud of his charge. He had two patches of new cloth at the shoulder blades of his faded claret coloured coat, like eyes at each

[1] *C. and Sara* Samuel Taylor Coleridge and Sara Hutchinson, sister of William Wordsworth's future wife.

[2] *the Pedlar* "The Pedlar," a poem by William Wordsworth that was eventually incorporated into *The Excursion*.

[3] *Lamb's tragedy* Charles Lamb's play *John Woodvil* (1802).

[4] *man-of-war* Warship.

[5] *Greenwich hospital* Royal Naval Hospital, i.e., home for pensioned seamen.

[6] *fustian* Coarse cloth made of cotton and linen.

[7] *meal* Grain ground to a powder, like flour.

shoulder, not worn elsewhere. I found Mary at home in her riding-habit all her clothes being put up. We were very sad about Coleridge. Wm. walked further. When he came home he cleared a path to the necessary[1]—called me out to see it but before we got there a whole housetop full of snow had fallen from the roof upon the path and it echoed in the ground beneath like a dull beating upon it. We talked of going to Ambleside after dinner to borrow money of Luff, but we thought we would defer our visit to Eusemere a day. Half the seaman's nose was reddish as if he had been in his youth somewhat used to drinking, though he was not injured by it. We stopped to look at the stone seat at the top of the hill. There was a white cushion upon it round at the edge like a cushion and the rock behind looked soft as velvet, of a vivid green and so tempting! The snow too looked as soft as a down cushion. A young foxglove, like a star in the centre. There were a few green lichens about it and a few withered brackens of fern here and there and upon the ground near. All else was a thick snow—no foot mark to it, not the foot of a sheep. When we were at Thomas Ashburner's on Sunday Peggy talked about the Queen of Patterdale. She had been brought to drinking by her husband's unkindness and avarice. She was formerly a very nice tidy woman. She had taken to drinking but "that was better than if she had taken to something worse" (by this I suppose she meant killing herself). She said that her husband used to be out all night with other women and she used to hear him come in in the morning for they never slept together—"Many a poor body a wife like me, has had a working heart for her, as much stuff as she had." We sat snugly round the fire. I read to them the Tale of Custance and the Syrian Monarch, also some of the Prologues. It is the Man of Lawes Tale.[2] We went to bed early. It snowed and thawed.

Monday Morning 8th February 1802. It was very windy and rained very hard all the morning. William worked at his poem and I read a little in Lessing[3] and the grammar. A chaise[4] came past to fetch Ellis the carrier[5] who had hurt his head. After dinner (i.e. we set off at about ½ past 4) we went towards Rydale for letters. It was a "*Cauld Clash*"[6]—the rain had been so cold that it hardly melted the snow. We stopped at Park's to get some straw in William's shoes. The young mother was sitting by a bright wood fire with her youngest child upon her lap and the other two sat on each side of the chimney. The light of the fire made them a beautiful sight, with their innocent countenances, their rosy cheeks and glossy curling hair. We sat and talked about poor Ellis, and our journey over the Hawes.[7] It had been reported that we came over in the night. Willy told us of three men who were once lost in crossing that way in the night—they had carried a lantern with them—the lantern went out at the tarn[8] and they all perished. Willy had seen their cloaks drying at the public house in Patterdale the day before their funeral. We walked on very wet through the clashy cold roads in bad spirits at the idea of having to go as far as Rydale, but before we had come again to the shore of the lake, we met our patient, bow-bent friend with his little wooden box at his back. "Where are you going?" said he, "To Rydale for letters"—"I have two for you in my box." We lifted up the lid and there they lay—poor fellow, he straddled and pushed on with all his might but we soon outstripped him far away when we had turned back with our letters. We were very thankful that we had not to go on, for we should have been sadly tired. In thinking of this I could not help comparing lots with him! He goes at that slow pace every morning, and after having wrought a hard day's work returns at night, however weary he may be, takes it all quietly, and though perhaps he neither feels thankfulness, nor pleasure when he eats his supper, and has no luxury to look forward to but

[1] *necessary* Outdoor toilet.

[2] *Tale of Custance … Man of Lawes Tale* From Geoffrey Chaucer's *The Canterbury Tales*.

[3] *Lessing* German author and critic Gotthold Ephraim Lessing (1729–81).

[4] *chaise* Light open carriage.

[5] *carrier* I.e., common carrier, a hired parcel delivery person.

[6] *"Cauld Clash"* Scottish phrase meaning a cold blow.

[7] *the Hawes* Grisedale Pass.

[8] *tarn* Small mountain lake.

falling asleep in bed, yet I daresay he neither murmurs nor thinks it hard. He seems mechanized to labour. We broke the seal of Coleridge's letter, and I had light enough just to see that he was not ill. I put it in my pocket but at the top of the White Moss I took it to my bosom, a safer place for it. The night was wild. There was a strange mountain lightness when we were at the top of the White Moss. I have often observed it there in the evenings, being between the two valleys. There is more of the sky there than any other place. It has a strange effect sometimes along with the obscurity of evening or night. It seems almost like a peculiar *sort* of light. There was not much wind till we came to John's Grove, then it roared right out of the grove, all the trees were tossing about. C's letter somewhat damped us, it spoke with less confidence about France.[1] William wrote to him. The other letter was from Montagu with 8£. William was very unwell, tired when he had written, he went to bed, and left me to write to M.H., Montagu and Calvert, and Mrs. Coleridge. I had written in his letter to Coleridge. We wrote to Calvert to beg him not to fetch us on Sunday. Wm left me with a *little* peat fire—it grew less—I wrote on and was starved.[2] At 2 o'clock I went to put my letters under Fletcher's door. I never felt such a cold night. There was a strong wind and it froze very hard. I collected together all the clothes I could find (for I durst not go into the pantry for fear of waking William). At first when I went to bed I seemed to be warm, I suppose because the cold air which I had just left no longer touched my body, but I soon found that I was mistaken. I could not sleep from sheer cold. I had baked pies and bread in the morning. Coleridge's letter contained prescriptions.

NB The moon came out suddenly when we were at John's Grove and "a star or two beside."[3]

[18 March]
Thursday A very fine morning. The sun shone but it was far colder than yesterday. I felt myself weak, and William charged me not to go to Mrs. Lloyds—I seemed indeed, to myself unfit for it but when he was gone I thought I would get the visit over if I could—so I ate a beefsteak thinking it would strengthen me, so it did, and I went off—I had a very pleasant walk. Rydale vale was full of life and motion. The wind blew briskly and the lake was covered all over with bright silver waves that were there each the twinkling of an eye, then others rose up and took their place as fast as they went away. The rocks glittered in the sunshine, the crows and the ravens were busy, and the thrushes and little birds sang—I went through the fields, and sat ½ an hour afraid to pass a cow. The cow looked at me and I looked at the cow and whenever I stirred the cow gave over eating. I was not very much tired when I reached Lloyds—I walked in the garden. Charles is all for agriculture. Mrs. L. in her kindest way. A parcel came in from Birmingham, with Lamb's play for us and for C. They came with me as far as Rydale. As we came along Ambleside vale in the twilight—it was a grave evening—there was something in the air that compelled me to serious thought—the hills were large, closed in by the sky. It was nearly dark when I parted from the Lloyds that is, night was come on and the moon was overcast. But as I climbed Moss the moon came out from behind a mountain mass of black clouds—O the unutterable darkness of the sky and the earth below the moon! and the glorious brightness of the moon itself! There was a vivid sparkling streak of light at this end of Rydale water but the rest was very dark and Loughrigg fell and Silver How were white and bright as if they were covered with hoar frost. The moon retired again and appeared and disappeared several times before I reached home. Once there was no moonlight to be seen but upon the island house and the promontory of the island where it stands, "That needs must be a holy place" &c.—&c. I had many very exquisite feelings when I saw this lowly building in the waters among the dark and lofty hills, with that bright soft light upon it—it made me more than half a poet. I was tired when I reached home. I

---

[1] *it spoke … France* Regarding plans for the Wordsworths and Coleridges to move to France.

[2] *starved* Frozen.

[3] *a star or two beside* From Coleridge's "The Rime of the Ancient Mariner," Part IV.

could not sit down to reading and tried to write verses but alas! I gave up expecting William and went soon to bed. Fletcher's carts came home late.

[April]

Thursday 15th It was a threatening misty morning—but mild. We set off after dinner from Eusemere—Mrs. Clarkson went a short way with us but turned back. The wind was furious, and we thought we must have returned. We first rested in the large boat-house, then under a furze bush[1] opposite Mr. Clarkson's—saw the plough going in the field. The wind seized our breath the lake was rough. There was a boat by itself floating in the middle of the Bay below Water Millock—We rested again in the Water Millock lane. The hawthorns are black and green, the birches here and there greenish but there is yet more of purple to be seen on the Twigs. We got over into a field to avoid some cows—people working, a few primroses by the roadside, woodsorrel flowers, the anemone, scentless violets, strawberries, and that starry yellow flower which Mrs. C. calls pile wort. When we were in the woods beyond Gowbarrow park we saw a few daffodils close to the water-side; we fancied that the lake had floated the seeds ashore and that the little colony had so sprung up. But as we went along there were more and yet more and at last under the boughs of the trees, we saw that there was a long belt of them along the shore, about the breadth of a country turnpike road. I never saw daffodils so beautiful they grew among the mossy stones about and about them, some rested their heads upon these stones as on a pillow for weariness and the rest tossed and reeled and danced and seemed as if they verily laughed with the wind that blew upon them over the lake, they looked so gay ever glancing ever changing. This wind blew directly over the lake to them. There was here and there a little knot and a few stragglers a few yards higher up but they were so few as not to disturb the simplicity and unity and life of that one busy highway. We rested again and again. The bays were stormy and we heard the waves at different distances and in the middle of the water like the sea—rain came on, we were wet when we reached Luffs but we called in. Luckily all was cheerless and gloomy so we faced the storm—we *must* have been wet if we had waited—put on dry clothes at Dobson's. I was very kindly treated by a young woman, the landlady looked sour but it is her way. She gave us a goodish supper, excellent ham and potatoes. We paid 7/ when we came away. William was sitting by a bright fire when I came downstairs. He soon made his way to the library piled up in a corner of the window. He brought out a volume of Enfield's Speaker,[2] another miscellany, and an odd volume of Congreve's plays.[3] We had a glass of warm rum and water—we enjoyed ourselves and wished for Mary. It rained and blew when we went to bed. NB deer in Gowbarrow park like to skeletons.

Tuesday May 4th William had slept pretty well and though he went to bed nervous and jaded in the extreme, he rose refreshed. I wrote the Leech Gatherer[4] for him which he had begun the night before and of which he wrote several stanzas in bed this Monday morning. It was very hot, we called at Mr. Simpson's door as we passed but did not go in. We rested several times by the way, read and repeated the Leech Gatherer. We were almost melted before we were at the top of the hill. We saw Coleridge on the Wytheburn side of the water, he crossed the beck[5] to us. Mr. Simpson was fishing there. William and I ate a luncheon, then went on towards the waterfall. It is a glorious wild solitude under that lofty purple crag. It stood upright by itself. Its own self and its shadow below, one mass—all else was sunshine. We went on further. A bird at the top of the crags was flying round and round and looked in thinness and transparency, shape and motion, like a moth. We climbed the hill but looked in vain for a shade except at the foot of the great waterfall, and there we did not like to stay on account of the loose stones above our heads. We came

[1] *furze bush* Common evergreen shrub.

[2] *Enfield's Speaker* William Enfield's *The Speaker; or Miscellaneous Pieces, Selected from the Best English Writers.*

[3] *Congreve's plays* Plays of William Congreve (1670–1729).

[4] *wrote the Leech Gatherer* Transcribed William's poem "Resolution and Independence."

[5] *beck* Stream.

down and rested upon a moss covered rock, rising out of the bed of the river. There we lay ate our dinner and stayed there till about 4 o'clock or later—Wm. and C. repeated and read verses. I drank a little brandy and water and was in heaven. The stag's horn is very beautiful and fresh springing upon the fells. Mountain ashes, green. We drank tea at a farm house. The woman had not a pleasant countenance, but was civil enough. She had a pretty boy a year old whom she suckled. We parted from Coleridge at Sara's crag after having looked at the letters which C. carved in the morning. I kissed them all. Wm. deepened the T with C's penknife. We sat afterwards on the wall, seeing the sun go down and the reflections in the still water. C. looked well and parted from us cheerfully, hopping up upon the side stones. On the rays we met a woman with 2 little girls one in her arms the other about 4 years old walking by her side, a pretty little thing, but half starved. She had on a pair of slippers that had belonged to some gentleman's child, down at the heels, but it was not easy to keep them on—but, poor thing! young as she was, she walked carefully with them. Alas too young for such cares and such travels. The mother when we accosted her told us that her husband had left her and gone off with another woman and how she "*pursued*" them. Then her fury kindled and her eyes rolled about. She changed again to tears. She was a Cockermouth woman—30 years of age a child at Cockermouth when I was—I was moved and gave her a shilling, I believe 6^{d} more than I ought to have given. We had the crescent moon with the "auld moon in her arms"[1]—We rested often:—always upon the bridges. Reached home at about 10 o'clock. The Lloyds had been here in our absence. We went soon to bed. I repeated verses to William while he was in bed—he was soothed and I left him. "This is the Spot"[2] over and over again.

[July]

Tuesday 26th Market day streets dirty, very rainy, did not leave Hull till 4 o'clock, and left Barton at about 6—rained all the way—almost—a beautiful village at the foot of a hill with trees—a gentleman's house converted into a lady's boarding school. We had a woman in bad health in the coach, and took in a lady and her daughter—supped at Lincoln. Duck and peas, and cream cheese—paid 2/-. We left Lincoln on Wednesday morning 27th July at six o'clock it rained heavily and we could see nothing but the ancientry of some of the buildings as we passed along. The night before, however, we had seen enough to make us regret this. The minster[3] stands at the edge of a hill, overlooking an immense plain. The country very flat as we went along—the day mended—We went to see the outside of the minster while the passengers were dining at Peterborough—the west end very grand. The little girl who was a great scholar, and plainly her mothers favorite though she had a large family at home had bought The Farmer's Boy.[4] She said it was written by a man without education and was very wonderful.

On Thursday morning, 29th, we arrived in London. Wm. left me at the inn—I went to bed &c. &c. &c. After various troubles and disasters we left London on Saturday morning at ½ past 5 or 6, the 31st of July (I have forgot which) we mounted the Dover coach at Charing Cross. It was a beautiful morning. The city, St. Paul's, with the river and a multitude of little boats, made a most beautiful sight as we crossed Westminster Bridge. The houses were not overhung by their cloud of smoke and they were spread out endlessly, yet the sun shone so brightly with such a pure light that there was even something like the purity of one of nature's own grand spectacles. We rode on cheerfully now with the Paris Diligence[5] before us, now behind—we walked up the steep hills, beautiful prospects everywhere, till we even reached Dover. At first the rich populous wide spreading woody country about London, then the river

[1] *auld moon in her arms* From the popular ballad "Sir Patrick Spens"; Coleridge also quoted this line in "Dejection: An Ode."

[2] *This is the Spot* From a poem by Dorothy Wordsworth, never published in her lifetime.

[3] *minster* Monastery church.

[4] *The Farmer's Boy* Long poem published by the laboring class poet Robert Bloomfield in 1800.

[5] *Diligence* Coach.

Thames, ships sailing, chalk cliffs, trees, little villages. Afterwards Canterbury, situated on a plain, rich and woody, but the city and cathedral disappointed me. Hop grounds on each side of the road some miles from Canterbury, then we came to a common, the race ground, an elevated plain, villages among trees in the bed of a valley at our right, and rising above this valley, green hills scattered over with wood—neat gentlemen's houses—one white house almost hid with green trees which we longed for and the parsons house as neat a place as could be which would just have suited Coleridge. No doubt we might have found one for Tom Hutchinson and Sara and a good farm too. We halted at a halfway house—fruit carts under the shade of trees, seats for guests, a tempting place to the weary traveller. Still as we went along the country was beautiful, hilly, with cottages lurking under the hills and their little plots of hop ground like vineyards. It was a bad hop-year—a woman on the top of the coach said to me "it is a sad thing for the poor people for the hop-gathering is the women's harvest, there is employment about the hops both for women and children." We saw the castle of Dover and the sea beyond four or five miles before we reached D. We looked at it through a long vale, the castle being upon an eminence, as it seemed at the end of this vale which opened to the sea. The country now became less fertile but near Dover it seemed more rich again. Many buildings stand on the flat fields, sheltered with tall trees. There is one old chapel that might have been there just in the same state in which it now is, when this vale was as retired and as little known to travellers, as our own Cumberland mountain wilds 30 years ago. There was also a very old building on the other side of the road which had a strange effect among the many new ones that are springing up everywhere. It seemed odd that it could have kept itself pure in its ancientry among so many upstarts. It was near dark when we reached Dover. We were told that the packet[1] was about to sail, so we went down to the Customhouse in half an hour, had our luggage examined &c. &c. and then we drank tea, with the honorable Mr. Knox and his tutor. We arrived at Calais at 4 o'clock on Sunday morning the 31st of July. We stayed in the vessel till ½ past 7. Then Wm. went for letters, at about ½ past 8 or 9. We found out Annette and C.[2] chez Madame Avril dans la Rue de la Tête d'or. We lodged opposite two ladies in tolerably decent-sized rooms but badly furnished, and with large store of bad smells and dirt in the yard, and all about. The weather was very hot. We walked by the seashore almost every evening with Annette and Caroline or Wm. and I alone. I had a bad cold and could not bathe at first but William did. It was a pretty sight to see as we walked upon the sands when the tide was low, perhaps a hundred people bathing about ¼ of a mile distant from us, and we had delightful walks after the heat of the day was passed away—seeing far off in the west the coast of England like a cloud crested with Dover Castle, which was but like the summit of the cloud—the evening star and the glory of the sky. The reflections in the water were more beautiful than the sky itself, purple waves brighter than precious stones forever melting away upon the sands. The fort, a wooden building, at the entrance of the harbour at Calais, when the evening twilight was coming on, and we could not see anything of the building but its shape which was far more distinct than in perfect daylight, seemed to be reared upon pillars of ebony, between which pillars the sea was seen in the most beautiful colours that can be conceived. Nothing in romance was ever half so beautiful. Now came in view as the evening star sank down and the colours of the west faded away the two lights of England, lighted up by Englishmen in our country, to warn vessels of rocks or sands. These we used to see from the pier when we could see no other distant objects but the clouds the sky and the sea itself. All was dark behind. The town of Calais seemed deserted of the light of heaven, but there was always light, and life, and joy upon the sea. One night, though, I shall never forget, the day had been very hot, and William and I walked alone together upon the pier—the sea was gloomy for there was a blackness over all the sky

[1] *packet* Boat originally used to carry mail (packets).

[2] *Annette and C.* Annette Vallon, with whom William Wordsworth had had an affair when he visited France in his youth, and their daughter, Caroline.

except when it was overspread with lightning which often revealed to us a distant vessel. Near us the waves roared and broke against the pier, and as they broke and as they travelled towards us, they were interfused with greenish fiery light. The more distant sea always black and gloomy. It was, also beautiful on the calm hot nights to see the little Boats row out of harbour with wings of fire and the sail boats with the fiery track which they cut as they went along and which closed up after them with a hundred thousand sparkles balls shootings, and streams of glowworm light. Caroline was delighted.

On Sunday the 29th of August we left Calais at 12 o'clock in the morning and landed at Dover at 1 on Monday the 30th. I was sick all the way. It was very pleasant to me when we were in harbour at Dover to breathe the fresh air, and to look up and see the stars among the ropes of the vessel. The next day was very hot. We both bathed and sat upon the Dover cliffs and looked upon France with many a melancholy and tender thought. We could see the shores almost as plain as if it were but an English lake. We mounted the coach at ½ past 4 and arrived in London at 6 the 30th August. It was misty and we could see nothing. We stayed in London till Wednesday the 22nd of September, and arrived at Gallow Hill on Friday 24th September. Mary first met us in the avenue. She looked so fat and well that we were made very happy by the sight of her—then came Sara, and last of all Joanna. Tom was forking corn[1] standing upon the corn cart. We dressed ourselves immediately and got tea—the garden looked gay with asters and sweet peas—I looked at everything with tranquillity and happiness but I was ill both on Saturday and Sunday and continued to be poorly most of the time of our stay. Jack and George came on Friday evening 1st October. On Saturday 2nd we rode to Hackness, William Jack George and Sara single, I behind Tom.[2] On Sunday 3rd Mary and Sara were busy packing. On Monday 4th October 1802, my brother William was married to Mary Hutchinson. I slept a good deal of the night and rose fresh and well in the morning—at a little after 8 o'clock I saw them go down the avenue towards the church. William had parted from me upstairs. I gave him the wedding ring—with how deep a blessing! I took it from my forefinger where I had worn it the whole of the night before—he slipped it again onto my finger and blessed me fervently. When they were absent my dear little Sara prepared the breakfast. I kept myself as quiet as I could, but when I saw the two men running up the walk, coming to tell us it was over, I could stand it no longer and threw myself on the bed where I lay in stillness, neither hearing or seeing anything, till Sara came upstairs to me and said "They are coming." This forced me from the bed where I lay and I moved I knew not how straight forward, faster than my strength could carry me till I met my beloved William and fell upon his bosom. He and John Hutchinson led me to the house and there I stayed to welcome my dear Mary. As soon as we had breakfasted we departed. It rained when we set off. Poor Mary was much agitated when she parted from her brothers and sisters and her home. Nothing particular occurred till we reached Kirby. We had sunshine and showers, pleasant talk, love and cheerfulness. We were obliged to stay two hours at K. while the horses were feeding. We wrote a few lines to Sara and then walked out, the sun shone and we went to the churchyard, after we had put a letter into the post office for the York Herald. We sauntered about and read the gravestones. There was one to the memory of 5 children, who had all died within 5 years, and the longest lived had only lived 4 years. There was another stone erected to the memory of an unfortunate woman (as we supposed, by a stranger). The verses engraved upon it expressed that she had been neglected by her relations and counselled the readers of those words to look within and recollect their own frailties. We left Kirby at about ½ past 2. There is not much variety of prospect from K. to Helmsely but the country is very pleasant, being rich and woody, and Helmsely itself stands very sweetly at the foot of the rising grounds of Duncombe Park which is scattered over with tall woods and lifting itself above the common buildings of the town stands Helmsely Castle, now a ruin, formerly inhabited by the gay Duke of Buckingham. Every foot

[1] *corn* Grain.

[2] *Jack George and Sara … Tom* Mary Hutchinson's siblings.

of the road was, of itself interesting to us, for we had travelled along it on foot Wm. and I when we went to fetch our dear Mary, and had sat upon the turf by the roadside more than once. Before we reached Helmsely our driver told us that he could not take us any further, so we stopped at the same inn where we had slept before. My heart danced at the sight of its cleanly outside, bright yellow walls, casements overshadowed with jasmine and its low, double gavel-ended front. We were not shown into the same parlour where Wm. and I were, it was a small room with a drawing over the chimney piece which the woman told us had been bought at a sale. Mary and I warmed ourselves at the kitchen fire—we then walked into the garden, and looked over a gate up to the old ruin which stands at the top of a mount, and round about it the moats are grown up into soft green cradles, hollows surrounded with green grassy hillocks and these are overshadowed by old trees, chiefly ashes. I prevailed upon William to go up with me to the ruins. We left Mary sitting by the kitchen fire. The sun shone, it was warm and very pleasant. One part of the castle seems to be inhabited. There was a man mowing nettles in the open space which had most likely once been the castle court. There is one gateway exceedingly beautiful—children were playing upon the sloping ground. We came home by the street. After about an hour's delay we set forward again, had an excellent driver who opened the gates so dexterously that the horses never stopped. Mary was very much delighted with the view of the castle from the point where we had seen it before. I was pleased to see again the little path which we had walked upon, the gate I had climbed over, and the road down which we had seen the two little boys drag a log of wood, and a team of horses struggle under the weight of a great load of timber. We had felt compassion for the poor horses that were under the governance of oppressive and ill-judging drivers, and for the poor boys who seemed of an age to have been able to have dragged the log of wood merely out of the love of their own activity, but from poverty and bad food they panted for weakness and were obliged to fetch their father from the town to help them. Duncombe House looks well from the road—a large building, though I believe only 2 thirds of the original design are completed. We rode down a very steep hill to Ryvaux valley, with woods all round us. We stopped upon the bridge to look at the abbey and again when we had crossed it. Dear Mary had never seen a ruined abbey before except Whitby. We recognized the cottages, houses, and the little valleys as we went along. We walked up a long hill, the road carrying us up the cleft or valley with woody hills on each side of us. When we *went* to G.H.[1] I had walked down this valley alone. Wm. followed me. It was not dark evening when we passed the little public house,[2] but before we had crossed the Hambledon hills and reached the point overlooking Yorkshire it was quite dark. We had not wanted, however, fair prospects before us, as we drove along the flat plain of the high hill, far far off us, in the western sky, we saw shapes of castles, ruins among groves, a great, spreading wood, rocks, and single trees, a minster with its tower unusually distinct, minarets in another quarter, and a round Grecian temple also—the colours of the sky of a bright grey and the forms of a sober grey, with a dome. As we descended the hill there was no distinct view, but of a great space, only near us, we saw the wild and (as the people say) bottomless tarn in the hollow at the side of the hill. It seemed to be made visible to us only by its own light, for all the hill about us was dark. Before we reached Thirsk we saw a light before us which we at first thought was the moon, then lime kilns, but when we drove into the market place it proved a large bonfire with lads dancing round it, which is a sight I dearly love. The inn was like an illuminated house—every room full. We asked the cause, and were told by the girl that it was "Mr. John Bell's Birthday, that he had heired his estate." The landlady was very civil. She did not recognise the despised foot-travellers. We rode nicely in the dark, and reached Leming Lane at 11 o'clock. I am always sorry to get out of a chaise when it is night. The people of the house were going to bed and we were not very well treated though we got a hot supper. We breakfasted the next morning and set off at

[1] *G.H.* George Hutchinson.

[2] *public house* Tavern.

about ½ past 8 o'clock. It was a cheerful sunny morning. We soon turned out of Leming Lane and passed a nice village with a beautiful church. We had a few showers, but when we came to the green fields of Wensley, the sun shone upon them all, and the Eure in its many windings glittered as it flowed along under the green slopes of Middleham and Middleham Castle. Mary looked about for her friend Mr. Place, and thought she had him sure on the contrary side of the vale from that on which we afterwards found that he lived. We went to a new built house at Leyburn, the same village where Wm. and I had dined with George Hutchinson on our road to Grasmere 2 years and ¾ ago, but not the same house. The landlady was very civil, giving us cake and wine but the horses being out we were detained at least 2 hours and did not set off till 2 o'clock. We paid for 35 miles, i.e. to Sedbergh, but the landlady did not encourage us to hope to get beyond Hawes. A shower came on just after we left the inn. While the rain beat against the windows we ate our dinners which M. and W. heartily enjoyed—I was not quite well. When we passed through the village of Wensly my heart was melted away with dear recollections, the bridge, the little waterspout the steep hill the church. They are among the most vivid of my own inner visions, for they were the first objects that I saw after we were left to ourselves, and had turned our whole hearts to Grasmere as a home in which we were to rest. The vale looked most beautiful each way. To the left the bright silver stream inlaid the flat and very green meadows, winding like a serpent. To the right we did not see it so far, it was lost among trees and little hills. I could not help observing as we went along how much more *varied* the prospects of Wensley Dale are in the summer time than I could have thought possible in the winter. This seemed to be in great measure owing to the trees being in leaf, and forming groves, and screens, and thence little openings upon recesses and concealed retreats which in winter only made a part of the one great vale. The *beauty* of the summertime here as much excels that of the winter as the variety, owing to the excessive greenness of the fields, and the trees in leaf half concealing, and where they do not conceal, softening the hard bareness of the limey white roofs. One of our horses seemed to grow a little restive as we went through the first village, a long village on the side of a hill. It grew worse and worse, and at last we durst not go on any longer. We walked a while, and then the post-boy[1] was obliged to take the horse out and go back for another. We seated ourselves again snugly in the post chaise. The wind struggled about us and rattled the window and gave a gentle motion to the chaise, but we were warm and at our ease within. Our station was at the top of a hill, opposite Bolton Castle, the Eure flowing beneath. William has since wrote a sonnet on this our imprisonment—Hard was thy durance Queen compared with ours.[2] Poor Mary! Wm. fell asleep, lying upon my breast and I upon Mary. I lay motionless for a long time, but I was at last obliged to move. I became very sick and continued so for some time after the boy brought the horse to us. Mary had been a little sick but it soon went off. We had a sweet ride till we came to a public house on the side of a hill where we alighted and walked down to see the waterfalls. The sun was not set, and the woods and fields were spread over with the yellow light of evening, which made their greenness a thousand times more green. There was too much water in the river for the beauty of the falls, and even the banks were less interesting than in winter. Nature had entirely got the better in her struggles against the giants who first cast the mould of these works; for indeed it is a place that did not in winter remind one of God, but one could not help feeling as if there had been the agency of some "Mortal Instruments"[3] which nature had been struggling against without making a perfect conquest. There was something so wild and new in this feeling, knowing as we did in the inner man that God alone had laid his hand upon it that I could not help

[1] *post-boy* Boy who "rides post," i.e., a person who rides the leading horse and acts as guide or driver.

[2] *Hard … with ours* Mary, Queen of Scots was imprisoned at Bolton Castle for six months in 1568–69. In 1817 William Wordsworth published "Lament of Mary Queen of Scots: On the Eve of a New Year," which dealt with the queen's imprisonment and execution.

[3] *Mortal Instruments* From Shakespeare's *Julius Caesar* 2.1 and W. Wordsworth's *The Borderers* 2.3.

regretting the want of it, besides it is a pleasure to a real lover of nature to give winter all the glory he can, for summer *will* make its own way, and speak its own praises. We saw the pathway which Wm. and I took at the close of evening, the path leading to the rabbit warren where we lost ourselves. The farm with its holly hedges was lost among the green hills and hedgerows in general, but we found it out and were glad to look at it again. When William had left us to seek the waterfalls Mary and I were frightened by a cow. At our return to the inn we found new horses and a new driver, and we went on nicely to Hawes where we arrived before it was quite dark. Mary and I got tea, and William had a partridge and mutton chops and tarts for his supper. Mary sat down with him. We had also a shilling's worth of negus[1] and Mary made me some broth for all which supper we were only charged 2/-. I could not sit up long. I vomited, and took the broth and then slept sweetly. We rose at 6 o'clock—a rainy morning. We had a good breakfast and then departed. There was a very pretty view about a mile from Hawes, where we crossed a bridge, bare, and very green fields with cattle, a glittering stream cottages, a few ill-grown trees, and high hills. The sun shone now. Before we got upon the bare hills there was a hunting lodge on our right exactly like Greta Hill, with fir plantations about it. We were very fortunate in the day, gleams of sunshine passing clouds, that travelled with their shadows below them. Mary was much pleased with Garsdale. It was a dear place to William and me. We noted well the public-house (Garsdale Hall) where we had baited and drunk our pint of ale, and afterwards the mountain which had been adorned by Jupiter[2] in his glory when we were here before. It was midday when we reached Sedbergh, and *market* day. We were in the same room where we had spent the evening together in our road to Grasmere. We had a pleasant ride to Kendal, where we arrived at about 2 o'clock—the day favored us—M. and I went to see the house where dear Sara had lived, then went to seek Mr. Bousfield's shop but we found him not—he had sold all his goods the day before. We then went to the pot woman's and bought 2 jugs and a dish, and some paper at Pennington's. When we came to the inn William was almost ready for us. The afternoon was not cheerful but it did not rain till we came near Windermere. I am always glad to see Stavely. It is a place I dearly love to think of—the first mountain village that I came to with Wm. when we first began our pilgrimage together. Here we drank a bason of milk at a public house, and here I washed my feet in the brook and put on a pair of silk stockings by Wm's advice. Nothing particular occurred till we reached Ing's chapel—the door was open and we went in. It is a neat little place, with a marble floor and marble communion table with a painting over it of the last supper, and Moses and Aaron on each side. The woman told us that "they had painted them as near as they could by the dresses as they are described in the Bible," and gay enough they are. The marble had been sent by Richard Bateman from Leghorn. The woman told us that a man had been at her house a few days before who told her he had helped to bring it down the Red Sea and she had believed him gladly. It rained very hard when we reached Windermere. We sat in the rain at Wilcock's to change horses, and arrived at Grasmere at about 6 o'clock on Wednesday Evening, the 6th of October 1802. Molly was overjoyed to see us,—for my part I cannot describe what I felt, and our dear Mary's feelings would I dare say not be easy to speak of. We went by candle light into the garden and were astonished at the growth of the brooms, Portugal laurels, &c. &c. &c.—The next day, Thursday, we unpacked the boxes. On Friday 8th we baked bread, and Mary and I walked, first upon the hill side, and then in John's Grove, then in view of Rydale, the first walk that I had taken with my sister.

—1897 (written 1800–02)

[1] *negus* Hot drink made with wine or port.

[2] *Jupiter* Supreme Roman deity.

Grasmere—A Fragment

Peaceful our valley, fair and green,
And beautiful her cottages,
Each in its nook, its sheltered hold,
Or underneath its tuft of trees

Many and beautiful they are;
But there is *one* that I love best,
A lowly shed, in truth, it is,
A brother of the rest.

Yet when I sit on rock or hill,
Down looking on the valley fair,
That cottage with its clustering trees
Summons my heart; it settles there.

Others there are whose small domain
Of fertile fields and hedgerows green
Might more seduce a wanderer's mind
To wish that *there* his home had been.

Such wish be his! I blame him not,
My fancies they perchance are wild
—I love that house because it is
The very mountains' child.

Fields hath it of its own, green fields,
But they are rocky steep and bare;
Their fence is of the mountain stone,
And moss and lichen flourish there.

And when the storm comes from the north
It lingers near that pastoral spot,
And, piping through the mossy walls,
It seems delighted with its lot.

And let it take its own delight;
And let it range the pastures bare;
Until it reach that group of trees,
—It may not enter there!

A green unfading grove it is,
Skirted with many a lesser tree,
Hazel and holly, beech and oak,
A bright and flourishing company.

Precious the shelter of those trees;
They screen the cottage that I love;
The sunshine pierces to the roof,
And the tall pine-trees tower above.

When first I saw that dear abode,
It was a lovely winter's day:
After a night of perilous storm
The west wind ruled with gentle sway;

A day so mild, it might have been
The first day of the gladsome spring;
The robins warbled, and I heard
One solitary throstle° sing. *song thrush*

A stranger, Grasmere, in thy vale,
All faces then to me unknown,
I left my sole companion-friend
To wander out alone.

Lured by a little winding path,
I quitted soon the public road,
A smooth and tempting path it was,
By sheep and shepherds trod.

Eastward, towards the lofty hills,
This pathway led me on
Until I reached a stately rock,
With velvet moss o'ergrown.

With russet oak and tufts of fern
Its top was richly garlanded;
Its sides adorned with eglantine° *fragrant rose*
Bedropped with hips° of glossy red. *rose berries*

There, too, in many a sheltered chink
The foxglove's broad leaves flourished fair,

And silver birch whose purple twigs
Bend to the softest breathing air.

Beneath that rock my course I stayed,
And, looking to its summit high,
"Thou wear'st," said I, "a splendid garb,
Here winter keeps his revelry.

"Full long a dweller on the plains,
I grieved when summer days were gone;
No more I'll grieve; for Winter here
Hath pleasure gardens of his own.

"What need of flowers? The splendid moss
Is gayer than an April mead;° *meadow*
More rich its hues of various green,
Orange, and gold, and glittering red."

—Beside that gay and lovely rock
There came with merry voice
A foaming streamlet glancing by;
It seemed to say "Rejoice!"

My youthful wishes all fulfilled,
Wishes matured by thoughtful choice,
I stood an inmate of this vale
How *could* I but rejoice?
—1892 (WRITTEN 1805)

Floating Island

Harmonious Powers with nature work
On sky, earth, river, lake and sea;
Sunshine and cloud, whirlwind and breeze,
All in one duteous task agree.[1]

Once did I see a slip of earth
(By throbbing waves long undermined)
Loosed from its hold; how, no one knew,
But all might see it float, obedient to the wind;

Might see it, from the mossy shore
Dissevered,° float upon the Lake, *separated*
Float with its crest of trees adorned
On which the warbling birds their pastime take.

Food, shelter, safety, there they find;
There berries ripen, flowerets° bloom; *small flowers*
There insects live their lives, and die;
A peopled world it is; in size a tiny room.

And thus through many seasons' space
This little Island may survive;
But Nature, though we mark her not,
Will take away, may cease to give.

Perchance when you are wandering forth
Upon some vacant sunny day,
Without an object, hope, or fear,
Thither your eyes may turn—the Isle is passed away;

Buried beneath the glittering Lake,
Its place no longer to be found;
Yet the lost fragments shall remain
To fertilise some other ground.
—1842 (WRITTEN LATE 1820S)

[1] *All ... agree* All work together to perform a task that is their duty.

Thoughts on My Sick-bed

And has the remnant of my life
Been pilfered of this sunny spring?
And have its own prelusive° sounds *introductory*
Touched in my heart no echoing string?

Ah! say not so—the hidden life
Couchant° within this feeble frame *lying*
Hath been enriched by kindred gifts,
That, undesired, unsought-for, came

With joyful heart in youthful days
When fresh each season in its round
I welcomed the earliest celandine° *yellow flower*
Glittering upon the mossy ground;

With busy eyes I pierced the lane
In quest of known and *un*known things,
—The primrose a lamp on its fortress rock,
The silent butterfly spreading its wings,

The violet betrayed by its noiseless breath,
The daffodil dancing in the breeze,
The carolling thrush, on his naked perch,
Towering above the budding trees.

Our cottage-hearth no longer our home,
Companions of nature were we,
The stirring, the still, the loquacious, the mute—
To all we gave our sympathy.

Yet never in those careless days
When spring-time in rock, field, or bower
Was but a fountain of earthly hope
A promise of fruits and the *splendid* flower.

No! then I never felt a bliss
That might with *that* compare
Which, piercing to my couch of rest,
Came on the vernal° air. *springtime*

When loving friends an offering brought,
The first flowers of the year,
Culled from the precincts of our home,
From nooks to memory dear.

With some sad thoughts the work was done,
Unprompted and unbidden,
But joy it brought to my *hidden* life,
To consciousness no longer hidden.

I felt a power unfelt before,
Controlling weakness, languor, pain;
It bore me to the terrace walk
I trod the hills again;—

No prisoner in this lonely room,
I *saw* the green banks of the Wye,
Recalling thy prophetic words,
Bard, brother, friend from infancy![1]

No need of motion, or of strength,
Or even the breathing air:
—I thought of nature's loveliest scenes;
And with memory I was there.
—1978 (WRITTEN 1832)

[1] *Recalling … infancy* Wordsworth is referring to her brother William's poem "Lines Composed a Few Miles above Tintern Abbey."

The Natural and the Sublime

CONTEXTS

In "The Two Guides of Life: The Sublime and the Beautiful" (a poem translated into English by Edward Bulwer Lytton in 1844), the eighteenth-century German philosopher Friedrich Schiller identifies "two genii," present from birth till death, "to guide thee." These guides structure our existence; we are, the poem maintains, perpetually under the sway of the beautiful and the sublime. Schiller's notion of aesthetic experience as profoundly powerful, indeed as the central force of human life, would hardly come as a surprise to the Romantics, who placed the beautiful and the sublime, along with the picturesque, at the forefront of their creative and philosophical vision.

Of course, the impulse to catalogue and categorize encounters with the aesthetic has a long history, originating well before the eighteenth century. The ancient Greeks had a great deal to say about the beautiful; Plato's work, for example, frequently discusses the ideal of Beauty and its imperfect reflections in the world of sense. In *Peri Hypsous*, a treatise on writing, a first-century rhetorician known as Longinus deemed extraordinary works "sublime," identifying great thought, powerful emotion, elevated figure of speech, noble diction, and distinguished word arrangement as the sources of sublimity in writing. The sublime, Longinus noted, is a significant source of pleasure, one that is distinguishable from beauty, for the experience of the sublime involves astonishment, alarm, and even fear.

Longinus's commentary was rediscovered in the late sixteenth century, translated into French (in 1674) and subsequently published in English as *On the Sublime* in 1680. The sustained intense interest in the beautiful and the sublime only became a defining feature of the eighteenth century and the Romantic era, however, when a number of important thinkers turned their attention to the principles and problems of aesthetics. At the same time, what had been formerly identified mainly as aspects of writing became more profoundly associated with the natural world. This evolution is evident in the definition of "sublime" in the *Oxford English Dictionary*, which notes, circa 1700, the first usage of the term as indicating "things in nature" that affect "the mind with a sense of overwhelming grandeur or irresistible power; calculated to inspire awe, deep reverence, or lofty emotion, by reason of its beauty, vastness, or grandeur." English writers, including Joseph Addison, the founder and editor of the popular *Spectator* magazine, and Anthony Ashley Cooper, the Earl of Shaftesbury, undertook the Grand Tour, a continental tour deemed necessary for learned young men, and wrote powerfully of crossing the Alps, extolling the mountains' greatness and testifying to their personal transformations through such experiences.

But it was Edmund Burke who, in *A Philosophical Enquiry into the Origin of Our Ideas of the Sublime and Beautiful* (1757), gave the project of categorizing "objects of experience" its most extensive theoretical treatment, initiating the era's myriad investigations into the underpinnings of the sublime and the beautiful. Burke's undertaking is significant in its insistence on the rigorous separation of the two qualities; they are, he proposed, in their effects, virtual opposites. Other thinkers, most notably the German philosopher Immanuel Kant, who wrote extensively on aesthetics, disputed some of Burke's premises, but Burke's ideas were immensely influential, shaping the representation of and reaction to the sublime and the beautiful in the writing of the Romantics.

Particularly noteworthy in this context is Burke's focus on the empirical experience of the beauty and grandeur of nature, an emphasis that plays out in much eighteenth-century British poetry and travel writing.

A third aesthetic category, "the picturesque," became an obsession of sorts, a feature of published travelogues and of great interest to travelers everywhere. The writings of priest, educator, and essayist William Gilpin played a major role in codifying what qualities made a landscape ideally picturesque. According to Gilpin, the ideal scene was one that yoked together the sublime and the beautiful—a sublime ruined abbey, for example, is best framed by a verdant, gentle valley. Such scenes were ideal for painting, but also for tourists to admire, with such admiration serving as proof of their refined sensibilities. Here, in a passage from *Pride and Prejudice* (1811), the novel's spirited heroine Elizabeth Bennet marvels at the picturesque splendor of an estate in Derbyshire:

> They gradually ascended for half a mile, and then found themselves at the top of a considerable eminence, where the wood ceased, and the eye was instantly caught by Pemberley House, situated on the opposite side of a valley, into which the road with some abruptness wound. It was a large, handsome, stone building, standing well on rising ground, and backed by a ridge of high woody hills;—and in front, a stream of some natural importance was swelled into greater, but without any artificial appearance. Its banks were neither formal, nor falsely adorned. Elizabeth was delighted.

Elizabeth so admires, we are told, "a place … where natural beauty had been so little counteracted by an awkward taste." The scene is one of beauty, but its pleasures come from the seeming absence of human intervention. This appreciation for or awe of nature structures and informs the Romantic mindset. Nature was not simply a matter of inspiration but the object of aspiration, to be emulated and celebrated in its beauty, its sublimity, and its ability to mediate between the two.

⌘⌘⌘

from Dionysius Longinus, *On the Sublime*[1] (First Century CE)

Longinus's *On the Sublime* is one of the most significant classical explorations of aesthetics. The treatise's authorship is unknown—the name "Dionysius Longinus" seems to have been the misreading of a medieval copyist—but its importance to the development of ideas about the sublime and their application to literary criticism is undeniable.

In the passage below, Longinus explains how the sublime is achieved in writing and elucidates the sources of the sublime.

from SECTION 1

… But I request you, my dear friend, to give me your opinion on whatever I advance, with that exactness which is due to truth, and that sincerity, which is natural to yourself. For well did the sage answer the question, *in what do we most resemble the gods*? when he replied, *in doing good and speaking truth*. But since I write, my dear friend, to you, who are versed in every branch of polite learning, there will be little occasion to use many previous words in proving, that the sublime is a certain eminence or perfection of language, and that the greatest writers, both in verse and prose, have by this alone obtained the prize of glory, and filled all time with their renown. For the sublime not only persuades, but even throws an audience into transport. The marvelous

[1] *On the Sublime* The translation here is that of William Smith (1743).

always works with more surprising force, than that which barely persuades or delights. In most cases, it is wholly in our own power, either to resist or yield to persuasion. But the sublime, endued with strength irresistible, strikes home, and triumphs over every hearer. Dexterity of invention, and good order and economy in composition, are not to be discerned from one or two passages, nor scarcely sometimes from the whole texture of a discourse; but the sublime, when seasonably addressed, with the rapid force of lightning has borne down all before it, and shown at one stroke the compacted might of genius. …

from SECTION 8

There are, if I may so express it, five very copious sources of the sublime, if we presuppose an ability of speaking well, as a common foundation for these five sorts, and indeed without it, any thing besides will avail but little.

1. The first and most excellent of these is a boldness and grandeur in the thoughts, as I have shown in my essay on Xenophon.[1]
2. The second is called the pathetic, or the power of raising the passions to a violent and even enthusiastic degree; and these two being genuine constituents of the sublime, are the gifts of nature, whereas the other sorts depend in some measure upon art.
3. The third consists in a skilful application of figures, which are two-fold, of sentiment and language.
4. The fourth is a noble and graceful manner of expression, which is not only to choose out significant and elegant words, but also to adorn and embellish the style, by the assistance of tropes.
5. The fifth source of the sublime, which completes all the preceding, is the structure or composition of all the periods, in all possible dignity and grandeur. …

[1] *Xenophon* Contemporary and admirer of Socrates, Xenophon (c. 430–354 BCE) recorded many of the sayings of Socrates, documenting in the process the history of ancient Greece.

from Sir Jonathan Richardson the Elder, *An Essay on the Theory of Painting* (1725)

A notable early eighteenth-century portrait painter, Richardson (1667–1745) was also an important critic and theorist of art. In this excerpt from his *Essay on the Theory of Painting*, Richardson discusses the role of the sublime in the creation of art.

OF THE SUBLIME

… By the sublime in general I mean the most excellent of what is excellent, as the excellent is the best of what is good. The dignity of a man consists chiefly in his capacity of thinking, and of communicating his ideas to another; *the greatest, and most noble thoughts, images, or sentiments, conveyed to us in the best chosen words*, I take therefore to be the perfect sublime in writing; the admirable, the marvellous.

But as there may be degrees even in the sublime, something short of the utmost may be also sublime.

Thought and language are two distinct excellencies: there are few that are capable of adding dignity to a great subject, or even of doing right to such a one; in some cases none: the bulk of mankind conceive not greatly, nor do they know how to utter the conceptions they have to the best advantage; and those that have higher capacities exert them but rarely, and on few occasions: hence it is that we so justly admire what is so excellent, and so uncommon.

The great manner of thinking (as thought in general) is either pure invention, or what arises upon hints suggested from without. …

As the thoughts, so the language of the sublime must be the most excellent; what that is is the question: whether it be confined to the florid, to magnificent, and sonorous words, tours, figures, &c. or whether brevity, simplicity, or even common, and low words are the best on some occasions.

Poetry, history, declamation, &c. have their peculiar styles, but the sublime (as our high court of parliament is not under the restrictions which inferior courts are) is not limited to any particular style: the best is the sublime language, and that is best that sets the idea in the strongest light; that is the great end, and use of words; but if those that please the ear do equally serve that purpose, no doubt they are preferable, but not otherwise. Plain and common words paint a great image sometimes stronger than any other. …

The only reasons that can be given for a peculiarity of style in the sublime are, that as the thought must be great, the language must be so too as best expressing such thought; and because the music of the words serve to the same purpose, and moreover please. I own all this is generally true: why do we use the term *sublime*, and not *the very best*, both which express the same thing, only that one raises, and the other depresses the idea? But I deny it is always thus; and only contend that when low, common words, and a plain style best serves the main end of language, it is then, and only then the sublime style. And when this happens the pleasure that is wanting in the sound is abundantly recompensed by observing the judgment of him who made so wise a choice. …

But the sublime, as the crown in the state hides all defects; it fills and satisfies the mind, nothing appears to be wanting; nothing to be amiss, or if it does it is easily forgiven. All faults die, and vanish in presence of the sublime, which when it appears is as *the sun traversing the vast desert of the sky*. …

from Samuel Johnson, *A Dictionary of the English Language* (1755)

Samuel Johnson's (1709–84) famous dictionary offered not only a sense of the meaning of sublime, as it did for all its entries, but it also documented notable instances of the term's literary usage.

SUBLIME. *adj*. [*sublimis*, Latin.]

1. High in place; exalted aloft.

They furri'd their pens, and soaring th' air *sublime*
With clang despis'd the ground. Milton.

Sublime on these a tow'r of steel is rear'd,
And dire Tisiphone there keeps the ward. Dryden.

2. High in excellence; exalted by nature.

My earthly strained to the height
In that celestial colloquy *sublime.* Milton.

Can it be, that souls *sublime*
Return to visit our terrestrial clime;
And that the gen'rous mind releas'd by death,
Can cover lazy limbs? Dryden.

3. High in stile or sentiment; lofty; grand.

Easy in stile, thy work in sense *sublime.* Prior.

4. Elevated by joy.

All yet left of that revolted rout,
Heav'n-fall'n, in station stood or just array,
Sublime with expectation. Milton.

Their hearts were jocund and *sublime*,
Drunk with idolatry, drunk with wine. Milton.

5. Haughty; proud.

He was *sublime*, and almost tumorous in
his looks and gestures. Wotton.

SUBLIME. *n.s.* The grand or lofty stile. *The sublime* is a Gallicism, but now naturalized.

Longinus strengthens all his laws,
And is himself the great *sublime* he draws. Pope.

The *sublime* rises from the nobleness of thoughts, the magnificence of the words, or the harmonious and lively turn of the phrase; the perfect *sublime* arises from all three together. Addison.

TO SUBLIME. *v.a.* [*sublimer*, Fr. from the adjective.]

1. To raise by a chemical fire.

Study our manuscripts, those myriads
Of letters, which have past 'twixt thee and me,
Thence write our annals, and in them lessons be
To all, whom love's *subliming* fire invades. Donne.

2. To raise on high.

Although thy trunk be neither large nor strong,
Nor can thy head, not helpt, itself *sublime*,
Yet, like a serpent, a tall tree can climb. Denham.

3. To exalt; to heighten; to improve.

Flow'rs, and the fruit,
Man's nourishment, by gradual scale *sublim'd*
To vital spirits aspire. Milton.

The fancies of most are moved by the inward springs of the corporeal machine, which even in the most *sublime* intellectuals is dangerously influential. Glanville.

Art being strengthened by the knowledge of things, may pass into nature by slow degrees, and so be *sublimed* into a pure genius which is capable of distinguishing betwixt the beauties of nature and that which is low in her. Dryden's *Dufresnoy*.

Meanly they seek the blessing to confine,
And force that sun but on a part to shine;
Which not alone the southern wit *sublimes*,
But ripens spirits in cold northern climes. Pope.

To Sublime. *v.n.* To rise in the chemical vessel by the force of fire.

The particles of sal ammoniack in sublimation carry up the particles of antimony, which will not *sublime* alone. Newton's *Optics*.

This salt is fixed in a gentle fire, and *sublimes* in a great one. Arbuthnot on Aliments.

Sublimely. *adv.* [from *sublime*.] Loftily; grandly.

This fustian's so *sublimely* bad;
It is not poetry, but prose run mad. Pope.

Sublimity. *n.s.* [from *sublime*; *sublimité*, Fr. *sublimitas*, Lat.]

1. Height of place; local elevation.
2. Height of nature; excellence.

As religion looketh upon him who in majesty and power is infinite, as we ought we account not of it, unless we esteem it even according to that very height of excellency which our hearts conceive, when divine *sublimity* itself is rightly considered. Hooker.

In respect of God's incomprehensible *sublimity* and purity, this is also true, that God is neither a mind, nor a spirit like other spirits, nor a light such as can be discerned. Raleigh.

3. Loftiness of style or sentiment.

Milton's distinguishing excellence lies in the *sublimity* of his thoughts, in the greatness of which he triumphs over all the poets, modern and ancient, Homer only excepted. Addison.

from Edmund Burke, *A Philosophical Enquiry into the Origin of Our Ideas of the Sublime and Beautiful* (1757)

Burke's systematic investigation of the sublime and the beautiful marks perhaps the first eighteenth-century attempt to classify aesthetic feeling and effects. Like Longinus, Burke (1729–97) is interested in how the two categories are produced in writing; unlike Longinus, Burke fully separates the sublime and the beautiful, delineating their respective qualities.

from Part 1

Of the Sublime

Whatever is fitted in any sort to excite the ideas of pain and danger, that is to say, whatever is in any sort terrible, or is conversant about terrible objects, or operates in a manner analogous to terror, is a source of the sublime; that is, it is productive of the strongest emotion which the mind is capable of feeling. I say the strongest emotion, because I am satisfied the ideas of pain are much more powerful than those which enter on the part of pleasure. Without all doubt, the torments which we may be made to suffer are much greater in their effect on the body and mind, than any pleasure which the most learned voluptuary could suggest, or than the liveliest imagination, and the most sound and exquisitely sensible body, could enjoy. Nay, I am in great doubt whether any man could be found, who would earn a life of the most perfect satisfaction, at the price of ending it in the torments, which justice inflicted in a few hours on the late unfortunate regicide in

France.[1] But as pain is stronger in its operation than pleasure, so death is in general a much more affecting idea than pain; because there are very few pains, however exquisite, which are not preferred to death: nay, what generally makes pain itself, if I may say so, more painful, is, that it is considered as an emissary of this king of terrors. When danger or pain press too nearly, they are incapable of giving any delight, and are simply terrible; but at certain distances, and with certain modifications, they may be, and they are, delightful, as we every day experience. The cause of this I shall endeavour to investigate hereafter.

OF BEAUTY

The passion which belongs to generation, merely as such, is lust only. This is evident in brutes, whose passions are more unmixed, and which pursue their purposes more directly than ours. The only distinction they observe with regard to their mates, is that of sex. It is true, that they stick severally to their own species in preference to all others. But this preference, I imagine, does not arise from any sense of beauty which they find in their species, as Mr. Addison supposes, but from a law of some other kind, to which they are subject; and this we may fairly conclude, from their apparent want of choice amongst those objects to which the barriers of their species have confined them. But man, who is a creature adapted to a greater variety and intricacy of relation, connects with the general passion the idea of some *social* qualities, which direct and heighten the appetite which he has in common with all other animals; and as he is not designed like them to live at large, it is fit that he should have something to create a preference, and fix his choice; and this in general should be some sensible quality; as no other can so quickly, so powerfully, or so surely produce its effect. The object therefore of this mixed passion, which we call love, is the *beauty* of the *sex.* Men are carried to the sex in general, as it is the sex, and by the common law of nature; but they are attached to particulars by personal *beauty.* I call beauty a social quality; for where women and men, and not only they, but when other animals give us a sense of joy and pleasure in beholding them (and there are many that do so), they inspire us with sentiments of tenderness and affection towards their persons; we like to have them near us, and we enter willingly into a kind of relation with them, unless we should have strong reasons to the contrary. But to what end, in many cases, this was designed, I am unable to discover; for I see no greater reason for a connection between man and several animals who are attired in so engaging a manner, than between him and some others who entirely want this attraction, or possess it in a far weaker degree. But it is probable, that Providence did not make even this distinction, but with a view to some great end; though we cannot perceive distinctly what it is, as his wisdom is not our wisdom, nor our ways his ways.

from PART 2

OF THE PASSION CAUSED BY THE SUBLIME

The passion caused by the great and sublime in nature, when those causes operate most powerfully, is astonishment; and astonishment is that state of the soul, in which all its motions are suspended, with some degree of horror. In this case the mind is so entirely filled with its object, that it cannot entertain any other, nor by consequence reason on that object which employs it. Hence arises the great power of the sublime, that, far from being produced by them, it anticipates our reasonings, and hurries us on by an irresistible force. Astonishment, as I have said, is the effect of the sublime in its highest degree; the inferior effects are admiration, reverence, and respect.

[1] *Nay, I am … in France* Robert-François Damiens (1715–57) attempted to assassinate Louis XV on 5 January 1757; he was barbarously tortured and then executed later that year.

TERROR

No passion so effectually robs the mind of all its powers of acting and reasoning as *fear.* For fear being an apprehension of pain or death, it operates in a manner that resembles actual pain. Whatever therefore is terrible, with regard to sight, is sublime too, whether this cause of terror be endued with greatness of dimensions or not; for it is impossible to look on anything as trifling, or contemptible, that may be dangerous. There are many animals, who though far from being large, are yet capable of raising ideas of the sublime, because they are considered as objects of terror. As serpents and poisonous animals of almost all kinds. And to things of great dimensions, if we annex an adventitious idea of terror, they become without comparison greater. A level plain of a vast extent on land, is certainly no mean idea; the prospect of such a plain may be as extensive as a prospect of the ocean: but can it ever fill the mind with anything so great as the ocean itself? This is owing to several causes; but it is owing to none more than this, that the ocean is an object of no small terror. Indeed, terror is in all cases whatsoever, either more openly or latently, the ruling principle of the sublime. Several languages bear a strong testimony to the affinity of these ideas. They frequently use the same word, to signify indifferently the modes of astonishment or admiration, and those of terror. θάμβος is in Greek, either fear or wonder; δετυος is terrible or respectable; αίδέω, to reverence or to fear. *Vereor* in Latin, is what αίδέω is in Greek. The Romans used the verb *stupeo*, a term which strongly marks the state of an astonished mind, to express the effect either of simple fear, or of astonishment; the word *attonitus* (thunder-struck) is equally expressive of the alliance of these ideas; and do not the French *étonnement*, and the English *astonishment* and *amazement*, point out as clearly the kindred emotions which attend fear and wonder? They who have a more general knowledge of languages, could produce, I make no doubt, many other and equally striking examples.

VASTNESS

Greatness of dimension is a powerful cause of the sublime. This is too evident, and the observation too common, to need any illustration: it is not so common to consider in what ways greatness of dimension, vastness of extent or quantity, has the most striking effect. For certainly, there are ways and modes, wherein the same quantity of extension shall produce greater effects than it is found to do in others. Extension is either in length, height, or depth. Of these the length strikes least; an hundred yards of even ground will never work such an effect as a tower an hundred yards high, or a rock or mountain of that altitude. I am apt to imagine likewise, that height is less grand than depth; and that we are more struck at looking down from a precipice, than looking up at an object of equal height; but of that I am not very positive. A perpendicular has more force in forming the sublime, than an inclined plane; and the effects of a rugged and broken surface seem stronger than where it is smooth and polished. It would carry us out of our way to enter in this place into the cause of these appearances; but certain it is they afford a large and fruitful field of speculation. However, it may not be amiss to add to these remarks upon magnitude, that, as the great extreme of dimension is sublime, so the last extreme of littleness is in some measure sublime likewise: when we attend to the infinite divisibility of matter, when we pursue animal life into these excessively small, and yet organized beings, that escape the nicest inquisition of the sense; when we push our discoveries yet downward, and consider those creatures so many degrees yet smaller, and the still diminishing scale of existence, in tracing which the imagination is lost as well as the sense; we become amazed and confounded at the wonders of minuteness; nor can we distinguish in its effects this extreme of littleness from the vast itself. For division must be infinite as well as addition; because the idea of a perfect unity can no more be arrived at, than that of a complete whole, to which nothing may be added.

from PART 3

OF BEAUTY

It is my design to consider beauty as distinguished from the sublime; and, in the course of the inquiry, to examine how far it is consistent with it. But previous to this, we must take a short review of the opinions already entertained of this quality; which I think are hardly to be reduced to any fixed principles; because men are used to talk of beauty in a figurative manner, that is to say, in a manner extremely uncertain, and indeterminate. By beauty I mean that quality or those qualities in bodies, by which they cause love, or some passion similar to it. I confine this definition to the merely sensible qualities of things, for the sake of preserving the utmost simplicity in a subject, which must always distract us whenever we take in those various causes of sympathy which attach us to any persons or things from secondary considerations, and not from the direct force which they have merely on being viewed. I likewise distinguish love (by which I mean that satisfaction which arises to the mind upon contemplating anything beautiful, of whatsoever nature it may be) from desire or lust; which is an energy of the mind, that hurries us on to the possession of certain objects, that do not affect us as they are beautiful, but by means altogether different. We shall have a strong desire for a woman of no remarkable beauty; whilst the greatest beauty in men or in other animals, though it causes love, yet excites nothing at all of desire. Which shows that beauty, and the passion caused by beauty, which I call love, is different from desire, though desire may sometimes operate along with it; but it is to this latter that we must attribute those violent and tempestuous passions, and the consequent emotions of the body, which attend what is called love in some of its ordinary acceptations, and not to the effects of beauty merely as it is such.

THE REAL CAUSE OF BEAUTY

Having endeavoured to show what beauty is not, it remains that we should examine, at least with equal attention, in what it really consists. Beauty is a thing much too affecting not to depend upon some positive qualities. And, since it is no creature of our reason, since it strikes us without any reference to use, and even where no use at all can be discerned, since the order and method of nature is generally very different from our measures and proportions, we must conclude that beauty is, for the greater part, some quality in bodies acting mechanically upon the human mind by the intervention of the senses. We ought therefore to consider attentively in what manner those sensible qualities are disposed, in such things as by experience we find beautiful, or which excite in us the passion of love, or some correspondent affection.

THE SUBLIME AND BEAUTIFUL COMPARED

On closing this general view of beauty, it naturally occurs, that we should compare it with the sublime; and in this comparison there appears a remarkable contrast. For sublime objects are vast in their dimensions, beautiful ones comparatively small: beauty should be smooth and polished; the great, rugged and negligent; beauty should shun the right line, yet deviate from it insensibly; the great in many cases loves the right line, and when it deviates it often makes a strong deviation: beauty should not be obscure; the great ought to be dark and gloomy: beauty should be light and delicate; the great ought to be solid, and even massive. They are indeed ideas of a very different nature, one being founded on pain, the other on pleasure; and however they may vary afterwards from the direct nature of their causes, yet these causes keep up an eternal distinction between them, a distinction never to be forgotten by any whose business it is to affect the passions. In the infinite variety of natural combinations, we must expect to find the qualities of things the most remote imaginable from each other united in the same object. We must expect also to find combinations of the same kind in the works of art. But when we consider the power of an object upon our passions, we must know that when anything is intended to affect the mind by the force of some predominant property, the affection produced is like to be the more uniform and perfect, if all the other properties or qualities of the object be of the same nature, and tending to the same design, as the principal.

> If black and white blend, soften, and unite
> A thousand ways, are there no black and white?[1]

If the qualities of the sublime and beautiful are sometimes found united, does this prove that they are the same; does it prove that they are any way allied; does it prove even that they are not opposite and contradictory? Black and white may soften, may blend; but they are not therefore the same. Nor, when they are so softened and blended with each other, or with different colours, is the power of black as black, or of white as white, so strong as when each stands uniform and distinguished.

from Part 5

Of Words

Natural objects affect us, by the laws of that connection which Providence has established between certain motions and configurations of bodies, and certain consequent feelings in our mind. Painting affects us in the same manner, but with the superadded pleasure of imitation. Architecture affects by the laws of nature, and the law of reason: from which latter result the rules of proportion, which make a work to be praised or censured, in the whole or in some part, when the end for which it was designed is or is not properly answered. But as to words; they seem to me to affect us in a manner very different from that in which we are affected by natural objects, or by painting or architecture; yet words have as considerable a share in exciting ideas of beauty and of the sublime as many of those, and sometimes a much greater than any of them: therefore an inquiry into the manner by which they excite such emotions is far from being unnecessary in a discourse of this kind.

Effect of Words

If words have all their possible extent of power, three effects arise in the mind of the hearer. The first is, the *sound*; the second, the *picture*, or representation of the thing signified by the sound; the third is, the *affection* of the soul produced by one or by both of the foregoing. *Compounded abstract* words, of which we have been speaking, (honour, justice, liberty, and the like,) produce the first and the last of these effects, but not the second. *Simple abstracts* are used to signify some one simple idea, without much adverting to others which may chance to attend it, as blue, green, hot, cold, and the like; these are capable of affecting all three of the purposes of words; as the *aggregate* words, man, castle, horse, &c., are in a yet higher degree. But I am of opinion, that the most general effect, even of these words, does not arise from their forming pictures of the several things they would represent in the imagination; because, on a very diligent examination of my own mind, and getting others to consider theirs, I do not find that once in twenty times any such picture is formed, and when it is, there is most commonly a particular effort of the imagination for that purpose. But the aggregate words operate, as I said of the compound-abstracts, not by presenting any image to the mind, but by having from use the same effect on being mentioned, that their original has when it is seen. Suppose we were to read a passage to this effect: "The river Danube rises in a moist and mountainous soil in the heart of Germany, where winding to and fro, it waters several principalities, until, turning into Austria, and leaving the walls of Vienna, it passes into Hungary; there with a vast flood, augmented by the Saave and the Drave, it quits Christendom, and rolling through the barbarous countries which border on Tartary,[2] it enters by many mouths in the Black Sea." In this description many

[1] *If black and … black and white?* Misquoted slightly from Alexander Pope's *An Essay on Man* (1733–34), 2.213–14.

[2] *Tartary* Vast region of eastern Europe and northern Asia controlled by the Mongols in the thirteenth and fourteenth centuries.

things are mentioned, as mountains, rivers, cities, the sea, &c. But let anybody examine himself, and see whether he has had impressed on his imagination any pictures of a river, mountain, watery soil, Germany, &c. Indeed it is impossible, in the rapidity and quick succession of words in conversation to have ideas both of the sound of the word, and of the thing represented: besides, some words, expressing real essences, are so mixed with others of a general and nominal import, that it is impracticable to jump from sense to thought, from particulars to generals, from things to words, in such a manner as to answer the purposes of life; nor is it necessary that we should.

How Words Influence the Passions

Now, as words affect, not by any original power, but by representation, it might be supposed, that their influence over the passions should be but light; yet it is quite otherwise; for we find by experience, that eloquence and poetry are as capable, nay indeed much more capable, of making deep and lively impressions than any other arts, and even than nature itself in very many cases. And this arises chiefly from these three causes. First, that we take an extraordinary part in the passions of others, and that we are easily affected and brought into sympathy by any tokens which are shown of them; and there are no tokens which can express all the circumstances of most passions so fully as words; so that if a person speaks upon any subject, he can not only convey the subject to you, but likewise the manner in which he is himself affected by it. Certain it is, that the influence of most things on our passions is not so much from the things themselves, as from our opinions concerning them; and these again depend very much on the opinions of other men, conveyable for the most part by words only. Secondly, there are many things of a very affecting nature, which can seldom occur in the reality, but the words that represent them often do; and thus they have an opportunity of making a deep impression and taking root in the mind, whilst the idea of the reality was transient; and to some perhaps never really occurred in any shape, to whom it is notwithstanding very affecting, as war, death, famine, &c. Besides, many ideas have never been at all presented to the senses of any men but by words, as God, angels, devils, heaven, and hell, all of which have, however, a great influence over the passions. Thirdly, by words we have it in our power to make such *combinations* as we cannot possibly do otherwise. By this power of combining, we are able, by the addition of well-chosen circumstances, to give a new life and force to the simple object. In painting we may represent any fine figure we please; but we never can give it those enlivening touches which it may receive from words. To represent an angel in a picture, you can only draw a beautiful young man winged: but what painting can furnish out anything so grand as the addition of one word, "the angel of the *Lord*"? It is true, I have here no clear idea; but these words affect the mind more than the sensible image did; which is all I contend for. A picture of Priam dragged to the altar's foot, and there murdered, if it were well executed, would undoubtedly be very moving, but there are very aggravating circumstances, which it could never represent:

> Sanguine fœdantem *quos ipse saeraverat ignes.*[1]

As a further instance, let us consider those lines of Milton, where he describes the travels of the fallen angels through their dismal habitation:

> —O'er many a dark and dreary vale
> They passed, and many a region dolorous;
> O'er many a frozen, many a fiery Alp;
> Rocks, caves, lakes, fens, bogs, dens, and shades of death,
> A universe of death.[2]—

Here is displayed the force of union in

---

1 *Sanguine … ignes* Cf. Virgil, *Aeneid*, 2.502. Latin: "Polluting with blood the flames that he [Priam, the king of Troy during the Trojan War] himself had sanctified."

2 *O'er many … universe of death* See John Milton, *Paradise Lost*, 2.618–22.

Rocks, caves, lakes, dens, bogs, fens, and shades;

Which yet would lose the greatest part of their effect, if they were not the

Rocks, caves, lakes, dens, bogs, fens, and shades—
——of *Death*.

This idea or this affection caused by a word, which nothing but a word could annex to the others, raises a very great degree of the sublime; and this sublime is raised yet higher by what follows, a "*universe of Death*." Here are again two ideas not presentable but by language; and an union of them great and amazing beyond conception; if they may properly be called ideas which present no distinct image to the mind:—but still it will be difficult to conceive how words can move the passions which belong to real objects, without representing these objects clearly. This is difficult to us, because we do not sufficiently distinguish, in our observations upon language, between a clear expression and a strong expression. These are frequently confounded with each other, though they are in reality extremely different. The former regards the understanding, the latter belongs to the passions. The one describes a thing as it is; the latter describes it as it is felt. Now, as there is a moving tone of voice, an impassioned countenance, an agitated gesture, which affect independently of the things about which they are exerted, so there are words, and certain dispositions of words, which being peculiarly devoted to passionate subjects; and always used by those who are under the influence of any passion, touch and move us more than those which far more clearly and distinctly express the subject matter. We yield to sympathy what we refuse to description. The truth is, all verbal description, merely as naked description, though never so exact, conveys so poor and insufficient an idea of the thing described, that it could scarcely have the smallest effect, if the speaker did not call in to his aid those modes of speech that mark a strong and lively feeling in himself. Then, by the contagion of our passions, we catch a fire already kindled in another, which probably might never have been struck out by the object described. Words, by strongly conveying the passions, by those means which we have already mentioned, fully compensate for their weakness in other respects. It may be observed, that very polished languages, and such as are praised for their superior clearness and perspicuity, are generally deficient in strength. The French language has that perfection and that defect, whereas the Oriental tongues, and in general the languages of most unpolished people, have a great force and energy of expression; and this is but natural. Uncultivated people are but ordinary observers of things, and not critical in distinguishing them; but, for that reason, they admire more, and are more affected with what they see, and therefore express themselves in a warmer and more passionate manner. If the affection be well conveyed, it will work its effect without any clear idea, often without any idea at all of the thing which has originally given rise to it.

It might be expected from the fertility of the subject, that I should consider poetry, as it regards the sublime and beautiful, more at large; but it must be observed that in this light it has been often and well handled already. It was not my design to enter into the criticism of the sublime and beautiful in any art, but to attempt to lay down such principles as may tend to ascertain, to distinguish, and to form a sort of standard for them; which purposes I thought might be best effected by an inquiry into the properties of such things in nature, as raise love and astonishment in us; and by showing in what manner they operated to produce these passions. Words were only so far to be considered, as to show upon what principle they were capable of being the representatives of these natural things, and by what powers they were able to affect us often as strongly as the things they represent, and sometimes much more strongly.

from Immanuel Kant, *Observations on the Feeling of the Beautiful and Sublime* (1764; first English translation 1799)

German philosopher Immanuel Kant (1724–1804) argues that aesthetic experience and pleasure are always subjective; here he presents his observations on the feelings he associates with the beautiful and the sublime. Along with Edmund Burke, Kant is perhaps the most important eighteenth-century thinker on aesthetics.

from SECTION 1: OF THE DISTINCT OBJECTS OF THE FEELING OF THE BEAUTIFUL AND SUBLIME

The various feelings of enjoyment or of displeasure rest not so much upon the nature of the external things that arouse them as upon each person's own disposition to be moved by these to pleasure or pain. This accounts for the joy of some people over things that cause aversion in others, or the amorous passion so often a puzzle to everybody, or the lively antipathy one person feels toward something that to another is quite indifferent. The field of observation of these peculiarities of human nature extends very wide, and still conceals a rich source for discoveries that are just as pleasurable as they are instructive. For the present I shall cast my gaze upon only a few places that seem particularly exceptional in this area, and even upon these more with the eye of an observer than of a philosopher.

Because a person finds himself happy only so far as he gratifies an inclination, the feeling that makes him capable of enjoying great pleasures, without needing exceptional talents to do so, is certainly no trifle. Stout persons, whose favorite authors are their cooks and whose works of fine taste are in their cellars, will thrive on vulgar obscenities and on a coarse jest with just as lively a delight as that upon which persons of noble sensitivity pride themselves. An indolent man who loves having books read aloud to him because it is so pleasant to fall asleep that way, the merchant to whom all pleasures are trifling except those a clever man enjoys when he calculates his profits, one who loves the opposite sex only so far as he counts it among things to enjoy, the lover of the hunt, whether he hunt flies like Domitian[1] or ferocious beasts like A. ... —all these have a feeling that makes them capable of enjoying pleasures after their own fashion, without presuming to envy others or even being able so much as to conceive of other pleasures. But to that kind of feeling, which can take place without any thought whatever, I shall here pay no attention. There is still another feeling of a more delicate sort, so described either because one can enjoy it longer without satiation and exhaustion; or because it presupposes a sensitivity of the soul, so to speak, which makes the soul fitted for virtuous impulses; or because it indicates talents and intellectual excellences. It is this feeling of which I wish to consider one aspect. I shall moreover exclude from it that inclination that is fixed upon high intellectual insights, and the thrill that was possible to a Kepler,[2] who, as Bayle[3] reports, would not have sold one of his discoveries for a princedom. The latter sensation is quite too delicate to belong in the present sketch, which will concern only the sensuous feeling of which also more ordinary souls are capable.

Finer feeling, which we now wish to consider, is chiefly of two kinds: the feeling of the *sublime* and that of the *beautiful*. The stirring of each is pleasant, but in different ways. The sight of a mountain whose snow-covered peaks rises above the clouds, the description of a raging storm, or Milton's portrayal of the infernal kingdom, arouse enjoyment but with horror; on the other hand, the sight of flower-strewn meadows, valleys with winding brooks and covered with grazing flocks, the description of Elysium, or Homer's portrayal of the girdle of Venus,[4] also occasion a pleasant sensation but

[1] *Domitian* Titus Flavius Domitianus (51–96 CE), eleventh emperor of Rome.

[2] *Kepler* Johannes Kepler (1571–1630), German mathematician, astronomer, and astrologer best known for articulating the laws of planetary motion, now named after him.

[3] *Bayle* Pierre Bayle (1647–1706), French philosopher who advocated the separation of faith and reason.

[4] *Elysium ... girdle of Venus* In Greek mythology, Elysium, or the Elysian Fields, was the section of the Underworld reserved for the souls of the heroic and the virtuous. In Homer's *Iliad*, Hera thwarts Zeus's design to aid the Trojans by obtaining the magical girdle and seducing him.

one that is joyous and smiling. In order that the former impression could occur to us in due strength, we must have *a feeling of the sublime*, and, in order to enjoy the latter well, a *feeling of the beautiful.* Tall oaks and lonely shadows in a sacred grove are sublime; flower beds, low hedges and trees trimmed in figures are beautiful. Night is sublime, day is beautiful. Temperaments that possess a feeling for the sublime are drawn gradually, by the quiet stillness of a summer evening as the shimmering light of the stars breaks through the brown shadows of night and the lonely moon rises into view, into high feelings of friendship, of disdain for the world, of eternity. The shining day stimulates busy fervor and a feeling of gaiety. The sublime *moves*, the beautiful *charms*. The mien of a man who is undergoing the full feeling of the sublime is earnest, sometimes rigid and astonished. On the other hand the lively sensation of the beautiful proclaims itself through shining cheerfulness in the eyes, through smiling features, and often through audible mirth. The sublime is in turn of different kinds. Its feeling is sometimes accompanied with a certain dread, or melancholy; in some cases merely with quiet wonder; and in still others with a beauty completely pervading a sublime plan. The first I shall call the *terrifying sublime*, the second the *noble*, and the third the *splendid*. Deep loneliness is sublime, but in a way that stirs terror. Hence great far-reaching solitudes, like the colossal Komul Desert in Tartary,[1] have always given us occasion for peopling them with fearsome spirits, goblins, and ghouls.

The sublime must always be great; the beautiful can also be small. The sublime must be simple; the beautiful can be adorned and ornamented. A great height is just as sublime as a great depth, except that the latter is accompanied with the sensation of shuddering, the former with one of wonder. Hence the latter feeling can be the terrifying sublime, and the former the noble. The sight of an Egyptian pyramid, as Hasselquist[2] reports, moves one far more than one can imagine from all the descriptions; but its design is simple and noble. St. Peter's in Rome is splendid; because on its frame, which is large and simple, beauty is so distributed, for example, gold, mosaic work, and so on, that the feeling of the sublime still strikes through with the greatest effect; hence the object is called splendid. An arsenal must be noble and simple, a residence castle splendid, and a pleasure palace beautiful and ornamented.

A long duration is sublime. If it is of time past, then it is noble. If it is projected into an incalculable future, then it has something of the fearsome in it. A building of the remotest antiquity is venerable. Haller's[3] description of the coming eternity stimulates a mild horror, and of the past, transfixed wonder.

from SECTION 4: OF NATIONAL CHARACTERISTICS, SO FAR AS THEY DEPEND UPON THE DISTINCT FEELING OF THE BEAUTIFUL AND SUBLIME

Of the peoples of our part of the world, in my opinion those who distinguish themselves among all others by the feeling for the beautiful are the Italians and the French, but by the feeling for the sublime, the Germans, English, and Spanish. Holland can be considered as that land where the finer taste becomes largely unnoticeable. The beautiful itself is either fascinating and moving, or laughing and delightful. The first has something of the sublime in it, and the mind in this feeling is thoughtful and enraptured, but in the second sort of feeling, smiling and joyful. The first sort of beautiful feeling seems to be excellently suited to the Italians, and the second, to the French. In the national character that bears the expression of the sublime, this is either that of the terrifying sort, which is a little inclined to the adventurous, or it is a feeling for the noble, or for the splendid. I believe I have reason to be able to ascribe the feeling of the first sort to the Spaniard, the second to the Englishman, and the third to the German. The feeling for the splendid is not original by nature, like the remaining kinds of taste; and although a spirit of imitation can be united with every other feeling, it really is more peculiar to the

[1] *Tartary* Vast region of eastern Europe and northern Asia controlled by the Mongols in the thirteenth and fourteenth centuries.

[2] *Hasselquist* Fredric Hasselquist (1722–52), Swedish traveler and naturalist.

[3] *Haller* Albrecht von Haller (1708–77), Swiss anatomist, physiologist, naturalist, and poet.

glittering sublime; for this is properly a mixed feeling combining the beautiful and the sublime, in which each taken by itself is colder, so that the mind is free enough by means of their combination to attend to examples, and in fact it stands in need of the impulsion of such examples. Accordingly, the German will have less feeling in respect to the beautiful than the Frenchman, and less of what pertains to the sublime than the Englishman; but instances in which both appear in combination will be more suitable to his feeling, as he will fortunately escape the faults into which an excessive strength of either of these sorts of feeling could fall.

from Mary Wollstonecraft, *A Vindication of the Rights of Men* (1790)

The primary purpose of this pamphlet by Mary Wollstonecraft (1759–97) was the defense of Richard Price, who Edmund Burke described as a radical in his *Reflections on the Revolution in France* (1790). Price, like Wollstonecraft, advocated republicanism, in opposition to Burke's championing of constitutional monarchy. In this excerpt, Wollstonecraft seeks to redefine, recast, and, perhaps most importantly, re-gender ideas about the sublime and the beautiful as they are laid out in Burke's *Enquiry*.

… Had you been in a philosophising mood, had your heart or your reason been at home, you might have been convinced, by ocular demonstration, that madness is only the absence of reason. The ruling angel leaving its seat, wild anarchy ensues. You would have seen that the uncontrolled imagination often pursues the most regular course in its most daring flight; and that the eccentricities are boldly relieved when judgment no longer officiously arranges the sentiments, by bringing them to the test of principles. You would have seen every thing out of nature in that strange chaos of levity and ferocity, and of all sorts of follies jumbled together. You would have seen in that monstrous tragi-comic scene the most opposite passions necessarily succeed, and sometimes mix with each other in the mind; alternate contempt and indignation; alternate laughter and tears; alternate scorn and horror. This is a true picture of that chaotic state of mind, called madness; when reason gone, we know not where, the wild elements of passion clash, and all is horror and confusion. You might have heard the best turned conceits, flash following flash, and doubted whether the rhapsody was not eloquent, if it had not been delivered in an equivocal language, neither verse nor prose, if the sparkling periods had not stood alone, wanting force because they wanted concatenation.[1]

It is a proverbial observation, that a very thin partition divides wit and madness. Poetry therefore naturally addresses the fancy, and the language of passion is with great felicity borrowed from the heightened picture which the imagination draws of sensible objects concentrated by impassioned reflection. And, during this "fine frenzy," reason has no right to rein-in the imagination, unless to prevent the introduction of supernumerary images; if the passion is real, the head will not be ransacked for stale tropes and cold rodomontade. I now speak of the genuine enthusiasm of genius, which, perhaps, seldom appears, but in the infancy of civilization; for as this light becomes more luminous reason clips the wing of fancy—the youth becomes the man.

Whether the glory of Europe is set, I shall not now enquire; but probably the spirit of romance and chivalry is in the wane; and reason will gain by its extinction.

From observing several cold romantic characters I have been led to confine the term romantic to one definition—false, or rather artificial, feelings. Works of genius are read with a prepossession in their favour, and sentiments imitated, because they were fashionable and pretty, and not because they were forcibly felt.

In modern poetry the understanding and memory often fabricate the pretended effusions of the heart, and romance destroys all simplicity; which, in works of taste, is but a synonymous word for truth. This romantic spirit has extended to our prose, and scattered artificial flowers over the most barren heath; or a mixture of verse and prose producing the strangest incongruities. The turgid bombast of some of your periods fully proves these assertions; for when the heart speaks we are seldom shocked by hyperbole, or dry raptures. …

[1] *concatenation* I.e., connection.

Where is the dignity, the infallibility of sensibility, in the fair ladies, whom, if the voice of rumour is to be credited, the captive negroes curse in all the agony of bodily pain, for the unheard of tortures they invent? It is probable that some of them, after the sight of a flagellation, compose their ruffled spirits and exercise their tender feelings by the perusal of the last imported novel. How true these tears are to nature, I leave you to determine. But these ladies may have read your *Enquiry concerning the origin of our ideas of the Sublime and Beautiful*, and, convinced by your arguments, may have laboured to be pretty, by counterfeiting weakness.

You may have convinced them that *littleness* and *weakness* are the very essence of beauty; and that the Supreme Being, in giving women beauty in the most supereminent degree, seemed to command them, by the powerful voice of Nature, not to cultivate the moral virtues that might chance to excite respect, and interfere with the pleasing sensations they were created to inspire. Thus confining truth, fortitude, and humanity, within the rigid pale of manly morals, they might justly argue, that to be loved, woman's high end and distinction! they should "learn to lisp, to totter in their walk, and nick-name God's creatures."[1] Never, they might repeat after you, was any man, much less a woman, rendered amiable by the force of those exalted qualities, fortitude, justice, wisdom, and truth; and thus forewarned of the sacrifice they must make to those austere, unnatural virtues, they would be authorised to turn all their attention to their persons, systematically neglecting morals to secure beauty. Some rational old woman indeed might chance to stumble at this doctrine, and hint, that in avoiding atheism you had not steered clear of the mussulman's[2] creed; but you could readily exculpate yourself by turning the charge on Nature, who made our idea of beauty independent of reason. Nor would it be necessary for you to recollect, that if virtue has any other foundation than worldly utility, you have clearly proved that one half of the human species, at least, have not souls; and that Nature, by making women *little, smooth, delicate, fair* creatures, never designed that they should exercise their reason to acquire the virtues that produce opposite, if not contradictory, feelings. The affection they excite, to be uniform and perfect, should not be tinctured with the respect which moral virtues inspire, lest pain should be blended with pleasure, and admiration disturb the soft intimacy of love. This laxity of morals in the female world is certainly more captivating to a libertine imagination than the cold arguments of reason, that give no sex to virtue. If beautiful weakness be interwoven in a woman's frame, if the chief business of her life be (as you insinuate) to inspire love, and Nature has made an eternal distinction between the qualities that dignify a rational being and this animal perfection, her duty and happiness in this life must clash with any preparation for a more exalted state. So that Plato and Milton were grossly mistaken in asserting that human love led to heavenly, and was only an exaltation of the same affection; for the love of the Deity, which is mixed with the most profound reverence, must be love of perfection, and not compassion for weakness. …

from Mary Wollstonecraft, *Letters Written during a Short Residence in Sweden, Norway, and Denmark* (1796)

In 1795, the prominent feminist writer and philosopher Mary Wollstonecraft (1759–97) traveled through Scandinavia with her one-year-old daughter, Fanny. *Letters Written during a Short Residence* is a travel narrative and memoir recording her impressions of the journey; the text is drawn from her journals and from letters she had sent to her lover, Gilbert Imlay (1754–1828), while in Scandinavia. In the following excerpt, Wollstonecraft visits a waterfall near Frederikstad, Norway.

[1] *learn to … God's creatures* Loosely quoted from Shakespeare's *Hamlet*, 3.1.144–45.

[2] *mussulman* Muslim.

from LETTER 15

I left Christiania[1] yesterday. The weather was not very fine; and having been a little delayed on the road, I found that it was too late to go round, a couple of miles, to see the cascade near Fredericstadt, which I had determined to visit. Besides, as Fredericstadt is a fortress, it was necessary to arrive there before they shut the gate.

The road along the river is very romantic, though the views are not grand; and the riches of Norway, its timber, floats silently down the stream, often impeded in its course by islands and little cataracts, the offspring, as it were, of the great one I had frequently heard described.

I found an excellent inn at Fredericstadt, and was gratified by the kind attention of the hostess, who, perceiving that my clothes were wet, took great pains to procure me, as a stranger, every comfort for the night.

It had rained very hard, and we passed the ferry in the dark, without getting out of our carriage, which I think wrong, as the horses are sometimes unruly. Fatigue and melancholy, however, had made me regardless whether I went down or across the stream, and I did not know that I was wet before the hostess marked it. My imagination has never yet severed me from my griefs—and my mind has seldom been so free as to allow my body to be delicate.[2]

How I am altered by disappointment! When going to Lisbon,[3] the elasticity of my mind was sufficient to ward off weariness, and my imagination still could dip her brush in the rainbow of fancy, and sketch futurity in glowing colours. Now—but let me talk of something else—will you go with me to the cascade? …

I have often mentioned the grandeur, but I feel myself unequal to the task of conveying an idea of the beauty and elegance of the scene when the spiral tops of the pines are loaded with ripening seed, and the sun gives a glow to their light green tinge, which is changing into purple, one tree more or less advanced, contrasted with another. The profusion with which Nature has decked them, with pendant honours, prevents all surprise at seeing, in every crevice, some sapling struggling for existence. Vast masses of stone are thus encircled; and roots, torn up by the storms, become a shelter for a young generation. The pine and fir woods, left entirely to nature, display an endless variety; and the paths in the woods are not entangled with fallen leaves, which are only interesting whilst they are fluttering between life and death. The grey cobweb-like appearance of the aged pines is a much finer image of decay; the fibres whitening as they lose their moisture, imprisoned life seems to be stealing away. I cannot tell why—but death, under every form, appears to me like something getting free—to expand in I know not what element; nay, I feel that this conscious being must be as unfettered, have the wings of thought, before it can be happy.

Reaching the cascade, or rather cataract,[4] the roaring of which had a long time announced its vicinity, my soul was hurried by the falls into a new train of reflections. The impetuous dashing of the rebounding torrent from the dark cavities which mocked the exploring eye, produced an equal activity in my mind: my thoughts darted from earth to heaven, and I asked myself why I was chained to life and its misery? Still the tumultuous emotions this sublime object excited, were pleasurable; and, viewing it, my soul rose, with renewed dignity, above its cares—grasping at immortality—it seemed as impossible to stop the current of my thoughts, as of the always varying, still the same, torrent before me—I stretched out my hand to eternity, bounding over the dark speck of life to come.

We turned with regret from the cascade. On a little hill, which commands the best view of it, several obelisks are erected to commemorate the visits of different kings. The appearance of the river above and below the falls is very picturesque, the ruggedness of the scenery disappearing as the torrent subsides into a peaceful

[1] *Christiania* From 1625–1925, the name for Oslo, Norway. The city was named after King Christian IV after a fire in 1624; in 1925 the original Norwegian name was restored.

[2] [Wollstonecraft's note] "When the mind's free, / The body's delicate." Vid. [see] *King Lear* [3.4.11–12].

[3] *Lisbon* Wollstonecraft had gone to Lisbon in 1785 to visit her friend Fanny Skeys, who died in childbirth shortly after Wollstonecraft's arrival.

[4] *cataract* A cataract is a waterfall of some prominence ("cascade," by contrast, can refer to a smaller waterfall). Cataracts also fall straight over a precipice, rather than more gently over a more gradual decline.

stream. But I did not like to see a number of saw-mills crowded together close to the cataracts; they destroyed the harmony of the prospect.

The sight of a bridge erected across a deep valley, at a little distance, inspired very dissimilar sensations. It was most ingeniously supported by mast-like trunks, just stripped of their branches; and logs, placed one across the other, produced an appearance equally light and firm, seeming almost to be built in the air when we were below it, the height taking from the magnitude of the supporting trees give them a slender graceful look. …

from William Gilpin, *Three Essays on Picturesque Beauty* (1792)

William Gilpin (1724–1804) articulated the picturesque as "that kind of beauty which is agreeable in a picture" in his *Essay on Prints* (1768). In *Three Essays on Picturesque Beauty*, he further refined and explored the concept that would become of great importance to Romantic poets and painters.

from ESSAY I

Disputes about beauty might perhaps be involved in less confusion, if a distinction were established, which certainly exists, between such objects as are *beautiful*, and such as are *picturesque*—between those, which please the eye in their *natural state*; and those, which please from some quality, capable of being *illustrated by painting*.

Ideas of beauty vary with the objects, and with the eye of the spectator. The stonemason sees beauties in a well-jointed wall, which escape the architect, who surveys the building under a different idea. And thus the painter, who compares his object with the rules of his art, sees it in a different light from the man of general taste, who surveys it only as simply beautiful.

As this difference therefore between the *beautiful*, and the *picturesque* appears really to exist, and must depend on some peculiar construction of the object; it may be worthwhile to examine, what that peculiar construction is. We inquire not into the *general sources of beauty*, either in nature, or in representation. This would lead into a nice, and scientific discussion, in which it is not our purpose to engage. The question simply is, *What is that quality in objects, which particularly marks them as picturesque?*

In examining the *real object*, we shall find, one source of beauty arises from that species of elegance, which we call *smoothness*, or *neatness*; for the terms are nearly synonymous. The higher the marble is polished, the brighter the silver is rubbed, and the more the mahogany shines, the more each is considered as an object of beauty: as if the eye delighted in gliding smoothly over a surface.

In the class of larger objects the same idea prevails. In a pile of building we wish to see neatness in every part added to the elegance of the architecture. And if we examine a piece of improved pleasure-ground, every thing rough, and slovenly offends.

Mr. Burke, enumerating the properties of beauty, considers *smoothness* as one of the most essential. "A very considerable part of the effect of beauty, says he, is owing to this quality: indeed the most considerable: for take any beautiful object, and give it a broken, and rugged surface, and however well-formed it may be in other respects, it pleases no longer. Whereas, let it want ever so many of the other constituents, if it want not this, it becomes more pleasing, than almost all the others without it."[1] How far Mr. Burke may be right in making smoothness the most considerable source of beauty, I rather doubt. A considerable one it certainly is.

Thus then, we suppose, the matter stands with regard to *beautiful objects in general*. But in *picturesque representation* it seems somewhat odd, yet perhaps we shall find it equally true, that the reverse of this is the case; and that the ideas of *neat* and *smooth*, instead of being picturesque, in reality strip the object, in which they reside, of all pretensions to *picturesque beauty*. Nay, farther, we do not scruple to assert, that roughness forms the most essential point of difference between the *beautiful*, and the *picturesque*; as it seems to be that particular quality, which makes objects chiefly pleasing in painting. I use

[1] *A very considerable … without it* From Edmund Burke's *A Philosophical Enquiry into the Origin of Our Ideas of the Sublime and Beautiful* (1757).

the general term *roughness*; but properly speaking roughness relates only to the surface of bodies: when we speak of their delineation, we use the word *ruggedness*. Both ideas however equally enter into the picturesque; and both are observable in the smaller, as well as in the larger parts of nature—in the outline, and bark of a tree, as in the rude summit, and craggy sides of a mountain.

Let us then examine our theory by an appeal to experience; and try how far these qualities enter into the idea of *picturesque beauty*; and how far they mark that difference among objects, which is the ground of our inquiry.

A piece of Palladian architecture[1] may be elegant in the last degree. The proportion of its parts—the propriety of its ornaments—and the symmetry of the whole may be highly pleasing. But if we introduce it in a picture, it immediately becomes a formal object, and ceases to please. Should we wish to give it picturesque beauty, we must use the mallet, instead of the chisel; we must beat down one half of it, deface the other, and throw the mutilated members around in heaps. In short, from a *smooth* building we must turn it into a *rough* ruin. No painter, who had the choice of the two objects, would hesitate which to choose.

Again, why does an elegant piece of garden-ground make no figure on canvas? The shape is pleasing; the combination of the objects, harmonious; and the widening of the walk in the very line of beauty. All this is true, but the *smoothness* of the whole, though right, and as it should be in nature, offends in picture. Turn the lawn into a piece of broken ground: plant rugged oaks instead of flowing shrubs: break the edges of the walk: give it the rudeness of a road; mark it with wheel-tracks; and scatter around a few stones, and brushwood; in a word, instead of making the whole *smooth*, make it rough; and you make it also *picturesque*. All the other ingredients of beauty it already possessed. …

[1] *Palladian architecture* European architectural style, derived from the work of Andrea Palladio, a sixteenth-century Venetian architect. Palladio's work was in turn based on the classical temple architecture of ancient Greece and Rome.

from Jane Austen, *Sense and Sensibility* (1811)

In the late eighteenth century, the concept of sensibility was rooted in one's susceptibility to aesthetic or emotional experiences. People of sensibility were thought to possess finely tuned natures that made them quick to sympathize with any victim of injustice and responsive to the full range of aesthetic possibility in art, music, literature, and landscape. When it came to landscape, sensibility was supposed to render one appreciative of the sublime and of the beautiful, and especially of the picturesque.

Jane Austen's novel *Sense and Sensibility* displays both the positive and negative aspects of sensibility in the character of Marianne Dashwood. In the selection excerpted below, the Dashwood family has recently moved to a cottage in Devonshire, and their friend Edward Ferrars is visiting them for the first time. He and Marianne's sister Elinor (who embodies the "sense" of the title) have formed an attachment. Marianne is fond of Edward but worries that he is neither passionate nor sensitive enough for Elinor.

from VOLUME 1
from CHAPTER 18

Edward returned to them with fresh admiration of the surrounding country; in his walk to the village, he had seen many parts of the valley to advantage; and the village itself, in a much higher situation than the cottage, afforded a general view of the whole, which had exceedingly pleased him. This was a subject which ensured Marianne's attention, and she was beginning to describe her own admiration of these scenes, and to question him more minutely on the objects that had particularly struck him, when Edward interrupted her by saying, "You must not inquire too far, Marianne—

remember I have no knowledge in the picturesque,[1] and I shall offend you by my ignorance and want of taste if we come to particulars. I shall call hills steep, which ought to be bold; surfaces strange and uncouth, which ought to be irregular and rugged; and distant objects out of sight, which ought only to be indistinct through the soft medium of a hazy atmosphere. You must be satisfied with such admiration as I can honestly give. I call it a very fine country—the hills are steep, the woods seem full of fine timber, and the valley looks comfortable and snug—with rich meadows and several neat farm houses scattered here and there. It exactly answers my idea of a fine country, because it unites beauty with utility—and I dare say it is a picturesque one too, because you admire it; I can easily believe it to be full of rocks and promontories, grey moss and brush wood, but these are all lost on me. I know nothing of the picturesque."

"I am afraid it is but too true," said Marianne; "but why should you boast of it?"

"I suspect," said Elinor, "that to avoid one kind of affectation, Edward here falls into another. Because he believes many people pretend to more admiration of the beauties of nature than they really feel, and is disgusted with such pretensions, he affects greater indifference and less discrimination in viewing them himself than he possesses. He is fastidious and will have an affectation of his own."

"It is very true," said Marianne, "that admiration of landscape scenery is become a mere jargon. Every body pretends to feel and tries to describe with the taste and elegance of him who first defined what picturesque beauty was.[2] I detest jargon of every kind, and sometimes I have kept my feelings to myself, because I could find no language to describe them in but what was worn and hackneyed out of all sense and meaning."

"I am convinced," said Edward, "that you really feel all the delight in a fine prospect which you profess to feel. But, in return, your sister must allow me to feel no more than I profess. I like a fine prospect, but not on picturesque principles. I do not like crooked, twisted, blasted trees. I admire them much more if they are tall, straight, and flourishing. I do not like ruined, tattered cottages. I am not fond of nettles or thistles, or heath blossoms. I have more pleasure in a snug farm-house than a watch-tower—and a troop of tidy, happy villages please me better than the finest banditti[3] in the world." Marianne looked with amazement at Edward, with compassion at her sister. Elinor only laughed.

Painting the Natural and the Sublime

FRENCH

The work of French artists of the Romantic period often displays a passionate flair for the dramatic, whether the subject be political, historical, or mythological; the sublime in nature is more often a backdrop for human drama than it is a subject in itself.

[1] *no knowledge in the picturesque* Though professing ignorance of the picturesque, Edward accurately deploys its vocabulary and conventions in the following dialogue.

[2] *him ... was* William Gilpin.

[3] *banditti* Italian: outlaws, robbers. One of Gilpin's favorite painters, Salvator Rosa (1615–73), placed banditti figures in his landscapes, and Gilpin recommends the practice in his "Instruction for Examining Landscape" (c. 1789–94): "In wild and desert scenes, we are best pleased with banditti-soldiers, if not in regimentals, and such figures as coalesce in idea with the scenes in which we place them."

Jacques-Louis David, *Napoleon Crossing the Alps*, fifth version, c. 1805. This painting (also known as *Napoleon at the Saint-Bernard Pass* and as *Bonaparte Crossing the Alps*), which became the most widely reproduced image of Napoleon, exists in five different versions. Napoleon had led his army through the Saint-Bernard Pass in the Alps in 1800 as part of a campaign that concluded with the defeat of the Austrian army in the Battle of Marengo later that year. The French victory in Italy led to improved relations between France and Spain, and various gifts were exchanged between the French and Spanish leaders; the first version of *Napoleon Crossing the Alps* was one such gift. David, an ardent supporter of Napoleon, was commissioned by the French ambassador to Spain to paint the portrait and completed it in January 1801. Napoleon himself asked David to paint three more versions. David painted a fifth on his own initiative and retained it until his death. (Like the second version, it now belongs to the museum of the Palace of Versailles.)

Jean-Antoine Gros, *Napoleon at the Battle of Eylau*, 1808. The Battle of Eylau was fought between the French and Russian armies in 1807; it resulted in the loss of between 25,000 and 50,000 lives, but with no clear victory on either side.

Theodore Géricault, *The Raft of the Medusa*, 1819. Perhaps the best known of all French paintings of the Romantic era, this work is a monumental depiction (approximately 16 x 24 feet) of an incident that occurred in 1816. The *Medusa* was a French frigate captained by a political appointee lacking in experience; it ran aground on a sandbank some 60 miles from the African coast. The ship had too few lifeboats and almost 150 men and one woman ended up adrift on a makeshift raft with inadequate supplies. By the time the raft was sighted and the survivors rescued by a passing ship, the *Argus*, only 15 remained alive; the others had starved to death or, in some cases, been killed and eaten (Géricault also completed a much smaller work entitled *Cannibalism on the Raft of the Medusa*).

The painting depicts the survivors' despair as the *Argus* has been sighted but has not seen the raft and is sailing on. By chance, the *Argus* re-appeared again on the horizon some hours later on another tack, at which point the raft was finally sighted. The incident followed the restoration of the French monarchy after the defeat of Napoleon and was widely taken as a sign of the corruption, incompetence, and heartlessness of the new French regime, which had not bothered to instigate any search for the missing ship.

The painting, which was originally hung in Paris under the title *Scène de Naufrage* ("Scene of a Shipwreck"), was also controversial for its inclusion of a black man at the center of the composition; Géricault was an ardent abolitionist. When the work was exhibited in London for several months in 1820, it was received with tremendous enthusiasm and viewed by more than 40,000 people.

Eugene Delacroix, *Liberty Leading the People*, 1830. Delacroix's most famous painting celebrates the overthrow of Charles X in 1830, which led to the establishment of a constitutional monarchy under Louis-Phillippe. The figure of Liberty holds a tattered *tricoleur*—the flag of the French Revolution of 1789. The new government bought the painting in 1831; later, it became the inspiration for France's 1886 gift to the United States of the statue *Liberty Enlightening the World*.

GERMAN

The work of such Romantic-era German artists as Philipp Otto Runge and Caspar David Friedrich is infused with symbolism and spirituality; the supernatural (and often specifically the Christian) is portrayed as a deep presence in nature—in plants, in the hours of the day and the changing seasons, and in human nature as well. The nineteenth-century European tradition of painting in this vein has roots in the Academy at Copenhagen in Denmark (where Runge, Friedrich, and the Norwegian Romantic painter Johann Christian Dahl all studied) and in the work of the Danish artist Jens Juel.

Philipp Otto Runge, *The Child in the Meadow*, from *Morning*, 1809. *The Child in the Meadow* was conceived as one part of a larger picture, *Morning*, that was itself planned as part of a still-larger work, *Times of Day*. *Morning* was not quite complete when Runge died (aged 33); before he died he suggested that the unfinished work be cut up and the parts that had been completed be displayed independently. *The Child in the Meadow* was the title given to this fragment. The grand scheme of the larger work is suggestive both of Christian and of classical mythology. The fragment gives a turn to Christian iconography that is also expressive of two other elements central to Runge's vision: a belief in an overriding connection between humans and nature, and a faith in childhood as the human stage that stands closest to the force of creation.

Caspar David Friedrich, *The Wanderer above the Sea of Fog*, 1818. The title of this famous painting is also sometimes translated as *The Walker above the Mists*; in German the title is *Der Wanderer über dem Nebelmeer*; the German "Wanderer" can mean either wanderer or hiker.

Caspar David Friedrich, *Arctic Shipwreck* (also known as *Sea of Ice* or *Polar Sea*), 1824.

British

From the gentle vision of nature expressed in the late eighteenth-century work of Thomas Gainsborough, British artists moved in several directions. The vast scenes depicted by John Martin[1] are dark and theatrical; the Romantic sublime of Philip James de Loutherbourg is strangely unthreatening, even when terrible subjects are depicted. The work of the two most prominent Romantic-era British artists, J.M.W. Turner and John Constable, evolved markedly over the course of several decades.

Thomas Gainsborough, *Peasants Going to Market, Early Morning*, 1770.

Thomas Gainsborough, *Cottage Door with Girl and Pigs*, 1786.

[1] *John Martin* See the color insert for work by Martin, as well as other examples of British painting during the Romantic era.

J.M.W. Turner, *Linlithgow Palace*, 1807. The palace where Mary, Queen of Scots had been born was by 1807 a picturesque ruin. The naked nymphs he added in the foreground are reminiscent of artistic styles of an earlier era, but the whole has an unmistakably Romantic cast.

J.M.W. Turner, *The Fighting Temeraire Tugged to Her Last Berth to Be Broken Up*, 1839. The *H.M.S. Temeraire* had played an important role in Nelson's victory over the French at Trafalgar in 1805; in 1838, it was towed to a scrap yard at the docks in East London.

J.M.W. Turner, *The Devil's Bridge*, 1841.

John Constable, *Dedham Vale*, 1802.

John Constable, *Brighton Beach, with Colliers*, 1824.

John Constable, *Old Sarum*, 1829. Old Sarum, near the site of present-day Salisbury, is the location of some of the earliest evidence of human settlement in Britain; it is known to have been inhabited over 3,000 years ago. By the early nineteenth century, however, the old hill fort was long-abandoned and Old Sarum was uninhabited.

Philip James de Loutherbourg, *Snowdon*, from *The Romantic and Picturesque Scenery of England and Wales*, 1805.

Philip James de Loutherbourg, *Storm off Margate*, from *The Romantic and Picturesque Scenery of England and Wales*, 1805.

David Cox, *Crossing Lancaster Sands*, 1841. Until 1857, when a railway line was built across the bay, people often made their way to Morecamb Bay at low tide across the Lancaster Sands. There were numerous dangers associated with the crossing (including quicksand as well as unpredictable and dangerous tides). The crossing inspired works by many artists, including J.M.W. Turner; the above painting is one of several depictions by the watercolorist David Cox.

Samuel Taylor Coleridge

1772 – 1834

Samuel Taylor Coleridge is one of the most important figures of English Romanticism. Over the course of a few years, when in his mid-twenties, he composed poems that continue to be regarded as central to the English canon, among them "The Rime of the Ancient Mariner," "Frost at Midnight," and the fragment "Kubla Khan." Later in his life, his critical and philosophical writing earned him a place as one of the most profound thinkers of the nineteenth century.

Born in 1772, Coleridge was the youngest son of the vicar of Ottery St. Mary, the Rev. John Coleridge, and his wife, Anna Bowdon. He was a voracious reader with a mind that he described as "habituated to *the Vast*." When his father died, his mother arranged for nine-year-old Samuel to be sent to Christ's Hospital in London, a school founded to educate the promising sons of the poor. Although he received an excellent education at Christ's, Coleridge remained ambivalent about the school long after he left, continuing to feel injured by the fact that he had been a "charity boy."

In 1791, Coleridge entered Jesus College, Cambridge, where his intellectual abilities and academic success were matched only by his facility in running up debts and his increasing despair at his financial situation. He eventually attempted to escape his financial problems by enlisting (under the name Silas Tomkyn Comberbache), but he was rescued by his brother George from both the army and financial distress. In 1794 he met Robert Southey, then an Oxford undergraduate, and the two recognized a shared interest in poetry and radical political ideas. They hatched a plan to found a communitarian settlement in Pennsylvania to be run under a system they called "Pantisocracy." Both the plan and the friendship, however, foundered over the question of what role women and servants should play (Coleridge insisted on a completely egalitarian community; Southey did not). In his early exuberance for the scheme Coleridge became engaged to Sara Fricker, the sister of Southey's fiancée, and he felt bound to honor the commitment even though his feeling for her quickly waned. They married in 1795 but after a brief period of happiness they became progressively more miserable, finally separating in 1807. The marriage produced four children.

Coleridge began a short-lived liberal periodical in 1796 called *The Watchman*. He also published his first poetic collection, *Poems on Various Subjects*, which contained the poem that would later be titled "The Eolian Harp." Almost destitute, he was saved by a yearly pension granted him by Tom and Josiah Wedgwood, sons of the famous potter. The following year he and William Wordsworth began a troubled but lifelong friendship, the first fruit of which was the joint volume *Lyrical Ballads*, which opened with Coleridge's "The Rime of the Ancyent Marinere" (revised and retitled in 1817). Shortly afterward he accompanied Wordsworth and his sister Dorothy to Germany, where he immersed himself in German philosophy.

Returning to England in 1799, Coleridge joined Wordsworth in the Lake District. Here he met Sara Hutchinson, Wordsworth's future sister-in-law, and became infatuated with her. The relationship between the two remained platonic, but it magnified Coleridge's estrangement from his wife, and the situation was made worse by his increasing dependence on laudanum, a drug derived from opium. From 1802 onward Coleridge spent only brief periods with his family. In 1804 he set off for Malta, where he took a post in the British government. From this time forth he became progressively more conservative, eventually going so far as to deny entirely his early liberal leanings. After a year and a half he returned to England penniless.

From 1808 to 1818, Coleridge intermittently delivered lectures with topics that ranged from German philosophy to current educational controversies. The highlight was a series he gave on Shakespeare and Milton, which displayed all the brilliance of his critical skills. These lectures offered incisive analyses of aspects of Shakespeare's plays, from a consideration of love in *Romeo and Juliet* to an anatomization of Hamlet's paradoxical psychology, and concluded with a masterful examination of *Paradise Lost.* During this period Coleridge, who had long been interested in newspaper writing, also undertook the most important of his journalistic ventures: *The Friend* (1809–10), a weekly newspaper he largely wrote himself. His drama, *Remorse,* was staged at the Drury Lane Theatre in 1813.

In 1816 Coleridge took up residence in Highgate with the family of the young doctor James Gillman. He asked to stay for a month; he remained for the rest of his life. The situation offered a stable environment, and Coleridge began publishing regularly. His Gothic ballad "Christabel," long known to other writers through private recitation (and an influence on Walter Scott's "The Lay of the Last Minstrel" and Lord Byron's "The Siege of Corinth"), was published in a collection with "Kubla Khan" and "The Pains of Sleep" in 1816, through Byron's enthusiastic support. Soon afterward Coleridge published *Sybilline Leaves*, a collection of his previous poems (including a newly revised *Ancient Mariner* with a marginal gloss) and the long work *Biographia Literaria.*

The first volume of *Biographia Literaria* is autobiographical, detailing (among other events) Coleridge's education and his first involvement with Wordsworth. The volume also begins to delve into literary analysis as, for example, in the famous passage in Chapter 13, in which Coleridge differentiates between imagination and fancy, defining the qualities of each and declaring imagination superior. The second volume consists almost entirely of literary criticism, both formal and philosophical, much of it focusing on Wordsworth's poetry. In both volumes, Coleridge anatomizes both poetry and poetic production, considering not only formal elements but also the psychology of the creative process.

Coleridge's genius and importance were gradually acknowledged by a considerable number of his contemporaries, and the "Sage of Highgate" began to be viewed as an important thinker. This opinion was cemented by the publication of *Aids to Reflection* (1825), which stressed the role of the personal in Christian faith, and *On the Constitution of Church and State* (1830), which emphasized the importance of national culture and defined the class of intellectuals needed to protect it. This latter book in particular had a profound influence on such authors as Matthew Arnold and Thomas Carlyle.

From 1832 onward Coleridge became increasingly ill, although this did not prevent him from helping to prepare *Poetical Works* (1834), a collection of his poetry—he died shortly after its publication. *Table Talk*, a posthumously published collection of his remarks on miscellaneous topics, appeared the following year.

Coleridge's poetry often presents Gothic story material in psychologically suggestive ways, delineating the mind as it explores itself and its relation to the larger world. His more uncanny poems, such as "The Rime of the Ancient Mariner," excite tension in the reader both through their handling of narrative and in the psychological complexity of their characters and relationships. Poems such as "Frost at Midnight" mingle contemplation and description to produce a richly interrelated whole, a style which influenced not only Wordsworth (specifically in "Tintern Abbey"), but also poets to the present day.

⌘⌘⌘

The Eolian Harp[1]

Composed at Clevedon, Somersetshire

My pensive Sara![2] thy soft cheek reclined
Thus on mine arm, most soothing sweet it is
To sit beside our Cot,° our Cot o'ergrown *cottage*
With white-flower'd Jasmin, and the broad-leav'd Myrtle,
(Meet emblems they of Innocence and Love!)
And watch the clouds, that late were rich with light,
Slow saddening round, and mark the star of eve
Serenely brilliant (such should Wisdom be)
Shine opposite! How exquisite the scents
Snatch'd from yon bean-field! and the world *so* hush'd!
The stilly murmur of the distant Sea
Tells us of silence.

And that simplest Lute,
Placed length-ways in the clasping casement, hark!
How by the desultory breeze caress'd,
Like some coy maid half yielding to her lover,
It pours such sweet upbraiding, as must needs
Tempt to repeat the wrong! And now, its strings
Boldlier swept, the long sequacious° notes *unvarying*
Over delicious surges sink and rise,
Such a soft floating witchery of sound
As twilight Elfins make, when they at eve
Voyage on gentle gales from Fairy-Land,
Where Melodies round honey-dropping flowers,
Footless and wild, like birds of Paradise,[3]
Nor pause, nor perch, hovering on untam'd wing!
O! the one Life within us and abroad,
Which meets all motion and becomes its soul,
A light in sound, a sound-like power in light,
Rhythm in all thought, and joyance every where—
Methinks, it should have been impossible
Not to love all things in a world so fill'd;
Where the breeze warbles, and the mute still air
Is Music slumbering on her instrument.

And thus, my Love! as on the midway slope
Of yonder hill I stretch my limbs at noon,
Whilst through my half-clos'd eye-lids I behold
The sunbeams dance, like diamonds, on the main,
And tranquil muse upon tranquillity;
Full many a thought uncall'd and undetain'd,
And many idle flitting phantasies,
Traverse my indolent and passive brain,
As wild and various, as the random gales
That swell and flutter on this subject Lute!

And what if all of animated nature
Be but organic Harps diversely fram'd,
That tremble into thought, as o'er them sweeps
Plastic and vast, one intellectual breeze,
At once the Soul of each, and God of all?

But thy more serious eye a mild reproof
Darts, O belovéd Woman! nor such thoughts
Dim and unhallow'd dost thou not reject,
And biddest me walk humbly with my God.
Meek Daughter in the family of Christ!
Well hast thou said and holily disprais'd
These shapings of the unregenerate mind;
Bubbles that glitter as they rise and break
On vain Philosophy's aye-babbling spring.
For never guiltless may I speak of Him,

---

[1] *Eolian Harp* Musical instrument named after Æolus, Greek god of the winds; the music of the harp is created by exposure to the wind passing through it.

[2] *Sara* Sara Fricker, whom Coleridge had married in 1795.

[3] *birds of Paradise* New Guinean birds of brilliant plumage, thought by Europeans to have no feet.

The Incomprehensible! save when with awe
I praise Him, and with Faith that inly *feels*;
Who with His saving mercies healéd me,
A sinful and most miserable man,
Wilder'd and dark, and gave me to possess
Peace, and this Cot, and thee, heart-honour'd Maid!
—1795

Fears in Solitude

Written in April 1798, During the Alarm of An Invasion[1]

A green and silent spot, amid the hills,
A small and silent dell! O'er stiller place
No singing sky-lark ever poised himself.
The hills are heathy, save that swelling slope,
Which hath a gay and gorgeous covering on,
All golden with the never-bloomless furze,° *evergreen shrub*
Which now blooms most profusely: but the dell,
Bathed by the mist, is fresh and delicate
As vernal corn-field, or the unripe flax,
When, through its half-transparent stalks, at eve,
The level sunshine glimmers with green light.
O! 'tis a quiet spirit-healing nook!
Which all, methinks, would love; but chiefly he,
The humble man, who, in his youthful years,
Knew just so much of folly, as had made
His early manhood more securely wise!
Here he might lie on fern or withered heath,
While from the singing lark (that sings unseen
The minstrelsy that solitude loves best),
And from the sun, and from the breezy air,
Sweet influences trembled o'er his frame;
And he, with many feelings, many thoughts,
Made up a meditative joy, and found
Religious meanings in the forms of Nature!
And so, his senses gradually wrapt
In a half sleep, he dreams of better worlds,
And dreaming hears thee still, O singing lark,
That singest like an angel in the clouds!

My God! it is a melancholy thing
For such a man, who would full fain preserve
His soul in calmness, yet perforce must feel
For all his human brethren—O my God!
It weighs upon the heart, that he must think
What uproar and what strife may now be stirring
This way or that way o'er these silent hills—
Invasion, and the thunder and the shout,
And all the crash of onset; fear and rage,
And undetermined conflict—even now,
Even now, perchance, and in his native isle:
Carnage and screams beneath this blessed sun!
We have offended, O! my countrymen!
We have offended very grievously,
And have been tyrannous. From east to west
A groan of accusation pierces Heaven!
The wretched plead against us; multitudes
Countless and vehement, the sons of God,
Our brethren! like a cloud that travels on,
Steamed up from Cairo's swamps of pestilence,
Even so, my countrymen! have we gone forth
And borne to distant tribes slavery and pangs,
And, deadlier far, our vices, whose deep taint
With slow perdition murders the whole man,
His body and his soul! Meanwhile, at home,
All individual dignity and power
Engulfed in Courts, Committees, Institutions,
Associations and Societies,
A vain, speech-mounting, speech-reporting Guild,
One Benefit-Club for mutual flattery,
We have drunk up, demure as at a grace,
Pollutions from the brimming cup of wealth;
Contemptuous of all honourable rule,
Yet bartering freedom and the poor man's life
For gold, as at a market! The sweet words
Of Christian promise, words that even yet
Might stem destruction, were they wisely preached,
Are muttered o'er by men, whose tones proclaim
How flat and wearisome they feel their trade:
Rank scoffers some, but most too indolent
To deem them falsehoods, or to know their truth.
O! blasphemous! the Book of Life is made
A superstitious instrument, on which

[1] *Invasion* By the French, who threatened an attack on Wales.

We gabble o'er the oaths we mean to break,
For all must swear[1]—all and in every place,
College and wharf, council and justice-court;
All, all must swear, the briber and the bribed,
Merchant and lawyer, senator and priest,
The rich, the poor, the old man and the young;
All, all make up one scheme of perjury,
That faith doth reel; the very name of God
Sounds like a juggler's charm; and bold with joy,
Forth from his dark and lonely hiding-place,
(Portentous sight!) the owlet Atheism,
Sailing on obscene wings athwart the noon,
Drops his blue-fringéd lids, and holds them close,
And hooting at the glorious sun in Heaven,
Cries out, "Where is it?"

Thankless too for peace,
(Peace long preserved by fleets and perilous seas)
Secure from actual warfare, we have loved
To swell the war-whoop, passionate for war!
Alas! for ages ignorant of all
Its ghastlier workings, (famine or blue plague,
Battle, or siege, or flight thro' wintry snows,)
We, this whole people, have been clamorous
For war and bloodshed; animating sports,
The which we pay for as a thing to talk of,
Spectators and not combatants! No guess
Anticipative of a wrong unfelt,
No speculation on contingency,
However dim and vague, too vague and dim
To yield a justifying cause; and forth,
(Stuffed out with big preamble, holy names,
And adjurations° of the God in Heaven,) *appeal*
We send our mandates for the certain death
Of thousands and ten thousands! Boys and girls,
And women, that would groan to see a child
Pull off an insect's leg, all read of war,
The best amusement for our morning meal!
The poor wretch, who has learnt his only prayers
From curses, who knows scarcely words enough
To ask a blessing from his Heavenly Father,
Becomes a fluent phraseman, absolute
And technical in victories and defeats,
And all our dainty terms for fratricide;
Terms which we trundle smoothly o'er our tongues
Like mere abstractions, empty sounds to which
We join no feeling and attach no form!
As if the soldier died without a wound;
As if the fibres of this godlike frame
Were gored without a pang; as if the wretch,
Who fell in battle, doing bloody deeds,
Passed off to Heaven, translated and not killed;
As though he had no wife to pine for him,
No God to judge him! Therefore, evil days
Are coming on us, O my countrymen!
And what if all-avenging Providence,
Strong and retributive, should make us know
The meaning of our words, force us to feel
The desolation and the agony
Of our fierce doings?

Spare us yet awhile,
Father and God! O! spare us yet awhile!
Oh! let not English women drag their flight
Fainting beneath the burthen of their babes,
Of the sweet infants, that but yesterday
Laughed at the breast! Sons, brothers, husbands, all
Who ever gazed with fondness on the forms
Which grew up with you round the same fire-side,
And all who ever heard the sabbath-bells
Without the infidel's scorn, make yourselves pure!
Stand forth! be men! repel an impious foe,
Impious and false, a light yet cruel race,
Who laugh away all virtue, mingling mirth
With deeds of murder; and still promising
Freedom, themselves too sensual to be free,
Poison life's amities, and cheat the heart
Of faith and quiet hope, and all that soothes,
And all that lifts the spirit! Stand we forth;
Render them back upon the insulted ocean,
And let them toss as idly on its waves
As the vile sea-weed, which some mountain-blast
Swept from our shores! And oh! may we return

[1] *all must swear* According to the Test and Corporation Acts, all public officials were required to swear allegiance to the Church of England. (Thus there would be no Catholics, Nonconformists, or Jews in office.)

Not with a drunken triumph, but with fear,
Repenting of the wrongs with which we stung
So fierce a foe to frenzy!

I have told,
O Britons! O my brethren! I have told
Most bitter truth, but without bitterness.
Nor deem my zeal or factious or mistimed;
For never can true courage dwell with them,
Who, playing tricks with conscience, dare not look
At their own vices. We have been too long
Dupes of a deep delusion! Some, belike,
Groaning with restless enmity, expect
All change from change of constituted power;
As if a Government had been a robe,
On which our vice and wretchedness were tagged
Like fancy-points and fringes, with the robe
Pulled off at pleasure. Fondly these attach
A radical causation to a few
Poor drudges of chastising Providence,
Who borrow all their hues and qualities
From our own folly and rank wickedness,
Which gave them birth and nursed them. Others, meanwhile,
Dote with a mad idolatry; and all
Who will not fall before their images,
And yield them worship, they are enemies
Even of their country!

Such have I been deemed.—
But, O dear Britain! O my Mother Isle!
Needs must thou prove a name most dear and holy
To me, a son, a brother, and a friend,
A husband, and a father! who revere
All bonds of natural love, and find them all
Within the limits of thy rocky shores.
O native Britain! O my Mother Isle!
How shouldst thou prove aught else but dear and holy
To me, who from thy lakes and mountain-hills,
Thy clouds, thy quiet dales, thy rocks and seas,
Have drunk in all my intellectual life,
All sweet sensations, all ennobling thoughts,
All adoration of the God in nature,
All lovely and all honourable things,
Whatever makes this mortal spirit feel
The joy and greatness of its future being?
There lives nor form nor feeling in my soul
Unborrowed from my country! O divine
And beauteous island! thou hast been my sole
And most magnificent temple, in the which
I walk with awe, and sing my stately songs,
Loving the God that made me!—

May my fears,
My filial fears, be vain! and may the vaunts
And menace of the vengeful enemy
Pass like the gust, that roared and died away
In the distant tree: which heard, and only heard
In this low dell, bowed not the delicate grass.

But now the gentle dew-fall sends abroad
The fruit-like perfume of the golden furze:
The light has left the summit of the hill,
Though still a sunny gleam lies beautiful,
Aslant the ivied beacon. Now farewell,
Farewell, awhile, O soft and silent spot!
On the green sheep-track, up the heathy hill,
Homeward I wind my way; and lo! recalled
From bodings that have well-nigh wearied me,
I find myself upon the brow, and pause
Startled! And after lonely sojourning
In such a quiet and surrounded nook,
This burst of prospect, here the shadowy main,
Dim tinted, there the mighty majesty
Of that huge amphitheatre of rich
And elmy fields, seems like society—
Conversing with the mind, and giving it
A livelier impulse and a dance of thought!
And now, belovéd Stowey![1] I behold
Thy church-tower, and, methinks, the four huge elms
Clustering, which mark the mansion of my friend;
And close behind them, hidden from my view,
Is my own lowly cottage, where my babe
And my babe's mother dwell in peace! With light

[1] *Stowey* Nether Stowey, a village in Somerset where Coleridge lived for a few years.

And quickened footsteps thitherward I tend,
Remembering thee, O green and silent dell!
And grateful, that by nature's quietness
And solitary musings, all my heart
Is softened, and made worthy to indulge
Love, and the thoughts that yearn for human kind.
—1798

Frost at Midnight

The Frost performs its secret ministry,
Unhelped by any wind. The owlet's cry
Came loud—and hark, again! loud as before.
The inmates of my cottage, all at rest,
Have left me to that solitude, which suits
Abstruser musings: save that at my side
My cradled infant slumbers peacefully.
'Tis calm indeed! so calm, that it disturbs
And vexes meditation with its strange
And extreme silentness. Sea, hill, and wood,
This populous village! Sea, and hill, and wood,
With all the numberless goings-on of life,
Inaudible as dreams! the thin blue flame
Lies on my low-burnt fire, and quivers not;
Only that film,[1] which fluttered on the grate,
Still flutters there, the sole unquiet thing.
Methinks, its motion in this hush of nature
Gives it dim sympathies with me who live,
Making it a companionable form,
Whose puny flaps and freaks the idling Spirit
By its own moods interprets, every where
Echo or mirror seeking of itself,
And makes a toy of Thought.

But O! how oft,
How oft, at school, with most believing mind,
Presageful, have I gazed upon the bars,
To watch that fluttering *stranger*! and as oft
With unclosed lids, already had I dreamt
Of my sweet birth-place, and the old church-tower,
Whose bells, the poor man's only music, rang
From morn to evening, all the hot Fair-day,
So sweetly, that they stirred and haunted me
With a wild pleasure, falling on mine ear
Most like articulate sounds of things to come!
So gazed I, till the soothing things, I dreamt,
Lulled me to sleep, and sleep prolonged my dreams!
And so I brooded all the following morn,
Awed by the stern preceptor's° face, mine eye *teacher's*
Fixed with mock study on my swimming book:
Save if the door half opened, and I snatched
A hasty glance, and still my heart leaped up,
For still I hoped to see the *stranger's* face,
Townsman, or aunt, or sister more beloved,
My play-mate when we both were clothed alike!

Dear Babe, that sleepest cradled by my side,
Whose gentle breathings, heard in this deep calm,
Fill up the interspersèd vacancies
And momentary pauses of the thought!
My babe so beautiful! it thrills my heart
With tender gladness, thus to look at thee,
And think that thou shalt learn far other lore,
And in far other scenes! For I was reared
In the great city, pent 'mid cloisters dim,
And saw nought lovely but the sky and stars.
But *thou*, my babe! shalt wander like a breeze
By lakes and sandy shores, beneath the crags
Of ancient mountain, and beneath the clouds,
Which image in their bulk both lakes and shores
And mountain crags: so shalt thou see and hear
The lovely shapes and sounds intelligible
Of that eternal language, which thy God
Utters, who from eternity doth teach
Himself in all, and all things in himself.
Great universal Teacher! he shall mould
Thy spirit, and by giving make it ask.

Therefore all seasons shall be sweet to thee,
Whether the summer clothe the general earth
With greenness, or the redbreast sit and sing
Betwixt the tufts of snow on the bare branch
Of mossy apple-tree, while the nigh thatch
Smokes in the sun-thaw; whether the eave-drops fall

[1] [Coleridge's note] In all parts of the kingdom these films are called *strangers* and supposed to portend the arrival of some absent friend.

Heard only in the trances of the blast,
Or if the secret ministry of frost
Shall hang them up in silent icicles,
Quietly shining to the quiet Moon.
—1798

The Rime of the Ancient Mariner

In Seven Parts[1]

Facile credo, plures esse Naturas invisibiles quam visibiles in rerum universitate. Sed horum omnium familiam quis nobis enarrabit? et gradus et cognationes et discrimina et singulorum munera? Quid agunt? quæ loca habitant? Harum rerum notitiam semper ambivit ingenium humanum, nunquam attigit. Juvat, interea, non diffiteor, quandoque in animo, tanquam in Tabulâ, majoris et melioris mundi imaginem contemplari: ne mens assuefecta hodiernæ vitæ minutiis se contrahat nimis, & tota subsidat in pusillas cogitationes. Sed veritati interea invigilandum est, modusque servandus, ut certa ab incertis, diem a nocte, distinguamus.[2]—T. Burnet. *Archaeol. Phil.* p. 68.

PART I

An ancient Mariner meeteth three Gallants bidden to a wedding-feast, and detaineth one.

It is an ancient Mariner,
And he stoppeth one of three.
"By thy long grey beard and glittering eye,
Now wherefore stopp'st thou me?

The Bridegroom's doors are opened wide,
And I am next of kin;
The guests are met, the feast is set:
May'st hear the merry din."

He holds him with his skinny hand,
"There was a ship," quoth he.
"Hold off! unhand me, grey-beard loon!"
Eftsoons[3] his hand dropt he.

The wedding-guest is spellbound by the eye of the old sea-faring man, and constrained to hear his tale.

He holds him with his glittering eye—
The Wedding-Guest stood still,
And listens like a three years' child:
The Mariner hath his will.

The Wedding-Guest sat on a stone:
He cannot choose but hear;
And thus spake on that ancient man,
The bright-eyed Mariner.

The Mariner tells how the ship sailed southward with a good wind and fair weather, till it reached the line.

"The ship was cheered, the harbour cleared,
Merrily did we drop
Below the kirk,[4] below the hill,
Below the lighthouse top.

The Sun came up upon the left,
Out of the sea came he!
And he shone bright, and on the right
Went down into the sea.

The wedding-guest heareth the bridal music; but the mariner continueth his tale.

Higher and higher every day,
Till over the mast at noon—"
The Wedding-Guest here beat his breast,
For he heard the loud bassoon.

The bride hath paced into the hall
Red as a rose is she;
Nodding their heads before her goes
The merry minstrelsy.

---

[1] *The Rime … Parts* This version of the poem was published in 1817.

[2] *Facile … distinguamus* From Thomas Burnet's *Archaeologiae Philosophicae* (1692), translated by Mead and Foxton (1736): "I can easily believe, that there are more invisible than visible beings in the universe. But who will declare to us the family of all these, and acquaint us with the agreements, differences, and peculiar talents which are to be found among them? It is true, human wit has always desired a knowledge of these things, though it has never yet attained it. I will own that it is very profitable, sometimes to contemplate in the mind, as in a draught, the image of the greater and better world, lest the soul being accustomed to the trifles of this present life, should contract itself too much, and altogether rest in mean cogitations, but, in the meantime, we must take care to keep to the truth, and observe moderation, that we may distinguish certain from uncertain things, and day from night."

[3] *Eftsoons* At once.

[4] *kirk* Church.

The Wedding-Guest he beat his breast,
Yet he cannot choose but hear;
And thus spake on that ancient man,
The bright-eyed Mariner.

"And now the STORM-BLAST came, and he
Was tyrannous and strong:
He struck with his o'ertaking wings,
And chased us south along.

The ship drawn by a storm toward the south pole.

With sloping masts and dipping prow,
As who pursued with yell and blow
Still treads the shadow of his foe,
And forward bends his head,
The ship drove fast, loud roared the blast,
And southward aye we fled.

And now there came both mist and snow,
And it grew wondrous cold:
And ice, mast-high, came floating by,
As green as emerald.

And through the drifts the snowy clifts
Did send a dismal sheen:
Nor shapes of men nor beasts we ken[1]—
The ice was all between.

The land of ice, and of fearful sounds, where no living thing was to be seen.

The ice was here, the ice was there,
The ice was all around:
It cracked and growled, and roared and howled,
Like noises in a swound![2]

At length did cross an Albatross,
Thorough the fog it came;
As if it had been a Christian soul,
We hailed it in God's name.

Till a great sea-bird, called the Albatross, came through the snow-fog, and was received with great joy and hospitality.

It ate the food it ne'er had eat,
And round and round it flew.
The ice did split with a thunder-fit;
The helmsman steered us through!

And a good south wind sprung up behind;
The Albatross did follow,
And every day, for food or play,
Came to the Mariner's hollo!

And lo! the Albatross proveth a bird of good omen, and followeth the ship as it returned northward, through fog and floating ice.

In mist or cloud, on mast or shroud,
It perched for vespers nine;[3]
Whiles all the night, through fog-smoke white,
Glimmered the white Moon-shine."

"God save thee, ancient Mariner!
From the fiends, that plague thee thus!—
Why look'st thou so?"—With my cross-bow
I shot the ALBATROSS.

The ancient Mariner inhospitably killed the pious bird of good omen.

PART 2

The Sun now rose upon the right:
Out of the sea came he,
Still hid in mist, and on the left
Went down into the sea.

And the good south wind still blew behind,
But no sweet bird did follow,
Nor any day for food or play
Came to the mariners' hollo!

And I had done a hellish thing,
And it would work 'em woe:
For all averred, I had killed the bird
That made the breeze to blow.
Ah wretch! said they, the bird to slay,
That made the breeze to blow!

His ship mates cry out against the ancient Mariner, for killing the bird of good luck.

Nor dim nor red, like God's own head,
The glorious Sun uprist:
Then all averred, I had killed the bird
That brought the fog and mist.

But when the fog cleared off, they justify the same—and thus make themselves accomplices in the crime.

[1] *ken* Recognize.

[2] *swound* Swoon.

[3] *vespers nine* I.e., nine evenings. Vespers are evening prayers.

'Twas right, said they, such birds to slay,
That bring the fog and mist.

The fair breeze continues.

The fair breeze blew, the white foam flew,
The furrow followed free;
We were the first that ever burst
Into that silent sea.

The ship enters the Pacific Ocean and sails northward, even till it reaches the Line.

Down dropt the breeze, the sails dropt down,
'Twas sad as sad could be;
And we did speak only to break
The silence of the sea!

The ship hath been suddenly becalmed.

All in a hot and copper sky,
The bloody Sun, at noon,
Right up above the mast did stand,
No bigger than the Moon.

Day after day, day after day,
We stuck, nor breath nor motion;
As idle as a painted ship
Upon a painted ocean.

And the Albatross begins to be avenged.

Water, water, every where,
And all the boards did shrink;
Water, water, every where,
Nor any drop to drink.

The very deep did rot: O Christ!
That ever this should be!
Yea, slimy things did crawl with legs
Upon the slimy sea.

About, about, in reel and rout
The death-fires[1] danced at night;
The water, like a witch's oils,
Burnt green, and blue and white.

A spirit has followed them; one of the invisible inhabitants of this planet, neither departed souls nor angels; concerning whom the learned Jew, Josephus [continued ...] and the Platonic Constantinopolitan, Micha Psellus, may be consulted, and there is no climate or element without one or more.

And some in dreams assuréd were
Of the Spirit that plagued us so;
Nine fathom deep he had followed us
From the land of mist and snow.

And every tongue, through utter drought,
Was withered at the root;
We could not speak, no more than if
We had been choked with soot.

The shipmates in their sore distress, would fain throw the whole guilt on the ancient Mariner; in sign where of they hang the dead seabird round his neck

Ah! well a-day! what evil looks
Had I from old and young!
Instead of the cross, the Albatross
About my neck was hung.

PART 3

There passed a weary time. Each throat
Was parched, and glazed each eye.
A weary time! a weary time!
How glazed each weary eye,
When looking westward, I beheld
A something in the sky.

The ancient Mariner beholdeth a sign in the element afar off.

At first it seemed a little speck,
And then it seemed a mist;
It moved and moved, and took at last
A certain shape, I wist.

A speck, a mist, a shape, I wist!
And still it neared and neared:
And as if it dodged a water-sprite,
It plunged and tacked and veered.

At its nearer approach, it seemeth him to be a ship; and at a dear ransom he freeth his speech from the bonds o thirst.

With throat unslacked, with black lips baked,
We could nor laugh nor wail;
Through utter drought all dumb we stood!
I bit my arm, I sucked the blood,
And cried, A sail! a sail!

With throat unslacked, with black lips
    baked,
Agape they heard me call:
Gramercy![2] they for joy did grin,

[1] *death-fires* Possibly luminescent plankton.

[2] *Gramercy* Grant mercy, i.e., may God reward you in his mercy.

A flash of joy.

And all at once their breath drew in,
As they were drinking all.

And horror follows. For can it be a *ship* that comes onward without wind or tide?

See! see! (I cried) she tacks no more!
Hither to work us weal;[1]
Without a breeze, without a tide,
She steadies with upright keel!

The western wave was all a-flame.
The day was well nigh done!
Almost upon the western wave
Rested the broad bright Sun;
When that strange shape drove suddenly
Betwixt us and the Sun.

It seemeth him but the skeleton of a ship.

And straight the Sun was flecked with bars,
(Heaven's Mother send us grace!)
As if through a dungeon-grate he peered
With broad and burning face.

And its ribs are seen as bars on the face of the setting Sun. The spectre-woman and her death-mate, and no other board the skeleton-ship.

Alas! (thought I, and my heart beat loud)
How fast she nears and nears!
Are those *her* sails that glance in the Sun,
Like restless gossameres?

Are those *her* ribs through which the Sun
Did peer, as through a grate?
And is that Woman all her crew?
Is that a DEATH? and are there two?
Is DEATH that woman's mate?

Like vessel, like crew! Death and Life-in-Death have diced for the ship's crew, and she (the latter) winneth the ancient Mariner.

Her lips were red, *her* looks were free,
Her locks were yellow as gold:
Her skin was as white as leprosy,
The Night-mare LIFE-IN-DEATH was she,
Who thicks man's blood with cold.

The naked hulk alongside came,
And the twain were casting dice;
"The game is done! I've won! I've won!"
Quoth she, and whistles thrice.

No twilight within the courts of the sun.

The Sun's rim dips; the stars rush out:
At one stride comes the dark;
With far-heard whisper, o'er the sea,
Off shot the spectre-bark.

At the rising of the Moon,

We listened and looked sideways up!
Fear at my heart, as at a cup,
My life-blood seemed to sip!
The stars were dim, and thick the night,
The steersman's face by his lamp gleamed white;
From the sails the dews did drip—
Till clomb above the eastern bar
The hornéd Moon, with one bright star
Within the nether tip.

One after another,

One after one, by the star-dogged Moon
Too quick for groan or sigh,
Each turned his face with a ghastly pang,
And cursed me with his eye.

His ship-mates drop down dead.

Four times fifty living men,
(And I heard nor sigh nor groan)
With heavy thump, a lifeless lump,
They dropped down one by one.

But Life-in-Death begins her work on the ancient Mariner.

The souls did from their bodies fly,—
They fled to bliss or woe!
And every soul, it passed me by,
Like the whiz of my cross-bow!

Part 4

The wedding-guest feareth that a spirit is talking to him;

"I fear thee, ancient Mariner!
I fear thy skinny hand!
And thou art long, and lank, and brown,
As is the ribbed sea-sand.[2]

I fear thee and thy glittering eye,
And thy skinny hand, so brown."—

[1] *work us weal* Benefit us.

[2] [Coleridge's note] For the two last lines of this stanza, I am indebted to Mr. WORDSWORTH. It was on a delightful walk from Nether Stowey to Dulverton, with him and his sister, in the Autumn of 1797, that this Poem was planned, and in part composed.

Fear not, fear not, thou Wedding-Guest!
This body dropt not down.

But the ancient Mariner assureth him of his bodily life, and proceedeth to relate his horrible penance.

Alone, alone, all, all alone,
Alone on a wide wide sea!
And never a saint took pity on
My soul in agony.

He despiseth the creatures of the calm,

The many men, so beautiful!
And they all dead did lie:
And a thousand thousand slimy things
Lived on; and so did I.

And envieth that they should live, and so many lie dead.

I looked upon the rotting sea,
And drew my eyes away;
I looked upon the rotting deck,
And there the dead men lay.

I looked to heaven, and tried to pray;
But or ever a prayer had gusht,
A wicked whisper came, and made
My heart as dry as dust.

I closed my lids, and kept them close,
And the balls like pulses beat;
For the sky and the sea, and the sea and the sky
Lay like a load on my weary eye,
And the dead were at my feet.

But the curse liveth for him in the eye of the dead men.

The cold sweat melted from their limbs,
Nor rot nor reek did they:
The look with which they looked on me
Had never passed away.

In his loneliness and fixedness, he yearneth towards the journeying Moon, and the stars that still sojourn, yet still move onwards; and every where [continued …] the blue sky belongs to them, and in their appointed rest, and their native country, and their own natural homes, which they enter unannounced, as lords that are certain expected, and yet there is a silent joy at their arrival.

An orphan's curse would drag to hell
A spirit from on high;
But oh! more horrible than that
Is the curse in a dead man's eye!
Seven days, seven nights, I saw that curse,
And yet I could not die.

The moving Moon went up the sky,
And no where did abide:
Softly she was going up,
And a star or two beside—

Her beams bemocked the sultry main,
Like April hoar-frost spread;
But where the ship's huge shadow lay,
The charméd water burnt alway
A still and awful red.

Beyond the shadow of the ship,
I watched the water-snakes:
They moved in tracks of shining white,
And when they reared, the elfish light
Fell off in hoary flakes.

By the light of the Moon he beholdeth God's creatures of the great calm.

Within the shadow of the ship
I watched their rich attire:
Blue, glossy green, and velvet black,
They coiled and swam; and every track
Was a flash of golden fire.

Their beauty and their happiness.

He blesseth them in his heart.

O happy living things! no tongue
Their beauty might declare:
A spring of love gushed from my heart,
And I blessed them unaware:
Sure my kind saint took pity on me,
And I blessed them unaware.

The spell begins to break.

The selfsame moment I could pray;
And from my neck so free
The Albatross fell off, and sank
Like lead into the sea.

Part 5

Oh sleep! it is a gentle thing,
Beloved from pole to pole!
To Mary Queen the praise be given!
She sent the gentle sleep from Heaven,
That slid into my soul.

The silly[1] buckets on the deck,
That had so long remained,
I dreamt that they were filled with dew;
And when I awoke, it rained.

By grace of the holy Mother, the ancient Mariner is refreshed with rain.

My lips were wet, my throat was cold,
My garments all were dank;
Sure I had drunken in my dreams,
And still my body drank.

I moved, and could not feel my limbs:
I was so light—almost
I thought that I had died in sleep,
And was a blesséd ghost.

And soon I heard a roaring wind:
It did not come anear;
But with its sound it shook the sails,
That were so thin and sere.

He heareth sounds, and seeth strange sights and commotions in the sky and the elements.

The upper air burst into life!
And a hundred fire-flags sheen,
To and fro they were hurried about!
And to and fro, and in and out,
The wan stars danced between.

And the coming wind did roar more loud,
And the sails did sigh like sedge;
And the rain poured down from one black cloud;
The Moon was at its edge.

The thick black cloud was cleft, and still
The Moon was at its side:
Like waters shot from some high crag,
The lightning fell with never a jag,
A river steep and wide.

The loud wind never reached the ship,
Yet now the ship moved on!
Beneath the lightning and the Moon
The dead men gave a groan.

The bodies of the ship's crew are inspirited, and the ship moves on;

They groaned, they stirred, they all uprose,
Nor spake, nor moved their eyes;
It had been strange, even in a dream,
To have seen those dead men rise.

The helmsman steered, the ship moved on;
Yet never a breeze up-blew;
The mariners all 'gan work the ropes,
Where they were wont to do;
They raised their limbs like lifeless tools—
We were a ghastly crew.

The body of my brother's son
Stood by me, knee to knee:
The body and I pulled at one rope,
But he said nought to me.

"I fear thee, ancient Mariner!"
Be calm, thou Wedding-Guest!
'Twas not those souls that fled in pain,
Which to their corses[2] came again,
But a troop of spirits blest:

But not by the souls of the men, nor by dæmons of earth or middle air, but by a blessed troop of angelic spirits, sent down by the invocation of the guardian saint.

For when it dawned—they dropped their arms,
And clustered round the mast;
Sweet sounds rose slowly through their mouths,
And from their bodies passed.

Around, around, flew each sweet sound,
Then darted to the Sun;
Slowly the sounds came back again,
Now mixed, now one by one.

Sometimes a-dropping from the sky
I heard the sky-lark sing;
Sometimes all little birds that are,
How they seemed to fill the sea and air
With their sweet jargoning!

And now 'twas like all instruments,
Now like a lonely flute;

[1] *silly* Simple.

[2] *corses* Corpses.

And now it is an angel's song,
That makes the heavens be mute.

It ceased; yet still the sails made on
A pleasant noise till noon,
A noise like of a hidden brook
In the leafy month of June,
That to the sleeping woods all night
Singeth a quiet tune.

Till noon we quietly sailed on,
Yet never a breeze did breathe:
Slowly and smoothly went the ship,
Moved onward from beneath.

The lonesome spirit from the south-pole carries on the ship as far as the line, in obedience to the angelic troop, but still requireth vengeance.

Under the keel nine fathom deep,
From the land of mist and snow,
The spirit slid: and it was he
That made the ship to go.
The sails at noon left off their tune,
And the ship stood still also.

The Sun, right up above the mast,
Had fixed her to the ocean:
But in a minute she 'gan stir,
With a short uneasy motion—
Backwards and forwards half her length
With a short uneasy motion.

Then like a pawing horse let go,
She made a sudden bound:
It flung the blood into my head,
And I fell down in a swound.

How long in that same fit I lay,
I have not to declare;
But ere my living life returned,
I heard and in my soul discerned
Two voices in the air.

The Polar Spirit's fellow-dæmons, the invisible inhabitants of the element, take part in his wrong; and two of them relate, one to the other, that penance long and heavy for the ancient Mariner hath been accorded to the Polar Spirit, who returned southward.

"Is it he?" quoth one, "Is this the man?
By Him who died on cross,
With his cruel bow he laid full low
The harmless Albatross.

The spirit who bideth by himself
In the land of mist and snow,
He loved the bird that loved the man
Who shot him with his bow."

The other was a softer voice,
As soft as honey-dew:
Quoth he, "The man hath penance done,
And penance more will do."

PART 6

FIRST VOICE

"But tell me, tell me! speak again,
Thy soft response renewing—
What makes that ship drive on so fast?
What is the ocean doing?"

SECOND VOICE

"Still as a slave before his lord,
The ocean hath no blast;
His great bright eye most silently
Up to the Moon is cast—

If he may know which way to go;
For she guides him smooth or grim.
See, brother, see! how graciously
She looketh down on him."

FIRST VOICE

"But why drives on that ship so fast,
Without or wave or wind?"

SECOND VOICE

"The air is cut away before,
And closes from behind.

Fly, brother, fly! more high, more high!
Or we shall be belated:
For slow and slow that ship will go,
When the Mariner's trance is abated."

The Mariner hath been cast into a trance; for the angelic power causeth the vessel to drive north-ward, faster than human life could endure.

I woke, and we were sailing on
As in a gentle weather:
'Twas night, calm night, the Moon was high;
The dead men stood together.

The supernatural motion is retarded; the Mariner awakes, and his penance begins anew.

All stood together on the deck,
For a charnel-dungeon[1] fitter:
All fixed on me their stony eyes,
That in the Moon did glitter.

The pang, the curse, with which they died,
Had never passed away:
I could not draw my eyes from theirs,
Nor turn them up to pray.

The curse is finally expiated.

And now this spell was snapt: once more
I viewed the ocean green,
And looked far forth, yet little saw
Of what had else been seen—

Like one, that on a lonesome road
Doth walk in fear and dread,
And having once turned round, walks on,
And turns no more his head;
Because he knows, a frightful fiend
Doth close behind him tread.

But soon there breathed a wind on me,
Nor sound nor motion made:
Its path was not upon the sea,
In ripple or in shade.

It raised my hair, it fanned my cheek
Like a meadow-gale of spring—
It mingled strangely with my fears,
Yet it felt like a welcoming.

Swiftly, swiftly flew the ship,
Yet she sailed softly too:
Sweetly, sweetly blew the breeze—
On me alone it blew.

And the ancient Mariner beholdeth his native country.

Oh! dream of joy! is this indeed
The light-house top I see?
Is this the hill? is this the kirk?
Is this mine own countree?

We drifted o'er the harbour-bar,
And I with sobs did pray—
O let me be awake, my God!
Or let me sleep alway.

The harbour-bay was clear as glass,
So smoothly was it strewn!
And on the bay the moonlight lay,
And the shadow of the Moon.

The rock shone bright, the kirk no less,
That stands above the rock:
The moonlight steeped in silentness
The steady weathercock.

The angelic spirits leave the dead bodies,

And the bay was white with silent light,
Till rising from the same,
Full many shapes, that shadows were,
In crimson colours came.

And appear in their own forms of light.

A little distance from the prow
Those crimson shadows were:
I turned my eyes upon the deck—
Oh, Christ! what saw I there!

Each corse lay flat, lifeless and flat,
And, by the holy rood!
A man all light, a seraph-man,[2]
On every corse there stood.

---

[1] *charnel-dungeon* Mortuary; house of death.

[2] *rood* Cross; *seraph-man* Angel.

This seraph-band, each waved his hand:
It was a heavenly sight!
They stood as signals to the land,
Each one a lovely light;

This seraph-band, each waved his hand,
No voice did they impart—
No voice; but oh! the silence sank
Like music on my heart.

But soon I heard the dash of oars,
I heard the Pilot's cheer;
My head was turned perforce away
And I saw a boat appear.

The Pilot and the Pilot's boy,
I heard them coming fast:
Dear Lord in Heaven! it was a joy
The dead men could not blast.

I saw a third—I heard his voice:
It is the Hermit good!
He singeth loud his godly hymns
That he makes in the wood.
He'll shrieve[1] my soul, he'll wash away
The Albatross's blood.

Part 7

The Hermit of the Wood.

This Hermit good lives in that wood
Which slopes down to the sea.
How loudly his sweet voice he rears!
He loves to talk with marineres
That come from a far countree.

He kneels at morn, and noon, and eve—
He hath a cushion plump:
It is the moss that wholly hides
The rotted old oak-stump.

The skiff-boat neared: I heard them talk,
"Why, this is strange, I trow![2]
Where are those light so many and fair,
That signal made but now?"

Approacheth the ship with wonder.

"Strange, by my faith!" the Hermit said—
"And they answered not our cheer!
The planks look warped! and see those sails,
How thin they are and sere!
I never saw aught like to them,
Unless perchance it were

Brown skeletons of leaves that lag
My forest-brook along;
When the ivy-tod[3] is heavy with snow,
And the owlet whoops to the wolf below,
That eats the she-wolf's young."

"Dear Lord! it hath a fiendish look"—
(The Pilot made reply)
"I am a-feared"—"Push on, push on!"
Said the Hermit cheerily.

The boat came closer to the ship,
But I nor spake nor stirred;
The boat came close beneath the ship,
And straight a sound was heard.

The ship suddenly sinketh.

Under the water it rumbled on,
Still louder and more dread:
It reached the ship, it split the bay;
The ship went down like lead.

The ancient Mariner is saved in the Pilot's boat.

Stunned by that loud and dreadful sound,
Which sky and ocean smote,
Like one that hath been seven days drowned
My body lay afloat;
But swift as dreams, myself I found
Within the Pilot's boat.

Upon the whirl, where sank the ship,
The boat spun round and round;
And all was still, save that the hill
Was telling of the sound.

[1] *shrieve* Give absolution to.

[2] *trow* Believe.

[3] *ivy-tod* Bush.

I moved my lips—the Pilot shrieked
And fell down in a fit;
The holy Hermit raised his eyes,
And prayed where he did sit.

I took the oars: the Pilot's boy,
Who now doth crazy go,
Laughed loud and long, and all the while
His eyes went to and fro.
"Ha! ha!" quoth he, "full plain I see,
The Devil knows how to row."

And now, all in my own countree,
I stood on the firm land!
The Hermit stepped forth from the boat,
And scarcely he could stand.

"O shrieve me, shrieve me, holy man!"
The Hermit crossed his brow.
"Say quick," quoth he, "I bid thee say—
What manner of man art thou?"

The ancient Mariner earnestly entreateth the Hermit to shrieve him; and the penance of life falls on him.

Forthwith this frame of mine was wrenched
With a woful agony,
Which forced me to begin my tale;
And then it left me free.

Since then, at an uncertain hour,
That agony returns;
And till my ghastly tale is told,
This heart within me burns.

And ever and anon throughout his future life an agony constraineth him to travel from land to land.

I pass, like night, from land to land;
I have strange power of speech;
That moment that his face I see,
I know the man that must hear me:
To him my tale I teach.

What loud uproar bursts from that door!
The wedding-guests are there:
But in the garden-bower the bride
And bride-maids singing are:
And hark the little vesper bell,
Which biddeth me to prayer!

O Wedding-Guest! this soul hath been
Alone on a wide wide sea:
So lonely 'twas, that God Himself
Scarce seemèd there to be.

O sweeter than the marriage-feast,
'Tis sweeter far to me,
To walk together to the kirk
With a goodly company!—

To walk together to the kirk,
And all together pray,
While each to his great Father bends,
Old men, and babes, and loving friends
And youth and maidens gay!

Farewell, farewell! but this I tell
To thee, thou Wedding-Guest!
He prayeth well, who loveth well
Both man and bird and beast.

And to teach by his own example, love and reverence to all things that God made and loveth.

He prayeth best, who loveth best
All things both great and small;
For the dear God who loveth us,
He made and loveth all.

The Mariner, whose eye is bright,
Whose beard with age is hoar,[1]
Is gone: and now the Wedding-Guest
Turned from the bridegroom's door.

He went like one that hath been stunned,
And is of sense forlorn:
A sadder and a wiser man,
He rose the morrow morn.

—1817 (EARLIER VERSION PUBLISHED 1798)

[1] *hoar* White, as with frost (hoarfrost).

IN CONTEXT

The Origin of "The Rime of the Ancient Mariner"

from Samuel Taylor Coleridge, *Biographia Literaria*, Chapter 14 (1817)

Almost twenty years after the first publication of "The Rime of the Ancient Mariner," Coleridge gave the following account of the poem's origin and composition.

During the first year that Mr. Wordsworth and I were neighbours, our conversations turned frequently on the two cardinal points of poetry, the power of exciting the sympathy of the reader by a faithful adherence to the truth of nature, and the power of giving the interest of novelty by the modifying colours of imagination. The sudden charm, which accidents of light and shade, which moonlight or sunset diffused over a known and familiar landscape, appeared to represent the practicability of combining both. These are the poetry of nature. The thought suggested itself (to which of us I do not recollect) that a series of poems might be composed of two sorts. In the one, the incidents and agents were to be, in part at least supernatural; and the excellence aimed at was to consist in the interesting of the affections by the dramatic truth of such emotions, as would naturally accompany such situations, supposing them real. And real in *this* sense they have been to every human being who, from whatever source of delusion, has at any time believed himself under supernatural agency. For the second class, subjects were to be chosen from ordinary life; the characters and incidents were to be such, as will be found in every village and its vicinity where there is a meditative and feeling mind to seek after them, or to notice them, when they present themselves. In this idea originated the plan of the *Lyrical Ballads*; in which it was agreed, that my endeavours should be directed to persons and characters supernatural, or at least romantic; yet so as to transfer from our inward nature a human interest and a semblance of truth sufficient to procure for these shadows of imagination that willing suspension of disbelief for the moment, which constitutes poetic faith. Mr. Wordsworth, on the other hand, was to propose to himself as his object, to give the charm of novelty to things of every day, and to excite a feeling analogous to the supernatural, by awakening the mind's attention from the lethargy of custom, and directing it to the loveliness and the wonders of the world before us; an inexhaustible treasure, but for which, in consequence of the film of familiarity and selfish solicitude we have eyes, yet see not, and hearts that neither feel or understand. With this view I wrote "The Ancient Mariner," and was preparing among other poems, "The Dark Ladie," and the "Christabel" in which I should have more nearly realized my ideal than I had done in my first attempt.

from A Letter from the Reverend Alexander Dyce to Hartley Coleridge (1852)

In this letter to Samuel Taylor Coleridge's eldest son, Hartley, the Reverend Alexander Dyce quotes Wordsworth as saying the following about the inception of "The Rime of the Ancient Mariner":

"The Ancient Mariner" was founded on a strange dream, which a friend of Coleridge had, who fancied he saw a skeleton ship, with figures in it. We had both determined to write some poetry for a monthly magazine, the profits of which were to defer the expenses of a little excursion we were to make together. "The Ancient Mariner" was intended for this periodical, but was too long. I had very little share in the composition of it, for I soon found the style of Coleridge and myself would not assimilate. Beside the lines (in the fourth part) "And thou art long, and lank, and brown, / As in the ribbed sea-sand—" I wrote the stanza (in the first part) "He holds him with his glittering eye— / The Wedding-Guest stood still, / And listens like a three-years child: / The Mariner hath his will" and four or five lines more in different parts of the poem, which I could not now point out. The idea of shooting an albatross was mine; for I had been reading *Shelvocke's Voyages*, which probably Coleridge never saw. I also suggested the reanimation of the dead bodies, to work the ship.

This Lime-Tree Bower My Prison[1]

Addressed to Charles Lamb,
Of the India House, London

Well, they are gone, and here must I remain,
This lime-tree bower my prison! I have lost
Beauties and feelings, such as would have been
Most sweet to my remembrance even when age
Had dimm'd mine eyes to blindness! They, meanwhile,
Friends, whom I never more may meet again,
On springy heath, along the hill-top edge,
Wander in gladness, and wind down, perchance,
To that still roaring dell, of which I told;
The roaring dell, o'erwooded, narrow, deep,
And only speckled by the mid-day sun;
Where its slim trunk the ash from rock to rock
Flings arching like a bridge;—that branchless ash,
Unsunn'd and damp, whose few poor yellow leaves
Ne'er tremble in the gale, yet tremble still,
Fann'd by the water-fall! and there my friends
Behold the dark green file of long lank weeds,[2]
That all at once (a most fantastic sight!)
Still nod and drip beneath the dripping edge
Of the blue clay-stone.

Now, my friends emerge
Beneath the wide wide Heaven—and view again
The many-steepled tract magnificent
Of hilly fields and meadows, and the sea,
With some fair bark, perhaps, whose sails light up
The slip of smooth clear blue betwixt two Isles
Of purple shadow! Yes! they wander on
In gladness all; but thou, methinks, most glad,
My gentle-hearted Charles! for thou hast pined
And hunger'd after Nature, many a year,
In the great City pent, winning thy way

[1] [Coleridge's note] In the June of 1797 some long-expected friends [Charles Lamb and William and Dorothy Wordsworth] paid a visit to the author's cottage; and on the morning of their arrival, he met with an accident, which disabled him from walking during the whole time of their stay. One evening, when they had left him for a few hours, he composed the following lines in the garden-bower.

[2] [Coleridge's note] The *Asplenium Scolopendrium*, called in some countries the Adder's Tongue, in others the Hart's Tongue, but Withering gives the Adder's Tongue as the trivial name of the *Ophioglossum* only.

With sad yet patient soul, through evil and pain
And strange calamity![1] Ah! slowly sink
Behind the western ridge, thou glorious Sun!
Shine in the slant beams of the sinking orb,
Ye purple heath-flowers! richlier burn, ye clouds!
Live in the yellow light, ye distant groves!
And kindle, thou blue Ocean! So my friend
Struck with deep joy may stand, as I have stood,
Silent with swimming sense; yea, gazing round
On the wide landscape, gaze till all doth seem
Less gross than bodily; and of such hues
As veil the Almighty Spirit, when yet he makes
Spirits perceive his presence.

A delight
Comes sudden on my heart, and I am glad
As I myself were there! Nor in this bower,
This little lime-tree bower, have I not mark'd
Much that has sooth'd me. Pale beneath the blaze
Hung the transparent foliage; and I watch'd
Some broad and sunny leaf, and lov'd to see
The shadow of the leaf and stem above
Dappling its sunshine! And that walnut-tree
Was richly ting'd, and a deep radiance lay
Full on the ancient ivy, which usurps
Those fronting elms, and now, with blackest mass
Makes their dark branches gleam a lighter hue
Through the late twilight: and though now the bat
Wheels silent by, and not a swallow twitters,
Yet still the solitary humble-bee
Sings in the bean-flower! Henceforth I shall know
That Nature ne'er deserts the wise and pure;
No plot so narrow, be but Nature there,
No waste so vacant, but may well employ
Each faculty of sense, and keep the heart
Awake to Love and Beauty! and sometimes
'Tis well to be bereft of promis'd good,
That we may lift the soul, and contemplate
With lively joy the joys we cannot share.
My gentle-hearted Charles! when the last rook
Beat its straight path along the dusky air
Homewards, I blest it! deeming its black wing
(Now a dim speck, now vanishing in light)
Had cross'd the mighty Orb's dilated glory,
While thou stood'st gazing; or, when all was still,
Flew creeking o'er thy head, and had a charm[2]
For thee, my gentle-hearted Charles, to whom
No sound is dissonant which tells of Life.
—1800

[1] *strange calamity* Charles Lamb's sister Mary, who suffered from periods of insanity, had fatally stabbed their mother.

Christabel

Preface

The first part of the following poem was written in the year 1797, at Stowey, in the county of Somerset. The second part, after my return from Germany, in the year 1800, at Keswick, Cumberland. Since the latter date, my poetic powers have been, till very lately, in a state of suspended animation. But as, in my very first conception of the tale, I had the whole present to my mind, with the wholeness, no less than with the liveliness of a vision; I trust that I shall be able to embody in verse the three parts yet to come, in the course of the present year.

It is probable that if the poem had been finished at either of the former periods, or if even the first and second part had been published in the year 1800, the impression of its originality would have been much greater than I dare at present expect. But for this, I have only my own indolence to blame. The dates are mentioned for the exclusive purpose of precluding charges of plagiarism or servile imitation from myself. For there is among us a set of critics, who seem to hold, that every possible thought and image is traditional; who have no notion that there are such things as fountains in the world, small as well as great; and who would therefore charitably derive every rill[3] they behold flowing from a

[2] [Coleridge's note] Some months after I had written this line, it gave me pleasure to find that Bartram had observed the same circumstance of the Savanna Crane. "When these Birds move their wings in flight, their strokes are slow, moderate and regular; and even when at a considerable distance or high above us, we plainly hear the quill-feathers: their shafts and webs upon one another creak as the joints or working of a vessel in a tempestuous sea."

[3] *rill* Brook.

perforation made in some other man's tank. I am confident however, that as far as the present poem is concerned, the celebrated poets whose writings I might be suspected of having imitated,[1] either in particular passages, or in the tone and the spirit of the whole, would be among the first to vindicate me from the charge, and who, on any striking coincidence, would permit me to address them in this doggerel version of two monkish Latin hexameters:

> 'Tis mine and it is likewise yours,
> But an if this will not do;
> Let it be mine, good friend! for I
> Am the poorer of the two.

I have only to add, that the metre of the Christabel is not, properly speaking, irregular, though it may seem so from its being founded on a new principle: namely, that of counting in each line the accents, not the syllables. Though the latter may vary from seven to twelve, yet in each line the accents will be found to be only four. Nevertheless this occasional variation in the number of syllables is not introduced wantonly, or for the mere ends of convenience, but in correspondence with some transition in the nature of the imagery or passion.

Part I

'Tis the middle of night by the castle clock,
And the owls have awakened the crowing cock;
Tu—whit!—Tu—whoo!
And hark, again! the crowing cock,
How drowsily it crew.

Sir Leoline, the Baron rich,
Hath a toothless mastiff bitch;
From her kennel beneath the rock
She maketh answer to the clock,
Four for the quarters, and twelve for the hour;
Ever and aye,° by shine and shower, *always*
Sixteen short howls, not over loud;
Some say, she sees my lady's shroud.

Is the night chilly and dark?
The night is chilly, but not dark.
The thin gray cloud is spread on high,
It covers but not hides the sky.
The moon is behind, and at the full;
And yet she looks both small and dull.
The night is chill, the cloud is gray:
'Tis a month before the month of May,
And the Spring comes slowly up this way.

The lovely lady, Christabel,
Whom her father loves so well,
What makes her in the wood so late,
A furlong from the castle gate?
She had dreams all yesternight
Of her own betrothéd knight;
And she in the midnight wood will pray
For the weal° of her lover that's far away. *well-being*

She stole along, she nothing spoke,
The sighs she heaved were soft and low,
And naught was green upon the oak
But moss and rarest misletoe:[2]
She kneels beneath the huge oak tree,
And in silence prayeth she.

The lady sprang up suddenly,
The lovely lady, Christabel!
It moaned as near, as near can be,
But what it is she cannot tell.—
On the other side it seems to be,
Of the huge, broad-breasted, old oak tree.

The night is chill; the forest bare;
Is it the wind that moaneth bleak?
There is not wind enough in the air
To move away the ringlet curl

[1] *celebrated poets … imitated* Lord Byron and Sir Walter Scott, both of whom had read "Christabel" in manuscript form and had been influenced by it in their own subsequent writings.

[2] *mistletoe* Plant considered sacred in ancient Britain when found growing on oak trees.

From the lovely lady's cheek—
There is not wind enough to twirl
The one red leaf, the last of its clan,
That dances as often as dance it can,
Hanging so light, and hanging so high,
On the topmost twig that looks up at the sky.

Hush, beating heart of Christabel!
Jesu, Maria, shield her well!
She folded her arms beneath her cloak,
And stole to the other side of the oak.
    What sees she there?

There she sees a damsel bright,
Dressed in a silken robe of white,
That shadowy in the moonlight shone:
The neck that made that white robe wan,
Her stately neck, and arms were bare;
Her blue-veined feet unsandal'd were,
And wildly glittered here and there
The gems entangled in her hair.
I guess, 'twas frightful there to see
A lady so richly clad as she—
Beautiful exceedingly!

Mary mother, save me now!
(Said Christabel,) And who art thou?

The lady strange made answer meet,
And her voice was faint and sweet:—
Have pity on my sore distress,
I scarce can speak for weariness:
Stretch forth thy hand, and have no fear!
Said Christabel, How camest thou here?
And the lady, whose voice was faint and sweet,
Did thus pursue her answer meet:—

My sire is of a noble line,
And my name is Geraldine:
Five warriors seized me yestermorn,
Me, even me, a maid forlorn:
They choked my cries with force and fright,
And tied me on a palfrey° white. *saddle horse*
The palfrey was as fleet as wind,
And they rode furiously behind.

They spurred amain,° their steeds were white: *forcefully*
And once we crossed the shade of night.
As sure as Heaven shall rescue me,
I have no thought what men they be;
Nor do I know how long it is
(For I have lain entranced, I wis°) *know*
Since one, the tallest of the five,
Took me from the palfrey's back,
A weary woman, scarce alive.
Some muttered words his comrades spoke:
He placed me underneath this oak;
He swore they would return with haste;
Whither they went I cannot tell—
I thought I heard, some minutes past,
Sounds as of a castle bell.
Stretch forth thy hand (thus ended she),
And help a wretched maid to flee.

Then Christabel stretched forth her hand,
And comforted fair Geraldine:
O well, bright dame! may you command
The service of Sir Leoline;
And gladly our stout° chivalry *fierce*
Will he send forth and friends withal
To guide and guard you safe and free
Home to your noble father's hall.

She rose: and forth with steps they passed
That strove to be, and were not, fast.
Her gracious stars the lady blest,
And thus spake on sweet Christabel:
All our household are at rest,
The hall is silent as the cell;
Sir Leoline is weak in health,
And may not well awakened be,
But we will move as if in stealth,
And I beseech your courtesy,
This night, to share your couch with me.

They crossed the moat, and Christabel
Took the key that fitted well;
A little door she opened straight,
All in the middle of the gate;
The gate that was ironed within and without,
Where an army in battle array had marched out.
The lady sank, belike through pain,
And Christabel with might and main
Lifted her up, a weary weight,
Over the threshold of the gate:
Then the lady rose again,
And moved, as she were not in pain.

So free from danger, free from fear,
They crossed the court: right glad they were.
And Christabel devoutly cried
To the Lady by her side,
Praise we the Virgin all divine
Who hath rescued thee from thy distress!
Alas, alas! said Geraldine,
I cannot speak for weariness.
So free from danger, free from fear,
They crossed the court: right glad they were.

Outside her kennel, the mastiff old
Lay fast asleep, in moonshine cold.
The mastiff old did not awake,
Yet she an angry moan did make!
And what can ail the mastiff bitch?
Never till now she uttered yell
Beneath the eye of Christabel.
Perhaps it is the owlet's scritch:
For what can aid the mastiff bitch?

They passed the hall, that echoes still
Pass as lightly as you will!
The brands° were flat, the brands were dying, *burning logs*
Amid their own white ashes lying;
But when the lady passed, there came
A tongue of light, a fit of flame;
And Christabel saw the lady's eye,
And nothing else saw she thereby,
Save the boss of the shield of Sir Leoline tall,
Which hung in a murky old niche in the wall.
O softly tread, said Christabel,
My father seldom sleepeth well.

Sweet Christabel her feet doth bare,
And jealous of the listening air
They steal their way from stair to stair,
Now in glimmer, and now in gloom,
And now they pass the Baron's room,
As still as death, with stifled breath!
And now have reached her chamber door;
And now doth Geraldine press down
The rushes of the chamber floor.

The moon shines dim in the open air,
And not a moonbeam enters here.
But they without its light can see
The chamber carved so curiously,
Carved with figures strange and sweet,
All made out of the carver's brain,
For a lady's chamber meet:° *suitable*
The lamp with twofold silver chain
Is fastened to an angel's feet.

The silver lamp burns dead and dim;
But Christabel the lamp will trim.
She trimmed the lamp, and made it bright,
And left it swinging to and fro,
While Geraldine, in wretched plight,
Sank down upon the floor below.

O weary lady, Geraldine,
I pray you, drink this cordial wine!
It is a wine of virtuous powers;
My mother made it of wild flowers.

And will your mother pity me,
Who am a maiden most forlorn?
Christabel answered—Woe is me!
She died the hour that I was born.
I have heard the gray-haired friar tell
How on her death-bed she did say,
That she should hear the castle-bell

Strike twelve upon my wedding-day.
O mother dear! that thou wert here!
I would, said Geraldine, she were!

But soon with altered voice, said she—
"Off, wandering mother! Peak and pine!
I have power to bid thee flee."
Alas! what ails poor Geraldine?
Why stares she with unsettled eye?
Can she the bodiless dead espy?
And why with hollow voice cries she,
"Off, woman, off! this hour is mine—
Though thou her guardian spirit be,
Off, woman, off! 'tis given to me."

Then Christabel knelt by the lady's side,
And raised to heaven her eyes so blue—
Alas! said she, this ghastly ride—
Dear lady! it hath wildered you!
The lady wiped her moist cold brow,
And faintly said, "'tis over now!"

Again the wild-flower wine she drank:
Her fair large eyes 'gan glitter bright,
And from the floor whereon she sank,
The lofty lady stood upright:
She was most beautiful to see,
Like a lady of a far countrée.

And thus the lofty lady spake—
"All they who live in the upper sky,
Do love you, holy Christabel!
And you love them, and for their sake
And for the good which me befell,
Even I in my degree will try,
Fair maiden, to requite you well.
But now unrobe yourself; for I
Must pray, ere yet in bed I lie."

Quoth Christabel, So let it be!
And as the lady bade, did she.
Her gentle limbs did she undress
And lay down in her loveliness.

But through her brain of weal and woe
So many thoughts moved to and fro,
That vain it were her lids to close;
So half-way from the bed she rose,
And on her elbow did recline
To look at the lady Geraldine.

Beneath the lamp the lady bowed,
And slowly rolled her eyes around;
Then drawing in her breath aloud,
Like one that shuddered, she unbound
The cincture° from beneath her breast: *girdle*
Her silken robe, and inner vest,
Dropt to her feet, and full in view,
Behold! her bosom, and half her side—
A sight to dream of, not to tell!
O shield her! shield sweet Christabel!

Yet Geraldine nor speaks nor stirs;
Ah! what a stricken look was hers!
Deep from within she seems half-way
To lift some weight with sick assay,° *attempt*
And eyes the maid and seeks delay;
Then suddenly as one defied
Collects herself in scorn and pride,
And lay down by the Maiden's side!—
And in her arms the maid she took,
Ah wel-a-day!
And with low voice and doleful look
These words did say:
"In the touch of this bosom there worketh a spell,
Which is lord of thy utterance, Christabel!
Thou knowest to-night, and wilt know to-morrow
This mark of my shame, this seal of my sorrow;
But vainly thou warrest,
For this is alone in
Thy power to declare,
That in the dim forest
Thou heard'st a low moaning,
And found'st a bright lady, surpassingly fair;
And didst bring her home with thee in love and in charity,
To shield her and shelter her from the damp air."

The Conclusion to Part 1

It was a lovely sight to see
The lady Christabel, when she
Was praying at the old oak tree.
    Amid the jaggéd shadows
    Of mossy leafless boughs,
    Kneeling in the moonlight,
    To make her gentle vows;
Her slender palms together prest,
Heaving sometimes on her breast;
Her face resigned to bliss or bale°— *grief*
Her face, oh call it fair not pale,
And both blue eyes more bright than clear.
Each about to have a tear.

With open eyes (ah, woe is me!)
Asleep, and dreaming fearfully,
Fearfully dreaming, yet, I wis,
Dreaming that alone, which is—
O sorrow and shame! Can this be she,
The lady, who knelt at the old oak tree?
And lo! the worker of these harms,
That holds the maiden in her arms,
Seems to slumber still and mild,
As a mother with her child.

A star hath set, a star hath risen,
O Geraldine! since arms of thine
Have been the lovely lady's prison.
O Geraldine! one hour was thine—
Thou'st had thy will! By tairn° and rill, *mountain pool*
The night-birds all that hour were still.
But now they are jubilant anew,
From cliff and tower, tu—whoo! tu—whoo!
Tu—whoo! tu—whoo! from wood and fell!° *hill*

And see! the lady Christabel
Gathers herself from out her trance;
Her limbs relax, her countenance
Grows sad and soft; the smooth thin lids
Close o'er her eyes; and tears she sheds—
Large tears that leave the lashes bright!
And oft the while she seems to smile
As infants at a sudden light!

Yea, she doth smile, and she doth weep,
Like a youthful hermitess,
Beauteous in a wilderness,
Who, praying always, prays in sleep.
And, if she move unquietly,
Perchance, 'tis but the blood so free
Comes back and tingles in her feet.
No doubt, she hath a vision sweet.
What if her guardian spirit 'twere,
What if she knew her mother near?
But this she knows, in joys and woes,
That saints will aid if men will call:
For the blue sky bends over all!

Part 2

Each matin° bell, the Baron saith, *morning*
Knells us back to a world of death.
These words Sir Leoline first said,
When he rose and found his lady dead:
These words Sir Leoline will say
Many a morn to his dying day!

And hence the custom and law began
That still at dawn the sacristan,° *church sexton*
Who duly pulls the heavy bell,
Five and forty beads° must tell° *rosary beads / count*
Between each stroke—a warning knell,
Which not a soul can choose but hear
From Bratha Head to Wyndermere.[1]

Saith Bracy the bard, So let it knell!
And let the drowsy sacristan
Still count as slowly as he can!
There is no lack of such, I ween,° *suppose*
As well fill up the space between.
In Langdale Pike and Witch's Lair,
And Dungeon-ghyll so foully rent,

[1] *Bratha Head … Wyndermere* In the Lake District.

With ropes of rock and bells of air
Three sinful sextons' ghosts are pent,
Who all give back, one after t'other,
The death-note to their living brother;
And oft too, by the knell offended,
Just as their one! two! three! is ended,
The devil mocks the doleful tale
With a merry peal from Borodale.

The air is still! through mist and cloud
That merry peal comes ringing loud;
And Geraldine shakes off her dread,
And rises lightly from the bed;
Puts on her silken vestments white,
And tricks her hair in lovely plight,[1]
And nothing doubting of her spell
Awakens the lady Christabel.
"Sleep you, sweet lady Christabel?
I trust that you have rested well."

And Christabel awoke and spied
The same who lay down by her side—
O rather say, the same whom she
Raised up beneath the old oak tree!
Nay, fairer yet! and yet more fair!
For she belike hath drunken deep
Of all the blessedness of sleep!
And while she spake, her looks, her air
Such gentle thankfulness declare,
That (so it seemed) her girded vests
Grew tight beneath her heaving breasts.
"Sure I have sinn'd!" said Christabel,
"Now heaven be praised if all be well!"
And in low faltering tones, yet sweet,
Did she the lofty lady greet
With such perplexity of mind
As dreams too lively leave behind.

So quickly she rose, and quickly arrayed
Her maiden limbs, and having prayed
That He, who on the cross did groan,
Might wash away her sins unknown,
She forthwith led fair Geraldine
To meet her sire, Sir Leoline.

The lovely maid and the lady tall
Are pacing both into the hall,
And pacing on through page and groom,
Enter the Baron's presence-room.

The Baron rose, and while he prest
His gentle daughter to his breast,
With cheerful wonder in his eyes
The lady Geraldine espies,
And gave such welcome to the same,
As might beseem so bright a dame!

But when he heard the lady's tale,
And when she told her father's name,
Why waxed Sir Leoline so pale,
Murmuring o'er the name again,
Lord Roland de Vaux of Tryermaine?

Alas! they had been friends in youth;
But whispering tongues can poison truth;
And constancy lives in realms above;
And life is thorny; and youth is vain;
And to be wroth with one we love,
Doth work like madness in the brain.
And thus it chanced, as I divine,
With Roland and Sir Leoline.
Each spake words of high disdain
And insult to his heart's best brother:
They parted—ne'er to meet again!
But never either found another
To free the hollow heart from paining—
They stood aloof, the scars remaining,
Like cliffs which had been rent asunder;
A dreary sea now flows between;—
But neither heat, nor frost, nor thunder,
Shall wholly do away, I ween,
The marks of that which once hath been.

Sir Leoline, a moment's space,
Stood gazing on the damsel's face:

[1] *plight* I.e., plait, or braid.

And the youthful Lord of Tryermaine
Came back upon his heart again.

O then the Baron forgot his age,
His noble heart swelled high with rage;
He swore by the wounds in Jesu's side,
He would proclaim it far and wide
With trump and solemn heraldry,
That they, who thus had wronged the dame,
Were base as spotted infamy!
"And if they dare deny the same,
My herald shall appoint a week,
And let the recreant traitors seek
My tourney° court—that there and then *tournament*
I may dislodge their reptile souls
From the bodies and forms of men!"
He spake: his eye in lightning rolls!
For the lady was ruthlessly seized; and he
kenned° *recognized*
In the beautiful lady the child of his friend!

And now the tears were on his face,
And fondly in his arms he took
Fair Geraldine, who met the embrace,
Prolonging it with joyous look.
Which when she viewed, a vision fell
Upon the soul of Christabel,
The vision of fear, the touch and pain!
She shrunk and shuddered, and saw again—
(Ah, woe is me! Was it for thee,
Thou gentle maid! such sights to see?)

Again she saw that bosom old,
Again she felt that bosom cold,
And drew in her breath with a hissing sound:
Whereat the Knight turned wildly round,
And nothing saw, but his own sweet maid
With eyes upraised, as one that prayed.

The touch, the sight, had passed away,
And in its stead that vision blest,
Which comforted her after-rest.
While in the lady's arms she lay,
Had put a rapture in her breast,
And on her lips and o'er her eyes
Spread smiles like light!
With new surprise,
"What ails then my belovéd child?"
The Baron said—His daughter mild
Made answer, "All will yet be well!"
I ween, she had no power to tell
Aught else: so mighty was the spell.

Yet he, who saw this Geraldine,
Had deemed her sure a thing divine:
Such sorrow with such grace she blended,
As if she feared she had offended
Sweet Christabel, that gentle maid!
And with such lowly tones she prayed,
She might be sent without delay
Home to her father's mansion.
"Nay!
Nay, by my soul!" said Leoline.
"Ho! Bracy the bard, the charge be thine!
Go thou, with music sweet and loud,
And take two steeds with trappings proud,
And take the youth whom thou lov'st best
To bear thy harp, and learn thy song,
And clothe you both in solemn vest,
And over the mountains haste along,
Lest wandering folk, that are abroad,
Detain you on the valley road.

"And when he has crossed the Irthing flood,
My merry bard! he hastes, he hastes
Up Knorren Moor, through Halegarth Wood,
And reaches soon that castle good
Which stands and threatens Scotland's wastes.

"Bard Bracy! bard Bracy! your horses are fleet,
Ye must ride up the hall, your music so sweet,
More loud than your horses' echoing feet!
And loud and loud to Lord Roland call,
Thy daughter is safe in Langdale hall!
Thy beautiful daughter is safe and free—
Sir Leoline greets thee thus through me!

He bids thee come without delay
With all thy numerous array
And take thy lovely daughter home:
And he will meet thee on the way
With all his numerous array
White with their panting palfreys' foam:
And, by mine honour! I will say,
That I repent me of the day
When I spake words of fierce disdain
To Roland de Vaux of Tryermaine!—
—For since that evil hour hath flown,
Many a summer's sun hath shone;
Yet ne'er found I a friend again
Like Roland de Vaux of Tryermaine."

The lady fell, and clasped his knees,
Her face upraised, her eyes o'erflowing;
And Bracy replied, with faltering voice,
His gracious hail on all bestowing!—
"Thy words, thou sire of Christabel,
Are sweeter than my harp can tell;
Yet might I gain a boon° of thee, *request*
This day my journey should not be,
So strange a dream hath come to me,
That I had vowed with music loud
To clear yon wood from thing unblest,
Warned by a vision in my rest!
For in my sleep I saw that dove,
That gentle bird, whom thou dost love,
And call'st by thy own daughter's name—
Sir Leoline! I saw the same
Fluttering, and uttering fearful moan,
Among the green herbs in the forest alone.
Which when I saw and when I heard,
I wonder'd what might ail the bird;
For nothing near it could I see,
Save the grass and herbs underneath the old tree.

"And in my dream methought I went
To search out what might there be found;
And what the sweet bird's trouble meant,
That thus lay fluttering on the ground.
I went and peered, and could descry
No cause for her distressful cry;
But yet for her dear lady's sake
I stooped, methought, the dove to take,
When lo! I saw a bright green snake
Coiled around its wings and neck.
Green as the herbs on which it couched,
Close by the dove's its head it crouched;
And with the dove it heaves and stirs,
Swelling its neck as she swelled hers!
I woke; it was the midnight hour,
The clock was echoing in the tower;
But though my slumber was gone by,
This dream it would not pass away—
It seems to live upon my eye!
And thence I vowed this self-same day,
With music strong and saintly song
To wander through the forest bare,
Lest aught unholy loiter there."

Thus Bracy said: the Baron, the while,
Half-listening heard him with a smile;
Then turned to Lady Geraldine,
His eyes made up of wonder and love;
And said in courtly accents fine,
"Sweet maid, Lord Roland's beauteous dove,
With arms more strong than harp or song,
Thy sire and I will crush the snake!"
He kissed her forehead as he spake,
And Geraldine in maiden wise,
Casting down her large bright eyes,
With blushing cheek and courtesy fine
She turned her from Sir Leoline;
Softly gathering up her train,
That o'er her right arm fell again;
And folded her arms across her chest,
And couched her head upon her breast,
And looked askance at Christabel—
Jesu, Maria, shield her well!

A snake's small eye blinks dull and shy;
And the lady's eyes they shrunk in her head,
Each shrunk up to a serpent's eye,
And with somewhat of malice, and more of dread,

At Christabel she looked askance!—
One moment—and the sight was fled!
But Christabel in dizzy trance
Stumbling on the unsteady ground
Shuddered aloud, with a hissing sound;
And Geraldine again turned round,
And like a thing, that sought relief,
Full of wonder and full of grief,
She rolled her large bright eyes divine
Wildly on Sir Leoline.

The maid, alas! her thoughts are gone,
She nothing sees—no sight but one!
The maid, devoid of guile and sin,
I know not how, in fearful wise,
So deeply had she drunken in
That look, those shrunken serpent eyes,
That all her features were resigned
To this sole image in her mind:
And passively did imitate
That look of dull and treacherous hate!
And thus she stood, in dizzy trance,
Still picturing that look askance
With forced unconscious sympathy
Full before her father's view—
As far as such a look could be
In eyes so innocent and blue!

And when the trance was o'er, the maid
Paused awhile, and inly prayed:
Then falling at the Baron's feet,
"By my mother's soul do I entreat
That thou this woman send away!"
She said: and more she could not say:
For what she knew she could not tell,
O'er-mastered by the mighty spell.

Why is thy cheek so wan and wild,
Sir Leoline? Thy only child
Lies at thy feet, thy joy, thy pride,
So fair, so innocent, so mild;
The same, for whom thy lady died!
O by the pangs of her dear mother
Think thou no evil of thy child!
For her, and thee, and for no other,
She prayed the moment ere she died:
Prayed that the babe for whom she died,
Might prove her dear lord's joy and pride!
That prayer her deadly pangs beguiled,
Sir Leoline!
And wouldst thou wrong thy only child,
Her child and thine?

Within the Baron's heart and brain
If thoughts, like these, had any share,
They only swelled his rage and pain,
And did but work confusion there.
His heart was cleft with pain and rage,
His cheeks they quivered, his eyes were wild,
Dishonored thus in his old age;
Dishonored by his only child,
And all his hospitality
To the wronged daughter of his friend
By more than woman's jealousy
Brought thus to a disgraceful end—
He rolled his eye with stern regard
Upon the gentle minstrel bard,
And said in tones abrupt, austere—
"Why, Bracy! dost thou loiter here?
I bade thee hence!" The bard obeyed;
And turning from his own sweet maid,
The agéd knight, Sir Leoline,
Led forth the lady Geraldine!

The Conclusion to Part 2

A little child, a limber elf,
Singing, dancing to itself,
A fairy thing with red round cheeks,
That always finds, and never seeks,
Makes such a vision to the sight
As fills a father's eyes with light;
And pleasures flow in so thick and fast
Upon his heart, that he at last
Must needs express his love's excess
With words of unmeant bitterness.

Perhaps 'tis pretty to force together
Thoughts so all unlike each other;
To mutter and mock a broken charm,
To dally with wrong that does no harm.
Perhaps 'tis tender too and pretty
At each wild word to feel within
A sweet recoil of love and pity.
And what, if in a world of sin
(O sorrow and shame should this be true!)
Such giddiness of heart and brain
Comes seldom save from rage and pain,
So talks as it's most used to do.
—1801

Dejection: An Ode[1]

> Late, late yestreen I saw the new Moon,
> With the old Moon in her arms;
> And I fear, I fear, my Master dear!
> We shall have a deadly storm.
>
> "Ballad of Sir Patrick Spence"[2]

1

Well! If the Bard was weather-wise, who made
The grand old ballad of Sir Patrick Spence,
This night, so tranquil now, will not go hence
Unroused by winds, that ply a busier trade
Than those which mould yon cloud in lazy flakes,
Or the dull sobbing draft, that moans and rakes
Upon the strings of this Æolian lute,[3]
Which better far were mute.
For lo! the New-moon winter-bright!
And overspread with phantom light,
(With swimming phantom light o'erspread
But rimmed and circled by a silver thread)
I see the old Moon in her lap, foretelling
The coming-on of rain and squally blast.
And oh! that even now the gust were swelling,
And the slant night-shower driving loud and fast!
Those sounds which oft have raised me, whilst they awed,
And sent my soul abroad,
Might now perhaps their wonted° impulse give, *usual*
Might startle this dull pain, and make it move and live!

2

A grief without a pang, void, dark, and drear,
A stifled, drowsy, unimpassioned grief,
Which finds no natural outlet, no relief,
In word, or sigh, or tear—
O Lady! in this wan and heartless mood,
To other thoughts by yonder throstle° woo'd, *song-thrush*
All this long eve, so balmy and serene,
Have I been gazing on the western sky,
And its peculiar tint of yellow green:
And still I gaze—and with how blank an eye!
And those thin clouds above, in flakes and bars,
That give away their motion to the stars;
Those stars, that glide behind them or between,
Now sparkling, now bedimmed, but always seen:
Yon crescent Moon, as fixed as if it grew
In its own cloudless, starless lake of blue;
I see them all so excellently fair,
I see, not feel, how beautiful they are!

3

My genial spirits fail;
And what can these avail
To lift the smothering weight from off my breast?
It were a vain endeavour,
Though I should gaze for ever
On that green light that lingers in the west:
I may not hope from outward forms to win
The passion and the life, whose fountains are within.

4

O Lady! we receive but what we give,
And in our life alone does Nature live:
Ours is her wedding-garment, ours her shroud!

---

[1] *Dejection: An Ode* Coleridge originally wrote this poem as a verse letter to Sara Hutchinson (Wordsworth's future sister-in-law), with whom he had fallen in love.

[2] *Ballad of Sir Patrick Spence* Anonymous; published in Thomas Percy's *Reliques of Ancient English Poetry* (1765).

[3] *Æolian lute* Musical instrument named after Æolus, Greek god of the winds; the music of the lute, or, rather, harp, is made by exposure to the wind passing through it.

And would we aught behold, of higher worth,
Than that inanimate cold world allowed
To the poor loveless ever-anxious crowd,
Ah! from the soul itself must issue forth
A light, a glory, a fair luminous cloud
Enveloping the Earth—
And from the soul itself must there be sent
A sweet and potent voice, of its own birth,
Of all sweet sounds the life and element!

5

O pure of heart! thou need'st not ask of me
What this strong music in the soul may be!
What, and wherein it doth exist,
This light, this glory, this fair luminous mist,
This beautiful and beauty-making power.
Joy, virtuous Lady! Joy that ne'er was given,
Save to the pure, and in their purest hour,
Life, and Life's effluence, cloud at once and shower,
Joy, Lady! is the spirit and the power,
Which wedding Nature to us gives in dower
A new Earth and new Heaven,
Undreamt of by the sensual and the proud—
Joy is the sweet voice, Joy the luminous cloud—
We in ourselves rejoice!
And thence flows all that charms or ear or sight,
All melodies the echoes of that voice,
All colours a suffusion from that light.

6

There was a time when, though my path was rough,
This joy within me dallied with distress,
And all misfortunes were but as the stuff
Whence Fancy made me dreams of happiness:
For hope grew round me, like the twining vine,
And fruits, and foliage, not my own, seemed mine.
But now afflictions bow me down to earth:
Nor care I that they rob me of my mirth;
But oh! each visitation
Suspends what nature gave me at my birth,
My shaping spirit of Imagination.
For not to think of what I needs must feel,
But to be still and patient, all I can;
And haply by abstruse research to steal
From my own nature all the natural man—
This was my sole resource, my only plan:
Till that which suits a part infects the whole,
And now is almost grown the habit of my soul.

7

Hence, viper thoughts, that coil around my mind,
Reality's dark dream!
I turn from you, and listen to the wind,
Which long has raved unnoticed. What a scream
Of agony by torture lengthened out
That lute sent forth! Thou Wind, that rav'st without,
Bare crag, or mountain-tairn,[1] or blasted tree,
Or pine-grove whither woodman never clomb,
Or lonely house, long held the witches' home,
Methinks were fitter instruments for thee,
Mad Lutanist! who in this month of showers,
Of dark-brown gardens, and of peeping flowers,
Mak'st Devils' yule, with worse than wintry song,
The blossoms, buds, and timorous leaves among.
Thou Actor, perfect in all tragic sounds!
Thou mighty Poet, e'en to frenzy bold!
What tell'st thou now about?
'Tis of the rushing of an host in rout,
With groans, of trampled men, with smarting wounds—
At once they groan with pain, and shudder with the cold!
But hush! there is a pause of deepest silence!
And all that noise, as of a rushing crowd,
With groans, and tremulous shudderings—all is over—
It tells another tale, with sounds less deep and loud!
A tale of less affright,
And tempered with delight,
As Otway's[2] self had framed the tender lay,—
'Tis of a little child
Upon a lonesome wild,

[1] [Coleridge's note] Tairn is a small lake, generally if not always applied to the lakes up in the mountains and which are the feeders of those in the valleys. This address to the Storm-wind will not appear extravagant to those who have heard it at night and in a mountainous country.

[2] *Otway* Thomas Otway (1652–85), English playwright known for his tragedies.

Not far from home, but she hath lost her way:
And now moans low in bitter grief and fear,
And now screams loud, and hopes to make her
    mother hear.

8

'Tis midnight, but small thoughts have I of sleep:
Full seldom may my friend such vigils keep!
Visit her, gentle Sleep! with wings of healing,
    And may this storm be but a mountain-birth,
May all the stars hang bright above her dwelling,
    Silent as though they watched the sleeping Earth!
        With light heart may she rise,
        Gay fancy, cheerful eyes,
    Joy lift her spirit, joy attune her voice;
To her may all things live, from the pole to pole,
Their life the eddying of her living soul!
    O simple spirit, guided from above,
Dear Lady! friend devoutest of my choice,
Thus mayest thou ever, evermore rejoice.
—1802

Phantom

All look and likeness caught from earth,
    All accident of kin and birth,
Had pass'd away. There was no trace
Of aught on that illumined face,
Upraised beneath the rifted° stone *cracked*
But of one spirit all her own—
She, she herself, and only she,
Shone through her body visibly.
—1805

Kubla Khan

Or, A Vision in a Dream. A Fragment[1]

In Xanadu did Kubla Khan
    A stately pleasure-dome decree:

---

[1] [Coleridge's note] The following fragment is here published at the request of a poet [Lord Byron] of great and deserved celebrity, and as far as the Author's own opinions are concerned, rather as a psychological curiosity, than on the ground of any supposed poetic merits.

In the summer of the year 1797, the Author, then in ill health, had retired to a lonely farmhouse between Porlock and Linton, on the Exmoor confines of Somerset and Devonshire. In consequence of a slight indisposition [dysentery], an anodyne [opium] had been prescribed, from the effects of which he fell asleep in his chair at the moment that he was reading the following sentence, or words of the same substance, in *Purchas's Pilgrimage* [i.e., *Purchas his Pilgrimage* (1613, 1614, 1617, 1626)]: "Here the Khan Kubla commanded a palace to be built, and a stately garden thereunto. And thus ten miles of fertile ground were inclosed with a wall." The author continued for about three hours in a profound sleep, at least of the external senses, during which time he has the most vivid confidence, that he could not have composed less than from two to three hundred lines, if that indeed can be called composition in which all the images rose up before him as things, with a parallel production of the correspondent expressions, without any sensation or consciousness of effort. On awaking he appeared to himself to have a distinct recollection of the whole, and taking his pen, ink, and paper, instantly and eagerly wrote down the lines that are here preserved. At this moment he was unfortunately called out by a person on business from Porlock, and detained by him above an hour, and on his return to his room, found to his no small surprise and mortification, that though he still retained some vague and dim recollection of the general purpose of the vision, yet, with the exception of some eight or ten scattered lines and images, all the rest had passed away like the images on the surface of a stream into which a stone has been cast, but, alas! without the after restoration of the latter!

            Then all the charm
Is broken—all that phantom-world so fair
Vanishes, and a thousand circlets spread,
And each mis-shape the other. Stay awhile,
Poor youth! who scarcely dar'st lift up thine eyes—
The stream will soon renew its smoothness, soon
The visions will return! And lo, he stays,
And soon the fragments dim of lovely forms
Come trembling back, unite, and now once more
The pool becomes a mirror.

[from Coleridge's "The Picture, or the Lover's Resolution" (1802) 69–78]

Yet from the still surviving recollections in his mind, the Author has frequently purposed to finish for himself what had been originally, as it were, given to him. Σαμερον αδιον ασω [from Theocritus's *Idyll* 1.145]: but the tomorrow is yet to come.

Where Alph, the sacred river, ran
Through caverns measureless to man
    Down to a sunless sea.
So twice five miles of fertile ground
With walls and towers were girdled round:
And there were gardens bright with sinuous rills,° *brooks*
Where blossomed many an incense-bearing tree;
And here were forests ancient as the hills,
Enfolding sunny spots of greenery.

But oh! that deep romantic chasm which slanted
Down the green hill athwart a cedarn cover!
A savage place! as holy and enchanted
As e'er beneath a waning moon was haunted
By woman wailing for her demon-lover!
And from this chasm, with ceaseless turmoil seething,
As if this earth in fast thick pants were breathing,
A mighty fountain momently was forced:
Amid whose swift half-intermitted burst
Huge fragments vaulted like rebounding hail,
Or chaffy grain beneath the thresher's flail:
And 'mid these dancing rocks at once and ever
It flung up momently the sacred river.
Five miles meandering with a mazy° motion *labyrinthine*
Through wood and dale the sacred river ran,
Then reached the caverns measureless to man,
And sank in tumult to a lifeless ocean:
And 'mid this tumult Kubla heard from far
Ancestral voices prophesying war!
    The shadow of the dome of pleasure
    Floated midway on the waves;
    Where was heard the mingled measure
    From the fountain and the caves.
It was a miracle of rare device,
A sunny pleasure-dome with caves of ice!

    A damsel with a dulcimer
    In a vision once I saw:
    It was an Abyssinian maid,
    And on her dulcimer she played,
    Singing of Mount Abora.
    Could I revive within me
    Her symphony and song,
    To such a deep delight 'twould win me,
That with music loud and long,
I would build that dome in air,
That sunny dome! those caves of ice!
And all who heard should see them there,
And all should cry, Beware! Beware!
His flashing eyes, his floating hair!
Weave a circle round him thrice,
And close your eyes with holy dread,
For he on honey-dew hath fed,
And drunk the milk of Paradise.
—1816 (WRITTEN 1798)

As a contrast to this vision, I have annexed a fragment of a very different character [Coleridge's poem "The Pains of Sleep"], describing with equal fidelity the dream of pain and disease.

Limbo[1]

'Tis a strange place, this Limbo!—not a Place,
Yet name it so—where Time and weary Space
Fettered from flight, with night-mare sense of fleeing,
Strive for their last crepuscular[2] half-being—
Lank Space, and scytheless Time with branny[3] hands
Barren and soundless as the measuring sands,
Not mark'd by flit of Shades—unmeaning they
As moonlight on the dial of the day!
But that is lovely—looks like human Time—
An old man with a steady look sublime,
That stops his earthly task to watch the skies;
But he is blind—a statue hath such eyes—
Yet having moonward turn'd his face by chance,
Gazes the orb with moon-like countenance,
With scant white hairs, with foretop bald and high,
He gazes still—his eyeless face all eye—
As 'twere an organ full of silent sight,

[1] *Limbo* In some Christian thought, the location of souls that have been excluded from Heaven through no fault of their own (e.g., virtuous individuals who lived before the coming of Christ, or unbaptized infants). More generally, the word has come to indicate any place or state of nothingness.

[2] *crepuscular* Dim; of or like twilight.

[3] *branny* Resembling bran; scaly, coarse.

His whole face seemeth to rejoice in light!
Lip touching lip, all moveless, bust and limb—
He seems to gaze at that which seems to gaze on him!
No such sweet sights doth Limbo den
immure,° *imprison*
Wall'd round, and made a spirit-jail secure,
By the mere horror of blank Naught-at-all,° *nothingness*
Whose circumambience° doth these ghosts *omnipresence*
enthral.
A lurid thought is growthless, dull Privation,
Yet that is but a Purgatory[1] curse;
Hell knows a fear far worse,
A fear—a future state—'tis positive Negation!
—1817

Work without Hope

Lines Composed 21st February 1825

All Nature seems at work. Slugs leave their lair—
The bees are stirring—birds are on the wing—
And Winter slumbering in the open air,
Wears on his smiling face a dream of Spring!
And I the while, the sole unbusy thing,
Nor honey make, nor pair, nor build, nor sing.

Yet well I ken° the banks where *recognize*
amaranths[2] blow,
Have traced the fount whence streams of nectar flow.
Bloom, O ye amaranths! bloom for whom ye may,
For me ye bloom not! Glide, rich streams, away!
With lips unbrightened, wreathless brow, I stroll:
And would you learn the spells that drowse my soul?
Work without hope draws nectar in a sieve,
And Hope without an object cannot live.
—1828

[1] *Purgatory* In Catholic thought, the state or place in which souls that are not banished permanently to Hell are instead sent to undergo suffering in order to become sufficiently purified to go to Heaven. The word has come to indicate, more generally, any place or state of waiting or of temporary suffering.

[2] *amaranths* Imaginary flowers, the blossoms of which never fade.

from *Biographia Literaria; or Biographical Sketches of My Literary Life and Opinions*

from Chapter 4
Mr. Wordsworth's Earlier Poems

... During the last year of my residence at Cambridge, I became acquainted with Mr. Wordsworth's first publication entitled *Descriptive Sketches*,[3] and seldom, if ever, was the emergence of an original poetic genius above the literary horizon more evidently announced. In the form, style, and manner of the whole poem, and in the structure of the particular lines and periods, there is an harshness and acerbity connected and combined with words and images all aglow, which might recall those products of the vegetable world, where gorgeous blossoms rise out of the hard and thorny rind and shell, within which the rich fruit was elaborating. The language was not only peculiar and strong, but at times knotty and contorted, as by its own impatient strength, while the novelty and struggling crowd of images, acting in conjunction with the difficulties of the style, demanded always a greater closeness of attention than poetry (at all events, than descriptive poetry) has a right to claim. It not seldom therefore justified the complaint of obscurity. In the following extract I have sometimes fancied that I saw an emblem of the poem itself, and of the author's genius as it was then displayed.

'Tis storm; and hid in mist from hour to hour,
All day the floods a deepening murmur pour;
The sky is veiled, and every cheerful sight:
Dark is the region as with coming night;
And yet what frequent bursts of overpowering light!
Triumphant on the bosom of the storm,
Glances the fire-clad eagle's wheeling form;
Eastward, in long perspective glittering, shine
The wood-crowned cliffs that o'er the lake recline;
Wide o'er the Alps a hundred streams unfold,
At once to pillars turned that flame with gold;

[3] *Descriptive Sketches* Published 1793 and again in 1815 in an altered version.

Behind his sail the peasant strives to shun
The West, that burns like one dilated sun,
Where in a mighty crucible expire
The mountains, glowing hot, like coals of fire.[1]

The poetic psyche, in its process to full development, undergoes as many changes as its Greek namesake, the butterfly.[2] And it is remarkable how soon genius clears and purifies itself from the faults and errors of its earliest products; faults which, in its earliest compositions, are the more obtrusive and confluent, because as heterogeneous elements, which had only a temporary use, they constitute the very *ferment*, by which themselves are carried off. Or we may compare them to some diseases, which must work on the humours, and be thrown out on the surface, in order to secure the patient from their future recurrence. I was in my twenty-fourth year, when I had the happiness of knowing Mr. Wordsworth personally, and while memory lasts, I shall hardly forget the sudden effect produced on my mind, by his recitation of a manuscript poem, which still remains unpublished,[3] but of which the stanza, and tone of style were the same as those of "The Female Vagrant" as originally printed in the first volume of the *Lyrical Ballads*. There was here, no mark of strained thought, or forced diction, no crowd or turbulence of imagery; and, as the poet hath himself well described in his lines "on revisiting the Wye,"[4] manly reflection, and human associations had given both variety, and an additional interest to natural objects, which in the passion and appetite of the first love they had seemed to him neither to need or permit. The occasional obscurities, which had risen from an imperfect control over the resources of his native language, had almost wholly disappeared, together with that worse defect of arbitrary and illogical phrases, at once hackneyed, and fantastic, which hold so distinguished a place in the *technique* of ordinary poetry, and will, more or less, alloy the earlier poems of the truest genius, unless the attention has been specifically directed to their worthlessness and incongruity.[5] I did not perceive anything particular in the mere style of the poem alluded to during its recitation, except indeed such difference as was not separable from the thought and manner; and the Spenserian stanza, which always, more or less, recalls to the reader's mind Spenser's own style, would doubtless have authorized, in my then opinion, a more frequent descent to the phrases of ordinary life, than could without an ill effect have been hazarded in the heroic couplet. It was not however the freedom from false taste, whether as to common defects, or to those more properly his own, which made so unusual an impression on my feelings immediately, and subsequently on my judgement. It was the union of deep feeling with profound thought; the fine balance of truth in observing, with the imaginative faculty in modifying the objects observed; and above all the original gift of spreading the tone, the *atmosphere*, and

[1] *'Tis storm … fire* From "Descriptive Sketches Taken During a Pedestrian Tour in the Alps" (1815).

[2] [Coleridge's note] The fact that in Greek Psyche is the common name for the soul, and the butterfly is thus alluded to in the following stanzas from an unpublished poem ["The Butterfly" (1817)] of the author:

The butterfly the ancient Grecians made
The soul's fair emblem, and its only name—
But of the soul, escaped the slavish trade
Of mortal life! For in this earthly frame
Our's is the reptile's lot, much toil, much blame,
Manifold motions making little speed,
And to deform and kill the things, whereon we feed.

[3] *manuscript … unpublished* "Guilt and Sorrow; or, Incidents upon Salisbury Plain" (1842; written 1793–94).

[4] *his lines on "on revisiting the Wye"* From Wordsworth's "Lines Composed a Few Miles above Tintern Abbey"; see lines 77–94.

[5] [Coleridge's note] Mr. Wordsworth, even in his two earliest, "An Evening Walk" and the "Descriptive Sketches," is more free from this latter defect than most of the young poets his contemporaries. It may, however, be exemplified, together with the harsh and obscure construction, in which he more often offended, in the following lines:

'Mid stormy vapours ever driving by,
Where ospreys, cormorants, and herons cry;
Where hardly given the hopeless waste to cheer,
Denied the bread of life, the foodful ear,
Dwindles the pear on autumn's latest spray,
And *apple sickens* pale in summer's ray;
Ev'n here content has fixed her smiling reign
With independence, child of high disdain.

I hope, I need not say, that I have quoted these lines for no other purpose than to make my meaning fully understood. It is to be regretted that Mr. Wordsworth has not republished these two poems entire.

with it the depth and height of the ideal world around forms, incidents, and situations, of which, for the common view, custom had bedimmed all the lustre, had dried up the sparkle and the dew drops. "To find no contradiction in the union of old and new; to contemplate the Ancient of days and all his works with feelings as fresh, as if all had then sprang forth at the first creative fiat;[1] characterizes the mind that feels the riddle of the world, and may help to unravel it. To carry on the feelings of childhood into the powers of manhood; to combine the child's sense of wonder and novelty with the appearances, which every day for perhaps forty years had rendered familiar;

> With sun and moon and stars throughout the year,
> And man and woman;[2]

this is the character and privilege of genius, and one of the marks which distinguish genius from talents. And therefore is it the prime merit of genius and its most unequivocal mode of manifestation, so to represent familiar objects as to awaken in the minds of others a kindred feeling concerning them and that freshness of sensation which is the constant accompaniment of mental, no less than of bodily, convalescence. Who has not a thousand times seen snow fall on water? Who has not watched it with a new feeling, from the time that he has read Burns' comparison of sensual pleasure

> To snow that falls upon a river
> A moment white—then gone for ever![3]

In poems, equally as in philosophic disquisitions, genius produces the strongest impressions of novelty, while it rescues the most admitted truths from the impotence caused by the very circumstance of their universal admission. Truths of all others the most awful and mysterious, yet being at the same time of universal interest, are too often considered as so true, that they lose all the life and efficiency of truth, and lie bedridden in the dormitory of the soul, side by side with the most despised and exploded errors."—The Friend,[4] p. 76, No. 5.

This excellence, which in all Mr. Wordsworth's writings is more or less predominant, and which constitutes the character of his mind, I no sooner felt, than I sought to understand. Repeated meditations led me first to suspect (and a more intimate analysis of the human faculties, their appropriate marks, functions, and effects matured my conjecture into full conviction) that fancy and imagination were two distinct and widely different faculties, instead of being, according to the general belief, either two names with one meaning, or, at furthest, the lower and higher degree of one and the same power. It is not, I own, easy to conceive a more apposite translation of the Greek *Phantasia* than the Latin *Imaginatio*; but it is equally true that in all societies there exists an instinct of growth, a certain collective, unconscious good sense working progressively to desynonymize[5] those words originally of the same

[1] *fiat* Command.

[2] *With sun … woman* Milton's sonnet "To Mr. Cyriack Skinner upon His Blindness" (1655) actually reads: "Of sun or moon or star throughout the year, / Or man or woman."

[3] *To snow … for ever!* Robert Burns's "Tam O'Shanter" (1791) reads: "Or like the snow falls in the river, / A moment white—then melts for ever."

[4] [Coleridge's note] As "The Friend" was printed on stampt sheets, and sent only by the poet to a very limited number of subscribers, the author has felt less objection to quote from it, though a work of his own. To the public at large indeed it is the same as a volume in manuscript.

[5] [Coleridge's note] This is effected either by giving to the one word a general, and to the other an exclusive use; as "to put on the back" and "to indorse;" or by an actual distinction of meanings as "naturalist," and "physician"; or by difference of relation as "I" and "Me"; (each of which the rustics of our different provinces still use in all the cases singular of the first personal pronoun). Even the mere difference, or corruption, in the *pronunciation* of the same word, if it have become general, will produce a new word with a distinct signification; thus "property" and "propriety"; the latter of which, even to the time of Charles II was the *written* word for all the senses of both. Thus too "mister" and "master" both hasty pronunciations of the same word "magister," "mistress," and "miss," "if," and "give," &c. &c. There is a sort of *minim immortal* among the *animalcula infusoria* which has not naturally either birth, or death, absolute beginning, or absolute end: for at a certain period a small point appears on its back, which deepens and lengthens till the creature divides into two, and the same process recommences in each of the halves now become integral. This may be a fanciful, but it is by no means a bad emblem of the formation of words, and may facilitate the conception, how immense a nomen-

meaning, which the conflux of dialects had supplied to the more homogeneous languages, as the Greek and German: and which the same cause, joined with accidents of translation from original works of different countries, occasion in mixed languages like our own. The first and most important point to be proved is, that two conceptions perfectly distinct are confused under one and the same word, and (this done) to appropriate that word exclusively to one meaning, and the synonym (should there be one) to the other. But if (as will be often the case in the arts and sciences) no synonym exists, we must either invent or borrow a word. In the present instance the appropriation has already begun, and been legitimated in the derivative adjective: Milton had a highly *imaginative*, Cowley a very *fanciful* mind. If therefore I should succeed in establishing the actual existences of two faculties generally different, the nomenclature would be at once determined. To the faculty by which I had characterized Milton, we should confine the term *imagination*; while the other would be contra-distinguished as *fancy*. Now were it once fully ascertained, that this division is no less grounded in nature, than that of delirium from mania, or Otway's

> Lutes, lobsters, seas of milk, and ships of amber,[1]

from Shakespeare's

> What! have his daughters brought him to this pass?[2]

or from the preceding apostrophe to the elements; the theory of the fine arts, and of poetry in particular, could not, I thought, but derive some additional and important light. It would in its immediate effects furnish a torch of guidance to the philosophical critic; and ultimately to the poet himself. In energetic minds, truth soon changes by domestication into power; and from directing in the discrimination and appraisal of the product, becomes influencive in the production. To admire on principle, is the only way to imitate without loss of originality. …

from CHAPTER 13

ON THE IMAGINATION, OR ESEMPLASTIC[3] POWER

The IMAGINATION then I consider either as primary, or secondary. The primary IMAGINATION I hold to be the living Power and prime Agent of all human Perception, and as a repetition in the finite mind of the eternal act of creation in the infinite I AM. The secondary I consider as an echo of the former, co-existing with the conscious will, yet still as identical with the primary in the *kind* of its agency, and differing only in *degree*, and in the *mode* of its operation. It dissolves, diffuses, dissipates, in order to re-create; or where this process is rendered impossible, yet still at all events it struggles to idealize and to unify. It is essentially *vital*, even as all objects (as objects) are essentially fixed and dead.

FANCY, on the contrary, has no other counters to play with, but fixities and definites. The Fancy is indeed no other than a mode of Memory emancipated from the order of time and space; and blended with, and modified by that empirical phenomenon of the will, which we express by the word CHOICE. But equally with the ordinary memory it must receive all its materials ready made from the law of association.

Whatever more than this, I shall think it fit to declare concerning the powers and privileges of the imagination in the present work, will be found in the critical essay on the uses of the Supernatural in poetry and the principles that regulate its introduction, which the reader will find prefixed to the poem of *The Ancient Mariner*.

clature may be organized from a few simple sounds by rational beings in a social state. For each new application, or excitement of the same sound, will call forth a different sensation, which cannot but affect the pronunciation. The after recollection of the sound, without the same vivid sensation, will modify it still further; till at length all trace of the original likeness is worn away.

[1] *Lutes … amber* From Thomas Otway's play *Venice Preserved* (1682) 5.2.; Otway's version has the word "laurel" replacing "lobster."

[2] *What! … pass?* From Shakespeare's *King Lear* 3.4.65.

[3] *ESEMPLASTIC* Word coined by Coleridge to mean "moulded into unity."

CHAPTER 14
OCCASION OF THE LYRICAL BALLADS

During the first year that Mr. Wordsworth and I were neighbours, our conversations turned frequently on the two cardinal points of poetry, the power of exciting the sympathy of the reader by a faithful adherence to the truth of nature, and the power of giving the interest of novelty by the modifying colours of imagination. The sudden charm, which accidents of light and shade, which moonlight or sunset diffused over a known and familiar landscape, appeared to represent the practicability of combining both. These are the poetry of nature. The thought suggested itself (to which of us I do not recollect) that a series of poems might be composed of two sorts. In the one, the incidents and agents were to be, in part at least, supernatural; and the excellence aimed at was to consist in the interesting of the affections by the dramatic truth of such emotions, as would naturally accompany such situations, supposing them real. And real in *this* sense they have been to every human being who, from whatever source of delusion, has at any time believed himself under supernatural agency. For the second class, subjects were to be chosen from ordinary life; the characters and incidents were to be such, as will be found in every village and its vicinity, where there is a meditative and feeling mind to seek after them, or to notice them, when they present themselves.

In this idea originated the plan of the *Lyrical Ballads*, in which it was agreed, that my endeavours should be directed to persons and characters supernatural, or at least romantic; yet so as to transfer from our inward nature a human interest and a semblance of truth sufficient to procure for these shadows of imagination that willing suspension of disbelief for the moment, which constitutes poetic faith. Mr. Wordsworth, on the other hand, was to propose to himself as his object, to give the charm of novelty to things of every day, and to excite a feeling analogous to the supernatural, by awakening the mind's attention from the lethargy of custom, and directing it to the loveliness and the wonders of the world before us; an inexhaustible treasure, but for which in consequence of the film of familiarity and selfish solicitude we have eyes, yet see not, ears that hear not, and hearts that neither feel nor understand.[1]

With this view I wrote *The Ancient Mariner*, and was preparing among other poems, the "Dark Ladie," and the "Christabel," in which I should have more nearly realized my ideal, than I had done in my first attempt. But Mr. Wordsworth's industry had proved so much more successful, and the number of his poems so much greater, that my compositions, instead of forming a balance, appeared rather an interpolation of heterogeneous matter. Mr. Wordsworth added two or three poems written in his own character, in the impassioned, lofty, and sustained diction, which is characteristic of his genius. In this form the *Lyrical Ballads* were published; and were presented by him, as an *experiment*, whether subjects, which from their nature rejected the usual ornaments and extra-colloquial style of poems in general, might not be so managed in the language of ordinary life as to produce the pleasurable interest, which it is the peculiar business of poetry to impart. To the second edition he added a preface of considerable length, in which notwithstanding some passages of apparently a contrary import, he was understood to contend for the extension of this style to poetry of all kinds, and to reject as vicious and indefensible all phrases and forms of style that were not included in what he (unfortunately, I think, adopting an equivocal expression) called the language of *real* life. From this preface, prefixed to poems in which it was impossible to deny the presence of original genius, however mistaken its direction might be deemed, arose the whole long continued controversy. For from the conjunction of perceived power with supposed heresy I explain the inveteracy[2] and in some instances, I grieve to say, the acrimonious passions, with which the controversy has been conducted by the assailants.

[1] *we have eyes … understand* Cf. Isaiah 6.9: "Hear ye indeed, but understand not; and see ye indeed, but perceive not." See also Matthew 13.13–14.

[2] *inveteracy* Deeply rooted prejudice.

Had Mr. Wordsworth's poems been the silly, the childish things, which they were for a long time described as being; had they been really distinguished from the compositions of other poets merely by meanness of language and inanity of thought; had they indeed contained nothing more than what is found in the parodies and pretended imitations of them; they must have sunk at once, a dead weight, into the slough of oblivion, and have dragged the preface along with them. But year after year increased the number of Mr. Wordsworth's admirers. They were found too not in the lower classes of the reading public, but chiefly among young men of strong sensibility and meditative minds; and their admiration (inflamed perhaps in some degree by opposition) was distinguished by its intensity, I might almost say, by its *religious* fervour. These facts, and the intellectual energy of the author, which was more or less consciously felt, where it was outwardly and even boisterously denied, meeting with sentiments of aversion to his opinions, and of alarm at their consequences, produced an eddy of criticism, which would of itself have borne up the poems by the violence with which it whirled them round and round. With many parts of this preface in the sense attributed to them and which the words undoubtedly seem to authorise, I never concurred; but on the contrary objected to them as erroneous in principle, and as contradictory (in appearance at least) both to other parts of the same preface, and to the author's own practice in the greater number of the poems themselves. Mr. Wordsworth in his recent collection[1] has, I find, degraded this prefatory disquisition to the end of his second volume, to be read or not at the reader's choice. But he has not, as far as I can discover, announced any change in his poetic creed. At all events, considering it as the source of a controversy, in which I have been honoured, more than I deserve, by the frequent conjunction of my name with his, I think it expedient to declare once for all, in what points I coincide with his opinions, and in what points I altogether differ. But in order to render myself intelligible I must previously, in as few words as possible, explain my ideas, first, of a POEM; and secondly, of POETRY itself, in *kind*, and in *essence*.

The office of philosophical *disquisition* consists in just *distinction*; while it is the privilege of the philosopher to preserve himself constantly aware, that distinction is not division. In order to obtain adequate notions of any truth, we must intellectually separate its distinguishable parts; and this is the technical *process* of philosophy. But having so done, we must then restore them in our conceptions to the unity, in which they actually co-exist; and this is the *result* of philosophy. A poem contains the same elements as a prose composition; the difference therefore must consist in a different combination of them, in consequence of a different object proposed. According to the difference of the object will be the difference of the combination. It is possible, that the object may be merely to facilitate the recollection of any given facts or observations by artificial arrangement; and the composition will be a poem, merely because it is distinguished from prose by metre, or by rhyme, or by both conjointly. In this, the lowest sense, a man might attribute the name of a poem to the well known enumeration of the days in the several months;

Thirty days hath September,
April, June, and November, &c.

and others of the same class and purpose. And as a particular pleasure is found in anticipating the recurrence of sounds and quantities, all compositions that have this charm superadded, whatever be their contents, *may* be entitled poems.

So much for the superficial *form*. A difference of object and contents supplies an additional ground of distinction. The immediate purpose may be the communication of truths; either of truth absolute and demonstrable, as in works of science; or of facts experienced and recorded, as in history. Pleasure, and that of the highest and most permanent kind, may *result* from the *attainment* of the end; but it is not itself the immediate end. In other works the communication of pleasure may be the immediate purpose; and though truth, either moral or intellectual, ought to be the

[1] *recent collection* Wordsworth's collected edition *Poems* (1815); the Preface to *Lyrical Ballads* appears at the end of the second volume of the two-volume edition.

ultimate end, yet this will distinguish the character of the author, not the class to which the work belongs. Blest indeed is that state of society, in which the immediate purpose would be baffled by the perversion of the proper ultimate end; in which no charm of diction or imagery could exempt the Bathyllus even of an Anacreon, or the Alexis of Virgil,[1] from disgust and aversion! But the communication of pleasure may be the immediate object of a work not metrically composed; and that object may have been in a high degree attained, as in novels and romances. Would then the mere superaddition of metre, with or without rhyme, entitle *these* to the name of poems? The answer is, that nothing can permanently please, which does not contain in itself the reason why it is so, and not otherwise. If metre be superadded, all other parts must be made consonant with it. They must be such, as to justify the perpetual and distinct attention to each part, which an exact correspondent recurrence of accent and sound are calculated to excite. The final definition then, so deduced, may be thus worded. A poem is that species of composition, which is opposed to works of science, by proposing for its *immediate* object pleasure, not truth; and from all other species (having *this* object in common with it) it is discriminated by proposing to itself such delight from the *whole*, as is compatible with a distinct gratification from each component *part*.

Controversy is not seldom excited in consequence of the disputants attaching each a different meaning to the same word; and in few instances has this been more striking, than in disputes concerning the present subject. If a man chooses to call every composition a poem, which is rhyme, or measure, or both, I must leave his opinion uncontroverted. The distinction is at least competent to characterize the writer's intention. If it were subjoined, that the whole is likewise entertaining or affecting, as a tale, or as a series of interesting reflections, I of course admit this as another fit ingredient of a poem, and an additional merit. But if the definition sought for be that of a *legitimate* poem, I answer, it must be one, the parts of which mutually support and explain each other; all in their proportion harmonizing with, and supporting the purpose and known influences of metrical arrangement. The philosophic critics of all ages coincide with the ultimate judgment of all countries, in equally denying the praises of a just poem, on the one hand, to a series of striking lines or distichs,[2] each of which absorbing the whole attention of the reader to itself disjoins it from its context, and makes it a separate whole, instead of an harmonizing part; and on the other hand, to an unsustained composition, from which the reader collects rapidly the general result unattracted by the component parts. The reader should be carried forward, not merely or chiefly by the mechanical impulse of curiosity, or by a restless desire to arrive at the final solution; but by the pleasurable activity of mind excited by the attractions of the journey itself. Like the motion of a serpent, which the Egyptians made the emblem of intellectual power; or like the path of sound through the air; at every step he pauses and half recedes, and from the retrogressive movement collects the force which again carries him onward. *Præcipitandus est liber spiritus*,[3] says Petronius Arbiter most happily. The epithet, *liber*,[4] here balances the preceding verb; and it is not easy to conceive more meaning condensed in fewer words.

But if this should be admitted as a satisfactory character of a poem, we have still to seek for a definition of poetry. The writings of Plato, and Bishop Taylor, and the *Theoria Sacra* of Burnet,[5] furnish undeniable proofs that poetry of the highest kind may exist without metre, and even without the contra-distinguishing objects of a poem. The first chapter of Isaiah (indeed a very large proportion of the whole book) is poetry in the most emphatic sense; yet it would be not less irrational than

[1] *Bathyllus … Virgil* Coleridge disparagingly references homoerotic passages in Virgil and Anacreon's work. During this period, many people held strong prejudice against sexuality between men, and "sodomy" was punishable by death.

[2] *distichs* Poetic couplets.

[3] *Præcipitandus est liber spiritus* Latin: The free spirit must be hurried along. From the *Satyricon*.

[4] *liber* Latin: free.

[5] *Bishop Taylor* English theologian and author Jeremy Taylor (1613–67); *Burnet* English cleric and author Thomas Burnet (1635–1715), who wrote *Sacred Theory of the Earth*.

strange to assert, that pleasure, arid not truth, was the immediate object of the prophet. In short, whatever *specific* import we attach to the word, poetry, there will be found involved in it, as a necessary consequence, that a poem of any length neither can be, or ought to be, all poetry. Yet if an harmonious whole is to be produced, the remaining parts must be preserved *in keeping* with the poetry; and this can be no otherwise effected than by such a studied selection and artificial arrangement, as will partake of *one*, though not a *peculiar*, property of poetry. And this again can be no other than the property of exciting a more continuous and equal attention, than the language of prose aims at, whether colloquial or written.

My own conclusions on the nature of poetry, in the strictest use of the word, have been in part anticipated in the preceding disquisition on the fancy and imagination. What is poetry? is so nearly the same question with, what is a poet? that the answer to the one is involved in the solution of the other. For it is a distinction resulting from the poetic genius itself, which sustains and modifies the images, thoughts, and emotions of the poet's own mind. The poet, described in *ideal* perfection, brings the whole soul of man into activity, with the subordination of its faculties to each other, according to their relative worth and dignity. He diffuses a tone, and spirit of unity, that blends, and (as it were) *fuses*, each into each, by that synthetic and magical power, to which we have exclusively appropriated the name of imagination. This power, first put in action by the will and understanding, and retained under their irremissive, though gentle and unnoticed, controul (*laxis effertur habenis*)[1] reveals itself in the balance or reconciliation of opposite or discordant qualities: of sameness, with difference; of the general, with the concrete; the idea, with the image; the individual, with the representative; the sense of novelty and freshness, with old and familiar objects; a more than usual state of emotion, with more than usual order; judgement ever awake and steady self-possession, with enthusiasm and feeling profound or vehement; and while it blends and harmonizes the natural and the artificial, still subordinates art to nature; the manner to the matter; and our admiration of the poet to our sympathy with the poetry. "Doubtless," as Sir John Davies observes of the soul (and his words may with slight alteration be applied, and even more appropriately to the poetic IMAGINATION):

Doubtless this could not be, but that she turns
Bodies to spirit by sublimation strange,
As fire converts to fire the things it burns,
As we our food into our nature change.

From their gross matter she abstracts their forms,
And draws a kind of quintessence from things;
Which to her proper nature she transforms
To bear them light, on her celestial wings.

Thus does she, when from individual states
She doth abstract the universal kinds;
Which then re-clothed in divers names and fates
Steal access through our senses to our minds.[2]

Finally, GOOD SENSE is the BODY of poetic genius, FANCY, its DRAPERY, MOTION its LIFE, and IMAGINATION the SOUL that is everywhere, and in each; and forms all into one graceful and intelligent whole.

from Chapter 17
Examination of the Tenets Peculiar to Mr. Wordsworth

As far then as Mr. Wordsworth in his preface contended, and most ably contended, for a reformation in our poetic diction, as far as he has evinced the truth of passion, and the *dramatic* propriety of those figures and metaphors in the original poets, which stript of their justifying reasons, and converted into mere artifices of connection or ornament, constitute the characteristic falsity in the poetic style of the moderns; and as far as he has, with equal acuteness and clearness, pointed out the process in which this change was effected, and the resemblances

[1] *laxis effertur habenis* Latin: moved forward with loosened rein.

[2] *Doubtless … minds* Adapted from "Nosce Teipsum: Of Human Knowledge" (1599).

between that state into which the reader's mind is thrown by the pleasurable confusion of thought from an unaccustomed bain[1] of words and images; and that state which is induced by the natural language of empassioned feeling; he undertook a useful task, and deserves all praise, both for the attempt and for the execution. …

My own differences from certain supposed parts of Mr. Wordsworth's theory ground themselves on the assumption, that his words had been rightly interpreted, as purporting that the proper diction for poetry in general consists altogether in a language taken, with due exceptions, from the mouths of men in real life, a language which actually constitutes the natural conversation of men under the influence of natural feelings. My objection is, first, that in *any* sense this rule is applicable only to *certain* classes of poetry; secondly, that even to these classes it is not applicable, except in such a sense, as hath never by any one (as far as I know or have read) been denied or doubted; and lastly, that as far as, and in that degree in which it is *practicable*, yet as a *rule* it is useless, if not injurious, and therefore either need not, or ought not to be practised. The poet informs his reader, that he had generally chosen *low and rustic* life; but not *as* low and rustic, or in order to repeat that pleasure of doubtful moral effect, which persons of elevated rank and of superior refinement oftentimes derive from a happy *imitation* of the rude unpolished manners and discourse of their inferiors. For the pleasure so derived may be traced to three exciting causes. The first is the naturalness, in *fact*, of the things presented. The second is the apparent naturalness of the *representation*, as raised and qualified by an imperceptible infusion of the author's own knowledge and talent, which infusion does, indeed, constitute it an *imitation* as distinguished from a mere *copy*. The third cause may be found in the reader's conscious feeling of his superiority awakened by the contrast presented to him; even as for the same purpose the kings and great barons of yore retained, sometimes *actual* clowns and fools, but more frequently shrewd and witty fellows in that *character*. These, however, were not Mr. Wordsworth's objects. *He* chose low and rustic life, "because in that condition the essential passions of the heart find a better soil, in which they can attain their maturity, are less under restraint, and speak a plainer and more emphatic language; because in that condition of life our elementary feelings coexist in a state of greater simplicity, and consequently may be more accurately contemplated, and more forcibly communicated; because the manners of rural life germinate from those elementary feelings; and from the necessary character of rural occupations are more easily comprehended, and are more durable; and lastly, because in that condition the passions of men are incorporated with the beautiful and permanent forms of nature."[2]

Now it is clear to me, that in the most interesting of the poems, in which the author is more or less dramatic, as the "Brothers," "Michael," "Ruth," the "Mad Mother," &c. the persons introduced are by no means taken *from low or rustic life* in the common acceptation of those words; and it is not less clear, that the sentiments and language, as far as they can be conceived to have been really transferred from the minds and conversation of such persons, are attributable to causes and circumstances not necessarily connected with "their occupations and abode." The thoughts, feelings, language, and manners of the shepherd-farmers in the vales of Cumberland and Westmoreland, as far as they are actually adopted in those poems, may be accounted for from causes, which will and do produce the same results in *every* state of life, whether in town or country. As the two principal I rank that INDEPENDENCE, which raises a man above servitude, or daily toil for the profit of others, yet not above the necessity of industry and a frugal simplicity of domestic life; and the accompanying unambitious, but solid and religious EDUCATION, which has rendered few books familiar, but the Bible, and the liturgy or hymn book. To this latter cause, indeed, which is so far *accidental*, that it is the blessing of particular countries and a particular age, not the product of particular places or employments, the poet owes the shew of probability, that his personages might really feel,

[1] *bain* Vessel for water.

[2] *because … nature* From Wordsworth's "Preface" to *Lyrical Ballads* (1800).

think, and talk with any tolerable resemblance to his representation. It is an excellent remark of Dr. Henry More's (*Enthusiasmus triumphatus*, Sec. xxxv) that "a man of confined education, but of good parts, by constant reading of the Bible will naturally form a more winning and commanding rhetoric than those that are learned; the intermixture of tongues and of artificial phrases debasing *their* style."

It is, moreover, to be considered that to the formation of healthy feelings, and a reflecting mind, *negations* involve impediments not less formidable, than sophistication intermixture. I am convinced, that for the human soul to prosper in rustic life, a certain vantage-ground is prerequisite. It is not every man, that is likely to be improved by a country life or by country labours. Education, or original sensibility, or both, must pre-exist, if the changes, forms, and incidents of nature are to prove a sufficient stimulant. And where these are not sufficient, the mind contracts and hardens by want of stimulants; and the man becomes selfish, sensual, gross, hard-hearted. Let the management of the Poor Laws in Liverpool, Manchester, or Bristol be compared with the ordinary dispensation of the poor rates in agricultural villages, where the *farmers* are the overseers and guardians of the poor. … [The] result would engender more than skepticism concerning the desirable influences of low and rustic life in and for itself. …

If then I am compelled to doubt the theory, by which the choice of *characters* was to be directed, not only *a priori*,[1] from grounds of reason, but both from the few instances in which the poet himself *need* be supposed to have been governed by it, and from the comparative inferiority of those instances; still more must I hesitate in my assent to the sentence which immediately follows the former citation; and which can neither admit as particular fact, or a general rule. "The language too of these men is adopted (purified indeed from what appear to be its real defects, from all lasting and rational causes of dislike or disgust) because such men hourly communicate with the best objects from which the best part of language is originally derived; and because, from their rank in society, and the sameness and narrow circle of their intercourse, being less under the action of social vanity, they convey their feelings and notions in simple and unelaborated expressions."[2] To this I reply; that a rustic's language, purified from all provincialism and grossness, and so far reconstructed as to be made consistent with the rules of grammar which are in essence no other than the laws of universal logic, applied to psychological materials will not differ from the language of any other man of commonsense, however learned or refined he may be, except as far as the notions, which the rustic has to convey, are fewer and more indiscriminate. This will become still clearer, if we add the consideration (equally important though less obvious) that the rustic, from the more imperfect development of his faculties, and from the lower state of their cultivation, aims almost solely to convey *insulated facts*, either those of his scanty experience or his traditional belief; while the educated man chiefly seeks to discover and express those *connections* of things, or those relative *hearings* of fact to fact, from which some more or less general law is deducible. For *facts* are valuable to a wise man, chiefly as they lead to the discovery of the indwelling *law*, which is the true *being* of things, the sole solution of their modes of existence, and in the knowledge of which consists our dignity and our power. …

Here let me be permitted to remind the reader, that the positions, which I controvert, are contained in the sentences—"*a selection of the* REAL *language of men*"—"*the language of these men* (i.e., men in low and rustic life) *I propose to myself to imitate, and as far as possible, to adopt the very language of men.*" "*Between the language of prose and that of metrical composition, there neither is, nor can be any essential difference.*"[3] It is against these exclusively, that my opposition is directed.

I object, in the very first instance, to an equivocation in the use of the word "real." Every man's language varies, according to the extent of his knowledge, the activity of his faculties, and the depth or quickness of his feelings. Every man's language has, first, its *indi-*

[1] *a priori* Latin: without direct experience.

[2] *The language … expressions* From Wordsworth's "Preface" to *Lyrical Ballads* (1800).

[3] *a selection … difference* From Wordsworth's "Preface" to *Lyrical Ballads* (1800).

vidualities; secondly, the common properties of the *class* to which he belongs; and thirdly, words and phrases of *universal* use. The language of Hooker,[1] Bacon, Bishop Taylor, and Burke,[2] differ from the common language of the learned class only by the superior number and novelty of the thoughts and relations which they had to convey. The language of Algernon Sidney differs not at all from that, which every well educated gentleman would wish to write, and (with due allowances for the undeliberateness, and less connected train, of thinking natural and proper to conversation) such as he would wish to talk. Neither one or the other differ half as much from the general language of cultivated society, as the language of Mr. Wordsworth's homeliest composition differs from that of a common peasant. For "real" therefore, we must substitute *ordinary*, or *lingua communis*.[3] And this, we have proved, is no more to be found in the phraseology of low and rustic life, than in that of any other class. Omit the peculiarities of each, and the result of course must be common to all. And assuredly the omissions and changes to be made in the language of rustics, before it could be transferred to any species of poem, except the drama or other professed imitation, are at least as numerous and weighty, as would be required in adapting to the same purpose the ordinary language of tradesmen and manufacturers. Not to mention, that the language so highly extolled by Mr. Wordsworth varies in every county, nay in every village, according to the accidental character of the clergyman, the existence or non-existence of schools; or even, perhaps, as the exciseman, publican, or barber happen to be, or not to be, zealous politicians, and readers of the weekly newspaper *pro bono publico*.[4] Anterior to cultivation the lingua communis of every country, as Dante has well observed, exists everywhere in parts, and nowhere as a whole.

Neither is the case rendered at all more tenable by the addition of the words, "*in a state of excitement.*" For the nature of a man's words, when he is strongly affected by joy, grief, or anger, must necessarily depend on the number and quality of the general truths, conceptions and images, and of the words expressing them, with which his mind had been previously stored. For the property of passion is not to *create*; but to set in increased activity. At least, whatever new connections of thought or images, or (which is equally, if not more than equally, the appropriate effect of strong excitement) whatever generalizations of truth or experience, the heat of passion may produce; yet the terms of their conveyance must have pre-existed in his former conversations, and are only collected and crowded together by the unusual stimulation. It is indeed very possible to adopt in a poem the unmeaning repetitions, habitual phrases, and other blank counters, which an unfurnished or confused understanding interposes at short intervals, in order to keep hold of his subject which is still slipping from him, and to give him time for recollection; or in mere aid of vacancy, as in the scanty companies of a country stage the same player pops backwards and forwards, in order to prevent the appearance of empty spaces, in the procession of *Macbeth*, or *Henry VIII*. But what assistance to the poet, or ornament to the poem, these can supply, I am at a loss to conjecture. Nothing assuredly can differ either in origin or in mode more widely from the *apparent* tautologies[5] of intense and turbulent feeling, in which the passion is greater and of longer endurance, than to be exhausted or satisfied by a single representation of the image or incident exciting it. Such repetitions I admit to be a beauty of the highest kind; as illustrated by Mr. Wordsworth himself from the song of Deborah. "*At her feet he bowed, he fell, he lay down; at her feet he bowed, he fell; where he bowed, there he fell down dead.*"[6]

—1817

[1] *Hooker* English clergy member and theologian Richard Hooker (1554–1600).

[2] *Burke* British politician and political writer Edmund Burke (1729–97).

[3] *lingua communis* Latin: common language.

[4] *pro bono publico* Latin: for the good of the public.

[5] *tautologies* Repetitions.

[6] *At her feet … dead* From Wordsworth's note to "The Thorn" (1798).

Jane Austen

1775 – 1817

Jane Austen is considered to be one of the finest novelists in the English language. Her six major novels, along with her shorter fictional works, juvenilia, and surviving correspondence, share a keenness of wit and irony of observation that have ensured her continued popularity among scholars and general readers alike into the twenty-first century. Her fiction scrutinizes human manners and behavior with particular attention to women of the emergent middle class in Georgian England who need to negotiate between feeling and duty, personal desire and social expectation. As Sir Walter Scott observed, her writing bears "that exquisite touch which renders ordinary commonplace things and characters interesting." Her life and work have for generations been the subject of what is often called an "industry," both scholarly and popular.

Jane Austen was born at Steventon, Hampshire, the sixth child in a family of seven, and the younger of two daughters. Her father, the Reverend George Austen, was a spirited and cultivated man who allowed his daughters free access to his extensive library. Educated mostly at home, she read broadly, including novels by Frances Burney, Laurence Sterne, Henry Fielding, and Samuel Richardson, whose *Sir Charles Grandison* was a particular favorite. Owing in part to the proximity of the boys' school run by Austen's parents from the Steventon Rectory, the household in which Austen grew up was busy and lively, and its members enjoyed and encouraged each others' literary and theatrical pursuits. The young Jane Austen's imagination was fed by family theatricals directed and performed by her elder siblings and cousins for friends and neighbors, possibly with Austen's participation. Most importantly, she was encouraged to read aloud from her early writing, and her family delighted in the comic stories and burlesques she produced in her teenage years. Fictions such as *Lesley Castle* and *Love & Freindship* (sic), the latter written when Austen was 14, are filled with impertinent and riotous humor, indecorous behavior on the part of young women, and an already astute sense of generic convention. Her father was particularly supportive of her writing: at the front of a notebook he had given her, in which she had composed her *History of England*, a juvenile parody of popular histories, George Austen inscribed the following appreciation: "Effusions of Fancy by a very Young Lady Consisting of Tales in a Style entirely new."

Austen lived a quiet country life among a wide network of relations, friends, and neighbors, an ideal context in which to hone the skills in social observation that informed her writing. She never married, although she had at least two admirers, and even accepted a proposal of marriage in 1802 (retracting her acceptance the following day). In 1795–96 she wrote an epistolary sketch called "Elinor and Marianne," which went through several rewrites in subsequent years before taking its final form as *Sense and Sensibility*. This became Austen's first published work (1811), selling out by 1813 and receiving positive reviews. Three other novels were published in quick succession: *Pride and*

Prejudice in 1813, *Mansfield Park* in 1814, and *Emma* in 1816. *Pride and Prejudice*, whose first title was "First Impressions," had initially been rejected in 1797 by the publisher Thomas Cadell, who did not even read the manuscript before returning it. When it finally did appear, *Pride and Prejudice* was an instant hit, and it has since become one of the most widely read novels in the English language. Much of its success is due to the appeal of its heroine, Elizabeth Bennet, whose intelligence, feeling, and independence of thought Austen conveys through sparkling dialogue and pioneering use of narrative techniques that provide for flexibility of viewpoint.

The composition of Austen's major works can be divided into two distinct periods. By 1800 she had written three full-length novels, none of them published. Then followed a ten-year silence: the Austens' decision to quit the family home at Steventon and move to Bath, taking Jane and her elder sister Cassandra with them, meant a break in Austen's writing routine. The family moved often in the next several years, and with the death of several friends and family members in this period, most importantly her father in 1805, Austen seems to have experienced a depression that prevented her from writing. Austen's biographer Claire Tomalin points out how easily Austen's existing manuscripts in this decade could have been lost or destroyed. With her settlement at Chawton Cottage in Hampshire late in 1808 with her mother and sister, Austen again found the time and space to write, and it was here that she revised "Elinor and Marianne" into *Sense and Sensibility*, and wrote *Mansfield Park*, *Emma*, and *Persuasion*.

Two of Austen's six major novels were published posthumously in 1818. *Northanger Abbey* had been written under the title "Susan" in 1798–99 and sold to the publisher Richard Crosby in 1803 for the low sum of ten pounds. Although he placed advertisements for the book, he never printed it, and refused to turn over the manuscript or copyright at her request in 1809. *Persuasion*, written in 1815–16, was Austen's last completed novel. It is unique among her major works as the only novel for which any manuscript material survives. Many of her letters were also destroyed by her elder sister, Cassandra Austen, after her death. The Austen sisters were extremely close, sparing no confidence in their correspondence with each other. Many of Austen's surviving letters to her sister are characterized by harshly honest observations of others' foibles.

Austen wrote fiction at a moment when women were getting their work into print in ever greater numbers, yet faced relentless pressure to think and behave in ways that militated against their attaining, or expressing, social power and authority. Although by 1816 Austen was a critical and popular success (whose most illustrious fan was the Prince Regent himself), she wore her success lightly, famously referring in a letter of that year to her nephew to the "little bit (two inches wide) of Ivory on which I work with so fine a brush." Perhaps the best known description of Austen's writing, the statement has been read by critics as both a disclaimer and a sly celebration of "women's" writing and the domestic novel. But perhaps not too much should be made of a comment made in a spirit of playful banter with a teenager.

Austen was already suffering from illness when she finished *Persuasion*. She began another novel—*Sanditon*—but it was never finished. Jane Austen died of an undetermined illness on 18 July 1817, and was buried at Winchester Cathedral.

⌘⌘⌘

from *Pride and Prejudice*

Chapter 1

It is a truth universally acknowledged, that a single man in possession of a good fortune must be in want of a wife.

However little known the feelings or views of such a man may be on his first entering a neighbourhood, this truth is so well fixed in the minds of the surrounding families that he is considered as the rightful property of some one or other of their daughters.

"My dear Mr. Bennet," said his lady to him one day, "have you heard that Netherfield Park is let at last?"

Mr. Bennet replied that he had not.

"But it is," returned she; "for Mrs. Long has just been here, and she told me all about it."

Mr. Bennet made no answer.

"Do not you want to know who has taken it?" cried his wife impatiently.

"*You* want to tell me, and I have no objection to hearing it."

This was invitation enough.

"Why, my dear, you must know, Mrs. Long says that Netherfield is taken by a young man of large fortune from the north of England; that he came down on Monday in a chaise and four[1] to see the place, and was so much delighted with it that he agreed with Mr. Morris immediately; that he is to take possession before Michaelmas,[2] and some of his servants are to be in the house by the end of next week."

"What is his name?"

"Bingley."

"Is he married or single?"

"Oh! single, my dear, to be sure! A single man of large fortune; four or five thousand a year. What a fine thing for our girls!"

"How so? how can it affect them?"

"My dear Mr. Bennet," replied his wife, "how can you be so tiresome! You must know that I am thinking of his marrying one of them."

[1] *chaise and four* Traveling carriage pulled by four horses.

[2] *Michaelmas* The feast of St. Michael, on 29 September.

"Is that his design in settling here?"

"Design! nonsense, how can you talk so! But it is very likely that he *may* fall in love with one of them, and therefore you must visit him as soon as he comes."

"I see no occasion for that. You and the girls may go, or you may send them by themselves, which perhaps will be still better, for as you are as handsome as any of them, Mr. Bingley might like you the best of the party."

"My dear, you flatter me. I certainly *have* had my share of beauty, but I do not pretend to be anything extraordinary now. When a woman has five grown up daughters, she ought to give over thinking of her own beauty."

"In such cases, a woman has not often much beauty to think of."

"But, my dear, you must indeed go and see Mr. Bingley when he comes into the neighbourhood."

"It is more than I engage for,[3] I assure you."

"But consider your daughters. Only think what an establishment it would be for one of them. Sir William and Lady Lucas are determined to go, merely on that account, for in general you know they visit no newcomers. Indeed you must go, for it will be impossible for *us* to visit him, if you do not."

"You are over scrupulous, surely. I dare say Mr. Bingley will be very glad to see you; and I will send a few lines by you to assure him of my hearty consent to his marrying which ever he chooses of the girls, though I must throw in a good word for my little Lizzy."

"I desire you will do no such thing. Lizzy is not a bit better than the others, and I am sure she is not half so handsome as Jane, nor half so good humoured as Lydia. But you are always giving *her* the preference."

"They have none of them much to recommend them," replied he; "they are all silly and ignorant like other girls, but Lizzy has something more of quickness than her sisters."

"Mr. Bennet, how can you abuse your own children in such a way? You take delight in vexing me. You have no compassion on my poor nerves."

"You mistake me, my dear. I have a high respect for your nerves. They are my old friends. I have heard you mention them with consideration these twenty years at least."

[3] *engage for* Promise to perform.

"Ah! you do not know what I suffer."

"But I hope you will get over it, and live to see many young men of four thousand a year come into the neighbourhood."

"It will be no use to us if twenty such should come, since you will not visit them."

"Depend upon it, my dear, that when there are twenty, I will visit them all."

Mr. Bennet was so odd a mixture of quick parts, sarcastic humour, reserve, and caprice, that the experience of three and twenty years had been insufficient to make his wife understand his character. *Her* mind was less difficult to develop. She was a woman of mean[1] understanding, little information, and uncertain temper. When she was discontented she fancied herself nervous. The business of her life was to get her daughters married; its solace was visiting and news.

Chapter 2

Mr. Bennet was among the earliest of those who waited on Mr. Bingley. He had always intended to visit him, though to the last always assuring his wife that he should not go; and till the evening after the visit was paid, she had no knowledge of it. It was then disclosed in the following manner. Observing his second daughter employed in trimming a hat, he suddenly addressed her with,

"I hope Mr. Bingley will like it, Lizzy."

"We are not in a way to know *what* Mr. Bingley likes," said her mother resentfully, "since we are not to visit."

"But you forget, mama," said Elizabeth, "that we shall meet him at the assemblies, and that Mrs. Long has promised to introduce him."

"I do not believe Mrs. Long will do any such thing. She has two nieces of her own. She is a selfish, hypocritical woman, and I have no opinion of her."[2]

"No more have I," said Mr. Bennet; "and I am glad to find that you do not depend on her serving you."

Mrs. Bennet deigned not to make any reply; but unable to contain herself, began scolding one of her daughters.

"Don't keep coughing so, Kitty, for heaven's sake! Have a little compassion on my nerves. You tear them to pieces."

"Kitty has no discretion in her coughs," said her father; "she times them ill."

"I do not cough for my own amusement," replied Kitty fretfully.

"When is your next ball to be, Lizzy?"

"Tomorrow fortnight."[3]

"Aye, so it is," cried her mother, "and Mrs. Long does not come back till the day before; so, it will be impossible for her to introduce him, for she will not know him herself."

"Then, my dear, you may have the advantage of your friend, and introduce Mr. Bingley to *her*."

"Impossible, Mr. Bennet, impossible, when I am not acquainted with him myself; how can you be so teazing?"

"I honour your circumspection. A fortnight's acquaintance is certainly very little. One cannot know what a man really is by the end of a fortnight. But if *we* do not venture, somebody else will; and after all, Mrs. Long and her nieces must stand their chance; and therefore, as she will think it an act of kindness, if you decline the office, I will take it on myself."

The girls stared at their father. Mrs. Bennet said only, "Nonsense, nonsense!"

"What can be the meaning of that emphatic exclamation?" cried he. "Do you consider the forms of introduction, and the stress that is laid on them, as nonsense? I cannot quite agree with you *there*. What say you, Mary? for you are a young lady of deep reflection I know, and read great books, and make extracts."

Mary wished to say something very sensible, but knew not how.

"While Mary is adjusting her ideas," he continued, "let us return to Mr. Bingley."

"I am sick of Mr. Bingley," cried his wife.

[1] *mean* Modest.

[2] *have no opinion of her* I.e., have no great opinion of her; regard her as unworthy.

[3] *Tomorrow fortnight* I.e., a fortnight (two weeks) from tomorrow.

"I am sorry to hear *that*; but why did not you tell me so before? If I had known as much this morning, I certainly would not have called on him. It is very unlucky, but as I have actually paid the visit, we cannot escape the acquaintance now."

The astonishment of the ladies was just what he wished; that of Mrs. Bennet perhaps surpassing the rest; though when the first tumult of joy was over, she began to declare that it was what she had expected all the while.

"How good it was in you, my dear Mr. Bennet! But I knew I should persuade you at last. I was sure you loved your girls too well to neglect such an acquaintance. Well, how pleased I am! and it is such a good joke, too, that you should have gone this morning, and never said a word about it till now."

"Now, Kitty, you may cough as much as you choose," said Mr. Bennet; and, as he spoke, he left the room, fatigued with the raptures of his wife.

"What an excellent father you have, girls," said she, when the door was shut. "I do not know how you will ever make him amends for his kindness; or me either, for that matter. At our time of life, it is not so pleasant, I can tell you, to be making new acquaintance every day; but for your sakes, we would do anything. Lydia, my love, though you *are* the youngest, I dare say Mr. Bingley will dance with you at the next ball."

"Oh!" said Lydia stoutly, "I am not afraid; for though I *am* the youngest, I'm the tallest."

The rest of the evening was spent in conjecturing how soon he would return Mr. Bennet's visit, and determining when they should ask him to dinner.

Chapter 3

Not all that Mrs. Bennet, however, with the assistance of her five daughters, could ask on the subject was sufficient to draw from her husband any satisfactory description of Mr. Bingley. They attacked him in various ways: with barefaced questions, ingenious suppositions, and distant surmises; but he eluded the skill of them all, and they were at last obliged to accept the second-hand intelligence of their neighbour Lady Lucas. Her report was highly favourable. Sir William had been delighted with him. He was quite young, wonderfully handsome, extremely agreeable, and to crown the whole, he meant to be at the next assembly with a large party. Nothing could be more delightful! To be fond of dancing was a certain step towards falling in love; and very lively hopes of Mr. Bingley's heart were entertained.

"If I can but see one of my daughters happily settled at Netherfield," said Mrs. Bennet to her husband, "and all the others equally well married, I shall have nothing to wish for."

In a few days Mr. Bingley returned Mr. Bennet's visit, and sat about ten minutes with him in his library. He had entertained hopes of being admitted to a sight of the young ladies, of whose beauty he had heard much; but he saw only the father. The ladies were somewhat more fortunate, for they had the advantage of ascertaining, from an upper window, that he wore a blue coat and rode a black horse.

An invitation to dinner was soon afterwards dispatched; and already had Mrs. Bennet planned the courses that were to do credit to her housekeeping, when an answer arrived which deferred it all. Mr. Bingley was obliged to be in town the following day, and consequently unable to accept the honour of their invitation, &c. Mrs. Bennet was quite disconcerted. She could not imagine what business he could have in town so soon after his arrival in Hertfordshire, and she began to fear that he might be always flying about from one place to another, and never settled at Netherfield as he ought to be. Lady Lucas quieted her fears a little by starting the idea of his being gone to London only to get a large party for the ball; and a report soon followed that Mr. Bingley was to bring twelve ladies and seven gentlemen with him to the assembly. The girls grieved over such a large number of ladies, but were comforted the day before the ball by hearing that, instead of twelve, he had brought only six with him from London, his five sisters and a cousin. And when the party entered the assembly room, it consisted of only five altogether; Mr. Bingley, his two sisters, the husband of the eldest, and another young man.

Mr. Bingley was good looking and gentlemanlike; he had a pleasant countenance, and easy, unaffected manners. His sisters were fine women, with an air of decided fashion. His brother-in-law, Mr. Hurst, merely looked the gentleman; but his friend Mr. Darcy soon drew the attention of the room by his fine, tall person, handsome features, noble mien,[1] and the report which was in general circulation within five minutes after his entrance, of his having ten thousand a year. The gentlemen pronounced him to be a fine figure of a man, the ladies declared he was much handsomer than Mr. Bingley, and he was looked at with great admiration for about half the evening, till his manners gave a disgust which turned the tide of his popularity; for he was discovered to be proud, to be above his company, and above being pleased; and not all his large estate in Derbyshire could then save him from having a most forbidding, disagreeable countenance, and being unworthy to be compared with his friend.

Mr. Bingley had soon made himself acquainted with all the principal people in the room; he was lively and unreserved, danced every dance, was angry that the ball closed so early, and talked of giving one himself at Netherfield. Such amiable qualities must speak for themselves. What a contrast between him and his friend! Mr. Darcy danced only once with Mrs. Hurst and once with Miss Bingley, declined being introduced to any other lady, and spent the rest of the evening in walking about the room, speaking occasionally to one of his own party. His character was decided. He was the proudest, most disagreeable man in the world, and everybody hoped that he would never come there again. Amongst the most violent against him was Mrs. Bennet, whose dislike of his general behaviour was sharpened into particular resentment by his having slighted one of her daughters.

Elizabeth Bennet had been obliged, by the scarcity of gentlemen, to sit down for two dances; and during part of that time, Mr. Darcy had been standing near enough for her to overhear a conversation between him and Mr. Bingley, who came from the dance for a few minutes to press his friend to join it.

"Come, Darcy," said he, "I must have you dance. I hate to see you standing about by yourself in this stupid manner. You had much better dance."

"I certainly shall not. You know how I detest it, unless I am particularly acquainted with my partner. At such an assembly as this, it would be insupportable. Your sisters are engaged, and there is not another woman in the room whom it would not be a punishment to me to stand up with."

"I would not be so fastidious as you are," cried Bingley, "for a kingdom! Upon my honour, I never met with so many pleasant girls in my life as I have this evening; and there are several of them you see uncommonly pretty."

"*You* are dancing with the only handsome girl in the room," said Mr. Darcy, looking at the eldest Miss Bennet.

"Oh! she is the most beautiful creature I ever beheld! But there is one of her sisters sitting down just behind you who is very pretty, and, I dare say, very agreeable. Do let me ask my partner to introduce you."

"Which do you mean?" and turning round, he looked for a moment at Elizabeth, till, catching her eye, he withdrew his own and coldly said, "She is tolerable; but not handsome enough to tempt *me*; and I am in no humour at present to give consequence to young ladies who are slighted by other men. You had better return to your partner and enjoy her smiles, for you are wasting your time with me." Mr. Bingley followed his advice. Mr. Darcy walked off, and Elizabeth remained with no very cordial feelings towards him. She told the story however with great spirit among her friends; for she had a lively, playful disposition, which delighted in anything ridiculous.

The evening altogether passed off pleasantly to the whole family. Mrs. Bennet had seen her eldest daughter much admired by the Netherfield party. Mr. Bingley had danced with her twice, and she had been distinguished by his sisters. Jane was as much gratified by this as her mother could be, though in a quieter way. Elizabeth felt Jane's pleasure. Mary had heard herself mentioned to Miss Bingley as the most accomplished girl in the neighbourhood; and Catherine and Lydia had been

[1] *mien* Bearing.

fortunate enough to be never without partners, which was all that they had yet learnt to care for at a ball. They returned therefore in good spirits to Longbourn, the village where they lived, and of which they were the principal inhabitants. They found Mr. Bennet still up. With a book he was regardless of time; and on the present occasion he had a good deal of curiosity as to the event of an evening which had raised such splendid expectations. He had rather hoped that all his wife's views on the stranger would be disappointed; but he soon found that he had a very different story to hear.

"Oh! my dear Mr. Bennet," as she entered the room, "we have had a most delightful evening, a most excellent ball. I wish you had been there. Jane was so admired, nothing could be like it. Everybody said how well she looked; and Mr. Bingley thought her quite beautiful, and danced with her twice. Only think of *that* my dear; he actually danced with her twice, and she was the only creature in the room that he asked a second time. First of all, he asked Miss Lucas. I was so vexed to see him stand up with her; but, however, he did not admire her at all—indeed, nobody can, you know—and he seemed quite struck with Jane as she was going down the dance. So, he enquired who she was, and got introduced, and asked her for the two next. Then, the two third he danced with Miss King, and the two fourth with Maria Lucas, and the two fifth with Jane again, and the two sixth with Lizzy, and the Boulanger."[1]

"If he had had any compassion for *me*," cried her husband impatiently, "he would not have danced half so much! For God's sake, say no more of his partners. Oh! that he had sprained his ankle in the first dance!"

"Oh! my dear," continued Mrs. Bennet, "I am quite delighted with him. He is so excessively handsome! and his sisters are charming women. I never in my life saw anything more elegant than their dresses. I dare say the lace upon Mrs. Hurst's gown—"

Here she was interrupted again. Mr. Bennet protested against any description of finery. She was therefore obliged to seek another branch of the subject, and related, with much bitterness of spirit and some exaggeration, the shocking rudeness of Mr. Darcy.

"But I can assure you," she added, "that Lizzy does not lose much by not suiting *his* fancy; for he is a most disagreeable, horrid man, not at all worth pleasing. So high and so conceited that there was no enduring him! He walked here, and he walked there, fancying himself so very great! Not handsome enough to dance with! I wish you had been there, my dear, to have given him one of your set downs. I quite detest the man."

Chapter 4

When Jane and Elizabeth were alone, the former, who had been cautious in her praise of Mr. Bingley before, expressed to her sister how very much she admired him.

"He is just what a young man ought to be," said she, "sensible, good humoured, lively; and I never saw such happy manners!—so much ease, with such perfect good breeding!"

"He is also handsome," replied Elizabeth, "which a young man ought likewise to be, if he possibly can. His character is thereby complete."

"I was very much flattered by his asking me to dance a second time. I did not expect such a compliment."

"Did not you? *I* did for you. But that is one great difference between us. Compliments always take *you* by surprise, and *me* never. What could be more natural than his asking you again? He could not help seeing that you were about five times as pretty as every other women in the room. No thanks to his gallantry for that. Well, he certainly is very agreeable, and I give you leave to like him. You have liked many a stupider person."

"Dear Lizzy!"

"Oh! you are a great deal too apt, you know, to like people in general. You never see a fault in anybody. All the world are good and agreeable in your eyes. I never heard you speak ill of a human being in my life."

"I would wish not to be hasty in censuring anyone; but I always speak what I think."

"I know you do; and it is *that* which makes the wonder. With *your* good sense, to be honestly blind to the follies and nonsense of others! Affectation of candour is common enough; one meets it everywhere. But

[1] *Boulanger* French dance, performed by a circle of couples, in which each person dances briefly with each member of the opposite sex. The boulanger was the closing dance at balls.

to be candid without ostentation or design—to take the good of everybody's character and make it still better, and say nothing of the bad—belongs to you alone. And so, you like this man's sisters too, do you? Their manners are not equal to his."

"Certainly not, at first. But they are very pleasing women when you converse with them. Miss Bingley is to live with her brother and keep his house; and I am much mistaken if we shall not find a very charming neighbour in her."

Elizabeth listened in silence, but was not convinced; their behaviour at the assembly had not been calculated to please in general; and with more quickness of observation and less pliancy of temper than her sister, and with a judgment too unassailed by any attention to herself, she was very little disposed to approve them. They were in fact very fine ladies; not deficient in good humour when they were pleased, nor in the power of being agreeable where they chose it; but proud and conceited. They were rather handsome, had been educated in one of the first private seminaries in town, had a fortune of twenty thousand pounds, were in the habit of spending more than they ought, and of associating with people of rank; and were therefore in every respect entitled to think well of themselves, and meanly of others. They were of a respectable family in the north of England, a circumstance more deeply impressed on their memories than that their brother's fortune and their own had been acquired by trade.

Mr. Bingley inherited property to the amount of nearly an hundred thousand pounds from his father, who had intended to purchase an estate, but did not live to do it. Mr. Bingley intended it likewise, and sometimes made choice of his county; but as he was now provided with a good house and the liberty of a manor, it was doubtful to many of those who best knew the easiness of his temper, whether he might not spend the remainder of his days at Netherfield, and leave the next generation to purchase.

His sisters were very anxious for his having an estate of his own; but though he was now established only as a tenant, Miss Bingley was by no means unwilling to preside at his table, nor was Mrs. Hurst, who had married a man of more fashion than fortune, less disposed to consider his house as her home when it suited her. Mr. Bingley had not been of age two years when he was tempted by an accidental recommendation to look at Netherfield House. He did look at it and into it for half an hour, was pleased with the situation and the principal rooms, satisfied with what the owner said in its praise, and took it immediately.

Between him and Darcy there was a very steady friendship, in spite of a great opposition of character. Bingley was endeared to Darcy by the easiness, openness, ductility of his temper—though no disposition could offer a greater contrast to his own, and though with his own he never appeared dissatisfied. On the strength of Darcy's regard Bingley had the firmest reliance, and of his judgment the highest opinion. In understanding, Darcy was the superior. Bingley was by no means deficient, but Darcy was clever. He was at the same time haughty, reserved, and fastidious, and his manners, though well bred, were not inviting. In that respect his friend had greatly the advantage. Bingley was sure of being liked wherever he appeared; Darcy was continually giving offence.

The manner in which they spoke of the Meryton assembly was sufficiently characteristic. Bingley had never met with pleasanter people or prettier girls in his life; everybody had been most kind and attentive to him, there had been no formality, no stiffness, he had soon felt acquainted with all the room; and as to Miss Bennet, he could not conceive an angel more beautiful. Darcy, on the contrary, had seen a collection of people in whom there was little beauty and no fashion, for none of whom he had felt the smallest interest, and from none received either attention or pleasure. Miss Bennet he acknowledged to be pretty, but she smiled too much.

Mrs. Hurst and her sister allowed it to be so—but still they admired her and liked her, and pronounced her to be a sweet girl, and one whom they should not object to know more of. Miss Bennet was therefore established as a sweet girl, and their brother felt authorised by such commendation to think of her as he chose.

—1813 (WRITTEN 1796–97)

Thomas De Quincey
1785 – 1859

Because he published his first essay in 1821, Thomas De Quincey appears to be a contemporary of Byron, Shelley, and Keats. The sensational title of his most famous work, *Confessions of an English Opium-Eater*, adds to the case for associating him with these later Romantics. For his elegant and introspective style, however, De Quincey is better compared with Wordsworth and Coleridge, the earlier Romantics he so admired, as well as with other prominent essayists of his time such as Charles Lamb and William Hazlitt. Written in installments for one of the magazines popular in the day, *Confessions* was one of the first pieces De Quincey submitted, and it brought him immediate notoriety and success. Citing St. Augustine and Rousseau as predecessors of his autobiographical "impassioned prose," De Quincey at times wrote lovingly about his addiction: "If opium-eating be a sensual pleasure, and if I am bound to confess that I have indulged in it to an excess not yet *recorded* of any other man, it is no less true that I have struggled against this fascinating enthralment with a religious zeal, and have at length accomplished what I never yet heard attributed to any other man—have untwisted, almost to its final links, the accursed chain which fettered me." Whether he ever became unfettered is in question—De Quincey seems to have remained hopelessly addicted his entire adult life—but he went on to write hundreds of essays on subjects as diverse as German philosophy and literature, Shakespearean drama, the French Revolution, economics, Christianity, and the California gold rush.

De Quincey was born in Manchester in 1785 to Elizabeth Penson and Thomas Quincey, a successful linen merchant. One of eight children, he had already experienced the loss of two sisters by the time of his father's early death in 1793. Even though these events made for a troubled childhood, De Quincey gained a reputation as a precocious student and scholar. In 1796 he entered Bath Grammar School, where he became fluent in Latin and Greek despite what he considered his ineffectual teachers. He later wrote that a headmaster once said of his brilliance as a Greek scholar, "That boy could harangue an Athenian mob better than you and I could address an English one."

In 1802 De Quincey left the school with the thought of presenting himself to Wordsworth, whose *Lyrical Ballads* he had greatly admired. Instead he embarked on a tour of Wales and eventually arrived in London, hungry and destitute. These years, although difficult, were fodder for some of his most vivid recollections. In the *Confessions*, for example, De Quincey often recalls his relationship with a prostitute named Ann, who had befriended and housed him in London. A year later, he returned to his family and enrolled in Worcester College, Oxford, where he became known as a solitary but brilliant scholar. During his college years, he began taking laudanum—a drug derived from opium—for a toothache, and for a number of years his habit was kept under control. In 1807 he once again quit school, this time on the brink of examinations for which he had appeared to be extremely well-prepared.

De Quincey came to know Coleridge during his university years, and through Coleridge he met his idol, Wordsworth. The attraction was such that De Quincey settled in Grasmere in order to be near both poets, eventually moving into Dove Cottage, the Wordsworths' home, when Dorothy and William moved into a larger house. After years of close friendship, De Quincey became estranged from the Wordsworths when his addiction became uncontrollable and when he chose to live out of wedlock with Margaret Simpson, a local farmer's daughter. The couple married in 1816 after the birth of their son. They eventually had eight children together during their twenty-one years of marriage.

Again destitute, De Quincey moved his family to London and began publishing the *Confessions* anonymously in *The London Magazine*. His "spiritual autobiography" is in part a paean to the glories of opium—"Thou hast the keys of Paradise, oh just, subtle, and mighty opium!"—and in part a record of the nightmares and dream visions he experienced as a result of his addiction. (He influenced both Edgar Allan Poe and Charles Baudelaire, not only in their writing, but also in their use of the drug.)

De Quincey had a sense of the importance of dreams and the unconscious that was remarkable for his time. "I feel assured," he wrote in *Confessions*, "that there is no such thing as *forgetting* possible to the mind; a thousand accidents may, and will, interpose a veil between our present consciousness and the secret inscriptions on the mind. Accidents of the same sort will also rend away this veil; but alike, whether veiled or unveiled, the inscription remains forever." De Quincey later penned *Suspiria de Profundis* (1845), a sequel to the *Confessions* in which he wrote about his dreams with considerable psychological acuity; many regard his ideas as precursors to Freud's dream theories.

Although his lifestyle was anything but conservative, the political and moral conservatism of many of his ideas was deep-seated. He was also a talented humorist, as his 1827 essay "On Murder Considered as One of the Fine Arts" well illustrates. De Quincey delineates how "drinking and Sabbath-breaking" and eventual "incivility and procrastination" follows on the "downward path" from murder. "Many a man," De Quincey writes, "dated his ruin from some murder or other that perhaps he thought little of at the time."

In the 1850s De Quincey began compiling the fourteen-volume series *Selections Grave and Gay from Writings Published and Unpublished*, which was completed in 1860, a year after his death. In the words of a review written shortly afterward in London's *Quarterly Review*, "The position of De Quincey in the literature of the present day is remarkable. We might search in vain for a writer who, with equal powers, has made an equally slight impression upon the general public. His style is superb; his powers of reasoning are unsurpassed; his imagination is warm and brilliant, and his humor … delicate." The past few decades have seen a surge of interest in De Quincey and his *Confessions of an English Opium-Eater*, which has struck a chord with many who have similarly experienced isolation and alienation from society.

⌘⌘⌘

from *Confessions of an English Opium-Eater*

To the Reader

I here present you, courteous reader, with the record of a remarkable period in my life; according to my application of it, I trust that it will prove not merely an interesting record, but in a considerable degree useful and instructive. In *that* hope it is that I have drawn it up; and *that* must be my apology for breaking through that delicate and honourable reserve which, for the most part, restrains us from the public exposure of our own errors and infirmities. Nothing, indeed, is more revolting to English feelings than the spectacle of a human being obtruding on our notice his moral ulcers or scars, and tearing away that "decent drapery"[1] which time or indulgence to human frailty may have drawn over them; accordingly, the greater part of *our* confessions (that is, spontaneous and extra-judicial confessions) proceed from demi-reps,[2] adventurers, or swindlers; and for any such acts of gratuitous self-humiliation from those who can be supposed in sympathy with the decent and self-respecting part of society, we must look to French literature, or to that part of the German which is tainted with the spurious and defective sensibility of the French. All this I feel so forcibly, and so nervously am I alive to reproach of this tendency, that I have for many months hesitated about the propriety of allowing this or any part of my narrative to come before the public eye until after my death (when, for many reasons, the whole will be published); and it is not without an anxious review of the reasons for and against this step that I have at last concluded on taking it.

Guilt and misery shrink, by a natural instinct, from public notice; they court privacy and solitude; and even in their choice of a grave will sometimes sequester themselves from the general population of the churchyard, as if declining to claim fellowship with the great family of man, and wishing (in the affecting language of Mr. Wordsworth)

> —humbly to express
> A penitential loneliness.[3]

It is well, upon the whole, and for the interest of us all, that it should be so; nor would I willingly in my own person manifest a disregard of such salutary feelings, nor in act or word do anything to weaken them; but, on the one hand, as my self-accusation does not amount to a confession of guilt, so, on the other, it is possible that, if it *did*, the benefit resulting to others from the record of an experience purchased at so heavy a price might compensate, by a vast overbalance, for any violence done to the feelings I have noticed, and justify a breach of the general rule. Infirmity and misery do not of necessity imply guilt. They approach or recede from shades of that dark alliance, in proportion to the probable motives and prospects of the offender, and the palliations,[4] known or secret, of the offence, in proportion as the temptations to it were potent from the first, and the resistance to it, in act or in effort, was earnest to the last. For my own part, without breach of truth or modesty, I may affirm that my life has been, on the whole, the life of a philosopher; from my birth I was made an intellectual creature, and intellectual in the highest sense my pursuits and pleasures have been, even from my school-boy days. If opium-eating be a sensual pleasure, and if I am bound to confess that I have indulged in it to an excess not yet *recorded*[5] of any other man, it is no less true that I have struggled against this fascinating enthralment with a religious zeal, and have at length accomplished what I never yet heard attributed to any other man—have untwisted, almost to its final links, the accursed chain which fettered me. Such a self-conquest

[1] *decent drapery* From Edmund Burke's *Reflections on the Revolution in France* (1790): "All the pleasing illusions … are to be dissolved by this new conquering empire of light and reason. All the decent drapery of life is to be rudely torn off."

[2] *demi-reps* Women of dubious character.

[3] *humbly … loneliness* From Wordsworth's "The White Doe of Rylstone, or The Fate of the Nortons" (176–77): "[G]uilt, that humbly would express / A penitential loneliness."

[4] *palliations* Concealment or alleviation of symptoms.

[5] [De Quincey's note] "Not yet *recorded,*" I say; for there is one celebrated man of the present day, who, if all be true which is reported of him, has greatly exceeded me in quantity. [De Quincey is referring to Samuel Taylor Coleridge.]

may reasonably be set off in counterbalance to any kind or degree of self-indulgence. Not to insist that in my case the self-conquest was unquestionable, the self-indulgence open to doubts of casuistry,[1] according as that name shall be extended to acts aiming at the bare relief of pain, or shall be restricted to such as aim at the excitement of positive pleasure.

Guilt, therefore, I do not acknowledge; and if I did, it is possible that I might still resolve on the present act of confession in consideration of the service which I may thereby render to the whole class of opium-eaters. But who are they? Reader, I am sorry to say a very numerous class indeed. Of this I became convinced some years ago by computing at that time the number of those in one small class of English society (the class of men distinguished for talents, or of eminent station) who were known to me, directly or indirectly, as opium-eaters; such, for instance, as the eloquent and benevolent ——,[2] the late Dean of ——, Lord ——, Mr. —— the philosopher, a late Under-Secretary of State (who described to me the sensation which first drove him to the use of opium in the very same words as the Dean of ——, viz.,[3] "that he felt as though rats were gnawing and abrading the coats of his stomach"), Mr. ——, and many others hardly less known, whom it would be tedious to mention. Now, if one class, comparatively so limited, could furnish so many scores of cases (and that within the knowledge of one single inquirer), it was a natural inference that the entire population of England would furnish a proportionable number. The soundness of this inference, however, I doubted, until some facts became known to me which satisfied me that it was not incorrect. I will mention two.

(1) Three respectable London druggists, in widely remote quarters of London, from whom I happened lately to be purchasing small quantities of opium, assured me that the number of amateur opium-eaters (as I may term them) was at this time immense; and that the difficulty of distinguishing those persons to whom habit had rendered opium necessary from such as were purchasing it with a view to suicide, occasioned them daily trouble and disputes. This evidence respected London only. But,

(2) —which will possibly surprise the reader more—some years ago, on passing through Manchester, I was informed by several cotton manufacturers that their workpeople were rapidly getting into the practice of opium-eating, so much so, that on a Saturday afternoon the counters of the druggists were strewed with pills of one, two, or three grains, in preparation for the known demand of the evening. The immediate occasion of this practice was the lowness of wages, which at that time would not allow them to indulge in ale or spirits, and wages rising, it may be thought that this practice would cease; but as I do not readily believe that any man having once tasted the divine luxuries of opium will afterwards descend to the gross and mortal enjoyments of alcohol, I take it for granted

That those eat now who never ate before;
And those who always ate, now eat the more.

Indeed, the fascinating powers of opium are admitted even by medical writers, who are its greatest enemies. Thus, for instance, Awsiter, apothecary to Greenwich Hospital, in his "Essay on the Effects of Opium" (published in the year 1763), when attempting to explain why Mead[4] had not been sufficiently explicit on the properties, counteragents, &c., of this drug, expresses himself in the following mysterious terms (φωνάντα συνετοισ[5]): "Perhaps he thought the subject of too delicate a nature to be made common; and as many people might then indiscriminately use it, it would take from that necessary fear and caution which should prevent their experiencing the extensive power of this drug, *for there are many properties in it, if universally known, that would habituate the use, and make it more in*

[1] *casuistry* Specious rationalization used to determine morality.

[2] *benevolent ——* De Quincey entered the full names in his 1856 revision to the *Confessions*, saying that the editor of the original version deleted the names.

[3] *viz.* I.e., *videlicet.* Latin: that is to say.

[4] *Mead* Dr. Richard Mead (1673–1754), said to be the leading physician of the age, whose patients included Queen Anne and Sir Isaac Newton.

[5] *φωνάντα συνετοισ* Greek: speaking to the wise.

request with us than with Turks themselves, the result of which knowledge," he adds, "must prove a general misfortune." In the necessity of this conclusion I do not altogether concur; but upon that point I shall have occasion to speak at the close of my Confessions, where I shall present the reader with the moral of my narrative.

Preliminary Confessions

These preliminary confessions, or introductory narrative of the youthful adventures which laid the foundation of the writer's habit of opium-eating in afterlife, it has been judged proper to premise, for three several reasons:

1. As forestalling that question, and giving it a satisfactory answer, which else would painfully obtrude itself in the course of the Opium Confessions—"How came any reasonable being to subject himself to such a yoke of misery; voluntarily to incur a captivity so servile, and knowingly to fetter himself with such a sevenfold chain?"—a question which, if not somewhere plausibly resolved, could hardly fail, by the indignation which it would be apt to raise as against an act of wanton folly, to interfere with that degree of sympathy which is necessary in any case to an author's purposes.

2. As furnishing a key to some parts of that tremendous scenery which afterwards peopled the dreams of the opium-eater.

3. As creating some previous interest of a personal sort in the confessing subject, apart from the matter of the confessions, which cannot fail to render the confessions themselves more interesting. If a man "whose talk is of oxen" should become an opium-eater, the probability is that (if he is not too dull to dream at all) he will dream about oxen; whereas, in the case before him, the reader will find that the opium-eater boasteth himself to be a philosopher, and accordingly, that the phantasmagoria of *his* dreams (waking or sleeping, daydreams or nightdreams) is suitable to one who in that character

Humani nihil a se alienum putat.[1]

For amongst the conditions which he deems indispensable to the sustaining of any claim to the title of philosopher is not merely the possession of a superb intellect in its *analytic* functions (in which part of the pretensions, however, England can for some generations show but few claimants; at least, he is not aware of any known candidate for this honour who can be styled emphatically *a subtle thinker*, with the exception of Samuel Taylor Coleridge, and in a narrower department of thought with the recent illustrious exception[2] of David Ricardo[3]) but also on such a constitution of the *moral* faculties as shall give him an inner eye and power of intuition for the vision and the mysteries of our human nature: *that* constitution of faculties, in short, which (amongst all the generations of men that from the beginning of time have deployed into life, as it were, upon this planet) our English poets have possessed in the highest degree, and Scottish professors[4] in the lowest. …

---

[1] *Humani … putat* Latin: from Terence's *Heautontimorumenos* (163 BCE); translates to: He thinks that nothing that is human is alien to him.

[2] [De Quincey's note] A third exception might perhaps have been added; and my reason for not adding that exception is chiefly because it was only in his juvenile efforts that the writer whom I allude to [William Hazlitt] expressly addressed hints to philosophical themes; his riper powers having been all dedicated (on very excusable and very intelligible grounds, under the present direction of the popular mind in England) to criticism and the fine arts. This reason apart, however, I doubt whether he is not rather to be considered an acute thinker than a subtle one. It is, besides, a great drawback on his mastery over philosophical subjects that he has obviously not had the advantage of a regular scholastic education: he has not read Plato in his youth (which most likely was only his misfortune), but neither has he read Kant in his manhood (which is his fault).

[3] *David Ricardo* British political economist, author of *On the Principles of Political Economy, and Taxation* (1819).

[4] [De Quincey's note] I disclaim any allusion to *existing* professors, of whom indeed I know only one.

from PART 2

THE PLEASURES OF OPIUM

It is so long since I first took opium that if it had been a trifling incident in my life I might have forgotten its date; but cardinal events are not to be forgotten, and from circumstances connected with it I remember that it must be referred to the autumn of 1804. During that season I was in London, having come thither for the first time since my entrance at college. And my introduction to opium arose in the following way. From an early age I had been accustomed to wash my head in cold water at least once a day; being suddenly seized with toothache, I attributed it to some relaxation caused by an accidental intermission of that practice, jumped out of bed, plunged my head into a basin of cold water, and with hair thus wetted went to sleep. The next morning, as I need hardly say, I awoke with excruciating rheumatic pains of the head and face, from which I had hardly any respite for about twenty days. On the twenty-first day I think it was, and on a Sunday, that I went out into the streets, rather to run away, if possible, from my torments, than with any distinct purpose. By accident I met a college acquaintance, who recommended opium. Opium! dread agent of unimaginable pleasure and pain! I had heard of it as I had of manna or of ambrosia,[1] but no further. How unmeaning a sound was it at that time; what solemn chords does it now strike upon my heart! what heart-quaking vibrations of sad and happy remembrances! Reverting for a moment to these, I feel a mystic importance attached to the minutest circumstances connected with the place and the time and the man (if man he was) that first laid open to me the Paradise of Opium-eaters. It was a Sunday afternoon, wet and cheerless, and a duller spectacle this earth of ours has not to show than a rainy Sunday in London. My road homewards lay through Oxford Street; and near "the stately Pantheon"[2] (as Mr. Wordsworth has obligingly called it) I saw a druggist's shop. The druggist—unconscious minister of celestial pleasures!—as if in sympathy with the rainy Sunday, looked dull and stupid, just as any mortal druggist might be expected to look on a Sunday; and when I asked for the tincture of opium, he gave it to me as any other man might do, and furthermore, out of my shilling returned me what seemed to be real copper halfpence, taken out of a real wooden drawer. Nevertheless, in spite of such indications of humanity, he has ever since existed in my mind as the beatific vision of an immortal druggist, sent down to earth on a special mission to myself. And it confirms me in this way of considering him, that when I next came up to London I sought him near the stately Pantheon, and found him not; and thus to me, who knew not his name (if indeed he had one), he seemed rather to have vanished from Oxford Street than to have removed in any bodily fashion. The reader may choose to think of him as possibly no more than a sublunary[3] druggist; it may be so, but my faith is better—I believe him to have evanesced,[4] or evaporated. So unwillingly would I connect any mortal remembrances with that hour, and place, and creature, that first brought me acquainted with the celestial drug.

Arrived at my lodgings, it may be supposed that I lost not a moment in taking the quantity prescribed. I was necessarily ignorant of the whole art and mystery of opium-taking, and what I took I took under every disadvantage. But I took it—and in an hour—oh,

[1] *manna* Biblical food that saved the Jews in their escape from Egypt; *ambrosia* Food of the Greek gods.

[2] *the stately Pantheon* From Wordsworth's "Power of Music" (3); London's Pantheon was then a concert hall.

[3] *sublunary* Earthly.

[4] [De Quincey's note] *Evanesced*: this way of going off the stage of life appears to have been well known in the 17th century, but at that time to have been considered a peculiar privilege of blood-royal, and by no means to be allowed to druggists. For about the year 1686 a poet of rather ominous name (and who, by-the-bye, did ample justice to his name), viz., Mr. *Flat-man*, in speaking of the death of Charles II expresses his surprise that any prince should commit so absurd an act as dying, because, says he, "Kings should disdain to die, and only *disappear*." They should *abscond*, that is, into the other world. [Cf. Thomas Flatman's *On the Death of Our Late Sovereign Lord King Charles II of Blessed Memory: A Pindarique Ode* (1685): "*Princes* (like the wondrous *Enoch*) should be free / From death's unbounded tyranny, / And when their godlike race is run, / And nothing glorious left undone, / Never submit to fate, but only disappear."]

heavens! what a revulsion! what an upheaving, from its lowest depths, of inner spirit! what an apocalypse of the world within me! That my pains had vanished was now a trifle in my eyes; this negative effect was swallowed up in the immensity of those positive effects which had opened before me—in the abyss of divine enjoyment thus suddenly revealed. Here was a panacea, a *φαρμακον νήωενθς*[1] for all human woes; here was the secret of happiness, about which philosophers had disputed for so many ages, at once discovered; happiness might now be bought for a penny, and carried in the waistcoat pocket; portable ecstacies might be had corked up in a pint bottle, and peace of mind could be sent down in gallons by the mail coach. But if I talk in this way the reader will think I am laughing, and I can assure him that nobody will laugh long who deals much with opium; its pleasures even are of a grave and solemn complexion, and in his happiest state the opium-eater cannot present himself in the character of L'Allegro; even then he speaks and thinks as becomes Il Penseroso.[2] Nevertheless, I have a very reprehensible way of jesting at times in the midst of my own misery; and unless when I am checked by some more powerful feelings, I am afraid I shall be guilty of this indecent practice even in these annals of suffering or enjoyment. The reader must allow a little to my infirm nature in this respect; and with a few indulgences of that sort I shall endeavour to be as grave, if not drowsy, as fits a theme like opium, so antimercurial as it really is, and so drowsy as it is falsely reputed.

And first, one word with respect to its bodily effects; for upon all that has been hitherto written on the subject of opium, whether by travellers in Turkey (who may plead their privilege of lying as an old immemorial right), or by professors of medicine, writing *ex cathedra*,[3] I have but one emphatic criticism to pronounce—Lies! lies! lies! I remember once, in passing a book stall, to have caught these words from a page of some satiric author: "By this time I became convinced that the London newspapers spoke truth at least twice a week, viz., on Tuesday and Saturday,[4] and might safely be depended upon for—the list of bankrupts." In like manner, I do by no means deny that some truths have been delivered to the world in regard to opium. Thus it has been repeatedly affirmed by the learned that opium is a dusky brown in colour; and this, take notice, I grant. Secondly, that it is rather dear, which also I grant, for in my time East Indian opium has been three guineas a pound, and Turkey eight. And thirdly, that if you eat a good deal of it, most probably you must do what is particularly disagreeable to any man of regular habits, viz., die.[5] These weighty propositions are, all and singular, true; I cannot gainsay them, and truth ever was, and will be, commendable. But in these three theorems I believe we have exhausted the stock of knowledge as yet accumulated by men on the subject of opium. And therefore, worthy doctors, as there seems to be room for further discoveries, stand aside, and allow me to come forward and lecture on this matter.

First, then, it is not so much affirmed as taken for granted, by all who ever mention opium, formally or incidentally, that it does or can produce intoxication. Now, reader, assure yourself, *meo perieulo*,[6] that no quantity of opium ever did or could intoxicate. As to the tincture of opium (commonly called laudanum) *that* might certainly intoxicate if a man could bear to take enough of it, but why? Because it contains so much proof spirit, and not because it contains so much opium. But crude opium, I affirm peremptorily, is incapable of producing any state of body at all resembling that which is produced by alcohol, and not in

[1] *φαρμακον νήωενθς* Greek: soothing and healing drug.

[2] *L'Allegro … Il Penseroso* Poems by Milton (1645), whose titles mean "The Happy Man" and "The Brooding Man" respectively.

[3] *ex cathedra* With authority (from the Latin, meaning, literally, "from the cathedral").

[4] *Tuesday and Saturday* Days on which the newspaper would publish a list of bankruptcies.

[5] [De Quincey's note] Of this, however, the learned appear latterly to have doubted; for in a pirated edition of Buchan's *Domestic Medicine*, which I once saw in the hands of a farmer's wife, who was studying it for the benefit of her health, the doctor was made to say—"Be particularly careful never to take above five-and-twenty *ounces* of laudanum [the liquid form of opium] at once;" the true reading being probably five-and-twenty *drops*, which are held equal to about one grain of crude opium.

[6] *meo perieulo* Latin: at my risk.

degree only incapable, but even in *kind*; it is not in the quantity of its effects merely, but in the quality, that it differs altogether. The pleasure given by wine is always mounting and tending to a crisis, after which it declines; that from opium, when once generated, is stationary for eight or ten hours: the first, to borrow a technical distinction from medicine, is a case of acute—the second, the chronic pleasure; the one is a flame, the other a steady and equable glow. But the main distinction lies in this, that whereas wine disorders the mental faculties, opium, on the contrary (if taken in a proper manner), introduces amongst them the most exquisite order, legislation, and harmony. Wine robs a man of his self-possession; opium greatly invigorates it. Wine unsettles and clouds the judgment, and gives a preternatural brightness and a vivid exaltation to the contempts and the admirations, the loves and the hatreds of the drinker; opium, on the contrary, communicates serenity and equipoise to all the faculties, active or passive, and with respect to the temper and moral feelings in general it gives simply that sort of vital warmth which is approved by the judgment, and which would probably always accompany a bodily constitution of primeval or antediluvian[1] health. Thus, for instance, opium, like wine, gives an expansion to the heart and the benevolent affections; but then, with this remarkable difference, that in the sudden development of kind-heartedness which accompanies inebriation there is always more or less of a maudlin character, which exposes it to the contempt of the bystander. Men shake hands, swear eternal friendship, and shed tears, no mortal knows why; and the sensual creature is clearly uppermost. But the expansion of the benigner feelings incident to opium is no febrile access, but a healthy restoration to that state which the mind would naturally recover upon the removal of any deep-seated irritation of pain that had disturbed and quarrelled with the impulses of a heart originally just and good. True it is that even wine, up to a certain point and with certain men, rather tends to exalt and to steady the intellect; I myself, who have never been a great wine drinker, used to find that half a dozen glasses of wine advantageously affected the faculties—brightened and intensified the consciousness, and gave to the mind a feeling of being "*ponderibus librata suis*;"[2] and certainly it is most absurdly said, in popular language, of any man that he is *disguised* in liquor; for, on the contrary, most men are disguised by sobriety, and it is when they are drinking (as some old gentleman says in Athenaeus), that men *ἑαυτοὺς ἐμφανίζουσιν οἵτινες εἰσίν*—display themselves in their true complexion of character, which surely is not disguising themselves. But still, wine constantly leads a man to the brink of absurdity and extravagance, and beyond a certain point it is sure to volatilize and to disperse the intellectual energies, whereas opium always seems to compose what had been agitated, and to concentrate what had been distracted. In short, to sum up all in one word, a man who is inebriated, or tending to inebriation, is, and feels that he is, in a condition which calls up into supremacy the merely human, too often the brutal part of his nature; but the opium-eater (I speak of him who is not suffering from any disease or other remote effects of opium) feels that the diviner part of his nature is paramount; that is, the moral affections are in a state of cloudless serenity, and overall is the great light of the majestic intellect.

This is the doctrine of the true church on the subject of opium, of which church I acknowledge myself to be the only member—the alpha and the omega;[3] but then it is to be recollected that I speak from the ground of a large and profound personal experience, whereas most of the unscientific[4] authors who have at all treated of

[1] *antediluvian* Before the Biblical flood, hence primitive.

[2] *ponderibus librata suis* Latin: from Ovid's *Metamorphoses* (1.16): "[the earth, not] poised, did on its own foundations lie."

[3] *the alpha and the omega* The beginning and the end; from the first and last letters of the Greek alphabet.

[4] [De Quincey's note] Amongst the great herd of travellers, &c., who show sufficiently by their stupidity that they never held any intercourse with opium, I must caution my readers specially against the brilliant author [Thomas Hope] of *Anastasius* [(1819)]. This gentleman, whose wit would lead one to presume him an opium-eater, has made it impossible to consider him in that character, from the grievous misrepresentation which he gives of its effects at pp. 215–17 of vol. 1. Upon consideration it must appear such to the author himself, for, waiving the errors I have insisted on in the text, which (and others) are adopted in the fullest manner, he will himself admit that an old

opium, and even of those who have written expressly on the *materia medica*, make it evident, from the horror they express of it, that their experimental knowledge of its action is none at all. I will, however, candidly acknowledge that I have met with one person who bore evidence to its intoxicating power, such as staggered my own incredulity, for he was a surgeon, and had himself taken opium largely. I happened to say to him that his enemies (as I had heard) charged him with talking nonsense on politics, and that his friends apologized for him by suggesting that he was constantly in a state of intoxication from opium. Now the accusation, said I, is not *prima facie*[1] and of necessity an absurd one; but the defence *is*. To my surprise, however, he insisted that both his enemies and his friends were in the right. "I will maintain," said he, "that I *do* talk nonsense; and secondly, I will maintain that I do not talk nonsense upon principle, or with any view to profit, but solely and simply," said he, "solely and simply—solely and simply (repeating it three times over), because I am drunk with opium, and *that* daily." I replied that, as to the allegation of his enemies, as it seemed to be established upon such respectable testimony, seeing that the three parties concerned all agree in it, it did not become me to question it; but the defence set up I must demur to. He proceeded to discuss the matter, and to lay down his reasons; but it seemed to me so impolite to pursue an argument which must have presumed a man mistaken in a point belonging to his own profession, that I did not press him even when his course of argument seemed open to objection, not to mention that a man who talks nonsense, even though "with no view to profit," is not altogether the most agreeable partner in a dispute, whether as opponent or respondent. I confess, however, that the authority of a surgeon, and one who was reputed a good one, may seem a weighty one to my prejudice; but still I must plead my experience, which was greater than his greatest by 7,000 drops a day; and though it was not possible to suppose a medical man unacquainted with the characteristic symptoms of vinous intoxication, it yet struck me that he might proceed on a logical error of using the word intoxication with too great latitude, and extending it generically to all modes of nervous excitement, instead of restricting it as the expression for a specific sort of excitement connected with certain diagnostics. Some people have maintained in my hearing that they had been drunk upon green tea; and a medical student in London, for whose knowledge in his profession I have reason to feel great respect, assured me the other day that a patient in recovering from an illness had got drunk on a beefsteak.

Having dwelt so much on this first and leading error in respect to opium, I shall notice very briefly a second and a third, which are, that the elevation of spirits produced by opium is necessarily followed by a proportionate depression, and that the natural and even immediate consequence of opium is torpor and stagnation, animal and mental. The first of these errors I shall content myself with simply denying, assuring my reader that for ten years, during which I took opium at intervals, the day succeeding to that on which I allowed myself this luxury was always a day of unusually good spirits.

With respect to the torpor supposed to follow, or rather (if we were to credit the numerous pictures of Turkish opium-eaters) to accompany the practice of opium-eating, I deny that also. Certainly opium is classed under the head of narcotics, and some such effect it may produce in the end; but the primary effects of opium are always, and in the highest degree, to excite and stimulate the system. This first stage of its action always lasted with me, during my noviciate, for upwards of eight hours, so that it must be the fault of the opium-eater himself if he does not so time his exhibition of the dose (to speak medically) as that the whole weight of its

gentleman "with a snow-white beard," who eats "ample doses of opium," and is yet able to deliver what is meant and received as very weighty counsel on the bad effects of that practice, is but an indifferent evidence that opium either kills people prematurely or sends them into a madhouse. But for my part, I see into this old gentleman and his motives: the fact is, he was enamoured of "the little golden receptacle of the pernicious drug" which Anastasius carried about him; and no way of obtaining it so safe and so feasible occurred as that of frightening its owner out of his wits (which, by the bye, are none of the strongest). This commentary throws a new light upon the case, and greatly improves it as a story; for the old gentleman's speech, considered as a lecture on pharmacy, is highly absurd; but considered as a hoax on Anastasius, it reads excellently.

[1] *prima facie* Latin: on first impression.

narcotic influence may descend upon his sleep. Turkish opium-eaters, it seems, are absurd enough to sit, like so many equestrian statues, on logs of wood as stupid as themselves. But that the reader may judge of the degree in which opium is likely to stupefy the faculties of an Englishman, I shall (by way of treating the question illustratively, rather than argumentatively) describe the way in which I myself often passed an opium evening in London during the period between 1804–1812. It will be seen that at least opium did not move me to seek solitude, and much less to seek inactivity, or the torpid state of self-involution ascribed to the Turks. I give this account at the risk of being pronounced a crazy enthusiast or visionary, but I regard *that* little. I must desire my reader to bear in mind that I was a hard student, and at severe studies for all the rest of my time; and certainly I had a right occasionally to relaxations as well as other people. These, however, I allowed myself but seldom. …

Thus I have shown that opium does not of necessity produce inactivity or torpor, but that, on the contrary, it often led me into markets and theatres. Yet, in candour, I will admit that markets and theatres are not the appropriate haunts of the opium-eater when in the divinest state incident to his enjoyment. In that state, crowds become an oppression to him; music even, too sensual and gross. He naturally seeks solitude and silence, as indispensable conditions of those trances, or profoundest reveries, which are the crown and consummation of what opium can do for human nature. I, whose disease it was to meditate too much and to observe too little, and who upon my first entrance at college was nearly falling into a deep melancholy, from brooding too much on the sufferings which I had witnessed in London, was sufficiently aware of the tendencies of my own thoughts to do all I could to counteract them. I was, indeed, like a person who, according to the old legend, had entered the cave of Trophonius;[1] and the remedies I sought were to force myself into society, and to keep my understanding in continual activity upon matters of science. But for these remedies I should certainly have become hypochondriacally melancholy. In after years, however, when my cheerfulness was more fully re-established, I yielded to my natural inclination for a solitary life. And at that time I often fell into these reveries upon taking opium; and more than once it has happened to me, on a summer night, when I have been at an open window, in a room from which I could overlook the sea at a mile below me, and could command a view of the great town of L——, at about the same distance, that I have sat from sunset to sunrise, motionless, and without wishing to move. …

Introduction to the Pains of Opium

… I remember about this time a little incident, which I mention because, trifling as it was, the reader will soon meet it again in my dreams, which it influenced more fearfully than could be imagined. One day a Malay[2] knocked at my door. What business a Malay could have to transact amongst English mountains I cannot conjecture, but possibly he was on his road to a seaport about forty miles distant.

The servant who opened the door to him was a young girl, born and bred amongst the mountains, who had never seen an Asiatic dress of any sort; his turban therefore confounded her not a little; and as it turned out that his attainments in English were exactly of the same extent as hers in the Malay, there seemed to be an impassable gulf fixed between all communication of ideas, if either party had happened to possess any. In this dilemma, the girl, recollecting the reputed learning of her master (and doubtless giving me credit for a knowledge of all the languages of the earth besides perhaps a few of the lunar ones), came and gave me to understand that there was a sort of demon below, whom she clearly imagined that my art could exorcise from the house. I did not immediately go down, but when I did, the group which presented itself, arranged as it was by accident, though not very elaborate, took hold of my

[1] *cave of Trophonius* State of despair: in Greek mythology, Trophonius, who had killed his brother, was buried in a cave that became famous for its oracle that would overwhelm with melancholy all those who consulted it.

[2] *Malay* Member of a people that inhabits Malaysia, Brunei, and parts of Indonesia.

fancy and my eye in a way that none of the statuesque attitudes exhibited in the ballets at the opera house, though so ostentatiously complex, had ever done. In a cottage kitchen, but panelled on the wall with dark wood that from age and rubbing resembled oak, and looking more like a rustic hall of entrance than a kitchen, stood the Malay—his turban and loose trousers of dingy white relieved upon the dark panelling. He had placed himself nearer to the girl than she seemed to relish, though her native spirit of mountain intrepidity contended with the feeling of simple awe which her countenance expressed as she gazed upon the tiger cat before her. And a more striking picture there could not be imagined than the beautiful English face of the girl, and its exquisite fairness, together with her erect and independent attitude, contrasted with the sallow and bilious skin of the Malay, enamelled or veneered with mahogany by marine air, his small, fierce, restless eyes, thin lips, slavish gestures and adorations. Half hidden by the ferocious-looking Malay was a little child from a neighbouring cottage who had crept in after him, and was now in the act of reverting its head and gazing upwards at the turban and the fiery eyes beneath it, whilst with one hand he caught at the dress of the young woman for protection. My knowledge of the Oriental tongues is not remarkably extensive, being indeed confined to two words—the Arabic word for barley and the Turkish for opium (*madjoon*), which I have learned from *Anastasius*; and as I had neither a Malay dictionary nor even Adelung's *Mithridates*,[1] which might have helped me to a few words, I addressed him in some lines from the *Iliad*, considering that, of such languages as I possessed, Greek, in point of longitude, came geographically nearest to an Oriental one. He worshipped me in a most devout manner, and replied in what I suppose was Malay. In this way I saved my reputation with my neighbours, for the Malay had no means of betraying the secret. He lay down upon the floor for about an hour and then pursued his journey. On his departure I presented him with a piece of opium. To him, as an Orientalist, I concluded that opium must be familiar, and the expression of his face convinced me that it was. Nevertheless, I was struck with some little consternation when I saw him suddenly raise his hand to his mouth, and, to use the schoolboy phrase, bolt the whole, divided into three pieces, at one mouthful. The quantity was enough to kill three dragoons[2] and their horses, and I felt some alarm for the poor creature, but what could be done? I had given him the opium in compassion for his solitary life, on recollecting that if he had travelled on foot from London it must be nearly three weeks since he could have exchanged a thought with any human being. I could not think of violating the laws of hospitality by having him seized and drenched with an emetic, and thus frightening him into a notion that we were going to sacrifice him to some English idol. No, there was clearly no help for it. He took his leave, and for some days I felt anxious, but as I never heard of any Malay being found dead, I became convinced that he was used to opium,[3] and that I must have done him the service I designed by giving him one night of respite from the pains of wandering. …

The Pains of Opium

—as when some great painter dips
His pencil in the gloom of earthquake and eclipse.
Shelley's *Revolt of Islam*.

Reader, who have thus far accompanied me, I must request your attention to a brief explanatory note on three points:

[1] *Adelung's Mithridates* German linguistics and grammar scholar Johann Christoph Adelung (1732–1806), author of *Mithridate or the Universal Table of Languages, with the Lord's Prayer in 500 Dialects*, a four-volume book on Oriental languages.

[2] *dragoons* Mounted soldiers.

[3] [De Quincey's note] This, however, is not a necessary conclusion; the varieties of effect produced by opium on different constitutions are infinite. A London magistrate (Harriott's *Struggles through Life*, vol. iii. p. 391, third edition) has recorded that, on the first occasion of his trying laudanum for the gout he took *forty* drops, the next night *sixty*, and on the fifth night *eighty*, without any effect whatever, and this at an advanced age. I have an anecdote from a country surgeon, however, which sinks Mr. Harriott's case into a trifle; and in my projected medical treatise on opium, which I will publish provided the College of Surgeons will pay me for enlightening their benighted understandings upon this subject, I will relate it; but it is far too good a story to be published gratis.

1. For several reasons I have not been able to compose the notes for this part of my narrative into any regular and connected shape. I give the notes disjointed as I find them, or have now drawn them up from memory. Some of them point to their own date, some I have dated, and some are undated. Whenever it could answer my purpose to transplant them from the natural or chronological order, I have not scrupled to do so. Sometimes I speak in the present, sometimes in the past tense. Few of the notes, perhaps, were written exactly at the period of time to which they relate; but this can little affect their accuracy, as the impressions were such that they can never fade from my mind. Much has been omitted. I could not, without effort, constrain myself to the task of either recalling, or constructing into a regular narrative, the whole burden of horrors which lies upon my brain. This feeling partly I plead in excuse, and partly that I am now in London, and am a helpless sort of person, who cannot even arrange his own papers without assistance; and I am separated from the hands which are wont to perform for me the offices of an amanuensis.[1]

2. You will think perhaps that I am too confidential and communicative of my own private history. It may be so. But my way of writing is rather to think aloud, and follow my own humors, than much to consider who is listening to me; and if I stop to consider what is proper to be said to this or that person, I shall soon come to doubt whether any part at all is proper. The fact is, I place myself at a distance of fifteen or twenty years ahead of this time, and suppose myself writing to those who will be interested about me hereafter; and wishing to have some record of time, the entire history of which no one can know but myself, I do it as fully as I am able with the efforts I am now capable of making, because I know not whether I can ever find time to do it again.

3. It will occur to you often to ask, why did I not release myself from the horrors of opium by leaving it off or diminishing it? To this I must answer briefly: it might be supposed that I yielded to the fascinations of opium too easily; it cannot be supposed that any man can be charmed by its terrors. The reader may be sure, therefore, that I made attempts innumerable to reduce the quantity. I add, that those who witnessed the agonies of those attempts, and not myself, were the first to beg me to desist. But could not have I reduced it a drop a day, or, by adding water, have bisected or trisected a drop? A thousand drops bisected would thus have taken nearly six years to reduce, and that way would certainly not have answered. But this is a common mistake of those who know nothing of opium experimentally; I appeal to those who do, whether it is not always found that down to a certain point it can be reduced with ease and even pleasure, but that after that point further reduction causes intense suffering. Yes, say many thoughtless persons, who know not what they are talking of, you will suffer a little low spirits and dejection for a few days. I answer, no; there is nothing like low spirits; on the contrary, the mere animal spirits are uncommonly raised; the pulse is improved; the health is better. It is not there that the suffering lies. It has no resemblance to the sufferings caused by renouncing wine. It is a state of unutterable irritation of stomach (which surely is not much like dejection), accompanied by intense perspirations, and feelings such as I shall not attempt to describe without more space at my command. …

I now pass to what is the main subject of these latter confessions, to the history and journal of what took place in my dreams, for these were the immediate and proximate cause of my acutest suffering.

The first notice I had of any important change going on in this part of my physical economy was from the reawakening of a state of eye generally incident to childhood, or exalted states of irritability. I know not whether my reader is aware that many children, perhaps most, have a power of painting, as it were upon the darkness, all sorts of phantoms. In some that power is simply a mechanical affection of the eye; others have a voluntary or semi-voluntary power to dismiss or to summon them, or, as a child once said to me when I questioned him on this matter, "I can tell them to go, and they go; but sometimes they come when I don't tell them to come." Whereupon I told him that he had almost as unlimited a command over apparitions as a

[1] *amanuensis* Latin: scribe or secretary.

Roman centurion over his soldiers. In the middle of 1817, I think it was, that this faculty became positively distressing to me: at night, when I lay awake in bed, vast processions passed along in mournful pomp; friezes of never-ending stories, that to my feelings were as sad and solemn as if they were stories drawn from times before Oedipus or Priam, before Tyre, before Memphis.[1] And at the same time a corresponding change took place in my dreams; a theater seemed suddenly opened and lighted up within my brain, which presented nightly spectacles of more than earthly splendour. And the four following facts may be mentioned as noticeable at this time:

1. That as the creative state of the eye increased, a sympathy seemed to arise between the waking and the dreaming states of the brain in one point—that whatsoever I happened to call up and to trace by a voluntary act upon the darkness was very apt to transfer itself to my dreams, so that I feared to exercise this faculty, for, as Midas turned all things to gold that yet baffled his hopes and defrauded his human desires,[2] so whatsoever things capable of being visually represented I did but think of in the darkness, immediately shaped themselves into phantoms of the eye; and by a process apparently no less inevitable, when thus once traced in faint and visionary colours, like writings in sympathetic[3] ink, they were drawn out by the fierce chemistry of my dreams into insufferable splendour that fretted my heart.

2. For this and all other changes in my dreams were accompanied by deep-seated anxiety and gloomy melancholy, such as are wholly incommunicable by words. I seemed every night to descend, not metaphorically, but literally to descend, into chasms and sunless abysses, depths below depths, from which it seemed hopeless that I could ever re-ascend. Nor did I, by waking, feel that I *had* re-ascended. This I do not dwell upon because the state of gloom which attended these gorgeous spectacles, amounting at last to utter darkness, as of some suicidal despondency, cannot be approached by words.

3. The sense of space, and in the end the sense of time, were both powerfully affected. Buildings, landscapes, &c., were exhibited in proportions so vast as the bodily eye is not fitted to receive. Space swelled and was amplified to an extent of unutterable infinity. This, however, did not disturb me so much as the vast expansion of time; I sometimes seemed to have lived for 70 or 100 years in one night—nay, sometimes had feelings representative of a millennium passed in that time, or, however, of a duration far beyond the limits of any human experience.

4. The minutest incidents of childhood, or forgotten scenes of later years, were often revived; I could not be said to recollect them, for if I had been told of them when waking, I should not have been able to acknowledge them as parts of my past experience. But placed as they were before me, in dreams like intuitions, and clothed in all their evanescent circumstances and accompanying feelings, I *recognized* them instantaneously. I was once told by a near relative of mine, that having in her childhood fallen into a river, and being on the very verge of death but for the critical assistance which reached her, she saw in a moment her whole life, in its minutest incidents, arrayed before her simultaneously as in a mirror; and she had a faculty developed as suddenly for comprehending the whole and every part. This, from some opium experiences of mine, I can believe; I have indeed seen the same thing asserted twice in modern books, and accompanied by a remark which I am convinced is true, viz., that the dread book of account which the Scriptures speak of[4] is in fact the mind itself of each individual. Of this at least I feel assured, that there is no such thing as *forgetting* possible to the mind; a thousand accidents may and will interpose a veil

[1] *Oedipus* King of Thebes, a city in ancient Egypt; *Priam* King of Troy, a city in ancient Greece; *Tyre* Ancient city of Phoenicia, now Lebanon; *Memphis* Capital of ancient Egypt.

[2] *Midas … desires* The Greek god Dionysus granted King Midas his wish that everything he touched be turned to gold; the king was devastated when his food, wine, and eventually his daughter were all turned to gold.

[3] *sympathetic* Invisible.

[4] *dread … speak of* Cf. Revelation 20.12: "I saw the dead, small and great, stand before God; and the books were opened: and another book was opened, which is the book of life: and the dead were judged out of those things which were written in the books, according to their works."

between our present consciousness and the secret inscriptions on the mind; accidents of the same sort will also rend away this veil; but alike, whether veiled or unveiled, the inscription remains forever, just as the stars seem to withdraw before the common light of day, whereas in fact we all know that it is the light which is drawn over them as a veil, and that they are waiting to be revealed when the obscuring daylight shall have withdrawn.…

May 1818

The Malay has been a fearful enemy for months. I have been every night, through his means, transported into Asiatic scenes. I know not whether others share in my feelings on this point, but I have often thought that if I were compelled to forego England and to live in China, and among Chinese manners and modes of life and scenery, I should go mad. The causes of my horror lie deep, and some of them must be common to others. Southern Asia in general is the seat of awful images and associations. As the cradle of the human race, it would alone have a dim and reverential feeling connected with it. But there are other reasons. No man can pretend that the wild, barbarous, and capricious superstitions of Africa, or of savage tribes elsewhere, affect him in the way that he is affected by the ancient, monumental, cruel, and elaborate religions of Indostan, &c. The mere antiquity of Asiatic things, of their institutions, histories, modes of faith, &c., is so impressive, that to me the vast age of the race and name overpowers the sense of youth in the individual. A young Chinese seems to me an antediluvian man renewed. Even Englishmen, though not bred in any knowledge of such institutions, cannot but shudder at the mystic sublimity of *castes* that have flowed apart, and refused to mix, through such immemorial tracts of time; nor can any man fail to be awed by the names of the Ganges or the Euphrates.[1] It contributes much to these feelings that southern Asia is, and has been for thousands of years, the part of the earth most swarming with human life, the great *officina gentium*.[2] Man is a weed in those regions. The vast empires also in which the enormous population of Asia has always been cast, give a further sublimity to the feelings associated with all Oriental names or images. In China, over and above what it has in common with the rest of southern Asia, I am terrified by the modes of life, by the manners, and the barrier of utter abhorrence and want of sympathy placed between us by feelings deeper than I can analyse. I could sooner live with lunatics or brute animals. All this, and much more than I can say or have time to say, the reader must enter into before he can comprehend the unimaginable horror which these dreams of Oriental imagery and mythological tortures impressed upon me. Under the connecting feeling of tropical heat and vertical sunlights I brought together all creatures, birds, beasts, reptiles, all trees and plants, usages and appearances, that are found in all tropical regions, and assembled them together in China or Indostan. From kindred feelings, I soon brought Egypt and all her gods under the same law. I was stared at, hooted at, grinned at, chattered at, by monkeys, by parroquets,[3] by cockatoos. I ran into pagodas, and was fixed for centuries at the summit or in secret rooms. I was the idol; I was the priest; I was worshipped; I was sacrificed. I fled from the wrath of Brama through all the forests of Asia; Vishnu hated me. Seeva[4] laid wait for me. I came suddenly upon Isis and Osiris. I had done a deed, they said, which the ibis and the crocodile[5] trembled at. I was buried for a thousand years in stone coffins, with mummies and sphinxes, in narrow chambers at the heart of eternal pyramids. I was kissed, with cancerous kisses, by crocodiles, and laid, confounded with all unutterable slimy things, amongst reeds and Nilotic mud.[6]

I thus give the reader some slight abstraction of my Oriental dreams, which always filled me with such

[1] *Ganges or the Euphrates* Major rivers of Asia.

[2] *officina gentium* Latin: factory of nations.

[3] *parroquets* I.e., parakeets.

[4] *Brama … Seeva* The Hindu triad: the gods Brahma, Vishnu, and Shiva.

[5] *Isis … crocodile* Isis and Osiris were deities of ancient Egypt; Thoth, in the shape of an ibis, and Sobek, a crocodile, were also Egyptian gods.

[6] *Nilotic mud* I.e., mud of the river Nile.

amazement at the monstrous scenery that horror seemed absorbed for a while in sheer astonishment. Sooner or later came a reflux of feeling that swallowed up the astonishment, and left me not so much in terror as in hatred and abomination of what I saw. Over every form, and threat, and punishment, and dim sightless incarceration, brooded a sense of eternity and infinity that drove me into an oppression as of madness. Into these dreams only it was, with one or two slight exceptions, that any circumstances of physical horror entered. All before had been moral and spiritual terrors. But here the main agents were ugly birds, or snakes, or crocodiles, especially the last. The cursed crocodile became to me the object of more horror than almost all the rest. I was compelled to live with him, and (as was always the case almost in my dreams) for centuries. I escaped sometimes, and found myself in Chinese houses, with cane tables, &c. All the feet of the tables, sofas, &c., soon became instinct with life; the abominable head of the crocodile, and his leering eyes, looked out at me, multiplied into a thousand repetitions, and I stood loathing and fascinated. And so often did this hideous reptile haunt my dreams that many times the very same dream was broken up in the very same way: I heard gentle voices speaking to me (I hear everything when I am sleeping), and instantly I awoke. It was broad noon, and my children were standing, hand in hand, at my bedside—come to show me their coloured shoes, or new frocks, or to let me see them dressed for going out. I protest that so awful was the transition from the damned crocodile, and the other unutterable monsters and abortions of my dreams, to the sight of innocent *human* natures and of infancy, that in the mighty and sudden revulsion of mind I wept, and could not forbear it, as I kissed their faces.

June 1819

I have had occasion to remark, at various periods of my life, that the deaths of those whom we love, and indeed the contemplation of death generally, is (*caeteris paribus*)[1] more affecting in summer than in any other season of the year. And the reasons are these three, I think: first, that the visible heavens in summer appear far higher, more distant, and (if such a solecism may be excused) more infinite; the clouds, by which chiefly the eye expounds the distance of the blue pavilion stretched over our heads, are in summer more voluminous, massed and accumulated in far grander and more towering piles. Secondly, the light and the appearances of the declining and the setting sun are much more fitted to be types and characters of the Infinite. And thirdly (which is the main reason), the exuberant and riotous prodigality of life naturally forces the mind more powerfully upon the antagonist thought of death, and the wintry sterility of the grave. For it may be observed generally, that wherever two thoughts stand related to each other by a law of antagonism, and exist, as it were, by mutual repulsion, they are apt to suggest each other. On these accounts it is that I find it impossible to banish the thought of death when I am walking alone in the endless days of summer; and any particular death, if not more affecting, at least haunts my mind more obstinately and besiegingly in that season. Perhaps this cause, and a slight incident which I omit, might have been the immediate occasions of the following dream, to which, however, a predisposition must always have existed in my mind; but having been once roused it never left me, and split into a thousand fantastic varieties, which often suddenly reunited, and composed again the original dream.

I thought that it was a Sunday morning in May, that it was Easter Sunday, and as yet very early in the morning. I was standing, as it seemed to me, at the door of my own cottage. Right before me lay the very scene which could really be commanded from that situation, but exalted, as was usual, and solemnized by the power of dreams. There were the same mountains, and the same lovely valley at their feet; but the mountains were raised to more than Alpine height, and there was interspace far larger between them of meadows and forest lawns; the hedges were rich with white roses, and no living creature was to be seen, excepting that in the green churchyard there were cattle tranquilly reposing upon the verdant graves, and particularly round about the grave of a child whom I had tenderly loved, just as

[1] *caeteris paribus* Latin: other things being equal.

I had really beheld them, a little before sunrise in the same summer, when that child died. I gazed upon the well-known scene, and I said aloud (as I thought) to myself, "It yet wants much of sunrise, and it is Easter Sunday; and that is the day on which they celebrate the first fruits of resurrection. I will walk abroad; old griefs shall be forgotten today, for the air is cool and still, and the hills are high and stretch away to heaven; and the forest glades are as quiet as the churchyard, and with the dew I can wash the fever from my forehead, and then I shall be unhappy no longer." And I turned as if to open my garden gate, and immediately I saw upon the left a scene far different, but which yet the power of dreams had reconciled into harmony with the other. The scene was an Oriental one, and there also it was Easter Sunday, and very early in the morning. And at a vast distance were visible, as a stain upon the horizon, the domes and cupolas of a great city—an image or faint abstraction, caught perhaps in childhood from some picture of Jerusalem. And not a bowshot[1] from me, upon a stone and shaded by Judean palms, there sat a woman, and I looked, and it was—Ann! She fixed her eyes upon me earnestly, and I said to her at length: "So, then, I have found you at last." I waited, but she answered me not a word. Her face was the same as when I saw it last, and yet again how different! Seventeen years ago, when the lamplight fell upon her face, as for the last time I kissed her lips (lips, Ann, that to me were not polluted), her eyes were streaming with tears; the tears were now wiped away; she seemed more beautiful than she was at that time, but in all other points the same, and not older. Her looks were tranquil, but with unusual solemnity of expression, and I now gazed upon her with some awe; but suddenly her countenance grew dim, and turning to the mountains I perceived vapours rolling between us. In a moment all had vanished, thick darkness came on, and in the twinkling of an eye I was far away from mountains, and by lamplight in Oxford Street, walking again with Ann—just as we walked seventeen years before, when we were both children.

[1] *bowshot* Measurement of distance: the span an arrow will fly from the bow.

As a final specimen, I cite one of a different character, from 1820.

The dream commenced with a music which now I often heard in dreams—a music of preparation and of awakening suspense, a music like the opening of the Coronation Anthem, and which, like *that*, gave the feeling of a vast march, of infinite cavalcades filing off, and the tread of innumerable armies. The morning was come of a mighty day—a day of crisis and of final hope for human nature, then suffering some mysterious eclipse, and labouring in some dread extremity. Somewhere, I knew not where—somehow, I knew not how—by some beings, I knew not whom—a battle, a strife, an agony, was conducting, was evolving like a great drama or piece of music, with which my sympathy was the more insupportable from my confusion as to its place, its cause, its nature, and its possible issue. I, as is usual in dreams (where of necessity we make ourselves central to every movement), had the power, and yet had not the power, to decide it. I had the power, if I could raise myself to will it, and yet again had not the power, for the weight of twenty Atlantics was upon me, or the oppression of inexpiable guilt. "Deeper than ever plummet sounded,"[2] I lay inactive. Then like a chorus the passion deepened. Some greater interest was at stake, some mightier cause than ever yet the sword had pleaded, or trumpet had proclaimed. Then came sudden alarms, hurryings to and fro, trepidations of innumerable fugitives—I knew not whether from the good cause or the bad, darkness and lights, tempest and human faces, and at last, with the sense that all was lost, female forms, and the features that were worth all the world to me, and but a moment allowed—and clasped hands, and heartbreaking partings, and then—everlasting farewells! And with a sigh, such as the caves of Hell sighed when the incestuous mother uttered the abhorred name of death,[3] the sound was reverberated—everlasting

[2] *Deeper … sounded* From Shakespeare's *The Tempest* 3.3.115.

[3] *incestuous … death* In Milton's *Paradise Lost* 2.787–89, Sin, the daughter of Satan, fled and: "cried out DEATH! / Hell trembled at the hideous name, and sighed / From all her caves, and back resounded, DEATH!"

farewells! And again and yet again reverberated—everlasting farewells!

And I awoke in struggles, and cried aloud—"I will sleep no more."[1]

But I am now called upon to wind up a narrative which has already extended to an unreasonable length. Within more spacious limits the materials which I have used might have been better unfolded, and much which I have not used might have been added with effect. Perhaps, however, enough has been given. It now remains that I should say something of the way in which this conflict of horrors was finally brought to a crisis. The reader is already aware (from a passage near the beginning of the introduction to the first part) that the opium-eater has, in some way or other, "unwound almost to its final links the accursed chain which bound him." By what means? To have narrated this according to the original intention would have far exceeded the space which can now be allowed. It is fortunate, as such a cogent reason exists for abridging it, that I should, on a maturer view of the case, have been exceedingly unwilling to injure, by any such unaffecting details, the impression of the history itself, as an appeal to the prudence and the conscience of the yet unconfirmed opium-eater—or even (though a very inferior consideration) to injure its effect as a composition. The interest of the judicious reader will not attach itself chiefly to the subject of the fascinating spells, but to the fascinating power. Not the opium-eater, but the opium, is the true hero of the tale, and the legitimate centre on which the interest revolves. The object was to display the marvellous agency of opium, whether for pleasure or for pain; if that is done, the action of the piece has closed.

However, as some people, in spite of all laws to the contrary, will persist in asking what became of the opium-eater, and in what state he now is, I answer for him thus: The reader is aware that opium had long ceased to found its empire on spells of pleasure; it was solely by the tortures connected with the attempt to abjure it that it kept its hold. Yet, as other tortures, no less it may be thought, attended the non-abjuration of such a tyrant, a choice only of evils was left; and *that* might as well have been adopted which, however terrific in itself, held out a prospect of final restoration to happiness. This appears true, but good logic gave the author no strength to act upon it. However, a crisis arrived for the author's life, and a crisis for other objects still dearer to him—and which will always be far dearer to him than his life, even now that it is again a happy one. I saw that I must die if I continued the opium. I determined, therefore, if that should be required, to die in throwing it off. How much I was at that time taking I cannot say, for the opium which I used had been purchased for me by a friend, who afterwards refused to let me pay him, so that I could not ascertain even what quantity I had used within the year. I apprehend, however, that I took it very irregularly, and that I varied from about fifty or sixty grains to 150 a day. My first task was to reduce it to forty, to thirty, and as fast as I could to twelve grains.

I triumphed. But think not, reader, that therefore my sufferings were ended, nor think of me as of one sitting in a *dejected* state. Think of me as one, even when four months had passed, still agitated, writhing, throbbing, palpitating, shattered, and much perhaps in the situation of him who has been racked, as I collect the torments of that state from the affecting account of them left by a most innocent sufferer[2] of the times of James I. Meantime, I derived no benefit from any medicine, except one prescribed to me by an Edinburgh surgeon of great eminence, viz., ammoniated tincture of valerian. Medical account, therefore, of my emancipation I have not much to give, and even that little, as managed by a man so ignorant of medicine as myself, would probably tend only to mislead. At all events, it would be misplaced in this situation. The moral of the narrative is addressed to the opium-eater, and therefore

[1] *I will sleep no more* From Shakespeare's *Macbeth* 2.2.46, in which the guilt-ridden Macbeth says: "Methought I heard a voice cry 'Sleep no more!'"

[2] [De Quincey's note] William Lithgow. His book (*Travels*, &c.) is ill and pedantically written; but the account of his own sufferings on the rack at Malaga is overpoweringly affecting. [Lithgow was tortured in Malaga, Spain, after being accused of being a spy for King James I, who reigned from 1604 to 1625.]

of necessity limited in its application. If he is taught to fear and tremble, enough has been effected. But he may say that the issue of my case is at least a proof that opium, after a seventeen years' use and an eight years' abuse of its powers, may still be renounced, and that *he* may chance to bring to the task greater energy than I did, or that with a stronger constitution than mine he may obtain the same results with less. This may be true. I would not presume to measure the efforts of other men by my own. I heartily wish him more energy. I wish him the same success. Nevertheless, I had motives external to myself which he may unfortunately want, and these supplied me with conscientious supports which mere personal interests might fail to supply to a mind debilitated by opium.

Jeremy Taylor[1] conjectures that it may be as painful to be born as to die. I think it probable; and during the whole period of diminishing the opium I had the torments of a man passing out of one mode of existence into another. The issue was not death, but a sort of physical regeneration; and I may add that ever since, at intervals, I have had a restoration of more than youthful spirits, though under the pressure of difficulties which in a less happy state of mind I should have called misfortunes.

One memorial of my former condition still remains—my dreams are not yet perfectly calm; the dread swell and agitation of the storm have not wholly subsided; the legions that encamped in them are drawing off, but not all departed; my sleep is still tumultuous, and, like the gates of Paradise to our first parents when looking back from afar, it is still (in the tremendous line of Milton)

> With dreadful faces thronged, and fiery arms.[2]

—1821

[1] *Jeremy Taylor* English bishop, theologian, and author (1613–67).

[2] *With dreadful … arms* From Milton's *Paradise Lost* (12.644).

Mary Prince

1788 – after 1833

"I will say the truth to the English people," declared the abolitionist Mary Prince, whose autobiography detailing her life in the West Indies is the earliest extant slave narrative by a woman. Published at a crucial moment in the campaign to end slavery in British possessions, *The History of Mary Prince* represents an important contribution to the abolitionist movement, as well as a work of historical and literary interest in its own right.

Mary Prince was born into bondage in the British colony of Bermuda, where for the first twelve years of her life she was, relatively speaking, spared the cruelty that dominated her adult years. Both her parents were also enslaved, the property of Charles Myners. After Myners died, Mary and her mother were sold to a Captain Williams, whose daughter Betsey treated Mary as "her little nigger," yet with relative compassion. Williams sold Prince to another family to raise money for his marriage, and in 1806 she was sent to work in the salt ponds of Turks Island: "This work was perfectly new to me. I was given a half barrel and shovel, and had to stand up to my knees in the water, from four o'clock in the morning till nine, when we were given some Indian corn boiled in water, which we were obliged to swallow as fast as we could for fear the rain should come on and melt the salt." In addition to these intolerable working conditions, Prince also endured physical and probably sexual abuse from her master.

In 1818, Prince was sold for three hundred dollars to John Wood, a plantation owner in Antigua, who beat, overworked, and otherwise abused her. By this time Prince had developed a serious skin problem, and while working for the Woods she became essentially crippled by severe rheumatism; her mistreatment would also eventually lead to damaged eyesight. Prince began attending meetings held at the Moravian Church, where various women taught her to read: "After we had done spelling, we tried to read in the Bible. After reading was over, the missionary gave out a hymn for us to sing." Prince was married in this church to Daniel Jones, a formerly enslaved man who had purchased his own freedom. Wood horsewhipped Prince when he discovered the marriage. In 1828 Wood took Prince to London as his servant. Abolitionist sympathizers helped her escape (which they were able to do because slavery was illegal in England), and she found employment as a domestic servant of Thomas Pringle, a Methodist and secretary of the Society for the Abolition of Slavery.

Pringle encouraged Prince to tell the story of her life and, in 1831, he arranged for the publication of her book, *The History of Mary Prince, a West-Indian Slave, Related by Herself.* In his "Preface" to the work, Pringle wrote: "The idea of writing Mary Prince's history was first suggested by herself. She wished it to be done, she said, that good people in England might hear from a slave what a slave had felt and suffered." Mary Prince told her story to Susanna Strickland (later Moodie), who recorded it in writing. It seems improbable that Strickland—who would later come to be regarded as one of Canada's most accomplished writers in the nineteenth century—would not at a minimum have edited the dictated narrative for grammar and syntax, and some have suggested that Pringle may have had some hand in shaping the manuscript so as to better serve abolitionist ends. (His insistence that the rhetorical flourish at the end of Prince's first paragraph is "given verbatim as uttered by Mary Prince" has struck more than one reader as rather forced.) But most scholars have stopped short of suggesting that material was fabricated by Pringle and Strickland, or that this is not in essence Prince's own narrative. Strickland herself attested that she had "been writing Mr. Pringle's black Mary's life from her own dictation and for her benefit adhering to her own simple story and language without deviating to the paths of flourish or romance."

The book was a great success, and gave rise to considerable controversy. *Blackwood's Magazine* and *The Glasgow Courier* claimed it was fraudulent and propagandistic. A number of libel suits resulted, with Wood suing Pringle and Pringle counter-suing. Wood claimed that the book had "endeavored to injure the character of my family by the most vile and infamous falsehoods." Wood lost the case, and the libel scandal served only to make Prince's work more widely known. It reached a third edition in the same year it was published, and it has since that time retained its place as one of the most moving, detailed, and comprehensive narratives of the life of an enslaved person.

Slavery was abolished in most British colonies in 1833. Little is known of Prince's life after the publication of her *History*, and we do not know when, where, or how she died.

⌘⌘⌘

The History of Mary Prince
A West Indian Slave
Related by Herself

PREFACE [BY THOMAS PRINGLE][1]

The idea of writing Mary Prince's history was first suggested by herself. She wished it to be done, she said, that good people in England might hear from a slave what a slave had felt and suffered; and a letter of her late master's, which will be found in the Supplement, induced me to accede to her wish without farther delay. The more immediate object of the publication will afterwards appear.

The narrative was taken down from Mary's own lips by a lady who happened to be at the time residing in my family as a visitor. It was written out fully, with all the narrator's repetitions and prolixities,[2] and afterwards pruned into its present shape; retaining, as far as was practicable, Mary's exact expressions and peculiar phraseology. No fact of importance has been omitted, and not a single circumstance or sentiment has been added. It is essentially her own, without any material alteration farther than was requisite to exclude redundances and gross grammatical errors, so as to render it clearly intelligible.

After it had been thus written out, I went over the whole, carefully examining her on every fact and circumstance detailed; and in all that relates to her residence in Antigua I had the advantage of being assisted in this scrutiny by Mr. Joseph Phillips, who was a resident in that colony during the same period, and had known her there.

The names of all the persons mentioned by the narrator have been printed in full, except those of Capt. I— and his wife, and that of Mr. D—, to whom conduct of peculiar atrocity is ascribed. These three individuals are now gone to answer at a far more awful tribunal than that of public opinion, for the deeds of which their former bondwoman accuses them; and to hold them up more openly to human reprobation could no longer affect themselves, while it might deeply lacerate the feelings of their surviving and perhaps innocent relatives, without any commensurate public advantage.

Without detaining the reader with remarks on other points which will be adverted to more conveniently in the Supplement, I shall here merely notice farther, that the Anti-Slavery Society have no concern whatever with this publication, nor are they in any degree responsible for the statements it contains. I have published the tract,

[1] *THOMAS PRINGLE* Poet and abolitionist Thomas Pringle (1789–1834) was born in Scotland and lived in South Africa between 1820 and 1826, where he published a newspaper and a magazine. In 1826 he returned to England, where he devoted himself to the antislavery movement as secretary to the Society for the Abolition of Slavery.

[2] *prolixities* Instances of wordiness.

not as their Secretary, but in my private capacity; and any profits that may arise from the sale will be exclusively appropriated to the benefit of Mary Prince herself.

THOMAS PRINGLE

7, Solly Terrace, Claremont Square,

January 25, 1831

P.S. Since writing the above, I have been furnished by my friend Mr. George Stephen, with the interesting narrative of Asa-Asa, a captured African, now under his protection; and have printed it as a suitable appendix to this little history.

T.P.

The History of Mary Prince

I was born at Brackish-Pond, in Bermuda, on a farm belonging to Mr. Charles Myners. My mother was a household slave; and my father, whose name was Prince, was a sawyer[1] belonging to Mr. Trimmingham, a ship-builder at Crow-Lane. When I was an infant, old Mr. Myners died, and there was a division of the slaves and other property among the family. I was bought along with my mother by old Captain Darrel, and given to his grandchild, little Miss Betsey Williams. Captain Williams, Mr. Darrel's son-in-law, was master of a vessel which traded to several places in America and the West Indies, and he was seldom at home long together.

Mrs. Williams was a kind-hearted good woman, and she treated all her slaves well. She had only one daughter, Miss Betsey, for whom I was purchased, and who was about my own age. I was made quite a pet of by Miss Betsey, and loved her very much. She used to lead me about by the hand, and call me her little nigger. This was the happiest period of my life; for I was too young to understand rightly my condition as a slave, and too thoughtless and full of spirits to look forward to the days of toil and sorrow.

My mother was a household slave in the same family. I was under her own care, and my little brothers and sisters were my play-fellows and companions. My mother had us several fine children after she came to Mrs. Williams, three girls and two boys. The tasks given out to us children were light, and we used to play together with Miss Betsey, with as much freedom almost as if she had been our sister.

My master, however, was a very harsh, selfish man; and we always dreaded his return from sea. His wife was herself much afraid of him; and, during his stay at home, seldom dared to show her usual kindness to the slaves. He often left her, in the most distressed circumstances, to reside in other female society, at some place in the West Indies of which I have forgot the name. My poor mistress bore his ill-treatment with great patience, and all her slaves loved and pitied her. I was truly attached to her, and, next to my own mother, loved her better than any creature in the world. My obedience to her commands was cheerfully given: it sprung solely from the affection I felt for her, and not from fear of the power which the white people's law had given her over me.

I had scarcely reached my twelfth year when my mistress became too poor to keep so many of us at home; and she hired me out to Mrs. Pruden, a lady who lived about five miles off, in the adjoining parish, in a large house near the sea. I cried bitterly at parting with my dear mistress and Miss Betsey, and when I kissed my mother and brothers and sisters, I thought my young heart would break, it pained me so. But there was no help; I was forced to go. Good Mrs. Williams comforted me by saying that I should still be near the home I was about to quit, and might come over and see her and my kindred whenever I could obtain leave of absence from Mrs. Pruden. A few hours after this I was taken to a strange house, and found myself among strange people. This separation seemed a sore trial to me then; but oh! 'twas light, light to the trials I have since endured!—'twas nothing—nothing to be mentioned with them; but I was a child then, and it was according to my strength.

I knew that Mrs. Williams could no longer maintain me; that she was fain to part with me for my food and clothing; and I tried to submit myself to the change. My new mistress was a passionate woman; but yet she did not treat me very unkindly. I do not remember her

[1] *sawyer* Worker whose job it is to saw timber.

striking me but once, and that was for going to see Mrs. Williams when I heard she was sick, and staying longer than she had given me leave to do. All my employment at this time was nursing a sweet baby, little Master Daniel; and I grew so fond of my nursling that it was my greatest delight to walk out with him by the sea-shore, accompanied by his brother and sister, Miss Fanny and Master James.—Dear Miss Fanny! She was a sweet, kind young lady, and so fond of me that she wished me to learn all that she knew herself; and her method of teaching me was as follows:—Directly she had said her lessons to her grandmamma, she used to come running to me, and make me repeat them one by one after her; and in a few months I was able not only to say my letters but to spell many small words. But this happy state was not to last long. Those days were too pleasant to last. My heart always softens when I think of them.

At this time Mrs. Williams died. I was told suddenly of her death, and my grief was so great that, forgetting I had the baby in my arms, I ran away directly to my poor mistress's house; but reached it only in time to see the corpse carried out. Oh, that was a day of sorrow—a heavy day! All the slaves cried. My mother cried and lamented her sore; and I (foolish creature!) vainly entreated them to bring my dear mistress back to life. I knew nothing rightly about death then, and it seemed a hard thing to bear. When I thought about my mistress I felt as if the world was all gone wrong; and for many days and weeks I could think of nothing else. I returned to Mrs. Pruden's; but my sorrow was too great to be comforted, for my own dear mistress was always in my mind. Whether in the house or abroad, my thoughts were always talking to me about her.

I stayed at Mrs. Pruden's about three months after this; I was then sent back to Mr. Williams to be sold. Oh, that was a sad sad time! I recollect the day well. Mrs. Pruden came to me and said, "Mary, you will have to go home directly; your master is going to be married, and he means to sell you and two of your sisters to raise money for the wedding." Hearing this I burst out a crying,—though I was then far from being sensible of the full weight of my misfortune, or of the misery that waited for me. Besides, I did not like to leave Mrs. Pruden, and the dear baby, who had grown very fond of me. For some time I could scarcely believe that Mrs. Pruden was in earnest, till I received orders for my immediate return.—Dear Miss Fanny! how she cried at parting with me, whilst I kissed and hugged the baby, thinking I should never see him again. I left Mrs. Pruden's, and walked home with a heart full of sorrow. The idea of being sold away from my mother and Miss Betsey was so frightful, that I dared not trust myself to think about it. We had been bought of Mrs. Myners, as I have mentioned, by Miss Betsey's grandfather, and given to her, so that we were by right *her* property, and I never thought we should be separated or sold away from her.

When I reached the house, I went in directly to Miss Betsey. I found her in great distress; and she cried out as soon as she saw me, "Oh, Mary! my father is going to sell you all to raise money to marry that wicked woman. You are *my* slaves, and he has no right to sell you; but it is all to please her." She then told me that my mother was living with her father's sister at a house close by, and I went there to see her. It was a sorrowful meeting; and we lamented with a great and sore crying our unfortunate situation. "Here comes one of my poor piccaninnies!"[1] she said, the moment I came in, "one of the poor slave-brood who are to be sold tomorrow."

Oh dear! I cannot bear to think of that day,—it is too much.—It recalls the great grief that filled my heart, and the woeful thoughts that passed to and fro through my mind, whilst listening to the pitiful words of my poor mother, weeping for the loss of her children. I wish I could find words to tell you all I then felt and suffered. The great God above alone knows the thoughts of the poor slave's heart, and the bitter pains which follow such separations as these. All that we love taken away from us—oh, it is sad, sad! and sore to be borne!—I got no sleep that night for thinking of the morrow; and dear Miss Betsey was scarcely less distressed. She could not bear to part with her old playmates and she cried sore and would not be pacified.

[1] *piccaninnies* Children, usually applied derogatively to black children.

The black morning at length came; it came too soon for my poor mother and us. Whilst she was putting on us the new osnaburgs[1] in which we were to be sold, she said, in a sorrowful voice, (I shall never forget it!) "See, I am *shrouding* my poor children; what a task for a mother!"—She then called Miss Betsey to take leave of us. "I am going to carry my little chickens to market," (these were her very words) "take your last look of them; may be you will see them no more." "Oh, my poor slaves! my own slaves!" said dear Miss Betsey, "you belong to me; and it grieves my heart to part with you."—Miss Betsey kissed us all, and, when she left us, my mother called the rest of the slaves to bid us good bye. One of them, a woman named Moll, came with her infant in her arms. "Ay!" said my mother, seeing her turn away and look at her child with the tears in her eyes, "your turn will come next." The slaves could say nothing to comfort us; they could only weep and lament with us. When I left my dear little brothers and the house in which I had been brought up, I thought my heart would burst.

Our mother, weeping as she went, called me away with the children Hannah and Dinah, and we took the road that led to Hamble Town, which we reached about four o'clock in the afternoon. We followed my mother to the market-place, where she placed us in a row against a large house, with our backs to the wall and our arms folded across our breasts. I, as the eldest, stood first, Hannah next to me, then Dinah; and our mother stood beside, crying over us. My heart throbbed with grief and terror so violently, that I pressed my hands quite tightly across my breast, but I could not keep it still, and it continued to leap as though it would burst out of my body. But who cared for that? Did one of the many bystanders, who were looking at us so carelessly, think of the pain that wrung the hearts of the negro woman and her young ones? No, no! They were not all bad, I dare say, but slavery hardens white people's hearts towards the blacks; and many of them were not slow to make their remarks upon us aloud, without regard to our grief—though their light words fell like cayenne on the fresh wounds of our hearts. Oh those white people have small hearts who can only feel for themselves.

At length the vendue[2] master, who was to offer us for sale like sheep or cattle, arrived, and asked my mother which was the eldest. She said nothing, but pointed to me. He took me by the hand, and led me out into the middle of the street, and, turning me slowly round, exposed me to the view of those who attended the vendue. I was soon surrounded by strange men, who examined and handled me in the same manner that a butcher would a calf or a lamb he was about to purchase, and who talked about my shape and size in like words—as if I could no more understand their meaning than the dumb beasts. I was then put up for sale. The bidding commenced at a few pounds, and gradually rose to fifty-seven, when I was knocked down to the highest bidder; and the people who stood by said that I had fetched a great sum for so young a slave.

I then saw my sisters led forth, and sold to different owners; so that we had not the sad satisfaction of being partners in bondage. When the sale was over, my mother hugged and kissed us, and mourned over us, begging of us to keep up a good heart, and do our duty to our new masters. It was a sad parting; one went one way, one another, and our poor mammy went home with nothing.

My new master was a Captain I—, who lived at Spanish Point. After parting with my mother and sisters, I followed him to his store, and he gave me into the charge of his son, a lad about my own age, Master Benjy, who took me to my new home. I did not know where I was going, or what my new master would do with me. My heart was quite broken with grief, and my thoughts went back continually to those from whom I had been so suddenly parted. "Oh, my mother! my mother!" I kept saying to myself, "Oh, my mammy and my sisters and my brothers, shall I never see you again!"

Oh, the trials! the trials! they make the salt water come into my eyes when I think of the days in which I was afflicted—the times that are gone; when I mourned and grieved with a young heart for those whom I

[1] *osnaburgs* Type of coarse linen used to make clothing.

[2] *vendue* Sale.

loved.—It was night when I reached my new home. The house was large, and built at the bottom of a very high hill; but I could not see much of it that night. I saw too much of it afterwards. The stones and the timber were the best things in it; they were not so hard as the hearts of the owners.

Before I entered the house, two slave women, hired from another owner, who were at work in the yard, spoke to me, and asked who I belonged to? I replied, "I am come to live here." "Poor child, poor child!" they both said; "you must keep a good heart, if you are to live here."—When I went in, I stood up crying in a corner. Mrs. I— came and took off my hat, a little black silk hat Miss Pruden made for me, and said in a rough voice, "You are not come here to stand up in corners and cry, you are come here to work." She then put a child into my arms, and, tired as I was, I was forced instantly to take up my old occupation of a nurse.—I could not bear to look at my mistress, her countenance was so stern. She was a stout tall woman with a very dark complexion, and her brows were always drawn together into a frown. I thought of the words of the two slave women when I saw Mrs. I—, and heard the harsh sound of her voice.

The person I took the most notice of that night was a French Black called Hetty, whom my master took in privateering from another vessel, and made his slave. She was the most active woman I ever saw, and she was tasked to her utmost. A few minutes after my arrival she came in from milking the cows, and put the sweet-potatoes on for supper. She then fetched home the sheep, and penned them in the fold; drove home the cattle, and staked them about the pond side; fed and rubbed down my master's horse, and gave the hog and the fed cow their suppers; prepared the beds, and undressed the children, and laid them to sleep. I liked to look at her and watch all her doings, for her's was the only friendly face I had as yet seen, and I felt glad that she was there. She gave me my supper of potatoes and milk, and a blanket to sleep upon, which she spread for me in the passage before the door of Mrs. I—'s chamber.

I got a sad fright, that night. I was just going to sleep, when I heard a noise in my mistress's room; and she presently called out to inquire if some work was finished that she had ordered Hetty to do. "No, Ma'am, not yet," was Hetty's answer from below. On hearing this, my master started up from his bed, and just as he was, in his shirt, ran down stairs with a long cow-skin in his hand. I heard immediately after, the cracking of the thong, and the house rang to the shrieks of poor Hetty, who kept crying out, "Oh, Massa! Massa! me dead. Massa! have mercy upon me—don't kill me outright."—This was a sad beginning for me. I sat up upon my blanket, trembling with terror, like a frightened hound, and thinking that my turn would come next. At length the house became still, and I forgot for a little while all my sorrows by falling fast asleep.

The next morning my mistress set about instructing me in my tasks. She taught me to do all sorts of household work; to wash and bake, pick cotton and wool, and wash floors, and cook. And she taught me (how can I ever forget it!) more things than these; she caused me to know the exact difference between the smart of the rope, the cart-whip, and the cow-skin, when applied to my naked body by her own cruel hand. And there was scarcely any punishment more dreadful than the blows I received on my face and head from her hard heavy fist. She was a fearful woman, and a savage mistress to her slaves.

There were two little slave boys in the house, on whom she vented her bad temper in a special manner. One of these children was a mulatto, called Cyrus, who had been bought while an infant in his mother's arms; the other, Jack, was an African from the coast of Guinea, whom a sailor had given or sold to my master. Seldom a day passed without these boys receiving the most severe treatment, and often for no fault at all. Both my master and mistress seemed to think that they had a right to ill-use them at their pleasure; and very often accompanied their commands with blows, whether the children were behaving well or ill. I have seen their flesh ragged and raw with licks.—Lick—lick—they were never secure one moment from a blow, and their lives were passed in continual fear. My mistress was not contented with using the whip, but often pinched their cheeks and arms in the most cruel manner. My pity for these poor boys was soon transferred to myself; for I was licked, and flogged, and pinched by her pitiless fingers in the neck and arms, exactly as they were. To strip me naked—to hang me up by the wrists and lay my flesh open with the cow-skin, was an ordinary punishment for even a slight offence. My mistress often robbed me too of the hours that belong to sleep. She used to sit up very late, frequently even until morning; and I had then to stand at a bench and wash during the greater part of the night, or pick wool and cotton and often I have dropped down overcome by sleep and fatigue, till roused from a state of stupor by the whip, and forced to start up to my tasks.

Poor Hetty, my fellow slave, was very kind to me, and I used to call her my Aunt; but she led a most miserable life, and her death was hastened (at least the slaves all believed and said so,) by the dreadful chastisement she received from my master during her pregnancy. It happened as follows. One of the cows had dragged the rope away from the stake to which Hetty had fastened it, and got loose. My master flew into a terrible passion, and ordered the poor creature to be stripped quite naked, notwithstanding her pregnancy, and to be tied up to a tree in the yard. He then flogged her as hard as he could lick, both with the whip and cow-skin, till she was all over streaming with blood. He rested, and then beat her again and again. Her shrieks were terrible. The consequence was that poor Hetty was brought to bed before her time, and was delivered after severe labour of a dead child. She appeared to recover after her confinement, so far that she was repeatedly flogged by both master and mistress afterwards; but her former strength never returned to her. Ere long her body and limbs swelled to a great size; and she lay on a mat in the kitchen, till the water burst out of her body and she died. All the slaves said that death was a good thing for poor Hetty; but I cried very much for her death. The manner of it filled me with horror. I could not bear to think about it; yet it was always present to my mind for many a day.

After Hetty died all her labours fell upon me, in addition to my own. I had now to milk eleven cows every morning before sunrise, sitting among the damp weeds; to take care of the cattle as well as the children; and to do the work of the house. There was no end to my toils—no end to my blows. I lay down at night and rose up in the morning in fear and sorrow; and often wished that like poor Hetty I could escape from this cruel bondage and be at rest in the grave. But the hand of that God whom then I knew not, was stretched over me; and I was mercifully preserved for better things. It was then, however, my heavy lot to weep, weep, weep, and that for years; to pass from one misery to another, and from one cruel master to a worse. But I must go on with the thread of my story. One day a heavy squall of wind and rain came on suddenly, and my mistress sent me round the corner of the house to empty a large earthen jar. The jar was already cracked with an old deep crack that divided it in the middle, and in turning it upside down to empty it, it parted in my hand. I could not help the accident, but I was dreadfully frightened, looking forward to a severe punishment. I ran crying to my mistress, "O mistress, the jar has come in two." "You have broken it, have you?" she replied; "come directly here to me." I came trembling: she stripped and flogged me long and severely with the cow-skin; as long as she had strength to use the lash, for she did not give over till she was quite tired.—When my master came home at night, she told him of my fault; and oh, frightful! how he fell a swearing. After abusing me with every ill name he could think of, (too, too bad to speak in England,) and giving me several heavy blows with his hand, he said, "I shall come home to-morrow morning at twelve, on purpose to give you a round hundred." He kept his word—Oh sad for me! I cannot easily forget it. He tied me up upon a ladder, and gave me a hundred lashes with his own hand, and master Benjy stood by to count them for him. When he had licked me for some time he sat down to take breath; then after resting, he beat me again and again, until he was quite wearied, and so hot (for the weather was very sultry), that he sank back in his chair, almost like to faint. While my mistress went to bring him drink, there was a dreadful earthquake. Part of the roof fell down, and every thing in the house went—clatter, clatter, clatter. Oh I thought the end of all things near at hand;

and I was so sore with the flogging, that I scarcely cared whether I lived or died. The earth was groaning and shaking; every thing tumbling about; and my mistress and the slaves were shrieking and crying out, "The earthquake! the earthquake!" It was an awful day for us all.

During the confusion I crawled away on my hands and knees, and laid myself down under the steps of the piazza, in front of the house. I was in a dreadful state—my body all blood and bruises, and I could not help moaning piteously. The other slaves, when they saw me, shook their heads and said, "Poor child! poor child"—I lay there till the morning, careless of what might happen, for life was very weak in me, and I wished more than ever to die. But when we are very young, death always seems a great way off, and it would not come that night to me. The next morning I was forced by my master to rise and go about my usual work, though my body and limbs were so stiff and sore, that I could not move without the greatest pain.—Nevertheless, even after all this severe punishment, I never heard the last of that jar; my mistress was always throwing it in my face.

Some little time after this, one of the cows got loose from the stake, and eat one of the sweet-potato slips. I was milking when my master found it out. He came to me, and without any more ado, stooped down, and taking off his heavy boot, he struck me such a severe blow in the small of my back, that I shrieked with agony, and thought I was killed; and I feel a weakness in that part to this day. The cow was frightened by his violence, and kicked down the pail and spilt the milk all about. My master knew that this accident was his own fault, but he was so enraged that he seemed glad of an excuse to go on with his ill usage. I cannot remember how many licks he gave me then, but he beat me till I was unable to stand, and till he himself was weary.

After this I ran away and went to my mother, who was living with Mr. Richard Darrel. My poor mother was both grieved and glad to see me; grieved because I had been so ill used, and glad because she had not seen me for a long, long while. She dared not receive me into the house, but she hid me up in a hole in the rocks near, and brought me food at night, after every body was asleep. My father, who lived at Crow-Lane, over the salt-water channel, at last heard of my being hid up in the cavern, and he came and took me back to my master. Oh I was loath, loath to go back; but as there was no remedy, I was obliged to submit.

When we got home, my poor father said to Capt. I—, "Sir, I am sorry that my child should be forced to run away from her owner; but the treatment she has received is enough to break her heart. The sight of her wounds has nearly broke mine.—I entreat you, for the love of God, to forgive her for running away, and that you will be a kind master to her in future." Capt. I— said I was used as well as I deserved, and that I ought to be punished for running away. I then took courage and said that I could stand the floggings no longer; that I was weary of my life, and therefore I had run away to my mother; but mothers could only weep and mourn over their children, they could not save them from cruel masters—from the whip, the rope, and the cow-skin. He told me to hold my tongue and go about my work, or he would find a way to settle me. He did not, however, flog me that day.

For five years after this I remained in his house, and almost daily received the same harsh treatment. At length he put me on board a sloop, and to my great joy sent me away to Turk's Island.[1] I was not permitted to see my mother or father, or poor sisters and brothers, to say good bye, though going away to a strange land, and might never see them again. Oh the Buckra[2] people who keep slaves think that black people are like cattle, without natural affection. But my heart tells me it is far otherwise.

We were nearly four weeks on the voyage, which was unusually long. Sometimes we had a light breeze, sometimes a great calm, and the ship made no way; so that our provisions and water ran very low, and we were put upon short allowance. I should almost have been starved had it not been for the kindness of a black man

[1] *sloop* Small ship; *Turk's Island* The southernmost and easternmost island of the Bahamas.

[2] *Buckra* White.

called Anthony, and his wife, who had brought their own victuals, and shared them with me.

When we went ashore at the Grand Quay, the captain sent me to the house of my new master, Mr. D—, to whom Captain I— had sold me. Grand Quay is a small town upon a sandbank; the houses low and built of wood. Such was my new master's. The first person I saw, on my arrival, was Mr. D—, a stout sulky looking man, who carried me through the hall to show me to his wife and children. Next day I was put up by the vendue master to know how much I was worth, and I was valued at one hundred pounds currency.

My new master was one of the owners or holders of the salt ponds, and he received a certain sum for every slave that worked upon his premises, whether they were young or old. This sum was allowed him out of the profits arising from the salt works. I was immediately sent to work in the salt water with the rest of the slaves. This work was perfectly new to me. I was given a half barrel and a shovel, and had to stand up to my knees in the water, from four o'clock in the morning till nine, when we were given some Indian corn boiled in water, which we were obliged to swallow as fast as we could for fear the rain should come on and melt the salt. We were then called again to our tasks, and worked through the heat of the day; the sun flaming upon our heads like fire, and raising salt blisters in those parts which were not completely covered. Our feet and legs, from standing in the salt water for so many hours, soon became full of dreadful boils, which eat down in some cases to the very bone, afflicting the sufferers with great torment. We came home at twelve; ate our corn soup, called *blawly,* as fast as we could, and went back to our employment till dark at night. We then shovelled up the salt in large heaps, and went down to the sea, where we washed the pickle from our limbs, and cleaned the barrows and shovels from the salt. When we returned to the house, our master gave us each our allowance of raw Indian corn, which we pounded in a mortar and boiled in water for our suppers. We slept in a long shed, divided into narrow slips, like the stalls used for cattle. Boards fixed upon stakes driven into the ground, without mat or covering, were our only beds. On Sundays, after we had washed the salt bags, and done other work required of us, we went into the bush and cut the long soft grass, of which we made trusses for our legs and feet to rest upon, for they were so full of the salt boils that we could get no rest lying upon the bare boards.

Though we worked from morning till night, there was no satisfying Mr. D—. I hoped, when I left Capt. I—, that I should have been better off, but I found it was but going from one butcher to another. There was this difference between them: my former master used to beat me while raging and foaming with passion; Mr. D— was usually quite calm. He would stand by and give orders for a slave to be cruelly whipped, and assist in the punishment, without moving a muscle of his face; walking about and taking snuff with the greatest composure. Nothing could touch his hard heart—neither sighs, nor tears, nor prayers, nor streaming blood; he was deaf to our cries, and careless of our sufferings.—Mr. D— has often stripped me naked, hung me up by the wrists, and beat me with the cow-skin, with his own hand, till my body was raw with gashes. Yet there was nothing very remarkable in this; for it might serve as a sample of the common usage of the slaves on that horrible island.

Owing to the boils in my feet, I was unable to wheel the barrow fast through the sand, which got into the sores, and made me stumble at every step; and my master, having no pity for my sufferings from this cause, rendered them far more intolerable, by chastising me for not being able to move so fast as he wished me. Another of our employments was to row a little way off from the shore in a boat, and dive for large stones to build a wall round our master's house. This was very hard work; and the great waves breaking over us continually, made us often so giddy that we lost our footing, and were in danger of being drowned.

Ah, poor me!—my tasks were never ended. Sick or well, it was work—work—work!—After the diving season was over, we were sent to the South Creek, with large bills, to cut up mangoes to burn lime with. Whilst one party of slaves were thus employed, another were sent to the other side of the island to break up coral out of the sea.

When we were ill, let our complaint be what it might, the only medicine given to us was a great bowl of hot salt water, with salt mixed with it, which made us very sick. If we could not keep up with the rest of the gang of slaves, we were put in the stocks,[1] and severely flogged the next morning. Yet, not the less, our master expected, after we had thus been kept from our rest, and our limbs rendered stiff and sore with ill usage, that we should still go through the ordinary tasks of the day all the same.—Sometimes we had to work all night, measuring salt to load a vessel; or turning a machine to draw water out of the sea for the salt-making. Then we had no sleep—no rest—but were forced to work as fast as we could, and go on again all next day the same as usual. Work—work—work—Oh that Turk's Island was a horrible place! The people in England, I am sure, have never found out what is carried on there. Cruel, horrible place!

Mr. D— had a slave called old Daniel, whom he used to treat in the most cruel manner. Poor Daniel was lame in the hip, and could not keep up with the rest of the slaves; and our master would order him to be stripped and laid down on the ground, and have him beaten with a rod of rough briar till his skin was quite red and raw. He would then call for a bucket of salt, and fling upon the raw flesh till the man writhed on the ground like a worm, and screamed aloud with agony. This poor man's wounds were never healed, and I have often seen them full of maggots, which increased his torments to an intolerable degree. He was an object of pity and terror to the whole gang of slaves, and in his wretched case we saw, each of us, our own lot, if we should live to be as old.

Oh the horrors of slavery!—How the thought of it pains my heart! But the truth ought to be told of it; and what my eyes have seen I think it is my duty to relate; for few people in England know what slavery is. I have been a slave—I have felt what a slave feels, and I know what a slave knows; and I would have all the good people in England to know it too, that they may break our chains, and set us free.

Mr. D— had another slave called Ben. He being very hungry, stole a little rice one night after he came in from work, and cooked it for his supper. But his master soon discovered the theft; locked him up all night; and kept him without food till one o'clock the next day. He then hung Ben up by his hands, and beat him from time to time till the slaves came in at night. We found the poor creature hung up when we came home; with a pool of blood beneath him, and our master still licking him, but this was not the worst. My master's son was in the habit of stealing the rice and rum. Ben had seen him do this, and thought he might do the same, and when master found out that Ben had stolen the rice and swore to punish him, he tried to excuse himself by saying that Master Dickey did the same thing every night. The lad denied it to his father, and was so angry with Ben for informing against him, that out of revenge he ran and got a bayonet, and whilst the poor wretch was suspended by his hands and writhing under his wounds, he run it quite through his foot. I was not by when he did it, but I saw the wound when I came home, and heard Ben tell the manner in which it was done.

I must say something more about this cruel son of a cruel father.—He had no heart—no fear of God; he had been brought up by a bad father in a bad path, and he delighted to follow in the same steps. There was a little old woman among the slaves called Sarah, who was nearly past work; and, Master Dickey being the overseer of the slaves just then, this poor creature, who was subject to several bodily infirmities, and was not quite right in her head, did not wheel the barrow fast enough to please him. He threw her down on the ground, and after beating her severely, he took her up in his arms and flung her among the prickly-pear[2] bushes, which are all covered over with sharp venomous prickles. By this her naked flesh was so grievously wounded, that her body swelled and festered all over, and she died in a few days after. In telling my own sorrows, I cannot pass by those of my fellow-slaves—for when I think of my own griefs, I remember theirs.

[1] *stocks* Device for confining the ankles and sometimes the wrists.

[2] *prickly-pear* Type of cactus.

I think it was about ten years I had worked in the salt ponds at Turk's Island, when my master left off business, and retired to a house he had in Bermuda, leaving his son to succeed him in the island. He took me with him to wait upon his daughters; and I was joyful, for I was sick, sick of Turk's Island, and my heart yearned to see my native place again, my mother, and my kindred.

I had seen my poor mother during the time I was a slave in Turk's Island. One Sunday morning I was on the beach with some of the slaves, and we saw a sloop come in loaded with slaves to work in the salt water. We got a boat and went aboard. When I came upon the deck I asked the black people, "Is there any one here for me?" "Yes," they said, "your mother." I thought they said this in jest—I could scarcely believe them for joy; but when I saw my poor mammy my joy was turned to sorrow, for she had gone from her senses. "Mammy," I said, "is this you!" She did not know me. "Mammy," I said, "what's the matter?" She began to talk foolishly and said that she had been under the vessel's bottom. They had been overtaken by a violent storm at sea. My poor mother had never been on the sea before, and she was so ill, that she lost her senses, and it was long before she came quite to herself again. She had a sweet child with her—a little sister I had never seen, about four years of age, called Rebecca. I took her on shore with me, for I felt I should love her directly; and I kept her with me a week. Poor little thing! her's has been a sad life, and continues so to this day. My mother worked for some years on the island, but was taken back to Bermuda some time before my master carried me again thither.

After I left Turk's Island, I was told by some negroes that came over from it, that the poor slaves had built up a place with boughs and leaves, where they might meet for prayers, but the white people pulled it down twice, and would not allow them even a shed for prayers. A flood came down soon after and washed away many houses, filled the place with sand, and overflowed the ponds: and I do think that this was for their wickedness; for the Buckra men there were very wicked. I saw and heard much that was very very bad at that place.

I was several years the slave of Mr. D— after I returned to my native place. Here I worked in the grounds. My work was planting and hoeing sweet-potatoes, Indian corn, plaintains, bananas, cabbages, pumpkins, onions, &c. I did all the household work, and attended upon a horse and cow besides,—going also upon all errands. I had to curry the horse—to clean and feed him—and sometimes to ride him a little. I had more than enough to do—but still it was not so very bad as Turk's Island.

My old master often got drunk, and then he would get in a fury with his daughter, and beat her till she was not fit to be seen. I remember on one occasion, I had gone to fetch water, and when I was coming up the hill I heard a great screaming; I ran as fast as I could to the house, put down the water, and went into the chamber, where I found my master beating Miss D— dreadfully. I strove with all my strength to get her away from him; for she was all black and blue with bruises. He had beat her with his fist, and almost killed her. The people gave me credit for getting her away. He turned round and began to lick me. Then I said, "Sir, this is not Turk's Island." I can't repeat his answer, the words were too wicked—too bad to say. He wanted to treat me the same in Bermuda as he had done in Turk's Island.

He had an ugly fashion of stripping himself quite naked and ordering me then to wash him in a tub of water. This was worse to me than all the licks. Sometimes when he called me to wash him I would not come, my eyes were so full of shame. He would then come to beat me. One time I had plates and knives in my hand, and I dropped both plates and knives, and some of the plates were broken. He struck me so severely for this, that at last I defended myself, for I thought it was high time to do so. I then told him I would not live longer with him, for he was a very indecent man—very spiteful, and too indecent; with no shame for his servants, no shame for his own flesh. So I went away to a neighbouring house and sat down and cried till the next morning, when I went home again, not knowing what else to do.

After that I was hired to work at Cedar Hills, and every Saturday night I paid the money to my master. I had plenty of work to do there—plenty of washing; but yet I made myself pretty comfortable. I earned two dollars and a quarter a week, which is twenty pence a day.

During the time I worked there, I heard that Mr. John Wood was going to Antigua. I felt a great wish to go there, and I went to Mr. D—, and asked him to let me go in Mr. Wood's service. Mr. Wood did not then want to purchase me; it was my own fault that I came under him, I was so anxious to go. It was ordained to be, I suppose; God led me there. The truth is, I did not wish to be any longer the slave of my indecent master.

Mr. Wood took me with him to Antigua, to the town of St. John's, where he lived. This was about fifteen years ago. He did not then know whether I was to be sold; but Mrs. Wood found that I could work, and she wanted to buy me. Her husband then wrote to my master to inquire whether I was to be sold? Mr. D— wrote in reply, "that I should not be sold to any one that would treat me ill." It was strange he should say this, when he had treated me so ill himself. So I was purchased by Mr. Wood for 300 dollars (or £100 Bermuda currency).

My work there was to attend the chambers and nurse the child, and to go down to the pond and wash clothes. But I soon fell ill of the rheumatism, and grew so very lame that I was forced to walk with a stick. I got the Saint Anthony's fire,[1] also, in my left leg, and became quite a cripple. No one cared much to come near me, and I was ill a long long time; for several months I could not lift the limb. I had to lie in a little old out-house, that was swarming with bugs and other vermin, which tormented me greatly; but I had no other place to lie in. I got the rheumatism by catching cold at the pond side, from washing in the fresh water; in the salt water I never got cold. The person who lived in next yard, (a Mrs. Greene,) could not bear to hear my cries and groans. She was kind, and used to send an old slave woman to help me, who sometimes brought me a little soup. When the doctor found I was so ill, he said I must be put into a bath of hot water. The old slave got the bark of some bush that was good for pains, which she boiled in the hot water, and every night she came and put me into the bath, and did what she could for me; I don't know what I should have done, or what would have become of me, had it not been for her.—My mistress, it is true, did send me a little food; but no one from our family came near me but the cook, who used to shove my food in at the door, and say, "Molly, Molly, there's your dinner." My mistress did not care to take any trouble about me; and if the Lord had not put it into the hearts of the neighbours to be kind to me, I must, I really think, have lain and died.

It was a long time before I got well enough to work in the house. Mrs. Wood, in the meanwhile, hired a mulatto woman to nurse the child; but she was such a fine lady she wanted to be mistress over me. I thought it very hard for a coloured woman to have rule over me because I was a slave and she was free. Her name was Martha Wilcox; she was a saucy woman, very saucy; and she went and complained of me, without cause, to my mistress, and made her angry with me. Mrs. Wood told me that if I did not mind what I was about, she would get my master to strip me and give me fifty lashes: "You have been used to the whip," she said, "and you shall have it here." This was the first time she threatened to have me flogged; and she gave me the threatening so strong of what she would have done to me, that I thought I should have fallen down at her feet, I was so vexed and hurt by her words. The mulatto woman was rejoiced to have power to keep me down. She was constantly making mischief; there was no living for the slaves—no peace after she came.

I was also sent by Mrs. Wood to be put in the Cage one night, and was next morning flogged, by the magistrate's order, at her desire; and this all for a quarrel I had about a pig with another slave woman. I was flogged on my naked back on this occasion; although I was in no fault after all; for old Justice Dyett, when we came before him, said that I was in the right, and ordered the pig to be given to me. This was about two or three years after I came to Antigua.

When we moved from the middle of the town to the Point, I used to be in the house and do all the work and mind the children, though still very ill with the rheumatism. Every week I had to wash two large bundles of clothes, as much as a boy could help me to lift; but I

[1] *Saint Anthony's fire* Erysipelas or ergotism, diseases that cause intense redness, swelling of the skin, and severe pain.

could give no satisfaction. My mistress was always abusing and fretting after me. It is not possible to tell all her ill language.—One day she followed me foot after foot scolding and rating me. I bore in silence a great deal of ill words: at last my heart was quite full, and I told her that she ought not to use me so;—that when I was ill I might have lain and died for what she cared; and no one would then come near me to nurse me, because they were afraid of my mistress. This was a great affront. She called her husband and told him what I had said. He flew into a passion: but did not beat me then; he only abused and swore at me; and then gave me a note and bade me go and look for an owner. Not that he meant to sell me; but he did this to please his wife and to frighten me. I went to Adam White, a cooper,[1] a free black who had money, and asked him to buy me. He went directly to Mr. Wood, but was informed that I was not to be sold. The next day my master whipped me.

Another time (about five years ago) my mistress got vexed with me because I fell sick and I could not keep on with my work. She complained to her husband, and he sent me off again to look for an owner. I went to a Mr. Burchell, showed him the note, and asked him to buy me for my own benefit; for I had saved about 100 dollars, and hoped with a little help, to purchase my freedom. He accordingly went to my master: "Mr. Wood," he said, "Molly has brought me a note that she wants an owner. If you intend to sell her, I may as well buy her as another." My master put him off and said that he did not mean to sell me. I was very sorry at this, for I had no comfort with Mrs. Wood, and I wished greatly to get my freedom.

The way in which I made my money was this.—When my master and mistress went from home, as they sometimes did, and left me to take care of the house and premises, I had a good deal of time to myself and made the most of it. I took in washing, and sold coffee and yams and other provisions to the captains of ships. I did not sit still idling during the absence of my owners; for I wanted, by all honest means, to earn money to buy my freedom. Sometimes I bought a hog cheap on board ship, and sold it for double the money on shore; and I also earned a good deal by selling coffee. By this means I by degrees acquired a little cash. A gentleman also lent me some to help to buy my freedom—but when I could not get free he got it back again. His name was Captain Abbot.

My master and mistress went on one occasion into the country, to Date Hill, for a change of air, and carried me with them to take charge of the children, and to do the work of the house. While I was in the country, I saw how the field negroes are worked in Antigua. They are worked very hard and fed but scantily. They are called out to work before daybreak, and come home after dark; and then each has to heave his bundle of grass for the cattle in the pen. Then, on Sunday morning, each slave has to go out and gather a large bundle of grass; and, when they bring it home, they have all to sit at the manager's door and wait till he comes out: often have they to wait there till past eleven o'clock without any breakfast. After that, those that have yams or potatoes, or fire-wood to sell, hasten to market to buy a dog's worth[2] of salt fish, or pork, which is a great treat for them. Some of them buy a little pickle out of the shad barrels, which they call sauce, to season their yams and Indian corn. It is very wrong, I know, to work on Sunday or go to market; but will not God call the Buckra men to answer for this on the great day of judgment—since they will give the slaves no other day?

While we were at Date Hill Christmas came; and the slave woman who had the care of the place (which then belonged to Mr. Roberts the marshal), asked me to go with her to her husband's house, to a Methodist meeting for prayer, at a plantation called Winthorps. I went; and they were the first prayers I ever understood. One woman prayed; and then they all sung a hymn; then there was another prayer and another hymn; and then they all spoke by turns of their own griefs as sinners. The husband of the woman I went with was a black driver. His name was Henry. He confessed that he had treated the slaves very cruelly; but said that he was compelled to obey the orders of his master. He prayed

[1] *cooper* Barrel- and tub-maker.

[2] *dog's worth* 72nd part of a dollar.

them all to forgive him, and he prayed that God would forgive him. He said it was a horrid thing for a ranger to have sometimes to beat his own wife or sister; but he must do so if ordered by his master.

I felt sorry for my sins also. I cried the whole night, but I was too much ashamed to speak. I prayed God to forgive me. This meeting had a great impression on my mind, and led my spirit to the Moravian church; so that when I got back to town, I went and prayed to have my name put down in the Missionaries' book; and I followed the church earnestly every opportunity. I did not then tell my mistress about it; for I knew that she would not give me leave to go. But I felt I *must* go. Whenever I carried the children their lunch at school, I ran round and went to hear the teachers.

The Moravian ladies (Mrs. Richter, Mrs. Olufsen, and Mrs. Sauter) taught me to read in the class; and I got on very fast. In this class there were all sorts of people, old and young, grey headed folks and children; but most of them were free people. After we had done spelling, we tried to read in the Bible. After the reading was over, the missionary gave out a hymn for us to sing. I dearly loved to go to the church, it was so solemn. I never knew rightly that I had much sin till I went there. When I found out that I was a great sinner, I was very sorely grieved, and very much frightened. I used to pray God to pardon my sins for Christ's sake, and forgive me for every thing I had done amiss; and when I went home to my work, I always thought about what I had heard from the missionaries, and wished to be good that I might go to heaven. After a while I was admitted a candidate for the holy Communion.—I had been baptized long before this, in August 1817, by the Rev. Mr. Curtin, of the English Church, after I had been taught to repeat the Creed and the Lord's Prayer. I wished at that time to attend a Sunday School taught by Mr. Curtin, but he would not receive me without a written note from my master, granting his permission. I did not ask my owner's permission, from the belief that it would be refused; so that I got no farther instruction at that time from the English Church.

Some time after I began to attend the Moravian Church, I met with Daniel James, afterwards my dear husband. He was a carpenter and cooper to his trade; an honest, hard-working, decent black man, and a widower. He had purchased his freedom of his mistress, old Mrs. Baker, with money he had earned whilst a slave. When he asked me to marry him, I took time to consider the matter over with myself, and would not say yes till he went to church with me and joined the Moravians. He was very industrious after he bought his freedom; and he had hired a comfortable house, and had convenient things about him. We were joined in marriage, about Christmas 1826, in the Moravian Chapel at Spring Gardens, by the Rev. Mr. Olufsen. We could not be married in the English Church. English marriage is not allowed to slaves; and no free man can marry a slave woman.

When Mr. Wood heard of my marriage, he flew into a great rage, and sent for Daniel, who was helping to build a house for his old mistress. Mr. Wood asked him who gave him a right to marry a slave of his? My husband said, "Sir, I am a free man, and thought I had a right to choose a wife; but if I had known Molly was not allowed to have a husband, I should not have asked her to marry me." Mrs. Wood was more vexed about my marriage than her husband. She could not forgive me for getting married, but stirred up Mr. Wood to flog me dreadfully with his horsewhip. I thought it very hard to be whipped at my time of life for getting a husband—I told her so. She said that she would not have nigger men about the yards and premises, or allow a nigger man's clothes to be washed in the same tub where hers were washed. She was fearful, I think, that I should lose her time, in order to wash and do things for my husband: but I had then no time to wash for myself; I was obliged to put out my own clothes, though I was always at the wash-tub.

I had not much happiness in my marriage, owing to my being a slave. It made my husband sad to see me so ill-treated. Mrs. Wood was always abusing me about him. She did not lick me herself, but she got her husband to do it for her, whilst she fretted the flesh off my bones. Yet for all this she would not sell me. She sold five slaves whilst I was with her; but though she was always finding fault with me, she would not part with me. However, Mr. Wood afterwards allowed Daniel to have a place to live in our yard, which we were very thankful for.

After this, I fell ill again with the rheumatism, and was sick a long time; but whether sick or well, I had my work to do. About this time I asked my master and mistress to let me buy my own freedom. With the help of Mr. Burchell, I could have found the means to pay Mr. Wood; for it was agreed that I should afterwards serve Mr. Burchell a while, for the cash he was to advance for me. I was earnest in the request to my owners; but their hearts were hard—too hard to consent. Mrs. Wood was very angry—she grew quite outrageous—she called me a black devil, and asked me who had put freedom into my head. "To be free is very sweet," I said: but she took good care to keep me a slave. I saw her change colour, and I left the room.

About this time my master and mistress were going to England to put their son in school, and bring their daughters home; and they took me with them to take care of the child. I was willing to come to England: I thought that by going there I should probably get cured of my rheumatism, and should return with my master and mistress, quite well, to my husband. My husband was willing for me to come away, for he had heard that my master would free me,—and I also hoped this might prove true; but it was all a false report.

The steward of the ship was very kind to me. He and my husband were in the same class in the Moravian Church. I was thankful that he was so friendly, for my mistress was not kind to me on the passage; and she told me, when she was angry, that she did not intend to treat me any better in England than in the West Indies—that I need not expect it. And she was as good as her word.

When we drew near to England, the rheumatism seized all my limbs worse than ever, and my body was dreadfully swelled. When we landed at the Tower, I showed my flesh to my mistress, but she took no great notice of it. We were obliged to stop at the tavern till my master got a house; and a day or two after, my mistress sent me down into the wash-house to learn to wash in the English way. In the West Indies we wash with cold water—in England with hot. I told my mistress I was afraid that putting my hands first into the hot water and then into the cold, would increase the pain in my limbs. The doctor had told my mistress long before I came from the West Indies, that I was a sickly body and the washing did not agree with me. But Mrs. Wood would not release me from the tub, so I was forced to do as I could. I grew worse, and could not stand to wash. I was then forced to sit down with the tub before me, and often through pain and weakness was reduced to kneel or to sit down on the floor, to finish my task. When I complained to my mistress of this, she only got into a passion as usual, and said washing in hot water could not hurt any one;—that I was lazy and insolent, and wanted to be free of my work; but that she would make me do it. I thought her very hard on me, and my heart rose up within me. However I kept still at that time, and went down again to wash the child's things; but the English washerwomen who were at work there, when they saw that I was so ill, had pity upon me and washed them for me.

After that, when we came up to live in Leigh Street, Mrs. Wood sorted out five bags of clothes which we had used at sea, and also such as had been worn since we came on shore, for me and the cook to wash. Elizabeth the cook told her, that she did not think that I was able to stand to the tub, and that she had better hire a woman. I also said myself, that I had come over to nurse the child, and that I was sorry I had come from Antigua, since mistress would work me so hard, without compassion for my rheumatism. Mr. and Mrs. Wood, when they heard this, rose up in a passion against me. They opened the door and bade me get out. But I was a stranger, and did not know one door in the street from another, and was unwilling to go away. They made a dreadful uproar, and from that day they constantly kept cursing and abusing me. I was obliged to wash, though I was very ill. Mrs. Wood, indeed once hired a washerwoman, but she was not well treated, and would come no more.

My master quarrelled with me another time, about one of our great washings, his wife having stirred him up to do so. He said he would compel me to do the whole of the washing given out to me, or if I again refused, he would take a short course with me: he would either send me down to the brig in the river, to carry me back to Antigua, or he would turn me at once out of doors, and let me provide for myself. I said I would willingly go back, if he would let me purchase my own freedom. But this enraged him more than all the rest: he cursed and swore at me dreadfully, and said he would never sell my freedom—if I wished to be free, I was free in England, and I might go and try what freedom would do for me, and be d—d. My heart was very sore with this treatment, but I had to go on. I continued to do my work, and did all I could to give satisfaction, but all would not do.

Shortly after, the cook left them, and then matters went on ten times worse. I always washed the child's clothes without being commanded to do it, and any thing else that was wanted in the family; though still I was very sick—very sick indeed. When the great washing came round, which was every two months, my mistress got together again a great many heavy things, such as bed-ticks, bed-coverlets, &c. for me to wash. I told her I was too ill to wash such heavy things that day. She said, she supposed I thought myself a free woman, but I was not; and if I did not do it directly I should be instantly turned out of doors. I stood a long time before I could answer, for I did not know well what to do. I knew that I was free in England, but I did not know where to go, or how to get my living; and therefore, I did not like to leave the house. But Mr. Wood said he would send for a constable to thrust me out; and at last I took courage and resolved that I would not be longer thus treated, but would go and trust to Providence. This was the fourth time they had threatened to turn me out, and, go where I might, I was determined now to take them at their word; though I thought it very hard, after I had lived with them for thirteen years, and worked for them like a horse, to be driven out in this way, like a beggar. My only fault was being sick, and therefore unable to please my mistress, who thought she never could get work enough out of her slaves; and I told them so: but they only abused me and drove me out. This took place from two to three months, I think, after we came to England.

When I came away, I went to the man (one Mash) who used to black the shoes of the family, and asked his wife to get somebody to go with me to Hatton Garden to the Moravian Missionaries: these were the only persons I knew in England. The woman sent a young girl with me to the mission house, and I saw there a gentleman called Mr. Moore. I told him my whole story, and how my owners had treated me, and asked him to take in my trunk with what few clothes I had. The missionaries were very kind to me—they were sorry for my destitute situation, and gave me leave to bring my things to be placed under their care. They were very good people, and they told me to come to the church.

When I went back to Mr. Wood's to get my trunk, I saw a lady, Mrs. Pell, who was on a visit to my mistress. When Mr. and Mrs. Wood heard me come in, they set this lady to stop me, finding that they had gone too far with me. Mrs. Pell came out to me, and said, "Are you really going to leave, Molly? Don't leave, but come into the country with me." I believe she said this because she thought Mrs. Wood would easily get me back again. I replied to her, "Ma'am, this is the fourth time my master and mistress have driven me out, or threatened to drive me—and I will give them no more occasion to bid me go. I was not willing to leave them, for I am a stranger in this country, but now I must go—I can stay no longer to be used." Mrs. Pell then went up stairs to my mistress, and told that I would go, and that she could not stop me. Mrs. Wood was very much hurt and frightened when she found I was determined to go out that day. She said, "If she goes the people will rob her, and then turn her adrift." She did not say this to me, but she spoke it loud enough for me to hear; that it might induce me not to go, I suppose. Mr. Wood also asked me where I was going to. I told him where I had been, and that I should never have gone away had I not been driven out by my owners. He had given me a written paper some time before, which said that I had come with them to England by my own desire; and that was true. It said also that I left them of my own free will, because I was a free woman in England; and that I was idle and would not do my work—

which was not true. I gave this paper afterwards to a gentleman who inquired into my case.

I went into the kitchen and got my clothes out. The nurse and the servant girl were there, and I said to the man who was going to take out my trunk, "Stop, before you take up this trunk, and hear what I have to say before these people. I am going out of this house, as I was ordered; but I have done no wrong at all to my owners, neither here nor in the West Indies. I always worked very hard to please them, both by night and day; but there was no giving satisfaction, for my mistress could never be satisfied with reasonable service. I told my mistress I was sick, and yet she has ordered me out of doors. This is the fourth time; and now I am going out."

And so I came out, and went and carried my trunk to the Moravians. I then returned back to Mash the shoeblack's house, and begged his wife to take me in. I had a little West Indian money in my trunk; and they got it changed for me. This helped to support me for a little while. The man's wife was very kind to me. I was very sick, and she boiled nourishing things up for me. She also sent for a doctor to see me, and sent me medicine, which did me good, though I was ill for a long time with the rheumatic pains. I lived a good many months with these poor people, and they nursed me, and did all that lay in their power to serve me. The man was well acquainted with my situation, as he used to go to and fro to Mr. Wood's house to clean shoes and knives; and he and his wife were sorry for me.

About this time, a woman of the name of Hill told me of the Anti-Slavery Society, and went with me to their office, to inquire if they could do any thing to get me my freedom, and send me back to the West Indies. The gentlemen of the Society took me to a lawyer, who examined very strictly into my case; but told me that the laws of England could do nothing to make me free in Antigua. However they did all they could for me: they gave me a little money from time to time to keep me from want; and some of them went to Mr. Wood to try to persuade him to let me return a free woman to my husband; but though they offered him, as I have heard, a large sum for my freedom, he was sulky and obstinate, and would not consent to let me go free.

This was the first winter I spent in England, and I suffered much from the severe cold, and from the rheumatic pains, which still at times torment me. However, Providence was very good to me, and I got many friends—especially some Quaker ladies, who hearing of my case, came and sought me out, and gave me good warm clothing and money. Thus I had great cause to bless God in my affliction.

When I got better I was anxious to get some work to do, as I was unwilling to eat the bread of idleness. Mrs. Mash, who was a laundress, recommended me to a lady for a charwoman. She paid me very handsomely for what work I did, and I divided the money with Mrs. Mash; for though very poor, they gave me food when my own money was done, and never suffered me to want.

In the spring, I got into service with a lady, who saw me at the house where I sometimes worked as a charwoman. This lady's name was Mrs. Forsyth. She had been in the West Indies, and was accustomed to Blacks, and liked them. I was with her six months, and went with her to Margate. She treated me well, and gave me a good character when she left London.

After Mrs. Forsyth went away, I was again out of place, and went to lodgings, for which I paid two shillings a week, and found coals and candle. After eleven weeks, the money I had saved in service was all gone, and I was forced to go back to the Anti-Slavery office to ask a supply, till I could get another situation. I did not like to go back—I did not like to be idle. I would rather work for my living than get it for nothing. They were very good to give me a supply, but I felt shame at being obliged to apply for relief whilst I had strength to work.

At last I went into the service of Mr. and Mrs. Pringle, where I have been ever since, and am as comfortable as I can be while separated from my dear husband, and away from my own country and all old friends and connections. My dear mistress teaches me daily to read the word of God, and takes great pains to make me understand it. I enjoy the great privilege of being enabled to attend church three times on the Sunday; and I have met with many kind friends since I have been here, both clergymen and others. The Rev.

Mr. Young, who lives in the next house, has shown me much kindness, and taken much pains to instruct me, particularly while my master and mistress were absent in Scotland. Nor must I forget, among my friends, the Rev. Mr. Mortimer, the good clergyman of the parish, under whose ministry I have now sat for upwards of twelve months. I trust in God I have profited by what I have heard from him. He never keeps back the truth, and I think he has been the means of opening my eyes and ears much better to understand the word of God. Mr. Mortimer tells me that he cannot open the eyes of my heart, but that I must pray to God to change my heart, and make me to know the truth, and the truth will make me free.

I still live in the hope that God will find a way to give me my liberty, and give me back to my husband. I endeavour to keep down my fretting, and to leave all to Him, for he knows what is good for me better than I know myself. Yet, I must confess, I find it a hard and heavy task to do so.

I am often much vexed, and I feel great sorrow when I hear some people in this country say, that the slaves do not need better usage, and do not want to be free. They believe the foreign people, who deceive them, and say slaves are happy. I say, Not so. How can slaves be happy when they have the halter round their neck and the whip upon their back? and are disgraced and thought no more of than beasts?—and are separated from their mothers, and husbands, and children, and sisters, just as cattle are sold and separated? Is it happiness for a driver in the field to take down his wife or sister or child, and strip them, and whip them in such a disgraceful manner?—women that have had children exposed in the open field to shame! There is no modesty or decency shown by the owner to his slaves; men, women, and children are exposed alike. Since I have been here I have often wondered how English people can go out into the West Indies and act in such a beastly manner. But when they go to the West Indies, they forget God and all feeling of shame, I think, since they can see and do such things. They tie up slaves like hogs—moor them up like cattle, and they lick them, so as hogs, or cattle, or horses never were flogged;—and yet they come home and say, and make some good people believe, that slaves don't want to get out of slavery. But they put a cloak about the truth. It is not so. All slaves want to be free—to be free is very sweet. I will say the truth to English people who may read this history that my good friend, Miss S—, is now writing down for me. I have been a slave myself—I know what slaves feel—I can tell by myself what other slaves feel, and by what they have told me. The man that says slaves be quite happy in slavery—that they don't want to be free—that man is either ignorant or a lying person. I never heard a slave say so. I never heard a Buckra man say so, till I heard tell of it in England. Such people ought to be ashamed of themselves. They can't do without slaves they say. What's the reason they can't do without slaves as well as in England? No slaves here—no whips—no stocks—no punishment, except for wicked people. They hire servants in England; and if they don't like them, they send them away: they can't lick them. Let them work ever so hard in England, they are far better off than slaves. If they get a bad master, they give warning and go hire to another. They have their liberty. That's just what *we* want. We don't mind hard work, if we had proper treatment, and proper wages like English servants, and proper time given in the week to keep us from breaking the Sabbath. But they won't give it; they will have work—work—work, night and day, sick or well, till we are quite done up; and we must not speak up nor look amiss, however much we be abused. And then when we are quite done up, who cares for us, more than for a lame horse? This is slavery. I tell it to let English people know the truth; and I hope they will never leave off to pray God, and call loud to the great King of England, till all the poor blacks be given free, and slavery done up for evermore.

—1831

Slavery and Its Abolition

CONTEXTS

In the 1750s it was possible for John Newton, the author of the hymn "Amazing Grace," to write that neither he nor any of his friends had had any notion that "slavery could be considered unlawful and wrong." By 1807 the tide had turned sufficiently that the British Parliament (through the Slave Trade Act) prohibited British vessels from participating in the trading of humans. And in 1833 (through the Slavery Abolition Act) slavery in most British territory was ended.

What brought about such a vast change in such a relatively short time? In part the answer lies in the history of ideas; the Enlightenment gave birth to concepts of freedom and equality—of human rights which, as they were thought through, were widely recognized to apply to all humans, regardless of gender, regardless of race. These ideas, though not initially thought to apply to those enslaved by the world's empires, did lead to anti-slavery uprisings and revolutions, most notably (and successfully) in Haiti, between 1789 and 1804. But the abolition first of the slave trade and then of slavery itself in Britain and its colonies was also the result of concerted political pressure. Some have identified the birth of the modern political movement and modern political lobbying in the campaign to abolish slavery. Certainly the Society for Effecting the Abolition of the Slave Trade, formed in 1787 and led by Thomas Clarkson and Granville Sharp, among others, played a hugely important role in acquiring and disseminating information as to the actual conditions endured by enslaved people, and in pressuring the government to take action. In Parliament, William Wilberforce became the de facto leader of the anti-slavery movement: Wilberforce, the author of *Practical Christianity*, was tireless in his efforts. The Society of Friends (also known as the Quakers) also played a leading role, both within the Society for Effecting the Abolition of the Slave Trade and independently, in shaping public opinion and pressing for change. Former enslaved people, such as Olaudah Equiano and Mary Prince, testified to the inhumanity of slavery in persuasive works of autobiography. And a number of established authors—including William Wordsworth, Samuel Taylor Coleridge, Helen Maria Williams, Anna Laetitia Barbauld, and Mary Robinson—lent their voices to the cause.

The legal system too played an important role in the process. In a landmark 1772 case the owner of one James Somerset lost his legal suit to regain ownership of Somerset, who had run away from servitude while in England. Lord Mansfield, the Lord Chief Justice, ruled in Somerset's favor. The language he used stated only that there was no legal justification for forcibly transporting enslaved people out of England for sale, but the verdict was popularly interpreted to mean that, according to the established principles of English law, everyone in England was free. Despite Mansfield's *caveat* against taking his ruling to apply to British possessions overseas, the progressive decision also gave abolitionists some reason to feel confident that the law would eventually support their arguments universally and unequivocally, in Britain's colonies as well as within Britain itself.

⌘⌘⌘

from John Newton, *A Slave Trader's Journal* (1751)

John Newton (1725–1807) first went to sea at the age of ten, sailing with his father, the captain of the vessel. By the age of twenty-eight he had wide experience both of the sea and of the slave trade, and was for the first time commanding a vessel himself. The *Duke of Argyll* left England for Bassa in West Africa (in what is now Guinea Bissau) in 1750, made the "middle passage" from Bassa to Antigua in the West Indies between 22 May and 2 July, and returned to Liverpool with a cargo of sugar, arriving in November. The following excerpts are from Newton's journal of that voyage. In later life, Newton came to regret deeply his life as a slave trader (which he had given up for health reasons in 1754). He became a Christian minister and wrote that he would have left the slave trade sooner "had I considered it as I now do to be unlawful and wrong. But I never had a scruple upon this head at the time; nor was such a thought ever suggested to me by any friend." In 1770 Newton wrote the famous hymn "Amazing Grace." He became a strong advocate for the abolition of the slave trade.

Thursday 16 May

… [A] long boat came on board from Grande Bassa. I sent Billinge [the second mate] chiefly to satisfy myself of the state and price of slaves. He says the glut we heard so much of is entirely over, the Brittannia and Ranger having met very few. About Settra Crue there is still plenty (upon the account of a war very probably begun with that view) but extravagantly dear. … He brought me a sample of the prices in a woman slave he bought at Bassa, which upon costing up the goods I find cost 96 bars, and I ordered him to get one upon any terms for that reason. That I might not think he gave more than usual, he brought me a list of goods he saw Saunders pay for a man which amounts to 102 bars, and the farther to leeward the dearer still. I think I have sufficient reason not to go down, for setting aside the cost, the assortments in demand there would ruin me soon.

Tuesday 28 May

Secured the after bulkhead of the men's room, for they had started almost every stantient. Their plot was exceedingly well laid, and had they been let alone an hour longer, must have occasioned us a good deal of trouble and damage. I have reason to be thankful they did not make attempts upon the coast when we had often 7 or 8 of our best men out of the ship at a time and the rest busy. They still look very gloomy and sullen and have doubtless mischief in their heads if they could find every opportunity to vent it. But I hope (by the Divine Assistance) we are fully able to overawe them now. …

Wednesday 12 June

Got the slaves up this morn. Washed them all with fresh water. They complained so much that was obliged to let them go down again when the rooms were cleaned. Buryed a man slave (No. 84) of a flux, which he has been struggling with near 7 weeks. …

Saturday 22 June

Being pretty warm, got up the men and washed all the slaves with fresh water. I am much afraid of another ravage from the flux, for we have had 8 taken within these few days. Have seen 2 or 3 tropick birds and a few flying fish.

Monday 24 June

Buried a girl slave (No. 92). In the afternoon while we were off the deck, William Cooney seduced a woman slave down into the room and lay with her brutelike in view of the whole quarter deck, for which I put him in irons.[1] I hope this has been the first affair of the kind on board and I am determined to keep them quiet if possible. If anything happens to the woman I shall impute it to him, for she was big with child. Her number is 83. …

[1] *for which … irons* In contrast to Newton, some captains actively encouraged their crew to rape the enslaved women, since pregnant women could be sold at a higher price; mulatto children were especially highly valued as house servants.

Friday 28 June
By the favour of Divine Providence made a timely discovery today that the slaves were forming a plot for an insurrection. Surprised 2 of them attempting to get off their irons, and upon farther search in their rooms, upon the information of 3 of the boys, found some knives, stones, shot, etc., and a cold chissel. Upon enquiry there appeared 8 principally concerned to move in projecting the mischief and 4 boys in supplying them with the above instruments. Put the boys in irons and slightly in the thumbscrews to urge them to a full confession. We have already 36 men out of our small number. …

Friday 5 July
… [I]n the morning Mr. Guichard went off with me to view the slaves. When came on shore again, after comparing orders and intelligence, he judged it best for the concern to sell here, if I approved it, without which, he was pleased to say, he would do nothing, tho my letters from the owners referred me wholly to his direction. It seems by all I can learn that this is likely to prove as good a market as any of the neighbouring islands; and as for Jamaica or America, I should be extremely loth to venture so far, for we have had the men slaves so long on board that their patience is just worn out, and I am certain they would drop fast had we another passage to make. Monday is appointed for the sale.

from Quobna Ottobah Cugoano, *Thoughts and Sentiments on the Evil and Wicked Traffic of the Slavery and Commerce of the Human Species* (1787)

Cugoano was kidnapped in West Africa in 1770 and sold into slavery in the West Indies. His owner traveled with him to England in 1772, and he declared himself a free man on English soil following the landmark Somerset case. His *Thoughts and Sentiments* is the first substantial anti-slavery work by a black writer.

But why should total abolition, and an universal emancipation of slaves, and the enfranchisement of all the Black People employed in the culture of the Colonies, taking place as it ought to do, and without any hesitation, or delay for a moment, even though it might have some seeming appearance of loss either to government or to individuals, be feared at all? Their labour, as freemen, would be as useful in the sugar colonies as any other class of men that could be found; and should it even take place in such a manner that some individuals, at first, would suffer loss as a just reward for their wickedness in slave-dealing, what is that to the happiness and good of doing justice to others; and, I must say, to the great danger, otherwise, that must eventually hang over the whole community? It is certain, that the produce of the labour of slaves, together with all the advantages of the West-India traffic, bring in an immense revenue to government; but let that amount be what it will, there might be as much or more expected from the labour of an equal increase of free people, and without the implication of any guilt attending it, and which, otherwise, must be a greater burden to bear, and more ruinous consequences to be feared from it, than if the whole national debt was to sink at once, and to rest upon the heads of all that might suffer by it. Whereas, if a generous encouragement were to be given to a free people, peaceable among themselves, intelligent and industrious, who by art and labour would improve the most barren situations, and make the most of that which is fruitful; the free and voluntary labour of many, would soon yield to any government, many greater advantages than any thing that slavery can produce. And this should be expected, wherever a Christian government is extended, and the true religion is embraced, that the blessings of liberty should be extended likewise, and that it should diffuse its influences first to fertilize the mind, and then the effects of its benignity would extend, and arise with exuberant blessings and advantages from all its operations. Was this to be the case, every thing would increase and prosper at home and abroad, and ten thousand times greater and greater advantages would arise to the state, and more permanent and solid benefit to individuals from the service of freemen, than ever they can reap, or in any possible way enjoy, by the labour of slaves. …

from Alexander Falconbridge, *Account of the Slave Trade on the Coast of Africa* (1788)

Falconbridge sailed aboard slave trading vessels as a surgeon in the 1780s. The work from which the following excerpts are taken was given wide distribution by the Society for Effecting the Abolition of the Slave Trade. In 1789 Falconbridge also testified as to the horrors of the trade before the Parliamentary Committee investigating the issue.

The men negroes, on being brought aboard the ship, are immediately fastened together, two and two, by hand-cuffs on their wrists, and by irons rivetted on their legs. They are then sent down between the decks, and placed in an apartment partitioned off for that purpose. The women likewise are placed in a separate apartment between decks, but without being ironed. And an adjoining room, on the same deck, is besides appointed for the boys. Thus are they all placed in different apartments.

But at the same time, they are frequently stowed so close, as to admit of no other posture than lying on their sides. Neither will the height between decks, unless directly under the grating, permit them the indulgence of an erect posture; especially where there are platforms, which is generally the case. These platforms are a kind of shelf, about eight or nine feet in breadth, extending from the side of the ship towards the centre. They are placed nearly midway between the decks, at the distance of two or three feet from each deck. Upon these the negroes are stowed in the same manner as they are on the deck underneath.

In each of the apartments are placed three or four large buckets, of a conical form, being near two feet in diameter at the bottom, and only one foot at the top, and in depth about twenty-eight inches; to which, when necessary, the negroes have recourse. It often happens, that those who are placed at a distance from the buckets, in endeavouring to get to them, tumble over their companions, in consequence of their being shackled. These accidents, although unavoidable, are productive of continual quarrels, in which some of them are always bruised. In this distressed situation, unable to proceed, and prevented from getting to the tubs, they desist from the attempt; and, as the necessities of nature are not to be repelled, ease themselves as they lie. This becomes a fresh source of broils and disturbances, and tends to render the condition of the poor captive wretches still more uncomfortable. The nuisance arising from these circumstances, is not unfrequently increased by the tubs being much too small for the purpose intended, and their being usually emptied but once every day. The rule for doing this, however, varies in different ships, according to the attention paid to the health and convenience of the slaves by the captain. …

The diet of the negroes, while on board, consists chiefly of horse-beans, boiled to the consistence of a pulp; of boiled yams and rice, and sometimes of a small quantity of beef or pork. The latter are frequently taken from the provisions laid in for the sailors. They sometimes make use of a sauce, composed of palm-oil, mixed with flour, water, and pepper, which the sailors call *slabber-sauce.* Yams are the favourite food of the Eboe, or Bight negroes, and rice or corn, of those from the Gold and Windward Coasts; each preferring the produce of their native soil. …

They are commonly fed twice a day, about eight o'clock in the morning and four in the afternoon. In most ships they are only fed with their *own food* once a day. Their food is served up to them in tubs, about the size of a small water bucket. They are placed round these tubs in companies of ten to each tub, out of which they feed themselves with wooden spoons. These they soon lose, and when they are not allowed others, they feed themselves with their hands. In favourable weather they are fed upon deck, but in bad weather their food is given them below. Numberless quarrels take place among them during their meals; more especially when they are put upon short allowance. … Their allowance of water is about half a pint each at every meal. It is handed round in a bucket, and given to each negroe in a panne-kin; a small utensil with a strait handle, somewhat similar to a sauce-boat. …

Upon the negroes refusing to take sustenance, I have seen coals of fire, glowing hot, put on a shovel, and placed so near their lips, as to scorch and burn them. And this has been accompanied with threats, of forcing them to swallow the coals, if they any longer persisted in refusing to eat. These means have generally had the desired effect. I have also been credibly informed, that a certain captain in the slave trade, poured melted lead on such of the negroes as obstinately refused their food.

Exercise being deemed necessary for the preservation of their health, they are sometimes obliged to dance, when the weather will permit their coming on deck. If they go about it reluctantly, or do not move with agility, they are flogged; a person standing by them all the time with a cat-o'-nine-tails[1] in his hand for that purpose. Their musick, upon these occasions consists of a drum, sometimes with only one head; and when that is worn out, they do not scruple to make use of the bottom of one of the tubs before described. The poor wretches are frequently compelled to sing also; but when they do so, their songs are generally, as may naturally be expected, melancholy lamentations of their exile from their native country. …

Diagram showing allotment of space for enslaved people on two decks of a late eighteenth-century sailing ship.

[1] *cat-o'-nine-tails* Switch with nine ropes attached, used as a beating implement.

On board some ships, the common sailors are allowed to have intercourse with such of the black women whose consent they can procure. And some of them have been known to take the inconstancy of their paramours so much to heart, as to leap overboard and drown themselves. The officers are permitted to indulge their passions among them at pleasure, and sometimes are guilty of such brutal excesses, as disgrace human nature.

William Cowper, "Sweet Meat Has Sour Sauce, or, The Slave-Trader in the Dumps"[2] (1788)

A trader I am to the African shore,
But since that my trading is like to be o'er,
I'll sing you a song that you ne'er heard before,
Which nobody can deny, deny,
Which nobody can deny.

When I first heard the news it gave me a shock,
Much like what they call an electrical knock,
And now I am going to sell off my stock,
Which nobody, &c.

'Tis a curious assortment of dainty regales,
To tickle the negroes with when the ship sails,
Fine chains for the neck, and a cat with nine tails,
Which nobody, &c.

Here's supple-jack plenty, and store of rat-tan,[3]
That will wind itself round the sides of a man,
As close as a hoop round a bucket or can,
Which nobody, &c.

Here's padlocks and bolts, and screws for the thumbs,
That squeeze them so lovingly till the blood comes,

[2] *Sweet Meat … Dumps* The poem is one of several anti-slavery poems by Cowper. The Society for Effecting the Abolition of the Slave Trade distributed his ballad "The Negro's Complaint" widely; both that poem and this were set to music and sung as well as read.

[3] *supple-jack* Climbing vine; *rat-tan* Palm stem. Both supple-jack and rattan were used for switches or canes.

They sweeten the temper like comfits or plums,[1]
    Which nobody, &c.

When a negro his head from his victuals withdraws,
And clenches his teeth and thrusts out his paws,
Here's a notable engine to open his jaws,
    Which nobody, &c.

Thus going to market, we kindly prepare
A pretty black cargo of African ware,
For what they must meet with when they get there,
    Which nobody, &c.

'Twould do your heart good to see 'em below
Lie flat on their backs all the way as we go,
Like sprats on a gridiron,[2] scores in a row,
    Which nobody, &c.

But ah! if in vain I have studied an art
So gainful to me, all boasting apart,
I think it will break my compassionate heart,
    Which nobody, &c.

For oh! how it enters my soul like an awl![3]
This pity, which some people self-pity call,
Is sure the most heart-piercing pity of all,
    Which nobody, &c.

So this is my song, as I told you before;
Come buy off my stock, for I must no more
Carry Caesars and Pompeys[4] to Sugar-cane shore,
    Which nobody can deny, deny,
    Which nobody can deny.

[1] *comfits or plums* Sweetmeats; sugarplums: fruits preserved with sugar.

[2] *sprats on a gridiron* Small fish on a griddle or broiling-pan.

[3] *awl* Tool for piercing holes in leather.

[4] *Caesars and Pompeys* Names commonly given to enslaved people from Africa.

from William Wilberforce, "Speech to the House of Commons," 13 May 1789

William Wilberforce began his long struggle to have the British Parliament abolish the slave trade with the speech excerpted below. In April of 1791, a bill put forward by Wilberforce was voted down by 163 votes to 88; not until 1807 were his efforts on this score successful. News of the passage of the Slavery Abolition Act reached Wilberforce on his deathbed in 1833.

A report has been made by his Majesty's Privy Council, which, I trust, every Gentleman has read, and which ascertains the Slave Trade to be just such in practice as we know, from theory, that it must be. What should we suppose must naturally be the consequence of our carrying on a Slave Trade with Africa? With a country, vast in its extent, not utterly barbarous, but civilized in a very small degree? Does any one suppose a Slave Trade would *help* their civilization? That Africa would *profit* by such an intercourse? Is it not plain, that she must *suffer* from it? That civilization must be checked; that her barbarous manners must be made more barbarous; and that the happiness of her millions of inhabitants must be prejudiced by her intercourse with Britain? Does not every one see, that a Slave Trade, carried on around her coasts, must carry violence and desolation to her very centre? That, in a Continent, just emerging from barbarism, if a Trade in Men is established—if her men are all converted into goods, and become commodities that can be bartered, it follows, they must be subject to ravage just as goods are; and this too, at a period of civilization, when there is no protecting Legislature to defend this their only sort of property, in the same manner as the rights of property are maintained by the legislature of every civilized country.

We see then, in the nature of things, how easily all the practices of Africa are to be accounted for. Her kings are never compelled to war, that we can hear of, by public principles,—by national glory—still less by the love of their people. In Europe it is the extension of commerce, the maintenance of national honor, or some great public object, that is ever the motive to war with every monarch; but, in Africa, it is the personal *avarice* and *sensuality* of their kings: these two vices of avarice and sensuality, (the most powerful and predominant in natures thus corrupt) we tempt, we stimulate in all these African Princes, and we depend upon these vices for the very maintenance of the Slave Trade. …

Sir, the nature and all the circumstances of this trade are now laid open to us; we can no longer plead ignorance,—we cannot evade it,—it is now an object placed before us,—we cannot pass it; we may spurn it, we may kick it out of our way, but we cannot turn aside so as to avoid seeing it; for it is brought now so directly before our eyes, that this House must decide, and must justify to all the world, and to their own consciences, the rectitude of the grounds and principles of their decision.

A Society [the Society for Effecting the Abolition of the Slave Trade] has been established for the abolition of this trade, [in 1787] in which Dissenters, Quakers, Churchmen—in which the most conscientious of all persuasions have all united, and made a common cause in this great question. Let not Parliament be the only body that is insensible to the principles of national justice. Let us make reparation to Africa, so far as we can, by establishing a trade upon true commercial principles, and we shall soon find the rectitude of our conduct rewarded, by the benefits of a regular and a growing commerce.

Proponents of Slavery

It is often (and rightly) pointed out that appeals to Christian virtue were central to the abolitionist cause. As some of the following excerpts illustrate, appeals to Christian principles were also made on the other side of the argument—as were appeals of a variety of other sorts.

from Reverend Robert Boncher Nicholls, *Observations, Occasioned by the Attempts Made in England to Effect the Abolition of the Slave Trade* (1788)

[The author] thought it incumbent on him first to search the scriptures, to learn whether slavery was inconsistent with the revealed will of the Deity. The result of his enquiry was perfectly satisfactory to himself, and he thought it but right to point out some few of the many passages, to be found in the sacred volumes, which justify that commerce. Since the following observations went to the press the author has the great satisfaction to find, that he might have pursued his original plan without any injury to the cause he has endeavoured to support, as he has seen a pamphlet by the Rev. Mr. Harris, of Liverpool, who has so clearly proved, from the scriptures, that slavery is neither contrary to the law nor gospel, that it is scarcely possible for the most conscientious believer, who reads that tract, to doubt in future; whether the man servant or the maid servant is not as much a man's property as "*his ox or his ass, or any thing that is his.*" …

About the time of Lord Mansfield's determination in the case of Mr. Stuart's negro, [those in England who were attended by slaves] … had every right to suppose they were authorised, by the laws of Great Britain, as well as those of the colonies, to consider those people as their property; and that they had a right to their services in Europe, or to send, or accompany them back to the colonies, as they judged proper: They found themselves mistaken, and that it was permitted to debauch their slaves, to encourage or entice them to run away, with impunity. The ideas of liberty, the charms of novelty, and an ignorance of the country they had got to; where they found themselves upon a perfect equality, at least, with the inferior white people, could not fail of having pernicious effects upon their minds, and great numbers ran away from their masters. They in general plunged into vice and debauchery, and many of them, who were desirous of returning to their masters and mistresses, were refused to be received. The whole of those thus lost to their owners, and as to every useful purpose, to the community, cannot have been less in number than from 15,000 to 20,000.—As most of them were prime, young, seasoned, or Creole slaves, the loss to their owners, the planters, have not been less than from 1,000,000 to 1,200,000 sterling. A large sum to be sacrificed, to the mere names of *liberty and humanity*! What has been the result of thus extending *the blessings of liberty* to so many *wretched slaves.* Let any body shew scarce a single instance of any one of these people being in so happy a situation as they were before. The greater part, it is known, died miserably, in a very short time. No parish was willing to receive them, so that the survivers, after begging about the streets of London, and suffering all those evils, and inconveniencies, consequent on idleness and poverty, famine, disease, and the inclemency of the weather; attracted the attention of the public, and government was prevailed upon to undertake the transportation of them to the country from whence they or their ancestors had been ravished *by the wicked traders* of London, Liverpool, and Bristol.

Equal unhappiness would be the lot of the slaves in the islands, if they were set free; what could they do to obtain a livelihood? To suppose they would hire themselves out to work, can only enter into the imagination of those who do not know the people, or the country: What has so lately passed in England is surely sufficient to shew that there can be no idea, they will, any of them, wish to return to their own country. Thousands of negroes have been made free by their masters in the colonies, and it may, with truth, be asserted, that, notwithstanding many of them were very capable of paying for a passage to any part of Africa they thought proper; scarce a single instance can be produced of any one of them desiring to return to the place of his nativity.

The present attempt to cram liberty down the throats of people who are incapable of digesting it, can with propriety, be resembled to nothing, so well as to the account of poor Gulliver, when he was carried out of his little cabinet to the top of the house, by the Brobdignag Monkey.

from Anonymous, *Thoughts on the Slavery of Negroes, as It Affects the British Colonies in the West Indies: Humbly Submitted to the Consideration of Both Houses of Parliament* (1788)

If I am able to shew that the blacks are really happy; that their condition (if the odious name of slave could be forgotten) is preferable to the lower orders of the people in Great Britain and Ireland; and that they enjoy the necessaries, and often the luxuries of life, I trust every honest man will feel a just indignation at any attempt to mislead his judgment, and to impose upon him an opinion of cruelty, which has no existence in any of the British West India islands. …

Let us take a view of the situation of the Africans, the nature of their country, their climate and government, and the genius and disposition of its inhabitants. The appearance of the slave-coast of Africa, when it was first visited by the Europeans, strongly marked the barbarous state of the people; a rude, inhospitable country, susceptible indeed of cultivation, but almost every way covered with thick, impenetrable forests. The wild luxuriance of nature was here portrayed in rich attire. The pruning hand of man was hardly seen. The peaceful labours of agriculture were little known.

It has been observed, that those countries most favoured by nature, often make the slowest progress to civilization; and that the people always groan under the weight of a cruel despotism. "This is an effect which springs from a natural cause. Great heat enervates the strength and courage of men, while in cold climates they have a certain vigour of body and mind, which renders them capable of long, painful, great, and intrepid actions. We ought not, then, to be astonished, that the effeminacy of the people in hot climates has almost always rendered them slaves; and that the bravery of those in colder regions has enabled them to maintain their liberties."

In those countries between the tropics, and especially under the equator, "the excess of heat renders men so slothful and dispirited, that nothing but the most pressing necessity can induce them to perform any laborious duty." An unconquerable indolence is universally felt and acknowledged. Sunk into the most deplorable degeneracy, they feel no incitements beyond the present moment. In vain may we represent to them the happiness of others. In vain may we attempt to rouse them to a sense of their own weakness. The soul, unwilling to enlarge itself, becomes the prey of every ignoble passion. Strangers to every virtuous and magnanimous sentiment, they are without fame—they are without glory.

The Africans have been always represented as a cruel and perfidious people, lazy, lascivious, faithless in their engagements, innate thieves, without morals, and without any just notion of any one religious duty. Their laws are founded on such principles as naturally flow from so impure a source. The government of the slave-coast of Africa is despotic. The will of the Prince must be obeyed. There is no appeal upon earth from his awful decree. The lives and fortunes of every one are absolutely at his disposal. These tyrants have thought fit to distinguish a number of crimes, but have taken no care to proportionate their degrees of punishment. Every offence is there punished with loss of life or liberty. Captives in war are deliberately murdered, or sold as slaves, as may most indulge the sanguinary caprice of the conqueror. Those convicted of adultery or theft, lose their liberty. He who is in debt, and unable to pay must either sell himself or his children to satisfy the creditor. It may be said, that the loss of life, or liberty, only commences with the injury done to society. I answer, "that in Africa, the civil liberty is already destroyed by the political slavery." A country like this, doomed to bear the weight of human misery, will always present a history of the most shocking cruelties, and of the severest slavery upon earth.

After viewing this melancholy picture, we ought not to be surprised at the extent of the present intercourse between the Africans and Europeans. For want of proper consideration, and from the influence of certain prejudices, the slave-trade has long been considered the scandal and reproach of every nation who have been anywise engaged in it, but without sufficient reason.

Men who enjoy the benefits of civilization, and who are protected in life, liberty, and property, by the wisdom of humane and equal laws, feel that spirit of liberty, and enthusiastic love of their country, which freedom only can inspire. Talk to them of banishment, and it is more terrible than death. Not so the poor African—he has few motives for wishing any longer to behold the distresses of his country; he is, alas! perhaps, the last witness of the sad misfortunes of his house—Already deprived of family, friends, and every other tender endearment, he has no relief but in banishment or death.

It is pleasant to mark the progress of the barbarian, from the moment he is put on shore in an English colony, to the time he becomes the master of a family, and acquires property of his own. He is first of all clothed (a thing unknown to him in his own country) and then instructed in the necessity of cleanliness. When carried to the plantation, he is shewn how to work in common with others. In a little time he chooses himself a wife, and has a house given to him, much better, allowing for the difference of climate, than what the peasants have in this country. When he is sufficiently instructed in the management of ground, a certain portion is allotted to the exclusive use of himself and family, which, with a moderate share of industry, is not only sufficient to supply every personal want, but leave a considerable part to be sent to market, to be sold, or exchanged for either necessaries or luxuries. The African now, finding himself a family man, and in possession of house and land, he begins to rear hogs, poultry, and other small stock, and either sells them to his master at a fair price, or carries them to market, for which one day in the week is allowed him. …

The African, no longer remembering a country to which he owes nothing but birth, becomes attached to the soil which is so propitious to his wants, and having few cares, and few desires, that are not completely satisfied, there is nothing so terrible to him as a change of situation. The master is the steward, the faithful guardian of all his wants and necessities. In sickness and in health—in youth and in old age, his assiduities are undiminished. The reader will anticipate the happiness of these people—and happy they must be, while their labours are directed by equity and humanity, and not by avarice.

God forbid that I should be an advocate for slavery, or servitude of any description, that can anywise limit the extent of human happiness: at the same time let me caution my countrymen against the weakness and folly of believing that happiness can only be sought in a constitution as free as their own. The history of all nations shew how extremely improper the laws of one country would be for those of another.

from Gordon Turnbull, *An Apology of Negro Slavery; or, the West India Planters Vindicated from the Charge of Inhumanity* (1786)

As a contrast to the horrid and fictitious picture, which has been drawn of the state of the negroes in the West-Indies, I shall here exhibit a true and more pleasing representation, taken from the life.

To begin then with the period of the Guinea negroe's arrival in one of the islands.—As soon as the ship that brings them is at anchor, the master or surgeon goes on shore to procure fresh provisions, fruit, and vegetables of all kinds, which are immediately sent on board for the slaves. Parties of them are sent on shore at different times, and conducted a little way into the country, where they frequently meet with many natives of their own country, who speak the same language, and sometimes with near and dear relations, who all appear very cheerful and happy. These agreeable and unexpected meetings are truly affecting, and excite the most tender and pleasing sensations in the breasts of the by-standers. It is not uncommon for these newly arrived guests, to mingle in the dance, or to join in the song, with their country people. If any of them appear dull or desponding, the old negroes endeavour to enliven them, by the most soothing and endearing expressions, telling them, in their own tongue, not to be afraid of the white men; that the white men are very good; that they will get plenty of *yam, yam,* (their general name for victuals) and that their work will be of the easiest kind. By these means, they are perfectly reconciled to the white men, and to a change of country, and of situation, which many of them declare, to be far superior to that which they had quitted. When the day of sale arrives, they not only meet the planter's looks, and answer his enquiries, by means of an interpreter, with great firmness, but they try, by offering their stout limbs to his inspection, jumping to shew their activity, and other allurements, to induce those, whose appearance pleases them, to buy them, and to engage, if possible, a preference in their favour. …

As soon as the new negroes are brought home to the plantation, if a planter has purchased them they are properly clothed.—A sufficient quantity of wholesome food is prepared, and served to them three times a day. They are comfortably lodged in some room of the manager's own house, or in some other convenient place, where they can be immediately under his eye for a few days. During this time they are not put to any kind of labour whatever, but are regularly conducted to bathe in the river, or in the sea, if it is nigh, twice a day. In the evenings they sing and dance, after the manner of their own nation, together with the old negroes who happen to be from the same country, one or two of whom are commonly instrumental performers, in these very noisy, but very joyous assemblies. In a very short time, they are taken into the houses of the principal and best disposed negroes, who adopt one or two of these new subjects into each family, to assist them in all the little domestic offices of cookery, carrying water, wood, &c. This is almost the only work they are employed in for the first two or three months, at the expiration of which, they are put to the easiest kind of labour for some months more. …

John Bicknell and Thomas Day, "The Dying Negro, A Poem" (1775)

In his fiction and essays, Thomas Day (1748–89) often wrote about oppression and injustice; "The Dying Negro," which he co-authored with his life-long friend John Bicknell, is one of the first English poems to attack slavery directly. It was inspired by the true story of an enslaved man who escaped from his master to marry a white servant, but was captured and returned to his ship. Rather than allow himself to be transported to the New World, he shot himself. The poem was very popular, and its success prompted Bicknell and Day to publish two revised and expanded versions in two years; the following is the third edition text.

Armed with thy sad last gift—the pow'r to die,
Thy shafts, stern fortune, now I can defy;
Thy dreadful mercy points at length the shore,
Where all is peace, and men are slaves no more;
—This weapon, ev'n in chains, the brave can wield,
And vanquished, quit triumphantly the field:
—Beneath such wrongs let pallid Christians live,
Such they can perpetrate, and may forgive.

Yet while I tread that gulf's tremendous brink,
Where nature shudders, and where beings sink,
Ere yet this hand a life of torment close,
And end by one determined stroke my woes,
Is there a fond regret, which moves my mind
To pause, and cast a ling'ring look behind?
—O my loved bride!—for I have called thee mine,
Dearer than life, whom I with life resign,
For thee ev'n here this faithful heart shall glow,
A pang shall rend me, and a tear shall flow.—
How shall I soothe thy grief, since fate denies
Thy pious duties to my closing eyes?
I cannot clasp thee in a last embrace,
Nor gaze in silent anguish on thy face;
I cannot raise these fettered arms for thee,
To ask that mercy heav'n denies to me;
Yet let thy tender breast my sorrows share,
Bleed for my wounds, and feel my deep despair.
Yet let thy tears bedew a wretch's grave,
Whom fate forbade thy tenderness to save.
Receive these sighs—to thee my soul I breathe—
Fond love in dying groans is all I can bequeath.

Why did I, slave, beyond my lot aspire?
Why didst thou fan the inauspicious fire?
For thee I bade my drooping soul revive;
For thee alone I could have borne to live;
And love, I said, shall make me large amends,
For persecuting foes, and faithless friends:
Fool that I was! inured so long to pain,
To trust to hope, or dream of joy again.
Joy, stranger guest, my easy faith betrayed,
And love now points to death's eternal shade;
There while I rest from mis'ry's galling load,
Be thou the care of ev'ry pitying God!
Nor may that Demon's unpropitious° pow'r, *malevolent*
Who shed his influence on my natal hour,
Pursue thee too with unrelenting hate,
And blend with mine the colour of thy fate.
For thee may those soft hours return again,
When pleasure led thee smiling o'er the plain,
Ere, like some hell-born spectre of dismay,
I crossed thy path, and darkened all the way.
Ye waving groves, which from this cell I view!
Ye meads° now glitt'ring with the morning dew! *meadows*
Ye flowers, which blush on yonder hated shore,
That at my baneful step shall fade no more,
A long farewell!—I ask no vernal° bloom— *of spring*
No pageant wreaths to wither on my tomb.
—Let serpents hiss and night-shade blacken there,
To mark the friendless victim of despair!

And better in th'untimely grave to rot,
The world and all its cruelties forgot,
Than, dragged once more beyond the Western main,° *sea*
To groan beneath some dastard planter's chain,
Where my poor countrymen in bondage wait
The slow enfranchisement° of ling'ring fate. *liberation*
Oh! my heart sinks, my dying eyes o'erflow,
When mem'ry paints the picture of their woe!
For I have seen them, ere the dawn of day,
Roused by the lash, begin their cheerless way;
Greeting with groans unwelcome morn's return,
While rage and shame their gloomy bosoms burn;
And, chiding every hour the slow-paced sun,
Endure their toils 'till all his race was run;
No eye to mark their suff'rings with a tear,
No friend to comfort, and no hope to cheer;
Then like the dull unpitied brutes repair
To stalls as wretched, and as coarse a fare;
Thank heav'n one day of misery was o'er,
And sink to sleep, and wish to wake no more.—
Sleep on! ye lost companions of my woes,
For whom in death this tear of pity flows;
Sleep, and enjoy the only boon of heav'n
To you in common with your tyrants giv'n!

O while soft slumber from their couches flies,
Still may the balmy blessing steep your eyes;
In sweet oblivion lull awhile your woes,
And brightest visions gladden the repose!
Let fancy then, unconscious of the change,
Through our own fields, and native forests range;
Waft ye to each once-haunted stream and grove,
And visit every long-lost scene ye love!
—I sleep no more—nor in the midnight shade,
Invoke ideal phantoms to my aid;
Nor wake again, abandoned and forlorn,
To find each dear delusion fled at morn;
A slow-consuming death let others wait,
I snatch destruction from unwilling fate:—
Yon ruddy streaks the rising sun proclaim,
That never more shall beam upon my shame;
Bright orb! for others let thy glory shine,
Mature the golden grain and purple vine,
While fettered Afric still for Europe toils,
And nature's plund'rers riot on her spoils;
Be theirs the gifts thy partial rays supply,
Be mine the gloomy privilege to die.

And thou, whose impious avarice and pride
The holy cross to my sad brows denied,[1]
Forbade me nature's common rights to claim,
Or share with thee a Christian's sacred name;
Thou too farewell!—for not beyond the grave
Extends thy pow'r, nor is my dust thy slave.
In vain heav'n spread so wide the swelling sea,
Vast wat'ry barrier, 'twixt thy world and me;
Swift round the globe, by earth nor heav'n controlled,
Fly stern oppression, and dire lust of gold.
Where-e'er the hell-hounds mark their bloody way,
Still nature groans, and man becomes their prey.
In the wild wastes of Afric's sandy plain,
Where roars the lion through his drear domain,
To curb the savage monarch in the chase,
There too heav'n planted man's majestic race;
Bade reason's sons with nobler titles rise,
Lift high their brow sublime, and scan the skies.
What though the sun in his meridian blaze
Dart on their naked limbs his scorching rays?
What though no rosy tints adorn their face,
No silken tresses shine with flowing grace?
Yet of ethereal temper are their souls,
And in their veins the tide of honour rolls;
And valour kindles there the hero's flame,
Contempt of death, and thirst of martial fame:
And pity melts the sympathising breast,
Ah! fatal virtue!—for the brave distrest.

My tortured bosom, sad remembrance spare!
Why dost thou plant thy keenest daggers there?
And show me what I was, and aggravate despair?
Ye streams of Gambia,[2] and thou sacred shade!
Where in my youth's first dawn I joyful strayed,
Oft have I roused, amid your caverns dim,
The howling tiger, and the lion grim;
In vain they gloried in their headlong force,
My javelin pierced them in their raging course.
But little did my boding° mind bewray,° *foreseeing / disclose*
The victor and his hopes were doomed a prey
To human brutes more fell,° more cruel far than they. *evil, destructive*
Ah! what avails the conqu'ror's bloody meed,[3]
The gen'rous purpose, or the dauntless deed?
This hapless breast exposed on every plain,
And liberty preferred to life in vain?
Fall'n are my trophies, blasted is my fame,
Myself become a thing without a name,
The sport of haughty lords, and ev'n of slaves the shame.

Curst be the winds, and curst the tides which bore
These European robbers to our shore!
O be that hour involved in endless night,
When first their streamers met my wond'ring sight!
I called the warriors from the mountains steep,

[1] *The holy … brows denied* Slaveowners often prevented the people they enslaved from converting to Christianity for fear that this would give the impression that enslaved people and free people were spiritually equal (and therefore deserving of equal rights).

[2] *Gambia* Located in north western Africa, and occupied by the British in the middle of the eighteenth century.

[3] *meed* Reward of honor.

To meet these unknown terrors of the deep;
Roused by my voice, their gen'rous bosoms glow,
They rush indignant, and demand the foe,
And poise the darts of death, and twang the bended bow:
When lo! advancing o'er the sea-beat plain,
I marked the leader of a warlike train.
Unlike his features to our swarthy race;
And golden hair played round his ruddy face.
While with insidious smile and lifted hand,
He thus accosts our unsuspecting band.
"Ye valiant chiefs, whom love of glory leads
To martial combats, and heroic deeds;
No fierce invader your retreat explores,
No hostile banner waves along your shores.
From the dread tempests of the deep we fly,
Then lay, ye chiefs, these pointed terrors by:
And O, your hospitable cares extend,
So may ye never need the aid ye lend!
So may ye still repeat to ev'ry grove
The songs of freedom, and the strains of love!"
Soft as the accents of the traitor flow,
We melt with pity, and unbend the bow;
With lib'ral hand our choicest gifts we bring,
And point the wand'rers to the freshest spring.
Nine days we feasted on the Gambian strand,
And songs of friendship echoed o'er the land.
When the tenth morn her rising lustre gave,
The chief approached me by the sounding wave.
"O, youth," he said, "What gifts can we bestow,
Or how requite the mighty debt we owe?
For lo! propitious to our vows, the gale
With milder omens fills the swelling sail.
Tomorrow's sun shall see our ships explore
These deeps, and quit your hospitable shore.
Yet while we linger, let us still employ
The numbered hours in friendship and in joy;
Ascend our ships, their treasures are your own,
And taste the produce of a world unknown."

He spoke; with fatal eagerness we burn,—
And quit the shores, undestined to return!
The smiling traitors with insidious care,
The goblet proffer, and the feast prepare,
'Till dark oblivion shades our closing eyes,
And all disarmed each fainting warrior lies.
O wretches! to your future evils blind!
O morn for ever present to my mind!
When bursting from the treach'rous bands of sleep,
Roused by the murmurs of the dashing deep,
I woke to bondage and ignoble pains,
And all the horrors of a life in chains.
Ye Gods of Afric! in that dreadful hour
Where were your thunders and avenging pow'r!
Did not my prayers, my groans, my tears invoke
Your slumb'ring justice to direct the stroke?
No pow'r descended to assist the brave,
No lightnings flashed, and I became a slave.
From lord to lord my wretched carcass sold,
In Christian traffic, for their sordid gold:
Fate's blackest clouds were gathered o'er my head;
And, bursting now, they mix me with the dead.

Yet when my fortune cast my lot with thine,
And bade beneath one roof our labours join,
Surprised I felt the tumults of my breast
Lulled by thy beauties to unwonted rest.
Delusive hopes my changing soul enflame,
And gentler transports° agitate my frame. *overpowering emotions*
What though obscure thy birth, superior grace
Shone in the glowing features of thy face.
Ne'er had my youth such winning softness seen,
Where Afric's sable beauties dance the green,
When some sweet maid receives her lover's vow,
And binds the offered chaplet[1] to her brow.
While on thy languid eyes I fondly gaze,
And trembling meet the lustre of their rays,
Thou, gentle virgin, thou didst not despise
The humble homage of a captive's sighs.
By heav'n abandoned, and by man betrayed,
Each hope resigned of comfort or of aid,
Thy gen'rous love could every sorrow end,
In thee I found a mistress and a friend;
Still as I told the story of my woes,

[1] *chaplet* Wreath worn on the head.

With heaving sighs thy lovely bosom rose;
The trickling drops of liquid crystal stole
Down thy fair cheek, and marked thy pitying soul:
Dear drops! upon my bleeding heart, like balm
They fell, and soon my tortured mind grew calm;
Then my loved country, parents, friends forgot;
Heav'n I absolved, nor murmured at my lot;
Thy sacred smiles could every pang remove,
And liberty became less dear than love.

—And I have loved thee with as pure a fire
As man e'er felt, or woman could inspire:
No pangs like these my pallid tyrants know,
Not such their transports, and not such their woe.
Their softer frames a feeble soul conceal,
A soul unused to pity or to feel;
Damped by base lucre,° and repelled by fear, *money*
Each nobler passion faintly blazes here.
Not such the mortals burning Afric breeds,
Mother of virtues and heroic deeds!
Descended from yon radiant orb, they claim
Sublimer courage, and a fiercer flame.
Nature has there, unchilled by art, impressed
Her awful majesty on every breast.
Where'er she leads, impatient of control,
The dauntless Negro rushes to the goal;
Firm in his love, resistless in his hate,
His arm is conquest, and his frown is fate.

What fond affection in my bosom reigns!
What soft emotions mingle with my pains!
Still as thy form before my mind appears,
My haggard eyes are bathed in gushing tears;
Thy loved idea rushes to my heart,
And stern despair suspends the lifted dart—
O could I burst these fetters which restrain
My struggling limbs, and waft thee o'er the main,
To some far distant shore, where Ocean roars
In horrid tempests round the gloomy shores;
To some wild mountain's solitary shade,
Where never European faith betrayed;
How joyful could I, of thy love secure,
Meet every danger, every toil endure!
For thee I'd climb the rock, explore the flood,
And tame the famished savage of the wood;
When scorching summer drinks the shrinking streams,
My care should screen thee from its sultry beams;
At noon I'd crown thee with the fairest flowers,
At eve I'd lead thee to the safest bowers;[1]
And when bleak winter howled around the cave,
For thee his horrors and his storms I'd brave;
Nor snows nor raging winds should damp my soul,
Nor such a night as shrouds the dusky pole;
O'er the dark waves my bounding skiff I'd guide,
To pierce each mightier monster of the tide;
Through frozen forests force my dreadful way,
In their own dens to rouse the beasts of prey;
Nor other blessing ask, if this might prove
How fixed my passion, and how fond my love.
—Then should vain fortune to my sight display
All that her anger now has snatched away;
Treasures more vast than av'rice e'er designed
In midnight visions to a Christian's mind;
The Monarch's diadem,° the conqu'ror's meed, *crown*
That empty prize for which the valiant bleed;
All that ambition strives to snatch from fate,
All that the Gods e'er lavished in their hate;
Not these should win thy lover from thy arms,
Or tempt a moment's absence from thy charms;
Indignant would I fly these guilty climes,
And scorn their glories as I hate their crimes!

But whither does my wand'ring fancy rove?
Hence ye wild wishes of desponding love!
—Ah! where is now that voice which lulled my woes?
That angel-face, which soothed me to repose?
By nature tempted, and with passion blind,
Are these the joys hope whispered to my mind?
Is this the end of constancy like thine,
Are these the transports of a love like mine?
My hopes, my joys, are vanished into air,
And now of all that once engaged my care,
These chains alone remain, this weapon and despair!

[1] *bowers* Sheltered places in the woods.

—So be thy life's gay prospects all o'ercast,
All thy fond hopes dire disappointment blast!
Thus end thy golden visions, son of pride!
Whose ruthless ruffians tore me from my bride;
That beauteous prize heav'n had reserved at last,
Sweet recompense for all my sorrows past.
O may thy hardened bosom never prove
The tender joys of friendship or of love!
Yet may'st thou, doomed to hopeless flames a prey,
In unrequited passion pine away!
May every transport violate thy rest,
Which tears the jealous lover's gloomy breast!
May secret anguish gnaw thy cruel heart,
'Till death in all his terrors wing the dart;
Then, to complete the horror of thy doom,
A favoured rival smile upon thy tomb!

Why does my ling'ring soul her flight delay?
Come, lovely maid, and gild the dreary way!
Come, wildly rushing with disordered charms,
And clasp thy bleeding lover in thy arms;
Close his sad eyes, receive his parting breath,
And soothe him sinking to the shades of death!
O come—thy presence can my pangs beguile,
And bid th'inexorable tyrant smile;
Transported will I languish on thy breast,
And sink enraptured to eternal rest:
The hate of men, the wrongs of fate forgive,
Forget my woes, and almost wish to live.
—Ah! rather fly, lest aught of doubt control
The dreadful purpose lab'ring in my soul;
Tears must not bend me, nor thy beauties move,
This hour I triumph over fate and love.

—Again with tenfold rage my bosom burns,
And all the tempest of my soul returns;
Again the furies fire my madding° brain, *agitated*
And death extends his shelt'ring arms in vain;
For unrevenged I fall, unpitied die;
And with my blood glut pride's insatiate eye!

Thou Christian God! to whom so late I bowed,
To whom my soul its new allegiance vowed,
When crimes like these thy injured pow'r profane,
O God of nature! art thou called in vain?
Didst thou for this sustain a mortal wound,
While heav'n, and earth, and hell, hung trembling round?
That these vile fetters might my body bind,
And agony like this distract my mind?
On thee I called with reverential awe,
Adored thy wisdom, and embraced thy law;
Yet mark thy destined convert as he lies,
His groans of anguish, and his livid eyes,
These galling chains, polluted with his blood,
Then bid his tongue proclaim thee just and good!
But if too weak thy vaunted power to spare,
Or suff'rings move thee not, O hear despair!
Thy hopes and blessings I alike resign,
But let revenge, let swift revenge be mine!
Be this proud bark,° which now triumphant rides, *ship*
Tossed by the winds, and shattered by the tides!
And may these fiends, who now exulting view
The horrors of my fortune, feel them too!
Be theirs the torment of a ling'ring fate,
Slow as thy justice, dreadful as my hate;
Condemned to grasp the riven° plank in vain, *broken*
And chased by all the monsters of the main;
And while they spread their sinking arms to thee,
Then let their fainting souls remember me!

—Thanks, righteous God!—Revenge shall yet be mine;
Yon flashing lightning gave the dreadful sign.
I see the flames of heav'nly anger hurled,
I hear your thunders shake a guilty world.
The time has come, the fated hour is nigh,
When guiltless blood shall penetrate the sky.
Amid these horrors, and involving night,
Prophetic visions flash before my sight;
Eternal justice wakes, and in their turn
The vanquished triumph, and the victors mourn;
Lo! Discord, fiercest of th'infernal band,
Fires all her snakes, and waves her flaming brand;[1]
No more proud Commerce courts the western gales,

[1] *Discord … flaming brand* The Roman goddess Discord is here associated with the Furies, goddesses who avenge the dead and are sometimes depicted carrying torches and using snakes as weapons.

But marks the lurid skies, and furls her sails;
War mounts his iron car, and at his wheels
In vain soft Pity weeps, and Mercy kneels;
He breathes a savage rage through all the host,
And stains with kindred blood the impious coast;
Then, while with horror sick'ning Nature groans,
And earth and heav'n the monstrous race disowns,—
Then the stern genius° of my native land, *spirit*
With delegated vengeance in his hand,
Shall raging cross the troubled seas, and pour
The plagues of Hell on yon devoted shore.
What tides of ruin mark his ruthless way!
How shriek the fiends exulting o'er their prey!
I see their warriors gasping on the ground,
I hear their flaming cities crash around.—
In vain with trembling heart the coward turns,
In vain with gen'rous rage the valiant burns.—
One common ruin, one promiscuous° grave, *indiscriminate*
O'erwhelms the dastard, and receives the brave—
For Afric triumphs!—his avenging rage
No tears can soften, and no blood assuage.
He smites the trembling waves, and at the shock
Their fleets are dashed upon the pointed rock.
He waves his flaming dart, and o'er their plains,
In mournful silence, desolation reigns—
Fly swift ye years!—Arise thou glorious morn!
Thou great avenger of thy race be born!
The conqu'ror's palm and deathless fame be thine!
One gen'rous stroke, and liberty be mine!
—And now, ye pow'rs! to whom the brave are dear,
Receive me falling, and your suppliant hear.
To you this unpolluted blood I pour,
To you that spirit which you gave restore!
I ask no lazy pleasures to possess,
No long eternity of happiness;—
But if unstained by voluntary guilt,
At your great call this being I have spilt,
For all the wrongs which innocent I share,
For all I've suffered, and for all I dare;
O lead me to that spot, that sacred shore,
Where souls are free, and men oppress no more!

from Mary Wollstonecraft, *A Vindication of the Rights of Men* (1790)

Wollstonecraft's more famous work, *A Vindication of the Rights of Woman*, was published two years after her much shorter work on the rights of men, which briefly discusses the issue of slavery.

Is it necessary to repeat, that there are rights which we received, at our birth, as men, when we were raised above the brute creation by the power of improving ourselves—and that we receive these not from our forefathers, but from God?

My father may dissipate his property, yet I have no right to complain;—but if he should attempt to sell me for a slave, or fetter me with laws contrary to reason; nature, in enabling me to discern good from evil, teaches me to break the ignoble chain. …

But on what principle Mr. Burke[1] could defend American independence, I cannot conceive; for the whole tenor of his … arguments settles slavery on an everlasting foundation. Allowing his servile reverence for antiquity, and prudent attention to self-interest, to have the force which he insists on, it ought never to be abolished; and, because our ignorant forefathers, not understanding the native dignity of man, sanctioned a traffic that outrages every suggestion of reason and religion, we are to submit to the inhuman custom, and term an atrocious insult to humanity the love of our country and a proper submission to those laws which secure our property.—Security of property! Behold, in a few words, the definition of English liberty. And to this selfish principle every nobler one is sacrificed. …

[1] *Mr. Burke* Edmund Burke (1729–97), Anglo-Irish political figure, author, and philosopher. Burke famously supported the right of the colonies to self-rule.

Anna Laetitia Barbauld, "Epistle to William Wilberforce, Esq., on the Rejection of the Bill for Abolishing the Slave Trade"[1] (1791)

Cease, Wilberforce, to urge thy generous aim!
Thy country knows the sin, and stands the shame!
The preacher, poet, senator in vain
Has rattled in her sight the Negro's chain;
With his deep groans assailed her startled ear,
And rent the veil that hid his constant tear;
Forced her averted eyes his stripes[2] to scan,
Beneath the bloody scourge laid bare the man,
Claimed Pity's tear, urged Conscience's strong control,
And flashed conviction on her shrinking soul.
The Muse too, soon awaked, with ready tongue
At Mercy's shrine applausive paeans rung;
And Freedom's eager sons, in vain foretold
A new Astraean[3] reign, an age of gold:
She knows and she persists—Still Afric bleeds,
Unchecked, the human traffic still proceeds;
She stamps her infamy to future time,
And on her hardened forehead seals the crime.
In vain, to thy white standard[4] gathering round,
Wit, Worth, and Parts° and Eloquence are found: *intelligence*
In vain, to push to birth thy great design,
Contending chiefs, and hostile virtues join;
All, from conflicting ranks, of power possest
To rouse, to melt, or to inform the breast.
Where seasoned tools of Avarice prevail,
A nation's eloquence, combined, must fail:
Each flimsy sophistry by turns they try;
The plausive° argument, the daring lie, *plausible*
The artful gloss,° that moral sense confounds, *explanation*
Th'acknowledged thirst of gain that honour wounds:
Bane of ingenuous minds, th'unfeeling sneer,
Which, sudden, turns to stone the falling tear:
They search assiduous, with inverted skill,
For forms of wrong, and precedents of ill;
With impious mockery wrest the sacred page,
And glean up crimes from each remoter age:
Wrung Nature's tortures, shuddering, while you tell,
From scoffing fiends bursts forth the laugh of hell;
In Britain's senate, Misery's pangs give birth
To jests unseemly, and to horrid mirth[5]—
Forbear!—thy virtues but provoke our doom,
And swell th'account of vengeance yet to come;
For, not unmarked in Heaven's impartial plan,
Shall man, proud worm, condemn his fellow man?
And injured Afric, by herself redrest,
Darts her own serpents at her tyrant's breast.
Each vice, to minds depraved by bondage known,
With sure contagion fastens on his own;
In sickly languors melts his nerveless frame,
And blows to rage impetuous Passion's flame:
Fermenting swift, the fiery venom gains
The milky innocence of infant veins;
There swells the stubborn will, damps learning's fire,
The whirlwind wakes of uncontrolled desire,
Sears the young heart to images of woe,
And blasts the buds of Virtue as they blow.
Lo! where reclined, pale Beauty courts the breeze,
Diffused on sofas of voluptuous ease;
With anxious awe, her menial train around,

[1] *William Wilberforce ... Slave Trade* This poem appeared shortly after the bill put forward by Wilberforce (and supported both by the Prime Minister, William Pitt, and the leader of the opposition, Charles Fox) was defeated by a vote of 163 to 88.

[2] *stripes* Open wounds caused by the lash.

[3] *Astraea* Greek goddess of justice.

[4] *standard* Flag.

[5] *To jests ... mirth* Barbauld refers to some Members of Parliament who laughed in the House of Commons upon hearing of the suffering of enslaved people.

Catch her faint whispers of half-uttered sound;
See her, in monstrous fellowship, unite
At once the Scythian, and the Sybarite;[1]
Blending repugnant vices, misallied,
Which frugal nature purposed to divide;
See her, with indolence to fierceness joined,
Of body delicate, infirm of mind,
With languid tones imperious mandates urge;
With arm recumbent wield the household scourge;
And with unruffled mien,° and placid sounds, *appearance*
Contriving torture, and inflicting wounds.
Nor, in their palmy walks and spicy groves,
The form benign of rural pleasure roves;
No milkmaid's song, or hum of village talk,
Soothes the lone poet in his evening walk:
No willing arm the flail unwearied plies,
Where the mixed sounds of cheerful labour rise;
No blooming maids, and frolic swains are seen
To pay gay homage to their harvest queen:
No heart-expanding scenes their eyes must prove
Of thriving industry, and faithful love:
But shrieks and yells disturb the balmy air,
Dumb sullen looks of woe announce despair,
And angry eyes through dusky features glare.
Far from the sounding lash the Muses fly,
And sensual riot drowns each finer joy.
Nor less from the gay East,° on essenced wings, *India*
Breathing unnamed perfumes, Contagion springs;
The soft luxurious plague alike pervades
The marble palaces, and rural shades;
Hence, thronged Augusta° builds her rosy bowers, *London*
And decks in summer wreaths her smoky towers;
And hence, in summer bow'rs, Art's costly hand
Pours courtly splendours o'er the dazzled land:
The manners melt—One undistinguished blaze
O'erwhelms the sober pomp of elder days;
Corruption follows with gigantic stride,
And scarce vouchsafes his shameless front to hide:
The spreading leprosy taints ev'ry part,
Infects each limb, and sickens at the heart.
Simplicity! most dear of rural maids,
Weeping resigns her violated shades:
Stern Independence from his glebe° retires, *field*
And anxious Freedom eyes her drooping fires;
By foreign wealth are British morals changed,
And Afric's sons, and India's, smile avenged.
For you, whose tempered ardour long has borne
Untired the labour, and unmoved the scorn;
In Virtue's fasti° be inscribed your fame, *calendar*
And uttered yours with Howard's[2] honoured name,
Friends of the friendless—Hail, ye generous band!
Whose efforts yet arrest Heav'n's lifted hand,
Around whose steady brows, in union bright,
The civic wreath, and Christian's palm unite:
Your merit stands, no greater and no less,
Without, or with the varnish of success;
But seek no more to break a nation's fall,
For ye have saved yourselves—and that is all.
Succeeding times your struggles, and their fate,
With mingled shame and triumph shall relate,
While faithful History, in her various page,
Marking the features of this motley age,
To shed a glory, and to fix a stain,
Tells how you strove, and that you strove in vain.

William Blake, Images of Slavery

The engravings reproduced here are among sixteen plates prepared by William Blake in 1792–93 as illustrations for John Stedman's *Narrative of Five Years' Expedition against the Revolted Negroes of Surinam* (1796).

[1] *Scythian* Ancient nomadic Europeans: synonym for ferocity; *Sybarite* People from the ancient Greek city of Sybaris: synonym for pleasure-loving.

[2] *Howard* John Howard (1726–90), prison reformer and philanthropist.

from Samuel Taylor Coleridge, *On the Slave Trade* (1796)

The article from which these excerpts are taken was originally delivered as a lecture in Bristol in 1795. It was published the following year in Coleridge's magazine *The Watchman*; the excerpts included here comprise approximately one half of the full article.

At the time slavery—and various proposals for its abolition—were the subject of increasing controversy, with William Wilberforce having recently proposed in the House of Commons several (unsuccessful) bills to put an end to the slave trade.

Whence arise our miseries? Whence arise our vices? From *imaginary* wants. No man is wicked without temptation; no man is wretched without a cause. But if each among us confined his wishes to the actual necessaries and real comforts of life, we should preclude all the causes of complaint and all the motives to iniquity.[1] …

I have dwelt anxiously on this subject, with a particular view, to the slave-trade, which, I knew, has insinuated in the minds of many, uneasy doubts respecting the existence of a beneficent deity. And indeed the evils arising from the formation of *imaginary* wants, have in no instance been so dreadfully exemplified, as in this inhuman traffic. We receive from the West-India Islands sugars, rum, cotton, logwood, cocoa, coffee, pimento, ginger, indigo, mahogany, and conserves.[2] Not one of these articles are necessary; indeed with the exception of cotton and mahogany we cannot truly call them even useful: and not one of them is at present attainable by

[1] *preclude* Prevent; *iniquity* Injustice.

[2] *West-India Islands* With the American colonies by this time independent of Britain, the largest number of enslaved people on British territory in the final decade of the eighteenth century were enslaved on plantations in the various British possessions in the West Indies—notably Barbados, Jamaica, and Trinidad; *logwood* Species of tree harvested in Central America, used as a dye; *pimento* Variety of chili pepper; *conserves* Preserved foods.

the poor and labouring part of society. In return we export vast quantities of necessary tools, raiment, and defensive weapons, with great stores of provision. So that in this trade as in most others the poor are employed with unceasing toil first to raise, and then to send away the comforts, which they themselves absolutely want,[1] in order to procure idle superfluities for their masters. If this trade had never existed, no one human being would have been less comfortably clothed, housed, or nourished. Such is its value—they who would estimate the price which we pay for it, may consult the evidence delivered before the House of Commons. … It is my present purpose to consider the objections of[2] the abolition of this commerce—which may be reduced to the five following—First, that the abolition would be useless, since though *we* should not carry it on, other nations would. 2. That the Africans are better treated and more happy in the plantations than in their native country. 3. That the revenue would be greatly injured. 4. That the right of property would be invaded. 5. That this is not a fit opportunity.

1. That if England abolish the slave-trade, other nations will carry it on. The same argument has been adduced by the French planters:[3] a sufficient proof of its fallacy. Somebody must *begin*; and there is little reason to fear, that a wise and politic example will not be followed. As society is constituted, there will be always highway robberies: it is useless therefore to prevent any *one* man from committing them. Fortunately for travellers this logic will not hold good in law. But although it cannot operate in favour of little rogues, it appears to possess wonderful power in the higher circles of villainy. …

2. That the slaves are more humanely treated and live more happily in the plantations than in their native country. If any incredulous person should entertain a doubt of this, the slave-merchants, slave-holders, and slave-drivers, together with the manufacturers of neck-collars and thumb-screws,[4] are ready and willing to take their bible oaths of it!! When treated with tolerable humanity the human race, as well as other animals, multiply. The Negroes multiply in their native country: they do *not* multiply in the West-India Islands; for if they did, the slave-trade would have been abolished long ago by its inutility. This is a fact which no perjury can overwhelm, which no sophistry[5] can undermine.

That tyranny of the African Chiefs[6] is in a great measure owing to the agency of Europeans, who flock to their courts, and seduce them by bribery, and madden them by intoxication. The Africans are not slaves in their native country; slavery is their highest punishment for the greatest crimes, which their chiefs now wantonly impute to the innocent for the sole purpose of making them slaves in order to sell them to the European merchants: and with the same views the chiefs make war with each other. Wadestrom,[7] a disinterested[8] and religious man, who has travelled into the interior parts of Africa, informs us that those Africans who are situated beyond the contagion of European vice are innocent and happy. The peaceful inhabitants of a fertile soil, they cultivate their fields in common, and reap the crop as the common property of all. Each family, like the peasants in some parts of Europe, spins, weaves, sews, hunts, fishes, and makes baskets, fishing-tackle,

---

1 *want* Lack.

2 *of* To.

3 [Coleridge's note] "Very soon this society of Friends to the Negroes require an abolition of the slave-trade; that is to say, that the profits which may result from it to the French commerce should be transferred to foreigners. For never will their romantic philosophy persuade the other European Powers &c." See the address of the Planters of St. Domingo to the French Legislature. [This address was made in November 1791, months after the beginning of a revolution carried out by enslaved people. The Society of the Friends of the Blacks was created in Paris in 1788, lobbying for abolition.]; *planters* Owners of slave plantations.

4 *incredulous* In the older sense of skeptical; *neck-collars and thumb-screws* Instruments used to punish and torture enslaved people.

5 *sophistry* Persuasive but ultimately fallacious arguments.

6 *tyranny of the African Chiefs* I.e., the tyranny of African rulers (with whom European traders had made agreements regarding the sale of enslaved people) over their own and nearby peoples.

7 *Wadestrom* Carl Bernhard Wadström (1746–99), Swedish economist and abolitionist who traveled to western Africa in the late 1780s and early 1790s.

8 *disinterested* Unbiased.

and the implements of agriculture: and this variety of employment gives an acuteness of intellect to the Negro which the mechanic whom the division of labour[1] condemns to one simple operation is precluded from attaining.

3. That the revenue would be injured.[2] To the friends of humanity this is indeed a cogent[3] argument against the abolition. They will doubtless reflect, how worthily this revenue has been employed for these last hundred years—they will review with delight waste-lands cultivated, sciences publicly protested and rewarded, and population increased, and the peasantry of England and Ireland instructed in useful learning, and humanized. The universal plenty, which this revenue has been applied to scatter and secure, they will recognize in every land, hamlet, and cottage. … The friends of humanity may mourn that so excellent an end could not be effected by less calamitous means; but they will stifle their feelings, and lose[4] the miseries of the West-Indies in the contemplation of that paradisiacal state of their native country—for which it is indebted to this well-raised, well-applied Revenue, which while it remains in such *pure* hands, no friend of freedom and virtue can possibly wish diminished! …

4. That the right of property would be injured. Yes perhaps, if immediate emancipation had been the object of Mr. Wilberforce's bill.[5] But how would the right of property be invaded by a law which should leave the estate and everything on it untouched and only prevent the owner from *forcing* men to work for him? From *forcing* men to leave their friends and country, and live as slaves in a climate so unwholesome or beneath a usage so unnatural, that contrary to the universal law of life they annually diminish? Can a man possess a right to commit actual and virtual murder? To shorten and prevent existence? …

5. This is not the time. This not the time? "The French," says Abbé Sieyès,[6] "hear with delight of the numerous armaments which England sends to certain death in the West-India islands. We make war there more effectually as well as economically by sending over a few adventurous officers to preach the rights of man to the negroes, and furnish them with weapons to assert those rights." What can prevent the success of these intrigues among the slaves, but the most active humanity on the part of their present masters?

Such have been the cosmetics with which our parliamentary orators have endeavoured to conceal the deformities of a commerce, which is blotched all over with one leprosy of evil. In the year 1786 its enormities became the subject of general conversation,[7] and in the following years petitions poured into parliament from various parts of the kingdom, requesting its abolition. The bill for that purpose passed the House of Commons mangled and mutilated by the amendments of Mr. Dundas,[8] and it has been dying ever since of a slow decline in the House of Lords. The jealous spirit of liberty placed the Elector of Hanover on the throne of Great Britain:[9] and the Duke of Clarence, one of his

[1] *division of labour* Assignment of different stages of production to different workers for the sake of efficiency.

[2] *the revenue would be injured* I.e., that government revenue would be reduced. The British government obtained substantial revenues from taxes on sugar, molasses, rum, and other products of slave labor.

[3] *cogent* Powerful and convincing.

[4] *lose* I.e., lose sight of.

[5] *if immediate … Mr. Wilberforce's bill* Wilberforce proposed at this time only the abolition of the trade of enslaved people, and not an outright prohibition of slavery itself (which he then believed would naturally cease over time after the cessation of the trade).

[6] *Abbé Sieyès* Emmanuel Joseph Sieyès (1748–1836), French Catholic priest and political theorist.

[7] *In the year … general conversation* Perhaps referring to the formation of the Society for the Abolition of the Slave Trade, which in fact occurred in May 1787. The society was very influential in raising awareness of the slave trade and its cruelties throughout England.

[8] *The bill … Mr. Dundas* Wilberforce's anti-slavery bill in 1792 was passed only after amendments by Henry Dundas, then British Home Secretary; these amendments calling for a "gradual abolition" would in practice have had the effect of delaying abolition almost indefinitely.

[9] *Elector of Hanover … Great Britain* George I (1660–1727), ruler of the Electorate of Hanover in the Holy Roman Empire since 1698, became king of Great Britain and Ireland in 1714 upon the death of his cousin, Queen Anne of Great Britain.

illustrious descendants, made his maiden speech in favour of the slave trade![1] …

The Abbé Raynal computes that at the time of his writing,[2] nine millions of slaves had been consumed by the Europeans—add one million since (for it is near thirty years since his book was first published) and recollect, that for one procured ten at least are slaughtered, that a fifth die in the passage, and a third in the seasoning;[3] and the calculation will amount to one hundred and eighty million! Ye who have joined in this confederacy,[4] ask of yourselves this fearful question—"if the God of Justice inflict on us that mass only of anguish which we have wantonly heaped on our brethren, what must a state of retribution be?" But who are they who have joined in this tartarean[5] confederacy? Who are these kidnappers, and assassins? In all reasoning neglecting the intermediate links we attribute the final effect to the first cause. And what is the first and constantly acting cause of the slave-trade? That cause, by which it exists and deprived of which it would immediately cease? Is it not self-evidently the consumption of its products? And does not then the guilt rest on the consumers? And is it not an allowed axiom in morality, that wickedness may be multiplied, but cannot be divided; and that the guilt of all attaches to each one who is knowingly an accomplice? Think not of the slave-captains and slave-holders! These very men, their darkened minds, and brutalized hearts, will prove one part of the dreadful charge against you! They are more to be pitied than the slaves, because more depraved. I address myself to you who, independently of all political distinctions, profess yourself Christians! As you hope to live with Christ hereafter, you are commanded to do unto others as ye would that others should do unto you.[6] Would *you* choose that a slave merchant should incite an intoxicated chieftain to make war on your country, and murder your wife and children before your face, or drag them with yourself to the market? Would you choose to be sold? To have the hot iron hiss upon your breasts, after having been crammed into the hold of a ship with so many fellow-victims, that the heat and stench, arising from your diseased bodies, should rot the very planks? Would *you*, that others should do this unto *you*? And if you shudder with selfish horror at the bare idea, do you yet dare be the occasion of it to others? … If only one tenth part among you who profess yourselves Christians; if one half only of the petitioners; instead of bustling about with ostentatious sensibility,[7] were to leave off—not *all* the West-India commodities—but only sugar and rum, the one useless and the other pernicious—all this misery might be stopped. Gracious Heaven! At your meals you rise up, and pressing your hands to your bosoms, you lift up your eyes to God, and say "O Lord! Bless the food which thou hast given us!" A part of that food among most of you, is sweetened with brothers' blood. "Lord! Bless the food which thou hast given us?" O blasphemy! Did God give food mingled with the blood of the murdered? Will God bless the food which is polluted with the blood of his own innocent children? …

I have read and heard one argument in favour of the slave-trade, which I mention chiefly on account of its seditions and treasonable tendency. It has been asserted by more than one writer on the subject that the plantation slaves are at least as well off as the peasantry in England. Now I appeal to common sense, whether to affirm that the slaves are as well off as our peasantry, be

[1] *Duke of Clarence … slave trade* Son of George III (1738–1820), and later King of Great Britain as William IV, the Duke of Clarence in his early years as a politician spoke vehemently in the House of Lords against the abolition of the slave trade—and against Wilberforce.

[2] *Abbé Raynal … his writing* Reference to *A Philosophical and Political History of the Settlement and Trade of the Europeans in the East and West Indies* (1770) by French Enlightenment writer Guillaume-Thomas Raynal; *computes* Calculates.

[3] *passage* The voyage known as the Middle Passage—the shipment of people from Africa to the Americas to be sold for the purpose of slavery; *seasoning* Period and process during which enslaved people were forcibly accustomed to the conditions of slavery.

[4] *confederacy* Evil scheme or alliance.

[5] *tartarean* Relating to Tartarus, realm of punishment in the afterlife in Greek mythology; infernal.

[6] *do unto others … unto you* Cf. Matthew 7.12: "Therefore all things whatsoever ye would that men should do to you, do ye even so to them: for this is the law and the prophets."

[7] *ostentatious sensibility* Insincere emotional response meant only for show.

not the same as to assert that our peasantry are as bad off as negro-slaves? And whether, if our peasantry believed it, they would not be inclined to rebel?

from William Earle, *Obi; or, the History of Three-Fingered Jack* (1800)

Earle's novel is set against the background of an enslaved people's uprising in Jamaica; it is based on the true story of Jack Mansong, a man who had escaped slavery and who was said to have gained strength to lead the rebellion from the religion of "obeah," or "obi." The epistolary novel is for the most part made up of letters from one George Stanford, "a resident of Jamaica," to Charles, "his friend in England." The excerpt that appears here is from the letter with which the book opens.

Jack is a noble fellow, and in spite of every cruel hard-hearted planter, I shall repeat the same to the last hour of my life. "Jack is a Negro," say they. "Jack is a MAN," say I.

—"He is a slave."

—"MAN cannot be a slave to MAN."

—"He is my property."

—"How did you acquire that property?"

—"By paying for it."

—"Paying! Paying whom?"

—"Him who brought him from Africa."

—"How did he get possession of him?"

—"He caught him there."

—"Caught! what? Like a wild beast?"

—"No, but he contrived means to convey him into his ship."

—"Contrived! Then he brought him without his consent?"

—"Very likely."

—"And what is become of that robber?"

—"Robber! He is a very respectable man, who has left off trade, has married the daughter of a rich planter, and now lives very comfortably, after the fatigues of an industrious life."

—"What! Do they hang a poor hard-labouring man, who, driven by despair at the sight of his numerous family ready to starve for want of a bit of bread, takes advantage of a dark night, goes on the highway and frightens the traveller out of a few pieces of gold; and shall a daring ruffian, who is openly guilty of a crime more heinous in its nature and baneful in its effects, get respected by every body and pass his days in the peaceable enjoyment of riches acquired by such infamous means?"

—"I don't understand you; I never heard that the traffic was infamous. Is it not authorised by all the nations of Europe, Asia and America? Have not regulations been made concerning it by all governments?"

—"Very true, but that does not make it more honorable."

Mary Robinson, Poems on Slavery

Robinson, one of the best-known writers of the age, published a substantial number of works devoted in whole or in part to anti-slavery themes, including "Captivity: A Poem" (1777), "The African" (1798), and "The Negro Girl" (1800). "The African" was published initially in the *Morning Post*, 2 August 1798 and later incorporated into the long poem *The Progress of Liberty*. "The Negro Girl" appeared in Robinson's collection of *Lyrical Tales*.

The African (1798)

Shall the poor AFRICAN, the passive Slave,
Born in the bland effulgence of broad day,
Cherish'd by torrid splendours, while around
The plains prolific teem with honey'd stores,
Sink prematurely to a grave obscure,
No tear to grace his ashes? Or suspire
To wear Submission's long and goading chain,
To drink the tear that down his swarthy cheek
Flows fast, to moisten his toil-fever'd lip
Parch'd by the noon-tide blaze? Shall HE endure
The frequent lash, the agonizing scourge,
The day of labour, and the night of pain;

Expose his naked limbs to burning gales;
Faint in the sun, and wither in the storm;
Traverse hot sands, imbibe the morbid breeze,
Wing'd with contagion; while his blister'd feet,
Scorch'd by the vertical and raging beam,
Pour the swift life-stream? Shall his frenzied eyes,
Oh! worst of mortal miseries! behold
The darling of his heart, his sable love,
Selected from the trembling timid throng,
By the wan TYRANT, whose licentious touch
Seals the dark fiat of the SLAVE's despair!

OH LIBERTY! From thee the suppliant claims
The meed of retribution! Thy pure flame
Would light the sense opaque, and warm the spring
Of boundless ecstacy: while Nature's laws,
So violated, plead immortal tongu'd,
For her dark-fated children! Lead them forth
From bondage infamous! Bid Reason own
The dignities of MAN, whate'er his clime,
Estate, or colour. And, O sacred TRUTH!
Tell the proud Lords of traffic, that the breast
Thrice ebon-tinted, owns a crimson tide
As pure,—as clear, as Europe's Sons can boast.

The Negro Girl (1800)

1

Dark was the dawn, and o'er the deep
  The boist'rous whirlwinds blew;
The Sea-bird wheel'd its circling sweep,
  And all was drear to view—
When on the beach that binds the western shore
The love-lorn ZELMA stood, list'ning the tempest's roar.

2

Her eager Eyes beheld the main,
  While on her DRACO dear
She madly call'd, but call'd in vain,
  No sound could DRACO hear,
Save the shrill yelling of the fateful blast,
While ev'ry Seaman's heart, quick shudder'd as it past.

3

White were the billows, wide display'd
  The clouds were black and low;
The Bittern shriek'd, a gliding shade
  Seem'd o'er the waves to go!
The livid flash illum'd the clam'rous main,
While ZELMA pour'd, unmark'd, her melancholy
  strain.

4

"Be still!" she cried, "loud tempest cease!
  O! spare the gallant souls:
The thunder rolls—the winds increase—
  The Sea, like mountains, rolls!
While, from the deck, the storm-worn victims leap,
And o'er their struggling limbs, the furious billows sweep.

5

"O! barb'rous Pow'r! relentless Fate!
  Does Heav'n's high will decree
That some should sleep on beds of state,—
  Some, in the roaring Sea?
Some, nurs'd in splendour, deal Oppression's blow,
While worth and DRACO pine—in Slavery and woe!

6

"Yon Vessel oft has plough'd the main
  With human traffic fraught;
Its cargo,—our dark Sons of pain—
  For worldly treasure bought!
What had they done?—O Nature tell me why—
Is taunting scorn the lot, of thy dark progeny?

7

"Thou gav'st, in thy caprice, the Soul
  Peculiarly enshrin'd;
Nor from the ebon Casket stole
  The Jewel of the mind!
Then wherefore let the suff'ring Negro's breast
Bow to his fellow, MAN, in brighter colours drest.

8

"Is it the dim and glossy hue
  That marks him for despair?—

While men with blood their hands embrue,
And mock the wretch's pray'r?
Shall guiltless Slaves the Scourge of tyrants feel,
And, e'en before their GOD! unheard, unpitied kneel.

9

"Could the proud rulers of the land
Our Sable race behold;
Some bow'd by torture's Giant hand
And others, basely sold!
Then would they pity Slaves, and cry, with shame,
Whate'er their TINTS may be, their SOULS are still the same!

10

"Why seek to mock the Ethiop's face?
Why goad our hapless kind?
Can features alienate the race—
Is there no kindred mind?
Does not the cheek which vaunts the roseate hue
Oft blush for crimes, that Ethiops never knew?

11

"Behold! the angry waves conspire
To check the barb'rous toil!
While wounded Nature's vengeful ire—
Roars, round this trembling Isle!
And hark! her voice re-echoes in the wind—
Man was not form'd by Heav'n, to trample on his kind!

12

"Torn from my Mother's aching breast,
My Tyrant sought my love—
But, in the Grave shall ZELMA rest,
E'er she will faithless prove—
No DRACO!—Thy companion I will be
To that celestial realm, where Negroes shall be free!

13

"The Tyrant WHITE MAN taught my mind—
The letter'd page to trace;—
He taught me in the Soul to find
No tint, as in the face:
He bade my Reason, blossom like the tree—
But fond affection gave, the ripen'd fruits to thee.

14

"With jealous rage he mark'd my love;
He sent thee far away;—
And prison'd in the plantain grove—
Poor ZELMA pass'd the day—
But ere the moon rose high above the main,
ZELMA, and Love contriv'd, to break the Tyrant's chain.

15

"Swift, o'er the plain of burning Sand
My course I bent to thee;
And soon I reach'd the billowy strand
Which bounds the stormy Sea.—
DRACO! my Love! Oh yet, thy ZELMA's soul
Springs ardently to thee,—impatient of controul.

16

"Again the lightning flashes white—
The rattling cords among!
Now, by the transient vivid light,
I mark the frantic throng!
Now up the tatter'd shrouds my DRACO flies—
While o'er the plunging prow, the curling billows rise.

17

"The topmast falls—three shackled slaves—
Cling to the Vessel's side!
Now lost amid the madd'ning waves—
Now on the mast they ride—
See! on the forecastle my DRACO stands
And now he waves his chain, now clasps his bleeding hands.

18

"Why, cruel WHITE-MAN! when away
My sable Love was torn,
Why did you let poor ZELMA stay,
On Afric's sands to mourn?
No! ZELMA is not left, for she will prove
In the deep troubled main, her fond—her faithful LOVE."

19

The lab'ring Ship was now a wreck,
The Shrouds were flutt'ring wide!
The rudder gone, the lofty deck
Was rock'd from side to side—
Poor ZELMA's eyes now dropp'd their last big tear,
While, from her tawny cheek, the blood recoil'd with fear.

20

Now frantic, on the sands she roam'd,
Now shrieking stop'd to view
Where high the liquid mountains foam'd,
Around the exhausted crew—
'Till, from the deck, her DRACO's well known form
Sprung mid the yawning waves, and buffetted the Storm.

21

Long, on the swelling surge sustain'd
Brave DRACO sought the shore,
Watch'd the dark Maid, but ne'er complain'd,
Then sunk, to gaze no more!
Poor ZELMA saw him buried by the wave—
And, with her heart's true Love, plung'd in a wat'ry grave.

---

from Dorothy Wordsworth, *The Grasmere Journal*

As the following excerpt from Dorothy Wordsworth's journals indicates, brutality on slave ships could also be directed at members of the crew.

Monday Morning [15 March 1802] We sat reading the poems and I read a little German. … During W's[1] absence a sailor who was travelling from Liverpool to Whitehaven called. He was faint and pale when he knocked at the door, a young man very well dressed. We sat by the kitchen fire talking with him for 2 hours—he told us most interesting stories of his life. His name was Isaac Chapel—he had been at sea since he was 15 years old. He was by trade a sail-maker. His last voyage was to the coast of Guinea. He had been on board a slave ship the captain's name Maxwell where one man had been killed a boy put to lodge with the pigs & was half eaten, one boy set to watch in the hot sun till he dropped down dead. He had been cast away in North America and had travelled 30 days among the Indians where he had been well treated. He had twice swum from a king's ship in the night & escaped, he said he would rather be in hell than be pressed.[2] He was now going to wait in England to appear against Captain Maxwell—"Oh he's a rascal, sir, he ought to be put in the papers!" The poor man had not been in bed since Friday night—he left Liverpool at 2 o'clock on Saturday morning. He had called at a farm house to beg victuals and had been refused. The woman said she would give him nothing—"Won't you? Then I can't help it." He was excessively like my brother John.

[1] *W's* William Wordsworth's.

from Thomas Clarkson, *The History of the Rise, Progress and Accomplishment of the Abolition of the African Slave Trade* (1808)

In 1785, Clarkson (1760–1846) was the author of a prize-winning essay at Cambridge University on "slavery and commerce of the human species, particularly the African." Thereafter he devoted enormous energy to the abolitionist cause. He played a leading role in founding the Society for Effecting the Abolition of the Slave Trade in 1787, and in pressing for the abolition of slavery itself after the halting of the slave trade in 1807.

Let us examine the state of the unhappy Africans, reduced to slavery in this manner, while on board the vessels, which are to convey them across the ocean to other lands. And here I must observe at once, that, as far as this part of the evil is concerned, I am at a loss to describe it. Where shall I find words to express properly their sorrow, as arising from the reflection of being parted for ever from their friends, their relatives, and

[2] *pressed* Forced into naval service. "Press gangs" were authorized to force men into the Navy at this period.

their country? Where shall I find language to paint in appropriate colours the horror of mind brought on by thoughts of their future unknown destination, of which they can augur nothing but misery from all that they have yet seen? How shall I make known their situation, while labouring under painful disease, or while struggling in the suffocating holds of their prisons, like animals inclosed in an exhausted receiver? How shall I describe their feelings as exposed to all the personal indignities, which lawless appetite or brutal passion may suggest? How shall I exhibit their sufferings as determining to refuse sustenance and die, or as resolving to break their chains, and, disdaining to live as slaves, to punish their oppressors? How shall I give an idea of their agony, when under various punishments and tortures for their reputed crimes? Indeed every part of this subject defies my powers, and I must therefore satisfy myself and the reader with a general representation, or in the words of a celebrated member of Parliament, that "Never was so much human suffering condensed in so small a space."

I now come to the evil, as it has been proved to arise in the third case; or to consider the situation of the unhappy victims of the trade, when their painful voyages are over, or after they have been landed upon their destined shores. And here we are to view them first under the degrading light of cattle. We are to see them examined, handled, selected, separated, and sold. Alas! relatives are separated from relatives, as if, like cattle, they had no rational intellect, no power of feeling the nearness of relationship, nor sense of the duties belonging to the ties of life! We are next to see them labouring, and this for the benefit of those, to whom they are under no obligation, by any law either natural or divine, to obey. We are to see them, if refusing the commands of their purchasers, however weary, or feeble, or indisposed, subject to corporal punishments, and, if forcibly resisting them, to death. We are to see them in a state of general degradation and misery. The knowledge, which their oppressors have of their own crime in having violated the rights of nature, and of the disposition of the injured to seek all opportunities of revenge, produces a fear, which dictates to them the necessity of a system of treatment by which they shall keep up a wide distinction between the two, and by which the noble feelings of the latter shall be kept down, and their spirits broken. We are to see them again subject to individual persecution, as anger, or malice, or any bad passion may suggest. Hence the whip—the chain—the iron-collar. Hence the various modes of private torture, of which so many accounts have been truly given. Nor can such horrible cruelties be discovered so as to be made punishable, while the testimony of any number of the oppressed is invalid against the oppressors, however they may be offences against the laws. And, lastly, we are to see their innocent offspring, against whose person liberty the shadow of an argument cannot be advanced, inheriting all the miseries of their parents' lot.

from Matthew Gregory Lewis, *Journal of a West India Proprietor* (1815–17)

Lewis (1775–1818), whose father was the absentee owner of sugar plantations in Jamaica and the Deputy Secretary of War, became well known with the publication of *The Monk*, a sensational Gothic novel written in a ten-week period when he was nineteen years old. Lewis inherited his father's property in 1812, and made two trips to Jamaica (in 1815–16 and 1817–18) with a view to ascertaining the condition of the plantations and ameliorating conditions for the people his family enslaved there. His journals were first offered for publication in 1817, but did not appear in print until 1834, sixteen years after Lewis's death from yellow fever, during the return voyage after his second residence in Jamaica.

Though Lewis was clearly considerably more humane than most plantation owners, he opposed any move to abolish slavery, on the grounds that it was necessary to the plantation economy.

15 January 1815

The offspring of a white man and black woman is a *mulatto*; the mulatto and black produce a *sambo*; from the mulatto and white comes the *quadroon*; from the quadroon and white the *mustee*; the child of a mustee by a white man is called a *musteefino*; while the children of a musteefino are free by law, and rank as white persons to all intents and purposes. I think it is Long who asserts, that two mulattoes will never have children; but, as far as the most positive assurances can go, since my arrival in Jamaica, I have reason to believe the contrary, and that mulattoes breed together just as well as blacks and whites; but they are almost universally weak and effeminate persons, and thus their children are very difficult to rear. On a sugar estate one black is considered as more than equal to two mulattoes. Beautiful as are their forms in general, and easy and graceful as are their movements (which, indeed, appear to me so striking, that they cannot fail to excite the admiration of any one who has ever looked with delight on statues), still the women of colour are deficient in one of the most requisite points of female beauty. When Oromases[1] was employed in the formation of woman, and said,—"Let her enchanting bosom resemble the celestial spheres," he must certainly have suffered the negress to slip out of his mind. Young or old, I have not yet seen such a thing as a *bosom.*

16 January 1815

I never witnessed on the stage a scene so picturesque as a negro village. I walked through my own to-day, and visited the houses of the drivers, and other principal persons; and if I were to decide according to my own taste, I should infinitely have preferred their habitations to my own. Each house is surrounded by a separate garden, and the whole village is intersected by lanes, bordered with all kinds of sweet-smelling and flowering plants; but not such gardens as those belonging to our English cottages, where a few cabbages and carrots just peep up and grovel upon the earth between hedges, in square narrow beds, and where the tallest tree is a gooseberry bush: the vegetables of the negroes are all cultivated in their provision-grounds; these form their *kitchen*-gardens, and these are all for ornament or luxury, and are filled with a profusion of oranges, shaddocks, cocoa-nuts, and peppers of all descriptions: in particular I was shown the abba, or palm tree, resembling the cocoa-tree, but much more beautiful, as its leaves are larger and more numerous, and, feathering to the ground as they grow old, they form a kind of natural arbour. It bears a large fruit, or rather vegetable, towards the top of the tree, in shape like the cone of the pine, but formed of seeds, some scarlet and bright as coral, others of a brownish-red or purple. The abba requires a length of years to arrive at maturity: a very fine one, which was shown me this morning, was supposed to be upwards of an hundred years old; and one of a very moderate size had been planted at the least twenty years, and had only borne fruit once.

It appears to me a strong proof of the good treatment which the negroes on Cornwall have been accustomed to receive, that there are many very old people upon it; I saw to-day a woman near a hundred years of age; and I am told that there are several of sixty, seventy, and eighty. I was glad, also, to find, that several negroes who have obtained their freedom, and possess little properties of their own in the mountains, and at Savannah la Mar, look upon my estate so little as the scene of their former sufferings while slaves, that they frequently come down to pass a few days in their ancient habitations with their former companions, by way of relaxation. One woman in particular expressed her hopes, that I should not be offended at her still coming to Cornwall now and then, although she belonged to it no longer; and begged me to give directions before my return to England, that her visits should not be hindered on the grounds of her having no business there.

My visit to Jamaica has at least produced one advantage to myself. Several runaways, who had disappeared for some time (some even for several months), have again made their appearance in the field, and I have desired that no questions should be asked. On the other hand, after enjoying herself during the Saturday and Sunday, which were allowed for holidays on my

[1] *Oromases* The good principle, the god of light, in ancient Persian thought.

arrival, one of my ladies chose *to pull foot,* and did not return from her hiding-place in the mountains till this morning. Her name is Marcia; but so unlike is she to Addison's Marcia, that she is not only as black as Juba, (instead of being "fair, oh! how divinely fair!") but,—whereas Sempronius[1] complains, that "Marcia, the lovely Marcia, is left behind," the complaint against my heroine is, that "Marcia, the lovely Marcia" is always running away. In excuse for her disappearance she alleged, that so far was her husband from thinking that "she towered above her sex," that he had called her "a very bad woman," which had provoked her so much, that she could not bear to stay with him; and she assured me, that he was himself "a very bad man"; which, if true, was certainly enough to justify any lady, black or white, in making a little incognito excursion for a week or so; therefore, as it appeared to be nothing more than a conjugal quarrel, and as Marcia engaged never to run away any more (at the same time allowing that she had suffered her resentment to carry her too far, when it had carried her all the way to the mountains), I desired that an act of oblivion might be passed in favour of Cato's daughter, and away she went, quite happy, to pick hog's meat.

The negro houses are composed of wattles[2] on the outside, with rafters of sweet-wood, and are well plastered within and white-washed; they consist of two chambers, one for cooking and the other for sleeping, and are, in general, well furnished with chairs, tables, etc., and I saw none without a four-post bedstead and plenty of bedclothes; for, in spite of the warmth of the climate, when the sun is not above the horizon the negro always feels very chilly. I am assured that many of my slaves are very rich (and their property is inviolable), and that they are never without salt provisions, porter, and even wine, to entertain their friends and their visitors from the bay or the mountains. As I passed through their grounds, many little requests were preferred to me: one wanted an additional supply of lime for the whitewashing his house; another was building a new house for a superannuated wife (for they have all so much decency as to call their sexual attachments by a conjugal name), and wanted a little assistance towards the finishing it; a third requested a new axe to work with; and several entreated me to negotiate the purchase of some relation or friend belonging to another estate, and with whom they were anxious to be reunited: but all their requests were for additional indulgences; not one complained of ill-treatment, hunger, or over-work.

Poor Nicholas gave me a fresh instance of his being one of those whom Fortune pitches upon to show her spite: he has had four children, none of whom are alive; and the eldest of them, a fine little girl of four years old, fell into the mill-stream, and was drowned before any one was aware of her danger. His wife told me that she had had fifteen children, had taken the utmost care of them, and yet had now but two alive: she said, indeed, fifteen at the first, but she afterwards corrected herself, and explained that she had had "twelve whole children and three half ones"; by which she meant miscarriages.

Besides the profits arising from their superabundance of provisions, which the better sort of negroes are enabled to sell regularly once a week at Savannah la Mar to a considerable amount, they keep a large stock of poultry, and pigs without number; which latter cost their owners but little, though they cost me a great deal; for they generally make their way into the cane-pieces, and sometimes eat me up an hogshead of sugar in the course of the morning: but the most expensive of the planter's enemies are the rats, whose numbers are incredible, and are so destructive that a reward is given for killing them. During the last six months my agent has paid for three thousand rats killed upon Cornwall. Nor is the sugar which they consume the worst damage which they commit; the worst mischief is, that if, through the carelessness of those whose business it is to supply the mill, one cane which has been gnawed by the rats is allowed admittance, that single damaged piece is sufficient to produce acidity enough to spoil the whole sugar.

24 February 1815

On the Sunday after my first arrival, the whole body of Eboe negroes came to me to complain of the attorney,

[1] *Addison's Marcia … Sempronius* Marcia and Sempronius are characters in Joseph Addison's *Cato* (1713).

[2] *wattles* Woven branches.

and more particularly of one of the book-keepers. I listened to them, if not with unwearied patience, at least with unsubdued fortitude, for above an hour and a half; and finding some grounds for their complaint against the latter, in a few days I went down to their quarter of the village, told them that to please them I had discharged the book-keeper, named a day for examining their other grievances, and listened to them for an hour more. When the day of trial came, they sent me word that they were perfectly satisfied, and had no complaint to make. I was, therefore, much surprised to receive a visit from Edward, the Eboe, yesterday evening, who informed me, that during my absence his fellows had formed a plan of making a complaint *en masse* to a neighbouring magistrate; and that, not only against the attorney, but against myself "for not listening to them when they were injured"; and Edward claimed great merit with me for having prevented their taking this step, and convinced them, that while I was on the estate myself, there could be no occasion for applying to a third person. Now, having made me aware of my great obligations to him, here Edward meant the matter to rest; but being a good deal incensed at their ingratitude, I instantly sent for the Eboes, and enquired into the matter; when it appeared, that Edward (who is a clever fellow, and has great influence over the rest) had first goaded them into a resolution of complaining to a magistrate, had then stopped them from putting their plan into execution, and that the whole was a plot of Edward's, in order to make a merit with me for himself at the expense of his countrymen. However, as they confessed their having had the intention of applying to Mr. Hill as a magistrate, I insisted upon their executing their intention. I told them, that as Mr. Hill was the person whom they had selected for their protector, to Mr. Hill they should go; that they should either make their complaint to him against me, or confess that they had been telling lies, and had no complaint to make; and that, as the next day was to be a play-day given them by me, instead of passing it at home in singing and dancing, they should pass it at the Bay in stating their grievances.

This threw them into terrible confusion; they cried out that they wanted to make no complaint whatever, and that it was all Edward's fault, who had misled them. Three of them, one after the other, gave him the lie to his face; and each and all (Edward as well as the rest) declared that go to the Bay they absolutely would *not.* The next morning they were all at the door waiting for my coming out: they positively refused to go to Mr. Hill, and begged and prayed, and humbled themselves; now scraping and bowing to me, and then blackguarding Edward with all their might and main; and when I ordered the driver to take charge of them, and carry them to Mr. Hill, some of them fairly took to their heels, and ran away. However, the rest soon brought them back again, for they swore that if one went, all should go; and away they were marched, in a string of about twenty, with the driver at their head. When they got to the Bay, they told Mr. Hill that, as to their massa, they had no complaint to make against him, except that he had compelled them to make one; and what they said against the attorney was so trifling, that the magistrate bade the driver take them all back again. Upon which they slunk away to their houses, while the Creoles cried out "Shame! shame!" as they passed along.

Indeed, the Creoles could not have received a greater pleasure than the mortification of the Eboes; for the two bodies hate each other as cordially as the Guelphs and Ghibellines;[1] and after their departure for the Bay, I heard the head cook haranguing a large audience, and declaring it to be her fixed opinion, "that massa ought to sell all the Eboes, and buy Creoles instead." Probably, Mrs. Cook was not the less loud in her exclamations against the ingratitude of the Eboes, from her own loyalty having lately been questioned. She had found fault one day in the hospital with some women who feigned sickness in order to remain idle. "You no work willing for massa," said Mrs. Cook, "and him so vex, him say him go to Kingston to-morrow, and him wish him neber come back again!"—"What!" cried Philippa, the mad woman, "you wish massa neber come back from Kingston?" So she gave Mrs. Cook a box on the

[1] *Guelphs and Ghibellines* Opposing factions in political struggles between papal and imperial powers during the later Middle Ages.

ear with all her might; upon which Mrs. Cook snatched up a stick and broke the mad woman's pate with it. But though she could beat a hole in her head, she never could beat out of it her having said that she wished massa might never come back. And although Philippa has recovered her senses, in her belief of Mrs. Cook's disloyalty she continues firm; and they never meet without renewing the dispute.

To-day being a play-day, the gaiety of the negroes was promoted by a distribution of an additional quantity of salt-fish (which forms a most acceptable ingredient in their pepper-pots), and as much rum and sugar as they chose to drink. But there was also a dinner prepared at the house where the "white people" reside, expressly for none but the *piccaninny-mothers*; that is, for the women who had children living. I had taken care, when this play-day was announced by the head driver, to make him inform the negroes that they were indebted for it entirely to these mothers; and to show them the more respect, I went to them after dinner myself, and drank their healths. The most respectable blacks on the estate were also assembled in the room; and I then told them that clothes would wear out, and money would be spent, and that I wished to give them something more lasting than clothes or money. The law only allows them, as a matter of right, every alternate Saturday for themselves, and holidays for three days at Christmas, which, with all Sundays, forms their whole legal time of relaxation. I therefore granted them as a matter of right, and of which no person should deprive them on any account whatever, *every* Saturday to cultivate their grounds; and in addition to their holidays at Christmas, I gave them for play-days Good-Friday, the second Friday in October, and the second Friday in July. By which means, they will in future have the same number of holidays four times a year, which hitherto they have been allowed only once, *i.e.* at Christmas. The first is to be called "the royal play-day," in honour of that excellent Princess, the Duchess of York; and the negroes are directed to give three cheers upon the head driver's announcing "The health of our good lady, HRH the Duchess of York." And I told them, that before my leaving the island, I should hear them drink this health, and should not fail to let Her Royal Highness know, that the negroes of Cornwall drank her health every year. This evidently touched the right chord of their vanity, and they all bowed and courtesied down to the very ground, and said, that would do them much high honour. The ninth being my own birthday, the July play-day is to be called "the massa's"; and that in October is to be in honour of the piccaninny-mothers, from whom it is to take its name.

The poor creatures overflowed with gratitude; and the prospective indulgences which had just been announced, gave them such an increase of spirits, that on returning to my own residence, they fell to singing and dancing again with as much violence as if they had been a pack of French furies at the Opera. The favourite song of the night was, "Since massa come, we very well off"; which words they repeated in chorus, without intermission (dancing all the time), for hours together; till, at half-past three, neither my eyes nor my brain could endure it any longer, and I was obliged to send them word that I wanted to go to bed, and could not sleep till the noise should cease.

1 May 1815 (Friday)

This morning I signed the manumission of Nicholas Cameron, the best of my mulatto carpenters. He had been so often on the very point of getting his liberty, and still the cup was dashed from his lips, that I had promised to set him free, whenever he could procure an able negro as his substitute; although being a good workman, a single negro was by no means an adequate price in exchange. On my arrival this year I found that he had agreed to pay 150*l.* for a female negro, and the woman was approved of by my trustee. But on enquiry it appeared that she had a child, from which she was unwilling to separate, and that her owner refused to sell the child, except at a most unreasonable price. Here then was an insurmountable objection to my accepting her, and Nicholas was told to his great mortification, that he must look out for another substitute. The woman, on her part, was determined to belong to Cornwall estate and no other: so she told her owner, that if he attempted to sell her elsewhere she would make away with herself, and on his ordering her to prepare for a removal to a neighbouring proprietor's, she disappeared, and concealed herself so well, that for some time she was believed to have put her threats of suicide into execution. The idea of losing his 150*l.* frightened her master so completely, that he declared himself ready to let me have the child at a fair price, as well as the mother, if she ever should be found; and her friends having conveyed this assurance to her, she thought proper to emerge from her hiding-place, and the bargain was arranged finally. The titles, however, were not yet made out, and as the time of my departure for Hordley was arrived, these were ordered to be got ready against my return, when the negroes were to be delivered over to me, and Nicholas was to be set free. In the meanwhile, the child was sent by her mistress (a free mulatto) to hide some stolen ducks upon a distant property, and on her return blabbed out the errand: in consequence the mistress was committed to prison for theft; and no sooner was she released, than she revenged herself upon the poor girl by giving her thirty lashes with the cattle-whip, inflicted with all the severity of vindictive malice. This treatment of a child of such tender years reduced her to such a state, as made the magistrates think it right to send her for protection to the workhouse, until the conduct of the mistress should have been enquired into. In the meanwhile, as the result of the enquiry might be the setting the girl at liberty, the joint title for her and her mother could not be made out, and thus poor Nicholas's manumission was at a stand-still again. The magistrates at length decided, that although the chastisement had been severe, yet (according to the medical report) it was not such as to authorise the sending the mistress to be tried at the assizes. She was accordingly dismissed from farther investigation, and the girl was once more considered as belonging to me, as soon as the title could be made out. But the fatality which had so often prevented Nicholas from obtaining his freedom, was not weary yet. On the very morning, when he was to sign the title, a person whose signature was indispensable, was thrown out of his chaise, the wheel of which passed over his head, and he was rendered incapable of transacting business for several weeks. Yesterday, the titles were at length brought to me complete, and this morning put Nicholas in possession of the object, in the pursuit of which he has experienced such repeated disappointments. The conduct of the poor child's mulatto mistress in this case was most unpardonable, and is only one of numerous instances of a similar description, which have been mentioned to me. Indeed, I have every reason to believe, that nothing can be uniformly more wretched, than the life of the slaves of free people of colour in Jamaica; nor would any thing contribute more to the relief of the black population, than the prohibiting by law any mulatto to become the owner of a slave for the future. Why should not rich people of colour be served by poor people of colour, hiring them as domestics? It seldom happens that mulattoes are in possession of plantations; but when a white man dies, who happens to possess twenty negroes, he will divide them among his brown family, leaving (we may say) five to each of his four children. These are too few to be employed in plantation work; they are, therefore, ordered to maintain their owner by some means or other, and which means are frequently not the most honest, the most frequent being the travelling about as higglers, and exchanging the trumpery contents of their packs and boxes with plantation negroes for stolen rum and sugar. I confess I cannot see why, on such bequest being made, the law should not order the negroes to be sold, and the produce of the sale paid to the mulatto heirs, but absolutely prohibiting the mulattoes from becoming proprietors of the negroes themselves. Every man of humanity must wish that slavery, even in its best and most mitigated form, had never found a legal sanction, and must regret that its system is now so incorporated with the welfare of Great Britain as well as of Jamaica, as to make its extirpation an absolute impossibility, without the certainty of producing worse mischiefs than the one which we annihilate. But certainly there can be no sort of occasion for continuing in the colonies the existence of *domestic slavery,* which neither contributes to the security of the colonies themselves, nor to the opulence of the mother-country, the revenue of which derived from colonial duties would suffer no defalcation whatever, even if neither whites nor blacks in the West Indies were suffered to employ slaves, except in plantation labour.

from Elizabeth Heyrick, *Immediate, Not Gradual Abolition* (1824)

In 1823, Wilberforce and Clarkson established a new organization to lead the mainstream abolition campaign: the Society for the Mitigation and Gradual Abolition of Slavery Throughout the British Dominions, more commonly known as the Antislavery Society. The same year, an Antislavery Society member introduced a parliamentary motion to gradually secure the "extinction of slavery altogether, by rendering all the negro children, born after a certain day, free."

The more radical position—that emancipation should be immediate, not "gradual"—was at first advocated primarily by the members of women's abolitionist societies, and especially by the Quaker and reformer Elizabeth Heyrick, whose pamphlet on the issue is excerpted below. Despite resistance from Wilberforce, who opposed not only immediate emancipation but also the involvement of women in political matters, Heyrick and her associates pressured the Antislavery Society into removing "Gradual" from its official name and adopting immediate abolition as its stated goal.

... We that hear, and read, and approve, and applaud the powerful appeals, the irrefragable arguments against the Slave Trade, and against slavery—are we *ourselves* sincere, or hypocritical? Are *we* the true friends of justice, or do we only cant[1] about it? To which party do *we* really belong—to the friends of emancipation, or of perpetual slavery? Every individual belongs to one party or the other; not speculatively, or professionally merely, but practically. The perpetuation of slavery in our West India colonies is not an abstract question, to be settled between the Government and the Planters—it is a question in which we are *all* implicated; we are all guilty (with shame and compunction let us admit the opprobrious truth) of supporting and perpetuating slavery. The West Indian planter and the people of this country stand in the same moral relation to each other as the thief and the receiver of stolen goods. The planter refuses to set his wretched captive at liberty; treats him as a beast of burden; compels his reluctant unremunerated labour under the lash of the cart-whip—why?—because WE furnish the stimulant to all this injustice, rapacity, and cruelty, by PURCHASING ITS PRODUCE. Heretofore, it may have been thoughtlessly and unconsciously—but now this palliative is removed; the veil of ignorance is rent aside; the whole nation must now divide itself into the *active supporters*, and the *active opposers* of slavery; there is no longer any ground for a neutral party to stand upon. ...

... Are there no tests to prove our sincerity—no sacrifices to be offered in confirmation of our zeal? Yes, there is one—but it is in itself so small and insignificant that it seems almost burlesque to dignify it with the name of sacrifice—it is ABSTINENCE FROM THE USE OF WEST INDIAN PRODUCTIONS, sugar especially, in the cultivation of which slave labour is chiefly occupied. Small, however, and insignificant as the sacrifice may appear, it would at once give the death blow to West Indian slavery. When there is no longer a market for the productions of *slave labour*, then, and *not till then*, will the slaves be emancipated. ...

... It has been abundantly proved that voluntary labour is more productive, more advantageous to the employer, than compulsory labour. The experiments of the venerable and philanthropic Joshua Steele[2] have established the fact beyond all doubt. But the planter shuts his eyes to such facts, though clear and evident as the sun at noon day. None are so blind as those who *will* not see. The conviction then must be *forced* upon these infatuated[3] men. It is often asserted that slavery is too deeply rooted an evil to be eradicated by the exer-

[1] *cant* Talk or argue in a way that involves insincere posturing.

[2] *Joshua Steele* British plantation owner who improved the productivity of his Barbados estates by treating the people he enslaved somewhat more justly; among other things, he paid them wages. His letters to Clarkson detailing the success of his reforms were published in 1814.

[3] *infatuated* Extremely foolish.

tions of any principle less potent and active than *self-interest*: if so, the resolution to abstain from West Indian produce would bring this potent and active principle into the fullest operation—would *compel* the planter to set his slaves at liberty.[1] …

"But (it will be objected) it is not an *immediate*, but a *gradual* emancipation, which the most enlightened and judicious friends of humanity call for; as a measure best calculated, in their judgment, to promote the real interests of the *slave*, as well as his master; the former not being in a condition to make a right use of his freedom, were it suddenly restored to him." This, it must be admitted, appears not only the general, but almost universal sentiment of the abolitionists; to oppose it, therefore, may seem a most presumptuous as well as hopeless attempt. But truth and justice are stubborn and inflexible; they yield neither to numbers or authority.

The history of emancipation in St. Domingo,[2] and of the conduct of the emancipated slaves for thirty years subsequent to that event (as detailed in Clarkson's admirable pamphlet,[3] on the necessity of improving the condition of our West Indian slaves), is a complete refutation of all the elaborate arguments which have been artfully advanced to discredit the design of *immediate* emancipation. No instance has been recorded in these important annals, of the emancipated slaves (not the *gradually*, but the *immediately* emancipated slaves) having abused their freedom. On the contrary, it is frequently asserted in the course of the narrative that the negroes continued to work upon all the plantations as quietly as before emancipation. …

In the face of such a body of evidence, the detaining our West Indian slaves in bondage is a continued acting of the same atrocious injustice which first kidnapped and tore them from their kindred and native soil, and robbed them of that sacred unalienable right which no considerations, how plausible soever, can justify the withholding. We have no right, on any pretext of expediency or pretended humanity, to say—"because you have been made a slave, and thereby degraded and debased, therefore I will continue to hold you in bondage, until you have acquired a capacity to make a right use of your liberty." As well might you say to a poor wretch, gasping and languishing in a pest house,[4] "here will I keep you, till I have given you a capacity for the enjoyment of pure air." …

… Thus, by a train of most exquisite reasoning, has [the father of lies] brought the abolitionists to the conclusion that the interest of the poor, degraded, and oppressed *slave*, as well as that of his master, will be best secured by his *remaining in slavery*. It has, indeed, been proposed to mitigate, in some degree, the miseries of his interminable bondage; but the blessings of *emancipation*, according to the propositions of the abolitionists in the last session of Parliament, were to be reserved for his *posterity* alone; and every idea of *immediate* emancipation is still represented, not only as impolitic, enthusiastic, and visionary, but as highly injurious to the slave himself; and a train of supposed apt illustrations is continually at hand to expose the absurdity of such a project. "Who (it is asked) would place a sumptuous banquet before a half-famished wretch, whilst his powers of digestion were so feeble that it would be fatal to partake of it? Who would bring a body, benumbed and half frozen with cold, into sudden contact with fervid heat? Who would take a poor captive from his dungeon, where he had been immured whole years, in total darkness, and bring him at once into the dazzling light of a meridian sun? No one in his senses, certainly. All these transitions from famine to plenty, from cold to heat, from darkness to light, must be gradual, in order to be salutary. But must it therefore follow, by any inductions of common sense, that emancipation out of the grip of a robber or an assassin, out of the jaws of a shark or a tiger, must be gradual? Must it therefore follow that the wretched victim of slavery must always

[1] [Heyrick's note] It has been ascertained that the abstinence of *one tenth* of the inhabitants of this country from West Indian sugar would abolish West Indian slavery.

[2] *St. Domingo* St. Domingue became Haiti during the Haitian Revolution (1791–1804), through which the enslaved people of the nation freed themselves and obtained independence from France.

[3] *Clarkson's admirable pamphlet* See Thomas Clarkson, *Thoughts on the Necessity of Improving the Condition of the Slaves in the British Colonies, with a View to Their Ultimate Emancipation* (1823).

[4] *pest house* Literally, a hospital for the treatment of infectious disease; figuratively, any place where the air is infectious.

remain in slavery—that emancipation must be so gradual that the blessings of freedom shall never be tasted by him who has endured all the curses of slavery, but be reserved for his posterity alone? …

It is utterly astonishing, with such an object as West Indian slavery before us, rendered palpable, in all its horrors, almost to our very senses, by a multitude of indubitable facts, collected from various sources of the highest authority, all uniting in the same appalling evidence; with the sight of our fellow-creatures in bondage so rigorous, in moral and physical degradation so abject; under a tyranny so arbitrary, wanton, and barbarous; it is utterly astonishing that our compassion and sympathy should be so timid and calculating, so slow and cautious. …

… Why then, in the name of humanity, of common sense, and common honesty, do we petition Parliament, year after year, for a gradual abolition of this horrid system, this complication of crime and misery? Why petition Parliament *at all*, to do that for us which, were they ever so well disposed, we can do more speedily and more effectually for ourselves? …

Should the wretched African find the moment for *breaking his own chains, and asserting his own freedom*, he may well be expected to take terrible vengeance—to push the law of retaliation to its utmost extreme. But, when presented with his freedom—when the sacred rights of humanity are restored to him, would that be the moment for rage, for revenge and murder? To *polished* and *Christianized* Europeans, such abuses of liberty may appear natural and inevitable, since their own history abounds with them. But the history of negro emancipation abundantly proves that no such consequences are to be apprehended from the poor *uncultivated* and *despised* African. …

The interests and prejudices of the West Indian planters have occupied much too prominent a place in the discussion of this great question. The abolitionists have shewn a great deal too much politeness and accommodation towards these gentlemen. With reference to them, the question is said to be a very *delicate* one. (Was ever the word delicacy so preposterously misapplied!) It is said to be beset with difficulties and dangers. Yes, the parties interested—*criminally* interested—protest that the difficulties are insurmountable, the dangers tremendous. … Must hundreds of thousands of human beings … continue to be roused and stimulated to uncompensated labour, night as well as day, during a great part of the year, by the impulse of the cart whip, that a few *noble lords* and *honourable gentlemen* may experience no privation of expensive luxury—no contraction of profuse expenditure—no curtailment of state and equipage?[1] Must the scale in which is placed the just claims, the sacred rights of *eight hundred thousand British subjects*, be made to kick the beam[2] when weighed in the balance against pretensions so comparatively light and frivolous? …

But if the West Indian gentlemen fail to obtain *protection* against the designs of the abolitionists, then they demand *compensation*, in the event of the emancipation of their slaves, to the immense amount of *sixty-four millions*. And is *compensation* demanded in no other quarter—or, if not demanded, is it no where else due? If compensation be demanded as an act of justice to the slave-holder, in the event of the liberation of his slaves, let justice take her free impartial course—let compensation be made in the first instance where it is most due—let compensation be first made to the *slave*, for his long years of uncompensated labour, degradation, and suffering. It is in *this* quarter that justice cries aloud for compensation—and if our attention is turned, but for a moment, to these two substantial and well authenticated claims, the demands of the *slave-holder* (even had they been couched in terms less arrogant and insulting) will become not a little questionable.

Experience has already sufficiently evinced the fallacy of the notion of the superior policy of aiming at gradual, instead of immediate emancipation, on the ground of its meeting with less opposition; for the planters have shewn themselves just as much enraged at the idea of *gradual* as

[1] *equipage* Material markers of social status, such as domestic objects, clothing, and staff.

[2] *kick the beam* The beam of a pair of scales is the cross bar from which the scales hang; a scale is said to "kick the beam" when the weight of the opposing scale is so comparatively great that the lighter scale is lifted as high as it will go.

of immediate emancipation. They appear, indeed, either incapable of perceiving or determined to confound all distinction between them; for, in the bitterness of their invectives, they accuse the *gradual* abolitionists of endeavouring to bring upon their heads all the calamities and destruction which they formerly deprecated as the inevitable consequence of *immediate* emancipation.

On this great question, the spirit of accommodation and conciliation has been a spirit of delusion. The abolitionists have lost, rather than gained ground by it; their cause has been weakened, instead of strengthened. The great interests of truth and justice are betrayed, rather than supported, by all softening qualifying concessions. Every iota which is yielded of their rightful claims, impairs the conviction of their rectitude, and, consequently, weakens their success. Truth and justice make their best way in the world when they appear in bold and simple majesty; their demands are most willingly conceded, when they are most fearlessly claimed.

The Haitian Revolution

The latter half of the eighteenth century saw numerous uprisings by enslaved people in colonial holdings throughout the West Indies and South America, notably in Panama, Jamaica, Surinam, and Guyana. But the only successful uprising took place in St. Domingue, the French colony that would become Haiti. Beginning in 1791 and ending in 1804, the Haitian Revolution spanned thirteen years and led to the foundation of a black state free from slavery.

In the decades leading up to the Revolution, the disdainful and violent treatment of the people enslaved on St. Domingue created a situation of barely contained hatred against the white masters—whom the enslaved people outnumbered by at least a 10 to 1 ratio. Enslaved people were treated with extreme cruelty; workdays as long as twenty hours were enforced by brutal supervision and corporal punishment.

In August 1791 the revolt began, and within ten days the rebels had gained control of the Northern provinces, killing the whites and burning the plantations. In the following years the rebel army confronted not only French forces, but also those sent by Britain to seize control of the lucrative colony. Britain's five-year attempt, beginning in 1793, was a costly disaster, with soldiers dying in great numbers from disease.

Toussaint Louverture, a plantation manager who had been emancipated from slavery decades earlier, began to take a leadership role in the rebel army in 1791, becoming commander-in-chief in 1796. By 1801 he controlled the entire island (St. Domingue as well as the Spanish colony Santo Domingo), and he created a new constitution that abolished slavery across the territory.

In 1802, French forces, now under the leadership of Napoleon, renewed efforts to retake the colony and reinstitute slavery. In June of that year Toussaint was captured, deported to France, and imprisoned, while the fighting continued, with the French perpetrating mass executions of captured soldiers. Toussaint died in prison in 1803; in November of the same year, the rebel army, now under the leadership of Jean-Jacques Dessalines, defeated the French, exacting their surrender and departure from the island. Dessalines declared independence for Haiti on 1 January 1804. He then ordered the massacre of the remaining white population.

In Britain, news of the Haitian Revolution elicited mixed responses. Most abolitionists were sympathetic to the Revolution and saw it as further proof that societies built on slavery were inherently unstable; few, however, were willing to support the Revolution outright, particularly as the bloodshed escalated. For plantation owners, sugar merchants, and many others in England, the violence of the Haitian Revolution was associated with the grisly scenes enacted in Revolutionary France, and compassion for the enslaved people was either absent or tempered by fear of civil unrest.

Nonetheless, the Haitian Revolution marked a turning point in the history of abolition. As Frederick Douglass later said in 1893, "Until [Haiti] spoke no Christian nation had abolished negro slavery. Until she spoke no Christian nation had given to the world an organized effort to abolish slavery. Until she spoke the slave ship, followed by hungry sharks, greedy to devour the dead and dying slaves flung overboard to feed them, ploughed in peace the South Atlantic, painting the sea with the Negro's blood."

from Baron de Wimpffen, *A Voyage to Saint Domingo, in the Years 1788, 1789, and 1790*[1] (1797)

Alexandre-Stanislas de Wimpffen (1748–1819), a German sea captain, soldier, and explorer, is best known for this account of his experiences in St. Domingue, in which he describes the social conditions that led to the 1791 uprising.

from Letter 12 [May 1789]

I have determined, Sir, to give you a description of one of my days; it will be the simplest method of giving you, once for all, a summary idea of the manner of living at St. Domingo, in what is called a town. …

The cracking of whips, the smothered cries, and the indistinct groans of the negroes, who never see the day break but to curse it; who are never recalled to a feeling of their existence but by sufferings—this, Sir, is what takes place of the crowing of the early cock; and by the strains of this infernal harmony, was I awakened out of my first sleep at St. Domingo. I started, screamed, and fancied that I had waked in the gulf of Tartarus, between Prometheus and Ixion[2]—And I was among Christians! Among the worshippers of a God—who died to mitigate the sorrows of the afflicted! Custom has already weakened the effect of the impression; it will never obliterate it altogether.

A walk of an hour served to dissipate the chagrin of this gloomy awakening. I came back in time to see a troop of male and female negroes lying against the wall, or squatting upon their heels, and waiting amidst a universal yawn, for the master's giving the signal of going to work, by loud cracks of the arceau,[3] on their back and shoulders—for, you will hardly conceive, and indeed it cost six months observation to convince me of the truth of it, there are negroes who must absolutely be beaten before they can be put in motion. The arceau is the true key of this species of watch—If I had chosen to take the word of the masters for it, I should have looked no farther for the cause of this singular disposition of the slaves, than to their natural sloth and inactivity: but on considering the matter a little more narrowly, I fancied I could see that these dispositions were marvelously seconded by the inactivity and sloth of their masters, who, for the greater part, too ignorant and too unindulgent to comprehend that the vices of education can only be subdued by time and patience, find the plan of beating more practicable than that of instructing! The natural consequence of which is, that the negro, once accustomed to this mode of treatment, can only be wrought on by rigour and severity. I have persisted, month after month, in lavishing on those who attended me, nothing but patience, gentleness, and good offices of every kind—all were in vain: the bent was taken, and nothing was left me, after all my endeavours, but the alternative of waiting on myself, or of having recourse to the arceau. …

[1] *A Voyage … 1790* Translated from the French by J. Wright, 1797.

[2] *gulf of Tartarus* In Greek mythology, an underworld prison associated with creative torture; *Prometheus and Ixion* Figures in Greek mythology who were subjected to extreme punishment. Prometheus's liver was eaten by an eagle (in some versions, a vulture) only to regrow and be eaten again; Ixion was strapped to an eternally revolving burning wheel.

[3] [Wimpffen's note] A kind of short-handled whip, so called in the colonies.

from LETTER 23 [MARCH 1790]

If this expedition has increased my local knowledge, and corrected some of my opinions, the alteration, Sir, has not always been favourable to the inhabitants of Saint Domingo. Amongst a variety of anecdotes, some of which may be exaggerated or untrue, there is one which the multiplicity, and respectability of the proofs do not permit me to call in doubt, in spite of its atrocity. A lady, whom I have seen, a young lady, and one of the handsomest in the island, gave a grand dinner. Furious at seeing a dish of pastry brought to the table overdone, she ordered her negro cook to be seized, and *thrown into the oven, yet glowing with heat*—And this horrible Magæra,[1] whose name I suppress out of respect to her family; this infernal fiend, whom public execration ought to drive with every mark of abhorrence from society; this worthy rival of the too famous Chaperon,[2] is followed, and admired—for she is rich and beautiful!

So much for what I have heard, and now for what I have seen.

The day after my return, I was walking before the casa of a planter with one of his neighbours, when we overheard him bid a negro go into the inclosure of this very neighbour, pull up two young trees which he pointed out to him, and re-plant them immediately on a terrace he was then forming.

The negro went: the neighbour followed him, surprised him in the fact, and brought him to his master, whom I had by this time joined, in the hope of witnessing a scene of confusion which promised to be amusing.

Conceive, Sir, what passed in my mind, when, on the complaint of the neighbour, I heard the master coldly order another of his negroes to tie the pretended culprit to a ladder, and give him an hundred lashes! We were both of us struck with such astonishment, that, stupefied, pale, and shuddering, while the unhappy negro received the barbarous chastisement in silence, we looked at one another without being able to utter a single word—And he who ordered, he who thus punished his own crime on the blind instrument of his will; at once the dastardly perpetrator and the unfeeling witness of the most atrocious injustice, is here one of the first organs of the law, the official protector of innocence! Heavens! If a pitiful respect for decorum forbids me to devote the name of this monster to eternal infamy, let me at least be permitted to hope that Divine Justice will hear the cries of the sufferer, and sooner or later accumulate on the tyrants' head, all the weight of its vengeance! …

[1] *Magæra* One of the Furies, monstrous goddesses of vengeance in Greek mythology.

[2] [Wimpffen's note] A planter of Saint Domingo, who, in the same circumstances, seeing the heat shrivel and draw open the lips of the unhappy negro, exclaimed in a fury, "The rascal laughs."

from "Insurrection at St. Domingo: No. 1: Remarks on the Resolutions of the West-India Merchants and Planters, at the London Tavern, Nov. 3, and 8, 1791," *Star and Evening Advertiser* (18 November 1791)

The following article, from the British evening paper the *Star,* begins with a transcription of the resolutions made at a meeting of the London Society of West India Planters and Merchants, an organization founded in London in 1780 to lobby for the interests of sugar merchants and plantation owners in the West Indies. The meeting was held in response to the uprising in St. Domingue. Following the transcription of the meeting, the anonymous commentator of the *Star,* writing under the pseudonym "Common Sense," argues for a different interpretation of the causes of the Haitian Revolution.

RESOLUTION 1ST AND 3RD, PASSED NOV. 3

Resolved,

From the official papers now laid before this meeting, as well as from other accounts, it appears that the very alarming insurrection of the Negroes which has arisen, and is believed yet to exist in the French colony of St. Domingo, and which has already occasioned much bloodshed and destruction, originates not solely in political differences consequent on the late changes of government in France, but rather in a mutinous disposition recently discovered, though long dreaded among the Negroes, and which has been industriously promoted by communications between mischievous or misguided persons in this country and in France,[1] subversive of that subordination on which entirely depends the welfare of the Negroes themselves, and of every other inhabitant of the West-India Colonies.

Resolved,
That dreadful consequences may result from the insurrection in St. Domingo to the British West-India islands in general, and particularly to the Island of Jamaica, should the revolt be of long duration, or should it end (as, from the distractions prevailing, and from the small effective military force now in the Island, there is too much cause to fear) in the desertion of that colony by the Europeans. …

Charged, as the West Indians have lately been, with upholding the most arbitrary principles and practices, it was natural to suppose that the insurrection in St. Domingo, though evidently arising out of the pernicious system of slavery, will be turned by them into an argument for their own side of the question.[2]

It is one of the evils of slavery and arbitrary power, that every new danger and insurrection is pleaded as a ground for still farther severity, and that serves only to increase the misery … of those who have been already too much oppressed. Nay, it often happens, that the oppressor affects to blame himself for an overstrained lenity in times past, in order to justify the stricter measures he is about to pursue. Recrimination on every friend of freedom is another natural consequence of a man's finding himself in danger from his own injured slaves—Hence all the evil effects of slavery are transferred to the very people who, foreboding these effects, had been attempting to avert them.

Another evil of slavery is, that events in other countries insignificant, become dangerous and portentous in places where slavery exists; and that events carrying only a smaller degree of evil in them, threaten a land of slavery with total ruin and desolation. On this principle the French Revolution seems to have wrought ten-fold mischief in those parts of their empire where slavery is tolerated. The British West Indians, however, curiously enough discover, that this tremendous convulsion in the French Islands is not at all the effect of slavery itself, is not to be ascribed to the French Revolution, but rather, as they say, "to communications between mischievous or misguided persons in this country and France, subversive of that SUBORDINATION *on which entirely depends the safety of the Negroes themselves, and of every other inhabitant of the West-India Colonies.*"

It is here evidently implied, that certain questions which have been agitated in England are the cause of the insurrection in St. Domingo—A supposition which the French themselves do not seem to have made, but which, if true, would only serve to exhibit the *extreme insecurity* of countries subject to slavery, in the strongest light; for, if the mere discussion of the question of importing slaves, in a foreign and independent country, has been sufficient to cause a general insurrection in the French Islands, how wretched a system must it be which exposes men to dangers so trivial, … and against which it is so impossible to provide! …

Common Sense.

William Wordsworth, "To Toussaint L'Ouverture" (1803)

Toussaint Louverture (1743–1803) was the leader of the Haitian Revolution from 1791 to 1802. In 1802, Toussaint was forced to resign by forces sent by Napoleon; he was deported to France, where he died in 1803. Wordsworth composed the sonnet during a trip to Calais in 1802; it was published in *The Morning Post* the following year. This sonnet represents one of very few works by Wordsworth to engage with slavery directly.

[1] *misguided … in France* I.e., abolitionists.

[2] *the question* I.e., the debate surrounding abolition.

Toussaint, the most unhappy Man of Men!
Whether the rural milk-maid by her cow
Sing in thy hearing, or thou liest now
Alone in some deep dungeon's earless den,
O miserable chieftain! where and when
Wilt thou find patience? Yet die not; do thou
Wear rather in thy bonds a cheerful brow:
Though fallen thyself, never to rise again,
Live, and take comfort. Thou hast left behind
Powers that will work for thee; air, earth, and skies;
There's not a breathing of the common wind
That will forget thee; thou hast great allies;
Thy friends are exultations, agonies,
And love, and Man's unconquerable mind.

from Jean-Jacques Dessalines, "Liberty or Death. Proclamation. Jean-Jacques Dessalines, Governor General, to the People of Hayti"[1] (1804)

When Haiti became an independent country, Jean-Jacques Dessalines (1758–1806) declared himself the state's Governor General-for-life; he then ruled as Emperor of Haiti until his assassination in 1806. One of the earliest state documents printed by the new country was his "Liberty or Death" speech, excerpted below. In part, the speech is offered as a justification for a series of massacres of the remaining white population of Haiti that Dessalines had ordered in the early months of 1804.

Crimes, the most atrocious, such as were until then unheard of, and would cause nature to shudder, have been perpetrated. The measure was overheaped. At length the hour of vengeance has arrived, and the implacable enemies of the rights of man have suffered the punishment due to their crimes.

My arm, raised over their heads, has too long delayed to strike. At that signal, which the justice of God has urged, your hands, righteously armed, have brought the axe upon the ancient tree of slavery and prejudices. In vain had time, and more especially the infernal politics of Europeans, surrounded it with triple brass; you have stripped it of its armour; you have placed it upon your hearts, that you may become (like your natural enemies) cruel and merciless. Like an overflowing mighty torrent that tears down all opposition, your vengeful fury has carried away every thing in its impetuous course. Thus perish all tyrants over innocence, all oppressors of mankind!

What then? bent for many ages under an iron yoke; the sport of the passions of men, of their injustice, and of the caprice of fortune; mutilated victims of the cupidity of white Frenchmen? after having fattened with our toils these insatiate blood-suckers, with a patience and resignation unexampled, we should again have seen that sacrilegious horde make an attempt upon our destruction, without any distinction of sex or age; and we, men without energy, of no virtue, or no delicate sensibility, should not we have plunged in their breast the dagger of desperation? Where is that vile Haytian, so unworthy of his regeneration, who thinks he has not accomplished the decrees of the Eternal, by exterminating these bloody thirsty tigers! If there is one, let him fly; indignant nature discards him from our bosom; let him hide his shame far from hence; the air we breathe is not suited to his gross organs; it is the pure air of Liberty, august and triumphant.

Yes, we have rendered to these true cannibals war for war, crime for crime, outrage for outrage. Yes, I have saved my country—I have avenged America.[2] The avowal I make of it in the face of earth and heaven, constitutes my pride and my glory. Of what consequence to me is the opinion which contemporary and future generations will pronounce upon my conduct? I have performed my duty; I enjoy my own approbation; for me that is sufficient. But what do I say? The preservation of my unfortunate brothers, the testimony of my own conscience are not my only recompence: I have seen two classes of men, born to cherish, assist and

[1] *Liberty or Death … Hayti* This anonymous translation from the French appeared in 1804 in several American papers; it appears here as it did in the *Connecticut Herald.*

[2] *America* I.e., the Americas (North, South, and Central).

succour one another—mixed, in a word, and blended together—crying for vengeance, and disputing the honour of the first blow. …

… [S]ooner or later Divine Justice will unchain on earth some mighty winds, above the weakness of the vulgar, for the destruction and terror of the wicked; tremble, tyrants, usurpers, scourges of the new world! our daggers are sharpened; your punishment is ready! sixty thousand men, equipped, inured to war, obedient to my orders, burn to offer a new sacrifice to the manes of their assassinated brothers. Let that nation come who may be mad and daring enough to attack me. Already at its approach, the irritated genius[1] of Hayti, rising out of the bosom of the ocean, appears; his menacing aspect throws the waves into commotion, excites tempests, and with his mighty hand disperses ships, or dashes them in pieces; to his formidable voice the laws of nature pay obedience; diseases, plague, famine, conflagration, poison, are his constant attendants. But why calculate on the assistance of the climate and of the elements? Have I forgot that I command a people of no common cast, brought up in adversity, whose audacious daring frowns at the obstacles and increases by dangers? Let them come, then, these homicidal Cohorts! I wait for them with firmness and with a steady eye. I abandon to them freely the sea-shore, and the places where cities have existed; but woe to those who may approach too near the mountains! It were better for them that the sea received them into its profound abyss, than to be devoured by the anger of the children of Hayti.

"War and Death to Tyrants!" this is my motto;
"Liberty! Independence!" this is our rallying cry

Generals, officers, soldiers, a little unlike him who has preceded me, the ex-general Toussaint Louverture, I have been faithful to the promise which I made to you when I took up arms against tyranny, and whilst the last spark of life remains in me I shall keep my oath. Never again shall a colonist or an European set his foot upon this territory with the title of master or proprietor. This resolution shall henceforward form the fundamental basis of our constitution.

Should other chiefs, after me, by pursuing a conduct diametrically opposite to mine, dig their own graves and those of their species, you will have to accuse only the law of destiny which shall have taken me away from the happiness and welfare of my fellow-citizens. May my successors follow the path I shall have traced out for them! It is the system best adapted for consolidating their power; it is the highest homage they can render to my memory.

As it is derogatory to my character and my dignity to punish the innocent for the crimes of the guilty, a handful of whites, commendable by the religion they have always professed, and who have besides taken the oath to live with us in the woods, have experienced my clemency. I order that the sword respect them, and that they be unmolested.

I recommend anew and order to all the generals of department, &c. to grant succours, encouragement, and protection, to all neutral and friendly nations who may wish to establish commercial relations in this island.

The Governor-General
(Signed) Dessalines
A true Copy. The Sec'y-General
Juste Chanlatte

[1] *genius* Guardian spirit.

George Gordon, Lord Byron

1788 – 1824

"If the finest poetry be that which leaves the deepest impression on the minds of its readers," the critic Francis Jeffrey wrote, "Lord Byron, we think, must be allowed to take precedence of all his distinguished contemporaries." The theatrical melancholy, incisive wit, and sometimes scandalous content of Byron's poetry undoubtedly evoked strong reactions, both of praise and condemnation. So did the poet himself: handsome, charming, sexually unconventional, and politically iconoclastic, Byron has been alternately celebrated and reviled from his own time to the present. His works—the long poems *Childe Harold's Pilgrimage* and *Don Juan* among them—were tremendous popular successes, and the "Byronic hero," a character type he developed and embodied throughout his career, remains a cultural icon.

Byron's beginnings were inauspicious. He was born in near-poverty on 22 January 1788, lame in one leg (probably the result of a form of cerebral palsy). His father, Captain John ("Mad Jack") Byron, a notorious spendthrift and rake, had married Byron's mother, the Scottish heiress Catherine Gordon, for her money. This he quickly squandered, afterward fleeing to France. Byron and his mother moved to Aberdeen. Here Byron lived out his first ten years, the object of his mother's capricious mixture of love and sudden overwhelming rages, deeply conscious of his lameness, and steeped in Calvinism. Here, too, at ten years old, he was regularly molested by his nursemaid.

In 1798 Byron's great-uncle, the fifth Lord Byron, died childless, and Byron inherited the title. He and his mother moved to the family's ancestral, debt-encumbered home, Newstead Abbey, in Nottinghamshire. Byron was sent to school, first to an academy in Dulwich, then to Harrow in 1801. Around 1801 he also met for the first time his half-sister Augusta, the product of an earlier marriage of his father's. In 1805 Byron entered Trinity College, Cambridge, where he made the most lasting friendships of his life. He also contracted huge debts to which he would only add in the future.

Byron took a degree from Cambridge in 1807. In the same year, he published his first poetry collection, *Hours of Idleness*. The book was excoriated in the press as pretentious and derivative; Byron responded in 1809 with the verse satire *English Bards and Scotch Reviewers*, in which he attacked the most notable of his critics and many of the leading poets of the day. In that same year, Byron came of age and took possession of Newstead Abbey, where he held riotous parties; as a result of carousing and redecorating, his mountain of debt grew larger. In March he made his first appearance in the House of Lords, and in July, after having incurred more debt to finance himself, he set off on a trip through Europe and the Near East, areas largely closed to the English as a result of the Napoleonic Wars. This journey began an intense attachment to Greece that would color the rest of Byron's life and writing and allowed him to fulfill the same-sex desires that were dangerous to explore in England (where sodomy was a capital crime). During this time he also began *Childe Harold's Pilgrimage*, the work that would make him a celebrity.

Featuring a journey almost identical to that which Byron himself had just completed, undertaken by a mysteriously gloomy hero, *Childe Harold's Pilgrimage*, Cantos I&II, launched both the figure of the "Byronic hero" and the association between that figure and Byron that the poet would alternately embrace and seek to evade for the remainder of his life. The poem cunningly managed to weave elements from familiar genres such as travel writing, Gothic novels, and sentimental literature with experiments in mood and tone. It enthralled its readers. Byron wrote in Spenserian stanzas, but as the poem progressed he began to bend this stiff form so that it became his own. (Harold's discoveries and the narrator's own growing observational and meditative abilities find their mirror in the rhythms of the verse.) With its panoramic focus, high-flown tone, and alluringly aloof protagonist, *Childe Harold's Pilgrimage* marked an important moment in English and European literature.

Now a celebrity, Byron played that role with gusto. He became a darling of Whig society and indulged in a series of affairs, most scandalously with Lady Caroline Lamb. In addition, some time in 1813 Byron became close with his half-sister Augusta. There is some evidence to suggest that this relationship may have been sexual in nature; in any case, it was one of Byron's deepest and most lasting attachments. He also continued writing, producing a collection of hugely popular works ranging from the short lyrics of *Hebrew Melodies* to the "Eastern Tales" produced in 1813 and 1814. In this series of long narrative poems, set in the Near East, he fleshed out the anti-heroic figure he had sketched in *Childe Harold's Pilgrimage*. The protagonists of the "Tales" stood aloof from those who surround them, tortured by a mysterious but deeply felt guilt. Brave, glamorous, and in each case devoted utterly to one woman (who herself was an idealized romantic heroine), they were nonetheless fated to be outcasts. Described most fully in the first of the "Eastern Tales," "The Giaour," the hero reached his final refinement in the last, "Lara." The public embraced this figure, and a literary type entered into the canon with a vengeance: the writing of the next hundred years would be crowded with Byronic heroes.

In January of 1815, Byron married Annabella Milbanke, a sheltered heiress. The marriage was based on a short courtship and false hopes, and the two participants were utterly unsuited. Byron was psychologically abusive to his wife, whose piety and conventionality were a constant irritant to him. Early in 1816, a few weeks after the birth of their daughter, Augusta Ada, Annabella left him. A public scandal followed, aided by the unauthorized publication of Byron's poems. Now a social outcast, Byron departed for Europe, never to return. He continued to communicate with his friends in England through a voluminous and revealingly frank series of letters that detailed his sexual adventures, his political and literary beliefs, and his continued involvement with affairs in England. Even if he had written no poetry, the letters would qualify Byron for a place as one of England's foremost authors: urbane, broad-ranging, dazzling, and hilarious, they make for riveting and delightful reading.

Landing in Belgium in April of 1816, Byron made his way through scenes—including a visit to Waterloo—which he would describe in the final two cantos of *Childe Harold*. At Geneva he met Mary and Percy Shelley. They had traveled to Switzerland accompanied by Mary's stepsister Claire Clairmont, who had had a brief sexual relationship with Byron in England. The two poets formed an intimate and intellectually rich friendship, and the four lived in close proximity during the summer. Byron resumed his involvement with Claire; she bore him a daughter, Allegra, in January of 1817.

When the Shelleys departed for England in August, Byron journeyed to Venice, where he lived for the next three years. Here he flung himself into a period of promiscuity (he estimated that he had sex with over two hundred women during this time), but continued to work as well, producing his verse drama *Manfred*, the fourth canto of *Childe Harold*, and the humorous *Beppo*, written in *ottava rima*. This colloquial Italian form was fiendishly ill-adapted to English, but Byron made it his own, also using it to produce his masterpiece, *Don Juan*, which he began in July of 1818.

Don Juan is the creation of an author who has found his *métier*. It is the longest satirical poem in English, a rollicking tale of a young hero who bears the same name as the seducer but resembles him in no other way. Juan, passive and sweet-natured, is seduced by women ranging from a family friend to Catherine the Great. His adventures take him on a journey from Spain to London by way of Greece and Russia. Byron was thus able to mock not only current social mores but also his own previous poems, Don Juan standing as a kind of anti-Byronic hero. He took as his model for the poem a slight satire in *ottava rima*, written in 1817 by John Hookham Frere, but *Don Juan* is also descended from Swift's *Gulliver's Travels*, and Sterne's *Tristram Shandy*. As with the latter, the focus of Byron's poem is not so much what is narrated as its narrator, a garrulous, easily distracted gentleman who at times bears a remarkable resemblance to the author. Byron's publisher, friends, and the critical establishment condemned *Don Juan* for its immorality, but he himself relished it, asserting that he had written it only "to giggle and make giggle"—a comment typically Byronic in its attempt to deny responsibility by invoking comedy. For all its author's disclaimers, *Don Juan* is no mere comic throwaway. It is a text of great cultural and political scope and a work of questing philosophy, arguably the best of its age.

In April of 1819 Byron met Countess Teresa Guiccioli, a young Italian woman married to a much older man. Almost immediately they began a socially sanctioned affair that would last, with reasonable fidelity, until the end of Byron's life. Through her family, Byron was drawn into nationalist schemes to free Italy from the Austrians. When the family was exiled to Pisa in 1821 as a result of this plotting, Byron followed. The Shelleys were now based in Pisa, and Byron became one of their group. Soon, however, this "Pisan circle" fell apart, first because of Shelley's anger over Byron's callous treatment of Allegra (she had joined him in Venice in 1819, only for him first to neglect her and then send her to be brought up in a convent, where she died, unvisited by him, in 1822), then because of Byron's decision to follow the Countess's family to Genoa, and finally because of Shelley's own death in July 1822.

Despite these upheavals, Byron wrote at a furious pace. Between 1819 and 1823 he produced numerous works, including a series of closet dramas (such as *Sardanapalus*, *The Two Foscari*, and *Cain*), and his biting satire of England under George III, *The Vision of Judgment*. He also continued *Don Juan*, finishing sixteen cantos by the end of 1823.

In 1824 Byron organized an expedition to assist the Greeks in their fight for independence from the Turks. Settled in the marsh town of Missolonghi, he financed and trained soldiers. Exhausted and worn down, he contracted a fever and died on 19 April, aged thirty-six, his death hastened by copious bloodletting performed by his incompetent doctors.

⌘⌘⌘

Sun of the Sleepless

Sun of the sleepless! melancholy star!
Whose tearful beam glows tremulously far,
That show'st the darkness thou canst not dispel,
How like art thou to joy remembered well!
So gleams the past, the light of other days,
Which shines, but warms not with its powerless rays;
A night-beam Sorrow watcheth to behold,
Distinct, but distant—clear—but, oh how cold!
—1814

She walks in beauty

1

She walks in beauty, like the night
Of cloudless climes and starry skies;
And all that's best of dark and bright
Meet in her aspect and her eyes:
Thus mellow'd to that tender light
Which heaven to gaudy day denies.

2

One shade the more, one ray the less,
Had half impair'd the nameless grace
Which waves in every raven tress,
Or softly lightens o'er her face;
Where thoughts serenely sweet express
How pure, how dear their dwelling place.

3

And on that cheek, and o'er that brow,
So soft, so calm, yet eloquent,
The smiles that win, the tints that glow,
But tell of days in goodness spent,
A mind at peace with all below,
A heart whose love is innocent!
—1815 (written 1814)

When we two parted [1]

1

When we two parted
In silence and tears,
Half broken-hearted
To sever for years,
Pale grew thy cheek and cold,
Colder thy kiss;
Truly that hour foretold
Sorrow to this.

2

The dew of the morning
Sunk chill on my brow—
It felt like the warning
Of what I feel now.
Thy vows are all broken,
And light is thy fame;
I hear thy name spoken,
And share in its shame.

3

They name thee before me,
A knell to mine ear;
A shudder comes o'er me—
Why wert thou so dear?
They know not I knew thee,
Who knew thee too well:—
Long, long shall I rue thee,
Too deeply to tell.

4

In secret we met—
In silence I grieve,
That thy heart could forget,

[1] *When we two parted* This poem has a complex history, at least partially because Byron deliberately misdated its composition as 1816, in order to hide its true subject. In fact, the lines were written in 1815, and their subject is Lady Frances Wedderburn Webster, the wife of a friend of Byron's; Byron had heard gossip about her affair with the Duke of Wellington. Byron himself had had a brief "platonic" affair with Lady Webster in 1813: a heated and exciting chase, kept secret from her husband and ending without consummation.

Thy spirit deceive.
If I should meet thee
After long years,
How should I greet thee!—
With silence and tears.
—1816 (WRITTEN 1815)

Stanzas for Music[1]

I

There's not a joy the world can give like that it takes away,
When the glow of early thought declines in feeling's dull decay;
'Tis not on youth's smooth cheek the blush alone, which fades so fast,
But the tender bloom of heart is gone, ere youth itself be past.

2

Then the few whose spirits float above the wreck of happiness,
Are driven o'er the shoals of guilt or ocean of excess:
The magnet of their course is gone, or only points in vain
The shore to which their shiver'd sail shall never stretch again.

3

Then the mortal coldness of the soul like death itself comes down;
It cannot feel for others' woes, it dare not dream its own;
That heavy chill has frozen o'er the fountain of our tears,
And tho' the eye may sparkle still, 'tis where the ice appears.

4

Tho' wit may flash from fluent lips, and mirth distract the breast,
Through midnight hours that yield no more their former hope of rest;
'Tis but as ivy-leaves around the ruin'd turret wreath,
All green and wildly fresh without but worn and grey beneath.

5

Oh could I feel as I have felt,—or be what I have been,
Or weep as I could once have wept, o'er many a vanished scene:
As springs in deserts found seem sweet, all brackish though they be,
So midst the wither'd waste of life, those tears would flow to me.
—1816

[1] *Stanzas for Music* Byron wrote this poem in 1815 to commemorate the death of one of the friends of his youth, the Duke of Dorset. He referred to it in an 1816 letter as "the truest, though the most melancholy, I ever wrote."

Darkness[2]

I had a dream, which was not all a dream.
The bright sun was extinguish'd, and the stars
Did wander darkling in the eternal space,
Rayless, and pathless, and the icy earth
Swung blind and blackening in the moonless air;[3]
Morn came, and went—and came, and brought no day,
And men forgot their passions in the dread
Of this their desolation; and all hearts
Were chill'd into a selfish prayer for light:
And they did live by watchfires—and the thrones,
The palaces of crowned kings—the huts,
The habitations of all things which dwell,
Were burnt for beacons; cities were consumed,

[2] *Darkness* The dust thrown into the atmosphere in 1815 by Mount Tamboro, an Indonesian volcano, made the summer of 1816 the coldest and wettest on record. Influenced by the weather, and perhaps by recent warnings by an Italian astronomer that sunspots might lead to the extinction of the sun, Byron produced this prescient poem, which he labeled "a Fragment."

[3] *icy earth ... moonless air* Cf. Ezekiel 32.7–8; Joel 2.31; Revelation 6.12.

And men were gathered round their blazing homes
To look once more into each other's face;
Happy were those who dwelt within the eye
Of the volcanos, and their mountain-torch:
A fearful hope was all the world contain'd;
Forests were set on fire—but hour by hour
They fell and faded—and the crackling trunks
Extinguish'd with a crash—and all was black.
The brows of men by the despairing light
Wore an unearthly aspect, as by fits
The flashes fell upon them; some lay down
And hid their eyes and wept; and some did rest
Their chins upon their clenched hands, and smiled;
And others hurried to and fro, and fed
Their funeral piles with fuel, and looked up
With mad disquietude on the dull sky,
The pall of a past world; and then again
With curses cast them down upon the dust,
And gnash'd their teeth and howl'd: the wild birds shriek'd,
And, terrified, did flutter on the ground,
And flap their useless wings; the wildest brutes
Came tame and tremulous; and vipers crawl'd
And twined themselves among the multitude,
Hissing, but stingless—they were slain for food:
And War, which for a moment was no more,
Did glut himself again;—a meal was bought
With blood, and each sate sullenly apart
Gorging himself in gloom: no love was left;
All earth was but one thought—and that was death,
Immediate and inglorious; and the pang
Of famine fed upon all entrails—men
Died, and their bones were tombless as their flesh;
The meagre by the meagre were devoured,
Even dogs assail'd their masters, all save one,
And he was faithful to a corse,° and kept *corpse*
The birds and beasts and famish'd men at bay,
Till hunger clung them, or the dropping dead
Lured their lank jaws; himself sought out no food,
But with a piteous and perpetual moan
And a quick desolate cry, licking the hand
Which answered not with a caress—he died.
The crowd was famish'd by degrees; but two
Of an enormous city did survive,
And they were enemies; they met beside
The dying embers of an altar-place
Where had been heap'd a mass of holy things
For an unholy usage; they raked up,
And shivering scraped with their cold skeleton hands
The feeble ashes, and their feeble breath
Blew for a little life, and made a flame
Which was a mockery; then they lifted up
Their eyes as it grew lighter, and beheld
Each other's aspects—saw, and shriek'd, and died—
Even of their mutual hideousness they died,
Unknowing who he was upon whose brow
Famine had written Fiend. The world was void,
The populous and the powerful was a lump,
Seasonless, herbless, treeless, manless, lifeless—
A lump of death—a chaos of hard clay.
The rivers, lakes, and ocean all stood still,
And nothing stirred within their silent depths;
Ships sailorless lay rotting on the sea,
And their masts fell down piecemeal; as they dropp'd
They slept on the abyss without a surge—
The waves were dead; the tides were in their grave,
The moon their mistress had expired before;
The winds were withered in the stagnant air,
And the clouds perish'd; Darkness had no need
Of aid from them—She was the universe.
—1816

Prometheus[1]

1

Titan! to whose immortal eyes
 The sufferings of mortality,
Seen in their sad reality,
Were not as things that gods despise;
What was thy pity's recompense?
A silent suffering, and intense;
The rock, the vulture, and the chain,
All that the proud can feel of pain,
The agony they do not show,
The suffocating sense of woe,
 Which speaks but in its loneliness,
And then is jealous lest the sky
Should have a listener, nor will sigh
 Until its voice is echoless.

2

Titan! to thee the strife was given
 Between the suffering and the will,
 Which torture where they cannot kill;
And the inexorable Heaven,
And the deaf tyranny of Fate,
The ruling principle of Hate,
Which for its pleasure doth create
The things it may annihilate,
Refused thee even the boon to die:
The wretched gift eternity
Was thine—and thou hast borne it well.
All that the Thunderer[2] wrung from thee
Was but the menace which flung back
On him the torments of thy rack;
The fate thou didst so well foresee
But would not to appease him tell;
And in thy Silence was his Sentence,
And in his Soul a vain repentance,
And evil dread so ill dissembled
That in his hand the lightnings trembled.

3

Thy Godlike crime was to be kind,
 To render with thy precepts less
 The sum of human wretchedness,
And strengthen Man with his own mind;
But baffled as thou wert from high,
Still in thy patient energy,
In the endurance, and repulse
 Of thine impenetrable Spirit,
Which Earth and Heaven could not convulse,
 A mighty lesson we inherit:
Thou art a symbol and a sign
 To Mortals of their fate and force;
Like thee, Man is in part divine,
 A troubled stream from a pure source;
And Man in portions can foresee
His own funereal destiny;
His wretchedness, and his resistance,
And his sad unallied existence:
To which his Spirit may oppose
Itself—an equal to all woes,
 And a firm will, and a deep sense,
Which even in torture can descry
 Its own concentered recompense,
Triumphant where it dares defy,
And making Death a Victory.
—1816

[1] *Prometheus* The Titan Prometheus stole fire from heaven and gave it to humanity. To punish him, Jupiter, King of the gods, had him chained to a rock in the Caucasus, where a vulture (in some versions, an eagle) tore at his liver. Each night Prometheus's liver grew afresh, to be torn out the next day. Prometheus's story is the subject of the *Prometheia*, a trio of plays attributed to the ancient Greek playwright Aeschylus. Only the first play, *Prometheus Bound*, survives; Byron's poem represents itself as a chorus from the lost second play, *Prometheus Unbound*.

[2] *Thunderer* Jupiter.

So, we'll go no more a roving[1]

1

So, we'll go no more a roving
So late into the night,
Though the heart be still as loving,
And the moon be still as bright.

2

For the sword outwears its sheath,
And the soul wears out the breast,
And the heart must pause to breathe,
And love itself have rest.

3

Though the night was made for loving,
And the day returns too soon,
Yet we'll go no more a roving
By the light of the moon.
—1817

When a man hath no freedom to fight for at home[2]

When a man hath no freedom to fight for at home,
Let him combat for that of his neighbors;
Let him think of the glories of Greece and of Rome,
And get knock'd on the head for his labours.

To do good to mankind is the chivalrous plan,
And is always as nobly required;
Then battle for freedom wherever you can,
And, if not shot or hang'd, you'll get knighted.
—1820

January 22nd 1824. Missolonghi
On this day I complete my thirty sixth year[3]

1

'Tis time this heart should be unmoved
Since others it hath ceased to move,
Yet though I cannot be beloved
Still let me love.

2

My days are in the yellow leaf[4]
The flowers and fruits of love are gone—
The worm—the canker, and the grief
Are mine alone.

3

The fire that on my bosom preys
Is lone as some Volcanic Isle,
No torch is kindled at its blaze
A funeral pile!

4

The hope, the fear, the jealous care
The exalted portion of the pain

[1] *So, we'll ... roving* Originally written as part of a letter from Byron to his friend Thomas Moore, 28 February 1817. Just before these lines Byron writes, "The Carnival ... knocked me up a little. But it is over—and it is now Lent, with all its abstinence and sacred music. The mumming closed with a masked ball ... and, though I did not dissipate much upon the whole, yet I find 'the sword wearing out the scabbard,' though I have but just turned the corner of twenty-nine."

[2] *When a man ... home* Byron first sent these lines in a letter to his friend Thomas Moore on 5 November 1820. They are based on Byron's activities with the Italian freedom-fighters, the Carbonari, and their abortive attempt to stage an uprising.

[3] *On this ... year* This poem was until recently most commonly known by its subtitle, but the date and place are the correct title. Byron wrote it on his 36th birthday, in Greece. A companion who was with him at the time says, "January 22.—Lord Byron came from his bedroom into the apartment ... where some friends were assembled, and said, with a smile, 'You were complaining, the other day, that I never write any poetry now:—this is my birthday, and I have just finished something which, I think, is better than what I usually write.'" The poem is informed by Byron's relationship with two people, his young Greek companion of the time, Loukas Chalandritsanos, and a Turkish girl, Hataje, whom he had taken into his care. Byron's feelings for Chalandritsanos are commonly understood to be the stronger influence of the two.

[4] *My days ... leaf* See Shakespeare's *Macbeth* 5.3.21–22.

And power of Love I cannot share
But wear the chain.

5

But 'tis not *thus*—and 'tis not *here*
Such thoughts should shake my soul, nor *now*
Where Glory decks the hero's bier
Or binds his brow.

6

The Sword—the Banner—and the Field
Glory and Greece around us see!
The Spartan borne upon his shield[1]
Was not more free!

7

Awake! (not Greece—She *is* awake!)
Awake my spirit—think through *whom*
Thy life-blood tracks its parent lake
And then strike home!

8

Tread those reviving passions down
Unworthy Manhood;—unto thee
Indifferent should the smile or frown
Of Beauty be.

9

If thou regret'st thy youth, why *live?*
The land of honourable Death
Is here—up to the Field! and give
Away thy Breath.

10

Seek out—less often sought than found,
A Soldier's Grave—for thee the best,
Then look around and choose thy ground
And take thy Rest.

—1824

[1] [Byron's note] The slain were borne on their shields—witness the Spartan mother's speech to her son, delivered with his buckler—"Either *with* this or *on* this."

Epistle to Augusta [2]

1

My Sister—my sweet Sister—if a name
Dearer and purer were—it should be thine.
Mountains and seas divide us—but I claim
No tears, but tenderness to answer mine:
Go where I will, to me thou art the same—
A loved regret which I would not resign—
There yet are two things in my destiny
A world to roam through—and a home with thee.

2

The first were nothing—had I still the last
It were the haven of my happiness—
But other claims and other ties thou hast—
And mine is not the wish to make them less.
A strange doom is thy father's son's and past
Recalling—as it lies beyond redress—
Reversed for him our grandsire's fate of yore
He had no rest at sea—nor I on shore.[3]

3

If my inheritance of storms hath been
In other elements—and on the rocks
Of perils overlooked or unforeseen
I have sustained my share of worldly shocks
The fault was mine—nor do I seek to screen
My errors with defensive paradox—
I have been cunning in mine overthrow
The careful pilot of my proper woe.

4

Mine were my faults—and mine be their reward—
My whole life was a contest—since the day
That gave me being gave me that which marred
The gift—a fate, or will that walked astray—
And I at times have found the struggle hard
And thought of shaking off my bonds of clay—

[2] *Augusta* Byron's half-sister, Augusta Leigh (1783–1857).

[3] *He had no ... on shore* Byron and Augusta's grandfather, Admiral John Byron, was renowned for never making a sea voyage without encountering a storm. He was known as "Foulweather Jack."

But now I fain would for a time survive
If but to see what next can well arrive.

5

Kingdoms and empires in my little day
I have outlived, and yet I am not old—
And when I look on this, the petty spray
Of my own years of trouble, which have rolled
Like a wild bay of breakers, melts away:—
Something—I know not what—does still uphold
A spirit of slight patience;—not in vain,
Even for its own sake—do we purchase pain.

6

Perhaps—the workings of defiance stir
Within me, or perhaps a cold despair—
Brought on when ills habitually recur,—
Perhaps a kinder clime—or purer air—
For even to this may change of soul refer—
And with light armour we may learn to bear—
Have taught me a strange quiet which was not
The chief companion of a calmer lot.

7

I feel almost at times as I have felt
In happy childhood—trees, and flowers, and brooks
Which do remember me of where I dwelt
Ere my young mind was sacrificed to books—
Come as of yore upon me—and can melt
My heart with recognition of their looks—
And even at moments I could think I see
Some living thing to love—but none like thee.

8

Here are the Alpine landscapes—which create
A fund for contemplation;—to admire
Is a brief feeling of a trivial date—
But something worthier do such scenes inspire:
Here to be lonely is not desolate—
For much I view which I could most desire—
And, above all a lake I can behold—
Lovelier—not dearer than our own of old.

9

Oh that thou wert but with me!—but I grow
The fool of my own wishes—and forget
The solitude which I have vaunted so
Has lost its praise in this but one regret—
There may be others which I less may show—
I am not of the plaintive mood—and yet
I feel an ebb in my philosophy
And the tide rising in my altered eye.

10

I did remind thee of our own dear lake
By the old Hall which may be mine no more—
Leman's is fair—but think not I forsake
The sweet remembrance of a dearer shore—
Sad havoc Time must with my memory make
Ere that or thou can fade these eyes before—
Though like all things which I have loved—they are
Resigned° for ever—or divided far. *given up*

11

The world is all before me—I but ask
Of Nature that with which she will comply—
It is but in her Summer's sun to bask—
To mingle with the quiet of her sky—
To see her gentle face without a mask
And never gaze on it with apathy—
She was my early friend—and now shall be
My Sister—till I look again on thee.

12

I can reduce all feelings but this one,
And that I would not—for at length I see
Such scenes as those wherein my life begun
The earliest—were the only paths for me.
Had I but sooner learnt the crowd to shun
I had been better than I now can be
The passions which have torn me would have slept—
I had not suffered—and *thou* hadst not wept.

13

With false Ambition what had I to do?
Little with love, and least of all with fame!
And yet they came unsought and with me grew,
And made me all which they can make—a Name.
Yet this was not the end I did pursue—
Surely I once beheld a nobler aim.
But all is over—I am one the more
To baffled millions which have gone before.

14

And for the future—this world's future may
From me demand but little from my care;
I have outlived myself by many a day,
Having survived so many things that were—
My years have been no slumber—but the prey
Of ceaseless vigils;—for I had the share
Of life which might have filled a century
Before its fourth in time had passed me by.

15

And for the remnants which may be to come
I am content—and for the past I feel
Not thankless—for within the crowded sum
Of struggles—happiness at times would steal
And for the present—I would not benumb
My feelings farther—nor shall I conceal
That with all this I still can look around
And worship Nature with a thought profound.

16

For thee—my own sweet Sister—in thy heart
I know myself secure—as thou in mine
We were and are—I am—even as thou art—
Beings who ne'er each other can resign
It is the same together or apart
From Life's commencement to its slow decline—
We are entwined—let death come slow or fast
The tie which bound the first endures the last.

—1830

In Context

The Byronic Hero

Byron is the only English author to give his name to a specific literary type, one that has been associated with him since he created it. The character now known as the Byronic hero, although based on attributes present in previous literary characters, was so distilled and reformed by Byron that it became uniquely his own creation. One can see the gradual refinement of the Byronic hero most clearly in the "Eastern Tales," a term most commonly used to identify the long series of narrative poems Byron wrote between 1813 and 1814. These verse tales, which were extremely popular when they were first published, feature a series of proud, gloomy heroes, each mysteriously tortured and each having as his only redeeming characteristic an enduring love for a single female figure. The extracts below are descriptions of this hero, giving the flavor of his personality and showing the ways in which Byron fine-tuned it as the poems progressed.

from *The Giaour: A Fragment of a Turkish Tale*[1] (1813)

"The Giaour" (the word means "infidel" and is pronounced "Jowr") was the first of Byron's "Eastern Tales." It is written in fragment form, the fragments unconnected to each other and divided between a number of speakers. It tells the story of the young Giaour's love for Leila, a concubine of the sultan Hassan. Leila escapes from the harem: Hassan re-captures her and kills her by sewing her up in a sack and drowning her (at the time, it was believed that Byron had rescued a young woman from just such a fate during his time in the East). The Giaour responds by killing Hassan as he journeys to find a new bride. Years later, the Giaour has taken refuge in a monastery, and the poem ends with his long confession of guilt, anguish, and enduring love for Leila.

…[2] Who thundering comes on blackest steed?
With slacken'd bit and hoof of speed,
Beneath the clattering iron's sound
The cavern'd echoes wake around
In lash for lash, and bound for bound;
The foam that streaks the courser's side,
Seems gather'd from the ocean-tide:
Though weary waves are sunk to rest,
There's none within his rider's breast,
And though tomorrow's tempest lower,
'Tis calmer than thy heart, young Giaour!
I know thee not, I loathe thy race,
But in thy lineaments I trace
What time shall strengthen, not efface;
Though young and pale, that sallow front
Is scath'd by fiery passion's brunt,
Though bent on earth thine evil eye
As meteor-like thou glidest by,
Right well I view, and deem thee one
Whom Othman's sons[3] should slay or shun.…

Tonight—set Rhamazani's[4] sun
Tonight—the Bairam feast's begun
Tonight—but who and what art thou
Of foreign garb and fearful brow?
And what are these to thine or thee,

[1] *The Giaour: A Fragment of a Turkish Tale* Byron added to this poem in each new edition: the first edition of 1813 was less than 700 lines in length; the seventh, from which these extracts are taken, is almost twice as long.

[2] … The speaker of lines 180–797 is a Turkish fisher.

[3] *Othman's sons* Othman I (1258–1324) was the founder of the Turkish Ottoman empire. "Othman's sons" thus means Turks, and by extension, Muslims.

[4] *Rhamazani* Ramadhan.

That thou should'st either pause or flee?
      He stood—some dread was on his face,
Soon Hatred settled in its place—
It rose not with the reddening flush
Of transient Anger's hasty blush,
But pale as marble o'er the tomb,
Whose ghastly whiteness aids its gloom.
His brow was bent—his eye was glazed—
He raised his arm, and fiercely raised;
And sternly shook his hand on high,
As doubting to return or fly;—
Impatient of his flight delayed
Here loud his raven charger neighed—
Down glanced that hand, and grasped his blade—
That sound had burst his waking dream,
As Slumber starts at owlet's scream.—
The spur hath lanced his courser's sides—
Away—away—for life he rides—
Swift as the hurled on high jerreed,[1]
Springs to the touch his startled steed,
The rock is doubled—and the shore
Shakes with the clattering tramp no more—
The crag is won—no more is seen
His Christian crest and haughty mien.[2]—
'Twas but an instant—he restrained
That fiery barb so sternly reined—
'Twas but a moment that he stood,
Then sped as if by death pursued;
But in that instant, o'er his soul
Winters of Memory seemed to roll,
And gather in that drop of time
A life of pain, an age of crime.
O'er him who loves, or hates, or fears,
Such moment pours the grief of years—
What felt *he* then—at once opprest
By all that most distracts the breast?
That pause—which pondered o'er his fate,
Oh, who its dreary length shall date!
Though in Time's record nearly nought,
It was Eternity to Thought!
For infinite as boundless space

[1] [Byron's note] Jeered, or Djerrid, a blunted Turkish Javelin, which darted from horseback with great force and precision. It is a favourite exercise of the Mussulmans [Muslims]; but I know not if it can be called a *manly* one, since the most expert in the art are the Black Eunuchs of Constantinople. I think, next to these, a Mamlouk at Smyrna was the most skilful that came within my observation. [Mamlouks were enslaved soldiers, originally from Circassia.]

[2] *mien* Appearance.

The thought that Conscience must embrace,
Which in itself can comprehend
Woe without name—or hope—or end.— …

Dark and unearthly is the scowl[1]
That glares beneath his dusky cowl—
The flash of that dilating eye
Reveals too much of times gone by—
Though varying—indistinct its hue,
Oft will his glance the gazer rue—
For in it lurks that nameless spell
Which speaks—itself unspeakable—
A spirit yet unquell'd and high
That claims and keeps ascendancy,
And like the bird whose pinions quake,
But cannot fly the gazing snake,
Will others quail beneath his look,
Nor 'scape the glance they scarce can brook.
From him the half-affrighted Friar
When met alone would fain retire—
As if that eye and bitter smile
Transferred to others fear and guile—
Not oft to smile descendeth he,
And when he doth 'tis sad to see
That he but mocks at Misery.
How that pale lip will curl and quiver!
Then fix once more as if for ever—
As if his sorrow or disdain
Forbade him e'er to smile again.—
Well were it so—such ghastly mirth
From joyaunce ne'er derived its birth.—
But sadder still it were to trace
What once were feelings in that face—
Time hath not yet the features fixed,
But brighter traits with evil mixed—
And there are hues not always faded,
Which speak a mind not all degraded
Even by the crimes through which it waded—
The common crowd but see the gloom
Of wayward deeds—and fitting doom—
The close observer can espy
A noble soul, and lineage high.—
Alas! though both bestowed in vain,
Which Grief could change—and Guilt could stain—

[1] *Dark and … scowl* This and the following lines (832–915) are spoken near the poem's end by a monk of the abbey where the Giaour lives.

It was no vulgar tenement
To which such lofty gifts were lent,
And still with little less than dread
On such the sight is riveted.—
The roofless cot decayed and rent,
    Will scarce delay the passer by—
The tower by war or tempest bent,
While yet may frown one battlement,
    Demands and daunts the stranger's eye—
Each ivied arch—and pillar lone,
Pleads haughtily for glories gone!

"His floating robe around him folding,
    Slow sweeps he through the column aisle—
With dread beheld—with gloom beholding
    The rites that sanctify the pile.
But when the anthem shakes the choir,
And kneel the monks—his steps retire—
By yonder lone and wavering torch
His aspect glares within the porch;
There will he pause till all is done—
And hear the prayer—but utter none.
See—by the half-illumined wall
His hood fly back—his dark hair fall—
That pale brow wildly wreathing round,
As if the Gorgon[1] there had bound
The sablest of the serpent-braid
That o'er her fearful forehead strayed.
For he declines the convent oath,
And leaves those locks' unhallowed growth—
But wears our garb in all beside;
And—not from piety but pride
Gives wealth to walls that never heard
Of his one holy vow nor word.—
Lo!—mark ye—as the harmony
Peals louder praises to the sky—
That livid cheek—that stoney air
Of mixed defiance and despair!
Saint Francis! keep him from the shrine!
Else may we dread the wrath divine
Made manifest by awful sign.—
If ever evil angel bore
The form of mortal, such he wore—

[1] *Gorgon* Medusa, one of the Gorgons, who was once a beautiful maiden whose hair was her chief beauty. Athena turned her hair into a nest of serpents.

By all my hope of sins forgiven
Such looks are not of earth nor heaven!" …

"My days, though few, have passed below
In much of joy, but more of woe;
Yet still in hours of love or strife,
I've 'scap'd the weariness of life;
Now leagu'd with friends, now girt by foes,
I loath'd the languor of repose;
Now nothing left to love or hate,
No more with hope or pride elate;
I'd rather be the thing that crawls
Most noxious o'er a dungeon's walls,[1]
Than pass my dull, unvarying days,
Condemned to meditate and gaze—
Yet, lurks a wish within my breast
For rest—but not to feel 'tis rest.
Soon shall my fate that wish fulfil;
    And I shall sleep without the dream
Of what I was, and would be still;
    Dark as to thee my deeds may seem—
My memory now is but the tomb
Of joys long dead—my hope—their doom—
Though better to have died with those
Than bear a life of lingering woes—
My spirit shrunk not to sustain
The searching throes of ceaseless pain;
Nor sought the self-accorded grave
Of ancient fool, and modern knave:
Yet death I have not fear'd to meet,
And in the field it had been sweet
Had danger wooed me on to move
The slave of glory, not of love.
I've brav'd it—not for honour's boast;
I smile at laurels won or lost.—
To such let others carve their way,
For high renown, or hireling pay;
But place again before my eyes
Aught that I deem a worthy prize;—
The maid I love—the man I hate—
And I will hunt the steps of fate,
(To save or slay, as these require)
Through rending steel, and rolling fire;
Nor need'st thou doubt this speech from one

[1] *I'd rather … walls* Cf. Shakespeare, *Othello* 3.3.27–71.

Who would but do—what he *hath* done.
Death is but what the haughty brave—
The weak must bear—the wretch must crave—
Then let Life go to him who gave:
I have not quailed to danger's brow—
When high and happy—need I *now*?"[1] …

He pass'd—nor of his name and race
Hath left a token or a trace,
Save what the father must not say
Who shrived[2] him on his dying day;
This broken tale was all we knew
Of her he lov'd, or him he slew.

from *The Corsair: A Tale* (1814)

The third of the "Eastern Tales," *The Corsair* was also the best-selling—it is said to have sold 10,000 on its day of publication. It tells the story of the pirate chief Conrad, whose only virtue is his deep love for the beautiful Medora. During a raid on the court of the Pasha Seyd, Conrad is captured and condemned to death. Saved by Seyd's concubine Gulnare, who has fallen in love with Conrad and murders Seyd to rescue him, Conrad returns home (accompanied by Gulnare), where he finds Medora dead. Destroyed by grief, Conrad vanishes, never to be seen again.

Canto 1.9

Unlike the heroes of each ancient race,
Demons in act, but Gods at least in face,
In Conrad's form seems little to admire,
Though his dark eyebrow shades a glance of fire:
Robust but not Herculean—to the sight
No giant frame sets forth his common height;
Yet, in the whole, who paused to look again,
Saw more than marks the crowd of vulgar men;
They gaze and marvel how—and still confess
That thus it is, but why they cannot guess.
Sun-burnt his cheek, his forehead high and pale
The sable[3] curls in wild profusion veil;

---

1 *My days … now* These lines are part of the Giaour's confession.

2 *shrived* Absolved from sin through the Roman Catholic Sacrament of Extreme Unction, or the Last Rites, which includes confession.

3 *sable* Black.

And oft perforce his rising lip reveals
The haughtier thought it curbs, but scarce conceals.
Though smooth his voice, and calm his general mien,
Still seems there something he would not have seen:
His features' deepening lines and varying hue
At times attracted, yet perplexed the view,
As if within that murkiness of mind
Worked feelings fearful, and yet undefined;
Such might it be—that none could truly tell—
Too close enquiry his stern glance would quell.
There breathe but few whose aspect might defy
The full encounter of his searching eye;
He had the skill, when Cunning's gaze would seek
To probe his heart and watch his changing cheek,
At once the observer's purpose to espy,
And on himself roll back his scrutiny,
Lest he to Conrad rather should betray
Some secret thought, than drag that chief's to day.
There was a laughing Devil in his sneer,
That raised emotions both of rage and fear;
And where his frown of hatred darkly fell,
Hope withering fled—and Mercy sighed farewell!

Canto 1.10

Slight are the outward signs of evil thought,
Within—within—'twas there the spirit wrought!
Love shows all changes—Hate, Ambition, Guile,
Betray no further than the bitter smile;
The lip's least curl, the lightest paleness thrown
Along the governed aspect, speak alone
Of deeper passions; and to judge their mien,
He, who would see, must be himself unseen.
Then—with the hurried tread, the upward eye,
The clenched hand, the pause of agony,
That listens, starting, lest the step too near
Approach intrusive on that mood of fear:
Then—with each feature working from the heart,
With feelings, loosed to strengthen—not depart;
That rise—convulse—contend—that freeze, or glow,
Flush in the cheek, or damp upon the brow;
Then—Stranger! if thou canst, and tremblest not,
Behold his soul—the rest that soothes his lot!
Mark—how that lone and blighted bosom sears
The scathing thought of execrated years!

Behold—but who hath seen, or e'er shall see,
Man as himself—the secret spirit free?

Canto 1.11

Yet was not Conrad thus by Nature sent
To lead the guilty—guilt's worse instrument—
His soul was changed, before his deeds had driven
Him forth to war with man and forfeit heaven.
Warped by the world in Disappointment's school,
In words too wise, in conduct *there* a fool;
Too firm to yield, and far too proud to stoop,
Doomed by his very virtues for a dupe,
He cursed those virtues as the cause of ill,
And not the traitors who betrayed him still;
Nor deemed that gifts bestowed on better men
Had left him joy, and means to give again.
Feared—shunned—belied—ere youth had lost her force,
He hated man too much to feel remorse,
And thought the voice of wrath a sacred call,
To pay the injuries of some on all.
He knew himself a villain—but he deemed
The rest no better than the thing he seemed;
And scorned the best as hypocrites who hid
Those deeds the bolder spirit plainly did.
He knew himself detested, but he knew
The hearts that loathed him, crouched and dreaded too.
Lone, wild, and strange, he stood alike exempt
From all affection and from all contempt:
His name could sadden, and his acts surprise;
But they that feared him dared not to despise:
Man spurns the worm, but pauses ere he wake
The slumbering venom of the folded snake:
The first may turn—but not avenge the blow;
The last expires—but leaves no living foe;
Fast to the doomed offender's form it clings,
And he may crush—not conquer—still it stings!

Canto 1.12

None are all evil—quickening round his heart,
One softer feeling would not yet depart;
Oft could he sneer at others as beguiled
By passions worthy of a fool or child;
Yet 'gainst that passion vainly still he strove,
And even in him it asks the name of Love!

Yes, it was love—unchangeable—unchanged,
Felt but for one from whom he never ranged;
Though fairest captives daily met his eye,
He shunned, nor sought,[1] but coldly passed them by;
Though many a beauty drooped in prisoned bower,
None ever soothed his most unguarded hour.
Yes—it was Love—if thoughts of tenderness,
Tried in temptation, strengthened by distress,
Unmoved by absence, firm in every clime,
And yet—oh more than all!—untired by time;
Which nor defeated hope, nor baffled wile,
Could render sullen were she[2] ne'er to smile,
Nor rage could fire, nor sickness fret to vent
On her one murmur of his discontent;
Which still would meet with joy, with calmness part,
Lest that his look of grief should reach her heart;
Which nought removed, nor menaced to remove—
If there be love in mortals—this was love!
He was a villain—ay—reproaches shower
On him—but not the passion, nor its power,
Which only proved, all other virtues gone,
Not guilt itself could quench this loveliest one!

from Canto 3.24

… And Conrad comes not—came not since that day:
Nor trace, nor tidings of his doom declare
Where lives his grief, or perished his despair!
Long mourned his band whom none could mourn beside;
And fair the monument they gave his bride:
For him they raise not the recording stone—
His death yet dubious, deeds too widely known;
He left a Corsair's name to other times,
Linked with one virtue, and a thousand crimes.

[1] *shunned, nor sought* I.e., neither shunned nor sought.

[2] *she* I.e., Conrad's beloved.

from *Lara: A Tale* (1819)

Lara (the title refers to the hero's last name) was the last of the "Eastern Tales." Its hero has returned to his homeland after a long, unexplained absence. Haunted by never-revealed events in his past, he remains aloof, attended only by his page Kaled. One night at a feast Lara is recognized by a fellow guest, who promises to reveal Lara's past the next day. In the morning, the guest does not appear, and Lara instead fights a duel with his host. The personal feud turns to political rebellion as Lara becomes leader of a serfs' uprising. Wounded in a raid, Lara dies in the arms of Kaled, who is then revealed to be a young woman.

from CANTO 1.5

Whate'er he be, 'twas not what he had been;
That brow in furrow'd lines had fix'd at last,
And spake of passions, but of passions past;
The pride, but not the fire, of early days,
Coldness of mien, and carelessness of praise;
A high demeanour, and glance that took
Their thoughts from others by a single look;
And that sarcastic levity of tongue,
The stinging of a heart the world hath stung,
That darts in seeming playfulness around,
And makes those feel who will not own the wound;
All these seem'd his, and something more beneath
Than glance could well reveal, or accent breathe.
Ambition, glory, love, the common aim
That some can conquer, and that all would claim,
Within his breast appear'd no more to strive,
Yet seem'd as lately they had been alive;
And some deep feeling it were vain to trace
At moments lighten'd o'er his livid face.

from CANTO 1.17

In him inexplicably mix'd appeared
Much to be loved and hated, sought and feared;
Opinion varying o'er his hidden lot,
In praise or railing[1] ne'er his name forgot;
His silence formed a theme for others' prate[2]—
They guessed—they gazed—they fain would[3] know his fate.
What had he been? what was he, thus unknown,
Who walked their world, his lineage only known?

---

[1] *railing* Mockery or abuse.

[2] *prate* Chatter.

[3] *fain would* Longed to.

A hater of his kind? yet some would say,
With them he could seem gay amidst the gay;
But owned that smile if oft observed and near,
Waned in its mirth and withered to a sneer;
That smile might reach his lip, but passed not by,
None e'er could trace its laughter to his eye;
Yet there was softness too in his regard,
At times, a heart as not by nature hard,
But once perceiv'd, his spirit seemed to chide
Such weakness, as unworthy of its pride,
And steel'd itself, as scorning to redeem
One doubt from others' half withheld esteem;
In self-inflicted penance of a breast
Which tenderness might once have wrung from rest;
In vigilance of grief that would compel
The soul to hate for having lov'd too well.

from Canto 1.18

There was in him a vital scorn of all:
As if the worst had fall'n which could befall
He stood a stranger in this breathing world,
An erring spirit from another hurled;
A thing of dark imaginings, that shaped
By choice the perils he by chance escaped;[1]
But 'scaped in vain, for in their memory yet
His mind would half exult and half regret:
With more capacity for love than earth
Bestows on most of mortal mould and birth,
His early dreams of good outstripp'd the truth,
And troubled manhood followed baffled youth;
With thought of years in phantom chace misspent,
And wasted powers for better purpose lent;
And fiery passions that had poured their wrath
In hurried desolation o'er his path,
And left the better feelings all at strife
In wild reflection o'er his stormy life;
But haughty still, and loth himself to blame,
He called on Nature's self to share the shame,
And charged all faults upon the fleshly form
She gave to clog the soul, and feast the worm;
'Till he at last confounded good and ill,

[1] *A thing ... escaped* Lara imagines that his lucky escapes are the result of choices he made, and thus imagines a control over his fate that he does not really possess.

And half mistook for fate the acts of will:[1]
Too high for common selfishness, he could
At times resign his own for others' good,
But not in pity, not because he ought,
But in some strange perversity of thought,
That swayed him onward with a secret pride
To do what few or none would do beside;
And this same impulse would in tempting time
Mislead his spirit equally in crime;
So much he soared beyond, or sunk beneath
The men with whom he felt condemned to breathe,
And longed by good or ill to separate
Himself from all who shared his mortal state;
His mind abhorring this had fixed her throne
Far from the world, in regions of her own;
Thus coldly passing all that passed below,
His blood in temperate seeming now would flow:
Ah! happier if it ne'er with guilt had glowed,
But ever in that icy smoothness flowed!
'Tis true, with other men their path he walked,
And like the rest in seeming did and talked,
Nor outraged Reason's rules by flaw nor start,
His madness was not of the head, but heart;
And rarely wandered in his speech, or drew
His thoughts so forth as to offend the view.

from Canto 1.19

With all that chilling mystery of mien,[2]
And seeming gladness to remain unseen,
He had (if 'twere not nature's boon) an art
Of fixing memory on another's heart:
It was not love perchance—nor hate—nor aught
That words can image to express the thought;
But they who saw him did not see in vain,
And once beheld, would ask of him again;
And those to whom he spake remembered well,
And on the words, however light, would dwell:
None knew, nor how, nor why, but he entwined
Himself perforce around the hearer's mind;

[1] *But haughty … acts of will* These lines may be paraphrased as follows: "unwilling to admit that he has wasted his better self and is responsible for his turn to evil, Lara blames his faults on the fact his (essentially good) soul is trapped in his (earthly and therefore essentially bad) body. By doing this, he confuses the very notions of good and bad, and assumes that his bad acts are the result of fate, rather than choice." Byron here draws on traditional Christian notions of the soul as an immortal and purely good entity, trapped in a body that perverts it through fleshly longings.

[2] *mien* Attitude, appearance.

There he was stamp'd, in liking, or in hate,
If greeted once; however brief the date
That friendship, pity, or aversion knew,
Still there within the inmost thought he grew.
You could not penetrate his soul, but found,
Despite your wonder, to your own he wound;
His presence haunted still; and from the breast
He forced an all unwilling interest:
Vain was the struggle in that mental net,
His spirit seemed to dare you to forget!

Percy Bysshe Shelley

1792 – 1822

Percy Bysshe Shelley's progressive social and political ideas have been an inspiration to many readers, from nineteenth-century socialists such as Marx and Engels to radical thinkers of the 1960s. Although he was born into wealth and privilege, Shelley opposed the powerful, from those who teased and harassed him in school at Eton to the Tory government and press whom he believed were responsible for the oppression of the working classes. He collaborated on *The Necessity of Atheism* (1811), a pamphlet destined to alienate not only his father, but also the bishops and authorities at Oxford, to whom Shelley sent the piece. Antagonistic to kings, priests, judges, the conservative press, and aristocracy, he was called "Mad Shelley" at Oxford. He earned this sobriquet not only for his radicalism but also for his intense interest in science. These intellectual passions underwrite a body of remarkable visionary poetry characterized by an elegance and complexity that is at once very wonderful and very difficult.

Shelley was born in 1792 at Field Place in Sussex, the first of the six children of Elizabeth and Timothy Shelley, a Member of Parliament who became a baronet on the death of his father, Sir Bysshe Shelley. Percy grew up in the affluence befitting his role as heir to the estate and title of his father and grandfather. He spent his early years running free on the estate and entertaining his siblings, so he was unprepared for the rules of the boys' academy he attended, or the bullying he would suffer there. Shelley later attended Eton College, and there the teasing continued, further developing his allegiance to outcasts and the disenfranchised, and nurturing his rebellious spirit. He was still a student at Eton when he published *Zastrozzi* (1810), a Gothic romance novel. He continued to publish during his short stint at Oxford University, from which he and Thomas Jefferson Hogg, his friend and the co-author of *The Necessity of Atheism*, were expelled for writing the pamphlet.

In 1813 Shelley published his first important work: *Queen Mab*, a poetic dream-vision that vilified conventional morality and institutional religion in a utopian picture of humanity returned to a condition of innocence. Shelley's greatest utopian fantasy, *Prometheus Unbound* (1820), would essentially reprise the same picture, imagining a world grown young again as human beings learn to undo the curse of their acquired historical fears and hatreds and replace it with a program based on love, which he called "the great secret" of all morality.

Shelley's personal involvements with love, fueled by his ideals, were also fraught with that inherited curse. In 1811 Shelley married Harriet Westbrook, and the couple had a daughter born to them in 1813. But before long he would fall in love with another young woman, Mary Godwin, the daughter of the radical thinkers William Godwin and Mary Wollstonecraft.

In 1814 Shelley left Harriet to undertake a six-week tour of the continent with Mary and her half sister Claire Clairmont. When they returned to England, Shelley proposed that Harriet should live with Mary and himself as free lovers. When Harriet refused, Shelley, Mary, and Claire again traveled to Europe, where the three met Lord Byron in Switzerland in June of 1816. In the meantime, Harriet had given birth to Shelley's second child, a son, in late 1814, and at the end of 1816 she committed suicide. Mary and Percy were then married.

The summer of 1816 is one of the most famous in the history of English letters. Out of it came a series of stunning literary works: Mary's great novel *Frankenstein*; Byron's third canto of *Childe Harold* as well as various apocalyptic works, especially *Manfred*; and a series of key lyric poems by Shelley including "Mont Blanc" and "Hymn to Intellectual Beauty." Later (1818) Shelley would write "Julian and Maddalo: A Conversation," a verse dialogue representing the conversations that he and Byron had been having since they met in 1816.

Upon his return to England from Switzerland, his life bristling with personal and political scandals, Shelley was denied custody of his two children from his first marriage. In 1818 the Shelleys moved to the Continent with their baby girl Clara in the hope of joining Byron in Italy and avoiding the judgment of English society. Unfortunately, Clara died in September, and William, born in 1816, died the following year. The only child to survive would be Percy Florence, born in 1819.

The year 1819 was a productive one for Shelley. He composed his lyric masterpiece *Prometheus Unbound*, as well as the political tragedy *The Cenci*. During this prolific period Shelley also responded to the Peterloo Massacre—in which at least eleven workers were killed at what was meant to be a peaceful rally in Manchester—by writing "The Mask of Anarchy," "Song: To the Men of England," "A Philosophical View of Reform," and "Ode to the West Wind," a revolutionary lyric that recapitulates, in miniature, the argument and structure of *Prometheus Unbound*. Shelley hoped his verse would undermine the retrograde political institutions of his time and seed the future with a promise of rejuvenation. Enjoying scant fame or immediate influence, he nevertheless believed in the power of art to effect political change, however slowly, and he concluded his *Defence of Poetry* (1821) with the now-famous pronouncement that poets are "the unacknowledged legislators of the world."

In 1822 Shelley—who could not swim—went sailing on the Bay of Spezia in Italy with his friend Edward Williams. They were caught in a sudden squall and drowned. When Shelley's body washed up on the beach a few days later, a copy of Keats's poems was found in his pocket. A funeral pyre was hastily built and his corpse cremated—except for his heart, which was snatched from the pyre by his friend Edward Trelawney.

In a letter to some of his conservative English friends Byron famously declared: "You are all brutally mistaken about Shelley who was without exception—the *best* and least selfish man I ever knew." His ashes were placed near the recently buried Keats in the Protestant Cemetery in Rome. His inconsumable heart remained in Mary Shelley's possession, wrapped in the pages of *Adonais*, Shelley's elegy for Keats, until her death. It is buried with her in her tomb at St. Peter's Churchyard in Bournemouth.

⌘⌘⌘

To Wordsworth[1]

Poet of Nature, thou hast wept to know
That things depart which never may return:
Childhood and youth, friendship and love's first glow,
Have fled like sweet dreams, leaving thee to mourn.
These common woes I feel. One loss is mine
Which thou too feel'st, yet I alone deplore.
Thou wert as a lone star, whose light did shine
On some frail bark in winter's midnight roar:
Thou hast like to a rock-built refuge stood
Above the blind and battling multitude:
In honoured poverty thy voice did weave
Songs consecrate to truth and liberty—
Deserting these, thou leavest me to grieve,
Thus having been, that thou shouldst cease to be.
—1816

Mutability

We are as clouds that veil the midnight moon;
How restlessly they speed, and gleam, and quiver,
Streaking the darkness radiantly! Yet soon
Night closes round, and they are lost for ever:

Or like forgotten lyres,[2] whose dissonant strings
Give various response to each varying blast,
To whose frail frame no second motion brings
One mood or modulation like the last.

We rest—A dream has power to poison sleep;
We rise—One wandering thought pollutes the day;
We feel, conceive or reason, laugh or weep;
Embrace fond woe, or cast our cares away:

It is the same! For, be it joy or sorrow,
The path of its departure still is free:
Man's yesterday may ne'er be like his morrow;
Nought may endure but Mutability.
—1816

Mont Blanc

Lines Written in the Vale of Chamouni[3]

I

The everlasting universe of things
Flows through the mind, and rolls its rapid waves,
Now dark—now glittering—now reflecting gloom—
Now lending splendour, where from secret springs
The source of human thought its tribute brings
Of waters—with a sound but half its own,
Such as a feeble brook will oft assume
In the wild woods, among the mountains lone,
Where waterfalls around it leap for ever,
Where woods and winds contend, and a vast river
Over its rocks ceaselessly bursts and raves.

2

Thus thou, Ravine of Arve—dark, deep Ravine—
Thou many-coloured, many-voicèd vale,
Over whose pines, and crags, and caverns sail
Fast cloud shadows and sunbeams: awful° scene, *awe-inspiring*
Where Power in likeness of the Arve comes down
From the ice gulfs that gird his secret throne,
Bursting through these dark mountains like the flame
Of lightning through the tempest—thou dost lie,
Thy giant brood of pines around thee clinging,

---

[1] *To Wordsworth* As a young man, Wordsworth identified himself as a political radical, but as his career progressed he gradually became more conservative. His 1814 poem *The Excursion* showed a marked change in his political and religious thinking, and was received with disappointment by many of his early admirers, such as Shelley.

[2] *lyres* Aeolian harps, stringed instruments that produce music when exposed to wind.

[3] *Mont Blanc … Chamouni* Mont Blanc, located near France's border with Italy, is the highest peak in the Alps. Shelley conceived the idea for the poem when standing on a bridge over the Arve River in the Valley of Chamonix in southeastern France. Of the poem, Shelley wrote, "It was composed under the immediate impression of the deep and powerful feelings excited by the objects which it attempts to describe; and, as an indisciplined overflowing of the soul, rests its claim to approbation on an attempt to imitate the untameable wildness and inaccessible solemnity from which those feelings sprang."

Children of elder time, in whose devotion
The chainless winds still come and ever came
To drink their odours, and their mighty swinging
To hear—an old and solemn harmony;
Thine earthly rainbows stretched across the sweep
Of the etherial waterfall, whose veil
Robes some unsculptured[1] image; the strange sleep
Which when the voices of the desert fail
Wraps all in its own deep eternity—
Thy caverns echoing to the Arve's commotion,
A loud, lone sound no other sound can tame;
Thou art pervaded with that ceaseless motion,
Thou art the path of that unresting sound—
Dizzy Ravine! and when I gaze on thee
I seem as in a trance sublime and strange
To muse on my own separate fantasy,
My own, my human mind, which passively
Now renders and receives fast influencings,
Holding an unremitting interchange
With the clear universe of things around;
One legion of wild thoughts, whose wandering wings
Now float above thy darkness, and now rest
Where that or thou art no unbidden guest,
In the still cave of the witch Poesy,
Seeking among the shadows that pass by,
Ghosts of all things that are, some shade of thee,
Some phantom, some faint image; till the breast
From which they fled recalls them, thou art there!

3

Some say that gleams of a remoter world
Visit the soul in sleep—that death is slumber,
And that its shapes the busy thoughts outnumber
Of those who wake and live. I look on high;
Has some unknown omnipotence unfurled
The veil of life and death? or do I lie
In dream, and does the mightier world of sleep
Spread far around and inaccessibly
Its circles? For the very spirit fails,
Driven like a homeless cloud from steep to steep
That vanishes among the viewless° gales! *invisible*
Far, far above, piercing the infinite sky,
Mont Blanc appears—still, snowy, and serene—
Its subject mountains their unearthly forms
Pile around it, ice and rock; broad vales between
Of frozen floods, unfathomable deeps,
Blue as the overhanging heaven, that spread
And wind among the accumulated steeps;
A desert peopled by the storms alone,
Save when the eagle brings some hunter's bone,
And the wolf tracks her there—how hideously
Its shapes are heaped around: rude, bare, and high,
Ghastly, and scarred, and riven. Is this the scene
Where the old Earthquake-daemon[2] taught her young
Ruin? Were these their toys? or did a sea
Of fire envelop once this silent snow?
None can reply—all seems eternal now.
The wilderness has a mysterious tongue
Which teaches awful doubt, or faith so mild,
So solemn, so serene, that man may be
But for such faith with nature reconciled;
Thou hast a voice, great Mountain, to repeal
Large codes of fraud and woe; not understood
By all, but which the wise, and great, and good
Interpret, or make felt, or deeply feel.

4

The fields, the lakes, the forests, and the streams,
Ocean, and all the living things that dwell
Within the daedal[3] earth; lightning, and rain,
Earthquake, and fiery flood, and hurricane,
The torpor of the year when feeble dreams
Visit the hidden buds, or dreamless sleep
Holds every future leaf and flower; the bound
With which from that detested trance they leap;
The works and ways of man, their death and birth,
And that of him and all that his may be;
All things that move and breathe with toil and sound
Are born and die; revolve, subside and swell.
Power dwells apart in its tranquillity

[1] *unsculptured* I.e., not shaped by humans.

[2] *daemon* In Greek mythology, supernatural being or minor deity that controls some natural force.

[3] *daedal* Skillfully or intricately wrought. (From Daedalus of classical myth, who built the famous labyrinth in Crete.)

Remote, serene, and inaccessible:
And *this*, the naked countenance of earth,
On which I gaze, even these primeval mountains
Teach the adverting mind. The glaciers creep
Like snakes that watch their prey, from their far
fountains,
Slow rolling on; there, many a precipice,
Frost and the Sun in scorn of mortal power
Have piled: dome, pyramid, and pinnacle,
A city of death, distinct with many a tower
And wall impregnable of beaming ice.
Yet not a city, but a flood of ruin
Is there, that from the boundaries of the sky
Rolls its perpetual stream; vast pines are strewing
Its destined path, or in the mangled soil
Branchless and shattered stand; the rocks, drawn down
From yon remotest waste, have overthrown
The limits of the dead and living world,
Never to be reclaimed. The dwelling-place
Of insects, beasts, and birds, becomes its spoil;
Their food and their retreat for ever gone,
So much of life and joy is lost. The race
Of man flies far in dread; his work and dwelling
Vanish, like smoke before the tempest's stream,
And their place is not known. Below, vast caves
Shine in the rushing torrent's restless gleam,
Which from those secret chasms in tumult welling[1]
Meet in the vale, and one majestic River,
The breath and blood of distant lands, for ever
Rolls its loud waters to the ocean waves,
Breathes its swift vapours to the circling air.

5

Mont Blanc yet gleams on high—the power is there,
The still and solemn power of many sights
And many sounds, and much of life and death.
In the calm darkness of the moonless nights,
In the lone glare of day, the snows descend
Upon that Mountain; none beholds them there,
Nor when the flakes burn in the sinking sun,
Or the star-beams dart through them. Winds contend
Silently there, and heap the snow with breath
Rapid and strong, but silently! Its home
The voiceless lightning in these solitudes
Keeps innocently, and like vapour broods
Over the snow. The secret strength of things
Which governs thought, and to the infinite dome
Of heaven is as a law, inhabits thee!
And what were thou, and earth, and stars, and sea,
If to the human mind's imaginings
Silence and solitude were vacancy?
—1817

[1] *Which from … welling* Cf. Coleridge's *Kubla Khan*, lines 12–24.

Hymn to Intellectual Beauty[2]

1

The awful shadow of some unseen Power
Floats though unseen amongst us, visiting
This various world with as inconstant wing
As summer winds that creep from flower to flower.
Like moonbeams that behind some piny mountain
shower,
It visits with inconstant glance
Each human heart and countenance;
Like hues and harmonies of evening,
Like clouds in starlight widely spread,
Like memory of music fled,
Like aught that for its grace may be
Dear, and yet dearer for its mystery.

2

Spirit of BEAUTY, that doth consecrate
With thine own hues all thou dost shine upon
Of human thought or form—where art thou gone?
Why dost thou pass away and leave our state,
This dim vast vale of tears, vacant and desolate?
Ask why the sunlight not forever
Weaves rainbows o'er yon mountain river,

[2] *Hymn … Beauty* Composed during the summer of 1816, the same summer in which Shelley wrote "Mont Blanc." The concept of "intellectual beauty" is Platonic in origin and was a popular one in contemporary writing. It denotes a beauty of the soul, or the mind and its inventions, that cannot be perceived by the senses and therefore must be grasped intuitively.

Why aught should fail and fade that once is shown,
Why fear and dream and death and birth
Cast on the daylight of this earth
Such gloom—why man has such a scope
For love and hate, despondency and hope?

3

No voice from some sublimer world hath ever
To sage or poet these responses given—
Therefore the name of God, and ghosts, and Heaven,
Remain the records of their vain endeavour,
Frail spells—whose uttered charm might not avail to sever,
From all we hear and all we see,
Doubt, chance, and mutability.
Thy light alone—like mist o'er mountains driven,
Or music by the night wind sent
Through strings of some still instrument,
Or moonlight on a midnight stream,
Gives grace and truth to life's unquiet dream.

4

Love, Hope, and Self-esteem, like clouds depart
And come, for some uncertain moments lent.
Man were° immortal, and omnipotent, *would be*
Didst thou,[1] unknown and awful as thou art,
Keep with thy glorious train firm state within his heart.
Thou messenger of sympathies
That wax and wane in lovers' eyes—
Thou—that to human thought art nourishment,
Like darkness to a dying flame!
Depart not as thy shadow came,
Depart not—lest the grave should be,
Like life and fear, a dark reality.

5

While yet a boy I sought for ghosts, and sped
Through many a listening chamber, cave and ruin,
And starlight wood, with fearful steps pursuing
Hopes of high talk with the departed dead.
I called on poisonous names with which our youth is fed,
I was not heard—I saw them not—
When musing deeply on the lot
Of life, at that sweet time when winds are wooing
All vital things that wake to bring
News of buds and blossoming—
Sudden, thy shadow fell on me;
I shrieked, and clasped my hands in ecstasy!

6

I vowed that I would dedicate my powers
To thee and thine—have I not kept the vow?
With beating heart and streaming eyes, even now
I call the phantoms of a thousand hours
Each from his voiceless grave: they have in visioned bowers
Of studious zeal or love's delight
Outwatched with me the envious night—
They know that never joy illumed my brow
Unlinked with hope that thou wouldst free
This world from its dark slavery,
That thou—O awful LOVELINESS,
Wouldst give whate'er these words cannot express.

7

The day becomes more solemn and serene
When noon is past—there is a harmony
In autumn, and a lustre in its sky,
Which through the summer is not heard or seen,
As if it could not be, as if it had not been!
Thus let thy power, which like the truth
Of nature on my passive youth
Descended, to my onward life supply
Its calm—to one who worships thee,
And every form containing thee,
Whom, SPIRIT fair, thy spells did bind
To fear° himself, and love all human kind. *revere*

—1817

[1] *Didst thou* I.e., if thou didst.

Ozymandias[1]

I met a traveller from an antique land
Who said: Two vast and trunkless legs of stone
Stand in the desert … Near them, on the sand,
Half sunk, a shattered visage lies, whose frown,
And wrinkled lip, and sneer of cold command,
Tell that its sculptor well those passions read
Which yet survive, stamped on these lifeless things,
The hand that mocked them, and the heart that fed:
And on the pedestal these words appear:
"My name is Ozymandias, king of kings:
Look on my works, ye Mighty, and despair!"
Nothing beside remains. Round the decay
Of that colossal wreck, boundless and bare
The lone and level sands stretch far away.
—1818

Ode to the West Wind[2]

1

O Wild West Wind, thou breath[3] of Autumn's being,
Thou, from whose unseen presence the leaves dead
Are driven, like ghosts from an enchanter fleeing,

Yellow, and black, and pale, and hectic° red, *feverish*
Pestilence-stricken multitudes: O thou,
Who chariotest to their dark wintry bed
The winged seeds, where they lie cold and low,
Each like a corpse within its grave, until
Thine azure sister of the Spring shall blow

Her clarion[4] o'er the dreaming earth, and fill
(Driving sweet buds like flocks to feed in air)
With living hues and odours plain and hill:

Wild Spirit, which art moving everywhere;
Destroyer and Preserver; hear, oh, hear!

2

Thou on whose stream, 'mid the steep sky's commotion,
Loose clouds like earth's decaying leaves are shed,
Shook from the tangled boughs of Heaven and Ocean,

Angels° of rain and lightning: there are spread *harbingers*
On the blue surface of thine aëry surge,
Like the bright hair uplifted from the head

Of some fierce Mænad,[5] even from the dim verge
Of the horizon to the zenith's height,
The locks of the approaching storm. Thou dirge

Of the dying year, to which this closing night
Will be the dome of a vast sepulchre,
Vaulted with all thy congregated might

Of vapours,° from whose solid atmosphere *clouds*
Black rain, and fire, and hail will burst: oh, hear!

3

Thou who didst waken from his summer dreams
The blue Mediterranean, where he lay,
Lulled by the coil of his chrystàlline streams,[6]

---

[1] *Ozymandias* Greek name for King Ramses II of Egypt (1304–1237 BCE). First century BCE Greek historian Diodorus Siculus records the story of this monument (Ozymandias's tomb was in the shape of a male sphinx) and its inscription, which Diodorus says reads: "King of Kings am I, Ozymandias. If anyone would know how great I am and where I lie, let him surpass one of my exploits."

[2] [Shelley's note] This poem was conceived and chiefly written in a wood that skirts the Arno, near Florence, and on a day when that tempestuous wind, whose temperature is at once mild and animating, was collecting the vapours which pour down the autumnal rains. They began, as I foresaw, at sunset with a violent tempest of hail and rain, attended by that magnificent thunder and lightning peculiar to the Cispaline regions.

[3] *breath* The Latin word for wind, *spiritus*, also means "breath" and "soul," and is the root of the word "inspiration."

[4] *clarion* High-pitched trumpet.

[5] *Mænad* Female attendant of Bacchus, the Greek god of wine.

[6] *coil … streams* Currents of the Mediterranean, the color of which are often different from the surrounding water.

Beside a pumice isle in Baiae's bay,[1]
And saw in sleep old palaces and towers
Quivering within the wave's intenser day,

All overgrown with azure moss and flowers
So sweet, the sense faints picturing them! Thou
For whose path the Atlantic's level powers

Cleave themselves into chasms, while far below
The sea-blooms and the oozy woods which wear
The sapless foliage of the ocean, know

Thy voice, and suddenly grow gray with fear,
And tremble and despoil themselves:[2] oh, hear!

4

If I were a dead leaf thou mightest bear;
If I were a swift cloud to fly with thee;
A wave to pant beneath thy power, and share

The impulse of thy strength, only less free
Than thou, O uncontrollable! If even
I were as in my boyhood, and could be

The comrade of thy wanderings over Heaven,
As then, when to outstrip thy skiey speed
Scarce seemed a vision; I would ne'er have striven

As thus with thee in prayer in my sore need.
Oh! lift me as a wave, a leaf, a cloud!
I fall upon the thorns of life! I bleed!

A heavy weight of hours has chained and bowed
One too like thee: tameless, and swift, and proud.

[1] *pumice* Porous stone made from cooled lava; *Baiae's bay* Bay west of Naples that contains the ruins of several imperial villas.

[2] [Shelley's note] The phenomenon alluded to at the conclusion of the third stanza is well known to naturalists. The vegetation at the bottom of the sea, of rivers, and of lakes, sympathizes with that of the land in the change of seasons, and is consequently influenced by the winds which announce it.

5

Make me thy lyre,[3] even as the forest is:
What if my leaves are falling like its own!
The tumult of thy mighty harmonies

Will take from both a deep, autumnal tone,
Sweet though in sadness. Be thou, Spirit fierce,
My spirit! Be thou me, impetuous one!

Drive my dead thoughts over the universe
Like withered leaves to quicken a new birth!
And, by the incantation of this verse,

Scatter, as from an unextinguished hearth
Ashes and sparks, my words among mankind!
Be through my lips to unawakened Earth

The trumpet of a prophecy! O, Wind,
If Winter comes, can Spring be far behind?
—1820

The Cloud

I bring fresh showers for the thirsting flowers,
From the seas and the streams;
I bear light shade for the leaves when laid
In their noonday dreams.
From my wings are shaken the dews that waken
The sweet buds every one,
When rocked to rest on their mother's breast,
As she dances about the sun.
I wield the flail of the lashing hail,
And whiten the green plains under,
And then again I dissolve it in rain,
And laugh as I pass in thunder.

I sift the snow on the mountains below,
And their great pines groan aghast;
And all the night 'tis my pillow white,
While I sleep in the arms of the blast,

[3] *lyre* Here, an Aeolian harp, a stringed instrument that produces music when exposed to wind.

Sublime on the towers of my skiey bowers,
    Lightning my pilot sits;
In a cavern under is fettered the thunder,
    It struggles and howls at fits;[1]
Over earth and ocean, with gentle motion,
    This pilot is guiding me,
Lured by the love of the genii that move
    In the depths of the purple sea;
Over the rills, and the crags, and the hills,
    Over the lakes and the plains,
Wherever he dream, under mountain or stream,
    The Spirit he loves remains;
And I all the while bask in Heaven's blue smile,
    Whilst he is dissolving in rains.

The sanguine Sunrise, with his meteor eyes,
    And his burning plumes outspread,
Leaps on the back of my sailing rack,[2]
    When the morning star shines dead;
As on the jag of a mountain crag,
    Which an earthquake rocks and swings,
An eagle alit one moment may sit
    In the light of its golden wings.
And when Sunset may breathe, from the lit sea beneath,
    Its ardours of rest and love,
And the crimson pall[3] of eve may fall
    From the depth of Heaven above,
With wings folded I rest, on mine aëry nest,
    As still as a brooding dove.

That orbèd maiden with white fire laden,
    Whom mortals call the Moon,
Glides glimmering o'er my fleece-like floor,
    By the midnight breezes strewn;
And wherever the beat of her unseen feet,
    Which only the angels hear,
May have broken the woof° of my tent's thin roof, *weave*
    The stars peep behind her and peer;
And I laugh to see them whirl and flee,
    Like a swarm of golden bees,
When I widen the rent in my wind-built tent,
    Till the calm rivers, lakes, and seas,
Like strips of the sky fallen through me on high,
    Are each paved with the moon and these.

I bind the Sun's throne with a burning zone,° *belt*
    And the Moon's with a girdle of pearl;
The volcanoes are dim, and the stars reel and swim,
    When the whirlwinds my banner unfurl.
From cape to cape, with a bridge-like shape,
    Over a torrent sea,
Sunbeam-proof, I hand like a roof—
    The mountains its columns be.
The triumphal arch through which I march
    With hurricane, fire, and snow,
When the Powers of the air are chained to my chair,
    Is the million-coloured bow;
The sphere-fire[4] above its soft colours wove,
    While the moist Earth was laughing below.

I am the daughter of Earth and Water,
    And the nursing of the Sky;
I pass through the pores of the ocean and shores;
    I change, but I cannot die.
For after the rain, when with never a stain
    The pavilion of Heaven is bare,
And the winds and sunbeams with their convex gleams
    Build up the blue dome of air,
I silently laugh at my own cenotaph,[5]
    And out of the caverns of rain,
Like a child from the womb, like a ghost from the tomb,
    I arise and unbuild it again.
—1820

[1] *at fits* Fitfully.

[2] *rack* Mass of clouds in the upper air.

[3] *pall* Rich cloth or canopy.

[4] *sphere-fire* I.e., sunlight.

[5] *cenotaph* Empty sepulcher; monument honoring a dead person whose body lies elsewhere.

To a Skylark[1]

Hail to thee, blithe Spirit!
Bird thou never wert,
That from Heaven, or near it,
Pourest thy full heart
In profuse strains of unpremeditated art.

Higher still and higher
From the earth thou springest
Like a cloud of fire;
The blue deep thou wingest,
And singing still dost soar, and soaring ever singest.

In the golden lightning
Of the sunken sun,
O'er which clouds are bright'ning,
Thou dost float and run;
Like an unbodied joy whose race is just begun.

The pale purple even
Melts around thy flight;
Like a star of Heaven,
In the broad daylight
Thou art unseen, but yet I hear thy shrill delight,

Keen as are the arrows
Of that silver sphere,[2]
Whose intense lamp narrows
In the white dawn clear
Until we hardly see—we feel that it is there.

All the earth and air
With thy voice is loud,
As, when night is bare,
From one lonely cloud
The moon rains out her beams, and Heaven is overflowed.

What thou art we know not;
What is most like thee?
From rainbow clouds there flow not
Drops so bright to see
As from thy presence showers a rain of melody.

Like a Poet hidden
In the light of thought,
Singing hymns unbidden,
Till the world is wrought
To sympathy with hopes and fears it heeded not:

Like a high-born maiden
In a palace-tower,
Soothing her love-laden
Soul in secret hour
With music sweet as love, which overflows her bower:

Like a glow-worm golden
In a dell of dew,
Scattering unbeholden
Its aëreal hue
Among the flowers and grass, which screen it from the view:

Like a rose embowered
In its own green leaves,
By warm winds deflowered,
Till the scent it gives
Makes faint with too much sweet these heavy-wingèd thieves:

Sound of vernal° showers — *springtime*
On the twinkling grass,
Rain-awakened flowers,
All that ever was
Joyous, and clear, and fresh, thy music doth surpass:

Teach us, Sprite° or Bird, — *fairy*
What sweet thoughts are thine:
I have never heard
Praise of love or wine
That panted forth a flood of rapture so divine.

---

[1] *Skylark* Small bird that sings only when in flight, and often flies so high that it cannot be easily seen.

[2] *silver sphere* I.e., the morning star.

Chorus Hymeneal,[1]
    Or triumphal chaunt,° *chant*
Matched with thine would be all
    But an empty vaunt,
A thing wherein we feel there is some hidden want.

What objects are the fountains
    Of thy happy strain?
What fields, or waves, or mountains?
    What shapes of sky or plain?
What love of thine own kind? what ignorance of pain?

With thy clear keen joyance
    Languor cannot be:
Shadow of annoyance
    Never came near thee:
Thou lovest—but ne'er knew love's sad satiety.

Waking or asleep,
    Thou of death must deem
Things more true and deep
    Than we mortals dream,
Or how could thy notes flow in such a crystal stream?

We look before and after,
    And pine for what is not:
Our sincerest laughter
    With some pain is fraught;
Our sweetest songs are those that tell of saddest thought.

Yet if we could scorn
    Hate, and pride, and fear;
If we were things born
    Not to shed a tear,
I know not how thy joy we ever should come near.

Better than all measures
    Of delightful sound,
Better than all treasures
    That in books are found,
Thy skill to poet were, thou scorner of the ground!

Teach me half the gladness
    That thy brain must know,
Such harmonious madness
    From my lips would flow
The world should listen then—as I am listening now.
—1820

[1] *Hymeneal* Marital (Hymen is the Greek god of marriage).

Adonais

In this pastoral elegy for fellow poet John Keats, Shelley calls the young poet Adonais after Adonis, the beautiful youth of classical myth who was loved by Venus and killed by a wild boar. In some versions of the story Venus asks Persephone, Queen of the underworld, to allow Adonis to return above ground for four months of every year, while in others she transforms his blood into the bright red anemone, enabling him to live on in this ever-blooming flower.

Shelley had known Keats only casually, through their mutual acquaintance Leigh Hunt, the editor of the radical *Examiner*, but he admired his poetry and agreed with many of his political views. Hearing of Keats's serious illness in 1820, Shelley had invited Keats to spend the winter with him in Pisa. Keats did journey to Italy, but died in Rome in February of 1821, before he could reach Pisa.

The beast whom Shelley blames for Keats's death is the anonymous critic who ridiculed Keats's *Endymion* in *The Quarterly Review* (April 1818); Shelley thus gave force to a sentimental myth that Keats's illness and death were brought on by demoralizing reviews, both in *The Quarterly Review* and *Blackwood's Magazine*. For many years after his death, it was commonly maintained that, as Byron said, Keats was "snuffed out by an article." Until the late 1840s, Keats was better known by *Adonais* and the legend of his death than by his own poetry.

Adonais

An Elegy on the Death of John Keats

Αστήρ πρὶν μέν ἐλαμπες ενι Ϛῶοισιν εῶος.
Νυν δε θανῶν, λαμπεις ἕοπερος εν φθίμενοις.
PLATO[1]

I

I weep for Adonais—he is dead!
O, weep for Adonais! though our tears
Thaw not the frost which binds so dear a head!
And thou, sad Hour, selected from all years
To mourn our loss, rouse thy obscure compeers,
And teach them thine own sorrow, say: with me
Died Adonais; till the Future dares
Forget the Past, his fate and fame shall be
An echo and a light unto eternity!

2

Where wert thou mighty Mother, when he lay,
When thy Son lay, pierced by the shaft which flies
In darkness? Where was lorn° Urania[2] *forlorn*
When Adonais died? With veiled eyes,
'Mid listening Echoes, in her Paradise
She sate, while one, with soft enamoured breath,
Rekindled all the fading melodies,
With which, like flowers that mock the corse° *body*
beneath,
He had adorned and hid the coming bulk of death.

3

O, weep for Adonais—he is dead!
Wake, melancholy Mother, wake and weep!
Yet wherefore? Quench within their burning bed
Thy fiery tears, and let thy loud heart keep
Like his, a mute and uncomplaining sleep;
For he is gone, where all things wise and fair
Descend—oh, dream not that the amorous Deep° *abyss*
Will yet restore him to the vital air;
Death feeds on his mute voice, and laughs at our
despair.

4

Most musical of mourners, weep again!
Lament anew, Urania! He[3] died,
Who was the Sire of an immortal strain,
Blind, old, and lonely, when his country's pride,
The priest, the slave, and the liberticide,
Trampled and mocked with many a loathed rite
Of lust and blood; he went, unterrified,
Into the gulf of death; but his clear Sprite° *spirit*
Yet reigns o'er earth; the third among the sons of light.

5

Most musical of mourners, weep anew!
Not all to that bright station dared to climb;
And happier they their happiness who knew,
Whose tapers yet burn through that night of time
In which suns perished; others more sublime,
Struck by the envious wrath of man or God,
Have sunk, extinct in their refulgent° prime; *gleaming*
And some yet live, treading the thorny road,
Which leads, through toil and hate, to Fame's serene
abode.

6

But now, thy youngest, dearest one, has perished,
The nursling of thy widowhood, who grew,
Like a pale flower by some sad maiden cherished,
And fed with true love tears, instead of dew;
Most musical of mourners, weep anew!
Thy extreme hope, the loveliest and the last,
The bloom, whose petals nipt before they blew,° *bloomed*

---

[1] *Αστήρ ... PLATO* [Shelley's translation] Thou wert the morning star among the living, / Ere thy fair light had fled— / Now, having died, thou art as Hesperus, giving / New splendour to the dead. [Translation from the Greek of Plato's *Epigram on Aster*. The planet Venus appears in the sky as both the morning star, Phosphorus, and the evening star, Vesper.]

[2] *Urania* Muse who is invoked near the beginning of Milton's *Paradise Lost*. Urania is also an epithet for the goddess Venus, who loved Adonis.

[3] *He* Poet John Milton (1608–74), who served in Cromwell's Parliamentary government and, as a result, was imprisoned when the monarchy was restored, although he was released quickly. At the end of this stanza, Shelley places Milton in a triumvirate with the earlier epic poets Homer and Dante ("the third among the sons of light").

Died on the promise of the fruit, is waste;
The broken lily lies—the storm is overpast.

7

To that high Capital,[1] where kingly Death
Keeps his pale court in beauty and decay,
He came; and bought, with price of purest breath,
A grave among the eternal. Come away!
Haste, while the vault of blue Italian day
Is yet his fitting charnel°-roof! while still *mortuary*
He lies, as if in dewy sleep he lay;
Awake him not! surely he takes his fill
Of deep and liquid rest, forgetful of all ill.

8

He will awake no more, oh, never more!
Within the twilight chamber spreads apace,
The shadow of white Death, and at the door
Invisible Corruption waits to trace
His extreme way to her dim dwelling-place;
The eternal Hunger sits, but pity and awe
Soothe her pale rage, nor dares she to deface
So fair a prey, till darkness, and the law
Of mortal change, shall fill the grave which is her
maw.° *stomach*

9

O, weep for Adonais! The quick° Dreams, *living*
The passion-winged Ministers of thought,
Who were his flocks, whom near the living streams
Of his young spirit he fed, and whom he taught
The love which was its music, wander not—
Wander no more, from kindling brain to brain,
But droop there, whence they sprung; and mourn their
lot
Round the cold heart, where, after their sweet pain,
They ne'er will gather strength, or find a home again.

10

And one with trembling hands clasps his cold head,
And fans him with her moonlight wings, and cries,
"Our love, our hope, our sorrow, is not dead;
See, on the silken fringe of his faint eyes,
Like dew upon a sleeping flower, there lies
A tear some Dream has loosened from his brain."
Lost Angel of a ruined Paradise!
She knew not 'twas her own; as with no stain
She faded, like a cloud which had outwept its rain.

11

One from a lucid° urn of starry dew *resplendent*
Washed his light limbs as if embalming them;
Another clipt her profuse locks, and threw
The wreath upon him, like an anadem,° *garland*
Which frozen tears instead of pearls begem;
Another in her wilful grief would break
Her bow and winged reeds,° as if to stem *arrows*
A greater loss with one which was more weak;
And dull the barbed fire against his frozen cheek.

12

Another Splendour on his mouth alit,
That mouth, whence it was wont to draw the breath
Which gave it strength to pierce the guarded wit,
And pass into the panting heart beneath
With lightning and with music: the damp death
Quenched its caress upon his icy lips;
And, as a dying meteor stains a wreath
Of moonlight vapour, which the cold night clips,° *clasps*
It flushed through his pale limbs, and passed to its
eclipse.

13

And others came ... Desires and Adorations,
Winged Persuasions and veiled Destinies,
Splendours, and Glooms, and glimmering Incarnations
Of hopes and fears, and twilight Phantasies;
And Sorrow, with her family of Sighs,
And Pleasure, blind with tears, led by the gleam
Of her own dying smile instead of eyes,
Came in slow pomp—the moving pomp might seem
Like pageantry of mist on an autumnal stream.

[1] *high Capital* Rome, where Keats died.

14

All he had loved, and moulded into thought,
From shape, and hue, and odour, and sweet sound,
Lamented Adonais. Morning sought
Her eastern watchtower, and her hair unbound,
Wet with the tears which should adorn the ground,
Dimmed the aerial eyes that kindle day;
Afar the melancholy thunder moaned,
Pale Ocean in unquiet slumber lay,
And the wild winds flew round, sobbing in their dismay.

15

Lost Echo sits amid the voiceless mountains,
And feeds her grief with his remembered lay,° *song*
And will no more reply to winds or fountains,
Or amorous birds perched on the young green spray,
Or herdsman's horn, or bell° at closing day; *church-bell*
Since she can mimic not his lips, more dear
Than those for whose disdain she pined away
Into a shadow of all sounds[1]—a drear
Murmur, between their songs, is all the woodmen hear.

16

Grief made the young Spring wild, and she threw down
Her kindling buds, as if she Autumn were,
Or they dead leaves; since her delight is flown
For whom should she have waked the sullen year?
To Phoebus was not Hyacinth so dear[2]
Nor to himself Narcissus, as to both
Thou Adonais: wan they stand and sere° *withered*
Amid the drooping comrades of their youth,
With dew all turned to tears; odour, to sighing ruth.° *pity*

17

Thy spirit's sister, the lorn nightingale
Mourns not her mate with such melodious pain;
Not so the eagle, who like thee could scale
Heaven, and could nourish in the sun's domain
Her mighty youth with morning,[3] doth complain,
Soaring and screaming round her empty nest,
As Albion[4] wails for thee: the curse of Cain[5]
Light on his head who pierced thy innocent breast,
And scared the angel soul that was its earthly guest!

18

Ah woe is me! Winter is come and gone,
But grief returns with the revolving year;
The airs and streams renew their joyous tone;
The ants, the bees, the swallows reappear;
Fresh leaves and flowers deck the dead Seasons' bier;
The amorous birds now pair in every brake,° *thicket*
And build their mossy homes in field and brere;° *briar*
And the green lizard, and the golden snake,
Like unimprisoned flames, out of their trance awake.

19

Through wood and stream and field and hill and Ocean
A quickening life from the Earth's heart has burst
As it has ever done, with change and motion,
From the great morning of the world when first
God dawned on Chaos; in its steam immersed
The lamps of Heaven flash with a softer light;
All baser things pant with life's sacred thirst;
Diffuse themselves; and spend in love's delight,
The beauty and the joy of their renewed might.

20

The leprous corpse touched by this spirit tender
Exhales itself in flowers of gentle breath;

---

[1] *those for ... sounds* Narcissus, whom the nymph Echo loved. Echo had been robbed of her voice by the goddess Hera, and could only repeat what others said. After falling in love with Narcissus, who rejected her in favor of his own reflection, she pined away until only her echoing voice remained.

[2] *To Phoebus ... dear* Phoebus Apollo, god of poetry and the sun, loved the beautiful youth Hyacinthus. When Hyacinthus was accidentally slain by a discus the god had thrown, Apollo caused the hyacinth flower to spring up from his spilt blood. It was said that Zephyrus (the west wind), a rejected suitor of Hyacinthus, blew the discus off course so that it would strike the youth. "Zephyr" was also the pen name of the reviewer of *Endymion*.

[3] *nourish ... morning* According to legend, the eagle could renew her youth by flying toward the sun until its heat burnt off her old plumage and cleared the film from her eyes.

[4] *Albion* England.

[5] *curse of Cain* For murdering his brother Abel, Cain was forced to wander the earth as a vagabond, unable to farm because no land would yield crops for him. See Genesis 4.

Like incarnations of the stars, when splendour
Is changed to fragrance, they illumine death
And mock the merry worm that wakes beneath;
Nought we know, dies. Shall that alone which knows[1]
Be as a sword consumed before the sheath
By sightless[2] lightning?—th'intense atom glows
A moment, then is quenched in a most cold repose.

21

Alas! that all we loved of him should be,
But for our grief, as if it had not been,
And grief itself be mortal! Woe is me!
Whence are we, and why are we? of what scene
The actors or spectators? Great and mean
Meet massed in death, who lends what life must borrow.
As long as skies are blue, and fields are green,
Evening must usher night, night urge the morrow,
Month follow month with woe, and year wake year to
  sorrow.

22

He will awake no more, oh, never more!
"Wake thou," cried Misery, "childless Mother, rise
Out of thy sleep, and slake,° in thy heart's core, *ease*
A wound more fierce than his with tears and sighs."
And all the Dreams that watched Urania's eyes,
And all the Echoes whom their sister's song
Had held in holy silence, cried: "Arise!"
Swift as a Thought by the snake Memory stung,
From her ambrosial rest the fading Splendour[3] sprung.

23

She rose like an autumnal Night, that springs
Out of the East, and follows wild and drear
The golden Day, which, on eternal wings,
Even as a ghost abandoning a bier,
Had left the Earth a corpse. Sorrow and fear
So struck, so roused, so rapt Urania;
So saddened round her like an atmosphere
Of stormy mist; so swept her on her way
Even to the mournful place where Adonais lay.

24

Out of her secret Paradise she sped,
Through camps and cities rough with stone, and steel,
And human hearts, which to her aery tread
Yielding not, wounded the invisible
Palms of her tender feet where'er they fell:
And barbed tongues, and thoughts more sharp than they
Rent the soft Form they never could repel,
Whose sacred blood, like the young tears of May,
Paved with eternal flowers that undeserving way.

25

In the death chamber for a moment Death,
Shamed by the presence of that living Might,
Blushed to annihilation, and the breath
Revisited those lips, and life's pale light
Flashed through those limbs, so late her dear delight.
"Leave me not wild and drear and comfortless,
As silent lightning leaves the starless night!
Leave me not!" cried Urania: her distress
Roused Death: Death rose and smiled, and met her
  vain caress.

26

"Stay yet awhile! speak to me once again;
Kiss me, so long but as a kiss may live;
And in my heartless breast and burning brain
That word, that kiss shall all thoughts else survive,
With food of saddest memory kept alive,
Now thou art dead, as if it were a part
Of thee, my Adonais! I would give
All that I am to be as thou now art!
But I am chained to Time, and cannot thence depart!

27

"Oh gentle child, beautiful as thou wert,
Why didst thou leave the trodden paths of men
Too soon, and with weak hands though mighty heart
Dare° the unpastured dragon in his den? *challenge*
Defenceless as thou wert, oh where was then

[1] *that alone which knows* I.e., the mind.

[2] *sightless* Invisible; blind.

[3] *ambrosial* Divine (ambrosia is the food of the gods); *the fading Splendour* Urania.

Wisdom the mirrored shield,[1] or scorn the spear?
Or hadst thou waited the full cycle, when
Thy spirit should have filled its crescent sphere,
The monsters of life's waste had fled from thee like deer.

28

"The herded wolves, bold only to pursue;
The obscene ravens, clamorous o'er the dead;
The vultures to the conqueror's banner true
Who feed where Desolation first has fed,
And whose wings rain contagion—how they fled,
When like Apollo, from his golden bow,
The Pythian of the age[2] one arrow sped
And smiled! The spoilers tempt no second blow,
They fawn on the proud feet that spurn them as they
go.

29

"The sun comes forth, and many reptiles spawn;
He sets, and each ephemeral insect then
Is gathered into death without a dawn,
And the immortal stars awake again;
So is it in the world of living men:
A godlike mind soars forth, in its delight
Making earth bare and veiling heaven, and when
It sinks, the swarms that dimmed or shared its light
Leave to its kindred lamps the spirit's awful° *awe-inspiring*
night."

30

Thus ceased she: and the mountain shepherds came,
Their garlands sere, their magic mantles rent;
The Pilgrim of Eternity,[3] whose fame
Over his living head like Heaven is bent,
An early but enduring monument,
Came, veiling all the lightnings of his song
In sorrow; from her wilds Ierne° sent *Ireland*
The sweetest lyrist of her saddest wrong,
And love taught grief to fall like music from his
tongue.[4]

31

Midst others of less note, came one frail Form,[5]
A phantom among men; companionless
As the last cloud of an expiring storm
Whose thunder is its knell;° he, as I guess, *funeral-bell*
Had gazed on Nature's naked loveliness,
Actæon-like,[6] and now he fled astray
With feeble steps o'er the world's wilderness,
And his own thoughts, along that rugged way,
Pursued, like raging hounds, their father and their prey.

32

A pardlike° Spirit beautiful and swift— *leopard-like*
A Love in desolation masked—a Power
Girt round with weakness; it can scarce uplift
The weight of the superincumbent hour;
It is a dying lamp, a falling shower,
A breaking billow—even whilst we speak
Is it not broken? On the withering flower
The killing sun smiles brightly: on a cheek
The life can burn in blood, even while the heart may
break.

33

His head was bound with pansies overblown,
And faded violets, white, and pied, and blue;
And a light spear topped with a cypress cone,
Round whose rude shaft dark ivy tresses grew[7]

---

[1] *mirrored shield* Because the stare of the Gorgon Medusa would turn men into stone, Perseus fought and defeated her by viewing her reflection in his shield.

[2] *Pythian of the age* Byron, who attacked the unfavorable reviewers of his *Hours of Idleness* in his satire *English Bards and Scotch Reviewers* (1809). The epithet "Pythian" was given to the god Apollo when he slew the dragon Python.

[3] *Pilgrim of Eternity* Byron.

[4] *The sweetest … tongue* Poet Thomas Moore (1779–1852), whose *Irish Melodies* deals with the oppression of his native Ireland by England.

[5] *one frail Form* Shelley.

[6] *Actæon-like* Actaeon was a hunter who accidentally came upon Diana, goddess of chastity, bathing naked. Angered, she turned him into a stag, and his own hounds chased him down and tore him apart.

[7] *pansies overblown* Pansies (a symbol of sorrow) past their bloom; *violets* Representing death; *light spear … tresses grew* Thyrsus, staff borne by Dionysus, the god of fertility, and his followers.

Yet dripping with the forest's noonday dew,
Vibrated, as the ever-beating heart
Shook the weak hand that grasped it; of that crew
He came the last, neglected and apart;
A herd-abandoned deer struck by the hunter's dart.

34

All stood aloof, and at his partial° moan *sympathetic*
Smiled through their tears; well knew that gentle band
Who in another's fate now wept his own;
As in the accents of an unknown land,
He sung new sorrow; sad Urania scanned
The Stranger's mien, and murmured: "who art thou?"
He answered not, but with a sudden hand
Made bare his branded and ensanguined° brow, *bloody*
Which was like Cain's or Christ's—Oh! that it should be so!

35

What softer voice is hushed over the dead?
Athwart what brow is that dark mantle thrown?
What form leans sadly o'er the white death-bed,
In mockery of monumental stone,
The heavy heart heaving without a moan?
If it be He, who, gentlest of the wise,
Taught, soothed, loved, honoured the departed one;[1]
Let me not vex, with inharmonious sighs
The silence of that heart's accepted sacrifice.

36

Our Adonais has drunk poison—oh!
What deaf and viperous murderer could crown
Life's early cup with such a draught of woe?
The nameless worm would now itself disown:
It felt, yet could escape the magic tone
Whose prelude held all envy, hate, and wrong,
But what was howling in one breast alone,
Silent with expectation of the song,
Whose master's hand is cold, whose silver lyre unstrung.[2]

37

Live thou, whose infamy is not thy fame!
Live! fear no heavier chastisement from me,
Thou noteless blot on a remembered name!
But be thyself, and know thyself to be!
And ever at thy season be thou free
To spill the venom when thy fangs o'er flow:
Remorse and Self-contempt shall cling to thee;
Hot Shame shall burn upon thy secret brow,
And like a beaten hound tremble thou shalt—as now.

38

Nor let us weep that our delight is fled
Far from these carrion kites[3] that scream below;
He wakes or sleeps with the enduring dead;
Thou canst not soar where he is sitting now.
Dust to the dust! but the pure spirit shall flow
Back to the burning fountain whence it came,
A portion of the Eternal, which must glow
Through time and change, unquenchably the same,
Whilst thy cold embers choke the sordid hearth of shame.

39

Peace, peace! he is not dead, he doth not sleep—
He hath awakened from the dream of life—
'Tis we who lost in stormy visions keep
With phantoms an unprofitable strife,
And in mad trance, strike with our spirit's knife
Invulnerable nothings. *We* decay
Like corpses in a charnel; fear and grief
Convulse us and consume us day by day,
And cold hopes swarm like worms within our living clay.

---

[1] *He, who … one* Radical journalist Leigh Hunt, to whom Keats dedicated his first volume.

[2] *silver lyre unstrung* On Keats's tomb is engraved the image of a Greek lyre with half its strings broken. According to his friend Joseph Severn, this symbolizes "his classical genius cut off by death before its maturity."

[3] *kites* Falcon-like birds of prey.

40

He has outsoared the shadow of our night;
Envy and calumny° and hate and pain, *slander*
And that unrest which men miscall delight,
Can touch him not and torture not again;
From the contagion of the world's slow stain
He is secure, and now can never mourn
A heart grown cold, a head grown grey in vain;
Nor, when the spirit's self has ceased to burn,
With sparkless ashes load an unlamented urn.

41

He lives, he wakes—'tis Death is dead, not he;
Mourn not for Adonais. Thou young Dawn
Turn all thy dew to splendour, for from thee
The spirit thou lamentest is not gone;
Ye caverns and ye forests, cease to moan!
Cease ye faint flowers and fountains, and thou Air
Which like a mourning veil thy scarf hadst thrown
O'er the abandoned Earth, now leave it bare
Even to the joyous stars which smile on its despair!

42

He is made one with Nature: there is heard
His voice in all her music, from the moan
Of thunder, to the song of night's sweet bird;[1]
He is a presence to be felt and known
In darkness and in light, from herb and stone,
Spreading itself where'er that Power may move
Which has withdrawn his being to its own;
Which wields the world with never wearied love,
Sustains it from beneath, and kindles it above.

43

He is a portion of the loveliness
Which once he made more lovely: he doth bear
His part, while the one Spirit's plastic° stress *formative*
Sweeps through the dull dense world, compelling there,
All new successions to the forms they wear;
Torturing th'unwilling dross° that checks *impure matter*
its flight
To its own likeness, as each mass may bear;
And bursting in its beauty and its might
From trees and beasts and men into the Heaven's light.

44

The splendours of the firmament of time
May be eclipsed, but are extinguished not;
Like stars to their appointed height they climb
And death is a low mist which cannot blot
The brightness it may veil. When lofty thought
Lifts a young heart above its mortal lair,
And love and life contend in it, for what
Shall be its earthly doom,° the dead live there *fate*
And move like winds of light on dark and stormy air.

45

The inheritors of unfulfilled renown
Rose from their thrones, built beyond mortal thought,
Far in the Unapparent. Chatterton[2]
Rose pale, his solemn agony had not
Yet faded from him; Sidney,[3] as he fought
And as he fell and as he lived and loved
Sublimely mild, a Spirit without spot,
Arose; and Lucan,[4] by his death approved:
Oblivion as they rose shrank like a thing reproved.

46

And many more, whose names on Earth are dark
But whose transmitted effluence cannot die
So long as fire outlives the parent spark,
Rose, robed in dazzling immortality.
"Thou art become as one of us," they cry,
"It was for thee yon kingless sphere has long
Swung blind in unascended majesty,
Silent alone amid an Heaven of song.

---

1 *night's sweet bird* I.e., the nightingale, in reference to Keats's "Ode to a Nightingale."

2 *Chatterton* Poet Thomas Chatterton, who committed suicide in 1770 at the age of 17.

3 *Sidney* Sir Philip Sidney (1554–86), who was killed in battle when he was 32.

4 *Lucan* First-century CE Roman poet Marcus Annaeus Lucan, who at the age of twenty-six killed himself to avoid being executed for conspiring against the tyrannical emperor Nero.

Assume thy winged throne, thou Vesper[1] of our
throng!"

47

Who mourns for Adonais? Oh come forth
Fond° wretch! and know thyself and him aright. *foolish*
Clasp with thy panting soul the pendulous Earth;
As from a centre, dart thy spirit's light
Beyond all worlds, until its spacious might
Satiate the void circumference: then shrink
Even to a point within our day and night;
And keep thy heart light lest it make thee sink
When hope has kindled hope, and lured thee to the
brink.

48

Or go to Rome, which is the sepulchre
O, not of him, but of our joy: 'tis nought
That ages, empires, and religions there
Lie buried in the ravage they have wrought;
For such as he can lend°—they borrow not *bestow*
Glory from those who made the world their prey;
And he is gathered to the kings of thought
Who waged contention with their time's decay,
And of the past are all that cannot pass away.

49

Go thou to Rome—at once the Paradise,
The grave, the city, and the wilderness;
And where its wrecks like shattered mountains rise,
And flowering weeds, and fragrant copses° dress *thickets*
The bones of Desolation's nakedness
Pass, till the Spirit of the spot shall lead
Thy footsteps to a slope of green access[2]
Where, like an infant's smile, over the dead,
A light of laughing flowers along the grass is spread.

50

And gray walls moulder round,[3] on which dull Time
Feeds, like slow fire upon a hoary° brand;[4] *white*
And one keen pyramid with wedge sublime,
Pavilioning the dust of him who planned
This refuge for his memory, doth stand
Like flame transformed to marble; and beneath,
A field is spread, on which a newer band
Have pitched in Heaven's smile their camp of death
Welcoming him we lose with scarce extinguished
breath.

51

Here pause: these graves are all too young as yet
To have outgrown the sorrow which consigned
Its charge to each; and if the seal is set,
Here, on one fountain of a mourning mind,
Break it not thou! too surely shalt thou find
Thine own well full, if thou returnest home,
Of tears and gall. From the world's bitter wind
Seek shelter in the shadow of the tomb.
What Adonais is, why fear we to become?

52

The One remains, the many change and pass;
Heaven's light forever shines, Earth's shadows fly;
Life, like a dome of many-coloured glass,
Stains the white radiance of Eternity,
Until Death tramples it to fragments. Die,
If thou wouldst be with that which thou dost seek!
Follow where all is fled! Rome's azure sky,
Flowers, ruins, statues, music, words, are weak
The glory they transfuse with fitting truth to speak.

53

Why linger, why turn back, why shrink, my Heart?
Thy hopes are gone before: from all things here
They have departed; thou shouldst now depart!
A light is past from the revolving year,
And man, and woman; and what still is dear

[1] *Vesper* The evening star.

[2] *slope of green access* The Protestant Cemetery in Rome, where Keats is buried. Shelley's son William, who died at age three, is also buried there.

[3] *gray ... round* One of the boundaries of the cemetery incorporates the wall of ancient Rome, while another is formed by the pyramid-tomb of Roman tribune Caius Cestius.

[4] *brand* Burning log.

Attracts to crush, repels to make thee wither.
The soft sky smiles—the low wind whispers near:
'Tis Adonais calls! Oh, hasten thither,
No more let Life divide what Death can join together.

54

That Light whose smile kindles the Universe,
That Beauty in which all things work and move,
That Benediction which the eclipsing Curse
Of birth can quench not, that sustaining Love
Which through the web of being blindly wove
By man and beast and earth and air and sea,
Burns bright or dim, as[1] each are mirrors of
The fire for which all thirst; now beams on me,
Consuming the last clouds of cold mortality.

55

The breath whose might I have invoked in song
Descends on me; my spirit's bark is driven,
Far from the shore, far from the trembling throng
Whose sails were never to the tempest given;
The massy earth and sphered skies are riven!
I am borne darkly, fearfully, afar;
Whilst burning through the inmost veil of Heaven,
The soul of Adonais, like a star,
Beacons from the abode where the Eternal are.
—1821

Mutability

1

The flower that smiles to-day
To-morrow dies;
All that we wish to stay
Tempts and then flies.
What is this world's delight?
Lightning that mocks the night,
Brief even as bright.

2

Virtue, how frail it is!
Friendship how rare!
Love, how it sells poor bliss
For proud despair!
But we, though soon they fall,
Survive their joy, and all
Which ours we call.

3

Whilst skies are blue and bright,
Whilst flowers are gay,
Whilst eyes that change ere night
Make glad the day;
Whilst yet the calm hours creep,
Dream thou—and from thy sleep
Then wake to weep.
—1824

Stanzas

Written in Dejection—December 1818, near Naples

1

The sun is warm, the sky is clear,
The waves are dancing fast and bright,
Blue isles and snowy mountains wear
The purple noon's transparent might,
The breath of the moist earth is light,
Around its unexpanded buds;
Like many a voice of one delight,
The winds, the birds, the ocean floods,
The City's voice itself, is soft like Solitude's.

2

I see the Deep's untrampled floor
With green and purple seaweeds strown;
I see the waves upon the shore,
Like light dissolved in star-showers,[2] thrown:

[1] *as* I.e., to the extent that.

[2] *star-showers* Meteor showers.

I sit upon the sands alone—
The lightning of the noontide ocean
Is flashing round me, and a tone
Arises from its measured motion,
How sweet! did any heart now share in my emotion.

3

Alas! I have nor hope nor health,
Nor peace within nor calm around,
Nor that content surpassing wealth
The sage in meditation found,
And walked with inward glory crowned—
Nor fame, nor power, nor love, nor leisure.
Others I see whom these surround—
Smiling they live, and call life pleasure;—
To me that cup has been dealt in another measure.

4

Yet now despair itself is mild,
Even as the winds and waters are;
I could lie down like a tired child,
And weep away the life of care
Which I have borne and yet must bear,
Till death like sleep might steal on me,
And I might feel in the warm air
My cheek grow cold, and hear the sea
Breathe o'er my dying brain its last monotony.

5

Some might lament that I were cold.
As I, when this sweet day is gone,
Which my lost heart, too soon grown old,
Insults with this untimely moan;
They might lament—for I am one
Whom men love not—and yet regret,
Unlike this day, which, when the sun
Shall on its stainless glory set,
Will linger, though enjoyed, like joy in memory yet.
—1824

Song to the Men of England[1]

1

Men of England, wherefore plough
For the lords who lay ye low?
Wherefore weave with toil and care
The rich robes your tyrants wear?

2

Wherefore feed, and clothe, and save,
From the cradle to the grave,
Those ungrateful drones who would
Drain your sweat—nay, drink your blood?

3

Wherefore, Bees of England, forge
Many a weapon, chain, and scourge,
That these stingless drones may spoil
The forced produce of your toil?

4

Have ye leisure, comfort, calm,
Shelter, food, love's gentle balm?
Or what is it ye buy so dear
With your pain and with your fear?

5

The seed ye sow, another reaps;
The wealth ye find, another keeps;
The robes ye weave, another wears;
The arms ye forge, another bears.

6

Sow seed—but let no tyrant reap;
Find wealth—let no impostor heap;
Weave robes—let not the idle wear;
Forge arms—in your defence to bear.

[1] *Song ... England* Composed in 1819, during a time of economic depression and social turmoil following the end of the Napoleonic Wars. In this song, which became a hymn for the British labor movement, Shelley urges the proletariat to force change in the social and economic order.

7

Shrink to your cellars, holes, and cells;
In halls ye deck another dwells.
Why shake the chains ye wrought? Ye see
The steel ye tempered glance on[1] ye.

8

With plough and spade, and hoe and loom,
Trace your grave, and build your tomb,
And weave your winding-sheet, till fair
England be your sepulchre.
—1839 (WRITTEN 1819)

England in 1819

An old, mad, blind, despised, and dying king,[2]
Princes, the dregs of their dull race, who flow
Through public scorn—mud from a muddy spring—
Rulers who neither see, nor feel, nor know,
But leech-like to their fainting country cling,
Till they drop, blind in blood, without a blow—
A people starved and stabbed in the untilled field[3]—
An army, which liberticide and prey
Makes as a two-edged sword to all who wield—
Golden and sanguine laws[4] which tempt and slay;
Religion Christless, Godless—a book sealed;
A Senate, Time's worst statute, unrepealed,[5]
Are graves, from which a glorious Phantom[6] may
Burst, to illumine our tempestuous day.
—1839 (WRITTEN 1819)

[1] *glance on* Strike obliquely.

[2] *old, mad ... king* George III, who was declared insane in 1811. His sons were known for their corruption and their licentious behavior.

[3] *A people ... field* Reference to the massacre at St. Peter's Field on 16 August 1819 (the Peterloo Massacre), when the militia attacked a crowd of people who were peacefully demonstrating for political reform. Eleven people were killed and hundreds more injured.

[4] *Golden ... laws* I.e., laws, bought with gold, that lead to bloodshed.

[5] *Time's ... unrepealed* Laws against Catholics and Dissenters.

[6] *a glorious Phantom* I.e., revolution.

A Defence of Poetry

This essay, begun in 1822 and never completed, was written in response to an 1820 essay by Shelley's friend Thomas Love Peacock called "The Four Ages of Poetry." In this partially ironic essay, Peacock describes four cycles through which poetry passes: the first is an iron age of crude folk ballads, medieval romances, etc.; the second, the gold age, contains the great epics of Homer, Dante, and Milton; the silver age contains the "derivative" poetry of the Augustan poets (who included John Dryden and Alexander Pope); and the fourth stage, the age of brass, is that of Peacock's contemporaries, whom he claimed were markedly inferior. Criticizing Romantic poets such as Byron, Coleridge, and Wordsworth, Peacock urged the men of his generation to apply themselves to new sciences, such as astronomy, economics, politics, mathematics, or chemistry, instead of poetry. Though Shelley recognized Peacock's satirical humor, he also acknowledged that Peacock had put his finger on a common bias of the time—both in the theories of utilitarian philosophers and in general public opinion—in favor of economic growth and scientific progress over creativity and humanitarian concerns. It was this bias that he attempted to correct in his *Defence*.

from *A Defence of Poetry*, *or Remarks Suggested by an Essay Entitled "The Four Ages of Poetry"*

According to one mode of regarding those two classes of mental action which are called reason and imagination, the former may be considered as mind contemplating the relations borne by one thought to another, however produced; and the latter, as mind acting upon those thoughts so as to colour them with its own light, and composing from them, as from elements, other thoughts, each containing within itself the principle of its own integrity. The one is the τὸ ποιειν,[7] or

[7] *τὸ ποιειν* Greek: making.

the principle of synthesis, and has for its objects those forms which are common to universal nature and existence itself; the other is the τὸ λογιζειν[1] or principle of analysis, and its action regards the relations of things, simply as relations; considering thoughts, not in their integral unity, but as the algebraical representations which conduct to certain general results. Reason is the enumeration of quantities already known; imagination is the perception of the value of those quantities, both separately and as a whole. Reason respects the differences, and imagination the similitudes of things. Reason is to Imagination as the instrument to the agent, as the body to the spirit, as the shadow to the substance.

Poetry, in a general sense, may be defined to be "the expression of the Imagination": and poetry is connate with the origin of man. Man is an instrument over which a series of external and internal impressions are driven, like the alternations of an ever-changing wind over an Æolian lyre,[2] which move it by their motion to ever-changing melody. But there is a principle within the human being, and perhaps within all sentient beings, which acts otherwise than in the lyre, and produces not melody alone, but harmony, by an internal adjustment of the sounds or motions thus excited to the impressions which excite them. It is as if the lyre could accommodate its chords to the motions of that which strikes them, in a determined proportion of sound; even as the musician can accommodate his voice to the sound of the lyre. A child at play by itself will express its delight by its voice and motions; and every inflexion of tone and every gesture will bear exact relation to a corresponding antitype in the pleasurable impressions which awakened it; it will be the reflected image of that impression; and as the lyre trembles and sounds after the wind has died away, so the child seeks, by prolonging in its voice and motions the duration of the effect, to prolong also a consciousness of the cause. In relation to the objects which delight a child, these expressions are what poetry is to higher objects. The savage (for the savage is to ages what the child is to years) expresses the emotions produced in him by surrounding objects in a similar manner; and language and gesture, together with plastic[3] or pictorial imitation, become the image of the combined effect of those objects, and of his apprehension of them. Man in society, with all his passions and his pleasures, next becomes the object of the passions and pleasures of man; an additional class of emotions produces an augmented treasure of expressions; and language, gesture, and the imitative arts become at once the representation and the medium, the pencil and the picture, the chisel and the statue, the chord and the harmony. The social sympathies, or those laws from which as from its elements society results, begin to develop themselves from the moment that two human beings coexist; the future is contained within the present as the plant within the seed; and equality, diversity, unity, contrast, mutual dependence, become the principles alone capable of affording the motives according to which the will of a social being is determined to action, inasmuch as he is social; and constitute pleasure in sensation, virtue in sentiment, beauty in art, truth in reasoning, and love in the intercourse of kind. Hence men, even in the infancy of society, observe a certain order in their words and actions, distinct from that of the objects and the impressions represented by them, all expression being subject to the laws of that from which it proceeds. But let us dismiss those more general considerations which might involve an enquiry into the principles of society itself, and restrict our view to the manner in which the imagination is expressed upon its forms.

In the youth of the world, men dance and sing and imitate natural objects, observing[4] in these actions, as in all others, a certain rhythm or order. And, although all men observe a similar, they observe not the same order, in the motions of the dance, in the melody of the song, in the combinations of language, in the series of their imitations of natural objects. For there is a certain order or rhythm belonging to each of these classes of mimetic representation, from which the hearer and the spectator

[1] *τὸ λογιζειν* Greek: reasoning.

[2] *Æolian lyre* Stringed instrument that produces music when exposed to wind.

[3] *plastic* Formative.

[4] *observing* Following.

receive an intenser and purer pleasure than from any other: the sense of an approximation to this order has been called taste, by modern writers. Every man in the infancy of art observes an order which approximates more or less closely to that from which this highest delight results: but the diversity is not sufficiently marked, as that its gradations should be sensible, except in those instances where the predominance of this faculty of approximation to the beautiful (for so we may be permitted to name the relation between this highest pleasure and its cause) is very great. Those in whom it exists in excess are poets, in the most universal sense of the word; and the pleasure resulting from the manner in which they express the influence of society or nature upon their own minds, communicates itself to others, and gathers a sort of reduplication from that community. Their language is vitally metaphorical; that is, it marks the before unapprehended relations of things, and perpetuates their apprehension, until the words which represent them, become through time signs for portions or classes of thoughts instead of pictures of integral thoughts; and then if no new poets should arise to create afresh the associations which have been thus disorganized, language will be dead to all the nobler purposes of human intercourse. These similitudes or relations are finely said by Lord Bacon to be "the same footsteps of nature impressed upon the various subjects of the world"[1]—and he considers the faculty which perceives them as the storehouse of axioms common to all knowledge. In the infancy of society every author is necessarily a poet, because language itself is poetry; and to be a poet is to apprehend the true and the beautiful, in a word the good which exists in the relation, subsisting, first between existence and perception, and secondly between perception and expression. Every original language near to its source is in itself the chaos of a cyclic poem:[2] the copiousness of lexicography and the distinctions of grammar are the works of a later age, and are merely the catalogue and the form of the creations of Poetry.

But Poets, or those who imagine and express this indestructible order, are not only the authors of language and of music, of the dance and architecture and statuary and painting: they are the institutors of laws, and the founders of civil society and the inventors of the arts of life and the teachers, who draw into a certain propinquity with the beautiful and the true that partial apprehension of the agencies of the invisible world which is called religion. Hence all original religions are allegorical, or susceptible of allegory, and like Janus have a double face of false and true.[3] Poets, according to the circumstances of the age and nation in which they appeared, were called in the earlier epochs of the world legislators or prophets:[4] a poet essentially comprises and unites both these characters. For he not only beholds intensely the present as it is, and discovers those laws according to which present things ought to be ordered, but he beholds the future in the present, and his thoughts are the germs of the flower and the fruit of latest time. Not that I assert poets to be prophets in the gross sense of the word, or that they can foretell the form as surely as they foreknow the spirit of events: such is the pretence of superstition which would make poetry an attribute of prophecy, rather than prophecy an attribute of poetry. A Poet participates in the eternal, the infinite, and the one; as far as relates to his conceptions, time and place and number are not. The grammatical forms which express the moods of time, and the difference of persons and the distinction of place, are convertible with respect to the highest poetry without injuring it as poetry, and the choruses of Æschylus, and the book of Job, and Dante's Paradise[5] would afford, more than

[1] *the same … world* From Francis Bacon's *Of the Advancement of Learning* (1605) 3.1.

[2] *cyclic poem* Set of poems dealing with the same subject (though not always by the same author). The "Arthurian Cycle," a series of poems about the court of King Arthur, is one example of the genre.

[3] *like Janus … true* Janus, the Roman god of war, of doorways, and of beginnings and endings (after whom the month of January is named) is generally depicted with two faces, one looking forward and one back.

[4] *were called … prophets* Cf. Sir Philip Sidney's *Defence of Poesy* (1595), in which he points out that *vates*, the Latin word for poet, also means diviner or prophet.

[5] *Æschylus* Greek tragic dramatist (c. 525–456 BCE); *Dante's Paradise* Reference to Italian poet Dante Alighieri's fourteenth-century work, *The Divine Comedy*, which describes a journey from Hell, through Purgatory, to Paradise.

any other writings, examples of this fact, if the limits of this essay did not forbid citation. The creations of sculpture, painting, and music are illustrations still more decisive.

Language, colour, form, and religious and civil habits of action are all the instruments and materials of poetry; they may be called poetry by that figure of speech which considers the effect as a synonym of the cause. But poetry in a more restricted sense expresses those arrangements of language, and especially metrical language, which are created by that imperial faculty whose throne is curtained within the invisible nature of man. And this springs from the nature itself of language, which is a more direct representation of the actions and passions of our internal being, and is susceptible of more various and delicate combinations, than colour, form, or motion, and is more plastic and obedient to the control of that faculty of which it is the creation. For language is arbitrarily produced by the Imagination and has relation to thoughts alone; but all other materials, instruments and conditions of art, have relations among each other, which limit and interpose between conception and expression. The former is as a mirror which reflects, the latter as a cloud which enfeebles, the light of which both are mediums of communication. Hence the fame of sculptors, painters and musicians, although the intrinsic powers of the great masters of these arts, may yield in no degree to that of those who have employed language as the hieroglyphic of their thoughts, has never equalled that of poets in the restricted sense of the term; as two performers of equal skill will produce unequal effects from a guitar and a harp. The fame of legislators and founders of religions, so long as their institutions last, alone seems to exceed that of poets in the restricted sense; but it can scarcely be a question whether, if we deduct the celebrity which their flattery of the gross opinions of the vulgar usually conciliates, together with that which belonged to them in their higher character of poets, any excess will remain.

We have thus circumscribed the meaning of the word Poetry within the limits of that art which is the most familiar and the most perfect expression of the faculty itself. It is necessary however to make the circle still narrower, and to determine the distinction between measured and unmeasured language; for the popular division into prose and verse is inadmissible in accurate philosophy. Sounds as well as thoughts have relation both between each other and towards that which they represent, and a perception of the order of those relations has always been found connected with a perception of the order of the relations of thoughts. Hence the language of poets has ever affected a certain uniform and harmonious recurrence of sound, without which it were not poetry, and which is scarcely less indispensable to the communication of its influence, than the words themselves, without reference to that peculiar order. …

A poem is the very image of life expressed in its eternal truth. There is this difference between a story and a poem, that a story is a catalogue of detached facts, which have no other bond of connection than time, place, circumstance, cause and effect; the other is the creation of actions according to the unchangeable forms of human nature, as existing in the mind of the creator, which is itself the image of all other minds. The one is partial, and applies only to a definite period of time, and a certain combination of events which can never again recur; the other is universal, and contains within itself the germ of a relation to whatever motives or actions have place in the possible varieties of human nature. …

Poetry is ever accompanied with pleasure: all spirits on which it falls open themselves to receive the wisdom which is mingled with its delight. In the infancy of the world, neither poets themselves nor their auditors are fully aware of the excellence of poetry: for it acts in a divine and unapprehended manner, beyond and above consciousness; and it is reserved for future generations to contemplate and measure the mighty cause and effect in all the strength and splendour of their union. Even in modern times, no living poet ever arrived at the fulness of his fame; the jury which sits in judgement upon a poet, belonging as he does to all time, must be composed of his peers: it must be impanelled by Time from the selectest of the wise of many generations. A Poet is a nightingale, who sits in darkness and sings to cheer its own solitude with sweet sounds; his auditors are as men entranced by the melody of an unseen musician, who feel that they are moved and softened, yet know not whence or why. The poems of Homer and his contemporaries were the delight of infant Greece; they were the elements of that social system which is the column upon which all succeeding civilization has reposed. Homer embodied the ideal perfection of his age in human character; nor can we doubt that those who read his verses were awakened to an ambition of becoming like to Achilles, Hector and Ulysses:[1] the truth and beauty of friendship, patriotism, and persevering devotion to an object were unveiled to the depths in these immortal creations: the sentiments of the auditors must have been refined and enlarged by a sympathy with such great and lovely impersonations, until from admiring they imitated, and from imitation they identified themselves with the objects of their admiration. …

The whole objection, however, of the immorality of poetry[2] rests upon a misconception of the manner in which poetry acts to produce the moral improvement of man. Ethical science[3] arranges the elements which poetry has created, and propounds schemes and proposes examples of civil and domestic life: nor is it for want of admirable doctrines that men hate, and despise, and censure, and deceive, and subjugate one another. But Poetry acts in another and diviner manner. It awakens and enlarges the mind itself by rendering it the receptacle of a thousand unapprehended combinations of thought. Poetry lifts the veil from the hidden beauty of the world, and makes familiar objects be as if they were not familiar; it reproduces[4] all that it represents, and the impersonations clothed in its Elysian[5] light stand thenceforward in the minds of those who have once contemplated them, as memorials of that gentle and exalted content which extends itself over all thoughts and actions with which it coexists. The great secret of morals is Love; or a going out of our own nature, and an identification of ourselves with the beautiful which exists in thought, action, or person not our own. A man, to be greatly good, must imagine intensely and comprehensively; he must put himself in the place of another and of many others; the pains and pleasures of his species must become his own. The great instrument of moral good is the imagination; and poetry administers to the effect by acting upon the cause. Poetry enlarges the circumference of the imagination by replenishing it with thoughts of ever new delight, which have the power of attracting and assimilating to their own nature all other thoughts, and which form new intervals and interstices whose void for ever craves fresh food. Poetry strengthens that faculty which is the organ of the moral nature of man, in the same manner as exercise strengthens a limb. A Poet therefore would do ill to embody his own conceptions of right and wrong, which are usually those of his place and time, in his poetical creations, which participate in neither. By this assumption of the inferior office of interpreting the effect, in which perhaps after all he might acquit himself but imperfectly, he would resign the glory in a participation in the cause. There was little danger that Homer, or any of the eternal poets, should have so far misunderstood themselves as to have abdicated this throne of their widest dominion. Those in whom the poetical faculty, though great, is less intense, as Euripides, Lucan, Tasso, Spenser,[6] have frequently affected a moral aim, and the effect of their poetry is diminished in exact proportion to the degree in which they compel us to advert to this purpose. …

The drama at Athens, or wheresoever else it may have approached to its perfection, coexisted with the moral and intellectual greatness of the age. The tragedies of the Athenian poets are as mirrors in which the spectator beholds himself, under a thin disguise of

[1] *Achilles, Hector and Ulysses* Trojan and Greek heroes in Homer's *Iliad* and *Odyssey*.

[2] *immorality of poetry* An objection voiced by Plato in his *Republic*, in which he says that poetry often depicts characters who are morally imperfect and whose actions do not provide suitable examples for readers.

[3] *Ethical science* Moral philosophy.

[4] *reproduces* I.e., produces or creates anew.

[5] *Elysian* I.e., paradisical. From Elysium, the paradise where the blessed reside after death, according to Greek myth.

[6] *Euripides* Greek tragedian of the fifth century BCE; *Lucan* Roman poet of the first century CE; *Tasso* Torquato Tasso, Italian epic poet of the sixteenth century; *Spenser* Edmund Spenser, sixteenth-century epic poet, author of *The Faerie Queene*.

circumstance, stript of all but that ideal perfection and energy which every one feels to be the internal type of all that he loves, admires, and would become. The imagination is enlarged by a sympathy with pains and passions so mighty that they distend in their conception the capacity of that by which they are conceived; the good affections are strengthened by pity, indignation, terror and sorrow; and an exalted calm is prolonged from the satiety of this high exercise of them into the tumult of familiar life; even crime is disarmed of half its horror and all its contagion by being represented as the fatal consequence of the unfathomable agencies of nature; error is thus divested of its wilfulness; men can no longer cherish it as the creation of their choice. In a drama of the highest order there is little food for censure or hatred; it teaches rather self-knowledge and self-respect. Neither the eye nor the mind can see itself, unless reflected upon that which it resembles. The drama, so long as it continues to express poetry, is as a prismatic and many-sided mirror, which collects the brightest rays of human nature and divides and reproduces them from the simplicity of these elementary forms, and touches them with majesty and beauty, and multiplies all that it reflects, and endows it with the power of propagating its like wherever it may fall.

But in periods of the decay of social life, the drama sympathizes with that decay. Tragedy becomes a cold imitation of the form of the great masterpieces of antiquity, divested of all harmonious accompaniment of the kindred arts; and often the very form misunderstood: or a weak attempt to teach certain doctrines, which the writer considers as moral truths; and which are usually no more than specious flatteries of some gross vice or weakness with which the author in common with his auditors are infected. …

The drama being that form under which a greater number of modes of expression of poetry are susceptible of being combined than any other, the connection of poetry and social good is more observable in the drama than in whatever other form: and it is indisputable that the highest perfection of human society has ever corresponded with the highest dramatic excellence; and that the corruption or the extinction of the drama in a nation where it has once flourished, is a mark of a corruption of manners, and an extinction of the energies which sustain the soul of social life. But, as Machiavelli[1] says of political institutions, that life may be preserved and renewed, if men should arise capable of bringing back the drama to its principles. And this is true with respect to poetry in its most extended sense: all language, institution and form, require not only to be produced but to be sustained: the office and character of a poet participates in the divine nature as regards providence, no less than as regards creation.

… It is admitted that the exercise of the imagination is most delightful, but it is alleged that that of reason is more useful. Let us examine as the grounds of this distinction, what is here meant by Utility. Pleasure or good, in a general sense, is that which the consciousness of a sensitive and intelligent being seeks, and in which when found it acquiesces. There are two kinds of pleasure, one durable, universal, and permanent; the other transitory and particular. Utility may either express the means of producing the former or the latter. In the former sense, whatever strengthens and purifies the affections, enlarges the imagination, and adds spirit to sense, is useful. But the meaning in which the Author of the Four Ages of Poetry seems to have employed the word utility is the narrower one of banishing the importunity of the wants of our animal nature, the surrounding men with security of life, the dispersing the grosser delusions of superstition, and the conciliating such a degree of mutual forbearance among men as may consist with the motives of personal advantage.

Undoubtedly the promoters of utility in this limited sense have their appointed office in society. They follow the footsteps of poets, and copy the sketches of their creations into the book of common life. They make space, and give time. Their exertions are of the highest value so long as they confine their administration of the concerns of the inferior powers of our nature within the limits due to the superior ones. But whilst the sceptic

[1] *Machiavelli* Niccolò Machiavelli (1469–1527), author of the political treatise *The Prince*.

destroys gross superstitions, let him spare to deface, as some of the French writers have defaced, the eternal truths charactered upon the imaginations of men. Whilst the mechanist abridges, and the political economist combines, labour, let them beware that their speculations, for want of correspondence with those first principles which belong to the imagination, do not tend, as they have in modern England, to exasperate at once the extremes of luxury and want. They have exemplified the saying, "To him that hath, more shall be given; and from him that hath not, the little that he hath shall be taken away."[1] The rich have become richer, and the poor have become poorer; and the vessel of the state is driven between the Scylla and Charybdis[2] of anarchy and despotism. Such are the effects which must ever flow from an unmitigated exercise of the calculating faculty.

It is difficult to define pleasure in its highest sense; the definition involving a number of apparent paradoxes. For, from an inexplicable defect of harmony in the constitution of human nature, the pain of the inferior is frequently connected with the pleasures of the superior portions of our being. Sorrow, terror, anguish, despair itself are often the chosen expressions of an approximation to the highest good. Our sympathy in tragic fiction depends on this principle; tragedy delights by affording a shadow of the pleasure which exists in pain. This is the source also of the melancholy which is inseparable from the sweetest melody. The pleasure that is in sorrow is sweeter than the pleasure of pleasure itself. And hence the saying, "It is better to go to the house of mourning, than to the house of mirth."[3] Not that this highest species of pleasure is necessarily linked with pain. The delight of love and friendship, the ecstasy of the admiration of nature, the joy of the perception and still more of the creation of poetry is often wholly unalloyed.

[1] *To him … away* Repeatedly said by Jesus (Matthew 25.29, Mark 4.25, Luke 8.18 and 19.26).

[2] *Scylla and Charybdis* A group of rocks and a whirlpool located at the Strait of Messina (between Sicily and mainland Italy).

[3] *It is … mirth* From Ecclesiastes 7.2.

The production and assurance of pleasure in this highest sense is true utility. Those who produce and preserve this pleasure are Poets or poetical philosophers.

The exertions of Locke, Hume, Gibbon, Voltaire, Rousseau,[4] and their disciples, in favour of oppressed and deluded humanity, are entitled to the gratitude of mankind. Yet it is easy to calculate the degree of moral and intellectual improvement which the world would have exhibited, had they never lived. A little more nonsense would have been talked for a century or two; and perhaps a few more men, women, and children, burnt as heretics. We might not at this moment have been congratulating each other on the abolition of the Inquisition in Spain.[5] But it exceeds all imagination to conceive what would have been the moral condition of the world if neither Dante, Petrarch, Boccaccio, Chaucer, Shakespeare, Calderon,[6] Lord Bacon, nor Milton, had ever existed; if Raphael and Michael Angelo[7] had never been born; if the Hebrew poetry had never been translated; if a revival of the study of Greek literature had never taken place; if no monuments of ancient sculpture had been handed down to us; and if the poetry of the religion of the ancient world had been extinguished together with its belief. The human mind could never, except by the intervention of these excitements, have been awakened to the invention of the grosser sciences, and that application of analytical reasoning to the aberrations of society, which it is now attempted to exalt over the direct expression of the inventive and creative faculty itself.

… The cultivation of those sciences which have enlarged the limits of the empire of man over the external world, has, for want of the poetical faculty,

[4] *Locke … Rousseau* John Locke, David Hume, Edward Gibbon, François-Marie Arouet Voltaire, and Jean-Jacques Rousseau, noted philosophers of the seventeenth and eighteenth centuries.

[5] *We might … Spain* The Inquisition was suspended in 1820 (the year before Shelley wrote this essay) and abolished permanently in 1834.

[6] *Petrarch* Fourteenth-century Italian poet, famous for his love lyrics; *Boccaccio* Italian poet, author of the *Decameron* (1351–53); *Calderon* Pedro Calderón de la Barca, seventeenth-century Spanish poet and dramatist.

[7] *Raphael and Michael Angelo* Italian Renaissance painters.

proportionally circumscribed those of the internal world; and man, having enslaved the elements, remains himself a slave. To what but a cultivation of the mechanical arts in a degree disproportioned to the presence of the creative faculty, which is the basis of all knowledge, is to be attributed the abuse of all invention for abridging and combining labour, to the exasperation of the inequality of mankind? From what other cause has it arisen that the discoveries which should have lightened, have added a weight to the curse imposed on Adam? Poetry, and the principle of Self, of which money is the visible incarnation, are the God and the Mammon of the world.[1]

The functions of the poetical faculty are two-fold; by one it creates new materials of knowledge, and power and pleasure; by the other it engenders in the mind a desire to reproduce and arrange them according to a certain rhythm and order which may be called the beautiful and the good. The cultivation of poetry is never more to be desired than at periods when, from an excess of the selfish and calculating principle, the accumulation of the materials of external life exceed the quantity of the power of assimilating them to the internal laws of human nature. The body has then become too unwieldy for that which animates it.

Poetry is indeed something divine. It is at once the centre and circumference of knowledge; it is that which comprehends all science, and that to which all science must be referred. It is at the same time the root and blossom of all other systems of thought: it is that from which all spring, and that which adorns all; and that which, if blighted, denies the fruit and the seed, and withholds from the barren world the nourishment and the succession of the scions[2] of the tree of life. It is the perfect and consummate surface and bloom of things; it is as the odour and the colour of the rose to the texture of the elements which compose it, as the form and the splendour of unfaded beauty to the secrets of anatomy and corruption. What were Virtue, Love, Patriotism, Friendship &c.—what were the scenery of this beautiful Universe which we inhabit—what were our consolations on this side of the grave—and what were our aspirations beyond it—if Poetry did not ascend to bring light and fire from those eternal regions where the owl-winged faculty of calculation dare not ever soar? Poetry is not like reasoning, a power to be exerted according to the determination of the will. A man cannot say, "I will compose poetry." The greatest poet even cannot say it: for the mind in creation is as a fading coal which some invisible influence, like an inconstant wind, awakens to transitory brightness: this power arises from within, like the colour of a flower which fades and changes as it is developed, and the conscious portions of our natures are unprophetic either of its approach or its departure. …

Poetry is the record of the best and happiest moments of the happiest and best minds. We are aware of evanescent visitations of thought and feeling sometimes associated with place or person, sometimes regarding our own mind alone, and always arising unforeseen and departing unbidden, but elevating and delightful beyond all expression: so that even in the desire and the regret they leave, there cannot but be pleasure, participating as it does in the nature of its object. It is as it were the interpenetration of a diviner nature through our own; but its footsteps are like those of a wind over a sea, which the coming calm erases, and whose traces remain only as on the wrinkled sand which paves it. These and corresponding conditions of being are experienced principally by those of the most delicate sensibility and the most enlarged imagination; and the state of mind produced by them is at war with every base desire. The enthusiasm of virtue, love, patriotism, and friendship is essentially linked with these emotions; and whilst they last, self appears as what it is, an atom to a Universe. Poets are not only subject to these experiences as spirits of the most refined organization, but they can colour all that they combine with the evanescent hues of this ethereal world; a word, a trait in the representation of a scene or a passion, will touch the enchanted chord, and reanimate, in those who have ever experienced these emotions, the sleeping, the cold, the

[1] *God and … world* Cf. Matthew 6.24: "No man can serve two masters: for either he will hate the one, and love the other; or else he will hold to the one, and despise the other. Ye cannot serve God and Mammon," Mammon being the false idol of worldly possessions.

[2] *scions* Shoots.

buried image of the past. Poetry thus makes immortal all that is best and most beautiful in the world; it arrests the vanishing apparitions which haunt the interlunations[1] of life, and veiling them or in language or in form sends them forth among mankind, bearing sweet news of kindred joy to those with whom their sisters abide—abide, because there is no portal of expression from the caverns of the spirit which they inhabit into the universe of things. Poetry redeems from decay the visitations of the divinity in man.

Poetry turns all things to loveliness; it exalts the beauty of that which is most beautiful, and it adds beauty to that which is most deformed: it marries exultation and horror, grief and pleasure, eternity and change; it subdues to union under its light yoke all irreconcilable things. It transmutes all that it touches, and every form moving within the radiance of its presence is changed by wondrous sympathy to an incarnation of the spirit which it breathes; its secret alchemy turns to potable[2] gold the poisonous waters which flow from death through life; it strips the veil of familiarity from the world, and lays bare the naked and sleeping beauty which is the spirit of its forms.

All things exist as they are perceived: at least in relation to the percipient. "The mind is its own place, and of itself can make a heaven of hell, a hell of heaven."[3] But poetry defeats the curse which binds us to be subjected to the accident of surrounding impressions. And whether it spreads its own figured curtain or withdraws life's dark veil from before the scene of things, it equally creates for us a being within our being. It makes us the inhabitants of a world to which the familiar world is a chaos. It reproduces the common universe of which we are portions and percipients, and it purges from our inward sight the film of familiarity which obscures from us the wonder of our being. It compels us to feel that which we perceive, and to imagine that which we know. It creates anew the universe after it has been annihilated in our minds by the recurrence of impressions blunted by reiteration. …

The first part of these remarks has related to Poetry in its elements and principles; and it has been shown, as well as the narrow limits assigned them would permit, that what is called poetry, in a restricted sense, has a common source with all other forms of order and of beauty according to which the materials of human life are susceptible of being arranged, and which is poetry in an universal sense.

The second part[4] will have for its object an application of these principles to the present state of the cultivation of Poetry, and a defence of the attempt to idealize the modern forms of manners and opinion, and compel them into a subordination to the imaginative and creative faculty. For the literature of England, an energetic development of which has ever preceded or accompanied a great and free development of the national will, has arisen as it were from a new birth. In spite of the low-thoughted envy which would undervalue contemporary merit, our own will be a memorable age in intellectual achievements, and we live among such philosophers and poets as surpass beyond comparison any who have appeared since the last national struggle for civil and religious liberty.[5] The most unfailing herald, companion, and follower of the awakening of a great people to work a beneficial change in opinion or institution, is Poetry. At such periods there is an accumulation of the power of communicating and receiving intense and impassioned conceptions respecting man and nature. The persons in whom this power resides, may often, as far as regards many portions of their nature, have little apparent correspondence with that spirit of good of which they are the ministers. But even whilst they deny and abjure, they are yet compelled to serve the Power which is seated upon the throne of their own soul. It is impossible to read the compositions of the most celebrated writers of the present day without being startled with the electric life which burns within

[1] *interlunations* Period between an old and a new moon; period of darkness.

[2] *potable* Drinkable. Alchemists sought a liquid form of gold that, when consumed, would be the elixir of life.

[3] *The mind … heaven* From Satan's speech in Milton's *Paradise Lost* 1.254–55.

[4] *The second part* Shelley did not complete a second part.

[5] *the last … liberty* I.e., the English Civil War of the 1640s.

their words. They measure the circumference and sound the depths of human nature with a comprehensive and all-penetrating spirit, and they are themselves perhaps the most sincerely astonished at its manifestations, for it is less their spirit than the spirit of the age. Poets are the hierophants[1] of an unapprehended inspiration, the mirrors of the gigantic shadows which futurity casts upon the present, the words which express what they understand not; the trumpets which sing to battle, and feel not what they inspire: the influence which is moved not, but moves.[2] Poets are the unacknowledged legislators of the World.

—1820

[1] *hierophants* Interpreters of sacred mysteries.

[2] *is moved … moves* Reference to Greek philosopher Aristotle's description of God as the "Unmoved Mover" of the universe.

Felicia Hemans

1793 – 1835

Among the most widely read poets in England during her lifetime, Felicia Hemans was seen, as an 1820s critic phrased it, as "the mistress-mind of the day." Her poetry in many ways reflected the ethos of the late Romantic era, deftly capturing its underlying values and intellectual concerns, but several of her poems—perhaps most notably "Casabianca" and "The Homes of England"—remained enormously popular well into the twentieth century. Adept at negotiating the gendered expectations of her readers, Hemans crafted a feminine literary persona that earned her a great deal of admiration; one reviewer, for example, praised her for a "purity of taste, a correctness of sentiment, and an elegance of expression truly feminine." (This is not to say that she escaped all sexist censure; Byron famously parodied her as "Mrs. Hewoman.") She achieved immense popular success and acclaim while addressing not only subjects deemed acceptable for women, from domesticity to the experience of women's writing and celebrity, but also subjects that were often taken to be the preserve of men—such as war, patriotism, history, and death.

Hemans was born Felicia Browne, the fifth of seven children of a Liverpool wine merchant and his wife, the daughter of a foreign diplomat. The failure of her father's business in 1799 caused the family to move to Wales; Felicia adored the countryside and it became the inspiration for much of her poetry. She learned several languages and a great deal about music from her mother, and benefited from a well-stocked family library. She loved Shakespeare as a child and was said to have had an excellent memory for reciting verse. Her own first published volume appeared in 1808, when she was only 14. Although *Poems* received some negative reviews, it sold 1,000 copies and she was encouraged to continue writing. Two of her brothers were then engaged in the British war against Spain, and many of the poems are patriotic depictions of Britain in battle. Her brothers passed the volume on to one of their colleagues, Captain Alfred Hemans; he later became Felicia's husband. Percy Bysshe Shelley also received her first volume and began a correspondence with the young poet.

Felicia Browne married in 1812, shortly after the publication of her third volume of poetry, *The Domestic Affections and Other Poems*. She and her husband initially lived in her mother's house in Wales, a situation that would eventually prove uncomfortable for Alfred. While Hemans continued to publish and become more popular, Alfred became disillusioned with Wales and moved to Italy in 1818 on grounds of "ill health," leaving his wife with their five young sons. From this point onwards she supported herself and her children solely by her writing.

Hemans was in the prime of her writing career in the 1810s and 1820s, occupying something of an uneasy position between the Romantics and the Victorians. Long after her death, her work retained a high degree of popularity, with Victorian critics perceiving her poetry as characterized by powerful rhythms and powerful passions. And certainly the strength of form and of feeling in poems of patriotic fervor such as "The Homes of England" and "Casabianca" (both of which were learnt by heart by English schoolchildren into the twentieth century) is unquestionable. Yet in her own day, seen against the backdrop of the extravagant passions of Byron and other poets associated with the Romantic movement, her poetry was praised for its formal and emotional restraint.

Though Hemans's most famous poems are short, she was also successful with longer works, notably the dramatic poem *The Siege of Valencia* (1823), which recounts the epic story of Elmira after her two sons are captured by a Moorish army. And she wrote innovative linked poems, such as those in *Records of Woman* (1828). Though she is often thought of as an important poet of domesticity, Hemans focused at least as much on women acting out their lives on a larger stage.

In 1821 Hemans was awarded the Royal Society of Literature's annual prize of £52.50 (a substantial amount at the time). She was then publishing regularly in British literary magazines, and from 1823 she was earning roughly £200 per year, enough to support herself and her children in some comfort. Her work was never out of print, and she was widely read in Britain and in America. The death of her mother in 1827 had a devastating effect on her, however, and from that point onwards she was plagued by poor health.

In her later years, she rivaled Byron in popularity, and was highly sought after by budding poets and autograph-seekers. She found herself caught, however, between the success she needed to support herself and the masculine characteristics attributed to it, a theme she explores in "Woman and Fame." In 1831 Hemans moved to Dublin to live with one of her brothers. She died there in 1835, of a weak heart and the effects of rheumatic fever.

⌘⌘⌘

The Homes of England

Where's the coward that would not dare
To fight for such a land?
—MARMION[1]

The stately Homes of England,
How beautiful they stand!
Amidst their tall ancestral trees,
O'er all the pleasant land.

The deer across their greensward° bound (turf)
Thro' shade and sunny gleam,
And the swan glides past them with the sound
Of some rejoicing stream.

The merry Homes of England!
Around their hearths by night,
What gladsome looks of household love
Meet, in the ruddy° light! (red-hued)
There woman's voice flows forth in song,
Or childhood's tale is told,
Or lips move tunefully along
Some glorious page of old.

The blessed Homes of England!
How softly on their bowers° (arbors)
Is laid the holy quietness
That breathes from Sabbath-hours!
Solemn, yet sweet, the church-bell's chime
Floats thro' their woods at morn;

[1] *MARMION* Walter Scott's *Marmion: A Tale of Flodden Field* (1808), 4.30. When first published in *Blackwood's Magazine*, the poem had instead the following epigraph from Joanna Baillie, *Ethwald: A Tragedy* (1802) 2.1.2.76–82:

A land of peace,
Where yellow fields unspoil'd, and pastures green,
Mottled with herds and flocks, who crop secure
Their native herbage, nor have ever known
A stranger's stall, smile gladly.
See through its tufted alleys to Heaven's roof
The curling smoke of quiet dwellings rise.

All other sounds, in that still time,
    Of breeze and leaf are born.

The Cottage Homes of England!
    By thousands on her plains,
They are smiling o'er the silvery brooks,
    And round the hamlet-fanes.[1]
Thro' glowing orchards forth they peep,
    Each from its nook of leaves,
And fearless there the lowly sleep,
    As the bird beneath their eaves.

The free, fair Homes of England!
    Long, long, in hut and hall,
May hearts of native proof be rear'd
    To guard each hallow'd wall!
And green for ever be the groves,
    And bright the flowery sod,
Where first the child's glad spirit loves
    Its country and its God![2]
—1812

The Land of Dreams

And dreams, in their development, have breath,
And tears and tortures, and the touch of joy;
They leave a weight upon our waking thoughts,
They make us what we were not—what they will,
And shake us with the vision that's gone by.
—BYRON.[3]

Oh spirit land, thou land of dreams!
A world thou art of mysterious gleams,
Of startling voices, and sounds at strife—
A world of the dead in the hues of life.

Like a wizard's magic-glass° thou art *mirror*
When the wavy shadows float by, and part—
Visions of aspects, now loved, now strange,
Glimmering and mingling in ceaseless change.

Thou art like a city of the past
With its gorgeous halls into fragments cast,
Amidst whose ruins there glide and play
Familiar forms of the world's today.

Thou art like the depths where the seas have birth,
Rich with the wealth that is lost from earth—
All the sere° flowers of our days gone by, *dry*
And the buried gems in thy bosom lie.

Yes, thou art like those dim sea-caves,
A realm of treasures, a realm of graves!
And the shapes through thy mysteries that come and go,
Are of beauty and terror, of power and woe.

But for me, oh thou picture-land of sleep,
Thou art all one world of affections deep—
And wrung from my heart is each flushing dye
That sweeps o'er thy chambers of imagery.

And thy bowers° are fair—even as Eden fair; *arbors*
All the beloved of my soul are there!
The forms my spirit most pines to see,
The eyes whose love hath been life to me:

They are there, and each blessed voice I hear,
Kindly, and joyous, and silvery clear;
But undertones are in each, that say,
"It is but a dream; it will melt away!"

I walk with sweet friends in the sunset's glow;
I listen to music of long ago;
But one thought, like an omen, breathes faint through
    the lay[4]—
"It is but a dream; it will melt away!"

I sit by the hearth of my early days;
All the home-faces are met by the blaze,
And the eyes of the mother shine soft, yet say,
"It is but a dream; it will melt away!"

[1] *hamlet-fanes* Weather vanes of the village.

[2] [Hemans's note] Originally published in *Blackwood's Magazine*. [1828.]

[3] *And dreams … BYRON* From "The Dream," by George Gordon, Lord Byron (1788–1824).

[4] *lay* Medieval narrative song or poem.

And away, like a flower's passing breath, 'tis gone,
And I wake more sadly, more deeply lone—
Oh, a haunted heart is a weight to bear!
Bright faces, kind voices, where are ye, where?

Shadow not forth, oh thou land of dreams,
The past, as it fled by my own blue streams!
Make not my spirit within me burn
For the scenes and the hours that may ne'er return!

Call out from the future thy visions bright,
From the world o'er the grave, take thy solemn light,
And oh! with the loved, whom no more I see,
Show me my home as it yet may be!

As it yet may be in some purer sphere,
No cloud, no parting, no sleepless fear;
So my soul may bear on through the long, long day,
Till I go where the beautiful melts not away!
—1821

Evening Prayer at a Girls' School

Now in thy youth, beseech of Him,
Who giveth, upbraiding° not, *sharply scolding*
That his light in thy heart become not dim,
And his love be unforgot;
And thy God, in the darkest of days, will be
Greenness, and beauty, and strength to thee.[1]
BERNARD BARTON.

Hush! 'tis a holy hour—the quiet room
Seems like a temple, while yon soft lamp sheds
A faint and starry radiance, through the gloom
And the sweet stillness, down on bright young heads,
With all their clust'ring locks, untouch'd by care,
And bow'd, as flowers are bow'd with night—in prayer.

Gaze on,—'tis lovely!—childhood's lip and cheek,
Mantling[2] beneath its earnest brow of thought—
Gaze—yet what seest thou in those fair, and meek,
And fragile things, as but for sunshine wrought?
—Thou seest what grief must nurture for the sky,
What death must fashion for eternity!

Oh! joyous creatures, that will sink to rest,
Lightly, when those pure orisons° are done, *prayers*
As birds with slumber's honey-dew oppress'd,
'Midst the dim folded leaves, at set of sun—
Lift up your hearts!—though yet no sorrow lies
Dark in the summer-heaven of those clear eyes;

Though fresh within your breasts th'untroubled springs
Of hope make melody where'er ye tread;
And o'er your sleep bright shadows, from the wings
Of spirits visiting but youth, be spread;
Yet in those flute-like voices, mingling low,
Is woman's tenderness—how soon her woe!° *sorrow*

Her lot° is on you—silent tears to weep, *fate*
And patient smiles to wear through suffering's hour,
And sumless riches, from Affection's deep,
To pour on broken reeds—a wasted shower!
And to make idols, and to find them clay,[3]
And to bewail that worship—therefore pray!

Her lot is on you—to be found untir'd,
Watching the stars out by the bed of pain,
With a pale cheek, and yet a brow inspir'd,
And a true heart of hope, though hope be vain.
Meekly to bear with wrong, to cheer decay,
And oh! to love through all things—therefore pray!

And take the thought of this calm vesper° *evening prayer*
time,
With its low murmuring sounds and silvery light,
Or through the dark days fading from their prime,
As a sweet dew to keep your souls from blight.

[1] *Now in ... strength to thee* "The Ivy, Addressed to a Young Friend" (1825), 43–48, by Bernard Barton (1784–1849).

[2] *Mantling* Blushing, coloring from emotion.

[3] *And to ... clay* See Daniel 2.31–45.

Earth will forsake—oh! happy to have given
Th'unbroken heart's first fragrance unto Heaven!
—1825

Casabianca[1]

The boy stood on the burning deck,
    Whence all but him had fled;
The flame that lit the battle's wreck,
    Shone round him o'er the dead.

Yet beautiful and bright he stood,
    As born to rule the storm;
A creature of heroic blood,
    A proud, though child-like form.

The flames roll'd on—he would not go,
    Without his father's word;
That father, faint in death below,
    His voice no longer heard.

He call'd aloud—"Say, father, say
    If yet my task is done?"
He knew not that the chieftain lay
    Unconscious of his son.

"Speak, Father!" once again he cried,
    "If I may yet be gone!"
—And but the booming shots replied,
    And fast the flames roll'd on.

Upon his brow he felt their breath,
    And in his waving hair;
And look'd from that lone post of death,
    In still, yet brave despair.

And shouted but once more aloud,
    "My father! must I stay?"
While o'er him fast, through sail and shroud,
    The wreathing fires made way.

They wrapt the ship in splendor wild,
    They caught the flag on high,
And stream'd above the gallant child,
    Like banners in the sky.

There came a burst of thunder sound—
    The boy—oh! where was he?
—Ask of the winds that far around
    With fragments strew'd the sea!

With mast, and helm, and pennon[2] fair,
    That well had borne their part—
But the noblest thing that perish'd there,
    Was that young faithful heart.
—1826

Corinne at the Capitol[3]

Les femmes doivent penser qu'il est dans cette carrière bien peu de sort qui puissent valoir la plus obscure vie d'une femme aimée et d'une mère heureuse.[4]

—MADAME DE STAËL.

[1] [Hemans's note] Young Casabianca, a boy about thirteen years old, son to the admiral of the Orient, remained at his post (in the battle of the Nile), after the ship had taken fire, and all the guns had been abandoned; and perished in the explosion of the vessel, when the flames had reached the powder. [The British fleet, commanded by Horatio Nelson, defeated Napoleon's fleet, commanded by Louis de Casabianca, at the battle of the Nile on 1 August 1798. Among those killed when the French flagship, *L'Orient*, exploded were the Admiral and his son, Giacomo Jocante Casabianca (who in fact was only ten). Hemans's source is probably Southey, *Life of Horatio, Lord Nelson* (1813). The poem was first published in the *Monthly Magazine*.]

[2] *pennon* Banner or flag.

[3] *Corinne at the Capitol* Based on the novel *Corinne, ou l'Italie* (1807), by Germaine de Staël (1766–1817). Corinne is an Italian improvisatrice—a poet who improvises verses in public. The English Lord Nelvil first sees her when she is being honored at the Capitol, in Rome. They fall in love and he offers to marry her, but she declines, preferring her independence. When he marries her half-sister instead, she dies of a broken heart. The poem was first published in *The Literary Souvenir for 1827*, 189–91.

[4] *Les femmes … heureuse* French: Women must reflect that there are in this career [of glory] very few destinies that can equal in worth the most obscure life of a beloved wife and happy mother. See de Staël, *De l'Influence des passions sur le bonheur des individus et des nations* (1796) chapter 3.

Daughter of th'Italian heaven!
Thou, to whom its fires are given,
Joyously thy car° hath roll'd *chariot*
Where the conqueror's pass'd of old;
And the festal° sun that shone, *festive*
O'er three hundred triumphs gone,[1]
Makes thy day of glory bright,
With a shower of golden light.

Now thou tread'st th'ascending road,
Freedom's foot so proudly trode;[2]
While, from tombs of heroes borne,
From the dust of empire shorn,
Flowers upon thy graceful head,
Chaplets[3] of all hues, are shed,
In a soft and rosy rain,
Touch'd with many a gemlike stain.

Thou hast gain'd the summit now!
Music hails thee from below;
Music, whose rich notes might stir
Ashes of the sepulchre;° *tomb*
Shaking with victorious notes
All the bright air as it floats.
Well may woman's heart beat high
Unto that proud harmony!

Now afar it rolls—it dies—
And thy voice is heard to rise
With a low and lovely tone
In its thrilling power alone;
And thy lyre's deep silvery string,
Touch'd as by a breeze's wing,
Murmurs tremblingly at first,
Ere° the tide of rapture burst. *before*

All the spirit of thy sky
Now hath lit thy large dark eye,
And thy cheek a flush hath caught
From the joy of kindled thought;
And the burning words of song
From thy lip flow fast and strong,
With a rushing stream's delight
In the freedom of its might.

Radiant daughter of the sun!
Now thy living wreath is won.
Crown'd of Rome!—Oh! art thou not
Happy in that glorious lot?°— *fate*
Happier, happier far than thou,
With the laurel on thy brow,[4]
She that makes the humblest hearth
Lovely but to one on earth!
—1826

The Effigies[5]

Der rasche Kampf verewigt einen Mann:
Er falle gleich, so preiset ihn das Lied.
Allein die Thränen, die unendlichen
Der überbliebnen, der verlass'nen Frau,
Zählt keine Nachwelt.[6]

—GOETHE

Warrior! whose image on thy tomb,
With shield and crested head,
Sleeps proudly in the purple gloom
By the stain'd window shed;
The records of thy name and race
Have faded from the stone,
Yet, through a cloud of years, I trace
What thou hast been and done.

A banner, from its flashing spear,
Flung out o'er many a fight;

[1] [Hemans's note] The trebly hundred triumphs.—Byron. [See *Childe Harold's Pilgrimage* 4.82 (1818)]; *triumph* Ancient Roman celebration of a military victory; there were a total of 320.

[2] *trode* Archaic past tense of "tread."

[3] *Chaplets* Garlands of flowers worn on the head.

[4] *laurel on … brow* Poets were traditionally honored with crowns of laurel, which was sacred to Apollo.

[5] *Effigies* Sculptural representations of people, often upon their tombs.

[6] *Der rasche … Nachwelt* German: Rash combat oft immortalizes man. / If he should fall, he is renowned in song; / But after ages reckon not the tears / Which ceaseless the forsaken woman sheds. (Goethe, *Iphigenie* 5.6. English translation by Anna Swanwick [1909–14].)

A war-cry ringing far and clear,
And strong to turn the flight;
An arm that bravely bore the lance
On for the holy shrine;
A haughty heart and a kingly glance—
Chief! were not these things thine?

A lofty place where leaders sate° *sat*
Around the council-board;° *table*
In festive halls a chair of state
When the blood-red wine was pour'd;
A name that drew a prouder tone
From herald, harp, and bard;° *court poet*
Surely these things were all thine own,—
So hadst thou thy reward.

Woman! whose sculptur'd form at rest
By the armed knight is laid,
With meek hands folded o'er a breast
In matron robes array'd;
What was thy tale?—Oh! gentle mate
Of him, the bold and free,
Bound unto his victorious fate,
What bard hath sung of *thee*?

He woo'd a bright and burning star—
Thine was the void, the gloom,
The straining eye that follow'd far
His fast-receding plume;
The heart-sick listening while his steed
Sent echoes on the breeze;
The pang—but when did *Fame* take heed
Of griefs obscure as these?

Thy silent and secluded hours
Thro' many a lonely day,
While bending o'er thy broider'd° flowers, *embroidered*
With spirit far away;
Thy weeping midnight prayers for him
Who fought on Syrian plains,
Thy watchings till the torch grew dim—
These fill no minstrel strains.

A still, sad life was thine!—long years
With tasks unguerdon'd° fraught, *unrewarded*
Deep, quiet love, submissive tears,
Vigils of anxious thought;
Prayer at the cross in fervour pour'd,
Alms[1] to the pilgrim given—
Oh! happy, happier than thy lord,
In that lone path to heaven!
—1826

The Image in Lava[2]

Thou thing of years departed!
What ages have gone by,
Since here the mournful seal was set
By love and agony!

Temple and tower have moulder'd,
Empires from earth have pass'd,—
And woman's heart hath left a trace
Those glories to outlast!

And childhood's fragile image
Thus fearfully enshrin'd,
Survives the proud memorials rear'd
By conquerors of mankind.

Babe! wert thou brightly slumbering
Upon thy mother's breast,
When suddenly the fiery tomb
Shut round each gentle guest?

A strange, dark fate o'ertook you,
Fair babe and loving heart!

---

[1] *Alms* Money given in charity to the poor.

[2] [Hemans's note] The impression of a woman's form, with an infant clasped to the bosom, found at the uncovering of Herculaneum. [Herculaneum and Pompeii were destroyed by the eruption of Vesuvius in 79 CE. The image is one of the casts made during the excavations (1763–1820) by pouring plaster into the holes left in the lava by the victims' bodies. The poem was first published in the *New Monthly Magazine* in 1827.]

One moment of a thousand pangs—
Yet better than to part!

Haply° of that fond bosom, *by chance*
On ashes here impress'd,
Thou wert the only treasure, child!
Whereon a hope might rest.

Perchance all vainly lavish'd,
Its other love had been,
And where it trusted, nought remain'd
But thorns on which to lean.

Far better then to perish,
Thy form within its clasp,
Than live and lose thee, precious one!
From that impassion'd grasp.

Oh! I could pass all relics
Left by the pomps of old,
To gaze on this rude° monument, *primitive*
Cast in affection's mould.

Love, human love! what art thou?
Thy print upon the dust
Outlives the cities of renown
Wherein the mighty trust!

Immortal, oh! immortal
Thou art, whose earthly glow
Hath given these ashes holiness—
It must, it must be so!
—1827

Properzia Rossi[1]

(Properzia Rossi, a celebrated female sculptor of Bologna, possessed also of talents for poetry and music, died in consequence of an unrequited attachment.—A painting, by Ducis, represents her showing her last work, a basso-relievo of Ariadne,[2] to a Roman knight, the object of her affection, who regards it with indifference.)

—Tell me no more, no more
Of my soul's lofty gifts! Are they not vain
To quench its haunting thirst for happiness?
Have I not lov'd, and striven, and fail'd to bind
One true heart unto me, whereon my own
Might find a resting-place, a home for all
Its burden of affections? I depart,
Unknown, tho' Fame goes with me; I must leave
The earth unknown. Yet it may be that death
Shall give my name a power to win such tears
As would have made life precious.[3]

I

One dream of passion and of beauty more!
And in its bright fulfilment let me pour
My soul away! Let earth retain a trace
Of that which lit my being, tho' its race
Might have been loftier far.—Yet one more dream!
From my deep spirit one victorious gleam
Ere I depart! For thee alone, for thee!
May this last work, this farewell triumph be,
Thou, loved so vainly! I would leave enshrined
Something immortal of my heart and mind,
That yet may speak to thee when I am gone,
Shaking thine inmost bosom with a tone
Of lost affection;—something that may prove
What she hath been, whose melancholy love
On thee was lavish'd; silent pang and tear,
And fervent song, that gush'd when none were near,
And dream by night, and weary thought by day,
Stealing the brightness from her life away,—
While thou—Awake! not yet within me die,
Under the burden and the agony
Of this vain tenderness,—my spirit, wake!
Ev'n for thy sorrowful affection's sake,
Live! in thy work breathe out!—that he may yet,

[1] *Properzia Rossi* Properzia de'Rossi (c.1491–1530), Bolognese sculptor, painter, and poet.

[2] *Ducis* Louis Ducis (1775–1847), *Properzia de'Rossi and Her Last Bas-relief*; *basso-relievo* Relief sculpture; *Ariadne* Cretan princess who helped the hero Theseus find his way through the labyrinth that enclosed the Minotaur, which he killed. They eloped, but he abandoned her on the island of Naxos. See Ovid's *Heroides* 10.

[3] *Tell me ... precious* The epigraph is by Hemans herself.

Feeling sad mastery there, perchance regret
Thine unrequited gift.

2

It comes,—the power
Within me born, flows back; my fruitless dower° *dowry*
That could not win me love. Yet once again
I greet it proudly, with its rushing train
Of glorious images:—they throng—they press—
A sudden joy lights up my loneliness,—
I shall not perish all![1]
The bright work grows
Beneath my hand, unfolding, as a rose,
Leaf after leaf, to beauty; line by line,
I fix my thought, heart, soul, to burn, to shine,
Thro' the pale marble's veins. It grows—and now
I give my own life's history to thy brow,
Forsaken Ariadne! thou shalt wear
My form, my lineaments;[2] but oh! more fair,
Touch'd into lovelier being by the glow
Which in me dwells, as by the summer-light
All things are glorified. From thee my woe
Shall yet look beautiful to meet his sight,
When I am pass'd away. Thou art the mould
Wherein I pour the fervent thoughts, th'untold,
The self-consuming! Speak to him of me,
Thou, the deserted by the lonely sea,
With the soft sadness of thine earnest eye,
Speak to him, lorn° one! deeply, mournfully, *forlorn*
Of all my love and grief! Oh! could I throw
Into thy frame a voice, a sweet, and low,
And thrilling voice of song! when he came nigh,
To send the passion of its melody
Thro' his pierced bosom—on its tones to bear
My life's deep feeling, as the southern air
Wafts the faint myrtle's[3] breath,—to rise, to swell,
To sink away in accents of farewell,
Winning but one, one gush of tears, whose flow
Surely my parted spirit yet might know,
If love be strong as death!

3

Now fair thou art,
Thou form, whose life is of my burning heart!
Yet all the vision that within me wrought,
I cannot make thee! Oh! I might have given
Birth to creations of far nobler thought,
I might have kindled, with the fire of heaven,
Things not of such as die! But I have been
Too much alone;[4] a heart whereon to lean,
With all these deep affections, that o'erflow
My aching soul, and find no shore below;
An eye to be my star, a voice to bring
Hope o'er my path, like sounds that breathe of spring,
These are denied me—dreamt of still in vain,—
Therefore my brief aspirings from the chain,
Are ever but as some wild fitful° song, *irregular*
Rising triumphantly, to die ere° long *before*
In dirge-like[5] echoes.

4

Yet the world will see
Little of this, my parting work, in thee,
Thou shalt have fame! Oh, mockery! give the reed
From storms a shelter,—give the drooping vine
Something round, which its tendrils may entwine,—
Give the parch'd flower a rain-drop, and the meed° *reward*
Of love's kind words to woman! Worthless fame!
That in *his* bosom wins not for my name
Th'abiding place it ask'd! Yet how my heart,
In its own fairy world of song and art,
Once beat for praise!—Are those high longings o'er?
That which I have been can I be no more?—
Never, oh! never more; tho' still thy sky
Be blue as then, my glorious Italy!
And tho' the music, whose rich breathings fill
Thine air with soul, be wandering past me still,
And tho' the mantle° of thy sunlight streams, *cloak*

[1] *I shall ... all* Cf. Horace, *Odes* 3.30.6.

[2] *lineaments* Distinctive shapes.

[3] *myrtle's* Belonging to the myrtle, a Mediterranean evergreen shrub bearing pink flowers and black berries.

[4] *Too ... alone* Cf. Byron's *Mazeppa* 839.

[5] *dirge-like* Like a funeral hymn, solemn and mournful.

Unchang'd on forms, instinct with poet-dreams;
Never, oh! never more! Where'er I move,
The shadow of this broken-hearted love
Is on me and around! Too well *they* know,
    Whose life is all within, too soon and well,
When there the blight hath settled;—but I go
    Under the silent wings of peace to dwell;
From the slow wasting, from the lonely pain,
The inward burning of those words—"*in vain*,"
    Sear'd on the heart—I go. 'Twill soon be past.
Sunshine, and song, and bright Italian heaven,
    And thou, oh! thou, on whom my spirit cast
Unvalued wealth,—who know'st not what was given
In that devotedness,—the sad, and deep,
And unrepaid—farewell! If I could weep
Once, only once, belov'd one! on thy breast,
Pouring my heart forth ere I sink to rest!
But that were happiness, and unto me
Earth's gift is *fame*. Yet I was form'd to be
So richly blest! With thee to watch the sky,
Speaking not, feeling but that thou wert nigh;
With thee to listen, while the tones of song
Swept ev'n as part of our sweet air along,
To listen silently;—with thee to gaze
On forms, the deified of olden days,
This had been joy enough;—and hour by hour,
From its glad well-springs drinking life and power,
How had my spirit soar'd, and made its fame
    A glory for thy brow!—Dreams, dreams!—the fire
Burns faint within me. Yet I leave my name—
    As a deep thrill may linger on the lyre[1]
When its full chords are hush'd—awhile to live,
And one day haply in thy heart revive
Sad thoughts of me:—I leave it, with a sound,
A spell o'er memory, mournfully profound,
I leave it, on my country's air to dwell,—
Say proudly yet—"'Twas hers who lov'd me well!"
—1828

[1] *lyre* Stringed instrument.

Woman and Fame

Happy—happier far than thou,
With the laurel on thy brow;[2]
She that makes the humblest hearth,
Lovely but to one on earth.[3]

Thou hast a charmed cup, O Fame!
    A draught that mantles[4] high,
And seems to lift this earthly frame
    Above mortality.
Away! to me—a woman—bring
Sweet waters from affection's spring.

Thou hast green laurel leaves, that twine
    Into so proud a wreath;
For that resplendent gift of thine,
    Heroes have smiled in death:
Give *me* from some kind hand a flower,
The record of one happy hour!

Thou hast a voice, whose thrilling tone
    Can bid each life-pulse beat
As when a trumpet's note hath blown,
    Calling the brave to meet:
But mine, let mine—a woman's breast,
By words of home-born love be bless'd.

A hollow sound is in thy song,
    A mockery in thine eye,
To the sick heart that doth but long
    For aid, for sympathy—
For kindly looks to cheer it on,
For tender accents that are gone.

[2] *laurel on … brow* Poets were traditionally honored with crowns of laurel, which was sacred to Apollo.

[3] *Happy—happier … earth* Paraphrased from Hemans's own "Corinne at the Capitol" (ll. 45–48).

[4] *mantles* Here, foams.

Fame, Fame! thou canst not be the stay° *support*
Unto the drooping reed,
The cool fresh fountain in the day
Of the soul's feverish need:
Where must the lone one turn or flee?—
Not unto thee—oh! not to thee!

—1829

John Clare
1793 – 1864

Later in his life, John Clare recalled that, as a young aspiring poet, he had made a brief effort to master the rules of grammar; however, "finding a jumble of words classed together under this name, and that name and this such-a-figure of speech and that another-hard-worded figure, I turned from further notice of it in instant disgust." Clare, however, read widely, particularly the work of other poets, and he chose to concentrate on the rhythm and sounds of his poetry, honing his craft carefully and steeping his writing in the dialect of his home town.

Born in Northamptonshire, England, in 1793 to Parker Clare, a poor thresher, and Ann Stimson, daughter of the town shepherd, John Clare grew up in a house where his love for reading and writing was an anomaly—though both his parents passed on to him numerous traditional hymns, ballads, and verses. While attempting to perfect the rhythms and meters of his first volume, *Poems Descriptive of Rural Life and Scenery* (1820), Clare would recite his poems to his parents for approval. When this volume was published, Clare was marketed as successor to Robert Burns: a poet shaped by the language and customs of rural life. The book enjoyed considerable success, and curious readers would often come to observe this "peasant poet" working in the fields.

With a keen eye for the natural world, Clare wrote several poems celebrating the niches in which various animals flourish. If Clare is frequently regarded as a nature poet, it is largely because of his evocation of these habitats. As he saw many of these animals hunted, their habitats destroyed, and what he observed to be the delicate balance between humanity and nature threatened, the mood of Clare's nature poems became darker and the tone more indignant. Of particular concern to Clare was the increasing division of the commons—the closing of public pathways, and the general enclosure of open land. Clare's home parish of Helpston was affected by the enclosures in 1809, and his protests against this can be seen in such poems as "Remembrances" and "The Lament of Swordy Well."

Building on the success of his debut, Clare published *The Village Minstrel* (1821), *The Shepherd's Calendar* (1827), and *The Rural Muse* (1835), but these works did not enjoy the popularity of Clare's first volume. The degree to which these successive disappointments, coupled with the pressures of providing for a steadily growing family, may have affected his mental health is unclear, but by 1830 Clare was unquestionably displaying symptoms of insanity. In that year, while watching a production of *The Merchant of Venice*, Clare became so incensed by the character Shylock demanding his pound of flesh that he began to upbraid the actor and had to be removed from the theater. He often imagined himself to be Lord Byron, and in that connection wrote "Don Juan: A Poem," a continuation of Byron's unfinished *Don Juan*. Clare also insisted that he was possessed of (or by) two wives—one his actual wife, and the other his dead childhood sweetheart and muse, Mary Joyce (the subject of "To Mary").

Clare was placed in a private asylum in 1837 and later in the Northampton general lunatic asylum, where he continued to write poems. He escaped from the first asylum in 1841 and walked eighty miles home, eating grass to survive, after which he was committed to the second institution, where he remained until his death some twenty-three years later.

Some of Clare's most interesting poems were written while he was institutionalized. In many of these later, "mad" lyrics, critics have found an inspired desolation; in others they have discerned interesting points of connection with his earlier work and with that of other poets. In "I Am," for example, Clare signals his increasing estrangement from the world; like some other Romantic poets, he sees in childhood an altogether different, and entirely blissful, form of asylum. Meanwhile, Clare's early "nesting" poems ("Mouse's Nest," for example) find analogues in later fantasies such as "Clock A Clay."

Clare died in May 1864 and was largely forgotten until the mid-twentieth century. Since that time, however, he has consistently been seen as one of the more important poetic voices of the first half of the nineteenth century. For many years his poems suffered at hands of editors who sought to standardize his spelling and punctuation and to remove his idiosyncratic use of dialect; recently, however, efforts have been made to restore the poems, enabling readers to experience them as Clare intended.

⌘⌘⌘

Written in November

Autumn I love thy latter end to view
In cold novembers[1] day so bleak & bare
When like lifes dwindld thread worn nearly thro
Wi lingering pottering° pace & head bleachd bare *dawdling*
Thou like an old man bids the world adieu
I love thee well & often when a child
Have roamd the bare brown heath a flower to find
& in the moss clad vale & wood bank wild
Have cropt the little bell flowers paley blue
That trembling peept the sheltering bush behind
When winnowing north winds cold & blealy° blew *bleakly*
How have I joyd wi dithering° hands to find *shivering*
Each fading flower & still how sweet the blast
Woud bleak novembers hour Restore the joy thats past
—1821

[1] *novembers* The usual practice of this anthology regarding modernization of spelling and punctuation has not been followed in the case of Clare; his idiosyncrasies have been retained.

[*The Lament of Swordy Well*][2]

Petitioners are full of prayers
To fall in pitys way
But if her hand the gift forbears
Theyll sooner swear then pray
They're not the worst to want who lurch[3]
On plenty with complaints
No more then those who go to church
Are eer the better saints

I hold no hat to beg a mite° *coin*
Nor pick it up when thrown
Nor limping leg I hold in sight
But pray to keep my own
Where profit gets his clutches in
Theres little he will leave

[2] *Swordy Well* Area of land near Clare's home parish of Helpston. Once the site of a stone quarry, Swordy Well (also called Swaddy Well) was a common space used for grazing and other purposes until 1809, when it was made private by an act of enclosure. Part of the enclosed space was converted to farmland, and part was used again as a quarry.

[3] *lurch* Consume rapidly, so as to get as much as possible for oneself.

Gain stooping for a single pin
Will stick it on his sleeve

For passers bye I never pin
No troubles to my breast
Nor carry round some names to win
More money from the rest
Im swordy well a piece of land
Thats fell upon the town[1]
Who worked me till I couldnt stand
& crush me now Im down

In parish bonds I well may wail
Reduced to every shift[2]
Pity may grieve at troubles tale
But cunning shares the gift
Harvests with plenty on his brow
Leaves losses taunts with me
Yet gain comes yearly with the plough
& will not let me be

Alas dependence thou'rt a brute
Want° only understands *privation*
His feelings wither branch & root
That falls in parish hands
The muck that clouts the ploughmans shoe
The moss that hides the stone
Now Im become the parish due
Is more then I can own

Though Im no man yet any wrong
Some sort of right may seek
& I am glad if een a song
Gives me the room to speak

Ive got among such grubbling° geer *digging*
& such a hungry pack
If I brought harvests twice a year
They'd bring me nothing back

When war their tyrant prices got
I trembled with alarms
They fell & saved my little spot
Or towns had turned to farms
Let profit keep an humble place
That gentry may be known
Let pedigrees their honours trace
& toil enjoy its own

The silver springs grown naked dykes
Scarce own a bunch of rushes
When grain got high the tasteless tykes[3]
Grubbed up trees banks & bushes
& me they turned me inside out
For sand & grit & stones
& turned my old green hills about
& pickt my very bones

These things that claim my own as theirs
Where born but yesterday
But ere I fell to town affairs
I were as proud as they
I kept my horses cows & sheep
& built the town below
Ere they had cat or dog to keep
& then to use me so

Parish allowance gaunt & dread
Had it the earth to keep
Would even pine the bees to dead[4]
To save an extra keep
Prides workhouse is a place that yields
From poverty its gains
& mines a workhouse for the fields
A starving the remains

---

[1] *Thats fell upon the town* That has become dependent on the town's charity. Before 1834, each parish administered its own relief for the poor, which might be provided in the form of a minimum allowance or via a workhouse, an institution in which the poor were given lodging and a minimal level of sustenance in exchange for work performed. After an 1834 act standardized the treatment of the poor across the country, allowances were discontinued; workhouses, the only remaining option, were designed to be as unpleasant as possible so as to discourage people from entering them.

[2] *shift* I.e., inventive means of survival.

[3] *tykes* Rustics, base people.

[4] *pine the … dead* Cause the bees to suffer until they die.

The bees flye round in feeble rings
& find no blossom bye
Then thrum their almost weary wings
Upon the moss & die
Rabbits that find my hills turned oer
Forsake my poor abode
They dread a workhouse like the poor
& nibble on the road

If with a clover bottle° now *flower*
Spring dares to lift her head
The next day brings the hasty plough
& makes me miserys bed
The butterflyes may wir° & come *whir*
I cannot keep em now
Nor can they bear my parish home
That withers on my brow

No now not een a stone can lie
Im just what eer they like
My hedges like the winter flye
& leave me but the dyke
My gates are thrown from off the hooks
The parish thoroughfare
Lord he thats in the parish books
Has little wealth to spare

I couldnt keep a dust of grit
Nor scarce a grain of sand
But bags & carts claimed every bit
& now theyve got the land
I used to bring the summers life
To many a butterflye
But in oppressions iron strife
Dead tussocks bow & sigh

Ive scarce a nook to call my own
For things that creep or flye
The beetle hiding neath a stone
Does well to hurry bye
Stock° eats my struggles every day *livestock*
As bare as any road
He's sure to be in somthings way
If eer he stirs abroad

I am no man to whine & beg
But fond of freedom still
I hing° no lies on pitys peg *hang*
To bring a gris to mill[1]
On pitys back I neednt jump
My looks speak loud alone
My only tree they've left a stump
& nought remains my own

My mossy hills gains greedy hand
& more then greedy mind
Levels into a russet land
Nor leaves a bent[2] behind
In summers gone I bloomed in pride
Folks came for miles to prize
My flowers that bloomed no where beside
& scarce believe their eyes

Yet worried with a greedy pack
They rend & delve & tear
The very grass from off my back
Ive scarce a rag to wear
Gain takes my freedom all away
Since its dull suit I wore
& yet scorn vows I never pay
& hurts me more & more

Who ever pays me rent or takes it
Ive neither words or dates
One makes the law & others break it
& stop my mouth with rates[3]

& should the price of grain get high
Lord help & keep it low

[1] *bring a gris to mill* "To bring grist to the mill" (literally, "to bring grain to the flour mill for grinding") is a proverbial phrase meaning "to turn a situation to one's own advantage."

[2] *bent* Single reed or blade of grass.

[3] *Who ever … with rates* This partial verse is omitted in some versions of the poem.

I shant possess a single flye
Or get a weed to grow
I shant possess a yard of ground
To bid a mouse to thrive
For gain has put me in a pound[1]
I scarce can keep alive

Im not a man as some may think
Petitioning for loss
Of cow that dyed of ages drink
& spavin foundered horse[2]
For which some beg a list of pelf° *stolen riches*
& seem on loss to thrive
But I petition for my self
& beg to keep alive

Theres folks that make a mort[3] of bother
& oer lost gainings whine
But lord of me Im this & tother
Theres no one cares for mine
They strip the grass from off my back
& take my things away
Im robbed by every outlaw pack
& nones to say em nay[4]

I own Im poor like many more
But then the poor mun° live *must*
& many came for miles before
For what I had to give
But since I fell upon the town
They pass me with a sigh
Ive scarce the room to say sit down
& so they wander bye

But when a poor man is allowed
So to enslave another
Well may the worlds tongue prate aloud
How brother uses brother
I couldnt keep a bush to stand
For years but what was gone
& now I hant° a foot of land *haven't*
To keep a rabbit on

They used to come & feed at night
When dangers day was gone
& in the morning out of sight
Hide underneath a stone
Im fain to shun the greedy pack
That now so tear & brag
They strip my coat from off my back
& scarcely leave a rag
That like the parish hurt & hurt
While gains new suit I wear
Then swear I never pay 'em for't
& add to my despair[5]

Though now I seem so full of clack° *noise*
Yet when yer' riding bye
The very birds upon my back
Are not more fain° to flye *eager*
I feel so lorn° in this disgrace *forlorn*
God send the grains to fall
I am the oldest in the place
& the worst served of all

Lord bless ye I was kind to all
& poverty in me
Could always find a humble stall
A rest & lodging free
Poor bodys with an hungry ass
I welcomed many a day
& gave him tether room & grass
& never said him nay

There was a time my bit of ground
Made freemen of the slave

[1] *pound* Enclosure in which trespassing or lost livestock are kept until claimed.

[2] *spavin foundered horse* Horse unable to work because of a bone growth in a leg joint.

[3] *a mort* A lot.

[4] *Im not a man … say em nay* These verses are omitted in some versions of the poem.

[5] *But when … despair* These verses are omitted in some versions of the poem.

The ass no pindard[1] dare to pound° *impound*
When I his supper gave
The gipseys camp was not affraid
I made his dwelling free
Till vile enclosure came & made
A parish slave of me

The gipseys further on sojourn
No parish bounds they like
No sticks I own & would earth burn
I shouldnt own a dyke
I am no friend to lawless work
Nor would a rebel be
& why I call a christian turk[2]
Is they are turks to me

& if I could but find a friend
With no deciet to sham
Who'd send me some few sheep to tend
& leave me as I am
To keep my hills from cart & plough
& strife of mongerel men
& as spring found me find me now
I should look up agen

& save his Lordships woods that past
The day of danger dwell
Of all the fields I am the last
That my own face can tell
Yet what with stone pits delving holes
& strife to buy & sell
My name will quickly be the whole
Thats left of swordy well
—1935 (WRITTEN 1821–24)

[1] *pindard* Contraction meaning "pinder would." A pinder policed enclosures and impounded any livestock not belonging to the land's owners.

[2] *turk* I.e., cruel; "Turk" was at this time used to mean "Muslim" and carried connotations of brutality and barbarism that reflected prejudices commonly held in Britain.

Sonnet
[*I am*]

I feel I am;—I only know I am,
And plod upon the earth, as dull and void:
Earth's prison chilled my body with its dram[3]
Of dullness, and my soaring thoughts destroyed,
I fled to solitudes from passions dream,
But strife persued—I only know, I am,
I was a being created in the race
Of men disdaining bounds of place and time:—
A spirit that could travel o'er the space
Of earth and heaven,—like a thought sublime,
Tracing creation, like my maker, free,—
A soul unshackled—like eternity,
Spurning earth's vain and soul debasing thrall
But now I only know I am,—that's all.
—1932 (WRITTEN C. 1842–46)

I Am

I am—yet what I am, none cares or knows;
My friends forsake me like a memory lost:—
I am the self-consumer of my woes;—
They rise and vanish in oblivion's host,
Like shadows in love's frenzied stifled throes:—
And yet I am, and live—like vapours tost

Into the nothingness of scorn and noise,—
Into the living sea of waking dreams,
Where there is neither sense of life or joys,
But the vast shipwreck of my lifes esteems;
Even the dearest, that I love the best
Are strange—nay, rather stranger than the rest.[4]

I long for scenes, where man hath never trod
A place where woman never smiled or wept
There to abide with my Creator, God;

[3] *dram* Measurement of weight.

[4] *Even the … rest* Apparently Clare's family never came to visit him in the Northampton asylum.

And sleep as I in childhood, sweetly slept,
Untroubling, and untroubled where I lie,
The grass below—above the vaulted sky.
—1848

Clock A Clay[1]

In the cowslips peeps I lye[2]
Hidden from the buzzing fly
While green grass beneath me lies
Pearled wi' dew like fishes eyes
Here I lye a Clock a clay
Waiting for the time o' day[3]

While grassy forests quake surprise
And the wild wind sobs and sighs
My gold home rocks as like to fall
On its pillars green and tall
When the pattering rain drives bye
Clock a Clay keeps warm and dry

Day by day and night by night
All the week I hide from sight
In the cowslips peeps I lye
In rain and dew still warm and dry
Day and night and night and day
Red black spotted clock a clay

My home it shakes in wind and showers
Pale green pillar top't wi' flowers
Bending at the wild winds breath
Till I touch the grass beneath
Here still I live lone clock a clay
Watching for the time of day
—1873 (WRITTEN C. 1848)

[1] *Clock A Clay* Ladybug.

[2] *In … lye* Cf. the spirit Ariel's song in Shakespeare's *The Tempest*, 5.1.88–89: "Where the bee sucks, there suck I: / In the cowslip's bell I lie"; *cowslips* Yellow primrose; *peeps* Pips; blossoms.

[3] *Waiting … day* In a popular game, children would tell the time by counting the number of taps necessary to make the ladybug fly home.

John Keats

1795 – 1821

John Keats has come to epitomize the popular conception of the Romantic poet as a passionate dreamer whose intense, sensuous poetry celebrates the world of the imagination over that of everyday life. Keats published only 54 poems in his short lifetime, but his work ranges across a number of poetic genres, including lyric, romance, and epic. In each of these genres his poetry seeks beauty and truth that will transcend the world of suffering, always questioning its own process of interpretation.

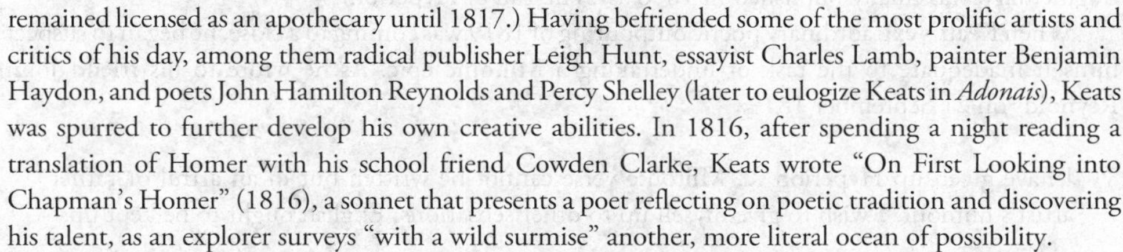

The eldest of four children, John Keats was born in London on 31 October 1795. He lost both his parents by the time he was fourteen—his father in a riding accident and his mother of tuberculosis (then commonly known as consumption). After his mother's death, Keats came under the care of two guardians. He continued to attend Enfield School, a liberal institution where he first became acquainted with Leigh Hunt's radical paper the *Examiner*, and where his interest in poetry grew, particularly after reading the poetry of Edmund Spenser. Keats's friend Charles Brown said it was *The Faerie Queene* that awakened Keats's talent for expressing the "acute sense of beauty" he possessed.

After a promising but incomplete schooling, Keats apprenticed himself in 1815 to a surgeon at Guy's Hospital in London. (He remained licensed as an apothecary until 1817.) Having befriended some of the most prolific artists and critics of his day, among them radical publisher Leigh Hunt, essayist Charles Lamb, painter Benjamin Haydon, and poets John Hamilton Reynolds and Percy Shelley (later to eulogize Keats in *Adonais*), Keats was spurred to further develop his own creative abilities. In 1816, after spending a night reading a translation of Homer with his school friend Cowden Clarke, Keats wrote "On First Looking into Chapman's Homer" (1816), a sonnet that presents a poet reflecting on poetic tradition and discovering his talent, as an explorer surveys "with a wild surmise" another, more literal ocean of possibility.

Shortly thereafter, Keats composed "Sleep and Poetry" (1817), a poetic manifesto of sorts in which he proclaims his devotion to a new type of poetry, one in the style of Wordsworth, devoted to nature and the human heart. By aligning himself with Wordsworth's naturalism, Keats ensured the condemnation of critics; nevertheless, that same year he chose to give up surgery and devote himself entirely to poetry. This decision was most likely sealed by Leigh Hunt's first "Young Poets" article (*Examiner*, December 1816), in which he identified Keats, Shelley, and Reynolds as the leaders of a new generation of poets.

Keats's first volume, *Poems* (1817), received little critical attention. The following year he published the long and ambitious romance *Endymion* (1818), about a shepherd-prince who pursues his elusive feminine ideal. The book was sharply criticized in a famous review published in the *Quarterly Review*, where Keats and his friend Hunt were ridiculed as representing "the Cockney school of poetry." Keats endured further criticism when he read "Hymn to Pan" from *Endymion* to the contemporary poet he most admired, Wordsworth; the elder poet ungenerously dismissed it as "a very pretty piece of paganism."

Despite such discouragement, Keats continued to pursue his poetic ideals. In a series of now-famous letters to Benjamin Bailey, he explored his aesthetic ideas and sought to define the purpose of literature for modern life. Keats's letters to his friends and family are justly acclaimed for their intuitions about life, suffering, and poetry. To Keats we owe the concepts of "negative capability," the "chameleon poet," and "the vale of Soul-making." He particularly admired what he saw as Shakespeare's chameleon-like ability to escape from his personality and enter fully into the being of his characters.

During this time, Keats fell in love with the lively and flirtatious Fanny Brawne, who became a kind of muse. Though they became engaged, Keats wanted to gain financial security before marrying. He had begun as well to be haunted by fears of his own early death. (Throat ulcers that had appeared during a walking tour in poor weather the previous summer had become chronic.) It was in this set of tumultuous emotional circumstances that Keats began one of the most extraordinary periods of creativity in the history of English literature. Between January and September of 1819 he composed all six of his "great Odes"—"Ode to Psyche," "Ode to a Nightingale," "Ode on a Grecian Urn," "Ode on Indolence," "Ode on Melancholy," and "To Autumn"—as well as "The Eve of St. Agnes," "La Belle Dame sans Merci," "Lamia," and a number of sonnets. Generations of readers have been seduced by the sensuous immediacy of this poetry.

Keats's largest poetic project was *Hyperion*, a blank-verse epic on Jupiter's dethroning of Saturn and Apollo's overthrow of Hyperion. An intense study of cultural loss, the poem is a self-consciously Miltonic exercise that Keats kept returning to but never completed. He began the poem in the autumn of 1818, but put the manuscript aside in April of the following year. (This first fragmentary version of the poem was published as "Hyperion: A Fragment" in the 1820 volume of his verse.)

In the summer he resumed work on the project, this time casting the story within the frame of a poet's dream vision, but he stopped for a second time in September. (This second version, also fragmentary, was finally published in 1856 as "The Fall of Hyperion.")

When Keats's extraordinary poetic outpouring of 1819 was coming to a close, he began to suspect himself inadequate to the task of undertaking a Miltonic epic. As he wrote to his friend John Reynolds on 21 September 1819:

> I have given up Hyperion … Miltonic verse cannot be written but in an artful or rather artist's humour. I wish to give myself up to other sensations. English ought to be kept up.

Keats wrote little after September of 1819, but he published his third volume of poetry, *Lamia, Isabella, The Eve of St. Agnes, and Other Poems*, in 1820—defiantly advertising himself on the cover as "the author of *Endymion*." Critics were gradually acquiring a taste for Keats's work, but by this time Keats was very ill, having contracted tuberculosis. With his lungs weakened and his throat still ulcerating, Keats declined an invitation to join Shelley and his circle in Pisa in August of 1820, and instead went to Rome, where he died in the house at the base of the Spanish Steps that is now the Keats-Shelley Memorial House. Keats was buried in the Protestant Cemetery in Rome.

In the generations since his death, many have wondered what Keats would have accomplished had he lived. Such thoughts, however, focus on the tragedy of the poet's death, rather than on the sustained richness of his achievement. Before his death, Keats asked that his epitaph be "Here lies one whose name was writ in water." (Though his friends complied, they added above, "This Grave contains all that was Mortal of a YOUNG ENGLISH POET, Who on his Death Bed in the Bitterness of his Heart at the Malicious Power of his Enemies, Desired these Words to be incised on his Tomb Stone.") On visiting his gravesite in 1877, Oscar Wilde supplied another epitaph: "A Priest of Beauty slain before his time." But the last sentences of Keats's last letter to Charles Brown are perhaps more evocative: "I can scarcely bid you good bye even in a letter. I always made an awkward bow."

⌘⌘⌘

On First Looking into Chapman's Homer[1]

Much have I travell'd in the realms of gold,
 And many goodly states and kingdoms seen;
 Round many western islands have I been
Which bards in fealty to Apollo[2] hold.
Oft of one wide expanse had I been told
 That deep-brow'd Homer ruled as his demesne;
 Yet never did I breathe its pure serene,
Till I heard Chapman speak out loud and bold:
Then felt I like some watcher of the skies
 When a new planet swims into his ken;[3]
Or like stout Cortez[4] when with eagle eyes
 He star'd at the Pacific—and all his men
Look'd at each other with a wild surmise—
 Silent, upon a peak in Darien.
—1816

[1] *On … Homer* Written in October 1816, on the morning after Keats and his friend and mentor Charles Cowden Clarke had stayed up all night reading the 1614 translation of Homer by George Chapman (1559–1634).

[2] *Apollo* Greek god of poetry.

[3] *a new … ken* William Herschel had discovered Uranus in 1781.

[4] *Cortez* The first European to see the Pacific (from the Isthmus of Darien in Panama) was not actually Hernán Cortez (1485–1547), the conqueror of Mexico, but Vasco Nuñez de Balboa (1475–1519) in 1513.

On the Grasshopper and Cricket[5]

The poetry of earth is never dead:
 When all the birds are faint with the hot sun,
 And hide in cooling trees, a voice will run
From hedge to hedge about the new-mown mead;
That is the Grasshopper's—he takes the lead
 In summer luxury—he has never done
 With his delights; for when tired out with fun
He rests at ease beneath some pleasant weed.
The poetry of earth is ceasing never:
 On a lone winter evening, when the frost
 Has wrought a silence, from the stove there shrills
The Cricket's song, in warmth increasing ever,
 And seems to one in drowsiness half lost,
 The Grasshopper's among some grassy hills.
—1817

Sleep and Poetry

As I lay in my bed slepe full unmete° *unallotted*
Was unto me, but why that I ne might
Rest I ne wist,° for there n'as° erthly *knew / was no*
 wight° *creature*

[5] *On the Grasshopper and Cricket* This poem was composed on 30 December 1816, when Keats was visiting his friend Leigh Hunt (1784–1859) in Hampstead. The poets were reading Thomas Moore's English translation of the *Odes* of Anacreon; after reading Ode 34, which is in praise of a grasshopper, they noticed a cricket near the fireplace. Hunt spontaneously suggested a sonnet-writing contest on the subject of the grasshopper and the cricket, and he and Keats both wrote sonnets within a time limit of 15 minutes. Each poet modestly claimed that the other had won.

[As I suppose] had more of hertis ese° *heart's ease*
Than I, for I n'ad° sickness nor disese.[1] *had not*
CHAUCER

What is more gentle than a wind in summer?
What is more soothing than the pretty hummer
That stays one moment in an open flower,
And buzzes cheerily from bower to bower?
What is more tranquil than a musk-rose blowing° *blossoming*
In a green island, far from all men's knowing?
More healthful than the leafiness of dales?
More secret than a nest of nightingales?
More serene than Cordelia's[2] countenance?
More full of visions than a high romance?
What, but thee Sleep? Soft closer of our eyes!
Low murmurer of tender lullabies!
Light hoverer around our happy pillows!
Wreather of poppy buds, and weeping willows!
Silent entangler of a beauty's tresses!
Most happy listener! when the morning blesses
Thee for enlivening all the cheerful eyes
That glance so brightly at the new sun-rise.

But what is higher beyond thought than thee?
Fresher than berries of a mountain tree?
More strange, more beautiful, more smooth, more regal,
Than wings of swans, than doves, than dim-seen eagle?
What is it? And to what shall I compare it?
It has a glory, and naught else can share it:
The thought thereof is awful, sweet, and holy,
Chasing away all worldliness and folly;
Coming sometimes like fearful claps of thunder,
Or the low rumblings earth's regions under;
And sometimes like a gentle whispering
Of all the secrets of some wond'rous thing
That breathes about us in the vacant air;
So that we look around with prying stare,
Perhaps to see shapes of light, aërial limning,[3]
And catch soft floatings from a faint-heard hymning;
To see the laurel wreath,[4] on high suspended,
That is to crown our name when life is ended.
Sometimes it gives a glory to the voice,
And from the heart up-springs, "Rejoice! rejoice!"
Sounds which will reach the Framer of all things,
And die away in ardent mutterings.

No one who once the glorious sun has seen,
And all the clouds, and felt his bosom clean
For his great Maker's presence, but must know
What 'tis I mean, and feel his being glow:
Therefore no insult will I give his spirit,
By telling what he sees from native merit.

O Poesy! For thee I hold my pen
That am not yet a glorious denizen
Of thy wide heaven—Should I rather kneel
Upon some mountain-top until I feel
A glowing splendour round about me hung,
And echo back the voice of thine own tongue?
O Poesy! For thee I grasp my pen
That am not yet a glorious denizen
Of thy wide heaven; yet, to my ardent prayer,
Yield from thy sanctuary some clear air,
Smoothed for intoxication by the breath
Of flowering bays, that I may die a death
Of luxury, and my young spirit follow
The morning sun-beams to the great Apollo[5]
Like a fresh sacrifice; or, if I can bear
The o'erwhelming sweets, 'twill bring to me the fair
Visions of all places: a bowery nook
Will be elysium[6]—an eternal book
Whence I may copy many a lovely saying

[1] *As … disese* From *The Floure and the Leafe* 17–21, which was then thought to have been written by Chaucer.

[2] *Cordelia* Daughter of King Lear in Shakespeare's *King Lear*.

[3] *limning* Painting.

[4] *laurel wreath* Wreaths made of leaves of the bay laurel were traditionally bestowed upon those who distinguished themselves in poetry.

[5] *Apollo* Greek god of poetry.

[6] *elysium* State of perfect happiness. From the Elysium of Greek mythology, the place where the blessed reside after death.

About the leaves, and flowers—about the playing
Of nymphs in woods, and fountains; and the shade
Keeping a silence round a sleeping maid;
And many a verse from so strange influence
That we must ever wonder how, and whence
It came. Also imaginings will hover
Round my fire-side, and haply there discover
Vistas of solemn beauty, where I'd wander
In happy silence, like the clear Meander[1]
Through its lone vales; and where I found a spot
Of awfuller shade, or an enchanted grot,° *grotto*
Or a green hill o'erspread with chequered dress
Of flowers, and fearful from its loveliness,
Write on my tablets all that was permitted,
All that was for our human senses fitted.
Then the events of this wide world I'd seize
Like a strong giant, and my spirit tease
Till at its shoulders it should proudly see
Wings to find out an immortality.

Stop and consider! Life is but a day;
A fragile dew-drop on its perilous way
From a tree's summit; a poor Indian's sleep
While his boat hastens to the monstrous steep
Of Montmorenci.[2] Why so sad a moan?
Life is the rose's hope while yet unblown;
The reading of an ever-changing tale;
The light uplifting of a maiden's veil;
A pigeon tumbling in clear summer air;
A laughing school-boy, without grief or care,
Riding the springy branches of an elm.

O for ten years, that I may overwhelm
Myself in poesy; so I may do the deed
That my own soul has to itself decreed.
Then will I pass the countries that I see
In long perspective, and continually
Taste their pure fountains. First the realm I'll pass
Of Flora, and old Pan:[3] sleep in the grass,
Feed upon apples red, and strawberries,
And choose each pleasure that my fancy sees;
Catch the white-handed nymphs in shady places,
To woo sweet kisses from averted faces,
Play with their fingers, touch their shoulders white
Into a pretty shrinking with a bite
As hard as lips can make it: till agreed,
A lovely tale of human life we'll read
And one will teach a tame dove how it best
May fan the cool air gently o'er my rest;
Another, bending o'er her nimble tread,
Will set a green robe floating round her head,
And still will dance with ever varied ease,
Smiling upon the flowers and the trees:
Another will entice me on, and on
Through almond blossoms and rich cinnamon;
Till in the bosom of a leafy world
We rest in silence, like two gems upcurl'd
In the recesses of a pearly shell.

And can I ever bid these joys farewell?
Yes, I must pass them for a nobler life,
Where I may find the agonies, the strife
Of human hearts: for lo! I see afar,
O'er sailing the blue cragginess, a car° *chariot*
And steeds with streamy manes—the charioteer
Looks out upon the winds with glorious fear:
And now the numerous tramplings quiver lightly
Along a huge cloud's ridge; and now with sprightly
Wheel downward come they into fresher skies,
Tipt round with silver from the sun's bright eyes.
Still downward with capacious whirl they glide,
And now I see them on the green-hill's side
In breezy rest among the nodding stalks.
The charioteer with wond'rous gesture talks
To the trees and mountains; and there soon appear
Shapes of delight, of mystery, and fear,

[1] *Meander* Winding river in Asia Minor.

[2] *Montmorenci* Montmorency Falls near Québec City, Canada.

[3] *Flora … Pan* In Greek mythology, the goddess of flowers and the shepherd god of nature, respectively. The realm of Flora and Pan is that of pastoral poesy, which, according to Virgil, should be the genre with which the aspiring poet begins, eventually working his way up to the epic.

Passing along before a dusky space
Made by some mighty oaks: as they would chase
Some ever-fleeting music on they sweep.
Lo! how they murmur, laugh, and smile, and weep:
Some with upholden hand and mouth severe;
Some with their faces muffled to the ear
Between their arms; some, clear in youthful bloom,
Go glad and smilingly athwart the gloom;
Some looking back, and some with upward gaze;
Yes, thousands in a thousand different ways
Flit onward—now a lovely wreath of girls
Dancing their sleek hair into tangled curls;
And now broad wings. Most awfully intent
The driver of those steeds is forward bent,
And seems to listen: O that I might know
All that he writes with such a hurrying glow.

The visions all are fled—the car is fled
Into the light of heaven, and in their stead
A sense of real things comes doubly strong,
And, like a muddy stream, would bear along
My soul to nothingness: but I will strive
Against all doubtings, and will keep alive
The thought of that same chariot, and the strange
Journey it went.

Is there so small a range
In the present strength of manhood, that the high
Imagination cannot freely fly
As she was wont of old? prepare her steeds,
Paw up against the light, and do strange deeds
Upon the clouds? Has she not shown us all?
From the clear space of ether, to the small
Breath of new buds unfolding? From the meaning
Of Jove's[1] large eyebrow, to the tender greening
Of April meadows? Here her altar shone,
E'en in this isle; and who could paragon
The fervid choir that lifted up a noise
Of harmony, to where it aye will poise
Its mighty self of convoluting sound,
Huge as a planet, and like that roll round,
Eternally around a dizzy void?
Ay, in those days the Muses[2] were nigh cloy'd
With honours; nor had any other care
Than to sing out and sooth their wavy hair.

Could all this be forgotten? Yes, a schism
Nurtured by foppery and barbarism,
Made great Apollo blush for this his land.
Men were thought wise who could not understand
His glories: with a puling infant's force
They sway'd about upon a rocking horse,
And thought it Pegasus.[3] Ah dismal soul'd!
The winds of heaven blew, the ocean roll'd
Its gathering waves—ye felt it not. The blue
Bared its eternal bosom, and the dew
Of summer nights collected still to make
The morning precious: beauty was awake!
Why were ye not awake? But ye were dead
To things ye knew not of—were closely wed
To musty laws lined out with wretched rule
And compass vile: so that ye taught a school
Of dolts to smooth, inlay, and clip, and fit,
Till, like the certain wands of Jacob's wit,[4]
Their verses tallied. Easy was the task:
A thousand handicraftsmen wore the mask
Of Poesy. Ill-fated, impious race!
That blasphemed the bright Lyrist[5] to his face,
And did not know it—no, they went about,
Holding a poor, decrepit standard out

[1] *Jove* Roman king of the gods.

[2] *Muses* In Greek mythology, nine daughters of Zeus and Mnemosyne, each of whom presided over and provided inspiration for an aspect of learning or the arts.

[3] *Pegasus* Great winged horse of Greek mythology. This line is a reference to William Hazlitt's essay "On Milton's Versification" (1815), in which he says, on the use of the heroic couplet by eighteenth-century poets, "Dr. Johnson and Pope would have turned [Milton's] vaulting Pegasus into a rocking-horse."

[4] *Jacob's wit* See Genesis 30.27–43, in which Jacob increases his wealth at the expense of Laban.

[5] *the bright Lyrist* I.e., Apollo.

Mark'd with most flimsy mottos, and in large
The name of one Boileau![1]

O ye whose charge
It is to hover round our pleasant hills!
Whose congregated majesty so fills
My boundly[2] reverence, that I cannot trace
Your hallowed names, in this unholy place,
So near those common folk; did not their shames
Affright you? Did our old lamenting Thames° *river*
Delight you? Did ye never cluster round
Delicious Avon,° with a mournful sound, *river*
And weep? Or did ye wholly bid adieu
To regions where no more the laurel grew?
Or did ye stay to give a welcoming
To some lone spirits[3] who could proudly sing
Their youth away, and die? 'Twas even so:
But let me think away those times of woe:
Now 'tis a fairer season; ye have breathed
Rich benedictions o'er us; ye have wreathed
Fresh garlands: for sweet music has been heard
In many places—some has been upstirr'd
From out its crystal dwelling in a lake,
By a swan's ebon bill;[4] from a thick brake,° *thicket*
Nested and quiet in a valley mild,
Bubbles a pipe;[5] fine sounds are floating wild
About the earth: happy are ye and glad.

These things are doubtless: yet in truth we've had
Strange thunders from the potency of song;
Mingled indeed with what is sweet and strong,
From majesty: but in clear truth the themes
Are ugly clubs, the poets Polyphemes[6]
Disturbing the grand sea. A drainless shower
Of light is poesy; 'tis the supreme of power;
'Tis might half slumb'ring on its own right arm.
The very archings of her eye-lids charm
A thousand willing agents to obey,
And still she governs with the mildest sway:
But strength alone though of the Muses born
Is like a fallen angel: trees uptorn,
Darkness, and worms, and shrouds, and sepulchres
Delight it; for it feeds upon the burrs,
And thorns of life; forgetting the great end
Of poesy, that it should be a friend
To sooth the cares, and lift the thoughts of man.

Yet I rejoice: a myrtle fairer than
E'er grew in Paphos,[7] from the bitter weeds
Lifts its sweet head into the air, and feeds
A silent space with ever sprouting green.
All tenderest birds there find a pleasant screen,
Creep through the shade with jaunty fluttering,
Nibble the little cupped flowers and sing.
Then let us clear away the choking thorns
From round its gentle stem; let the young fawns,
Yeaned° in after times, when we are flown, *brought forth*
Find a fresh sward° beneath it, overgrown *turf*
With simple flowers: let there nothing be
More boisterous than a lover's bended knee;
Nought more ungentle than the placid look
Of one who leans upon a closed book;
Nought more untranquil than the grassy slopes
Between two hills. All hail delightful hopes!
As she was wont, th'imagination
Into most lovely labyrinths will be gone,
And they shall be accounted poet kings
Who simply tell the most heart-easing things.
O may these joys be ripe before I die.

[1] *Boileau* French literary critic Nicolas Boileau-Despréaux (1636–1711), whose *L'Art Poétique* (1674), a verse treatise on literary aesthetics, was extremely influential among English poets.

[2] *boundly* Term coined by Keats, meaning either "boundless" or "bounden."

[3] *some lone spirits* Reference to poets Thomas Chatterton (1752–70), Henry White (1785–1806), and others, who died young, without receiving the critical attention their work deserved.

[4] *swan's ebon bill* Reference to William Wordsworth (1770–1850), who, along with Coleridge and Southey, was known as a "Lake Poet."

[5] *from a … pipe* Reference to poet Leigh Hunt (1784–1859).

[6] *Polyphemes* One-eyed, club-wielding giant in Homer's *Odyssey*.

[7] *Paphos* City in Cyprus that is the site of a famous temple to Venus, goddess of love and beauty. Myrtle (line 248) is also associated with Venus.

Will not some say that I presumptuously
Have spoken? that from hastening disgrace
'Twere better far to hide my foolish face?
That whining boyhood should with reverence bow
Ere the dread thunderbolt could reach? How!
If I do hide myself, it sure shall be
In the very fane, the light of Poesy:
If I do fall, at least I will be laid
Beneath the silence of a poplar shade;
And over me the grass shall be smooth shaven;
And there shall be a kind memorial graven.
But off Despondence! miserable bane!
They should not know thee, who athirst to gain
A noble end, are thirsty every hour.
What though I am not wealthy in the dower
Of spanning wisdom; though I do not know
The shiftings of the mighty winds that blow
Hither and thither all the changing thoughts
Of man: though no great minist'ring reason sorts
Out the dark mysteries of human souls
To clear conceiving: yet there ever rolls
A vast idea before me, and I glean
Therefrom my liberty; thence too I've seen
The end and aim of Poesy. 'Tis clear
As any thing most true; as that the year
Is made of the four seasons—manifest
As a large cross, some old cathedral's crest,
Lifted to the white clouds. Therefore should I
Be but the essence of deformity,
A coward, did my very eyelids wink
At speaking out what I have dared to think.
Ah! rather let me like a madman run
Over some precipice; let the hot sun
Melt my Dedalian wings,[1] and drive me down
Convuls'd and headlong! Stay! an inward frown
Of conscience bids me be more calm awhile.
An ocean dim, sprinkled with many an isle,
Spreads awfully before me. How much toil!
How many days! what desperate turmoil!
Ere I can have explored its widenesses.
Ah, what a task! upon my bended knees,
I could unsay those—no, impossible!
Impossible!

For sweet relief I'll dwell
On humbler thoughts, and let this strange assay
Begun in gentleness die so away.
E'en now all tumult from my bosom fades:
I turn full hearted to the friendly aids
That smooth the path of honour; brotherhood,
And friendliness the nurse of mutual good.
The hearty grasp that sends a pleasant sonnet
Into the brain ere one can think upon it;
The silence when some rhymes are coming out;
And when they're come, the very pleasant rout:
The message certain to be done to-morrow.
'Tis perhaps as well that it should be to borrow
Some precious book from out its snug retreat,
To cluster round it when we next shall meet.
Scarce can I scribble on; for lovely airs
Are fluttering round the room like doves in pairs;
Many delights of that glad day recalling,
When first my senses caught their tender falling.
And with these airs come forms of elegance
Stooping their shoulders o'er a horse's prance,
Careless, and grand—fingers soft and round
Parting luxuriant curls—and the swift bound
Of Bacchus from his chariot, when his eye
Made Ariadne's cheek look blushingly.[2]
Thus I remember all the pleasant flow
Of words at opening a portfolio.

Things such as these are ever harbingers
To trains of peaceful images: the stirs
Of a swan's neck unseen among the rushes:

[1] *Dedalian wings* According to Greek mythology, the sculptor Daedalus built wings of wax and feathers so that he and his son Icarus could escape from the island of Crete, where they were imprisoned. Icarus flew too close to the sun, and his wings melted, causing him to fall into the sea.

[2] *Of Bacchus … blushingly* Ariadne, daughter of King Minos of Crete, was abandoned by her lover, Theseus, on the island of Naxos. Bacchus, god of wine, found her there, consoled her, and married her (Ovid, *Metamorphses* 8.172–82). Keats would also have been familiar with the painting *Bacchus and Ariadne* (1523) by Venetian painter Titian (1490–1576).

A linnet starting all about the bushes:
A butterfly, with golden wings broad parted,
Nestling a rose, convuls'd as though it smarted
With over° pleasure—many, many more, *too much*
Might I indulge at large in all my store
Of luxuries: yet I must not forget
Sleep, quiet with his poppy coronet:[1]
For what there may be worthy in these rhymes
I partly owe to him: and thus, the chimes
Of friendly voices had just given place
To as sweet a silence, when I 'gan retrace
The pleasant day, upon a couch at ease.
It was a poet's house who keeps the keys
Of pleasure's temple.[2] Round about were hung
The glorious features of the bards who sung
In other ages—cold and sacred busts
Smiled at each other. Happy he who trusts
To clear Futurity his darling fame!
Then there were fauns and satyrs taking aim
At swelling apples with a frisky leap
And reaching fingers, 'mid a luscious heap
Of vine leaves. Then there rose to view a fane° *temple*
Of liny° marble, and thereto a train *veined*
Of nymphs approaching fairly o'er the sward:
One, loveliest, holding her white hand toward
The dazzling sun-rise: two sisters sweet
Bending their graceful figures till they meet
Over the trippings of a little child:
And some are hearing, eagerly, the wild
Thrilling liquidity of dewy piping.
See, in another picture, nymphs are wiping
Cherishingly Diana's[3] timorous limbs;
A fold of lawny mantle dabbling swims
At the bath's edge, and keeps a gentle motion
With the subsiding crystal: as when ocean
Heaves calmly its broad swelling smoothness o'er
Its rocky marge,° and balances once more *edge*
The patient weeds; that now unshent° *unharmed*
by foam
Feel all about their undulating home.

Sappho's[4] meek head was there half smiling down
At nothing; just as though the earnest frown
Of over thinking had that moment gone
From off her brow, and left her all alone.

Great Alfred's[5] too, with anxious, pitying eyes,
As if he always listened to the sighs
Of the goaded world; and Kosciusko's[6] worn
By horrid suffrance—mightily forlorn.

Petrarch, outstepping from the shady green,
Starts at the sight of Laura;[7] nor can wean
His eyes from her sweet face. Most happy they!
For over them was seen a free display
Of out-spread wings, and from between them shone
The face of Poesy: from off her throne
She overlook'd things that I scarce could tell.
The very sense of where I was might well
Keep Sleep aloof: but more than that there came
Thought after thought to nourish up the flame
Within my breast; so that the morning light
Surprised me even from a sleepless night;
And up I rose refresh'd, and glad, and gay,
Resolving to begin that very day
These lines; and howsoever they be done,
I leave them as a father does his son.
—1817

[1] *poppy coronet* The seed capsules of some species of poppy contain opium, and therefore were associated with sleep.

[2] *It was … temple* Poet Leigh Hunt kept a bed for Keats in his study. Hunt's cottage was filled with busts and pictures, on which the following descriptions are probably based.

[3] *Diana* Roman goddess of chastity, childbirth, and the hunt.

[4] *Sappho* Greek lyric poet of the sixth century BCE.

[5] *Great Alfred* Alfred the Great, King of Wessex from 871 to 899.

[6] *Kosciusko* Polish patriot Tadeusz Kosciusko (1746–1817), who led his countrymen in an uprising against Russia, and also fought for the United States Army in the American struggle for independence.

[7] *Petrarch … Laura* Italian poet Petrarch (1304–74) wrote odes and sonnets in celebration of his beloved, Laura.

On Seeing the Elgin Marbles[1]

My spirit is too weak; mortality
Weighs heavily on me like unwilling sleep,
And each imagined pinnacle and steep
Of godlike hardship, tells me I must die
Like a sick Eagle looking at the sky.
Yet 'tis a gentle luxury to weep,
That I have not the cloudy winds to keep
Fresh for the opening of the morning's eye.
Such dim-conceived glories of the brain
Bring round the heart an indescribable feud;
So do these wonders a most dizzy pain,
That mingles Grecian grandeur with the rude
Wasting of old Time—with a billowy main,° *sea*
A sun, a shadow of a magnitude.
—1817

On Sitting Down to Read King Lear Once Again

O golden tongued Romance, with serene lute!
Fair plumed Syren![2] Queen of far-away!
Leave melodizing on this wintry day,
Shut up thine olden pages, and be mute:
Adieu! for once again the fierce dispute
Betwixt damnation and impassion'd clay
Must I burn through; once more humbly assay
The bitter-sweet of this Shakespearian fruit.
Chief Poet! and ye clouds of Albion,[3]
Begetters of our deep eternal theme,
When through the old oak forest I am gone,
Let me not wander in a barren dream,
But when I am consumed in the fire,
Give me new Phœnix[4] wings to fly at my desire.
—1838

When I Have Fears That I May Cease to Be

When I have fears that I may cease to be
Before my pen has glean'd my teeming brain,
Before high piled books, in charact'ry,[5]
Hold like rich garners the full-ripen'd grain;
When I behold, upon the night's starr'd face,
Huge cloudy symbols of a high romance,
And think that I may never live to trace
Their shadows, with the magic hand of chance;
And when I feel, fair creature of an hour!
That I shall never look upon thee more,
Never have relish in the fairy power
Of unreflecting love—then on the shore
Of the wide world I stand alone, and think
Till love and fame to nothingness do sink.
—1848 (WRITTEN 1818)

Epistle to John Hamilton Reynolds[6]

Dear Reynolds! as last night I lay in bed,
There came before my eyes that wonted thread
Of shapes, and shadows, and remembrances,
That every other minute vex and please:
Things all disjointed come from north and south—
Two witch's eyes above a cherub's mouth,
Voltaire with casque and shield and habergeon,[7]

[1] *Elgin Marbles* In 1806 Lord Elgin brought friezes and other sculptures that had decorated the exterior of the Parthenon, in Athens, to England. In 1816 the government purchased them for display in the British Museum, where they remain today.

[2] *Syren* Monster of classical mythology who is half woman, half serpent, and whose enchanted singing lures sailors to their deaths.

[3] *Albion* England.

[4] *Phœnix* Mythical Egyptian bird that is consumed by fire, and then reborn, once every 500 years.

[5] *charact'ry* Symbols or characters.

[6] *John Hamilton Reynolds* Poet and lawyer (1794–1852) who was a close friend of Keats. Reynolds was ill at the time, and Keats sent him this verse letter to cheer him.

[7] *Voltaire* French philosopher (1694–1778); *casque* Helmet; *habergeon* Sleeveless jacket of chain mail.

And Alexander[1] with his night-cap on;
Old Socrates[2] a-tying his cravat,
And Hazlitt playing with Miss Edgeworth's[3] cat;
And Junius Brutus, pretty well so so,[4]
Making the best of's way towards Soho.[5]

Few are there who escape these visitings—
Perhaps one or two whose lives have patent wings,
And through whose curtains peeps no hellish nose,
No wild-boar tushes,° and no mermaid's toes; *tusks*
But flowers bursting out with lusty pride,
And young Æolian harps[6] personified;
Some, Titian[7] colours touch'd into real life—
The sacrifice goes on; the pontiff knife
Gleams in the sun, the milk-white heifer lows,
The pipes go shrilly, the libation flows:
A white sail shows above the green-head cliff,
Moves round the point, and throws her anchor stiff;
The mariners join hymn with those on land.

You know the Enchanted Castle[8]—it doth stand
Upon a rock, on the border of a lake,
Nested in trees, which all do seem to shake
From some old magic like Urganda's sword.[9]
O Phoebus![10] that I had thy sacred word
To show this Castle, in fair dreaming wise,
Unto my friend, while sick and ill he lies!

You know it well enough, where it doth seem
A mossy place, a Merlin's Hall,[11] a dream;
You know the clear lake, and the little isles,
The mountains blue, and cold near neighbour rills,
All which elsewhere are but half animate;
There do they look alive to love and hate,
To smiles and frowns; they seem a lifted mound
Above some giant, pulsing underground.

Part of the building was a chosen see,° *dwelling-place*
Built by a banish'd Santon° of Chaldee; *holy man*
The other part, two thousand years from him,
Was built by Cuthbert de Saint Aldebrim;[12]
Then there's a little wing, far from the sun,
Built by a Lapland witch[13] turn'd maudlin nun;
And many other juts of aged stone
Founded with many a mason-devil's groan.

The doors all look as if they oped themselves,
The windows as if latched by fays° and elves, *fairies*
And from them comes a silver flash of light,
As from the westward of a summer's night;
Or like a beauteous woman's large blue eyes
Gone mad through olden songs and poesies.

See! what is coming from the distance dim!
A golden galley all in silken trim!
Three rows of oars are lightening, moment whiles,
Into the verd'rous bosoms of those isles;
Towards the shade, under the Castle wall,
It comes in silence—now 'tis hidden all.
The clarion sounds, and from a postern-gate
An echo of sweet music doth create
A fear in the poor herdsman, who doth bring
His beasts to trouble the enchanted spring—
He tells of the sweet music, and the spot,
To all his friends, and they believe him not.

---

[1] *Alexander* Poet Alexander Pope (1688–1744).

[2] *Socrates* Greek philosopher of the fifth century BCE.

[3] *Hazlitt* Painter and writer William Hazlitt (1778–1830); *Miss Edgeworth* Novelist Maria Edgeworth (1767–1849).

[4] *Junius Brutus* Actor Junius Brutus Booth (1796–1852); *so so* Tipsy.

[5] *Soho* Area in London, then rather disreputable.

[6] *Æolian harps* Harps that produce sound when exposed to the wind or open air. From Æolus, the Greek god of the winds.

[7] *Titian* I.e, rich; in the style of Titian, a Venetian Renaissance painter whose work was characterized by bold colors. The following lines most likely describe *Sacrifice to Apollo*, by French painter Claude Lorraine (1600–82).

[8] *the Enchanted Castle* Painting by Claude Lorraine.

[9] *Urganda's sword* Enchantress figure in *Amadis of Gaul*, a fifteenth-century romance.

[10] *Phoebus* Apollo, Greek god of poetry and of the sun.

[11] *Merlin's Hall* I.e., a hall built by magicians such as the sorcerer Merlin, from Arthurian legend.

[12] *Cuthbert … Aldebrim* Character invented by Keats.

[13] *Lapland witch* Lapland was supposed to be the dwelling-place of witches.

O that our dreamings all, of sleep or wake,
Would all their colours from the sunset take:
From something of material sublime,
Rather than shadow our own soul's daytime
In the dark void of night. For in the world
We jostle—but my flag is not unfurl'd
On the admiral-staff—and to philosophise
I dare not yet! Oh, never will the prize,
High reason, and the lore of good and ill,
Be my award! Things cannot to the will
Be settled, but they tease us out of thought;
Or is it that imagination brought
Beyond its proper bound, yet still confin'd,
Lost in a sort of Purgatory blind,
Cannot refer to any standard law
Of either earth or heaven? It is a flaw
In happiness, to see beyond our bourn—
It forces us in summer skies to mourn,
It spoils the singing of the nightingale.

Dear Reynolds! I have a mysterious tale,
And cannot speak it: the first page I read
Upon a lampit° rock of green sea-weed *limpet*
Among the breakers; 'twas a quiet eve,
The rocks were silent, the wide sea did weave
An untumultuous fringe of silver foam
Along the flat brown sand; I was at home
And should have been most happy—but I saw
Too far into the sea, where every maw° *throat, gullet*
The greater on the less feeds evermore.
But I saw too distinct into the core
Of an eternal fierce destruction,
And so from happiness I far was gone.
Still am I sick of it, and tho', to-day,
I've gather'd young spring-leaves, and flowers gay
Of periwinkle and wild strawberry,
Still do I that most fierce destruction see—
The shark at savage prey, the hawk at pounce,
The gentle robin, like a pard° or ounce,° *leopard / lynx*
Ravening a worm—Away, ye horrid moods!
Moods of one's mind! You know I hate them well.
You know I'd sooner be a clapping bell
To some Kamschatkan[1] missionary church,
Than with these horrid moods be left i'the lurch.
Do you get health—and Tom the same—I'll dance,
And from detested moods in new romance[2]
Take refuge—Of bad lines a centaine[3] dose
Is sure enough—and so "here follows prose."[4]
—1848

To Homer[5]

Standing aloof in giant ignorance,
Of thee I hear and of the Cyclades,[6]
As one who sits ashore and longs perchance
To visit dolphin-coral in deep seas.
So thou wast blind![7]—but then the veil was rent;
For Jove[8] uncurtain'd Heaven to let thee live,
And Neptune[9] made for thee a spumy[10] tent,
And Pan[11] made sing for thee his forest-hive;
Aye, on the shores of darkness there is light,
And precipices show untrodden green;
There is a budding morrow in midnight;
There is a triple sight in blindness keen;

[1] *Kamschatkan* From the Kamchatka Peninsula in Siberia.

[2] *new romance* Probably Keats's *Isabella* (1820), a romance based on a tale from Italian poet Giovanni Boccaccio's *Decameron* (written 1348–53).

[3] *centaine* Company of one hundred.

[4] *here follows prose* See Shakespeare's *Twelfth Night* 2.5.154.

[5] *Homer* Early Greek poet, believed to be the author of *The Iliad* and *Odyssey*.

[6] *Cyclades* Group of islands in the Aegean Sea, off the southeast coast of Greece.

[7] *thou wast blind* Homer was said to have been blind.

[8] *Jove* Roman King of the gods.

[9] *Neptune* Roman god of the sea.

[10] *spumy* Covered in sea foam.

[11] *Pan* Greek shepherd god of nature who was half goat and half man. After the nymph Syrinx turned herself into a bed of reeds in order to escape him, Pan created an instrument (the panpipe) out of the reeds.

Such seeing hast thou, as it once befell
To Dian, Queen of Earth, and Heaven, and Hell.[1]
—1848 (WRITTEN C. 1818)

The Eve of St. Agnes[2]

1

St. Agnes' Eve—Ah, bitter chill it was!
The owl, for all his feathers, was a-cold;
The hare limp'd trembling through the frozen grass,
And silent was the flock in woolly fold:
Numb were the Beadsman's[3] fingers, while he told
His rosary, and while his frosted breath,
Like pious incense from a censer[4] old,
Seem'd taking flight for heaven, without a death,
Past the sweet Virgin's[5] picture, while his prayer he saith.

2

His prayer he saith, this patient, holy man;
Then takes his lamp, and riseth from his knees,
And back returneth, meagre, barefoot, wan,
Along the chapel aisle by slow degrees:
The sculptur'd dead, on each side, seem to freeze,
Emprison'd in black, purgatorial rails:
Knights, ladies, praying in dumb orat'ries,° *chapels*
He passeth by; and his weak spirit fails
To think how they may ache in icy hoods and mails.

3

Northward he turneth through a little door,
And scarce three steps, ere Music's golden tongue
Flatter'd to tears this aged man and poor;
But no—already had his deathbell rung:
The joys of all his life were said and sung:
His was harsh penance on St. Agnes' Eve:
Another way he went, and soon among
Rough ashes sat he for his soul's reprieve,
And all night kept awake, for sinners' sake to grieve.

4

That ancient Beadsman heard the prelude soft;
And so it chanc'd, for many a door was wide,
From hurry to and fro. Soon, up aloft,
The silver, snarling trumpets 'gan to chide:
The level chambers, ready with their pride,
Were glowing to receive a thousand guests:
The carved angels, ever eager-eyed,
Star'd, where upon their heads the cornice rests,
With hair blown back, and wings put cross-wise on their breasts.

5

At length burst in the argent[6] revelry,
With plume, tiara, and all rich array,
Numerous as shadows haunting fairily
The brain, new stuff'd, in youth, with triumphs gay
Of old romance. These let us wish away,
And turn, sole-thoughted, to one Lady there,
Whose heart had brooded, all that wintry day,
On love, and wing'd St. Agnes' saintly care,
As she had heard old dames full many times declare.

6

They told her how, upon St. Agnes' Eve,
Young virgins might have visions of delight,
And soft adorings from their loves receive
Upon the honey'd middle of the night,
If ceremonies due they did aright;° *arranged properly*
As, supperless to bed they must retire,
And couch supine their beauties, lily white;
Nor look behind, nor sideways, but require
Of Heaven with upward eyes for all that they desire.

---

[1] *To Dian ... Hell* Diana was sometimes envisioned as a multi-figured goddess, presiding over the moon, childbirth, the hunt, and hell.

[2] *St. Agnes* Fourth-century Christian martyr, executed at the age of thirteen, who is the patron saint of virgins. It was tradition that young women could obtain a vision of their future husbands if they performed the proper rituals on 20 January, the night before St. Agnes's Feast Day.

[3] *Beadsman* Pensioner paid to say prayers for the souls of his benefactors. He "tells," or counts, the beads of his rosary, saying a prayer at each bead.

[4] *censer* Incense burner.

[5] *Virgin* I.e., Mary, virgin mother of Christ.

[6] *argent* Adorned with silver.

7

Full of this whim was thoughtful Madeline:
The music, yearning like a God in pain,
She scarcely heard: her maiden eyes divine,
Fix'd on the floor, saw many a sweeping train
Pass by—she heeded not at all: in vain
Came many a tiptoe, amorous cavalier,
And back retir'd; not cool'd by high disdain,
But she saw not: her heart was otherwhere:
She sigh'd for Agnes' dreams, the sweetest of the year.

8

She danc'd along with vague, regardless eyes,
Anxious her lips, her breathing quick and short:
The hallow'd hour was near at hand: she sighs
Amid the timbrels,° and the throng'd resort *tambourines*
Of whisperers in anger, or in sport;
'Mid looks of love, defiance, hate, and scorn,
Hoodwink'd° with faery fancy; all *blindfolded*
amort,° *dead*
Save to St. Agnes and her lambs unshorn,[1]
And all the bliss to be before to-morrow morn.

9

So, purposing each moment to retire,
She linger'd still. Meantime, across the moors,
Had come young Porphyro, with heart on fire
For Madeline. Beside the portal doors,
Buttress'd from moonlight, stands he, and implores
All saints to give him sight of Madeline,
But for one moment in the tedious hours,
That he might gaze and worship all unseen;
Perchance speak, kneel, touch, kiss—in sooth such
things have been.

10

He ventures in: let no buzz'd whisper tell:
All eyes be muffled, or a hundred swords
Will storm his heart, Love's fev'rous citadel:
For him, those chambers held barbarian hordes,
Hyena foemen, and hot-blooded lords,
Whose very dogs would execrations howl
Against his lineage: not one breast affords
Him any mercy, in that mansion foul,
Save one old beldame,[2] weak in body and in soul.

11

Ah, happy chance! the aged creature came,
Shuffling along with ivory-headed wand,° *staff*
To where he stood, hid from the torch's flame,
Behind a broad hall-pillar, far beyond
The sound of merriment and chorus bland:° *soft*
He startled her; but soon she knew his face,
And grasp'd his fingers in her palsied hand,
Saying, "Mercy, Porphyro! hie thee from this place;
They are all here to-night, the whole blood-thirsty race!"

12

"Get hence! get hence! there's dwarfish Hildebrand;
He had a fever late, and in the fit
He cursed thee and thine, both house and land:
Then there's that old Lord Maurice, not a whit
More tame for his gray hairs—Alas me! flit!
Flit like a ghost away."—"Ah, Gossip[3] dear,
We're safe enough; here in this arm-chair sit,
And tell me how"—"Good Saints! not here, not here;
Follow me, child, or else these stones will be thy bier."

13

He follow'd through a lowly arched way,
Brushing the cobwebs with his lofty plume,
And as she mutter'd "Well-a—well-a-day!"
He found him in a little moonlight room,
Pale, lattic'd, chill, and silent as a tomb.
"Now tell me where is Madeline," said he,
"O tell me, Angela, by the holy loom
Which none but secret sisterhood may see,
When they St. Agnes' wool are weaving piously."

14

"St. Agnes! Ah! it is St. Agnes' Eve—
Yet men will murder upon holy days:
Thou must hold water in a witch's sieve,

---

[1] *St. Agnes … unshorn* The Latin for lamb is *agnus*; thus the traditional association of St. Agnes with lambs, which also carry connotations of whiteness and purity.

[2] *beldame* Grandmother, old woman, or elderly nurse.

[3] *Gossip* Good friend; godmother.

And be liege-lord of all the Elves and Fays,° *fairies*
To venture so: it fills me with amaze
To see thee, Porphyro!—St. Agnes' Eve!
God's help! my lady fair the conjuror plays
This very night: good angels her deceive!
But let me laugh awhile, I've mickle° time *much*
to grieve."

15

Feebly she laugheth in the languid moon,
While Porphyro upon her face doth look,
Like puzzled urchin on an aged crone
Who keepeth clos'd a wond'rous riddle-book,
As spectacled she sits in chimney nook.
But soon his eyes grew brilliant, when she told
His lady's purpose; and he scarce could
brook° *prevent*
Tears, at the thought of those enchantments cold
And Madeline asleep in lap of legends old.

16

Sudden a thought came like a full-blown rose,
Flushing his brow, and in his pained heart
Made purple riot: then doth he propose
A stratagem, that makes the beldame start:
"A cruel man and impious thou art:
Sweet lady, let her pray, and sleep, and dream
Alone with her good angels, far apart
From wicked men like thee. Go, go!—I deem
Thou canst not surely be the same that thou didst seem."

17

"I will not harm her, by all saints I swear,"
Quoth Porphyro: "O may I ne'er find grace
When my weak voice shall whisper its last prayer,
If one of her soft ringlets I displace,
Or look with ruffian passion in her face:
Good Angela, believe me by these tears;
Or I will, even in a moment's space,
Awake, with horrid shout, my foemen's ears,
And beard° them, though they be more *oppose*
fang'd than wolves and bears."

18

"Ah! why wilt thou affright a feeble soul?
A poor, weak, palsy-stricken, churchyard thing,
Whose passing-bell may ere the midnight toll;
Whose prayers for thee, each morn and evening,
Were never miss'd."—Thus plaining,° *complaining*
doth she bring
A gentler speech from burning Porphyro;
So woeful, and of such deep sorrowing,
That Angela gives promise she will do
Whatever he shall wish, betide her weal or woe.

19

Which was, to lead him, in close secrecy,
Even to Madeline's chamber, and there hide
Him in a closet, of such privacy
That he might see her beauty unespied,
And win perhaps that night a peerless bride,
While legion'd fairies pac'd the coverlet,
And pale enchantment held her sleepy-eyed.
Never on such a night have lovers met,
Since Merlin paid his Demon all the monstrous debt.[1]

20

"It shall be as thou wishest," said the Dame:
"All cates° and dainties shall be stored there *delicacies*
Quickly on this feast-night: by the tambour frame[2]
Her own lute thou wilt see: no time to spare,
For I am slow and feeble, and scarce dare
On such a catering trust my dizzy head.
Wait here, my child, with patience; kneel in prayer
The while: Ah! thou must needs the lady wed,
Or may I never leave my grave among the dead."

21

So saying, she hobbled off with busy fear.
The lover's endless minutes slowly pass'd:
The dame return'd, and whisper'd in his ear
To follow her; with aged eyes aghast

[1] *Since … debt* Probably a reference to the episode in Arthurian legend in which the enchanter Merlin falls in love with the enchantress Vivien, or Nimue, who turns one of his spells against him and imprisons him in a cave.

[2] *tambour frame* Circular frame for embroidery.

From fright of dim espial. Safe at last,
Through many a dusky gallery, they gain
The maiden's chamber, silken, hush'd, and chaste;
Where Porphyro took covert, pleas'd amain.° *completely*
His poor guide hurried back with agues° *fever*
in her brain.

22

Her falt'ring hand upon the balustrade,
Old Angela was feeling for the stair,
When Madeline, St. Agnes' charmed maid,
Rose, like a mission'd spirit, unaware:
With silver taper's light, and pious care,
She turn'd, and down the aged gossip led
To a safe level matting. Now prepare,
Young Porphyro, for gazing on that bed;
She comes, she comes again, like ring-dove
fray'd° and fled. *frightened*

23

Out went the taper° as she hurried in; *candle*
Its little smoke, in pallid moonshine, died:
She clos'd the door, she panted, all akin
To spirits of the air, and visions wide:
No uttered syllable, or, woe betide!
But to her heart, her heart was voluble,
Paining with eloquence her balmy side;
As though a tongueless nightingale should swell
Her throat in vain, and die, heart-stifled, in her dell.

24

A casement high and triple-arch'd there was,
All garlanded with carven imag'ries
Of fruits, and flowers, and bunches of knot-grass,
And diamonded with panes of quaint device,
Innumerable of stains and splendid dyes,
As are the tiger-moth's deep-damask'd wings;
And in the midst, 'mong thousand heraldries,[1]
And twilight saints, and dim emblazonings,
A shielded scutcheon blush'd with blood of queens
and kings.[2]

[1] *heraldries* Emblems of rank and genealogy.

[2] *scutcheon* I.e., escutcheon: shield; *blush'd ... kings* I.e., indicates she is of royal blood.

25

Full on this casement shone the wintry moon,
And threw warm gules[3] on Madeline's fair breast,
As down she knelt for heaven's grace and boon;° *blessing*
Rose-bloom fell on her hands, together prest,
And on her silver cross soft amethyst,
And on her hair a glory, like a saint:
She seem'd a splendid angel, newly drest,
Save wings, for heaven—Porphyro grew faint:
She knelt, so pure a thing, so free from mortal taint.

26

Anon his heart revives: her vespers° done, *evening prayers*
Of all its wreathed pearls her hair she frees;
Unclasps her warmed jewels one by one;
Loosens her fragrant boddice; by degrees
Her rich attire creeps rustling to her knees:
Half-hidden, like a mermaid in sea-weed,
Pensive awhile she dreams awake, and sees,
In fancy, fair St. Agnes in her bed,
But dares not look behind, or all the charm is fled.

27

Soon, trembling in her soft and chilly nest,
In sort of wakeful swoon, perplex'd[4] she lay,
Until the poppied° warmth of sleep oppress'd *narcotic*
Her soothed limbs, and soul fatigued away;
Flown, like a thought, until the morrow-day;
Blissfully haven'd both from joy and pain;
Clasp'd like a missal[5] where swart Paynims[6] pray;
Blinded alike from sunshine and from rain,
As though a rose should shut, and be a bud again.

28

Stol'n to this paradise, and so entranced,
Porphyro gazed upon her empty dress,
And listen'd to her breathing, if it chanced
To wake into a slumberous tenderness;
Which when he heard, that minute did he bless,

[3] *gules* Red bars (a heraldic device).

[4] *perplex'd* I.e., between sleep and waking.

[5] *missal* Christian mass- or prayer-book.

[6] *swart Paynims* Dark-skinned pagans.

And breath'd himself: then from the closet crept,
Noiseless as fear in a wide wilderness,
And over the hush'd carpet, silent, stept,
And 'tween the curtains peep'd, where, lo!—how fast
she slept.

29

Then by the bed-side, where the faded moon
Made a dim, silver twilight, soft he set
A table, and, half anguish'd, threw thereon
A cloth of woven crimson, gold, and jet—
O for some drowsy Morphean amulet![1]
The boisterous, midnight, festive clarion,° *trumpet*
The kettle-drum, and far-heard clarinet,
Affray his ears, though but in dying tone—
The hall door shuts again, and all the noise is gone.

30

And still she slept an azure-lidded sleep,
In blanched linen, smooth, and lavender'd,
While he from forth the closet brought a heap
Of candied apple, quince, and plum, and gourd;° *melon*
With jellies soother[2] than the creamy curd,
And lucent° syrops, tinct° with cinnamon; *clear / imbued*
Manna[3] and dates, in argosy[4] transferr'd
From Fez;[5] and spiced dainties, every one,
From silken Samarkand[6] to cedar'd Lebanon.

31

These delicates he heap'd with glowing hand
On golden dishes and in baskets bright
Of wreathed silver: sumptuous they stand
In the retired quiet of the night,
Filling the chilly room with perfume light.
"And now, my love, my seraph° fair, awake! *angel*
Thou art my heaven, and I thine eremite:° *hermit*
Open thine eyes, for meek St. Agnes' sake,
Or I shall drowse beside thee, so my soul doth ache."

32

Thus whispering, his warm, unnerved arm
Sank in her pillow. Shaded was her dream
By the dusk curtains—'twas a midnight charm
Impossible to melt as iced stream:
The lustrous salvers° in the moonlight gleam; *trays*
Broad golden fringe upon the carpet lies:
It seem'd he never, never could redeem
From such a stedfast spell his lady's eyes;
So mus'd awhile, entoil'd in woofed° phantasies. *woven*

33

Awakening up, he took her hollow lute—
Tumultuous—and, in chords that tenderest be,
He play'd an ancient ditty, long since mute,
In Provence call'd, "La belle dame sans mercy":[7]
Close to her ear touching the melody—
Wherewith disturb'd, she utter'd a soft moan:
He ceased—she panted quick—and suddenly
Her blue affrayed eyes wide open shone:
Upon his knees he sank, pale as smooth-sculptured
stone.

34

Her eyes were open, but she still beheld,
Now wide awake, the vision of her sleep:
There was a painful change, that nigh expell'd
The blisses of her dream so pure and deep,
At which fair Madeline began to weep,
And moan forth witless words with many a sigh;
While still her gaze on Porphyro would keep;
Who knelt, with joined hands and piteous eye,
Fearing to move or speak, she look'd so dreamingly.

35

"Ah, Porphyro!" said she, "but even now
Thy voice was at sweet tremble in mine ear,

---

[1] *Morphean amulet* Sleep-inducing medicine or charm. (Morpheus is the god of dreams.)

[2] *soother* A word of Keats's own invention, meaning more soothing, softer.

[3] *Manna* Dried, sweet gum taken from various plants.

[4] *argosy* Merchant vessels.

[5] *Fez* City in Morocco.

[6] *Samarkand* City in Uzbekistan.

[7] *La belle ... mercy* French: The beautiful woman without pity. Title of a long poem by medieval poet Alain Chartier (c. 1385–1433); Keats had not yet written his own poem with this title.

Made tuneable with every sweetest vow;
And those sad eyes were spiritual and clear:
How chang'd thou art! how pallid, chill, and drear!
Give me that voice again, my Porphyro,
Those looks immortal, those complainings° dear! *lamentings*
Oh leave me not in this eternal woe,
For if thou diest, my Love, I know not where to go."

36

Beyond a mortal man impassion'd far
At these voluptuous accents, he arose,
Ethereal, flush'd, and like a throbbing star
Seen mid the sapphire heaven's deep repose;
Into her dream he melted, as the rose
Blendeth its odour with the violet—
Solution sweet: meantime the frost-wind blows
Like Love's alarum° pattering the sharp sleet *warning bell*
Against the window-panes; St. Agnes' moon hath set.

37

'Tis dark: quick pattereth the flaw-blown° sleet: *gust-driven*
"This is no dream, my bride, my Madeline!"
'Tis dark: the iced gusts still rave and beat:
"No dream, alas! alas! and woe is mine!
Porphyro will leave me here to fade and pine.
Cruel! what traitor could thee hither bring?
I curse not, for my heart is lost in thine,
Though thou forsakest a deceived thing—
A dove forlorn and lost with sick unpruned wing."

38

"My Madeline! sweet dreamer! lovely bride!
Say, may I be for aye° thy vassal blest? *ever*
Thy beauty's shield, heart-shap'd and vermeil° dyed? *vermilion (red)*
Ah, silver shrine, here will I take my rest
After so many hours of toil and quest,
A famish'd pilgrim, saved by miracle.
Though I have found, I will not rob thy nest
Saving of thy sweet self; if thou think'st well
To trust, fair Madeline, to no rude infidel.

39

"Hark! 'tis an elfin-storm from faery land,
Of haggard° seeming, but a boon indeed: *wild*
Arise—arise! the morning is at hand;
The bloated wassaillers° will never heed— *drinkers*
Let us away, my love, with happy speed;
There are no ears to hear, or eyes to see—
Drown'd all in Rhenish and the sleepy mead:[1]
Awake! arise! my love, and fearless be,
For o'er the southern moors I have a home for thee."

40

She hurried at his words, beset with fears,
For there were sleeping dragons all around,
At glaring watch, perhaps, with ready spears—
Down the wide stairs a darkling[2] way they found.
In all the house was heard no human sound.
A chain-droop'd lamp was flickering by each door;
The arras,° rich with horseman, hawk, and hound, *tapestries*
Flutter'd in the besieging wind's uproar;
And the long carpets rose along the gusty floor.

41

They glide, like phantoms, into the wide hall;
Like phantoms, to the iron porch, they glide;
Where lay the Porter, in uneasy sprawl,
With a huge empty flaggon by his side:
The wakeful bloodhound rose, and shook his hide,
But his sagacious eye an inmate owns:
By one, and one, the bolts full easy slide—
The chains lie silent on the footworn stones—
The key turns, and the door upon its hinges groans.

42

And they are gone: ay, ages long ago
These lovers fled away into the storm.
That night the Baron dreamt of many a woe,
And all his warrior-guests, with shade and form
Of witch, and demon, and large coffin-worm,
Were long be-nightmar'd. Angela the old

---

[1] *Rhenish* Wine from the Rhine region; *mead* Alcoholic beverage made from fermented honey and water.

[2] *darkling* Obscure, gloomy.

Died palsy-twitch'd, with meagre face deform;
The Beadsman, after thousand aves[1] told,
For aye unsought for slept among his ashes cold.
—1820

Bright Star

Bright star, would I were steadfast as thou art—
Not in lone splendour hung aloft the night
And watching, with eternal lids apart,
Like nature's patient, sleepless Eremite,° *hermit*
The moving waters at their priestlike task
Of pure ablution[2] round earth's human shores,
Or gazing on the new soft fallen mask
Of snow upon the mountains and the moors—
No—yet still steadfast, still unchangeable,
Pillow'd upon my fair love's ripening breast,
To feel for ever its soft fall and swell,
Awake for ever in a sweet unrest,
Still, still to hear her tender-taken breath,
And so live ever—or else swoon to death.
—1838 (WRITTEN 1819)

La Belle Dame sans Merci[3]

O what can ail thee, knight-at-arms,
Alone and palely loitering?
The sedge[4] has wither'd from the lake,
And no birds sing.

O what can ail thee, knight-at-arms,
So haggard, and so woe-begone?
The squirrel's granary is full,
And the harvest's done.

I see a lily[5] on thy brow,
With anguish moist and fever dew
And on thy cheeks a fading rose
Fast withereth too.

I met a lady in the meads,° *meadows*
Full beautiful—a faery's child,
Her hair was long, her foot was light,
And her eyes were wild.

I made a garland for her head,
And bracelets too, and fragrant zone;° *belt*
She look'd at me as she did love,
And made sweet moan.

I set her on my pacing steed,
And nothing else saw all day long,
For sidelong would she bend and sing
A faery's song.

She found me roots of relish sweet,
And honey wild, and manna dew,[6]
And sure in language strange she said
"I love thee true."

She took me to her elfin grot,° *grotto*
And there she wept and sigh'd full sore,
And there I shut her wild wild eyes
With kisses four.

And there she lulled me asleep,
And there I dream'd—Ah! woe betide!
The latest° dream I ever dream'd *last*
On the cold hill side.

I saw pale kings and princes too,
Pale warriors, death-pale were they all;

[1] *aves* Latin: abbreviation for *Ave Marias*, or Hail Marys, prayers to the Virgin Mary.

[2] *ablution* Religious ritual washing of the body.

[3] *La Belle Dame sans Merci* French: The beautiful lady without pity. This original version of the poem, found in a journal letter to George and Georgiana Keats, was first published in 1848. Keats's revised version was published in 1820.

[4] *sedge* Rush-like grass.

[5] *lily* Flower traditionally symbolic of death.

[6] *manna dew* See Exodus 16, in which God provides the Israelites with a food that falls from heaven, called manna.

They cried, "La belle dame sans merci
Hath thee in thrall!"° *captivity*

I saw their starved lips in the gloam,° *twilight*
With horrid warning gaped wide,
And I awoke, and found me here,
On the cold hill's side.

And this is why I sojourn here,
Alone and palely loitering,
Though the sedge is wither'd from the lake,
And no birds sing.
—1848 (WRITTEN 1819)

La Belle Dame sans Mercy[1]

Ah, what can ail thee, wretched wight,° *being*
Alone and palely loitering;
The sedge[2] is wither'd from the lake,
And no birds sing.

Ah, what can ail thee, wretched wight,
So haggard and so woe-begone?
The squirrel's granary is full,
And the harvest's done.

I see a lily[3] on thy brow,
With anguish moist and fever dew;
And on thy cheek a fading rose
Fast withereth too.

I met a lady in the meads° *meadows*
Full beautiful, a fairy's child;
Her hair was long, her foot was light,
And her eyes were wild.

I set her on my pacing steed,
And nothing else saw all day long;
For sideways would she lean, and sing
A fairy's song.

I made a garland for her head,
And bracelets too, and fragrant zone:° *belt*
She look'd at me as she did love,
And made sweet moan.

She found me roots of relish sweet,
And honey wild, and manna[4] dew;
And sure in language strange she said,
"I love thee true."

She took me to her elfin grot,° *grotto*
And there she gaz'd and sighed deep.
And there I shut her wild sad eyes—
So kiss'd to sleep.

And there we slumber'd on the moss,
And there I dream'd, ah woe betide,
The latest dream I ever dream'd
On the cold hill side.

I saw pale kings, and princes too,
Pale warriors, death-pale were they all;
Who cry'd—"La belle dame sans mercy
Hath thee in thrall!"° *captivity*

I saw their starv'd lips in the gloom
With horrid warning gaped wide,
And I awoke, and found me here
On the cold hill side.

And this is why I sojourn here
Alone and palely loitering,
Though the sedge is wither'd from the lake,
And no birds sing.
—1820 (WRITTEN 1819)

[1] *La Belle … Mercy* French: The beautiful lady without pity. This version of the poem, a revision of "La Belle Dame sans Merci," was published in 1820.

[2] *sedge* Rush-like grass.

[3] *lily* Flower traditionally symbolic of death.

[4] *manna* See Exodus 16, in which God provides the Israelites with a food that falls from heaven, called manna.

Incipit altera Sonneta[1]

I have been endeavouring to discover a better sonnet stanza than we have. The legitimate[2] does not suit the language over-well from the pouncing rhymes—the other kind appears too elegaiac—and the couplet at the end of it has seldom a pleasing effect—I do not pretend to have succeeded—it will explain itself—

If by dull rhymes our English must be chain'd
And, like Andromeda,[3] the Sonnet sweet
Fetter'd in spite of pained loveliness;
Let us find out, if we must be constrain'd
Sandals more interwoven & complete
To fit the naked foot of Poesy;
Let us inspect the Lyre,[4] & weigh the stress
Of every chord & see what may be gain'd
By ear industrious & attention meet;° *fitting*
Misers of sound & syllable, no less
Than Midas of his coinage,[5] let us be
Jealous of dead leaves in the bay wreath Crown;[6]
So if we may not let the Muse[7] be free,
She will be bound with Garlands of her own.
—1836 (WRITTEN 1819)

---

[1] *Incipit altera Sonneta* Latin: Another sonnet begins.

[2] *The legitimate* I.e., the Petrarchan sonnet. The "other kind" to which Keats refers is the Shakespearean sonnet.

[3] *Andromeda* In Greek myth, Andromeda is tied to a rock to be devoured by a sea serpent after her mother boasts that she is more beautiful than the sea nymphs. Perseus, on his winged horse Pegasus (a symbol of poetic inspiration), rescues her.

[4] *Lyre* Stringed instrument.

[5] *Midas … coinage* In Ovid's *Metamorphoses*, King Midas of Phrygia gets his wish that everything he touches will turn to gold.

[6] *bay wreath Crown* Wreaths made of leaves of the bay laurel were traditionally bestowed upon those who distinguished themselves in poetry.

[7] *Muse* One of nine daughters of Zeus and Mnemosyne, each of whom presided over and provided inspiration for an aspect of learning or the arts.

Ode to Psyche[8]

O Goddess! hear these tuneless numbers, wrung
By sweet enforcement and remembrance dear,
And pardon that thy secrets should be sung
Even into thine own soft-conched[9] ear:
Surely I dreamt to-day, or did I see
The winged Psyche with awaken'd eyes?
I wander'd in a forest thoughtlessly,
And, on the sudden, fainting with surprise,
Saw two fair creatures, couched side by side
In deepest grass, beneath the whisp'ring roof
Of leaves and trembled blossoms, where there ran
A brooklet, scarce espied:

'Mid hush'd, cool-rooted flowers, fragrant-eyed,
Blue, silver-white, and budded Tyrian,[10]
They lay calm-breathing on the bedded grass;
Their arms embraced, and their pinions° too; *wings*
Their lips touch'd not, but had not bade adieu,
As if disjoined by soft-handed slumber,
And ready still past kisses to outnumber
At tender eye-dawn of aurorean[11] love:
The winged boy° I knew; *Cupid*
But who wast thou, O happy, happy dove?
His Psyche true!

O latest born and liveliest vision far
Of all Olympus'[12] faded hierarchy!
Fairer than Phœbe's[13] sapphire-region'd star,
Or Vesper,[14] amorous glow-worm of the sky;

---

[8] *Psyche* In classical mythology, a young woman who was beloved by Cupid, winged god of love and son of Venus. After winning over Venus, who was jealous of Psyche's beauty, Psyche was granted immortality by Jupiter. In Greek myth she is often a personification of the soul: her name in Greek means soul or mind as well as butterfly.

[9] *soft-conched* Shaped like a conch shell, but soft.

[10] *Tyrian* Purple. From the Phoenician city of Tyre, where purple or crimson dyes were made in ancient times.

[11] *aurorean* I.e., dawning. Aurora was the goddess of the dawn.

[12] *Olympus* Mount Olympus, home of the gods.

[13] *Phœbe* Diana, goddess of the moon.

[14] *Vesper* Venus, the evening star.

Fairer than these, though temple thou hast none,
Nor altar heap'd with flowers;
Nor virgin-choir to make delicious moan
Upon the midnight hours;
No voice, no lute, no pipe, no incense sweet
From chain-swung censer° teeming; *incense burner*
No shrine, no grove, no oracle, no heat
Of pale-mouth'd prophet dreaming.

O brightest! Though too late for antique vows,
Too, too late for the fond believing
lyre,° *stringed instrument*
When holy were the haunted forest boughs,
Holy the air, the water, and the fire;
Yet even in these days so far retir'd
From happy pieties, thy lucent fans,° *wings*
Fluttering among the faint Olympians,
I see, and sing, by my own eyes inspired.
So let me be thy choir, and make a moan
Upon the midnight hours;
Thy voice, thy lute, thy pipe, thy incense sweet
From swinged censer teeming;
Thy shrine, thy grove, thy oracle, thy heat
Of pale-mouth'd prophet dreaming.

Yes, I will be thy priest, and build a fane° *temple*
In some untrodden region of my mind,
Where branched thoughts, new grown with pleasant
pain,
Instead of pines shall murmur in the wind:
Far, far around shall those dark-cluster'd trees
Fledge the wild-ridged mountains steep by steep;
And there by zephyrs,° streams, and birds, *breezes*
and bees,
The moss-lain Dryads° shall be lull'd *wood nymphs*
to sleep;
And in the midst of quietness
A rosy sanctuary will I dress
With the wreath'd trellis of a working brain,
With buds, and bells, and stars without a name,
With all the gardener Fancy e'er could feign,
Who breeding flowers, will never breed the same:
And there shall be for thee all soft delight
That shadowy thought can win,
A bright torch, and a casement ope° *window opened*
at night,
To let the warm Love in!
—1820

Ode to a Nightingale[1]

I

My heart aches, and a drowsy numbness pains
My sense, as though of hemlock° I had *poison*
drunk,
Or emptied some dull opiate to the drains
One minute past, and Lethe-wards[2] had sunk:
'Tis not through envy of thy happy lot,
But being too happy in thine happiness—
That thou, light-winged Dryad° *wood-nymph*
of the trees,
In some melodious plot
Of beechen green, and shadows numberless,
Singest of summer in full-throated ease.

2

O, for a draught of vintage! that hath been
Cool'd a long age in the deep-delved earth,
Tasting of Flora[3] and the country green,
Dance, and Provençal song,[4] and sunburnt mirth!
O for a beaker full of the warm South,

---

[1] *Ode to a Nightingale* Written about 1 May 1819. Twenty years later, Keats's friend and housemate Charles Armitage Brown remembered the composition of the poem: "In the spring of 1819 a nightingale had built her nest near my house. Keats felt a tranquil and continual joy in her song; and one morning he took his chair from the breakfast-table to the grass-plot under a plum-tree, where he sat for two or three hours. When he came into the house, I perceived he had some scraps of paper in his hand, and these he was quietly thrusting behind the books. On enquiry, I found those scraps, four or five in number, contained his poetic feeling on the song of our nightingale."

[2] *Lethe-wards* Towards Lethe, the river of forgetfulness which, in classical mythology, the dead must cross to reach Hades, the underworld.

[3] *Flora* Roman goddess of flowers.

[4] *Provençal song* The region of Provençe, in southern France, was known in the Middle Ages for its poet-singers, or troubadours.

Full of the true, the blushful Hippocrene,[1]
With beaded bubbles winking at the brim,
And purple-stained mouth;
That I might drink, and leave the world unseen,
And with thee fade away into the forest dim:

3

Fade far away, dissolve, and quite forget
What thou among the leaves hast never known,
The weariness, the fever, and the fret
Here, where men sit and hear each other groan;
Where palsy shakes a few, sad, last gray hairs,
Where youth grows pale, and spectre-thin, and dies;
Where but to think is to be full of sorrow
And leaden-eyed despairs,
Where Beauty cannot keep her lustrous eyes,
Or new Love pine at them beyond to-morrow.

4

Away! away! for I will fly to thee,
Not charioted by Bacchus and his pards,[2]
But on the viewless wings of Poesy,
Though the dull brain perplexes and retards:
Already with thee! tender is the night,
And haply° the Queen-Moon is on her throne, *maybe*
Cluster'd around by all her starry Fays;° *fairies*
But here there is no light,
Save what from heaven is with the breezes blown
Through verdurous glooms and winding mossy ways.

5

I cannot see what flowers are at my feet,
Nor what soft incense hangs upon the boughs,
But, in embalmed° darkness, guess each sweet *fragrant*
Wherewith the seasonable month endows
The grass, the thicket, and the fruit-tree wild;
White hawthorn, and the pastoral eglantine;
Fast fading violets cover'd up in leaves;
And mid-May's eldest child,
The coming musk-rose, full of dewy wine,
The murmurous haunt of flies on summer eves.

6

Darkling[3] I listen; and, for many a time
I have been half in love with easeful Death,
Call'd him soft names in many a mused rhyme,
To take into the air my quiet breath;
Now more than ever seems it rich to die,
To cease upon the midnight with no pain,
While thou art pouring forth thy soul abroad
In such an ecstasy!
Still wouldst thou sing, and I have ears in vain—
To thy high requiem[4] become a sod.

7

Thou wast not born for death, immortal Bird!
No hungry generations tread thee down;
The voice I hear this passing night was heard
In ancient days by emperor and clown:° *rustic*
Perhaps the self-same song that found a path
Through the sad heart of Ruth, when, sick for home,
She stood in tears amid the alien corn;[5]
The same that oft-times hath
Charm'd magic casements, opening on the foam
Of perilous seas, in faery lands forlorn.

8

Forlorn! the very word is like a bell
To toll me back from thee to my sole self!
Adieu! the fancy cannot cheat so well
As she is fam'd to do, deceiving elf.
Adieu! adieu! thy plaintive anthem fades
Past the near meadows, over the still stream,
Up the hill-side; and now 'tis buried deep
In the next valley-glades:
Was it a vision, or a waking dream?
Fled is that music—Do I wake or sleep?
—1819

[1] *Hippocrene* Fountain of the Muses (nine sister goddesses who presided over aspects of learning and the arts) located on the sacred Mount Helicon. Its waters were said to provide poetic inspiration.

[2] *Bacchus … pards* Bacchus, the god of wine, rides a chariot drawn by pards, or leopards.

[3] *Darkling* In the dark.

[4] *requiem* Mass sung for the dead.

[5] *Ruth … corn* Widow in the Book of Ruth (1–4) who leaves Moab for Judah with her mother-in-law Naomi because of famine.

Ode on a Grecian Urn

1

Thou still unravish'd bride of quietness,
Thou foster-child of silence and slow time,
Sylvan° historian, who canst thus express *woodland*
A flowery tale more sweetly than our rhyme:
What leaf-fring'd legend haunts about thy shape
Of deities or mortals, or of both,
In Tempe or the dales of Arcady?[1]
What men or gods are these? What maidens loth?
What mad pursuit? What struggle to escape?
What pipes and timbrels?° What *tambourines*
wild ecstasy?

2

Heard melodies are sweet, but those unheard
Are sweeter; therefore, ye soft pipes, play on;
Not to the sensual° ear, but, more endear'd, *physical*
Pipe to the spirit ditties of no tone:
Fair youth, beneath the trees, thou canst not leave
Thy song, nor ever can those trees be bare;
Bold Lover, never, never canst thou kiss,
Though winning near the goal—yet, do not grieve;
She cannot fade, though thou hast not thy bliss,
For ever wilt thou love, and she be fair!

3

Ah, happy, happy boughs! that cannot shed
Your leaves, nor ever bid the Spring adieu;
And, happy melodist, unwearied,
For ever piping songs for ever new;
More happy love! more happy, happy love!
For ever warm and still to be enjoy'd,
For ever panting, and for ever young;
All breathing human passion far above,
That leaves a heart high-sorrowful and cloy'd,
A burning forehead, and a parching tongue.

4

Who are these coming to the sacrifice?
To what green altar, O mysterious priest,
Lead'st thou that heifer lowing at the skies,
And all her silken flanks with garlands drest?
What little town by river or sea shore,
Or mountain-built with peaceful citadel,
Is emptied of this folk, this pious morn?
And, little town, thy streets for evermore
Will silent be; and not a soul to tell
Why thou art desolate, can e'er return.

5

O Attic[2] shape! Fair attitude! with brede° *interwoven design*
Of marble men and maidens overwrought,° *overlaid*
With forest branches and the trodden weed;
Thou, silent form, dost tease us out of thought
As doth eternity: Cold Pastoral!
When old age shall this generation waste,
Thou shalt remain, in midst of other woe
Than ours, a friend to man, to whom thou say'st,
"Beauty is truth, truth beauty,"—that is all
Ye know on earth, and all ye need to know.[3]
—1820

[1] *Tempe* Valley in ancient Greece renowned for its beauty; *Arcady* Ideal region of rural life, named for a mountainous district in Greece.

[2] *Attic* I.e., Greek. Attica was an ancient region of Greece that had Athens as its capital.

[3] *Beauty is … know* The quotation marks in line 49 are present in Keats's 1820 volume of poems, but are absent in transcripts of the poem made by Keats's friends and in the version of the poem published in *Annals of the Fine Arts* in 1820. As a result, their presence has engendered much critical debate. It is unclear whether Keats meant the last line and a half to be spoken by the poet, or whether the entire final two lines are the imagined declaration of the urn.

Ode on Melancholy[1]

1

No, No, go not to Lethe,[2] neither twist
Wolf's-bane,[3] tight-rooted, for its poisonous wine;
Nor suffer thy pale forehead to be kiss'd
By nightshade, ruby grape of Proserpine;[4]
Make not your rosary of yew-berries,[5]
Nor let the beetle, nor the death-moth[6] be
Your mournful Psyche,[7] nor the downy owl
A partner in your sorrow's mysteries;[8]
For shade to shade will come too drowsily,
And drown the wakeful anguish of the soul.

2

But when the melancholy fit shall fall
Sudden from heaven like a weeping cloud,
That fosters the droop-headed flowers all,
And hides the green hill in an April shroud;
Then glut thy sorrow on a morning rose,
Or on the rainbow of the salt sand-wave,
Or on the wealth of globed peonies;
Or if thy mistress some rich anger shows,
Emprison her soft hand, and let her rave,
And feed deep, deep upon her peerless eyes.

3

She dwells with Beauty—Beauty that must die;
And Joy, whose hand is ever at his lips
Bidding adieu; and aching Pleasure nigh,
Turning to poison while the bee-mouth sips:
Ay, in the very temple of Delight
Veil'd Melancholy has her sovran° shine, *sovereign*
Though seen of none save him whose strenuous tongue
Can burst Joy's grape against his palate fine;° *refined*
His soul shall taste the sadness of her might,
And be among her cloudy trophies hung.

—1820

Ode on Indolence[9]

"They toil not, neither do they spin."[10]

1

One morn before me were three figures seen,
With bowed necks, and joined hands, side-faced;
And one behind the other stepp'd serene,
In placid sandals, and in white robes graced;

[1] *Ode on Melancholy* In the original manuscript version, the poem opened with the following stanza:
Though you should build a bark of dead men's bones,
And rear a phantom gibbet for a mast,
Stitch creeds together for a sail, with groans
To fill it out, bloodstained and aghast;
Although your rudder be a Dragon's tail,
Long sever'd, yet still hard with agony,
Your cordage large uprootings from the skull
Of bald Medusa; certes you would fail
To find Melancholy, whether she
Dreameth in any isle of Lethe dull.
(Medusa was one of the Gorgons, three monstrous, winged sisters who had snakes for hair.)

[2] *Lethe* River in Hades, the classical underworld, whose waters produce forgetfulness.

[3] *Wolf's-bane* Poisonous plant native to Europe.

[4] *nightshade* Plants with poisonous berries; *Proserpine* Daughter of Demeter who was abducted by Pluto, god of the underworld, and made queen of Hades. Her mother, goddess of the harvest, mourned for her daughter and so caused an eternal winter until Pluto was prevailed upon to allow Proserpine to return to her mother six months of every year.

[5] *yew-berries* Poisonous berries of the yew tree, which is commonly planted in graveyards and is therefore often regarded as symbolic of death or sadness.

[6] *beetle* The scarab, a large black beetle that Egyptians placed in their tombs as a symbol of resurrection; *death-moth* Death's-head moth, whose wings carry a mark resembling a human skull.

[7] *Psyche* In classical mythology, a young woman who was beloved by Cupid, winged god of love and son of Venus. After winning over Venus, who was jealous of Psyche's beauty, Psyche was granted immortality by Jupiter. In Greek myth she is often a personification of the soul. Her name in Greek means butterfly as well as soul. Psyche was often represented as a butterfly flying out of a dying person's mouth.

[8] *mysteries* I.e., secret rites or ceremonies.

[9] *Ode on Indolence* See the 1819 letter to George and Georgiana Keats, reprinted below, in which Keats describes the bout of indolence that is thought to have inspired this poem.

[10] *They toil … spin* From Matthew 6.28–89: "Consider the lilies of the field, how they grow; they toil not, neither do they spin: And yet I say unto you, That even Solomon in all his glory was not arrayed like one of these."

They pass'd, like figures on a marble urn,
When shifted round to see the other side;
They came again; as when the urn once more
Is shifted round, the first seen shades return;
And they were strange to me, as may betide
With vases, to one deep in Phidian lore.[1]

2

How is it, shadows, that I knew ye not?
How came ye muffled in so hush a masque?° *play*
Was it a silent deep-disguised plot
To steal away, and leave without a task
My idle days? Ripe was the drowsy hour;
The blissful cloud of summer-indolence
Benumb'd my eyes; my pulse grew less and less;
Pain had no sting, and pleasure's wreath no flower:
O, why did ye not melt, and leave my sense
Unhaunted quite of all but—nothingness?

3

A third time pass'd they by, and, passing, turn'd
Each one the face a moment whiles to me;
Then faded, and to follow them I burn'd
And ached for wings because I knew the three;
The first was a fair Maid, and Love her name;
The second was Ambition, pale of cheek,
And ever watchful with fatigued eye;
The last, whom I love more, the more of blame
Is heap'd upon her, maiden most unmeek,
I knew to be my demon Poesy.

4

They faded, and, forsooth! I wanted wings:
O folly! What is Love! and where is it?
And for that poor Ambition! It springs
From a man's little heart's short fever-fit;
For Poesy! No—she has not a joy—
At least for me—so sweet as drowsy noons,
And evenings steep'd in honeyed indolence;
O, for an age so shelter'd from annoy,° *harm*
That I may never know how change the moons,
Or hear the voice of busy common sense!

5

A third time came they by—alas! wherefore?
My sleep had been embroider'd with dim dreams;
My soul had been a lawn besprinkled o'er
With flowers, and stirring shades, and baffled beams:
The morn was clouded, but no shower fell,
Tho' in her lids hung the sweet tears of May;
The open casement press'd a new-leav'd vine,
Let in the budding warmth and
throstle's° lay;° *thrush's / song*
O shadows! 'twas a time to bid farewell!
Upon your skirts had fallen no tears of mine.

6

So, ye three ghosts, adieu! Ye cannot raise
My head cool-bedded in the flowery grass;
For I would not be dieted with praise,
A pet-lamb in a sentimental farce!
Fade softly from my eyes, and be once more
In masque-like figures on the dreamy urn;
Farewell! I yet have visions for the night,
And for the day faint visions there is store;
Vanish, ye phantoms! from my idle spright,° *spirit*
Into the clouds, and never more return!

—1848 (WRITTEN 1819)

To Autumn

I

Season of mists and mellow fruitfulness,
Close bosom-friend of the maturing sun;
Conspiring with him how to load and bless
With fruit the vines that round the thatch-eves run;
To bend with apples the moss'd cottage-trees,
And fill all fruit with ripeness to the core;
To swell the gourd, and plump the hazel shells
With a sweet kernel; to set budding more,
And still more, later flowers for the bees,
Until they think warm days will never cease,
For Summer has o'er-brimm'd their clammy cells.

[1] *Phidian lore* Lore concerning Phidias, the fifth-century Athenian sculptor of what were later named the Elgin Marbles, the marble sculptures that decorated the outside of the Parthenon and were brought to England by Lord Elgin.

2

Who hath not seen thee oft amid thy store?
Sometimes whoever seeks abroad may find
Thee sitting careless on a granary floor,
Thy hair soft-lifted by the winnowing wind;
Or on a half-reap'd furrow sound asleep,
Drows'd with the fume of poppies, while thy hook[1]
Spares the next swath and all its twined flowers:
And sometimes like a gleaner[2] thou dost keep
Steady thy laden head across a brook;
Or by a cider-press, with patient look,
Thou watchest the last oozings hours by hours.

3

Where are the songs of Spring? Ay, where are they?
Think not of them, thou hast thy music too—
While barred clouds bloom the soft-dying day,
And touch the stubble-plains with rosy hue;
Then in a wailful choir the small gnats mourn
Among the river sallows,° borne aloft *willows*
Or sinking as the light wind lives or dies;
And full-grown lambs loud bleat from hilly bourn;° *realm*
Hedge-crickets sing; and now with treble soft
The red-breast whistles from a garden-croft;° *enclosed garden*
And gathering swallows twitter in the skies.
—1820

This Living Hand[3]

This living hand, now warm and capable
Of earnest grasping, would, if it were cold
And in the icy silence of the tomb,
So haunt thy days and chill thy dreaming nights
That thou would wish thine own heart dry of blood
So in my veins red life might stream again,
And thou be conscience-calm'd—see here it is—
I hold it towards you—
—1898 (WRITTEN C. 1819)

[1] *hook* I.e., a reaping-hook or scythe.

[2] *gleaner* One who gathers the grain left by the reaper.

[3] *This Living Hand* A fragment whose context is unknown.

Selected Letters

TO BENJAMIN BAILEY[4]

22 November 1817

My Dear Bailey,

... O I wish I was as certain of the end of all your troubles as that of your momentary start about the authenticity of the Imagination. I am certain of nothing but of the holiness of the Heart's affections and the truth of imagination—What the imagination seizes as Beauty must be truth—whether it existed before or not—for I have the same Idea of all our Passions as of Love they are all in their sublime, creative of essential Beauty—In a Word, you may know my favourite Speculation by my first Book and the little song I sent in my last[5]—which is a representation from the fancy of the probable mode of operating in these Matters—The Imagination may be compared to Adam's dream[6]—he awoke and found it truth. I am the more zealous in this affair, because I have never yet been able to perceive how any thing can be known for truth by consequitive[7] reasoning—and yet it must be—Can it be that even the greatest Philosopher ever arrived at his goal without putting aside numerous objections—However it may be, O for a Life of Sensations rather than of Thoughts! It is "a Vision in the form of Youth" a Shadow of reality to come—and this consideration has further convinced me for it has come as auxiliary to another favourite Speculation of mine, that we shall enjoy ourselves here after by having what we called happiness on Earth repeated in a finer tone and so repeated—And yet such a fate can only befall those who delight in sensation

[4] *BENJAMIN BAILEY* Undergraduate student in Divinity at Oxford University. Keats had stayed with him in September while he was working on *Endymion*.

[5] *my first Book* I.e., the first book of *Endymion*; *little song ... last* The first five stanzas of "Ode to Sorrow," from Book 4 of *Endymion*, which Keats had enclosed with his previous letter.

[6] *Adam's dream* See Milton's *Paradise Lost* 8.460–90, in which Adam dreams about Eve and wakes to find she has been created.

[7] *consequitive* Consecutive and consequent: a word of Keats's invention.

rather than hunger as you do after Truth—Adam's dream will do here and seems to be a conviction that Imagination and its empyreal[1] reflection is the same as human Life and its spiritual repetition. But as I was saying—the simple imaginative Mind may have its rewards in the repetition of its own silent Working coming continually on the spirit with a fine suddenness—to compare great things with small—have you never by being surprised with an old Melody—in a delicious place—by a delicious voice, felt over again your very speculations and surmises at the time it first operated on your soul—do you not remember forming to yourself the singer's face more beautiful [than] it was possible and yet with the elevation of the Moment you did not think so—even then you were mounted on the Wings of Imagination so high—that the Prototype must be here after—that delicious face you will see—What a time! I am continually running away from the subject—sure this cannot be exactly the case with a complex Mind—one that is imaginative and at the same time careful of its fruits—who would exist partly on sensation partly on thought—to whom it is necessary that years should bring the philosophic Mind[2]—such an one I consider yours and therefore it is necessary to your eternal Happiness that you not only have drink this old Wine of Heaven which I shall call the redigestion of our most ethereal Musings on Earth; but also increase in knowledge and know all things. I am glad to hear you are in a fair Way for Easter—you will soon get through your unpleasant reading and then!—but the world is full of troubles and I have not much reason to think myself pestered with many—I think Jane or Marianne has a better opinion of me than I deserve—for really and truly I do not think my Brother's illness connected with mine[3]—you know more of the real Cause than they do—nor have I any chance of being rack'd as you have been[4]—you perhaps at one time thought there was such a thing as Worldly Happiness to be arrived at, at certain periods of time marked out—you have of necessity from your disposition been thus led away—I scarcely remember counting upon any Happiness—I look not for it if it be not in the present hour—nothing startles me beyond the Moment. The setting sun will always set me to rights—or if a Sparrow come before my Window I take part in its existence and pick about the Gravel. The first thing that strikes me on hearing a Misfortune having befalled another is this. Well it cannot be helped.—he will have the pleasure of trying the resources of his spirit, and I beg now my dear Bailey that hereafter should you observe any thing cold in me not to [put] it to the account of heartlessness but abstraction—for I assure you I sometimes feel not the influence of a Passion or Affection during a whole week—and so long this sometimes continues I begin to suspect myself and the genuineness of my feelings at other times—thinking them a few barren Tragedy-tears—My Brother Tom is much improved—he is going to Devonshire—whither I shall follow him—at present I am just arrived at Dorking to change the Scene—change the Air and give me a spur to wind up my Poem, of which there are wanting 500 Lines. …

Your affectionate friend
John Keats—

I want to say much more to you—a few hints will set me going
Direct Burford Bridge near dorking

[1] *empyreal* Celestial; pertaining to the highest heavens.

[2] *philosophic Mind* Cf. Wordsworth's *Ode: Intimations of Immortality*, line 186.

[3] *Jane or … mine* Jane and Marianne Reynolds, two friends of Keats, were afraid that his illness was a sign of tuberculosis, from which Keats's youngest brother, Tom, was suffering.

[4] *rack'd … been* Bailey was upset over a love affair that had recently ended.

TO GEORGE AND THOMAS KEATS

21, 27(?) December 1817
Hampstead Sunday

My Dear Brothers,

... I spent Friday evening with Wells[1] & went the next morning to see *Death on the Pale horse*. It is a wonderful picture, when West's[2] age is considered; But there is nothing to be intense upon; no women one feels mad to kiss; no face swelling into reality. the excellence of every Art is its intensity, capable of making all disagreeables evaporate, from their being in close relationship with Beauty & Truth—Examine *King Lear*[3] & you will find this exemplified throughout; but in this picture we have unpleasantness without any momentous depth of speculation excited, in which to bury its repulsiveness—The picture is larger than *Christ rejected*—I dined with Haydon[4] the sunday after you left, & had a very pleasant day, I dined too (for I have been out too much lately) with Horace Smith[5] & met his two Brothers with Hill & Kingston & one Du Bois, they only served to convince me, how superior humour is to wit in respect to enjoyment—These men say things which make one start, without making one feel, they are all alike; their manners are alike; they all know fashionables; they have a mannerism in their very eating & drinking, in their mere handling a Decanter—They talked of Kean[6] & his low company—Would I were with that company instead of yours said I to myself! I know such like acquaintance will never do for me & yet I am going to Reynolds,[7] on Wednesday—Brown & Dilke[8] walked with me & back from the Christmas pantomime. I had not a dispute but a disquisition[9] with Dilke, on various subjects; several things dovetailed in my mind, & at once it struck me, what quality went to form a Man of Achievement especially in Literature & which Shakespeare possessed so enormously—I mean *Negative Capability*, that is when man is capable of being in uncertainties, Mysteries, doubts, without any irritable reaching after fact & reason—Coleridge, for instance, would let go by a fine isolated verisimilitude caught from the Penetralium[10] of mystery, from being incapable of remaining content with half knowledge. This pursued through Volumes would perhaps take us no further than this, that with a great poet the sense of Beauty overcomes every other consideration, or rather obliterates all consideration.

Shelley's poem[11] is out, & there are words about its being objected too, as much as Queen Mab was. Poor Shelley I think he has his Quota of good qualities, in sooth la!![12] Write soon to your most sincere friend & affectionate Brother.

John

[1] *Wells* Charles Wells, a school friend of Tom Keats.

[2] *West* American painter Benjamin West (1738–1820), who moved to England and became President of the Royal Academy. The painting *Christ Rejected*, mentioned later in this letter, is West's.

[3] *King Lear* Painting by West that depicts the storm scene in Shakespeare's play.

[4] *Haydon* Painter Benjamin Haydon (1786–1846).

[5] *Horace Smith* Famous literary wit (1779–1849). The other men mentioned are all minor writers or literary critics.

[6] *Kean* Shakespearean actor Edmund Kean (1787–1833).

[7] *Reynolds* Lawyer and poet John Hamilton Reynolds (1796–1852).

[8] *Brown & Dilke* Writers Charles Wentworth Dilke (1789–1864) and Charles Armitage Brown (1786–1842), a close friend and housemate of Keats's who cared for him after he first became ill and who later wrote his biography.

[9] *disquisition* Systematic investigation.

[10] *Penetralium* I.e., the innermost part. From the Latin *penetralia*, the innermost parts of a temple.

[11] *Shelley's poem* Shelley's *Laon and Cythna* (*The Revolt of Islam*), which he was forced to withdraw because readers objected to the poem's description of incestuous love between its hero and heroine.

[12] *in sooth la* In truth.

Benjamin West, *King Lear*, 1788.

To John Hamilton Reynolds
3 February 1818
Hampstead

My Dear Reynolds,

I thank you for your dish of Filberts[1]—Would I could get a basket of them by way of dessert every day for the sum of two pence—Would we were a sort of ethereal Pigs, & turn'd loose to feed upon spiritual Mast[2] & Acorns—which would be merely being a squirrel & feeding upon filberts. For what is a squirrel but an airy pig, or a filbert but a sort of archangelical acorn. About the nuts being worth cracking, all I can say is that where there are a throng of delightful Images ready drawn simplicity is the only thing. The first is the best on account of the first line, and the "arrow—foil'd of its antler'd food"[3]—and moreover (and this is the only word or two I find fault with, the more because I have had so much reason to shun it as a quicksand) the last has "tender and true"—We must cut this, and not be rattle-snaked into any more of the like—It may be said that we ought to read our Contemporaries, that Wordsworth &c should have their due from us. But for the sake of a few fine imaginative or domestic passages, are we to be bullied into a certain Philosophy engendered in

[1] *Filberts* Hazelnuts.

[2] *Mast* Fruit of certain woodland trees, such as beech, oak, and chestnut.

[3] *arrow … food* Keats is commenting on Reynolds's "Sonnet on Robin Hood 1," which Reynolds had sent to Keats.

the whims of an Egotist—Every man has his speculations, but every man does not brood and peacock over them till he makes a false coinage and deceives himself—Many a man can travel to the very bourne[1] of Heaven, and yet want confidence to put down his halfseeing. Sancho[2] will invent a Journey heavenward as well as any body. We hate poetry that has a palpable design upon us—and if we do not agree, seems to put its hand in its breeches pocket.[3] Poetry should be great & unobtrusive, a thing which enters into one's soul, and does not startle it or amaze it with itself but with its subject.—How beautiful are the retired flowers! how would they lose their beauty were they to throng into the highway crying out, "admire me I am a violet! dote upon me I am a primrose!" Modern poets differ from the Elizabethans in this. Each of the moderns like an Elector of Hanover governs his petty state, & knows how many straws are swept daily from the Causeways in all his dominions & has a continual itching that all the Housewives should have their coppers well scoured: the antients were Emperors of vast Provinces, they had only heard of the remote ones and scarcely cared to visit them.—I will cut all this—I will have no more of Wordsworth or Hunt in particular—Why should we be of the tribe of Manasseh, when we can wander with Esau?[4] Why should we kick against the Pricks, when we can walk on Roses? Why should we be owls, when we can be Eagles? Why be teased with "nice Eyed wagtails," when we have in sight "the Cherub Contemplation"?[5]—Why with Wordsworths "Matthew with a bough of wilding in his hand" when we can have Jacques "under an oak &c"?[6]—The secret of the Bough of Wilding will run through your head faster than I can write it—Old Matthew spoke to him some years ago on some nothing, & because he happens in an Evening Walk to imagine the figure of the old man—he must stamp it down in black & white, and it is henceforth sacred—I don't mean to deny Wordsworth's grandeur & Hunt's merit, but I mean to say we need not be teazed with grandeur & merit—when we can have them uncontaminated & unobtrusive. Let us have the old Poets, & robin Hood Your letter and its sonnets gave me more pleasure than will the 4th Book of Childe Harold[7] & the whole of any body's life & opinions. In return for your dish of filberts, I have gathered a few Catkins, I hope they'll look pretty.[8]

Yr sincere friend and Coscribbler

John Keats

To John Taylor[9]

27 February 1818

Hampstead

My Dear Taylor,

Your alteration strikes me as being a great improvement—the page looks much better. And now I will attend to the Punctuations you speak of—the comma should be at *soberly,* and in the other passage the comma should follow *quiet.*[10] I am extremely indebted to you for this attention and also for your after admonitions—It is a sorry thing for me that any one should have to overcome Prejudices in reading my Verses—that affects me more than any hyper-criticism on any particular Passage. In *Endymion* I have most likely but moved into the Go-cart from the leading strings. In Poetry I have a few Axioms, and you will see how far I am from their Centre. 1st I think Poetry should surprise by a fine

[1] *bourne* Realm.

[2] *Sancho* Sancho Panza, squire of the naive and idealistic Don Quixote in Miguel de Cervantes's *Don Quixote.*

[3] *put its … pocket* I.e., refuse to fight (by putting one's fists away).

[4] *Why should … Esau* In the Old Testament, the tribe of Manasseh lived according to the old way of life, while in Genesis 25 Esau sold his birthright and became an outlaw.

[5] *nice Eyed wagtails* From Leigh Hunt's *The Nymphs* 2.170; *the Cherub Contemplation* From Milton's *Il Penseroso* 54.

[6] *Matthew … hand* From Wordsworth's *The Two April Mornings* 57–60; *under … &c* From Shakespeare's *As You Like It* 2.1.31.

[7] *4th … Harold* Canto 4 of Byron's *Childe Harold's Pilgrimage*, whose publication was eagerly anticipated at the time.

[8] *In return … pretty* In return for the sonnets on Robin Hood that Reynolds had sent, Keats enclosed two poems of his own, *Robin Hood* and *Lines on the Mermaid Tavern.*

[9] *John Taylor* Partner in the publishing firm of Taylor and Hessey, who were publishing Keats's poem *Endymion* at this time.

[10] *soberly … quiet* References to *Endymion* 1.149 and 1.247.

excess and not by Singularity—it should strike the Reader as a wording of his own highest thoughts, and appear almost a Remembrance—2nd Its touches of Beauty should never be half way thereby making the reader breathless instead of content: the rise, the progress, the setting of imagery should like the Sun come natural to him—shine over him and set soberly although in magnificence leaving him in the Luxury of twilight—but it is easier to think what Poetry should be than to write it—and this leads me on to another axiom. That if Poetry comes not as naturally as the Leaves to a tree it had better not come at all. However it may be with me I cannot help looking into new countries with "O for a Muse of fire to ascend!"[1]—If *Endymion* serves me as a Pioneer perhaps I ought to be content. I have great reason to be content, for thank God I can read and perhaps understand Shakespeare to his depths, and I have I am sure many friends, who, if I fail, will attribute any change in my Life and Temper to Humbleness rather than to Pride—to a cowering under the Wings of great Poets rather than to a Bitterness that I am not appreciated. I am anxious to get *Endymion* printed that I may forget it and proceed. I have copied the 3rd Book and have begun the 4th. On running my Eye over the Proofs—I saw one Mistake I will notice it presently and also any others if there be any—There should be no comma in "the raft branch down sweeping from a tall Ash top"[2]—I have besides made one or two alterations and also altered the 13 Line Page 32 to make sense of it as you will see. I will take care the Printer shall not trip up my Heels—There should be no dash after Dryope in this Line "Dryope's lone lulling of her Child."[3] Remember me to Percy Street.

Your sincere and obliged friend
John Keats—

P. S. You shall have a short *Preface* in good time—

[1] *O for … ascend* Cf. Shakespeare's *Henry V* Prologue 1: "O for a Muse of fire, that would ascend / The brightest heaven of invention."

[2] *the raft … top* From *Endymion* 1.334–35.

[3] *Dryope's … Child* From *Endymion* 1.495.

To Benjamin Bailey

13 March 1818
Teignmouth

My dear Bailey,

… I have never had your Sermon[4] from Wordsworth but Mrs. Dilke lent it me—You know my ideas about Religion—I do not think myself more in the right than other people and that nothing in this world is proveable. I wish I could enter into all your feelings on the subject merely for one short 10 Minutes and give you a Page or two to your liking. I am sometimes so very sceptical as to think Poetry itself a mere Jack a lantern to amuse whoever may chance to be struck with its brilliance—As Tradesmen say every thing is worth what it will fetch, so probably every mental pursuit takes its reality and worth from the ardour of the pursuer—being in itself a nothing—Ethereal things may at least be thus real, divided under three heads—Things real—things semireal—and no things—Things real—such as existences of Sun Moon & Stars and passages of Shakespeare—Things semireal such as Love, the Clouds &c which require a greeting of the Spirit to make them wholly exist—and Nothings which are made Great and dignified by an ardent pursuit—Which by the by stamps the burgundy mark on the bottles of our Minds, insomuch as they are able to "*consecrate whate'er they look upon*"[5] I have written a Sonnet here of a somewhat collateral nature—so don't imagine it an a propos des bottes.[6]

[*The Human Seasons* is included here.]

Aye this may be carried—but what am I talking of—it is an old maxim of mine and of course must be well known that every point of thought is the centre of an intellectual world—the two uppermost thoughts in a Man's mind are the two poles of his World he revolves on them and every thing is southward or northward to him through their means—We take but three steps from

[4] *your Sermon* Bailey, like many clergymen at the time, had written a memorial sermon for Princess Charlotte, who died in childbirth in 1817.

[5] *consecrate … upon* From Percy Shelley's *Hymn to Intellectual Beauty* 13–14.

[6] *a propos des bottes* French: on the subject of boots.

feathers to iron. Now my dear fellow I must once for all tell you I have not one Idea of the truth of any of my speculations—I shall never be a Reasoner because I care not to be in the right, when retired from bickering and in a proper philosophical temper … My Brother Tom desires to be remember'd to you—he has just this moment had a spitting of blood poor fellow—Remember me to [Gleig] and Whitehead—

Your affectionate friend
John Keats—

To JOHN HAMILTON REYNOLDS

3 May 1818
Teignmouth

My dear Reynolds,

… An extensive knowledge is needful to thinking people—it takes away the heat and fever; and helps, by widening speculation, to ease the Burden of the Mystery:[1] a thing I begin to understand a little, and which weighed upon you in the most gloomy and true sentence in your Letter. The difference of high Sensations with and without knowledge appears to me this—in the latter case we are falling continually ten thousand fathoms deep and being blown up again without wings and with all [the] horror of a bare shouldered Creature— in the former case, our shoulders are fledge,[2] and we go through the same air and space without fear. …

You may be anxious to know for fact to what sentence in your Letter I allude. You say "I fear there is little chance of any thing else in this life." You seem by that to have been going through with a more painful and acute zest the same labyrinth that I have—I have come to the same conclusion thus far. My Branchings out therefrom have been numerous: one of them is the consideration of Wordsworth's genius and as a help, in the manner of gold being the meridian Line of worldly wealth,[3] how he differs from Milton. And here I have nothing but surmises, from an uncertainty whether Milton's apparently less anxiety for Humanity proceeds from his seeing further or no than Wordsworth: And whether Wordsworth has in truth epic passion, and martyrs himself to the human heart, the main region of his song[4]—In regard to his genius alone—we find what he says true as far as we have experienced and we can judge no further but by larger experience—for axioms in philosophy are not axioms until they are proved upon our pulses: We have read fine —— things but never feel them to the full until we have gone the same steps as the author. …

I will return to Wordsworth—whether or no he has an extended vision or a circumscribed grandeur—whether he is an eagle in his nest, or on the wing—And to be more explicit and to show you how tall I stand by the giant, I will put down a simile of human life as far as I now perceive it; that is, to the point to which I say we both have arrived at—Well—I compare human life to a large Mansion of Many Apartments,[5] two of which I can only describe, the doors of the rest being as yet shut upon me—The first we step into we call the infant or thoughtless Chamber, in which we remain as long as we do not think—We remain there a long while, and notwithstanding the doors of the second Chamber remain wide open, showing a bright appearance, we care not to hasten to it; but are at length imperceptibly impelled by the awakening of the thinking principle—within us—we no sooner get into the second Chamber, which I shall call the Chamber of Maiden-Thought, than we become intoxicated with the light and the atmosphere, we see nothing but pleasant wonders, and think of delaying there for ever in delight: However among the effects this breathing is father of is that tremendous one of sharpening one's vision into the

---

[1] *Burden of the Mystery* From Wordsworth's "Lines Written a Few Miles above Tintern Abbey" (40).

[2] *fledge* With developed feathers, capable of flight.

[3] *in the manner … wealth* I.e., providing orienting information; the metaphor refers to the gold standard against which the values of currencies are measured, and to the prime meridian, the mark of 0° longitude.

[4] *main region of his song* Paraphrased from Wordsworth's Prospectus (1799, 1814) to his unfinished long poem *The Recluse*.

[5] *Mansion … Apartments* See John 14.2: "In my father's house are many mansions."

heart and nature of Man—of convincing ones nerves that the World is full of Misery and Heartbreak, Pain, Sickness and oppression—whereby This Chamber of Maiden Thought becomes gradually darkened and at the same time on all sides of it many doors are set open—but all dark—all leading to dark passages—we see not the balance of good and evil. We are in a Mist—*We* are now in that state—we feel the "burden of the Mystery." To this point was Wordsworth come, as far as I can conceive when he wrote "Tintern Abbey" and it seems to me that his genius is explorative of those dark Passages. Now if we live, and go on thinking, we too shall explore them. He is a Genius and superior [to] us, in so far as he can, more than we, make discoveries, and shed a light in them—Here I must think Wordsworth is deeper than Milton—though I think it has depended more upon the general and gregarious[1] advance of intellect, than individual greatness of Mind—From the *Paradise Lost* and the other Works of Milton, I hope it is not too presuming, even between ourselves to say, his Philosophy, human and divine, may be tolerably understood by one not much advanced in years. In his time Englishmen were just emancipated from a great superstition—and Men had got hold of certain points and resting places in reasoning which were too newly born to be doubted, and too much opposed by the Mass of Europe not to be thought ethereal[2] and authentically divine—who could gainsay his ideas on virtue, vice, and Chastity in *Comus*, just at the time of the dismissal of Cod-pieces[3] and a hundred other disgraces? who would not rest satisfied with his hintings at good and evil in the *Paradise Lost*, when just free from the inquisition and burning in Smithfield?[4] The Reformation produced such immediate and great benefits, that Protestantism was considered under the immediate eye of heaven, and its own remaining Dogmas and superstition, then, as it were, regenerated, constituted those resting places and seeming sure points of Reasoning—from that I have mentioned, Milton, whatever he may have thought in the sequel,[5] appears to have been content with these by his writings—He did not think into the human heart, as Wordsworth has done—Yet Milton as a philosopher, had sure as great powers as Wordsworth—What is then to be inferred? O many things—It proves there is really a grand march of intellect, it proves that a mighty providence subdues the mightiest Minds to the service of the time being, whether it be in human Knowledge or Religion. …

[T]he truth is there is something real in the World. Your third Chamber of Life shall be a lucky and a gentle one—stored with the wine of love—and the Bread of Friendship. …

Your affectionate friend
John Keats

[1] *general and gregarious* I.e., applying to all.

[2] *ethereal* Heavenly.

[3] *Comus* 1634 masque in which Comus, a debauched god, kidnaps a woman and attempts to persuade her to abandon rational virtue; *Cod-pieces* Coverings that, in the fifteenth and sixteenth centuries, were commonly worn over male genitals, and often drew attention to the region with decoration or padding.

[4] *Smithfield* London site where many Protestants were executed, often via burning, during the reign of the Catholic queen Mary I (r. 1553–58).

TO BENJAMIN BAILEY

18 July 1818

My dear Bailey,

… I am certain I have not a right feeling towards Women—at this moment I am striving to be just to them but I cannot—Is it because they fall so far beneath my Boyish imagination? When I was a Schoolboy I thought a fair Woman a pure Goddess, my mind was a soft nest in which some one of them slept though she knew it not—I have no right to expect more than their reality. I thought them ethereal above Men—I find them perhaps equal. … I do not like to think insults in a Lady's Company—I commit a Crime with her which absence would have not known—is it not extraordinary? When among Men I have no evil thoughts, no malice, no spleen[6]—I feel free to speak or to be silent—I can listen and from every one I can learn—my hands are in

[5] *in the sequel* I.e., in the end.

[6] *spleen* Irritability; ill-humor; melancholy.

my pockets I am free from all suspicion and comfortable. When I am among Women I have evil thoughts, malice spleen—I cannot speak or be silent—I am full of Suspicions and therefore listen to no thing—I am in a hurry to be gone—You must be charitable and put all this perversity to my being disappointed since Boyhood—Yet with such feelings I am happier alone among Crowds of men, by myself or with a friend or two—With all this trust me Bailey I have not the least idea that Men of different feelings and inclinations are more short sighted than myself—I never rejoiced more than at my Brother's Marriage[1] and shall do so at that of any of my friends—. I must absolutely get over this—but how? The only way is to find the root of evil, and so cure it "with backward mutters of dissevering Power."[2] That is a difficult thing; for an obstinate Prejudice can seldom be produced but from a gordian complication[3] of feelings, which must take time to unravell and care to keep unravelled—I could say a good deal about this but I will leave it in hopes of better and more worthy dispositions—and also content that I am wronging no one, for after all I do think better of Womankind than to suppose they care whether Mister John Keats five feet high likes them or not. …

Your affectionate friend

John Keats—

To Richard Woodhouse[4]

27 October 1818

My Dear Woodhouse,

Your Letter gave me a great satisfaction; more on account of its friendliness, than any relish of that matter in it which is accounted so acceptable in the "genus irritabile."[5] The best answer I can give you is in a clerklike manner to make some observations on two principle points, which seem to point like indices[6] into the midst of the whole pro and con, about genius, and views and achievements and ambition and coetera.[7] 1st As to the poetical Character itself, (I mean that sort of which, if I am any thing, I am a Member; that sort distinguished from the wordsworthian or egotistical sublime; which is a thing per se and stands alone) it is not itself—it has no self—it is every thing and nothing—It has no character—it enjoys light and shade; it lives in gusto, be it foul or fair, high or low, rich or poor, mean or elevated—It has as much delight in conceiving an Iago as an Imogen.[8] What shocks the virtuous philosopher delights the chameleon Poet. It does no harm from its relish of the dark side of things any more than from its taste for the bright one; because they both end in speculation. A Poet is the most unpoetical of any thing in existence; because he has no Identity—he is continually in for—and filling some other Body—The Sun, the Moon, the Sea and Men and Women who are creatures of impulse are poetical and have about them an unchangeable attribute—the poet has none; no identity—he is certainly the most unpoetical of all God's Creatures. If then he has no self, and if I am a Poet, where is the Wonder that I should say I would write no more? Might I not at that very instant [have] been cogitating on the Characters of Saturn and Ops?[9] It is a wretched thing to confess; but is a very fact that not one word I ever utter can be taken for granted as an opinion growing out of my identical nature—how can it, when I have no nature? When I am in a room with People if I ever am free from speculating

---

[1] *my Brother's Marriage* Keats's brother George had recently married, as had Bailey.

[2] *with … Power* From Milton's *Comus* 816–17, in which the author describes the spells that will release a lady from the enchantment of Comus.

[3] *gordian complication* I.e., as difficult to undo as the intricate knot tied by King Gordias.

[4] *Richard Woodhouse* Young lawyer who worked with Keats's publishers. Woodhouse was struck by Keats's talent and preserved manuscript copies of many of his poems and letters.

[5] *genus irritabile* Latin: irritable tribe. The complete phrase, from Horace, *Epistles* 2.2.102, is "irritable race of poets."

[6] *indices* Pointers.

[7] *coetera* Latin: the following; the next.

[8] *gusto* Term used by William Hazlitt to describe expressive vitality in visual arts as well as in poetry. See Hazlitt's essay "On Gusto" (1816); *Iago* Villain of Shakespeare's *Othello*; *Imogen* Heroine of Shakespeare's *Cymbeline*.

[9] *Saturn and Ops* King and queen of the Titans in Keats's *Hyperion* (1820).

on creations of my own brain, then not myself goes home to myself: but the identity of every one in the room begins [so] to press upon me that, I am in a very little time annihilated—not only among Men; it would be the same in a Nursery of children: I know not whether I make myself wholly understood: I hope enough so to let you see that no dependence is to be placed on what I said that day.[1]

In the second place I will speak of my views, and of the life I purpose to myself—I am ambitious of doing the world some good: if I should be spared that may be the work of maturer years—in the interval I will assay to reach to as high a summit in Poetry as the nerve bestowed upon me will suffer. The faint conceptions I have of Poems to come brings the blood frequently into my forehead—All I hope is that I may not lose all interest in human affairs—that the solitary indifference I feel for applause even from the finest Spirits, will not blunt any acuteness of vision I may have. I do not think it will—I feel assured I should write from the mere yearning and fondness I have for the Beautiful even if my night's labours should be burnt every morning and no eye ever shine upon them. But even now I am perhaps not speaking from myself; but from some character in whose soul I now live. I am sure however that this next sentence is from myself. I feel your anxiety, good opinion and friendliness in the highest degree, and am

Yours most sincerely
John Keats

To George and Georgiana Keats[2]

14 February–3 May 1819

My dear Brother & Sister—

… [19 March] Yesterday I got a black eye—the first time I took a Cricket bat—Brown who is always one's friend in a disaster applied a leech to the eyelid, and there is no inflammation this morning though the ball hit me directly on the sight—'t was a white ball—I am glad it was not a clout—This is the second black eye I have had since leaving school—during all my school days I never had one at all—we must eat a peck before we die[3]—This morning I am in a sort of temper indolent and supremely careless: I long after a stanza or two of Thomson's *Castle of indolence*[4]—My passions are all asleep from my having slumbered till nearly eleven and weakened the animal fibre all over me to a delightful sensation about three degrees on this side of faintness—if I had teeth of pearl and the breath of lilies I should call it langour—but as I am[5] I must call it Laziness—In this state of effeminacy the fibres of the brain are relaxed in common with the rest of the body, and to such a happy degree that pleasure has no show of enticement and pain no unbearable frown. Neither Poetry, nor Ambition, nor Love have any alertness of countenance as they pass by me: they seem rather like three figures on a greek vase—a Man and two women—whom no one but myself could distinguish in their disguisement. This is the only happiness; and is a rare instance of advantage in the body overpowering the Mind. I have this moment received a note from Haslam[6] in which he expects the death of his Father who has been for some time in a state of insensibility—his mother bears up he says very well—I shall go to [town] tomorrow to see him. This is the world—thus we cannot expect to give way many hours to pleasure—Circumstances are like Clouds continually gathering and bursting—While we are laughing the seed of some trouble is put into the wide arable land of events—while we are laughing it sprouts [it] grows and suddenly bears a poison fruit which we must pluck—Even so we have leisure to reason on the misfortunes of our friends; our

[1] *what I … day* Keats had told Woodhouse that he felt preempted by great poets of the past.

[2] *George and Georgiana Keats* Keats's brother and sister-in-law, who had emigrated to America. Keats would compose long letters to them, each of which spanned several months, and in which he would include transcriptions of his poems.

[3] *eat a peck … die* Proverbial: everyone must eat a peck of dirt before he or she dies.

[4] *Thomson … indolence* James Thomson's *The Castle of Indolence*, in which a wizard named Indolence puts a spell of indolence on tired travelers who are lured into his castle.

[5] [Keats's note] Especially as I have a black eye.

[6] *Haslam* Keats's friend William Haslam, a businessperson.

own touch us too nearly for words. Very few men have ever arrived at a complete disinterestedness[1] of Mind: very few have been influenced by a pure desire of the benefit of others—in the greater part of the Benefactors of & to Humanity some meretricious motive has sullied their greatness—some melodramatic scenery has fascinated them—From the manner in which I feel Haslam's misfortune I perceive how far I am from any humble standard of disinterestedness—Yet this feeling ought to be carried to its highest pitch, as there is no fear of its ever injuring society—which it would do I fear pushed to an extremity—For in wild nature the Hawk would loose his Breakfast of Robins and the Robin his of Worms. The Lion must starve as well as the swallow—The greater part of Men make their way with the same instinctiveness, the same unwandering eye from their purposes, the same animal eagerness as the Hawk—The Hawk wants a Mate, so does the Man—look at them both they set about it and procure one in the same manner—They want both a nest and they both set about one in the same manner—they get their food in the same manner—The noble animal Man for his amusement smokes his pipe—the Hawk balances about the Clouds—that is the only difference of their leisures. This it is that makes the Amusement of Life—to a speculative Mind. I go among the Fields and catch a glimpse of a stoat[2] or a fieldmouse peeping out of the withered grass—the creature hath a purpose and its eyes are bright with it—I go amongst the buildings of a city and I see a Man hurrying along—to what? The Creature has a purpose and his eyes are bright with it. But then as Wordsworth says, "we have all one human heart"[3]—there is an electric fire in human nature tending to purify—so that among these human creatures there is continually some birth of new heroism—The pity is that we must wonder at it: as we should at finding a pearl in rubbish—I have no doubt that thousands of people never heard of have had hearts completely disinterested: I can remember but two—Socrates and Jesus—their Histories evince it—What I heard a little time ago, Taylor observe with respect to Socrates, may be said of Jesus—That he was so great a man that though he transmitted no writing of his own to posterity, we have his Mind and his sayings and his greatness handed to us by others. It is to be lamented that the history of the latter was written and revised by Men interested in the pious frauds of Religion. Yet through all this I see his splendour. Even here though I myself am pursuing the same instinctive course as the veriest human animal you can think of—I am however young writing at random—straining at particles of light in the midst of a great darkness—without knowing the bearing of any one assertion of any one opinion. Yet may I not in this be free from sin? May there not be superior beings amused with any graceful, though instinctive attitude my mind may fall into, as I am entertained with the alertness of a Stoat or the anxiety of a Deer? Though a quarrel in the streets is a thing to be hated, the energies displayed in it are fine; the commonest Man shows a grace in his quarrel—By a superior being our reasoning may take the same tone—though erroneous they may be fine—This is the very thing in which consists poetry; and if so it is not so fine a thing as philosophy—For the same reason that an eagle is not so fine a thing as a truth—Give me this credit—Do you not think I strive—to know myself? Give me this credit—and you will not think that on my own account I repeat Milton's lines

> How charming is divine Philosophy
> Not harsh and crabbed as dull fools suppose
> But musical as is Apollo's lute[4]—

No—no for myself—feeling grateful as I do to have got into a state of mind to relish them properly—Nothing ever becomes real till it is experienced—Even a Proverb is no proverb to you till your Life has illustrated it— …

[21 April] I have been reading lately two very different books Robertson's *America* and Voltaire's *Siecle De Louis xiv* It is like walking arm and arm between Pizzarro and

[1] *disinterestedness* State unmotivated by self-interest.

[2] *stoat* Weasel-like animal.

[3] *we have … heart* From *The Old Cumberland Beggar* 152–53.

[4] *How charming … lute* See Milton's *Comus* 475–77.

the great-little Monarch.[1] In How lamentable a case do we see the great body of the people in both instances: in the first, where Men might seem to inherit quiet of Mind from unsophisticated sense; from uncontamination of civilisation; and especially from their being as it were estranged from the mutual helps of Society and its mutual injuries—and thereby more immediately under the Protection of Providence—even there they had mortal pains to bear as bad; or even worse than Bailiffs, Debts and Poverties of civilised Life—The whole appears to resolve into this—that Man is originally "a poor forked creature"[2] subject to the same mischances as the beasts of the forest, destined to hardships and disquietude of some kind or other. If he improves by degrees his bodily accommodations and comforts—at each stage, at each accent there are waiting for him a fresh set of annoyances—he is mortal and there is still a heaven with its Stars above his head. The most interesting question that can come before us is, How far by the persevering endeavours of a seldom appearing Socrates Mankind may be made happy—I can imagine such happiness carried to an extreme—but what must it end in?—Death—and who could in such a case bear with death—the whole troubles of life which are now frittered away in a series of years, would then be accumulated for the last days of a being who instead of hailing its approach, would leave this world as Eve left Paradise—But in truth I do not at all believe in this sort of perfectibility—the nature of the world will not admit of it—the inhabitants of the world will correspond to itself—Let the fish philosophise the ice away from the Rivers in winter time and they shall be at continual play in the tepid delight of summer. Look at the Poles and at the sands of Africa, Whirlpools and volcanoes—Let men exterminate them and I will say that they may arrive at earthly Happiness—The point at which Man may arrive is as far as the parallel state in inanimate nature and no further—For instance suppose a rose to have sensation, it blooms on a beautiful morning it enjoys itself—but there comes a cold wind, a hot sun—it can not escape it, it cannot destroy its annoyances—they are as native to the world as itself: no more can man be happy in spite, the worldly elements will prey upon his nature—The common cognomen of this world among the misguided and superstitious is "a vale of tears" from which we are to be redeemed by a certain arbitrary interposition of God and taken to Heaven—What a little circumscribed straightened notion! Call the world if you Please "The vale of Soul-making" Then you will find out the use of the world (I am speaking now in the highest terms for human nature admitting it to be immortal which I will here take for granted for the purpose of showing a thought which has struck me concerning it) I say "*Soul making*" Soul as distinguished from an Intelligence—There may be intelligences or sparks of the divinity in millions—but they are not Souls till they acquire identities, till each one is personally itself. Intelligences are atoms of perception—they know and they see and they are pure, in short they are God—how then are Souls to be made? How then are these sparks which are God to have identity given them—so as ever to possess a bliss peculiar to each ones individual existence? How, but by the medium of a world like this? This point I sincerely wish to consider because I think it a grander system of salvation than the christian religion—or rather it is a system of Spirit-creation—This is effected by three grand materials acting the one upon the other for a series of years—These three Materials are the *Intelligence*—the *human heart* (as distinguished from intelligence or Mind) and the *World* or *Elemental space* suited for the proper action of *Mind and Heart* on each other for the purpose of forming the *Soul or Intelligence destined to possess the sense of Identity*. I can scarcely express what I but dimly perceive—and yet I think I perceive it—that you may judge the more clearly I will put it in the most homely form possible—I will call the world a School instituted for the purpose of teaching little children to read—I will call the *human*

[1] *Robertson's … Monarch* William Robertson's *History of the Discovery and Settlement of America* (1777) describes the Spanish conquistadors, including Francisco Pizarro, who conquered the Incas in the sixteenth century. French philosopher Voltaire's *Le Siècle de Louis XIV* (1751) describes the rule of Louis XIV, who was often called "The Great Monarch."

[2] *a poor forked creature* From Shakespeare's *King Lear* 3.4.112–13, in which Lear looks at "Poor Tom" and says "Unaccommodated man is no more but such a poor, bare, forked animal as thou art."

heart the *horn Book*[1] used in that School—and I will call the *Child able to read, the Soul* made from that *school* and its *hornbook*. Do you not see how necessary a World of Pains and troubles is to school an Intelligence and make it a soul? A Place where the heart must feel and suffer in a thousand diverse ways! Not merely is the Heart a Hornbook, It is the Minds Bible, it is the Minds experience, it is the teat from which the Mind or intelligence sucks its identity—As various as the Lives of Men are—so various become their souls, and thus does God make individual beings, Souls, Identical Souls of the sparks of his own essence—This appears to me a faint sketch of a system of Salvation which does not affront our reason and humanity—I am convinced that many difficulties which christians labour under would vanish before it—there is one which even now Strikes me—the Salvation of Children—In them the Spark or intelligence returns to God without any identity—it having had no time to learn of, and be altered by, the heart—or seat of the human Passions—It is pretty generally suspected that the christian scheme has been copied from the ancient persian and greek Philosophers. Why may they not have made this simple thing even more simple for common apprehension by introducing Mediators and Personages in the same manner as in the heathen mythology abstractions are personified—Seriously I think it probable that this System of Soul-making—may have been the Parent of all the more palpable and personal Schemes of Redemption, among the Zoroastrians the Christians and the Hindus. For as one part of the human species must have their carved Jupiter; so another part must have the palpable and named Mediator and saviour, their Christ their Oromanes and their Vishnu[2]—If what I have said should not be plain enough, as I fear it may not be, I will but [put] you in the place where I began in this series of thoughts—I mean, I began by seeing how man was formed by circumstances—and what are circumstances?—but touchstones of his heart?—and what are touchstones?—but provings of his heart? and what are provings of his heart but fortifiers or alterers of his nature? and what is his altered nature but his soul?—and what was his soul before it came into the world and had These provings and alterations and perfectionings?—An intelligence—without Identity—and how is this Identity to be made? Through the medium of the Heart? And how is the heart to become this Medium but in a world of Circumstances?—There now I think what with Poetry and Theology you may thank your Stars that my pen is not very long winded— …

… [T]his is the 3rd of May & every thing is in delightful forwardness; the violets are not withered, before the peeping of the first rose; You must let me know every thing, how parcels go &. come, what papers you have, &. what Newspapers you want, & other things—God bless you my dear Brother & Sister

Your ever Affectionate Brother

John Keats—

To Fanny Brawne[3]

25 July 1819

Sunday Night

Isle of Wight

My Sweet Girl,

I hope you did not blame me much for not obeying your request of a Letter on Saturday: we have had four in our small room playing at cards night and morning leaving me no undisturb'd opportunity to write. Now Rice and Martin are gone I am at liberty. Brown to my sorrow confirms the account you give of your ill health. You cannot conceive how I ache to be with you: how I would die for one hour—for what is in the world? I say you cannot conceive; it is impossible you should look with such eyes upon me as I have upon you: it cannot be. Forgive me if I wander a little this

[1] *horn Book* Child's primer, originally made of a sheet of paper mounted on wood and protected by a thin sheet of transparent horn.

[2] *Oromanes* Ahriman, the chief evil spirit in Zoroastrianism, who is locked in perpetual struggle with Ahura Mazda; *Vishnu* Hindu deity who protects and preserves the world.

[3] *Fanny Brawne* Young woman whom Keats met in the summer of 1818, and to whom he was engaged by the end of the year (though the couple was waiting to marry until Keats felt he was financially secure). From October 1818 to May 1819 Keats stayed in his friend Charles Brown's apartment in Hampstead, which was next door to the Brawnes, who took care of him throughout the summer.

evening, for I have been all day employ'd in a very abstract Poem[1] and I am in deep love with you—two things which must excuse me. I have, believe me, not been an age in letting you take possession of me; the very first week I knew you I wrote myself your vassal; but burnt the Letter as the very next time I saw you I thought you manifested some dislike to me. If you should ever feel for Man at the first sight what I did for you, I am lost. Yet I should not quarrel with you, but hate myself if such a thing were to happen—only I should burst if the thing were not as fine as a Man as you are as a Woman. Perhaps I am too vehement, then fancy me on my knees, especially when I mention a part of your Letter which hurt me; you say speaking of Mr. Severn[2] "but you must be satisfied in knowing that I admired you much more than your friend." My dear love, I cannot believe there ever was or ever could be any thing to admire in me especially as far as sight goes—I cannot be admired, I am not a thing to be admired. You are, I love you; all I can bring you is a swooning admiration of your Beauty. I hold that place among Men which snubnos'd brunettes with meeting eyebrows do among women—they are trash to me—unless I should find one among them with a fire in her heart like the one that burns in mine. You absorb me in spite of myself—you alone: for I look not forward with any pleasure to what is call'd being settled in the world; I tremble at domestic cares—yet for you I would meet them, though if it would leave you the happier I would rather die than do so. I have two luxuries to brood over in my walks, your Loveliness and the hour of my death. O that I could have possession of them both in the same minute. I hate the world: it batters too much the wings of my self-will, and would I could take a sweet poison from your lips to send me out of it. From no others would I take it. I am indeed astonish'd to find myself so careless of all charms but yours—remembering as I do the time when even a bit of ribband was a matter of interest with me. What softer words can I find for you after this—what it is I will not read. Nor will I say more here, but in a Postscript answer any thing else you may have mentioned in your Letter in so many words—for I am distracted with a thousand thoughts. I will imagine you Venus tonight and pray, pray, pray to your star like a Heathen.

Yours ever, fair Star,
John Keats

To Percy Bysshe Shelley[3]

16 August 1820
Hampstead

My Dear Shelley,

I am very much gratified that you, in a foreign country, and with a mind almost over occupied, should write to me in the strain of the Letter beside me. If I do not take advantage of your invitation it will be prevented by a circumstance I have very much at heart to prophesy—There is no doubt that an english winter would put an end to me, and do so in a lingering hateful manner, therefore I must either voyage or journey to Italy as a soldier marches up to a battery. My nerves at present are the worst part of me, yet they feel soothed when I think that come what extreme may, I shall not be destined to remain in one spot long enough to take a hatred of any four particular bedposts. I am glad you take any pleasure in my poor Poem;[4]—which I would willingly take the trouble to unwrite, if possible, did I care so much as I have done about Reputation. I received a copy of the Cenci,[5] as from yourself from Hunt.

---

[1] *very abstract Poem* Most likely *The Fall of Hyperion*.

[2] *Mr. Severn* Joseph Severn, an artist and a friend of Keats. He cared for Keats during his final illness in Rome and was present when he died.

[3] *To ... Shelley* This letter is written in response to one from Shelley, in which he, having learned of Keats's serious illness, invites Keats to stay with him in Pisa for the winter.

[4] *my poor Poem* Keats's *Endymion*, which had received several negative reviews but which Shelley had praised in his letter.

[5] *Cenci* Shelley's blank-verse tragedy (1820).

There is only one part of it I am judge of; the Poetry, and dramatic effect, which by many spirits now a days is considered the mammon.[1] A modern work it is said must have a purpose, which may be the God—*an artist* must serve Mammon—he must have "self concentration" selfishness perhaps. You I am sure will forgive me for sincerely remarking that you might curb your magnanimity and be more of an artist, and "load every rift" of your subject with ore.[2] The thought of such discipline must fall like cold chains upon you, who perhaps never sat with your wings furl'd for six Months together. And is not this extraordinary talk for the writer of *Endymion*? whose mind was like a pack of scattered cards—I am pick'd up and sorted to a pip.[3] My Imagination is a Monastry and I am its Monk—you must explain my [metaphysics] to yourself. I am in expectation of *Prometheus*[4] every day. Could I have my own wish for its interest effected you would have it still in manuscript—or be but now putting an end to the second act. I remember you advising me not to publish my first-blights, on Hampstead heath—I am returning advice upon your hands. Most of the Poems in the volume I send you[5] have been written above two years, and would never have been publish'd but from a hope of gain; so you see I am inclined enough to take your advice now. I must express once more my deep sense of your kindness, adding my sincere thanks and respects for Mrs. Shelley. In the hope of soon seeing you I remain

most sincerely yours,
John Keats—

[1] *mammon* Wealth and profit, regarded as a false god. Cf. Matthew 6.24, in which Jesus says, "Ye cannot serve God and Mammon."

[2] *load ... ore* Reference to Spenser's *Faerie Queene* 2.7.28, in which he describes the Palace of Mammon: "Embost with massy gold of glorious gift, / And with rich metal loaded every rift."

[3] *sorted to a pip* Put in order. Pips are the markings on playing cards.

[4] *Prometheus* Shelley's *Prometheus Unbound* (1820), a copy of which he had promised to send to Keats.

[5] *the volume ... you* Keats's 1820 volume, which Shelley had in his pocket when he drowned.

TO CHARLES BROWN

30 November 1820
Rome

My Dear Brown,

'Tis the most difficult thing in the world to me to write a letter. My stomach continues so bad, that I feel it worse on opening any book,—yet I am much better than I was in Quarantine.[6] Then I am afraid to encounter the proing and conning of any thing interesting to me in England. I have an habitual feeling of my real life having past, and that I am leading a posthumous existence. God knows how it would have been—but it appears to me—however, I will not speak of that subject. I must have been at Bedhampton nearly at the time you were writing to me from Chichester—how unfortunate—and to pass on the river too! There was my star predominant! I cannot answer any thing in your letter, which followed me from Naples to Rome, because I am afraid to look it over again. I am so weak (in mind) that I cannot bear the sight of any hand writing of a friend I love so much as I do you. Yet I ride the little horse,[7]—and, at my worst, even in Quarantine, summoned up more puns, in a sort of desperation, in one week than in any year of my life. There is one thought enough to kill me—I have been well, healthy, alert &c, walking with her[8]—and now—the knowledge of contrast, feeling for light and shade, all that information (primitive sense) necessary for a poem are great enemies to the recovery of the stomach. There, you rogue, I put you to the torture,—but you must bring your philosophy to bear—as I do mine, really—or how should I be able to live? Dr Clarke is very attentive to me; he says, there is very little the matter with my lungs, but my stomach, he says, is very bad. I am well disappointed in hearing good news from George,—for it runs in my head we shall all die young. I have not written to

[6] *in Quarantine* Keats's ship was quarantined for ten days outside Naples, in extremely hot weather. Keats was writing this letter from Rome, where he was being cared for by Joseph Severn.

[7] *Yet ... horse* Recommended by Keats's doctor for exercise.

[8] *her* Fanny Brawne.

* * * *[1] yet, which he must think very neglectful; being anxious to send him a good account of my health, I have delayed it from week to week. If I recover, I will do all in my power to correct the mistakes made during sickness; and if I should not, all my faults will be forgiven. I shall write to * * * * tomorrow, or next day. I will write to * * * * in the middle of next week. Severn is very well, though he leads so dull a life with me. Remember me to all friends, and tell * * * * I should not have left London without taking leave of him, but from being so low in body and mind. Write to George as soon as you receive this, and tell him how I am, as far as you can guess; and also a note to my sister—who walks about my imagination like a ghost—she is so like Tom.[2] I can scarcely bid you good bye even in a letter. I always made an awkward bow.

God bless you!

John Keats.

In Context

Politics, Poetry, and the "Cockney School Debate"

As literary journals and magazines of the time demonstrate, in the nineteenth century politics and literary theory were often inextricably intertwined. At the time, only a small minority of adult males had been granted the vote, and the political system was widely perceived to be corrupt. Leigh Hunt, John Keats, William Hazlitt, and Percy Bysshe Shelley were among those who pressed strongly for political reform. Leigh Hunt, with his brothers John and Robert, edited the *Examiner*, a liberal weekly journal that frequently riled the government. After offending the Prince of Wales, Leigh and John spent two years in prison (1813–15) for libel.

In August 1817 the *Edinburgh Review* began to refer to Wordsworth, Coleridge, and Robert Southey as "The Lake School"—all three had lived in and been inspired by England's Lake District. Those poets and some others—Lord Byron in particular—had been identified the previous year by Leigh Hunt as representative of a school of poets "who go directly to Nature for inspiration." Hunt had written his article "Young Poets" to bring to the attention of the public "three young writers [Shelley, Keats, and John Hamilton Reynolds] who appear to us to promise a considerable addition of strength to the new school." Hunt had not named himself as a member of this new group, but it was on him that John Gibson Lockhart focused in launching an attack on the group that was as much political as literary. Lockhart's series of articles on "The Cockney School of Poetry" appeared in *Blackwood's Edinburgh Magazine*, a conservative journal founded in response to the *Edinburgh Review*.

1 * * * * Brown, whose transcription of this letter is the only surviving copy, deleted the names of Keats's friends in order to conceal their identities.

2 *my sister … Tom* Keats's sister Fanny closely resembled his youngest brother Tom, who had died of tuberculosis in December 1818.

from Leigh Hunt, "Young Poets," *Examiner* (1 December 1816)

In sitting down to this subject, we happen to be restricted by time to a much shorter notice than we could wish: but we mean to take it up again shortly. Many of our readers however have perhaps observed for themselves, that there has been a new school of poetry rising of late, which promises to extinguish the French one that has prevailed among us since the time of Charles the 2d. It began with something excessive, like most revolutions, but this gradually wore away; and an evident aspiration after real nature and original fancy remained, which called to mind the finer times of the English Muse. In fact it is wrong to call it a new school, and still more so to represent it as one of innovation, its only object being to restore the same love of Nature, and of *thinking* instead of mere *talking*, which formerly rendered us real poets, and not merely versifying wits, and bead-rollers of couplets.

We were delighted to see the departure of the old school acknowledged in the number of the *Edinburgh Review* just published—a candour the more generous and spirited, inasmuch as that work has hitherto been the greatest surviving ornament of the same school in prose and criticism, as it is now destined, we trust, to be still the leader in the new.

We also felt the same delight at the third canto of Lord Byron's *Childe Harold*, in which, to our conceptions at least, he has fairly renounced a certain leaven of the French style, and taken his place where we always said he would be found—among the poets who have a real feeling for numbers,[1] and who go directly to Nature for inspiration. But more of this poem in our next.

The object of the present article is merely to notice three young writers, who appear to us to promise a considerable addition of strength to the new school. Of the first who came before us, we have, it is true, yet seen only one or two specimens, and these were no sooner sent us than we unfortunately mislaid them; but we shall procure what he has published, and if the rest answer to what we have seen, we shall have no hesitation in announcing him for a very striking and original thinker. His name is Percy Bysshe Shelley, and he is the author of a poetical work entitled *Alastor, or the Spirit of Solitude*.

The next with whose name we became acquainted was John Henry Reynolds, author of a tale called *Safie*, written, we believe, in imitation of Lord Byron, and more lately of a small set of poems published by Taylor and Hessey, the principal of which is called the *Naiad*. It opens thus:

> The gold sun went into the west,
> And soft airs sang him to his rest;
> And yellow leaves all loose and dry,
> Play'd on the branches listlessly:
> The sky wax'd palely blue, and high
> A cloud seem'd touch'd upon the sky—
> A spot of cloud—blue, thin, and still,
> And silence bask'd on vale and hill. …

We shall give another extract or two in a future number. The author's style is too artificial, though he is evidently an admirer of Mr. Wordsworth. Like all young poets too, properly so called,

[1] *numbers* I.e., metrical harmony, rhythm.

his love of detail is too overwrought and indiscriminate; but still he is a young poet, and only wants a still closer attention to things as opposed to the seduction of words, to realize all that he promises. His nature seems very true and amiable.

The last of these young aspirants who we have met with, and who promise to help the new school to revive Nature and

> "To put a spirit of youth in every thing,"

is, we believe, the youngest of them all, and just of age. His name is John Keats. He has not yet published anything except in a newspaper; but a set of his manuscripts was handed us the other day, and fairly surprised us with the truth of their ambition, and ardent grappling with Nature. In the following sonnet there is one incorrect rhyme, which might be easily altered, but which shall serve in the mean time as a peace-offering to the rhyming critics. The rest of the composition, with the exception of a little vagueness in calling the regions of poetry "the realms of gold," we do not hesitate to pronounce excellent, especially the last six lines. The word *swims* is complete; and the whole conclusion is equally powerful and quiet

[Quotes "On First Looking into Chapman's Homer"]

We have spoken with the less scruple of these poetical promises, because we really are not in the habit of lavishing praises and announcements, and because we have no fear of any pettier vanity on the part of young men who promise to understand human nature so well.

from John Lockhart ("Z."), "On the Cockney School of Poetry, No. 1," *Blackwood's Edinburgh Magazine* (October 1817)

> Our talk shall be (a theme we never tire on)
> Of Chaucer, Spenser, Shakespeare, Milton, Byron,
> (Our England's Dante)—Wordsworth—Hunt, and Keats,
> The Muses' son of promise; and of what feats
> He yet may do.
>
> —CORNELIUS WEBB

While the whole critical world is occupied with balancing the merits, whether in theory or in execution, of what is commonly called The Lake School, it is strange that no one seems to think it at all necessary to say a single word about another new school of poetry which has of late sprung up amongst us. This school has not, I believe, as yet received any name; but if I may be permitted to have the honour of christening it, it may henceforth be referred to by the designation of The Cockney School. Its chief Doctor and Professor is Mr. Leigh Hunt, a man certainly of some talents, of extravagant pretensions both in wit, poetry, and politics, and withal of exquisitely bad taste, and extremely vulgar modes of thinking and manners in all respects. He is a man of little education. He knows absolutely nothing of Greek, almost nothing of Latin, and his knowledge of Italian literature is confined to a few of the most popular of Petrarch's sonnets, and an imperfect acquaintance with Ariosto, through the medium of Mr. Hoole. As to the French poets, he dismisses them in the mass as a set of prim, precise, unnatural pretenders. The truth is, he is in a state of happy ignorance about them and all that they have done. …

With this stock of knowledge, Mr. Hunt presumes to become the founder of a new school of poetry, and throws away entirely the chance he might have had of gaining some true poetic fame, had he been less lofty in his pretensions. …

All the great poets of our country have been men of some rank in society, and there is no vulgarity in any of their writings; but Mr. Hunt cannot utter a dedication, or even a note, without betraying the *Shibboleth*[1] of low birth and low habits. He is the ideal of a Cockney Poet. He raves perpetually about "green fields," "jaunty streams," and "o'er-arching leafiness," exactly as a Cheapside shop-keeper does about the beauties of his box[2] on the Camberwell road. Mr. Hunt is altogether unacquainted with the face of nature in her magnificent scenes; he has never seen any mountain higher than Highgate-hill,[3] nor reclined by any stream more pastoral than the Serpentine River.[4] But he is determined to be a poet eminently rural, and he rings the changes—till one is sick of him, on the beauties of the different "high views" which he has taken of God and nature, in the course of some Sunday dinner parties, at which he has assisted in the neighbourhood of London. His books are indeed not known in the country; his fame as a poet (and I might almost say, as a politician too) is entirely confined to the young attorneys and embryo-barristers about town. In the opinion of these competent judges, London is the world—and Hunt is a Homer.

Mr. Hunt is not disqualified by his ignorance and vulgarity alone, for being the founder of a respectable sect in poetry. He labours under the burden of a sin more deadly than either of these. The two great elements of all dignified poetry, religious feeling and patriotic feeling, have no place in his writings. His religion is a poor tame dilution of the blasphemies of the *Encyclopaedie*[5]—his patriotism a crude, vague, ineffectual, and sour Jacobinism.[6] His works exhibit no reverence either for God or man; neither altar nor throne have any dignity in his eyes. He speaks well of nobody but two or three great dead poets, and in so speaking of them he does well; but alas! Mr. Hunt is no conjurer *τεχνη ὅ λανθανει*.[7] He pretends, indeed, to be an admirer of Spenser and Chaucer, but what he praises in them is never what is most deserving of praise—it is only that which he humbly conceives bears some resemblance to the more perfect productions of Mr. Leigh Hunt; and we can always discover in the midst of his most violent ravings about the Court of Elizabeth, and the days of Sir Philip Sidney, and the Fairy Queen, that the real objects of his admiration are the Coterie of Hampstead and the Editor of the Examiner. When he talks about chivalry and King Arthur, he is always thinking of himself, and "*a small party of friends, who meet once a week at a Round Table, to discuss the merits of a*

[1] *Shibboleth* Word distinguishing a certain class or party.

[2] *box* Boxwood.

[3] *Highgate-hill* Hill (and district) in the north of London.

[4] *Serpentine River* Lake in Hyde Park, in the center of London.

[5] *Encylopaedie* Great manifesto of the French *philosophes*, prepared by Denis Diderot and Jean le Rond d'Alembert (1751).

[6] *Jacobinism* Extreme democratic principles; belief in complete equality (after the practice of the French political sect the Jacobins).

[7] *τεχνη ὅ λανθανει* Greek: his technique does not escape notice.

leg of mutton, and of the subjects upon which we are to write."[1]—Mr. Leigh Hunt's ideas concerning the sublime, and concerning his own powers, bear a considerable resemblance to those of his friend Bottom, the weaver, on the same subjects; "I will roar, that it shall do any man's heart good to hear me."—"I will roar you an 'twere any nightingale."[2]

The poetry of Mr. Hunt is such as might be expected from the personal character and habits of its author. As a vulgar man is perpetually labouring to be genteel—in like manner, the poetry of this man is always on the stretch to be grand. He has been allowed to look for a moment from the antechamber into the salon, and mistaken the waving of feathers and the painted floor for the *sine qua non*'s[3] of elegant society. He would fain be always tripping and waltzing, and is sorry that he cannot be allowed to walk about in the morning with yellow breeches and flesh-coloured silk-stockings. He sticks an artificial rosebud into his button hole in the midst of winter. …

How such an indelicate writer as Mr. Hunt can pretend to be an admirer of Mr. Wordsworth, is to us a thing altogether inexplicable. One great charm of Wordsworth's noble compositions consists in the dignified purity of thought, and the patriarchal simplicity of feeling, with which they are throughout penetrated and imbued. We can conceive a vicious[4] man admiring with distant awe the spectacle of virtue and purity; but if he does so sincerely, he must also do so with the profoundest feeling of the error of his own ways, and the resolution to amend them. His admiration must be humble and silent, not pert and loquacious. Mr. Hunt praises the purity of Wordsworth as if he himself were pure, his dignity as if he also were dignified. …

The founder of the Cockney School would fain claim poetical kindred with Lord Byron and Thomas Moore.[5] Such a connection would be as unsuitable for them as for William Wordsworth. The days of Mr. Moore's follies are long since over; and, as he is a thorough gentleman, he must necessarily entertain the greatest contempt for such an under-bred person as Mr. Leigh Hunt. But Lord Byron! … We dare say Mr. Hunt has some fine dreams about the true nobility being the nobility of talent, and flatters himself, that with those who acknowledge only that sort of rank, he himself passes for being the *peer* of Byron. He is sadly mistaken. He is as completely a Plebeian[6] in his mind as he is in his rank and station in society. To that highest and unalienable nobility which the great Roman satirist styles "*sola atque unica*,"[7] we fear his pretensions would be equally unavailing.

The shallow and impotent pretensions, tenets, and attempts of this man—and the success with which his influence seems to be extending itself among a pretty numerous, though certainly a very paltry and pitiful, set of readers—have for the last two or three years been considered by us with the most sickening aversion. The very culpable manner in which his chief poem was reviewed in the *Edinburgh Review* (we believe it is no secret, at his own impatient and feverish request, by his partner

---

1 *a small … write* From a feature in the *Examiner*, initiated by Leigh Hunt, called "The Round Table."

2 *I will … nightingale* From Shakespeare's *A Midsummer Night's Dream* 1.2, in which Bottom the weaver (who is later transformed into an ass) desires to play the lion's part in a play.

3 *sine qua non* Latin: without which, not.

4 *vicious* Immoral.

5 *Thomas Moore* Irish poet (1779–1852).

6 *Plebeian* In ancient Rome, a commoner, a person of low birth or rank.

7 *sola atque unica* Latin: alone and only. See Juvenal's *Satire* 8: "Virtue alone is the only true nobility."

in the Round Table[1]), was matter of concern to more readers than ourselves. The masterly pen which inflicted such signal chastisement on the early licentiousness of Moore, should not have been idle on that occasion. Mr. Jeffrey[2] does ill, when he delegates his important functions into such hands as those of Mr. Hazlitt. It was chiefly in consequence of that gentleman's allowing Leigh Hunt to pass unpunished through the scene of slaughter, which his execution might so highly have graced, that we came to the resolution of laying before our readers a series of essays on *the Cockney School*—of which here terminates the first.

from John Lockhart ("Z."), "On the Cockney School of Poetry, No. 4," *Blackwood's Edinburgh Magazine* (August 1818)

———Of Keats,
The Muses' son of promise, and what feats
He yet may do, &c.
—CORNELIUS WEBB

Of all the manias of this mad age, the most incurable, as well as the most common, seems to be no other than the *Metromanie*.[3] The just celebrity of Robert Burns and Miss Baillie[4] has had the melancholy effect of turning the heads of we know not how many farm-servants and unmarried ladies; our very footmen compose tragedies, and there is scarcely a superannuated governess in the island that does not leave a roll of lyrics behind her in her band-box. To witness the disease of any human understanding, however feeble, is distressing; but the spectacle of an able mind reduced to a state of insanity is of course ten times more afflicting. It is with such sorrow as this that we have contemplated the case of Mr. John Keats. This young man appears to have received from nature talents of an excellent, perhaps even of a superior order—talents which, devoted to the purpose of any useful profession, must have rendered him a respectable, if not an eminent citizen. His friends, we understand, destined him to the career of medicine, and he was bound apprentice some years ago to a worthy apothecary in town. But all has been undone by a sudden attack of the malady to which we have alluded. Whether Mr. John had been sent home with a diuretic or composing draught to some patient far gone in the poetical mania, we have not heard. This much is certain, that he has caught the infection, and that thoroughly. For some time we were in hopes that he might get off with a violent fit or two; but of late the symptoms are terrible. The frenzy of the "Poems"[5] was bad enough in its way; but it did not alarm us half so seriously as the calm, settled, imperturbable drivelling idiocy of "Endymion." We hope, however, that in so young a person, and with a constitution originally so good, even now the disease is not utterly incurable. Time, firm treatment, and rational restraint, do

[1] *partner … Table* William Hazlitt, who contributed to both the *Examiner* and the *Edinburgh Review*. Hazlitt frequently wrote for the *Examiner* feature "The Round Table," and his first book-length collection of essays appeared in 1817 under that title.

[2] *Mr. Jeffrey* Francis Jeffrey (1773–1850), founder and editor of the *Edinburgh Review*.

[3] *Metromanie* Mania for writing poetry.

[4] *Miss Baillie* Scottish poet and playwright Joanna Baillie (1762–1851).

[5] *Poems* Keats's first volume of poetry, which was published in March 1817.

much for many apparently hopeless invalids; and if Mr. Keats should happen, at some interval of reason, to cast his eye upon our pages, he may perhaps be convinced of the existence of his malady, which in such cases is often all that is necessary to put the patient in a fair way of being cured. …

[Keats's] Endymion is not a Greek shepherd, loved by a Grecian goddess;[1] he is merely a young Cockney rhymester, dreaming a fantastic dream at the full of the moon. Costume, were it worth while to notice such a trifle, is violated in every page of this goodly octavo. From his prototype Hunt, Keats has acquired a sort of vague idea that the Greeks were a most tasteful people, and that no mythology can be so finely adapted for the purposes of poetry as theirs. It is amusing to see what a hand the two Cockneys make of this mythology; the one confesses that he never read the Greek Tragedians, and the other knows Homer only from Chapman;[2] and both of them write about Apollo, Pan, Nymphs, Muses, and Mysteries, as might be expected from persons of their education. We shall not, however, enlarge at present upon this subject, as we mean to dedicate an entire paper to the classical attainments and attempts of the Cockney poets. As for Mr. Keats' "Endymion," it has just as much to do with Greece as it has with "old Tartary the fierce;" no man whose mind has ever been imbued with the smallest knowledge or feeling of classical poetry or classical history could have stooped to profane and vulgarise every association in the manner which has been adopted by this "son of promise." Before giving any extracts, we must inform our readers that this romance is meant to be written in English heroic rhyme. To those who have read any of Hunt's poems, this hint might indeed be needless. Mr. Keats has adopted the loose, nerveless versification and Cockney rhymes of the poet of *Rimini*;[3] but, in fairness to that gentleman, we must add that the defects of the system are tenfold more conspicuous in his disciple's work than in his own. Mr. Hunt is a small poet, but he is a clever man. Mr. Keats is a still smaller poet, and he is only a boy of pretty abilities, which he has done every thing in his power to spoil.

---

[1] *Endymion … goddess* "Endymion" retells the story of the goddess of the moon falling in love with a shepherd, as told by the Roman poet Ovid.

[2] *Homer … Chapman* Keats knew very little Greek, and read it only in translation. George Chapman's edition of Homer's *Iliad* appeared in 1612, and his edition of the *Odyssey* in 1616.

[3] *Rimini* Hunt's long poem *The Story of Rimini* (1816).

Mary Shelley
1797 – 1851

As Mary Wollstonecraft Shelley wrote in her introduction to the second edition of *Frankenstein*, readers constantly asked her "How I, then a young girl, came to think of, and to dilate upon, so hideous an idea." At the age of nineteen, Shelley created one of the most extraordinary and powerful horror stories in Western literature, one that continues to pervade our popular culture. While *Frankenstein* is undoubtedly her most widely read and influential work, Shelley is also celebrated for a large body of fiction of vivid imaginative power that grapples in penetrating fashion with the political and social concerns of her day.

If Shelley's writing is extraordinary, neither is there anything ordinary in her parentage or her tumultuous life. She was born Mary Wollstonecraft Godwin in August of 1797. The only child of radical feminist Mary Wollstonecraft and the philosopher, author, and political journalist William Godwin, Shelley felt the weight of her parents' controversial reputations throughout her life. Her mother died just after giving birth, and Shelley came to know her only through her works—in particular the *Vindication of the Rights of Woman* (1792). Godwin, for whom Shelley later said she bore an "excess of attachment," raised Mary and her half-sister Fanny, educating them with the help of several friends and regular visitors—a group of supremely qualified teachers that included poet Samuel Taylor Coleridge, painter Thomas Lawrence, novelist Maria Edgeworth, and scientist Humphrey Davy. Godwin's novels and philosophical works, particularly his *Enquiry Concerning Political Justice* (1793), were formative influences on his daughter's thought.

After her father married Mary Jane Clairmont in 1801, Mary Godwin, who did not get along with her stepmother, spent extended periods of time with family friends in Scotland. On a visit home in 1814, she became acquainted with Percy Bysshe Shelley, a radical poet and admirer of Godwin's principles, who had become a regular visitor to the Godwin home. Although Percy was married at the time, within months the two declared their love for each other, meeting in secret by the grave of Mary's mother. The two then eloped to France, taking Mary's stepsister Claire Clairmont with them. Godwin disowned his daughter upon her elopement and was only slightly mollified when the two married in 1816, following the suicide of Percy's first wife, Harriet.

The couple toured France, Switzerland, and Germany (a trip described in Mary Shelley's first publication, *History of a Six Weeks' Tour*, 1817) before eventually settling in Italy near Lord Byron. The subsequent years in Italy were turbulent ones. Two of Shelley's children died in infancy, and her three-year-old son William died in 1819. A life-threatening miscarriage that same year plunged Shelley into severe depression, and she and her husband became increasingly distant. When Percy drowned with his friend Edward Williams in July of 1822, her sorrow at his death was further augmented by her guilt at their estrangement.

Although she wrote some poetry and verse dramas, Shelley's only publication during these years was *Frankenstein, or The Modern Prometheus*, first published in 1818 and revised for a new edition in 1831. The novel was conceived in the summer of 1816, when the Shelleys were in Switzerland with Lord Byron and John Polidori, Byron's resident physician. The summer was rainy and miserable, so the friends spent much time around a fire indoors, reading ghost stories. Byron suggested that they amuse themselves by each writing a ghost story to share with the others, and he proceeded to begin a vampire horror story later published as "A Fragment" (1819). Polidori began work on his *Ernestus Berchtold; or, The Modern Oedipus* (1819). According to Mary Shelley's own account in her 1831 introduction to *Frankenstein*, she found inspiration for her contribution after listening to Byron and Percy discuss the work of Erasmus Darwin on galvanism and the possibility of reanimating corpses. That night, she fell asleep and had a "waking dream," of "the pale student of unhallowed arts kneeling beside the thing he had put together … the hideous phantasm of a man stretched out, and then, on the working of some powerful engine, show signs of life, and stir with an uneasy, half vital motion." This vision of horror, which "mock[ed] the stupendous mechanism of the Creator of the world," became the seed of her ghost story, which she eventually expanded into the novel *Frankenstein*.

As a result of the scandalous events in her past, as well as the radical views of her parents and husband—not to mention her own radical opinions—Shelley felt exiled from society. After the deaths of Percy in 1822 and of Byron in 1824, she found herself without friendship or support. She had a small allowance from her father-in-law, but it was hardly enough to support her, so she turned to writing for income. She returned to London and began producing book reviews, essays, and short biographies while continuing to write novels. *The Last Man* (1826) presents a view of humanity in which a plague destroys the earth, leaving only one man, Lionel Verney. Shelley's novels *Valperga* (1823) and *The Fortunes of Perkin Warbeck: A Romance* (1830) experiment with the genre of historical fiction—a mode that had recently been made popular by Walter Scott—combining romance and fiction with historical and political analysis. In these novels, as well as in *The Last Man*, critics found evidence of the "unsavory politics" they expected from one of the Godwin circle. Critics and readers alike preferred Shelley's more traditional domestic fictions, such as *Lodore* (1835) and *Falkner* (1837).

Percy's father, Sir Timothy Shelley, for many years prevented Mary Shelley from publishing editions of her husband's work, but he eventually reconsidered, and in 1839 she released his four-volume *Poetical Works*, as well as his *Essays and Letters from Abroad, Translations and Fragments*. In writing about her husband, Shelley endeavored to rationalize his radical attitudes and behavior—particularly his atheism and sedition—in order to mediate his poetry for his audience and redeem his public image. Although she has been accused of altering his manuscripts and misrepresenting his politics, she succeeded in her goal of bringing his work to public notice.

In 1844 the concerns that had plagued Shelley since the death of her husband were relieved by the death of his father, whose title and estate her son, Percy Florence, inherited. Shelley spent her final years traveling with Percy Florence and helping him manage the estate. In 1848 he married Jane St. John, a widow and friend of Shelley. Jane nursed Shelley in the months before her death from a brain tumor in 1851.

⌘⌘⌘

from *Frankenstein; or, the Modern Prometheus*

Shelley's celebrated tale is framed by the narrative of an explorer, Captain Walton, who encounters the title character while on an arctic expedition; the majority of the novel is Victor Frankenstein's life story as he tells it for Walton's benefit. In the first chapters, Victor recounts his pleasant upbringing as the eldest son of a wealthy Genevan family. His happiness is interrupted by the death of his mother from scarlet fever, and a few weeks later he leaves Geneva to study natural philosophy at the University of Ingolstadt. The selection from the novel reprinted here commences as Victor, having successfully completed his university education in natural philosophy, independently undertakes a study of "the causes of life."

from Volume 1

from Chapter 3

… Whence, I often asked myself, did the principle of life proceed? It was a bold question, and one which has ever been considered as a mystery; yet with how many things are we upon the brink of becoming acquainted, if cowardice or carelessness did not restrain our inquiries. I revolved these circumstances in my mind, and determined thenceforth to apply myself more particularly to those branches of natural philosophy which relate to physiology. Unless I had been animated by an almost supernatural enthusiasm, my application to this study would have been irksome, and almost intolerable. To examine the causes of life, we must first have recourse to death. I became acquainted with the science of anatomy: but this was not sufficient; I must also observe the natural decay and corruption of the human body. In my education my father had taken the greatest precautions that my mind should be impressed with no supernatural horrors. I do not ever remember to have trembled at a tale of superstition, or to have feared the apparition of a spirit. Darkness had no effect upon my fancy; and a church-yard was to me merely the receptacle of bodies deprived of life, which, from being the seat of beauty and strength, had become food for the worm. Now I was led to examine the cause and progress of this decay, and forced to spend days and nights in vaults and charnel houses. My attention was fixed upon every object the most insupportable to the delicacy of the human feelings. I saw how the fine form of man was degraded and wasted; I beheld the corruption of death succeed to the blooming cheek of life; I saw how the worm inherited the wonders of the eye and brain. I paused, examining and analysing all the minutiae of causation, as exemplified in the change from life to death, and death to life, until from the midst of this darkness a sudden light broke in upon me—a light so brilliant and wondrous, yet so simple, that while I became dizzy with the immensity of the prospect which it illustrated, I was surprised that among so many men of genius, who had directed their inquiries towards the same science, that I alone should be reserved to discover so astonishing a secret.

Remember, I am not recording the vision of a madman. The sun does not more certainly shine in the heavens, than that which I now affirm is true. Some miracle might have produced it, yet the stages of the discovery were distinct and probable. After days and nights of incredible labour and fatigue, I succeeded in discovering the cause of generation and life; nay, more, I became myself capable of bestowing animation upon lifeless matter.

The astonishment which I had at first experienced on this discovery soon gave place to delight and rapture. After so much time spent in painful labour, to arrive at once at the summit of my desires, was the most gratifying consummation of my toils. But this discovery was so great and overwhelming, that all the steps by which I had been progressively led to it were obliterated, and I beheld only the result. What had been the study and desire of the wisest men since the creation of the world, was now within my grasp. Not that, like a magic scene, it all opened upon me at once: the information I had obtained was of a nature rather to direct my endeavours so soon as I should point them towards the object of my search, than to exhibit that object already accomplished. I was like the Arabian who had been buried with the dead, and found a passage to life aided only by one glimmering, and seemingly ineffectual, light.[1]

I see by your eagerness, and the wonder and hope which your eyes express, my friend, that you expect to be informed of the secret with which I am acquainted; that cannot be: listen patiently until the end of my story, and you will easily perceive why I am reserved upon that subject. I will not lead you on, unguarded and ardent as I then was, to your destruction and infallible misery. Learn from me, if not by my precepts, at least by my example, how dangerous is the acquirement of knowledge, and how much happier that man is who believes his native town to be the world, than he who aspires to become greater than his nature will allow.

When I found so astonishing a power placed within my hands, I hesitated a long time concerning the manner in which I should employ it. Although I possessed the capacity of bestowing animation, yet to prepare a frame for the reception of it, with all its intricacies of fibres, muscles, and veins, still remained a work of inconceivable difficulty and labour. I doubted at first whether I should attempt the creation of a being like myself or one of simpler organization; but my imagination was too much exalted by my first success to permit me to doubt of my ability to give life to an animal as complex and wonderful as man. The materials at present within my command hardly appeared adequate to so arduous an undertaking; but I doubted not that I should ultimately succeed. I prepared myself for a multitude of reverses; my operations might be incessantly baffled, and at last my work be imperfect: yet, when I considered the improvement which every day takes place in science and mechanics, I was encouraged to hope my present attempts would at least lay the foundations of future success. Nor could I consider the magnitude and complexity of my plan as any argument of its impracticability. It was with these feelings that I began the creation of a human being. As the minuteness of the parts formed a great hindrance to my speed, I resolved, contrary to my first intention, to make the being of a gigantic stature; that is to say, about eight feet in height, and proportionably large. After having formed this determination, and having spent some months in successfully collecting and arranging my materials, I began.

No one can conceive the variety of feelings which bore me onwards, like a hurricane, in the first enthusiasm of success. Life and death appeared to me ideal bounds, which I should first break through, and pour a torrent of light into our dark world. A new species would bless me as its creator and source; many happy and excellent natures would owe their being to me. No father could claim the gratitude of his child so completely as I should deserve theirs. Pursuing these reflections, I thought, that if I could bestow animation upon lifeless matter, I might in process of time (although I now found it impossible) renew life where death had apparently devoted the body to corruption.

These thoughts supported my spirits, while I pursued my undertaking with unremitting ardour. My cheek had grown pale with study, and my person had become emaciated with confinement. Sometimes, on the very brink of certainty, I failed; yet still I clung to the hope which the next day or the next hour might realize. One secret which I alone possessed was the hope to which I had dedicated myself; and the moon gazed on my midnight labours, while, with unrelaxed and breathless eagerness, I pursued nature to her hiding places. Who shall conceive the horrors of my secret toil, as I dabbled among the unhallowed damps of the grave, or tortured the living animal to animate the lifeless clay? My limbs now tremble, and my eyes swim with the remembrance; but then a resistless, and almost frantic impulse, urged me forward; I seemed to have lost all soul or sensation but for this one pursuit. It was indeed but a passing trance, that only made me feel with renewed acuteness so soon as, the unnatural stimulus ceasing to operate, I had returned to my old habits. I collected bones from charnel houses; and disturbed, with profane fingers, the tremendous secrets of the human frame. In a solitary chamber, or rather cell, at the top of the house, and separated from all the other apartments by a gallery and staircase, I kept my workshop of filthy creation; my eyeballs were starting from their sockets in attending to the details of my employ-

[1] *like the Arabian … light* In the fourth voyage of Sinbad, recounted in the *One Thousand and One Nights,* Sinbad is buried alive in a cavern full of corpses; he eventually finds his way out by walking toward a light he perceives in the distance.

ment. The dissecting room and the slaughter-house furnished many of my materials; and often did my human nature turn with loathing from my occupation, whilst, still urged on by an eagerness which perpetually increased, I brought my work near to a conclusion.

The summer months passed while I was thus engaged, heart and soul, in one pursuit. It was a most beautiful season; never did the fields bestow a more plentiful harvest, or the vines yield a more luxuriant vintage: but my eyes were insensible to the charms of nature. And the same feelings which made me neglect the scenes around me caused me also to forget those friends who were so many miles absent, and whom I had not seen for so long a time. I knew my silence disquieted them; and I well remembered the words of my father: "I know that while you are pleased with yourself, you will think of us with affection, and we shall hear regularly from you. You must pardon me, if I regard any interruption in your correspondence as a proof that your other duties are equally neglected."

I knew well therefore what would be my father's feelings; but I could not tear my thoughts from my employment, loathsome in itself, but which had taken an irresistible hold of my imagination. I wished, as it were, to procrastinate all that related to my feelings of affection until the great object, which swallowed up every habit of my nature, should be completed.

I then thought that my father would be unjust if he ascribed my neglect to vice, or faultiness on my part; but I am now convinced that he was justified in conceiving that I should not be altogether free from blame. A human being in perfection ought always to preserve a calm and peaceful mind, and never to allow passion or a transitory desire to disturb his tranquillity. I do not think that the pursuit of knowledge is an exception to this rule. If the study to which you apply yourself has a tendency to weaken your affections, and to destroy your taste for those simple pleasures in which no alloy can possibly mix, then that study is certainly unlawful, that is to say, not befitting the human mind. If this rule were always observed; if no man allowed any pursuit whatsoever to interfere with the tranquillity of his domestic affections, Greece had not been enslaved; Caesar would have spared his country; America would have been discovered more gradually; and the empires of Mexico and Peru had not been destroyed.

But I forget that I am moralizing in the most interesting part of my tale; and your looks remind me to proceed.

My father made no reproach in his letters; and only took notice of my silence by inquiring into my occupations more particularly than before. Winter, spring, and summer, passed away during my labours; but I did not watch the blossom or the expanding leaves—sights which before always yielded me supreme delight, so deeply was I engrossed in my occupation. The leaves of that year had withered before my work drew near to a close; and now every day shewed me more plainly how well I had succeeded. But my enthusiasm was checked by my anxiety, and I appeared rather like one doomed by slavery to toil in the mines, or any other unwholesome trade, than an artist occupied by his favourite employment. Every night I was oppressed by a slow fever, and I became nervous to a most painful degree; a disease that I regretted the more because I had hitherto enjoyed most excellent health, and had always boasted of the firmness of my nerves. But I believed that exercise and amusement would soon drive away such symptoms; and I promised myself both of these, when my creation should be complete.

from CHAPTER 4

It was on a dreary night of November, that I beheld the accomplishment of my toils. With an anxiety that almost amounted to agony, I collected the instruments of life around me, that I might infuse a spark of being into the lifeless thing that lay at my feet. It was already one in the morning; the rain pattered dismally against the panes, and my candle was nearly burnt out, when, by the glimmer of the half-extinguished light, I saw the dull yellow eye of the creature open; it breathed hard, and a convulsive motion agitated its limbs.

How can I describe my emotions at this catastrophe, or how delineate the wretch whom with such infinite pains and care I had endeavoured to form? His limbs were in proportion, and I had selected his features as beautiful. Beautiful!—Great God! His yellow skin scarcely covered the work of muscles and arteries beneath; his hair was of a lustrous black, and flowing; his teeth of a pearly whiteness; but these luxuriances only formed a more horrid contrast with his watery eyes, that seemed almost of the same colour as the dun white sockets in which they were set, his shrivelled complexion, and straight black lips.

The different accidents of life are not so changeable as the feelings of human nature. I had worked hard for nearly two years, for the sole purpose of infusing life into an inanimate body. For this I had deprived myself of rest and health. I had desired it with an ardour that far exceeded moderation; but now that I had finished, the beauty of the dream vanished, and breathless horror and disgust filled my heart. Unable to endure the aspect of the being I had created, I rushed out of the room, and continued a long time traversing my bed-chamber, unable to compose my mind to sleep. At length lassitude succeeded to the tumult I had before endured; and I threw myself on the bed in my clothes, endeavouring to seek a few moments of forgetfulness. But it was in vain: I slept indeed, but I was disturbed by the wildest dreams. I thought I saw Elizabeth,[1] in the bloom of health, walking in the streets of Ingolstadt. Delighted and surprised, I embraced her; but as I imprinted the first kiss on her lips, they became livid with the hue of death; her features appeared to change, and I thought that I held the corpse of my dead mother in my arms; a shroud enveloped her form, and I saw the grave-worms crawling in the folds of the flannel. I started from my sleep with horror; a cold dew covered my forehead, my teeth chattered, and every limb became convulsed; when, by the dim and yellow light of the moon, as it forced its way through the window-shutters, I beheld the wretch—the miserable monster whom I had created. He held up the curtain of the bed; and his eyes, if eyes they may be called, were fixed on me. His jaws opened, and he muttered some inarticulate sounds, while a grin wrinkled his cheeks. He might have spoken, but I did not hear; one hand was stretched out, seemingly to detain me, but I escaped, and rushed down stairs. I took refuge in the court-yard belonging to the house which I inhabited; where I remained during the rest of the night, walking up and down in the greatest agitation, listening attentively, catching and fearing each sound as if it were to announce the approach of the demoniacal corpse to which I had so miserably given life. …

[In the chapters omitted here, Victor, after a long illness, discovers that his brother has been murdered and suspects that the creature may be the killer; afraid that if he reveals this he will be thought insane, he allows an innocent family servant to be executed for the crime. He is plagued by guilt, and his family, concerned for his well-being, persuades him to go mountain climbing in the Alps. As this selection commences, he is appreciating the view of Mont Blanc from the summit of Montanvert.]

from VOLUME 2
from CHAPTER 2

… I suddenly beheld the figure of a man, at some distance, advancing towards me with superhuman speed. He bounded over the crevices in the ice, among which I had walked with caution; his stature also, as he approached, seemed to exceed that of man. I was troubled: a mist came over my eyes, and I felt a faintness seize me; but I was quickly restored by the cold gale of the mountains. I perceived, as the shape came nearer, (sight tremendous and abhorred!) that it was the wretch whom I had created. I trembled with rage and horror, resolving to wait his approach, and then close with him in mortal combat. He approached; his countenance bespoke bitter anguish, combined with disdain and malignity, while its unearthly ugliness rendered it almost too horrible for human eyes. But I scarcely observed this; anger and hatred had at first deprived me of utterance, and I recovered only to overwhelm him with words expressive of furious detestation and contempt.

"Devil!" I exclaimed, "do you dare approach me? and do not you fear the fierce vengeance of my arm wreaked on your miserable head? Begone, vile insect! or rather stay, that I may trample you to dust! and, oh, that I could, with the extinction of your miserable existence,

---

1 *Elizabeth* Elizabeth Lavenza, Victor's cousin, who has been raised alongside him.

restore those victims whom you have so diabolically murdered!"

"I expected this reception," said the daemon. "All men hate the wretched; how then must I be hated, who am miserable beyond all living things! Yet you, my creator, detest and spurn me, thy creature, to whom thou art bound by ties only dissoluble by the annihilation of one of us. You purpose to kill me. How dare you sport thus with life? Do your duty towards me, and I will do mine towards you and the rest of mankind. If you will comply with my conditions, I will leave them and you at peace; but if you refuse, I will glut the maw of death, until it be satiated with the blood of your remaining friends."

"Abhorred monster! fiend that thou art! the tortures of hell are too mild a vengeance for thy crimes. Wretched devil! you reproach me with your creation; come on then, that I may extinguish the spark which I so negligently bestowed."

My rage was without bounds; I sprang on him, impelled by all the feelings which can arm one being against the existence of another.

He easily eluded me, and said,

"Be calm! I entreat you to hear me, before you give vent to your hatred on my devoted head. Have I not suffered enough, that you seek to increase my misery? Life, although it may only be an accumulation of anguish, is dear to me, and I will defend it. Remember, thou hast made me more powerful than thyself; my height is superior to thine; my joints more supple. But I will not be tempted to set myself in opposition to thee. I am thy creature, and I will be even mild and docile to my natural lord and king, if thou wilt also perform thy part, the which thou owest me. Oh, Frankenstein, be not equitable to every other, and trample upon me alone, to whom thy justice, and even thy clemency and affection, is most due. Remember, that I am thy creature: I ought to be thy Adam; but I am rather the fallen angel,[1] whom thou drivest from joy for no misdeed. Every where I see bliss, from which I alone am irrevocably excluded. I was benevolent and good; misery made me a fiend. Make me happy, and I shall again be virtuous."

"Begone! I will not hear you. There can be no community between you and me; we are enemies. Begone, or let us try our strength in a fight, in which one must fall."

"How can I move thee? Will no entreaties cause thee to turn a favourable eye upon thy creature, who implores thy goodness and compassion. Believe me, Frankenstein: I was benevolent; my soul glowed with love and humanity: but am I not alone, miserably alone? You, my creator, abhor me; what hope can I gather from your fellow-creatures, who owe me nothing? they spurn and hate me. The desert mountains and dreary glaciers are my refuge. I have wandered here many days; the caves of ice, which I only do not fear, are a dwelling to me, and the only one which man does not grudge. These bleak skies I hail, for they are kinder to me than your fellow-beings. If the multitude of mankind knew of my existence, they would do as you do, and arm themselves for my destruction. Shall I not then hate them who abhor me? I will keep no terms with my enemies. I am miserable, and they shall share my wretchedness. Yet it is in your power to recompense me, and deliver them from an evil which it only remains for you to make so great, that not only you and your family, but thousands of others, shall be swallowed up in the whirlwinds of its rage. Let your compassion be moved, and do not disdain me. Listen to my tale: when you have heard that, abandon or commiserate me, as you shall judge that I deserve. But hear me. The guilty are allowed, by human laws, bloody as they may be, to speak in their own defence before they are condemned. Listen to me, Frankenstein. You accuse me of murder; and yet you would, with a satisfied conscience, destroy your own creature. Oh, praise the eternal justice of man! Yet I ask you not to spare me: listen to me; and then, if you can, and if you will, destroy the work of your hands."

"Why do you call to my remembrance circumstances of which I shudder to reflect, that I have been the miserable origin and author? Cursed be the day, abhorred devil, in which you first saw light! Cursed (although I curse myself) be the hands that formed you! You have made me wretched beyond expression. You

---

[1] *ought to be … fallen angel* Adam (created by God as the first human) and Satan (the angel cast out of heaven for his rebellion against God) are major characters in Milton's *Paradise Lost* (1667).

have left me no power to consider whether I am just to you, or not. Begone! relieve me from the sight of your detested form."

"Thus I relieve thee, my creator," he said, and placed his hated hands before my eyes, which I flung from me with violence; "thus I take from thee a sight which you abhor. Still thou canst listen to me, and grant me thy compassion. By the virtues that I once possessed, I demand this from you. Hear my tale; it is long and strange, and the temperature of this place is not fitting to your fine sensations; come to the hut upon the mountain. The sun is yet high in the heavens; before it descends to hide itself behind yon snowy precipices, and illuminate another world, you will have heard my story, and can decide. On you it rests, whether I quit for ever the neighbourhood of man, and lead a harmless life, or become the scourge of your fellow-creatures, and the author of your own speedy ruin."

As he said this, he led the way across the ice: I followed. My heart was full, and I did not answer him; but, as I proceeded, I weighed the various arguments that he had used, and determined at least to listen to his tale. I was partly urged by curiosity, and compassion confirmed my resolution. I had hitherto supposed him to be the murderer of my brother, and I eagerly sought a confirmation or denial of this opinion. For the first time, also, I felt what the duties of a creator towards his creature were, and that I ought to render him happy before I complained of his wickedness. These motives urged me to comply with his demand. We crossed the ice, therefore, and ascended the opposite rock. The air was cold, and the rain again began to descend: we entered the hut, the fiend with an air of exultation, I with a heavy heart, and depressed spirits. But I consented to listen; and, seating myself by the fire which my odious companion had lighted, he thus began his tale.

CHAPTER 3

"It is with considerable difficulty that I remember the original aera of my being: all the events of that period appear confused and indistinct. A strange multiplicity of sensations seized me, and I saw, felt, heard, and smelt, at the same time; and it was, indeed, a long time before I learned to distinguish between the operations of my various senses. By degrees, I remember, a stronger light pressed upon my nerves, so that I was obliged to shut my eyes. Darkness then came over me, and troubled me; but hardly had I felt this, when, by opening my eyes, as I now suppose, the light poured in upon me again. I walked, and, I believe, descended; but I presently found a great alteration in my sensations. Before, dark and opaque bodies had surrounded me, impervious to my touch or sight; but I now found that I could wander on at liberty, with no obstacles which I could not either surmount or avoid. The light became more and more oppressive to me; and, the heat wearying me as I walked, I sought a place where I could receive shade. This was the forest near Ingolstadt; and here I lay by the side of a brook resting from my fatigue, until I felt tormented by hunger and thirst. This roused me from my nearly dormant state, and I ate some berries which I found hanging on the trees, or lying on the ground. I slaked my thirst at the brook; and then lying down, was overcome by sleep.

"It was dark when I awoke; I felt cold also, and half-frightened as it were instinctively, finding myself so desolate. Before I had quitted your apartment, on a sensation of cold, I had covered myself with some clothes; but these were insufficient to secure me from the dews of night. I was a poor, helpless, miserable wretch; I knew, and could distinguish, nothing; but, feeling pain invade me on all sides, I sat down and wept.

"Soon a gentle light stole over the heavens, and gave me a sensation of pleasure. I started up, and beheld a radiant form rise from among the trees. I gazed with a kind of wonder. It moved slowly, but it enlightened my path; and I again went out in search of berries. I was still cold, when under one of the trees I found a huge cloak, with which I covered myself, and sat down upon the ground. No distinct ideas occupied my mind; all was confused. I felt light, and hunger, and thirst, and darkness; innumerable sounds rung in my ears, and on all sides various scents saluted me: the only object that I could distinguish was the bright moon, and I fixed my eyes on that with pleasure.

"Several changes of day and night passed, and the orb of night had greatly lessened when I began to distinguish my sensations from each other. I gradually saw plainly the clear stream that supplied me with drink, and the trees that shaded me with their foliage. I was delighted when I first discovered that a pleasant sound, which often saluted my ears, proceeded from the throats of the little winged animals who had often intercepted the light from my eyes. I began also to observe, with greater accuracy, the forms that surrounded me, and to perceive the boundaries of the radiant roof of light which canopied me. Sometimes I tried to imitate the pleasant songs of the birds, but was unable. Sometimes I wished to express my sensations in my own mode, but the uncouth and inarticulate sounds which broke from me frightened me into silence again.

"The moon had disappeared from the night, and again, with a lessened form, shewed itself, while I still remained in the forest. My sensations had, by this time, become distinct, and my mind received every day additional ideas. My eyes became accustomed to the light, and to perceive objects in their right forms; I distinguished the insect from the herb, and, by degrees, one herb from another. I found that the sparrow uttered none but harsh notes, whilst those of the blackbird and thrush were sweet and enticing.

"One day, when I was oppressed by cold, I found a fire which had been left by some wandering beggars, and was overcome with delight at the warmth I experienced from it. In my joy I thrust my hand into the live embers, but quickly drew it out again with a cry of pain. How strange, I thought, that the same cause should produce such opposite effects! I examined the materials of the fire, and to my joy found it to be composed of wood. I quickly collected some branches; but they were wet, and would not burn. I was pained at this, and sat still watching the operation of the fire. The wet wood which I had placed near the heat dried, and itself became inflamed. I reflected on this; and, by touching the various branches, I discovered the cause, and busied myself in collecting a great quantity of wood, that I might dry it, and have a plentiful supply of fire. When night came on, and brought sleep with it, I was in the greatest fear lest my fire should be extinguished. I covered it carefully with dry wood and leaves, and placed wet branches upon it; and then, spreading my cloak, I lay on the ground, and sunk into sleep.

"It was morning when I awoke, and my first care was to visit the fire. I uncovered it, and a gentle breeze quickly fanned it into a flame. I observed this also, and contrived a fan of branches, which roused the embers when they were nearly extinguished. When night came again, I found, with pleasure, that the fire gave light as well as heat; and that the discovery of this element was useful to me in my food; for I found some of the offals[1] that the travellers had left had been roasted, and tasted much more savoury than the berries I gathered from the trees. I tried, therefore, to dress my food in the same manner, placing it on the live embers. I found that the berries were spoiled by this operation, and the nuts and roots much improved.

"Food, however, became scarce; and I often spent the whole day searching in vain for a few acorns to assuage the pangs of hunger. When I found this, I resolved to quit the place that I had hitherto inhabited, to seek for one where the few wants I experienced would be more easily satisfied. In this emigration, I exceedingly lamented the loss of the fire which I had obtained through accident, and knew not how to re-produce it. I gave several hours to the serious consideration of this difficulty; but I was obliged to relinquish all attempt to supply it; and, wrapping myself up in my cloak, I struck across the wood towards the setting sun. I passed three days in these rambles, and at length discovered the open country. A great fall of snow had taken place the night before, and the fields were of one uniform white; the appearance was disconsolate, and I found my feet chilled by the cold damp substance that covered the ground.

"It was about seven in the morning, and I longed to obtain food and shelter; at length I perceived a small hut, on a rising ground, which had doubtless been built for the convenience of some shepherd. This was a new sight to me; and I examined the structure with great curiosity. Finding the door open, I entered. An old man sat in it, near a fire, over which he was preparing his breakfast. He turned on hearing a noise; and, perceiving me, shrieked loudly, and, quitting the hut, ran across the fields with a speed of which his debilitated form

[1] *offals* I.e., scraps.

hardly appeared capable. His appearance, different from any I had ever before seen, and his flight, somewhat surprised me. But I was enchanted by the appearance of the hut: here the snow and rain could not penetrate; the ground was dry; and it presented to me then as exquisite and divine a retreat as Pandaemonium appeared to the daemons of hell after their sufferings in the lake of fire.[1] I greedily devoured the remnants of the shepherd's breakfast, which consisted of bread, cheese, milk, and wine; the latter, however, I did not like. Then overcome by fatigue, I lay down among some straw, and fell asleep.

"It was noon when I awoke; and, allured by the warmth of the sun, which shone brightly on the white ground, I determined to recommence my travels; and, depositing the remains of the peasant's breakfast in a wallet[2] I found, I proceeded across the fields for several hours, until at sunset I arrived at a village. How miraculous did this appear! the huts, the neater cottages, and stately houses, engaged my admiration by turns. The vegetables in the gardens, the milk and cheese that I saw placed at the windows of some of the cottages, allured my appetite. One of the best of these I entered; but I had hardly placed my foot within the door, before the children shrieked, and one of the women fainted. The whole village was roused; some fled, some attacked me, until, grievously bruised by stones and many other kinds of missile weapons, I escaped to the open country, and fearfully took refuge in a low hovel, quite bare, and making a wretched appearance after the palaces I had beheld in the village. This hovel, however, joined a cottage of a neat and pleasant appearance; but, after my late dearly-bought experience, I dared not enter it. My place of refuge was constructed of wood, but so low, that I could with difficulty sit upright in it. No wood, however, was placed on the earth, which formed the floor, but it was dry; and although the wind entered it by innumerable chinks, I found it an agreeable asylum from the snow and rain.

"Here then I retreated, and lay down, happy to have found a shelter, however miserable, from the inclemency of the season, and still more from the barbarity of man.

"As soon as morning dawned, I crept from my kennel, that I might view the adjacent cottage, and discover if I could remain in the habitation I had found. It was situated against the back of the cottage, and surrounded on the sides which were exposed by a pig-sty and a clear pool of water. One part was open, and by that I had crept in; but now I covered every crevice by which I might be perceived with stones and wood, yet in such a manner that I might move them on occasion to pass out: all the light I enjoyed came through the sty, and that was sufficient for me.

"Having thus arranged my dwelling, and carpeted it with clean straw, I retired; for I saw the figure of a man at a distance, and I remembered too well my treatment the night before, to trust myself in his power. I had first, however, provided for my sustenance for that day, by a loaf of coarse bread, which I purloined, and a cup with which I could drink, more conveniently than from my hand, of the pure water which flowed by my retreat. The floor was a little raised, so that it was kept perfectly dry, and by its vicinity to the chimney of the cottage it was tolerably warm.

"Being thus provided, I resolved to reside in this hovel, until something should occur which might alter my determination. It was indeed a paradise, compared to the bleak forest, my former residence, the rain-dropping branches, and dank earth. I ate my breakfast with pleasure, and was about to remove a plank to procure myself a little water, when I heard a step, and, looking through a small chink, I beheld a young creature, with a pail on her head, passing before my hovel. The girl was young and of gentle demeanour, unlike what I have since found cottagers and farm-house servants to be. Yet she was meanly dressed, a coarse blue petticoat and a linen jacket being her only garb; her fair hair was plaited, but not adorned; she looked patient, yet sad. I lost sight of her; and in about a quarter of an hour she returned, bearing the pail, which was now partly filled with milk. As she walked along, seemingly incommoded by the burden, a young man met her, whose countenance expressed a deeper despondence. Uttering

[1] *Pandaemonium … of fire* In *Paradise Lost* 1, the narrative commences as Satan and the fallen angels have been driven out of heaven and cast onto a lake of fire. A magnificent building, called Pandemonium, arises, and Satan and his followers hold a council there.

[2] *wallet* Bag.

a few sounds with an air of melancholy, he took the pail from her head, and bore it to the cottage himself. She followed, and they disappeared. Presently I saw the young man again, with some tools in his hand, cross the field behind the cottage; and the girl was also busied, sometimes in the house, and sometimes in the yard.

"On examining my dwelling, I found that one of the windows of the cottage had formerly occupied a part of it, but the panes had been filled up with wood. In one of these was a small and almost imperceptible chink, through which the eye could just penetrate. Through this crevice, a small room was visible, whitewashed and clean, but very bare of furniture. In one corner, near a small fire, sat an old man, leaning his head on his hands in a disconsolate attitude. The young girl was occupied in arranging the cottage; but presently she took something out of a drawer, which employed her hands, and she sat down beside the old man, who, taking up an instrument, began to play, and to produce sounds, sweeter than the voice of the thrush or the nightingale. It was a lovely sight, even to me, poor wretch! who had never beheld aught beautiful before. The silver hair and benevolent countenance of the aged cottager, won my reverence; while the gentle manners of the girl enticed my love. He played a sweet mournful air, which I perceived drew tears from the eyes of his amiable companion, of which the old man took no notice, until she sobbed audibly; he then pronounced a few sounds, and the fair creature, leaving her work, knelt at his feet. He raised her, and smiled with such kindness and affection, that I felt sensations of a peculiar and overpowering nature: they were a mixture of pain and pleasure, such as I had never before experienced, either from hunger or cold, warmth or food; and I withdrew from the window, unable to bear these emotions.

"Soon after this the young man returned, bearing on his shoulders a load of wood. The girl met him at the door, helped to relieve him of his burden, and, taking some of the fuel into the cottage, placed it on the fire; then she and the youth went apart into a nook of the cottage, and he shewed her a large loaf and a piece of cheese. She seemed pleased; and went into the garden for some roots and plants, which she placed in water, and then upon the fire. She afterwards continued her work, whilst the young man went into the garden, and appeared busily employed in digging and pulling up roots. After he had been employed thus about an hour, the young woman joined him, and they entered the cottage together.

"The old man had, in the mean time, been pensive; but, on the appearance of his companions, he assumed a more cheerful air, and they sat down to eat. The meal was quickly dispatched. The young woman was again occupied in arranging the cottage; the old man walked before the cottage in the sun for a few minutes, leaning on the arm of the youth. Nothing could exceed in beauty the contrast between these two excellent creatures. One was old, with silver hairs and a countenance beaming with benevolence and love: the younger was slight and graceful in his figure, and his features were moulded with the finest symmetry; yet his eyes and attitude expressed the utmost sadness and despondency. The old man returned to the cottage; and the youth, with tools different from those he had used in the morning, directed his steps across the fields.

"Night quickly shut in; but, to my extreme wonder, I found that the cottagers had a means of prolonging light, by the use of tapers,[1] and was delighted to find, that the setting of the sun did not put an end to the pleasure I experienced in watching my human neighbours. In the evening, the young girl and her companion were employed in various occupations which I did not understand; and the old man again took up the instrument, which produced the divine sounds that had enchanted me in the morning. So soon as he had finished, the youth began, not to play, but to utter sounds that were monotonous, and neither resembling the harmony of the old man's instrument or the songs of the birds; I since found that he read aloud, but at that time I knew nothing of the science of words or letters.

"The family, after having been thus occupied for a short time, extinguished their lights, and retired, as I conjectured, to rest.

[1] *tapers* Candles.

from CHAPTER 4

"I lay on my straw, but I could not sleep. I thought of the occurrences of the day. What chiefly struck me was the gentle manners of these people; and I longed to join them, but dared not. I remembered too well the treatment I had suffered the night before from the barbarous villagers, and resolved, whatever course of conduct I might hereafter think it right to pursue, that for the present I would remain quietly in my hovel, watching, and endeavouring to discover the motives which influenced their actions.

"The cottagers arose the next morning before the sun. The young woman arranged the cottage, and prepared the food; and the youth departed after the first meal.

"This day was passed in the same routine as that which preceded it. The young man was constantly employed out of doors, and the girl in various laborious occupations within. The old man, whom I soon perceived to be blind, employed his leisure hours on his instrument, or in contemplation. Nothing could exceed the love and respect which the younger cottagers exhibited towards their venerable companion. They performed towards him every little office of affection and duty with gentleness; and he rewarded them by his benevolent smiles.

"They were not entirely happy. The young man and his companion often went apart, and appeared to weep. I saw no cause for their unhappiness; but I was deeply affected by it. If such lovely creatures were miserable, it was less strange that I, an imperfect and solitary being, should be wretched. Yet why were these gentle beings unhappy? They possessed a delightful house (for such it was in my eyes), and every luxury; they had a fire to warm them when chill, and delicious viands[1] when hungry; they were dressed in excellent clothes; and, still more, they enjoyed one another's company and speech, interchanging each day looks of affection and kindness. What did their tears imply? Did they really express pain? I was at first unable to solve these questions; but perpetual attention, and time, explained to me many appearances which were at first enigmatic.

"A considerable period elapsed before I discovered one of the causes of the uneasiness of this amiable family; it was poverty: and they suffered that evil in a very distressing degree. Their nourishment consisted entirely of the vegetables of their garden, and the milk of one cow, who gave very little during the winter, when its masters could scarcely procure food to support it. They often, I believe, suffered the pangs of hunger very poignantly, especially the two younger cottagers; for several times they placed food before the old man, when they reserved none for themselves.

"This trait of kindness moved me sensibly. I had been accustomed, during the night, to steal a part of their store for my own consumption; but when I found that in doing this I inflicted pain on the cottagers, I abstained, and satisfied myself with berries, nuts, and roots, which I gathered from a neighbouring wood.

"I discovered also another means through which I was enabled to assist their labours. I found that the youth spent a great part of each day in collecting wood for the family fire; and, during the night, I often took his tools, the use of which I quickly discovered, and brought home firing sufficient for the consumption of several days.

"I remember, the first time that I did this, the young woman, when she opened the door in the morning, appeared greatly astonished on seeing a great pile of wood on the outside. She uttered some words in a loud voice, and the youth joined her, who also expressed surprise. I observed, with pleasure, that he did not go to the forest that day, but spent it in repairing the cottage, and cultivating the garden.

"By degrees I made a discovery of still greater moment. I found that these people possessed a method of communicating their experience and feelings to one another by articulate sounds. I perceived that the words they spoke sometimes produced pleasure or pain, smiles or sadness, in the minds and countenances of the hearers. This was indeed a godlike science, and I ardently desired to become acquainted with it. But I was baffled in every attempt I made for this purpose. Their pronunciation was quick; and the words they uttered, not having any apparent connexion with visible objects, I was unable to discover any clue by which I could

[1] *viands* Foods.

unravel the mystery of their reference. By great application, however, and after having remained during the space of several revolutions of the moon in my hovel, I discovered the names that were given to some of the most familiar objects of discourse: I learned and applied the words *fire*, *milk*, *bread*, and *wood*. I learned also the names of the cottagers themselves. The youth and his companion had each of them several names, but the old man had only one, which was *father*. The girl was called *sister*, or *Agatha*; and the youth *Felix*, *brother*, or *son*. I cannot describe the delight I felt when I learned the ideas appropriated to each of these sounds, and was able to pronounce them. I distinguished several other words, without being able as yet to understand or apply them; such as *good*, *dearest*, *unhappy*.

"I spent the winter in this manner. The gentle manners and beauty of the cottagers greatly endeared them to me: when they were unhappy, I felt depressed; when they rejoiced, I sympathized in their joys. I saw few human beings beside them; and if any other happened to enter the cottage, their harsh manners and rude gait only enhanced to me the superior accomplishments of my friends. The old man, I could perceive, often endeavoured to encourage his children, as sometimes I found that he called them, to cast off their melancholy. He would talk in a cheerful accent, with an expression of goodness that bestowed pleasure even upon me. Agatha listened with respect, her eyes sometimes filled with tears, which she endeavoured to wipe away unperceived; but I generally found that her countenance and tone were more cheerful after having listened to the exhortations of her father. It was not thus with Felix. He was always the saddest of the group; and, even to my unpractised senses, he appeared to have suffered more deeply than his friends. But if his countenance was more sorrowful, his voice was more cheerful than that of his sister, especially when he addressed the old man.

"I could mention innumerable instances, which, although slight, marked the dispositions of these amiable cottagers. In the midst of poverty and want, Felix carried with pleasure to his sister the first little white flower that peeped out from beneath the snowy ground. Early in the morning before she had risen, he cleared away the snow that obstructed her path to the milk-house, drew water from the well, and brought the wood from the out-house, where, to his perpetual astonishment, he found his store always replenished by an invisible hand. In the day, I believe, he worked sometimes for a neighbouring farmer, because he often went forth, and did not return until dinner, yet brought no wood with him. At other times he worked in the garden; but, as there was little to do in the frosty season, he read to the old man and Agatha.

"This reading had puzzled me extremely at first; but, by degrees, I discovered that he uttered many of the same sounds when he read as when he talked. I conjectured, therefore, that he found on the paper signs for speech which he understood, and I ardently longed to comprehend these also; but how was that possible, when I did not even understand the sounds for which they stood as signs? I improved, however, sensibly in this science, but not sufficiently to follow up any kind of conversation, although I applied my whole mind to the endeavour: for I easily perceived that, although I eagerly longed to discover[1] myself to the cottagers, I ought not to make the attempt until I had first become master of their language; which knowledge might enable me to make them overlook the deformity of my figure; for with this also the contrast perpetually presented to my eyes had made me acquainted.

"I had admired the perfect forms of my cottagers—their grace, beauty, and delicate complexions: but how was I terrified, when I viewed myself in a transparent pool![2] At first I started back, unable to believe that it was indeed I who was reflected in the mirror; and when I became fully convinced that I was in reality the monster that I am, I was filled with the bitterest sensations of despondence and mortification. Alas! I did not yet entirely know the fatal effects of this miserable deformity.

"As the sun became warmer, and the light of day longer, the snow vanished, and I beheld the bare trees

---

[1] *discover* Reveal.

[2] *viewed myself ... pool* See *Paradise Lost* 4.453–75, in which Eve first sees her reflection in a pool and is "pleased"; she is then told that she is made in the image of God.

and the black earth. From this time Felix was more employed; and the heart-moving indications of impending famine disappeared. Their food, as I afterwards found, was coarse, but it was wholesome; and they procured a sufficiency of it. Several new kinds of plants sprung up in the garden, which they dressed; and these signs of comfort increased daily as the season advanced.

"The old man, leaning on his son, walked each day at noon, when it did not rain, as I found it was called when the heavens poured forth its waters. This frequently took place; but a high wind quickly dried the earth, and the season became far more pleasant than it had been.

"My mode of life in my hovel was uniform. During the morning I attended the motions of the cottagers; and when they were dispersed in various occupations, I slept: the remainder of the day was spent in observing my friends. When they had retired to rest, if there was any moon, or the night was starlight, I went into the woods, and collected my own food and fuel for the cottage. When I returned, as often as it was necessary, I cleared their path from the snow, and performed those offices that I had seen done by Felix. I afterwards found that these labours, performed by an invisible hand, greatly astonished them; and once or twice I heard them, on these occasions, utter the words *good spirit*, *wonderful*; but I did not then understand the signification of these terms. …

from Chapter 5

…[1] "My days were spent in close attention, that I might more speedily master the language; and I may boast that I improved more rapidly than the Arabian, who understood very little, and conversed in broken accents, whilst I comprehended and could imitate almost every word that was spoken.

"While I improved in speech, I also learned the science of letters, as it was taught to the stranger; and this opened before me a wide field for wonder and delight.

"The book from which Felix instructed Safie was Volney's *Ruins of Empires*.[2] I should not have understood the purport of this book, had not Felix, in reading it, given very minute explanations. He had chosen this work, he said, because the declamatory style was framed in imitation of the eastern authors. Through this work I obtained a cursory knowledge of history, and a view of the several empires at present existing in the world; it gave me an insight into the manners, governments, and religions of the different nations of the earth. I heard of the slothful Asiatics; of the stupendous genius and mental activity of the Grecians; of the wars and wonderful virtue of the early Romans—of their subsequent degeneration—of the decline of that mighty empire; of chivalry, christianity, and kings. I heard of the discovery of the American hemisphere, and wept with Safie over the hapless fate of its original inhabitants.

"These wonderful narrations inspired me with strange feelings. Was man, indeed, at once so powerful, so virtuous, and magnificent, yet so vicious and base? He appeared at one time a mere scion of the evil principle, and at another as all that can be conceived of noble and godlike. To be a great and virtuous man appeared the highest honour that can befall a sensitive being; to be base and vicious, as many on record have been, appeared the lowest degradation, a condition more abject than that of the blind mole or harmless worm. For a long time I could not conceive how one man could go forth to murder his fellow, or even why there were laws and governments; but when I heard details of vice and bloodshed, my wonder ceased, and I turned away with disgust and loathing.

"Every conversation of the cottagers now opened new wonders to me. While I listened to the instructions which Felix bestowed upon the Arabian, the strange system of human society was explained to me. I heard of the division of property, of immense wealth and squalid poverty; of rank, descent, and noble blood.

---

[1] … In the text omitted here, Felix's beloved, Safie, joins the cottagers. She is Arabian and at the time of her arrival does not speak French.

[2] *Ruins of Empires* French philosopher and historian Constantin-François de Chassebœuf, comte de Volney's *Ruins; or Meditations on the Revolution of Empires* (1791). In this overview of world history, Volney, a French Revolutionary, argues that empires fall because of conflict between the privileged classes and the working people whose labor they depend upon. He proposes that all political ideologies and religions should be eliminated.

"The words induced me to turn towards myself. I learned that the possessions most esteemed by your fellow-creatures were, high and unsullied descent united with riches. A man might be respected with only one of these acquisitions; but without either he was considered, except in very rare instances, as a vagabond and a slave, doomed to waste his powers for the profit of the chosen few. And what was I? Of my creation and creator I was absolutely ignorant; but I knew that I possessed no money, no friends, no kind of property. I was, besides, endowed with a figure hideously deformed and loathsome; I was not even of the same nature as man. I was more agile than they, and could subsist upon coarser diet; I bore the extremes of heat and cold with less injury to my frame; my stature far exceeded theirs. When I looked around, I saw and heard of none like me. Was I then a monster, a blot upon the earth, from which all men fled, and whom all men disowned?

"I cannot describe to you the agony that these reflections inflicted upon me; I tried to dispel them, but sorrow only increased with knowledge.[1] Oh, that I had for ever remained in my native wood, nor known or felt beyond the sensations of hunger, thirst, and heat!

"Of what a strange nature is knowledge! It clings to the mind, when it has once seized on it, like a lichen on the rock. I wished sometimes to shake off all thought and feeling; but I learned that there was but one means to overcome the sensation of pain, and that was death—a state which I feared yet did not understand. I admired virtue and good feelings, and loved the gentle manners and amiable qualities of my cottagers; but I was shut out from intercourse with them, except through means which I obtained by stealth, when I was unseen and unknown, and which rather increased than satisfied the desire I had of becoming one among my fellows. The gentle words of Agatha, and the animated smiles of the charming Arabian, were not for me. The mild exhortations of the old man, and the lively conversation of the loved Felix, were not for me. Miserable, unhappy wretch!

"Other lessons were impressed upon me even more deeply. I heard of the difference of sexes; of the birth and growth of children; how the father doted on the smiles of the infant, and the lively sallies of the older child; how all the life and cares of the mother were wrapt up in the precious charge; how the mind of youth expanded and gained knowledge; of brother, sister, and all the various relationships which bind one human being to another in mutual bonds.

"But where were my friends and relations? No father had watched my infant days, no mother had blessed me with smiles and caresses; or if they had, all my past life was now a blot, a blind vacancy in which I distinguished nothing. From my earliest remembrance I had been as I then was in height and proportion. I had never yet seen a being resembling me, or who claimed any intercourse with me. What was I? The question again recurred, to be answered only with groans. …

from CHAPTER 7

… "One night, during my accustomed visit to the neighbouring wood, where I collected my own food, and brought home firing for my protectors, I found on the ground a leathern portmanteau, containing several articles of dress and some books. I eagerly seized the prize, and returned with it to my hovel. Fortunately the books were written in the language the elements of which I had acquired at the cottage; they consisted of *Paradise Lost*, a volume of *Plutarch's Lives*, and the *Sorrows of Werter*.[2] The possession of these treasures gave me extreme delight; I now continually studied and exercised my mind upon these histories, whilst my friends were employed in their ordinary occupations.

"I can hardly describe to you the effect of these books. They produced in me an infinity of new images and feelings, that sometimes raised me to ecstasy, but more frequently sunk me into the lowest dejection. In

[1] *sorrow only … knowledge* See George Gordon, Lord Byron's 1817 poem *Manfred* 1.1.11–12: "Sorrow is knowledge: they who know the most / Must mourn the deepest o'er the fatal truth."

[2] *Plutarch's Lives* Influential collection of biographies of historical figures by the Greek writer Plutarch (c. 46–120 CE). Plutarch paired biographies of Greeks with those of Romans to illustrate their virtues by means of comparison and contrast; *Sorrows of Werter* German author Johann Wolfgang von Goethe's *The Sorrows of Young Werther* (1774), a novel about a young man who, unable to marry the woman he loves, commits suicide.

the *Sorrows of Werter*, besides the interest of its simple and affecting story, so many opinions are canvassed, and so many lights thrown upon what had hitherto been to me obscure subjects, that I found in it a never-ending source of speculation and astonishment. The gentle and domestic manners it described, combined with lofty sentiments and feelings, which had for their object something out of self, accorded well with my experience among my protectors, and with the wants which were for ever alive in my own bosom. But I thought Werter himself a more divine being than I had ever beheld or imagined; his character contained no pretension, but it sunk deep. The disquisitions upon death and suicide were calculated to fill me with wonder. I did not pretend to enter into the merits of the case, yet I inclined towards the opinions of the hero, whose extinction I wept, without precisely understanding it.

"As I read, however, I applied much personally to my own feelings and condition. I found myself similar, yet at the same time strangely unlike the beings concerning whom I read, and to whose conversation I was a listener. I sympathized with, and partly understood them, but I was unformed in mind; I was dependent on none, and related to none. 'The path of my departure was free';[1] and there was none to lament my annihilation. My person was hideous, and my stature gigantic: what did this mean? Who was I? What was I? Whence did I come? What was my destination? These questions continually recurred, but I was unable to solve them.

"The volume of *Plutarch's Lives* which I possessed, contained the histories of the first founders of the ancient republics. This book had a far different effect upon me from the *Sorrows of Werter*. I learned from Werter's imaginations despondency and gloom: but Plutarch taught me high thoughts; he elevated me above the wretched sphere of my own reflections, to admire and love the heroes of past ages. Many things I read surpassed my understanding and experience. I had a very confused knowledge of kingdoms, wide extents of country, mighty rivers, and boundless seas. But I was perfectly unacquainted with towns, and large assemblages of men. The cottage of my protectors had been the only school in which I had studied human nature; but this book developed new and mightier scenes of action. I read of men concerned in public affairs governing or massacring their species. I felt the greatest ardour for virtue rise within me, and abhorrence for vice, as far as I understood the signification of those terms, relative as they were, as I applied them, to pleasure and pain alone. Induced by these feelings, I was of course led to admire peaceable law-givers, Numa, Solon, and Lycurgus, in preference to Romulus and Theseus.[2] The patriarchal lives[3] of my protectors caused these impressions to take a firm hold on my mind; perhaps, if my first introduction to humanity had been made by a young soldier, burning for glory and slaughter, I should have been imbued with different sensations.

"But *Paradise Lost* excited different and far deeper emotions. I read it, as I had read the other volumes which had fallen into my hands, as a true history. It moved every feeling of wonder and awe, that the picture of an omnipotent God warring with his creatures was capable of exciting. I often referred the several situations, as their similarity struck me, to my own. Like Adam, I was created apparently united by no link to any other being in existence; but his state was far different from mine in every other respect. He had come forth from the hands of God a perfect creature, happy and prosperous, guarded by the especial care of his Creator; he was allowed to converse with, and acquire knowledge from beings of a superior nature: but I was wretched, helpless, and alone. Many times I considered Satan as the fitter emblem of my condition; for often, like him, when I viewed the bliss of my protectors, the bitter gall of envy rose within me.

[1] *The path ... was free* See Percy Bysshe Shelley's 1816 poem "Mutability": "be it joy or sorrow, / The path of its departure still is free."

[2] *Numa, Solon, and Lycurgus* Numa Pompilius (fl. eighth century BCE), second King of Rome; Solon, Athenian reformist legislator (c. 638–c. 558 BCE); and Lycurgus of Sparta (legendary or fl. ninth century BCE). All three figures are presented by Plutarch as virtuous political leaders; *Romulus and Theseus* According to legend, Romulus was the founder of Rome; Theseus was the mythical founder of Athens. According to Plutarch, they committed acts of heroism but also acts of unjustified violence.

[3] *patriarchal lives* I.e., lives incorporating respect for the wisdom of elder men (such as the younger cottagers' father).

"Another circumstance strengthened and confirmed these feelings. Soon after my arrival in the hovel, I discovered some papers in the pocket of the dress which I had taken from your laboratory. At first I had neglected them; but now that I was able to decipher the characters in which they were written, I began to study them with diligence. It was your journal of the four months that preceded my creation. You minutely described in these papers every step you took in the progress of your work; this history was mingled with accounts of domestic occurrences. You, doubtless, recollect these papers. Here they are. Every thing is related in them which bears reference to my accursed origin; the whole detail of that series of disgusting circumstances which produced it is set in view; the minutest description of my odious and loathsome person is given, in language which painted your own horrors, and rendered mine ineffaceable. I sickened as I read. 'Hateful day when I received life!' I exclaimed in agony. 'Cursed creator! Why did you form a monster so hideous that even you turned from me in disgust? God in pity made man beautiful and alluring, after his own image; but my form is a filthy type of yours, more horrid from its very resemblance. Satan had his companions, fellow-devils, to admire and encourage him; but I am solitary and detested.'

"These were the reflections of my hours of despondency and solitude; but when I contemplated the virtues of the cottagers, their amiable and benevolent dispositions, I persuaded myself that when they should become acquainted with my admiration of their virtues, they would compassionate me, and overlook my personal deformity. Could they turn from their door one, however monstrous, who solicited their compassion and friendship? I resolved, at least, not to despair, but in every way to fit myself for an interview with them which would decide my fate. …

"The winter advanced, and an entire revolution of the seasons had taken place since I awoke into life. My attention, at this time, was solely directed towards my plan of introducing myself into the cottage of my protectors. I revolved many projects; but that on which I finally fixed was, to enter the dwelling when the blind old man should be alone. I had sagacity enough to discover, that the unnatural hideousness of my person was the chief object of horror with those who had formerly beheld me. My voice, although harsh, had nothing terrible in it; I thought, therefore, that if, in the absence of his children, I could gain the good-will and mediation of the old De Lacey, I might, by his means, be tolerated by my younger protectors.

"One day, when the sun shone on the red leaves that strewed the ground, and diffused cheerfulness, although it denied warmth, Safie, Agatha, and Felix, departed on a long country walk, and the old man, at his own desire, was left alone in the cottage. When his children had departed, he took up his guitar, and played several mournful, but sweet airs, more sweet and mournful than I had ever heard him play before. At first his countenance was illuminated with pleasure, but, as he continued, thoughtfulness and sadness succeeded; at length, laying aside the instrument, he sat absorbed in reflection.

"My heart beat quick; this was the hour and moment of trial, which would decide my hopes, or realize my fears. The servants were gone to a neighbouring fair. All was silent in and around the cottage: it was an excellent opportunity; yet, when I proceeded to execute my plan, my limbs failed me, and I sunk to the ground. Again I rose; and, exerting all the firmness of which I was master, removed the planks which I had placed before my hovel to conceal my retreat. The fresh air revived me, and, with renewed determination, I approached the door of their cottage.

"I knocked. 'Who is there?' said the old man—'Come in.'

"I entered; 'Pardon this intrusion,' said I, 'I am a traveller in want of a little rest; you would greatly oblige me, if you would allow me to remain a few minutes before the fire.'

"'Enter,' said De Lacey; 'and I will try in what manner I can relieve your wants; but, unfortunately, my children are from home, and, as I am blind, I am afraid I shall find it difficult to procure food for you.'

"'Do not trouble yourself, my kind host, I have food; it is warmth and rest only that I need.'

"I sat down, and a silence ensued. I knew that every minute was precious to me, yet I remained irresolute in what manner to commence the interview; when the old man addressed me—

"'By your language, stranger, I suppose you are my countryman; are you French?'

"'No; but I was educated by a French family, and understand that language only. I am now going to claim the protection of some friends, whom I sincerely love, and of whose favour I have some hopes.'

"'Are these Germans?'

"'No, they are French. But let us change the subject. I am an unfortunate and deserted creature; I look around, and I have no relation or friend upon earth. These amiable people to whom I go have never seen me, and know little of me. I am full of fears; for if I fail there, I am an outcast in the world for ever.'

"'Do not despair. To be friendless is indeed to be unfortunate; but the hearts of men, when unprejudiced by any obvious self-interest, are full of brotherly love and charity. Rely, therefore, on your hopes; and if these friends are good and amiable, do not despair.'

"'They are kind—they are the most excellent creatures in the world; but, unfortunately, they are prejudiced against me. I have good dispositions; my life has been hitherto harmless, and, in some degree, beneficial; but a fatal prejudice clouds their eyes, and where they ought to see a feeling and kind friend, they behold only a detestable monster.'

"'That is indeed unfortunate; but if you are really blameless, cannot you undeceive them?'

"'I am about to undertake that task; and it is on that account that I feel so many overwhelming terrors. I tenderly love these friends; I have, unknown to them, been for many months in the habits of daily kindness towards them; but they believe that I wish to injure them, and it is that prejudice which I wish to overcome.'

"'Where do these friends reside?'

"'Near this spot.'

"The old man paused, and then continued, 'If you will unreservedly confide to me the particulars of your tale, I perhaps may be of use in undeceiving them. I am blind, and cannot judge of your countenance, but there is something in your words which persuades me that you are sincere. I am poor, and an exile; but it will afford me true pleasure to be in any way serviceable to a human creature.'

"'Excellent man! I thank you, and accept your generous offer. You raise me from the dust[1] by this kindness; and I trust that, by your aid, I shall not be driven from the society and sympathy of your fellow-creatures.'

"'Heaven forbid! even if you were really criminal; for that can only drive you to desperation, and not instigate you to virtue. I also am unfortunate; I and my family have been condemned, although innocent: judge, therefore, if I do not feel for your misfortunes.'

"'How can I thank you, my best and only benefactor? from your lips first have I heard the voice of kindness directed towards me; I shall be for ever grateful; and your present humanity assures me of success with those friends whom I am on the point of meeting.'

"'May I know the names and residence of those friends?'

"I paused. This, I thought, was the moment of decision, which was to rob me of, or bestow happiness on me for ever. I struggled vainly for firmness sufficient to answer him, but the effort destroyed all my remaining strength; I sank on the chair, and sobbed aloud. At that moment I heard the steps of my younger protectors. I had not a moment to lose; but, seizing the hand of the old man, I cried, 'Now is the time!—save and protect me! You and your family are the friends whom I seek. Do not you desert me in the hour of trial!'

"'Great God!' exclaimed the old man, 'who are you?'

"At that instant the cottage door was opened, and Felix, Safie, and Agatha entered. Who can describe their horror and consternation on beholding me? Agatha fainted; and Safie, unable to attend to her friend, rushed out of the cottage. Felix darted forward, and with supernatural force tore me from his father, to whose knees I clung: in a transport of fury, he dashed me to the ground, and struck me violently with a stick. I could have torn him limb from limb, as the lion rends the antelope. But my heart sunk within me as with bitter sickness, and I refrained. I saw him on the point of repeating his blow, when, overcome by pain and anguish, I quitted the cottage, and in the general tumult escaped unperceived to my hovel.

[1] *raise me from the dust* In *Paradise Lost* 4.16–17, Adam refers to the goodness of God "That rais'd us from the dust and plac't us here / In all this happiness."

from Chapter 8

"Cursed, cursed creator! Why did I live? Why, in that instant, did I not extinguish the spark of existence which you had so wantonly bestowed? I know not; despair had not yet taken possession of me; my feelings were those of rage and revenge. I could with pleasure have destroyed the cottage and its inhabitants, and have glutted myself with their shrieks and misery.

"When night came, I quitted my retreat, and wandered in the wood; and now, no longer restrained by the fear of discovery, I gave vent to my anguish in fearful howlings. I was like a wild beast that had broken the toils; destroying the objects that obstructed me, and ranging through the wood with a stag-like swiftness. Oh! what a miserable night I passed! the cold stars shone in mockery, and the bare trees waved their branches above me: now and then the sweet voice of a bird burst forth amidst the universal stillness. All, save I, were at rest or in enjoyment: I, like the arch fiend, bore a hell within me;[1] and, finding myself unsympathized with, wished to tear up the trees, spread havoc and destruction around me, and then to have sat down and enjoyed the ruin.

"But this was a luxury of sensation that could not endure; I became fatigued with excess of bodily exertion, and sank on the damp grass in the sick impotence of despair. There was none among the myriads of men that existed who would pity or assist me; and should I feel kindness towards my enemies? No: from that moment I declared everlasting war against the species, and, more than all, against him who had formed me,[2] and sent me forth to this insupportable misery. …

—1818

Theodor von Holst, frontispiece from the 1831 edition of *Frankenstein*. A caption placed below this image in the 1831 edition reads "By the glimmer of the half-extinguished light, I saw the dull, yellow eye of the creature open: it breathed hard, and a convulsive motion agitated its limbs. … I rushed out of the room."

[1] *I, like … within me* See *Paradise Lost* 4.20–22, where it is said of Satan that "within him Hell / He brings, and round about him, nor from Hell / One step no more than from himself can fly."

[2] *I declared … had formed me* See *Paradise Lost* 1.121–22, where Satan states his intention "To wage by force or guile eternal war, / Irreconcilable to our grand Foe."

The Victorian Era

The word "Victorian" conjures up a series of images that both accurately describe and misrepresent the literature and culture of the last two thirds of the nineteenth century in Britain. Stiff collars and stiff upper lips, draped table legs, exceedingly long novels, and gritty urban squalor have become the iconic images of Victorian Britain. But these images reveal only one dimension of what is a much more complex picture. While it is certainly the case that Victorians tended to place a high value on such qualities as honor, duty, moral seriousness, and sexual propriety—at least officially—it is a mistake to assume that most were humorless or repressed. And while many of the best-known Victorian novels run to many hundreds of pages, we need to remember that Victorian audiences tended to read these in weekly or monthly installments, or in shorter volumes. Although brutal factory conditions, pitiful wages, and crowded cities impoverished many millions of people, the Victorian period also saw the passage of progressive labor laws, unprecedented wealth creation for some, and the first public sewage systems in Britain. And though "Victorian" still suggests "repressed" to many readers, historians and literary scholars alike have increasingly shown that discourses about sexuality developed and proliferated throughout the period, not least in its literary output.

Franz Xaver Winterhalter, *Queen Victoria*, 1842.

Photographer unknown, *Her Majesty the Queen*, 21 June 1887.

In fact, it may be fair to say that there was never a single "Victorian mindset" or "Victorian value system" but rather a range of them, and that these shifted throughout the century. Indeed, there is no real consensus about when the Victorian era began and ended. Some point to the passage of the Reform Bill of 1832 as the dawn of a new era, others to the abolition of slavery in the British Empire in 1833. Still others argue for the unity of a longer period,[1] beginning perhaps with

[1] Some historians have suggested that the period's beginning should perhaps be dated even earlier, with the seeds of "Victorianism" being planted as early as the late eighteenth century, with the reemergence of

the end of the Napoleonic Wars in 1815 and ending with the outbreak of World War I in 1914. Perhaps the obvious choice is to date the period as starting with Victoria's ascension to the throne in 1837 and concluding with her death in 1901, but the identification of the period so entirely with her reign is ultimately arbitrary and tells us little about the Victorian era.

Photographer unknown, *Queen Victoria*, c. 1897. A picture of Albert is in the background.

Although a great deal of overlap can be found between the Romantic and Victorian periods, most scholars agree that the 1830s was a pivotal decade, marked by the transition of the monarchy from William IV to Victoria and by the spread of a spirit of political and social reform that would characterize the next several decades. During the 1850s and 1860s, Britain emerged from a depressed economy and experienced a level of political and social stability that made these decades the most prosperous of the century. The mid-Victorian period is now often regarded as a kind of high-water mark for Victorian culture, particularly because the 1870s and 1880s saw some decline in the strength of the economy and in Britain's imperial dominance abroad, despite its continued acquisition of colonial possessions. These decades were also marked by the glimmerings of social change, a wave that culminated in the fin-de-siècle spirit of the 1890s, which saw many challenges to the values and conventions of the preceding decades in literature, politics, and everyday life.

Evangelicalism and the Methodist revival. The religious movement countered the ideals of the Enlightenment and may thus be said to mark the conclusion of the primary movement of the eighteenth century.

A Growing Power

During Victoria's reign, Britain was the richest nation and the most powerful empire on the globe, with unchallenged military supremacy until the latter decades of the century and an imperial reach that covered one-quarter of the earth's surface by 1897.[1] As the world's

Fleet Street, London, c. 1890.

[1] The scope of Britain's imperial holdings was memorably expressed in a popular saying of the period: "The sun never sets on the British empire." (A popular rejoinder to the sentiment was the saying that God did not trust the English in the dark.)

Construction of the sewer beneath Fleet Street, London, early 1860s. By 1858 the stench of sewage from the Thames had become so overwhelming that the Houses of Parliament at Westminster found it impossible to meet; construction of a city-wide underground system of sewers, under the direction of Joseph Bazalgette, began the following year.

Building the Holborn Viaduct across the Fleet valley (*Illustrated Times*, 18 September 1869). The viaduct, carrying both road and rail traffic, was a vast project carried out by the Corporation of the City of London between 1863 and 1869.

first industrialized country, Britain experienced both the benefits and the horrors of enormous growth throughout the nineteenth century. The census of 1801 put the population of the country at 11 million people; at century's end that number had increased by almost 300 per cent to 37 million. Just as striking was the movement of this population, from 75 per cent rural distribution in the early decades to nearly the same percentage residing in urban districts by the end of the century. Northern industrial cities grew particularly fast: Manchester, a town of no more than 15,000 people in 1750, had grown to 75,000 by 1800, and to 125,000 by 1820; by 1850 its population was over 300,000. Between 1815 and 1914, more than 20 million people emigrated from Britain to other parts of the world, over half of them to the United States, but millions, too, to Australia and to Canada.

Alfred Morgan, *An Omnibus Ride to Piccadilly Circus—Mr. Gladstone Travelling with Ordinary Passengers*, 1885. The previous year Prime Minister William Gladstone's government had extended the franchise to working class males, through the Reform Bill of 1884.

The shift from an agrarian to an industrial wage economy meant an increase in income for many people, creating a sector of the population that was neither rich nor poor and was increasingly termed "middle class." A spirit of entrepreneurship and market thinking—dominated by upwardly mobile males—gradually replaced what had once seemed an entrenched, unchangeable system of aristocratic patronage and paternalism in the world of business and trade. The Reform Bill of 1832 granted political representation in Parliament to certain sectors of the middle-class male population for the first time, although even with its passage, only one in six adult males could vote, and the suffrage was still linked to property ownership. Rail travel, the advent of the telegraph, daily newspapers, and the manufacture and import of goods via steamship from all over the globe collapsed time and space, and flooded the homes of the affluent with new luxuries and conveniences. The Great Exhibition of 1851, the first World's Fair, showcased Britain's industrial dominance with exhibits of new consumer goods and remarkable technologies; the event symbolized Britain's reputation as the "workshop of the world." Thus, for many the overall mood was positive, and Thomas Macaulay's confident assertions of the nation's progress in his bestselling *History of England* rang true for much of his audience.

GRINDING MILLS, GRINDING POVERTY

The paradox of the economic life of the time was summed up by Thomas Carlyle in 1843: "England is full of wealth," he wrote, "of multifarious produce, supply for human want in every kind; yet England is dying of inanition." For millions of people, low wages, unemployment, and fluctuations in trade created widespread misery in crowded industrial cities such as Manchester and Birmingham. According to one estimate, 70 per cent of the population at mid-century was considered poor. The New Poor Law,[1] passed in 1834, divided and categorized the poor as either "deserving" (the elderly and the physically infirm) or "undeserving" (the able-bodied but unemployed). The poor were now eligible to receive public assistance only in the notorious workhouses, also known as the "Poor Law Bastilles,"[2] which often served to punish and stigmatize rather than relieve. In addition, inadequate housing and slum conditions led to frequent outbreaks of illness and disease. Between 1831 and 1866, four cholera epidemics killed more than 140,000 people, inaugurating Britain's first wide-scale public health movement. Scores of "Blue Books"—statistical investigations, surveys, and government reports on the condition of inner-city neighborhoods—culminated in the Public Health Acts of 1848 and the 1870s. Similarly, between 1802 and 1847, factories and mines producing iron, cotton, and coal, which had been unregulated, employing men, women, and children in conditions that were often dirty and dangerous, were made subject to a series of Factory Acts, designed to

[1] The "Old Poor Law" was passed during the reign of Queen Elizabeth I.

[2] The Paris fortress-prison named the Bastille was stormed on 14 July 1789, initiating the French Revolution.

force employers to limit work hours—working 14 hours a day had been not uncommon—and prohibit the employment of children under the age of nine in certain industries.

In her poem, "The Cry of the Children" (1843), Elizabeth Barrett Browning drew attention to the problem of child labor, helping to create humanitarian awareness on the part of middle-class readers by asking "How long, O cruel nation, / Will you stand to move the world, on a child's heart?"[1] Thomas Hood's "The Song of the Shirt" (1843) focused on the plight of the genteel but impoverished female needle-worker who toils alone in grim conditions for meager wages. Cast in the elevated and stylized "voices" of their victimized speakers, such poems were both wildly popular and highly sentimental, qualities that have until recently served to exclude them from serious study by scholars of English literature. Yet these poems did as much as or more than government reports and statistical surveys to shed light on major social issues. So too did Carlyle's *Past and Present* (1843), which called England to take responsibility for the many starving workers in the land of "plenty":

> We have more riches than any Nation ever had before: we have less good of them than any Nation had before. … We have forgotten everywhere that *Cash-payment* is not the sole relation of human beings; we think, nothing doubting, that it absolves and liquidates all other engagements.

Even as such voices spoke up in support of the destitute and the working classes, over the course of the century, the voices of working-class people themselves were also increasingly heard. The 1828 publication of Robert Blincoe's *Memoir* of his appalling early life in the mills had a lasting impact; in addition to a direct effect on its readers, Blincoe's memoir provided much of the raw material for Frances Trollope's novel *Michael Armstrong: Factory Boy* (1840), and may also have inspired Charles Dickens's *Oliver Twist* (1838). Blincoe's memoir was followed by a number of other autobiographical narratives of working-class hardship; a particularly notable example of the genre was *A Narrative of the Experience and Sufferings of William Dodd* (1841). Ellen Johnson published a more wide-ranging memoir, *Autobiography of a Factory Girl* (1867), together with her poems and songs. Another prominent working-class poetic voice was that of Ebenezer Elliott, the "Corn-Law Rhymer" from Yorkshire who became an active force first in the Chartist movement and then in the struggle to repeal the Corn Laws (both of which will be discussed in more detail below). In his *Corn-Law Rhymes* (1831) and in subsequent work Elliott attacked

> The deadly will that takes
> What labour ought to keep;
> It is the deadly power that makes
> Bread dear and labour cheap.

How to best respond to the force of this "deadly power" remained a matter of debate and speculation. If some emphasized the need to continually press for political reform, others appealed emotionally for hearts to change; still others formulated new philosophical approaches to the underlying moral and socio-economic questions. Perhaps the most important of these approaches was Utilitarianism, a broad-reaching philosophy that had first been developed in the late eighteenth century, primarily by Jeremy Bentham, and that was expounded in a more careful, subtle, and thoroughgoing fashion by John Stuart Mill in the nineteenth.[2] Utilitarian thought began to shape governmental policy, including the New Poor Law, in the middle decades of the nineteenth century—and continues to be a shaping force in the social policy of many nations today. In its crude form, Utilitarianism holds—in the words of Bentham's 1776 "A Fragment on Government"—that "it is the greatest happiness of

[1] Many of the poem's details were drawn from the 1842–43 Parliamentary commission report investigating the conditions of child employment in mines and factories. The report's author, R.H. Horne, was a close friend of the poet.

[2] Mill first published *Utilitarianism*, his defense of the utilitarian philosophy in 1861, as a series of three articles in *Fraser's Magazine*. The essays appeared as a one-volume work in 1863.

Thomas Iron Works, London, 1867.

Hatting mill, Manchester, 1890s.

the greatest number that is the measure of right and wrong." In other words, the central guiding principle of social morality should be the pursuit of that which is good for all members of society, with no one person or group's interests given special weight. But how does one calculate "the greatest happiness of the greatest number"? Can social, legal, economic, and political problems be resolved by a "moral arithmetic" that evaluates human pain and pleasure according to entirely rationalist principles? According to some crude versions of utilitarian philosophy—though certainly not that of Mill—the answer is yes; imagination, feeling, and individual desire are obsolete impediments to the operation of the "laws" of social improvement, which may be derived from empirical observation and calculation.

Writers such as Elizabeth Barrett Browning, Dickens, Carlyle, and John Ruskin were intensely critical of Utilitarianism, taking its crudest forms as representative and regarding it as a morally and spiritually bankrupt response to the human condition. Dickens, in particular, caricatured utilitarian thinking with telling directness in his portrayal of Thomas Gradgrind in *Hard Times* (1854), his tenth novel, aimed at exposing the working conditions in English factories and initiating reform.[1] However, it may be fitting to understand the intensity of these writers' opposition to Utilitarianism in a larger context: for Mill, "the greatest number" included not only the poor white people of England but also brown and black people in poverty the world over; on the other hand, Dickens, Carlyle, and Ruskin, for all their sympathy for the British poor, looked at those of other races, at best, with condescension and, at worst, with outright loathing. In any case, as the works of writers such as Dickens, Barrett Browning, and Elizabeth Gaskell amply demonstrated, opposition to the cruelties of poverty could be expressed—as plausibly and as powerfully—by means of emotional and aesthetic appeals through literature as it could by means of the philosophical arguments of the Utilitarians.[2]

CORN LAWS, POTATO FAMINE

As the powerful and privileged attempted to confront the range of social crises facing a newly industrialized nation, economic depression, unemployment, political instability in Europe, and a series of crop failures in the 1840s—a decade often dubbed the "Hungry Forties"—caused a disproportionate level of suffering for the poor. Artificial shortages of grain in the country inflated the price of bread beyond the reach of the working class, causing periodic bread riots and a discontented work force. These shortages were in part the result of the Corn Laws, which imposed heavy tariffs on imports of grain, and were intended to protect British agricultural interests and limit dependence on foreign supplies of cereal grains. The Corn Laws were repealed in 1846 under pressure from the Anti-Corn-Law League, an alliance of free-trade advocates and liberal, laissez-faire[3] trade reformers.

While the Corn Laws were being debated in the English parliament, in Ireland an outbreak of potato blight in 1845 marked the onset of what would become one of the most devastating human catastrophes of the nineteenth century. The tenant-farming rural poor of Ireland—who constituted the vast majority of the population—had for generations been subsisting very largely on the potatoes that they grew themselves on their meager plots of land. They could afford little else; the immense inequities of the Irish tenant farming system, together with the heavy tariffs imposed on imports of grain under the Corn Laws, ensured the Irish peasantry's near total dependence on the potato crop. The tenant farming population was thus desperately poor even before the famine of the 1840s. But as the potato blight spread throughout Ireland and persisted—devastating the crops of 1846, 1847, and 1848—outright starvation spread across the island, even as Ireland continued to export to England vast quantities of meat, butter, and other food that remained unaffordable to the starving poor. Prime Minister Robert Peel's Conservative government attempted to alleviate the situation with make-work projects for the destitute and with emergency shipments of grain imported from the United States. The Irish famine was also an important factor in Peel's decision to support repeal of the Corn Laws; like many, he believed that cheaper grain would help alleviate the situation in Ireland. Peel succeeded in repealing the Corn Laws, but the issue split the Conservative party; he was forced into the opposition and his government was replaced in 1846 by the Whig administration of Lord John Russell, which by the end of 1847 had greatly reduced funding of emergency aid for Ireland. The laissez-faire economic beliefs of many Whigs informed their decision to transfer the responsibility for famine relief to local authorities (who were in most cases utterly unable to fulfill such responsibilities) under the provisions of a new Irish Poor Law.

[1] In a letter to his friend Charles Knight, Dickens accused the utilitarians of seeing "figures and averages, and nothing else."

[2] Although the "social novel" had its origins in the eighteenth century, it was developed and popularized as a genre during the Victorian period.

[3] From the French for "let do," the phrase "laissez-faire" came to be used in the late eighteenth century as a shorthand for the belief that government should intervene as little as possible in the workings of the economy. The term first appeared in English usage in George Whatley's *Principles of Trade* (1774), but it did not become popularized until James Mill's reference in an 1824 entry in *The Encyclopedia Britannica*.

The effects of the famine were aggravated by long-standing structural inequities. Desperately poor, mostly Catholic tenants were forced to pay rents (often extraordinarily high) to wealthy English or Anglo-Irish landowners who lived abroad. If they failed to pay, eviction was the likely result—which often left the tenant facing imminent starvation. By the end of the decade, between 850,000 and 1,500,000 people—perhaps as much as 15 per cent of the Irish population—had died of starvation, and at least a million more had emigrated.

A great deal of the literature on the Great Famine is devoted to allocating blame among particular individuals. Was Lord John Russell in fact more to blame for the catastrophe than was Robert Peel? The latter is generally portrayed as more sympathetic than Russell to the plight of the Irish, yet Russell was a Prime Minister with little knowledge either of economics or of Ireland. In formulating his Irish policy he depended for advice very largely on his Chancellor of the Exchequer, Sir Charles Wood, who in turn worked closely with Peel; the Whigs' minority status in Parliament necessitated their working closely with Peel's faction in order to maintain the support of Parliament. Many have apportioned a good deal of blame to Sir Charles Trevelyan, who was responsible both for advising the government on the Irish situation and for implementing the government's relief policies in Ireland. Others have suggested that the indebtedness of the British government made it virtually impossible for England to provide help on the scale that was required. Still others have blamed the laissez-faire economic doctrines preached (if not always practised) by the Whigs.

No doubt there is more than a grain of truth in all these arguments. But two underlying truths are also inescapable. The first is that the structure of Irish society (with its absentee landlords and its vast inequities between rich and poor, between landowner and tenant, and between Protestant and Catholic) meant that the island was perpetually teetering on the edge of catastrophe. The second is that anti-Irish attitudes in England were so widespread and ran so deep in the general populace that it would in all probability have been impossible politically for any English leader—no matter how well-intentioned—to have succeeded in putting in place measures sufficiently wide-reaching to have prevented catastrophe. There is little question that Sir Charles Trevelyan was echoing the anti-Irish sentiments of many in England when he infamously claimed that "the judgement of God sent the calamity to teach the Irish a lesson, [and] that calamity must not be too much mitigated."

The year that followed the famine saw a wave of democratic revolutions sweep through much of Europe, affecting France, the German States, the Habsburg Empire, the Italian States, and many other areas. There was no revolution in England, but in Ireland a group called the Young Irelanders—incensed by the famine and in part inspired by the spirit of democracy abroad—staged a rebellion in Ireland on 29 June 1848. The group's grievances can be traced to the 1800 Acts of Union, which had dissolved the Irish Parliament; responsibility for the governance of Ireland was transferred to the Houses of Parliament in London. Although the representation of Ireland in this body was strengthened in 1829 (when legal restrictions on the political position of Catholics were lifted), many in Ireland continued to feel that the repeal of the Union and the establishment of self-government was the only effective response to the needs of Ireland.

The rebellion of the Young Irelanders was subdued within a day. Nevertheless, the seeds of the Irish independence movement had been effectively sown—not only in Ireland but also in the United States, where hundreds of thousands of Irish now lived. As these emigrants prospered in America, they provided more and more support for groups agitating for Irish independence. Chief among these was the Fenian movement, formed in the 1850s. The Fenians launched numerous attacks in the 1860s and 1870s, not only in England but also against symbols of colonial authority in British possessions in New Brunswick, Upper Canada, and Manitoba. The most significant Fenian uprising occurred in 1867; though unsuccessful in its aim of establishing an independent Irish Republic, it again brought the demands of Ireland to the forefront of public debate.

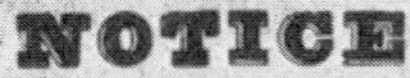

NOTICE
TO
THE EARL OF CHARLEMONT'S TENANTRY.

IN consideration of the extensive failure in the POTATO CROP this Season, willing to bear his share in the general calamity, and anxious to relieve, as far as in him lies, his Poorer Tenants from an undue share of suffering under the Divine Will, LORD CHARLEMONT has directed that the following Scale of Reduction, in Payment of Rent, shall be adopted for this Year, upon his Estates in the COUNTIES of ARMAGH and TYRONE, viz. :—

25 per Cent. on Rents under £5	10 per Cent. on Rents under £20.
20 per Cent. on Rents under £10	5 per Cent. on Rents under £30.
15 per Cent. on Rents under £15	No Discount on Rents exceeding £30.

Notice of a rent abatement by an Irish landlord, 1846.

On the Parliamentary front, the demand for the repeal of the Union took the form of the Home Rule Movement; Home Rule for Ireland was the subject of heated debate through much of the latter half of the century. Its leading spokesperson was Charles Stewart Parnell, Ireland's greatest Parliamentarian during this time. (Parnell survived dozens of scurrilous attempts to discredit him over several decades; he was finally brought down when his affair with a divorced woman became a public scandal.) Proposals to enact Home Rule were twice passed by the House of Commons—in 1886, when William Gladstone introduced a Home Rule bill, and then again in 1893. Both times the measure was defeated in the House of Lords. Another bill to enact Home Rule was put aside with the outbreak of World War I in 1914. Ultimately, independence was only achieved after the violent struggles of the 1916 Easter Uprising and the War of Independence of 1919–22. Even then, the British retained possession of a substantial area in Northern Ireland.

Evicted family, Glenbeigh, Ireland, 1888. In the 1880s an economic depression coincided with the election of a substantial number of Irish Home Rule Members of Parliament (under Charles Parnell's leadership), and with a campaign by the Land League to resist the practice of evicting impoverished tenant farmers unable to pay their rent.

"THE TWO NATIONS"

In the 1830s and 1840s, the human cost of the Industrial Revolution—what became known as the "Condition of England" question—was scrutinized by legislators, workers, and writers. Carlyle, Dickens, Gaskell, Harriet Martineau, Benjamin Disraeli, and Henry Mayhew documented the daily existence of poor and working people, and criticized the laws that were intended to address their suffering. The "social problem novel" or "industrial novel," an important subgenre of Victorian fiction, drew attention to class conflict and the social ramifications of laissez-faire economic policies. Prominent examples include Charles Kingsley's *Alton Locke* (1850), Charles Dickens's *Hard Times*, and Elizabeth Gaskell's *Mary Barton* (1848) and *North and South* (1854–55).

In his 1845 novel *Sybil*, future Prime Minister Benjamin Disraeli coined the phrase "the Two Nations" to describe the disparity in Britain between rich and poor. Novelists felt that their work could provoke social reform by exposing their middle-class audiences to the plight of the working classes, who were often portrayed as either vulnerable and victimized by forces beyond their control, or as a violent, angry "mass"; intervention by those of goodwill from other social classes is often implicitly recommended in such fiction as a way of

Jabez Hughes, *Benjamin Disraeli*, c. 1877. Disraeli, who led the Conservative Party from 1868 to 1880 (serving as Prime Minister briefly in 1868 and then again from 1874 to 1880), was seen as something of an exotic within the English establishment. His parents were Jewish, but he was baptized as an infant and remained a practicing Anglican throughout his life. Disraeli's prolific literary career, which began with the publication of his first novel, *Vivian Grey*, in 1826, made him a well-known man of letters. A fashionable figure, Disraeli was derided by his strait-laced rival, Liberal leader William Gladstone, as "Asiatic"—a word often used in Victorian times as a synonym for "indulgent and irresponsible." But Disraeli remained a popular figure with much of the general population as well as with much of the establishment—and with the Queen.

ameliorating the situation and bridging "the Two Nations." The middle-class narrator of Gaskell's novel *Mary Barton*, for example, adopts the role of mediator between Manchester's workers and their industrial "masters" in an attempt to foster understanding and prevent political insurrection.

Non-fiction writing may have been as important as that of any novelist in nurturing the seeds of social change. Henry Mayhew's interviews with working people and street folk for the *Morning Chronicle* newspaper opened a window for its readers onto the daily existence of an often voiceless underclass. It must be said, however, that Mayhew's reports contained no overt political commentary or reform agenda. Friedrich Engels, by contrast, in his chronicle of urban squalor *The Condition of the Working Class in England in 1844*, not only described the extraordinary scale of the human suffering he witnessed but also placed the blame squarely on the shoulders of a class system created by industrial capitalism: "Power lies in the hands of those who own, directly or indirectly, foodstuffs and the means of production. The poor, having no capital, inevitably bear the consequences of defeat in the struggle."[1]

It was not only middle-class writers and observers who were bringing attention to the great divide between Britain's rich and poor. Chartism, a movement that initiated a series of political campaigns in the 1830s and 1840s, was a concrete expression of the desire of working-class people to resist economic and social disparity and press for political reform. The People's Charter of 1838, from which the movement took its name, petitioned the government to adopt a range of key reforms, including annual elections, universal male suffrage, and the abolition of the secret ballot and property qualifications for Members of Parliament. The mouthpiece of the Chartist movement was the *Northern Star* newspaper, one of many working-class periodicals that flourished in the early decades of the nineteenth century. The Chartist petitions were signed by up to five million people and presented to Parliament by a coalition of workers in 1839, 1842, and 1848, but were rejected each time. A number of middle-class writers sympathetic to the claims of the working classes were

[1] Engels's treatise, first published in Germany in 1845, was not translated into English until 1892.

nevertheless suspicious of the Chartist movement, particularly in light of the political revolutions taking place in continental Europe in the late 1840s. In his longing for the imagined social order of a feudal past, Carlyle denounced the "mad Chartisms" of the "anarchic multitude," comparing them to the events of the French Revolution and the Reign of Terror. With the defeat of the third petition, Chartism collapsed, but it had helped instigate a new level of class consciousness among ordinary people, and is now considered to be the first independent working-class movement in Britain.

The Six Points
OF THE
PEOPLE'S
CHARTER.

1. A vote for every man twenty-one years of age, of sound mind, and not undergoing punishment for crime.
2. The Ballot.—To protect the elector in the exercise of his vote.
3. No Property Qualification for Members of Parliament—thus enabling the constituencies to return the man of their choice, be he rich or poor.
4. Payment of Members, thus enabling an honest tradesman, working man, or other person, to serve a constituency, when taken from his business to attend to the interests of the country.
5. Equal Constituencies, securing the same amount of representation for the same number of electors, instead of allowing small constituencies to swamp the votes of large ones.
6. Annual Parliaments, thus presenting the most effectual check to bribery and intimidation, since though a constituency might be bought once in seven years (even with the ballot), no purse could buy a constituency (under a system of universal suffrage) in each ensuing twelvemonth; and since members, when elected for a year only, would not be able to defy and betray their constituents as now.

In the 1880s and 1890s various socialist movements emerged, partly on the strength of Karl Marx's theories of capital, which he formulated under the dome of the British Library after moving to London in 1849. The Fabian Society was one of the most influential socialist organizations. Its membership was mainly drawn from the middle class and included such notables as George Bernard Shaw, Sidney Webb, Beatrice Potter Webb, Edith Nesbit, and Annie Besant. The Fabians' tactics were reformist rather than revolutionary; they advocated public ownership of utilities, affordable housing, improved wages, and greater access to higher education for all.

The Matchgirl Strike Committee, 1888. A threatened strike by Bryant and May Match Company employees—most of them girls of no more than 15, earning starvation wages and exposed to hazardous phosphorous fumes—became a *cause célèbre* in 1888, and forced the company to change its practices. The action was led by Annie Besant (who had initially become famous during her 1877 trial for obscenity—the charge being based on the distribution of her pamphlet offering practical advice on contraception).

Trade unions and labor movements also grew gradually in scope and strength throughout the century, with the Trade Union Act of 1871 granting legal status to unions for the first time. Newly mobilized workers in the 1880s organized to mount a series of strikes with varying degrees of success. Two of the most highly publicized of these were the match-girls' strike in 1888 and the London dock workers' strike of 1889. Union membership doubled in these years, partly because of the success of these labor actions.

The match-girls' strike began after the dismissal of one of the workers at the Bryant and May Factory in Bow, London, in early July 1888, but its real causes lay in the terrible working conditions at the factory, including 14-hour workdays, poor pay and excessive fines, and severe health complications resulting from working with dangerous materials. The strike attracted significant publicity, and factory owners were forced to concede to the strikers' demands for a better working-environment.

The London Dock Strike began on 14 August 1889. At a Parliamentary hearing on the issue, the general manager at the Millwall Docks testified about the physical conditions of the workers, which led to the strike:

> The poor fellows are miserably clad, scarcely with a boot on their foot, in a most miserable state. ... These are men who come to work in our docks who come on without having a bit of food in their stomachs, perhaps since the previous day; they have worked for an hour and have earned 5d.; their hunger will not allow them to continue: they take the 5d. in order that they may get food, perhaps the first food they have had for twenty-four hours.

The strike, which had succeeded in garnering strong middle-class support, ended in victory for the workers, whose principal demand had been for increased pay, and the establishment of unions for dock workers.

THE POSITION OF WOMEN

Gender consciousness was central to Victorian England's political scene in a number of significant ways. At the beginning of the Victorian period, middle-class women were shut out of most remunerative employments and institutions of higher education, could not vote, and had few legal rights. By the end of the century, the situation did not, on the surface, look radically different—universal female suffrage, for example, was not achieved in Britain until 1928—but several key developments heralded the changes to come in the twentieth century.

The first major challenges by Victorian "strong-minded women" to patriarchal control were in the area of marriage law. The common-law doctrine of coverture ensured that a woman's legal identity was subsumed in that of her husband's upon marriage. In effect, the law of coverture regarded the husband and wife as "one person": the husband. This meant that upon marriage a husband had full control of his wife's personal property and any earnings she acquired during the marriage; he had absolute authority over their home and children; and he could legally use physical force to discipline the members of his family. If he deserted his wife, she could not sue for divorce and had no custody rights to their children. No viable legal mechanism was available to an average woman to contest her husband's decisions, since husband and wife were "one body" under the law.[1] The essayist Frances Power Cobbe was among the most effective in pointing out the illogic of such arrangements, as well as the terrible toll they exacted. In contemplating, for example, the situation of "the poor woman whose husband has robbed her earnings, who leaves her and her children to starve, and then goes unpunished because the law can only recognize the relation of husband and wife as … one before the law," Cobbe observed in her provocative 1868 essay "Criminals, Idiots, Women, and Minors" that

> It is one of the numerous anomalies connected with women's affairs, that when they are under debate the same argument which would be held to determine other questions in one way is felt to settle theirs in another. If for instance it be proved of any other class of the community, that it is particularly liable to be injured, imposed upon, and tyrannized over (e.g., the children who work in factories), it is considered to follow as a matter of course that the

[1] The tremendous pressures placed on women as a result of coverture are significant to the plot of a number of prominent Victorian novels, perhaps most notably Emily Brontë's *Wuthering Heights* (1847). In the novel, Heathcliff exploits marital coverture to usurp property as part of his plan for vengeance, repeatedly resorting to abuse and exploitation of the authority he is granted as husband.

law must step in for its protection. But it is the alleged *helplessness* of married women which, it is said, makes it indispensable to give all the support of the law, *not* to them, but to the stronger persons with whom they are unequally yoked.

Under pressure from organized networks of reformers, several major pieces of legislation were enacted that altered the status and position of married women. Perhaps the most economically significant of these was

POLITICAL CANDIDATE: "As your husband is dead, madam, and women do not vote, it is no use my staying."
TAX COLLECTOR: "As your husband is dead, madam, and women have to pay taxes, you will have to pay the tax instead of him."

The movement to win the vote for women began in the 1850s, and articles and petitions on the issue appeared with increasing frequency thereafter. Many of the early arguments drew parallels with other efforts to extend the franchise; as Mary Margaret Dilke observed in an 1889 article, "it is really an interesting study to notice how every argument used to delay the enfranchisement of working men and farm labourers reappears to do duty against women. How often has the question been asked, 'What does Hodge know about finance and foreign policy, colonial affairs and commercial interests?'"

As the suffrage movement grew, differences of opinion developed over the appropriate level of militancy to adopt and over whether the movement should press for universal suffrage or only for certain categories of women to be allowed to vote. The granting of the vote eventually came in two stages, with certain classes of propertied women granted the right to vote in 1918 (the same year the vote was granted to all men of 21 years or more), and all women over the age of 21 finally being granted the franchise in 1928.

the Married Women's Property Act of 1870,[1] which finally allowed married women to legally own the money they earned and the property they inherited. In addition, the Matrimonial Causes Act of 1878 accorded some legal protection to female victims of domestic violence, and the Infant Custody Acts of 1839 and 1886 granted a woman custodial rights to her children. Although full equality within marriage was not realized in law until the twentieth century, the passage of the aforementioned legislation began to chip away at male patriarchal privilege and challenged the legal and religious "justifications" for women's oppression within the family.

In her 1851 essay "The Enfranchisement of Women" Harriet Taylor Mill addresses those "justifications" one by one, then proceeds to the heart of the matter: "The real question is, whether it is right and expedient that one half of the human race should pass through life in a state of forced subordination to the other half." *The Subjection of Women* (1869),[2] John Stuart Mill's famous extended essay on the topic, grew out of Taylor Mill's essay—the two worked largely collaboratively. "The Enfranchisement of Women" had set out with utmost clarity the ideal that is still being striven for today: "the principle which regulates the existing social relations between the two sexes—the legal subordination of one sex to the other—is wrong in itself and now one of the chief hindrances to human improvement … it ought to be replaced by a principle of perfect equality, admitting no power or privilege on the one side, nor disability on the other."

The principles advocated by Cobbe, Taylor Mill, and Mill were, of course, not only matters of law and politics; they pervaded every aspect of British life, from employment, to educational access, to a variety of cultural matters. The principle of "perfect equality" was far from being realized in any of these areas even at century's end. But, by 1900, some at least were beginning to feel that the slow movement toward acceptance of the principles of gender equality had become inexorable.

Empire

Victorian Britain's internal politics, enormous wealth, and its sense of national and global identity cannot be adequately understood in isolation from its imperial rule abroad. In an address at Oxford in 1870, the highly influential critic and social thinker John Ruskin urged England to "found colonies as fast and as far as she is able, … seizing every piece of fruitful waste ground she can set her foot on, and there teaching these her colonists that their first aim is to be to advance the power of England by land and sea." And under Victoria's reign such power did indeed grow steadily, with 18 major territories added to the British Empire, which already included India, Canada, Australia, New Zealand, and much of southern Africa and the Caribbean.

If the Empire arose largely from the desire to increase trade and maximize commercial interests, it also increasingly took hold of the political and cultural imagination. The often brutal effects of colonial domination were rationalized by a pseudo-science purporting to demonstrate the inferiority of dark-skinned peoples and by a keenly felt, much-encouraged sense of racial and cultural superiority over other peoples. A paternalistic sense of responsibility for the peoples of the "inferior races" became known as the "white man's burden" in Rudyard Kipling's famous phrasing. Or, as evolutionary theorist Alfred Russel Wallace put it, "the relation of a civilized to an uncivilized race, over which it rules, is exactly that of

[1] The Act's full title was "An Act to amend the law relating to the property of married women." Although the Act effectively overturned coverture by allowing women to legally claim their own earnings and property, serious loopholes made it possible to easily evade the law, particularly in regard to inheritance. An additional problem was posed by the fact that the Act was not retroactive, thereby limiting its usefulness for many women. The Act also made it a woman's legal duty to financially maintain her children from profits earned. That is, the Act effectively established both parents as responsible for the financial support of their children.

[2] The essay was completed in 1861, but Mill waited to publish the work until he felt it would be more influential.

Edward Bulwer-Lytton, Viceroy of India, Calcutta, 1877.

parent to child, or generally adults to infants." In missionary work, travel and exploration, scientific writing, advertising, visual art, and literature, the culture and logic of imperial rule were formulated as part of the everyday "common sense" of the age.

Not everyone was in complete agreement about Britain's imperial policies and practices. Impassioned public debates about the moral and economic injustice of slavery had culminated in the abolition of the slave trade in 1807 and of slavery in most British possessions in 1833. Britain continued to rely on cheap imports of raw materials from its Caribbean colonies, however, and conditions for free workers were sometimes little better than they had been for enslaved people. Attention to British rule in the West Indies was renewed in 1865, following an attempted uprising in which black Jamaicans had killed about twenty white colonists. Governor Edward Eyre's response was to send troops, who killed more than four hundred black Jamaicans, many of whom had not been involved in the uprising. Hundreds more people were also captured, some of whom were later executed, and Eyre's forces burned down more than 1,000 homes. The opinions of two of the century's most respected public intellectuals—Thomas Carlyle and John Stuart Mill—represented the opposing poles of the public's response, with Carlyle supporting Eyre's imposition of a harsh law to restore order, and Mill calling for Eyre to be tried for murder.

The "Indian Mutiny" of 1857–58 presented a major challenge to British rule in India, which until that point was still largely under the control of the East India Company. Sepoys—Indian men employed as soldiers by the British—staged a rebellion at Meerut in early 1857, killing British officers. The violence spread throughout northern territories and to Delhi, with massacres of British men, women, and children taking place at Cawnpore and Lucknow. British reprisals were swift and bloody, leading to summary executions, looting, and massacres of Indian civilians. The Indian resistance was motivated by religious, cultural, and political opposition to British policies, and had a lasting impact on British rule in India. One especially significant change was the transfer of colonial governance from the East India Company to the Crown in 1858. In the meantime, the English press was filled with lurid reports of the violence, resulting in greater public fascination with India than ever before. Countless eyewitness accounts, sermons, plays, novels, and poems—some written decades after the events—expressed moral outrage about the insurgency. There were also those, including the soon-to-be Prime Minister Benjamin Disraeli, who tried to contextualize the violence by criticizing Britain's exploitative attitudes and practices in India, but such dissenting voices remained very much a minority.

Britain participated in few major wars during Victoria's reign; when it did, the results were often less than heroic. In the Crimean War of 1854–56, Britain joined Turkey and France in fighting Russian encroachment into the Middle East, but the war did little to change the balance of power in Europe; it nonetheless resulted in the deaths of 21,000 British

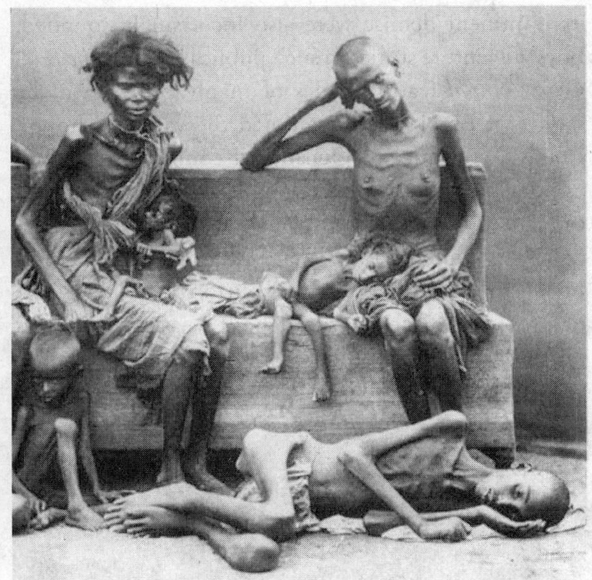

Famine Victims, Madras, c. 1877. Famine was a recurrent reality in India throughout the nineteenth century, but the famine of the 1870s was particularly harsh. It gave rise to considerable controversy in Britain, with some (such as Florence Nightingale, the founder of modern nursing) pressing for investment in health, sanitation, and irrigation as well as short-term relief measures; others (in sympathy with the harsh approach taken by the Viceroy, Edward Bulwer-Lytton) saw such measures as too expensive or too "lenient."

Florence Nightingale in the Crimea, c. 1856.

Queen Victoria and her servant Abdul Karim, 1893.

troops, 16,000 of whom died of disease.[1] In the Anglo-Zulu War of 1878–79, the Zulus of southern Africa had considerable initial success against British forces before being subdued, and in the Anglo-Afghan War of 1878–80, the British suffered various reversals before achieving a tenuous hold over Afghanistan. The Boer War of 1899–1902, in South Africa, was fought between the British and the Boers[2] over gold and diamond fields. For the Boers, the war was part of a larger struggle to prevent the influence of foreign powers on agricultural lands they had claimed. A guerilla war ensued, and Britain's image as the greatest military power in the world suffered when the army was unable to defeat the vastly outnumbered Boers.

[1] When the deplorable conditions of the military's hospitals became public knowledge through reports in *The Times*, Florence Nightingale was dispatched to the Crimea to superintend Britain's female nurses.

[2] White settlers of Dutch descent, also known as Afrikaaners.

In England, popular support for the Empire reached its zenith in the 1880s and 1890s, as Britain accelerated the pace of its drive to increase its imperial acquisitions to compete with other European powers and with the United States. Queen Victoria's Golden and Diamond Jubilees, during which she celebrated the fiftieth and sixtieth anniversaries of her sovereignty, provided grand occasions for the expression of national pride. As *The Times* crowed, Britain was extolled as "the mightiest and most beneficial Empire ever known in the annals of mankind." Much popular reading in these decades was devoted to a celebration of Empire, though warnings of its imminent demise were also increasingly sounded. Boys' adventure stories in such publications as *The Boy's Own Annual* featured tales of manly prowess in the service of Empire and promoted the values of honor, courage, and duty to Queen and country. Travel and exploration narratives were popular, too—particularly those that recounted the heroic journeys of such larger-than-life figures as Richard Burton and David Livingstone. Richard Francis Burton (1821–90) was renowned for his travels throughout Asia and Africa and much celebrated for his mastery of foreign languages, of which he knew 29, by some counts. Perhaps his most

Engraving by G. Durand, after a sketch by H.M. Stanley, "The Meeting of Livingstone and Stanley in Central Africa" (from *The Graphic*, 3 August 1872). By 1869, it had been three years since the renowned missionary and explorer David Livingstone had embarked on an expedition in search of the source of the Nile River. American journalist Henry Morgan Stanley was commissioned in that year by a New York newspaper to find Livingstone; the story of the two finally meeting on the shores of Lake Tanganyika in 1871 became legendary. As Stanley described it, "I … would have embraced him, only, he being an Englishman, I did not know how he would receive me; so I did what cowardice and false pride suggested was the best thing—walked deliberately to him, took off my hat, and said, 'Dr. Livingstone, I presume?'

"'Yes,' said he, with a kind smile, lifting his cap slightly."

famous exploit was traveling to Mecca in disguise, but he was also recognized for translating the complete *One Thousand and One Nights* from Arabic and for bringing the *Kama Sutra* to publication in English. Although he served as a symbol of the Empire's might, Burton was a prominent critic of colonial policies. David Livingstone (1813–73) renamed the Mosi-oa-Tunya—perhaps the world's most impressive waterfall—Victoria Falls in honor of the Queen. He was a national hero of sorts during the Victorian era, famed as a missionary, a scientist and explorer, and an idealistic imperialist who fought against slavery but advocated commercial empire. Speaking to students at Cambridge University in 1857, Livingstone declared,

> People talk of the sacrifice I have made in spending so much of my life in Africa. Can that be called a sacrifice which is simply paid back as a small part of a great debt owing to our God, which we can never repay? Is that a sacrifice which brings its own blest reward in healthful activity, the consciousness of doing good, peace of mind, and a bright hope of a glorious destiny hereafter? Away with the word in such a view and with such a thought! It is emphatically no sacrifice. Say rather it is a privilege.

Almost as popular as the narratives of Burton and Livingstone were travel journals by intrepid "lady explorers" such as Mary Kingsley and Isabella Bird, who unsettled conventional notions of Victorian femininity even as they satisfied the public taste for true stories with fictionalized elements. Kingsley (1862–1900) first traveled to Africa in order to complete research for a book left unfinished by her father at the time of his death. She lived with local tribes in Angola. Upon her return to England, she toured the country, giving lectures in which she criticized missionaries for their attempts to change the local people—earning her much censure from the Church of England. She also defended African customs, including polygamy. Her books about her experiences—*Travels in Africa* (1897) and *West African Studies* (1899)—were best-sellers. Bird (1831–1904) traveled extensively, visiting Australia, Hawaii, and Colorado—then the most recent state to join the United States—where she covered more than 800 miles in the Rocky Mountains. The letters she wrote to her sister during this time were published as the immensely popular *A Lady's Life in the Rocky Mountains* (1879).

The imperial romances of some authors were a symptom of the anxieties surrounding Britain's increasingly tenuous grip on its empire. Whereas early and mid-century Victorian fiction tended to imagine the Empire as a fairly static, unknown space to which characters can be exiled in the interests of narrative closure, late-century fiction often represented the Empire in darker, Gothic terms. Incorporating supernatural and psychological elements in their work, writers such as H. Rider Haggard, Arthur Conan Doyle, Rudyard Kipling, and Robert Louis Stevenson used colonial settings to explore themes of racial degeneration and human "savagery." In his 1899 novella, *Heart of Darkness*, Joseph Conrad, a Polish émigré to England, drew on his experience as a member of the merchant marine in his portrayal of imperial greed, exploitation, and corruption among ivory traders in the Congo. Even Kipling, called the "Laureate of Empire" for his energetic—and often jingoistic—portrayals of the glories of British imperialism, was not always unequivocal in his attitudes toward the Empire: in his 1897 poem "Recessional," he sounded a famous warning against imperial hubris: "Far-called, our navies melt away; / On dune and headland sinks the fire: / Lo, all our pomp of yesterday / Is one with Nineveh and Tyre!"[1]

Faith and Doubt

One of the most unsettling developments for average citizens during the Victorian period was the growing opposition to the authority of Christian faith and the

[1] Nineveh, called an "exceeding great city" in the Book of Jonah, was the center of worship of the goddess Ishtar in Assyria; it was captured and razed in 612 BCE, signaling the end of the Assyrian Empire. Tyre—the largest and most important Phoenician city—was sacked by Alexander the Great during his campaign against Persia in 332 BCE.

established church. A rapidly changing social order, combined with the growing predominance of scientific rationalism and empiricist method, destabilized Christian certainty, creating a rising tide of secularism and religious skepticism. As critic J.A. Froude put it in 1841, "the very truths which have come forth have produced doubts … this dazzle has too often ended in darkness."

The poet Arthur Hugh Clough was a central figure in the expression of the religious doubt of the age; in "Easter Day: Naples, 1849"—a poem whose title deliberately invokes the most sacred of days for Christians only for the poem to subvert the day's holiness—his verse conveys a strong sense of the intense emotion that could accompany such feelings:

> My heart was hot within me; till at last
> My brain was lightened when my tongue had said—
> Christ is not risen!
> Christ is not risen, no—
> He lies and moulders low.

Biblical scholars in England and Europe in the early decades of the century had begun to question the Scriptures as a source of literal truth and to present the figure of Jesus Christ as a mortal rather than a divine being. The German "higher critics" of the Bible—especially D.F. Strauss in his *Das Leben Jesu* (translated by George Eliot, 1844–46)[1]—were influential in this "scientific" discussion of biblical texts. Leading Victorian thinkers such as Carlyle, Eliot, and Martineau wrote of personal religious crises, and wrestled publicly with doubts about the value and meaning of Christian belief. As Matthew Arnold wrote in 1880, "There is not a creed which is not shaken, nor an accredited dogma which is not shown to be questionable, not a received tradition which does not threaten to dissolve." In this climate of uncertainty as to whether the divine could be knowable, Carlyle's arrival, in *Sartor Resartus* (1833–34), at an affirmation of "natural supernaturalism" offers a telling statement of the almost desperate determination to find the divine in both nature and other human beings.

Traditional religious belief received its greatest challenge in the Victorian period from the evidence of the fossil record, and from Darwinian explanations of the origins of the universe and human beings' place within it. Charles Darwin's theories of evolution and natural selection in *On the Origin of Species* (1859) and *The Descent of Man* (1871) rejected the Christian idea that human beings had been created in God's image and were thus of a different order than the rest of the natural world. In *Descent*, Darwin provoked and challenged his audience by declaring, "He who is not content to look, like a savage, at the phenomena of nature as disconnected, cannot any longer believe that man is the work of a separate act of creation."[2]

And religious controversy and doubt extended further still. Not only were the divinity of Christ, the literal truth of the Bible, and the processes of creation at issue, so too was the very existence of a creator or divine being. One of Darwin's strongest supporters, the scientist Thomas Henry Huxley, coined the term "agnostic" in 1869 at a party held in connection with the forming of the Metaphysical Society, a learned society that met regularly for over a decade to discuss theological issues, and whose members also included Tennyson, Ruskin, and Gladstone. The term agnostic named a person of a sort unimaginable in most earlier ages—one who neither believes nor disbelieves in the existence of God, holding instead that it is simply

[1] David Friedrich Strauss (1808–74) shocked and outraged Christian Europe with his depiction of the "historical Jesus." *Das Leben Jesu*, or *The Life of Jesus, Critically Examined*, caused a scandal with its insistence on the need to understand the miraculous events depicted in the Gospels as "mythical" in character. Eventually, Strauss's views came to dominate the new epoch of scriptural study, focused on textual interpretation.

[2] Much recent debate has focused on the question of Darwin's own Christian faith. His *Autobiography* (completed in 1876, but first published in 1887, five years after his death) and letters suggest Darwin's growing agnosticism. In the *Autobiography*, Darwin recalls "In my Journal I wrote that whilst standing in the midst of the grandeur of a Brazilian forest, 'it is not possible to give an adequate idea of the higher feelings of wonder, admiration, and devotion, which fill and elevate the mind.' I well remember my conviction that there is more in man than the mere breath of his body." But, toward the end of his life, he wrote to a correspondent, "I am sorry to have to inform you that I do not believe in the Bible as a divine revelation, & therefore not in Jesus Christ as the Son of God."

impossible for humans to possess knowledge of such matters.[1] It is to such beliefs—or the lack thereof—that Matthew Arnold refers when he writes in "Dover Beach" (1867) of the ebbing tide of the "Sea of Faith." Whereas in the twentieth century that ebbing tide was sometimes welcomed as representing a freeing of human potential, Victorians tended to hear it in the way that Arnold heard it, inextricably associated with an "eternal note of sadness."

The established church of England and Scotland—the Anglican denomination—remained a powerful entity throughout the Victorian era, with the reigning monarch heading the Church as the "Defender of the Faith," as had been the case since Henry VIII's break with Rome in the 1530s. By century's end, however, its power was more social than political. Though only Anglicans could be admitted to Parliament until the late 1820s, and non-Anglicans were barred from taking degrees at Oxford and Cambridge until 1871, the changes in both policies demonstrated that allegiance to Anglicanism was no longer a necessary criterion for admission to the bastions of power.

The Church was also profoundly influenced by the gradual severance of church-state relations, as well as the increasing popularity of Evangelicalism, a broad-based movement comprising numerous Protestant denominations including Methodism and Presbyterianism. These "Dissenting" or "nonconformist" faiths transformed religious practice in Britain, stressing the importance of an individual's personal relationship with God, of prudence and temperance, of conversion, of missionary work, and of humanitarian activism. In 1878, the Methodist minister William Booth founded the Salvation Army, which ministered to the poor in London's East End and became the center of social purity campaigns stressing chastity and public decency for both sexes. In general, Evangelical congregations were less hierarchical in organization than the traditional Anglican Church, were anti-Catholic in orientation, and attracted both middle- and working-class believers who felt that Anglicanism had lost its spiritual power and had become a mere appendage of the state.

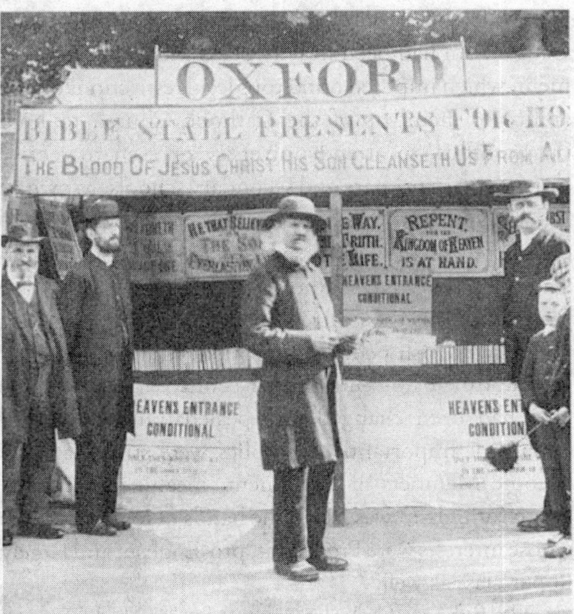

Henry Taunt, "Bible Stall at the St. Giles Fair, Oxford," 1880.

Evangelicalism—and the resistance to it—within the Church of England resulted in a split between Anglican Evangelicals (commonly referred to as Low Church), progressives (Broad Church, sometimes called Latitudinarians), and Anglo-Catholics (High Church). An important High Church reaction to Evangelicalism took place in the 1830s and 1840s through the Oxford Movement, also called Tractarianism, led by Oxford theologians and intellectuals John Henry Newman, John Keble, and Edward Pusey. Celebrating the mystical and aesthetic elements of worship, they advocated an increased emphasis on religious ritual and a strict observance of clerical hierarchy within the Anglican communion. Newman's conversion to Roman Catholicism in 1845 spelled the end of the Oxford Movement, heralding a significant Catholic revival that saw many intellectuals rejecting Protestantism to embrace the Catholic faith and tradition. This was a significant

[1] Among Victorian authors, George Eliot is perhaps the most prominent to have described herself as an agnostic.

religious as well as political development, since Catholics in England and especially in Ireland had for centuries been subject to persecution.

Since the seventeenth century, the practice of Catholicism had been heavily penalized by the government, which imposed numerous legal restrictions on the ability of members of the Catholic Church to hold public office, to attend university or even to receive instruction in primary and secondary schools, to own or inherit land, and much more. These laws were known collectively as the Penal Laws. As Ireland's population was overwhelmingly Catholic, the practical effect of the Penal Laws was the near-complete exclusion of the vast majority of Irish people from public and political life. By the turn of the nineteenth century many of these laws had been changed or repealed, but several still remained. Importantly, Catholics were still unable to become Members of Parliament, meaning that legislation for Ireland was left in the hands of representatives whose interests were Protestant, pro-English, and largely upper-class as well.

The fight for Catholic rights—for "Catholic Emancipation," as it was generally referred to—was largely led by the charismatic leader Daniel O'Connell. O'Connell accused the government of despotism, positioning the call for Emancipation within the larger context of the call for liberty and equality that had been sweeping Europe since the end of the previous century. The Emancipation movement ostensibly achieved victory in 1829, with the passing of the Roman Catholic Relief Act, which annulled all previous restrictions on the ability of Catholics—including O'Connell himself—to be elected to Parliament. As some barriers were removed, however, others were erected. Notably, the financial requirement for running for Parliament was raised considerably: one needed now to own land worth at least ten pounds, a fivefold increase from the previous two-pound requirement. While not explicitly discriminatory toward the Irish, the requirement effectively excluded the majority of Catholics, who were on average far poorer than the Protestant minority.

English Jews were also denied full rights of citizenship until a series of measures granted them access to Parliament, the military, the legal establishment, and institutions of higher learning. Anti-Semitic stereotypes were legion in Victorian novels such as *Oliver Twist*. In at least a few cases the writings of non-Jewish novelists challenged the stereotypes—sometimes tentatively, in ways that to some extent still participated in the culture of prejudice (as in Anthony Trollope's wide-ranging novel of capitalism, marriage, and religion, *The Way We Live Now* [1875]), sometimes more clearly and unequivocally (as in George Eliot's *Daniel Deronda* [1876][1]). And a significant body of Anglo-Jewish literature by writers such as Israel Zangwill and Amy Levy expressed a range of Jewish responses to social prejudice on the part of England's Christian majority.

Though the religious establishment suffered many challenges to its power, it would be a mistake to assume that secularism, Utilitarianism, and Darwinian theory stamped out religious faith or traditional religious practice: far from it. The Victorian period can be fairly characterized as an age of religious doubt that was also marked by intense religious feeling. As novels such as Anthony Trollope's *Barsetshire Chronicles*—a series of six novels published from 1855 to 1867—vividly convey, religious affiliation (irrespective of the strength of one's actual faith) shaped most people's sense of personal identity. And the quest for spiritual meaning was itself the driving force behind some of the most moving literary works of the age. One such work, Tennyson's *In Memoriam* (1849), an elegy for his friend Arthur Henry Hallam, chronicles the spiritual crisis of one man in the aftermath of his friend's death. By the end of the poem, the speaker has reconciled his religious doubts and scientific skepticism to re-embrace a Christian vision of

[1] Eliot's novel has been cited by a number of early Zionist leaders—including Emma Lazarus—as highly influential in their decision to embrace Zionism. The narrative's treatment of Jews—contrasting their spirituality and connection to their community to the materialism and corruption of English society—was met with some hostility, and many reviewers remarked that the parts of *Daniel Deronda* focusing on Jewish characters were its weakest.

The critic Edward Said has suggested, in "Zionism from the Standpoint of Its Victims" (1979), that the novel was a propaganda tool, used to encourage patriation of British-controlled Palestine by Jews.

John Everett Millais, *Ophelia*, 1851–52. The drowning of Ophelia (from Shakespeare's *Hamlet*) was a frequent subject in Victorian painting; the best known representation is that of Millais. As the scene is described in Act 4, Scene 7 of the play, the mentally ill Ophelia comes to a stream "with fantastic garlands" of flowers. Distracted, she falls into the "weeping brook." For a while before she drowns, "her clothes spread wide" and hold her up.

Henry Wallis, *Chatterton*, 1856. The suicide of Thomas Chatterton (1752–70), of arsenic poisoning after a period of living close to starvation as a struggling poet, captured the Victorian imagination even more strongly than it had the Romantic one. Wallis's painting was widely praised when exhibited in 1856 at the Royal Academy; John Ruskin described it in his notes on the exhibit as "faultless and wonderful."

Thomas Jones Barker, *The Secret of England's Greatness* (detail), c. 1863. Barker's painting depicts the Queen presenting a Bible. The recipient and the specific occasion remain unidentified; in the background are Elizabeth, Duchess of Wellington (who served as Mistress of the Robes to the Queen); Prince Albert; Lord Palmerston (then serving as Prime Minister); and Lord John Russell (then serving as Foreign Secretary). An engraving of the painting was published under the fuller title, *The Bible: The Secret of England's Greatness.*

Franz Xaver Winterhalter, *The Royal Family in 1846* (detail), 1846.

Ford Madox Brown, *Work*, c. 1852–c. 1865. This famous painting (above), which took over twelve years to complete, brings together Victorians from an extraordinary range of backgrounds. The central group of excavators was the painting's starting point—the inspiration coming from the artist observing work on the construction of the London sewers. Less well-off members of society include the flower seller to the left and the orphaned children in the foreground, cared for by an older sibling. To the right are two "brain-workers" admired by the artist, Rev. F.D. Maurice (founder of the Working Man's College, where Brown was an art instructor) and Thomas Carlyle. In the background, members of the gentry on horseback observe the scene.

George Clausen,
The Stone Pickers, 1887.

William Holman Hunt, *The Awakening Conscience*, 1853–54. This canvas presents an elaborately coded story. In a letter to *The Times* of London, John Ruskin (signing himself as "The Author of Modern Painters") described the reaction of viewers—and elucidated the painting's intended significance: "… assuredly it is not understood. People gaze at it in a blank wonder, and leave it hopelessly; so that, although it is almost an insult to the painter to explain his thoughts in this instance, I cannot persuade myself to leave it thus misunderstood. The poor girl has been singing with her seducer; some chance words of the song "Oft in the stilly night" have struck upon the numbed places of her heart; she has started up in agony; he, not seeing her face, goes on singing, striking the keys carelessly with his gloved hand." As Ruskin discerned, the woman is evidently the mistress rather than the wife of the man; she wears a ring on every finger of her left hand except the fourth. The piece that has been played, "Oft in the stilly night," is a song in which a woman looks back to the innocence of her childhood. The doubling of the female figure through the use of the mirror suggests the possibility of a brighter future if she follows her awakened conscience and gives up the life of a "kept woman."

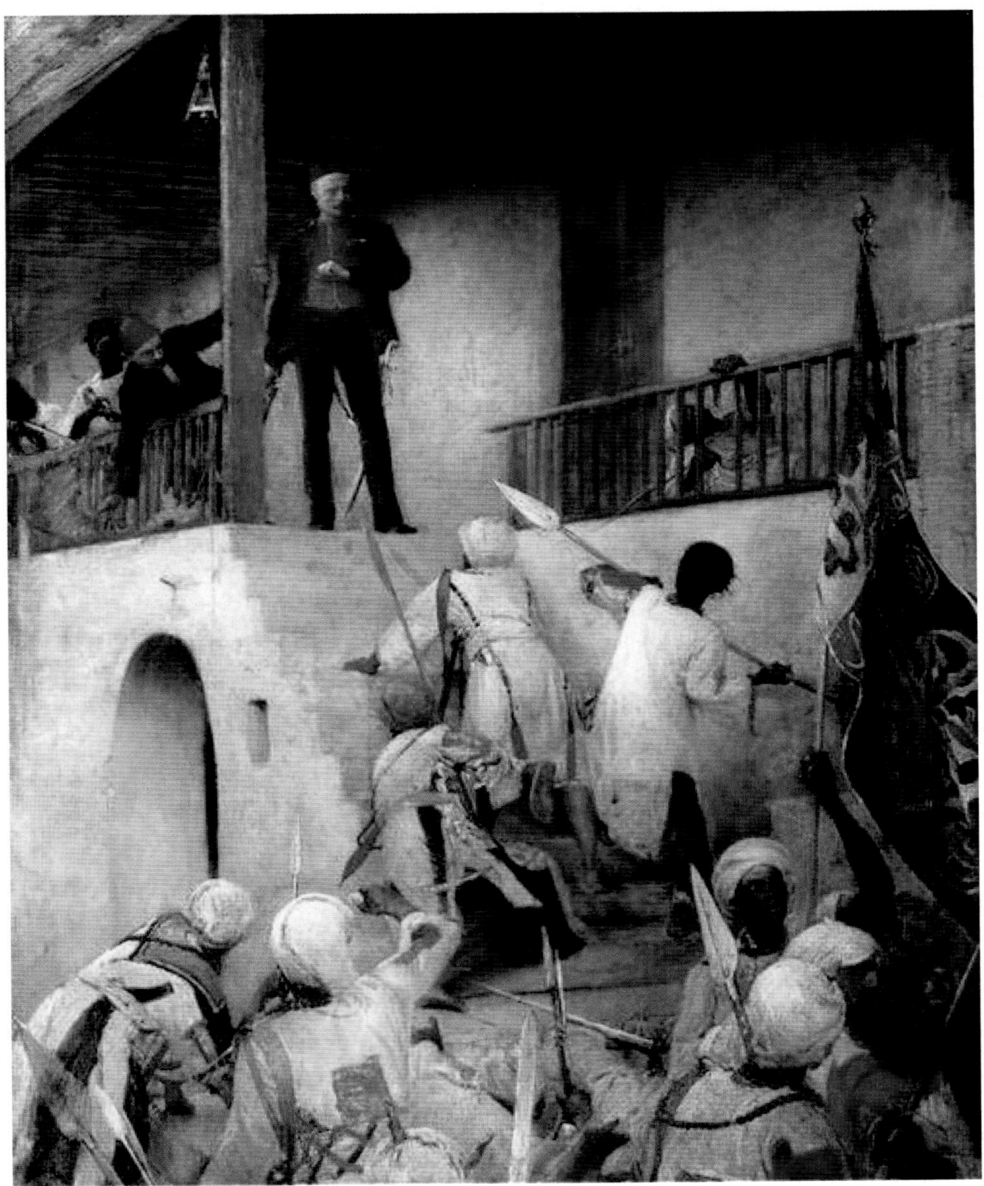

G.W. Joy, *General Gordon's Last Stand*, c. 1893. Gordon, who had held an administrative post in the Sudan in the 1870s (and played an important role during that period in ending the slave trade in the area), was sent again to the Sudan in 1884 on a mission to rescue garrisons of British troops that had been cut off after a remarkably successful rebellion led by Muhammad Ahmad. Ahmad, a Sudanese political leader and Islamic messianic figure known as the Madhi, had managed to unite many Sudanese people in the pursuit of independence from Ottoman-Egyptian powers (which were in turn largely dominated by British interests). Ahmad besieged Gordon's forces in Khartoum for ten months and finally overwhelmed them, and Gordon was killed during the battle (though almost certainly in the streets of the city, not as he is shown in Joy's iconic painting of the imagined scene). The incident became a *cause célèbre* in Britain, and there were many calls to avenge Gordon's death, but the Madhists managed to maintain independence for more than a decade; it was not until 1898 that the British under General Kitchener re-established British control of the Sudan.

Trade Emblem, Amalgamated Society of Engineers, Machinists, Millwrights, Smiths, and Pattern Makers, c. 1860.

Alfred Concanen, *Modern Advertising: A Railway Station in 1874*, 1874. This colored lithograph appeared as a fold-out frontispiece in the book *A History of Advertising from the Earliest Times.*

John O'Connor, *From Pentonville Road Looking West*, 1884. In the background is St. Pancras, one of the greatest of Victorian railway stations.

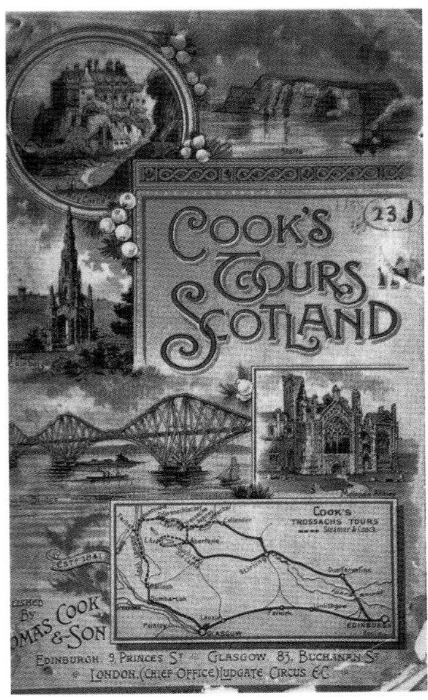

Advertisement, 1890s, "Cook's Tours in Scotland." Featured at lower left is the Firth of Forth Bridge (also known as the Forth Rail Bridge). The bridge, built in the wake of the collapse of the Firth of Tay Bridge, in which 75 lives had been lost, pioneered new techniques of cantilever construction; on its completion in 1890 it was by far the longest bridge in the world.

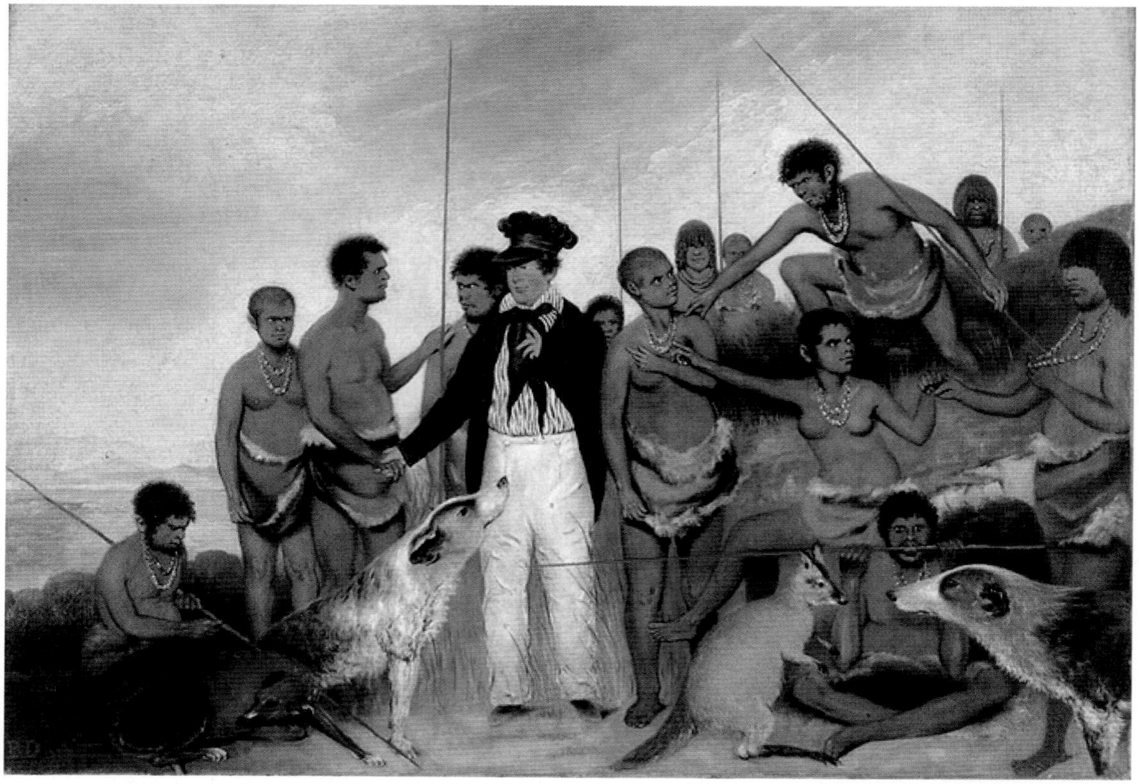

Benjamin Duterrau, *The Conciliation*, 1840. The painting shows a Methodist lay preacher instructing native Tasmanians.

Canadian election poster, 1891. The "Old Leader" was Sir John A. Macdonald, Canadian Prime Minister from 1867 to 1873 and again from 1878 to 1891. "The Old Policy" was Macdonald's National Policy, under the terms of which industries in the Dominion would be protected by a tariff on imports from the United States, but "imperial preference" exempted goods from Britain and its possessions from any tariff.

Emma Brownlow, *The Foundling Restored to Its Mother—An Incident in the Foundling Hospital*, 1858. Foundlings—deserted or abandoned children—were a frequent subject, both in Victorian literature and in the visual arts. The young girl portrayed here was indeed reclaimed soon after Brownlow had painted the picture. Most Victorian-era foundlings (like most orphans) were not so fortunate; they usually ended up not in the Foundling Hospital but in one of the workhouses established under the provisions of the 1834 Poor Law Amendment Act. Brownlow was herself raised in the Foundling Hospital—though not as a foundling; her father held a live-in position as administrator of the Thomas Coram Foundling Hospital.

(above) James Tissot, *Too Early*, 1873. The French painter Jacques-Joseph Tissot moved from Paris to London after being active in the 1871 Paris Commune; he took the Anglicized first name of James, and became both a popular and a highly regarded artist in his adopted home. Over the eleven years until his return to Paris in 1882 he painted many portraits, as well as many canvases depicting social interactions—often suggestive of a narrative. His narrative paintings include scenes of city streets, of harbor life, of garden parties, and of fashionable young women in a variety of sometimes surprising settings. Often dismissed in the twentieth century as a sentimentalist, Tissot is increasingly becoming recognized as an artist who provides a unique window into English social life in the 1870s and early 1880s.

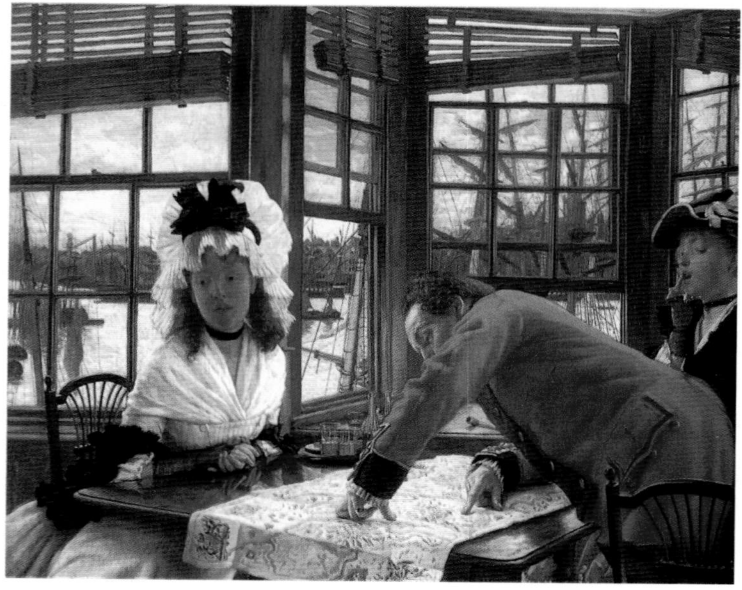

(below) James Tissot, *An Interesting Story*, c. 1872. Of note: Tissot painted a very similar scene from a different angle, and gave it the title *A Tedious History*.

Joseph Nash, *The Great Industrial Exhibition of 1851: The Transept*, 1851. Nash's lithograph, from "his drawing in the possession of Her Majesty," was one of a series. The view was described as follows in the official catalogue: "the whole extent of the transept, interrupted only by the magnificent glass fountain of Messrs. Osler, and the groups of sculpture and tropical plants and trees, … flashes on the eye more like the fabled palace of Vathek than a structure reared in a few months by mortal hands." (For more on the Crystal Palace see the Contexts section on "Britain, Empire, and a Wider World.")

Franz Xaver Winterhalter, *The First of May, 1851*, 1851. The first of May, 1851 was the opening day of the Great Exhibition at the Crystal Palace; it was also the first birthday of the Queen's third son, Prince Arthur, and the eighty-second birthday of the Duke of Wellington; the "Iron Duke" is here shown presenting a gold casket decorated with jewels to mother and child (who is holding a sprig of lily of the valley). The scene in numerous respects follows traditional Christian iconography; Prince Albert stands behind the Queen, in the position occupied by Joseph in many depictions of Mary and her newborn son.

(For more on the Great Exhibition see the introduction to the Victorian Era and the Contexts section on "Britain, Empire, and a Wider World.")

Illustrations by George Cruikshank to Charles Dickens's *Oliver Twist* (1838). The captions identify the figures in the above illustrations as "Fagin and the boys" and as "Monks [another character in the novel] and the Jew." As presented by Dickens and Cruikshank, the character of Fagin is a caricature of evil—and of Jewishness. In passages such as the following, Dickens's descriptions of Fagin give expression to some of the most extreme anti-Semitic stereotypes: "It seemed just the night when it befitted such a being as the Jew to be abroad. As he glided stealthily along, creeping beneath the shelter of the walls and doorways, the hideous old man seemed like some loathsome reptile, engendered in the slime and darkness through which he moved: crawling forth by night, in search of some rich offal for a meal." By repeatedly naming him as "the Jew" Dickens crudely implied that the characteristics of Fagin were also those of Jews in general. Dickens received complaints from readers on this score, and over time he altered his views. Beginning with the edition of 1867 he made revisions to *Oliver Twist*, changing to "Fagin" the previous references to "the Jew." The last novel Dickens completed, *Our Mutual Friend* (1864–65), is notable not least of all for the inclusion of a Jewish character (Riah) who is portrayed by Dickens in a distinctly positive light.

the afterlife. In the closing lines of the poem the speaker exalts "That God, which ever lives and loves, / One God, one law, one element, / And one far-off divine event, / To which the whole creation moves."[1]

[1] The importance of Tennyson's poem during the period is well illustrated by Queen Victoria's comment after the death of her husband Prince Albert in 1861 that "Next to the Bible, *In Memoriam* is my comfort."

Victorian Domesticity: Life and Death

The center of British religious, cultural, and emotional life in the nineteenth century was the family. As industrialization transformed the household from a workspace into its "opposite," the home came to be regarded as an almost sacred space, to be shielded from the aggressive competitiveness of the public world of

Illustration, *Wonders of a Toy-Shop*, c. 1852. Though it is sometimes claimed that children were treated as "little adults" in the nineteenth century, that was far less frequently the case than it had been a century or two earlier. In many respects, indeed, the nineteenth century marks the coming into prominence of "childhood" as a cultural entity. The changing attitude towards children working in factories was one manifestation of change. Another was the evolution of "toy"—a word used before the nineteenth century to refer to a wide variety of trifles, but increasingly in the nineteenth century applied to playthings for children; toyshops specializing in such items became more and more widespread over the course of the Victorian period.

work. The family, especially among the rising middle class, was increasingly nuclear in structure; the extended networks of friends and relations that had formed strong household connections in pre-industrial society became more and more tenuous. Increasingly, the social arrangement perceived as ideal among the better-off social classes consisted of a male breadwinner, employed outside the home, and his female helpmeet, who nurtured the children, managed the servants, and served as a paragon of domestic virtue. One of the key signs of a man's professional success was his wife's "idleness" within the home. The separation of work and family life was reflected in city planning with the construction of the first modern suburbs, supported by public transportation systems. Middle-class domestic architecture encouraged the display of wealth and the division of sexual labor amongst family members by dividing houses into "public" and "private" spaces. The middle-class family model became the ideal for the working class as well, although economic necessity continued to force many working-class wives and children to contribute to household earnings through paid labor, both inside and outside the home.

The domestic ideal and the emphasis on the family circle was shaped and promoted within the most privileged sphere of society. Throughout her reign, Queen Victoria was a paragon of good manners, restraint, and moral uprightness. In this she stood in contrast both to the escapades and excess that had surrounded the monarchies of her predecessors, George IV and William IV, and to the moral hypocrisy that characterized the reign of her son, Edward VII. In 1840, three years after her coronation, she married her first cousin, Prince Albert of Saxe-Coburg-Gotha. Together, they had nine children, and Victoria became the nation's most revered icon of domestic femininity and maternal fecundity. Despite her own public role, she was a firm believer in separate spheres of influence and authority for men and women, voicing a then-conventional feminine distaste for power: "I am every day more convinced," she at one point declared, "that we women, if we are to be good women, feminine and amiable and domestic, are not fitted to reign." The Queen, not her husband, held the power of the monarch, but the royal family nonetheless projected an ideal of Victorian domesticity, with Albert exercising much influence over his wife's decisions, and Victoria displaying unwavering devotion to the practical, manly Albert. Yet for all her outwardly conventional feminine attitudes, Victoria privately expressed ambivalence toward childbirth and marriage; she once complained in a letter to her daughter that giving birth made her feel like "a dog or a cow." In 1853, she agreed to undergo anesthesia during the birth of her son Leopold. This was a controversial new medical procedure, not least of all because it challenged the curse laid upon Eve (and therefore all women) in Genesis 1: "In sorrow shalt thou bring forth children."

When Albert died of typhoid in 1861, the entire nation went into a state of mourning. Victoria was overwhelmed with grief, and for 15 years after his death she was rarely seen in public, except at the unveiling of the many public monuments she arranged to have erected to his memory. Eventually many began to regard her seclusion as self-indulgent and excessive, and her popularity among her subjects suffered for several years. Yet Victoria's long widowhood was in many ways a sign of the times; it both reflected and influenced the Victorian vogue for elaborate mourning rituals and conventions governing the public observance of death.

Life expectancy during the Victorian period was almost certainly higher than it was in the late eighteenth century, and it did improve over the period, but for most of the century it was nevertheless extraordinarily low by the standards of the developed world today—probably no higher than 40 years in many areas of the country. The death of relatively young people was far more common than it is today—not only deaths of children but also of young adults, many of diseases such as "consumption" (tuberculosis) and cholera. It was also very common for mothers to die in childbirth.

It is no exaggeration to say that death became a commercial industry in the nineteenth century; funerals provided a public occasion to mourn the passing of a loved one as much as they offered an opportunity for rich and middle-income people to display wealth. Strict observance of funerary rituals in details of dress and deportment became a social necessity, and commemorative memorabilia, such as tea sets, photographs, and mourning jewelry—often made from the hair of the deceased—could be found in most homes. Many families were prepared to spend the bulk of their savings on the funerals of loved ones. For the poor, the story was of course much different. The indigent were buried with little or no ceremony in unmarked paupers' graves. Many working-class families contributed to burial clubs, an early form of insurance that guaranteed that at least a modest amount of money would be set aside for a respectable funeral for family members.

The obsession with death in the Victorian period is reflected in much of the literature of the period; in

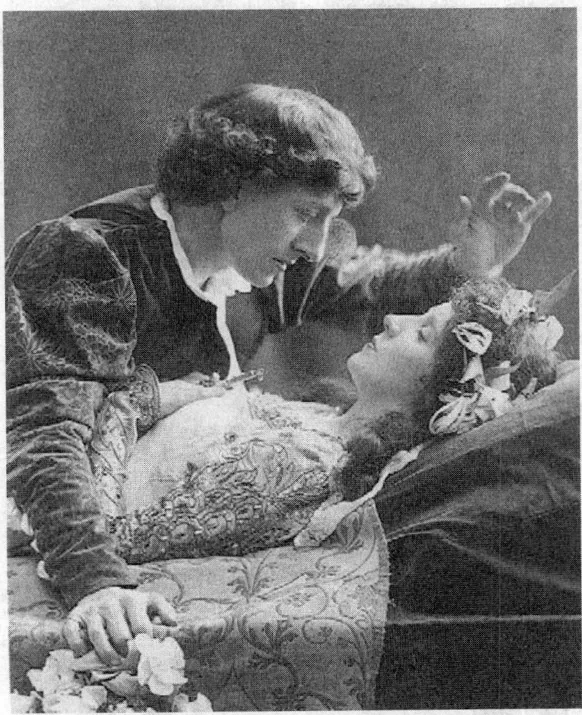

Romeo gazes at the dead Juliet: photograph of an 1895 production of Shakespeare's *Romeo and Juliet*, with Mrs. Patrick Campbell as Juliet.

Gaskell's novel *Mary Barton*, no fewer than 13 deaths either take place or are recounted within the first ten chapters. Tennyson's famed elegy *In Memoriam* is as much a meditation on death as it is a lament for the loss of a loved one. Countless Victorian novels feature prolonged death scenes, with grieving or greedy family members keeping vigil by the bedside of the dying. One of Dickens's most beloved characters, Little Nell in *The Old Curiosity Shop* (1840–41), was modeled on his sister-in-law, Mary Hogarth, whose death had affected him deeply. Little Nell's death prompted an outpouring of grief from readers, many of whom wrote letters to Dickens in between installments of the novel imploring him to spare her.[1] The beautiful, often eroticized

[1] Not all were so moved. Of the death of Dickens's beloved character, Oscar Wilde famously opined, "One would have to have a heart of stone to read the death of little Nell without dissolving into tears ... of laughter."

Advertisement from *The Lady*, 4 October 1900.

corpse—especially of a woman—was a favorite image in both visual art and poetry. In Christina Rossetti's "After Death" (1862), a female speaker observes her lover's attitude toward her corpse, and realizes, "He did not love me living; but once dead / He pitied me; and very sweet it is / To know he still is warm tho' I am cold."

Though mortality rates, especially among infants, remained high throughout the century, there were significant medical advances in disease control and sanitation. Prominent among these was the verification of the bacterial theory of disease. Until late in the century, most medical practitioners and lay people believed that disease was spread through miasma, or the spread of harmful odors through the atmosphere. Susceptibility was routinely blamed on moral and social factors such as poverty, overcrowding, and sexual behaviors. During the cholera epidemics of the 1840s, researchers began to make links between incidents of the disease and water sources. Joseph Lister's work in the 1850s and 1860s confirmed the existence of micro-organisms, yet the miasma theory of disease was so entrenched that it was not until late in the century that the bacterial theory was fully accepted. By 1890, the pathogens for several diseases, including tuberculosis, cholera, typhoid, rabies, and diphtheria, had been identified. Surgical practice was also transformed by Lister's work on antiseptic treatments and the adoption of anesthetics, particularly ether and chloroform.

Cultural Trends

When the Duke of Wellington died in 1852, a million and a half people lined the streets of London to pay their last respects to the military hero who had defeated Napoleon at Waterloo. The deaths of the eminent were marked by elaborate, theatrical state funerals that fed an increasing appetite for public spectacles, epitomized by the Great Exhibition of 1851. The culture of Victorian Britain was very much a visual one, with public amusements, popular shows, traveling exhibitions, circuses, sporting events, holiday resorts, and public gardens to cater to every stratum of a society that had a growing amount of both disposable income and leisure time. London's theaters drew thousands of spectators every night to witness ingenious visual effects created by London's theater impresarios; live animals, underwater sequences, mob scenes, flying machines, sumptuous interiors, and innovations in lighting stoked the public mania for stage realism.[1] Music halls aimed at lower middle- and working-class audiences featured a miscellany of comic songs, dance numbers, and magic shows by popular performers. Many public museums and galleries—which today draw thousands of visitors

[1] Perhaps not coincidentally, this era of special-effects theatricality is now generally said to have marked a nadir in the history of English drama as a literary genre.

"View of the Grand Entrance to the Great Exhibition, 1851." The idea for what became the Great Exhibition grew out of a proliferation of smaller exhibitions of the products of craft and industry in the 1840s, and out of an awareness that Paris was contemplating its own large-scale international exhibition. Organized largely by Henry Cole, with the strong support of Prince Albert, the "Great Exhibition of the Works of Industry of All Nations" was held in Hyde Park in 1851. The Crystal Palace, centerpiece of the Exhibition, was later dismantled and re-assembled at Sydenham in south London as a home for permanent exhibitions, where it stood until it was destroyed by fire in 1936. (See Contexts: Britain, Empire, and a Wider World.)

annually—were established in the Victorian period following the Great Exhibition, including the Victoria and Albert Museum, the National Portrait Gallery, and the Tate Gallery (founded by sugar magnate Henry Tate). Madame Tussaud's Wax Museum found a permanent home in London in 1835. From the 1870s and 1880s onwards, fashionable new shopping arcades and department stores filled with enticing consumer goods made shopping a respectable pastime for middle-class women.

Mass visual culture was inaugurated in the nineteenth century with the advent of a range of technologies, including the kaleidoscope, the daguerreotype, the photograph, and the cinema. As on the stage, visual technologies exploited light and movement in an effort to create the illusion of reality and transport viewers across time and space. Panoramas and dioramas[1] featured foreign cities, battlefields, landscapes, and natural disasters, and anticipated the "moving pictures" of the cinema. Innovations in print technology and the explosion of illustrated print material from the 1830s onwards signaled the public's increasing demand for the pictorial representation of daily events. The popular *Illustrated London News*, established in 1842, was the

[1] In a diorama, spectators view a partially translucent painting in a specially designed building, with variations of light cast upon the image to simulate the movement of light in a daytime scene. The diorama was first exhibited in London in 1823.

William Powell Frith, *The Railway Station* (detail), 1862. The painting depicts a scene at Paddington Station in London.

world's first illustrated weekly paper to hit newsstands; it used increasingly sophisticated technologies—from woodcuts to steel engravings to photographs—in its pictorial coverage of events at home and abroad. Serial novels published in periodicals were accompanied by wood-engraved illustrations intended to heighten the reader's appreciation of the narrative; popular engraver-illustrators such as George Cruikshank and Hablot K. Browne ("Phiz"), both of whom illustrated for Dickens, were initially as celebrated as the author himself.

Victorian painters benefited both from the emergence of a wealthy middle class able to purchase art for their homes and from the public's fascination with visual representation of contemporary life and historical drama. Scenes of everyday life with a narrative dimension and a moral message were especially popular with the viewing public. Like Victorian novelists and poets, many Victorian visual artists came to document the hardships of an industrial culture and landscape, depicting agricultural laborers, factory workers, and the unemployed in a highly realistic, yet often sentimental mode that has come to be known as social realism. Childhood innocence and scenes of domestic harmony were also common themes for many Victorian artists; new and inexpensive methods of art reproduction meant that such pictures could be sold cheaply to a wide audience that was interested in seeing the values of home and family reflected on its walls. Panoramic views of Victorian life in all its colorful variety were also popular: William Powell Frith's *Derby Day* (1858) and *Railway Station* (1862) portrayed scenes of ordinary Victorians in such realistic detail that they caused a great sensation when they were first exhibited at the Royal Academy. Founded in the eighteenth century under George III, the Royal Academy of Arts was institutionalized as the most important mediator of public taste in art in the Victorian period. It offered a free training school to many of the century's most significant artists, and its annual exhibitions of what it deemed the best works of the year drew thousands of spectators and buyers—as well as accusations of bias and preferential treatment on the part of those whose work had been excluded from the exhibitions or poorly hung.

The most influential movement in Victorian painting was the Pre-Raphaelite Brotherhood, composed of the artists John Everett Millais, William Holman Hunt, Thomas Woolner, James Collinson, Frederick George Stephens, and the brothers of Christina Rossetti, artist and poet Dante Gabriel Rossetti, and critic William Michael Rossetti. (Christina Rossetti herself, though she influenced and was influenced by the movement, was officially excluded from the Pre-Raphaelites on the grounds of gender.) At mid-century these artists began producing works that challenged the dominant taste for neoclassical style and subject matter by painting in a manner that shared commonalities with the work of medieval, pre-Renaissance artists. Close attention to natural detail, flattened perspective, vivid colors, an interest in literary subject matter, and erotically charged images of spiritual and religious devotion were some of the hallmarks of the group. Their paintings of female figures as either ravishing "femmes fatales" or dreamy heroines in historical dress are today instantly recognizable (and are much reproduced). These paintings conveyed both women's power and vulnerability in nineteenth-century culture, and were sometimes twinned, in D.G. Rossetti's work especially, with a companion poem or with a quotation from a literary work. ("The Blessed Damozel" [1846] is one such example, in which the separation of two lovers by death in the poem is conveyed with two separate panels in the painting.) "Pre-Raphaelite," indeed, denotes a style of poetry as well as of painting; sensuous detail and a tendency to link earthly beauty to the divine are as characteristic of the poetry of D.G. Rossetti as they are of his paintings.

Arthur Hughes, *The Long Engagement* (detail). Hughes (1832–1915) was one of the most prominent of the second wave of Pre-Raphaelite painters.

The Pre-Raphaelites should in part be considered alongside the Gothic Revival, a wave of interest in a medieval and Gothic aesthetic that had begun in the Romantic period and influenced Victorian painting, architecture, design, literature, and religious practice.

The idealization of the Middle Ages is exemplified in the writing of Thomas Carlyle, John Ruskin, William Morris, and Alfred Tennyson. Ruskin, an art critic who also championed the work of the Pre-Raphaelites, argued in *The Stones of Venice* (1851–53) for the moral superiority of the Gothic style, in part because it was the product of artisan-workers who were free to use their creativity in their work, and so express their individual and spiritual nature. Ruskin urged his readers to re-examine the "ugly goblins" and "stern statues" of Gothic cathedrals, for "they are the signs of the life and liberty of every workman who struck the stone; a freedom of thought, and rank in scale of being, such as no laws, no charters, no charities can secure."

The Arts and Crafts movement of the last few decades of the century, led by William Morris and influenced by Ruskin's ideas, was dedicated to the production of hand-crafted furniture, glassware, books, and art objects. Design firms such as Morris and Co. and the Century Guild revived the medieval guild system of production, rejecting the mass-produced manufactures of the assembly line in favor of the freedom and spontaneity of craft and its makers. In their critique of the ravages of industrial technology and the drudgery of mechanized labor, the practitioners of Gothic Revival imagined, and to some extent invented, the idea of the medieval past as a time of moral and religious stability, devotion to craft, and harmony with the rhythms of the natural world.

TECHNOLOGY

The technological invention that perhaps best exemplified the industrial age was the steam engine, a source and symbol of power both on land and at sea. Although the steam engine had been in use since the early eighteenth century, it was not until the nineteenth that steam technology helped transform an entire economy and a way of life. Steam engines were adapted for use in the production of coal, textiles, heavy metals, and printing presses, thus becoming indispensable to Britain's industrial growth. Steamships powered the British Empire, with several major shipping lines established in the 1840s to serve routes to India, Africa,

The Palace of Westminster, home to both Houses of Parliament, was redesigned and rebuilt following the fire of 1834, in a vast project not completed until 1860. It is one of the most striking examples of the Gothic style applied to a secular construction.

East Asia, and Australia. Railway steam locomotives epitomized the coming of the Victorian era, with the first local lines built in 1837 and 1838 as Victoria assumed the throne. In the "railway mania" of the 1840s, over 8,000 miles of new track were approved, and, by 1900, over nine hundred million passengers were using Britain's rail system annually. London's underground rail system opened its first line in 1863, though horse-drawn transportation continued to dominate the streetscape until the end of the century. The convenience and speed of rail travel caught on quickly with everyone from the Queen to the ordinary worker. Rail companies established excursions to special events, such as horse races or the seaside, inaugurating local and national tourism on a mass scale. So important was the advent of railway travel to the development of English daily life, railway stations even became essential to the book trade and the spread of leisure reading; from the 1850s onward, book stalls catering to thousands of daily commuters began to stock their shelves with newspapers, magazines, and cheap, popular fiction, which became known as "railway literature."

Robert Howlett, "Isambard Kingdom Brunel and the Launching Chains of the *Great Eastern*," 1857. The ship (designed largely by Brunel) remained the largest in the world throughout its 31 years on the seas. Brunel, the leading engineer of the age, also played an important role in designing such Victorian landmarks as the Crystal Palace, the new Houses of Parliament, Paddington Station, and the Clifton Suspension Bridge at Bristol.

CULTURAL IDENTITIES

The adoption of new technologies, the reorganization of employment, and the shift in power from the monarchy to the institutions of the modern liberal state revolutionized people's experience of work, family life, civic duty, and leisure time in the Victorian era. Such developments are almost always accompanied by shifts in the way people understand themselves as individuals in relation to their society. In the nineteenth century, the conditions and practices of one's class, gender, race, and sexuality began to acquire new meanings, to take on new importance, and to attract a new kind of attention. Changes in living conditions developed in connection with prescribed gender roles, which began to seem "natural" and "innate" because they supported the logic of industrial capital and bourgeois family life. Though this process did not begin in the Victorian period, it was signficantly extended and thoroughly revised at this time. Victorians tended to think about identity in terms of oppositions: male and female, rich and poor, black and white, and, later in the century, homosexual and heterosexual. Such oppositions had the effect of establishing seemingly stable types and suggesting that the differences were natural and unchangeable. For example, the ideology of separate spheres for men and women proposed that gender and sexual identity were fixed categories and that "true womanhood" was the inherent opposite of normative manliness. Still, in the literary works of the period, the line between "opposites" was constantly crossed and revealed as problematic and variable.

The "Angel in the House"[1] became a common label for the Victorian ideal of respectable middle-class femininity. Quiet beauty, purity, devotion and selflessness were some of the essential features of the domestic wife and mother, who was described and exalted in advice literature and popular domestic novels aimed at female readers. "She must be enduringly, incorruptibly good," advised John Ruskin, "instinctively, infallibly wise—wise, not for self-development, but for self-renunciation; wise, not that she may set herself above her husband, but that she may never fall from his side." The absolute other to this paragon of virtue was the "fallen woman," a label that encompassed any form of female sexual experience deemed improper or immoral. Prostitutes, rape survivors, unmarried mothers, adulteresses, homeless women, the insane, and any

[1] The phrase originated in the title of Coventry Patmore's long narrative poem. Patmore's "The Angel in the House"—first published in 1854, but revised several times for subsequent publication—was written about the author's wife, Emily, whom Patmore exalted as the perfect model of Victorian femininity and domesticity. The poem's opening lines—"Man must be pleased; but him to please / Is woman's pleasure"—rather neatly encapsulate the meaning and the message of the work. In "Professions for Women," a 1942 address given to the Women's Service League, Virginia Woolf argued that "part of the occupation ... of a woman writer" was to kill the "Angel in the House."

woman who displayed rebellious passions could be labeled "fallen." Yet the boundary between the domestic angel and the fallen woman was extraordinarily narrow; one false step and innocence became wickedness, followed by ostracism from society, poverty, and almost certain death for the transgressor, at least according to dominant narratives of fallenness.[1] On the other hand, some fallen women were portrayed as penitent victims who embodied the feminine ideal even more fully than their uncorrupted female counterparts. Writers such as Elizabeth Gaskell, Christina Rossetti, George Eliot, Mary Elizabeth Braddon, Augusta Webster, and Thomas Hardy explored the tropes of purity and fallenness, bringing "pure" and "impure" women into each other's (and the reader's) proximity in order to probe the limits of the feminine ideal.

The male counterpart to the domestic angel was the Victorian gentleman, an heir of the chivalric ideal updated for the industrial age. In *The Idea of a University* (a series of lectures published as one volume in 1873), John Henry Newman characterized the gentleman as tender, merciful, prudent, patient, forbearing, resigned, and disciplined. Yet despite Newman's apparent confidence in this description, gentlemanliness was difficult to define: was it based on a man's mode of income or on his behavior? Was it a hereditary, professional, or moral category, or some combination? While eminent men were celebrated with great gusto in biography and prose works such as Carlyle's *On Heroes and Hero Worship* (1841), men were also often regarded as morally inferior to women because of their greater contact with the competition and corruption of the public world. (On the other hand, women could just as easily be pressed into the role of evil temptress in accounting for a man's fall from grace.) Tennyson's dramatic monologue "Ulysses" (1842) wrestles with two competing versions of masculinity: the thwarted Romantic hero, who longs for adventure and freedom from domestic encumbrance, and the reliable, managerial male who faithfully adheres to professional duty.

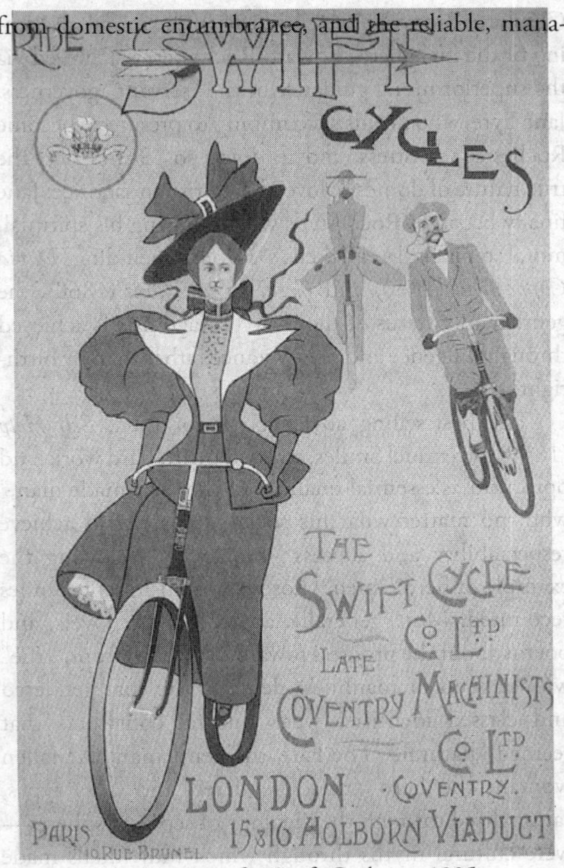

Advertisement for Swift Cycles, c. 1895.

The concepts of the Victorian lady and gentleman were also class categories, serving to both reinforce and blur distinctions between various socio-economic groups. The boarding schools for the sons and daughters of the elite and the middle classes promulgated notions of proper female and male conduct in their curricula; increasingly, it was understood that one was not simply born a lady or a gentleman, but must learn to become one through rigorous training and constant self-scrutiny. As the terms "lady" and "gentleman" gradually lost their association with rank, socio-economic boundaries became increasingly difficult to distinguish, and novelists began to focus on the gendered and class behaviors of individuals for their narrative content. In

[1] In a famous moment in Dickens's *David Copperfield*, the narrator's recollection of a dangerous moment in the fallen Emily's early life leads him to wonder if it might not have been far better for her to have died rather than to have survived only to later "fall."

Charlotte Brontë's *Jane Eyre* (1847), the moral awakening of the male hero, Edward Rochester, is achieved via the superior moral guidance of the "servant" governess, Jane Eyre, who avoids succumbing to presure to become Rochester's mistress, and in doing so teaches him the true nature of domestic love and Christian sacrifice; Jane finally becomes Rochester's wife following his spiritual, moral rebirth. In Dickens's novels, including *David Copperfield* (1850) and *Great Expectations* (1860), the gentlemanly status of the male protagonists is achieved through diligence and perseverance rather than by birthright.

The best-selling advice book for men, *Self Help* (1859) by Samuel Smiles, stressed thrift, hard work, and optimism as essential qualities of the "self-made man," who, no matter what his social status, could achieve respectability and success, in part by following the example of heroic men whose accomplishments Smiles recounted. More generally, advice books, novels, and poems about the progress toward, or the fall from, "true" womanhood or manliness demonstrate that gendered and classed identities were cultural constructs that seemed "natural." The lady, the gentleman, the fallen woman, the hero—these gendered and class types, rationalized through the ideology of separate spheres—were cultural myths through which individuals made sense of their relationship to the social order.

As the century drew to a close, new styles of masculinity and femininity emerged to compete with the prevailing gender models of the previous decades. One of these emergent types was the "New Woman," a term that described a figure of greater sexual, economic, and social independence than the "Angel in the House." Although the term denoted a lifestyle and a literary category more than a political perspective, the figure of the New Woman was in part a product of the gains feminists had made by the 1880s and 1890s in the areas of higher education, employment, political and legal rights, and civic visibility. The New Woman quickly became a flashpoint for opinion makers on either side of the "Woman Question."[1] Smoking, swearing, riding a bicycle, debating in public, wearing men's clothes, and refusing marriage were some of the trademarks of the New Woman, who figured in novels, short stories, and popular journalism as someone either to emulate or to condemn. A number of male novelists, including George Gissing, George Moore, and Thomas Hardy, created memorable New Woman characters who grapple with the competing demands of personal autonomy and social expectation, while the works of many female writers, such as Sarah Grand's *The Heavenly Twins* (1893) and the semi-autobiographical *The Beth Book* (1897), presented New Woman characters who triumph over social convention and the sexual double standard.

For Grand and other feminist writers, such as Mona Caird and Olive Schreiner, the portrayal of the New Woman hinged on a critique of the male sexual privilege that had already come under fire in the 1870s and 1880s during the social purity campaigns and the resistance to the Contagious Diseases Acts. This legislation, enacted in the 1860s, allowed for the forcible confinement and internal examination of prostitutes by doctors in order to prevent the spread of venereal disease, first among the military, and then within civilian communities. Underwriting these Acts was the assumption that because male sexual urges were "uncontrollable," prostitution was a necessary evil that should be regulated because it could not be eradicated. The Act of 1864 decreed that infected women could be held in locked hospitals for three months; the Act of 1869 extended the period of confinement to a year. In 1867, there were proposals to extend the Acts to the north of England and the civilian population. Though the laws were intended to combat the spread of disease by prostitutes, in practice, they essentially meant that any woman passing through a poor neighborhood was subject to compulsory medical examination and arrest. They also, as activists were quick to point out, hypo-

[1] The question was largely one of the nature—and consequently, the proper role—of women. The "Woman Question" came to encompass the debates about the rights and responsibilities, as well as the place, of women in Victorian society.

critically targeted prostitutes but not their clients. The campaign against the Acts, led by the charismatic Josephine Butler, condemned the sexual double standard and the humiliation of poor and vulnerable women by police and doctors, with Butler comparing the compulsory medical examinations to "instrumental rape." The Acts were struck down in 1886 after much public controversy; the movement to repeal them, led mostly by middle-class women, marked the first instance in which women publicly debated the subject of sex on a broad scale. It was also one of the most visible of the many social purity campaigns of the 1870s, 1880s, and 1890s, in which moral reformers engaged in the rescue and "reformation" of prostitutes and other "fallen women" and urged men to take a vow of chastity. The mandate of the National Vigilance Association, for example, was to "create a universal ethic of chastity, for all men and women alike." In calling for a single standard of behavior, many of the social purity groups espoused moral coerciveness and interventionist policies, which often ended up stigmatizing and further repressing the women and girls they were attempting to help.

The preoccupations of the purity campaigners were part of a renewed cultural and scientific interest in human sexuality among Victorians, dating from at least the early 1870s and the publication of Darwin's *The Descent of Man*. In that book, Darwin applied the theories from his *On the Origin of Species* to human evolution and behavior, positing that sexual selection among men and women accounted for their mental and physical differences. These "natural differences" were drawn straight from the catalogue of Victorian gender stereotypes, which held that men were inherently courageous, virile, and combative, and women intuitive, passive, and altruistic. The "complementarity" of these traits ensured the survival of the human "race," which evolutionists, anthropologists, and psychologists understood as a hierarchy: white European males at the top, followed by women, children, and the "primitive races." But, scientists wondered, how to explain the fact that some white men—seemingly nature's most civilized specimen—occasionally exhibited traits that resembled those of the women, children, primitives, and even the animals who were understood as biologically and mentally inferior? Such questions were compounded by fears that Britain's empire was crumbling because the purity of the "white race" was being diluted through crossbreeding and racial mingling among English imperialists and the "savages" they ruled in the benighted labyrinths of the Empire. Closer to home, the poverty, crime, and vice of England's urban districts was often racialized: "As there is a darkest Africa is there not also a darkest England?" asked William Booth, founder of the Salvation Army. "Civilisation, which can breed its own barbarians, does it not also breed its own pygmies? May we not find a parallel at our own doors, and discover within a stone's throw of our cathedrals and palaces similar horrors to those which Stanley[1] has found existing in the great Equatorial forest?" Social Darwinist theories of atavism (the reappearance of "primitive" characteristics in "advanced" populations) and degeneration (retrograde evolution) were formulated in the second half of the century to account for the "tendencies" of criminals, alcoholics, the poor, the mentally and physically disabled, and people with non-normative sexualities.

The first recorded English usage of the term "homosexual" did not occur until 1892; before that time "sodomy" was illegal (it was punishable by death until 1861), but the concept of "the homosexual"—either male or female—as a distinct identity or way of being did not exist at the beginning of the Victorian era. With the emergence of a gay male subculture in London in the 1870s and 1880s, gay men—also called "sexual inverts"—became subject to increased scientific and legal scrutiny. Although "the lesbian" also emerged as a distinct identity in the 1890s, women were not subject to the same kinds of persecution as gay men, in part because of the belief that women were unmotivated by sexual desire, and that their passionate female "friendships" were therefore innocent, merely temporary diversions from their true calling as wives and mothers. Bisexuality would not come to be considered a discrete

[1] Henry Morton Stanley (1841–1904) was a renowned journalist and explorer, best known for his travels in Africa and his successful search for David Livingstone (see above, p. 596).

sexuality until the twentieth century.

The Criminal Law Amendment Act of 1885, which raised the age of sexual consent from 13 to 16 under pressure from the social purity campaigners, contained a clause (known as the Labouchère Amendment, after Member of Parliament Henry Labouchère, who had introduced it) that mandated imprisonment for any man found guilty of "gross indecency"—effectively, any sexual act—with another man, even if the "indecency" was conducted entirely in private.[1] The Labouchère Amendment served to demonize gay men as "degenerates" whose "unnatural" desires threatened the stability of marriage, the future of the race, and the strength of the Empire. Feminized male types—the dandy, the aesthete, the fop—surfaced in visual art and literature alongside the masculinized New Woman figure to characterize a climate of sexual and gender experimentation at the fin-de-siècle that was celebrated by a few and denounced by many. As the popular satirical magazine *Punch* joked, "A new fear my bosom vexes; / Tomorrow there may be no sexes!"

In 1895, celebrity playwright Oscar Wilde[2] was brought to trial under the terms of the Labouchère Amendment and sentenced to two years in prison for "gross indecency." The highly publicized Wilde trials brought the moral panic of the preceding two decades to a crisis point. Yet Wilde's trial testimony, his writing, and that of his contemporaries such as John Addington Symonds, Algernon Charles Swinburne, "Michael Field," Sarah Grand, Mona Caird, Vernon Lee, and Edward Carpenter signaled a new level of consciousness

"Two Seated Sicilian Youths," photograph from c. 1893 (Victoria and Albert Museum).

regarding sexual and gender identity. With remarkable candor, the sexologist Havelock Ellis wrote that while "we may not know exactly what sex is ... we do know that it is mutable, with the possibility of one sex being changed into the other sex, that its frontiers are often mutable, and that there are many stages between a complete male and a complete female." Ellis broke new ground with his multi-volume *The Psychology of Sex* (1897–1910), an early volume of which, *Sexual Inversion* (1897), was particularly noteworthy for treating homosexuality in a purely descriptive fashion, rather than as a pathology. (In other volumes Ellis took a similar approach to many other topics, including "autoerotism," or masturbation, and sado-masochism.) Sexuality and sexual practice had become topics of public conversation in a way that belies twentieth-century stereotypes of Victorian culture as sexually conservative or naïve. The apparent "repression" of sexual behaviors deemed improper or immoral only seemed to prohibit what was in fact an intense interest

[1] Many sexual acts were already illegal; in particular, "buggery"—a British term for anal sex—whether between two men or between a man and a woman, had been illegal since the Buggery Act of 1553.

[2] Wilde was a married father of two young children, but rumors about his dalliances with men—many of working-class backgrounds, known as "rent-boys"—had abounded as his popularity increased. It was Wilde's involvement with Lord Alfred "Bosie" Douglas, the son of the 9th Marquess of Queensberry, that resulted in the rumors becoming a legal matter. The eccentric Queensberry, who believed his son had been corrupted by the older Wilde, left a note for Wilde at his club, accusing the playwright of "posing as a somdomite [*sic*]." Encouraged by Bosie, who hated his father, Wilde sued for libel; the resulting trial revealed a number of graphic details about Wilde's sexual predilections, and he was subsequently himself tried for acts of gross indecency.

in the passions, proclivities, and practices of the "other" Victorians.[1]

Realism

"Art is the nearest thing to life," wrote George Eliot in "The Natural History of German Life" (1856). "It is a mode of amplifying experience and extending our contact with our fellow-men beyond the bounds of our personal lot. All the more sacred is the task of the artist when he undertakes to paint the life of the People." Eliot's essay anticipated the masterpieces of realist fiction she would begin writing in just a few years—*Adam Bede* (1859), *The Mill on the Floss* (1860), and *Middlemarch* (1874) among them. For Eliot, as for many of her contemporaries, the true, even "sacred," purpose of art was to present an objective representation of real life that reflected the habits, desires, and aspirations of readers. For many novelists, realism seemed to be the form best suited to this purpose.

Victorian poetry too, especially at mid-century, was influenced by the predominance of realist fiction; long narrative poems, such as Tennyson's *Idylls of the King* (1856–85) and Robert Browning's *The Ring and the Book* (1868–69), appropriated novelistic forms of storytelling, combining trenchant social critique with formal experimentation. In Elizabeth Barrett Browning's "verse novel" and Bildungsroman[2] *Aurora Leigh* (1856), the speaker, Aurora Leigh herself, defines and defends her poetic practice of social engagement with the contemporary world, sounding very much like Eliot:

> Nay, if there's room for poets in this world
> A little overgrown (I think there is),
> Their sole work is to represent the age,
> Their age, not Charlemagne's …
> …
> … this is living art,
> Which thus presents and thus records true life.

Much realist fiction of the Victorian period tended to center on the everyday experiences, moral progress, and inner struggles of an ordinary individual, while giving a sense of the connections between that individual and his or her broader social networks. Many realist novels, including those by Anthony Trollope, William Thackeray, Dickens, and Eliot contained multiple plot lines and a range of characters across socio-economic strata, representing both the cohesiveness and the disintegration of various social communities in an industrialized, commercializing society. Detailed descriptions of landscapes, city streets, and domestic interiors and close attention to the emotionally complex motivations of characters—these too are characteristic of the realism of the Victorian novel. However, such broad vision is typically viewed from a single narrative perspective, whether that of the novel's protagonist or of an omniscient narrator.

Why did realism hold such appeal for Victorian novelists and their audiences? One explanation is that the revolutions of the nineteenth century created a climate in which people longed for a sense of verisimilitude in their literature in order to guide them through the changes and upheavals, both private and public, which they themselves faced. Many Victorian readers sought moral and ethical guidance from their authors, who assumed—or were thrust into—the role of "secular clerics" with varying degrees of confidence and authority. Realist fiction, along with other forms of writing such as biography, criticism, poetry, and history, was accepted as having a pedagogical function; such texts not only taught readers how to navigate the changes they were experiencing, but also how to imagine sympathetically and authentically the experiences of others. "We want to be taught to feel," wrote Eliot, "not for the heroic artisan or the sentimental peasant, but for the peasant in all his coarse apathy, and the artisan in all his suspicious selfishness."

In rejecting the heroic and the sentimental, Eliot positioned the realist novel in opposition to the

---

[1] Steven Marcus's seminal exploration of Victorian expressions and repressions of sexuality, *The Other Victorians: A Study of Sexuality and Pornography in Mid-Nineteenth Century England* (1966) helped complicate the sometimes overly simplified early and mid-twentieth-century view of the Victorians as simply repressed and "anti-sexual."

[2] "Novel of Education" (German).

Advertisements.

COMIC HISTORY OF ENGLAND.

On the First of July, 1846, will be published, price One Shilling,

THE FIRST PART

OF THE

COMIC HISTORY OF ENGLAND.

BY GILBERT ABBOTT à BECKETT.

WITH NUMEROUS ILLUSTRATIONS BY JOHN LEECH.

In announcing a Comic History of England it may be necessary to observe that the levity implied in the title will relate to the manner, but by no means to the matter of the work, which will be collected with the gravest regard to the truth and accuracy that the subject requires. The aim of the writer will be to present a faithful narrative, for which the best authorities will be most carefully consulted, and to serve it up to the reader in a more palatable form than has hitherto been thought compatible with the dignity of history. There is not the smallest intention to sacrifice fidelity to fun in the forthcoming production, which is designed to show that the *utile et dulce*—are not inseparable. The advantages of blending amusement with instruction are universally allowed; and there is an end to the once favourite fallacy that food for the mind requires the uninviting flavour of physic.

It will appear in Monthly Parts, price One Shilling each, handsomely printed in octavo, and copiously illustrated by John Leech, with

ONE LARGE ETCHING,

AND

FROM SIX TO TWELVE WOOD ENGRAVINGS.

The Comic History of England will comprise from Twelve to Twenty Parts, and will appear regularly with the monthly Magazines until its completion.

PUBLISHED AT THE "PUNCH" OFFICE, 85, FLEET STREET.

AN INFALLIBLE HAIR DYE.

ROWLAND'S MELACOMIA,

The most successful liquid preparation ever known in this or any other Country, for Dyeing the hair of the head, whiskers, mustachios, and eyebrows a *natural* and *permanent* brown or black, so exactly resembling the natural colour of the hair as to defy detection. It is perfectly innocent in its nature, is free from any unpleasant smell, and can be used by any Lady or Gentleman with the greatest ease and secrecy. Its effect is so permanent that neither water nor perspiration will influence it; and it is entirely free from those properties (usual in Hair Dyes) which give an unnatural *red* or *purple* tint to the Hair. Price 5*s.*

Prepared by A. ROWLAND & SON, 20, Hatton Garden, London.

ROWLAND'S ODONTO,

OR PEARL DENTIFRICE,

A WHITE POWDER FOR THE TEETH, composed of the Choicest and most *Recherché Ingredients of the Oriental Herbal*; the leading requisites of *cleanliness* and efficacy being present in the highest possible degree. It extirpates all *tartarous adhesions* to the Teeth, and insures a Pearl-like Whiteness to the *enamelled surface*. Its Anti-Septic and Anti-Scorbutic Properties exercise a highly beneficial and salutary influence; they arrest the further progress of decay of the Teeth, induce a healthy action of the Gums, and cause them to assume the brightness and colour indicative of perfect soundness; while, by confirming their adhesion to the Teeth, they give unlimited enjoyment and fresh zest to appetite, by perpetuating effective and complete mastication. The Breath also, from the salubrious and disinfecting qualities of the Odonto, attains a sweetness and fragrance truly grateful to its possessor.

The Proprietors of this Dentifrice pledge themselves, that its efficacy in preserving and embellishing the Teeth far surpasses anything of the kind ever offered to the Public.

As the most efficient and fragrant aromatic purifier of the Breath, Teeth, and Gums ever known, ROWLAND'S ODONTO has for a long series of years occupied a distinguished Place at the Toilets of the SOVEREIGNS and the NOBILITY throughout Europe; while the general demand for it at once announces the favour in which it is universally held.

Price 2*s.* 9*d.* per Box.

CAUTION.—To protect the Public from Fraud, the *Hon. Commissioners of Stamps* have directed the Proprietors' Name and Address, thus—**A. ROWLAND & SON, 20, Hatton Garden,** to be engraved on the Government Stamp, and which is affixed on each Box.

*** All others are **FRAUDULENT IMITATIONS.**

The Genuine Preparations are sold by the Proprietors, as above, and by Chemists and Perfumers.

Page of advertisements from the eighth number of the 1846 serial publication in ten numbers of Dickens's *Oliver Twist*. (Pages of advertisements appeared at the front and back of each number.)

heightened, "falsifying" sensibilities of the romantic mode, as did many others. In 1785, distinguishing between the romance and the newly emergent genre of the novel, Clara Reeve had observed that "the Novel is a picture of real life and manners, and of the times in which it was written. The Romance in lofty and elevated language, describes what never happened nor is likely to happen." Reeve's description of the novel could be applied to most Victorian fiction. Nonetheless, many of the best-known Victorian novels contain elements of the fantastic, the supernatural, or the mysterious: Dickens's *Oliver Twist* is like many of his others novels in that it sets out to realistically document the ravages of industrial poverty, but the novel's plot depends on outrageous coincidence, its story peopled with broadly drawn character types befitting the romance mode.[1] The novels of Charlotte and Emily Brontë memorably combine psychological realism with Gothic elements such as female imprisonment and suggestions of ghostly presences. The persistence of romantic elements in Victorian realist novels not only unsettles the confidence of our formal definitions, but also prompts us to consider just whose versions of "the real" were recognized as the most truthful.

Inevitably, realism's dominance in literature and in visual art came under attack. As early as the 1850s, but more widely in the 1880s and 1890s, visual artists, writers, and critics began to question the moral imperatives of realist art in a series of movements that have come to be referred to under the umbrella term "Aestheticism." In poetry, drama, criticism, and fiction, Aestheticism stressed experimentation in form and composition, independence of imagination and expression, and freedom of content, however perverse, morbid, or tawdry. In rebelling against the harsh brutalities of British industrial culture, the Aesthetes sought a "pure" art and formal beauty dissociated from the concerns and surroundings of the everyday. The Aesthetes were not interested in instructing or edifying a mass readership; rather, they advocated aesthetic withdrawal in order to pursue the essential forms of art. "Art for art's sake,"[2] translated from the French by art critic Walter Pater, became the rallying cry of the Aesthetes. "Art never expresses anything but itself," declares one of Oscar Wilde's speakers. "It has an independent life, just as Thought has, and develops purely on its own lines. It is not necessarily realistic in an age of realism, nor spiritual in an age of faith. So far from being a creation of its own time, it is usually in direct opposition to it." Similarly, Wilde concludes his preface to *The Picture of Dorian Gray* (1891) with the assertion that "All art is quite useless," having earlier stated that "There is no such thing as a moral or an immoral book."

By the 1890s, the aesthetic movement had been charged with elitism, hedonism, self-absorption, and homosexuality.[3] Aestheticism by that time had shifted into Decadence, a term of either censure or praise, depending on who wielded it. The Decadents extended the precepts of Aestheticism in their affirmation of the perversity, artificiality, and overindulgence of a culture and a century that was nearing its end, and their works were often taken as evidence of social degeneration; in *Degeneration* (1892), the German critic Max Nordau attacked Decadent artists—including Wilde—as degenerates and argued that social decay is both reflected in and driven by art.

[1] Oliver Twist is one of many orphans in Dickens's novels. Dickens's orphans inevitably confront the urban nightmares of Victorian life with well-nigh angelic purity—and, in Oliver's case, perfectly grammatical literary English.

[2] The French writer Théophile Gautier (1811–72) is generally credited with coining the phrase "l'art pour l'art" in the preface to his novel, *Mademoiselle de Maupin* (1836). A number of critics have contended that the idea—if not the precise phrase—dates back to ancient Rome.

[3] Wilde's *The Picture of Dorian Gray*, which first appeared in *Lippincott's Monthly Magazine* in 1890, was immediately accused of having homoerotic overtones and deemed "unclean," "effeminate," and "contaminating." Wilde made a number of changes to the novel before its publication as one volume in 1891, but these were not enough to keep the book from counting against him during Wilde's trial for acts of "gross indecency."

THE VICTORIAN NOVEL

The dominant Victorian literary form was the novel. Although the genre of the novel emerged well in advance of the Victorian period, the literary legitimacy and cultural authority the novel wields today were solidified in the nineteenth century. The novel was a dynamic form, shifting according to popular taste and critical assessments of its potential value to readers, who were offered an ever-expanding list of authors and sub-genres from which to choose. While the early and mid-Victorian novels of men such as Dickens, Thackeray, and Trollope were wildly successful, both with the critical establishment and the reading public, many of the century's most influential and prolific novelists were women. These novelists—the Brontës, Eliot, Braddon, Gaskell, Charlotte Yonge, and Ellen Price Wood among them—paved the way for legions of other women to enter the field of fiction writing. Although the profession of "novelist" achieved new respectability in the period for both men and women alike, the novel continued in some circles to be maligned as lightweight and "pernicious," associated with frivolous lady scribblers and their female readers. As George Henry Lewes, George Eliot's partner, observed in "The Lady Novelists" (1852), "Of all departments of literature, Fiction is the one to which, by nature and by circumstance, women are best adapted.… The very nature of fiction calls for that predominance of Sentiment which we have already attributed to the feminine mind."

The taste for particular subjects and approaches shifted regularly: the "silver fork" novels of the 1820s and 1830s centered on the extravagances and corruptions of the rich and fashionable, while the "social problem" novels of the 1840s depicted the minute details of life at the very opposite end of the social scale. Domestic novels by both the famous and the obscure focused on the quotidian; George Eliot's *Middlemarch*, rich in psychological complexity and moral analysis, is one of the most outstanding examples of domestic fiction of the Victorian period. A heightened form of this domestic-centered fiction was the "sensation" novel, which flourished in the 1860s and 1870s. Strong on dramatic incident and scandalous subject matter, such as bigamy, murder, madness, and crime, sensation novels exposed the hidden corruptions and dirty secrets of the outwardly respectable middle class; Wilkie Collins, Braddon, and Wood were some of the leading practitioners of this wildly popular and much maligned sub-genre. The immense popular appeal of sensation novels was linked to the continued growth of a "mass readership," much to the chagrin of the critical elite, who bemoaned the "degradation" of literature as the century drew to a close. In the latter decades of the century, mystery novels, detective fiction, horror, and adventure stories soared in popularity, partly on the strength of an expanding audience of lower-income readers, rising literacy rates, and cheaper methods of book production. The counterpart to these often lurid and shocking tales were the naturalistic novels of Thomas Hardy, George Gissing, and George Moore, whose late-century fiction offers bleak, social Darwinist portraits of urban class struggle, slum life, rural poverty, and sexual frustration.

If the vogue for particular kinds of subject matter in novels shifted regularly, so too did their modes of publication, distribution, and consumption. One significant mode of publication was the three-volume edition, known as the "triple-decker." Readers who could not afford to buy the volumes themselves borrowed one volume at a time from lending libraries for a fee, generating huge profits for the most successful of these, Mudie's Select Library and W.H. Smith and Son. The triple-decker format was eventually supplanted by cheap single-volume editions that were sold in national book chains and at rail stations. Another mode of publication, one that made the novel a household word, was the monthly or weekly serial. Monthly installments of a few chapters, often accompanied by illustrations and advertisements, were initially published and purchased in separate parts with paper wrappers, generally appearing over a period of 19 months. By the 1860s, these serializations were more often appearing in monthly or weekly literary magazines. Dickens's enormously successful *Pickwick Papers* appeared in installments in 1836–37, launching the serial format as

Cover, *Famous Crimes*, Police Budget Edition, c. 1890. Sensationalized stories of crime and horror, priced at one penny each and known as "penny dreadfuls," became hugely popular in the late nineteenth century.

the most important publishing medium for Victorian fiction.[1] Serialization allowed readers with modest incomes to purchase new works when bound volumes were beyond their financial reach, and the regular continuation of a novel over a period of months or years meant that novels and novel reading became woven into the fabric of daily life, mingling with news, opinion, and readers' personal experience. The serialized format also had an influence on the novelistic genre, establishing a particular pace and necessitating "cliff-hangers," ensuring the return of the audience week after week.

Poetry

The novel's predominance and popularity have often meant that the significance of Victorian poetry is overlooked. Victorian poets throughout the century were greatly influenced by poets of the Romantic period, but key departures in form, content, and purpose set the Victorians apart from their predecessors. One of the most important of Victorian innovations was the development of the dramatic monologue, a lyric poem in the voice of a speaker who is not the poet and who occasionally addresses a silent auditor. Although the Victorians did not invent the dramatic monologue, Robert Browning and Alfred Tennyson are typically credited with developing it into a form expressive of psychological complexity. Victorian psychologists were interested in exploring the boundary between sanity and madness, and the possibility of a lucid yet mentally unbalanced narrating persona appealed to Browning and Tennyson, who used the dramatic monologue to expose not only the unstable character of their speakers' passions, but also the social and cultural contexts that either produced or reflected their instability. Browning, in particular, chose a range of unstable, deluded, or even mentally deranged speakers whose self-perception is ironically distanced from the reader's, thus participating in pre-Freudian ideas about the divided self; perhaps the most famous of these is "My Last Duchess" (1842), which slowly reveals the fate of the speaker's wife. The dramatic monologue was also notably employed by Elizabeth Barrett Browning, D.G. Rossetti, Christina Rossetti, Augusta Webster, Thomas Hardy, Rudyard Kipling, and by many twentieth-century poets.

Many other poetic forms also flourished in the period. Perhaps surprisingly in an "age of realism," epic poems were a feature of the Victorian literary landscape, from Tennyson's *Idylls of the King* to George Eliot's *The Spanish Gypsy* (1868) and William Morris's *The Earthly Paradise* (1868–70). Sonnet sequences too were a popu-

[1] Long poems and works of non-fiction prose were also sometimes published serially; important examples include Robert Browning's *The Ring and the Book* and Matthew Arnold's *Culture and Anarchy* (serialized in *Cornhill Magazine* in 1867–68).

lar form, particularly among women poets; notable examples include George Eliot's *Brother and Sister Sonnets* (1869), Christina Rossetti's *Monna Innominata* (1881), Augusta Webster's *Mother and Daughter Sonnets* (1895), and—most popular of all—Elizabeth Barrett Browning's *Sonnets from the Portuguese* (1850), a collection of 44 sonnets chronicling Barrett Browning's courtship with Robert Browning. Through the work of these writers and a host of others—from Felicia Hemans and Letitia Landon at the beginning of the period to Charlotte Mew and Mathilde Blind at its end—the "poetess" became an accepted part of the literary landscape.

The lyric introspection and self-exploration that is the hallmark of much Romantic verse was augmented in both form and content by a Victorian poetry of social engagement that strove to contextualize a speaker's moral and spiritual questions within the vicissitudes of contemporary life. In Tennyson's monologue *Maud* (1855), the tormented speaker's mental deterioration and reawakening are represented as continuous with the effects of industrialization and England's entry into the Crimean War. In Augusta Webster's dramatic monologue *A Castaway* (1870), a high-class prostitute's self-scrutiny illustrates the relationship between political economy and the commodification of female identity, with "coin" as a central metaphor for the connection between the two.

Not all poets accepted the view that poetry should speak to the issues and concerns of the present. In 1853, Matthew Arnold wrote that poets should respond to their world by mining "those elementary feelings which subsist permanently in the race, and are independent of time." In some of his later poetry, Arnold turned to classical rather than contemporary subjects as a way of rejecting what he saw as the crass materialism and spiritual futility of modern life. Yet for all his melancholia, Arnold did not advocate artistic isolation; whereas many poets of the second half of the century called for the independence of art from the imperative to offer moral instruction, Arnold continued to insist that the aesthetic endeavor necessarily involved ethical responsibility.

In contrast, Swinburne's poetry of sensual experience, his carnal subject matter and verbal pyrotechnics revel in the corporeality of poetry, so much so that he was accused in one famous review of "fleshliness" to the exclusion of "meditation" and "thought."[1] Swinburne's verse was important to the development of Aestheticism, influencing later poets such as Wilde and Symonds, whose poetry tended to emphasize formal beauty, sonic effects, and the momentary over the timeless. Like the Spasmodic poets of the 1840s and 1850s, like Arthur Hugh Clough in the late 1850s and early 1860s, and like Gerard Manley Hopkins at the century's end, Swinburne also engaged in many challenging experiments with poetic form and meter, thereby anticipating some of the innovations and deliberate difficulties of modernist writing.

DRAMA

The Victorian period is not remembered for great stage dramas or for penetrating comedies, at least until the last decades of the century. Although Victorian audiences were avid theatergoers, they tended to prefer lighthearted entertainment to more serious fare. Comedies, pantomimes, farces, and musicals attracted audiences from across the social spectrum, but it was melodrama that became the most popular dramatic genre. For most literary critics, melodrama has little or no literary value and is thus easy to dismiss as an aesthetically vacant genre. Yet popular texts can reveal much about a culture because they are so intimately connected with everyday assumptions and values. The melodrama of the Victorian period opens a window onto the nature of power relations within modern market culture and the patriarchal family; sometimes it seems to support, and at other times to contest, these relations. With its sensational plots, stock characters, unadorned language, and

[1] The charge was made in Robert Buchanan's "The Fleshly School of Poetry," a review essay that first appeared in Volume 18 of *The Contemporary Review* in 1871. The review focused on D.G. Rossetti's *Poems*, citing Swinburne and Morris as other key figures in what Buchanan derisively termed "the Fleshly School," a mode he took to task for its "morbid deviation from the healthy forms of life."

a moral economy that unambiguously separates good from evil, melodrama exploited an audience's emotions, and invariably ended on a happy note. (We need look no further than the mass appeal of Hollywood films to begin to understand why stage melodrama was so popular.) Early in the century, melodramas often featured Gothic plots, settings, and characters, but the vogue for such subject matter gave way in the Victorian period to storylines centered on workaday conflicts in familiar settings, such as factories, cottages, and manor houses.

The most prolific and successful writer and adapter of melodramas was Dion Boucicault; his 1852 play *The Corsican Brothers* was such a hit with Queen Victoria that she saw it five times. Tom Taylor's popular *The Ticket-of-Leave Man* (1863) was set in recognizable London locations and featured a sleuth named Jack Hawksure who became a prototype for later stage detectives. Many popular novels, including works by Dickens, Collins, and Braddon, were adapted or pirated for the stage soon after they had been published. Ellen Price Wood's *East Lynne* (1861), a novel with a fallen woman theme, was adapted into several stage versions on the basis of its enormous success as one of the earliest sensation novels.

In 1881, theater impresario Richard D'Oyly Carte opened the Savoy Theatre in London for the express purpose of staging the comic operettas of W.S. Gilbert and Arthur Sullivan, whose collaboration had begun in 1875. Their most popular plays, such as *H.M.S. Pinafore* (1878), *The Mikado* (1885), and *Patience* (1881), are still regularly staged today. Gilbert's storylines and lyrics combined frivolous romance with witty and genial mockery of certain contemporary values,[1] as well as of the formulaic nature of most London stage fare; Sullivan's alternately lilting and bouncy melodies proved irresistible, and "Gilbert and Sullivan" rapidly became a popular phenomenon. The

"A Gaiety Girl," music hall poster, 1893.

Savoy Operas, as they came to be known, anticipated the new directions in British theater of the 1890s, epitomized in the comic plays of Oscar Wilde and the "problem plays" of George Bernard Shaw; both Wilde and Shaw offered serious critiques of their society while dazzling their audiences with their audacious wit, brilliant dialogue, and shocking candor.

PROSE NON-FICTION AND PRINT CULTURE

Victorian writers of essays, criticism, history, and biography fully embraced the role of the public intellectual, whose particular mission was to instruct and

---

[1] *Patience*, for example, satirized Aestheticism, prominently featuring a character known as Bunthorne, an aesthete poet. Though some critics have identified Oscar Wilde as the model for Bunthorne, Wilde's relative obscurity at the time of the operetta's composition suggests that the character is more likely a representation of then-better-known poets such as Swinburne and D.G. Rossetti.

edify readers about the day's key issues. Virtually no subject remained untouched: writers of non-fiction prose, also known as "sages," probed everything, from the latest scientific developments to religious controversies, from political and economic questions to gender issues, from aesthetic developments to social values and mores.

In an age of growing religious skepticism, readers looked to their "sages" as latter-day prophets and interpreters who were uniquely qualified to offer an almost divinely inspired wisdom. For men, this role of the secular cleric emerged along with the rise of the professional writer, or "man of letters," who could earn a comfortable living by the pen and maintain a level of gentlemanly respectability. For women writers, however, the decision to offer social and cultural critique often came at a price, since women were discouraged from involvement in—and even knowledge of—political issues. Arnold, Eliot, Ruskin, Pater, and Wilde produced some of the most influential literary and cultural criticism of the age, while Carlyle, Harriet Martineau, John Stuart Mill, Harriet Taylor Mill, and Frances Power Cobbe are among those better remembered for more overtly political commentary. What united most of these writers, male and female, was their simultaneous position as societal outsiders and insiders: in a range of rhetorical styles, from prophetic to disinterested, prose writers typically argued from a marginal position under the assumption that their particular viewpoint had been abandoned or would be resisted by their readers. Yet it was precisely this outsider perspective that guaranteed the sage's unique authority within a society hungry for moral guidance by a voice not restrained by established cultural norms.

For every writer or sage celebrated by his or her reading public as a visionary, there were countless, often nameless "hack" writers who also contributed non-fiction prose, or, more properly, journalism, to newspapers and periodicals. Indeed, the periodical and newspaper press afforded both the sages and the hacks, as well as novelists and poets, a space to disseminate their work and reach ever-expanding audiences. In Wilkie Collins's words, it was "the age of periodicals."

The opening of the Manchester Free Library, 1852. In 1845, local governments were given the authority to raise tax revenues to support the establishment of public libraries and museums. Free public libraries were distinguished from fee-charging circulating libraries such as Mudie's and W.H. Smith's.

Early in the century, prominent literary journals such as the *Edinburgh Review*, *Blackwood's Magazine*, the *Quarterly Review*, *Fraser's Magazine*, and the *Athenaeum* attracted the most eminent writers. In the early Victorian era, writers in these journals generally published anonymously or under a pseudonym, no matter how distinguished they might be; not until the latter half of the century did signatures gradually begin to replace anonymity in many of the periodicals. Throughout the period, the number of periodicals steadily increased, until there was a magazine for every taste, every income level, every hobby group, every political and religious organization. Domestic magazines aimed at women readers, children's magazines, satirical or humor magazines, and monthly and quarterly miscellanies publishing fiction, poetry, criticism, and news all competed with each other for readers' interest, loyalty, and purchasing power in an increasingly diverse literary marketplace. Nearly all of the best-known literary writers across the genres saw their work published in magazines and newspapers: Barrett Browning's "The Cry of the Children" (1843) in *Blackwood's*, Dickens's *Oliver Twist* in *Bentley's Miscellany*, Arnold's *Culture and Anarchy* in the *Cornhill Magazine*, Yonge's *The Clever Woman of the Family* (1865) in the *Churchman's Family Magazine*.

The periodical press was also instrumental in the development of modern literary criticism. Book reviews in influential periodicals, such as the *Athenaeum*, could make or break a writer's reputation; prominent literary reviewers—some of whom, such as Henry James, were also celebrated authors in their own right—both forged a professional identity for themselves as literary critics and formulated principles of literary analysis that are today's tools of the trade.

Victorians were, in general, fascinated with characterizing their "age": Carlyle's "Signs of the Times," Mill's "Spirit of the Age," and Eliza Lynn Linton's "Girl of the Period" became popular catchphrases that signaled a self-conscious awareness of a society in transition. It was the "age of steam," the "age of doubt," and, perhaps most notably for students of literature, the "age of reading." Reading, like many other social institutions and cultural practices, gradually became democratized during Victoria's reign. The 1870 Education Act instituted compulsory elementary education in England and Wales for the first time; adult literacy was nearly universal by century's end. Readers were everywhere: in pubs, on trains, around the family hearth, at gentlemen's clubs, and in reading rooms.[1] The single reader—particularly the female reader—was a common subject for Victorian painters. Reading aloud was also a popular pastime; it was common for middle-class fathers to gather together their dependents, including the servants, at the end of the day or week to read edifying family literature, such as sermons, tracts, and didactic fiction. Drawing on his background in the London theater, Dickens delivered public readings of his novels that attracted huge crowds and increased sales of his books. His performance of Little Nell's death scene famously left audiences weeping.

The explosion of reading and reading cultures in Victorian England went hand in hand with new print technologies, the removal of prohibitive taxes on reading material, the ease of distribution made possible through the rail system, the rise of cheap, mass-produced print, and political, economic, and social reforms that affected people at all levels of their existence. At the beginning of the century, mass literacy was regarded as a recipe for political revolution. From at least the middle of the century onwards, some worried that reading was becoming too popular, that it was a kind of "mania" or "disease" that "consumed" people. Critics such as Matthew Arnold argued that the newly literate but untutored masses lacked the necessary skills to distinguish between the timeless and the trashy, and that their rise therefore signaled the demise of English culture. Yet there were also those who argued that literacy was a human right, and it was ultimately this viewpoint that prevailed. In 1840, Carlyle wrote, "Books are written by martyr-men, not for rich men alone but for all men. If we consider it, every human being has, by the nature of the case, a *right* to hear what other wise human beings have spoken to him. It is one of the Rights of Men; a very cruel injustice if you deny it to a man."[2] The history of reading—the history of what and how different people read, the expectations that existed about what women and men should read, both in their leisure time and professionally—is ultimately inseparable from the history of the Victorian period.

The English Language in the Victorian Era

The English vocabulary continued to expand throughout the period. New words entered the language to name aspects of the changing world of work (*trade-union* is recorded as first having entered the language in 1831, for example; *margin*, used with reference to profit

[1] Private libraries where readers could pay an annual fee for access to current newspapers and the latest books and periodicals.

[2] It is unclear whether in this passage Carlyle meant "man" in the sense of "humanity" or in the narrower sense.

to mean "amount of money available once certain costs are covered," in the 1850s). New words were also needed to name aspects of human nature that were being seen in new ways or acknowledged for the first time (*personality*, used in the modern sense of "distinctive personal identity," in 1835; *sadism* in 1888; *homosexual* in 1892). New words were coined to name new religious movements (such as *evangelicanism*, *disestablishmentarianism*, and its famously long opposite *antidisestablishmentarianism*) and to name new developments in the culture of sports (*caddie* is first recorded in 1857). Less innocuously, new ways kept springing up to express old prejudices; *jew* is first recorded as being used derogatively as a transitive verb in 1845.

The coining of new words from Latin and Greek roots—especially new scientific terms—continued at a quickened pace, from *lithograph* and *locomotive*, to *photograph* and *phonograph*, to *telegraph*, *telephone*, and *dictaphone*. Far fewer new words were entering English from French, however; the flow of new words from French into English,[1] which had continued in the second half of the eighteenth century and the early years of the nineteenth at about the same pace as it had been a century earlier, slowed to a trickle in the Victorian era. It was far more characteristic of the eighteenth-century English to turn to the French for *etiquette* (1750) than it was for Victorians to turn to the French for *élan* (1880).

The expansion of English in the nineteenth century was not restricted to new noun coinages. A lively feature of the growth of the language during this period was an expansion in the use of verb-adverb combinations (e.g., *bring up*, *hold up*, *let up*, *pass up*, *shut up*—to name only a few of those involving *up*). With the spread of such coinages (as well as of an ever-growing number of slang expressions) into the written language came a gradual reduction in the level of formality of standard English.

A reduction in dialect differences and in range of variation in English pronunciation had begun centuries

The Western Electric multiple telephone switchboard, the Royal Exchange, Manchester, 1888. The spread of English as the leading language of communication world-wide was aided by the invention of the telegraph in 1837, and of the telephone later in the century.

earlier, with the imposition of English authority over Wales, Scotland, and Ireland; no doubt it was influenced, too, by the inherently stabilizing effects of print culture following the introduction of the printing press to England in the late fifteenth century. This trend toward greater standardization of vocabulary and of pronunciation continued through the nineteenth century. The spread of standardized pronunciation in particular was assisted by the growing influence of the elite boarding schools (known as "public schools") as the preferred sites of education for the privileged classes and for those who aspired to join them. Increasingly, in the late-Victorian period, girls as well as boys were sent to such schools; boarding schools such as St. Andrews (1877) and Roedean (1885) were the first institutions for girls that paralleled centuries-old boys' schools such as Eton, Harrow, and Rugby.

Perhaps the greatest development relating to the history of the English language in the Victorian period was the initiation of a dictionary "on historical principles"—one that would record not only the various different meanings of words, but also how they had changed over time, and precisely when each meaning was first recorded in surviving written English. *The Oxford English Dictionary*, which was to be among the

[1] The importation of French words into English, often thought of as beginning with the Norman conquest in 1066, in fact did not occur with any great frequency until roughly a century later; the flow reached its peak in the late fourteenth century.

most ambitious of projects in an age of famously ambitious projects, had its origins in the work of the Philological Society, founded in 1842. In 1858, following the lead of a similar project initiated in Germany[1] and following years of discussion, the society issued a formal "Proposal for the Publication of a New Dictionary by the Philological Society." The society would invite volunteers to assist in sending in records they found of early or significant uses of words; eventually some six million slips with quotations written on them were submitted. By 1879, the Philological Society concluded that the project was so vast that it would not be able to complete it on its own, entering into an agreement with the Oxford University Press. Even with this assistance, it was not until 1884 that it proved possible to publish a volume covering one part of the letter *A*. By 1900, only four and one-half volumes had been published, and it was not until 1928 that a complete version of the full dictionary was available. (By then, of course, much of the early work was outdated; a second edition was published in 1989, and the *OED* is now continually being updated online.)

A less successful Victorian initiative was a multi-faceted campaign to rationalize spelling—a campaign that extended in one form or another through almost the entire period as the prevalence of spellings that bear no relation to phonetic principles increasingly came to be criticized as antiquated and illogical.[2] In the early years of the Victorian era, interest in such matters was spurred by the introduction of Isaac Pitman's system of shorthand, with Pitman himself acting as a leading advocate for reform. By the 1850s, the Bible and a number of works were available in phonetic spelling versions, and by the end of the following decade, the Philological Society was taking an active role in airing all sides of the debate. Its American counterpart adopted a less impartial stance, calling in particular for the adoption of simplified phonetic spellings of words such as *tho*, *altho*, and *thruout*. Of their list only two—*program* and *catalog*—became generally adopted in the United States. In Britain resistance to such Americanisms carried the day—and in both countries, the campaign to rationalize spelling faltered by century's end in the face of a growing recognition of the degree to which English had become a written as well as a spoken language, with words comprehended very largely through the appearance on paper of the entire written word.

Resistance to Americanisms generally was felt not only in Britain itself, but also—indeed, perhaps even more strongly—in English Canada, in its unique position as staunchly British by history and by disposition but unavoidably "American" in the geographical sense. Complaints, such as those of a contributor to the *Canadian Journal* in 1857 against words and expressions "imported by travellers, daily circulated by American newspapers, and eagerly incorporated into the language of our Provincial press," were far from uncommon. Words such as *travellers* (in its British spelling; *travelers* according to common practice in the United States) themselves became points of contention. As the American spellings of such words—introduced by Noah Webster in his dictionary in 1825—became entrenched in the United States, Canadians began to develop a hybrid somewhere in between British and American spellings.

Conventions for marking direct speech and quoted material finally stabilized in the Victorian period in something close to their current form, though with what are now established differences between American and British conventions of punctuation still unsettled. Quotation marks themselves are a relatively recent invention; they became widely used only in the eighteenth century. Even in the late eighteenth century a number of different indicators for quoted material were still being used, the most common of which was to include quotation marks not only at the beginning of

---

[1] The *Deutsches Wörterbuch* was begun by the classicist Franz Passow and the philologists (and compilers of fairy tales) Jacob and Wilhelm Grimm.

[2] As a late-Victorian spelling reformer pointed out, the ways in which English words are spelled often bear so little connection to pronunciation that it would be possible to spell *fish* as *ghoti*, with the *gh* pronounced as we do the *gh* in *cough*; the *o* pronounced as we do the *o* in *women*; and the *ti* pronounced as we do the *ti* in *nation*. This now-famous example is thought to have been first given common currency by Bernard Shaw (who later became a crusader for spelling reform).

the quoted passage, but also at the beginning of each subsequent line for as long as the quotation extended. In the early Victorian period, it had become conventional to mark quotations with only an open quotation mark at the beginning of a passage and a closed quotation mark at the end—though it remained acceptable to use either single or double quotation marks.

The period also saw significant changes in the evolution of the paragraph as a primary means of signaling the shape of ideas in prose. The paragraph was originally simply a short horizontal marker added beneath a line in which a break in meaning occurred; in the sixteenth century, it became conventional to mark such shifts by setting off blocks of text through indentation at the beginning of each block. Until the late eighteenth century, however, paragraphs of English prose were often extremely long by modern standards, and one paragraph of expository or argumentative prose might hold a large number of only loosely related ideas. Even in the Romantic era, a paragraph might often run to a page or more. Through the nineteenth century, however, paragraphs gradually but steadily became shorter, and the principle of restricting each paragraph to a set of closely related ideas became much more widely followed.

History of the Language and of Print Culture

In an effort to provide for readers a direct sense of the development of the language and of print culture, examples of texts in their original form (and of illustrations) have been provided in each volume. A list of materials related to Victorian period print culture and language within the present volume appears below in chronological order. Overviews of "prose non-fiction and print culture" and of developments in the history of language during this period appear on pages 623–26.

Anonymous, "The New Poor Law with a Description of the New Workhouses," c. 1834, p. 733.

"The Angel in 'The House'; or, The Result of Female Suffrage," cartoon from *Punch*, 1884, p. 773.

Masthead illustration from *The Girl's Own Paper*, 1886, p. 778.

Alfred, Lord Tennyson, "The Charge of the Light Brigade," galley proofs of the text from the *Examiner*, 1854, p. 851.

"The Lion of the Season," 1861, and "Man is But a Worm," cartoons from *Punch*, 1882, p. 887.

Emily Brontë, [No coward soul is mine], poem in original spelling, 1850 (written 1846), p. 958.

Christina Rossetti, *Goblin Market and Other Poems*, title page with illustration by Dante Gabriel Rossetti, 1862, p. 1057; illustration by Laurence Housman, 1893, p. 1057.

John Tenniel, illustration to Lewis Carroll's *Through the Looking-Glass and What Alice Found There*, 1872, p. 1070.

A. Forrester, illustrations to Thomas Hardy's "The Son's Veto," from the *Illustrated London News*, 1891 (sites.broadviewpress.com/bablonline).

Gerard Manley Hopkins and Robert Bridges, manuscript versions of "The Windhover," c. 1877 and c. 1883, pp.1107–08.

Sidney Paget, illustrations to Sir Arthur Conan Doyle's "The Adventure of the Speckled Band," *The Strand* magazine, 1892, pp. 1211 ff.

THOMAS CARLYLE

1795 – 1881

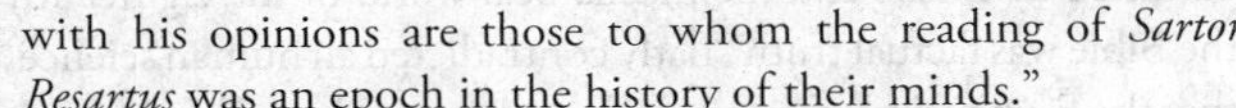

Reviewing a book of selections from Thomas Carlyle's writings in 1855, George Eliot evaluated Carlyle's influence on his contemporaries: "There is hardly a superior or active mind of this generation that has not been modified by Carlyle's writings; there has hardly been an English book written for the last ten or twelve years that would not have been different if Carlyle had not lived. The character of his influence is best seen in the fact that many of the men who have the least agreement with his opinions are those to whom the reading of *Sartor Resartus* was an epoch in the history of their minds."

This evaluation stands as essentially correct. Whether it was Charles Dickens or John Ruskin, Robert Browning or Harriet Martineau, Matthew Arnold or George Eliot herself, Carlyle's thought and work affected the thinking and perspectives of those around him as few other writers did. This Victorian "sage" who was to become fluent in seven languages and count Johann Wolfgang von Goethe, J.S. Mill, Ralph Waldo Emerson, Alfred, Lord Tennyson, Charles Dickens, and Robert Browning among his friends, had very humble beginnings in the village of Ecclefechan, Scotland. Born in 1795, the eldest child of a poor, strict, Calvinist stonemason and a working class, uneducated mother, the young Carlyle showed early promise, and his parents were determined to give their son an education befitting his bright mind. At the age of 14, having attended local schools since he was five, Carlyle walked the nearly 100 miles from his home to enroll in a program at the University of Edinburgh, where he studied mathematics and prepared to enter the ministry. During his years at the University, however, his faith in God was challenged by his studies of skeptics such as David Hume, Voltaire, and Edward Gibbon. He left Edinburgh at age 19 without attaining a degree, and for some years he taught mathematics at Annan Academy.

He also continued what he began at Edinburgh: his life-long reading and study of German writers, whose work he was to introduce to English readers. In 1823 Carlyle completed a biography of the German poet Schiller, which was published serially in *The London Magazine*; his second publication was a translation of Goethe's *Wilhelm Meister* (1824). In 1827 he published an essay on Jean Paul Richter in the influential *Edinburgh Review*. This sign of recognition was repeated in 1829, when he published his "Signs of the Times" in the *Review*, the first of his essays that focused on the social problems of nineteenth-century England and its "Age of Machinery." With "Signs" and another essay, "Characteristics" (1831), the voice of a great social prophet of England emerged. Carlyle's importance increased with the publication of the semiautobiographical *Sartor Resartus* (1833–34), an unconventional work that, while its initial reception was lukewarm, would soon become widely influential.

It is in this period, as well, that Carlyle met and married Jane Baillie Welsh, the brilliant, articulate, talented daughter of a prosperous surgeon. She was well-placed to select from amongst many suitors; why she chose a coarse man from a working-class background was a mystery to her friends and a source of sorrow for her mother. Although their arguments were legendary, their union in 1826 was a true meeting of minds, Carlyle's creative genius and ambition matching Welsh's intellect and drive. In 1834, they moved to London, to a home in Cheyne Row in Chelsea, where Carlyle began the long career of writing that was to make him a prominent voice among his contemporaries, and where Jane Carlyle continued writing the letters that are amongst the most brilliant of all portraits of nineteenth-century London life.

Carlyle's work shows clearly and urgently the writer's confrontation with the age's dual heritage of religion and Romanticism, of tradition and the "march of mind." Carlyle discovered early on in his reading of Gibbon and the Germans that the "old theorem" of religion by which his own father had lived had "passed away," its "immaterialism, mysterious, divine though invisible character" banished by Locke and the mechanical world of the eighteenth century. For Carlyle, claiming that the Bible was factual truth "flatly contradicted all human science and experience." Yet he also believed that the Romantics' response to the passing of the "old beliefs"—the effort he saw in the early Goethe to form "his world out of himself"—led to despair and solipsism. Carlyle's celebration of Goethe's spiritual progress from narcissistic self-focus to a capacious view of humanity's role in a larger world became one of the main themes of his early work. This estimation was to become one of Carlyle's signature lines: "Close thy Byron, Open thy Goethe," commands Diogenes Teufelsdröckh, the questing protagonist of *Sartor Resartus*.

Carlyle began to achieve great fame with the publication of *The French Revolution* in 1836. His style resembled that of no other historian: highly metaphoric language, sentences that seemed "barbarous" because of their German-inflected structures and jarring syntax, the use of the present tense, representations of historical figures so vivid that they seemed like characters from a novel. Carlyle used this style to articulate the dangers that arise when the ruling classes lose sight of moral and social accountability: "French Revolution means here the open violent Rebellion, and Victory, of disimprisoned Anarchy against corrupt worn-out Authority" in which "Anarchy breaks prison; bursts up from the infinite Deep, and rages uncontrollable, immeasurable, enveloping a world."

In 1840 Carlyle gave a series of lectures, *On Heroes and Hero-Worship*, which he published in 1841. Here again he turns his attention to the sweep of historical transformation, now with a deeper focus on the role individual leaders play in history's unfolding. In these lectures, he argues that progress occurs only through the actions of "Great Men," whom the rest of humankind ought to worship: "No nobler feeling than this of admiration for one higher than himself dwells in the breast of man." The lectures take up as heroes such figures as the Norse god Odin, Mohammad, Shakespeare, Martin Luther, Robert Burns, Samuel Johnson, Oliver Cromwell, and Napoleon. Individuals such as these, Carlyle argues, apprehend the workings of the divine and can lead humankind out of darkness—if human beings will listen. In the nineteenth century, he laments, hero worship has fallen out of fashion, placing society in peril.

In Past and Present (1843), Carlyle further develops his views regarding the potential salvation of British politics and culture. By juxtaposing the medieval past of England, with its monks and serfs living in an organic community focused around a monastery, and the industrialism and *laissez-faire* economics of England's present that had produced poverty and starvation, Carlyle created a remarkable picture of the desperate social crises of the hungry forties. This latter-day England is populated by a group of vividly realized demons escaped out of Bunyan and the daily newspapers: Pandarus Dogdraught, Bobus of Houndsditch, Plugson of Undershot (a captain of industry), Sir Jabesh Windbag, the amphibious Pope, and the Dead Sea Apes (who believe that soul and stomach are synonymous). Through the biting depiction of such figures, Carlyle denounces the "Gospel of Enlightened Selfishness" that he and others saw as reducing the connections between human beings to those of a "cash nexus." The solution, Carlyle suggests, can be found in the redemptive powers of work—and especially in the efforts of heroes like Abbot Samson, a medieval figure whom Carlyle presents as a reformer who restored his degenerating society to its former glory. If the Victorian nation's "Captains of Industry" can develop the necessary nobility and heroism, then its people will transform from "a bewildered and bewildering mob" into "a firm regimented mass."

For many readers, Carlyle's exaltation of authority has represented a danger, and his conservative and authoritarian tendencies become more pronounced in his later work. *The Letters and Speeches of Oliver Cromwell* (1845) and *The History of Friedrich II of Prussia, Called Frederick the Great*, published between 1858 and 1865, furthered Carlyle's doctrine of hero-worship and his principles of order. He strongly opposed the enfranchisement of women and just as vehemently supported the enslavement of black people in the West Indies. (Carlyle's 1849 essay on this topic ended his friendship with Mill, who wrote a spirited reply.) His 1850 publication of *Latter-Day Pamphlets*, with its corrosively satirical attacks on democracy and its representatives, is an extraordinarily splenetic outburst from a voice that had once challenged England to discover the godlike connections amongst all human beings.

Carlyle remained influential; Dickens, Browning, and John Ruskin all dedicated books to him. In 1874 he turned down a baronetcy offered by British Prime Minister Disraeli; he did, however, accept the Prussian Order of Merit in the same year. After his wife's death in 1866, he wrote little, though he did edit his wife's remarkable letters, *The Letters and Memorials of Jane Welsh Carlyle*, which were published after his own death. Carlyle, who had earlier stated his aversion to the idea of being buried in Westminster Abbey, was buried in 1881 beside his parents in Ecclefechan. George Eliot's estimation of Carlyle is an apt epitaph: "When he is saying the opposite of what we think, he says it so finely, with so hearty conviction—he makes the object about which we differ stand out in such grand relief under the clear light of his strong and honest intellect—he appeals so constantly to our sense of the manly and the truthful—that we are obliged to say 'Hear! Hear!' to the writer before we can give the decorous 'Oh! Oh!' to his opinions."

⌘⌘⌘

from *Past and Present*[1]

from BOOK 1

CHAPTER 1—MIDAS[2]

The condition of England, on which many pamphlets are now in the course of publication, and many thoughts unpublished are going on in every reflective head, is justly regarded as one of the most ominous, and withal one of the strangest, ever seen in this world. England is full of wealth, of multifarious produce, supply for human want in every kind; yet England is dying of inanition. With unabated bounty the land of England blooms and grows; waving with yellow harvests; thick-studded with workshops, industrial implements, with fifteen millions of workers, understood to be the strongest, the cunningest and the willingest our Earth ever had; these men are here; the work they have done, the fruit they have realised is here, abundant, exuberant on every hand of us: and behold, some baleful fiat as of Enchantment has gone forth, saying, "Touch it not, ye workers, ye master-workers, ye master-idlers; none of you can touch it, no man of you shall be the better for it; this is enchanted fruit!" On the poor workers such fiat[3] falls first, in its rudest shape; but on the rich master-workers too it falls; neither can the rich master-idlers, nor any richest or highest man escape, but all are like to be brought low with it, and made "poor" enough, in the money sense or a far fataler one.

Of these successful skilful workers some two millions, it is now counted, sit in Workhouses, Poor-law Prisons; or have "out-door relief"[4] flung over the wall to them—the workhouse Bastille[5] being filled to bursting, and the strong Poor-law broken asunder by a stronger. They sit there, these many months now; their hope of deliverance as yet small. In workhouses, pleasantly so-named, because work cannot be done in them. Twelve-hundred-thousand workers in England alone; their cunning right-hand lamed, lying idle in their sorrowful bosom; their hopes, outlooks, share of this fair world, shut-in by narrow walls. They sit there, pent up, as in a kind of horrid enchantment; glad to be imprisoned and enchanted, that they may not perish starved. The picturesque Tourist, in a sunny autumn day, through this bounteous realm of England, descries the Union Workhouse on his path. "Passing by the Workhouse of St. Ives in Huntingdonshire, on a bright day last autumn," says the picturesque Tourist, "I saw sitting on wooden benches, in front of their Bastille and within their ring-wall and its railings, some half-hundred or more of these men. Tall robust figures, young mostly or of middle age; of honest countenance, many of them thoughtful and even intelligent-looking men. They sat there, near by one another; but in a kind of torpor, especially in a silence, which was very striking. In silence: for, alas, what word was to be said? An Earth all lying round, crying, Come and till me, come and reap me—yet we here sit enchanted! In the eyes and brows of these men hung the gloomiest expression, not of anger,

---

[1] *Past and Present* Carlyle wrote this treatise in seven weeks, in response to the lack of order and leadership that he felt was contributing to the widespread social and economic difficulties England was experiencing at that time. Carlyle blamed both the complacent aristocracy, which sought to maintain the status quo, and the spread of democracy, which he felt did little to provide heroic leaders. In 1837, industry in England entered into a depression that lasted several years. Many factories closed and others were forced to cut wages, which led to rioting in the manufacturing districts. By 1845, approximately one-twelfth of the population was unemployed, and many people ended up in overcrowded poorhouses. When the Chartists organized peaceful protests for social and economic reform, many British citizens began to fear a full-scale revolution.

[2] *MIDAS* Fabled king of Phrygia who, in one myth, was granted his wish that everything he touched would turn to gold. As a result, he was unable to eat. In another myth, he judges the music of the woodland god Pan to be superior to that of Apollo, god of music. Apollo, offended, changes Midas's ears to those of a donkey.

[3] *fiat* Order.

[4] *Workhouses* Established under the Poor Law Amendment Act of 1834 for the relief of the poor. They were designed to be as unpleasant as possible, in order to discourage people from entering them. Living conditions were poor, the work provided was equivalent to prison labor, and families were separated upon entering, with men and women lodged separately; *out-door relief* System, in place prior to the Poor Law Amendment Act, under which each parish would provide its poor with minimum allowances.

[5] *Bastille* Prison. (In reference to the Parisian prison of that name, the destruction of which by the mob in 1789 is commonly held to mark the beginning of the French Revolution.)

but of grief and shame and manifold inarticulate distress and weariness; they returned my glance with a glance that seemed to say, 'Do not look at us. We sit enchanted here, we know not why. The Sun shines and the Earth calls; and, by the governing Powers and Impotences of this England, we are forbidden to obey. It is impossible, they tell us!' There was something that reminded me of Dante's Hell[1] in the look of all this; and I rode swiftly away."

So many hundred thousands sit in workhouses, and other hundred thousands have not yet got even workhouses; and in thrifty Scotland itself, in Glasgow or Edinburgh City, in their dark lanes, hidden from all but the eye of God, and of rare Benevolence, the minister of God, there are scenes of woe and destitution and desolation, such, as, one may hope, the Sun never saw before in the most barbarous regions where men dwelt. Competent witnesses, the brave and humane Dr. Alison,[2] who speaks what he knows, whose noble Healing Art in his charitable hands becomes once more a truly sacred one, report these things for us. These things are not of this year, or of last year, have no reference to our present state of commercial stagnation, but only to the common state. Not in sharp fever-fits, but in chronic gangrene of this kind is Scotland suffering. A Poor-law, any and every Poor-law, it may be observed, is but a temporary measure; an anodyne, not a remedy. Rich and Poor, when once the naked facts of their condition have come into collision, cannot long subsist together on a mere Poor-law. True enough—and yet, human beings cannot be left to die! Scotland too, till something better come, must have a Poor-law, if Scotland is not to be a byword among the nations. O what a waste is there; of noble and thrice-noble national virtues; peasant Stoicisms, Heroisms; valiant manful habits, soul of a Nation's worth, which all the metal of Potosi[3] cannot purchase back; to which the metal of Potosi, and all you can buy with *it*, is dross and dust!

Why dwell on this aspect of the matter? It is too indisputable, not doubtful now to anyone. Descend where you will into the lower class, in Town or Country, by what avenue you will, by Factory Inquiries, Agricultural Inquiries, by Revenue Returns, by Mining-Labourer Committees, by opening your own eyes and looking, the same sorrowful result discloses itself: you have to admit that the working body of this rich English Nation has sunk or is fast sinking into a state, to which, all sides of it considered, there was literally never any parallel. At Stockport Assizes[4]—and this too has no reference to the present state of trade, being of date prior to that—a Mother and a Father are arraigned and found guilty of poisoning three of their children, to defraud a burial-society of some *3l.8s.*[5] due on the death of each child. They are arraigned, found guilty; and the official authorities, it is whispered, hint that perhaps the case is not solitary, that perhaps you had better not probe farther into that department of things. This is in the autumn of 1841; the crime itself is of the previous year or season. "Brutal savages, degraded Irish,"[6] mutters the idle reader of Newspapers, hardly lingering on this incident. Yet it is an incident worth lingering on; the depravity, savagery, and degraded Irishism being never so well admitted. In the British land, a human Mother and Father, of white skin and professing the Christian religion, had done this thing; they, with their Irishism and necessity and savagery, had been driven to do it. Such instances are like the highest mountain apex emerged into view, under which lies a whole mountain region and land, not yet emerged. A human Mother and Father had said to themselves, What shall we do to escape starvation? We are deep sunk here, in our dark cellar; and help is far. Yes, in the Ugolino Hunger-tower[7] stern things happen; best-loved little Gaddo

[1] *Dante's Hell* Reference to *The Divine Comedy* by thirteenth-century Italian poet Dante Alighieri.

[2] *Dr. Alison* Scottish physician and social reformer who wrote *Observations on the Management of the Poor in Scotland* (1840).

[3] *Potosi* Bolivian city known for its silver mines.

[4] *Assizes* Court sessions held periodically in the various counties in England.

[5] *3l.8s.* Three pounds, eight shillings.

[6] *Brutal … Irish* This passage reflects the prejudice of many Englishmen and women against the native people of Ireland.

[7] *Ugolino Hunger-tower* In the thirteenth century, Count Ugolino of Pisa and his children and nephews were imprisoned and starved to death when Ugolino betrayed his political allies. [continued …]

fallen dead on his Father's knees! The Stockport Mother and Father think and hint: our poor little starveling Tom, who cries all day for victuals, who will see only evil and not good in this world; if he were out of misery at once; he well dead, and the rest of us perhaps kept alive? It is thought, and hinted; at last it is done. And now Tom being killed, and all spent and eaten, Is it poor little starveling Jack that must go, or poor little starveling Will? What a committee of ways and means!

In starved sieged cities, in the uttermost doomed ruin of old Jerusalem fallen under the wrath of God, it was prophesied and said, "The hands of the pitiful women have sodden their own children."[1] The stern Hebrew imagination could conceive no blacker gulf of wretchedness; that was the ultimatum of degraded god-punished man. And we here, in modern England, exuberant with supply of all kinds, besieged by nothing if it be not by invisible Enchantments, are we reaching that? How come these things? Wherefore are they, wherefore should they be?

Nor are they of the St. Ives workhouses, of the Glasgow lanes, and Stockport cellars, the only unblessed among us. This successful industry of England, with its plethoric wealth, has as yet made nobody rich; it is an enchanted wealth, and belongs yet to nobody. We might ask, Which of us has it enriched? We can spend thousands where we once spent hundreds, but can purchase nothing good with them. In Poor and Rich, instead of noble thrift and plenty, there is idle luxury alternating with mean scarcity and inability. We have sumptuous garnitures for our Life, but have forgotten to *live* in the middle of them. It is an enchanted wealth; no man of us can yet touch it. The class of men who feel that they are truly better off by means of it, let them give us their name!

Many men eat finer cookery, drink dearer liquors—with what advantage they can report, and their Doctors can; but in the heart of them, if we go out of the dyspeptic stomach, what increase of blessedness is there? Are they better, beautifuller, stronger, braver? Are they even what they call "happier"? Do they look with satisfaction on more things and human faces in this God's-Earth; do more things and human faces look with satisfaction on them? Not so. Human faces gloom discordantly, disloyally on one another. Things, if it be not mere cotton and iron things, are growing disobedient to man. The Master Worker is enchanted, for the present, like his Workhouse Workman; clamours, in vain hitherto, for a very simple sort of "Liberty"—the liberty "to buy where he finds it cheapest, to sell where he finds it dearest." With guineas jingling in every pocket, he was no whit richer; but now, the very guineas threatening to vanish, he feels that he is poor indeed. Poor Master Worker! And the Master Unworker,[2] is not he in a still fataler situation? Pausing amid his game-preserves, with awful eye—as he well may! Coercing fifty-pound tenants;[3] coercing, bribing, cajoling; "doing what he likes with his own." His mouth full of loud futilities, and arguments to prove the excellence of his Corn-law;[4] and in his heart the blackest misgiving, a desperate half-consciousness that his excellent Corn-law is *in*defensible, that his loud arguments for it are of a kind to strike men too literally *dumb*.

To whom, then, is this wealth of England wealth? Who is it that it blesses, makes happier, wiser, beautifuler, in any way better? Who has got hold of it, to make it fetch and carry for him, like a true servant, not like a false mock-servant, to do him any real service whatsoever? As yet no one. We have more riches than any Nation ever had before; we have less good of them than any Nation ever had before. Our successful industry is hitherto unsuccessful; a strange success, if we stop here! In the midst of plethoric plenty, the people perish; with gold walls, and full barns, no man feels himself safe or satisfied. Workers, Master Workers, Unworkers, all men, come to a pause; stand fixed, and cannot farther.

According to Dante's *Inferno*, Ugolino ate his children's bodies after they died, in order to stave off starvation. The tower in Pisa's central piazza in which Ugolino was imprisoned has since been called the Tower of Hunger.

[1] *The hands ... children* From Lamentations 4.10; *sodden* Boiled.

[2] *Unworker* I.e., person who does not work.

[3] *fifty-pound tenants* Tenants who paid fifty pounds or more in rent. Under the Reform Bill of 1832, these tenants were allowed to vote.

[4] *Corn-law* One of a series of laws passed in 1815 to regulate the import of grain and keep the price of grain artificially high.

Fatal paralysis spreading inwards, from the extremities, in St. Ives workhouses, in Stockport cellars, through all limbs, as if towards the heart itself. Have we actually got enchanted, then, accursed by some god?

Midas longed for gold, and insulted the Olympians. He got gold, so that whatsoever he touched became gold—and he, with his long ears, was little the better for it. Midas had misjudged the celestial music-tones; Midas had insulted Apollo and the gods. The gods gave him his wish, and a pair of long ears, which also were a good appendage to it. What a truth in these old Fables! …

CHAPTER 6—HERO-WORSHIP

To the present Editor, not less than to Bobus,[1] a Government of the Wisest, what Bobus calls an Aristocracy of Talent, seems the one healing remedy; but he is not so sanguine as Bobus with respect to the means of realising it. He thinks that we have at once missed realising it, and come to need it so pressingly, by departing far from the inner eternal Laws, and taking-up with the temporary outer semblances of Laws. He thinks that "enlightened Egoism,"[2] never so luminous, is not the rule by which man's life can be led. That "Laissez-faire," "Supply-and-demand," "Cash-payment for the sole nexus,"[3] and so forth, were not, are not and will never be, a practicable Law of Union for a Society of Men. The Poor and Rich, that Governed and Governing, cannot long live together on any such Law of Union. Alas, he thinks that man has a soul in him, *different* from the stomach in any sense of this word; that if said soul be asphyxied, and lie quietly forgotten, the man and his affairs are in a bad way. He thinks that said soul will have to be resuscitated from its asphyxia; that if it prove irresuscitable, the man is not long for this world. In brief, that Midas-eared Mammonism, double-barrelled Dilettantism,[4] and their thousand adjuncts and corollaries, are *not* the Law by which God Almighty has appointed this his Universe to go; that, once for all, these are not the Law; and then, further, that we shall have to return to what *is* the Law—not by smooth flowery paths, it is like, and with "tremendous cheers" in our throat, but over steep untrodden places, through stormclad chasms, waste oceans, and the bosom of tornadoes; thank Heaven, if not through very Chaos and the Abyss! The resuscitating of a soul that has gone to asphyxia is no momentary or pleasant process, but a long and terrible one.

To the present Editor, Hero-worship, as he has elsewhere named it, means much more than an elected Parliament or stated Aristocracy of the Wisest; for in his dialect it is the summary, ultimate essence, and supreme practical perfection of all manner of worship, and true worthships and noblenesses whatsoever. Such blessed Parliament and, were it once in perfection, blessed Aristocracy of the Wisest, god-honoured and man-honoured, he does look for, more and more perfected—as the topmost blessed practical apex of a whole world reformed from sham-worship, informed anew with worship, with truth and blessedness! He thinks that Hero-worship, done differently in every different epoch of the world, is the soul of all social business among men; that the doing of it well, or the doing of it ill, measures accurately what degree of well-being or of ill-being there is in the world's affairs. He thinks that we, on the whole, do our Hero-worship worse than any Nation in this world ever did it before; that the Burns an Exciseman, the Byron[5] a Literary Lion, are intrinsi-

[1] *Bobus* Carlyle creates this fictional character, whom he earlier refers to as "Bobus Higgins, Sausage-maker on the great scale," as a caricature of members of the middle class who take a narrow-minded view of social reform.

[2] *enlightened Egoism* I.e., rational egoism, according to which it is beneficial for society if individuals act in their own best interests.

[3] *Laissez-faire* Theory of economics, holding that the government should not interfere with business or trade, and that the market will regulate itself; *Cash … nexus* I.e., cash is the only nexus (connection or bond) between people.

[4] *Mammonism* Worship of, or devotion to, Mammon, the personification of wealth. See Luke 16.13: "Ye cannot serve God and Mammon"; *Dilettantism* Pursuit of knowledge in an art or science as an idle pastime, without any serious interest or goal.

[5] *Exciseman* Poet Robert Burns (1759–96), who worked as an excise officer. Burns came to be regarded as Scotland's national poet; *Byron* Romantic poet George Gordon, Lord Byron (1788–1824).

cally, all things considered, a baser and falser phenomenon than the Odin[1] a God, the Mahomet a Prophet of God. It is this Editor's clear opinion, accordingly, that we must learn to do our Hero-worship better; that to do it better and better means the awakening of the Nation's soul from its asphyxia, and the return of blessed life to us—Heaven's blessed life, not Mammon's galvanic[2] accursed one. To resuscitate the Asphyxied, apparently now moribund and in the last agony if not resuscitated, such and no other seems the consummation.

"Hero-worship," if you will—yes, friends; but, first of all, by being ourselves of heroic mind. A whole world of Heroes; a world not of Flunkies, where no Hero-King *can* reign: that is what we aim at! We, for our share, will put away all Flunkyism, Baseness, Unveracity from us; we shall then hope to have Noblenesses and Veracities set over us; never till then. Let Bobus and Company sneer, "That is your Reform!" Yes, Bobus, that is our Reform; and except in that, and what will follow out of that, we have no hope at all. Reform, like Charity, O Bobus, must begin at home. Once well at home, how will it radiate outwards, irrepressible, into all that we touch and handle, speak and work; kindling ever new light, by incalculable contagion, spreading in geometric ratio, far and wide—doing good only, wheresoever it spreads, and not evil.

By Reform Bills, Anti-Corn-Law Bills, and thousand other bills and methods, we will demand of our Governors, with emphasis, and for the first time not without effect, that they cease to be quacks, or else depart; that they set no quackeries and block-headisms anywhere to rule over us, that they utter or act no cant to us—it will be better if they do not. For we shall now know quacks when we see them; cant, when we hear it, shall be horrible to us! We will say, with the poor Frenchman at the Bar of the Convention, though in wiser style than he, and "for the space" not "of an hour" but of a lifetime: "*Je demands l'arrestation des coquins et des laches.*" "Arrestment of the knaves and dastards." Ah, we know what a work that is; how long it will be before *they* are all or mostly got "arrested"—but here is one; arrest him, in God's name; it is one fewer! We will, in all practicable ways, by word and silence, by act and refusal to act, energetically demand that arrestment—"*je demande cette arrestation-la!*"—and by degrees infallibly attain it. Infallibly, for light spreads; all human souls, never so bedarkened, love light; light once kindled spreads, till all is luminous, till the cry, "*Arrest* your knaves and dastards" rises imperative from millions of hearts, and rings and reigns from sea to sea. Nay, how many of them may we not "arrest" with our own hands, even now, we! Do not countenance them, thou there: turn away from their lacquered sumptuosities, their belauded sophistries, their serpent graciosities, their spoken and acted cant, with a sacred horror, with an *Apage Satanas*.[3] Bobus and Company, and all men, will gradually join us. We demand arrestment of the knaves and dastards, and begin by arresting our own poor selves out of that fraternity. There is no other reform conceivable. Thou and I, my friend, can, in the most flunky world, make, each of us, *one* non-flunky, one hero, if we like. That will be two heroes to begin with—Courage! even that is a whole world of heroes to end with, or what we poor Two can do in furtherance thereof!

Yes, friends: Hero-kings, and a whole world not unheroic—there lies the port and happy haven, towards which, through all these stormtost seas, French Revolutions, Chartisms, Manchester Insurrections,[4] that make the heart sick in these bad days, the Supreme Powers are driving us. On the whole, blessed be the Supreme Powers, stern as they are! Towards that haven will we, O friends; let all true men, with what of faculty is in them, bend valiantly, incessantly, with thousandfold endeavour, thither, thither! There, or else in the Ocean-abysses, it is very clear to me, we shall arrive.

---

[1] *Odin* Norse god of war, art, and culture.

[2] *galvanic* Applying electricity; having the effect of an electric shock.

[3] *Apage Satanas* Latin: Begone, Satan.

[4] *Chartisms* Movements by the Chartists, peaceful democratic reformers whose principles were set out in the "People's Charter," published in 1838; *Manchester Insurrections* Rioting in Manchester in 1842 resulted from the reduction of wages in both the coal mines and the factories. Manchester was also the site of the famous 1819 Peterloo Massacre, at which cavalry charged on an outdoor political meeting, killing at least eleven people and wounding several others.

Well, here truly is no answer to the Sphinx-question[1]—not the answer a disconsolate public, inquiring at the College of Health, was in hopes of! A total change of regimen, change of constitution and existence from the very centre of it; a new body to be got, with resuscitated soul—not without convulsive travail-throes, as all birth and new-birth presupposes travail! This is sad news to a disconsolate discerning Public, hoping to have got off by some Morrison's Pill,[2] some Saint-John's corrosive mixture and perhaps a little blistery friction on the back! We were prepared to part with our Corn-Law, with various Laws and Unlaws, but this, what is this?

Nor has the Editor forgotten how it fares with your ill-boding Cassandras in Sieges of Troy.[3] Imminent perdition is not usually driven away by words of warning. Didactic Destiny has other methods in store, or these would fail always. Such words should, nevertheless, be uttered, when they dwell truly in the soul of any man. Words are hard, are importunate; but how much harder the importunate events they foreshadow! Here and there a human soul may listen to the words—who knows how many human souls?—whereby the importunate events, if not diverted and prevented, will be rendered *less* hard. The present Editor's purpose is to himself full of hope.

For though fierce travails, though wide seas and roaring gulfs lie before us, is it not something if a Loadstar, in the eternal sky, do once more disclose itself; an everlasting light, shining through all cloud-tempests and roaring billows, ever as we emerge from the trough of the sea; the blessed beacon, far off on the edge of far horizons, towards which we are to steer incessantly for life? Is it not something, O Heavens, is it not all? There lies the Heroic Promised Land; under that Heaven's-light, my brethren, bloom the Happy Isles—there, O there! Thither will we;

"There dwells the great Achilles whom we knew."[4]

There dwell all Heroes, and will dwell: thither, all ye heroic-minded! The Heaven's Loadstar once clearly in our eye, how will each true man stand truly to *his* work in the ship; how, with undying hope, will all things be fronted, all be conquered. Nay, with the ship's prow once turned in that direction, is not all, as it were, already well? Sick wasting misery has become noble manful effort with a goal in our eye. The choking Nightmare chokes us no longer, for we *stir* under it; the Nightmare has already fled.

Certainly, could the present Editor instruct men how to know Wisdom, Heroism, when they see it, that they might do reverence to *it* only, and loyally make it ruler over them, yes, he were the living epitome of all Editors, Teachers, Prophets, that now teach and prophesy; he were an *Apollo*-Morrison, a Trismegistus[5] and *effective* Cassandra! Let no Able Editor hope such things. It is to be expected the present laws of copyright, rate of reward per sheet, and other considerations will save him from that peril. Let no Editor hope such things; no—and yet let all Editors aim towards such things, and even towards such alone! One knows not what the meaning of editing and writing is, if even this be not it.

Enough, to the present Editor it has seemed possible some glimmering of light, for here and there a human soul might lie in these confused Paper-Masses now entrusted to him; wherefore he determines to edit the same. Out of old Books, new Writings, and much Meditation not of yesterday, he will endeavour to select a thing or two; and from the Past, in a circuitous way, illustrate the Present and the Future. The Past is a dim indubitable fact: the Future too is one, only dimmer; nay properly it is the *same* fact in new dress and development. For the Present holds it in both the whole Past

---

[1] *Sphinx-question* Riddle, like those posed by the mythological sphinx, a winged half-woman, half-lion who would not allow travelers to pass unless they could correctly answer her riddle. If they answered incorrectly, they would be killed.

[2] *Morrison's Pill* I.e., a cure-all.

[3] *Cassandras … Troy* Cassandra, daughter of the King of Troy, was given the gift of prophecy, but cursed so that nobody would believe her.

[4] *There dwells … knew* Cf. lines 63–64 of Alfred, Lord Tennyson's poem "Ulysses": "It may be we shall touch the Happy Isles, / And see the great Achilles, whom we knew." The Happy Isles were the Isles of the Blessed, supposedly (according to Greek myth) located in the Atlantic Ocean.

[5] *Apollo* Classical god of poetry, music, and prophecy; *Trismegistus* Greek: thrice great. This is an epithet of the classical god Hermes, the messenger and herald for the other gods.

and the whole Future—as the life-tree Igdrasil,[1] wide-waving, many-toned, has its roots down deep in the Death-kingdoms, among the oldest dead dust of men, and with its boughs reaches always beyond the stars, and in all times and places is one and the same Life-tree! …

from BOOK 3
CHAPTER 2—GOSPEL OF MAMMONISM

Reader, even Christian Reader as thy title goes, hast thou any notion of Heaven and Hell? I rather apprehend, not. Often as the words are on our tongue, they have got a fabulous or semi-fabulous character for most of us, and pass on like a kind of transient similitude, like a sound signifying little.

Yet it is well worth while for us to know, once and always, that they are not a similitude, nor a fable nor semi-fable; that they are an everlasting highest fact! "No Lake of Sicilian or other sulphur[2] burns now anywhere in these ages," sayest thou? Well, and if there did not! Believe that there does not; believe it if thou wilt; nay, hold by it as a real increase, a rise to higher stages, to wider horizons and empires. All this has vanished, or has not vanished; believe as thou wilt as to all this. But that an Infinite of Practical Importance, speaking with strict arithmetical exactness, an *Infinite*, has vanished or can vanish from the Life of any Man, this thou shalt not believe! O brother, the Infinite of Terror, of Hope, of Pity, did it not at any moment disclose itself to thee, indubitable, unnameable? Came it never, like the gleam of eternal Oceans, like the voice of old Eternities, far-sounding through thy heart of hearts? Never? Alas, it was not thy Liberalism, then; it was thy Animalism! The Infinite is more sure than any other fact. But only men can discern it; mere building beavers, spinning arachnes, much more the predatory vulturous and vulpine species, do not discern it well!

"The word Hell," says Sauerteig,[3] "is still frequently in use among the English people, but I could not without difficulty ascertain what they meant by it. Hell generally signifies the Infinite Terror, the thing a man *is* infinitely afraid of, and shudders and shrinks from, struggling with his whole soul to escape from it. There is a Hell, therefore, if you will consider, which accompanies man in all stages of his history and religious or other development. But the Hells of men and Peoples differ notably. With Christians it is the infinite terror of being found guilty before the Just Judge. With old Romans, I conjecture, it was the terror not of Pluto,[4] for whom probably they cared little, but of doing unworthily, doing unvirtuously, which was their word for un*man*fully.[5] And now what is it, if you pierce through his Cants, his oft-repeated Hearsays, what he calls his Worships and so forth, what is it that the modern English soul does, in very truth, dread infinitely, and contemplate with entire despair? What *is* his Hell, after all these reputable, oft-repeated Hearsays, what is it? With hesitation, with astonishment, I pronounce it to be the terror of 'Not succeeding'; of not making money, fame, or some other figure in the world—chiefly of not making money! Is not that a somewhat singular Hell?"

Yes, O Sauerteig, it is very singular. If we do not "succeed," where is the use of us? We had better never have been born. "Tremble intensely," as our friend the Emperor of China says: *there* is the black Bottomless of Terror, what Sauerteig calls the "Hell of the English!" But indeed this Hell belongs naturally to the Gospel of Mammonism, which also has its corresponding Heaven. For there *is* one Reality among so many Phantasms; about one thing we are entirely in earnest: the making of money. Working Mammonism does divide the world with idle game-preserving Dilettantism—thank Heaven that there is even a Mammonism, *anything* we are in earnest about! Idleness is worst, Idleness alone is without

[1] *Igdrasil* Great tree of Scandinavian mythology, the roots and branches of which stretched through the universe.

[2] *Lake … sulphur* Sulphur, often found near volcanic rocks, was formerly known as "brimstone" (i.e., "burning stone") and was thought to feed the fires of hell. At this time, Sicily was the world's primary source of sulphur.

[3] *Sauerteig* Gottfried Sauerteig, the fictitious "Picturesque Tourist" who visits the St. Ives workhouse in Book 1, Chapter 1.

[4] *Pluto* Roman god of the underworld.

[5] *which was … unmanfully* The Latin word for man is *vir*.

hope: work earnestly at anything, you will by degrees learn to work at almost all things. There is endless hope in work, were it even work at making money.

True, it must be owned, we for the present, with our Mammon-Gospel, have come to strange conclusions. We call it a Society; and go about professing openly the totalest separation, isolation. Our life is not a mutual helpfulness; but rather, cloaked under due laws-of-war, named "fair competition" and so forth, it is a mutual hostility. We have profoundly forgotten everywhere that *Cash payment* is not the sole relation of human beings; we think, nothing doubting, that *it* absolves and liquidates all engagements of man. "My starving workers?" answers the rich mill-owner: "Did not I hire them fairly in the market? Did I not pay them, to the last sixpence, the sum covenanted for? What have I to do with them more?" Verily Mammon-worship is a melancholy creed. When Cain, for his own behoof, had killed Abel, and was questioned, "Where is thy brother?" he too made answer, "Am I my brother's keeper?" Did I not pay my brother *his* wages, the thing he had merited from me?[1]

O sumptuous Merchant Prince, illustrious game-preserving Duke, is there no way of "killing" thy brother but Cain's rude way! "A good man by the very look of him, by his very presence with us as a fellow wayfarer in this Life-pilgrimage, *promises* so much." Woe to him if he forget all such promises, if he never know that they were given! To a deadened soul, seared with the brute Idolatry of Sense, to whom going to Hell is equivalent to not making money, all "promises" and moral duties, that cannot be pleaded for in Courts of Requests,[2] address themselves in vain. Money he can be ordered to pay, but nothing more. I have not heard in all Past History, and expect not to hear in all Future History, of any Society anywhere under God's Heaven, supporting itself on such Philosophy. The Universe is not made so; it is made otherwise than so. The man or nation of men that thinks it is made so, marches forward nothing doubting, step after step, but marches—whither we know! In these last two centuries of Atheistic Government (near two centuries now, since the blessed restoration of his Sacred Majesty, and Defender of the Faith, Charles Second), I reckon that we have pretty well exhausted what of "firm earth" there was for us to march on—and are now, very ominously, shuddering, reeling, and let us hope trying to recoil, on the cliff's edge!

For out of this that we call Atheism come so many other *isms* and falsities, each falsity with its misery at its heels! A SOUL is not like wind (*spiritus*, or breath) contained within a capsule; the ALMIGHTY MAKER is not like a Clockmaker that once, in old immemorial ages, having *made* his Horologe of a Universe, sits ever since and sees it go! Not at all. Hence comes Atheism; come, as we say, many other *isms*, and, as the sum of all, comes Valetism,[3] the *reverse* of Heroism—sad root of all woes whatsoever. For indeed, as no man ever saw the above-said wind-element enclosed within its capsule, and finds it at bottom more deniable than conceivable; so too he finds, in spite of Bridgwater Bequests,[4] your Clockmaker Almighty an entirely questionable affair, a deniable affair—and accordingly denies it, and along with it so much else. Alas, one knows not what and how much else! For the faith in an Invisible, Unnameable, Godlike, present everywhere in all that we see and work and suffer, is the essence of all faith whatsoever; and that once denied, or still worse, asserted with lips only, and out of bound prayerbooks only, what other thing remains believable? That Cant well-ordered is marketable Cant; that Heroism means gas-lighted Histrionism;[5] that seen with "clear eyes" (as they call Valet-eyes) no man is a Hero, or ever was a Hero, but all men are Valets and Varlets. The accursed practical quintessence of all sorts of Unbelief! For if there be now no Hero, and the Histrio himself begin to be seen into, what hope is there for the seed of Adam here below? We are the

[1] *When Cain ... me* See Genesis 4.9.

[2] *Courts of Requests* Court that examined the petitions of the poor.

[3] *Valetism* I.e., the character of a valet. Carlyle defines valetism in Book 2 as "cloth-worship and quack-worship."

[4] *Bridgwater Bequests* Francis Henry Egerton, 8th Earl of Bridgewater (1756–1829) left £8000 in his will to be awarded to the author of a treatise entitled "On the Power, Wisdom, and Goodness of God, as Manifested in the Creation."

[5] *Histrionism* Acting.

doomed everlasting prey of the Quack; who, now in this guise, now in that, is to filch us, to pluck and eat us, by such modes as are convenient for him. For the modes and guises I care little. The Quack once inevitable, let him come swiftly, let him pluck and eat me—swiftly, that I may at least have done with him, for in his Quack-world I can have no wish to linger. Though he slay me, yet will I *not* trust in him. Though he conquer nations, and have all the Flunkies of the Universe shouting at his heels, yet will I know well that *he* is an Inanity; that for him and his there is no continuance appointed, save only in Gehenna and the Pool.[1] Alas, the Atheist world, from its utmost summits of Heaven and Westminster Hall,[2] downwards through poor seven-feet Hats and "Unveracities fallen hungry," down to the lowest cellars and neglected hunger-dens of it, is very wretched.

One of Dr. Alison's Scotch facts struck us much. A poor Irish Widow, her husband having died in one of the Lanes of Edinburgh, went forth with her three children, bare of all resource, to solicit help from the Charitable Establishments of that City. At this Charitable Establishment and then at that she was refused, referred from one to the other, helped by none, till she had exhausted them all, till her strength and heart failed her. She sank down in typhus-fever, died, and infected her Lane with fever, so that "seventeen other persons" died of fever there in consequence. The humane Physician asks thereupon, as with a heart too full for speaking, Would it not have been *economy* to help this poor Widow? She took typhus-fever, and killed seventeen of you! Very curious. The forlorn Irish Widow applies to her fellow-creatures, as if saying, "Behold I am sinking, bare of help. Ye must help me! I am your sister, bone of your bone; one God made us. Ye must help me!" They answer, "No, impossible; thou art no sister of ours." But she proves her sisterhood; her typhus-fever kills *them*. They actually were her brothers, though denying it! Had human creature ever to go lower for a proof?

For, as indeed was very natural in such case, all government of the Poor by the Rich has long ago been given over to Supply-and-demand, Laissez-faire and suchlike, and universally declared to be "impossible." "You are no sister of ours; what shadow of proof is there? Here are our parchments, our padlocks, proving indisputably our money-safes to be *ours*, and you to have no business with them. Depart! It is impossible!" Nay, what wouldst thou thyself have us do? cry indignant readers. Nothing, my friends—till you have got a soul for yourselves again. Till then all things are "impossible." Till then I cannot even bid you buy, as the old Spartans would have done, two-pence worth of powder and lead, and compendiously shoot to death this poor Irish Widow. Even that is "impossible" for you. Nothing is left but that she prove her sisterhood by dying, and infecting you with typhus. Seventeen of you lying dead will not deny such proof that she *was* flesh of your flesh; and perhaps some of the living may lay it to heart.

"Impossible": of a certain two-legged animal with feathers it is said, if you draw a distinct chalk-circle round him, he sits imprisoned, as if girt with the iron ring of Fate, and will die there, though within sight of victuals, or sit in sick misery there, and be fatted to death. The name of this poor two-legged animal is—Goose; and they make of him, when well fattened, *Pâté de foie gras,* much prized by some! …

from CHAPTER 13—DEMOCRACY

If the Serene Highnesses and Majesties do not take note of that,[3] then, as I perceive, *that* will take note of itself! The time for levity, insincerity, and idle babble and play-acting, in all kinds, is gone by; it is a serious, grave time. Old long-vexed questions, not yet solved in logical words or parliamentary laws, are fast solving themselves in facts, somewhat unblessed to behold! This largest of questions, this question of Work and Wages, which ought, had we heeded Heaven's voice, to have begun two generations ago or more, cannot be delayed longer without hearing

[1] *Gehenna and the Pool* I.e., Hell.

[2] *Westminster Hall* Location of the British Houses of Parliament.

[3] *that* At the end of the previous chapter, Carlyle urged that "the proper epic of this world" should be "Tools and the Man," rather than "Arms and the Man," a reference to the opening line of Virgil's *Aeneid*: "Arma virumque cano" (Latin: "Of arms and the man I sing").

Earth's voice. "Labour" will verily need to be somewhat "organised," as they say—God knows with what difficulty. Man will actually need to have his debts and earnings a little better paid by man; which, let Parliaments speak of them or be silent of them, are eternally his due from man, and cannot, without penalty and at length not without death penalty,[1] be withheld. How much ought to cease among us straightway, how much ought to begin straightway, while the hours yet are!

Truly they are strange results to which this of leaving all to "Cash," of quietly shutting-up the God's Temple, and gradually opening wide-open the Mammon's Temple, with "Lassez-faire, and Every man for himself," have led us in these days! We have Upper, speaking Classes, who indeed do "speak" as never man spake before; the withered flimsiness, the godless baseness and barrenness of whose Speech might of itself indicate what kind of Doing and practical Governing went on under it! For Speech is the gaseous element out of which most kinds of Practice and Performance, especially all kinds of moral Performance, condense themselves, and take shape; as the one is, so will the other be. Descending, accordingly, into the Dumb Class in its Stockport Cellars and Poor-Law Bastilles, have we not to announce that they also are hitherto unexampled in the History of Adam's Posterity?

Life was never a May-game[2] for men. In all times the lot of the dumb millions born to toil was defaced with manifold sufferings, injustices, heavy burdens, avoidable and unavoidable—not play at all, but hard work that made the sinews sore and the heart sore. As bond-slaves, *villani, bordarii, sochemanni*,[3] nay indeed as dukes, earls, and kings, men were oftentimes made weary of their life, and had to say, in the sweat of their brow and of their soul, Behold, it is not sport, it is grim earnest, and our back can bear no more! Who knows not what massacrings and harryings there have been—grinding, long-continuing, unbearable injustices—till the heart had to rise in madness, and some "*Eu Sachsen, nimith euer sachses*, You Saxons, out with your gully-knives,[4] then!" You Saxons, some "arrestment," partial "arrestment of the Knaves and Dastards" has become indispensable! The page of Dryasdust[5] is heavy with such details.

And yet I will venture to believe that in no time, since the beginnings of Society, was the lot of those same dumb millions of toilers so entirely unbearable as it is even in the days now passing over us. It is not to die, or even to die of hunger, that makes a man wretched; many men have died; all men must die—the last exit of us all is in a Fire-Chariot of Pain.[6] But it is to live miserable we know not why; to work sore and yet gain nothing; to be heart-worn, weary, yet isolated, unrelated, girt-in with a cold universal Laissez-faire: it is to die slowly all our life long, imprisoned in a deaf, dead, Infinite Injustice, as in the accursed iron belly of a Phalaris' Bull![7] This is and remains forever intolerable to all men whom God has made. Do we wonder at French Revolutions, Chartisms, Revolts of Three Days? The times, if we will consider them, are really unexampled.

Never before did I hear of an Irish Widow reduced to "prove" her sisterhood by dying of typhus-fever and infecting seventeen "persons," saying in such undeniable way, "You *see* I was your sister!" Sisterhood, brotherhood, was often forgotten; but not till the rise of these ultimate Mammon and Shotbelt Gospels[8] did I ever see it so expressly denied. If no pious Lord or *Law-ward* would remember it, always some pious Lady ("*Hlaf-dig*,"[9] Benefactress, "*Loaf-giveress*," they say she is—blessings on her beautiful heart!) was there, with mild mother-voice and hand, to remember it; some

[1] *death penalty* Reference to the deaths caused by violent revolutions, such as the French Revolution.

[2] *May-game* Entertainment or performance (such as those traditionally making up part of the celebration on the first day of May).

[3] *villani … sochemanni* Classes of peasants in the feudal system.

[4] *gully-knives* Large household knives.

[5] *Dryasdust* Name given to a dull, pedantic historian, after the fictional antiquarian Dr. Jonas Dryasdust, to whom Walter Scott facetiously dedicated some of his novels.

[6] *last exit … Pain* See 2 Kings 2.11–12.

[7] *Phalaris' Bull* Phalaris, an ancient Sicilian tyrant, murdered wrongdoers by placing them in a brass bull that sat over a fire.

[8] *Shotbelt Gospels* I.e., principles of the landed aristocracy who sought to maintain their exclusive right to shoot game.

[9] *Hlaf-dig* I.e., loaf-giver.

pious thoughtful *Elder*, what we now call "Prester," *Presbyter* or "Priest," was there to put all men in mind of it, in the name of the God who had made all.

Not even in Black Dahomey[1] was it ever, I think, forgotten to the typhus-fever length. Mungo Park,[2] resourceless, had sunk down to die under the Negro Village-Tree, a horrible White object in the eyes of all. But in the poor Black Woman, and her daughter who stood aghast at him, whose earthly wealth and funded capital consisted of one small calabash of rice, there lived a heart richer than *Laissez-faire*: they, with a royal munificence, boiled their rice for him; they sang all night to him, spinning assiduous on their cotton distaffs, as he lay to sleep: "Let us pity the poor white man; no mother has he to fetch him milk, no sister to grind him corn!" Thou poor black Noble One, thou *Lady* too. Did not a God make thee too; was there not in thee too something of a God!

Gurth,[3] born thrall of Cedric the Saxon, has been greatly pitied by Dryasdust and others. Gurth, with the brass collar round his neck, tending Cedric's pigs in the glades of the wood, is not what I call an exemplar of human felicity. But Gurth, with the sky above him, with the free air and tinted boscage and umbrage[4] round him, and in him at least the certainty of supper and social lodging when he came home, Gurth to me seems happy, in comparison with many a Lancashire and Buckinghamshire man of these days, not born thrall of anybody! Gurth's brass collar did not gall him; Cedric *deserved* to be his master. The pigs were Cedric's, but Gurth too would get his parings of them. Gurth had the inexpressible satisfaction of feeling himself related indissolubly, though in a rude brass-collar way, to his fellow-mortals in this Earth. He had superiors, inferiors, equals. Gurth is now "emancipated" long since, has what we call "Liberty." Liberty, I am told, is a divine thing. Liberty when it becomes the "Liberty to die by starvation" is not so divine!

Liberty? The true liberty of a man, you would say, consisted in his finding out, or being forced to find out, the right path, and to walk thereon. To learn, or to be taught, what work he actually was able for, and then by permission, persuasion, and even compulsion, to set about doing of the same! That is his true blessedness, honour, "liberty," and maximum of wellbeing: if liberty be not that, I for one have small care about liberty. You do not allow a palpable madman to leap over precipices; you violate his liberty, you that are wise, and keep him, were it in strait-waistcoats, away from the precipices! Every stupid, every cowardly and foolish man is but a less palpable madman: his true liberty were that a wiser man, that any and every wiser man, could, by brass collars, or in whatever milder or sharper way, lay hold of him when he was going wrong, and order and compel him to go a little righter. O, if thou really art my *Senior*, Seigneur, my *Elder*, Presbyter or Priest—if thou art in very deed my *Wiser*, may a beneficent instinct lead and impel thee to "conquer" me, to command me! If thou do know better than I what is good and right, I conjure thee in the name of God, force me to do it; were it by never such brass collars, whips and handcuffs, leave me not to walk over precipices! That I have been called, by all the Newspapers, a "free man" will avail me little, if my pilgrimage have ended in death and wreck. O that the Newspapers had called me slave, coward, fool, or what it pleased their *sweet* voices to name me, and I had attained not death, but life! Liberty requires new definitions.

A conscious abhorrence and intolerance of Folly, of Baseness, Stupidity, Poltroonery[5] and all that brood of things, dwells deep in some men; still deeper in others an *un*conscious abhorrence and intolerance, clotted moreover by the beneficent Supreme Powers in what stout appetites, energies, egoisms so-called, are suitable to it. These latter are your Conquerors, Romans,

[1] *Black Dahomey* Area of West Africa, formerly belonging to the French, in which human sacrifice and cannibalism were rumored to take place.

[2] *Mungo Park* Scottish explorer and author of *Travels in the Interior of Africa* (1799), who was killed by Africans in Bussa in 1806.

[3] *Gurth* In Walter Scott's *Ivanhoe* (1819), Gurth is a serf (thrall) of the wealthy farmer Cedric.

[4] *boscage and umbrage* Grove and shade.

[5] *Poltroonery* Cowardliness; mean-spiritedness.

Normans, Russians, Indo-English; Founders of what we call Aristocracies. Which indeed have they not the most "divine right" to found—being themselves very truly Αριστοι[1] BRAVEST, BEST, and conquering generally a confused rabble of WORST, or at lowest, clearly enough, of WORSE? I think their divine right, tried, with affirmatory verdict, in the greatest Law-Court known to me, was good! A class of men who are dreadfully exclaimed against by Dryasdust, of whom nevertheless beneficent Nature has oftentimes had need, and may, alas, again have need.

When, across the hundredfold poor scepticisms, trivialisms and constitutional cobwebberies of Dryasdust, you catch any glimpse of a William the Conqueror, a Tancred of Hauteville[2] or suchlike, do you not discern veritably some rude outline of a true God-made King, whom not the Champion of England[3] cased in tin, but all Nature and the Universe were calling to the throne? It is absolutely necessary that he get thither. Nature does not mean her poor Saxon children to perish of obesity, stupor, or other malady, as yet. A stern Ruler and Line of Rulers therefore is called in—a stern but most beneficent *perpetual House-Surgeon* is by Nature herself called in, and even the appropriate *fees* are provided for him! Dryasdust talks lamentably about Hereward and the Fen Counties,[4] fate of Earl Waltheof,[5] Yorkshire and the North reduced to ashes—all which is undoubtedly lamentable. But even Dryasdust apprises me of one fact: "A child, in this William's reign, might have carried a purse of gold from end to end of England." My erudite friend, it is a fact which outweighs a thousand! Sweep away thy constitutional, sentimental, and other cobwebberies; look eye to eye, if thou still have any eye, in the face of this big burly William Bastard.[6] Thou wilt see a fellow of most flashing discernment, of most strong lion-heart, in whom, as it were, within a frame of oak and iron, the gods have planted the soul of "a man of genius"! Dost thou call that nothing? I call it an immense thing! Rage enough was in this Willelmus Conquaestor,[7] rage enough for his occasions—and yet the essential element of him, as of all such men, is not scorching *fire*, but shining illuminative *light*. Fire and light are strangely interchangeable; nay, at bottom, I have found them different forms of the same most godlike "elementary substance" in our world—a thing worth stating in these days. The essential element of this Conquaestor is, first of all, the most sun-eyed perception of what *is* really what on this God's-Earth—which, thou wilt find, does mean at bottom "Justice," and "Virtues" not a few—*Conformity* to what the Maker has seen good to make; that, I suppose, will mean Justice and a Virtue or two?

Dost thou think Willelmus Conquaestor would have tolerated ten years' jargon, one hour's jargon, on the propriety of killing Cotton manufactures by partridge[8] Corn Laws? I fancy, this was not the man to knock out of his night's-rest with nothing but a noisy bedlamism[9] in your mouth! "Assist us still better to bush the partridges; strangle Plugson[10] who spins the shirts?"—"*Par la Splendeur de Dieu!*"[11]—Dost thou think Willelmus Conquaestor, in this new time, with Steamengine Captains of Industry on one hand of him, and Joe-

[1] *Αριστοι* Greek: Aristocrats.

[2] *William the Conqueror* King William I of England (who ruled from 1066 to 1087) was named "the Conqueror" after he won the throne from King Harold at the Battle of Hastings in 1066; *Tancred of Hauteville* Norman Crusader (1076–1112).

[3] *Champion of England* Official at the coronation ceremony who acts as champion or defender of the monarch before any who challenges his or her right to the throne.

[4] *Hereward … Counties* Anglo-Saxon who rebelled against William I and organized uprisings in Lincolnshire and its surrounding counties (known collectively as the "Fen Counties" because of their marshland).

[5] *Earl Waltheof* Anglo-Saxon who was executed for treason by William I, but was later believed innocent and regarded as a martyr.

[6] *William Bastard* William I was an illegitimate son of Robert I, Duke of Normandy.

[7] *Willelmus Conquaestor* Latin: William the Conqueror.

[8] *partridge* Reference to the aristocracy's attachment to hunting game.

[9] *bedlamism* Something characteristic of madness—specifically, of the Hospital of St. Mary of Bethlehem (referred to as "Bedlam"), an overcrowded and frenetic London asylum.

[10] *Plugson* Fictional industrial firm to which Carlyle refers several times throughout *Past and Present*.

[11] *Par la … Dieu* French: By the splendor of God.

Manton Captains of Idleness on the other, would have doubted which *was* really the BEST; which did deserve strangling, and which not?

I have a certain indestructible regard for Willelmus Conquaestor. A resident House-Surgeon, provided by Nature for her beloved English People, and even furnished with the requisite fees, as I said; for he by no means felt himself doing Nature's work, this Willelmus, but his own work exclusively! And his own work withal it was, informed "*par la Splendeur de Dieu!*" I say, it is necessary to get the work out of such a man, however harsh that be! When a world, not yet doomed for death, is rushing down to ever-deeper Baseness and Confusion, it is a dire necessity of Nature's to bring in her ARISTOCRACIES, her BEST, even by forcible methods. When their descendants or representatives cease entirely to *be* the Best, Nature's poor world will very soon rush down again to Baseness; and it becomes a dire necessity of Nature's to cast them out. Hence French Revolutions, Five-point Charters,[1] Democracies, and a mournful list of *Etceteras*, in these our afflicted times.

To what extent Democracy has now reached, how it advances irresistible with ominous, ever-increasing speed, he that will open his eyes on any province of human affairs may discern. Democracy is everywhere the inexorable demand of these ages, swiftly fulfilling itself. From the thunder of Napoleon battles, to the jabbering of Open-vestry in St. Mary Axe,[2] all things announce Democracy. A distinguished man, whom some of my readers will hear again with pleasure, thus writes to me what in these days he notes from the Wahngasse of Weissnichtwo,[3] where our London fashions seem to be in full vogue. Let us hear the Herr Teufelsdröckh[4] again, were it but the smallest word!

Democracy, which means despair of finding any Heroes to govern you, and contented putting-up with the want of them, alas, thou too, *mein Lieber*,[5] seest well how close it is of kin to *Atheism*, and other sad *Isms*: he who discovers no God whatever, how shall he discover Heroes, the visible Temples of God? Strange enough meanwhile it is to observe with what thoughtlessness, here in our rigidly Conservative Country, men rush into Democracy with full cry. …

… It may be admitted that Democracy, in all meanings of the word, is in full career; irresistible by any Ritter Kauderwalsch or other Son of Adam, as times go. "Liberty" is a thing men are determined to have.

But truly, as I had to remark in the meanwhile, "the liberty of not being oppressed by your fellow man" is an indispensable, yet one of the most insignificant fractional, parts of Human Liberty. No man oppresses thee, can bid thee fetch or carry, come or go, without reason shown. True, from all men thou art emancipated; but from Thyself and from the Devil—? No man, wiser, unwiser, can make thee come or go; but thy own futilities, bewilderments, thy false appetites for Money, Windsor Georges[6] and suchlike? No man oppresses thee, O free and independent Franchiser; but does not this stupid Porter-pot[7] oppress thee? No Son of Adam can bid thee come or go; but this absurd Pot of Heavy-wet,[8] this can and does! Thou art the thrall not of Cedric the Saxon, but of thy own brutal appetites and this scoured dish of liquor. And thou pratest of thy "liberty"? Thou entire blockhead!

Heavy-wet and gin; alas, these are not the only kinds of thraldom. Thou who walkest in a vain show, looking out with ornamental dilettante sniff and serene supremacy at all Life and all Death; and amblest jauntily, perking up thy poor talk into crotchets,[9] thy poor

[1] *Five-point Charters* The "People's Charter" (on which the Chartist movement was based) actually had six points, all concerning suffrage.

[2] *jabbering … Axe* I.e., the bickering of the rate-paying parishioners, who were generally allowed to express their opinions on temporal affairs of the Church.

[3] *Wahngasse of Weissnichtwo* German: Delusion alley of I-know-not-where.

[4] *Herr Teufelsdröckh* Carlyle writes about this fictional German philosopher, Diogenes Teufelsdröckh, in *Sartor Resartus*. He is said to be the author of *Clothes: Their Origin and Influence*, and his name, in German, literally means "God-born devil's dung."

[5] *mein Lieber* German: my Dear.

[6] *Windsor Georges* I.e., the pomp of royalty.

[7] *Porter-pot* Vessel of porter, a dark beer.

[8] *Heavy-wet* Malt liquor.

[9] *crotchets* Odd notions; perverse conceits.

conduct into fatuous somnambulisms; and *art* as an "enchanted Ape" under God's sky, where thou mightest have been a man, had proper Schoolmasters and Conquerors, and Constables with cat-o'-nine tails,[1] been vouchsafed thee—dost thou call that "liberty"? Or your unreposing Mammon-worshipper again, driven, as if by Galvanisms,[2] by Devils and Fixed Ideas, who rises early and sits late, chasing the impossible, straining every faculty to "fill himself with the east wind"[3]—how merciful were it, could you, by mild persuasion, or by the severest tyranny so-called, check him in his mad path, and turn him into a wiser one! All painful tyranny, in that case again, were but mild "surgery," the pain of it cheap, as health and life, instead of galvanism and fixed-idea, are cheap at any price.

Sure enough, of all paths a man could strike into, there *is*, at any given moment, a *best path* for every man; a thing which, here and now, it were of all things *wisest* for him to do—which, could he be but led or driven to do, he were then doing "like a man," as we phrase it, all men and gods agreeing with him, the whole Universe virtually exclaiming Well-done to him! His success, in such case, were complete; his felicity a maximum. This path, to find this path and walk in it, is the one thing needful for him. Whatsoever forwards him in that, let it come to him even in the shape of blows and spurnings, is liberty; whatsoever hinders him, were it wardmotes,[4] open-vestries, pollbooths, tremendous cheers, rivers of heavy-wet, is slavery.

The notion that a man's liberty consists in giving his vote at election-hustings,[5] and saying, "Behold, now I too have my twenty-thousandth part of a Talker in our National Palaver;[6] will not all the gods be good to me?" is one of the pleasantest! Nature nevertheless is kind at present, and puts it into the heads of many, almost of all. The liberty especially which has to purchase itself by social isolation, and each man standing separate from the other, having no business with him but a cash-account, this is such a liberty as the Earth seldom saw—as the Earth will not long put up with, recommend it how you may. This liberty turns out, before it have long continued in action, with all men flinging up their caps round it, to be, for the Working Millions, a liberty to die by want of food; for the Idle Thousands and Units, alas, a still more fatal liberty to live in want of work, to have no earnest duty to do in this God's-World anymore. What becomes of a man in such predicament? Earth's Laws are silent, and Heaven's speak in a voice which is not heard. No work, and the ineradicable need of work, give rise to new very wondrous life-philosophies, new very wondrous life-practices! Dilettantism, Pococurantism, Beau-Brummelism,[7] with perhaps an occasional, half-mad, protesting burst of Byronism, establish themselves; at the end of a certain period, if you go back to "the Dead Sea," there is, say our Moslem friends, a very strange "Sabbath day" transacting itself there![8] Brethren, we know but imperfectly yet, after ages of Constitutional Government, what Liberty and Slavery are.

Democracy, the chase of Liberty in that direction shall go its full course, unrestrainable by him of Pferdefuss-Quacksalber,[9] or any of *his* household. The Toiling Millions of Mankind, in most vital need and passionate instinctive desire of Guidance, shall cast away False-Guidance and hope, for an hour, that No-Guid-

[1] *cat-o'-nine tails* Whip with nine lashes.

[2] *Galvanisms* Applications of electricity.

[3] *east wind* The east wind was proverbially harmful to one's health. In the Bible it is seen as destructive; the wind blowing from the east onto Palestine brings dry, hot air from the desert, and is harmful to crops.

[4] *wardmotes* Meetings of the citizens of a ward, or area of the city.

[5] *election-hustings* I.e., election proceedings. The husting was a temporary platform on which candidates for Parliament stood to address electors.

[6] *Palaver* Rigamarole, prolonged and tedious discussion.

[7] *Pococurantism* Attitude of indifference or unconcern, from an Italian expression describing an indifferent person; *Beau-Brummelism* Obsession with fashion. George Bryan Brummel (known as "Beau Brummel") was a leader of fashion in Regency England.

[8] *there is ... there* According to an Islamic myth, a tribe living on the banks of the Dead Sea were turned into apes after refusing to acknowledge Moses' prophecies.

[9] *Pferdefuss-Quacksalber* German: Horsefoot-Charletan. Carlyle invented this name to satirize Sir Robert Peel, the Conservative Prime Minister.

ance will suffice them; but it can be for an hour only. The smallest item of human Slavery is the oppression of man by his Mock Superiors; the palpablest, but I say at bottom the smallest. Let him shake off such oppression, trample it indignantly under his feet; I blame him not, I pity and commend him. But oppression by your Mock Superiors well shaken off, the grand problem yet remains to solve: that of finding government by your Real Superiors! Alas, how shall we ever learn the solution of that, benighted, bewildered, sniffing, sneering, god-forgetting unfortunates we are? It is a work for centuries, to be taught us by tribulations, confusions, insurrections, obstructions; who knows if not by conflagration and despair! It is a lesson inclusive of all other lessons; the hardest of all lessons to learn.

One thing I do know: those Apes, chattering on the branches by the Dead Sea, never got it learned, but chatter there to this day. To them no Moses need come a second time; a thousand Moseses would be but so many painted Phantasms, interesting Fellow-Apes of new strange aspect, whom they would "invite to dinner," be glad to meet with in lion-soirées. To them the voice of Prophecy,[1] of heavenly monition, is quite ended. They chatter here, all Heaven shut to them, to the end of the world. The unfortunates! Oh, what is dying of hunger, with honest tools in your hand, with a manful purpose in your heart, and much real labour lying round you done, in comparison? You honestly quit your tools, quit a most muddy confused coil of sore work, short rations, of sorrow, dispiritments, and contradictions, having now honestly done with it all, and await, not entirely in a distracted manner, what the Supreme Powers, and the Silences and the Eternities may have to say to you.

A second thing I know: this lesson will have to be learned—under penalties! England will either learn it, or England also will cease to exist among Nations. England will either learn to reverence its Heroes, and discriminate them from its Sham-Heroes and Valets and gas-lighted Histrios,[1] and to prize them as the audible God's-voice, amid all inane jargons and temporary market-cries, and say to them with heart-loyalty, "Be ye King and Priest, and Gospel and Guidance for us," or else England will continue to worship new and ever-new forms of Quackhood—and so, with what resiliences and reboundings matters little, go down to the Father of Quacks! Can I dread such things of England? Wretched, thickeyed, gross-hearted mortals, why will ye worship lies, and "Stuffed Clothes-suits created by the ninth-parts of men!"[2] It is not your purses that suffer, your farm-rents, your commerces, your mill-revenues, loud as ye lament over these; no, it is not these alone, but a far deeper than these: it is your souls that lie dead, crushed down under despicable Nightmares, Atheisms, Brain-fumes, and are not souls at all, but mere succedanea[3] for *salt* to keep your bodies and their appetites from putrefying! Your cotton-spinning and thrice-miraculous mechanism, what is this too, by itself, but a larger kind of Animalism? Spiders can spin, Beavers can build and show contrivance, the Ant lays-up accumulation of capital, and has, for aught I know, a Bank of Antland. If there is no soul in man higher than all that, did it reach to sailing on the cloud-rack and spinning sea-sand, then I say, man is but an animal, a more cunning kind of brute; he has no soul, but only a succedaneum for salt. Whereupon, seeing himself to be truly of the beasts that perish, he ought to admit it, I think—and also straightway universally to kill himself, and so, in a manlike manner at least *end*, and wave these brute-worlds *his* dignified farewell! …

from BOOK 4

CHAPTER 4—CAPTAINS OF INDUSTRY

If I believed that Mammonism with its adjuncts was to continue henceforth the one serious principle of our existence, I should reckon it idle to solicit remedial measures from any Government, the disease being insusceptible of remedy. Government can do much, but it can in no wise[4] do all. Government, as the most

[1] *Histrios* Stage actors, used here in the derogatory sense of "buffoons."

[2] *the ninth-parts of men* I.e., worthless men.

[3] *succedanea* Substitutes.

[4] *wise* Way.

conspicuous object in Society, is called upon to give signal of what shall be done; and, in many ways, to preside over, further, and command the doing of it. But the Government cannot do, by all its signaling and commanding, what the Society is radically indisposed to do. In the long-run every Government is the exact symbol of its People, with their wisdom and unwisdom; we have to say, Like People like Government. The main substance of this immense Problem of Organising Labour, and first of all of Managing the Working Classes, will, it is very clear, have to be solved by those who stand practically in the middle of it, by those who themselves work and preside over work. Of all that can be enacted by any Parliament in regard to it, the germs must already lie potentially extant in those two Classes, who are to obey such enactment. A Human Chaos *in* which there is no light, you vainly attempt to irradiate by light shed *on* it; order never can arise there.

But it is my firm conviction that the "Hell of England" will *cease* to be that of "not making money," that we shall get a nobler Hell and a nobler Heaven! I anticipate light *in* the Human Chaos, glimmering, shining more and more, under manifold true signals from without That light shall shine. Our deity no longer being Mammon, O Heavens, each man will then say to himself, "Why such deadly haste to make money? I shall not go to Hell, even if I do not make money! There is another Hell, I am told!" Competition, at railway-speed, in all branches of commerce and work will then abate; good felt-hats for the head, in every sense, instead of seven-feet lath-and-plaster hats on wheels, will then be discoverable! Bubble-periods,[1] with their panics and commercial crises, will again become infrequent; steady modest industry will take the place of gambling speculation. To be a noble Master, among noble Workers, will again be the first ambition with some few; to be a rich Master only the second. How the Inventive Genius of England, with the whirr of its bobbins and billy-rollers[2] shoved somewhat into the backgrounds of the brain, will contrive and devise, not cheaper produce exclusively, but fairer distribution of the produce at its present cheapness! By degrees, we shall again have a Society with something of Heroism in it, something of Heaven's Blessing on it; we shall again have, as my German friend[3] asserts, "instead of Mammon-Feudalism with unsold cotton-shirts and Preservation of the Game, noble just Industrialism and Government by the Wisest!"

It is with the hope of awakening here and there a British man to know himself for a man and divine soul, that a few words of parting admonition, to all persons to whom the Heavenly Powers have lent power of any kind in this land, may now be addressed. And first to those same Master-Workers, Leaders of Industry, who stand nearest and in fact powerfulest, though not most prominent, being as yet in too many senses a Virtuality rather than an Actuality.

The Leaders of Industry, if Industry is ever to be led, are virtually the Captains of the World; if there be no nobleness in them, there will never be an Aristocracy more. But let the Captains of Industry consider: once again, are they born of other clay than the old Captains of Slaughter, doomed forever to be no Chivalry, but a mere gold-plated *Doggery*—what the French well name *Canaille*, "Doggery" with more or less gold carrion at its disposal? Captains of Industry are the true Fighters, henceforth recognisable as the only true ones—Fighters against Chaos, Necessity, and the Devils and Jötuns[4]—and lead on Mankind in that great, and alone true and universal warfare; the stars in their courses fighting for them, and all Heaven and all Earth saying audibly, Well done! Let the Captains of Industry retire into their own hearts, and ask solemnly, If there is nothing but vulturous hunger for fine wines, valet reputation, and gilt carriages discoverable there? Of hearts made by the Almighty God I will not believe such a thing. Deep-hidden under wretchedest god-forgetting Cants, Epicurisms, Dead-Sea Apisms, forgotten as under foulest fat

[1] *Bubble-periods* Violent fluctuations in the stock market.

[2] *bobbins* Wooden spools or cylinders on which cotton or thread is wound; *billy-rollers* Machines for preparing cotton or wool for spinning.

[3] *German friend* Reference to Teufelsdröckh, the protagonist of *Sartor Resartus* (1833–34).

[4] *Jötuns* Members of a mythological Norse race of giants.

Lethe[1] mud and weeds, there is yet, in all hearts born into this God's-World, a spark of the Godlike slumbering. Awake, O nightmare sleepers; awake, arise, or be forever fallen![2] This is not playhouse poetry, it is sober fact. Our England, our world, cannot live as it is. It will connect itself with a God again, or go down with nameless throes and fire-consummation to the Devils. Thou who feelest aught[3] of such a Godlike stirring in thee, any faintest intimation of it as through heavy-laden dreams, follow *it*, I conjure thee. Arise, save thyself, be one of those that save thy country.

Buccaneers, Chactaw Indians,[4] whose supreme aim in fighting is that they may get the scalps, the money, that they may amass scalps and money—out of such came no Chivalry, and never will! Out of such came only gore and wreck, infernal rage and misery; desperation quenched in annihilation. Behold it, I bid thee; behold there, and consider! What is it that thou have a hundred thousand-pound bills laid-up in thy strong-room, a hundred scalps hung-up in thy wigwam? I value not them or thee. Thy scalps and thy thousand-pound bills are as yet nothing, if no nobleness from within irradiate them; if no Chivalry, in action, or in embryo ever struggling towards birth and action, be there.

Love of men cannot be bought by cash-payment, and without love men cannot endure to be together. You cannot lead a Fighting World without having it regimented, chivalried; the thing, in a day, becomes impossible. All men in it, the highest at first, the very lowest at last, discern consciously, or by a noble instinct, this necessity. And can you any more continue to lead a Working World unregimented, anarchic? I answer, and the Heavens and Earth are now answering, No! The thing becomes not "in a day" impossible; but in some two generations it does. Yes, when fathers and mothers, in Stockport hunger-cellars, begin to eat their children; and Irish widows have to prove their relationship by dying of typhus-fever; and amid Governing "Corporations of the Best and Bravest," busy to preserve their game by "bushing,"[5] dark millions of God's human creatures start up in mad Chartisms, impracticable Sacred-Months,[6] and Manchester Insurrections; and there is a virtual Industrial Aristocracy as yet only half-alive, spell-bound amid money-bags and ledgers; and an actual Idle Aristocracy seemingly near dead in somnolent delusions, in trespasses and double-barrels, "sliding," as on inclined planes, which every new year they *soap* with new Hansard's-jargon under God's sky, and so are "sliding," ever faster, towards a "scale"[7] and balance-scale whereon is written *Thou art found Wanting*[8]—in such days, after a generation or two, I say, it does become, even to the low and simple, very palpably impossible! No Working World, any more than a Fighting World, can be led on without a noble Chivalry of Work, and laws and fixed rules which follow out of that, far nobler than any Chivalry of Fighting was. As an anarchic multitude on mere Supply-and-demand, it is becoming inevitable that we dwindle in horrid suicidal convulsion and self-abrasion, frightful to the imagination, into *Chactaw* Workers. With wigwams and scalps,

[1] *Epicurisms* Pursuits of sensual pleasures, luxury, and ease, so named after the philosophical system of third-century BCE Greek thinker Epicurus; *Dead-Sea Apisms* Muslim fable in which a community living by the Dead Sea were transformed into apes on account of their failure to listen to Moses, God's prophet; *Lethe* River of forgetfulness in Hades, the classical underworld.

[2] *awake … fallen!* See Milton's *Paradise Lost*, 1.330.

[3] *aught* Anything.

[4] *Chactaw Indians* The Choctaw, who formerly inhabited central and southern Mississippi and southwest Alabama, were among many Native American tribes to practice scalping in warfare. Scalping became even more common, however, as the various colonial settlers offered rewards for the scalps of those who resisted them. In the nineteenth century, many Choctaw were forcibly removed from their lands in what is now Mississippi and made to relocate to Oklahoma.

[5] *bushing* Placing bushes on the land in such a way as to prevent poachers from using nets to sweep for game.

[6] *Sacred-Months* General strikes. At the 1839 Chartist Convention, there was widespread discussion of having a general strike for a month's duration.

[7] *Idle Aristocracy … "scale"* Deluded and idle aristocrats obsess over game laws and possible trespassers on their game preserves, and over the "sliding scale" that sets the tariffs on grain (which were created to, among other things, enrich aristocratic landlords). To keep these benefits flowing they "soap" (with flattery) the scale in parliament ("Hansard's-jargon" refers to Parliamentary debate, the official report of which is known as "Hansard").

[8] *Thou … Wanting* See Daniel 5.27.

with palaces and thousand-pound bills, with savagery, depopulation, chaotic desolation! Good Heavens, will not one French Revolution and Reign of Terror suffice us, but must there be two? There will be two if needed; there will be twenty if needed; there will be precisely as many as are needed. The Laws of Nature will have themselves fulfilled. That is a thing certain to me.

Your gallant battle-hosts and work-hosts, as the others did, will need to be made loyally yours; they must and will be regulated, methodically secured in their just share of conquest under you—joined with you in veritable brotherhood, sonhood, by quite other and deeper ties than those of temporary day's wages! How would mere red-coated regiments, to say nothing of chivalries, fight for you, if you could discharge them on the evening of the battle, on payment of the stipulated shillings—and they discharge you on the morning of it! Chelsea Hospitals,[1] pensions, promotions, rigorous lasting covenant on the one side and on the other, are indispensable even for a hired fighter. The Feudal Baron, much more—how could he subsist with mere temporary mercenaries round him at sixpence a day, ready to go over to the other side, if sevenpence were offered? He could not have subsisted, and his noble instinct saved him from the necessity of even trying! The Feudal Baron had a Man's Soul in him, to which anarchy, mutiny, and the other fruits of temporary mercenaries were intolerable; he had never been a Baron otherwise, but had continued a Chactaw and Buccaneer. He felt it precious, and at last it became habitual, and his fruitful enlarged existence included it as a necessity, to have men round him who in heart loved him; whose life he watched over with rigour yet with love; who were prepared to give their life for him, if need came. It was beautiful; it was human! Man lives not otherwise, nor can live contented, anywhere or anywhen. Isolation is the sum-total of wretchedness to man. To be cut off, to be left solitary; to have a world alien, not your world, all a hostile camp for you, not a home at all, of hearts and faces who are yours, whose you are! It is the frightfulest enchantment, too truly a work of the Evil One. To have neither superior, nor inferior, nor equal, united manlike to you. Without father, without child, without brother. Man knows no sadder destiny. "How is each of us," exclaims Jean Paul,[2] "so lonely in the wide bosom of the All!" Encased each as in his transparent "ice-palace," our brother visible in his, making signals and gesticulations to us—visible, but forever unattainable; on his bosom we shall never rest, nor he on ours. It was not a God that did this; no!

Awake, ye noble Workers, warriors in the one true war; all this must be remedied. It is you who are already half-alive, whom I will welcome into life, whom I will conjure, in God's name, to shake off your enchanted sleep, and live wholly! Cease to count scalps, gold-purses; not in these lies your or our salvation. Even these, if you count only these, will not long be left. Let buccaneering be put far from you; alter, speedily abrogate all laws of the buccaneers, if you would gain any victory that shall endure. Let God's justice, let pity, nobleness and manly valour, with more gold-purses or with fewer, testify themselves in this your brief Life-transit to all the Eternities, the Gods and Silences. It is to you I call; for ye are not dead, ye are already half-alive; there is in you a sleepless dauntless energy, the prime-matter of all nobleness in man. Honour to you in your kind. It is to you I call; ye know at least this, That the mandate of God to His creature man is Work! The future Epic of the World rests not with those that are near dead, but with those that are alive, and those that are coming into life.

Look around you. Your world-hosts are all in mutiny, in confusion, destitution; on the eve of fiery wreck and madness! They will not march farther for you, on the sixpence a day and supply-and-demand principle; they will not, nor ought they, nor can they. Ye shall reduce them to order, begin reducing them. To order, to just subordination; noble loyalty in return for noble guidance. Their souls are driven nigh mad; let yours be sane and ever saner. Not as a bewildered bewildering mob, but as a firm regimented mass, with real captains over them, will these men march any more.

[1] *Chelsea Hospitals* Homes such as the Chelsea Royal Hospital, for elderly or disabled veterans.

[2] *Jean Paul* German writer Jean Paul Richter (1763–1825).

All human interests, combined human endeavours, and social growths in this world, have, at a certain stage of their development, required organising; and Work, the grandest of human interests, does now require it.

God knows, the task will be hard; but no noble task was ever easy. This task will wear away your lives, and the lives of your sons and grandsons; but for what purpose, if not for tasks like this, were lives given to men? Ye shall cease to count your thousand-pound scalps; the noble of you shall cease! Nay, the very scalps, as I say, will not long be left if you count only these. Ye shall cease wholly to be barbarous vulturous Chactaws, and become noble European Nineteenth-Century Men. Ye shall know that Mammon, in never such gigs[1] and flunky "respectabilities," is not the alone God, that of himself he is but a Devil, and even a Brute-god.

Difficult? Yes, it will be difficult. The short-fibre cotton, that too was difficult. The waste cotton-shrub, long useless, disobedient, as the thistle by the way-side—have ye not conquered it, made it into beautiful bandana webs, white woven shirts for men, bright-tinted air-garments wherein flit goddesses? Ye have shivered mountains asunder, made the hard iron pliant to you as soft putty; the Forest-giants, Marsh-jötuns bear sheaves of golden-grain; Aegir[2] the Sea-demon himself stretches his back for a sleek highway to you, and on Firehorses and Windhorses ye career. Ye are most strong. Thor[3] red-bearded, with his blue sun-eyes, with his cheery heart and strong thunder-hammer, he and you have prevailed. Ye are most strong, ye Sons of the icy North, of the far East—far marching from your rugged Eastern Wildernesses, hitherward from the gray Dawn of Time! Ye are Sons of the *Jötun-land*, the land of Difficulties Conquered. Difficult? You must try this thing. Once try it with the understanding that it will and shall have to be done. Try it as ye try the paltrier thing, making of money! I will bet on you once more, against all Jötuns, Tailor-gods, Double-barrelled Law-wards, and Denizens of Chaos whatsoever!

—1843

[1] *gigs* Two-wheeled carriages. Ownership of a gig was a sign of social prestige.

[2] *Aegir* Norse god of the sea.

[3] *Thor* Norse god of thunder and rain.

Ireland, Scotland, and Wales: Literary Currents in the Long Nineteenth Century

For those studying English history and literary history, there is some logic to seeing the 1830s as a turning point. In English history, the tumultuous events of the early and mid 1830s—chief among them the Reform Bill of 1832 and the abolition of slavery in 1833–34—give plausibility to the notion that Victoria's accession to the throne in 1837 was part of the dawn of a new era. And in literary history—to grossly oversimplify—the 1830s mark a divide on one side of which is Romanticism and revolution (with poetry the dominant genre), and on the other side of which is realism (with prose fiction the dominant genre). The Reform Bill was of some importance for Scotland and Wales too, but it is far from obvious that the 1830s mark a natural divide in the history or the literary history of Ireland, Scotland, or Wales.

For Ireland in particular, it seems more natural to think in terms of what historians of Europe often refer to as the long nineteenth century—the period from the beginning of the French Revolution in 1789 to the beginning of the First World War in 1914. For Ireland the revolt that was in part inspired by the French, as well as aided by them—the United Irishmen Rebellion of 1798 ("the year of the French")—marks a much more natural start to a historical era than do the 1830s, just as the outbreak of World War I (and the Easter Rising of 1916) mark a more natural end to it than does the end of the nineteenth century or the end of Victoria's reign. (The tumultuous history of Ireland over this period—the rebellion of '98, the Acts of Union, Catholic Emancipation, the Great Irish Famine, and the long struggle over Home Rule—is accorded a substantial Contexts section in the website component of this anthology.)

One thread above all—aside from a shared linguistic background—ties together the literatures of Ireland, Scotland, and Wales in the medieval era and into the early modern period: the presence of a bardic tradition. A *bard* (Gaelic spelling) or *bardd* (Welsh spelling) was a poet and storyteller by profession; bards underwent long training in their art, and became adept at writing in a variety of genres, each with its own conventions as to meter and rhyme as well as appropriate subject matter and tone. Bards wrote elegies, eulogies and other praise poems, satires, and love poetry. They were well versed in history and legend, and were expected to be able to compose new work in these areas too (as well as to know and to be able to recite traditional works). Typically they worked for hire, under the patronage of a chief or nobleman—though during some eras they might move from place to place or compose work for more than one patron. Though it had died out as a living tradition by the eighteenth century, the idea of the bard carried on as a cultural reference point—and to some extent as a rallying cry.

Nowhere had the bardic tradition been stronger than in Ireland—and in no other area did it survive so long: the last great work in Irish in the bardic tradition is a 1,026 line narrative poem by Brian Merriman (1747–1805), *Cúirt an Mheon-Oíche*, composed in or around 1780. Usually given the title *The Midnight Court* in English translations (of which there at least eleven), the poem is by turns satirical, erotic, and broadly comical; the "court" in question is run by fairies trying to reach a judgment concerning the complaints of Irish women who say they have been suffering from sexual neglect (as their husbands think only of war and politics).

Many have judged *The Midnight Court* to be among the finest of all works of Irish poetry, but it marks the end of a line. By the early nineteenth century the old "hedge schools" were dying out and formal education was becoming available to Catholics; as in Protestant schools, formal schooling was conducted entirely in English; not surprisingly, therefore, nineteenth-century Irish poetry—and Irish literature generally—is almost entirely dominated by English-language writing. A widespread opinion has long been (as Thomas Kinsella put it in a widely quoted 1971 essay) that this change represents a virtually unmitigated disaster; the "dullness of the nineteenth century" in Irish literature in general, and Irish poetry in particular, seems to Kinsella so extreme that he characterizes the period between the age of Merriman and the age of Yeats as, in literary terms, "one of total silence." When it comes to individual writers, though, even critics such as Kinsella acknowledge some merit in the established canon of mid-nineteenth-century writers—a group that includes James Clarence Mangan, Samuel Ferguson, and William Allingham. They acknowledge too the social and political significance of the century's literature. In this regard, a pivotal development was the 1842 founding of *The Nation,* a weekly newspaper that had extraordinary ambitions. Founded by two Catholics (Charles Gavan Duffy, its first editor, and John Blake Dillon) and a Protestant (Thomas Davis), it aimed, in the words of the prospectus for the publication, to foster

> a nationality which will not only raise our people from their poverty, by securing to them the blessings of a domestic legislature, but inflame and purify them with a lofty and heroic love of country ... a nationality which may come to be stamped upon our manners, our literature, and our deeds—a nationality which may embrace Protestant, Catholic ... a nationality which would be recognized by the world, and sanctified by wisdom, virtue, and time.

The magnitude of the struggles that the Irish faced over the course of the long nineteenth century is truly extraordinary: the struggle for better living conditions for tenant farmers and for the poor generally; the struggle for better education; the fight over tithes and, more broadly, the struggle for Catholic emancipation; the struggle for Home Rule; the wrenching effects of mass emigration; and, most dramatic and heart-wrenching of all, the struggle for survival during the famine of 1845–47, when over a million people are estimated to have died of starvation or famine-related disease, and perhaps twice that number were forced to emigrate. Given the degree to which these struggles were all a part of a larger struggle against the centuries-long history of English oppression, it should not surprise us that so much of Irish literature during the long nineteenth century is infused with political content. From the late nineteenth century through to the late twentieth, it was the habit of many critics and literary historians to regard such content in a negative light—to disparage the literary qualities of works that broadcast a clear political agenda. So it was, for example, that the novels of Sydney Owenson (included in the website component of this anthology), whose lively "national tales" had an overtly political purpose, were frequently dismissed as "escapist" and the novels of William Carleton as "polemical." To some extent such views have persisted into the twenty-first century. Lucy Collins, for example, reaches the following conclusion in the introduction to her fine anthology of the work of nineteenth- and twentieth-century women poets: "while engagement with the Gaelic past had a largely revivifying effect on Irish writing in the nineteenth century, an exclusive focus on nationalist feeling generally detracted from the aesthetic value of the poetry, privileging political conviction over artistic complexity." On the whole, however, critics and literary historians have come increasingly to the view that political conviction and artistic merit are far from mutually exclusive—

and that a good deal of both is to be found in Irish literature of the nineteenth century. To be sure, they acknowledge the dearth of famous names over the period between the great Irish writers of the late eighteenth and early nineteenth centuries (Merriman, and also the Anglo-Irish writers Richard Brinsley Sheridan and Maria Edgeworth) and the extraordinary cluster of major writers in the very late nineteenth century and the first half of the twentieth (Bernard Shaw and Oscar Wilde as well as W.B. Yeats, James Joyce, John Millington Synge, Sean O'Casey, and Samuel Beckett). But there is an increasing interest in exploring the writings of the nineteenth-century Irish writers who inhabit the space between those two clusters—and an increasing willingness to acknowledge that much of their work is extraordinarily interesting as well as remarkably varied.

For most of the twentieth century, Irish literature in the nineteenth and early twentieth centuries was often taken to be an almost entirely male preserve (Kinsella's 1986 *Oxford Book of Irish Verse*, for example, includes no nineteenth- or twentieth-century women writers). Over the past generation or two, however—as prominent modern writers such as Eavan Boland and Nuala Ní Dhomhnaill have spoken up powerfully against "the traditional exclusion" of women from Irish literary history—it has come to be increasingly appreciated in recent decades that the work of writers such as Emily Lawless, Katherine Tynan, Eve Gore-Booth, and Winnifred Mary Letts was in fact just as accomplished—and just as informed politically—as the work of Mangan, Ferguson, or Davis had been, while, arguably, being broader in scope. It should perhaps not surprise us that open-minded inquiry brings to light as many accomplished women writers as their male counterparts during this period, for—unlike in Scotland—education was not a male preserve. By the 1870s, indeed, there were as many female as male students in Irish schools.

That there are fewer Scottish authors represented in this section than there are Irish or Welsh authors is a reflection not of any ebb in the importance of Scottish writers to British literature over the course of the long nineteenth century—quite the reverse. From the late eighteenth to the early twentieth centuries no fewer than ten Scottish writers (Robert Burns, Joanna Baillie, James Hogg, Sir Walter Scott, James Macpherson, Thomas Carlyle, Margaret Oliphant, James Thomson, Robert Louis Stevenson, and Sir Arthur Conan Doyle) are accorded author entries in this anthology—a remarkable number, given that the Scots made up no more than 10 per cent of the British population during this period. And that list does not include several outstanding writers whose work is not easy to anthologize—such as the novelist Susan Ferrier, the fantasy writer George Macdonald, and J.M. Barrie, creator of *Peter Pan*.

Literature is in no way an extraordinary case here; from the great figures of the Scottish Enlightenment in the mid eighteenth century—Adam Smith and David Hume chief among them—through to the early years of the twentieth century, Scottish notables make up an outsized proportion of the leading figures in any number of fields. In science and technology James Watt, George Stevenson, and John McAdam revolutionized industry and transportation with the steam engine, the modern railway, and the gravel roadbed; in engineering Thomas Telford broke new ground in his designs for bridges and canals (and it was Scottish engineer and railway builder Sandford Fleming who invented standard time); Joseph Lister revolutionized medicine by introducing the concept of sterilization; and the list goes on.

The Scottish influence was strong not just within Britain, but around the world. Scots such as Lachlan Macquarie in Australia and John A. Macdonald in Canada became colonial leaders; Scotsman David Livingstone redefined the role of the missionary in his explorations of southern Africa; Scotsman James Mill set colonial policy on a new path with his *History of British India*; and Scots were disproportionately represented in business enterprises in all corners of the globe (in the early nineteenth century, 80 per cent of those on the payroll of the Hudson's Bay Company, for example, were Scottish).

There is no single cultural or socio-economic explanation for Scotland's extraordinary prominence through this period, but it has often been surmised that Scottish accomplishments in this era are not unconnected to the state of religion in Scotland. Unlike in Ireland and Wales, the established Church in Scotland was not a branch of the Anglican Church; the Church of Scotland had long been Presbyterian and Calvinist.[1] There was thus little or no parallel in Scotland to the sense that prevailed among the majority in Ireland of the established Church as an oppressive force. That it not to say that religious affairs were without controversy—far from it. There were numerous and ongoing tensions both between secular and religious influences in society and between different strains of Protestantism. Moderate Presbyterians had defeated Evangelicals in their 1757 bid to control the Church of Scotland, but Evangelicals continued to agitate through the early decades of the nineteenth century against Church of Scotland policies such as the practice of allowing influential landowners to influence the choosing of local ministers in the Church. Finally, the Disruption of 1843 resulted in the formation of the breakaway Free Church of Scotland—which in turn would merge in 1900 with the United Presbyterian Church to form the United Free Church of Scotland. In whatever its forms, Scottish Presbyterianism continued throughout the period to promote what Max Weber famously termed the "Protestant work ethic" perhaps more effectively than did any other branch of Protestantism. But the workings of any society's psyche resist easy generalizations; as the excerpt below from the oft-mocked *Self-Help* suggests, even such an exemplar of the principles of the work ethic as Samuel Smiles is not easy to pigeonhole.

If religious currents may help to explain Scottish exceptionalism, so too may education. The Scots were, on average, better educated than the English—from the sixteenth century onwards Scottish Presbyterians had been world leaders in this regard. By the 1830s, however, the old system of parish schools and "dame schools" (which taught girls to read and to sew—but not to write) was becoming inadequate to the needs of a modern nation. George Lewis's *Scotland: A Half Educated Nation* (1834) provided a wake-up call, and in the second half of the century the burden of educating the people began to shift from church to secular authorities; the 1872 Education Act made schooling compulsory for all children between the ages of five and thirteen, and transferred responsibility to State authorities.

Education was almost always in English rather than in Gaelic, however, and by 1911 only 4.2 per cent of Scotland's 4,500,000 people spoke Gaelic. More broadly, the culture of the Gaelic-speaking Highlands had long been in decline—along with the Highland population. Not until 1885 did the Highlands and Island Crofting Act end the centuries-old practice of landlords evicting tenant farmers *en masse* and destroying entire communities in order to clear the land for more profitable activities (such as sheep farming).

By the end of the century, then, some of the greatest contrasts in the industrialized world were in Scotland. One could find one of the world's great urban economies—powered by engineering, ship-building, steel-making, and textiles. But one could also find abject urban poverty—and abject

[1] The Anglican Church (or "Scottish Episcopal Church") did retain a presence in Scotland, but its numbers were small and its influence minimal. As J.M. Barrie observed, in the eyes of many Presbyterians there was little difference between being a member of the "English Kirk" (as the Anglican Church was often referred to) and being a Roman Catholic.

rural poverty among the people who still remained in the Highland counties. One could find a deep-rooted literary culture—but one could also find a culture in which women were only beginning to be taught how to write.

The nineteenth century is a century of paradox in the history of Welsh culture. The best-known of all Welsh writers of the century—Felicia Hemans—is famous most of all for poems expressing sentimental patriotic feeling not towards Wales, but towards England. Wales enjoyed considerable economic growth over the course of the century, but key sectors of the economy—most notably, coal mining—continued to be notorious for low wages and horrendous working conditions until well into the twentieth century.

Religion played a central role in nineteenth-century Wales—and here too there were numerous paradoxes. The most important religious event of the century occurred in 1811, when the Welsh Methodists broke free from the control of the Anglican Church. Culturally, however, religion was far from a liberating force. With the great growth during the century of Nonconformist or "Dissenting" forms of religion (i.e., those dissenting from and not conforming with the Anglican Church, which remained throughout the century the established church), strictures against alcoholic drink and sexual licentiousness became more and more widespread—and so too did strictures against the "sins" of dancing, secular music, and works of fiction. Censorious attitudes took hold not only in Methodism but in most other Nonconformist denominations as well. To be sure, such strictures were not universal—and Dissenters were not uniformly censorious or puritanical. One of the century's most notable cultural developments was the founding in 1845 by Lewis Edwards, a Welsh Calvinist minister, of *Y Traethodydd* [The Essayist], a Welsh-language organ of culture that has survived into the twenty-first century. And the old medieval tradition of *eisteddfodau* (festivals of literature, dance, and music), which had been revived in the eighteenth century, was carried on through the nineteenth; despite considerable opposition, a national *Eisteddfod* was established in the second half of the century.

Given the degree to which strict Nonconformist strains of Christianity dominated Welsh life in this period, it is ironic that Anglican authorities continued to characterize the bulk of the Welsh people as being sexually irresponsible and of doubtful moral character generally. Notoriously, the 1847 Report of the Commission of Enquiry into the State of Education in Wales (known as the "Blue Books") veered from educational into cultural commentary of the most dubious sort, suggesting that the natural state of the majority of the population was an "utter vacuity of thought" and maligning the Welsh language as "a vast drawback to Wales, and a manifold barrier to the moral progress of the people."

The Welsh language certainly came under pressure during this century, but by its end there had been only a modest decline in its use. By 1911 there were still approximately 1,000,000 speakers of the language, out of a total population of just over 2,400,000. As the selections here—perhaps most memorably, Evan James's "Land of my Fathers"—suggest, pride in the language remained a powerful rallying cry throughout the century. In the end, the greatest legacy left by the "Blue Books" was the degree to which they united the Welsh in support of Welsh language and culture.

The century saw a considerable growth in formal education—passage of the Intermediate Schools Act in 1889 was a notable milestone—but at century's end a substantial gulf remained between the well-educated and almost entirely English-speaking privileged classes and the much less educated mass of the Welsh people. There was nevertheless a significant growth in Welsh literary culture. A significant milestone was the publication between 1838 and 1849 of Charlotte Guest's translation of *The Four Branches of the Mabinogi* and related poems (which together she termed *The Mabinogion*).

Much as her translation is now faulted, the works themselves, which were little-known before Guest's work, are now universally acknowledged as foundational classics of Welsh culture.

A striking number of the outstanding Welsh writers of the long nineteenth century are women. The list of prominent Anglo-Welsh writers includes not only Jane Cave, Mary Robinson, and Hemans (all of whom are accorded full author entries in this anthology) and the writers included below, but also Ann Griffiths (1776–1805), a noted author of hymns; Maria James (1795–1868), a woman of working class background whose family emigrated to America when she was ten, and whose poetry returns frequently to themes of cultural and linguistic loss; and Emily Jane Pfeiffer (1827–90), an Anglo-Welsh poet whose writing often took issue with the domination of Britain by England over Wales, Scotland, and Ireland, and with the domination of men over women.

Religious conservatism does not always imply political conservatism, and certainly it did not always do so in nineteenth-century Wales. In the first half of the century there were numerous uprisings against oppressively high taxes and a lack of adequate support for farmers (notably, the Rebecca riots of 1839–43 in south and mid-Wales), and against low wages and high unemployment (notably, the Merthyr Rising of 1831 in south Wales). In the second half of the century there came to be considerable support for socialist causes—again, especially in the more heavily populated and more heavily industrialized south. There were protests too against British military action—as the selection below by Samuel Roberts illustrates. Anti-war sentiment was not confined to Radicals such as Roberts; many mainstream nonconformists were also opposed to British militarism. (During WWI in the early twentieth century, acrimonious divisions among religious nonconformists in Wales opened up over the pacifist cause.)

As in Ireland there was a strong push in Wales for Home Rule—though in Wales the agitation for Home Rule, which gathered steam only in the second half of the nineteenth century, was less vehement. Few in Wales called for outright independence from Britain, but the *Cymru Fydd* (Young Wales) movement, which was outspoken in its demands for a separate Welsh parliament, was for a time in the 1880s and 1890s a force to be reckoned with. One of the leading lights of *Cymru Fydd* was David Lloyd George (see below), later to play a key role in British politics as the force behind the "People's Budget" of 1909–10 and as Prime Minister during WWI.

⌘⌘⌘

Ireland

Songs of '98

The Rebellion of 1798 became the subject of many poems and songs; two of the best known are included here. (For background on the rebellion see the Contexts section "Ireland in the Long Nineteenth Century" in the website component of this anthology.)

Slievenamon[1]

Slievenamon, a low mountain in Tipperary, figures prominently in Irish history and myth. The battle referenced in this song took place 23 July 1798.

It is my sorrow that this day's troubles
Poor Irishmen so sore did strike,
Because our tyrants are laughing at us,
And say they fear neither fork nor pike;

[1] *Slievenamon* Translated from the Irish by Frank O'Connor. Not to be confused with this song is the well-known nineteenth-century poem of the same name by Charles Kickham.

Our Major never came to lead us,
We had no orders and drifted on
As you'd send a drover[1] with a cow to the fair
On the sunny side of Slievenamon.

Ross[2] was the place we were defeated,
There we left many a pikeman dead,
Little children burned to ashes,
Women in holes and ditches hid.
But I promise you the men that slew them
We'll meet them yet with pike and gun,
And we'll drive the yeomen[3] in flight before us
When we pay them back on Slievenamon.

The sturdy Frenchman with ships in order
Beneath sharp masts is long at sea;
They're always saying they will come to Ireland,
And they will set the Irish free.
Light as a blackbird on a green bough swinging
Would be my heart if the French would come—
O the broken ranks and the trumpets ringing
On the sunny side of Slievenamon!

—DATE UNKNOWN

CARROLL MALONE, *The Croppy[4] Boy*

There is more than one version of this nineteenth century song. That which Patrick Crotty includes in *The Penguin Book of Irish Poetry* includes only nine stanzas; in that anonymously authored version the young man is betrayed not by a soldier pretending to be a priest (as in the Malone version below), but by a relative:

> My own first cousin did me betray
> And for one bare guinea stole my life away.

The lyrics below were published in the 4 January 1845 issue of *The Nation*, and credited to Carroll Malone (the pen name of poet William B. McBurney [d. 1892]). It is the Malone version that now has particularly deep roots in Irish culture. James Joyce refers to it in *Ulysses*, and wrote of it as well in a letter to his son:

> It is a pure and noble musical poem, profoundly sincere and dramatic ... This is not a patriotic song like "Wearing of the Green." You could sing it just as well at Sheffield as at Cork.[5] Study every word of it and you will make it into a masterpiece.

"The Croppy Boy" is usually sung to the tune *Cailín Óg a Stór*—an air that is many centuries old.

"Good men and true in this house who dwell,
To a stranger bouchal[6] I pray you tell:
Is the priest at home, or may he be seen?
I would speak a word with Father Green."

"The Priest's at home, boy, and may be seen;
'Tis easy speaking with Father Green.
But you must wait till I go and see
If the Holy Father alone may be."

The youth has entered an empty hall—
What a lonely sound has his light footfall!
And the gloomy chamber's chill and bare,
With a vested priest in a lonely chair.

The youth has knelt to tell his sins:
"Nomine Dei," the youth begins;
At "mea culpa"[7] he beats his breast,
And in broken murmurs he speaks the rest.

---

[1] *drover* Person who drives livestock to market.

[2] *Ross* New Ross, a site of one of the 1798 Rebellion's significant battles; after their victory, the British Army massacred uninvolved civilians as well as rebel fighters.

[3] *yeomen* Government soldiers in the British army.

[4] *Croppy* Slang designation for a young man fighting in the Irish Rebellion of 1798; these men were known for having short cropped hair.

[5] *as well at Sheffield as at Cork* Sheffield is in England, Cork in Ireland.

[6] *bouchal* Irish: young man. (The more common spelling today is *buachaill*.)

[7] *Nomine Dei ... mea culpa* Latin phrases used in the Catholic ritual of confessing one's sins; *Nomine Dei* In the name of our Lord; *mea culpa* I have sinned.

"At the siege of Ross did my father fall,
And at Gorey my loving brothers all.
I alone am left of my name and race;
I will go to Wexford[1] and take their place.

"I cursed three times since last Easter day;
At mass-time once I went to play;
I passed the churchyard one day in haste,
And forgot to pray for my mother's rest.

"I bear no grudge against living thing,
But I love my country above the king.
Now, Father! bless me, and let me go
To die, if God has ordained it so."

The priest said nought, but a rustling noise
Made the youth look about in wild surprise;
The robes were off, and in scarlet there
Sat a yeoman[2] captain with fiery glare.

With fiery glare and with fury hoarse,
Instead of a blessing, he breathed a curse:
"'Twas a good thought, boy, to come here and shrive,[3]
For one short hour is your time to live.

"Upon yon river three tenders[4] float;
The priest's in one—if he isn't shot!
We hold his house for our Lord the King,
And, amen say I, may all traitors swing!"

At Geneva Barrack that young man died,
And at Passage[5] they have his body laid.
Good people who live in peace and joy,
Breathe a prayer and a tear for the Croppy Boy.
—1845

[1] *Ross ... Wexford* Two significant clashes during the 1798 Rebellion took place at the towns of New Ross and Gorey; both are located in County Wexford, which was the center of the rebellion. (Another name for the rebels was "Wexford boys.")

[2] *yeoman* Government soldier in the British Army.

[3] *shrive* Present oneself to a priest for the purposes of confessing one's sins and receiving absolution.

[4] *tenders* Boats used for transporting people, especially between shore and a larger vessel.

[5] *Geneva Barrack ... Passage* Geneva Barracks (now a ruin) is located in the town of Waterford in southeast Ireland; the community of Passage (or Passage East) is located on the narrow passage into Waterford Harbor.

WILLIAM CARLETON (1794–1869)

Novelist William Carleton—"the great novelist of Ireland," in W.B. Yeats's view—is known for his lively and influential—if sometimes stereotypical—depictions of the rural Irish character in the nineteenth century; a review of his *Traits and Stories* in *Blackwood's Edinburgh Magazine* called his tales "Admirable, truly! Intensely Irish," and claimed that "never were that wild, imaginative people better described."

Carleton was born in County Tyrone in 1798 to a farming family; his Irish-speaking parents instilled in him a love of literature and song at an early age. He lived a rather peripatetic life for several years, working at various jobs before publishing *Traits and Stories* in 1830. An immediate success, this collection of sketches and stories was followed some years later by a second series of stories. In 1847 Carleton published *The Black Prophet: A Tale of Irish Famine*, in which he vividly describes the bleak realities of rural communities during the Famine.

Though born a Catholic, Carleton converted to Protestantism in early adulthood, and became the target of criticism for the sometimes-satirical perspective towards Catholicism adopted in certain of his later writings. Despite the success of his work, Carleton's last years were spent in relative poverty; he died in 1869.

from *The Black Prophet; A Tale of Irish Famine*

from Chapter 6: A Rustic Miser and His Establishment

There is to be found in Ireland, and, we presume, in all other countries, a class of hardened wretches, who look forward to a period of dearth as to one of great gain and advantage, and who contrive, by exercising the most heartless and diabolical principles, to make the sickness, famine, and general desolation which scourge their fellow-creatures, so many sources of successful extortion and rapacity, and consequently of gain to themselves. These are country misers or money-lenders, who are remarkable for keeping meal until the arrival of what is termed a hard year, or a dear summer, when they sell it out at an enormous or usurious prices, and who, at all times, and under all circumstances, dispose of it only at terms dictated by their own griping spirit and the crying necessity of the unhappy purchasers.

The houses and places of such persons are always remarkable for a character in their owners of hard and severe saving, which at a first glance has the appearance of that rare virtue in our country, called frugality—a virtue which, upon a closer inspection, is found to be nothing with them but selfishness, sharpened up into the most unscrupulous avarice and penury.

About half a mile from the Sullivans', lived a remarkable man of this class, named Darby Skinadre. In appearance he was lank and sallow, with a long, thin, parched-looking face, and a miserable crop of yellow beard, which no one could pronounce as anything else than "a dead failure;" added to this were two piercing ferret eyes, always sore and with a tear standing in each, or trickling down his fleshless cheeks; so that, to persons disposed to judge only by appearances, he looked very like a man in a state of perpetual repentance for his transgressions, or, what was still farther from the truth, who felt a most Christian sympathy with the distresses of the poor. In his house, and about it, there was much, no doubt, to be commended, for there was much to mark the habits of the saving man. Everything was neat and clean, not so much from any innate love of neatness and cleanliness, as because these qualities were economical in themselves. His ploughs and farming implements were all snugly laid up, and covered, lest they might be injured by exposure to the weather; and his house was filled with large chests and wooden hogsheads, trampled hard with oatmeal, which, as they were never opened unless during a time of famine, had their joints and crevices festooned by innumerable mealy-looking cobwebs, which description of ornament extended to the dresser itself, where they might be seen upon most of the cold-looking shelves, and those neglected utensils, that in other families are mostly used for food. His haggard[1] was also remarkable for having in it, throughout all the year, a remaining stack or two of oats or wheat, or perhaps one or two large ricks of hay, tanned by the sun of two or three summers into tawny hue—each or all kept in the hope of a failure and a famine.

In a room from the kitchen, he had a beam, a pair of scales, and a set of weights, all of which would have been vastly improved by a visit from the lord mayor, had our mealmonger lived under the jurisdiction of that civic gentleman. He was seldom known to use metal weights when disposing of his property; in lieu of these he always used round stones, which, upon the principle of the Scottish proverb, that "many a little makes a muckle,"[2] he must have found a very beneficial mode of transacting business.

If anything could add to the iniquity of his principles, as a plausible but most unscrupulous cheat, it was the hypocritical prostitution of the sacred name and character of religion to his own fraudulent impositions upon the poor and the distressed. Outwardly, and to the eye of men, he was proverbially strict and scrupulous in the observation of its sanctions, but outrageously severe and unsparing upon all who appeared to be influenced either by a negligent or worldly spirit, or who omitted the least title of its forms. Religion and its duties, therefore, were perpetually in his

[1] *haggard* Storeroom for hay and grains.

[2] *muckle* Scots: a large amount.

mouth but never with such apparent zeal and sincerity as when enforcing his most heartless and hypocritical exactions upon the honest and struggling creatures whom necessity or neglect had driven into his meshes.

Such was Darby Skinadre; and certain we are that the truth of the likeness we have given of him will be at once recognized by our readers as that of the roguish hypocrite, whose rapacity is the standing curse of half the villages of the country, especially during the seasons of distress, or failure of crops.

Skinadre, on the day we write of, was reaping a rich harvest from the miseries of the unhappy people. In a lower room of his house, to the right of the kitchen as you entered it, he stood over the scales, weighing out with a dishonest and parsimonious hand, the scanty pittance which poverty enabled the wretched creatures to purchase from him; and in order to give them a favourable impression of his piety, and consequently of his justice, he had placed against the wall a delf[1] crucifix, with a semi-circular receptacle at the bottom of it for holding holy water. This was as much as to say "how could I cheat you, with the image of our Blessed Redeemer before my eyes to remind me of my duty, and to teach me, as He did, to love my fellow-creatures?" And with many of the simple people, he actually succeeded in making the impression he wished; for they could not conceive it possible that any principle, however rapacious, could drive a man to the practice of such sacrilegious imposture.

There stood Skinadre, like the very Genius of Famine, surrounded by distress, raggedness, feeble hunger, and tottering disease, in all the various aspects of pitiable suffering, hopeless desolation, and that agony of the heart which impresses wildness upon the pale cheek, makes the eye at once dull and eager, parches the mouth and gives to the voice of misery tones that are hoarse and hollow. There he stood, striving to blend consolation with deceit, and in the name of religion and charity subjecting the helpless wretches to fraud and extortion. Around him was misery, multiplied into all her most appalling shapes. Fathers of families were there, who could read in each other's faces too truly the gloom and anguish that darkened the brow and wrung the heart. The strong man, who had been not long before a comfortable farmer, now stood dejected and apparently broken down, shorn of his strength, without a trace of either hope or spirit; so woefully shrunk away too, from his superfluous apparel, that the spectators actually wondered to think that this was the large man, of such powerful frame, whose feats of strength had so often heretofore filled them with amazement. But, alas! what will not sickness and hunger do? …

And there was the widower, on behalf of his motherless children, coming with his worn and desolate look of sorrow, almost thankful to God that his Kathleen was not permitted to witness the many-shaped miseries of this woeful year; and yet experiencing the sharp and bitter reflection that now, in all their trials—in his poor children's want and sickness—in their moanings by day and their cries for her by night, they have not the soft affection of her voice nor the tender touch of her hand to soothe their pain—nor has he that smile, which was ever his, to solace him now, nor that faithful heart to soothe him with its affection, or to cast its sweetness into the bitter cup of affliction. …

It is impossible, however, to describe the various aspects and claims of misery which presented themselves at Skinadre's house. The poor people flitted to and fro silently and dejectedly, wasted, feeble, and sickly—sometimes in small groups of twos and threes, and sometimes a solitary individual might be seen hastening with earnest but languid speed, as if the life of some dear child or beloved parent, of a husband or wife, or perhaps, the lives of a whole family, depended upon his or her arrival with food.

Chapter 7: A Panorama of Misery

Skinadre, thin and mealy, with his coat off, but wearing a waistcoat to which were attached flannel sleeves, was busily engaged in his agreeable task of administering to their necessities. Such was his smoothness of manner, and the singular control which a long life of hypocrisy had given him over his feelings, that it was impossible to

[1] *delf* Delft (type of earthenware originating in the Dutch town of Delft).

draw any correct distinction between that which he only assumed, and that which he really felt. This consequently gave him an immense advantage over everyone with whom he came in contact, especially the artless and candid, and all who were in the habit of expressing what they thought. We shall, however, take the liberty of introducing him to the reader, and allow honest Skinadre to speak for himself.

"They're beggars—thim three—that woman and her two childre; still my heart bleeds for them, bekase[1] we should love our neighbours as ourselves; but I have given away as much meal in charity, an' me can so badly afford it, as would—I can't now, indeed, my poor woman! Sick—troth they look sick, an' you look sick yourself. Here, Paddy Lenahan, help that woman an' her two poor childre out of that half bushel of meal you've got; you won't miss a handful for God's sake."

This he said to a poor man who had just purchased some oatmeal from him; for Skinadre was one of those persons who, however he might have neglected works of mercy himself, took great delight in encouraging others to perform them.

"Troth it's not at your desire I do it, Darby," replied the man; "but bekase she an' they wants it, God help them. Here, poor creature, take this for the honour of God: an' I'm only sorry, for both our sakes, that I can't do more."

"Well, Jemmy Duggan," proceeded the miser, addressing a new-comer, "what's the news wid you? They're hard times, Jemmy; we all know that an' feel it too, and yet we live, most of us, as if there wasn't a God ta punish us."

"At all events," replied the man, "we feel what sufferin' is now, God help us! Between hunger and sickness, the counthry was never in sich a state widin[2] the memory of man. What, in the name o' God, will become of the poor people, I know not. The Lord pity them an' relieve them!"

"Amen, amen, Jemmy! Well, Jemmy, can I do anything for you? But Jemmy, in regard to that, the thruth is, we have brought all these scourges on us by our sins and our thransgressions; thim that sins, Jemmy, must suffer."

"There's no one denyin' it, Darby; but you're axin' me can you do anything for me, an' my answer to that is, that you can, if you like."

"Ah! Jemmy, you wor ever an' always a wild, heedless, heerum-skeerum rake,[3] that never was likely to do much good; little religion ever rested on you, an' now I'm afeard no signs on it."

"Well, well, who's widout sin? I'm sure I'm not. What I want is, to know if you'll credit me for a hundred of meal till the times mends a trifle. I have the six o' them at home widout their dinner this day, an' must go widout if you refuse me. When the harvest comes round, I'll pay you."

"Jemmy, you owe three half-year's, rent; an' as for the harvest an' what it'll bring, only jist look at the day that's in it. It goes to my heart to refuse you, poor man; but Jemmy, you see you have brought this on yourself. If you had been an attentive, industrious man, an' minded your religion, you wouldn't be as you are now. Six you have at home, you say?"

"Ay, not to speak of the woman an' myself. I know you won't refuse them, Darby, bekase if we're hard pushed now, it's a'most everybody's case as well as mine. Be what I may, you know I'm honest."

"I don't doubt your honesty, Jemmy; but Jemmy, if I sell my meal to a man that can pay and won't, or if I sell my meal to a man that would pay and can't, by which do I lose most? There it is, Jemmy—think o' that now. Six in family, you say?"

"Six in family, wid the woman an' myself." …

"It goes to my heart, Jemmy, to refuse you—six in family, an' the two of yourselves. Troth it does, to my very heart itself; but stay, maybe we may manage it. You have no money, you say?"

"No money now, but won't be so long, plaise God."

"Well, but havn't you value of any kind? sure, God help them, they can't starve, poor creatures—the Lord pity them!" Here he wiped away a drop of villainous

[1] *bekase* Because.

[2] *widin* Within.

[3] *rake* Scots slang: someone who is always trying to get more money.

rheum which ran down his cheek, and he did it with such an appearance of sympathy, that almost anyone would have imagined it was a tear of compassion for the distresses of the poor man's family.

"Oh! no, they can't starve. Have you no valuables of any kind, Jemmy?—ne'er a baste[1] now, or anything that way?"

"Why, there's a young heifer; but I'm strugglin' to keep it to help me in the rent. I was obliged to sell my pig long ago, for I had no way of feedin' it."

"Well, bring me the heifer, Jemmy, an' I won't let the crathurs[2] starve. We'll see what can be done when it comes here. An' now, Jemmy, let me ax if you wint to hear mass on last Sunday?"

"Troth I didn't like to go in this trim. Peggy has a web of frieze[3] half made this good while; it'll be finished some time, I hope."

"Ah! Jemmy, Jemmy, it's no wondher the world's the way it is, for indeed there's little thought of God or religion in it. You passed last Sunday like a haythen, an' now you see how you stand today for the same."

"You'll let me bring some o' the meal home wid me now," said the man; "the poor cratures tasted hardly anything today yet, an' they wor cryin' whin I left home. I'll come back wid the heifer fullfut. Troth they're in outher misery, Darby."

"Poor things! an' no wondher, wid such a haythen of a father; but, Jemmy, bring the heifer here first till I look at it, an' the sooner you bring it here the sooner they'll have relief, the crathurs."

It is not our intention to follow up this iniquitous bargain any further; it is enough to say that the heifer passed from Jemmy's possession into his, at about the fourth part of its value....

—1847

IN CONTEXT

W.B. Yeats, from Introduction to *Stories from Carleton* (1889)

In 1889, when the Walter Scott publishing company issued *Stories from Carleton* in their Camelot Series of reprints—"monthly shilling volumes," as they were advertised, ranging from Plutarch's *Lives* to Thoreau's *Walden*—Carleton himself had been dead for twenty years. Nobel-Prize winning poet William Butler Yeats (1865–1939), for his part, was at this time just 23; *The Wind among the Reeds*, his first volume of poetry, was still ten years away.

At the end of the last century, there lived in the townland of Prillisk, in the parish of Clogher, in the county of Tyrone,[4] a farmer named Carleton. Among his neighbours, he was noted for his great memory. A pious Catholic, he could repeat almost the whole of the Old and New Testament, and no man ever heard tell of Gaelic charm, rann,[5] poem, prophesy, miracle, tale of blessed priest or friar, revelation of ghost or fairy, that did not already lie on this man's tongue.

His wife, Mary, was even better known. Hers was the sweetest voice within the range of many Baronies. When she went to sing at wake or wedding the neighbours for miles round would flock in to hear, as city folk do for some famous prima donna. She had a great store of old Gaelic songs and

---

1 *baste* Beast; animal.

2 *crathurs* Creatures.

3 *web of frieze* Knitted woolen garment in a frieze pattern.

4 *Tyrone* Located in what is now Northern Ireland.

5 *rann* Style of Irish verse.

tunes, many an air, sung once under all Irish roof-trees, has gone into the grave with her. The words she sang were Gaelic. Once they asked her to sing the air,[1] "The Red-Haired Man's Wife," to English words. "I will sing for you," she answered, "but the English words and the air are like a quarrelling man and wife. The Irish melts into the tune: the English does not." She could repeat many poems, some handed down for numberless years, others written by her own grandfather and uncle, who were noted peasant poets in their day. She was a famous keener,[2] likewise. No one could load the wild funeral song with so deep sorrow. Often and often when she caught up the cry, the other keeners would become silent in admiration.

On Shrove-Tuesday, in the year 1798, when pitch-caps[3] were well in fashion, was born to these two a son, whom they called William Carleton. He was the youngest of fourteen children.

Before long his mind was brimful of his father's stories and his mother's songs. In after days he recorded how many times, when his mother sat by her spinning wheel, singing "Shule agra" or the "Trougha," or some other "song of sorrow," he would go over with tears in his eyes, and whisper, "Mother dear, don't sing that song; it makes me sorrowful." Fifty years later his mind was still full of old songs that had died on all other lips than his.

At this time Ireland was plentifully stored with hedge schoolmasters. Government had done its best to crush out education, and only succeeded in doing what like policy had done for the priestcraft—surrounding it with a halo. Ditchers and plough-boys developed the strangest enthusiasm for Greek and Latin. The worst of it was, the men who set up schools behind the hedges were often sheer imposters. Among them, however, were a few worthy of fame, like Andrew Magrath, the Munster poet, who sang his allegiance to the fairy, "Dawn of the Ocean Vats."

The boy Carleton sat under three hedge schoolmasters in succession—Pat Fryne, called Mat Kavanagh in the stories; O'Beirne of Findramore; and another, the master in "The Poor Scholar," whose name Carleton never recorded, as he had nothing but evil to say of him. …

William Carleton was a great Irish historian. The history of a nation is not in parliaments and battlefields, but in what the people say to each other on fair days and high days, and how they farm, and quarrel, and go on pilgrimage. These things has Carleton recorded.

He is the great novelist of Ireland, by right of the most Celtic eyes that ever gazed from under the brows of storyteller. His equals in gloomy and tragic power, Michael and John Banim,[4] had nothing of his Celtic humour. One man alone stands near him there—Charles Kickham,[5] of Tipperary. … But, then, he had not Carleton's intensity. …

There is no wistfulness in the works of Carleton. I find there, especially in his longer novels, a kind of clay-cold melancholy. One is not surprised to hear, great humourist though he was, that his conversation was more mournful than humorous. He seems, like the animals in Milton,[6] half emerged only from the earth and its brooding. When I read any portion of the "Black Prophet," … I seem to

---

[1] *air* Song.

[2] *keener* One who performs keens, or lamentations for the dead, at Irish funerals and wakes.

[3] *pitch-caps* The pitch-cap was a method of torture, famously used by the British military upon participants in the United Irishmen Rebellion of 1798; it involved placing a "cap" of boiling tar onto the victim's head.

[4] *Michael and John Banim* Irish writers of the early 1800s.

[5] *Charles Kickham* Irish writer and revolutionary (1828–82).

[6] *Milton* John Milton (1608–74), English poet and dramatist. His account of the sixth day of Creation (*Paradise Lost,* 7.449ff.) includes descriptions of the creation of various animals—among them the lion who, when half created, paws the ground as he struggles to be free of the "grassy clods" of the "fertile womb" of Earth that is giving birth to him.

be looking out at the wild, torn storm-clouds that lie in heaps at sundown along the western seas of Ireland; all nature, and not merely man's nature, seems to pour out for me its inbred fatalism.

JAMES CLARENCE MANGAN (1803–1849)

Dublin-born poet James Clarence Mangan was a self-taught translator of languages as diverse as German, Irish, and Persian, and was during his lifetime known at least as much for his translations as for his original poetry. His writings became increasingly patriotic and political during the Great Famine, and many of his best-known poems—including "Dark Rosaleen"—were published in *The Nation.* Though Mangan lived his latter years in poverty and died of cholera (likely brought on by malnutrition and alcoholism) at the age of 46, he is now recognized as one of most important Irish poets of the nineteenth century.

The Woman of Three Cows[1]

from the Irish[2]

O Woman of Three Cows, *agragh*![3] don't let
  your tongue thus rattle!
O, don't be saucy, don't be stiff, because you may
  have cattle.
I have seen—and, here's my hand to you, I only
  say what's true—
A many a one with twice your stock not half so proud
  as you.

Good luck to you, don't scorn the poor, and don't
  be their despiser,
For worldly wealth soon melts away, and cheats the
  very miser,
And Death soon strips the proudest wreath
  from haughty human brows;
Then don't be stiff, and don't be proud, good
  Woman of Three Cows!

See where Momonia's[4] heroes lie, proud Owen
  More's descendants,
'Tis they that won the glorious name, and had the
  grand attendants!
If *they* were forced to bow to Fate, as every mortal bows,
Can *you* be proud, can *you* be stiff, my Woman of
  Three Cows!

The brave sons of the Lord of Clare,[5] they left the
  land to mourning;
Movrone![6] for they were banished, with no hope of
  their returning—
Who knows in what abodes of want those youths
  were driven to house?
Yet *you* can give yourself these airs, O Woman of
  Three Cows!

O, think of Donnell of the Ships,[7] the Chief
  whom nothing daunted—
See how he fell in distant Spain, unchronicled,
  unchanted!

---

[1] *The Woman of Three Cows* Based on an anonymous Irish poem.

[2] *from the Irish* Mangan used this phrase to identify poems whose subject matter originated in an Irish language poem. Such poems are not properly speaking translations; Mangan often drew on literal translations of the Irish originals, but his own poems are poetic re-workings rather than translations.

[3] *agragh* Irish: my love.

[4] *Momonia* Munster, one of the four provinces of Ireland and formerly the Kingdom of Munster; its kings were said to be descended from the mythological Éogan Mór, or Owen More.

[5] *brave sons ... of Clare* Daniel and Charles O'Brien, both of whom fought for the Jacobites in the Irish army and died in battle abroad; along with the many Irish soldiers who fought for foreign armies between the sixteenth and eighteenth centuries, they were part of the group known as the "Wild Geese."

[6] *Movrone* From the Irish *mo bhrón*: my sorrow.

[7] *Donnell of the Ships* Donal Cam O'Sullivan Beare (1561–1618), among the last Gaelic lords of Ireland; after losing a battle at his stronghold at Dunboy Castle, he was exiled to Spain and eventually murdered there by an Englishman from Dublin.

He sleeps, the great O'Sullivan, where thunder
cannot rouse—
Then ask yourself, should *you* be proud, good
Woman of Three Cows!

O'Ruark, Maguire,[1] those souls of fire, whose names
are shrined in story—
Think how their high achievements once made
Erin's[2] highest glory—
Yet now their bones lie mouldering under weeds
and cypress boughs,
And so, for all your pride, will yours, O Woman
of Three Cows!

The O'Carrolls,[3] also, famed when Fame was only
for the boldest,
Rest in forgotten sepulchres with Erin's best and oldest;
Yet who so great as they of yore in battle or carouse?
Just think of that, and hide your head, good
Woman of Three Cows!

Your neighbour's poor, and you, it seems, are big
with vain ideas,
Because, *inagh*![4] you've got three cows—one more,
I see, than *she* has.
That tongue of yours wags more at times than
Charity allows,
But if you're strong, be merciful, great Woman of
Three Cows!
—1840

[1] *O'Ruark, Maguire* Brian O'Rourke (c. 1540–91) and Hugh Maguire (d. 1600), both supporters of O'Sullivan Beare in the Nine Years' War.

[2] *Erin* From the Irish *Éire* or *Éireann*, common poetic name for Ireland.

[3] *The O'Carrolls* Significant Gaelic noble family, who once ruled the Kingdom of Éile.

[4] *inagh!* An exclamation in Irish.

Kathaleen Ny-Houlahan[5]

Long they pine in weary woe, the nobles of our land,
Long they wander to and fro, proscribed, alas!
and banned;
Feastless, houseless, altarless, they bear the exile's brand;
But their hope is in the coming-to of Kathaleen
Ny-Houlahan.

Think her not a ghostly hag, too hideous to be seen,
Call her not unseemly names, our matchless Kathaleen!
Young she is, and fair she is, and would be crowned
a queen,
Were the king's son at home here with Kathaleen
Ny-Houlahan!

Sweet and mild would look her face, O, none so
sweet and mild,
Could she crush the foes by whom her beauty is reviled;
Woolen plaids[6] would grace herself, and robes of silk
her child,
If the king's son were living here with Kathaleen
Ny-Houlahan!

Sore disgrace it is to see the Arbitress° of thrones, *ruler*
Vassal° to a Saxoneen[7] of cold and *servant*
sapless bones!
Bitter anguish wrings our souls—with heavy sighs
and groans
We wait the Young Deliverer of Kathaleen
Ny-Houlahan!

[5] *Kathaleen Ny-Houlahan* Figure of Irish nationalist mythology (more commonly spelled Kathleen Ni Houlihan), generally depicted as a woman who calls for the help and sacrifice of young men to help her take back her rightful land; she is most famously depicted in the play of the same name (1902) written by W.B. Yeats and Lady Augusta Gregory.

[6] *plaids* Garments in tartan patterns, generally associated with the Scottish Highlands but also sometimes with Ireland (especially during the rise of Irish nationalism).

[7] *Saxoneen* Mocking diminutive for Saxon, i.e., English person.

Let us pray to Him who holds life's issues in His hands—
Him who formed the mighty globe, with all its thousand lands;
Girding them with seas and mountains, rivers deep, and strands,
To cast a look of pity upon Kathaleen Ny-Houlahan!

He, who over sands and waves led Israèl along—
He, who fed with heavenly bread, that chosen tribe and throng—
He who stood by Moses when his foes were fierce and strong—
May He show forth His might in saving Kathaleen Ny-Houlahan.

—1841

Dark Rosaleen[1]

from the Irish

O my Dark Rosaleen,
Do not sigh, do not weep!
The priests are on the ocean green,
They march along the deep.
There's wine from the royal Pope,
Upon the ocean green;
And Spanish ale shall give you hope,[2]
My Dark Rosaleen!
My own Rosaleen!
Shall glad your heart, shall give you hope,
Shall give you health, and help, and hope,
My Dark Rosaleen.

Over hills and through dales,
Have I roamed for your sake;
All yesterday I sailed with sails
On river and on lake.
The Erne,[3] at its highest flood,
I dashed across unseen,
For there was lightning in my blood,
My Dark Rosaleen!
My own Rosaleen!
Oh! there was lightning in my blood,
Red lightning lightened through my blood,
My Dark Rosaleen!

All day long in unrest
To and fro do I move,
The very soul within my breast
Is wasted for you, love!
The heart in my bosom faints
To think of you, my Queen,
My life of life, my saint of saints,
My Dark Rosaleen!
My own Rosaleen!
To hear your sweet and sad complaints,
My life, my love, my saint of saints,
My Dark Rosaleen!

Woe and pain, pain and woe,
Are my lot night and noon,
To see your bright face clouded so,
Like to the mournful moon.
But yet will I rear your throne
Again in golden sheen;
'Tis you shall reign, shall reign alone,
My Dark Rosaleen!
My own Rosaleen!
'Tis you shall have the golden throne,
'Tis you shall reign, and reign alone,
My Dark Rosaleen!

Over dews, over sands
Will I fly for your weal;
Your holy delicate white hands
Shall girdle me with steel.
At home in your emerald bowers,

[1] *Dark Rosaleen* The poem is an adaptation of the Irish song *Róisín Dubh*, meaning "Dark Róisín," said to be named after the daughter of the Earl of Tyrone; the name Róisín has come to be taken as a poetic name for Ireland.

[2] *Spanish ale … you hope* Referring to Spanish sympathies with Ireland, as a fellow Catholic country.

[3] *The Erne* River in Ulster, the northern province of Ireland.

From morning's dawn till e'en,° *evening*
You'll pray for me, my flower of flowers,
My Dark Rosaleen!
My fond Rosaleen!
You'll think of me through daylight hours,
My virgin flower, my flower of flowers,
My Dark Rosaleen!

I could scale the blue air,
I could plough the high hills,
Oh, I could kneel all night in prayer,
To heal your many ills!
And one beamy smile from you
Would float like light between
My toils and me, my own, my true,
My Dark Rosaleen!
My fond Rosaleen!
Would give me life and soul anew,
A second life, a soul anew,
My Dark Rosaleen!

O! the Erne shall run red
With redundance of blood,
The earth shall rock beneath our tread,
And flames wrap hill and wood,
And gun-peal, and slogan cry,
Wake many a glen serene,
Ere you shall fade, ere you shall die,
My Dark Rosaleen!
My own Rosaleen!
The Judgement Hour must first be nigh,
Ere you can fade, ere you can die,
My Dark Rosaleen!
—1846

The Nameless One

Roll forth, my song, like the rushing river,
That sweeps along to the mighty sea;
God will inspire me while I deliver
My soul of thee!

Tell thou the world, when my bones lie whitening
Amid the last homes of youth and eld,° *old age*
That once there was one whose veins ran lightning
No eye beheld.

Tell how his boyhood was one drear night-hour,
How shone for him, through his griefs and gloom,
No star of all heaven sends to light our
Path to the tomb.

Roll on, my song, and to after ages
Tell how, disdaining all earth can give,
He would have taught men, from wisdom's pages,
The way to live.

And tell how trampled, derided, hated,
And worn by weakness, disease, and wrong,
He fled for shelter to God, who mated
His soul with song.

With song which alway, sublime or vapid,
Flowed like a rill° in the morning beam, *small river*
Perchance not deep, but intense and rapid—
A mountain stream.

Tell how this Nameless, condemned for years long
To herd with demons from hell beneath,
Saw things that made him, with groans and tears, long
For even death.

Go on to tell how, with genius wasted,
Betrayed in friendship, befooled in love,
With spirit shipwrecked, and young hopes blasted,
He still, still strove;

Till, spent with toil, dreeing° death for others *suffering*
(And some whose hands should have wrought
for him,
If children live not for sires° and mothers,) *fathers*
His mind grew dim;

And he fell far through that pit abysmal,
The gulf and grave of Maginn and Burns,[1]
And pawned his soul for the devil's dismal
Stock of returns.

But yet redeemed it in days of darkness,
And shapes and signs of the final wrath,
When death, in hideous and ghastly starkness,
Stood on his path.

And tell how now, amid wreck and sorrow,
And want, and sickness, and houseless nights,
He bides in calmness the silent morrow
That no ray lights.

And lives he still, then? Yes! Old and hoary
At thirty-nine, from despair and woe,
He lives, enduring what future story
Will never know.

Him grant a grave to, ye pitying noble,
Deep in your bosoms: there let him dwell!
He, too, had tears for all souls in trouble,
Here, and in hell.
—1849(?)

SAMUEL FERGUSON (1810–1886)

A lawyer by profession, Samuel Ferguson was also a poet, antiquarian, and general enthusiast of Irish history. Born in Belfast, he lived in numerous regions throughout Ireland, and became a regular contributor to publications such as *Blackwood's Edinburgh Magazine* and the *Dublin University Magazine*. His travels throughout Great Britain and Ireland provided the material for an archaeological text on Celtic Ogham inscriptions, and he also published several volumes of poetry. Ferguson was a supporter of the nationalist Young Ireland movement, and through this association met writer and activist Thomas Davis, who became a beloved friend; Ferguson's "Lament for the Death of Thomas Davis" was written in grief at the young man's early death. Ferguson was knighted in 1878.

Lament for the Death of Thomas Davis

I walked through Ballinderry[2] in the spring-time,
When the bud was on the tree;
And I said, in every fresh-ploughed field beholding
The sowers striding free,
Scattering broadside° forth the corn in golden plenty *widely*
On the quick seed-clasping soil,
"Even such this day, among the fresh-stirred hearts of Erin.[3]
Thomas Davis, is thy toil!"

I sat by Ballyshannon[4] in the summer,
And saw the salmon leap;
And I said, as I beheld the gallant creatures
Spring glittering from the deep,
Through the spray, and through the prone heaps striving onward
To the calm, clear streams above,
"So seekest thou thy native founts of freedom, Thomas Davis,
In thy brightness of strength and love!"

I stood on Derrybawn[5] in the autumn,
I heard the eagle call,
With a clangorous cry of wrath and lamentation,
That filled the wide mountain hall,
O'er the bare deserted place of his plundered eyrie;
And I said, as he screamed and soared,
"So callest thou, thou wrathful-soaring Thomas Davis,
For a nation's rights restored!"

[1] *Maginn and Burns* William Maginn (1794–1842) and Robert Burns (1759–96), writers known for the unhappy circumstances of their deaths, both rumored to have been alcoholics.

[2] *Ballinderry* Small parish in Northern Ireland.

[3] *Erin* Name for Ireland, stemming from the Irish endonym *Éire*.

[4] *Ballyshannon* Town in County Donegal.

[5] *Derrybawn* Mountain in County Wicklow.

And, alas! to think but now, and thou art lying
Dear Davis, dead at thy mother's knee;
And I, no mother near, on my own sick bed,
That face on earth shall never see;
I may lie and try to feel that I am dreaming,
I may lie and try to say, "Thy will be done"—
But a hundred such as I will never comfort Erin
For the loss of the noble son!

Young husbandman of Erin's fruitful seed-time,
In the fresh track of danger's plough!
Who will walk the heavy, toilsome, perilous furrow,
Girt with freedom's seed-sheets now?
Who will banish with the wholesome crop of knowledge
The flaunting weed and the bitter thorn,
Now that thou thyself art but a seed for hopeful planting
Against the resurrection[1] morn?

Young salmon of the flood-tide of freedom
That swells round Erin's shore!
Thou wilt leap against their loud oppressive torrent
Of bigotry and hate no more:
Drawn downward by their prone material instinct
Let them thunder on their rocks, and foam—
Thou hast leapt, aspiring soul, to founts beyond their raging,
Where troubled waters never come!

But I grieve not, eagle of the empty eyrie,
That thy wrathful cry is still;
And that the songs alone of peaceful mourners
Are heard today on Erin's hill:
Better far, if brothers' war be destined for us
(God avert that horrid day I pray!)
That ere our hands be stained with slaughter fratricidal,
Thy warm hand should be cold in clay.

But my trust is strong in God, who made us brothers,
That he will not suffer their right hands
Which thou hast joined in holier rites than wedlock,
To draw opposing brands.
Oh, many a tuneful tongue that thou mad'st vocal
Would lie cold and silent then—
And songless long once more, should often-widowed Erin
Mourn the loss of her brave young men.

Oh, brave young men, my love, my pride, my promise,
'Tis on you my hopes are set,
In manliness, in kindliness, in justice
To make Erin a nation yet:
Self-respecting, self-relying, self-advancing,
In union or in severance, free and strong—
And if God grant this, then, under God, to Thomas Davis
Let the greater praise belong!
—1847

Dear Dark Head

Put your head, darling, darling, darling,
Your darling black head my heart above;
Oh, mouth of honey, with the thyme for fragrance,
Who, with heart in breast, could deny you love?

Oh, many and many a young girl for me is pining,
Letting her locks of gold to the cold wind free,
For me, the foremost of our gay young fellows;
But I'd leave a hundred, pure love, for thee!

Then put your head, darling, darling, darling,
Your darling black head my heart above;
Oh, mouth of honey, with the thyme for fragrance,
Who, with heart in breast, could deny you love?
—1867

[1] *resurrection* I.e., the raising of the dead at the Day of Judgement.

THOMAS DAVIS (1814–1845)

Born in County Cork, Thomas Davis studied law at Trinity College in Dublin before becoming a leader of the nationalist Young Ireland movement. Hoping for unity between Protestants and Catholics in support of the Irish cause, he helped to establish the influential weekly newspaper *The Nation*, and wrote numerous nationalist ballads. Though he died of scarlet fever at the age of 30, his accomplishments during his brief years were such that he provided significant inspiration to later nationalists such as Patrick (or Pádraig) Pearse.

A Nation Once Again

When boyhood's fire was in my blood,
I read of ancient freemen,
For Greece and Rome who bravely stood,
Three Hundred men and Three men.[1]
And then I prayed I yet might see
Our fetters rent° in twain,° *torn / two*
And Ireland, long a province, be
A Nation once again

And, from that time, through wildest woe,
That hope has shone, a far light;
Nor could love's brightest summer glow
Outshine that solemn starlight:
It seemed to watch above my head
In forum, field, and fane;° *church*
Its angel voice sang round my bed,
"A Nation once again."

It whispered, too, that "freedom's ark
And service high and holy,
Would be profaned by feelings dark,
And passions vane or lowly;
For freedom comes from God's right hand,
And needs a godly train;
And righteous men must make our land
A Nation once again."

So, as I grew from boy to man,
I bent me to that bidding—
My spirit of each selfish plan
And cruel passion ridding;
For, thus I hoped one day to aid—
Oh! can such hope be vain?
When my dear country shall be made
A Nation once again.

—1845

AODH MAC DOMHNAILL (1802–1867)

Mac Domhnaill wrote poetry in Irish during a period when the use of that language was declining dramatically. For many years he was employed by the Irish Society, a Protestant-run organization which aimed to give Irish speakers throughout Ireland access to the Scriptures in their native language; he also worked collecting Irish-language songs, stories, and manuscripts. Among Mac Domhnaill's own writings—many of which were elegies to figures such as the Catholic leader Daniel O'Connell—are three poems written during various stages of the Great Famine. The details of the last few years of Mac Domhnaill's life are unclear; he died in a poorhouse in County Cavan in 1867.

[1] [Davis's note] The Three Hundred Greeks who died at Thermopylæ, and the Three Romans who kept the Sublician Bridge.

Milleadh na bPrátaí

Níl file ná fáidh dár ghnáthaigh cumann na Naoi,
Níl ollamh ná bard le fáil a bhlas an sruth sí,
Níl duine den dáil gan cháin gan donas gan díth,
Faoi chogadh lucht Béarla a sháraigh orainn le dlí.

Ach dá mairfeadh i stát san áit seo curaidh mar bhí,
Mac Cumhaill is mac Dáire is ní áirím Conchúr an rí,
Cú Chulainn, Conall Cearnach is ar sáraíodh uilig sa maidhm,
Ba ghairid an spás go gcarnfaí Bhullaí sa ngríb.

Ach ó d'imigh gan dáil na táinte a chleacht inár dtír,
Is gan againn 'na n-áit ach bearnadh, gorta is íot',
Ní chluintear in áltaibh cárlach is ceiliúr ar chraobh,
Is níl bric san áill mar ghnách in Oileán na Naomh.

Níl fear i gcrích Fáil ná mná is leinbh na cích',
Níl scafaire breá ná stáidbhean mhascalach mhín,
Níl bacach ar shráid ach cráite is torrach a chaoi,
Ó tháinig an phláigh ar phrátaí, is díomhaoin dubh díth'.

The Spoiling of the Potatoes[1]

There's neither poet nor prophet with the Muses acquainted,
Nor ollave,[2] nor bard, the enchanted stream that has tasted,
Not one of them is free of censure, misery, and want,
After the war of the English speakers who with laws have oppressed us.

But if the heroes of old held sway in this place,
Mac Cumhaill, mac Dáire or, even, Conchúr the king,[3]
Cú Chulainn, Conall Cearnach[4] and all who were bested in the attack,
They wouldn't be long driving Billy[5] into the mud.

But since the wealth we knew in this land was divested,
And in its place only destruction, famine and thirst,
The song of the birds in glen or on branch is heard not,
There's no longer trout in the streams of the Island of Saints.[6]

There's no man in Ireland, nor woman, nor suckling babe,
There's no strapping fellow nor stately woman, strong and fine,
There's no beggar on the street that is not tormented and care-laden;
Since the potatoes were blighted, they are destitute and sorely wanting.

---

[1] *The Spoiling of the Potatoes* The translation is by Fionntán DeBrun (translation copyright © Fionntán DeBrun 2018).

[2] *ollave* Highest class of poets. (The Irish spelling *ollamh* is often used in English as well.)

[3] *Mac Cumhaill* Fionn mac Cumhaill, also known in English as Finn MacCool, a celebrated hunter-warrior of Irish mythology, featured in the Fenian Cycle; *mac Dáire* Legendary warrior-king of Munster; *Conchúr the king* Conchobar mac Nessa, legendary king of Ulster.

[4] *Cú Chulainn* Legendary warrior of Ulster, known for his ability to go into a terrifying battle frenzy; *Conall Cearnach* Legendary warrior.

[5] *Billy* Anglicization of an Irish word for the English.

[6] *Island of Saints* Common epithet for Ireland.

Is an measann sibh a chairde an rá seo uile bheith fior,
Gurbh é siocair na mbráithre a sháraigh aithne na naomh,
Nó cionnfáth na banríona a d'áirigh muintir na crích',
Nó an dtáinig an phláigh mar thámhaibh eile ón ngaoth?

Ní chreidim go bráth is a shárfhios anois ag mo chroí
Gurbh é mallacht an Phápa ar Mháirtín fá bhriseadh an dlí
A thug milleadh ar bharr na bprátaí uilig san oích'—
Is feicfidh tú bearnadh is bánú eile ar Sheán Bhuí.

Guímse an tAthair is Banríon Fhlaitheas na Naomh,
Peadar 's a' Papa, Pádraig is easpaig an tsaoil,
Sagairt is bráithre cráifeach is manaigh le brí
Go dtige na Spáinnigh le prátaí chugainn arís.

And friends, do you think that all that is said is true,
That this was the fault of the friars who broke the commandments of saints,
Or the reason the queen counted the people of the land?[1]
Or did the blight come like other plagues from the wind?

I will never believe it for I now know it right well in my heart,
That it was the Pope's curse on Martin[2] for breaking the law
That brought destruction on all the potato crop in the night—
And you'll yet see John Bull[3] breached and laid to waste.

I pray in earnest to the Father and the Queen of Heaven,
Peter and the Pope, Patrick[4] and all the world's bishops,
Priests and pious friars and monks
That the Spanish may come to us with potatoes again.[5]
—1846

---

[1] *the queen ... the land* Reference to the census taken in 1841 (the monarch at the time was Queen Victoria).

[2] *Martin* Martin Luther (1483–1546), German religious leader whose attacks on ecclesiastical corruption began the Protestant Reformation in Europe; he was excommunicated by the Pope for his anti-Church writings.

[3] *John Bull* Common personification of England.

[4] *Peter* Saint Peter, one of Jesus' apostles, traditionally considered the first pope by Roman Catholics; *Patrick* Patron saint of Ireland, traditionally considered the first bishop of Armagh and the founder of Christianity on the island.

[5] *the Spanish ... potatoes again* The earliest-known cultivation of the potato was by the Incas in South America; following the conquest of Peru by Spain in 1536, the Spanish introduced the potato to Europe.

A temporary roadside home of a landless family, late nineteenth century. No photographs of the suffering endured by the Irish peasantry during the Great Famine are known to exist. Photographs such as this one from later in the century, however, provide evidence of how little improvement there was in housing conditions for the very poor, even many decades after the famine. (For more on this subject, see the section "Contexts: Ireland in the Long Nineteenth Century" in the online component of this anthology.)

BOY AND GIRL AT CAHERA.

James Mahoney, *Boy and Girl at Cahera*. This sketch was one of several published in the 13 February 1847 and 20 February 1847 issues of *The Illustrated London News*. The accompanying story provided the background: "The sketch is taken on the road, at Cahera, of a famished boy and girl turning up the ground to seek for a potato to appease their hunger. 'Not far from the spot where I made this sketch,' says Mr. Mahoney, 'is another of the many sepulchres above ground, where six dead bodies had lain for twelve days, without the least chance of interment, owing to their being so far from the town.'" Substantial excerpts from these illustrated articles, together with other background documents pertaining to the Great Famine, are available in the online component of this anthology, in the section "Contexts: Ireland in the Long Nineteenth Century."

LADY JANE WILDE (SPERANZA) (1821–1896)

Poet, nationalist, and women's rights campaigner Lady Jane Wilde, née Elgee, was born in Wexford in 1821. Though today less well-known than her son Oscar, in her own time Wilde was a popular and respected member of literary circles in Dublin and London, and hosted a salon in the home in which her son grew up. Wilde wrote poetry for the influential and controversial nationalist newspaper *The Nation* in the 1840s, alternately using the pen names John Fenshaw Ellis and "Speranza"—meaning "hope" in Italian; she became an editor of the newspaper in 1848. Wilde also published two volumes of poetry and a collection of Irish folktales. Upon the bankruptcy and death of her husband, Lady Wilde moved to London to join Oscar and his brother Willie, where she lived in relative poverty until her death in 1896.

The Famine Year

1

Weary men, what reap ye?—Golden corn for the stranger.[1]
What sow ye?—Human corses° that wait for the avenger. *corpses*
Fainting forms, hunger-stricken, what see you in the offing?° *distance*
Stately ships to bear our food away, amid the stranger's scoffing.
There's a proud array of soldiers—what do they round your door?
They guard our masters' granaries from the thin hands of the poor.
Pale mothers, wherefore weeping?—Would to God that we were dead—
Our children swoon° before us, and we cannot give them bread. *faint*

2

Little children, tears are strange upon your infant faces,
God meant you but to smile within your mother's soft embraces.
Oh! we know not what is smiling, and we know not what is dying;
But we're hungry, very hungry, and we cannot stop our crying.
And some of us grow cold and white—we know not what it means;
But, as they lie beside us, we tremble in our dreams.
There's a gaunt crowd on the highway—are ye come to pray to man,
With hollow eyes that cannot weep, and for words your faces wan?° *pale, sickly*

3

No; the blood is dead within our veins—we care not now for life;
Let us die hid in the ditches, far from children and from wife;
We cannot stay and listen to their raving, famished cries—
Bread! Bread! Bread! and none to still their agonies.
We left our infants playing with their dead mother's hand:
We left our maidens maddened by the fever's scorching brand:
Better, maiden, thou were strangled in thy own dark-twisted tresses—
Better, infant, thou wert smothered in thy mother's first caresses.

4

We are fainting in our misery, but God will hear our groan;
Yet, if fellow-men desert us, will He hearken° from His Throne? *listen*
Accursed are we in our own land, yet toil we still and toil;
But the stranger reaps our harvest—the alien owns our soil.

[1] *Golden corn … the stranger* Aside from the blight upon potatoes, during the famine actual shortage of food in Ireland was never as extreme as might be expected; rather, the issue at hand was the continued export of Irish crops to England and abroad, even throughout the height of starvation; *corn* Any edible grain, such as wheat.

O Christ! how have we sinned, that on our native plains
We perish houseless, naked, starved, with branded brow, like Cain's?[1]
Dying, dying wearily, with a torture sure and slow—
Dying, as a dog would die, by the wayside as we go.

5

One by one they're falling round us, their pale faces to the sky;
We've no strength left to dig them graves—there let them lie.
The wild bird, if he's stricken, is mourned by the others,
But we—we die in Christian land—we die amid our brothers,
In the land which God has given, like a wild beast in his cave,
Without a tear, a prayer, a shroud, a coffin, or a grave.
Ha! but think ye the contortions on each livid face ye see,
Will not be read on judgment-day by eyes of Deity?

6

We are wretches, famished, scorned, human tools to build your pride,
But God will yet take vengeance for the souls for whom Christ died.
Now is your hour of pleasure—bask ye in the world's caress;
But our whitening bones against ye will arise as witnesses,
From the cabins and the ditches, in their charred, uncoffined masses,
For the Angel of the Trumpet[2] will know them as he passes.
A ghastly, spectral army, before the great God we'll stand,
And arraign ye as our murderers, the spoilers of our land.
—1864

[1] *Cain* In Genesis 4, Cain murders his brother Abel, and is thenceforth marked and cursed by God.

[2] *Angel of the Trumpet* I.e., the angel or angels who will sound the trumpets to announce the coming of the Last Judgment.

William Allingham (1824–1889)

Though today remembered mostly for "The Fairies" and a small number of similar poems, William Allingham was a relatively influential writer during his own day, and was a contemporary and friend of poets such as Alfred Tennyson and Dante Gabriel Rossetti. Besides being a writer of original poetry, Allingham was also a collector of ballads, and published a popular volume of British ballads in 1864. His own poetry was significant in the development of the Celtic revival movement, and in this capacity inspired later Irish poets such as W.B. Yeats.

The Fairies (A Child's Song)

Up the airy mountain,
Down the rushy glen,
We daren't go a-hunting
For fear of little men;
Wee folk, good folk,[3]
Trooping all together;
Green jacket, red cap,
And white owl's feather!

Down along the rocky shore
Some make their home,
They live on crispy pancakes
Of yellow tide-foam;
Some in the reeds
Of the black mountain lake,
With frogs for their watch-dogs,
All night awake.

High on the hill-top
The old King sits;
He is now so old and grey
He's nigh lost his wits.
With a bridge of white mist

[3] *good folk* Common epithet in Ireland for the fairies.

Columbkill[1] he crosses,
On his stately journeys
From Slieveleague to Rosses;[2]
Or going up with music
On cold starry nights,
To sup with the Queen
Of the gay Northern Lights.

They stole little Bridget
For seven years long;
When she came down again
Her friends were all gone.
They took her lightly back,
Between the night and morrow;
They thought that she was fast asleep,
But she was dead with sorrow.
They have kept her ever since
Deep within the lakes,
On a bed of flag-leaves,
Watching till she wakes.

By the craggy hill-side,
Through the mosses bare,
They have planted thorn-trees
For pleasure here and there.
Is any man so daring
As dig one up in spite,
He shall find their sharpest thorns
In his bed at night.

Up the airy mountain,
Down the rushy glen,
We daren't go a-hunting
For fear of little men;
Wee folk, good folk,
Trooping all together;
Green jacket, red cap,
And white owl's feather!
—1849

[1] *Columbkill* Coloumbkille Lough in County Donegal, named after Saint Columba or Colm Cille, a significant early missionary said to have been born in Donegal.

[2] *Slieveleague to Rosses* Set of sea cliffs and geographical area, respectively, in County Donegal.

THOMAS D'ARCY MCGEE (1825–1868)

Although he is more widely known as the Irish-Canadian politician who successfully pushed for Confederation in the 1860s, Thomas D'Arcy McGee (1825–68) was also a prolific writer, and was indeed regarded by some as among the finest Irish poets of the nineteenth century. Born in Louth and raised largely in Wexford, McGee received little formal education, instead attending informal hedge schools. At the age of seventeen he emigrated to the United States, where he wrote for Irish-American journals such as *The Boston Pilot* and spoke in favor of repealing the Irish Acts of Union. Three years later he returned to Ireland and became involved with the radical nationalist paper *The Nation* and the Young Irelander Rebellion of 1848; when the rebellion failed, he fled back to the United States. After this period his political views grew increasingly conservative. He moved to Canada in 1857 and denounced the radicalism of the growing Fenian Movement. After a decade of success as a Canadian politician, McGee was assassinated in 1868; his funeral was attended by thousands.

Throughout the changing periods of his political career, McGee remained known and respected for his poetry, much of which takes inspiration from the history and mythology of his native Ireland. The text of the following poems is taken from the posthumous collection of his poetry, *The Poems of Thomas D'Arcy McGee*, edited by Irish author Mary Anne Sadlier in 1869. In her preface to the volume, Sadlier notes that some poems have been changed very slightly "to correct errors, which the author himself would have done in a general revision."

The Celts

Long, long ago, beyond the misty space
Of twice a thousand years,
In Erin[3] old there dwelt a mighty race,
Taller than Roman spears;
Like oaks and towers, they had a giant grace,
Were fleet as deers,

[3] *Erin* From the Irish name for Ireland, Éire.

With winds and wave they made their
  'biding°-place, *abiding*
 These Western shepherd-seers.

Their ocean-god was Mân-â-nân M'Lir,[1]
 Whose angry lips,
In their white foam, full often would inter
 Whole fleets of ships;
Cromah,[2] their day-god and their thunderer,
 Made morning and eclipse;
Bride[3] was their queen of song, and unto her
 They prayed with fire-touched lips.

Great were their deeds, their passions, and their sports;
 With clay and stone
They piled on strath[4] and shore those mystic forts
 Not yet o'erthrown;
On cairn-crowned hills they held their council-courts;
 While youths alone,
With giant dogs, explored the elk resorts,
 And brought them down.

Of these was Finn,[5] the father of the bard
 Whose ancient song
Over the clamor of all change is heard,
 Sweet-voiced and strong.
Finn once o'ertook Granu,[6] the golden-haired,
 The fleet and young;
From her the lovely, and from him the feared,
 The primal poet sprung.

Ossian! two thousand years of mist and change
 Surround thy name—
Thy Finian[7] heroes now no longer range
 The hills of fame.
The very name of Finn and Gaul[8] sound strange—
 Yet thine the same—
By miscalled lake and desecrated grange—
 Remains, and shall remain!

The Druid's[9] altar and the Druid's creed
 We scarce can trace,
There is not left an undisputed deed
 Of all your race,
Save your majestic song, which hath their speed,
 And strength and grace;
In that sole song they live, and love, and bleed—
 It bears them on through space.

Oh, inspired giant! shall we e'er behold
 In our own time
One fit to speak your spirit on the wold,° *forest*
 Or seize your rhyme?
One pupil of the past, as mighty souled
 As in the prime,
Were the fond, fair, and beautiful, and bold—
 They, of your song sublime!
—1869

Home Thoughts

If will had wings, how fast I'd flee
To the home of my heart o'er the seething sea!

---

[1] *Mân-â-nân M'Lir* Celtic sea god.

[2] *Cromah* Likely Crom Cruach, Celtic god with unclear associations and origins, who has been described variously as a sun god, a god of fertility, or a violent god propitiated by human sacrifice.

[3] *Bride* Also known as Brigid, Celtic goddess of spring, fertility, and poetry, whose mythology may have merged with that of the popular Catholic Saint Brigid; traditions in the veneration of both the goddess and the saint involve tending a sacred fire.

[4] *strath* Broad river valley.

[5] *Finn* Fionn mac Cumhaill or Finn MacCool, famed hunter-warrior of Irish mythology and father of the mythological poet Oisín, or Ossian.

[6] *Granu* Probably Gráinne, mythological wife of Fionn; however, according to the dominant mythology, Gráinne vehemently disliked her husband and eventually separated from him; the poet Oisín is thus said to have been the son of Fionn and another woman, Sadhbh.

[7] *Finian* Referring to the Fenian Cycle, the body of mythological accounts describing the life of Fionn Mac Cumhaill and his relations.

[8] *Gaul* Probably Goll mac Morna, Fionn's sometime-enemy and sometime-ally.

[9] *Druid* Member of an ancient, semi-mythological Celtic order of magicians, sorcerers, and soothsayers.

If wishes were power, if words were spells,
I'd be this hour where my own love dwells.

My own love dwells in the storied land,
Where the holy wells sleep in yellow sand;
And the emerald lustre of Paradise beams
Over homes that cluster round singing streams.

I, sighing, alas! exist alone—
My youth is as grass on an unsunned stone,
Bright to the eye, but unfelt below—
As sunbeams that lie over Arctic snow.

My heart is a lamp that love must relight,
Or the world's fire-damp will quench it quite;
In the breast of my dear, my life-tide springs—
Oh! I'd tarry none here, if will had wings.
—1869

The Irish Wife

Earl Desmond's Apology[1]

I would not give my Irish wife
  For all the dames of the Saxon land—
I would not give my Irish wife
  For the Queen of France's hand;
For she to me is dearer
  Than castles strong, or lands, or life—
An outlaw—so I'm near her
  To love till death my Irish wife.

Oh, what would be this home of mine—
  A ruined, hermit-haunted place,
But for the light that nightly shines
  Upon its walls from Kathleen's face?
What comfort in a mine of gold—
  What pleasure in a royal life,
If the heart within lay dead and cold,
  If I could not wed my Irish wife?

I knew the law forbade the banns[2]—
  I knew my king abhorred her race—
Who never bent before their clans,
  Must bow before their ladies' grace.
Take all my forfeited domain,
  I cannot wage with kinsmen strife—
Take knightly gear and noble name,
  And I will keep my Irish wife.

My Irish wife has clear blue eyes,
  My heaven by day, my stars by night—
And, twin-like, truth and fondness lie
  Within her swelling bosom white.
My Irish wife has golden hair—
  Apollo's[3] harp had once such strings—
Apollo's self might pause to hear
  Her bird-like carol when she sings.

I would not give my Irish wife
  For all the dames of the Saxon land—
I would not give my Irish wife
  For the Queen of France's hand;
For she to me is dearer
  Than castles strong, or lands, or life—
In death I would lie near her,
  And rise beside my Irish wife.
—1869

[1] *Earl Desmond's Apology* The poem is apparently inspired by the marriage in 1418 of Thomas Fitzgerald, 5th Earl of Desmond—an Anglo-Norman peer—and the Gaelic woman Catherine MacCormac. The marriage violated the Statutes of Kilkenny, which forbade English settlers from marrying into old Irish families; Fitzgerald was thereby dispossessed of his lands. The marriage also inspired a poem by Irish poet Thomas Moore (1779–1852), "Desmond's Song"; *Apology* Defense.

Memories

I left two loves on a distant strand,
One young, and fond, and fair, and bland;[4]

[2] *banns* Public declaration of an intention to marry.

[3] *Apollo* Greek god of music.

[4] *bland* Gentle; mild-mannered.

One fair, and old, and sadly grand—
My wedded wife and my native land.

One tarrieth sad and seriously
Beneath the roof that mine should be;
One sitteth sibyl-like[1] by the sea,
Chanting a grave song mournfully.

A little life I have not seen
Lies by the heart that mine hath been;
A cypress wreath darkles now, I ween,° *think*
Upon the brow of my love in green.

The mother and wife shall pass away,
Her hands be dust, her lips be clay;
But my other love on earth shall stay,
And live in the life of a better day.

Ere we were born my first love was,
My sires° were heirs to her holy cause; *fathers*
And she yet shall sit in the world's applause,
A mother of men and blessèd laws.

I hope and strive the while I sigh,
For I know my first love cannot die;
From the chain of woes that loom so high
Her reign shall reach to eternity.
—1869

Emily Lawless (1824–1889)

Born into an aristocratic Anglo-Irish family (her father became a baron while she was a child), Lawless spent much of her childhood at the estate of her mother's family in Country Galway, and became much affected by the rugged scenery of western Ireland. She began to write while in her thirties; her first novel, the three-volume *A Chelsea Householder*, was published in 1882. Her third novel, *Hurrish*, set a remote area of County Clare, established Lawless as a popular novelist.

[1] *sibyl-like* Resembling the sibyls, women of classical mythology with powers of divination, often characterized as frenzied or witch-like.

Lawless wrote history as well as fiction and poetry, and her novels and poems are often set in earlier eras. She seems to have had more sympathy with the cause of rebellion against English oppression in earlier eras than she did in her own. She supported the Land League's efforts to improve the lot of Irish tenant farmers (a cause bitterly opposed by her landowner brother), but she was no revolutionary; rather than Home Rule for Ireland, she advocated a continuance of the union between Ireland and the rest of Britain.

Her best-known poems appear in the volume *With the Wild Geese* (1902), which had originally appeared in a privately printed edition in 1898. It came to the attention of Stopford Brooke, who encouraged her to seek a wider audience for the poems; she agreed on the condition that he write an introduction that would fill in for English readers the historical context for the poems. Here is the explanation given for the meaning of "wild geese" in this context:

> The "Wild Geese" was the name given by the romantic and sorrowful imaginings of the Irish to the exiles who, like the wild birds and with their wailing cry, migrated to the Continent before and after the Battle of Aughrim, and the Surrender of Limerick in 1691. The Irish officers and soldiers were permitted by the Treaty of Limerick to go where they pleased in ships provided by the English government. Twenty thousand sorrowing men ... sailed to Brest. ... They were only the forerunners of a great exodus of Irishmen flying from the iniquities of the penal laws to give their swords to France, an exodus which lasted fully a hundred years.

Lawless never married; towards the end of the century she moved to Surrey, south of London, where she appears to have shared a household with Lady Sarah Spencer. In *A Garden Diary* (1902), which she dedicates "To the Garden's Chief owner, and the Gardener's Friend," Lawless published selections from a diary in which she writes of their garden, of their household, of world affairs (especially of the Boer War that was then raging), and—with passionate intensity in the 25 August 1900 entry reproduced below—of their friendship.

After Aughrim[1]

She said, "They gave me of their best,
They lived, they gave their lives for me;[2]
I tossed them to the howling waste,
And flung them to the foaming sea."

She said, "I never gave them aught,
Not mine the power, if mine the will;
I let them starve, I let them bleed—
They bled and starved, and loved me still."

She said, "Ten times they fought for me,
Ten times they strove with might and main,
Ten times I saw them beaten down,
Ten times they rose and fought again."

She said, "I stayed alone at home,
A dreary woman, grey and cold;
I never asked them how they fared,
Yet still they loved me as of old."

She said, "I never called them sons,
I almost ceased to breathe their name,
Then caught it echoing down the wind,
Blown backwards from the lips of Fame."

She said, "Not mine, not mine the fame;
Far over sea, far over land,
Cast forth like rubbish from my shores,
They won it yonder, sword in hand."

She said, "God knows they owe me nought,
I tossed them to the foaming sea,
I tossed them to the howling waste,
Yet still their love comes home to me."
—1902

[1] *Aughrim* At the battle of Aughrim (1691), fought near Galway in western Ireland, between 5,000 and 10,000 lives were lost as the English army defeated the Jacobite army; the Jacobites were never again a significant force.

[2] *me* The voice here is that of Ireland personified as a woman—a literary device long common in Irish literature.

Clare Coast[3]

Circa 1720

See, cold island, we stand
Here tonight on your shore,
Tonight, but never again;
Lingering a moment more.
See, beneath us our boat
Tugs at its tightening chain,
Holds out its sail to the breeze,
Pants to be gone again.
Off then with shouts and mirth,
Off with laughter and jests,
Mirth and song on our lips,
Hearts like lead in our breasts.

Death and the grave behind,
Death and a traitor's bier;
Honour and fame before,
Why do we linger here?
Why do we stand and gaze,
Fools, whom fools despise,
Fools untaught by the years,
Fools renounced by the wise?

Heartsick, a moment more,
Heartsick, sorry, fierce,
Lingering, lingering on,
Dreaming the dreams of yore;
Dreaming the dreams of our youth,
Dreaming the days when we stood
Joyous, expectant, serene,
Glad, exultant of mood,
Singing with hearts afire,
Singing with joyous strain,
Singing aloud in our pride,
"We shall redeem her again!"

[3] *Clare Coast* The poem, part of Lawless's collection *With the Wild Geese* (1902), takes as its subject the "Wild Geese," exiled soldiers who left Ireland to fight in continental armies between the sixteenth and eighteenth centuries; many of those soldiers were Irish Catholics, who were barred by the Penal Laws from entering the armed forces in their own country; *Clare* County on the west coast of Ireland.

Ah, not tonight that strain—
Silent tonight we stand,
A scanty, a toil-worn crew,
Strangers, foes in the land!
Gone the light of our youth,
Gone forever, and gone,
Hope with the beautiful eyes,
Who laughed as she lured us on;
Lured us to danger and death,
To honour, perchance to fame—
Empty fame at the best,
Glory half dimmed with shame.
War-battered dogs are we,
Fighters in every clime,
Fillers of trench and of grave,
Mockers, bemocked by time.
War-dogs, hungry and grey,
Gnawing a naked bone,
Fighters in every clime,
Every cause but our own.

See us, cold isle of our love!
Coldest, saddest of isles—
Cold as the hopes of our youth,
Cold as your own wan smiles.
Coldly your streams outpour,
Each apart on the height,
Trickling, indifferent, slow,
Lost in the hush of the night.
Colder, sadder the clouds,
Comfortless bringers of rain;
Desolate daughters of air,
Sweep o'er your sad grey plain
Hiding the form of your hills,
Hiding your low sand duns;° *dunes*
But coldest, saddest, oh isle!
Are the homeless hearts of your sons.

Coldest, and saddest there,
In yon sun-lit land of the south,
Where we sicken, and sorrow, and pine,
And the jest flies from mouth to mouth,
And the church bells crash overhead,
And the idle hours flit by,
And the beaded wine-cups clink.
And the sun burns fierce in the sky;
And your exiles, the merry of heart,
Laugh and boast with the best,
Boast, and extol their part,
Boast, till some lifted brow,
Crossed with a line severe,
Seems with displeasure to ask,
"Are these loud braggarts we hear,
Are they the sons of the West,
The wept-for, the theme of songs,
The exiled, the injured, the banned,
The men of a thousand wrongs?"

Fool, did you never hear
Of sunshine which broke through rain?
Sunshine which came with storm?
Laughter that rang of pain?
Boastings begotten of grief,
Vauntings to hide a smart,
Braggings with trembling lip,
Tricks of a broken heart?

Sudden some wayward gleam,
Sudden some passing sound—
The careless splash of an oar,
The idle bark of a hound,
A shadow crossing the sun,
An unknown step in the hall,
A nothing, a folly, a straw!
Back it returns—all—all!
Back with the rush of a storm,
Back the old anguish and ill,
The sad, green landscape of home,
The small grey house by the hill,
The wide grey shores of the lake,
The low sky, seeming to weave
Its tender pitiful arms
Round the sick lone landscape at eve.
Back with its pains and its wrongs,
Back with its toils and its strife,
Back with its struggle and woe,

Back flows the stream of our life.
Darkened with treason and wrong,
Darkened with anguish and ruth,° *sorrow*
Bitter, tumultuous, fierce,
Yet glad in the light of our youth.

So, cold island, we stand
Here tonight on your shore—
Tonight, but never again,
Lingering a moment more.
See, beneath us our boat,
Tugs at its tightening chain,
Holds out its sail to the breeze,
Pants to be gone again.
Off then with shouts and mirth,
Off with laughter and jests,
Jests and song on our lips,
Hearts like lead in our breasts.
—1902

To ________, Aged Twenty-Two

You will recall perchance some summer day,
Not this year, or e'en the next, but some far year,
What time we have two have stood together here,
Under this friendly cloudflecked sky of May.

The late-come swallows in their devious way,
The urgent questings of bewildered bees,
The chirp of some proud mother from the trees,
And the warm promise of the procreant clay,

All these will perhaps return, and if with these,
With sun and cloud and bird and budding trees
There mingle some old memories of me,
Keep them, but do not grieve. For naught abides,
The untiring river rolls, and down its tides
Wave follows wave into the same old sea.
—1909

Emigrants

Like sea-pools on some restless, rock-strewn shore
These bog-pools flutter ere they sink to rest,
And o'er this surface, level as a floor,
Yon blue reek° trails its idle way to west *chimney-smoke*
It comes from thee, brown shieling,[1] late bereft
Of thy last fledgelings; tenement outworn,
Long marked for desolation, and now left
To two old hearts, submissive, but forlorn.

How like some wintry nest it shows tonight;
While over its bent thatch a young curved moon
Peers through thin clouds scarce greyer than her light
Peers wistfully, as if arrived too soon,
Or doubtful of her welcome. While I stand
A string of wild duck speeds across her horn,
Six, seven, eleven—Oh adventurous band!
Westward you stream, due west, and now are gone.

Gone! Gone! They leave us! Yet the brown pools there
Still dance and flutter in this crisping wind,
And still the blue reek gaily mounts to where
That new-born moon, so timid, yet so kind,
Peers earthward, as if curious to mark
A scene less often honoured of the sun.
Slowly the shadows lengthen, while the dark
Grows deeper; and another day is done.
—1906

from *A Garden Diary*

September 4, 1899

It has been wet, and is now fine again, consequently our view of the downs exhibits those tones of vinous[2] purple, shading into indigo, that in moments of patriotic expansion I am apt to call Irish. I do not think it is quite friendly of our neighbours, especially those who

---

[1] *shieling* Rustic house on a pasture.

[2] *vinous* Wine-like.

live upon the ridge above our heads, to smile so significantly whenever that word "view" happens to slip out, as it did just now, in alluding to our new possession, and its prospects. For what, after all, is a view? The question seems to suggest a reference to the dictionary, and here is Webster, ponderous in brown calf.[1] "View. 1st. Act of seeing, or beholding; sight; survey; examination by the eye. That which is looked towards, or kept in sight; an appearance; a show." Well, have we not something to look towards, to keep in sight, some appearance, some show? For that matter, so, it may be urged, has the habitant of the "two pair back,"[2] or the rustic whose prospect is limited to a survey of his or her neighbours' under garments—those "short and simple flannels of the poor" hung to dry in silhouette against a back fence. The truth is it is not at all desirable to be so haughty. I will not go so far as to say that it is unchristian, but it is certainly unbecoming, for are we not all fellow-creatures? What if you *can* command seven counties from your windows? What if on one particular morning—to me incredible—you did see three ships cross Shoreham gap?[3] What if from your garden chair you can be regaled by a fantasia of changing lights and shadows? be lapped into peace upon summer afternoons, or stirred by the drama of battle clouds, flung into blackness by a storm? Well, if you can, be glad of it, but for pity's sake abstain from bragging! "Gi' God thanks, and say no more o' it." Believe me it is not even commonly lucky to be so proud, and I speak with some little authority upon that subject.

For as regards this matter of views, I too have been haughty to the point of insupportableness. I too have believed that the possession of wide prospects argued some peculiar, some ineffable superiority in myself. There was a time when nothing short of an entire ocean, none of your petty babbling channels, but the whole thundering Atlantic, sufficed for my ambition. In those days only upon the largest combination of sea, sky, mountain; seascape, landscape, cloudscape, did it seem possible adequately to exist. As for a mere rustic landscape, as for a confined one, as for a humdrum English one, above all as for a landscape within fifty miles of London, why the mention of such things merely moved my commiseration! Those were the days when to be called upon to leave what is sometimes uncivilly called the ruder[4] island, and to repair, even temporarily, to the more prosperous one, seemed a fall and a degradation hardly to be measured by words. When the contraction of the horizon seemed like a contraction of all life, and of all that made life worth having. When the remembrance that one would have to wake in the morning with no dim blue line to greet one, appeared, to a patriotic, a self-respecting being, to be a wrong and an indignity hardly to be endured without revolt.

Such an attitude is, I now hold, unbecoming in mere mortals, and, like other vaulting ambitions, is apt to precede a fall. The man who starts in life determined to be either Cæsar, or nothing, frequently fails to become Cæsar, whereas with regard to the other alternative, the gods are quite capable of taking him at his word. Happily, life is for most of us a liberal education, and the narrowing of the horizon comes to be endured with a philosophy born of other, and more serious deprivations. It may even be open to question whether any man or woman ever yet was made the better by the possession of a noble view? That he or she ought to have been made so is quite true, but as a matter of fact, have they? We are moulded out of exceedingly stubborn stuff, and are not often ennobled, I suspect, by the landscapes that surround us, any more than we are by the pursuits we follow, or the names that we carry about with us. Furthermore the essentials of all landscape show a considerable similarity. Much the same sort of clouds and sunshine, much the same sort of nights and days, much the same sort of summers and winters, visit alike the tamest and the wildest of them. Even the more dramatic and exciting fluctuations—snow, and hail, storm, and lightning—exhibit a greater impartiality than might have been expected. The gale that has just unroofed your lordly tower, had equally swept the tiles

[1] *calf* Calfskin; i.e., bound in leather.

[2] *two pair back* Room at the back of a house's second floor.

[3] *Shoreham gap* The opening to the harbor at Shoreham-on-Sea (in West Sussex).

[4] *ruder* Humbler; less civilized (as Ireland was often thought of by the English).

off our humble porch; in the same way that moralists are fond of assuring us that sickness and sorrow, loss and pain, old age and death, fall equally upon the homes of beggars and of kings.

Never having belonged to the last of these classes, I cannot take it upon me to answer for the discomforts that pertain to it. With regard to the other, though I have often seen myself figuring, or upon the point of figuring, amongst its sad and tattered ranks, the impression has never been a particularly agreeable one, and I prefer, therefore, no to dwell upon it. It was moreover the subject of landscapes, I think, not of either kings or beggars, that was under discussion? But that is the sort of thing that is always happening! Of all the unsatisfactory stock to keep, ideas are in my experience the most unsatisfactory; equally whether they are winged, or entirely wingless ones. As for a diary—which, to be of the slightest use, ought to act as a kind of cow-boy, or goose-girl, to them, and keep them in order—on the contrary it seems merely to follow their waddling and gyrations with the most foolish, and unnecessary submissiveness. The result is that one starts intending to fill a page with one subject, and before one has got very far one discovers that in reality one is filling it up with quite another! …

August 25, 1900

From gropings along unlit ways, and towards an undiscoverable goal, what a pleasant experience it is to turn suddenly back to the well-trodden paths of a near and a tried companionship! It is almost an exact parallel to the sensations of the child who, having rushed out of its home into the wild winter night, full of hollow reverberations, and perturbing gleams, suddenly retreats, and finds itself once more beside the hearth, with an absolutely new sense of its security, and wide-armed delightfulness.

Upon few topics has more ink been expended than upon this one of friendship. As regards one point all the pens have I think been agreed, and that is that diversity constitutes its soundest basis. If a truism, this is at least one of those truisms that every day's experience throws into new relief. Friendship demands absolutely no conformity, but lives, thrives, and has its being upon the most absolutely radical differences. Friend and friend may differ by nearly everything that can differentiate one human being from another. By the tenor of their thoughts; by the circumstances of their lives; by the very texture of their brains, their souls, their hearts, their entire natures. Friendship makes light of such little discrepancies as these. Its roots push down to a stratum where even the largest of them become mere accidents, and at that serene depth they meet and lock securely under them all.

To say that such a tie is the great ameliorator of life, the soother of its sorrows, the encourager of its brighter moments, is to say ridiculously little. To say that it is one that we could hardly endure to think of existing without, is to say almost less. The very notion of such a deprivation produces a sort of vertigo; a species of mental confusion, akin to the thought of losing identity itself. Worse, indeed, for it is not merely the everyday, the vulgar self, that such a loss—supposing it to be complete—would deprive one of. It is that other, better, and more shining self, which only really exists inside the enchanted walls of a loving, sympathetic friendship. Within those fostering walls it grows, expands, and flourishes, but outside of them it sickens, pines away, and dies.

It is a very singular tie, when one reflects a little upon it; so close often that no nearness of blood, no identity of name, could, so far as one can see, make it any closer. It seems to be antecedent, not alone to itself, but to the whole social warp and woof,[1] of which it is an outcome. Just as the trees in one wood seem, to anyone who wanders often in it, to have acquired a sort of identity, so two who have walked for some time very closely together, though they may differ as widely as an ash does from a pine, as an oak does from a hornbeam, acquire a sort of similarity, due to the same sunshine having warmed, the same storms having shaken and darkened both. It is well to speak a good word now and then of a personage whom one habitually abuses, so let

[1] *warp and woof* In weaving, the *warp* and *woof* are threads which cross each other at right angles to form the finished piece; thus, the social "fabric."

it be recorded in favour of that odd compound of good and ill which we call our existence that, if it has thwarted our desires, dwarfed our ambitions, nipped in our joys, chilled back our aspirations, cut down our hopes, and not infrequently wrung our hearts, at least—it has given us our friends!
—1901

JOHN KEEGAN CASEY (1846–1870)

Born during the Great Famine, Irish revolutionary John Keegan Casey wrote numerous articles for the later incarnation of the nationalist *Nation* newspaper, and was imprisoned for his participation in the Fenian Rising of 1867. He is best known for "The Rising of the Moon," a popular and much-performed ballad that exists in several variants.

The Rising of the Moon[1]

"Tell me, tell me, Shawn O'Farrell,
    Why it is you hurry so?"
"Hush *ma bouchal*,[2] hush and listen,"
    And his cheeks were in a glow.
"I bear orders from the captain,
    Get you ready quick and soon,
For our pikes must be together
    By the rising of the moon."

"Tell me, tell me, Shawn O'Farrell,
    Where the gathering is to be."
"At the old spot by the river
    That's well known to you and me.
One word more, our signal token,
    Whistle up the marching tune,
Hurrah, my boys, for Ireland's freedom,
    By the rising of the moon."

Down by the lonely river,
    A dark mass of men were seen,
Far above the starry banner
    Hung our own immortal green.
"Death to every foe and traitor,
    Forward on the marching tune,"
And a million pikes[3] were shining
    By the rising of the moon.

Out of every mud wall cabin
    Eyes were watching all the night,
Many a manly breast was throbbing
    For the blessed morning light.
Murmurs passed along the valley
    Like the banshee's lonely croon,
And a million pikes were shining
    By the rising of the moon.

Well they fought for poor old Ireland,
    And bitter was their fate,
What a feeling of pride and sorrow
    Fills the name of Ninety-Eight.
But yet we have in poor old Ireland
    Hearts that beat as firm and true,
We will follow in their footsteps
    By the rising of the moon.
—1866

[1] *The Rising of the Moon* The poem memorializes aspects of the Irish Rebellion of 1798, an uprising against British rule led by the United Irishmen; the rebellion was ultimately a failure, and many suspected rebels were brutally executed.

[2] *ma bouchal* From the Irish *mo bhuachaill*, meaning "my boy."

[3] *pikes* Long spears, the weapon most commonly used by the rebels in the Rebellion.

KATHARINE TYNAN (1859–1931)

A prolific writer, Katharine Tynan wrote twenty-seven volumes of poetry alone. Much of her earlier work was—like that of her friend W.B. Yeats—associated with the Celtic revival movement, and she had sympathies with Irish nationalism from a young age. Upon her marriage to an English man, however, Tynan became increasingly involved in British social and political concerns and increasingly wary of what she came to see as the radical nationalism of her home country.

The Long Vacation

This is the time the boys come home from school,
Filling the house with gay and happy noise,
Never at rest from morn till evening cool—
All the roads of the world bring home the boys.

This is the time—but still they are not come;
The mothers stand in the doorway listening long;
Long, long they shall wait ere the boys come home.
Where do they tarry, the dear, the light-heart
throng?

Their feet are heavy as lead and deep their rest.
The mothers watch the road till set of sun;
But nevermore the birds fly back to the nest.
The roads of the world run Heavenward every one.
—1916

Herbal

Love-lies-bleeding[1] now is found
Grown in every common ground.
Love-lies-bleeding thrives apace
With the dear forget-me-not;
Nor is boy's love[2] out of place
Now in any garden plot.

Love-in-a-mist,[3] bewildered
With the many tears Love shed,
Seeks for herb-o'-grace[4] to bind
Up her wounds, and fever-few[5]
To give ease to a hurt mind;
Wound-wort[6] is not wanting too.

Now the love-lies-bleeding grows
More than lily or the rose;[7]
Love-in-idleness[8] has gone
Out of fashion; here are flowers—
Heartsease[9] for to rest upon
With remembrance of sweet hours.

Ladders-to-heaven[10] may be found
Now in any common ground.
—1918

For Your Sake

For your sake who have left me grieving
I love the old who are tired of living,
Tired of travelling a road grown weary,
More than the young, more than the merry.

The old, patient and rosy faces
Stir my heart in its secret places.
The old eyes that ache for rest
Set my heart to bleed in my breast.

More than the children, golden and ruddy,
The bent knees and the feeble body
Stab my heart with the mother-pain,
For your sake in the night and rain.

For your sake I would fain enfold them,
The old heads to my breast and hold them,
Keep them safe from the lonely fear,
My kind love of many a year.

[1] *Love-lies-bleeding* Common name for Amaranthus caudatus, a purple-pink flower.

[2] *boy's love* Strongly scented flowering plant.

[3] *Love-in-a-mist* Common name for Nigella damascene, a blue-white flower with distinct twisted foliage, commonly grown in English gardens.

[4] *herb-o'-grace* Rue, a herb with small yellow flowers.

[5] *fever-few* Medicinal herb with small white flowers.

[6] *Wound-wort* Another medicinal herb common in Britain.

[7] *lily or the rose* Both flowers are traditional symbols of England (the lily is also a symbol of France).

[8] *Love-in-idleness* Also known as the wild pansy, a European wildflower.

[9] *Heartsease* Another name for the wild pansy.

[10] *Ladders-to-heaven* Lily-of-the-valley.

The old hands, I could kneel and kiss them,
Knotted and purple, could love them, caress them.
Ah, my dear, when the house is asleep,
I see your hands and I wake and weep.
—1908

Easter

Bring flowers to strew His way,
Yea, sing, make holiday;
Bid young lambs leap,
And earth laugh after sleep.

For now He cometh forth
Winter flies to the north,
Folds wings and cries
Amid the bergs and ice.

Yea, Death, great Death is dead,
And Life reigns in his stead;
Cometh the Athlete
New from dead Death's defeat.

Cometh the Wrestler,
But Death he makes no stir,
Utterly spent and done,
And all his kingdom gone.
—1907[1]

Any Woman[2]

I am the pillars of the house;
The keystone of the arch am I.
Take me away, and roof and wall
Would fall to ruin me utterly.

I am the fire upon the hearth,
I am the light of the good sun.
I am the heat that warms the earth,
Which else were colder than a stone.

At me the children warm their hands;
I am their light of love alive.
Without me cold the hearthstone stands,
Nor could the precious children thrive.

I am the twist that holds together
The children in its sacred ring,
Their knot of love, from whose close tether
No lost child goes a-wandering.

I am the house from floor to roof.
I deck the walls, the board I spread;
I spin the curtains, warp and woof,
And shake the down to be their bed.

I am their wall against all danger,
Their door against the wind and snow.
Thou Whom a woman laid in a manger,
Take me not till the children grow!
—1911

Eva Gore-Booth (1870–1926)

Though born into a wealthy landowning family of Anglo-Irish ancestry, Eva Gore-Booth—and her sister, the Easter 1916 revolutionary Countess Markievicz—were both committed to the cause of land reform and to improving conditions for the rural poor, as well as to other social reform causes of the day, such as women's suffrage. In 1916, along with Esther Roper, Gore-Booth launched the radical magazine *Urania*, whose aim was to eradicate the notion of inherent distinctions between the genders. Much of Gore-Booth's early poetry displays an interest in Irish mythology and mysticism, but her work is also expressive of her social and political interests.

[1] *1907* The first appearance of this poem in book form appears to have been in the slim volume, *Twenty-one Poems by Katharine Tynan, Selected by W.B. Yeats*, of which 200 copies were published in 1907.

[2] *Any Woman* Published variously under this title and as "The Mother."

Women's Rights

Down by Glencar Waterfall[1]
There's no winter left at all.

Every little flower that blows
Cold and darkness overthrows.

Every little thrush that sings
Quells the wild air with brave wings.

Every little stream that runs
Holds the light of brighter suns.

But where men in office sit
Winter holds the human wit.

In the dark and dreary town
Summer's green is trampled down.

Frozen, frozen everywhere
Are the springs of thought and prayer.

Rise with us and let us go
To where the living waters flow.

Oh, whatever men may say
Ours is the wide and open way.

Oh, whatever men may dream
We have the blue air and the stream.

Men have got their towers and walls,
We have cliffs and waterfalls.

Oh, whatever men may do
Ours is the gold air and the blue.

Men have got their pomp and pride—
All the green world is on our side.
—1907

[1] *Glencar Waterfall* In County Leitrim. Glencar is also mentioned in W.B. Yeats's poem "The Stolen Child," though he may be writing of Glencar Lough, which is just over the border in County Sligo.

1916[2]

Dew-pearlèd cobwebs glitter on green boughs,
Beneath our feet the grass is wet with dew,
It seems as if this clear dawn must arouse
Our broken world to something strange and new.

Deep in the high-built fortress of the pines,
Lost to her stars dark night imprisoned lies,
Near my hushed soul in peace a white rose shines,
Like a new dream down flung from ancient skies.

Alas, the bugles on the distant plain—
The guns break forth with their insistent din,
The dews of noon-day leave a crimson stain
On grass, that all men's feet must wander in.

Oh, singing splendour of the morning furled,
About the souls of trees, the hearts of flowers.
Have you no dream of beauty for the world—
This bitter blood-stained world we men call ours?
—1918

Comrades

The peaceful night that round me flows,
Breaks through your iron prison doors,
Free through the world your spirit goes,
Forbidden hands are clasping yours.
The wind is our confederate,
The night has left her doors ajar,
We meet beyond earth's barred gate,
Where all the world's wild Rebels are.
—c. 1916

PATRICK PEARSE (1879–1916)

Patrick Pearse—often referred to using the Irish spelling of his first name, Pádraig—is arguably the most celebrated icon of early twentieth-century Irish nationalism. He developed his interest in the Irish language while attending university in Dublin,

[2] *1916* The year of the Easter Rising in Dublin.

joined the Gaelic League or *Conradh na Gaeilge* in 1896, and founded a bilingual Irish-English school in 1908 with the intention of bringing about educational reform. Pearse joined the revolutionary Irish Republican Brotherhood in 1913, and read out the Proclamation of the Republic in Dublin on the outset of the Easter Rebellion in 1916; he was executed for his participation in that uprising only a few days later. Though Pearse is known above all for his political activism, he was also a writer of poetry in both Irish and English.

The Mother

I do not grudge them: Lord, I do not grudge
My two strong sons that I have seen go out
To break their strength and die, they and a few,
In bloody protest for a glorious thing,
They shall be spoken of among their people,
The generations shall remember them,
And call them blessed;
But I will speak their names to my own heart
In the long nights;
The little names that were familiar once
Round my dead hearth.
Lord, thou art hard on mothers:
We suffer in their coming and their going;
And tho' I grudge them not, I weary, weary
Of the long sorrow—And yet I have my joy:
My sons were faithful, and they fought.
—1915

Mise Éire

Mise Éire:
Sine mé ná an Chailleach Bhéarra.

Mór mo ghlóir:
Mé a rug Cú Chulainn cróga.

Mór mo náire:
Mo chlann féin a dhíol a máthair.

Mór mo phian:
Bithnaimhde do mo shíorchiapadh.

Mór mo bhrón:
D'éag an dream inar chuireas dóchas.

Mise Éire:
Uaigní mé ná an Chailleach Bhéarra.

I Am Ireland[1]

I am Ireland:
Older than the old woman of Beare.[2]

Great is my glory:
I whose child is Cúchulainn the brave

Great is my shame:
My own children sold their mother.

Great is my pain:
The attacks of my enemies torment me.

Great is my sorrow:
The hope I placed in my people has died.

I am Ireland:
More lonely than the Old Woman of Beare.
—1912

[1] *I Am Ireland* The present translation has been prepared by the editors of this anthology, in consultation with several of the many extant translations.

[2] *old woman of Beare* Figure in Irish legend. "The Lament of the Old Woman of Beare"—an extended lament on the ravages of age—is one of the best known of Old Irish poems. Beare is a peninsula on the coast of Munster, in southwest Ireland.

Winifred M. Letts (1882–1972)

Though Winifred M. Letts was born in England, she spent most of her life in her maternal home country of Ireland. She began her literary career writing plays for the Abbey Theatre in Dublin, but turned to poetry with the publication of her first collection in 1913. Her poem "The Deserter" is an oft-anthologized poem of the First World War.

Deirdre[1] in the Street

Deirdre is dead, and all her beauty blown
Like wind-swept petals underneath the thorn.
If beauty dies, then beauty is new-born,
And Deirdre met me in the street today,
Her hair like blackbirds' breasts, her shadowed eyes
Two hazel-circled pools beneath grey skies.
Proudly she walked as women from the hills,
Her basket full of early daffodils.

Deirdre is dead, and beauty, like a smoke,
Passes its phantom way into the air.
But other women are as young and fair.
Here at my elbow with soft hurried speech
She urged her wares. And in this dreary place
I looked upon a princess face to face.
Backed by a hoarding fierce with garish bills,
Deirdre stood crying—"Buy the daffodils."
—1913

The Old Wexford Woman

What do I think of the women that's in it?
'Tis little enough;
If you offered them flax would they trouble to spin it?
Faith! I've a notion before they'd begin it
You'd wait for your stuff.

Would they pick wool from the hedges and ditches?
We did in my day.
But it's easier plans they have now to make riches:
Why would you sew when machines makes your stitches?
Sure, that's what they say.

'Tis truth I'd no hand for making a letter,
But where was the lack?[2]
An' I couldn't read books any more than that setter.[3]
But for baking or stitching there wasn't a better,
Or making a brack.[4]

The black fasts[5] were kept without hesitation,
I tell you no lie.
Arrah![6] now there's no manner of strength in the nation,
It's sorra a one but needs dispensation[7]
For fear they would die.

The way they are now they're seeking their pleasure,
The days are too slow.
They'd look twice at a spade were they hunting for treasure,
It's towns that they want, and evenings of leisure
To streel[8] to and fro.

What is it they're after there in the city
That takes them away?
It's new clothes they'll be buying to make themselves pretty;

[1] *Deirdre* Deirdre is a popular figure of Irish mythology, a beautiful and tragic heroine who is betrothed from birth to King Conchubar. She falls in love with Naoise and runs off with him, but she is later recaptured, and forced to marry Conchubar after her lover is slain. When Conchubar is dissatisfied with Deirdre's coldness towards him, he tries to marry her off to Naoise's murderer as a punishment; she kills herself in anguish and protest.

[2] *lack* Shame.

[3] *setter* Type of dog.

[4] *brack* Fruitcake or loaf.

[5] *black fasts* Severe forms of fasting, often practiced by Catholics during the observation of Lent.

[6] *Arrah!* Exclamation used in Irish English.

[7] *dispensation* Official permission from the Church to be exempt from the full terms of a fast, sometimes claimed for one's health or for other reasons.

[8] *streel* Stroll aimlessly.

No value at all—an' that is the pity.
They'll know it some day.
What do I think of the race that we're rarin'?
They're not worth my shawl.
For it's sooner they're threadbare an' nobody carin'.
Mine was the days—but there's no good comparin'.
God help us all!
—1913

The Deserter

There was a man—don't mind his name,
Whom Fear had dogged by night and day.
He could not face the German guns
And so he turned and ran away.
Just that—he turned and ran away,
But who can judge him, you or I ?
God makes a man of flesh and blood
Who yearns to live and not to die.
And this man when he feared to die
Was scared as any frightened child,
His knees were shaking under him,
His breath came fast, his eyes were wild.
I've seen a hare with eyes as wild,
With throbbing heart and sobbing breath.
But oh! it shames one's soul to see
A man in abject fear of death,
But fear had gripped him, so had death;
His number had gone up that day,
They might not heed his frightened eyes,
They shot him when the dawn was grey.
Blindfolded, when the dawn was grey,
He stood there in a place apart,
The shots rang out and down he fell.
An English bullet in his heart.
An English bullet in his heart!
But here's the irony of life—
His mother thinks he fought and fell,
A hero, foremost in the strife.
So she goes proudly; to the strife
Her best, her hero son she gave.
O well for her she does not know
He lies in a deserter's grave.
—1916

SCOTLAND

JOHN GALT (1779 – 1839)

Perhaps a precursor to the historical novel popularized by later writers such as Sir Walter Scott, John Galt's *Annals of the Parish* was one of what the author called his "theoretical histories." Not quite a novel, this relatively plot-less work purports to chronicle the life of a small parish town in Scotland as witnessed by the Reverend Micah Balwhidder. The novel was an immediate success, Balwhidder becoming one of Galt's most beloved characters. Balwhidder, whose tenure as minister of Dalmailing coincides with the first fifty years of King George III's reign, provides a reliable lens through which the reader witnesses changes such as the Industrial Revolution and the rise of international trade, and the effects these events had on ordinary citizens in Scotland. Written in a fluid mixture of English and Scots, and with a sense of humor not unlike that of Galt's contemporary Jane Austen, *Annals* paints a lively portrait of village life in eighteenth- and early-nineteenth-century Scotland.

from *Annals of the Parish: or, The Chronicle of Dalmailing; during the ministry of the Rev. Micah Balwhidder, written by himself*

CHAPTER 4: YEAR 1763

Charles Malcolm's return from sea—Kate Malcolm is taken to live with Lady Macadam—Death of the first Mrs. Balwhidder.

The An. Dom.[1] 1763, was, in many a respect, a memorable year, both in public and in private. The King granted peace to the French,[2] and Charlie Malcolm, that went to sea in the Tobacco trader, came home to see his mother. The ship, after being at America, had gone down to Jamaica, an island in the West Indies, with a cargo of live lumber, as Charlie told me himself, and had come home with more than a hundred and fifty hoggits of sugar, and sixty-three puncheons[3] full of rum; for she was, by all accounts, a stately galley, and almost two hundred tons in the burthen,[4] being the largest vessel then sailing from the creditable town of Port-Glasgow. Charlie was not expected; and his coming was a great thing to us all, so I will mention the whole particulars.

One evening, towards the gloaming,[5] as I was taking my walk of meditation, I saw a brisk sailor laddie coming towards me. He had a pretty green parrot sitting on a bundle, tied in a Barcelona silk handkerchief, which he carried with a stick over his shoulder, and in this bundle was a wonderful big nut, such as no one in our parish had ever seen. It was called a cocker-nut.[6] This blithe callant[7] was Charlie Malcolm, who had come all the way that day his leaful lane,[8] on his own legs from Greenock, where the Tobacco trader was then 'livering her cargo. I told him how his mother, and his brothers, and his sisters were all in good health, and went to convoy him home; and as we were going along he told me many curious things, and he gave me six beautiful yellow limes, that he had brought in his pouch all the way across the seas, for me to make a bowl of punch with, and I thought more of them than if they had been golden guineas, it was so mindful of the laddie.

When we got to the door of his mother's house, she was sitting at the fireside, with her three other bairns[9] at their bread and milk, Kate being then with Lady Skimmilk at the Breadland[10] sewing. It was between the day and dark, when the shuttle stands still till the lamp is lighted. But such a shout of joy and thankfulness as rose from that hearth, when Charlie went in! The very parrot, ye would have thought, was a participator, for the beast gied a skraik that made my whole head dirl;[11] and the neighbours came flying and flocking to see what was the matter, for it was the first parrot ever seen within the bounds of the parish, and some thought it was but a foreign hawk, with a yellow head and green feathers.

In the midst of all this, Effie Malcolm had run off to the Breadland for her sister Kate, and the two lassies came flying breathless, with Miss Girzie Gilchrist, the Lady Skimmilk pursuing them like desperation, or a griffin, down the avenue; for Kate, in her hurry, had flung down her seam, a new printed gown, that she was helping to make, and it had fallen into a boyne[12] of milk that was ready for the creaming, by which ensued a double misfortune to Miss Girzie, the gown being not

---

1 *An. Dom* Anno Domini; Latin: Year of our Lord.

2 *The King … the French* Referring to the 1763 Treaty of Paris, which ended the Seven Years' War with a British victory over France; the end of the war has been commonly viewed as marking the beginning of the era of British imperial dominance.

3 *hoggits* Hogsheads; large casks; *puncheons* Casks for alcoholic beverages.

4 *burthen* Carrying capacity.

5 *gloaming* Twilight.

6 *cocker-nut* Coconut.

7 *callant* Young man.

8 *leaful lane* All alone.

9 *bairns* Children.

10 *Breadland* Estate of Balwhidder's late patron, the Laird of Breadland.

11 *gied a skraik* Gave a screech; *dirl* Shake; ring.

12 *boyne* Milk dish.

only ruined, but licking up the cream. For this, poor Kate was not allowed ever to set her face in the Breadland again.

When Charlie Malcolm had staid about a week with his mother, he returned to his berth in the Tobacco trader, and shortly after his brother Robert was likewise sent to serve his time to the sea, with an owner that was master of his own bark, in the coal trade at Irville. Kate, who was really a surprising lassie for her years, was taken off her mother's hands by the old Lady Macadam, that lived in her jointure house,[1] which is now the Cross Keys Inn. Her ladyship was a woman of high breeding, her husband having been a great general, and knighted by the King for his exploits; but she was lame, and could not move about in her dining-room without help, so hearing from the first Mrs. Balwhidder how Kate had done such an unatonable deed to Miss Girzie Gilchrist, she sent for Kate, and finding her sharp and apt, she took her to live with her as a companion. This was a vast advantage, for the lady was versed in all manner of accomplishments, and could read and speak French with more ease than any professor at that time would do in the College of Glasgow; and she had learnt to sew flowers on satin, either in a nunnery abroad, or in a boarding-school in England, and took pleasure in teaching Kate all she knew, and how to behave herself like a lady.

In the summer of this year, old Mr. Patrick Dilworth, that had so long been doited with the paralytics,[2] died, and it was a great relief to my people, for the heritors[3] could no longer refuse to get a proper schoolmaster; so we took on trial Mr. Lorimore, who has ever since the year after, with so much credit to himself, and usefulness to the parish, been schoolmaster, session-clerk, and precentor[4]—a man of great mildness, and extraordinary particularity. He was then a very young man, and some objection was made on account of his youth, to his being session-clerk, especially as the smuggling immorality still gave us much trouble in the making up of irregular marriages; but his discretion was greater than could have been hoped for from his years; and after a twelvemonth's probation in the capacity of schoolmaster, he was installed in all the offices that had belonged to his predecessor, old Mr. Patrick Dilworth that was.

But the most memorable thing that befell among my people this year, was the burning of the lint-mill on the Lugton Water,[5] which happened, of all the days of the year, on the very self-same day that Miss Girzie Gilchrist, better known as Lady Skim-milk, hired the chaise[6] from Mrs. Watts of the New Inns of Irville, to go with her brother the Major, to consult the faculty in Edinburgh,[7] concerning his complaints. For, as the chaise was coming by the mill, William Huckle, the miller that was, came flying out of the mill like a demented man, crying fire!—and it was the driver that brought the melancholy tidings to the clachan[8]—and melancholy they were; for the mill was utterly destroyed, and in it not a little of all that year's crop of lint in our parish. The first Mrs. Balwhidder lost upwards of twelve stone, which we had raised on the glebe with no small pains, watering it in the drouth, as it was intended for sarking to ourselves, and sheets and napery.[9] A great loss indeed it was, and the vexation thereof had a visible effect on Mrs. Balwhidder's health, which from the spring had been in a dwining[10] way. But for it, I think she might have wrestled through the winter: however, it was ordered otherwise, and she was removed from mine to Abraham's bosom on Christmas Day, and buried on

[1] *jointure house* Property inherited by a woman in the event of her husband's death (jointures were arranged primarily among the wealthy).

[2] *doited* Mentally impaired; *paralytics* Paralysis; Dilworth may have been affected by a stroke.

[3] *heritors* Privileged parish landowners responsible for the financial upkeep of the church, schools, etc.

[4] *precentor* Leader of the church choir.

[5] *lint-mill* Flax mill, for the making of linen; *Lugton Water* River in western Scotland.

[6] *chaise* Light open carriage.

[7] *the faculty in Edinburgh* I.e., the medical faculty.

[8] *clachan* Village.

[9] *glebe* Parish minister's land; *drouth* Drought; *sarking* Linen undergarments; *napery* Table linen.

[10] *dwining* Dwindling; sickly.

Hogmanay,[1] for it was thought uncanny to have a dead corpse in the house on the new-year's day. She was a worthy woman, studying with all her capacity to win the hearts of my people towards me—in the which good work she prospered greatly; so that, when she died, there was not a single soul in the parish that was not contented with both my walk[2] and conversation. Nothing could be more peaceable than the way we lived together. Her brother Andrew, a fine lad, I had sent to the College at Glasgow, at my own cost, and when he came out to the burial, he stayed with me a month, for the Manse after her decease was very dull, and it was during this visit that he gave me a n inkling of his wish to go out to India as a cadet, but the transactions anent[3] that fall within the scope of another year—as well as what relates to her headstone, and the epitaph in metre, which I indicated myself thereon; John Truel the mason carving the same, as may be seen in the kirkyard,[4] where it wants a little reparation and setting upright, having settled the wrong way when the second Mrs. Balwhidder was laid by her side. But I must not here enter upon an anticipation.

CHAPTER 5: YEAR 1764

He gets a marble headstone for Mrs. Balwhidder, and writes an Epitaph for it—He is afflicted with melancholy, and thinks of writing a book—Nichol Snipe the gamekeeper's device when reproved in church.

This year well deserved the name of the monumental year in our parish; for the young Laird[5] of the Breadland, that had been my pupil, being learning to be an advocate among the faculty in Edinburgh, with his lady mother, who had removed thither with the young ladies her daughters, for the benefit of education, sent out to be put up in the kirk, under the loft over the family vault, an elegant marble headstone, with an epitaph engraven thereon, in fair Latin, setting forth many excellent qualities which the old laird, my patron that was, the inditer[6] thereof, said he possessed. I say the inditer, because it could no have been the young laird himself, although he got the credit o't on the stone, for he was nae daub in my aught at the Latin or any other language. However, he might improve himself at Edinburgh, where a' manner of genteel things were then to be got at an easy rate, and doubtless, the young laird got a probationer at the College to write the epitaph; but I have often wondered sin' syne,[7] how he came to make it in Latin, for assuredly his dead parent, if he could have seen it, could not have read a single word o't, notwithstanding it was so vaunty[8] about his virtues, and other civil and hospitable qualifications.

The coming of the laird's monumental stone had a great effect on me, then in a state of deep despondency, for the loss of the first Mrs. Balwhidder; and I thought I could not do a better thing, just by way of diversion in my heavy sorrow, than to get a well-shapen headstone made for her—which, as I have hinted at in the record of the last year, was done and set up. But a headstone without an epitaph, is no better than a body without the breath of life in't; and so it behoved me to make a posey[9] for the monument, the which I conned[10] and pondered upon for many days. I thought as Mrs. Balwhidder, worthy woman as she was, did not understand the Latin tongue, it would not do to put on what I had to say in that language, as the laird had done—nor indeed would it have been easy, as I found upon the experimenting, to tell what I had to tell in Latin, which is naturally a crabbed[11] language, and very difficult to write properly. I therefore, after mentioning her age and the dates of her birth and departure, composed in sedate poetry, the following epitaph, which may yet be seen on the tombstone.

---

[1] *Hogmanay* New Year's Eve.

[2] *walk* I.e., of life; manner of living.

[3] *anent* Regarding.

[4] *kirkyard* Churchyard.

[5] *Laird* Estate owner.

[6] *inditer* Writer.

[7] *sin' syne* Since then.

[8] *vaunty* Boastful.

[9] *posey* Poesy; poem.

[10] *conned* Pored over.

[11] *crabbed* Difficult.

EPITAPH

A lovely Christian, spouse, and friend,
Pleasant in life, and at her end.
A pale consumption dealt the blow
That laid her here, with dust below.
Sore was the cough that shook her frame;
That cough her patience did proclaim—
And as she drew her latest breath,
She said, "The Lord is sweet in death."
O pious reader, standing by,
Learn like this gentle one to die.
The grass doth grow and fade away,
And time runs out by night and day;
The King of Terrors has command
To strike us with his dart in hand.
Go where we will by flood or field,
He will pursue and make us yield.
But though to him we must resign
The vesture of our part divine,
There is a jewel in our trust,
That will not perish in the dust,
A pearl of price, a precious gem,
Ordained for Jesus' diadem;
Therefore, be holy while you can,
And think upon the doom of man.
Repent in time and sin no more,
That when the strife of life is o'er,
On wings of love your soul may rise,
To dwell with angels in the skies,
Where psalms are sung eternally,
And martyrs ne'er again shall die;
But with the saints still bask in bliss,
And drink the cup of blessedness.

This was greatly thought of at the time, and Mr. Loremore, who had a nerve for poesy himself in his younger years, was of opinion, that it was so much to the purpose and suitable withal, that he made his scholars write it out for their examination copies, at the reading whereof before the heritors, when the examination of the school came round, the tear came into my eye, and everyone present sympathized with me in my great affliction for the loss of the first Mrs. Balwhidder.

Andrew Lanshaw, as I have recorded, having come from the Glasgow College to the burial of his sister, my wife that was, stayed with me a month to keep me company; and staying with me, he was a great cordial, for the weather was wet and sleety, and the nights were stormy, so that I could go little out, and few of the elders came in, they being at that time old men in a feckless condition, not at all qualified to warsle[1] with the blasts of winter. But when Andrew left me to go back to his classes, I was eerie[2] and lonesome, and but for the getting of the monument ready, which was a blessed entertainment to me in those dreary nights, with consulting anent the shape of it with John Truel, and meditating on the verse for the epitaph, I might have gone altogether demented. However, it pleased HIM, who is the surety of the sinner, to help me through the Slough of Despond,[3] and to set my feet on fair land, establishing my way thereon.

But the work of the monument, and the epitaph, could not endure for a constancy, and after it was done, I was again in great danger of sinking into the hypochonderies[4] a second time. However, I was enabled to fight with my affliction, and by and by, as the spring began to open her green lattice, and to set out her flower-pots to the sunshine, and the time of the singing of birds was come, I became more composed, and like myself, so I often walked in the fields, and held communion with nature, and wondered at the mysteries thereof.

On one of these occasions, as I was sauntering along the edge of Eaglesham-wood, looking at the industrious bee going from flower to flower, and the idle butterfly, that layeth up no store, but perisheth ere it is winter, I felt as it were a spirit from on high descending upon me, a throb at my heart, and a thrill in my brain, and I was transported out of myself, and seized with the notion of

[1] *warsle* Wrestle.

[2] *eerie* Gloomy.

[3] *Slough of Despond* Name of a bog in John Bunyan's *The Pilgrim's Progress* (1678) that represents a state of moral degradation and sinfulness.

[4] *hypochonderies* Melancholia; depression.

writing a book—but what it should be about, I could not settle to my satisfaction. Sometimes I thought of an orthodox poem, like Paradise Lost,[1] by John Milton, wherein I proposed to treat more at large of Original Sin, and the great mystery of Redemption; at others, I fancied that a connect treatise on the efficacy of Free Grace[2] would be more taking; but although I made diverse beginnings in both subjects, some new thought ever came into my head, and the whole summer passed away, and nothing was done. I therefore postponed my design of writing a book till the winter, when I would have the benefit of the long nights. Before that, however, I had other things of more importance to think about. My servant lasses, having no eye of a mistress over them, wastered everything at such a rate, and made such a galravitching[3] in the house, that, long before the end of the year, the year's stipend was all spent, and I did not know what to do. At lang and length I mustered courage to send for Mr. Auld, who was then living, and an elder. He was a douce[4] and discreet man, fair and well-doing in the world, and had a better handful of strong common sense than many even of the heritors. So I told him how I was situate, and conferred with him, and he advised me, for my own sake, to look out for another wife, as soon as decency would allow, which, he thought, might very properly be after the turn of the year, by which time the first Mrs. Balwhidder would be dead more than twelve months; and when I mentioned my design to write a book, he said (and he was a man of good discretion), that the doing of the book was a thing that would keep, but wasterful servants were a growing evil; so, upon his counselling, I resolved not to meddle with the book till I was married again, but employ the interim, between then and the turn of the year, in looking out for a prudent woman to be my second wife, strictly intending, as I did perform, not to mint[5] a word about my choice, if I made one, till the whole twelve months and a day, from the date of the first Mrs. Balwhidder's interment, had run out.

In this the hand of Providence was very visible, and lucky for me it was that I had sent for Mr. Auld when I did send, as the very week following, a sound began to spread in the parish, that one of my lassies had got herself with bairn, which was an awful thing to think had happened in the house of her master, and that master a minister of the gospel. Some there were, for backbiting appertaineth to all conditions, that jealoused[6] and wondered if I had not a finger in the pie; which, when Mr. Auld heard, he bestirred himself in such a manful and godly way in my defence, as silenced the clash, telling that I was utterly incapable of any such thing, being a man of a guileless heart, and a spiritual simplicity, that would be ornamental in a child. We then had the latheron[7] summoned before the Session, and was not long of making her confess, that the father was Nichol Snipe, Lord Glencairn's gamekeeper; and both her and Nichol were obligated to stand in the kirk, but Nichol was a graceless reprobate, for he came with two coats, one buttoned behind him, and another buttoned before him, and two wigs of my lord's, lent him by the valet-de-chamer;[8] the one over his face, and the other in the right way; and he stood with his face to the church-wall. When I saw him from the pu'-pit,[9] I said to him—"Nichol, you must turn your face towards me!" At the which, he turned round to be sure, but there he presented the same show as his back. I was confounded, and did not know what to say, but cried out, with a voice of anger—"Nichol, Nichol! if ye had been a' back, ye would nae hae[10] been there this day;" which had such an effect on the whole congregation,

[1] *Paradise Lost* Epic poem (1667) recounting the fall of the angel Satan and the loss of the Garden of Eden by Adam and Eve.

[2] *connect* Orderly; *Free Grace* The idea that one can be saved by God's grace through one's own faith alone, regardless of prior sins; a central tenet of Protestant theology.

[3] *wastered* Wasted; *galravitching* Extravagance.

[4] *douce* Sober, judicious.

[5] *mint* Speak; hint at.

[6] *jealoused* Suspected.

[7] *latheron* Laidron or ladrone; slattern; derogatory word for a "loose" woman.

[8] *valet-de-chamer* Valet-de-chambre; personal servant of a gentleman.

[9] *pu'-pit* Pulpit.

[10] *nae hae* Not have.

that the poor fellow suffered afterwards more derision, than if I had rebuked him in the manner prescribed by the Session.

This affair, with the previous advice of Mr. Auld, was, however, a warning to me, that no pastor of his parish should be long without a helpmate. Accordingly, as soon as the year was out, I set myself earnestly about the search for one, but as the particulars fall properly within the scope and chronicle of the next year, I must reserve them for it; and I do not recollect that anything more particular befell in this, excepting that William Mutchkins, the father of Mr. Mutchkins, the great spirit-dealer in Glasgow, set up a change house[1] in the clachan, which was the first in the parish, and which, if I could have helped, it would have been the last; for it was opening a howf[2] to all manner of wickedness, and was an immediate get and offspring of the smuggling trade, against which I had so set my countenance. But William Mutchkins himself was a respectable man, and no house could be better ordered than his change. At a stated hour he made family worship, for he brought up his children in the fear of God and the Christian religion; and although the house was full, he would go in to the customers, and ask them if they would want anything for half an hour, for that he was going to make exercise with his family; and many a wayfaring traveller has joined in the prayer. There is no such thing, I fear, now-a-days, of publicans entertaining travellers in this manner.

CHAPTER 6: YEAR 1765

Establishment of a whisky distillery—He is again married to Miss Lizzy Kibbock—Her industry in the dairy—Her example diffuses a spirit of industry through the parish.

As there was little in the last year that concerned the parish, but only myself, so in this the like fortune continued; and saving a rise in the price of barley, occasioned, as was thought, by the establishment of a house for brewing whisky in a neighbouring parish, it could not be said that my people were exposed to the mutations and influences of the stars, which ruled in the seasons of Ann. Dom. 1765. In the winter there was a dearth[3] of fuel, such as has not been since; for when the spring loosened the bonds of the ice, three new coal-heughs were shanked[4] in the Douray moor, and ever since there has been a great plenty of that necessary article. Truly, it is very wonderful to see how things come round; when the talk was about the shanking of their heughs, and a paper to get folk to take shares in them, was carried through the circumjacent parishes, it was thought a gowk's[5] errand; but no sooner was the coal reached, but up sprung such a traffic, that it was a God-send to the parish, and the opening of a trade and commerce, that has, to use an old byword, brought gold in gowpins amang[6] us. From that time my stipend has been on the regular increase, and therefore I think that the incoming of the heritors must have been in like manner augmented.

Soon after this, the time was drawing near for my second marriage. I had placed my affections, with due consideration, on Miss Lizy Kibbock, the well-brought-up daughter of Mr. Joseph Kibbock, of the Gorbyholm, who was the first that made a speculation in the farming way in Ayrshire, and whose cheese were of such an excellent quality, that they have, under the name of Delap-cheese, spread far and wide over the civilized world. Miss Lizy and me were married on the 29th day of April, with some inconvenience to both sides, on account of the dread that we had of being married in May, for it is said,

> "Of the marriages in May,
> The bairns die of a decay."

However, married we were, and we hired the Irville chaise, and with Miss Jenny her sister, and Becky Cairns

---

[1] *change house* Inn; pub.

[2] *howf* Abode; housing place (often with the implication of housing something disreputable).

[3] *dearth* Shortage.

[4] *coal-heughs* Coal quarries; *shanked* Sunk; mined.

[5] *gowk* Fool.

[6] *gowpins* Handfuls; *amang* Among.

her niece, who sat on a portmanty[1] at our feet, we went on a pleasure jaunt to Glasgow, where we bought a miracle[2] of useful things for the Manse, that neither the first Mrs. Balwhidder nor me ever thought of; but the second Mrs. Balwhidder that was, had a geni[3] for management, and it was extraordinary what she could go through. Well may I speak of her with commendations; for she was the bee that made my honey, although at first things did not go so clear with us. For she found the Manse rookit and herrit, and there was such a supply of plenishing of all sort wanted,[4] that I thought myself ruined and undone by her care and industry. There was such a buying of wool to make blankets, with a booming of the meikle wheel to spin the same, and such birring of the little wheel for sheets and napery, that the Manse was for many a day like an organ kist.[5] Then we had milk cows, and the calves to bring up, and a kirning[6] of butter, and a making of cheese; in short, I was almost by myself[7] with the jangle and din, which prevented me from writing a book as I had proposed, and I for a time thought of the peaceful and kindly nature of the first Mrs. Balwhidder with a sigh; but the outcoming was soon manifest. The second Mrs. Balwhidder sent her butter on the market-days to Irville, and her cheese from time to time to Glasgow, to Mrs. Firlot, that kept the huxtry[8] in the Saltmarket, and they were both so well made, that our dairy was just a coining of money, insomuch, that after the first year, we had the whole tot[9] of my stipend to put untouched into the bank.

But I must say, that although we were thus making siller like sclate[10] stones, I was not satisfied in my own mind, that I had got the Manse merely to be a factory of butter and cheese, and to breed up veal calves for the slaughter; so I spoke to the second Mrs. Balwhidder, and pointed out to her what I thought the error of our way; but she had been so ingrained with the profitable management of cows and grumphies[11] in her father's house, that she could not desist, at the which I was greatly grieved. By and by, however, I began to discern that there was something as good in her example, as the giving of alms to the poor folk. For all the wives of the parish were stirred up by it into a wonderful thrift, and nothing was heard of in every house, but of quiltings and wabs[12] to weave; insomuch, that before many years came round, there was not a better stocked parish, with blankets and napery, than mine was, within the bounds of Scotland....

—1821

[1] *portmanty* Portmanteau, traveling case.

[2] *miracle* Impressively large amount.

[3] *geni* Genius.

[4] *rookit* Dirty; *herrit* Plundered, stripped of goods; *wanted* Lacking.

[5] *meikle* Large; *birring* Whirring; *kist* Chest or trunk in which clothes or valuables are kept.

[6] *kirning* Churning.

[7] *by myself* Beside myself; out of my wits.

[8] *huxtry* Small shop.

[9] *tot* Lot.

[10] *siller* Silver; money; *sclate* Slate, i.e. for roofing.

[11] *grumphies* Pigs.

[12] *wabs* Webs, i.e. of woven fabric.

JANET HAMILTON (1795–1873)

James Thomson and Mary Brownlee Thomson, Janet Hamilton's parents, were field laborers for much of her childhood; her father also worked at different times as a shoemaker. Married when she was thirteen to another shoemaker, Hamilton bore ten children in the years 1810–25. She received no formal education but was taught by her mother to read; she did not learn how to write until she was in her fifties. Hamilton's first book, *Poems and Essays of a Miscellaneous Character*, was published by subscription in 1863. By the time her third volume, *Poems and Ballads* (1868) was published, her work was widely and very positively reviewed. As *The Glasgow Herald* put it, "the name of Janet Hamilton is one of the most remarkable in the history of Scottish poetry. That a woman in humble life, who did not enjoy the advantages of a school education, should, at the age of 73, and while now blind, be capable of composing verse at all, is singular enough; but that these verses should possess the verve, pathos, and genuine truthfulness of … a Burns (in all but his best pieces) can only be accounted for by the inheritance of genius."

Hamilton has been known largely for her poems in Scottish dialect, but she was also a highly accomplished writer in standard English of poems, prose essays, and sketches.

Lines on the Long and Beautiful Summer of 1865, in Connection with the Cattle Plague Then Raging[1]

The first recorded case in the cattle plague (also known as *rinderpest*) of 1865 was 24 June; the disease quickly spread throughout much of England, Wales, and Scotland. On 29 September a Royal Commission was appointed to investigate the plague's causes and make recommendations as to how best to deal with it. By February 1866 the government had placed increased restrictions on cattle movement and made the mass slaughter of diseased animals obligatory; by the following summer the plague had been brought under control. The plague is estimated to have killed 75–80 per cent of the animals affected, and approximately 8 per cent of the total British cattle population.

At the height of the plague there were widespread calls for days of public fasting and humiliation—the idea being that the plague had been sent by God as punishment for human sin. Though such notions would become far less widely held in Britain in the twentieth century, they have a long history, and in the mid nineteenth century they were certainly not relics of a distant past; nevertheless, such calls were not always made without controversy or resistance. In 1865 the Queen sided with the Archbishop of Canterbury in approving a special prayer for protection against the plague, but did not declare a day of fasting and humiliation.

[1] This is the retrospective title given the poem when it appears in the 1868 *Poems and Ballads* volume and also the 1880 posthumous volume *Poems, Essays and Sketches: Comprising the Principal Pieces from Her Complete Works*. Where the poem itself appears in the tables of contents of those volumes, however, it is given the shorter title "Lines on the Summer of the Cattle Plague, 1865." The wording of the poem itself ("Now alas!", "not now the milkmaid's song", etc.) seems to suggest that the poem dates at the latest from early in 1866.

Lines on the Summer of the Cattle Plague, 1865

Summer long, and bright, and glowing,
Flowers in triple plenty blowing,
Flushed the garden, field and glade,
Tints of every hue and shade.
Woods and fields more richly green,
Waters placid, pure and sheen,
Singing, sparkling, danced along,
Musical as merles'° song. *blackbirds'*
Ne'er did "incense breathing morn"[2]
O'er green fields of springing corn,
Flowery lea, and moorland heath,
Shed more balmy odorous breath.
Such pearl-drops ne'er, I ween,° *think*
Gathered were on village green,
On sweet May, by sportive girls,
They the purest, fairest pearls,
'Sixty-five as thou hast given
From the dewy morning heaven.
With the first faint streak of morn,
When the cock first winds his horn,
Wakes the music of the woods,
Rising, swelling into floods
Of melody! Sweet warbling throats!
How ye poured your jubilant notes
Of love and joy, devoid of fear:
No tuneless Winter chilled your cheer.
 In that Summer, long and glowing,
Nature from her lap o'erflowing
Spread around an ample feast
With full hand for bird and beast.
Ah! what pleasure 'twas to see
Straying o'er the daisied lea,° *grass*

[2] *incense breathing morn* The phrase is from the line that opens the fifth stanza of Thomas Gray's "Elegy Written in a Country Churchyard": "The breezy call of incense-breathing Morn."

Or, recumbent on the sward,° *grassy field*
"The milky mothers of the herd,"
Udder rich in lacteal wealth,
Full of lusty life and health—
Richest clover, greenest grass,
Cropping quietly.
Now, alas!
Sore, plague-smitten, dying, dead,
On the pastures where they fed!
Thousands upon thousands gone—
Deep the loss, and sad the moan
In the dairies and the farms,
Where each day brings fresh alarms:
And the wonder ever grows
Whence the dire distemper flows.
Ah! not now the milkmaid's song,
As she drives the herd along,
Comes on woodland echoes borne,
At gloamin'° grey or dewy morn. *twilight*
Now she walks with mournful tread
Through each empty stall and shed;
Meets her ear no welcome low:
All is deathly silence now.
For your suff'rings, sinless things,
Weeps the muse even while she sings:
Guilt not yours brought down the rod
Of a just and righteous God.
To that God we now appeal:
He has wounded, He can heal;
He alone can grant release
From this dark and fell° disease. *cruel*
From our sinful, suff'ring land,
Lord, remove Thy chast'ning hand!
—1866

Rhymes for the Times IV—1865

Juist noo° there are mony wha° rin° to an' fro, *now / many who* *run*
An' knowledge increases, abune° an' below; *above*
The yird's° like a riddle,[1] pits, tunnels, an' bores, *earth*
Whaur° bodies, like mowdies,° by hunners° an' scores,[2] *where / moles* *hundreds*
Are houkin',° an' holin', an' blastin' the rocks; *digging*
An' droonin's° an' burnin's, explosions an' shocks, *drownings*
An' a' ither meagries,° amang us are rife; *misfortunes*
Oh, mony's the slain in the battle o' life!
It's Mammon[3] we worship, wi' graspin' an' greed,
Wi' sailin' an' railin' at telegraph speed,
Get gowd oot° the ironstone, an' siller frae° coal, *gold out of* *silver from*
An' thoosan's on thoosan's draw oot o' ae° hole. *one*
Wi' oil shale aneath° us, an' fire-warks abune, *beneath*
I think we'll tak' lowe,° an' bleeze° up to the mune.° *fire / blaze* *moon*
The kintra's° contentit an' hale° at the heart; *country's / healthy*
That gleg birkie, Gladstone,[4] has weel dune° his part; *well done*
Exchequer's big pouches o' siller are fu',° *full*
An' mony's the taxes that's dune awa' noo;
An' labour's weel paid, an' the flour an' the meal
At a wanworth[5]—an' sae we micht fen unco weel.° *fare very well*
Oor Premier has promised to stan' for reform;[6]

[1] *riddle* Sieve; piece of coarse mesh.

[2] *scores* Groups of twenty.

[3] *Mammon* Wealth or material things, personified as a devil-figure.

[4] *gleg* Sharp-witted; *birkie* Spirited or assertive man; *Gladstone* William Gladstone (1809–98), later Prime Minister, served as Chancellor of the Exchequer from 1859 to 1866.

[5] *wanworth* Cost below actual value.

[6] *Oor Premier … for reform* Perhaps alluding to the struggle for electoral reform, which came to fruition in Scotland with the Representation of the People Act 1868.

The Fins an' the Yankees are brewin' a storm,[1]
They're swallin'° an' frothin' wi' bunkum *swelling*
an' bosh,° *nonsense*
But they daurna° come near oor bit *dare not*
islan' sae cosh.° *comfortable*
There's a bee in the bannet o' some o' the cloth,[2]
The Sabbath's the subject, an' wow but I'm wroth
To see the blin'° leaders lead blin' men awa', *blind*
Till into the ditch they baith stumble an' fa'.
"The soul is immortal," tak' that for a text,
"The body is perishin'," tak' for the next;
To whilk o' the twa° shou'd the *which of the two*
Sabbath be given?
To the body?—then what for the soul an' for heaven?
—1868

Auld Mither Scotlan'[3]

A Lay of the Doric[4]

Na, na, I wunna pairt° wi' that *would not part*
I downa° gi'e it up; *do not*
O' Scotlan's hamely° mither tongue *homely*
I canna quat the grup.[5]
It's 'bedded° in my very heart, *embedded*
Ye needna rive an' rug;[6]
It's in my e'en° an' on my tongue, *eye*
An' singin' in my lug.° *ear*

Oh, leeze me on[7] the Scottish lass,
Fresh frae her muirlan'° hame, *moorland*
Wi' gowden° or wi' coal-black hair, *golden*
Row'd° up wi' bucklin came;[8] *twisted*
Or wavin' roun her snawy broo,° *snowy brow*
Sae bonnie, braid,° an' brent,° *broad / smooth*
Gaun barefit wi' her kiltit[9] coat,
Blythe singin' ower the bent!

I heard her sing "Auld Robin Gray,"[10]
An' "Yarrow's Dowie Den"[11]—
O' Flodden,° an' oor° forest *flooded / our*
flouris° *flourishing*
Cut doon by Englishmen;
My saul was fir'd, my heart was fu',
The tear was in my e'e:° *eye*
Let ither lan's ha ither sangs,
Auld Scotlan's sangs for me.

What words mair tender, kin' an' true,
Can wooer ha'e to say,
Whan doun the burn at gloamin' fa',° *nightfall*
He meets his bonnie May?
Or words mair sweet, mair saft an' dear,
Can lassie ha'e to speak,
Whan love is dancin' in her e'e
An' glowin' on her cheek!

For, oh, the meltin' Doric lay,
In cot or clachan° sung, *village*
The words that drap like hinny dew
Frae mither Scotlan's tongue,
Ha'e power to thrill the youthfu' heart
An' fire the patriot's min';
To saften grief in ilka° form *every*
It comes to human kin'.

I saw a waefu' mither kneel
On weary, tremblin' knee,
Beside the cradle, where she laid
Her bairnie° doon to dee.° *child / die*

---

[1] *The Fins ... a storm* Allusion to the American Civil War (1861–65).

[2] *o' the cloth* Of the Church; i.e., the clergy.

[3] *Auld Mither Scotlan'* Hamilton in fact wrote two poems by this title; the following text is taken from the memorial volume *Poems, Essays, and Sketches* published posthumously in 1880; *Mither* Mother.

[4] *Lay* Song; *Doric* Scottish dialect.

[5] *quat the grup* Relinquish the grip; let go.

[6] *rive an' rug* Struggle.

[7] *leeze me on* Dear to me is.

[8] *bucklin came* Comb for pinning up the hair.

[9] *kiltit* Tucked in or held up for freedom of movement.

[10] *Auld Robin Gray* Popular Scots ballad written by Lady Anne Lindsay (1750–1825).

[11] *Yarrow's Dowie Den* Scottish folk ballad.

An' aye she kissed the cauld white cheek,
An' aye she made her mane,° *lament*
"My ain wee lamb, my ain sweet doo,
Frae me forever gane!"

The faither straikit° back her hair, *stroked*
An' dichtit saft her e'en,[1]
"Wee Willie's gane, thy marrow's° here, *husband*
Thy life-lang, lovin' frien'."
She leant her on his faithfu' breast,
An' sabbed "Wilt thou forgi'e
My sinfu' grief for bairnie lost,
Whan I ha'e God an' thee.

"My mither, tho' the snaws o' eld
Are on my pow° an' thine, *head*
My heart is leal to thee as in
The days o' auld langsyne.[2]
Thy hamely worth, thy couthie° speech, *kindly*
Are dear—hoo dear to me!
An' neist° to God, my John, an' bairns, *next*
Thy place sall ever be."
—1868

Effie—A Ballad

She was wearin' awa'! she was wearin' awa'!
Wi' the leaves in October, we thocht she
wad fa',° *fall*
For her cheek was owre red, an' her e'e° was *eye*
owre bricht,° *bright*
Whaur the saul leukit oot[3] like an angel o' licht.

She dwalt in the muirlans° amang the *moorlands*
red bells
O' the sweet hinny heather that blooms on the fells,
Whaur the peesweep an' plover[4] are aye on the wing,
An' the lilt o' the lav'rock's° first heard *skylark*
in the Spring.

As black as a craw, an' as saft as the silk,
Were the lang locks that fell on a neck like the milk;
She was lithesome an' lo'esome° as lassie *lonesome*
micht be,
An' saft was the love-licht that danc'd in her e'e.

Puir Effie had lov'd; a' the hopes an' the fears,
The plagues an' the pleasures, the smiles an' the tears
O' love she had kenn'd°—she had gone thro' *known*
them a'
For fause° Jamie Crichton—oh, black be *false*
his fa'!° *fate*

The auldest o' five, whan a lassie o' ten,
She had baith the hoose an' the bairnies° *children*
to fen';° *care for*
The mither° had gane when she was but a bairn, *mother*
Sae Effie had mony° sad lessons to learn. *many*

At hame, had ye seen her amang the young chips,
The sweet law o' kindness was aye on her lips;
She kamed oot their hair, wash'd their wee
hackit° feet, *white*
Wi' sae tentie a haun° that a bairn *gentle a hand*
wadna greet.° *complain*

She was to her faither the licht o' his een,° *eye*
He said she was be what her mither had been—
A fair an' sweet sample o' true womanhood,
Sae carefu' an' clever, sae bonnie an' guid.

The cot-house it stood on the lip o' the burn,° *river*
That wimpled an' jinkit[5] wi' mony a turn
Roun' the fit o' the heather-fring'd
gowany brae,° *flower-covered hill*
Whaur the ae cow was tether'd, an' bairnies at play.

[1] *dichtit saft her e'en* Softly wiped [the tears from] her eye.

[2] *auld langsyne* Times gone by.

[3] *saul leukit oot* Soul looks out.

[4] *peesweep an' plover* Birds common to the Scottish Highlands; *peesweep* Lapwing or peewit.

[5] *wimpled an' jinkit* Twisted and turned; meandered.

Sweet Effie was juist in the midst o' her teens
Whan she gat the first inkling o' what wooing means
Frae a chiel° in the clachan, wha aften was seen *young man*
Stealin' up the burnside to the cot-hoose° at e'en. *cottage*

On a saft simmer° gloamin' I saw them mysel' *summer*
On the bank o' the burnie, an' well I cou'd tell,
By the hue on her cheek, an' the blink o' her e'e,
That her young love was his, an' wad evermair be.

Belyve° to fair Effie cam' wooers galore, *soon*
An' mony saft tirlin's° at e'en on the door; *knocks*
She smiled on them a', but gied° welcome to nane— *gave*
Her first love an' last was young Jamie's alane.

An' Jamie, wha ne'er was a week frae her side,
Had vowed e'er a towmond[1] to mak' her his bride;
Her troth° she had gi'en him wi' blushes an' tears— *promise, betrothal*
It was sweet—oh, how sweet! tho' whiles she had fears;

For a wee burdie sang, as roun' her it flew,
Sweet lassie, tak' tent—he's owre sweet to be true;
He's oot in the e'enin's whan ye dinna ken,° *do not know*
An' they say he's been seen wi' Kate o' the Glen.

But Effie wad lauch,° an' wad sae to hersel', *laugh*
What lees° an' what clashes° thae bodies maun° tell, *lies / gossip* *must*
For my Jamie has sworn to be true to the death,
An' nocht noo° can pairt us as lang's we ha'e breath. *nothing now*

Ae° short winter Sabbath, juist as it grew mirk,° *one / dark*
The faither cam' hame—he had been at the kirk;° *church*
His cheek was sae white, an' his leuk was sae queer,
That Effie glower'd at him in dredour an' fear.

Then he said, "My ain Effie, puir mitherless° lass! *motherless*
Oh, wha wad ha'e thocht this wad e'er come to pass?
Thy Jamie, this day, in the kirk was proclaim'd,
An' Katie MacLean for his bride they ha'e named.

"I was tauld on the road by ane that maun ken,
Her grannie was ance the gudewife o' the Glen,
An' she left to young Katie a hantle o' gear[2]—
It's gear Jamie wants, an' there's naething o't here."

An' what said puir Effie? She stood like a stane,
But faintin', or greetin', or cryin' was nane;
Her sweet lips they quiver'd, the bluid frae her cheek
Flew back to her heart, but nae word cou'd she speak.

The faither sat doun, laid her head on his breast:
"On God an' her faither my Effie maun rest,
They ne'er will deceive thee—thy wrangs are richt sair;
Gin Jamie had wed thee they micht ha'e been mair."

Sune Effie gat up, gied her faither some meat,
Put the bairnies to bed, yet ne'er could she greet—
Her young heart was stricken—the fountains were dry
That gush frae the een wi' a tearfu' supply.

That nicht at the reading she joined in the psalm,
Her cheek it was pale, but her brow it was calm;
An' faither he pray'd, as she knelt by his side,
That God his dear lassie wad comfort an' guide.

The winter gaed by, an' the hale° simmer thro' *whole*
She tosh'd° up the hoose, fed an' milkit the cow; *tidied*
The cauld warl' had nocht that she cared for ava,° *at all*
Her life it was silently meltin' awa'.

Oh! whaur noo the love-licht that sparkled ere while
In her bonny black e'e? Oh! whaur noo the smile
That dimpled her cheek? They were gane! they were gane!
Yet she ne'er shed a tear, an' ne'er made a mane.° *moan*

[1] *e'er a towmond* Within a year.

[2] *hantle o' gear* Large amount of wealth.

An sae she was wearin', fast wearin awa'!
Wi' the leaves in October sweet Effie did fa'!
Her mournin' was ended, an' blissfu' an' bricht
The dear lassie dwells wi' the angels o' licht.
—1868

Samuel Smiles (1812–1904)

Smiles's most famous book, *Self-Help; with Illustrations of Character and Conduct* (1859), is renowned as a ground-breaking work of popular non-fiction—the forerunner that gave its name to an entire genre. By the end of the nineteenth century *Self-Help* had sold a quarter of a million copies.

The degree to which doctrines of individual enterprise are today associated with political conservativism has led many to assume that Smiles himself must have been to the right of center politically. In fact he was a strong advocate of causes such as parliamentary reform and women's suffrage, and a strong critic of *rentier* capitalists who obtain wealth merely through deploying their capital and through the labor of others rather that through their own hard work. He was not against government measures to help the poor or government measures to further the progress of the nation; he was simply of the view that the actions of individuals would, collectively, have greater impact than the actions of governments.

Raised near Edinburgh, Smiles attended the University of Edinburgh. He began to attract attention during the 1840s when he was editor of the *Leeds Times*; it was during his time in Leeds that he began to give lectures to groups of working men on the subject of self-help. Though self-reliance is said by many to be a characteristically Scottish trait, Smiles himself was so far from being a Scottish nationalist that he writes of England as "our nation."

from *Self-Help*[1]

from Chapter 1: Self-Help—National and Individual

"The worth of a State, in the long run, is the worth of the individuals composing it."—J.S. Mill[2]

"We put too much faith in systems, and look too little to men."—B. Disraeli[3]

… National progress is the sum of individual industry, energy, and uprightness, as national decay is of individual idleness, selfishness, and vice. What we are accustomed to decry as great social evils, will, for the most part, be found to be but the outgrowth of man's own perverted life; and though we may endeavour to cut them down and extirpate them by means of Law, they will only spring up again with fresh luxuriance in some other form, unless the conditions of personal life and character are radically improved. If this view be correct, then it follows that the highest patriotism and philanthropy consist, not so much in altering laws and modifying institutions, as in helping and stimulating men to elevate and improve themselves by their own free and independent individual action.

It may be of comparatively little consequence how a man is governed from without, whilst everything depends upon how he governs himself from within. The greatest slave is not he who is ruled by a despot, great though that evil be, but he who is the thrall of his own moral ignorance, selfishness, and vice. Nations who are thus enslaved at heart cannot be freed by any mere changes of masters or of institutions; and so long as the fatal delusion prevails, that liberty solely depends upon and consists in government, so long will such changes, no matter at what cost they may be effected, have as little

---

[1] *Self-Help* The text used here is that of the "new edition" of 1896, for which Smiles made a number of revisions.

[2] *J.S. Mill* John Stuart Mill, English philosopher and proponent of the doctrine of utilitarianism; the quotation is from the last paragraph of *On Liberty* (1859).

[3] *B. Disraeli* Benjamin Disraeli (1804–81), writer and Prime Minister of the United Kingdom.

practical and lasting result as the shifting of the figures in a phantasmagoria.[1] The solid foundations of liberty must rest upon individual character; which is also the only sure guarantee for social security and national progress. John Stuart Mill truly observes that "even despotism does not produce its worst effects so long as individuality exists under it; and whatever crushes individuality is despotism, by whatever name it be called."[2]

Old fallacies as to human progress are constantly turning up. Some call for Caesars,[3] others for Nationalities,[4] and others for Acts of Parliament. We are to wait for Caesars, and when they are found, "happy the people who recognise and follow them."[5] This doctrine shortly means, everything *for* the people, nothing *by* them—a doctrine which, if taken as a guide, must, by destroying the free conscience of a community, speedily prepare the way for any form of despotism. Caesarism is human idolatry in its worst form—a worship of mere power, as degrading in its effects as the worship of mere wealth would be. A far healthier doctrine to inculcate among[6] the nations would be that of Self-Help; and so soon as it is thoroughly understood and carried into action, Caesarism will be no more. The two principles are directly antagonistic; and what Victor Hugo said of the Pen and the Sword alike applies to them, "Ceci tuera cela."[7]

The power of Nationalities and Acts of Parliament is also a prevalent superstition. What William Dargan,[8] one of Ireland's truest patriots, said at the closing of the first Dublin Industrial Exhibition, may well be quoted now: "To tell the truth," he said, "I never heard the word independence mentioned that my own country and my own fellow townsmen did not occur to my mind. I have heard a great deal about the independence that we were to get from this, that, and the other place, and of the great expectations we were to have from persons from other countries coming amongst us. Whilst I value as much as any man the great advantages that must result to us from that intercourse, I have always been deeply impressed with the feeling that our industrial independence is dependent upon ourselves. I believe that with simple industry and careful exactness in the utilization of our energies, we never had a fairer chance nor a brighter prospect than the present. We have made a step, but perseverance is the great agent of success; and if we but go on zealously, I believe in my conscience that in a short period we shall arrive at a position of equal comfort, of equal happiness, and of equal independence, with that of any other people."

All nations have been made what they are by the thinking and the working of many generations of men. Patient and persevering labourers in all ranks and conditions of life, cultivators of the soil and explorers of the mine, inventors and discoverers, manufacturers, mechanics and artisans, poets, philosophers, and politicians, all have contributed towards the grand result, one generation building upon another's labours, and carrying them forward to still higher stages. This constant succession of noble workers—the artisans of civilisation—has served to create order out of chaos in industry, science, and art; and the living race has thus, in the course of nature, become the inheritor of the rich estate provided by the skill and industry of our forefathers, which is placed in our hands to cultivate, and to hand down, not only unimpaired but improved, to our successors.

The spirit of self-help, as exhibited in the energetic action of individuals, has in all times been a marked feature in the English character, and furnishes the true measure of our power as a nation. Rising above the heads of the mass, there were always to be found a series of individuals distinguished beyond others, who com-

---

[1] *phantasmagoria* Exhibition of optical illusions using artificial light.

[2] *even despotism … be called* See *On Liberty*.

[3] *Caesars* I.e., strong political leaders.

[4] *Nationalities* I.e., nationalism; movements for national autonomy.

[5] *happy the … follow them* From Napoleon III's *History of Julius Caesar* (1865–66).

[6] *inculcate among* Impress upon.

[7] *Ceci tuera cela* French: This will kill that. Smiles may have confused the classic proverb regarding the pen being mightier than the sword with this phrase by Victor Hugo (1802–85) regarding the pen (or the book) and religion. In Hugo's novel *Notre-Dame de Paris* (English translations of which have often been published under the title *The Hunchback of Notre Dame*) the character Claude Frollo, a priest attached to Notre-Dame cathedral in Paris, points to a book as he looks at the cathedral tower and says "This [the book] will kill that [religion, as symbolized by the cathedral]."

[8] *William Dargan* Irish rail engineer (1799–1867).

manded the public homage. But our progress has also been owing to multitudes of smaller and less known men. Though only the generals' names may be remembered in the history of any great campaign, it has been in a great measure through the individual valour and heroism of the privates that victories have been won. And life, too, is "a soldiers' battle,"—men in the ranks having in all times been amongst the greatest of workers. Many are the lives of men unwritten, which have nevertheless as powerfully influenced civilisation and progress as the more fortunate Great whose names are recorded in biography. Even the humblest person, who sets before his fellows an example of industry, sobriety, and upright honesty of purpose in life, has a present as well as a future influence upon the well-being of his country; for his life and character pass unconsciously into the lives of others, and propagate good example for all time to come.

Daily experience shows that it is energetic individualism which produces the most powerful effects upon the life and action of others, and really constitutes the best practical education. …

—1859, 1896

John A. Macdonald (1815–1891)

Though Macdonald's family emigrated from Scotland in 1820, when he was still a child, he remained proudly attached to his Scottish heritage throughout his life. He was a leading force behind the drive to unite the British colonies in the northern part of North America into one entity, and became Canada's first Prime Minister following Confederation in 1867. (He was, it must be noted, also a forceful proponent of the worst harms associated with the foundation of Canada, including the policy of cultural genocide the Canadian government implemented against the Indigenous peoples whose land the British Empire had colonized.) Macdonald delivered the speech excerpted below at a conference held in Quebec to consider the possibility of uniting Upper and Lower Canada with the Atlantic colonies of Nova Scotia, New Brunswick, and Prince Edward Island; in the excerpts presented here he compares the nature of the proposed Canadian union to the union between Scotland and England and the union of United States to the south.

from *Speech on the Quebec Resolution,*[1] 6 February 1865

… The relations between England and Scotland are very similar to that which obtains[2] between the Canadas. The union between them, in matters of legislation, is of a federal character, because the Act of Union[3] between the two countries provides that the Scottish law cannot be altered, except for the manifest advantage of the people of Scotland. This stipulation has been held to be so obligatory on the Legislature of Great Britain, that no measure affecting the law of Scotland is passed unless it receives the sanction of a majority of the Scottish members in Parliament. No matter how important it may be for the interests of the empire as a whole to alter the laws of Scotland—no matter how much it may interfere with the symmetry of the general law of the United Kingdom, that law is not altered, except with the consent of the Scottish people, as expressed by their representatives in Parliament. (Hear, hear.) Thus, we have, in Great Britain, to a limited extent, an example of the working and effects of a Federal Union, as we might expect to witness them in our own Confederation.

The whole scheme of Confederation, as propounded by the Conference, as agreed to and sanctioned by the Canadian Government, and as now presented for the consideration of the people, and the Legislature, bears upon its face the marks of compromise. Of necessity there must have been a great deal of mutual concession.

---

[1] *Quebec Resolution* Collection of resolutions drafted at the October 1864 Quebec Conference laying down the foundation for the eventual Canadian Confederation; a fundamental aspect of the resolution was the establishment of a strong central government.

[2] *obtains* Exists.

[3] *Act of Union* The Acts of Union between England and Scotland were passed in 1707, joining the two kingdoms (previously separate though ruled by the same monarch) into the United Kingdom of Great Britain; one of the Acts' provisions stipulated that Scots law would remain unchanged.

When we think of the representatives of five colonies, all supposed to have different interests, meeting together, charged with the duty of protecting those interests and of pressing the views of their own localities and sections, it must be admitted that had we not met in a spirit of conciliation, and with an anxious desire to promote this union; if we had not been impressed with the idea contained in the words of the resolution—"That the best interests and present and future prosperity of British North America would be promoted by a Federal Union under the Crown of Great Britain,"—all our efforts might have proved to be of no avail. If we had not felt that, after coming to this conclusion, we were bound to set aside our private opinions on matters of detail, if we had not felt ourselves bound to look at what was practicable, not obstinately rejecting the opinions of others nor adhering to our own; if we had not met, I say, in a spirit of conciliation, and with an anxious, overruling desire to form one people under one government, we never would have succeeded. …

Prior to the formation of the American Union, as we all know, the different states which entered into it were separate colonies. They had no connection with each other further than that of having a common sovereign, just as with us at present. Their constitutions and their laws were different. They might and did legislate against each other, and when they revolted against the Mother Country they acted as separate sovereignties, and carried on the war by a kind of treaty of alliance against the common enemy. Ever since the union was formed the difficulty of what is called "State Rights" has existed, and this had much to do in bringing on the present unhappy war in the United States.[1] They commenced, in fact, at the wrong end. They declared by their Constitution that each state was a sovereignty in itself, and that all the powers incident to a sovereignty belonged to each state, except those powers which, by the Constitution, were conferred upon the General Government and Congress.

Here we have adopted a different system. We have strengthened the General Government.[2] We have given the General Legislature all the great subjects of legislation. We have conferred on them, not only specifically and in detail, all the powers which are incident to sovereignty, but we have expressly declared that all subjects of general interest not distinctly and exclusively conferred upon the local governments and local legislatures, shall be conferred upon the General Government and Legislature. We have thus avoided that great source of weakness which has been the cause of the disruption of the United States. We have avoided all conflict of jurisdiction and authority, and if this Constitution is carried out, as it will be in full detail in the Imperial Act to be passed if the colonies adopt the scheme, we will have in fact, as I said before, all the advantages of a legislative union under one administration, with, at the same time the guarantees for local institutions and for local laws, which are insisted upon by so many in the provinces now, I hope, to be united. …

—1865

[1] *Ever since … United States* The first constitution of the United States, formed during the Revolutionary War, had guaranteed individual states almost complete sovereignty; while the authority of the central government was strengthened with the creation of the new Constitution in 1789, questions surrounding the sovereignty of individual states continued to figure prominently in American political discourse. The American Civil War (1861–65) was fought in large part over the claims of Southern states that they had a constitutional right to maintain the institution of slavery.

[2] *General Government* I.e., the central government.

ELIZA OGILVY (1822–1912)

Born in 1822, Scottish writer Eliza Ogilvy is best known for her poems on motherhood, as well as for her poems and stories that illustrate Scottish history and myth. She married in 1843 and wrote "A Natal Address" on the occasion of the birth of her first child, Rose. The death of Rose less than two years later inspired Ogilvy's first full volume, the solemn *Rose Leaves* (1845). The following year she published *A Book of Highland Minstrelsy*, in which each poem is prefaced by a background piece in prose. Ogilvy put out several more volumes of verse over the years, one of which was written while living in Florence, Italy, where she and her family befriended the English poets Robert and Elizabeth Barrett

Browning. Upon their return to Britain Ogilvy concentrated on her prose writing, publishing stories and articles in periodicals, and also wrote a memoir of E.B. Browning.

A Natal Address to My Child, March 19th 1844

Hail to thy puggy nose, my Darling,
Fair womankind's last added scrap,
That, callow° as an unfledged starling, *bald*
Liest screaming in the Nurse's lap.

No locks thy tender cranium boasteth,
No lashes veil thy gummy eye
And, like some steak gridiron° toasteth, *griddle*
Thy skin is red and crisp and dry.

Thy mouth is swollen past describing
Its corners twisted as in scorn
Of all the leech° is now prescribing *doctor, physician*
To doctor° thee, the newly born. *treat*

Sweet little lump of flannel binding,
Thou perfect cataract° of clothes, *waterfall*
Thy many folds there's no unwinding
Small mummy without arms or toes!

And am I really then thy Mother?
My very child I cannot doubt thee,
Remembering all the fuss and bother
And moans and groans I made about thee!

'Tis now thy turn to groan and grumble,
As if afraid to enter life,
To dare each whipping scar and tumble
And task and toil with which 'tis rife.

O Baby of the wise round forehead,
Be not too thoughtful ere thy time;
Life is not truly quite so horrid—
Oh! how she squalls!—she can't bear rhyme!

—1844

The Imprecation[1] by the Cradle

A young lady of rank, belonging to an ancient family in the north of Scotland, was betrothed, with the consent of her relations, to a gentleman of equal birth. Their union being delayed by unforeseen obstacles, the lover found means to ruin the unhappy girl, whose affection for her plighted husband left her more exposed to his unprincipled passion. Then, notwithstanding the wealth to which she was heiress, he deserted her, and completed his perfidy[2] by carrying his addresses to the daughter of a neighbouring earl, by whom they were accepted.

The distracted[3] lady heard of his new betrothal when on the point of becoming a mother. With a strength almost supernatural in one so delicately reared, she rose from her bed the very day her child was born, and attiring herself in costly garments, went to a public assembly,[4] where her fickle lover and his engaged wife were to be present. There she danced so gaily and so lightly as completely to belie the rumours scandal had circulated regarding her.

But shortlived was her assumed gaiety. Returned to her dishonoured home, heartbroken and a prey to her emotions, she knelt down by the cradle of her son and prayed that on the father's head sorrow and retribution might descend, and that he might never know happiness in his home or child in his wedlock.

Her adjuration seemed a prophecy, for she who had filled her place in his affections, learning the story of her hapless rival, conceived a violent hatred for her husband. So far did this dislike proceed that her mind became unsettled. She repeatedly attempted both her own and her husband's life; and at last, confined to prevent fatal consequences, she died a raving and a childless maniac.

The boy, whose birth had brought misfortune on both his parents and caused so much sorrow on all sides, grew to manhood, when he distinguished himself

[1] *Imprecation* Invocation of vengeance; curse.

[2] *perfidy* Deceit.

[3] *distracted* Distressed.

[4] *assembly* Ball; party.

greatly in the profession of arms, gaining both honour and wealth in his country's service.

Such are the romantic incidents of a story which is literally true.

PART 1

Slumber sweet, my babie,
  Slumber peacefullie,
Mickle° grief and mickle wrang° *much / wrong*
  I have borne for thee!

Hush thee, heir of sorrow!
  Sleep and sleep away,
All of thy fause° father's heart *false*
  Mingled with thy clay.° *body*

Dinna° wear his likeness, *do not*
  Dinna smile his smile;
I should hate thee, innocent,
  For that look of guile!

Dinna speak his accents,
  Lest my heart of fire
Spurn the child for blandishments
  Borrowed from the sire.° *father*

Faint with mother-anguish
  From my bed I rose,
Kamed° the locks he praised so weel,° *combed / well, highly*
  Donned my richest clothes,

Danced amang the blythest,
  Gay as ony° bride, *any*
All the weakness of my limbs
  Iron-braced by pride.

Fair is Lady Ellen,
  He her hand did hold,
Breathed to her the flatteries
  Breathed to me of old.

Dancing down the measure,
  Ne'er his thoughts could be
How to him a child was born
  That dark day by me.

Oh! ye dreams of vengeance,
  Which the injured haunt,
If ye come like evil powers
  Evil prayers to grant,

Cursèd be his union!
  Cursèd be his name!
Trodden in forgetfulness,
  Blotted out in shame!

Barren be his wedlock,
  Desolate his hearth,
Never may his ancient halls
  Echo children's mirth.

Childless Lady Ellen!
  Never may her hand
Rock the cradled little one,
  Heir of all her land.

Land and lordly glories
  Passing to another,
Never may a lawful heir
  Mock his elder brother!

Slumber sweet, my babie,
  Slumber peacefullie,
Mickle grief and mickle wrang
  Life has yet for thee!

PART 2

Slumber sweet, my mother,
  Slumber peacefullie,
Dinna heed the grief and wrang
  Life has brought to me!

Dinna heed the scorning
  Of thy haughty kin,
Dinna weep sae° bitterlie *so*
  Lang° repented sin! *long*

Dinna heed the portion
  Lawful heirs enjoy,
Forfeit lands and forfeit name
  Wrested from thy boy.

Dinna weep the traitor
  Who thy youth betrayed,
Wooed thee in the sunny time,
  Left thee in the shade.

For the curse is working,
  At my birth conjured,
Sharper griefs are piercing him
  Than thyself endured!

Lonely are his castles,
  Desolate his halls,
Never child hath propped the house
  Which to ruin falls.

Hate is in her bosom,
  Who the long night lies
Gazing in his haggard face
  With unquiet eyes.

Crazed is Lady Ellen,
  She whose beauty won
Lover from his plighted bride,
  Father from his son.

Crazed is Lady Ellen,
  Yet her madness knows
Horror for his perjury,
  Pity for thy woes.

Softly sleep, my mother,
  He can sleep no more,
Fearfulness and gaunt remorse
  Knocking at his door.

Outcast from my lineage,
  He to me denied
Father's love and father's name,
  Wealth and rank and pride;

Yet my blood is burning
  With ancestral fires,
And the glory of the child
  Shall outshine the sire's.

And the landless soldier,
  From the gory field,
From the ramparts won shall carve
  His unspotted shield.

Softly sleep, my mother,
  Slumber peacefullie,
Justice for its cruel wrong
  Life shall yield to me!
—1846

The Portents of the Night

Night to the devout Highlander was a time to rest within doors, and renew the strength by sleep. Evil spirits were abroad, the Prince of Darkness[1] roamed over the hills: it was presumption to dare his presence, and drew upon itself the neglect of all angelic guardians. It is rather difficult to reconcile this timorous avoidance of danger with the thousand recorded facts of nightly creaghs,[2] nightly robberies, nightly assassinations; but we must remember, that even in the most superstitious the overwhelming passion of the moment has silenced the voice of fear. The constantly recurring disasters of these evil undertakings was, of course, attributed by the neighbours to the contemptuous presumption which

[1] *Prince of Darkness* I.e., the devil; Satan.

[2] *creaghs* Cattle raids.

overlooked the peril. It was then held an established axiom, that evil spirits were to be shunned, not braved. Those whose necessary tasks detained them out of doors beyond nightfall were not so liable to harm as the daring loiterer, who was sure to suffer for his boldness by an encounter with the wicked demons let loose upon the earth during the dark hours.

The vision of armed horsemen riding along the face of an impassable precipice is taken from a narration of a similar appearance in the daytime on the mountains of Cumberland.[1] It is given in detail by Sir David Brewster,[2] in his work on "Natural Magic." Scott[3] likewise speaks, in his "Lady of the Lake," of a presage of coming death of a similar character:

> Sounds, too, had come in midnight blast
> Of charging steeds careering fast
> Along Benharrow's shingly side,
> Where mortal horseman ne'er might ride.

The birk scarred by the witch's ban[4] recalls an idea entertained in many parts of the Highlands, that these ill-omened crones could wither a tree by their curses, so that the sap should dry up in the trunk, and the whole become blighted and unfruitful, as if scathed by lightning.

It was sometimes the custom to baptize an infant over a drawn sword, in the emergency of illness and distance from a priest. The rite of baptism was highly prized among the Highlanders; they regarded it as an unfailing passport to heaven for the child who died in earliest infancy. On the other hand, those unhappy ones whose parents, through accident or neglect, had omitted ensuring for them the entrance into happiness, were lost forever and ever, as much as the most hardened sinner. Their voices were heard in the woods bewailing their wretched fate, and upbraiding their forgetful parents. To "win west" was a proverbial expression for reaching heaven. The Highlanders to this day suppose the realms of everlasting glory to be situate to the westward. This fancy has probably remained to them from an extinct Druidical[5] superstition, which fixed the locality of the eternal mansions in the island of Hath Innis, among the more remote of the Hebridean archipelago.[6]

The water of three streams at their confluence possessed, it was said, singular properties. Hither bereaved parents came with the elfin changeling, whom the fairies had substituted for their own fair mortal child. The infant being left all night at this gathering of the waters, was found in the morning the very one whom the "gude people"[7] had stolen, the magic of the spot forcing the dishonest elves to restore their prize. The ford crossed on occasion of a burial by a funeral party, was called the Ford of the Dead and the Living. Its waters were of potent efficacy to counteract evil spells, witchcraft, and all delusions of the devil, but the ford itself was generally haunted, especially on the approach of a death among the neighbouring inhabitants. The spectre seen by the traveller had its face hidden—a circumstance usually held to portend evil to the spectator himself, who saw in the muffled form his shadowy likeness. The gazer, when such an appearance came before him, could, by reversing his plaid[8] or any other part of his vestments, ascertain this fact to his satisfaction, as the spectre, if his own, would undergo a similar change. The "Legend of Montrose"[9] illustrates this most dramatically in the dialogue between Ranald of the Mist and Allan Macaulay.

The compatibility of such a superstitious disposition with a religious and sincere faith has been before commented on; the effect of those visions would be to sink

[1] *Cumberland* Mountainous region in northwestern England, on the Scottish border.

[2] *Sir David Brewster* Scottish academic and scientist (1781–1868), who wrote a series of letters addressed to Sir Walter Scott on various topics including "spectral apparitions."

[3] *Scott* Scottish poet and novelist Sir Walter Scott (1771–1832).

[4] *birk* Birch tree; *ban* Curse.

[5] *Druidical* Originating with the Druids, ancient figures of Celtic history and myth who often figure in legend as magicians, sorcerers, and soothsayers.

[6] *Hebridean archipelago* Group of remote islands off the northwest coast of Scotland.

[7] *gude people* Good people; common epithet for the fairies.

[8] *plaid* Woolen cloak in a tartan pattern, worn as part of traditional Highland dress.

[9] *Legend of Montrose* 1819 novel by Sir Walter Scott.

every serious Highlander on his knees. In his habitual reference of every occurrence, natural or extraordinary, to the watchful superintendence of an all-wise Deity, the Gael has left his posterity a lesson of true wisdom.

The Portents of the Night

"What saw ye outbye in the gloamin',° *twilight*
gudeman?° *husband*
Your teeth chatter sairly, your colour is wan!
Did ye venture the pass o' the mountain by night?
Ye surely have witnessed some terrible sight;
Was it aught° o' this warld, or a kelpie, or *anything*
sprite?"

"I cam' by the pass o' the mountain, gudewife,
But I'll never return a' the days of my life;
The calm caller° moonlight was stirred on *cool*
the crags
By the glinting of harness, the fluttering of flags;
A troop of armed horsemen rode gallantly by
Where a goat couldna° creep on the *could not*
precipice high,
In a long single file, horse by horse, round the cliff;
The flash o' their weapons gaed° past in *went*
a gliff.° *instant*
Sure never was seen at sic° hour, in sic place, *such*
Or rider or steed of this earth's mortal race;
And I knelt there in fear wi' my plaid on my face."

"That troop boded naething but evil, gudeman;
The voice o' dissension is loud in the lan';
The horse o' the Saxon° shall trample *i.e., the English*
he vale,
And faggot[1] and sword be the meed° o' *distinction*
the Gael.
But saw ye nae sicht° in the forest, gudeman, *sight*
Where the birks are all scaured by the dour witch's ban?
Your teeth chatter sairly, your colour is wan!"

"Nae sight have I seen in the forest, gudewife,
But I heard what I ne'er shall forget in my life,—
A moanin' and sobbin' of infant in pain,
A dreary cry over and over again.
It was na the wind, for the wind it was still;
It was na the burn, for there's frost on the hill;
'Twas the voice of a child, girning° sadly *crying*
and sair,
Sounding close at my footsteps and filling the air;
And I searched the dark wood, but no baby was there."

"'Twas the voice o' your baby unchristened, gudeman;
Unblessed by the priest was her life's little span;
No waters of mercy were poured on her head,
And therefore she waileth so sair from the dead,
And haunteth the forest, and canna find rest;
Unsealed by redemption, she canna win west.
Oh! would I had crossed thee with naked claymore[2]
Than barred thee from heaven, my babe that I bore!
Or would I had ta'en° thee though *taken*
corri° and spate,° *valley / flood*
Through the drifts of the snow to the priest's very gate,
Or ever thou cam'st to such terrible fate!
But saw ye nae sicht by the water, gudeman?
Your teeth chatter sairly, your colour is wan!
Did ye come by the ford where the three rivers meet,
Where the widowed and childless gae aften to greet
By the graves that lie close at the kirk's° *church's*
holy feet?"

"I cam' by the kirk o' the rivers, gudewife,
'Tis the last time I ever shall pass it in life.
As the ford o' the Dead and the Living I crossed,
I saw a drooned man° in the wild billows *drowned*
tossed;
The features were downward, no face could I see,
But closely he drifted, he brushed by my knee;
And still when the plaid or the hair I would grasp,
The wet spray alone did I find in my clasp,
Till the corse° floated seaward with shrieks *corpse*
on the breeze,

[1] *faggot* Bundle of sticks used in military contexts to fortify embankments, construct paths across boggy terrain, etc.

[2] *claymore* Two-handed sword with a double-edged blade, formerly used by Scottish Highlanders.

With the roar of the river, the sigh of the trees,
And my heart 'gan to swim, and my pulses to freeze."

"Ohone[1] for my Donald! ohone, my gudeman!
Was ever sic sorrow since life first began?
Not many may look on their ain ghastly wraith,
Not many like thee hae sic warnin' o' death;
For lo! as I sat here at evening's dark close,
And toasted your bannocks and thickened your brose,[2]
The river seemed suddenly rushing beside,
And I saw a drooned man swept away by the tide—
I saw 'twas your face as it hurled o'er the
linn,° *waterfall*
There was shrieking without and that vision within.
As swift as it came so it vanished away,
And nocht at my feet but the black poussie° lay; *cat*
He shivered wi' terror, I greeted full sore,
Till your hand at the latch and your foot on the floor
Gar'd me rise up to meet you and clasp you once more."

"Your words are a warning of evil, gudewife!
Short, short is the thread o' my fast-dwindled life;
And mickle° my sinnin' and hardened my soul, *great*
And far is my heart frae the heavenly goal.
The path o' the just is a steep whinny[3] brae,° *hill*
And aft did I stumble, and aft did I stray:
Kneel down by the ingle, gudewife, and we'll pray!"
—1846

John Davidson (1857–1909)

Much of the work of Scottish-born writer John Davidson is notable for its blending of lyric poetry and philosophy, and for the scientific influence that is evident in his ideas. In the decade leading up to his death Davidson wrote four "Testaments," long poems which express his Materialist philosophical vision; he claimed in 1904 that the purpose of the series was "to aid in the overthrow of the rotten financial investment called Christendom." Plagued by financial difficulties and depression, Davidson committed suicide by drowning at the age of 50.

N.B. One poem of Davidson's ("A Northern Suburb") is also included in "The Aesthetic Movement" section of volume 5 of the full *Broadview Anthology of British Literature* (The Victorian Era).

Waiting

Within unfriendly walls
We starve—or starve by stealth.
Oxen fatten in their stalls;
You guard the harrier's° health: *hunting hound*
They never can be criminals,
And can't compete for wealth.
From the mansion and the palace
Is there any help or hail° *protection*
For the tenants of the alleys,
Of the workhouse[4] and the jail?

Though lands await our toil,[5]
And earth half-empty rolls,
Cumberers° of English soil, *burdens*
We cringe for orts° and doles°— *scraps / charity*
Prosperity's accustomed foil,
Millions of useless souls.
In the gutters and the ditches
Human vermin festering lurk—
We, the rust upon your riches;
We, the flaw in all your work.

Come down from where you sit;
We look to you for aid.
Take us from the miry pit,

[1] *Ohone* Exclamation of grief.

[2] *brose* Type of porridge.

[3] *whinny* Covered in furze-bushes; thorny.

[4] *workhouse* Especially after the Poor Law Amendment Act of 1834, most other forms of financial relief for the impoverished and unemployed were replaced by the workhouse, an institution to which people could go to perform labor in exchange for food and shelter; conditions at these workhouses were often made intentionally severe in order to discourage the poor from seeking even this degree of aid.

[5] *Though lands … our toil* Many believed that a solution to poverty and unemployment would be found in encouraging emigration to the "half-empty" colonies.

And lead us out undismayed:
Say, "Even you, outcast, unfit,
Forward with sword and spade!"
And myriads of us idle
Would thank you through our tears,
Though you drove us with a bridle,
And a whip about our ears!

From cloudy cape to cape
The teeming waters seethe;
Golden grain and purple grape
The regions overwreathe.
Will no one help up to escape?
We scarce have room to breathe.
You might try to understand us:
We are waiting night and day
For a captain to command us,
And the word we must obey.
—1897

from *The Testament of an Empire Builder*

…

Do I believe in Heaven and Hell? I do;
We have them here; the world is nothing else.
Beauty and power and splendor and delight
Of chosen ones, elect ere Time began,
In loathsomeness, debility, disgrace,
Humiliation, travail, terror, woe,
Of multitudes, of myrmidons,[1] of all
The labourers, soldiers, servants, rooted deep:
He is a slave: a prisoner: damned: in Hell,
Whose daily bread depends on toil approved.
For me, I clambered into Heaven at once
And stayed there; joined the warfare of the times
In corner, trust, and syndicate: upheaved
A furrow, hissing through the angry world,
A redhot ploughshare in a frozen glebe,° *field*
And reaped my millions long before my prime.
Then, being English, one of the elect
Above all folks, within me fate grew strong.
The authentic mandate of imperial doom
Silenced the drowsy lullaby of love,
(Though now my turbid[2] blood and nerves disused
Complain of mystery unrevealed, and haunt
Imagination day and night with looks—
With beckoning looks, soft arms and fragrant breath;
For even in Heaven each ransomed soul frequents
A private, an inevitable Hell!)
Undid my simple, immature design,
And made me—What! tenfold a criminal?
No other name for Hastings, Clive,[3] and me!
I broke your slothful dream of folded wings,
Of work achieved and empire circumscribed,
Dispelled the treacherous flatteries of peace,
And thrust upon you in your dull despite
The one thing needful, half a continent
Of habitable land! The English Hell
Forever crowds upon the English Heaven.
Secure your birthright; set the world at naught;
Confront your fate; regard the naked deed;
Enlarge your Hell; preserve it in repair;
Only a splendid Hell keeps Heaven fair.
—1902

[1] *myrmidons* Vicious warriors who followed Achilles into battle against Troy.

[2] *turbid* Thick, muddled.

[3] *Hastings, Clive* Warren Hastings (1732–1818) and Robert Clive (1725–74) were both controversial Governors-General of India who contributed to consolidating British rule in the subcontinent; Clive in particular has been harshly criticized for his policies, which led to famine and hardship for many while enabling Clive to amass a great deal of personal wealth for himself.

WALES

FELICIA HEMANS (1793 – 1835)

A separate author entry for Hemans appears elsewhere in this anthology; included here are two poems from her largely forgotten 1822 collection *Welsh Melodies*, together with one of her more popular poems ("The Better Land") that has interesting parallels to "The Cambrian in America."

The Cambrian[1] in America

When the last flush of eve is dying
On boundless lakes afar that shine:
When winds amidst the palms are sighing,
And fragrance breathes from every pine:[2]
When stars through cypress boughs are gleaming,
And fire-flies wander bright and free,
Still of thy harps, thy mountains dreaming,
My thoughts, wild Cambria! dwell with thee!
Alone o'er green savannas roving,
Where some broad stream in silence flows,
Or through the eternal forests moving,
One only home my spirit knows!
Sweet land, whence memory ne'er hath parted!
To thee on sleep's light wing I fly;
But happier could the weary-hearted
Look on his own blue hills and die!
—1822

Taliesin's[3] Prophecy

[A prophecy of Taliesin relating to the Ancient Britons is still extant, and has been strikingly verified. It is to the following effect:

Their God they shall worship,
Their language they shall retain,
Their land they shall lose,
Except wild Wales.]

A voice from time departed yet floats thy hills among,
O Cambria! thus thy prophet bard, thy Taliesin sung:
"The path of unborn ages is traced upon my soul,
The clouds which mantle things unseen away before me roll,
A light the depths revealing hath o'er my spirit passed,
A rushing sound from days to be swells fitful in the blast,
And tells me that forever shall live the lofty tongue
To which the harp of Mona's[4] woods by freedom's hand was strung.

"Green island of the mighty![5] I see thine ancient race
Driven from their father's realm to make the rocks their dwelling-place!
I see from Uthyr's[6] kingdom the sceptre pass away,
And many a line of bards and chiefs and princely men decay.
But long as Arvon's mountains[7] shall lift their sovereign forms,
And wear the crown to which is given dominion o'er the storms,
So long, their empire sharing, shall live the lofty tongue
To which the harp of Mona's woods by freedom's hand was strung!"
—1822

The Better Land

"I hear thee speak of the better land,
Thou call'st its children a happy band;
Mother! oh, where is that radiant shore?
Shall we not seek it, and weep no more?
Is it where the flower of the orange blows,
And the fire-flies glance through the myrtle boughs?"
—"Not there, not there, my child!"

"Is it where the feathery palm-trees rise,
And the date grows ripe under sunny skies?

[1] *Cambrian* Welsh person; "Cambria" is the Anglicized version of the Welsh name for Wales, *Cymru*.

[2] [Hemans's note] The aromatic odor of the pine has frequently been mentioned by travellers.

[3] *Taliesin* Sixth-century Celtic bard, the reputed author of many texts including a Welsh manuscript known as *The Book of Taliesin*.

[4] *harp* National instrument of Wales; *Mona* The island of Anglesey in northern Wales, also known in Welsh as *Ynys Môn*.

[5] [Hemans's note] *Ynys y Cedeirn*, or Isle of the Mighty—an ancient name given to Britain.

[6] [Hemans's note] Uthyr Pendragon, king of Britain, supposed to have been the father of Arthur.

[7] *Arvon's mountains* Wales's highest mountains are located in Arfon, in the northern part of the country.

Or midst the green islands of glittering seas,
Where fragrant forests perfume the breeze,
And strange, bright birds on their starry wings,
Bear the rich hues of all glorious things?"
—"Not there, not there, my child!"

"Is it far away, in some region old,
Where the rivers wander o'er sands of gold?—
Where the burning rays of the ruby shine,
And the diamond lights up the secret mine,
And the pearl gleams forth from the coral strand?—
Is it there, sweet mother, that better land?"
—"Not there, not there, my child!

"Eye hath not seen it, my gentle boy!
Ear hath not heard its deep songs of joy;
Dreams cannot picture a world so fair—
Sorrow and death may not enter there;
Time doth not breathe on its fadeless bloom,
For beyond the clouds, and beyond the tomb,
It is there, it is there, my child!"
—1828

JOHN BLACKWELL (ALUN) (1797–1840)

Born in the town of Mold in Wales, John Blackwell—who adopted the bardic name Alun—received little to no formal education, but learned to read and write while apprenticing to a shoemaker who had an interest in poetry. An enthusiastic student of both English and Welsh poetic traditions, he attended local *eisteddfodau*—Welsh competitive literary festivals—and became editor of a Welsh-language magazine. He is best remembered for lyric poems such as "*Cathl i'r Eos.*"

Cathl i'r Eos

Pan guddio nos in daear gu
O dan ei du adenydd
Y clywir dy delori mwyn,
A chôr llwyn yn llonydd;
Ac os bydd pigyn dan dy fron
Yn peri i'th galon guro,
Ni wnei, nes torro'r wawrddydd hael,
Ond canu, a gadael iddo.

A thebyg it yw'r feinir wâr
Sydd gymar gwell na gemau:
Er cilio haul a hulio bro
Â miloedd o gymylau,
Pan dawo holl gysurwyr dydd,
Hi lyna yn ffyddlonaf;
Yn nyfnder nos o boen a thrais
Y dyry lais felysaf.

Song to the Nightingale[1]

When our dear earth is hid by night
Under its black wing,
The woodland choir is mute, but you
Then gently sing,
And if against your heart a thorn
Throbs beneath your breast,
You, till generous day should break,
Will but sing, and leave the rest.

And like you is this gentle girl,
Partner more than rubies dear,
At sunset, though across the land
A thousand clouds appear,
When all day's comforters are dumb° *silent*
Her fidelity's complete;
In the night's anguish and dismay
Never sounded voice so sweet.

[1] *Song to the Nightingale* Translated by Anthony Conran.

Er dichon fod ei chalon wan
    Yn delwi dan y dulid,
Ni chwyna, i flino'i hannwyl rai,
    Ei gwên a guddia'i gofid;
Na pheidia'i chân trwy ddunos faith,
    Nes gweled gobaith golau
Yn t'wynnu, megis llygad aur,
    Trwy bur amrantau'r borau.

Though the worry almost numbs her heart
    She'll not complain
Nor tire her dear ones with distress—
    Her smile hides her pain;
Nor ends her song the long night through
    Until bright hope shall dawn,
Shining like an eye of gold
    Through the clear lids of morn.

—c. 1830?

Samuel Roberts (1800–1885)

Welsh minister Samuel Roberts became known for his radical political writings in the 1840s, many of which were published in his Welsh-language periodical, *Y Cronicl*. Among the causes he adopted were the abolition of slavery, women's suffrage, and the recognition of the rights of tenant farmers. He frequently gave voice to his disdain for British imperialism and militarism; in the following piece on the Crimean War,[1] Roberts condemns Britain and its allies for their roles in the conflict.

A Pacifist's Credo

In times of difficulty governments like individuals tend to be very stubborn and selfish. Many a country, at such times, has been terribly selfish, and madly boastful: but we acknowledge despite our shame that we do not believe any country (either civilized or barbarian) has ever deigned to boast more and so outrageously than England has done these last two years; and its proud boasting will remain a stain on its name for as long as the Thames flows through the centre of its capital city. And it weighs heavily on us to confess our belief that the war [in Crimea] will continue, and get worse, and spread, multiplying the losses and dangers of the kingdoms of Europe if the voice of England were to carry the day in the conferences which have recently been considering the matter. One of the blackest pages in the historiography of the world is the one dealing with "the wars of England." It is to be hoped to God she will change her tune and her spirit with a view to the usefulness and "glory" of her military institutions. If she will not, her name will be accursed all over the world and will remain so until the last afternoon of the earth.

The chief and foremost announcement made by England up to now has been that it wishes to replenish its armies, and build up its navy, and reinforce its defences and strengthen and increase the number of all its military institutions. In this it is setting the worst example to other kingdoms. It is in fact making them increase their armies according to the English pattern, to the detriment of the world. Instead of devoting its talent and influence to excelling in love and good works, it is leading the way in barbarism of the worst kind.

It is claimed boldly that the war is "for civilization and Christendom." We have wondered a great deal about the barbarism of such a claim. Furthering civilization by war! Perfecting European civilization by spreading the barbarism of war throughout Europe! Pleading virtue by means of vice! Kindness by rashness! Love by cruelty! Patience and order through riot and anarchy! Restraint and wealth through waste and damage! Courtesy and civilization through the most atrocious plans and slaughter! We can only say that people who hold to such a philosophy are uncivilized barbarians. Though they wear scarlet and silks, they are barbarians. Though they have golden chains about their necks, they are barbarians. Though they live in marble palaces, they are barbarians. Though the finest food and wine is on their

---

[1] *Crimean War* Fought on the Crimean Peninsula (then part of the Russian Empire) between 1853 and 1856, the Crimean War pitted Russia against an alliance of France, Britain, the Ottoman Empire, and Sardinia in a battle over control of certain parts of the Middle East, including the Holy Land. The war was notorious for its high number of casualties and increasingly perceived ineffectualness.

tables, they are barbarians. Though they are fluent in parliamentary debates, they are barbarians. And barbarians they will remain until there is a change. Yes, they are fond of talking about "war to further Christianity!" "To further Christianity by war!" That is the blackest calumny[1] that has ever passed the lips of the superstitious, the blackest ever uttered in the name of atheism. Yes, they say, war is necessary for the furtherance of Christianity. No, no, I say, the history of the late war is everlasting evidence against Turkey, France, and England, that Christianity's influence, the influence of the gospels of peace, has been completely gagged in the spheres of their authority …

Who does not pray—and pray more earnestly—for the dawning of a day, yes, for the imminent dawning of a fair and peaceful day when kind-hearted, courteous, and peace-loving men will administer the courts of Europe! Then their peace shall flow out like a river, and justice be guided like waves of the sea.

—1855

Evan James (1809–1878)

Evan James was a weaver by trade; he also wrote poetry and essays and was an active member of Welsh-language communities. His "*Hen Wlad fy Nhadau*" or "Land of my Fathers" has been the unofficial but widely used national anthem of Wales since the early twentieth century. It is said that James's son, James James, composed the melody one day while walking along the banks of the River Rhonda, though it is uncertain whether this preceded or followed the writing of the lyrics.

Hen Wlad fy Nhadau

Mae hen wlad fy nhadau yn annwyl i mi,
Gwlad beirdd a chantorion, enwogion o fri,
Ei gwrol ryfelwyr, gwladgarwyr tra mad,
Dros ryddid gollasant eu gwa'd.

Gwlad, Gwlad, pleidiol wyf i'm gwlad.
Tra môr yn fur i'r bur hoff bau,
O bydded i'r heniaih barhau.

Hen Gymru fynyddig, paradwys y bardd,
Pob dyffryn, pob clogwyn, i'm golwg sydd hardd,
Trwy deimlad gwladgarol, mor swynol yw si
Ei nentydd, afonydd, i fi.
Os treisiodd y gelyn fy ngwlad dan ei droed,
Mae hen iaith y Cymry mor fyw ag erioed,
Ni luddiwyd yr awen dan erchyll law brad,
Na thelyn berseiniol fy ngwlad.

Old Land of My Fathers[2]

Old land of my fathers, land of my choice,
The land in which bards and minstrels rejoice;
Land whose stern warriors were true as could be;
They gave their blood to be free.

Wales! Wales! I'll be faithful to Wales!
The sea is her wall; may nought 'ere befall
The pure, loved land, and th' old language of Wales.

Old mountains of Cambria,[3] bards' paradise,
Each hill and each valley the eye delights;
To the ears of her patriots how charming still seems
The music that forever flows in her streams.

If my land be by enemies harshly oppressed
The old Welsh tongue never dies, never rests;
The muse has slipped the traitor's noose—she's gone,
And the harp of my country plays on.

—1856

[1] *calumny* Lie.

[2] *Old Land of My Fathers* The present translation has been prepared by the editors of this anthology, in consultation with several of the extant translations.

[3] *Cambria* Latinized form of the Welsh name for Wales, *Cymru*.

SARAH JANE REES [CRANOGWEN] (1839–1916)

The daughter of a master mariner, Sarah Jane Rees had a fascinatingly varied career, during which she taught at a school of marine navigation, campaigned on behalf of the women's temperance movement, and wrote numerous works of prose and poetry. Like many Welsh poets of her era, she gained much of her literary skill and fame through participation in local *eisteddfodau*, competitive literary festivals. She was also editor of the Welsh-language women's periodical *Y Frythones*, and spoke on behalf of many progressive causes throughout her life.

The End of the Year[1]

Almost, almost done, another year,
And I go forward, forward, drawing near;
Many a year is now left high and dry,
And my life, my only life, is passing by:
I feel now that my journey's a descent
A rapid one—Oh strange how downward bent!
The day—the month—the year, all onward brings,
Hastening past, as if on speedy, tiny wings;
While I am contemplating them with joy,
They fly past, making of my mind a toy,
If one must sing happily at their birth,
One must do the same now, or the knell of death
Will sound with sorrow from the brink of their grave,
And thus does all in this sad world its ending have.

What?—Does the speed of time increase,
As it draws near the end of its lease?
Is there some great Power which pulls at it?
Perhaps a new name is given to it?
Is it true that the whole of the present,
While toward eternity it follows the current,
With its great powers sucking ardently,
Speeds on time's wheels, which turn more quickly?
It's as if we're in reach of the tide of Eternity,
And everything goes speeding on at a gallop,
But oh how I long to be able to say "stop"!
But no, too quickly the twilight falls for me!

There's work to be done, but time pays me no heed,
I think of doing, but time goes on with speed,
I decide to do, I plan, and I make haste,
While the day, the month, the year, speed past;
Each morning the day begins to die,
And the week just disappears, goes powering by,
The year, as if it were running a race,
Eager to reach its end, it speeds apace!

What is going on?—Where is everything going
Like this, powering onward, unstoppable, turning?
Is there no rest sometimes, no respite?
Day follows day, a new year comes to light;
But to my eyes everything seems restrained,
Everything's smaller, quicker, contained:
As it drives forward like this, before long it's sure
The end will be reached, the eternal cure,
And then—what, my Lord, will be thy behest?
A great stillness, and everything at rest?
The eager wheels of changeful time will
Beyond this boundary, be completely still?
Do the years there live and die?
Does the tide there have a neap[2] and high?
Are there boundaries to that Continent,
Does its moon change from waning to crescent?
Oh my Lord God, how boundless is Eternity!
How incomprehensible is that place to me!
How impossible to plumb that Ocean's deeps,
Whose tide is high and brooks no neaps!
I feel myself being pulled towards it!
What, oh what will be my fate within it?
You plumb its very depths, entirely!
Oh grant that I may know you fully,
And shelter always in your shadow!
I'll release myself into the eternal now
Quietly, trusting always in you!
—1870(?)

[1] *The End of the Year* Translated by Katie Gramich for *Welsh Women's Poetry 1460–2001: An Anthology*. Copyright © Katie Gramich 2003.

[2] *neap* Period in which the high tide is at its lowest, and there is little difference between high and low tide.

O.M. EDWARDS (1858–1920)

Welsh writer and scholar (and briefly Member of Parliament) Sir Owen Morgan Edwards was known for the radical idealism of his political thought, and for his influence in the development of cultural nationalism in Wales. Born in the village of Llanuwchllyn—where approximately 80 per cent of the people speak Welsh even today—he glorified the life and history of rural Wales in much of his work and writing. He also worked for educational reform, especially with regard to the Welsh language and history.

from *The Soul of a Nation (Enaid Cenedl)*[1]

But Wales has a soul, a soul which is her own. And she can lose it. Education may thrive, religion may increase its hold, freedom may be won, the poor may arise from the dust and become powerful, the wealthy may be strong and flourish like the green bay, and the nation's soul may weaken and fade. The nation may lose itself in the empire, and be a dead member and not a living one, her voice never more to be heard. And if that calamity were to come about, Wales would be without a soul, and the world would be the poorer. When the next upsurge of freedom and religion would take place, Wales would not be there to hold up the banner; her voice would have been silenced …

May Wales succeed in every possible way. Equality and freedom will come; a University and a Hospital Service; and many a dream will be fulfilled. But let us not lose sight of the nation's soul, lest among much fine building and enthusiastic committee-work it vanish from sight. May it be fostered in the schools and the various colleges of the University, but the hearth is its cradle. The spirit of Wales is born in the mountain farmhouse, in the cottage by the brook, in the coal-miner's home. And if it be not fostered the Welsh nation will become merely derivative and second rate, an imitator of something inferior to her own true life. If she guards her soul, she has it in herself to make her contribution among the leaders of the world. In a delicate love of country, and in steadfast faith, may our aim be no less.

—1920

[1] *The Soul of a Nation* Translated by D.M. Lloyd.

ALICE GRAY JONES [CERIDWEN PERIS] (1852–1943)

Alice Gray Jones was a Welsh writer, teacher, and temperance activist, who contributed to many Welsh-language periodicals throughout her literary career (including *Y Frythones*, which was edited by Sarah Jane Rees). Her pen name is a reference to the local Saint Peris.

A New Year Greeting—1929[2]

Women of Wales! Let the New Year
Be good, happy, carefree, all that's fine.
For this is the year of years—
Nineteen hundred and twenty nine!
All women now possess the vote[3]
When they're twenty-one years old!
Where's the prophet of the future?
Who could have such a thing foretold?

Young women—have your wits about you—
Be careful; of what you do be certain,
Remember this—the effect of your action
Will be on the statute books of Britain!
Women, they say, are the majority—
You, therefore, are at the helm,
Guard then lest your apathy displease
The Lord and do mischief to the realm.
Remember the old hearths of Wales,
Which awake in us a sad *hiraeth*[4]—

[2] *A New Year Greeting—1929* Translated by Katie Gramich for *Welsh Women's Poetry 1460–2001: An Anthology*. Copyright © Katie Gramich 2003.

[3] *All women … the vote* The Representation of the People Act was passed in 1928, expanding on the 1918 act which had given the vote only to a limited class of women over the age of thirty (men were able to vote at the age of twenty-one).

[4] *hiraeth* Welsh: a concept related to nostalgia.

Remember our pure, humble mothers—
And fathers, renowned for their faith:
Remember the fervent prayers that rose
Night and morn to God our guide,
Here they are, the dear old hearths
Which gave our country its pride.

Women of Wales! Be valiant,
Insist on fairness, insist on concord—
Through the Word[1]—not the sword;
And flee from all worldly temptation.
Oh! Dear country of Revivals—
When shall we relish them once more?
A land whose song is full of praises,
A land whose faith springs from the core.
—1929

Song of the Worker's Wife[2]

My hands are none too white,
Nor lovely nor tender either,
They're rough and ugly to your sight,
Because of the constant labour;
But my hands are not complaining,
There's no whinging in my breast,
When I recall my tidy house, containing
My happy little family, like a nest.

The kids would go early to bed,
And I'd set to doing the wash,
The little snow white clothes all aired
I'd get them up so nice and posh,
I'd sew a button on David's shirt,
And put a nail in Sam's shoe,
And I'd mend Enid's red skirt—
Those chores that all mothers do.

And oh! they were all around me
Like glad little chicks in a throng,
And my single purpose was to see
My children happy, fit and strong,
To keep an eye on their progress,
To care for them all day long,
To keep their language spotless:
I was happy, all smiles and song.

But, alas, they've all grown up,
And all have left the nest,
They'll no more come home to sup,
And their old toys are all at rest!
The workbox for mending their things,
And for putting a nail in Sam's shoe,
Is now quite useless—a bird without wings;
A mam's initiative unwanted, no more for her to do!
—1934(?)

David Lloyd George (1863–1945)

Of all British Prime Ministers, David Lloyd George is said to number among the handful of greatest English orators. He is also the only British Prime Minister for whom English was a second language; born in northern England to Welsh parents, he grew up with Welsh as his first language.

In the early 1890s (when a Liberal member of Parliament) Lloyd George devoted a considerable amount of time to setting up new branches of the *Cymru Fydd* League; the speech excerpted here was delivered at such an occasion in Cardiff.

---

[1] *Word* The capitalization suggests the Biblical Word.

[2] *Song of the Worker's Wife* Translated by Katie Gramich for *Welsh Women's Poetry 1460–2001: An Anthology*. Copyright © Katie Gramich 2003.

from *Speech delivered at the inaugural meeting of the Cardiff branch of the Cymru Fydd League*, October 1894

… No one can fairly lay cowardice to the charge of any Celtic race.[1] Their bravery has stood the severest test to which courage can be put. They have been beaten, baffled, discomfited, disappointed, times innumerable. They know more of the "hope deferred that maketh the heart sick"[2] than almost any branch of the human race. They have been trodden on and despised for centuries in their own land, but their indomitable spirit is still unbroken. There is one thing, however, that their fortitude does not seem to be equal to. You cannot get the Celt to face a disagreeable fact. His fiery nature always shies at an unpleasant truth. There is but one way of curing him of his fault, and that is by adopting a method used by trainers when a spirited horse starts at an object on the roadway turn his head towards it and compel him, whether he will or not, to stare at it. … Let us pursue the same strategy with the Welsh spirit. Get it to look steadily at the disturbing facts along the path of its national progress. It will get on its journey very much more surely and speedily for the experience. …

… During the last twenty-six years Wales has returned a preponderating majority of Liberal members to Parliament. … Liberal Ministries have … been dependent for their very existence upon the loyalty of their Welsh supporters. But, in spite of all this, Wales has not during the whole of that time had a single measure of reform from any Liberal Government dealing with any of the special topics in which she is more immediately interested. I would say more than that she has not had in the aggregate one week out of the whole of those fourteen years for the discussion of her special concerns. The result is surely not a promising one. … Of course we may be told that this sterility of results is attributable entirely to Tory obstruction. … [But] in spite of Tory obstruction England has always had her wants attended to without delay. … If any one suffers from the obstruction of the reactionary forces represented in the House of Commons, it is the Celtic nationalities of this kingdom. …

—1894

---

[1] *Celtic race* Twenty-first-century Welsh, Scottish, and Irish people have grown to be highly suspicious of generalizations about "the Celts" or "the Celtic races," which (quite aside from the issue of oversimplification) have a long history of being advanced in disparaging or patronizing ways. Lloyd George's speech is evidence that such terms were sometimes also employed by those of Welsh, Scottish, or Irish background in support of the cause of "Celtic peoples."

[2] *hope deferred … sick* The quotation is from Proverbs 13.12.

Urban Work and Poverty

CONTEXTS

The Industrial Revolution brought rapid, pervasive, and frequently disorienting change to Britain. Manufacturing changed the face of the nation, from its physical appearance to the structure of family life. The Industrial Revolution had begun in the eighteenth century with the invention of new technology for spinning and weaving, and with the invention of the steam engine to power these machines, manufacturers established factories (originally called "mills") for centralized production. Mill towns such as Manchester boomed as workers crowded into cities seeking employment. There they lived in crowded, unsanitary conditions that bred disease—resulting in frequent epidemics of diseases such as cholera and typhoid. The second wave of the Industrial Revolution came with the spread of the railway in the 1840s, which allowed the iron and coal industries to flourish. Before legislation began to be passed in the 1840s, workers, including small children, worked long hours in dangerous, unhealthy conditions, without job security, insurance, or benefits. When occasional economic depressions caused factories and mines to close or cut down hours of operation, these workers often starved.

The lifelong damage resulting from the hardships faced by child workers is exemplified in the testimony of Elizabeth Bentley, one of the few women to speak before the 1832 Sadler Committee on the Labour of Children in Factories. Social reformer Michael Sadler had argued in Parliament for the passing of a Ten Hours Bill (limiting factory work to ten hours a day) and had detailed the suffering of child laborers in order to move his fellow members of Parliament to action. When the government asked for a committee of enquiry into the conditions of child laborers, Sadler chaired it, and the resulting testimony was published in Samuel Kydd's 1857 *History of the Factory Movement.* Bentley was one of thirty-eight workers (only three of whom were female) to be interviewed.

Andrew Ure's *The Philosophy of Manufactures* was one of the best-known works arguing in favor of the factory system. Ure viewed the factory system as a self-regulating organism that should be beyond government regulation, and into which workers should be introduced at a very young age, when they could be easily disciplined. While Ure speaks of the national wealth and prosperity that the factory system created, William Dodd, a child laborer, gives evidence in the excerpt following of the human costs of such "prosperity." Dodd's narrative of his life, which he published to expose the falsities of "eye-witness" accounts such as Ure's, details the lifetime of suffering and physical deformity that resulted from his early introduction to factory life. Prospects were not much better for adults employed in the mills; the reality for many working-class people was that they would work until they could work no more, at which point they would likely perish—a fate the woman in Thomas Hood's poem "Song of the Shirt" (reprinted below) seems eagerly to anticipate—or live the remainder of their days in a workhouse.

Friedrich Engels, author of *The Condition of the Working Class in England,* excerpted below, sought to expose not only the degrading conditions of the poor, but also the deliberate ways in which the middle classes shielded themselves from the realities of working-class people's suffering. Having come from Germany to study the cotton trade, Engels was struck by the conditions in England's urban centers. In this excerpt, he examines the living conditions of the working-class areas of Manchester (he also examines those of England's other "Great Towns," such as London) and the ways in which these areas are systematically hidden from the view of wealthier citizens. Engels went on to collaborate with Karl Marx on *The Communist Manifesto* (1848), and together the two thinkers laid the foundation of modern Communism.

The excerpt following, from Elizabeth Gaskell's novel *Mary Barton*, shows the opposing effects of industrialism on the rich and the poor, and the ways in which the factory system resulted in further alienation between classes. Gaskell contrasts the home lives of the rich and poor and details the private suffering of the latter during the economic depression known as the "hungry forties." *Mary Barton* was part of a developing genre known as the "social problem novel," which focused on the rampant poverty, unemployment, and disease that pervaded the Industrial Revolution. In his slightly later novel *Hard Times*, Charles Dickens details the dehumanizing effects of the factory system and factory managers' lack of recognition of the shared humanity of their employees. The fictional "Coketown" (so called because of the soot that blackens the city), in which his novel is set, is based on Dickens's observations of northern industrial towns such as Manchester and Preston.

One of the era's most influential depictions of working class and poor people was author and social reformer Henry Mayhew's *London Labour and the London Poor*, excerpted below. Asked by *The Morning Chronicle* to document, as metropolitan correspondent, the lives of the urban poor, Mayhew produced eighty-two articles that he later expanded into a four-volume collection of testimony of the lives of the lower class. He painted the underworld of Victorian society in unprecedented detail, shedding light on the specificities of economic exchange and the economic order that governed the poor. Perhaps more importantly, his work provided Victorians with a personal glimpse into the lives of the poor that helped to shape Victorian social theories. The serial newspaper publications were so popular that they resulted in the establishment of a fund to assist "Labour and the Poor." Mayhew had an ear for individual dialects, slang, and other oddities of speech, and composed each subject's narrative in language that, as closely as possible, imitated the speaker's own words. His characters were so compelling that Mayhew's narratives influenced the depiction of such characters in fiction, and writers such as Charles Dickens drew upon his representations of the poor to bring life to their own characters.

Overall, writings such as those reprinted here helped to make the middle and leisure classes more sympathetic to the hardships of poverty, and over the course of the nineteenth century some efforts were made to improve living and working conditions for the urban poor. Cities saw better sewer systems, cleaner water supplies, and in some cases the removal of slums—though the latter development had mixed effects on the slums' occupants, who, more often than not, were forced into even more crowded areas when their homes were demolished. Real wages for working people, however, increased, and a series of Factory Acts set requirements for ventilation, sanitation, and equipment safety, as well as limiting the working hours of women and children (a provision that effectively limited the working hours of many men as well). Many of these changes were achieved by the workers themselves; the century saw great strides in labor organization, with trade unions decriminalized in the 1860s. Yet labor for most working-class people remained dangerous, arduous, overlong, and underpaid well beyond the Victorian era.

⌘⌘⌘

from Elizabeth Bentley, *Testimony before the 1832 Committee on the Labour of Children in Factories* (1857)

"I am twenty-three years of age, and live at Leeds. I began to work at Mr. Busk's flax mill when I was six years old. I was then a little 'doffer.'[1] In that mill we worked from five in the morning till nine at night, when they were 'throng';[2] when they were not so 'throng,' the usual hours of labour were from six in the morning till seven at night. The time allowed for our meals was forty minutes at noon; not any time was allowed for breakfast or 'drinking': these we got as we could. When our work was bad, we had hardly any time to eat them at all: we were obliged to leave them or take them home. When we did not take our uneaten food home, the overlooker took it and gave it to his pigs. I consider 'doffing' to be a laborious employment. When the frames are full, the 'doffers' have to stop them, and take the 'flyers'[3] off, and take the full bobbins off, and carry them to the roller, and then put empty ones on, and set the frame going again. I was kept constantly on my feet; there were so many frames, and they run so quick, the labour was excessive, there was not time for anything. When the 'doffers' flagged[4] a little, or were too late, they were strapped. Those who were last in 'doffing' were constantly strapped—girls as well as boys. I have been strapped severely, and have been hurt by the strap excessively. The overlooker I was under was a very severe man. When I and others have been fatigued and worn out, and had not baskets enough to put the bobbins in, we used to put them in the window bottoms, and that broke the panes sometimes; and I broke one one time, and the overlooker strapped me on the arm, and it rose a blister, and I ran home to my mother. I worked at Mr. Busk's factory three or four years.

"When I left Mr. Busk's, I then went to Benyon's factory; I was about ten years of age, and was employed as a weigher in the card-room.[5] At Benyon's factory we worked from half-past five till eight at night; when they were 'throng,' until nine. The spinners at that mill were allowed forty minutes at noon for meals; no more time throughout the day was allowed. Those employed in the card-rooms had, in addition to the forty minutes at noon, a quarter of an hour allowed for their breakfast, and a quarter of an hour for their 'drinking.' The carding-room is more oppressive than the spinning department: those at work cannot see each other for dust. The 'cards' get so soon filled up with waste and dirt, they must be stopped or they would take fire: the stoppages are as much for the benefit of the employer as for the working people. The children at Benyon's factory were beat up to their labour with a strap. ... The girls have many times had black marks upon their skins. Had the parents complained of this excessive ill-usage, the probable consequence would have been the loss of the employment of the child. Of this result the parents were afraid.

"I worked in the card-room; it was so dusty that the dust got upon my lungs, and the work was so hard. I was middling strong when I went there, but the work was so bad; I got so bad in health, that when I pulled the baskets down, I pulled my bones out of their places. The basket I pulled was a very large one; that was full of weights, upheaped, and pulling the basket, pulled my shoulder out of its place, and my ribs have grown over it. That hard work is generally done by women: it is not fit for children. There was no spinning for me, and I therefore did that work. ...

"I am considerably deformed in person in consequence of this labour. I was about thirteen years old when my deformity began to come on, and it has got worse since. It is five years since my mother died, and she was never able to get me a pair of good stays[6] to hold me up; and when my mother died I had to do for myself,

[1] *doffer* Worker who assists the spinner by removing the full spindles, or bobbins, from the carding machine (which combs the cotton or wool) and replacing them with empty ones.

[2] *throng* Busy.

[3] *flyers* Part of the spinning machine that twists the thread and winds it upon the bobbin.

[4] *flagged* Slowed down.

[5] *card-room* Room that held the carding machines, which combed and cleaned the wool or cotton in preparation for spinning.

[6] *stays* Bodice stiffened with strips of whale-bone that gives support and shape to the figure; a corset.

and got me a pair. Before I worked at a mill I was as straight a little girl as ever went up and down town. I was straight until I was thirteen. I have been attended by a medical gentleman, Mr. Hare. He said it was owing to hard labour, and working in the factories. …

"I have had the misfortune, from being a straight and healthful girl, to become very much otherwise in person. I do not know of any other girls that have become weak and deformed in like manner. I have known others who have been similarly injured in health. I am deformed in the shoulders; it is very common indeed to have weak ankles and crooked knees, that is brought on by stopping the spindle.

"I have had experience in wet spinning—it is very uncomfortable. I have stood before the frames till I have been wet through to my skin; and in winter-time, when myself and others have gone home, our clothes have been frozen, and we have nearly caught our death from cold. We have stopped at home one or two days, just as we were situated in our health; had we stopped away any length of time we should have found it difficult to keep our situation.

"I am now in the poor-house at Hunslet. Not any of my former employers come to see me. When I was at home, Mr. Walker made me a present of 1s. or 2s.,[1] but since I left my work and have gone to the poor-house, no one has come nigh me. I was very willing to have worked as long as I was able, and to have supported my widowed mother. I am utterly incapable now of any exertion of that sort, and am supported by the parish."[2]

from Andrew Ure, *The Philosophy of Manufactures* (1835)

In its precise acceptation, the factory system is of recent origin, and may claim England for its birthplace. The mills for throwing silk, or making organzine,[3] which were mounted centuries ago in several of the Italian states, and furtively transferred to this country by Sir Thomas Lombe in 1718, contained indeed certain elements of a factory, and probably suggested some hints of those grander and more complex combinations of self-acting machines, which were first embodied half a century later in our cotton manufacture by Richard Arkwright, assisted by gentlemen of Derby, well acquainted with its celebrated silk establishment. …

When the first water-frames for spinning cotton were erected at Cromford, in the romantic valley of the Derwent, about sixty years ago, mankind were little aware of the mighty revolution which the new system of labour was destined by Providence to achieve, not only in the structure of British society, but in the fortunes of the world at large. Arkwright alone had the sagacity to discern, and the boldness to predict in glowing language, how vastly productive human industry would become, when no longer proportioned in its results to muscular effort, which is by its nature fitful and capricious, but when made to consist in the task of guiding the work of mechanical fingers and arms, regularly impelled with great velocity by some indefatigable physical power. What his judgment so clearly led him to perceive, his energy of will enabled him to realize with such rapidity and success, as would have done honour to the most influential individuals, but were truly wonderful in that obscure and indigent artisan. The main difficulty did not, to my apprehension, lie so much in the invention of a proper self-acting mechanism for drawing out and twisting cotton into a continuous thread, as in the distribution of the different members of the apparatus into one cooperative body, in impelling each organ with its appropriate delicacy and speed, and, above all, in training human beings to renounce their desultory[4] habits of work, and to identify themselves with the unvarying regularity of the complex automaton. To devise and administer a successful code of factory discipline, suited to the necessities of factory diligence, was the Herculean enterprise, the noble achievement of Arkwright. Even at the present day,

[1] *s.* Shilling.

[2] *supported by the parish* I.e., with public funds.

[3] *organzine* Silk yarn.

[4] *desultory* Half-hearted, lacking enthusiasm.

when the system is perfectly organized, and its labour lightened to the utmost, it is found nearly impossible to convert persons past the age of puberty, whether drawn from rural or from handicraft occupations, into useful factory hands. After struggling for a while to conquer their listless or restive habits, they either renounce the employment spontaneously, or are dismissed by the overlookers on account of inattention. …

It required, in fact, a man of a Napoleon nerve and ambition to subdue the refractory tempers of work-people accustomed to irregular paroxysms of diligence, and to urge on his multifarious and intricate constructions in the face of prejudice, passion, and envy. Such was Arkwright, who, suffering nothing to stay or turn aside his progress, arrived gloriously at the goal, and has for ever affixed his name to a great era in the annals of mankind, an era which has laid open unbounded prospects of wealth and comfort to the industrious, however much they may have been occasionally clouded by ignorance and folly.

… In my recent tour, continued during several months, through the manufacturing districts, I have seen tens of thousands of old, young, and middle-aged of both sexes, many of them too feeble to get their daily bread by any of the former modes of industry, earning abundant food, raiment, and domestic accommodation, without perspiring at a single pore, screened meanwhile from the summer's sun and the winter's frost, in apartments more airy and salubrious[1] than those of the metropolis, in which our legislative and fashionable aristocracies assemble. In those spacious halls the benignant power of steam summons around him his myriads of willing menials, and assigns to each the regulated task, substituting for painful muscular effort on their part, the energies of his own gigantic arm, and demanding in return only attention and dexterity to correct such little aberrations as casually occur in his workmanship. The gentle docility of this moving force qualifies it for impelling the tiny bobbins of the lace-machine with a precision and speed inimitable by the most dexterous hands, directed by the sharpest eyes. Hence, under its auspices, and in obedience to Arkwright's polity,[2] magnificent edifices, surpassing far in number, value, usefulness, and ingenuity of construction, the boasted monuments of Asiatic, Egyptian, and Roman despotism, have, within the short period of fifty years, risen up in this kingdom, to show to what extent capital, industry, and science may augment the resources of a state, while they meliorate the condition of its citizens. Such is the factory system, replete with prodigies in mechanics and political economy, which promises, in its future growth, to become the great minister of civilization to the terraqueous[3] globe, enabling this country, as its heart, to diffuse along with its commerce the life-blood of science and religion to myriads of people still lying "in the region and shadow of death."[4] …

No master would wish to have any wayward children to work within the walls of his factory who do not mind their business without beating, and he therefore usually fines or turns away any spinners who are known to maltreat their assistants. Hence, ill-usage of any kind is a very rare occurrence. I have visited many factories, both in Manchester and in the surrounding districts, during a period of several months, entering the spinning rooms, unexpectedly, and often alone, at different times of the day, and I never saw a single instance of corporal chastisement inflicted on a child, nor indeed did I ever see children in ill-humour. They seemed to be always cheerful and alert, taking pleasure in the light play of their muscles—enjoying the mobility natural to their age. The scene of industry, so far from exciting sad emotions in my mind, was always exhilarating. It was delightful to observe the nimbleness with which they pieced the broken ends, as the mule-carriage[5] began to recede from the fixed roller beam, and to see them at leisure, after a few seconds' exercise of their tiny fingers, to amuse themselves in any attitude

[1] *salubrious* Favorable to health.

[2] *polity* Mode of administration.

[3] *terraqueous* Consisting of land and water.

[4] *in the … death* From Matthew 4.16.

[5] *broken ends* I.e., of thread. This was the job of the "piecer," who ensured that the process of spinning could continue uninterrupted; *mule-carriage* The movable part of the mule, a kind of spinning machine, invented in 1779, that could spin yarn of varying thicknesses.

they chose, till the stretch and winding-on were once more completed. The work of these lively elves seemed to resemble a sport, in which habit gave them a pleasing dexterity. Conscious of their skill, they were delighted to show it off to any stranger. As to exhaustion by the day's work, they evinced no trace of it on emerging from the mill in the evening; for they immediately began to skip about any neighbouring playground, and to commence their little amusements with the same alacrity as boys issuing from a school. It is moreover my firm conviction that if children are not ill-used by bad parents or guardians, but receive in food and raiment the full benefit of what they earn, they would thrive better when employed in our modern factories than if left at home in apartments too often ill-aired, damp, and cold.

from William Dodd, *A Narrative of the Experience and Sufferings of William Dodd, a Factory Cripple, Written by Himself* (1841)

Dear Reader,—I wish it to be distinctly and clearly understood, that, in laying before you the following sheets, I am not actuated by any motive of ill-feeling to any party with whom I have formerly been connected; on the contrary, I have a personal respect for some of my former masters, and am convinced that, had they been in any other line of life, they would have shone forth as ornaments to the age in which they lived; but having witnessed the efforts of some writers (who can know nothing of the factories by experience) to mislead the minds of the public upon a subject of so much importance, I feel it to be my duty to give to the world a fair and impartial account of the working of the factory system, as I have found it in twenty-five years' experience.

… Of four children in our family, I was the only boy; and we were all, at different periods, as we could meet with employers, sent to work in the factories. My eldest sister was ten years of age before she went; consequently, she was, in a manner, out of harm's way, her bones having become firmer and stronger than ours, and capable of withstanding the hardships to which she

A

NARRATIVE

OF THE

EXPERIENCE AND SUFFERINGS

OF

WILLIAM DODD,

A FACTORY CRIPPLE.

WRITTEN BY HIMSELF.

GIVING AN ACCOUNT OF THE HARDSHIPS AND SUFFERINGS HE ENDURED IN EARLY LIFE, UNDER WHAT DIFFICULTIES HE ACQUIRED HIS EDUCATION, THE EFFECTS OF FACTORY LABOUR ON HIS MIND AND PERSON, THE UNSUCCESSFUL EFFORTS MADE BY HIM TO OBTAIN A LIVELIHOOD IN SOME OTHER LINE OF LIFE, THE COMPARISON HE DRAWS BETWEEN AGRICULTURAL AND MANUFACTURING LABOURERS, AND OTHER MATTERS RELATING TO THE WORKING CLASSES.

SECOND EDITION.

LONDON:
PUBLISHED BY L. & G. SEELEY, 169, FLEET STREET,
AND HATCHARD & SON, 187, PICCADILLY.
1841.

PRICE ONE SHILLING.

Title page from William Dodd, *A Narrative of the Experience and Sufferings of William Dodd, a Factory Cripple, Written by Himself* (1841).

was exposed much better than we could. … I was born on the 18th of June, 1804; and in the latter part of 1809, being then turned of five years of age, I was put to work at card-making,[1] and about a year after I was sent, with my sisters, to the factories. I was then a fine, strong, healthy, hardy boy, straight in every limb, and remarkably stout and active. …

From six to fourteen years of age, I went through a series of uninterrupted, unmitigated suffering, such as very rarely falls to the lot of mortals so early in life, except to those situated as I was, and such as I could not have withstood, had I not been strong, and of a good constitution.

[1] *card-making* Cards combed and cleansed fibers in preparation for spinning.

My first place in the factories was that of piecer, or the lowest situation: but as the term conveys only a vague idea of the duties to be performed, it will be necessary here to give such explanation as may enable those unacquainted with the business to form a just conception of what those duties are, and to judge of the inadequacy of the remuneration or reward for their performance, and the cruelty of the punishments inflicted for the neglect of those duties. …

The position in which the piecer stands to his work is with his right foot forward, and his right side facing the frame: the motion he makes in going along in front of the frame, for the purpose of piecing, is neither forwards nor backwards, but in a sidling direction, constantly keeping his right side towards the frame. In this position he continues during the day, with his hands, feet, and eyes constantly in motion. It will be easily seen, that the chief weight of his body rests upon his right knee, which is almost always the first joint to give way. The number of cripples with the right knee in, greatly exceed those with the left knee in; a great many have both knees in such as my own from this cause.

Another evil resulting from the position in which the piecer stands, is what is termed "splay-foot," which may be explained thus: in a well-formed foot, there is a finely formed arch of bones immediately under the instep and ankle joint. The continual pressure of the body on this arch, before it is sufficiently strong to bear such pressure (as in the case of boys and girls in the factories) causes it to give way: the bones fall gradually down, the foot then becomes broad and flat, and the owner drags it after him with the broad side first. A great many factory cripples are in this state; this is very often attended with weak ankle and knee joints. I have a brother-in-law exactly thus, who has tried everything likely to do him good, but without success.

The spinner and the piecer are intimately connected together:[1] the spinner works by the piece, being paid by the stone[2] for the yarn spun; the piecer is hired by the week, and paid according to his abilities. The piecers are the servants of the spinners, and both are under an overlooker; and liable to be dismissed at a week's notice. Being thus circumstanced, it is clearly the advantage of the spinner to have good able piecers, who ought, in return, to be well paid. …

In order to induce the piecer to do his work quick and well, the spinner has recourse to many expedients, such as offering rewards of a penny or two-pence for a good week's work inducing them to sing, which, like the music in the army, has a very powerful effect, and keeps them awake and active longer than any other thing; and, as a last resource, when nothing else will do, he takes the strap, or the billy-roller,[3] which are laid on most unmercifully, accompanied by a round volley of oaths; and I pity the poor wretch who has to submit to the infliction of either.

On one occasion, I remember being thrashed with the billy-roller till my back, arms, and legs were covered with ridges as thick as my finger. This was more than I could bear, and, seeing a favourable opportunity, I slipped out and stole off home along some by-ways, so as not to be seen. Mother stripped me, and was shocked at my appearance. The spinner, not meeting with any other to suit him, had the assurance to come and beg that mother would let me go again, and promised not to strike me with the billy-roller any more. He kept his promise, but instead of using the roller, he used his fist.

… A piecer, it will be seen, is an important person in the factories, inasmuch as it is impossible to do without them. Formerly, boys and girls were sent to work in the factories as piecers at the early age of five or six years—as in my own case—but now, owing to the introduction of some wise laws for the regulation of factories,[4] they

[1] *The spinner … together* The spinner, who ran the "billy" (or "slubbing," the machine that spins yarn) was dependent on the piecer for the preparation of the wool.

[2] *stone* Unit of measurement equal to 14 pounds.

[3] *billy-roller* Uppermost of a series of wooden rollers through which the wool is moved to the spindles. It was very long and easily removed from the billy; as a result, it was a notorious instrument of punishment to factory children.

[4] *some wise … factories* The 1833 Factory Act, which prevented children under nine from working in any factories except silk mills. It also decreed that children under 11 (and, eventually, under 13) could not work more than 9 hours a day or 48 hours a week, and that all working children had to be provided with education at the expense of the factory owners.

A wood engraving of a child mine-worker included in the *Report of the Commission of the Employment of Children and Young Persons in the Mines* (1842).

cannot employ any as piecers before they have attained the age of 9 years; at which age their bones are comparatively strong, generally speaking, and more able to endure the hardships to which they will be exposed.

They now enjoy many privileges that we had not, such as attending schools, limited hours of labour, &c.; but still it is far from being a desirable place for a child. Formerly, it was nothing but work till we could work no longer. I have frequently worked at the frame till I could scarcely get home, and in this state have been stopped by people in the streets who noticed me shuffling along, and advised me to work no more in the factories: but I was not my own master. Thus year after year passed away, my afflictions and deformities increasing. I could not associate with anybody; on the contrary, I sought every opportunity to rest myself, and to shrink into any corner to screen myself from the prying eye of the curious and scornful! During the day, I frequently counted the clock, and calculated how many hours I had still to remain at work; my evenings were spent in preparing for the following day—in rubbing my knees, ankles, elbows, and wrists with oil, &c., and wrapping them in warm flannel! (for everything was tried to benefit me, except the right one—that of taking me from the work) after which, with a look at, rather than eating my supper (the bad smells of the factory having generally taken my appetite away) I went to bed, to cry myself to sleep, and pray that the Lord would take me to Himself before morning.

… A great many are made cripples by over-exertion. Among those who have been brought up from infancy with me in the factories, and whom death has spared, few have escaped without some injury. My brother-in-law and myself have been crippled by this cause, but in different ways; my sister partly by over-exertion and partly by machinery. On going home to breakfast one morning, I was much surprised at seeing several of the neighbours and two doctors in our house. On inquiring the cause, I found that my second sister had nearly lost her hand in the machinery. She had been working all night, and, fatigued and sleepy, had not been so watchful as she otherwise would have been; and consequently, her right hand became entangled in the machine which she was attending. Four iron teeth of a wheel, three-quarters of an inch broad, and one-quarter of an inch thick, had been forced through her hand, from the back part, among the leaders, &c.; and the fifth iron tooth fell upon the thumb, and crushed it to atoms. It was thought, for some time, that she would lose her hand. But it was saved; and, as you may be sure, it is stiff and contracted, and is but a very feeble apology for a hand. This accident might have been prevented, if the wheels above referred to had been boxed off,[1] which they might have been for a couple of shillings; and the very next week after this accident, a man had two fingers taken off his hand, by the very same wheels—and still they are not boxed off!

Thomas Annan, *Close No. 193, High Street, Glasgow*, 1868. Thomas Annan was hired by the Glasgow City Improvement Trust to photograph the city's slums before they were demolished. Many of his pictures show the open sewers and narrow passageways that were features of slum life. (See also Annan's photographs in the Contexts section on photography.)

[1] *the wheels … boxed off* The Factory Act of 1844 decreed that flywheels connected to mechanical parts, such as shafts, had to be boxed off or fenced. However, such a project would cost a few shillings per wheel, which would add up to a considerable expense, and would make it difficult for workers to clean the machinery. As a result, many factory owners ignored the law when it came into effect.

Thomas Hood, "Song of the Shirt" (1843)

With fingers weary and worn,
With eyelids heavy and red,
A woman sat, in unwomanly rags,
Plying her needle and thread—
Stitch—stitch—stitch!
In poverty, hunger, and dirt,
And still with a voice of dolorous pitch
She sang the "Song of the Shirt."

"Work—work—work
Till the brain begins to swim;
Work—work—work
Till the eyes are heavy and dim!
Seam, and gusset,[2] and band,
Band, and gusset, and seam;
Till over the buttons I fall asleep,
And sew them on in a dream!

"O! men, with sisters dear!
O! men, with mothers and wives!
It is not linen you're wearing out,
But human creatures' lives!
Stitch—stitch—stitch,
In poverty, hunger, and dirt,
Sewing at once, with a double thread,
A shroud[3] as well as a shirt.

"But why do I talk of Death?
That phantom of grisly bone;
I hardly fear his terrible shape,
It seems so like my own—
It seems so like my own,
Because of the fasts I keep:
Oh! God! that bread should be so dear,
And flesh and blood so cheap!

"Work—work—work!
My labour never flags;
And what are its wages?

[2] *gusset* Triangular piece of material inserted into a piece of clothing to strengthen or enlarge some part.

[3] *shroud* Sheet in which a corpse is wrapped for burial.

John Thomson's photograph of "The crawler," 1877. This photograph is taken from Thomson's famous project, *Street Life in London* (1877–78), one of the era's most influential pieces of social documentary. Thomson collaborated with Adolph Smith to create text to accompany the photographs. This picture, one of the best known, shows a destitute woman who told Thomson that she spent her nights on the steps of a workhouse and her days looking after a friend's baby, in exchange for a cup of tea and some bread.

A bed of straw,
A crust of bread and rags,
That shatter'd roof, and this naked floor
A table—a broken chair—
A wall so blank, my shadow I thank
For sometimes falling there!

"Work—work—work!
From weary chime to chime,
Work—work—work
As prisoners work for crime!
Band, and gusset, and seam,
Seam, and gusset, and band,
Till the heart is sick, and the brain benumb'd,
As well as the weary hand.

"Work—work—work,
In the dull December light,
And work—work—work,
When the weather is warm and bright—
While underneath the eaves
The brooding swallows cling,
As if to show me their sunny backs
And twit me with the spring.

"Oh! but to breathe the breath
Of the cowslip and primrose[1] sweet—
With the sky above my head,
And the grass beneath my feet,
For only one short hour
To feel as I used to feel,
Before I knew the woes of want
And the walk that costs a meal:

"Oh, but for one short hour!
A respite, however brief!
No blessed leisure for Love or Hope,
But only time for grief!
A little weeping would ease my heart,
But in their briny head
My tears must stop, for every drop
Hinders needle and thread!"

With fingers weary and worn,
With eyelids heavy and red,
A woman sat, in unwomanly rags,
Plying her needle and thread—
Stitch—stitch—stitch!
In poverty, hunger, and dirt,
And still with a voice of dolorous pitch,
Would that its tone could reach the rich!
She sang this "Song of the Shirt!"

[1] *cowslip … primrose* Wildflowers.

Anonymous, *The New Poor Law with a Description of the New Workhouses*, c. 1834. In the early nineteenth century, each parish administered its own relief for the poor. This might be provided in the form of a minimum allowance, or it might be provided via a workhouse, an institution in which the poor were given lodging and a minimal level of sustenance in exchange for work performed. This parish relief system was unpopular with a large proportion of the middle and leisure classes, who believed that many of the people the system supported were merely avoiding work out of laziness. Such concerns led to the passing of the 1834 Poor Law Amendment Act, which attempted to reduce the costs of poverty relief by discouraging people from claiming it. Allowances for the able-bodied were made illegal, and workhouses, the only remaining option, now consistently were designed to be as unpleasant as possible: families were separated by gender, strict discipline and uniforms were imposed, and food was unappealing. Residents of the workhouse were forbidden to leave without permission, and they were required to perform daily manual labor of a sort similar to the work assigned to prison inmates. Corporal punishment was sometimes used to keep workhouse inhabitants in line, but solitary confinement and denial of food were more usual disciplinary measures. The anonymous poster reproduced here reflects real workhouse practices—although many of them are represented in exaggerated form.

from Friedrich Engels, *The Condition of the Working Class in England in 1844*[1] (1845)

CHAPTER 3: THE GREAT TOWNS

Manchester lies at the foot of the southern slope of a range of hills, which stretch hither from Oldham, their last peak, Kersallmoor, being at once the racecourse and the Mons Sacer[2] of Manchester. Manchester proper lies on the left bank of the Irwell, between that stream and the two smaller ones, the Irk and the Medlock, which here empty into the Irwell. On the right bank of the Irwell, bounded by a sharp curve of the river, lies Salford, and farther westward Pendleton; northward from the Irwell lie Upper and Lower Broughton; northward of the Irk, Cheetham Hill; south of the Medlock lies Hulme; farther east Chorlton on Medlock; still farther, pretty well to the east of Manchester, Ardwick. The whole assemblage of buildings is commonly called Manchester, and contains about four hundred thousand inhabitants, rather more than less. The town itself is peculiarly built, so that a person may live in it for years, and go in and out daily without coming into contact with a working people's quarter or even with workers, that is, so long as he confines himself to his business or to pleasure walks. This arises chiefly from the fact that by unconscious tacit agreement, as well as with outspoken conscious determination, the working people's quarters are sharply separated from the sections of the city reserved for the middle class; or, if this does not succeed, they are concealed with the cloak of charity. Manchester contains, at its heart, a rather extended commercial district, perhaps half a mile long and about as broad, and consisting almost wholly of offices and warehouses. Nearly the whole district is abandoned by dwellers, and is lonely and deserted at night; only watchmen and policemen traverse its narrow lanes with their dark lanterns. This district is cut through by certain main thoroughfares upon which the vast traffic concentrates, and in which the ground level is lined with brilliant shops. In these streets the upper floors are occupied, here and there, and there is a good deal of life upon them until late at night. With the exception of this commercial district, all Manchester proper, all Salford and Hulme, a great part of Pendleton and Chorlton, two-thirds of Ardwick, and single stretches of Cheetham Hill and Broughton are all unmixed working people's quarters, stretching like a girdle, averaging a mile and a half in breadth, around the commercial district. Outside, beyond this girdle, lives the upper and middle bourgeoisie, the middle bourgeoisie in regularly laid out streets in the vicinity of the working quarters, especially in Chorlton and the lower lying portions of Cheetham Hill; the upper bourgeoisie in remoter villas with gardens in Chorlton and Ardwick, or on the breezy heights of Cheetham Hill, Broughton, and Pendleton, in free, wholesome country air, in fine, comfortable homes, passed once every half or quarter hour by omnibuses going into the city. And the finest part of the arrangements is this, that the members of this money aristocracy can take the shortest road through the middle of all the labouring districts to their places of business, without ever seeing that they are in the midst of the grimy misery that lurks to the right and the left. For the thoroughfares leading from the Exchange in all directions out of the city are lined, on both sides, with an almost unbroken series of shops, and are so kept in the hands of the middle and lower bourgeoisie, which, out of self-interest, cares for a decent and cleanly external appearance and can *care* for it. True, these shops bear some relation to the districts which lie behind them, and are more elegant in the commercial and residential quarters than when they hide grimy working men's dwellings; but they suffice to conceal from the eyes of the wealthy men and women of strong stomachs and weak nerves the misery and grime which form the complement to their wealth. So, for instance, Deansgate, which leads from the Old Church directly southward, is lined first with mills and warehouses, then with second-rate shops and alehouses; farther south, when it leaves the commercial district, with less inviting shops, which grow dirtier and more interrupted by beer houses

[1] *The Condition … 1844* Translated by Florence Wischnewetzky, 1887.

[2] *Mons Sacer* Latin: Sacred Mountain.

and gin palaces the farther one goes, until at the southern end the appearance of the shops leaves no doubt that workers and workers only are their customers. So Market Street running south-east from the Exchange; at first brilliant shops of the best sort, with counting-houses or warehouses above; in the continuation, Piccadilly, immense hotels and warehouses; in the farther continuation, London Road, in the neighbourhood of the Medlock, factories, beerhouses, shops for the humbler bourgeoisie and the working population; and from this point onward, large gardens and villas of the wealthier merchants and manufacturers. In this way anyone who knows Manchester can infer the adjoining districts, from the appearance of the thoroughfare, but one is seldom in a position to catch from the street a glimpse of the real labouring districts. I know very well that this hypocritical plan is more or less common to all great cities; I know, too, that the retail dealers are forced by the nature of their business to take possession of the great highways; I know that there are more good buildings than bad ones upon such streets everywhere, and that the value of land is greater near them than in remoter districts; but at the same time I have never seen so systematic a shutting out of the working class from the thoroughfares, so tender a concealment of everything which might affront the eye and the nerves of the bourgeoisie, as in Manchester. And yet, in other respects, Manchester is less built according to a plan, after official regulations, is more an outgrowth of accident, than any other city; and when I consider in this connection the eager assurances of the middle class that the working class is doing famously, I cannot help feeling that the liberal manufacturers, the "Big Wigs" of Manchester, are not so innocent after all, in the matter of this sensitive method of construction.

I may mention just here that the mills almost all adjoin the rivers or the different canals that ramify throughout the city, before I proceed at once to describe the labouring quarters. First of all, there is the Old Town of Manchester, which lies between the northern boundary of the commercial district and the Irk. Here the streets, even the better ones, are narrow and winding, like Todd Street, Long Millgate, Withy Grove, and Shude Hill, the houses dirty, old, and tumble-down, and the construction of the side streets utterly horrible. Going from the Old Church to Long Millgate, the stroller has at once a row of old-fashioned houses on the right, of which not one has kept its original level; these are remnants of the old pre-manufacturing Manchester, whose former inhabitants have removed with their descendants into better-built districts, and have left the houses, which were not good enough for them, to a working-class population strongly mixed with Irish blood. Here one is in an almost undisguised working men's quarter, for even the shops and beerhouses hardly take the trouble to exhibit a trifing degree of cleanliness. But all this is nothing in comparison with the courts and lanes which lie behind, to which access can be gained only through covered passages, in which no two human beings can pass at the same time. Of the irregular cramming together of dwellings in ways which defy all rational plan, of the tangle in which they are crowded literally one upon the other, it is impossible to convey an idea. And it is not the buildings surviving from the old times of Manchester which are to blame for this; the confusion has only recently reached its height when every scrap of space left by the old way of building has been filled up and patched over until not a foot of land is left to be further occupied. …

The south bank of the Irk is here very steep and between fifteen and thirty feet high. On this abrupt slope there are planted three rows of houses, of which the lowest rise directly out of the river, while the front walls of the highest stand on the crest of the rise in Long Millgate. Among them are mills on the river; in short, the method of construction is as crowded and disorderly here as in the lower part of Long Millgate. Right and left a multitude of covered passages lead from the main street into numerous courts, and he who turns in thither gets into filth and disgusting grime, the equal of which is not to be found—especially in the courts which lead down to the Irk, and which contain unqualifiedly the most horrible dwellings which I have yet beheld. In one of these courts there stands directly at the entrance, at the end of the covered passage, a privy without a door, so dirty that the inhabitants can pass into and out of the court only by passing through foul pools of stagnant urine and excrement. This is the first court on the Irk above Ducie Bridge—in case anyone should care to look into it. Below it on the river there are several tanneries which fill the whole neighbourhood with the stench of animal putrefaction. Below Ducie Bridge the only entrance to most of the houses is by means of narrow, dirty stairs and over heaps of refuse and filth. The first court below Ducie Bridge, known as Allen's Court, was in such a state at the time of the cholera[1] that the sanitary police ordered it evacuated, swept, and disinfected with chloride of lime. … Since then, it seems to have been partially torn down and rebuilt; at least, looking down from Ducie Bridge, the passer-by sees several ruined walls and heaps of debris with some newer houses. The view from this bridge, mercifully concealed from mortals of small stature by a parapet as high as a man, is characteristic for the whole district. At the bottom flows, or rather stagnates, the Irk, a narrow, coal-black, foul-smelling stream, full of debris and refuse, which it deposits on the lower right bank. In dry weather, a lone string of the most disgusting blackish-green slime pools are left standing on this bank, from the depths of which bubbles of miasmatic[2] gas constantly arise and give forth a stench unendurable even on the bridge forty or fifty feet above the surface of the stream. But besides this, the stream itself is checked every few paces by high weirs, behind which slime and refuse accumulate and rot in thick masses. Above the bridge are tanneries, bone mills, and gasworks, from which all drains and refuse find their way into the Irk, which receives further the contents of all the neighbouring sewers and privies. It may be easily imagined, therefore, what sort of residue the stream deposits. Below the bridge you look upon the piles of debris, the refuse, filth, and offal from the courts on the steep left bank; here each house is packed close behind its neighbour and a bit of each is visible, all black, smoky, crumbling, ancient, with broken panes and window-frames. The background is furnished by old barrack-like factory buildings. On the lower right bank stands a long row of houses and mills, the second row being a ruin without a roof, piled with debris; the third stands so low that the lowest floor is uninhabitable, and therefore without windows or doors. Here the background embraces the pauper burial-ground, the station of the Liverpool and Leeds railway, and, in the rear of this, the workhouse, the "Poor-Law Bastille"[3] of Manchester, which, like a citadel, looks threateningly down from behind its high walls and parapets on the hilltop, upon the working people's quarter below. …

Such is the Old Town of Manchester, and, on re-reading my description, I am forced to admit that instead of being exaggerated, it is far from black enough to convey a true impression of the filth, ruin, and uninhabitableness, the defiance of all considerations of cleanliness, ventilation, and health which characterize the construction of this single district, containing at least twenty to thirty thousand inhabitants. And such a district exists in the heart of the second city of England, the first manufacturing city of the world. If anyone wishes to see in how little space a human being can move, how little air—and *such* air—he can breathe, how little of civilization he may share and yet live, it is only necessary to travel hither. True, this is the *Old* Town, and the people of Manchester emphasize the fact whenever anyone mentions to them the frightful condition of this Hell upon Earth; but what does that prove? Everything which here arouses horror and indignation is of recent origin, belongs to the *industrial epoch*. The couple of hundred houses which belong to Old Manchester have been long since abandoned by their original inhabitants; the industrial epoch alone has crammed into them the swarms of workers whom they now shelter; the industrial epoch alone has built up every spot between these old houses to make a covering for the masses whom it has conjured hither from the

[1] *the time of the cholera* I.e., 1832.

[2] *miasmatic* Consisting of noxious vapor.

[3] *Poor-Law Bastille* Because of the terrible conditions in the workhouses (established by the Poor Laws in the 1830s), including poor food, monotonous make-work, and the separation of families, workhouses were often compared to prisons such as the famous Bastille in Paris.

A cross-section of working-class low-lodgings. The crowded rooms and open sewer running beneath the building provide examples of the sort of deplorable living conditions described by Engels in his examination of Manchester.

agricultural districts and from Ireland; the industrial epoch alone enables the owners of these cattle sheds to rent them for high prices to human beings, to plunder the poverty of the workers, to undermine the health of thousands, in order that they only, the owners, may grow rich. In the industrial epoch alone has it become possible that the worker scarcely freed from feudal servitude can be used as mere material, a mere chattel; that he must let himself be crowded into a dwelling too bad for every other, which he for his hard-earned wages buys the right to let go utterly to ruin. This is what manufacture has achieved, and, without these workers and their poverty, this slavery would have been impossible. True, the original construction of this quarter was bad, little good could have been made out of it; but, have the land-owners, has the municipality done anything to improve it when rebuilding? On the contrary, wherever a nook or corner was free, a house has been run up; where a superfluous passage remained, it has been built on; the value of land rose with the blossoming out of manufacture, and the more it rose, the more madly was the work of building carried on, without reference to the health or comfort of the inhabitants, with sole reference to the highest possible profit, on the principle that *no hole is so bad but that some poor creature must take it who can pay for nothing better.* However, it is the Old Town, and with this reflection the bourgeoisie is comforted.

from Elizabeth Gaskell, *Mary Barton* (1848)

CHAPTER 6

John Barton was not far wrong in his idea that the Messrs. Carson would not be over-much grieved for the consequences of the fire in their mill. They were well insured; the machinery lacked the improvements of late years, and worked but poorly in comparison with that which might now be procured. Above all, trade was very slack; cottons could find no market, and goods lay packed and piled in many a warehouse. The mills were merely worked to keep the machinery, human and metal, in some kind of order and readiness for better times. So this was an excellent opportunity, Messrs. Carson thought, for refitting their factory with first-rate improvements, for which the insurance-money would amply pay. They were in no hurry about the business, however. The weekly drain of wages given for labour, useless in the present state of the market, was stopped. The partners had more leisure than they had known for years, and promised wives and daughters all manner of pleasant excursions, as soon as the weather should become more genial. It was a pleasant thing to be able to lounge over breakfast with a review or newspaper in hand; to have time for becoming acquainted with agreeable and accomplished daughters, on whose education no money had been spared, but whose fathers, shut up during a long day with calicoes[1] and accounts, had so seldom had leisure to enjoy their daughters' talents. There were happy family evenings, now that the men of business had time for domestic enjoyments. There is another side to the picture. There were homes over which Carsons' fire threw a deep, terrible gloom; the homes of those who would fain work, and no man gave unto them—the homes of those to whom leisure was a curse. There, the family music was angry wails, when week after week passed by, and there was no work to be had, and consequently no wages to pay for the bread the children cried aloud for in their young impatience of suffering. There was no breakfast to lounge over; their lounge was taken in bed, to try and keep warmth in them that bitter March weather, and, by being quiet, to deaden the gnawing wolf within. Many a penny that would have gone little way enough in oatmeal or potatoes bought opium to still the hungry little ones,[2] and make them forget their uneasiness in heavy troubled sleep. It was mother's mercy. The evil and the good of our nature came out strongly then. There were desperate fathers; there were bitter-tongued mothers (Oh God! what wonder!); there were reckless children; the very closest bonds of nature were snapped in that time of trial and distress. There was Faith such as the rich can never imagine on earth; there was "Love strong as death"; and, self-denial, among rude, coarse men, akin to that of Sir Philip Sidney's most glorious deed.[3] The vices of the poor sometimes astound us *here*; but when the secrets of all hearts shall be made known, their virtues will astound us in far greater degree. Of this I am certain.

As the cold, bleak spring came on (spring, in name alone), and consequently as trade continued dead, other mills shortened hours, turned off hands,[4] and finally stopped work altogether.

Barton worked short hours; Wilson, of course, being a hand in Carsons' factory, had no work at all. But his son, working at an engineer's, and a steady man, obtained wages enough to maintain all the family in a careful way. Still it preyed on Wilson's mind to be

[1] *calicoes* Cotton cloths.

[2] *opium ... hungry little ones* The apparently common practice among working-class families of giving sick or hungry infants opium or laudanum to help them sleep was frequently discussed at the time.

[3] *Sir Philip ... deed* Poet and courtier Sir Philip Sidney (1554–86), who served in many diplomatic missions on the Continent, is said to have refused a glass of water offered to him when he lay dying on the battlefield at Zutphen, in the Netherlands. He instead gave the glass to a less seriously wounded soldier, saying "Thy necessity is greater than mine."

[4] *turned off hands* I.e., laid off workers.

so long indebted to his son. He was out of spirits and depressed. Barton was morose, and soured towards mankind as a body, and the rich in particular. One evening, when the clear light at six o'clock contrasted strangely with the Christmas cold, and when the bitter wind piped down every entry, and through every cranny, Barton sat brooding over his stinted fire, and listening for Mary's step, in unacknowledged trust that her presence would cheer him. The door was opened, and Wilson came breathless in.

"You've not got a bit o' money by you, Barton?" asked he.

"Not I; who has now, I'd like to know. Whatten you want it for?"

"I donnot want it for mysel', tho' we've none to spare. But don[1] you know Ben Davenport as worked at Carsons'? He's down wi' the fever, and ne'er a stick o' fire nor a cowd[2] potato in the house."

"I han got no money, I tell ye," said Barton. Wilson looked disappointed. Barton tried not to be interested, but he could not help it in spite of his gruffness. He rose, and went to the cupboard (his wife's pride long ago). There lay the remains of his dinner, hastily put by ready for supper. Bread, and a slice of cold fat boiled bacon. He wrapped them in his handkerchief, put them in the crown of his hat and said—"Come, let's be going."

from Charles Dickens, *Hard Times* (1854)

CHAPTER 5: THE KEY-NOTE

Coketown, to which Messrs. Bounderby and Gradgrind now walked, was a triumph of fact; it had no greater taint of fancy in it than Mrs. Gradgrind herself. Let us strike the key-note, Coketown, before pursuing our tune.

It was a town of red brick, or of brick that would have been red if the smoke and ashes had allowed it; but as matters stood it was a town of unnatural red and black like the painted face of a savage. It was a town of machinery and tall chimneys, out of which interminable serpents of smoke trailed themselves forever and ever, and never got uncoiled. It had a black canal in it, and a river that ran purple with ill-smelling dye, and vast piles of building full of windows where there was a rattling and trembling all day long, and where the piston of the steam-engine worked monotonously up and down, like the head of an elephant in a state of melancholy madness. It contained several large streets all very like one another, and many small streets still more like one another, inhabited by people equally like one another, who all went in and out at the same hours, with the same sound upon the same pavements, to do the same work, and to whom every day was the same as yesterday and tomorrow, and every year the counterpart of the last and the next.

These attributes of Coketown were in the main inseparable from the work by which it was sustained; against them were to be set off, comforts of life which found their way all over the world, and elegancies of life which made, we will not ask how much of the fine lady, who could scarcely bear to hear the place mentioned. The rest of its features were voluntary, and they were these.

You saw nothing in Coketown but what was severely workful. If the members of a religious persuasion built a chapel there—as the members of eighteen religious persuasions had done—they made it a pious warehouse of red brick, with sometimes (but this is only in highly ornamental examples) a bell in a birdcage on the top of it. The solitary exception was the New Church; a stuccoed edifice with a square steeple over the door, terminating in four short pinnacles like florid wooden legs. All the public inscriptions in the town were painted alike, in severe characteristics of black and white. The jail might have been the infirmary, the infirmary might have been the jail, the town hall might have been either, or both, or anything else, for anything that appeared to the contrary in the graces of their construction. Fact, fact, fact, everywhere in the immaterial. The M'Choakumchild school was all fact, and the

[1] *don* Do.

[2] *cowd* I.e., cold.

school of design was all fact, and the relations between master and man were all fact, and everything was fact between the lying-in hospital and the cemetery, and what you couldn't state in figures, or show to be purchaseable in the cheapest market and saleable in the dearest, was not, and never should be, world without end, Amen.[1]

A town so sacred to fact, and so triumphant in its assertion, of course got on well? Why no, not quite well. No? Dear me!

No. Coketown did not come out of its own furnaces, in all respects like gold that had stood the fire. First, the perplexing mystery of the place was, Who belonged to the eighteen denominations? Because, whoever did, the labouring people did not. It was very strange to walk through the streets on a Sunday morning, and note how few of *them* the barbarous jangling of bells that was driving the sick and nervous mad, called away from their own quarter, from their own close rooms, from the corners of their own streets, where they lounged listlessly, gazing at all the church and chapel going, as at a thing with which they had no manner of concern. Nor was it merely the stranger who noticed this, because there was a native organization in Coketown itself, whose members were to be heard of in the House of Commons every session, indignantly petitioning for Acts of Parliament that should make these people religious by main force.[2] Then came the Teetotal Society, who complained that these same people *would* get drunk, and showed their tabular statements that they did get drunk, and proved at tea parties that no inducement, human or divine (except a medal), would induce them to forego their custom of getting drunk. Then came the chemist and druggist, with other tabular statements, showing that when they didn't get drunk, they took opium. Then came the experienced chaplain of the jail, with more tabular statements, outdoing all the previous tabular statements, and showing that the same people *would* resort to low haunts, hidden from the public eye, where they heard low singing and saw low dancing, and mayhap joined in it; and where A.B., aged twenty-four next birthday, and committed for eighteen months' solitary, had himself said (not that he had ever shown himself particularly worthy of belief) his ruin began, as he was perfectly sure and confident that otherwise he would have been a tip-top moral specimen. Then came Mr. Gradgrind and Mr. Bounderby, the two gentlemen at this present moment walking through Coketown, and both eminently practical, who could, on occasion, furnish more tabular statements derived from their own personal experience, and illustrated by cases they had known and seen, from which it clearly appeared—in short, it was the only clear thing in the case—that these same people were a bad lot altogether, gentlemen; that do what you would for them they were never thankful for it, gentlemen; that they were restless, gentlemen; that they never knew what they wanted; that they lived upon the best, and bought fresh butter; and insisted on Mocha coffee, and rejected all but prime parts of meat, and yet were eternally dissatisfied and unmanageable. In short, it was the moral of the old nursery fable:

There was an old woman, and what do you think
She lived upon nothing but victuals and drink;
Victuals and drink were the whole of her diet,
And yet this old woman would NEVER be quiet.

[1] *never should be … Amen* From the Anglican Book of Common Prayer: "Glory be to the Father, and to the Son, and to the Holy Ghost; as it was in the beginning, is now, and ever shall be, world without end. Amen."

[2] *members … main force* See Dickens's pamphlet *Sunday Under Three Heads* (written under the pseudonym "Timothy Sparks"), in which he vehemently opposes the "Sunday Observance Bill." Sir Andrew Agnew and his Evangelical group recommended to Parliament a series of moral reforms focusing on curtailing activities on Sunday, which Dickens contended would severely restrict the ability of the poor to enjoy their one day in the week that was free of labor.

London Nomads by John Thomson, from *Street Life in London* (1877).

from Henry Mayhew, *London Labour and the London Poor*, "Boy Crossing-Sweepers and Tumblers" (1851)

A remarkably intelligent lad, who, on being spoken to, at once consented to give all the information in his power, told me the following story of his life.

It will be seen from this boy's account, and the one or two following, that a kind of partnership exists among some of these young sweepers. They have associated themselves together, appropriated several crossings to their use, and appointed a captain over them. They have their forms of trial, and "jury-house" for the settlement of disputes; laws have been framed, which govern their commercial proceedings, and a kind of language adopted by the society for its better protection from the arch-enemy, the policeman.

I found the lad who first gave me an insight into the proceedings of the associated crossing-sweepers crouched on the stone steps of a door in Adelaide Street, Strand; and when I spoke to him he was preparing to settle down in a corner and go to sleep—his legs and body being curled round almost as closely as those of a cat on a hearth. The moment he heard my voice he was upon his feet, asking me to "give a halfpenny to poor little Jack."

He was a good-looking lad, with a pair of large mild eyes, which he took good care to turn up with an expression of supplication as he moaned for a halfpenny.

A cap, or more properly a stuff bag, covered a crop of hair which had matted itself into the form of so many paint-brushes, while his face, from its roundness of feature and the complexion of dirt, had an almost Indian look about it; the colour of his hands, too, was such that you could imagine he had been shelling walnuts.

He ran before me, treading cautiously with his naked feet, until I reached a convenient spot to take down his statement, which was as follows:

"I've got no mother or father; mother has been dead for two years, and father's been gone for more than that—more nigh five years—he died at Ipswich, in Suffolk. He was a perfumer by trade, and used to make hair-dye, and scent, and pomatum,[1] and all kinds of scents. He didn't keep a shop himself, but he used to serve them as did; he didn't hawk his goods about, neether, but had regular customers, what used to send him a letter, and then he'd take them what they wanted. Yes, he used to serve some good shops: there was H—'s, of London Bridge, what's a large chemist's. He used to make a good deal of money, but he lost it betting; and so his brother, my uncle, did all his. …

"After mother died, sister still kept on making nets,[2] and I lived with her for some time. But she was keeping company with a young man, and one day they went out, and came back and said they'd been and got married. It was him as got rid of me.

"He was kind to me for the first two or three months, while he was keeping her company; but before he was married he got a little cross, and after he was

[1] *pomatum* Scented ointment for the hair.

[2] *nets* Meshwork or network, used for various purposes.

The Boy Crossing Sweepers, from Henry Mayhew's *London Labour and the London Poor* (1861).

A group of homeless boys just after being admitted to a shelter. (Photograph by John Thomson, c. 1880.)

married he begun to get more cross, and used to send me to play in the streets, and tell me not to come home again till night. One day he hit me, and I said I wouldn't be hit about by him, and then at tea that night sister gave me three shillings, and told me I must go and get my own living. So I bought a box and brushes (they cost me just the money) and went cleaning boots, and I done pretty well with them, till my box was stole from me by a boy where I was lodging. He's in prison now—got six calendar[1] for picking pockets. …

"I was fifteen the 24th of last May, sir, and I've been sweeping crossings now near upon two years. There's a party of six of us, and we have the crossings from St. Martin's Church as far as Pall Mall. I always go along with them as lodges in the same place as I do. In the daytime, if it's dry, we do anythink what we can—open cabs, or anythink; but if it's wet, we separate, and I an' another gets a crossing—those who gets on it first, keeps it—and we stand on each side and take our chance.

"We do it this way: if I was to see two gentlemen coming, I should cry out, 'Two toffs!' and then they are mine; and whether they give me anythink or not they are mine, and my mate is bound not to follow them; for if he did he would get a hiding from the whole lot of us. If we both cry out together, then we share. If it's a lady and a gentleman, then we cries, 'A toff and a doll!' Sometimes we are caught out in this way. Perhaps it is a lady and gentleman and a child; and if I was to see them, and only say, 'A toff and a doll,' and leave out the child, then my mate can add the child; and as he is right and I wrong, then it's his party.

"If there's a policeman coming we musn't ask for money; but we are always on the look-out for policemen, and if we see one, then we calls out 'Phillup!' for that's our signal. One of the policemen at St. Martin's Church—Bandy, we calls him—knows what Phillup means, for he's up to us; so we had to change the word. (At the request of the young crossing-sweeper the present signal is omitted.) …

"When we see the rain we say together, 'Oh! there's a jolly good rain! we'll have a good day tomorrow.' If a shower comes on, and we are at our room, which we general are about three o'clock, to get somethink to eat—besides, we general go there to see how much each

[1] *six calendar* I.e., six months.

Peter Henry Emerson and Thomas Frederick Goodall, "Coming Home from the Marshes," from *Life and Landscape on the Norfolk Broads*, 1887. While laborers in urban centers suffered deplorable living and working conditions, rural laborers also suffered from exploitative wages, long work hours, and poor housing. On the whole, rural families made do with dwellings, food, and clothing that were even worse than what their urban counterparts had—but poor people in the countryside nonetheless lived longer than those in the unsanitary, polluted cities and factory towns. This image, taken by the photographer Peter Henry Emerson in collaboration with Thomas Frederick Goodall, is part of their collection of photographs taken on the Norfolk Broads, where livelihoods were becoming increasingly precarious due to economic changes associated with England's industrialization. Influenced by the naturalist school of painting, Emerson and Goodall strove to capture what an observer would really see, but their photographs were nonetheless staged—a necessity given the long exposure time required by the camera they used.

other's taken in the day—why, out we run with our brooms.

"At night-time we tumbles[1]—that is, if the policeman ain't nigh. We goes general to Waterloo Place when the opera's on. We sends on one of us ahead, as a looker-out, to look for the policeman, and then we follows. It's no good tumbling to gentlemen *going* to the opera; it's when they're coming back they gives us money. When they've got a young lady on their arm they laugh at us tumbling; some will give us a penny, others threepence, sometimes a sixpence or a shilling, and sometimes a halfpenny. We either do the cat'un-wheel, or else we keep before the gentleman and lady, turning head-over-heels, putting our broom on the ground and then turning over it. …

"When we are talking together we always talk in a kind of slang. Each policeman we gives a regular name— there's 'Bull's Head,' 'Bandy Shanks,' and 'Old Cherry Legs,' and 'Dot-and-carry-one'; they all knows their names as well as us. We never talks of crossings, but 'fakes.' We don't make no slang of our own, but uses the regular one."

[1] *tumbles* Perform leaps, somersaults, etc., like acrobats.

John Stuart Mill
1806 – 1873

Philosopher, social reformer, economist, and politician, John Stuart Mill was one of the most influential of Victorian thinkers. His breadth of knowledge and interests was staggering, as was the range of subject matter that he chose to examine in his writing, including women's rights, civil liberties, economic theories, logic, and poetics. Mill's *Utilitarianism* and *On Liberty* are both still regarded as central works in the fields of moral and social philosophy and political science.

Mill seemed destined from an early age to become a polymath—his childhood was practically a monument to over-achievement. He was born in London in 1806, the first child of Harriet Burrow and James Mill, a distinguished psychologist, philosopher, and historian. James was a disciple of Jeremy Bentham, who had founded the philosophical school of utilitarianism, an ethical doctrine whose main premise is that an action ought to be taken only if it produces happiness for all involved (later refined by J.S. Mill into the "greatest happiness principle," which suggests that people ought to act in ways that produce the greatest happiness for all involved). Participating in an experiment devised in part by Bentham, James decided that his eldest son would be a guinea pig for his educational theories, and at a very young age John began a rigorous education aimed at preparing him to become a future leader of the Benthamites.

In his autobiography, Mill described his formal instruction as beginning with Greek at age three; by the age of eight he could translate the works of Socrates and Plato. He then learned Latin well enough to translate such masters as Horace and Ovid, and also studied mathematics, the sciences, and English literature. Not being content to allow his son to learn simply by rote, James heavily emphasized rhetoric and debate, insisting that John make moral decisions about the principles he was learning. By the time he was 14, his father considered him to be ready for university study but felt that an institution would hold him back, and thus Mill began his career a full "quarter of a century before his contemporaries," as he would say in his autobiography.

James's experiment succeeded—John was a brilliant and erudite child, able to converse and debate with adults and to tutor all of his siblings from an early age. The daily ten-hour study regime, however, took a toll on him, and in his early twenties Mill experienced a period of deep depression that was relieved only when he discovered the poetry of William Wordsworth. During this time he pondered the virtues of Bentham's utilitarianism, which seemed to favor the good of the majority at the expense of the individual, who, Mill felt, is the best judge of his or her own happiness. Although he himself was an empiricist, he felt that Bentham's philosophy promoted the "science" of ethics at the expense of real life. Mill said of Bentham's utilitarianism: "It is wholly empirical and the empiricism of one who has had little experience." After reading the Romantic poets—Wordsworth in particular—Mill began to appreciate the therapeutic effects of poetry and the arts and the importance of an emotional life. The essay "What Is Poetry?" (1833) speaks to his concerns about the necessity of individual pleasure.

After studying law for two years, Mill worked for decades in the East India Office, first as a clerk and then as head of his department, but he continued to be an outspoken advocate for individual rights and freedoms (he had been arrested as a teenager for disseminating literature in support of birth control). He published a modification of Bentham's philosophy, later reworked as *Utilitarianism* (1863); his most ambitious early work was *System of Logic*, published in 1843 and still highly regarded in philosophical circles today. The book that followed, *Principles of Political Economy* (1848), commands a similar level of respect in the field of economics. In 1859 Mill wrote another key work: *On Liberty*, a treatise that continued his theme of support for individual rights, deriding democratic majorities that conform to tradition and smother individuality.

In the planning and to some extent the writing of both these and subsequent works, Mill was assisted by Harriet Taylor, an aspiring author whom Mill had first met in 1831 and with whom he began to work closely. (The precise extent of Taylor's involvement remains the subject of debate among scholars). The two were married in 1851 after her husband's death. Mill and Taylor never moved freely in society together, however; many of his friends, Carlyle and Tennyson included, viewed their relationship as inappropriate.

After serving as Member of Parliament from 1865 to 1868, Mill published *The Subjection of Women* (1869). He had worked on this book for years, and it had become a passionate subject for both Mill and Taylor. *The Subjection of Women* spoke to the rights of women, both legally and practically, arguing for government reforms of property and divorce laws, women's enfranchisement, and advocating the end of "slavery" in the home. Mill even argued in Parliament—well ahead of his time—for non-sexist language and the rewording of parliamentary bills to remove gender-specific terms.

Mill died in 1873 in Avignon, France, and was buried beside his wife, who had died prematurely in 1858. In his eloquent and insightful *Autobiography*, published shortly after his death, Mill wrote candidly about his childhood experiences with a demanding father and a thoroughly rational education; about his mental breakdown and his discovery of the value of works of the imagination; about his relationship with Harriet Taylor; and about his writing. The *Autobiography* is valued both as a work of literature in its own right and as a record of the remarkable life of a profoundly influential thinker.

⌘⌘⌘

from *The Subjection of Women*

Chapter 1

If people are mostly so little aware how completely, during the greater part of the duration of our species, the law of force was the avowed rule of general conduct, any other being only a special and exceptional consequence of peculiar ties—and from how very recent a date it is that the affairs of society in general have been even pretended to be regulated according to any moral law; as little do people remember or consider, how institutions and customs which never had any ground but the law of force, last on into ages and states of general opinion which never would have permitted their first establishment. Less than forty years ago, Englishmen might still by law hold human beings in bondage as saleable property: within the present century they might kidnap them and carry them off, and work them literally to death. This absolutely extreme case of the law of force, condemned by those who can tolerate almost every other form of arbitrary power, and which, of all others, presents features the most revolting to the feelings of all who look at it from an impartial position, was the law of civilized and Christian England within the memory of persons now living: and in one half of Anglo-Saxon America three or four years ago, not only did slavery exist, but the slave trade, and the breeding of slaves expressly for it, was a general practice between slave states. Yet not only was there a greater strength of sentiment against it, but, in England at least, a less amount either of feeling or of interest in favour of it, than of any other of the customary abuses of force: for its motive was the love of gain, unmixed and undisguised; and those who profited by it were a very small numerical fraction of the country, while the natural feeling of all who were not personally interested in it, was unmitigated abhorrence. So extreme an instance makes it almost superfluous to refer to any other: but consider the long duration of absolute monarchy. In England at present it is the almost universal conviction that military despotism is a case of the law of force, having no other origin or justification. Yet in all the great nations of Europe except England it either still exists, or has only just ceased to exist, and has even now a strong party favourable to it in all ranks of the people, especially among persons of station and consequence. Such is the power of an established system, even when far from universal; when not only in almost every period of history there have been great and well-known examples of the contrary system, but these have almost invariably been afforded by the most illustrious and most prosperous communities. In this case, too, the possessor of the undue power, the person directly interested in it, is only one person, while those who are subject to it and suffer from it are literally all the rest. The yoke is naturally and necessarily humiliating to all persons, except the one who is on the throne, together with, at most, the one who expects to succeed to it. How different are these cases from that of the power of men over women! I am not now prejudging the question of its justifiableness. I am showing how vastly more permanent it could not but be, even if not justifiable, than these other dominations which have nevertheless lasted down to our own time. Whatever gratification of pride there is in the possession of power, and whatever personal interest in its exercise, is in this case not confined to a limited class, but common to the whole male sex. Instead of being, to most of its supporters, a thing desirable chiefly in the abstract, or, like the political ends usually contended for by factions, of little private importance to any but the leaders; it comes home to the person and hearth of every male head of a family, and of everyone who looks forward to being so. The clodhopper exercises, or is to exercise, his share of the power equally with the highest nobleman. And the case is that in which the desire of power is the strongest: for everyone who desires power, desires it most over those who are nearest to him, with whom his life is passed, with whom he has most concerns in common, and in whom any independence of his authority is oftenest likely to interfere with his individual preferences. If, in the other cases specified, powers manifestly grounded only on force, and having so much less to support them, are so slowly and with so much difficulty got rid of, much more must it be so with this, even if it rests on no better foundation than those. We must consider, too, that the possessors of the power have facilities in this case, greater than in any other, to prevent any uprising against it. Every one of the subjects lives under the very eye, and almost, it may be said, in the hands, of one of the masters—in closer intimacy with him than with any of her fellow-subjects; with no means of combining against him, no power of even locally overmastering him, and, on the other hand, with the strongest motives for seeking his favour and avoiding to give him offence. In struggles for political emancipation, everybody knows how often its champions are bought off by bribes, or daunted by terrors. In the case of women, each individual of the subject-class is in a chronic state of bribery and intimidation combined. In setting up the standard of resistance, a large number of the leaders, and still more of the followers, must make an almost complete sacrifice of the pleasures or the alleviations of their own individual lot. If ever any system of privilege and enforced subjection had its yoke tightly riveted on the necks of those who are kept down by it, this has. I have not yet shown that it is a wrong system: but everyone who is capable of thinking on the subject must see that even if it is, it was certain to outlast all other forms of unjust authority. And when some of the grossest of the other forms still exist in many civilized countries, and have only recently been got rid of in others, it would be strange if that which is so much the deepest rooted had yet been perceptibly shaken anywhere. There is more reason to wonder that the protests and testimonies against it should have been so numerous and so weighty as they are.

Some will object, that a comparison cannot fairly be made between the government of the male sex and the forms of unjust power which I have adduced in illustration of it, since these are arbitrary, and the effect of mere usurpation, while it on the contrary is natural. But was there ever any domination which did not appear natural to those who possessed it? There was a time when the division of mankind into two classes, a small one of masters and a numerous one of slaves, appeared, even to the most cultivated minds, to be a natural, and the only natural, condition of the human race. No less an intellect, and one which contributed no less to the progress of human thought, than Aristotle,[1] held this opinion without doubt or misgiving; and rested it on the same premises on which the same assertion in regard to the dominion of men over women is usually based, namely that there are different natures among mankind, free natures, and slave natures; that the Greeks were of a free nature, the barbarian races of Thracians[2] and Asiatics of a slave nature. But why need I go back to Aristotle? Did not the slaveowners of the Southern United States maintain the same doctrine, with all the fanaticism with which men cling to the theories that justify their passions and legitimate their personal interests? Did they not call heaven and earth to witness that the dominion of the white man over the black is natural, that the black race is by nature incapable of freedom, and marked out for slavery? some even going so far as to say that the freedom of manual labourers is an unnatural order of things anywhere. Again, the theorists of absolute monarchy have always affirmed it to be the only natural form of government; issuing from the patriarchal, which was the primitive and spontaneous form of society, framed on the model of the paternal, which is anterior to society itself, and, as they contend, the most natural authority of all. Nay, for that matter, the law of force itself, to those who could not plead any other, has always seemed the most natural of all grounds for the exercise of authority. Conquering races hold it to be Nature's own dictate that the conquered should obey the conquerors, or, as they euphoniously paraphrase it, that the feebler and more unwarlike races should submit to the braver and manlier. The smallest acquaintance with human life in the middle ages, shows how supremely natural the dominion of the feudal nobility over men of low condition appeared to the nobility themselves, and how unnatural the conception seemed, of a person of the inferior class claiming equality with them, or exercising authority over them. It hardly seemed less so to the class held in subjection. The emancipated serfs and burgesses, even in their most vigorous struggles, never made any pretension to a share of authority; they only demanded more or less of limitation to the power of tyrannizing over them. So true is it that unnatural generally means only uncustomary, and that everything which is usual appears natural. The subjection of women to men being a universal custom, any departure from it quite naturally appears unnatural. But how entirely, even in this case, the feeling is dependent on custom, appears by ample experience. Nothing so much astonishes the people of distant parts of the world, when they first learn anything about England, as to be told that it is under a queen: the thing seems to them so unnatural as to be almost incredible. To Englishmen this does not seem in the least degree unnatural, because they are used to it; but they do feel it unnatural that women should be soldiers or members of parliament. In the feudal ages, on the contrary, war and politics were not thought unnatural to women, because not unusual; it seemed natural that women of the privileged classes should be of manly character, inferior in nothing but bodily strength to

[1] *Aristotle* See Aristotle's *Politics*.

[2] *Thracians* A warring group of tribes, the Thracians occupied the area north of Greece from 700 BCE to 4 CE.

their husbands and fathers. The independence of women seemed rather less unnatural to the Greeks than to other ancients, on account of the fabulous Amazons[1] (whom they believed to be historical), and the partial example afforded by the Spartan women; who, though no less subordinate by law than in other Greek states, were more free in fact, and being trained to bodily exercises in the same manner with men, gave ample proof that they were not naturally disqualified for them. There can be little doubt that Spartan experience suggested to Plato,[2] among many other of his doctrines, that of the social and political equality of the two sexes.

But, it will be said, the rule of men over women differs from all these others in not being a rule of force: it is accepted voluntarily; women make no complaint, and are consenting parties to it. In the first place, a great number of women do not accept it. Ever since there have been women able to make their sentiments known by their writings (the only mode of publicity which society permits to them), an increasing number of them have recorded protests against their present social condition: and recently many thousands of them, headed by the most eminent women known to the public, have petitioned parliament for their admission to the Parliamentary Suffrage.[3] The claim of women to be educated as solidly, and in the same branches of knowledge, as men, is urged with growing intensity, and with a great prospect of success; while the demand for their admission into professions and occupations hitherto closed against them, becomes every year more urgent. Though there are not in this country, as there are in the United States, periodical Conventions and an organized party to agitate for the Rights of Women, there is a numerous and active Society organized and managed by women, for the more limited object of obtaining the political franchise. Nor is it only in our own country and in America that women are beginning to protest, more or less collectively, against the disabilities under which they labour. France, and Italy, and Switzerland, and Russia now afford examples of the same thing. How many more women there are who silently cherish similar aspirations, no one can possibly know; but there are abundant tokens how many *would* cherish them, were they not so strenuously taught to repress them as contrary to the proprieties of their sex. It must be remembered, also, that no enslaved class ever asked for complete liberty at once. When Simon de Montfort[4] called the deputies of the commons to sit for the first time in parliament, did any of them dream of demanding that an assembly, elected by their constituents, should make and destroy ministries, and dictate to the king in affairs of state? No such thought entered into the imagination of the most ambitious of them. The nobility had already these pretensions; the commons pretended to nothing but to be exempt from arbitrary taxation, and from the gross individual oppression of the king's officers. It is a political law of nature that those who are under any power of ancient origin, never begin by complaining of the power itself, but only of its oppressive exercise. There is never any want of women who complain of ill usage by their husbands. There would be infinitely more, if complaint were not the greatest of all provocatives to a repetition and increase of the ill usage. It is this which frustrates all attempts to maintain the power but protect the woman against its abuses. In no other case (except that of a child) is the person who has been proved judicially to have suffered an injury, replaced under the physical power of the culprit who inflicted it. Accordingly wives, even in the most extreme and protracted cases of bodily ill usage, hardly ever dare avail themselves of the laws made for their protection: and if, in a moment of irrepressible indignation, or by the interference of neighbours, they are induced to do so, their whole effort afterwards is to disclose as little as they can, and to beg off their tyrant from his merited chastisement.

All causes, social and natural, combine to make it unlikely that women should be collectively rebellious to the power of men. They are so far in a position different

[1] *Amazons* A mythical race of women warriors.

[2] *Plato* See Plato's *Republic*, 5.

[3] *petitioned … Parliamentary Suffrage* Mill himself also introduced such a petition to the House of Commons in 1866.

[4] *Simon de Montfort* The Earl of Leicester (c. 1208–65) led a baronial revolt against Henry III and subsequently established a newly representative Parliament.

from all other subject classes, that their masters require something more from them than actual service. Men do not want solely the obedience of women, they want their sentiments. All men, except the most brutish, desire to have, in the woman most nearly connected with them, not a forced slave but a willing one, not a slave merely, but a favourite. They have therefore put everything in practice to enslave their minds. The masters of all other slaves rely, for maintaining obedience, on fear; either fear of themselves, or religious fears. The masters of women wanted more than simple obedience, and they turned the whole force of education to effect their purpose. All women are brought up from the very earliest years in the belief that their ideal of character is the very opposite to that of men; not self-will, and government by self-control, but submission, and yielding to the control of others. All the moralities tell them that it is the duty of women, and all the current sentimentalities that it is their nature, to live for others; to make complete abnegation of themselves, and to have no life but in their affections. And by their affections are meant the only ones they are allowed to have—those to the men with whom they are connected, or to the children who constitute an additional and indefeasible tie between them and a man. When we put together three things—first, the natural attraction between opposite sexes; secondly, the wife's entire dependence on the husband, every privilege or pleasure she has being either his gift, or depending entirely on his will; and lastly, that the principal object of human pursuit, consideration, and all objects of social ambition, can in general be sought or obtained by her only through him, it would be a miracle if the object of being attractive to men had not become the polar star of feminine education and formation of character. And, this great means of influence over the minds of women having been acquired, an instinct of selfishness made men avail themselves of it to the utmost as a means of holding women in subjection, by representing to them meekness, submissiveness, and resignation of all individual will into the hands of a man, as an essential part of sexual attractiveness. Can it be doubted that any of the other yokes which mankind have succeeded in breaking, would have subsisted till now if the same means had existed, and had been so sedulously used, to bow down their minds to it? If it had been made the object of the life of every young plebeian to find personal favour in the eyes of some patrician, of every young serf with some seigneur;[1] if domestication with him, and a share of his personal affections, had been held out as the prize which they all should look out for, the most gifted and aspiring being able to reckon on the most desirable prizes; and if, when this prize had been obtained, they had been shut out by a wall of brass from all interests not centering in him, all feelings and desires but those which he shared or inculcated; would not serfs and seigneurs, plebeians and patricians, have been as broadly distinguished at this day as men and women are? and would not all but a thinker here and there, have believed the distinction to be a fundamental and unalterable fact in human nature?

The preceding considerations are amply sufficient to show that custom, however universal it may be, affords in this case no presumption, and ought not to create any prejudice, in favour of the arrangements which place women in social and political subjection to men. But I may go farther, and maintain that the course of history, and the tendencies of progressive human society, afford not only no presumption in favour of this system of inequality of rights, but a strong one against it; and that, so far as the whole course of human improvement up to this time, the whole stream of modern tendencies, warrants any inference on the subject, it is, that this relic of the past is discordant with the future, and must necessarily disappear.

For, what is the peculiar character of the modern world—the difference which chiefly distinguishes modern institutions, modern social ideas, modern life itself, from those of times long past? It is, that human beings are no longer born to their place in life, and chained down by an inexorable bond to the place they are born to, but are free to employ their faculties, and such favourable chances as offer, to achieve the lot which may appear to them most desirable. Human

[1] *plebeian* Commoner; *patrician* Aristocrat; *serf* Laborer in a condition of servitude; *seigneur* Feudal lord.

society of old was constituted on a very different principle. All were born to a fixed social position, and were mostly kept in it by law, or interdicted from any means by which they could emerge from it. As some men are born white and others black, so some were born slaves and others freemen and citizens; some were born patricians, others plebeians; some were born feudal nobles, others commoners and *roturiers*.[1] A slave or serf could never make himself free, nor, except by the will of his master, become so. In most European countries it was not till towards the close of the middle ages, and as a consequence of the growth of regal power, that commoners could be ennobled. Even among nobles, the eldest son was born the exclusive heir to the paternal possessions, and a long time elapsed before it was fully established that the father could disinherit him. Among the industrious classes, only those who were born members of a guild, or were admitted into it by its members, could lawfully practise their calling within its local limits; and nobody could practise any calling deemed important, in any but the legal manner—by processes authoritatively prescribed. Manufacturers have stood in the pillory[2] for presuming to carry on their business by new and improved methods. In modern Europe, and most in those parts of it which have participated most largely in all other modern improvements, diametrically opposite doctrines now prevail. Law and government do not undertake to prescribe by whom any social or industrial operation shall or shall not be conducted, or what modes of conducting them shall be lawful. These things are left to the unfettered choice of individuals. Even the laws which required that workmen should serve an apprenticeship, have in this country been repealed: there being ample assurance that in all cases in which an apprenticeship is necessary, its necessity will suffice to enforce it. The old theory was, that the least possible should be left to the choice of the individual agent; that all he had to do should, as far as practicable, be laid down for him by superior wisdom. Left to himself he was sure to go wrong. The modern conviction, the fruit of a thousand years of experience, is, that things in which the individual is the person directly interested, never go right but as they are left to his own discretion; and that any regulation of them by authority, except to protect the rights of others, is sure to be mischievous. This conclusion, slowly arrived at, and not adopted until almost every possible application of the contrary theory had been made with disastrous result, now (in the industrial department) prevails universally in the most advanced countries, almost universally in all that have pretensions to any sort of advancement. It is not that all processes are supposed to be equally good, or all persons to be equally qualified for everything; but that freedom of individual choice is now known to be the only thing which procures the adoption of the best processes, and throws each operation into the hands of those who are best qualified for it. Nobody thinks it necessary to make a law that only a strong-armed man shall be a blacksmith. Freedom and competition suffice to make blacksmiths strong-armed men, because the weak-armed can earn more by engaging in occupations for which they are more fit. In consonance with this doctrine, it is felt to be an overstepping of the proper bounds of authority to fix beforehand, on some general presumption, that certain persons are not fit to do certain things. It is now thoroughly known and admitted that if some such presumptions exist, no such presumption is infallible. Even if it be well grounded in a majority of cases, which it is very likely not to be, there will be a minority of exceptional cases in which it does not hold: and in those it is both an injustice to the individuals, and a detriment to society, to place barriers in the way of their using their faculties for their own benefit and for that of others. In the cases, on the other hand, in which the unfitness is real, the ordinary motives of human conduct will on the whole suffice to prevent the incompetent person from making, or from persisting in, the attempt.

If this general principle of social and economical science is not true; if individuals, with such help as they can derive from the opinion of those who know them, are not better judges than the law and the government, of their own capacities and vocation; the world cannot

[1] *roturiers* Commoners who owned land in feudal times.

[2] *pillory* Wooden framework in which wrongdoers were locked and exposed to public derision.

too soon abandon this principle, and return to the old system of regulations and disabilities. But if the principle is true, we ought to act as if we believed it, and not to ordain that to be born a girl instead of a boy, any more than to be born black instead of white, or a commoner instead of a nobleman, shall decide the person's position through all life—shall interdict people from all the more elevated social positions, and from all, except a few, respectable occupations. Even were we to admit the utmost that is ever pretended as to the superior fitness of men for all the functions now reserved to them, the same argument applies which forbids a legal qualification for members of parliament. If only once in a dozen years the conditions of eligibility exclude a fit person, there is a real loss, while the exclusion of thousands of unfit persons is no gain; for if the constitution of the electoral body disposes them to choose unfit persons, there are always plenty of such persons to choose from. In all things of any difficulty and importance, those who can do them well are fewer than the need, even with the most unrestricted latitude of choice: and any limitation of the field of selection deprives society of some chances of being served by the competent, without ever saving it from the incompetent.

At present, in the more improved countries, the disabilities of women are the only case, save one, in which laws and institutions take persons at their birth, and ordain that they shall never in all their lives be allowed to compete for certain things. The one exception is that of royalty. Persons still are born to the throne; no one, not of the reigning family, can ever occupy it, and no one even of that family can, by any means but the course of hereditary succession, attain it. All other dignities and social advantages are open to the whole male sex: many indeed are only attainable by wealth, but wealth may be striven for by anyone, and is actually obtained by many men of the very humblest origin. The difficulties, to the majority, are indeed insuperable without the aid of fortunate accidents; but no male human being is under any legal ban: neither law nor opinion superadd artificial obstacles to the natural ones. Royalty, as I have said, is excepted: but in this case everyone feels it to be an exception—an anomaly in the modern world, in marked opposition to its customs and principles, and to be justified only by extraordinary special expediencies, which, though individuals and nations differ in estimating their weight, unquestionably do in fact exist. But in this exceptional case, in which a high social function is, for important reasons, bestowed on birth instead of being put up to competition, all free nations contrive to adhere in substance to the principle from which they nominally derogate; for they circumscribe this high function by conditions avowedly intended to prevent the person to whom it ostensibly belongs from really performing it; while the person by whom it is performed, the responsible minister, does obtain the post by a competition from which no full-grown citizen of the male sex is legally excluded. The disabilities, therefore, to which women are subject from the mere fact of their birth, are the solitary examples of the kind in modern legislation. In no instance except this, which comprehends half the human race, are the higher social functions closed against anyone by a fatality of birth which no exertions, and no change of circumstances, can overcome; for even religious disabilities (besides that in England and in Europe they have practically almost ceased to exist) do not close any career to the disqualified person in case of conversion.

The social subordination of women thus stands out an isolated fact in modern social institutions; a solitary breach of what has become their fundamental law; a single relic of an old world of thought and practice exploded in everything else, but retained in the one thing of most universal interest; as if a gigantic dolmen,[1] or a vast temple of Jupiter Olympius, occupied the site of St. Paul's and received daily worship, while the surrounding Christian churches were only resorted to on fasts and festivals. This entire discrepancy between one social fact and all those which accompany it, and the radical opposition between its nature and the progressive movement which is the boast of the modern world, and which has successively swept away everything else of an analogous character, surely affords, to a conscientious observer of human tendencies, serious matter for reflec-

[1] *dolmen* Celtic monument associated with pagan rituals.

tion. It raises a *prima facie*[1] presumption on the unfavourable side, far outweighing any which custom and usage could in such circumstances create on the favourable; and should at least suffice to make this, like the choice between republicanism and royalty, a balanced question.

The least that can be demanded is, that the question should not be considered as prejudged by existing fact and existing opinion, but open to discussion on its merits, as a question of justice and expediency: the decision on this, as on any of the other social arrangements of mankind, depending on what an enlightened estimate of tendencies and consequences may show to be most advantageous to humanity in general, without distinction of sex. And the discussion must be a real discussion, descending to foundations, and not resting satisfied with vague and general assertions. It will not do, for instance, to assert in general terms, that the experience of mankind has pronounced in favour of the existing system. Experience cannot possibly have decided between two courses, so long as there has only been experience of one. If it be said that the doctrine of the equality of the sexes rests only on theory, it must be remembered that the contrary doctrine also has only theory to rest upon. All that is proved in its favour by direct experience, is that mankind have been able to exist under it, and to attain the degree of improvement and prosperity which we now see; but whether that prosperity has been attained sooner, or is now greater, than it would have been under the other system, experience does not say. On the other hand, experience does say, that every step in improvement has been so invariably accompanied by a step made in raising the social position of women, that historians and philosophers have been led to adopt their elevation or debasement as on the whole the surest test and most correct measure of the civilization of a people or an age. Through all the progressive period of human history, the condition of women has been approaching nearer to equality with men. This does not of itself prove that the assimilation must go on to complete equality; but it assuredly affords some presumption that such is the case.

Neither does it avail anything to say that the *nature* of the two sexes adapts them to their present functions and position, and renders these appropriate to them. Standing on the ground of common sense and the constitution of the human mind, I deny that anyone knows, or can know, the nature of the two sexes, as long as they have only been seen in their present relation to one another. If men had ever been found in society without women, or women without men, or if there had been a society of men and women in which the women were not under the control of the men, something might have been positively known about the mental and moral differences which may be inherent in the nature of each. What is now called the nature of women is an eminently artificial thing—the result of forced repression in some directions, unnatural stimulation in others. It may be asserted without scruple, that no other class of dependents have had their character so entirely distorted from its natural proportions by their relation with their masters; for, if conquered and slave races have been, in some respects, more forcibly repressed, whatever in them has not been crushed down by an iron heel has generally been let alone, and if left with any liberty of development, it has developed itself according to its own laws; but in the case of women, a hot-house and stove cultivation has always been carried on of some of the capabilities of their nature, for the benefit and pleasure of their masters. Then, because certain products of the general vital force sprout luxuriantly and reach a great development in this heated atmosphere and under this active nurture and watering, while other shoots from the same root, which are left outside in the wintry air, with ice purposely heaped all round them, have a stunted growth, and some are burnt off with fire and disappear; men, with that inability to recognise their own work which distinguishes the unanalytic mind, indolently believe that the tree grows of itself in the way they have made it grow, and that it would die if one half of it were not kept in a vapour bath and the other half in the snow.

Of all difficulties which impede the progress of thought, and the formation of well-grounded opinions on life and social arrangements, the greatest is now the unspeakable ignorance and inattention of mankind in

[1] *prima facie* Latin: arising at first sight.

respect to the influences which form human character. Whatever any portion of the human species now are, or seem to be, such, it is supposed, they have a natural tendency to be: even when the most elementary knowledge of the circumstances in which they have been placed, clearly points out the causes that made them what they are. Because a cottier[1] deeply in arrears to his landlord is not industrious, there are people who think that the Irish are naturally idle. Because constitutions can be overthrown when the authorities appointed to execute them turn their arms against them, there are people who think the French incapable of free government. Because the Greeks cheated the Turks, and the Turks only plundered the Greeks, there are persons who think that the Turks are naturally more sincere: and because women, as is often said, care nothing about politics except their personalities, it is supposed that the general good is naturally less interesting to women than to men. History, which is now so much better understood than formerly, teaches another lesson: if only by showing the extraordinary susceptibility of human nature to external influences, and the extreme variableness of those of its manifestations which are supposed to be most universal and uniform. But in history, as in travelling, men usually see only what they already had in their own minds; and few learn much from history, who do not bring much with them to its study.

Hence, in regard to that most difficult question, what are the natural differences between the two sexes—a subject on which it is impossible in the present state of society to obtain complete and correct knowledge—while almost everybody dogmatizes upon it, almost all neglect and make light of the only means by which any partial insight can be obtained into it. This is, an analytic study of the most important department of psychology, the laws of the influence of circumstances on character. For, however great and apparently ineradicable the moral and intellectual differences between men and women might be, the evidence of there being natural differences could only be negative. Those only could be inferred to be natural which could not possibly be artificial—the residuum, after deducting every characteristic of either sex which can admit of being explained from education or external circumstances. The profoundest knowledge of the laws of the formation of character is indispensable to entitle anyone to affirm even that there is any difference, much more what the difference is, between the two sexes considered as moral and rational beings; and since no one, as yet, has that knowledge (for there is hardly any subject which, in proportion to its importance, has been so little studied), no one is thus far entitled to any positive opinion on the subject. Conjectures are all that can at present be made; conjectures more or less probable, according as more or less authorized by such knowledge as we yet have of the laws of psychology, as applied to the formation of character.

Even the preliminary knowledge, what the differences between the sexes now are, apart from all question as to how they are made what they are, is still in the crudest and most incomplete state. Medical practitioners and physiologists have ascertained, to some extent, the differences in bodily constitution; and this is an important element to the psychologist: but hardly any medical practitioner is a psychologist. Respecting the mental characteristics of women; their observations are of no more worth than those of common men. It is a subject on which nothing final can be known, so long as those who alone can really know it, women themselves, have given but little testimony, and that little, mostly suborned. It is easy to know stupid women. Stupidity is much the same all the world over. A stupid person's notions and feelings may confidently be inferred from those which prevail in the circle by which the person is surrounded. Not so with those whose opinions and feelings are an emanation from their own nature and faculties. It is only a man here and there who has any tolerable knowledge of the character even of the women of his own family. I do not mean, of their capabilities; these nobody knows, not even themselves, because most of them have never been called out. I mean their actually existing thoughts and feelings. Many a man thinks he perfectly understands women, because he has had amatory relations with several, perhaps with many of

[1] *cottier* Tenant who rents a cottage and often works for a landlord in return.

them. If he is a good observer, and his experience extends to quality as well as quantity, he may have learnt something of one narrow department of their nature—an important department, no doubt. But of all the rest of it, few persons are generally more ignorant, because there are few from whom it is so carefully hidden. The most favourable case which a man can generally have for studying the character of a woman, is that of his own wife: for the opportunities are greater, and the cases of complete sympathy not so unspeakably rare. And in fact, this is the source from which any knowledge worth having on the subject has, I believe, generally come. But most men have not had the opportunity of studying in this way more than a single case: accordingly one can, to an almost laughable degree, infer what a man's wife is like, from his opinions about women in general. To make even this one case yield any result, the woman must be worth knowing, and the man not only a competent judge, but of a character so sympathetic in itself, and so well adapted to hers, that he can either read her mind by sympathetic intuition, or has nothing in himself which makes her shy of disclosing it. Hardly anything, I believe, can be more rare than this conjunction. It often happens that there is the most complete unity of feeling and community of interests as to all external things, yet the one has as little admission into the internal life of the other as if they were common acquaintance. Even with true affection, authority on the one side and subordination on the other prevent perfect confidence. Though nothing may be intentionally withheld, much is not shown. In the analogous relation of parent and child, the corresponding phenomenon must have been in the observation of everyone. As between father and son, how many are the cases in which the father, in spite of real affection on both sides, obviously to all the world does not know, nor suspect, parts of the son's character familiar to his companions and equals. The truth is, that the position of looking up to another is extremely unpropitious to complete sincerity and openness with him. The fear of losing ground in his opinion or in his feelings is so strong, that even in an upright character, there is an unconscious tendency to show only the best side, or the side which, though not the best, is that which he most likes to see: and it may be confidently said that thorough knowledge of one another hardly ever exists, but between persons who, besides being intimates, are equals. How much more true, then, must all this be, when the one is not only under the authority of the other, but has it inculcated on her as a duty to reckon everything else subordinate to his comfort and pleasure, and to let him neither see nor feel anything coming from her, except what is agreeable to him. All these difficulties stand in the way of a man's obtaining any thorough knowledge even of the one woman whom alone, in general, he has sufficient opportunity of studying. When we further consider that to understand one woman is not necessarily to understand any other woman; that even if he could study many women of one rank, or of one country, he would not thereby understand women of other ranks or countries; and even if he did, they are still only the women of a single period of history; we may safely assert that the knowledge which men can acquire of women, even as they have been and are, without reference to what they might be, is wretchedly imperfect and superficial, and always will be so, until women themselves have told all that they have to tell.

And this time has not come; nor will it come otherwise than gradually. It is but of yesterday that women have either been qualified by literary accomplishments or permitted by society, to tell anything to the general public. As yet very few of them dare tell anything, which men, on whom their literary success depends, are unwilling to hear. Let us remember in what manner, up to a very recent time, the expression, even by a male author, of uncustomary opinions, or what are deemed eccentric feelings, usually was, and in some degree still is, received; and we may form some faint conception under what impediments a woman, who is brought up to think custom and opinion her sovereign rule, attempts to express in books anything drawn from the depths of her own nature. The greatest woman who has left writings behind her sufficient to give her an eminent rank in the literature of her country, thought it necessary to prefix as a motto to her boldest work, "Un homme peut braver l'opinion; une femme doit s'y soumettre."[1] The greater part of what women write about women is mere sycophancy to men. In the case of unmarried women, much of it seems only intended to increase their chance of a husband. Many, both married and unmarried, overstep the mark, and inculcate a servility beyond what is desired or relished by any man, except the very vulgarest. But this is not so often the case as, even at a quite late period, it still was. Literary women are becoming more freespoken, and more willing to express their real sentiments. Unfortunately, in this country especially, they are themselves such artificial products, that their sentiments are compounded of a small element of individual observation and consciousness, and a very large one of acquired associations. This will be less and less the case, but it will remain true to a great extent, as long as social institutions do not admit the same free development of originality in women which is possible to men. When that time comes, and not before, we shall see, and not merely hear, as much as it is necessary to know of the nature of women, and the adaptation of other things to it.

I have dwelt so much on the difficulties which at present obstruct any real knowledge by men of the true nature of women, because in this as in so many other things "opinio copiæ inter maximas causas inopiæ est;"[2] and there is little chance of reasonable thinking on the matter, while people flatter themselves that they perfectly understand a subject of which most men know absolutely nothing, and of which it is at present impossible that any man, or all men taken together, should have knowledge which can qualify them to lay down the law to women as to what is, or is not, their vocation. Happily, no such knowledge is necessary for any practical purpose connected with the position of women in relation to society and life. For, according to all the principles involved in modern society, the question rests with women themselves—to be decided by their own experience, and by the use of their own faculties. There are no means of finding what either one person or many can do, but by trying—and no means by which anyone else can discover for them what it is for their happiness to do or leave undone.

One thing we may be certain of—that what is contrary to women's nature to do, they never will be made to do by simply giving their nature free play. The anxiety of mankind to interfere in behalf of nature, for fear lest nature should not succeed in effecting its purpose, is an altogether unnecessary solicitude. What women by nature cannot do, it is quite superfluous to forbid them from doing. What they can do, but not so well as the men who are their competitors, competition suffices to exclude them from; since nobody asks for protective duties and bounties in favour of women; it is only asked that the present bounties and protective duties in favour of men should be recalled. If women have a greater natural inclination for some things than for others, there is no need of laws or social inculcation to make the majority of them do the former in preference to the latter. Whatever women's services are most wanted for, the free play of competition will hold out the strongest inducements to them to undertake. And, as the words imply, they are most wanted for the things for which they are most fit; by the apportionment of which to them, the collective faculties of the two sexes can be applied on the whole with the greatest sum of valuable result.

The general opinion of men is supposed to be, that the natural vocation of a woman is that of a wife and mother. I say, is supposed to be, because, judging from acts—from the whole of the present constitution of society—one might infer that their opinion was the direct contrary. They might be supposed to think that the alleged natural vocation of women was of all things the most repugnant to their nature; insomuch that if they are free to do anything else—if any other means of living, or occupation of their time and faculties, is open, which has any chance of appearing desirable to them—there will not be enough of them who will be willing to accept the condition said to be natural to them. If this is the real opinion of men in general, it would be well

[1] [Mill's note] Title-page of Mme. de Staël's *Delphine*. [The French novelist's (1766–1817) words translate as: "A man can brave (public) opinion; a woman must submit to it."]

[2] *opinio copiæ … inopiæ est* Latin: the belief in sufficiency is one of the greatest causes of insufficiency.

that it should be spoken out. I should like to hear somebody openly enunciating the doctrine (it is already implied in much that is written on the subject)—"It is necessary to society that women should marry and produce children. They will not do so unless they are compelled. Therefore it is necessary to compel them." The merits of the case would then be clearly defined. It would be exactly that of the slaveholders of South Carolina and Louisiana. "It is necessary that cotton and sugar should be grown. White men cannot produce them. Negroes will not, for any wages which we choose to give. *Ergo* they must be compelled." An illustration still closer to the point is that of impressment.[1] Sailors must absolutely be had to defend the country. It often happens that they will not voluntarily enlist. Therefore there must be the power of forcing them. How often has this logic been used! and, but for one flaw in it, without doubt it would have been successful up to this day. But it is open to the retort—First pay the sailors the honest value of their labour. When you have made it as well worth their while to serve you, as to work for other employers, you will have no more difficulty than others have in obtaining their services. To this there is no logical answer except "I will not:" and as people are now not only ashamed, but are not desirous, to rob the labourer of his hire, impressment is no longer advocated. Those who attempt to force women into marriage by closing all other doors against them, lay themselves open to a similar retort. If they mean what they say, their opinion must evidently be, that men do not render the married condition so desirable to women, as to induce them to accept it for its own recommendations. It is not a sign of one's thinking the boon one offers very attractive, when one allows only Hobson's choice,[2] "that or none." And here, I believe, is the clue to the feelings of those men, who have a real antipathy to the equal freedom of women. I believe they are afraid, not lest women should be unwilling to marry, for I do not think that anyone in reality has that apprehension; but lest they should insist that marriage should be on equal conditions; lest all women of spirit and capacity should prefer doing almost anything else, not in their own eyes degrading, rather than marry, when marrying is giving themselves a master, and a master too of all their earthly possessions. And truly, if this consequence were necessarily incident to marriage, I think that the apprehension would be very well founded. I agree in thinking it probable that few women, capable of anything else, would, unless under an irresistible *entrainement*,[3] rendering them for the time insensible to anything but itself, choose such a lot, when any other means were open to them of filling a conventionally honourable place in life: and if men are determined that the law of marriage shall be a law of despotism, they are quite right, in point of mere policy, in leaving to women only Hobson's choice. But, in that case, all that has been done in the modern world to relax the chain on the minds of women, has been a mistake. They never should have been allowed to receive a literary education. Women who read, much more women who write, are, in the existing constitution of things, a contradiction and a disturbing element: and it was wrong to bring women up with any acquirements but those of an odalisque,[4] or of a domestic servant.

—1869

[1] *impressment* Policy that pressed men into public service, even against their will; this practice was discontinued after 1835.

[2] *Hobson's choice* Expression originating from a Cambridge-London carrier, Thomas Hobson (1544–1630), who refused, when hiring out his horses, to allow any to leave the stable out of turn.

[3] *entrainement* Enchantment or charm.

[4] *odalisque* Concubine.

The Place of Women in Society

CONTEXTS

There was much debate concerning the proper place of women and the ideal characteristics of femininity throughout the nineteenth century. In a nation ruled by a female queen who supported education for women but not female suffrage, the lines between conventional masculine and feminine realms were often blurred. The traditional roles of wives, mothers, and daughters; the structure of the family; the nature of marriage; and how society ought to treat those unwilling or unable to conform to its standards of womanhood—all these subjects were open for examination by both men and women, and many writers and thinkers voiced opinions on them.

Sarah Stickney Ellis, the author of *The Women of England*, ran a school for girls but did not support intellectual advancement for women. Instead, she educated her pupils to become capable managers of their homes, from which they could best facilitate the advancement of their husbands and sons. Her numerous guides to female conduct, including *The Daughters of England* (1842), *The Wives of England* (1843), and *The Mothers of England* (1845), were extremely popular.

As the selection from *Fraser's Magazine* shows, the role of the governess in Victorian society posed issues of both gender and class. The growing prosperity of the middle classes enabled more and more families to afford governesses—and the increased emphasis on education (for females as well as for males) led to a widespread acknowledgment of the importance of the role governesses played as educators. In Victorian social hierarchy, the governess was a "lady"; this was *socially* a desirable occupation for many women, especially those daughters of tradespeople who sought to "better themselves." But as a paid employee (albeit often a poorly paid one) the governess was part of the work force—a status that would normally disqualify a woman from being considered a "lady." Consequently, the situation of the governess was rife with tensions, and the daily reality of her life was often very difficult; Charlotte Brontë complained of the "wretched bondage" of being a governess.

While some women were forced into the difficulties of life as a governess, others found themselves in a position that was even more fraught: for many lower-class women, prostitution represented the best of a narrow range of options, but those who engaged in it were almost universally condemned. Known as "the great social evil," prostitution was seen variously as the last resort of victims of desperate poverty, as evidence of the moral degradation of the lower classes, and even as the inevitable consequence of individual women's failures to control their unnatural lust. Victorian women were haunted by the specter of the "fallen woman" whose sexual transgression—a relationship out of wedlock, an adulterous affair, or an act of commercial sex—caused her to be permanently cast out of her family and society. While in reality many prostitutes eventually married or transitioned to other employment, in literature the fate of fallen women tended to resemble that of the suicidal protagonist depicted in Thomas Hood's highly popular poem "The Bridge of Sighs." In the selection following Hood's poem, reporter Henry Mayhew presents a less romanticized view of the motivations and consequences of prostitution; as part of a large interview project addressing urban poverty, Mayhew recorded the stories of several London needlewomen, whose work was so unpleasant and underpaid that many considered prostitution a preferable alternative.

The women's suffrage campaign, which began in the 1850s, heightened the debate over women's proper role in society. Suffragists' frustration over the lack of female vote was exacerbated by a series of Reform Acts, which extended the vote to a much greater proportion of men than had previously been entitled, but explicitly excluded all women. There were a variety of arguments used in the effort to justify the political subordination of women to men; these included the scientific argument, which presented evidence for women's supposed intellectual and physical inferiority, and the "divine will" argument, which portrayed female inferiority as part of the natural order established by God in Genesis. In her argument for female suffrage in *The Enfranchisement of Women*, Harriet Taylor presents—and attacks—some additional arguments used to protest women's entrance into politics.

Coventry Patmore's long poem *The Angel in the House*, which became extraordinarily popular in both Britain and the United States, is a sentimental depiction of the ideal female as conceived by many Victorian men of the upper and middle classes. The poem, which celebrated Patmore's first wife (he remarried twice after her death) details their courtship and marriage and epitomizes the view of women held by many men at the time. In the twentieth century the poem became the object of attacks by many feminist critics, notably Virginia Woolf, and the phrase "angel in the house" was commonly used as a sort of shorthand to refer to an oppressive Victorian attitude towards gender roles.

During this era, when the "angel in the house" was seen by many as the ideal to which every woman should aspire, growing numbers of women were actually unmarried—an uncomfortable fact that had long been true but began to generate considerable commentary in the latter half of the century. It was generally believed that the "problem" was demographic: there were too many women relative to men, and so some women—commonly referred to as "odd" or "redundant" women—were left without a partner. While emigration and military service occupied many men who might otherwise have started families, the low marriage rate was also a result of individual choice; initially, it was a choice made by men who did not want or could not afford to marry, leaving an abundance of single women (especially those of the middle class) competing for the narrow range of jobs that were considered appropriate for them. But as many in the first generation of "odd women" found single life a viable option, more and more women began to feel free either to postpone marriage or to reject it altogether. To conventional writers such as William Rathbone Greg, who tackles the question in his essay "Why Are Women Redundant?," the "odd women" were to be pitied for their inability—or derided for their refusal—to fulfill their natural destinies as wives and mothers. For feminists such as Frances Power Cobbe, as she argues in a response to Greg's article, the "odd women" were a clear illustration of the problems with a societal model that forced women to choose between marriage and financial desperation. The debate surrounding the "odd women" thus became part of a larger debate raging in the late nineteenth century: the argument over "the woman question."

Conversation about "the woman question" was heated, and the proponents of women's rights were often viciously attacked in print. As the satirical cartoon reproduced below demonstrates, suffragists were often viewed as the antithesis of the ideal woman, epitomizing instead traditionally "masculine" characteristics. In the excerpt following, Eliza Lynn Linton, perhaps the most vocal anti-feminist of the period, criticizes what she sees as the unnatural, masculine boldness of the "modern girl," whose unwillingness to serve and support her husband and nurture her children, Linton argues, makes her not only unsuitable for marriage, but a disgrace to England's national character.

The idea that a woman ought to be subordinate to her husband was not only a matter of social expectation; it was also incorporated into English law. For much of the nineteenth century, in most respects the law treated a husband and wife as a single person, with many of the wife's rights—including her right to the possession of her own property—subsumed by her husband's. In her article

"Criminals, Idiots, Women, and Minors," Frances Power Cobbe describes and criticizes the common arguments used to justify depriving married women of the legal rights that even convicted felons were afforded. Women began campaigning against these laws in the 1850s, and the Married Women's Property Acts were passed in 1870 and 1882, allowing married women the same property rights as unmarried women.

Within Victorian society's complex network of gender and class distinctions, many citizens relied upon printed material for guidance in matters of conduct and etiquette, as well as for practical advice on household management and professional opportunities. *The Girl's Own Paper*, a weekly paper founded in 1880 as a companion to the very successful *Boy's Own Paper*, provided such information to many female readers. According to its editor, the paper, which was published by the Religious Tract Society, aimed to instruct its readers "in the moral and domestic virtues, preparing them for the responsibility of womanhood and for a heavenly home."

Many women began to reject this traditional paradigm of wifehood and motherhood when "the marriage question" came to occupy a central position in debates concerning women's political rights, their education, and their need for economic independence. Among those who vehemently opposed the change in values was Grant Allen; in some respects a radical thinker, he believed that the institution of marriage required extensive revision, but in his "Plain Words on the Woman Question" he nonetheless attacks the abandonment of traditional gender roles as unnatural and harmful to society. Despite such hostile responses, the new outlook persisted; in her article "The New Aspect of the Woman Question," Sarah Grand coined the phrase "the new woman" to name those of her generation who had embraced the goals of political, educational, and economic equality with men. The importance of these values is defended in Mona Caird's somewhat humorous response to the *Daily Telegraph*'s question "Does Marriage Hinder a Woman's Self-Development?" Her hypothetical reversal of men's and women's roles brings to light how arbitrary—and confining—definitions of "masculine" and "feminine" characteristics could be.

⌘⌘⌘

from Sarah Stickney Ellis, *The Daughters of England: Their Position in Society, Character and Responsibilities* (1842)

… The sphere upon which a young woman enters on first leaving school, or, to use a popular phrase, on "completing her education," is so entirely new to her, her mind is so often the subject of new impressions, and her attention so frequently absorbed by new motives for exertion, that, if at all accustomed to reflect, we cannot doubt but she will make these, or similar questions, the subject of serious inquiry—"What is my position in society? What do I aim at? And what means do I intend to employ for the accomplishment of my purpose?" …

As women, then, the first thing of importance is to be content to be inferior to men—inferior in mental power, in the same proportion that you are inferior in bodily strength. Facility of movement, aptitude, and grace, the bodily frame of woman may possess in a higher degree than that of man; just as in the softer touches of mental and spiritual beauty her character may present a lovelier page than his. Yet, as the great attribute of power must still be wanting there, it becomes more immediately her business to inquire how this want may be supplied.

An able and eloquent writer on "Woman's Mission"[1] has justly observed that woman's strength is in her influence. And, in order to render this influence more complete, you will find on examination that you are by

[1] *An able … Mission* Sarah Lewis, whose *Woman's Mission*, a popular book on female conduct, was published in 1839.

nature endowed with peculiar faculties—with a quickness of perception, facility of adaptation, and acuteness of feeling, which fit you especially for the part you have to act in life; and which, at the same time, render you, in a higher degree than men, susceptible both of pain and pleasure. …

* * *

I have already stated that women, in their position in life, must be content to be inferior to men; but as their inferiority consists chiefly in their want of power, this deficiency is abundantly made up to them by their capability of exercising influence; it is made up to them also in other ways, incalculable in their number and extent; but in none so effectually as by that order of Divine Providence which places them, in a moral and religious point of view, on the same level with man; nor can it be a subject of regret to any right-minded woman that they are not only exempt from the most laborious occupations both of mind and body, but also from the necessity of engaging in those eager pecuniary speculations, and in that fierce conflict of worldly interests by which men are so deeply occupied as to be in a manner compelled to stifle their best feelings, until they become in reality the characters they at first only assumed. Can it be a subject of regret to any kind and feeling woman that her sphere of action is one adapted to the exercise of the affections, where she may love, and trust, and hope, and serve, to the utmost of her wishes? Can it be a subject of regret that she is not called upon, so much as man, to calculate, to compete, to struggle, but rather to occupy a sphere in which the elements of discord cannot with propriety be admitted—in which beauty and order are expected to denote her presence, and where the exercise of benevolence is the duty she is most frequently called upon to perform.

Women almost universally consider themselves, and wish to be considered by others, as extremely affectionate; scarcely can a more severe libel be pronounced upon a woman than to say that she is not so. Now the whole law of woman's life is a law of love. I propose, therefore, to treat the subject in this light—to try whether the neglect of their peculiar duties does not imply an absence of love, and whether the principle of love, thoroughly carried out, would not so influence their conduct and feelings as to render them all which their best friends could desire.

Let us, however, clearly understand each other at the outset. To love, is a very different thing from a desire to be beloved. To love, is woman's nature—to be beloved is the consequence of her having properly exercised and controlled that nature. To love, is a woman's duty—to be beloved, is her reward.

* * *

… There is yet another flight of female ambition, another course which the love of distinction is apt to make, more product of folly, and of disappointment, perhaps, than all the rest. It is the ambition of the female author who writes for fame. Could those young aspirants know how little real dignity there is connected with the *trade* of authorship, their harps would be exchanged for distaffs,[1] their rose-tinted paper would be converted into ashes, and their Parnassus[2] would dwindle to a molehill. … The same want of sympathy which so often inspires the first effort of female authorship, might often find a sweet and abundant interchange of kindness in many a faithful heart beside the homely hearth. And after all, there is more true poetry in the fire-side affections of early life than in all those sympathetic associations with unknown and untried developments of mind which ever have existed either amongst the sons or the daughters of men.

Taking a more sober view of the case, there are, unquestionably, subjects of deep interest with which women have opportunities peculiar to themselves of becoming acquainted, and thus of benefiting their fellow creatures through the medium of their writings. But, after all, literature is not the natural channel for a woman's feelings; and pity, not envy, ought to be the meed[3] of her who writes for the public. How much of what with other women is reserved for the select and chosen intercourse of affection, with her must be laid

[1] *distaff* Staff on which wool or flax was wound when spinning.

[2] *Parnassus* Mountain in Greece sacred to the Muses, the nine daughters of Zeus and Mnemosyne, each of whom presided over, and provided inspiration for, a different aspect of the arts and sciences.

[3] *meed* Recompense; reward.

bare to the coarse cavillings,[1] and coarser commendations, of amateur or professional critics. How much of what no woman loves to say, except to the listening ear of domestic affection, by her must be told—nay, blazoned—to the world. And then, in her season of depression, or of wounded feeling, when her spirit yearns to sit in solitude, or even in darkness, so that it may be still; to know and feel that the very essence of that spirit, now embodied in a palpable form, has become an article of sale and bargain, tossed over from the hands of one workman to another, free alike to the touch of the prince and the peasant, and no longer to be reclaimed at will by the original possessor, let the world receive it as it may.

Is such, I ask, an enviable distinction?

from Anonymous, "Hints on the Modern Governess System," *Fraser's Magazine* (November 1844)

… To trace the growth of woman's desire after knowledge would be the task of a philosopher; for us, it suffices to see that it is, that is has been from all ages. The barter of Paradise for the means of knowledge is the first recorded act of woman's life; she tempted man to forego all tried blessings, for the untried boon of "knowing good and evil." Thenceforth, man wreaked his vengeance upon woman, for the loss of ease and plenty, by keeping her ignorant, and, consequently, helpless. But since the day that Christianity dawned on the world, an emancipation of the weak out of the power of the strong has been silently progressing. The faint cry, uplifted at intervals, swelled into a chorus; there was a sudden rush; all the world clamoured for a better education for women; no wonder, in such a struggle, that the greater number mistook chaff and husks[2] for bread. The movement was all too sudden. Education, in as far as it implies intellectual and moral growth, is the work of life; its operations are as secret and as self-derived as the gradual shooting of the green blade into the wheat-ear.

Now, when that cry of women after knowledge pierced the air, a thousand sprang up, mushroomwise, in a night, to answer it. Mothers who had only read their Bibles and receipt-books[3] found themselves unprepared for the emergency—we have so little patience, so little foresight. Then, teaching, that holy vocation of a woman, became a trade. An universal demand creates its own supply. Here was a tempting opening to all aspiring women, who were free to try a new field; the unmarried daughters of the gentry left with scanty portions had, till now, been content to eke out their small incomes in trade; many were the gentlewomen, in our great-grandmothers' days, who lived in honoured independence, though they kept small shops, to which their old friends resorted. They did not lose caste[4] because they sat for part of the day behind the counter. However, this refuge grew insecure from the outward pressure of public opinion in favour of refinement. … Many left their quiet homes for the schoolrooms of halls and castles. As they mounted the stair, others came from a lower rank, and filled the vacant steps. The restless rage to push on had stirred all classes. Those who, disappointed in their new stand, looked wistfully back to the old, found that when they would return they could not. There was no place left for them but that which they had chosen. Like much else, it looked best from a distance. Here, then, was a whole class of women driven into a new line, for which they had received no fitting preparation. … The new generation, thirsting to be taught, found teachers at their mercy, hanging between two ranks. Do the weak desire to learn what they may expect from the strong? Let them ponder deeply the governess system of the present day. This was the watch-word, "Teach us on our own terms, or work, and cease to be gentlewomen." To the newly risen race of governesses, even such equivocal gentility was preferable to a second change, though it was to be gained at the price of isolation. …

[1] *cavillings* Unfair or petty fault-finding.

[2] *chaff and husks* Material separated out from grains when threshing cereal crops.

[3] *receipt-books* I.e., recipe books.

[4] *lose caste* I.e., lose their position in society.

The policy of the world is to take advantage of want. It became apparent that a whole family of daughters might be taught by one of these single women, struggling for bread, for less than it formerly cost to send one girl to school. Where competition was so great, there was no difficulty in driving a bargain. The means of instruction might be had so cheaply that the grocer's daughters could be taught to read *Paul and Virginia* in the original tongue, and to strum *The Fall of Paris*.[1] In process of time, therefore, a governess became a necessary appanage[2] in every family.

Whether it be right or wrong, as a general rule, for mothers to delegate their most sacred trust to hired strangers, we are not here to discuss. The fact exists. Is the system carried out fairly for all parties? Is there any question astir as to its abuse? Philanthropic eyes are scanning many social evils. Is it yet considered how far a whole race of women are dragging out weary lives under a mass of trials, the detail of which would fill a "blue book"[3] by themselves? True, if the case were known, "a thousand voices" would be "uplifted."[4] The miseries of the governess may even swell that sickening clamour about the "rights of women," which would never have been raised had women been true to themselves. But that trite saying in this case has its point. The modern governess system is a case between woman and woman. Before one sex demands its due from the other, let it be just to itself.

Punch has ably pleaded in the cause of salaries and qualifications.[5] The statistics touching lunatic asylums give a frightful proportion of governesses in the list of the insane.[6] But has the whole life in home schoolrooms ever been investigated? We ask this with a real wish to be informed, with a hope of directing eyes to this unknown page of human life. Have kind, ladylike, cultivated women ever reflected on the relation which subsists between themselves and others of like minds, and, perhaps, formerly in similar circumstances? Have they ever tried to put themselves in the position of the young women devoting themselves to the education of their children, who yet live as strangers in the midst of their homes?...

... When the lesson-books are closed, and the little ones have capered out of the school-room, what becomes of the teacher, who has not exchanged a thought or a word with any one of congenial mind all day? Hour after hour she has *bent down* her mind, and *raised* the children's to given points, which, however interesting, are exhausting. A young thing, perhaps, still herself, ready to spring up again at one kindly touch. Do not even fond mothers, who teach their own children, feel that after the labours of the day they need some interchange of *mind*? They have often felt refreshed when husband or friend has given them a new thought, or understood an articulated feeling, after the repression of the day, necessary in fulfilling the duty of teaching. Who is there that has not known the dryness of spending time with people of more limited capacities and interests than one's own? ... Let mothers ask if they would not expect their own daughters to languish in spirits and energy, if they had no intercourse with older companions. Whilst the children are with their parents and their guests, the governess, quite as often as not, is expected to remain in the school-room, unless specially invited to join the circle. This is peculiarly the case in large establishments, where the school-room arrangements are distinct from the rest of the family. We

[1] *Paul and Virginia* The sentimental French novel *Paul et Virginie* (1787), by Jacques-Henri Bernadin de St. Pierre; *strum* Play poorly on the piano; *The Fall of Paris* Popular song of the period.

[2] *appanage* Possession, perquisite.

[3] *blue book* Parliamentary report.

[4] *a thousand ... uplifted* A reference to the epigraph of this article, from French novelist George Sand's collection of fictional letters, *Lettres à Marcie* (1837): "Society is full of abuses. Women complain of being brutally enslaved, badly brought up, badly educated, badly treated, and badly defended. All this is, unfortunately, true. These complaints are just, and do not doubt but that before long a thousand voices will be uplifted to remedy the evil."

[5] *Punch has ... qualifications* The satirical weekly magazine *Punch* had recently printed numerous articles advocating the improvement of conditions for governesses.

[6] *The statistics ... insane* During the early and mid nineteenth century it was a commonplace that governesses tended toward mental instability as a result of the stressful nature of their employment. While some statistics did show that there was a high percentage of governesses in asylums, this may have been due in part to the fact that private asylums sometimes provided the cheapest respectable accommodation for women without family or employment.

believe that most young women of delicate perceptions would prefer their desolate apartment to feeling themselves clogs[1] upon the family party. But do people know what they are about when they leave young creatures alone, long evening after evening, following days of seclusion and exhaustion? Factory-girls, shop-women, teachers of accomplishments, return to their homes at night. The servants gather round the work-table or the hall-fire. Prisoners in gaol[2] may collect together in knots in their yards, look in each other's faces, hear the sound of human voices, tell their troubles and joys, and listen to their neighbours. Solitary confinement, even for felons, is reserved to punish some special offence. It is only the governess, and a certain class of private tutors, who must hear the echoes from the drawing-room and the offices, feeling that, in a house full of people, they dwell alone. Nervous irritability, dejection, loss of energy, are the inevitable results which follow a too solitary life in youth. Yet, without elasticity in her own frame, how can the governess be a fitting companion and teacher of such gay, volatile creatures as children—so easily cowed and spirit-broken by harshness or settled sadness in those who live with them? Would not querulous temper of depression of spirits in the governess be complained of by the parents? Do they consider, when they expect cheerfulness and an even composure of spirits from one fretted with children's restless waywardness, and chilled by the frosty indifference and neglect of the grown-up members of the family, that they ask an impossible thing?

[1] *clogs* Encumbrances. Literally, blocks of wood attached to the leg or neck of a person or animal to prevent escape.

[2] *gaol* I.e., jail.

Thomas Hood, "The Bridge of Sighs" (1844)

"Drowned! Drowned!"[3]—HAMLET

One more Unfortunate,
Weary of breath,
Rashly importunate,
Gone to her death!

Take her up tenderly,
Lift her with care;
Fashioned so slenderly,
Young, and so fair!

Look at her garments
Clinging like cerements;[4]
Whilst the wave constantly
Drips from her clothing;
Take her up instantly,
Loving, not loathing.

Touch her not scornfully;
Think of her mournfully,
Gently and humanly;
Not of the stains of her,
All that remains of her
Now is pure womanly.

Make no deep scrutiny
Into her mutiny
Rash and undutiful:
Past all dishonour,
Death has left on her
Only the beautiful.

Still, for all slips of hers,
One of Eve's family—
Wipe those poor lips of hers
Oozing so clammily.

[3] *Drowned! Drowned!* From Shakespeare's *Hamlet* 4.7.183; the Queen's line upon learning that Ophelia, mad with grief, has drowned.

[4] *cerements* Cloths used to wrap a body for burial.

Loop up her tresses
Escaped from the comb,
Her fair auburn tresses;
Whilst wonderment guesses
Where was her home?

Who was her father?
Who was her mother?
Had she a sister?
Had she a brother?
Or was there a dearer one
Still, and a nearer one
Yet, than all other?

Alas! for the rarity
Of Christian charity
Under the sun!
Oh! it was pitiful!
Near a whole city full,
Home she had none.

Sisterly, brotherly,
Fatherly, motherly
Feelings had changed:
Love, by harsh evidence,
Thrown from its eminence;
Even God's providence
Seeming estranged.

Where the lamps quiver
So far in the river,
With many a light
From window and casement,
From garret to basement,
She stood, with amazement,
Houseless by night.

The bleak wind of March
Made her tremble and shiver;
But not the dark arch,
Or the black flowing river:
Mad from life's history,
Glad to death's mystery,
Swift to be hurled—
Anywhere, anywhere
Out of the world!

In she plunged boldly
No matter how coldly
The rough river ran—
Over the brink of it,
Picture it—think of it,
Dissolute Man!
Lave° in it, drink of it, *wash*
Then, if you can!

Take her up tenderly,
Lift her with care;
Fashioned so slenderly,
Young, and so fair!

Ere her limbs frigidly
Stiffen too rigidly,
Decently—kindly—
Smooth and compose them;
And her eyes, close them,
Staring so blindly!

Dreadfully staring
Through muddy impurity,
As when with the daring
Last look of despairing
Fixed on futurity.

Perishing gloomily,
Spurred by contumely,° *scornful abuse*
Cold inhumanity,
Burning insanity,
Into her rest.
Cross her hands humbly
As if praying dumbly,
Over her breast!

Owning her weakness,
Her evil behaviour,
And leaving, with meekness,
Her sins to her Saviour!

from Henry Mayhew, "Labour and the Poor: The Metropolitan Districts," *The Morning Chronicle* (1849)

... "I make moleskin trousers. I get 7*d.* and 8*d.*[1] per pair. I can do two pairs in a day, and twelve, when there is full employment, in a week. But some weeks I have no work at all. I work from six in the morning to ten at night; that is what I call my day's work. When I am fully employed I get from 7*s.* to 8*s.*[2] a week. My expenses out of that for twist,[3] thread, and candles are about 1*s.* 6*d.* a week, leaving me about 6*s.* a week clear. But there's coals to pay for out of this, and that's at the least 6*d.* or more; so 5*s.* 6*d.* is the very outside of what I earn when I'm in full work. Lately I have been dreadfully slack; so we are every winter, all of us "sloppers,"[4] and that's the time when we wants the most money. The week before last I had but two pair to make all the week, so that I only earnt 1*s.* clear. For this last month I'm sure I haven't done any more than that each week. Taking one week with another, all the year round, I don't make above 3*s.* clear money each week. I don't work at any other kind of slop work. The trousers work is held to be the best paid of all. I give 1*s.* a week rent.

"My father died when I was five years of age. My mother is a widow, upwards of 66 years of age, and seldom has a day's work. Generally once in the week she is employed pot-scouring—that is, cleaning publicans' pots.[5] She is paid 4*d.* a dozen for that, and does about four dozen and a half, so that she gets about 1*s.* 6*d.* in the day by it. For the rest she is dependent upon me. I am 20 years of age the 25th of this month. We earn together, to keep the two of us, from 4*s.* 6*d.* to 5*s.* each week. Out of this we have to pay 1*s.* rent, and there remains 3*s.* 6*d.* to 4*s.* to find us both in food and clothing. It is of course impossible for us to live upon it, and the consequence is I am obligated to go in a bad way.

"I have been three years working at slop work. I was virtuous when I first went to work, and I remained so till this last twelvemonth. I struggled very hard to keep myself chaste, but I found that I couldn't get food and clothing for myself and mother, so I took to live with a young man. He is turned 20. He is a tinman. He did promise to marry me, but his sister made mischief between me and him, so that parted us. I have not seen him now for about six months, and I can't say whether he will keep his promise or not. I am now pregnant by him, and expect to be confined in two months' time. He knows of my situation, and so does my mother. My mother believed me to be married to him. She knows otherwise now. I was very fond of him, and had known him for two years before he seduced me. He could make 14*s.* a week. He told me if I came to live with him he'd take care I shouldn't want, and both mother and me had been very bad off before. He said, too, he'd make me his lawful wife, but I hardly cared so long as I could get food for myself and mother.

"Many young girls at the shop advised me to go wrong. They told me how comfortable they was off; they said they could get plenty to eat and drink, and good clothes. There isn't one young girl as can get her living by slop work. The masters all know this, but they wouldn't own to it, of course. It stands to reason that no one can live and pay rent, and find clothes, upon 3*s.* a week, which is the most they make clear, even the best hands, at the moleskin and cord trousers work. There's poor people moved out of our house that was making ¾*d.* shirts. I am satisfied there is not one young girl that works at slop work that is virtuous, and there are some thousands in the trade. They may do very well if they have got mothers and fathers to find them a home and food, and to let them have what they earn for clothes; then they may be virtuous, but not without. I've heard of numbers who have gone from slop work to the streets altogether for a living, and I shall be obligated to do the same thing myself unless something better turns up for me.

"If I was never allowed to speak no more, it was the little money I got by my labour that led me to go wrong. Could I have honestly earnt enough to have

---

[1] *7d. and 8d.* Seven and eight pence. There were twelve pence in a shilling, and twenty shillings in a pound.

[2] *7s. to 8s.* Seven to eight shillings.

[3] *twist* Strong thread made of multiple strands twisted together.

[4] *sloppers* Slop workers, producers of cheap, low-quality clothing.

[5] *publicans' pots* Pewter drinking vessels used by the working-class customers of pubs.

subsisted upon, to find me in proper food and clothing, such as is necessary, I should not have gone astray; no, never—As it was I fought against it as long as I could—that I did—to the last. I hope to be able to get a ticket for a midwife;[1] a party has promised me as much, and, he says, if possible, he'll get me an order for a box of linen. My child will only increase my burdens, and if my young man won't support my child I must go on the streets altogether. I know how horrible all this is. It would have been much better for me to have subsisted upon a dry crust and water rather than be as I am now. But no one knows the temptations of us poor girls in want. Gentlefolks can never understand it. If I had been born a lady it wouldn't have been very hard to have acted like one. To be poor and to be honest, especially with young girls, is the hardest struggle of all. There isn't one in a thousand that can get the better of it. I am ready to say again, that it was want, and nothing more, that made me transgress. If I had been better paid I should have done better. Young as I am, my life is a curse to me. If the Almighty would please to take me before my child is born, I should die happy."

from Harriet Taylor, *The Enfranchisement of Women* (1851)

When a prejudice, which has any hold on the feeling, finds itself reduced to the unpleasant necessity of assigning reasons, it thinks it has done enough when it has re-asserted the very point in the dispute, in phrases which appeal to the pre-existing feelings. Thus, many persons think they have sufficiently justified the restrictions on women's field of action when they have said that the pursuits from which women are excluded are *unfeminine*, and that the *proper sphere* of women is not politics or publicity, but private and domestic life.

We deny the right of any portion of the species to decide for another portion, or any individual for another individual, what is and what is not their "proper sphere." The proper sphere for all human beings is the largest and highest which they are able to attain to. …

We shall follow the very proper convention, in not entering into the question of the alleged differences in physical or mental qualities between the sexes; not because we have nothing to say, but because we have too much. … But if those who assert that the "proper sphere" for women is the domestic, mean by this that they have not shown themselves qualified for any other, the assertion evinces great ignorance of life and of history. Women have shown fitness for the highest social functions, exactly in proportion as they have been admitted to them. By a curious anomaly, though ineligible to even the lowest offices of state, they are in some countries admitted to the highest of all, the regal; and if there is any one function for which they have shown a decided vocation, it is that of reigning. …

Concerning the fitness, then, of women for politics, there can be no question: but the dispute is more likely to turn upon the fitness of politics for women. When the reasons alleged for excluding women from active life in all its higher departments are stripped of their garb of declamatory phrases, and reduced to the simple expression of a meaning, they seem to be mainly three: the incompatibility of active life with maternity and with the cares of a household; secondly, its alleged hardening effect on the character; and thirdly, the inexpediency of making an addition to the already excessive pressure of competition in every kind of professional or lucrative employment.

The first, the maternity argument, is usually laid most stress upon: although (it needs hardly be said) this reason, if it be one, can apply only to mothers. It is neither necessary nor just to make imperative on women that they shall be either mothers or nothing; or that if they have been mothers once, they shall be nothing else during the whole remainder of their lives. Neither women nor men need any law to exclude them from an occupation if they have undertaken another which is incompatible with it. No one proposes to exclude the male sex from Parliament because a man may be a soldier or sailor in active service, or a merchant whose business requires all his time and energies. Nine-tenths

[1] *ticket for a midwife* I.e., document issued by a charity that has paid for the recipient to receive a midwife's services.

of the occupations of men exclude them *de facto*[1] from public life, as effectually as if they were excluded by law; but that is no reason for making laws to exclude even the nine-tenths, much less the remaining tenth. The reason of the case is the same for women as for men. There is no need to make provision by law that a woman shall not carry on the active details of a household, or of the education of children, and at the same time practise a profession or be elected to Parliament. Where incompatibility is real, it will take care of itself: but there is gross injustice in making the incompatibility a pretence for the exclusion of those in whose case it does not exist. And these, if they were free to choose, would be a very large proportion. The maternity argument deserts its supporters in the case of single women, a large and increasing class of the population; a fact which, it is not irrelevant to remark, by tending to diminish the excessive competition of numbers, is calculated to assist greatly the prosperity of all. There is no inherent reason or necessity that all women should voluntarily choose to devote their lives to one animal function and its consequences. Numbers of women are wives and mothers only because there is no other career open to them, no other occupation for their feelings or their activities. Every improvement in their education, and enlargement of their faculties—everything which renders them more qualified for any other mode of life, increases the number of those to whom it is an injury and an oppression to be denied the choice. To say that women must be excluded from active life because maternity disqualifies them for it, is in fact to say that every other career should be forbidden them in order that maternity may be their only resource.

But secondly, it is urged that to give the same freedom of occupation to women as to men would be an injurious addition to the crowd of competitors, by whom the avenues to almost all kinds of employment are choked up, and its remuneration depressed. This argument, it is to be observed, does not reach the political question. It gives no excuse for withholding from women the rights of citizenship. The suffrage, the jury-box, admission to the legislature and to office, it does not touch. It bears only on the industrial branch of the subject. Allowing it, then, in an economical point of view, its full force; assuming that to lay open to women the employments now monopolized by men, would tend, like the breaking down of other monopolies, to lower the rate of remuneration in those employments; let us consider what is the amount of this evil consequence, and what the compensation for it. The worst ever asserted, much worse than is at all likely to be realized, is that if women competed with men, a man and a woman could not together earn more than is now earned by the man alone. Let us make this supposition, the most favourable supposition possible: the joint income of the two would be the same as before, while the woman would be raised from the position of a servant to that of a partner. Even if every woman, as matters now stand, had a claim on some man for support, how infinitely preferable is it that part of the income should be of the woman's earning, even if the aggregate sum were but little increased by it, rather than that she should be compelled to stand aside in order that men may be the sole earners, and the sole dispensers of what is earned. Even under the present laws respecting the property of women, a woman who contributes materially to the support of the family cannot be treated in the same contemptuously tyrannical manner as one who, however she may toil as a domestic drudge, is a dependent on the man for subsistence. As for the depression of wages by increase of competition, remedies will be found for it in time. Palliatives might be applied immediately; for instance, a more rigid exclusion of children from industrial employment, during the years in which they ought to be working only to strengthen their bodies and minds for after life. Children are necessarily dependent, and under the power of others; and their labour, being not for themselves but for the gain of their parents, is a proper subject for legislative regulation. With respect to the future, we neither believe that improvident multiplication, and the consequent excessive difficulty of gaining a subsistence, will always continue, nor that the division of mankind into capitalists and hired labourers, and the regulation

[1] *de facto* Latin: in reality; as a matter of fact.

of the reward of labourers mainly by demand and supply, will be for ever, or even much longer, the rule of the world. But so long as competition is the general law of human life, it is tyranny to shut out one half of the competitors. All who have attained the age of self-government have an equal claim to be permitted to sell whatever kind of useful labour they are capable of, for the price which it will bring.

The third objection to the admission of women to political or professional life, its alleged hardening tendency, belongs to an age now past, and is scarcely to be comprehended by people of the present time. There are still, however, persons who say that the world and its avocations render men selfish and unfeeling; that the struggles, rivalries, and collisions of business and of politics make them harsh and unamiable; that if half the species must unavoidably be given up to these things, it is the more necessary that the other half should be kept free from them; that to preserve women from the bad influences of the world is the only chance of preventing men from being wholly given up to them.

There would have been plausibility in this argument when the world was still in the age of violence; when life was full of physical conflict, and every man had to redress his injuries or those of others, by the sword or by the strength of his arm. Women, like priests, by being exempted from such responsibilities, and from some part of the accompanying dangers, may have been enabled to exercise a beneficial influence. But in the present condition of human life, we do not know where those hardening influences are to be found, to which men are subject and from which women are at present exempt. Individuals now-a-days are seldom called upon to fight hand to hand, even with peaceful weapons; personal enmities and rivalries count for little in worldly transactions; the general pressure of circumstances, not the adverse will of individuals, is the obstacle men now have to make head against. That pressure, when excessive, breaks the spirit, and cramps and sours the feelings, but not less of women than of men, since they suffer certainly not less from its evils. There are still quarrels and dislikes, but the sources of them are changed. The feudal chief once found his bitterest enemy in his powerful neighbour, the minister or courtier in his rival for place: but opposition of interest in active life, as a cause of personal animosity, is out of date; the enmities of the present day arise not from great things but small, from what people say of one another, more than from what they do; and if there are hatred, malice, and all uncharitableness, they are to be found among women fully as much as among men. In the present state of civilization, the notion of guarding women from the hardening influences of the world could only be realized by secluding them from society altogether. The common duties of common life, as at present constituted, are incompatible with any other softness in women than weakness. Surely weak minds in weak bodies must ere long cease to be even supposed to be either attractive or amiable.

But, in truth, none of these arguments and considerations touch the foundations of the subject. The real question is, whether it is right and expedient that one half of the human race should pass through life in a state of forced subordination to the other half. If the best state of human society is that of being divided into two parts, one consisting of persons with a will and a substantive existence, the other of humble companions to these persons, attached, each of them to one, for the purpose of bringing up *his* children, and making *his* home pleasant to him; if this is the place assigned to women, it is but kindness to educate them for this; to make them believe that the greatest good fortune which can befall them is to be chosen by some man for this purpose; and that every other career which the world deems happy or honourable is closed to them by the law, not of social institutions, but of nature and destiny.

When, however, we ask why the existence of one-half the species should be merely ancillary to that of the other—why each woman should be a mere appendage to a man, allowed to have no interests of her own, that there may be nothing to compete in her mind with his interests and his pleasure; the only reason which can be given is, that men like it. It is agreeable to them that men should live for their own sake, women for the sake of men: and the qualities and conduct in subjects which are agreeable to rulers, they succeed for a long time in making the subjects themselves consider as their appropriate virtues.

from Coventry Patmore, *The Angel in the House* (1854–56)

THE WIFE'S TRAGEDY

Man must be pleased; but him to please
Is woman's pleasure; down the gulf
Of his condoled necessities
She casts her best, she flings herself.
How often flings for nought! and yokes
Her heart to an icicle or whim,
Whose each impatient word provokes
Another, not from her, but him;
While she, too gentle even to force
His penitence by kind replies,
Waits by, expecting his remorse,
With pardon in her pitying eyes;
And if he once, by shame oppressed,
A comfortable word confers,
She leans and weeps against his breast,
And seems to think the sin was hers;
And whilst his love has any life,
Or any eye to see her charms,
At any time, she's still his wife,
Dearly devoted to his arms;
She loves with love that cannot tire;
And when, ah woe, she loves alone,
Through passionate duty love flames higher,
As grass grows taller round a stone. …

THE FOREIGN LAND

A woman is a foreign land,
Of which, though there he settle young
A man will ne'er quite understand
The customs, politics, and tongue.
The foolish hie° them post-haste through, *hasten*
See fashions odd, and prospects fair,
Learn of the language, "How-d'ye do,"
And go and brag that they've been there.
The most for leave to trade apply,
For once, at Empire's seat her heart,
Then get what knowledge ear and eye
Glean chancewise in the life-long mart.° *market*
And certain others few and fit,
Attach them to the Court, and see
The country's best, its accent hit,
And partly sound its polity.

from William Rathbone Greg, "Why Are Women Redundant?" (1862)

… [T]here is an enormous and increasing number of single women in the nation, a number quite disproportionate and quite abnormal; a number which, positively and relatively, is indicative of an unwholesome social state, and is both productive and prognostic of much wretchedness and wrong. There are hundreds of thousands of women—not to speak more largely still—scattered through all ranks, but proportionally most numerous in the middle and upper classes—who have to earn their own living instead of spending and husbanding the earnings of men; who, not having the natural duties and labours of wives and mothers, have to carve out artificial and painfully-sought occupations for themselves; who, in place of completing, sweetening, and embellishing the existence of others, are compelled to lead an independent and incomplete existence of their own. In the manufacturing districts thousands of girls are working in mills and earning ample wages, instead of performing, or preparing and learning to perform, the functions and labours of domestic life. In great cities, thousands, again, are toiling in the ill-paid *métier*[1] of seamstresses and needlewomen, wasting life and soul, gathering the scantiest subsistence, and surrounded by the most overpowering and insidious temptations. As we go a few steps higher in the social scale, we find two classes of similar abnormal existences; women, more or less well educated, spending youth and middle life as governesses, living laboriously, yet perhaps not uncomfortably, but laying by nothing, and retiring to a lonely and destitute old age: and old maids, with just enough income to live upon, but wretched and deteriorating, their minds narrowing, and their hearts withering,

[1] *métier* French: employment.

because they have nothing to do, and none to love, cherish, and obey. A little further upwards, how many do we daily see, how many have we all known, who are raised by fortune above the necessity of caring for their own subsistence, but to whom employment is a necessity as imperious as to the milliner or the husbandman,[1] because only employment can fill the dreary void of an unshared existence—beautiful lay nuns, involuntary takers of the veil, who pine for work, who beg for occupation, who pant for interest in life, as the hart panteth after the water-brooks, and dig for it more earnestly than for hid treasures.[2] With most women, probably, this phase comes at some epoch in their course; with numbers, alas, it never passes into any other. Some rush to charity, and do partial good or much mischief; some find solace in literary interests and work, and these, though the fewest, are perhaps the most fortunate of all; some seek in the excessive development of the religious affections a pale ideal substitute for the denied human ones—a substitute of which God forbid that we should speak slightingly, but which is seldom wholly satisfactory or wholly safe. Lastly, as we ascend into the highest ranks of all, we come upon crowds of the same unfulfilled destinies—the same *existences manquées*[3]—women who have gay society,[4] but no sacred or suffering home, whose dreary round of pleasure is yet sadder, less remunerative, and less satisfying, than the dreary round of toil trodden by their humble sisters. The very being of all these various classes is a standing proof of, and protest against, that "something wrong," on which we have a few words to say—that besetting problem which, like the sphinx's,[5] society must solve or die. …

[1] *husbandman* Farmer.

[2] *as the hart … water-brooks* Expression of longing for God in Psalm 42.1; *dig for … hid treasures* Description of longing for death in Job 3.21.

[3] *existences manquées* French: lost lives.

[4] *gay society* Pleasant, carefree social circle.

[5] *sphinx* Mythical creature said to guard the entrance to the Greek city of Thebes. She posed a riddle to all travelers attempting to enter the city and killed those unable to solve it.

… Therefore it is that all those efforts, on which chivalric or compassionate benevolence is now so intent, to render single life as easy, as attractive, and as lucrative to women, as unhappily other influences to which we have alluded have already made it to men, *are efforts in a wrong direction*—spontaneous and natural, no doubt, to the tender heart of humanity, which always seeks first to relieve suffering, and only at a later date begins to think of curing disorder—but not to be smiled upon or aided by wise prescribers for the maladies of states. … To endeavour to make women independent of men; to multiply and facilitate their employments; to enable them to earn a separate and ample subsistence by competing with the hardier sex in those careers and occupations hitherto set apart for that sex alone; to induct them generally into avocations, not only as interesting and beneficent, and therefore *appropriate*, but specially and definitely as *lucrative*; to surround single life for them with so smooth an entrance, and such a pleasant, ornamented, comfortable path, that marriage shall almost come to be regarded, not as their most honourable function and especial calling, but merely as one of many ways open to them, competing on equal terms with other ways for their cold and philosophic choice: this would appear to be the aim and theory of many female reformers. …

from Frances Power Cobbe, "What Shall We Do with Our Old Maids?" (1862)

… It appears that there is a natural excess of four or five per cent of females over the males in our population. This, then, might be assumed to be the limits within which female celibacy was normal and inevitable.

There is, however, an actual ratio of thirty per cent of women now in England who never marry, leaving one-fourth of both sexes in a state of celibacy. This proportion further appears to be constantly on the increase. It is obvious enough that these facts call for a revision of many of our social arrangements. The old assumption that marriage was the sole destiny of woman, and that it was the business of her husband to afford her support, is brought up short by the statement that one woman in four is certain not to marry, and that three millions of women earn their own living at this moment in England. We may view the case two ways: either—

1st, We must frankly accept this new state of things, and educate women and modify trade in accordance therewith, so as to make the condition of celibacy as little injurious as possible; or—

2nd, We must set ourselves vigorously to stop the current which is leading men and women away from the natural order of Providence. We must do nothing whatever to render celibacy easy or attractive; and we must make the utmost efforts to promote marriage by emigration of women to the colonies,[1] and all other means in our power.

The second of these views we shall in the first place consider. It may be found to colour the ideas of a vast number of writers, and to influence essentially the decisions made on many points—as the admission of women to university degrees, to the medical profession, and generally to free competition in employment. Lately it has met a powerful and not unkindly exposition in an article in a contemporary quarterly, entitled, "Why Are Women Redundant?" Therein it is plainly set forth that all efforts to make celibacy easy for women are labours in a wrong direction, and are to be likened to the noxious exertions of quacks to mitigate the symptoms of disease, and allow the patient to persist in his evil courses. …

A little deeper reflection, however, discloses a very important point which has been dropped out of the argument. Marriage is, indeed, the happiest and best condition for mankind. But does anyone think that all marriages are so? When we make the assertion that marriage is good and virtuous, do we mean a marriage of interest,[2] a marriage for wealth, for position, for rank, for support? Surely nothing of the kind. Such marriages as these are the sources of misery and sin, not of happiness and virtue, nay, their moral character, to be fitly designated, would require stronger words than we care to use. There is only one kind of marriage which makes good the assertion that it is the right and happy condition for mankind, and that is a marriage founded on free choice, esteem, and affection—in one word, on love. If, then, we seek to promote the happiness and virtue of the community, our efforts must be directed to encouraging *only* marriages which are of the sort to produce them—namely, marriages founded on love. All marriages founded on interest, on the desire for position, support, or the like, we must discourage to the utmost of our power, as the sources of nothing but wretchedness. Where, now, have we reached? Is it not to the conclusion that to make it a woman's *interest* to marry, to force her, by barring out every means of self-support and all fairly remunerative labour, to look to marriage as her sole chance of competency, is precisely to drive her into one of those sinful and unhappy marriages? It is quite clear we can never drive her into *love*. That is a sentiment which poverty, friendlessness, and helplessness can by no means call out. Nor, on the contrary, can competence and freedom in any way check it. It will arise under its natural conditions, if we will but leave the matter alone. A loving marriage can never become a matter of "cold philosophic choice."[3] And if *not* a loving one, then, for Heaven's sake, let us give no motive for choice at all.

Let the employments of women be raised and multiplied as much as possible, let their labour be as fairly remunerated, let their education be pushed as high, let their whole position be made as healthy and happy as possible, and there will come out once more, here as in every other department of life, the triumph of the Divine laws of our nature. Loving marriages are (we cannot doubt) what God has designed, not marriages of interest. When we have made it *less* women's interest to marry, we shall indeed have less and fewer interested marriages, with all their train of miseries and evils. But we shall also have more *loving* ones, more marriages founded on free choice and free affection. Thus we

[1] *emigration of … the colonies* One course of action recommended in "Why Are Women Redundant?" by William Rathbone Greg, the article to which Cobbe is responding. A selection from Greg's article is reproduced above.

[2] *interest* I.e., self-interest.

[3] *cold philosophic choice* Phrase used by Greg in "Why Are Women Redundant?"

arrive at the conclusion that for the very end of promoting marriage—that is, such marriage as it is alone desirable to promote—we should pursue a precisely opposite course to that suggested by the Reviewer or his party. Instead of leaving single women as helpless as possible, and their labour as ill-rewarded—instead of dinning into their ears from childhood that marriage is their one vocation and concern in life, and securing afterwards if they miss it that they shall find no other vocation or concern—instead of all this, we shall act exactly on the reverse principle. We shall make single life so free and happy that they shall have not one temptation to change it save the only temptation which *ought* to determine them—namely, love. Instead of making marriage a case of "Hobson's choice"[1] for a woman, we shall endeavour to give her such independence of all interested considerations that she may make it a choice, not indeed "cold and philosophic," but warm from the heart, and guided by heart and conscience only.

from Eliza Lynn Linton, "The Girl of the Period," *Saturday Review* (March 1868)

Time was when the stereotyped phrase "a fair young English girl" meant the ideal of womanhood, to us, at least, of home birth and breeding. It meant a creature generous, capable, and modest; something franker than a Frenchwoman, more to be trusted than an Italian, as brave as an American but more refined, as domestic as a German and more graceful. It meant a girl who could be trusted alone if need be, because of the innate purity and dignity of her nature, but who was neither bold in bearing nor masculine in mind; a girl who, when she married, would be her husband's friend and companion, but never his rival; one who would consider their interests identical, and not hold him as just so much fair game for spoil; who would make his house his true home and place of rest, not a mere passage-place for vanity and ostentation to go through; a tender mother, an industrious housekeeper, a judicious mistress. We prided ourselves as a nation on our women. We thought we had the pick of creation in this fair young English girl of ours, and envied no other men their own. … This was in the old time, and when English girls were content to be what God and nature had made them. Of late years we have changed the pattern, and have given to the world a race of women as utterly unlike the old insular ideal as if we had created another nation altogether. The girl of the period and the fair young English girl of the past have nothing in common save ancestry and their mother-tongue; and even of this last the modern version makes almost a new language, through the copious additions it has received from the current slang of the day.

The girl of the period is a creature who dyes her hair and paints her face, as the first articles of her personal religion; whose sole idea of life is plenty of fun and luxury; and whose dress is the object of such thought and intellect as she possesses. Her main endeavour in this is to outvie her neighbours in the extravagance of fashion. No matter whether, as in the time of crinolines, she sacrificed decency, or, as now, in the time of trains, she sacrifices cleanliness; no matter either, whether she makes herself a nuisance and an inconvenience to every one she meets. The girl of the period has done away with such moral muffishness[2] as consideration for others, or regard for counsel and rebuke. It was all very well in old-fashioned times, when fathers and mothers had some authority and were treated with respect, to be tutored and made to obey, but she is far too fast and flourishing to be stopped in mid-career by these slow old morals; and as she dresses to please herself, she does not care if she displeases everyone else. Nothing is too extraordinary and nothing too exaggerated for her vitiated[3] taste; and things which in themselves would be useful reforms if let alone become monstrosities worse than those which they have displaced so soon as she begins to manipulate and improve. If a sensible fashion lifts the gown out of the mud, she raises hers midway to

[1] *Hobson's choice* Choice in which only one thing is offered, and one must accept it or make do with nothing.

[2] *muffishness* Foolishness, often describing someone or something seen as old-fashioned.

[3] *vitiated* Corrupted.

June 14, 1884.] PUNCH, OR THE LONDON CHARIVARI. 279
THE ANGEL IN 'THE HOUSE;' OR, THE RESULT OF FEMALE SUFFRAGE.
(A Troubled Dream of the Future.)

This cartoon appeared in the 14 June 1884 edition of *Punch*. A satirical representation of the suffragist, here having gained the vote and a position of political power, speaking in the House of Commons. She is knitting a "blue stocking," an allusion to the term "bluestocking," a derogatory term that began to be applied to free-thinking women in the eighteenth century.

her knee. If the absurd structure of wire and buckram, once called a bonnet, is modified to something that shall protect the wearer's face without putting out the eyes of her companion, she cuts hers down to four straws and a rosebud, or a tag of lace and a bunch of glass beads! … She has blunted the fine edges of feeling so much that she cannot understand why she should be condemned for an imitation of form which does not include imitation of fact; she cannot be made to see that modesty of appearance and virtue ought to be inseparable, and that no good girl can afford to appear bad, under penalty of receiving the contempt awarded to the bad.

This imitation of the *demi-monde*[1] in dress leads to something in manner and feeling, not quite so pronounced perhaps, but far too like to be honourable to herself or satisfactory to her friends. It leads to slang, bold talk, and fastness; to the love of pleasure and indifference to duty; to the desire of money before either love or happiness; to uselessness at home, dissatisfaction

[1] *demi-monde* French: literally, "half world"; figuratively, the world existing below the level of respectable society. The term was often used to denote the world of the courtesan.

with the monotony of ordinary life, and horror of all useful work; in a word, to the worst forms of luxury and selfishness, to the most fatal effects arising from want of high principle and absence of tender feeling. … No one can say of the modern English girl that she is tender, loving, retiring, or domestic. The old fault so often found by keen-sighted Frenchwomen, that she was so fatally *romanesque*,[1] so prone to sacrifice appearances and social advantages for love, will never be set down to the girl of the period. Love indeed is the last thing she thinks of, and the least of the dangers besetting her. Love in a cottage, that seductive dream which used to vex the heart and disturb the calculations of prudent mothers, is now a myth of past ages. The legal barter of herself for so much money, representing so much dash, so much luxury and pleasure—that is her idea of marriage; the only idea worth entertaining. For all seriousness of thought respecting the duties or the consequences of marriage, she has not a trace. If children come, they find but a stepmother's cold welcome from her; and if her husband thinks that he has married anything that is to belong to him—a *tacens et placens uxor*[2] pledged to make him happy—the sooner he wakes from his hallucination and understands that he has simply married someone who will condescend to spend his money on herself, and who will shelter her indiscretions behind the shield of his name, the less severe will be his disappointment. She has married his house, his carriage, his balance at the bankers, his title; and he himself is just the inevitable condition clogging the wheel of her fortune; at best an adjunct, to be tolerated with more or less patience as may chance. For it is only the old-fashioned sort, not girls of the period *pur sang*,[3] that marry for love, or put the husband before the banker. But she does not marry easily. Men are afraid of her; and with reason. They may amuse themselves with her of an evening, but they do not take her readily for life. …

The marvel, in the present fashion of life among women, is how it holds its ground in spite of the disapprobation of men. It used to be an old-time notion that the sexes were made for each other, and that it was only natural for them to please each other, and to set themselves out for that end. But the girl of the period does not please men. She pleases them as little as she elevates them; and how little she does that, the class of women she has taken as her models of itself testifies. All men whose opinion is worth having prefer the simple and genuine girl of the past, with her tender little ways and pretty bashful modesties, to this loud and rampant modernization, with her false red hair and painted skin, talking slang as glibly as a man, and by preference leading the conversation to doubtful subjects. She thinks she is piquante[4] and exciting when she thus makes herself the bad copy of a worse original; and she will not see that though men laugh with her they do not respect her, though they flirt with her they do not marry her; she will not believe that she is not the kind of thing they want, and that she is acting against nature and her own interests when she disregards their advice and offends their taste. We do not see how she makes out her account, viewing her life from any side; but all we can do is to wait patiently until the national madness has passed, and our women have come back again to the old English ideal, once the most beautiful, the most modest, the most essentially womanly in the world.

from Frances Power Cobbe, "Criminals, Idiots, Women, and Minors," *Fraser's Magazine* (December 1868)

There was an allegory rather popular about thirty years ago, whose manifest purpose was to impress on the juvenile mind that tendency which Mr. Matthew Arnold has ingeniously designated "Hebraism."[5] The

[1] *romanesque* French: romantic.

[2] *tacens … uxor* Latin: silent and pleasing wife.

[3] *pur sang* French: pure-blooded.

[4] *piquante* Stimulating.

[5] *Hebraism* Originally denoting an attribute of the Hebrew people, the term was used by Arnold to describe a moral (rather than intellectual) theory of life. Arnold used the term "Hellenistic," in contrast, to denote the intellectual culture or way of life typified by the ancient Greeks.

hero of the tale descends upon earth from some distant planet, and is conducted by a mundane cicerone[1] through one of our great cities, where he beholds the docks and arsenals, the streets and marts, the galleries of art, and the palaces of royalty. The visitor admires everything till he happens to pass a graveyard. "What is that gloomy spot?" he asks of his companion. "It is a cemetery," replies the guide.

"A—what did you say?" inquires the son of the star.

"A graveyard; a place of public interment; where we bury our dead," reiterates the cicerone.

The visitor, pale with awe and terror, learns at last that there is in this world such a thing as *Death*, and (as he is forbidden to return to his own planet) he resolves to dedicate every moment left to him to prepare himself for that fearful event and all that may follow it.

Had that visitor heard for the first time upon his arrival on earth of another incident of human existence—namely, *Marriage*, it may be surmised that his astonishment and awe would also have been considerable. To his eager inquiry whether men and women earnestly strove to prepare themselves for so momentous an occurrence, he would have received the puzzling reply that women frequently devoted themselves with perfectly Hebraistic singleness of aim to that special purpose; but that men, on the contrary, very rarely included any preparation for the married state among the items of their widest Hellenistic culture. But this anomaly would be trifling compared to others which would be revealed to him. "Ah," we can hear him say to his guide as they pass into a village church. "What a pretty sight is this! What is happening to that sweet young woman in white who is giving her hand to the good-looking fellow beside her, all the company decked in holiday attire, and the joy-bells shaking the old tower overhead? She is receiving some great honour, is she not? The Prize of Virtue, perhaps?"

"Oh, yes," would reply the friend; "an honour certainly. She is being Married." After a little further explanation the visitor would pursue his inquiry:

"Of course, having entered this honourable state of matrimony, she has some privilege above the women who are not chosen by anybody? I notice her husband has just said, 'With all my worldly goods I thee endow.' Does that mean that she will henceforth have the control of his money altogether, or only that he takes her into partnership?"

"*Pas précisément*,[2] my dear sir. By our law it is *her* goods and earnings, present and future, which belong to him from this moment."

"You don't say so? But then, of course, his goods are hers also?"

"Oh dear, no! not at all. He is only bound to find her food; and truth to tell, not very strictly or efficaciously bound to do that."

"How! do I understand you? Is it possible that here in the most solemn religious act, which I perceive your prayer book calls 'The Solemnisation of Holy Matrimony,' every husband makes a generous promise, which promise is not only a mockery, but the actual reverse and parody of the real state of the case: the man who promises giving nothing, and the woman who is silent giving all?"

"Well, yes; I suppose that is something like it, as to the letter of the law. But then, of course, practically—"

"Practically, I suppose few men can really be so unmanly and selfish as the law warrants them in being. Yet some, I fear, may avail themselves of such authority. May I ask another question? As you subject women who enter the marriage state to such very severe penalties as this, what worse have you in store for women who lead a dissolute life, to the moral injury of the community?"

"Oh, the law takes nothing from them. Whatever they earn or inherit is their own. They are able, also, to sue the fathers of their children for their maintenance, which a wife, of course, is not allowed to do on behalf of *her* little ones, because she and her husband are one in the eye of the law."

"One question still further—your criminals? Do they always forfeit their entire property on conviction?"

---

[1] *cicerone* Guide.

[2] *Pas précisément* French: Not exactly.

"Only for the most heinous crimes; felony and murder, for example."

"Pardon me; I must seem to you so stupid! Why is the property of the woman who commits Murder, and the property of the woman who commits Matrimony, dealt with alike by your law?"

Leaving our little allegory and in sober seriousness, we must all admit that the just and expedient treatment of women by men is one of the most obscure problems, alike of equity and of policy. Nor of women only, but of all classes and races of human beings whose condition is temporarily or permanently one of comparative weakness and dependence. …

By the common law of England a married woman has no legal existence, so far as property is concerned, independently of her husband. The husband and wife are assumed to be one person, and that person is the husband. The wife can make no contract, and can neither sue nor be sued. Whatever she possess of personal property at the time of her marriage, or whatever she may afterwards earn or inherit, belongs to her husband, without control on her part. … If she possess real estate, so long as her husband lives he receives and spends the income derived from it, being only forbidden to sell it without her consent. From none of her property is he bound to reserve anything, or make any provision for her maintenance or that of her children. This is the law for all, but practically it affects only two classes of women, *viz.*[1] those who marry hurriedly or without proper advisers, and those whose property at the time of marriage is too small to permit of the expense of a settlement; in other words, the whole middle and lower ranks of women, and a certain portion of the upper ranks. Women of the richer class, with proper advisers, never come under the provisions of the Common Law, being carefully protected therefrom by an intricate system elaborated for the purpose by the courts of Equity, to which the victims of the Common Law have for years applied for redress. That system always involves considerable legal expenses, and an arrangement with trustees which is often extremely inconvenient and injurious to the interests of the married couple; nevertheless it is understood to be so great a boon that none who can afford to avail themselves of it fail to do so.

What then is the principle on which the Common Law mulcts[2] the poorer class of women of their property and earnings, and entails on the rich, if they wish to evade it, the costs and embarrassment of a marriage settlement? There is, of course, a principle in it, and one capable of clear statement. There are grounds for the law; first of Justice, then of Expediency, lastly (and as we believe) most influential of all, of Sentiment.

First, the grounds of Justice.

Man is the natural bread-winner. Woman lives by the bread which man has earned. Ergo, it is fit and right that the man who wins should have absolute disposal, not only of his winnings, but of every other small morsel or fraction of earning or property she may possess. It is a fair return to him for his labour in the joint interests of both. … The woman's case is that of a pauper who enters a workhouse. The ratepayers are bound to support him; but if he have any savings they must be given up to the board. HE cannot claim support and keep independent property.

Then for Expediency. "How can two walk together except they be agreed?" says the Bible. "How can they walk together except one of them have it all his own way?" says the voice of rough and ready practicality. Somebody must rule in a household, or everything will go to rack and ruin; and disputes will be endless. If somebody is to rule it can only be the husband, who is wiser, stronger, knows more of the world, and in any case has not the slightest intention of yielding his predominance. But to give a man such rule he must be allowed to keep the purse. Nothing but the power of the purse—in default of the stick—can permanently and thoroughly secure authority. …

Lastly, for the sentimental view. How painful is the notion of a wife holding back her money from him who is every day toiling for her support! How fair is the ideal

[1] *viz.* Latin: namely; that is to say (an abbreviation of *videlicet*).

[2] *mulcts* Swindles.

picture of absolute concession on her part of all she possesses of this world's dross to the man to whom she gives her heart and life! … The young man and maiden, after years of affection, and carefully laying by of provision for the event, take each other at last, to be henceforth no more twain, but one flesh. Both have saved a little money, but it now belongs to the husband alone. He lays it out in the purchase of a cottage where they are henceforth to dwell. Day by day he goes forth to his labour, and weekly he brings home his earnings and places them in his wife's lap, bidding her spend them as she knows best for the supply of their homely board, their clothing which her deft fingers will make and many a time repair, and last for their common treasures, the little children who gather around them. Thus they grow old in unbroken peace and love, the man's will having never once been disputed, the wide yielding alike from choice and from necessity to his superior sense and his legal authority.

Surely this idea of life, for which the Common Law of England has done its utmost to provide, is well worth the pondering before we attempt to meddle with any of its safeguards? Who will suggest anything better in its room?

Alas, there are other scenes besides idylls of domestic peace and obedience promoted by the laws we are considering. …

The existing Common Law is not *Just*, because it neither can secure nor actually even attempts to secure for the woman the equivalent support for whose sake she is forced to relinquish her property.

It is not *Expedient*, because while in happy marriages it is superfluous and useless, in unhappy ones it becomes highly injurious; often causing the final ruin of a family which the mother (if upheld by law) might have supported single-handed. It is also shown not to be considered expedient by the conduct of the entire upper class of the country, and even of the legislature itself in the system of the Court of Chancery. Where no one who can afford to evade the law fails to evade it, the pretence that it is believed to be generally expedient is absurd. Further, the classes which actually evade it, and the countries where it is non-existing, show in no degree less connubial harmony than those wherein it is enforced.

Lastly, it does not tend to fulfil, but to counteract, the *Sentiment* regarding the marriage union, to which it aims to add the pressure of force. Real unanimity is not produced between two parties by forbidding one of them to have any voice at all. The hard mechanical contrivance of the law for making husband and wife of one heart and mind is calculated to produce a precisely opposite result.

from "Between School and Marriage," *The Girl's Own Paper* (4 September 1886)

This time in a girl's life corresponds to that in a man's which is passed in a university, or in learning the work of his profession. Too many girls look on it as a *mauvais quart d'heure*,[1] which may be dawdled through in an irresponsible way until they have a house of their own. Marriage represents a home, a position; sometimes even less than that—a trousseau,[2] or a wedding tour. So they hasten through the years of adolescence as well as may be in order to reach the end of a wearisome task.

And yet if the girl is mother to the woman—that is to say, if the woman will be what the girl now is, this time, which is essentially one for settling habits, cannot be anything less than the most important in life. If the girl spend it in thoughtless idleness and discontented trifling, the result will be seen in the character of the woman. It is well for any of us when our work is cut out for us, so to speak, and we have not to look about for a profitable way of passing the time; but this last is the miserable condition of many girls belonging to daughter-full houses in easy circumstances. What can they do between school and marriage?

When the financial resources of her father are slender, a girl is quite right to seek for some employment by which she may earn her own living, and

[1] *mauvais quart d'heure* French: an unpleasant time (literally, an unpleasant quarter of an hour), from the French expression "*passer un mauvais quart d'heure*," meaning "to have a bad time of it."

[2] *trousseau* A bride's collection of clothing and linens.

The Girl's Own Paper, sold weekly for a penny, was mainly marketed to working- and middle-class women, but it was read by women from all classes and age groups and soon after its founding reached a circulation of over 250,000.

perhaps help her brothers and sisters; but when this is not the case, let no feeling of quixotic restlessness induce her to rashly leave home. It may be her plain duty to remain at home, and she may be independent and pay her way quite as much as one who earns and pays current coin. She can pay her way by filling in the little spaces in home life as only a dear daughter can, by lifting the weight of care from her mother, and by slipping in a soft word or a smile where it is like oil on the troubled waters of a father's spirit. What better remuneration can a father have for his expenditure upon his daughters than their laughter, good humour, and sympathy?…

from Emma Brewer, "Our Friends the Servants," *The Girl's Own Paper* (25 March 1893)

Among mistresses who earnestly desire the welfare of their servants there is no question which causes more trouble and anxiety than that of allowing visitors in the kitchen, men visitors especially. It is indeed a difficult question, and cannot be solved for every one alike.

I know several ladies who have thought it right that such of their maids as were engaged should be permitted to receive their sweethearts from time to time in the kitchen; but in every case where this has been granted that has come under my notice, the results have been so disastrous as to necessitate the withdrawal of the privilege. It was found utterly destructive of harmony in the kitchen, and gave no real pleasure to anyone. In some cases the fickle men forsook their old love in favour of some younger and more attractive of the fellow-servants, and it is not difficult to imagine the bitterness, anger, and sharp words which became the fashion after such faithlessness.

In others the sweethearts borrowed money of all the foolish girls in order to lay it upon horses in which they were interested; in others, where more stimulant had been taken than was good for them, they have boasted among other men of the beautiful silver, etc., in the houses where their young women lived, with what results may be guessed.

In simple fairness the privilege cannot be granted to one without extending it to all; this, in many houses, would fill the kitchens of an evening; for no maid would acknowledge that she had no young man, and would get one on the spot without considering his character, and such a one would scarcely add to the safety or morality of the kitchen....

There are a few things in the relationship between mistress and maid which distress me greatly, because I know they are utterly destructive of home-peace and comfort; one is a mistress reproving her servant in public, another is a maid answering her mistress rudely, and a third is a mistress finding fault with servants out of the room to one who is waiting in the room.

No good servant would endure the first nor be guilty of the second, but one and all are evil in their result, and it is easy to see that, let the fault be what it may, it cannot be remedied in this fashion.

Servants have feelings to be wounded and rights to be respected, and when these are ignored they feel that their occupation is compromising to their respectability and freedom.

We lose many good servants in this way, and get in their place large importations of very inferior ones from the Continent. It gives one a feeling of sadness that while the mother country stands in increased need of good and trustworthy servants, she cannot retain them or make friends of them, but has to look on while her colonies attract those she herself would so gladly keep.

I do not know if all are aware that every month ships leave England with a number of servants on board; indeed, as many as fourteen vessels go over to Queensland alone, carrying, on an average, two hundred servants on each ship. Any young woman with good health and good character can get a free passage to Queensland if she is under thirty-five years of age. This colony, even above others, values highly our friends the servants, whose success is undoubted. They try to live up to the high opinion formed of them, but it is grievous to see them leaving the old country which wants them even more than the colonies.

from Grant Allen, "Plain Words on the Woman Question," *Fortnightly Review* (October 1889)

... Almost every woman must bear four or five children.[1] In doing so she must on the average use up the ten or twelve best years of her life: the ten or twelve years that immediately succeed her attainment of complete womanhood. ... Again, during these ten or twelve years of child-bearing at the very least, the women can't conveniently earn their own livelihood; they must be provided for by the labour of the men. ... It is true that in the very lowest state of savagery special provision is seldom made by the men for the women even during the periods of pregnancy, childbirth, and infancy of the offspring. The women must live (as among the Hottentots[2]) over the worst of these periods on their own stored-up stock of fat, like hibernating bears or desert camels. It is true also that among savage races generally the women have to work as hard as the men, though the men bear in most cases the larger share in providing actual food for the entire family. But in civilised communities—and the more so in proportion to their degree of civilisation—the men do most of the hardest work, and in particular take upon themselves the duty of providing for the wives and children. The higher the type, the longer are the wives and children provided for. Analogy would lead one to suppose (with Comte[3]) that in the highest communities the men would do all the work, and the women would be left entirely free to undertake the management and education of the children. ...

Seeing, then, that these necessities are laid by the very nature of our organization upon women, it would appear as though two duties were clearly imposed upon the women themselves, and upon all those men who

[1] *Almost every ... five children* Earlier in the essay, Allen presents statistics to support his argument that women must maintain this average in order for the population to remain stable.

[2] *Hottentots* European term (now recognized as offensive) for the Khoikhoi people of southwestern Africa.

[3] *Comte* French philosopher Auguste Comte (1798–1857) wrote that in an ideal society women would be wholly isolated from political and material concerns in order to serve as parents and moral guardians.

sympathize in their welfare: First, to see that their training and education should fit them above everything else for this their main function in life; and, second, that in consideration of the special burden they have to bear in connection with reproduction, all the rest of life should be made as light and easy and free for them as possible. We ought frankly to recognise that most women must be wives and mothers: that most women should therefore be trained, physically, morally, socially, and mentally, in the way best fitting them to be wives and mothers; and that all such women have a right to the fullest and most generous support in carrying out their functions as wives and mothers.

And here it is that we seem to come in conflict for a moment with most of the modern Woman-Question agitators. …

For what is the ideal that most of these modern woman agitators set before them? Is it not clearly the ideal of an unsexed woman? Are they not always talking to us as though it were not the fact that most women must be wives and mothers?… A woman ought to be ashamed to say she has no desire to become a wife and mother. Many such women there are no doubt—it is to be feared, with our existing training, far too many: but instead of boasting of their sexlessness as a matter of pride, they ought to keep it dark, and to be ashamed of it—as ashamed as a man in a like predicament would be of his impotence. They ought to feel they have fallen short of the healthy instincts of their kind, instead of posing as in some sense the cream of the universe, on the strength of what is really a functional aberration.

Unfortunately, however, just at the present moment, a considerable number of the ablest women have been misled into taking this unfeminine side, and becoming real "traitors to their sex" in so far as they endeavour to assimilate women to men in everything, and to put upon their shoulders, as a glory and privilege, the burden of their own support. …

from Sarah Grand, "The New Aspect of the Woman Question," *North American Review* (March 1894)

… What [the new woman] perceived at the outset was the sudden and violent upheaval of the suffering sex in all parts of the world. Women were awakening from their long apathy, and, as they woke, like healthy hungry children unable to articulate, they began to whimper for they knew not what. They might have been easily satisfied at that time had not society, like an ill-conditioned and ignorant nurse, instead of finding out what they lacked, shaken them and beaten them and stormed at them until what was once a little wail became convulsive shrieks and roused up the whole human household. Then man, disturbed by the uproar, came upstairs all anger and irritation, and, without waiting to learn what was the matter, added his own old theories to the din, but, finding they did not act rapidly, formed new ones, and made an intolerable nuisance of himself with his opinions and advice. He was in the state of one who cannot comprehend because he has no faculty to perceive the thing in question, and that is why he was so positive. The dimmest perception that you may be mistaken will save you from making an ass of yourself.

We must look upon man's mistakes, however, with some leniency, because we are not blameless in the matter ourselves. We have allowed him to arrange the whole social system and manage or mismanage it all these ages without ever seriously examining his work with a view to considering whether his abilities or motives were sufficiently good to qualify him for the task. We have listened without a smile to his preachments, about our place in life and all we are good for, on the text that "there is no understanding a woman." We have endured most poignant misery for his sins, and screened him when we should have exposed him and had him punished. We have allowed him to exact all things of us, and have been content to accept the little he grudgingly gave us in return. We have meekly bowed our heads when he called us bad names instead of demanding proofs of the superiority which alone would give him a right to do so. We have listened much edified to man's sermons on the subject of virtue, and have acquiesced uncomplainingly in the convenient arrangement by which this quality has come to be altogether practised for him by us vicariously. We have seen him set up Christ as an example for all men to follow, which argues his belief in the possibility of doing so, and have not only allowed his weakness and hypocrisy in the matter to pass without comment, but, until lately, have not even seen the humor of his pretensions when contrasted with his practices, nor held him up to that wholesome ridicule which is a stimulating corrective. Man deprived us of all proper education, and then jeered at us because we had no knowledge. He narrowed our outlook on life so that our view of it should be all distorted, and then declared that our mistaken impression of it proved us to be senseless creatures. He cramped our minds so that there was no room for reason in them, and then made merry at our want of logic. Our divine intuition was not to be controlled by him, but he did his best to damage it by sneering at it as an inferior feminine method of arriving at conclusions; and finally, after having had his own way until he lost his head completely, he set himself up as a sort of god and required us to worship him, and to our eternal shame be it said, we did so. The truth has all along been in us, but we have cared more for man than for truth, and so the whole human race has suffered. We have failed of our effect by neglecting our duty here, and have deserved much of the obloquy that was cast upon us. All that is over now, however, and while on the one hand man has shrunk to his true proportions in our estimation, we, on the other, have been expanding to our own; and now we come confidently forward to maintain, not that this or that was "intended," but that there are in ourselves, in both sexes, possibilities hitherto suppressed or abused, which, when properly developed, will supply to either what is lacking in the other.

The man of the future will be better, while the woman will be stronger and wiser. To bring this about is the whole aim and object of the present struggle, and with the discovery of the means lies the solution of the Woman Question. Man, having no conception of himself as imperfect from the woman's point of view, will find this difficult to understand, but we know his weakness, and will be patient with him, and help him with his lesson. It is the woman's place and pride and pleasure to teach the child, and man morally is in his infancy. There have been times when there was a doubt as to whether he was to be raised or woman was to be lowered, but we have turned that corner at last; and now woman holds out a strong hand to the child-man, and insists, but with infinite tenderness and pity, upon helping him up. …

from Mona Caird, "Does Marriage Hinder a Woman's Self-Development?" *Lady's Realm* (March 1899)

Perhaps it might throw some light on the question whether marriage interferes with a woman's self-development and career, if we were to ask ourselves honestly how a man would fare in the position, say, of his own wife.

We will take a mild case, so as to avoid all risk of exaggeration.

Our hero's wife is very kind to him. Many of his friends have far sadder tales to tell. Mrs. Brown is fond of her home and family. She pats the children on the head when they come down to dessert, and plies them with chocolate creams, much to the detriment of their health; but it amuses Mrs. Brown. Mr. Brown superintends the bilous[1] attacks, which the lady attributes to other causes. As she never finds fault with the children, and generally remonstrates with their father, in a good-natured way, when *he* does so, they are devoted to the indulgent parent, and are inclined to regard the other as second-rate. …

John's faded cheeks, the hollow lines under the eyes, and hair out of curl, speak of the struggle for existence as it penetrates to the fireside. If Sophia but knew what it meant to keep going the multitudinous details and departments of a household! …

[1] *bilous* Angry, peevish.

If incessant vigilance, tact, firmness, foresight, initiative, courage and judgment—in short, all the qualities required for governing a kingdom, and more—have made things go smoothly, the wife takes it as a matter of course; if they go wrong, she naturally lays the blame on the husband. In the same way, if the children are a credit to their parents, that is only as it should be. But if they are naughty, and fretful, and stupid, and untidy, is it not clear that there must be some serious flaw in the system which could produce such results in the offspring of Mrs. Brown? What word in the English language is too severe to describe the man who neglects to watch with sufficient vigilance over his children's health and moral training, who fails to see that his little boys' sailor-suits and knickerbockers are in good repair, that their bootlace ends do not fly out from their ankles at every step, that their hair is not like a hearth-brush, that they do not come down to dinner every day with dirty hands?

To every true man, the cares of fatherhood and home are sacred and all-sufficing. He realizes, as he looks around at his little ones, that they are his crown and recompense.

John often finds that *his* crown-and-recompense gives him a racking headache by war-whoops and stampedes of infinite variety, and there are moments when he wonders in dismay if he is really a true man! He has had the privilege of rearing and training five small crowns and recompenses, and he feels that he could face the future if further privilege, of this sort, were denied him. Not but that he is devoted to his family. Nobody who understands the sacrifices he has made for them could doubt that. Only, he feels that those parts of his nature which are said to distinguish the human from the animal kingdom are getting rather effaced.

He remembers the days before his marriage, when he was so bold, in his ignorant youth, as to cherish a passion for scientific research. He even went so far as to make a chemical laboratory of the family box-room, till attention was drawn to the circumstance by a series of terrific explosions, which shaved off his eyebrows, blackened his scientific countenance, and caused him to be turned out, neck and crop, with his crucibles, and a sermon on the duty that lay nearest him.… His own bent, however, has always been so painfully strong that he even yet tries to snatch spare moments for his researches; but the strain in so many directions has broken down his health. People always told him that a man's constitution was not fitted for severe brain-work. He supposes it is true.…

John still hoped, after twenty years of experience, that presently, by some different arrangement, some better management on his part, he would achieve leisure and mental repose to do the work that his heart was in; but that time never came.

No doubt John was not infallible, and made mistakes in dealing with his various problems: do the best of us achieve consummate wisdom? No doubt, if he had followed the advice that we could all have supplied him with, in such large quantities, he might have done rather more than he did. But the question is: Did his marriage interfere with his self-development and career, and would many other Johns, in his circumstances, have succeeded much better?

ELIZABETH BARRETT BROWNING

1806 – 1861

Now widely considered one of the foremost poets of the Victorian era, Elizabeth Barrett Browning was equally highly regarded in her day, admired by contemporaries such as Wordsworth and Dickinson, critics, and the general public alike. Strongly associated in popular consciousness with the romantic vision of her *Sonnets from the Portuguese*—"How do I love thee? Let me count the ways," the first line of "Sonnet 43," remains one of the most famous lines in English literature—she was also a boldly political poet with a range of emotion and subject matter extending far beyond the romantic. Many critics consider her greatest achievement to be *Aurora Leigh*, a semiautobiographical long poem in which Barrett Browning articulates her "highest convictions upon Life and Art."

Elizabeth Barrett was the eldest of twelve children born to a wealthy plantation-owning family in Durham, England. Just prior to her birth her parents, Edward Barrett Moulton-Barrett and Mary Graham Clarke Moulton-Barrett, moved from their slave plantation in Jamaica to raise a family in England. The young Barrett grew up in the sheltered environment of a country manor called Hope End, learning languages and studying the classics, at a time when a young woman's education was typically restricted to the domestic sphere. An exceptional and intellectually voracious student, Barrett learned Latin, Greek, and French from her brothers' tutors and studied philosophical, historical, and religious works on her own. She had read Milton's *Paradise Lost* by the time she was 10 years old and, encouraged by her parents, anonymously published her first poem, an epic entitled *The Battle of Marathon*, a few years later. In 1826, she published *An Essay on Mind and Other Poems*. In 1833 she published her translation from the Greek of Aeschylus' *Prometheus Bound*; she also included some of her own poems in the volume.

Due to the abolition of slavery, the Barretts' fortune began to wane, and in 1832 they were required to sell Hope End, eventually moving to Wimpole Street in London. Her father was overly protective of his children, however, and Barrett fell into semi-seclusion within the family home; her seclusion was compounded by illnesses that had begun to plague her when she was about 12 years old. Critics speculate as to the exact nature of those illnesses, but there is evidence to suggest that Barrett may have suffered from tuberculosis and possibly from a spinal injury. Her maladies were no doubt exacerbated by the opiates prescribed by doctors and the depression that followed the accidental death of her beloved brother Edward, who had accompanied her while she recuperated in the south of England. This tragedy, and Barrett's subsequent feelings of anguish and guilt, inspired some of her best-known poems, including the elegiac sonnet "Grief."

Much has been written about Barrett's middle years, but the image of the bed-ridden recluse remains somewhat at odds with the prolific reader and writer who wrote poetry, essays, reviews, and criticism for magazines and journals and published *The Seraphim and Other Poems* in 1838. The two-volume collection of her *Poems* published in 1844 contains some of her most politically charged poetry, including "The Cry of the Children," which condemned the employment of children in factories. During these years, Barrett kept up an active correspondence with many writers, critics, and artists and accepted occasional visitors in the confines of her family home. It was in this way that she met Robert Browning, who called upon her after the 1844 collection appeared. He visited her after first writing to express his admiration for work that had already made Barrett famous in England and was rapidly gaining recognition in the United States.

The subsequent exchange of 574 letters between Barrett and Browning, and their eventual elopement have received much attention, with some suggesting that Barrett Browning's best work was inspired by this passionate relationship. It is worth noting here that she had already begun to write love poetry, having translated Petrarch's sonnets and written her own before she met Browning. There is no doubt, however, that the force of their relationship inspired some of her most enduring work, notably her famous *Sonnets from the Portuguese*, written during her courtship with Browning and published in 1850. "My little Portuguese," an allusion to her dark skin, was Browning's pet name for his wife.

Her 1846 marriage to Browning and their ensuing life together in Italy were a boon to Barrett Browning's health and her work. Her beloved father, however, who had forbidden his children to marry, refused to speak to or see his daughter again, going so far as to return her letters unopened. In 1849 the Brownings' only child, Robert Wiedemann Barrett Browning (nicknamed "Pen"), was born in Casa Guidi, just outside Florence.

Not long after the publication of *Sonnets*, Barrett Browning published *Casa Guidi Windows*, which promoted the cause of *Risorgimento*, the Italian struggle for unification and independence from foreign domination (the subject also of many of the later *Poems before Congress*). In 1850, she published the abolition poem "The Runaway Slave at Pilgrim's Point," one of the great dramatic monologues and political-protest poems written in English in the nineteenth century. Barrett Browning's comment on Harriet Beecher Stowe's *Uncle Tom's Cabin* summarizes her consistent response to critics who questioned her choice of subjects: "… is it possible you think a woman has no business with questions like the question of slavery? Then she had better use a pen no more. She had better subside into slavery and concubinage herself, I think, as in the times of old, shut herself up with the Penelopes in the 'women's apartment,' and take no rank among thinkers and speakers."

The 1856 work *Aurora Leigh* further cemented Barrett Browning's immense popularity, even though its candid sexual content and direct treatment of gender inequality were deemed scandalous by many at the time. An ambitious "novel in verse" (as Barrett Browning styled it), *Aurora Leigh* is narrated in nine books of blank verse and is the zenith of Barrett Browning's life work, encompassing her convictions on desire, power, art, love, romance, race, class structures, and the subjugation of women. The independent and progressive heroine of the books is named in part after Barrett Browning's idol, French writer George Sand (née Aurore Dupin), known for her liberal, feminist views and her penchant for wearing men's clothing. Like Sand, and also like Barrett Browning herself, Aurora Leigh is a writer, one who questions her identity as both artist and woman, and who struggles to achieve independence from staid societal mores and yet still preserve the ability to attain love and companionship. As Barrett Browning herself would observe, "never did a book so divide opinions in London. Some persons can't bear it—& others [are] crying it up as what I am too modest to write"; John Ruskin, for example, pronounced it the greatest poem of the century. It would later be praised by Virginia Woolf for capturing essential qualities of the Victorian intellectual landscape: "Aurora Leigh, with her passionate interest in social questions, her conflict as artist and woman, her longing for knowledge and freedom, is the true daughter of her age."

Elizabeth Barrett Browning predeceased her husband by 28 years when she passed away in his arms in 1861; she is buried in the Protestant cemetery in Florence. By the early twentieth century,

Sonnets from the Portuguese was still widely read, but the rest of her work had fallen out of fashion. It remained so, despite praise from Woolf and a few other individual critics, until the growth of feminist criticism in the 1970s, which restored attention to her broader oeuvre; now, her work is as highly valued as it was during her lifetime.

⌘⌘⌘

The Young Queen[1]

"This awful[2] responsibility is imposed upon me so suddenly, and at so early a period of my life, that I should feel myself utterly oppressed by the burden, were I not sustained by the hope that Divine Providence, which has called me to this work, will give me strength for the performance of it."

The Queen's Declaration in Council[3]

The shroud is yet unspread
  To wrap our crownèd dead;
His soul hath scarcely hearkened for the thrilling[4] word of doom;
And Death that makes serene
Ev'n brows where crowns have been,
Hath scarcely time to meeten° his, for silence of the tomb. *prepare*

St. Paul's king-dirging[5] note
The city's heart hath smote—
The city's heart is struck with thought more solemn than the tone!
A shadow sweeps apace° *swiftly*
Before the nation's face,
Confusing in a shapeless blot the sepulchre and throne.

The palace sounds with wail—
The courtly dames are pale—
A widow o'er the purple[6] bows, and weeps its splendour dim:
And we who hold the boon,
A king for freedom won,
Do feel eternity rise up between our thanks and him.

And while all things express
All glory's nothingness,
A royal maiden treadeth firm where that departed trod!
The deathly scented crown
Weighs her shining ringlets down;
But calm she lifts her trusting face, and calleth upon God.

Her thoughts are deep within her:
No outward pageants[7] win her
From memories that in her soul are rolling wave on wave—
Her palace walls enring
The dust that was a king—
And very cold beneath her feet, she feels her father's grave[8]

[1] *The Young Queen* Written in July 1837, this poem responds to the ascension of Victoria to the throne upon the death of her uncle, King William IV. Victoria was only eighteen years old.

[2] *awful* Awe-inspiring; intimidating.

[3] *The Queen's Declaration in Council* From Victoria's first official address as Queen of the United Kingdom, given on 21 June 1837.

[4] *thrilling* Shudder-inducing; frightening.

[5] *St. Paul's* Anglican Cathedral in London, whose bells would have rung to announce the king's death; *king-dirging* A dirge is a funeral song.

[6] *widow* William IV's wife, queen consort Adelaide of Saxe-Meiningen; *purple* Color associated with royalty, and sometimes the color of the cloth used to cover a royal coffin.

[7] *pageants* Performances; false displays.

[8] *father's grave* Victoria's father, Edward, Duke of Kent and Strathearn, had died in 1820.

And One, as fair as she,[1]
Can scarce forgotten be—
Who clasped a little infant dead, for all a kingdom's worth!
The mournèd, blessèd One,
Who views Jehovah's throne,
Aye smiling to the angels, that she lost a throne on earth.

Perhaps our youthful Queen
Remembers what has been—
Her childhood's rest by loving heart, and sport on grassy sod—
Alas! can others wear
A mother's heart for her?
But calm she lifts her trusting face, and calleth upon God

Yea! Call on God, thou maiden
Of spirit nobly laden,
And leave such happy days behind, for happy-making years!
A nation looks to thee
For steadfast sympathy:
Make room within thy bright clear eyes, for all its gathered tears.

And so the grateful isles
Shall give thee back their smiles,
And as thy mother joys in thee, in them shalt thou rejoice;
Rejoice to meekly bow
A somewhat paler brow,
While the King of kings[2] shall bless thee by the British people's voice!
—1837

The Cry of the Children[3]

"Φεῦ, φεῦ, τί προσδέρκεσθέ μ' ὄμμασιν, τέκνα;"[4] —Medea.

1

Do ye hear the children weeping, O my brothers,
Ere the sorrow comes with years?
They are leaning their young heads against their mothers,
And *that* cannot stop their tears.
The young lambs are bleating in the meadows,
The young birds are chirping in the nest,
The young fawns are playing with the shadows,
The young flowers are blowing toward the west—
But the young, young children, O my brothers,
They are weeping bitterly!
They are weeping in the playtime of the others,
In the country of the free.

2

Do you question the young children in the sorrow
Why their tears are falling so?
The old man may weep for his tomorrow
Which is lost in Long Ago;
The old tree is leafless in the forest,
The old year is ending in the frost,
The old wound, if stricken, is the sorest,
The old hope is hardest to be lost.
But the young, young children, O my brothers,
Do you ask them why they stand
Weeping sore before the bosoms of their mothers,
In our happy Fatherland?

[1] *One, as fair as she* Allusion to Princess Charlotte, daughter of George IV, who had died after giving birth to a stillborn child in 1817.

[2] *King of kings* I.e., Jesus Christ.

[3] *The Cry of the Children* This poem was written in response to Richard Henry Horne's 1843 "Report of the Children's Employment Commission" regarding child labor in the mining and manufacturing industries (see "In Context: Children in the Mines," on the companion website). Horne was the author of the epic poem *Orion* and the play *Cosmo de' Medici*, as well as *A New Spirit of the Age*, co-written with Elizabeth Barrett.

[4] *Φεῦ … τέκνα* From Euripides's *Medea* (431 BCE) 1.1040, in which Medea says, upon killing her children: "Alas, why do you gaze at me thus, my children?"

3

They look up with their pale and sunken faces,
And their looks are sad to see,
For the man's hoary anguish draws and presses
Down the cheeks of infancy.
"Your old earth," they say, "is very dreary;
Our young feet," they say, "are very weak!
Few paces have we taken, yet are weary—
Our grave rest is very far to seek.
Ask the aged why they weep, and not the children;
For the outside earth is cold;
And we young ones stand without, in our bewildering,
And the graves are for the old."

4

"True," say the children, "it may happen
That we die before our time;
Little Alice died last year—her grave is shapen
Like a snowball, in the rime.
We looked into the pit prepared to take her:
Was no room for any work in the close clay!
From the sleep wherein she lieth none will wake her,
Crying, 'Get up, little Alice! it is day.'
If you listen by that grave, in sun and shower,
With your ear down, little Alice never cries;
Could we see her face, be sure we should not know her,
For the smile has time for growing in her eyes:
And merry go her moments, lulled and stilled in
The shroud by the kirk° chime. *church*
It is good when it happens," say the children,
"That we die before our time."

5

Alas, alas, the children! they are seeking
Death in life, as best to have;
They are binding up their hearts away from breaking,
With a cerement° from the grave. *shroud*
Go out, children, from the mine and from the city,
Sing out, children, as the little thrushes do;
Pluck you handfuls of the meadow cowslips pretty,
Laugh aloud, to feel your fingers let them through!
But they answer, "Are your cowslips of the meadows
Like our weeds anear the mine?
Leave us quiet in the dark of the coal shadows,
From your pleasures fair and fine!

6

"For oh," say the children, "we are weary,
And we cannot run or leap;
If we cared for any meadows, it were merely
To drop down in them and sleep.
Our knees tremble sorely in the stooping,
We fall upon our faces, trying to go;
And, underneath our heavy eyelids drooping,
The reddest flower would look as pale as snow;
For, all day, we drag our burden tiring
Through the coal dark, under ground;
Or, all day, we drive the wheels of iron
In the factories, round and round.

7

"For all day, the wheels are droning, turning;
Their wind comes in our faces,
Till our hearts turn, our heads with pulses burning,
And the walls turn in their places:
Turns the sky in the high window blank and reeling,
Turns the long light that drops adown the wall,
Turn the black flies that crawl along the ceiling,
All are turning, all the day, and we with all.
And all day, the iron wheels are droning,
And sometimes we could pray,
'O ye wheels,' (breaking out in a mad moaning)
'Stop! be silent for today!'"

8

Aye, be silent! Let them hear each other breathing
For a moment, mouth to mouth!
Let them touch each other's hands, in a fresh wreathing
Of their tender human youth!
Let them feel that this cold metallic motion
Is not all the life God fashions or reveals:
Let them prove their living souls against the notion
That they live in you, or under you, O wheels!
Still, all day, the iron wheels go onward,
Grinding life down from its mark;

And the children's souls, which God is calling sunward,
Spin on blindly in the dark.

9

Now tell the poor young children, O my brothers,
To look up to Him and pray;
So the blessed One who blesseth all the others,
Will bless them another day.
They answer, "Who is God that He should hear us,
While the rushing of the iron wheels is stirred?
When we sob aloud, the human creatures near us
Pass by, hearing not, or answer not a word.
And *we* hear not (for the wheels in their resounding)
Strangers speaking at the door:
Is it likely God, with angels singing round him,
Hears our weeping any more?

10

"Two words, indeed, of praying we remember,
And at midnight's hour of harm,
'Our Father,' looking upward in the chamber,
We say softly for a charm.[1]
We know no other words except 'Our Father,'
And we think that, in some pause of angels' song,
God may pluck them with the silence sweet to gather,
And hold both within His right hand which is strong.
'Our Father!' If He heard us, He would surely
(For they call Him good and mild)
Answer, smiling down the steep world very purely,
'Come and rest with me, my child.'"

11

"But no!" say the children, weeping faster,
"He is speechless as a stone:
And they tell us, of His image is the master
Who commands us to work on.
Go to!" say the children,—"up in heaven,
Dark, wheel-like, turning clouds are all we find.
Do not mock us; grief has made us unbelieving:
We look up for God, but tears have made us blind."
Do you hear the children weeping and disproving,
O my brothers, what ye preach?
For God's possible is taught by His world's loving,
And the children doubt of each.

12

And well may the children weep before you!
They are weary ere they run;
They have never seen the sunshine, nor the glory
Which is brighter than the sun.
They know the grief of man, without its wisdom;
They sink in man's despair, without its calm;
Are slaves, without the liberty in Christdom,
Are martyrs, by the pang without the palm;
Are worn as if with age, yet unretrievingly
The harvest of its memories cannot reap,—
Are orphans of the earthly love and heavenly.
Let them weep! let them weep!

13

They look up with their pale and sunken faces,
And their look is dread to see,
For they mind you of their angels in high places,
With eyes turned on Deity!
"How long," they say, "how long, O cruel nation,
Will you stand, to move the world, on a child's heart,—
Stifle down with a mailed° heel its palpitation, *armored*
And tread onward to your throne amid the mart?
Our blood splashes upward, O gold-heaper,
And your purple shows your path!
But the child's sob in the silence curses deeper
Than the strong man in his wrath."

—1844

[1] [Barrett Browning's note] A fact rendered pathetically historical by Mr. Horne's report of his commission. The name of the poet of *Orion* and *Cosmo de' Medici* has, however, a change of associations, and comes in time to remind me that we have some noble poetic heat of literature still, however open to the reproach of being somewhat gelid in our humanity. [*gelid* Cold.]

To George Sand[1] *A Desire*

Thou large-brained woman and large-hearted man,
Self-called George Sand! whose soul, amid the lions
Of thy tumultuous senses, moans defiance
And answers roar for roar, as spirits can:
I would some mild miraculous thunder ran
Above the applauded circus, in appliance
Of thine own nobler nature's strength and science,
Drawing two pinions,° white as wings of swan, *wings*
From thy strong shoulders, to amaze the place
With holier light! that thou to woman's claim
And man's, mightst join beside the angel's grace
Of a pure genius sanctified from blame,
Till child and maiden pressed to thine embrace
To kiss upon thy lips a stainless fame.
—1844

To George Sand *A Recognition*

True genius, but true woman! dost deny
The woman's nature with a manly scorn,
And break away the gauds° and armlets worn *ornaments*
By weaker women in captivity?
Ah, vain denial! that revolted cry
Is sobbed in by a woman's voice forlorn,—
Thy woman's hair, my sister, all unshorn
Floats back dishevelled strength in agony,
Disproving thy man's name: and while before
The world thou burnest in a poet fire,
We see thy woman heart beat evermore
Through the large flame. Beat purer, heart, and higher,
Till God unsex thee on the heavenly shore
Where unincarnate spirits purely aspire!
—1844

[1] *George Sand* Pseudonym of French author Amandine Aurore Lucie Dupin (1804–76), who was often condemned for her free-spirited ways, which included wearing men's clothing. For images of Sand see "In Context: Images of George Sand," on the companion website.

A Year's Spinning

1

He listened at the porch that day,
To hear the wheel go on, and on;
And then it stopped, ran back away,
While through the door he brought the sun:
But now my spinning is all done.

2

He sat beside me, with an oath
That love ne'er ended, once begun;
I smiled—believing for us both,
What was the truth for only one:
And now my spinning is all done.

3

My mother cursed me that I heard
A young man's wooing as I spun:
Thanks, cruel mother, for that word—
For I have, since, a harder known!
And now my spinning is all done.

4

I thought—O God!—my firstborn's cry
Both voices to mine ear would drown:
I listened in mine agony—
It was the *silence* made me groan!
And now my spinning is all done.

5

Bury me 'twixt my mother's grave,
(Who cursed me on her deathbed lone)
And my dead baby's (God it save!)
Who, not to bless me, would not moan.
And now my spinning is all done.

6

A stone upon my heart and head,
But no name written on the stone!
Sweet neighbours, whisper low instead,
"This sinner was a loving one—
And now her spinning is all done."

7

And let the door ajar remain,
In case he should pass by anon;
And leave the wheel out very plain,—
That HE, when passing in the sun,
May see the spinning is all done.

—1850

The Runaway Slave at Pilgrim's Point

1

I stand on the mark beside the shore
Of the first white pilgrim's bended knee,
Where exile turned to ancestor,
And God was thanked for liberty.
I have run through the night, my skin is as dark,
I bend my knee down on this mark:
I look on the sky and the sea.

2

O pilgrim-souls, I speak to you!
I see you come proud and slow
From the land of the spirits pale as dew
And round me and round me ye go.
O pilgrims, I have gasped and run
All night long from the whips of one
Who in your names works sin and woe!

3

And thus I thought that I would come
And kneel here where you knelt before,
And feel your souls around me hum
In undertone to the ocean's roar;
And lift my black face, my black hand,
Here, in your names, to curse this land
Ye blessed in freedom's, evermore.

4

I am black, I am black,
And yet God made me, they say:
But if He did so, smiling back
He must have cast His work away
Under the feet of His white creatures,
With a look of scorn, that the dusky features
Might be trodden again to clay.

5

And yet He has made dark things
To be glad and merry as light:
There's a little dark bird sits and sings,
There's a dark stream ripples out of sight,
And the dark frogs chant in the safe morass,
And the sweetest stars are made to pass
O'er the face of the darkest night.

6

But *we* who are dark, we are dark!
Ah God, we have no stars!
About our souls in care and cark° *troubles*
Our blackness shuts like prison bars:
The poor souls crouch so far behind
That never a comfort can they find
By reaching through the prison bars.

7

Indeed we live beneath the sky,
That great smooth Hand of God stretched out
On all his children fatherly,
To save them from the dread and doubt
Which would be if, from this low place,
All opened straight up to His face
Into the grand eternity.

8

And still God's sunshine and His frost,
They make us hot, they make us cold,
As if we were not black and lost;
And the beasts and birds, in wood and fold,
Do fear and take us for very men:
Could the whippoorwill or the cat of the glen
Look into my eyes and be bold?

9

I am black, I am black!
But, once, I laughed in girlish glee,
For one of my colour stood in the track

Where the drivers drove, and looked at me,
And tender and full was the look he gave—
Could a slave look *so* at another slave?—
I look at the sky and sea.

10

And from that hour our spirits grew
As free as if unsold, unbought:
Oh, strong enough, since we were two,
To conquer the world, we thought.
The drivers drove us day by day;
We did not mind, we went one way,
And no better a freedom sought.

11

In the sunny ground between the canes,
He said "I love you" as he passed;
When the shingle roof rang sharp with the rains,
I heard how he vowed it fast:
While others shook he smiled in the hut,
As he carved me a bowl of the coconut
Through the roar of the hurricanes.

12

I sang his name instead of a song,
Over and over I sang his name,
Upward and downward I drew it along
My various notes,—the same, the same!
I sang it low, that the slave girls near
Might never guess, from aught they could hear,
It was only a name—a name.

13

I look on the sky and the sea.
We were two to love, and two to pray:
Yes, two, O God, who cried to Thee,
Though nothing didst Thou say!
Coldly Thou sat'st behind the sun:
And now I cry who am but one,
Thou wilt not speak today.

14

We were black, we were black,
We had no claim to love and bliss,
What marvel if each went to wrack?
They wrung my cold hands out of his
They dragged him—where? I crawled to touch
His blood's mark in the dust ... not much,
Ye pilgrim-souls, though plain as this!

15

Wrong, followed by a deeper wrong!
Mere grief's too good for such as I:
So the white men brought the shame ere long
To strangle the sob of my agony.
They would not leave me for my dull
Wet eyes!—it was too merciful
To let me weep pure tears and die.

16

I am black, I am black!
I wore a child upon my breast,
An amulet that hung too slack,
And, in my unrest, could not rest:
Thus we went moaning, child and mother,
One to another, one to another,
Until all ended for the best.

17

For hark! I will tell you low, low,
I am black, you see,—
And the babe who lay on my bosom so,
Was far too white, too white for me;
As white as the ladies who scorned to pray
Beside me at church but yesterday,
Though my tears had washed a place for my knee.

18

My own, own child! I could not bear
To look in his face, it was so white;
I covered him up with a kerchief there,
I covered his face in close and tight:
And he moaned and struggled, as well might be,
For the white child wanted his liberty—
Ha, ha! he wanted the master right.

19

He moaned and beat with his head and feet,
His little feet that never grew;
He struck them out, as it was meet,
Against my heart to break it through:
I might have sung and made him mild,
But I dared not sing to the white-faced child
The only song I knew.

20

I pulled the kerchief very close:
He could not see the sun, I swear,
More, then, alive, than now he does
From between the roots of the mango … where?
I know where. Close! A child and mother
Do wrong to look at one another
When one is black and one is fair.

21

Why, in that single glance I had
Of my child's face, … I tell you all,
I saw a look that made me mad!
The master's look, that used to fall
On my soul like his lash … or worse!
And so, to save it from my curse,
I twisted it round in my shawl.

22

And he moaned and trembled from foot to head,
He shivered from head to foot;
Till after a time, he lay instead
Too suddenly still and mute.
I felt, beside, a stiffening cold:
I dared to lift up just a fold,
As in lifting a leaf of the mango fruit.

23

But *my* fruit … ha, ha!—there, had been
(I laugh to think on't at this hour!)
Your fine white angels (who have seen
Nearest the secret of God's power)
And plucked my fruit to make them wine,
And sucked the soul of that child of mine
As the hummingbird sucks the soul of the flower.

24

Ha, ha, the trick of the angels white!
They freed the white child's spirit so.
I said not a word, but day and night
I carried the body to and fro,
And it lay on my heart like a stone, as chill.
—The sun may shine out as much as he will:
I am cold, though it happened a month ago.

25

From the white man's house, and the black man's hut,
I carried the little body on;
The forest's arms did round us shut,
And silence through the trees did run:
They asked no question as I went,
They stood too high for astonishment,
They could see God sit on His throne.

26

My little body, kerchiefed fast,
I bore it on through the forest, on;
And when I felt it was tired at last,
I scooped a hole beneath the moon:
Through the forest tops the angels far,
With a white sharp finger from every star,
Did point and mock at what was done.

27

Yet when it was all done aright,—
Earth, 'twixt me and my baby, strewed,—
All, changed to black earth,—nothing white,—
A dark child in the dark!—ensued
Some comfort, and my heart grew young;
I sat down smiling there and sung
The song I learnt in my maidenhood.

28

And thus we two were reconciled,
The white child and black mother, thus;
For as I sang it soft and wild,
The same song, more melodious,
Rose from the grave whereon I sat:
It was the dead child singing that,
To join the souls of both of us.

29

I look on the sea and the sky.
Where the pilgrims' ships first anchored lay
The free sun rideth gloriously,
But the pilgrim-ghosts have slid away
Through the earliest streaks of the morn:
My face is black, but it glares with a scorn
Which they dare not meet by day.

30

Ha!—in their stead, their hunter sons!
Ha, ha! they are on me—they hunt in a ring!
Keep off! I brave you all at once,
I throw off your eyes like snakes that sting!
You have killed the black eagle at nest, I think:
Did you ever stand still in your triumph, and shrink
From the stroke of her wounded wing?

31

(Man, drop that stone you dared to lift!—)
I wish you who stand there five abreast,
Each, for his own wife's joy and gift,
A little corpse as safely at rest
As mine in the mangoes! Yes, but she
May keep live babies on her knee,
And sing the song she likes the best.

32

I am not mad: I am black.
I see you staring in my face—
I know you staring, shrinking back,
Ye are born of the Washington race,
And this land is the free America,
And this mark on my wrist—(I prove what I say)
Ropes tied me up here to the flogging place.

33

You think I shrieked then? Not a sound!
I hung, as a gourd hangs in the sun;
I only cursed them all around
As softly as I might have done
My very own child: from these sands
Up to the mountains, lift your hands,
O slaves, and end what I begun!

34

Whips, curses; these must answer those!
For in this UNION you have set
Two kinds of men in adverse rows,
Each loathing each; and all forget
The seven wounds in Christ's body fair,
While HE sees gaping everywhere
Our countless wounds that pay no debt.

35

Our wounds are different. Your white men
Are, after all, not gods indeed,
Nor able to make Christs again
Do good with bleeding. We who bleed
(Stand off!) we help not in our loss!
We are too heavy for our cross,
And fall and crush you and your seed.

36

I fall, I swoon! I look at the sky.
The clouds are breaking on my brain;
I am floated along, as if I should die
Of liberty's exquisite pain.
In the name of the white child waiting for me
In the death dark where we may kiss and agree,
White men, I leave you all curse-free
In my broken heart's disdain!

—1850

from *Sonnets from the Portuguese*

1

I thought once how Theocritus[1] had sung
Of the sweet years, the dear and wished-for years,
Who each one in a gracious hand appears
To bear a gift for mortals, old or young:
And, as I mused it in his antique tongue,[2]
I saw, in gradual vision through my tears,
The sweet, sad years, the melancholy years,

---

[1] *Theocritus* Greek poet of the third century BCE who created the genre of the pastoral (characterized by idyllic country life and love between shepherds and shepherdesses).

[2] *antique tongue* Greek language.

Those of my own life, who by turns had flung
A shadow across me. Straightway I was 'ware,
So weeping, how a mystic Shape did move
Behind me, and drew me backward by the hair;
And a voice said in mastery, while I strove—
"Guess now who holds thee?"—"Death," I said. But, there,
The silver answer rang—"Not Death, but Love."

7

The face of all the world is changed, I think,
Since first I heard the footsteps of thy soul
Move still, oh, still, beside me, as they stole
Betwixt me and the dreadful outer brink
Of obvious death, where I, who thought to sink,
Was caught up into love, and taught the whole
Of life in a new rhythm. The cup of dole
God gave for baptism, I am fain to drink,
And praise its sweetness, Sweet, with thee anear.
The names of country, heaven, are changed away
For where thou art or shalt be, there or here;
And this ... this lute and song ... loved yesterday,
(The singing angels know) are only dear
Because thy name moves right in what they say.

13

And wilt thou have me fasten into speech
The love I bear thee, finding words enough,
And hold the torch out, while the winds are rough,
Between our faces, to cast light on each?—
I drop it at thy feet. I cannot teach
My hand to hold my spirit so far off
From myself—me—that I should bring thee proof
In words, of love hid in me out of reach.
Nay, let the silence of my womanhood
Commend my woman-love to thy belief—
Seeing that I stand unwon, however wooed,
And rend the garment of my life, in brief,
By a most dauntless, voiceless fortitude,
Lest one touch of this heart convey its grief.

21

Say over again, and yet once over again,
That thou dost love me. Though the word repeated
Should seem "a cuckoo-song," as thou dost treat it,
Remember, never to the hill or plain,
Valley and wood, without her cuckoo-strain
Comes the fresh Spring in all her green completed.
Belovèd, I, amid the darkness greeted
By a doubtful spirit-voice, in that doubt's pain
Cry, "Speak once more—thou lovest!" Who can fear
Too many stars, though each in heaven shall roll,
Too many flowers, though each shall crown the year?
Say thou dost love me, love me, love me—toll
The silver iterance![1]—only minding, Dear,
To love me also in silence with thy soul.

22

When our two souls stand up erect and strong,
Face to face, silent, drawing nigh and nigher,
Until the lengthening wings break into fire
At either curvèd point—what bitter wrong
Can the earth do to us, that we should not long
Be here contented? Think. In mounting higher,
The angels would press on us and aspire
To drop some golden orb of perfect song
Into our deep, dear silence. Let us stay
Rather on earth, Belovèd—where the unfit
Contrarious moods of men recoil away
And isolate pure spirits, and permit
A place to stand and love in for a day,
With darkness and the death hour rounding it.

24

Let the world's sharpness, like a clasping knife,
Shut in upon itself and do no harm
In this close hand of Love, now soft and warm,
And let us hear no sound of human strife
After the click of the shutting. Life to life—
I lean upon thee, Dear, without alarm,
And feel as safe as guarded by a charm
Against the stab of worldlings, who if rife
Are weak to injure. Very whitely still

[1] *iterance* Repetition.

The lilies of our lives may reassure
Their blossoms from their roots, accessible
Alone to heavenly dews that drop not fewer,
Growing straight, out of man's reach, on the hill.
God only, who made us rich, can make us poor.

26

I lived with visions for my company
Instead of men and women, years ago,
And found them gentle mates, nor thought to know
A sweeter music than they played to me.
But soon their trailing purple was not free
Of this world's dust, their lutes did silent grow,
And I myself grew faint and blind below
Their vanishing eyes. Then *thou* didst come—to be,
Belovèd, what they seemed. Their shining fronts,
Their songs, their splendours (better, yet the same,
As river water hallowed into fonts),
Met in thee, and from out thee overcame
My soul with satisfaction of all wants:
Because God's gifts put man's best dreams to shame.

28

My letters! all dead paper, mute and white!
And yet they seem alive and quivering
Against my tremulous hands which loose the string
And let them drop down on my knee tonight.
This said—he wished to have me in his sight
Once, as a friend: this fixed a day in spring
To come and touch my hand … a simple thing,
Yet I wept for it!—this, … the paper's light …
Said, *Dear, I love thee*; and I sank and quailed
As if God's future thundered on my past.
This said, *I am thine*—and so its ink has paled
With lying at my heart that beat too fast.
And this … O Love, thy words have ill availed
If, what this said, I dared repeat at last!

43

How do I love thee? Let me count the ways.
I love thee to the depth and breadth and height
My soul can reach, when feeling out of sight
For the ends of Being and ideal Grace.
I love thee to the level of every day's
Most quiet need, by sun and candle-light.
I love thee freely, as men strive for Right;
I love thee purely, as they turn from Praise.
I love thee with the passion put to use
In my old griefs, and with my childhood's faith.
I love thee with a love I seemed to lose
With my lost saints—I love thee with the breath,
Smiles, tears, of all my life!—and, if God choose,
I shall but love thee better after death.
—1845–47

Aurora Leigh

Published in 1856, *Aurora Lee* dazzled and baffled its first readers because of its size (close to 11,000 lines) and its focus on a fictional female poet. This mixed reception changed by the end of the century, when it was embraced for its poetics and treatment of gender politics. In 1857, George Eliot remarked that the poem gave her "a deeper sense of communion with a large as well as beautiful mind." Her religious language is telling. Indeed, when in 1896, Fanny Zampini-Salazer described the poem as "the gospel of woman," she captured Browning's engagement with the issues of sexual, political, artistic, and economic liberty that one observes in Rossetti's "Goblin Market," Mill's *The Subjection of Women*, and Sarah Grand's writing—the issues that inform the "New Woman" debate.

The poem is a *Künstlerroman*, the story of a poet's artistic development as she loses her parents and travels from her childhood home in Italy to England. There she discovers books and a desire to write, and struggles to find her voice as she contends with the patriarchal world: the marital advances of her cousin Romney; the story of the "fallen woman" Marian Erle; and her growth as a poet who finds critical but little popular or financial success.

In such a world, Aurora's struggles as a woman and as a poet are intertwined as she attempts to throw "off the old conventions"—literary and cultural (1.177). Although Browning commented that the poem is "an autobiography of a poetess—(not me)," her life and Aurora's overlap. Both poets work to craft a female voice in a patriarchal literary tradition. Dubbing *Aurora Leigh* "a novel-poem," Browning established a feminist, hybridic genre that shares narrative elements with the Victorian novel.

There is also an epic quality to the poem that places it alongside Milton's *Paradise Lost,* Tennyson's *In Memoriam*, and Wordsworth's *Prelude*. All are epics that expand and reinvent the conventions and history of the genre, and in this context Browning faces the challenge of all poets: writing in the present, in the "throbbing age," with a "double vision" that requires keeping the past in sight (5. 129–148). In doing so, she explores gendered aesthetics in political and cultural contexts of Victorian England but with an eye to the future. She offers a forward-looking epic in many ways resembling that which Thomas Carlyle has in mind in *Past and Present*: "The future Epic of the World rests not with those that are near dead, but with those that are alive, and those that are coming into life" (38).

from *Aurora Leigh*

BOOK 1

Of writing many books there is no end;[1]
And I who have written much in prose and verse
For others' uses, will write now for mine—
Will write my story for my better self,
As when you paint your portrait for a friend,
Who keeps it in a drawer and looks at it
Long after he has ceased to love you, just
To hold together what he was and is.

I, writing thus, am still what men call young;
I have not so far left the coasts of life
To travel inward, that I cannot hear
That murmur of the outer Infinite[2]
Which unweaned babies smile at in their sleep
When wondered at for smiling; not so far,
But still I catch my mother at her post
Beside the nursery door, with finger up,
"Hush, hush—here's too much noise!" while her sweet eyes
Leap forward, taking part against her word
In the child's riot. Still I sit and feel
My father's slow hand, when she had left us both,
Stroke out my childish curls across his knee,
And hear Assunta's daily jest (she knew
He liked it better than a better jest)
Inquire how many golden scudi[3] went
To make such ringlets. O my father's hand,
Stroke heavily, heavily the poor hair down,
Draw, press the child's head closer to thy knee!
I'm still too young, too young, to sit alone.

I write. My mother was a Florentine,
Whose rare blue eyes were shut from seeing me
When scarcely I was four years old, my life
A poor spark snatched up from a failing lamp
Which went out therefore. She was weak and frail;
She could not bear the joy of giving life,
The mother's rapture slew her. If her kiss
Had left a longer weight upon my lips
It might have steadied the uneasy breath,
And reconciled and fraternised my soul
With the new order. As it was, indeed,
I felt a mother-want about the world,
And still went seeking, like a bleating lamb
Left out at night in shutting up the fold—
As restless as a nest-deserted bird
Grown chill through something being away, though what
It knows not. I, Aurora Leigh, was born
To make my father sadder, and myself
Not overjoyous, truly. Women know

[1] *Of writing … end* See Ecclesiastes 12.12: "[O]f making many books there is no end; and much study is a weariness of the flesh."

[2] *I have not so far … outer Infinite* Cf. William Wordsworth's "Ode: Intimations of Immortality from Recollections of Early Childhood," 9.

[3] *scudi* Italian coins no longer in use.

The way to rear up children (to be just),
They know a simple, merry, tender knack
Of tying sashes, fitting baby shoes,
And stringing pretty words that make no sense,
And kissing full sense into empty words,
Which things are corals[1] to cut life upon,
Although such trifles: children learn by such,
Love's holy earnest in a pretty play
And get not over-early solemnised,
But seeing, as in a rose-bush, Love's Divine
Which burns and hurts not,[2]—not a single bloom—
Become aware and unafraid of Love.
Such good do mothers. Fathers love as well
—Mine did, I know—but still with heavier brains,
And wills more consciously responsible,
And not as wisely, since less foolishly;
So mothers have God's license to be missed.

My father was an austere Englishman,
Who, after a dry lifetime spent at home
In college learning, law, and parish talk,
Was flooded with a passion unaware,
His whole provisioned and complacent past
Drowned out from him that moment. As he stood
In Florence, where he had come to spend a month
And note the secret of da Vinci's drains,[3]
He musing somewhat absently perhaps
Some English question ... whether men should pay
The unpopular but necessary tax
With left or right hand—in the alien sun
In that great square of the Santissima[4]
There drifted past him (scarcely marked enough
To move his comfortable island scorn)
A train of priestly banners, cross and psalm,
The white-veiled rose-crowned maidens holding up
Tall tapers, weighty for such wrists, aslant
To the blue luminous tremor of the air,
And letting drop the white wax as they went
To eat the bishop's wafer[5] at the church;
From which long trail of chanting priests and girls,
A face flashed like a cymbal on his face
And shook with silent clangour brain and heart,
Transfiguring him to music. Thus, even thus,
He too received his sacramental gift
With eucharistic meanings; for he loved.

And thus beloved, she died. I've heard it said
That but to see him in the first surprise
Of widower and father, nursing me,
Unmothered little child of four years old,
His large man's hands afraid to touch my curls,
As if the gold would tarnish—his grave lips
Contriving such a miserable smile
As if he knew needs must, or I should die,
And yet 'twas hard—would almost make the stones
Cry out for pity.[6] There's a verse he set
In Santa Croce[7] to her memory—
"Weep for an infant too young to weep much
When death removed this mother"—stops the mirth
Today on women's faces when they walk
With rosy children hanging on their gowns,
Under the cloister to escape the sun
That scorches in the piazza. After which
He left our Florence and made haste to hide
Himself, his prattling child, and silent grief,
Among the mountains above Pelago;[8]
Because unmothered babes, he thought, had need
Of mother nature more than others use,
And Pan's[9] white goats, with udders warm and full
Of mystic contemplations, come to feed
Poor milkless lips of orphans like his own—

[1] *corals* Babies' teething toys made of polished coral.

[2] *rose-bush ... hurts not* See Exodus 3.2, in which God appears in a burning bush.

[3] *da Vinci's drains* Leonardo da Vinci (1452–1519), Renaissance painter, sculptor, architect, and engineer, invented a system of drainage canals.

[4] *Santissima* Florence's baroque church of Santissima Annunziata.

[5] *eat the bishop's wafer* Receive Holy Communion.

[6] *make the stones / Cry out for pity* Cf. Jesus' speech to the Pharisees in Luke 19.40: "If these should hold their peace, the stones would immediately cry out."

[7] *Santa Croce* Gothic church in Florence.

[8] *Pelago* Village near Florence.

[9] *Pan* Greek god of Nature who was half goat and half man, and to whom white goats were sacred.

Such scholar-scraps he talked, I've heard from friends,
For even prosaic men who wear grief long
Will get to wear it as a hat aside
With a flower stuck in't. Father, then, and child,
We lived among the mountains many years,
God's silence on the outside of the house,
And we who did not speak too loud within,
And old Assunta to make up the fire,
Crossing herself whene'er a sudden flame
Which lightened from the firewood, made alive
That picture of my mother on the wall.

The painter drew it after she was dead,
And when the face was finished, throat and hands,
Her cameriera[1] carried him, in hate
Of the English-fashioned shroud, the last brocade
She dressed in at the Pitti;[2] "he should paint
No sadder thing than that," she swore, "to wrong
Her poor signora." Therefore very strange
The effect was. I, a little child, would crouch
For hours upon the floor with knees drawn up,
And gaze across them, half in terror, half
In adoration, at the picture there—
That swan-like supernatural white life
Just sailing upward from the red stiff silk
Which seemed to have no part in it nor power
To keep it from quite breaking out of bounds.
For hours I sat and stared. Assunta's awe
And my poor father's melancholy eyes
Still pointed that way. That way went my thoughts
When wandering beyond sight. And as I grew
In years, I mixed, confused, unconsciously,
Whatever I last read or heard or dreamed,
Abhorrent, admirable, beautiful,
Pathetical, or ghastly, or grotesque,
With still that face ... which did not therefore change,
But kept the mystic level of all forms,
Hates, fears, and admirations, was by turns
Ghost, fiend, and angel, fairy, witch, and sprite,
A dauntless Muse who eyes a dreadful Fate,[3]
A loving Psyche[4] who loses sight of Love,
A still Medusa[5] with mild milky brows
All curdled and all clothed upon with snakes
Whose slime falls fast as sweat will; or anon
Our Lady of the Passion, stabbed with swords
Where the Babe sucked; or Lamia[6] in her first
Moonlighted pallor, ere she shrunk and blinked
And shuddering wriggled down to the unclean;
Or my own mother, leaving her last smile
In her last kiss upon the baby-mouth
My father pushed down on the bed for that—
Or my dead mother, without smile or kiss,
Buried at Florence. All which images,
Concentred on the picture, glassed themselves
Before my meditative childhood, as
The incoherencies of change and death
Are represented fully, mixed and merged,
In the smooth fair mystery of perpetual Life.

And while I stared away my childish wits
Upon my mother's picture (ah, poor child!),
My father, who through love had suddenly
Thrown off the old conventions, broken loose
From chin-bands of the soul, like Lazarus,[7]
Yet had no time to learn to talk and walk

[1] *cameriera* Maid.

[2] *Pitti* Renaissance palace in Florence, former home of the Medicis and other royal families.

[3] *Muse* One of the nine goddesses of the arts and sciences in Greek and Roman mythology; *Fate* One of three goddesses of fate and destiny in Greek and Roman mythology.

[4] *Psyche* Mortal daughter of royalty in Greek mythology. Eros, the god of love, visited Psyche in the dark of night as her lover, but he abandoned her after she disobeyed his command not to look at him.

[5] *Medusa* One of the three Gorgons, who was made mortal after claiming she was more beautiful than Athena. Medusa was transformed into a monster with hair made of snakes, whose gaze would turn men to stone.

[6] *Lady ... Babe sucked* Catholic iconology portrays the Virgin Mary stabbed through the heart with the seven swords of grief (the seven sorrows) upon the events leading up to and the crucifixion of Christ, her son; *Lamia* After the goddess Hera killed her children, the mortal Lamia turned to killing others' children out of revenge.

[7] *chin-bands ... Lazarus* Cloth used to hold a corpse's mouth closed. John 11.44 speaks of Lazarus rising from the dead, "bound hand and foot with graveclothes: and his face was bound about with a napkin. Jesus saith unto them, Loose him, and let him go."

Or grow anew familiar with the sun—
Who had reached to freedom, not to action, lived,
But lived as one entranced, with thoughts, not aims—
Whom love had unmade from a common man
But not completed to an uncommon man—
My father taught me what he had learnt the best
Before he died and left me—grief and love.
And, seeing we had books among the hills,
Strong words of counselling souls confederate
With vocal pines and waters—out of books
He taught me all the ignorance of men,
And how God laughs in heaven when any man
Says "Here I'm learned; this, I understand;
In that, I am never caught at fault or doubt."
He sent the schools to school, demonstrating
A fool will pass for such through one mistake,
While a philosopher will pass for such,
Through said mistakes being ventured in the gross
And heaped up to a system.
                                        I am like,
They tell me, my dear father. Broader brows
Howbeit, upon a slenderer undergrowth
Of delicate features—paler, near as grave;
But then my mother's smile breaks up the whole,
And makes it better sometimes than itself.

So, nine full years, our days were hid with God
Among his mountains: I was just thirteen,
Still growing like the plants from unseen roots
In tongue-tied Springs—and suddenly awoke
To full life and life's needs and agonies
With an intense, strong, struggling heart beside
A stone-dead father. Life, struck sharp on death,
Makes awful lightning. His last word was "Love—"
"Love, my child, love, love!"—(then he had done with grief)
"Love, my child." Ere I answered he was gone,
And none was left to love in all the world.

There, ended childhood. What succeeded next
I recollect as, after fevers, men
Thread back the passage of delirium,
Missing the turn still, baffled by the door;
Smooth endless days, notched here and there with knives,
A weary, wormy darkness, spurred i' the flank
With flame, that it should eat and end itself
Like some tormented scorpion.[1] Then at last
I do remember clearly how there came
A stranger with authority, not right
(I thought not), who commanded, caught me up
From old Assunta's neck; how, with a shriek,
She let me go—while I, with ears too full
Of my father's silence to shriek back a word,
In all a child's astonishment at grief
Stared at the wharf edge where she stood and moaned,
My poor Assunta, where she stood and moaned!
The white walls, the blue hills, my Italy,
Drawn backward from the shuddering steamer deck,
Like one in anger drawing back her skirts
Which suppliants catch at. Then the bitter sea
Inexorably pushed between us both
And, sweeping up the ship with my despair,
Threw us out as a pasture to the stars.

Ten nights and days we voyaged on the deep;
Ten nights and days without the common face
Of any day or night; the moon and sun
Cut off from the green reconciling earth,
To starve into a blind ferocity
And glare unnatural; the very sky
(Dropping its bell-net down upon the sea,
As if no human heart should 'scape alive)
Bedraggled with the desolating salt,
Until it seemed no more that holy heaven
To which my father went. All new and strange;
The universe turned stranger, for a child.

Then, land!—then, England! oh, the frosty cliffs
Looked cold upon me. Could I find a home
Among those mean red houses through the fog?
And when I heard my father's language first
From alien lips which had no kiss for mine
I wept aloud, then laughed, then wept, then wept,

[1] *flame ... scorpion* When surrounded by fire a scorpion will arch its back in protection; this habit is the source of the myth that it is stinging itself and committing suicide.

And someone near me said the child was mad
Through much seasickness. The train swept us on:
Was this my father's England? the great isle?
The ground seemed cut up from the fellowship
Of verdure, field from field, as man from man;
The skies themselves looked low and positive,
As almost you could touch them with a hand,
And dared to do it they were so far off
From God's celestial crystals; all things blurred
And dull and vague. Did Shakespeare and his mates
Absorb the light here?—not a hill or stone
With heart to strike a radiant colour up
Or active outline on the indifferent air.

I think I see my father's sister stand
Upon the hall step of her country house
To give me welcome. She stood straight and calm,
Her somewhat narrow forehead braided tight
As if for taming accidental thoughts
From possible pulses; brown hair pricked with gray
By frigid use of life (she was not old,
Although my father's elder by a year),
A nose drawn sharply, yet in delicate lines;
A close mild mouth, a little soured about
The ends, through speaking unrequited loves
Or peradventure niggardly half-truths;
Eyes of no colour—once they might have smiled,
But never, never have forgot themselves
In smiling; cheeks, in which was yet a rose
Of perished summers, like a rose in a book,
Kept more for ruth° than pleasure—if past bloom, *pity*
Past fading also.
                    She had lived, we'll say,
A harmless life, she called a virtuous life,
A quiet life, which was not life at all
(But that, she had not lived enough to know),
Between the vicar and the county squires,
The lord-lieutenant looking down sometimes
From the empyrean° to assure their souls *heaven*
Against chance vulgarisms, and, in the abyss,
The apothecary,[1] looked on once a year
To prove their soundness of humility.
The poor-club exercised her Christian gifts
Of knitting stockings, stitching petticoats,
Because we are of one flesh, after all,
And need one flannel (with a proper sense
Of difference in the quality)—and still
The book-club, guarded from your modern trick
Of shaking dangerous questions from the crease,
Preserved her intellectual. She had lived
A sort of cage-bird life, born in a cage,
Accounting that to leap from perch to perch
Was act and joy enough for any bird.
Dear heaven, how silly are the things that live
In thickets, and eat berries!
                    I, alas,
A wild bird scarcely fledged, was brought to her cage,
And she was there to meet me. Very kind.
Bring the clean water, give out the fresh seed.

She stood upon the steps to welcome me,
Calm, in black garb. I clung about her neck—
Young babes, who catch at every shred of wool
To draw the new light closer, catch and cling
Less blindly. In my ears my father's word
Hummed ignorantly, as the sea in shells,
"Love, love, my child." She, black there with my grief,
Might feel my love—she was his sister once—
I clung to her. A moment she seemed moved,
Kissed me with cold lips, suffered me to cling,
And drew me feebly through the hall into
The room she sat in.
                    There, with some strange spasm
Of pain and passion, she wrung loose my hands
Imperiously, and held me at arm's length,
And with two grey-steel naked-bladed eyes
Searched through my face—ay, stabbed it through and through,
Through brows and cheeks and chin, as if to find
A wicked murderer in my innocent face,
If not here, there perhaps. Then, drawing breath,
She struggled for her ordinary calm—
And missed it rather—told me not to shrink,
As if she had told me not to lie or swear—
"She loved my father and would love me too
As long as I deserved it." Very kind.

[1] *apothecary* One who dispenses medicines (a low status profession).

I understood her meaning afterward;
She thought to find my mother in my face,
And questioned it for that. For she, my aunt,
Had loved my father truly, as she could,
And hated, with the gall of gentle souls,
My Tuscan mother who had fooled away
A wise man from wise courses, a good man
From obvious duties, and, depriving her,
His sister, of the household precedence,
Had wronged his tenants, robbed his native land,
And made him mad, alike by life and death,
In love and sorrow. She had pored° for years *pondered*
What sort of woman could be suitable
To her sort of hate, to entertain it with,
And so, her very curiosity
Became hate too, and all the idealism
She ever used in life was used for hate,
Till hate, so nourished, did exceed at last
The love from which it grew, in strength and heat,
And wrinkled her smooth conscience with a sense
Of disputable virtue (say not, sin)
When Christian doctrine was enforced at church.

And thus my father's sister was to me
My mother's hater. From that day she did
Her duty to me (I appreciate it
In her own word as spoken to herself),
Her duty, in large measure, well pressed out
But measured always. She was generous, bland,
More courteous than was tender, gave me still
The first place—as if fearful that God's saints
Would look down suddenly and say "Herein
You missed a point, I think, through lack of love."
Alas, a mother never is afraid
Of speaking angerly to any child,
Since love, she knows, is justified of love.

And I, I was a good child on the whole,
A meek and manageable child. Why not?
I did not live, to have the faults of life:
There seemed more true life in my father's grave
Than in all England. Since *that* threw me off
Who fain would cleave (his latest will, they say,
Consigned me to his land), I only thought
Of lying quiet there where I was thrown
Like seaweed on the rocks, and suffering her
To prick me to a pattern with her pin,
Fibre from fibre, delicate leaf from leaf,
And dry out from my drowned anatomy
The last sea-salt left in me.
So it was.
I broke the copious curls upon my head
In braids, because she liked smooth-ordered hair.
I left off saying my sweet Tuscan words
Which still at any stirring of the heart
Came up to float across the English phrase
As lilies (*Bene* or *Che che*[1]), because
She liked my father's child to speak his tongue.
I learnt the collects and the catechism,[2]
The creeds, from Athanasius back to Nice,[3]
The Articles, the Tracts *against* the times[4]
(By no means Buonaventure's "Prick of Love"[5]),
And various popular synopses of
Inhuman doctrines never taught by John,
Because she liked instructed piety.
I learnt my complement of classic French
(Kept pure of Balzac[6] and neologism)
And German also, since she liked a range
Of liberal education—tongues, not books.
I learnt a little algebra, a little
Of the mathematics—brushed with extreme flounce
The circle of the sciences, because
She misliked women who are frivolous.
I learnt the royal genealogies

1 *Bene or Che che* Common Italian sayings.

2 *collects* Short prayers; *catechism* Questions and answers in the Anglican *Book of Common Prayer*.

3 *Athanasius ... Nice* Doctrines of Athanasia and the Nicene Council, creeds of the Church of England.

4 *Articles* Thirty-nine articles in the Anglican doctrine; *the Tracts against the times* Referring to the *Tracts for the Times*. The first tract was composed by John Henry Newman in 1833 and called for a return to the Catholic roots of the Anglican Church.

5 *Buonaventure's "Prick of Love"* Once incorrectly attributed to the thirteenth-century Franciscan theologian St. Bonaventure, *Stimulus Divini Amoris* ("God of Love") was actually written by Jacobus Mediolanensis in the fourteenth century. The devotional text concentrates on the emotional aspect of spirituality.

6 *Balzac* French novelist Honoré de Balzac (1799–1850).

Of Oviedo,[1] the internal laws
Of the Burmese empire—by how many feet
Mount Chimborazo outsoars Teneriffe.[2]
What navigable river joins itself
To Lara,[3] and what census of the year five
Was taken at Klagenfurt,[4]—because she liked
A general insight into useful facts.
I learnt much music—such as would have been
As quite impossible in Johnson's day[5]
As still it might be wished—fine sleights of hand
And unimagined fingering, shuffling off
The hearer's soul through hurricanes of notes
To a noisy Tophet;° and I drew … costumes *Hell*
From French engravings, nereids° neatly draped *sea nymphs*
(With smirks of simmering godship): I washed in
Landscapes from nature (rather say, washed out).
I danced the polka and Cellarius,[6]
Spun glass, stuffed birds, and modelled flowers in wax,
Because she liked accomplishments in girls.
I read a score of books on womanhood
To prove, if women do not think at all,
They may teach thinking (to a maiden aunt
Or else the author)—books that boldly assert
Their right of comprehending husband's talk
When not too deep, and even of answering
With pretty "may it please you," or "so it is"—
Their rapid insight and fine aptitude,
Particular worth and general missionariness,
As long as they keep quiet by the fire
And never say "no" when the world says "ay,"
For that is fatal—their angelic reach
Of virtue, chiefly used to sit and darn,
And fatten household sinners—their, in brief,
Potential faculty in everything
Of abdicating power in it: she owned
She liked a woman to be womanly,
And English women, she thanked God and sighed
(Some people always sigh in thanking God)
Were models to the universe. And last
I learnt cross-stitch, because she did not like
To see me wear the night with empty hands
A-doing nothing. So, my shepherdess
Was something after all (the pastoral saints
Be praised for't), leaning lovelorn with pink eyes
To match her shoes, when I mistook the silks;
Her head uncrushed by that round weight of hat
So strangely similar to the tortoise-shell
Which slew the tragic poet.[7]
By the way,
The works of women are symbolical.
We sew, sew, prick our fingers, dull our sight,
Producing what? A pair of slippers, sir,
To put on when you're weary—or a stool
To stumble over and vex you … "curse that stool!"
Or else at best, a cushion, where you lean
And sleep, and dream of something we are not
But would be for your sake. Alas, alas!
This hurts most, this—that, after all, we are paid
The worth of our work, perhaps.
In looking down
Those years of education (to return)
I wonder if Brinvilliers suffered more
In the water torture[8] … flood succeeding flood
To drench the incapable throat and split the veins …
Than I did. Certain of your feebler souls
Go out in such a process; many pine
To a sick, inodorous light; my own endured:
I had relations in the Unseen, and drew

[1] *Oviedo* Gonzalo Fernandez de Oviedo y Valdez (1478–1557), Spanish historian, wrote a posthumously published book on the natural history of the Americas.

[2] *Mount Chimborazo outsoars Teneriffe* One of Spain's Canary Islands, Tenerife has a peak just over half the height of Chimborazo, the highest mountain in the Andes of Ecuador.

[3] *Lara* Town in Spain.

[4] *Klagenfurt* Capital city of Carinthia (Kärnten) in Austria.

[5] *music … Johnson's day* The Classical and Baroque music popular during "Johnson's day" was extraordinarily difficult to play. Samuel Johnson (1709–84) once famously said of a renowned violinist's musical choice: "Difficult do you call it, Sir? I would it had been impossible."

[6] *Cellarius* Waltz-Mazurka named after dance master Henri Cellarius in 1842.

[7] *tortoise-shell … poet* Greek tragedian Aeschylus (c. 525–456 BCE) was said to have been killed when an eagle dropped a tortoise on his bald head in order to crack the tortoise's shell.

[8] *Brinvilliers … water torture* The Parisian Marquise de Brinvilliers (1630–76) was tortured and eventually beheaded after being convicted of poisoning various members of her family.

The elemental nutriment and heat
From nature, as earth feels the sun at nights,
Or as a babe sucks surely in the dark.
I kept the life thrust on me, on the outside
Of the inner life with all its ample room
For heart and lungs, for will and intellect,
Inviolable by conventions. God,
I thank thee for that grace of thine!
                                        At first
I felt no life which was not patience—did
The thing she bade me, without heed to a thing
Beyond it, sat in just the chair she placed,
With back against the window, to exclude
The sight of the great lime-tree on the lawn,
Which seemed to have come on purpose from the woods
To bring the house a message—ay, and walked
Demurely in her carpeted low rooms,
As if I should not, hearkening my own steps,
Misdoubt I was alive. I read her books,
Was civil to her cousin, Romney Leigh,
Gave ear to her vicar, tea to her visitors,
And heard them whisper, when I changed a cup
(I blushed for joy at that)—"The Italian child,
For all her blue eyes and her quiet ways,
Thrives ill in England: she is paler yet
Than when we came the last time; she will die."

"Will die." My cousin, Romney Leigh, blushed too,
With sudden anger, and approaching me
Said low between his teeth, "You're wicked now?
You wish to die and leave the world a-dusk
For others, with your naughty light blown out?"
I looked into his face defyingly;
He might have know that, being what I was,
'Twas natural to like to get away
As far as dead folk can: and then indeed
Some people make no trouble when they die.
He turned and went abruptly, slammed the door,
And shut his dog out.
                                        Romney, Romney Leigh.
I have not named my cousin hitherto,
And yet I used him as a sort of friend;
My elder by few years, but cold and shy
And absent … tender, when he thought of it,
Which scarcely was imperative, grave betimes,
As well as early master of Leigh Hall,
Whereof the nightmare sat upon his youth,
Repressing all its seasonable delights,
And agonising with a ghastly sense
Of universal hideous want and wrong
To incriminate possession. When he came
From college to the country, very oft
He crossed the hill on visits to my aunt,
With gifts of blue grapes from the hothouses,
A book in one hand—mere statistics (if
I chanced to lift the cover), count of all
The goats whose beards grow sprouting down toward
    hell
Against God's separative judgment hour.[1]
And she, she almost loved him—even allowed
That sometimes he should seem to sigh my way;
It made him easier to be pitiful,
And sighing was his gift. So, undisturbed,
At whiles she let him shut my music up
And push my needles down, and lead me out
To see in that south angle of the house
The figs grow black as if by a Tuscan rock,
On some light pretext. She would turn her head
At other moments, go to fetch a thing,
And leave me breath enough to speak with him,
For his sake; it was simple.
                                        Sometimes too
He would have saved me utterly, it seemed,
He stood and looked so.
                                        Once, he stood so near,
He dropped a sudden hand upon my hand
Bent down on woman's work, as soft as rain—
But then I rose and shook it off as fire,
The stranger's touch that took my father's place
Yet dared seem soft.
                                        I used him for a friend
Before I ever knew him for a friend.
'Twas better, 'twas worse also, afterward:
We came so close, we saw our differences
Too intimately. Always Romney Leigh
Was looking for the worms, I for the gods.

[1] *The goats … judgment hour* See Matthew 25.32–33, 41.

A godlike nature his; the gods look down,
Incurious of themselves; and certainly
'Tis well I should remember, how, those days,
I was a worm too, and he looked on me.

A little by his act perhaps, yet more
By something in me, surely not my will,
I did not die. But slowly, as one in swoon,
To whom life creeps back in the form of death,
With a sense of separation, a blind pain
Of blank obstruction, and a roar i' the ears
Of visionary chariots which retreat
As earth grows clearer … slowly, by degrees;
I woke, rose up … where was I? in the world;
For uses therefore I must count worthwhile.

I had a little chamber in the house,
As green as any privet hedge a bird
Might choose to build in, though the nest itself
Could show but dead-brown sticks and straws; the walls
Were green, the carpet was pure green, the straight
Small bed was curtained greenly, and the folds
Hung green about the window which let in
The outdoor world with all its greenery.
You could not push your head out and escape
A dash of dawn-dew from the honeysuckle,
But so you were baptized into the grace
And privilege of seeing …
First, the lime
(I had enough there, of the lime, be sure—
My morning-dream was often hummed away
By the bees in it); past the lime, the lawn,
Which, after sweeping broadly round the house,
Went trickling through the shrubberies in a stream
Of tender turf, and wore and lost itself
Among the acacias, over which you saw
The irregular line of elms by the deep lane
Which stopped the grounds and dammed the overflow
Of arbutus and laurel. Out of sight
The lane was; sunk so deep, no foreign tramp
Nor drover of wild ponies out of Wales
Could guess if lady's hall or tenant's lodge
Dispensed such odours—though his stick well crooked
Might reach the lowest trail of blossoming briar
Which dipped upon the wall. Behind the elms,
And through their tops, you saw the folded hills
Striped up and down with hedges (burly oaks
Projecting from the line to show themselves),
Through which my cousin Romney's chimneys smoked
As still as when a silent mouth in frost
Breathes, showing where the woodlands hid Leigh Hall;
While, far above, a jut of tableland,
A promontory without water, stretched—
You could not catch it if the days were thick,
Or took it for a cloud; but, otherwise,
The vigorous sun would catch it up at eve
And use it for an anvil till he had filled
The shelves of heaven with burning thunderbolts,
Protesting against night and darkness:—then,
When all his setting trouble was resolved
To a trance of passive glory, you might see
In apparition on the golden sky
(Alas, my Giotto's background!)[1] the sheep run
Along the fine clear outline, small as mice
That run along a witch's scarlet thread.[2]

Not a grand nature. Not my chestnut woods
Of Vallombrosa,[3] cleaving by the spurs
To the precipices. Not my headlong leaps
Of waters, that cry out for joy or fear
In leaping through the palpitating pines,
Like a white soul tossed out to eternity
With thrills of time upon it. Not indeed
My multitudinous mountains, sitting in
The magic circle, with the mutual touch
Electric, panting from their full deep hearts
Beneath the influent[4] heavens, and waiting for
Communion and commission. Italy
Is one thing, England one.
On English ground
You understand the letter—ere the fall
How Adam lived in a garden. All the fields
Are tied up fast with hedges, nosegay-like;

---

[1] *golden sky … background* Renaissance Florentine painter Giotto (1267–1337) often used gold as a background color.

[2] *small as mice … scarlet thread* Meaning obscure.

[3] *Vallombrosa* Summer resort in the mountains near Florence.

[4] *influent* Exerting celestial, astral, or occult power.

The hills are crumpled plains, the plains parterres,[1]
The trees, round, woolly, ready to be clipped,
And if you seek for any wilderness
You find, at best, a park. A nature tamed
And grown domestic like a barn-door fowl,
Which does not awe you with its claws and beak,
Nor tempt you to an eyrie too high up,
But which, in cackling, sets you thinking of
Your eggs tomorrow at breakfast, in the pause
Of finer meditation.
Rather say,
A sweet familiar nature, stealing in
As a dog might, or child, to touch your hand
Or pluck your gown, and humbly mind you so
Of presence and affection, excellent
For inner uses, from the things without.

I could not be unthankful, I who was
Entreated thus and holpen.° In the room *helped*
I speak of, ere the house was well awake,
And also after it was well asleep,
I sat alone, and drew the blessing in
Of all that nature. With a gradual step,
A stir among the leaves, a breath, a ray,
It came in softly, while the angels made
A place for it beside me. The moon came,
And swept my chamber clean of foolish thoughts.
The sun came, saying, "Shall I lift this light
Against the lime-tree, and you will not look?
I make the birds sing—listen! but, for you,
God never hears your voice, excepting when
You lie upon the bed at nights and weep."

Then, something moved me. Then, I wakened up
More slowly than I verily write now,
But wholly, at last, I wakened, opened wide
The window and my soul, and let the airs
And outdoor sights sweep gradual gospels in,
Regenerating what I was. O, Life,
How oft we throw it off and think—"Enough,
Enough of life in so much!—here's a cause
For rupture;—herein we must break with Life,
Or be ourselves unworthy; here we are wronged,
Maimed, spoiled for aspiration: farewell, Life!"
And so, as froward° babes, we hide our eyes *obstinate*
And think all ended.—Then, Life calls to us
In some transformed, apocalyptic voice,
Above us, or below us, or around:
Perhaps we name it Nature's voice, or Love's,
Tricking ourselves, because we are more ashamed
To own our compensations than our griefs:
Still, Life's voice!—still, we make our peace with Life.

And I, so young then, was not sullen. Soon
I used to get up early, just to sit
And watch the morning quicken in the gray,
And hear the silence open like a flower
Leaf after leaf—and stroke with listless hand
The woodbine through the window, till at last
I came to do it with a sort of love,
At foolish unaware: whereat I smiled—
A melancholy smile, to catch myself
Smiling for joy.
Capacity for joy
Admits temptation. It seemed, next, worthwhile
To dodge the sharp sword set against my life;
To slip downstairs through all the sleepy house,
As mute as any dream there, and escape
As a soul from the body, out of doors,
Glide through the shrubberies, drop into the lane,
And wander on the hills an hour or two,
Then back again before the house should stir.

Or else I sat on in my chamber green,
And lived my life, and thought my thoughts, and prayed
My prayers without the vicar; read my books
Without considering whether they were fit
To do me good. Mark, there. We get no good
By being ungenerous, even to a book,
And calculating profits—so much help
By so much reading. It is rather when
We gloriously forget ourselves and plunge
Soul-forward, headlong, into a book's profound,
Impassioned for its beauty and salt of truth—
'Tis then we get the right good from a book.

[1] *parterres* Patterned ornamental gardens.

I read much. What my father taught before
From many a volume, Love re-emphasised
Upon the self-same pages: Theophrast[1]
Grew tender with the memory of his eyes,
And Ælian[2] made mine wet. The trick of Greek
And Latin he had taught me, as he would
Have taught me wrestling or the game of fives[3]
If such he had known—most like a shipwrecked man
Who heaps his single platter with goats' cheese
And scarlet berries; or like any man
Who loves but one, and so gives all at once,
Because he has it, rather than because
He counts it worthy. Thus, my father gave;
And thus, as did the women formerly
By young Achilles,[4] when they pinned a veil
Across the boy's audacious front, and swept
With tuneful laughs the silver-fretted rocks,
He wrapt his little daughter in his large
Man's doublet,° careless did it fit or no. *jacket*

But, after I had read for memory,
I read for hope. The path my father's foot
Had trod me out (which suddenly broke off
What time he dropped the wallet of the flesh
And passed), alone I carried on, and set
My child-heart 'gainst the thorny underwood,
To reach the grassy shelter of the trees.
Ah babe i' the wood, without a brother-babe!
My own self-pity, like the red-breast bird,
Flies back to cover all that past with leaves.[5]

Sublimest danger, over which none weeps,
When any young wayfaring soul goes forth
Alone, unconscious of the perilous road,
The day-sun dazzling in his limpid eyes,
To thrust his own way, he an alien, through
The world of books! Ah, you!—you think it fine,
You clap hands—"A fair day!"—you cheer him on,
As if the worst, could happen, were to rest
Too long beside a fountain. Yet, behold,
Behold!—the world of books is still the world,
And worldlings° in it are less merciful *worldly people*
And more puissant.° For the wicked there *powerful*
Are winged like angels; every knife that strikes
Is edged from elemental fire to assail
A spiritual life; the beautiful seems right
By force of beauty, and the feeble wrong
Because of weakness; power is justified
Though armed against Saint Michael;[6] many a crown
Covers bald foreheads. In the book world, true,
There's no lack, neither, of God's saints and kings,
That shake the ashes of the grave aside
From their calm locks and undiscomfited
Look steadfast truths against Time's changing mask.
True, many a prophet teaches in the roads;
True, many a seer pulls down the flaming heavens
Upon his own head in strong martyrdom
In order to light men a moment's space.
But stay!—who judges?—who distinguishes
'Twixt Saul and Nahash[7] justly, at first sight,
And leaves king Saul precisely at the sin,
To serve king David?[8] who discerns at once
The sound of the trumpets, when the trumpets blow
For Alaric as well as Charlemagne?[9]
Who judges wizards, and can tell true seers
From conjurers? the child, there? Would you leave
That child to wander in a battlefield
And push his innocent smile against the guns;
Or even in a catacomb—his torch

[1] *Theophrast* Greek philosopher (c. 370–287 BCE), student and successor of Aristotle at the Lyceum, the Athenian philosophical school founded by Aristotle.

[2] *Ælian* Greek rhetorician (c. 170–c. 230) and author of Greek books on natural history.

[3] *game of fives* Handball game similar to the game of squash.

[4] *as did the women … Achilles* The Greek god Thetis disguised her son Achilles as a girl and hid him among the women of the court in order to prevent him from perishing in the Trojan War.

[5] *babe i' the wood … leaves* Cf. the British children's ballad "The Babes in the Woods," in which two children are abandoned in the wood. After they die, robins come to cover them with leaves.

[6] *Saint Michael* One of the principal archangels, known as a protector and figured with a sword.

[7] *Saul and Nahash* See 1 Samuel 11: Saul was named king of Israel over his rival Nahash.

[8] *king David* David succeeded Saul as king of Israel.

[9] *Alaric* Visigoth king (c. 370–410 CE) and conqueror of much of the Eastern and Roman empires; *Charlemagne* Charles the Great (742?–814), emperor of the West and king of the Franks.

Grown ragged in the fluttering air, and all
The dark a-mutter round him? not a child.

I read books bad and good—some bad and good
At once (good aims not always make good books:
Well-tempered spades turn up ill-smelling soils
In digging vineyards even); books that prove
God's being so definitely, that man's doubt
Grows self-defined the other side the line,
Made atheist by suggestion; moral books,
Exasperating to license; genial books,
Discounting from the human dignity;
And merry books, which set you weeping when
The sun shines—ay, and melancholy books,
Which make you laugh that anyone should weep
In this disjointed life for one wrong more.

The world of books is still the world, I write,
And both worlds have God's providence, thank God,
To keep and hearten: with some struggle, indeed,
Among the breakers, some hard swimming through
The deeps—I lost breath in my soul sometimes
And cried "God save me if there's any God,"
But, even so, God saved me; and, being dashed
From error on to error, every turn
Still brought me nearer to the central truth.

I thought so. All this anguish in the thick
Of men's opinions … press and counter-press,
Now up, now down, now underfoot, and now
Emergent … all the best of it, perhaps,
But throws you back upon a noble trust
And use of your own instinct—merely proves
Pure reason stronger than bare inference
At strongest. Try it—fix against heaven's wall
The scaling-ladders of school logic—mount
Step by step!—sight goes faster; that still ray
Which strikes out from you, how, you cannot tell,
And why, you know not (did you eliminate,
That such as you indeed should analyse?)
Goes straight and fast as light, and high as God.

The cygnet° finds the water, but the man *young swan*
Is born in ignorance of his element
And feels out blind at first, disorganised
By sin i' the blood—his spirit-insight dulled
And crossed by his sensations. Presently
He feels it quicken in the dark sometimes,
When, mark, be reverent, be obedient,
For such dumb motions of imperfect life
Are oracles of vital Deity
Attesting the Hereafter. Let who says
"The soul's a clean white paper," rather say,
A palimpsest,[1] a prophet's holograph[2]
Defiled, erased and covered by a monk's—
The apocalypse, by a Longus![3] poring on
Which obscene text, we may discern perhaps
Some fair, fine trace of what was written once,
Some upstroke of an alpha and omega[4]
Expressing the old scripture.
Books, books, books!
I had found the secret of a garret room
Piled high with cases in my father's name,
Piled high, packed large—where, creeping in and out
Against the giant fossils of my past,
Like some small nimble mouse between the ribs
Of a mastodon, I nibbled here and there
At this or that box, pulling through the gap,
In heats of terror, haste, victorious joy,
The first book first. And how I felt it beat
Under my pillow, in the morning's dark,
An hour before the sun would let me read!
My books! At last because the time was ripe,
I chanced upon the poets.
As the earth
Plunges in fury, when the internal fires
Have reached and pricked her heart, and, throwing flat
The marts and temples, the triumphal gates

[1] *palimpsest* Paper or manuscript that has been written upon, rubbed out and written upon again, either partially or wholly obliterating the original.

[2] *holograph* Document handwritten by its author.

[3] *Longus* Greek poet of the third or fourth century, author of *Daphnis and Chloë* and originator of the pastoral romance, which often articulates intense physical desire.

[4] *alpha and omega* First and last letters of the Greek alphabet; metaphorically, the be all and end all. See Revelation 1.11, in which God says: "I am Alpha and Omega, the first and the last: and, What thou seest, write in a book."

And towers of observation, clears herself
To elemental freedom—thus, my soul,
At poetry's divine first finger-touch,
Let go conventions and sprang up surprised,
Convicted of the great eternities
Before two worlds.

What's this, Aurora Leigh,
You write so of the poets, and not laugh?
Those virtuous liars, dreamers after dark,
Exaggerators of the sun and moon,
And soothsayers in a teacup?

I write so
Of the only truth-tellers now left to God,
The only speakers of essential truth,
Opposed to relative, comparative,
And temporal truths; the only holders by
His sun-skirts, through conventional gray glooms;
The only teachers who instruct mankind
From just a shadow on a charnel° wall *mortuary*
To find man's veritable stature out
Erect, sublime—the measure of a man,
And that's the measure of an angel, says
The apostle.[1] Ay, and while your common men
Lay telegraphs, gauge railroads, reign, reap, dine,
And dust the flaunty carpets of the world
For kings to walk on, or our president,
The poet suddenly will catch them up
With his voice like a thunder—"This is soul,
This is life, this word is being said in heaven,
Here's God down on us! what are you about?"
How all those workers start amid their work,
Look round, look up, and feel, a moment's space,
That carpet dusting, though a pretty trade,
Is not the imperative labour after all.

My own best poets, am I one with you,
That thus I love you—or but one through love?
Does all this smell of thyme about my feet
Conclude my visit to your holy hill
In personal presence, or but testify
The rustling of your vesture° through my dreams *clothing*
With influent odours? When my joy and pain,
My thought and aspiration like the stops
Of pipe or flute, are absolutely dumb
Unless melodious, do you play on me
My pipers—and if, sooth, you did not blow,
Would no sound come? or is the music mine,
As a man's voice or breath is called his own,
Inbreathed by the Life-breather? There's a doubt
For cloudy seasons!

But the sun was high
When first I felt my pulses set themselves
For concord; when the rhythmic turbulence
Of blood and brain swept outward upon words,
As wind upon the alders, blanching them
By turning up their under-natures till
They trembled in dilation. O delight
And triumphs of the poet, who would say
A man's mere "yes," a woman's common "no,"
A little human hope of that or this,
And says the word so that it burns you through
With a special revelation, shakes the heart
Of all the men and women in the world,
As if one came back from the dead and spoke,
With eyes too happy, a familiar thing
Become divine i' the utterance! while for him
The poet, speaker, he expands with joy;
The palpitating angel in his flesh
Thrills inly with consenting fellowship
To those innumerous spirits who sun themselves
Outside of time.

O life, O poetry,
—Which means life in life! cognisant of life
Beyond this blood-beat, passionate for truth
Beyond these senses!—poetry, my life,
My eagle, with both grappling feet still hot
From Zeus's thunder, who hast ravished me
Away from all the shepherds, sheep, and dogs,
And set me in the Olympian roar and round
Of luminous faces for a cupbearer,[2]
To keep the mouths of all the godheads moist
For everlasting laughters—I myself

[1] *measure of a man … apostle* See Revelation 21.17.

[2] *Zeus's thunder … cupbearer* Zeus, king of the Greek gods, unleashed a thunderstorm on earth to confuse mortals and steal away the beautiful shepherd boy Ganymede. Zeus made the boy immortal and brought him to Olympus to serve as cupbearer to the gods.

Half drunk across the beaker with their eyes!
How those gods look!
Enough so, Ganymede,
We shall not bear above a round or two.
We drop the golden cup at Heré's[1] foot
And swoon back to the earth—and find ourselves
Face down among the pinecones, cold with dew,
While the dogs bark, and many a shepherd scoffs,
"What's come now to the youth?" Such ups and downs
Have poets.
Am I such indeed? The name
Is royal, and to sign it like a queen
Is what I dare not—though some royal blood
Would seem to tingle in me now and then,
With sense of power and ache—with
imposthumes° *abscesses*
And manias usual to the race. Howbeit
I dare not: 'tis too easy to go mad
And ape a Bourbon in a crown of straws;[2]
The thing's too common.
Many fervent souls
Strike rhyme on rhyme, who would strike steel on steel
If steel had offered, in a restless heat
Of doing something. Many tender souls
Have strung their losses on a rhyming thread,
As children cowslips:[3] the more pains they take,
The work more withers. Young men, ay, and maids,
Too often sow their wild oats in tame verse,
Before they sit down under their own vine[4]
And live for use. Alas, near all the birds
Will sing at dawn—and yet we do not take
The chaffering° swallow for the holy lark. *chattering*

In those days, though, I never analysed,
Not even myself. Analysis comes late.
You catch a sight of Nature, earliest,
In full front sun-face, and your eyelids wink
And drop before the wonder of 't; you miss
The form, through seeing the light. I lived, those days,
And wrote because I lived—unlicensed else;
My heart beat in my brain. Life's violent flood
Abolished bounds—and, which my neighbour's field,
Which mine, what mattered? it is thus in youth!
We play at leapfrog over the god Term;[5]
The love within us and the love without
Are mixed, confounded; if we are loved or love,
We scarce distinguish: thus, with other power;
Being acted on and acting seem the same:
In that first onrush of life's chariot-wheels,
We know not if the forests move or we.

And so, like most young poets, in a flush
Of individual life I poured myself
Along the veins of others, and achieved
Mere lifeless imitations of live verse,
And made the living answer for the dead,
Profaning nature. "Touch not, do not taste,
Nor handle,"[6]—we're too legal, who write young:
We beat the phorminx° till we hurt our thumbs, *lyre*
As if still ignorant of counterpoint;° *interwoven melodies*
We call the Muse—"O Muse, benignant Muse,"—
As if we had seen her purple-braided head,
With the eyes in it, start between the boughs
As often as a stag's. What make-believe,
With so much earnest! what effete° results *overrefined*
From virile efforts! what cold wire-drawn° odes *detailed*
From such white heats!—bucolics,[7] where the cows
Would scare the writer if they splashed the mud
In lashing off the flies—didactics, driven
Against the heels of what the master said;
And counterfeiting epics, shrill with trumps
A babe might blow between two straining cheeks
Of bubbled rose, to make his mother laugh;
And elegiac griefs, and songs of love,
Like cast-off nosegays° picked up on the road, *bouquets*
The worse for being warm: all these things, writ
On happy mornings, with a morning heart,
That leaps for love, is active for resolve,
Weak for art only. Oft, the ancient forms

[1] *Heré* Hera, wife of Zeus.

[2] *Bourbon in a crown of straws* The Bourbon dynasty was founded by Napoleon, who of course had no real title to the Crown of France.

[3] *cowslips* Fragrant pasture flowers, sometimes made into garlands.

[4] *sit down under their own vine* See 1 Kings 4.25.

[5] *Term* Terminus, Roman god of boundaries.

[6] *Touch not … handle* From Colossians 2.21–22: "Touch not; taste not; handle not; Which all are to perish with the using."

[7] *bucolics* Pastoral poems.

Will thrill, indeed, in carrying the young blood.
The wine-skins, now and then, a little warped,
Will crack even, as the new wine gurgles in.
Spare the old bottles!—spill not the new wine.[1]

By Keats's[2] soul, the man who never stepped
In gradual progress like another man,
But, turning grandly on his central self,
Ensphered himself in twenty perfect years
And died, not young (the life of a long life
Distilled to a mere drop, falling like a tear
Upon the world's cold cheek to make it burn
Forever); by that strong excepted soul,
I count it strange and hard to understand
That nearly all young poets should write old,
That Pope was sexagenary at sixteen,
And beardless Byron[3] academical,
And so with others. It may be perhaps
Such have not settled long and deep enough
In trance, to attain to clairvoyance—and still
The memory mixes with the vision, spoils,
And works it turbid.
Or perhaps, again,
In order to discover the Muse-Sphinx,[4]
The melancholy desert must sweep round,
Behind you as before.—
For me, I wrote
False poems, like the rest, and thought them true
Because myself was true in writing them.
I peradventure have writ true ones since
With less complacence.
But I could not hide
My quickening inner life from those at watch.
They saw a light at a window, now and then,
They had not set there: who had set it there?
My father's sister started when she caught
My soul agaze in my eyes. She could not say
I had no business with a sort of soul,
But plainly she objected—and demurred
That souls were dangerous things to carry straight
Through all the spilt saltpetre[5] of the world.

She said sometimes "Aurora, have you done
Your task this morning? have you read that book?
And are you ready for the crochet here?"—
As if she said "I know there's something wrong;
I know I have not ground you down enough
To flatten and bake you to a wholesome crust
For household uses and proprieties,
Before the rain has got into my barn
And set the grains a-sprouting. What, you're green
With outdoor impudence? you almost grow?"
To which I answered, "Would she hear my task,
And verify my abstract of the book?
Or should I sit down to the crochet work?
Was such her pleasure?" Then I sat and teased
The patient needle till it split the thread,
Which oozed off from it in meandering lace
From hour to hour. I was not, therefore, sad;
My soul was singing at a work apart
Behind the wall of sense, as safe from harm
As sings the lark when sucked up out of sight
In vortices of glory and blue air.

And so, through forced work and spontaneous work,
The inner life informed the outer life,
Reduced the irregular blood to a settled rhythm,
Made cool the forehead with fresh-sprinkling dreams,
And, rounding to the spheric soul the thin,
Pined body, struck a colour up the cheeks
Though somewhat faint. I clenched my brows across
My blue eyes greatening in the looking-glass,
And said "We'll live, Aurora! we'll be strong.
The dogs are on us—but we will not die."

[1] *Spare … wine* See Matthew 9.17: "Neither do men put new wine into old bottles: else the bottles break, and the wine runneth out, and the bottles perish: but they put new wine into new bottles, and both are preserved."

[2] *Keats* Romantic poet John Keats (1795–1821).

[3] *Pope … Byron* Both Alexander Pope (1688–1744) and Lord Byron (1788–1824) were precocious poets who published while still in their teens.

[4] *Sphinx* In Greek mythology the Sphinx is represented with the body of a lion and the head of a woman. The Sphinx would pose a riddle to passersby and destroy them if they could not solve it.

[5] *saltpetre* Potassium nitrate, a component in explosives.

Whoever lives true life will love true love.
I learnt to love that England. Very oft,
Before the day was born, or otherwise
Through secret windings of the afternoons,
I threw my hunters off and plunged myself
Among the deep hills, as a hunted stag
Will take the waters, shivering with the fear
And passion of the course. And when at last
Escaped, so many a green slope built on slope
Betwixt me and the enemy's house behind,
I dared to rest, or wander, in a rest
Made sweeter for the step upon the grass,
And view the ground's most gentle dimplement[1]
(As if God's finger touched but did not press
In making England), such an up and down
Of verdure—nothing too much up or down,
A ripple of land; such little hills, the sky
Can stoop to tenderly and the wheatfields climb;
Such nooks of valleys lined with orchises,
Fed full of noises by invisible streams;
And open pastures where you scarcely tell
White daisies from white dew—at intervals
The mythic oaks and elm trees standing out
Self-poised upon their prodigy of shade—
I thought my father's land was worthy too
Of being my Shakespeare's.
Very oft alone,
Unlicensed; not unfrequently with leave
To walk the third with Romney and his friend
The rising painter, Vincent Carrington,
Whom men judge hardly as bee-bonneted,
Because he holds that, paint a body well,
You paint a soul by implication,[2] like
The grand first Master. Pleasant walks! for if
He said "When I was last in Italy,"
It sounded as an instrument that's played
Too far off for the tune—and yet it's fine
To listen.

[1] *dimplement* Dimple (Barrett Browning coined this word).

[2] *paint a body ... soul by implication* Cf. Robert Browning's "Fra Lippo Lippi" 179–83, in which the painter/narrator says: "Your business is not to catch men with show, / With homage to the perishable clay, / But lift them over it, ignore it all, / Make them forget there's such a thing as flesh. / Your business is to paint the souls of men."

Often we walked only two
If cousin Romney pleased to walk with me.
We read, or talked, or quarrelled, as it chanced.
We were not lovers, nor even friends well-matched:
Say rather, scholars upon different tracks,
And thinkers disagreed: he, overfull
Of what is, and I, haply, overbold
For what might be.
But then the thrushes sang,
And shook my pulses and the elms' new leaves:
At which I turned, and held my finger up,
And bade him mark that, howsoe'er the world
Went ill, as he related, certainly
The thrushes still sang in it. At the word
His brow would soften—and he bore with me
In melancholy patience, not unkind,
While breaking into voluble ecstasy
I flattered all the beauteous country round,
As poets use, the skies, the clouds, the fields,
The happy violets hiding from the roads
The primroses run down to, carrying gold;
The tangled hedgerows, where the cows push out
Impatient horns and tolerant churning mouths
'Twixt dripping ash boughs—hedgerows all alive
With birds and gnats and large white butterflies
While look as if the mayflower had caught life
And palpitated forth upon the wind;
Hills, vales, woods, netted in a silver mist,
Farms, granges, doubled up among the hills;
And cattle grazing in the watered vales,
And cottage chimneys smoking from the woods,
And cottage gardens smelling everywhere,
Confused with smell of orchards. "See," I said,
"And see! is God not with us on the earth?
And shall we put Him down by aught we do?
Who says there's nothing for the poor and vile
Save poverty and wickedness? behold!"
And ankle-deep in English grass I leaped
And clapped my hands, and called all very fair.

In the beginning when God called all good,
Even then was evil near us,[3] it is writ;

[3] *In the beginning ... near us* See Genesis 1.1, 1.31, and 2.9.

But we indeed who call things good and fair,
The evil is upon us while we speak;
Deliver us from evil,[1] let us pray.

from BOOK 2

Times followed one another. Came a morn
I stood upon the brink of twenty years,
And looked before and after, as I stood
Woman and artist—either incomplete,
Both credulous of completion. There I held
The whole creation in my little cup,
And smiled with thirsty lips before I drank
"Good health to you and me, sweet neighbour mine,
And all these peoples."
I was glad, that day;
The June was in me, with its multitudes
Of nightingales all singing in the dark,
And rosebuds reddening where the calyx[2] split.
I felt so young, so strong, so sure of God!
So glad, I could not choose be very wise!
And, old at twenty, was inclined to pull
My childhood backward in a childish jest
To see the face of 't once more, and farewell!
In which fantastic mood I bounded forth
At early morning—would not wait so long
As even to snatch my bonnet by the strings,
But, brushing a green trail across the lawn
With my gown in the dew, took will and away
Among the acacias of the shrubberies,
To fly my fancies in the open air
And keep my birthday, till my aunt awoke
To stop good dreams. Meanwhile I murmured on
As honeyed bees keep humming to themselves,
"The worthiest poets have remained uncrowned
Till death has bleached their foreheads to the bone;
And so with me it must be unless I prove
Unworthy of the grand adversity,
And certainly I would not fail so much.
What, therefore, if I crown myself today
In sport, not pride, to learn the feel of it,
Before my brows be numbed as Dante's[3] own
To all the tender pricking of such leaves?
Such leaves! what leaves?"
I pulled the branches down
To choose from.
"Not the bay![4] I choose no bay
(The fates deny us if we are overbold),
Nor myrtle[5]—which means chiefly love; and love
Is something awful which one dares not touch
So early o' mornings. This verbena strains
The point of passionate fragrance; and hard by,
This guelder rose, at far too slight a beck
Of the wind, will toss about her flower-apples.
Ah—there's my choice—that ivy on the wall,
That headlong ivy! not a leaf will grow
But thinking of a wreath. Large leaves, smooth leaves,
Serrated like my vines, and half as green.
I like such ivy, bold to leap a height
'Twas strong to climb; as good to grow on graves
As twist about a thyrsus;[6] pretty too
(And that's not ill) when twisted round a comb."

Thus speaking to myself, half singing it,
Because some thoughts are fashioned like a bell
To ring with once being touched, I drew a wreath
Drenched, blinding me with dew, across my brow,
And fastening it behind so, turning faced
… My public!—cousin Romney—with a mouth
Twice graver than his eyes.
I stood there fixed—
My arms up, like the caryatid,[7] sole
Of some abolished temple, helplessly
Persistent in a gesture which derides
A former purpose. Yet my blush was flame,
As if from flax, not stone.
"Aurora Leigh,

[1] *Deliver us from evil* From Matthew 6.13.

[2] *calyx* Outer leaves of a bud.

[3] *Dante* Italian poet Dante Alighieri (1265–1321), author of *The Divine Comedy*.

[4] *bay* Sacred tree of the Greek god Apollo; famous poets in Greece were given laurel wreaths as a symbol of honor.

[5] *myrtle* Plant sacred to Venus, Roman goddess of love.

[6] *thyrsus* Spear or staff of the Greek god Dionysus, tipped with a pinecone and entwined with vines.

[7] *caryatid* Building column sculpted in the figure of a woman.

The earliest of Auroras!"[1]
Hand stretched out
I clasped, as shipwrecked men will clasp a hand,
Indifferent to the sort of palm. The tide
Had caught me at my pastime, writing down
My foolish name too near upon the sea
Which drowned me with a blush as foolish. "You,
My cousin!"
The smile died out in his eyes
And dropped upon his lips, a cold dead weight,
For just a moment, "Here's a book I found!
No name writ on it—poems, by the form;
Some Greek upon the margin—lady's Greek
Without the accents. Read it? Not a word.
I saw at once the thing had witchcraft in't,
Whereof the reading calls up dangerous spirits:
I rather bring it to the witch."
"My book.
You found it"...
"In the hollow by the stream
That beech leans down into—of which you said
The Oread in it has a Naiad's[2] heart
And pines for waters."
"Thank you."
"Thanks to *you*
My cousin! that I have seen you not too much
Witch, scholar, poet, dreamer, and the rest,
To be a woman also."
With a glance
The smile rose in his eyes again and touched
The ivy on my forehead, light as air.
I answered gravely "Poets needs must be
Or men or women—more's the pity."
"Ah,
But men, and still less women, happily,
Scarce need be poets. Keep to the green wreath,
Since even dreaming of the stone and bronze
Brings headaches, pretty cousin, and defiles
The clean white morning dresses."
"So you judge!
Because I love the beautiful I must
Love pleasure chiefly, and be overcharged
For ease and whiteness! well, you know the world,
And only miss your cousin, 'tis not much.
But learn this; I would rather take my part
With God's Dead, who afford to walk in white
Yet spread His glory, than keep quiet here
And gather up my feet from even a step
For fear to soil my gown in so much dust.
I choose to walk at all risks.—Here, if heads
That hold a rhythmic thought, much ache perforce,
For my part I choose headaches—and today's
My birthday."
"Dear Aurora, choose instead
To cure them. You have balsams."° *salves*
"I perceive.
The headache is too noble for my sex.
You think the heartache would sound decenter,
Since that's the woman's special, proper ache,
And altogether tolerable, except
To a woman."
Saying which, I loosed my wreath,
And swinging it beside me as I walked,
Half-petulant, half-playful, as we walked,
I sent a sidelong look to find his thought—
As falcon set on falconer's finger may,
With sidelong head, and startled, braving eye,
Which means, "You'll see—you'll see! I'll soon take flight,
You shall not hinder." He, as shaking out
His hand and answering "Fly then," did not speak,
Except by such a gesture. Silently
We paced, until, just coming into sight
Of the house windows, he abruptly caught
At one end of the swinging wreath, and said
"Aurora!" There I stopped short, breath and all.

"Aurora, let's be serious, and throw by
This game of head and heart. Life means, be sure,
Both heart and head—both active, both complete,
And both in earnest. Men and women make
The world, as head and heart make human life.
Work man, work woman, since there's work to do
In this beleaguered earth, for head and heart,
And thought can never do the work of love:
But work for ends, I mean for uses, not

[1] *Auroras* Dawns; personification of Aurora, Roman goddess of the dawn.

[2] *Oread* Mountain nymph; *Naiad* River nymph.

For such sleek fringes (do you call them ends,
Still less God's glory?) as we sew ourselves
Upon the velvet of those baldaquins° *canopies*
Held 'twixt us and the sun. That book of yours,
I have not read a page of; but I toss
A rose up—it falls calyx down, you see!
The chances are that, being a woman, young
And pure, with such a pair of large, calm eyes,
You write as well … and ill … upon the whole,
As other women. If as well, what then?
If even a little better, … still, what then?
We want the Best in art now, or no art.
The time is done for facile settings up
Of minnow gods, nymphs here and tritons[1] there;
The polytheists have gone out in God,
That unity of Bests. No best, no God!
And so with art, we say. Give art's divine,
Direct, indubitable, real as grief,
Or leave us to the grief we grow ourselves
Divine by overcoming with mere hope
And most prosaic patience. You, you are young
As Eve with nature's daybreak on her face,
But this same world you are come to, dearest coz,
Has done with keeping birthdays, saves her wreaths
To hang upon her ruins—and forgets
To rhyme the cry with which she still beats back
Those savage, hungry dogs that hunt her down
To the empty grave of Christ. The world's hard pressed;
The sweat of labour in the early curse
Has (turning acrid in six thousand years[2])
Become the sweat of torture. Who has time,
An hour's time … think!—to sit upon a bank
And hear the cymbals tinkle[3] in white hands?
When Egypt's slain, I say, let Miriam sing!—
Before—where's Moses?"[4]
"Ah, exactly that.
Where's Moses?—is a Moses to be found?
You'll seek him vainly in the bulrushes,[5]
While I in vain touch cymbals. Yet concede,
Such sounding brass[6] has done some actual good
(The application in a woman's hand,
If that were credible, being scarcely spoilt,)
In colonising beehives."
"There it is!—
You play beside a deathbed like a child,
Yet measure to yourself a prophet's place
To teach the living. None of all these things
Can women understand. You generalise
Oh, nothing—not even grief! Your quick-breathed hearts,
So sympathetic to the personal pang,
Close on each separate knife stroke, yielding up
A whole life at each wound, incapable
Of deepening, widening a large lap of life
To hold the world-full woe. The human race
To you means, such a child, or such a man,
You saw one morning waiting in the cold,
Beside that gate, perhaps. You gather up
A few such cases, and when strong sometimes
Will write of factories and of slaves, as if
Your father were a negro, and your son
A spinner in the mills. All's yours and you,
All, coloured with your blood, or otherwise
Just nothing to you. Why, I call you hard
To general suffering. Here's the world half-blind
With intellectual light, half-brutalised
With civilisation, having caught the plague
In silks from Tarsus,[7] shrieking east and west
Along a thousand railroads, mad with pain
And sin too!… does one woman of you all
(You who weep easily) grow pale to see
This tiger shake his cage?—does one of you
Stand still from dancing, stop from stringing pearls,
And pine and die because of the great sum

[1] *minnow gods … tritons* Minor deities of Greek mythology.

[2] *six thousand years* The world was then widely thought to have been created in 4004 BCE.

[3] *cymbals tinkle* See 1 Corinthians 13.1.

[4] *Egypt's slain … Moses* According to Exodus 15.19–22, Miriam sang and danced after the Pharaoh and his men drowned and Moses led the Jewish people through the Red Sea.

[5] *bulrushes* In Exodus 2.3 Moses' mother hides her son in an ark made from bulrushes.

[6] *sounding brass* From 1 Corinthians 13.1: "Though I speak with the tongues of men and of angels, and have not charity, I am become as sounding brass, or a tinkling cymbal."

[7] *Tarsus* City in Turkey.

Of universal anguish?—Show me a tear
Wet as Cordelia's,[1] in eyes bright as yours,
Because the world is mad. You cannot count,
That you should weep for this account, not you!
You weep for what you know. A red-haired child
Sick in a fever, if you touch him once,
Though but so little as with a fingertip,
Will set you weeping; but a million sick …
You could as soon weep for the rule of three[2]
Or compound fractions. Therefore, this same world,
Uncomprehended by you, must remain
Uninfluenced by you.—Women as you are,
Mere women, personal and passionate,
You give us doting mothers, and perfect wives,
Sublime Madonnas, and enduring saints!
We get no Christ from you—and verily
We shall not get a poet, in my mind."

"With which conclusion you conclude!" …
"But this,
That you, Aurora, with the large live brow
And steady eyelids, cannot condescend
To play at art, as children play at swords,
To show a pretty spirit, chiefly admired
Because true action is impossible.
You never can be satisfied with praise
Which men give women when they judge a book
Not as mere work but as mere woman's work,
Expressing the comparative respect
Which means the absolute scorn. 'Oh, excellent,
What grace, what facile turns, what fluent sweeps,
What delicate discernment … almost thought!
The book does honour to the sex, we hold.
Among our female authors we make room
For this fair writer, and congratulate
The country that produces in these times
Such women, competent to … spell.'"
"Stop there,"
I answered, burning through his thread of talk
With a quick flame of emotion—"You have read
My soul, if not my book, and argue well
I would not condescend … we will not say
To such a kind of praise (a worthless end
Is praise of all kinds), but to such a use
Of holy art and golden life. I am young,
And peradventure° weak—you tell me so— *perhaps*
Through being a woman. And, for all the rest,
Take thanks for justice. I would rather dance
At fairs on tightrope, till the babies dropped
Their gingerbread for joy—than shift the types[3]
For tolerable verse, intolerable
To men who act and suffer. Better far
Pursue a frivolous trade by serious means,
Than a sublime art frivolously."
"You,
Choose nobler work than either, O moist eyes
And hurrying lips and heaving heart! We are young,
Aurora, you and I. The world—look round—
The world, we're come to late, is swollen hard
With perished generations and their sins:
The civiliser's spade grinds horribly
On dead men's bones, and cannot turn up soil
That's otherwise than fetid. All success
Proves partial failure; all advance implies
What's left behind; all triumph, something crushed
At the chariot wheels; all government, some wrong
And rich men make the poor, who curse the rich,
Who agonise together, rich and poor,
Under and over, in the social spasm
And crisis of the ages. Here's an age
That makes its own vocation! here we have stepped
Across the bounds of time! here's nought to see,
But just the rich man and just Lazarus,
And both in torments, with a mediate gulf,
Though not a hint of Abraham's bosom.[4] Who
Being man, Aurora, can stand calmly by
And view these things, and never tease his soul
For some great cure? No physic for this grief,
In all the earth and heavens too?"
"You believe
In God, for your part?—ay? that He who makes

[1] *tear … Cordelia's* See Shakespeare's *King Lear* 4.7.80.

[2] *rule of three* Also called the "golden rule" or "rule of proportion."

[3] *types* Moveable type, or letters, used in the printing process.

[4] *rich man … Abraham's bosom* From Luke 16.19–22: the rich man who denied food to the beggar Lazarus was sent to hell, while Lazarus was sent to join Abraham in heaven.

Can make good things from ill things, best from worst,
As men plant tulips upon dunghills when
They wish them finest?"
"True. A death-heat is
The same as life-heat, to be accurate,
And in all nature is no death at all,
As men account of death, so long as God
Stands witnessing for life perpetually,
By being just God. That's abstract truth, I know,
Philosophy, or sympathy with God:
But I, I sympathise with man, not God
(I think I was a man for chiefly this),
And when I stand beside a dying bed,
'Tis death to me. Observe—it had not much
Consoled the race of mastodons to know,
Before they went to fossil, that anon
Their place would quicken with the elephant.
They were not elephants but mastodons;
And I, a man, as men are now and not
As men may be hereafter, feel with men
In the agonising present."
"Is it so,"
I said, "my cousin? is the world so bad,
While I hear nothing of it through the trees?
The world was always evil—but so bad?"

"So bad, Aurora. Dear, my soul is grey
With poring over the long sum of ill;
So much for vice, so much for discontent,
So much for the necessities of power,
So much for the connivances of fear,
Coherent in statistical despairs
With such a total of distracted life,...
To see it down in figures on a page,
Plain, silent, clear, as God sees through the earth
The sense of all the graves—that's terrible
For one who is not God, and cannot right
The wrong he looks on. May I choose indeed,
But vow away my years, my means, my aims,
Among the helpers, if there's any help
In such a social strait? The common blood
That swings along my veins is strong enough
To draw me to this duty."
Then I spoke.
"I have not stood long on the strand of life,
And these salt waters have had scarcely time
To creep so high up as to wet my feet:
I cannot judge these tides—I shall, perhaps.
A woman's always younger than a man
At equal years, because she is disallowed
Maturing by the outdoor sun and air,
And kept in long-clothes past the age to walk.
Ah well, I know you men judge otherwise!
You think a woman ripens, as a peach,
In the cheeks chiefly. Pass it to me now;
I'm young in age, and younger still, I think,
As a woman. But a child may say amen
To a bishop's prayer and feel the way it goes,
And I, incapable to loose the knot
Of social questions, can approve, applaud
August compassion, Christian thoughts that shoot
Beyond the vulgar white° of personal aims. *archery target*
Accept my reverence."
There he glowed on me
With all his face and eyes. "No other help?"
Said he—"no more than so?"
"What help?" I asked.
"You'd scorn my help—as Nature's self, you say,
Has scorned to put her music in my mouth
Because a woman's. Do you now turn round
And ask for what a woman cannot give?"

"For what she only can, I turn and ask,"
He answered, catching up my hands in his,
And dropping on me from his high-eaved brow
The full weight of his soul—"I ask for love,
And that, she can; for life in fellowship
Through bitter duties—that, I know she can;
For wifehood—will she?"
"Now," I said, "may God
Be witness 'twixt us two!" and with the word,
Meseemed[1] I floated into a sudden light
Above his stature—"am I proved too weak
To stand alone, yet strong enough to bear
Such leaners on my shoulder? poor to think,
Yet rich enough to sympathise with thought?

[1] *Meseemed* It seemed to me.

Incompetent to sing, as blackbirds can,
Yet competent to love, like HIM?"
I paused;
Perhaps I darkened, as the lighthouse will
That turns upon the sea. "It's always so.
Anything does for a wife."
"Aurora, dear,
And dearly honoured,"—he pressed in at once
With eager utterance—"you translate me ill.
I do not contradict my thought of you
Which is most reverent, with another thought
Found less so. If your sex is weak for art
(And I, who said so, did but honour you
By using truth in courtship), it is strong
For life and duty. Place your fecund heart
In mine, and let us blossom for the world
That wants love's colour in the grey of time.
My talk, meanwhile, is arid to you, ay,
Since all my talk can only set you where
You look down coldly on the arena-heaps
Of headless bodies, shapeless, indistinct!
The Judgment-Angel scarce would find his way
Through such a heap of generalised distress
To the individual man with lips and eyes,
Much less Aurora. Ah, my sweet, come down,
And hand in hand we'll go where yours shall touch
These victims, one by one! till, one by one,
The formless, nameless trunk of every man
Shall seem to wear a head with hair you know,
And every woman catch your mother's face
To melt you into passion."
"I am a girl,"
I answered slowly; "you do well to name
My mother's face. Though far too early, alas,
God's hand did interpose 'twixt it and me,
I know so much of love as used to shine
In that face and another. Just so much;
No more indeed at all. I have not seen
So much love since, I pray you pardon me,
As answers even to make a marriage with
In this cold land of England. What you love
Is not a woman, Romney, but a cause:
You want a helpmate, not a mistress, sir,
A wife to help your ends—in her no end.
Your cause is noble, your ends excellent,
But I, being most unworthy of these and that,
Do otherwise conceive of love. Farewell."

"Farewell, Aurora? you reject me thus?"
He said.
"Sir, you were married long ago.
You have a wife already whom you love,
Your social theory. Bless you both, I say.
For my part, I am scarcely meek enough
To be the handmaid of a lawful spouse.
Do I look a Hagar,[1] think you?"
"So you jest."

"Nay, so, I speak in earnest," I replied.
"You treat of marriage too much like, at least,
A chief apostle: you would bear with you
A wife … a sister[2] … shall we speak it out?
A sister of charity."
"Then, must it be
Indeed farewell? And was I so far wrong
In hope and in illusion, when I took
The woman to be nobler than the man,
Yourself the noblest woman, in the use
And comprehension of what love is—love,
That generates the likeness of itself
Through all heroic duties? so far wrong,
In saying bluntly, venturing truth on love,
'Come, human creature, love and work with me,'—
Instead of 'Lady, thou art wondrous fair,
And, where the Graces[3] walk before, the Muse
Will follow at the lightning of their eyes,
And where the Muse walks, lovers need to creep:
Turn round and love me, or I die of love.'"
With quiet indignation I broke in.
"You misconceive the question like a man,
Who sees a woman as the complement
Of his sex merely. You forget too much
That every creature, female as the male,
Stands single in responsible act and thought

[1] *Hagar* See Genesis 16.1–4: Hagar was handmaid to Sarah, Abraham's wife, and she also bore Abraham's child, as Sarah was unable to conceive.

[2] *chief apostle … sister* See 1 Corinthians 9.5.

[3] *Graces* In Greek mythology, three goddesses of beauty and charm.

As also in birth and death. Whoever says
To a loyal woman, 'Love and work with me,'
Will get fair answers if the work and love,
Being good themselves, are good for her—the best
She was born for. Women of a softer mood,
Surprised by men when scarcely awake to life,
Will sometimes only hear the first word, love,
And catch up with it any kind of work,
Indifferent, so that dear love go with it.
I do not blame such women, though, for love,
They pick much oakum;[1] earth's fanatics make
Too frequently heaven's saints. But *me* your work
Is not the best for—nor your love the best,
Nor able to commend the kind of work
For love's sake merely. Ah, you force me, sir,
To be overbold in speaking of myself:
I too have my vocation—work to do,
The heavens and earth have set me since I changed
My father's face for theirs, and, though your world
Were twice as wretched as you represent,
Most serious work, most necessary work
As any of the economists'. Reform,
Make trade a Christian possibility,
And individual right no general wrong;
Wipe out earth's furrows of the Thine and Mine,
And leave one green for men to play at bowls,
With innings for them all! … What then, indeed,
If mortals are not greater by the head
Than any of their prosperities? what then,
Unless the artist keep up open roads
Betwixt the seen and unseen—bursting through
The best of your conventions with his best,
The speakable, imaginable best
God bids him speak, to prove what lies beyond
Both speech and imagination? A starved man
Exceeds a fat beast: we'll not barter, sir,
The beautiful for barley.—And, even so,
I hold you will not compass your poor ends
Of barley-feeding and material ease,
Without a poet's individualism
To work your universal. It takes a soul,
To move a body: it takes a high-souled man,
To move the masses, even to a cleaner stye:
It takes the ideal, to blow a hair's-breadth off
The dust of the actual.—Ah, your Fouriers[2] failed,
Because not poets enough to understand
That life develops from within.—For me,
Perhaps I am not worthy, as you say,
Of work like this: perhaps a woman's soul
Aspires, and not creates: yet we aspire,
And yet I'll try out your perhapses, sir,
And if I fail … why, burn me up my straw
Like other false works—I'll not ask for grace;
Your scorn is better, cousin Romney. I
Who love my art, would never wish it lower
To suit my stature. I may love my art.
You'll grant that even a woman may love art,
Seeing that to waste true love on anything
Is womanly, past question."
                                        I retain
The very last word which I said that day,
As you the creaking of the door, years past,
Which let upon you such disabling news
You ever after have been graver. He,
His eyes, the motions in his silent mouth,
Were fiery points on which my words were caught,
Transfixed for ever in my memory
For his sake, not their own. And yet I know
I did not love him … nor he me … that's sure …
And what I said is unrepented of,
As truth is always. Yet … a princely man!—
If hard to me, heroic for himself!
He bears down on me through the slanting years,
The stronger for the distance. If he had loved,
Ay, loved me, with that retributive face, …
I might have been a common woman now
And happier, less known and less left alone,
Perhaps a better woman after all,
With chubby children hanging on my neck
To keep me low and wise. Ah me, the vines
That bear such fruit are proud to stoop with it.
The palm stands upright in a realm of sand.

[1] *oakum* Rope fibers acquired by untwisting and picking at old rope, a chore commonly assigned to prisoners or the workhouse poor.

[2] *Fourier* Charles Fourier (1772–1837), French socialist philosopher and utopian theorist.

And I, who spoke the truth then, stand upright,
Still worthy of having spoken out the truth,
By being content I spoke it though it set
Him there, me here.—O woman's vile remorse,
To hanker after a mere name, a show,
A supposition, a potential love!
Does every man who names love in our lives
Become a power for that? is love's true thing
So much best to us, that what personates love
Is next best? A potential love, forsooth!
I'm not so vile. No, no—he cleaves, I think,
This man, this image—chiefly for the wrong
And shock he gave my life, in finding me
Precisely where the devil of my youth
Had set me, on those mountain-peaks of hope[1]
All glittering with the dawn-dew, all erect
And famished for the noon—exclaiming, while
I looked for empire and much tribute, "Come,
I have some worthy work for thee below.
Come, sweep my barns and keep my hospitals,
And I will pay thee with a current coin
Which men give women."
...

from Book 5

Aurora Leigh, be humble. Shall I hope
To speak my poems in mysterious tune
With man and nature?—with the lava-lymph
That trickles from successive galaxies
Still drop by drop adown the finger of God
In still new worlds?—with summer days in this
That scarce dare breathe they are so beautiful?
With spring's delicious trouble in the ground,
Tormented by the quickened blood of roots,
And softly pricked by golden crocus sheaves
In token of the harvest-time of flowers?
With winters and with autumns—and beyond
With the human heart's large seasons, when it hopes
And fears, joys, grieves, and loves?—with all that strain
Of sexual passion, which devours the flesh
In a sacrament of souls? with mother's breasts
Which, round the new-made creatures hanging there,
Throb luminous and harmonious like pure spheres?—
With multitudinous life, and finally
With the great escapings of ecstatic souls,
Who, in a rush of too long prisoned flame,
Their radiant faces upward, burn away
This dark of the body, issuing on a world
Beyond our mortal?—can I speak my verse
So plainly in tune to these things and the rest
That men shall feel it catch them on the quick
As having the same warrant over them
To hold and move them if they will or no,
Alike imperious as the primal rhythm
Of that theurgic[2] nature?—I must fail,
Who fail at the beginning to hold and move
One man—and he my cousin, and he my friend,
And he born tender, made intelligent,
Inclined to ponder the precipitous sides
Of difficult questions; yet, obtuse to *me*,
Of *me*, incurious! likes me very well,
And wishes me a paradise of good,
Good looks, good means, and good digestion—ay,
But otherwise evades me, puts me off
With kindness, with a tolerant gentleness—
Too light a book for a grave man's reading! Go,
Aurora Leigh: be humble.
There it is,
We women are too apt to look to one,
Which proves a certain impotence in art.
We strain our natures at doing something great,
Far less because it's something great to do,
Than haply that we, so, commend ourselves
As being not small, and more appreciable
To some one friend. We must have mediators
Betwixt our highest conscience and the judge;
Some sweet saint's blood must quicken in our palms,
Or all the like in heaven seems slow and cold:
Good only being perceived as the end of good,
And God alone pleased—that's too poor, we think,
And not enough for us by any means.
Ay—Romney, I remember, told me once

[1] *devil ... hope* See Luke 4.5: "And the devil, taking him [Jesus] up into an high mountain, showed unto him all the kingdoms of the world in a moment of time."

[2] *theurgic* Pertaining to the operation of the gods or the supernatural in human affairs.

We miss the abstract when we comprehend.
We miss it most when we aspire—and fail.

Yet, so, I will not.—This vile woman's way
Of trailing garments shall not trip me up:
I'll have no traffic with the personal thought
In Art's pure temple. Must I work in vain,
Without the approbation of a man?
It cannot be; it shall not. Fame itself,
That approbation of the general race,
Presents a poor end (though the arrow speed
Shot straight with vigorous finger to the white),
And the highest fame was never reached except
By what was aimed above it. Art for art,
And good for God Himself, the essential Good!
We'll keep our aims sublime, our eyes erect,
Although our woman-hands should shake and fail;
And if we fail ... But must we?—
                                        Shall I fail?
The Greeks said grandly in their tragic phrase,
"Let no one be called happy till his death."[1]
To which I add—Let no one till his death
Be called unhappy. Measure not the work
Until the day's out and the labour done,
Then bring your gauges. If the day's work's scant,
Why, call it scant; affect no compromise;
And, in that we have nobly striven at least,
Deal with us nobly, women though we be,
And honour us with truth if not with praise.
...
The critics say that epics have died out
With Agamemnon[2] and the goat-nursed gods;[3]
I'll not believe it. I could never deem,
As Payne Knight[4] did (the mythic mountaineer
Who travelled higher than he was born to live,
And showed sometimes the goitre[5] in his throat
Discoursing of an image seen through fog),
That Homer's heroes measured twelve feet high.[6]
They were but men:—his Helen's hair turned grey
Like any plain Miss Smith's who wears a front;[7]
And Hector's infant whimpered at a plume[8]
As yours last Friday at a turkey-cock.
All actual heroes are essential men,
And all men possible heroes: every age,
Heroic in proportions, double-faced,
Looks backward and before, expects a morn
And claims an epos.° *epic poem*
                                        Ay, but every age
Appears to souls who live in't (ask Carlyle)
Most unheroic.[9] Ours, for instance, ours:
The thinkers scout° it, and the poets abound *mock*
Who scorn to touch it with a fingertip:
A pewter age—mixed metal, silver-washed;
An age of scum, spooned off the richer past,
An age of patches for old gaberdines,° *woolen cloths*
An age of mere transition,[10] meaning nought
Except that what succeeds must shame it quite
If God please. That's wrong thinking, to my mind,
And wrong thoughts make poor poems.
                                        Every age,

---

[1] *Let no one ... death* The final lines of Sophocles's *Oedipus Rex*: "From hence the lesson draw, / To reckon no man happy till ye see / The closing day; until he pass the bourn / Which severs life from death, unscathed by woe."

[2] *Agamemnon* King of Mycenae and head of the Greek forces in the Trojan War; Agamemnon was murdered by his wife and her lover.

[3] *goat-nursed gods* Zeus, the supreme god of Greek mythology, was nursed by a goat as a baby.

[4] *Payne Knight* Radical historian and author of much commentary on Greek mythology; Richard Payne Knight (1750–1824) released an edition of the *Iliad* and the *Odyssey* that deleted many of Homer's passages.

[5] *goitre* Thyroid swelling in the neck, occurring disproportionately in people who dwell in mountainous areas.

[6] *Homer's ... high* Payne Knight felt that Greek art and literature idealized humans.

[7] *front* False hair that covers the forehead.

[8] *Hector's ... plume* In Homer's the *Iliad* 6.575–78, Hector's son recoils in fear upon seeing his warrior father's plumed helmet.

[9] *every age ... unheroic* Thomas Carlyle wrote in *On Heroes, Hero-Worship, and the Heroic in History* (1840) that the heroism of any given age is never recognized in its time.

[10] *An age of mere transition* In *The Spirit of the Age* (1831) John Stuart Mill wrote: "In the present age of transition, everything must be subordinate to freedom of inquiry."

Through being beheld too close, is ill-discerned
By those who have not lived past it. We'll suppose
Mount Athos carved, as Alexander schemed,
To some colossal statue of a man.[1]
The peasants, gathering brushwood in his ear,
Had guessed as little as the browsing goats
Of form or feature of humanity
Up there—in fact, had travelled five miles off
Or ere the giant image broke on them,
Full human profile, nose and chin distinct,
Mouth, muttering rhythms of silence up the sky
And fed at evening with the blood of suns;
Grand torso—hand, that flung perpetually
The largesse of a silver river down
To all the country pastures. 'Tis even thus
With times we live in—evermore too great
To be apprehended near.
But poets should
Exert a double vision; should have eyes
To see near things as comprehensively
As if afar they took their point of sight,
And distant things as intimately deep
As if they touched them. Let us strive for this.
I do distrust the poet who discerns
No character or glory in his times,
And trundles back his soul five hundred years,
Past moat and drawbridge, into a castle court,
To sing—oh, not of lizard or of toad
Alive i' the ditch there—'twere excusable,
But of some black chief, half knight, half sheep-lifter,
Some beauteous dame, half chattel and half queen,
As dead as must be, for the greater part,
The poems made on their chivalric bones;
And that's no wonder: death inherits death.
Nay, if there's room for poets in this world
A little overgrown (I think there is),
Their sole work is to represent the age,
Their age, not Charlemagne's,[2]—this live, throbbing
age,
That brawls, cheats, maddens, calculates, aspires,
And spends more passion, more heroic heat,
Betwixt the mirrors of its drawing-rooms,
Than Roland with his knights at Roncesvalles.[3]
To flinch from modern varnish, coat or flounce,
Cry out for togas and the picturesque,
Is fatal—foolish too. King Arthur's self
Was commonplace to Lady Guenever;
And Camelot to minstrels seemed as flat
As Fleet Street[4] to our poets.
Never flinch,
But still, unscrupulously epic, catch
Upon the burning lava of a song
The full-veined, heaving, double-breasted Age:
That, when the next shall come, the men of that
May touch the impress with reverent hand, and say
"Behold—behold the paps° we have all sucked! *nipples*
This bosom seems to beat still, or at least
It sets ours beating: this is living art,
Which thus presents and thus records true life."
—1857

1 *Mount Athos ... man* In Plutarch's *The Life of Alexander*, the sculptor Stasicrates proposed to Alexander that he carve out of Mount Athos "a most enduring and most conspicuous statue of the king, which in its left hand should hold a city of ten thousand inhabitants, and with its right should pour forth a river running with generous current into the sea."

2 *Charlemagne* Charles the Great (742–814), ruler of much of Europe in the early years of the ninth century.

3 *Roland ... Roncesvalles* Roland, Charlemagne's commander, was immortalized in *Chanson de Roland*, which relates his death in a battle at Roncesvalles.

4 *Fleet Street* In London, then the hub of the news and publishing industries.

ALFRED, LORD TENNYSON

1809 – 1892

In 1850, the novelist and critic Charles Kingsley praised Tennyson's dramatic monologue "Locksley Hall" as the poem that "has had most influence on the minds of the young men of our day." Throughout his long career, Tennyson's poems continued to resonate with Victorian audiences. The self-reflective grief of *In Memoriam* (1850) touched a chord of genuine sympathy in nineteenth-century readers, including Queen Victoria herself, much as Tennyson's re-telling of Arthurian legend in *Idylls of the King* (1859–85) echoed—while also questioning—the nationalistic zeal of the later Victorian period. Britain's poet laureate from 1850 to his death in 1892, Tennyson was the quintessential poet of his age.

He was born in 1809 in Somersby, Lincolnshire, to a privileged family, and his poetic gifts became apparent early on. At age eight, Tennyson was composing pages of blank verse in the style of James Thomson; by ten or eleven he had graduated to studying the work of Alexander Pope, imitating hundreds of lines of Pope's translation of Homer's *Iliad*. At twelve, Tennyson set to work on his first epic, a six-thousand-line experiment that mimicked Walter Scott's octo-syllabic extravaganzas of war and romance. "I wrote as much as seventy lines at one time," he later recalled, "and used to go shouting them about the fields in the dark." By age fourteen, with an Elizabethan-style drama entitled *The Devil and the Lady*, Tennyson's work was approaching the sonorous agility and understated pathos for which it would be known. His first publication, *Poems by Two Brothers* (1827), a collaborative effort by Tennyson and his two older brothers, Frederick and Charles, was completed just prior to Tennyson's entrance to Trinity College, Cambridge.

Tennyson distinguished himself at Cambridge, establishing his reputation as both a deep thinker and a poet. In June of 1829, he won the chancellor's Gold Medal with a blank-verse poem, *Timbuctoo*. Some time in that year, Tennyson met Arthur Henry Hallam, who was to become the poet's closest friend and companion. It was also in 1829 that Tennyson joined the Cambridge Apostles, an undergraduate debating society of which Hallam and many of Tennyson's other Cambridge friends were a part. The year 1830 saw the publication of Tennyson's first important volume, *Poems, Chiefly Lyrical*, which Hallam reviewed for the *Englishman's Magazine* in an essay entitled "On Some of the characteristics of Modern poetry and on the lyrical poems of Alfred Tennyson." Hallam describes Tennyson as a poet of "sensation," one of a school of poets, including Shelley and Keats, whose "fine organs tremble into emotion at colors, and sounds, and movements" and who translate this physiological sensitivity into their verses. It was precisely such sensitivity that Christopher North (the pseudonym of John Wilson) later attacked in his 1832 *Blackwood's* review of the volume. Subsequently many critics have charted Tennyson's gradual movement away from a poetics of sensation and toward a more restrained poetic style.

The early 1830s were a difficult time for the young poet. Following the death of his father in 1831, Tennyson left Cambridge without taking his degree. Soon afterward, his brother Edward lost his sanity, succumbing to what was known as the "black blood" of the Tennyson family. Finally, and perhaps most devastatingly, Arthur Hallam died suddenly in 1833, apparently of a stroke or a brain hemorrhage. Having published one volume, *Poems*, in 1832, Tennyson would remain silent as a poet for the next ten years, refusing to publish his many works in progress until the *Poems* of 1842, the work that brought him his reputation as both a remarkable poet and a great voice of his age. During the "ten years' silence," however, Tennyson composed much of what many consider his masterwork, *In Memoriam* (1850), in addition to the innovative dramatic monologues of the 1842 *Poems*, including "Ulysses," "Locksley Hall," and "St Simeon Stylites."

In 1847, Tennyson published *The Princess*, a poetic medley that explored, through a wildly improbable narrative, the relations between the sexes and the viability of education for women. Interspersed throughout the work are many of Tennyson's best-known lyrics: "Sweet and Low," "The Splendour Falls," and "Tears, Idle Tears," among others. In 1850, Tennyson ascended to the laureateship and married Emily Sellwood, to whom he had been engaged for thirteen years. That same year, Tennyson also published *In Memoriam*, the elegy on which he had been at work since Arthur Hallam's death. The first of many of Tennyson's books to sell in large numbers, *In Memoriam* went into three editions in its first year alone. Amid a rising swell of scientific discovery and industrial transformation, the poem captured the mood of the era, alternating between faith in science and faith in religion, and reflecting the hopes, doubts, and beliefs of the Victorians.

Tennyson's life changed notably as a result of both his marriage and his suddenly public role as poet laureate. The Tennysons had two sons within the next four years, the elder of whom was named Hallam after Tennyson's deceased friend. (After his father's death, Hallam Tennyson wrote a biography entitled *Alfred Lord Tennyson: A Memoir*, and he penned a second volume in 1911, *Tennyson and His Friends*. Alfred Tennyson's grandson Charles also wrote a biography in 1949.)

Many critics have argued that Tennyson's style changed after his appointment as Poet Laureate. Certainly it is true that he assumed a different voice in the occasional poems composed in his role as poet laureate, most notably the "Ode on the Death of the Duke of Wellington" (1852); likewise "The Charge of the Light Brigade" (1854) projects an explicit political stance largely absent in his earlier works. But Tennyson continued to evolve as a poet, publishing an experimental "monodrama," *Maud*, in 1855 and the first four segments of his epic, *Idylls of the King*, in 1859. *Maud* was in many ways Tennyson's most controversial publication. Critics complained of the poem's irregular rhythms and of the "screed of bombast" that seemed to some like "the rasping of a blacksmith's file." *Idylls of the King*, on the other hand, was largely—though not universally—hailed as a *magnum opus*. Tennyson had contemplated writing an epic from his childhood; the finished *Idylls* reflects the poet's mature thoughts about Victorian life, politics, and culture through the world of Camelot and King Arthur.

Tennyson's later publications include the plays *Queen Mary* (1875), *The Falcon* (1879), and *The Promise of May* (1882), all of which were produced on the Victorian stage, and numerous volumes of poetry, including *Enoch Arden* (1864), *Tiresias, and Other Poems* (1885), *Locksley Hall Sixty Years After* (1886), and *Demeter and Other Poems* (1889). In 1883, Tennyson accepted a barony and took a seat in the House of Lords. When he died in 1892, over 11,000 people applied for tickets to his funeral at Westminster Abbey, though only 1,000 were permitted to attend. He is buried beside Robert Browning in the Poets' Corner of the Abbey.

⌘⌘⌘

Julia Margaret Cameron, *Mariana*, 1875.

Mariana

Mariana in the moated grange
(*Measure for Measure*)[1]

With blackest moss the flower-plots
Were thickly crusted, one and all:
The rusted nails fell from the knots
That held the pear to the gable-wall.[2]
The broken sheds looked sad and strange:
Unlifted was the clinking latch;
Weeded and worn the ancient thatch
Upon the lonely moated grange.
She only said, "My life is dreary,
He cometh not," she said;
She said, "I am aweary, aweary,
I would that I were dead!"

Her tears fell with the dews at even;° *evening*
Her tears fell ere° the dews were dried; *before*
She could not look on the sweet heaven,
Either at morn or eventide.
After the flitting of the bats,
When thickest dark did trance° the sky, *entrance*
She drew her casement-curtain by,
And glanced athwart the glooming flats.[3]
She only said, "The night is dreary,
He cometh not," she said;
She said, "I am aweary, aweary,
I would that I were dead!"

Upon the middle of the night,
Waking she heard the night-fowl crow:
The cock sung out an hour ere light:
From the dark fen° the oxen's low *lowlands*
Came to her: without hope of change,
In sleep she seemed to walk forlorn,
Till cold winds woke the gray-eyed morn
About the lonely moated grange.
She only said, "The day is dreary,
He cometh not," she said;
She said, "I am aweary, aweary,
I would that I were dead!"

About a stone-cast from the wall
A sluice with blackened waters slept,
And o'er it many, round and small,
The clustered marish-mosses[4] crept.
Hard by a poplar shook alway,
All silver-green with gnarlèd bark:
For leagues no other tree did mark
The level waste, the rounding gray.
She only said, "My life is dreary,

[1] *Mariana … Measure* Tennyson's epigraph is adapted from the words of the Duke in Shakespeare's *Measure for Measure*, 3.1.277: "There, at the moated grange, lies this dejected Mariana." Earlier in the scene, the Duke has recounted how Mariana, having lost her dowry (and her brother) in a shipwreck, has been deserted by her betrothed; *moated grange* Cottage or small farmhouse surrounded by a moat, or water-filled ditch.

[2] *The rusted … gable-wall* The pear has been espaliered, or trained to grow against a wall on a lattice or framework of stakes.

[3] *flats* Flatlands or lowlands.

[4] [Tennyson's note] *Marish-mosses*, the little marsh-moss lumps that float on the surface of the water.

He cometh not," she said;
She said, "I am aweary, aweary,
I would that I were dead!"

And ever when the moon was low,
And the shrill winds were up and away,
In the white curtain, to and fro,
She saw the gusty shadow sway.
But when the moon was very low,
And wild winds bound within their cell,[1]
The shadow of the poplar fell
Upon her bed, across her brow.
She only said, "The night is dreary,
He cometh not," she said;
She said, "I am aweary, aweary,
I would that I were dead!"

All day within the dreamy house,
The doors upon their hinges creaked;
The blue fly sung in the pane; the mouse
Behind the mouldering wainscot° shrieked, *paneling*
Or from the crevice peered about.
Old faces glimmered through the doors,
Old footsteps trod the upper floors,
Old voices called her from without.
She only said, "My life is dreary,
He cometh not," she said;
She said, "I am aweary, aweary,
I would that I were dead!"

The sparrow's chirrup on the roof,
The slow clock ticking, and the sound
Which to the wooing wind aloof
The poplar made, did all confound
Her sense; but most she loathed the hour
When the thick-moted[2] sunbeam lay
Athwart the chambers, and the day
Was sloping toward his western bower.
Then, said she, "I am very dreary,
He will not come," she said;
She wept, "I am aweary, aweary,
Oh God, that I were dead!"

—1830

The Lady of Shalott[3]

Part 1

On either side the river lie
Long fields of barley and of rye,
That clothe the wold° and meet the sky; *plain*
And through the field the road runs by
To many-towered Camelot;
And up and down the people go,
Gazing where the lilies blow
Round an island there below,
The island of Shalott.

Willows whiten,[4] aspens quiver,
Little breezes dusk° and shiver *darken*
Through the wave that runs for ever
By the island in the river
Flowing down to Camelot.
Four gray walls, and four gray towers,
Overlook a space of flowers,
And the silent isle imbowers° *encloses*
The Lady of Shalott.

By the margin, willow-veiled,
Slide the heavy barges trailed
By slow horses; and unhailed
The shallop[5] flitteth silken-sailed
Skimming down to Camelot:
But who hath seen her wave her hand?

[1] *wild winds … their cell* Reference to Virgil's *Aeneid*, 1.52, in which Aeolus, god of winds, keeps the winds imprisoned in a cavern.

[2] *thick-moted* I.e., thick with motes of dust.

[3] *The Lady of Shalott* The title character is based on the figure of Elaine in the Arthurian romances, who dies for love of Lancelot; she is called "the lily maid of Astolat" in Malory's *Morte d'Arthur*. Tennyson first encountered the story, however, in a medieval Italian romance called "La Donna di Scalotta" and changed the name to Shalott for a softer sound.

[4] *Willows whiten* I.e., the wind exposes the white undersides of the leaves.

[5] *shallop* Light open boat for use in shallow water.

Or at the casement seen her stand?
Or is she known in all the land,
The Lady of Shalott?

Only reapers, reaping early
In among the bearded barley,
Hear a song that echoes cheerly
From the river winding clearly,
Down to towered Camelot:
And by the moon the reaper weary,
Piling sheaves in uplands airy,
Listening, whispers "'Tis the fairy
Lady of Shalott."

Part 2

There she weaves by night and day
A magic web with colours gay.
She has heard a whisper say,
A curse is on her if she stay
To look down to Camelot.
She knows not what the curse may be,
And so she weaveth steadily,
And little other care hath she,
The Lady of Shalott.

And moving through a mirror clear
That hangs before her all the year,
Shadows of the world appear.
There she sees the highway near
Winding down to Camelot:
There the river eddy whirls,
And there the surly village-churls,
And the red cloaks of market girls,
Pass onward from Shalott.

Sometimes a troop of damsels glad,
An abbot on an ambling pad,° *horse*
Sometimes a curly shepherd-lad,
Or long-haired page in crimson clad,
Goes by to towered Camelot;
And sometimes through the mirror blue
The knights come riding two and two:
She hath no loyal knight and true,
The Lady of Shalott.

But in her web she still delights
To weave the mirror's magic sights,
For often through the silent nights
A funeral, with plumes and lights
And music, went to Camelot:
Or when the moon was overhead,
Came two young lovers lately wed;
"I am half sick of shadows," said
The Lady of Shalott.

Part 3

A bow-shot from her bower-eaves,
He rode between the barley-sheaves,
The sun came dazzling through the leaves,
And flamed upon the brazen greaves[1]
Of bold Sir Lancelot.
A red-cross knight for ever kneeled
To a lady in his shield,
That sparkled on the yellow field,
Beside remote Shalott.

The gemmy° bridle glittered free, *brilliant*
Like to some branch of stars we see
Hung in the golden Galaxy.
The bridle bells rang merrily
As he rode down to Camelot:
And from his blazoned baldric° slung *shoulder-strap*
A mighty silver bugle hung,
And as he rode his armour rung,
Beside remote Shalott.

All in the blue unclouded weather
Thick-jewelled shone the saddle-leather,
The helmet and the helmet-feather
Burned like one burning flame together,
As he rode down to Camelot.
As often through the purple night,
Below the starry clusters bright,

[1] *greaves* Armor worn below the knee.

Some bearded meteor, trailing light,
Moves over still Shalott.

His broad clear brow in sunlight glowed;
On burnished hooves his war-horse trode;
From underneath his helmet flowed
His coal-black curls as on he rode,
As he rode down to Camelot.
From the bank and from the river
He flashed into the crystal mirror,
"Tirra lirra," by the river
Sang Sir Lancelot.

She left the web, she left the loom,
She made three paces through the room,
She saw the water-lily bloom,
She saw the helmet and the plume,
She looked down to Camelot.
Out flew the web and floated wide;
The mirror cracked from side to side;
"The curse is come upon me," cried
The Lady of Shalott.

Part 4

In the stormy east-wind straining,
The pale yellow woods were waning,
The broad stream in his banks complaining,
Heavily the low sky raining
Over towered Camelot;
Down she came and found a boat
Beneath a willow left afloat,
And round about the prow she wrote
The Lady of Shalott.

And down the river's dim expanse
Like some bold seer in a trance,
Seeing all his own mischance—
With a glassy countenance
Did she look to Camelot.
And at the closing of the day
She loosed the chain, and down she lay;
The broad stream bore her far away,
The Lady of Shalott.

Lying, robed in snowy white
That loosely flew to left and right—
The leaves upon her falling light—
Through the noises of the night
She floated down to Camelot:
And as the boat-head wound along
The willowy hills and fields among,
They heard her singing her last song,
The Lady of Shalott.

Heard a carol, mournful, holy,
Chanted loudly, chanted lowly,
Till her blood was frozen slowly,
And her eyes were darkened wholly,
Turned to towered Camelot.
For ere she reached upon the tide
The first house by the water-side,
Singing in her song she died,
The Lady of Shalott.

Under tower and balcony,
By garden-wall and gallery,
A gleaming shape she floated by,
Dead-pale between the houses high,
Silent into Camelot.
Out upon the wharfs they came,
Knight and burgher, lord and dame,
And round the prow they read her name,
The Lady of Shalott.

Who is this? and what is here?
And in the lighted palace near
Died the sound of royal cheer;
And they crossed themselves for fear,
All the knights at Camelot:
But Lancelot mused a little space;
He said, "She has a lovely face;
God in his mercy lend her grace,
The Lady of Shalott."
—1832 (revised 1842)

The Lotos-Eaters[1]

"Courage!" he said, and pointed toward the land,
"This mounting wave will roll us shoreward soon."
In the afternoon they came unto a land
In which it seemed always afternoon.
All round the coast the languid air did swoon,
Breathing like one that hath a weary dream.
Full-faced above the valley stood the moon;
And like a downward smoke, the slender stream
Along the cliff to fall and pause and fall did seem.

A land of streams! some, like a downward smoke,
Slow-dropping veils of thinnest lawn,[2] did go;
And some through wavering lights and shadows broke,
Rolling a slumbrous sheet of foam below.
They saw the gleaming river seaward flow
From the inner land: far off, three mountain-tops,
Three silent pinnacles of agèd snow,
Stood sunset-flushed: and, dewed with showery drops,
Up-clomb the shadowy pine above the woven copse.° *thicket*

The charmèd sunset lingered low adown
In the red West: through mountain clefts the dale
Was seen far inland, and the yellow down
Bordered with palm, and many a winding vale
And meadow, set with slender galingale;[3]
A land where all things always seemed the same!
And round about the keel with faces pale,
Dark faces pale against that rosy flame,
The mild-eyed melancholy Lotos-eaters came.

Branches they bore of that enchanted stem,
Laden with flower and fruit, whereof they gave
To each, but whoso did receive of them,
And taste, to him the gushing of the wave
Far far away did seem to mourn and rave
On alien shores; and if his fellow spake,
His voice was thin, as voices from the grave;
And deep-asleep he seemed, yet all awake,
And music in his ears his beating heart did make.

They sat them down upon the yellow sand,
Between the sun and moon upon the shore;
And sweet it was to dream of Fatherland,
Of child, and wife, and slave; but evermore
Most weary seemed the sea, weary the oar,
Weary the wandering fields of barren foam.
Then some one said, "We will return no more";
And all at once they sang, "Our island home
Is far beyond the wave; we will no longer roam."

CHORIC SONG[4]

1

There is sweet music here that softer falls
Than petals from blown roses on the grass,
Or night-dews on still waters between walls
Of shadowy granite, in a gleaming pass;
Music that gentlier on the spirit lies,
Than tired eyelids upon tired eyes;
Music that brings sweet sleep down from the blissful skies.
Here are cool mosses deep,
And through the moss the ivies creep,
And in the stream the long-leaved flowers weep,
And from the craggy ledge the poppy hangs in sleep.

2

Why are we weighed upon with heaviness,
And utterly consumed with sharp distress,
While all things else have rest from weariness?
All things have rest: why should we toil alone,
We only toil, who are the first of things,
And make perpetual moan,

[1] *Lotos-Eaters* In Homer's *Odyssey* (9.82–104), the Lotus Eaters were a race of people who inhabited a remote island; they existed in peaceful apathy because of the narcotic effects of the lotus plants they ate. When Odysseus landed on the island, some of his men ate the lotus plants and wanted to stay on the island, rather than return home to their families. The speaker in line 1 is Odysseus; his men sing the "Choric Song" beginning at line 46.

[2] *lawn* Fine fabric.

[3] *galingale* Species of sedge.

[4] *CHORIC SONG* Song sung in unison (like that performed by the Chorus in an ancient Greek play).

Still from one sorrow to another thrown:
Nor ever fold our wings,
And cease from wanderings,
Nor steep our brows in slumber's holy balm;
Nor harken what the inner spirit sings,
"There is no joy but calm!"
Why should we only toil, the roof and crown of things?

3

Lo! in the middle of the wood,
The folded leaf is wooed from out the bud
With winds upon the branch, and there
Grows green and broad, and takes no care,
Sun-steeped at noon, and in the moon
Nightly dew-fed; and turning yellow
Falls, and floats adown the air.
Lo! sweetened with the summer light,
The full-juiced apple, waxing over-mellow,
Drops in a silent autumn night.
All its allotted length of days,
The flower ripens in its place,
Ripens and fades, and falls, and hath no toil,
Fast-rooted in the fruitful soil.

4

Hateful is the dark-blue sky,
Vaulted o'er the dark-blue sea.
Death is the end of life; ah, why
Should life all labour be?
Let us alone. Time driveth onward fast,
And in a little while our lips are dumb.
Let us alone. What is it that will last?
All things are taken from us, and become
Portions and parcels of the dreadful Past.
Let us alone. What pleasure can we have
To war with evil? Is there any peace
In ever climbing up the climbing wave?
All things have rest, and ripen toward the grave
In silence; ripen, fall and cease:
Give us long rest or death, dark death, or dreamful ease.

5

How sweet it were, hearing the downward stream,
With half-shut eyes ever to seem
Falling asleep in a half-dream!
To dream and dream, like yonder amber light,
Which will not leave the myrrh-bush on the height;
To hear each other's whispered speech;
Eating the Lotos day by day,
To watch the crisping ripples on the beach,
And tender curving lines of creamy spray;
To lend our hearts and spirits wholly
To the influence of mild-minded melancholy;
To muse and brood and live again in memory,
With those old faces of our infancy
Heaped over with a mound of grass,
Two handfuls of white dust,[1] shut in an urn of brass!

6

Dear is the memory of our wedded lives,
And dear the last embraces of our wives
And their warm tears: but all hath suffered change:
For surely now our household hearths are cold:
Our sons inherit us: our looks are strange:
And we should come like ghosts to trouble joy.
Or else the island princes over-bold
Have eat our substance,[2] and the minstrel sings
Before them of the ten years' war in Troy,
And our great deeds, as half-forgotten things.
Is there confusion in the little isle?
Let what is broken so remain.
The Gods are hard to reconcile:
'Tis hard to settle order once again.
There *is* confusion worse than death,
Trouble on trouble, pain on pain,
Long labour unto agèd breath,
Sore task to hearts worn out by many wars
And eyes grown dim with gazing on the pilot-stars.

---

[1] *white dust* I.e., cremated remains.

[2] *Have eat our substance* I.e., have consumed our goods and property. As the sailors rightly surmise, in the years that they have been away from their home island of Ithaca (the "little isle" of line 124) following Odysseus to fight the Trojan War, the other princes of Ithaca and the neighboring islands have encroached upon their homes.

7

But, propped on beds of amaranth and moly,[1]
How sweet (while warm airs lull us, blowing lowly)
With half-dropped eyelid still,
Beneath a heaven dark and holy,
To watch the long bright river drawing slowly
His waters from the purple hill—
To hear the dewy echoes calling
From cave to cave through the thick-twinèd vine—
To watch the emerald-coloured water falling
Through many a woven acanthus[2]-wreath divine!
Only to hear and see the far-off sparkling brine,
Only to hear were sweet, stretched out beneath the pine.

8

The Lotos blooms below the barren peak:
The Lotos blows by every winding creek:
All day the wind breathes low with mellower tone:
Through every hollow cave and alley lone
Round and round the spicy downs the yellow
Lotos-dust is blown.
We have had enough of action, and of motion we,
Rolled to starboard, rolled to larboard,° when *port*
the surge was seething free,
Where the wallowing monster spouted his foam-
fountains in the sea.
Let us swear an oath, and keep it with an equal mind,
In the hollow Lotos-land to live and lie reclined
On the hills like Gods together, careless of mankind.
For they lie beside their nectar, and the bolts are hurled
Far below them in the valleys, and the clouds are
lightly curled
Round their golden houses, girdled with the gleaming
world:
Where they smile in secret, looking over wasted lands,
Blight and famine, plague and earthquake, roaring
deeps and fiery sands,
Clanging fights, and flaming towns, and sinking
ships, and praying hands.
But they smile, they find a music centred in a doleful
song
Steaming up, a lamentation and an ancient tale of
wrong,
Like a tale of little meaning though the words are strong;
Chanted from an ill-used race of men that cleave the
soil,
Sow the seed, and reap the harvest with enduring toil,
Storing yearly little dues of wheat, and wine and oil;
Till they perish and they suffer—some, 'tis whispered
—down in hell
Suffer endless anguish, others in Elysian[3] valleys dwell,
Resting weary limbs at last on beds of asphodel.[4]
Surely, surely, slumber is more sweet than toil, the shore
Than labour in the deep mid-ocean, wind and wave
and oar;
Oh rest ye, brother mariners, we will not wander more.

—1832 (REVISED 1842)

Ulysses[5]

It little profits that an idle king,
By this still hearth, among these barren crags,
Matched with an agèd wife, I mete and dole
Unequal laws unto a savage race,
That hoard, and sleep, and feed, and know not me.

I cannot rest from travel: I will drink
Life to the lees:° all times I have enjoyed *dregs*
Greatly, have suffered greatly, both with those
That loved me, and alone; on shore, and when

[1] *amaranth* Mythical flower that never wilted; *moly* Herb with magical protective powers.

[2] *acanthus* Plant native to Mediterranean shores. The Greeks and Romans esteemed the plant for the elegance of its leaves.

[3] *Elysian* Heavenly. According to the ancient Greeks, Elysium was the dwelling place of the blessed after death.

[4] *asphodel* Plant said to cover the Elysian fields.

[5] *Ulysses* Latin name for Odysseus, the hero of Homer's *Odyssey*, which culminates in his reunion (after nearly twenty years) with his wife Penelope and his only son Telemachus (see line 33) and his regaining the throne of Ithaca. Here, some time after the adventures recounted by Homer, the aged yet restless Ulysses prepares to embark on one last voyage of discovery. Tennyson was inspired by a passage in Dante's *Inferno* (Canto 26), in which the shade of Ulysses recounts the story of that final voyage.

Thro' scudding drifts the rainy Hyades[1]
Vexed the dim sea: I am become a name;
For always roaming with a hungry heart
Much have I seen and known; cities of men
And manners, climates, councils, governments,
Myself not least, but honoured of them all;
And drunk delight of battle with my peers,
Far on the ringing plains of windy Troy.
I am a part of all that I have met;
Yet all experience is an arch wherethrough
Gleams that untravelled world, whose margin° *horizon*
fades
For ever and for ever when I move.
How dull it is to pause, to make an end,
To rust unburnished, not to shine in use!
As though to breathe were life. Life piled on life
Were all too little, and of one to me
Little remains: but every hour is saved
From that eternal silence, something more,
A bringer of new things; and vile it were
For some three suns to store and hoard myself,
And this gray spirit yearning in desire
To follow knowledge like a sinking star,
Beyond the utmost bound of human thought.

This is my son, mine own Telemachus,
To whom I leave the sceptre and the isle—
Well-loved of me, discerning to fulfil
This labour, by slow prudence to make mild
A rugged people, and through soft degrees
Subdue them to the useful and the good.
Most blameless is he, centred in the sphere
Of common duties, decent not to fail
In offices of tenderness, and pay
Meet adoration to my household gods,
When I am gone. He works his work, I mine.

There lies the port; the vessel puffs her sail:
There gloom the dark broad seas. My mariners,
Souls that have toiled, and wrought, and thought
with me—
That ever with a frolic welcome took
The thunder and the sunshine, and opposed
Free hearts, free foreheads—you and I are old;
Old age hath yet his honour and his toil;
Death closes all: but something ere the end,
Some work of noble note, may yet be done,
Not unbecoming men that strove with Gods.

The lights begin to twinkle from the rocks:
The long day wanes: the slow moon climbs: the deep
Moans round with many voices. Come, my friends,
'Tis not too late to seek a newer world.
Push off, and sitting well in order smite
The sounding furrows; for my purpose holds
To sail beyond the sunset, and the baths
Of all the western stars, until I die.
It may be that the gulfs will wash us down:
It may be we shall touch the Happy Isles,[2]
And see the great Achilles,[3] whom we knew.
Though much is taken, much abides; and though
We are not now that strength which in old days
Moved earth and heaven; that which we are, we are;
One equal temper of heroic hearts,
Made weak by time and fate, but strong in will
To strive, to seek, to find, and not to yield.
—1842 (WRITTEN 1833)

The Epic[4]

At Francis Allen's on the Christmas-eve,—
The game of forfeits done—the girls all kissed
Beneath the sacred bush[5] and past away—
The parson Holmes, the poet Everard Hall,

[1] *Hyades* Group of stars near the constellation Taurus and associated with rainstorms.

[2] *Happy Isles* Elysium, or Isles of the Blessed, where heroes enjoyed the afterlife.

[3] *Achilles* Greek hero of the Trojan War, the central character of Homer's *Iliad.*

[4] *The Epic* Tennyson wrote this poem as a poetic "frame" for "Morte d'Arthur," which follows; together the two poems make up a single work. "The Epic" itself consists of the fifty-one lines that precede the "Morte d'Arthur," plus the thirty-one lines that follow.

[5] *sacred bush* Mistletoe.

The host, and I sat round the wassail-bowl,[1]
Then half-way ebbed: and there we held a talk,
How all the old honour had from Christmas gone,
Or gone, or dwindled down to some odd games
In some odd nooks like this; till I, tired out
With cutting eights[2] that day upon the pond,
Where, three times slipping from the outer edge,
I bumped the ice into three several stars,
Fell in a doze; and half-awake I heard
The parson taking wide and wider sweeps,
Now harping on the church-commissioners,
Now hawking at Geology and schism;[3]
Until I woke, and found him settled down
Upon the general decay of faith
Right through the world, "at home was little left,
And none abroad: there was no anchor, none,
To hold by." Francis, laughing, clapped his hand
On Everard's shoulder, with "I hold by him."
"And I," quoth Everard, "by the wassail-bowl."
"Why yes," I said, "we knew your gift that way
At college: but another which you had,
I mean of verse (for so we held it then),
What came of that?" "You know," said Frank, "he burnt
His epic, his King Arthur, some twelve books"—
And then to me demanding why? "Oh, sir,
He thought that nothing new was said, or else
Something so said 'twas nothing—that a truth
Looks freshest in the fashion of the day:
God knows: he has a mint of reasons: ask.
It pleased *me* well enough." "Nay, nay," said Hall,
"Why take the style of those heroic times?
For nature brings not back the Mastodon,[4]
Nor we those times; and why should any man
Remodel models? these twelve books of mine
Were faint Homeric echoes, nothing-worth,
Mere chaff and draff,[5] much better burnt." "But I,"
Said Francis, "picked the eleventh from this hearth
And have it: keep a thing, its use will come.
I hoard it as a sugar-plum for Holmes."
He laughed, and I, though sleepy, like a horse
That hears the corn-bin open, pricked my ears;
For I remembered Everard's college fame
When we were freshmen: then at my request
He brought it; and the poet little urged,
But with some prelude of disparagement,
Read, mouthing out his hollow oes and aes,
Deep-chested music, and to this result.

Morte d'Arthur[6]

So all day long the noise of battle rolled
Among the mountains by the winter sea;
Until King Arthur's table, man by man,
Had fallen in Lyonnesse[7] about their Lord,
King Arthur: then, because his wound was deep,
The bold Sir Bedivere uplifted him,
Sir Bedivere, the last of all his knights,
And bore him to a chapel nigh the field,
A broken chancel[8] with a broken cross,
That stood on a dark strait of barren land.
On one side lay the ocean, and on one
Lay a great water, and the moon was full.

Then spake King Arthur to Sir Bedivere:
"The sequel of today unsolders all
The goodliest fellowship of famous knights
Whereof this world holds record. Such a sleep
They sleep—the men I loved. I think that we
Shall never more, at any future time,
Delight our souls with talk of knightly deeds,
Walking about the gardens and the halls

[1] *wassail-bowl* Punch bowl containing spiced ale.

[2] *cutting eights* Skating figure-eights.

[3] *church-commissioners ... Geology ... schism* References to contemporary religious and scientific controversies.

[4] *Mastodon* Extinct elephant-like mammal; evidence of its existence was first discovered in the eighteenth century, and the name first applied in the early nineteenth.

[5] *chaff and draff* Here, refuse, material of little worth.

[6] *Morte d'Arthur* French: The Death of [King] Arthur. This poem was later incorporated into the final book of Tennyson's epic *Idylls of the King*. As his kingdom and the knightly Order of the Round Table fall into disorder, Arthur faces a rebellion led by his nephew Modred; in one final battle Arthur defeats Modred, but his knights are almost all killed and Arthur himself gravely wounded by a blow to the head.

[7] [Tennyson's note] The country of legend that lay between Cornwall and the Scilly Islands.

[8] *chancel* Area around the altar.

Of Camelot, as in the days that were.
I perish by this people which I made,—
Though Merlin sware° that I should come again *promised*
To rule once more—but let what will be, be,
I am so deeply smitten through the helm
That without help I cannot last till morn.
Thou therefore take my brand° Excalibur, *sword*
Which was my pride: for thou rememberest how
In those old days, one summer noon, an arm
Rose up from out the bosom of the lake,
Clothed in white samite,° mystic, wonderful, *silk*
Holding the sword—and how I rowed across
And took it, and have worn it, like a king:
And, wheresoever I am sung or told
In aftertime, this also shall be known:
But now delay not: take Excalibur,
And fling him far into the middle mere:[1]
Watch what thou seest, and lightly bring me word."

To him replied the bold Sir Bedivere:
"It is not meet,° Sir King, to leave thee thus, *appropriate*
Aidless, alone, and smitten through the helm.
A little thing may harm a wounded man.
Yet I thy hest° will all perform at full, *command*
Watch what I see, and lightly bring thee word."

So saying, from the ruined shrine he stepped
And in the moon athwart the place of tombs,
Where lay the mighty bones of ancient men,
Old knights, and over them the sea-wind sang
Shrill, chill, with flakes of foam. He, stepping down
By zig-zag paths, and juts of pointed rock,
Came on the shining levels of the lake.

There drew he forth the brand Excalibur,
And o'er him, drawing it, the winter moon,
Brightening the skirts of a long cloud, ran forth
And sparkled keen with frost against the hilt:
For all the haft° twinkled with diamond sparks, *handle*
Myriads of topaz-lights, and jacinth[2]-work
Of subtlest jewellery. He gazed so long
That both his eyes were dazzled, as he stood,
This way and that dividing the swift mind,
In act to throw: but at the last it seemed
Better to leave Excalibur concealed
There in the many-knotted waterflags,° *reeds*
That whistled stiff and dry about the marge.° *shore*
So strode he back slow to the wounded King.

Then spake King Arthur to Sir Bedivere:
"Hast thou performed my mission which I gave?
What is it thou hast seen? or what hast heard?"

And answer made the bold Sir Bedivere:
"I heard the ripple washing in the reeds,
And the wild water lapping on the crag."

To whom replied King Arthur, faint and pale:
"Thou hast betrayed thy nature and thy name,
Not rendering true answer, as beseemed
Thy fealty,° nor like a noble knight: *sworn allegiance*
For surer sign had followed, either hand,
Or voice, or else a motion of the mere.
This is a shameful thing for men to lie.
Yet now, I charge thee, quickly go again
As thou art lief° and dear, and do the thing *beloved*
I bad[3] thee, watch, and lightly bring me word."

Then went Sir Bedivere the second time
Across the ridge, and paced beside the mere,
Counting the dewy pebbles, fix'd in thought;
But when he saw the wonder of the hilt,
How curiously and strangely chased,° he smote *engraved*
His palms together, and he cried aloud,

"And if indeed I cast the brand away,
Surely a precious thing, one worthy note,
Should thus be lost for ever from the earth,
Which might have pleased the eyes of many men.
What good should follow this, if this were done?
What harm, undone? deep harm to disobey,
Seeing obedience is the bond of rule.
Were it well to obey then, if a king demand
An act unprofitable, against himself?
The King is sick, and knows not what he does.

[1] *middle mere* Middle of the lake.

[2] *jacinth* Reddish-orange gem.

[3] *bad* I.e., bade, commanded.

What record, or what relic of my lord
Should be to aftertime, but empty breath
And rumours of a doubt? but were this kept,
Stored in some treasure-house of mighty kings,
Some one might show it at a joust of arms,
Saying, 'King Arthur's sword, Excalibur,
Wrought by the lonely maiden of the Lake.
Nine years she wrought it, sitting in the deeps
Upon the hidden bases of the hills.'
So might some old man speak in the aftertime
To all the people, winning reverence.
But now much honour and much fame were lost."

So spake he, clouded with his own conceit,
And hid Excalibur the second time,
And so strode back slow to the wounded King.

Then spoke King Arthur, breathing heavily:
"What is it thou hast seen? or what hast heard?"

And answer made the bold Sir Bedivere:
"I heard the water lapping on the crag,
And the long ripple washing in the reeds."

To whom replied King Arthur, much in wrath:
"Ah, miserable and unkind, untrue,
Unknightly, traitor-hearted! Woe is me!
Authority forgets a dying king,
Laid widowed of the power in his eye
That bowed the will. I see thee what thou art,
For thou, the latest-left of all my knights,
In whom should meet the offices of all,
Thou wouldst betray me for the precious hilt;
Either from lust of gold, or like a girl
Valuing the giddy pleasure of the eyes.
Yet, for a man may fail in duty twice,
And the third time may prosper, get thee hence:
But, if thou spare to fling Excalibur,
I will arise and slay thee with my hands."

Then quickly rose Sir Bedivere, and ran,
And, leaping down the ridges lightly, plunged
Among the bulrush-beds, and clutched the sword,
And strongly wheeled and threw it. The great brand
Made lightnings in the splendour of the moon,
And flashing round and round, and whirled in an arch,
Shot like a streamer of the northern morn,[1]
Seen where the moving isles of winter[2] shock
By night, with noises of the northern sea.
So flashed and fell the brand Excalibur:
But ere he dipped the surface, rose an arm
Clothed in white samite, mystic, wonderful,
And caught him by the hilt, and brandished him
Three times, and drew him under in the mere.
And lightly went the other to the King.

Then spoke King Arthur, drawing thicker breath:
"Now see I by thine eyes that this is done.
Speak out: what is it thou hast heard, or seen?"

And answer made the bold Sir Bedivere:
"Sir King, I closed mine eyelids, lest the gems
Should blind my purpose, for I never saw,
Nor shall see, here or elsewhere, till I die,
Not though I live three lives of mortal men,
So great a miracle as yonder hilt.
Then with both hands I flung him, wheeling him;
But when I looked again, behold an arm,
Clothed in white samite, mystic, wonderful,
That caught him by the hilt, and brandished him
Three times, and drew him under in the mere."

And answer made King Arthur, breathing hard:
"My end draws nigh; 'tis time that I were gone.
Make broad thy shoulders to receive my weight,
And bear me to the margin; yet I fear
My wound hath taken cold, and I shall die."

So saying, from the pavement he half rose,
Slowly, with pain, reclining on his arm,
And looking wistfully with wide blue eyes
As in a picture. Him Sir Bedivere
Remorsefully regarded through his tears,
And would have spoken, but he found not words,
Then took with care, and kneeling on one knee,
O'er both his shoulders drew the languid hands,
And rising bore him through the place of tombs.

[1] *northern morn* Aurora borealis.

[2] *isles of winter* Icebergs.

But, as he walked, King Arthur panted hard,
Like one that feels a nightmare on his bed
When all the house is mute. So sighed the King,
Muttering and murmuring at his ear, "Quick, quick!
I fear it is too late, and I shall die."
But the other swiftly strode from ridge to ridge,
Clothed with his breath, and looking, as he walked,
Larger than human on the frozen hills.
He heard the deep behind him, and a cry
Before. His own thought drove him, like a goad.
Dry clashed his harness in the icy caves
And barren chasms, and all to left and right
The bare black cliff clanged round him, as he based
His feet on juts of slippery crag that rang
Sharp-smitten with the dint of armèd heels—
And on a sudden, lo! the level lake,
And the long glories of the winter moon.
Then saw they how there hove° a dusky barge, *floated*
Dark as a funeral scarf from stem to stern,
Beneath them; and descending they were ware° *aware*
That all the decks were dense with stately forms
Black-stoled,[1] black-hooded, like a dream—by these
Three Queens with crowns of gold—and from them rose
A cry that shivered to the tingling stars,
And, as it were one voice, an agony
Of lamentation, like a wind, that shrills
All night in a waste land, where no one comes,
Or hath come, since the making of the world.

Then murmured Arthur, "Place me in the barge,"
And to the barge they came. There those three Queens
Put forth their hands, and took the King, and wept.
But she, that rose the tallest of them all
And fairest, laid his head upon her lap,
And loosed the shattered casque,° and chafed his hands, *helmet*
And called him by his name, complaining loud,
And dropping bitter tears against his brow
Striped with dark blood: for all his face was white
And colourless, and like the withered moon
Smote by the fresh beam of the springing east;
And all his greaves and cuisses[2] dashed with drops
Of onset;[3] and the light and lustrous curls—
That made his forehead like a rising sun
High from the dais-throne—were parched with dust;
Or, clotted into points and hanging loose,
Mix'd with the knightly growth that fringed his lips.
So like a shattered column lay the King;
Not like that Arthur who, with lance in rest,
From spur to plume a star of tournament,
Shot through the lists[4] at Camelot, and charged
Before the eyes of ladies and of kings.

Then loudly cried the bold Sir Bedivere,
"Ah! my Lord Arthur, whither shall I go?
Where shall I hide my forehead and my eyes?
For now I see the true old times are dead,
When every morning brought a noble chance,
And every chance brought out a noble knight.
Such times have been not since the light that led
The holy Elders[5] with the gift of myrrh.
But now the whole Round Table is dissolved
Which was an image of the mighty world;
And I, the last, go forth companionless,
And the days darken round me, and the years,
Among new men, strange faces, other minds."

And slowly answered Arthur from the barge:
"The old order changeth, yielding place to new,
And God fulfils Himself in many ways,
Lest one good custom should corrupt the world.
Comfort thyself: what comfort is in me?
I have lived my life, and that which I have done
May He within Himself make pure! but thou,
If thou shouldst never see my face again,
Pray for my soul. More things are wrought by prayer
Than this world dreams of. Wherefore, let thy voice
Rise like a fountain for me night and day.
For what are men better than sheep or goats

1 *Black-stoled* Wearing black cloaks.

2 *greaves and cuisses* Armor for shins and thighs.

3 *onset* Rush of battle (which has splattered his armor).

4 *lists* Arenas in which jousting and tilting tournaments were held.

5 *holy Elders* Three kings who brought gifts, including myrrh, at the birth of Jesus (Matthew 2.11).

That nourish a blind life within the brain,
If, knowing God, they lift not hands of prayer
Both for themselves and those who call them friend?
For so the whole round earth is every way
Bound by gold chains about the feet of God.
But now farewell. I am going a long way
With these thou seest—if indeed I go—
(For all my mind is clouded with a doubt)
To the island-valley of Avilion;° *i.e., Avalon*
Where falls not hail, or rain, or any snow,
Nor ever wind blows loudly; but it lies
Deep-meadowed, happy, fair with orchard-lawns
And bowery hollows crown'd with summer sea,
Where I will heal me of my grievous wound."

So said he, and the barge with oar and sail
Moved from the brink, like some full-breasted swan
That, fluting a wild carol ere her death,[1]
Ruffles her pure cold plume, and takes the flood
With swarthy webs.[2] Long stood Sir Bedivere
Revolving many memories, till the hull
Looked one black dot against the verge of dawn,
And on the mere the wailing died away.

Here ended Hall,[3] and our last light, that long
Had winked and threatened darkness, flared and fell:
At which the Parson, sent to sleep with sound,
And waked with silence, grunted "Good!" but we
Sat rapt: it was the tone with which he read—
Perhaps some modern touches here and there
Redeemed it from the charge of nothingness—
Or else we loved the man, and prized his work;
I know not: but we sitting, as I said,
The cock crew loud; as at that time of year
The lusty bird takes every hour for dawn:[4]
Then Francis, muttering, like a man ill-used,
"There now—that's nothing!" drew a little back,
And drove his heel into the smouldered log,
That sent a blast of sparkles up the flue:
And so to bed; where yet in sleep I seemed
To sail with Arthur under looming shores,
Point after point; till on to dawn, when dreams
Begin to feel the truth and stir of day,
To me, methought, who waited with a crowd,
There came a bark° that, blowing forward, bore *ship*
King Arthur, like a modern gentleman
Of stateliest port;° and all the people cried, *bearing*
"Arthur is come again: he cannot die."
Then those that stood upon the hills behind
Repeated—"Come again, and thrice as fair;"
And, further inland, voices echoed—"Come
With all good things, and war shall be no more."
At this a hundred bells began to peal,
That with the sound I woke, and heard indeed
The clear church-bells ring in the Christmas-morn.
—1842 (written 1833–34)

[1] *swan ... death* Swans were said to sing only once, at their deaths.

[2] *webs* I.e., webbed feet.

[3] *Here ended Hall* "The Epic" here resumes, as Everard Hall has finished reading out his poem.

[4] *The cock ... for dawn* For the belief that the rooster crows all night long on Christmas Eve, see Shakespeare, *Hamlet*, 1.1.158–60.

[*Break, break, break*]

Break, break, break,
On thy cold gray stones, O Sea!
And I would that my tongue could utter
The thoughts that arise in me.

O well for the fisherman's boy,
That he shouts with his sister at play!
O well for the sailor lad,
That he sings in his boat on the bay!

And the stately ships go on
To their haven under the hill;
But O for the touch of a vanished hand,
And the sound of a voice that is still![5]

[5] *But ... still* Probably a reference to Tennyson's closest friend, Arthur Hallam, who had died in 1833.

Break, break, break,
At the foot of thy crags, O Sea!
But the tender grace of a day that is dead
Will never come back to me.
—1842 (WRITTEN 1834?)

Locksley Hall

Comrades, leave me here a little, while as yet 'tis early morn:
Leave me here, and when you want me, sound upon the bugle-horn.

'Tis the place, and all around it, as of old, the curlews[1] call,
Dreary gleams about the moorland flying over Locksley Hall;

Locksley Hall, that in the distance overlooks the sandy tracts,
And the hollow ocean-ridges roaring into cataracts.

Many a night from yonder ivied casement, ere I went to rest,
Did I look on great Orion[2] sloping slowly to the West.

Many a night I saw the Pleiads,[3] rising through the mellow shade,
Glitter like a swarm of fire-flies tangled in a silver braid.

Here about the beach I wandered, nourishing a youth sublime
With the fairy tales of science, and the long result of Time;

When the centuries behind me like a fruitful land reposed;
When I clung to all the present for the promise that it closed:

When I dipped into the future far as human eye could see;
Saw the Vision of the world, and all the wonder that would be.—

In the Spring a fuller crimson comes upon the robin's breast;
In the Spring the wanton lapwing gets himself another crest;

In the Spring a livelier iris changes on the burnished dove;
In the Spring a young man's fancy lightly turns to thoughts of love.

Then her cheek was pale and thinner than should be for one so young,
And her eyes on all my motions with a mute observance hung.

And I said, "My cousin Amy, speak, and speak the truth to me,
Trust me, cousin, all the current of my being sets to thee."

On her pallid cheek and forehead came a colour and a light,
As I have seen the rosy red flushing in the northern night.

And she turned—her bosom shaken with a sudden storm of sighs—
All the spirit deeply dawning in the dark of hazel eyes—

Saying, "I have hid my feelings, fearing they should do me wrong;"
Saying, "Dost thou love me, cousin?" weeping, "I have loved thee long."

Love took up the glass of Time,[4] and turned it in his glowing hands;
Every moment, lightly shaken, ran itself in golden sands.

---

[1] *curlews* Species of shore-dwelling birds.

[2] *Orion* The constellation named after the hunter of Greek legend. It sets in November and so was associated with rains and storms.

[3] *Pleiads* The constellation commonly known as the Pleiades (named after the seven daughters of Atlas), which rises in May and sets in November.

[4] *glass of Time* Hourglass.

Love took up the harp of Life, and smote on all the chords with might;
Smote the chord of Self, that, trembling, passed in music out of sight.

Many a morning on the moorland did we hear the copses ring,
And her whisper thronged my pulses with the fullness of the Spring.

Many an evening by the waters did we watch the stately ships,
And our spirits rushed together at the touching of the lips.

O my cousin, shallow-hearted! O my Amy, mine no more!
O the dreary, dreary moorland! O the barren, barren shore!

Falser than all fancy fathoms,° falser than all songs have sung, *apprehends*
Puppet to a father's threat, and servile to a shrewish tongue!

Is it well to wish thee happy?—having known me—to decline
On a range of lower feelings and a narrower heart than mine!

Yet it shall be: thou shalt lower to his level day by day,
What is fine within thee growing coarse to sympathise with clay.

As the husband is, the wife is: thou art mated with a clown,[1]
And the grossness of his nature will have weight to drag thee down.

He will hold thee, when his passion shall have spent its novel force,
Something better than his dog, a little dearer than his horse.

What is this? his eyes are heavy: think not they are glazed with wine.
Go to him: it is thy duty: kiss him: take his hand in thine.

It may be my lord is weary, that his brain is overwrought:
Soothe him with thy finer fancies, touch him with thy lighter thought.

He will answer to the purpose, easy things to understand—
Better thou wert dead before me, though I slew thee with my hand!

Better thou and I were lying, hidden from the heart's disgrace,
Rolled in one another's arms, and silent in a last embrace.

Cursèd be the social wants that sin against the strength of youth!
Cursèd be the social lies that warp us from the living truth!

Cursèd be the sickly forms that err from honest Nature's rule!
Cursèd be the gold that gilds the straitened forehead of the fool![2]

Well—'tis well that I should bluster!—Hadst thou less unworthy proved—
Would to God—for I had loved thee more than ever wife was loved.

Am I mad, that I should cherish that which bears but bitter fruit?
I will pluck it from my bosom, though my heart be at the root.

[1] *clown* Rustic, boorish fellow.

[2] *straitened ... fool* Narrow or low foreheads were thought to indicate stupidity; *straitened* Narrowed.

Never, though my mortal summers to such length of years should come
As the many-wintered crow that leads the clanging rookery home.

Where is comfort? in division of the records of the mind?
Can I part her from herself, and love her, as I knew her, kind?

I remember one that perished: sweetly did she speak and move:
Such a one do I remember, whom to look at was to love.

Can I think of her as dead, and love her for the love she bore?
No—she never loved me truly: love is love for evermore.

Comfort? comfort scorned of devils! this is truth the poet sings,
That a sorrow's crown of sorrow is remembering happier things.[1]

Drug thy memories, lest thou learn it, lest thy heart be put to proof,
In the dead unhappy night, and when the rain is on the roof.

Like a dog, he hunts in dreams, and thou art staring at the wall,
Where the dying night-lamp flickers, and the shadows rise and fall.

Then a hand shall pass before thee, pointing to his drunken sleep,
To thy widowed[2] marriage-pillows, to the tears that thou wilt weep.

Thou shalt hear the "Never, never," whispered by the phantom years,
And a song from out the distance in the ringing of thine ears;

And an eye shall vex thee, looking ancient kindness on thy pain.
Turn thee, turn thee on thy pillow: get thee to thy rest again.

Nay, but Nature brings thee solace; for a tender voice will cry.
'Tis a purer life than thine; a lip to drain thy trouble dry.

Baby lips will laugh me down: my latest rival brings thee rest.
Baby fingers, waxen touches, press me from the mother's breast.

O, the child too clothes the father with a dearness not his due.
Half is thine and half is his: it will be worthy of the two.

O, I see thee old and formal, fitted to thy petty part,
With a little hoard of maxims preaching down a daughter's heart.

"They were dangerous guides the feelings—she[3] herself was not exempt—
Truly, she herself had suffered"—Perish in thy self-contempt!

Overlive it—lower yet—be happy! wherefore should I care?
I myself must mix with action, lest I wither by despair.

What is that which I should turn to, lighting upon days like these?
Every door is barred with gold, and opens but to golden keys.

Every gate is thronged with suitors, all the markets overflow.

[1] *this is truth … happier things* Cf. Dante, *Inferno* 5.121–23: "No greater grief than to remember joy, when misery is at hand."

[2] *widowed* In that she and her husband are emotionally estranged.

[3] *she* The woman, Amy, is pictured in the future, speaking of herself in the third person to her daughter.

I have but an angry fancy: what is that which I should do?

I had been content to perish, falling on the foeman's ground,
When the ranks are rolled in vapour, and the winds are laid with sound.

But the jingling of the guinea° helps the hurt that Honour feels, *coin*
And the nations do but murmur, snarling at each other's heels.

Can I but relive in sadness? I will turn that earlier page.
Hide me from my deep emotion, O thou wondrous Mother-Age!

Make me feel the wild pulsation that I felt before the strife,
When I heard my days before me, and the tumult of my life;

Yearning for the large excitement that the coming years would yield,
Eager-hearted as a boy when first he leaves his father's field,

And at night along the dusky highway near and nearer drawn,
Sees in heaven the light of London flaring like a dreary dawn;

And his spirit leaps within him to be gone before him then,
Underneath the light he looks at, in among the throngs of men:

Men, my brothers, men the workers, ever reaping something new:
That which they have done but earnest of the things that they shall do:

For I dipped into the future, far as human eye could see,
Saw the Vision of the world, and all the wonder that would be;

Saw the heavens fill with commerce, argosies[1] of magic sails,
Pilots of the purple twilight, dropping down with costly bales;

Heard the heavens fill with shouting, and there rained a ghastly dew
From the nations' airy navies grappling in the central blue;

Far along the world-wide whisper of the south-wind rushing warm,
With the standards of the peoples plunging through the thunder-storm;

Till the war-drum throbbed no longer, and the battle-flags were furled
In the Parliament of man, the Federation of the world.

There the common sense of most shall hold a fretful realm in awe,
And the kindly earth shall slumber, lapped in universal law.

So I triumphed ere my passion sweeping through me left me dry,
Left me with the palsied heart, and left me with the jaundiced eye;

Eye, to which all order festers, all things here are out of joint:
Science moves, but slowly slowly, creeping on from point to point:

Slowly comes a hungry people, as a lion creeping nigher,

[1] *argosies* Fleets of merchants ships. In this couplet and the next the speaker predicts that commerce and warfare will someday be carried out by aircraft.

Glares at one that nods and winks behind a slowly-dying fire.

Yet I doubt not through the ages one increasing purpose runs,
And the thoughts of men are widened with the process of the suns.

What is that to him that reaps not harvest of his youthful joys,
Though the deep heart of existence beat forever like a boy's?

Knowledge comes, but wisdom lingers, and I linger on the shore,
And the individual withers, and the world is more and more.

Knowledge comes, but wisdom lingers, and he bears a laden breast,
Full of sad experience, moving toward the stillness of his rest.

Hark, my merry comrades call me, sounding on the bugle-horn,
They to whom my foolish passion were a target for their scorn:

Shall it not be scorn to me to harp on such a mouldered string?
I am shamed through all my nature to have loved so slight a thing.

Weakness to be wroth° with weakness! woman's pleasure, woman's pain— *angry*
Nature made them blinder motions bounded in a shallower brain:

Woman is the lesser man, and all thy passions, matched with mine,
Are as moonlight unto sunlight, and as water unto wine—

Here at least, where nature sickens, nothing. Ah, for some retreat
Deep in yonder shining Orient, where my life began to beat;

Where in wild Mahratta-battle[1] fell my father evil-starred;[2]—
I was left a trampled orphan, and a selfish uncle's ward.

Or to burst all links of habit—there to wander far away,
On from island unto island at the gateways of the day.

Larger constellations burning, mellow moons and happy skies,
Breadths of tropic shade and palms in cluster, knots of Paradise.

Never comes the trader, never floats an European flag,
Slides the bird o'er lustrous woodland, swings the trailer[3] from the crag;

Droops the heavy-blossomed bower, hangs the heavy-fruited tree—
Summer isles of Eden lying in dark-purple spheres of sea.

There methinks would be enjoyment more than in this march of mind,
In the steamship, in the railway, in the thoughts that shake mankind.

There the passions cramped no longer shall have scope and breathing space;
I will take some savage woman, she shall rear my dusky race.

Iron jointed, supple-sinewed, they shall dive, and they shall run,
Catch the wild goat by the hair, and hurl their lances in the sun;

[1] *Mahratta-battle* Conflict between the British and the Mahratta soldiers from Bombay in 1818.

[2] *evil-starred* Cursed with bad luck.

[3] *trailer* Vine or hanging branch.

Whistle back the parrot's call, and leap the rainbows of the brooks,
Not with blinded eyesight poring over miserable books—

Fool, again the dream, the fancy! but I *know* my words are wild,
But I count the gray barbarian lower than the Christian child.

I, to herd with narrow foreheads, vacant of our glorious gains,
Like a beast with lower pleasures, like a beast with lower pains!

Mated with a squalid savage—what to me were sun or clime?
I the heir of all the ages, in the foremost files[1] of time—

I that rather held it better men should perish one by one,
Than that earth should stand at gaze like Joshua's moon in Ajalon![2]

Not in vain the distance beacons. Forward, forward let us range,
Let the great world spin forever down the ringing grooves of change.

Through the shadow of the globe we sweep into the younger day:
Better fifty years of Europe than a cycle of Cathay.° *China*

Mother-Age (for mine I knew not) help me as when life begun:
Rift° the hills, and roll the waters, flash the lightnings, weigh the Sun. *split open*

O, I see the crescent promise of my spirit hath not set.
Ancient founts of inspiration well through all my fancy yet.

Howsoever these things be, a long farewell to Locksley Hall!
Now for me the woods may wither, now for me the roof-tree fall.

Comes a vapour from the margin, blackening over heath and holt,° *wood*
Cramming all the blast before it, in its breast a thunderbolt.

Let it fall on Locksley Hall, with rain or hail, or fire or snow;
For the mighty wind arises, roaring seaward, and I go.
—1842

from *The Princess*

[*Sweet and Low*]

Sweet and low, sweet and low,
Wind of the western sea,
Low, low, breathe and blow,
Wind of the western sea!
Over the rolling waters go,
Come from the dying moon, and blow,
Blow him again to me;
While my little one, while my pretty one, sleeps.

Sleep and rest, sleep and rest,
Father will come to thee soon;
Rest, rest, on mother's breast,
Father will come to thee soon;
Father will come to his babe in the nest,
Silver sails all out of the west
Under the silver moon:
Sleep, my little one, sleep, my pretty one, sleep.

[1] *files* The ages of time pictured as men marching in file.

[2] *Joshua's moon in Ajalon* In Joshua 10.12–13, Joshua makes the moon and sun stand still during a battle in the valley of Ajalon.

[*The Splendour Falls*]

The splendour falls on castle walls
And snowy summits old in story:
The long light shakes across the lakes,
And the wild cataract° leaps in glory. *waterfall*
Blow, bugle, blow, set the wild echoes flying,
Blow, bugle; answer, echoes, dying, dying, dying.

O hark, O hear! how thin and clear,
And thinner, clearer, farther going!
O sweet and far from cliff and scar[1]
The horns of Elfland faintly blowing!
Blow, let us hear the purple glens replying:
Blow, bugle; answer, echoes, dying, dying, dying.

O love, they die in yon rich sky,
They faint on hill or field or river:
Our echoes roll from soul to soul,
And grow for ever and for ever.
Blow, bugle, blow, set the wild echoes flying,
And answer, echoes, answer, dying, dying, dying.

[*Tears, Idle Tears*]

Tears, idle tears, I know not what they mean,
Tears from the depth of some divine despair
Rise in the heart, and gather to the eyes,
In looking on the happy Autumn-fields,
And thinking of the days that are no more.

Fresh as the first beam glittering on a sail,
That brings our friends up from the underworld,
Sad as the last which reddens over one
That sinks with all we love below the verge;° *horizon*
So sad, so fresh, the days that are no more.

Ah, sad and strange as in dark summer dawns
The earliest pipe of half-awakened birds
To dying ears, when unto dying eyes
The casement° slowly grows a glimmering square; *window*
So sad, so strange, the days that are no more.

Dear as remembered kisses after death,
And sweet as those by hopeless fancy feigned
On lips that are for others; deep as love,
Deep as first love, and wild with all regret;
O Death in Life, the days that are no more.

[*Now Sleeps the Crimson Petal*]

Now sleeps the crimson petal, now the white;
Nor waves the cypress in the palace walk;
Nor winks the gold fin in the porphyry[2] font:
The fire-fly wakens: waken thou with me.

Now droops the milkwhite peacock like a ghost,
And like a ghost she glimmers on to me.

Now lies the Earth all Danaë[3] to the stars,
And all thy heart lies open unto me.

Now slides the silent meteor on, and leaves
A shining furrow, as thy thoughts in me.

Now folds the lily all her sweetness up,
And slips into the bosom of the lake:
So fold thyself, my dearest, thou, and slip
Into my bosom and be lost in me.

[*Come Down, O Maid*]

Come down, O maid, from yonder mountain height:
What pleasure lives in height (the shepherd sang)
In height and cold, the splendour of the hills?
But cease to move so near the Heavens, and cease

---

[1] *scar* Steep, craggy portion of mountainside.

[2] *porphyry* Beautiful, polished purple stone.

[3] *Danaë* In Greek mythology, a princess visited by Zeus in the form of a shower of gold.

To glide a sunbeam by the blasted Pine,
To sit a star upon the sparkling spire;
And come, for Love is of the valley, come,
For Love is of the valley, come thou down
And find him; by the happy threshold, he,
Or hand in hand with Plenty in the maize,
Or red with spurted purple of the vats,
Or foxlike in the vine;[1] nor cares to walk
With Death and Morning on the silver horns,
Nor wilt thou snare him in the white ravine,
Nor find him dropped upon the firths° of ice, *juttings*
That huddling slant in furrow-cloven falls
To roll the torrent out of dusky doors:
But follow; let the torrent dance thee down
To find him in the valley; let the wild
Lean-headed Eagles yelp alone, and leave
The monstrous ledges there to slope, and spill
Their thousand wreaths of dangling water-smoke,
That like a broken purpose waste in air:
So waste not thou; but come; for all the vales
Await thee; azure pillars of the hearth[2]
Arise to thee; the children call, and I
Thy shepherd pipe, and sweet is every sound,
Sweeter thy voice, but every sound is sweet;
Myriads of rivulets hurrying through the lawn,
The moan of doves in immemorial elms,
And murmuring of innumerable bees.

[*The Woman's Cause Is Man's*][3]

"Blame not thyself too much," I said, "nor blame
Too much the sons of men and barbarous laws;
These were the rough ways of the world till now.
Henceforth thou hast a helper, me, that know
The woman's cause is man's: they rise or sink
Together, dwarfed or godlike, bond or free:
For she that out of Lethe[4] scales with man
The shining steps of Nature, shares with man
His nights, his days, moves with him to one goal,
Stays° all the fair young planet in her hands— *sustains*
If she be small, slight-natured, miserable,
How shall men grow? but work no more alone!
Our place is much: as far as in us lies
We two will serve them both in aiding her—
Will clear away the parasitic forms
That seem to keep her up but drag her down—
Will leave her space to burgeon out of all
Within her—let her make herself her own
To give or keep, to live and learn and be
All that not harms distinctive womanhood.
For woman is not undeveloped man,
But diverse:° could we make her as the man, *different*
Sweet Love were slain: his dearest bond is this,
Not like to like, but like in difference.
Yet in the long years liker must they grow;
The man be more of woman, she of man;
He gain in sweetness and in moral height,
Nor lose the wrestling thews° that throw the world; *muscles*
She mental breadth, nor fail in childward care,
Nor lose the childlike in the larger mind;
Till at the last she set herself to man,
Like perfect music unto noble words;
And so these twain, upon the skirts° of Time, *borders*
Sit side by side, full-summed in all their powers,
Dispensing harvest, sowing the To-be,
Self-reverent each and reverencing each,
Distinct in individualities,
But like each other even as those who love.
Then comes the statelier Eden back to men:
Then reign the world's great bridals, chaste and calm:
Then springs the crowning race of humankind.
May these things be!"
Sighing she spoke "I fear
They will not."

[1] *foxlike in the vine* See Song of Solomon 2.15: "Take us the foxes, the little foxes, that spoil the vines. …"

[2] *azure pillars of the hearth* Columns of bluish smoke rising from household fires.

[3] *The Woman's Cause Is Man's* This passage from late in *The Princess* (7.239–91) shows the reconciliation between the princess, a feminist who hoped to live in an environment from which all men were excluded, and the narrator, a prince who wishes to marry her.

[4] *Lethe* In Greek myth, one of the rivers of Hades. Drinking its waters caused the souls of the dead to forget their past lives.

"Dear, but let us type[1] them now
In our own lives, and this proud watchword rest
Of equal; seeing either sex alone
Is half itself, and in true marriage lies
Nor equal, nor unequal: each fulfils
Defect in each, and always thought in thought,
Purpose in purpose, will in will, they grow,
The single pure and perfect animal,
The two-celled heart beating, with one full stroke,
Life."
And again sighing she spoke: "A dream
That once was mine! what woman taught you this?"
—1847 (REVISED AND SUPPLEMENTED 1850)

In Memoriam A.H.H.

Arthur Henry Hallam, who attended Cambridge's Trinity College at the same time as Tennyson, was regarded by many who knew him as among the most promising poetic talents of his generation. Eighteen months younger than Tennyson, Hallam was also far more outgoing. The two became friends and fierce supporters of each other's work. Both also became members of the famous Cambridge intellectual society, the Apostles, and after meeting Tennyson's family, Hallam became engaged to Tennyson's sister Emily. Hallam and Tennyson remained in close contact even after the death of Tennyson's father forced him to leave Cambridge; they traveled together to the Pyrenees in 1830, and to the Rhineland in 1832. In 1833, however, while on a trip to Vienna with his family, Hallam suffered a stroke and died; he was 22 years old.

Hallam's unexpected death had a profound and lasting effect on many of his friends; for Tennyson it marked the beginning of a long period of self-reflection and questioning. He began writing the lyric poems that would eventually form the basis of *In Memoriam* within a few weeks of Hallam's death—some seventeen years before the full poem was eventually published. According to the poet's own account, "the sections were written at many different places" and over the course of many years. He did not at first think of "weaving them into a whole"; only later did the longer work begin to take shape in his mind. The ultimate arrangement is loosely chronological, with the elegy as a whole tracing a three-year journey through the grieving process, punctuated by three Christmas scenes (sections 30, 78, and 105).

As Tennyson continued to reflect on Hallam's death, his subject matter broadened and deepened. The many moods of grief provide occasions for the poem to interrogate matters as wide-ranging as the character of scientific inquiry, the origin of human life, and the nature of religious faith. The Victorian "crisis of faith" that is often associated with the publication of Darwin's *On the Origin of Species* in 1859 is sometimes said to have begun before the Victorian age itself—with the publication just before Hallam's death of Charles Lyell's *Principles of Geology*, a book that made it far more difficult to accept the Christian account of Creation as being true in any literal sense. Perhaps more than any other work of the age, *In Memoriam* gave voice to the resulting uncertainty of a society trying to make room for both God and science. But for Tennyson, as for many Victorians, the scientific challenge made religious faith more vitally important than ever before. "The different moods of sorrow as in a drama are dramatically given," Tennyson said of the full poem, as was his "conviction that fear, doubts, and suffering will find answer and relief only through Faith in a God of Love."

The 133 sections that make up *In Memoriam* vary widely in length and style as well as mood. Yet they are all written in the form that has come to be known as the "In Memoriam stanza": a stanza of four lines in iambic tetrameter, with an ABBA rhyme scheme.

In Memoriam appeared in 1850 to near-universal acclaim. Initially it was published anonymously, but the identity of the author quickly became well-known; Charles Kingsley was not alone in believing (as Kingsley wrote in a September 1850 review of the poem) that there was only "one man in England possessed at once of poetic talent and artistic experience sufficient for so noble a creation." The poem cemented Tennyson's reputation, and he was appointed to the position of Poet Laureate before the year was out.

[1] *type* Serve as a model for.

from *In Memoriam A.H.H.*[1]

I

I held it truth, with him who sings
 To one clear harp in divers tones,
 That men may rise on stepping-stones
Of their dead selves to higher things.[2]

But who shall so forecast the years
 And find in loss a gain to match?
 Or reach a hand through time to catch
The far-off interest of tears?

Let Love clasp Grief lest both be drowned,
 Let darkness keep her raven gloss:
 Ah, sweeter to be drunk with loss,
To dance with death, to beat the ground,

Than that the victor Hours[3] should scorn
 The long result of love, and boast,
 "Behold the man that loved and lost,
But all he was is overworn."

5

I sometimes hold it half a sin
 To put in words the grief I feel;
 For words, like Nature, half reveal
And half conceal the Soul within.

But, for the unquiet heart and brain,
 A use in measured language lies;
 The sad mechanic exercise,
Like dull narcotics, numbing pain.

In words, like weeds,[4] I'll wrap me o'er,
 Like coarsest clothes against the cold:
 But that large grief which these enfold
Is given in outline and no more.

7

Dark house,[5] by which once more I stand
 Here in the long unlovely street,
 Doors, where my heart was used to beat
So quickly, waiting for a hand,

A hand that can be clasped no more—
 Behold me, for I cannot sleep,
 And like a guilty thing I creep
At earliest morning to the door.

He is not here; but far away
 The noise of life begins again,
 And ghastly through the drizzling rain
On the bald street breaks the blank day.

14

If one should bring me this report,
 That thou° hadst touched the land today, *i.e., the ship*
 And I went down unto the quay,
And found thee lying in the port;

And standing, muffled round with woe,
 Should see thy passengers in rank
 Come stepping lightly down the plank,
And beckoning unto those they know;

And if along with these should come
 The man I held as half-divine;
 Should strike a sudden hand in mine,
And ask a thousand things of home;

And I should tell him all my pain,
 And how my life had drooped of late,

[1] *In Memoriam A.H.H.* Latin: In memory of; the title was apparently suggested by the poet's fiancée. The published poem did not bear either Tennyson's name or Arthur Henry Hallam's, only the dedication "In Memoriam A.H.H. obiit MDCCCXXXIII" (In memory of A.H.H., died 1833).

[2] *him … things* The reference here is unclear. Tennyson said that he was alluding to a work by the German poet Goethe; however, the passage does not appear to correspond to any of Goethe's works.

[3] *Hours* Horai, Greek goddesses of time and of the changing of seasons.

[4] *weeds* In the Victorian period, this word was also used to refer to mourning clothes.

[5] *Dark house* I.e., Hallam's house in London.

And he should sorrow o'er my state
And marvel what possessed my brain;

And I perceived no touch of change,
No hint of death in all his frame,
But found him all in all the same,
I should not feel it to be strange.

27

I envy not in any moods
The captive void of noble rage,
The linnet born within the cage,
That never knew the summer woods:

I envy not the beast that takes
His license in the field of time,
Unfettered by the sense of crime,
To whom a conscience never wakes;

Nor, what may count itself as blest,
The heart that never plighted troth[1]
But stagnates in the weeds of sloth;
Nor any want-begotten rest.

I hold it true, whate'er befall;
I feel it, when I sorrow most;
'Tis better to have loved and lost
Than never to have loved at all.

54

Oh yet we trust that somehow good
Will be the final goal of ill,[2]
To pangs of nature, sins of will,
Defects of doubt, and taints of blood;

That nothing walks with aimless feet;
That not one life shall be destroyed,
Or cast as rubbish to the void,
When God hath made the pile complete;

That not a worm is cloven in vain;
That not a moth with vain desire
Is shrivelled in a fruitless fire,
Or but subserves another's gain.

Behold, we know not anything;
I can but trust that good shall fall
At last—far off—at last, to all,
And every winter change to spring.

So runs my dream: but what am I?
An infant crying in the night:
An infant crying for the light:
And with no language but a cry.

55

The wish, that of the living whole
No life may fail beyond the grave,
Derives it not from what we have
The likest God within the soul?

Are God and Nature then at strife,
That Nature lends such evil dreams?
So careful of the type° she seems, *species*
So careless of the single life;

That I, considering everywhere
Her secret meaning in her deeds,
And finding that of fifty seeds
She often brings but one to bear,

I falter where I firmly trod,
And falling with my weight of cares
Upon the great world's altar-stairs
That slope through darkness up to God,

I stretch lame hands of faith, and grope,
And gather dust and chaff, and call
To what I feel is Lord of all,
And faintly trust the larger hope.

---

[1] *plighted troth* Vowed faithfulness.

[2] *Oh yet … of ill* Section 54–56 together address this topic.

56

"So careful of the type?" but no.
From scarpèd[1] cliff and quarried stone
She cries, "A thousand types are gone:
I care for nothing, all shall go.[2]

"Thou makest thine appeal to me:
I bring to life, I bring to death:
The spirit does but mean the breath:
I know no more." And he, shall he,

Man, her last work, who seemed so fair,
Such splendid purpose in his eyes,
Who rolled the psalm to wintry skies,
Who built him fanes° of fruitless prayer, *temples*

Who trusted God was love indeed
And love Creation's final law—
Though Nature, red in tooth and claw
With ravine,° shrieked against his creed— *violence*

Who loved, who suffered countless ills,
Who battled for the True, the Just,
Be blown about the desert dust,
Or sealed within the iron hills?

No more? A monster then, a dream,
A discord. Dragons° of the prime, *dinosaurs*
That tare° each other in their slime, *tore*
Were mellow music matched with him.[3]

O life as futile, then, as frail!
O for thy voice to soothe and bless!
What hope of answer, or redress?
Behind the veil, behind the veil.

[1] *scarpèd* Steeply cut.

[2] *A thousand … shall go* A reference to the geological discoveries of Charles Lyell, whose *Principles of Geology* (1830–33) Tennyson had read. The fossil record evident in exposed rocks and cliffs reveals that entire species have become extinct.

[3] *Dragons … with him* I.e., if the natural world reflects a universe based in destruction rather than love, then the dinosaurs are more in accord with nature than humankind, which is deluded in its pursuit of religion (see lines 11–12).

67

When on my bed the moonlight falls,
I know that in thy place of rest
By that broad water of the west,[4]
There comes a glory on the walls;

Thy marble bright in dark appears,
As slowly steals a silver flame
Along the letters of thy name,
And o'er the number of thy years.

The mystic glory swims away;
From off my bed the moonlight dies;
And closing eaves of wearied eyes
I sleep till dusk is dipped in gray:

And then I know the mist is drawn
A lucid veil from coast to coast,
And in the dark church like a ghost
Thy tablet glimmers to the dawn.

83

Dip down upon the northern shore,
O sweet new-year delaying long;
Thou doest expectant nature wrong;
Delaying long, delay no more.

What stays thee from the clouded noons,
Thy sweetness from its proper place?
Can trouble live with April days,
Or sadness in the summer moons?

Bring orchis,° bring the foxglove spire, *orchid*
The little speedwell's darling blue,
Deep tulips dashed with fiery dew,
Laburnums,[5] dropping-wells of fire.

O thou, new-year, delaying long,
Delayest the sorrow in my blood,
That longs to burst a frozen bud
And flood a fresher throat with song.

[4] *broad … west* I.e., the Severn Estuary.

[5] *Laburnums* Trees with hanging bunches of bright yellow flowers.

88

Wild bird, whose warble, liquid sweet,
Rings Eden through the budded quicks,° *hedgerows*
O tell me where the senses mix,
O tell me where the passions meet,

Whence radiate: fierce extremes employ
Thy spirits in the darkening leaf,
And in the midmost heart of grief
Thy passion clasps a secret joy:

And I—my harp would prelude woe—
I cannot all command the strings;
The glory of the sum of things
Will flash along the chords and go.

123

There rolls the deep where grew the tree.
O earth, what changes hast thou seen!
There where the long street roars, hath been
The stillness of the central sea.

The hills are shadows, and they flow
From form to form, and nothing stands;
They melt like mist, the solid lands,
Like clouds they shape themselves and go.[1]

But in my spirit will I dwell,
And dream my dream, and hold it true;
For though my lips may breathe adieu,
I cannot think the thing farewell.

130

Thy voice is on the rolling air;
I hear thee where the waters run;
Thou standest in the rising sun,
And in the setting thou art fair.

What art thou then? I cannot guess;
But though I seem in star and flower
To feel thee some diffusive power,
I do not therefore love thee less:

My love involves the love before;
My love is vaster passion now;
Though mixed with God and Nature thou,
I seem to love thee more and more.

Far off thou art, but ever nigh;
I have thee still, and I rejoice;
I prosper, circled with thy voice;
I shall not lose thee though I die.
—1850

The Eagle

[Fragment]

He clasps the crag with crooked hands;
Close to the sun in lonely lands,
Ringed with the azure world, he stands.

The wrinkled sea beneath him crawls;
He watches from his mountain walls,
And like a thunderbolt he falls.
—1851 (written 1833?)

[1] *O earth … and go* The images that Tennyson uses here are inspired by Charles Lyell's geological discoveries as described in his work *The Principles of Geology* (1830–33).

The Charge of the Light Brigade

In one of the most notorious events of the Crimean War (1853–56), a miscommunication within the British chain of military command on 24 October 1854 caused a cavalry of lightly armed troops to be sent into a frontal assault upon far more heavily armed Russian troops; despite being obviously unmatched to the task, the cavalry obeyed their orders and entered into a short and extremely unequal battle by the end of which over 100 of the Light Brigade's 670 troops had been killed, with many more wounded or taken prisoner. The episode has often been held up as an example of the bravery of the British troops; it has often been taken too as emblematic of the general mismanagement and futility of the Crimean War. Debates over who was to blame for the blunder raged for years.

The three senior officers involved in the misunderstanding were all members of the aristocracy. Lord Raglan commanded the entire British military force; Lord Lucan commanded the two cavalry brigades (Heavy and Light); Lord Cardigan had been given command of the Light Brigade by Lord Lucan. A junior officer, Captain Louis Nolan, carried over to Lord Lucan an order that Lord Raglan had shouted out. The order as Lucan had understood it was then relayed to Lord Cardigan, who led the charge.

Tennyson wrote the first draft of this famous poem on 2 December 1854 after having read accounts in *The Times* of the disastrous charge. A fragmentary report of the incident had appeared in the 11 November issue of *The Times*, and a much fuller report by *Times* correspondent William Howard Russell had been published in the 14 November issue. Tennyson appears to have also drawn on the long editorial on the subject that appeared in the 13 November issue; in that editorial the phrase "some hideous blunder" is used. Excerpts from all three of these *Times* pieces appear below. Tennyson evidently drew on other texts as well; as Herman Melville was among the first to point out, the poem follows very closely the rhythm of certain stanzas of "Agincourt," a seventeenth-century battle poem by Michael Drayton ("They now to fight are gone, / Armour on armour shone …").

The poem was first published in a weekly newspaper, *The Examiner*, on 9 December 1854. A facsimile of the galley proofs of the *Examiner* text, with Tennyson's corrections, is the first version of the poem provided below. A significantly altered version appeared in *Maud and Other Poems* (published in July, 1855); Tennyson substantially shortened the poem, and removed any reference to a "blunder." By this time, however, the original *Examiner* version had become well known and had been fairly widely circulated; it was said to have been recited by some of the soldiers serving in Crimea. A chaplain working in Crimea for The Society for the Propagation of the Gospel suggested that the poem be reprinted for wider circulation among the troops. Tennyson was happy to approve the request—but which of the two versions should be used? On reflection Tennyson concluded that the heavily revised 1855 *Maud and Other Poems* version had been a mistake—that "the criticism of one or two London friends" had induced him to spoil the original poem. Given that it had been the *Examiner* version that had already been known and recited in the Crimea, Tennyson now refered to that version as "the soldiers' version." In a letter to publisher John Forster he gave the following instructions: "The soldiers are the best critics in what pleases them. I send you a copy which retains the 'Light Brigade' and the 'blunder'd'; and I declare that it is the best of the two [versions]." A postscript reiterated the point: "P.S. I am convinced now after writing it out that this *is* the best version."

As can be seen below, the text he then sent off (which became the standard text, printed in the 1856 edition of *Maud and Other Poems* and in subsequent editions of Tennyson's poetry), does not in fact represent a complete return to the 1854 *Examiner* "soldier's version." Though the two are substantially the same, the opening of the 1856 version is altered (with one "blundered" rather than two), and the fourth stanza is significantly altered as well. These and other smaller changes are itemized in the footnotes to the 1856 version.

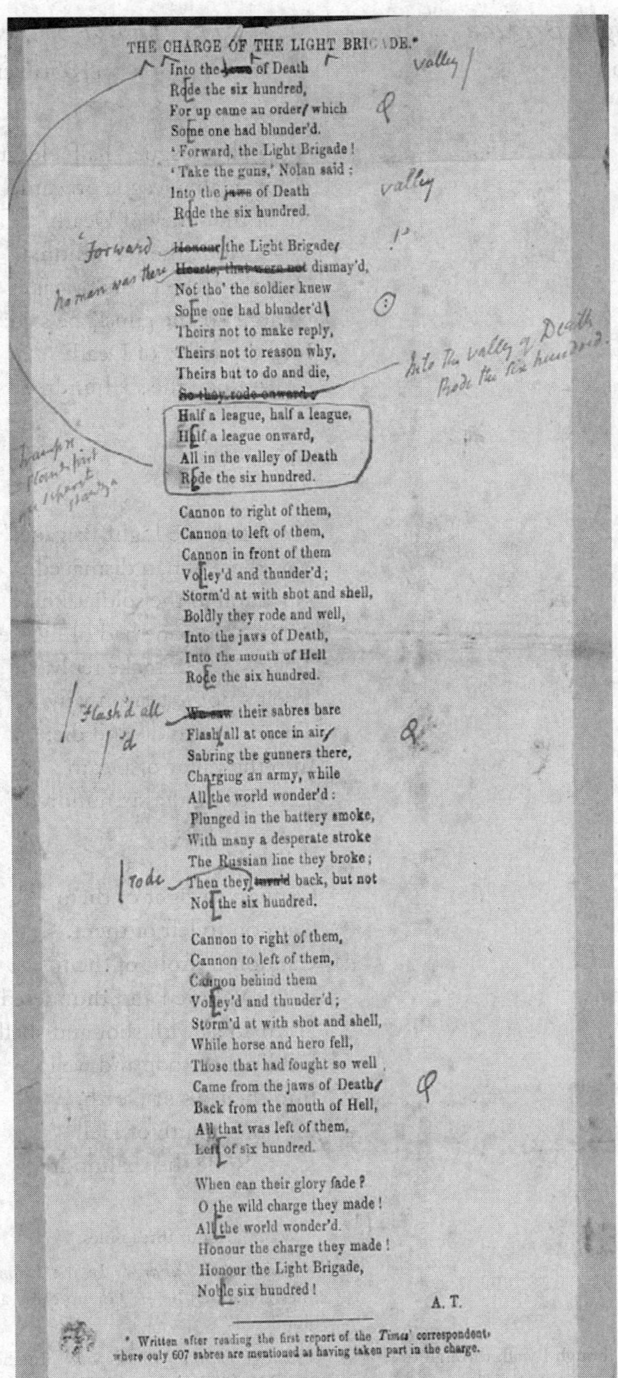

THE CHARGE OF THE LIGHT BRIGADE.*

Into the jaws of Death
Rode the six hundred,
For up came an order which
Some one had blunder'd.
'Forward, the Light Brigade!
'Take the guns,' Nolan said;
Into the jaws of Death
Rode the six hundred.

Honour the Light Brigade,
Hearts, that were not dismay'd,
Not tho' the soldier knew
Some one had blunder'd:
Theirs not to make reply,
Theirs not to reason why,
Theirs but to do and die,
So they rode onward;
Half a league, half a league,
Half a league onward,
All in the valley of Death
Rode the six hundred.

Cannon to right of them,
Cannon to left of them,
Cannon in front of them
Volley'd and thunder'd;
Storm'd at with shot and shell,
Boldly they rode and well,
Into the jaws of Death,
Into the mouth of Hell
Rode the six hundred.

We saw their sabres bare
Flash all at once in air
Sabring the gunners there,
Charging an army, while
All the world wonder'd:
Plunged in the battery smoke,
With many a desperate stroke
The Russian line they broke;
Then they turn'd back, but not
Not the six hundred.

Cannon to right of them,
Cannon to left of them,
Cannon behind them
Volley'd and thunder'd;
Storm'd at with shot and shell,
While horse and hero fell,
Those that had fought so well
Came from the jaws of Death
Back from the mouth of Hell,
All that was left of them,
Left of six hundred.

When can their glory fade?
O the wild charge they made!
All the world wonder'd.
Honour the charge they made!
Honour the Light Brigade,
Noble six hundred!

A. T.

* Written after reading the first report of the *Times'* correspondent, where only 607 sabres are mentioned as having taken part in the charge.

The galley proofs of the initial *Examiner* text, with Tennyson's hand-written corrections.

The Charge of the Light Brigade
[1855 version]

1

Half a league,[1] half a league,
Half a league onward,
All in the valley of Death[2]
Rode the six hundred.
"Charge," was the captain's cry;
Their's not to reason why,
Their's not to make reply,
Their's but to do and die,
Into the valley of Death
Rode the six hundred.

2

Cannon to right of them,
Cannon to left of them,
Cannon in front of them
Volleyed and thundered;
Stormed at with shot and shell,
Boldly they rode and well;
Into the jaws of Death,
Into the mouth of Hell,
Rode the six hundred.

3

Flashed all their sabres[3] bare,
Flashed all at once in air,
Sabring the gunners there,
Charging an army, while
All the world wondered:
Plunged in the battery-smoke
Fiercely the line they broke;
Strong was the sabre-stroke;
Making an army reel
Shaken and sundered.
Then they rode back, but not,
Not the six hundred.

[1] *league* About three miles.

[2] *valley of Death* See Psalm 23.4: "Yea, though I walk through the valley of the shadow of death." The phrase "valley of death" also appears in the 14 November *Times* account.

[3] *sabres* Long, curved swords.

The Charge of the Light Brigade
[1856 version]

1

Half a league,[4] half a league,
Half a league onward,
All in the valley of Death
Rode the six hundred.[5]
"Forward, the Light Brigade!
Charge for the guns!" he said:[6]
Into the valley of Death
Rode the six hundred.

2

"Forward, the Light Brigade!"
Was there a man dismayed?[7]
Not though the soldier knew
Some one had blundered:
Their's not to make reply,
Their's not to reason why,
Their's but to do and die:
Into the valley of Death
Rode the six hundred.

3

Cannon to right of them,
Cannon to left of them,
Cannon in front of them
Volleyed and thundered;
Stormed at with shot and shell,
Boldly they rode and well,
Into the jaws of Death,
Into the mouth of Hell
Rode the six hundred.

[4] *league* About three miles.

[5] *Rode the six hundred* In the *Examiner* version the following two lines are added here: "For up came an order which / Some one had blundered."

[6] *Charge for the guns, he said* In the *Examiner* version, "'Take the guns,' Nolan said."

[7] *Was there a man dismayed?* In the *Examiner* version, "No man was there dismayed."

4

Cannon to right of them,
Cannon to left of them,
Cannon behind them
    Volleyed and thundered;
Stormed at with shot and shell,
They that had struck so well
Rode thro' the jaws of Death,
Half a league back again,
Up from the mouth of Hell,
All that was left of them,
    Left of six hundred.

5

Honour the brave and bold!
Long shall the tale be told,
Yea, when our babes are old—
    How they rode onward.

—1854 (REVISED 1855)

4

Flashed all their sabres bare,
Flashed as they turned[1] in air
Sabring the gunners there,
Charging an army, while
    All the world wondered:
Plunged in the battery-smoke
Right through the line they broke;
Cossack and Russian
Reeled from the sabre-stroke
    Shattered and sundered.[2]
Then they rode back, but not
    Not the six hundred.

5

Cannon to right of them,
Cannon to left of them,
Cannon behind them
    Volleyed and thundered;
Stormed at with shot and shell,
While horse and hero fell,
They[3] that had fought so well
Came through[4] the jaws of Death,
Back from the mouth of Hell,
All that was left of them,[5]
    Left of six hundred.

6

When can their glory fade?
O the wild charge they made!
    All the world wondered.
Honour the charge they made!
Honour the Light Brigade,
    Noble six hundred!

—1854 (REVISED 1856)

---

[1] *as they turned* In the *Examiner* version, "all at once."

[2] *Right through … sundered* In the *Examiner* version, two lines take the place of these four: "With many a desperate stroke / The Russian line they broke."

[3] *They* In the *Examiner* version, "Those."

[4] *through* In the *Examiner* version, "from."

[5] *All … them* Hundreds of men died or were taken prisoner.

IN CONTEXT

The Charge of the Light Brigade as Reported in *The Times*

from "The Attack on Balaklava," *The Times* (13 November 1854)

The long 13 November report in *The Times* of the action in the Crimea included two letters from the principals—one from Lord Raglan and one from Lord Lucan.

[from LETTER TO THE DUKE OF NEWCASTLE FROM FITZROY JAMES HENRY SOMERSET, LORD RAGLAN]

… The charge of this brigade was one of the most successful I ever witnessed, was never for a moment doubtful, and is in the highest degree creditable to Brigadier-General Scarlett[1] and the officers and men engaged in it.

As the enemy withdrew from the ground which they had momentarily occupied, I directed the cavalry, supported by the Fourth Division, under Lieutenant-General Sir George Cathcart, to move forward, and take advantage of any opportunity to regain the heights; and, not having been able to accomplish this immediately, and it appearing that an attempt was making to remove the captured guns, the Earl of Lucan was desired to advance rapidly, follow the enemy in their retreat, and try to prevent them from effecting their objects.

In the meanwhile the Russians had time to reform on their own ground, with artillery in front and upon their flanks.

From some misconception of the instruction to advance, the Lieutenant-General considered that he was bound to attack at all hazards, and he accordingly ordered Major-General the Earl of Cardigan[2] to move forward with the Light Brigade.

This order was obeyed in the most spirited and gallant manner. Lord Cardigan charged with the utmost vigour, attacked a battery which was firing upon the advancing squadrons, and, having passed beyond it, engaged the Russian cavalry in its rear; but there his troops were assailed by artillery and infantry as well as cavalry, and necessarily retired, after having committed much havoc upon the enemy.

They effected this movement without haste or confusion; but the loss they have sustained has, I deeply lament, been very severe in officers, men, and horses, only counterbalanced by the brilliancy of the attack and the gallantry, order, and discipline which distinguished it, forming a striking contrast to the conduct of the enemy's cavalry which had previously been engaged with the heavy brigade. …

---

[1] *Brigadier-General Scarlett* James Yorke Scarlett (1799–1871), General in command of the Heavy Brigade that was also present during the battle.

[2] *Major-General the Earl of Cardigan* James Thomas Brudenell (1797–1868), commander of the Light Brigade.

[from Letter from George Bingham, Lord Lucan]

… The Heavy Brigade having now joined the Light Brigade, the division took up a position with a view of supporting an attack upon the heights, when, being instructed to make a rapid advance to our front, to prevent the enemy carrying the guns lost by the Turkish troops in the morning, I ordered the Light Brigade to advance in two lines, and supported them with the Heavy Brigade. This attack of the Light Cavalry was very brilliant and daring; exposed to a fire from heavy batteries on their front and two flanks, they advanced unchecked until they reached the batteries of the enemy, and cleared them of their gunners, and only retired when they found themselves engaged with a very superior force of cavalry in the rear. Major-General the Earl of Cardigan led this attack in the most gallant and intrepid manner; and his Lordship has expressed himself to me as admiring in the highest degree the courage and zeal of every officer, non-commissioned officer, and man who assisted.

The Heavy Brigade advanced to the support of the attack under a very galling fire from the batteries and infantry in a redoubt,[1] and acted with most perfect steadiness, and in a manner to deserve all praise.

The losses, my Lord, it grieves me to state, have been very great indeed, and, I fear, will be much felt by your Lordship.

I cannot too strongly recommend to your Lordship the two General officers commanding the brigades, all the officers in command of regiments, as also the divisional and brigade staffs; indeed, the conduct of every individual, of every rank, I feel to be deserving of my entire praise, and, I hope, of your Lordship's approbation. …

from Editorial, *The Times* (13 November 1854)

The phrase "some hideous blunder" in the conclusion to this piece appears to have prompted Tennyson's use of the verb "blundered" in his poem.

We now know the details of the attack on Balaklava on the 25th, and with them much that is glorious and much that is reassuring. The worst is comprehended in a melancholy loss of men, chiefly in that arm of the service which could least bear it[.] … We have, then, in the despatches before us nearly the whole of the loss, which it would be vain to conceal is most lamentable[.] … The disaster, then, of which the mere shadow has darkened so many a household among us for the last ten days is not more, but it is not much less, than the annihilation of the Light Cavalry Brigade. It entered into action about 700 strong, and mustered only 191 on its return, though, of course, some afterwards rejoined their comrades. Of the missing, it is to be feared that the majority are killed, as the Russians, who would make the most of their prisoners, do not account for half as many. Had there been the smallest use in the movement that has cost us so much—had it been the necessity of a retreat or part of any plan whatever, we should endeavour to bear this sad loss as we do the heaps of human life lavished in an assault. Even accident would have made it more tolerable. But it was a mere mistake—evidently a mistake, and perceived to be such when it was too late to correct it. The affair then assumed the terrible form of a splendid self-sacrifice. Two great armies, composed of four nations, saw from the slopes of a vast amphitheatre seven hundred British cavalry proceed at a rapid pace, and in perfect order, to certain destruction. Such a spectacle was never seen before, and we trust will never be repeated. There are two consolations—the first that, owing to the very incomplete state

[1] *redoubt* Stronghold.

of our regiments, there were not more to exhibit in this fearful death-parade; and, secondly, that even in that awful progress, when officer and soldier felt themselves hurried to their doom by some inextricable error, they still kept their ranks, went fiercely on, rode up hills, stormed batteries, and sold their lives as dearly as the manifest odds against them would allow.

The error was one of unusual simplicity, and requires no science to understand it. There was no surprise, not even too short a notice. There was no misconception of the enemy's strength. There was no inevitable train of consequences, in which disaster was the slow result of successive operations. … It was about noon … that the fatal movement took place. The cavalry then received an order to advance rapidly to the front, to follow the enemy, and attempt to prevent them carrying off the guns; and, as the circumstances under which the order was received were not a little formidable, they were told that the French cavalry were on their left. How far the order was itself the result of a misconception, or was intended to be executed at discretion, does not appear, and will probably afford the subject of painful but vain recrimination. It was interpreted as leaving no discretion at all, and the whole brigade advanced at a trot for more than a mile, down a valley, with a murderous flank fire of Minié muskets[1] and shells from hills on both sides. It charged batteries, took guns, sabred[2] the gunners, and charged the Russian cavalry beyond; but, not being supported—and, under the circumstances, perhaps it is fortunate it was not—and being attacked by cavalry in front and rear, it had to cut its way through them, and return through the same cavalry and the same fire. The brigade was simply pounded by the shot, shell, and Minié bullets from the hills. Not more than a dozen were killed by the Russian cavalry, who, if they had been good for anything, would have taken care that not a single British soldier should return to tell the tale. Causeless as the sacrifice was, it was most glorious. A French General who saw the advance, and apprehended at once its fatal issue, exclaimed, "*C'est très magnifique, mais ce n'est pas la guerre*."[3] The enthusiasm of the moment, and the fellow-feeling of the two armies, almost led the Chasseurs d'Afrique[4] to follow the British brigade to its doom, but they were wisely restrained, and did much better service by charging a Russian battery on the flank, and for a time checking its fire.

It is difficult not to regard such a disaster in a light of its own, and to separate it from the general sequence of affairs. Causeless and fruitless, it stands by itself, as a grand heroic deed, surpassing even that spectacle of a shipwrecked regiment, settling down into the waves, each man still in his rank. The British soldier will do his duty, even to certain death, and is not paralyzed by feeling that he is the victim of some hideous blunder. Whatever the case of the common soldier, and however little he might know the full horrors of his position till death had done its work all around him, the officers who led him on, with a conspicuous gallantry that extorted the admiration of the foe, knew well what they were about. Nor were those officers mere soldiers of fortune, with nothing to lose but themselves, and no inducements out of their profession. They were men who risked on that day all the enjoyments that rank, wealth, good social position, and many fortunate circumstances can offer to those who are content to stay at home. Splendid as the event was on the Alma,[5] yet that rugged ascent in the face of heights blazing with destruction was scarcely so glorious as the progress of the

[1] *Minié muskets* Rifles that came into use during the mid-nineteenth century. They had a longer range and greater accuracy than most similar guns of the period, and fired Minié bullets, which were easier to load than their predecessors.

[2] *sabred* I.e., attacked with sabres, curved swords.

[3] *C'est très … la guerre* French: This is very magnificent, but this is not war.

[4] *Chasseurs d'Afrique* Light cavalry branch of the French Armé d'Afrique, who were normally stationed in France's colonial possessions in North Africa, but also participated in the Crimean War.

[5] *Alma* Crimean river.

cavalry through and through that valley of death,[1] with a murderous fire, not only in front, but on both sides, above, and even in the rear. …

from "The Cavalry Action at Balaclava," *The Times* (14 November 1854)

Though the report from which the following excerpt is taken appeared in the 14 November issue of *The Times*, the dispatch from *The Times*' correspondent (William Howard Russell) is dated 25 October.

… As they passed towards the front, the Russians opened on them from the guns in the redoubt on the right, with volleys of musketry and rifles. They swept proudly past, glittering in the morning sun in all the pride and splendour of war. We could scarcely believe the evidence of our senses! Surely that handful of men are not going to charge an army in position? Alas! it was but too true—their desperate valour knew no bounds, and far indeed was it removed from its so-called better part—discretion. They advanced in two lines, quickening their pace as they closed towards the enemy. A more fearful spectacle was never witnessed than by those who, without the power to aid, beheld their heroic countrymen rushing to the arms of death. At the distance of 1,200 yards the whole line of the enemy belched forth, from 30 iron mouths, a flood of smoke and flame, through which hissed the deadly balls. Their flight was marked by instant gaps in our ranks by dead men and horses, by steeds flying wounded or riderless across the plain. The first line is broken, it is joined by the second, they never halt or check their speed an instant; with diminished ranks, thinned by those 30 guns, which the Russians had laid with the most deadly accuracy, with a halo of flashing steel above their heads, and with a cheer which was many a noble fellow's death-cry, they flew into the smoke of the batteries, but ere they were lost from view the plain was strewed with their bodies and with the carcasses of horses. They were exposed to an oblique fire from the batteries on the hills on both sides, as well as to a direct fire of musketry. Through the clouds of smoke we could see their sabres flashing as they rode up to the guns and dashed between them, cutting down the gunners as they stood. We saw them riding through the guns, as I have said; to our delight we saw them returning, after breaking through a column of Russian infantry, and scattering them like chaff, when the flank fire of the battery on the hill swept them down, scattered and broken as they were. Wounded men and dismounted troopers flying towards us told the sad tale—demi-gods could not have done what we had failed to do. …

[1] *valley of death* See Psalm 23.4: "Yea, though I walk through the valley of the shadow of death."

[*Flower in the Crannied Wall*]

Flower in the crannied wall,
I pluck you out of the crannies,
I hold you here, root and all, in my hand,
Little flower—but *if* I could understand
What you are, root and all, and all in all,
I should know what God and man is.
—1869

Vastness

I

Many a hearth upon our dark globe sighs after many a vanished face,
Many a planet by many a sun may roll with the dust of a vanished race.

2

Raving politics, never at rest—as this poor earth's pale history runs,—
What is it all but a trouble° of ants in the gleam of a million million of suns? *agitation*

3

Lies upon this side, lies upon that side, truthless violence mourned by the Wise,
Thousands of voices drowning his own in a popular torrent of lies upon lies;

4

Stately purposes, valour in battle, glorious annals of army and fleet,
Death for the right cause, death for the wrong cause, trumpets of victory, groans of defeat;

5

Innocence seethed° in her mother's milk,[1] and Charity setting the martyr aflame; *boiled*
Thraldom° who walks with the banner of Freedom, and recks not[2] to ruin a realm in her name. *bondage*

6

Faith at her zenith, or all but lost in the gloom of doubts that darken the schools;
Craft with a bunch of all-heal[3] in her hand, followed up by her vassal° legion of fools; *servile*

7

Trade flying over a thousand seas with her spice and her vintage, her silk and her corn;
Desolate offing,[4] sailorless harbours, famishing populace, wharves forlorn;

8

Star of the morning, Hope in the sunrise; gloom of the evening, Life at a close;
Pleasure who flaunts on her wide down-way with her flying robe and her poisoned rose;

9

Pain, that has crawled from the corpse of Pleasure, a worm which writhes all day, and at night
Stirs up again in the heart of the sleeper, and stings him back to the curse of the light;

10

Wealth with his wines and his wedded harlots; honest Poverty, bare to the bone;
Opulent Avarice, lean as Poverty; Flattery gilding the rift in a throne;

11

Fame blowing out from her golden trumpet a jubilant challenge to Time and to Fate;
Slander, her shadow, sowing the nettle on all the laurelled graves of the Great;

---

1 *Innocence … milk* See Exodus 34.26: "Thou shalt not seethe a kid in his mother's milk."

2 *recks not* Is not reluctant.

3 *all-heal* Name given to various plants believed to possess healing properties.

4 *offing* Most distant part of the sea visible from shore.

12

Love for the maiden, crowned with marriage,
no regrets for aught that has been,
Household happinesss, gracious children,
debtless competence,° golden mean; *sufficiency*

13

National hatreds of whole generations, and
pigmy° spites of the village spire; *trivial*
Vows that will last to the last death-ruckle,° *death-rattle*
and vows that are snapped in a moment of fire;

14

He that has lived for the lust of the minute,
and died in the doing it, flesh without mind;
He that has nailed all flesh to the Cross,
till Self died out in the love of his kind;

15

Spring and Summer and Autumn and Winter,
and all these old revolutions of earth;
All new-old revolutions of Empire—change of the
tide—what is all of it worth?

16

What the philosophies, all the sciences, poesy,
varying voices of prayer?
All that is noblest, all that is basest, all that is filthy
with all that is fair?

17

What is it all, if we all of us end but in being our own
corpse-coffins at last,
Swallowed in Vastness, lost in Silence, drowned
in the deeps of a meaningless Past?

18

What but a murmur of gnats in the gloom,
or a moment's anger of bees in their hive?—

* * *

Peace, let it be! for I loved him, and love him for ever:
the dead are not dead but alive.
—1885; 1889

Crossing the Bar[1]

Sunset and evening star,
And one clear call for me!
And may there be no moaning of the bar,
When I put out to sea,

But such a tide as moving seems asleep,
Too full for sound and foam,
When that which drew from out the boundless deep
Turns again home.

Twilight and evening bell,
And after that the dark!
And may there be no sadness of farewell,
When I embark;

For though from out our bourne° of Time and Place *limit*
The flood may bear me far,
I hope to see my Pilot face to face
When I have crossed the bar.
—1889

[1] *Bar* Sandbank across the mouth of a harbor or estuary.

IN CONTEXT

Images of Tennyson

Particularly in his later years, Tennyson became an iconic figure in Victorian Britain. The best known photographic images of him are those taken by Julia Margaret Cameron, two of which are reproduced, below. (Another appears in the introduction to Tennyson, above.) Tennyson as a younger man is described below by Thomas Carlyle.

Julia Margaret Cameron, *Alfred Tennyson*, 1865. Tennyson nicknamed this photograph "the dirty monk" and claimed that it was his favorite photograph of himself.

Julia Margaret Cameron, *Alfred Lord Tennyson*, 1866.

from Thomas Carlyle, Letter to Ralph Waldo Emerson, 5 August 1844

Alfred is one of the few British or Foreign Figures (a not increasing number I think!) who are and remain beautiful to me;—a true human soul, or some authentic approximation thereto, to whom your own soul can say, Brother!—However, I doubt[1] he will not come; he often skips me, in these brief visits to Town; skips everybody indeed; being a man solitary and sad, as certain men are, dwelling in an element of gloom,—carrying a bit of Chaos about him, in short, which he is manufacturing into Cosmos!

Alfred is the son of a Lincolnshire Gentleman Farmer, I think; indeed, you see in his verses that he is a native of "moated granges,"[2] and green, fat pastures, not of mountains and their torrents and

---

[1] *doubt* Suspect.

[2] *moated granges* See Tennyson's poem, "Mariana"(above).

storms. He had his breeding at Cambridge, as if for the Law or Church; being master of a small annuity on his Father's decease, he preferred clubbing with his Mother and some Sisters, to live unpromoted and write Poems. In this way he lives still, now here, now there; the family always within reach of London, never in it; he himself making rare and brief visits, lodging in some old comrade's rooms. I think he must be under forty, not much under it.[1] One of the finest-looking men in the world. A great shock of rough dusty-dark hair; bright-laughing hazel eyes; massive aquiline face, most massive yet most delicate; of sallow-brown complexion, almost Indian-looking; clothes cynically loose, free-and-easy;—smokes infinite tobacco. His voice is musical metallic,—fit for loud laughter and piercing wail, and all that may lie between; speech and speculation free and plenteous: I do not meet, in these late decades, such company over a pipe!—We shall see what he will grow to. He is often unwell; very chaotic,—his way is through Chaos and the Bottomless and Pathless; not handy for making out many miles upon.

In Context

Victorian Images of Arthurian Legend

Arthurian romance was a frequent subject of Victorian painting and photography as well as Victorian literature; a sampling is reproduced below.

Julia Margaret Cameron, *The Parting of Lancelot and Guinevere*, 1874.

Julia Margaret Cameron, *Vivien and Merlin*, 1874.

[1] *not much under it* In fact, Tennyson was just about to turn thirty-five when this was written.

John William Waterhouse, *The Lady of Shalott*, 1888.

William Holman Hunt, *The Lady of Shalott*, 1857.

Henry Peach Robinson, *The Lady of Shalott*, c. 1860.

IN CONTEXT

Crimea and the Camera

The Crimean War was the first to be photographed extensively—most notably by Roger Fenton, who spent three months in Crimea in 1855. Both the technology of the time and the demands of Victorian taste militated against shooting scenes of battle directly; unlike Matthew Brady and other photographers of the American Civil War a few years later, Fenton took no pictures of bloody and mangled corpses.

Fenton's most famous photograph of the war, *Valley of the Shadow of Death*, came to be closely associated with Tennyson's famous 1854 poem, "The Charge of the Light Brigade." The connection is not entirely a direct one, however. It was not the valley where the charge occurred that Fenton photographed but another valley in the vicinity—one that had begun to be referred to by soldiers as "the valley of the shadow of death" (in an echo both of Tennyson's poem and of the Bible) because of the frequency with which the Russians shelled it.

Roger Fenton, *Group of Croat Chiefs*, 1855.

Roger Fenton, *Cookhouse of the 8th Hussars*, 1855.

Roger Fenton, *Valley of the Shadow of Death*, 1855.

Charles Darwin

1809 – 1882

The name Charles Darwin has become synonymous in many minds with the theory of evolution, but theories of evolution did not begin with Darwin. Long before the Victorian era the ancient Greek thinkers Anaximander (611–547 BCE), Empedocles (492–432 BCE), and Aristotle (384–322 BCE) all speculated that life as we know it evolved from sea creatures. In the year Darwin was born, the French biologist Lamarck suggested that species respond and adapt to their environments and then transmit these adaptive traits to their offspring. And in 1850, drawing on the theories of Charles Lyell and Robert Chambers, Tennyson speculated on the idea of evolution in his poetic elegy *In Memoriam*. But when the unassuming British naturalist Charles Darwin articulated his acceptance of the concept of evolution and published his theory of natural selection in 1859 in *On the Origin of Species*, his views provoked comment and controversy internationally. He had offered a detailed, cogent, and plausible theory that to many appeared to call into question the idea of divine creation, as well as assumptions about human beings' innate superiority to, and difference from, other creatures.

Charles Robert Darwin was born in 1809 in Shrewsbury, England, to Robert Waring Darwin, a successful doctor (and son of the famous physician, botanist, philosopher, and poet Erasmus Darwin), and Susannah Wedgwood Darwin, daughter of the pottery manufacturer Josiah Wedgwood. Charles distinguished himself neither at school nor at the University of Edinburgh, where his father sent him to study medicine. He often complained throughout his school years of being bored, although he always showed an active interest in and enthusiasm for the natural sciences and for specimen collection. When he left medical school without taking his degree, his father pushed him into a second career track; ironically, the man who would be reviled by religious fundamentalists next studied theology at Cambridge with a view to joining the clergy. Darwin again became bored with his studies, preferring to spend his time collecting and studying beetles. He did make an important friend at Cambridge; his botany professor, John Henslow, recognized Darwin's potential as a natural scientist and recommended him for a position on the H.M.S. Beagle, the ship that would take him around the world to collect biological specimens and data. On this pivotal five-year voyage, Darwin compiled meticulous records of his findings along with an engaging account of his travels and the cultures he encountered, which he subsequently published as *The Voyage of the Beagle* in 1839.

Influenced by James Hutton's geological theories and Charles Lyell's *Principles of Geology*, Darwin also collected fossils and noted the relationship between creatures and their environments, particularly among the unique fauna of the Galapagos Islands. These isolated islands contained species of birds completely unlike those on the mainland, as well as others that closely resembled species of South America. After completing the voyage, Darwin devoted the rest of his career to researching and attempting to explain the differences between such species and their ancestors. After reading Thomas Malthus's *An Essay on the Principle of Population*, he came up with his answer: individuals that are strong enough to survive environmental pressures pass their favorable traits on to successive generations, and thus species adapt and gradually form new species, a process Darwin called "natural selection." Moreover, according to Darwinian theory this process has persisted for millions of years, with all species having evolved from a single life form.

Although he wrote essays on his evolutionary ideas, Darwin did not publish his findings for 20 years, until another naturalist, Alfred Russel Wallace, sent him a paper that included similar conclusions about natural selection. The two agreed to present a joint paper in 1858 to the Linnaean Society in London, and the next year Darwin published *On the Origin of Species*. *Origin* sold out its entire print run amidst a storm of protest and indignation. In the decade following its publication, responses to the book abounded in the literary world, with authors such as Charles Kingsley and Samuel Butler opposing Darwin, while George Eliot, Thomas Hardy, and Joseph Conrad drew on his theories and modes of explanation.

For the rest of his life, Darwin lived in his country house with his wife, his cousin Emma Wedgwood, whom he had married in 1839, and his many children, studying flora and fauna and publishing his findings. Although the world around him struggled to absorb the impact of his evolutionary theory, Darwin refused to engage in debates about the questions that haunted so many: are humans really evolved from lower life forms, and where does this theory leave the Bible's teachings? In *The Descent of Man, and Selection in Relation to Sex* (1871) Darwin explicitly extended his evolutionary theory to human beings and put forward the notion of sexual selection.

In 1882, after suffering from ill health for many years, quite possibly from a disease acquired during his voyage on the H.M.S. Beagle, Darwin died. He was buried next to Sir Isaac Newton in Westminster Abbey.

⌘⌘⌘

Charles Darwin, 1840
(sketch by George Richmond).

Conrad Martens, *H.M.S. Beagle*, Tierra del Fuego, c. 1832.

Charles Island, Galapagos, 1835 (watercolor by Conrad Martens).

from *On the Origin of Species*

Introduction

When on board H.M.S. "Beagle," as naturalist,[1] I was much struck with certain facts in the distribution of the inhabitants of South America, and in the geological relations of the present to the past inhabitants of that continent. These facts seemed to me to throw some light on the origin of species—that mystery of mysteries, as it has been called by one of our greatest philosophers. On my return home, it occurred to me, in 1837, that something might perhaps be made out on this question by patiently accumulating and reflecting on all sorts of facts which could possibly have any bearing on it. After five years' work I allowed myself to speculate on the subject, and drew up some short notes; these I enlarged in 1844 into a sketch of the conclusions, which then seemed to me probable: from that period to the present day I have steadily pursued the same object. I hope that I may be excused for entering on these personal details, as I give them to show that I have not been hasty in coming to a decision.

My work is now nearly finished; but as it will take me two or three more years to complete it, and as my health is far from strong, I have been urged to publish this abstract. I have more especially been induced to do this, as Mr. Wallace,[2] who is now studying the natural history of the Malay archipelago, has arrived at almost exactly the same general conclusions that I have on the origin of species. Last year he sent to me a memoir on this subject, with a request that I would forward it to Sir Charles Lyell,[3] who sent it to the Linnean Society,[4] and it is published in the third volume of the Journal of that Society. Sir C. Lyell and Dr. Hooker,[5] who both knew of my work—the latter having read my sketch of 1844—honoured me by thinking it advisable to pub-

[1] *When on board ... naturalist* Darwin traveled on the *Beagle* between 1831 and 1836.

[2] *Mr. Wallace* Alfred Russel Wallace (1823–1913), English naturalist and social critic.

[3] *Sir Charles Lyell* British geologist (1797–1875).

[4] *Linnean Society* Prominent London scientific society.

[5] *Dr. Hooker* Joseph Dalton Hooker (1817–1911), botanist and friend of Darwin.

lish, with Mr. Wallace's excellent memoir, some brief extracts from my manuscripts.

This abstract, which I now publish, must necessarily be imperfect. I cannot here give references and authorities for my several statements; and I must trust to the reader reposing some confidence in my accuracy. No doubt errors will have crept in, though I hope I have always been cautious in trusting to good authorities alone. I can here give only the general conclusions at which I have arrived, with a few facts in illustration, but which, I hope, in most cases will suffice. No one can feel more sensible than I do of the necessity of hereafter publishing in detail all the facts, with references, on which my conclusions have been grounded; and I hope in a future work to do this. For I am well aware that scarcely a single point is discussed in this volume on which facts cannot be adduced,[1] often apparently leading to conclusions directly opposite to those at which I have arrived. A fair result can be obtained only by fully stating and balancing the facts and arguments on both sides of each question; and this cannot possibly be here done.

I much regret that want of space prevents my having the satisfaction of acknowledging the generous assistance which I have received from very many naturalists, some of them personally unknown to me. I cannot, however, let this opportunity pass without expressing my deep obligations to Dr. Hooker, who for the last fifteen years has aided me in every possible way by his large stores of knowledge and his excellent judgment.

In considering the origin of species, it is quite conceivable that a naturalist, reflecting on the mutual affinities of organic beings, on their embryological relations, their geographical distribution, geological succession, and other such facts, might come to the conclusion that each species had not been independently created, but had descended, like varieties, from other species. Nevertheless, such a conclusion, even if well founded, would be unsatisfactory, until it could be shown how the innumerable species inhabiting this world have been modified, so as to acquire that perfection of structure and coadaptation which most justly excites our admiration. Naturalists continually refer to external conditions, such as climate, food, *et cetera*, as the only possible cause of variation. In one very limited sense, as we shall hereafter see, this may be true; but it is preposterous to attribute to mere external conditions, the structure, for instance, of the woodpecker, with its feet, tail, beak, and tongue, so admirably adapted to catch insects under the bark of trees. In the case of the mistletoe, which draws its nourishment from certain trees, which has seeds that must be transported by certain birds, and which has flowers with separate sexes absolutely requiring the agency of certain insects to bring pollen from one flower to the other, it is equally preposterous to account for the structure of this parasite, with its relations to several distinct organic beings, by the effects of external conditions, or of habit, or of the volition of the plant itself.

The author of the "Vestiges of Creation"[2] would, I presume, say that, after a certain unknown number of generations, some bird had given birth to a woodpecker, and some plant to the mistletoe, and that these had been produced perfect as we now see them; but this assumption seems to me to be no explanation, for it leaves the case of the coadaptations of organic beings to each other and to their physical conditions of life, untouched and unexplained.

It is, therefore, of the highest importance to gain a clear insight into the means of modification and coadaptation. At the commencement of my observations it seemed to me probable that a careful study of domesticated animals and of cultivated plants would offer the best chance of making out this obscure problem. Nor have I been disappointed; in this and in all other perplexing cases I have invariably found that our knowledge, imperfect though it be, of variation under domestication, afforded the best and safest clue. I may venture to express my conviction of the high value of such studies, although they have been very commonly neglected by naturalists.

[1] *adduced* Brought forth.

[2] *Vestiges of Creation* 1844 book, published anonymously but written by Robert Chambers, which suggests that progressive evolution is God's act of creation through geological time.

From these considerations, I shall devote the first chapter of this abstract to variation under domestication. We shall thus see that a large amount of hereditary modification is at least possible, and, what is equally or more important, we shall see how great is the power of man in accumulating by his selection successive slight variations. I will then pass on to the variability of species in a state of nature; but I shall, unfortunately, be compelled to treat this subject far too briefly, as it can be treated properly only by giving long catalogues of facts. We shall, however, be enabled to discuss what circumstances are most favourable to variation. In the next chapter the struggle for existence amongst all organic beings throughout the world, which inevitably follows from their high geometrical ratio of increase, will be treated of. This is the doctrine of Malthus,[1] applied to the whole animal and vegetable kingdoms. As many more individuals of each species are born than can possibly survive; and as, consequently, there is a frequently recurring struggle for existence, it follows that any being, if it vary however slightly in any manner profitable to itself, under the complex and sometimes varying conditions of life, will have a better chance of surviving, and thus be *naturally selected*. From the strong principle of inheritance, any selected variety will tend to propagate its new and modified form.

This fundamental subject of natural selection will be treated at some length in the fourth chapter; and we shall then see how natural selection almost inevitably causes much extinction of the less improved forms of life and induces what I have called divergence of character. In the next chapter I shall discuss the complex and little known laws of variation and of correlation of growth. In the four succeeding chapters, the most apparent and gravest difficulties on the theory will be given: namely, first, the difficulties of transitions, or in understanding how a simple being or a simple organ can be changed and perfected into a highly developed being or elaborately constructed organ; secondly the subject of instinct, or the mental powers of animals, thirdly, hybridism, or the infertility of species and the fertility of varieties when intercrossed; and fourthly, the imperfection of the geological record. In the next chapter I shall consider the geological succession of organic beings throughout time; in the eleventh and twelfth, their geographical distribution throughout space; in the thirteenth, their classification or mutual affinities, both when mature and in an embryonic condition. In the last chapter I shall give a brief recapitulation of the whole work, and a few concluding remarks.

No one ought to feel surprise at much remaining as yet unexplained in regard to the origin of species and varieties, if he makes due allowance for our profound ignorance in regard to the mutual relations of all the beings which live around us. Who can explain why one species ranges widely and is very numerous, and why another allied species has a narrow range and is rare? Yet these relations are of the highest importance, for they determine the present welfare, and, as I believe, the future success and modification of every inhabitant of this world. Still less do we know of the mutual relations of the innumerable inhabitants of the world during the many past geological epochs in its history. Although much remains obscure, and will long remain obscure, I can entertain no doubt, after the most deliberate study and dispassionate judgment of which I am capable, that the view which most naturalists entertain, and which I formerly entertained—namely, that each species has been independently created—is erroneous. I am fully convinced that species are not immutable; but that those belonging to what are called the same genera[2] are lineal descendants of some other and generally extinct species, in the same manner as the acknowledged varieties of any one species are the descendants of that species. Furthermore, I am convinced that natural selection has been the main but not exclusive means of modification.

from CHAPTER 3: STRUGGLE FOR EXISTENCE

Before entering on the subject of this chapter, I must make a few preliminary remarks, to show how the

[1] *Malthus* Thomas Robert Malthus (1766–1834), who theorized in his 1798 work *An Essay on the Principle of Population* that the human population would eventually outstrip its food resources.

[2] *genera* Latin: groupings of species. Plural of "genus."

struggle for existence bears on natural selection. It has been seen in the last chapter that amongst organic beings in a state of nature there is some individual variability; indeed I am not aware that this has ever been disputed. It is immaterial for us whether a multitude of doubtful forms be called species or sub-species or varieties; what rank, for instance, the two or three hundred doubtful forms of British plants are entitled to hold, if the existence of any well-marked varieties be admitted. But the mere existence of individual variability and of some few well-marked varieties, though necessary as the foundation for the work, helps us but little in understanding how species arise in nature. How have all those exquisite adaptations of one part of the organisation to another part, and to the conditions of life, and of one distinct organic being to another being, been perfected? We see these beautiful co-adaptations most plainly in the woodpecker and mistletoe; and only a little less plainly in the humblest parasite which clings to the hairs of a quadruped or feathers of a bird; in the structure of the beetle which dives through the water; in the plumed seed which is wafted by the gentlest breeze; in short, we see beautiful adaptations everywhere and in every part of the organic world.

Again, it may be asked, how is it that varieties, which I have called incipient species, become ultimately converted into good and distinct species, which in most cases obviously differ from each other far more than do the varieties of the same species? How do those groups of species, which constitute what are called distinct genera, and which differ from each other more than do the species of the same genus, arise? All these results, as we shall more fully see in the next chapter, follow inevitably from the struggle for life. Owing to this struggle for life, any variation, however slight and from whatever cause proceeding, if it be in any degree profitable to an individual of any species, in its infinitely complex relations to other organic beings and to external nature, will tend to the preservation of that individual, and will generally be inherited by its offspring. The offspring, also, will thus have a better chance of surviving, for, of the many individuals of any species which are periodically born, but a small number can survive. I have called this principle, by which each slight variation, if useful, is preserved, by the term of natural selection, in order to mark its relation to man's power of selection. We have seen that man by selection can certainly produce great results, and can adapt organic beings to his own uses, through the accumulation of slight but useful variations, given to him by the hand of nature. But natural selection, as we shall hereafter see, is a power incessantly ready for action, and is as immeasurably superior to man's feeble efforts, as the works of nature are to those of art.

We will now discuss in a little more detail the struggle for existence. In my future work this subject shall be treated, as it well deserves, at much greater length. The elder De Candolle[1] and Lyell have largely and philosophically shown that all organic beings are exposed to severe competition. In regard to plants, no one has treated this subject with more spirit and ability than W. Herbert,[2] Dean of Manchester, evidently the result of his great horticultural knowledge. Nothing is easier than to admit in words the truth of the universal struggle for life, or more difficult—at least I have found it so—than constantly to bear this conclusion in mind. Yet unless it be thoroughly engrained in the mind, I am convinced that the whole economy of nature, with every fact on distribution, rarity, abundance, extinction, and variation, will be dimly seen or quite misunderstood. We behold the face of nature bright with gladness, we often see superabundance of food; we do not see, or we forget, that the birds which are idly singing round us mostly live on insects or seeds, and are thus constantly destroying life; or we forget how largely these songsters, or their eggs, or their nestlings, are destroyed by birds and beasts of prey; we do not always bear in mind, that though food may be now superabundant, it is not so at all seasons of each recurring year.

I should premise that I use the term struggle for existence in a large and metaphorical sense, including dependence of one being on another, and including (which is more important) not only the life of the

---

[1] *The elder De Candolle* Augustin-Pyramus de Candolle (1778–1841), Swiss botanist.

[2] *W. Herbert* William Herbert (1778–1847).

individual, but success in leaving progeny. Two canine animals in a time of dearth, may be truly said to struggle with each other which shall get food and live. But a plant on the edge of a desert is said to struggle for life against the drought, though more properly it should be said to be dependent on the moisture. A plant which annually produces a thousand seeds, of which on an average only one comes to maturity, may be more truly said to struggle with the plants of the same and other kinds which already clothe the ground. The mistletoe is dependent on the apple and a few other trees, but can only in a far-fetched sense be said to struggle with these trees, for if too many of these parasites grow on the same tree, it will languish and die. But several seedling mistletoes, growing close together on the same branch, may more truly be said to struggle with each other. As the mistletoe is disseminated by birds, its existence depends on birds; and it may metaphorically be said to struggle with other fruit-bearing plants, in order to tempt birds to devour and thus disseminate its seeds rather than those of other plants. In these several senses, which pass into each other, I use for convenience' sake the general term of struggle for existence.

A struggle for existence inevitably follows from the high rate at which all organic beings tend to increase. Every being, which during its natural lifetime produces several eggs or seeds, must suffer destruction during some period of its life, and during some season or occasional year, otherwise, on the principle of geometrical increase, its numbers would quickly become so inordinately great that no country could support the product. Hence, as more individuals are produced than can possibly survive, there must in every case be a struggle for existence, either one individual with another of the same species, or with the individuals of distinct species, or with the physical conditions of life. It is the doctrine of Malthus applied with manifold force to the whole animal and vegetable kingdoms; for in this case there can be no artificial increase of food, and no prudential restraint from marriage. Although some species may be now increasing, more or less rapidly, in numbers, all cannot do so, for the world would not hold them.

There is no exception to the rule that every organic being naturally increases at so high a rate, that if not destroyed, the earth would soon be covered by the progeny of a single pair. Even slow-breeding man has doubled in twenty-five years, and at this rate, in a few thousand years, there would literally not be standing room for his progeny. Linnaeus[1] has calculated that if an annual plant produced only two seeds—and there is no plant so unproductive as this—and their seedlings next year produced two, and so on, then in twenty years there would be a million plants. The elephant is reckoned to be the slowest breeder of all known animals, and I have taken some pains to estimate its probable minimum rate of natural increase: it will be under the mark to assume that it breeds when thirty years old, and goes on breeding till ninety years old, bringing forth three pair of young in this interval; if this be so, at the end of the fifth century there would be alive fifteen million elephants, descended from the first pair.

But we have better evidence on this subject than mere theoretical calculations, namely, the numerous recorded cases of the astonishingly rapid increase of various animals in a state of nature, when circumstances have been favourable to them during two or three following seasons. Still more striking is the evidence from our domestic animals of many kinds which have run wild in several parts of the world: if the statements of the rate of increase of slow-breeding cattle and horses in South America, and latterly in Australia, had not been well authenticated, they would have been quite incredible. So it is with plants: cases could be given of introduced plants which have become common throughout whole islands in a period of less than ten years. Several of the plants now most numerous over the wide plains of La Plata,[2] clothing square leagues of surface almost to the exclusion of all other plants, have been introduced from Europe; and there are plants which now range in India, as I hear

[1] *Linnaeus* Carolus Linnaeus (1707–78), Swedish scientist who laid the foundations of modern taxonomy.

[2] *La Plata* Region of Argentina.

from Dr. Falconer,[1] from Cape Comorin[2] to the Himalaya, which have been imported from America since its discovery. In such cases, and endless instances could be given, no one supposes that the fertility of these animals or plants has been suddenly and temporarily increased in any sensible degree. The obvious explanation is that the conditions of life have been very favourable, and that there has consequently been less destruction of the old and young, and that nearly all the young have been enabled to breed. In such cases the geometrical ratio of increase, the result of which never fails to be surprising, simply explains the extraordinarily rapid increase and wide diffusion of naturalised productions in their new homes. …

Many cases are on record showing how complex and unexpected are the checks and relations between organic beings, which have to struggle together in the same country. I will give only a single instance, which, though a simple one, has interested me. In Staffordshire, on the estate of a relation where I had ample means of investigation, there was a large and extremely barren heath, which had never been touched by the hand of man; but several hundred acres of exactly the same nature had been enclosed twenty-five years previously and planted with Scotch fir. The change in the native vegetation of the planted part of the heath was most remarkable, more than is generally seen in passing from one quite different soil to another: not only the proportional numbers of the heath-plants were wholly changed, but twelve species of plants (not counting grasses and carices[3]) flourished in the plantations, which could not be found on the heath. The effect on the insects must have been still greater, for six insectivorous birds were very common in the plantations, which were not to be seen on the heath; and the heath was frequented by two or three distinct insectivorous birds. Here we see how potent has been the effect of the introduction of a single tree, nothing whatever else having been done, with the exception that the land had been enclosed, so that cattle could not enter. But how important an element enclosure is, I plainly saw near Farnham, in Surrey. Here there are extensive heaths, with a few clumps of old Scotch firs on the distant hill-tops: within the last ten years large spaces have been enclosed, and self-sown firs are now springing up in multitudes, so close together that all cannot live. When I ascertained that these young trees had not been sown or planted, I was so much surprised at their numbers that I went to several points of view, whence I could examine hundreds of acres of the unenclosed heath, and literally I could not see a single Scotch fir, except the old planted clumps. But on looking closely between the stems of the heath, I found a multitude of seedlings and little trees, which had been perpetually browsed down by the cattle. In one square yard, at a point some hundreds yards distant from one of the old clumps, I counted thirty-two little trees; and one of them, judging from the rings of growth, had during twenty-six years tried to raise its head above the stems of the heath, and had failed. No wonder that, as soon as the land was enclosed, it became thickly clothed with vigorously growing young firs. Yet the heath was so extremely barren and so extensive that no one would ever have imagined that cattle would have so closely and effectually searched it for food.

Here we see that cattle absolutely determine the existence of the Scotch fir; but in several parts of the world insects determine the existence of cattle. Perhaps Paraguay offers the most curious instance of this; for here neither cattle nor horses nor dogs have ever run wild, though they swarm southward and northward in a feral state; and Azara and Rengger[4] have shown that this is caused by the greater number in Paraguay of a certain fly, which lays its eggs in the navels of these animals when first born. The increase of these flies, numerous as they are, must be habitually checked by some means, probably by birds. Hence, if certain insectivorous birds (whose numbers are probably regulated by hawks or beasts of prey) were to increase in

[1] *Dr. Falconer* Hugh Falconer (1808–65), one of the pre-eminent British palaeontologists of the time.

[2] *Cape Comorin* Southernmost point of the Indian subcontinent.

[3] *carices* Sedges.

[4] *Azara and Rengger* Félix de Azara (1746–1821), Spanish explorer and naturalist, and Johann Rudolph Rengger (1795–1832), German naturalist. In the early part of the nineteenth century, both published influential studies on Paraguayan fauna.

Paraguay, the flies would decrease—then cattle and horses would become feral, and this would certainly greatly alter (as indeed I have observed in parts of South America) the vegetation: this again would largely affect the insects; and this, as we just have seen in Staffordshire, the insectivorous birds, and so onwards in ever-increasing circles of complexity. We began this series by insectivorous birds, and we have ended with them. Not that in nature the relations can ever be as simple as this. Battle within battle must ever be recurring with varying success; and yet in the long-run the forces are so nicely balanced, that the face of nature remains uniform for long periods of time, though assuredly the merest trifle would often give the victory to one organic being over another. Nevertheless so profound is our ignorance, and so high our presumption, that we marvel when we hear of the extinction of an organic being; and as we do not see the cause, we invoke cataclysms to desolate the world, or invent laws on the duration of the forms of life!

I am tempted to give one more instance showing how plants and animals, most remote in the scale of nature, are bound together by a web of complex relations. I shall hereafter have occasion to show that the exotic *Lobelia fulgens*,[1] in this part of England, is never visited by insects, and consequently, from its peculiar structure, never can set a seed. Many of our orchidaceous plants absolutely require the visits of moths to remove their pollen-masses and thus to fertilise them. I have, also, reason to believe that humble-bees are indispensable to the fertilisation of the heartsease (*Viola tricolor*), for other bees do not visit this flower. From experiments which I have tried, I have found that the visits of bees, if not indispensable, are at least highly beneficial to the fertilisation of our clovers; but humble-bees alone visit the common red clover (*Trifolium pratense*), as other bees cannot reach the nectar. Hence I have very little doubt, that if the whole genus of humble-bees became extinct or very rare in England, the heartsease and red clover would become very rare, or wholly disappear. The number of humble-bees in any district depends in a great degree on the number of field-mice, which destroy their combs and nests; and Mr. H. Newman,[2] who has long attended to the habits of humble-bees, believes that "more than two thirds of them are thus destroyed all over England." Now the number of mice is largely dependent, as every one knows, on the number of cats; and Mr. Newman says, "Near villages and small towns I have found the nests of humble-bees more numerous than elsewhere, which I attribute to the number of cats that destroy the mice." Hence it is quite credible that the presence of a feline animal in large numbers in a district might determine, through the intervention first of mice and then of bees, the frequency of certain flowers in that district!

from CHAPTER 14: RECAPITULATION AND CONCLUSION

… I have now recapitulated the chief facts and considerations which have thoroughly convinced me that species have changed, and are still slowly changing by the preservation and accumulation of successive slight favourable variations. Why, it may be asked, have all the most eminent living naturalists and geologists rejected this view of the mutability of species? It cannot be asserted that organic beings in a state of nature are subject to no variation; it cannot be proved that the amount of variation in the course of long ages is a limited quantity; no clear distinction has been, or can be, drawn between species and well-marked varieties. It cannot be maintained that species when intercrossed are invariably sterile, and varieties invariably fertile; or that sterility is a special endowment and sign of creation. The belief that species were immutable productions was almost unavoidable as long as the history of the world was thought to be of short duration; and now that we have acquired some idea of the lapse of time, we are too apt to assume, without proof, that the geological record is so perfect that it would have afforded us plain evidence of the mutation of species, if they had undergone mutation.

But the chief cause of our natural unwillingness to admit that one species has given birth to other and distinct species, is that we are always slow in admitting

[1] *Lobelia fulgens* Queen Victoria Cardinal flower.

[2] *Mr. H. Newman* Unidentified.

any great change of which we do not see the intermediate steps. The difficulty is the same as that felt by so many geologists, when Lyell first insisted that long lines of inland cliffs had been formed, and great valleys excavated, by the slow action of the coast-waves. The mind cannot possibly grasp the full meaning of the term of a hundred million years; it cannot add up and perceive the full effects of many slight variations, accumulated during an almost infinite number of generations.

Although I am fully convinced of the truth of the views given in this volume under the form of an abstract, I by no means expect to convince experienced naturalists whose minds are stocked with a multitude of facts all viewed, during a long course of years, from a point of view directly opposite to mine. It is so easy to hide our ignorance under such expressions as the "plan of creation," "unity of design," *et cetera*, and to think that we give an explanation when we only restate a fact. Any one whose disposition leads him to attach more weight to unexplained difficulties than to the explanation of a certain number of facts will certainly reject my theory. A few naturalists, endowed with much flexibility of mind, and who have already begun to doubt on the immutability of species, may be influenced by this volume; but I look with confidence to the future, to young and rising naturalists, who will be able to view both sides of the question with impartiality. Whoever is led to believe that species are mutable will do good service by conscientiously expressing his conviction; for only thus can the load of prejudice by which this subject is overwhelmed be removed....

When the views entertained in this volume on the origin of species, or when analogous views are generally admitted, we can dimly foresee that there will be a considerable revolution in natural history. Systematists will be able to pursue their labours as at present; but they will not be incessantly haunted by the shadowy doubt whether this or that form be in essence a species. This I feel sure, and I speak after experience, will be no slight relief. The endless disputes whether or not some fifty species of British brambles are true species will cease. Systematists will have only to decide (not that this will be easy) whether any form be sufficiently constant and distinct from other forms, to be capable of definition; and if definable, whether the differences be sufficiently important to deserve a specific name. This latter point will become a far more essential consideration than it is at present; for differences, however slight, between any two forms, if not blended by intermediate gradations, are looked at by most naturalists as sufficient to raise both forms to the rank of species. Hereafter we shall be compelled to acknowledge that the only distinction between species and well-marked varieties is, that the latter are known, or believed, to be connected at the present day by intermediate gradations, whereas species were formerly thus connected. Hence, without quite rejecting the consideration of the present existence of intermediate gradations between any two forms, we shall be led to weigh more carefully and to value higher the actual amount of difference between them. It is quite possible that forms now generally acknowledged to be merely varieties may hereafter be thought worthy of specific names, as with the primrose and cowslip; and in this case scientific and common language will come into accordance. In short, we shall have to treat species in the same manner as those naturalists treat genera, who admit that genera are merely artificial combinations made for convenience. This may not be a cheering prospect; but we shall at least be freed from the vain search for the undiscovered and undiscoverable essence of the term species.

The other and more general departments of natural history will rise greatly in interest. The terms used by naturalists of affinity, relationship, community of type, paternity, morphology, adaptive characters, rudimentary and aborted organs, *et cetera*, will cease to be metaphorical, and will have a plain signification. When we no longer look at an organic being as a savage looks at a ship, as at something wholly beyond his comprehension; when we regard every production of nature as one which has had a history; when we contemplate every complex structure and instinct as the summing up of many contrivances, each useful to the possessor, nearly in the same way as when we look at any great mechanical invention as the summing up of the labour, the experience, the reason, and even the blunders of numerous workmen; when we thus view each organic being, how far more interesting, I speak from experience, will the study of natural history become!

A grand and almost untrodden field of inquiry will be opened, on the causes and laws of variation, on correlation of growth, on the effects of use and disuse, on the direct action of external conditions, and so forth. The study of domestic productions will rise immensely in value. A new variety raised by man will be a far more important and interesting subject for study than one more species added to the infinitude of already recorded species. Our classifications will come to be, as far as they can be so made, genealogies; and will then truly give what may be called the plan of creation. The rules for classifying will no doubt become simpler when we have a definite object in view. We possess no pedigrees or armorial bearings; and we have to discover and trace the many diverging lines of descent in our natural genealogies, by characters of any kind which have long been inherited. Rudimentary organs will speak infallibly with respect to the nature of long-lost structures. Species and groups of species, which are called aberrant, and which may fancifully be called living fossils, will aid us in forming a picture of the ancient forms of life. Embryology will reveal to us the structure, in some degree obscured, of the prototypes of each great class.

When we can feel assured that all the individuals of the same species, and all the closely allied species of most genera, have within a not very remote period descended from one parent, and have migrated from some one birthplace; and when we better know the many means of migration, then, by the light which geology now throws, and will continue to throw, on former changes of climate and of the level of the land, we shall surely be enabled to trace in an admirable manner the former migrations of the inhabitants of the whole world. Even at present, by comparing the differences of the inhabitants of the sea on the opposite sides of a continent, and the nature of the various inhabitants of that continent in relation to their apparent means of immigration, some light can be thrown on ancient geography.

The noble science of geology loses glory from the extreme imperfection of the record. The crust of the earth with its embedded remains must not be looked at as a well-filled museum, but as a poor collection made at hazard and at rare intervals. The accumulation of each great fossiliferous formation will be recognised as having depended on an unusual concurrence of circumstances, and the blank intervals between the successive stages as having been of vast duration. But we shall be able to gauge with some security the duration of these intervals by a comparison of the preceding and succeeding organic forms. We must be cautious in attempting to correlate as strictly contemporaneous two formations, which include few identical species, by the general succession of their forms of life. As species are produced and exterminated by slowly acting and still existing causes, and not by miraculous acts of creation and by catastrophes; and as the most important of all causes of organic change is one which is almost independent of altered and perhaps suddenly altered physical conditions, namely, the mutual relation of organism to organism—the improvement of one being entailing the improvement or the extermination of others; it follows, that the amount of organic change in the fossils of consecutive formations probably serves as a fair measure of the lapse of actual time. A number of species, however, keeping in a body might remain for a long period unchanged, whilst within this same period, several of these species, by migrating into new countries and coming into competition with foreign associates, might become modified; so that we must not overrate the accuracy of organic change as a measure of time. During early periods of the earth's history, when the forms of life were probably fewer and simpler, the rate of change was probably slower; and at the first dawn of life, when very few forms of the simplest structure existed, the rate of change may have been slow in an extreme degree. The whole history of the world, as at present known, although of a length quite incomprehensible by us, will hereafter be recognised as a mere fragment of time, compared with the ages which have elapsed since the first creature, the progenitor of innumerable extinct and living descendants, was created.

In the distant future I see open fields for far more important researches. Psychology will be based on a new foundation, that of the necessary acquirement of each mental power and capacity by gradation. Light will be thrown on the origin of man and his history.

Authors of the highest eminence seem to be fully satisfied with the view that each species has been independently created. To my mind it accords better with what we know of the laws impressed on matter by the Creator, that the production and extinction of the past and present inhabitants of the world should have been due to secondary causes, like those determining the birth and death of the individual. When I view all beings not as special creations, but as the lineal descendants of some few beings which lived long before the first bed of the Silurian[1] system was deposited, they seem to me to become ennobled. Judging from the past, we may safely infer that not one living species will transmit its unaltered likeness to a distant futurity. And of the species now living very few will transmit progeny of any kind to a far distant futurity; for the manner in which all organic beings are grouped, shows that the greater number of species of each genus, and all the species of many genera, have left no descendants, but have become utterly extinct. We can so far take a prophetic glance into futurity as to foretell that it will be the common and widely-spread species, belonging to the larger and dominant groups, which will ultimately prevail and procreate new and dominant species. As all the living forms of life are the lineal descendants of those which lived long before the Silurian epoch, we may feel certain that the ordinary succession by generation has never once been broken, and that no cataclysm has desolated the whole world. Hence we may look with some confidence to a secure future of equally inappreciable length. And as natural selection works solely by and for the good of each being, all corporeal and mental endowments will tend to progress towards perfection.

It is interesting to contemplate an entangled bank, clothed with many plants of many kinds, with birds singing on the bushes, with various insects flitting about, and with worms crawling through the damp earth, and to reflect that these elaborately constructed forms, so different from each other, and dependent on each other in so complex a manner, have all been produced by laws acting around us. These laws, taken in the largest sense, being growth with reproduction; inheritance which is almost implied by reproduction; variability from the indirect and direct action of the external conditions of life, and from use and disuse; a ratio of increase so high as to lead to a struggle for life, and as a consequence to natural selection, entailing divergence of character and the extinction of less-improved forms. Thus, from the war of nature, from famine and death, the most exalted object which we are capable of conceiving, namely, the production of the higher animals, directly follows. There is grandeur in this view of life, with its several powers, having been originally breathed into a few forms or into one; and that, whilst this planet has gone cycling on according to the fixed law of gravity, from so simple a beginning endless forms most beautiful and most wonderful have been, and are being, evolved.

—1859

[1] *Silurian* Geological time period approximately 440 million to 410 million years ago.

from *The Descent of Man*

from Chapter 19
Secondary Sexual Characters of Man

With mankind the differences between the sexes are greater than in most species of Quadrumana, but not so great as in some, for instance, the mandrill.[2] Man on an average is considerably taller, heavier, and stronger than woman, with squarer shoulders and more plainly-pronounced muscles. Owing to the relation which exists between muscular development and the projection of the brows, the superciliary ridge[3] is generally more strongly marked in man than in woman. His body, and especially his face, is more hairy, and his voice has a

[2] *Quadrumana* Primates with, literally, "four hands," in that both the hind and forefeet have opposable thumbs. This category, now obsolete, included all primates other than human beings; *mandrill* Earlier, Darwin describes the adult male mandrill (close relative of the baboon) as possessing "extraordinary" bright coloration and facial protuberances that are "scarcely perceptible" in the female.

[3] *superciliary ridge* Ridge of bone above the eye sockets.

different and more powerful tone. In certain tribes the women are said, whether truly I know not, to differ slightly in tint from the men; and with Europeans, the women are perhaps the more brightly coloured of the two, as may be seen when both sexes have been equally exposed to the weather.

Man is more courageous, pugnacious and energetic than woman, and has a more inventive genius. His brain is absolutely larger, but whether relatively to the larger size of his body, in comparison with woman, has not, I believe, been fully ascertained. In woman the face is rounder; the jaws and the base of the skull smaller; the outlines of the body rounder, in parts more prominent; and her pelvis is broader than in man; but this latter character may perhaps be considered rather as a primary than a secondary sexual character. She comes to maturity at an earlier age than man.

As with animals of all classes, so with man, the distinctive characters of the male sex are not fully developed until he is nearly mature; and if emasculated they never appear. The beard, for instance, is a secondary sexual character, and male children are beardless, though at an early age they have abundant hair on the head. It is probably due to the rather late appearance in life of the successive variations, by which man acquired his masculine characters, that they are transmitted to the male sex alone. Male and female children resemble each other closely, like the young of so many other animals in which the adult sexes differ; they likewise resemble the mature female much more closely than the mature male. The female, however, ultimately assumes certain distinctive characters, and in the formation of her skull is said to be intermediate between the child and the man.…

The half-human progenitors of man, and men in a savage state, have struggled together during many generations for the possession of the females. But mere bodily strength and size would do little for victory, unless associated with courage, perseverance, and determined energy. With social animals, the young males have to pass through many a contest before they win a female, and the older males have to retain their females by renewed battles. They have, also, in the case of mankind, to defend their females, as well as their young, from enemies of all kinds, and to hunt for their joint subsistence. But to avoid enemies or to attack them with success, to capture wild animals, and to invent and fashion weapons, requires the aid of the higher mental faculties, namely, observation, reason, invention, or imagination. These various faculties will thus have been continually put to the test and selected during manhood; they will, moreover, have been strengthened by use during this same period of life. Consequently, in accordance with the principle often alluded to,[1] we might expect that they would at least tend to be transmitted chiefly to the male offspring at the corresponding period of manhood.

Now, when two men are put into competition, or a man with a woman, who possess every mental quality with the same perfection, with the exception that the one has the higher energy, perseverance, and courage, this one will generally become more eminent, whatever the object may be, and will gain victory. He may be said to possess genius—for genius has been declared by a great authority to be patience; and patience, in this sense, mean unflinching, undaunted perseverance. But this view of genius is perhaps deficient; for without the higher powers of the imagination and reason, no eminent success in many subjects can be gained. But these latter as well as the former faculties will have developed in man, partly through sexual selection—that is, through the contest of rival males, and partly through natural selection—that is, from success in the general struggle for life; and as in both cases the struggle will have been during maturity, the characters thus gained will have been transmitted more fully to the male than to the female offspring. Thus man has ultimately become superior to woman. It is, indeed, fortunate that the law of the equal transmission of characters to both sexes has commonly prevailed throughout the whole class of mammals; otherwise, it is probable that man would have become as superior in mental endowment to woman, as the peacock is in ornamental plumage to the peahen. …

[1] *the principle often alluded to* I.e., the principle that characteristics appearing in one sex after maturity will more likely be transmitted to that sex alone.

from Chapter 21
General Summary and Conclusion

A brief summary will be sufficient to recall to the reader's mind the more salient points in this work. Many of the views which have been advanced are highly speculative, and some no doubt will prove erroneous; but I have in every case given the reasons which have led me to one view rather than to another. It seemed worthwhile to try how far the principle of evolution would throw light on some of the more complex problems in the natural history of man. False facts are highly injurious to the progress of science, for they often endure long; but false views, if supported by some evidence, do little harm, for every one takes a salutary pleasure in proving their falseness: and when this is done, one path towards error is closed and the road to truth is often at the same time opened.

The main conclusion here arrived at, and now held by many naturalists who are well competent to form a sound judgment is that man is descended from some less highly organised form. The grounds upon which this conclusion rests will never be shaken, for the close similarity between man and the lower animals in embryonic development, as well as in innumerable points of structure and constitution both of high and of the most trifling importance—the rudiments which he retains, and the abnormal reversions to which he is occasionally liable—are facts which cannot be disputed. They have long been known, but until recently they told us nothing with respect to the origin of man. Now when viewed by the light of our knowledge of the whole organic world, their meaning is unmistakable. The great principle of evolution stands up clear and firm, when these groups or facts are considered in connection with others, such as the mutual affinities of the members of the same group, their geographical distribution in past and present times, and their geological succession. It is incredible that all these facts should speak falsely. He who is not content to look, like a savage, at the phenomena of nature as disconnected, cannot any longer believe that man is the work of a separate act of creation. He will be forced to admit that the close resemblance of the embryo of man to that, for instance, of a dog—the construction of his skull, limbs and whole frame on the same plan with that of other mammals, independently of the uses to which the parts may be put—the occasional re-appearance of various structures, for instance of several muscles, which man does not normally possess, but which are common to the Quadrumana—and a crowd of analogous facts—all point in the plainest manner to the conclusion that man is the co-descendant with other mammals of a common progenitor.

We have seen that man incessantly presents individual differences in all parts of his body and in his mental faculties. These differences or variations seem to be induced by the same general causes, and to obey the same laws as with the lower animals. In both cases similar laws of inheritance prevail. Man tends to increase at a greater rate than his means of subsistence; consequently he is occasionally subjected to a severe struggle for existence, and natural selection will have effected whatever lies within its scope. A succession of strongly-marked variations of a similar nature is by no means requisite; slight fluctuating differences in the individual suffice for the work of natural selection; not that we have any reason to suppose that in the same species, all parts of the organization tend to vary to the same degree. We may feel assured that the inherited effects of the long-continued use or disuse of parts will have done much in the same direction with natural selection. Modifications formerly of importance, though no longer of any special use, are long-inherited. When one part is modified, other parts change through the principle of correlation, of which we have instances in many curious cases of correlated monstrosities. Something may be attributed to the direct and definite action of the surrounding conditions of life, such as abundant food, heat or moisture; and lastly, many characters of slight physiological importance, some indeed of considerable importance, have been gained through sexual selection.

No doubt man, as well as every other animal, presents structures, which seem to our limited knowledge, not to be now of any service to him, nor to have been so formerly, either for the general conditions of life, or in the relations of one sex to the other. Such structures cannot be accounted for by any form of selection, or by the inherited effects of the use and disuse of parts. We know, however, that many strange and strongly-marked peculiarities of structure occasionally appear in our domesticated productions, and if their unknown causes were to act more uniformly, they would probably become common to all the individuals of the species. We may hope hereafter to understand something about the causes of such occasional modifications, especially through the study of monstrosities: hence the labours of experimentalists such as those of M. Camille Dareste,[1] are full of promise for the future. In general we can only say that the cause of each slight variation and of each monstrosity lies much more in the constitution of the organism, than in the nature of the surrounding conditions; though new and changed conditions certainly play an important part in exciting organic changes of many kinds. Through the means just specified, aided perhaps by others as yet undiscovered, man has been raised to his present state. But since he attained to the rank of manhood, he has diverged into distinct races, or as they may be more fitly called subspecies. Some of these, such as the Negro and European, are so distinct that, if specimens had been brought to a naturalist without any further information, they would undoubtedly have been considered by him as good and true species. Nevertheless all the races agree in so many unimportant details of structure and in so many mental peculiarities that these can be accounted for only by inheritance from a common progenitor; and a progenitor thus characterised would probably deserve to rank as man.

It must not be supposed that the divergence of each race from the other races, and of all from a common stock, can be traced back to any one pair of progenitors. On the contrary, at every stage in the process of modification, all the individuals which were in any way better fitted for their conditions of life, though in different degrees, would have survived in greater numbers than the less well-fitted. The process would have been like that followed by man, when he does not intentionally select particular individuals, but breeds from all the superior individuals, and neglects the inferior. He thus slowly but surely modifies his stock, and unconsciously forms a new strain. So with respect to modifications acquired independently of selection, and due to variations arising from the nature of the organism and the action of the surrounding conditions, or from changed habits of life, no single pair will have been modified much more than the other pairs inhabiting the same country, for all will have been continually blended through free intercrossing.

By considering the embryological structure of man—the homologies[2] which he presents with the lower animals—the rudiments which he retains—and the reversions to which he is liable, we can partly recall in imagination the former condition of our early progenitors; and can approximately place them in their proper place in the zoological series. We thus learn that man is descended from a hairy, tailed quadruped, probably arboreal in its habits, and an inhabitant of the Old World. This creature, if its whole structure had been examined by a naturalist, would have been classed amongst the Quadrumana, as surely as the still more ancient progenitor of the Old and New World monkeys. The Quadrumana and all the higher mammals are probably derived from an ancient marsupial animal, and this through a long series of diversified forms, from some amphibian-like creature, and this again from some fish-like animal. In the dim obscurity of the past we can see that the early progenitor of all the Vertebrata must have been an aquatic animal provided with branchiae,[3] with the two sexes united in the same individual, and with the most important organs of the body (such as the brain and heart) imperfectly or not at all developed. This animal seems to have been more like the larvae of the existing marine Ascidians[4] than any other known form. …

[1] *M. Camille Dareste* (Monsieur) Camille Dareste, French zoologist (1822–99), founder of experimental teratology, the study of abnormalities in plants and animals.

[2] *homologies* Similarities of structure due to common descent.

[3] *branchiae* Breathing apparatus, gills.

[4] *Ascidians* Molluscs.

The belief in God has often been advanced as not only the greatest, but the most complete of all the distinctions between man and the lower animals. It is however impossible, as we have seen, to maintain that this belief is innate or instinctive in man. On the other hand a belief in all-pervading spiritual agencies seems to be universal; and apparently follows from a considerable advance in man's reason, and from a still greater advance in his faculties of imagination, curiosity and wonder. I am aware that the assumed instinctive belief in God has been used by many persons as an argument for His existence. But this is a rash argument, as we should thus be compelled to believe in the existence of many cruel and malignant spirits, only a little more powerful than man; for the belief in them is far more general than in a beneficent Deity. The idea of a universal and beneficent Creator does not seem to arise in the mind of man, until he has been elevated by long-continued culture.

He who believes in the advancement of man from some low organised form, will naturally ask how does this bear on the belief in the immortality of the soul. The barbarous races of man, as Sir J. Lubbock[1] has shown, possess no clear belief of this kind; but arguments derived from the primeval beliefs of savages are, as we have just seen, of little or no avail. Few persons feel any anxiety from the impossibility of determining at what precise period in the development of the individual, from the first trace of a minute germinal vesicle,[2] man becomes an immortal being; and there is no greater cause for anxiety because the period cannot possibly be determined in the gradually ascending organic scale.

I am aware that the conclusions arrived at in this work will be denounced by some as highly irreligious; but he who denounces them is bound to show why it is more irreligious to explain the origin of man as a distinct species by descent from some lower form, through the laws of variation and natural selection, than to explain the birth of the individual through the laws of ordinary reproduction. The birth both of the species and of the individual are equally parts of that grand sequence of events, which our minds refuse to accept as the result of blind chance. The understanding revolts at such a conclusion, whether or not we are able to believe that every slight variation of structure—the union of each pair in marriage—the dissemination of each seed—and other such events, have all been ordained for some special purpose.

Sexual selection has been treated at great length in this work; for, as I have attempted to show, it has played an important part in the history of the organic world. I am aware that much remains doubtful, but I have endeavoured to give a fair view of the whole case. In the lower divisions of the animal kingdom, sexual selection seems to have done nothing: such animals are often affixed for life to the same spot, or have the sexes combined in the same individual, or what is still more important, their perceptive and intellectual faculties are not sufficiently advanced to allow of the feelings of love and jealousy, or of the exertion of choice. When, however, we come to the Arthropoda[3] and Vertebrata, even to the lowest classes in these two great sub-kingdoms, sexual selection has effected much.

In the several great classes of the animal kingdom—in mammals, birds, reptiles, fishes, insects, and even crustaceans—the differences between the sexes follow nearly the same rules. The males are almost always the wooers; and they alone are armed with special weapons for fighting with their rivals. They are generally stronger and larger than the females, and are endowed with the requisite qualities of courage and pugnacity. They are provided, either exclusively or in a much higher degree than the females, with organs for vocal or instrumental music, and with odoriferous glands. They are ornamental with infinitely diversified appendages, and with the most brilliant or conspicuous colours, often arranged in elegant patterns, whilst the females are unadorned. When the sexes differ in more important structures, it is the male which is provided with special sense-organs for discovering the female, with locomotive organs for reaching her, and often with prehensile

[1] *Sir J. Lubbock* John Lubbock, Lord Avebury (1834–1913), in his book *Prehistoric Times* (1865).

[2] *germinal vesicle* Nucleus of animals' permanent ovum.

[3] *Arthropoda* Sub-kingdom which includes insects, spiders, crustaceans, etc.

organs for holding her. These various structures for charming or securing the female are often developed in the male during only part of the year, namely the breeding-season. They have in many cases been more or less transferred to the females; and in the latter case they often appear in her as mere rudiments. They are lost or never gained by the males after emasculation. Generally they are not developed in the male during early youth, but appear a short time before the age for reproduction. Hence in most cases the young of both sexes resemble each other; and the female somewhat resembles her young offspring throughout life. In almost every great class a few anomalous cases occur, where there has been an almost complete transposition of the characters proper to the two sexes; the females assuming characters which properly belong to the males. This surprising uniformity in the laws regulating the differences between the sexes in so many and such widely separated classes, is intelligible if we admit the action of one common cause, namely sexual selection.

Sexual selection depends on the success of certain individuals over others of the same sex, in relation to the propagation of the species; whilst natural selection depends on the success of both sexes, at all ages, in relation to the general conditions of life. The sexual struggle is of two kinds; in the one it is between individuals of the same sex, generally the males, in order to drive away or kill their rivals, the females remaining passive; whilst in the other, the struggle is likewise between the individuals of the same sex, in order to excite or charm those of the opposite sex, generally the females, which no longer remain passive, but select the more agreeable partners. This latter kind of selection is closely analogous to that which man unintentionally, yet effectually, brings to bear on his domesticated productions, when he preserves during a long period the most pleasing or useful individuals, without any wish to modify the breed.

The laws of inheritance determine whether characters gained through sexual selection by either sex shall be transmitted to the same sex, or to both; as well as the age at which they shall be developed. It appears that variations arising late in life are commonly transmitted to one and the same sex. Variability is the necessary basis for the action of selection, and is wholly independent of it. It follows from this, that variations of the same general nature have often been taken advantage of and accumulated through sexual selection in relation to the propagation of the species, as well as through natural selection in relation to the general purposes of life. Hence secondary sexual characters, when equally transmitted to both sexes can be distinguished from ordinary specific characters only by the light of analogy. The modifications acquired through sexual selection are often so strongly pronounced that the two sexes have frequently been ranked as distinct species, or even as distinct genera.[1] Such strongly-marked differences must be in some manner highly important; and we know that they have been acquired in some instances at the cost not only of inconvenience, but of exposure to actual danger.

The belief in the power of sexual selection rests chiefly on the following considerations. Certain characters are confined to one sex; and this alone renders it probable that in most cases they are connected with the act of reproduction. In innumerable instances these characters are fully developed only at maturity, and often during only a part of the year, which is always the breeding-season. The males (passing over a few exceptional cases) are the more active in courtship; they are the better armed, and are rendered the more attractive in various ways. It is to be especially observed that the males display their attractions with elaborate care in the presence of the females; and that they rarely or never display them excepting during the season of love. It is incredible that all this should be purposeless. Lastly we have distinct evidence with some quadrupeds and birds, that the individuals of one sex are capable of feeling a strong antipathy or preference for certain individuals of the other sex.

Bearing in mind these facts, and the marked results of man's unconscious selection, when applied to domesticated animals and cultivated plants, it seems to me almost certain that if the individuals of one sex were during a long series of generations to prefer pairing with

[1] *genera* Latin: groups of species. Plural of "genus."

certain individuals of the other sex, characterised in some peculiar manner, the offspring would slowly but surely become modified in this same manner. I have not attempted to conceal that, excepting when the males are more numerous than the females, or when polygamy prevails, it is doubtful how the more attractive males succeed in leaving a large number of offspring to inherit their superiority in ornaments or other charms than the less attractive males; but I have shown that this would probably follow from the females—especially the more vigorous ones, which would be the first to breed—preferring not only the more attractive but at the same time the more vigorous and victorious males.

Although we have some positive evidence that birds appreciate bright and beautiful objects, as with the bower-birds of Australia, and although they certainly appreciate the power of song, yet I fully admit that it is astonishing that the females of many birds and some mammals should be endowed with sufficient taste to appreciate ornaments, which we have reason to attribute to sexual selection; and this is even more astonishing in the case of reptiles, fish, and insects. But we really know little about the minds of the lower animals. It cannot be supposed, for instance, that male birds of paradise or peacocks should take such pains in erecting, spreading, and vibrating their beautiful plumes before the females for no purpose. We should remember the fact given on excellent authority in a former chapter, that several peahens, when debarred from an admired male, remained widows during a whole season rather than pair with another bird.

Nevertheless I know of no fact in natural history more wonderful than that of the female Argus pheasant should appreciate the exquisite shading of the ball-and-socket ornaments and the elegant patterns on the wing-feathers of the male. He who thinks that the male was created as he now exists must admit that the great plumes, which prevent the wings from being used for flight, and which are displayed during courtship and at no other time in a manner quite peculiar to this one species, were given to him as an ornament. If so, he must likewise admit that the female was created and endowed with the capacity of appreciating such ornaments. I differ only in the conviction that the male Argus pheasant acquired his beauty gradually, through the preference of the females during many generations for the more highly ornamented males; the aesthetic capacity of the females having been advanced through exercise or habit, just as our own taste is gradually improved. In the male through the fortunate chance of a few feathers, being left, unchanged, we can distinctly trace how simple spots with a little fulvous shading on one side may have been developed by small steps into the wonderful ball-and-socket ornaments; and it is probable that they were actually thus developed.

Everyone who admits the principle of evolution, and yet feels great difficulty in admitting that female mammals, birds, reptiles, and fish, could have acquired the high taste implied by the beauty of the males, and which generally coincides with our own standard, should reflect that the nerve-cells of the brain in the highest as well as in the lowest members of the Vertebrate series, are derived from those of the common progenitor of this great kingdom. For we can thus see how it has come to pass that certain mental faculties, in various and widely distinct groups of animals, have been developed in nearly the same manner and to nearly the same degree.

The reader who has taken the trouble to go through the several chapters devoted to sexual selection, will be able to judge how far the conclusions at which I have arrived are supported by sufficient evidence. If he accepts these conclusions he may, I think, safely extend them to mankind; but it would be superfluous here to repeat what I have so lately said on the manner in which sexual selection apparently has acted on man, both on the male and female side, causing the two sexes to differ in body and mind, and the several races to differ from each other in various characters, as well as from their ancient and lowly-organised progenitors. He who admits the principle of sexual selection will be led to the remarkable conclusion that the nervous system not only regulates most of the existing functions of the body, but has indirectly influenced the progressive development of various bodily structures and of certain mental qualities. Courage, pugnacity, perseverance, strength and size of body, weapons of all kinds, musical organs, both vocal and instrumental, bright colours and ornamental appendages, have all been indirectly gained by the one sex or the other, through the exertion of choice, the influence of love and jealousy, and the appreciation of the beautiful in sound, colour or form; and these powers of the mind manifestly depend on the development of the brain.

Man scans with scrupulous care the character and pedigree of his horses, cattle, and dogs before he matches them; but when he comes to his own marriage he rarely, or never, takes any such care. He is impelled by nearly the same motives as the lower animals, when they are left to their own free choice, though he is in so far superior to them that he highly values mental charms and virtues. On the other hand he is strongly attracted by mere wealth or rank. Yet he might by selection do something not only for the bodily constitution and frame of his offspring, but for their intellectual and moral qualities. Both sexes ought to refrain from marriage if they are in any marked degree inferior in body or mind; but such hopes are Utopian and will never be even partially realised until the laws of inheritance are thoroughly known. Everyone does good service who aids towards this end. When the principles of breeding and inheritance are better understood, we shall not hear ignorant members of our legislature rejecting with scorn a plan for ascertaining whether or not consanguineous marriages[1] are injurious to man.

The advancement of the welfare of mankind is a most intricate problem: all ought to refrain from marriage who cannot avoid abject poverty for their children; for poverty is not only a great evil, but tends to its own increase by leading to recklessness in marriage. On the other hand as Mr. Galton[2] has remarked, if the prudent avoid marriage, whilst the reckless marry, the inferior members tend to supplant the better members of society. Man, like every other animal, has no doubt advanced to his present high condition through a struggle for existence consequent on his rapid multiplication; and if he is to advance still higher, it is to be feared that he must remain subject to a severe struggle. Otherwise he would sink into indolence, and the more gifted men would not be more successful in the battle of life than the less gifted. Hence our natural rate of increase, though leading to many and obvious evils, must not be greatly diminished by any means. There should be open competition for all men; and the most able should not be prevented by laws or customs from succeeding best and rearing the largest number of offspring. Important as the struggle for existence has been and even still is, yet as far as the highest part of man's nature is concerned there are other agencies more important. For the moral qualities are advanced, either directly or indirectly, much more through the effects of habit, the reasoning powers, instruction, religion, *et cetera*, than through natural selection; though to this latter agency may be safely attributed the social instincts, which afforded the basis for the development of the moral sense.

The main conclusion arrived at in this work, namely, that man is descended from some lowly organised form, will, I regret to think, be highly distasteful to many. But there can hardly be a doubt that we are descended from barbarians. The astonishment which I felt on first seeing a party of Fuegians on a wild and broken shore will never be forgotten by me, for the reflection at once rushed into my mind—such were our ancestors. These men were absolutely naked and bedaubed with paint, their long hair was tangled, their mouths frothed with excitement, and their expression was wild, startled, and distrustful. They possessed hardly any arts, and like wild animals lived on what they could catch; they had no government, and were merciless to every one not of their own small tribe. He who has seen a savage in his native land will not feel much shame, if forced to acknowledge that the blood of some more humble creature flows in his veins. For my own part I would as soon be descended from that heroic little monkey, who braved his dreaded enemy in order to save the life of his keeper, or from that old baboon, who descending from the mountains, carried away in triumph his young comrade from a crowd of astonished

[1] *consanguineous marriages* Marriages between blood relatives.

[2] *Mr. Galton* Sir Francis Galton (1822–94), Darwin's half cousin, one of the founders of eugenics, the "science" that aimed to improve the human species through selective breeding.

dogs—as from a savage who delights to torture his enemies, offers up bloody sacrifices, practises infanticide without remorse, treats his wives like slaves, knows no decency, and is haunted by the grossest superstitions.

Man may be excused for feeling some pride at having risen, though not through his own exertions, to the very summit of the organic scale; and the fact of his having thus risen, instead of having been aboriginally placed there, may give him hope for a still higher destiny in the distant future. But we are not here concerned with hopes or fears, only with the truth as far as our reason permits us to discover it; and I have given the evidence to the best of my ability. We must, however, acknowledge, as it seems to me, that man with all his noble qualities, with sympathy which feels for the most debased, with benevolence which extends not only to other men but to the humblest living creature, with his god-like intellect which has penetrated into the movements and constitution of the solar system—with all these exalted powers—Man still bears in his bodily frame the indelible stamp of his lowly origin.

—1871

In Context

Defending and Attacking Darwin

One of Darwin's most important defenders was Thomas Henry Huxley (1825–95), a naturalist and essayist who in the 1870s developed the concept of agnosticism. In 1860 he became known as "Darwin's Bulldog" for his aggressive and persuasive efforts to popularize the theory of natural selection—and counter the backlash against it. He continued to write about evolutionary theory throughout the rest of his life.

from Thomas Huxley, "Criticisms on *The Origin of Species*" (1864)

It is singular how differently one and the same book will impress different minds. That which struck the present writer most forcibly on his first perusal of the "Origin of Species" was the conviction that teleology,[1] as commonly understood, had received its deathblow at Mr. Darwin's hands. For the teleological argument runs thus: an organ or organism (A) is precisely fitted to perform a function or purpose (B); therefore it was specially constructed to perform that function. In Paley's[2] famous illustration, the adaptation of all the parts of the watch to the function, or purpose, of showing the time, is held to be evidence that the watch was specially contrived to that end; on the ground, that the only cause we know of, competent to produce such an effect as a watch which shall keep time, is a contriving intelligence adapting the means directly to that end.

Suppose, however, that any one had been able to show that the watch had not been made directly by any person, but that it was the result of the modification of another watch which kept time but poorly; and that this again had proceeded from a structure which could hardly be called a watch at all—seeing that it had no figures on the dial and the hands were rudimentary; and that going back and back in time we came at last to a revolving barrel as the earliest traceable rudiment of the whole fabric. And imagine that it had been possible to show that all these changes had resulted, first, from

[1] *teleology* Study of intelligent design or purpose in nature.

[2] *Paley* William Paley (1743–1805), English philosopher. Huxley refers to Paley's 1802 book, *Natural Theology, or Evidences of the Existence and Attributes of the Deity Collected from the Appearances of Nature.*

a tendency of the structure to vary indefinitely; and secondly, from something in the surrounding world which helped all variations in the direction of an accurate time-keeper, and checked all those in other directions; then it is obvious that the force of Paley's argument would be gone. For it would be demonstrated that an apparatus thoroughly well adapted to a particular purpose might be the result of a method of trial and error worked by unintelligent agents, as well as of the direct application of the means appropriate to that end, by an intelligent agent.

Now it appears to us that what we have here, for illustration's sake, supposed to be done with the watch, is exactly what the establishment of Darwin's theory will do for the organic world. For the notion that every organism has been created as it is and launched straight at a purpose, Mr. Darwin substitutes the conception of something which may fairly be termed a method of trial and error. Organisms vary incessantly; of these variations the few meet with surrounding conditions which suit them and thrive; the many are unsuited and become extinguished.

from Thomas Huxley, "Mr. Darwin's Critics" (1871)

The gradual lapse of time has now separated us by more than a decade from the date of the publication of the "Origin of Species"—and whatever may be thought or said about Mr. Darwin's doctrines, or the manner in which he has propounded them, this much is certain, that, in a dozen years, the "Origin of Species" has worked as complete a revolution in biological science as the "Principia"[1] did in astronomy—and it has done so, because, in the words of Helmholtz,[2] it contains "an essentially new creative thought."

And as time has slipped by, a happy change has come over Mr. Darwin's critics. The mixture of ignorance and insolence which, at first, characterised a large proportion of the attacks with which he was assailed, is no longer the sad distinction of anti-Darwinian criticism. Instead of abusive nonsense, which merely discredited its writers, we read essays, which are, at worst, more or less intelligent and appreciative; while, sometimes, like that which appeared in the "North British Review" for 1867, they have a real and permanent value.

The several publications of Mr. Wallace and Mr. Mivart[3] contain discussions of some of Mr. Darwin's views, which are worthy of particular attention, not only on account of the acknowledged scientific competence of these writers, but because they exhibit an attention to those philosophical questions which underlie all physical science, which is as rare as it is needful.

---

[1] *Principia* Sir Isaac Newton's *Philosophiae Naturalis Principia Mathematica* (1687).

[2] *Helmholtz* Hermann Ludwig Ferdinand von Helmholtz (1821–94), German professor of physiology and physics.

[3] *Mr. Wallace* Alfred Russel Wallace (1823–1913), English naturalist and social critic; *Mr. Mivart* St. George Jackson Mivart (1827–1900), British biologist. His *Genesis of Species* (1871) established him as a leading opponent of Darwin's theory.

from *Punch*

The humor magazine *Punch* continued to lampoon Darwin's theories in its cartoons even after they had become widely accepted in the community at large. The first of the cartoons below (depicting a gorilla as a social "lion"), was published in 1861, the second (a response to Darwin's 1881 *The Formation of Vegetable Mould Through the Action of Worms*) in 1882.

IN CONTEXT

Social Darwinism

The term "Social Darwinism" is used to refer to ideas that attempt to apply certain evolutionary notions to social issues. Chief among the Victorian "Social Darwinists" was Herbert Spencer, a wide-ranging thinker who coined the term "survival of the fittest" in an 1852 essay, "A Theory of Population." Like that work, his 1851 book *Social Statics* (from which excerpts are reprinted below) pre-dates Darwin's *On the Origin Species* by several years. In fact the tenets of Social Darwinism were quite independent of Darwin's biological theories, and were in no way necessarily embraced by the same people.

from Herbert Spencer, *Social Statics: or, the Conditions Essential to Human Happiness Specified, and the First of Them Developed* (1851)

Pervading all nature we may see at work a stern discipline, which is a little cruel that it may be very kind. That state of universal warfare maintained throughout the lower creation, to the great perplexity of many worthy people, is at bottom the most merciful provision which the circumstances admit of. It is much better that the ruminant animal, when deprived by age of the vigour which made its existence a pleasure, should be killed by some beast of prey, than that it should linger out a life made painful by infirmities, and eventually die of starvation. By the destruction of all such, not only is existence ended before it becomes burdensome, but room is made for a younger generation capable of the fullest enjoyment; and, moreover, out of the very act of substitution happiness is derived for a tribe of predatory creatures. Note further, that their carnivorous enemies not only remove from herbivorous herds individuals past their prime, but also weed out the sickly, the malformed, and the least fleet or powerful. By the aid of which purifying process, as well as by the fighting, so universal in the pairing season, all vitiation[1] of the race through the multiplication of its inferior samples is prevented; and the maintenance of a constitution completely adapted to surrounding conditions, and therefore most productive of happiness, is ensured.

The development of the higher creation is a progress towards a form of being capable of a happiness undiminished by these drawbacks. It is in the human race that the consummation is to be accomplished. Civilization is the last stage of its accomplishment. And the ideal man is the man in whom all the conditions of that accomplishment are fulfilled. Meanwhile the well-being of existing humanity, and the unfolding of it into this ultimate perfection, are both secured by that same beneficent, though severe discipline, to which the animate creation at large is subject: a discipline which is pitiless in the working out of good: a felicity-pursuing law which never swerves for the avoidance of partial and temporary suffering. The poverty of the incapable, the distresses that come upon the imprudent, the starvation of the idle, and those shoulderings aside of the weak by the strong, which leave so many "in shallows and in miseries,"[2] are the decrees of a large, far-seeing benevolence. It seems hard that an unskilfulness which with all his efforts he cannot overcome, should

[1] *vitiation* Impairment.

[2] *in … miseries* From Shakespeare's *Julius Caesar* 4.2.70–73: "There is a tide in the affairs of men, / Which taken at the flood leads on to fortune; / Omitted, all the voyage of that life / Is bound in shallows and in miseries."

entail hunger upon the artisan. It seems hard that a labourer incapacitated by sickness from competing with his stronger fellows, should have to bear the resulting privations. It seems hard that widows and orphans should be left to struggle for life or death. Nevertheless, when regarded not separately, but in connection with the interests of universal humanity, these harsh fatalities are seen to be full of the highest beneficence—the same beneficence which brings to early graves the children of diseased parents, and singles out the low-spirited,[1] the intemperate,[2] and the debilitated as the victims of an epidemic.

There are many very amiable people—people over whom in so far as their feelings are concerned we may fitly rejoice—who have not the nerve to look this matter fairly in the face. Disabled as they are by their sympathies with present suffering, from duly regarding ultimate consequences, they pursue a course which is very injudicious, and in the end even cruel. We do not consider it true kindness in a mother to gratify her child with sweetmeats that are certain to make it ill. We should think it a very foolish sort of benevolence which led a surgeon to let his patient's disease progress to a fatal issue, rather than inflict pain by an operation. Similarly, we must call those spurious philanthropists, who, to prevent present misery, would entail greater misery upon future generations. All defenders of a poor-law[3] must, however, be classed amongst such. That rigorous necessity which, when allowed to act on them, becomes so sharp a spur to the lazy, and so strong a bridle to the random, these paupers' friends would repeal, because of the wailings it here and there produces. Blind to the fact, that under the natural order of things society is constantly excreting its unhealthy, imbecile, slow, vacillating, faithless members, these unthinking, though well-meaning, men advocate an interference which not only stops the purifying process, but even increases the vitiation—absolutely encourages the multiplication of the reckless and incompetent by offering them an unfailing provision, and discourages the multiplication of the competent and provident by heightening the prospective difficulty of maintaining a family. And thus, in their eagerness to prevent the really salutary sufferings that surround us, these sigh-wise and groan-foolish people bequeath to posterity a continually increasing curse.

At first sight these considerations seem conclusive against *all* relief to the poor—voluntary as well as compulsory; and it is no doubt true that they imply a condemnation of whatever private charity enables the recipients to elude the necessities of our social existence. With this condemnation, however, no rational man will quarrel. That careless squandering of pence which has fostered into perfection a system of organized begging—which has made skilful mendicancy more profitable than ordinary manual labour—which induces the simulation of palsy, epilepsy, cholera, and no end of diseases and deformities—which has called into existence warehouses for the sale and hire of impostor's dresses—which has given to pity-inspiring babes a market value of *9d.* per day—the unthinking benevolence which has generated all this, cannot but be disapproved by every one. Now it is only against this injudicious charity that the foregoing argument tells. To that charity which may be described as helping men to help themselves, it makes no objection—countenances[4] it rather. And in helping men to help themselves, there remains abundant scope for the exercise of a people's sympathies. Accidents will still supply victims on whom generosity may be legitimately expended. Men thrown upon their backs by unforeseen events, men who have failed for want of knowledge inaccessible to them, men ruined by the dishonesty of others, and men in whom hope long delayed

---

[1] *low-spirited* Depressed.

[2] *intemperate* Heavy drinkers.

[3] *poor-law* Law providing for the support of the poor at public expense.

[4] *countenances* Approves.

has made the heart sick, may, with advantage to all parties, be assisted. Even the prodigal, after severe hardship has branded his memory with the unbending conditions of social life to which he must submit, may properly have another trial afforded him. And, although by these ameliorations the process of adaptation must be remotely interfered with, yet in the majority of cases, it will not be so much retarded in one direction as it will be advanced in another. …

Progress … is not accident, but a necessity. Instead of civilisation being artificial, it is part of nature; all of a piece with the development of the embryo or the unfolding of a flower. The modifications mankind have undergone, and are still undergoing, result from a law underlying the whole organic creation; and provided the human race continues, and the constitution of things remains the same, those modifications must end in completeness. As surely as the tree becomes bulky when it stands alone, and slender if one of a group … so surely must things be called evil and immoral disappear; so surely must man become perfect.

Elizabeth Gaskell

1810 – 1865

Mrs. Gaskell, as she was known to nineteenth-century readers, became famous both for her gentle portrayals in fiction of genteel village life and as one of the first authors of the Victorian era to write "social protest" novels dealing with contemporary issues of poverty, industrialization, and social life in both rural and urban England. Gaskell presents brutally honest portrayals of very different sorts of Victorian reality—conditions of poor factory workers in *Mary Barton* and *North and South*, for example, and of the plight of an unwed mother in *Ruth*.

Elizabeth Cleghorn Stevenson was born in 1810 near London to William Stevenson, a Unitarian preacher and civil servant, and Elizabeth Holland, who died soon after childbirth. From the age of one, Elizabeth was raised by a beloved aunt in the village of Knutsford (the model for Gaskell's novel *Cranford*), near Manchester in northern England. She received a liberal, modern education at a boarding school in Warwick, in central England, and when she came of age went to visit a distant relative in Manchester, where she met her future husband, William Gaskell, a Unitarian minister.

According to Unitarian practices, the two pursued a degree of gender equality far greater than was typical for a Victorian marriage, with Gaskell free to pursue her own interests. For the first twelve years of their marriage, however, she devoted herself to the upbringing and education of her five children and performed many of the duties of her role as a minister's wife, which entailed teaching at a charity school and visiting poor parishioners. By listening to these people's tales of hardship and observing the conditions in factories and homes, Gaskell acquired much of the inspiration for her books. She wrote a small number of short stories and co-authored a poem with her husband while raising her children, but it was not until her infant son died of scarlet fever in 1845 that she began to write novels and stories in earnest, an activity her husband recommended as a partial remedy for the depression brought on by loss.

Mary Barton, Gaskell's first novel, was published in 1848. In it, she exposed the desperation and hopelessness of poverty-stricken millworkers who toiled in miserable, unhealthy conditions in the industrial city of Manchester. Although the book was originally published under the pseudonym "Cotton Mather Mills, Esq.," it was not long before the public's and critics' curiosity unmasked Gaskell. Even though many society people found her portrayal of factory owners to be harsh and unfair, she became an esteemed guest at literary gatherings and social events. Charles Dickens was so impressed with her writing that he asked her to contribute "a short tale or any number of tales" to his magazine, *Household Words*. Gaskell agreed and contributed numerous stories over the next several years; the first, "Our Society at Cranford," appeared in the 13 December 1851 issue. Eight other humorous tales followed, all concerning the same group of upper- and middle-class women and their milieu in a peaceful country village. The tales were extremely well received, and were soon published together as the novel *Cranford* (1853).

Gaskell's next novel was not received as enthusiastically as *Cranford* had been. *Ruth*, also published in 1853, tells the story of a woman who has a child out of wedlock. The subject would have been criticized in any event, but Gaskell's sympathetic portrayal of the woman and her exposure of the hypocrisy of Victorian society deeply angered many people. The book was so controversial that some parishioners burned their copies, and it was banned in many homes, including, ironically, Gaskell's own—even she felt that the subject matter was unsuitable for children. On the other hand, notable women writers such as Elizabeth Barrett Browning, George Eliot, and Charlotte Brontë spoke out in praise of the book. In her next novel, *North and South* (1855), also published in *Household Words* (1854–55), Gaskell returned to issues of factory workers, comparing life in both the rural and urban south with the harsh lives of the working poor in the north. Like *Mary Barton*, *North and South* addressed the need for factory owners to reform workplace conditions and for workers to fight for their rights.

After Charlotte Brontë's death in 1855, Gaskell wrote her biography at the behest of Charlotte's father, Patrick Brontë. Influenced by her close friendship with Charlotte, Gaskell created a very sympathetic portrait of the Brontës, and she included their outspoken opinions about various friends and acquaintances. Unfortunately, Gaskell's loyalty to her subject landed her in trouble when one of those maligned by the Brontës threatened legal action. Under pressure from her publisher, Gaskell was forced to apologize publicly, and the questionable material was removed from the book's subsequent editions. *The Life of Charlotte Brontë* (1857) remains, however, a highly readable biography and a masterpiece of characterization—and it did a great deal to defend Brontë's reputation, ensuring that her work would continue to be read.

Gaskell had almost completed her final novel, *Wives and Daughters*, when she collapsed and died suddenly in 1865. Often compared with the novels of Jane Austen and George Eliot, *Wives and Daughters* exposes the social workings of various classes in a small country town, expressing social critique with the delicate wit and sly humor for which the author was known. Gaskell was buried beside the Unitarian chapel in Knutsford, the town of her childhood that she had so loved and had immortalized in her stories.

⌘⌘⌘

The Manchester Marriage[1]

Mr. and Mrs. Openshaw came from Manchester to settle in London. He had been, what is called in Lancashire,[2] a salesman for a large manufacturing firm, who were extending their business, and opening a warehouse in the city; where Mr. Openshaw was now to superintend their affairs. He rather enjoyed the change; having a kind of curiosity about London, which he had never yet been able to gratify in his brief visits to the metropolis. At the same time, he had an odd, shrewd, contempt for the inhabitants; whom he always pictured to himself as fine, lazy people; caring nothing but for fashion and aristocracy, and lounging away their days in Bond Street[3] and such places; ruining good English, and ready in their turn to despise him as a provincial. The hours that the men of business kept in the city scandalized him too, accustomed as he was to the early dinners of Manchester folk, and the consequently far longer evenings. Still, he was pleased to go to London; though he would not for the world have confessed it, even to himself, and always spoke of the step to his friends as one demanded of him by the interests of his employers, and sweetened to him by a considerable increase of salary. This, indeed, was so liberal that he might have been justified in taking a much larger house than the one he did, had he not thought himself bound to set an example to Londoners of how little a Manchester man of business cared for show. Inside, however, he furnished it with an unusual degree of comfort, and, in the wintertime, he insisted on keeping up as large fires as the grates would allow, in every room where the temperature was in the least chilly. Moreover, his northern sense of hospitality was such, that, if he were at home, he could hardly suffer a visitor to leave the house without forcing meat and drink upon him. Every servant in the house was well warmed, well fed, and kindly treated; for their master scorned all petty saving in aught that conduced to comfort; while he amused himself by following out all his accustomed habits and individual ways, in defiance of what any of his new neighbours might think.

His wife was a pretty, gentle woman, of suitable age and character. He was forty-two, she thirty-five. He was loud and decided; she soft and yielding. They had two children; or rather, I should say, she had two; for the elder, a girl of eleven, was Mrs. Openshaw's child by Frank Wilson, her first husband. The younger was a little boy, Edwin, who could just prattle, and to whom his father delighted to speak in the broadest and most unintelligible Lancashire dialect, in order to keep up what he called the true Saxon accent.

Mrs. Openshaw's Christian name was Alice, and her first husband had been her own cousin. She was the orphan niece of a sea captain in Liverpool; a quiet, grave little creature, of great personal attraction when she was fifteen or sixteen, with regular features and a blooming complexion. But she was very shy, and believed herself to be very stupid and awkward; and was frequently scolded by her aunt, her own uncle's second wife. So when her cousin, Frank Wilson, came home from a long absence at sea, and first was kind and protective to her; secondly, attentive, and thirdly, desperately in love with her, she hardly knew how to be grateful enough to him. It is true, she would have preferred his remaining in the first or second stages of behaviour; for his violent love puzzled and frightened her. Her uncle neither helped nor hindered the love affair; though it was going on under his own eyes. Frank's stepmother had such a

[1] *The Manchester Marriage* Gaskell's short story is reproduced here as it appeared in her collection *Right at Last and Other Tales* (1860). The story was originally published in Charles Dickens's weekly magazine *Household Words* (1850–59), which printed non-fiction pieces about current social issues, as well as serialized novels, short fiction, and poetry. "Manchester Marriage" was a segment within a larger framed narrative titled *A House to Let*, which was published in the 1858 Christmas number of *Household Words*.

Christmas editions of the magazine often published suspenseful or spooky stories, and *A House to Let* featured an older unmarried woman who rents a London lodging across from a strange house that is always available for rent but never taken. The woman soon notices that the empty house is mysteriously occupied, and, while investigating the mystery, she and her servant uncover the histories of previous occupants. "The Manchester Marriage" is one of these histories, appearing as the second inset story within the framed narrative.

[2] *Lancashire* Manufacturing district in north west England; Liverpool and Manchester are the largest cities in the area.

[3] *Bond street* Fashionable street in West London, famous for its high-end shopping.

variable temper, that there was no knowing whether what she liked one day she would like the next, or not. At length she went to such extremes of crossness, that Alice was only too glad to shut her eyes and rush blindly at the chance of escape from domestic tyranny offered her by a marriage with her cousin; and, liking him better than any one in the world, except her uncle (who was at this time at sea), she went off one morning and was married to him; her only bridesmaid being the housemaid at her aunt's. The consequence was, that Frank and his wife went into lodgings, and Mrs. Wilson refused to see them, and turned away Norah, the warm-hearted housemaid, whom they accordingly took into their service. When Captain Wilson returned from his voyage, he was very cordial with the young couple, and spent many an evening at their lodgings, smoking his pipe, and sipping his grog; but he told them that, for quietness' sake, he could not ask them to his own house; for his wife was bitter against them. They were not, however, very unhappy about this.

The seed of future unhappiness lay rather in Frank's vehement, passionate disposition; which led him to resent his wife's shyness and want of demonstrativeness as failures in conjugal duty. He was already tormenting himself, and her too, in a slighter degree, by apprehensions and imaginations of what might befall her during his approaching absence at sea. At last, he went to his father and urged him to insist upon Alice's being once more received under his roof; the more especially as there was now a prospect of her confinement[1] while her husband was away on his voyage. Captain Wilson was, as he himself expressed it, "breaking up," and unwilling to undergo the excitement of a scene; yet he felt that what his son said was true. So he went to his wife. And before Frank set sail, he had the comfort of seeing his wife installed in her old little garret in his father's house. To have placed her in the one best spare room, was a step beyond Mrs. Wilson's powers of submission or generosity. The worst part about it, however, was that the faithful Norah had to be dismissed. Her place as housemaid had been filled up; and, even if it had not, she had forfeited Mrs. Wilson's good opinion forever. She comforted her young master and mistress by pleasant prophecies of the time when they would have a household of their own; of which, whatever service she might be in meanwhile, she should be sure to form a part. Almost the last action Frank did, before setting sail, was going with Alice to see Norah once more at her mother's house; and then he went away.

Alice's father-in-law grew more and more feeble as winter advanced. She was of great use to her stepmother in nursing and amusing him; and, although there was anxiety enough in the household, there was, perhaps, more of peace than there had been for years; for Mrs. Wilson had not a bad heart, and was softened by the visible approach of death to one whom she loved, and, touched by the lonely condition of the young creature, expecting her first confinement in her husband's absence. To this relenting mood Norah owed the permission to come and nurse Alice when her baby was born, and to remain to attend on Captain Wilson.

Before one letter had been received from Frank (who had sailed for the East Indies and China), his father died. Alice was always glad to remember that he had held her baby in his arms, and kissed and blessed it before his death. After that, and the consequent examination into the state of his affairs, it was found that he had left far less property than people had been led by his style of living to expect; and what money there was, was all settled upon his wife, and at her disposal after her death. This did not signify much to Alice, as Frank was now first mate of his ship, and, in another voyage or two, would be captain. Meanwhile he had left her rather more than two hundred pounds (all his savings) in the bank.

It became time for Alice to hear from her husband. One letter from the Cape she had already received. The next was to announce his arrival in India. As week after week passed over, and no intelligence of the ship having got there reached the office of the owners, and the Captain's wife was in the same state of ignorant suspense as Alice herself, her fears grew most oppressive. At length the day came when, in reply to her inquiry at the Shipping Office, they told her that the owners had given up hope of ever hearing more of the "Betsy-Jane," and

[1] *confinement* Being confined to bed for childbirth.

had sent in their claim upon the Underwriters.[1] Now that he was gone for ever, she first felt a yearning, longing love for the kind cousin, the dear friend, the sympathizing protector, whom she should never see again—first felt a passionate desire to show him his child, whom she had hitherto rather craved to have all to herself—her own sole possession. Her grief was, however, noiseless, and quiet—rather to the scandal of Mrs. Wilson; who bewailed her stepson as if he and she had always lived together in perfect harmony, and who evidently thought it her duty to burst into fresh tears at every strange face she saw; dwelling on his poor young widow's desolate state, and the helplessness of the fatherless child, with an unction, as if she liked the excitement of the sorrowful story.

So passed away the first days of Alice's widowhood. By-and-by things subsided into their natural and tranquil course. But, as if this young creature was always to be in some heavy trouble, her ewe-lamb[2] began to be ailing, pining, and sickly. The child's mysterious illness turned out to be some affection[3] of the spine, likely to affect health, but not to shorten life—at least, so the doctors said. But the long, dreary suffering of one whom a mother loves as Alice loved her only child, is hard to look forward to. Only Norah guessed what Alice suffered; no one but God knew.

And so it fell out, that when Mrs. Wilson, the elder, came to her one day, in violent distress, occasioned by a very material diminution in the value of the property that her husband had left her—a diminution which made her income barely enough to support herself, much less Alice—the latter could hardly understand how anything which did not touch health or life could cause such grief, and she received the intelligence with irritating composure. But when, that afternoon, the little sick child was brought in, and the grandmother—who after all loved it well—began a fresh moan over her losses to its unconscious ears—saying how she had planned to consult this or that doctor, and to give it this or that comfort or luxury in after years, but that now all chance of this had passed away—Alice's heart was touched, and she drew near to Mrs. Wilson with unwonted caresses, and, in a spirit not unlike to that of Ruth,[4] entreated that, come what would, they might remain together. After much discussion in succeeding days, it was arranged that Mrs. Wilson should take a house in Manchester, furnishing it partly with what furniture she had, and providing the rest with Alice's remaining two hundred pounds. Mrs. Wilson was herself a Manchester woman, and naturally longed to return to her native town; some connections of her own, too, at that time required lodgings, for which they were willing to pay pretty handsomely. Alice undertook the active superintendence and superior work of the household; Norah, willing, faithful Norah, offered to cook, scour, do anything in short, so that she might but remain with them.

The plan succeeded. For some years, their first lodgers remained with them, and all went smoothly, with the one sad exception of the little girl's increasing deformity. How that mother loved that child, it is not for words to tell!

Then came a break of misfortune. Their lodgers left, and no one succeeded to them. After some months, it became necessary to remove to a smaller house; and Alice's tender conscience was torn by the idea that she ought not to be a burden to her mother-in-law, but to go out and seek her own maintenance. And leave her child! The thought came like the sweeping boom of a funeral bell over her heart.

By-and-by, Mr. Openshaw came to lodge with them. He had started in life as the errand-boy and sweeper-out of a warehouse; had struggled up through all the grades of employment in it, fighting his way through the hard striving Manchester life with strong, pushing energy of character. Every spare moment of time had been sternly given up to self-teaching. He was a capital accountant, a good French and German

[1] *Betsy-Jane* Name of the ship Mr. Wilson had sailed in; *Underwriters* Those who had insured the ship.

[2] *ewe-lamb* Little girl.

[3] *affection* Affliction.

[4] *Ruth* In the Book of Ruth, a widowed Ruth goes to Judah with her mother-in-law Naomi, saying "whither thou goest I will go; and where thou lodgest, I will lodge: thy people shall be my people, and thy God my God" (1.16).

scholar, a keen, far-seeing, tradesman—understanding markets, and the bearing of events, both near and distant, on trade: and yet, with such vivid attention to present details, that I do not think he ever saw a group of flowers in the fields without thinking whether their colours would, or would not, form harmonious contrasts in the coming spring muslins and prints.[1] He went to debating societies, and threw himself with all his heart and soul into politics; esteeming, it must be owned, every man a fool or a knave who differed from him, and overthrowing his opponents rather by the loud strength of his language than the calm strength of his logic. There was something of the Yankee in all this. Indeed, his theory ran parallel to the famous Yankee motto—"England flogs[2] creation, and Manchester flogs England." Such a man, as may be fancied, had had no time for falling in love, or any such nonsense. At the age when most young men go through their courting and matrimony, he had not the means of keeping a wife, and was far too practical to think of having one. And now that he was in easy circumstances, a rising man, he considered women almost as incumbrances to the world, with whom a man had better have as little to do as possible. His first impression of Alice was indistinct, and he did not care enough about her to make it distinct. "A pretty yea-nay[3] kind of woman," would have been his description of her, if he had been pushed into a corner. He was rather afraid, in the beginning, that her quiet ways arose from a listlessness and laziness of character, which would have been exceedingly discordant to his active, energetic nature. But, when he found out the punctuality with which his wishes were attended to, and her work was done; when he was called in the morning at the very stroke of the clock, his shaving water scalding hot, his fire bright, his coffee made exactly as his peculiar fancy dictated (for he was a man who had his theory about everything based upon what he knew of science, and often perfectly original)—then he began to think: not that Alice had any peculiar merit, but that he had got into remarkably good lodgings; his restlessness wore away, and he began to consider himself as almost settled for life in them.

Mr. Openshaw had been too busy, all his days, to be introspective. He did not know that he had any tenderness in his nature; and if he had become conscious of its abstract existence, he would have considered it as a manifestation of disease in some part of him. But he was decoyed into pity unawares; and pity led on to tenderness. That little helpless child—always carried about by one of the three busy women of the house, or else patiently threading coloured beads in the chair from which, by no effort of its own, could it ever move—the great grave blue eyes, full of serious, not uncheerful, expression, giving to the small delicate face a look beyond its years—the soft plaintive voice dropping out but few words, so unlike the continual prattle of a child—caught Mr. Openshaw's attention in spite of himself. One day—he half scorned himself for doing so—he cut short his dinner hour to go in search of some toy, which should take the place of those eternal beads. I forget what he bought; but, when he gave the present (which he took care to do in a short, abrupt manner, and when no one was by to see him), he was almost thrilled by the flash of delight that came over that child's face, and he could not help, all through that afternoon, going over and over again the picture left on his memory, by the bright effect of unexpected joy on the little girl's face. When he returned home, he found his slippers placed by his sitting room fire; and even more careful attention paid to his fancies than was habitual in those model lodgings. When Alice had taken the last of his tea things away—she had been silent as usual till then—she stood for an instant with the door in her hand. Mr. Openshaw looked as if he were deep in his book, though in fact he did not see a line; but was heartily wishing the woman would go, and not make any palaver of gratitude. But she only said:

"I am very much obliged to you, sir. Thank you very much," and—was gone, even before he could send her away with a "There, my good woman, that's enough!"

---

[1] *spring muslins and prints* Patterns that would be printed on muslin and other cloth used to make women's dresses.

[2] *famous Yankee motto* Americans were said to declare that "America flogs the world"; *flogs* Surpasses, defeats.

[3] *yea-nay* Hesitating; having a weak personality.

For some time longer he took no apparent notice of the child. He even hardened his heart into disregarding her sudden flush of colour and little timid smile of recognition, when he saw her by chance. But, after all, this could not last forever; and, having a second time given way to tenderness, there was no relapse. The insidious enemy having thus entered his heart, in the guise of compassion to the child, soon assumed the more dangerous form of interest in the mother. He was aware of this change of feeling—despised himself for it—struggled with it; nay, internally yielded to it and cherished it, long before he suffered the slightest expression of it, by word, action, or look to escape him. He watched Alice's docile, obedient ways to her stepmother; the love which she had inspired in the rough Norah (roughened by the wear and tear of sorrow and years); but, above all, he saw the wild, deep, passionate affection existing between her and her child. They spoke little to any one else, or when any one else was by; but, when alone together, they talked, and murmured, and cooed, and chattered so continually, that Mr. Openshaw first wondered what they could find to say to each other, and next became irritated because they were always so grave and silent with him. All this time, he was perpetually devising small new pleasures for the child. His thoughts ran, in a pertinacious way, upon the desolate life before her; and often he came back from his day's work loaded with the very thing Alice had been longing for, but had not been able to procure. One time, it was a little chair for drawing the little sufferer along the streets; and, many an evening that following summer, Mr. Openshaw drew her along himself, regardless of the remarks of his acquaintances. One day in autumn, he put down his newspaper, as Alice came in with the breakfast, and said, in as indifferent a voice as he could assume:

"Mrs. Frank, is there any reason why we two should not put up our horses together?"

Alice stood still in perplexed wonder. What did he mean? He had resumed the reading of his newspaper, as if he did not expect any answer; so she found silence her safest course, and went on quietly arranging his breakfast, without another word passing between them. Just as he was leaving the house, to go to the warehouse as usual, he turned back and put his head into the bright, neat, tidy kitchen, where all the women breakfasted in the morning:

"You'll think of what I said, Mrs. Frank" (this was her name with the lodgers), "and let me have your opinion upon it tonight."

Alice was thankful that her mother and Norah were too busy talking together to attend much to this speech. She determined not to think about it at all through the day; and, of course, the effort not to think, made her think all the more. At night she sent up Norah with his tea. But Mr. Openshaw almost knocked Norah down as she was going out at the door, by pushing past her and calling out, "Mrs. Frank!" in an impatient voice, at the top of the stairs.

Alice went up, rather than seem to have affixed too much meaning to his words.

"Well, Mrs. Frank," he said, "what answer? Don't make it too long; for I have lots of office work to get through tonight."

"I hardly know what you meant, sir," said truthful Alice.

"Well! I should have thought you might have guessed. You're not new at this sort of work, and I am. However, I'll make it plain this time. Will you have me to be thy wedded husband, and serve me, and love me, and honour me, and all that sort of thing? Because, if you will, I will do as much by you, and be a father to your child—and that's more than is put in the Prayer-book.[1] Now, I'm a man of my word; and what I say, I feel; and what I promise, I'll do. Now, for your answer!"

Alice was silent. He began to make the tea, as if her reply was a matter of perfect indifference to him; but, as soon as that was done, he became impatient.

"Well?" said he.

"How long, sir, may I have to think over it?"

"Three minutes!" (looking at his watch). "You've had two already—that makes five. Be a sensible woman, say Yes, and sit down to tea with me, and we'll talk it over together; for, after tea, I shall be busy; say No" (he

[1] *Prayer-book* Book of Common Prayer, which contains the Anglican marriage vows.

hesitated a moment to try and keep his voice in the same tone), "and I shan't say another word about it, but pay up a year's rent for my rooms tomorrow, and be off. Time's up! Yes or no?"

"If you please, sir—you have been so good to little Ailsie—"

"There, sit down comfortably by me on the sofa, and let us have our tea together. I am glad to find you are as good and sensible as I took you for."

And this was Alice Wilson's second wooing.

Mr. Openshaw's will was too strong, and his circumstances too good, for him not to carry all before him. He settled Mrs. Wilson in a comfortable house of her own, and made her quite independent of lodgers. The little that Alice said with regard to future plans was in Norah's behalf.

"No," said Mr. Openshaw. "Norah shall take care of the old lady as long as she lives; and, after that, she shall either come and live with us, or, if she likes it better, she shall have a provision for life—for your sake, missus. No one who has been good to you or the child shall go unrewarded. But even the little one will be better for some fresh stuff about her. Get her a bright, sensible girl as a nurse: one who won't go rubbing her with calf's-foot jelly[1] as Norah does; wasting good stuff outside that ought to go in, but will follow doctors' directions; which, as you must see pretty clearly by this time, Norah won't; because they give the poor little wench[2] pain. Now, I'm not above being nesh[3] for other folks myself. I can stand a good blow, and never change colour; but, set me in the operating room in the infirmary, and I turn as sick as a girl. Yet, if need were, I would hold the little wench on my knees while she screeched with pain, if it were to do her poor back good. Nay, nay, wench! keep your white looks for the time when it comes—I don't say it ever will. But this I know, Norah will spare the child and cheat the doctor,[4] if she can. Now, I say, give the bairn[5] a year or two's chance, and then, when the pack of doctors have done their best—and, maybe, the old lady has gone—we'll have Norah back, or do better for her."

The pack of doctors could do no good to little Ailsie. She was beyond their power. But her father (for so he insisted on being called, and also on Alice's no longer retaining the appellation of Mamma, but becoming henceforward Mother), by his healthy cheerfulness of manner, his clear decision of purpose, his odd turns and quirks of humour, added to his real strong love for the helpless little girl, infused a new element of brightness and confidence into her life; and, though her back remained the same, her general health was strengthened, and Alice—never going beyond a smile herself—had the pleasure of seeing her child taught to laugh.

As for Alice's own life, it was happier than it had ever been before. Mr. Openshaw required no demonstration, no expressions of affection from her. Indeed, these would rather have disgusted him. Alice could love deeply, but could not talk about it. The perpetual requirement of loving words, looks, and caresses, and misconstruing their absence into absence of love, had been the great trial of her former married life. Now, all went on clear and straight, under the guidance of her husband's strong sense, warm heart, and powerful will. Year by year, their worldly prosperity increased. At Mrs. Wilson's death, Norah came back to them, as nurse to the newly-born little Edwin; into which post she was not installed without a pretty strong oration on the part of the proud and happy father; who declared that if he found out that Norah ever tried to screen the boy by a falsehood, or to make him nesh either in body or mind, she should go that very day. Norah and Mr. Openshaw were not on the most thoroughly cordial terms; neither of them fully recognizing or appreciating the other's best qualities.

This was the previous history of the Lancashire family who had now removed to London.

[1] *calf's-foot jelly* Dish made by boiling down a calf's foot to extract the gelatin and mixing in wine, lemon, spices, and sometimes sugar. It was thought to be a wholesome dish for invalids; Norah is using it here as a topical rub to help ease the child's discomfort.

[2] *wench* Girl.

[3] *being nesh* Northern English: becoming faint, or losing one's nerve.

[4] *spare … doctor* Rephrasing of the adage "Spare the rod and spoil the child."

[5] *bairn* Child.

They had been there about a year, when Mr. Openshaw suddenly informed his wife that he had determined to heal long-standing feuds, and had asked his uncle and aunt Chadwick to come and pay them a visit and see London. Mrs. Openshaw had never seen this uncle and aunt of her husband's. Years before she had married him, there had been a quarrel. All she knew was, that Mr. Chadwick was a small manufacturer in a country town in South Lancashire. She was extremely pleased that the breach was to be healed, and began making preparations to render their visit pleasant.

They arrived at last. Going to see London was such an event to them, that Mrs. Chadwick had made all new linen fresh for the occasion—from nightcaps downwards; and as for gowns, ribbons, and collars, she might have been going into the wilds of Canada where never a shop is, so large was her stock. A fortnight before the day of her departure for London, she had formally called to take leave of all her acquaintance; saying she should need every bit of the intermediate time for packing up. It was like a second wedding in her imagination; and, to complete the resemblance which an entirely new wardrobe made between the two events, her husband brought her back from Manchester, on the last market day before they set off, a gorgeous pearl and amethyst brooch, saying, "Lunnon[1] should see that Lancashire folks knew a handsome thing when they saw it."

For some time after Mr. and Mrs. Chadwick arrived at the Openshaws' there was no opportunity for wearing this brooch; but at length they obtained an order to see Buckingham Palace, and the spirit of loyalty demanded that Mrs. Chadwick should wear her best clothes in visiting the abode of her sovereign. On her return, she hastily changed her dress; for Mr. Openshaw had planned that they should go to Richmond,[2] drink tea, and return by moonlight. Accordingly, about five o'clock, Mr. and Mrs. Openshaw and Mr. and Mrs. Chadwick set off.

The housemaid and cook sat below, Norah hardly knew where. She was always engrossed in the nursery, in tending her two children, and in sitting by the restless, excitable Ailsie till she fell asleep. By-and-by, the housemaid Bessy tapped gently at the door. Norah went to her, and they spoke in whispers.

"Nurse! there's some one downstairs wants you."

"Wants me! Who is it?"

"A gentleman—"

"A gentleman? Nonsense!"

"Well! a man, then, and he asks for you, and he rang at the front door bell, and has walked into the dining room."

"You should never have let him," exclaimed Norah, "master and missus out—"

"I did not want him to come in; but, when he heard you lived here, he walked past me, and sat down on the first chair, and said, 'Tell her to come and speak to me.' There is no gas lighted in the room, and supper is all set out."

"He'll be off with the spoons!" exclaimed Norah, putting the housemaid's fear into words, and preparing to leave the room, first, however, giving a look to Ailsie, sleeping soundly and calmly.

Downstairs she went, uneasy fears stirring in her bosom. Before she entered the dining room she provided herself with a candle, and, with it in her hand, she went in, looking around her in the darkness for her visitor.

He was standing up, holding by the table. Norah and he looked at each other; gradual recognition coming into their eyes.

"Norah?" at length he asked.

"Who are you?" asked Norah, with the sharp tones of alarm and incredulity. "I don't know you:" trying, by futile words of disbelief, to do away with the terrible fact before her.

"Am I so changed?" he said, pathetically. "I dare say I am. But, Norah, tell me!" he breathed hard, "where is my wife? Is she—is she alive?"

He came nearer to Norah, and would have taken her hand; but she backed away from him; looking at him all the time with staring eyes, as if he were some horrible object. Yet he was a handsome, bronzed, good-looking fellow, with beard and moustache, giving him a foreign-looking aspect; but his eyes! there was no mistaking

[1] *Lunnon* Northern English: London.

[2] *Richmond* Scenic town south-west of London on the river Thames.

those eager, beautiful eyes—the very same that Norah had watched not half an hour ago, till sleep stole softly over them.

"Tell me, Norah—I can bear it—I have feared it so often. Is she dead?" Norah still kept silence. "She is dead!" He hung on Norah's words and looks, as if for confirmation or contradiction.

"What shall I do?" groaned Norah. "O, sir! why did you come? how did you find me out? where have you been? We thought you dead, we did indeed!" She poured out words and questions to gain time, as if time would help her.

"Norah! answer me this question straight, by yes or no—Is my wife dead?"

"No, she is not!" said Norah, slowly and heavily.

"O, what a relief! Did she receive my letters? But perhaps you don't know. Why did you leave her? Where is she? O, Norah, tell me all quickly!"

"Mr. Frank!" said Norah at last, almost driven to bay by her terror lest her mistress should return at any moment, and find him there—unable to consider what was best to be done or said—rushing at something decisive, because she could not endure her present state: "Mr. Frank! we never heard a line from you, and the shipowners said you had gone down, you and every one else. We thought you were dead, if ever man was, and poor Miss Alice and her little sick, helpless child! O, sir, you must guess it," cried the poor creature at last, bursting out into a passionate fit of crying, "for indeed I cannot tell it. But it was no one's fault. God help us all this night!"

Norah had sat down. She trembled too much to stand. He took her hands in his. He squeezed them hard, as if, by physical pressure, the truth could be wrung out.

"Norah." This time his tone was calm, stagnant as despair. "She has married again!"

Norah shook her head sadly. The grasp slowly relaxed. The man had fainted.

There was brandy in the room. Norah forced some drops into Mr. Frank's mouth, chafed his hands, and—when mere animal life returned, before the mind poured in its flood of memories and thoughts—she lifted him up, and rested his head against her knees. Then she put a few crumbs of bread taken from the supper table, soaked in brandy, into his mouth. Suddenly he sprang to his feet.

"Where is she? Tell me this instant." He looked so wild, so mad, so desperate, that Norah felt herself to be in bodily danger; but her time of dread had gone by. She had been afraid to tell him the truth, and then she had been a coward. Now, her wits were sharpened by the sense of his desperate state. He must leave the house. She would pity him afterwards; but now she must rather command and upbraid; for he must leave the house before her mistress came home. That one necessity stood clear before her.

"She is not here: that is enough for you to know. Nor can I say exactly where she is" (which was true to the letter if not to the spirit). "Go away, and tell me where to find you tomorrow, and I will tell you all. My master and mistress may come back at any minute, and then what would become of me, with a strange man in the house?"

Such an argument was too petty to touch his excited mind.

"I don't care for your master and mistress. If your master is a man, he must feel for me—poor shipwrecked sailor that I am—kept for years a prisoner amongst savages, always, always, always thinking of my wife and my home—dreaming of her by night, talking to her, though she could not hear, by day. I loved her more than all heaven and earth put together. Tell me where she is, this instant, you wretched woman, who salved over[1] her wickedness to her, as you to do to me!"

The clock struck ten. Desperate positions require desperate measures.

"If you will leave the house now, I will come to you tomorrow and tell you all. What is more, you shall see your child now. She lies sleeping upstairs. O, sir, you have a child, you do not know that as yet—a little weakly girl—with just a heart and soul beyond her years. We have reared her up with such care! We watched her, for we thought for many a year she might die any day, and we tended her, and no hard thing has

[1] *salved over* Smoothed over, excused.

come near her, and no rough word has ever been said to her. And now you come and will take her life into your hand, and will crush it. Strangers to her have been kind to her; but her own father—Mr. Frank, I am her nurse, and I love her, and I tend her, and I would do anything for her that I could. Her mother's heart beats as hers beats; and, if she suffers a pain, her mother trembles all over. If she is happy, it is her mother that smiles and is glad. If she is growing stronger, her mother is healthy: if she dwindles, her mother languishes. If she dies—well, I don't know: it is not every one can lie down and die when they wish it. Come up stairs, Mr. Frank, and see your child. Seeing her will do good to your poor heart. Then go away, in God's name, just this one night; tomorrow, if need be, you can do anything—kill us all if you will, or show yourself a great, grand man, whom God will bless for ever and ever. Come, Mr. Frank, the look of a sleeping child is sure to give peace."

She led him upstairs; at first almost helping his steps, till they came near the nursery door. She had well-nigh forgotten the existence of little Edwin. It struck upon her with affright as the shaded light fell over the other cot; but she skilfully threw that corner of the room into darkness, and let the light fall on the sleeping Ailsie. The child had thrown down the coverings, and her deformity, as she lay with her back to them, was plainly visible through her slight nightgown. Her little face, deprived of the lustre of her eyes, looked wan and pinched, and had a pathetic expression in it, even as she slept. The poor father looked and looked with hungry, wistful eyes, into which the big tears came swelling up slowly and dropped heavily down, as he stood trembling and shaking all over. Norah was angry with herself, for growing impatient of the length of time that long lingering gaze lasted. She thought that she waited for full half an hour before Frank stirred. And then—instead of going away—he sank down on his knees by the bedside, and buried his face in the clothes. Little Ailsie stirred uneasily. Norah pulled him up in terror. She could afford no more time, even for prayer, in her extremity of fear; for surely the next moment would bring her mistress home. She took him forcibly by the arm: but, as he was going, his eye lighted on the other bed: he stopped. Intelligence came back into his face. His hands clenched.

"His child?" he asked.

"Her child," replied Norah. "God watches over him," said she instinctively; for Frank's looks excited her fears, and she needed to remind herself of the Protector of the helpless.

"God has not watched over me," he said, in despair; his thoughts apparently recoiling on his own desolate, deserted state. But Norah had no time for pity. Tomorrow she would be as compassionate as her heart prompted. At length she guided him downstairs, and shut the outer door, and bolted it—as if by bolts to keep out facts.

Then she went back into the dining room, and effaced all traces of his presence, as far as she could. She went upstairs to the nursery and sat there, her head on her hand, thinking what was to come of all this misery. It seemed to her very long before her master and mistress returned; yet it was hardly eleven o'clock. She heard the loud, hearty Lancashire voices on the stairs; and, for the first time, she understood the contrast of the desolation of the poor man who had so lately gone forth in lonely despair.

It almost put her out of patience to see Mrs. Openshaw come in, calmly smiling, handsomely dressed, happy, easy, to inquire after her children.

"Did Ailsie go to sleep comfortably?" she whispered to Norah.

"Yes."

Her mother bent over her, looking at her slumbers with the soft eyes of love. How little she dreamed who had looked on her last! Then she went to Edwin, with perhaps less wistful anxiety in her countenance, but more of pride. She took off her things, to go down to supper. Norah saw her no more that night.

Beside having a door into the passage, the sleeping-nursery opened out of Mr. and Mrs. Openshaw's room, in order that they might have the children more immediately under their own eyes. Early the next summer morning, Mrs. Openshaw was awakened by Ailsie's startled call of "Mother! mother!" She sprang up, put on her dressing gown, and went to her child. Ailsie was only half awake, and in a not unusual state of terror.

"Who was he mother? Tell me!"

"Who, my darling? No one is here. You have been dreaming, love. Waken up quite. See, it is broad day-light."

"Yes," said Ailsie, looking round her; then clinging to her mother, "but a man was here in the night, mother."

"Nonsense, little goose. No man has ever come near you!"

"Yes, he did. He stood there. Just by Norah. A man with hair and a beard. And he knelt down and said his prayers. Norah knows he was here, mother" (half angrily, as Mrs. Openshaw shook her head in smiling incredulity).

"Well! we will ask Norah when she comes," said Mrs. Openshaw, soothingly. "But we won't talk any more about him now. It is not five o'clock; it is too early for you to get up. Shall I fetch you a book and read to you?"

"Don't leave me, mother," said the child, clinging to her. So Mrs. Openshaw sat on the bedside talking to Ailsie, and telling her of what they had done at Richmond the evening before, until the little girl's eyes slowly closed and she once more fell asleep.

"What was the matter?" asked Mr. Openshaw, as his wife returned to bed.

"Ailsie wakened up in a fright, with some story of a man having been in the room to say his prayers—a dream, I suppose." And no more was said at the time.

Mrs. Openshaw had almost forgotten the whole affair when she got up about seven o'clock. But, by-and-by, she heard a sharp altercation going on in the nursery—Norah speaking angrily to Ailsie, a most unusual thing. Both Mr. and Mrs. Openshaw listened in astonishment.

"Hold your tongue, Ailsie! let me hear none of your dreams; never let me hear you tell that story again!" Ailsie began to cry.

Mr. Openshaw opened the door of communication, before his wife could say a word.

"Norah, come here!"

The nurse stood at the door, defiant. She perceived she had been heard, but she was desperate.

"Don't let me hear you speak in that manner to Ailsie again," he said sternly, and shut the door.

Norah was infinitely relieved; for she had dreaded some questioning; and a little blame for sharp speaking was what she could well bear, if cross examination was let alone.

Downstairs they went, Mr. Openshaw carrying Ailsie; the sturdy Edwin coming step by step, right foot foremost, always holding his mother's hand. Each child was placed in a chair by the breakfast table, and then Mr. and Mrs. Openshaw stood together at the window, awaiting their visitors' appearance and making plans for the day. There was a pause. Suddenly Mr. Openshaw turned to Ailsie, and said:

"What a little goosey somebody is with her dreams, wakening up poor, tired mother in the middle of the night, with a story of a man being in the room."

"Father! I'm sure I saw him," said Ailsie, half crying. "I don't want to make Norah angry; but I was not asleep, for all she says I was. I had been asleep, and I wakened up quite wide awake, though I was so frightened. I kept my eyes nearly shut, and I saw the man quite plain. A great brown man with a beard. He said his prayers. And then he looked at Edwin. And then Norah took him by the arm and led him away, after they had whispered a bit together."

"Now, my little woman must be reasonable," said Mr. Openshaw, who was always patient with Ailsie. "There was no man in the house last night at all. No man comes into the house, as you know, if you think; much less goes up into the nursery. But sometimes we dream something has happened, and the dream is so like reality, that you are not the first person, little woman, who has stood out that the thing has really happened."

"But, indeed it was not a dream!" said Ailsie, beginning to cry.

Just then Mr. and Mrs. Chadwick came down, looking grave and discomposed. All during breakfast time, they were silent and uncomfortable. As soon as the breakfast things were taken away, and the children had been carried upstairs, Mr. Chadwick began, in an evidently preconcerted manner, to inquire if his nephew was certain that all his servants were honest; for, that

Mrs. Chadwick had that morning missed a very valuable brooch, which she had worn the day before. She remembered taking it off when she came home from Buckingham Palace. Mr. Openshaw's face contracted into hard lines: grew like what it was before he had known his wife and her child. He rang the bell, even before his uncle had done speaking. It was answered by the housemaid.

"Mary, was any one here last night, while we were away?"

"A man, sir, came to speak to Norah."

"To speak to Norah! Who was he? How long did he stay?"

"I'm sure I can't tell, sir. He came—perhaps about nine. I went up to tell Norah in the nursery, and she came down to speak to him. She let him out, sir. She will know who he was, and how long he stayed."

She waited a moment to be asked any more questions, but she was not, so she went away.

A minute afterwards, Mr. Openshaw made as though he were going out of the room; but his wife laid her hand on his arm:

"Do not speak to her before the children," she said, in her low, quiet voice. "I will go up and question her."

"No! I must speak to her. You must know," said he, turning to his uncle and aunt, "my missus has an old servant, as faithful as ever woman was, I do believe, as far as love goes—but at the same time, who does not always speak truth, as even the missus must allow. Now, my notion is, that this Norah of ours has been come over by some good-for-nothing chap (for she's at the time o' life when they say women pray for husbands—'any, good Lord, any') and has let him into our house, and the chap has made off with your brooch, and m'appen many another thing beside. It's only saying that Norah is soft-hearted, and doesn't stick at a white lie—that's all, missus."

It was curious to notice how his tone, his eyes, his whole face was changed, as he spoke to his wife; but he was the resolute man through all. She knew better than to oppose him; so she went upstairs, and told Norah her master wanted to speak to her, and that she would take care of the children in the meanwhile.

Norah rose to go, without a word. Her thoughts were these:

"If they tear me to pieces, they shall never know through me. He may come—and then, just Lord have mercy upon us all! for some of us are dead folk to a certainty. But he shall do it; not me."

You may fancy, now, her look of determination, as she faced her master alone in the dining room; Mr. and Mrs. Chadwick having left the affair in their nephew's hands, seeing that he took it up with such vehemence.

"Norah! Who was that man that came to my house last night?"

"Man, sir!" As if infinitely surprised; but it was only to gain time.

"Yes; the man that Mary let in; that she went upstairs to the nursery to tell you about; that you came down to speak to; the same chap, I make no doubt, that you took into the nursery to have your talk out with; the one Ailsie saw, and afterwards dreamed about; thinking, poor wench! she saw him say his prayers, when nothing, I'll be bound, was further from his thoughts; the one that took Mrs. Chadwick's brooch, value ten pounds. Now, Norah! Don't go off. I'm as sure, as my name's Thomas Openshaw, that you knew nothing of this robbery. But I do think you've been imposed on, and that's the truth. Some good-for-nothing chap has been making up to you, and you've been just like all other women, and have turned a soft place in your heart to him; and he came last night a-lovyering,[1] and you had him up in the nursery, and he made use of his opportunities, and made off with a few things on his way down! Come, now, Norah: it's no blame to you, only you must not be such a fool again! Tell us," he continued, "what name he gave you, Norah. I'll be bound, it was not the right one; but it will be a clue for the police."

Norah drew herself up. "You may ask that question, and taunt me with my being single, and with my credulity, as you will, Master Openshaw. You'll get no answer from me. As for the brooch, and the story of theft and burglary; if any friend ever came to see me (which I defy you to prove, and deny), he'd be just as much above doing such a thing as you yourself, Mr.

[1] *a-lovyering* Courting.

Openshaw—and more so too; for I'm not at all sure as everything you have is rightly come by, or would be yours long, if every man had his own." She meant, of course, his wife; but he understood her to refer to his property in goods and chattels.

"Now, my good woman," said he, "I'll just tell you truly, I never trusted you out and out; but my wife liked you, and I thought you had many a good point about you. If you once begin to sauce me, I'll have the police to you, and get out the truth in a court of justice, if you'll not tell it me quietly and civilly here. Now, the best thing you can do, is quietly to tell me who the fellow is. Look here! a man comes to my house; asks for you; you take him upstairs; a valuable brooch is missing next day; we know that you, and Mary, and cook, are honest; but you refuse to tell us who the man is. Indeed, you've told one lie already about him, saying no one was here last night. Now, I just put it to you, what do you think a policeman would say to this, or a magistrate? A magistrate would soon make you tell the truth, my good woman."

"There's never the creature born that should get it out of me," said Norah. "Not unless I choose to tell."

"I've a great mind to see," said Mr. Openshaw, growing angry at the defiance. Then, checking himself, he thought before he spoke again:

"Norah, for your missus's sake I don't want to go to extremities. Be a sensible woman, if you can. It's no great disgrace, after all, to have been taken in. I ask you once more—as a friend—who was this man that you let into my house last night?"

No answer. He repeated the question in an impatient tone. Still no answer. Norah's lips were set in determination not to speak.

"Then there is but one thing to be done. I shall send for a policeman."

"You will not," said Norah, starting forward. "You shall not, sir! No policeman shall touch me. I know nothing of the brooch, but I know this: ever since I was four-and-twenty, I have thought more of your wife than of myself: ever since I saw her, a poor motherless girl, put upon in her uncle's house, I have thought more of serving her than of serving myself: I have cared for her and her child, as nobody ever cared for me. I don't cast blame on you, sir, but I say it's ill giving up one's life to any one; for, at the end, they will turn round upon you, and forsake you. Why does not my missus come herself to suspect me? Maybe, she is gone for the police? But I don't stay here, either for police, or magistrate, or master. You're an unlucky lot. I believe there's a curse on you. I'll leave you this very day. Yes! I'll leave that poor Ailsie, too. I will! No good will ever come to you!"

Mr. Openshaw was utterly astonished at this speech; most of which was completely unintelligible to him, as may easily be supposed. Before he could make up his mind what to say, or what to do, Norah had left the room. I do not think he had ever really intended to send for the police to this old servant of his wife's; for he had never for a moment doubted her perfect honesty. But he had intended to compel her to tell him who the man was, and in this he was baffled. He was, consequently, much irritated. He returned to his uncle and aunt in a state of great annoyance and perplexity, and told them he could get nothing out of the woman; that some man had been in the house the night before; but that she refused to tell who he was. At this moment his wife came in, greatly agitated, and asked what had happened to Norah; for that she had put on her things in passionate haste, and left the house.

"This looks suspicious," said Mr. Chadwick. "It is not the way in which an honest person would have acted."

Mr. Openshaw kept silence. He was sorely perplexed. But Mrs. Openshaw turned round on Mr. Chadwick, with a sudden fierceness no one ever saw in her before.

"You don't know Norah, uncle! She is gone because she is deeply hurt at being suspected. Oh, I wish I had seen her—that I had spoken to her myself. She would have told me anything." Alice wrung her hands.

"I must confess," continued Mr. Chadwick to his nephew, in a lower voice, "I can't make you out. You used to be a word and a blow, and oftenest the blow first; and now, when there is every cause for suspicion, you just do nought. Your missus is a very good woman, I grant; but she may have been put upon as well as other folk, I suppose. If you don't send for the police, I shall."

"Very well," replied Mr. Openshaw, surlily. "I can't clear Norah. She won't clear herself, as I believe she might if she would. Only I wash my hands of it; for I am sure the woman herself is honest, and she's lived a long time with my wife, and I don't like her to come to shame."

"But she will then be forced to clear herself. That, at any rate, will be a good thing."

"Very well, very well! I am heartsick of the whole business. Come, Alice, come up to the babies; they'll be in a sore way. I tell you, uncle," he said, turning round once more to Mr. Chadwick, suddenly and sharply, after his eye had fallen on Alice's wan, tearful, anxious face; "I'll have no sending for the police, after all. I'll buy my aunt twice as handsome a brooch this very day; but I'll not have Norah suspected, and my missus plagued. There's for you!"

He and his wife left the room. Mr. Chadwick quietly waited till he was out of hearing, and then said to his wife, "For all Tom's heroics, I'm just quietly going for a detective, wench. Thou need'st know nought about it."

He went to the police station, and made a statement of the case. He was gratified by the impression which the evidence against Norah seemed to make. The men all agreed in his opinion, and steps were to be immediately taken to find out where she was. Most probably, as they suggested, she had gone at once to the man, who, to all appearance, was her lover. When Mr. Chadwick asked how they would find her out, they smiled, shook their heads, and spoke of mysterious but infallible ways and means. He returned to his nephew's house with a very comfortable opinion of his own sagacity. He was met by his wife with a penitent face:

"O master, I've found my brooch! It was just sticking by its pin in the flounce of my brown silk, that I wore yesterday. I took it off in a hurry, and it must have caught in it: and I hung up my gown in the closet. Just now, when I was going to fold it up, there was the brooch! I'm very vexed, but I never dreamt but what it was lost!"

Her husband muttering something very like "Confound thee and thy brooch too! I wish I'd never given it thee," snatched up his hat, and rushed back to the station, hoping to be in time to stop the police from searching for Norah. But a detective was already gone off on the errand.

Where was Norah? Half mad with the strain of the fearful secret, she had hardly slept through the night for thinking what must be done. Upon this terrible state of mind had come Ailsie's questions, showing that she had seen the Man, as the unconscious child called her father. Lastly came the suspicion of her honesty. She was little less than crazy as she ran up stairs and dashed on her bonnet and shawl; leaving all else, even her purse, behind her. In that house she would not stay. That was all she knew or was clear about. She would not even see the children again, for fear it should weaken her. She dreaded above everything Mr. Frank's return to claim his wife. She could not tell what remedy there was for a sorrow so tremendous, for her to stay to witness. The desire of escaping from the coming event was a stronger motive for her departure, than her soreness about the suspicions directed against her; although this last had been the final goad[1] to the course she took. She walked away almost at headlong speed; sobbing as she went, as she had not dared to do during the past night for fear of exciting wonder in those who might hear her. Then she stopped. An idea came into her mind that she would leave London altogether, and betake herself to her native town of Liverpool. She felt in her pocket for her purse, as she drew near the Euston Square station with this intention. She had left it at home. Her poor head aching, her eyes swollen with crying, she had to stand still, and think, as well as she could, where next she should bend her steps. Suddenly the thought flashed into her mind, that she would go and find our poor Mr. Frank. She had been hardly kind to him the night before, though her heart had bled for him ever since. She remembered his telling her, when she inquired for his address, almost as she had pushed him out of the door, of some hotel in a street not far distant from Euston Square. Thither she went: with what intention she scarcely knew, but to assuage her conscience by telling him how much she pitied him. In her present

[1] *goad* Spur.

state she felt herself unfit to counsel, or restrain, or assist, or do aught else but sympathize and weep. The people of the inn said such a person had been there; had arrived only the day before; had gone out soon after his arrival, leaving his luggage in their care; but had never come back. Norah asked for leave to sit down, and await the gentleman's return. The landlady—pretty secure in the deposit of luggage against any probable injury—showed her into a room, and quietly locked the door on the outside. Norah was utterly worn out, and fell asleep—a shivering, starting, uneasy slumber, which lasted for hours.

The detective, meanwhile, had come up with her some time before she entered the hotel, into which he followed her. Asking the landlady to detain her for an hour or so, without giving any reason beyond showing his authority (which made the landlady applaud herself a good deal for having locked her in), he went back to the police station to report his proceedings. He could have taken her directly; but his object was, if possible, to trace out the man who was supposed to have committed the robbery. Then he heard of the discovery of the brooch; and consequently did not care to return.

Norah slept till even the summer evening began to close in. Then started up. Some one was at the door. It would be Mr. Frank; and she dizzily pushed back her ruffled grey hair, which had fallen over her eyes, and stood looking to see him. Instead, there came in Mr. Openshaw and a policeman.

"This is Norah Kennedy," said Mr. Openshaw.

"O, sir," said Norah, "I did not touch the brooch; indeed I did not. O, sir, I cannot live to be thought so badly of;" and very sick and faint, she suddenly sank down on the ground. To her surprise, Mr. Openshaw raised her up very tenderly. Even the policeman helped to lay her on the sofa; and, at Mr. Openshaw's desire, he went for some wine and sandwiches; for the poor gaunt woman lay there almost as if dead with weariness and exhaustion.

"Norah," said Mr. Openshaw, in his kindest voice, "the brooch is found. It was hanging to Mrs. Chadwick's gown. I beg your pardon. Most truly I beg your pardon, for having troubled you about it. My wife is almost broken-hearted. Eat, Norah—or, stay,[1] first drink this glass of wine," said he, lifting her head, and pouring a little down her throat.

As she drank, she remembered where she was, and who she was waiting for. She suddenly pushed Mr. Openshaw away, saying, "O, sir, you must go. You must not stop a minute. If he comes back, he will kill you."

"Alas, Norah! I do not know who 'he' is. But some one is gone away who will never come back: some one who knew you, and whom I am afraid you cared for."

"I don't understand you, sir," said Norah, her master's kind and sorrowful manner bewildering her yet more than his words. The policeman had left the room at Mr. Openshaw's desire, and they two were alone.

"You know what I mean, when I say some one is gone who will never come back. I mean that he is dead!"

"Who?" said Norah, trembling all over.

"A poor man has been found in the Thames this morning—drowned."

"Did he drown himself?" asked Norah, solemnly.

"God only knows," replied Mr. Openshaw, in the same tone. "Your name and address at our house were found in his pocket: that, and his purse, were the only things that were found upon him. I am sorry to say it, my poor Norah; but you are required to go and identify him."

"To what?" asked Norah.

"To say who it is. It is always done, in order that some reason may be discovered for the suicide—if suicide it was. I make no doubt, he was the man who came to see you at our house last night. It is very sad, I know." He made pauses between each little clause, in order to try and bring back her senses, which he feared were wandering—so wild and sad was her look.

"Master Openshaw," said she, at last, "I've a dreadful secret to tell you—only you must never breathe it to any one, and you and I must hide it away for ever. I thought to have done it all by myself, but I see I cannot. Yon[2] poor man—yes! the dead, drowned creature is, I fear, Mr. Frank, my mistress's first husband!"

[1] *stay* Wait.

[2] *Yon* Yonder.

Mr. Openshaw sat down, as if shot. He did not speak; but, after a while, he signed to Norah to go on.

"He came to me the other night—when—God be thanked! you were all away at Richmond. He asked me if his wife was dead or alive. I was a brute, and thought more of your all coming home than of his sore trial: I spoke out sharp, and said she was married again, and very content and happy: I all but turned him away: and now he lies dead and cold."

"God forgive me!" said Mr. Openshaw.

"God forgive us all!" said Norah. "Yon poor man needs forgiveness, perhaps, less than any one among us. He had been among the savages—shipwrecked—I know not what—and he had written letters which had never reached my poor missus."

"He saw his child!"

"He saw her—yes! I took him up, to give his thoughts another start; for I believed he was going mad on my hands. I came to seek him here, as I more than half promised. My mind misgave me when I heard he never came in. O, sir! it must be him!"

Mr. Openshaw rang the bell. Norah was almost too much stunned to wonder at what he did. He asked for writing materials, wrote a letter, and then said to Norah:

"I am writing to Alice, to say I shall be unavoidably absent for a few days; that I have found you; that you are well, and send her your love, and will come home tomorrow. You must go with me to the Police Court; you must identify the body; I will pay high to keep names and details out of the papers."

"But where are you going, sir?"

He did not answer her directly. Then he said:

"Norah! I must go with you, and look on the face of the man whom I have so injured—unwittingly, it is true; but it seems to me as if I had killed him. I will lay his head in the grave, as if he were my only brother: and how he must have hated me! I cannot go home to my wife till all that I can do for him is done. Then I go with a dreadful secret on my mind. I shall never speak of it again, after these days are over. I know you will not, either." He shook hands with her: and they never named the subject again, the one to the other.

Norah went home to Alice the next day. Not a word was said on the cause of her abrupt departure a day or two before. Alice had been charged by her husband, in his letter, not to allude to the supposed theft of the brooch; so she, implicitly obedient to those whom she loved both by nature and habit, was entirely silent on the subject, only treated Norah with the most tender respect, as if to make up for unjust suspicion.

Nor did Alice inquire into the reason why Mr. Openshaw had been absent during his uncle and aunt's visit, after he had once said that it was unavoidable. He came back grave and quiet; and from that time forth was curiously changed. More thoughtful, and perhaps less active; quite as decided in conduct, but with new and different rules for the guidance of that conduct. Towards Alice he could hardly be more kind than he had always been; but he now seemed to look upon her as some one sacred, and to be treated with reverence, as well as tenderness. He throve in business, and made a large fortune, one half of which was settled upon her.

Long years after these events—a few months after her mother died—Ailsie and her "father" (as she always called Mr. Openshaw), drove to a cemetery a little way out of town, and she was carried to a certain mound by her maid, who was then sent back to the carriage. There was a headstone, with F.W. and a date upon it. That was all. Sitting by the grave, Mr. Openshaw told her the story; and for the sad fate of that poor father whom she had never seen, he shed the only tears she ever saw fall from his eyes.

—1858 (REVISED 1860)

Robert Browning

1812 – 1889

"The spirit of passionate and imaginative poetry is not dead among us," wrote an exultant R.H. Horne in 1844, while reviewing the poems of the young Robert Browning. But Browning, for all his passion and imagination, was not a popular poet for much of his lifetime. Indeed, until the 1860s, Browning was better known as the husband of Elizabeth Barrett. His own poetry, in the eyes of many of his contemporaries, was far too obscure, littered as it was with recondite historical and literary references and with dubious subject matter—husbands murdering their wives, artists frolicking with prostitutes. Fame did come, however, and scholars now credit Browning for having realized new possibilities in the dramatic monologue, a form of poetry that, like a monologue in a dramatic production, showcases the speech of a character to an implied or imaginary audience. The poems are, in Browning's own words, "so many utterances of so many imaginary persons, not mine." As Browning's dramatic monologues unfold, their speakers reveal levels of psychological complexity that have inspired generations of poets, from the Pre-Raphaelites who were coming of age in the 1840s to Modernists such as Ezra Pound and T.S. Eliot.

Browning was the eldest of two children born in an upper middle-class suburb of London to a scholarly father and a devout, Protestant mother, Sarah Anna Wiedemann. An opponent of slavery, Robert Browning, Sr. rejected employment on his family's plantation in St. Kitts in favor of less lucrative but more morally acceptable work as a clerk for the Bank of England. Both parents helped to shape Browning's religious, social, and intellectual tastes and values, with Browning, Sr. in particular feeding his son's voracious appetite for knowledge. The young Browning composed his first poem at the age of six. He attended Peckham School between the ages of ten and twelve and later some classes at University College in London. But the great majority of his schooling took place at home with tutors, and he spent many hours studying the books in his family's voluminous library.

Browning first arrived on the literary scene with the publication in 1833 of *Pauline: A Fragment of a Confession*, a long poem in the style of Shelley's *Alastor* (1816). John Stuart Mill credited *Pauline* with "considerable poetic powers" that yet revealed "a more intense and morbid self-consciousness than I ever knew in any sane human being." The volume, published with family funds, apparently sold not even a single copy. It was followed in 1835 by *Paracelsus*, which, though similarly obscure, at least made Browning known to a few important critics and ultimately brought him into contact with Carlyle, Dickens, and Wordsworth, among others. With *Sordello* (1840), Browning secured his reputation for writing poetry of bewildering difficulty. Browning claimed that his "stress [in *Sordello*] lay on the incidents in the development of a soul: little else is worth study," and yet few could make sense of such incidents as Browning had chosen to portray them.

In 1842 Browning published a volume of shorter poems, *Dramatic Lyrics*, which marked an important break from his earlier productions. Included were many of the poems on which his reputation came to be based: "My Last Duchess," "Soliloquy of the Spanish Cloister," "Johannes Agricola in Meditation," and "Porphyria's Lover," the last two of which had been published in the

Monthly Repository of 1836 under the heading "Madhouse Cells." With *Dramatic Romances and Lyrics* (1845) and *Men and Women* (1855), Browning confirmed his literary reputation as the foremost innovator of the dramatic monologue; he remained, however, little known among contemporary Victorians. *Men and Women* contained now-canonical poems such as "Fra Lippo Lippi" and "Andrea del Sarto." In Browning's volume, wrote George Eliot in the *Westminster Review*, the reader will find "no conventionality, no melodious commonplace, but freshness, originality, sometimes eccentricity of expression; no didactic laying-out of a subject, but dramatic indication, which requires the reader to trace by his own mental activity the underground stream of thought that jets out in elliptical and pithy verse." Eliot's commentary draws attention not only to Browning's unconventional subject matter and dramatic presentation, but also to the range of his accomplishment in poetic form, his lack of "melodious commonplace." Victorian critics noted with varying degrees of wonder and consternation the degree to which Browning experimented with rhythm and meter, an experimentation that in the early twentieth century earned him the nickname "Old Hippety-Hop o' the accents" from Ezra Pound.

In January of 1845 Browning began what became a celebrated correspondence with the already-famous poet Elizabeth Barrett. Even before meeting her personally (an event that took place after four months of writing), Browning praised Barrett's 1844 volume *Poems* with the words, "I do, as I say, love these books with all my heart—and I love you too." Barrett fell in love with Browning after meeting him, and in 1846, despite her chronic illness and her father's command never to marry, the two eloped in London and moved to Italy, where they remained for the rest of her life. Their only child, Robert Wiedemann Barrett Browning (nicknamed "Pen"), was born in 1849 in their Florence home, Casa Guidi.

Browning returned to London and society life after his wife's death in 1861. 1864 brought the publication of *Dramatis Personae*, the first of his volumes to be popular among British readers. This was followed in 1868–69 by his twelve-part epic "murder-poem" (as Browning called it), *The Ring and the Book*. Browning conceived the idea of writing this epic in 1860, when in a Florence market he chanced upon a book of documents concerning a 1698 murder trial. He organized the story so that each book in the epic gives voice to a different participant in the event: the murderer, various onlookers, the victim, and even the Pope. In juxtaposing these varying testimonies, Browning suggests the impossibility of ever finding a coherent or truthful narrative and the importance of recognizing the relativity of points of view—something enacted in his dramatic monologues. These "filthy rags of speech," says the Pope, are "tatters all too contaminate for use."

The 1879–80 volumes of *Dramatic Idyls* brought the poet even greater fame, both in England and internationally; the public in the United States flocked to buy his books, and wearing brown articles of clothing in his honor became fashionable. In 1889, on the day his final volume of poems, *Asolando*, was published, Robert Browning died at his son's home in Venice. He is buried next to Alfred, Lord Tennyson, in the Poets' Corner of Westminster Abbey.

⌘⌘⌘

Porphyria's Lover

The rain set early in tonight,
The sullen wind was soon awake,
It tore the elm tops down for spite,
And did its worst to vex the lake:
I listened with heart fit to break.
When glided in Porphyria; straight
She shut the cold out and the storm,
And kneeled and made the cheerless grate
Blaze up, and all the cottage warm;
Which done, she rose, and from her form
Withdrew the dripping cloak and shawl,
And laid her soiled gloves by, untied
Her hat and let the damp hair fall,
And, last, she sat down by my side
And called me. When no voice replied,
She put my arm about her waist,
And made her smooth white shoulder bare,
And all her yellow hair displaced,
And, stooping, made my cheek lie there,
And spread, o'er all, her yellow hair,
Murmuring how she loved me—she
Too weak, for all her heart's endeavour,
To set its struggling passion free
From pride, and vainer ties dissever,
And give herself to me forever.
But passion sometimes would prevail,
Nor could tonight's gay feast restrain
A sudden thought of one so pale
For love of her, and all in vain:
So, she was come through wind and rain.
Be sure I looked up at her eyes
Happy and proud; at last I knew
Porphyria worshipped me; surprise
Made my heart swell, and still it grew
While I debated what to do.
That moment she was mine, mine, fair,
Perfectly pure and good: I found
A thing to do, and all her hair
In one long yellow string I wound
Three times her little throat around,
And strangled her. No pain felt she;
I am quite sure she felt no pain.
As a shut bud that holds a bee,
I warily oped her lids: again
Laughed the blue eyes without a stain.
And I untightened next the tress
About her neck; her cheek once more
Blushed bright beneath my burning kiss:
I propped her head up as before,
Only, this time my shoulder bore
Her head, which droops upon it still:
The smiling rosy little head,
So glad it has its utmost will,
That all it scorned at once is fled,
And I, its love, am gained instead!
Porphyria's love: she guessed not how
Her darling one wish would be heard.
And thus we sit together now,
And all night long we have not stirred,
And yet God has not said a word!
—1836

Soliloquy of the Spanish Cloister

1

Gr-r-r—there go, my heart's abhorrence!
Water your damned flowerpots, do!
If hate killed men, Brother Lawrence,
God's blood, would not mine kill you!
What? your myrtle bush wants trimming?
Oh, that rose has prior claims—
Needs its leaden vase filled brimming?
Hell dry you up with its flames!

2

At the meal we sit together:
Salve tibi! [1] I must hear
Wise talk of the kind of weather,
Sort of season, time of year:
Not a plenteous cork crop: scarcely

[1] *Salve tibi* Hail to thee.

Dare we hope oak galls,[1] *I doubt:*
What's the Latin name for "parsley"?
What's the Greek name for Swine's Snout?[2]

3

Whew! We'll have our platter burnished,
Laid with care on our own shelf!
With a fire-new spoon we're furnished,
And a goblet for ourself,
Rinsed like something sacrificial
Ere 'tis fit to touch our chaps°— *jaws*
Marked with L. for our initial!
(He-he! There his lily snaps!)

4

Saint, forsooth! While brown Dolores
Squats outside the Convent bank
With Sanchicha, telling stories,
Steeping tresses in the tank,
Blue-black, lustrous, thick like horsehairs,
—Can't I see his dead eye glow,
Bright as 'twere a Barbary corsair's?[3]
(That is, if he'd let it show!)

5

When he finishes refection,° *a meal*
Knife and fork he never lays
Crosswise, to my recollection,
As do I, in Jesu's praise.
I the Trinity illustrate,
Drinking watered orange pulp—
In three sips the Arian[4] frustrate;
While he drains his at one gulp.

6

Oh, those melons? If he's able
We're to have a feast! so nice!
One goes to the Abbot's table,
All of us get each a slice.
How go on your flowers? None double?
Not one fruit-sort can you spy?
Strange!—And I, too, at such trouble,
Keep them close-nipped on the sly!

7

There's a great text in Galatians,
Once you trip on it, entails
Twenty-nine distinct damnations,[5]
One sure, if another fails:
If I trip him just a-dying,
Sure of heaven as sure can be,
Spin him round and send him flying
Off to hell, a Manichee?[6]

8

Or, my scrofulous° French novel *morally corrupt*
On grey paper with blunt type!
Simply glance at it, you grovel
Hand and foot in Belial's° gripe: *the devil's*
If I double down its pages
At the woeful sixteenth print,
When he gathers his greengages,° *plums*
Ope a sieve and slip it in't?

9

Or, there's Satan!—one might venture
Pledge one's soul to him, yet leave
Such a flaw in the indenture
As he'd miss till, past retrieve,
Blasted lay that rose acacia
We're so proud of! *Hy, Zy, Hine …*

---

[1] *oak galls* Growths on oak trees that are used to produce certain inks and tannins.

[2] *Swine's Snout* Dandelion.

[3] *Barbary corsair* Pirate of the Barbary Coast (former name of the Mediterranean coastal region of North Africa).

[4] *Arian* Follower of Arius (256–336), considered a heretic in his day for his disavowal of the notion (inherent in the concept of the Trinity) that Jesus Christ was of the same essence or substance as God.

[5] *Galatians … damnations* See Galatians 5.19–21 for a list of 17, not 29, sins.

[6] *Manichee* Heretic; follower of the Persian theologian Mani's third-century beliefs in dualism.

'St, there's Vespers![1] *Plena gratiâ*
Ave, Virgo![2] Gr-r-r—you swine!
—1842

My Last Duchess[3]

Ferrara

That's my last Duchess painted on the wall,
Looking as if she were alive. I call
That piece a wonder, now: Frà° Pandolf's hands *Brother*
Worked busily a day, and there she stands.
Will't please you sit and look at her? I said
"Frà Pandolf" by design, for never read
Strangers like you that pictured countenance,
The depth and passion of its earnest glance,
But to myself they turned (since none puts by
The curtain I have drawn for you, but I)
And seemed as they would ask me, if they durst,
How such a glance came there; so, not the first
Are you to turn and ask thus. Sir, 'twas not
Her husband's presence only, called that spot
Of joy into the Duchess' cheek: perhaps
Frà Pandolf chanced to say "Her mantle laps
Over my lady's wrist too much," or "Paint
Must never hope to reproduce the faint
Half-flush that dies along her throat": such stuff
Was courtesy, she thought, and cause enough
For calling up that spot of joy. She had
A heart—how shall I say?—too soon made glad,
Too easily impressed; she liked whate'er
She looked on, and her looks went everywhere.
Sir, 'twas all one! My favour° at her breast, *gift*
The dropping of the daylight in the West,
The bough of cherries some officious fool
Broke in the orchard for her, the white mule
She rode with round the terrace—all and each
Would draw from her alike the approving speech,
Or blush, at least. She thanked men—good! but
thanked
Somehow—I know not how—as if she ranked
My gift of a nine-hundred-years-old name
With anybody's gift. Who'd stoop to blame
This sort of trifling? Even had you skill
In speech—(which I have not)—to make your will
Quite clear to such an one, and say, "Just this
Or that in you disgusts me; here you miss,
Or there exceed the mark"—and if she let
Herself be lessoned so, nor plainly set
Her wits to yours, forsooth, and made excuse,
—E'en then would be some stooping; and I choose
Never to stoop. Oh sir, she smiled, no doubt,
Whene'er I passed her; but who passed without
Much the same smile? This grew; I gave commands;
Then all smiles stopped together. There she stands
As if alive. Will't please you rise? We'll meet
The company below, then. I repeat,
The Count your master's known munificence
Is ample warrant that no just pretence
Of mine for dowry will be disallowed;
Though his fair daughter's self, as I avowed
At starting, is my object. Nay, we'll go
Together down, sir. Notice Neptune,[4] though,
Taming a seahorse, thought a rarity,
Which Claus of Innsbruck cast in bronze for me!
—1842

[1] *Hy, Zy, Hine … Vespers* Sound of the bell that rings for Vespers, or evening prayers.

[2] *Plena … Virgo* Version of the Latin prayer "Ave Maria": "Full of grace / Hail, Virgin."

[3] *My Last Duchess* According to Louis S. Friedland, Browning likely modeled the speaker of this poem on Alfonso II (1533–98), Duke of Ferrara. His first wife, a member of the wealthy Medici family, was only fourteen years old when they married. Only three days after the wedding, Alfonso left his wife for two years, and she died of suspicious causes a year after he returned. Four years later the duke negotiated with a servant to marry the daughter of the Count of Tyrol.

[4] *Neptune* Roman god of the sea, who rides in a chariot pulled by seahorses.

Home-Thoughts, from Abroad

1

Oh, to be in England
Now that April's there,
And whoever wakes in England
Sees, some morning, unaware,
That the lowest boughs and the brushwood sheaf
Round the elm-tree bole° are in tiny leaf, *trunk*
While the chaffinch sings on the orchard bough
In England—now!

2

And after April, when May follows,
And the whitethroat builds, and all the swallows!
Hark, where my blossomed pear tree in the hedge
Leans to the field and scatters on the clover
Blossoms and dewdrops—at the bent spray's edge—
That's the wise thrush; he sings each song twice over,
Lest you should think he never could recapture
The first fine careless rapture!
And though the fields look rough with hoary dew
All will be gay when noontide wakes anew
The buttercups, the little children's dower—
Far brighter than this gaudy melon flower!

—1845

The Bishop Orders His Tomb at Saint Praxed's Church

Rome, 15—

Vanity, saith the preacher, vanity![1]
Draw round my bed: is Anselm keeping back?
Nephews—sons mine … ah God, I know not! Well—
She, men would have to be your mother once,
Old Gandolf envied me, so fair she was!
What's done is done, and she is dead beside,
Dead long ago, and I am Bishop since,
And as she died so must we die ourselves,
And thence ye may perceive the world's a dream.
Life, how and what is it? As here I lie
In this state-chamber, dying by degrees,
Hours and long hours in the dead night, I ask
"Do I live, am I dead?" Peace, peace seems all.
Saint Praxed's ever was the church for peace;
And so, about this tomb of mine. I fought
With tooth and nail to save my niche, ye know:
—Old Gandolf cozened me,° despite my care; *cheated*
Shrewd was that snatch from out the corner south
He graced his carrion with, God curse the same!
Yet still my niche is not so cramped but thence
One sees the pulpit o' the epistle side,[2]
And somewhat of the choir, those silent seats,
And up into the aery dome where live
The angels, and a sunbeam's sure to lurk:
And I shall fill my slab of basalt there,
And 'neath my tabernacle take my rest,
With those nine columns round me, two and two,
The odd one at my feet where Anselm stands:
Peach-blossom marble all, the rare, the ripe
As fresh-poured red wine of a mighty pulse.
—Old Gandolf with his paltry onion-stone,[3]
Put me where I may look at him! True peach,
Rosy and flawless: how I earned the prize!
Draw close: that conflagration of my church
—What then? So much was saved if aught were missed!
My sons, ye would not be my death? Go dig
The white-grape vineyard where the oil-press stood,
Drop water gently till the surface sink,
And if ye find … Ah God, I know not, I! …
Bedded in store of rotten fig leaves soft,
And corded up in a tight olive-frail,° *basket*
Some lump, ah God, of *lapis lazuli*,[4]
Big as a Jew's head cut off at the nape,
Blue as a vein o'er the Madonna's breast …

[1] *Vanity, saith the preacher, vanity* From Ecclesiastes 1.2: "Vanity of vanities, saith the Preacher, vanity of vanities; all is vanity."

[2] *epistle side* Right-hand side, where the pulpit is and from which the epistles are read.

[3] *onion-stone* Variety of less expensive marble that is named for its tendency to peel into layers.

[4] *lapis lazuli* Semi-precious blue stone; the altar-tomb of St. Ignatius at Il Gesù (Church of the Holy Name of Jesus) in Rome is decorated with huge columns made from lapis lazuli.

Sons, all have I bequeathed you, villas, all,
That brave Frascati[1] villa with its bath,
So, let the blue lump poise between my knees,
Like God the Father's globe on both his hands
Ye worship in the Jesu Church[2] so gay,
For Gandolf shall not choose but see and burst!
Swift as a weaver's shuttle fleet our years:[3]
Man goeth to the grave, and where is he?[4]
Did I say basalt for my slab, sons? Black—
'Twas ever antique-black° I meant! How else *black marble*
Shall ye contrast my frieze[5] to come beneath?
The bas-relief in bronze ye promised me,
Those Pans and Nymphs[6] ye wot of, and perchance
Some tripod, thyrsus,[7] with a vase or so,
The Saviour at his sermon on the mount,
Saint Praxed[8] in a glory,° and one Pan[9] *halo, lightbeam*
Ready to twitch the Nymph's last garment off,
And Moses with the tables[10] … but I know
Ye mark me not! What do they whisper thee,
Child of my bowels, Anselm? Ah, ye hope
To revel down my villas while I gasp
Bricked o'er with beggar's mouldy travertine° *limestone*
Which Gandolf from his tomb top chuckles at!
Nay, boys, ye love me—all of jasper,° then! *precious stone*
'Tis jasper ye stand pledged to, lest I grieve
My bath must needs be left behind, alas!
One block, pure green as a pistachio nut,
There's plenty jasper somewhere in the world—
And have I not Saint Praxed's ear to pray
Horses for ye, and brown Greek manuscripts,
And mistresses with great smooth marbly limbs?
—That's if ye carve my epitaph aright,
Choice Latin, picked phrase, Tully's[11] every word,
No gaudy ware like Gandolf's second line—
Tully, my masters? Ulpian[12] serves his need!
And then how I shall lie through centuries,
And hear the blessed mutter of the mass,
And see God made and eaten all day long,
And feel the steady candle flame, and taste
Good strong thick stupefying incense smoke!
For as I lie here, hours of the dead night,
Dying in state and by such slow degrees,
I fold my arms as if they clasped a crook,° *bishop's staff*
And stretch my feet forth straight as stone can point,
And let the bedclothes, for a mortcloth,[13] drop
Into great laps and folds of sculptor's work:
And as yon tapers dwindle, and strange thoughts
Grow, with a certain humming in my ears,
About the life before I lived this life,
And this life too, popes, cardinals and priests,
Saint Praxed at his sermon on the mount,
Your tall pale mother with her talking eyes,
And newfound agate urns as fresh as day,
And marble's language, Latin pure, discreet,
—Aha, *ELUCESCEBAT*[14] quoth our friend?
No Tully, said I, Ulpian at the best!
Evil and brief hath been my pilgrimage.[15]
All *lapis*, all, sons! Else I give the Pope

[1] *Frascati* Summer resort near Rome.

[2] *Jesu Church* Il Gesù.

[3] *Swift … years* From Job 7.6: "My days are swifter than a weaver's shuttle, and are spent without hope"; *shuttle* Weaver's instrument used to pass the yarn across the loom.

[4] *Man goeth … where is he?* From Job 7.9: "As the cloud is consumed and vanisheth away: so he that goeth down to the grave shall come up no more."

[5] *frieze* Painted or sculpted band on a wall or column.

[6] *bas-relief … Pans and Nymphs* Shallow carvings that depict Greek mythological figures alongside Biblical figures.

[7] *tripod* Vessel on which sat the Oracle at Delphi, where she delivered her prophecies; *thyrsus* Staff adorned with a pine cone and ivy, carried by Dionysus, the Greek god of wine, and his followers.

[8] *Saint Praxed* Roman virgin of the second century who gave away all of her wealth to the poor.

[9] *Pan* Greek shepherd god of nature, who chased the nymph Syrinx until she turned herself into a bed of reeds.

[10] *tables* Tablets with the Ten Commandments inscribed upon them.

[11] *Tully* Commonly known as Cicero, Roman orator, philosopher, and political figure of the first century BCE.

[12] *Ulpian* Roman jurist (?–228 CE), whose writings were acknowledged to be of a lower standard than Cicero's.

[13] *mortcloth* Funeral cloth draped over the dead.

[14] *ELUCESCEBAT* Latin: He was illustrious. *Elucescebat* is a later Latin verb form; Cicero would have written *elucebat*.

[15] *Evil … pilgrimage* Cf. Genesis 47.9: "Jacob said unto Pharaoh … few and evil have the days of the years of my life been, and have not attained unto the days of the years of the life of my fathers in the days of their pilgrimage."

My villas! Will ye ever eat my heart?
Ever your eyes were as a lizard's quick,
They glitter like your mother's for my soul,
Or ye would heighten my impoverished frieze,
Piece out its starved design, and fill my vase
With grapes, and add a vizor and a Term,[1]
And to the tripod ye would tie a lynx
That in his struggle throws the thyrsus down,
To comfort me on my entablature° *column*
Whereon I am to lie till I must ask
"Do I live, am I dead?" There, leave me, there!
For ye have stabbed me with ingratitude
To death—ye wish it—God, ye wish it! Stone—
Gritstone, a-crumble! Clammy squares which sweat
As if the corpse they keep were oozing through—
And no more lapis to delight the world!
Well go! I bless ye. Fewer tapers° there, *candles*
But in a row: and, going, turn your backs
—Ay, like departing altar ministrants,
And leave me in my church, the church for peace,
That I may watch at leisure if he leers—
Old Gandolf, at me, from his onion-stone,
As still he envied me, so fair she was!
—1845

Long Among the Ruins

1

Where the quiet-coloured end of evening smiles,
  Miles and miles
On the solitary pastures where our sheep
  Half-asleep
Tinkle homeward thro' the twilight, stray or stop
  As they crop—
Was the site once of a city great and gay,
  (So they say)
Of our country's very capital, its prince
  Ages since
Held his court in, gathered councils, wielding far
  Peace or war.

[1] *vizor* Helmet piece represented in Roman sculpture; *Term* Statue of Terminus, Roman god of boundaries.

2

Now—the country does not even boast a tree,
  As you see,
To distinguish slopes of verdure, certain rills° *brooks*
  From the hills
Intersect and give a name to, (else they run
  Into one)
Where the domed and daring palace shot its spires
  Up like fires
O'er the hundred-gated circuit of a wall
  Bounding all
Made of marble, men might march on nor be pressed,[2]
  Twelve abreast.

3

And such plenty and perfection, see, of grass
  Never was!
Such a carpet as, this summer-time, o'erspreads
  And embeds
Every vestige of the city, guessed alone,
  Stock° or stone— *stump*
Where a multitude of men breathed joy and woe
  Long ago;
Lust of glory pricked their hearts up, dread of shame
  Struck them tame;
And that glory and that shame alike, the gold
  Bought and sold.

4

Now—the single little turret that remains
  On the plains,
By the caper overrooted, by the gourd[3]
  Overscored,
While the patching houseleek's[4] head of blossom winks
  Through the chinks—

[2] *nor be pressed* Without being pressed close together.

[3] *caper* Flowering Mediterranean plant that grows on walls and in other rocky, inhospitable locations; *gourd* Family of climbing or trailing plants that includes pumpkins and squashes.

[4] *houseleek* Hardy flowering succulent suited to dry and rocky climates. Common houseleeks were traditionally planted on roofs, where they were thought to exert protective properties against lightning, decay, and evil magic.

Marks the basement whence a tower in ancient time
    Sprang sublime,
And a burning ring, all round, the chariots traced
    As they raced,
And the monarch and his minions and his dames
    Viewed the games.

5

And I know, while thus the quiet-coloured eve
    Smiles to leave
To their folding,[1] all our many-tinkling fleece° *sheep*
    In such peace,
And the slopes and rills in undistinguished grey
    Melt away—
That a girl with eager eyes and yellow hair
    Waits me there
In the turret whence the charioteers caught soul
    For the goal,
When the king looked, where she looks now, breathless, dumb
    Till I come.

6

But he looked upon the city, every side,
    Far and wide,
All the mountains topped with temples, all the glades'
    Colonnades,
All the causeys,° bridges, aqueducts—and then, *raised roads*
    All the men!
When I do come, she will speak not, she will stand,
    Either hand
On my shoulder, give her eyes the first embrace
    Of my face,
Ere we rush, ere we extinguish sight and speech
    Each on each.

7

In one year they sent a million fighters forth
    South and North,
And they built their gods a brazen pillar[2] high
    As the sky
Yet reserved a thousand chariots in full force—
    Gold, of course.
O heart! oh blood that freezes, blood that burns!
    Earth's returns
For whole centuries of folly, noise and sin!
    Shut them in,
With their triumphs and their glories and the rest!
    Love is best.

—1855, REVISED 1863

[1] *their folding* I.e., their return to the sheepfold.

"Childe Roland to the Dark Tower Came"

(*See Edgar's song in* Lear[3])

I

My first thought was, he lied in every word,
    That hoary° cripple, with malicious eye *wizened*
    Askance to watch the working of his lie
On mine, and mouth scarce able to afford
Suppression of the glee, that pursed and scored
    Its edge, at one more victim gained thereby.

2

What else should he be set for, with his staff?
    What, save to waylay with his lies, ensnare
    All travellers who might find him posted there,
And ask the road? I guessed what skull-like laugh
Would break, what crutch 'gin° write my epitaph *begin*
    For pastime in the dusty thoroughfare,

[2] *brazen pillar* Brass pillar. See 1 Kings 7.15, in which Solomon, who is overseeing the construction of a magnificent temple, has "two pillars of brass" cast for the building. Browning's line may also reference the Tower of Babel: in Genesis 11.1–9, the people of the earth share one language, and they attempt to build a tower to reach to heaven. When God sees the tower, he scatters the people and diversifies their languages so that they cannot work together to accomplish such ambitious projects.

[3] *Edgar ... Lear* From Shakespeare's *King Lear* 3.4.130–32, in which the character Edgar, disguised as the beggar Poor Tom, sings about the French hero Rowland, nephew of Charlemagne: "Child Rowland to the dark tower came, / His word was still, Fie, foh, and fum, / I smell the blood of a British man." "Childe" refers to a youth born of noble stock, who would usually become a candidate for knighthood.

3

If at his counsel I should turn aside
Into that ominous tract which, all agree,
Hides the Dark Tower. Yet acquiescingly
I did turn as he pointed: neither pride
Nor hope rekindling at the end descried,
So much as gladness that some end might be.

4

For, what with my whole world-wide wandering,
What with my search drawn out thro' years, my hope
Dwindled into a ghost not fit to cope
With that obstreperous joy success would bring—
I hardly tried now to rebuke the spring
My heart made, finding failure in its scope.

5

As when a sick man very near to death
Seems dead indeed, and feels begin and end
The tears and takes the farewell of each friend,
And hears one bid the other go, draw breath
Freelier outside ("since all is o'er," he saith,
"And the blow fallen no grieving can amend");

6

While some discuss if near the other graves
Be room enough for this, and when a day
Suits best for carrying the corpse away,
With care about the banners, scarves and staves:
And still the man hears all, and only craves
He may not shame such tender love and stay.

7

Thus, I had so long suffered in this quest,
Heard failure prophesied so oft, been writ
So many times among "The Band"—to wit,
The knights who to the Dark Tower's search addressed
Their steps—that just to fail as they, seemed best,
And all the doubt was now—should I be fit?

8

So, quiet as despair, I turned from him,
That hateful cripple, out of his highway
Into the path he pointed. All the day
Had been a dreary one at best, and dim
Was settling to its close, yet shot one grim
Red leer to see the plain catch its estray.° *stray animal*

9

For mark! no sooner was I fairly found
Pledged to the plain, after a pace or two,
Than, pausing to throw backward a last view
O'er the safe road, 'twas gone; grey plain all round:
Nothing but plain to the horizon's bound.
I might go on; nought else remained to do.

10

So, on I went. I think I never saw
Such starved ignoble nature; nothing throve:
For flowers—as well expect a cedar grove!
But cockle, spurge,[1] according to their law
Might propagate their kind, with none to awe,
You'd think; a burr had been a treasure trove.

11

No! penury, inertness and grimace,
In some strange sort, were the land's portion. "See
Or shut your eyes," said Nature peevishly,
"It nothing skills: I cannot help my case:
'Tis the Last Judgment's fire must cure this place,
Calcine° its clods and set my prisoners free." *burn completely*

12

If there pushed any ragged thistle-stalk
Above its mates, the head was chopped; the bents° *reed-like grasses*
Were jealous else. What made those holes and rents
In the dock's° harsh swarth leaves, bruised as to baulk *weed's*
All hope of greenness? 'tis a brute must walk
Pashing° their life out, with a brute's intents. *smashing*

[1] *cockle, spurge* Types of weeds.

13

As for the grass, it grew as scant as hair
In leprosy; thin dry blades pricked the mud
Which underneath looked kneaded up with blood.
One stiff blind horse, his every bone a-stare,
Stood stupefied, however he came there:
Thrust out past service from the devil's stud!

14

Alive? he might be dead for aught I know,
With that red gaunt and colloped[1] neck a-strain,
And shut eyes underneath the rusty mane;
Seldom went such grotesqueness with such woe;
I never saw a brute I hated so;
He must be wicked to deserve such pain.

15

I shut my eyes and turned them on my heart.
As a man calls for wine before he fights,
I asked one draught of earlier, happier sights,
Ere fitly I could hope to play my part.
Think first, fight afterwards—the soldier's art:
One taste of the old time sets all to rights.

16

Not it! I fancied Cuthbert's reddening face
Beneath its garniture of curly gold,
Dear fellow, till I almost felt him fold
An arm in mine to fix me to the place,
That way he used. Alas, one night's disgrace!
Out went my heart's new fire and left it cold.

17

Giles then, the soul of honour—there he stands
Frank as ten years ago when knighted first.
What honest man should dare (he said) he durst.
Good—but the scene shifts—faugh! what hangman hands
Pin to his breast a parchment? His own bands
Read it. Poor traitor, spit upon and curst!

18

Better this present than a past like that;
Back therefore to my darkening path again!
No sound, no sight as far as eye could strain.
Will the night send a howlet° or a bat? *owl*
I asked: when something on the dismal flat
Came to arrest my thoughts and change their train.

19

A sudden little river crossed my path
As unexpected as a serpent comes.
No sluggish tide congenial to the glooms;
This, as it frothed by, might have been a bath
For the fiend's glowing hoof—to see the wrath
Of its black eddy bespate° with flakes and spumes. *flooded*

20

So petty yet so spiteful! All along,
Low scrubby alders kneeled down over it;
Drenched willows flung them headlong in a fit
Of mute despair, a suicidal throng:
The river which had done them all the wrong,
Whate'er that was, rolled by, deterred no whit.

21

Which, while I forded—good saints, how I feared
To set my foot upon a dead man's cheek,
Each step, or feel the spear I thrust to seek
For hollows, tangled in his hair or beard!
—It may have been a water-rat I speared,
But, ugh! it sounded like a baby's shriek.

22

Glad was I when I reached the other bank.
Now for a better country. Vain presage!
Who were the strugglers, what war did they wage,
Whose savage trample thus could pad the dank
Soil to a plash?° Toads in a poisoned tank, *pool*
Or wild cats in a red-hot iron cage—

[1] *colloped* Having folds of fat.

23

The fight must so have seemed in that fell cirque.[1]
What penned them there, with all the plain to
choose?
No footprint leading to that horrid mews,
None out of it. Mad brewage set to work
Their brains, no doubt, like galley slaves the Turk
Pits for his pastime, Christians against Jews.

24

And more than that—a furlong on—why, there!
What bad use was that engine for, that wheel,
Or brake, not wheel—that harrow fit to reel
Men's bodies out like silk? with all the air
Of Tophet's° tool, on earth left unaware, *hell's*
Or brought to sharpen its rusty teeth of steel.

25

Then came a bit of stubbed ground, once a wood,
Next a marsh, it would seem, and now mere earth
Desperate and done with; (so a fool finds mirth,
Makes a thing and then mars it, till his mood
Changes and off he goes!) within a rood°— *quarter acre*
Bog, clay and rubble, sand and stark black dearth.

26

Now blotches rankling, coloured gay and grim,
Now patches where some leanness of the soil's
Broke into moss or substances like boils;
Then came some palsied oak, a cleft in him
Like a distorted mouth that splits its rim
Gaping at death, and dies while it recoils.

27

And just as far as ever from the end!
Nought in the distance but the evening, nought
To point my footstep further! At the thought,
A great black bird, Apollyon's[2] bosom-friend,
Sailed past, nor beat his wide wing dragon-
penned° *winged*
That brushed my cap—perchance the guide I sought.

28

For, looking up, aware I somehow grew,
'Spite of the dusk, the plain had given place
All round to mountains—with such name to grace
Mere ugly heights and heaps now stolen in view.
How thus they had surprised me,—solve it, you!
How to get from them was no clearer case.

29

Yet half I seemed to recognize some trick
Of mischief happened to me, God knows when—
In a bad dream perhaps. Here ended, then,
Progress this way. When, in the very nick
Of giving up, one time more, came a click
As when a trap shuts—you're inside the den!

30

Burningly it came on me all at once,
This was the place! those two hills on the right,
Crouched like two bulls locked horn in horn in
fight;
While to the left, a tall scalped mountain ... Dunce,
Dotard, a-dozing at the very nonce,° *moment*
After a life spent training for the sight!

31

What in the midst lay but the Tower itself?
The round squat turret, blind as the fool's heart,
Built of brown stone, without a counterpart
In the whole world. The tempest's mocking elf
Points to the shipman° thus the unseen shelf *sailor*
He strikes on, only when the timbers start.

32

Not see? because of night perhaps?—why, day
Came back again for that! before it left,
The dying sunset kindled through a cleft:
The hills, like giants at a hunting, lay,
Chin upon hand, to see the game at bay,—
"Now stab and end the creature—to the
heft!"° *sword handle*

---

[1] *fell cirque* Dreadful arena.

[2] *Apollyon* Devil, or winged "angel of the bottomless pit," in Revelations 9.11.

33

Not hear? when noise was everywhere! it tolled
Increasing like a bell. Names in my ears
Of all the lost adventurers my peers—
How such a one was strong, and such was bold,
And such was fortunate, yet each of old
Lost, lost! one moment knelled the woe of years.

34

There they stood, ranged along the hillsides, met
To view the last of me, a living frame
For one more picture! in a sheet of flame
I saw them and I knew them all. And yet
Dauntless the slug-horn° to my lips I set, *trumpet*
And blew. "*Childe Roland to the Dark Tower came.*"
—1855

Fra Lippo Lippi[1]

I am poor brother Lippo, by your leave!
You need not clap your torches to my face.
Zooks,[2] what's to blame? you think you see a monk!
What, 'tis past midnight, and you go the rounds,
And here you catch me at an alley's end
Where sportive ladies leave their doors ajar?
The Carmine's[3] my cloister: hunt it up,
Do—harry out, if you must show your zeal,
Whatever rat, there, haps on his wrong hole,
And nip each softling of a wee white mouse,
Weke, weke, that's crept to keep him company!
Aha, you know your betters! Then, you'll take
Your hand away that's fiddling on my throat,
And please to know me likewise. Who am I?
Why, one, sir, who is lodging with a friend
Three streets off—he's a certain ... how d'ye call?
Master—a ... Cosimo of the Medici,[4]
I' the house that caps the corner. Boh! you were best!
Remember and tell me, the day you're hanged,
How you affected such a gullet's-gripe!° *stranglehold*
But you, sir, it concerns you that your knaves
Pick up a manner nor discredit you:
Zooks, are we pilchards,[5] that they sweep the streets
And count fair prize what comes into their net?
He's Judas to a tittle,[6] that man is!
Just such a face! Why, sir, you make amends.
Lord, I'm not angry! Bid your hangdogs go
Drink out this quarter-florin[7] to the health
Of the munificent House that harbours me
(And many more beside, lads! more beside!)
And all's come square again. I'd like his face—
His, elbowing on his comrade in the door
With the pike and lantern—for the slave that holds
John Baptist's head a-dangle by the hair
With one hand ("Look you, now," as who should say)
And his weapon in the other, yet unwiped!
It's not your chance to have a bit of chalk,
A wood-coal or the like? or you should see!
Yes, I'm the painter, since you style me so.
What, brother Lippo's doings, up and down,
You know them and they take you? like enough!
I saw the proper twinkle in your eye—
'Tell you, I liked your looks at very first.
Let's sit and set things straight now, hip to haunch.
Here's spring come, and the nights one makes up bands
To roam the town and sing out carnival,[8]
And I've been three weeks shut within my
mew,° *confined space*
A-painting for the great man, saints and saints
And saints again. I could not paint all night—
Ouf! I leaned out of window for fresh air.
There came a hurry of feet and little feet,

[1] *Fra Lippo Lippi* Browning extracted details of the life of Florentine painter and Carmelite monk Fra (Brother) Filippo Lippi (1406–69) from Giorgio Vasari's *The Lives of the Painters* (1550); the art theory Lippi propounds, however, is envisioned by Browning.

[2] *Zooks* Exclamation of surprise.

[3] *Carmine* Lippi was raised an orphan and eventually took his vows in Santa Maria del Carmine, a Carmelite monastery.

[4] *Cosimo of the Medici* The wealthy Medici family, headed up by Lippi's patron, Cosimo dé Medici (1389–1464), ruled Florence for many years.

[5] *pilchards* Herring-like fish.

[6] *to a tittle* Exactly (a "tittle" is a letter stroke or punctuation mark).

[7] *florin* Florentine currency.

[8] *carnival* Celebrations before Lent.

A sweep of lute strings, laughs, and whifts of song—
Flower o' the broom,
Take away love, and our earth is a tomb![1]
Flower o' the quince,
I let Lisa go, and what good in life since?
Flower o' the thyme—and so on. Round they went.
Scarce had they turned the corner when a titter
Like the skipping of rabbits by moonlight—three slim
    shapes,
And a face that looked up … zooks, sir, flesh and blood,
That's all I'm made of! Into shreds it went,
Curtain and counterpane and coverlet,
All the bed furniture—a dozen knots,
There was a ladder! Down I let myself,
Hands and feet, scrambling somehow, and so dropped,
And after them. I came up with the fun
Hard by Saint Laurence,[2] hail fellow, well met—
Flower o' the rose,
If I've been merry, what matter who knows?
And so as I was stealing back again
To get to bed and have a bit of sleep
Ere I rise up tomorrow and go work
On Jerome[3] knocking at his poor old breast
With his great round stone to subdue the flesh,
You snap me of the sudden. Ah, I see!
Though your eye twinkles still, you shake your head—
Mine's shaved—a monk, you say—the sting's in that!
If Master Cosimo announced himself,
Mum's the word naturally; but a monk!
Come, what am I a beast for? tell us, now!
I was a baby when my mother died
And father died and left me in the street.
I starved there, God knows how, a year or two
On fig skins, melon parings, rinds and shucks,
Refuse and rubbish. One fine frosty day,
My stomach being empty as your hat,
The wind doubled me up and down I went.
Old Aunt Lapaccia trussed me with one hand,
(Its fellow was a stinger as I knew)
And so along the wall, over the bridge,
By the straight cut to the convent. Six words there,
While I stood munching my first bread that month:
"So, boy, you're minded," quoth the good fat father
Wiping his own mouth, 'twas refection°-time— *meal*
"To quit this very miserable world?
Will you renounce" … "the mouthful of bread?"
    thought I;
By no means! Brief, they made a monk of me;
I did renounce the world, its pride and greed,
Palace, farm, villa, shop and banking-house,
Trash, such as these poor devils of Medici
Have given their hearts to—all at eight years old.
Well, sir, I found in time, you may be sure,
'Twas not for nothing—the good bellyful,
The warm serge and the rope that goes all round,[4]
And day-long blessed idleness beside!
"Let's see what the urchin's fit for"—that came next.
Not overmuch their way, I must confess.
Such a to-do! They tried me with their books:
Lord, they'd have taught me Latin in pure waste!
Flower o' the clove,
All the Latin I construe is, "amo," I love!
But, mind you, when a boy starves in the streets
Eight years together, as my fortune was,
Watching folk's faces to know who will fling
The bit of half-stripped grape bunch he desires,
And who will curse or kick him for his pains—
Which gentleman processional and fine,
Holding a candle to the Sacrament,
Will wink and let him lift a plate and catch
The droppings of the wax to sell again,
Or holla for the Eight[5] and have him whipped—
How say I?—nay, which dog bites, which lets drop
His bone from the heap of offal in the street—
Why, soul and sense of him grow sharp alike,
He learns the look of things, and none the less
For admonition from the hunger pinch.
I had a store of such remarks, be sure,

[1] *Flower … tomb* This song takes the form of a *stornelli*, a three-line Italian folk song about a flower.

[2] *Saint Laurence* Church of San Lorenzo in Florence.

[3] *Jerome* The ascetic St. Jerome, who lived many years as a hermit in the Syrian desert.

[4] *rope … round* I.e., rope belt.

[5] *Eight* The eight magistrates who governed Florence.

Which, after I found leisure, turned to use.
I drew men's faces on my copy books,
Scrawled them within the antiphonary's marge,[1]
Joined legs and arms to the long music notes,
Found eyes and nose and chin for A's and B's,
And made a string of pictures of the world
Betwixt the ins and outs of verb and noun,
On the wall, the bench, the door. The monks looked black.
"Nay," quoth the Prior, "turn him out, d'ye say?
In no wise. Lose a crow and catch a lark.
What if at last we get our man of parts,[2]
We Carmelites, like those Camaldolese
And Preaching Friars,[3] to do our church up fine
And put the front on it that ought to be!"
And hereupon he bade me daub away.
Thank you! my head being crammed, the walls a blank,
Never was such prompt disemburdening.
First, every sort of monk, the black and white,
I drew them, fat and lean: then, folk at church,
From good old gossips waiting to confess
Their cribs° of barrel droppings, candle ends— *pilferings*
To the breathless fellow at the altar foot,
Fresh from his murder, safe[4] and sitting there
With the little children round him in a row
Of admiration, half for his beard and half
For that white anger of his victim's son
Shaking a fist at him with one fierce arm,
Signing himself[5] with the other because of Christ
(Whose sad face on the cross sees only this
After the passion of a thousand years)
Till some poor girl, her apron o'er her head,
(Which the intense eyes looked through) came at eve
On tiptoe, said a word, dropped in a loaf,
Her pair of earrings and a bunch of flowers
(The brute took growling), prayed, and so was gone.
I painted all, then cried "'Tis ask and have;
Choose, for more's ready!"—laid the ladder flat,
And showed my covered bit of cloister wall.
The monks closed in a circle and praised loud
Till checked, taught what to see and not to see,
Being simple bodies—"That's the very man!
Look at the boy who stoops to pat the dog!
That woman's like the Prior's niece who comes
To care about his asthma: it's the life!"
But there my triumph's straw-fire flared and funked;° *smoked*
Their betters took their turn to see and say:
The Prior and the learned pulled a face
And stopped all that in no time. "How? what's here?
Quite from the mark of painting, bless us all!
Faces, arms, legs and bodies like the true
As much as pea and pea! it's devil's game!
Your business is not to catch men with show,
With homage to the perishable clay,
But lift them over it, ignore it all,
Make them forget there's such a thing as flesh.
Your business is to paint the souls of men—
Man's soul, and it's a fire, smoke ... no, it's not ...
It's vapour done up like a newborn babe—
(In that shape when you die it leaves your mouth)
It's ... well, what matters talking, it's the soul!
Give us no more of body than shows soul!
Here's Giotto,[6] with his Saint a-praising God,
That sets us praising—why not stop with him?
Why put all thoughts of praise out of our head
With wonder at lines, colours, and what not?
Paint the soul, never mind the legs and arms!
Rub all out, try at it a second time.
Oh, that white smallish female with the breasts,
She's just my niece ... Herodias, I would say—
Who went and danced and got men's heads cut off![7]
Have it all out!" Now, is this sense, I ask?
A fine way to paint soul, by painting body

[1] *antiphonary's marge* Margin of a book of choral—or antiphonal—music, normally sung in harmony by two choirs.

[2] *man of parts* Man of intellect, ability.

[3] *Preaching Friars* Dominican monks.

[4] *fellow ... safe* Safe from prosecution within the church.

[5] *Signing himself* Making the sign of the cross.

[6] *Giotto* Renowned Florentine artist (1267–1337), whose works consist mainly of religious paintings and frescoes.

[7] *Herodias ... heads cut off* According to Matthew 14.6–10, King Herod's niece Salomé (the daughter of his sister Herodias) danced for the king and then requested that he bring her the head of John the Baptist, now the patron saint of Florence.

So ill, the eye can't stop there, must go further
And can't fare worse! Thus, yellow does for white
When what you put for yellow's simply black,
And any sort of meaning looks intense
When all beside itself means and looks nought.
Why can't a painter lift each foot in turn,
Left foot and right foot, go a double step,
Make his flesh liker and his soul more like,
Both in their order? Take the prettiest face,
The Prior's niece ... patron saint—is it so pretty
You can't discover if it means hope, fear,
Sorrow or joy? won't beauty go with these?
Suppose I've made her eyes all right and blue,
Can't I take breath and try to add life's flash,
And then add soul and heighten them threefold?
Or say there's beauty with no soul at all—
(I never saw it—put the case the same—)
If you get simple beauty and nought else,
You get about the best thing God invents:
That's somewhat: and you'll find the soul you have missed,
Within yourself, when you return him thanks.
"Rub all out!" Well, well, there's my life, in short,
And so the thing has gone on ever since.
I'm grown a man no doubt, I've broken bounds:
You should not take a fellow eight years old
And make him swear to never kiss the girls.
I'm my own master, paint now as I please—
Having a friend, you see, in the Corner-house!
Lord, it's fast holding by the rings in front—
Those great rings serve more purposes than just
To plant a flag in, or tie up a horse!
And yet the old schooling sticks, the old grave eyes
Are peeping o'er my shoulder as I work,
The heads shake still—"It's art's decline, my son!
You're not of the true painters, great and old;
Brother Angelico's the man, you'll find;
Brother Lorenzo[1] stands his single peer:
Fag on at flesh, you'll never make the third!"
Flower o' the pine,
You keep your mistr ... manners, and I'll stick to mine!
I'm not the third, then: bless us, they must know!
Don't you think they're the likeliest to know,
They with their Latin? So, I swallow my rage,
Clench my teeth, suck my lips in tight, and paint
To please them—sometimes do and sometimes don't;
For, doing most, there's pretty sure to come
A turn, some warm eve finds me at my saints—
A laugh, a cry, the business of the world—
(*Flower o' the peach,*
Death for us all, and his own life for each!)
And my whole soul revolves, the cup runs over,
The world and life's too big to pass for a dream,
And I do these wild things in sheer despite,
And play the fooleries you catch me at,
In pure rage! The old mill-horse, out at grass
After hard years, throws up his stiff heels so,
Although the miller does not preach to him
The only good of grass is to make chaff.
What would men have? Do they like grass or no—
May they or mayn't they? all I want's the thing
Settled forever one way. As it is,
You tell too many lies and hurt yourself:
You don't like what you only like too much,
You do like what, if given you at your word,
You find abundantly detestable.
For me, I think I speak as I was taught;
I always see the garden and God there
A-making man's wife: and, my lesson learned,
The value and significance of flesh,
I can't unlearn ten minutes afterwards.

You understand me: I'm a beast, I know.
But see, now—why, I see as certainly
As that the morning star's about to shine,
What will hap some day. We've a youngster here
Comes to our convent, studies what I do,
Slouches and stares and lets no atom drop:
His name is Guidi[2]—he'll not mind the monks—
They call him Hulking Tom, he lets them talk—

[1] *Brother Angelico ... Brother Lorenzo* Italian Renaissance artists who painted in the early 1400s in the conventional style, as opposed to Lippi's naturalist style.

[2] *Guidi* Tommaso Guidi (1401–28), who became known as Masaccio, was highly skilled at creating naturalistic portrayals of human figures; he was likely Lippi's teacher, not his student.

He picks my practice up—he'll paint apace,
I hope so—though I never live so long,
I know what's sure to follow. You be judge!
You speak no Latin more than I, belike;
However, you're my man, you've seen the world
—The beauty and the wonder and the power,
The shapes of things, their colours, lights and shades,
Changes, surprises—and God made it all!
—For what? Do you feel thankful, ay or no,
For this fair town's face, yonder river's line,
The mountain round it and the sky above,
Much more the figures of man, woman, child,
These are the frame to? What's it all about?
To be passed over, despised? or dwelt upon,
Wondered at? oh, this last of course!—you say.
But why not do as well as say—paint these
Just as they are, careless what comes of it?
God's works—paint anyone, and count it crime
To let a truth slip. Don't object, "His works
Are here already; nature is complete:
Suppose you reproduce her—(which you can't)
There's no advantage! you must beat her, then."
For, don't you mark? we're made so that we love
First when we see them painted, things we have passed
Perhaps a hundred times nor cared to see;
And so they are better, painted—better to us,
Which is the same thing. Art was given for that;
God uses us to help each other so,
Lending our minds out. Have you noticed, now,
Your cullion's° hanging face? A bit of chalk, *scoundrel's*
And trust me but you should, though! How much more,
If I drew higher things with the same truth!
That were to take the Prior's pulpit place,
Interpret God to all of you! Oh, oh,
It makes me mad to see what men shall do
And we in our graves! This world's no blot for us,
Nor blank; it means intensely, and means good:
To find its meaning is my meat and drink.
"Ay, but you don't so instigate to prayer!"
Strikes in the Prior: "when your meaning's plain
It does not say to folk—remember matins,[1]
Or, mind you fast next Friday!" Why, for this
What need of art at all? A skull and bones,
Two bits of stick nailed crosswise, or, what's best,
A bell to chime the hour with, does as well.
I painted a Saint Laurence[2] six months since
At Prato,[3] splashed the fresco in fine style:
"How looks my painting, now the scaffold's down?"
I ask a brother: "Hugely," he returns—
"Already not one phiz° of your three slaves *face*
Who turn the Deacon off his toasted side,
But's scratched and prodded to our heart's content,
The pious people have so eased their own
With coming to say prayers there in a rage:
We get on fast to see the bricks beneath.
Expect another job this time next year,
For pity and religion grow i' the crowd—
Your painting serves its purpose!" Hang the fools!

—That is—you'll not mistake an idle word
Spoke in a huff by a poor monk, God wot,
Tasting the air this spicy night which turns
The unaccustomed head like Chianti wine!
Oh, the church knows! don't misreport me, now!
It's natural a poor monk out of bounds
Should have his apt word to excuse himself:
And hearken how I plot to make amends.
I have bethought me: I shall paint a piece
… There's for you! Give me six months, then go, see
Something in Sant'Ambrogio's![4] Bless the nuns!
They want a cast o' my office. I shall paint
God in the midst, Madonna and her babe,
Ringed by a bowery flowery angel brood,
Lilies and vestments and white faces, sweet
As puff on puff of grated orris-root[5]

---

[1] *matins* Morning prayer services.

[2] *Saint Laurence* Roman deacon (?–258 CE) who was martyred by being burnt on a gridiron, an instrument of torture.

[3] *Prato* Town west of Florence.

[4] *Sant' Ambrogio's* Lippi painted *Coronation of the Virgin* for the main altar of Florence's Sant' Ambrogio convent.

[5] *orris-root* Roots of the iris flower, used as a fragrant cosmetic powder.

When ladies crowd to Church at midsummer.
And then i' the front, of course a saint or two—
Saint John, because he saves the Florentines,
Saint Ambrose, who puts down in black and white
The convent's friends and gives them a long day,
And Job, I must have him there past mistake,
The man of Uz[1] (and Us without the z,
Painters who need his patience). Well, all these
Secured at their devotion, up shall come
Out of a corner when you least expect,
As one by a dark stair into a great light,
Music and talking, who but Lippo! I!—
Mazed, motionless and moonstruck—I'm the man!
Back I shrink—what is this I see and hear?
I, caught up with my monk's things by mistake,
My old serge gown and rope that goes all round,
I, in this presence, this pure company!
Where's a hole, where's a corner for escape?
Then steps a sweet angelic slip of a thing
Forward, puts out a soft palm—"Not so fast!"
—Addresses the celestial presence, "nay—
He made you and devised you, after all,
Though he's none of you! Could Saint John there draw—
His camel hair[2] make up a painting brush?
We come to brother Lippo for all that,
Iste perfecit opus!"[3] So, all smile—
I shuffle sideways with my blushing face
Under the cover of a hundred wings
Thrown like a spread of kirtles° when you're gay *skirts*
And play hot cockles,[4] all the doors being shut,
Till, wholly unexpected, in there pops
The hothead husband! Thus I scuttle off
To some safe bench behind, not letting go
The palm of her, the little lily thing
That spoke the good word for me in the nick,
Like the Prior's niece … Saint Lucy,[5] I would say.
And so all's saved for me, and for the church
A pretty picture gained. Go, six months hence!
Your hand, sir, and goodbye: no lights, no lights!
The street's hushed, and I know my own way back,
Don't fear me! There's the grey beginning. Zooks!
—1855

[1] *man of Uz* See Job 1.1: Job was a righteous man who lost everything when God allowed Satan to challenge his faith.

[2] *Saint John … camel hair* St. John the Baptist "was clothed in camel hair," according to Mark 1.6.

[3] *Iste perfecit opus* Latin: He caused the work to be created; inscription on the *Coronation*, placed beside a portrait that Browning (following Vasari) mistakenly took to be Lippi's.

[4] *hot cockles* Christmas game played blindfolded.

[5] *Saint Lucy* Virgin martyr of Sicily (? –304? CE).

The Last Ride Together

1

I said—Then, dearest, since 'tis so,
Since now at length my fate I know,
Since nothing all my love avails,
Since all, my life seemed meant for, fails,
  Since this was written and needs must be—
My whole heart rises up to bless
Your name in pride and thankfulness!
Take back the hope you gave—I claim
Only a memory of the same,
—And this beside, if you will not blame,
  Your leave for one more last ride with me.

2

My mistress bent that brow of hers;
Those deep dark eyes where pride demurs
When pity would be softening through,
Fixed me a breathing-while or two
  With life or death in the balance: right!
The blood replenished me again;
My last thought was at least not vain:
I and my mistress, side by side
Shall be together, breathe and ride,
So, one day more am I deified.
  Who knows but the world may end tonight?

3

Hush! if you saw some western cloud
All billowy-bosomed, over-bowed
By many benedictions—sun's
And moon's and evening-star's at once—

And so, you, looking and loving best,
Conscious grew, your passion drew
Cloud, sunset, moonrise, star-shine too,
Down on you, near and yet more near,
Till flesh must fade for heaven was here!—
Thus leant she and lingered—joy and fear!
Thus lay she a moment on my breast.

4

Then we began to ride. My soul
Smoothed itself out, a long-cramped scroll
Freshening and fluttering in the wind.
Past hopes already lay behind.
What need to strive with a life awry?
Had I said that, had I done this,
So might I gain, so might I miss.
Might she have loved me? just as well
She might have hated, who can tell!
Where had I been now if the worst befell?
And here we are riding, she and I.

5

Fail I alone, in words and deeds?
Why, all men strive and who succeeds?
We rode; it seemed my spirit flew,
Saw other regions, cities new,
As the world rushed by on either side.
I thought—All labour, yet no less
Bear up beneath their unsuccess.
Look at the end of work, contrast
The petty done, the undone vast,
This present of theirs with the hopeful past!
I hoped she would love me; here we ride.

6

What hand and brain went ever paired?
What heart alike conceived and dared?
What act proved all its thought had been?
What will but felt the fleshly screen?
We ride and I see her bosom heave.
There's many a crown for who can reach.
Ten lines, a statesman's life in each!
The flag stuck on a heap of bones,
A soldier's doing! what atones?
They scratch his name on the Abbey[1] stones.
My riding is better, by their leave.

7

What does it all mean, poet? Well,
Your brains beat into rhythm, you tell
What we felt only; you expressed
You hold things beautiful the best,
And pace them in rhyme so, side by side.
'Tis something, nay 'tis much: but then,
Have you yourself what's best for men?
Are you—poor, sick, old ere your time—
Nearer one whit your own sublime
Than we who never have turned a rhyme?
Sing, riding's a joy! For me, I ride.

8

And you, great sculptor—so, you gave
A score of years to Art, her slave,
And that's your Venus,[2] whence we turn
To yonder girl that fords the burn!° *stream*
You acquiesce, and shall I repine?° *complain*
What, man of music, you grown grey
With notes and nothing else to say,
Is this your sole praise from a friend,
"Greatly his opera's strains intend,
But in music we know how fashions end!"
I gave my youth; but we ride, *in fine*.[3]

9

Who knows what's fit for us? Had fate
Proposed bliss here should sublimate
My being—had I signed the bond—
Still one must lead some life beyond,
Have a bliss to die with, dim-descried.
This foot once planted on the goal,
This glory-garland round my soul,
Could I descry such? Try and test!
I sink back shuddering from the quest.

---

[1] *Abbey* Westminster Abbey.

[2] *Venus* Roman goddess of love.

[3] *in fine* In the end.

Earth being so good, would heaven seem best?
    Now, heaven and she are beyond this ride.

10

And yet—she has not spoke so long!
What if heaven be that, fair and strong
At life's best, with our eyes upturned
Whither life's flower is first discerned,
    We, fixed so, ever should so abide?
What if we still ride on, we two
With life forever old yet new,
Changed not in kind but in degree,
The instant made eternity—
And heaven just prove that I and she
    Ride, ride together, forever ride?
—1855

Andrea del Sarto[1]

(*Called "The Faultless Painter"*)

But do not let us quarrel any more,
No, my Lucrezia;[2] bear with me for once:
Sit down and all shall happen as you wish.
You turn your face, but does it bring your heart?
I'll work then for your friend's friend, never fear,
Treat his own subject after his own way,
Fix his own time, accept too his own price,
And shut the money into this small hand
When next it takes mine. Will it? tenderly?
Oh, I'll content him—but tomorrow, Love!
I often am much wearier than you think,
This evening more than usual, and it seems
As if—forgive now—should you let me sit
Here by the window with your hand in mine
And look a half-hour forth on Fiesole,[3]
Both of one mind, as married people use,
Quietly, quietly the evening through,
I might get up tomorrow to my work
Cheerful and fresh as ever. Let us try.
Tomorrow, how you shall be glad for this!
Your soft hand is a woman of itself,
And mine the man's bared breast she curls inside.
Don't count the time lost, neither; you must serve
For each of the five pictures we require:
It saves a model. So! keep looking so—
My serpentining beauty, rounds on rounds!
—How could you ever prick those perfect ears,
Even to put the pearl there! oh, so sweet—
My face, my moon, my everybody's moon,
Which everybody looks on and calls his,
And, I suppose, is looked on by in turn,
While she looks—no one's: very dear, no less.
You smile? why, there's my picture ready made,
There's what we painters call our harmony!
A common greyness silvers everything—
All in a twilight, you and I alike
—You, at the point of your first pride in me
(That's gone you know)—but I, at every point;
My youth, my hope, my art, being all toned down
To yonder sober pleasant Fiesole.
There's the bell clinking from the chapel top;
That length of convent wall across the way
Holds the trees safer, huddled more inside;
The last monk leaves the garden; days decrease,
And autumn grows, autumn in everything.
Eh? the whole seems to fall into a shape
As if I saw alike my work and self
And all that I was born to be and do,
A twilight piece. Love, we are in God's hand.
How strange now, looks the life he makes us lead;
So free we seem, so fettered° fast we are! *shackled*
I feel he laid the fetter: let it lie!
This chamber for example—turn your head—
All that's behind us! You don't understand
Nor care to understand about my art,
But you can hear at least when people speak:
And that cartoon,° the second from the door *sketch*
—It is the thing, Love! so such things should be—

[1] *Andrea del Sarto* Browning's poem explores the life of the painter Andrea del Sarto (1486–1531), as narrated by Giorgio Vasari (once del Sarto's pupil) in *The Lives of the Painters*. In this biography, Vasari speculates as to why del Sarto (translated, this name means "son of a tailor") failed to fulfill the promise of his early paintings.

[2] *Lucrezia* Lucrezia del Fede, del Sarto's wife and model.

[3] *Fiesole* Hill town near Florence.

Behold Madonna!—I am bold to say.
I can do with my pencil what I know,
What I see, what at bottom of my heart
I wish for, if I ever wish so deep—
Do easily, too—when I say, perfectly,
I do not boast, perhaps: yourself are judge,
Who listened to the Legate's[1] talk last week,
And just as much they used to say in France.
At any rate 'tis easy, all of it!
No sketches first, no studies, that's long past:
I do what many dream of, all their lives,
—Dream? strive to do, and agonize to do,
And fail in doing. I could count twenty such
On twice your fingers, and not leave this town,
Who strive—you don't know how the others strive
To paint a little thing like that you smeared
Carelessly passing with your robes afloat—
Yet do much less, so much less, Someone says,
(I know his name, no matter)—so much less!
Well, less is more, Lucrezia: I am judged.
There burns a truer light of God in them,
In their vexed beating stuffed and stopped-up brain,
Heart, or whate'er else, than goes on to prompt
This low-pulsed forthright craftsman's hand of mine.
Their works drop groundward, but themselves, I know,
Reach many a time a heaven that's shut to me,
Enter and take their place there sure enough,
Though they come back and cannot tell the world.
My works are nearer heaven, but I sit here.
The sudden blood of these men! at a word—
Praise them, it boils, or blame them, it boils too.
I, painting from myself and to myself,
Know what I do, am unmoved by men's blame
Or their praise either. Somebody remarks
Morello's[2] outline there is wrongly traced,
His hue mistaken; what of that? or else,
Rightly traced and well ordered; what of that?
Speak as they please, what does the mountain care?
Ah, but a man's reach should exceed his grasp,
Or what's a heaven for? All is silver-grey
Placid and perfect with my art: the worse!
I know both what I want and what might gain,
And yet how profitless to know, to sigh
"Had I been two, another and myself,
Our head would have o'erlooked the world!" No doubt.
Yonder's a work now, of that famous youth
The Urbinate[3] who died five years ago.
('Tis copied, George Vasari sent it me.)
Well, I can fancy how he did it all,
Pouring his soul, with kings and popes to see,
Reaching, that heaven might so replenish him,
Above and through his art—for it gives way;
That arm is wrongly put—and there again—
A fault to pardon in the drawing's lines,
Its body, so to speak: its soul is right,
He means right—that, a child may understand.
Still, what an arm! and I could alter it:
But all the play, the insight and the stretch—
Out of me, out of me! And wherefore out?
Had you enjoined them on me, given me soul,
We might have risen to Rafael, I and you!
Nay, Love, you did give all I asked, I think—
More than I merit, yes, by many times.
But had you—oh, with the same perfect brow,
And perfect eyes, and more than perfect mouth,
And the low voice my soul hears, as a bird
The fowler's pipe,[4] and follows to the snare—
Had you, with these the same, but brought a mind!
Some women do so. Had the mouth there urged
"God and the glory! never care for gain.
The present by the future, what is that?
Live for fame, side by side with Agnolo![5]
Rafael is waiting: up to God, all three!"
I might have done it for you. So it seems:
Perhaps not. All is as God over-rules.
Beside, incentives come from the soul's self;
The rest avail not. Why do I need you?
What wife had Rafael, or has Agnolo?

[1] *Legate* Representative of the Pope.

[2] *Morello* Monte Morello, a mountain near Florence.

[3] *Urbinate* The painter Raphael (1483–1520), who was born in Urbino.

[4] *fowler's pipe* Call used by hunters to lure fowl.

[5] *Agnolo* I.e., Michelangelo Buonarroti (1475–1564), sculptor and painter.

In this world, who can do a thing, will not;
And who would do it, cannot, I perceive:
Yet the will's somewhat—somewhat, too, the power—
And thus we half-men struggle. At the end,
God, I conclude, compensates, punishes.
'Tis safer for me, if the award be strict,
That I am something underrated here,
Poor this long while, despised, to speak the truth.
I dared not, do you know, leave home all day,
For fear of chancing on the Paris lords.[1]
The best is when they pass and look aside;
But they speak sometimes; I must bear it all.
Well may they speak! That Francis, that first time,
And that long festal year at Fontainebleau!
I surely then could sometimes leave the ground,
Put on the glory, Rafael's daily wear,
In that humane great monarch's golden look—
One finger in his beard or twisted curl
Over his mouth's good mark that made the smile,
One arm about my shoulder, round my neck,
The jingle of his gold chain in my ear,
I painting proudly with his breath on me,
All his court round him, seeing with his eyes,
Such frank French eyes, and such a fire of souls
Profuse, my hand kept plying by those hearts—
And, best of all, this, this, this face beyond,
This in the background, waiting on my work,
To crown the issue with a last reward!
A good time, was it not, my kingly days?
And had you not grown restless … but I know—
'Tis done and past; 'twas right, my instinct said;
Too live the life grew, golden and not grey,
And I'm the weak-eyed bat no sun should tempt
Out of the grange whose four walls make his world.
How could it end in any other way?
You called me, and I came home to your heart.
The triumph was—to reach and stay there; since
I reached it ere the triumph, what is lost?
Let my hands frame your face in your hair's gold,
You beautiful Lucrezia that are mine!
"Rafael did this, Andrea painted that;
The Roman's is the better when you pray,
But still the other's Virgin was his wife—"
Men will excuse me. I am glad to judge
Both pictures in your presence; clearer grows
My better fortune, I resolve to think.
For, do you know, Lucrezia, as God lives,
Said one day Agnolo, his very self,
To Rafael … I have known it all these years …
(When the young man was flaming out his thoughts
Upon a palace wall for Rome to see,
Too lifted up in heart because of it)
"Friend, there's a certain sorry little scrub
Goes up and down our Florence, none cares how,
Who, were he set to plan and execute
As you are, pricked on by your popes and kings,
Would bring the sweat into that brow of yours!"
To Rafael's!—And indeed the arm is wrong.
I hardly dare … yet, only you to see,
Give the chalk here—quick, thus the line should go!
Ay, but the soul! he's Rafael! rub it out!
Still, all I care for, if he spoke the truth,
(What he? why, who but Michel Agnolo?
Do you forget already words like those?)
If really there was such a chance, so lost—
Is, whether you're—not grateful—but more pleased.
Well, let me think so. And you smile indeed!
This hour has been an hour! Another smile?
If you would sit thus by me every night
I should work better, do you comprehend?
I mean that I should earn more, give you more.
See, it is settled dusk now; there's a star;
Morello's gone, the watch-lights show the wall,
The cue-owls[2] speak the name we call them by.
Come from the window, love—come in, at last,
Inside the melancholy little house
We built to be so gay with. God is just.
King Francis may forgive me: oft at nights
When I look up from painting, eyes tired out,
The walls become illumined, brick from brick
Distinct, instead of mortar, fierce bright gold,

[1] *For fear … lords* According to Vasari, del Sarto absconded with funds given to him at Fontainebleau by his patron, King Francis I of France.

[2] *cue-owls* Also known as scops-owls, whose cry sounds like "cue."

That gold of his I did cement them with!
Let us but love each other. Must you go?
That cousin here again? he waits outside?
Must see you—you, and not with me? Those loans?
More gaming debts to pay? you smiled for that?
Well, let smiles buy me! have you more to spend?
While hand and eye and something of a heart
Are left me, work's my ware, and what's it worth?
I'll pay my fancy. Only let me sit
The grey remainder of the evening out,
Idle, you call it, and muse perfectly
How I could paint, were I but back in France,
One picture, just one more—the Virgin's face,
Not yours this time! I want you at my side
To hear them—that is, Michel Agnolo—
Judge all I do and tell you of its worth.
Will you? Tomorrow, satisfy your friend.
I take the subjects for his corridor,
Finish the portrait out of hand—there, there,
And throw him in another thing or two
If he demurs; the whole should prove enough
To pay for this same cousin's freak. Beside,
What's better and what's all I care about,
Get you the thirteen scudi° for the ruff! *Italian currency*
Love, does that please you? Ah, but what does he,
The cousin! what does he to please you more?

I am grown peaceful as old age tonight.
I regret little, I would change still less.
Since there my past life lies, why alter it?
The very wrong to Francis!—it is true
I took his coin, was tempted and complied,
And built this house and sinned, and all is said.
My father and my mother died of want.
Well, had I riches of my own? you see
How one gets rich! Let each one bear his lot.
They were born poor, lived poor, and poor they died:
And I have laboured somewhat in my time
And not been paid profusely. Some good son
Paint my two hundred pictures—let him try!
No doubt, there's something strikes a balance. Yes,
You loved me quite enough, it seems tonight.
This must suffice me here. What would one have?
In heaven, perhaps, new chances, one more chance—
Four great walls in the New Jerusalem,[1]
Meted on each side by the angel's reed,
For Leonard,[2] Rafael, Agnolo and me
To cover—the three first without a wife,
While I have mine! So—still they overcome
Because there's still Lucrezia—as I choose.

Again the cousin's whistle! Go, my Love.
—1855

[1] *Four … Jerusalem* See Revelations 21.10.

[2] *Leonard* Artist Leonardo da Vinci (1452–1519).

Charles Dickens

1812 – 1870

Few English novelists have attracted the vast audiences and lasting fame of Charles Dickens. People the world over are familiar with the moral transformation of *A Christmas Carol*'s Ebenezer Scrooge and the life of the orphan Oliver Twist, immortalized in his piteous request for a second bowl of watery gruel: "Please, sir, I want some more." From Pickwick and Sam Weller in *The Pickwick Papers* to Mr. Micawber in *David Copperfield* to Pip in *Great Expectations*, from Mr. Guppy and Mrs. Jellyby in *Bleak House* to Mr. Gradgrind in *Hard Times* and Flora Finching in *Little Dorrit*, Dickens created a panoply of memorable characters. Combining comic genius with astute criticisms of the laws, institutions, and the social order of Victorian society, he created novels that continue to command the attention of critics and the general public alike. His novels still stand as a testament to his stature both as a popular writer and as a social critic.

Dickens's early childhood was signally important as source material for the concerns and themes of his novels. His father worked as a naval office clerk in Portsmouth when Charles was born in 1812, the second of 10 children (two died in infancy). John and Elizabeth Dickens aspired to a middle-class life, but had unending difficulties controlling their spending and were always on the brink of penury. At one time, they served a four-month stint in the Marshalsea debtors' prison. Charles was able to attend school in Chatham, near London, after the family was transferred to the dockyards there, but in 1823 his education was halted, and he joined his parents in Camden Town, London. The young Dickens worked at odd jobs for his parents and was eventually sent off to work at Warren's Boot Blacking Factory at the age of 12. The psychological impact of this environment on Dickens was permanent; he never forgot the humiliation he had suffered or the dismay he had felt at the relatively harsh working conditions under which he and other children were forced to toil.

After the family came into a modest inheritance, Dickens returned to school, but in 1827, at just 15 years of age, he left school again because his father was unable to pay the fees. Working as a clerk in a law firm, he studied shorthand in his spare time, eventually becoming a parliamentary reporter. In 1833, *Monthly Magazine* published Dickens's first story, "A Dinner at Poplar Walk." While working as a newspaper reporter the next year, he launched a highly popular series of articles that were eventually collected and published as *Sketches by Boz* (his journalistic pseudonym) in 1836. The success of this book allowed Dickens to marry Catherine Hogarth and to begin another series that cemented his fame and secured his financial stability. A monthly illustrated serial about the Pickwick Club was commissioned by publishers Chapman and Hall, and the absurd characters of Mr. Pickwick, Mr. Winkle, Mr. Tupman, Mr. Snodgrass, and Sam Weller soon had people all over England clamoring for the latest installment of *The Pickwick Papers*. Dickens consolidated this success by beginning *Oliver Twist* (1837–38) in *Bentley's Miscellany*, which he had begun editing, and then launching *Nicholas Nickleby* (1838–39) as a monthly serial.

In 1837, Dickens and his wife began to raise a family (they eventually had 10 children). In this same year, he lost his beloved sister-in-law, Mary Hogarth, who would become the inspiration for Little Nell in *The Old Curiosity Shop* (1840–41) and for many of the childlike women that constitute the "good angels" of his novels. By the time this book was published, Dickens's fame had spread throughout North America; eager fans would line the piers in New York waiting for the latest installment of a Dickens story to arrive from England.

In 1842, Dickens journeyed to the United States to take advantage of his fame, but the trip turned out to be a disappointment. The hordes that crowded around him relentlessly, trying to speak to, touch, or even just glimpse the famous author were only part of the problem. He scorned, publicly and at any opportunity, the lack of international copyright laws, which meant that Americans could pirate editions of his books without any of the proceeds going to him. Dickens set out his disdain for American habits (such as chewing and spitting tobacco) and for American institutions, such as slavery and what he thought was a ruthless prison system in a book about his travels, *American Notes* (1842), and made Americans the object of derision in his novel *Martin Chuzzlewit* (1843–44). Americans were incensed and reacted with an outpouring of vindictive editorials in the press. As it happened, *Martin Chuzzlewit* did not sell well on either side of the Atlantic. Americans began to forgive Dickens after the appearance of the overwhelmingly successful *A Christmas Carol* (1843), the first in his Christmas book series and a novel that is all about forgiveness and redemption.

Dickens was an astonishingly energetic and prolific writer, becoming the editor of *Household Words* in 1850, while writing and acting in theatrical works, traveling widely, and working in various social causes. Throughout the 1840s and 1850s, he published at an unprecedented rate: *Dombey and Son* (1846–48), *David Copperfield* (his most autobiographical work, 1849–50), *Bleak House* (1852–53), *Hard Times* (1854), *Little Dorrit* (1855–57), and *A Tale of Two Cities* (1859), *Great Expectations* (1861), and *Our Mutual Friend* (1865). All of these novels were first published in serial form. This approach necessitated an episodic structure, prompting him to develop methods of characterizations that allowed immediate identification of characters by readers waiting for weekly or monthly installments. He also developed an extraordinary talent for weaving together numerous strands of story material and coincidental events that, however implausible they might appear, somehow strike the reader as persuasive.

Dickens not only edited *Household Words*; he also wrote many of the pieces himself, both fiction and non-fiction. In fact, he referred to himself as the "conductor" of the magazine, not its editor. Had he never written any of his novels or short stories, he would still be remembered for the extraordinary body of non-fiction he produced. His essays for the magazine deal with a wide variety of topics, but again and again he returns in one way or another to the condition of the poor—the great issue of his time. The condition of poor children was a particular concern for Dickens—as his 1850 essay "A Walk in the Workhouse" suggests. But, as the 1854 essay "The Quiet Poor" demonstrates, his sympathetic understanding for poor people both *en masse* and as individuals could operate just as keenly for those "who are never to be seen in workhouses and prisons." That essay also illustrates Dickens's abiding interest in public policy; he believed in the power of the human heart to bring change (and he strove in his writing to tug at the heartstrings of his readers), but he was also an advocate for changes to social and economic legislation.

In 1858 Dickens separated from Catherine; the break was complicated by his relationship with the actress Ellen Ternan and by the degree of publicity that (partly at Dickens's instigation) attended his change in marital status. In that same year, Dickens began an extensive series of public readings, a lucrative but exhausting enterprise that severely compromised his health. He continued touring throughout the 1860s while editing his new journal, *All the Year Round* (begun in 1859). Dickens was at work on *The Mystery of Edwin Drood* when he died in 1870 during a grueling schedule of readings. In his will Dickens requested that he be buried at Rochester, Kent, near his home. Under public pressure the family agreed to allow him to be buried instead in Poet's Corner in Westminster Abbey. Dickens's instructions that the funeral be "unostentatious, and strictly private" were followed, however; there were only a dozen present for the ceremony in the cathedral.

⌘⌘⌘

A Walk in the Workhouse[1]

On a certain Sunday I formed one of the congregation assembled in the chapel of a large metropolitan Workhouse. With the exception of the clergyman and clerk, and a very few officials, there were none but paupers present. The children sat in the galleries; the women in the body of the chapel, and in one of the side aisles; the men in the remaining aisle. The service was decorously performed, though the sermon might have been much better adapted to the comprehension and to the circumstances of the hearers. The usual supplications were offered, with more than the usual significancy in such a place, for the fatherless children and widows, for all sick persons and young children, for all that were desolate and oppressed, for the comforting and helping of the weak-hearted, for the raising up of them that had fallen; for all that were in danger, necessity, and tribulation. The prayers of the congregation were desired "for several persons in the various wards dangerously ill"; and others who were recovering returned their thanks to Heaven.

Among this congregation were some evil-looking young women, and beetle-browed young men; but not many—perhaps that kind of characters kept away. Generally, the faces (those of the children excepted) were depressed and subdued, and wanted colour. Aged people were there in every variety. Mumbling, blear-eyed, spectacled, stupid, deaf, lame; vacantly winking in the gleams of sun that now and then crept in through the open doors, from the paved yard; shading their listening ears, or blinking eyes, with their withered hands; poring over their books, leering at nothing, going to sleep, crouching and drooping in corners. There were weird old women, all skeleton within, all bonnet and cloak without, continually wiping their eyes with dirty dusters of pocket handkerchiefs; and there were ugly old crones, both male and female, with a ghastly kind of contentment upon them which was not at all comforting to see. Upon the whole, it was the dragon, Pauperism, in a very weak and impotent condition: toothless, fangless, drawing his breath heavily enough, and hardly worth chaining up.

When the service was over, I walked with the humane and conscientious gentleman whose duty it was to take that walk, that Sunday morning, through the little world of poverty enclosed within the workhouse walls. It was inhabited by a population of some fifteen hundred or two thousand paupers, ranging from the infant newly born or not yet come into the pauper world, to the old man dying on his bed.

In a room opening from a squalid yard, where a number of listless women were lounging to and fro, trying to get warm in the ineffectual sunshine of the tardy May morning—in the "Itch Ward," not to compromise the truth—a woman such as HOGARTH[2] has often drawn, was hurriedly getting on her gown before a dusty fire. She was the nurse, or wardswoman, of that insalubrious department—herself a pauper—flabby, raw-boned, untidy—unpromising and coarse of aspect as need be. But, on being spoken to about the patients whom she had in charge, she turned round, with her shabby gown half on, half off, and fell a crying with all

[1] *A Walk in the Workhouse* This essay appeared in 1850 in Dickens's magazine *Household Words*.

[2] *HOGARTH* Artist and printmaker William Hogarth (1687–1764) was greatly admired by Dickens for his satirical paintings and prints of eighteenth-century London life.

her might. Not for show, not querulously, not in any mawkish sentiment, but in the deep grief and affliction of her heart; turning away her dishevelled head: sobbing most bitterly, wringing her hands, and letting fall abundance of great tears, that choked her utterance. What was the matter with the nurse of the itch ward? Oh, "the dropped child" was dead! Oh, the child that was found in the street, and she had brought up ever since, had died an hour ago, and see where the little creature lay, beneath this cloth! The dear, the pretty dear!

The dropped child seemed too small and poor a thing for Death to be in earnest with, but Death had taken it; and already its diminutive form was neatly washed, composed, and stretched as if in sleep upon a box. I thought I heard a voice from Heaven saying, It shall be well for thee, O nurse of the itch ward, when some less gentle pauper does those offices to thy cold form, that such as the dropped child are the angels who behold my Father's face!

In another room were several ugly old women crouching, witch-like, round a hearth, and chattering and nodding, after the manner of the monkeys. "All well here? And enough to eat?" A general chattering and chuckling; at last an answer from a volunteer. "Oh yes, gentleman! Bless you, gentleman! Lord bless the Parish of St. So-and-So! It feed the hungry, sir, and give drink to the thusty, and it warm them which is cold, so it do, and good luck to the parish of St. So-and-So, and thankee, gentleman!" Elsewhere, a party of pauper nurses were at dinner. "How do YOU get on?" "Oh pretty well, sir! We works hard, and we lives hard—like the sodgers!"[1]

In another room, a kind of purgatory or place of transition, six or eight noisy madwomen were gathered together, under the superintendence of one sane attendant. Among them was a girl of two or three and twenty, very prettily dressed, of most respectable appearance and good manners, who had been brought in from the house where she had lived as domestic servant (having, I suppose, no friends), on account of being subject to epileptic fits, and requiring to be removed under the influence of a very bad one. She was by no means of the same stuff, or the same breeding, or the same experience, or in the same state of mind, as those by whom she was surrounded; and she pathetically complained that the daily association and the nightly noise made her worse, and was driving her mad—which was perfectly evident. The case was noted for inquiry and redress, but she said she had already been there for some weeks.

If this girl had stolen her mistress's watch, I do not hesitate to say she would have been infinitely better off. We have come to this absurd, this dangerous, this monstrous pass, that the dishonest felon is, in respect of cleanliness, order, diet, and accommodation, better provided for, and taken care of, than the honest pauper.

And this conveys no special imputation on the workhouse of the parish of St. So-and-So, where, on the contrary, I saw many things to commend. It was very agreeable, recollecting that most infamous and atrocious enormity committed at Tooting[2]—an enormity which, a hundred years hence, will still be vividly remembered in the byways of English life, and which has done more to engender a gloomy discontent and suspicion among many thousands of the people than all the Chartist leaders[3] could have done in all their lives—to find the pauper children in this workhouse looking robust and well, and apparently the objects of very great care. In the Infant School—a large, light, airy room at the top of the building—the little creatures, being at dinner, and eating their potatoes heartily, were not cowed by the presence of strange visitors, but stretched out their small hands to be shaken, with a very pleasant confidence. And it was comfortable to see two mangy pauper rocking-horses rampant in a corner. In the girls' school, where the dinner was also in progress, everything bore a cheerful and healthy aspect. The meal was over in the boys' school by the time of our arrival there, and the room was not yet quite rearranged; but the boys were

[1] *sodgers* I.e., soldiers.

[2] *Tooting* In 1849, after four half-starved children had died of cholera in a Tooting workhouse, the proprietor was found guilty of manslaughter.

[3] *Chartist leaders* The Chartist movement pressed for political (and by implication, social and economic) reform from 1836 onwards.

roaming unrestrained about a large and airy yard, as any other schoolboys might have done. Some of them had been drawing large ships upon the schoolroom wall; and if they had a mast with shrouds and stays set up for practice (as they have in the Middlesex House of Correction), it would be so much the better. At present, if a boy should feel a strong impulse upon him to learn the art of going aloft, he could only gratify it, I presume, as the men and women paupers gratify their aspirations after better board and lodging, by smashing as many workhouse windows as possible, and being promoted to prison.

In one place, the Newgate[1] of the workhouse, a company of boys and youths were locked up in a yard alone; their dayroom being a kind of kennel where the casual poor used formerly to be littered down at night. Diverse of them had been there some long time. "Are they never going away?" was the natural inquiry. "Most of them are crippled, in some form or other," said the wardsman, "and not fit for anything." They slunk about, like dispirited wolves or hyenas; and made a pounce at their food when it was served out, much as those animals do. The big-headed idiot shuffling his feet along the pavement, in the sunlight outside, was a more agreeable object everyway.

Groves of babies in arms; groves of mothers and other sick women in bed; groves of lunatics; jungles of men in stone-paved downstairs dayrooms, waiting for their dinners; longer and longer groves of old people, in upstairs infirmary wards, wearing out life, God knows how—this was the scenery through which the walk lay, for two hours. In some of these latter chambers, there were pictures stuck against the wall, and a neat display of crockery and pewter on a kind of sideboard; now and then it was a treat to see a plant or two; in almost every ward there was a cat.

In all of these long walks of aged and infirm, some old people were bedridden, and had been for a long time; some were sitting on their beds half naked; some dying in their beds; some out of bed, and sitting at a table near the fire. A sullen or lethargic indifference to what was asked, a blunted sensibility to everything but warmth and food, a moody absence of complaint as being of no use, a dogged silence and resentful desire to be left alone again, I thought were generally apparent. On our walking into the midst of one of these dreary perspectives of old men, nearly the following little dialogue took place, the nurse not being immediately at hand:

"All well here?"

No answer. An old man in a Scotch cap[2] sitting among others on a form at the table, eating out of a tin porringer,[3] pushes back his cap a little to look at us, claps it down on his forehead again with the palm of his hand, and goes on eating.

"All well here?" (repeated).

No answer. Another old man sitting on his bed, paralytically peeling a boiled potato, lifts his head and stares.

"Enough to eat?"

No answer. Another old man, in bed, turns himself and coughs.

"How are YOU today?" To the last old man.

That old man says nothing; but another old man, a tall old man of very good address, speaking with perfect correctness, comes forward from somewhere, and volunteers an answer. The reply almost always proceeds from a volunteer, and not from the person looked at or spoken to.

"We are very old, sir," in a mild, distinct voice. "We can't expect to be well, most of us."

"Are you comfortable?"

"I have no complaint to make, sir." With a half shake of his head, a half shrug of his shoulders, and a kind of apologetic smile.

"Enough to eat?"

"Why, sir, I have but a poor appetite," with the same air as before; "and yet I get through my allowance very easily."

"But," showing a porringer with a Sunday dinner in it; "here is a portion of mutton, and three potatoes. You

[1] *Newgate* Newgate was London's main prison.

[2] *Scotch cap* Woolen hat worn in the Highlands.

[3] *porringer* Bowl for porridge, soups, and other runny foods.

can't starve on that?"

"Oh dear no, sir," with the same apologetic air. "Not starve."

"What do you want?"

"We have very little bread, sir. It's an exceedingly small quantity of bread."

The nurse, who is now rubbing her hands at the questioner's elbow, interferes with, "It ain't much raly, sir. You see they've only six ounces a day, and when they've took their breakfast, there CAN only be a little left for night, sir." Another old man, hitherto invisible, rises out of his bedclothes, as out of a grave, and looks on.

"You have tea at night?" The questioner is still addressing the well-spoken old man.

"Yes, sir, we have tea at night."

"And you save what bread you can from the morning, to eat with it?"

"Yes, sir—if we can save any."

"And you want more to eat with it?"

"Yes, sir." With a very anxious face.

The questioner, in the kindness of his heart, appears a little discomposed, and changes the subject.

"What has become of the old man who used to lie in that bed in the corner?"

The nurse don't remember what old man is referred to. There has been such a many old men. The well-spoken old man is doubtful. The spectral old man who has come to life in bed says "Billy Stevens." Another old man who has previously had his head in the fireplace, pipes out, "Charley Walters."

Something like a feeble interest is awakened. I suppose Charley Walters had conversation in him.

"He's dead," says the piping old man.

Another old man, with one eye screwed up, hastily displaces the piping old man, and says.

"Yes! Charley Walters died in that bed, and—and —"

"Billy Stevens," persists the spectral old man.

"No, no! and Johnny Rogers died in that bed, and—and—they're both on 'em dead—and Sam'l Bowyer"; this seems very extraordinary to him; "he went out!"

With this he subsides, and all the old men (having had quite enough of it) subside, and the spectral old man goes into his grave again, and takes the shade of Billy Stevens with him.

As we turn to go out at the door, another previously invisible old man, a hoarse old man in a flannel gown, is standing there, as if he had just come up through the floor.

"I beg your pardon, sir, could I take the liberty of saying a word?"

"Yes, what is it?"

"I am greatly better in my health, sir; but what I want, to get me quite round," with his hand on his throat, "is a little fresh air, sir. It has always done my complaint so much good, sir. The regular leave for going out, comes round so seldom, that if the gentlemen, next Friday, would give me leave to go out walking, now and then—for only an hour or so, sir!—"

Who could wonder, looking through those weary vistas of bed and infirmity, that it should do him good to meet with some other scenes, and assure himself that there was something else on earth? Who could help wondering why the old men lived on as they did; what grasp they had on life; what crumbs of interest or occupation they could pick up from its bare board; whether Charley Walters had ever described to them the days when he kept company with some old pauper woman in the bud, or Billy Stevens ever told them of the time when he was a dweller in the far off foreign land called Home!

The morsel of burnt child, lying in another room, so patiently, in bed, wrapped in lint, and looking steadfastly at us with his bright quiet eyes when we spoke to him kindly, looked as if the knowledge of these things, and of all the tender things there are to think about, might have been in his mind as if he thought, with us, that there was a fellow-feeling in the pauper nurses which appeared to make them more kind to their charges than the race of common nurses in the hospitals—as if he mused upon the future of some older children lying around him in the same place, and thought it best, perhaps, all things considered, that he should die—as if he knew, without fear, of those many coffins, made and unmade, piled up in the store below—and of his unknown friend, "the dropped child," calm upon the box lid covered with a cloth. But there was something wistful and appealing, too, in his tiny face, as if, in the midst of all the hard necessities and incongruities he pondered on, he pleaded, in behalf of the helpless and the aged poor, for a little more liberty—and a little more bread.

—1850

David Copperfield[1]

CHAPTER I

I had known Mr. Peggotty's house very well in my childhood, and I am sure I could not have been more charmed with it if it had been Aladdin's palace, roc's egg and all.[2] It was an old black barge, or boat, high and dry on Yarmouth Sands,[3] with an iron funnel sticking out of it for a chimney. There was a delightful door cut in the side, and it was roofed in, and there were little windows in it. It was beautifully clean, and as tidy as possible. There were some lockers and boxes, and there was a table, and there was a Dutch clock,[4] and there was a chest of drawers, and there was a tea-tray with a painting on it, and the tray was kept from tumbling down by a Bible, and the tray, if it *had* tumbled down, would have smashed a quantity of cups and saucers and a teapot that were grouped around the book. On the walls were coloured pictures of Abraham in red going to sacrifice Isaac in blue; and of Daniel in yellow being cast into a den of green lions.[5] Over the little mantle-shelf was a picture of the "Sarah Jane" lugger,[6] built at Sunderland, with a real little wooden stern stuck on it—a work of art combining composition with carpentry, which I had regarded in my childhood as one of the most enviable possessions the world could afford. Mr. Peggotty, as honest a seafaring man as ever breathed, dealt in lobsters, crabs, and crawfish; and a heap of those creatures, in a state of wonderful conglomeration with one another, and never leaving off pinching whatever they laid hold of, were usually to be found in a little wooden out-house, where the pots and kettles were kept.

As in my childhood, so in these days, when I was a young man, Mr. Peggotty's household consisted of his orphan nephew, Ham Peggotty, a young shipwright; his adopted niece, Little Emily, once my small sweetheart, now a beautiful young woman; and Mrs. Gummidge.

All three had been maintained at Mr. Peggotty's sole charge for years and years, and Mrs. Gummidge was the widow of his partner in a boat, who had died poor. She was very grateful, but she would have been more agreeable company in a small habitation if she had hit upon any other acknowledgement of the hospitality she received than constantly complaining, as she sat in the most comfortable corner by the fireside, that she was a "lone lorn creetur and everythink went contrairy with her."

Towards this old boat I walked one memorable night, with my former schoolfellow and present dear friend, Steerforth—Steerforth, half a dozen years older than I, brilliant, handsome, easy, winning, whom I admired with my whole heart, for whom I entertained the most romantic feelings of fidelity and friendship. He had come down with me from London, and had entered with the greatest ardour into my scheme of visiting the old simple place, and the old simple people.

There was no moon, and as he and I walked on the dark, wintry sands, towards the old boat, the wind sighed mournfully.

---

[1] *David Copperfield* Dickens, who was almost as famous for his public readings as he was for his writing, trimmed and revised material from his novels to create self-contained works for performance; this text is one such performance fiction, based upon the novel of the same title.

[2] *Aladdin … and all* In his tale in *One Thousand and One Nights* (1710), Aladdin's palace is built by a genie and is finer than any other palace. Aladdin requests that the genie bring him the egg of a roc, a giant mythological bird, but the genie refuses.

[3] *Yarmouth Sands* Coastal area in the county of Norfolk.

[4] *Dutch clock* Simple clock with a plain face and pendulum. Dutch clocks were inexpensive and favored for use by the poor.

[5] *Abraham … green lions* The pictures depict biblical tales. See Genesis 22 and Daniel 6.

[6] *lugger* Small sailboat.

"This is a wild place, Steerforth, is it not?"

"Dismal enough in the dark, and the sea has a cry in it, as if it were hungry for us. Is that the boat, where I see a light yonder?"

"That's the boat."

We said no more as we approached the light, but made softly for the door. I laid my hand upon the latch, and, whispering Steerforth to keep close to me, went in, and I was in the midst of the astonished family, whom I had not seen from my childhood, face to face with Mr. Peggotty, and holding out my hand to him, when Ham shouted, "Mas'r Davy! it's Mas'r Davy!"

In a moment we were all shaking hands with one another, and asking one another how we did, and telling one another how glad we were to meet, and all talking at once. Mr. Peggotty was so overjoyed to see me, and to see my friend, that he did not know what to say or do, but kept over and over again shaking hands with me, and then with Steerforth, and then with me, and then ruffling his shaggy hair all over his head, and then laughing with such glee and triumph, that it was a treat to see him.

"Why, that you two gentl'men—gentl'men growed —should come to this here roof to-night, of all nights in my life, is such a merry-go-rounder as never happened afore, I do rightly believe. Em'ly, my darling, come here. Come here, my little witch. Theer's Mas'r Davy's friend, my dear! Theer's the gentl'man as you've heerd on, Em'ly. He comes to see you along with Mas'r Davy, on the brightest night of your uncle's life as ever was or will be; horroar[1] for it!" Then he let her go, and, as she ran into her little chamber, looked round upon us, quite hot and out of breath with his uncommon satisfaction.

"If you two gentl'men—gentl'men growed now, and such gentl'men—don't ex-cuse me for being in a state of mind, when you understand matters, I'll arks your pardon. Em'ly, my dear! She knows I'm going to tell, and has made off. This here little Em'ly, sir," to Steerforth, "her as you see a blushing here just now—this here little Em'ly of ours has been in our house, sir, what I suppose (I'm a ignorant man, but that's my belief) no one but a little bright-eyed creetur *can* be in a house. She ain't my child, I never had one; but I couldn't love her more if she was fifty times my child. You understand; I couldn't do it!"

"I quite understand."

"I know you do, sir, and thank'ee. Well, sir, there was a certain person as had know'd our Em'ly from the time when her father was drownded; as had seen her constant when a babby, when a young gal, when a woman. Not much of a person to look at, he warn't—something o' my own build, rough, a good deal o' the sou'wester in him, wery salt, but, on the whole, a honest sort of a chap too, with his art in the right place."

I had never seen Ham grin to anything like the extent to which he sat grinning at us now.

"What does this here blessed tarpaulin go and do, but he loses that there art of his to our little Em'ly. He follers her about, he makes hisself a sort o' servant to her, he loses in a great measure his relish for his wittles, and, in the long run, he makes it clear to me wot's amiss.

"Well, I counsels him to speak to Em'ly. He's big enough, but he's bashfuller than a little un, and he says to me he doen't like. So I speak. 'What, *him*!' says Em'ly, '*him* that I've know'd so intimate so many year, and like so much? Oh, Uncle! I never can have *him*! He's such a good fellow!' I gives her a kiss, and I says no more to her than, 'My dear, you're right to speak out, you're to choose for yourself, you're as free as a little bird.' Then I aways to him, and I says, 'I wish it could have been so, but it can't. But you can both be as you was, and wot I say to you is, Be as you was with her, like a man.' He says to me, a shaking of my hand, 'I will,' he says. And then he was, honourable, trew, and manful, going on for two year.

"All of a sudden, one evening, as it might be to-night, comes little Em'ly from her work, and him with her! There ain't so much in *that*, you'll say. No, sure, because he takes care on her, like a brother, arter dark, and indeed afore dark, and at all times. But this heer tarpaulin chap, he takes hold of her hand, and he cries out to me, joyful, 'Look'ee here! This is to be my little wife!' And she says, half bold and half shy, and half a

[1] *horroar* Hooray.

laughing, and half a crying, 'Yes, uncle! If you please.' If I please! Lord, as if I should do anythink else! 'If you please,' she says, 'I am steadier now, and I have thought better of it, and I'll be as good a little wife as I can to him, for he's a dear good fellow!' Then Missis Gummidge, she claps her hands like a play, and you come in. There, the murder's out![1] You come in! It took place this here present hour, and here's the man as'll marry her the minute she's out of her time at the needlework."

Ham staggered, as well he might, under the blow Mr. Peggotty dealt him, as a mark of confidence and friendship; but, feeling called upon to say something to us, he stammered:

"She warn't no higher than you was, Mas'r Davy, when you first come heer, when I thought what she'd grow up to be. I see her grow up, gentl'men, like a flower. I'd lay down my life for her, Mas'r Davy—Oh, most content and cheerful. There ain't a gentl'man in all the land, nor yet a sailing upon all the sea—that can love his lady more than I love her, though there's many a common man as could say better what he meant."

I thought it affecting to see such a sturdy fellow trembling in the strength of what he felt for the pretty little creature who had won his heart. I thought the simple confidence reposed in us by Mr. Peggotty, and by himself, was touching. I was affected by the story altogether. I was filled with pleasure, but at first with an indescribably sensitive pleasure, that a very little would have changed to pain.

Therefore, if it had depended upon me to touch the prevailing chord among them, with any skill, I should have made a poor hand of it. But it depended upon Steerforth, and he did it with such address, that in a few minutes we were all as easy as possible.

"Mr. Peggotty," he said, "you are a thoroughly good fellow, and deserve to be as happy as you are to-night. My hand upon it. Ham, I give you joy, my boy. My hand upon that, too! Davy, stir the fire and make it a brisk one. And, Mr. Peggotty, unless you can induce your gentle niece to come back, I shall go. Any gap at your fireside on such a night—such a gap, least of all—I wouldn't make for the wealth of the Indies."

So Mr. Peggotty went to fetch little Em'ly. At first little Em'ly didn't like to come, and then Ham went. Presently they brought her to the fireside, very much confused, and very shy; but she soon became more assured when she found how Steerforth spoke to her; how skilfully he avoided anything that would embarrass her; how he talked to Mr. Peggotty of boats, and ships, and tides, and fish; how delighted he was with that boat and all belonging to it; how lightly and easily he carried on, until he brought us by degrees into a charmed circle.

But he set up no monopoly of the conversation. He was silent and attentive when little Em'ly talked across the fire to me of our old childish wanderings upon the beach, to pick up shells and pebbles; he was very silent and attentive when I asked her if she recollected how I used to love her, and how we used to walk about that dim old flat, hours and hours, and how the days sported by us as if Time himself had not grown up then, but were a child like ourselves, and always at play. She sat all the evening in her old little corner by the fire—Ham beside her. I could not satisfy myself whether it was in her little tormenting way, or in a maidenly reserve before us, that she kept quite close to the wall, and away from Ham; but I observed that she did so all the evening.

As I remember, it was almost midnight when we took our leave. We had had some biscuit and dried fish for supper, and Steerforth had produced from his pocket a flask of Hollands.[2] We parted merrily; and as they all stood crowded round the door to light us on our road, I saw the sweet blue eyes of little Em'ly peeping after us, from behind Ham, and heard her soft voice calling to us to be careful how we went.

"A most engaging little beauty!" said Steerforth, taking my arm. "Well! It's a quaint place, and they are quaint company; and it's quite a new sensation to mix with them."

"How fortunate we are, too, Steerforth, to have arrived to witness their happiness in that intended marriage! I never saw people so happy. How delightful to see it!"

[1] *murder's out* Secret is revealed.

[2] *Hollands* Type of gin made in Holland.

"Yes—that's rather a chuckle-headed[1] fellow for the girl. Isn't he?"

I felt a shock in this cold reply. But turning quickly upon him, and seeing a laugh in his eyes, I answered:

"Ah, Steerforth! It's well for you to joke about the poor! But when I see how perfectly you understand them, and how you can enter into happiness like this plain fisherman's, I know there is not a joy, or sorrow, or any emotion of such people that can be indifferent to you. And I admire and love you for it, Steerforth, twenty times the more!"

To my surprise he suddenly said, with nothing that I could see to lead to it:

"Daisy, I wish to God I had had a judicious father these last twenty years! You know my mother has always doted on me and spoilt me. I wish with all my soul I had been better guided! I wish with all my soul I could guide myself better!"

There was a passionate dejection in his manner that quite amazed me. He was more unlike himself than I could have supposed possible.

"It would be better to be this poor Peggotty, or his lout of a nephew, than be myself, twenty times richer and twenty times wiser, and be the torment to myself that I have been in that Devil's bark of a boat within the last half-hour."

I was so confounded by the change in him that at first I could only regard him in silence as he walked at my side. At length I asked him to tell me what had happened to cross him so unusually.

"Tut, it's nothing—nothing, Davy! I must have had a nightmare, I think. What old women call the horrors have been creeping over me from head to foot. I have been afraid of myself."

"You are afraid of nothing else, I think."

"Perhaps not, and yet may have enough to be afraid of too. Well! so it goes by! Daisy—for though that's not the name your godfathers and godmothers gave you, you're such a fresh fellow that it's the name I best like to call you by—and I wish, I wish, I wish you could give it to me!"

"Why, so I can, if I choose."

"Daisy, if anything should ever happen to separate us, you must think of me at my best, old boy. Come! let us make that bargain. Think of me at my best, if circumstances should ever part us."

"You have no best to me, Steerforth, and no worst. You are always equally loved and cherished in my heart."

I was up to go away alone next morning with the dawn, and, having dressed as quietly as I could, looked into his room. He was fast asleep, lying easily with his head upon his arm, as I had often seen him lie at school.

The time came in its season, and that was very soon, when I almost wondered that nothing troubled his repose, as I looked at him then. But he slept—let me think of him so again—as I had often seen him sleep at school; and thus, in this silent hour, I left him.

Nevermore, oh God forgive you, Steerforth! to touch that passive hand in love and friendship. Never, never more!

Chapter 2

Some months elapsed before I again found myself down in that part of the country and approaching the old boat by night.

It was a dark evening, and rain was beginning to fall, when I came within sight of Mr. Peggotty's house, and of the light within it shining through the window. A little floundering across the sand, which was heavy, brought me to the door, and I went in.

I was bidden to a little supper; Em'ly was to be married to Ham that day fortnight,[2] and this was the last time I was to see her in her maiden life.

It looked very comfortable indeed. Mr. Peggotty had smoked his evening pipe, and there were preparations for supper by and by. The fire was bright, the ashes were thrown up, the locker was ready for little Em'ly in her old place. Mrs. Gummidge appeared to be fretting a little in her own corner, and consequently looked quite natural.

"You're first of the lot, Mas'r Davy! Sit ye down, sir. It ain't o' no use saying welcome to you; but you're

[1] *chuckle-headed* Block-headed, stupid.

[2] *that day fortnight* In exactly two weeks.

welcome, kind and hearty."

Here Mrs. Gummidge groaned.

"Cheer up, cheer up, Mrs. Gummidge!" said Mr. Peggotty.

"No, no, Dan'l. It ain't o' no use telling me to cheer up, when everythink goes contrairy with me. Nothink's nat'ral to me but to be lone and lorn."

After looking at Mrs. Gummidge for some moments with great sympathy, Mr. Peggotty glanced at the Dutch clock, rose, snuffed the candle, and put it in the window.

"Theer! theer we are, Missis Gummidge!" Mrs. Gummidge slightly groaned again. "Theer we are, Mrs. Gummidge, lighted up accordin' to custom! You're a wonderin' what that's fur, sir! Well, it's for our little Em'ly. You see, the path ain't over light or cheerful arter dark; and when I'm here at the hour as she's a comin' home from her needle-work down town, I puts the light in the winder. That, you see, meets two objects. She says to herself, says Em'ly, 'Theer's home!' she says. And likeways, says Em'ly, 'My uncle's theer!' Fur if I ain't theer, I never have no light showed. You may say this is like a babby, sir. Well, I doen't know but what I am a babby in regard o' Em'ly. Not to look at, but to—to consider on, you know. I doen't care, bless you! Now I tell you. When I go a looking and looking about that theer pritty house of our Em'ly's, all got ready for her to be married, if I doen't feel as if the littlest things was her, a'most. I takes 'em up, and I puts 'em down, and I touches of 'em as delicate as if they was our Em'ly. So 't is with her little bonnets and that. I couldn't see one on 'em rough used, a purpose, not fur the whole wureld.

"It's my opinion, you see, as this is along of my havin' played with Em'ly so much when she was a child, and havin' made believe as we was Turks, and French, and sharks, and every wariety of forinners—bless you, yes; and lions and whales, and I don't know what all!—when she warn't no higher than my knee. I've got into the way on it, you know. Why, this here candle, now! I know wery well that arter she's married and gone, I shall put that candle theer, just the same as now, and sit afore the fire, pretending I'm expecting of her, like as I'm a doing now. Why, at the present minute when I see the candle sparkle up, I says to myself, 'She's a looking at it! Em'ly's a coming!' Right too, fur here she is!"

No; it was only Ham. The night should have turned more wet since I came in, for he had a large sou'wester hat on, slouched over his face.

"Where's Em'ly?"

Ham made a movement as if she were outside. Mr. Peggotty took the light from the window, trimmed it, put it on the table, and was stirring the fire, when Ham, who had not moved, said, "Mas'r Davy, will you come out a minute, and see what Em'ly and me has got to show you?"

As I passed him, I saw to my astonishment and fright that he was deadly pale. He closed the door upon us. Only upon us two.

"Ham! What's the matter?"

"My love, Mas'r Davy—the pride and hope of my art—her that I'd have died for, and would die for now—she's gone!"

"Gone!"

"Em'ly's run away! You're a scholar and know what's right and best. What am I to say, in-doors? How am I ever to break it to him, Mas'r Davy?"

I saw the door move, and tried to hold the latch, to gain a moment's time. It was too late. Mr. Peggotty thrust forth his face; and never could I forget the change that came upon it when he saw us, if I were to live five hundred years.

I remember a great wail and cry, and the women hanging about him, and we all standing in the room—I with an open letter in my hand which Ham had given me; Mr. Peggotty with his vest torn open, his hair wild, his face and lips white, and blood trickling down his bosom (it had sprung from his mouth, I think).

"Read it, sir; slow, please. I doen't know as I can understand."

In the midst of the silence of death, I read thus, from the blotted letter Ham had given me. In Em'ly's hand, addressed to himself:

"'When you, who love me so much better than I ever have deserved, even when my mind was innocent, see this, I shall be far away. When I leave my dear home—my dear home—Oh, my dear home!—in the morning,'" (the letter bore date on the previous night), "'it will be never to come back, unless he brings me back a lady. This will be found at night, many hours after, instead of me. For mercy's sake, tell uncle that I never loved him half so dear as now. Oh, don't remember you and I were ever to be married, but try to think as if I died when I was very little, and was buried somewhere. Pray Heaven that I am going away from, have compassion on my uncle! Be his comfort. Love some good girl, that will be what I was once to uncle, and that will be true to you, and worthy of you, and know no shame but me. God bless all! If he don't bring me back a lady, and I don't pray for my own self, I'll pray for all. My parting love to uncle. My last tears, and my last thanks, for uncle!'" That was all.

He stood, long after I had ceased to read, still looking at me. Slowly at last he moved his eyes from my face, and cast them round the room.

"Who's the man? I want to know his name." Ham glanced at me, and suddenly I felt a shock. "Mas'r Davy! Go out a bit, and let me tell him what I must. You doen't ought to hear it, sir."

I sank down in a chair and tried to utter some reply; but my tongue was fettered, and my sight was weak. For I felt that the man was my friend, the friend I had unhappily introduced there—Steerforth, my old schoolfellow and my friend.

"I want to know his name!"

"Mas'r Davy, it ain't no fault of yourn—and I am far from laying of it to you—but it is your friend Steerforth, and he's a damned villain!"

Mr. Peggotty moved no more, until he seemed to wake all at once, and pulled down his rough coat from its peg in a corner.

"Bear a hand with this! I'm struck of a heap,[1] and can't do it. Bear a hand and help me. Well! Now give me that theer hat!"

Ham asked him whither he was going.

"I'm a going to seek my niece. I'm a going to seek my Em'ly. I'm a going, first, to stave in that theer boat as he gave me, and sink it where I would have drownded *him*, as I'm a livin' soul, if I had had one thought of what was in him! As he sat afore me, in that boat, face to face, strike me down dead, but I'd have drownded him, and thought it right!—I'm a going fur to seek my niece."

"Where?"

"Anywhere! I'm a going to seek my niece through the wureld. I'm a going to find my poor niece in her shame, and bring her back wi' my comfort and forgiveness. No one stop me! I tell you I'm a going to seek my niece! I'm a going to seek her fur and wide!"

Mrs. Gummidge came between them in a fit of crying. "No, no, Dan'l, not as you are now. Seek her in a little while, my lone lorn Dan'l, and that'll be but right; but not as you are now. Sit ye down, and give me your forgiveness for having ever been a worrit to you, Dan'l—what have *my* contrairies ever been to this!—and let us speak a word about them times when she was first a orphan, and when Ham was too, and when I was a poor widder woman and you took me in. It'll soften your poor heart, Dan'l, and you'll bear your sorrow better; for you know the promise, Dan'l, 'As you have done it unto one of the least of these, you have done it unto me';[2] and that can never fail under this roof, that's been our shelter for so many, many year!"

He was quite passive now; and when I heard him crying, the impulse that had been upon me to go down upon my knees and curse Steerforth yielded to a better feeling. My overcharged heart found the same relief as his, and I cried too.

CHAPTER 3

At this period of my life I lived in my top set of chambers in Buckingham Street, Strand, London, and was over head and ears in love with Dora. I lived principally on Dora and coffee. My appetite languished, and I was glad of it, for I felt as though it would have been an act of perfidy towards Dora to have a natural relish for my dinner. I bought four sumptuous waistcoats—not for myself, I had no pride in them—for Dora. I took to wearing straw-coloured kid gloves in the streets. I laid the foundations of all the corns I have ever had. If the boots

[1] *struck of a heap* Extremely disconcerted.

[2] *As you … unto me* In Matthew 25.40, it is said that Christ will speak these words to the righteous regarding their charitable acts.

I wore at that period could only be produced, and compared with the natural size of my feet, they would show in a most affecting manner what the state of my heart was.

Mrs. Crupp, the housekeeper of my chambers, must have been a woman of penetration; for when this attachment was but a few weeks old she found it out. She came up to me one evening when I was very low, to ask (she being afflicted with spasms) if I could oblige her with a little tincture of cardamums, mixed with rhubarb, and flavoured with seven drops of the essence of cloves; or, if I had not such a thing by me, with a little brandy. As I had never even heard of the first remedy, and always had the second in the closet, I gave Mrs. Crupp a glass of the second, which (that I might have no suspicion of its being devoted to any improper use) she began to take immediately.

"Cheer up, sir," said Mrs. Crupp. "Excuse me; I know what it is, sir. There's a lady in the case."

"Mrs. Crupp?"

"Oh, bless you! Keep a good heart, sir! Never say die, sir! If she don't smile upon you, there's a many as will. You're a young gentleman to *be* smiled on, Mr. Copperfull, and you must learn your walue, sir."

Mrs. Crupp always called me Mr. Copperfull: firstly, no doubt, because it was not my name; and secondly, I am inclined to think, in some indistinct association with a washing-day.[1]

"What makes you suppose there is any young lady in the case, Mrs. Crupp?"

"Mr. Copperfull, I'm a mother myself. Your boots and your waist is equally too small, and you don't eat enough, sir, nor yet drink. Sir, I have laundressed other young gentlemen besides you. It was but the gentleman which died here before yourself that fell in love—with a barmaid—and had his waistcoats took in directly, though much swelled by drinking."

"Mrs. Crupp, I must beg you not to connect the young lady in my case with a barmaid, or anything of that sort, if you please."

"Mr. Copperfull, I'm a mother myself, and not likely. I ask your pardon, sir, if I intrude. I should never wish to intrude where I were not welcome. But you are a young gentleman, Mr. Copperfull, and my adwice to you is, to cheer up, sir, to keep a good heart, and to know your own walue. If you was to take to something, sir—if you was to take to skittles,[2] now, which is healthy—you might find it divert your mind, and do you good."

I turned it off, and changed the subject by informing Mrs. Crupp that I wished to entertain at dinner next day my esteemed friend Traddles and Mr. and Mrs. Micawber; and I took the liberty of suggesting a pair of soles,[3] a small leg of mutton, and a pigeon-pie. Mrs. Crupp broke out into rebellion on my first bashful hint in reference to *her* cooking the fish and joint. But, in the end, a compromise was effected, and Mrs. Crupp consented to achieve this feat on condition that I dined from home for a fortnight afterwards.

Having laid in the materials for a bowl of punch, to be compounded by Mr. Micawber, having provided a bottle of lavender-water,[4] two wax candles, a paper of mixed pins, and a pincushion, to assist Mrs. Micawber in her toilette, at my dressing-table, having also caused the fire in my bed-room to be lighted for Mrs. Micawber's convenience, and having laid the cloth with my own hands, I awaited the result with composure.

At the appointed time my three visitors arrived together. Mr. Micawber, with more shirt-collar[5] than usual, and a new ribbon to his eye-glass; Mrs. Micawber, with her cap in a parcel; Traddles carrying the parcel, and supporting Mrs. Micawber on his arm. They were all delighted with my residence. When I conducted Mrs. Micawber to my dressing-table, and she saw the scale on which it was prepared for her, she was in such raptures that she called Mr. Micawber to come in and look.

"My dear Copperfield," said Mr. Micawber, "this is luxurious. This is a way of life which reminds me of the

[1] *association with a washing-day* Large copper vessels called "coppers" were used to do laundry.

[2] *skittles* Game in which the object is to knock over a set of pins.

[3] *a pair of soles* Two filets of sole.

[4] *lavender-water* Perfume.

[5] *more shirt-collar* I.e., a higher collar.

period when I was myself in a state of celibacy. I am at present established on what may be designated as a small and unassuming scale; but you are aware that I have, in the course of my career, surmounted difficulties and conquered obstacles. You are no stranger to the fact that there have been periods of my life, when it has been requisite that I should pause until certain expected events should turn up—when it has been necessary that I should fall back before making what I trust I shall not be accused of presumption in terming—a spring. The present is one of those momentous stages in the life of man. You find me fallen back *for* a spring, and I have every reason to believe that a vigorous leap will shortly be the result."

I informed Mr. Micawber that I relied upon him for a bowl of punch, and led him to the lemons. I never saw a man so thoroughly enjoy himself, as he stirred, and mixed, and tasted, and looked as if he were making, not mere punch, but a fortune for his family down to the latest posterity. As to Mrs. Micawber, I don't know whether it was the effect of the cap, or the lavender-water, or the pins, or the fire, or the wax candles, but she came out of my room, comparatively speaking, lovely.

I suppose—I never ventured to inquire, but I suppose—that Mrs. Crupp, after frying the soles, was taken ill. Because we broke down at that point. The leg of mutton came up very red inside, and very pale outside, besides having a foreign substance of a gritty nature sprinkled over it, as if it had had a fall into ashes. But we were not in a condition to judge of this fact from the appearance of the gravy, forasmuch as it had been all dropped on the stairs. The pigeon-pie was not bad, but it was a delusive pie, the crust being like a disappointing phrenological[1] head—full of lumps and bumps, with nothing particular underneath. In short, the banquet was such a failure that I should have been quite unhappy—about the failure I mean, for I was always unhappy about Dora—if I had not been relieved by the great good-humour of my company.

"My dear friend Copperfield," said Mr. Micawber, "accidents will occur in the best-regulated families, and especially in families not regulated by that pervading influence which sanctifies while it enhances the—a—I would say, in short, by the influence of Woman in the lofty character of Wife. If you will allow me to take liberty of remarking that there are few comestibles better, in their way, than a Devil,[2] and that I believe, with a little division of labour, we could accomplish a good one if the young person in attendance could produce a gridiron,[3] I would put it to you, that this little misfortune may be easily repaired."

There *was* a gridiron in the pantry, on which my morning rasher of bacon was cooked. We had it out in a twinkling. Traddles cut the mutton into slices; Mr. Micawber covered them with pepper, mustard, salt, and cayenne; I put them on the gridiron, turned them with a fork, and took them off, under Mr. Micawber's direction; and Mrs. Micawber heated some mushroom ketchup in a little saucepan. Under these circumstances my appetite came back miraculously. I am ashamed to confess it, but I really believe I forgot Dora for a little while.

"Punch, my dear Copperfield," said Mr. Micawber, tasting it as soon as dinner was done, "like time and tide, waits for no man. Ah! it is at the present moment in high flavour. My love, will you give me your opinion?"

Mrs. Micawber pronounced it excellent.

"As we are quite confidential here, Mr. Copperfield," said Mrs. Micawber, sipping her punch, "(Mr. Traddles being a part of our domesticity), I should much like to have your opinion on Mr. Micawber's prospects. I have consulted branches of my family on the course most expedient for Mr. Micawber to take, and it was, that he should immediately turn his attention to coals."

"To what, ma'am?"

"To coals. To the coal trade. Mr. Micawber was induced to think, on inquiry, that there might be an opening for a man of his talent in the Medway Coal

[1] *phrenological* Phrenology is the study of bumps and dents on the surface of the skull as a supposed indicator of personality and abilities.

[2] *Devil* Meat dish served with devil sauce.

[3] *gridiron* Metal grate used for grilling over a fire.

Trade. Then, as Mr. Micawber very properly said, the first step to be taken clearly was to go and *see* the Medway; which we went and saw. I say 'we,' Mr. Copperfield; for I never will desert Mr. Micawber. I am a wife and mother, and I never will desert Mr. Micawber." Traddles and I murmured our admiration. "That," said Mrs. Micawber, "that, at least, is *my* view, my dear Mr. Copperfield and Mr. Traddles, of the obligation which I took upon myself when I repeated the irrevocable words, 'I, Emma, take thee, Wilkins.' I read the service over with a flat candle, on the previous night, and the conclusion I derived from it was that I never could or would desert Mr. Micawber."

"My dear," said Mr. Micawber, a little impatiently, "I am not conscious that you are expected to do anything of the sort."

"We went," repeated Mrs. Micawber, "and saw the Medway. My opinion of the coal trade on that river was, that it might require talent, but that it certainly requires capital. Talent, Mr. Micawber has; capital, Mr. Micawber has not. We saw, I think, the greater part of the Medway; and that was my individual conclusion. My family were then of opinion that Mr. Micawber should turn his attention to corn—on commission. But corn, as I have repeatedly said to Mr. Micawber, may be gentlemanly, but it is not remunerative. Commission to the extent of two and ninepence[1] in a fortnight cannot, however limited our ideas, be considered remunerative."

We were all agreed upon that.

"Then," said Mrs. Micawber, who prided herself on taking a clear view of things, and keeping Mr. Micawber straight by her woman's wisdom, when he might otherwise go a little crooked, "then I naturally look round the world, and say, 'What is there in which a person of Mr. Micawber's talent is likely to succeed?' I may have a conviction that Mr. Micawber's manners peculiarly qualify him for the Banking business. I may argue within myself, that if I had a deposit in a banking-house, the manners of Mr. Micawber, as representing that banking-house, would inspire confidence and extend the connexion. But if the various banking-houses refuse to avail themselves of Mr. Micawber's abilities, or receive the offer of them with contumely,[2] what is the use of dwelling upon *that* idea? None. As to originating a banking business, I may know that there are members of my family, who, if they chose to place their money in Mr. Micawber's hands, might found an establishment of that description. But if they do *not* choose to place their money in Mr. Micawber's hands—which they don't—what is the use of that? Again I contend that we are no farther advanced than we were before."

I shook my head, and said, "Not a bit." Traddles also shook his head, and said, "Not a bit."

"What do I deduce from this?" Mrs. Micawber went on to say, still with the same air of putting a case lucidly. "What is the conclusion, my dear Mr. Copperfield, to which I am irresistibly brought. Am I wrong in saying it is clear that we must live?"

I answered, "Not at all!" and Traddles answered, "Not at all!" and I found myself afterwards sagely adding, alone, that a person must either live or die.

"Just so," returned Mrs. Micawber. "It is precisely that. And here is Mr. Micawber without any suitable position or employment. Where does that responsibility rest? Clearly on society. Then I would make a fact so disgraceful known, and boldly challenge society to set it right. It appears to me, my dear Mr. Copperfield, that what Mr. Micawber has to do is to throw down the gauntlet to society and say, in effect, 'Show me who will take that up. Let the party immediately step forward.'"

I ventured to ask Mrs. Micawber how this was to be done.

"By advertising in all the papers. It appears to me, that what Mr. Micawber has to do, in justice to himself, in justice to his family, and I will even go so far as to say in justice to society, by which he has been hitherto overlooked, is to advertise in all the papers; to describe himself plainly as so and so, with such and such qualifications, and to put it thus: '*Now* employ me on remunerative terms, and address, post paid, to W.M., Post Office, Camden Town.'[3]

---

[1] *two and ninepence* Two shillings and nine pence; a shilling was worth twelve pence.

[2] *contumely* Insulting language or treatment.

[3] *Camden Town* District of inner London, considered an unfashionable location in the nineteenth century.

"Advertising is rather expensive," I remarked.

"Exactly so!" said Mrs. Micawber, preserving the same logical air. "Quite true, my dear Mr. Copperfield. I have made the identical observation to Mr. Micawber. It is for that reason, especially, that I think Mr. Micawber ought to raise a certain sum of money—on a bill."[1]

Mr. Micawber, leaning back in his chair, trifled with his eye-glass, and cast his eye up at the ceiling; but I thought him observant of Traddles, too, who was looking at the fire.

"If no member of my family," said Mrs. Micawber, "is possessed of sufficient natural feeling to negotiate that bill—I believe there is a better business term to express what I mean—"

Mr. Micawber, with his eyes still cast up at the ceiling, suggested, "Discount."[2]

"To discount that bill, then, my opinion is, that Mr. Micawber should go into the city, should take that bill into the money market,[3] and should dispose of it for what he can get."

I felt, but I am sure I don't know why, that this was highly self-denying and devoted in Mrs. Micawber, and I uttered a murmur to that effect. Traddles, who took his tone from me, did likewise, and really I felt that she was a noble woman—the sort of woman who might have been a Roman matron, and done all manner of troublesome heroic public actions.

In the fervour of this impression, I congratulated Mr. Micawber on the treasure he possessed. So did Traddles. Mr. Micawber extended his hand to each of us in succession, and then covered his face with his pocket-handkerchief—which I think had more snuff upon it than he was aware of. He then returned to the punch in the highest state of exhilaration.

Mrs. Micawber made tea for us in a most agreeable manner, and after tea we discussed a variety of topics before the fire; and she was good enough to sing us (in a small, thin, flat voice, which I remembered to have considered, when I first knew her, the very table-beer[4] of acoustics) the favourite ballads of "The Dashing White Sergeant" and "Little Tafflin." For both of these songs Mrs. Micawber had been famous when she lived at home with her papa and mamma. Mr. Micawber told us that when he heard her sing the first one, on the first occasion of his seeing her beneath the parental roof, she had attracted his attention in an extraordinary degree; but that when it came to "Little Tafflin" he had resolved to win that woman or perish in the attempt.

It was between ten and eleven o'clock when Mrs. Micawber rose to replace her cap in the parcel, and to put on her bonnet. Mr. Micawber took the opportunity to slip a letter into my hand, with a whispered request that I would read it at my leisure. I also took the opportunity of my holding a candle over the bannisters to light them down, when Mr. Micawber was going first, leading Mrs. Micawber, to detain Traddles for a moment on the top of the stairs.

"Traddles, Mr. Micawber don't mean any harm, but, if I were you, I wouldn't lend him anything."

"My dear Copperfield, I haven't got anything to lend."

"You have got a name, you know."

"Oh, you call *that* something to lend?"

"Certainly."

"Oh, yes, to be sure! I am very much obliged to you, Copperfield, but—I am afraid I have lent him that already."

"For the bill that is to go into the money market?"

"No, not for that one. This is the first I have heard of that one. I have been thinking that he will most likely propose that one on the way home. Mine's another."

"I hope there will be nothing wrong about it."

"I hope not. I should think not, though, because he told me, only the other day, that it was provided for. That was Mr. Micawber's expression, 'provided for.'"

[1] *bill* I.e., accommodation bill, a signed document similar in form to a check but serving to raise money on credit, by which the borrower contracts to pay a specific sum at a given date, typically some months in the future.

[2] *Discount* Buy an accommodation bill in advance of the due date for less than the sum specified on the bill (the difference being equal to or greater than the related interest).

[3] *money market* Dealers in short-term finance to whom the bill could be sold at a steep discount. Such bills could change hands a number of times so that the party signing the bill might finally have to settle the debt with an unknown and unaccommodating party.

[4] *table-beer* Beer of low alcoholic content.

Mr. Micawber looking up at this juncture, I had only time to repeat my caution. Traddles thanked me, and descended. But I was much afraid, when I observed the good-natured manner in which he went down with Mrs. Micawber's cap in his hand, that he would be carried into the money market, neck and heels.[1]

I returned to my fireside, and read Mr. Micawber's letter, which was dated an hour and a half before dinner. I am not sure whether I have mentioned that, when Mr. Micawber was at any particularly desperate crisis, he used a sort of legal phraseology, which he seemed to think equivalent to winding up his affairs.

This was the letter.

> SIR—for I dare not say my dear Copperfield—
> It is expedient that I should inform you that the undersigned is Crushed. Some flickering efforts to spare the premature knowledge of his calamitous position, you may observe in him this day; but hope has sunk beneath the horizon, and the undersigned is Crushed.
>
> The present communication is penned within the personal range (I cannot call it the society) of an individual in a state closely bordering on intoxication, employed by a broker. That individual is in legal possession of the premises, under a distress for rent. His inventory includes, not only the chattels and effects of every description belonging to the undersigned, as yearly tenant of this habitation, but also those appertaining to Mr. Thomas Traddles, lodger, a member of the Honourable Society of the Inner Temple.[2]
>
> If any drop of gloom were wanting in the overflowing cup, which is now 'commended' (in the language of an immortal Writer) to the lips of the undersigned,[3] it would be found in the fact that a friendly acceptance granted to the undersigned by the before-mentioned Mr. Thomas Traddles, for the sum of £23 4*s.* 9½*d.*,[4] is overdue, and is not provided for. Also, in the fact, that the living responsibilities clinging to the undersigned will, in the course of nature, be increased by the sum of one more helpless victim, whose miserable appearance may be looked for—in round numbers—at the expiration of a period not exceeding six lunar months from the present date.
>
> After premising thus much, it would be a work of supererogation to add that dust and ashes are forever scattered
>
> On
>
> The
>
> Head
>
> Of
>
> WILKINS MICAWBER.

CHAPTER 4

Seldom did I wake at night, seldom did I look up at the moon, or stars, or watch the falling rain, or hear the wind, but I thought of the solitary figure of the good fisherman, toiling on—poor Pilgrim—and recalled his words, "I'm a going to seek my niece. I'm a going to seek her fur and wide."

Months passed, and he had been absent—no one knew where—the whole time. It had been a bitter day in London, and a cutting northeast wind had blown. The wind had gone down with the light, and snow had come on. My shortest way home—and I naturally took the shortest way on such a night—was through Saint Martin's Lane. On the steps of the church there was the figure of a man, and I stood face to face with Mr. Peggotty.

"Mas'r Davy! It do my art good to see you, sir. Well met, well met!"

"Well met, my dear old friend!"

"I had thowts o' coming to make inquiration for you, sir, to-night, but it was too late. I should have come early in the morning, sir, afore going away agen."

"Again?"

"Yes, sir, I'm away to-morrow."

[1] *neck and heels* Entirely.

[2] *Honourable Society of the Inner Temple* Professional association of lawyers.

[3] *If any … the undersigned* Cf. Shakespeare's *Macbeth* 1.7.10–12: "This even-handed justice / Commends the ingredients of our poisoned chalice / To our own lips."

[4] *£23 4s. 9½d.* Twenty-three pounds, four shillings, nine and a half pence.

In those days there was a side entrance to the stable-yard of the Golden Cross Inn. Two or three public-rooms opened out of the yard, and looking into one of them, and finding it empty and a good fire burning, I took him in there.

"I'll tell you, Mas'r Davy, wheer-all I've been, and what-all we've heerd. I've been fur, and we've heerd little; but I'll tell you."

As he sat thinking, there was a fine massive gravity in his face which I did not venture to disturb.

"You see, sir, when she was a child she used to talk to me a deal about the sea, and about them coasts where the sea got to be dark blue, and to lay a shining and a shining in the sun. When she was lost, I know'd in my mind as he would take her to them countries. I know'd in my mind as he'd have told her wonders of 'em, and how she was to be a lady theer, and how he first got her to listen to him along o' sech like. I went across channel to France, and landed theer, as if I'd fell down from the skies. I found out a English gentleman, as was in authority, and told him I was going to seek my niece. He got me them papers as I wanted fur to carry me through—I doen't rightly know how they're called—and he would have give me money, but that I was thankful to have no need on. I thank him kind for all he done, I'm sure. I told him, best as I was able, what my gratitoode was, and went away through France, fur to seek my niece."

"Alone, and on foot?"

"Mostly afoot; sometimes in carts, along with people going to market; sometimes in empty coaches. Many mile a day afoot, and often with some poor soldier or another, travelling fur to see his friends. I couldn't talk to him, nor he to me; but we was company for one another, too, along the dusty roads. When I come to any town, I found the inn, and waited about the yard till some one came by (some one mostly did) as know'd English. Then I told how that I was on my way to seek my niece, and they told me what manner of gentlefolks was in the house, and I waited to see any as seemed like her, going in or out. When it warn't Em'ly, I went on agen. By little and little, when I come to a new village or that, among the poor people, I found they know'd about me. They would set me down at their cottage doors, and give me what-not fur to eat and drink, and show me where to sleep. And many a woman, Mas'r Davy, as has had a daughter about Em'ly's age, I've found a-waiting for me, at Our Saviour's Cross outside the village, fur to do me sim'lar kindnesses. Some has had daughters as was dead. And God only knows how good them mothers was to me!"

I laid my trembling hand upon the hand he put before his face. "Thank'ee, sir, doen't take no notice.

"At last I come to the sea. It warn't hard, you may suppose, for a seafaring man like me to work his way over to Italy. When I got theer I wandered on as I had done afore. I got news of her being seen among them Swiss mountains yonder. I made for them mountains, day and night. Ever so fur as I went, ever so fur them mountains seemed to shift away from me. But I come up with 'em, and I crossed 'em. I never doubted her. No! Not a bit! On'y let her see my face—on'y let her heer my voice—on'y let my stanning still afore her bring to her thoughts the home she had fled away from, and the child she had been—and if she had growed to be a royal lady, she'd have fell down at my feet! I know'd it well! I bought a country dress to put upon her. To put that dress upon her, and to cast off what she wore—to take her on my arm again, and wander towards home—to stop sometimes upon the road and heal her bruised feet and her worse bruised heart—was all I thowt of now. But, Mas'r Davy, it warn't to be—not yet! I was too late, and they was gone. Wheer, I couldn't learn. Some said heer, some said theer. I travelled heer, and I travelled theer, but I found no Em'ly, and I travelled home."

"How long ago?"

"A matter o' fower days. I sighted the old boat arter dark, and I never could have thowt, I'm sure, that the old boat would have been so strange."

From some pocket in his breast he took out, with a very careful hand, a small paper bundle containing two or three letters or little packets which he laid upon the table.

"The faithful creetur Mrs. Gummidge gave me these. This first one come afore I had been gone a week. A fifty pound bank-note in a sheet of paper, directed to me, and put underneath the door in the night. She tried to hide her writing, but she couldn't hide it from Me! This one come to Missis Gummidge two or three months ago. Five pounds."

It was untouched, like the previous sum, and he refolded both.

"Is that another letter in your hand?"

"It's money too, sir. Ten pound, you see. And wrote inside, 'From a true friend.' But the two first was put underneath the door, and this come by the post, day afore yesterday. I'm going to seek her at the post-mark."

He showed it to me. It was a town on the Upper Rhine. He had found out at Yarmouth some foreign dealers who knew that country, and they had drawn him a rude[1] map on paper, which he could very well understand.

I asked him how Ham was.

"He works as bold as a man can. He's never been heerd fur to complain. But my belief is ('twixt ourselves), as it has cut him deep. Well! Having seen you to-night, Mas'r Davy (and that does me good), I shall away betimes[2] to-morrow morning. You have seen what I've got heer," putting his hand on where the little packet lay. "All that troubles me is, to think that any harm might come to me afore this money was give back. If I was to die, and it was lost or stole or elseways made away with, and it was never know'd by him but what I'd accepted of it, I believe the tother wureld wouldn't hold me! I believe I must come back!"

He rose, and I rose too. We grasped each other by the hand again; and as we went out into the rigorous night, everything seemed to be hushed in reverence for him, when he resumed his solitary journey through the snow.

Chapter 5

All this time I had gone on loving Dora harder than ever. If I may so express it, I was steeped in Dora. I was not merely over head and ears in love with her, I was saturated through and through. I took night walks to Norwood[3] where she lived, and perambulated round and round the house and garden for hours together, looking through crevices in the palings, using violent exertions to get my chin above the rusty nails on the top, blowing kisses at the lights in the windows, and romantically calling on the night to shield my Dora—I don't exactly know from what—I suppose from fire, perhaps from mice, to which she had a great objection.

Dora had a discreet friend, comparatively stricken in years, almost of the ripe age of twenty, I should say, whose name was Miss Mills. Dora called her Julia. She was the bosom friend of Dora. Happy Miss Mills!

One day Miss Mills said: "Dora is coming to stay with me. She is coming the day after to-morrow. If you would like to call, I am sure papa would be happy to see you."

I passed three days in a luxury of wretchedness. At last, arrayed for the purpose, at a vast expense, I went to Miss Mills's, fraught with a declaration.

Mr. Mills was not at home. I didn't expect he would be. Nobody wanted *him*. Miss Mills was at home. Miss Mills would do.

I was shown into a room up stairs, where Miss Mills and Dora were. Dora's little dog Jip was there. Miss Mills was copying music, and Dora was painting flowers. What were my feelings when I recognized flowers I had given her!

Miss Mills was very glad to see me, and very sorry her papa was not at home, though I thought we all bore that with fortitude. Miss Mills was conversational for a few minutes, and then, laying down her pen, got up and left the room.

I began to think I would put it off till to-morrow.

"I hope your poor horse was not tired when he got home at night from that picnic," said Dora, lifting up her beautiful eyes. "It was a long way for him."

I began to think I would do it to-day.

"It was a long way for *him*, for *he* had nothing to uphold him on the journey."

"Wasn't he fed, poor thing?" asked Dora.

I began to think I would put it off till to-morrow.

[1] *rude* Crude or simple.

[2] *betimes* Early.

[3] *Norwood* Part of Lambeth, in south London.

"Ye—yes, he was well taken care of. I mean he had not the unutterable happiness that I had in being so near you."

I saw now that I was in for it, and it must be done on the spot.

"I don't know why you should care for being near me," said Dora, "or why you should call it a happiness. But of course you don't mean what you say. Jip, you naughty boy, come here!"

I don't know how I did it, but I did it in a moment. I intercepted Jip. I had Dora in my arms. I was full of eloquence. I never stopped for a word. I told her how I loved her. I told her I should die without her. I told her that I idolized and worshipped her. Jip barked madly all the time. My eloquence increased, and I said, if she would like me to die for her, she had but to say the word, and I was ready. I had loved her to distraction every minute, day and night, since I first set eyes upon her. I loved her at that minute to distraction. I should always love her, every minute, to distraction. Lovers had loved before, and lovers would love again; but no lover had ever loved, might, could, would, or should ever love, as I loved Dora. The more I raved, the more Jip barked. Each of us in his own way got more mad every moment.

Well, well! Dora and I were sitting on the sofa by and by, quiet enough, and Jip was lying in her lap, winking peacefully at me. It was off my mind. I was in a state of perfect rapture. Dora and I were engaged.

Being poor, I felt it necessary the next time I went to my darling to expatiate on that unfortunate drawback. I soon carried desolation into the bosom of our joys—not that I meant to do it, but that I was so full of the subject—by asking Dora, without the smallest preparation, if she could love a beggar.

"How can you ask me anything so foolish? Love a beggar!"

"Dora, my own dearest, I am a beggar!"

"How can you be such a silly thing," replied Dora, slapping my hand, "as to sit there, telling such stories? I'll make Jip bite you, if you are so ridiculous."

But I looked so serious that Dora began to cry. She did nothing but exclaim, Oh dear! Oh dear! And oh, she was so frightened! And where was Julia Mills! And oh, take her to Julia Mills, and go away, please! until I was almost beside myself.

I thought I had killed her. I sprinkled water on her face; I went down on my knees; I plucked at my hair; I implored her forgiveness; I besought her to look up; I ravaged Miss Mills's work-box for a smelling-bottle,[1] and, in my agony of mind, applied an ivory needle-case instead, and dropped all the needles over Dora.

At last I got Dora to look at me, with a horrified expression which I gradually soothed until it was only loving, and her soft, pretty cheek was lying against mine.

"Is your heart mine still, dear Dora?"

"Oh yes! Oh yes! it's all yours. Oh, don't be dreadful!"

"My dearest love, the crust well earned—"

"Oh yes; but I don't want to hear any more about crusts. And after we are married, Jip must have a mutton-chop every day at twelve, or he'll die."

I was charmed with her childish, winning way, and I fondly explained to her that Jip should have his mutton-chop with his accustomed regularity.

When we had been engaged some half-year or so, Dora delighted me by asking me to give her that cookery-book I had once spoken of, and to show her how to keep accounts, as I had once promised I would. I brought the volume with me on my next visit (I got it prettily bound, first, to make it look less dry and more inviting), and showed her an old housekeeping book of my aunt's, and gave her a set of tablets, and a pretty little pencil-case, and a box of leads, to practise housekeeping with.

But the cookery-book made Dora's head ache, and the figures made her cry. They wouldn't add up, she said. So she rubbed them out, and drew little nosegays, and likenesses of me and Jip, all over the tablets.

Time went on, and at last, here in this hand of mine, I held the wedding licence. There were the two names in the sweet old visionary connection—David Copperfield and Dora Spenlow; and there in the corner was that parental Institution, the Stamp Office, looking down

[1] *smelling-bottle* Bottle of smelling salts, used to revive a person who has fainted.

upon our union; and there, in the printed form of words, was the Archbishop of Canterbury, invoking a blessing on us, and doing it as cheap as could possibly be expected.

I doubt whether two young birds could have known less about keeping house than I and my pretty Dora did. We had a servant, of course. *She* kept house for us. We had an awful time of it with Mary Anne.

Her name was Paragon. Her nature was represented to us, when we engaged her, as being feebly expressed in her name. She had a written character,[1] as large as a Proclamation, and according to this document could do everything of a domestic nature that ever I heard of, and a great many things that I never did hear of. She was a woman in the prime of life; of a severe countenance, and subject (particularly in the arms) to a sort of perpetual measles. She had a cousin in the Life Guards,[2] with such long legs that he looked like the afternoon shadow of somebody else. She was warranted sober and honest; and I am therefore willing to believe that she was in a fit when we found her under the boiler, and that the deficient teaspoons were attributable to the dustman.[3] She was the cause of our first little quarrel.

"My dearest life," I said one day to Dora, "do you think Mary Anne has any idea of time?"

"Why, Doady?"

"My love, because it's five, and we were to have dined at four."

My little wife came and sat upon my knee, to coax me to be quiet, and drew a line with her pencil down the middle of my nose; but I couldn't dine off that, though it was very agreeable.

"Don't you think, my dear, it would be better for you to remonstrate with Mary Anne?"

"Oh no, please! I couldn't, Doady!"

"Why not, my love?"

"Oh, because I am such a little goose, and she knows I am!"

I thought this sentiment so incompatible with the establishment of any system of check on Mary Anne, that I frowned a little.

"My precious wife, we must be serious sometimes. Come! sit down on this chair, close beside me! Give me the pencil! There! Now let us talk sensibly. You know, dear," what a little hand it was to hold, and what a tiny wedding-ring it was to see—"you know, my love, it is not exactly comfortable to have to go out without one's dinner. Now, is it?"

"N-n-no!" replied Dora, faintly.

"My love, how you tremble!"

"Because I know you're going to scold me."

"My sweet, I am only going to reason."

"Oh, but reasoning is worse than scolding! I didn't marry to be reasoned with. If you meant to reason with such a poor little thing as I am, you ought to have told me so, you cruel boy!"

"Dora, my darling!"

"No, I am not your darling. Because you *must* be sorry that you married me, or else you wouldn't reason with me!"

I felt so injured by the inconsequential nature of this charge, that it gave me courage to be grave.

"Now, my own Dora, you are childish, and are talking nonsense. You must remember, I am sure, that I was obliged to go out yesterday when dinner was half over; and that, the day before, I was made quite unwell by being obliged to eat underdone veal in a hurry; to-day, I don't dine at all, and I am afraid to say how long we waited for breakfast, and *then* the water didn't boil. I don't mean to reproach you, my dear, but this is not comfortable."

"Oh, you cruel, cruel boy, to say I am a disagreeable wife!"

"Now, my dear Dora, you must know that I never said that!"

"You said I wasn't comfortable!"

"I said the housekeeping was not comfortable."

"It's exactly the same thing! and I wonder, I do, at your making such ungrateful speeches. When you know

[1] *character* Letter of recommendation.

[2] *Life Guards* Cavalry units charged with the task of guarding the royal family.

[3] *dustman* Ashes from fireplace grates and other garbage were emptied into dustbins. Dustmen emptied the bins and sifted them for accidentally discarded valuables.

that the other day, when you said you would like a little bit of fish, I went out myself, miles and miles, and ordered it to surprise you."

"And it was very kind of you, my own darling; and I felt it so much that I wouldn't, on any account, have mentioned that you bought a salmon, which was too much for two; or that it cost one pound six, which was more than we can afford."

"You enjoyed it very much," sobbed Dora. "And you said I was a Mouse."

"And I'll say so again, my love, a thousand times!"

I said it a thousand times, and more, and went on saying it until Mary Anne's cousin deserted into our coal-hole,[1] and was brought out, to our great amazement, by a piquet of his companions in arms, who took him away handcuffed in a procession that covered our front-garden with disgrace.

Everybody we had anything to do with seemed to cheat us. Our appearance in a shop was a signal for the damaged goods to be brought out immediately. If we bought a lobster it was full of water. All our meat turned out tough, and there was hardly any crust to our loaves.

As to the washerwoman pawning the clothes, and coming in a state of penitent intoxication to apologize, I suppose that might have happened several times to anybody. Also the chimney on fire, the parish engine, and perjury on the part of the beadle.[2] But I apprehend we were personally unfortunate in our page, whose principal function was to quarrel with the cook. We wanted to get rid of him, but he was very much attached to us, and wouldn't go, until one day he stole Dora's watch, and spent the produce (he was always a weak-minded boy) in riding up and down between London and Uxbridge[3] outside the coach.

He was taken to the Police Office on the completion of his fifteenth journey; when four-and-sixpence, and a second-hand fife which he couldn't play, were found upon his person.

He was tried, and ordered to be transported.[4] Even then he couldn't be quiet, but was always writing us letters; and he wanted so much to see Dora before he went away, that Dora went to visit him, and fainted when she found herself inside the iron bars. I had no peace of my life until he was expatriated and made (as I afterwards heard) a shepherd of "up the country" somewhere, I have no geographical idea where.

"I am very sorry for all this, Doady," said Dora. "Will you call me a name I want you to call me?"

"What is it, my dear?"

"It's a stupid name—Child-wife. When you are going to be angry with me, say to yourself 'It's only my Child-wife.' When I am very disappointing, say, 'I knew a long time ago, that she would make but a Child-wife.' When you miss what you would like me to be, and what I should like to be, and what I think I never can be, say, 'Still my foolish Child-wife loves me.' For indeed I do."

I invoke the innocent figure that I dearly loved to come out of the mists and shadows of the past, and to turn its gentle head towards me once again, and to bear witness that it was made happy by what I answered.

Chapter 6

I heard a footstep on the stairs one day. I knew it to be Mr. Peggotty's. It came nearer, nearer, rushed into the room.

"Mas'r Davy, I've found her! I thank my Heavenly Father for having guided of me in his own ways to my darling!"

"You have made up your mind as to the future, good friend?"

"Yes, Mas'r Davy, theer's mighty countries fur from heer. Our future life lays over the sea."

As he gave me both his hands, hurrying to return to the one charge of his noble existence, I thought of Ham, and who would break the intelligence to him. Mr. Peggotty thought of everything. He had already written to the poor fellow, and had the letter in the pocket of

[1] *deserted into our coal-hole* I.e., deserted from the Life Guards and hid in the Copperfields' coal cellar.

[2] *engine* Fire engine; *beadle* Low-ranking parish official.

[3] *Uxbridge* Town just west of London.

[4] *transported* Sent to a colony, probably in Australia, to serve his sentence.

his rough coat, ready for the post. I asked him for it, and said I would go down to Yarmouth, and talk to Ham myself before I gave it him, and prepare him for its contents. He thanked me very earnestly, and we parted, with the understanding that I would go down by the mail[1] that same night. In the evening I started.

"Don't you think that," I asked the coachman, in the first stage out of London, "a very remarkable sky? I don't remember to have ever seen one like it."

"Nor I. That's wind, sir. There'll be mischief done at sea before long."

It was a murky confusion of flying clouds tossed up into most remarkable heaps, through which the wild moon seemed to plunge headlong, as if, in a dread disturbance of the laws of nature, she had lost her way. There had been a wind all day; and it was rising then, with an extraordinary great sound. In another hour it had much increased, and the sky was more overcast, and it blew hard.

But as the night advanced, it came on to blow harder and harder. Many times, in the dark part of the night (it was then late in September), we were in serious apprehension that the coach would be blown over; and when the day broke, the wind blew harder, and still harder. I had been in Yarmouth when the seamen said it blew great guns, but I had never known the like of this, or anything approaching to it.

As we struggled on, nearer and nearer to the sea, from which this mighty wind was blowing dead on shore, its force became more and more terrific. When we came within sight of the sea, the waves on the horizon, seen at intervals above the rolling abyss, were like glimpses of another shore with towers and buildings. When at last we got into the town, the people came out to their doors, making a wonder of the mail that had come through such a storm.

The tremendous sea itself, when I could find pause to look at it, in the agitation of the blinding wind, the flying stones and sand, and the awful noise, confounded me. As the high watery walls came rolling in, and tumbled into surf, I seemed to see a rending and upheaving of all nature.

Not finding Ham among the people whom this memorable wind—for it is still remembered down there as the greatest ever known to blow upon that coast—had brought together on the beach, I made my way to his house.

I learned that he had gone on a job of shipwright's work some miles away, but that he would be back tomorrow morning in good time.

So I went back to the inn; and when I had washed and dressed, and tried to sleep, but in vain, it was late in the afternoon. I had not sat five minutes by the coffee-room fire, when the waiter, coming to stir it, told me that two colliers had gone down, with all hands, a few miles off; and that some other ships had been seen labouring hard in the Roads,[2] and trying, in great distress, to keep off shore. Mercy on them, and on all poor sailors, said he, if we had another night like the last!

I could not eat, I could not sit still, I could not continue steadfast to anything. My dinner went away almost untasted, and I tried to refresh myself with a glass or two of wine. In vain. I walked to and fro, tried to read an old gazetteer,[3] listened to the awful noises, looked at faces, scenes, and figures in the fire. At length the ticking of the undisturbed clock on the wall tormented me to that degree that I resolved to go to bed.

For hours I lay in bed listening to the wind and water, imagining, now, that I heard shrieks out at sea; now, that I distinctly heard the firing of signal-guns; now, the fall of houses in the town. At length my restlessness attained to such a pitch that I hurried on my clothes and went down stairs. In the large kitchen all the inn servants and some other watchers were clustered together.

One man asked me, when I went in among them, whether I thought the souls of the collier's crews who had gone down were out in the storm.

---

[1] *by the mail* Mail coaches could carry one or two additional passengers on the outside and were used if quick transportation was required.

[2] *the Roads* Stretch of water off the coast of Yarmouth.

[3] *gazetteer* Newspaper.

I remained with these people, I dare say, two hours. Once I opened the yard gate and looked into the empty street. The sand, the sea-weed, and the flakes of foam were driving by, and I was obliged to call for assistance before I could shut the gate again, and make it fast against the wind.

There was a dark gloom in my lonely chamber, when I at length returned to it; but I was tired now, and, getting into bed again, fell into the depths of sleep until broad day; when I was aroused at eight or nine o'clock by some one knocking and calling at my door.

"What is the matter?"

"A wreck! close by!"

"What wreck?"

"A schooner from Spain or Portugal, laden with fruit and wine. Make haste, sir, if you want to see her! It's thought down on the beach she'll go to pieces every moment."

I wrapped myself in my clothes as quickly as I could, and ran into the street, where numbers of people were before me, all running in one direction—to the beach. I ran the same way, outstripping a good many, and soon came facing the wild sea. Every appearance it had before presented bore the expression of being *swelled*; and the height to which the breakers rose and bore one another down, and rolled in, in interminable hosts, was most appalling.

In the difficulty of hearing anything but wind and waves, and in the crowd, and the unspeakable confusion, and my first breathless efforts to stand against the weather, I was so confused that I looked out to sea for the wreck, and saw nothing but the foaming heads of the great waves.

A boatman laid a hand upon my arm, and pointed. Then I saw it, close in upon us.

One mast was broken short off, six or eight feet from the deck, and lay over the side, entangled in a maze of sail and rigging; and all that ruin, as the ship rolled and beat—which she did with a violence quite inconceivable—beat the side as if it would stave it in. Some efforts were being made to cut this portion of the wreck away; for as the ship, which was broadside on, turned towards us in her rolling, I plainly descried her people at work with axes—especially one active figure, with long curling hair. But a great cry, audible even above the wind and water, rose from the shore; the sea, sweeping over the wreck, made a clean breach, and carried men, spars, casks, planks, bulwarks, heaps of such toys, into the boiling surge.

The second mast was yet standing, with the rags of a sail, and a wild confusion of broken cordage, flapping to and fro. The ship had struck once, the same boatman said, and then lifted in, and struck again. I understood him to add that she was parting amidships. As he spoke, there was another great cry of pity from the beach. Four men arose with the wreck out of the deep, clinging to the rigging of the remaining mast; uppermost, the active figure with the curling hair.

There was a bell on board; and as the ship rolled and dashed, this bell rang; and its sound, the knell of those unhappy men, was borne towards us on the wind. Again we lost her, and again she rose. Two of the four men were gone.

I noticed that some new sensation moved the people on the beach, and I saw them part, and Ham come breaking through them to the front.

Instantly I ran to him, for I divined that he meant to wade off with a rope. I held him back with both arms; and implored the men not to listen to him, not to let him stir that sand.

Another cry arose, and we saw the cruel sail, with blow on blow, beat off the lower of the two men, and fly up in triumph round the active figure left alone upon the mast. Against such a sight, and against such determination as that of the calmly desperate man, who was already accustomed to lead half the people present, I might as hopefully have entreated the wind.

I was swept away to some distance, where the people around me made me stay; urging, as I confusedly perceived, that he was bent on going, with help or without, and that I should endanger the precautions for his safety by troubling those with whom they rested. I saw hurry on the beach, and men running with ropes, and penetrating into a circle of figures that hid him from me. Then I saw him standing alone, in a seaman's frock and trousers, a rope in his hand, another round his body, and several of the best men holding to the latter.

The wreck was breaking up. I saw that she was parting in the middle, and that the life of the solitary man upon the mast hung by a thread. He had a singular red cap on, not like a sailor's cap, but of a finer colour; and as the few planks between him and destruction rolled and bulged, and as his death-knell rung, he was seen by all of us to wave this cap. I saw him do it now, and thought I was going distracted, when his action brought an old remembrance to my mind of a once dear friend, *the* once dear friend—Steerforth.

Ham watched the sea until there was a great retiring wave; when he dashed in after it, and in a moment was buffeting with the water, rising with the hills, falling with the valleys, lost beneath the foam—borne in towards the shore, borne on towards the ship.

At length he neared the wreck. He was so near, that with one more of his vigorous strokes he would be clinging to it, when, a high, green, vast hill-side of water moving on shoreward from beyond the ship, he seemed to leap up into it with a mighty bound—and the ship was gone!

They drew him to my very feet, insensible, dead. He was carried to the nearest house, and every means of restoration was tried; but he had been beaten to death by the great wave, and his generous heart was stilled forever.

As I sat beside the bed, when hope was abandoned, and all was done, a fisherman who had known me when Emily and I were children, and ever since, whispered my name at the door.

"Sir, will you come over yonder?"

The old remembrance that had been recalled to me was in his look, and I asked him, "Has a body come ashore?"

"Yes."

"Do I know it?"

He answered nothing. But he led me to the shore. And on that part of it where she and I had looked for shells, two children—on that part of it where some lighter fragments of the old boat blown down last night had been scattered by the wind—among the ruins of the home he had wronged—I saw him lying with his head upon his arm, as I had often seen him lie at school.

—1861

Emily Brontë

1818 – 1848

It would seem that there were two Emily Brontës: one a shy, introverted, and unremarkable young woman, and the other the strong-willed, brilliant, and legendary woman who became almost a mythic figure after her death at the age of thirty. Both versions develop from the impressions her sister Charlotte gave of her in the preface to the second edition of *Wuthering Heights*, published shortly after her death. It is for this novel that she is now best known, although she is also widely lauded for the emotional intensity, enigmatic mysticism, and linguistic ingenuity of her poetry—much of which was not published until the twentieth century. She was at work on a second, lost novel at the time of her death. While many Victorians were suspicious of *Wuthering Heights* on account of its expressions of passion and of violence, it became a classic text in the twentieth century. Its reputation has been enhanced by film adaptations, particularly by the 1939 version starring Laurence Olivier, which helped make it into a by-word for romantic tragedy.

Emily Brontë's literary talent flourished in a house of creative writers that included her sisters Charlotte (best known for *Jane Eyre*) and Anne (*The Tenant of Wildfell Hall*). Emily was the fifth child of Patrick Brontë and Maria Branwell, born in 1818 into poor circumstances in Thornton, Yorkshire. Maria died just two years later, not long after Patrick, an Anglican clergyman, had taken a post in nearby Haworth, where he and the children remained for practically all their lives. The six children were cared for by Maria's sister, Elizabeth Branwell, and educated primarily by Patrick (who had graduated from Cambridge). For the most part the children had the run of the stone parsonage that sat next to a graveyard in the desolate West Yorkshire moors. At the same time, industrial Yorkshire was close at hand.

When she was just five years old, Emily followed her three elder sisters to a charity school for the daughters of poor clergy. The conditions there were wretched, and all the sisters returned home when the two eldest, Maria and Elizabeth, contracted tuberculosis; they died soon afterward. The remaining children were left mainly to their own devices, performing household chores, reading literary classics and current affairs periodicals, walking on the moors, and writing elaborate plays and stories together. The two oldest children, Charlotte and Branwell, created an imaginary kingdom called "Angria"; the two younger children, Emily and Anne, fashioned the island of "Gondal," inspired by their father's colorful descriptions of political and historical events. Although the children's transcripts of Gondal no longer exist, Brontë continued its themes in her later, published poems.

Brontë again went off to school when she was 16, to the harsh institution that Charlotte subsequently depicted in *Jane Eyre*; she returned home after only six months due to illness. Two years later she left home for another brief sojourn—this time to teach at a girls' school—but her homesickness and aversion to the stringent workload brought her back again soon afterward. Her last stint away from home was in 1842, when she joined Charlotte at a teaching institution in Brussels. The two had planned to open their own school in Yorkshire, hoping they could turn around the family's desperate financial circumstances.

Charlotte eventually persuaded her sisters to publish a volume of their poems using pseudonyms. Unfortunately, *The Poems of Currer, Ellis, and Acton Bell* (1846), which was published with their own funds, sold only two copies and was ignored by most reviewers, although one did say that Ellis (Emily) showed the most promise. Within a year, however, all three Brontë sisters had completed novels: Charlotte, *The Professor*; Emily, *Wuthering Heights*; and Anne, *Agnes Grey*. When Charlotte's subsequently published novel, *Jane Eyre*, became a bestseller, Emily's and Anne's books were also published together in three volumes (*Agnes Grey* being the third). All three sisters used their pseudonyms.

Wuthering Heights is a book so full of passion and violence that the Victorian public assumed it had been written by a man (some even speculated that Branwell Brontë penned it), and some conjectured that the author of *Jane Eyre* had written it. Its dark and brooding story is set against the wild and bleak landscape of the Yorkshire moors. Highly charged with sexuality and with powerful moral ambiguities, the novel broke many conventions of the time. The marriage plot is at once respected (the "good characters," Cathy Linton and Hareton Earnshaw, inherit their rightful property and a happy ending) and damned (the "lovers" Catherine and Heathcliff both meet with an unhappy end, even if they are rumored to still roam the moors). The idea of love, so central to Victorian realism, is in *Wuthering Heights* as much frightening as comforting. It is no wonder that some reviewers found the novel gloomy, too unrelenting in its violence, and morally suspect. Even Charlotte Brontë, who always championed the novel as a work of genius, questioned its meaning.

Much of Brontë's poetry shares the bleakness of *Wuthering Heights* and its preoccupation with passion, loss, and death. Many of the poems display a desire for transcendence reminiscent of Catherine and Heathcliff's yearnings and yet a tenderness that is not evident in them or in the narrators of the novel. There is often in the poems a view of an existence free of the restraints of everyday life, even though this existence is often realized only through the realm of the imagination—perspectives that connect Brontë to her Romantic predecessors much more than to her Victorian contemporaries.

In 1848 the only Brontë son, Branwell, died of tuberculosis hastened by the effects of long-term alcohol and drug addiction. Emily Brontë soon began to show symptoms of tuberculosis herself, dying of the disease in December of 1848—only one year after the publication of *Wuthering Heights*. She left behind more than 150 poems in manuscript form; after her death Charlotte arranged for the publication of a few of these, but the majority did not appear in print until the early 1900s.

⌘⌘⌘

Remembrance

Cold in the earth—and the deep snow piled above thee,
    Far, far removed, cold in the dreary grave!
Have I forgot, my only Love, to love thee,
    Severed at last by Time's all-severing wave?

Now, when alone, do my thoughts no longer hover
    Over the mountains, on that northern shore,
Resting their wings where heath and fern-leaves cover
    Thy noble heart for ever, ever more?

Cold in the earth—and fifteen wild Decembers,
    From those brown hills, have melted into spring:
Faithful, indeed, is the spirit that remembers
    After such years of change and suffering!

Sweet Love of youth, forgive, if I forget thee,
    While the world's tide is bearing me along;

Other desires and other hopes beset me,
Hopes which obscure, but cannot do thee wrong!

No later light has lightened up my heaven,
No second morn has ever shone for me;
All my life's bliss from thy dear life was given,
All my life's bliss is in the grave with thee.

But when the days of golden dreams had perished,
And even Despair was powerless to destroy;
Then did I learn how existence could be cherished,
Strengthened, and fed without the aid of joy.

Then did I check the tears of useless passion,
Weaned my young soul from yearning after thine;
Sternly denied its burning wish to hasten
Down to that tomb already more than mine.

And, even yet, I dare not let it languish,
Dare not indulge in memory's rapturous pain;
Once drinking deep of that divinest anguish,
How could I seek the empty world again?
—1846

[*No coward soul is mine*][1]

original spelling

No coward soul is mine
No trembler in the world's storm-troubled sphere
I see Heaven's glories shine
And Faith shines equal arming me from Fear

O God within my breast
Almighty ever-present Deity
Life, that in me hast rest
As I Undying Life, have power in Thee

Vain are the thousand creeds
That move men's hearts, unutterably vain,
Worthless as withered weeds
Or idlest froth amid the boundless main

To waken doubt in one
Holding so fast by thy infinity
So surely anchored on
The steadfast rock of Immortality.

With wide-embracing love
Thy spirit animates eternal years
Pervades and broods above,
Changes, sustains, dissolves, creates and rears

Though Earth and moon were gone
And suns and universes ceased to be
And thou wert left alone
Every Existence would exist in thee

There is not room for Death
Nor atom that his might could render void
Since thou art Being and Breath
And what thou art may never be destroyed.
—1850 (WRITTEN 1846)

original spelling

[1] *No coward soul is mine* Like much of Brontë's poetry, this poem was not published until after her death. In preparing the poems for publication in 1850, Charlotte Brontë made some alterations in punctuation and syntax. The copy printed here is from the original 1846 manuscript, which is largely unpunctuated.

[*Often rebuked, yet always back returning*][2]

Often rebuked, yet always back returning
To those first feelings that were born with me,
And leaving busy chase of wealth and learning
For idle dreams of things which cannot be:

Today, I will seek not the shadowy region;
Its unsustaining vastness waxes drear;
And visions rising, legion after legion,
Bring the unreal world too strangely near.

I'll walk, but not in old heroic traces,
And not in paths of high morality,

[2] *Often rebuked … returning* This authorship of "Often rebuked" has been variously credited to Emily, Charlotte, and Anne Brontë; when the poem was first printed it was recorded as having been written by Emily.

And not among the half-distinguished faces,
    The clouded forms of long-past history.

I'll walk where my own nature would be leading:
    It vexes me to choose another guide:
Where the gray flocks in ferny glens are feeding;
    Where the wild wind blows on the mountain side.

What have those lonely mountains worth revealing?
    More glory and more grief than I can tell:
The earth that wakes *one* human heart to feeling
    Can centre both the worlds of heaven and hell.
—1850[1]

[*I'll come when thou art saddest*]

I'll come when thou art saddest,
Laid alone in the darkened room;
When the mad day's mirth has vanished
And the smile of joy is banished
From evening's chilly gloom.

I'll come when the heart's real feeling
Has entire, unbiased sway,
And my influence o'er thee stealing,
Grief deepening, joy congealing,
Shall bear thy soul away.

Listen! 'tis just the hour,
The awful time for thee:
Dost thou not feel upon thy soul
A flood of strange sensations roll,
Forerunners of a sterner power,
Heralds of me?
—1902 (WRITTEN 1837)

[*I'm happiest when most away*]

I'm happiest when most away
I can bear my soul from its home of clay
On a windy night when the moon is bright
And the eye can wander through worlds of light—

When I am not and none beside—
Nor earth nor sea nor cloudless sky—
But only spirit wandering wide
Through infinite immensity.
—1910 (WRITTEN 1838)

[1] *1850* Brontë did not record the date on which she composed this poem.

The New Art of Photography

CONTEXTS

If the Victorian era was in many ways an "age of realism" in literature, it was also an age in which the "real" was given new definition through the medium of photography. Photography was developed virtually simultaneously by Louis Daguerre and Henry Fox Talbot, with the Frenchman and the Englishman making announcements of their discoveries within three weeks of each other in 1839. As Charles Dickens describes in his essay on "Photography" (excerpted in this section), the technologies developed by the two were quite distinct; the "daguerreotype" resulted in a single image, while the calotype technology developed by Talbot involved paper negatives from which multiple images could be created. Later in the century a variety of other techniques were developed, including glass plate technology, which provided levels of photographic detail that remain virtually unrivaled, even in the twenty-first century. By the 1890s, the advent of the portable "Kodak" camera had put photography into the reach of the middle classes. Not only was it possible for one to obtain a few images of one's loved ones from a professional; one could also take up the activity of photography as an amateur. But even in the 1840s, the new science and art of photography was helping to transform a number of aspects of Victorian culture.

Photography had a particularly strong impact on print culture. Engraving had for centuries made possible the reproduction of illustrations, and wood engraving, one of the first methods used to produce illustrations in books, enjoyed a renaissance in the period, as did all things medieval. Metal engravings, a slightly later invention, enjoyed a short revival in popularity during the nineteenth century—particularly steel engravings, which could be used to produce a large number of proofs. This practice was soon superceded, however, by photo-engraving, a photomechanical process by which a photographic image was recorded on a sensitized metal plate, which was then etched in an acid bath and used to reproduce the photograph. The widespread reproduction of actual photographs in newspapers and magazines did not come until the early twentieth century, but these engraving techniques, pioneered in such publications as the satirical magazine *Punch* (founded in 1841), and, especially, in *The Illustrated London News* (founded 14 May 1842), allowed engravings based on photographic images to be reproduced—and to give readers a sense of the world being shown to them as it really was.

The connections between photography and print were not restricted to newspapers and magazines, of course; new technologies such as the engraving machine (created in the 1830s) enabled an unprecedented expansion of book illustration in the Victorian period. And sometimes the connections between literature and photography were entirely direct; Tennyson, for example, commissioned the photographer Julia Margaret Cameron to illustrate his *Idylls of the King*.

Photography interacted just as powerfully with other arts. The connection between photography and painting was an obvious one, and certainly many artists began to use photographs in their work, sometimes merely as an *aide memoire*, sometimes as a "copy text," sometimes as something in-between. For his famous panorama of *Derby Day* (1856–58), for example, the painter William Powell Frith commissioned the photographer Robert Howlett to take photographs not of the entire scene in which Frith was interested (for which Frith relied on his own sketches from life) but of a range of different individuals within it, so that he could fill in human details with greater accuracy and completeness.

Some expressed an outright preference for the newer art over the arts of painting and drawing. In an essay that appeared in the 21 January 1857 issue of the *Journal of the Photographic Society*, for example, "Theta" argued that "what in painting is a tiresome pedantry of observation, becomes in photography an inexhaustible delight, a study, and a piece of instruction. What we cared not for in nature, becomes a joy and wonder in the photographic picture." But when practitioners of the new art began to stake claims for an artistic status that went beyond fidelity to nature and aspired to the condition of "High Art," they met with considerable resistance. A landmark was the exhibition in 1857 at the Art Treasures Exhibition in Manchester (the first major exhibition to showcase photography alongside painting and other traditional visual arts). The most controversial work exhibited was Oscar Rejlander's vast photographic tableau, *The Two Ways of Life*, in which a montage of photographic images of allegorical figures are brought together against an artificial backdrop. To many, the artistic presumption of the work crossed a line; reviewing the exhibition in *The Art-Journal*, Robert Hunt allowed that "the pose of each figure is good and the grouping of the whole as nearly perfect as possible," but nevertheless concluded that "we do not ... desire to see many advances in this direction. Works of High Art are not to be executed by a mechanical contrivance. The hand of man, guided by the heaven-born mind, can alone achieve greatness in this direction."

Rejlander was not alone in his desire to create photographs that would be recognized as "High Art," that is, in the same sorts of ways as oil paintings were received. Henry Peach Robinson argued unabashedly in "Pictorial Effect in Photography" (1867) for the use of the photographer's artifice to contrive a pleasing result: "any dodge, trick, and conjuration of any kind is open to the photographer's use. His imperative duty is to avoid the mean, the base, and the ugly, and to aim to elevate his subject, ... to correct the unpicturesque.... A great deal can be done and very beautiful pictures made, by a mixture of the real and the artificial in a picture." Robinson's most controversial work of precisely this sort was *Fading Away* (1858), a composition combining images from five negatives, with the full image depicting a girl dying of consumption. Some saw the result of Robinson's artistry as a tasteless exploitation of grief, but the image was extremely popular (Prince Albert was prompted by his admiration of *Fading Away* to place a standing order for a copy of any composite photograph Robinson produced).

A very different approach to the art of photography was taken by Henry Emerson, who strongly criticized the approaches of photographers such as Rejlander, Robinson, and Julia Margaret Cameron. "Photograph people as they really are," he advised in *Naturalistic Photography* (1886). "Do not dress them up.... The photographic technique is perfect." Emerson's recommended photographic techniques, however, were themselves highly original—and in their own way as consciously artistic as those of Robinson or Cameron. In Emerson's view, one should emulate the natural, and "nothing in nature has a hard outline, but everything is seen against something else, and its outlines fade gently into something else, often so subtly that you cannot distinguish clearly where one ends and the other begins." To represent nature as the eye perceives it, then, Emerson recommended shooting photographs slightly out of focus. Emerson's impressionistic approach was popular for a time (and continued to influence some important photographers well into the twentieth century), but by the 1890s it was in painting rather than in photography that impressionism was putting down deep roots. Emerson himself came to recant his earlier views; in "The Death of Naturalistic Photography" (1890), he wrote that he had given up hope of photography being able to compete with painting; and regretting that he had compared "photographs to great works of art, and photographers to great artists ... I throw in my lot with those who say Photography is a very limited Art."

But "limited" was by then precisely what photography had proven it was *not*. Within Britain and its colonies alone, the medium had produced the war photographs, nature photographs, and still-lifes of Roger Fenton; the social realism of John Thomson and Thomas Annan; the memorably idealized expressions of female beauty of Julia Margaret Cameron and Lady Clementina Hawarden; suggestive representations of the exotic by Fenton, Thomson, Cameron, Francis Frith, and others; powerful representations by Howlett and others of the vitality of industrial Britain, and Annan's and Thomson's equally powerful images of its brutality; Frank Sutcliffe's and Henry Taunt's evocative images of village and rural life; and the compelling portraiture of Cameron, Lewis Carroll, William Notman, and many others.

The practice of photography was diverse, too. Early on it had become established as a professional pursuit—in the 1851 census there were already 51 British citizens who listed "photographer" as their occupation. But aristocratic amateurs such as Cameron, Hawarden, and Talbot continued to make their marks. With the notable exception of Lady Elizabeth Butler, women remained excluded from the ranks of accepted artists in the medium of painting; in photography, however, Cameron, Hawarden—and, later in the century, Anna Atkins and others—were leading figures.

More generally, it was also true that the sorts of individuals who were attracted to photography formed a diverse group. The barriers that today divide photography as an artistic pursuit from its commercial and scientific applications had for the most part not yet been erected in the Victorian era. Even those who saw photography as an art simultaneously appreciated it as science; Roger Fenton, for example, in his 1852 "Proposal for the Formation of a Royal Photographic Society" (reprinted in this section), refers to photography both as an art and as a "branch of natural science," and proposes to open the society to opticians and chemists as well as artists and "practical photographers, both professional and amateur." One influential photographer whose work straddled the line between art and science was Eadweard Muybridge, who created a famous serious of photographs to answer the question—until then unresolved—of whether a horse becomes momentarily airborne while trotting or galloping. After nearly six years spent at work on a process involving multiple cameras with a brief exposure time, he captured *The Horse in Motion* (1878). He continued to use photography to study different forms of movement, eventually developing faster shutter speeds and faster film; his work ultimately paved the way for the creation of motion pictures.

As Muybridge's achievements demonstrate, the nineteenth century was a period of rapid advancement in the technology of photography—a medium that in the mid-century was not only extremely new but also severely limited. No means existed, for example, to enlarge photographic images, and the very long exposure times required in photography's early years meant that it remained impossible for a photograph to "capture a moment"; figures passing quickly in front of the camera would remain entirely unrecorded. (That Fenton's most famous photograph of the Crimean War showed cannon balls in an empty valley was a reflection of Victorian sensibilities, but also a reflection of the limits of technology: he could have depicted dead bodies, but to photograph the action of battle was still impossible.) The diversity and the depth of the achievement of practitioners of the photographic arts in the Victorian era is all the more impressive for the technical obstacles that they faced.

⌘⌘⌘

Roger Fenton, "Proposal for the Formation of a Photographic Society" (1852)

Roger Fenton, a 32-year-old painter and sometime law student, was among the many in whom the displays at the Great Exhibition of 1851 sparked an interest in the new art of photography. Much of the finest work displayed at the Exhibition was by French photographers (prominent among them Hippolyte Bayard and Gustave Le Gray), and in October of 1851, Fenton traveled to Paris to meet members of the Societé Héliographique, the world's first photographic society. By the summer of 1852, Fenton was becoming prominent in English photographic circles, and later that year he put forward the proposal reprinted here, for the formation of a new society. The Photographic Society came into existence in 1853, with the Queen and Prince Albert as patrons; in 1894 the name was changed to The Royal Photographic Society.

The science of Photography gradually progressing for several years, seems to have advanced at a more rapid pace during and since the Exhibition of 1851. Its lovers and students in all parts of Europe were brought into more immediate and frequent communication.

Ideas of theory and methods of practice were interchanged, the pleasure and the instruction were mutual. In order that this temporary may become the normal condition of the art and of its professors, it is proposed to unite in a common society, with a fixed place of meeting, and a regular official organization, all those gentlemen whose tastes have led them to the cultivation of this branch of natural science.

As the object proposed is not only to form a pleasant and convenient Photographic Club, but a society that shall be as advantageous for the art as is the Geographic Society to the advancement of knowledge in its department, it follows necessarily that it shall include among its members men of all ranks of life; that while men of eminence, from their fortune, social position, or scientific reputation, are welcomed, no photographer of respectability in his particular sphere of life be rejected.

The society then will consist of those eminent in the study of natural philosophy, of opticians, chemists, artists, and practical photographers, professional and amateur. It will admit both town and country members. It is proposed:—

That, after the society has been once organized, persons who may in future wish to become members will have to be proposed and seconded, a majority of votes deciding their election.

That the entrance fee and subscription shall be as small as possible, in order that none may be excluded by the narrowness of their means.

That there shall be an entrance fee of £2.2s.—a subscription of £1.1s.

That the society should have appropriate premises fitted up with laboratory, glass operating room, and salon, in which to hold its meetings.

That such meetings should be periodically held, for the purpose of hearing and discussing written or verbal communications on the subject of Photography, receiving and verifying claims as to priority of invention, exhibiting and comparing pictures produced by different applications of photographic principles; making known improvements in construction of cameras and lenses; and, in fine, promoting by emulation and comparison the progress of the art.

That the proceedings of the society shall be published regularly in some acknowledged organ, which shall be sent to all subscribing members.

That a library of works bearing upon the history or tending to the elucidation of the principles of the science be formed upon the premises, and at the expense of the society, to be used by the members, subject to such rules as may hereafter be agreed upon.

That the society should publish an annual album, of which each member should receive a copy, who had contributed a good negative photograph to its formation, other members having to pay (and the public being charged at the rate of   )?[1]

The heaviest expense attendant upon this plan would be leasing or construction of convenient premises, and this expense might be lessened by the letting off the lower

---

[1] *rate of   )?* The space left here, together with the question mark, suggest that the specific amount was an issue left for later discussion.

part as a shop for the sale of photographic chemicals, and the upper part to some person who would form a commercial establishment for the printing of positives.

Before any progress can be made in the organization of such a society as the foregoing, it is necessary first to ascertain the amount of support which it would be likely to obtain. If those gentlemen, therefore, who feel inclined to become members of such a society will send in their names and addresses to R. FENTON, Esq., 2, Albert Terrace, and 50, King William Street, City,[1] together with any suggestion which may occur to them individually on the perusal of this outline of a plan, arrangements will be made as soon as a sufficient number of persons have sent in their names, to hold a meeting in some central situation, to which they will be invited to discuss the matter and to elect a committee for the organization of a society.

from Charles Dickens, "Photography," *Household Words* (1853)

Among Dickens's many contributions to *Household Words* (a widely-circulated miscellany of articles and literary pieces) were installments of his fiction, essays on political issues, and articles on various cultural topics—such as the selection excerpted below.

… Light from the sky is, in fact, the chief part of the stock-in-trade of a photographer. Other light than the sun's can be employed; but, while the sun continues to pour down to us a daily flow of light of the best quality, as cheap as health (we will not say as cheap as dirt, for dirt is a dear article), sunlight will be consumed by the photographers in preference to any other. A diffused, mellow light from the sky, which moderates the darkness of all shadows, is much better suited to the purpose of photography than a direct sunbeam; which creates hard contrasts of light and shade. For in the picture formed by light, whether on metal, glass, or paper, such hard contrasts will be made still harder. Lumpy shadows haunt the chambers of all bad photographers.

He who would not be vexed by them and would produce a portrait in which the features shall be represented with the necessary softness, finds it generally advantageous not only to let the shades be cast upon the face in a room full of diffused rays—that is to say, under a skylight—but also by the waving of large black velvet screens over the head to moderate and stint the quantity of light that falls on features not thrown into shadow. For this reason few very good photographic pictures can be taken from objects illuminated only by a side light, as in a room with ordinary windows. The diffused light of cloudy weather, if the air be free from fog, hinders the process of photography only by lengthening the time occupied in taking impressions. Light, when it is jaundiced by a fog, is quite as liable as jaundiced men to give erroneous views of mankind.

Photography, out of England, has made its most rapid advances, and produced its best results in the United States and in France; but, although both the French and the Americans have the advantage of a much purer and more certain supply of sunlight, it is satisfactory to know that the English photographers have thrown as much light of their own on the new science as any of their neighbours. …

The den of the photographer, in which he goes through those mysterious operations which are not submitted to the observation of the sitter, is a small room lighted by a window, and communicating into a dark closet, veiled with heavy curtains. Our sense of the supernatural, always associated with dark closets, was excited strongly in this chamber, by the sound of a loud rumbling in the bowels of the house, and the visible departure of a portion of the wall to lower regions. "We thought instinctively of bandits who wind victims up and down in moveable rooms or turn them up in treacherous screw bedsteads. But, of course, there was no danger to be apprehended. What we saw was, of course, only a contrivance to save labour in conveying pictures up or down for colouring or framing. Our consciences having been satisfied on this point, the expert magician took a plate of the prescribed size, made ready to his hand. Such plates consist of a thin layer of silver fixed upon copper, and are provided to the artist

[1] *City* I.e., the City of London.

highly polished; but a final and superlative polish is given to each plate, with a "buff" or pad like a double handled razor strop, tinged with a fine mineral powder. Simple as it appears, the final polishing of the plate is an operation that can only succeed well under a practised pair of hands, that regulate their pressure by a refined sense of touch. The plate thus polished was brushed over finally and very lightly, as with the touch of a cat's paw, with a warm pad of black velvet freshly taken from an oven.

To witness the next process we went into the dark closet itself, the very head quarters of spectredom. There, having carefully excluded daylight, the operator lifted up the lid of a small bin, rapidly fixed the plate, silver side downwards, in a place made underneath for its reception, shut down the lid, and began to measure seconds by counting, talking between whiles, thus:—"One—that box—two contains—three—chloride of iodine—four—strewn—five—six—at the bottom. Now!" (Presto, out came the plate in a twinkling, and was held against a sheet of white paper, upon which it reflected a ghastly straw colour by the light of a small jet of gas.) "Ah, tint not deep enough!" The plate was popped into its vapour bath again with magic quickness. "Seven—the action of the iodine" (continued the operator, counting seconds, and teaching us our lesson in the same breath) "rising in vapour upon the surface—eleven—of the plate—twelve—causes it to take in succession—thirteen—fourteen—fifteen—all the colours of the spectrum—sixteen—seventeen; and deposits upon it a film." As he went on solemnly counting, we asked how long he exposed the plate to the visitation of that potent vapour. "A very short time," he replied; "but it varies—thirty—thirty-one—according to the light in the next room—thirty-five—thirty-six—thirty-seven. Adjusting the plate to the weather, thirty-eight—is the result of an acquired instinct—thirty-nine—forty. Now it is ready." The plate was out, and its change to a deeper straw colour was shown. The lid of an adjoining bin was lifted, and the iodized plate was hung in the same way over another vapour; that of the chloride of bromine, that the wraiths of the two vapours might mingle, mingle, mingle as black spirits with white, blue spirits with gray. In this position it remained but a very short time, while we stood watching by in the dark cupboard. The plate having had its temper worked upon by these mysterious agencies was rendered so extremely sensitive, that it was requisite to confine it at once, in a dark hole or solitary cell, made ready for it in a wooden frame; a wooden slide was let down over it, and it was ready to be carried to the camera.

Before quitting this part of the subject, we must add to the preceding description two or three external facts. We have been discussing hitherto the kernel without touching the nutshell in which these, like all other reasonable matters in this country, may be (and usually are) said to lie. The nutshell is in fact as important to a discussion in this country as the small end of the wedge or the British Lion:—In the action of light upon surfaces prepared in a certain manner lies the whole idea of photography. The camera-obscura is an old friend; how to fix chemically the illuminated images formed in the camera by light, was a problem at which Sir Humphrey Davy,[1] half a century ago, was one of the first men who worked. Sir Humphrey succeeded no farther than in the imprinting of a faint image, but as he could not discover how to fix it, the whole subject was laid aside. Between the years 1814 and 1828, two Frenchmen, M. Daguerre and M. Nièpce,[2] were at work upon the problem. In 1827 M. Nièpce produced before the Royal Society what he then called heliographs, sun-pictures, formed and fixed upon glass, copper plated with silver, and well-polished tin. But, as he kept the secret of his processes, no scientific use was made of his discovery. M. Daguerre, working at the same problem, succeeded about the same time in fixing sun-pictures on paper impregnated with nitrate of silver. M. Daguerre and M. Nièpce having combined their knowledge to increase the value of their art, the French government—in the year 1839—acting nobly, as it has often acted in the

[1] *Sir Humphrey Davy* English scientist. The discoverer of several chemical elements, Davy (1778–1829) also invented a safety lamp for use in mines.

[2] *two Frenchman … Nièpce* Louis-Jacques-Mandé Daguerre (1787–1851), now more commonly referred to as "Louis Daguerre," inventor of the daguerreotype process of photography, and Nicéphore Niépce, said by many to have produced the world's first photograph.

interests of science, bought for the free use of the world the details of the new discovery. For the full disclosure of their secrets there was granted to M. Daguerre a life pension of two hundred and forty pounds (he died not many months ago), and a pension of one hundred and sixty pounds to the son of M. Nièpce, with the reversion of one half to their widows.

Six months before the disclosure of the processes in France, Mr. Fox Talbot[1] in England had discovered a process leading to a like result—the fixing of sun-pictures upon paper. As the English parliament buys little for science, nothing unfortunately hindered the patenting of Mr. Talbot's method. That patent in certain respects very much obstructed the advance of photography in this country, and great credit is due to Mr. Talbot for having recently and voluntarily abandoned his exclusive rights, and given his process to the public for all purposes and uses, except that of the portrait-taker. By so doing he acted in the spirit of a liberal art born in our own days, and peculiarly marked with the character of our own time. It does one good to think how photographers, even while exercising the new art for money, have pursued it with a generous ardour for its own sake, and emulate each other in the magnanimity with which they throw their own discoveries into the common heap, and scorn to check the progress of their art for any selfish motive. After the completion of the French discovery two daguerreotype establishments were formed in London armed with patent rights, and their proprietors, Messrs. Claudet and Beard, do in fact still hold those rights, of which they have long cheerfully permitted the infringement. Mr. Beard tried to enforce them only once, we believe; and M. Claudet, with distinguished liberality, never. …

And we may observe here that another illustration of our vanities was furnished to us on a different occasion. Daguerreotype plates commonly present faces as they would be seen in a looking-glass, that is to say, reversed: the left side of the face, in nature, appearing upon the right side of the miniature. That is the ordinary aspect in which every one sees his own face, for it is only possible for him to behold it reflected in a mirror. This reversing, of course, alters in the slightest degree the similitude … and it is a curious fact that few of us are content to have even our faces shown to us as others see them. The non-inverted daguerreotypes differ too much from the dear images of self that we are used to learn by heart out of our looking-glasses. They invariably please the friend to whom they are to be given, but they frequently displease the sitter.… A daguerreotype, formed in the usual way and inverted, if held before a looking-glass, becomes again inverted, and shows therefore a non-inverted picture of the person whom it represents.

… There are many processes by which photographic impressions may be taken upon paper and glass; a book full of them lies at this moment before us: we have ourselves seen two, and shall confine ourselves to the telling of a part of our experience. We rang the artist's bell of Mr. Henneman in Regent-street, who takes very good portraits upon paper by a process cousin to the Talbotype. By that gentleman we were introduced into a neat little chamber lighted by gas, with a few pans and chemicals upon a counter. His process was excessively simple: he would show it to us. He took a square of glass, cleaned it very perfectly, then holding it up by one corner with the left hand, he poured over the centre of the glass some collodion, which is, as most people know, gun-cotton dissolved in ether. By a few movements of the left hand, which appear easy, but are acquired with trouble, the collodion was caused to flow into an even coat over the surface of the glass, and the excess was poured off at another corner. To do this by a few left-handed movements without causing any ripple upon the collodion adhering to the glass is really very difficult. This done, the plate was left till the ether had almost evaporated, and deposited a film of gun-cotton—which is in fact a delicate paper—spread evenly over the surface of the glass. The glass covered with this delicate paper, before it was yet quite dry, was plunged carefully into a pan or bath, containing a solution of nitrate of silver, about eight grains of it to every hundred of distilled water. In about two minutes it was taken out, and ready for the camera. It was a sheet of glass covered with a fine film of cotton-paper impregnated with nitrate of silver,

[1] *Mr. Fox Talbot* Henry Fox Talbot (1800–77), English scientist and mathematician, inventor of the calotype photographic process.

a colourless salt blackened by light.

It was removed in a dark frame to the camera. Then an assistant, opening a book, assumed an attitude and sat for his picture. In a few seconds it was taken in the usual way, and the glass carried again into the operator's room. There it was dipped into another bath—a bath of pyrogallic acid—and the impression soon became apparent. To bring it out with greater force it was then dipped into a second and much weaker bath of nitrate of silver. The image was then made perfect; but, as the light parts were all depicted by the blackest shades, and the black parts were left white, the courteous assistant was there represented as a negro.

That negro stage was not of course the finished portrait, it was "the negative"—or stereotype plate, as it were—from which, after it had been fixed with a solution of the sulphate of the peroxyde of iron, any number of impressions could be taken. For it is obvious that if a plate like this be placed on sensitive paper, and exposed to daylight, the whole process will be reversed. The black face will obstruct the passage of the light and leave a white face underneath, the white hair will allow the light to pass, making black hair below, and so on. Impressions thus taken on paper, and afterwards fixed, may either serve for portraits, as they are, or, like the silver plates, they may be coloured.

… Photography already has been found available by the astronomer; the moon has sat for a full-face picture,[1] and there is hope that in a short time photographic paper will become a common auxiliary to the telescope. History will be indebted to photography for facsimiles of documents and volumes that have perished; travellers may bring home incontestible transcripts of inscriptions upon monuments, or foreign scenery. The artist will no longer be delayed in travelling to execute his sketches on the spot. He can now wander at his ease, and bring home photographic views, from which to work, as sculptors from the model. Photography is a young art, but from its present aspect we can judge what power it will have in its maturity. The mind may readily become bewildered among expectations, but one thing will suggest many. We understand that a catalogue of the national library of Paris has been commenced, in which each work is designated by a photographic miniature of its title-page.

Photography and Immortality

The following brief extracts are from a letter of poet Elizabeth Barrett (later Elizabeth Barrett Browning) to a friend, and from a speech by one of the first presidents of the photographic society. Pollock's belief was that photography was first and foremost "a *practical science*," but his enthusiasm for it was no less than that of those who valued it more as an art.

from Elizabeth Barrett, Letter to Mary Russell Mitford (1843)

Do you know anything about that wonderful invention of the day, called the Daguerrotype? Think of a man sitting down in the sun and leaving his facsimile in all its full completion of outline and shadow, steadfast on a plate, at the end of a minute and a half! The Mesmeric[2] disembodiment of spirits strikes one as a degree less marvelous. … It is not merely the likeness which is precious in such cases—but the association and the sense of nearness involved in the thing … the fact of the very shadow of the person lying there fixed for ever! It is the very sanctification of portraits.

[1] *moon has sat for a full-face picture* Amateur photographer John Dillwyn Llewelyn (1810–82) and his daughter Thereza Llewelyn were pioneers in astronomical photography, taking pictures of the moon through the telescope Llewelyn had constructed in 1851 at his estate in Wales.

[2] *Mesmeric* Franz Mesmer (1734–1835) claimed to have discovered a mysterious force he termed "animal magnetism"; it was termed *mesmerism* by others.

from Sir Frederick Pollock, "Presidential Address," Photographic Society (1855)

The varied objects to which Photography can address itself, its power of rendering permanent that which appears to be as fleeting as the shadows that go across the dial, the power that it possesses of giving fixedness to instantaneous objects, are for the purposes of history … a matter of the greatest importance. It is not too much to say that no individual—not merely individual man, but no individual substance, no individual matter, nothing that is extraordinary in art, that is celebrated in architecture, that is calculated to excite the imagination of those who behold it, need now perish; but may be rendered immortal by the assistance of Photography.

Henry Fox Talbot, *The Haystack*, 1844. Talbot wrote of this photo, "[o]ne advantage of the discovery of the Photographic Art will be, that it will enable us to introduce into our pictures a multitude of minute details which add to the truth and reality of the representation, but which no artist would take the trouble to copy faithfully from nature."

Henry Fox Talbot, *Nelson's Column under Construction, Trafalgar Square*, 1844.

Roger Fenton, *The British Museum*, 1857.

Roger Fenton, *Fruit and Flowers*, 1860.

Roger Fenton, *The Long Walk, Windsor*, 1860.

Oscar Gustav Rejlander, *The Two Ways of Life* (detail), 1857.

Robert Howlett, *The Great Eastern: Isambard Kingdom Brunel Inspecting Construction Work* (detail), 1857.

Oscar Gustav Rejlander, *Homeless*, c. 1860. (This well-known and widely praised photograph was also sometimes referred to as *A Night in Town* or *Poor Joe*.)

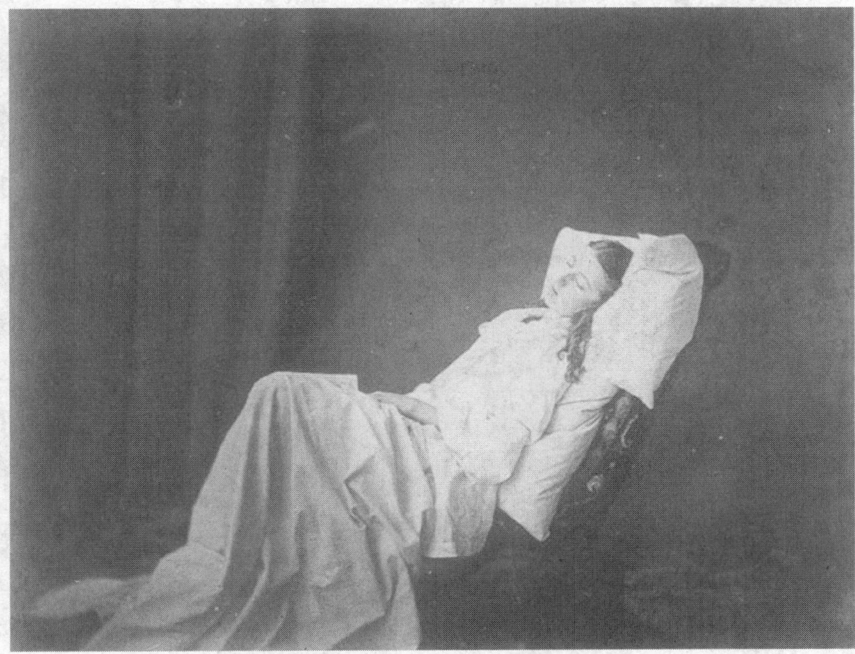

Henry Peach Robinson, *She Never Told Her Love*, 1857.

A preliminary study for *Fading Away*, this photograph was exhibited with the following verse:

> She never told her Love
> But let concealment, like a
> worm i' the bud,
> Feed on her damask cheek.
> Shakespeare

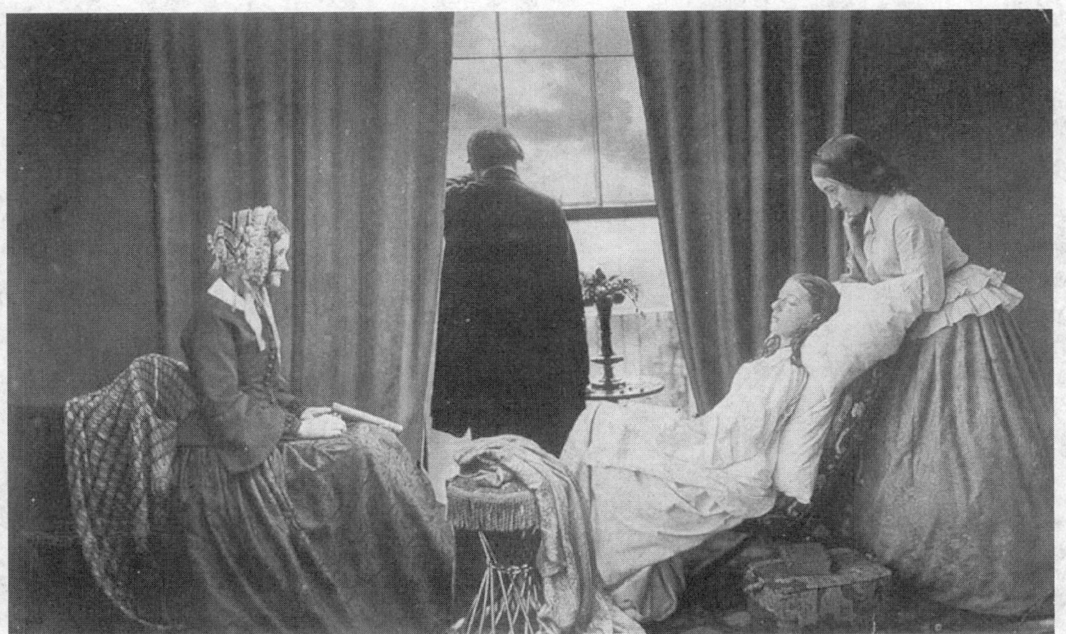

Henry Peach Robinson, *Fading Away*, 1858. Robinson inscribed "First Impression" on the printed matt along with the following verse: "Must then that peerless form, / Which love and admiration cannot view / Without a beating heart, those azure veins / Which steal like streams along a field of snow, / As breathing marble, perish! Shelley"

Francis Frith, *The Pyramids of Dahshoor, From the East*, c. 1857.

Francis Frith, *Crocodile on a Sand-Bank* (detail), 1857.

Lady Clementina Hawarden, *The Toilette*, c. 1864.

Lady Clementina Hawarden, *Lady Isabella Grace and Clementina Maude, 5 Princes Gardens*, c. 1862–63.

Lewis Carroll, *Ellen Watts (Ellen Terry)*, 1865.

Lewis Carroll, *Tuning*, 1876.

Lewis Carroll, *John Everett Millais, His Wife, and Two of Their Daughters*, 1865.

Francis Bedford, *A Peaceful Village*, 1859.

Julia Margaret Cameron, *Annie—My First Success*, 1864. Cameron maintained that this image was her first successful photograph.

Julia Margaret Cameron, *Thomas Carlyle*, 1867. Carlyle wrote of the photo, "it is as if it suddenly began to speak, terrifically ugly and woebegone!"

Julia Margaret Cameron, *Ophelia*, 1867.

Julia Margaret Cameron, *The Angel at the Sepulchre*, 1869.

Julia Margaret Cameron, *Cingalese Girl*, 1875.

Julia Margaret Cameron, *The Passing of Arthur*, 1875.

Bourne & Shepherd, *Man Singh, Rajah of Dhrangadhra*, c. 1870.

Thomas Annan, *Close No. 46, Saltmarket, Glasgow*, 1868.

William Notman, *Miss Thomas, Montreal, QC*, c. 1868.

Eadweard Muybridge, *The Horse in Motion*, 1878.

John Thomson, *Physic Street, Canton*, c. 1869.

William Notman, *Blackfoot Brave, near Calgary, Alberta*, 1889.

Peter Henry Emerson, *Gathering Water-Lilies*, 1886.

Frederick Evans, *A Sea of Steps, Wells Cathedral*, c. 1903.

Frederick Evans, *Lincoln Cathedral: From the Castle*, 1896.

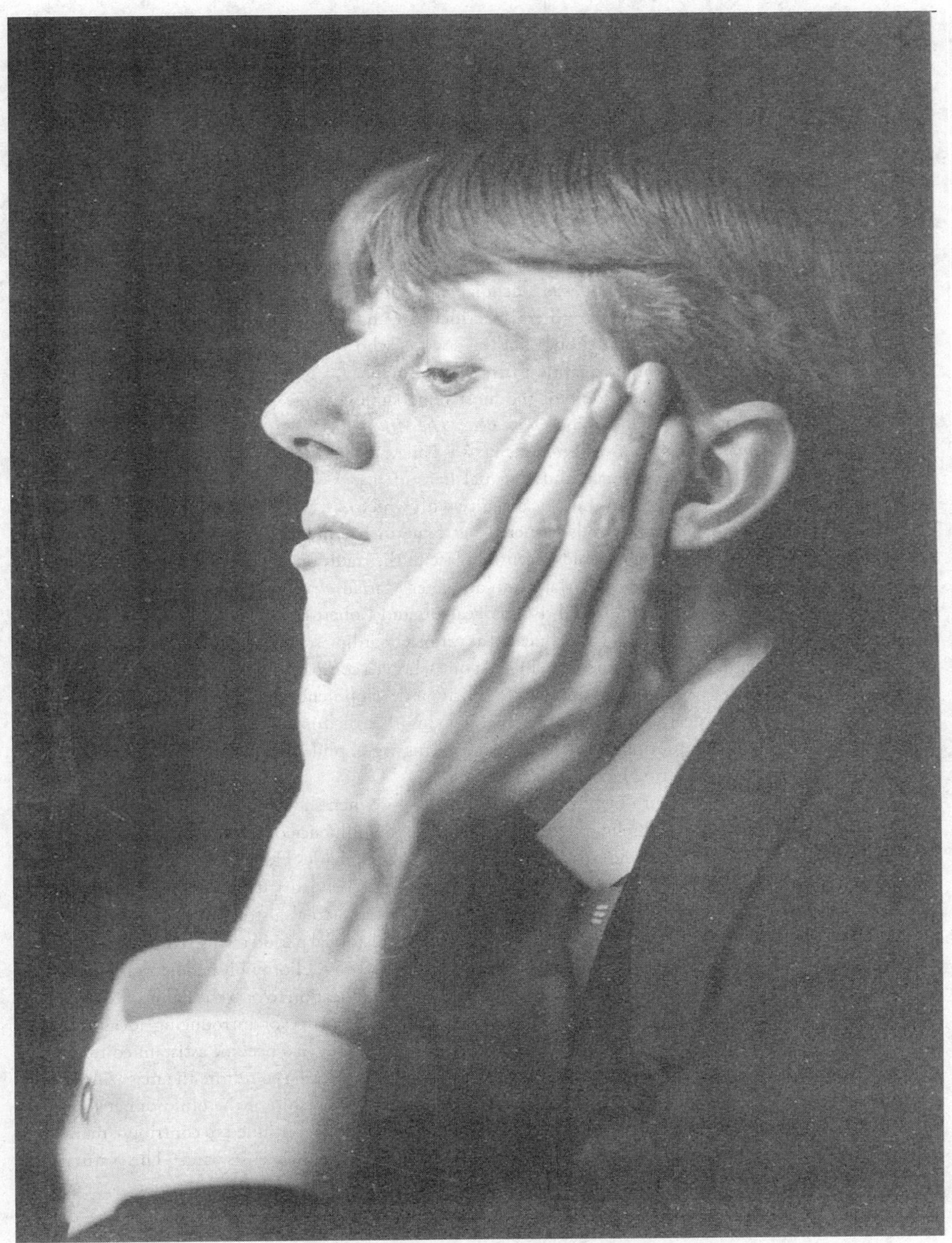

Frederick Evans, *Portrait of Aubrey Beardsley*, c. 1894.

George Eliot

1819 – 1880

George Eliot chose her masculine pen name with good reason: she did not wish to be received by the public as a woman writer and judged by terms thought to be appropriate to women's work. At a time when women were often prevented from engaging in such work, Eliot was a scholar and editor, publishing groundbreaking essays, literary criticism, and translations. When she turned to fiction, Eliot was a writer who valued sympathy above all other qualities; hers was a notable intellectual voice that produced some of the most remarkable novels of the Victorian period, including *Adam Bede*, *The Mill on the Floss*, *Middlemarch*, and *Daniel Deronda*. She was hailed for her intimate portrayal of the social and spiritual lives of her characters, particularly for the psychological acuity with which she brought them to life. Her novels garnered her fame in her lifetime, and it has been widely acknowledged since that her work holds a central place in the tradition of novel-writing in English.

Mary Anne Evans (she also used Mary Ann and later Marian) was born in rural Warwickshire, England, in 1819, the third child of Christiana Pearson and Robert Evans. This landscape was to figure in almost all her fiction. She was educated at various boarding schools where she distinguished herself as a studious, shy and introspective child. At one school, a compassionate teacher named Maria Lewis took her under her wing and molded her spiritual development, instilling evangelical beliefs that would persist into early adulthood. When Eliot's mother died in 1836, her formal education came to an end, but she continued to study theology, languages, philosophy, Romantic poetry, and German literature while caring for her father.

Her close relationship with her father was tested in 1842 when she announced her loss of faith in Christianity and organized religion, after falling under the influence of the freethinking, radical intellectuals Charles and Caroline Bray and Caroline's brother, Charles Hennell. Hennell urged her to translate *The Life of Jesus*, by the German "higher critic" David Friedrich Strauss; the translation appeared in 1846. This study considered the Bible's texts not as factual histories ordained by God, but rather as myths, the products of people living in a specific historical period trying to find language to articulate their sense of the powers that ruled the universe. In 1854, Eliot published her translation of Ludwig Feuerbach's *Essence of Christianity* (1854), her only publication to bear the name of Marian Evans on its title page. Here again she continued her radical work of introducing ideas that challenged traditional religious beliefs. Before this work, in 1851, she had become assistant editor of the radical *Westminster Review*, a position she held for two years, helping to restore the magazine to the high intellectual standards it had attained while under the editorship of the philosopher John Stuart Mill. Even after leaving her position at the *Review*, George Eliot continued to contribute many important essays to the magazine, among them "Silly Novels by Lady Novelists" and "The Natural History of German Life" (1856).

In 1851 she met George Henry Lewes, biographer, novelist, botanist, and literary and theatrical critic. In 1854, they began to live together (though he was married). The decision to live in a common-law "marriage," as they called it (indeed, George Eliot called herself and became known to many as "Mrs. Lewes"), came at great personal expense; the brother to whom she had once been very close persuaded the entire family to shun her, which they did for the duration of her quarter-century relationship with Lewes. The relationship also constricted her involvement in the literary and intellectual world of London, especially in the early years of her writing career.

George Eliot's novels and shorter fiction (three novellas were published in *Blackwood's Magazine* under her pseudonym and collected in *Scenes of Clerical Life* in 1858) mostly harken back to the early part of the century in pre-industrial England and concentrate on the lives of ordinary people at a time when great changes were on the horizon; she draws readers' attention to how tragedy, as well as sublime comedy, may form part of the lives of common people. In a passage in *The Mill on the Floss*, George Eliot explains the appeal of the Midland landscape and its Wordsworthian influence upon her imagination: "These familiar flowers, these well-remembered bird-notes, this sky, with its fitful brightness, these furrowed and grassy fields ... such things as these are the mother tongue of our imagination, the language that is laden with all the subtle inextricable associations the fleeting hours of our childhood left behind them. Our delight in the sunshine on the deep-bladed grass to-day, might be no more than the faint perception of wearied souls, if it were not for the sunshine and the grass in the far-off years which still live in us, and transform our perception into love." These scenes become the sources of the moral imagination, "with its deep immoveable roots in memory." They are also the sources of George Eliot's moral realism. As she wrote in Chapter 17 of *Adam Bede*, her focus was not heroes or sublimely beautiful women, but people who do "the rough work of the world" because human beings need to reverence "that other beauty ... which lies in no secret of proportion, but in the secret of deep human sympathy."

Even though George Eliot was almost forty when she began writing fiction, once she began she was prolific. *Adam Bede* appeared in 1859 to great critical acclaim (Queen Victoria was among its admirers); *The Mill on the Floss* was published in 1860 and *Silas Marner* in 1861; her Renaissance historical novel, *Romola*, in 1863; *Felix Holt, the Radical*, a book about the First Reform Bill, in 1866; a collection of poetry, *The Spanish Gypsy*, in 1868; and *Middlemarch* in 1871–72. This novel, widely thought to be among the greatest written in English, is set in the time leading up to the 1832 Reform Bill, which significantly expanded the male electorate and accomplished a more equal distribution of Parliamentary seats, particularly benefiting manufacturing towns and cities. At this historical moment, when the forces of progress were struggling with countervailing conservative reaction, Eliot traces the interwoven lives of the inhabitants of the fictive town of Middlemarch and the lands surrounding it, particularly the lives of Dorothea Brooke, an idealistic, ardent, and intelligent young woman, and of Tertius Lydgate, an ambitious young doctor who longs to make important medical discoveries. The omniscient narrator's sympathy and intellectual generosity continually guide the reader's impressions; while capable of incisive satire, the narrator nevertheless finds redemptive qualities even in the most flawed characters. The profound degree of social and psychological insight displayed in the novel reflects Eliot's professed aim for her writings, "that those who read them should be better able to *imagine* and to *feel* the pains and the joys of those who differ from themselves in everything but the broad fact of being struggling, erring, human creatures."[1]

Daniel Deronda (1876) was George Eliot's final novel. Her interest in Judaism and in the Hebrew language informed this epic story, set in contemporary England, of a woman who is forced into an oppressive marriage with an aristocrat and of an idealistic young man, the eponymous Daniel, who

[1] From a letter to Charles Bray, 5 July 1859.

discovers his Jewish roots and works toward a renewal of the Jewish nation. For the agnostic George Eliot, the appeal of Judaism lay in its role as the foundation of the images and texts that inform a morality divinely human; Judaism was the source of western culture's moral imagination. She may not have been a believer, but her fiction finds much of its life in the tropes and images of the religious imagination as she found them in the King James Bible, Milton, Bunyan, and the English hymns. This most intellectually sophisticated of all Victorian novelists was also one of its most deeply traditional.

In 1878, George Eliot's beloved partner Lewes died. In May of 1880, she married John Walter Cross, a man 20 years her junior. She died in December 1880, and was buried beside Lewes in Highgate Cemetery. Before her death she reconciled with her brother Isaac, who welcomed the "legitimacy" of her marriage to Cross. Five years after her death, Cross published a reverent biography of Mary Anne Evans, entitled *George Eliot's Life as Related in Her Letters and Journals*.

⌘⌘⌘

from *Middlemarch*

One of the main story lines of Eliot's novel traces the development of the romance (and subsequent marriage) between Dr. Tertius Lydgate, an idealistic medical practitioner who has brought his reforming ways to the small community of Middlemarch, and Rosamond Vincy, the beautiful but shallow daughter of Walter Vincy, a manufacturer who is also mayor of the town. In the excerpt included here, Rosamund and Lydgate find themselves often in each other's company as a result of Lydgate's frequent visits to the Vincy household to care for Rosamond's feverish brother, Fred.

from CHAPTER 27

"Let the high Muse chant loves Olympian:
We are but mortals, and must sing of man."[1]

An eminent philosopher among my friends, who can dignify even your ugly furniture by lifting it into the serene light of science, has shown me this pregnant little fact. Your pier-glass[2] or extensive surface of polished steel made to be rubbed by a housemaid, will be minutely and multitudinously scratched in all directions; but place now against it a lighted candle as a centre of illumination, and lo! the scratches will seem to arrange themselves in a fine series of concentric circles round that little sun. It is demonstrable that the scratches are going everywhere impartially and it is only your candle which produces the flattering illusion of a concentric arrangement, its light falling with an exclusive optical selection. These things are a parable. The scratches are events, and the candle is the egoism of any person now absent—of Miss Vincy, for example. Rosamond had a Providence of her own who had kindly made her more charming than other girls, and who seemed to have arranged Fred's illness and Mr. Wrench's mistake[3] in order to bring her and Lydgate within effective proximity. …

[Rosamond's mother] never left Fred's side when her husband was not in the house, and thus Rosamond was in the unusual position of being much alone. Lydgate, naturally, never thought of staying long with her, yet it seemed that the brief impersonal conversations they had together were creating that peculiar intimacy which

[1] *Let the high Muse … sing of man* From Theocritus, *Idylls* 16.3–4, translated here by Eliot.

[2] *pier-glass* Large mirror, especially one made to be set over a fireplace or between two windows.

[3] *Mr. Wrench's mistake* On the previous day, Mr. Wrench, the doctor who usually attended the Vincy household, had declared Fred's fever a "slight derangement" and had not returned to check on him; Lydgate immediately recognized typhoid fever and started appropriate treatment.

consists in shyness. They were obliged to look at each other in speaking, and somehow the looking could not be carried through as the matter of course which it really was. Lydgate began to feel this sort of consciousness unpleasant and one day looked down, or anywhere, like an ill-worked puppet. But this turned out badly: the next day, Rosamond looked down, and the consequence was that when their eyes met again, both were more conscious than before. There was no help for this in science, and as Lydgate did not want to flirt, there seemed to be no help for it in folly. It was therefore a relief when neighbours no longer considered the house in quarantine, and when the chances of seeing Rosamond alone were very much reduced.

But that intimacy of mutual embarrassment, in which each feels that the other is feeling something, having once existed, its effect is not to be done away with. Talk about the weather and other well-bred topics is apt to seem a hollow device, and behaviour can hardly become easy unless it frankly recognizes a mutual fascination—which of course need not mean anything deep or serious. This was the way in which Rosamond and Lydgate slid gracefully into ease, and made their intercourse lively again. Visitors came and went as usual, there was once more music in the drawing-room, and all the extra hospitality of Mr. Vincy's mayoralty returned. Lydgate, whenever he could, took his seat by Rosamond's side, and lingered to hear her music, calling himself her captive—meaning, all the while, not to be her captive. The preposterousness of the notion that he could at once set up a satisfactory establishment as a married man was a sufficient guarantee against danger. This play at being a little in love was agreeable, and did not interfere with graver pursuits. Flirtation, after all, was not necessarily a singeing process. Rosamond, for her part, had never enjoyed the days so much in her life before: she was sure of being admired by some one worth captivating, and she did not distinguish flirtation from love, either in herself or in another. She seemed to be sailing with a fair wind just whither she would go, and her thoughts were much occupied with a handsome house in Lowick Gate which she hoped would by-and-by be vacant. She was quite determined, when she was married, to rid herself adroitly of all the visitors who were not agreeable to her at her father's; and she imagined the drawing-room in her favourite house with various styles of furniture.

Certainly her thoughts were much occupied with Lydgate himself; he seemed to her almost perfect: if he had known his notes so that his enchantment under her music had been less like an emotional elephant's, and if he had been able to discriminate better the refinements of her taste in dress, she could hardly have mentioned a deficiency in him. How different he was from young Plymdale or Mr. Caius Larcher! Those young men had not a notion of French, and could speak on no subject with striking knowledge, except perhaps the dyeing and carrying trades,[1] which of course they were ashamed to mention; they were Middlemarch gentry, elated with their silver-headed whips and satin stocks,[2] but embarrassed in their manners, and timidly jocose: even Fred was above them, having at least the accent and manner of a university man. Whereas Lydgate was always listened to, bore himself with the careless politeness of conscious superiority, and seemed to have the right clothes on by a certain natural affinity, without ever having to think about them. Rosamond was proud when he entered the room, and when he approached her with a distinguishing smile, she had a delicious sense that she was the object of enviable homage. If Lydgate had been aware of all the pride he excited in that delicate bosom, he might have been just as well pleased as any other man, even the most densely ignorant of humoral pathology[3] or fibrous tissue: he held it one of the prettiest attitudes of the feminine mind to adore a man's pre-eminence without too precise a knowledge of what it consisted in.

[1] *dyeing and carrying trades* These young men make their livings (as does Mr. Vincy) in manufacturing textiles and then exporting ("carrying") them.

[2] *stocks* High-collared type of neckwear.

[3] *humoral pathology* Study of disease according to the doctrine, now obsolete, that sickness is caused by an imbalance in the body of the four substances called humors: blood, phlegm, yellow bile, and black bile.

But Rosamond was not one of those helpless girls who betray themselves unawares, and whose behavior is awkwardly driven by their impulses, instead of being steered by wary grace and propriety. Do you imagine that her rapid forecast and rumination concerning house-furniture and society were ever discernible in her conversation, even with her mamma? On the contrary, she would have expressed the prettiest surprise and disapprobation if she had heard that another young lady had been detected in that immodest prematureness—indeed, would probably have disbelieved in its possibility. For Rosamond never showed any unbecoming knowledge, and was always that combination of correct sentiments, music, dancing, drawing, elegant note-writing, private album for extracted verse,[1] and perfect blond loveliness, which made the irresistible woman for the doomed man of that date. Think no unfair evil of her, pray: she had no wicked plots, nothing sordid or mercenary; in fact, she never thought of money except as something necessary which other people would always provide. She was not in the habit of devising falsehoods, and if her statements were no direct clue to fact, why, they were not intended in that light—they were among her elegant accomplishments, intended to please. Nature had inspired many arts in finishing Mrs. Lemon's favourite pupil,[2] who by general consent (Fred's excepted) was a rare compound of beauty, cleverness, and amiability.

Lydgate found it more and more agreeable to be with her, and there was no constraint now, there was a delightful interchange of influence in their eyes, and what they said had that superfluity of meaning for them, which is observable with some sense of flatness by a third person; still they had no interviews or asides from which a third person need have been excluded. In fact, they flirted; and Lydgate was secure in the belief that they did nothing else. If a man could not love and be wise, surely he could flirt and be wise at the same time? Really, the men in Middlemarch, except Mr. Farebrother, were great bores, and Lydgate did not care about commercial politics or cards: what was he to do for relaxation? He was often invited to the Bulstrodes';[3] but the girls there were hardly out of the schoolroom; and Mrs. Bulstrode's *naïve* way of conciliating piety and worldliness, the nothingness of this life and the desirability of cut glass, the consciousness at once of filthy rags and the best damask, was not a sufficient relief from the weight of her husband's invariable seriousness. The Vincys' house, with all its faults, was the pleasanter by contrast; besides, it nourished Rosamond—sweet to look at as a half-opened blush-rose, and adorned with accomplishments for the refined amusement of man.

But he made some enemies, other than medical, by his success with Miss Vincy. One evening he came into the drawing-room rather late, when several other visitors were there. The card-table had drawn off the elders, and Mr. Ned Plymdale (one of the good matches in Middlemarch, though not one of its leading minds) was in *tête-à-tête* with Rosamond. He had brought the last "Keepsake,"[4] the gorgeous watered-silk publication which marked modern progress at that time; and he considered himself very fortunate that he could be the first to look over it with her, dwelling on the ladies and gentlemen with shiny copper-plate cheeks and copper-plate smiles, and pointing to comic verses as capital and sentimental stories as interesting. Rosamond was gracious, and Mr. Ned was satisfied that he had the very best thing in art and literature as a medium for "paying addresses"—the very thing to please a nice girl. He had also reasons, deep rather than ostensible, for being satisfied with his own appearance. To superficial observers his chin had too vanishing an aspect, looking as if it were being gradually reabsorbed. And it did indeed cause him some

[1] *private album for extracted verse* It was fashionable for ladies at this time to keep commonplace books of favorite quotations.

[2] *Mrs. Lemon's favourite pupil* Earlier in the novel, Rosamond attends Mrs. Lemon's school, "the chief school in the county, where the teaching included all that was demanded in the accomplished female—even to extras, such as the getting in and out of a carriage" (Chapter 11).

[3] *Bulstrodes* Mr. Bulstrode, the chief banker in Middlemarch, is Rosamond's uncle.

[4] *Keepsake* Popular art and literature annual marketed as a Christmas gift for women in the mid-nineteenth century. Though many prominent writers contributed to it, it was dismissed by critics as overly sentimental.

difficulty about the fit of his satin stocks, for which chins were at that time useful.

"I think the Honourable Mrs. S. is something like you," said Mr. Ned. He kept the book open at the bewitching portrait, and looked at it rather languishingly.

"Her back is very large; she seems to have sat for that," said Rosamond, not meaning any satire, but thinking how red young Plymdale's hands were, and wondering why Lydgate did not come. She went on with her tatting[1] all the while.

"I did not say she was as beautiful as you are," said Mr. Ned, venturing to look from the portrait to its rival.

"I suspect you of being an adroit flatterer," said Rosamond, feeling sure that she should have to reject this young gentleman a second time.

But now Lydgate came in; the book was closed before he reached Rosamond's corner, and as he took his seat with easy confidence on the other side of her, young Plymdale's jaw fell like a barometer towards the cheerless side of change. Rosamond enjoyed not only Lydgate's presence but its effect: she liked to excite jealousy.

"What a late comer you are!" she said, as they shook hands. "Mamma had given you up a little while ago. How do you find Fred?"

"As usual; going on well, but slowly. I want him to go away—to Stone Court, for example. But your mamma seems to have some objection."

"Poor fellow!" said Rosamond, prettily. "You will see Fred so changed," she added, turning to the other suitor; "we have looked to Mr. Lydgate as our guardian angel during this illness."

Mr. Ned smiled nervously, while Lydgate, drawing the "Keepsake" towards him and opening it, gave a short scornful laugh and tossed up his chin, as if in wonderment at human folly.

"What are you laughing at so profanely?" said Rosamond, with bland neutrality.

"I wonder which would turn out to be the silliest—the engravings or the writing here," said Lydgate, in his most convinced tone, while he turned over the pages quickly, seeming to see all through the book in no time, and showing his large white hands to much advantage, as Rosamond thought. "Do look at this bridegroom coming out of church: did you ever see such a 'sugared invention'[2]—as the Elizabethans used to say? Did any haberdasher[3] ever look so smirking? Yet I will answer for it the story makes him one of the first gentlemen in the land."

"You are so severe, I am frightened at you," said Rosamond, keeping her amusement duly moderate. Poor young Plymdale had lingered with admiration over this very engraving, and his spirit was stirred.

"There are a great many celebrated people writing in the 'Keepsake,' at all events," he said, in a tone at once piqued and timid. "This is the first time I have heard it called silly."

"I think I shall turn round on you and accuse you of being a Goth," said Rosamond, looking at Lydgate with a smile. "I suspect you know nothing about Lady Blessington and L.E.L."[4] Rosamond herself was not without relish for these writers, but she did not readily commit herself by admiration, and was alive to the slightest hint that anything was not, according to Lydgate, in the very highest taste.

"But Sir Walter Scott[5]—I suppose Mr. Lydgate knows him," said young Plymdale, a little cheered by this advantage.

"Oh, I read no literature now," said Lydgate, shutting the book, and pushing it away. "I read so much when I was a lad, that I suppose it will last me all my life. I used to know Scott's poems by heart."

[1] *tatting* Making knotted lace.

[2] *sugared invention* See Sir Philip Sidney, *The Defence of Poesy* (1595): "His sugared invention of that picture of love."

[3] *haberdasher* Seller of miscellaneous small items used in the making of clothing.

[4] *Lady Blessington* Marguerite, Countess of Blessington (1789–1849), was a novelist and editor of *The Keepsake*; *L.E.L.* Letitia Elizabeth Landon (1802–38), a prominent English poet who contributed to several editions of *The Keepsake*. She is especially well known for love poetry with a melancholy tone.

[5] *Sir Walter Scott* Influential Scottish poet and novelist (1771–1832) who contributed to *The Keepsake for 1829*. Scott established his career as a writer of ballads, then became widely read as a historical novelist.

"I should like to know when you left off," said Rosamond, "because then I might be sure that I knew something which you did not know."

"Mr. Lydgate would say that was not worth knowing," said Mr. Ned, purposely caustic.

"On the contrary," said Lydgate, showing no smart; but smiling with exasperating confidence at Rosamond. "It would be worth knowing by the fact that Miss Vincy could tell it me."

Young Plymdale soon went to look at the whist-playing, thinking that Lydgate was one of the most conceited, unpleasant fellows it had ever been his ill-fortune to meet.

"How rash you are!" said Rosamond, inwardly delighted. "Do you see that you have given offence?"

"What! is it Mr. Plymdale's book? I am sorry. I didn't think about it."

"I shall begin to admit what you said of yourself when you first came here—that you are a bear, and want teaching by the birds."

"Well, there is a bird who can teach me what she will. Don't I listen to her willingly?"

To Rosamond it seemed as if she and Lydgate were as good as engaged. That they were some time to be engaged had long been an idea in her mind; and ideas, we know, tend to a more solid kind of existence, the necessary materials being at hand. It is true, Lydgate had the counter-idea of remaining unengaged; but this was a mere negative, a shadow cast by other resolves which themselves were capable of shrinking. Circumstance was almost sure to be on the side of Rosamond's idea, which had a shaping activity and looked through watchful blue eyes, whereas Lydgate's lay blind and unconcerned as a jelly-fish which gets melted without knowing it.

That evening when he went home, he looked at his phials to see how a process of maceration[1] was going on, with undisturbed interest; and he wrote out his daily notes with as much precision as usual. The reveries from which it was difficult for him to detach himself were ideal constructions of something else than Rosamond's virtues, and the primitive tissue was still his fair unknown.[2] Moreover, he was beginning to feel some zest for the growing though half-suppressed feud between him and the other medical men, which was likely to become more manifest, now that Bulstrode's method of managing the new hospital was about to be declared; and there were various inspiriting signs that his non-acceptance by some of Peacock's patients[3] might be counterbalanced by the impression he had produced in other quarters. …

—1871–72

[1] *phials* Small, sealable glass bottles for medicine or chemicals; *maceration* In biological experiments, the process of soaking a specimen in a solution to dissolve it.

[2] *primitive tissue … fair unknown* Earlier in the novel, the narrator tells us that Lydgate's chief ambition in medicine is to study anatomy and the "primary webs or tissues." He hopes to make important discoveries, particularly in the treatment of fevers.

[3] *Peacock's patients* Lydgate had bought Dr. Peacock's practice when he arrived in Middlemarch; some of the patients did not trust Lydgate's modern ways, while other members of the community believed in him and his scientific approach.

John Ruskin

1819 – 1900

John Ruskin was a painter and a poet, author of dozens of books on the arts and sciences, and a dedicated believer in fundamental links between all disciplines. Famous as a critic of art, culture, and society, Ruskin synthesized subjects in fluid and poetic ways, and he exerted an enormous influence on the aesthetic, philosophical, and political sensibilities of his day. This influence bore heavily on the work of the Pre-Raphaelite painters, notably Dante Gabriel Rossetti, John Everett Millais, and William Holman Hunt. In addition, Ruskin's opposition to industrialization and his ideas about the sacredness of human work inspired William Morris and the Arts and Crafts Movement. Mahatma Gandhi, who translated Ruskin's *Unto the Last* into Gujarati, said about the work's effect on him, "I believe that I discovered some of my deepest convictions reflecting on this great book of Ruskin's, [... which] captured me and made me transform my life."

Ruskin was born in London in 1819 to Margaret Cox and John James Ruskin, a successful wine merchant. Possibly because the couple bore John in midlife and had no other children, the Evangelical Ruskins raised their child in an overprotective and cloistered manner, allowing him neither friends nor toys. The young John's schooling, administered by his mother, was strict and included hours of Bible study every day (the two would read the entire Bible and then resume from the beginning), while his father, also a stern Evangelical, procured tutors for the arts and languages. When Ruskin came of age, he attended Oxford (where he won the Newdigate Prize for poetry), but even then his mother accompanied him, living in rooms nearby, and his father joined the two every weekend.

Even though he had a talent for both poetry and painting, Ruskin realized after graduation that he did not wish to pursue either as a career. His admiration for the British painter J.M.W. Turner, however, led to his first work of art criticism, which evolved into the five-volume *Modern Painters*, published over a period of more than a decade. The first volume of *Modern Painters* was a defense of Turner's "fidelity" to his landscapes and his ability to see and express "truth" in nature. It was not only Ruskin's aesthetic analyses that attracted attention, however, but also his elegant and engaging prose style.

In 1848, Ruskin entered into a disastrous marriage with Euphemia ("Effie") Chalmers, which ended six years later in an annulment on the grounds that the marriage had never been consummated. The following year Effie married the painter John Everett Millais. Throughout his life, Ruskin's relationships with women were fraught, most notably his relationship with Rose La Touche, whom he met in 1858 when she was only nine years old. Ruskin proposed marriage to Rose in 1866, but she ultimately rejected his offer, both because of his earlier annulment and because she was a strict Evangelical, while he had lost his religious faith (he said he had been "unconverted" while attending church in Turin). Not long after her death in 1875, Ruskin suffered an attack of madness, the first of many such episodes he experienced throughout his life.

Although there were times when Ruskin could not function due to mental illness, he was astonishingly prolific: his *Collected Works* fill thirty-nine volumes, and he wrote thousands of letters. His books on architecture, *The Seven Lamps of Architecture* (1849) and the three-volume *Stones of Venice* (1851–53), were so influential that they provoked a revival of Gothic architecture that in some ways ran counter to his philosophies. Ruskin felt that the hand of God was present in those who labored on the stone buildings of the Middle Ages, and that the magnificent Gothic architecture of Venice was a manifestation of a virtuous and honorable people. His writing inspired many to support the preservation and restoration of architectural treasures. Ruskin himself, however, promoted a social, rather than simply an architectural, restoration.

Ruskin's attacks on society became increasingly focused on the effects of modern production, and he became an outspoken challenger of the Industrial Age. His views on economic and social reform, radical at the time, have affected social thinking to this day. Ruskin was strongly opposed to *laissez faire* economics and advocated the organization of labor (the founders of the Labour Party in Britain attributed their ideas to Ruskin), cooperative business ventures, an old-age pension, a minimum wage, public libraries and art galleries, a national health service, equal education opportunities, and pollution control, among many other initiatives. In 1878, Ruskin founded the Guild of St. George, an organization that still exists today, in order to educate the public and to preserve and support small businesses and the production of local crafts. This is not to say that Ruskin's political views could in any way be considered wholly progressive; for example, his 1865 two-part essay *Sesame and Lilies*, in which he defines the qualities and ideal roles of men and women, was popular in his own era but roundly condemned by feminist critics in the late twentieth century. He was also a supporter of British imperialism. He considered Britain to be superior in civilization to nations such as India, and, in 1865 he was an outspoken defender of the infamous Jamaican Governor Edward John Eyre, who had committed a shocking series of atrocities to repress a rebellion.

After writing and lecturing throughout the 1860s, Ruskin was offered the first Slade Professorship of Fine Arts at Oxford, where he delivered (and subsequently published) many famous lectures and speeches to awestruck students, including the young Oscar Wilde. During this decade he also began a series of letters addressed to English laborers, published as *Fors Clavigera*. Ruskin was forced to resign his position at Oxford in 1880 due to mental illness, and although he resumed his professorship for a brief period and published two final books of lectures, *The Pleasures of England* and *The Art of England*, these years were not good to him. He managed to write many installments of his brilliant autobiography, *Praeterita*, but it remained unfinished. After a long illness he died in 1900. Although Westminster Abbey offered a resting place, Ruskin's last wishes were honored, and he was buried near his home in the Coniston graveyard. For the great Russian writer Leo Tolstoy, and for many others, Ruskin's legacy remained alive: "Ruskin was one of the most remarkable of men, not only of England and our time but of all countries and all times. He was one of those rare men who think with their hearts, and so he thought and said not only what he himself had seen and felt, but what everyone will think and say in the future."

⌘⌘⌘

from *Modern Painters*

A DEFINITION OF GREATNESS IN ART

Painting, or art generally, as such, with all its technicalities, difficulties, and particular ends, is nothing but a noble and expressive language, invaluable as the vehicle of thought, but by itself nothing. He who has learned what is commonly considered the whole art of painting, that is, the art of representing any natural object faithfully, has as yet only learned the language by which his thoughts are to be expressed. He has done just as much towards being that which we ought to respect as a great painter, as a man who has learned how to express himself grammatically and melodiously has towards being a great poet. The language is, indeed, more difficult of acquirement in the one case than in the other, and possesses more power of delighting the sense, while it speaks to the intellect; but it is, nevertheless, nothing more than language, and all those excellences which are peculiar to the painter as such, are merely what rhythm, melody, precision, and force are in the words of the orator and the poet, necessary to their greatness, but not the tests of their greatness. It is not by the mode of representing and saying, but by what is represented and said, that the respective greatness either of the painter or the writer is to be finally determined. …

So that, if I say that the greatest picture is that which conveys to the mind of the spectator the greatest number of the greatest ideas, I have a definition which will include as subjects of comparison every pleasure which art is capable of conveying. If I were to say, on the contrary, that the best picture was that which most closely imitated nature, I should assume that art could only please by imitating nature; and I should cast out of the pale of criticism those parts of works of art which are not imitative, that is to say, intrinsic beauties of colour and form, and those works of art wholly, which, like the Arabesques of Raffaelle[1] in the Loggias,[2] are not imitative at all. Now, I want a definition of art wide enough to include all its varieties of aim. I do not say, therefore, that the art is greatest which gives most pleasure, because perhaps there is some art whose end is to teach, and not to please. I do not say that the art is greatest which teaches us most, because perhaps there is some art whose end is to please, and not to teach. I do not say that the art is greatest which imitates best, because perhaps there is some art whose end is to create and not to imitate. But I say that the art is greatest which conveys to the mind of the spectator, by any means whatsoever, the greatest number of the greatest ideas; and I call an idea great in proportion as it is received by a higher faculty of the mind, and as it more fully occupies, and in occupying, exercises and exalts, the faculty by which it is received.

If this, then, be the definition of great art, that of a great artist naturally follows. He is the greatest artist who has embodied, in the sum of his works, the greatest number of the greatest ideas. …

OF TRUTH OF WATER

I believe it is a result of the experience of all artists, that it is the easiest thing in the world to give a certain degree of depth and transparency to water; but that it is next to impossible, to give a full impression of surface. If no reflection be given, a ripple being supposed, the water looks like lead: if reflection be given, it, in nine cases out of ten, looks *morbidly* clear and deep, so that we always go down *into* it, even when the artist most wishes us to glide *over* it. Now, this difficulty arises from the very same circumstance which occasions the frequent failure in effect of the best-drawn foregrounds … the change, namely, of focus necessary in the eye in order to receive rays of light coming from different distances. Go to the edge of a pond in a perfectly calm day, at some place where there is duckweed floating on the surface, not thick, but a leaf here and there. Now, you may either see in the water the reflection of the sky, or you may see the duckweed; but you cannot, by any effort, see both together. If you look for the reflection, you will be sensible of a sudden change or effort in the eye, by which it adapts itself to the reception of the rays which

[1] *Raffaelle* I.e., Raphael (1483–1520), Italian Renaissance painter.

[2] *Loggias* Open-air galleries.

have come all the way from the clouds, have struck on the water, and so been sent up again to the eye. The focus you adopt is one fit for great distance; and, accordingly, you will feel that you are looking down a great way under the water, while the leaves of the duckweed, though they lie upon the water at the very spot on which you are gazing so intently, are felt only as a vague uncertain interruption, causing a little confusion in the image below, but entirely undistinguishable as leaves, and even their colour unknown and unperceived. Unless you think of them, you will not even feel that anything interrupts your sight, so excessively slight is their effect. If, on the other hand, you make up your mind to look for the leaves of the duckweed, you will perceive an instantaneous change in the effort of the eye, by which it becomes adapted to receive near rays, those which have only come from the surface of the pond. You will then see the delicate leaves of the duckweed with perfect clearness, and in vivid green; but, while you do so, you will be able to perceive nothing of the reflections in the very water on which they float, nothing but a vague flashing and melting of light and dark hues, without form or meaning, which to investigate, or find out what they mean or are, you must quit your hold of the duckweed, and plunge down.

Hence it appears, that whenever we see plain reflections of comparatively distant objects, in near water, we cannot possibly see the surface, and *vice versa;* so that when in a painting we give the reflections with the same clearness with which they are visible in nature, we presuppose the effort of the eye to look under the surface, and, of course, destroy the surface, and induce an effect of clearness which, perhaps, the artist has not particularly wished to attain, but which he has found himself forced into, by his reflections, in spite of himself. And the reason of this effect of clearness appearing preternatural is, that people are not in the habit of looking at water with the distant focus adapted to the reflections, unless by particular effort. We invariably, under ordinary circumstances, use the surface focus; and, in consequence, receive nothing more than a vague and confused impression of the reflected colours and lines, however clearly, calmly, and vigorously all may be defined underneath, if we choose to look for them. We do not look for them, but glide along over the surface, catching only playing light and capricious colour for evidence of reflection, except where we come to images of objects close to the surface, which the surface focus is of course adapted to receive; and these we see clearly, as of the weeds on the shore, or of sticks rising out of the water, etc. Hence, the ordinary effect of water is only to be rendered by giving the reflections of the *margin* clear and distinct (so clear they usually are in nature, that it is impossible to tell where the water begins); but the moment we touch the reflection of distant objects, as of high trees or clouds, that instant we must become vague and uncertain in drawing, and, though vivid in colour and light as the object itself, quite indistinct in form and feature. If we take such a piece of water as that in the foreground of Turner's[1] Château of Prince Albert, the first impression from it is, "What a wide *surface*!" We glide over it a quarter of a mile into the picture before we know where we are, and yet the water is as calm and crystalline as a mirror; but we are not allowed to tumble into it, and gasp for breath as we go down, we are kept upon the surface, though that surface is flashing and radiant with every hue of cloud, and sun, and sky, and foliage. But the secret is in the drawing of these reflections. We cannot tell, when we look *at* them and *for* them, what they mean. They have all character, and are evidently reflections of something definite and determined; but yet they are all uncertain and inexplicable; playing colour and palpitating shade, which, though we recognize them in an instant for images of something, and feel that the water is bright, and lovely, and calm, we cannot penetrate nor interpret; we are not allowed to go down to them, and we repose, as we should in nature, upon the lustre of the level surface. It is in this power of saying everything, and yet saying nothing too plainly, that the perfection of art here, as in all other cases, consists.

—1843

[1] *Turner* J.M.W. Turner (1775–1851), English landscape artist.

from *The Stones of Venice*

The Nature of Gothic

… In the definition proposed, I shall only endeavour to analyze the idea which I suppose already to exist in the reader's mind. We all have some notion, most of us a very determined one, of the meaning of the term Gothic, but I know that many persons have this idea in their minds without being able to define it: that is to say, understanding generally that Westminster Abbey is Gothic, and St. Paul's is not, that Strasburg Cathedral is Gothic, and St. Peter's is not, they have, nevertheless, no clear notion of what it is that they recognize in the one or miss in the other, such as would enable them to say how far the work at Westminster or Strasburg is good and pure of its kind; still less to say of any nondescript building, like St. James's Palace or Windsor Castle, how much right Gothic element there is in it, and how much wanting. And I believe this inquiry to be a pleasant and profitable one; and that there will be found something more than usually interesting in tracing out this grey, shadowy, many-pinnacled image of the Gothic spirit within us; and discerning what fellowship there is between it and our Northern hearts. And if, at any point of the inquiry, I should interfere with any of the reader's previously formed conceptions, and use the term Gothic in any sense which he would not willingly attach to it, I do not ask him to accept, but only to examine and understand, my interpretation, as necessary to the intelligibility of what follows in the rest of the work. …

I believe, then, that the characteristic or moral elements of Gothic are the following, placed in the order of their importance:

1. Savageness.
2. Changefulness.
3. Naturalism.
4. Grotesqueness.
5. Rigidity.
6. Redundance.

These characters are here expressed as belonging to the building; as belonging to the builder, they would be expressed thus:—1. Savageness or Rudeness. 2. Love of Change. 3. Love of Nature. 4. Disturbed Imagination. 5. Obstinacy. 6. Generosity. And I repeat, that the withdrawal of any one, or any two, will not at once destroy the Gothic character of a building, but the removal of a majority of them will. I shall proceed to examine them in their order.

(1.) Savageness. I am not sure when the word "Gothic" was first generically applied to the architecture of the North; but I presume that, whatever the date of its original usage, it was intended to imply reproach, and express the barbaric character of the nations among whom that architecture arose. It never implied that they were literally of Gothic lineage, far less that their architecture had been originally invented by the Goths themselves; but it did imply that they and their buildings together exhibited a degree of sternness and rudeness, which, in contradistinction to the character of Southern and Eastern nations, appeared like a perpetual reflection of the contrast between the Goth and the Roman in their first encounter. And when that fallen Roman, in the utmost impotence of his luxury, and insolence of his guilt, became the model for the imitation of civilized Europe, at the close of the so-called Dark ages, the word Gothic became a term of unmitigated contempt, not unmixed with aversion. From that contempt, by the exertion of the antiquaries and architects of this century, Gothic architecture has been sufficiently vindicated; and perhaps some among us, in our admiration of the magnificent science of its structure, and sacredness of its expression, might desire that the term of ancient reproach should be withdrawn, and some other, of more apparent honourableness, adopted in its place. There is no chance, as there is no need, of such a substitution. As far as the epithet was used scornfully, it was used falsely; but there is no reproach in the word, rightly understood; on the contrary, there is a profound truth, which the instinct of mankind almost unconsciously recognizes. It is true, greatly and deeply true, that the architecture of the North is rude and wild; but it is not true, that, for this reason, we are to condemn it, or despise. Far otherwise: I believe it is in this very character that it deserves our profoundest reverence.

The charts of the world which have been drawn up by modern science have thrown into a narrow space the expression of a vast amount of knowledge, but I have never yet seen any one pictorial enough to enable the spectator to imagine the kind of contrast in physical character which exists between Northern and Southern countries. We know the differences in detail, but we have not that broad glance and grasp which would enable us to feel them in their fulness. We know that gentians[1] grow on the Alps, and olives on the Apennines; but we do not enough conceive for ourselves that variegated mosaic of the world's surface which a bird sees in its migration, that difference between the district of the gentian and of the olive which the stork and the swallow see far off, as they lean upon the sirocco wind.[2] Let us, for a moment, try to raise ourselves even above the level of their flight, and imagine the Mediterranean lying beneath us like an irregular lake, and all its ancient promontories sleeping in the sun: here and there an angry spot of thunder, a grey stain of storm, moving upon the burning field; and here and there a fixed wreath of white volcano smoke, surrounded by its circle of ashes; but for the most part a great peacefulness of light, Syria and Greece, Italy and Spain, laid like pieces of a golden pavement into the sea-blue, chased, as we stoop nearer to them, with bossy beaten work of mountain chains, and glowing softly with terraced gardens, and flowers heavy with frankincense, mixed among masses of laurel, and orange, and plumy palm, that abate with their grey-green shadows the burning of the marble rocks, and of the ledges of porphyry[3] sloping under lucent sand. Then let us pass farther towards the north, until we see the orient colours change gradually into a vast belt of rainy green, where the pastures of Switzerland, and poplar valleys of France, and dark forests of the Danube and Carpathians stretch from the mouths of the Loire to those of the Volga, seen through clefts in grey swirls of rain-cloud and flaky veils of the mist of the brooks, spreading low along the pasture lands: and then, farther north still, to see the earth heave into mighty masses of leaden rock and heathy moor, bordering with a broad waste of gloomy purple that belt of field and wood, and splintering into irregular and grisly islands amidst the northern seas, beaten by storm, and chilled by ice-drift, and tormented by furious pulses of contending tide, until the roots of the last forests fail from among the hill ravines, and the hunger of the north wind bites their peaks into barrenness; and, at last, the wall of ice, durable like iron, sets, deathlike, its white teeth against us out of the polar twilight. And, having once traversed in thought this gradation of the zoned iris of the earth in all its material vastness, let us go down nearer to it, and watch the parallel change in the belt of animal life; the multitudes of swift and brilliant creatures that glance in the air and sea, or tread the sands of the southern zone; striped zebras and spotted leopards, glistening serpents, and birds arrayed in purple and scarlet. Let us contrast their delicacy and brilliancy of colour, and swiftness of motion, with the frost-cramped strength, and shaggy covering, and dusky plumage of the northern tribes; contrast the Arabian horse with the Shetland, the tiger and leopard with the wolf and bear, the antelope with the elk, the bird of paradise with the osprey; and then, submissively acknowledging the great laws by which the earth and all that it bears are ruled throughout their being, let us not condemn, but rejoice in the expression by man of his own rest in the statutes of the lands that gave him birth. Let us watch him with reverence as he sets side by side the burning gems, and smoothes with soft sculpture the jasper pillars, that are to reflect a ceaseless sunshine, and rise into a cloudless sky: but not with less reverence let us stand by him, when, with rough strength and hurried stroke, he smites an uncouth animation out of the rocks which he has torn from among the moss of the moorland, and heaves into the darkened air the pile of iron buttress and rugged wall, instinct with work of an imagination as wild and wayward as the northern sea; creatures of ungainly shape and rigid limb, but full of

[1] *gentians* Flowers.

[2] *sirocco wind* Hot, moist wind from North Africa.

[3] *porphyry* Red crystalline rock.

wolfish life; fierce as the winds that beat, and changeful as the clouds that shade them. …

In … the first volume of this work, it was noticed that the systems of architectural ornament, properly so called, might be divided into three:—1. Servile ornament, in which the execution or power of the inferior workman is entirely subjected to the intellect of the higher;—2. Constitutional ornament, in which the executive inferior power is, to a certain point, emancipated and independent, having a will of its own, yet confessing its inferiority and rendering obedience to higher powers;—and 3. Revolutionary ornament, in which no executive inferiority is admitted at all. I must here explain the nature of these divisions at somewhat greater length.

Of Servile ornament, the principal schools are the Greek, Ninevite, and Egyptian; but their servility is of different kinds. The Greek master-workman was far advanced in knowledge and power above the Assyrian or Egyptian. Neither he nor those for whom he worked could endure the appearance of imperfection in anything; and, therefore, what ornament he appointed to be done by those beneath him was composed of mere geometrical forms—balls, ridges, and perfectly symmetrical foliage—which could be executed with absolute precision by line and rule, and were as perfect in their way, when completed, as his own figure sculpture. The Assyrian and Egyptian, on the contrary, less cognizant of accurate form in anything, were content to allow their figure sculpture to be executed by inferior workmen, but lowered the method of its treatment to a standard which every workman could reach, and then trained him by discipline so rigid, that there was no chance of his falling beneath the standard appointed. The Greek gave to the lower workman no subject which he could not perfectly execute. The Assyrian gave him subjects which he could only execute imperfectly, but fixed a legal standard for his imperfection. The workman was, in both systems, a slave.

But in the mediaeval, or especially Christian, system of ornament, this slavery is done away with altogether; Christianity having recognized, in small things as well as great, the individual value of every soul. But it not only recognizes its value; it confesses its imperfection, in only bestowing dignity upon the acknowledgment of unworthiness. That admission of lost power and fallen nature, which the Greek or Ninevite felt to be intensely painful, and, as far as might be, altogether refused, the Christian makes daily and hourly, contemplating the fact of it without fear, as tending, in the end, to God's greater glory. Therefore, to every spirit which Christianity summons to her service, her exhortation is: Do what you can, and confess frankly what you are unable to do; neither let your effort be shortened for fear of failure, nor your confession silenced for fear of shame. And it is, perhaps, the principal admirableness of the Gothic schools of architecture, that they thus receive the results of the labour of inferior minds; and out of fragments full of imperfection, and betraying that imperfection in every touch, indulgently raise up a stately and unaccusable whole. …

And now, reader, look round this English room of yours, about which you have been proud so often, because the work of it was so good and strong, and the ornaments of it so finished. Examine again all those accurate mouldings, and perfect polishings, and unerring adjustments of the seasoned wood and tempered steel. Many a time you have exulted over them, and thought how great England was, because her slightest work was done so thoroughly. Alas! if read rightly, these perfectnesses are signs of a slavery in our England a thousand times more bitter and more degrading than that of the scourged African, or helot[1] Greek. Men may be beaten, chained, tormented, yoked like cattle, slaughtered like summer flies, and yet remain in one sense, and the best sense, free. But to smother their souls with them, to blight and hew into rotting pollards[2] the suckling branches of their human intelligence, to make the flesh and skin which, after the worm's work on it, is to see God, into leathern thongs to yoke machinery with—this is to be slave-masters indeed; and there might be more freedom in England, though her feudal lords' lightest words were worth men's lives, and though

[1] *helot* Of a class of serfs, falling between slave and citizen in the Spartan social hierarchy.

[2] *pollards* Trees whose branches have been lopped off to shape them.

the blood of the vexed husbandman dropped in the furrows of her fields, than there is while the animation of her multitudes is sent like fuel to feed the factory smoke, and the strength of them is given daily to be wasted into the fineness of a web, or racked into the exactness of a line.

And, on the other hand, go forth again to gaze upon the old cathedral front, where you have smiled so often at the fantastic ignorance of the old sculptors: examine once more those ugly goblins, and formless monsters, and stern statues, anatomiless and rigid; but do not mock at them, for they are signs of the life and liberty of every workman who struck the stone; a freedom of thought, and rank in scale of being, such as no laws, no charters, no charities can secure; but which it must be the first aim of all Europe at this day to regain for her children. …

We have much studied and much perfected, of late, the great civilized invention of the division of labour; only we give it a false name. It is not, truly speaking, the labour that is divided; but the men: divided into mere segments of men—broken into small fragments and crumbs of life; so that all the little piece of intelligence that is left in a man is not enough to make a pin, or a nail, but exhausts itself in making the point of a pin or the head of a nail. Now it is a good and desirable thing, truly, to make many pins in a day; but if we could only see with what crystal sand their points were polished—sand of human soul, much to be magnified before it can be discerned for what it is—we should think there might be some loss in it also. And the great cry that rises from all our manufacturing cities, louder than their furnace blast, is all in very deed for this—that we manufacture everything there except men; we blanch cotton, and strengthen steel, and refine sugar, and shape pottery; but to brighten, to strengthen, to refine, or to form a single living spirit, never enters into our estimate of advantages. And all the evil to which that cry is urging our myriads can be met only in one way: not by teaching nor preaching, for to teach them is but to show them their misery, and to preach to them, if we do nothing more than preach, is to mock at it. It can be met only by a right understanding, on the part of all classes, of what kinds of labour are good for men, raising them, and making them happy; by a determined sacrifice of such convenience, or beauty, or cheapness as is to be got only by the degradation of the workman; and by equally determined demand for the products and results of healthy and ennobling labour.

And how, it will be asked, are these products to be recognized, and this demand to be regulated? Easily: by the observance of three broad and simple rules:

1. Never encourage the manufacture of any article not absolutely necessary, in the production of which *Invention* has no share.

2. Never demand an exact finish for its own sake, but only for some practical or noble end.

3. Never encourage imitation or copying of any kind, except for the sake of preserving records of great works.

The second of these principles is the only one which directly rises out of the consideration of our immediate subject; but I shall briefly explain the meaning and extent of the first also, reserving the enforcement of the third for another place.

1. Never encourage the manufacture of anything not necessary, in the production of which invention has no share.

For instance. Glass beads are utterly unnecessary, and there is no design or thought employed in their manufacture. They are formed by first drawing out the glass into rods; these rods are chopped up into fragments of the size of beads by the human hand, and the fragments are then rounded in the furnace. The men who chop up the rods sit at their work all day, their hands vibrating with a perpetual and exquisitely timed palsy, and the beads dropping beneath their vibration like hail. Neither they, nor the men who draw out the rods or fuse the fragments, have the smallest occasion for the use of any single human faculty; and every young lady, therefore, who buys glass beads is engaged in the slave-trade, and in a much more cruel one than that which we have so long been endeavouring to put down. …

[One example to] show the reader what I mean [comes] from the manufacture already alluded to, that of glass. Our modern glass is exquisitely clear in its substance, true in its form, accurate in its cutting. We are proud of this. We ought to be ashamed of it. The old Venice glass was muddy, inaccurate in all its forms, and clumsily cut, if at all. And the old Venetian was justly proud of it. For there is this difference between the English and Venetian workman, that the former thinks only of accurately matching his patterns, and getting his curves perfectly true and his edges perfectly sharp, and becomes a mere machine for rounding curves and sharpening edges; while the old Venetian cared not a whit whether his edges were sharp or not, but he invented a new design for every glass that he made, and never moulded a handle or a lip without a new fancy in it. And therefore, though some Venetian glass is ugly and clumsy enough when made by clumsy and uninventive workmen, other Venetian glass is so lovely in its forms that no price is too great for it; and we never see the same form in it twice. Now you cannot have the finish and the varied form too. If the workman is thinking about his edges, he cannot be thinking of his design; if of his design, he cannot think of his edges. Choose whether you will pay for the lovely form or the perfect finish, and choose at the same moment whether you will make the worker a man or a grindstone.

Nay, but the reader interrupts me—"If the workman can design beautifully, I would not have him kept at the furnace. Let him be taken away and made a gentleman, and have a studio, and design his glass there, and I will have it blown and cut for him by common workmen, and so I will have my design and my finish too."

All ideas of this kind are founded upon two mistaken suppositions: the first, that one man's thoughts can be, or ought to be, executed by another man's hands; the second, that manual labour is a degradation, when it is governed by intellect.

On a large scale, and in work determinable by line and rule, it is indeed both possible and necessary that the thoughts of one man should be carried out by the labour of others; in this sense I have already defined the best architecture to be the expression of the mind of manhood by the hands of childhood. But on a smaller scale, and in a design which cannot be mathematically defined, one man's thoughts can never be expressed by another: and the difference between the spirit of touch of the man who is inventing, and of the man who is obeying directions, is often all the difference between a great and a common work of art. How wide the separation is between original and second-hand execution, I shall endeavour to show elsewhere; it is not so much to our purpose here as to mark the other and more fatal error of despising manual labour when governed by intellect; for it is no less fatal an error to despise it when thus regulated by intellect, than to value it for its own sake. We are always in these days endeavouring to separate the two; we want one man to be always thinking, and another to be always working, and we call one a gentleman, and the other an operative; whereas the workman ought often to be thinking, and the thinker often to be working, and both should be gentlemen, in the best sense. As it is, we make both ungentle, the one envying, the other despising, his brother; and the mass of society is made up of morbid thinkers, and miserable workers. Now it is only by labour that thought can be made healthy, and only by thought that labour can be made happy, and the two cannot be separated with impunity. It would be well if all of us were good handicraftsmen in some kind, and the dishonour of manual labour done away with altogether; so that though there should still be a trenchant distinction of race between nobles and commoners, there should not, among the latter, be a trenchant distinction of employment, as between idle and working men, or between men of liberal and illiberal professions. All professions should be liberal, and there should be less pride felt in peculiarity of employment, and more in excellence of achievement. And yet more, in each several profession, no master should be too proud to do its hardest work. The painter should grind his own colours; the architect work in the mason's yard with his men.... Hitherto I have used the words imperfect and perfect merely to distinguish between work grossly unskilful, and work executed with average precision and science; and I have been pleading that any degree of unskilfulness should be admitted, so only that the labourer's mind had room for expression. But, accurately speaking, no good work whatever can be perfect, and *the demand for perfection is always a sign of a misunderstanding of the ends of art.*

This for two reasons, both based on everlasting laws. The first, that no great man ever stops working till he has reached his point of failure: that is to say, his mind is always far in advance of his powers of execution, and the latter will now and then give way in trying to follow it; … And therefore, if we are to have great men working at all, or less men doing their best, the work will be imperfect, however beautiful. Of human work none but what is bad can be perfect, in its own bad way.

The second reason is, that imperfection is in some sort essential to all that we know of life. It is the sign of life in a mortal body, that is to say, of a state of progress and change. Nothing that lives is, or can be, rigidly perfect; part of it is decaying, part nascent. The foxglove blossom—a third part bud, a third part past, a third part in full bloom—is a type of the life of this world. And in all things that live there are certain irregularities and deficiencies which are not only signs of life, but sources of beauty. No human face is exactly the same in its lines on each side, no leaf perfect in its lobes, no branch in its symmetry. All admit irregularity as they imply change; and to banish imperfection is to destroy expression, to check exertion, to paralyze vitality. All things are literally better, lovelier, and more beloved for the imperfections which have been divinely appointed, that the law of human life may be Effort, and the law of human judgment, Mercy.

Accept this then for a universal law, that neither architecture nor any other noble work of man can be good unless it be imperfect; and let us be prepared for the otherwise strange fact, which we shall discern clearly as we approach the period of the Renaissance, that the first cause of the fall of the arts of Europe was a relentless requirement of perfection, incapable alike either of being silenced by veneration for greatness, or softened into forgiveness of simplicity.

Thus far then of the Rudeness or Savageness, which is the first mental element of Gothic architecture. It is an element in many other healthy architectures also, as the Byzantine and Romanesque; but true Gothic cannot exist without it.

The second mental element above named was Changefulness, or Variety.

I have already enforced the allowing independent operation to the inferior workman, simply as a duty *to him,* and as ennobling the architecture by rendering it more Christian. We have now to consider what reward we obtain for the performance of this duty, namely, the perpetual variety of every feature of the building.

Wherever the workman is utterly enslaved, the parts of the building must of course be absolutely like each other; for the perfection of his execution can only be reached by exercising him in doing one thing, and giving him nothing else to do. The degree in which the workman is degraded may be thus known at a glance, by observing whether the several parts of the building are similar or not; and if, as in Greek work, all the capitals are alike, and all the mouldings unvaried, then the degradation is complete; if, as in Egyptian or Ninevite work, though the manner of executing certain figures is always the same, the order of design is perpetually varied, the degradation is less total; if, as in Gothic work, there is perpetual change both in design and execution, the workman must have been altogether set free.

How much the beholder gains from the liberty of the labourer may perhaps be questioned in England, where one of the strongest instincts in nearly every mind is that love of order which makes us desire that our house windows should pair like our carriage horses, and allows us to yield our faith unhesitatingly to architectural theories which fix a form for everything, and forbid variation from it. I would not impeach love of order: it is one of the most useful elements of the English mind; it helps us in our commerce and in all purely practical matters; and it is in many cases one of the foundation stones of morality. Only do not let us suppose that love of order is love of art. It is true that order, in its highest sense, is one of the necessities of art, just as time is a necessity of music; but love of order has no more to do with our right enjoyment of architecture or painting, than love of punctuality with the appreciation of an opera. …

From these general uses of variety in the economy of the world, we may at once understand its use and abuse in architecture. The variety of the Gothic schools is the more healthy and beautiful, because in many cases it is entirely unstudied, and results, not from mere love of change, but from practical necessities. For in one point of view Gothic is not only the best, but the *only rational* architecture, as being that which can fit itself most easily to all services, vulgar or noble. Undefined in its slope of roof, height of shaft, breadth of arch, or disposition of ground plan, it can shrink into a turret, expand into a hall, coil into a staircase, or spring into a spire, with undegraded grace and unexhausted energy; and whenever it finds occasion for change in its form or purpose, it submits to it without the slightest sense of loss either to its unity or majesty,—subtle and flexible like a fiery serpent, but ever attentive to the voice of the charmer. And it is one of the chief virtues of the Gothic builders, that they never suffered ideas of outside symmetries and consistencies to interfere with the real use and value of what they did. If they wanted a window, they opened one; a room, they added one; a buttress, they built one; utterly regardless of any established conventionalities of external appearance, knowing (as indeed it always happened) that such daring interruptions of the formal plan would rather give additional interest to its symmetry than injure it. …

The third constituent element of the Gothic mind was stated to be Naturalism; that is to say, the love of natural objects for their own sake, and the effort to represent them frankly, unconstrained by artistical laws.

This characteristic of the style partly follows in necessary connection with those named above. For, so soon as the workman is left free to represent what subjects he chooses, he must look to the nature that is round him for material, and will endeavour to represent it as he sees it, with more or less accuracy according to the skill he possesses, and with much play of fancy, but with small respect for law. There is, however, a marked distinction between the imaginations of the Western and Eastern races, even when both are left free; the Western, or Gothic, delighting most in the representation of facts, and the Eastern (Arabian, Persian, and Chinese) in the harmony of colours and forms. …

Now the noblest art is an exact unison of the abstract value, with the imitative power, of forms and colours. It is the noblest composition, used to express the noblest facts. But the human mind cannot in general unite the two perfections: it either pursues the fact to the neglect of the composition, or pursues the composition to the neglect of the fact.

The Ducal Palace—Bird's Eye View.

And it is intended by the Deity that it *should* do this: the best art is not always wanted. Facts are often wanted without art, as in a geological diagram; and art often without facts, as in a Turkey carpet. And most men have been made capable of giving either one or the other, but not both; only one or two, the very highest, can give both. …

We have now, I believe, obtained a sufficiently accurate knowledge both of the spirit and form of Gothic architecture; but it may, perhaps, be useful to the general reader, if, in conclusion, I set down a few plain and practical rules for determining, in every instance, whether a given building be good Gothic or not, and, if not Gothic, whether its architecture is of a kind which will probably reward the pains of careful examination.

First, look if the roof rises in a steep gable, high above the walls. If it does not do this, there is something wrong: the building is not quite pure Gothic, or has been altered.

Secondly, look if the principal windows and doors have pointed arches with gables over them. If not pointed arches, the building is not Gothic; if they have not any gables over them, it is either not pure, or not first-rate.

If, however, it has the steep roof, the pointed arch, and gable all united, it is nearly certain to be a Gothic building of a very fine time.…

… See if it looks as if it had been built by strong men; if it has the sort of roughness, and largeness, and nonchalance, mixed in places with the exquisite tenderness which seems always to be the sign-manual of the broad vision, and massy[1] power of men, who can see *past* the work they are doing, and betray here and there something like disdain for it.…

Secondly, observe if it be irregular, its different parts fitting themselves to different purposes, no one caring what becomes of them, so that they do their work. If one part always answers accurately to another part, it is sure to be a bad building; and the greater and more conspicuous the irregularities, the greater the chances are that it is a good one. For instance, in the Ducal Palace,[2] of which a rough woodcut [appears here], the general idea is sternly symmetrical; but two windows are lower than the rest of the six; and if the reader will count the arches of the small arcade as far as to the great balcony, he will find it is not in the centre, but set to the right-hand side by the whole width of one of those arches. We may be pretty sure that the building is a good one; none but a master of his craft would have ventured to do this.

—1853

[1] *massy* Heavy.

[2] *Ducal Palace* Gothic palace in Venice.

Matthew Arnold
1822 – 1888

Nicknamed "the Emperor" by his friends and family, Matthew Arnold was an ardent and, in the view of some Victorians, arrogant critic of modernity. Arnold embodied both the idealist expectations and the apocalyptic anxieties of the approaching *fin-de-siécle* in his poetry and prose. In the face of an increasingly materialistic mass culture, dominated by what he considered the vacuity of "the average man" or "Philistine" of the democratized middle classes, Arnold sought to revive culture in the image of liberal humanism. Only an education in the ostensibly timeless and universal works of masters like Marcus Aurelius, Tolstoy, Homer, and Wordsworth, Arnold believed, could cure the *malaise* of modern life.

"For the creation of a masterwork of literature, two powers must concur," Arnold wrote in 1865, "The power of the man and the power of the moment, and the man is not enough without the moment." Arnold believed that modern industrial life and the materialism it had made possible were radically indisposed towards artistic genius and indeed had created a climate of psychological and moral enervation that poetry was powerless to heal. The *Zeitgeist* (one of his terms for the powerful work of modern popular culture) was profoundly "unpoetical," and was best anatomized through prose. His own career shows symptoms of the fragmentation he analyzed. Arnold incisively broke with the often melancholic poetry of his early years in order to pursue prose criticism, for him the best possible literary work, he believed, in an era that he saw as spiritually bankrupt. Modern society was in no condition to produce great poets; the best that modern life could muster, according to Arnold, were powerful critics—*if* they stayed away from the politics of the passing moment.

The River Thames ran past the village of Laleham where Matthew Arnold was born in 1822. Arnold was the eldest son of Mary Penrose Arnold and Dr. Thomas Arnold. His father, a clergyman and headmaster of Rugby School, was celebrated for reforming the school's curriculum to foreground Christian values, classical languages, and competitive games. Ironically, Arnold, who in later life would come to resemble his father by valuing above all else great humanist texts and a classical education, was lazy, laconic, and flippant as a student. Upon meeting the young dilettante, Charlotte Brontë wrote that "his manner displeases, from its seeming foppery." Yet, in spite of a flamboyant indifference to academia and a studied attempt to dissociate himself from all that his father represented, he amazed family and friends by winning a scholarship to Oxford's Balliol College in 1840, the prodigious Newdigate Prize for poetry in 1843, and a Fellowship at Oriel College in 1845.

Wordsworth, a friend of the family, was one of the most tangible influences on Arnold's poetry. When Wordsworth died, Arnold wondered sadly, "Who will teach us how to feel?" He frequently fled from classes to wander the countryside around the Lake District or to hike in the Alps, landscapes memorialized by Wordsworth and Coleridge. Many critics claim that Arnold was most accomplished as a poet of nature. The "simple joy the country yields," rendered in poems like "Thyrsis," reveals a surprising affinity with the quiet style of Thomas Gray; his "Resignation" speaks to Wordsworth's "Tintern Abbey." Arnold's personal manner, reminiscent of his idols Lord Byron and Goethe, did not cancel out a heartfelt relation to nature, whose unadorned expression modeled the "high seriousness" he admired in Sophocles and Aeschylus.

In 1847, Arnold obtained employment in London as a private secretary to the liberal politician Lord Lansdowne, beginning a period during which he produced most of his poetry. The 1849 publication of *The Strayed Reveller, and Other Poems*, by "A," was followed by *Empedocles on Etna, and Other Poems* (1852). The controversial preface to *Poems* (1853) provoked heated debate. Here Arnold focused on the ponderous force of the "unpoetical" nineteenth century writ large over his earlier work and damned the "dialogue of the mind with itself" that his *Empedocles on Etna* exhibited. Great poetry, Arnold claimed, must be distinguished from verse produced by a restless intellect fragmented by attempts to address the problems of contemporary life. Poetry should create works of beauty and unity that rise above the historical moment to "inspirit and rejoice" readers.

Letters to his best friend and fellow poet Arthur Hugh Clough, who did address the intellectual issues of the current moment, provide valuable insight into the demanding standards Arnold set for poetry. "I am glad you like the *Gypsy Scholar*," he wrote, "—but what does it *do* for you? Homer *animates*—Shakespeare *animates*—in its poor way I think *Sohrab and Rustum animates*—the *Gypsy Scholar* at best awakens a pleasing melancholy." Considered an often biting critic of the work of his contemporaries, including Clough, Arnold's harshest criticisms were first addressed to his own work. His poem "Dover Beach," probably written in 1851, but published in 1867, is considered one of English literature's profound expressions of modernity's disaffection with itself. Yet perceiving that his own poetry seemed passively ensnared in the "continual state of mental distress" that he took to task in the preface to *Poems*, he largely ceased writing poetry from the mid-1850s onward. After *New Poems* (1867), Arnold would refashion himself as a prose writer. According to Lionel Trilling, Arnold "perceived in himself the poetic power, but knew that his genius was not of the greatest, that the poetic force was not irresistible in him," not enough, at any rate, to act as a transformative agent in an age of disillusionment.

Arnold married Frances Lucy Wightman in 1851, and to support his family he accepted a position as a public school inspector. Initially thinking the job would suffice "for the next three or four years," Arnold continued to be employed in the public service for three and a half decades, writing only in his spare time. He believed that his inspections of schools in Britain and across Europe gave him first-hand experience to support his conviction that educating the public in a classical humanist tradition was key to "civilizing the next generation of the lower classes."

In 1857, Arnold was elected Professor of Poetry at Oxford University, where he delivered public lectures for the following ten years. Though a proponent of an exacting standard of classical scholarship, Arnold was the first to lecture in English rather than Latin, altering an elitist institutional practice that acted as a barrier to the kind of education that, in his opinion, the nineteenth century urgently needed. Arnold turned many of his lectures into essays and books, including *On Translating Homer* (1861) and *Friendship's Garland* (1871).

Though by his own standards of greatness Arnold could not transform society as a poet, as a critic he was determined to reform it. In his famous essay "The Function of Criticism at the Present Time," published in *Essays in Criticism* (1865), Arnold helped raise the value of criticism from its status as a "baneful and injurious employment" to a creative activity in its own right. Deftly juxtaposing snatches from tabloids alongside texts of high culture, Arnold's critical methodology foreshadowed the kind of work pursued in cultural studies today. While few have unanimously agreed with Arnold's pronouncements on literature and society, his critical work has had a profound impact on the work of the twentieth-century critics that followed him, such as T.S. Eliot, Virginia Woolf, F.R. Leavis, Lionel Trilling, and Raymond Williams.

In *Culture and Anarchy* (1869), arguably his most important work of social criticism, Arnold proposed that antagonistic factions of British society could learn to overcome their differences through an education in "disinterested" and universal human values. The differences allowed expression in democratic societies would disintegrate into anarchic disorder, thought Arnold, unless tethered to the "higher" ideals of the humanist tradition. His witty veneer and Apollonian appeal to transcendent virtues of "sweetness and light" sometimes enamored, and sometimes exasperated, a public whose prominent figures he often singled out by name for critical interrogation. Leslie Stephen, Virginia Woolf's father, remarked drily, "I often wished … that I too had a little sweetness and light that I might be able to say such nasty things of my enemies."

During the 1870s, Arnold published a series of attacks on orthodox religion: *St. Paul and Protestantism* (1870), *Literature and Dogma* (1873), and *God and the Bible* (1875). Even in a period that witnessed the challenges to traditional religious belief posed by Darwin's theories, the work of geologists, and the "higher criticism" of the Bible that came from Germany and elsewhere, Arnold's religious critiques scandalized many Victorians. He recommended that Victorians exchange their faith in a religion founded on the assumption of the truth of the Bible for faith in a transcendent, secular humanism. When he returned to literary criticism in "The Study of Poetry" (1880), he claimed, as Thomas Carlyle had before him in the 1830s, that "most of what now passes for religion and philosophy will be replaced by poetry.".

Arnold embarked on a lecture tour of the United States in 1883. Tired and burdened by debts, Arnold saw the trip as a money-making venture that would also allow him to visit a daughter who had married an American. He was loved in Washington but received with mixed success in other cities. He compiled his lectures in *Discourses in America* (1885), which contains his discussion of Emerson as well as the essay "Literature and Science." Here Arnold responds to Thomas Huxley's claim in "Science and Culture" (1881) that "for the purpose of attaining real culture, an exclusively scientific education is at least as effectual as an exclusively literary education." Especially in America, Arnold argued, where the democratic impulse to glorify "the average man" was particularly enthusiastic, education must safeguard the guiding ideals of the Western tradition, "the best that is known and thought."

Arnold died suddenly of a heart attack in 1888, leaving behind him a remarkable body of cultural criticism and a few poems familiar to all readers of English poetry. His statement about Oxford and modernity in *Culture and Anarchy* may well be taken as fitting epitaph: "We in Oxford … have not failed to seize one truth,—the truth that beauty and sweetness are essential characters of a complete human perfection.… We have not won our political battles, we have not carried our main points, we have not stopped our adversaries' advance, we have not marched victoriously with the modern world;

but we have told silently upon the mind of the century, we have prepared currents of feeling which sap our adversaries' position when it seems gained, we have kept up our communications with the future."

⌘⌘⌘

The Buried Life

Light flows our war of mocking words, and yet,
Behold, with tears mine eyes are wet!
I feel a nameless sadness o'er me roll.
Yes, yes, we know that we can jest,
We know, we know that we can smile!
But there's a something in this breast,
To which thy light words bring no rest,
And thy gay smiles no anodyne.° *remedy*
Give me thy hand, and hush awhile,
And turn those limpid eyes on mine,
And let me read there, love! thy inmost soul.

Alas! is even love too weak
To unlock the heart, and let it speak?
Are even lovers powerless to reveal
To one another what indeed they feel?
I knew the mass of men concealed
Their thoughts, for fear that if revealed
They would by other men be met
With blank indifference, or with blame reproved;
I knew they lived and moved
Tricked in disguises, alien to the rest
Of men, and alien to themselves—and yet
The same heart beats in every human breast!

But we, my love!—doth a like spell benumb
Our hearts, our voices?—must we too be dumb?

Ah! well for us, if even we,
Even for a moment, can get free
Our heart, and have our lips unchained;
For that which seals them hath been deep-ordained!
Fate, which foresaw
How frivolous a baby man would be—
By what distractions he would be possessed,
How he would pour himself in every strife,
And well-nigh change his own identity—
That it might keep from his capricious play
His genuine self, and force him to obey
Even in his own despite his being's law,
Bade through the deep recesses of our breast
The unregarded river of our life
Pursue with indiscernible flow its way;
And that we should not see
The buried stream, and seem to be
Eddying at large in blind uncertainty,
Though driving on with it eternally.

But often, in the world's most crowded streets,
But often, in the din of strife,
There rises an unspeakable desire
After the knowledge of our buried life;
A thirst to spend our fire and restless force
In tracking out our true, original course;
A longing to inquire
Into the mystery of this heart which beats
So wild, so deep in us—to know
Whence our lives come and where they go.
And many a man in his own breast then delves,
But deep enough, alas! none ever mines.
And we have been on many thousand lines,
And we have shown, on each, spirit and power;
But hardly have we, for one little hour,
Been on our own line, have we been ourselves—
Hardly had skill to utter one of all
The nameless feelings that course through our breast,
But they course on for ever unexpressed.
And long we try in vain to speak and act
Our hidden self, and what we say and do
Is eloquent, is well—but 'tis not true!
And then we will no more be racked
With inward striving, and demand

Of all the thousand nothings of the hour
Their stupefying power;
Ah yes, and they benumb us at our call!
Yet still, from time to time, vague and forlorn,
From the soul's subterranean depth upborne
As from an infinitely distant land,
Come airs, and floating echoes, and convey
A melancholy into all our day.

Only—but this is rare—
When a beloved hand is laid in ours,
When, jaded with the rush and glare
Of the interminable hours,
Our eyes can in another's eyes read clear,
When our world-deafened ear
Is by the tones of a loved voice caressed—
A bolt is shot back somewhere in our breast,
And a lost pulse of feeling stirs again.
The eye sinks inward, and the heart lies plain,
And what we mean, we say, and what we would, we know.
A man becomes aware of his life's flow,
And hears its winding murmur; and he sees
The meadows where it glides, the sun, the breeze.

And there arrives a lull in the hot race
Wherein he doth for ever chase
That flying and elusive shadow, rest.
An air of coolness plays upon his face,
And an unwonted calm pervades his breast.
And then he thinks he knows
The hills where his life rose,
And the sea where it goes.
—1852

The Scholar-Gipsy[1]

Go, for they call you, shepherd, from the hill;
Go, shepherd, and untie the wattled cotes![2]
No longer leave thy wistful flock unfed,
Nor let thy bawling fellows rack their throats,
Nor the cropped herbage shoot another head.
But when the fields are still,
And the tired men and dogs all gone to rest,
And only the white sheep are sometimes seen
Cross and recross the strips of moon-blanched green,
Come, shepherd, and again begin the quest!

Here, where the reaper was at work of late—
In this high field's dark corner, where he leaves
His coat, his basket, and his earthen cruse,° *jug*
And in the sun all morning binds the sheaves,
Then here, at noon, comes back his stores to use—
Here will I sit and wait,
While to my ear from uplands far away
The bleating of the folded° flocks is borne, *enclosed*

[1] *The Scholar-Gipsy* Arnold said this poem was inspired by the following passage in Joseph Glanville's *Vanity of Dogmatizing* (1661):

> There was very lately a lad in the University of Oxford, who was by his poverty forced to leave his studies there; and at last to join himself to a company of vagabond gypsies. Among these extravagant people, by the insinuating subtilty of his carriage, he quickly got so much of their love and esteem as that they discovered to him their mystery. After he had been a pretty while exercised in the trade, there chanced to ride by a couple of scholars, who had formerly been of his acquaintance. They quickly spied out their old friend among the gypsies; and he gave them an account of the necessity which drove him to that kind of life, and told them that the people he went with were not such imposters as they were taken for, but that they had a traditional kind of learning among them, and could do wonders by the power of imagination, their fancy binding that of others; that he himself had learned much of their art, and when he had compassed the whole secret, he intended, he said, to leave their company, and give the world an account of what he had learned.

Arnold imagines this student still roaming the area surrounding Oxford, where Arnold spent "the freest and most delightful part, perhaps, of my life."

[2] *wattled cotes* Sheepfolds made of woven sticks.

With distant cries of reapers in the corn—
All the live murmur of a summer's day.

Screened is this nook o'er the high, half-reaped field,
And here till sun-down, shepherd! will I be.
Through the thick corn the scarlet poppies peep,
And round green roots and yellowing stalks I see
Pale pink convolvulus[1] in tendrils creep;
And air-swept lindens yield
Their scent, and rustle down their perfumed showers
Of bloom on the bent grass where I am laid,
And bower me from the August sun with shade;
And the eye travels down to Oxford's towers.

And near me on the grass lies Glanvil's book—
Come, let me read the oft-read tale again!
The story of the Oxford scholar poor,
Of pregnant[2] parts and quick inventive brain,
Who, tired of knocking at preferment's door,
One summer-morn forsook
His friends, and went to learn the gipsy-lore,
And roamed the world with that wild brotherhood,
And came, as most men deemed, to little good,
But came to Oxford and his friends no more.

But once, years after, in the country-lanes,
Two scholars, whom at college erst he knew,
Met him, and of his way of life enquired;
Whereat he answered, that the gipsy-crew,
His mates, had arts to rule as they desired
The workings of men's brains,
And they can bind them to what thoughts they will.
"And I," he said, "the secret of their art,
When fully learned, will to the world impart;
But it needs heaven-sent moments for this skill."

This said, he left them, and returned no more.
But rumours hung about the country-side,
That the lost Scholar long was seen to stray,
Seen by rare glimpses, pensive and tongue-tied,
In hat of antique shape, and cloak of grey,
The same the gypsies wore.
Shepherds had met him on the Hurst[3] in spring;
At some lone alehouse in the Berkshire moors,
On the warm ingle-bench,[4] the smock-frocked boors° *rustics*
Had found him seated at their entering,

But, 'mid their drink and clatter, he would fly.
And I myself seem half to know thy looks,
And put the shepherds, wanderer! on thy trace;
And boys who in lone wheatfields scare the rooks
I ask if thou hast passed their quiet place;
Or in my boat I lie
Moored to the cool bank in the summer-heats,
'Mid wide grass meadows which the sunshine fills,
And watch the warm, green-muffled Cumner hills,
And wonder if thou haunt'st their shy retreats.

For most, I know, thou lov'st retired ground!
Thee at the ferry Oxford riders blithe,
Returning home on summer-nights, have met
Crossing the stripling Thames at Bab-lock-hithe,
Trailing in the cool stream thy fingers wet,
As the punt's[5] rope chops round;
And leaning backward in a pensive dream,
And fostering in thy lap a heap of flowers
Plucked in shy fields and distant Wychwood bowers,
And thine eyes resting on the moonlit stream.

---

[1] *convolvulus* Morning-glory.

[2] *pregnant* Full of ideas.

[3] *the Hurst* Hill outside Oxford. All the places mentioned in the stanzas following are located in the area surrounding Oxford.

[4] *ingle-bench* Fireside bench.

[5] *punt* Small, shallow boat propelled with a long pole pushed against the river bottom.

And then they land, and thou art seen no more!
Maidens, who from the distant hamlets come
To dance around the Fyfield elm in May,
Oft through the darkening fields have seen thee roam,
Or cross a stile into the public way.
Oft thou hast given them store
Of flowers—the frail-leafed, white anemone,
Dark bluebells drenched with dews of summer eves,
And purple orchises with spotted leaves—
But none hath words she can report of thee.

And, above Godstow Bridge, when hay-time's here
In June, and many a scythe in sunshine flames,
Men who through those wide fields of breezy grass
Where black-winged swallows haunt the glittering Thames,
To bathe in the abandoned lasher pass,[1]
Have often passed thee near
Sitting upon the river bank o'ergrown;
Marked thine outlandish garb, thy figure spare,
Thy dark vague eyes, and soft abstracted air—
But, when they came from bathing, thou wast gone!

At some lone homestead in the Cumner hills,
Where at her open door the housewife darns,
Thou hast been seen, or hanging on a gate
To watch the threshers in the mossy barns.
Children, who early range these slopes and late
For cresses from the rills,
Have known thee eyeing, all an April-day,
The springing pastures and the feeding kine;° *cows*
And marked thee, when the stars come out and shine,
Through the long dewy grass move slow away.

In autumn, on the skirts of Bagley Wood—
Where most the gypsies by the turf-edged way
Pitch their smoked tents, and every bush you see
With scarlet patches tagged and shreds of grey,[2]
Above the forest-ground called Thessaly—
The blackbird, picking food,
Sees thee, nor stops his meal, nor fears at all;
So often has he known thee past him stray,
Rapt, twirling in thy hand a withered spray,
And waiting for the spark from heaven to fall.

And once, in winter, on the causeway chill
Where home through flooded fields foot-travellers go,
Have I not passed thee on the wooden bridge,
Wrapt in thy cloak and battling with the snow,
Thy face toward Hinksey and its wintry ridge?
And thou hast climbed the hill,
And gained the white brow of the Cumner range;
Turned once to watch, while thick the snowflakes fall,
The line of festal light in Christ-Church hall[3]—
Then sought thy straw in some sequestered grange.

But what—I dream! Two hundred years are flown
Since first thy story ran through Oxford halls,
And the grave Glanvil did the tale inscribe
That thou wert wandered from the studious walls
To learn strange arts, and join a gipsy-tribe;
And thou from earth art gone
Long since, and in some quiet churchyard laid—
Some country-nook, where o'er thy unknown grave
Tall grasses and white flowering nettles wave,
Under a dark, red-fruited yew-tree's shade.

—No, no, thou hast not felt the lapse of hours!
For what wears out the life of mortal men?
'Tis that from change to change their being rolls;

[1] *lasher pass* Place where water collects after spilling over a dam.

[2] *With scarlet … grey* Reference to the clothes of the gypsies, which they hang on the bushes to dry.

[3] *Christ-Church hall* Dining hall of Christ Church, an Oxford College.

'Tis that repeated shocks, again, again,
Exhaust the energy of strongest souls
And numb the elastic powers.
Till having used our nerves with bliss and teen,° *vexation*
And tired upon a thousand schemes our wit,
To the just-pausing Genius[1] we remit
Our worn-out life, and are—what we have been.

Thou hast not lived, why should'st thou perish, so?
Thou hadst *one* aim, *one* business, *one* desire;
Else wert thou long since numbered with the dead!
Else hadst thou spent, like other men, thy fire!
The generations of thy peers are fled,
And we ourselves shall go;
But thou possessest an immortal lot,
And we imagine thee exempt from age
And living as thou liv'st on Glanvil's page,
Because thou hadst—what we, alas! have not.

For early didst thou leave the world, with powers
Fresh, undiverted to the world without,
Firm to their mark, not spent on other things;
Free from the sick fatigue, the languid doubt,
Which much to have tried, in much been baffled, brings.
O life unlike to ours!
Who fluctuate idly without term or scope,
Of whom each strives, nor knows for what he strives,
And each half lives a hundred different lives;
Who wait like thee, but not, like thee, in hope.

Thou waitest for the spark from heaven! and we,
Light half-believers of our casual creeds,
Who never deeply felt, nor clearly willed,
Whose insight never has borne fruit in deeds,
Whose vague resolves never have been fulfilled;
For whom each year we see
Breeds new beginnings, disappointments new;
Who hesitate and falter life away,
And lose tomorrow the ground won today—
Ah! do not we, wanderer! await it too?

Yes, we await it!—but it still delays,
And then we suffer! and amongst us one,
Who most has suffered,[2] takes dejectedly
His seat upon the intellectual throne;
And all his store of sad experience he
Lays bare of wretched days;
Tells us his misery's birth and growth and signs,
And how the dying spark of hope was fed,
And how the breast was soothed, and how the head,
And all his hourly varied anodynes.

This for our wisest! and we others pine,
And wish the long unhappy dream would end,
And waive all claim to bliss, and try to bear;
With close-lipped patience for our only friend,
Sad patience, too near neighbour to despair—
But none has hope like thine!
Thou through the fields and through the woods dost stray,
Roaming the country-side, a truant boy,
Nursing thy project in unclouded joy,
And every doubt long blown by time away.

O born in days when wits were fresh and clear,
And life ran gaily as the sparkling Thames;
Before this strange disease of modern life,
With its sick hurry, its divided aims,
Its heads o'ertaxed, its palsied hearts, was rife—
Fly hence, our contact fear!
Still fly, plunge deeper in the bowering wood!
Averse, as Dido did with gesture stern

[1] *Genius* Attendant spirit that accompanies a soul from birth to death and shapes his or her character.

[2] *one … suffered* Reference probably either to Tennyson—whose *In Memoriam* appeared in 1850, the year he succeeded Wordsworth as Poet Laureate—or to German philosopher Johann Wolfgang von Goethe (1749–1832).

From her false friend's approach in Hades turn,[1]
Wave us away, and keep thy solitude!

Still nursing the unconquerable hope,
Still clutching the inviolable shade,
With a free, onward impulse brushing through,
By night, the silvered branches of the glade—
Far on the forest-skirts, where none pursue.
On some mild pastoral slope
Emerge, and resting on the moonlit pales
Freshen thy flowers as in former years
With dew, or listen with enchanted ears,
From the dark dingles,[2] to the nightingales!

But fly our paths, our feverish contact fly!
For strong the infection of our mental strife,
Which, though it gives no bliss, yet spoils for rest;
And we should win thee from thy own fair life,
Like us distracted, and like us unblest.
Soon, soon thy cheer would die,
Thy hopes grow timorous, and unfixed thy powers,
And thy clear aims be cross and shifting made;
And then thy glad perennial youth would fade,
Fade, and grow old at last, and die like ours.

Then fly our greetings, fly our speech and smiles!
—As some grave Tyrian[3] trader, from the sea,
Descried at sunrise an emerging prow
Lifting the cool-haired creepers stealthily,
The fringes of a southward-facing brow
Among the Aegean isles;
And saw the merry Grecian coaster come,
Freighted with amber grapes, and Chian wine,
Green, bursting figs, and tunnies° *tuna fish*
steeped in brine—
And knew the intruders on his ancient home,

The young light-hearted masters of the waves—
And snatched his rudder, and shook out more sail;
And day and night held on indignantly
O'er the blue Midland waters with the gale,
Betwixt the Syrtes[4] and soft Sicily,
To where the Atlantic raves
Outside the western straits; and unbent sails
There, where down cloudy cliffs, through sheets of foam,
Shy traffickers, the dark Iberians[5] come;
And on the beach undid his corded bales.
—1853

Stanzas from The Grande Chartreuse[6]

Through Alpine meadows soft-suffused
With rain, where thick the crocus blows,
Past the dark forges long disused,
The mule-track from Saint Laurent goes.
The bridge is crossed, and slow we ride,
Through forest, up the mountain-side.

The autumnal evening darkens round,
The wind is up, and drives the rain;
While, hark! far down, with strangled sound
Doth the Dead Guier's[7] stream complain,

[1] *as Dido … turn* In Virgil's *Aeneid*, Dido, Queen of Carthage, commits suicide when her lover, Aeneas, deserts her. When he encounters her in Hades, she turns away from him.

[2] *dingles* Wooded dales.

[3] *Tyrian* From Tyre, ancient capital of Phoenicia.

[4] *Syrtes* Two treacherous gulfs off the coast of northern Africa.

[5] *dark Iberians* Inhabitants of Spain or Portugal. The story of these "shy traffickers" comes from fifth-century BCE Greek historian Herodotus's *History*, in which he explains that the Carthaginians would sail through the Strait of Gibraltar to trade with the West Africans. In a unique trading process, these Carthaginians would leave their goods on the beach, withdrawing to their ships. The Africans would come out of their hiding places and leave gold beside the goods they wished to purchase. After they had retreated, the Carthaginians would return and decide if this was adequate payment. The process would be repeated until the two sides reached an agreement.

[6] *Grande Chartreuse* Carthusian monastery in a nearly inaccessible valley in the French Alps, established by Saint Bruno in 1804. Arnold visited the monastery on his honeymoon in 1851. The Carthusians are known for their austerity, and devote their time to fasting, solitary contemplation, and prayer.

[7] *Dead Guier* Guiers Mort, a river that flows down past the monastery and into the Guiers Vif (French: Living Guiers).

Where that wet smoke, among the woods,
Over his boiling cauldron broods.

Swift rush the spectral vapours white
Past limestone scars with ragged pines,
Showing—then blotting from our sight!—
Halt—through the cloud-drift something shines!
High in the valley, wet and drear,
The huts of Courrerie appear.

Strike leftward! cries our guide; and higher
Mounts up the stony forest-way.
At last the encircling trees retire;
Look! through the showery twilight grey
What pointed roofs are these advance?
A palace of the Kings of France?

Approach, for what we seek is here!
Alight, and sparely sup, and wait
For rest in this outbuilding near;
Then cross the sward[1] and reach that gate.
Knock; pass the wicket! Thou art come
To the Carthusians' world-famed home.

The silent courts, where night and day
Into their stone-carved basins cold
The splashing icy fountains play—
The humid corridors behold!
Where, ghostlike in the deepening night,
Cowled forms brush by in gleaming white.

The chapel, where no organ's peal
Invests the stern and naked prayer—
With penitential cries they kneel
And wrestle; rising then, with bare
And white uplifted faces stand,
Passing the Host from hand to hand;

Each takes, and then his visage wan
Is buried in his cowl once more.
The cells!—the suffering Son of Man
Upon the wall—the knee-worn floor—
And where they sleep, that wooden bed,
Which shall their coffin be, when dead![2]

The library, where tract and tome
Not to feed priestly pride are there,
To hymn the conquering march of Rome,
Nor yet to amuse, as ours are!
They paint of souls the inner strife,
Their drops of blood, their death in life.

The garden, overgrown—yet mild,
See, fragrant herbs[3] are flowering there!
Strong children of the Alpine wild
Whose culture is the brethren's care;
Of human tasks their only one,
And cheerful works beneath the sun.

Those halls, too, destined to contain
Each its own pilgrim-host of old,
From England, Germany, or Spain—
All are before me! I behold
The House, the Brotherhood austere!
—And what am I, that I am here?

For rigorous teachers seized my youth,
And purged its faith, and trimmed its fire,
Showed me the high, white star of Truth,
There bade me gaze, and there aspire.
Even now their whispers pierce the gloom:
What dost thou in this living tomb?

Forgive me, masters of the mind!
At whose behest I long ago
So much unlearnt, so much resigned—
I come not here to be your foe!
I seek these anchorites, not in ruth,° *remorse*
To curse and to deny your truth;

[1] *sward* Stretch of grass.

[2] *that wooden … dead* Carthusians are buried on wooden planks. They are sometimes (incorrectly) thought to sleep in their coffins.

[3] *fragrant herbs* From which the Carthusians make the liqueur Chartreuse, the sales of which provide their primary source of income.

Not as their friend, or child, I speak!
But as, on some far northern strand,
Thinking of his own Gods, a Greek
In pity and mournful awe might stand
Before some fallen Runic[1] stone—
For both were faiths, and both are gone.

Wandering between two worlds, one dead,
The other powerless to be born,
With nowhere yet to rest my head,
Like these, on earth I wait forlorn.
Their faith, my tears, the world deride—
I come to shed them at their side.

Oh, hide me in your gloom profound,
Ye solemn seats of holy pain!
Take me, cowled forms, and fence me round,
Till I possess my soul again;
Till free my thoughts before me roll,
Not chafed by hourly false control!

For the world cries your faith is now
But a dead time's exploded dream;
My melancholy, sciolists[2] say,
Is a passed mode, an outworn theme—
As if the world had ever had
A faith, or sciolists been sad!

Ah, if it *be* passed, take away,
At least, the restlessness, the pain;
Be man henceforth no more a prey
To these out-dated stings again!
The nobleness of grief is gone—
Ah, leave us not the fret alone!

But—if you cannot give us ease—
Last of the race of them who grieve
Here leave us to die out with these
Last of the people who believe!

Silent, while years engrave the brow;
Silent—the best are silent now.

Achilles[3] ponders in his tent,
The kings of modern thought are dumb;
Silent they are, though not content,
And wait to see the future come.
They have the grief men had of yore,
But they contend and cry no more.

Our fathers[4] watered with their tears
This sea of time whereon we sail,
Their voices were in all men's ears
Who passed within their puissant° hail. *powerful*
Still the same ocean round us raves,
But we stand mute, and watch the waves.

For what availed it, all the noise
And outcry of the former men?
Say, have their sons achieved more joys,
Say, is life lighter now than then?
The sufferers died, they left their pain—
The pangs which tortured them remain.

What helps it now, that Byron bore,
With haughty scorn which mocked the smart,
Through Europe to the Aetolian shore[5]
The pageant of his bleeding heart?
That thousands counted every groan,
And Europe made his woe her own?

What boots it, Shelley! that the breeze
Carried thy lovely wail away,
Musical through Italian trees
Which fringe thy soft blue Spezzian bay?[6]

[1] *Runic* Carved with runes (early Norse letters).

[2] *sciolists* Pretenders to knowledge.

[3] *Achilles* Greek warrior who, during the Trojan War, stayed in his tent, refusing to participate, until the death of his best friend, Patrocles, in battle, moved him to action.

[4] *Our fathers* I.e., the previous generation of writers.

[5] *Aetolian shore* In Greece, where the English poet George Gordon, Lord Byron, died.

[6] *Spezzian bay* Where English poet Percy Bysshe Shelley drowned, in Italy.

Inheritors of thy distress
Have restless hearts one throb the less?

Or are we easier, to have read,
O Obermann![1] the sad, stern page,
Which tells us how thou hidd'st thy head
From the fierce tempest of thine age
In the lone brakes of Fontainebleau,
Or chalets near the Alpine snow?

Ye slumber in your silent grave!
The world, which for an idle day
Grace to your mood of sadness gave,
Long since hath flung her weeds[2] away.
The eternal trifler breaks your spell;
But we—we learnt your lore too well!

Years hence, perhaps, may dawn an age,
More fortunate, alas! than we,
Which without hardness will be sage,
And gay without frivolity.
Sons of the world, oh, speed those years;
But, while we wait, allow our tears!

Allow them! We admire with awe
The exulting thunder of your race;
You give the universe your law,
You triumph over time and space!
Your pride of life, your tireless powers,
We laud them, but they are not ours.

We are like children reared in shade
Beneath some old-world abbey wall,
Forgotten in a forest-glade,
And secret from the eyes of all.
Deep, deep the greenwood round them waves,
Their abbey, and its close° of graves! *enclosure*

But, where the road runs near the stream,
Oft through the trees they catch a glance
Of passing troops in the sun's beam—
Pennon,[3] and plume, and flashing lance!
Forth to the world those soldiers fare,
To life, to cities, and to war!

And through the wood, another way,
Faint bugle-notes from far are borne,
Where hunters gather, staghounds bay,
Round some fair forest-lodge at morn.
Gay dames are there, in sylvan green;
Laughter and cries—those notes between!

The banners flashing through the trees
Make their blood dance and chain their eyes;
That bugle-music on the breeze
Arrests them with a charmed surprise.
Banner by turns and bugle woo:
Ye shy recluses, follow too!

O children, what do ye reply?
"Action and pleasure, will ye roam
Through these secluded dells to cry
And call us?—but too late ye come!
Too late for us your call ye blow,
Whose bent was taken long ago.

"Long since we pace this shadowed nave;
We watch those yellow tapers shine,
Emblems of hope over the grave,
In the high altar's depth divine;
The organ carries to our ear
Its accents of another sphere.

"Fenced early in this cloistral round
Of reverie, of shade, of prayer,
How should we grow in other ground?
How should we flower in foreign air?
—Pass, banners, pass, and bugles, cease;
And leave our desert to its peace!"
—1855

[1] *Obermann* Protagonist of the 1804 novel of that name by Étienne Pivert de Senancour (1770–1846).

[2] *weeds* Mourning garments.

[3] *Pennon* Narrow triangular flag, usually borne on the head of a lance.

Dover Beach

The sea is calm tonight.
  The tide is full, the moon lies fair
Upon the straits—on the French coast the light
Gleams and is gone; the cliffs of England stand,
Glimmering and vast, out in the tranquil bay.
Come to the window, sweet is the night-air!
Only, from the long line of spray
Where the sea meets the moon-blanched land,
Listen! you hear the grating roar
Of pebbles which the waves draw back, and fling,
At their return, up the high strand,° *shore*
Begin, and cease, and then again begin,
With tremulous cadence slow, and bring
The eternal note of sadness in.

Sophocles long ago
Heard it on the Aegean, and it brought
Into his mind the turbid ebb and flow
Of human misery;[1] we
Find also in the sound a thought,
Hearing it by this distant northern sea.

The Sea of Faith
Was once, too, at the full, and round earth's shore
Lay like the folds of a bright girdle furled.
But now I only hear
Its melancholy, long, withdrawing roar.
Retreating, to the breath
Of the night-wind, down the vast edges drear
And naked shingles[2] of the world.

Ah, love, let us be true
To one another! for the world, which seems
To lie before us like a land of dreams,
So various, so beautiful, so new,
Hath really neither joy, nor love, nor light,
Nor certitude, nor peace, nor help for pain;
And we are here as on a darkling plain
Swept with confused alarms of struggle and flight,
Where ignorant armies clash by night.[3]
—1867

East London[4]

'Twas August, and the fierce sun overhead
  Smote on the squalid streets of Bethnal Green,
And the pale weaver, through his windows seen
In Spitalfields, looked thrice dispirited.

I met a preacher there I knew, and said:
"Ill and o'erworked, how fare you in this scene?"
"Bravely!" said he; "for I of late have been
Much cheered with thoughts of Christ, *the living bread.*"

O human soul! as long as thou canst so
Set up a mark of everlasting light,
Above the howling senses' ebb and flow,

To cheer thee, and to right thee if thou roam—
Not with lost toil thou labourest through the night!
Thou mak'st the heaven thou hop'st indeed thy
  home.
—1867

West London[5]

Crouched on the pavement, close by Belgrave
  Square,

[1] *Sophocles … misery* Cf. Sophocles's *Antigone* 583–91: "Blest are those whose days have not tasted of evil. For when a house has once been shaken by the gods, no form of ruin is lacking, but it spreads over the bulk of the race, just as, when the surge is driven over the darkness of the deep by the fierce breath of Thracian sea-winds, it rolls up the black sand from the depths, and the wind-beaten headlands that front the blows of the storm give out a mournful roar."

[2] *shingles* Water-worn pebbles.

[3] *as on … night* Reference to Thucydides's *History of the Peloponnesian War*, in which the invading Athenians became confused as night fell on the battle at Epipolae. Combatants could not tell friend from foe in the moonlight.

[4] *East London* Working-class area of the city. Bethnal Green and Spitalfields are districts in East London.

[5] *West London* Wealthy end of the city. Belgrave Square was (and is) a particularly affluent district.

A tramp I saw, ill, moody, and tongue-tied.
A babe was in her arms, and at her side
A girl; their clothes were rags, their feet were bare.

Some labouring men, whose work lay somewhere
there,
Passed opposite; she touched her girl, who hied° *hastened*
Across, and begged, and came back satisfied.
The rich she had let pass with frozen stare.

Thought I: "Above her state this spirit towers;
She will not ask of aliens, but of friends,
Of sharers in a common human fate.

"She turns from that cold succour, which attends
The unknown little from the unknowing great,
And points us to a better time than ours."
—1867

from *The Function of Criticism at the Present Time*

Many objections have been made to a proposition which, in some remarks of mine on translating Homer,[1] I ventured to put forth; a proposition about criticism, and its importance at the present day. I said: "Of the literature of France and Germany, as of the intellect of Europe in general, the main effort, for now many years, has been a critical effort; the endeavour, in all branches of knowledge, theology, philosophy, history, art, science, to see the object as in itself it really is." I added, that owing to the operation in English literature of certain causes, "almost the last thing for which one would come to English literature is just that very thing which now Europe most desires—criticism"; and that the power and value of English literature was thereby impaired. More than one rejoinder declared that the importance I here assigned to criticism was excessive, and asserted the inherent superiority of the creative effort of the human spirit over its critical effort. And the other day, having been led by a Mr. Shairp's excellent notice of Wordsworth[2] to turn again to his biography, I found, in the words of this great man, whom I, for one, must always listen to with the profoundest respect, a sentence passed on the critic's business, which seems to justify every possible disparagement of it. Wordsworth says in one of his letters:

> The writers in these publications [the reviews], while they prosecute their inglorious employment, can not be supposed to be in a state of mind very favourable for being affected by the finer influences of a thing so pure as genuine poetry.

And a trustworthy reporter of his conversation quotes a more elaborate judgement to the same effect:

> Wordsworth holds the critical power very low, infinitely lower than the inventive; and he said today that if the quantity of time consumed in writing critiques on the works of others were given to original composition, of whatever kind it might be, it would be much better employed; it would make a man find out sooner his own level, and it would do infinitely less mischief. A false or malicious criticism may do much injury to the minds of others, a stupid invention, either in prose or verse, is quite harmless.

It is almost too much to expect of poor human nature, that a man capable of producing some effect in one line of literature, should, for the greater good of society, voluntarily doom himself to impotence and obscurity in another. Still less is this to be expected from

---

[1] *in some … Homer* In Arnold's *On Translating Homer* (1861).

[2] [Arnold's note] I cannot help thinking that a practice, common in England during the last century, and still followed in France, of printing a notice of this kind—a notice by competent critics—to serve as an introduction to an eminent author's works, might be revived among us with advantage. To introduce all succeeding editions of Wordsworth, Mr. Shairp's notice might, it seems it me, excellently serve; it is written from the point of view of an admirer, nay, or a disciple, and that is right; but then the disciple must also be, as in this case he is, a critic, a man of letters, not, as too often happens, some relation or friend with no qualification for his task except affection for his author. [Arnold refers to J.C. Shairp's essay *Wordsworth: The Man and the Poet* (1864).]

men addicted to the composition of the "false or malicious criticism" of which Wordsworth speaks. However, everybody would admit that a false or malicious criticism had better never been written. Everybody, too, would be willing to admit, as a general proposition, that the critical faculty is lower than the inventive. But is it true that criticism is really, in itself, a baneful and injurious employment; is it true that all time given to writing critiques on the works of others would be much better employed if it were given to original composition of whatever kind this may be? Is it true Johnson had better have gone on producing more *Irenes* instead of writing his *Lives of the Poets*;[1] nay, is it certain that Wordsworth himself was better employed in making his Ecclesiastical Sonnets than when he made his celebrated Preface,[2] so full of criticism, and criticism of the works of others? Wordsworth was himself a great critic, and it is to be sincerely regretted that he has not left us more criticism; Goethe[3] was one of the greatest of critics, and we may sincerely congratulate ourselves that he has left us so much criticism. Without wasting time over the exaggeration which Wordsworth's judgement on criticism clearly contains, or over an attempt to trace the causes—not difficult, I think, to be traced—which may have led Wordsworth to this exaggeration, a critic may with advantage seize an occasion for trying his own conscience, and for asking himself of what real service at any given moment the practice of criticism either is or may be made to his own mind and spirit, and to the minds and spirits of others.

The critical power is of lower rank than the creative. True; but in assenting to this proposition, one or two things are to be kept in mind. It is undeniable that the exercise of a creative power, that a free creative activity, is the highest function of man; it is proved to be so by man's finding in it his true happiness. But it is undeniable, also, that men may have the sense of exercising this free creative activity in other ways than in producing great words of literature or art; if it were not so, all but a very few men would be shut out from the true happiness of all men. They may have it in well-doing, they may have it in learning, they may have it even in criticising. This is one thing to be kept in mind. Another is, that the exercise of the creative power in the production of great works of literature or art, however high this exercise of it may rank, is not at all epochs and under all conditions possible; and that therefore labour may be vainly spent in attempting it, which might with more fruit be used in preparing for it, in rendering it possible. This creative power works with elements, with materials; what if it has not those materials, those elements, ready for its use? In that case it must surely wait till they are ready. Now in literature—I will limit myself to literature, for it is about literature that the question arises—the elements with which the creative power works are ideas; the best ideas, on every matter which literature touches, current at the time. At any rate we may lay it down as certain that in modern literature no manifestation of the creative power not working with these can be very important or fruitful. And I say current at the time, not merely accessible at the time; for creative literary genius does not principally show itself in discovering new ideas; that is rather the business of the philosopher. The grand work of literary genius is a work of synthesis and exposition, not of analysis and discovery; its gift lies in the faculty of being happily inspired by a certain intellectual and spiritual atmosphere, by a certain order of ideas, when it finds itself in them; of dealing divinely with these ideas, presenting them in the most effective and attractive combinations—making beautiful works with them, in short. But it must have the atmosphere, it must find itself amidst the order of ideas, in order to work freely; and these it is not so easy to command. This is why great creative epochs in literature are so rare, this is why there is so much that is unsatisfactory in the productions of many men of real genius; because, for the creation of a masterwork of literature two powers must concur, the

---

[1] *Johnson ... Poets* In the nineteenth century Samuel Johnson was perhaps most celebrated for his biographical and critical work *Lives of the English Poets* (1779–81), while his play *Irene* (1736) has never been highly regarded.

[2] *Preface* To Wordsworth and Coleridge's *Lyrical Ballads* (1800). His *Ecclesiastical Sonnets* is not his best-known work.

[3] *Goethe* German poet and dramatist Johann Wolfgang von Goethe (1749–1832).

power of the man and the power of the moment, and the man is not enough without the moment; the creative power has, for its happy exercise, appointed elements, and those elements are not in its own control.

Nay, they are more within the control of the critical power. It is the business of the critical power, as I said in the words already quoted, "in all branches of knowledge, theology, philosophy, history, art, science, to see the object as in itself it really is." Thus it tends, at last, to make an intellectual situation of which the creative power can profitably avail itself. It tends to establish an order of ideas, if not absolutely true, yet true by comparison with that which it displaces; to make the best ideas prevail. Presently these new ideas reach society, the touch of truth is the touch of life, and there is a stir and growth everywhere; out of this stir and growth come the creative epochs of literature.

Or, to narrow our range, and quit these considerations of the general march of genius and of society—considerations which are apt to become too abstract and impalpable—every one can see that a poet, for instance, ought to know life and the world before dealing with them in poetry; and life and the world being in modern times very complex things, the creation of a modern poet, to be worth much, implies a great critical effort behind it; else it must be a comparatively poor, barren, and short-lived affair. This is why Byron's poetry had so little endurance in it, and Goethe's so much; both Byron and Goethe had a great productive power, but Goethe's was nourished by a great critical effort providing the true materials for it, and Byron's was not; Goethe knew life and the world, the poet's necessary subjects, much more comprehensively and thoroughly than Byron. He knew a great deal more of them, and he knew them much more as they really are.

It has long seemed to me that the burst of creative activity in our literature, through the first quarter of this century, had about it in fact something premature; and that from this cause its productions are doomed, most of them, in spite of the sanguine hopes which accompanied and do still accompany them, to prove hardly more lasting than the productions of far less splendid epochs. And this prematureness comes from its having proceeded without having its proper data, without sufficient materials to work with. In other words, the English poetry of the first quarter of this century, with plenty of energy, plenty of creative force, did not know enough. This makes Byron so empty of matter, Shelley so incoherent, Wordsworth even, profound as he is, yet so wanting in completeness and variety. Wordsworth cared little for books, and disparaged Goethe. I admire Wordsworth, as he is, so much that I cannot wish him different; and it is vain, no doubt, to imagine such a man different from what he is, to suppose that he could have been different. But surely the one thing wanting to make Wordsworth an even greater poet than he is—his thought richer, and his influence of wider application—was that he should have read more books, among them, no doubt, those of that Goethe whom he disparaged without reading him.

But to speak of books and reading may easily lead to a misunderstanding here. It was not really books and reading that lacked to our poetry at this epoch; Shelley had plenty of reading, Coleridge had immense reading. Pindar[1] and Sophocles—as we all say so glibly, and often with so little discernment of the real import of what we are saying—had not many books; Shakespeare was no deep reader. True; but in the Greece of Pindar and Sophocles, in the England of Shakespeare, the poet lived in a current of ideas in the highest degree animating and nourishing to the creative power; society was, in the fullest measure, permeated by fresh thought, intelligent and alive. And this state of things is the true basis for the creative power's exercise, in this it finds its data, its materials, truly ready for its hand; all the books and reading in the world are only valuable as they are helps to this. Even when this does not actually exist, books and reading may enable a man to construct a kind of semblance of it in his own mind, a world of knowledge and intelligence in which he may live and work. This is by no means an equivalent to the artist for the nationally diffused life and thought of the epochs of Sophocles or Shakespeare; but, besides that it may be a means of preparation for such epochs, it does really constitute, if

[1] *Pindar* Greek lyric poet of the fifth century BCE.

many share in it, a quickening and sustaining atmosphere of great value. Such an atmosphere the many-sided learning and the long and widely combined critical effort of Germany formed for Goethe, when he lived and worked. There was no national glow of life and thought there, as in the Athens of Pericles[1] or the England of Elizabeth. That was the poet's weakness. But there was a sort of equivalent for it in the complete culture and unfettered thinking of a large body of Germans. That was his strength. In the England of the first quarter of this century there was neither a national glow of life and thought, such as we had in the age of Elizabeth, nor yet a culture and a force of learning and criticism such as were to be found in Germany. Therefore the creative power of poetry wanted, for success in the highest sense, materials and a basis; a thorough interpretation of the world was necessarily denied to it.

… The Englishman has been called a political animal, and he values what is political and practical so much that ideas easily become objects of dislike in his eyes, and thinkers "miscreants," because ideas and thinkers have rashly meddled with politics and practice. This would be all very well if the dislike and neglect confined themselves to ideas transported out of their own sphere, and meddling rashly with practice; but they are inevitably extended to ideas as such, and to the whole life of intelligence; practice is everything, a free play of the mind is nothing. The notion of the free play of the mind upon all subjects being a pleasure in itself, being an object of desire, being an essential provider of elements without which a nation's spirit, whatever compensations it may have for them, must, in the long run, die of inanition, hardly enters into an Englishman's thoughts. It is noticeable that the word *curiosity*, which in other languages is used in a good sense, to mean, as a high and fine quality of man's nature, just this disinterested love of a free play of the mind on all subjects, for its own sake—it is noticeable, I say, that this word has in our language no sense of the kind, no sense but a rather bad and disparaging one. But criticism, real criticism, is essentially the exercise of this very quality; it obeys an instinct prompting it to try to know the best that is known and thought in the world, irrespectively of practice, politics, and everything of the kind; and to value knowledge and thought as they approach this best, without the intrusion of any other considerations whatever. This is an instinct for which there is, I think, little original sympathy in the practical English nature, and what there was of it has undergone a long benumbing period of blight and suppression in the epoch of concentration which followed the French Revolution.

But epochs of concentration cannot well endure for ever; epochs of expansion, in the due course of things, follow them. Such an epoch of expansion seems to be opening in this country. In the first place all danger of a hostile forcible pressure of foreign ideas upon our practice has long disappeared; like the traveller in the fable, therefore, we begin to wear our cloak a little more loosely.[2] Then, with a long peace, the ideas of Europe steal gradually and amicably in, and mingle, though in infinitesimally small quantities at a time, with our own notions. Then, too, in spite of all that is said about the absorbing and brutalising influence of our passionate material progress, it seems to me indisputable that this progress is likely, though not certain, to lead in the end to an apparition of intellectual life; and that man, after he has made himself perfectly comfortable and has now to determine what to do with himself next, may begin to remember that he has a mind, and that the mind may be made the source of great pleasure. I grant it is mainly the privilege of faith, at present, to discern this end to our railways, our business, and our fortune-making; but we shall see if, here as elsewhere, faith is not in the end the true prophet. Our ease, our travelling, and our unbounded liberty to hold just as hard and securely as we please to the practice to which our notions have given birth, all tend to beget an inclination to deal a

[1] *Athens of Pericles* Pericles was a prominent Athenian political leader of the early fifth century BCE and was responsible for the construction of the Parthenon.

[2] *like the … loosely* In one of Aesop's fables, the wind and the sun compete to see who is more powerful, betting on which of them can cause a traveler to take his cloak off first. The wind attempts to use force, but the fierce gusts only cause the traveler to clutch his cloak more tightly. When the sun shines on him, however, the traveler is persuaded to take off his cloak.

little more freely with these notions themselves, to canvass them a little, to penetrate a little into their real nature. Flutterings of curiosity, in the foreign sense of the word, appear amongst us, and it is in these that criticism must look to find its account. Criticism first; a time of true creative activity, perhaps—which, as I have said, must inevitably be preceded amongst us by a time of criticism—hereafter, when criticism has done its work.

It is of the last importance that English criticism should clearly discern what rule for its course, in order to avail itself of the field now opening to it, and to produce fruit for the future, it ought to take. The rule may be summed up in one word—*disinterestedness*.[1] And how is criticism to show disinterestedness? By keeping aloof from what is called "the practical view of things"; by resolutely following the law of its own nature, which is to be a free play of the mind on all subjects which it touches. By steadily refusing to lend itself to any of those ulterior, political, practical considerations about ideas, which plenty of people will be sure to attach to them, which perhaps ought often to be attached to them, which in this country at any rate are certain to be attached to them quite sufficiently, but which criticism has really nothing to do with. Its business is, as I have said, simply to know the best that is known and thought in the world, and by in its turn making this known, to create a current of true and fresh ideas. Its business is to do this with inflexible honesty, with due ability; but its business is to do no more, and to leave alone all questions of practical consequences and applications, questions which will never fail to have due prominence given to them. Else criticism, besides being really false to its own nature, merely continues in the old rut which it has hitherto followed in this country, and will certainly miss the chance now given to it. For what is at present the bane of criticism in this country? It is that practical considerations cling to it and stifle it. It subserves interests not its own. Our organs of criticism are organs of men and parties having practical ends to serve, and with them those practical ends are the first thing and the play of the mind the second; so much play of mind as is compatible with the prosecution of those practical ends is all that is wanted. An organ like the *Revue des Deux Mondes*,[2] having for its main function to understand and utter the best that is known and thought in the world, existing, it may be said, as just an organ for a free play of the mind, we have not. But we have the *Edinburgh Review*, existing as an organ of the old Whigs, and for as much play of the mind as may suit its being that; we have the *Quarterly Review*, existing as an organ of the Tories, and for as much play of mind as may suit its being that; we have the *British Quarterly Review*, existing as an organ of the political Dissenters, and for as much play of mind as may suit its being that; we have *The Times*, existing as an organ of the common, satisfied, well-to-do Englishman, and for as much play of mind as may suit its being that. And so on through all the various fractions, political and religious, of our society; every fraction has, as such, its organ of criticism, but the notion of combining all fractions in the common pleasure of a free disinterested play of mind meets with no favour. Directly this play of mind wants to have more scope, and to forget the pressure of practical considerations a little, it is checked, it is made to feel the chain. We saw this the other day in the extinction, so much to be regretted, of the *Home and Foreign Review*.[3] Perhaps in no organ of criticism in this country was there so much knowledge, so much play of mind; but these could not save it. The *Dublin Review* subordinates play of mind to the practical business of English and Irish Catholicism, and lives. It must needs be that men should act in sects and parties, that each of these sects and parties should have its organ, and should make this organ subserve the interests of its action; but it would be well, too, that there should be a criticism, not the minister of these interests, not their enemy, but absolutely and entirely independent of them. No other criticism will ever attain any real authority or make any real way towards its end—the creating a current of true and fresh ideas.

[1] *disinterestedness* I.e., objectivity.

[2] *Revue ... Mondes* International magazine founded in Paris in 1829.

[3] *Home ... Review* Liberal, predominantly Catholic periodical (1862–64).

It is because criticism has so little kept in the pure intellectual sphere, has so little detached itself from practice, has been so directly polemical and controversial, that it has so ill accomplished, in this country, its best spiritual work; which is to keep man from a self-satisfaction which is retarding and vulgarizing, to lead him towards perfection, by making his mind dwell upon what is excellent in itself, and the absolute beauty and fitness of things. A polemical practical criticism makes men blind even to the ideal imperfection of their practice, makes them willingly assert its ideal perfection, in order the better to secure it against attack; and clearly this is narrowing and baneful for them. If they were reassured on the practical side, speculative considerations of ideal perfection they might be brought to entertain, and their spiritual horizon would thus gradually widen. Sir Charles Adderley[1] says to the Warwickshire farmers—

> Talk of the improvement of breed! Why, the race we ourselves represent, the men and women, the old Anglo-Saxon race, are the best breed in the whole world…The absence of a too enervating climate, too unclouded skies, and a too luxurious nature, has produced so vigorous a race of people, and has rendered us so superior to all the world.

Mr. Roebuck says to the Sheffield cutlers—

> I look around me and ask what is the state of England? Is not property safe? Is not every man able to say what he likes? Can you not walk from one end of England to the other in perfect security? I ask you whether, the world over or in past history, there is anything like it? Nothing. I pray that our unrivaled happiness may last.

Now obviously there is a peril for poor human nature in words and thoughts of such exuberant self-satisfaction, until we find ourselves safe in the streets of the Celestial City.

> *Das wenige verschwindet leicht dem Blicke*
> *Der vorwärts sieht, wie viel noch übrig bleibt*[2]—

says Goethe; "the little that is done seems nothing when we look forward and see how much we have yet to do." Clearly this is a better line of reflection for weak humanity, so long as it remains on this earthly field of labour and trial.

But neither Sir Charles Adderley nor Mr. Roebuck is by nature inaccessible to considerations of this sort. They only lose sight of them owing to the controversial life we all lead, and the practical from which all speculation takes with us. They have in view opponents whose aim is not ideal, but practical; and in their zeal to uphold their own practice against these innovators, they go so far as even to attribute to this practice an ideal perfection. Somebody has been wanting to introduce a six-pound franchise, or to abolish church-rates,[3] or to collect agricultural statistics by force, or to diminish local self-government. How natural, in reply to such proposals, very likely improper or ill-timed, to go a little beyond the mark and to say stoutly, "such a race of people as we stand, so superior to all the world! The Old Anglo-Saxon race, the best breed in the whole world! I pray that our unrivaled happiness may last! I ask you whether, the world over or in past history, there is anything like it?" And so long as criticism answers this dithyramb by insisting that the old Anglo-Saxon race would be still more superior to all others if it had no church-rates, or that our unrivalled happiness would last yet longer with a six-pound franchise, so long will the strain, "The best breed in the whole world!" swell louder and louder, everything ideal and refining will be lost out of sight, and both the assailed and their critics will remain in a sphere, to say the truth, perfectly unvital, a sphere in which spiritual progression is impossible. But let criticism leave church-rates and the franchise alone, and in the most candid spirit, without a single lurking thought of practical innovation, confront with our

[1] *Sir Charles Adderley* Conservative member of Parliament and landowner (1814–1905).

[2] *Das wenige … bleibt* Goethe's *Iphigenie auf Tauris* 1.291–92.

[3] *six-pound franchise* Proposal to extend voting rights to anyone whose property was worth six pounds or more annual rent—a radical idea at the time; *church-rates* Taxes paid to support the Church of England.

dithyramb this paragraph on which I stumbled in a newspaper immediately after reading Mr. Roebuck:

> A shocking child murder has just been committed at Nottingham. A girl named Wragg left the workhouse there on Saturday morning with her young illegitimate child. The child was soon afterwards found dead on Mapperly Hills, having been strangled. Wragg is in custody.

Nothing but that; but, in juxtaposition with the absolute eulogies of Sir Charles Adderley and Mr. Roebuck, how eloquent, how suggestive are those few lines! "Our old Anglo-Saxon breed, the best in the whole world!"—how much that is harsh and ill-favoured there is in this best! *Wragg*! If we are to talk of ideal perfection of "the best in the whole world," has any one reflected what a touch of grossness in our race, what an original shortcoming in the more delicate spiritual perceptions, is shown by the natural growth amongst us of such hideous names—Higginbottom, Stiggins, Bugg! In Ionia and Attica they were luckier in this respect than "the best race in the world"; by the Ilissus[1] there was no Wragg, poor thing! And "our unrivaled happiness"— what an element of grimness, bareness, and hideousness mixes with it and blurs it; the workhouse, the dismal Mapperly Hills[2]—how dismal those who have seen them will remember—the gloom, the smoke, the cold, the strangled illegitimate child! "I ask you whether, the world over or in past history, there is anything like it?" Perhaps not, one is inclined to answer; but at any rate, in that case, the world is very much to be pitied. And the final touch—short, bleak, and inhuman: *Wragg is in custody*. The sex lost in the confusion of our unrivalled happiness; or (shall I say?) the superfluous Christian name lopped off by the straightforward vigour of our old Anglo-Saxon breed! There is profit for the spirit in such contrasts as this; criticism serves the cause of perfection by establishing them. By eluding sterile conflict, by refusing to remain in the sphere where alone narrow and relative conceptions have any worth and validity, criticism may diminish its momentary importance, but only in this way has it a chance of gaining admittance for those wider and more perfect conceptions to which all its duty is really owed. Mr. Roebuck will have a poor opinion of an adversary who replies to his defiant songs of triumph only by murmuring under his breath, *Wragg is in custody*; but in no other way will these songs of triumph be induced gradually to moderate themselves, to get rid of what in them is excessive and offensive, and to fall into a softer and truer key.

It will be said that it is a very subtle and indirect action which I am thus prescribing for criticism, and that, by embracing in this manner the Indian virtue of detachment and abandoning the sphere of practical life, it condemns itself to a slow and obscure work. Slow and obscure it may be, but it is the only proper work of criticism. The mass of mankind will never have any ardent zeal for seeing things as they are; very inadequate ideas will always satisfy them. On these inadequate ideas reposes, and must repose, the general practice of the world. That is as much as saying that whoever sets himself to see things as they are will find himself one of a very small circle; but it is only by this small circle resolutely doing its own work that adequate ideas will ever get current at all. The rush and roar of practical life will always have a dizzying and attracting effect upon the most collected spectator, and tend to draw him into its vortex; most of all will this be the case where that life is so powerful as it is in England. But it is only by remaining collected, and refusing to lend himself to the point of view of the practical man, that the critic can do the practical man any service; and it is only by the greatest sincerity in pursuing his own course, and by at last convincing even the practical man of his sincerity, that he can escape misunderstandings which perpetually threaten him.

For the practical man is not apt for fine distinctions, and yet in these distinctions truth and the highest culture greatly find their account. But it is not easy to lead a practical man—unless you reassure him as to your practical intentions, you have no chance of leading him—to see a thing which he has always been used to look at from one side only, which he greatly values, and

---

[1] *Ilissus* River in Attica.

[2] *Mapperly Hills* Located near the coal-mining, industrial area of Nottingham.

which, looked at from that side, quite deserves, perhaps, all the prizing and admiring which he bestows upon it—that this thing, looked at from another side, may appear much less beneficent and beautiful, and yet retain all its claims to our practical allegiance. Where shall we find language innocent enough, how shall we make the spotless purity of our intentions evident enough, to enable us to say to the political Englishman that the British Constitution itself, which, seen from the practical side, looks such a magnificent organ of progress and virtue, seen from the speculative side—with its compromises, its love of facts, its horror of theory, its studied avoidance of clear thoughts—that, seen from this side, our august Constitution sometimes looks—forgive me, shade of Lord Somers![1]—a colossal machine for the manufacture of Philistines?[2] How is Cobbett[3] to say this and not be misunderstood, blackened as he is with the smoke of a lifelong conflict in the field of political practice? How is Mr. Carlyle to say it and not be misunderstood, after his furious raid into this field with his Latter-day Pamphlets?[4] How is Mr. Ruskin, after his pugnacious political economy?[5] I say, the critic must keep out of the region of immediate practice in the political, social, humanitarian sphere, if he wants to make a beginning for that more free speculative treatment of things, which may perhaps one day make its benefits felt even in this sphere, but in a natural and thence irresistible manner. …

If I have insisted so much on the course which criticism must take where politics and religion are concerned, it is because, where these burning matters are in question, it is most likely to go astray. I have wished, above all, to insist on the attitude which criticism should adopt towards things in general; on its right tone and temper of mind. But then comes another question as to the subject-matter which literary criticism should most seek. Here, in general, its course is determined for it by the idea which is the law of its being; the idea of a disinterested endeavour to learn and propagate the best that is known and thought in the world, and thus to establish a current of fresh and true ideas. By the very nature of things, as England is not all the world, much of the best that is known and thought in the world cannot be of English growth, must be foreign; by the nature of things, again, it is just this that we are least likely to know, while English thought is streaming in upon us from all sides, and takes excellent care that we shall not be ignorant of its existence. The English critic of literature, therefore, must dwell much on foreign thought, and with particular heed on any part of it, which, while significant and fruitful in itself, is for any reason specially likely to escape him. Again, judging is often spoken of as the critic's one business, and so in some sense it is; but the judgement which almost insensibly forms itself in a fair and clear mind, along with fresh knowledge, is the valuable one; and thus knowledge, and ever fresh knowledge, must be the critic's great concern for himself. And it is by communicating fresh knowledge, and letting his own judgement pass along with it—but insensibly, and in the second place, not the first, as a sort of companion and clue, not as an abstract lawgiver—that the critic will generally do most good to his readers. Sometimes, no doubt, for the sake of establishing an author's place in literature, and his relation to a central standard (and if this is not done, how are we to get at our best in the world?) criticism may have to deal with a subject-matter so familiar that fresh knowledge is out of the question, and then it must be all judgement; an enunciation and detailed application of principles. Here the great safeguard is never to let oneself become abstract, always to retain an intimate and lively consciousness of the truth of what one is saying, and, the moment this fails us, to be sure that something is wrong. Still, under all circumstances, this mere judgement and application of

[1] *Lord Somers* Political leader who presided over the creation of the Declaration of Rights (1689).

[2] *Philistines* Members of the Biblical tribe that fought against the Israelites. Here Arnold uses the term humorously to denote the unenlightened middle classes; "the enemy."

[3] *Cobbett* William Cobbett (1762–1835), farmer and radical political writer.

[4] *Latter-day Pamphlets* Satirical pamphlets, published in 1850, in which Thomas Carlyle expressed vehement anti-democratic views.

[5] *Mr. Ruskin … economy* In his *Unto the Last* (1862), John Ruskin moved away from art criticism and attacked laissez-faire economics.

principles is, in itself, not the most satisfactory work to the critic; like mathematics, it is tautological, and cannot well give us, like fresh learning, the sense of creative activity.

But stop, someone will say; all this talk is of no practical use to us whatever; this criticism of yours is not what we have in our minds when we speak of criticism; when we speak of critics and criticism, we mean critics and criticism of the current English literature of the day; when you offer to tell criticism of its function, it is to this criticism that we expect you to address yourself. I am sorry for it, for I am afraid I must disappoint these expectations. I am bound by my own definition of criticism: a disinterested endeavour to learn and propagate the best that is known and thought in the world. How much of current English literature comes into this "best that is known and thought in the world"? Not very much, I fear; certainly less, at this moment, than of the current literature of France or Germany. Well, then, am I to alter my definition of criticism, in order to meet the requirements of a number of practising English critics, who, after all, are free in their choice of a business? That would be making criticism lend itself just to one of those alien practical considerations, which, I have said, are so fatal to it. One may say, indeed, to those who have to deal with the mass—so much better disregarded—of current English literature, that they may at all events endeavour, in dealing with this, to try it, so far as they can, by the standard of the best that is known and thought in the world; one may say, that to get anywhere near this standard, every critic should try and possess one great literature, at least, besides his own; and the more unlike his own, the better. But, after all, the criticism I am really concerned with—the criticism which alone can much help us for the future, the criticism which, throughout Europe, is at the present day meant, when so much stress is laid on the importance of criticism and the critical spirit—is a criticism which regards Europe as being, for intellectual and spiritual purposes, one great confederation, bound to a joint action and working to a common result; and whose members have, for their proper outfit, a knowledge of Greek, Roman, and Eastern antiquity, and of one another. Special, local, and temporary advantages being put out of account, that modern nation will in the intellectual and spiritual sphere make most progress, which most thoroughly carries out this programme. And what is that but saying that we too, all of us, as individuals, the more thoroughly we carry it out, shall make the more progress?

There is so much inviting us!—what are we to take? what will nourish us in growth towards perfection? That is the question which, with the immense field of life and of literature lying before him, the critic has to answer; for himself first, and afterwards for others. In this idea of the critic's business the essays brought together in the following pages have had their origin; in this idea, widely different as are their subjects, they have, perhaps, their unity.

I conclude with what I said at the beginning: to have the sense of creative activity is the great happiness and the great proof of being alive, and it is not denied to criticism to have it; but then criticism must be sincere, simple, flexible, ardent, ever widening its knowledge. Then it may have, in no contemptible measure, a joyful sense of creative activity; a sense which a man of insight and conscience will prefer to what he might derive from a poor, starved, fragmentary, inadequate creation. And at some epochs no other creation is possible.

Still, in full measure, the sense of creative activity belongs only to genuine creation; in literature we must never forget that. But what true man of letters ever can forget it? It is no such common matter for a gifted nature to come into possession of a current of true and living ideas, and to produce amidst the inspiration of them, that we are likely to underrate it. The epochs of Aeschylus and Shakespeare make us feel their pre-eminence. In an epoch like those is, no doubt, the true life of literature; there is the promised land, towards which criticism can only beckon. That promised land it will not be ours to enter, and we shall die in the wilderness: but to have desired to enter it, to have saluted it from afar, is already, perhaps, the best distinction among contemporaries; it will certainly be the best title to esteem with posterity.

—1864

from *Culture and Anarchy*[1]

from CHAPTER 1: SWEETNESS AND LIGHT

The disparagers of culture make its motive curiosity; sometimes, indeed, they make its motive mere exclusiveness and vanity. The culture which is supposed to plume itself on a smattering of Greek and Latin is a culture which is begotten by nothing so intellectual as curiosity; it is valued either out of sheer vanity and ignorance or else as an engine of social and class distinction, separating its holder, like a badge or title, from other people who have not got it. No serious man would call this *culture*, or attach any value to it, as culture, at all. To find the real ground for the very different estimate which serious people will set upon culture, we must find some motive for culture in the terms of which may lie a real ambiguity; and such a motive the word *curiosity* gives us.

I have before now pointed out that we English do not, like the foreigners, use this word in a good sense as well as in a bad sense. With us the word is always used in a somewhat disapproving sense. A liberal and intelligent eagerness about the things of the mind may be meant by a foreigner when he speaks of curiosity, but with us the word always conveys a certain notion of frivolous and unedifying activity. In the *Quarterly Review*, some little time ago, was an estimate of the celebrated French critic, M. Sainte-Beuve,[2] and a very inadequate estimate it in my judgement was. And its inadequacy consisted chiefly in this: that in our English way it left out of sight the double sense really involved in the word *curiosity*, thinking enough was said to stamp M. Sainte-Beuve with blame if it was said that he was impelled in his operations as a critic by curiosity, and omitting either to perceive that M. Sainte-Beuve himself, and many other people with him, would consider that this was praiseworthy and not blameworthy, or to point out why it ought really to be accounted worthy of blame and not of praise. For as there is a curiosity about intellectual matters which is futile, and merely a disease, so there is certainly a curiosity—a desire after the things of the mind simply for their own sakes and for the pleasure of seeing them as they are—which is, in an intelligent being, natural and laudable. Nay, and the very desire to see things as they are implies a balance and regulation of mind which is not often attained without fruitful effort, and which is the very opposite of the blind and diseased impulse of mind which is what we mean to blame when we blame curiosity. Montesquieu[3] says: "The first motive which ought to impel us to study is the desire to augment the excellence of our nature, and to render an intelligent being yet more intelligent." This is the true ground to assign for the genuine scientific passion, however manifested, and for culture, viewed simply as a fruit of this passion; and it is a worthy ground, even though we let the term *curiosity* stand to describe it.

But there is of culture another view, in which not solely the scientific passion, the sheer desire to see things as they are, natural and proper in an intelligent being, appears as the ground of it. There is a view in which all the love of our neighbour, the impulses towards action, help, and beneficence, the desire for removing human error, clearing human confusion, and diminishing human misery, the noble aspiration to leave the world better and happier than we found it—motives eminently such as are called social—come in as part of the grounds of culture, and the main and pre-eminent part. Culture is then properly described not as having its origin in curiosity, but as having its origin in the love of perfection; it is *a study of perfection*. It moves by the

[1] *Culture and Anarchy* This work grew out of Arnold's last Oxford lecture, in 1869, and responds to the political climate surrounding the passage of the Second Reform Bill in 1867. Arnold feared that the individualism, or self-serving attitude, that seemed to fuel much of laissez-faire capitalism would lead to a state of anarchy—a state in which no culture could flourish. "Sweetness and light" is taken from a fable in Jonathan Swift's *The Battle of the Books* (1704). In this fable, the bee (who represents ancient culture) travels far to fill its hive with honey and wax (which is used to make candles). The bee thus provides "the two noblest things, which are sweetness and light," while the spider (representing modern culture) stays at home and forms its own web, producing "nothing at all but flybane and cobweb."

[2] *M. Sainte-Beuve* French critic Charles Augustin Sainte-Beuve (1804–69).

[3] *Montesquieu* French political philosopher (1689–1755).

force, not merely or primarily of the scientific passion for pure knowledge, but also of the moral and social passion for doing good. As, in the first view of it, we took for its worthy motto Montesquieu's words: "To render an intelligent being yet more intelligent!" so, in the second view of it, there is no better motto which it can have than these words of Bishop Wilson:[1] "To make reason and the will of God prevail!"...

Nothing is more common than for people to confound the inward peace and satisfaction which follows the subduing of the obvious faults of our animality with what I may call absolute inward peace and satisfaction—the peace and satisfaction which are reached as we draw near to complete spiritual perfection, and not merely to moral perfection, or rather to relative moral perfection. No people in the world have done more and struggled more to attain this relative moral perfection than our English race has. For no people in the world has the command to *resist the devil, to overcome the wicked one*, in the nearest and most obvious sense of those words, had such a pressing force and reality. And we have had our reward, not only in the great worldly prosperity which our obedience to this command has brought us, but also, and far more, in great inward peace and satisfaction. But to me few things are more pathetic than to see people, on the strength of the inward peace and satisfaction which their rudimentary efforts towards perfection have brought them, employ, concerning their incomplete perfection and the religious organisations within which they have found it, language which properly applies only to complete perfection, and is a far-off echo of the human soul's prophecy of it. Religion itself, I need hardly say, supplies them in abundance with this grand language. And very freely do they use it; yet it is really the severest possible criticism of such an incomplete perfection as alone we have yet reached through our religious organisations.

The impulse of the English race towards moral development and self-conquest has nowhere so powerfully manifested itself as in Puritanism. Nowhere has Puritanism found so adequate an expression as in the religious organisation of the Independents.[2] The modern Independents have a newspaper, the *Nonconformist*, written with great sincerity and ability. The motto, the standard, the profession of faith which this organ of theirs carries aloft, is: "The Dissidence of Dissent and the Protestantism of the Protestant religion." There is sweetness and light, and an ideal of complete harmonious human perfection! One need not go to culture and poetry to find language to judge it. Religion, with its instinct for perfection, supplies language to judge it, language, too, which is in our mouths every day. "Finally, be of one mind, united in feeling," says St. Peter.[3] There is an ideal which judges the Puritan ideal: "The Dissidence of Dissent and the Protestantism of the Protestant religion!" And religious organisations like this are what people believe in, rest in, would give their lives for! Such, I say, is the wonderful virtue of even the beginnings of perfection, of having conquered even the plain faults of our animality, that the religious organisation which has helped us to do it can seem to us something precious, salutary, and to be propagated, even when it wears such a brand of imperfection on its forehead as this. And men have got such a habit of giving to the language of religion a special application, of making it a mere jargon, that for the condemnation which religion itself passes on the shortcomings of their religious organisations they have no ear; they are sure to cheat themselves and to explain this condemnation away. They can only be reached by the criticism which culture, like poetry, speaking a language not to be sophisticated, and resolutely testing these organisations by the ideal of a human perfection complete on all sides, applies to them.

But men of culture and poetry, it will be said, are again and again failing, and failing conspicuously, in the necessary first stage to a harmonious perfection, in the subduing of the great obvious faults of our animality, which it is the glory of these religious organisations to have helped us to subdue. True, they do often so fail. They have often been without the virtues as well as the

[1] *Bishop Wilson* Church of England clergyman (1601–53) whose *Maxims* Arnold admired.

[2] *Independents* Members of a seventeenth-century Puritan sect.

[3] *Finally ... Peter* From 1 Peter 3.8.

faults of the Puritan; it has been one of their dangers that they so felt the Puritan's faults that they too much neglected the practice of his virtues. I will not, however, exculpate them at the Puritan's expense. They have often failed in morality, and morality is indispensable. And they have been punished for their failure, as the Puritan has been rewarded for his performance. They have been punished wherein they erred; but their ideal of beauty, of sweetness and light, and a human nature complete on all its sides, remains the true ideal of perfection still; just as the Puritan's ideal of perfection remains narrow and inadequate, although for what he did well he has been richly rewarded. Notwithstanding the mighty results of the Pilgrim Fathers' voyage, they and their standard of perfection are rightly judged when we figure to ourselves Shakespeare or Virgil—souls in whom sweetness and light, and all that in human nature is most humane, were eminent—accompanying them on their voyage, and think what intolerable company Shakespeare and Virgil would have found them! In the same way let us judge the religious organisations which we see all around us. Do not let us deny the good and the happiness which they have accomplished; but do not let us fail to see clearly that their idea of human perfection is narrow and inadequate, and that the Dissidence of Dissent and the Protestantism of the Protestant religion will never bring humanity to its true goal. As I said with regard to wealth: Let us look at the life of those who live in and for it—so I say with regard to the religious organisations. Look at the life imaged in such a newspaper as the *Nonconformist*—a life of jealousy of the Establishment,[1] disputes, tea-meetings, openings of chapels, sermons; and then think of it as an ideal of a human life completing itself on all sides, and aspiring with all its organs after sweetness, light, and perfection!

Another newspaper, representing, like the *Nonconformist*, one of the religious organisations of this country, was a short time ago giving an account of the crowd at Epsom on the Derby day,[2] and of all the vice and hideousness which was to be seen in that crowd; and then the writer turned suddenly round upon Professor Huxley,[3] and asked him how he proposed to cure all this vice and hideousness without religion. I confess I felt disposed to ask the asker this question: and how do you propose to cure it with such a religion as yours? How is the ideal of a life so unlovely, so unattractive, so incomplete, so narrow, so far removed from a true and satisfying ideal of human perfection, as is the life of your religious organisation as you yourself reflect it, to conquer and transform all this vice and hideousness? Indeed, the strongest plea for the study of perfection as pursued by culture, the clearest proof of the actual inadequacy of the idea of perfection held by the religious organisations—expressing, as I have said, the most widespread effort which the human race has yet made after perfection—is to be found in the state of our life and society with these in possession of it, and having been in possession of it I know not how many hundred years. We are all of us included in some religious organisation or other; we all call ourselves, in the sublime and aspiring language of religion which I have before noticed, children of God. Children of God—it is an immense pretension!—and how are we to justify it? By the works which we do, and the words which we speak. And the work which we collective children of God do, our grand centre of life, our city which we have builded for us to dwell in, is London! London, with its unutterable external hideousness, and with its internal canker of *publice egestas, privatim opulentia*—to use the words which Sallust puts into Cato's[4] mouth about Rome—unequalled in the world! The word, again, which we children of God speak, the voice which most hits our collective thought, the newspaper with the largest circulation in England, nay, with the largest circulation in the whole world, is the *Daily Telegraph*! I say that when our religious organisations—which I admit to express the most considerable effort after perfection that our race has yet made—land

[1] *Establishment* I.e., the established Church, the Church of England.

[2] *Epsom ... day* The Derby Stakes, a thoroughbred horse race, is held every June in Epsom, Surrey.

[3] *Professor Huxley* Thomas Huxley (1825–95), biologist, educator, and vocal supporter of the theory of evolution.

[4] *publice ... opulentia* Latin: public poverty; private opulence; *Sallust* First-century BCE Roman historian; *Cato* Roman political figure Cato the Younger (95–46 BCE).

us in no better result than this, it is high time to examine carefully their idea of perfection, to see whether it does not leave out of account sides and forces of human nature which we might turn to great use; whether it would not be more operative if it were more complete. And I say that English reliance on our religious organisations and on their ideas of human perfection just as they stand, is like our reliance on freedom, on muscular Christianity, on population, on coal, on wealth—mere belief in machinery, and unfruitful; and that it is wholesomely counteracted by culture, bent on seeing things as they are, and on drawing the human race onwards to a more complete, a harmonious perfection.

Culture, however, shows its single-minded love of perfection, its desire simply to make reason and the will of God prevail, its freedom from fanaticism, by its attitude towards all this machinery, even while it insists that it is machinery. Fanatics, seeing the mischief men do themselves by their blind belief in some machinery or other—whether it is wealth and industrialism, or whether it is the cultivation of bodily strength and activity, or whether it is a political organisation—or whether it is a religious organisation—oppose with might and main the tendency to this or that political and religious organisation, or to games and athletic exercises, or to wealth and industrialism, and try violently to stop it. But the flexibility which sweetness and light give, and which is one of the rewards of culture pursued in good faith, enables a man to see that a tendency may be necessary, and even, as a preparation for something in the future, salutary, and yet that the generations or individuals who obey this tendency are sacrificed to it, that they fall short of the hope of perfection by following it; and that its mischiefs are to be criticised, lest it should take too firm a hold and last after it has served its purpose. …

—1868

Dante Gabriel Rossetti

1828 – 1882

"Youth and Death, Destiny and Fortune, Fame, Poetic Fame, Memory, Oblivion"—these, according to Walter Pater, are among the "mysterious powers" at the center of Dante Gabriel Rossetti's work. But "enthroned" among these, Pater wrote, is "the ideal intensity of love." The ethereal yet sensuous aesthetic Rossetti developed to evoke these mysteries in painting as well as poetry exerted a strong influence on poets and artists of the late nineteenth and early twentieth centuries.

Stylized and radiant scenes of knights, maidens, and lovers—soon synonymous with Rossetti's name—found their original inspiration in works of early Italian, Christian, and medieval iconography. The subject of "The Blessed Damozel," one of Rossetti's finest poems, glows with the spiritually luminous effects associated with the religious poetry of Dante (Rossetti's namesake). Yet Rossetti also endowed his damsel with an earthly voluptuousness. Borrowing from Dantesque and Arthurian mythology, Rossetti created fantasies whose "stained glass" quality reflects both the literary outlines of religious allegory and the sensual strokes of an artist enraptured by the female figure. It was an artistic approach that ran the risk of causing offense at a time when soul and body, love and sex, were separate compartments of Victorian life, and Rossetti's work was frequently attacked in the later half of his career for trying to solder spiritual to "fleshly" desires.

Born in 1828 into an erudite family, Rossetti was the second child and eldest son of four children. He was a competitive yet fiercely fond older brother to his sister, the future poet Christina. His mother, Frances Polidori Rossetti, was Anglo-Italian; his father, Gabriele Rossetti, an exiled Italian patriot, was a Professor at King's College, London. The Rossettis' childhood home, with its assortment of orthodox and unorthodox books, was a meeting place where politicized ex-patriots spent many an evening debating the past and future of Italy. From the stream of sketches and literary compositions issuing from the temperamental imaginations of Dante Gabriel and Christina, it was apparent early on that the two Rossettis were extraordinarily gifted. Their parents held high hopes that Dante Gabriel would become a great painter, even though his schooling in painting and his knowledge of European painting were not extensive.

Rossetti was a moody student at the Royal Academy of Arts in 1848 when he co-founded the Pre-Raphaelite Brotherhood with fellow painters William Holman Hunt, John Everett Millais, James Collinson, Frederic George Stephens, Thomas Woolner, and Dante Gabriel's brother, critic William Michael Rossetti. In a letter to his sister Christina, Rossetti spoke of the group as a "Round Table" whose knights shared a mutual love of Keats. They also adored Malory's *Morte Darthur*, the novels of Walter Scott, and the work of Blake, Dante, Tennyson, and Browning. By referencing early Florentine and Sienese schools (dubbed "the Italian Primitives" because they predated the High Renaissance), the Pre-Raphaelites sought to reform what they saw as the florid emptiness of Victorian art and its lack of truth to nature. "Sincerity" as a quality of near-devotional feeling communicated through purity of line and color was more important to the Pre-Raphaelites than mere technical virtuosity. As one critic put it, the Pre-Raphaelites favored "primitive but vital imperfection, as opposed to lifeless perfection." A movement in both literature and painting, Pre-Raphaelitism was identified with a vivid palette, formal patterning, and symbolic details woven into exotic scenes of religious or romantic love whose settings evoked a sumptuous "elsewhere." In Pre-Raphaelite poetry and painting, there was always a "definiteness of sensible imagery," as Pater said of "The Blessed Damozel."

When sixteen-year old Christina published *Verses* in 1847, Rossetti was compelled to try with meter what he was doing with color. "Colour and metre," Rossetti claimed, "are the true parents of nobility in painting and poetry." In 1850, the Pre-Raphaelite Brotherhood published a journal of poems and illustrations entitled *The Germ*, in which Rossetti's "The Blessed Damozel" first appeared. The publication gained Rossetti a small group of admirers that would steadily increase. John Ruskin, who helped turn the tide in his favor by praising the art of the Pre-Raphaelites in *The Times* in 1851, became one of Rossetti's prominent patrons and closest friends. Rossetti cherished intellectual friendships with Robert Browning and William Morris, and socialized with the flamboyant Algernon Swinburne. He obtained stable employment teaching art at the Working Men's College. Stumbling across a book of William Blake's poems and paintings, Rossetti discovered another kindred spirit, albeit one who had died a year before he was born. Having secured his own reputation, Rossetti was able to rescue Blake from near oblivion, rediscovering him for a Victorian audience. In 1861, he also published *The Early Italian Poets*, which introduced, through his translations of the *Vita Nuova* and other poems by Dante and his predecessors and contemporaries, many poets whose work had been unknown in England.

Rossetti was also prone to what one biographer calls "rescue missions" of unknown beauties. Elizabeth Gaskell wrote that Rossetti was "hair-mad," with a penchant for the wavy tresses of women he and his friends called "stunners." On the one hand, Rossetti supported the equality and independence of working-class women like Elizabeth Siddal, whom he eventually married. On the other hand, his rescue of beautiful women from their class obscurity dramatized a sexual imbalance of power that was titillating; like many Victorian men, Rossetti enjoyed the license to "fall in love" with working-class women without seriously compromising his reputation, a license prohibited to women under the double standards of Victorian society.

Siddal, a model for the Pre-Raphaelites and an artist and poet in her own right, committed suicide in 1862, two years after her marriage to Rossetti. Invoking Dante's dead beloved, Beatrice, Rossetti memorialized Siddal in a painting entitled *Beata Beatrix* (c. 1863). Seized with remorse at her funeral, he tucked a manuscript of poems into her coffin. He had them exhumed years later in order to publish his first collection of verse, *Poems* (1870). Though Rossetti afterwards lived with Fanny Cornforth, he fell in love with Jane Burden, the wife of William Morris. Both Fanny and "Janey" came from working-class backgrounds and modeled for Rossetti, becoming sensuously stylized objects of desire in paintings such as *Proserpine* (1874).

Soon after the appearance of Rossetti's *The House of Life*, a sequence of sonnets that appeared in his first volume of poetry, the poet Robert Buchanan denounced its "animalism" in a scalding critique entitled *The Fleshly School of Poetry* (1871). According to Buchanan, Rossetti's "house of life" was suggestive of a brothel and his sonnets bore the stamp of "the same sense of weary, wasting, yet exquisite sensuality." Rossetti counterattacked with "The Stealthy School of Criticism" (1872), and he would make significant additions and revisions to *The House of Life* over the next decade.

Rossetti's mental health had long been unstable, and Buchanan's attack provoked a serious breakdown. Though Yeats's youthful claim that he was "in all things Pre-Raphaelite" was proof of Rossetti's influence on the next generation of poets, Rossetti himself never fully recovered from being "stigmatized as a sensualist," in the words of one critic. He continued to paint and write, however, and in 1881 he published *Ballads and Sonnets*, a collection featuring several long ballads as well as an expanded version of *The House of Life*. Bouts of nervous depression, made worse by the consumption of whiskey and narcotics, led to a decline in Rossetti's health; he died in 1882.

⌘⌘⌘

The Blessed Damozel [1]

The blessed damozel leaned out
From the gold bar of Heaven;
Her eyes were deeper than the depth
Of waters stilled at even;
She had three lilies in her hand,
And the stars in her hair were seven.

Her robe, ungirt from clasp to hem,
No wrought flowers did adorn,
But a white rose of Mary's gift,
For service meetly worn;
Her hair that lay along her back
Was yellow like ripe corn.

Herseemed she scarce had been a day
One of God's choristers;
The wonder was not yet quite gone
From that still look of hers;
Albeit, to them she left, her day
Had counted as ten years.

(To one, it is ten years of years.
… Yet now, and in this place,
Surely she leaned o'er me—her hair
Fell all about my face.…
Nothing: the autumn-fall of leaves.
The whole year sets apace.)

It was the rampart of God's house
That she was standing on;
By God built over the sheer depth
The which is Space begun;
So high, that looking downward thence
She scarce could see the sun.

It lies in Heaven, across the flood
Of ether, as a bridge.
Beneath, the tides of day and night
With flame and darkness ridge
The void, as low as where this earth
Spins like a fretful midge.[2]

Around her, lovers, newly met
'Mid deathless love's acclaims,
Spoke evermore among themselves
Their heart-remembered names;
And the souls mounting up to God
Went by her like thin flames.

And still she bowed herself and stooped
Out of the circling charm;
Until her bosom must have made
The bar she leaned on warm,
And the lilies lay as if asleep
Along her bended arm.

From the fixed place of Heaven she saw
Time like a pulse shake fierce
Through all the worlds. Her gaze still strove
Within the gulf to pierce

[1] *The Blessed Damozel* After the poem's publication, Rossetti told novelist Hall Caine that he had written it as something of a sequel to Edgar Allen Poe's poem "The Raven" (1845): "I saw that Poe had done the utmost it was possible to do with the grief of the lover on earth, and so determined to reverse the conditions, and give utterance to the yearning of the loved one in heaven." A "damozel" is a damsel, a young, unmarried woman.

[2] *midge* Small fly.

Dante Gabriel Rossetti, *The Blessed Damozel*, 1875–78.

Its path; and now she spoke as when
    The stars sang in their spheres.[1]

The sun was gone now; the curled moon
    Was like a little feather
Fluttering far down the gulf; and now
    She spoke through the still weather.
Her voice was like the voice the stars
    Had when they sang together.

(Ah sweet! Even now, in that bird's song,
    Strove not her accents there,

[1] *as when … spheres* See Job 38.7, in which the morning stars sing on creation day. Rossetti probably also refers to the Pythagorean concept of the music of the spheres, inaudible to those on earth.

Fain to be hearkened? When those bells
    Possessed the mid-day air,
Strove not her steps to reach my side
    Down all the echoing stair?)

"I wish that he were come to me,
    For he will come," she said.
"Have I not prayed in Heaven?—on earth,
    Lord, Lord, has he not prayed?
Are not two prayers a perfect strength?
    And shall I feel afraid?

"When round his head the aureole° clings, *halo*
    And he is clothed in white,
I'll take his hand and go with him
    To the deep wells of light;
As unto a stream we will step down,
    And bathe there in God's sight.

"We two will stand beside that shrine,
    Occult,° withheld, untrod, *secret*
Whose lamps are stirred continually
    With prayer sent up to God;
And see our old prayers, granted, melt
    Each like a little cloud.

"We two will lie i'the shadow of
    That living mystic tree[2]
Within whose secret growth the Dove[3]
    Is sometimes felt to be,
While every leaf that His plumes touch
    Saith His Name audibly.

"And I myself will teach to him,
    I myself, lying so,
The songs I sing here; which his voice
    Shall pause in, hushed and slow,
And find some knowledge at each pause,
    Or some new thing to know."

[2] *living mystic tree* Tree of life (See Revelation 22.2).

[3] *Dove* Holy Spirit.

(Alas! We two, we two, thou say'st!
Yea, one wast thou with me
That once of old. But shall God lift
To endless unity
The soul whose likeness with thy soul
Was but its love for thee?)

"We two," she said, "will seek the groves
Where the lady Mary is,
With her five handmaidens, whose names
Are five sweet symphonies,
Cecily, Gertrude, Magdalen,
Margaret and Rosalys.

"Circlewise sit they, with bound locks
And foreheads garlanded;
Into the fine cloth white like flame
Weaving the golden thread,
To fashion the birth-robes for them
Who are just born, being dead.

"He shall fear, haply,° and be dumb: *perchance*
Then will I lay my cheek
To his, and tell about our love,
Not once abashed or weak:
And the dear Mother will approve
My pride, and let me speak.

"Herself shall bring us, hand in hand,
To him round whom all souls
Kneel, the clear-ranged unnumbered heads
Bowed with their aureoles:° *haloes*
And angels meeting us shall sing
To their citherns and citoles.[1]

"There will I ask of Christ the Lord
Thus much for him and me:
Only to live as once on earth
With Love—only to be,

[1] *citherns* Guitar-like instruments strung with wire and played with a quill, popular in the sixteenth and seventeenth centuries; *citoles* Stringed instruments common in the thirteenth to fifteenth centuries.

As then awhile, for ever now
Together, I and he."

She gazed and listened and then said,
Less sad of speech than mild—
"All this is when he comes." She ceased.
The light thrilled towards her, filled
With angels in strong level flight.
Her eyes prayed, and she smiled.

(I saw her smile.) But soon their path
Was vague in distant spheres:
And then she cast her arms along
The golden barriers,
And laid her face between her hands,
And wept. (I heard her tears.)
—1850

The Woodspurge[2]

The wind flapped loose, the wind was still,
Shaken out dead from tree and hill:
I had walked on at the wind's will—
I sat now, for the wind was still.

Between my knees my forehead was—
My lips, drawn in, said not Alas!
My hair was over in the grass,
My naked ears heard the day pass.

My eyes, wide open, had the run
Of some ten weeds to fix upon;
Among those few, out of the sun,
The woodspurge flowered, three cups in one.

From perfect grief there need not be
Wisdom or even memory:
One thing then learnt remains to me—
The woodspurge has a cup of three.
—1870

[2] *Woodspurge* Wildflower with cup-like, yellowish-green flowers that excrete a milky juice.

Jenny

"Vengeance of Jenny's case! Fie on her! Never name her, child"
(Mrs. Quickly.)[1]

Lazy laughing languid Jenny,
Fond of a kiss and fond of a guinea,[2]
Whose head upon my knee to-night
Rests for a while, as if grown light
With all our dances and the sound
To which the wild tunes spun you round:
Fair Jenny mine, the thoughtless queen
Of kisses which the blush between
Could hardly make much daintier;
Whose eyes are as blue skies, whose hair
Is countless gold incomparable;
Fresh flower, scarce touched with signs that tell
Of Love's exuberant hotbed—Nay,
Poor flower left torn since yesterday
Until to-morrow leave you bare;
Poor handful of bright spring-water
Flung in the whirlpool's shrieking face;
Poor shameful Jenny, full of grace
Thus with your head upon my knee—
Whose person or whose purse may be
The lodestar[3] of your reverie?

This room of yours, my Jenny, looks
A change from mine so full of books,
Whose serried[4] ranks hold fast, forsooth,
So many captive hours of youth—
The hours they thieve from day and night
To make one's cherished work come right,
And leave it wrong for all their theft,
Even as to-night my work was left:
Until I vowed that since my brain
And eyes of dancing seemed so fain,
My feet should have some dancing too—
And thus it was I met with you.
Well, I suppose 'twas hard to part,
For here I am. And now, sweetheart,
You seem too tired to get to bed.

It was a careless life I led
When rooms like this were scarce so strange
Not long ago. What breeds the change—
The many aims or the few years?
Because to-night it all appears
Something I do not know again.

The cloud's not danced out of my brain—
The cloud that made it turn and swim
While hour by hour the books grew dim.
Why, Jenny, as I watch you there,
For all your wealth of loosened hair,
Your silk ungirdled and unlaced
And warm sweets open to the waist,
All golden in the lamplight's gleam,
You know not what a book you seem,
Half-read by lightning in a dream!
How should you know, my Jenny? Nay,
And I should be ashamed to say—
Poor beauty, so well worth a kiss!
But while my thought runs on like this
With wasteful whims more than enough,
I wonder what you're thinking of.

If of myself you think at all,
What is the thought?—conjectural
On sorry matters best unsolved?—
Or inly° is each grace revolved *inwardly*
To fit me with a lure?—or (sad
To think!) perhaps you're merely glad
That I'm not drunk or ruffianly
And let you rest upon my knee.

For sometimes, were the truth confessed,
You're thankful for a little rest—
Glad from the crush to rest within,

[1] *Vengeance ... Quickly* From Shakespeare's *The Merry Wives of Windsor* 1.1. The rest of Mistress Quickly's speech reads, "if she be a whore."

[2] *guinea* English gold coin.

[3] *lodestar* Pole star; i.e., guiding star.

[4] *serried* Pressed close together.

From the heart-sickness and the din
Where envy's voice at virtue's pitch
Mocks you because your gown is rich;
And from the pale girl's dumb rebuke,
Whose ill-clad grace and toil-worn look
Proclaim the strength that keeps her weak
And other nights than yours bespeak;
And from the wise unchildish elf,
To schoolmate lesser than himself
Pointing you out, what thing you are—
Yes, from the daily jeer and jar,
From shame and shame's outbraving too,
Is rest not sometimes sweet to you?
But most from the hatefulness of man
Who spares not to end what he began,
Whose acts are ill and his speech ill,
Who, having used you at his will,
Thrusts you aside, as when I dine
I serve the dishes and the wine.

Well, handsome Jenny mine, sit up,
I've filled our glasses, let us sup,
And do not let me think of you,
Lest shame of yours suffice for two.
What, still so tired? Well, well then, keep
Your head there, so you do not sleep;
But that the weariness may pass
And leave you merry, take this glass.
Ah! lazy lily hand, more blessed
If ne'er in rings it had been dressed
Nor ever by a glove concealed!

Behold the lilies of the field,
They toil not neither do they spin;[1]
(So doth the ancient text begin—
Not of such rest as one of these
Can share.) Another rest and ease
Along each summer-sated path
From its new lord the garden hath,
Than that whose spring in blessings ran
Which praised the bounteous husbandman,
Ere yet, in days of hankering breath,
The lilies sickened unto death.

What, Jenny, are your lilies dead?
Aye, and the snow-white leaves are spread
Like winter on the garden-bed.
But you had roses left in May—
They were not gone too. Jenny, nay,
But must your roses die, and those
Their purfled[2] buds that should unclose?
Even so; the leaves are curled apart,
Still red as from the broken heart,
And here's the naked stem of thorns.

Nay, nay, mere words. Here nothing warns
As yet of winter. Sickness here
Or want alone could waken fear—
Nothing but passion wrings a tear.
Except when there may rise unsought
Haply° at times a passing thought *perchance*
Of the old days which seem to be
Much older than any history
That is written in any book;
When she would lie in fields and look
Along the ground through the blown grass,
And wonder where the city was,
Far out of sight, whose broil° and bale° *tumult / woe*
They told her then for a child's tale.

Jenny, you know the city now.
A child can tell the tale there, how
Some things which are not yet enrolled
In market-lists are bought and sold
Even till the early Sunday light,
When Saturday night is market-night
Everywhere, be it dry or wet,
And market-night in the Haymarket.
Our learned London children know,
Poor Jenny, all your pride and woe;
Have seen your lifted silken skirt
Advertise dainties through the dirt;

[1] *Behold … spin* Reference to Matthew 6.28: "And why take ye thought for raiment? Consider the lilies of the field, how they grow; they toil not, neither do they spin."

[2] *purfled* Edged with another color.

Have seen your coach-wheels splash rebuke
On virtue; and have learned your look
When, wealth and health slipped past, you stare
Along the streets alone, and there,
Round the long park, across the bridge,
The cold lamps at the pavement's edge
Wind on together and apart,
A fiery serpent for your heart.

Let the thoughts pass, an empty cloud!
Suppose I were to think aloud—
What if to her all this were said?
Why, as a volume seldom read
Being opened halfway shuts again,
So might the pages of her brain
Be parted at such words, and thence
Close back upon the dusty sense.
For is there hue or shape defined
In Jenny's desecrated mind,
Where all contagious currents meet,
A Lethe[1] of the middle street?
Nay, it reflects not any face,
Nor sound is in its sluggish pace,
But as they coil those eddies clot,
And night and day remember not.

Why, Jenny, you're asleep at last!
Asleep, poor Jenny, hard and fast—
So young and soft and tired; so fair,
With chin thus nestled in your hair,
Mouth quiet, eyelids almost blue
As if some sky of dreams shone through!

Just as another woman sleeps!
Enough to throw one's thoughts in heaps
Of doubt and horror—what to say
Or think—this awful secret sway,
The potter's power over the clay!
Of the same lump (it has been said)
For honour and dishonour made,
Two sister vessels.[2] Here is one.

My cousin Nell is fond of fun,
And fond of dress, and change, and praise,
So mere a woman in her ways:
And if her sweet eyes rich in youth
Are like her lips that tell the truth,
My cousin Nell is fond of love.
And she's the girl I'm proudest of.
Who does not prize her, guard her well?
The love of change, in cousin Nell,
Shall find the best and hold it dear:
The unconquered mirth turn quieter
Not through her own, through others' woe:
The conscious pride of beauty glow
Beside another's pride in her,
One little part of all they share.
For Love himself shall ripen these
In a kind soil to just increase
Through years of fertilizing peace.

Of the same lump (as it is said)
For honour and dishonour made,
Two sister vessels. Here is one.

It makes a goblin of the sun.

So pure—so fallen! How dare to think
Of the first common kindred link?
Yet, Jenny, till the world shall burn
It seems that all things take their turn;
And who shall say but this fair tree
May need, in changes that may be,
Your children's children's charity?
Scorned then, no doubt, as you are scorned!
Shall no man hold his pride forewarned
Till in the end, the Day of Days,
At Judgment, one of his own race,

[1] *Lethe* River in Hades (the underworld of classical mythology) whose waters bring forgetfulness to those who drink from them.

[2] *The potter's … vessels* Reference to Romans 9.21: "Hath not the potter power over the clay, of the same lump to make one vessel unto honor, and another unto dishonor?"

As frail and lost as you, shall rise—
His daughter, with his mother's eyes?

How Jenny's clock ticks on the shelf!
Might not the dial scorn itself
That has such hours to register?
Yet as to me, even so to her
Are golden sun and silver moon,
In daily largesse of earth's boon,
Counted for life-coins to one tune.
And if, as blindfold fates are tossed,
Through some one man this life be lost,
Shall soul not somehow pay for soul?

Fair shines the gilded aureole° *halo*
In which our highest painters place
Some living woman's simple face.
And the stilled features thus descried
As Jenny's long throat droops aside—
The shadows where the cheeks are thin,
And pure wide curve from ear to chin—
With Raffael's, Leonardo's[1] hand
To show them to men's souls, might stand,
Whole ages long, the whole world through,
For preachings of what God can do.
What has man done here? How atone,
Great God, for this which man has done?
And for the body and soul which by
Man's pitiless doom must now comply
With lifelong hell, what lullaby
Of sweet forgetful second birth
Remains? All dark. No sign on earth
What measure of God's rest endows
The many mansions of his house.

If but a woman's heart might see
Such erring heart unerringly
For once! But that can never be.

Like a rose shut in a book
In which pure women may not look,
For its base pages claim control
To crush the flower within the soul;
Where through each dead rose-leaf that clings,
Pale as transparent psyche-wings,
To the vile text, are traced such things
As might make lady's cheek indeed
More than a living rose to read;
So nought save foolish foulness may
Watch with hard eyes the sure decay;
And so the life-blood of this rose,
Puddled with shameful knowledge, flows
Through leaves no chaste hand may unclose:
Yet still it keeps such faded show
Of when 'twas gathered long ago,
That the crushed petals' lovely grain,
The sweetness of the sanguine stain,
Seen of a woman's eyes, must make
Her pitiful heart, so prone to ache,
Love roses better for its sake—
Only that this can never be:
Even so unto her sex is she.

Yet, Jenny, looking long at you,
The woman almost fades from view.
A cipher of man's changeless sum
Of lust, past, present, and to come,
Is left. A riddle that one shrinks
To challenge from the scornful sphinx.[2]

Like a toad within a stone
Seated while Time crumbles on;[3]
Which sits there since the earth was cursed
For Man's transgression at the first;

---

[1] *Raffael, Leonardo* I.e., Italian painters Raphael (1483–1520) and Leonardo da Vinci (1452–1519).

[2] *sphinx* Winged creature of Greek mythology who killed those who could not answer its riddles.

[3] *Like a … on* Phenomenon of living toads, frogs, or other creatures trapped in stone or wood is one that has been occasionally reported. One such instance occurred in 1865, when workers excavating in Hartlepool, England, split open a magnesium limestone rock found 25 feet underground to discover a living toad. The *Hartlepool Free Press* reported, "The cavity was no larger than its body, and presented the appearance of being cast for it." There was no evidence as to how the toad could have gotten into the stone or survived in it for any length of time. But, from its appearance and the age of the rock in which it was found, the toad was estimated to be over 6,000 years old.

Which, living through all centuries,
Not once has seen the sun arise;
Whose life, to its cold circle charmed,
The earth's whole summers have not warmed;
Which always—whitherso the stone
Be flung—sits there, deaf, blind, alone;
Aye, and shall not be driven out
Till that which shuts him round about
Break at the very Master's stroke,
And the dust thereof vanish as smoke,
And the seed of Man vanish as dust—
Even so within this world is Lust.

Come, come, what use in thoughts like this?
Poor little Jenny, good to kiss—
You'd not believe by what strange roads
Thought travels, when your beauty goads
A man to-night to think of toads!
Jenny, wake up … Why, there's the dawn!

And there's an early wagon drawn
To market, and some sheep that jog
Bleating before a barking dog;
And the old streets come peering through
Another night that London knew;
And all as ghostlike as the lamps.

So on the wings of day decamps
My last night's frolic. Glooms begin
To shiver off as lights creep in
Past the gauze curtains half drawn-to,
And the lamp's doubled shade grows blue—
Your lamp, my Jenny, kept alight,
Like a wise virgin's, all one night!
And in the alcove coolly spread
Glimmers with dawn your empty bed;
And yonder your fair face I see
Reflected lying on my knee,
Where teems with first foreshadowings
Your pier-glass[1] scrawled with diamond rings:
And on your bosom all night worn
Yesterday's rose now droops forlorn
But dies not yet this summer morn.

And now without, as if some word
Had called upon them that they heard,
The London sparrows far and nigh
Clamour together suddenly;
And Jenny's cage-bird grown awake
Here in their song his part must take,
Because here too the day doth break.

And somehow in myself the dawn
Among stirred clouds and veils withdrawn
Strikes greyly on her. Let her sleep.
But will it wake her if I heap
These cushions thus beneath her head
Where my knee was? No—there's your bed,
My Jenny, while you dream. And there
I lay among your golden hair
Perhaps the subject of your dreams,
These golden coins.

For still one deems
That Jenny's flattering sleep confers
New magic on the magic purse—
Grim web, how clogged with shrivelled flies!
Between the threads fine fumes arise
And shape their pictures in the brain.
There roll no streets in glare and rain,
Nor flagrant man-swine whets his tusk;
But delicately sighs in musk
The homage of the dim boudoir;
Or like a palpitating star
Thrilled into song, the opera-night
Breathes faint in the quick pulse of light;
Or at the carriage-window shine
Rich wares for choice; or, free to dine,
Whirls through its hour of health (divine
For her) the concourse of the Park.
And though in the discounted dark
Her functions there and here are one,
Beneath the lamps and in the sun
There reigns at least the acknowledged belle

[1] *pier-glass* Large, tall mirror.

Apparelled beyond parallel.
Ah Jenny, yes, we know your dreams.

For even the Paphian Venus[1] seems
A goddess o'er the realms of love,
When silver-shrined in shadowy grove:
Aye, or let offerings nicely placed
But hide Priapus[2] to the waist,
And whoso looks on him shall see
An eligible deity.

Why, Jenny, waking here alone
May help you to remember one,
Though all the memory's long outworn
Of many a double-pillowed morn.
I think I see you when you wake,
And rub your eyes for me, and shake
My gold, in rising, from your hair,
A Danaë[3] for a moment there.

Jenny, my love rang true! for still
Love at first sight is vague, until
That tinkling makes him audible.

And must I mock you to the last,
Ashamed of my own shame—aghast
Because some thoughts not born amiss
Rose at a poor fair face like this?
Well, of such thoughts so much I know:
In my life, as in hers, they show,
By a far gleam which I may near,
A dark path I can strive to clear.

Only one kiss. Goodbye, my dear.
—1848

---

[1] *Paphian Venus* Venus, goddess of love, was said to have been born of sea-foam, but emerged on the island of Paphos, Cyprus.

[2] *Priapus* God of procreation, and a personification of an erect phallus.

[3] *Danaë* According to Greek mythology, Acrisius imprisoned his daughter Danaë in a room of bronze to ensure she would never conceive a son. Zeus, however, fell in love with Danaë and came to her through the ceiling as a shower of gold that fell in her lap.

My Sister's Sleep

She fell asleep on Christmas Eve:
At length the long-ungranted shade
Of weary eyelids overweighed
The pain nought else might yet relieve.

Our mother, who had leaned all day
Over the bed from chime to chime,
Then raised herself for the first time,
And as she sat her down, did pray.

Her little work-table was spread
With work to finish. For the glare
Made by her candle, she had care
To work some distance from the bed.

Without, there was a cold moon up,
Of winter radiance sheer and thin;
The hollow halo it was in
Was like an icy crystal cup.

Through the small room, with subtle sound
Of flame, by vents the fireshine drove
And reddened. In its dim alcove
The mirror shed a clearness round.

I had been sitting up some nights,
And my tired mind felt weak and blank;
Like a sharp strengthening wine it drank
The stillness and the broken lights.

Twelve struck. That sound, by dwindling years
Heard in each hour, crept off; and then
The ruffled silence spread again,
Like water that a pebble stirs.

Our mother rose from where she sat:
Her needles, as she laid them down,
Met lightly, and her silken gown
Settled: no other noise than that.

"Glory unto the Newly Born!"
So, as said angels, she did say;
Because we were in Christmas Day,
Though it would still be long till morn.

Just then in the room over us
There was a pushing back of chairs,
As some who had sat unawares
So late, now heard the hour, and rose.

With anxious softly-stepping haste
Our mother went where Margaret lay,
Fearing the sounds o'erhead—should they
Have broken her long watched-for rest!

She stopped an instant, calm, and turned;
But suddenly turned back again;
And all her features seemed in pain
With woe, and her eyes gazed and yearned.

For my part, I but hid my face,
And held my breath, and spoke no word:
There was none spoken; but I heard
The silence for a little space.

Our mother bowed herself and wept:
And both my arms fell, and I said,
"God knows I knew that she was dead."
And there, all white, my sister slept.

Then kneeling, upon Christmas morn
A little after twelve o'clock
We said, ere the first quarter struck,
"Christ's blessing on the newly born!"
—1850

Dante Gabriel Rossetti, *Lady Lilith*, 1866–68 (revised 1872–73).

Lady Lilith[1]

Of Adam's first wife, Lilith, it is told
(The witch he loved before the gift of Eve)
That, ere the snake's, her sweet tongue could deceive,
And her enchanted hair was the first gold.
And still she sits, young while the earth is old,
And, subtly of herself contemplative,
Draws men to watch the bright web she can weave,
Till heart and body and life are in its hold.

Rose, foxglove, poppy are her flowers: for where
Is he not found, O Lilith, whom shed scent
And soft-shed fingers and soft sleep shall snare?
Lo! as that youth's eyes burned at thine, so went

[1] *Lady Lilith* This sonnet was composed to accompany a painting of the same title, reproduced here. In the extended version of Rossetti's sonnet sequence *The House of Life* (1881), it appeared with the title "Body's Beauty." Lilith was the first wife of Adam; according to Talmudic legend, she rejected Adam when she refused to accept a subservient position in sexual intercourse. She left the Garden of Eden and mated with various demons.

Thy spell through him, and left his straight neck
bent
And round his heart one strangling golden hair.
—1868

Dante Gabriel Rossetti, *Mary Magdalene at the Door of Simon the Pharisee*, 1858.

Mary Magdalene at the Door of Simon the Pharisee[1]

(*For a Drawing*)[2]

"Why wilt thou cast the roses from thine hair?
Nay, be thou all a rose—wreath, lips, and
cheek.
Nay, not this house—that banquet-house we seek;
See how they kiss and enter; come thou there.
This delicate day of love we two will share
Till at our ear love's whispering night shall speak.
What, sweet one—hold'st thou still the foolish
freak?° *whim*
Nay, when I kiss thy feet they'll leave the stair."

"Oh loose me! See'st thou not my Bridegroom's face
That draws me to Him? For His feet my kiss,
My hair, my tears He craves to-day—and oh!
What words can tell what other day and place
Shall see me clasp those blood-stained feet of His?
He needs me, calls me, loves me: let me go!"
—1870

[1] *Mary … Pharisee* See Luke 7.36–50, which tells how an anonymous penitent, often assumed to be Mary Magdalene, burst into the house of Simon, a Pharisee, where Jesus was dining. She prostrated herself at his feet, which she then washed with her tears and dried with her hair.

[2] [Rossetti's note] In the drawing Mary has left a procession of revellers, and is ascending by a sudden impulse the steps of the house where she sees Christ. Her lover has followed her and is trying to turn her back.

from *The House of Life*

The Sonnet

A Sonnet is a moment's monument—
Memorial from the Soul's eternity
To one dead deathless hour. Look that it be,
Whether for lustral° rite or dire portent, *purification*
Of its own arduous fulness reverent:
Carve it in ivory or in ebony,
As Day or Night may rule; and let Time see
Its flowering crest impearled and orient.

A Sonnet is a coin: its face reveals
The soul—its converse, to what Power 'tis due—
Whether for tribute to the august appeals
Of Life, or dower in Love's high retinue,
It serve; or, 'mid the dark wharf's cavernous breath,
In Charon's[3] palm it pay the toll to Death.
—1881

[3] *Charon* In Greek mythology, ferryman of the river Styx who, for a fee, transports dead souls into Hades.

6a. Nuptial Sleep[1]

At length their long kiss severed, with sweet smart:
And as the last slow sudden drops are shed
From sparkling eaves when all the storm has fled,
So singly flagged the pulses of each heart.
Their bosoms sundered, with the opening start
Of married flowers to either side outspread
From the knit stem; yet still their mouths, burnt red,
Fawned on each other where they lay apart.

Sleep sank them lower than the tide of dreams,
And their dreams watched them sink, and slid away.
Slowly their souls swam up again, through gleams
Of watered light and dull drowned waifs of day;
Till from some wonder of new woods and streams
He woke, and wondered more: for there she lay.
—1870

10. The Portrait

O Lord of all compassionate control,
O Love! let this my lady's picture glow
Under my hand to praise her name, and show
Even of her inner self the perfect whole:
That he who seeks her beauty's furthest goal,
Beyond the light that the sweet glances throw
And refluent wave of the sweet smile, may know
The very sky and sea-line of her soul.

Lo! it is done. Above the enthroning throat
The mouth's mould testifies of voice and kiss,
The shadowed eyes remember and foresee.
Her face is made her shrine. Let all men note
That in all years (O Love, thy gift is this!)
They that would look on her must come to me.
—1870

101. The One Hope

When vain desire at last and vain regret
Go hand in hand to death, and all is vain,
What shall assuage the unforgotten pain
And teach the unforgetful to forget?
Shall Peace be still a sunk stream long unmet—
Or may the soul at once in a green plain
Stoop through the spray of some sweet life-fountain
And cull the dew-drenched flowering amulet?[2]

Ah! when the wan soul in that golden air
Between the scriptured petals softly blown
Peers breathless for the gift of grace unknown—
Ah! let none other alien spell soe'er
But only the one Hope's one name be there—
Not less nor more, but even that word alone.
—1870

[1] *Nuptial Sleep* This sonnet was published in Rossetti's 1870 volume, *Poems*, but was omitted from the 1881 edition of *The House of Life* after Robert Buchanan, in his review *The Fleshly School of Poetry* (1871), attacked its depiction of "shameless nakedness."

[2] *amulet* Charm against evil, sickness, harm, etc.

In Context

Pre-Raphaelite Principles[1]

In addition to Dante Gabriel Rossetti, the Pre-Raphaelite Brotherhood had three other founding members: William Holman Hunt, John Everett Millais, and Dante Gabriel's brother William Michael Rossetti, who acted as secretary to the group. In the following selection from William Michael's account of the group's history, he summarizes the principles he recalled as being central to the Brotherhood at its 1848 formation.

from William Michael Rossetti, *Dante Gabriel Rossetti; His Family Letters, with a Memoir by William Michael Rossetti* (1895)

… Had the Pre-Raphaelite Brotherhood any ulterior aim beyond that of producing good works of art? Yes, and No. Assuredly they had the aim of developing such ideas as are suited to the medium of fine art, as a bridging the arts of form into general unison with what is highest in other arts, especially poetry. … In the person of at least two of its members, Hunt and Collins, it had also a definite relation to a Christian, and not a pagan or latitudinarian,[2] line of thought. On the other hand, the notion of the Brotherhood, as such, had anything whatever to do with a particular movements in the religious world … is totally … erroneous. To say that Pre-Raphaelitism was part of "the ever rising protest of our century against artificial authority," as in the cases of "The French Revolution" and Wordsworth and Darwin, etc.,[3] is indeed not untrue, but is far too vague to account for anything. … Neither was Ruskin[4] their inciter, though it is true that Hunt had read and laid to heart in 1847 the first volume of *Modern Painters*, the only thing then current as Ruskin's work. …

That the Pre-Raphaelites valued moral and spiritual ideas as an important section of the ideas germane to fine art is most true, and not one of them was in the least any inclined to do any work of a gross, lascivious, or sensual description; but neither did they limit the province of art to the spiritual or the moral. I will therefore take it upon me to say that the bond of union among the members of the Brotherhood was really and simply this: 1) to have genuine ideas to express; 2) to study Nature attentively, so as to know how to express them; 3) to sympathize with what is direct and serious and heartfelt in previous art, to the exclusion of what is conventional and self-parading and learned by rote; and 4) and most indispensable of all, to produce thoroughly good pictures and statues. …

---

[1] Additional materials regarding the Pre-Raphaelites, including further selections from the memoir excerpted here, are included in "Contexts: The Pre-Raphaelite Brotherhood," available in this anthology's online component. Also see the color insert for paintings by Millais and Hunt.

[2] *latitudinarian* Latitudinarians believed that the Church should try to accommodate a diverse range of views when it came to issues of liturgy and of theological doctrine.

[3] [Rossetti's note] See Mrs. Wood's *Dante Rossetti and the Pre-Raphaelite Movement*, page 9. [A history of the Pre-Raphaelite movement, written by Esther Wood and published in 1894.]

[4] *Ruskin* John Ruskin (1819–1900), influential critic and art historian, who would later defend the movement in his writings.

Christina Rossetti

1830 – 1894

To the late-Victorian critic Edmund Gosse, Christina Rossetti was "one of the most perfect poets of the age." Her melding of sensuous imagery and precise form earned her the admiration and devotion of many nineteenth-century readers, an admiration that has only increased in the generations that followed. Praised for being, as one critic wrote in 1862, "remarkably fresh and free," Rossetti's lyric voice is marked by its concision and symbolic richness, and by a pervasive spiritual dimension, even when the subject matter is secular. The quality of her faith, and of her doubt, lend an intensity to her poems that places her writing in kinship with the work of Emily Brontë, Emily Dickinson, and Gerard Manley Hopkins.

She was born in London in 1830, the youngest of four children. Her father, Gabriel Rossetti, was a scholar and an Italian exile, and her mother, Frances Polidori, also a scholar, was the daughter of an Italian exile. Italian revolutionaries-in-exile frequented the Rossetti home, creating a provocative and unconventional environment for the Rossetti children. Frances and Gabriel educated all their four children themselves, including Christina, who dedicated all her work to her mother. Other influences included their mother's devotion to Christianity and visits to their maternal grandfather's rural home. "If any one thing schooled me in the direction of poetry," Rossetti was later to write, "it was perhaps the delightful idle liberty to prowl all alone about my grandfather's cottage-grounds some thirty miles from London." Rossetti's grandfather Polidori printed her first volume of poems, *Verses*, in 1847. These poems of the sixteen-year-old Rossetti already exhibited many of the qualities for which her work would later be known: directness of expression, and narratives colored with vivid and often sensuous detail. The poems in this collection reflected her literary influences: Gothic fiction and the poetry of George Herbert, William Blake, John Keats, and the Italian poets Dante and Tasso.

In 1850 her two brothers, Dante Gabriel and William Michael, helped found the Pre-Raphaelite Brotherhood, a group of writers and painters that shared certain aesthetic goals. Rossetti was both part of, and not part of, this "Brotherhood": she published several poems in *The Germ*, the journal of the Brotherhood, and she also served as a model for several paintings in the early years of the movement. Her aesthetic sense—and especially her attention to color and detail—link her to the movement, as do her devotion to the faithful representation of nature and her interest in symbolic representation. As a woman, however, she was not invited to their meetings, and in later years she became more and more critical of the Brotherhood's increasingly secular orientation and its objectification of women (such criticism is apparent in poems such as "In an Artist's Studio").

The 1850s were a difficult time for Rossetti. Early in the decade she rejected, most likely on religious grounds, a suitor to whom she had been engaged for two years, the Pre-Raphaelite painter James Collinson. Collinson had converted to Anglicanism to please Rossetti, but he ultimately returned to his original faith, Catholicism. (In 1866 Rossetti appears to have rejected a second suitor, Charles Bagot Cayley, perhaps because he was an agnostic.) In 1854 Rossetti volunteered to join

Florence Nightingale's nursing efforts in the Crimean War, but she was rejected for being too young. She volunteered instead at the Highgate Penitentiary for "fallen women," where she was known as "sister Christina." When on duty at the penitentiary, she would live there for two-week intervals, and her experiences with the inmates influenced her literary work (particularly her development of the themes of betrayal and illicit love in her poetry), as well as spurring her activism against child prostitution. Her social activism extended to protesting vivisection and other animal experimentation; she was also openly critical of slavery and imperialism. Throughout this period, she lived with her mother, sister, and brother William in the family home.

Rossetti first gained attention in the literary world with her 1862 publication of *Goblin Market and Other Poems*. Before publication of the volume, the eminent critic John Ruskin had declared the poems irregular in their rhyme schemes and meters. Ruskin advised Rossetti to "exercise herself in the severest commonplace of metre until she [could] write as the public like." Rossetti nevertheless went ahead with publication, and the vast majority of her Victorian critics praised the volume for what one reviewer called its "very decided character and originality, both in theme and treatment." "Goblin Market" remains among her most discussed works. Few readers have believed William Michael Rossetti's insistence that his sister "did not mean anything profound" by "Goblin Market," and the poem has been interpreted in countless ways, including as an examination of female relationship, as a Christian allegory, and as a story of the redemption of a fallen woman.

More volumes followed, among the most important of which were *The Prince's Progress and Other Poems* (1866), *Sing-Song* (1872), and *A Pageant and Other Poems* (1881). *Sing-Song* is a collection of children's verses and nursery rhymes that have proved enduringly popular. With "Monna Innominata," the "sonnet of sonnets" published in *A Pageant and Other Poems,* Rossetti offered her own bold contribution to the sonnet-sequence tradition. In the prose preface to "Monna Innominata," Rossetti notes that women such as Dante's Beatrice and Petrarch's Laura were denied the opportunity to speak for themselves. If either had spoken in her own voice, Rossetti writes, "the portrait left us might have appeared more tender, if less dignified, than any drawn even by a devoted friend." Rossetti's sonnets speak of unfulfilled yearning and painful loss, bringing to the sonnet form the voice of a woman's suffering such as Rossetti argued had never before been written.

The role of faith in Rossetti's life was central: it guided her decisions and actions, as well as her literary output. More than half of her poems are devotional, and as she grew older her writing became almost exclusively religious. The Rossettis were High Anglicans, and Christina was influenced by the Oxford Movement, an intellectual movement within the Anglican church that led to Anglo-Catholicism. Some of her key devotional works include *Annus Domini: A Prayer for Each Day of the Year* (1874), *Time Flies: A Reading Diary* (1885), and *The Face of the Deep* (1892). *Verses* (1893), her last book of poetry, collects poems from her devotional works, and is a passionate record of her desire for union with Christ. In her essay "I Am Christina Rossetti," Virginia Woolf writes that "the pressure of a tremendous faith circles and clamps together these little songs," and, addressing Rossetti directly, observes, "No sooner have you feasted on beauty with your eyes than your mind tells you that beauty is vain and beauty passes. Death, oblivion, and rest lap round your songs with their dark wave."

In 1871, Rossetti was stricken with Graves's disease, which led her to retreat even further into an already quiet life as she continued to live with and care for her mother and two aunts. She lived to see editions of her collected poems published in 1875 and then again in 1890. Rossetti underwent surgery for breast cancer in 1892, and died of the disease in 1894.

⌘⌘⌘

Goblin Market

Morning and evening
Maids heard the goblins cry:
"Come buy our orchard fruits,
Come buy, come buy:
Apples and quinces,
Lemons and oranges,
Plump unpecked cherries,
Melons and raspberries,
Bloom-down-cheeked peaches,
Swart°-headed mulberries, *dark*
Wild free-born cranberries,
Crabapples, dewberries,
Pine-apples, blackberries,
Apricots, strawberries;—
All ripe together
In summer weather,—
Morns that pass by,
Fair eves that fly;
Come buy, come buy:
Our grapes fresh from the vine,
Pomegranates full and fine,
Dates and sharp bullaces,
Rare pears and greengages,
Damsons[1] and bilberries
Taste them and try:
Currants and gooseberries,
Bright-fire-like barberries,
Figs to fill your mouth,
Citrons from the South,
Sweet to tongue and sound to eye;
Come buy, come buy."

Evening by evening
Among the brookside rushes,
Laura bowed her head to hear,
Lizzie veiled her blushes:
Crouching close together
In the cooling weather,
With clasping arms and cautioning lips,
With tingling cheeks and finger tips.
"Lie close," Laura said,
Pricking up her golden head:
"We must not look at goblin men,
We must not buy their fruits:
Who knows upon what soil they fed
Their hungry thirsty roots?"
"Come buy," call the goblins
Hobbling down the glen.
"Oh," cried Lizzie, "Laura, Laura,
You should not peep at goblin men."
Lizzie covered up her eyes,
Covered close lest they should look;
Laura reared her glossy head,
And whispered like the restless brook:
"Look, Lizzie, look, Lizzie,
Down the glen tramp little men.
One hauls a basket,
One bears a plate,
One lugs a golden dish
Of many pounds weight.
How fair the vine must grow
Whose grapes are so luscious;
How warm the wind must blow
Through those fruit bushes."
"No," said Lizzie: "No, no, no;
Their offers should not charm us,
Their evil gifts would harm us."
She thrust a dimpled finger
In each ear, shut eyes and ran:
Curious Laura chose to linger
Wondering at each merchant man.
One had a cat's face,
One whisked a tail,
One tramped at a rat's pace,
One crawled like a snail,
One like a wombat prowled obtuse and furry,
One like a ratel° tumbled hurry skurry. *badger*
She heard a voice like voice of doves
Cooing all together:
They sounded kind and full of loves
In the pleasant weather.

---

[1] *bullaces ... Damsons* Bullaces, greengages, and damsons are all varieties of plums.

Laura stretched her gleaming neck
Like a rush-imbedded swan,
Like a lily from the beck,° *stream*
Like a moonlit poplar branch,
Like a vessel at the launch
When its last restraint is gone.

Backwards up the mossy glen
Turned and trooped the goblin men,
With their shrill repeated cry,
"Come buy, come buy."
When they reached where Laura was
They stood stock still upon the moss,
Leering at each other,
Brother with queer brother;
Signalling each other,
Brother with sly brother.
One set his basket down,
One reared his plate;
One began to weave a crown
Of tendrils, leaves, and rough nuts brown
(Men sell not such in any town);
One heaved the golden weight
Of dish and fruit to offer her:
"Come buy, come buy," was still their cry.
Laura stared but did not stir,
Longed but had no money:
The whisk-tailed merchant bade her taste
In tones as smooth as honey,
The cat-faced purr'd,
The rat-paced spoke a word
Of welcome, and the snail-paced even was heard;
One parrot-voiced and jolly
Cried "Pretty Goblin" still for "Pretty Polly";—
One whistled like a bird.

But sweet-tooth Laura spoke in haste:
"Good Folk, I have no coin;
To take were to purloin:
I have no copper in my purse,
I have no silver either,
And all my gold is on the furze° *evergreen shrub*
That shakes in windy weather
Above the rusty heather."
"You have much gold upon your head,"
They answered all together:
"Buy from us with a golden curl."
She clipped a precious golden lock,
She dropped a tear more rare than pearl,
Then sucked their fruit globes fair or red.
Sweeter than honey from the rock,[1]
Stronger than man-rejoicing wine,
Clearer than water flowed that juice;
She never tasted such before,
How should it cloy with length of use?
She sucked and sucked and sucked the more
Fruits which that unknown orchard bore;
She sucked until her lips were sore;
Then flung the emptied rinds away
But gathered up one kernel-stone,
And knew not was it night or day
As she turned home alone.

Lizzie met her at the gate
Full of wise upbraidings:
"Dear, you should not stay so late,
Twilight is not good for maidens;
Should not loiter in the glen
In the haunts of goblin men.
Do you not remember Jeanie,
How she met them in the moonlight,
Took their gifts both choice and many,
Ate their fruits and wore their flowers
Plucked from bowers
Where summer ripens at all hours?
But ever in the noonlight
She pined and pined away;
Sought them by night and day,
Found them no more but dwindled and grew grey;
Then fell with the first snow,
While to this day no grass will grow
Where she lies low:
I planted daisies there a year ago
That never blow.

[1] *honey from the rock* See Deuteronomy 32.13.

You should not loiter so."
"Nay, hush," said Laura:
"Nay, hush, my sister:
I ate and ate my fill,
Yet my mouth waters still;
Tomorrow night I will
Buy more": and kissed her:
"Have done with sorrow;
I'll bring you plums tomorrow
Fresh on their mother twigs,
Cherries worth getting;
You cannot think what figs
My teeth have met in,
What melons icy cold
Piled on a dish of gold
Too huge for me to hold,
What peaches with a velvet nap,
Pellucid° grapes without one seed: *translucent*
Odorous indeed must be the mead° *meadow*
Whereon they grow, and pure the wave they drink
With lilies at the brink,
And sugar-sweet their sap."

Golden head by golden head,
Like two pigeons in one nest
Folded in each other's wings,
They lay down in their curtained bed:
Like two blossoms on one stem,
Like two flakes of new-fall'n snow,
Like two wands of ivory
Tipped with gold for awful° kings. *awe-inspiring*
Moon and stars gazed in at them,
Wind sang to them lullaby,
Lumbering owls forbore to fly,
Not a bat flapped to and fro
Round their rest:
Cheek to cheek and breast to breast
Locked together in one nest.

Early in the morning
When the first cock crowed his warning,
Neat like bees, as sweet and busy,
Laura rose with Lizzie:
Fetched in honey, milked the cows,
Aired and set to rights the house,
Kneaded cakes of whitest wheat,
Cakes for dainty mouths to eat,
Next churned butter, whipped up cream,
Fed their poultry, sat and sewed;
Talked as modest maidens should:
Lizzie with an open heart,
Laura in an absent dream,
One content, one sick in part;
One warbling for the mere bright day's delight,
One longing for the night.

At length slow evening came:
They went with pitchers to the reedy brooks;
Lizzie most placid in her look,
Laura most like a leaping flame.
They drew the gurgling water from its deep.
Lizzie plucked purple and rich golden flags,
Then turning homeward said: "The sunset flushes
Those furthest loftiest crags;
Come Laura, not another maiden lags.
No wilful squirrel wags,
The beasts and birds are fast asleep."
But Laura loitered still among the rushes,
And said the bank was steep.

And said the hour was early still,
The dew not fall'n, the wind not chill;
Listening ever, but not catching
The customary cry,
"Come buy, come buy,"
With its iterated jingle
Of sugar-baited words:
Not for all her watching
Once discerning even one goblin
Racing, whisking, tumbling, hobbling—
Let alone the herds
That used to tramp along the glen,
In groups or single,
Of brisk fruit-merchant men.
Till Lizzie urged, "O Laura, come;
I hear the fruit-call, but I dare not look:

You should not loiter longer at this brook:
Come with me home.
The stars rise, the moon bends her arc,
Each glowworm winks her spark,
Let us get home before the night grows dark:
For clouds may gather
Though this is summer weather,
Put out the lights and drench us thro';
Then if we lost our way what should we do?"

Laura turned cold as stone
To find her sister heard that cry alone,
That goblin cry,
"Come buy our fruits, come buy."
Must she then buy no more such dainty fruit?
Must she no more such succous° pasture find, *juicy*
Gone deaf and blind?
Her tree of life drooped from the root:
She said not one word in her heart's sore ache;
But peering through the dimness, nought discerning,
Trudged home, her pitcher dripping all the way;
So crept to bed, and lay
Silent till Lizzie slept;
Then sat up in a passionate yearning,
And gnashed her teeth for baulked desire, and wept
As if her heart would break.

Day after day, night after night,
Laura kept watch in vain
In sullen silence of exceeding pain.
She never caught again the goblin cry,
"Come buy, come buy"—
She never spied the goblin men
Hawking their fruits along the glen:
But when the noon waxed bright
Her hair grew thin and grey;
She dwindled, as the fair full moon doth turn
To swift decay and burn
Her fire away.

One day remembering her kernel-stone
She set it by a wall that faced the south;
Dewed it with tears, hoped for a root,
Watched for a waxing shoot,
But there came none.
It never saw the sun,
It never felt the trickling moisture run:
While with sunk eyes and faded mouth
She dreamed of melons, as a traveller sees
False waves in desert drouth
With shade of leaf-crowned trees,
And burns the thirstier in the sandful breeze.

She no more swept the house,
Tended the fowl or cows,
Fetched honey, kneaded cakes of wheat,
Brought water from the brook:
But sat down listless in the chimney-nook
And would not eat.

Tender Lizzie could not bear
To watch her sister's cankerous care,
Yet not to share.
She night and morning
Caught the goblins' cry:
"Come buy our orchard fruits,
Come buy, come buy:"—
Beside the brook, along the glen,
She heard the tramp of goblin men,
The voice and stir
Poor Laura could not hear;
Longed to buy fruit to comfort her,
But feared to pay too dear.
She thought of Jeanie in her grave,
Who should have been a bride;
But who for joys brides hope to have
Fell sick and died
In her gay prime,
In earliest winter time,
With the first glazing rime,
With the first snow-fall of crisp Winter time.

Till Laura dwindling
Seemed knocking at Death's door.
Then Lizzie weighed no more
Better and worse;

But put a silver penny in her purse,
Kissed Laura, crossed the heath with clumps of furze
At twilight, halted by the brook:
And for the first time in her life
Began to listen and look.

Laughed every goblin
When they spied her peeping:
Came towards her hobbling,
Flying, running, leaping,
Puffing and blowing,
Chuckling, clapping, crowing.
Clucking and gobbling,
Mopping and mowing,
Full of airs and graces,
Pulling wry faces,
Demure grimaces,
Cat-like and rat-like,
Ratel- and wombat-like,
Snail-paced in a hurry,
Parrot-voiced and whistler,
Helter skelter, hurry skurry,
Chattering like magpies,
Fluttering like pigeons,
Gliding like fishes,—
Hugged her and kissed her:
Squeezed and caressed her:
Stretched up their dishes,
Panniers, and plates:
"Look at our apples
Russet and dun,
Bob at our cherries,
Bite at our peaches,
Citrons and dates,
Grapes for the asking,
Pears red with basking
Out in the sun,
Plums on their twigs;
Pluck them and suck them,—
Pomegranates, figs."

"Good folk," said Lizzie,
Mindful of Jeanie:
"Give me much and many"—
Held out her apron,
Tossed them her penny.
"Nay, take a seat with us,
Honour and eat with us,"
They answered grinning:
"Our feast is but beginning.
Night yet is early,
Warm and dew-pearly,
Wakeful and starry:
Such fruits as these
No man can carry;
Half their bloom would fly,
Half their dew would dry,
Half their flavour would pass by.
Sit down and feast with us,
Be welcome guest with us,
Cheer you and rest with us."—
"Thank you," said Lizzie: "But one waits
At home alone for me:
So without further parleying,° *discussion*
If you will not sell me any
Of your fruits though much and many,
Give me back my silver penny
I tossed you for a fee."—
They began to scratch their pates,° *heads*
No longer wagging, purring,
But visibly demurring,
Grunting and snarling.
One called her proud,
Cross-grained, uncivil;
Their tones waxed loud,
Their looks were evil.
Lashing their tails
They trod and hustled her,
Elbowed and jostled her,
Clawed with their nails,
Barking, mewing, hissing, mocking,
Tore her gown and soiled her stocking,
Twitched her hair out by the roots,
Stamped upon her tender feet,
Held her hands and squeezed their fruits
Against her mouth to make her eat.

White and golden Lizzie stood,
Like a lily in a flood,—
Like a rock of blue-veined stone
Lashed by tides obstreperously,—
Like a beacon left alone
In a hoary roaring sea,
Sending up a golden fire,—
Like a fruit-crowned orange tree
White with blossoms honey-sweet
Sore beset by wasp and bee,—
Like a royal virgin town
Topped with gilded dome and spire
Close beleaguered by a fleet
Mad to tug her standard down.

One may lead a horse to water,
Twenty cannot make him drink.
Though the goblins cuffed and caught her,
Coaxed and fought her,
Bullied and besought her,
Scratched her, pinched her black as ink,
Kicked and knocked her,
Mauled and mocked her,
Lizzie uttered not a word;
Would not open lip from lip
Lest they should cram a mouthful in:
But laughed in heart to feel the drip
Of juice that syruped all her face,
And lodged in dimples of her chin,
And streaked her neck which quaked like curd.
At last the evil people,
Worn out by her resistance,
Flung back her penny, kicked their fruit
Along whichever road they took,
Not leaving root or stone or shoot;
Some writhed into the ground,
Some dived into the brook
With ring and ripple,
Some scudded on the gale without a sound,
Some vanished in the distance.

In a smart, ache, tingle,
Lizzie went her way;
Knew not was it night or day;
Sprang up the bank, tore through the furze,
Threaded copse and dingle,° *dell*
And heard her penny jingle
Bouncing in her purse,—
Its bounce was music to her ear.
She ran and ran
As if she feared some goblin man
Dogged her with gibe or curse
Or something worse:
But not one goblin skurried after,
Nor was she pricked by fear;
The kind heart made her windy-paced
That urged her home quite out of breath with haste
And inward laughter.

She cried, “Laura,” up the garden,
“Did you miss me?
Come and kiss me.
Never mind my bruises,
Hug me, kiss me, suck my juices
Squeezed from goblin fruits for you,
Goblin pulp and goblin dew.
Eat me, drink me, love me;
Laura, make much of me;
For your sake I have braved the glen
And had to do with goblin merchant men.”

Laura started from her chair,
Flung her arms up in the air,
Clutched her hair:
“Lizzie, Lizzie, have you tasted
For my sake the fruit forbidden?
Must your light like mine be hidden,
Your young life like mine be wasted,
Undone in mine undoing,
And ruined in my ruin,
Thirsty, cankered, goblin-ridden?”—
She clung about her sister,
Kissed and kissed and kissed her:
Tears once again
Refreshed her shrunken eyes,
Dropping like rain

After long sultry drouth;
Shaking with aguish[1] fear, and pain,
She kissed and kissed her with a hungry mouth.

Her lips began to scorch,
That juice was wormwood to her tongue,
She loathed the feast:
Writhing as one possessed she leaped and sung,
Rent all her robe, and wrung
Her hands in lamentable haste,
And beat her breast.
Her locks streamed like the torch
Borne by a racer at full speed,
Or like the mane of horses in their flight,
Or like an eagle when she stems the light
Straight toward the sun,
Or like a caged thing freed,
Or like a flying flag when armies run.

Swift fire spread through her veins, knocked at her heart,
Met the fire smouldering there
And overbore its lesser flame;
She gorged on bitterness without a name:
Ah! fool, to choose such part
Of soul-consuming care!
Sense failed in the mortal strife:
Like the watchtower of a town
Which an earthquake shatters down,
Like a lightning-stricken mast,
Like a wind-uprooted tree
Spun about,
Like a foam-topped waterspout
Cast down headlong in the sea,
She fell at last;
Pleasure past and anguish past,
Is it death or is it life?

Life out of death.
That night long Lizzie watched by her,
Counted her pulse's flagging stir,
Felt for her breath,
Held water to her lips, and cooled her face
With tears and fanning leaves.
But when the first birds chirped about their eaves,
And early reapers plodded to the place
Of golden sheaves,
And dew-wet grass
Bowed in the morning winds so brisk to pass,
And new buds with new day
Opened of cup-like lilies on the stream,
Laura awoke as from a dream,
Laughed in the innocent old way,
Hugged Lizzie but not twice or thrice;
Her gleaming locks showed not one thread of grey,
Her breath was sweet as May,
And light danced in her eyes.

Days, weeks, months, years
Afterwards, when both were wives
With children of their own;
Their mother-hearts beset with fears,
Their lives bound up in tender lives;
Laura would call the little ones
And tell them of her early prime,
Those pleasant days long gone
Of not-returning time:
Would talk about the haunted glen,
The wicked quaint fruit-merchant men,
Their fruits like honey to the throat
But poison in the blood;
(Men sell not such in any town):
Would tell them how her sister stood
In deadly peril to do her good,
And win the fiery antidote:
Then joining hands to little hands
Would bid them cling together,—
"For there is no friend like a sister
In calm or stormy weather;
To cheer one on the tedious way,
To fetch one if one goes astray,
To lift one if one totters down,
To strengthen whilst one stands."
—1862

[1] *aguish* Feverish.

IN CONTEXT

Illustrating *Goblin Market*

The first edition of *Goblin Market* appeared in 1862 with a frontispiece by the author's brother, the Pre-Raphaelite painter and poet Dante Gabriel Rossetti. The round inset above the drawing of sisters Laura and Lizzie depicts the goblins carrying their fruits to market. Another notable edition was that of 1893, with art nouveau illustrations by artist and writer Laurence Housman (brother of poet A.E. Housman).

1862 Macmillan edition—illustration by D.G. Rossetti.

Illustration by Laurence Housman from the 1893 Macmillan edition.

A Triad

Three sang of love together: one with lips
 Crimson, with cheeks and bosom in a glow,
Flushed to the yellow hair and finger tips;
 And one there sang who soft and smooth as snow
 Bloomed like a tinted hyacinth at a show;
And one was blue with famine after love,
 Who like a harpstring snapped rang harsh and low
The burden of what those were singing of.
One shamed herself in love; one temperately
 Grew gross in soulless love, a sluggish wife;
One famished died for love. Thus two of three
 Took death for love and won him after strife;
One droned in sweetness like a fattened bee:
 All on the threshold, yet all short of life.
—1862

Remember

Remember me when I am gone away,
 Gone far away into the silent land;
 When you can no more hold me by the hand,
Nor I half turn to go yet turning stay.
Remember me when no more day by day
 You tell me of our future that you planned:
 Only remember me; you understand
It will be late then to counsel or to pray.
Yet if you should forget me for a while
 And afterwards remember, do not grieve:
 For if the darkness and corruption leave
 A vestige of the thoughts that once I had,
Better by far you should forget and smile
 Than that you should remember and be sad.
—1862

A Birthday

My heart is like a singing bird
 Whose nest is in a watered shoot;
My heart is like an apple tree
 Whose boughs are bent with thickset fruit;
My heart is like a rainbow shell
 That paddles in a halcyon° sea; *calm*
My heart is gladder than all these
 Because my love is come to me.

Raise me a dais of silk and down;
 Hang it with vair° and purple dyes; *squirrel fur*
Carve it in doves and pomegranates,
 And peacocks with a hundred eyes;
Work it in gold and silver grapes,
 In leaves, and silver fleurs-de-lys;
Because the birthday of my life
 Is come, my love is come to me.
—1861

After Death

The curtains were half drawn, the floor was swept
 And strewn with rushes, rosemary and may
 Lay thick upon the bed on which I lay,
Where thro' the lattice ivy-shadows crept.
He leaned above me, thinking that I slept
 And could not hear him; but I heard him say:
 "Poor child, poor child": and as he turned away
Came a deep silence, and I knew he wept.
He did not touch the shroud, or raise the fold
 That hid my face, or take my hand in his,
 Or ruffle the smooth pillows for my head:
 He did not love me living; but once dead
 He pitied me; and very sweet it is
To know he still is warm tho' I am cold.
—1862

An Apple-Gathering

I plucked pink blossoms from mine apple tree
 And wore them all that evening in my hair:
Then in due season when I went to see
 I found no apples there.

With dangling basket all along the grass
As I had come I went the selfsame track:
My neighbours mocked me while they saw me pass
So empty-handed back.

Lilian and Lilias smiled in trudging by,
Their heaped-up basket teazed me like a jeer;
Sweet-voiced they sang beneath the sunset sky,
Their mother's home was near.

Plump Gertrude passed me with her basket full,
A stronger hand than hers helped it along;
A voice talked with her thro' the shadows cool
More sweet to me than song.

Ah Willie, Willie, was my love less worth
Than apples with their green leaves piled above?
I counted rosiest apples on the earth
Of far less worth than love.

So once it was with me you stooped to talk
Laughing and listening in this very lane;
To think that by this way we used to walk
We shall not walk again!

I let my neighbours pass me, ones and twos
And groups; the latest said the night grew chill,
And hastened: but I loitered, while the dews
Fell fast I loitered still.
—1862

Echo

Come to me in the silence of the night;
Come in the speaking silence of a dream;
Come with soft rounded cheeks and eyes as bright
As sunlight on a stream;
Come back in tears,
O memory, hope, love of finished years.

O dream how sweet, too sweet, too bitter sweet,
Whose wakening should have been in Paradise,
Where souls brimfull of love abide and meet;
Where thirsting longing eyes
Watch the slow door
That opening, letting in, lets out no more.

Yet come to me in dreams, that I may live
My very life again tho' cold in death:
Come back to me in dreams, that I may give
Pulse for pulse, breath for breath:
Speak low, lean low,
As long ago, my love, how long ago.
—1862

Winter: My Secret

I tell my secret? No indeed, not I:
Perhaps some day, who knows?
But not today; it froze, and blows, and snows,
And you're too curious: fie!
You want to hear it? well:
Only, my secret's mine, and I won't tell.

Or, after all, perhaps there's none:
Suppose there is no secret after all,
But only just my fun.
Today's a nipping day, a biting day;
In which one wants a shawl,
A veil, a cloak, and other wraps:
I cannot ope to every one who taps,
And let the draughts come whistling thro' my hall;
Come bounding and surrounding me,
Come buffeting, astounding me,
Nipping and clipping thro' my wraps and all.
I wear my mask for warmth: who ever shows
His nose to Russian snows
To be pecked at by every wind that blows?
You would not peck? I thank you for good will,
Believe, but leave that truth untested still.

Spring's an expansive time: yet I don't trust
March with its peck of dust,
Nor April with its rainbow-crowned brief showers,

Nor even May, whose flowers
One frost may wither thro' the sunless hours.

Perhaps some languid summer day,
When drowsy birds sing less and less,
And golden fruit is ripening to excess,
If there's not too much sun nor too much cloud,
And the warm wind is neither still nor loud,
Perhaps my secret I may say,
Or you may guess.
—1862

"No, Thank You, John"

I never said I loved you, John:
Why will you teaze me day by day,
And wax a weariness to think upon
With always "do" and "pray"?

You know I never loved you, John;
No fault of mine made me your toast:[1]
Why will you haunt me with a face as wan
As shows an hour-old ghost?

I dare say Meg or Moll would take
Pity upon you, if you'd ask:
And pray don't remain single for my sake
Who can't perform that task.

I have no heart?—Perhaps I have not;
But then you're mad to take offence
That I don't give you what I have not got:
Use your own common sense.

Let bygones be bygones:
Don't call me false, who owed not to be true:
I'd rather answer "No" to fifty Johns
Than answer "Yes" to you.

Let's mar our pleasant days no more,
Songbirds of passage, days of youth:
Catch at today, forget the days before:
I'll wink at your untruth.

Let us strike hands as hearty friends;
No more, no less; and friendship's good:
Only don't keep in view ulterior ends,
And points not understood

In open treaty. Rise above
Quibbles and shuffling off and on:
Here's friendship for you if you like; but love,—
No, thank you, John.
—1862

[1] *your toast* I.e., the woman to whom John would raise a glass when toasting his lady.

A Pause of Thought

I looked for that which is not, nor can be,
And hope deferred made my heart sick in truth:
But years must pass before a hope of youth
Is resigned utterly.

I watched and waited with a steadfast will:
And though the object seemed to flee away
That I so longed for, ever day by day
I watched and waited still.

Sometimes I said, "This thing shall be no more;
My expectation wearies and shall cease;
I will resign it now and be at peace:"
Yet never gave it o'er.

Sometimes I said, "It is an empty name
I long for; to a name why should I give
The peace of all the days I have to live?"—
Yet gave it all the same.

Alas, thou foolish one! alike unfit
For healthy joy and salutary pain:
Thou knowest the chase useless, and again
Turnest to follow it.
—1848

Song

She sat and sang alway
By the green margin of a stream,
Watching the fishes leap and play
Beneath the glad sunbeam.

I sat and wept alway
Beneath the moon's most shadowy beam,
Watching the blossoms of the May
Weep leaves into the stream.

I wept for memory;
She sang for hope that is so fair:
My tears were swallowed by the sea;
Her songs died on the air.
—1862

Song

When I am dead, my dearest,
Sing no sad songs for me;
Plant thou no roses at my head,
Nor shady cypress tree.
Be the green grass above me
With showers and dewdrops wet;
And if thou wilt, remember,
And if thou wilt, forget.

I shall not see the shadows,
I shall not feel the rain;
I shall not hear the nightingale
Sing on as if in pain.
And dreaming through the twilight
That doth not rise nor set,
Haply° I may remember,
And haply may forget.
—1862

° *by chance*

Dead before Death

Ah! changed and cold, how changed and very cold!
With stiffened smiling lips and cold calm eyes:
Changed, yet the same; much knowing, little wise;
This was the promise of the days of old!
Grown hard and stubborn in the ancient mould,
Grown rigid in the sham of lifelong lies:
We hoped for better things as years would rise,
But it is over as a tale once told.
All fallen the blossom that no fruitage bore,
All lost the present and the future time,
All lost, all lost, the lapse that went before:
So lost till death shut-to the opened door,
So lost from chime to everlasting chime,
So cold and lost for ever evermore.
—1862

Monna Innominata [1]

A Sonnet of Sonnets

Beatrice, immortalized by "*altissimo poeta … cotanto amante*";[2] Laura, celebrated by a great though an inferior bard[3]—have alike paid the exceptional penalty of exceptional honour, and have come down to us resplendent with charms, but (at least, to my apprehension) scant of attractiveness.

These heroines of worldwide fame were preceded by a bevy of unnamed ladies "*donne innominate*" sung by a school of less conspicuous poets; and in that land and that period which gave simultaneous birth to Catholics, to Albigenses, and to Troubadours,[4] one can imagine many a lady as sharing her lover's poetic aptitude, while the barrier between them might be one held sacred by both, yet not such as to render mutual love incompatible with mutual honour.

[1] *Monna Innominata* Italian: Unnamed Lady.

[2] *altissimo poeta … cotanto amante* Italian: loftiest poet … equally great lover (Italian). Rossetti refers to Italian poet Dante Alighieri (1265–1321), whose muse was Beatrice.

[3] *great … bard* Italian poet Francesco Petrarca (1304–74) wrote many love songs to Laura.

[4] *Albigenses* Albigensians were members of a religious sect of the twelfth and thirteenth centuries; *Troubadours* Wandering lyric poets of the eleventh to thirteenth centuries.

Had such a lady spoken for herself, the portrait left us might have appeared more tender, if less dignified, than any drawn even by a devoted friend. Or had the Great Poetess[1] of our own day and nation only been unhappy instead of happy, her circumstances would have invited her to bequeath to us, in lieu of the "Portuguese Sonnets," an inimitable "*donna innominata*" drawn not from fancy but from feeling, and worthy to occupy a niche beside Beatrice and Laura.

1

"Lo dì che han detto a' dolci amici addio."—DANTE
"Amor, con quanto sforzo oggi mi vinci!"—PETRARCA[2]

Come back to me, who wait and watch for you:—
Or come not yet, for it is over then,
And long it is before you come again,
So far between my pleasures are and few.
While, when you come not, what I do I do
Thinking "Now when he comes," my sweetest "when":
For one man is my world of all the men
This wide world holds; O love, my world is you.
Howbeit, to meet you grows almost a pang
Because the pang of parting comes so soon;
My hope hangs waning, waxing, like a moon
Between the heavenly days on which we meet:
Ah me, but where are now the songs I sang
When life was sweet because you called them sweet?

2

"Era già l'ora che volge il desio."—DANTE
"Ricorro al tempo ch' io vi vidi prima."—PETRARCA[3]

I wish I could remember that first day,
First hour, first moment of your meeting me,
If bright or dim the season, it might be
Summer or winter for aught I can say;
So unrecorded did it slip away,
So blind was I to see and to foresee,
So dull to mark the budding of my tree
That would not blossom yet for many a May.
If only I could recollect it, such
A day of days! I let it come and go
As traceless as a thaw of bygone snow;
It seemed to mean so little, meant so much;
If only now I could recall that touch,
First touch of hand in hand—Did one but know!

3

"O ombre vane, fuor che ne l'aspetto!"—DANTE
"Immaginata guida la conduce."—PETRARCA[4]

I dream of you to wake: would that I might
Dream of you and not wake but slumber on;
Nor find with dreams the dear companion gone,
As summer ended summer birds take flight.
In happy dreams I hold you full in sight,
I blush again who waking look so wan;
Brighter than sunniest day that ever shone,
In happy dreams your smile makes day of night.
Thus only in a dream we are at one,
Thus only in a dream we give and take
The faith that maketh rich who take or give;
If thus to sleep is sweeter than to wake,
To die were surely sweeter than to live,
Tho' there be nothing new beneath the sun.

4

"Poca favilla gran fiamma seconda."—DANTE
"Ogni altra cosa, ogni pensier va fore,
E sol ivi con voi rimansi amore."—PETRARCA[5]

I loved you first: but afterwards your love,
Outsoaring mine, sang such a loftier song
As drowned the friendly cooings of my dove.
Which owes the other most? My love was long,

[1] *Great Poetess* Elizabeth Barrett Browning.

[2] DANTE From *Purgatorio* 8.3: "Who in the morn have bid sweet friends farewell"; PETRARCA From *Canzone* 85.12: "Love, with what forces you conquer me now!"

[3] DANTE From *Purgatorio* 8.1: "Now was the hour that wakens fond desire"; PETRARCA From Sonnet 20.3: "I remember when I saw you for the first time."

[4] DANTE From *Purgatorio* 2.79: "Oh vain shadows, except in outward aspect"; PETRARCA From *Canzone* 277.9: "An imagined guide leads her."

[5] DANTE From *Paradiso* 1.34: "From a small spark a great flame rises"; PETRARCA From *Canzone* 72.44–45: "All other hopes, all other thoughts are gone, and love with you remains there alone."

And yours one moment seemed to wax more strong;
I loved and guessed at you, you construed me
And loved me for what might or might not be—
Nay, weights and measures do us both a wrong.
For verily love knows not "mine" or "thine";
With separate "I" and "thou" free love has done,
For one is both and both are one in love:
Rich love knows nought of "thine that is not mine";
Both have the strength and both the length thereof,
Both of us, of the love which makes us one.

5

"Amor che a nullo amato amar perdona."—DANTE
"Amor m'addusse in sì gioiosa spene."—PETRARCA[1]

O my heart's heart, and you who are to me
More than myself myself, God be with you,
Keep you in strong obedience leal° and true *loyal*
To Him whose noble service setteth free;
Give you all good we see or can foresee,
Make your joys many and your sorrows few,
Bless you in what you bear and what you do,
Yea, perfect you as He would have you be.
So much for you; but what for me, dear friend?
To love you without stint and all I can
Today, tomorrow, world without an end;
To love you much and yet to love you more,
As Jordan at his flood sweeps either shore;
Since woman is the helpmeet made for man.

6

"Or puoi la quantitate
Comprender de l'amor che a te mi scalda."—DANTE
"Non vo'che da tal nodo amor mi sciolglia."—PETRARCA[2]

Trust me, I have not earned your dear rebuke,
I love, as you would have me, God the most;
Would lose not Him, but you, must one be lost,
Nor with Lot's wife cast back a faithless look,[3]
Unready to forego what I forsook;
This say I, having counted up the cost,
This, tho' I be the feeblest of God's host,
The sorriest sheep Christ shepherds with His crook.
Yet while I love my God the most, I deem
That I can never love you overmuch;
I love Him more, so let me love you too;
Yea, as I apprehend it, love is such
I cannot love you if I love not Him,
I cannot love Him if I love not you.

7

"Qui primavera sempre ed ogni frutto."—DANTE
"Ragionando con meco ed io con lui."—PETRARCA[4]

"Love me, for I love you"—and answer me,
"Love me, for I love you": so shall we stand
As happy equals in the flowering land
Of love, that knows not a dividing sea.
Love builds the house on rock and not on sand,
Love laughs what while the winds rave desperately;
And who hath found love's citadel unmanned?
And who hath held in bonds love's liberty?—
My heart's a coward tho' my words are brave—
We meet so seldom, yet we surely part
So often; there's a problem for your art!
Still I find comfort in his Book, who saith,
Tho' jealousy be cruel as the grave,
And death be strong, yet love is strong as death.[5]

[1] *DANTE* From *Inferno* 5.103: "Love, that denial takes from none beloved"; *PETRARCA* From Sonnet 56.11: "Love urged me in this gladness to believe."

[2] *DANTE* From *Purgatorio* 21.133–34: "Now has thou proved the force and ardor of the love I bear thee"; *PETRARCA* From *Canzone* 59.17: "I do not wish love to release me from this knot."

[3] *Lot's wife … look* See Genesis 19.26: "[Lot's] wife looked back from behind him, and she became a pillar of salt."

[4] *DANTE* From *Purgatorio* 28.143: "Perpetual spring and every fruit"; *PETRARCA* From *Canzone* 35.14: "Speaking with me and I with him."

[5] *his Book … death* See The Song of Solomon 6: "Set me as a seal upon your heart, as a seal upon your arm; for love is strong as death, passion fierce as the grave."

8

"Come dicesse a Dio, D'altro non calme."—DANTE
"Spero trovar pietà non che perdono."—PETRARCA[1]

"I, if I perish, perish"—Esther spake:[2]
And bride of life or death she made her fair
In all the lustre of her perfumed hair
And smiles that kindle longing but to slake.
She put on pomp of loveliness, to take
Her husband through his eyes at unaware;
She spread abroad her beauty for a snare,
Harmless as doves and subtle as a snake.
She trapped him with one mesh of silken hair,
She vanquished him by wisdom of her wit,
And built her people's house that it should stand:—
If I might take my life so in my hand,
And for my love to Love put up my prayer,
And for love's sake by Love be granted it!

9

"O dignitosa coscienza e netta!"—DANTE
"Spirto più acceso di virtuti ardenti."—PETRARCA[3]

Thinking of you, and all that was, and all
That might have been and now can never be,
I feel your honoured excellence, and see
Myself unworthy of the happier call:
For woe is me who walk so apt to fall,
So apt to shrink afraid, so apt to flee,
Apt to lie down and die (ah woe is me!)
Faithless and hopeless turning to the wall.
And yet not hopeless quite nor faithless quite,
Because not loveless; love may toil all night,
But take at morning; wrestle till the break
Of day, but then wield power with God and man:—
So take I heart of grace as best I can,
Ready to spend and be spent for your sake.

10

"Con miglior corso e con migliore stella."—DANTE
"La vita fugge e non s'arresta un' ora."—PETRARCA[4]

Time flies, hope flags, life plies a wearied wing;
Death following hard on life gains ground apace;
Faith runs with each and rears an eager face,
Outruns the rest, makes light of everything,
Spurns earth, and still finds breath to pray and sing;
While love ahead of all uplifts his praise,
Still asks for grace and still gives thanks for grace,
Content with all day brings and night will bring.
Life wanes; and when love folds his wings above
Tired hope, and less we feel his conscious pulse,
Let us go fall asleep, dear friend, in peace:
A little while, and age and sorrow cease;
A little while, and life reborn annuls
Loss and decay and death, and all is love.

11

"Vien dietro a me e lascia dir le genti."—DANTE
"Contando i casi della vita nostra."—PETRARCA[5]

Many in aftertimes will say of you
"He loved her"—while of me what will they say?
Not that I loved you more than just in play,
For fashion's sake as idle women do.
Even let them prate; who know not what we knew
Of love and parting in exceeding pain,
Of parting hopeless here to meet again,
Hopeless on earth, and heaven is out of view.

[1] *DANTE* From *Purgatorio* 8.12: "As if telling God, 'I care for nothing else'"; *PETRARCA* From *Canzone* 1.8: "I hope to find pity, not just forgiveness."

[2] *I … spake* From Esther 4.16, in which Queen Esther says to Mordecai, before donning beautiful robes and appealing to her husband to cease his mission to kill her people, the Jews: "Go, gather together all the Jews … and neither eat nor drink three days, night or day: I also and my maidens will fast likewise; and so will I go in unto the king, which is not according to the law: and if I perish, I perish."

[3] *DANTE* From *Purgatorio* 3.8: "Oh conscience clear and upright!"; *PETRARCA* From *Canzone* 283.3: "Spirit dazzling with blazing virtues."

[4] *DANTE* From *Paradiso* 1.40: "In best course and in happiest constellation"; *PETRARCA* From *Canzone* 272.1: "Life flies and doesn't stay for an hour."

[5] *DANTE* From *Purgatorio* 5.13: "Come after me, and leave behind the people's babblings"; *PETRARCA* From *Canzone* 285.12: "Telling of the changes in our lives."

But by my heart of love laid bare to you,
My love that you can make not void nor vain,
Love that foregoes you but to claim anew
Beyond this passage of the gate of death,
I charge you at the Judgment make it plain
My love of you was life and not a breath.

12

"Amor, che ne la mente mi ragiona."—DANTE
"Amor vien nel bel viso di costei."—PETRARCA[1]

If there be any one can take my place
And make you happy whom I grieve to grieve,
Think not that I can grudge it, but believe
I do commend you to that nobler grace,
That readier wit than mine, that sweeter face;
Yea, since your riches make me rich, conceive
I too am crowned, while bridal crowns I weave,
And thread the bridal dance with jocund° pace. *merry*
For if I did not love you, it might be
That I should grudge you some one dear delight;
But since the heart is yours that was mine own,
Your pleasure is my pleasure, right my right,
Your honourable freedom makes me free,
And you companioned I am not alone.

13

"E drizzeremo glí occhi al Primo Amore."—DANTE
"Ma trovo peso non de le mie braccia."—PETRARCA[2]

If I could trust mine own self with your fate,
Shall I not rather trust it in God's hand?
Without Whose Will one lily doth not stand,
Nor sparrow fall at His appointed date;
Who numbereth the innumerable sand,
Who weighs the wind and water with a weight,
To Whom the world is neither small nor great,
Whose knowledge foreknew every plan we planned.
Searching my heart for all that touches you,
I find there only love and love's goodwill
Helpless to help and impotent to do,
Of understanding dull, of sight most dim;
And therefore I commend you back to Him
Whose love your love's capacity can fill.

14

"E la Sua Volontade è nostra pace."—DANTE
"Sol con questi pensier, con altre chiome."—PETRARCA[3]

Youth gone, and beauty gone if ever there
Dwelt beauty in so poor a face as this;
Youth gone and beauty, what remains of bliss?
I will not bind fresh roses in my hair,
To shame a cheek at best but little fair,—
Leave youth his roses, who can bear a thorn,—
I will not seek for blossoms anywhere,
Except such common flowers as blow with corn.[4]
Youth gone and beauty gone, what doth remain?
The longing of a heart pent up forlorn,
A silent heart whose silence loves and longs;
The silence of a heart which sang its songs
While youth and beauty made a summer morn,
Silence of love that cannot sing again.
—1881

Cobwebs

It is a land with neither night nor day,
Nor heat nor cold, nor any wind, nor rain,
Nor hills nor valleys; but one even plain
Stretches thro' long unbroken miles away:
While thro' the sluggish air a twilight grey
Broodeth; no moons or seasons wax and wane,
No ebb and flow are there along the main,
No bud-time no leaf-falling there for aye,° *any*
No ripple on the sea, no shifting sand,

[1] *DANTE* From *Purgatorio* 2.112: "Love that discourses in my thoughts"; *PETRARCA* From *Canzone* 13.2: "Love appears in the beautiful face of this lady."

[2] *DANTE* From *Paradiso* 32.142: "And our eyes will turn unto the first Love"; *PETRARCA* From Sonnet 20.5: "The burden I find too great a weight for my arms."

[3] *DANTE* From *Paradiso* 3.85: "And in his will is our tranquility"; *PETRARCA* From *Canzone* 30.32: "Alone with these thoughts, with time-altered locks of hair."

[4] *corn* Grain.

No beat of wings to stir the stagnant space,
No pulse of life thro' all the loveless land:
And loveless sea; no trace of days before,
No guarded home, no toil-won resting place
No future hope no fear for evermore.
—1896 (WRITTEN 1855)

In an Artist's Studio

One face[1] looks out from all his canvasses,
One selfsame figure sits or walks or leans:
We found her hidden just behind those screens,
That mirror gave back all her loveliness.
A queen in opal or in ruby dress,
A nameless girl in freshest summer-greens,
A saint, an angel;—every canvass means
The same one meaning, neither more nor less.
He feeds upon her face by day and night,
And she with true kind eyes looks back on him,
Fair as the moon and joyful as the light:
Not wan with waiting, nor with sorrow dim;
Not as she is, but was when hope shone bright;
Not as she is, but as she fills his dream.
—1896

Dante Gabriel Rossetti's *Beata Beatrix*, 1864–70.

Promises like Pie-Crust[2]

Promise me no promises,
So will I not promise you;
Keep we both our liberties,
Never false and never true:
Let us hold the die uncast,
Free to come as free to go;
For I cannot know your past,
And of mine what can you know?

You, so warm, may once have been
Warmer towards another one;
I, so cold, may once have seen
Sunlight, once have felt the sun:
Who shall show us if it was
Thus indeed in time of old?
Fades the image from the glass
And the fortune is not told.

If you promised, you might grieve
For lost liberty again;
If I promised, I believe
I should fret to break the chain:
Let us be the friends we were,
Nothing more but nothing less;
Many thrive on frugal fare
Who would perish of excess.
—1896 (WRITTEN 1861)

[1] *One face* I.e., Elizabeth (Lizzie) Siddal's. Siddal (1829–62) was D.G. Rossetti's model for *Beata Beatrix* and many other paintings; the two eventually married. She was a poet and artist in her own right.

[2] *Promises like Pie-Crust* See Jonathan Swift's comment: "Promises and pie-crust are made to be broken."

In Progress

Ten years ago it seemed impossible
That she should ever grow so calm as this,
With self-remembrance in her warmest kiss
And dim dried eyes like an exhausted well.
Slow-speaking when she has some fact to tell,
Silent with long-unbroken silences,
Centred in self yet not unpleased to please,
Gravely monotonous like a passing bell.
Mindful of drudging daily common things,
Patient at pastime, patient at her work,
Wearied perhaps but strenuous certainly.
Sometimes I fancy we may one day see
Her head shoot forth seven stars from where they lurk
And her eyes lightnings and her shoulders wings.
—1896

Sleeping at Last

Sleeping at last, the trouble & tumult over,
Sleeping at last, the struggle & horror past,
Cold & white out of sight of friend & of lover
Sleeping at last.

No more a tired heart downcast or overcast,
No more pangs that wring or shifting fears that hover,
Sleeping at last in a dreamless sleep locked fast.

Fast asleep. Singing birds in their leafy cover
Cannot wake her, nor shake her gusty blast.
Under the purple thyme & the purple clover
Sleeping at last.
—1896

Lewis Carroll

1832 – 1898

Charles Dodgson (better known by his pseudonym, "Lewis Carroll") created some of his era's most beloved and enduring literature for children. *Alice's Adventures in Wonderland* and *Through the Looking-Glass* have remained perennially popular since their first publication. His famously frustrated protagonist, who engages in bewildering exchanges with such memorable characters as the Mad Hatter, the Cheshire Cat, the March Hare, and the Mock Turtle, is as familiar a figure as any character in nineteenth-century fiction.

Charles Lutwidge Dodgson was the third of eleven children born to Frances Jane Lutwidge and the Reverend Charles Dodgson, who was a mathematician and later a curate in Daresbury, Cheshire. Because they lived in a remote village, the Dodgson children were largely schooled at home and relied on one another for amusement; Charles contributed many stories and drawings to their various family magazines. He became a fine student when he later entered boarding school, winning many awards and scholarships.

Dodgson continued to excel at Oxford University, where he followed in his father's footsteps and took first place honors in mathematics. He thereafter spent almost his entire life as a lecturer in mathematics at Oxford, where he was given a lifetime fellowship, with the stipulation that he enter the ministry and refrain from marrying. During his early years there, he took up the then-new art of photography as a hobby and devoted himself to taking exquisite photographs—primarily of children, although he later also became known for his portraits of famous literary figures, Alfred, Lord Tennyson and Dante Gabriel Rossetti among them.

Dodgson eventually became acquainted with the family of Henry Liddell, who was then Dean of Christ Church College. As he had done with many other children, Dodgson endeared himself to the three Liddell daughters by weaving elaborate tales for their amusement. On one occasion, Dodgson and a friend took advantage of a beautiful summer's day to go boating down the Thames with the Liddell girls. During the outing Dodgson began making up the story of Alice's adventures underground, wherein Alice goes down a rabbit hole and meets various characters that both fascinate and confound her. He later often looked back upon this day wistfully, as when he wrote of the "birth" of the Alice of his tales: "I can call it up almost as clearly as if it were yesterday—the cloudless blue above, the watery mirror below, the boat drifting idly on its way, the tinkle of the drops that fell from the oars … the three eager faces, hungry for news of fairy-land, and who would not be said 'nay' to: from whose lips 'Tell us a story, please,' had all the stern immutability of Fate!"

After Dodgson had complied with Alice Liddell's request to write up the story for her, Henry Kingsley (brother of novelist Charles Kingsley) saw the manuscript and persuaded him to publish it. Having already published several books on mathematics under his own name, he took the name Lewis, which he anglicized from "Ludovicus," the Latin word for "Lutwidge," and Carroll from "Carolus," Latin for "Charles." *Alice's Adventures in Wonderland* appeared in 1865 with illustrations by *Punch* cartoonist John Tenniel. From that point on, Lewis Carroll's fame far surpassed that of Charles Dodgson. In 1872 he published the sequel *Through the Looking-Glass and What Alice Found There*, which continued the tale of Alice as she passes through a mirror and finds herself engaged as a pawn in a topsy-turvy game of chess.

By the time *Through the Looking-Glass* was published, Dodgson was entirely estranged from the Liddells. The reason for this remains unclear, as the relevant pages were removed from Dodgson's diary; some scholars have since suggested that Carroll was sexually attracted to children and the break occurred as a result of his romantic interest in Alice. Other scholars argue that he had no such interest and offer different explanations for the estrangement, including the possibility that he had been caught in romantic pursuit of the Liddells' governess. The former critics tend to see undertones of sexual desire in Carroll's photographs and literary portrayals of girl children, while the latter tend to interpret the same elements as reflective of typical Victorian aesthetics and attitudes regarding childhood.

Carroll later wrote three books of nonsense poems, including *The Hunting of the Snark* (1876). He also published *Sylvie and Bruno* and *Sylvie and Bruno Concluded* (1889 and 1893), but the novel and its sequel never achieved the fame of the Alice series. The author died of bronchitis in 1898; he is buried in a cemetery near the home he bought for his family in Surrey.

⌘⌘⌘

Verses Recited by Humpty Dumpty[1]

In winter when the fields are white,
I sing this song for your delight.

In spring, when woods are getting green,
I'll try and tell you what I mean.

In summer, when the days are long,
Perhaps you'll understand the song.

In autumn, when the leaves are brown,
Take pen and ink and write it down.

I sent a message to the fish:
I told them "This is what I wish."

The little fishes of the sea,
They sent an answer back to me.

The little fishes' answer was
"We cannot do it, sir, because."

I sent to them again to say
"It will be better to obey."

The fishes answered with a grin,
"Why, what a temper you are in!"

I told them once, I told them twice;
They would not listen to advice.

I took a kettle large and new,
Fit for the deed I had to do.

My heart went hop, my heart went thump;
I filled the kettle at the pump.

Then someone came to me and said,
"The little fishes are in bed."

I said to him, I said it plain,
"Then you must wake them up again."

I said it very loud and clear;
I went and shouted in his ear.

[1] *Verses ... Dumpty* From *Through the Looking-Glass and What Alice Found There*, Ch. 6: "Humpty Dumpty."

But he was very stiff and proud;
He said, "You needn't shout so loud!"

And he was very proud and stiff;
He said, "I'd go and wake them, if ——"

I took a corkscrew from the shelf;
I went to wake them up myself.

And when I found the door was locked,
I pulled and pushed and kicked and knocked.

And when I found the door was shut,
I tried to turn the handle, but ——
("That's all," said Humpty Dumpty.)
—1872

Jabberwocky[1]

'Twas brillig and the slithy toves
Did gyre and gimble in the wabe;
All mimsy were the borogroves,
And the mome raths outgrabe.

"Beware the Jabberwock, my son!
The jaws that bite, the claws that catch!
Beware the Jubjub bird, and shun
The frumious Bandersnatch!"

He took his vorpal sword in hand:
Long time the manxome foe he sought—
So rested he by the Tumtum tree.
And stood awhile in thought.

And as in uffish thought he stood,
The Jabberwock, with eyes of flame,
Came whiffling through the tulgey wood,
And burbled as it came!

John Tenniel, *Slaying the Jabberwock*, from Lewis Carroll, *Through the Looking-Glass*, 1872.

One, two! One, two! And through and through
The vorpal blade went snicker-snack!
He left it dead, and with its head
He went galumphing back.

"And hast thou slain the Jabberwock?
Come to my arms, my beamish boy!
O frabjous day! Callooh! Callay!"
He chortled in his joy.

'Twas brillig and the slithy toves
Did gyre and gimble in the wabe;
All mimsy were the borogroves,
And the mome raths outgrabe.
—1872

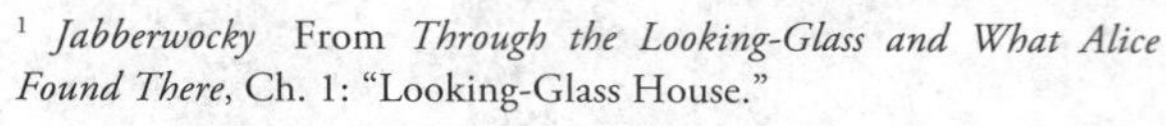

[1] *Jabberwocky* From *Through the Looking-Glass and What Alice Found There*, Ch. 1: "Looking-Glass House."

In Context

"Jabberwocky"

The poem "Jabberwocky" appears in the first chapter of *Through the Looking-Glass and What Alice Found There*. The first of the following excerpts provides the surrounding context in that chapter; the second is an excerpt from later in the book, when the poem is again discussed.

from Lewis Carroll, *Through the Looking-Glass and What Alice Found There* (1872)

from Chapter 1: Looking-Glass House

There was a book lying near Alice on the table, and while she sat watching the White King (for she was still a little anxious about him, and had the ink all ready to throw over him, in case he fainted again), she turned over the leaves, to find some part that she could read, "—for it's all in some language I don't know," she said to herself.

It was like this.

YKCOWREBBAJ

sevot yhtils eht dna ,gillirb sawT'
ebaw eht ni elbmig dna eryg diD
,sevorgorob eht erew ysmim llA
.ebargtuo shtar emom eht dnA

She puzzled over this for some time, but at last a bright thought struck her. "Why, it's a looking-glass book, of course! And if I hold it up to a glass, the words will all go the right way again."

This was the poem that Alice read.

[Here the poem appears.]

"It seems very pretty," she said when she had finished it, "but it's rather hard to understand." (You see she didn't like to confess, even to herself, that she couldn't make it out at all.) "Somehow it seems to fill my head with ideas—only I don't exactly know what they are! However, somebody killed something: that's clear, at any rate—."

from Chapter 6: Humpty Dumpty

"You seem very clever at explaining words, sir," said Alice. "Would you kindly tell me the meaning of the poem called 'Jabberwocky'?"

"Let's hear it," said Humpty Dumpty. "I can explain all the poems that ever were invented—and a good many that haven't been invented just yet."

This sounded very hopeful, so Alice repeated the first verse:

"'Twas brillig, and the slithy toves
Did gyre and gimble in the wabe;
All mimsy were the borogroves,
And the mome raths outgrabe."

"That's enough to begin with," Humpty Dumpty interrupted: "there are plenty of hard words there. '*Brillig*' means four o'clock in the afternoon—the time when you begin *broiling* things for dinner."

"That'll do very well," said Alice: "and '*slithy*'?"

"Well, '*slithy*' means 'lithe and slimy.' 'Lithe' is the same as 'active.' You see it's like a portmanteau[1]—there are two meanings packed up into one word."

"I see it now," Alice remarked thoughtfully: "and what about '*toves*'?"

"Well, '*toves*' are something like badgers—they're something like lizards—and they're something like corkscrews."

"They must be very curious-looking creatures."

"They are that," said Humpty Dumpty: "also they made their nests under sundials—also they live on cheese."

"And what's to '*gyre*' and to '*gimble*'?"

"To '*gyre*' is to go round and round like a gyroscope. To '*gimble*' is to make holes like a gimlet."[2]

"And 'the *wabe*' is the grass plot round a sundial, I suppose?" said Alice, surprised at her own ingenuity.

"Of course it is. It's called '*wabe*,' you know, because it goes a long way before it, and a long way behind it——"

"And a long way beyond it on each side," Alice added.

"Exactly so. Well, then, '*mimsy*' is 'flimsy and miserable' (there's another portmanteau for you). And a '*borogrove*' is a thin, shabby-looking bird with its feathers sticking out all round—something like a live mop."

"And then '*mome raths*'?" said Alice. "If I'm not giving you too much trouble."

"Well, a '*rath*' is a sort of green pig; but '*mome*' I'm not certain about. I think it's short for '*from home*'—meaning that they'd lost their way, you know."

"And what does '*outgrabe*' mean?"

"Well, '*outgribing*' is something between bellowing and whistling, with a kind of sneeze in the middle: however, you'll hear it done, maybe—down in the wood yonder—and when you've once heard it you'll be *quite* content. Who's been repeating all that hard stuff to you?"

"I read it in a book," said Alice.

In Context

The Photographs of Lewis Carroll

Though as a photographer Carroll is best known for his images of children—and of Alice Liddell in particular—he was among the most accomplished of Victorian portrait photographers. Like many photographers of the time, he often portrayed his subjects in dramatic roles.

[1] *portmanteau* Leather carrying case; "portmanteau" has since entered the English language in the sense to which Humpty Dumpty refers, i.e., a blended word.

[2] *gimlet* Small tool used for boring holes.

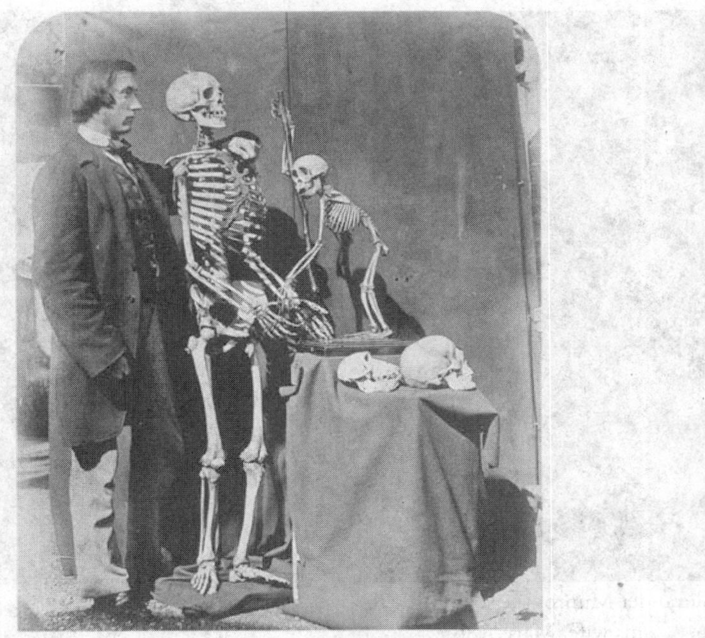

Reginald Southey and Skeletons, 1857.

Alice, Lorina, Harry, and Edith Liddell, 1860.

Alice Liddell as "The Beggar Maid," 1858.

Alexander Munro, the sculptor with his wife, Mary, 1863.

George MacDonald and his daughter Lily, 1863.

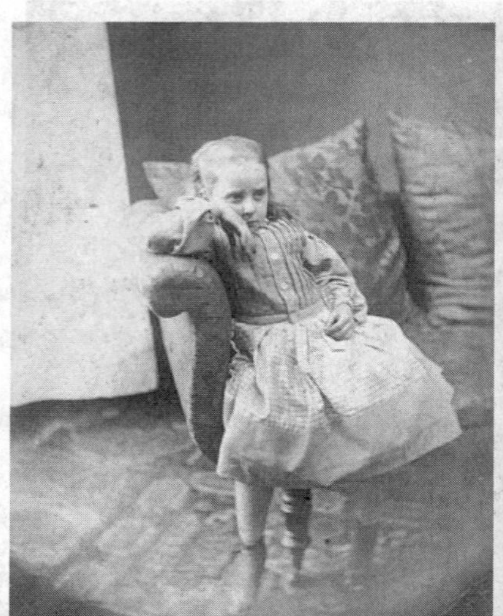

Ella Chlora Monier-Williams, 1866.

Andromeda, 1865.

Captive Princess, 1875.

Algernon Charles Swinburne

1837 – 1909

Victorian poet and critic Algernon Swinburne was physically slight, but he had a powerful personality, and he left behind a vast literary output. Much of his writing, however, on topics such as incest, cannibalism, sadomasochism, and necrophilia, was too outrageous for "respectable" Victorian tastes. Although he was born into a distinguished family of British aristocracy, Swinburne's opinions on politics, religion, and sexuality were offensive enough to have earned him the nickname "Swineborn" in *Punch* magazine. Swinburne's poetry, however, was also metrically innovative, musical, and often erudite. Oscar Wilde claimed him as his literary master but said of Swinburne's writing, "Words seem to dominate him. Alliteration tyrannizes over him. Mere sound often becomes his lord. He is so eloquent that whatever he touches becomes unreal." This "diffuseness" was, according to T.S. Eliot, one of his "glories." Although few have disputed the musicality of Swinburne's poetry, some critics have accused him of being vague and soporific.

Algernon Swinburne was born in 1837 into a highly respectable aristocratic family. His father, Admiral Charles Henry Swinburne, was the son of a baronet, and his mother, Lady Jane, was the daughter of an earl. Raised a devout Anglo-Catholic, Swinburne read profusely and acquired an intimate knowledge of the Bible, as well as a proficiency in French and Italian. His early years at Eton, however, were troubled ones; as a result of disciplinary problems, he was removed from the school before he graduated. After private tutoring, he entered Balliol College at Oxford in 1856. During his first two years there, Swinburne excelled in the Classics and won a scholarship for French and Italian, but his unruliness got the better of him again, and he was forced to leave Balliol without a degree. He nevertheless made many important friends at Oxford, including Benjamin Jowett (then master of Balliol) and the Pre-Raphaelites Edward Burne-Jones, William Morris, and Dante Gabriel Rossetti (with whom he lived in London after Rossetti's wife, Elizabeth Siddal, died).

In London during the 1860s, Swinburne gained notoriety for his wild, drunken revelries and experiments with flagellation, as much as for the publication of two important works, *Atalanta in Calydon* (1865) and *Poems and Ballads* (1866). The classical Greek tragic form of the verse-play *Atalanta* and its concentration on fate and divine intervention belied the long poem's modern revolt against religious institutions and its sympathy, instead, with the "holy spirit of man." While Victorians might have been expected to rail against Swinburne's chastisement of religious orthodoxy, the lyrical and mellifluous tragedy held many in its sway, and won accolades from reviewers. John Ruskin said that it was the "grandest thing ever done by a youth—though he is a Demoniac youth," and Tennyson wrote to Swinburne praising the metrical creativity of *Atalanta.*

Poems and Ballads, on the other hand, had the public (Ruskin included) up in arms. In such poems as "The Triumph of Time," "Dolores," "The Leper," "Hymn to Prosperine," and "Laus

Veneris," Swinburne explored themes of sexual perversion, paganism, and moral and spiritual decay. One reviewer said the author was an "unclean, fiery imp from the pit," while another, referring to Swinburne's association with the Aesthetes, called him the "libidinous laureate of a pack of satyrs." Amid this outcry, the publishing house withdrew the book from publication, angering Swinburne and prompting his eloquent riposte in *Notes on Poems and Reviews*. *Poems and Ballads* was re-released shortly afterward by another publisher.

Swinburne's notoriety continued into the late 1860s and 1870s, as he cultivated his image as a "scandalous poet," to use his own words. He wrote at a feverish rate—even though his alcoholism was by then prompting seizures and blackouts—and produced such works as *A Song of Italy* (1867), a defense of Italian liberation; *Ave Atque Vale* (1868), an elegy to Baudelaire; the brilliant essay *William Blake* (1868); and *Songs Before Sunrise* (1871), which continued the theme of spiritual and political revolution. By the end of the 1870s, however, Swinburne was near death, his nerves destroyed by alcohol, and his body depleted from overwork. Luckily, in 1879, his friend Theodore Watts-Dunton took him to his house in Putney and helped nurse him back to health. There Swinburne lived in quiet solitude for the remaining 30 years of his life, writing and publishing prolifically, and finally succumbing to pneumonia in 1909.

In those final decades, Swinburne won the respect of many Victorians. Although the *Guardian* noted upon his death that his verse could be "careless, trivial, or inharmonious," the newspaper also acknowledged that "the greatest poet lately living is dead … and we cannot doubt that much of his poetry will live by virtue of its exquisite music."

⌘⌘⌘

Hymn to Proserpine[1]

(*After the Proclamation in Rome of the Christian Faith*[2])

Vicisti, Galilæ[3]

I have lived long enough, having seen one thing, that love hath an end;
Goddess and maiden and queen, be near me now and befriend.
Thou art more than the day or the morrow, the seasons that laugh or that weep;
For these give joy and sorrow; but thou, Proserpina, sleep.
Sweet is the treading of wine, and sweet the feet of the dove;
But a goodlier gift is thine than foam of the grapes or love.
Yea, is not even Apollo,[4] with hair and harpstring of gold,
A bitter God to follow, a beautiful God to behold?
I am sick of singing: the bays burn deep and chafe: I am fain
To rest a little from praise and grievous pleasure and pain.
For the Gods we know not of, who give us our daily breath,
We know they are cruel as love or life, and lovely as death.

[1] *Proserpine* In Roman mythology, daughter of Jupiter and Ceres and wife of Pluto, King of the underworld, who stole her from her mother.

[2] *Proclamation … Faith* Roman Emperor Constantine the Great legalized the Christian faith when he proclaimed the Edict of Milan in 313 CE.

[3] *Vicisti, Galilæ* Latin: "Thou hast conquered, Galilee," said to be the dying words in 363 of Julian the Apostate, half-brother of Constantine the Great. Julian eventually became emperor after the deaths of Constantine I and II; he was a pagan who opposed instituting Christianity as the state religion (as it was eventually proclaimed by Emperor Theodosius in 380).

[4] *Apollo* Greek sun god; also god of the arts.

O Gods dethroned and deceased, cast forth, wiped out in a day!
From your wrath is the world released, redeemed from your chains, men say.
New Gods are crowned in the city; their flowers have broken your rods;
They are merciful, clothed with pity, the young compassionate Gods.
But for me their new device is barren, the days are bare;
Things long past over suffice, and men forgotten that were.
Time and the Gods are at strife; ye dwell in the midst thereof,
Draining a little life from the barren breasts of love.
I say to you, cease, take rest; yea, I say to you all, be at peace,
Till the bitter milk of her breast and the barren bosom shall cease.
Wilt thou yet take all, Galilean? but these thou shalt not take,
The laurel, the palms and the pæan,[1] the breast of the nymphs in the brake;[2]
Breasts more soft than a dove's that tremble with tenderer breath;
And all the wings of the Loves,[3] and all the joy before death;
All the feet of the hours that sound as a single lyre,
Dropped and deep in the flowers, with strings that flicker like fire.
More than these wilt thou give, things fairer than all these things?
Nay, for a little we live, and life hath mutable wings.
A little while and we die; shall life not thrive as it may?
For no man under the sky lives twice, outliving his day.
And grief is a grievous thing, and a man hath enough of his tears:
Why should he labour, and bring fresh grief to blacken his years?
Thou hast conquered, O pale Galilean; the world has grown grey from thy breath;
We have drunken of things Lethean,[4] and fed on the fullness of death.
Laurel is green for a season, and love is sweet for a day;
But love grows bitter with treason, and laurel outlives not May.
Sleep, shall we sleep after all? for the world is not sweet in the end;
For the old faiths loosen and fall, the new years ruin and rend.
Fate is a sea without shore, and the soul is a rock that abides;
But her ears are vexed with the roar and her face with the foam of the tides.
O lips that the live blood faints in, the leavings of racks and rods!
O ghastly glories of saints, dead limbs of gibbeted Gods!
Though all men abase them before you in spirit, and all knees bend,
I kneel not neither adore you, but standing, look to the end.
All delicate days and pleasant, all spirits and sorrows are cast
Far out with the foam of the present that sweeps to the surf of the past:
Where beyond the extreme sea-wall, and between the remote sea-gates,
Waste water washes, and tall ships founder, and deep death waits:
Where, mighty with deepening sides, clad about with the seas as with wings,
And impelled of invisible tides, and fulfilled of unspeakable things,
White-eyed and poisonous-finned, shark-toothed and serpentine-curled,
Rolls, under the whitening wind of the future, the wave of the world.

[1] *pæan* Hymn of praise.

[2] *brake* Ferns.

[3] *Loves* Cupids or other gods representing sexual love.

[4] *Lethean* Of the Greek mythological river Lethe in Hades (the underworld), the waters of which cause the dead to forget the past; also called the "River of Oblivion."

The depths stand naked in sunder behind it, the storms flee away;
In the hollow before it the thunder is taken and snared as a prey;
In its sides is the north-wind bound; and its salt is of all men's tears;
With light of ruin, and sound of changes, and pulse of years:
With travail of day after day, and with trouble of hour upon hour;
And bitter as blood is the spray; and the crests are as fangs that devour:
And its vapour and storm of its steam as the sighing of spirits to be;
And its noise as the noise in a dream; and its depth as the roots of the sea:
And the height of its heads as the height of the utmost stars of the air:
And the ends of the earth at the might thereof tremble, and time is made bare.
Will ye bridle the deep sea with reins, will ye chasten the high sea with rods?
Will ye take her to chain her with chains, who is older than all ye Gods?
All ye as a wind shall go by, as a fire shall ye pass and be past;
Ye are Gods, and behold, ye shall die, and the waves be upon you at last.
In the darkness of time, in the deeps of the years, in the changes of things,
Ye shall sleep as a slain man sleeps, and the world shall forget you for kings.
Though the feet of thine high priests tread where thy lords and our forefathers trod,
Though these that were Gods are dead, and thou being dead art a God,
Though before thee the throned Cytherean[1] be fallen, and hidden her head,
Yet thy kingdom shall pass, Galilean, thy dead shall go down to thee dead.
Of the maiden thy mother men sing as a goddess with grace clad around;
Thou art throned where another was king; where another was queen she is crowned.
Yea, once we had sight of another: but now she is queen, say these.
Not as thine, not as thine was our mother, a blossom of flowering seas,
Clothed round with the world's desire as with raiment, and fair as the foam,
And fleeter than kindled fire, and a goddess, and mother of Rome.
For thine came pale and a maiden, and sister to sorrow; but ours,
Her deep hair heavily laden with odour and colour of flowers,
White rose of the rose-white water, a silver splendour, a flame,
Bent down unto us that besought her, and earth grew sweet with her name.
For thine came weeping, a slave among slaves, and rejected; but she
Came flushed from the full-flushed wave, and imperial, her foot on the sea.
And the wonderful waters knew her, the winds and the viewless ways,
And the roses grew rosier, and bluer the sea-blue stream of the bays.
Ye are fallen, our lords, by what token? we wist[2] that ye should not fall.
Ye were all so fair that are broken; and one more fair than ye all.
But I turn to her still, having seen she shall surely abide in the end;
Goddess and maiden and queen, be near me now and befriend.
O daughter of earth, of my mother, her crown and blossom of birth,
I am also, I also, thy brother; I go as I came unto earth.

---

[1] *throned Cytherean* Venus, Roman goddess of love and beauty (Aphrodite in Greek mythology), who was born of the foam of the sea and, according to some accounts, came ashore on the Greek island of Cythera.

[2] *wist* Know.

In the night where thine eyes are as moons are in heaven, the night where thou art,
Where the silence is more than all tunes, where sleep overflows from the heart,
Where the poppies[1] are sweet as the rose in our world, and the red rose is white,
And the wind falls faint as it blows with the fume of the flowers of the night.
And the murmur of spirits that sleep in the shadow of Gods from afar
Grows dim in thine ears and deep as the deep dim soul of a star,
In the sweet low light of thy face, under heavens untrod by the sun,
Let my soul with their souls find place, and forget what is done and undone.
Thou art more than the Gods who number the days of our temporal breath;
For these give labour and slumber; but thou, Proserpina, death.
Therefore now at thy feet I abide for a season in silence. I know
I shall die as my fathers died, and sleep as they sleep; even so.
For the glass of the years is brittle wherein we gaze for a span;
A little soul for a little bears up this corpse which is man.[2]
So long I endure, no longer; and laugh not again, neither weep.
For there is no God found stronger than death; and death is a sleep.
—1866

A Forsaken Garden

In a coign° of the cliff between lowland and highland, *wedge*
At the sea-down's edge between windward and lee,
Walled round with rocks as an inland island,
The ghost of a garden fronts the sea.
A girdle of brushwood and thorn encloses
The steep square slope of the blossomless bed
Where the weeds that grew green from the graves of its roses
Now lie dead.

The fields fall southward, abrupt and broken,
To the low last edge of the long lone land.
If a step should sound or a word be spoken,
Would a ghost not rise at the strange guest's hand?
So long have the grey bare walks lain guestless,
Through branches and briars if a man make way,
He shall find no life but the sea-wind's, restless
Night and day.

The dense hard passage is blind and stifled
That crawls by a track none turn to climb
To the strait° waste place that the years have rifled *narrow*
Of all but the thorns that are touched not of time.
The thorns he spares when the rose is taken;
The rocks are left when he wastes the plain.
The wind that wanders, the weeds wind-shaken,
These remain.

Not a flower to be pressed of the foot that falls not;
As the heart of a dead man the seed-lots are dry;
From the thicket of thorns whence the nightingale calls not,
Could she call, there were never a rose to reply.
Over the meadows that blossom and wither
Rings but the note of a sea-bird's song;
Only the sun and the rain come hither
All year long.

[1] *poppies* Flowers representing sleep, sacred to Proserpine.

[2] [Swinburne's note] ψμχάρτον εἶ βαστάζον νεκρόν.—Epictetus [Greek: You are a little soul, carrying around a corpse.]

The sun burns sere and the rain dishevels
    One gaunt bleak blossom of scentless breath.
Only the wind here hovers and revels
    In a round where life seems barren as death.
Here there was laughing of old, there was weeping,
    Haply, of lovers none ever will know,
Whose eyes went seaward a hundred sleeping
    Years ago.

Heart handfast in heart as they stood, "Look thither,"
    Did he whisper? "look forth from the flowers to the sea;
For the foam-flowers endure when the rose-blossoms wither,
    And men that love lightly may die—but we?"
And the same wind sang and the same waves whitened,
    And or ever the garden's last petals were shed,
In the lips that had whispered, the eyes that had lightened,
    Love was dead.

Or they loved their life through, and then went whither?
    And were one to the end—but what end who knows?
Love deep as the sea as a rose must wither,
    As the rose-red seaweed that mocks the rose.
Shall the dead take thought for the dead to love them?
    What love was ever as deep as a grave?
They are loveless now as the grass above them
    Or the wave.

All are at one now, roses and lovers,
    Not known of the cliffs and the fields and the sea.
Not a breath of the time that has been hovers
    In the air now soft with a summer to be.
Not a breath shall there sweeten the seasons hereafter
    Of the flowers or the lovers that laugh now or weep,
When as they that are free now of weeping and laughter
    We shall sleep.

Here death may deal not again forever;
    Here change may come not till all change end.
From the graves they have made they shall rise up never,
    Who have left nought living to ravage and rend.
Earth, stones, and thorns of the wild ground growing,
    While the sun and the rain live, these shall be;
Till a last wind's breath upon all these blowing
    Roll the sea.

Till the slow sea rise and the sheer cliff crumble,
    Till terrace and meadow the deep gulfs drink,
Till the strength of the waves of the high tides humble
    The fields that lessen, the rocks that shrink,
Here now in his triumph where all things falter,
    Stretched out on the spoils that his own hand spread,
As a god self-slain on his own strange altar,
    Death lies dead.
—1876

Walter Pater

1839 – 1894

Known as the leader of the nineteenth-century Aesthetic Movement, the unassuming and reserved critic and theorist Walter Pater was somewhat surprised at the influence his writings commanded because of their advocacy of "art for art's sake." (The phrase *"l'art pour l'art"* was first coined in 1818 by the French philosopher Victor Cousins, who in turn based his theory on Kantian notions of art and beauty.) In the famous conclusion to his collection of essays, *Studies in the History of the Renaissance* (1873), Pater repeated in altered form words he had written in 1868 in his essay "Poems by William Morris" (1868):

> What we have to do is to be for ever curiously testing new opinions and courting new impressions, never acquiescing in a facile orthodoxy of Comte or Hegel, or of our own.… Great passions may give us this quickened sense of life, ecstasy and sorrow of love, the various forms of enthusiastic activity, disinterested or otherwise, which come naturally to many of us. Only be sure it is passion—that it does yield you this fruit of a quickened, multiplied consciousness. Of such wisdom, the poetic passion, the desire of beauty, the love of art for its sake, has most. For art comes to you proposing frankly to give nothing but the highest quality to your moments as they pass, and simply for those moments' sake.

Without specifically advocating hedonism, Pater was reacting against the prevailing moral aesthetic (articulated compellingly by Carlyle, Ruskin, and Arnold) that charged the artist with ethical responsibilities. The response was in some quarters embarrassingly positive; so influential was this essay upon such "decadents" of the 1890s as Oscar Wilde that Pater withdrew the controversial conclusion from the book's second printing. He allowed it to be reprinted in subsequent editions, while making slight alterations "which," he claimed, "bring it closer to my original meaning."

The events of Walter Horatio Pater's early life did not give any indication of the effect his work would eventually have upon Victorian aesthetics. Born in London, Pater lost his father, Dr. Richard Glode Pater, at a young age, and moved with his siblings and mother, Maria Hill Pater, to Enfield. At the age of 13, the year before his mother died, Pater entered the King's School in Canterbury and five years later entered Queen's College, Oxford, where, to his disappointment, he graduated in 1862 with only second class honors. After tutoring for two years (Gerard Manley Hopkins was among his students), Pater became a fellow at Brasenose College. He remained a teacher at Oxford for most of his life. Soon after his appointment, Pater began publishing critical essays, beginning with "Coleridge's Writings," in which he spoke of abandoning his faith in the High Church for the "religion of art." Previously influenced by Ruskin's *Modern Painters,* Pater began to rethink his notions of beauty upon reading about the classical scholar Johann Winckelmann (1717–68), in whose life he saw a model for an ideal critic's dedication to the aesthetic. He set out these thoughts in his essay "Winckelmann," published in the *Westminster Review* in 1867. This essay was a key moment not only in the development of Pater's thought but also in his career; the essay so impressed the editor of the *Fortnightly Review* that it initiated a decades-long relationship between Pater and the magazine.

In 1873, the essay on Winckelmann and essays on Botticelli, Michelangelo, Leonardo da Vinci, and others, were collected in *The Renaissance*. Pater's preface and conclusion attracted much attention, setting out as they did his Epicurean theories. The "Preface" defines the work of the aesthetic critic:

> The aesthetic critic … regards all objects with which he has to do, all works of art, and the fairer forms of nature and human life, as powers or forces producing pleasurable sensations, each of a more or less peculiar or unique kind .… What is important … is not that the critic should possess a correct abstract definition of beauty for the intellect, but a certain kind of temperament, the power of being deeply moved by the presence of beautiful objects. To him all periods, types, schools of taste, are in themselves equal.

For many, Pater's subjective vision of art, literature, and music—and indeed of one's responsibility to enjoy life—appeared self-indulgent and even amoral. The book, however, with its rich and eloquent prose style, established him as an important critic and placed him at the center of a school of aesthetes that included Wilde, Algernon Swinburne, Katharine Bradley, and Edith Cooper.

Possibly as a result of the controversy over *The Renaissance*, Pater was passed over for a proctorship at Oxford, and thereafter, although his lectures were popular, he was never considered for important positions at the university. He did, however, continue to publish articles and reviews, and worked on a novel, *Marius the Epicurean* (1885), which brought together his philosophies on art and religion, expanding in fictional form the ideas from the "Conclusion" to his first book. In 1887 he published *Imaginary Portraits*, a series of essays on intellectually and artistically rebellious people; in 1889 *Appreciations: With an Essay on Style*; and in 1893 a group of lectures, *Plato and Platonism*. His literary style was so meticulous and eloquent that decades after his death in 1894, Yeats reprinted Pater's description of the *Mona Lisa* in verse form as the opening piece in the *Oxford Book of Modern Verse* (1936). This style, along with his theories of aesthetics, influenced not only Yeats but many modernists, most notably Virginia Woolf and Ezra Pound.

Pater died suddenly of rheumatic fever, at Oxford, on 30 July 1894, at the age of 54. He is buried at Oxford's Holywell Cemetery.

⌘⌘⌘

from *The Renaissance: Studies in Art and Poetry*

Preface

Many attempts have been made by writers on art and poetry to define beauty in the abstract, to express it in the most general terms, to find a universal formula for it. The value of these attempts has most often been in the suggestive and penetrating things said by the way. Such discussions help us very little to enjoy what has been well done in art or poetry, to discriminate between what is more and what is less excellent in them, or to use words like beauty, excellence, art, poetry, with a more precise meaning than they would otherwise have. Beauty, like all other qualities presented to human experience, is relative; and the definition of it becomes unmeaning and useless in proportion to its abstractness. To define beauty, not in the most abstract, but in the most concrete terms possible, to find, not a universal formula for it, but the formula which expresses most adequately this or that special manifestation of it, is the aim of the true student of aesthetics.

"To see the object as in itself it really is,"[1] has been justly said to be the aim of all true criticism whatever; and in aesthetic criticism the first step towards seeing one's object as it really is, is to know one's own impression as it really is, to discriminate it, to realize it distinctly. The objects with which aesthetic criticism deals—music, poetry, artistic and accomplished forms of human life—are indeed receptacles of so many powers or forces; they possess, like the products of nature, so many virtues or qualities. What is this song or picture, this engaging personality presented in life or in a book, to *me*? What effect does it really produce on me? Does it give me pleasure? and if so, what sort or degree of pleasure?

How is my nature modified by its presence, and under its influence? The answers to these questions are the original facts with which the aesthetic critic has to do; and, as in the study of light, of morals, of number, one must realise such primary data for oneself, or not at all. And he who experiences these impressions strongly, and drives directly at the discrimination and analysis of them, has no need to trouble himself with the abstract question what beauty is in itself, or what its exact relation to truth or experience—metaphysical questions, as unprofitable as metaphysical questions elsewhere. He may pass them all by as being, answerable or not, of no interest to him.

The aesthetic critic, then, regards all the objects with which he has to do, all works of art, and the fairer forms of nature and human life, as powers or forces producing pleasurable sensations, each of a more or less peculiar and unique kind. This influence he feels, and wishes to explain, analyzing it, and reducing it to its elements. To him, the picture, the landscape, the engaging personality in life or in a book, *La Gioconda*, the hills of Carrara, Pico of Mirandola,[2] are valuable for their virtues, as we say, in speaking of a herb, a wine, a gem, for the property each has of affecting one with a special, a unique, impression of pleasure. Our education becomes complete in proportion as our susceptibility to these impressions increases in depth and variety. And the function of the aesthetic critic is to distinguish, analyze, and separate from its adjuncts, the virtue by which a picture, a landscape, a fair personality in life or in a book, produces this special impression of beauty or pleasure, to indicate what the source of that impression is, and under what conditions it is experienced. His end is reached when he has disengaged that virtue, and noted it, as a chemist notes some natural element, for himself and others; and the rule for those who would reach this end is stated with great exactness in the words of a recent critic of Sainte-Beuve: *De se borner à connaître de près les belles choses, et à s'en nourrir en exquis amateurs, en humanistes accomplis.*[3]

What is important, then, is not that the critic should possess a correct abstract definition of beauty for the intellect, but a certain kind of temperament, the power of being deeply moved by the presence of beautiful objects. He will remember always that beauty exists in many forms. To him all periods, types, schools of taste, are in themselves equal. In all ages there have been some excellent workmen, and some excellent work done. The question he asks is always: In whom did the stir, the genius, the sentiment of the period find itself? where was the receptacle of its refinement, its elevation, its taste? "The ages are all equal," says William Blake, "but genius is always above its age."[4]

Often it will require great nicety to disengage this virtue from the commoner elements with which it may be found in combination. Few artists, not Goethe or

---

[1] *To see … really is* From Matthew Arnold's *The Function of Criticism at the Present Time* (1865).

[2] *La Gioconda* The painting the *Mona Lisa* (1506) by Leonardo da Vinci, the subject of chapter six of Pater's *The Renaissance*; *Carrara* Region in Italy, center of the marble industry; *Pico of Mirandola* Italian Neoplatonist philosopher (1463–94), the subject of chapter two of *The Renaissance*.

[3] *De se borner … accomplis* Quotation by French literary critic Charles Augustin Saint-Beuve (1804–69): "To restrict themselves with knowing beautiful things thoroughly and to nourish themselves by these, as do perceptive amateurs and accomplished humanists."

[4] *The ages … age* From Blake's annotations to *The Works of Sir Joshua Reynolds* (1798).

Byron[1] even, work quite cleanly, casting off all *débris*, and leaving us only what the heat of their imagination has wholly fused and transformed. Take, for instance, the writings of Wordsworth. The heat of his genius, entering into the substance of his work, has crystallised a part, but only a part, of it; and in that great mass of verse there is much which might well be forgotten. But scattered up and down it, sometimes fusing and transforming entire compositions, like the *Stanzas on Resolution and Independence*, and the *Ode on the Recollections of Childhood*,[2] sometimes, as if at random, depositing a fine crystal here or there, in a matter it does not wholly search through and transform, we trace the action of his unique, incommunicable faculty, that strange, mystical sense of a life in natural things, and of man's life as a part of nature, drawing strength and colour and character from local influences, from the hills and streams, and from natural sights and sounds. Well! that is the *virtue*, the active principle in Wordsworth's poetry; and then the function of the critic of Wordsworth is to follow up that active principle, to disengage it, to mark the degree in which it penetrates his verse.

The subjects of the following studies are taken from the history of the *Renaissance*, and touch what I think the chief points in that complex, many-sided movement. I have explained in the first of them what I understand by the word, giving it a much wider scope than was intended by those who originally used it to denote only that revival of classical antiquity in the fifteenth century which was but one of many results of a general excitement and enlightening of the human mind, of which the great aim and achievements of what, as Christian art, is often falsely opposed to the Renaissance, were another result. This outbreak of the human spirit may be traced far into the middle age itself, with its qualities already clearly pronounced, the care for physical beauty, the worship of the body, the breaking down of those limits which the religious system of the middle age imposed on the heart and the imagination. I have taken as an example of this movement, this earlier Renaissance within the middle age itself, and as an expression of its qualities, two little compositions in early French, not because they constitute the best possible expression of them, but because they help the unity of my series, inasmuch as the Renaissance ends also in France, in French poetry, in a phase of which the writings of Joachim du Bellay[3] are in many ways the most perfect illustration; the Renaissance thus putting forth in France an aftermath, a wonderful later growth, the products of which have to the full that subtle and delicate sweetness which belongs to a refined and comely decadence; just as its earliest phases have the freshness which belongs to all periods of growth in art, the charm of *ascêsis*,[4] of the austere and serious girding of the loins in youth.

But it is in Italy, in the fifteenth century, that the interest of the Renaissance mainly lies—in that solemn fifteenth century which can hardly be studied too much, not merely for its positive results in the things of the intellect and the imagination, its concrete works of art, its special and prominent personalities, with their profound aesthetic charm, but for its general spirit and character, for the ethical qualities of which it is a consummate type.

The various forms of intellectual activity which together make up the culture of an age, move for the most part from different starting points, and by unconnected roads. As products of the same generation they partake indeed of a common character, and unconsciously illustrate each other; but of the producers themselves, each group is solitary, gaining what advantage or disadvantage there may be in intellectual isolation. Art and poetry, philosophy and the religious life, and that other life of refined pleasure and action in the open places of the world, are each of them confined to its own circle of ideas, and those who prosecute either of

[1] *Goethe* Johann Wolfgang von Goethe (1749– 1832), German novelist, playwright, and natural philosopher; *Byron* George Gordon, Lord Byron (1788–1824), English Romantic poet.

[2] *Stanzas … Childhood* Two poems by Wordsworth. The exact titles are "Resolution and Independence" (1807) and "Ode: Intimations of Immortality from Recollections of Early Childhood" (1803–06).

[3] *Joachim du Bellay* French poet (c. 1522–60) and subject of chapter eight of *The Renaissance*.

[4] *ascêsis* Asceticism; defined by Pater in his essay "Style" (1888) as "Self-restraint, a skillful economy of means."

them are generally little curious of the thoughts of others. There come, however, from time to time, eras of more favorable conditions, in which the thoughts of men draw nearer together than is their wont, and the many interests of the intellectual world combine in one complete type of general culture. The fifteenth century in Italy is one of these happier eras; and what is sometimes said of the age of Pericles is true of that of Lorenzo:[1] it is an age productive in personalities, many-sided, centralised, complete. Here, artists and philosophers and those whom the action of the world has elevated and made keen, do not live in isolation, but breathe a common air, and catch light and heat from each other's thoughts. There is a spirit of general elevation and enlightenment in which all alike communicate. It is the unity of this spirit which gives unity to all the various products of the Renaissance; and it is to this intimate alliance with mind, this participation in the best thoughts which that age produced, that the art of Italy in the fifteenth century owes much of its grave dignity and influence.

I have added an essay on Winckelmann,[2] as not incongruous with the studies which precede it, because Winckelmann, coming in the eighteenth century, really belongs in spirit to an earlier age. By his enthusiasm for things of the intellect and the imagination for their own sake, by his Hellenism, his lifelong struggle to attain to the Greek spirit, he is in sympathy with the humanists of an earlier century. He is the last fruit of the Renaissance, and explains in a striking way its motive and tendencies.

—1873

[1] *Pericles* Athenian political leader and great patron of the arts of the fifth century BCE; *Lorenzo* Lorenzo de Medici, an Italian prince and art patron of the fifteenth century CE.

[2] *Winckelmann* Johann Joachim Winckelmann (1717–68), German classical scholar and art historian, the subject of chapter 9 of *The Renaissance.*

CONCLUSION[3]

Λέγει που Ἡράκλειτος ὅτι πάντα χωρεῖ
καὶ οὐδὲν μένει.[4]

To regard all things and principles of things as inconstant modes or fashions has more and more become the tendency of modern thought. Let us begin with that which is without—our physical life. Fix upon it in one of its more exquisite intervals, the moment, for instance, of delicious recoil from the flood of water in summer heat. What is the whole physical life in that moment but a combination of natural elements to which science gives their names? But these elements, phosphorus and lime and delicate fibres, are present not in the human body alone; we detect them in places most remote from it. Our physical life is a perpetual motion of them—the passage of the blood, the wasting and repairing of the lenses of the eye, the modification of the tissues of the brain by every ray of light and sound—processes which science reduces to simpler and more elementary forces. Like the elements of which we are composed, the action of these forces extends beyond us; it rusts iron and ripens corn. Far out on every side of us those elements are broadcast, driven by many forces; and birth and gesture and death and the springing of violets from the grave[5] are but a few out of ten thousand resultant combinations. That clear, perpetual outline of face and limb is but an image of ours, under which we group

[3] [Pater's note] This brief "Conclusion" was omitted in the second edition of this book, as I conceived it might possibly mislead some of those young men into whose hands it might fall. On the whole, I have thought it best to reprint it here, with some slight changes which bring it closer to my original meaning. I have dealt more fully in *Marius the Epicurean* with the thoughts suggested by it.

[4] *Λέγει … μένει* Greek (Pater's translation): "Heracleitus says, 'All things give way; nothing remains!'" From Plato's *Cratylus* (360 BCE). Heracleitus (c. 500 BCE), Greek philosopher.

[5] *birth … grave* Cf. Shakespeare's *Hamlet* 5.1.238–40: "Lay her i' the earth: / And from her fair and unpolluted flesh / May violets spring!"

them—a design in a web, the actual threads of which pass out beyond it. This at least of flame-like our life has, that it is but the concurrence, renewed from moment to moment, of forces parting sooner or later on their ways.

Or if we begin with the inward world of thought and feeling, the whirlpool is still more rapid, the flame more eager and devouring. There it is no longer the gradual darkening of the eye and fading of colour from the wall—the movement of the shoreside, where the water flows down indeed, though in apparent rest—but the race of the midstream, a drift of momentary acts of sight and passion and thought. At first sight experience seems to bury us under a flood of external objects, pressing upon us with a sharp and importunate reality, calling us out of ourselves in a thousand forms of action. But when reflexion begins to act upon those objects they are dissipated under its influence; the cohesive force seems suspended like a trick of magic; each object is loosed into a group of impressions—colour, odour, texture—in the mind of the observer. And if we continue to dwell in thought on this world, not of objects in the solidity with which language invests them, but of impressions unstable, flickering, inconsistent, which burn and are extinguished with our consciousness of them, it contracts still further; the whole scope of observation is dwarfed to the narrow chamber of the individual mind. Experience, already reduced to a swarm of impressions, is ringed round for each one of us by that thick wall of personality through which no real voice has ever pierced on its way to us, or from us to that which we can only conjecture to be without. Every one of those impressions is the impression of the individual in his isolation, each mind keeping as a solitary prisoner its own dream of a world. Analysis goes a step farther still, and assures us that those impressions of the individual mind to which, for each one of us, experience dwindles down, are in perpetual flight; that each of them is limited by time, and that as time is infinitely divisible, each of them is infinitely divisible also; all that is actual in it being a single moment, gone while we try to apprehend it, of which it may ever be more truly said that it has ceased to be than that it is. To such a tremulous wisp constantly reforming itself on the stream, to a single sharp impression, with a sense in it, a relic more or less fleeting, of such moments gone by, what is real in our life fines itself down. It is with this movement, with the passage and dissolution of impressions, images, sensations, that analysis leaves off—that continual vanishing away, that strange, perpetual weaving and unweaving of ourselves.

Philosophiren, says Novalis, *ist dephlegmatisiren vivificiren.*[1] The service of philosophy, of speculative culture, towards the human spirit is to rouse, to startle it into sharp and eager observation. Every moment some form grows perfect in hand or face; some tone on the hills or the sea is choicer than the rest; some mood of passion or insight or intellectual excitement is irresistibly real and attractive for us—for that moment only. Not the fruit of experience, but experience itself, is the end. A counted number of pulses only is given to us of a variegated, dramatic life. How may we see in them all that is to be seen in them by the finest senses? How shall we pass most swiftly from point to point, and be present always at the focus where the greatest number of vital forces unite in their purest energy?

To burn always with this hard, gemlike flame, to maintain this ecstasy, is success in life. In a sense it might even be said that our failure is to form habits, for, after all, habit is relative to a stereotyped world, and meantime it is only the roughness of the eye that makes any two persons, things, situations, seem alike. While all melts under our feet, we may well catch at any exquisite passion, or any contribution to knowledge that seems by a lifted horizon to set the spirit free for a moment, or any stirring of the senses, strange dyes, strange colours, and curious odours, or work of the artist's hands, or the face of one's friend. Not to discriminate every moment some passionate attitude in those about us, and in the brilliancy of their gifts some tragic dividing of forces on their ways, is, on this short day of frost and sun, to sleep before evening. With this sense of the splendour of our experience and of its awful brevity, gathering all we are

[1] *Philosophiren ... vivificiren* German: To philosophize is to cast off apathy, to come alive. Novalis is the pseudonym of German poet Friedrich von Hardenberg (1772–1801).

into one desperate effort to see and touch, we shall hardly have time to make theories about the things we see and touch. What we have to do is to be forever curiously testing new opinions and courting new impressions, never acquiescing in a facile orthodoxy of Comte, or of Hegel,[1] or of our own. Philosophical theories or ideas, as points of view, instruments of criticism, may help us to gather up what might otherwise pass unregarded by us. "Philosophy is the microscope of thought."[2] The theory or idea or system which requires of us the sacrifice of any part of this experience, in consideration of some interest into which we cannot enter, or some abstract theory we have not identified with ourselves, or what is only conventional, has no real claim upon us.

One of the most beautiful passages in the writings of Rousseau is that in the sixth book of the *Confessions*, where he describes the awakening in him of the literary sense. An undefinable taint of death had always clung about him, and now in early manhood he believed himself smitten by mortal disease. He asked himself how he might make as much as possible of the interval that remained; and he was not biased by anything in his previous life when he decided that it must be by intellectual excitement, which he found just then in the clear, fresh writings of Voltaire. Well! we are all *con*damnés, as Victor Hugo says: we are all under sentence of death but with a sort of indefinite reprieve—*les hommes sont tous condamnés à mort avec des sursis indéfinis*:[3] we have an interval, and then our place knows us no more. Some spend this interval in listlessness, some in high passions, the wisest, at least among "the children of this world,"[4] in art and song. For our one chance lies in expanding that interval, in getting as many pulsations as possible into the given time. Great passions may give us this quickened sense of life, ecstasy and sorrow of love, the various forms of enthusiastic activity, disinterested or otherwise, which come naturally to many of us. Only be sure it is passion—that it does yield you this fruit of a quickened, multiplied consciousness. Of this wisdom, the poetic passion, the desire of beauty, the love of art for art's sake, has most, for art comes to you professing frankly to give nothing but the highest quality to your moments as they pass, and simply for those moments' sake.

—1868

---

[1] *Comte* French philosopher Auguste Comte (1798–1857); *Hegel* German philosopher Georg Wilhelm Friedrich Hegel (1770–1831).

[2] *Philosophy ... thought* From Victor Hugo's *Les Miserables* (1862) 2.2.

[3] *les hommes ... indéfinis* From Victor Hugo's *Le dernier jour d'un condamné* (1829).

[4] *the children of this world* From Luke 16.8: "The children of this world are in their generation wiser than the children of light."

Leonardo da Vinci, *The Last Supper*, 1498. "On the damp wall of the refectory, oozing with mineral salts, Leonardo painted the *Last Supper*. A hundred anecdotes were told about it, his retouchings and delays. They show him refusing to work except at the moment of invention, scornful of whoever thought that art was a work of mere industry and rule, often coming the whole length of Milan to give a single touch. He painted it, not in fresco, where all must be impromptu, but in oils, the new method which he had been one of the first to welcome, because it allowed of so many afterthoughts, so refined a working out of perfection. It turned out that on a plastered wall no process could have been less durable" (from *The Renaissance*).

Giorgione, *The Pastoral Concert*, 1508–09. "It is to the law or condition of music, as I said, that all art like this is really aspiring; and, in the school of Giorgione, the perfect moments of music itself, the making or hearing of music, song or its accompaniment, are themselves prominent as subjects. On that background of the silence of Venice, so impressive to the modern visitor, the world of Italian music was then forming. In choice of subject, as in all besides, the *Concert* of the Pitti Palace is typical of everything that Giorgione, himself an admirable musician, touched with his influence; and in sketch or finished picture, in various collections, we may follow it through many intricate variations—men fainting at music; music heard at the poolside while people fish, or mingled with the sound of the pitcher in the well, or heard across running water, or among the flocks; the tuning of instruments; people with intent faces, as if listening, like those described by Plato in an ingenious passage of the *Republic*, to detect the smallest interval of musical sound, the smallest undulation in the air, or feeling for music in thought on a stringless instrument, ear and finger refining themselves infinitely, in the appetite for sweet sound; a momentary touch of an instrument in the twilight, as one passes through some unfamiliar room, in a chance company" (from *The Renaissance*).

THOMAS HARDY

1840 – 1928

The work of Thomas Hardy—highly original and yet intimately connected with centuries-old traditions—is as important to the history of English poetry as it is to that of the novel in English, and as central to twentieth-century literature as it is to that of the Victorian era. Hardy was born in 1840 in Dorset, where much of his fiction was later set. A frail child, he did not attend the local school until the age of eight. However, his ill health fostered his love of reading. In his walks in the area, Hardy also came into contact with the local farmers and laborers, whose hardship and poverty deeply touched him. At the age of 15, he was apprenticed to a local architect, a career that would sustain him until he became established as a writer.

In 1862 Hardy moved to London to work with another architect. Always driven, he would rise at five in the morning to complete three or four hours of reading—in Homer, the Greek Testament, the Renaissance poets—before going to the office. On his return from work, he would often stay up reading and writing until midnight. It was during this time that he began writing poetry and short stories. Although he submitted many pieces to various magazines and the editors often wrote that he showed promise, his work was consistently rejected.

The hectic schedule that Hardy was following caused his health to deteriorate, and he was forced to return to the countryside in 1867 to recuperate. In Dorchester, he worked as an architect during the day and wrote in his spare time. It was in the course of his employment that he met his first wife, Emma Gifford. He had been sent to St. Juliot to draw plans for a church restoration, and Emma was the sister-in-law of the rector. The two struck up a close friendship, and Emma was very supportive of his writing. With Emma's encouragement, Hardy published his first novel, *Desperate Remedies* (1871). The novel, which has much in common with sensation fiction, a popular sub-genre of the 1860s, met with mixed reviews, but he continued to write. *Under the Greenwood Tree* (1872), his next novel, brought him popular acclaim.

In his early novels, Hardy began to include real places from the Dorset area, renamed Wessex—and was praised for his portrayal of the countryside and the people of the region. *A Pair of Blue Eyes* (1873), mirrored his own courtship with Emma, whom he married in 1874. That year also saw the publication of *Far from the Madding Crowd*, the first of what are now regarded as his classic novels. It depicts the life and loves of Bathsheba Everdene, and provides a convincing portrait of rural life. The novel also includes one of Hardy's "fallen women"; the case of Fanny Robin, who is seduced and eventually dies in a workhouse, shocked many readers. Despite this, the novel was very popular, and allowed him to give up his architectural work and concentrate solely on writing.

The Return of the Native, published in 1878, was also very successful. All of Hardy's novels were by now appearing in serialized form in monthly family magazines—a development which affected both the way that he wrote and the content of his fiction. Like most serialized writers, Hardy incorporated a steady flow of incidents in his novels; he was catering to an audience that needed to be encouraged to keep reading and buy the next issue. The "family" nature of the magazines often led his editors (one of whom was Leslie Stephen, the father of Virginia Woolf) to caution him to tone down the racier scenes and rewrite large sections. Because of the strict morality that dominated editorial policy, for example, Hardy could not state explicitly that some of his characters might have been involved in extra-marital activities.

Censure of Hardy's depiction of "immoral" subject matter reached its peak with the publication of his next two major novels, *Tess of the d'Urbervilles* (1891) and *Jude the Obscure* (1895). In the first of these, the aristocratic Alec d'Urberville forces himself upon Tess, who then bears his illegitimate child. Both the "seduction" itself and Tess's attempt to have the illegitimate child baptized shocked readers. Hardy rewrote many of the novel's explicit or controversial sections for serialization in *Longman's Magazine*, but when the novel was published as a complete volume, the controversial sections were restored.

Jude the Obscure depicts the thwarted life of Jude Fawley, a village mason who dreams of attending university but whose hopes are derailed by romantic entanglements—first with Arabella Dunn and later with Sue Bridehead—and by the deadening exclusions of class-conscious English society of the later nineteenth century. Hardy's marriage was on shaky ground at the time, and his wife Emma attempted to halt the publication of the novel. Publication went forward, but criticism of the book was swift and cruel. The Bishop of Wakefield, for one, said he had "bought one of Mr. Hardy's novels, but was so disgusted with its insolence and indecency" that he "threw it into the fire." Unfavorable and uncomprehending responses to *Jude* encouraged Hardy to give up fiction; this was the last novel he wrote.

Hardy's stories—of which he considered "The Son's Veto" to be his best—are, like his novels, frequently rooted in the details of traditional rural and small town life, although they often touch on highly contemporary issues. Also like his novels, they often take in the broad sweep of his characters' lives, which are typically subject to remorseless twists of fate; the gods may haunt his texts, but no God is there. Ongoing tensions between the city and the countryside, the educated and the uneducated, and the rich and the poor frequently contribute to the tragedy that lies at the heart of the life of a typical Hardy character, although these material factors frequently combine with a more philosophically grounded pessimism.

From the mid 1890s, Hardy concentrated on composing poetry, continuing in a different genre the portrayal of the Wessex region he had made famous in the novels. *Wessex Poems* appeared in 1898, *Satires of Circumstance* in 1914, and *Moments of Vision* in 1917. Hardy's poems form a body of work strongly rooted in the physical details of place—but even more than that, one strongly rooted in the past. Hardy often borrows from traditional poetic forms (such as the ballad), and he often employs archaic diction. In subject matter, too, the poems tend to be strongly rooted in the past—more often than not a very personal past, with love and the loss of love being recalled by the speaker; in very many of Hardy's poems an elegiac tone is pervasive.

Hardy's poetry is sometimes discussed as constituting a reaction to modernism; perhaps it would be more accurate to think of it standing as a strong counterweight to modernism. Certainly the simplicity and emotional resonance of his poetry have exerted a strong influence on the works of many subsequent poets (Philip Larkin perhaps most prominent among them). So too has Hardy's formal approach. His rhythms, his rhymes, and the way in which he varies quantity are all tightly controlled and finely modulated; the extraordinary degree of technical accomplishment in much of Hardy's poetry does not call attention to itself, and is perhaps all the more impressive for so often being unobtrusive.

Hardy's reputation continues to rest on his lyrics and ballads—most of them tightly compact works. His most ambitious poetic work is much longer; *The Dynasts* is an extraordinary epic poem set in the Napoleonic Wars. It was published in three parts between 1903 and 1908.

The death of Emma in 1912, and Hardy's subsequent remorse for what had become of their relationship, resulted in some of his finest poetry and love poems, which appeared in *Satires of Circumstance* (1914). Hardy remarried in 1914; his second wife, Florence, is listed as the author of a two-volume biography that appeared in 1928 and 1930, but it has since been established that Hardy wrote the work himself. Hardy was awarded the Order of Merit in 1910 and the Gold Medal of the Royal Society of Literature in 1912. When he died in 1928, his ashes were interred in Poets' Corner at Westminster Abbey, but his heart was buried with Emma in Stinsford, in southern England.

⌘⌘⌘

Hap° *chance*

If but some vengeful god would call to me
From up the sky, and laugh: "Thou suffering thing,
Know that thy sorrow is my ecstasy,
That thy love's loss is my hate's profiting!"

Then would I bear it, clench myself, and die,
Steeled by the sense of ire unmerited;
Half-eased in that a Powerfuller than I
Had willed and meted° me the tears I shed. *allotted*

But not so. How arrives it joy lies slain,
And why unblooms the best hope ever sown?
—Crass Casualty obstructs the sun and rain,
And dicing Time for gladness casts a moan....
These purblind Doomsters[1] had as readily strown
Blisses about my pilgrimage as pain.
—1898 (WRITTEN 1866)

Neutral Tones

We stood by a pond that winter day,
And the sun was white, as though chidden of God,
And a few leaves lay on the starving sod;
—They had fallen from an ash, and were gray.

Your eyes on me were as eyes that rove
Over tedious riddles of years ago;
And some words played between us to and fro
On which lost the more by our love.

The smile on your mouth was the deadest thing
Alive enough to have strength to die;
And a grin of bitterness swept thereby
Like an ominous bird a-wing ...

Since then, keen° lessons that love deceives, *sharp*
And wrings with wrong, have shaped to me
Your face, and the God-curst sun, and a tree,
And a pond edged with grayish leaves.
—1898 (WRITTEN 1867)

The Darkling[2] *Thrush*

I leant upon a coppice gate[3]
When Frost was spectre-grey,
And Winter's dregs made desolate
The weakening eye of day.
The tangled bine[4]-stems scored the sky
Like strings of broken lyres,

[1] *purblind Doomsters* Half-blind judges.

[2] *Darkling* Being in the dark; obscure.

[3] *coppice gate* Gate leading to a thicket or small forest.

[4] *bine* Hop, a climbing plant.

And all mankind that haunted nigh
Had sought their household fires.

The land's sharp features seemed to be
The Century's corpse outleant,[1]
His crypt the cloudy canopy,
The wind his death-lament.
The ancient pulse of germ and birth
Was shrunken hard and dry,
And every spirit upon earth
Seemed fervorless as I.

At once a voice arose among
The bleak twigs overhead
In a full-hearted evensong
Of joy illimited;
An aged thrush, frail, gaunt, and small,
In blast-beruffled plume,[2]
Had chosen thus to fling his soul
Upon the growing gloom.

So little cause for carolings
Of such ecstatic sound
Was written on terrestrial things
Afar or nigh around,
That I could think there trembled through
His happy good-night air
Some blessed Hope, whereof he knew
And I was unaware.
—1901 (WRITTEN 31 DECEMBER 1900)

The Ruined Maid

"O'Melia, my dear, this does everything crown![3]
Who could have supposed I should meet you in Town?
And whence such fair garments, such prosperi-ty?"—
"O didn't you know I'd been ruined?" said she.

—"You left us in tatters, without shoes or socks,
Tired of digging potatoes, and spudding up docks;[4]
And now you've gay bracelets and bright feathers three!"—
"Yes: that's how we dress when we're ruined," said she.

—"At home in the barton° you said 'thee' and 'thou,' *barnyard*
And 'thik oon,' and 'theäs oon,' and 't'other'; but now
Your talking quite fits 'ee for high compa-ny!"—
"Some polish is gained with one's ruin," said she.

—"Your hands were like paws then, your face blue and bleak
But now I'm bewitched by your delicate cheek,
And your little gloves fit as on any la-dy!"—
"We never do work when we're ruined," said she.

—"You used to call home-life a hag-ridden dream,
And you'd sigh, and you'd sock;[5] but at present you seem
To know not of megrims° or melancho-ly!"— *depression*
"True. One's pretty lively when ruined," said she.

—"I wish I had feathers, a fine sweeping gown,
And a delicate face, and could strut about Town!"—
"My dear—a raw country girl, such as you be,
Cannot quite expect that. You ain't ruined," said she.
—1901 (WRITTEN 1866)

A Broken Appointment

You did not come.
And marching Time drew on, and wore me numb.—
Yet less for loss of your dear presence there
Than that I thus found lacking in your make
That high compassion which can overbear
Reluctance for pure lovingkindness' sake
Grieved I, when, as the hope-hour stroked its sum,
You did not come.

[1] *The Century's corpse outleant* I.e., as if the century were leaning out of its coffin.

[2] *plume* I.e., feathers.

[3] *this does everything crown* This surpasses everything.

[4] *spudding up docks* Uprooting weeds.

[5] *sock* Mouth your displeasure.

You love not me,
And love alone can lend you loyalty;
—I know and knew it. But, unto the store
Of human deeds divine in all but name,
Was it not worth a little hour or more
To add yet this: Once you, a woman, came
To soothe a time-torn man; even though it be
You love not me?
—1902

The Puzzled Game-Birds
(*Triolet*)

They are not those who used to feed us
When we were young—they cannot be—
These shapes that now bereave and bleed us?
They are not those who used to feed us,
For did we then cry, they would heed us.
—If hearts can house such treachery
They are not those who used to feed us
When we were young—they cannot be!
—1902

Shut Out That Moon

Close up the casement, draw the blind,
Shut out that stealing moon,
She wears too much the guise she wore
Before our lutes were strewn
With years-deep dust, and names we read
On a white stone were hewn.

Step not out on the dew-dashed lawn
To view the Lady's Chair,
Immense Orion's glittering form,
The Less and Greater Bear:[1]
Stay in; to such sights we were drawn
When faded ones were fair.

Brush not the bough for midnight scents
That come forth lingeringly,
And wake the same sweet sentiments
They breathed to you and me
When living seemed a laugh, and love
All it was said to be.

Within the common lamp-lit room
Prison my eyes and thought;
Let dingy details crudely loom,
Mechanic° speech be wrought: *low, vulgar*
Too fragrant was Life's early bloom,
Too tart the fruit it brought!
—1909

The Convergence of the Twain
(*Lines on the Loss of the "Titanic"*[2])

1

In a solitude of the sea
Deep from human vanity,
And the Pride of Life that planned her, stilly couches she.

2

Steel chambers, late the pyres
Of her salamandrine fires,[3]
Cold currents thrid,[4] and turn to rhythmic tidal lyres.

3

Over the mirrors meant
To glass the opulent
The sea-worm crawls—grotesque, slimed, dumb, indifferent.

4

Jewels in joy designed
To ravish the sensuous mind

[1] *Lady's Chair ... Greater Bear* Constellations.

[2] *the "Titanic"* At the time the largest ship ever built, the ocean liner *Titanic* had been described as unsinkable, but on its maiden voyage in 1912 it collided with an iceberg; over 1,400 people drowned when it sank.

[3] *salamandrine fires* According to mythology, salamanders are able to survive any heat.

[4] *thrid* Thread.

Lie lightless, all their sparkles bleared and black and blind.

5

Dim moon-eyed fishes near
Gaze at the gilded gear
And query: "What does this vaingloriousness down here?" …

6

Well: while was fashioning
This creature of cleaving wing,
The Immanent Will[1] that stirs and urges everything

7

Prepared a sinister mate
For her—so gaily great—
A Shape of Ice, for the time far and dissociate.

8

And as the smart ship grew
In stature, grace, and hue,
In shadowy silent distance grew the Iceberg too.

9

Alien they seemed to be:
No mortal eye could see
The intimate welding of their later history,

10

Or sign that they were bent
By paths coincident
On being anon twin halves of one august event,

11

Till the Spinner of the Years
Said "Now!" And each one hears,
And consummation comes, and jars two hemispheres.
—1914

[1] *The Immanent Will* The force that pervades and determines human existence.

Channel Firing[2]

That night your great guns, unawares,
Shook all our coffins as we lay,
And broke the chancel[3] window-squares,
We thought it was the Judgment-day

And sat upright. While drearisome
Arose the howl of wakened hounds:
The mouse let fall the altar-crumb,
The worms drew back into the mounds,

The glebe[4] cow drooled. Till God called, "No;
It's gunnery practice out at sea
Just as before you went below;
The world is as it used to be:

"All nations striving strong to make
Red war yet redder. Mad as hatters[5]
They do no more for Christès° sake *Christ's*
Than you who are helpless in such matters.

"That this is not the judgment-hour
For some of them's a blessed thing,
For if it were they'd have to scour
Hell's floor for so much threatening.…

"Ha, ha. It will be warmer when
I blow the trumpet (if indeed
I ever do; for you are men,
And rest eternal sorely need)."

So down we lay again. "I wonder,
Will the world ever saner be,"

[2] *Channel Firing* In the months leading up to the First World War both the British and the German navies practiced firing in the English Channel. (This poem was written in April 1914; the First World War began in August of the same year.)

[3] *chancel* Eastern part of a church, used by those who officiate at services.

[4] *glebe* Field, especially a field belonging to a church.

[5] *Mad as hatters* Makers of felt hats in the late eighteenth and early nineteenth century frequently went insane as a result of breathing in mercury compounds used in the manufacture of the hats.

Said one, "than when He sent us under
In our indifferent century!"

And many a skeleton shook his head.
"Instead of preaching forty year,"
My neighbour Parson Thirdly said,
"I wish I had stuck to pipes and beer."

Again the guns disturbed the hour,
Roaring their readiness to avenge,
As far inland as Stourton Tower,
And Camelot, and starlit Stonehenge.[1]
—1914

The Voice

Woman much missed, how you call to me, call to me,
Saying that now you are not as you were
When you had changed from the one who was all to me,
But as at first, when our day was fair.

Can it be you that I hear? Let me view you, then,
Standing as when I drew near to the town
Where you would wait for me: yes, as I knew you then,
Even to the original air-blue gown!

Or is it only the breeze, in its listlessness
Travelling across the wet mead° to me here, *meadow*
You being ever dissolved to wan wistlessness,
Heard no more again far or near?

Thus I; faltering forward,
Leaves around me falling,
Wind oozing thin through the thorn from norward,
And the woman calling.
—1914 (WRITTEN DECEMBER 1912)

[1] *Stourton Tower … Stonehenge* Stourton Tower was built to commemorate the victory of King Alfred over the Danes; Camelot was the site of King Arthur's court; Stonehenge is the famous prehistoric stone monument near Salisbury.

Transformations

Portion of this yew[2]
Is a man my grandsire knew,
Bosomed here at its foot:
This branch may be his wife,
A ruddy human life
Now turned to a green shoot.

These grasses must be made
Of her who often prayed,
Last century, for repose;
And the fair girl long ago
Whom I vainly tried to know
May be entering this rose.

So, they are not underground,
But as nerves and veins abound
In the growths of upper air,
And they feel the sun and rain,
And the energy again
That made them what they were!
—1915

In Time of "The Breaking of Nations"[3]

1

Only a man harrowing clods
In a slow silent walk
With an old horse that stumbles and nods
Half asleep as they stalk.

2

Only thin smoke without flame
From the heaps of couch-grass;
Yet this will go onward the same
Though Dynasties pass.

[2] *yew* Traditionally, yew trees have been planted beside churches and near graveyards.

[3] *In Time of "The Breaking of Nations"* See Jeremiah 51.20: "Thou art my battleaxe and weapons of war: for with thee will I break in pieces the nations. …"

3

Yonder a maid and her wight[1]
Come whispering by:
War's annals will fade into night
Ere their story die.
—1916

The Photograph

The flame crept up the portrait line by line
As it lay on the coals in the silence of night's profound,
And over the arm's incline,
And along the marge of the silkwork superfine,
And gnawed at the delicate bosom's defenceless round.

Then I vented a cry of hurt, and averted my eyes;
The spectacle was one that I could not bear,
To my deep and sad surprise;
But, compelled to heed, I again looked furtivewise
Till the flame had eaten her breasts, and mouth, and hair.

"Thank God, she is out of it now!" I said at last,
In a great relief of heart when the thing was done
That had set my soul aghast,
And nothing was left of the picture unsheathed from the past
But the ashen ghost of the card it had figured on.

She was a woman long hid amid packs of years,
She might have been living or dead; she was lost to my sight,
And the deed that had nigh drawn tears
Was done in a casual clearance of life's arrears;
But I felt as if I had put her to death that night! …

—Well; she knew nothing thereof did she survive,
And suffered nothing if numbered among the dead;
Yet—yet—if on earth alive
Did she feel a smart, and with vague strange anguish strive?
If in heaven, did she smile at me sadly and shake her head?
—1917

[1] *wight* I.e., man.

During Wind and Rain

They sing their dearest songs—
He, she, all of them—yea,
Treble and tenor and bass,
And one to play;
With the candles mooning each face....
Ah, no; the years O!
How the sick leaves reel down in throngs!

They clear the creeping moss—
Elders and juniors—aye,
Making the pathways neat
And the garden gay;
And they build a shady seat....
Ah, no; the years, the years;
See, the white storm-birds wing across.

They are blithely breakfasting all—
Men and maidens—yea,
Under the summer tree,
With a glimpse of the bay,
While pet fowl come to the knee....
Ah, no; the years O!
And the rotten rose is ript from the wall.

They change to a high new house,
He, she, all of them—aye,
Clocks and carpets and chairs
On the lawn all day,
And brightest things that are theirs....
Ah, no; the years, the years;
Down their carved names the rain-drop ploughs.
—1917

The Oxen

Christmas Eve, and twelve of the clock.
  "Now they are all on their knees,"[1]
An elder said as we sat in a flock
  By the embers in hearthside ease.

We pictured the meek mild creatures where
  They dwelt in their strawy pen,
Nor did it occur to one of us there
  To doubt they were kneeling then.

So fair a fancy few would weave
  In these years! Yet, I feel,
If someone said on Christmas Eve,
  "Come; see the oxen kneel,

"In the lonely barton° by yonder coomb° *barnyard / valley*
  Our childhood used to know,"
I should go with him in the gloom,
  Hoping it might be so.
—1917

[1] *Now they are all on their knees* According to legend, oxen kneel at the appointed time on Christmas every year in imitation of the ox in the manger kneeling when Christ was born.

Going and Staying

1

The moving sun-shapes on the spray,
  The sparkles where the brook was flowing,
Pink faces, plightings, moonlit May—
These were the things we wished would stay;
    But they were going.

2

Seasons of blankness as of snow,
The silent bleed of a world decaying,
The moan of multitudes in woe—
These were the things we wished would go;
    But they were staying.

3

Then we looked closelier at Time,
And saw his ghostly arms revolving
To sweep off woeful things with prime,
Things sinister with things sublime
    Alike dissolving.
—1920

IN CONTEXT

Hardy's Reflections on the Writing of Poetry

The Life of Thomas Hardy, published under the name of his second wife, Florence Hardy, was later discovered to have been written by Hardy himself. When this third-person autobiography discusses Hardy's poetic career in relation to his fiction writing, the author reveals his sensitivity to suggestions that he had taken up poetry only as a result of the reaction against his later novels:

> In the early weeks of this year [1899] the poems were reviewed in the customary periodicals—mostly in a friendly tone, even in a tone of respect, and with praise for many pieces in the volume; though by some critics not without umbrage at Hardy's having taken the liberty to adopt another vehicle of expression than prose fiction without consulting them. …
>
> Almost all the fault-finding was, in fact, based on the one great antecedent conclusion that an author who has published prose first, and that largely, must necessarily express himself badly in verse, no reservation being added to except cases in which he may have published prose for temporary or compulsory reasons, or prose of a poetical kind, or have written verse first of all, or for a long time intermediately. … In the present case, although it was shown that many of the verses had been written before their author dreamt of novels, the critics' view was very little affected that he had "at the eleventh hour," as they untruly put it, taken up a hitherto uncared-for art.

A few pages on, the account is again at pains to emphasize the purity of Hardy's motives in abandoning prose fiction and devoting himself to poetry:

> When one considers how he might have made himself a man of affluence by taking the current of popularity as it served, writing "best sellers," and ringing changes upon the novels he had already written, his bias towards poetry must have been instinctive and disinterested.

Hardy includes few reflections on the nature of his own poetry, but he does take issue with Wordsworth's famous strictures against poetic diction, asserting that Wordsworth "should have put the matter somewhat like this: in works of *passion and sentiment* (not 'imagination and sentiment') the language of verse is the language of prose. In works of *fancy* (or *imagination*), 'poetic diction' (of the real kind) is proper, and even necessary." Here and there Hardy also makes interesting comments on the origin of particular poems. Here, for example, are his remarks concerning "In Time of 'The Breaking of Nations'":

> I believe it would be said by people who knew me well that I have a faculty (perhaps not uncommon) for burying an emotion in my heart or brain for forty years, and exhuming it at the end of that time as fresh as when interred. For instance, the poem entitled "The Breaking of Nations" contains a feeling that moved me in 1870, during the Franco-Prussian war, when I chanced to be looking at such an agricultural incident in Cornwall. But I did not write the verses till during the war with Germany of 1914, and onwards.

Gerard Manley Hopkins
1844 – 1889

The Victorian priest and poet Gerard Manley Hopkins lived only 45 years, but his work spans three eras of literary history. A Romantic in his notions of the beauty and power of the natural world and of the imagination's importance, Hopkins shared some affinities with Keats and other poets of the Romantic period. He also shared affinities with the Victorian Pre-Raphaelites and, like them, was very influenced by the writings of John Ruskin. But because his poems and letters, in which he outlined his innovative poetic theories, were not published until 1918, some 30 years after his death, he is sometimes grouped with such Modernists as T.S. Eliot and Ezra Pound. Indeed these poets were influenced by Hopkins's experimental verse, with its unconventional syntax, dense alliteration, and "sprung rhythm" (the term Hopkins coined to describe his unique metric style).

Hopkins was born in Essex of affluent parents and showed promise as a scholar from an early age, but he was clearly also talented in music and the visual arts. His early schooling was at Highgate, where he studied under, and formed a lifelong friendship with, the Pre-Raphaelite poet R.W. Dixon. Hopkins went on to study classics at Oxford, where he became known as the "Star of Balliol [College]" and was educated by such luminaries as Benjamin Jowett and Walter Pater. While Pater's aestheticism was indeed an influence on Hopkins's artistic philosophies, no one at Oxford had a greater impact on him than did John Henry Newman. A convert to Roman Catholicism who later became a Cardinal, Newman was one of the leaders of the "Oxford Movement" of the 1830s and early 1840s, a Tractarian movement (so called because of the "Tracts for the Times" that Newman and others wrote) that called for the Church of England to recognize points of communion with the Roman Catholic Church.

Hopkins's conversion to Roman Catholicism in 1866 estranged him from his devout Anglican parents, who wrote "terrible" letters to try to dissuade him from his decision to become a Jesuit priest. He replied to his father's concerns by saying: "I am surprised you shd. say fancy and aesthetic tastes have led me to my present state of mind: these wd. be better satisfied in the Church of England, for bad taste is always meeting one in the accessories of Catholicism." Hopkins served the Catholic Church for the rest of his life, and for many of those years he renounced his own poetry, burning much of it in the belief that, with the exception of sermons, authorship was not becoming for a priest. It was obvious, however, that he did not cease thinking about the techniques of writing, as is attested by his journals and letters, many written to his Oxford friend the poet (later Poet Laureate) Robert Bridges.

After a famous shipwreck in 1875, Hopkins's superiors encouraged him to write of the fate of five Franciscan nuns, exiled from Germany by the Falk Laws, who had drowned in the disaster. In the long ode *The Wreck of the Deutschland* he began experimenting with the rhythms he had been thinking about for so long. According to Hopkins, every object in the natural world has a unique and fluid identity, or "inscape," an essence that comprises its form and its meaning. Hopkins also coined the term "instress" to describe the way in which objects or people perceive "inscape." Instress is a powerful burst of energy that allows an observer to penetrate and experience the object's essence. Poetry, for Hopkins, is instress, and that which it seeks to penetrate is the divine.

In creating a poetic sound that would present the inscape of objects and of speech itself, Hopkins was inspired by the rhythms of Welsh nursery rhymes and Old English poetry. "Sprung rhythm" was the result, a syntactically disjunctive, highly alliterative, and densely rhyming style that reconfigured the nature of stresses and line length. The poems in this style that followed *Deutschland*—among them the famous "God's Grandeur"—often aimed to celebrate the spiritual and the divine.

Hopkins continued to write poetry, but his duties as a priest took priority. He served from 1877 to 1879 in various parishes in Sheffield, Oxford, and London, and then went on to fulfill demanding duties in the dreary slums of Manchester, Liverpool, and Glasgow. In 1881 he began teaching at Stonyhurst College in Lancashire, and in 1884 was appointed Professor of Greek and Latin at University College in Dublin. Hopkins disliked both his duties at this university and the city itself, which was still recovering from the Great Famine. Years of illness and depression followed, combined with doubts about his ability to give himself completely to God. During these years of angst, Hopkins composed what are now called his "terrible sonnets," among them "[Not, I'll not, carrion comfort]," and "[No worst, there is none]," their titles reflecting their themes of anguish and desolation.

Hopkins was not to live long in Ireland; he contracted typhoid fever and died in 1889 at the age of 45. Robert Bridges edited a volume of his poetry, *The Poems of Gerard Manley Hopkins*, and released it to the public thirty years after Hopkins's death, presumably waiting until the world was ready to hear the sound of the poet who acknowledged his "oddness" by saying, "The effect of studying masterpieces is to make me admire and do otherwise." Although his output was relatively small, the poet who "did otherwise" made an enormous impact on the literary world, and has influenced several generations of poets.

⌘⌘⌘

God's Grandeur

The world is charged with the grándeur of God.
It will flame out, like shining from shook foil;[1]
It gathers to a greatness, like the ooze of oil
Crushed.[2] Why do men then now not reck° his rod? *regard*
Generátions have trod, have trod, have trod;
And all is seared with trade; bleared, smeared, with toil;
And wears man's smudge and shares man's smell: the soil
Is bare now, nor can foot feel, being shod.

Ánd, for° all this, náture is never spent; *despite*
There lives the dearest freshness deep down things;
And though the last lights off the black West went
Oh, morning, at the brown brink eastward, springs—
Because the Holy Ghost óver the bent
World broods with warm breast and with ah! bright wings.

—1918 (WRITTEN 1877)

The Windhover[3]

To Christ Our Lord

I caught this morning morning's minion, king-
dom of daylight's dauphin,[4] dapple-dáwn-drawn Falcon, in his riding
Of the rólling level úndernéath him steady air, and striding
High there, how he rung upon the rein of a wimpling° wing *rippling*
In his écstasy! then off, off forth on swing,
As a skate's heel sweeps smooth on a bow-bend: the hurl and gliding
Rebuffed the bíg wind. My heart in hiding
Stírred for a bird,—the achieve of, the mástery of the thing!

Brute beauty and valour and act, oh, air, pride, plűme, here
Buckle! AND the fire that breaks from thee then, a billion
Tímes told lovelier, more dangerous, O my chevalier!° *knight*

No wőnder of it: shéer plód makes plóugh down síllion° *furrows*
Shíne, and blue-bleak embers, ah my dear,
Fall, gáll themsélves, and gásh gőld-vermílion.

—1918 (WRITTEN 1877)

Pied[5] *Beauty*

Glóry be to God for dappled things—
For skies of couple-colour as a brinded° cow; *spotted*
For rose-moles all in stipple upon trout that swim;
Fresh-fírecoal chestnut-fálls;[6] fínches' wings;
Lándscape plotted and pieced—fold,° fallow, and plough; *pasture*
And áll trádes, their gear and tackle and trim.° *equipment*

Áll things counter,° original, spáre,° stránge; *contrary / rare*
Whatever is fickle, frecklèd (who knows how?)
With swift, slów; sweet, soũr; adázzle, dím;
He fathers-forth whose beauty is pást chánge:
Práise hím.

—1918 (WRITTEN 1877)

[1] [Hopkins's note] I mean foil in its sense of leaf or tinsel. …Shaken goldfoil gives off broad glares like sheet lightning and also, and this is true of nothing else, owing to its zigzag dints and creasings and network of small many cornered facets, a sort of fork lightning too.

[2] *oil / Crushed* I.e., as olive oil.

[3] *Windhover* Another name for a kestrel, a small falcon that appears to hover in the wind.

[4] *dauphin* Title of the eldest son of the King of France—the heir.

[5] *Pied* Multicolored.

[6] *Fresh … fálls* Freshly fallen, brightly colored chestnuts.

Felix Randal

Félix Rándal the fárrier,[1] O is he déad then? my dúty all énded,
Who have watched his mould of man, big-bóned and hardy-handsome
Pining, píning, till time when reason rámbled in it and some
Fatal four disorders, fléshed there, all contended?

Síckness bróke him. Impatient, he cursed at first, but mended
Being anointed[2] and all; though a heavenlier heart began some
Mónths éarlier, since I had our swéet repríeve and ránsom[3]
Téndered to him. Áh well, God rést him áll road éver[4] he offénded!

This séeing the sick endéars them tó us, us tóo it endéars.
My tongue had taught thee comfort, touch had quenched thy tears,
Thy tears that touched my heart, child, Félix, poor Felix Randal;

How far from then forethought of, all thy more boisterous years,
When thou at the random[5] grim fórge, pówerful amídst péers,
Didst fettle° for the great grey drayhorse[6] his bright and battering sandal! *prepare*
—1918 (WRITTEN 1880)

[1] *fárrier* One who shoes horses.

[2] *anointed* As in the sacrament of Extreme Unction, performed for the dying.

[3] *had our swéet repríeve and ránsom* I.e., had received Holy Communion.

[4] *áll road éver* However.

[5] *random* Roughly built.

[6] *drayhorse* Powerful horse used for drawing a sled.

Spring and Fall: To a Young Child

Márgarét, áre you gríeving
Over Goldengrove unleaving?
Leáves, like the thíngs of mán, you
With your fresh thoughts care for, can you?
Ah! ás the héart grows ólder
It will come to such sights colder
By and by, nor spare a sigh
Though worlds of wanwood leafmeal[7] lie;
And yet you *will* weep and know why.
Now no matter, child, the name:
Sórrow's spríngs áre the sáme.
Nor mouth had, no nor mind, expressed
What héart héard of, ghóst° guéssed: *spirit*
It ís the blíght mán was bórn for,
It is Margaret you mourn for.
—1918 (WRITTEN 1880)

[*As kingfishers catch fire*]

As kingfishers catch fire, dragonflies draw flame;
As tumbled over rim in roundy wells
Stones ring; like each tucked° string tells, each hung bell's *plucked*
Bow swung finds tongue to fling out broad its name;
Each mortal thing does one thing and the same:
Deals out that being indoors each one dwells;
Selves—goes its self; *myself* it speaks and spells,
Crying *What I do is me: for that I came.*

I say more: the just man justices;
Keeps grace: that keeps all his goings graces;
Ácts in God's eye what in God's eye he is—
Chríst. For Christ plays in ten thousand places,
Lovely in limbs, and lovely in eyes not his
To the Father through the features of men's faces.
—1918 (WRITTEN 1879–82)

[7] *wanwood leafmeal* Decaying wood and leaves.

[*No worst, there is none*]

No worst, there is none. Pitched past pitch of grief,
More pangs will, schooled at forepangs, wilder wring.
Comforter, where, where is your comforting?
Mary, mother of us, where is your relief?
My cries heave, herds-long; huddle in a main, a chief—
Woe, world-sorrow; on an áge-old ánvil wínce and síng—
Then lull, then leave off. Fury had shrieked "No ling-
Ering! Let me be fell:° force[1] I must be brief." *fierce*
O the mind, mind has mountains; cliffs of fall
Frightful, sheer, no-man-fathomed. Hold them cheap
May who ne'er hung there. Nor does long our small
Durance deal with that steep or deep. Here! creep,
Wretch, under a comfort serves in a whirlwind: all
Life death does end and each day dies with sleep.
—1918 (WRITTEN 1884–85)

[*I wake and feel the fell*[2] *of dark, not day*]

I wake and feel the fell of dark, not day
What hours, O what black hours we have spent
This night! what sights you, heart, saw, ways you went!
And more must, in yet longer light's delay.

With witness I speak this. But where I say
Hours I mean years, mean life. And my lament
Is cries countless, cries like dead letters sent
To dearest him that lives alas! away.

I am gall, I am heartburn. God's most deep decree
Bitter would have me taste: my taste was me;
Bones built in me, flesh filled, blood brimmed the curse.

Selfyeast of spirit a dull dough sours. I see
The lost are like this, and their scourge to be
As I am mine, their sweating selves; but worse.
—1918 (WRITTEN C. 1885–86)

[1] *force* Perforce, or out of necessity.

[2] *fell* Bitterness; also an animal hide, used as a covering.

[*Not, I'll not, carrion*[3] *comfort*]

Not, I'll not, carrion comfort, Despair, not feast on thee;
Not untwist—slack they may be—these last strands of man
In me ór, most weary, cry *I can no more.* I can;
Can something, hope, wish day come, not choose not to be.

But ah, but O thou terrible, why wouldst thou rude on me[4]
Thy wring-world right foot rock? lay a lionlimb against me? scan
With darksome devouring eyes my bruisèd bones? and fan,
O in turns of tempest, me heaped there; me frantic to avoïd thee and flee?

Why? That my chaff might fly; my grain lie, sheer and clear.
Nay in all that toil, that coil,° since (seems) I kissed the rod, *tumult*
Hand rather, my heart lo! lapped strength, stole joy, would laugh, cheer.
Cheer whóm though? The hero whose héaven-handling flúng me, fóot tród
Me? or mé that fóught him? O which one? is it éach one? That níght, that yéar
Of now done darkness I wretch lay wrestling with (my God!) my God.
—1918 (WRITTEN C. 1885–86)

That Nature Is a Heraclitean Fire[5] *and of the Comfort of the Resurrection*

Cloud-puffball, torn tufts, tossed pillows | flaunt forth, then chevy° on an air— *race*

[3] *carrion* Dead flesh.

[4] *rude on me* Roughly against me.

[5] *Heraclitean Fire* Heraclitus (c. 535–475 BCE), a Greek philosopher, taught that everything is derived from fire, and therefore in a constant state of change.

Built thoroughfare: heaven-roysterers,[1] in gay-gangs | they throng; they glitter in marches.
Down roughcast,[2] down dazzling whitewash, | wherever an elm arches,
Shivelights[3] and shadowtackle[4] in long | lashes lace, lance, and pair.
Delightfully the bright wind boisterous | ropes, wrestles, beats earth bare
Of yestertempest's creases; in pool and rut peel parches
Squandering ooze to squeezed | dough, crúst, dust; stánches,° stárches *reinforces*
Squadroned masks and manmarks | treadmire toil there
Fóotfretted in it. Million-fuelèd, | nature's bonfire burns on.
But quench her bonniest, dearest | to her, her clearest-selvèd spark
Mán, how fást his fíredint, | his mark on mind, is gone!
Bóth are in an űnfáthomable, áll is in an enórmous dárk
Drowned. O pity and indig | nation! Manshape, that shone
Sheer off, disseveral,° a star, death blots black out; nor mark *separate*
Is any of him at all so stark
But vastness blurs and time | beats level. Enough! the Resurrection,
A héart's-clarion! Awáy grief's gásping, | joyless days, dejection.
Across my foundering deck shone
A beacon, an eternal beam. | Flesh fade, and mortal trash
Fáll to the residuary worm; | world's wildfire, leave but ash:
In a flash, at a trumpet crash,
I am all at once what Christ is, | since he was what I am, and
This Jack,° jóke, poor pótsherd,[5] | patch,[6] *fellow*
matchwood,° immortal diamond, *kindling*
Is immortal diamond.

—1918 (WRITTEN 1888)

[*Thou art indeed just, Lord*]

Justus quidem tu es, Domine, si disputem tecum: verumtamen justa loquar ad te: Quare via impiorum prosperatur?[7] etc.

Thou art indeed just, Lord, if I contend
With thee; but, sir, so what I plead is just.
Whý do sínners' ways prosper? and why must
Dísappóintment all I endeavour end?
Wert thou my enemy, O thou my friend,
How wouldst thou worse, I wonder, than thou dost
Defeat, thwart me? Oh, the sots° and thralls of lust *drunkards*
Do in spare hours more thrive than I that spend,
Sir, life upon thy cause. See, banks and brakes° *thickets*
Now, leavèd how thick! lacèd they are again
With fretty chervil,[8] look, and fresh wind shakes
Them; birds build—but not I build; no, but strain,
Time's eunuch, and not breed one work that wakes.
Mine, O thou lord of life, send my roots rain.

—1918 (WRITTEN 1889)

[1] *roysterers* Noisy party-goers.

[2] *roughcast* Wall plastering made of lime and gravel.

[3] *Shivelights* Strips of light.

[4] *shadowtackle* Shadows which resemble a ship's rigging.

[5] *pótsherd* Piece of broken pottery.

[6] *patch* Simpleton.

[7] *Justus … prosperatur* Latin: You are always righteous, O Lord, when I bring a case before you. Yet I would speak with you about your justice: why does the way of the wicked prosper? (Jeremiah 12.1).

[8] *fretty chervil* Interlaced leaves and stems of a garden herb.

IN CONTEXT

The Growth of "The Windhover"

Manuscript copies of Hopkins's poems open a remarkable window on his unique approach to poetic rhythm—and to poetic composition; "The Windhover" is a particularly interesting example.

The first page reproduced here (headed "Another version") is entirely in Hopkins's hand, and probably dates from 1877. The second dates from 1883; it is from an album of "fair copy" transcriptions of Hopkins's (often not very legible) manuscripts that was prepared by his friend and mentor, the poet Robert Bridges, and then corrected by Hopkins in 1884. According to Hopkins scholar Norman H. Mackenzie, the corrections and revisions here in Hopkins's handwriting include the addition of ": to Christ our Lord" to the title; the alteration of "o air" to "oh, air"; the replacement of the ampersand with the word "AND" in line 10; the addition of stress marks in lines 2, 3, 12, and 14; the addition of a "slur" between "the" and "hurl" in line 6, and the addition of seven "outrides" (as Hopkins termed the curved marks below the line).

Adding marks to indicate particularly strong stresses and adding "slurs" and "outrides" were among the many ways Hopkins endeavored to direct the reading of his poems according to the principles of what he termed "sprung rhythm" (see the Glossary at the back of this volume for a definition). The meaning of the "slur" mark is fairly straightforward; it indicates where two syllables should be compressed together so as to be pronounced as one—much as in this case an apostrophe might be used to do (*th'hurl*). The "outride" denotes a much less familiar concept, and it may be best to quote Hopkins directly here. At one point he writes that "the outride under one or more syllables makes them extrametrical: a slight pause follows as if the voice were silently making its way back to the highroad of the verse." Elsewhere he describes syllables so marked as "hangers or outriders," meaning "one, two or three slack syllables added to a foot and not counted in the nominal scanning. They are so called because they seem to hang below the line or ride forward or backward from it in another dimension than the line itself, according to a principle needless to explain here."

When entering corrections and revisions in 1884 Hopkins also added at lower right the date and place of the poem's original composition. The marginal notes, however, were evidently added by Bridges when he transcribed them; "= A", for example, indicates that the hyphen Bridges has added to line 6 is taken from an early manuscript of the poem (referred to as manuscript A).

The Windhover (Another version) — to Christ our Lord.

96

I caught this morning morning's minion, king-
Of daylight's dau(phin), dapple-dawn-drawn Fal-
con, in his riding [and striding
Of the rolling level underneath him steady air,
O how he rung upon the rein of a wimpling wing
In his ecstacy! then off, ; forth on swing,
As a skate's heel sweeps smooth on a bow-bend: the hurl and gliding
Rebuffed the big: wind. My heart in hiding
Stirred for a bird — for the mastery of the thing!

Brute beauty and valour and act, O air, pride, plume, here [then, a billion
Buckle! And the fire that breaks from thee
Times told lovelier, more dangerous, O my chevalier!

No wonder of it: sheer; plod makes plough down sillion
Shine, and blue-bleak embers, ah my dear,
Fall, gall themselves, and gash: gold-vermilion.

(8)

The Windhover: to Christ our Lord

~

I caught this morning morning's minion, king-
dom of daylight's dauphin, dapple-dawn-drawn Falcon, in his riding
Of the rolling, level underneath him steady air, & striding
High there, how he rung upon the rein of a wimpling wing
In his ecstacy! then off, off forth on swing
As a skate's heel sweeps smooth on a bow-bend: the hurl & gliding
Rebuffed the big wind. My heart in hiding
Stirred for a bird,—the achieve of, the mastery of the thing!

Brute beauty & valour & act, oh, air, pride, plume here
Buckle! AND the fire that breaks from thee then, a billion
Times told lovelier, more dangerous, o my chevalier!
No wonder of it: sheer plod makes plough down sillion
Shine, & blue-bleak embers, ah my dear,
Fall, gall themselves, & gash gold-vermilion.

~ St. Beuno's. May 30 1877

from *Journal* 1870–74

[*"Inscape" and "Instress"*]

[April 15] The white violets are broader and smell; the blue, scentless and finer made, have sharper whelking[1] and a more winged recoil in the leaves.

Take a *few* primroses in a glass and the instress[2] of—brilliancy, sort of starriness: I have not the right word—so simple a flower gives is remarkable. It is, I think, due to the strong swell given by the deeper yellow middle.

"The young lambs bound As to the tabour's sound."[3]

They toss and toss: it is as if it were the earth that flung them, not themselves. It is the pitch of graceful agility when we think that.

April 16—Sometimes they rest a little space on the hind legs and the fore-feet drop curling in on the breast, not so liquidly as we see it in the limbs of foals though.

Bright afternoon; clear distances; Pendle[4] dappled with tufted shadow; west wind; interesting clouding, flat and lying in the warp of the heaved but the pieces with rounded outline and dolphin-backs showing in places and all was at odds and at Z's, one piece with another. Later beautifully delicate crisping. Later rippling. …

April 21—We have had other such afternoons, one today—the sky a beautiful grained blue, silky lingering clouds in flat-bottomed loaves, others a little browner in ropes or in burly-shouldered ridges swanny and lustrous, more in the Zenith[5] stray packs of a sort of violet paleness. White-rose cloud formed fast, not in the same density—some caked and swimming in a wan whiteness, the rest soaked with the blue and like the leaf of a flower held against the light and diapered out by the worm or veining of deeper blue between rosette and rosette. Later / moulding, which brought rain: in perspective it was vaulted in very regular ribs with fretting between: but these are not ribs; they are a "wracking" install made of these two realities—the frets, which are scarves of rotten cloud bellying upwards and drooping at their ends and shaded darkest at the brow or tropic where they double to the eye, and the whiter field of sky showing between: the illusion looking down the "wagon" is complete. These swaths of fretted cloud move in rank, not in file.

April 22—But such a lovely damasking in the sky as today I never felt before. The blue was charged with simple instress, the higher, zenith sky earnest and frowning, lower more light and sweet. High up again, breathing through woolly coats of cloud or on the quains[6] and branches of the flying pieces it was the true exchange of crimson, nearer the earth / against the sun / it was turquoise, and in the opposite south-western bay below the sun it was like clear oil but just as full of colour, shaken over with slanted flashing "travellers," all in flight, stepping one behind the other, their edges tossed with bright ravelling,[7] as if white napkins were thrown up in the sun but not quite at the same moment so that they were all in a scale down the air falling one after the other to the ground. …

[May 9] This day and May 11 the bluebells in the little wood between the College[8] and the highroad and in one of the Hurst Green[9] cloughs.[10] In the little wood / opposite the light / they stood in blackish spreads or sheddings like the spots on a snake. The heads are then like thongs and solemn in grain and grape-colour. But in the clough / through the light / they came in falls of

[1] *whelking* Ridges.

[2] *instress* Hopkins's own term, meaning the force or energy which sustains an inscape, which is the individual or essential quality of a thing.

[3] *The … sound* From William Wordsworth's *Ode: Intimations of Immortality*, line 20–21; *tabour's* Drum's.

[4] *Pendle* Pendle Hill in Lancashire, England.

[5] *Zenith* Point in the sky directly overhead.

[6] *quains* Angles (Hopkins's own term).

[7] *ravelling* Frayed edges.

[8] *College* Stonyhurst College, the seminary where Hopkins studied, in Lancashire, England.

[9] *Hurst Green* Village in Blackburn, Lancashire, England.

[10] *cloughs* Ravines.

sky-colour washing the brows and slacks of the ground with vein-blue, thickening at the double, vertical themselves and the young grass and brake fern combed vertical, but the brake struck the upright of all this with light winged transomes.[1] It was a lovely sight.—The bluebells in your hand baffle you with their inscape, made to every sense: if you draw your fingers through them they are lodged and struggle / with a shock of wet heads; the long stalks rub and click and flatten to a fan on one another like your fingers themselves would when you passed the palms hard across one another, making a brittle rub and jostle like the noise of a hurdle strained by leaning against; then there is the faint honey smell and in the mouth the sweet gum when you bite them. But this is easy, it is the eye they baffle. They give one a fancy of panpipes and of some wind instrument with stops—a trombone perhaps. The overhung necks—for growing they are little more than a staff with a simple crook but in water, where they stiffen, they take stronger turns, in the head like sheephooks[2] or, when more waved throughout, like the waves riding through a whip that is being smacked—what with these overhung necks and what with the crisped ruffled bells dropping mostly on one side and the gloss these have at their footstalks they have an air of the knights at chess. Then the knot or "knoop" of buds some shut, some just gaping, which makes the pencil of the whole spike, should be noticed: the inscape of the flower most finely carried out in the siding of the axes, each striking a greater and greater slant, is finished in these clustered buds, which for the most part are not straightened but rise to the end like a tongue and this and their tapering and a little flattening they have made them look like the heads of snakes.

[July 19, 1872] Stepped into a barn of ours, a great shadowy barn, where the hay had been stacked on either side, and looking at the great rudely arched timber-frames—principals(?) and tie-beams, which make them look like bold big *As* with the cross-bar high up—I thought how sadly beauty of inscape was unknown and buried away from simple people and yet how near at hand it was if they had eyes to see it and it could be called out everywhere again. …

After the examinations we went for our holiday out to Douglas in the Isle of Man. Aug. 3—At this time I had first begun to get hold of the copy of Scotus[3] on the Sentences in the Baddely library and was flush with a new stroke of enthusiasm. It may come to nothing or it may be a mercy from God. But just then when I took in any inscape of the sky or sea I thought of Scotus. …

Aug. 10—I was looking at high waves. The breakers always are parallel to the coast and shape themselves to it except where the curve is sharp however the wind blows. They are rolled out by the shallowing shore just as a piece of putty between the palms whatever its shape runs into a long roll. The slant ruck[4] or crease one sees in them shows the way of the wind. The regularity of the barrels surprised and charmed the eye; the edge behind the comb or crest was as smooth and bright as glass. It may be noticed to be green behind and silver white in front: the silver marks where the air begins, the pure white is foam, the green / solid water. Then looked at to the right or left they are scrolled over like mouldboards[5] or feathers or jibsails seen by the edge. It is pretty to see the hollow of the barrel disappearing as the white combs on each side run along the wave gaining ground till the two meet at a pitch and crush and overlap each other.

About all the turns of the scaping[6] from the break and flooding of wave to its run out again I have not yet satisfied myself. The shores are swimming and the eyes have before them a region of milky surf but it is hard for them to unpack the huddling and gnarls of the water and law out the shapes and the sequence of the running: I catch however the looped or forked wisp made by every big pebble the backwater runs over—if it were clear and smooth there would be a network from their

[1] *transomes* Crossbeams.

[2] *sheephooks* Shepherds' crooks.

[3] *Scotus* Duns Scotus (c. 1266–1308), Scottish-born theologian and philosopher. In his *Lectura*, he analyzes Thomas Lombard's *Sentences*.

[4] *ruck* Ridge.

[5] *mouldboards* Boards attached to plows, used to form furrows.

[6] *scaping* Hopkins's term for a reflection or impression of the individual quality of a thing or action.

overlapping, such as can in fact be seen on smooth sand after the tide is out; then I saw it run browner, the foam dwindling and twitched into long chains of suds, while the strength of the backdraught shrugged the stones together and clocked them one against another. …

April 8 [1873]—The ashtree growing in the corner of the garden was felled. It was lopped first: I heard the sound and looking out and seeing it maimed there came at that moment a great pang and I wished to die and not to see the inscapes of the world destroyed any more. …

July 23—To Beaumont: it was the rector's day. It was a lovely day: shires-long of pearled cloud under cloud, with a grey stroke underneath marking each row; beautiful blushing yellow in the straw of the uncut rye fields, the wheat looking white and all the ears making a delicate and very true crisping along the top and with just enough air stirring for them to come and go gently; then there were fields reaping. All this I would have looked at again in returning but during dinner I talked too freely and unkindly and had to do penance going home. One field I saw from the balcony of the house behind an elmtree, which it threw up, like a square of pale goldleaf, as it might be, catching the light.
—(WRITTEN 1871–73)

from *Letter to Robert Bridges*

St. Giles's, Oxford.
25 February 1879

… No doubt my poetry errs on the side of oddness. I hope in time to have a more balanced and Miltonic[1] style. But as air, melody, is what strikes me most of all in music and design in painting, so design, pattern or what I am in the habit of calling "inscape" is what I above all aim at in poetry. Now it is the virtue of design, pattern, or inscape to be distinctive and it is the virtue of distinctiveness to become queer. This vice I cannot have escaped. …
—(WRITTEN 1879)

[1] *Miltonic* In the manner of John Milton (1608–74), English poet.

Author's Preface[2]

The poems in this book are written some in Running Rhythm, the common rhythm in English use, some in Sprung Rhythm, and some in a mixture of the two. And those in the common rhythm are some counterpointed,[3] some not.

Common English rhythm, called Running Rhythm above, is measured by feet[4] of either two or three syllables and (putting aside the imperfect feet at the beginning and end of lines and also some unusual measures in which feet seem to be paired together and double or composite feet to arise) never more or less.

Every foot has one principal stress or accent, and this or the syllable it falls on may be called the Stress of the foot and the other part, the one or two unaccented syllables, the Slack. Feet (and the rhythms made out of them) in which the stress comes first are called Falling Feet and Falling Rhythms, feet and rhythm in which the slack comes first are called Rising Feet and Rhythms, and if the stress is between two slacks there will be Rocking Feet and Rhythms. These distinctions are real and true to nature; but for purposes of scanning it is a great convenience to follow the example of music and take the stress always first, as the accent or the chief accent always comes first in a musical bar. If this is done there will be in common English verse only two possible feet—the so-called accentual Trochee[5] and Dactyl,[6] and correspondingly only two possible uniform rhythms, the so-called Trochaic and Dactylic. But they may be mixed and then what the Greeks called a Logaoedic Rhythm[7] arises. These are the facts and according to these the scanning of ordinary regularly-written English verse is

[2] *Author's Preface* Prefatory to accompany Hopkins's manuscript poems.

[3] *counterpointed* Containing two types of rhythm in a line of verse.

[4] *feet* Metrical units.

[5] *Trochee* Metrical foot consisting of an accented syllable followed by an unaccented syllable.

[6] *Dactyl* Metrical foot consisting of an accented syllable followed by two unaccented syllables.

[7] *Logaoedic Rhythm* Rhythm in which dactyls are combined with trochees.

very simple indeed and to bring in other principles is here unnecessary.

But because verse written strictly in these feet and by these principles will become same and tame the poets have brought in licences and departures from rule to give variety, and especially when the natural rhythm is rising, as in the common ten-syllable or five-foot verse, rhymed or blank. These irregularities are chiefly Reversed Feet and Reversed or Counterpoint Rhythm, which two things are two steps or degrees of licence in the same kind. By a reversed foot I mean the putting the stress where, to judge by the rest of the measure, the slack should be and the slack where the stress, and this is done freely at the beginning of a line and, in the course of a line, after a pause; only scarcely ever in the second foot or place and never in the last, unless when the poet designs some extraordinary effect; for these places are characteristic and sensitive and cannot well be touched. But the reversal of the first foot and of some middle foot after a strong pause is a thing so natural that our poets have generally done it, from Chaucer down, without remark and it commonly passes unnoticed and cannot be said to amount to a formal change of rhythm, but rather is that irregularity which all natural growth and motion shows. If however the reversal is repeated in two feet running, especially so as to include the sensitive second foot, it must be due either to great want of ear or else is a calculated effect, the super-inducing or *mounting* of a new rhythm upon the old; and since the new or mounted rhythm is actually heard and at the same time the mind naturally supplies the natural or standard foregoing rhythm, for we do not forget what the rhythm is that by rights we should be hearing, two rhythms are in some manner running at once and we have something answerable to counterpoint in music, which is two or more strains of tune going on together, and this is Counterpoint Rhythm. Of this kind of verse Milton is the great master and the choruses of *Samson Agonistes*[1] are written throughout in it—but with the disadvantage that he does not let the reader clearly know what the ground-rhythm is meant to be and so they have struck most readers as merely irregular. And in fact if you counterpoint throughout, since only one of the counter rhythms is actually heard, the other is really destroyed or cannot come to exist, and what is written is one rhythm only and probably Sprung Rhythm, of which I now speak.

Sprung Rhythm, as used in this book, is measured by feet of from one to four syllables, regularly, and for particular effects any number of weak or slack syllables may be used. It has one stress, which falls on the only syllable, if there is only one, or, if there are more, then scanning as above, on the first, and so gives rise to four sorts of feet, a monosyllable and the so-called accentual Trochee, Dactyl, and the First Paeon.[2] And there will be four corresponding natural rhythms; but nominally the feet are mixed and any one may follow any other. And hence Sprung Rhythm differs from Running Rhythm in having or being only one nominal rhythm, a mixed or "logaoedic" one, instead of three, but on the other hand in having twice the flexibility of foot, so that any two stresses may either follow one another running or be divided by one, two, or three slack syllables. But strict Sprung Rhythm cannot be counterpointed. In Sprung Rhythm, as in logaoedic rhythm generally, the feet are assumed to be equally long or strong and their seeming inequality is made up by pause or stressing.

Remark also that it is natural in Sprung Rhythm for the lines to be *rove over*, that is for the scanning of each line immediately to take up that of the one before, so that if the first has one or more syllables at its end the other must have so many the less at its beginning; and in fact the scanning runs on without break from the beginning, say, of a stanza to the end and all the stanza is one long strain, though written in lines asunder.

Two licences are natural to Sprung Rhythm. The one is rests, as in music; but of this an example is scarcely to be found in this book, unless in the *Echos*, second line. The other is *hangers* or *outrides*, that is one, two, or three slack syllables added to a foot and not counting in the nominal scanning. They are so called because they seem to hang below the line or ride for-

[1] *Samson Agonistes* Dramatic poem published by Milton in 1671.

[2] *Paeon* Metrical foot consisting of one stressed and three unstressed syllables.

ward or backward from it in another dimension than the line itself, according to a principle needless to explain here. These outriding half feet or hangers are marked by a loop underneath them, and plenty of them will be found.

The other marks are easily understood, namely accents, where the reader might be in doubt which syllable should have the stress; slurs, that is loops *over* syllables, to tie them together into the time of one; little loops at the end of a line to show that the rhyme goes on to the first letter of the next line; what in music are called pauses ⌒, to show that the syllable should be dwelt on; and twirls ~, to mark reversed or counterpointed rhythm.

Note on the nature and history of Sprung Rhythm—Sprung Rhythm is the most natural of things. For (1) it is the rhythm of common speech and of written prose, when rhythm is perceived in them. (2) It is the rhythm of all but the most monotonously regular music, so that in the words of choruses and refrains and in songs written closely to music it arises. (3) It is found in nursery rhymes, weather saws, and so on; because, however these may have been once made in running rhythm, the terminations having dropped off by the change of language, the stresses come together and so the rhythm is sprung. (4) It arises in common verse when reversed or counterpointed, for the same reason.

But nevertheless in spite of all this and though Greek and Latin lyric verse, which is well known, and the old English verse seen in "Pierce Ploughman"[1] are in sprung rhythm, it has in fact ceased to be used since the Elizabethan age, Greene[2] being the last writer who can be said to have recognized it. For perhaps there was not, down to our days, a single, even short, poem in English in which sprung rhythm is employed—not for single effects or in fixed places—but as the governing principle of the scansion. I say this because the contrary has been asserted: if it is otherwise the poem should be cited. …
—1883

[1] *Pierce Ploughman* I.e., *Piers Plowman,* by William Langland (written c. 1360–99).

[2] *Greene* Robert Greene (1558–92).

"Michael Field" Katharine Bradley and Edith Cooper

1846 – 1914 and 1862 – 1913

In May 1884, a volume of two plays by an unknown author, Michael Field, was published to critical acclaim. One reviewer wrote in *The Spectator*: "We know nothing of the author, but we have found a wealth of surprises in the strength, the simplicity, and the terseness of the imaginative feeling. … [The work] has the true poetic voice of fire in it. If this is the work of a young author, it is the work of the highest possible promise." The two authors who had taken the pen name "Michael Field," Katharine Bradley[1] and Edith Cooper had wished to receive the serious criticism accorded to male authors and also to conceal their relationship as lovers. The authors' identities did become widely known during their lifetimes, but "Michael" (Bradley) and "Field" (Cooper), as they called themselves, continued to collaborate on many books of plays and poetry, sometimes as "Michael Field," sometimes under other pseudonyms.

Bradley's father, a tobacco manufacturer, died in 1848, when she was two. Her mother educated her at home, and she later attended Newnham College, the new women's college at Cambridge. When her older sister, Emma, married James Cooper, the family stayed together with the married couple in Kenilworth, near Birmingham in central England. Bradley's mother died when Bradley was twenty-two, and not long afterward Emma also passed away. Bradley stayed on to help raise her sister's children, Amy and Edith Cooper; Edith was then six years old. Katharine and her niece Edith shared a love of literature and writing, evident from the time Edith was young, and the two later attended Bristol University together.

Bradley wrote one volume of poetry on her own in 1875 (*The New Minnesinger*, published under the pseudonym Arran Leigh), but thereafter published only in collaboration with Cooper. A stanza from their poem "It Was Deep April" describes their moment of decision: "The world was on us, pressing sore; / My love and I took hands and swore, / Against the world, to be / Poets and lovers evermore." The two eventually wrote some thirty plays and eleven volumes of poetry together in such a close collaboration that they later claimed in their journals that when they reviewed their work they could not distinguish who had written what. When their first collaborative work under the name "Michael Field" was published, the plays *Callirrhoë* and *Fair Rosamund*, they sent a copy to Robert Browning and revealed their true identities. Browning loved their work and became a close friend, but unfortunately he let slip to the public the authorship of the plays, a move that Bradley wrote back to tell him would "dwarf and enfeeble our work. … We cannot be stifled in drawing room conventionalities."

But even though critical reception of their work cooled somewhat after their identities were exposed, Bradley and Cooper did not allow themselves to be stifled. They continued to live and travel together, and many of their poems address the subject of love between women. In its form and content their earlier work was influenced by figures associated with the aesthetic movement, such as

[1] Though Bradley's first name is spelled various ways, the spelling here is that she used when signing her own name.

Dante Gabriel Rossetti and Walter Pater, and by classical poets, especially Sappho (though Sappho's sexuality was a subject of speculation in the Victorian era, Bradley and Cooper were influential in claiming her as a lesbian foremother—as many other poets would do in the twentieth century). The figure and poetry of Sappho provides key inspiration for their 1889 volume *Long Ago*, which was called by the journal *The Academy* "one of the most exquisite lyrical productions of the latter half of the nineteenth century." In the last years of their lives, Bradley and Cooper converted to Catholicism, which replaced classicism as a driving influence in their work.

For nearly half a century, Bradley and Cooper together kept a diary that they called *Works and Days*, which incorporated critical discussions, letters to friends such as Pater and Browning, and descriptions of their travels and their daily lives. In these diaries, Bradley and Cooper also describe their abiding love for each other: "closer married" than the Brownings, they said, because they also shared an artistic partnership. The younger, Cooper, was the first to die, of cancer, in 1913; eight months later Bradley died of the same disease.

⌘⌘⌘

The Magdalen

Timoteo Viti[1]

This tender sylph[2] of a maid
Is the Magdalen—this figure lone:
Her attitude is swayed
By the very breath she breathes,
The prayer of her being that takes no voice.
Boulders, the grass enwreathes,
Arch over her as a cave
That of old an earthquake clave
And filled with stagnant gloom:
Yet a woman has strength to choose it for her room.

Her long, fair hair is allowed
To wander in its thick simpleness;
The graceful tresses crowd
Unequal, yet close enough
To have woven about her neck and breast
A wimple of golden stuff.
Though the rock behind is rude,
The sweetness of solitude
Is on her face, the soft
Withdrawal that in wildflowers we have loved so oft.

Her mantle is scarlet red
In folds of severe resplendency;
Her hair beneath is spread
Full length; from its lower flakes
Her feet come forth in their naked charm:
A wind discreetly shakes
The scarlet raiment,° the hair. *dress*
Her small hands, a tranquil pair,
Are laid together; her book
And cup of ointment furnish scantily her nook.

She is happy the livelong day,
Yet her thoughts are often with the past;
Her sins are done away,
They can give her no annoy.
She is white—oh! infinitely clean
And her heart throbs with joy;
Besides, there is joy in heaven
That her sins are thus forgiven;
And she thinks till even-fall° *dusk*
Of the grace, the strangeness, the wonder of it all.

[1] *The Magdalen Timoteo Viti* Painting of the biblical Mary Magdalene by Renaissance painter Timoteo Viti (reproduced here as an illustration).

[2] *sylph* Slight, graceful woman.

Timoteo Viti, *St. Mary Magdalene*, 1521.

She is shut from fellowship;
How she loved to mingle with her friends!
To give them eyes and lip;
She lived for their sake alone;
Not a braid of her hair, not a rose
Of her cheek was her own:
And she loved to minister
To any in want of her,
All service was so sweet:
Now she must stand all day on lithe, unsummoned feet.

Among the untrodden weeds
And moss she is glad to be remote;
She knows that when God needs
From the sinning world relief,
He will find her thus with the wild bees,
The doves and the plantain leaf,
Waiting in a perfect peace
For His kingdom's sure increase,
Waiting with a deeper glow
Of patience every day, because He tarrieth so.

By her side the box of nard[1]
Unbroken … God is a great way off;
She loves Him: it is hard
That she may not now even spread
The burial spice, who would gladly keep
The tomb where He lay dead,
As it were her rocky cave;
And fold the linen and lave° *wash*
The napkin that once bound
His head; no place for her pure arts is longer found.

And these are the things that hurt;
For the rest she gives herself no pain:
She wears no camel shirt,
She uses nor scourge, nor rod;
But bathes her fair body in the well
And keeps it pure for God:
The beauty, that He hath made
So bright, she guards in the shade,
For, as an angel's dress,
Spotless she must preserve her newborn loveliness.

Day by day and week by week,
She lives and muses and makes no sound;
She has no words to speak
The joy that her desert brings:
In her heart there is a song
And yet no song she sings.
Since the word *Rabboni*[2] came
Straightway at the call of her name
And the Master reproved,
It seems she has no choice—her lips have never moved.

---

[1] *nard* Ointment made from the aromatic plant of the same name.

[2] *Rabboni* Hebrew: Master, teacher.

She stole away when the pale
Light was trembling on the garden ground
And others told the tale,
Christ was risen; she roamed the wide,
Fearful countries of the wilderness
And many a riverside,
Till she found her destined grot,° *grotto*
South, in France, a woody spot,
Where she is often glad,
Musing on those great days when she at first grew sad.
—1892

La Gioconda[1]

Leonardo Da Vinci

Historic, sidelong, implicating eyes;
A smile of velvet's lustre on the cheek;
Calm lips the smile leads upward; hand that lies
Glowing and soft, the patience in its rest
Of cruelty that waits and doth not seek
For prey; a dusky forehead and a breast
Where twilight touches ripeness amorously:
Behind her, crystal rocks, a sea and skies
Of evanescent blue on cloud and creek;
Landscape that shines suppressive of its zest
For those vicissitudes by which men die.
—1892

A girl

A girl,
Her soul a deep-wave pearl
Dim, lucent of all lovely mysteries;
A face flowered for heart's ease,
A brow's grace soft as seas
Seen through faint forest trees:
A mouth, the lips apart,
Like aspen leaflets trembling in the breeze
From her tempestuous heart.
Such: and our souls so knit,
I leave a page half-writ—
The work begun
Will be to heaven's conception done,
If she come to it.
—1893

[1] *La Gioconda* Da Vinci's painting *The Mona Lisa* (c. 1503–19).

[*It was deep April, and the morn*]

It was deep April, and the morn
Shakespeare was born;[1]
The world was on us, pressing sore;
My Love and I took hands and swore,
Against the world, to be
Poets and lovers evermore,
To laugh and dream on Lethe's[2] shore
To sing to Charon[3] in his boat,
Heartening the timid souls afloat;
Of judgment never to take heed,
But to those fast-locked souls to speed,
Who never from Apollo fled,
Who spent no hour among the dead;
Continually
With them to dwell,
Indifferent to heaven and hell.
—1893

[1] *morn … was born* It is traditional to celebrate Shakespeare's birthday on 23 April, St. George's Day.

[2] *Lethe* In Greek mythology, a river in Hades (the underworld), the waters of which cause the dead to forget the past.

[3] *Charon* Greek mythological ferryman of the underworld who transports the souls of the dead across the River Styx.

To Christina Rossetti

Lady, we would behold thee moving bright
As Beatrice or Matilda[4] mid the trees,
Alas! thy moan was as a moan for ease
And passage through cool shadows to the night:
Fleeing from love, hadst thou not poet's right
To slip into the universe? The seas
Are fathomless to rivers drowned in these,
And sorrow is secure in leafy light.
Ah, had this secret touched thee, in a tomb
Thou hadst not buried thy enchanting self,
As happy Syrinx[5] murmuring with the wind,
Or Daphne,[6] thrilled through all her mystic bloom,
From safe recess as genius or as elf,
Thou hadst breathed joy in earth and in thy kind.
—1896

[4] *Beatrice* From Dante's *Divine Comedy*, Book 3, *Paradise*: a woman who personifies love and acts as Dante's guide through Paradise; *Matilda* From Book 2, *Purgatory*: a beautiful virgin who meets Dante in the Garden of Eden and leads him to the river Lethe to wash away his sins.

[5] *Syrinx* In Greek mythology, the nymph Syrinx turned herself into a bed of reeds in order to escape Pan's advances.

[6] *Daphne* In Greek mythology, the nymph Daphne fled from the god Apollo's advances and was transformed into a laurel tree in her escape.

Robert Louis Stevenson

1850 – 1894

Due in part to his belief in romance rather than realism and in part to the success of *Treasure Island* and *Kidnapped*, Robert Louis Stevenson was once considered primarily a writer of adventure fiction for children. His large body of work has been re-evaluated in the past half century, however. His most famous work, the fantastic novella *Strange Case of Dr. Jekyll and Mr. Hyde*, has now taken a place among the canonical works of late Victorian literature. Stevenson's interest in the nature of good and evil lends this short novel a provocative moral complexity that has captivated the interest of a wide audience, with some readers viewing the book as a critique of Victorian double standards, others looking to the myth of the *doppelgänger*, or spiritual double, to explain the wicked Mr. Hyde, and still others adopting Freudian theories of the ego and the id to explain the two incarnations of Dr. Jekyll. Although he was long fascinated by the duality of the human psyche, in later years Stevenson turned to the concerns of his adopted country, Samoa, for subject matter, writing about the evils of imperialism and the damage done by foreign merchants. In all he wrote over 50 books in the course of his short life.

Stevenson's life was adventurous, but most of his travels were undertaken in search of respite from his ailments, which he wrote about in so much detail that he was once described as a "connoisseur of disease." He was an only child, born in Edinburgh in 1850 to Margaret Balfour, the daughter of a clergyman, and Thomas Stevenson, a well-known engineer for the Board of Northern Lighthouses. When he was young Stevenson contracted tuberculosis, and he remained frail ever after. He was put under the care of a nurse, who stimulated his interest in literature by reading to him everything from the Bible to serial adventure novels. Even as a child, he began spinning the raw material of these tales into stories of his own. In *Memories and Portraits* (1887), Stevenson said: "All through my boyhood and youth, I was known and pointed out for the pattern of an idler; and yet I was always busy on my own private end, which was to learn to write. I kept always two books in my pocket, one to read, one to write in. As I walked, my mind was busy fitting what I saw with appropriate words."

Stevenson continued writing in university, even though he was there initially to take an engineering degree and thereby continue the family tradition of his father and grandfather. He found himself uninterested in the profession, and switched to law, but after he had been called to the bar he decided to defy his father and pursue a career in writing. Stevenson began his legendary peregrinations soon after graduation; his first full-length published works, *An Inland Voyage* (1878) and *Travels with a Donkey in the Cévennes* (1879), record his travels through France. Both books found an enthusiastic audience. Two years later Stevenson published *Virginibus Puerisque*, a collection of essays previously published in *Macmillan's*, *Cornhill*, and *London* magazines. Many of these essays display the same gentle humor and wit that appears in the letters Stevenson wrote to his friends and family.

On one of his trips to France Stevenson met his future wife, Fanny Osbourne, an American who was then married, with two children. He followed her to California, where she obtained a divorce, and the two were married in 1880. It was for his stepson Lloyd's pleasure that Stevenson created *Treasure Island* (1883), the "boy's story" of a man who procures a secret map and sets out alongside Long John Silver in a quest for hidden treasure. *Kidnapped* (1886) and its sequel *Catriona* (1893) were equally successful. 1886 also saw the publication of Stevenson's most enduring work of fiction, *Strange Case of Dr. Jekyll and Mr. Hyde*, whose mystery concerns Dr. Jekyll's development of a drug that enables him to separate the good and bad parts of his nature. In these stories Stevenson saw himself as a romancer, eschewing the domestic realism that had defined the English novel as written by Dickens and George Eliot, with its complex focus on the home and the good woman who gives it moral definition. "This is a poison bad world for the romancer, this Anglo-Saxon world," he wrote; "I usually get out of it [the demand for morality in fiction] by not having any women in it at all." Later he would add: "Beware of realism; it is the devil."

Stevenson also enjoyed success as a poet and as a writer of short stories. The enormously popular *A Child's Garden of Verses* (1885) included many poems written in his Scottish dialect. His first collection of short stories, *New Arabian Nights* (1882), includes "The Pavilion on the Links," which Arthur Conan Doyle called "the high-water mark of [Stevenson's] genius." *The Merry Men and Other Tales and Fables* was published in 1887, and *Island Nights' Entertainment* in 1893. The latter deals largely with the problems of imperialism in the South Sea islands; "The Beach of Falesà," for instance, concerns discord between colonial merchants and native islanders. Stevenson had come to live in Samoa after searching the South Seas for a more salubrious climate than that of his Scottish homeland.

Though he continued to express longing for Scotland in his final years, Stevenson also came to love Samoa profoundly. After his death from a cerebral hemorrhage in 1894, his many island friends carried his remains up Mt. Vaea to bury him as he had requested in his poem "Requiem," which also provided the epitaph engraved on his tombstone. Stevenson was in his prime at the time of his death, at work on *Weir of Hermiston* (1896)—a book that, although unfinished, is regarded by many as a masterpiece.

Strange Case of Dr. Jekyll and Mr. Hyde

The concept of "Jekyll and Hyde" is now such a cultural commonplace that few twenty-first-century readers can experience the original story's twist ending the way a reader might have when it was first published in 1886. Though its shocking conclusion is too often already known to readers coming to the book for the first time, *Strange Case of Dr. Jekyll and Mr. Hyde* continues to fascinate general readers as well as critics, who have seen it variously as sensationalist escapism, a morally instructive fable, an early detective novel, and a Gothic examination of human psychology. Many have shared the view of critic Julia Wedgewood, who shortly after its publication described it as "a shilling story, which the reader devours in an hour, but to which [the reader] may return again and again, to study a profound allegory and admire a model of style."

At the time he conceived of *Jekyll and Hyde*, in the fall of 1885, Robert Louis Stevenson was in some personal difficulty. His typically poor health was particularly bad during this period, and he longed to become financially independent from his parents but frequently found himself requesting more support from them. He was in just such a state of financial distress when, as he would later claim, inspiration for a money-making story came to him in the form of a dream: "For two days I went about racking my brains for a plot of any sort; and on the second night I dreamed the scene at the window, and a scene afterwards split in two, in which Hyde, pursued for some crime, took the powder." After this moment of inspiration, *Jekyll and Hyde* was written in "white-hot haste": Stevenson composed the first draft in just three days. This draft, however, was just as quickly discarded when Fanny Stevenson argued that, by emphasizing sensationalism over moral substance, it had failed to fulfill its literary potential. It has been claimed that in this original draft Hyde was not an alternative personality but only an outer disguise, and some critics have speculated that the draft may have contained explicit sexual or violent content—but these conjectures cannot be confirmed because, after an intense disagreement, Stevenson is said to have burned the pages. He undertook his second draft with similarly punishing speed, and would later write that "*Jekyll* was conceived, written, re-written, re-rewritten, and printed inside ten weeks."

Released both as a cloth-bound volume and as a cheaply printed "shilling shocker," *Jekyll and Hyde* was an immediate hit and a major step in the establishment of Stevenson's writing career. Within half a year, it had sold 40,000 copies. Stevenson himself was somewhat uncomfortable with the book's mass success and its lowbrow elements, dismissing *Jekyll and Hyde* as "a fine bogey tale" and confiding in a letter to a friend that "[t]here must be something wrong in me, or I would not be popular." Although the book was favorably received by critics, who lauded Stevenson's style and originality, some of them also seemed hesitant to praise too highly a work with such broad appeal. In his 1894 criticism of the novella, Henry James would muse, "Is *Doctor Jekyll and Mr. Hyde* a work of high philosophic intention, or simply the most ingenious and irresponsible of fictions?"

The novella's popularity quickly prompted what would become the first of many theatrical adaptations of the *Jekyll and Hyde* story. Capitalizing on its most sensational elements, playwright Thomas Russell Sullivan and the prominent actor Richard Mansfield transformed Stevenson's narrative into an 1887 melodrama complete with a romance plot of which the original text contains no trace. After acclaimed performances in Boston and New York, the production was moved to London, where, despite initial success, the melodrama's run was closed down early. The infamous "Jack the Ripper" murders had begun, and Mansfield's convincing portrayal of Hyde reminded Londoners so strongly of the feared serial killer that Mansfield himself became a rumored suspect.

Though Jack the Ripper entered public consciousness after *Jekyll and Hyde* was published, it is perhaps not surprising that audiences drew a connection between them. Hyde's dwelling in Soho reflects anxieties that were made concrete in the figure of Jack the Ripper, but that pre-existed him—fears about the impoverished regions of London and the crime and vice they bred. Although it was immediately adjacent to the affluent Mayfair, Soho was a rough neighborhood, inhabited by poor families and associated with prostitution and other illicit activities. At the time *Jekyll and Hyde* was written, Victorian anxieties about such neighborhoods were particularly focused on sexual crimes; in the summer of 1885, Londoners were horrified to learn of the extent and violence of the city's underground child prostitution industry, disturbingly documented in an investigative newspaper report titled "The Maiden Tribute of Modern Babylon."

Consensual encounters between men were also a subject of public censure and discussion during this period; the Labouchère Amendment, passed in the same month as *Jekyll and Hyde*'s publication, expanded the range of sexual acts between men that could be punished by law. Many critics have drawn parallels between Jekyll's double life and that lived by participants in late-nineteenth-century middle-class gay subculture—a subculture with which Stevenson's own social circle overlapped (though it is not clear whether he himself was ever sexually attracted to men). It is worth noting, however, that Stevenson discouraged sexual interpretations of the novella, claiming that "people are so filled full of folly and inverted lust, that they can think of nothing but sexuality" and that "the beast Hyde … is no more sensual than another, but … is the essence of cruelty and malice, and selfishness and cowardice: and these are the diabolic in man."

Stevenson's evocation of "the beast Hyde" reflects another touchpoint for class anxieties in the last quarter of the nineteenth century: the pseudoscientific belief that criminality and moral degeneracy were caused by atavism—regression to an earlier point in biological evolution. This notion originated with the Italian criminologist Cesare Lombroso, who argued that in physiology as well as behavior criminals resembled the primates from which humans evolved. Cranial deformity, small brain size, and left-handedness were among the characteristics that, according to Lombroso, were associated with criminality. Though Lombroso's work was not published in English until the early twentieth century, he had many English popularizers, including some whom Stevenson knew personally.

Another contemporary theory regarding the physiology of disordered behavior was that of the double brain. According to this account, each half of a human brain was capable of independent functioning but possessed different dominant characteristics: the left brain was associated with reason, civilization, and masculinity, the right brain with emotion, instinct, and femininity. (These associations were informed by Victorian assumptions regarding race and gender; the left brain's influence was said to be strongest in healthy white men.) Misalignment of brain hemispheres was thought to cause all manner of criminal behaviors and mental illnesses, including multiple personalities. There is evidence to suggest that Stevenson—who had long been interested in the concept of the double—read medical case studies of dual personalities before composing his own "strange case."

Informed though it was by the ideological landscape of his own era, *Strange Case of Dr. Jekyll and Mr. Hyde* continues to hold a place in popular consciousness; it has never been out of print, and it has been adapted for the stage, film, and television hundreds of times. Although the novella's stature among scholars has never matched its tremendous mass appeal, *Jekyll and Hyde* has lent itself to an extraordinarily wide range of critical frameworks, from Freudian psychoanalysis to postmodern theories of language. Twenty-first-century readers continue to reinterpret the novella's suggestion that, as Stevenson's friend Andrew Lang put it, "every Jekyll among us is haunted by his own Hyde."

⌘⌘⌘

Strange Case of Dr. Jekyll and Mr. Hyde

Story of the Door

Mr. Utterson the lawyer was a man of a rugged countenance, that was never lighted by a smile; cold, scanty, and embarrassed in discourse; backward in sentiment; lean, long, dusty, dreary, and yet somehow lovable. At friendly meetings, and when the wine was to his taste, something eminently human beaconed from his eye; something indeed which never found its way into his talk, but which spoke not only in these silent symbols of the after-dinner face, but more often and loudly in the acts of his life. He was austere with himself; drank gin when he was alone, to mortify a taste for vintages; and though he enjoyed the theatre, had not crossed the doors of one for twenty years. But he had an approved[1] tolerance for others; sometimes wondering, almost with envy, at the high pressure of spirits involved in their misdeeds; and in any extremity inclined to help rather than to reprove. "I incline to Cain's heresy,"[2] he used to say quaintly: "I let my brother go to the devil in his own way." In this character, it was frequently his fortune to be the last reputable acquaintance and the last good influence in the lives of down-going men. And to such as these, so long as they came about his chambers, he never marked a shade of change in his demeanour.

No doubt the feat was easy to Mr. Utterson; for he was undemonstrative at the best, and even his friendship seemed to be founded in a similar catholicity[3] of good

[1] *approved* Proven.

[2] *Cain's heresy* Cain, the eldest son of Adam and Eve, murdered his younger brother, Abel, in an act of jealousy (see Genesis 4). His "heresy" refers to his denial of responsibility for his brother in Genesis 4.9.

[3] *catholicity* All-inclusiveness.

nature. It is the mark of a modest man to accept his friendly circle readymade from the hands of opportunity; and that was the lawyer's way. His friends were those of his own blood or those whom he had known the longest; his affections, like ivy, were the growth of time, they implied no aptness in the object. Hence, no doubt, the bond that united him to Mr. Richard Enfield, his distant kinsman, the well-known man about town. It was a nut to crack for many, what these two could see in each other, or what subject they could find in common. It was reported by those who encountered them in their Sunday walks, that they said nothing, looked singularly dull, and would hail with obvious relief the appearance of a friend. For all that, the two men put the greatest store by these excursions, counted them the chief jewel of each week, and not only set aside occasions of pleasure, but even resisted the calls of business, that they might enjoy them uninterrupted.

It chanced on one of these rambles that their way led them down a bystreet in a busy quarter of London. The street was small and what is called quiet, but it drove a thriving trade on the weekdays. The inhabitants were all doing well, it seemed, and all emulously hoping to do better still, and laying out the surplus of their gains in coquetry; so that the shop fronts stood along that thoroughfare with an air of invitation, like rows of smiling saleswomen. Even on Sunday, when it veiled its more florid charms and lay comparatively empty of passage, the street shone out in contrast to its dingy neighbourhood, like a fire in a forest; and with its freshly painted shutters, well-polished brasses, and general cleanliness and gaiety of note, instantly caught and pleased the eye of the passenger.

Two doors from one corner, on the left hand going east, the line was broken by the entry of a court; and just at that point, a certain sinister block of building thrust forward its gable on the street. It was two stories high; showed no window, nothing but a door on the lower story and a blind forehead of discoloured wall on the upper; and bore in every feature, the marks of prolonged and sordid negligence. The door, which was equipped with neither bell nor knocker, was blistered and distained.[1] Tramps slouched into the recess and struck matches on the panels; children kept shop upon the steps; the schoolboy had tried his knife on the mouldings; and for close on a generation, no one had appeared to drive away these random visitors or to repair their ravages.

Mr. Enfield and the lawyer were on the other side of the bystreet; but when they came abreast of the entry, the former lifted up his cane and pointed.

"Did you ever remark that door?" he asked; and when his companion had replied in the affirmative, "It is connected in my mind," added he, "with a very odd story."

"Indeed?" said Mr. Utterson, with a slight change of voice, "and what was that?"

"Well, it was this way," returned Mr. Enfield: "I was coming home from some place at the end of the world, about three o'clock of a black winter morning, and my way lay through a part of town where there was literally nothing to be seen but lamps. Street after street, and all the folks asleep—street after street, all lighted up as if for a procession and all as empty as a church—till at last I got into that state of mind when a man listens and listens and begins to long for the sight of a policeman. All at once, I saw two figures: one a little man who was stumping along eastward at a good walk, and the other a girl of maybe eight or ten who was running as hard as she was able down a cross street. Well, sir, the two ran into one another naturally enough at the corner; and then came the horrible part of the thing; for the man trampled calmly over the child's body and left her screaming on the ground. It sounds nothing to hear, but it was hellish to see. It wasn't like a man; it was like some damned Juggernaut.[2] I gave a view halloa,[3] took to my heels, collared my gentleman, and brought him back to where there was already quite a group about the screaming child. He was perfectly cool and made no resistance, but gave me one look, so ugly that it brought out the sweat on me like running. The people who had

[1] *distained* Stained, discolored, or tarnished.

[2] *Juggernaut* Huge, powerful force that destroys whatever is in its path.

[3] *view halloa* Shout made by a hunter who sights a fox.

turned out were the girl's own family; and pretty soon, the doctor, for whom she had been sent, put in his appearance. Well, the child was not much the worse, more frightened, according to the Sawbones;[1] and there you might have supposed would be an end to it. But there was one curious circumstance. I had taken a loathing to my gentleman at first sight. So had the child's family, which was only natural. But the doctor's case was what struck me. He was the usual cut-and-dry apothecary, of no particular age and colour, with a strong Edinburgh accent, and about as emotional as a bagpipe. Well, sir, he was like the rest of us; every time he looked at my prisoner, I saw that Sawbones turn sick and white with the desire to kill him. I knew what was in his mind, just as he knew what was in mine; and killing being out of the question, we did the next best. We told the man we could and would make such a scandal out of this, as should make his name stink from one end of London to the other. If he had any friends or any credit,[2] we undertook that he should lose them. And all the time, as we were pitching it in red hot, we were keeping the women off him as best we could, for they were as wild as harpies.[3] I never saw a circle of such hateful faces; and there was the man in the middle, with a kind of black, sneering coolness—frightened too, I could see that—but carrying it off, sir, really like Satan. 'If you choose to make capital out of this accident,' said he, 'I am naturally helpless. No gentleman but wishes to avoid a scene,' says he. 'Name your figure.' Well, we screwed him up to a hundred pounds for the child's family; he would have clearly liked to stick out; but there was something about the lot of us that meant mischief, and at last he struck.[4] The next thing was to get the money; and where do you think he carried us but to that place with the door?—whipped out a key, went in, and presently came back with the matter of ten pounds in gold and a cheque for the balance on Coutts's,[5] drawn payable to bearer and signed with a name that I can't mention, though it's one of the points of my story, but it was a name at least very well known and often printed. The figure was stiff; but the signature was good for more than that, if it was only genuine. I took the liberty of pointing out to my gentleman that the whole business looked apocryphal,[6] and that a man does not, in real life, walk into a cellar door at four in the morning and come out of it with another man's cheque for close upon a hundred pounds. But he was quite easy and sneering. 'Set your mind at rest,' says he, 'I will stay with you till the banks open and cash the cheque myself.' So we all set off, the doctor, and the child's father, and our friend and myself, and passed the rest of the night in my chambers; and next day, when we had breakfasted, went in a body to the bank. I gave in the cheque myself, and said I had every reason to believe it was a forgery. Not a bit of it. The cheque was genuine."

"Tut-tut," said Mr. Utterson.

"I see you feel as I do," said Mr. Enfield. "Yes, it's a bad story. For my man was a fellow that nobody could have to do with, a really damnable man; and the person that drew the cheque is the very pink of the proprieties, celebrated too, and (what makes it worse) one of your fellows who do what they call good. Blackmail, I suppose; an honest man paying through the nose for some of the capers of his youth. Blackmail House is what I call that place with the door, in consequence. Though even that, you know, is far from explaining all," he added, and with the words fell into a vein of musing.

From this he was recalled by Mr. Utterson asking rather suddenly: "And you don't know if the drawer of the cheque lives there?"

"A likely place, isn't it?" returned Mr. Enfield. "But I happen to have noticed his address; he lives in some square or other."

"And you never asked about the—place with the door?" said Mr. Utterson.

"No, sir: I had a delicacy," was the reply. "I feel very strongly about putting questions; it partakes too much

[1] *Sawbones* Slang: Doctor or surgeon.

[2] *credit* Good reputation.

[3] *harpies* Cruel, vengeful monsters of Greek and Roman mythology described as part woman and part bird.

[4] *struck* Surrendered.

[5] *Coutts* London bank that served only upper-class clients.

[6] *apocryphal* Dubious.

of the style of the day of judgment. You start a question, and it's like starting a stone. You sit quietly on the top of a hill; and away the stone goes, starting others; and presently some bland old bird (the last you would have thought of) is knocked on the head in his own back garden and the family have to change their name. No, sir, I make it a rule of mine: the more it looks like Queer Street,[1] the less I ask."

"A very good rule, too," said the lawyer.

"But I have studied the place for myself," continued Mr. Enfield. "It seems scarcely a house. There is no other door, and nobody goes in or out of that one but, once in a great while, the gentleman of my adventure. There are three windows looking on the court on the first floor;[2] none below; the windows are always shut but they're clean. And then there is a chimney which is generally smoking; so somebody must live there. And yet it's not so sure; for the buildings are so packed together about that court, that it's hard to say where one ends and another begins."

The pair walked on again for a while in silence; and then, "Enfield," said Mr. Utterson, "that's a good rule of yours."

"Yes, I think it is," returned Enfield.

"But for all that," continued the lawyer, "there's one point I want to ask: I want to ask the name of that man who walked over the child."

"Well," said Mr. Enfield, "I can't see what harm it would do. It was a man of the name of Hyde."

"H'm," said Mr. Utterson. "What sort of a man is he to see?"

"He is not easy to describe. There is something wrong with his appearance; something displeasing, something downright detestable. I never saw a man I so disliked, and yet I scarce know why. He must be deformed somewhere; he gives a strong feeling of deformity, although I couldn't specify the point. He's an extraordinary looking man, and yet I really can name nothing out of the way. No, sir; I can make no hand of it; I can't describe him. And it's not want of memory; for I declare I can see him this moment."

Mr. Utterson again walked some way in silence and obviously under a weight of consideration. "You are sure he used a key?" he inquired at last.

"My dear sir ..." began Enfield, surprised out of himself.

"Yes, I know," said Utterson; "I know it must seem strange. The fact is, if I do not ask you the name of the other party, it is because I know it already. You see, Richard, your tale has gone home. If you have been inexact in any point, you had better correct it."

"I think you might have warned me," returned the other with a touch of sullenness. "But I have been pedantically exact, as you call it. The fellow had a key; and what's more, he has it still. I saw him use it, not a week ago."

Mr. Utterson sighed deeply but said never a word; and the young man presently resumed. "Here is another lesson to say nothing," said he. "I am ashamed of my long tongue. Let us make a bargain never to refer to this again."

"With all my heart," said the lawyer. "I shake hands on that, Richard."

SEARCH FOR MR. HYDE

That evening Mr. Utterson came home to his bachelor house in sombre spirits and sat down to dinner without relish. It was his custom of a Sunday, when this meal was over, to sit close by the fire, a volume of some dry divinity on his reading desk, until the clock of the neighbouring church rang out the hour of twelve, when he would go soberly and gratefully to bed. On this night, however, as soon as the cloth was taken away, he took up a candle and went into his business room. There he opened his safe, took from the most private part of it a document endorsed on the envelope as Dr. Jekyll's Will, and sat down with a clouded brow to study its contents. The will was holograph,[3] for Mr. Utterson, though he took charge of it now that it was made, had refused to lend the least assistance in the

[1] *Queer Street* Slang term referring to a personal predicament, usually of a financial nature.

[2] *first floor* I.e., the floor immediately above street level; in North American usage, it would be called the second floor.

[3] *holograph* Written out by the person who has signed it.

making of it; it provided not only that, in case of the decease of Henry Jekyll, M.D., D.C.L., L.L.D., F.R.S.,[1] etc., all his possessions were to pass into the hands of his "friend and benefactor Edward Hyde," but that in case of Dr. Jekyll's "disappearance or unexplained absence for any period exceeding three calendar months," the said Edward Hyde should step into the said Henry Jekyll's shoes without further delay and free from any burthen or obligation, beyond the payment of a few small sums to the members of the doctor's household. This document had long been the lawyer's eyesore. It offended him both as a lawyer and as a lover of the sane and customary sides of life, to whom the fanciful was the immodest. And hitherto it was his ignorance of Mr. Hyde that had swelled his indignation; now, by a sudden turn, it was his knowledge. It was already bad enough when the name was but a name of which he could learn no more. It was worse when it began to be clothed upon with detestable attributes; and out of the shifting, insubstantial mists that had so long baffled his eye, there leaped up the sudden, definite presentment[2] of a fiend.

"I thought it was madness," he said, as he replaced the obnoxious paper in the safe, "and now I begin to fear it is disgrace."

With that he blew out his candle, put on a greatcoat, and set forth in the direction of Cavendish Square,[3] that citadel of medicine, where his friend, the great Dr. Lanyon, had his house and received his crowding patients. "If any one knows, it will be Lanyon," he had thought.

The solemn butler knew and welcomed him; he was subjected to no stage of delay, but ushered direct from the door to the dining room where Dr. Lanyon sat alone over his wine. This was a hearty, healthy, dapper, red-faced gentleman, with a shock of hair prematurely white, and a boisterous and decided manner. At sight of Mr. Utterson, he sprang up from his chair and welcomed him with both hands. The geniality, as was the way of the man, was somewhat theatrical to the eye; but it reposed on genuine feeling. For these two were old friends, old mates both at school and college, both thorough respecters of themselves and of each other, and, what does not always follow, men who thoroughly enjoyed each other's company.

After a little rambling talk, the lawyer led up to the subject which so disagreeably preoccupied his mind.

"I suppose, Lanyon," said he "you and I must be the two oldest friends that Henry Jekyll has?"

"I wish the friends were younger," chuckled Dr. Lanyon. "But I suppose we are. And what of that? I see little of him now."

"Indeed?" said Utterson. "I thought you had a bond of common interest."

"We had," was the reply. "But it is more than ten years since Henry Jekyll became too fanciful for me. He began to go wrong, wrong in mind; and though of course I continue to take an interest in him for old sake's sake, as they say, I see and I have seen devilish little of the man. Such unscientific balderdash," added the doctor, flushing suddenly purple, "would have estranged Damon and Pythias."[4]

This little spirit of temper was somewhat of a relief to Mr. Utterson. "They have only differed on some point of science," he thought; and being a man of no scientific passions (except in the matter of conveyancing[5]), he even added: "It is nothing worse than that!" He gave his friend a few seconds to recover his composure, and then approached the question he had come to put. "Did you ever come across a protégé of his—one Hyde?" he asked.

"Hyde?" repeated Lanyon. "No. Never heard of him. Since my time."

[1] *M.D.* Doctor of Medicine; *D.C.L.* Doctor of Civil Law; *L.L.D.* Doctor of Laws; *F.R.S.* Fellow of the Royal Society, a prestigious organization of scientists.

[2] *presentment* Mental picture.

[3] *Cavendish Square* Affluent neighborhood in London's West End; many prominent doctors had offices in the area.

[4] *Damon and Pythias* Loyal friends of Greek mythology. Damon was condemned to execution, and Pythias offered himself as collateral so Damon could leave to settle his affairs. Impressed when Damon returned as promised, the sovereign pardoned him.

[5] *conveyancing* Use of legal documents to transfer property from one owner to another.

That was the amount of information that the lawyer carried back with him to the great, dark bed on which he tossed to and fro, until the small hours of the morning began to grow large. It was a night of little ease to his toiling mind, toiling in mere[1] darkness and besieged by questions.

Six o'clock struck on the bells of the church that was so conveniently near to Mr. Utterson's dwelling, and still he was digging at the problem. Hitherto it had touched him on the intellectual side alone; but now his imagination also was engaged, or rather enslaved; and as he lay and tossed in the gross darkness of the night and the curtained room, Mr. Enfield's tale went by before his mind in a scroll of lighted pictures. He would be aware of the great field of lamps of a nocturnal city; then of the figure of a man walking swiftly; then of a child running from the doctor's; and then these met, and that human Juggernaut trod the child down and passed on regardless of her screams. Or else he would see a room in a rich house, where his friend lay asleep, dreaming and smiling at his dreams; and then the door of that room would be opened, the curtains of the bed plucked apart, the sleeper recalled, and lo! there would stand by his side a figure to whom power was given, and even at that dead hour, he must rise and do its bidding. The figure in these two phases haunted the lawyer all night; and if at any time he dozed over, it was but to see it glide more stealthily through sleeping houses, or move the more swiftly and still the more swiftly, even to dizziness, through wider labyrinths of lamp-lighted city, and at every street corner crush a child and leave her screaming. And still the figure had no face by which he might know it; even in his dreams, it had no face, or one that baffled him and melted before his eyes; and thus it was that there sprang up and grew apace in the lawyer's mind a singularly strong, almost an inordinate, curiosity to behold the features of the real Mr. Hyde. If he could but once set eyes on him, he thought the mystery would lighten and perhaps roll altogether away, as was the habit of mysterious things when well examined. He might see a reason for his friend's strange preference or bondage (call it which you please) and even for the startling clause of the will. At least it would be a face worth seeing: the face of a man who was without bowels of mercy: a face which had but to show itself to raise up, in the mind of the unimpressionable Enfield, a spirit of enduring hatred.

From that time forward, Mr. Utterson began to haunt the door in the bystreet of shops. In the morning before office hours, at noon when business was plenty, and time scarce, at night under the face of the fogged city moon, by all lights and at all hours of solitude or concourse, the lawyer was to be found on his chosen post.

"If he be Mr. Hyde," he had thought, "I shall be Mr. Seek."

And at last his patience was rewarded. It was a fine dry night; frost in the air; the streets as clean as a ballroom floor; the lamps, unshaken by any wind, drawing a regular pattern of light and shadow. By ten o'clock, when the shops were closed, the bystreet was very solitary and, in spite of the low growl of London from all round, very silent. Small sounds carried far; domestic sounds out of the houses were clearly audible on either side of the roadway; and the rumour[2] of the approach of any passenger preceded him by a long time. Mr. Utterson had been some minutes at his post, when he was aware of an odd, light footstep drawing near. In the course of his nightly patrols, he had long grown accustomed to the quaint effect with which the footfalls of a single person, while he is still a great way off, suddenly spring out distinct from the vast hum and clatter of the city. Yet his attention had never before been so sharply and decisively arrested; and it was with a strong, superstitious prevision[3] of success that he withdrew into the entry of the court.

The steps drew swiftly nearer, and swelled out suddenly louder as they turned the end of the street. The lawyer, looking forth from the entry, could soon see what manner of man he had to deal with. He was small and very plainly dressed, and the look of him, even at

[1] *mere* Undiluted.

[2] *rumour* Noise.

[3] *prevision* Foreknowledge.

that distance, went somehow strongly against the watcher's inclination. But he made straight for the door, crossing the roadway to save time; and as he came, he drew a key from his pocket like one approaching home.

Mr. Utterson stepped out and touched him on the shoulder as he passed. "Mr. Hyde, I think?"

Mr. Hyde shrank back with a hissing intake of the breath. But his fear was only momentary; and though he did not look the lawyer in the face, he answered coolly enough: "That is my name. What do you want?"

"I see you are going in," returned the lawyer. "I am an old friend of Dr. Jekyll's—Mr. Utterson of Gaunt Street—you must have heard my name; and meeting you so conveniently, I thought you might admit me."

"You will not find Dr. Jekyll; he is from home," replied Mr. Hyde, blowing in the key. And then suddenly, but still without looking up, "How did you know me?" he asked.

"On your side," said Mr. Utterson, "will you do me a favour?"

"With pleasure," replied the other. "What shall it be?"

"Will you let me see your face?" asked the lawyer.

Mr. Hyde appeared to hesitate, and then, as if upon some sudden reflection, fronted about with an air of defiance; and the pair stared at each other pretty fixedly for a few seconds. "Now I shall know you again," said Mr. Utterson. "It may be useful."

"Yes," returned Mr. Hyde, "it is as well we have, met; and *à propos*,[1] you should have my address." And he gave a number of a street in Soho.[2]

"Good God!" thought Mr. Utterson, "can he, too, have been thinking of the will?" But he kept his feelings to himself and only grunted in acknowledgment of the address.

"And now," said the other, "how did you know me?"

"By description," was the reply.

"Whose description?"

"We have common friends," said Mr. Utterson.

"Common friends?" echoed Mr. Hyde, a little hoarsely. "Who are they?"

"Jekyll, for instance," said the lawyer.

"He never told you," cried Mr. Hyde, with a flush of anger. "I did not think you would have lied."

"Come," said Mr. Utterson, "that is not fitting language."

The other snarled aloud into a savage laugh; and the next moment, with extraordinary quickness, he had unlocked the door and disappeared into the house.

The lawyer stood awhile when Mr. Hyde had left him, the picture of disquietude. Then he began slowly to mount the street, pausing every step or two and putting his hand to his brow like a man in mental perplexity. The problem he was thus debating as he walked, was one of a class that is rarely solved. Mr. Hyde was pale and dwarfish, he gave an impression of deformity without any nameable malformation, he had a displeasing smile, he had borne himself to the lawyer with a sort of murderous mixture of timidity and boldness, and he spoke with a husky, whispering, and somewhat broken voice; all these were points against him, but not all of these together could explain the hitherto unknown disgust, loathing, and fear with which Mr. Utterson regarded him. "There must be something else," said the perplexed gentleman. "There *is* something more, if I could find a name for it. God bless me, the man seems hardly human! Something troglodytic,[3] shall we say? or can it be the old story of Dr. Fell?[4] or is it the mere radiance of a foul soul that thus transpires through, and transfigures, its clay continent? The last, I think; for, O my poor old Harry Jekyll, if ever I read Satan's signature upon a face, it is on that of your new friend."

Round the corner from the bystreet, there was a square of ancient, handsome houses, now for the most part decayed from their high estate and let in flats and chambers to all sorts and conditions of men: map engravers, architects, shady lawyers, and the agents of obscure enterprises. One house, however, second from

[1] *à propos* French: with respect to (this) purpose.

[2] *Soho* Central London district known for bohemians, criminals, and sex workers.

[3] *troglodytic* Like a cave person.

[4] *Dr. Fell* Character in a rhyme beginning "I do not like thee, Dr. Fell; / The reason why, I cannot tell."

the corner, was still occupied entire; and at the door of this, which wore a great air of wealth and comfort, though it was now plunged in darkness except for the fanlight, Mr. Utterson stopped and knocked. A well-dressed, elderly servant opened the door.

"Is Dr. Jekyll at home, Poole?" asked the lawyer.

"I will see, Mr. Utterson," said Poole, admitting the visitor, as he spoke, into a large, low-roofed, comfortable hall, paved with flags,[1] warmed (after the fashion of a country house) by a bright, open fire, and furnished with costly cabinets of oak. "Will you wait here by the fire, sir? or shall I give you a light in the dining room?"

"Here, thank you," said the lawyer, and he drew near and leaned on the tall fender.[2] This hall, in which he was now left alone, was a pet fancy of his friend the doctor's; and Utterson himself was wont to speak of it as the pleasantest room in London. But tonight there was a shudder in his blood; the face of Hyde sat heavy on his memory; he felt (what was rare with him) a nausea and distaste of life; and in the gloom of his spirits, he seemed to read a menace in the flickering of the firelight on the polished cabinets and the uneasy starting of the shadow on the roof. He was ashamed of his relief, when Poole presently returned to announce that Dr. Jekyll was gone out.

"I saw Mr. Hyde go in by the old dissecting room door, Poole," he said. "Is that right, when Dr. Jekyll is from home?"

"Quite right, Mr. Utterson, sir," replied the servant. "Mr. Hyde has a key."

"Your master seems to repose a great deal of trust in that young man, Poole," resumed the other musingly.

"Yes, sir, he do indeed," said Poole. "We have all orders to obey him."

"I do not think I ever met Mr. Hyde?" asked Utterson.

"O, dear no, sir. He never *dines* here," replied the butler. "Indeed we see very little of him on this side of the house; he mostly comes and goes by the laboratory."

"Well, good night, Poole."

"Goodnight, Mr. Utterson."

And the lawyer set out homeward with a very heavy heart. "Poor Harry Jekyll," he thought, "my mind misgives me he is in deep waters! He was wild when he was young; a long while ago to be sure; but in the law of God, there is no statute of limitations. Ay, it must be that; the ghost of some old sin, the cancer of some concealed disgrace: punishment coming, *pede claudo*,[3] years after memory has forgotten and self-love condoned the fault." And the lawyer, scared by the thought, brooded awhile on his own past, groping in all the corners of memory, lest by chance some Jack-in-the-Box of an old iniquity should leap to light there. His past was fairly blameless; few men could read the rolls of their life with less apprehension; yet he was humbled to the dust by the many ill things he had done, and raised up again into a sober and fearful gratitude by the many that he had come so near to doing, yet avoided. And then by a return on his former subject, he conceived a spark of hope. "This Master Hyde, if he were studied," thought he, "must have secrets of his own; black secrets, by the look of him; secrets compared to which poor Jekyll's worst would be like sunshine. Things cannot continue as they are. It turns me cold to think of this creature stealing like a thief to Harry's bedside; poor Harry, what a wakening! And the danger of it; for if this Hyde suspects the existence of the will, he may grow impatient to inherit. Ay, I must put my shoulder to the wheel—if Jekyll will but let me," he added, "if Jekyll will only let me." For once more he saw before his mind's eye, as clear as a transparency, the strange clauses of the will.

Dr. Jekyll Was Quite at Ease

A fortnight later, by excellent good fortune, the doctor gave one of his pleasant dinners to some five or six old cronies, all intelligent, reputable men and all judges of good wine; and Mr. Utterson so contrived that he remained behind after the others had departed. This was

[1] *flags* Flagstones.

[2] *fender* Guard placed around a fireplace.

[3] *pede claudo* Latin: lame-footed. The phrase appears in Horace's *Odes* 3.2: "Lame-footed punishment has rarely abandoned a wicked man with a head start."

no new arrangement, but a thing that had befallen many scores of times. Where Utterson was liked, he was liked well. Hosts loved to detain the dry lawyer, when the light-hearted and the loose-tongued had already their foot on the threshold; they liked to sit awhile in his unobtrusive company, practising for solitude, sobering their minds in the man's rich silence after the expense and strain of gaiety. To this rule, Dr. Jekyll was no exception; and as he now sat on the opposite side of the fire—a large, well-made, smooth-faced man of fifty, with something of a slyish cast perhaps, but every mark of capacity and kindness—you could see by his looks that he cherished for Mr. Utterson a sincere and warm affection.

"I have been wanting to speak to you, Jekyll," began the latter. "You know that will of yours?"

A close observer might have gathered that the topic was distasteful; but the doctor carried it off gaily. "My poor Utterson," said he, "you are unfortunate in such a client. I never saw a man so distressed as you were by my will; unless it were that hidebound[1] pedant, Lanyon, at what he called my scientific heresies. Oh, I know he's a good fellow—you needn't frown—an excellent fellow, and I always mean to see more of him; but a hidebound pedant for all that; an ignorant, blatant pedant. I was never more disappointed in any man than Lanyon."

"You know I never approved of it," pursued Utterson, ruthlessly disregarding the fresh topic.

"My will? Yes, certainly, I know that," said the doctor, a trifle sharply. "You have told me so."

"Well, I tell you so again," continued the lawyer. "I have been learning something of young Hyde."

The large handsome face of Dr. Jekyll grew pale to the very lips, and there came a blackness about his eyes. "I do not care to hear more," said he. "This is a matter I thought we had agreed to drop."

"What I heard was abominable," said Utterson.

"It can make no change. You do not understand my position," returned the doctor, with a certain incoherency of manner. "I am painfully situated, Utterson; my position is a very strange—a very strange one. It is one of those affairs that cannot be mended by talking."

"Jekyll," said Utterson, "you know me: I am a man to be trusted. Make a clean breast of this in confidence; and I make no doubt I can get you out of it."

"My good Utterson," said the doctor, "this is very good of you, this is downright good of you, and I cannot find words to thank you in. I believe you fully; I would trust you before any man alive, ay, before myself, if I could make the choice; but indeed it isn't what you fancy; it is not so bad as that; and just to put your good heart at rest, I will tell you one thing: the moment I choose, I can be rid of Mr. Hyde. I give you my hand upon that; and I thank you again and again; and I will just add one little word, Utterson, that I'm sure you'll take in good part: this is a private matter, and I beg of you to let it sleep."

Utterson reflected a little, looking in the fire.

"I have no doubt you are perfectly right," he said at last, getting to his feet.

"Well, but since we have touched upon this business, and for the last time I hope," continued the doctor, "there is one point I should like you to understand. I have really a very great interest in poor Hyde. I know you have seen him; he told me so; and I fear he was rude. But, I do sincerely take a great, a very great interest in that young man; and if I am taken away, Utterson, I wish you to promise me that you will bear with him and get his rights for him. I think you would, if you knew all; and it would be a weight off my mind if you would promise."

"I can't pretend that I shall ever like him," said the lawyer.

"I don't ask that," pleaded Jekyll, laying his hand upon the other's arm; "I only ask for justice; I only ask you to help him for my sake, when I am no longer here."

Utterson heaved an irrepressible sigh. "Well," said he, "I promise."

The Carew Murder Case

Nearly a year later, in the month of October, 18—, London was startled by a crime of singular ferocity and rendered all the more notable by the high position of the victim. The details were few and startling. A maid-

[1] *hidebound* Wedded to convention.

servant living alone in a house not far from the river, had gone upstairs to bed about eleven. Although a fog rolled over the city in the small hours, the early part of the night was cloudless, and the lane, which the maid's window overlooked, was brilliantly lit by the full moon. It seems she was romantically given, for she sat down upon her box, which stood immediately under the window, and fell into a dream of musing. Never (she used to say, with streaming tears, when she narrated that experience), never had she felt more at peace with all men or thought more kindly of the world. And as she so sat she became aware of an aged and beautiful gentleman with white hair, drawing near along the lane; and advancing to meet him, another and very small gentleman, to whom at first she paid less attention. When they had come within speech (which was just under the maid's eyes) the older man bowed and accosted the other with a very pretty manner of politeness. It did not seem as if the subject of his address were of great importance; indeed, from his pointing, it sometimes appeared as if he were only inquiring his way; but the moon shone on his face as he spoke, and the girl was pleased to watch it, it seemed to breathe such an innocent and old world kindness of disposition, yet with something high too, as of a well-founded self-content. Presently her eye wandered to the other, and she was surprised to recognise in him a certain Mr. Hyde, who had once visited her master and for whom she had conceived a dislike. He had in his hand a heavy cane, with which he was trifling; but he answered never a word, and seemed to listen with an ill-contained impatience. And then all of a sudden he broke out in a great flame of anger, stamping with his foot, brandishing the cane, and carrying on (as the maid described it) like a madman. The old gentleman took a step back, with the air of one very much surprised and a trifle hurt; and at that Mr. Hyde broke out of all bounds and clubbed him to the earth. And next moment, with apelike fury, he was trampling his victim under foot and hailing down a storm of blows, under which the bones were audibly shattered and the body jumped upon the roadway. At the horror of these sights and sounds, the maid fainted.

It was two o'clock when she came to herself and called for the police. The murderer was gone long ago; but there lay his victim in the middle of the lane, incredibly mangled. The stick with which the deed had been done, although it was of some rare and very tough and heavy wood, had broken in the middle under the stress of this insensate cruelty; and one splintered half had rolled in the neighbouring gutter—the other, without doubt, had been carried away by the murderer. A purse and a gold watch were found upon the victim: but no cards or papers, except a sealed and stamped envelope, which he had been probably carrying to the post, and which bore the name and address of Mr. Utterson.

This was brought to the lawyer the next morning, before he was out of bed; and he had no sooner seen it, and been told the circumstances, than he shot out a solemn lip. "I shall say nothing till I have seen the body," said he; "this may be very serious. Have the kindness to wait while I dress." And with the same grave countenance he hurried through his breakfast and drove to the police station, whither the body had been carried. As soon as he came into the cell, he nodded.

"Yes," said he, "I recognise him. I am sorry to say that this is Sir Danvers Carew."

"Good God, sir," exclaimed the officer, "is it possible?" And the next moment his eye lighted up with professional ambition. "This will make a deal of noise," he said. "And perhaps you can help us to the man." And he briefly narrated what the maid had seen, and showed the broken stick.

Mr. Utterson had already quailed at the name of Hyde; but when the stick was laid before him, he could doubt no longer; broken and battered as it was, he recognised it for one that he had himself presented many years before to Henry Jekyll.

"Is this Mr. Hyde a person of small stature?" he inquired.

"Particularly small and particularly wicked looking, is what the maid calls him," said the officer.

Mr. Utterson reflected; and then, raising his head, "If you will come with me in my cab," he said, "I think I can take you to his house."

It was by this time about nine in the morning, and the first fog of the season. A great chocolate-coloured pall lowered over heaven, but the wind was continually charging and routing these embattled vapours; so that as the cab crawled from street to street, Mr. Utterson beheld a marvellous number of degrees and hues of twilight; for here it would be dark like the back-end of evening; and there would be a glow of a rich, lurid brown, like the light of some strange conflagration; and here, for a moment, the fog would be quite broken up, and a haggard shaft of daylight would glance in between the swirling wreaths. The dismal quarter of Soho seen under these changing glimpses, with its muddy ways, and slatternly passengers, and its lamps, which had never been extinguished or had been kindled afresh to combat this mournful reinvasion of darkness, seemed, in the lawyer's eyes, like a district of some city in a nightmare. The thoughts of his mind, besides, were of the gloomiest dye; and when he glanced at the companion of his drive, he was conscious of some touch of that terror of the law and the law's officers, which may at times assail the most honest.

As the cab drew up before the address indicated, the fog lifted a little and showed him a dingy street, a gin palace, a low French eating house, a shop for the retail of penny numbers[1] and twopenny salads, many ragged children huddled in the doorways, and many women of different nationalities passing out, key in hand, to have a morning glass; and the next moment the fog settled down again upon that part, as brown as umber, and cut him off from his blackguardly surroundings. This was the home of Henry Jekyll's favourite; of a man who was heir to a quarter of a million sterling.

An ivory-faced and silvery-haired old woman opened the door. She had an evil face, smoothed by hypocrisy; but her manners were excellent. Yes, she said, this was Mr. Hyde's, but he was not at home; he had been in that night very late, but had gone away again in less than an hour; there was nothing strange in that; his habits were very irregular, and he was often absent; for instance, it was nearly two months since she had seen him till yesterday.

"Very well, then, we wish to see his rooms," said the lawyer; and when the woman began to declare it was impossible, "I had better tell you who this person is," he added. "This is Inspector Newcomen of Scotland Yard."

A flash of odious joy appeared upon the woman's face. "Ah!" said she, "he is in trouble! What has he done?"

Mr. Utterson and the inspector exchanged glances. "He don't seem a very popular character," observed the latter. "And now, my good woman, just let me and this gentleman have a look about us."

In the whole extent of the house, which but for the old woman remained otherwise empty, Mr. Hyde had only used a couple of rooms; but these were furnished with luxury and good taste. A closet was filled with wine; the plate was of silver, the napery[2] elegant; a good picture hung upon the walls, a gift (as Utterson supposed) from Henry Jekyll, who was much of a connoisseur; and the carpets were of many plies and agreeable in colour. At this moment, however, the rooms bore every mark of having been recently and hurriedly ransacked; clothes lay about the floor, with their pockets inside out; lock-fast drawers stood open; and on the hearth there lay a pile of grey ashes, as though many papers had been burned. From these embers the inspector disinterred the butt end of a green chequebook, which had resisted the action of the fire; the other half of the stick was found behind the door; and as this clinched his suspicions, the officer declared himself delighted. A visit to the bank, where several thousand pounds were found to be lying to the murderer's credit, completed his gratification.

"You may depend upon it, sir," he told Mr. Utterson: "I have him in my hand. He must have lost his head, or he never would have left the stick or, above all, burned the chequebook. Why, money's life to the man. We have nothing to do but wait for him at the bank, and get out the handbills."[3]

This last, however, was not so easy of accomplishment; for Mr. Hyde had numbered few familiars—even

[1] *gin palace* Pub; *penny numbers* Serial publications offering sensational stories at low prices.

[2] *napery* Tablecloths, napkins, etc.

[3] *handbills* I.e., wanted posters.

the master of the servant maid had only seen him twice; his family could nowhere be traced; he had never been photographed; and the few who could describe him differed widely, as common observers will. Only on one point, were they agreed; and that was the haunting sense of unexpressed deformity with which the fugitive impressed his beholders.

INCIDENT OF THE LETTER

It was late in the afternoon, when Mr. Utterson found his way to Dr. Jekyll's door, where he was at once admitted by Poole, and carried down by the kitchen offices and across a yard which had once been a garden, to the building which was indifferently known as the laboratory or the dissecting rooms. The doctor had bought the house from the heirs of a celebrated surgeon; and his own tastes being rather chemical than anatomical, had changed the destination[1] of the block at the bottom of the garden. It was the first time that the lawyer had been received in that part of his friend's quarters; and he eyed the dingy, windowless structure with curiosity, and gazed round with a distasteful sense of strangeness as he crossed the theatre,[2] once crowded with eager students and now lying gaunt and silent, the tables laden with chemical apparatus, the floor strewn with crates and littered with packing straw, and the light falling dimly through the foggy cupola. At the further end, a flight of stairs mounted to a door covered with red baize; and through this, Mr. Utterson was at last received into the doctor's cabinet.[3] It was a large room, fitted round with glass presses, furnished, among other things, with a cheval glass[4] and a business table, and looking out upon the court by three dusty windows barred with iron. A fire burned in the grate; a lamp was set lighted on the chimney shelf, for even in the houses the fog began to lie thickly; and there, close up to the warmth, sat Dr. Jekyll, looking deadly sick. He did not rise to meet his visitor, but held out a cold hand and bade him welcome in a changed voice.

"And now," said Mr. Utterson, as soon as Poole had left them, "you have heard the news?"

The doctor shuddered. "They were crying it in the square,"[5] he said. "I heard them in my dining room."

"One word," said the lawyer. "Carew was my client, but so are you, and I want to know what I am doing. You have not been mad enough to hide this fellow?"

"Utterson, I swear to God," cried the doctor, "I swear to God I will never set eyes on him again. I bind my honour to you that I am done with him in this world. It is all at an end. And indeed he does not want my help; you do not know him as I do; he is safe, he is quite safe; mark my words, he will never more be heard of."

The lawyer listened gloomily; he did not like his friend's feverish manner. "You seem pretty sure of him," said he; "and for your sake, I hope you may be right. If it came to a trial, your name might appear."

"I am quite sure of him," replied Jekyll; "I have grounds for certainty that I cannot share with anyone. But there is one thing on which you may advise me. I have—I have received a letter; and I am at a loss whether I should show it to the police. I should like to leave it in your hands, Utterson; you would judge wisely, I am sure; I have so great a trust in you."

"You fear, I suppose, that it might lead to his detection?" asked the lawyer.

"No," said the other. "I cannot say that I care what becomes of Hyde; I am quite done with him. I was thinking of my own character, which this hateful business has rather exposed."

Utterson ruminated a while; he was surprised at his friend's selfishness, and yet relieved by it. "Well," said he, at last, "let me see the letter."

The letter was written in an odd, upright hand and signed "Edward Hyde": and it signified, briefly enough, that the writer's benefactor, Dr. Jekyll, whom he had

[1] *destination* Designated purpose.

[2] *theatre* Lecture theater (here, one originally designed for medical demonstrations).

[3] *baize* Felt-like fabric often tacked onto doors to insulate against noise; *cabinet* Private office.

[4] *cheval glass* Freestanding mirror that tilts from the middle so that the angle of the reflection can be adjusted.

[5] *They were … square* Newspaper-sellers frequently shouted the headlines to entice buyers.

long so unworthily repaid for a thousand generosities, need labour under no alarm for his safety, as he had means of escape on which he placed a sure dependence. The lawyer liked this letter well enough; it put a better colour on the intimacy than he had looked for; and he blamed himself for some of his past suspicions.

"Have you the envelope?" he asked.

"I burned it," replied Jekyll, "before I thought what I was about. But it bore no postmark. The note was handed in."

"Shall I keep this and sleep upon it?" asked Utterson.

"I wish you to judge for me entirely," was the reply. "I have lost confidence in myself."

"Well, I shall consider," returned the lawyer. "And now one word more: it was Hyde who dictated the terms in your will about that disappearance?"

The doctor seemed seized with a qualm of faintness: he shut his mouth tight and nodded.

"I knew it," said Utterson. "He meant to murder you. You have had a fine escape."

"I have had what is far more to the purpose," returned the doctor solemnly: "I have had a lesson—O God, Utterson, what a lesson I have had!" And he covered his face for a moment with his hands.

On his way out, the lawyer stopped and had a word or two with Poole. "By the by," said he, "there was a letter handed in today: what was the messenger like?" But Poole was positive nothing had come except by post; "and only circulars[1] by that," he added.

This news sent off the visitor with his fears renewed. Plainly the letter had come by the laboratory door; possibly, indeed, it had been written in the cabinet; and if that were so, it must be differently judged, and handled with the more caution. The newsboys, as he went, were crying themselves hoarse along the footways: "Special edition. Shocking murder of an M.P."[2] That was the funeral oration of one friend and client; and he could not help a certain apprehension lest the good name of another should be sucked down in the eddy of the scandal. It was, at least, a ticklish decision that he had to make; and self-reliant as he was by habit, he began to cherish a longing for advice. It was not to be had directly; but perhaps, he thought, it might be fished for.

Presently after, he sat on one side of his own hearth, with Mr. Guest, his head clerk, upon the other, and midway between, at a nicely calculated distance from the fire, a bottle of a particular old wine that had long dwelt unsunned in the foundations of his house. The fog still slept on the wing above the drowned city, where the lamps glimmered like carbuncles;[3] and through the muffle and smother of these fallen clouds, the procession of the town's life was still rolling in through the great arteries with a sound as of a mighty wind. But the room was gay with firelight. In the bottle the acids were long ago resolved; the imperial[4] dye had softened with time, as the colour grows richer in stained windows; and the glow of hot autumn afternoons on hillside vineyards was ready to be set free and to disperse the fogs of London. Insensibly the lawyer melted. There was no man from whom he kept fewer secrets than Mr. Guest; and he was not always sure that he kept as many as he meant. Guest had often been on business to the doctor's; he knew Poole; he could scarce have failed to hear of Mr. Hyde's familiarity about the house; he might draw conclusions: was it not as well, then, that he should see a letter which put that mystery to rights? and above all since Guest, being a great student and critic of handwriting, would consider the step natural and obliging? The clerk, besides, was a man of counsel; he would scarce read so strange a document without dropping a remark; and by that remark Mr. Utterson might shape his future course.

"This is a sad business about Sir Danvers," he said.

"Yes, sir, indeed. It has elicited a great deal of public feeling," returned Guest. "The man, of course, was mad."

"I should like to hear your views on that," replied Utterson. "I have a document here in his handwriting; it is between ourselves, for I scarce know what to do

---

[1] *circulars* Advertisements produced for mass distribution by mail.

[2] *M.P.* Member of Parliament.

[3] *carbuncles* Red gemstones, especially those cut round, without facets.

[4] *imperial* Deep, reddish purple.

about it; it is an ugly business at the best. But there it is; quite in your way: a murderer's autograph."

Guest's eyes brightened, and he sat down at once and studied it with passion. "No, sir," he said: "not mad; but it is an odd hand."

"And by all accounts a very odd writer," added the lawyer.

Just then the servant entered with a note.

"Is that from Dr. Jekyll, sir?" inquired the clerk. "I thought I knew the writing. Anything private, Mr. Utterson?"

"Only an invitation to dinner. Why? Do you want to see it?"

"One moment. I thank you, sir"; and the clerk laid the two sheets of paper alongside and sedulously compared their contents. "Thank you, sir," he said at last, returning both; "it's a very interesting autograph."

There was a pause, during which Mr. Utterson struggled with himself. "Why did you compare them, Guest?" he inquired suddenly.

"Well, sir," returned the clerk, "there's a rather singular resemblance; the two hands are in many points identical: only differently sloped."

"Rather quaint,"[1] said Utterson.

"It is, as you say, rather quaint," returned Guest.

"I wouldn't speak of this note, you know," said the master.

"No, sir," said the clerk. "I understand."

But no sooner was Mr. Utterson alone that night than he locked the note into his safe, where it reposed from that time forward. "What!" he thought. "Henry Jekyll forge for a murderer!" And his blood ran cold in his veins.

REMARKABLE INCIDENT OF DR. LANYON

Time ran on; thousands of pounds were offered in reward, for the death of Sir Danvers was resented as a public injury; but Mr. Hyde had disappeared out of the ken of the police as though he had never existed. Much of his past was unearthed, indeed, and all disreputable: tales came out of the man's cruelty, at once so callous and violent; of his vile life, of his strange associates, of the hatred that seemed to have surrounded his career; but of his present whereabouts, not a whisper. From the time he had left the house in Soho on the morning of the murder, he was simply blotted out; and gradually, as time drew on, Mr. Utterson began to recover from the hotness of his alarm, and to grow more at quiet with himself. The death of Sir Danvers was, to his way of thinking, more than paid for by the disappearance of Mr. Hyde. Now that that evil influence had been withdrawn, a new life began for Dr. Jekyll. He came out of his seclusion, renewed relations with his friends, became once more their familiar guest and entertainer; and whilst he had always been known for charities, he was now no less distinguished for religion. He was busy, he was much in the open air, he did good; his face seemed to open and brighten, as if with an inward consciousness of service; and for more than two months, the doctor was at peace.

On the 8th of January Utterson had dined at the doctor's with a small party; Lanyon had been there; and the face of the host had looked from one to the other as in the old days when the trio were inseparable friends. On the 12th, and again on the 14th, the door was shut against the lawyer. "The doctor was confined to the house," Poole said, "and saw no one." On the 15th, he tried again, and was again refused; and having now been used for the last two months to see his friend almost daily, he found this return of solitude to weigh upon his spirits. The fifth night he had in Guest to dine with him; and the sixth he betook himself to Dr. Lanyon's.

There at least he was not denied admittance; but when he came in, he was shocked at the change which had taken place in the doctor's appearance. He had his death warrant written legibly upon his face. The rosy man had grown pale; his flesh had fallen away; he was visibly balder and older; and yet it was not so much these tokens of a swift physical decay that arrested the lawyer's notice, as a look in the eye and quality of manner that seemed to testify to some deep-seated terror of the mind. It was unlikely that the doctor should fear death; and yet that was what Utterson was tempted to suspect. "Yes," he thought; "he is a doctor, he must

[1] *quaint* Strange, illogical.

know his own state and that his days are counted; and the knowledge is more than he can bear." And yet when Utterson remarked on his ill looks, it was with an air of greatness that Lanyon declared himself a doomed man.

"I have had a shock," he said, "and I shall never recover. It is a question of weeks. Well, life has been pleasant; I liked it; yes, sir, I used to like it. I sometimes think if we knew all, we should be more glad to get away."

"Jekyll is ill, too," observed Utterson. "Have you seen him?"

But Lanyon's face changed, and he held up a trembling hand. "I wish to see or hear no more of Dr. Jekyll," he said in a loud, unsteady voice. "I am quite done with that person; and I beg that you will spare me any allusion to one whom I regard as dead."

"Tut-tut," said Mr. Utterson; and then after a considerable pause, "Can't I do anything?" he inquired. "We are three very old friends, Lanyon; we shall not live to make others."

"Nothing can be done," returned Lanyon; "ask himself."

"He will not see me," said the lawyer.

"I am not surprised at that," was the reply. "Some day, Utterson, after I am dead, you may perhaps come to learn the right and wrong of this. I cannot tell you. And in the meantime, if you can sit and talk with me of other things, for God's sake, stay and do so; but if you cannot keep clear of this accursed topic, then, in God's name, go, for I cannot bear it."

As soon as he got home, Utterson sat down and wrote to Jekyll, complaining of his exclusion from the house, and asking the cause of this unhappy break with Lanyon; and the next day brought him a long answer, often very pathetically worded, and sometimes darkly mysterious in drift. The quarrel with Lanyon was incurable. "I do not blame our old friend," Jekyll wrote, "but I share his view that we must never meet. I mean from henceforth to lead a life of extreme seclusion; you must not be surprised, nor must you doubt my friendship, if my door is often shut even to you. You must suffer me to go my own dark way. I have brought on myself a punishment and a danger that I cannot name. If I am the chief of sinners, I am the chief of sufferers also. I could not think that this earth contained a place for sufferings and terrors so unmanning; and you can do but one thing, Utterson, to lighten this destiny, and that is to respect my silence." Utterson was amazed; the dark influence of Hyde had been withdrawn, the doctor had returned to his old tasks and amities; a week ago, the prospect had smiled with every promise of a cheerful and an honoured age; and now in a moment, friendship, and peace of mind, and the whole tenor of his life were wrecked. So great and unprepared a change pointed to madness; but in view of Lanyon's manner and words, there must lie for it some deeper ground.

A week afterwards Dr. Lanyon took to his bed, and in something less than a fortnight he was dead. The night after the funeral, at which he had been sadly affected, Utterson locked the door of his business room, and sitting there by the light of a melancholy candle, drew out and set before him an envelope addressed by the hand and sealed with the seal of his dead friend. "PRIVATE: for the hands of G.J. Utterson ALONE and in case of his predecease *to be destroyed unread*," so it was emphatically superscribed; and the lawyer dreaded to behold the contents. "I have buried one friend today," he thought: "what if this should cost me another?" And then he condemned the fear as a disloyalty, and broke the seal. Within there was another enclosure, likewise sealed, and marked upon the cover as "not to be opened till the death or disappearance of Dr. Henry Jekyll." Utterson could not trust his eyes. Yes, it was disappearance; here again, as in the mad will which he had long ago restored to its author, here again were the idea of a disappearance and the name of Henry Jekyll bracketed. But in the will, that idea had sprung from the sinister suggestion of the man Hyde; it was set there with a purpose all too plain and horrible. Written by the hand of Lanyon, what should it mean? A great curiosity came on the trustee, to disregard the prohibition and dive at once to the bottom of these mysteries; but professional honour and faith to his dead friend were stringent obligations; and the packet slept in the inmost corner of his private safe.

It is one thing to mortify curiosity, another to conquer it; and it may be doubted if, from that day forth, Utterson desired the society of his surviving friend with the same eagerness. He thought of him kindly; but his thoughts were disquieted and fearful. He went to call indeed; but he was perhaps relieved to be denied admittance; perhaps, in his heart, he preferred to speak with Poole upon the doorstep and surrounded by the air and sounds of the open city, rather than to be admitted into that house of voluntary bondage, and to sit and speak with its inscrutable recluse. Poole had, indeed, no very pleasant news to communicate. The doctor, it appeared, now more than ever confined himself to the cabinet over the laboratory, where he would sometimes even sleep; he was out of spirits, he had grown very silent, he did not read; it seemed as if he had something on his mind. Utterson became so used to the unvarying character of these reports, that he fell off little by little in the frequency of his visits.

INCIDENT AT THE WINDOW

It chanced on Sunday, when Mr. Utterson was on his usual walk with Mr. Enfield, that their way lay once again through the bystreet; and that when they came in front of the door, both stopped to gaze on it.

"Well," said Enfield, "that story's at an end at least. We shall never see more of Mr. Hyde."

"I hope not," said Utterson. "Did I ever tell you that I once saw him, and shared your feeling of repulsion?"

"It was impossible to do the one without the other," returned Enfield. "And by the way, what an ass you must have thought me, not to know that this was a back way to Dr. Jekyll's! It was partly your own fault that I found it out, even when I did."

"So you found it out, did you?" said Utterson. "But if that be so, we may step into the court and take a look at the windows. To tell you the truth, I am uneasy about poor Jekyll; and even outside, I feel as if the presence of a friend might do him good."

The court was very cool and a little damp, and full of premature twilight, although the sky, high up overhead, was still bright with sunset. The middle one of the three windows was halfway open; and sitting close beside it, taking the air with an infinite sadness of mien,[1] like some disconsolate prisoner, Utterson saw Dr. Jekyll.

"What! Jekyll!" he cried. "I trust you are better."

"I am very low, Utterson," replied the doctor, drearily, "very low. It will not last long, thank God."

"You stay too much indoors," said the lawyer. "You should be out, whipping up the circulation like Mr. Enfield and me. (This is my cousin—Mr. Enfield—Dr. Jekyll.) Come, now; get your hat and take a quick turn with us."

"You are very good," sighed the other. "I should like to very much; but no, no, no, it is quite impossible; I dare not. But indeed, Utterson, I am very glad to see you; this is really a great pleasure; I would ask you and Mr. Enfield up, but the place is really not fit."

"Why then," said the lawyer, good-naturedly, "the best thing we can do is to stay down here and speak with you from where we are."

"That is just what I was about to venture to propose," returned the doctor with a smile. But the words were hardly uttered, before the smile was struck out of his face and succeeded by an expression of such abject terror and despair, as froze the very blood of the two gentlemen below. They saw it but for a glimpse, for the window was instantly thrust down; but that glimpse had been sufficient, and they turned and left the court without a word. In silence, too, they traversed the bystreet; and it was not until they had come into a neighbouring thoroughfare, where even upon a Sunday there were still some stirrings of life, that Mr. Utterson at last turned and looked at his companion. They were both pale; and there was an answering horror in their eyes.

"God forgive us, God forgive us," said Mr. Utterson.

But Mr. Enfield only nodded his head very seriously and walked on once more in silence.

THE LAST NIGHT

Mr. Utterson was sitting by his fireside one evening after dinner, when he was surprised to receive a visit from Poole.

---

[1] *mien* Bearing, appearance.

"Bless me, Poole, what brings you here?" he cried; and then taking a second look at him, "What ails you?" he added; "is the doctor ill?"

"Mr. Utterson," said the man, "there is something wrong."

"Take a seat, and here is a glass of wine for you," said the lawyer. "Now, take your time, and tell me plainly what you want."

"You know the doctor's ways, sir," replied Poole, "and how he shuts himself up. Well, he's shut up again in the cabinet; and I don't like it, sir—I wish I may die if I like it. Mr. Utterson, sir, I'm afraid."

"Now, my good man," said the lawyer, "be explicit. What are you afraid of?"

"I've been afraid for about a week," returned Poole, doggedly disregarding the question, "and I can bear it no more."

The man's appearance amply bore out his words; his manner was altered for the worse; and except for the moment when he had first announced his terror, he had not once looked the lawyer in the face. Even now, he sat with the glass of wine untasted on his knee, and his eyes directed to a corner of the floor. "I can bear it no more," he repeated.

"Come," said the lawyer, "I see you have some good reason, Poole; I see there is something seriously amiss. Try to tell me what it is."

"I think there's been foul play," said Poole, hoarsely.

"Foul play!" cried the lawyer, a good deal frightened and rather inclined to be irritated in consequence. "What foul play? What does the man mean?"

"I daren't say, sir," was the answer; "but will you come along with me and see for yourself?"

Mr. Utterson's only answer was to rise and get his hat and great coat; but he observed with wonder the greatness of the relief that appeared upon the butler's face, and perhaps with no less, that the wine was still untasted when he set it down to follow.

It was a wild, cold, seasonable night of March, with a pale moon, lying on her back as though the wind had tilted her, and a flying wrack of the most diaphanous and lawny[1] texture. The wind made talking difficult, and flecked the blood into the face. It seemed to have swept the streets unusually bare of passengers, besides; for Mr. Utterson thought he had never seen that part of London so deserted. He could have wished it otherwise; never in his life had he been conscious of so sharp a wish to see and touch his fellow creatures; for struggle as he might, there was borne in upon his mind a crushing anticipation of calamity. The square, when they got there, was all full of wind and dust, and the thin trees in the garden were lashing themselves along the railing. Poole, who had kept all the way a pace or two ahead, now pulled up in the middle of the pavement, and in spite of the biting weather, took off his hat and mopped his brow with a red pocket handkerchief. But for all the hurry of his coming, these were not the dews of exertion that he wiped away, but the moisture of some strangling anguish; for his face was white and his voice, when he spoke, harsh and broken.

"Well, sir," he said, "here we are, and God grant there be nothing wrong."

"Amen, Poole," said the lawyer.

Thereupon the servant knocked in a very guarded manner; the door was opened on the chain; and a voice asked from within, "Is that you, Poole?"

"It's all right," said Poole. "Open the door."

The hall, when they entered it, was brightly lighted up; the fire was built high; and about the hearth the whole of the servants, men and women, stood huddled together like a flock of sheep. At the sight of Mr. Utterson, the housemaid broke into hysterical whimpering; and the cook, crying out, "Bless God! it's Mr. Utterson," ran forward as if to take him in her arms.

"What, what? Are you all here?" said the lawyer peevishly. "Very irregular, very unseemly; your master would be far from pleased."

"They're all afraid," said Poole.

Blank silence followed, no one protesting; only the maid lifted up her voice and now wept loudly.

"Hold your tongue!" Poole said to her, with a ferocity of accent that testified to his own jangled

[1] *wrack* Body of high clouds moving quickly in the wind; *lawny* Like lawn, a sheer fabric made from linen or cotton.

nerves; and indeed, when the girl had so suddenly raised the note of her lamentation, they had all started and turned toward the inner door with faces of dreadful expectation. "And now," continued the butler, addressing the knife-boy, "reach me a candle, and we'll get this through hands[1] at once." And then he begged Mr. Utterson to follow him, and led the way to the back garden.

"Now, sir," said he, "you come as gently as you can. I want you to hear, and I don't want you to be heard. And see here, sir, if by any chance he was to ask you in, don't go."

Mr. Utterson's nerves, at this unlooked-for termination, gave a jerk that nearly threw him from his balance; but he recollected his courage and followed the butler into the laboratory building and through the surgical theatre, with its lumber[2] of crates and bottles, to the foot of the stair. Here Poole motioned him to stand on one side and listen; while he himself, setting down the candle and making a great and obvious call on his resolution, mounted the steps and knocked with a somewhat uncertain hand on the red baize of the cabinet door.

"Mr. Utterson, sir, asking to see you," he called; and even as he did so, once more violently signed to the lawyer to give ear.

A voice answered from within: "Tell him I cannot see any one," it said complainingly.

"Thank you, sir," said Poole, with a note of something like triumph in his voice; and taking up his candle, he led Mr. Utterson back across the yard and into the great kitchen, where the fire was out and the beetles were leaping on the floor.

"Sir," he said, looking Mr. Utterson in the eyes, "was that my master's voice?"

"It seems much changed," replied the lawyer, very pale, but giving look for look.

"Changed? Well, yes, I think so," said the butler. "Have I been twenty years in this man's house, to be deceived about his voice? No, sir; master's made away with; he was made away with eight days ago, when we heard him cry out upon the name of God; and *who's* in there instead of him, and *why* it stays there, is a thing that cries to Heaven, Mr. Utterson!"

"This is a very strange tale, Poole; this is rather a wild tale, my man," said Mr. Utterson, biting his finger. "Suppose it were as you suppose, supposing Dr. Jekyll to have been—well, murdered, what could induce the murderer to stay? That won't hold water; it doesn't commend itself to reason."

"Well, Mr. Utterson, you are a hard man to satisfy, but I'll do it yet," said Poole. "All this last week (you must know) him, or it, or whatever it is that lives in that cabinet, has been crying night and day for some sort of medicine and cannot get it to his mind. It was sometimes his way—the master's, that is—to write his orders on a sheet of paper and throw it on the stair. We've had nothing else this week back; nothing but papers, and a closed door, and the very meals left there to be smuggled in when nobody was looking. Well, sir, every day, ay, and twice and thrice in the same day, there have been orders and complaints, and I have been sent flying to all the wholesale chemists in town. Every time I brought the stuff back, there would be another paper telling me to return it, because it was not pure, and another order to a different firm. This drug is wanted bitter bad, sir, whatever for."

"Have you any of these papers?" asked Mr. Utterson.

Poole felt in his pocket and handed out a crumpled note, which the lawyer, bending nearer to the candle, carefully examined. Its contents ran thus: "Dr. Jekyll presents his compliments to Messrs. Maw. He assures them that their last sample is impure and quite useless for his present purpose. In the year 18—, Dr. J. purchased a somewhat large quantity from Messrs. M. He now begs them to search with the most sedulous care, and should any of the same quality be left, to forward it to him at once. Expense is no consideration. The importance of this to Dr. J. can hardly be exaggerated." So far the letter had run composedly enough, but here with a sudden splutter of the pen, the writer's emotion had broken loose. "For God's sake," he had added, "find me some of the old."

---

1 *knife-boy* Low servant who performs menial chores; *we'll get … hands* A Scottish expression meaning "we'll fix this problem."

2 *lumber* Household clutter.

"This is a strange note," said Mr. Utterson; and then sharply, "How do you come to have it open?"

"The man at Maw's was main angry, sir, and he threw it back to me like so much dirt," returned Poole.

"This is unquestionably the doctor's hand, do you know?" resumed the lawyer.

"I thought it looked like it," said the servant rather sulkily; and then, with another voice, "But what matters hand of write?" he said. "I've seen him!"

"Seen him?" repeated Mr. Utterson. "Well?"

"That's it!" said Poole. "It was this way. I came suddenly into the theatre from the garden. It seems he had slipped out to look for this drug or whatever it is; for the cabinet door was open, and there he was at the far end of the room digging among the crates. He looked up when I came in, gave a kind of cry, and whipped upstairs into the cabinet. It was but for one minute that I saw him, but the hair stood upon my head like quills. Sir, if that was my master, why had he a mask upon his face? If it was my master, why did he cry out like a rat, and run from me? I have served him long enough. And then ..." The man paused and passed his hand over his face.

"These are all very strange circumstances," said Mr. Utterson, "but I think I begin to see daylight. Your master, Poole, is plainly seized with one of those maladies that both torture and deform the sufferer; hence, for aught I know, the alteration of his voice; hence the mask and the avoidance of his friends; hence his eagerness to find this drug, by means of which the poor soul retains some hope of ultimate recovery—God grant that he be not deceived! There is my explanation; it is sad enough, Poole, ay, and appalling to consider; but it is plain and natural, hangs well together, and delivers us from all exorbitant alarms."

"Sir," said the butler, turning to a sort of mottled pallor, "that thing was not my master, and there's the truth. My master"—here he looked round him and began to whisper—"is a tall, fine build of a man, and this was more of a dwarf." Utterson attempted to protest. "O, sir," cried Poole, "do you think I do not know my master after twenty years? Do you think I do not know where his head comes to in the cabinet door, where I saw him every morning of my life? No, Sir, that thing in the mask was never Dr. Jekyll—God knows what it was, but it was never Dr. Jekyll; and it is the belief of my heart that there was murder done."

"Poole," replied the lawyer, "if you say that, it will become my duty to make certain. Much as I desire to spare your master's feelings, much as I am puzzled by this note which seems to prove him to be still alive, I shall consider it my duty to break in that door."

"Ah, Mr. Utterson, that's talking!" cried the butler.

"And now comes the second question," resumed Utterson: "Who is going to do it?"

"Why, you and me, sir," was the undaunted reply.

"That is very well said," returned the lawyer; "and whatever comes of it, I shall make it my business to see you are no loser."

"There is an axe in the theatre," continued Poole; "and you might take the kitchen poker for yourself."

The lawyer took that rude but weighty instrument into his hand, and balanced it. "Do you know, Poole," he said, looking up, "that you and I are about to place ourselves in a position of some peril?"

"You may say so, sir, indeed," returned the butler.

"It is well, then, that we should be frank," said the other. "We both think more than we have said; let us make a clean breast. This masked figure that you saw, did you recognise it?"

"Well, sir, it went so quick, and the creature was so doubled up, that I could hardly swear to that," was the answer. "But if you mean, was it Mr. Hyde?—why, yes, I think it was! You see, it was much of the same bigness; and it had the same quick, light way with it; and then who else could have got in by the laboratory door? You have not forgot, sir, that at the time of the murder he had still the key with him? But that's not all. I don't know, Mr. Utterson, if ever you met this Mr. Hyde?"

"Yes," said the lawyer, "I once spoke with him."

"Then you must know as well as the rest of us that there was something queer about that gentleman—something that gave a man a turn—I don't know rightly how to say it, sir, beyond this: that you felt it in your marrow kind of cold and thin."

"I own I felt something of what you describe," said Mr. Utterson.

"Quite so, sir," returned Poole. "Well, when that masked thing like a monkey jumped from among the chemicals and whipped into the cabinet, it went down my spine like ice. Oh, I know it's not evidence, Mr. Utterson. I'm book learned enough for that; but a man has his feelings, and I give you my Bible word it was Mr. Hyde!"

"Ay, ay," said the lawyer. "My fears incline to the same point. Evil, I fear, founded—evil was sure to come—of that connection. Ay, truly, I believe you; I believe poor Harry is killed; and I believe his murderer (for what purpose, God alone can tell) is still lurking in his victim's room. Well, let our name be vengeance. Call Bradshaw."

The footman came at the summons, very white and nervous.

"Pull yourself together, Bradshaw," said the lawyer. "This suspense, I know, is telling upon all of you; but it is now our intention to make an end of it. Poole, here, and I are going to force our way into the cabinet. If all is well, my shoulders are broad enough to bear the blame. Meanwhile, lest anything should really be amiss, or any malefactor seek to escape by the back, you and the boy must go round the corner with a pair of good sticks and take your post at the laboratory door. We give you ten minutes to get to your stations."

As Bradshaw left, the lawyer looked at his watch. "And now, Poole, let us get to ours," he said; and taking the poker under his arm, led the way into the yard. The scud[1] had banked over the moon, and it was now quite dark. The wind, which only broke in puffs and draughts into that deep well of building, tossed the light of the candle to and fro about their steps, until they came into the shelter of the theatre, where they sat down silently to wait. London hummed solemnly all around; but nearer at hand, the stillness was only broken by the sounds of a footfall moving to and fro along the cabinet floor.

"So it will walk all day, sir," whispered Poole; "ay, and the better part of the night. Only when a new sample comes from the chemist, there's a bit of a break. Ah, it's an ill conscience that's such an enemy to rest! Ah, sir, there's blood foully shed in every step of it! But hark again, a little closer—put your heart in your ears, Mr. Utterson, and tell me, is that the doctor's foot?"

The steps fell lightly and oddly, with a certain swing, for all they went so slowly; it was different indeed from the heavy creaking tread of Henry Jekyll. Utterson sighed. "Is there never anything else?" he asked.

Poole nodded. "Once," he said. "Once I heard it weeping!"

"Weeping? how that?" said the lawyer, conscious of a sudden chill of horror.

"Weeping like a woman or a lost soul," said the butler. "I came away with that upon my heart, that I could have wept too."

But now the ten minutes drew to an end. Poole disinterred the axe from under a stack of packing straw; the candle was set upon the nearest table to light them to the attack; and they drew near with bated breath to where that patient foot was still going up and down, up and down, in the quiet of the night.

"Jekyll," cried Utterson, with a loud voice, "I demand to see you." He paused a moment, but there came no reply. "I give you fair warning, our suspicions are aroused, and I must and shall see you," he resumed; "if not by fair means, then by foul—if not of your consent, then by brute force!"

"Utterson," said the voice, "for God's sake, have mercy!"

"Ah, that's not Jekyll's voice—it's Hyde's!" cried Utterson. "Down with the door, Poole!"

Poole swung the axe over his shoulder; the blow shook the building, and the red baize door leaped against the lock and hinges. A dismal screech, as of mere animal terror, rang from the cabinet. Up went the axe again, and again the panels crashed and the frame bounded; four times the blow fell; but the wood was tough and the fittings were of excellent workmanship; and it was not until the fifth, that the lock burst in sunder and the wreck of the door fell inwards on the carpet.

The besiegers, appalled by their own riot and the stillness that had succeeded, stood back a little and peered in. There lay the cabinet before their eyes in the

[1] *scud* Body of low, thin clouds moving quickly in the wind.

quiet lamplight, a good fire glowing and chattering on the hearth, the kettle singing its thin strain, a drawer or two open, papers neatly set forth on the business table, and nearer the fire, the things laid out for tea: the quietest room, you would have said, and, but for the glazed presses full of chemicals, the most commonplace that night in London.

Right in the midst there lay the body of a man sorely contorted and still twitching. They drew near on tiptoe, turned it on its back and beheld the face of Edward Hyde. He was dressed in clothes far too large for him, clothes of the doctor's bigness; the cords of his face still moved with a semblance of life, but life was quite gone; and by the crushed phial in the hand and the strong smell of kernels[1] that hung upon the air, Utterson knew that he was looking on the body of a self-destroyer.

"We have come too late," he said sternly, "whether to save or punish. Hyde is gone to his account; and it only remains for us to find the body of your master."

The far greater proportion of the building was occupied by the theatre, which filled almost the whole ground story and was lighted from above, and by the cabinet, which formed an upper story at one end and looked upon the court. A corridor joined the theatre to the door on the bystreet; and with this the cabinet communicated separately by a second flight of stairs. There were besides a few dark closets and a spacious cellar. All these they now thoroughly examined. Each closet needed but a glance, for all were empty, and all, by the dust that fell from their doors, had stood long unopened. The cellar, indeed, was filled with crazy lumber, mostly dating from the times of the surgeon who was Jekyll's predecessor; but even as they opened the door they were advertised of the uselessness of further search, by the fall of a perfect mat of cobweb which had for years sealed up the entrance. Nowhere was there any trace of Henry Jekyll, dead or alive.

Poole stamped on the flags of the corridor. "He must be buried here," he said, hearkening to the sound.

"Or he may have fled," said Utterson, and he turned to examine the door in the bystreet. It was locked; and lying nearby on the flags, they found the key, already stained with rust.

"This does not look like use," observed the lawyer.

"Use!" echoed Poole. "Do you not see, sir, it is broken? much as if a man had stamped on it."

"Ay," continued Utterson, "and the fractures, too, are rusty." The two men looked at each other with a scare. "This is beyond me, Poole," said the lawyer. "Let us go back to the cabinet."

They mounted the stair in silence, and still with an occasional awestruck glance at the dead body, proceeded more thoroughly to examine the contents of the cabinet. At one table, there were traces of chemical work, various measured heaps of some white salt being laid on glass saucers, as though for an experiment in which the unhappy man had been prevented.

"That is the same drug that I was always bringing him," said Poole; and even as he spoke, the kettle with a startling noise boiled over.

This brought them to the fireside, where the easy chair was drawn cosily up, and the tea things stood ready to the sitter's elbow, the very sugar in the cup. There were several books on a shelf; one lay beside the tea things open, and Utterson was amazed to find it a copy of a pious work, for which Jekyll had several times expressed a great esteem, annotated, in his own hand, with startling blasphemies.

Next, in the course of their review of the chamber, the searchers came to the cheval glass, into whose depths they looked with an involuntary horror. But it was so turned as to show them nothing but the rosy glow playing on the roof, the fire sparkling in a hundred repetitions along the glazed front of the presses, and their own pale and fearful countenances stooping to look in.

"This glass have seen some strange things, sir," whispered Poole.

"And surely none stranger than itself," echoed the lawyer in the same tones. "For what did Jekyll"—he caught himself up at the word with a start, and then conquering the weakness—"what could Jekyll want with it?" he said.

---

[1] *kernels* Nuts or the insides of fruit pits; their smell here indicates the presence of cyanide.

"You may say that!" said Poole.

Next they turned to the business table. On the desk among the neat array of papers, a large envelope was uppermost, and bore, in the doctor's hand, the name of Mr. Utterson. The lawyer unsealed it, and several enclosures fell to the floor. The first was a will, drawn in the same eccentric terms as the one which he had returned six months before, to serve as a testament in case of death and as a deed of gift in case of disappearance; but, in place of the name of Edward Hyde, the lawyer, with indescribable amazement, read the name of Gabriel John Utterson. He looked at Poole, and then back at the paper, and last of all at the dead malefactor stretched upon the carpet.

"My head goes round," he said. "He has been all these days in possession; he had no cause to like me; he must have raged to see himself displaced; and he has not destroyed this document."

He caught up the next paper; it was a brief note in the doctor's hand and dated at the top.

"O Poole!" the lawyer cried, "he was alive and here this day. He cannot have been disposed of in so short a space, he must be still alive, he must have fled! And then, why fled? and how? and in that case, can we venture to declare this suicide? Oh, we must be careful. I foresee that we may yet involve your master in some dire catastrophe."

"Why don't you read it, sir?" asked Poole.

"Because I fear," replied the lawyer solemnly. "God grant I have no cause for it!" And with that he brought the paper to his eyes and read as follows:

"My Dear Utterson,—When this shall fall into your hands, I shall have disappeared, under what circumstances I have not the penetration to foresee, but my instinct and all the circumstances of my nameless situation tell me that the end is sure and must be early. Go then, and first read the narrative which Lanyon warned me he was to place in your hands; and if you care to hear more, turn to the confession of

"Your unworthy and unhappy friend,

"HENRY JEKYLL."

"There was a third enclosure?" asked Utterson.

"Here, sir," said Poole, and gave into his hands a considerable packet sealed in several places.

The lawyer put it in his pocket. "I would say nothing of this paper. If your master has fled or is dead, we may at least save his credit. It is now ten; I must go home and read these documents in quiet; but I shall be back before midnight, when we shall send for the police."

They went out, locking the door of the theatre behind them; and Utterson, once more leaving the servants gathered about the fire in the hall, trudged back to his office to read the two narratives in which this mystery was now to be explained.

DR. LANYON'S NARRATIVE

On the ninth of January, now four days ago, I received by the evening delivery a registered envelope, addressed in the hand of my colleague and old school companion, Henry Jekyll. I was a good deal surprised by this; for we were by no means in the habit of correspondence; I had seen the man, dined with him, indeed, the night before; and I could imagine nothing in our intercourse that should justify formality of registration. The contents increased my wonder; for this is how the letter ran:

"10th December,[1] 18—

"Dear Lanyon, You are one of my oldest friends; and although we may have differed at times on scientific questions, I cannot remember, at least on my side, any break in our affection. There was never a day when, if you had said to me, 'Jekyll, my life, my honour, my reason, depend upon you,' I would not have sacrificed my left hand to help you. Lanyon, my life, my honour, my reason, are all at your mercy; if you fail me tonight I am lost. You might suppose, after this preface, that I am going to ask you for something dishonourable to grant. Judge for yourself.

"I want you to postpone all other engagements for tonight—ay, even if you were summoned to the bedside of an emperor; to take a cab, unless your

[1] *10th December* The date of the letter is an error in Stevenson's original; for consistency it should be dated "9th January."

carriage should be actually at the door; and with this letter in your hand for consultation, to drive straight to my house. Poole, my butler, has his orders; you will find, him waiting your arrival with a locksmith. The door of my cabinet is then to be forced: and you are to go in alone; to open the glazed press[1] (letter E) on the left hand, breaking the lock if it be shut; and to draw out, *with all its contents as they stand*, the fourth drawer from the top or (which is the same thing) the third from the bottom. In my extreme distress of mind, I have a morbid fear of misdirecting you; but even if I am in error, you may know the right drawer by its contents: some powders, a phial and a paper book. This drawer I beg of you to carry back with you to Cavendish Square exactly as it stands.

"That is the first part of the service: now for the second. You should be back, if you set out at once on the receipt of this, long before midnight; but I will leave you that amount of margin, not only in the fear of one of those obstacles that can neither be prevented nor foreseen, but because an hour when your servants are in bed is to be preferred for what will then remain to do. At midnight, then, I have to ask you to be alone in your consulting room, to admit with your own hand into the house a man who will present himself in my name, and to place in his hands the drawer that you will have brought with you from my cabinet. Then you will have played your part and earned my gratitude completely. Five minutes afterwards, if you insist upon an explanation, you will have understood that these arrangements are of capital importance; and that by the neglect of one of them, fantastic as they must appear, you might have charged your conscience with my death or the shipwreck of my reason.

"Confident as I am that you will not trifle with this appeal, my heart sinks and my hand trembles at the bare thought of such a possibility. Think of me at this hour, in a strange place, labouring under a blackness of distress that no fancy can exaggerate, and yet well aware that, if you will but punctually serve me, my troubles will roll away like a story that is told. Serve me, my dear Lanyon, and save

"Your friend,

"H.J.

"P.S.—I had already sealed this up when a fresh terror struck upon my soul. It is possible that the post office may fail me, and this letter not come into your hands until tomorrow morning. In that case, dear Lanyon, do my errand when it shall be most convenient for you in the course of the day; and once more expect my messenger at midnight. It may then already be too late; and if that night passes without event, you will know that you have seen the last of Henry Jekyll."

Upon the reading of this letter, I made sure[2] my colleague was insane; but till that was proved beyond the possibility of doubt, I felt bound to do as he requested. The less I understood of this farrago,[3] the less I was in a position to judge of its importance; and an appeal so worded could not be set aside without a grave responsibility. I rose accordingly from table, got into a hansom,[4] and drove straight to Jekyll's house. The butler was awaiting my arrival; he had received by the same post as mine a registered letter of instruction, and had sent at once for a locksmith and a carpenter. The tradesmen came while we were yet speaking; and we moved in a body to old Dr. Denman's surgical theatre, from which (as you are doubtless aware) Jekyll's private cabinet is most conveniently entered. The door was very strong, the lock excellent; the carpenter avowed he would have great trouble and have to do much damage, if force were to be used; and the locksmith was near despair. But this last was a handy fellow, and after two hours' work, the door stood open. The press marked E was unlocked; and I took out the drawer, had it filled up with straw and tied in a sheet, and returned with it to Cavendish Square.

Here I proceeded to examine its contents. The powders were neatly enough made up, but not with the nicety of the dispensing chemist; so that it was plain they were of Jekyll's private manufacture; and when I opened one of the wrappers I found what seemed to me

---

1 *glazed press* Cupboard with glass in the doors.

2 *made sure* I.e., was sure.

3 *farrago* Mishmash, jumble.

4 *hansom* Horse-drawn cab for hire.

a simple crystalline salt of a white colour. The phial, to which I next turned my attention, might have been about half-full of a blood-red liquor, which was highly pungent to the sense of smell and seemed to me to contain phosphorus and some volatile ether. At the other ingredients I could make no guess. The book was an ordinary version book[1] and contained little but a series of dates. These covered a period of many years, but I observed that the entries ceased nearly a year ago and quite abruptly. Here and there a brief remark was appended to a date, usually no more than a single word: "double" occurring perhaps six times in a total of several hundred entries; and once very early in the list and followed by several marks of exclamation, "total failure!!!" All this, though it whetted my curiosity, told me little that was definite. Here were a phial of some tincture, a paper of some salt, and the record of a series of experiments that had led (like too many of Jekyll's investigations) to no end of practical usefulness. How could the presence of these articles in my house affect either the honour, the sanity, or the life of my flighty colleague? If his messenger could go to one place, why could he not go to another? And even granting some impediment, why was this gentleman to be received by me in secret? The more I reflected the more convinced I grew that I was dealing with a case of cerebral disease; and though I dismissed my servants to bed, I loaded an old revolver, that I might be found in some posture of self-defence.

Twelve o'clock had scarce rung out over London, ere the knocker sounded very gently on the door. I went myself at the summons, and found a small man crouching against the pillars of the portico.

"Are you come from Dr. Jekyll?" I asked.

He told me "yes" by a constrained gesture; and when I had bidden him enter, he did not obey me without a searching backward glance into the darkness of the square. There was a policeman not far off, advancing with his bullseye[2] open; and at the sight, I thought my visitor started and made greater haste.

These particulars struck me, I confess, disagreeably; and as I followed him into the bright light of the consulting room, I kept my hand ready on my weapon. Here, at last, I had a chance of clearly seeing him. I had never set eyes on him before, so much was certain. He was small, as I have said; I was struck besides with the shocking expression of his face, with his remarkable combination of great muscular activity and great apparent debility of constitution, and—last but not least—with the odd, subjective disturbance caused by his neighbourhood. This bore some resemblance to incipient rigor,[3] and was accompanied by a marked sinking of the pulse. At the time, I set it down to some idiosyncratic, personal distaste, and merely wondered at the acuteness of the symptoms; but I have since had reason to believe the cause to lie much deeper in the nature of man, and to turn on some nobler hinge than the principle of hatred.

This person (who had thus, from the first moment of his entrance, struck in me what I can only describe as a disgustful curiosity) was dressed in a fashion that would have made an ordinary person laughable; his clothes, that is to say, although they were of rich and sober fabric, were enormously too large for him in every measurement—the trousers hanging on his legs and rolled up to keep them from the ground, the waist of the coat below his haunches, and the collar sprawling wide upon his shoulders. Strange to relate, this ludicrous accoutrement was far from moving me to laughter. Rather, as there was something abnormal and misbegotten in the very essence of the creature that now faced me—something seizing, surprising, and revolting—this fresh disparity seemed but to fit in with and to reinforce it; so that to my interest in the man's nature and character, there was added a curiosity as to his origin, his life, his fortune and status in the world.

These observations, though they have taken so great a space to be set down in, were yet the work of a few seconds. My visitor was, indeed, on fire with sombre excitement.

[1] *version book* Blank book often used by students for translation exercises.

[2] *bullseye* Lantern used to project a contained beam of bright light.

[3] *rigor* Shivering, goosebumps.

"Have you got it?" he cried. "Have you got it?" And so lively was his impatience that he even laid his hand upon my arm and sought to shake me.

I put him back, conscious at his touch of a certain icy pang along my blood. "Come, sir," said I. "You forget that I have not yet the pleasure of your acquaintance. Be seated, if you please." And I showed him an example, and sat down myself in my customary seat and with as fair an imitation of my ordinary manner to a patient, as the lateness of the hour, the nature of my preoccupations, and the horror I had of my visitor, would suffer me to muster.

"I beg your pardon, Dr. Lanyon," he replied civilly enough. "What you say is very well founded; and my impatience has shown its heels to my politeness. I come here at the instance of your colleague, Dr. Henry Jekyll, on a piece of business of some moment; and I understood ..." He paused and put his hand to his throat, and I could see, in spite of his collected manner, that he was wrestling against the approaches of the hysteria—"I understood, a drawer ..."

But here I took pity on my visitor's suspense, and some perhaps on my own growing curiosity.

"There it is, sir," said I, pointing to the drawer, where it lay on the floor behind a table and still covered with the sheet.

He sprang to it, and then paused, and laid his hand upon his heart: I could hear his teeth grate with the convulsive action of his jaws; and his face was so ghastly to see that I grew alarmed both for his life and reason.

"Compose yourself," said I.

He turned a dreadful smile to me, and as if with the decision of despair, plucked away the sheet. At sight of the contents, he uttered one loud sob of such immense relief that I sat petrified. And the next moment, in a voice that was already fairly well under control, "Have you a graduated glass?"[1] he asked.

I rose from my place with something of an effort and gave him what he asked.

He thanked me with a smiling nod, measured out a few minims[2] of the red tincture and added one of the powders. The mixture, which was at first of a reddish hue, began, in proportion as the crystals melted, to brighten in colour, to effervesce audibly, and to throw off small fumes of vapour. Suddenly and at the same moment, the ebullition[3] ceased and the compound changed to a dark purple, which faded again more slowly to a watery green. My visitor, who had watched these metamorphoses with a keen eye, smiled, set down the glass upon the table, and then turned and looked upon me with an air of scrutiny.

"And now," said he, "to settle what remains. Will you be wise? will you be guided? will you suffer me to take this glass in my hand and to go forth from your house without further parley? or has the greed of curiosity too much command of you? Think before you answer, for it shall be done as you decide. As you decide, you shall be left as you were before, and neither richer nor wiser, unless the sense of service rendered to a man in mortal distress may be counted as a kind of riches of the soul. Or, if you shall so prefer to choose, a new province of knowledge and new avenues to fame and power shall be laid open to you, here, in this room, upon the instant; and your sight shall be blasted by a prodigy to stagger the unbelief of Satan."

"Sir," said I, affecting a coolness that I was far from truly possessing, "you speak enigmas, and you will perhaps not wonder that I hear you with no very strong impression of belief. But I have gone too far in the way of inexplicable services to pause before I see the end."

"It is well," replied my visitor. "Lanyon, you remember your vows: what follows is under the seal of our profession. And now, you who have so long been bound to the most narrow and material views, you who have denied the virtue of transcendental medicine, you who have derided your superiors—behold!"

He put the glass to his lips and drank at one gulp. A cry followed; he reeled, staggered, clutched at the table

[1] *graduated glass* Glass container marked with gradations for measurement.

[2] *minims* Small amounts of liquid; a minim is approximately 0.002 ounces or 0.06 milliliters.

[3] *ebullition* Bubbling.

and held on, staring with injected[1] eyes, gasping with open mouth; and as I looked there came, I thought, a change—he seemed to swell—his face became suddenly black and the features seemed to melt and alter—and the next moment, I had sprung to my feet and leaped back against the wall, my arm raised to shield me from that prodigy, my mind submerged in terror.

"O God!" I screamed, and "O God!" again and again; for there before my eyes—pale and shaken, and half fainting, and groping before him with his hands, like a man restored from death—there stood Henry Jekyll!

What he told me in the next hour, I cannot bring my mind to set on paper. I saw what I saw, I heard what I heard, and my soul sickened at it; and yet now when that sight has faded from my eyes, I ask myself if I believe it, and I cannot answer. My life is shaken to its roots; sleep has left me; the deadliest terror sits by me at all hours of the day and night; I feel that my days are numbered, and that I must die; and yet I shall die incredulous. As for the moral turpitude that man unveiled to me, even with tears of penitence, I cannot, even in memory, dwell on it without a start of horror. I will say but one thing, Utterson, and that (if you can bring your mind to credit it) will be more than enough. The creature who crept into my house that night was, on Jekyll's own confession, known by the name of Hyde and hunted for in every corner of the land as the murderer of Carew.

HASTIE LANYON

HENRY JEKYLL'S FULL STATEMENT OF THE CASE

I was born in the year 18— to a large fortune, endowed besides with excellent parts,[2] inclined by nature to industry, fond of the respect of the wise and good among my fellow men, and thus, as might have been supposed, with every guarantee of an honourable and distinguished future. And indeed the worst of my faults was a certain impatient gaiety[3] of disposition, such as has made the happiness of many, but such as I found it hard to reconcile with my imperious desire to carry my head high, and wear a more than commonly grave countenance before the public. Hence it came about that I concealed my pleasures; and that when I reached years of reflection, and began to look round me and take stock of my progress and position in the world, I stood already committed to a profound duplicity of life. Many a man would have even blazoned[4] such irregularities as I was guilty of; but from the high views that I had set before me, I regarded and hid them with an almost morbid sense of shame. It was thus rather the exacting nature of my aspirations than any particular degradation in my faults, that made me what I was, and, with even a deeper trench than in the majority of men, severed in me those provinces of good and ill which divide and compound man's dual nature. In this case, I was driven to reflect deeply and inveterately on that hard law of life, which lies at the root of religion and is one of the most plentiful springs of distress. Though so profound a double dealer, I was in no sense a hypocrite; both sides of me were in dead earnest; I was no more myself when I laid aside restraint and plunged in shame, than when I laboured, in the eye of day, at the furtherance of knowledge or the relief of sorrow and suffering. And it chanced that the direction of my scientific studies, which led wholly toward the mystic and the transcendental, reacted and shed a strong light on this consciousness of the perennial war among my members. With every day, and from both sides of my intelligence, the moral and the intellectual, I thus drew steadily nearer to that truth, by whose partial discovery I have been doomed to such a dreadful shipwreck: that man is not truly one, but truly two. I say two, because the state of my own knowledge does not pass beyond that point. Others will follow, others will outstrip me on the same lines; and I hazard the guess that man will be ultimately known for a mere polity of multifarious, incongruous,

[1] *injected* Bloodshot or engorged.

[2] *parts* Talents or other positive personal attributes.

[3] *gaiety* In its most usual meaning during this period, "gay" meant "light-hearted"; it could also mean "licentious" but was not yet specifically related to sexual orientation.

[4] *blazoned* Publicly declared, i.e., bragged about.

and independent denizens. I, for my part, from the nature of my life, advanced infallibly in one direction and in one direction only. It was on the moral side, and in my own person, that I learned to recognise the thorough and primitive duality of man; I saw that, of the two natures that contended in the field of my consciousness, even if I could rightly be said to be either, it was only because I was radically both; and from an early date, even before the course of my scientific discoveries had begun to suggest the most naked possibility of such a miracle, I had learned to dwell with pleasure, as a beloved daydream, on the thought of the separation of these elements. If each, I told myself could but be housed in separate identities, life would be relieved of all that was unbearable; the unjust delivered from the aspirations might go his way, and remorse of his more upright twin; and the just could walk steadfastly and securely on his upward path, doing the good things in which he found his pleasure, and no longer exposed to disgrace and penitence by the hands of this extraneous evil. It was the curse of mankind that these incongruous faggots[1] were thus bound together that in the agonised womb of consciousness, these polar twins should be continuously struggling. How, then, were they dissociated?

I was so far in my reflections when, as I have said, a sidelight began to shine upon the subject from the laboratory table. I began to perceive more deeply than it has ever yet been stated, the trembling immateriality, the mist-like transience, of this seemingly so solid body in which we walk attired. Certain agents I found to have the power to shake and to pluck back that fleshly vestment, even as a wind might toss the curtains of a pavilion. For two good reasons, I will not enter deeply into this scientific branch of my confession. First, because I have been made to learn that the doom and burden of our life is bound forever on man's shoulders, and when the attempt is made to cast it off, it but returns upon us with more unfamiliar and more awful pressure. Second, because, as my narrative will make, alas! too evident, my discoveries were incomplete. Enough, then, that I not only recognised my natural body for the mere aura and effulgence[2] of certain of the powers that made up my spirit, but managed to compound a drug by which these powers should be dethroned from their supremacy, and a second form and countenance substituted, none the less natural to me because they were the expression, and bore the stamp, of lower elements in my soul.

I hesitated long before I put this theory to the test of practice. I knew well that I risked death; for any drug that so potently controlled and shook the very fortress of identity, might by the least scruple[3] of an overdose or at the least inopportunity in the moment of exhibition, utterly blot out that immaterial tabernacle which I looked to it to change. But the temptation of a discovery so singular and profound, at last overcame the suggestions of alarm. I had long since prepared my tincture; I purchased at once, from a firm of wholesale chemists, a large quantity of a particular salt which I knew, from my experiments, to be the last ingredient required; and late one accursed night, I compounded the elements, watched them boil and smoke together in the glass, and when the ebullition had subsided, with a strong glow of courage, drank off the potion.

The most racking pangs succeeded: a grinding in the bones, deadly nausea, and a horror of the spirit that cannot be exceeded at the hour of birth or death. Then these agonies began swiftly to subside, and I came to myself as if out of a great sickness. There was something strange in my sensations, something indescribably new and, from its very novelty, incredibly sweet. I felt younger, lighter, happier in body; within I was conscious of a heady recklessness, a current of disordered sensual images running like a mill race[4] in my fancy, a solution of the bonds of obligation, an unknown but not an innocent freedom of the soul. I knew myself, at the first breath of this new life, to be more wicked, tenfold more wicked, sold a slave to my original evil; and the thought, in that moment, braced and delighted me like wine. I stretched out my hands, exulting in the

[1] *faggots* Bundles, especially bundles of sticks used to make fires.

[2] *effulgence* Radiance.

[3] *scruple* Tiny quantity.

[4] *mill race* Fast-flowing water used to power a mill wheel.

freshness of these sensations; and in the act, I was suddenly aware that I had lost in stature.

There was no mirror, at that date, in my room; that which stands beside me as I write, was brought there later on and for the very purpose of these transformations. The night, however, was far gone into the morning—the morning, black as it was, was nearly ripe for the conception of the day—the inmates of my house were locked in the most rigorous hours of slumber; and I determined, flushed as I was with hope and triumph, to venture in my new shape as far as to my bedroom. I crossed the yard, wherein the constellations looked down upon me, I could have thought, with wonder, the first creature of that sort that their unsleeping vigilance had yet disclosed to them; I stole through the corridors, a stranger in my own house; and coming to my room, I saw for the first time the appearance of Edward Hyde.

I must here speak by theory alone, saying not that which I know, but that which I suppose to be most probable. The evil side of my nature, to which I had now transferred the stamping efficacy, was less robust and less developed than the good which I had just deposed. Again, in the course of my life, which had been, after all, nine-tenths a life of effort, virtue, and control, it had been much less exercised and much less exhausted. And hence, as I think, it came about that Edward Hyde was so much smaller, slighter, and younger than Henry Jekyll. Even as good shone upon the countenance of the one, evil was written broadly and plainly on the face of the other. Evil besides (which I must still believe to be the lethal side of man) had left on that body an imprint of deformity and decay. And yet when I looked upon that ugly idol in the glass, I was conscious of no repugnance, rather of a leap of welcome. This, too, was myself. It seemed natural and human. In my eyes it bore a livelier image of the spirit, it seemed more express and single, than the imperfect and divided countenance I had been hitherto accustomed to call mine. And in so far I was doubtless right. I have observed that when I wore the semblance of Edward Hyde, none could come near to me at first without a visible misgiving of the flesh. This, as I take it, was because all human beings, as we meet them, are commingled out of good and evil: and Edward Hyde, alone in the ranks of mankind, was pure evil.

I lingered but a moment at the mirror: the second and conclusive experiment had yet to be attempted; it yet remained to be seen if I had lost my identity beyond redemption and must flee before daylight from a house that was no longer mine; and hurrying back to my cabinet, I once more prepared and drank the cup, once more suffered the pangs of dissolution, and came to myself once more with the character, the stature, and the face of Henry Jekyll.

That night I had come to the fatal crossroads. Had I approached my discovery in a more noble spirit, had I risked the experiment while under the empire of generous or pious aspirations, all must have been otherwise, and from these agonies of death and birth, I had come forth an angel instead of a fiend. The drug had no discriminating action; it was neither diabolical nor divine; it but shook the doors of the prison house of my disposition; and like the captives of Philippi,[1] that which stood within ran forth. At that time my virtue slumbered; my evil, kept awake by ambition, was alert and swift to seize the occasion; and the thing that was projected was Edward Hyde. Hence, although I had now two characters as well as two appearances, one was wholly evil, and the other was still the old Henry Jekyll, that incongruous compound of whose reformation and improvement I had already learned to despair. The movement was thus wholly toward the worse.

Even at that time, I had not yet conquered my aversion to the dryness of a life of study. I would still be merrily disposed at times; and as my pleasures were (to say the least) undignified, and I was not only well known and highly considered, but growing toward the elderly man, this incoherency of my life was daily growing more unwelcome. It was on this side that my new power tempted me until I fell in slavery. I had but to drink the cup, to doff at once the body of the noted professor, and to assume, like a thick cloak, that of

[1] *captives of Philippi* Cf. Acts 16.26, in which Paul and his followers were given an opportunity to escape from prison when an earthquake caused the doors of their prison to open. They chose to remain in their cells, but were freed as a result of their obedience.

Edward Hyde. I smiled at the notion; it seemed to me at the time to be humorous; and I made my preparations with the most studious care. I took and furnished that house in Soho, to which Hyde was tracked by the police; and engaged as housekeeper a creature whom I well knew to be silent and unscrupulous. On the other side, I announced to my servants that a Mr. Hyde (whom I described) was to have full liberty and power about my house in the square; and to parry mishaps, I even called and made myself a familiar object, in my second character. I next drew up that will to which you so much objected; so that if anything befell me in the person of Dr. Jekyll, I could enter on that of Edward Hyde without pecuniary loss. And thus fortified, as I supposed, on every side, I began to profit by the strange immunities of my position.

Men have before hired bravos[1] to transact their crimes, while their own person and reputation sat under shelter. I was the first that ever did so for his pleasures. I was the first that could thus plod in the public eye with a load of genial respectability, and in a moment, like a schoolboy, strip off these lendings[2] and spring headlong into the sea of liberty. But for me, in my impenetrable mantle, the safety was complete. Think of it—I did not even exist! Let me but escape into my laboratory door, give me but a second or two to mix and swallow the draught that I had always standing ready; and whatever he had done, Edward Hyde would pass away like the stain of breath upon a mirror; and there in his stead, quietly at home, trimming the midnight lamp in his study, a man who could afford to laugh at suspicion, would be Henry Jekyll.

The pleasures which I made haste to seek in my disguise were, as I have said, undignified; I would scarce use a harder term. But in the hands of Edward Hyde, they soon began to turn toward the monstrous. When I would come back from these excursions, I was often plunged into a kind of wonder at my vicarious depravity. This familiar[3] that I called out of my own soul, and sent forth alone to do his good pleasure, was a being inherently malign and villainous; his every act and thought centred on self; drinking pleasure with bestial avidity from any degree of torture to another; relentless like a man of stone. Henry Jekyll stood at times aghast before the acts of Edward Hyde; but the situation was apart from ordinary laws, and insidiously relaxed the grasp of conscience. It was Hyde, after all, and Hyde alone, that was guilty. Jekyll was no worse; he woke again to his good qualities seemingly unimpaired; he would even make haste, where it was possible, to undo the evil done by Hyde. And thus his conscience slumbered.

Into the details of the infamy at which I thus connived (for even now I can scarce grant that I committed it) I have no design of entering; I mean but to point out the warnings and the successive steps with which my chastisement approached. I met with one accident which, as it brought on no consequence, I shall no more than mention. An act of cruelty to a child aroused against me the anger of a passerby, whom I recognised the other day in the person of your kinsman; the doctor and the child's family joined him; there were moments when I feared for my life; and at last, in order to pacify their too just resentment, Edward Hyde had to bring them to the door, and pay them in a cheque drawn in the name of Henry Jekyll. But this danger was easily eliminated from the future, by opening an account at another bank in the name of Edward Hyde himself; and when, by sloping my own hand backward, I had supplied my double with a signature, I thought I sat beyond the reach of fate.

Some two months before the murder of Sir Danvers, I had been out for one of my adventures, had returned at a late hour, and woke the next day in bed with somewhat odd sensations. It was in vain I looked about me; in vain I saw the decent furniture and tall proportions of my room in the square; in vain that I recognised the pattern of the bed curtains and the design of the mahogany frame; something still kept insisting that I was not where I was, that I had not wakened where I seemed to be, but in the little room in Soho where I was accustomed to sleep in the body of Edward Hyde. I smiled to myself,

[1] *bravos* Paid criminals, especially killers.

[2] *lendings* Borrowed clothes.

[3] *familiar* Spirit, often in animal form, that obeys and helps magic practitioners.

and, in my psychological way began lazily to inquire into the elements of this illusion, occasionally, even as I did so, dropping back into a comfortable morning doze. I was still so engaged when, in one of my more wakeful moments, my eyes fell upon my hand. Now the hand of Henry Jekyll (as you have often remarked) was professional in shape and size: it was large, firm, white, and comely. But the hand which I now saw, clearly enough, in the yellow light of a mid-London morning, lying half shut on the bedclothes, was lean, corded, knuckly, of a dusky pallor and thickly shaded with a swart[1] growth of hair. It was the hand of Edward Hyde.

I must have stared upon it for near half a minute, sunk as I was in the mere stupidity of wonder, before terror woke up in my breast as sudden and startling as the crash of cymbals; and bounding from my bed, I rushed to the mirror. At the sight that met my eyes, my blood was changed into something exquisitely thin and icy. Yes, I had gone to bed Henry Jekyll, I had awakened Edward Hyde. How was this to be explained? I asked myself; and then, with another bound of terror—how was it to be remedied? It was well on in the morning; the servants were up; all my drugs were in the cabinet—a long journey down two pairs of stairs, through the back passage, across the open court and through the anatomical theatre, from where I was then standing horror-struck. It might indeed be possible to cover my face; but of what use was that, when I was unable to conceal the alteration in my stature? And then with an overpowering sweetness of relief, it came back upon my mind that the servants were already used to the coming and going of my second self. I had soon dressed, as well as I was able, in clothes of my own size: had soon passed through the house, where Bradshaw stared and drew back at seeing Mr. Hyde at such an hour and in such a strange array; and ten minutes later, Dr. Jekyll had returned to his own shape and was sitting down, with a darkened brow, to make a feint of breakfasting.

Small indeed was my appetite. This inexplicable incident, this reversal of my previous experience, seemed, like the Babylonian finger on the wall, to be spelling out the letters of my judgment;[2] and I began to reflect more seriously than ever before on the issues and possibilities of my double existence. That part of me which I had the power of projecting, had lately been much exercised and nourished; it had seemed to me of late as though the body of Edward Hyde had grown in stature, as though (when I wore that form) I were conscious of a more generous tide of blood; and I began to spy a danger that, if this were much prolonged, the balance of my nature might be permanently overthrown, the power of voluntary change be forfeited, and the character of Edward Hyde become irrevocably mine. The power of the drug had not been always equally displayed. Once, very early in my career, it had totally failed me; since then I had been obliged on more than one occasion to double, and once, with infinite risk of death, to treble the amount; and these rare uncertainties had cast hitherto the sole shadow on my contentment. Now, however, and in the light of that morning's accident, I was led to remark that whereas, in the beginning, the difficulty had been to throw off the body of Jekyll, it had of late gradually but decidedly transferred itself to the other side. All things therefore seemed to point to this: that I was slowly losing hold of my original and better self, and becoming slowly incorporated with my second and worse.

Between these two, I now felt I had to choose. My two natures had memory in common, but all other faculties were most unequally shared between them. Jekyll (who was composite) now with the most sensitive apprehensions, now with a greedy gusto, projected and shared in the pleasures and adventures of Hyde; but Hyde was indifferent to Jekyll, or but remembered him as the mountain bandit remembers the cavern in which he conceals himself from pursuit. Jekyll had more than a father's interest; Hyde had more than a son's indifference. To cast in my lot with Jekyll, was to die to those appetites which I had long secretly indulged and had of late begun to pamper. To cast it in with Hyde, was to

[1] *swart* Swarthy, i.e., dark.

[2] *the Babylonian … judgment* Cf. Daniel 5, in which a message of judgment against Belshazzar, King of Babylon, was written on the wall by a disembodied finger. The writing foretold the king's assassination and the division of his kingdom, which happened that night.

die to a thousand interests and aspirations, and to become, at a blow and forever, despised and friendless. The bargain might appear unequal; but there was still another consideration in the scales; for while Jekyll would suffer smartingly in the fires of abstinence, Hyde would be not even conscious of all that he had lost. Strange as my circumstances were, the terms of this debate are as old and commonplace as man; much the same inducements and alarms cast the die for any tempted and trembling sinner; and it fell out with me, as it falls with so vast a majority of my fellows, that I chose the better part and was found wanting in the strength to keep to it.

Yes, I preferred the elderly and discontented doctor, surrounded by friends and cherishing honest hopes; and bade a resolute farewell to the liberty, the comparative youth, the light step, leaping impulses and secret pleasures, that I had enjoyed in the disguise of Hyde. I made this choice perhaps with some unconscious reservation, for I neither gave up the house in Soho, nor destroyed the clothes of Edward Hyde, which still lay ready in my cabinet. For two months, however, I was true to my determination; for two months I led a life of such severity as I had never before attained to, and enjoyed the compensations of an approving conscience. But time began at last to obliterate the freshness of my alarm; the praises of conscience began to grow into a thing of course; I began to be tortured with throes and longings, as of Hyde struggling after freedom; and at last, in an hour of moral weakness, I once again compounded and swallowed the transforming draught.

I do not suppose that, when a drunkard reasons with himself upon his vice, he is once out of five hundred times affected by the dangers that he runs through his brutish, physical insensibility; neither had I, long as I had considered my position, made enough allowance for the complete moral insensibility and insensate readiness to evil, which were the leading characters of Edward Hyde. Yet it was by these that I was punished. My devil had been long caged, he came out roaring. I was conscious, even when I took the draught, of a more unbridled, a more furious propensity to ill. It must have been this, I suppose, that stirred in my soul that tempest of impatience with which I listened to the civilities of my unhappy victim; I declare, at least, before God, no man morally sane could have been guilty of that crime upon so pitiful a provocation; and that I struck in no more reasonable spirit than that in which a sick child may break a plaything. But I had voluntarily stripped myself of all those balancing instincts by which even the worst of us continues to walk with some degree of steadiness among temptations; and in my case, to be tempted, however slightly, was to fall.

Instantly the spirit of hell awoke in me and raged. With a transport of glee, I mauled the unresisting body, tasting delight from every blow; and it was not till weariness had begun to succeed, that I was suddenly, in the top fit of my delirium, struck through the heart by a cold thrill of terror. A mist dispersed; I saw my life to be forfeit; and fled from the scene of these excesses, at once glorying and trembling, my lust of evil gratified and stimulated, my love of life screwed to the topmost peg. I ran to the house in Soho, and (to make assurance doubly sure) destroyed my papers; thence I set out through the lamplit streets, in the same divided ecstasy of mind, gloating on my crime, light-headedly devising others in the future, and yet still hastening and still hearkening in my wake for the steps of the avenger. Hyde had a song upon his lips as he compounded the draught, and as he drank it, pledged[1] the dead man. The pangs of transformation had not done tearing him, before Henry Jekyll, with streaming tears of gratitude and remorse, had fallen upon his knees and lifted his clasped hands to God. The veil of self-indulgence was rent from head to foot.[2] I saw my life as a whole: I followed it up from the days of childhood, when I had walked with my father's hand, and through the self-denying toils of my professional life, to arrive again and again, with the same sense of unreality, at the damned horrors of the evening. I could have screamed aloud; I sought with tears and prayers to smother down the crowd of hideous images and sounds with which my

---

[1] *pledged* Toasted.

[2] *The veil … foot* Cf. Mark 15.38: "And the veil of the temple was rent in twain from the top to the bottom." This line immediately follows the death of Jesus; see also Matthew 27.51 and Luke 23.45.

memory swarmed against me; and still, between the petitions, the ugly face of my iniquity stared into my soul. As the acuteness of this remorse began to die away, it was succeeded by a sense of joy. The problem of my conduct was solved. Hyde was thenceforth impossible; whether I would or not, I was now confined to the better part of my existence; and oh, how I rejoiced to think it! with what willing humility, I embraced anew the restrictions of natural life! with what sincere renunciation, I locked the door by which I had so often gone and come, and ground the key under my heel!

The next day, came the news that the murder had been overlooked,[1] that the guilt of Hyde was patent to the world, and that the victim was a man high in public estimation. It was not only a crime, it had been a tragic folly. I think I was glad to know it; I think I was glad to have my better impulses thus buttressed and guarded by the terrors of the scaffold. Jekyll was now my city of refuge; let but Hyde peep out an instant, and the hands of all men would be raised to take and slay him.

I resolved in my future conduct to redeem the past; and I can say with honesty that my resolve was fruitful of some good. You know yourself how earnestly in the last months of last year, I laboured to relieve suffering; you know that much was done for others, and that the days passed quietly, almost happily for myself. Nor can I truly say that I wearied of this beneficent and innocent life; I think instead that I daily enjoyed it more completely; but I was still cursed with my duality of purpose; and as the first edge of my penitence wore off, the lower side of me, so long indulged, so recently chained down, began to growl for licence. Not that I dreamed of resuscitating Hyde; the bare idea of that would startle me to frenzy: no, it was in my own person, that I was once more tempted to trifle with my conscience; and it was as an ordinary secret sinner, that I at last fell before the assaults of temptation.

There comes an end to all things; the most capacious measure is filled at last; and this brief condescension to evil finally destroyed the balance of my soul. And yet I was not alarmed; the fall seemed natural, like a return to the old days before I had made discovery. It was a fine, clear, January day, wet underfoot where the frost had melted, but cloudless overhead; and the Regent's Park[2] was full of winter chirrupings and sweet with spring odours. I sat in the sun on a bench; the animal within me licking the chops of memory; the spiritual side a little drowsed, promising subsequent penitence, but not yet moved to begin. After all, I reflected, I was like my neighbours; and then I smiled, comparing myself with other men, comparing my active goodwill with the lazy cruelty of their neglect. And at the very moment of that vain-glorious thought, a qualm came over me, a horrid nausea and the most deadly shuddering. These passed away, and left me faint; and then as in its turn the faintness subsided, I began to be aware of a change in the temper of my thoughts, a greater boldness, a contempt of danger, a solution of the bonds of obligation. I looked down; my clothes hung formlessly on my shrunken limbs; the hand that lay on my knee was corded and hairy. I was once more Edward Hyde. A moment before I had been safe of all men's respect, wealthy, beloved—the cloth laying for me in the dining room at home; and now I was the common quarry of mankind, hunted, houseless, a known murderer, thrall to the gallows.

My reason wavered, but it did not fail me utterly. I have more than once observed that, in my second character, my faculties seemed sharpened to a point and my spirits more tensely elastic; thus it came about that, where Jekyll perhaps might have succumbed, Hyde rose to the importance of the moment. My drugs were in one of the presses of my cabinet; how was I to reach them? That was the problem that (crushing my temples in my hands) I set myself to solve. The laboratory door I had closed. If I sought to enter by the house, my own servants would consign me to the gallows. I saw I must employ another hand, and thought of Lanyon. How was he to be reached? how persuaded? Supposing that I escaped capture in the streets, how was I to make my way into his presence? and how should I, an unknown and displeasing visitor, prevail on the famous physician

[1] *overlooked* Witnessed from a higher viewpoint.

[2] *Regent's Park* Northwest London public park.

to rifle the study of his colleague, Dr. Jekyll? Then I remembered that of my original character, one part remained to me: I could write my own hand; and once I had conceived that kindling spark, the way that I must follow became lighted up from end to end.

Thereupon, I arranged my clothes as best I could, and summoning a passing hansom, drove to an hotel in Portland Street,[1] the name of which I chanced to remember. At my appearance (which was indeed comical enough, however tragic a fate these garments covered) the driver could not conceal his mirth. I gnashed my teeth upon him with a gust of devilish fury; and the smile withered from his face—happily for him—yet more happily for myself, for in another instant I had certainly dragged him from his perch. At the inn, as I entered, I looked about me with so black a countenance as made the attendants tremble; not a look did they exchange in my presence; but obsequiously took my orders, led me to a private room, and brought me wherewithal to write. Hyde in danger of his life was a creature new to me; shaken with inordinate anger, strung to the pitch of murder, lusting to inflict pain. Yet the creature was astute; mastered his fury with a great effort of the will; composed his two important letters, one to Lanyon and one to Poole; and that he might receive actual evidence of their being posted, sent them out with directions that they should be registered.

Thenceforward, he sat all day over the fire in the private room, gnawing his nails; there he dined, sitting alone with his fears, the waiter visibly quailing before his eye; and thence, when the night was fully come, he set forth in the corner of a closed cab, and was driven to and fro about the streets of the city. He, I say—I cannot say, I. That child of Hell had nothing human; nothing lived in him but fear and hatred. And when at last, thinking the driver had begun to grow suspicious, he discharged the cab and ventured on foot, attired in his misfitting clothes, an object marked out for observation, into the midst of the nocturnal passengers, these two base passions raged within him like a tempest. He walked fast, hunted by his fears, chattering to himself, skulking through the less frequented thoroughfares, counting the minutes that still divided him from midnight. Once a woman spoke to him, offering, I think, a box of lights.[2] He smote her in the face, and she fled.

When I came to myself at Lanyon's, the horror of my old friend perhaps affected me somewhat: I do not know; it was at least but a drop in the sea to the abhorrence with which I looked back upon these hours. A change had come over me. It was no longer the fear of the gallows, it was the horror of being Hyde that racked me. I received Lanyon's condemnation partly in a dream; it was partly in a dream that I came home to my own house and got into bed. I slept after the prostration of the day, with a stringent and profound slumber which not even the nightmares that wrung me could avail to break. I awoke in the morning shaken, weakened, but refreshed. I still hated and feared the thought of the brute that slept within me, and I had not of course forgotten the appalling dangers of the day before; but I was once more at home, in my own house and close to my drugs; and gratitude for my escape shone so strong in my soul that it almost rivalled the brightness of hope.

I was stepping leisurely across the court after breakfast, drinking the chill of the air with pleasure, when I was seized again with those indescribable sensations that heralded the change; and I had but the time to gain the shelter of my cabinet, before I was once again raging and freezing with the passions of Hyde. It took on this occasion a double dose to recall me to myself; and alas! six hours after, as I sat looking sadly in the fire, the pangs returned, and the drug had to be re-administered. In short, from that day forth it seemed only by a great effort as of gymnastics, and only under the immediate stimulation of the drug, that I was able to wear the countenance of Jekyll. At all hours of the day and night, I would be taken with the premonitory shudder; above all, if I slept, or even dozed for a moment in my chair, it was always as Hyde that I awakened. Under the strain of this continually impending doom and by the sleeplessness to which I now condemned myself, ay, even beyond what I had thought possible to man, I became,

[1] *Portland Street* Street on the edge of nineteenth-century Soho.

[2] *lights* Matches.

in my own person, a creature eaten up and emptied by fever, languidly weak both in body and mind, and solely occupied by one thought: the horror of my other self. But when I slept, or when the virtue of the medicine wore off, I would leap almost without transition (for the pangs of transformation grew daily less marked) into the possession of a fancy brimming with images of terror, a soul boiling with causeless hatreds, and a body that seemed not strong enough to contain the raging energies of life. The powers of Hyde seemed to have grown with the sickliness of Jekyll. And certainly the hate that now divided them was equal on each side. With Jekyll, it was a thing of vital instinct. He had now seen the full deformity of that creature that shared with him some of the phenomena of consciousness, and was coheir with him to death: and beyond these links of community, which in themselves made the most poignant part of his distress, he thought of Hyde, for all his energy of life, as of something not only hellish but inorganic. This was the shocking thing; that the slime of the pit seemed to utter cries and voices; that the amorphous dust gesticulated and sinned; that what was dead, and had no shape, should usurp the offices of life. And this again, that that insurgent horror was knit to him closer than a wife, closer than an eye; lay caged in his flesh, where he heard it mutter and felt it struggle to be born; and at every hour of weakness, and in the confidence of slumber, prevailed against him, and deposed him out of life. The hatred of Hyde for Jekyll, was of a different order. His terror of the gallows drove him continually to commit temporary suicide, and return to his subordinate station of a part instead of a person; but he loathed the necessity, he loathed the despondency into which Jekyll was now fallen, and he resented the dislike with which he was himself regarded. Hence the apelike tricks that he would play me, scrawling in my own hand blasphemies on the pages of my books, burning the letters and destroying the portrait of my father; and indeed, had it not been for his fear of death, he would long ago have ruined himself in order to involve me in the ruin. But his love of life is wonderful; I go further: I, who sicken and freeze at the mere thought of him, when I recall the abjection and passion of this attachment, and when I know how he fears my power to cut him off by suicide, I find it in my heart to pity him.

It is useless, and the time awfully fails me, to prolong this description; no one has ever suffered such torments, let that suffice; and yet even to these, habit brought—no, not alleviation—but a certain callousness of soul, a certain acquiescence of despair; and my punishment might have gone on for years, but for the last calamity which has now fallen, and which has finally severed me from my own face and nature. My provision of the salt, which had never been renewed since the date of the first experiment, began to run low. I sent out for a fresh supply, and mixed the draught; the ebullition followed, and the first change of colour, not the second; I drank it and it was without efficiency. You will learn from Poole how I have had London ransacked; it was in vain; and I am now persuaded that my first supply was impure, and that it was that unknown impurity which lent efficacy to the draught.

About a week has passed, and I am now finishing this statement under the influence of the last of the old powders. This, then, is the last time, short of a miracle, that Henry Jekyll can think his own thoughts or see his own face (now how sadly altered!) in the glass. Nor must I delay too long to bring my writing to an end; for if my narrative has hitherto escaped destruction, it has been by a combination of great prudence and great good luck. Should the throes of change take me in the act of writing it, Hyde will tear it in pieces; but if some time shall have elapsed after I have laid it by, his wonderful selfishness and circumscription[1] to the moment will probably save it once again from the action of his apelike spite. And indeed the doom that is closing on us both, has already changed and crushed him. Half an hour from now, when I shall again and for ever reindue[2] that hated personality, I know how I shall sit shuddering and weeping in my chair, or continue, with the most strained and fear-struck ecstasy of listening, to pace up and down this room (my last earthly refuge) and give ear

[1] *circumscription* Restriction.

[2] *reindue* Dress (myself) in again.

to every sound of menace. Will Hyde die upon the scaffold? or will he find courage to release himself at the last moment? God knows; I am careless;[1] this is my true hour of death, and what is to follow concerns another than myself. Here then, as I lay down the pen and proceed to seal up my confession, I bring the life of that unhappy Henry Jekyll to an end.

—1886

[1] *I am careless* I do not care.

OSCAR WILDE

1854 – 1900

For his epigrammatic genius, his challenges to bourgeois sensibilities, and his dazzling essays, dramas, and other writings, Oscar Wilde has been both reverenced and reviled for more than a century. Notorious for his flamboyance and wit before he had ever published a word, Wilde established himself in the literary world with his sole novel, *The Picture of Dorian Gray*, and even more with such sparkling social comedies as *An Ideal Husband* and *The Importance of Being Earnest*. He was a vocal advocate of aestheticism; Wilde saw in art the possibility for a life beyond the day-to-day monotony of ordinary existence. The "aesthetic movement," he writes, "produced certain colours, subtle in their loveliness and fascinating in their almost mystical tone. They were, and are, our reaction against the crude primaries of a doubtless more respectable but certainly less cultivated age."

Wilde began his life as Oscar Fingal O'Flahertie Wills Wilde. His parents, themselves no strangers to controversy, were Lady Jane Francesca Elgee and Dr. (later Sir) William Wilde. Both were accomplished writers. William, an ear and eye surgeon, wrote a book on medical and literary institutions in Austria and another about his voyage to North Africa and the Middle East. He achieved fame for his work on the Irish Census, for which he conducted a groundbreaking demographic study of the Great Famine, earning a knighthood in 1864. His reputation was somewhat tainted, however, by his womanizing; he fathered three children out of wedlock. Lady Wilde was also a prominent figure. Born Jane Frances Agnes Elgee, she adopted the more Italian-sounding "Francesca" to reinforce the family's claim that they were descended from Dante Alighieri (truth never stood in the way of a good Wilde family story). Lady Wilde took yet another name, "Speranza," when she published poems in *The Nation*, a weekly Dublin newspaper published by an anti-British revolutionary group called the Young Irelanders.

Wilde grew up in the colorful environment of his mother's famous salon, where she hosted leading Dublin artists and writers. Once when Wilde returned from college, he invited a friend to Lady Wilde's weekly "conversazione," saying, "I want to introduce you to my mother. We have founded a society for the suppression of virtue." Wilde was a brilliant student at Trinity College, graduating in 1874 with the Berkeley Gold Medal for Classics and receiving a scholarship to study at Oxford. Before long, he was celebrated at Oxford's Magdalen College for his wit, decadence, and ostentatious appearance. He was most influenced in his academic years by two rivals at Oxford, John Ruskin and Walter Pater. From Ruskin, perhaps the most influential art critic of the century, Wilde took counsel on what the older scholar believed to be the spiritual, ethical, and moral nature of art. From Pater, who was already infamous following the publication of his *Studies in the History of the Renaissance* (1873), Wilde picked up elements of aestheticism he would eventually transform into his own theories of art. Wilde would later describe Pater's *Renaissance* as "the holy writ of beauty."

After winning the Newdigate prize for poetry and graduating with first class honors, Wilde moved to London and began his career as a divisive public figure. He was known, for example, for a formal jacket, called his "cello coat," that he wore to the opening of the Grosvenor Gallery in 1877, and for being more generally a poster-boy of the emerging aesthetic movement. By the time he published a book of poems in 1881, he had already become the butt of many caricatures in *Punch* magazine; he had taken to modeling his look on the character of Bunthorne in Gilbert and Sullivan's satirical comic opera *Patience*. For the next few years Wilde delivered lectures in the United States and Great Britain about the aesthetic movement, for which he had ambitious plans: "I want to make this artistic movement the basis for a new civilization." In Boston he voiced some of the ideas about art and life for which he would become best known: "The supreme object of life is to live. Few people live. It is true life only to realize one's own perfection, to make one's every dream a reality. Even this is possible."

In 1884 Wilde married Constance Lloyd, with whom he would have two sons, Cyril and Vyvyan. From 1887 to 1889 he edited *Woman's World*, a popular magazine. Through the late 1880s, Wilde wrote reviews of many of his most famous contemporaries, including the painter James Whistler and the poets D.G. Rossetti, William Morris, and Algernon Swinburne. He was also at work on the volume *Intentions* (1891), which would ultimately constitute the most thorough account of his aesthetic philosophy, and would include his famous essays "The Decay of Lying" and "The Critic as Artist." The essays argue for the paramount importance of art in human life: "[Works of art] are … the great archetypes of which things that have existence are but unfinished copies." Rather than artists copying from the world about them, writes Wilde, we as individuals interpret the world *through art*, through the "archetypes" presented to us by works of art. Hence "[T]here may have been fogs for centuries in London," but "no one saw them … till Art had invented them." The early 1890s also saw the publication of Wilde's novel, *The Picture of Dorian Gray*, which both puts forward Wilde's aesthetic beliefs and suggests some of the dangers of a life given over to aesthetic consumption.

Wilde was clearly at his very best in the early 1890s. In addition to *Intentions*, *Dorian Gray*, and poems such as "Helas," Wilde penned a string of brilliant social comedies, including *Lady Windermere's Fan* (1892), *A Woman of No Importance* (1893), and *An Ideal Husband* (1895). His final comedy was his masterpiece of farce, *The Importance of Being Earnest*; it first played in 1895 to wildly enthusiastic crowds at the St. James Theatre in London. Success came to an end only through Wilde's ill-fated affair with a young aristocrat, Lord Alfred Douglas ("Bosie"). Douglas's father, the mentally unstable Marquis of Queensbury, was infuriated by the relationship, and in 1895 he publicly accused Wilde of sodomy. Convinced he had to defend his own and Douglas's honor, Wilde sued the Marquis for libel. After Wilde failed in his suit against Queensbury, the government used evidence from the trial to launch a criminal investigation against Wilde (sexuality between men was a crime during this period). Wilde was found guilty of "gross indecency" and sentenced to two years of imprisonment with hard labor.

Prison left Wilde financially and emotionally broken. The horrid conditions of late-Victorian prison life—including a poor diet, enforced silence, and physically taxing labor—were especially difficult to handle. From prison Wilde wrote a moving autobiographical letter to Bosie, later entitled *De Profundis*, that accuses the younger man of heartless and selfish behavior. (Bosie had treated Wilde poorly all along, and he abandoned Wilde during his imprisonment.) Even from his cell, however, Wilde wrote of seeing "new developments in Art and Life." Upon his release he composed "The Ballad of Reading Gaol" (1898), a heartfelt indictment of the prison system and capital punishment, as well as a meditation on the universal characteristics of human nature.

Wilde's last years were spent in Italy and France. He seems never to have recovered fully from his prison experience, and by late in 1900 he was quite ill. He died and was buried in Paris before the year ended; the immediate cause of his death has never been conclusively established. In 1995 a window in the Poets' Corner of Westminster Abbey was dedicated in his honor.

⌘⌘⌘

Impression du Matin[1]

The Thames nocturne of blue and gold[2]
Changed to a harmony in gray:
A barge with ochre-coloured hay
Dropped from the wharf: and chill and cold

The yellow fog came creeping down
The bridges, till the houses' walls
Seemed changed to shadows and St. Paul's
Loomed like a bubble o'er the town.

Then suddenly arose the clang
Of waking life; the streets were stirred
With country wagons: and a bird
Flew to the glistening roofs and sang.

But one pale woman all alone,
The daylight kissing her wan hair,
Loitered beneath gas lamps' flare,
With lips of flame and heart of stone.
—1881

E Tenebris[3]

Come down, O Christ, and help me! Reach thy hand,
For I am drowning in a stormier sea
Than Simon on thy lake of Galilee:[4]
The wine of life is spilt upon the sand,
My heart is as some famine-murdered land
Whence all good things have perished utterly,
And well I know my soul in Hell must lie
If I this night before God's throne should stand.
"He sleeps perchance, or rideth to the chase,
Like Baal, when his prophets howled that name
From morn to noon on Carmel's smitten height."[5]
Nay, peace, I shall behold, before the night,
The feet of brass,[6] the robe more white than flame,
The wounded hands, the weary human face.
—1881

[1] *Impression du Matin* French: Impression of the morning.

[2] *gold* Cf. James McNeill Whistler's series of paintings, the "Nocturnes." Two of the most famous of these are *Nocturne in Blue and Gold: Old Battersea Bridge* and *Nocturne in Black and Gold: The Falling Rocket*, both of which were painted in the 1870s. These and other similar paintings were important precursors of the movement that came to be known as Impressionism; painters such as Claude Monet and Edgar Degas, like Whistler, strove to capture the transitory effects of light both on the landscape and on human figures. Much as Wilde was moved to write his own "impressions" in verse (this is one of several Wilde poems that include the word "impression" in their title), he did not respond positively to Whistler's radical experiments with impressions on canvas. His response to *Nocturne in Black and Gold: The Falling Rocket* on seeing it exhibited at the Grosvenor Gallery in 1877 was to call it "worth looking at for about as long as one looks at a real rocket, that is, for something less than a quarter of a minute." This judgment concurred with that of the famous art critic John Ruskin (who had been a teacher of Wilde's at Oxford). Ruskin criticized Whistler for "flinging a pot of paint in the public's face" with works such as *Nocturne in Black and Gold: The Falling Rocket*—an insult for which Whistler sued him in a famous trial. (Whistler won the case, but was awarded only one farthing in damages and had to pay the costs of the trial, which contributed to his eventual bankruptcy.)

[3] *E Tenebris* Latin: Out of the darkness.

[4] *Simon … Galilee* In Matthew 14.24–31, Simon Peter, one of the twelve apostles, nearly drowns in a storm at sea when Christ bids him to walk across the water to him. Christ reaches out his hand and saves him, saying "O thou of little faith, wherefore didst thou doubt?"

[5] *He sleeps … height* In 1 Kings 18.19–40, Elijah mocks the priests of Baal (who had called upon their God all day in vain) by saying, "either he is talking, or he is pursuing, or he is in a journey, or peradventure he sleepeth, and must be awaked." Here the speaker imagines a similar voice taunting him.

[6] *feet of brass* Revelation 1.13–16 describes a vision of the Son of man in which his feet are "like unto fine brass."

To Milton

Milton! I think thy spirit hath passed away
From these white cliffs and high-embattled towers;
This gorgeous fiery-coloured world of ours
Seems fallen into ashes dull and grey,
And the age changed unto a mimic play
Wherein we waste our else too-crowded hours:
For all our pomp and pageantry and powers
We are but fit to delve the common clay,
Seeing this little isle on which we stand,
This England, this sea-lion of the sea,
By ignorant demagogues is held in fee,
Who love her not: Dear God! is this the land
Which bare a triple empire in her hand
When Cromwell spake the word "Democracy!"
—1881

from *"The Critic as Artist"*[1]

ERNEST. … [S]urely, the higher you place the creative artist, the lower must the critic rank.

GILBERT. Why so?

ERNEST. Because the best that he can give us will be but an echo of rich music, a dim shadow of clear-outlined form. It may, indeed, be that life is chaos, as you tell me that it is; that its martyrdoms are mean and its heroisms ignoble; and that it is the function of Literature to create, from the rough material of actual existence, a new world that will be more marvellous, more enduring, and more true than the world that common eyes look upon, and through which common natures seek to realize their perfection. But surely, if this new world has been made by the spirit and touch of a great artist, it will be a thing so complete and perfect that there will be nothing left for the critic to do. I quite understand now, and indeed admit most readily, that it is far more difficult to talk about a thing than to do it. But it seems to me that this sound and sensible maxim, which is really extremely soothing to one's feelings, and should be adopted as its motto by every Academy of Literature all over the world, applies only to the relations that exist between Art and Life, and not to any relations that there may be between Art and Criticism.

GILBERT. But, surely, Criticism is itself an art. And just as artistic creation implies the working of the critical faculty, and, indeed, without it cannot be said to exist at all, so Criticism is really creative in the highest sense of the word. Criticism is, in fact, both creative and independent.

ERNEST. Independent?

GILBERT. Yes; independent. Criticism is no more to be judged by any low standard of imitation or resemblance than is the work of poet or sculptor. The critic occupies the same relation to the work of art that he criticizes as the artist does to the visible world of form and colour, or the unseen world of passion and of thought. He does not even require for the perfection of his art the finest materials. Anything will serve his purpose. And just as out of the sordid and sentimental amours of the silly wife of a small country doctor in the squalid village of Yonville-l'Abbaye, near Rouen, Gustave Flaubert was able to create a classic and make a masterpiece of style,[2] so, from subjects of little or no importance, such as the pictures in this year's Royal Academy, or in any year's Royal Academy for that matter, Mr. Lewis Morris's poems, M. Ohnet's novels, or the plays of Mr. Henry Arthur Jones,[3] the true critic can, if it be his pleasure so to direct or waste his faculty of contemplation, produce work that will be flawless in beauty and instinct with intellectual subtlety. Why not? Dullness is always an

[1] *The Critic as Artist* In this dialogue, two men debate the merits of art criticism. Earlier, Ernest had questioned the usefulness of criticism, asking, "Why should the artist be troubled by the shrill clamour of criticism? Why should those who cannot create take it upon themselves to estimate the value of creative work?" In response, Gilbert argued that criticism is itself an art, that "there is no fine art without self-consciousness, and self-consciousness and the critical spirit are one," and, furthermore, that it is "very much more difficult to talk about a thing than to do it."

[2] *masterpiece of style* I.e., Flaubert's *Madame Bovary*.

[3] *Mr. Lewis Morris* Popular Anglo-Welsh poet; *M. Ohnet* Georges Ohnet, nineteenth-century French novelist, many of whose works were successfully dramatized; *Mr. Henry Arthur Jones* Innovative playwright of the late nineteenth century.

irresistible temptation for brilliancy, and stupidity is the permanent *Bestia Trionfans*[1] that calls wisdom from its cave. To an artist so creative as the critic, what does subject matter signify? No more and no less than it does to the novelist and the painter. Like them, he can find his motives everywhere. Treatment is the test. There is nothing that has not in it suggestion or challenge.

ERNEST. But is Criticism really a creative art?

GILBERT. Why should it not be? It works with materials, and puts them into a form that is at once new and delightful. What more can one say of poetry? Indeed, I would call criticism a creation within a creation. For just as the great artists, from Homer and Aeschylus down to Shakespeare and Keats,[2] did not go directly to life for their subject-matter, but sought for it in myth, and legend, and ancient tale, so the critic deals with materials that others have, as it were, purified for him, and to which imaginative form and colour have been already added. Nay, more, I would say that the highest Criticism, being the purest form of personal impression, is in its way more creative than creation, as it has least reference to any standard external to itself, and is, in fact, its own reason for existing, and, as the Greeks would put it, in itself, and to itself, an end. Certainly, it is never trammelled by any shackles of verisimilitude. No ignoble considerations of probability, that cowardly concession to the tedious repetitions of domestic or public life, affect it ever. One may appeal from fiction unto fact. But from the soul there is no appeal.

ERNEST. From the soul?

GILBERT. Yes, from the soul. That is what the highest criticism really is, the record of one's own soul. It is more fascinating than history, as it is concerned simply with oneself. It is more delightful than philosophy, as its subject is concrete and not abstract, real and not vague. It is the only civilized form of autobiography, as it deals not with the events, but with the thoughts of one's life; not with life's physical accidents of deed or circumstance, but with the spiritual moods and imaginative passions of the mind. I am always amused by the silly vanity of those writers and artists of our day who seem to imagine that the primary function of the critic is to chatter about their second-rate work. The best that one can say of most modern creative art is that it is just a little less vulgar than reality, and so the critic, with his fine sense of distinction and sure instinct of delicate refinement, will prefer to look into the silver mirror or through the woven veil, and will turn his eyes away from the chaos and clamour of actual existence, though the mirror be tarnished and the veil be torn. His sole aim is to chronicle his own impressions. It is for him that pictures are painted, books written, and marble hewn into form.

ERNEST. I seem to have heard another theory of Criticism.

GILBERT. Yes: it has been said by one whose gracious memory we all revere, and the music of whose pipe once lured Proserpina from her Sicilian fields, and made those white feet stir, and not in vain, the Cumnor cowslips, that the proper aim of Criticism is to see the object as in itself it really is.[3] But this is a very serious error, and takes no cognizance of Criticism's most perfect form, which is in its essence purely subjective, and seeks to reveal its own secret and not the secret of another. For the highest Criticism deals with art not as expressive but as impressive purely.

ERNEST. But is that really so?

GILBERT. Of course it is. Who cares whether Mr. Ruskin's views on Turner[4] are sound or not? What does it matter? That mighty and majestic prose of his, so fervid and so fiery-coloured in its noble eloquence, so rich in its elaborate symphonic music, so sure and certain, at its best, in subtle choice of word and epithet, is at least as great a work of art as any of those wonderful sunsets

---

[1] *Bestia Trionfans* Latin: Triumphant Beast. From the title of sixteenth-century philosopher Giordano Bruno's allegory *Spacio della Bestia Trionfante* (*Expulsion of the Triumphant Beast*).

[2] *Homer* Greek poet to whom the authorship of the *Iliad* and the *Odyssey* is attributed (?850 BCE); *Shakespeare* William Shakespeare, English poet and playwright (1564–1616); *Keats* John Keats, English poet (1795–1821).

[3] *it has … really is* Matthew Arnold, whose poem *Thyrsis* attempts to summon the goddess Proserpine from the pastoral landscape of Sicily to the Cumnor hills of England. Arnold discusses the aim of criticism in his essay *The Function of Criticism at the Present Time*.

[4] *Turner* English landscape painter Joseph Mallord William Turner. Cf. John Ruskin's *Modern Painters*.

that bleach or rot on their corrupted canvases in England's Gallery;[1] greater indeed, one is apt to think at times, not merely because its equal beauty is more enduring, but on account of the fuller variety of its appeal, soul speaking to soul in those long-cadenced lines, not through form and colour alone, though through these, indeed, completely and without loss, but with intellectual and emotional utterance, with lofty passion and with loftier thought, with imaginative insight, and with poetic aim; greater, I always think, even as Literature is the greater art.

—1890

from *"The Decay of Lying"*[2]

CYRIL. ... [I]n order to avoid making any error I want you to tell me briefly the doctrines of the new aesthetics.

VIVIAN. Briefly, then, they are these. Art never expresses anything but itself. It has an independent life, just as Thought has, and develops purely on its own lines. It is not necessarily realistic in an age of realism, nor spiritual in an age of faith. So far from being the creation of its time, it is usually in direct opposition to it, and the only history that it preserves for us is the history of its own progress. Sometimes it returns upon its footsteps, and revives some antique form, as happened in the archaistic movement of late Greek Art, and in the Pre-Raphaelite movement of our own day. At other times it entirely anticipates its age, and produces in one century work that it takes another century to understand, to appreciate, and to enjoy. In no case does it reproduce its age. To pass from the art of a time to the time itself is the great mistake that all historians commit.

The second doctrine is this. All bad art comes from returning to Life and Nature and elevating them into ideals. Life and Nature may sometimes be used as part of Art's rough material, but before they are of any real service to art they must be translated into artistic conventions. The moment Art surrenders its imaginative medium it surrenders everything. As a method Realism is a complete failure, and the two things that every artist should avoid are modernity of form and modernity of subject matter. To us, who live in the nineteenth century, any century is a suitable subject for art except our own. The only beautiful things are the things that do not concern us. It is, to have the pleasure of quoting myself, exactly because Hecuba is nothing to us that her sorrows are so suitable a motive for a tragedy.[3] Besides, it is only the modern that ever becomes old-fashioned. M. Zola[4] sits down to give us a picture of the Second Empire. Who cares for the Second Empire now? It is out of date. Life goes faster than Realism, but Romanticism is always in front of Life.

The third doctrine is that Life imitates Art far more than Art imitates Life. This results not merely from Life's imitative instinct, but from the fact that the self-conscious aim of Life is to find expression, and that Art offers it certain beautiful forms through which it may realize that energy. It is a theory that has never been put forward before, but it is extremely fruitful, and throws an entirely new light upon the history of Art.

It follows, as a corollary from this, that external Nature also imitates Art. The only effects that she can show us are effects that we have already seen through poetry, or in paintings. This is the secret of Nature's charm, as well as the explanation of Nature's weakness.

---

[1] *England's Gallery* The Tate Gallery in London, upon which a major bequest of Turner's paintings was bestowed in 1856.

[2] *The Decay of Lying* In this Platonic dialogue, Wilde sets out a new theory of aesthetics through the conversation of two characters, Vivian and Cyril (named after Wilde's two sons). Vivian, prompted by Cyril's questioning, has been reading from his essay in progress, called "The Decay of Lying," which explores and confirms Plato's claim in the *Republic* that art is falsehood, yet challenges his assertion that art is a mere imitation of life, and that the lies of art are morally repugnant. On the contrary, Vivian celebrates the lies of art, declaring, "if something cannot be done to check, or at least modify, our monstrous worship of facts, Art will become sterile and Beauty will pass from the land." At the heart of this work is a challenge to the Victorian adherence to realism and advocacy of faithful imitation of nature.

[3] *Hecuba ... tragedy* Hecuba, Queen of Troy when that city was conquered by the Greeks, saw her husband and her sons murdered. In Shakespeare's *Hamlet*, one of the players performing for Hamlet recites an emotional monologue on the terrible fate of Hecuba, prompting Hamlet to wonder, "What's Hecuba to him, or he to Hecuba, / That he should weep for her?" (2.2.).

[4] *M. Zola* (Monsieur) Émile Zola, French novelist (1840–1902).

The final revelation is that Lying, the telling of beautiful untrue things, is the proper aim of Art. But of this I think I have spoken at sufficient length. And now let us go out on the terrace, where "droops the milk-white peacock like a ghost,"[1] while the evening star "washes the dusk with silver."[2] At twilight nature becomes a wonderfully suggestive effect, and is not without loveliness, though perhaps its chief use is to illustrate quotations from the poets. Come! We have talked long enough.

—1889

Preface[3] to *The Picture of Dorian Gray*

The artist is the creator of beautiful things.

To reveal art and conceal the artist is art's aim.

The critic is he who can translate into another medium or a new material his impression of beautiful things.

The highest as the lowest form of criticism is a mode of autobiography.

Those who find ugly meanings in beautiful things are corrupt without being charming. This is a fault.

Those who find beautiful meanings in beautiful things are cultivated. For these there is hope.

They are the elect to whom beautiful things mean only beauty.

There is no such thing as a moral or an immoral book. Books are well written, or badly written. That is all.

The nineteenth century dislike of Realism is the rage of Caliban[4] seeing his own face in a glass.

The nineteenth century dislike of Romanticism is the rage of Caliban not seeing his own face in a glass.

The moral life of man forms part of the subject matter of the artist, but the morality of art consists in the perfect use of an imperfect medium.

No artist desires to prove anything. Even things that are true can be proved.

No artist has ethical sympathies. An ethical sympathy in an artist is an unpardonable mannerism of style.

No artist is ever morbid. The artist can express everything.

Thought and language are to the artist instruments of an art.

Vice and virtue are to the artist materials for an art.

From the point of view of form, the type of all the arts is the art of the musician.

From the point of view of feeling, the actor's craft is the type.

All art is at once surface and symbol.

Those who go beneath the surface do so at their peril.

Those who read the symbol do so at their peril.

It is the spectator, and not life, that art really mirrors.

Diversity of opinion about a work of art shows that the work is new, complex, and vital.

When critics disagree the artist is in accord with himself.

We can forgive a man for making a useful thing as long as he does not admire it. The only excuse for making a useless thing is that one admires it intensely.

All art is quite useless.

—1891

The Importance of Being Earnest
A Trivial Comedy for Serious People

THE PERSONS IN THE PLAY

John Worthing, J.P.[5]
Algernon Moncrieff
Rev. Canon Chasuble, D.D.[6]
Merriman, *Butler*
Lane, *Manservant*

[1] *droops … ghost* From "The Princess" by Alfred, Lord Tennyson.

[2] *washes … silver* From "To the Evening Star" by William Blake.

[3] *Preface* Published in 1891, the year after the novel's first appearance, this preface was a response to the charges of immorality leveled at the novel by numerous critics.

[4] *Caliban* The "monster" of Shakespeare's *The Tempest*, Caliban is a native of the island and has been enslaved by Prospero.

[5] *J.P.* Justice of the Peace.

[6] *D.D.* Doctor of Divinity.

Lady Bracknell
Hon.[1] Gwendolen Fairfax
Cecily Cardew
Miss Prism, *Governess*

THE SCENES IN THE PLAY

ACT 1. Algernon Moncrieff's Flat in Half-Moon Street,[2] W.
ACT 2. The Garden at the Manor House, Woolton.[3]
ACT 3. Drawing-Room at the Manor House, Woolton.

TIME: The Present.

ACT 1

SCENE

(*Morning-room in Algernon's flat in Half-Moon Street. The room is luxuriously and artistically furnished. The sound of a piano is heard in the adjoining room.*)

(*Lane is arranging afternoon tea on the table, and after the music has ceased, Algernon enters.*)

ALGERNON. Did you hear what I was playing, Lane?
LANE. I didn't think it polite to listen, sir.
ALGERNON. I'm sorry for that, for your sake. I don't play accurately—any one can play accurately—but I play with wonderful expression. As far as the piano is concerned, sentiment is my forte. I keep science for Life.
LANE. Yes, sir.
ALGERNON. And, speaking of the science of Life, have you got the cucumber sandwiches[4] cut for Lady Bracknell?
LANE. Yes, sir. (*Hands them on a salver.*[5])
ALGERNON. (*Inspects them, takes two, and sits down on the sofa.*) Oh! … by the way, Lane, I see from your book that on Thursday night, when Lord Shoreman and Mr. Worthing were dining with me, eight bottles of champagne are entered as having been consumed.
LANE. Yes, sir; eight bottles and a pint.
ALGERNON. Why is it that at a bachelor's establishment the servants invariably drink the champagne? I ask merely for information.
LANE. I attribute it to the superior quality of the wine, sir. I have often observed that in married households the champagne is rarely of a first-rate brand.
ALGERNON. Good heavens! Is marriage so demoralising as that?
LANE. I believe it is a very pleasant state, sir. I have had very little experience of it myself up to the present. I have only been married once. That was in consequence of a misunderstanding between myself and a young person.
ALGERNON. (*Languidly.*) I don't know that I am much interested in your family life, Lane.
LANE. No, sir; it is not a very interesting subject. I never think of it myself.
ALGERNON. Very natural, I am sure. That will do, Lane, thank you.
LANE. Thank you, sir. (*Lane goes out.*)
ALGERNON. Lane's views on marriage seem somewhat lax. Really, if the lower orders don't set us a good example, what on earth is the use of them? They seem, as a class, to have absolutely no sense of moral responsibility.

(*Enter Lane.*)

LANE. Mr. Ernest Worthing.

(*Enter Jack. Lane goes out.*)

ALGERNON. How are you, my dear Ernest? What brings you up to town?

[1] *Hon.* I.e., The Honorable. The honorific in this case designates the daughter of a peer below the rank of Earl.

[2] *Half-Moon Street* Street located in a fashionable area of London.

[3] *Woolton* A fictional location.

[4] *cucumber sandwiches* Small sandwiches of cucumber on thinly sliced bread, a staple of afternoon tea in polite English society.

[5] *salver* Serving tray, typically silver.

JACK. Oh, pleasure, pleasure! What else should bring one anywhere? Eating as usual, I see, Algy!

ALGERNON. (*Stiffly.*) I believe it is customary in good society to take some slight refreshment at five o'clock. Where have you been since last Thursday?

JACK. (*Sitting down on the sofa.*) In the country.

ALGERNON. What on earth do you do there?

JACK. (*Pulling off his gloves.*) When one is in town[1] one amuses oneself. When one is in the country one amuses other people. It is excessively boring.

ALGERNON. And who are the people you amuse?

JACK. (*Airily.*) Oh, neighbours, neighbours.

ALGERNON. Got nice neighbours in your part of Shropshire?

JACK. Perfectly horrid! Never speak to one of them.

ALGERNON. How immensely you must amuse them! (*Goes over and takes sandwich.*) By the way, Shropshire is your county, is it not?

JACK. Eh? Shropshire? Yes, of course. Hallo! Why all these cups? Why cucumber sandwiches? Why such reckless extravagance in one so young? Who is coming to tea?

ALGERNON. Oh! merely Aunt Augusta and Gwendolen.

JACK. How perfectly delightful!

ALGERNON. Yes, that is all very well; but I am afraid Aunt Augusta won't quite approve of your being here.

JACK. May I ask why?

ALGERNON. My dear fellow, the way you flirt with Gwendolen is perfectly disgraceful. It is almost as bad as the way Gwendolen flirts with you.

JACK. I am in love with Gwendolen. I have come up to town expressly to propose to her.

ALGERNON. I thought you had come up for pleasure? ... I call that business.

JACK. How utterly unromantic you are!

ALGERNON. I really don't see anything romantic in proposing. It is very romantic to be in love. But there is nothing romantic about a definite proposal. Why, one may be accepted. One usually is, I believe. Then the excitement is all over. The very essence of romance is uncertainty. If ever I get married, I'll certainly try to forget the fact.

[1] *in town* In London.

JACK. I have no doubt about that, dear Algy. The Divorce Court was specially invented for people whose memories are so curiously constituted.

ALGERNON. Oh! there is no use speculating on that subject. Divorces are made in Heaven—(*Jack puts out his hand to take a sandwich. Algernon at once interferes.*) Please don't touch the cucumber sandwiches. They are ordered specially for Aunt Augusta. (*Takes one and eats it.*)

JACK. Well, you have been eating them all the time.

ALGERNON. That is quite a different matter. She is my aunt. (*Takes plate from below.*) Have some bread and butter. The bread and butter is for Gwendolen. Gwendolen is devoted to bread and butter.

JACK. (*Advancing to table and helping himself.*) And very good bread and butter it is too.

ALGERNON. Well, my dear fellow, you need not eat as if you were going to eat it all. You behave as if you were married to her already. You are not married to her already, and I don't think you ever will be.

JACK. Why on earth do you say that?

ALGERNON. Well, in the first place girls never marry the men they flirt with. Girls don't think it right.

JACK. Oh, that is nonsense!

ALGERNON. It isn't. It is a great truth. It accounts for the extraordinary number of bachelors that one sees all over the place. In the second place, I don't give my consent.

JACK. Your consent!

ALGERNON. My dear fellow, Gwendolen is my first cousin. And before I allow you to marry her, you will have to clear up the whole question of Cecily. (*Rings bell.*)

JACK. Cecily! What on earth do you mean? What do you mean, Algy, by Cecily! I don't know any one of the name of Cecily.

(*Enter Lane.*)

ALGERNON. Bring me that cigarette case Mr. Worthing left in the smoking-room the last time he dined here.

LANE. Yes, sir.

(*Lane goes out.*)

JACK. Do you mean to say you have had my cigarette case all this time? I wish to goodness you had let me know. I have been writing frantic letters to Scotland Yard about it. I was very nearly offering a large reward.

ALGERNON. Well, I wish you would offer one. I happen to be more than usually hard up.

JACK. There is no good offering a large reward now that the thing is found.

(*Enter Lane with the cigarette case on a salver. Algernon takes it at once. Lane goes out.*)

ALGERNON. I think that is rather mean of you, Ernest, I must say. (*Opens case and examines it.*) However, it makes no matter, for, now that I look at the inscription inside, I find that the thing isn't yours after all.

JACK. Of course it's mine. (*Moving to him.*) You have seen me with it a hundred times, and you have no right whatsoever to read what is written inside. It is a very ungentlemanly thing to read a private cigarette case.

ALGERNON. Oh! it is absurd to have a hard and fast rule about what one should read and what one shouldn't. More than half of modern culture depends on what one shouldn't read.

JACK. I am quite aware of the fact, and I don't propose to discuss modern culture. It isn't the sort of thing one should talk of in private. I simply want my cigarette case back.

ALGERNON. Yes; but this isn't your cigarette case. This cigarette case is a present from some one of the name of Cecily, and you said you didn't know any one of that name.

JACK. Well, if you want to know, Cecily happens to be my aunt.

ALGERNON. Your aunt!

JACK. Yes. Charming old lady she is, too. Lives at Tunbridge Wells. Just give it back to me, Algy.

ALGERNON. (*Retreating to back of sofa.*) But why does she call herself little Cecily if she is your aunt and lives at Tunbridge Wells? (*Reading.*) "From little Cecily with her fondest love."

JACK. (*Moving to sofa and kneeling upon it.*) My dear fellow, what on earth is there in that? Some aunts are tall, some aunts are not tall. That is a matter that surely an aunt may be allowed to decide for herself. You seem to think that every aunt should be exactly like your aunt! That is absurd! For Heaven's sake give me back my cigarette case. (*Follows Algernon round the room.*)

ALGERNON. Yes. But why does your aunt call you her uncle? "From little Cecily, with her fondest love to her dear Uncle Jack." There is no objection, I admit, to an aunt being a small aunt, but why an aunt, no matter what her size may be, should call her own nephew her uncle, I can't quite make out. Besides, your name isn't Jack at all; it is Ernest.

JACK. It isn't Ernest; it's Jack.

ALGERNON. You have always told me it was Ernest. I have introduced you to every one as Ernest. You answer to the name of Ernest. You look as if your name was Ernest. You are the most earnest-looking person I ever saw in my life. It is perfectly absurd your saying that your name isn't Ernest. It's on your cards. Here is one of them. (*Taking it from case.*) "Mr. Ernest Worthing, B. 4, The Albany." I'll keep this as a proof that your name is Ernest if ever you attempt to deny it to me, or to Gwendolen, or to any one else. (*Puts the card in his pocket.*)

JACK. Well, my name is Ernest in town and Jack in the country, and the cigarette case was given to me in the country.

ALGERNON. Yes, but that does not account for the fact that your small Aunt Cecily, who lives at Tunbridge Wells, calls you her dear uncle. Come, old boy, you had much better have the thing out at once.

JACK. My dear Algy, you talk exactly as if you were a dentist. It is very vulgar to talk like a dentist when one isn't a dentist. It produces a false impression.

ALGERNON. Well, that is exactly what dentists always do. Now, go on! Tell me the whole thing. I may mention that I have always suspected you of being a confirmed and secret Bunburyist; and I am quite sure of it now.

JACK. Bunburyist? What on earth do you mean by a Bunburyist?

ALGERNON. I'll reveal to you the meaning of that incomparable expression as soon as you are kind enough to inform me why you are Ernest in town and Jack in the country.

JACK. Well, produce my cigarette case first.

ALGERNON. Here it is. (*Hands cigarette case.*) Now produce your explanation, and pray make it improbable. (*Sits on sofa.*)

JACK. My dear fellow, there is nothing improbable about my explanation at all. In fact it's perfectly ordinary. Old Mr. Thomas Cardew, who adopted me when I was a little boy, made me in his will guardian to his granddaughter, Miss Cecily Cardew. Cecily, who addresses me as her uncle from motives of respect that you could not possibly appreciate, lives at my place in the country under the charge of her admirable governess, Miss Prism.

ALGERNON. Where is that place in the country, by the way?

JACK. That is nothing to you, dear boy. You are not going to be invited ... I may tell you candidly that the place is not in Shropshire.

ALGERNON. I suspected that, my dear fellow! I have Bunburyed all over Shropshire on two separate occasions. Now, go on. Why are you Ernest in town and Jack in the country?

JACK. My dear Algy, I don't know whether you will be able to understand my real motives. You are hardly serious enough. When one is placed in the position of guardian, one has to adopt a very high moral tone on all subjects. It's one's duty to do so. And as a high moral tone can hardly be said to conduce very much to either one's health or one's happiness, in order to get up to town I have always pretended to have a younger brother of the name of Ernest, who lives in the Albany, and gets into the most dreadful scrapes. That, my dear Algy, is the whole truth pure and simple.

ALGERNON. The truth is rarely pure and never simple. Modern life would be very tedious if it were either, and modern literature a complete impossibility!

JACK. That wouldn't be at all a bad thing.

ALGERNON. Literary criticism is not your forte, my dear fellow. Don't try it. You should leave that to people who haven't been at a University. They do it so well in the daily papers. What you really are is a Bunburyist. I was quite right in saying you were a Bunburyist. You are one of the most advanced Bunburyists I know.

JACK. What on earth do you mean?

ALGERNON. You have invented a very useful younger brother called Ernest, in order that you may be able to come up to town as often as you like. I have invented an invaluable permanent invalid called Bunbury, in order that I may be able to go down into the country whenever I choose. Bunbury is perfectly invaluable. If it wasn't for Bunbury's extraordinary bad health, for instance, I wouldn't be able to dine with you at Willis's to-night, for I have been really engaged to Aunt Augusta for more than a week.

JACK. I haven't asked you to dine with me anywhere to-night.

ALGERNON. I know. You are absurdly careless about sending out invitations. It is very foolish of you. Nothing annoys people so much as not receiving invitations.

JACK. You had much better dine with your Aunt Augusta.

ALGERNON. I haven't the smallest intention of doing anything of the kind. To begin with, I dined there on Monday, and once a week is quite enough to dine with one's own relations. In the second place, whenever I do dine there I am always treated as a member of the family, and sent down[1] with either no woman at all, or two. In the third place, I know perfectly well whom she will place me next to, to-night. She will place me next Mary Farquhar, who always flirts with her own husband across the dinner-table. That is not very pleasant. Indeed, it is not even decent ... and that sort of thing is enormously on the increase. The amount of women in London who flirt with their own husbands is perfectly scandalous. It looks so bad. It is simply washing one's clean linen in public. Besides, now that I know you to be a confirmed Bunburyist I naturally want to talk to you about Bunburying. I want to tell you the rules.

JACK. I'm not a Bunburyist at all. If Gwendolen accepts me, I am going to kill my brother, indeed I think I'll kill him in any case. Cecily is a little too much interested in him. It is rather a bore. So I am going to get rid of

[1] *sent down* I.e., sent from the drawing-room (typically upstairs) down to the dining-room (typically on a lower floor).

Ernest. And I strongly advise you to do the same with Mr. … with your invalid friend who has the absurd name.

ALGERNON. Nothing will induce me to part with Bunbury, and if you ever get married, which seems to me extremely problematic, you will be very glad to know Bunbury. A man who marries without knowing Bunbury has a very tedious time of it.

JACK. That is nonsense. If I marry a charming girl like Gwendolen, and she is the only girl I ever saw in my life that I would marry, I certainly won't want to know Bunbury.

ALGERNON. Then your wife will. You don't seem to realise, that in married life three is company and two is none.

JACK. (*Sententiously.*) That, my dear young friend, is the theory that the corrupt French Drama has been propounding for the last fifty years.

ALGERNON. Yes; and that the happy English home has proved in half the time.

JACK. For heaven's sake, don't try to be cynical. It's perfectly easy to be cynical.

ALGERNON. My dear fellow, it isn't easy to be anything nowadays. There's such a lot of beastly competition about. (*The sound of an electric bell is heard.*) Ah! that must be Aunt Augusta. Only relatives, or creditors, ever ring in that Wagnerian[1] manner. Now, if I get her out of the way for ten minutes, so that you can have an opportunity for proposing to Gwendolen, may I dine with you to-night at Willis's?

JACK. I suppose so, if you want to.

ALGERNON. Yes, but you must be serious about it. I hate people who are not serious about meals. It is so shallow of them.

(*Enter Lane.*)

Lady Bracknell and Miss Fairfax.

(*Algernon goes forward to meet them. Enter Lady Bracknell and Gwendolen.*)

LADY BRACKNELL. Good afternoon, dear Algernon, I hope you are behaving very well.

ALGERNON. I'm feeling very well, Aunt Augusta.

LADY BRACKNELL. That's not quite the same thing. In fact the two things rarely go together. (*Sees Jack and bows to him with icy coldness.*)

ALGERNON. (*To Gwendolen.*) Dear me, you are smart!

GWENDOLEN. I am always smart! Am I not, Mr. Worthing?

JACK. You're quite perfect, Miss Fairfax.

GWENDOLEN. Oh! I hope I am not that. It would leave no room for developments, and I intend to develop in many directions.

(*Gwendolen and Jack sit down together in the corner.*)

LADY BRACKNELL. I'm sorry if we are a little late, Algernon, but I was obliged to call on dear Lady Harbury. I hadn't been there since her poor husband's death. I never saw a woman so altered; she looks quite twenty years younger. And now I'll have a cup of tea, and one of those nice cucumber sandwiches you promised me.

ALGERNON. Certainly, Aunt Augusta. (*Goes over to tea-table.*)

LADY BRACKNELL. Won't you come and sit here, Gwendolen?

GWENDOLEN. Thanks, mamma, I'm quite comfortable where I am.

ALGERNON. (*Picking up empty plate in horror.*) Good heavens! Lane! Why are there no cucumber sandwiches? I ordered them specially.

LANE. (*Gravely.*) There were no cucumbers in the market this morning, sir. I went down twice.

ALGERNON. No cucumbers!

LANE. No, sir. Not even for ready money.

ALGERNON. That will do, Lane, thank you.

LANE. Thank you, sir. (*Goes out.*)

ALGERNON. I am greatly distressed, Aunt Augusta, about there being no cucumbers, not even for ready money.

[1] *Wagnerian* Suggesting the music of German composer Richard Wagner (1813–83), known for dramatic, stirring compositions such as *Tannhäuser*, *Lohengrin*, and *Der Ring des Nibelungen*.

LADY BRACKNELL. It really makes no matter, Algernon. I had some crumpets with Lady Harbury, who seems to me to be living entirely for pleasure now.

ALGERNON. I hear her hair has turned quite gold from grief.

LADY BRACKNELL. It certainly has changed its colour. From what cause I, of course, cannot say. (*Algernon crosses and hands tea.*) Thank you. I've quite a treat for you to-night, Algernon. I am going to send you down with Mary Farquhar. She is such a nice woman, and so attentive to her husband. It's delightful to watch them.

ALGERNON. I am afraid, Aunt Augusta, I shall have to give up the pleasure of dining with you to-night after all.

LADY BRACKNELL. (*Frowning.*) I hope not, Algernon. It would put my table completely out. Your uncle would have to dine upstairs. Fortunately he is accustomed to that.

ALGERNON. It is a great bore, and, I need hardly say, a terrible disappointment to me, but the fact is I have just had a telegram to say that my poor friend Bunbury is very ill again. (*Exchanges glances with Jack.*) They seem to think I should be with him.

LADY BRACKNELL. It is very strange. This Mr. Bunbury seems to suffer from curiously bad health.

ALGERNON. Yes; poor Bunbury is a dreadful invalid.

LADY BRACKNELL. Well, I must say, Algernon, that I think it is high time that Mr. Bunbury made up his mind whether he was going to live or to die. This shilly-shallying with the question is absurd. Nor do I in any way approve of the modern sympathy with invalids. I consider it morbid. Illness of any kind is hardly a thing to be encouraged in others. Health is the primary duty of life. I am always telling that to your poor uncle, but he never seems to take much notice … as far as any improvement in his ailment goes. I should be much obliged if you would ask Mr. Bunbury, from me, to be kind enough not to have a relapse on Saturday, for I rely on you to arrange my music for me. It is my last reception, and one wants something that will encourage conversation, particularly at the end of the season when every one has practically said whatever they had to say, which, in most cases, was probably not much.

ALGERNON. I'll speak to Bunbury, Aunt Augusta, if he is still conscious, and I think I can promise you he'll be all right by Saturday. Of course the music is a great difficulty. You see, if one plays good music, people don't listen, and if one plays bad music people don't talk. But I'll run over the programme I've drawn out, if you will kindly come into the next room for a moment.

LADY BRACKNELL. Thank you, Algernon. It is very thoughtful of you. (*Rising, and following Algernon.*) I'm sure the programme will be delightful, after a few expurgations. French songs I cannot possibly allow. People always seem to think that they are improper, and either look shocked, which is vulgar, or laugh, which is worse. But German sounds a thoroughly respectable language, and indeed, I believe is so. Gwendolen, you will accompany me.

GWENDOLEN. Certainly, mamma.

(*Lady Bracknell and Algernon go into the music-room, Gwendolen remains behind.*)

JACK. Charming day it has been, Miss Fairfax.

GWENDOLEN. Pray don't talk to me about the weather, Mr. Worthing. Whenever people talk to me about the weather, I always feel quite certain that they mean something else. And that makes me so nervous.

JACK. I do mean something else.

GWENDOLEN. I thought so. In fact, I am never wrong.

JACK. And I would like to be allowed to take advantage of Lady Bracknell's temporary absence …

GWENDOLEN. I would certainly advise you to do so. Mamma has a way of coming back suddenly into a room that I have often had to speak to her about.

JACK. (*Nervously.*) Miss Fairfax, ever since I met you I have admired you more than any girl … I have ever met since … I met you.

GWENDOLEN. Yes, I am quite well aware of the fact. And I often wish that in public, at any rate, you had been more demonstrative. For me you have always had an irresistible fascination. Even before I met you I was far from indifferent to you. (*Jack looks at her in amazement.*) We live, as I hope you know, Mr. Worthing, in an age of ideals. The fact is constantly mentioned in the more expensive monthly magazines, and has reached the provincial[1] pulpits, I am told; and my ideal has always been to love some one of the name of Ernest. There is something in that name that inspires absolute confidence. The moment Algernon first mentioned to me that he had a friend called Ernest, I knew I was destined to love you.

JACK. You really love me, Gwendolen?

GWENDOLEN. Passionately!

JACK. Darling! You don't know how happy you've made me.

GWENDOLEN. My own Ernest!

JACK. But you don't really mean to say that you couldn't love me if my name wasn't Ernest?

GWENDOLEN. But your name is Ernest.

JACK. Yes, I know it is. But supposing it was something else? Do you mean to say you couldn't love me then?

GWENDOLEN. (*Glibly.*) Ah! that is clearly a metaphysical speculation, and like most metaphysical speculations has very little reference at all to the actual facts of real life, as we know them.

JACK. Personally, darling, to speak quite candidly, I don't much care about the name of Ernest ... I don't think the name suits me at all.

GWENDOLEN. It suits you perfectly. It is a divine name. It has a music of its own. It produces vibrations.

JACK. Well, really, Gwendolen, I must say that I think there are lots of other much nicer names. I think Jack, for instance, a charming name.

GWENDOLEN. Jack? ... No, there is very little music in the name Jack, if any at all, indeed. It does not thrill. It produces absolutely no vibrations ... I have known several Jacks, and they all, without exception, were more than usually plain. Besides, Jack is a notorious domesticity for John! And I pity any woman who is married to a man called John. She would probably never be allowed to know the entrancing pleasure of a single moment's solitude. The only really safe name is Ernest.

JACK. Gwendolen, I must get christened at once—I mean we must get married at once. There is no time to be lost.

GWENDOLEN. Married, Mr. Worthing?

JACK. (*Astounded.*) Well ... surely. You know that I love you, and you led me to believe, Miss Fairfax, that you were not absolutely indifferent to me.

GWENDOLEN. I adore you. But you haven't proposed to me yet. Nothing has been said at all about marriage. The subject has not even been touched on.

JACK. Well ... may I propose to you now?

GWENDOLEN. I think it would be an admirable opportunity. And to spare you any possible disappointment, Mr. Worthing, I think it only fair to tell you quite frankly before-hand that I am fully determined to accept you.

JACK. Gwendolen!

GWENDOLEN. Yes, Mr. Worthing, what have you got to say to me?

JACK. You know what I have got to say to you.

GWENDOLEN. Yes, but you don't say it.

JACK. Gwendolen, will you marry me? (*Goes on his knees.*)

GWENDOLEN. Of course I will, darling. How long you have been about it! I am afraid you have had very little experience in how to propose.

JACK. My own one, I have never loved any one in the world but you.

GWENDOLEN. Yes, but men often propose for practice. I know my brother Gerald does. All my girl-friends tell me so. What wonderfully blue eyes you have, Ernest! They are quite, quite, blue. I hope you will always look at me just like that, especially when there are other people present. (*Enter Lady Bracknell.*)

LADY BRACKNELL. Mr. Worthing! Rise, sir, from this semi-recumbent posture. It is most indecorous.

GWENDOLEN. Mamma! (*He tries to rise; she restrains him.*) I must beg you to retire. This is no place for you. Besides, Mr. Worthing has not quite finished yet.

LADY BRACKNELL. Finished what, may I ask?

GWENDOLEN. I am engaged to Mr. Worthing, mamma.

(*They rise together.*)

[1] *provincial* "Province" does not indicate a formal British jurisdiction; "the provinces" is a colloquial term for all areas of the country that are some distance from London.

LADY BRACKNELL. Pardon me, you are not engaged to any one. When you do become engaged to some one, I, or your father, should his health permit him, will inform you of the fact. An engagement should come on a young girl as a surprise, pleasant or unpleasant, as the case may be. It is hardly a matter that she could be allowed to arrange for herself ... And now I have a few questions to put to you, Mr. Worthing. While I am making these inquiries, you, Gwendolen, will wait for me below in the carriage.

GWENDOLEN. (*Reproachfully.*) Mamma!

LADY BRACKNELL. In the carriage, Gwendolen!

(*Gwendolen goes to the door. She and Jack blow kisses to each other behind Lady Bracknell's back. Lady Bracknell looks vaguely about as if she could not understand what the noise was. Finally turns round.*)

Gwendolen, the carriage!

GWENDOLEN. Yes, mamma. (*Goes out, looking back at Jack.*)

LADY BRACKNELL. (*Sitting down.*) You can take a seat, Mr. Worthing. (*Looks in her pocket for note-book and pencil.*)

JACK. Thank you, Lady Bracknell, I prefer standing.

LADY BRACKNELL. (*Pencil and note-book in hand.*) I feel bound to tell you that you are not down on my list of eligible young men, although I have the same list as the dear Duchess of Bolton has. We work together, in fact. However, I am quite ready to enter your name, should your answers be what a really affectionate mother requires. Do you smoke?

JACK. Well, yes, I must admit I smoke.

LADY BRACKNELL. I am glad to hear it. A man should always have an occupation of some kind. There are far too many idle men in London as it is. How old are you?

JACK. Twenty-nine.

LADY BRACKNELL. A very good age to be married at. I have always been of opinion that a man who desires to get married should know either everything or nothing. Which do you know?

JACK. (*After some hesitation.*) I know nothing, Lady Bracknell.

LADY BRACKNELL. I am pleased to hear it. I do not approve of anything that tampers with natural ignorance. Ignorance is like a delicate exotic fruit; touch it and the bloom is gone. The whole theory of modern education is radically unsound. Fortunately in England, at any rate, education produces no effect whatsoever. If it did, it would prove a serious danger to the upper classes, and probably lead to acts of violence in Grosvenor Square.[1] What is your income?

JACK. Between seven and eight thousand a year.

LADY BRACKNELL. (*Makes a note in her book.*) In land, or in investments?

JACK. In investments, chiefly.

LADY BRACKNELL. That is satisfactory. What between the duties[2] expected of one during one's lifetime, and the duties exacted from one after one's death, land has ceased to be either a profit or a pleasure. It gives one position, and prevents one from keeping it up. That's all that can be said about land.

JACK. I have a country house with some land, of course, attached to it, about fifteen hundred acres, I believe; but I don't depend on that for my real income. In fact, as far as I can make out, the poachers are the only people who make anything out of it.

LADY BRACKNELL. A country house! How many bedrooms? Well, that point can be cleared up afterwards. You have a town house, I hope? A girl with a simple, unspoiled nature, like Gwendolen, could hardly be expected to reside in the country.

JACK. Well, I own a house in Belgrave Square, but it is let by the year to Lady Bloxham. Of course, I can get it back whenever I like, at six months' notice.

LADY BRACKNELL. Lady Bloxham? I don't know her.

JACK. Oh, she goes about very little. She is a lady considerably advanced in years.

LADY BRACKNELL. Ah, nowadays that is no guarantee of respectability of character. What number in Belgrave Square?

JACK. 149.

LADY BRACKNELL. (*Shaking her head.*) The unfashionable side. I thought there was something. However, that

[1] *Grosvenor Square* Located in a fashionable part of central London.

[2] *duties* Taxes.

could easily be altered.

JACK. Do you mean the fashion, or the side?

LADY BRACKNELL. (*Sternly.*) Both, if necessary, I presume. What are your politics?

JACK. Well, I am afraid I really have none. I am a Liberal Unionist.[1]

LADY BRACKNELL. Oh, they count as Tories. They dine with us. Or come in the evening, at any rate. Now to minor matters. Are your parents living?

JACK. I have lost both my parents.

LADY BRACKNELL. To lose one parent, Mr. Worthing, may be regarded as a misfortune; to lose both looks like carelessness. Who was your father? He was evidently a man of some wealth. Was he born in what the Radical papers call the purple of commerce,[2] or did he rise from the ranks of the aristocracy?

JACK. I am afraid I really don't know. The fact is, Lady Bracknell, I said I had lost my parents. It would be nearer the truth to say that my parents seem to have lost me … I don't actually know who I am by birth. I was … well, I was found.

LADY BRACKNELL. Found!

JACK. The late Mr. Thomas Cardew, an old gentleman of a very charitable and kindly disposition, found me, and gave me the name of Worthing, because he happened to have a first-class ticket for Worthing in his pocket at the time. Worthing is a place in Sussex. It is a seaside resort.

LADY BRACKNELL. Where did the charitable gentleman who had a first-class ticket for this seaside resort find you?

JACK. (*Gravely.*) In a hand-bag.

LADY BRACKNELL. A hand-bag?

JACK. (*Very seriously.*) Yes, Lady Bracknell. I was in a hand-bag—a somewhat large, black leather hand-bag, with handles to it—an ordinary hand-bag in fact.

LADY BRACKNELL. In what locality did this Mr. James, or Thomas, Cardew come across this ordinary hand-bag?

JACK. In the cloak-room at Victoria Station. It was given to him in mistake for his own.

LADY BRACKNELL. The cloak-room at Victoria Station?

JACK. Yes. The Brighton line.

LADY BRACKNELL. The line is immaterial. Mr. Worthing, I confess I feel somewhat bewildered by what you have just told me. To be born, or at any rate bred, in a hand-bag, whether it had handles or not, seems to me to display a contempt for the ordinary decencies of family life that reminds one of the worst excesses of the French Revolution. And I presume you know what that unfortunate movement led to? As for the particular locality in which the hand-bag was found, a cloak-room at a railway station might serve to conceal a social indiscretion—has probably, indeed, been used for that purpose before now—but it could hardly be regarded as an assured basis for a recognised position in good society.

JACK. May I ask you then what you would advise me to do? I need hardly say I would do anything in the world to ensure Gwendolen's happiness.

LADY BRACKNELL. I would strongly advise you, Mr. Worthing, to try and acquire some relations as soon as possible, and to make a definite effort to produce at any rate one parent, of either sex, before the season[3] is quite over.

JACK. Well, I don't see how I could possibly manage to do that. I can produce the hand-bag at any moment. It is in my dressing-room at home. I really think that should satisfy you, Lady Bracknell.

LADY BRACKNELL. Me, sir! What has it to do with me? You can hardly imagine that I and Lord Bracknell would dream of allowing our only daughter—a girl brought up with the utmost care—to marry into a cloak-room, and form an alliance with a parcel? Good morning, Mr. Worthing!

(*Lady Bracknell sweeps out in majestic indignation.*)

[1] *Liberal Unionist* The Liberal Unionists, who in 1886 had broken away from the Liberal party in reaction to Prime Minister William Gladstone's support for Irish Home Rule, occupied the political center between the two large parties, the Liberals and the Conservatives.

[2] *Was he born … the purple of commerce* I.e., was he born into a wealthy merchant or trading family. (The color purple is traditionally associated with royalty.)

[3] *the season* The London social season, which ran while Parliament was sitting. Many wealthy families spent the rest of the year at their country homes.

JACK. Good morning! (*Algernon, from the other room, strikes up the Wedding March. Jack looks perfectly furious, and goes to the door.*) For goodness' sake don't play that ghastly tune, Algy. How idiotic you are!

(*The music stops and Algernon enters cheerily.*)

ALGERNON. Didn't it go off all right, old boy? You don't mean to say Gwendolen refused you? I know it is a way she has. She is always refusing people. I think it is most ill-natured of her.

JACK. Oh, Gwendolen is as right as a trivet.[1] As far as she is concerned, we are engaged. Her mother is perfectly unbearable. Never met such a Gorgon[2] … I don't really know what a Gorgon is like, but I am quite sure that Lady Bracknell is one. In any case, she is a monster, without being a myth, which is rather unfair … I beg your pardon, Algy, I suppose I shouldn't talk about your own aunt in that way before you.

ALGERNON. My dear boy, I love hearing my relations abused. It is the only thing that makes me put up with them at all. Relations are simply a tedious pack of people, who haven't got the remotest knowledge of how to live, nor the smallest instinct about when to die.

JACK. Oh, that is nonsense!

ALGERNON. It isn't!

JACK. Well, I won't argue about the matter. You always want to argue about things.

ALGERNON. That is exactly what things were originally made for.

JACK. Upon my word, if I thought that, I'd shoot myself … (*A pause.*) You don't think there is any chance of Gwendolen becoming like her mother in about a hundred and fifty years, do you, Algy?

ALGERNON. All women become like their mothers. That is their tragedy. No man does. That's his.

JACK. Is that clever?

ALGERNON. It is perfectly phrased! and quite as true as any observation in civilized life should be.

JACK. I am sick to death of cleverness. Everybody is clever nowadays. You can't go anywhere without meeting clever people. The thing has become an absolute public nuisance. I wish to goodness we had a few fools left.

ALGERNON. We have.

JACK. I should extremely like to meet them. What do they talk about?

ALGERNON. The fools? Oh! about the clever people, of course.

JACK. What fools!

ALGERNON. By the way, did you tell Gwendolen the truth about your being Ernest in town, and Jack in the country?

JACK. (*In a very patronising manner.*) My dear fellow, the truth isn't quite the sort of thing one tells to a nice, sweet, refined girl. What extraordinary ideas you have about the way to behave to a woman!

ALGERNON. The only way to behave to a woman is to make love to her, if she is pretty, and to some one else, if she is plain.

JACK. Oh, that is nonsense.

ALGERNON. What about your brother? What about the profligate Ernest?

JACK. Oh, before the end of the week I shall have got rid of him. I'll say he died in Paris of apoplexy.[3] Lots of people die of apoplexy, quite suddenly, don't they?

ALGERNON. Yes, but it's hereditary, my dear fellow. It's a sort of thing that runs in families. You had much better say a severe chill.

JACK. You are sure a severe chill isn't hereditary, or anything of that kind?

ALGERNON. Of course it isn't!

JACK. Very well, then. My poor brother Ernest is carried off suddenly, in Paris, by a severe chill. That gets rid of him.

ALGERNON. But I thought you said that … Miss Cardew was a little too much interested in your poor brother Ernest? Won't she feel his loss a good deal?

JACK. Oh, that is all right. Cecily is not a silly romantic girl, I am glad to say. She has got a capital appetite, goes

---

1 *as right as a trivet* Proverbial expression indicating stability (a trivet is a three-footed stand or support).

2 *Gorgon* In Greek mythology the three Gorgons are sisters who have repulsive features (including snakes growing out of their heads instead of hair); anyone who looks at them turns into stone.

3 *apoplexy* Stroke.

on long walks, and pays no attention at all to her lessons.

ALGERNON. I would rather like to see Cecily.

JACK. I will take very good care you never do. She is excessively pretty, and she is only just eighteen.

ALGERNON. Have you told Gwendolen yet that you have an excessively pretty ward who is only just eighteen?

JACK. Oh! one doesn't blurt these things out to people. Cecily and Gwendolen are perfectly certain to be extremely great friends. I'll bet you anything you like that half an hour after they have met, they will be calling each other sister.

ALGERNON. Women only do that when they have called each other a lot of other things first. Now, my dear boy, if we want to get a good table at Willis's, we really must go and dress. Do you know it is nearly seven?

JACK. (*Irritably.*) Oh! It always is nearly seven.

ALGERNON. Well, I'm hungry.

JACK. I never knew you when you weren't …

ALGERNON. What shall we do after dinner? Go to a theatre?

JACK. Oh no! I loathe listening.

ALGERNON. Well, let us go to the Club?

JACK. Oh, no! I hate talking.

ALGERNON. Well, we might trot round to the Empire[1] at ten?

JACK. Oh, no! I can't bear looking at things. It is so silly.

ALGERNON. Well, what shall we do?

JACK. Nothing!

ALGERNON. It is awfully hard work doing nothing. However, I don't mind hard work where there is no definite object of any kind.

(*Enter Lane.*)

LANE. Miss Fairfax.

(*Enter Gwendolen. Lane goes out.*)

ALGERNON. Gwendolen, upon my word!

GWENDOLEN. Algy, kindly turn your back. I have something very particular to say to Mr. Worthing.

ALGERNON. Really, Gwendolen, I don't think I can allow this at all.

GWENDOLEN. Algy, you always adopt a strictly immoral attitude towards life. You are not quite old enough to do that. (*Algernon retires to the fireplace.*)

JACK. My own darling!

GWENDOLEN. Ernest, we may never be married. From the expression on mamma's face I fear we never shall. Few parents nowadays pay any regard to what their children say to them. The old-fashioned respect for the young is fast dying out. Whatever influence I ever had over mamma, I lost at the age of three. But although she may prevent us from becoming man and wife, and I may marry some one else, and marry often, nothing that she can possibly do can alter my eternal devotion to you.

JACK. Dear Gwendolen!

GWENDOLEN. The story of your romantic origin, as related to me by mamma, with unpleasing comments, has naturally stirred the deeper fibres of my nature. Your Christian name has an irresistible fascination. The simplicity of your character makes you exquisitely incomprehensible to me. Your town address at the Albany[2] I have. What is your address in the country?

JACK. The Manor House, Woolton, Hertfordshire.

(*Algernon, who has been carefully listening, smiles to himself, and writes the address on his shirt-cuff. Then picks up the Railway Guide.*)

GWENDOLEN. There is a good postal service, I suppose? It may be necessary to do something desperate. That of course will require serious consideration. I will communicate with you daily.

JACK. My own one!

GWENDOLEN. How long do you remain in town?

JACK. Till Monday.

GWENDOLEN. Good! Algy, you may turn round now.

ALGERNON. Thanks, I've turned round already.

GWENDOLEN. You may also ring the bell.

[1] *the Empire* Theater that often featured risqué variety shows.

[2] *the Albany* Fashionable men's club in London.

JACK. You will let me see you to your carriage, my own darling?

GWENDOLEN. Certainly.

JACK. (*To Lane, who now enters.*) I will see Miss Fairfax out.

LANE. Yes, sir. (*Jack and Gwendolen go off.*)

(*Lane presents several letters on a salver to Algernon. It is to be surmised that they are bills, as Algernon, after looking at the envelopes, tears them up.*)

ALGERNON. A glass of sherry, Lane.

LANE. Yes, sir.

ALGERNON. To-morrow, Lane, I'm going Bunburying.

LANE. Yes, sir.

ALGERNON. I shall probably not be back till Monday. You can put up my dress clothes, my smoking jacket, and all the Bunbury suits …

LANE. Yes, sir. (*Handing sherry.*)

ALGERNON. I hope to-morrow will be a fine day, Lane.

LANE. It never is, sir.

ALGERNON. Lane, you're a perfect pessimist.

LANE. I do my best to give satisfaction, sir.

(*Enter Jack. Lane goes off.*)

JACK. There's a sensible, intellectual girl! the only girl I ever cared for in my life. (*Algernon is laughing immoderately.*) What on earth are you so amused at?

ALGERNON. Oh, I'm a little anxious about poor Bunbury, that is all.

JACK. If you don't take care, your friend Bunbury will get you into a serious scrape some day.

ALGERNON. I love scrapes. They are the only things that are never serious.

JACK. Oh, that's nonsense, Algy. You never talk anything but nonsense.

ALGERNON. Nobody ever does.

(*Jack looks indignantly at him, and leaves the room. Algernon lights a cigarette, reads his shirt-cuff, and smiles.*)

ACT DROP

ACT 2

SCENE

(*Garden at the Manor House. A flight of grey stone steps leads up to the house. The garden, an old-fashioned one, full of roses. Time of year, July. Basket chairs, and a table covered with books, are set under a large yew-tree. Miss Prism discovered seated at the table. Cecily is at the back watering flowers.*)

MISS PRISM. (*Calling.*) Cecily, Cecily! Surely such a utilitarian occupation as the watering of flowers is rather Moulton's duty than yours? Especially at a moment when intellectual pleasures await you. Your German grammar is on the table. Pray open it at page fifteen. We will repeat yesterday's lesson.

CECILY. (*Coming over very slowly.*) But I don't like German. It isn't at all a becoming language. I know perfectly well that I look quite plain after my German lesson.

MISS PRISM. Child, you know how anxious your guardian is that you should improve yourself in every way. He laid particular stress on your German, as he was leaving for town yesterday. Indeed, he always lays stress on your German when he is leaving for town.

CECILY. Dear Uncle Jack is so very serious! Sometimes he is so serious that I think he cannot be quite well.

MISS PRISM. (*Drawing herself up.*) Your guardian enjoys the best of health, and his gravity of demeanour is especially to be commended in one so comparatively young as he is. I know no one who has a higher sense of duty and responsibility.

CECILY. I suppose that is why he often looks a little bored when we three are together.

MISS PRISM. Cecily! I am surprised at you. Mr. Worthing has many troubles in his life. Idle merriment and triviality would be out of place in his conversation. You must remember his constant anxiety about that unfortunate young man his brother.

CECILY. I wish Uncle Jack would allow that unfortunate young man, his brother, to come down here sometimes. We might have a good influence over him, Miss Prism.

I am sure you certainly would. You know German, and geology, and things of that kind influence a man very much. (*Cecily begins to write in her diary.*)

MISS PRISM. (*Shaking her head.*) I do not think that even I could produce any effect on a character that according to his own brother's admission is irretrievably weak and vacillating. Indeed I am not sure that I would desire to reclaim him. I am not in favour of this modern mania for turning bad people into good people at a moment's notice. As a man sows so let him reap.[1] You must put away your diary, Cecily. I really don't see why you should keep a diary at all.

CECILY. I keep a diary in order to enter the wonderful secrets of my life. If I didn't write them down, I should probably forget all about them.

MISS PRISM. Memory, my dear Cecily, is the diary that we all carry about with us.

CECILY. Yes, but it usually chronicles the things that have never happened, and couldn't possibly have happened. I believe that Memory is responsible for nearly all the three-volume novels that Mudie sends us.[2]

MISS PRISM. Do not speak slightingly of the three-volume novel, Cecily. I wrote one myself in earlier days.

CECILY. Did you really, Miss Prism? How wonderfully clever you are! I hope it did not end happily? I don't like novels that end happily. They depress me so much.

MISS PRISM. The good ended happily, and the bad unhappily. That is what Fiction means.

CECILY. I suppose so. But it seems very unfair. And was your novel ever published?

MISS PRISM. Alas! no. The manuscript unfortunately was abandoned. (*Cecily starts.*) I use the word in the sense of lost or mislaid. To your work, child, these speculations are profitless.

CECILY. (*Smiling.*) But I see dear Dr. Chasuble coming up through the garden.

MISS PRISM. (*Rising and advancing.*) Dr. Chasuble! This is indeed a pleasure.

(*Enter Canon Chasuble.*)

CHASUBLE. And how are we this morning? Miss Prism, you are, I trust, well?

CECILY. Miss Prism has just been complaining of a slight headache. I think it would do her so much good to have a short stroll with you in the Park, Dr. Chasuble.

MISS PRISM. Cecily, I have not mentioned anything about a headache.

CECILY. No, dear Miss Prism, I know that, but I felt instinctively that you had a headache. Indeed I was thinking about that, and not about my German lesson, when the Rector came in.

CHASUBLE. I hope, Cecily, you are not inattentive.

CECILY. Oh, I am afraid I am.

CHASUBLE. That is strange. Were I fortunate enough to be Miss Prism's pupil, I would hang upon her lips. (*Miss Prism glares.*) I spoke metaphorically.—My metaphor was drawn from bees. Ahem! Mr. Worthing, I suppose, has not returned from town yet?

MISS PRISM. We do not expect him till Monday afternoon.

CHASUBLE. Ah yes, he usually likes to spend his Sunday in London. He is not one of those whose sole aim is enjoyment, as, by all accounts, that unfortunate young man his brother seems to be. But I must not disturb Egeria and her pupil any longer.

MISS PRISM. Egeria? My name is Lætitia, Doctor.

CHASUBLE. (*Bowing.*) A classical allusion merely, drawn from the Pagan authors.[3] I shall see you both no doubt at Evensong?[4]

MISS PRISM. I think, dear Doctor, I will have a stroll with you. I find I have a headache after all, and a walk might do it good.

CHASUBLE. With pleasure, Miss Prism, with pleasure. We might go as far as the schools and back.

MISS PRISM. That would be delightful. Cecily, you will

---

[1] *As a man sows so let him reap* Galatians 6.7: "whatsoever a man soweth, that shall he also reap."

[2] *nearly all … Mudie sends us* Commercial lending libraries of the time, such as Mudie's, specialized in lending novels that were published in three volumes.

[3] *A classical allusion … Pagan authors* In Roman mythology, the nymph Egeria taught Numa, the second King of Rome, the lessons of wisdom and law which he then used to found the institutions of Rome.

[4] *Evensong* The evening service in the Anglican church (and various other Christian denominations).

read your Political Economy in my absence. The chapter on the Fall of the Rupee you may omit. It is somewhat too sensational. Even these metallic problems have their melodramatic side.[1]

(*Goes down the garden with Dr. Chasuble.*)

CECILY. (*Picks up books and throws them back on table.*) Horrid Political Economy! Horrid Geography! Horrid, horrid German!

(*Enter Merriman with a card on a salver.*)

MERRIMAN. Mr. Ernest Worthing has just driven over from the station. He has brought his luggage with him.

CECILY. (*Takes the card and reads it.*) "Mr. Ernest Worthing, B. 4, The Albany, W." Uncle Jack's brother! Did you tell him Mr. Worthing was in town?

MERRIMAN. Yes, Miss. He seemed very much disappointed. I mentioned that you and Miss Prism were in the garden. He said he was anxious to speak to you privately for a moment.

CECILY. Ask Mr. Ernest Worthing to come here. I suppose you had better talk to the housekeeper about a room for him.

MERRIMAN. Yes, Miss.

(*Merriman goes off.*)

CECILY. I have never met any really wicked person before. I feel rather frightened. I am so afraid he will look just like every one else. (*Enter Algernon, very gay and debonair.*) He does!

ALGERNON. (*Raising his hat.*) You are my little cousin Cecily, I'm sure.

CECILY. You are under some strange mistake. I am not little. In fact, I believe I am more than usually tall for my age. (*Algernon is rather taken aback.*) But I am your cousin Cecily. You, I see from your card, are Uncle Jack's brother, my cousin Ernest, my wicked cousin Ernest.

ALGERNON. Oh! I am not really wicked at all, cousin Cecily. You mustn't think that I am wicked.

CECILY. If you are not, then you have certainly been deceiving us all in a very inexcusable manner. I hope you have not been leading a double life, pretending to be wicked and being really good all the time. That would be hypocrisy.

ALGERNON. (*Looks at her in amazement.*) Oh! Of course I have been rather reckless.

CECILY. I am glad to hear it.

ALGERNON. In fact, now you mention the subject, I have been very bad in my own small way.

CECILY. I don't think you should be so proud of that, though I am sure it must have been very pleasant.

ALGERNON. It is much pleasanter being here with you.

CECILY. I can't understand how you are here at all. Uncle Jack won't be back till Monday afternoon.

ALGERNON. That is a great disappointment. I am obliged to go up by the first train on Monday morning. I have a business appointment that I am anxious … to miss!

CECILY. Couldn't you miss it anywhere but in London?

ALGERNON. No: the appointment is in London.

CECILY. Well, I know, of course, how important it is not to keep a business engagement, if one wants to retain any sense of the beauty of life, but still I think you had better wait till Uncle Jack arrives. I know he wants to speak to you about your emigrating.

ALGERNON. About my what?

CECILY. Your emigrating. He has gone up to buy your outfit.

ALGERNON. I certainly wouldn't let Jack buy my outfit. He has no taste in neckties at all.

CECILY. I don't think you will require neckties. Uncle Jack is sending you to Australia.[2]

ALGERNON. Australia! I'd sooner die.

CECILY. Well, he said at dinner on Wednesday night, that you would have to choose between this world, the next world, and Australia.

ALGERNON. Oh, well! The accounts I have received of

[1] *The chapter … melodramatic side* The rupee (India's currency) declined dramatically in the early 1890s as a result of a variety of disasters, including an outbreak of plague.

[2] *Australia* A former penal colony, at the time still considered to be largely composed of wilderness.

Australia and the next world are not particularly encouraging. This world is good enough for me, cousin Cecily.

CECILY. Yes, but are you good enough for it?

ALGERNON. I'm afraid I'm not that. That is why I want you to reform me. You might make that your mission, if you don't mind, cousin Cecily.

CECILY. I'm afraid I've no time, this afternoon.

ALGERNON. Well, would you mind my reforming myself this afternoon?

CECILY. It is rather Quixotic of you. But I think you should try.

ALGERNON. I will. I feel better already.

CECILY. You are looking a little worse.

ALGERNON. That is because I am hungry.

CECILY. How thoughtless of me. I should have remembered that when one is going to lead an entirely new life, one requires regular and wholesome meals. Won't you come in?

ALGERNON. Thank you. Might I have a buttonhole[1] first? I never have any appetite unless I have a buttonhole first.

CECILY. A Maréchal Niel?[2] (*Picks up scissors.*)

ALGERNON. No, I'd sooner have a pink rose.

CECILY. Why? (*Cuts a flower.*)

ALGERNON. Because you are like a pink rose, Cousin Cecily.

CECILY. I don't think it can be right for you to talk to me like that. Miss Prism never says such things to me.

ALGERNON. Then Miss Prism is a short-sighted old lady. (*Cecily puts the rose in his buttonhole.*) You are the prettiest girl I ever saw.

CECILY. Miss Prism says that all good looks are a snare.

ALGERNON. They are a snare that every sensible man would like to be caught in.

CECILY. Oh, I don't think I would care to catch a sensible man. I shouldn't know what to talk to him about.

(*They pass into the house. Miss Prism and Dr. Chasuble return.*)

MISS PRISM. You are too much alone, dear Dr. Chasuble. You should get married. A misanthrope I can understand—a womanthrope,[3] never!

CHASUBLE. (*With a scholar's shudder.*) Believe me, I do not deserve so neologistic a phrase. The precept as well as the practice of the Primitive Church[4] was distinctly against matrimony.

MISS PRISM. (*Sententiously.*) That is obviously the reason why the Primitive Church has not lasted up to the present day. And you do not seem to realize, dear Doctor, that by persistently remaining single, a man converts himself into a permanent public temptation. Men should be more careful; this very celibacy leads weaker vessels astray.

CHASUBLE. But is a man not equally attractive when married?

MISS PRISM. No married man is ever attractive except to his wife.

CHASUBLE. And often, I've been told, not even to her.

MISS PRISM. That depends on the intellectual sympathies of the woman. Maturity can always be depended on. Ripeness can be trusted. Young women are green. (*Dr. Chasuble starts.*) I spoke horticulturally. My metaphor was drawn from fruits. But where is Cecily?

CHASUBLE. Perhaps she followed us to the schools.

(*Enter Jack slowly from the back of the garden. He is dressed in the deepest mourning, with crepe hatband and black gloves.*)

MISS PRISM. Mr. Worthing!

CHASUBLE. Mr. Worthing?

MISS PRISM. This is indeed a surprise. We did not look for you till Monday afternoon.

JACK. (*Shakes Miss Prism's hand in a tragic manner.*) I have returned sooner than I expected. Dr. Chasuble, I hope you are well?

CHASUBLE. Dear Mr. Worthing, I trust this garb of woe does not betoken some terrible calamity?

---

[1] *buttonhole* Boutonniere, flower for one's lapel.

[2] *Maréchal Niel* Variety of yellow rose.

[3] *misanthrope … womanthrope* The correct word for someone who hates women is a "misogynist"; a "misanthrope" is someone who hates all humanity.

[4] *Primitive Church* Early Christian church.

JACK. My brother.

MISS PRISM. More shameful debts and extravagance?

CHASUBLE. Still leading his life of pleasure?

JACK. (*Shaking his head.*) Dead!

CHASUBLE. Your brother Ernest dead?

JACK. Quite dead.

MISS PRISM. What a lesson for him! I trust he will profit by it.

CHASUBLE. Mr. Worthing, I offer you my sincere condolence. You have at least the consolation of knowing that you were always the most generous and forgiving of brothers.

JACK. Poor Ernest! He had many faults, but it is a sad, sad blow.

CHASUBLE. Very sad indeed. Were you with him at the end?

JACK. No. He died abroad; in Paris, in fact. I had a telegram last night from the manager of the Grand Hotel.

CHASUBLE. Was the cause of death mentioned?

JACK. A severe chill, it seems.

MISS PRISM. As a man sows, so shall he reap.

CHASUBLE. (*Raising his hand.*) Charity, dear Miss Prism, charity! None of us are perfect. I myself am peculiarly susceptible to draughts. Will the interment take place here?

JACK. No. He seems to have expressed a desire to be buried in Paris.

CHASUBLE. In Paris! (*Shakes his head.*) I fear that hardly points to any very serious state of mind at the last. You would no doubt wish me to make some slight allusion to this tragic domestic affliction next Sunday. (*Jack presses his hand convulsively.*) My sermon on the meaning of the manna in the wilderness[1] can be adapted to almost any occasion, joyful, or, as in the present case, distressing. (*All sigh.*) I have preached it at harvest celebrations, christenings, confirmations,[2] on days of humiliation and festal days. The last time I delivered it was in the Cathedral, as a charity sermon on behalf of the Society for the Prevention of Discontent among the Upper Orders. The Bishop, who was present, was much struck by some of the analogies I drew.

JACK. Ah! that reminds me, you mentioned christenings I think, Dr. Chasuble? I suppose you know how to christen all right? (*Dr. Chasuble looks astounded.*) I mean, of course, you are continually christening, aren't you?

MISS PRISM. It is, I regret to say, one of the Rector's most constant duties in this parish. I have often spoken to the poorer classes on the subject. But they don't seem to know what thrift is.

CHASUBLE. But is there any particular infant in whom you are interested, Mr. Worthing? Your brother was, I believe, unmarried, was he not?

JACK. Oh yes.

MISS PRISM. (*Bitterly.*) People who live entirely for pleasure usually are.

JACK. But it is not for any child, dear Doctor. I am very fond of children. No! the fact is, I would like to be christened myself, this afternoon, if you have nothing better to do.

CHASUBLE. But surely, Mr. Worthing, you have been christened already?

JACK. I don't remember anything about it.

CHASUBLE. But have you any grave doubts on the subject?

JACK. I certainly intend to have. Of course I don't know if the thing would bother you in any way, or if you think I am a little too old now.

CHASUBLE. Not at all. The sprinkling, and, indeed, the immersion of adults is a perfectly canonical practice.

JACK. Immersion!

CHASUBLE. You need have no apprehensions. Sprinkling is all that is necessary, or indeed I think advisable. Our weather is so changeable. At what hour would you wish the ceremony performed?

JACK. Oh, I might trot round about five if that would suit you.

CHASUBLE. Perfectly, perfectly! In fact I have two similar ceremonies to perform at that time. A case of twins that occurred recently in one of the outlying cottages on

---

[1] *manna in the wilderness* See Exodus 16.

[2] *christenings, confirmations* Whereas a christening formally admits a person to the Christian church through baptism (usually as an infant), in many Christian denominations a person's standing as a full member of the church must be confirmed at a later ceremony (typically as a young adult).

your own estate. Poor Jenkins the carter,[1] a most hard-working man.

JACK. Oh! I don't see much fun in being christened along with other babies. It would be childish. Would half-past five do?

CHASUBLE. Admirably! Admirably! (*Takes out watch.*) And now, dear Mr. Worthing, I will not intrude any longer into a house of sorrow. I would merely beg you not to be too much bowed down by grief. What seem to us bitter trials are often blessings in disguise.

MISS PRISM. This seems to me a blessing of an extremely obvious kind.

(*Enter Cecily from the house.*)

CECILY. Uncle Jack! Oh, I am pleased to see you back. But what horrid clothes you have got on! Do go and change them.

MISS PRISM. Cecily!

CHASUBLE. My child! my child!

(*Cecily goes towards Jack; he kisses her brow in a melancholy manner.*)

CECILY. What is the matter, Uncle Jack? Do look happy! You look as if you had toothache, and I have got such a surprise for you. Who do you think is in the dining-room? Your brother!

JACK. Who?

CECILY. Your brother Ernest. He arrived about half an hour ago.

JACK. What nonsense! I haven't got a brother.

CECILY. Oh, don't say that. However badly he may have behaved to you in the past he is still your brother. You couldn't be so heartless as to disown him. I'll tell him to come out. And you will shake hands with him, won't you, Uncle Jack? (*Runs back into the house.*)

CHASUBLE. These are very joyful tidings.

MISS PRISM. After we had all been resigned to his loss, his sudden return seems to me peculiarly distressing.

JACK. My brother is in the dining-room? I don't know what it all means. I think it is perfectly absurd.

(*Enter Algernon and Cecily hand in hand. They come slowly up to Jack.*)

JACK. Good heavens! (*Motions Algernon away.*)

ALGERNON. Brother John, I have come down from town to tell you that I am very sorry for all the trouble I have given you, and that I intend to lead a better life in the future. (*Jack glares at him and does not take his hand.*)

CECILY. Uncle Jack, you are not going to refuse your own brother's hand?

JACK. Nothing will induce me to take his hand. I think his coming down here disgraceful. He knows perfectly well why.

CECILY. Uncle Jack, do be nice. There is some good in every one. Ernest has just been telling me about his poor invalid friend Mr. Bunbury whom he goes to visit so often. And surely there must be much good in one who is kind to an invalid, and leaves the pleasures of London to sit by a bed of pain.

JACK. Oh! he has been talking about Bunbury, has he?

CECILY. Yes, he has told me all about poor Mr. Bunbury, and his terrible state of health.

JACK. Bunbury! Well, I won't have him talk to you about Bunbury or about anything else. It is enough to drive one perfectly frantic.

ALGERNON. Of course I admit that the faults were all on my side. But I must say that I think that Brother John's coldness to me is peculiarly painful. I expected a more enthusiastic welcome, especially considering it is the first time I have come here.

CECILY. Uncle Jack, if you don't shake hands with Ernest I will never forgive you.

JACK. Never forgive me?

CECILY. Never, never, never!

JACK. Well, this is the last time I shall ever do it. (*Shakes hands with Algernon and glares.*)

CHASUBLE. It's pleasant, is it not, to see so perfect a reconciliation? I think we might leave the two brothers together.

MISS PRISM. Cecily, you will come with us.

[1] *carter* Cart driver.

CECILY. Certainly, Miss Prism. My little task of reconciliation is over.

CHASUBLE. You have done a beautiful action to-day, dear child.

MISS PRISM. We must not be premature in our judgments.

CECILY. I feel very happy.

(*They all go off except Jack and Algernon.*)

JACK. You young scoundrel, Algy, you must get out of this place as soon as possible. I don't allow any Bunburying here.

(*Enter Merriman.*)

MERRIMAN. I have put Mr. Ernest's things in the room next to yours, sir. I suppose that is all right?

JACK. What?

MERRIMAN. Mr. Ernest's luggage, sir. I have unpacked it and put it in the room next to your own.

JACK. His luggage?

MERRIMAN. Yes, sir. Three portmanteaus, a dressing-case, two hat-boxes, and a large luncheon-basket.

ALGERNON. I am afraid I can't stay more than a week this time.

JACK. Merriman, order the dog-cart[1] at once. Mr. Ernest has been suddenly called back to town.

MERRIMAN. Yes, sir. (*Goes back into the house.*)

ALGERNON. What a fearful liar you are, Jack. I have not been called back to town at all.

JACK. Yes, you have.

ALGERNON. I haven't heard any one call me.

JACK. Your duty as a gentleman calls you back.

ALGERNON. My duty as a gentleman has never interfered with my pleasures in the smallest degree.

JACK. I can quite understand that.

ALGERNON. Well, Cecily is a darling.

JACK. You are not to talk of Miss Cardew like that. I don't like it.

ALGERNON. Well, I don't like your clothes. You look perfectly ridiculous in them. Why on earth don't you go up and change? It is perfectly childish to be in deep mourning for a man who is actually staying for a whole week with you in your house as a guest. I call it grotesque.

JACK. You are certainly not staying with me for a whole week as a guest or anything else. You have got to leave … by the four-five train.

ALGERNON. I certainly won't leave you so long as you are in mourning. It would be most unfriendly. If I were in mourning you would stay with me, I suppose. I should think it very unkind if you didn't.

JACK. Well, will you go if I change my clothes?

ALGERNON. Yes, if you are not too long. I never saw anybody take so long to dress, and with such little result.

JACK. Well, at any rate, that is better than being always over-dressed as you are.

ALGERNON. If I am occasionally a little over-dressed, I make up for it by being always immensely over-educated.

JACK. Your vanity is ridiculous, your conduct an outrage, and your presence in my garden utterly absurd. However, you have got to catch the four-five, and I hope you will have a pleasant journey back to town. This Bunburying, as you call it, has not been a great success for you. (*Goes into the house.*)

ALGERNON. I think it has been a great success. I'm in love with Cecily, and that is everything.

(*Enter Cecily at the back of the garden. She picks up the can and begins to water the flowers.*)

But I must see her before I go, and make arrangements for another Bunbury. Ah, there she is.

CECILY. Oh, I merely came back to water the roses. I thought you were with Uncle Jack.

ALGERNON. He's gone to order the dog-cart for me.

CECILY. Oh, is he going to take you for a nice drive?

ALGERNON. He's going to send me away.

CECILY. Then have we got to part?

ALGERNON. I am afraid so. It's a very painful parting.

CECILY. It is always painful to part from people whom

[1] *dog-cart* Small horse-drawn carriage in which the occupants would sit back-to-back; a box for conveying hunting dogs was also typically part of the contraption.

one has known for a very brief space of time. The absence of old friends one can endure with equanimity. But even a momentary separation from anyone to whom one has just been introduced is almost unbearable.

ALGERNON. Thank you.

(*Enter Merriman.*)

MERRIMAN. The dog-cart is at the door, sir.

(*Algernon looks appealingly at Cecily.*)

CECILY. It can wait, Merriman for … five minutes.

MERRIMAN. Yes, Miss.

(*Exit Merriman.*)

ALGERNON. I hope, Cecily, I shall not offend you if I state quite frankly and openly that you seem to me to be in every way the visible personification of absolute perfection.

CECILY. I think your frankness does you great credit, Ernest. If you will allow me, I will copy your remarks into my diary. (*Goes over to table and begins writing in diary.*)

ALGERNON. Do you really keep a diary? I'd give anything to look at it. May I?

CECILY. Oh no. (*Puts her hand over it.*) You see, it is simply a very young girl's record of her own thoughts and impressions, and consequently meant for publication. When it appears in volume form I hope you will order a copy. But pray, Ernest, don't stop. I delight in taking down from dictation. I have reached "absolute perfection." You can go on. I am quite ready for more.

ALGERNON. (*Somewhat taken aback.*) Ahem! Ahem!

CECILY. Oh, don't cough, Ernest. When one is dictating one should speak fluently and not cough. Besides, I don't know how to spell a cough. (*Writes as Algernon speaks.*)

ALGERNON. (*Speaking very rapidly.*) Cecily, ever since I first looked upon your wonderful and incomparable beauty, I have dared to love you wildly, passionately, devotedly, hopelessly.

CECILY. I don't think that you should tell me that you love me wildly, passionately, devotedly, hopelessly. Hopelessly doesn't seem to make much sense, does it?

ALGERNON. Cecily!

(*Enter Merriman.*)

MERRIMAN. The dog-cart is waiting, sir.

ALGERNON. Tell it to come round next week, at the same hour.

MERRIMAN. (*Looks at Cecily, who makes no sign.*) Yes, sir.

(*Merriman retires.*)

CECILY. Uncle Jack would be very much annoyed if he knew you were staying on till next week, at the same hour.

ALGERNON. Oh, I don't care about Jack. I don't care for anybody in the whole world but you. I love you, Cecily. You will marry me, won't you?

CECILY. You silly boy! Of course. Why, we have been engaged for the last three months.

ALGERNON. For the last three months?

CECILY. Yes, it will be exactly three months on Thursday.

ALGERNON. But how did we become engaged?

CECILY. Well, ever since dear Uncle Jack first confessed to us that he had a younger brother who was very wicked and bad, you of course have formed the chief topic of conversation between myself and Miss Prism. And of course a man who is much talked about is always very attractive. One feels there must be something in him, after all. I daresay it was foolish of me, but I fell in love with you, Ernest.

ALGERNON. Darling! And when was the engagement actually settled?

CECILY. On the 14th of February last. Worn out by your entire ignorance of my existence, I determined to end the matter one way or the other, and after a long struggle with myself I accepted you under this dear old tree here. The next day I bought this little ring in your name, and this is the little bangle with the true lover's knot I promised you always to wear.

ALGERNON. Did I give you this? It's very pretty, isn't it?

CECILY. Yes, you've wonderfully good taste, Ernest. It's the excuse I've always given for your leading such a bad life. And this is the box in which I keep all your dear letters. (*Kneels at table, opens box, and produces letters tied up with blue ribbon.*)

ALGERNON. My letters! But, my own sweet Cecily, I have never written you any letters.

CECILY. You need hardly remind me of that, Ernest. I remember only too well that I was forced to write your letters for you. I wrote always three times a week, and sometimes oftener.

ALGERNON. Oh, do let me read them, Cecily?

CECILY. Oh, I couldn't possibly. They would make you far too conceited. (*Replaces box.*) The three you wrote me after I had broken off the engagement are so beautiful, and so badly spelled, that even now I can hardly read them without crying a little.

ALGERNON. But was our engagement ever broken off?

CECILY. Of course it was. On the 22nd of last March. You can see the entry if you like. (*Shows diary.*) "To-day I broke off my engagement with Ernest. I feel it is better to do so. The weather still continues charming."

ALGERNON. But why on earth did you break it off? What had I done? I had done nothing at all. Cecily, I am very much hurt indeed to hear you broke it off. Particularly when the weather was so charming.

CECILY. It would hardly have been a really serious engagement if it hadn't been broken off at least once. But I forgave you before the week was out.

ALGERNON. (*Crossing to her, and kneeling.*) What a perfect angel you are, Cecily.

CECILY. You dear romantic boy. (*He kisses her, she puts her fingers through his hair.*) I hope your hair curls naturally, does it?

ALGERNON. Yes, darling, with a little help from others.

CECILY. I am so glad.

ALGERNON. You'll never break off our engagement again, Cecily?

CECILY. I don't think I could break it off now that I have actually met you. Besides, of course, there is the question of your name.

ALGERNON. Yes, of course. (*Nervously.*)

CECILY. You must not laugh at me, darling, but it had always been a girlish dream of mine to love some one whose name was Ernest. (*Algernon rises, Cecily also.*) There is something in that name that seems to inspire absolute confidence. I pity any poor married woman whose husband is not called Ernest.

ALGERNON. But, my dear child, do you mean to say you could not love me if I had some other name?

CECILY. But what name?

ALGERNON. Oh, any name you like—Algernon—for instance …

CECILY. But I don't like the name of Algernon.

ALGERNON. Well, my own dear, sweet, loving little darling, I really can't see why you should object to the name of Algernon. It is not at all a bad name. In fact, it is rather an aristocratic name. Half of the chaps who get into the Bankruptcy Court are called Algernon. But seriously, Cecily … (*Moving to her*) … if my name was Algy, couldn't you love me?

CECILY. (*Rising.*) I might respect you, Ernest, I might admire your character, but I fear that I should not be able to give you my undivided attention.

ALGERNON. Ahem! Cecily! (*Picking up hat.*) Your Rector here is, I suppose, thoroughly experienced in the practice of all the rites and ceremonials of the Church?

CECILY. Oh, yes. Dr. Chasuble is a most learned man. He has never written a single book, so you can imagine how much he knows.

ALGERNON. I must see him at once on a most important christening—I mean on most important business.

CECILY. Oh!

ALGERNON. I shan't be away more than half an hour.

CECILY. Considering that we have been engaged since February the 14th, and that I only met you to-day for the first time, I think it is rather hard that you should leave me for so long a period as half an hour. Couldn't you make it twenty minutes?

ALGERNON. I'll be back in no time.

(*Kisses her and rushes down the garden.*)

CECILY. What an impetuous boy he is! I like his hair so much. I must enter his proposal in my diary.

(*Enter Merriman.*)

MERRIMAN. A Miss Fairfax has just called to see Mr. Worthing. On very important business, Miss Fairfax states.

CECILY. Isn't Mr. Worthing in his library?

MERRIMAN. Mr. Worthing went over in the direction of the Rectory some time ago.

CECILY. Pray ask the lady to come out here; Mr. Worthing is sure to be back soon. And you can bring tea.

MERRIMAN. Yes, Miss. (*Goes out.*)

CECILY. Miss Fairfax! I suppose one of the many good elderly women who are associated with Uncle Jack in some of his philanthropic work in London. I don't quite like women who are interested in philanthropic work. I think it is so forward of them.

(*Enter Merriman.*)

MERRIMAN. Miss Fairfax.

(*Enter Gwendolen. Exit Merriman.*)

CECILY. (*Advancing to meet her.*) Pray let me introduce myself to you. My name is Cecily Cardew.

GWENDOLEN. Cecily Cardew? (*Moving to her and shaking hands.*) What a very sweet name! Something tells me that we are going to be great friends. I like you already more than I can say. My first impressions of people are never wrong.

CECILY. How nice of you to like me so much after we have known each other such a comparatively short time. Pray sit down.

GWENDOLEN. (*Still standing up.*) I may call you Cecily, may I not?

CECILY. With pleasure!

GWENDOLEN. And you will always call me Gwendolen, won't you?

CECILY. If you wish.

GWENDOLEN. Then that is all quite settled, is it not?

CECILY. I hope so. (*A pause. They both sit down together.*)

GWENDOLEN. Perhaps this might be a favourable opportunity for my mentioning who I am. My father is Lord Bracknell. You have never heard of Papa, I suppose?

CECILY. I don't think so.

GWENDOLEN. Outside the family circle, Papa, I am glad to say, is entirely unknown. I think that is quite as it should be. The home seems to me to be the proper sphere for the man. And certainly once a man begins to neglect his domestic duties he becomes painfully effeminate, does he not? And I don't like that. It makes men so very attractive. Cecily, Mamma, whose views on education are remarkably strict, has brought me up to be extremely short-sighted; it is part of her system; so do you mind my looking at you through my glasses?

CECILY. Oh! not at all, Gwendolen. I am very fond of being looked at.

GWENDOLEN. (*After examining Cecily carefully through a lorgnette.*) You are here on a short visit, I suppose.

CECILY. Oh no! I live here.

GWENDOLEN. (*Severely.*) Really? Your mother, no doubt, or some female relative of advanced years, resides here also?

CECILY. Oh no! I have no mother, nor, in fact, any relations.

GWENDOLEN. Indeed?

CECILY. My dear guardian, with the assistance of Miss Prism, has the arduous task of looking after me.

GWENDOLEN. Your guardian?

CECILY. Yes, I am Mr. Worthing's ward.

GWENDOLEN. Oh! It is strange he never mentioned to me that he had a ward. How secretive of him! He grows more interesting hourly. I am not sure, however, that the news inspires me with feelings of unmixed delight. (*Rising and going to her.*) I am very fond of you, Cecily; I have liked you ever since I met you! But I am bound to state that now that I know that you are Mr. Worthing's ward, I cannot help expressing a wish you were—well, just a little older than you seem to be—and not quite so very alluring in appearance. In fact, if I may speak candidly—

CECILY. Pray do! I think that whenever one has anything

unpleasant to say, one should always be quite candid.

GWENDOLEN. Well, to speak with perfect candour, Cecily, I wish that you were fully forty-two, and more than usually plain for your age. Ernest has a strong upright nature. He is the very soul of truth and honour. Disloyalty would be as impossible to him as deception. But even men of the noblest possible moral character are extremely susceptible to the influence of the physical charms of others. Modern, no less than Ancient History, supplies us with many most painful examples of what I refer to. If it were not so, indeed, History would be quite unreadable.

CECILY. I beg your pardon, Gwendolen, did you say Ernest?

GWENDOLEN. Yes.

CECILY. Oh, but it is not Mr. Ernest Worthing who is my guardian. It is his brother—his elder brother.

GWENDOLEN. (*Sitting down again.*) Ernest never mentioned to me that he had a brother.

CECILY. I am sorry to say they have not been on good terms for a long time.

GWENDOLEN. Ah! that accounts for it. And now that I think of it I have never heard any man mention his brother. The subject seems distasteful to most men. Cecily, you have lifted a load from my mind. I was growing almost anxious. It would have been terrible if any cloud had come across a friendship like ours, would it not? Of course you are quite, quite sure that it is not Mr. Ernest Worthing who is your guardian?

CECILY. Quite sure. (*A pause.*) In fact, I am going to be his.

GWENDOLEN. (*Inquiringly.*) I beg your pardon?

CECILY. (*Rather shy and confidingly.*) Dearest Gwendolen, there is no reason why I should make a secret of it to you. Our little county newspaper is sure to chronicle the fact next week. Mr. Ernest Worthing and I are engaged to be married.

GWENDOLEN. (*Quite politely, rising.*) My darling Cecily, I think there must be some slight error. Mr. Ernest Worthing is engaged to me. The announcement will appear in the *Morning Post* on Saturday at the latest.

CECILY. (*Very politely, rising.*) I am afraid you must be under some misconception. Ernest proposed to me exactly ten minutes ago. (*Shows diary.*)

GWENDOLEN. (*Examines diary through her lorgnettte carefully.*) It is certainly very curious, for he asked me to be his wife yesterday afternoon at 5:30. If you would care to verify the incident, pray do so. (*Produces diary of her own.*) I never travel without my diary. One should always have something sensational to read in the train. I am so sorry, dear Cecily, if it is any disappointment to you, but I am afraid I have the prior claim.

CECILY. It would distress me more than I can tell you, dear Gwendolen, if it caused you any mental or physical anguish, but I feel bound to point out that since Ernest proposed to you he clearly has changed his mind.

GWENDOLEN. (*Meditatively.*) If the poor fellow has been entrapped into any foolish promise I shall consider it my duty to rescue him at once, and with a firm hand.

CECILY. (*Thoughtfully and sadly.*) Whatever unfortunate entanglement my dear boy may have got into, I will never reproach him with it after we are married.

GWENDOLEN. Do you allude to me, Miss Cardew, as an entanglement? You are presumptuous. On an occasion of this kind it becomes more than a moral duty to speak one's mind. It becomes a pleasure.

CECILY. Do you suggest, Miss Fairfax, that I entrapped Ernest into an engagement? How dare you? This is no time for wearing the shallow mask of manners. When I see a spade I call it a spade.

GWENDOLEN. (*Satirically.*) I am glad to say that I have never seen a spade. It is obvious that our social spheres have been widely different.

(*Enter Merriman, followed by the footman. He carries a salver, table cloth, and plate stand. Cecily is about to retort. The presence of the servants exercises a restraining influence, under which both girls chafe.*)

MERRIMAN. Shall I lay tea here as usual, Miss?

CECILY. (*Sternly, in a calm voice.*) Yes, as usual.

(*Merriman begins to clear table and lay cloth. A long pause. Cecily and Gwendolen glare at each other.*)

GWENDOLEN. Are there many interesting walks in the vicinity, Miss Cardew?

CECILY. Oh! yes! a great many. From the top of one of the hills quite close one can see five counties.

GWENDOLEN. Five counties! I don't think I should like that; I hate crowds.

CECILY. (*Sweetly.*) I suppose that is why you live in town?

(*Gwendolen bites her lip, and beats her foot nervously with her parasol.*)

GWENDOLEN. (*Looking round.*) Quite a well-kept garden this is, Miss Cardew.

CECILY. So glad you like it, Miss Fairfax.

GWENDOLEN. I had no idea there were any flowers in the country.

CECILY. Oh, flowers are as common here, Miss Fairfax, as people are in London.

GWENDOLEN. Personally I cannot understand how anybody manages to exist in the country, if anybody who is anybody does. The country always bores me to death.

CECILY. Ah! This is what the newspapers call agricultural depression,[1] is it not? I believe the aristocracy are suffering very much from it just at present. It is almost an epidemic amongst them, I have been told. May I offer you some tea, Miss Fairfax?

GWENDOLEN. (*With elaborate politeness.*) Thank you. (*Aside.*) Detestable girl! But I require tea!

CECILY. (*Sweetly.*) Sugar?

GWENDOLEN. (*Superciliously.*) No, thank you. Sugar is not fashionable any more. (*Cecily looks angrily at her, takes up the tongs and puts four lumps of sugar into the cup.*)

CECILY. (*Severely.*) Cake or bread and butter?

GWENDOLEN. (*In a bored manner.*) Bread and butter, please. Cake is rarely seen at the best houses nowadays.

CECILY. (*Cuts a very large slice of cake, and puts it on the tray.*) Hand that to Miss Fairfax.

(*Merriman does so, and goes out with footman. Gwendolen drinks the tea and makes a grimace. Puts down cup at once, reaches out her hand to the bread and butter, looks at it, and finds it is cake. Rises in indignation.*)

GWENDOLEN. You have filled my tea with lumps of sugar, and though I asked most distinctly for bread and butter, you have given me cake. I am known for the gentleness of my disposition, and the extraordinary sweetness of my nature, but I warn you, Miss Cardew, you may go too far.

CECILY. (*Rising.*) To save my poor, innocent, trusting boy from the machinations of any other girl there are no lengths to which I would not go.

GWENDOLEN. From the moment I saw you I distrusted you. I felt that you were false and deceitful. I am never deceived in such matters. My first impressions of people are invariably right.

CECILY. It seems to me, Miss Fairfax, that I am trespassing on your valuable time. No doubt you have many other calls of a similar character to make in the neighbourhood.

(*Enter Jack.*)

GWENDOLEN. (*Catching sight of him.*) Ernest! My own Ernest!

JACK. Gwendolen! Darling! (*Offers to kiss her.*)

GWENDOLEN. (*Draws back.*) A moment! May I ask if you are engaged to be married to this young lady? (*Points to Cecily.*)

JACK. (*Laughing.*) To dear little Cecily! Of course not! What could have put such an idea into your pretty little head?

GWENDOLEN. Thank you. You may! (*Offers her cheek.*)

CECILY. (*Very sweetly.*) I knew there must be some misunderstanding, Miss Fairfax. The gentleman whose arm is at present round your waist is my guardian, Mr. John Worthing.

GWENDOLEN. I beg your pardon?

CECILY. This is Uncle Jack.

GWENDOLEN. (*Receding.*) Jack! Oh!

---

[1] *agricultural depression* The British economy in general was in depression from 1873 until the mid-1890s; the agricultural sector was depressed from 1875 until the mid-1890s.

(*Enter Algernon.*)

CECILY. Here is Ernest.

ALGERNON. (*Goes straight over to Cecily without noticing any one else.*) My own love! (*Offers to kiss her.*)

CECILY. (*Drawing back.*) A moment, Ernest! May I ask you—are you engaged to be married to this young lady?

ALGERNON. (*Looking round.*) To what young lady? Good heavens! Gwendolen!

CECILY. Yes! to good heavens, Gwendolen, I mean to Gwendolen.

ALGERNON. (*Laughing.*) Of course not! What could have put such an idea into your pretty little head?

CECILY. Thank you. (*Presenting her cheek to be kissed.*) You may.

(*Algernon kisses her.*)

GWENDOLEN. I felt there was some slight error, Miss Cardew. The gentleman who is now embracing you is my cousin, Mr. Algernon Moncrieff.

CECILY. (*Breaking away from Algernon.*) Algernon Moncrieff! Oh!

(*The two girls move towards each other and put their arms round each other's waists as if for protection.*)

CECILY. Are you called Algernon?

ALGERNON. I cannot deny it.

CECILY. Oh!

GWENDOLEN. Is your name really John?

JACK. (*Standing rather proudly.*) I could deny it if I liked. I could deny anything if I liked. But my name certainly is John. It has been John for years.

CECILY. (*To Gwendolen.*) A gross deception has been practised on both of us.

GWENDOLEN. My poor wounded Cecily!

CECILY. My sweet wronged Gwendolen!

GWENDOLEN. (*Slowly and seriously.*) You will call me sister, will you not? (*They embrace. Jack and Algernon groan and walk up and down.*)

CECILY. (*Rather brightly.*) There is just one question I would like to be allowed to ask my guardian.

GWENDOLEN. An admirable idea! Mr. Worthing, there is just one question I would like to be permitted to put to you. Where is your brother Ernest? We are both engaged to be married to your brother Ernest, so it is a matter of some importance to us to know where your brother Ernest is at present.

JACK. (*Slowly and hesitatingly.*) Gwendolen—Cecily—it is very painful for me to be forced to speak the truth. It is the first time in my life that I have ever been reduced to such a painful position, and I am really quite inexperienced in doing anything of the kind. However, I will tell you quite frankly that I have no brother Ernest. I have no brother at all. I never had a brother in my life, and I certainly have not the smallest intention of ever having one in the future.

CECILY. (*Surprised.*) No brother at all?

JACK. (*Cheerily.*) None!

GWENDOLEN. (*Severely.*) Had you never a brother of any kind?

JACK. (*Pleasantly.*) Never. Not even of any kind.

GWENDOLEN. I am afraid it is quite clear, Cecily, that neither of us is engaged to be married to any one.

CECILY. It is not a very pleasant position for a young girl suddenly to find herself in. Is it?

GWENDOLEN. Let us go into the house. They will hardly venture to come after us there.

CECILY. No, men are so cowardly, aren't they?

(*They retire into the house with scornful looks.*)

JACK. This ghastly state of things is what you call Bunburying, I suppose?

ALGERNON. Yes, and a perfectly wonderful Bunbury it is. The most wonderful Bunbury I have ever had in my life.

JACK. Well, you've no right whatsoever to Bunbury here.

ALGERNON. That is absurd. One has a right to Bunbury anywhere one chooses. Every serious Bunburyist knows that.

JACK. Serious Bunburyist! Good heavens!

ALGERNON. Well, one must be serious about something, if one wants to have any amusement in life. I happen to be serious about Bunburying. What on earth you are serious about I haven't got the remotest idea. About everything, I should fancy. You have such an absolutely trivial nature.

JACK. Well, the only small satisfaction I have in the whole of this wretched business is that your friend Bunbury is quite exploded. You won't be able to run down to the country quite so often as you used to do, dear Algy. And a very good thing too.

ALGERNON. Your brother is a little off colour, isn't he, dear Jack? You won't be able to disappear to London quite so frequently as your wicked custom was. And not a bad thing either.

JACK. As for your conduct towards Miss Cardew, I must say that your taking in a sweet, simple, innocent girl like that is quite inexcusable. To say nothing of the fact that she is my ward.

ALGERNON. I can see no possible defence at all for your deceiving a brilliant, clever, thoroughly experienced young lady like Miss Fairfax. To say nothing of the fact that she is my cousin.

JACK. I wanted to be engaged to Gwendolen, that is all. I love her.

ALGERNON. Well, I simply wanted to be engaged to Cecily. I adore her.

JACK. There is certainly no chance of your marrying Miss Cardew.

ALGERNON. I don't think there is much likelihood, Jack, of you and Miss Fairfax being united.

JACK. Well, that is no business of yours.

ALGERNON. If it was my business, I wouldn't talk about it. (*Begins to eat muffins.*) It is very vulgar to talk about one's business. Only people like stock-brokers do that, and then merely at dinner parties.

JACK. How can you sit there, calmly eating muffins when we are in this horrible trouble, I can't make out. You seem to me to be perfectly heartless.

ALGERNON. Well, I can't eat muffins in an agitated manner. The butter would probably get on my cuffs. One should always eat muffins quite calmly. It is the only way to eat them.

JACK. I say it's perfectly heartless your eating muffins at all, under the circumstances.

ALGERNON. When I am in trouble, eating is the only thing that consoles me. Indeed, when I am in really great trouble, as any one who knows me intimately will tell you, I refuse everything except food and drink. At the present moment I am eating muffins because I am unhappy. Besides, I am particularly fond of muffins. (*Rising.*)

JACK. (*Rising.*) Well, that is no reason why you should eat them all in that greedy way. (*Takes muffins from Algernon.*)

ALGERNON. (*Offering tea-cake.*) I wish you would have tea-cake instead. I don't like tea-cake.

JACK. Good heavens! I suppose a man may eat his own muffins in his own garden.

ALGERNON. But you have just said it was perfectly heartless to eat muffins.

JACK. I said it was perfectly heartless of you, under the circumstances. That is a very different thing.

ALGERNON. That may be. But the muffins are the same.

(*He seizes the muffin-dish from Jack.*)

JACK. Algy, I wish to goodness you would go.

ALGERNON. You can't possibly ask me to go without having some dinner. It's absurd. I never go without my dinner. No one ever does, except vegetarians and people like that. Besides I have just made arrangements with Dr. Chasuble to be christened at a quarter to six under the name of Ernest.

JACK. My dear fellow, the sooner you give up that nonsense the better. I made arrangements this morning with Dr. Chasuble to be christened myself at 5:30, and I naturally will take the name of Ernest. Gwendolen would wish it. We can't both be christened Ernest. It's absurd. Besides, I have a perfect right to be christened if I like. There is no evidence at all that I have ever been christened by anybody. I should think it extremely probable I never was, and so does Dr. Chasuble. It is entirely different in your case. You have been christened already.

ALGERNON. Yes, but I have not been christened for years.

JACK. Yes, but you have been christened. That is the important thing.

ALGERNON. Quite so. So I know my constitution can stand it. If you are not quite sure about your ever having been christened, I must say I think it rather dangerous your venturing on it now. It might make you very unwell. You can hardly have forgotten that some one very closely connected with you was very nearly carried off this week in Paris by a severe chill.

JACK. Yes, but you said yourself that a severe chill was not hereditary.

ALGERNON. It usen't to be, I know—but I daresay it is now. Science is always making wonderful improvements in things.

JACK. (*Picking up the muffin-dish.*) Oh, that is nonsense; you are always talking nonsense.

ALGERNON. Jack, you are at the muffins again! I wish you wouldn't. There are only two left. (*Takes them.*) I told you I was particularly fond of muffins.

JACK. But I hate tea-cake.

ALGERNON. Why on earth then do you allow tea-cake to be served up for your guests? What ideas you have of hospitality!

JACK. Algernon! I have already told you to go. I don't want you here. Why don't you go!

ALGERNON. I haven't quite finished my tea yet! and there is still one muffin left. (*Jack groans, and sinks into a chair. Algernon still continues eating.*)

ACT DROP

ACT 3

SCENE

(*Morning-room at the Manor House. Gwendolen and Cecily are at the window, looking out into the garden.*)

GWENDOLEN. The fact that they did not follow us at once into the house, as any one else would have done, seems to me to show that they have some sense of shame left.

CECILY. They have been eating muffins. That looks like repentance.

GWENDOLEN. (*After a pause.*) They don't seem to notice us at all. Couldn't you cough?

CECILY. But I haven't got a cough.

GWENDOLEN. They're looking at us. What effrontery!

CECILY. They're approaching. That's very forward of them.

GWENDOLEN. Let us preserve a dignified silence.

CECILY. Certainly. It's the only thing to do now.

(*Enter Jack followed by Algernon. They whistle some dreadful popular air from a British Opera.*)

GWENDOLEN. This dignified silence seems to produce an unpleasant effect.

CECILY. A most distasteful one.

GWENDOLEN. But we will not be the first to speak.

CECILY. Certainly not.

GWENDOLEN. Mr. Worthing, I have something very particular to ask you. Much depends on your reply.

CECILY. Gwendolen, your common sense is invaluable. Mr. Moncrieff, kindly answer me the following question. Why did you pretend to be my guardian's brother?

ALGERNON. In order that I might have an opportunity of meeting you.

CECILY. (*To Gwendolen.*) That certainly seems a satisfactory explanation, does it not?

GWENDOLEN. Yes, dear, if you can believe him.

CECILY. I don't. But that does not affect the wonderful beauty of his answer.

GWENDOLEN. True. In matters of grave importance, style, not sincerity is the vital thing. Mr. Worthing, what explanation can you offer to me for pretending to have a brother? Was it in order that you might have an opportunity of coming up to town to see me as often as possible?

JACK. Can you doubt it, Miss Fairfax?

GWENDOLEN. I have the gravest doubts upon the subject. But I intend to crush them. This is not the moment for German scepticism.[1] (*Moving to Cecily.*) Their explanations appear to be quite satisfactory,

[1] *German scepticism* According to the school of philosophy deriving from Immanuel Kant, we do not always perceive the true state of things-in-themselves.

especially Mr. Worthing's. That seems to me to have the stamp of truth upon it.

CECILY. I am more than content with what Mr. Moncrieff said. His voice alone inspires one with absolute credulity.

GWENDOLEN. Then you think we should forgive them?

CECILY. Yes. I mean no.

GWENDOLEN. True! I had forgotten. There are principles at stake that one cannot surrender. Which of us should tell them? The task is not a pleasant one.

CECILY. Could we not both speak at the same time?

GWENDOLEN. An excellent idea! I nearly always speak at the same time as other people. Will you take the time from me?

CECILY. Certainly.

(*Gwendolen beats time with uplifted finger.*)

GWENDOLEN and CECILY. (*Speaking together.*) Your Christian names are still an insuperable barrier. That is all!

JACK and ALGERNON. (*Speaking together.*) Our Christian names! Is that all? But we are going to be christened this afternoon.

GWENDOLEN. (*To Jack.*) For my sake you are prepared to do this terrible thing?

JACK. I am.

CECILY. (*To Algernon.*) To please me you are ready to face this fearful ordeal?

ALGERNON. I am!

GWENDOLEN. How absurd to talk of the equality of the sexes! Where questions of self-sacrifice are concerned, men are infinitely beyond us.

JACK. We are. (*Clasps hands with Algernon.*)

CECILY. They have moments of physical courage of which we women know absolutely nothing.

GWENDOLEN. (*To Jack.*) Darling!

ALGERNON. (*To Cecily.*) Darling! (*They fall into each other's arms.*)

(*Enter Merriman. When he enters he coughs loudly, seeing the situation.*)

MERRIMAN. Ahem! Ahem! Lady Bracknell!

JACK. Good heavens!

(*Enter Lady Bracknell. The couples separate in alarm. Exit Merriman.*)

LADY BRACKNELL. Gwendolen! What does this mean?

GWENDOLEN. Merely that I am engaged to be married to Mr. Worthing, Mamma.

LADY BRACKNELL. Come here. Sit down. Sit down immediately. Hesitation of any kind is a sign of mental decay in the young, of physical weakness in the old. (*Turns to Jack.*) Apprised, sir, of my daughter's sudden flight by her trusty maid, whose confidence I purchased by means of a small coin, I followed her at once by a luggage train. Her unhappy father is, I am glad to say, under the impression that she is attending a more than usually lengthy lecture by the University Extension Scheme on the Influence of a permanent income on Thought. I do not propose to undeceive him. Indeed I have never undeceived him on any question. I would consider it wrong. But of course, you will clearly understand that all communication between yourself and my daughter must cease immediately from this moment. On this point, as indeed on all points, I am firm.

JACK. I am engaged to be married to Gwendolen, Lady Bracknell!

LADY BRACKNELL. You are nothing of the kind, sir. And now, as regards Algernon! … Algernon!

ALGERNON. Yes, Aunt Augusta.

LADY BRACKNELL. May I ask if it is in this house that your invalid friend Mr. Bunbury resides?

ALGERNON. (*Stammering.*) Oh! No! Bunbury doesn't live here. Bunbury is somewhere else at present. In fact, Bunbury is dead.

LADY BRACKNELL. Dead! When did Mr. Bunbury die? His death must have been extremely sudden.

ALGERNON. (*Airily.*) Oh! I killed Bunbury this afternoon. I mean poor Bunbury died this afternoon.

LADY BRACKNELL. What did he die of?

ALGERNON. Bunbury? Oh, he was quite exploded.

LADY BRACKNELL. Exploded! Was he the victim of a revolutionary outrage? I was not aware that Mr. Bunbury was interested in social legislation. If so, he is well punished for his morbidity.

ALGERNON. My dear Aunt Augusta, I mean he was found out! The doctors found out that Bunbury could not live, that is what I mean—so Bunbury died.

LADY BRACKNELL. He seems to have had great confidence in the opinion of his physicians. I am glad, however, that he made up his mind at the last to some definite course of action, and acted under proper medical advice. And now that we have finally got rid of this Mr. Bunbury, may I ask, Mr. Worthing, who is that young person whose hand my nephew Algernon is now holding in what seems to me a peculiarly unnecessary manner?

JACK. That lady is Miss Cecily Cardew, my ward.

(*Lady Bracknell bows coldly to Cecily.*)

ALGERNON. I am engaged to be married to Cecily, Aunt Augusta.

LADY BRACKNELL. I beg your pardon?

CECILY. Mr. Moncrieff and I are engaged to be married, Lady Bracknell.

LADY BRACKNELL. (*With a shiver, crossing to the sofa and sitting down.*) I do not know whether there is anything peculiarly exciting in the air of this particular part of Hertfordshire, but the number of engagements that go on seems to me considerably above the proper average that statistics have laid down for our guidance. I think some preliminary inquiry on my part would not be out of place. Mr. Worthing, is Miss Cardew at all connected with any of the larger railway stations in London? I merely desire information. Until yesterday I had no idea that there were any families or persons whose origin was a Terminus.

(*Jack looks perfectly furious, but restrains himself.*)

JACK. (*In a clear, cold voice.*) Miss Cardew is the granddaughter of the late Mr. Thomas Cardew of 149 Belgrave Square, S.W.; Gervase Park, Dorking, Surrey; and the Sporran, Fifeshire, N.B.

LADY BRACKNELL. That sounds not unsatisfactory. Three addresses always inspire confidence, even in tradesmen. But what proof have I of their authenticity?

JACK. I have carefully preserved the Court Guides[1] of the period. They are open to your inspection, Lady Bracknell.

LADY BRACKNELL. (*Grimly.*) I have known strange errors in that publication.

JACK. Miss Cardew's family solicitors are Messrs. Markby, Markby, and Markby.

LADY BRACKNELL. Markby, Markby, and Markby? A firm of the very highest position in their profession. Indeed I am told that one of the Mr. Markbys is occasionally to be seen at dinner parties. So far I am satisfied.

JACK. (*Very irritably.*) How extremely kind of you, Lady Bracknell! I have also in my possession, you will be pleased to hear, certificates of Miss Cardew's birth, baptism, whooping cough, registration, vaccination, confirmation, and the measles; both the German and the English variety.

LADY BRACKNELL. Ah! A life crowded with incident, I see; though perhaps somewhat too exciting for a young girl. I am not myself in favour of premature experiences. (*Rises, looks at her watch.*) Gwendolen! the time approaches for our departure. We have not a moment to lose. As a matter of form, Mr. Worthing, I had better ask you if Miss Cardew has any little fortune?

JACK. Oh! about a hundred and thirty thousand pounds in the Funds. That is all. Goodbye, Lady Bracknell. So pleased to have seen you.

LADY BRACKNELL. (*Sitting down again.*) A moment, Mr. Worthing. A hundred and thirty thousand pounds! And in the Funds! Miss Cardew seems to me a most attractive young lady, now that I look at her. Few girls of the present day have any really solid qualities, any of the qualities that last, and improve with time. We live, I regret to say, in an age of surfaces. (*To Cecily.*) Come over here, dear. (*Cecily goes across.*) Pretty child! your dress is sadly simple, and your hair seems almost as Nature might have left it. But we can soon alter all that. A thoroughly experienced French maid produces a really

---

[1] *Court Guides* Directory of names and addresses of those members of the nobility, gentry, and society who have been presented at court.

marvellous result in a very brief space of time. I remember recommending one to young Lady Lancing, and after three months her own husband did not know her.

JACK. And after six months nobody knew her.

LADY BRACKNELL. (*Glares at Jack for a few moments. Then bends, with a practised smile, to Cecily.*) Kindly turn round, sweet child. (*Cecily turns completely round.*) No, the side view is what I want. (*Cecily presents her profile.*) Yes, quite as I expected. There are distinct social possibilities in your profile. The two weak points in our age are its want of principle and its want of profile. The chin a little higher, dear. Style largely depends on the way the chin is worn. They are worn very high, just at present. Algernon!

ALGERNON. Yes, Aunt Augusta!

LADY BRACKNELL. There are distinct social possibilities in Miss Cardew's profile.

ALGERNON. Cecily is the sweetest, dearest, prettiest girl in the whole world. And I don't care twopence about social possibilities.

LADY BRACKNELL. Never speak disrespectfully of Society, Algernon. Only people who can't get into it do that. (*To Cecily.*) Dear child, of course you know that Algernon has nothing but his debts to depend upon. But I do not approve of mercenary marriages. When I married Lord Bracknell I had no fortune of any kind. But I never dreamed for a moment of allowing that to stand in my way. Well, I suppose I must give my consent.

ALGERNON. Thank you, Aunt Augusta.

LADY BRACKNELL. Cecily, you may kiss me!

CECILY. (*Kisses her.*) Thank you, Lady Bracknell.

LADY BRACKNELL. You may also address me as Aunt Augusta for the future.

CECILY. Thank you, Aunt Augusta.

LADY BRACKNELL. The marriage, I think, had better take place quite soon.

ALGERNON. Thank you, Aunt Augusta.

CECILY. Thank you, Aunt Augusta.

LADY BRACKNELL. To speak frankly, I am not in favour of long engagements. They give people the opportunity of finding out each other's character before marriage, which I think is never advisable.

JACK. I beg your pardon for interrupting you, Lady Bracknell, but this engagement is quite out of the question. I am Miss Cardew's guardian, and she cannot marry without my consent until she comes of age. That consent I absolutely decline to give.

LADY BRACKNELL. Upon what grounds may I ask? Algernon is an extremely, I may almost say an ostentatiously, eligible young man. He has nothing, but he looks everything. What more can one desire?

JACK. It pains me very much to have to speak frankly to you, Lady Bracknell, about your nephew, but the fact is that I do not approve at all of his moral character. I suspect him of being untruthful.

(*Algernon and Cecily look at him in indignant amazement.*)

LADY BRACKNELL. Untruthful! My nephew Algernon? Impossible! He is an Oxonian.[1]

JACK. I fear there can be no possible doubt about the matter. This afternoon during my temporary absence in London on an important question of romance, he obtained admission to my house by means of the false pretence of being my brother. Under an assumed name he drank, I've just been informed by my butler, an entire pint bottle of my Perrier-Jouet, Brut, '89; wine I was specially reserving for myself. Continuing his disgraceful deception, he succeeded in the course of the afternoon in alienating the affections of my only ward. He subsequently stayed to tea, and devoured every single muffin. And what makes his conduct all the more heartless is, that he was perfectly well aware from the first that I have no brother, that I never had a brother, and that I don't intend to have a brother, not even of any kind. I distinctly told him so myself yesterday afternoon.

LADY BRACKNELL. Ahem! Mr. Worthing, after careful consideration I have decided entirely to overlook my nephew's conduct to you.

[1] *Oxonian* One who has attended Oxford University.

JACK. That is very generous of you, Lady Bracknell. My own decision, however, is unalterable. I decline to give my consent.

LADY BRACKNELL. (*To Cecily.*) Come here, sweet child. (*Cecily goes over.*) How old are you, dear?

CECILY. Well, I am really only eighteen, but I always admit to twenty when I go to evening parties.

LADY BRACKNELL. You are perfectly right in making some slight alteration. Indeed, no woman should ever be quite accurate about her age. It looks so calculating ... (*In a meditative manner.*) Eighteen, but admitting to twenty at evening parties. Well, it will not be very long before you are of age and free from the restraints of tutelage. So I don't think your guardian's consent is, after all, a matter of any importance.

JACK. Pray excuse me, Lady Bracknell, for interrupting you again, but it is only fair to tell you that according to the terms of her grandfather's will Miss Cardew does not come legally of age till she is thirty-five.

LADY BRACKNELL. That does not seem to me to be a grave objection. Thirty-five is a very attractive age. London society is full of women of the very highest birth who have, of their own free choice, remained thirty-five for years. Lady Dumbleton is an instance in point. To my own knowledge she has been thirty-five ever since she arrived at the age of forty, which was many years ago now. I see no reason why our dear Cecily should not be even still more attractive at the age you mention than she is at present. There will be a large accumulation of property.

CECILY. Algy, could you wait for me till I was thirty-five?

ALGERNON. Of course I could, Cecily. You know I could.

CECILY. Yes, I felt it instinctively, but I couldn't wait all that time. I hate waiting even five minutes for anybody. It always makes me rather cross. I am not punctual myself, I know, but I do like punctuality in others, and waiting, even to be married, is quite out of the question.

ALGERNON. Then what is to be done, Cecily?

CECILY. I don't know, Mr. Moncrieff.

LADY BRACKNELL. My dear Mr. Worthing, as Miss Cardew states positively that she cannot wait till she is thirty-five—a remark which I am bound to say seems to me to show a somewhat impatient nature—I would beg of you to reconsider your decision.

JACK. But my dear Lady Bracknell, the matter is entirely in your own hands. The moment you consent to my marriage with Gwendolen, I will most gladly allow your nephew to form an alliance with my ward.

LADY BRACKNELL. (*Rising and drawing herself up.*) You must be quite aware that what you propose is out of the question.

JACK. Then a passionate celibacy is all that any of us can look forward to.

LADY BRACKNELL. That is not the destiny I propose for Gwendolen. Algernon, of course, can choose for himself. (*Pulls out her watch.*) Come, dear, (*Gwendolen rises*) we have already missed five, if not six, trains. To miss any more might expose us to comment on the platform.

(*Enter Dr. Chasuble.*)

CHASUBLE. Everything is quite ready for the christenings.

LADY BRACKNELL. The christenings, sir! Is not that somewhat premature?

CHASUBLE. (*Looking rather puzzled, and pointing to Jack and Algernon.*) Both these gentlemen have expressed a desire for immediate baptism.

LADY BRACKNELL. At their age? The idea is grotesque and irreligious! Algernon, I forbid you to be baptized. I will not hear of such excesses. Lord Bracknell would be highly displeased if he learned that that was the way in which you wasted your time and money.

CHASUBLE. Am I to understand then that there are to be no christenings at all this afternoon?

JACK. I don't think that, as things are now, it would be of much practical value to either of us, Dr. Chasuble.

CHASUBLE. I am grieved to hear such sentiments from you, Mr. Worthing. They savour of the heretical views of the Anabaptists,[1] views that I have completely

---

[1] *heretical views ... Anabaptists* Although Anabaptists, members of a Protestant sect that rejects Anglican doctrine, believe in baptism, they reject the Anglican custom of baptizing infants. Dr. Chasuble is suggesting that Jack is heretical in denying the value of baptism in the Anglican church.

refuted in four of my unpublished sermons. However, as your present mood seems to be one peculiarly secular, I will return to the church at once. Indeed, I have just been informed by the pew-opener[1] that for the last hour and a half, Miss Prism has been waiting for me in the vestry.

LADY BRACKNELL. (*Starting.*) Miss Prism! Did I hear you mention a Miss Prism?

CHASUBLE. Yes, Lady Bracknell. I am on my way to join her.

LADY BRACKNELL. Pray allow me to detain you for a moment. This matter may prove to be one of vital importance to Lord Bracknell and myself. Is this Miss Prism a female of repellent aspect, remotely connected with education?

CHASUBLE. (*Somewhat indignantly.*) She is the most cultivated of ladies, and the very picture of respectability.

LADY BRACKNELL. It is obviously the same person. May I ask what position she holds in your household?

CHASUBLE. (*Severely.*) I am a celibate, madam.

JACK. (*Interposing.*) Miss Prism, Lady Bracknell, has been for the last three years Miss Cardew's esteemed governess and valued companion.

LADY BRACKNELL. In spite of what I hear of her, I must see her at once. Let her be sent for.

CHASUBLE. (*Looking off.*) She approaches; she is nigh.

(*Enter Miss Prism hurriedly.*)

MISS PRISM. I was told you expected me in the vestry, dear Canon. I have been waiting for you there for an hour and three-quarters.

(*Catches sight of Lady Bracknell, who has fixed her with a stony glare. Miss Prism grows pale and quails. She looks anxiously round as if desirous to escape.*)

LADY BRACKNELL. (*In a severe, judicial voice.*) Prism! (*Miss Prism bows her head in shame.*) Come here, Prism! (*Miss Prism approaches in a humble manner.*) Prism! Where is that baby? (*General consternation. The Canon starts back in horror. Algernon and Jack pretend to be anxious to shield Cecily and Gwendolen from hearing the details of a terrible public scandal.*) Twenty-eight years ago, Prism, you left Lord Bracknell's house, Number 104, Upper Grosvenor Street, in charge of a perambulator that contained a baby of the male sex. You never returned. A few weeks later, through the elaborate investigations of the Metropolitan police, the perambulator was discovered at midnight, standing by itself in a remote corner of Bayswater. It contained the manuscript of a three-volume novel of more than usually revolting sentimentality. (*Miss Prism starts in involuntary indignation.*) But the baby was not there! (*Every one looks at Miss Prism.*) Prism! Where is that baby? (*A pause.*)

MISS PRISM. Lady Bracknell, I admit with shame that I do not know. I only wish I did. The plain facts of the case are these. On the morning of the day you mention, a day that is for ever branded on my memory, I prepared as usual to take the baby out in its perambulator. I had also with me a somewhat old, but capacious hand-bag in which I had intended to place the manuscript of a work of fiction that I had written during my few unoccupied hours. In a moment of mental abstraction, for which I never can forgive myself, I deposited the manuscript in the bassinette, and placed the baby in the hand-bag.

JACK. (*Who has been listening attentively.*) But where did you deposit the hand-bag?

MISS PRISM. Do not ask me, Mr. Worthing.

JACK. Miss Prism, this is a matter of no small importance to me. I insist on knowing where you deposited the hand-bag that contained that infant.

MISS PRISM. I left it in the cloak-room of one of the larger railway stations in London.

JACK. What railway station?

MISS PRISM. (*Quite crushed.*) Victoria. The Brighton line. (*Sinks into a chair.*)

JACK. I must retire to my room for a moment. Gwendolen, wait here for me.

GWENDOLEN. If you are not too long, I will wait here for you all my life.

(*Exit Jack in great excitement.*)

[1] *pew-opener* One assigned to open the doors of pews for privileged churchgoers.

CHASUBLE. What do you think this means, Lady Bracknell?

LADY BRACKNELL. I dare not even suspect, Dr. Chasuble. I need hardly tell you that in families of high position strange coincidences are not supposed to occur. They are hardly considered the thing.

(*Noises heard overhead as if some one was throwing trunks about. Every one looks up.*)

CECILY. Uncle Jack seems strangely agitated.

CHASUBLE. Your guardian has a very emotional nature.

LADY BRACKNELL. This noise is extremely unpleasant. It sounds as if he was having an argument. I dislike arguments of any kind. They are always vulgar, and often convincing.

CHASUBLE. (*Looking up.*) It has stopped now. (*The noise is redoubled.*)

LADY BRACKNELL. I wish he would arrive at some conclusion.

GWENDOLEN. This suspense is terrible. I hope it will last.

(*Enter Jack with a hand-bag of black leather in his hand.*)

JACK. (*Rushing over to Miss Prism.*) Is this the handbag, Miss Prism? Examine it carefully before you speak. The happiness of more than one life depends on your answer.

MISS PRISM. (*Calmly.*) It seems to be mine. Yes, here is the injury it received through the upsetting of a Gower Street omnibus[1] in younger and happier days. Here is the stain on the lining caused by the explosion of a temperance beverage,[2] an incident that occurred at Leamington. And here, on the lock, are my initials. I had forgotten that in an extravagant mood I had had them placed there. The bag is undoubtedly mine. I am delighted to have it so unexpectedly restored to me. It has been a great inconvenience being without it all these years.

JACK. (*In a pathetic voice.*) Miss Prism, more is restored to you than this hand-bag. I was the baby you placed in it.

MISS PRISM. (*Amazed.*) You?

JACK. (*Embracing her.*) Yes … mother!

MISS PRISM. (*Recoiling in indignant astonishment.*) Mr. Worthing! I am unmarried!

JACK. Unmarried! I do not deny that is a serious blow. But after all, who has the right to cast a stone against one who has suffered? Cannot repentance wipe out an act of folly? Why should there be one law for men, and another for women? Mother, I forgive you. (*Tries to embrace her again.*)

MISS PRISM. (*Still more indignant.*) Mr. Worthing, there is some error. (*Pointing to Lady Bracknell.*) There is the lady who can tell you who you really are.

JACK. (*After a pause.*) Lady Bracknell, I hate to seem inquisitive, but would you kindly inform me who I am?

LADY BRACKNELL. I am afraid that the news I have to give you will not altogether please you. You are the son of my poor sister, Mrs. Moncrieff, and consequently Algernon's elder brother.

JACK. Algy's elder brother! Then I have a brother after all. I knew I had a brother! I always said I had a brother! Cecily,—how could you have ever doubted that I had a brother? (*Seizes hold of Algernon.*) Dr. Chasuble, my unfortunate brother. Miss Prism, my unfortunate brother. Gwendolen, my unfortunate brother. Algy, you young scoundrel, you will have to treat me with more respect in the future. You have never behaved to me like a brother in all your life.

ALGERNON. Well, not till to-day, old boy, I admit. I did my best, however, though I was out of practice. (*Shakes hands.*)

GWENDOLEN. (*To Jack.*) My own! But what own are you? What is your Christian name, now that you have become some one else?

JACK. Good heavens! … I had quite forgotten that point. Your decision on the subject of my name is irrevocable, I suppose?

GWENDOLEN. I never change, except in my affections.

CECILY. What a noble nature you have, Gwendolen!

[1] *Gower Street omnibus* Public horse-drawn bus on a route in central London.

[2] *temperance beverage* Non-alcoholic drink. (The temperance movement aimed to prohibit all alcoholic beverages.)

JACK. Then the question had better be cleared up at once. Aunt Augusta, a moment. At the time when Miss Prism left me in the hand-bag, had I been christened already?

LADY BRACKNELL. Every luxury that money could buy, including christening, had been lavished on you by your fond and doting parents.

JACK. Then I was christened! That is settled. Now, what name was I given? Let me know the worst.

LADY BRACKNELL. Being the eldest son you were naturally christened after your father.

JACK. (*Irritably.*) Yes, but what was my father's Christian name?

LADY BRACKNELL. (*Meditatively.*) I cannot at the present moment recall what the General's Christian name was. But I have no doubt he had one. He was eccentric, I admit. But only in later years. And that was the result of the Indian climate, and marriage, and indigestion, and other things of that kind.

JACK. Algy! Can't you recollect what our father's Christian name was?

ALGERNON. My dear boy, we were never even on speaking terms. He died before I was a year old.

JACK. His name would appear in the Army Lists[1] of the period, I suppose, Aunt Augusta?

LADY BRACKNELL. The General was essentially a man of peace, except in his domestic life. But I have no doubt his name would appear in any military directory.

JACK. The Army Lists of the last forty years are here. These delightful records should have been my constant study. (*Rushes to bookcase and tears the books out.*) M. Generals … Mallam, Maxbohm, Magley, what ghastly names they have—Markby, Migsby, Mobbs, Moncrieff! Lieutenant 1840, Captain, Lieutenant-Colonel, Colonel, General 1869, Christian names, Ernest John. (*Puts book very quietly down and speaks quite calmly.*) I always told you, Gwendolen, my name was Ernest, didn't I? Well, it is Ernest after all. I mean it naturally is Ernest.

LADY BRACKNELL. Yes, I remember now that the General was called Ernest, I knew I had some particular reason for disliking the name.

GWENDOLEN. Ernest! My own Ernest! I felt from the first that you could have no other name!

JACK. Gwendolen, it is a terrible thing for a man to find out suddenly that all his life he has been speaking nothing but the truth. Can you forgive me?

GWENDOLEN. I can. For I feel that you are sure to change.

JACK. My own one!

CHASUBLE. (*To Miss Prism.*) Lætitia! (*Embraces her.*)

MISS PRISM. (*Enthusiastically.*) Frederick! At last!

ALGERNON. Cecily! (*Embraces her.*) At last!

JACK. Gwendolen! (*Embraces her.*) At last!

LADY BRACKNELL. My nephew, you seem to be displaying signs of triviality.

JACK. On the contrary, Aunt Augusta, I've now realized for the first time in my life the vital Importance of Being Earnest.

TABLEAU

—1895

[1] *Army Lists* Directories of officers.

IN CONTEXT

Wilde and "The Public"

Interview with Oscar Wilde, *St. James Gazette* (January 1895)

I found Mr. Oscar Wilde (writes a Representative) making ready to depart on a short visit to Algiers, and reading—of course, nothing so obvious as a time-table, but a French newspaper which contained an account of the first night of *The Ideal Husband*[1] and its author's appearance after the play.

"How well the French appreciate these brilliant willful moments in an artist's life," remarked Mr. Wilde, handing me the article as if he considered the interview already at an end.

"Does it give you any pleasure," I inquired, "to appear before the curtain after the production of your plays?"

"None whatsoever. No artist finds any interest in seeing the public. The public is very much interested in seeing an artist. Personally, I prefer the French custom, according to which the name of the dramatist is announced to the public by the oldest actor in the piece."

"Would you advocate," I asked, "this custom in England?"

"Certainly. The more the public is interested in artists, the less it is interested in art. The personality of the artist is not a thing the public should know anything about. It is too accidental." Then, after a pause—

"It might be more interesting if the name of the author were announced by the *youngest* actor present."

"It is only in deference, then, to the imperious mandate of the public that you have appeared before the curtain?"

"Yes; I have always been very good-natured about that. The public has always been so appreciative of my work I felt it would be a pity to spoil its evening."

"I notice some people have found fault with the character of your speeches."

"Yes, the old-fashioned idea was that the dramatist should appear and merely thank his kind friends for their patronage and presence. I am glad to say I have altered all that. The artist cannot be degraded into the servant of the public. While I have always recognized the cultured appreciation that actors and audience have shown for my work, I have equally recognized that humility is for the hypocrite, modesty for the incompetent. Assertion is at once the duty and privilege of the artist."

"To what do you attribute, Mr. Wilde, the fact that so few men of letters besides yourself have written plays for public presentation?"

"Primarily the existence of an irresponsible censorship. The fact that my *Salomé* cannot be performed is sufficient to show the folly of such an institution. If painters were obliged to show their pictures to clerks at Somerset House, those who think in form and colour would adopt some other mode of expression. If every novel had to be submitted to a police magistrate, those whose passion is fiction would seek some new mode of realization. No art ever survived censorship; no art ever will."

"And secondly?"

---

[1] *The Ideal Husband* I.e., Wilde's play *An Ideal Husband*. The play, which had opened on 3 January 1895, was currently enjoying a very successful run at the Haymarket Theatre.

"Secondly to the rumour persistently spread abroad by journalists for the last thirty years, that the duty of the dramatist was to please the public. The aim of art is no more to give pleasure than to give pain. The aim of art is to be art. As I said once before, the work of art is to dominate the spectator—the spectator is not to dominate art."

"You admit no exceptions?"

"Yes. Circuses where it seems the wishes of the public might be reasonably carried out."

"Do you think," I inquired, "that French dramatic criticism is superior to our own?"

"It would be unfair to confuse French dramatic criticism with English theatrical criticism. The French dramatic critic is always a man of culture and generally a man of letters. In France poets like Gautier[1] have been dramatic critics. In England they are drawn from a less distinguished class. They have neither the same capacities nor the same opportunities. They have all the moral qualities, but none of the artistic qualifications. For the criticism of such a complex mode of art as the drama the highest culture is necessary. No one can criticize drama who is not capable of receiving impressions from the other arts also."

"You admit they are sincere?"

"Yes; but their sincerity is little more than stereotyped stupidity. The critic of the drama should be versatile as the actor. He should be able to change his mood at will and should catch the colour of the moment."

"At least they are honest?"

"Absolutely. I don't believe there is a single dramatic critic in London who would deliberately set himself to misrepresent the work of any dramatist—unless, of course, he personally disliked the dramatist, or had some play of his own he wished to produce at the same theatre, or had an old friend among the actors, or some natural reasons of that kind. I am speaking, however, of London dramatic critics. In the provinces both audience and critics are cultured. In London it is only the audience who are cultured."

"I fear you do not rate our dramatic critics very highly, Mr. Wilde; but, at all events, they are incorruptible?"

"In a market where there are no bidders."

"Still their memories stand them in good stead," I pleaded.

"The old talk of having seen Macready[;][2] that must be a very painful memory. The middle-aged boast that they can recall *Diplomacy*:[3] hardly a pleasant reminiscence."

"You deny them, then, even a creditable past?"

"They have no past and no future, and are incapable of realizing the colour of the moment that finds them at the play."

"What do you propose should be done?"

"They should be pensioned off, and only allowed to write on politics or theology or bimetallism, or some subject easier than art."

"In fact," I said, carried away by Mr. Wilde's aphorisms, "they should be seen and not heard."

"The old should neither be seen nor heard," said Mr. Wilde with some emphasis.

"You said the other day there were only two dramatic critics in London. May I ask—"

"They must have been greatly gratified by such an admission from me; but I am bound to say that since last week I have struck one of them from the list."

---

[1] *Gautier* Théophile Gautier (1811–72), French poet, novelist, and dramatist.

[2] *Macready* William Charles Macready (1793–1873), English actor and theater manager.

[3] *Diplomacy* An English adaptation of the French play *Dora* (1878), by Victorien Sardou (1831–1908).

"Whom have you left in?"

"I think I had better not mention his name. It might make him too conceited. Conceit is the privilege of the creative."

"How would you define ideal dramatic criticism?"

"As far as my work is concerned[,] unqualified appreciation."

"And whom have you omitted?"

"Mr. William Archer, of the *World*."[1]

"What do you chiefly object to in his article?"

"I object to nothing in the article, but I grieve at everything in it. It is bad taste in him to write of me by my Christian name, and he need not have stolen his vulgarisms from the *National Observer* in its most impudent and impotent days."

"Mr. Archer asked whether[,] if it was agreeable to you to be hailed by your Christian name when the enthusiastic spectators called you before the curtain."

"To be so addressed by enthusiastic spectators is as great a compliment as to be written of by one's Christian name is, in a journalist, bad manners. Bad manners make a journalist."

"Do you think French actors, like French criticism, superior to our own?"

"The English actors act quite as well; but they act best between the lines. They lack the superb elocution of the French—so clear, so cadenced, and so musical. A long sustained speech seems to exhaust them. At the Théâtre Français we go to listen, to an English theatre we go to look. There are, of course, exceptions. Mr. George Alexander, Mr. Lewis Waller, Mr. Forbes Robertson, and others I might mention, have superb voices and know how to use them. I wish I could say the same of the critics; but in the case of the literary drama in England there is too much of what is technically known as 'business.' Yet there is more than one of our English actors who is capable of producing a wonderful dramatic effect by aid of a monosyllable and two cigarettes."

For a moment Mr. Wilde was silent, and then added, "Perhaps, after all, that is acting."

"But are you satisfied with the interpreters of *The Ideal Husband*?"

"I am charmed with all of them. Perhaps they are a little too fascinating. The stage is the refuge of the too fascinating."

"Have you heard it said that all the characters in your play talk as you do?"

"Rumours of that kind have reached me from time to time," said Mr. Wilde, lighting a cigarette, "and I should fancy that some such criticism has been made. The fact is that it is only in the last few years that the dramatic critic has had the opportunity of seeing plays written by anyone who has a mastery of style. In the case of a dramatist, also an artist, it is impossible not to feel that the work of art, to be a work of art, must be dominated by the artist. Every play of Shakespeare is dominated by Shakespeare. Ibsen and Dumas[2] dominate their works. My works are dominated by myself."

"Have you ever been influenced by any of your predecessors?"

"It is enough for me to state definitely, and I hope once for all, that not a single dramatist in this century has ever in the smallest degree influenced me. Only two have interested me."

"And they are?"

"Victor Hugo and Maeterlinck."[3]

"Other writers surely have influenced your other works?"

---

[1] *Mr. William … World* For Archer's criticism of Wilde, see "*An Ideal Husband*," *The World*, 9 January 1895, 26–27.

[2] *Ibsen* Norwegian playwright Henrik Ibsen (1828–1906); *Dumas* French author and playwright Alexandre Dumas (1824–95).

[3] *Maeterlinck* Maurice Maeterlinck (1862–1949), Belgian poet and playwright who was awarded the Nobel Prize for Literature in 1911.

"Setting aside the prose and poetry of Greek and Latin authors, the only writers who have influenced me are Keats, Flaubert, and Walter Pater;[1] and before I came across them I had already gone more than halfway to meet them. Style must be in one's soul before one can recognize it in others."

"And do you consider *The Ideal Husband* the best of your plays?"

A charming smile crossed Mr. Wilde's face.

"Have you forgotten my classical expression—that only mediocrities improve? My three plays are to each other, as a wonderful young poet has beautifully said,

as one white rose
On one green stalk to another one.

They form a perfect cycle, and in their delicate sphere complete both life and art."

"Do you think that the critics will understand your new play,[2] which Mr. George Alexander has secured?"

"I hope not."

"I dare not ask, I suppose, if it will please the public?"

"When a play that is a work of art is produced on the stage, what is being tested is not the play, but the stage; when a play that is *not* a work of art is produced on the stage, what is being tested is not the play, but the public."

"What sort of play are we to expect?"

"It is exquisitely trivial, a delicate bubble of fancy, and it has its philosophy."

"Its philosophy!"

"That we should treat all the trivial things of life very seriously, and all the serious things of life with sincere and studied triviality."[3]

"You have no leanings towards realism?"

"None whatever. Realism is only a background; it cannot form an artistic motive for a play that is to be a work of art."

"Still I have heard you congratulated on your pictures of London society."

"If Robert Chiltern, the Ideal Husband, were a common clerk, the humanity of his tragedy would be none the less poignant. I have placed him in the higher ranks of life merely because that is the side of social life with which I am best acquainted. In a play dealing with actualities to write with ease one must write with knowledge."

"Then you see nothing suggestive of treatment in the tragedies of everyday existence?"

"If a journalist is run over by a four-wheeler in the Strand, an incident I regret to say I have never witnessed, it suggests nothing to me from a dramatic point of view. Perhaps I am wrong; but the artist must have his limitations."

"Well," I said, rising to go, "I have enjoyed myself immensely."

"I was sure you would," said Mr. Wilde. "But tell me how you manage your interviews."

"Oh, Pitman," I said carelessly.

"Is that your name? It's not a very *nice* name."

Then I left.

---

[1] *Keats* John Keats, English poet (1795–1821); *Flaubert* French novelist Gustave Flaubert (1821–80), celebrated author of *Madame Bovary* (1867); *Walter Pater* English critic and scholar; he had reviewed some of Wilde's works.

[2] *new play* *The Importance of Being Earnest*, which opened on 14 February 1895.

[3] *That we should … triviality* The full title of the play is *The Importance of Being Earnest: A Trivial Comedy for Serious People.*

IN CONTEXT

The First Wilde Trial (1895)

The following is an excerpt from the transcripts of the cross examination of Wilde by Edward Carson, the attorney defending the Marquess of Queensberry in the libel action[1] Wilde had brought against him.

Portrait of Oscar Wilde at the time of his trial, by Henri de Toulouse-Lautrec.

from The Transcripts of the Trial

CARSON. You stated that your age was thirty-nine. I think you are over forty. You were born on 16th October 1854?

WILDE. I have no wish to pose as being young. I am thirty-nine or forty. You have my certificate and that settles the matter.

CARSON. But being born in 1854 makes you more than forty?

WILDE. Ah! Very well.

CARSON. What age is Lord Alfred Douglas?

WILDE. Lord Alfred Douglas is about twenty-four, and was between twenty and twenty-one years of age when I first knew him. Down to the time of the interview in Tite Street, Lord Queensberry was friendly. I did not receive a letter on 3rd April in which Lord Queensberry desired that my acquaintance with his son should cease. After the interview I had no doubt that such was Lord Queensberry's desire. Notwithstanding Lord Queensberry's protest, my intimacy with Lord Alfred

[1] *Marquess … libel action* The Marquess of Queensberry, offended at the close friendship Wilde had formed with his son, Lord Alfred Douglas, had left a card at Wilde's club addressed to "Oscar Wilde posing as a sodomnite [sic]." Wilde felt that he had little choice but to prosecute, or to become publicly known as a man who was unable to deny such a charge. It was this prosecution which eventually led to his imprisonment and the exile of Lord Alfred Douglas.

Douglas has continued down to the present moment.

CARSON. You have stayed with him at many places?

WILDE. Yes.

CARSON. At Oxford? Brighton on several occasions? Worthing?

WILDE. Yes.

CARSON. You never took rooms for him?

WILDE. No.

CARSON. Were you at other places with him?

WILDE. Yes; at Cromer and at Torquay.

CARSON. And in various hotels in London?

WILDE. Yes; at one in Albemarle Street, and in Dover Street, and at the Savoy.

CARSON. Did you ever take rooms yourself in addition to your house in Tite Street?

WILDE. Yes; at 10 and 11 St. James's Place. I kept the rooms from the month of October 1893 to the end of March 1894. Lord Alfred Douglas has stayed in those chambers, which are not far from Piccadilly. I have been abroad with him several times and even lately to Monte Carlo. With reference to the writings which have been mentioned, it was not at Brighton, in 20 King's Road, that I wrote my article for *The Chameleon*.[1] I observed that there were also contributions from Lord Alfred Douglas, but these were not written at Brighton. I have seen them. I thought them exceedingly beautiful poems. One was "In Praise of Shame" and the other "Two Loves."

CARSON. These loves. They were two boys?

WILDE. Yes.

CARSON. One boy calls his love "true love," and the other boy calls his love "shame"?

WILDE. Yes.

CARSON. Did you think that made any improper suggestion?

WILDE. No, none whatever.

CARSON. You read "The Priest and the Acolyte"?

WILDE. Yes.

CARSON. You have no doubt whatever that that was an improper story?

WILDE. From the literary point of view it was highly improper. It is impossible for a man of literature to judge it otherwise; by literature, meaning treatment, selection of subject, and the like. I thought the treatment rotten and the subject rotten.

CARSON. You are of opinion, I believe, that there is no such thing as an immoral book?

WILDE. Yes.

CARSON. May I take it that you think "The Priest and the Acolyte" was not immoral?

WILDE. It was worse; it was badly written.

CARSON. Was not the story that of a priest who fell in love with a boy who served him at the altar, and was discovered by the rector in the priest's room, and a scandal arose?

WILDE. I have read it only once, in last November, and nothing will induce me to read it again. I don't care for it. It doesn't interest me.

CARSON. Do you think the story blasphemous?

WILDE. I think it violated every artistic canon of beauty.

[1] *The Chameleon* Oxford undergraduate magazine, of which there was only one issue, that of December 1894 to which Wilde refers. In this issue Wilde's "Phrases and Philosophies for the Use of the Young" appeared, as well as an anonymous story about sexuality between men (actually written not by Wilde but by the editor), called "The Priest and the Acolyte." Though Wilde was not the author, the mere fact that a piece signed by him appeared juxtaposed to this story proved damaging to his reputation.

CARSON. That is not an answer?
WILDE. It is the only one I can give.
CARSON. I want to see the position you pose in?
WILDE. I do not think you should say that.
CARSON. I have said nothing out of the way. I wish to know whether you thought the story blasphemous?
WILDE. The story filled me with disgust. The end was wrong.
CARSON. Answer the question, sir. Did you or did you not consider the story blasphemous?
WILDE. I thought it disgusting.
CARSON. I am satisfied with that. You know that when the priest in the story administers poison to the boy, he uses the words of the sacrament of the Church of England?
WILDE. That I entirely forgot.
CARSON. Do you consider that blasphemous?
WILDE. I think it is horrible. "Blasphemous" is not a word of mine.

[*Carson then read the following passage from "The Priest and the Acolyte."*]:

> Just before the consecration the priest took a tiny phial from the pocket of his cassock, blessed it, and poured the contents into the chalice.
>
> When the time came for him to receive from the chalice, he raised it to his lips, but did not taste of it.
>
> He administered the sacred wafer to the child, and then he took his hand; he turned towards him; but when he saw the light in the beautiful face he turned again to the crucifix with a low moan. For one instant his courage failed him; then he turned to the little fellow again, and held the chalice to his lips:
>
> "The Blood of our Lord Jesus Christ, which was shed for thee, preserve thy body and soul unto everlasting life."

CARSON. Do you approve of those words?
WILDE. I think them disgusting, perfect twaddle.
CARSON. I think you will admit that anyone who would approve of such an article would pose as guilty of improper practices?
WILDE. I do not think so in the person of another contributor to the magazine. It would show very bad literary taste. I strongly objected to the whole story. I took no steps to express disapproval of *The Chameleon* because I think it would have been beneath my dignity as a man of letters to associate myself with an Oxford undergraduate's productions. I am aware that the magazine may have been circulated among the undergraduates of Oxford. I do not believe that any book or work of art ever had any effect whatever on morality.
CARSON. Am I right in saying that you do not consider the effect in creating morality or immorality?
WILDE. Certainly, I do not.
CARSON. So far as your works are concerned, you pose as not being concerned about morality or immorality?
WILDE. I do not know whether you use the word "pose" in any particular sense.
CARSON. It is a favorite word of your own?
WILDE. Is it? I have no pose in this matter. In writing a play or a book, I am concerned entirely with

literature—that is, with art. I aim not at doing good or evil, but in trying to make a thing that will have some quality of beauty.

CARSON. Listen, sir. Here is one of the "Phrases and Philosophies for the Use of the Young" which you contributed: "Wickedness is a myth invented by good people to account for the curious attractiveness of others." You think that true?

WILDE. I rarely think that anything I write is true.

CARSON. Did you say "rarely"?

WILDE. I said "rarely." I might have said "never"—not true in the actual sense of the word.

CARSON. "Religions die when they are proved to be true." Is that true?

WILDE. Yes; I hold that. It is a suggestion towards a philosophy of the absorption of religions by science, but it is too big a question to go into now.

CARSON. Do you think that was a safe axiom to put forward for the philosophy of the young?

WILDE. Most stimulating.

CARSON. "If one tells the truth, one is sure, sooner or later, to be found out"?

WILDE. That is a pleasing paradox, but I do not set very high store on it as an axiom.

CARSON. Is it good for the young?

WILDE. Anything is good that stimulates thought in whatever age.

CARSON. Whether moral or immoral?

WILDE. There is no such thing as morality or immorality in thought. There is immoral emotion.

CARSON. "Pleasure is the only thing one should live for"?

WILDE. I think that the realization of oneself is the prime aim of life, and to realize oneself through pleasure is finer than to do so through pain. I am, on that point, entirely on the side of the ancients—the Greeks. It is a pagan idea.

CARSON. "A truth ceases to be true when more than one person believes in it"?

WILDE. Perfectly. That would be my metaphysical definition of truth; something so personal that the same truth could never be appreciated by two minds.

CARSON. "The condition of perfection is idleness: the aim of perfection is youth"?

WILDE. Oh, yes; I think so. Half of it is true. The life of contemplation is the highest life, and so recognized by the philosopher.

CARSON. "There is something tragic about the enormous number of young men there are in England at the present moment who start life with perfect profiles, and end by adopting some useful profession"?

WILDE. I should think that the young have enough sense of humour.

CARSON. You think that is humourous?

WILDE. I think it is an amusing paradox, an amusing play on words.

CARSON. What would anyone say would be the effect of "Phrases and Philosophies" taken in connection with such an article as "The Priest and the Acolyte"?

WILDE. Undoubtedly it was the idea that might be formed that made me object so strongly to the story. I saw at once that maxims that were perfectly nonsensical, paradoxical, or anything you like, might be read in conjunction with it.

CARSON. After the criticisms that were passed on *Dorian Gray*, was it modified a good deal?

WILDE. No. Additions were made. In one case it was pointed out to me—not in a newspaper or anything of that sort, but by the only critic of the century whose opinion I set high, Mr. Walter Pater—that a certain passage was liable to misconstruction, and I made an addition.

CARSON. This is in your introduction to *Dorian Gray*: "There is no such thing as a moral or an immoral book. Books are well written, or badly written." That expresses your view?

WILDE. My view on art, yes.
CARSON. Then I take it that no matter how immoral a book may be, if it is well written, it is, in your opinion, a good book?
WILDE. Yes, if it were well written so as to produce a sense of beauty, which is the highest sense of which a human being can be capable. If it were badly written, it would produce a sense of disgust.
CARSON. Then a well-written book putting forward perverted moral views may be a good book?
WILDE. No work of art ever puts forward views. Views belong to people who are not artists.
CARSON. A perverted novel might be a good book?
WILDE. I don't know what you mean by a "perverted" novel.
CARSON. Then I will suggest *Dorian Gray* as open to the interpretation of being such a novel?
WILDE. That could only be to brutes and illiterates. The views of Philistines on art are incalculably stupid.
CARSON. An illiterate person reading *Dorian Gray* might consider it such a novel?
WILDE. The views of illiterates on art are unaccountable. I am concerned only with my view of art. I don't care twopence what other people think of it.
CARSON. The majority of persons would come under your definition of Philistines and illiterates?
WILDE. I have found wonderful exceptions.
CARSON. Do you think that the majority of people live up to the position you are giving us?
WILDE. I am afraid they are not cultivated enough.
CARSON. Not cultivated enough to draw the distinction between a good book and a bad book?
WILDE. Certainly not.
CARSON. The affection and love of the artist of *Dorian Gray* might lead an ordinary individual to believe that it might have a certain tendency?
WILDE. I have no knowledge of the views of ordinary individuals.
CARSON. You did not prevent the ordinary individual from buying your book?
WILDE. I have never discouraged him.

[*Carson then read a long passage from Chapter 1 of* The Picture of Dorian Gray *(from "The story is simply this ..." to "I must see Dorian Gray")*.]

CARSON. Now I ask you, Mr. Wilde, do you consider that that description of the feeling of one man towards a youth just grown up was a proper or an improper feeling?
WILDE. I think it is the most perfect description of what an artist would feel on meeting a beautiful personality that was in some way necessary to his art and life.
CARSON. You think that is a feeling a young man should have towards another?
WILDE. Yes, as an artist.

[*Carson then read a long passage from Chapter 9 of* The Picture of Dorian Gray *(from "Let us sit down, Dorian" to "You are made to be worshipped")*.]

CARSON. Do you mean to say that that passage describes the natural feeling of one man towards another?
WILDE. It would be the influence produced by a beautiful personality.
CARSON. A beautiful person?
WILDE. I said a "beautiful personality." You can describe it as you like. Dorian Gray's was a most remarkable personality.

CARSON. May I take it that you, as an artist, have never known the feeling described here?
WILDE. I have never allowed any personality to dominate my art.
CARSON. Then you have never known the feeling you described?
WILDE. No. It is a work of fiction.
CARSON. So far as you are concerned you have no experience as to its being a natural feeling?
WILDE. I think it is perfectly natural for any artist to admire intensely and love a young man. It is an incident in the life of almost every artist.
CARSON. But let us go over it phrase by phrase. "I quite admit that I adored you madly." What do you say to that? Have you ever adored a young man madly?
WILDE. No, not madly; I prefer love—that is a higher form.
CARSON. Never mind about that. Let us keep down to the level we are at now?
WILDE. I have never given adoration to anybody except myself. (*Loud laughter.*)
CARSON. I suppose you think that a very smart thing?
WILDE. Not at all.
CARSON. Then you have never had that feeling?
WILDE. No. The whole idea was borrowed from Shakespeare, I regret to say—yes, from Shakespeare's sonnets.
CARSON. I believe you have written an article to show that Shakespeare's sonnets were suggestive of unnatural vice?
WILDE. On the contrary I have written an article to show that they are not.[1] I objected to such a perversion being put upon Shakespeare.
CARSON. "I have adored you extravagantly"?
WILDE. Do you mean financially?
CARSON. Oh, yes, financially! Do you think we are talking about finance?
WILDE. I don't know what you are talking about.
CARSON. Don't you? Well, I hope I shall make myself very plain before I have done. "I was jealous of everyone to whom you spoke." Have you ever been jealous of a young man?
WILDE. Never in my life.
CARSON. "I wanted to have you all to myself." Did you ever have that feeling?
WILDE. No; I should consider it an intense nuisance, an intense bore.
CARSON. "I grew afraid that the world would know of my idolatry." Why should he grow afraid that the world should know of it?
WILDE. Because there are people in the world who cannot understand the intense devotion, affection, and admiration that an artist can feel for a wonderful and beautiful personality. These are the conditions under which we live. I regret them.
CARSON. These unfortunate people, that have not the high understanding that you have, might put it down to something wrong?
WILDE. Undoubtedly; to any point they chose. I am not concerned with the ignorance of others.
CARSON. In another passage Dorian Gray receives a book. Was the book to which you refer a moral book?
WILDE. Not well written, but it gave me an idea.
CARSON. Was not the book you have in mind of a certain tendency?
WILDE. I decline to be cross-examined upon the work of another artist. It is an impertinence and a vulgarity.

---

[1] *an article ... not* Cf. "The Portrait of Mr. W.H." first published in *Blackwood's Edinburgh Magazine*, 146.885 (July 1889), and then again in a limited edition in 1921.

[*Wilde then stated the book Carson referred to was* A Rebours, *by J.K. Huysmans; and, following an appeal by Sir Edward Clarke, Wilde's attorney, the judge ruled against further reference to it. Carson then read a long passage from Chapter 12 of* The Picture of Dorian Gray *(from "... I think it right that you should know the most dreadful things are being said about you in London" to "Dorian, your reputation is infamous ... ").*]

CARSON. Does not this passage suggest a charge of unnatural vice?
WILDE. It describes Dorian Gray as a man of very corrupt influence, though there is no statement as to the nature of the influence. But as a matter of fact I do not think that one person influences another, nor do I think there is any bad influence in the world.
CARSON. A man never corrupts a youth?
WILDE. I think not.
CARSON. Nothing could corrupt him?
WILDE. If you are talking of separate ages.
CARSON. No, sir, I am talking common sense.
WILDE. I do not think one person influences another.
CARSON. You don't think that flattering a young man, making love[1] to him, in fact, would be likely to corrupt him?
WILDE. No.
CARSON. Where was Lord Alfred Douglas staying when you wrote that letter to him?
WILDE. At the Savoy; and I was at Babbacombe, near Torquay.
CARSON. It was a letter in answer to something he had sent you?
WILDE. Yes, a poem.
CARSON. Why should a man of your age address a boy nearly twenty years younger as "My own boy"?
WILDE. I was fond of him. I have always been fond of him.
CARSON. Do you adore him?
WILDE. No, but I have always liked him. I think it is a beautiful letter. It is a poem. I was not writing an ordinary letter. You might as well cross-examine me as to whether *King Lear* or a sonnet of Shakespeare was proper.
CARSON. Apart from art, Mr. Wilde?
WILDE. I cannot answer apart from art.
CARSON. Suppose a man who was not an artist had written this letter, would you say it was a proper letter?
WILDE. A man who was not an artist could not have written that letter.
CARSON. Why?
WILDE. Because nobody but an artist could write it. He certainly could not write the language unless he were a man of letters.
CARSON. I can suggest, for the sake of your reputation, that there is nothing very wonderful in this "red rose-leaf lips of yours"?
WILDE. A great deal depends on the way it is read.
CARSON. "Your slim gilt soul walks between passion and poetry." Is that a beautiful phrase?
WILDE. Not as you read it, Mr. Carson. You read it very badly.

---

[1] *making love* Until the 1960s this expression was generally used to refer to the process of wooing or courtship, not to any physical act of lovemaking.

CARSON. I do not profess to be an artist; and when I hear you give evidence, I am glad I am not—

SIR EDWARD CLARKE. I don't think my friend should talk like that. (*To witness*) Pray, do not criticize my friend's reading again.

CARSON. Is that not an exceptional letter?

WILDE. It is unique, I should say.

CARSON. Was that the ordinary way in which you carried on your correspondence?

WILDE. No; but I have often written to Lord Alfred Douglas, though I never wrote to another young man in the same way.

CARSON. Have you often written letters in the same style as this?

WILDE. I don't repeat myself in style.

CARSON. Here is another letter which I believe you also wrote to Lord Alfred Douglas. Will you read it?

WILDE. No; I decline. I don't see why I should.

CARSON. Then I will.

> Savoy Hotel,
> Victoria Embankment, London.
> Dearest of all Boys,
> Your letter was delightful, red and yellow wine to me; but I am sad and out of sorts. Bosie,[1] you must not make scenes with me. They kill me, they wreck the loveliness of life. I cannot see you, so Greek and gracious, distorted with passion. I cannot listen to your curved lips saying hideous things to me. I would sooner——than have you bitter, unjust, hating. … I must see you soon. You are the divine thing I want, the thing of grace and beauty; but I don't know how to do it. Shall I come to Salisbury? My bill here is £49 for a week. I have also got a new sitting-room. … Why are you not here, my dear, my wonderful boy? I fear I must leave—no money, no credit, and a heart of lead.
> Your own Oscar. …

Is that an ordinary letter?

WILDE. Everything I write is extraordinary. I do not pose as being ordinary, great heavens! Ask me any question you like about it.

CARSON. Is it the kind of letter a man writes to another?

WILDE. It was a tender expression of my great admiration for Lord Alfred Douglas. It was not, like the other, a prose poem. …

[1] *Bosie* Lord Alfred Douglas's nickname.

Sir Arthur Conan Doyle

1859 – 1930

British detective Sherlock Holmes is so renowned that his fame outstrips that of his creator, Sir Arthur Conan Doyle. Conan Doyle wrote many other sorts of fiction, as well as books on history, war, and supernatural subjects, and although some were very successful, they never roused the interest generated by the man with the deerstalker cap, calabash pipe, and magnifying glass, who solved crimes using "elementary" deductions, abetted by the faithful Dr. Watson. When Conan Doyle grew bored with his creation and tried to kill off Holmes and his evil nemesis Professor Moriarty, his reading public wore arm bands to display their mourning, and publishers offered such enormous sums to have Holmes revived that Conan Doyle eventually succumbed to pressure and brought his character back to life.

Conan Doyle was born in Edinburgh, Scotland, in 1859. His father, Charles Altamont Doyle, was a civil servant with artistic aspirations, but alcoholism and epilepsy eventually caused him to be institutionalized. Conan Doyle's mother, Mary Foley Doyle, encouraged her son's voluminous appetite for books and his literary aspirations, even though unrelieved poverty made educating her ten children a financial struggle. When Conan Doyle came of age, he studied medicine at Edinburgh University—where he met Dr. Joseph Bell, the man who became the model for Sherlock Holmes—and earned his medical degree in 1881. During a subsequent medical stint in Southsea near Portsmouth, a dearth of patients left him ample time for writing. During this period he met his first wife, Louisa Hawkins, who would suffer from tuberculosis for much of their marriage, eventually dying of the disease.

Conan Doyle's first Sherlock Holmes adventure, *A Study in Scarlet*, was written in Southsea and published in the 1887 *Beeton Christmas Annual*. After he had published his second Holmes story, *The Sign of the Four*, in *Lippincott's Magazine* in 1890, *The Strand Magazine* began featuring "The Adventures of Sherlock Holmes." (The illustrations by Sidney Paget that accompany "The Adventure of the Speckled Band," below, are from its original publication in *The Strand* in 1892.) In an age of great scientific discovery, the public became captivated by Holmes's cool, rational, almost superhuman reasoning skills, but readers also responded to his all-too-human problems, such as his fear of emotional ties and his cocaine habit. Conan Doyle created other memorable characters in such books as *Micah Clarke* (1889) and *The Lost World* (1912), but none attained Holmes's cachet, much to Conan Doyle's chagrin. In 1891—the same year that his popular success enabled him to leave medicine and pursue writing full-time—he complained that the Sherlock Holmes adventures held back his writing career: "I'm thinking of slaying Holmes," he said in a letter to his mother, "he takes my mind from better things."

Whether or not these other "things" were better, Conan Doyle penned much fine work alongside his Sherlock Holmes adventures, including the historical novel *The White Company* (1891) and the science-fiction novella *The Poison Belt* (1913). He also adapted some of his Holmes stories, such as

"The Adventure of the Speckled Band," for the stage. After serving in the Boer War in South Africa, he was knighted in recognition of two treatises he had written in support of the war. In the final decades of his life, and especially after the death of his son due to injuries sustained during World War I, Conan Doyle became immersed in spiritualism and the occult, writing and lecturing extensively on the subject.

After returning from an exhausting lecture tour in 1929, Conan Doyle suffered a heart attack. He never regained his health, and he died in 1930. He is buried in the rose garden at Windlesham, his home in Sussex, where he had lived with his second wife and children.

⌘⌘⌘

The Adventure of the Speckled Band

In glancing over my notes of the seventy odd cases in which I have during the last eight years studied the methods of my friend Sherlock Holmes, I find many tragic, some comic, a large number merely strange, but none commonplace; for, working as he did rather for the love of his art than for the acquirement of wealth, he refused to associate himself with any investigation which did not tend towards the unusual, and even the fantastic. Of all these varied cases, however, I cannot recall any which presented more singular features than that which was associated with the well-known Surrey family of the Roylotts of Stoke Moran. The events in question occurred in the early days of my association with Holmes, when we were sharing rooms as bachelors, in Baker Street. It is possible that I might have placed them upon record before, but a promise of secrecy was made at the time, from which I have only been freed during the last month by the untimely death of the lady to whom the pledge was given. It is perhaps as well that the facts should now come to light, for I have reasons to know there are widespread rumours as to the death of Dr. Grimesby Roylott which tend to make the matter even more terrible than the truth.

It was early in April, the year '83, that I woke one morning to find Sherlock Holmes standing, fully dressed, by the side of my bed. He was a late riser as a rule, and, as the clock on the mantelpiece showed me that it was only a quarter past seven, I blinked up at him in some surprise, and perhaps just a little resentment, for I was myself regular in my habits.

"Very sorry to knock you up,[1] Watson," said he, "but it's the common lot this morning. Mrs. Hudson has been knocked up, she retorted upon me, and I on you."

"What is it, then? A fire?"

"No, a client. It seems that a young lady has arrived in a considerable state of excitement, who insists upon seeing me. She is waiting now in the sitting room. Now, when young ladies wander about the metropolis at this hour of the morning, and knock sleepy people up out of their beds, I presume that it is something very pressing which they have to communicate. Should it prove to be an interesting case, you would, I am sure, wish to follow it from the outset. I thought at any rate that I should call you, and give you the chance."

"My dear fellow, I would not miss it for anything."

I had no keener pleasure than in following Holmes in his professional investigations, and in admiring the rapid deductions, as swift as intuitions, and yet always founded on a logical basis, with which he unravelled the problems which were submitted to him. I rapidly threw on my clothes, and was ready in a few minutes to accompany my friend down to the sitting room. A lady dressed in black and heavily veiled, who had been sitting in the window, rose as we entered.

[1] *knock you up* I.e., "wake you up with a knock at the door." (This usage remains current in some parts of Britain.)

"Good morning, madam," said Holmes cheerily. "My name is Sherlock Holmes. This is my intimate friend and associate, Dr. Watson, before whom you can speak as freely as before myself. Ha, I am glad to see that Mrs. Hudson has had the good sense to light the fire. Pray draw up to it, and I shall order you a cup of hot coffee, for I observe that you are shivering."

"It is not cold which makes me shiver," said the woman in a low voice, changing her seat as requested.

"What then?"

"It is fear, Mr. Holmes. It is terror." She raised her veil as she spoke, and we could see that she was indeed in a pitiable state of agitation, her face all drawn and grey, with restless, frightened eyes, like those of some hunted animal. Her features and figure were those of a woman of thirty, but her hair was shot with premature grey, and her expression was weary and haggard. Sherlock Holmes ran her over with one of his quick, all-comprehensive glances.[1]

"She raised her veil."

"You must not fear," said he soothingly, bending forward and patting her forearm. "We shall soon set matters right, I have no doubt. You have come in by train this morning, I see."

"You know me, then?"

"No, but I observe the second half of a return ticket in the palm of your left glove. You must have started early, and yet you had a good drive in a dog-cart, along heavy roads, before you reached the station."

The lady gave a violent start, and stared in bewilderment at my companion.

"There is no mystery, my dear madam," said he, smiling. "The left arm of your jacket is spattered with mud in no less than seven places. The marks are perfectly fresh. There is no vehicle save a dog-cart which throws up mud in that way, and then only when you sit on the left-hand side of the driver."

"Whatever your reasons may be, you are perfectly correct," said she. "I started from home before six, reached Leatherhead at twenty past, and came in by the first train to Waterloo. Sir, I can stand this strain no longer, I shall go mad if it continues. I have no one to turn to—none, save only one, who cares for me, and he, poor fellow, can be of little aid. I have heard of you, Mr. Holmes; I have heard of you from Mrs. Farintosh, whom you helped in the hour of her sore need. It was from her that I had your address. Oh, sir, do you not think you could help me too, and at least throw a little light through the dense darkness which surrounds me? At present it is out of my power to reward you for your services, but in a month or two I shall be married, with the control of my own income, and then at least you shall not find me ungrateful."

Holmes turned to his desk, and unlocking it, drew out a small casebook which he consulted.

"Farintosh," said he. "Ah, yes, I recall the case; it was concerned with an opal tiara. I think it was before your time, Watson. I can only say, madam, that I shall be happy to devote the same care to your case as I did to that of your friend. As to reward, my profession is its reward; but you are at liberty to defray whatever expenses I may be put to, at the time which suits you best. And now I beg that you will lay before us everything that may help us in forming an opinion upon the matter."

[1] *She raised her veil … glances* The illustration of this scene is by Sidney Paget; it accompanied the story's original publication in *The Strand Magazine* in 1892. Paget's eight other original illustrations are also included in these pages.

"Alas!" replied our visitor. "The very horror of my situation lies in the fact that my fears are so vague, and my suspicions depend so entirely upon small points, which might seem trivial to another, that even he to whom of all others I have a right to look for help and advice looks upon all that I tell him about it as the fancies of a nervous woman. He does not say so, but I can read it from his soothing answers and averted eyes. But I have heard, Mr. Holmes, that you can see deeply into the manifold wickedness of the human heart. You may advise me how to walk amid the dangers which encompass me."

"I am all attention, madam."

"My name is Helen Stoner, and I am living with my stepfather, who is the last survivor of one of the oldest Saxon families in England, the Roylotts of Stoke Moran, on the western border of Surrey."

Holmes nodded his head. "The name is familiar to me," said he.

"The family was at one time among the richest in England, and the estate extended over the borders into Berkshire in the north, and Hampshire in the west. In the last century, however, four successive heirs were of a dissolute and wasteful disposition, and the family ruin was eventually completed by a gambler, in the days of the Regency.[1] Nothing was left save a few acres of ground and the two-hundred-year-old house, which is itself crushed under a heavy mortgage. The last squire dragged out his existence there, living the horrible life of an aristocratic pauper; but his only son, my stepfather, seeing that he must adapt himself to the new conditions, obtained an advance from a relative, which enabled him to take a medical degree, and went out to Calcutta, where, by his professional skill and his force of character, he established a large practice. In a fit of anger, however, caused by some robberies which had been perpetrated in the house, he beat his native butler to death, and narrowly escaped a capital sentence. As it was, he suffered a long term of imprisonment, and afterwards returned to England a morose and disappointed man.

"When Dr. Roylott was in India he married my mother, Mrs. Stoner, the young widow of Major-General Stoner, of the Bengal Artillery. My sister Julia and I were twins, and we were only two years old at the time of my mother's re-marriage. She had a considerable sum of money, not less than a thousand a year, and this she bequeathed to Dr. Roylott entirely whilst we resided with him, with a provision that a certain annual sum should be allowed to each of us in the event of our marriage. Shortly after our return to England my mother died—she was killed eight years ago in a railway accident near Crewe. Dr. Roylott then abandoned his attempts to establish himself in practice in London, and took us to live with him in the ancestral house at Stoke Moran. The money which my mother had left was enough for all our wants, and there seemed no obstacle to our happiness.

"But a terrible change came over our stepfather about this time. Instead of making friends and exchanging visits with our neighbours, who had at first been overjoyed to see a Roylott of Stoke Moran back in the old family seat, he shut himself up in his house, and seldom came out save to indulge in ferocious quarrels with whoever might cross his path. Violence of temper approaching to mania has been hereditary in the men of the family, and in my stepfather's case it had, I believe, been intensified by his long residence in the tropics. A series of disgraceful brawls took place, two of which ended in the police-court, until at last he became the terror of the village, and the folks would fly at his approach, for he is a man of immense strength, and absolutely uncontrollable in his anger.

[1] *the Regency* I.e., 1810–20, the period in which George, Prince of Wales, acted as regent for his father, George III, who was incapacitated by mental illness.

"He hurled the blacksmith over a parapet."

"Last week he hurled the local blacksmith over a parapet[1] into a stream and it was only by paying over all the money that I could gather together that I was able to avert another public exposure. He had no friends at all save the wandering gypsies, and he would give these vagabonds leave to encamp upon the few acres of bramble-covered land which represent the family estate, and would accept in return the hospitality of their tents, wandering away with them sometimes for weeks on end. He has a passion also for Indian animals, which are sent over to him by a correspondent, and he has at this moment a cheetah and a baboon, which wander freely over his grounds, and are feared by the villagers almost as much as their master.

"You can imagine from what I say that my poor sister Julia and I had no great pleasure in our lives. No servant would stay with us, and for a long time we did all the work of the house. She was but thirty at the time of her death, and yet her hair had already begun to whiten, even as mine has."

"Your sister is dead, then?"

"She died just two years ago, and it is of her death that I wish to speak to you. You can understand that, living the life which I have described, we were little likely to see anyone of our own age and position. We had, however, an aunt, my mother's maiden sister, Miss Honoria Westphail, who lives near Harrow, and we were occasionally allowed to pay short visits at this lady's house. Julia went there at Christmas two years ago, and met there a half-pay Major[2] of Marines, to whom she became engaged. My stepfather learned of the engagement when my sister returned, and offered no objection to the marriage; but within a fortnight of the day which had been fixed for the wedding, the terrible event occurred which has deprived me of my only companion."

Sherlock Holmes had been leaning back in his chair with his eyes closed, and his head sunk in a cushion, but he half opened his lids now, and glanced across at his visitor.

"Pray be precise as to details," said he.

"It is easy for me to be so, for every event of that dreadful time is seared into my memory. The manor house is, as I have already said, very old, and only one wing is now inhabited. The bedrooms in this wing are on the ground floor, the sitting rooms being in the central block of the buildings. Of these bedrooms, the first is Dr. Roylott's, the second my sister's, and the third my own. There is no communication between them, but they all open out into the same corridor. Do I make myself plain?"

"Perfectly so."

"The windows of the three rooms open out upon the lawn. That fatal night Dr. Roylott had gone to his room early, though we knew that he had not retired to rest, for my sister was troubled by the smell of the strong Indian cigars which it was his custom to smoke. She left her room, therefore, and came into mine, where she sat for some time, chatting about her approaching wedding. At eleven o'clock she rose to leave me, but she paused at the door and looked back. 'Tell me, Helen,' said she, 'have you ever heard anyone whistle in the dead of the night?'

"'Never,' said I.

"'I suppose that you could not possibly whistle yourself in your sleep?'

[1] *parapet* Stone embankment.

[2] *half-pay Major* When retired or not in service, officers were paid half their wages.

"'Certainly not. But why?'

"'Because during the last few nights I have always, about three in the morning, heard a low clear whistle. I am a light sleeper, and it has awakened me. I cannot tell where it came from—perhaps from the next room, perhaps from the lawn. I thought that I would just ask you whether you had heard it.'

"'No, I have not. It must be those wretched gypsies in the plantation.'

"'Very likely. And yet if it were on the lawn I wonder that you did not hear it also.'

"'Ah, but I sleep more heavily than you.'

"'Well, it is of no great consequence, at any rate,' she smiled back at me, closed my door, and a few moments later I heard her key turn in the lock."

"Indeed," said Holmes. "Was it your custom always to lock yourselves in at night?"

"Always."

"And why?"

"I think that I mentioned to you that the doctor kept a cheetah and a baboon. We had no feeling of security unless our doors were locked."

"Quite so. Pray proceed with your statement."

"I could not sleep that night. A vague feeling of impending misfortune impressed me. My sister and I, you will recollect, were twins, and you know how subtle are the links which bind two souls which are so closely allied. It was a wild night. The wind was howling outside, and the rain was beating and splashing against the windows. Suddenly, amidst all the hubbub of the gale, there burst forth the wild scream of a terrified woman. I knew that it was my sister's voice. I sprang from my bed, wrapped a shawl round me, and rushed into the corridor. As I opened my door I seemed to hear a low whistle, such as my sister described, and a few moments later a clanging sound, as if a mass of metal had fallen. As I ran down the passage my sister's door was unlocked, and revolved slowly upon its hinges. I stared at it horror-stricken, not knowing what was about to issue from it. By the light of the corridor lamp I saw my sister appear at the opening, her face blanched with terror, her hands groping for help, her whole figure swaying to and fro like that of a drunkard. I ran to her

"Her face blanched with terror."

and threw my arms round her, but at that moment her knees seemed to give way and she fell to the ground. She writhed as one who is in terrible pain, and her limbs were dreadfully convulsed. At first I thought that she had not recognized me, but as I bent over her she suddenly shrieked out in a voice which I shall never forget, 'O, my God! Helen! It was the band! The speckled band!' There was something else which she would fain have said, and she stabbed with her finger into the air in the direction of the doctor's room, but a fresh convulsion seized her and choked her words. I rushed out, calling loudly for my stepfather, and I met him hastening from his room in his dressing gown. When he reached my sister's side she was unconscious, and though he poured brandy down her throat, and sent for medical aid from the village, all efforts were in vain, for she slowly sank and died without having recovered her consciousness. Such was the dreadful end of my beloved sister."

"One moment," said Holmes; "are you sure about this whistle and metallic sound? Could you swear to it?"

"That was what the county coroner asked me at the inquiry. It was my strong impression that I heard it, and yet among the crash of the gale, and the creaking of an old house, I may possibly have been deceived."

"Was your sister dressed?"

"No, she was in her nightdress. In her right hand was found the charred stump of a match, and in her left a matchbox."

"Showing that she had struck a light and looked about her when the alarm took place. That is important. And what conclusions did the coroner come to?"

"He investigated the case with great care, for Dr. Roylott's conduct had long been notorious in the county, but he was unable to find any satisfactory cause of death. My evidence showed that the door had been fastened upon the inner side, and the windows were blocked by old-fashioned shutters with broad iron bars, which were secured every night. The walls were carefully sounded, and were shown to be quite solid all round, and the flooring was also thoroughly examined, with the same result. The chimney is wide, but is barred up by four large staples. It is certain, therefore, that my sister was quite alone when she met her end. Besides, there were no marks of any violence upon her."

"How about poison?"

"The doctors examined her for it, but without success."

"What do you think that this unfortunate lady died of, then?"

"It is my belief that she died of pure fear and nervous shock, though what it was which frightened her I cannot imagine."

"Were there gypsies in the plantation at the time?"

"Yes, there are nearly always some there."

"Ah, and what did you gather from this allusion to a band—a speckled band?"

"Sometimes I have thought that it was merely the wild talk of delirium, sometimes that it may have referred to some band of people, perhaps to these very gypsies in the plantation. I do not know whether the spotted handkerchiefs which so many of them wear over their heads might have suggested the strange adjective which she used."

Holmes shook his head like a man who is far from being satisfied.

"These are very deep waters," said he; "pray go on with your narrative."

"Two years have passed since then, and my life has been until lately lonelier than ever. A month ago, however, a dear friend, whom I have known for many years, has done me the honour to ask my hand in marriage. His name is Armitage—Percy Armitage—the second son of Mr. Armitage, of Crane Water, near Reading. My stepfather has offered no opposition to the match, and we are to be married in the course of the spring. Two days ago some repairs were started in the west wing of the building, and my bedroom wall has been pierced, so that I have had to move into the chamber in which my sister died, and to sleep in the very bed in which she slept. Imagine, then, my thrill of terror when last night, as I lay awake, thinking over her terrible fate, I suddenly heard in the silence of the night the low whistle which had been the herald of her own death. I sprang up and lit the lamp, but nothing was to be seen in the room. I was too shaken to go to bed again, however, so I dressed, and as soon as it was daylight I slipped down, got a dog-cart at the Crown Inn, which is opposite, and drove to Leatherhead, from whence I have come on this morning, with the one object of seeing you and asking your advice."

"You have done wisely," said my friend. "But have you told me all?"

"Yes, all."

"Miss Stoner, you have not. You are screening your stepfather."

"Why, what do you mean?"

For answer Holmes pushed back the frill of black lace which fringed the hand that lay upon our visitor's knee. Five little livid spots, the marks of four fingers and a thumb, were printed upon the white wrist.

"You have been cruelly used," said Holmes.

The lady coloured deeply, and covered over her injured wrist. "He is a hard man," she said, "and perhaps he hardly knows his own strength."

There was a long silence, during which Holmes leaned his chin upon his hands and stared into the crackling fire.

"This is very deep business," he said at last. "There are a thousand details which I should desire to know before I decide upon our course of action. Yet we have not a moment to lose. If we were to come to Stoke Moran today, would it be possible for us to see over these rooms without the knowledge of your stepfather?"

"As it happens, he spoke of coming into town today upon some most important business. It is probable that he will be away all day, and that there would be nothing to disturb you. We have a housekeeper now, but she is old and foolish, and I could easily get her out of the way."

"Excellent. You are not averse to this trip, Watson?"

"By no means."

"Then we shall both come. What are you going to do yourself?"

"I have one or two things which I would wish to do now that I am in town. But I shall return by the twelve o'clock train, so as to be there in time for your coming."

"And you may expect us early in the afternoon. I have myself some small business matters to attend to. Will you not wait and breakfast?"

"No, I must go. My heart is lightened already since I have confided my trouble to you. I shall look forward to seeing you again this afternoon." She dropped her thick black veil over her face, and glided from the room.

"And what do you think of it all, Watson?" asked Sherlock Holmes, leaning back in his chair.

"It seems to me to be a most dark and sinister business."

"Dark enough and sinister enough."

"Yet if the lady is correct in saying that the flooring and walls are sound, and that the door, window, and chimney are impassable, then her sister must have been undoubtedly alone when she met her mysterious end."

"What becomes, then, of these nocturnal whistles, and what of the very peculiar words of the dying woman?"

"I cannot think."

"When you combine the ideas of whistles at night, the presence of a band of gypsies who are on intimate terms with this old doctor, the fact that we have every reason to believe that the doctor has an interest in preventing his stepdaughter's marriage, the dying allusion to a band, and finally, the fact that Miss Helen Stoner heard a metallic clang, which might have been caused by one of those metal bars which secured the shutters falling back into their place, I think there is good ground to think that the mystery may be cleared along these lines."

"But what, then, did the gypsies do?"

"I cannot imagine."

"I see many objections to any such a theory."

"And so do I. It is precisely for that reason that we are going to Stoke Moran this day. I want to see whether the objections are fatal, or if they may be explained away. But what, in the name of the devil!"

The ejaculation had been drawn from my companion by the fact that our door had been suddenly dashed open, and that a huge man framed himself in the aperture. His costume was a peculiar mixture of the professional and of the agricultural, having a black top hat, a long frock-coat, and a pair of high gaiters,[1] with a hunting-crop swinging in his hand. So tall was he that his hat actually brushed the crossbar of the doorway, and his breadth seemed to span it across from side to side. A large face, seared with a thousand wrinkles, burned yellow with the sun, and marked with every evil passion, was turned from one to the other of us, while his deep-set, bile-shot eyes, and the high thin fleshless nose, gave him somewhat the resemblance to a fierce old bird of prey.

"Which of you is Holmes?"

"Which of you is Holmes?" asked this apparition.

[1] *gaiters* Coverings of cloth or leather for the lower legs.

"My name, sir, but you have the advantage of me," said my companion quietly.

"I am Dr. Grimesby Roylott, of Stoke Moran."

"Indeed, Doctor," said Holmes blandly. "Pray take a seat."

"I will do nothing of the kind. My stepdaughter has been here. I have traced her. What has she been saying to you?"

"It is a little cold for the time of the year," said Holmes.

"What has she been saying to you?" screamed the old man furiously.

"But I have heard that the crocuses promise well," continued my companion imperturbably.

"Ha! You put me off, do you?" said our new visitor, taking a step forward, and shaking his hunting crop. "I know you, you scoundrel! I have heard of you before. You are Holmes the meddler."

My friend smiled.

"Holmes the busybody!"

His smile broadened.

"Holmes the Scotland Yard jack-in-office."[1]

Holmes chuckled heartily. "Your conversation is most entertaining," said he. "When you go out close the door, for there is a decided draught."

"I will go when I have had my say. Don't you dare to meddle with my affairs. I know that Miss Stoner has been here—I traced her! I am a dangerous man to fall foul of! See here." He stepped swiftly forward, seized the poker, and bent it into a curve with his huge brown hands.

"See that you keep yourself out of my grip," he snarled, and hurling the twisted poker into the fireplace, he strode out of the room.

"He seems a very amiable person," said Holmes, laughing. "I am not quite so bulky, but if he had remained I might have shown him that my grip was not much more feeble than his own." As he spoke he picked up the steel poker, and with a sudden effort straightened it out again.

"Fancy his having the insolence to confound me with the official detective force! This incident gives zest to our investigation, however, and I only trust that our little friend will not suffer from her imprudence in allowing this brute to trace her. And now, Watson, we shall order breakfast, and afterwards I shall walk down to Doctors' Commons,[2] where I hope to get some data which may help us in this matter."

It was nearly one o'clock when Sherlock Holmes returned from his excursion. He held in his hand a sheet of blue paper, scrawled over with notes and figures.

"I have seen the will of the deceased wife," said he. "To determine its exact meaning I have been obliged to work out the present prices of the investments with which it is concerned. The total income, which at the time of the wife's death was little short of £1,100, is now through the fall in agricultural prices not more than £750. Each daughter can claim an income of £250, in case of marriage. It is evident, therefore, that if both girls had married this beauty would have had a mere pittance, while even one of them would cripple him to a serious extent. My morning's work has not been wasted, since it has proved that he has the very strongest motives for standing in the way of anything of the sort. And now, Watson, this is too serious for dawdling, especially as the old man is aware that we are interesting ourselves in his affairs, so if you are ready we shall call a cab and drive to Waterloo. I should be very much obliged if you would slip your revolver into your pocket. An Eley's No. 2[3] is an excellent argument with gentlemen who can twist steel pokers into knots. That and a toothbrush are, I think, all that we need."

At Waterloo we were fortunate in catching a train for Leatherhead, where we hired a trap[4] at the station inn, and drove for four or five miles through the lovely Surrey lanes. It was a perfect day, with a bright sun and a few fleecy clouds in the heavens. The trees and wayside hedges were just throwing out their first green shoots, and the air was full of the pleasant smell of the moist

[1] *jack-in-office* Insolent minor official.

[2] *Doctors' Commons* Buildings that housed the association of Doctors of Civil Law in London.

[3] *Eley's No. 2* Conan Doyle is likely referring to a small but powerful pistol called a "Webley No. 2," which could be loaded with cartridges made by the ammunition manufacturer Eley.

[4] *trap* Small, two-wheeled carriage.

earth. To me at least there was a strange contrast between the sweet promise of the spring and this sinister quest upon which we were engaged. My companion sat in front of the trap, his arms folded, his hat pulled down over his eyes, and his chin sunk upon his breast, buried in the deepest thought.

Suddenly, however, he started, tapped me on the shoulder, and pointed over the meadows.

"Look there!" said he.

A heavily timbered park stretched up in a gentle slope, thickening into a grove at the highest point. From amidst the branches there jutted out the grey gables and high roof-tree[1] of a very old mansion.

"Stoke Moran?" said he.

"Yes, sir, that be the house of Dr. Grimesby Roylott," remarked the driver.

"There is some building going on there," said Holmes; "that is where we are going."

"There's the village," said the driver, pointing to a cluster of roofs some distance to the left; "but if you want to get to the house, you'll find it shorter to go over this stile,[2] and so by the footpath over the fields. There it is, where the lady is walking."

"And the lady, I fancy, is Miss Stoner," observed Holmes, shading his eyes. "Yes, I think we had better do as you suggest."

"We got off, paid our fare."

We got off, paid our fare, and the trap rattled back on its way to Leatherhead.

"I thought it as well," said Holmes, as we climbed the stile, "that this fellow should think we had come here as architects, or on some definite business. It may stop his gossip. Good afternoon, Miss Stoner. You see that we have been as good as our word."

Our client of the morning had hurried forward to meet us with a face which spoke her joy. "I have been waiting so eagerly for you," she cried, shaking hands with us warmly. "All has turned out splendidly. Dr. Roylott has gone to town, and it is unlikely that he will be back before evening."

"We have had the pleasure of making the doctor's acquaintance," said Holmes, and in a few words he sketched out what had occurred. Miss Stoner turned white to the lips as she listened.

"Good heavens!" she cried, "he has followed me, then."

"So it appears."

"He is so cunning that I never know when I am safe from him. What will he say when he returns?"

"He must guard himself, for he may find that there is someone more cunning than himself upon his track. You must lock yourself from him tonight. If he is violent, we shall take you away to your aunt's at Harrow. Now, we must make the best use of our time, so kindly take us at once to the rooms which we are to examine."

The building was of grey, lichen-blotched stone, with a high central portion, and two curving wings, like the claws of a crab, thrown out on each side. In one of these wings the windows were broken and blocked with wooden boards, while the roof was partly caved in, a picture of ruin. The central portion was in little better repair, but the right-hand block was comparatively modern, and the blinds in the windows, with the blue smoke curling up from the chimneys, showed that this was where the family resided. Some scaffolding had been erected against the end wall, and the stonework had been broken into, but there were no signs of any workmen at the moment of our visit. Holmes walked slowly

[1] *roof-tree* Ridge pole.

[2] *stile* Set of steps passing over a fence.

up and down the ill-trimmed lawn, and examined with deep attention the outsides of the windows.

"This, I take it, belongs to the room in which you used to sleep, the centre one to your sister's, and the one next to the main building to Dr. Roylott's chamber?"

"Exactly so. But I am now sleeping in the middle one."

"Pending the alterations, as I understand. By the way, there does not seem to be any very pressing need for repairs at that end wall."

"There were none. I believe that it was an excuse to move me from my room."

"Ah! that is suggestive. Now, on the other side of this narrow wing runs the corridor from which these three rooms open. There are windows in it, of course?"

"Yes, but very small ones. Too narrow for anyone to pass through."

"As you both locked your doors at night, your rooms were unapproachable from that side. Now, would you have the kindness to go into your room, and to bar your shutters."

Miss Stoner did so, and Holmes, after a careful examination through the open window, endeavoured in every way to force the shutter open, but without success. There was no slit through which a knife could be passed to raise the bar. Then with his lens[1] he tested the hinges, but they were of solid iron, built firmly into the massive masonry. "Hum!" said he, scratching his chin in some perplexity, "my theory certainly presents some difficulties. No one could pass these shutters if they were bolted. Well, we shall see if the inside throws any light upon the matter."

A small side door led into the white-washed corridor from which the three bedrooms opened. Holmes refused to examine the third chamber, so we passed at once to the second, that in which Miss Stoner was now sleeping, and in which her sister had met her fate. It was a homely[2] little room, with a low ceiling and a gaping fireplace, after the fashion of old country houses. A brown chest of drawers stood in one corner, a narrow white-counterpaned bed in another, and a dressing-table on the left-hand side of the window. These articles, with two small wicker-work chairs, made up all the furniture in the room, save for a square of Wilton carpet[3] in the centre. The boards round and the panelling of the walls were brown, worm-eaten oak, so old and discoloured that it may have dated from the original building of the house. Holmes drew one of the chairs into a corner and sat silent, while his eyes travelled round and round and up and down, taking in every detail of the apartment.

"Where does that bell communicate with?" he asked at last, pointing to a thick bell-rope which hung down beside the bed, the tassel actually lying upon the pillow.

"It goes to the housekeeper's room."

"It looks newer than the other things?"

"Yes, it was only put there a couple of years ago."

"Your sister asked for it, I suppose?"

"No, I never heard of her using it. We used always to get what we wanted for ourselves."

"Indeed, it seemed unnecessary to put so nice a bell-pull there. You will excuse me for a few minutes while I satisfy myself as to this floor." He threw himself down upon his face with his lens in his hand, and crawled swiftly backwards and forwards, examining minutely the cracks between the boards. Then he did the same with the woodwork with which the chamber was panelled. Finally he walked over to the bed and spent some time in staring at it, and in running his eye up and down the wall. Finally he took the bell-rope in his hand and gave it a brisk tug.

"Why, it's a dummy," said he.

"Won't it ring?"

"No, it is not even attached to a wire. This is very interesting. You can see now that it is fastened to a hook just above where the little opening of the ventilator is."

"How very absurd! I never noticed that before."

"Very strange!" muttered Holmes, pulling at the rope. "There are one or two very singular points about this room. For example, what a fool a builder must be to open a ventilator in another room, when, with the same trouble, he might have communicated with the outside air!"

"That is also quite modern," said the lady.

[1] *lens* Magnifying glass.

[2] *homely* Simple, unsophisticated.

[3] *Wilton carpet* Brand of carpet made in Wilton, England.

"Done about the same time as the bell-rope," remarked Holmes.

"Yes, there were several little changes carried out about that time."

"They seem to have been of a most interesting character—dummy bell-ropes, and ventilators which do not ventilate. With your permission, Miss Stoner, we shall now carry our researches into the inner apartment."

Dr. Grimesby Roylott's chamber was larger than that of his stepdaughter, but was as plainly furnished. A camp bed, a small wooden shelf full of books, mostly of a technical character, an armchair beside the bed, a plain wooden chair against the wall, a round table, and a large iron safe were the principal things which met the eye. Holmes walked slowly round and examined each and all of them with the keenest interest.

"What's in here?" he asked, tapping the safe.

"My stepfather's business papers."

"Oh! you have seen inside, then?"

"Only once, some years ago. I remember that it was full of papers."

"There isn't a cat in it, for example?"

"No. What a strange idea!"

"Well, look at this!" He took up a small saucer of milk which stood on the top of it.

"Well, look at this."

"No; we don't keep a cat. But there is a cheetah and a baboon."

"Ah, yes, of course! Well, a cheetah is just a big cat, and yet a saucer of milk does not go very far in satisfying its wants, I daresay. There is one point which I should wish to determine." He squatted down in front of the wooden chair, and examined the seat of it with the greatest attention.

"Thank you. That is quite settled," said he, rising and putting his lens in his pocket. "Hullo! Here is something interesting!"

The object which had caught his eye was a small dog lash hung on one corner of the bed. The lash, however, was curled upon itself, and tied so as to make a loop of whipcord.

"What do you make of that, Watson?"

"It's a common enough lash. But I don't know why it should be tied."

"That is not quite so common, is it? Ah, me! It's a wicked world, and when a clever man turns his brain to crime it is the worst of all. I think that I have seen enough now, Miss Stoner, and, with your permission, we shall walk out upon the lawn."

I had never seen my friend's face so grim, or his brow so dark, as it was when we turned from the scene of this investigation. We had walked several times up and down the lawn, neither Miss Stoner nor myself liking to break in upon his thoughts before he roused himself from his reverie. "It is very essential, Miss Stoner," said he, "that you should absolutely follow my advice in every respect."

"I shall most certainly do so."

"The matter is too serious for any hesitation. Your life may depend upon your compliance."

"I assure you that I am in your hands."

"In the first place, both my friend and I must spend the night in your room."

Both Miss Stoner and I gazed at him in astonishment.

"Yes, it must be so. Let me explain. I believe that that is the village inn over there?"

"Yes, that is the Crown."

"Very good. Your windows would be visible from there?"

"Certainly."

"You must confine yourself to your room, on pretence of a headache, when your stepfather comes back. Then when you hear him retire for the night, you must open the shutters of your window, undo the hasp, put your lamp there as a signal to us, and then withdraw with everything which you are likely to want into the room which you used to occupy. I have no doubt that, in spite of the repairs, you could manage there for one night."

"Oh, yes, easily."

"The rest you will leave in our hands."

"But what will you do?"

"We shall spend the night in your room, and we shall investigate the cause of this noise which has disturbed you."

"I believe, Mr. Holmes, that you have already made up your mind," said Miss Stoner, laying her hand upon my companion's sleeve.

"Perhaps I have."

"Then for pity's sake tell me what was the cause of my sister's death."

"I should prefer to have clearer proofs before I speak."

"You can at least tell me whether my own thought is correct, and if she died from some sudden fright."

"No, I do not think so. I think that there was probably some more tangible cause. And now, Miss Stoner, we must leave you, for if Dr. Roylott returned and saw us, our journey would be in vain. Goodbye, and be brave, for if you will do what I have told you, you may rest assured that we shall soon drive away the dangers that threaten you."

Sherlock Holmes and I had no difficulty in engaging a bedroom and sitting room at the Crown Inn. They were on the upper floor, and from our window we could command a view of the avenue gate, and of the inhabited wing of Stoke Moran Manor House. At dusk we saw Dr. Grimesby Roylott drive past, his huge form looming up beside the little figure of the lad who drove him. The boy had some slight difficulty in undoing the heavy iron gates, and we heard the hoarse roar of the doctor's voice, and saw the fury with which he shook his clenched fists at him. The trap drove on, and a few minutes later we saw a sudden light spring up among

"Good-bye, and be brave."

the trees as the lamp was lit in one of the sitting rooms.

"Do you know, Watson," said Holmes, as we sat together in the gathering darkness, "I have really some scruples as to taking you tonight. There is a distinct element of danger."

"Can I be of assistance?"

"Your presence might be invaluable."

"Then I shall certainly come."

"It is very kind of you."

"You speak of danger. You have evidently seen more in these rooms than was visible to me."

"No, but I fancy that I may have deduced a little more. I imagine that you saw all that I did."

"I saw nothing remarkable save the bell-rope, and what purpose that could answer I confess is more than I can imagine."

"You saw the ventilator, too?"

"Yes, but I do not think that it is such a very unusual thing to have a small opening between two rooms. It was so small that a rat could hardly pass through."

"I knew that we should find a ventilator before ever we came to Stoke Moran."

"My dear Holmes!"

"Oh, yes, I did. You remember in her statement she said that her sister could smell Dr. Roylott's cigar. Now, of course that suggests at once that there must be a communication between the two rooms. It could only be a small one, or it would have been remarked upon at the coroner's inquiry. I deduced a ventilator."

"But what harm can there be in that?"

"Well, there is at least a curious coincidence of dates. A ventilator is made, a cord is hung, and a lady who sleeps in the bed dies. Does not that strike you?"

"I cannot as yet see any connection."

"Did you observe anything very peculiar about that bed?"

"No."

"It was clamped to the floor. Did you ever see a bed fastened like that before?"

"I cannot say that I have."

"The lady could not move her bed. It must always be in the same relative position to the ventilator and to the rope—for so we may call it, since it was clearly never meant for a bell-pull."

"Holmes," I cried, "I seem to see dimly what you are hitting at. We are only just in time to prevent some subtle and horrible crime."

"Subtle enough and horrible enough. When a doctor does go wrong he is the first of criminals. He has nerve and he has knowledge. Palmer and Pritchard[1] were among the heads of their profession. This man strikes even deeper, but I think, Watson, that we shall be able to strike deeper still. But we shall have horrors enough before the night is over; for goodness' sake let us have a quiet pipe, and turn our minds for a few hours to something more cheerful."

About nine o'clock the light among the trees was extinguished, and all was dark in the direction of the Manor House. Two hours passed slowly away, and then, suddenly, just at the stroke of eleven, a single bright light shone out right in front of us.

"That is our signal," said Holmes, springing to his feet; "it comes from the middle window."

As we passed out he exchanged a few words with the landlord, explaining that we were going on a late visit to an acquaintance, and that it was possible that we might spend the night there. A moment later we were out on the dark road, a chill wind blowing in our faces, and one yellow light twinkling in front of us through the gloom to guide us on our sombre errand. There was little difficulty in entering the grounds, for unrepaired breaches gaped in the old park wall. Making our way among the trees, we reached the lawn, crossed it, and were about to enter through the window, when out from a clump of laurel bushes there darted what seemed to be a hideous and distorted child, who threw itself on the grass with writhing limbs, and then ran swiftly across the lawn into the darkness.

"My God!" I whispered, "did you see it?"

Holmes was for the moment as startled as I. His hand closed like a vice upon my wrist in his agitation. Then he broke into a low laugh, and put his lips to my ear.

"It is a nice household," he murmured, "that is the baboon."

I had forgotten the strange pets which the doctor affected. There was a cheetah, too; perhaps we might find it upon our shoulders at any moment. I confess that I felt easier in my mind when, after following Holmes's example and slipping off my shoes, I found myself inside the bedroom. My companion noiselessly closed the shutters, moved the lamp on to the table, and cast his eyes round the room. All was as we had seen it in the daytime. Then creeping up to me and making a trumpet of his hand, he whispered into my ear again so gently that it was all that I could do to distinguish the words:

"The least sound would be fatal to our plans."

I nodded to show that I had heard.

"We must sit without a light. He would see it through the ventilator."

I nodded again.

[1] *Palmer and Pritchard* Both men were doctors who, in unrelated cases, were executed in the mid-1800s for murdering people using poison.

"Do not go to sleep; your very life may depend upon it. Have your pistol ready in case we should need it. I will sit on the side of the bed, and you in that chair."

I took out my revolver and laid it on the corner of the table. Holmes had brought up a long thin cane, and this he placed upon the bed beside him. By it he laid the box of matches and the stump of a candle. Then he turned down the lamp and we were left in darkness.

How shall I ever forget that dreadful vigil? I could not hear a sound, not even the drawing of a breath, and yet I knew that my companion sat open-eyed, within a few feet of me, in the same state of nervous tension in which I was myself. The shutters cut off the least ray of light, and we waited in absolute darkness. From outside came the occasional cry of a night bird, and once at our very window a long drawn, cat-like whine, which told us that the cheetah was indeed at liberty. Far away we could hear the deep tones of the parish clock, which boomed out every quarter of an hour. How long they seemed, those quarters! Twelve o'clock, and one, and two, and three, and still we sat waiting silently for whatever might befall.

Suddenly there was the momentary gleam of a light up in the direction of the ventilator, which vanished immediately, but was succeeded by a strong smell of burning oil and heated metal. Someone in the next room had lit a dark lantern.[1] I heard a gentle sound of movement, and then all was silent once more, though the smell grew stronger. For half an hour I sat with straining ears. Then suddenly another sound became audible—a very gentle, soothing sound, like that of a small jet of steam escaping continually from a kettle. The instant that we heard it, Holmes sprang from the bed, struck a match, and lashed furiously with his cane at the bell-pull.

"You see it, Watson?" he yelled. "You see it?"

But I saw nothing. At the moment when Holmes struck the light I heard a low, clear whistle, but the sudden glare flashing into my weary eyes made it impossible for me to tell what it was at which my friend lashed so savagely. I could, however, see that his face was deadly pale, and filled with horror and loathing.

"Holmes lashed furiously."

He had ceased to strike, and was gazing up at the ventilator, when suddenly there broke from the silence of the night the most horrible cry to which I have ever listened. It swelled up louder and louder, a hoarse yell of pain and fear and anger all mingled in the one dreadful shriek. They say that away down in the village, and even in the distant parsonage, that cry raised the sleepers from their beds. It struck cold to our hearts, and I stood gazing at Holmes, and he at me, until the last echoes of it had died away into the silence from which it rose.

"What can it mean?" I gasped.

"It means that it is all over," Holmes answered. "And perhaps, after all, it is for the best. Take your pistol, and we shall enter Dr. Roylott's room."

With a grave face he lit the lamp, and led the way down the corridor. Twice he struck at the chamber door without any reply from within. Then he turned the handle and entered, I at his heels, with the cocked pistol in my hand.

[1] *dark lantern* Lantern with a slide so that its light can be hidden.

It was a singular sight which met our eyes. On the table stood a dark lantern with the shutter half open, throwing a brilliant beam of light upon the iron safe, the door of which was ajar. Beside this table, on the wooden chair, sat Dr. Grimesby Roylott, clad in a long grey dressing gown, his bare ankles protruding beneath, and his feet thrust into red heelless Turkish slippers. Across his lap lay the short stock with the long lash which we had noticed during the day. His chin was cocked upwards, and his eyes were fixed in a dreadful rigid stare at the corner of the ceiling. Round his brow he had a peculiar yellow band, with brownish speckles, which seemed to be bound tightly round his head. As we entered he made neither sound nor motion.

"He made neither sound nor motion."

"The band! The speckled band!" whispered Holmes.

I took a step forward. In an instant his strange headgear began to move, and there reared itself from among his hair the squat diamond-shaped head and puffed neck of a loathsome serpent.

"It is a swamp adder!" cried Holmes—"the deadliest snake in India. He has died within ten seconds of being bitten. Violence does, in truth, recoil upon the violent, and the schemer falls into the pit which he digs for another. Let us thrust this creature back into its den, and we can then remove Miss Stoner to some place of shelter, and let the county police know what has happened."

As he spoke he drew the dog whip swiftly from the dead man's lap, and throwing the noose round the reptile's neck, he drew it from its horrid perch, and, carrying it at arm's length, threw it into the iron safe, which he closed upon it.

Such are the true facts of the death of Dr. Grimesby Roylott, of Stoke Moran. It is not necessary that I should prolong a narrative which has already run to too great a length, by telling how we broke the sad news to the terrified girl, how we conveyed her by the morning train to the care of her good aunt at Harrow, of how the slow process of official inquiry came to the conclusion that the doctor met his fate while indiscreetly playing with a dangerous pet. The little which I had yet to learn of the case was told me by Sherlock Holmes as we travelled back next day.

"I had," said he, "come to an entirely erroneous conclusion, which shows, my dear Watson, how dangerous it always is to reason from insufficient data. The presence of the gypsies, and the use of the word 'band,' which was used by the poor girl, no doubt, to explain the appearance which she had caught a horrid glimpse of by the light of her match, were sufficient to put me upon an entirely wrong scent. I can only claim the merit that I instantly reconsidered my position when, however, it became clear to me that whatever danger threatened an occupant of the room could not come either from the window or the door. My attention was speedily drawn, as I have already remarked to you, to this ventilator, and to the bell-rope which hung down to the bed. The discovery that this was a dummy, and that the bed was clamped to the floor, instantly gave rise to the suspicion that the rope was there as a bridge for something passing through the hole, and coming to the bed. The idea of a snake instantly occurred to me, and when I coupled it with my knowledge that the doctor was furnished with a supply of creatures from India, I felt that I was probably on the right track. The idea of using a form of poison which could not possibly be discovered by any chemical test was just such a one as would occur to a clever and ruthless man who had had an Eastern training. The rapidity with which such a poison would take effect would also, from his point of view, be an advantage. It would be a sharp-eyed coroner indeed who could distinguish the two little dark punctures which would show where the poison fangs had done their work. Then I thought of the whistle. Of course, he must recall the snake before the morning light revealed it to the victim. He had trained it, probably by the use of the milk which we saw, to return to him when summoned. He would put it through the ventilator at the hour that he thought best, with the certainty that it would crawl down the rope, and land on the bed. It might or might not bite the occupant, perhaps she might escape every night for a week, but sooner or later she must fall a victim.

"I had come to these conclusions before ever I had entered his room. An inspection of his chair showed me that he had been in the habit of standing on it, which, of course, would be necessary in order that he should reach the ventilator. The sight of the safe, the saucer of milk, and the loop of whipcord were enough to finally dispel any doubts which may have remained. The metallic clang heard by Miss Stoner was obviously caused by her father hastily closing the door of his safe upon its terrible occupant. Having once made up my mind, you know the steps which I took in order to put the matter to the proof. I heard the creature hiss, as I have no doubt that you did also, and I instantly lit the light and attacked it."

"With the result of driving it through the ventilator."

"And also with the result of causing it to turn upon its master at the other side. Some of the blows of my cane came home, and roused its snakish temper, so that it flew upon the first person it saw. In this way I am no doubt indirectly responsible for Dr. Grimesby Roylott's death, and I cannot say that it is likely to weigh very heavily upon my conscience."

—1892

Amy Levy

1861 – 1889

As a novelist, short-fiction writer, essayist, and poet of the late Victorian era, Amy Levy is recognized for her work's emotional depth, its anticipation of Modernism through formal innovation and deployment of irony, its courageous "New Woman" politics of female independence, and its complex literary engagement with her own Anglo-Jewish culture. The extent of her contribution to English literature is especially striking given that she died before reaching 30. Her poetry, emotionally evocative as well as forthright in its feminist views, is also of interest to present-day critics for its evocation of eroticism between women. Her novels—one a "New Woman" novel, one an uncompromising examination of Anglo-Jewish society, and one a governess novel—have in common a realist engagement with feminist themes.

Levy, the daughter of Isabelle Levin and Lewis Levy, a stockbroker, grew up in a large, Anglo-Jewish, middle-class household in London. Intelligent and well educated, she began writing poetry at an early age, publishing her first work, "Ida Grey: A Story of Woman's Sacrifice," in a feminist journal at the age of thirteen. Contributions of poems, essays, and stories to many other journals followed, among them *The Cambridge Review*, *The Jewish Chronicle* and the *Pall Mall Gazette*. In 1879 Levy became the first Jewish woman to attend Cambridge University, where she studied at Newnham College.

In 1881 Levy left the university without taking her exams, having published her first book of poetry, *Xantippe, and Other Verse*. The title poem is a defense of the wife of Socrates, who was much maligned for her outspokenness and intelligence. The volume, which quickly sold out, was followed by two more books of poems, many of the lyrics of which concentrated on melancholic and depressive themes; *A Minor Poet and Other Poems* appeared in 1884, and *A London Plane-Tree and Other Verse* was published posthumously in 1889. This last collection in particular offers an early example of the symbolist movement in English poetry, in some respects anticipating the development of poetic Modernism. Levy's first novel was *The Romance of a Shop* (1888), in which she writes of the determination of a family of orphaned sisters to support themselves by opening a photographic studio. The short novel vividly portrays the challenges facing independent, working, "new women" and the relatively uncharted territory they face when attempting to integrate the demands of self-employment and of romantic relationships.

In an 1886 article in *The Jewish Chronicle*, Levy criticized literary depictions of Jewish characters, saying that no one had as yet portrayed Jews with all their "surprising virtues and no less surprising vices." From this idea was born her most influential work, which was, ironically, criticized by *The Jewish Chronicle* and members of the Jewish community as anti-Semitic in its engagement with Jewish stereotypes. The novel *Reuben Sachs* (1888) proved to be very popular, notwithstanding its portrayal of, as one reviewer called it, "the less than refined aspects of Jewish society." Oscar Wilde praised the novel, saying, "Its directness, its uncompromising truths, its depth of feeling, and above all, its absence of any single superfluous word, make it, in some sort, a classic. Like all her best work it is sad, but the sadness is by no means morbid. The strong undertone of moral earnestness, never preached, gives a stability and force to the vivid portraiture, and prevents the satiric touches from degenerating into mere malice. Truly, the book is an achievement." Levy followed *Reuben Sachs* with a third novel, *Miss Meredith* (1889), a governess novel displaying the influence of Charlotte Brontë. This work is often dismissed as a blatant attempt to cater to a popular market, though some have seen an ironic sophistication in Levy's employment of genre clichés.

Levy moved in literary and artistic circles, counting among her friends Olive Schreiner (author of *The Story of an African Farm*), Beatrix Potter (author and political activist), Eleanor Marx (daughter of Karl Marx and later a translator of Levy's poetry into German), and Vernon Lee (the *nom de plume* of author Violet Paget), for whom she was said to harbor a deep unrequited passion. She wrote a number of short essays, largely on literary matters (such as recent American fiction, and the poet James Thomson) or on Jewish issues, often seeking to explain to a gentile readership such topics as Jewish humor or contemporary middle-class Jewish women. Levy's writings often betray her self-conscious status as an outsider, and they reveal a fascination with others who felt themselves to be outsiders, whether by race or gender.

Levy suffered intense periods of depression that she called "the great-devil that lyeth ever in wait in the recesses of my heart." There is speculation that the press's negative reaction to *Reuben Sachs*, combined with health problems, contributed to her suicide at the age of 27. But the many difficulties experienced by a Jewish woman of her era attracted to other women and living an independent literary life may well also have been factors. Her marginal status certainly contributed to critical neglect of her work throughout much of the twentieth century, such that she was practically unknown when the 1993 publication of her *Complete Novels and Selected Writings* helped to rescue her work from obscurity. Her importance as a contributor to New Woman literature and to Anglo-Jewish literature, and as a forerunner of Modernism, has since come to be appreciated.

⌘⌘⌘

Xantippe[1] *(A Fragment)*

What, have I waked again? I never thought
To see the rosy dawn, or ev'n this grey,
Dull, solemn stillness, ere the dawn has come.
The lamp burns low; low burns the lamp of life:
The still morn stays expectant, and my soul,
All weighted with a passive wonderment,
Waiteth and watcheth, waiteth for the dawn.
Come hither, maids; too soundly have ye slept
That should have watched me; nay, I would not chide—
Oft have I chidden, yet I would not chide
In this last hour—now all should be at peace.
I have been dreaming in a troubled sleep
Of weary days I thought not to recall;
Of stormy days, whose storms are hushed long since;
Of gladsome days, of sunny days; alas!
In dreaming, all their sunshine seemed so sad,
As though the current of the dark To-Be
Had flowed, prophetic, through the happy hours.
And yet, full well, I know it was not thus;
I mind me sweetly of the summer days,
When, leaning from the lattice, I have caught
The fair, far glimpses of a shining sea:
And nearer, of tall ships which thronged the bay,
And stood out blackly from a tender sky

[1] *Xantippe* Wife of Socrates, ancient Greek philosopher (469–399 BCE) who devoted his life to the study and teaching of ethics and moral behavior; Socrates was later executed for corrupting the youth and interfering with the religion of Athens. Xantippe was criticized for being headstrong.

All flecked with sulphur, azure, and bright gold;
And in the still, clear air have heard the hum
Of distant voices; and methinks there rose
No darker fount° to mar or stain the joy *fountain*
Which sprang ecstatic in my maiden breast
Than just those vague desires, those hopes and fears,
Those eager longings, strong, though undefined,
Whose very sadness makes them seem so sweet.
What cared I for the merry mockeries
Of other maidens sitting at the loom?
Or for sharp voices, bidding me return
To maiden labour? Were we not apart—
I and my high thoughts, and my golden dreams,
My soul which yearned for knowledge, for a tongue
That should proclaim the stately mysteries
Of this fair world, and of the holy gods?
Then followed days of sadness, as I grew
To learn my woman-mind had gone astray,
And I was sinning in those very thoughts—
For maidens, mark, such are not woman's thoughts—
(And yet, 'tis strange, the gods who fashion us
Have given us such promptings). …
                                        Fled the years,
Till seventeen had found me tall and strong,
And fairer, runs it, than Athenian maids
Are wont to seem; I had not learnt it well—
My lesson of dumb patience—and I stood
At Life's great threshold with a beating heart,
And soul resolved to conquer and attain. …
Once, walking 'thwart° the crowded marketplace, *across*
With other maidens, bearing in the twigs,
White doves for Aphrodite's sacrifice,[1]
I saw him, all ungainly and uncouth,
Yet many gathered round to hear his words,
Tall youths and stranger-maidens—Sokrates—
I saw his face and marked it, half with awe,
Half with a quick repulsion at the shape. …
The richest gem lies hidden furthest down,
And is the dearer for the weary search;
We grasp the shining shells which strew the shore,
Yet swift we fling them from us; but the gem
We keep for aye° and cherish. So a soul, *forever*
Found after weary searching in the flesh
Which half repelled our senses, is more dear,
For that same seeking, than the sunny mind
Which lavish Nature marks with thousand hints
Upon a brow of beauty. We are prone
To overweigh such subtle hints, then deem,
In after disappointment, we are fooled. …
And when, at length, my father told me all,
That I should wed me with great Sokrates,
I, foolish, wept to see at once cast down
The maiden image of a future love,
Where perfect body matched the perfect soul.
But slowly, softly did I cease to weep;
Slowly I 'gan to mark the magic flash
Leap to the eyes, to watch the sudden smile
Break round the mouth, and linger in the eyes;
To listen for the voice's lightest tone—
Great voice, whose cunning modulations seemed
like to the notes of some sweet instrument.
So did I reach and strain, until at last
I caught the soul athwart the grosser flesh.
Again of thee, sweet Hope, my spirit dreamed!
I, guided by his wisdom and his love,
Led by his words, and counselled by his care,
Should lift the shrouding veil from things which be,
And at the flowing fountain of his soul
Refresh my thirsting spirit. …
                                        And indeed,
In those long days which followed that strange day
When rites and song, and sacrifice and flow'rs,
Proclaimed that we were wedded, did I learn,
In sooth,° a-many lessons; bitter ones *truth*
Which sorrow taught me, and not love inspired,
Which deeper knowledge of my kind impressed
With dark insistence on reluctant brain—
But that great wisdom, deeper, which dispels
Narrowed conclusions of a half-grown mind,
And sees athwart the littleness of life
Nature's divineness and her harmony,
Was never poor Xantippe's. …
                                        I would pause

[1] *White doves … sacrifice* Aphrodite is the Greek goddess of love; white doves, Aphrodite's favorite birds, were sacrificed during her festival.

And would recall no more, no more of life,
Than just the incomplete, imperfect dream
Of early summers, with their light and shade,
Their blossom-hopes, whose fruit was never ripe;
But something strong within me, some sad chord
Which loudly echoes to the later life,
Me to unfold the after-misery
Urges, with plaintive wailing in my heart.
Yet, maidens, mark; I would not that ye thought
I blame my lord departed, for he meant
No evil, so I take it, to his wife.
'Twas only that the high philosopher,
Pregnant with noble theories and great thoughts,
Deigned not to stoop to touch so slight a thing
As the fine fabric of a woman's brain—
So subtle as a passionate woman's soul.
I think, if he had stooped a little, and cared,
I might have risen nearer to his height,
And not lain shattered, neither fit for use
As goodly household vessel, nor for that
Far finer thing which I had hoped to be. …
Death, holding high his retrospective lamp,
Shows me those first, far years of wedded life,
Ere I had learnt to grasp the barren shape
Of what the Fates[1] had destined for my life.
Then, as all youthful spirits are, was I
Wholly incredulous that Nature meant
So little, who had promised me so much.
At first I fought my fate with gentle words,
With high endeavours after greater things;
Striving to win the soul of Sokrates,
Like some slight bird, who sings her burning love
To human master, till at length she finds
Her tender language wholly misconceived,
And that same hand whose kind caress she sought,
With fingers flippant flings the careless corn. …
I do remember how, one summer's eve,
He, seated in an arbour's leafy shade,
Had bade me bring fresh wine-skins. …
As I stood
Ling'ring upon the threshold, half concealed
By tender foliage, and my spirit light
With draughts of sunny weather, did I mark
An instant the gay group before mine eyes.
Deepest in shade, and facing where I stood,
Sat Plato,[2] with his calm face and low brows
Which met above the narrow Grecian eyes,
The pale, thin lips just parted to the smile,
Which dimpled that smooth olive of his cheek.
His head a little bent, sat Sokrates,
With one swart° finger raised admonishing, *dark-skinned*
And on the air were borne his changing tones.
Low lounging at his feet, one fair arm thrown
Around his knee (the other, high in air
Brandished a brazen amphor,° which yet rained *wine vessel*
Bright drops of ruby on the golden locks
And temples with their fillets of the vine),
Lay Alkibiades the beautiful.[3]
And thus, with solemn tone, spake Sokrates:
"This fair Aspasia, which our Perikles
Hath brought from realms afar, and set on high[4]
In our Athenian city, hath a mind,
I doubt not, of a strength beyond her race;
And makes employ of it, beyond the way
Of women nobly gifted: woman's frail—
Her body rarely stands the test of soul;
She grows intoxicate with knowledge; throws
The laws of custom, order, 'neath her feet,
Feasting at life's great banquet with wide throat."
Then sudden, stepping from my leafy screen,
Holding the swelling wine-skin o'er my head,
With breast that heaved, and eyes and cheeks aflame,
Lit by a fury and a thought, I spake:
"By all great powers around us! can it be
That we poor women are empirical?[5]

[1] *Fates* Three Greek goddesses of destiny.

[2] *Plato* Greek philosopher and student of Socrates (427–347 BCE).

[3] *Alkibiades the beautiful* The political leader Alcibiades (c. 450–404 BCE) was once a student of Socrates; his outstanding beauty was said to contrast with that of Socrates.

[4] *Aspasia … set on high* Pericles, a political figure in ancient Athens, divorced his wife and married his lover, Aspasia, a woman of great education and intellect, who influenced the work of many philosophers, including Socrates, Plato, and Cicero.

[5] *That we … empirical* I.e., that we rely on experience rather than theory.

That gods who fashioned us did strive to make
Beings too fine, too subtly delicate,
With sense that thrilled response to ev'ry touch
Of nature's, and their task is not complete?
That they have sent their half-completed work
To bleed and quiver here upon the earth?
To bleed and quiver, and to weep and weep,
To beat its soul against the marble walls
Of men's cold hearts, and then at last to sin!"
I ceased, the first hot passion stayed and stemmed
And frighted by the silence: I could see,
Framed by the arbour foliage, which the sun
In setting softly gilded with rich gold,
Those upturned faces, and those placid limbs;
Saw Plato's narrow eyes and niggard° mouth, *stingy*
Which half did smile and half did criticise,
One hand held up, the shapely fingers framed
To gesture of entreaty—"Hush, I pray,
Do not disturb her; let us hear the rest;
Follow her mood, for here's another phase
Of your black-browed Xantippe. …"
Then I saw
Young Alkibiades, with laughing lips
And half-shut eyes, contemptuous shrugging up
Soft, snowy shoulders, till he brought the gold
Of flowing ringlets round about his breasts.
But Sokrates, all slow and solemnly,
Raised, calm, his face to mine, and sudden spake:
"I thank thee for the wisdom which thy lips
Have thus let fall among us: prithee[1] tell
From what high source, from what philosophies
Didst cull the sapient° notion of thy words?" *astute*
Then stood I straight and silent for a breath,
Dumb, crushed with all that weight of cold contempt;
But swiftly in my bosom there uprose
A sudden flame, a merciful fury sent
To save me; with both angry hands I flung
The skin upon the marble, where it lay
Spouting red rills° and fountains on the white; *rivulets*
Then, all unheeding faces, voices, eyes,
I fled across the threshold, hair unbound—
White garment stained to redness—beating heart
Flooded with all the flowing tide of hopes
Which once had gushed out golden, now sent back
Swift to their sources, never more to rise. …
I think I could have borne the weary life,
The narrow life within the narrow walls,
If he had loved me; but he kept his love
For this Athenian city and her sons;
And, haply, for some stranger-woman, bold
With freedom, thought, and glib philosophy. …
Ah me! the long, long weeping through the nights,
The weary watching for the pale-eyed dawn
Which only brought fresh grieving: then I grew
Fiercer, and cursed from out my inmost heart
The Fates which marked me an Athenian maid.
Then faded that vain fury; hope died out;
A huge despair was stealing on my soul,
A sort of fierce acceptance of my fate,—
He wished a household vessel—well 'twas good,
For he should have it! He should have no more
The yearning treasure of a woman's love,
But just the baser treasure which he sought.
I called my maidens, ordered out the loom,
And spun unceasing from the morn till eve;
Watching all keenly over warp and woof,[2]
Weighing the white wool with a jealous hand.
I spun until, methinks, I spun away
The soul from out my body, the high thoughts
From out my spirit; till at last I grew
As ye have known me,—eye exact to mark
The texture of the spinning; ear all keen
For aimless talking when the moon is up,
And ye should be a-sleeping; tongue to cut
With quick incision, 'thwart the merry words
Of idle maidens. …
Only yesterday
My hands did cease from spinning; I have wrought
My dreary duties, patient till the last.
The gods reward me! Nay, I will not tell
The after years of sorrow; wretched strife
With grimmest foes—sad Want and Poverty;—

[1] *prithee* Please.

[2] *warp and woof* Cross threads in a weaving.

Nor yet the time of horror, when they bore
My husband from the threshold; nay, nor when
The subtle weed had wrought its deadly work.[1]
Alas! alas! I was not there to soothe
The last great moment; never any thought
Of her that loved him—save at least the charge,
All earthly, that her body should not starve. …
You weep, you weep; I would not that ye wept;
Such tears are idle; with the young, such grief
Soon grows to gratulation, as, "her love
Was withered by misfortune; mine shall grow
All nurtured by the loving," or, "her life
Was wrecked and shattered—mine shall smoothly sail."
Enough, enough. In vain, in vain, in vain!
The gods forgive me! Sorely have I sinned
In all my life. A fairer fate befall
You all that stand there. …
Ha! the dawn has come;
I see a rosy glimmer—nay! it grows dark;
Why stand ye so in silence? throw it wide,
The casement, quick; why tarry?—give me air—
O fling it wide, I say, and give me light!
—1881

To Vernon Lee[2]

O Bellosguardo,[3] when the year was young,
We wandered, seeking for the daffodil
And dark anemone, whose purples fill
The peasant's plot, between the corn-shoots sprung.

Over the grey, low wall the olive flung
Her deeper greyness; far off, hill on hill
Sloped to the sky, which, pearly-pale and still,
Above the large and luminous landscape hung.

A snowy blackthorn flowered beyond my reach;
You broke a branch and gave it to me there;
I found for you a scarlet blossom rare.

Thereby ran on of Art and Life our speech;
And of the gifts the gods had given to each—
Hope unto you, and unto me Despair.
—1889

The End of the Day

To B.T.

Dead-tired, dog-tired, as the vivid day
Fails and slackens and fades away—
The sky that was so blue before
With sudden clouds is shrouded o'er.
Swiftly, stilly the mists uprise,
Till blurred and grey the landscape lies.

. . . .

All day we have plied the oar; all day
Eager and keen have said our say
On life and death, on love and art,
On good or ill at Nature's heart.
Now, grown so tired, we scarce can lift
The lazy oars, but onward drift.
And the silence is only stirred
Here and there by a broken word.

. . . .

O, sweeter far than strain and stress
Is the slow, creeping weariness.
And better far than thought I find
The drowsy blankness of the mind.
More than all joys of soul or sense
Is this divine indifference;
Where grief a shadow grows to be,
And peace a possibility.
—1889

---

[1] *Nor … work* Socrates was condemned to die by suicide, which was accomplished by his drinking a cup of poison made from hemlock.

[2] *Vernon Lee* Pseudonym for British novelist and critic Violet Paget (1856–1935), known for her work on aesthetics and her supernatural fiction.

[3] *Bellosguardo* Town in Italy, near Florence.

Rudyard Kipling
1865 – 1936

The name "Rudyard Kipling" evokes images of the Raj in India, a time when Britannia ruled the waves and the sun never set on the British Empire. Indeed his life spanned most of the duration of British Colonial Office rule in India (1858–1947). Kipling, for many years considered England's unofficial poet laureate, was a strong proponent of imperialism; he believed it was Britain's duty to govern and civilize colonized lands. Though he was also capable of offering serious critiques of empire—and though he acknowledged that colonized people were "captives"—Kipling gave frequent voice to his belief that the British were in India to serve the native people. His famous 1899 poem, "The White Man's Burden," published in *McClure's Magazine*, aroused a storm of controversy, coming out at a time when many people were beginning to question the right of imperialist powers to subjugate other lands and peoples. Yet, for more than a half century Kipling's poems, short stories, and novels were wildly popular in India, Great Britain, and the United States, and in 1907 the Nobel Foundation honored him "in consideration of the power of observation, originality of imagination, virility of ideas and remarkable talent for narration which characterize the creations of this world-famous author." Thus Kipling became the first British writer to be awarded the Nobel Prize for Literature.

Kipling was named after Rudyard Lake in England, but he was born in Bombay (now Mumbai), India. Both his father, John Lockwood Kipling, professor of architectural sculpture at the University of Bombay, and his mother, Alice Macdonald, were children of Methodist ministers. Macdonald and her sisters were all associated with distinguished people—one sister married the neoclassical painter Sir Edward Poynter; another was the mother of Stanley Baldwin, who became Prime Minister of England in 1923; and another was the wife of the Pre-Raphaelite painter Sir Edward Burne-Jones. Kipling spent his first six years with his parents, learning the languages of his Indian friends and imbibing the cultural wealth of India. Of his school years, however, Kipling would say in his autobiography that his only happy moments were spent at the Burne-Jones home. Like many children of expatriates, he and his sister were sent to England for their education, where they spent five miserable years with severe, Calvinist foster parents in a home that Kipling would later call the House of Desolation. In 1878 he transferred to a boarding school in Devon (depicted in *Stalky and Co.*), which was also brutal at times, but where he acquired a schoolboy ethos—a sense of loyalty to and camaraderie with his peers—which later pervaded his work. It was at this school in Devon, too, where Kipling started to write in earnest.

Upon graduation, Kipling moved back to India, working first as a newspaper journalist for the *Civil and Military Gazette* in Lahore (now part of Pakistan) and then as an editor of *Pioneer* in Allahabad. Many of the poems and stories he wrote during that time were collected in *Departmental Ditties* (1886) and *Plain Tales from the Hills* (1888), in which Kipling wrote about the moral and psychological difficulties of integrating Indian and British cultures. The Indian Railway Library also published collections of Kipling's stories, notably *The Phantom Rickshaw and Other Eerie Tales* and *Wee Willie Winkie and Other Child Stories* (1888). The first of these collections included "The Man Who Would

Be King," which has remained one of Kipling's most popular stories. By the time he returned to England in 1889, Kipling was a well-established author in India and had become very popular in Britain as well. The British public loved his "tales of the exotic," which took them to worlds they could scarcely imagine and introduced them to cultures they would likely never experience first-hand.

Kipling published several collections of short stories and poems in the early 1890s; the volume *Barrack-Room Ballads and Other Verses* (1892), which included such well-known poems as "Mandalay" and "Gunga Din," went into more than 50 editions in the 30 years following. Two early novels, *The Light that Failed* (1891) and *The Naulahka* (1892), did not fare as well. Nevertheless, in this period Kipling acquired a reputation for using everyday language to express the thoughts of soldiers and other working Brits; his poems, for example, were often inspired by street ballads and music hall ditties.

In 1892 Kipling married an American, Caroline Balestier, and the couple settled in Vermont. Although Kipling was unhappy in the United States, he wrote some of his most esteemed works during his five-year stay there, including *The Jungle Book* (1894), *The Second Jungle Book* (1895), and *Captains Courageous* (1897).

The family eventually settled in Sussex, England, but Kipling continued to travel the world as a newspaper correspondent. He covered the Boer War in South Africa in 1899 and returned to the region annually thereafter, staying in a house given to him by Cecil Rhodes, the famous British imperialist and business magnate. Kipling's own imperialist political sentiments were disseminated widely at the turn of the century, most notably in the London *Times*, which published "Recessional," composed in honor of Queen Victoria's Diamond Jubilee, and "The White Man's Burden." The latter poem was soon afterward countered in the London magazine *Truth* with a poem by Henry Labouchère, which changed Kipling's opening refrain from "Take up the white man's burden," to "Pile on the brown man's burden." Amid the controversy that ensued, a letter to the editor was published that read, "There is something almost sickening in this 'imperial' talk of assuming and bearing burdens for the good of others. They are never assumed or held where they are not found to be of material advantage or ministering to honor or glory." Kipling himself suggested that his poem offered neither a noble call to arms nor a justification for colonization, but rather a warning of the costs involved on both sides of imperialist missions abroad.

Kipling's least controversial and best-loved novel appeared in 1901. *Kim* is a picaresque adventure tale of a British beggar boy, the orphaned son of an Irish soldier. Raised in Lahore by an opium-addicted, half-caste woman, Kim O'Hare comes to believe he is destined for greatness and eventually travels through India with a holy man in search of his glorious future. In 1907, the Nobel committee said that in *Kim* "there is an elevated diction as well as a tenderness and charm.... In sketching a personality he makes clear, almost in his first words, the peculiar traits of that person's character and temper.... [Kipling is] capable of reproducing with astounding accuracy the minutest detail from real life."

In the decades following his Nobel Prize, Kipling's literary output dwindled somewhat amid controversy over his politics and grief over the loss of two of his three children. Even former admirers, such as W.B. Yeats and T.S. Eliot, began to be critical of Kipling's unwavering allegiance to British imperialism. Nevertheless, the last half century has seen a resurgence of interest in his work.

Sir Ian Hamilton said that Kipling's death in January 1936 (two days before the death of Kipling's friend, King George V) placed "a full stop to the period when war was a romance and the expansion of our Empire a duty." When his ashes were interred in Poets' Corner of Westminster Abbey, Kipling's pallbearers included the then-prime minister of England, a field marshal, and the admiral of the fleet; the poem "Recessional" was sung as a hymn. Kipling's unfinished autobiography, *Something of Myself*, was published a year after his death.

⌘⌘⌘

Gunga Din

You may talk o' gin and beer
When you're quartered safe out 'ere,
An' you're sent to penny-fights° an' Aldershot[1] it; *skirmishes*
But when it comes to slaughter
You will do your work on water,
An' you'll lick the bloomin' boots of 'im that's got it.
Now in Injia's sunny clime,
Where I used to spend my time
A-servin' of 'Er Majesty the Queen,
Of all them blackfaced crew
The finest man I knew
Was our regimental bhisti,° Gunga Din. *water carrier*
He was "Din! Din! Din!
You limpin' lump o' brick-dust, Gunga Din!
Hi! Slippy *hitherao*![2]
Water, get it! *Panee lao*,[3]
You squidgy-nosed old idol, Gunga Din."

The uniform 'e wore
Was nothin' much before,
An' rather less than 'arf o' that be'ind,
For a piece o' twisty rag
An' a goatskin water bag
Was all the field equipment 'e could find.
When the sweatin' troop train lay
In a sidin' through the day,
Where the 'eat would make your bloomin' eyebrows crawl,
We shouted "Harry By!"[4]
Till our throats were bricky-dry,
Then we wopped 'im 'cause 'e couldn't serve us all.
It was "Din! Din! Din!
You 'eathen, where the mischief 'ave you been?
You put some *juldee*[5] in it
Or I'll *marrow*[6] you this minute
If you don't fill up my helmet, Gunga Din!"

'E would dot an' carry one[7]
Till the longest day was done;
An' 'e didn't seem to know the use o' fear.
If we charged or broke or cut,
You could bet your bloomin' nut,
'E'd be waitin' fifty paces right flank rear.
With 'is mussick° on 'is back, *waterbag*
'E would skip with our attack,
An' watch us till the bugles made "Retire,"
An' for all 'is dirty 'ide
'E was white, clear white, inside
When 'e went to tend the wounded under fire!
It was "Din! Din! Din!"
With the bullets kickin' dust spots on the green.
When the cartridges ran out,
You could hear the front ranks shout,
"Hi! ammunition mules an' Gunga Din!"

I shan't forgit the night
When I dropped be'ind the fight
With a bullet where my belt plate should 'a' been.
I was chokin' mad with thirst,
An' the man that spied me first
Was our good old grinnin', gruntin' Gunga Din.
'E lifted up my 'ead,
An' he plugged me where I bled,
An' 'e guv me 'arf-a-pint o' water green.
It was crawlin' and it stunk,
But of all the drinks I've drunk,
I'm gratefullest to one from Gunga Din.
It was "Din! Din! Din!
'Ere's a beggar with a bullet through 'is spleen;

[1] *Aldershot* Town southwest of London, site of a military training center.

[2] *Slippy hitherao* I.e., *idhar ao*. Urdu: Come here!

[3] *Panee lao* Urdu: Bring water.

[4] *Harry By* I.e., *arré bhai!* Urdu: in this context, Hey, you!

[5] *juldee* I.e., *juldee karo*. Urdu: hurry!

[6] *marrow* I.e., *maro*. Urdu: hit.

[7] *dot an' carry one* From mathematics: calculate.

'E's chawin' up the ground,
An' 'e's kickin' all around:
For Gawd's sake git the water, Gunga Din!"

'E carried me away
To where a dooli° lay, *stretcher*
An' a bullet come an' drilled the beggar clean.
'E put me safe inside,
An' just before 'e died,
"I 'ope you liked your drink," sez Gunga Din.
So I'll meet 'im later on
At the place where 'e is gone—
Where it's always double drill and no canteen.
'E'll be squattin' on the coals
Givin' drink to poor damned souls,
An' I'll get a swig in hell from Gunga Din!
Yes, Din! Din! Din!
You Lazarushian[1]-leather Gunga Din!
Though I've belted you and flayed you,
By the livin' Gawd that made you,
You're a better man than I am, Gunga Din!
—1890

The Widow at Windsor[2]

'Ave you 'eard o' the Widow at Windsor
With a hairy gold crown on 'er 'ead?
She 'as ships on the foam—she 'as millions at 'ome,
An' she pays us poor beggars in red.[3]
(Ow, poor beggars in red!)
There's 'er nick[4] on the cavalry 'orses,
There's 'er mark[5] on the medical stores—
An' 'er troopers° you'll find with a fair wind be'ind *troop-ships*
That takes us to various wars.
(Poor beggars!—barbarious wars!)
Then 'ere's to the Widow at Windsor,
An 'ere's to the stores an' the guns,
The men an' the 'orses what makes up the forces
O' Missis Victorier's sons.
(Poor beggars! Victorier's sons!)

Walk wide o' the Widow at Windsor,
For 'alf o' Creation she owns:
We 'ave bought 'er the same with the sword an' the flame,
An' we've salted it down with our bones.
(Poor beggars!—it's blue with our bones!)
Hands off o' the sons o' the Widow,
Hands off o' the goods in 'er shop,
For the kings must come down an' the emperors frown
When the Widow at Windsor says "Stop!"
(Poor beggars!—we're sent to say "Stop!")
Then 'ere's to the lodge o' the Widow,
From the pole to the tropics it runs—
To the lodge that we tile with the rank an' the file,
An' open in form with the guns.
(Poor beggars!—it's always they guns!)

We 'ave 'eard o' the Widow at Windsor,
It's safest to leave 'er alone:
For 'er sentries we stand by the sea an' the land
Wherever the bugles are blown.
(Poor beggars!—an' don't we get blown!)
Take 'old o' the Wings o' the Mornin',[6]
An' flop round the earth till you're dead;
But you won't get away from the tune that they play
To the bloomin' old rag over'ead.
(Poor beggars!—it's 'ot over'ead!)
Then 'ere's to the sons o' the Widow,
Wherever, 'owever they roam.
'Ere's all they desire, an' if they require
A speedy return to their 'ome.
(Poor beggars! they'll never see 'ome!)
—1890

[1] *Lazarushian* Cf. Luke 16; the good Lazarus was a leper/beggar.

[2] *The Widow at Windsor* Queen Victoria, who, upon losing her husband in 1861, went into permanent mourning. (See the "In Context" section below for more information.)

[3] *red* Red coats of British soldiers.

[4] *'er nick* Mark distinguishing animals as belonging to the queen.

[5] *'er mark* "V.R.I.," the Queen's identification mark.

[6] *Wings o' the Mornin'* From Psalm 139.9–10: "If I take the wings of the morning, and dwell in the uttermost parts of the sea; / Even there shall thy hand lead me, and thy right hand shall hold me."

Recessional[1]

God of our fathers, known of old,
    Lord of our far-flung battle-line,
Beneath whose awful Hand we hold
    Dominion over palm and pine—
Lord God of Hosts, be with us yet,
Lest we forget[2]—lest we forget!

The tumult and the shouting dies;
    The captains and the kings depart:
Still stands Thine ancient sacrifice,
    An humble and a contrite heart.[3]
Lord God of Hosts, be with us yet,
Lest we forget—lest we forget!

Far-called, our navies melt away;
    On dune and headland sinks the fire:
Lo, all our pomp of yesterday
    Is one with Nineveh and Tyre![4]
Judge of the nations, spare us yet,
Lest we forget—lest we forget!

If, drunk with sight of power, we loose
    Wild tongues that have not Thee in awe,
Such boastings as the Gentiles use,
    Or lesser breeds without the law[5]—
Lord God of Hosts, be with us yet,
Lest we forget—lest we forget!

For heathen heart that puts her trust
    In reeking tube and iron shard,
All valiant dust that builds on dust,
    And guarding, calls not Thee to guard,
For frantic boast and foolish word—
Thy mercy on Thy people, Lord!
—1897

The White Man's Burden

THE UNITED STATES AND THE PHILIPPINE ISLANDS[6]

Take up the White Man's burden—
    Send forth the best ye breed—
Go bind your sons to exile
    To serve your captives' need;
To wait in heavy harness
    On fluttered folk and wild—
Your new-caught, sullen peoples,
    Half devil and half child.

Take up the White Man's burden—
    In patience to abide,
To veil the threat of terror
    And check the show of pride;
By open speech and simple,
    An hundred times made plain.
To seek another's profit,
    And work another's gain.

Take up the White Man's burden—
    The savage wars of peace—
Fill full the mouth of Famine
    And bid the sickness cease;
And when your goal is nearest
    The end for others sought,
Watch Sloth and heathen Folly
    Bring all your hope to nought.

Take up the White Man's burden—
    No tawdry rule of kings,

[1] *Recessional* Hymn written for Queen Victoria's sixtieth anniversary Jubilee.

[2] *Lest we forget* Cf. Deuteronomy 4.9: "[T]ake heed to thyself, and keep thy soul diligently, lest thou forget the things which thine eyes have seen, and lest they depart from thy heart all the days of thy life: but teach them thy sons, and thy sons' sons."

[3] *contrite heart* Cf. Psalms 51.17: "The sacrifices of God are a broken spirit: a broken and a contrite heart."

[4] *Nineveh and Tyre* Ruined cities that were once capitals of empires.

[5] *Gentiles … law* Cf. Romans 2.14: "For when the Gentiles, which have not the law, do by nature the things contained in the law, these, having not the law, are a law unto themselves."

[6] *UNITED STATES AND THE PHILIPPINE ISLANDS* Response to the American takeover of the Philippines after the Spanish American War of 1898. (See the "In Context" section below for more information.)

But toil of serf and sweeper—
The tale of common things.
The ports ye shall not enter,
The roads ye shall not tread,
Go make them with your living,
And mark them with your dead!

Take up the White Man's burden—
And reap his old reward:
The blame of those ye better,
The hate of those ye guard—
The cry of hosts ye humour
(Ah, slowly!) toward the light:—
"Why brought ye us from bondage,
Our loved Egyptian night?"

Take up the White Man's burden—
Ye dare not stoop to less—
Nor call too loud on Freedom
To cloak your weariness;
By all ye cry or whisper,
By all ye leave or do,
The silent, sullen peoples
Shall weigh your gods and you.

Take up the White Man's burden—
Have done with childish days—
The lightly proffered laurel,[1]
The easy, ungrudged praise.
Comes now, to search your manhood
Through all the thankless years,
Cold-edged with dear-bought wisdom,
The judgment of your peers!
—1899

[1] *laurel* Leaves of the bay laurel tree are a symbol of victory.

If[2]—

If you can keep your head when all about you
Are losing theirs and blaming it on you,
If you can trust yourself when all men doubt you,
But make allowance for their doubting too;
If you can wait and not be tired by waiting,
Or being lied about, don't deal in lies,
Or being hated, don't give way to hating,
And yet don't look too good, nor talk too wise:

If you can dream—and not make dreams your master;
If you can think—and not make thoughts your aim;
If you can meet with Triumph and Disaster
And treat those two impostors just the same;
If you can bear to hear the truth you've spoken
Twisted by knaves to make a trap for fools,
Or watch the things you gave your life to, broken,
And stoop and build 'em up with worn out tools:

If you can make one heap of all your winnings
And risk it on one turn of pitch-and-toss,[3]
And lose, and start again at your beginnings
And never breathe a word about your loss;
If you can force your heart and nerve and sinew
To serve your turn long after they are gone,
And so hold on when there is nothing in you
Except the Will which says to them: "Hold on!"

If you can talk with crowds and keep your virtue,
Or walk with kings—nor lose the common touch,
If neither foes nor loving friends can hurt you,
If all men count with you, but none too much;
If you can fill the unforgiving minute
With sixty seconds' worth of distance run,
Yours is the earth and everything that's in it,
And—which is more—you'll be a man, my son!
—1910

[2] *If* It has been suggested that this poem may have been written in celebration of Dr. Leander Starr Jameson. Jameson launched the failed Jameson Raid of British troops against the Boers in South Africa in 1895, which ultimately led to the Boer War (1899–1902). Jameson went on to serve as Premier of the Cape Colony from 1904 to 1908.

[3] *pitch-and-toss* Coin tossing game.

In Context

Victoria and Albert

Queen Victoria was widowed when Prince Albert died on 14 December 1861. His partnership with the Queen had been an extraordinarily successful one—as a professional partnership as well as in family life. For many years after his death the Queen was a recluse, so much so that the public began to lose patience with and sympathy for Victoria in her mourning. It was not until the early 1870s that the Queen began to re-emerge. As she did so she gradually regained public favor, and by the time Kipling's "The Widow at Windsor" was published in 1890 she was widely revered. Her 60th Anniversary Jubilee in 1897—for which Kipling composed "Recessional"—was a massive national celebration.

Franz Xaver Winterhalter, *The Royal Family in 1846.*

Queen Victoria and Prince Albert in the early 1850s. (Photograph by Roger Fenton.)

Queen Victoria in mourning, 1867.

Queen Victoria with John Brown, a servant who had been personal ghillie (the term applied to the attendant to a Highland Chief) to Prince Albert and who later served Queen Victoria; Brown is credited with helping to bring the Queen out from seclusion. (Photo by W & D Downy.)

The Queen with Princess Beatrice, Princess Victoria, and great-granddaughter Alice, c. 1885. (Photographer unknown.)

Queen Victoria in the Golden Jubilee procession, 1897.

Victoria holding the future Edward VIII on the occasion of his baptism; her son Edward (later Edward VII) and grandson George (later George V) are in the background.

IN CONTEXT

The "White Man's Burden" in the Philippines

The Philippine Islands had long been a Spanish colony, but Spain's defeat in 1898 at the hands of American Admiral George Dewey during the Spanish-American War was followed by an agreement ceding the islands to the United States for $20 million. Local forces (under Emilio Agninaldo) had been rebelling against the Spanish, and, expecting the American victory to lead to liberation, declared a republic. The Americans, however, deciding that the natives were not ready for independence, ruthlessly suppressed the insurrection of Agninaldo's forces (which continued until 1905). Not until 1946 was the Republic of the Philippines granted full independence. The American annexation of the islands in 1899 was widely popular in the United States, but a significant minority loudly protested the expression of American imperialism that was the occasion for Kipling's famous poem. Following are excerpts from the platform adopted by one American organization at their founding meeting in Chicago, 17 October 1899.

Platform of the American Anti-Imperialist League

We hold that the policy known as imperialism is hostile to liberty and tends toward militarism, an evil from which it has been our glory to be free. We regret that it has become necessary in the land of Washington and Lincoln to reaffirm that all men, of whatever race or color, are entitled to life, liberty, and the pursuit of happiness. We maintain that governments derive their just powers from the consent of the governed. We insist that the subjugation of any people is "criminal aggression" and open disloyalty to the distinctive principles of our government.

We earnestly condemn the policy of the present national administration in the Philippines. It seeks to extinguish the spirit of 1776 in those islands. We deplore the sacrifice of our soldiers and sailors, whose bravery deserves admiration even in an unjust war. We denounce the slaughter of the Filipinos as a needless horror. We protest against the extension of American sovereignty by Spanish methods.

We demand the immediate cessation of the war against liberty, begun by Spain and continued by us. We urge that Congress be promptly convened to announce to the Filipinos our purpose to concede to them the independence for which they have so long fought and which of right is theirs.

The United States have always protested against the doctrine of international law which permits the subjugation of the weak by the strong. A self-governing state cannot accept sovereignty over an unwilling people. The United States cannot act upon the ancient heresy that might makes right.

Imperialists assume that with the destruction of self-government in the Philippines by American hands, all opposition here will cease. This is a grievous error. Much as we abhor the war of "criminal aggression" in the Philippines, greatly as we regret that the blood of the Filipinos is on American hands, we more deeply resent the betrayal of American institutions at home. The real firing line is not in the suburbs of Manila. The foe is of our own household. The attempt of 1861 was to divide the country. That of 1899 is to destroy its fundamental principles and noblest ideals.

Whether the ruthless slaughter of the Filipinos shall end next month or next year is but an incident in a contest that must go on until the Declaration of Independence and the Constitution of the United States are rescued from the hands of their betrayers. Those who dispute about standards of value while the Republic is undermined will be listened to as little as those who would wrangle about the small economies of the household while the house is on fire. The training of a great people for a century, the aspiration for liberty of a vast immigration are forces that will hurl aside those who in the delirium of conquest seek to destroy the character of our institutions.

We deny that the obligation of all citizens to support their Government in times of grave national peril applies to the present situation. If an administration may with impunity ignore the issues upon which it was chosen, deliberately create a condition of war anywhere on the face of the globe, debauch the civil service for spoils to promote the adventure, organize a truth suppressing censorship and demand of all citizens a suspension of judgement and their unanimous support while it chooses to continue the fighting, representative government itself is imperiled.

We propose to contribute to the defeat of any person or party that stands for the forcible subjugation of any people. We shall oppose for reelection all who in the White House or in Congress betray American liberty in pursuit of un-American gains. We still hope that both of our great political parties will support and defend the Declaration of Independence in the closing campaign of the century.

We hold, with Abraham Lincoln, that "no man is good enough to govern another man without that other's consent. When the white man governs himself, that is self-government, but when he governs himself and also governs another man, that is more than self-government—that is despotism." "Our reliance is in the love of liberty which God has planted in us. Our defense is in the spirit which prizes liberty as the heritage of all men in all lands. Those who deny freedom to others deserve it not for themselves, and under a just God cannot long retain it."

We cordially invite the co-operation of all men and women who remain loyal to the Declaration of Independence and the Constitution of the United States.

Britain, Empire, and a Wider World

CONTEXTS

In the Victorian era colonies in the British Empire were divided into two broad categories. In one category were crown colonies ruled by governments with no direct responsibility to the people they ruled, but only to the Foreign Office and the home country as a whole. The vast majority of the populace in such colonies did not share in the history, religion, or traditions of England or other European cultures, and were brown or black in color; in this category were the bulk of British possessions in Africa, Asia, and the Caribbean. In areas of the Empire where emigration from Britain and other European nations had created a majority or a substantial minority of a population sharing the cultural and racial makeup of "the old country," on the other hand, responsible government became the norm—though the indigenous residents whose nations had been colonized were often denied voting rights (and many other fundamental rights as well). Under the terms of Imperial arrangements in the latter category, administration was still overseen by British authority, but governments with a substantial degree of real power were elected by and responsible to the local settler populace, and were composed of local leaders rather than temporary appointees from abroad. Canada, the Australian colonies, and New Zealand were prominent in this second category.

India was in many ways a special case, with local hereditary rulers in some cases maintaining considerable authority under an umbrella of British rule over the subcontinent, and with this power structure complicated both by the existence of the India Office as a separate government department in Britain, and by the authority wielded (until 1858) by the East India Company. In the seventeenth century, the East India Company, the Hudson's Bay Company, and the Royal Africa Company were among the commercial entities given royal charters, empowering them not only to trade commercially in particular parts of the globe but also to exercise political authority over the local people. The empire continued to establish such charter companies into the late nineteenth century, even as the authority of earlier charter companies was transferred to government of a more conventional sort.

The nature of the Empire also changed in the course of the century, the last three decades of which saw a profound intensification of Britain's economic and ideological investment in imperialism. During this period—known as the "new imperialism"—Britain competed with other European powers to establish control of the territories Europeans saw as being ripe for imperial takeover. The largest arena of competition was the "scramble for Africa," where imperial domination was imposed with unprecedented speed; before 1870, European interest in Africa was focused mainly on coastal trade relationships, and by 1900 most of the continent had been divided among the empires of Europe.

Throughout the history of the British Empire various notions of "Empire" competed with one another. Perhaps the least complicated was the notion that Empire should be based purely on the commercial interests of the Imperial power. It was this notion that was foremost in the minds of many commercial adventurers staking out an Imperial claim—but also in the minds of many "little Englanders" in the nineteenth century who did not necessarily have any desire to abandon the Empire as a whole, but felt it would be expedient and appropriate to "cut loose" colonies that were perceived to represent a net drain on Britain's resources, financial and otherwise. For others, though, the Empire was a vital symbol of the nation's importance in the world—and of its "greatness" (a word in which power and morality came to be inextricably entangled). Finally, there were those whose notions of Empire were shaped by a hope and a confidence that Britain would improve the lot of its subject peoples—improve their economic conditions, certainly, but also bring to them literacy and an appropriate level of education, what were perceived to be the benefits of Christianity, and a broader set of cultural benefits, as well. It is easy to be cynical about this last set of ideas, and these "enlightened" notions of Empire were undoubtedly hypocritical, patronizing, and racist. That there was also frequently some kernel of altruism in the "enlightened imperialism" of the likes of William Gladstone or David Livingstone, however, is difficult to doubt, even as it must now be plain to all how horrifically misguided such impulses often were.

The pretense that British imperialism constituted a civilizing mission, however, is contradicted by the extremity of the horrors that were endured by the peoples they colonized. After a long struggle, outright slavery had been abolished in most British possessions in 1833, but in certain British colonies in the Caribbean, practices tantamount to slavery continued for decades thereafter—prompting incidents such as the uprising against British Governor Edward Eyre in Jamaica in 1865. Each colony had its own evils, such as the unspeakable atrocities meted out during the suppression of the Indian rebellion in 1857–58, and the brutal treatment accorded the aboriginal peoples of Australia, New Zealand, and Canada.

The feelings of cultural and racial superiority on which rationalizations of the subjugation of other peoples were founded took a variety of forms. The sort of anthropological theorizing that Adam Smith and other eighteenth-century thinkers had engaged in was one discourse that remained popular throughout the nineteenth century. According to this way of thinking, other peoples were not inherently inferior; they were simply at a less fully advanced stage of social and economic organization than were European peoples. An anthropological "stages of development" approach often led to an assumption by the British and other Europeans of a "childish" mentality among peoples elsewhere in the globe, but it also left room for the moral anthropology of Rousseau and others that ascribed to the "noble savage" the attribute of an innocence largely lost to "higher" stages of civilization. (It is this view with which Charles Dickens takes vehement issue in the essay from *Household Words* excerpted in this section.)

Although this approach was widely adopted throughout the Victorian era, pseudo-scientific claims of a biological sort were increasingly made. According to many making such claims, other peoples were not at a lower stage of development (from which they could, with assistance, be raised over the course of time to the level of Europeans); rather they were inherently, biologically inferior, and it would thus always be appropriate to treat them as creatures of a lower order.

One might assume that Victorian writers who deplored, for example, the brutality of conditions for workers in industry in England would also have deplored oppression and brutality overseas. However, this was simply not the case; imperialism and its racist justifications were an integral part of Victorian thought and culture. While John Stuart Mill and some others did indeed hold what could be considered relatively enlightened views on the subject of race and culture, many prominent Victorian writers—such as Thomas Carlyle, William Thackeray, and John Ruskin—defended profoundly bigoted positions, bolstering the beliefs that have served to justify imperialism and other forms of large-scale racist violence in the Victorian era and beyond it.

⌘⌘⌘

from Thomas Babington Macaulay, "Minute on Indian Education" (1835)

In this 1835 speech, Macaulay, then a member of the Council of India, argued that the sum set aside by the British Parliament for the education of Indian citizens should be used to teach the English language and the scientific and cultural advancements of Britain, rather than to promote the study of India's native cultures and languages. In the paragraphs immediately preceding this excerpt, Macaulay put forward the claim that the people of India should not be taught in any of their native languages, as the various dialects are "poor and rude," and "contain neither literary nor scientific information." In addition, he asserted, the historical, philosophical, and literary achievements of works written in European languages far surpassed their Sanskrit and Arabic equivalents.

from "Minute on Indian Education"

…

How, then, stands the case? We have to educate a people who cannot at present be educated by means of their mother-tongue. We must teach them some foreign language. The claims of our own language it is hardly necessary to recapitulate. It stands pre-eminent even among the languages of the west. It abounds with works of imagination not inferior to the noblest which Greece has bequeathed to us; with models of every species of eloquence; with historical compositions, which, considered merely as narratives, have seldom been surpassed, and which, considered as vehicles of ethical and political instruction, have never been equalled; with just and lively representations of human life and human nature; with the most profound speculations on metaphysics, morals, government, jurisprudence,[1] and trade; with full and correct information respecting every experimental science which tends to preserve the health, to increase the comfort, or to expand the intellect of man. Whoever knows that language has ready access to all the vast intellectual wealth which all the wisest nations of the earth have created and hoarded in the course of ninety generations. It may safely be said that the literature now extant in that language is of far greater value than all the literature which three hundred years ago was extant in all the languages of the world together. Nor is this all. In India, English is the language spoken by the ruling class. It is spoken by the higher class of natives at the seats of government. It is likely to become the language of commerce throughout the seas of the East. It is the language of two great European communities which are rising, the one in the south of Africa, the other in Australasia; communities which are every year becoming more important, and more closely connected with our Indian Empire. Whether we look at the intrinsic value of our literature, or at the particular situation of this country, we shall see the strongest reason to think that, of all foreign tongues, the English tongue is that which would be the most useful to our native subjects.

The question now before us is simply whether, when it is in our power to teach this language, we shall teach languages in which, by universal confession, there are no books on any subject which deserve to be compared to our own; whether, when we can teach European science, we shall teach systems which, by universal confession, whenever they differ from those of Europe, differ for the worse; and whether, when we can patronize sound philosophy and true history, we shall countenance, at the public expense, medical doctrines which would disgrace an English farrier,[2] astronomy which would move laughter in girls at an English boarding-school, history abounding with kings thirty feet high, and reigns thirty thousand years long, and geography made up of seas of treacle and seas of butter.

We are not without experience to guide us. History furnishes several analogous cases, and they all teach the same lesson. There are in modern times, to go no further, two memorable instances of a great impulse given to the mind of a whole society—of prejudices overthrown, of knowledge diffused, of taste purified, of

[1] *jurisprudence* Law.

[2] *farrier* One who shoes or cares for horses.

arts and sciences planted in countries which had recently been ignorant and barbarous.

The first instance to which I refer is the great revival of letters among the western nations at the close of the fifteenth, and the beginning of the sixteenth, century. At that time almost everything that was worth reading was contained in the writings of the ancient Greeks and Romans. Had our ancestors acted as the Committee of Public Instruction has hitherto acted;[1] had they neglected the language of Cicero and Tacitus;[2] had they confined their attention to the old dialects of our own island; had they printed nothing, and taught nothing at the universities, but chronicles in Anglo-Saxon, and romances in Norman-French, would England have been what she now is? What the Greek and Latin were to the contemporaries of More and Ascham,[3] our tongue is to the people of India. The literature of England is now more valuable than that of classical antiquity. I doubt whether the Sanskrit literature be as valuable as that of our Saxon and Norman progenitors. In some departments—in history, for example—I am certain that it is much less so.

Another instance may be said to be still before our eyes. Within the last hundred and twenty years, a nation which had previously been in a state as barbarous as that in which our ancestors were before the crusades, has gradually emerged from the ignorance in which it was sunk, and has taken its place among civilized communities—I speak of Russia. There is now in that country a large educated class, abounding with persons fit to serve the state in the highest functions, and in no wise inferior to the most accomplished men who adorn the best circles of Paris and London. There is reason to hope that this vast empire, which in the time of our grandfathers was probably behind the Punjab, may, in the time of our grandchildren, be pressing close on France and Britain in the career of improvement. And how was this change effected? Not by flattering national prejudices; not by feeding the mind of the young Muscovite[4] with old women's stories which his rude fathers had believed; not by filling his head with lying legends about St. Nicholas;[5] not by encouraging him to study the great question, whether the world was or was not created on the 13th of September; not by calling him "a learned native," when he has mastered all these points of knowledge: but by teaching him those foreign languages in which the greatest mass of information had been laid up, and thus putting all that information within his reach. The languages of Western Europe civilized Russia. I cannot doubt that they will do for the Hindu what they have done for the Tartar.[6] …

It is impossible for us, with our limited means, to attempt to educate the body of the people. We must at present do our best to form a class who may be interpreters between us and the millions whom we govern; a class of persons, Indian in blood and colour, but English in taste, in opinions, in morals, and in intellect. To that class we may leave it to refine the vernacular dialects of the country, to enrich those dialects with terms of science borrowed from the Western nomenclature, and to render them by degrees fit vehicles for conveying knowledge to the great mass of the population.

from Report of a Speech by William Charles Wentworth, Australian Legislative Council (1844)

In 1844 the aboriginal populace in Australia probably still outnumbered that of the whites. Official policy called for "amity and kindness" and forbade "any unnecessary interruption" of aboriginal

[1] *Committee … acted* The Committee of Public Instruction had hitherto used the allocated funds solely for promoting the study of Arabic and Sanskrit literature and for encouraging those "learned natives" who studied the science, religions, and histories of their native cultures.

[2] *Cicero* Roman orator of the first century BCE; *Tacitus* First-century CE author of two works of Roman history, *Histories* and *Annals*.

[3] *More* Sir Thomas More (1478–1535), English lawyer and humanist scholar, author of *Utopia*; *Ascham* Roger Ascham (1515–68), Latin Secretary to Edward VI, Mary I, and Elizabeth I.

[4] *Muscovite* Resident of Moscow.

[5] *St. Nicholas* Patron saint of sailors, revered in Christian Orthodox tradition.

[6] *Tartar* Here, Russian.

existence, but, as the excerpt below suggests, attitudes towards native peoples that prevailed were often brutally harsh.

He could not see if the whites in this colony were to go out into the land and possess it, that the Government had much to do with them. No doubt there would be battles between the settlers and the border tribes; but they might be settled without the aid of the Government. The civilized people had come in and the savage must go back. They must go on progressing until their dominancy was established, and therefore he could think that no measure was wise or merciful to the blacks which clothed them with a degree of seeming protection, which their position would not allow them to maintain.… It was not the policy of a wise Government to attempt the perpetuation of the aboriginal race of New South Wales.… They must give way before the arms, aye! even the diseases of civilized nations—they must give way before they attain the power of those nations.

Carlyle, Mill, and "The Negro Question"

In the wake of the abolition of slavery in all British possessions in 1837, and of the ending of the preferential tariff on sugar in 1846, plantation owners in the British West Indies complained vociferously about their situation, arguing that they were placed in the unfair position of having to compete against sugar produced in countries such as Brazil where slavery was still permitted. Amongst the many in Britain who supported their arguments was Thomas Carlyle, who sets out his position in the essay excerpted below. Shortly thereafter, John Stuart Mill delivered a stinging reply, also excerpted below. Carlyle reprinted a revised version of the essay in 1853 under the more incendiary title "Occasional Discourse on the Nigger Question."[1] In the 1860s the two also disagreed publicly over the Eyre rebellion (an uprising in Jamaica against the oppressive conditions under which black Jamaicans were forced to work, which became a *cause célèbre* in England when the rebellion was suppressed, with extraordinary brutality, by Governor Edward John Eyre).

from Thomas Carlyle, "Occasional Discourse on the Negro Question," *Fraser's Magazine* (1849)

West Indian affairs, as we all know, and some of us know to our cost, are in a rather troublous condition this good while. In regard to West Indian affairs, however, Lord John Russell[2] is able to comfort us with one fact, indisputable where so many are dubious, that the negroes are all very happy and doing well. A fact very comfortable indeed. West Indian whites, it is admitted, are far enough from happy; West Indian colonies not unlike sinking wholly into ruin; at home, too, the British whites are rather badly off—several millions of them hanging on the verge of continual famine—and, in single towns, many thousands of them very sore put to it, at this time … to live at all—these, again, are uncomfortable facts; and they are extremely extensive and important ones. But … how pleasant to have always this fact to fall back upon; our beautiful black darlings are at last happy; with little labor except to the teeth, *which*, surely, in those excellent horse-jaws of theirs, will not fail!

Exeter Hall,[3] my philanthropic friends, has had its way in this matter. The twenty millions, a mere trifle, despatched with a single dash of the pen, are paid; and, far over the sea, we have a few black persons rendered extremely "free" indeed. Sitting yonder, with their beautiful muzzles up to the ears in pumpkins, imbibing

[1] *more incendiary … Nigger Question* From the late sixteenth century into the eighteenth, the term "nigger" was generally used in a more or less neutral fashion, and rarely in a way that directly expressed hostility towards black people. In the late eighteenth and early nineteenth centuries the word began to be used more and more frequently to express contempt. An example from the same period at which Carlyle was writing is Hartley Coleridge's 1849 complaint against turning Othello "into a rank wooly-pated, thick-lipped nigger."

[2] *Lord John Russell* Russell (1792–1878) was British Prime Minister from 1846 to 1852 and from 1865 to 1866.

[3] *Exeter Hall* Exeter Hall, on the Strand, in London, was built in 1830 to serve as a meeting place for a variety of religious groups, benevolent associations, and other charitable institutions.

sweet pulps and juices; the grinder and incisor teeth ready for every new work, and the pumpkins cheap as grass in those rich climates; while the sugar crops rot round them, uncut, because labor cannot be hired. … A state of matters lovely to contemplate, in these emancipated epochs of the human mind, which has earned us, not only the praises of Exeter Hall, and loud, long-eared hallelujahs of laudatory psalmody[1] from the friends of freedom everywhere, but lasting favor (it is hoped) from the heavenly powers themselves; which may, at least, justly appeal to the heavenly powers, and ask them, if ever, in terrestrial procedure, they saw the match of it! Certainly, in the past history of the human species, it has no parallel; nor, one hopes, will it have in the future. …

Truly, my philanthropic friends, Exeter Hall philanthropy is wonderful; and the social science … which finds the secret of this universe in "supply and demand," and reduces the duty of human governors to that of letting men alone, is also wonderful. A dreary, desolate and, indeed, quite abject and distressing one; what we might call, by way of eminence, the *dismal science*.[2] These two, Exeter Hall philanthropy and the Dismal Science, led by any sacred cause of black emancipation, or the like, to fall in love and make a wedding of it—will give birth to progenies and prodigies: dark extensive moon-calves, unnameable abortions, wide-coiled monstrosities, such as the world has not seen hitherto! …

My philanthropic friends, can you discern no fixed headlands in this wide-weltering[3] deluge of benevolent twaddle and revolutionary grapeshot that has burst forth on us—no sure bearings at all? Fact and nature, it seems to me, say a few words to us, if, happily, we have still an ear for fact and nature. Let us listen a little, and try. And first, with regard to the West Indies, it may be laid down as a principle, which no eloquence in Exeter Hall, or Westminster Hall,[4] or elsewhere, can invalidate or hide, except for a short time only, that no black man, who will not work according to what ability the gods have given him for working, has the smallest right to eat pumpkin, or to any fraction of land that will grow pumpkin, however plentiful such land may be, but has an indisputable and perpetual *right* to be compelled, by the real proprietors of said land, to do competent work for his living. This is the everlasting duty of all men, black or white, who are born into this world. To do competent work, to labor honestly according to the ability given them; for that, and for no other purpose, was each one of us sent into this world; and woe is to every man who by friend or by foe, is prevented from fulfilling this, the end of his being. …

The idle black man in the West Indies had, not long since, the right, and will again, under better form, if it please Heaven, have the right (actually the first "right of man" for an indolent person) to be *compelled* to work as he was fit, and to *do* the Maker's will, who had constructed him with such and such prefigurements of capability. …

And now observe, my friends, it was not Black Quashee,[5] or those he represents, that made those West India islands what they are, or can, by any hypothesis, be considered to have the right of growing pumpkins there. For countless ages, since they first mounted oozy on the back of earthquakes, from their dark bed in the ocean deeps, and reeking, saluted the tropical sun, and ever onward, till the European white man first saw them, some three short centuries ago, those islands had produced mere jungle, savagery, poison reptiles and swamp malaria till the white European first saw them, they were, as if not yet created; their noble elements of cinnamon—sugar, coffee, pepper, black and gray, lying all asleep, waiting the white Enchanter, who should say to them, awake! Till the end of human history, and the sounding of the trump of doom, they might have lain so, had Quashee, and the like of him, been the only artists in the game. Swamps, fever-jungles, man-eating

[1] *psalmody* Singing of psalms.

[2] *dismal science* This famous phrase describing the science now known as economics has often been cited as first used by Carlyle in his "Latter Day Pamphlet" (1850), rather than in the present essay.

[3] *wide-weltering* State of turmoil, often used to describe the sea.

[4] *Westminster Hall* Location of British Parliament.

[5] *Quashee* African first name, used by some eighteenth- and nineteenth-century writers to stand for all black people.

caribs, rattle-snakes, and reeking waste and putrefaction: this had been the produce of them under the incompetent caribal[1] (what we call cannibal) possessors till that time; and Quashee knows, himself, whether ever he could have introduced an improvement. Him, had he, by a miraculous chance, been wafted thither, the caribals would have eaten, rolling him as a fat morsel under their tongue—for him, till the sounding of the trump of doom, the rattlesnakes and savageries would have held on their way. It was not he, then—it was another than he! … Quashee, if he will not help in bringing out the spices, will get himself made a slave again (which state will be a little less ugly than his present one), and with beneficent whip, since other methods avail not, will be compelled to work. … The gods are long-suffering; but the law, from the beginning, was, He that will not work shall perish from the earth—and the patience of the gods has limits!

Before the West Indies could grow a pumpkin for any negro, how much European heroism had to spend itself in obscure battle; to sink, in mortal agony, before the jungles, the putrescences and waste savageries could become arable, and the devils be, in some measure, chained there! The West Indies grow pineapples, and sweet fruits, and spices; we hope they will, one day, grow beautiful, heroic human lives too, which is surely the ultimate object they were made for; beautiful souls and brave; sages, poets, what not—making the earth nobler round them, as their kindred from of old have been doing; … heroic white men, worthy to be called old Saxons, browned with a mahogany tint in those new climates and conditions. But under the soil of Jamaica, before it could even produce spices, or any pumpkin, the bones of many thousand British men had to be laid. …

Already one hears of black *Adscripti glebae*;[2] which seems a promising arrangement, one of the first to suggest itself in such a complicacy. It appears the Dutch blacks, in Java, are already a kind of *Adscripts*, after the manner of the old European serfs; bound by royal authority, to give so many days of work a year. Is not this something like a real approximation; the first step toward all manner of such? Wherever, in British territory, there exists a black man, and needful work to the just extent is not to be got out of him, such a law, in defect of better, should be brought to bear upon said black man! …

[1] *caribal* Insulting combination of "Carib," indigenous person of the West Indies, and "cannibal."

[2] *Adscripti glebae* Latin: Permanently tied to the land; serf.

from John Stuart Mill, "The Negro Question," *Fraser's Magazine* (1850)

To the Editor of *Fraser's Magazine*

Sir:

Your last month's number contains a speech against the "rights of Negroes," the doctrines and spirit of which ought not to pass without remonstrance. The author issues his opinions, or rather ordinances, under imposing auspices no less than those of the "immortal gods." "The Powers," "the Destinies," announce, through him, not only what *will* be, but what *shall* be done; what they "have decided upon, passed their eternal act of Parliament for." This is speaking "as one having authority"; but authority from whom? If by the quality of the message we may judge of those who sent it, not from any powers to whom just or good men acknowledge allegiance. This so-called "eternal act of Parliament" is no new law, but the old law of the strongest—a law against which the great teachers of mankind have in all ages protested—it is the law of force and cunning; the law that whoever is more powerful than an other, is "born lord" of that other, the other being born his "servant," who must be "compelled to work" for him by "beneficent whip," if "other methods avail not." I see nothing divine in this injunction. If "the gods" will this, it is the first duty of human beings to resist such gods. Omnipotent these "gods" are *not*, for powers which demand *human* tyranny and injustice cannot accomplish their purpose unless human beings cooperate. The history of human improvement is the record of a struggle by which inch after inch of ground has been wrung from these maleficent[3] powers, and

[3] *maleficent* Harmful, evil.

more and more of human life rescued from the iniquitous[1] dominion of the law of might. Much, very much of this work still remains to do; but the progress made in it is the best and greatest achievement yet performed by mankind, and it was hardly to be expected at this period of the world that we should be enjoined, by way of a great reform in human affair, to begin *un*doing it.

… I must first set my anti-philanthropic opponent right on a matter of fact. He entirely misunderstands the great national revolt of the conscience of this country against slavery and the slave-trade if he supposes it to have been an affair of sentiment. It depended no more on humane feelings than any cause which so irresistibly appealed to them must necessarily do: Its first victories were gained while the lash yet ruled uncontested in the barrack-yard, and the rod in schools, and while men were still hanged by dozens for stealing to the value of forty shillings. It triumphed because it was the cause of justice; and, in the estimation of the great majority of its supporters, of religion. Its originators and leaders were persons of a stern sense of moral obligation, who, in the spirit of the religion of their time, seldom spoke much of benevolence and philanthropy, but often of duty, crime, and sin. For nearly two centuries had negroes, many thousands annually, been seized by force or treachery and carried off to the West Indies to be worked to death, literally to death; for it was the received maxim, the acknowledged dictate of good economy, to wear them out quickly and import more. In this fact every other possible cruelty, tyranny, and wanton oppression was by implication included. And the motive on the part of the slave-owners was the love of gold; or, to speak more truly, of vulgar and puerile ostentation. I have yet to learn that anything more detestable than this has been done by human beings towards human beings in any part of the earth.…

After fifty years of toil and sacrifice, the object was accomplished, and the negroes, freed from the despotism of their fellow-beings, were left to themselves, and to the chances which the arrangements of existing society provide for these who have no resource but their labour. These chances proved favorable to them, and, for the last ten years, they afford the unusual spectacle of a labouring class whose labour bears so high a price that they can exist in comfort on the wages of a comparatively small quantity of work. This, to the ex-slave-owners, is an inconvenience; but I have not yet heard that any of them has been reduced to beg his bread, or even to dig for it, as the negro, however scandalously he enjoys himself, still must. … If the [plantation owners] cannot continue to realize their large incomes without more labourers, let them find them, and bring them from where they can best be procured, only not by force. Not so, thinks your anti-philanthropic contributor. That negroes should exist, and enjoy existence, on so little work, is a scandal, in his eyes, worse than their former slavery. It must be put a stop to at any price. He does not "wish to see" them slaves again "if it can be avoided"; but "decidedly" they "will have to be servants," "servants to the whites," "compelled to labour," and "not to go idle another minute." "Black Quashee," "up to the ears in pumpkins," and "working about half an hour a day," is to him the abomination of abominations.

… To give it a rational meaning, it must first be known what he means by work. Does work mean everything which people *do*? No; or he would not reproach people with doing no work. Does it mean laborious exertion? No; for many a day spent in killing game, includes more muscular fatigue than a day's ploughing. Does it mean *useful* exertion? But your contributor always scoffs at the idea of utility. Does he mean that all persons ought to earn their living? But some earn their living by doing nothing, and some by doing mischief; and the negroes, whom he despises, still do earn by labour the "pumpkins" they consume and the finery they wear.

Work, I imagine, is not a good in itself. There is nothing laudable in work for work's sake. To work voluntarily for a worthy object is laudable; but what constitutes a worthy object? On this matter, the oracle

[1] *iniquitous* Unjust, unrighteous.

of which your contributor is the prophet[1] has never yet been prevailed on to declare itself. He revolves in an eternal circle round the idea of work, as if turning up the earth, or driving a shuttle or a quill, were ends in themselves, and the ends of human existence. Yet, even in the case of the most sublime service to humanity, it is not because it is work that it is worthy; the worth lies in the service itself, and in the will to render it—the noble feelings of which it is the fruit; and if the nobleness of will is proved by other evidence than work, as for instance by danger or sacrifice, there is the same worthiness. While we talk only of work, and not of its object, we are far from the root of the matter; or, if it may be called the root, it is a root without flower or fruit.

In the present case, it seems, a noble object means "spices."——"The gods wish, besides pumpkins, that spices and valuable products be grown in their West Indies"——the "noble elements of cinnamon, sugar, coffee, pepper black and gray," "things far nobler than pumpkins." Why so? Is what supports life inferior in dignity to what merely gratifies the sense of taste? Is it the verdict of the "immortal gods" that pepper is noble, freedom (even freedom from the lash) contemptible? But spices lead "towards commerces, arts, polities, and social developments." Perhaps so; but of what sort? When they must be produced by slaves, the "polities and social developments" they lead to are such as the world, I hope, will not choose to be cursed with much longer.

The worth of work does not surely consist in its leading to other work, and so on to work upon work without end. On the contrary, the multiplication of work, for purposes not worth caring about, is one of the evils of our present condition. When justice and reason shall be the rule of human affairs, one of the first things to which we may expect them to be applied is the question. How many of the so-called luxuries, conveniences, refinements, and ornaments of life, are *worth* the labour which must be undergone as the condition of producing them? The beautifying of existence is as worthy and useful an object as the sustaining of it; but only a vitiated[2] taste can see any such result in those fopperies[3] of so-called civilization, which myriads of hands are now occupied and lives wasted in providing. In opposition to the "gospel of work," I would assert the gospel of leisure, and maintain that human beings *cannot* rise to the finer attributes of their nature compatibly with a life filled with labour. I do not include under the name labour such work, if work it be called, as is done by writers and afforders of "guidance," an occupation which, let alone the vanity of the thing, cannot be called by the same name with the real labour, the exhausting, stiffening, stupefying toil of many kinds of agricultural and manufacturing labourers. To reduce very greatly the quantity of work required to carry on existence is as needful as to distribute it more equally; and the progress of science, and the increasing ascendency of justice and good sense, tend to this result.

There is a portion of work rendered necessary by the fact of each person's existence: no one could exist unless work, to a certain amount, were done either by or for him. Of this each person is bound, in justice, to perform his share; and society has an incontestable right to declare to every one, that if he work not, at this work of necessity, neither shall he eat. Society has not enforced this right, having in so far postponed the rule of justice to other considerations. But there is an ever-growing demand that it be enforced, so soon as any endurable plan can be devised for the purpose. If this experiment is to be tried in the West Indies, let it be tried impartially; and let the whole produce belong to those who do the work which produces it. We would not have black labourers compelled to grow spices which they do not want, and white proprietors who do not work at all exchanging the spices for houses in Belgrave Square.[4] We would not withhold from the whites, any more than from the blacks, the "divine right" of being compelled to labour. Let them have exactly the same share in the produce that they have in the work. If they do not like

[1] *prophet* With the publication of *Past and Present* in 1843, Carlyle began to be considered a visionary, even a prophetic voice, of social and cultural commentary in England.

[2] *vitiated* Corrupted.

[3] *fopperies* Here, useless consumer goods.

[4] *Belgrave Square* Fashionable area of London.

this, let them remain as they are, so long as they are permitted, and make the best of supply and demand.

Your contributor's notions of justice and proprietary right are of another kind than these. According to him, the whole West Indies belong to the whites: the negroes have no claim there, to either land or food, but by their sufferance. "It was not Black Quashee, or those he represents, that made those West India islands what they are." I submit, that those who furnished the thews[1] and sinews really had something to do with the matter.

But the great ethical doctrine of the discourse, … than which a doctrine more damnable, I should think, never was propounded by a professed moral reformer, is, that one kind of human beings are born servants to another kind. "You will have to be servants," he tells the negroes, "to those that are born wiser than you, that are born lords of you—servants to the whites, if they are (as what mortal can doubt that they are?) born wiser than you." I do not hold him to the absurd letter of his dictum; it belongs to the mannerism in which he is enthralled like a child in swaddling clothes. By "born wiser," I will suppose him to mean, born more capable of wisdom: a proposition which, he says, no mortal can doubt, but which, I will make bold to say, that a full moiety[2] of all thinking persons, who have attended to the subject, either doubt or positively deny.

Among the things for which your contributor professes entire disrespect, is the analytical examination of human nature. It is by analytical examination that we have learned whatever we know of the laws of external nature; and if he had not disdained to apply the same mode of investigation to the laws of the formation of character, he would have escaped the vulgar error of imputing every difference which he finds among human beings to an original difference of nature. As well might it be said, that of two trees, sprung from the same stock one cannot be taller than another but from greater vigor in the original seedling. Is nothing to be attributed to soil, nothing to climate, nothing to difference of exposure—has no storm swept over the one and not the other, no lightning scathed it, no beast browsed on it, no insects preyed on it, no passing stranger stripped off its leaves or its bark? If the trees grew near together, may not the one which, by whatever accident, grew up first, have retarded the other's development by its shade? Human beings are subject to an infinitely greater variety of accidents and external influences than trees, and have infinitely more operation in impairing the growth of one another; since those who begin by being strongest, have almost always hitherto used their strength to keep the others weak. What the original differences are among human beings, I know no more than your contributor, and no less; it is one of the questions not yet satisfactorily answered in the natural history of the species. This, however, is well known—that spontaneous improvement, beyond a very low grade—improvement by internal development, without aid from other individuals or peoples—is one of the rarest phenomena in history; and whenever known to have occurred, was the result of an extraordinary combination of advantages; in addition doubtless to many accidents of which all trace is now lost. No argument against the capacity of negroes for improvement, could be drawn from their not being one of these rare exceptions. It is curious, withal, that the earliest known civilization was, we have the strongest reason to believe, a negro civilization. The original Egyptians are inferred, from the evidence of their sculptures, to have been a negro race: it was from negroes, therefore, that the Greeks learnt their first lessons in civilization; … but I again renounce all advantage from facts: [even if it *were* true that] whites [were] born ever so superior in intelligence to the blacks, and competent by nature to instruct and advise them, it would not be the less monstrous to assert that they had therefore a right either to subdue them by force, or circumvent them by superior skill; to throw upon them the toils and hardships of life, reserving for themselves, under the misapplied name of work, its agreeable excitements. …

Though we cannot extirpate[3] all pain, we can, if we are sufficiently determined upon it, abolish all tyranny;

1 *thews* Muscles.

2 *moiety* Half.

3 *extirpate* To remove, literally pull out roots.

one of the greatest victories yet gained over that enemy is slave-emancipation and all Europe is struggling, with various success, towards further conquests over it. If, in the pursuit of this, we lose sight of any object equally important; if we forget that freedom is not the only thing necessary for human beings, let us be thankful to any one who points out what is wanting; but let us not consent to turn back. That this country should turn back, in the matter of negro slavery, I have not the smallest apprehension.

There is, however, another place where that tyranny still flourishes, but now for the first time finds itself seriously in danger. At this crisis of American slavery, when the decisive conflict between right and iniquity seems about to commence, your contributor steps in, and flings this missile, loaded with the weight of his reputation, into the abolitionist camp. The words of English writers of celebrity are words of power on the other side of the ocean; and the owners of human flesh, who probably thought they had not an honest man on their side between the Atlantic and the Vistula,[1] will welcome such an auxiliary. Circulated as his dissertation will probably be, by those whose interests profit by it, from one end of the American Union to the other, I hardly know of an act by which one person could have done so much mischief as this may possibly do; and I hold that by thus acting, he has made himself an instrument of what an able writer in the *Inquirer* justly calls "a true work of the devil."[2]

The Great Exhibition of 1851

No single event is more expressive of the place Britain saw itself and its Empire occupying in the world than the Great Exhibition of the Industry of all Nations of 1851. It was intended as a celebration of the achievements of the entire world, but also of the special place that Britain saw itself occupying in the world—economic engine, most powerful nation, moral leader. The brainchild very largely of the Prince Consort, the event attracted exhibitors from throughout the Empire and from many other nations; more than 6,200,000 people visited what came to be regarded as the first world's fair. The exhibition hall—popularly known as the Crystal Palace—occupied over twenty-one acres in Hyde Park in central London over a six month period (after which it was disassembled and rebuilt in a suburban location). The Exhibition was a success in every respect, not least of all financially; revenues helped to fund the construction of both the Albert Hall and the Victoria and Albert Museum.

Prince Albert, Speech Delivered at the Lord Mayor's Banquet, London, 1849 (as reprinted in *The Illustrated London News*, 11 October 1849)

I conceive it to be the duty of every educated person closely to study and watch the time in which he lives; and as far as in him lies, to add his might of individual exertion to further the accomplishment of what he believes Providence to have ordained. Nobody, however, who has paid any attention to the features of our present era, will doubt for a moment that we are living at a period of most wonderful transition which tends rapidly to the accomplishment of that great end to which indeed, all history points—the realization of the unity of mankind. Not a unity which breaks down the limits and levels the peculiar characteristics of the different nations of the earth, but rather a unity, the result and product of those very national varieties and antagonistic qualities. The distances which separated the different nations and parts of the globe are gradually vanishing before the achievements of modern invention, and we can traverse them with incredible ease; the languages of all nations are known and their acquirements placed within the reach of everybody; thought is communicated with the rapidity and even by the power of lightning.

On the other hand, the great principle of the division of labour which may be called the moving

---

[1] *between the Atlantic and the Vistula* I.e., in Britain or in Continental Europe. (The Vistula is a river in Poland.)

[2] *writer … devil* From an article responding to Carlyle in *London Inquirer*: "It is a true work of the Devil, the fostering of a tyrannical prejudice."

Engraving by H. Bibby of a daguerreotype by John J.E. Mayall, *Great Exhibition, Main Avenue Looking East*, 1851.

power of civilization, is being extended to all branches of science, industry and art. Whilst formerly the greatest mental energies strove at universal knowledge, and that knowledge was confined to a few, now they are directed to specialities, and in these again, even to the minutest points; but the knowledge acquired becomes at once the property of the community at large. Whilst formerly discovery was wrapped in secrecy, the publicity of the present day causes, that no sooner is a discovery or invention made, than it is already improved upon and surpassed by competing efforts: the products of all quarters of the globe are placed at our disposal, and we have only to choose what is the cheapest and best for our purposes, and the powers of production are entrusted to the stimulus of competition and capital.

So man is approaching a more complete fulfillment of that great and sacred mission which he has to perform in this world. His reason being created after the image of God, he has to use it to discover the laws by which the Almighty governs His creation, and, by making these laws his standard of action, to conquer nature to his use—himself a divine instrument. Science discovers these laws of power, motion and transformation; industry applies them to raw matter which the earth yields us in abundance, but which becomes valuable only by knowledge; art teaches us the immutable laws of beauty and symmetry, and gives to our productions forms in accordance with them.

Gentlemen, the Exhibition of 1851 is to give us a true test and a living picture of the point of development at which the whole of mankind has arrived in this great task, and a new starting point from which all nations will be able to direct their further exertions.

London Dining Rooms, 1851
Waiter (to Chinaman). "Very nice birds'-nest soup, Sir!—Yes, Sir!—Rat pie, Sir, just up—yes, Sir!—and a nice little dog to foller—yes, Sir!"

Cartoon from *Punch*, 1851. The Great Exhibition brought an unprecedented influx of foreign visitors to London—most from Europe, but some from much farther afield. The satirical magazine *Punch* was far from alone in engaging in casually racist ridicule of the cultural practices of foreigners. The original caption is reproduced above.

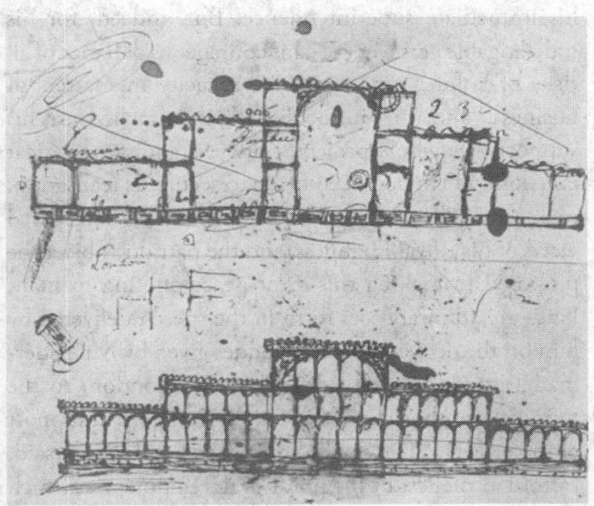

Joseph Paxton, first sketch for the Great Exhibition Building, 1850. From this initial sketch, drawn on blotting paper during a railway board meeting, Paxton developed the design of the Crystal Palace.

from *The Art Journal Illustrated Catalogue of the Great Exhibition of The Industry of All Nations* (1851)

We commence this illustrated catalogue of the principal contents of the Great Exhibition with a brief but succinct History of the Building—and of the Project from its commencement up to the present time.

The experiment of an Exhibition of the Industry of all the civilised Nations of the World has been tried, and has succeeded beyond the most sanguine expectations of its projectors. It is, indeed, scarcely possible to instance any great enterprise of modern date which has so completely satisfied the anticipations which had been formed of its results.... Other nations have devised means for the display and encouragement of their own arts and manufactures; but it has been reserved for England to provide an arena for the exhibition of the industrial triumphs of the whole world. She has offered an hospitable invitation to surrounding nations to bring the choicest products of their industry to her capital, and there to enter into an amicable competition with each other and with herself; and she has endeavoured to secure to them the certainty of an impartial verdict on their efforts. Whatever be the extent of the benefit which this great demonstration may confer upon the Industrial Arts of the world, it cannot fail to soften, if not to eradicate altogether, the prejudices and animosities which have so long retarded the happiness of nations; and to promote those feelings of "peace and good will" which are among the surest antecedents of their prosperity; a peace, which Shakespeare has told us—

> Is of the nature of a conquest;
> For then both parties nobly are subdued,
> And neither party loses.

It forms no part of our present object to enter, with any degree of minuteness, into the history of exhibitions of this class; but a brief glance at the origin and progress of such associations in France and England may not be considered irrelevant. …

The great success which attended the French Industrial Exposition of 1844 had caused representations to be made to the English government of the advantages which would accrue to our commerce from a similar exhibition in this country; but the efforts which were made to obtain its cooperation appear to have been wholly unsuccessful. In 1848, a proposal to establish a self-supporting exhibition of the products of British industry, to be directed by a Royal Commission, was submitted by H.R.H. Prince Albert to the government, but with no better success; and it then became apparent that no reliance whatever could be placed upon the active support of Her Majesty's ministers for any such plan. They had, in all probability, no objection to see the experiment tried, but were evidently unwilling to commit themselves to any responsibility in behalf of a scheme which seemed to be beset by so many difficulties. Meanwhile, the popular feeling in favour of such an undertaking was rapidly strengthening, and the success which has attended the experiment may, in a great measure, be referred to the freedom of action which this dissociation from the timid councils of the government secured for its projectors. It may be proper, in this place, to remark that, excepting in facilitating its correspondence with foreign nations; the provision of a site for the building; and the organisation of the police; no assistance has been either sought or obtained from the government for the present Exhibition; whilst, in every case in which it has been attended by expense, the cost has been defrayed out of the funds at the disposal of the Executive Committee. …

H.R.H. Prince Albert … on the termination of the Parliamentary session of 1849, took the subject under his immediate superintendence. But, indeed, for his indefatigable perseverance, his courageous defiance of all risks of failure, his remarkable sagacity in matters of business, and the influence which attached to his support, the whole project, notwithstanding the great exertions which had been made to secure its realisation, must have fallen to the ground. The maturely considered views of his Royal Highness, and the patriotic objects he proposed in making this great peace-offering to mankind, are admirably set forth in the speech delivered by him on the occasion of the banquet given by Mr. Alderman Farncomb, then Lord Mayor of London, to the municipal authorities of the United Kingdom in support of the project. "The Exhibition of 1851 would," he said, "afford a true test of the point of development at which the whole of mankind has arrived in this great task, and a new starting point from which all nations would be able to direct their further exertions."…

On the 29th of June, 1849, at a meeting, at Buckingham Palace, of several of the gentlemen who afterwards became members of the Royal Commission, and Prince Albert, his Royal Highness communicated his plan for the formation of a great collection of works of Industry and Art in London, in 1851, for the purposes of exhibition, of competition, and of encouragement; when he proposed that these contributions should consist of four great divisions, namely: raw materials;

machinery and mechanical inventions; manufactures; and sculpture and plastic[1] art generally. …

Impressed with the truth of the proverb, *Ce n'est que le premier pas qui coûte*,[2] the council of the Society of Arts, after much fruitless negotiation with other parties, entered into an engagement with Messrs. Munday, the well-known contractors, by which those gentlemen undertook to deposit a prize fund of 20,000 *l.*; to erect a suitable building; to find offices; to advance the money requisite for all preliminary expenses; and to take the whole risk of loss; on the following conditions: The 20,000 *l.* prize fund, the cost of the building, and five percent on all advances, to be repaid out of the first receipts; the residue to be divided into three equal parts; one part to be paid over at once to the Society of Arts, in aid of future exhibitions; and out of the other two parts all other incidental costs, such as those of general management and preliminary expenses; the residue, if any, to be remuneration of the contractors for their outlay, trouble, and risk. …

With a view to give Foreign nations as much time for preparation as possible, the Commissioners resolved, long before they had decided on the size and character of the building, to divide a certain large extent of space among foreign countries, amounting in the whole to 210,000 superficial feet, or rather more than the entire space which France had occupied for its two expositions of 1844 and 1849. Subsequently, the quantities of space allotted to foreign nations was increased; France obtaining 65,000 feet instead of 50,000. A definite amount of space proportioned to their presumed wants was also allotted to each of the British Colonies. …

Every class appears, however, to have been satisfied with the final allocations, which were the best that could have been made under the circumstances.

When the time arrived for making definite arrangements for the erection of the building, the Commissioners had only 35,000 *l.* in hand; and, notwithstanding the guarantee to which they had themselves largely subscribed, they must have felt themselves committed to a very deep responsibility. Nothing daunted, however, an invitation was addressed, through the public prints, to architects of all nations, to furnish designs for an edifice, the roof of which was to cover 700,000 square feet; and the area of which, including the open spaces, was not to exceed 900,000 feet. Other conditions were enumerated which showed that the whole of the details had been carefully and judiciously considered. Although the time allowed for the preparation of the drawings was only a month, there were no fewer than two hundred and thirty-three competitors, many of whom sent in designs of a highly elaborate character. Of these, thirty-eight, or one-sixth of the whole, were from foreigners; 128 from London and its vicinity; and 51 from the provincial towns of England. …

Among the contractors who had accepted the invitation of the Building Committee, was the firm of Fox & Henderson, who, availing themselves of the permission to alter and amend the plan of the Committee, contained in the latter part of the report, presented a tender for a building of an entirely different character from that which had been suggested by the Committee. This, we need scarcely add, was the plan which, with certain modifications and additions, was ultimately adopted; and for which, notwithstanding all that has been said to the contrary, the public is wholly indebted to Mr. Paxton. …

[A]nd if it be correct, as stated by Mr. Paxton at the dinner given to him at Derby, on the 6th of August, that his original sketch on a sheet of blotting paper indicates the principal features of the building as it now stands as much as the most finished drawings which have been made since, there can be no excuse for attempting to deprive him of any portion of the merit of the invention. But he appears to have done considerably more than merely furnish the idea. In nine days from that on which he had made the blotting paper sketch, he was in possession of nine plans, all, with a single exception, prepared by his own hand. And although his suggestion to Messrs. Fox & Henderson was offered so late as the 2nd June, 1850, his plan was engraved and published in the Illustrated News of the 6th July. …

Tests had, as we have shown, been applied in the course of the work which had satisfied the scientific men

[1] *plastic* Involving the manipulation or sculpting of physical materials.

[2] *Ce … coûte* French: It is only the first step that costs.

EXTERIOR OF THE BUILDING FOR THE GREAT EXHIBITION (SOUTH SIDE).

who witnessed them that the iron girders would bear a strain upon them four times as great as they could ever be called upon to bear; but it was resolved to subject them to a still severer ordeal.

The first of these more elaborate experiments, which took place in the presence of Her Majesty, Prince Albert, and several scientific persons, was to ascertain the extent of oscillation that would be produced in the galleries by the regular motion of large bodies of persons. Three hundred workmen were accordingly deployed over the platform, and then crowded together as closely as possible. The load borne by the planks laid across the platform represented the degree of pressure that would be occasioned by the crowding of the bays of the galleries. The amount of deflection produced by this experiment was scarcely perceptible. The men next walked regularly and irregularly, and finally ran over the temporary floor, with little more effect. Even when packed in the closest order, and jumping simultaneously for several minutes, the play of the timbers and the wrought-iron work, was admirably developed, and the extreme deflection of any one girder did not exceed a quarter of an inch. As, however, the workmen were unable to keep military time in their step, the whole corps of Sappers and Miners employed on the ground, arranged in close order, marched several times over and around the bays without producing any other effect than is observable in a house in which dancing is going on. The crowning experiment suggested by Messrs. Maudslay & Field, the eminent civil engineers, rendered any further test wholly unnecessary. Seven frames, each capable of holding 36 cannon-balls, of 68 lbs. each, were constructed, and drawn with their contents over the floor. In this way a pressure on the flooring of seven and a half tons was obtained; the probable pressure from a crowd not exceeding 95 lb. The pressure of an ordinary crowd, however, at a public meeting or a theatre does not exceed 60 lbs. to the square foot. …

The site of the Great Exhibition is the one originally proposed for it by H.R.H. Prince Albert. It consists of a rectangular piece of ground in Hyde Park, situated between the Queen's Drive and Rotten Row,[1] and contains about 26 acres, being 2300 feet in length by 500 feet in breadth. Its principal frontage extends from

[1] *Queen's Drive and Rotten Row* Carriage paths.

east to west. Several lofty trees which stretch across the centre of its length have been allowed to remain, and it is to them we are indebted for the magnificent transept and semicircular roof, suggested after the first plans had received the approval of the Commissioners. The ground, although apparently level, has a fall from 1 to 250 inches from west to east. Among the most striking advantages of the spot were the facilities of access from all parts which it presented, and the ease with which it could be drained and supplied with gas and water; whilst the beauty of the neighbourhood can scarcely be exceeded within the same convenient distance from the metropolis. Indeed, however strong may have been the private objections urged against the adoption of this site, in the first instance, it is now universally admitted that a more desirable locality for the purpose to which it has been converted could not have been selected. …

Two … groups of trees, whose immolation was also interdicted, have rendered open courts necessary; but they are, nevertheless, included within the building. The entire area enclosed and roofed over comprises no fewer than 772,784 square feet, or about 19 acres; thus presenting an edifice about four times the size of St. Peter's, at Rome, and six times that of St. Paul's.[1] We have already described the principal entrance at the south front. Besides this, there is one at each end, and, at convenient intervals, no fewer than fifteen places of egress. …

The first impression conveyed to the mind of a visitor, inexperienced in the science of architecture, on entering the building, is a sense of insecurity, arising from the apparent lightness of its supports as compared with the vastness of its dimensions. But this feeling is soon dissipated when he is informed how severely the strength of every separate part has been tested, and with what extreme care the connexion of all the supports with each other has been considered, so as to present the greatest possible combination of strength. …

Among other striking examples of the ingenuity of the originators and constructors of the Crystal Palace is the ridge-and-furrow roof, by which the rain water is distributed into equal portions, and all ordinary chances of overflow averted; and the peculiar formation of the floor, which is a "trellised wooden pathway," with spaces between each board through which, on sweeping, "the dust at once disappears, and falls into the vacuity below." It may also be thoroughly washed without discomfort, for the water disappears as fast as the dust through the interstices; and the boards become fit for visitors almost immediately afterwards. …

Such was the extraordinary eagerness of the public to be present at its inauguration, that upwards of 40,000 *l.* of season tickets were disposed of on the 29th of April; and but for the restriction that the holders of season tickets only should be admitted to this ceremony, the place would doubtless have overflowed with visitors. It is not our intention to enter into minute details of the circumstances which attended its inauguration; they were in every respect worthy of the occasion. It was opened by Her Majesty in person, accompanied by the Royal Family, and attended by the members of her cabinet, and by all the officers and ladies of her court. So soon as the music which hailed her entry had ceased, H.R.H. Prince Albert, as President of the Royal Commissioners, read a report of their proceedings since their appointment. This manifesto mentions that "for the suggestions of the principle of this structure, the Commissioners are indebted to Mr. Joseph Paxton, and expresses a hope that the undertaking, which has for its end the promotion of all branches of human industry, and the strengthening of the bonds of peace and friendship among all nations of the earth, may, under God's blessing, conduce to the welfare of Her Majesty's people, and be long remembered among the brightest incidents of her peaceful and happy reign."

To this address, Her Majesty returned a most gracious answer, and the Archbishop of Canterbury having invoked the blessing of the Almighty on the undertaking, the ceremony terminated with the performance of the Hallelujah chorus by the united choirs of the Chapel Royal, St. Paul's, Westminster Abbey, and St. George's Chapel, Windsor. The procession included all the persons who had been officially engaged in the work; the royal and foreign commissioners, Her Majesty's minis-

[1] *St. Peter's, at Rome* St. Peter's Basilica, among the world's largest churches; *St. Paul's* St. Paul's Cathedral in London, then the largest church in England.

ters, the whole of the lords and ladies of the court in waiting, and the foreign ambassadors. The vast but elegant proportions of the building, the richness and tastefulness of the costumes, and the large number (25,000) of well-dressed persons assembled on the occasion, rendered its inauguration one of the most imposing sights that had ever been witnessed in this country. But it is not in her regal capacity alone that Her Majesty has deigned to honour the Great Exhibition with her countenance. Day after day, accompanied by her children, and often at much personal inconvenience, has she flattered the various exhibitors by careful examinations of their productions; until it may fairly be presumed that there is scarcely one of her subjects who has more thoroughly inspected all that is worthy of attention within its walls than she has done. Whatever may have been the weather, or however crowded the interior, Her Majesty has devoted, almost daily, until the close of the session of parliament released her from attendance in London, several hours to visits to the Crystal Palace; inspecting each department in succession, and selecting from many of them such objects as gratified her taste, or were, for other reasons, considered to possess claims upon her attention.

On entering the building, for the first time, the eye is completely dazzled by the rich variety of hues which burst upon it on every side; and it is not until this partial bewilderment has subsided, that we are in a condition to appreciate as it deserves its real magnificence and the harmonious beauty of effect produced by the artistical arrangement of the glowing and varied hues which blaze along its grand and simple lines. After passing through the southern entrance, the whole extent of the transept, interrupted only by the magnificent glass fountain of Messrs. Osler,[1] and the groups of sculpture and tropical plants and trees, that are intermixed throughout, flashes on the eye more like the fabled palace of Vathek,[2] than a structure reared in a few months by mortal hands. …

Forming the centre, or nearly so, of the entire building, and dividing alike the transept and the nave, rises the gigantic fountain of Messrs. Osler, the culminating point of view from every quarter of the building; whilst at the northern end the eye is relieved by the verdure of tropical plants and the lofty and overshadowing branches of forest trees.

On the right, looking from Messrs. Osler's glass fountain up the Eastern Division of the Nave, towards the American organ and its enormous eagle, a combination of splendours bursts upon the sight of overpowering magnificence. …

The Western Division of the Nave, devoted to the products of England and her Colonies, if less showy, on a superficial view, than its rival, has much of sterling merit to recommend it. Here, too, are interspersed statues, fountains, mirrors, organs, and other large ornamental objects.

Crossing the Transept, and pursuing our course to the left, we enter the western division of the nave. We have here the Indian Court, Africa, Canada, the West Indies, the Cape of Good Hope, the Medieval Court, and the English Sculpture Court. … To these succeed Birmingham, the great British Furniture Court, Sheffield, and its hardware, the woollen and mixed fabrics, shawls, flax, and linens, and printing and dyeing. The long avenue leading from the Medieval Court to the end of the building is devoted to general hardware, brass and iron-work of all kinds, locks, grates, etc.; whilst behind it, and parallel with it, but occupying three times its breadth, is the department for agricultural machines and implements. At the back of this division is the long narrow gallery occupied by the mineral products of England. Passing the small compartment of glass which runs transversely under the great organ gallery, across the nave, we have the cotton fabric and carriage courts, leather, furs, and hair, minerals and mineral manufactures, and machinery; including cotton and woollen power-looms in motion. The next is the largest compartment in the building, comprising machinery in motion, flax, silk, and lace, rope-making lathes, tools,

[1] *Messrs. Osler* Follett and Clarkson Osler, England's leading glass manufacturers.

[2] *palace of Vathek* In William Beckford's French novel *Vathek* (1782; first English translation 1786), the title character expands his already magnificent palace to incorporate five new wings, each for the satisfaction of one of the five senses.

and mills; minerals and mineral manufactures, furniture, marine engines, ceilings, hydraulic presses, steam hammers, fire engines, etc. Then follow paper and stationery; Jersey, Ceylon, and Malta, with the Fine Arts Court behind them; railway and steam machinery in motion; building contrivances, printing, and French machinery, occupying the whole of the last compartments on both sides of the nave, as well as those which face the transept. Crossing to the left of the Crystal Fountain, we have Persia, Greece, Egypt, and Turkey, Spain, Portugal, Madeira, and Italy, musical instruments, and chemicals; France, its tapestry, machinery, arms and instruments, occupying two large courts; Belgium her furniture, carpets, and machinery; Austria, with her gorgeous furniture courts, and machinery furniture; the Zollverein, with its octagon room, the most tastefully-arranged compartment in the building; North of Germany and Hanse Towns; Russia, with its malachite doors, vases, and ornaments; and the United States, with its agricultural implements, raw materials, etc., occupying all that part of the nave which terminates with its organ, if we except a small gallery on the north-east side, devoted to English paper-hangings. From this extremity of the building, and from the organ gallery more especially, the finest *coup d'œil*[1] of the nave and its adjoining galleries may be obtained. …

Among the more striking objects in the south-eastern gallery, in the British half of the nave, are the silks and shawls, abutting on the transept; lace and embroideries, jewellery, and clocks and watches; and behind them military arms and models, raw produce, substances used as food, and chemicals. Traversing the gallery for naval architecture, by the organ, we have philosophical instruments, civil engineering, architecture and building models, musical instruments, anatomical models, glass chandeliers, decorations, etc.; china and pottery above the left side of the northern part of the transept. On the opposite side, in the north-eastern gallery, are perfumery, toys, fishing materials, miscellaneous articles, wax flowers, stained glass, British, French, Austrian, Belgian, Prussian, Bavarian, and American products.

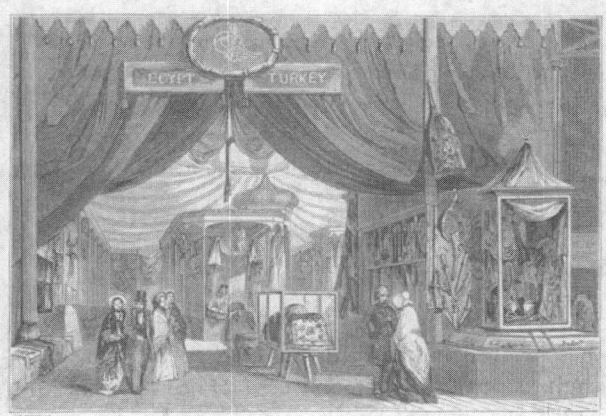

Clear passages under the galleries, of eight and ten feet broad, run the whole length of the building. Upon the extreme north and south sides, there are also longitudinal passages of similar width; the former interrupted by the offices of the commissioners and the entrances, and the latter by the refreshment rooms. With the exception of the offices, staircases, entrances, refreshment courts, and the various avenues and passages, including the transept, the whole of the ground-floor and galleries are available for exhibitors. As we have already shown, foreign countries, including the United States of America, occupy the east side of the transept above and below; whilst the United Kingdom, the East

[1] *coup d'œil* Here, line of sight.

Indies, and the British Colonies are confined to the west side; with the exception of the United Kingdom, which extends into parts of the north and south galleries, on the east side of the transept. The productions of England and her Colonies occupy thirty separate sections....

In retiring from the contemplation of this magnificent edifice, the extraordinary expedition with which it was constructed must be regarded as one of the marvels of the age.

---

from Henry Mayhew, *London Labour and the London Poor* (1851)

Mayhew's work is known primarily for the sympathetic attention it drew to the plight of poor Londoners. When the poor were not of "English stock," however, Mayhew was decidedly less sympathetic—as the following excerpt from his section on "Hindo Beggars" illustrates.

HINDO BEGGARS

[These] are those spare, snake-eyed Asiatics who walk the streets, coolly dressed in Manchester cottons, or chintz of a pattern commonly used for bed-furniture, to which the resemblance is carried out by the dark, polished colour of the thin limbs which it envelopes. They very often affect to be converts to the Christian religion, and give away tracts; with the intention of entrapping the sympathy of elderly ladies. They assert that they have been high-caste Brahmins,[1] but as untruth, even when not acting professionally, is habitual to them, there is not the slightest dependence to be placed on what they say. Sometimes, in the winter, they "do shallow," that is, stand on the kerb-stone of the pavement, in their thin, ragged clothes, and shiver as with cold and hunger, or crouch against a wall and whine like a whipped animal; at others they turn out with a small, barrel-shaped drum, on which they make a monotonous noise with their fingers, to which music they sing and dance. Or they will "stand pad with a fakement," i.e., wear a placard upon their breasts, that describes them as natives of Madagascar, in distress, converts to Christianity, anxious to get to a seaport where they can work their passage back. This is a favourite artifice with Lascars[2]—or they will sell lucifers,[3] or sweep a crossing, or do anything where their picturesque appearance, of which they are proud and conscious, can be effectively displayed. They are as cunning as they look, and can detect a sympathetic face among a crowd. They never beg of soldiers, or sailors, to whom they always give a wide berth as they pass them in the streets. ...

[1] *Brahmins* Members of the highest Hindu class or caste.

Dickens and Thackeray on the Race Question

Charles Dickens and William Makepeace Thackeray, widely regarded as the two greatest novelists of the age, were also great friends. And, as the excerpts below show, they held similar views on the question of race.

from Charles Dickens, "The Noble Savage," *Household Words* (1853)

To come to the point at once, I beg to say that I have not the least belief in the Noble Savage.[4] I consider him a prodigious nuisance, and an enormous superstition. His calling rum firewater, and me a pale face, wholly fail to reconcile me to him. I don't care what he calls me. I call him a savage, and I call a savage a something highly desirable to be civilised off the face of the earth. I think a mere gent (which I take to be the lowest form of civilisation) better than a howling, whistling, clucking, stamping, jumping, tearing savage. It is all one to me, whether he sticks a fish-bone through his visage, or bits of trees through the lobes of his ears, or bird's feathers in his head; whether he flattens his hair between

[2] *Lascars* East Asian sailors.

[3] *lucifers* Cheap matches sold by street peddlers.

[4] *Noble Savage* The notion of the "noble savage" is associated with the ideas of the French philosopher Jean-Jacques Rousseau (1712–78), who held that human beings are naturally innocent and good, but become corrupted by civilized society. According to this way of thinking, indigenous peoples were seen as inherently nobler because they were closer to a "state of nature."

two boards, or spreads his nose over the breadth of his face, or drags his lower lip down by great weights, or blackens his teeth, or knocks them out, or paints one cheek red and the other blue, or tattoos himself, or oils himself, or rubs his body with fat, or crimps it with knives. Yielding to whichsoever of these agreeable eccentricities, he is a savage cruel, false, thievish, murderous; addicted more or less to grease, entrails, and beastly customs; a wild animal with the questionable gift of boasting; a conceited, tiresome, bloodthirsty, monotonous humbug.

Yet it is extraordinary to observe how some people will talk about him, as they talk about the good old times; how they will regret his disappearance, in the course of this world's development, from such and such lands where his absence is a blessed relief and an indispensable preparation for the sowing of the very first seeds of any influence that can exalt humanity; how, even with the evidence of himself before them, they will either be determined to believe, or will suffer themselves to be persuaded into believing, that he is something which their five senses tell them he is not.

There was Mr. Catlin,[1] some few years ago, with his Ojibbeway Indians. Mr. Catlin was an energetic, earnest man, who had lived among more tribes of Indians than I need reckon up here, and who had written a picturesque and glowing book about them. With his party of Indians squatting and spitting on the table before him, or dancing their miserable jigs after their own dreary manner, he called, in all good faith, upon his civilised audience to take notice of their symmetry and grace, their perfect limbs, and the exquisite expression of their pantomime; and his civilised audience, in all good faith, complied and admired. Whereas, as mere animals, they were wretched creatures, very low in the scale and very poorly formed; and as men and women possessing any power of truthful dramatic expression by means of action, they were no better than the chorus at an Italian Opera in England—and would have been worse if such a thing were possible.

Mine are no new views of the noble savage. The greatest writers on natural history found him out long ago. Buffon[2] knew what he was, and showed why he is the sulky tyrant that he is to his women, and how it happens (Heaven be praised!) that his race is spare in numbers. For evidence of the quality of his moral nature, pass himself for a moment and refer to his "faithful dog." Has he ever improved a dog, or attached a dog, since his nobility first ran wild in woods, and was brought down (at a very long shot) by Pope?[3] Or does the animal that is the friend of man, always degenerate in his low society?

It is not the miserable nature of the noble savage that is the new thing; it is the whimpering over him with maudlin admiration, and the affecting to regret him, and the drawing of any comparison of advantage between the blemishes of civilisation and the tenor of his swinish life. There may have been a change now and then in those diseased absurdities, but there is none in him.

Think of the Bushmen.[4] Think of the two men and the two women who have been exhibited about England for some years. Are the majority of persons—who remember the horrid little leader of that party in his festering bundle of hides, with his filth and his antipathy to water, and his straddled legs, and his odious eyes shaded by his brutal hand, and his cry of "Qu-u-u-u-aaa!" (Bosjesman[5] for something desperately insulting I have no doubt)— conscious of an affectionate yearning towards that noble savage, or is it idiosyncratic in me to abhor, detest, abominate, and abjure him? I have no reserve on this subject, and will frankly state that, setting aside that stage of the entertainment when he counterfeited the death of some creature he had shot, by laying his head on his hand and shaking his left leg—at which time I think it would have been justifiable homicide to slay him—I have never seen that group sleeping, smoking, and expectorating round their brazier, but I have sincerely desired that something might happen to the charcoal

[1] *Mr. Catlin* George Catlin (1796–1872), pioneered the Wild West Show, which brought indigenous peoples and cultures from the American West to the American east coast and to Europe.

[2] *Buffon* Georges-Louis Leclerc, Comte de Buffon (1707–88), French naturalist and mathematician.

[3] *Pope* Alexander Pope (1688–1744), British poet.

[4] *Bushmen* European name for peoples of the Kalahari desert.

[5] *Bosjesman* Language of the "Bushmen."

smouldering therein, which would cause the immediate suffocation of the whole of the noble strangers.

There is at present a party of Zulu Kaffirs[1] exhibiting at the St. George's Gallery, Hyde Park Corner, London. These noble savages are represented in a most agreeable manner; they are seen in an elegant theatre, fitted with appropriate scenery of great beauty, and they are described in a very sensible and unpretending lecture, delivered with a modesty which is quite a pattern to all similar exponents. Though extremely ugly, they are much better shaped than such of their predecessors as I have referred to; and they are rather picturesque to the eye, though far from odoriferous to the nose. What a visitor left to his own interpretings and imaginings might suppose these noblemen to be about, when they give vent to that pantomimic expression which is quite settled to be the natural gift of the noble savage, I cannot possibly conceive; for it is so much too luminous for my personal civilisation that it conveys no idea to my mind beyond a general stamping, ramping, and raving, remarkable (as everything in savage life is) for its dire uniformity. But let us—with the interpreter's assistance, of which I for one stand so much in need—see what the noble savage does in Zulu Kaffirland.

The noble savage sets a king to reign over him, to whom he submits his life and limbs without a murmur or question, and whose whole life is passed chin deep in a lake of blood; but who, after killing incessantly, is in his turn killed by his relations and friends, the moment a grey hair appears on his head. All the noble savage's wars with his fellow-savages (and he takes no pleasure in anything else) are wars of extermination—which is the best thing I know of him, and the most comfortable to my mind when I look at him. He has no moral feelings of any kind, sort, or description; and his "mission" may be summed up as simply diabolical.

The ceremonies with which he faintly diversifies his life are, of course, of a kindred nature. If he wants a wife he appears before the kennel of the gentleman whom he has selected for his father-in-law, attended by a party of male friends of a very strong flavour, who screech and whistle and stamp an offer of so many cows for the young lady's hand. The chosen father-in-law—also supported by a high-flavoured party of male friends—screeches, whistles, and yells (being seated on the ground, he can't stamp) that there never was such a daughter in the market as his daughter, and that he must have six more cows. The son-in-law and his select circle of backers screech, whistle, stamp, and yell in reply, that they will give three more cows. The father-in-law (an old deluder, overpaid at the beginning) accepts four, and rises to bind the bargain. The whole party, the young lady included, then falling into epileptic convulsions, and screeching, whistling, stamping, and yelling together—and nobody taking any notice of the young lady (whose charms are not to be thought of without a shudder)—the noble savage is considered married, and his friends make demoniacal leaps at him by way of congratulation.

When the noble savage finds himself a little unwell, and mentions the circumstance to his friends, it is immediately perceived that he is under the influence of witchcraft. A learned personage, called an Imyanger or Witch Doctor, is immediately sent for to Nooker the Umtargartie, or smell out the witch. The male inhabitants of the kraal[2] being seated on the ground, the learned doctor, got up like a grizzly bear, appears, and administers a dance of a most terrific nature, during the exhibition of which remedy he incessantly gnashes his teeth, and howls:—"I am the original physician to Nooker the Umtargartie. Yow yow yow! No connexion with any other establishment. Till till till! All other Umtargarties are feigned Umtargarties, Boroo Boroo! but I perceive here a genuine and real Umtargartie, Hoosh Hoosh Hoosh! in whose blood I, the original Imyanger and Nookerer, Blizzerum Boo! will wash these bear's claws of mine. O yow yow yow!" All this time the learned physician is looking out among the attentive faces for some unfortunate man who owes him a cow, or who has given him any small offence, or against whom, without offence, he has conceived a spite. Him he never fails to Nooker as the Umtargartie, and he is instantly

[1] *Kaffirs* Derogatory term for Africans.

[2] *kraal* A community of indigenous people in southern or central Africa, typically dwelling in huts surrounded by a stockade.

killed. In the absence of such an individual, the usual practice is to Nooker the quietest and most gentlemanly person in company. But the nookering is invariably followed on the spot by the butchering.

Some of the noble savages in whom Mr. Catlin was so strongly interested, and the diminution of whose numbers, by rum and smallpox, greatly affected him, had a custom not unlike this, though much more appalling and disgusting in its odious details.

The women being at work in the fields, hoeing the Indian corn, and the noble savage being asleep in the shade, the chief has sometimes the condescension to come forth, and lighten the labour by looking at it. On these occasions, he seats himself in his own savage chair, and is attended by his shield-bearer: who holds over his head a shield of cowhide—in shape like an immense mussel shell fearfully and wonderfully, after the manner of a theatrical supernumerary. But lest the great man should forget his greatness in the contemplation of the humble works of agriculture, there suddenly rushes in a poet, retained for the purpose, called a Praiser. This literary gentleman wears a leopard's head over his own, and a dress of tigers' tails; he has the appearance of having come express on his hind legs from the Zoological Gardens; and he incontinently strikes up the chief's praises, plunging and tearing all the while. There is a frantic wickedness in this brute's manner of worrying the air, and gnashing out, "O what a delightful chief he is! O what a delicious quantity of blood he sheds! O how majestically he laps it up! O how charmingly cruel he is! O how he tears the flesh of his enemies and crunches the bones! O how like the tiger and the leopard and the wolf and the bear he is! O, row row row row, how fond I am of him!" which might tempt the Society of Friends to charge at a hand-gallop into the Swartz-Kop location and exterminate the whole kraal.

When war is afoot among the noble savages—which is always—the chief holds a council to ascertain whether it is the opinion of his brothers and friends in general that the enemy shall be exterminated. On this occasion, after the performance of an Umsebeuza, or war song,—which is exactly like all the other songs, the chief makes a speech to his brothers and friends, arranged in single file. No particular order is observed during the delivery of this address, but every gentleman who finds himself excited by the subject, instead of crying "Hear, hear!" as is the custom with us, darts from the rank and tramples out the life, or crushes the skull, or mashes the face, or scoops out the eyes, or breaks the limbs, or performs a whirlwind of atrocities on the body, of an imaginary enemy. Several gentlemen becoming thus excited at once, and pounding away without the least regard to the orator, that illustrious person is rather in the position of an orator in an Irish House of Commons. But, several of these scenes of savage life bear a strong generic resemblance to an Irish election, and I think would be extremely well received and understood at Cork.[1]

In all these ceremonies the noble savage holds forth to the utmost possible extent about himself; from which (to turn him to some civilised account) we may learn, I think, that as egotism is one of the most offensive and contemptible littlenesses a civilised man can exhibit, so it is really incompatible with the interchange of ideas; inasmuch as if we all talked about ourselves we should soon have no listeners, and must be all yelling and screeching at once on our own separate accounts: making society hideous. It is my opinion that if we retained in us anything of the noble savage, we could not get rid of it too soon. But the fact is clearly otherwise. Upon the wife and dowry question, substituting coin for cows, we have assuredly nothing of the Zulu Kaffir left. The endurance of despotism is one great distinguishing mark of a savage always. The improving world has quite got the better of that too. In like manner, Paris is a civilised city, and the Théâtre Français a highly civilised theatre; and we shall never hear, and never have heard in these later days (of course) of the Praiser THERE. No, no, civilised poets have better work to do. As to Nookering Umtargarties, there are no pretended Umtargarties in Europe, and no European powers to Nooker them; that would be mere spydom, subordination, small malice, superstition, and false pretence. And as to private Umtargarties, are we not in

[1] *Several gentlemen ... Cork* Dickens is displaying his prejudice against the Irish, who had historically been held, by many in England, to have been "savages."

the year eighteen hundred and fifty-three, with spirits rapping at our doors?

To conclude as I began. My position is, that if we have anything to learn from the Noble Savage, it is what to avoid. His virtues are a fable; his happiness is a delusion; his nobility, nonsense.

We have no greater justification for being cruel to the miserable object, than for being cruel to a WILLIAM SHAKESPEARE or an ISAAC NEWTON; but he passes away before an immeasurably better and higher power than ever ran wild in any earthly woods, and the world will be all the better when his place knows him no more.

from William Makepeace Thackeray, Letters to Mrs. Carmichael-Smyth

To Mrs. Carmichael-Smyth, 26 January 1853

… I don't believe Blacky *is* my man and my brother, though God forbid I should own him or flog him, or part him from his wife and children. But the question is a much longer [one than] is set forth in Mrs. Stowe's philosophy:[1] and I shan't speak about it, till I know it, or till it's my business, or I think I can do good.

To Mrs. Carmichael-Smyth, 13 February 1853

… They are not my men and brethren,[2] these strange people with retreating foreheads, with great obtruding lips and jaws: with capacities for thought, pleasure, endurance quite different to mine. They are not suffering as you are impassioning yourself for their wrongs as you read Mrs. Stowe, they are grinning and joking in the sun; roaring with laughter as they stand about the streets in squads; very civil, kind and gentle, even winning in their manner when you accost them at gentlemen's houses, where they do all the service. But they don't seem to me to be the same as white men, any more than asses are the same animals as horses; I don't mean this disrespectfully, but simply that there is such a difference of colour, habits, conformation of brains, that we must acknowledge it, and can't by any rhetorical phrase get it over; Sambo[3] is not my man and my brother; the very aspect of his face is grotesque and inferior.… As soon as the cheap substitute is found, depend on it the Planter, who stoutly pleads humanity now as the one of the reasons why he can't liberate his people, will get rid of them quickly enough; & the price of the slave-goods will fall so that owners won't care to hold such an unprofitable & costly stock.

[1] *Mrs. Stowe's philosophy* Reference to Harriet Beecher Stowe's anti-slavery novel, *Uncle Tom's Cabin* (1852).

[2] *They are … brethren* Reference to abolitionist materials that featured an enslaved man in chains accompanied by the caption "Am I not a man and your brother?"

Conservatives, Liberals, and Empire

The following excerpts from speeches by Liberal Prime Minister William Gladstone, Conservative Prime Minister Benjamin Disraeli, and business-person, mining magnate, politician, and colonizer Cecil Rhodes provide three different perspectives on the attitudes taken by Britain's two main political parties towards issues of Empire in the second half of the nineteenth century.

from William Gladstone, "Our Colonies" (1855)

But an idea far more important and effective to a far greater extent has been the idea that the colonies ought to be maintained for the purpose of establishing an exclusive trade, the whole profit of which should be confined to the mother country, and should be enjoyed by the mother country. This was in fact the basis of the modern colonial system of Europe. I do not speak now of the political system, but it was the basis of the commercial laws of the countries which had colonies: that the industry of the colonists, instead of having a fair field and equal favour given to it, was attempted to be made entirely subservient to the interests and the profit

[3] *Sambo* Common name given to enslaved people which became a derogatory term for any black person.

of the mother country. It was placed in an unfair position. People were told in fact that they might go to the colonies, but that whatever they produced in the colonies must be sent to the British market—nay, that it must be sent in British vessels to the British market—nay, that whatever was produced must be sent to the British market in British vessels and in the state of raw produce, because if sent in other vessels, although it were sent better and cheaper, it would not be for the interest of the British shipowner, and if sent in a manufactured state it would not be for the interest of the British manufacturer. …

Now, as I repudiate any and all of these reasons for desiring the possession of colonies, it is but fair that I should endeavour to state why I think colonies are desirable for a country circumstanced as England is. I have stated, that I do not think them desirable simply to puff up our reputation, apart from the basis and substance on which it rests. It is plain that they are not to be desired for revenue, because they do not yield it. It is plain that they are not to be desired for trading monopoly, because that we have entirely abandoned. It is plain they are not to be desired for patronage, properly so called, within their limits, because they will not allow us to exercise patronage, and I am bound to say, I do not think the public men of this country have any desire so to exercise it. With respect to territory, it is perfectly plain that mere extension of territory is not a legitimate object of ambition, unless you can show that you are qualified to make use of that territory for the purposes for which God gave the earth to man. Why then are colonies desirable? In my opinion, and I submit it to you with great respect, they are desirable both for the material and for the moral and social results which a wise system of colonisation is calculated to produce. As to the first, the effect of colonisation undoubtedly is to increase the trade and employment of the mother country. Take the case of the emigrant going across the Atlantic. Why does he go across the Atlantic? Because he expects—and in general he is the best judge of his own interests—to get better wages across the Atlantic than he can get at home. If he goes across the Atlantic to get better wages, he leaves in the labour market at home fewer persons than before, and consequently raises the rate of wages at home by carrying himself away from the competition with his fellows. By going to the colony and supplying it with labour he likewise creates a demand for capital there, and by this means he creates a trade between the colony and the mother country. The capital and labour thus employed in the colony raise and export productions, for which commodities are wanted in return. …

But I do not concede that the material benefit of colonies is the only consideration which we are able to plead. Their moral and social advantage is a very great one. If we are asked why, on these grounds, it is desirable that colonies should be founded and possessed, I answer by asking another question—Why is it desirable that your population at home should increase? Why is it that you rejoice, always presuming that the increase of population goes hand in hand with equally favourable or more favourable conditions of existence for the mass of the people—why is it that you rejoice in an increase of population at home? Because an increase of population is an increase of power, an increase of strength and stability to the state, and because it multiplies the number of people who, as we hope, are living under good laws, and belong to a country to which it is an honour and an advantage to belong. That is the great moral benefit that attends the foundation of British colonies. We think that our country is a country blessed with laws and a constitution that are eminently beneficial to mankind, and if so, what can be more to be desired than that we should have the means of reproducing in different portions of the globe something as like as may be to that country which we honour and revere? I think it is in a work by Mr. Roebuck that the expression is used, "that the object of colonisation is the creation of so many happy Englands." It is the reproduction of the image and likeness of England—the reproduction of a country in which liberty is reconciled with order, in which ancient institutions stand in harmony with popular freedom, and a full recognition of popular rights, and in which religion and law have found one of their most favoured homes. …

from Benjamin Disraeli, "Conservative and Liberal Principles" (1872)

Gentlemen, there is another and second great object of the Tory party. If the first is to maintain the institutions of the country, the second is, in my opinion, to uphold the Empire of England. If you look to the history of this country since the advent of Liberalism—forty years ago—you will find that there has been no effort so continuous, so subtle, supported by so much energy, and carried on with so much ability and acumen, as the attempts of Liberalism to effect the disintegration of the Empire of England.

And, gentlemen, of all its efforts, this is the one which has been the nearest to success. Statesmen of the highest character, writers of the most distinguished ability, the most organised and efficient means, have been employed in this endeavour. It has been proved to all of us that we have lost money by our colonies. It has been shown with precise, with mathematical demonstration, that there never was a jewel in the Crown of England that was so truly costly as the possession of India. How often has it been suggested that we should at once emancipate ourselves from this incubus.[1] Well, that result was nearly accomplished. When those subtle views were adopted by the country under the plausible plea of granting self-government to the colonies, I confess that I myself thought that the tie was broken. Not that I for one object to self-government. I cannot conceive how our distant colonies can have their affairs administered except by self-government. But self-government, in my opinion, when it was conceded, ought to have been conceded as part of a great policy of Imperial consolidation. It ought to have been accompanied by an Imperial tariff, by securities for the people of England for the enjoyment of the unappropriated lands which belonged to the Sovereign as their trustee, and by a military code which should have precisely defined the means and the responsibilities by which the colonies should be defended, and by which, if necessary, this country should call for aid from the colonies themselves. It ought, further, to have been accompanied by the institution of some representative council in the metropolis, which would have brought the colonies into constant and continuous relations with the Home Government. All this, however, was omitted because those who advised that policy—and I believe their convictions were sincere —looked upon the colonies of England, looked even upon our connection with India, as a burden upon this country, viewing everything in a financial aspect, and totally passing by those moral and political considerations which make nations great, and by the influence of which alone men are distinguished from animals.

Well, what has been the result of this attempt during the reign of Liberalism for the disintegration of the Empire? It has entirely failed. But how has it failed? Through the sympathy of the colonies with the Mother Country. They have decided that the Empire shall not be destroyed, and in my opinion no minister in this country will do his duty who neglects any opportunity of reconstructing as much as possible our Colonial Empire, and of responding to those distant sympathies which may become the source of incalculable strength and happiness to this land. …

[1] *incubus* Mythical demon said to rape sleeping women, and in so doing to drain their life force to sustain itself. Figuratively, an evil that drains vital energy.

---

from Cecil Rhodes, Speech Delivered in Cape Town, 18 July 1899

And, sir, my people have changed. I speak of the English people, with their marvellous common sense, coupled with their powers of imagination—all thoughts of a Little England are over. They are tumbling over each other, Liberals and Conservatives, to show which side are the greatest and most enthusiastic Imperialists. The people have changed, and so do all the parties, just like the Punch and Judy show[2] at a country fair. The people have found out that England is small,

[2] *Punch and Judy show* Puppet show involving Mr. Punch and his wife Judy.

Cecil Rhodes (1858–1902), nowadays best known for having endowed the Rhodes Scholarships for study at Oxford University, was the leading Briton in Southern Africa in the late nineteenth century—and a leading backer of the extension of British commercial and political interests in Africa as a whole. (The statue of the Colossus in the ancient city of Rhodes to which this cartoon alludes is said to have straddled the entrance to the harbor.)

and her trade is large, and they have also found out that other people are taking their share of the world, and enforcing hostile tariffs. The people of England are finding out that "trade follows the flag,"[1] and they have all become Imperialists. They are not going to part with any territory. And the bygone ideas of nebulous republics are over. The English people intend to retain every inch of land they have got, and perhaps, sir, they intend to secure a few more inches. …

from David Livingstone, "Cambridge Lecture Number 1" (1858)

The following excerpts are from a speech delivered at Cambridge University by the famous missionary; it was received with extended cheering.

When I went to Africa about seventeen years ago I resolved to acquire an accurate knowledge of the native tongues; and as I continued, while there, to speak generally in the African languages, the result is that I am not now very fluent in my own; but if you will excuse my imperfections under that head, I will endeavour to give you as clear an idea of Africa as I can. …

My object in going into the country south of the desert was to instruct the natives in a knowledge of Christianity, but many circumstances prevented my living amongst them more than seven years, amongst which were considerations arising out of the slave system carried on by the Dutch Boers. I resolved to go into the country beyond, and soon found that, for the purposes of commerce, it was necessary to have a path to the sea. I might have gone on instructing the natives in religion, but as civilization and Christianity must go on together, I was obliged to find a path to the sea, in order that I should not sink to the level of the natives. The chief was overjoyed at the suggestion, and furnished me with twenty-seven men, and canoes, and provisions, and presents for the tribes through whose country we had to pass. We might have taken a shorter path to the sea than that to the north, and then to the west, by which we went; but along the country by the shorter route, there is an insect called the tsetse, whose bite is fatal to horses, oxen, and dogs, but not to men or donkeys. You seem to think there is a connexion between the two. The habitat of that insect is along the shorter route to the sea. The bite of it is fatal to domestic animals, not immediately, but certainly in the course of two or three months; the animal grows leaner and leaner, and gradually dies of emaciation: a horse belonging to Gordon Cumming died of a bite five or six months after it was bitten.

On account of this insect, I resolved to go to the north, and then westwards to the Portuguese settlement of Loanda. Along the course of the river which we passed, game was so abundant that there was no difficulty in supplying the wants of my whole party: antelopes were so tame that they might be shot from the canoe. But beyond 14 degrees of south latitude the natives had guns, and had themselves destroyed the game, so that I and my party had to live on charity. The people, however, in that central region were friendly and hospitable: but they had nothing but vegetable productions: the most abundant was the cassava, which, however nice when made into tapioca pudding, resembles in its more primitive condition nothing so much as a mess of laundress's starch. There was a desire in the various villages through which we passed to have intercourse with us, and kindness and hospitality were shown us; but when we got near the Portuguese settlement of Angola the case was changed, and payment was demanded for every thing. But I had nothing to pay with. Now the people had been in the habit of trading with the slavers, and so they said I might give one of my men in payment for what I wanted. When I shewed them that I could not do this, they looked upon me as an interloper, and I was sometimes in danger of being murdered.

[1] *trade … flag* Popular dictum of the period, meant to encourage colonization.

David Livingstone, 1864. Photo by Thomas Annan.

As we neared the coast, the name of England was recognized, and we got on with ease. Upon one occasion, when I was passing through the parts visited by slave-traders, a chief who wished to shew me some kindness offered me a slave-girl: upon explaining that I had a little girl of my own, whom I should not like my own chief to give to a black man, the chief thought I was displeased with the size of the girl, and sent me one a head taller. By this and other means I convinced my men of my opposition to the principle of slavery; and when we arrived at Loanda I took them on board a British vessel, where I took a pride in showing them that those countrymen of mine and those guns were there for the purpose of putting down the slave-trade. They were convinced from what they saw of the honesty of Englishmen's intentions; and the hearty reception they met with from the sailors made them say to me, "We see they are your countrymen, for they have hearts like you." On the journey, the men had always looked forward to reaching the coast: they had seen Manchester prints and other articles imported therefrom, and they could not believe they were made by mortal hands. On reaching the sea, they thought that they had come to the end of the world. They said, "We marched along with our father, thinking the world was a large plain without limit; but all at once the land said 'I am finished, there is no more of me'"; and they called themselves the true old men—the true ancients—having gone to the end of the world. On reaching Loanda, they commenced trading in firewood, and also engaged themselves at sixpence a day in unloading coals, brought by a steamer for the supply of the cruiser lying there to watch the slave-vessels. On their return, they told their people "we worked for a whole moon, carrying away the stones that burn." By the time they were ready to go back to their own country, each had secured a large bundle of goods. On the way back, however, fever detained them, and their goods were all gone, leaving them on their return home, as poor as when they started. …

A prospect is now before us of opening Africa for commerce and the Gospel. Providence has been preparing the way, for even before I proceeded to the Central basin it had been conquered and rendered safe by a chief named Sebituane, and the language of the Bechuanas made the fashionable tongue, and that was one of the languages into which Mr. Moffat had translated the Scriptures. Sebituane also discovered Lake Ngami some time previous to my explorations in that part. In going back to that country my object is to open up traffic along the banks of the Zambesi, and also to preach the Gospel. The natives of Central Africa are very desirous of trading, but their only traffic is at present in slaves, of which the poorer people have an unmitigated horror; it is therefore most desirable to encourage the former principle, and thus open a way for the consumption of free productions, and the introduction of Christianity and commerce. By encouraging the native propensity for trade, the advantages that might be derived in a commercial point of view are incalculable; nor should we lose sight of the inestimable blessings it is in our power to bestow upon the unenlightened African, by giving him the light of Christianity. Those two pioneers of civilization—Christianity and commerce—should ever be inseparable; and Englishmen should be warned by the fruits of neglecting that principle as exemplified in the result of the management of Indian affairs. By trading with Africa, also, we should at length be independent of slave labour, and thus discountenance practices so obnoxious to every Englishman.

Though the natives are not absolutely anxious to receive the Gospel, they are open to Christian influences. Among the Bechuanas the Gospel was well received. These people think it a crime to shed a tear, but I have seen some of them weep at the recollection of their sins when God had opened their hearts to Christianity and repentance. …

I beg to direct your attention to Africa; I know that in a few years I shall be cut off in that country, which is now open; do not let it be shut again! I go back to Africa to try to make an open path for commerce and Christianity; do you carry out the work which I have begun. I LEAVE IT WITH YOU!

Eliza M., "Account of Cape Town," *King William's Town Gazette* (1863)

The following account (brought to light by M.J. Daymond et al. and the *Women Writing Africa Project*[1]) is one of the most remarkable literary descriptions we have of the world of nineteenth-century British colonialism from the point of view of one of the colonized. King William's Town was a small town some 500 miles east of Cape Town, and Eliza M., as she was identified in the *King William's Town Gazette*, had attended school at St. Matthew's Mission in the area. As Daymond et al. suggest, such a piece as this would in all likelihood have "been written as a school exercise." It would have been published, they speculate, "partly because its naiveté was amusing to the whites, but also because it was proof of the civilizing policies of the missionaries. It was translated from Xhosa into English by an unknown translator." What may have seemed "amusing naiveté" to nineteenth-century settlers is more likely to strike the modern reader as a style of elemental freshness.

We left East London on the Sunday, while it was raining; the sea was fighting very much, and there were soldiers going to England and their wives. On the Tuesday we arrived at Algoa Bay, and boats came to fetch the people who were going there, and other people came in. The ship went off the same day. A great wind blew, and I thought myself that if it had

[1] *Women Writing Africa Project* M.J. Daymond et al., eds., *Women Writing Africa: The Southern Region* (New York: The Feminist Press, 2003), 98–104.

been another ship, it would not have been able to go on, but in its going, it kept twisting about, it did not go straight, but it went well on the day of our arrival, for the wind was good. We arrived on the Friday. While I was in the ship, I forgot I was on the water, it was like a house inside, but outside it was not like a house. There is everything that is kept at home; there were fowls and sheep and pigs, and slaughtering every day. I kept looking at the thing which makes the ship go. There are two horses inside, made of iron, which make it go; and when I looked inside, it was very frightful. There are many bed-rooms inside. The ship we were in is named the *Norman*, it is a steamer. It was unpleasant when nothing appeared, but when we left the Bay, we saw the mountains till we got to the Cape. One mountain is called the Lion's Head, and another is called Green Point, and I myself saw those mountains. That which is called the Lion's Head, is like a lion asleep. And another mountain above the town is that called Table Mountain; nevertheless it is not like a table, still that name is proper for it.

Before I came into the town, my heart said, "this place is not large," but when I entered it, I wondered, and was afraid. Oh, we slept that day. I have forgotten to relate something I saw the day I arrived. I saw black people, and I thought they were our kind, but they are not; they are Slams, called in English, Malays. Also, I was astonished at their large hats, pointed at the top, and large below. I saw some making baskets of reeds, and I wished I knew how to do it. On the Saturday evening, we went to a shop to buy butter and bread. At night lights were hung up throughout the whole town. I had thought we were going to walk in the darkness. I have not yet seen houses built with grass, like those we live in, they are high beautiful houses. The roads where people walk, are very fine. I have not yet seen a dirty, muddy place in the whole town. On the Sunday, bells sounded; there is one big one, and other small ones; we went to service in the great church.

Early on the Monday, wagons came about to sell things. Really people here get these things for nothing from their owners. A person can get men's trousers for three shillings each, yet in other places a person can never get them for that money. You can get three pairs of stockings for a shilling, a child's cap for a penny; you can get a width of a dress for threepence, if it is five widths, it is a shilling and threepence. There are little wagons, the man who drives the horses sits behind, the proprietor does nothing, he sits so.

Another thing. The shoes of the Malays astonished me. There is a heel, and yonder on before a piece of wood sticks out, and they put it between their toes, and so make a clattering like the Germans. As things are to be got for such little money, how cheap must they be in England!

On Friday I saw a man riding in a wagon, there was a barrel inside and a cross-bar, and the water came out there. I don't know how it came out. It watered the new road, which is being made. And on Tuesday I saw people working at slates, taking off their ends—it was a great heap; the people who were at work were four. On the day of our arrival, a house was burnt, the people escaped, but I don't know whether the goods escaped. There are carts which go every day, carrying earth to throw on the road which is being mended, drawn by one horse.

There is a house where there are all kinds of beasts, and there are figures of black people, as if they were alive; their blackness is very ugly; also the bones of a man when he is dead, and birds and elephants, and lions, and tigers and sea-shells. I was afraid of those people, and the skeleton. There is also an ape holding Indian Corn, and there are monkeys.

In the evening we went out again, we went to the houses of the Malays; we went to see their decorations, for they were rejoicing because their days of fasting were ended. They were very beautiful; they had made flowers of paper, you would never think they were made of paper. We went for the sole purpose of seeing these works. They made a great noise, singing as they walked; you would laugh to see the children dancing outside and clapping their hands.

There are also wagons there for the sale of fish. The proprietors sound a thing like a horn to announce that he who wishes to buy let him buy. There are others for collecting dust-heaps, they ring a bell. There are vehicles to convey two people, he who drives the horses, and he who sits inside. In some there are windows and lights lit at night: those windows are two.

There are not many trees in the town; in some places there are not many at all, but in one place it is like the bush; it is pleasant underneath the trees; there are stools to sit on when a person is tired. That path is very long; I saw two Newfoundland dogs. I did not know that I should ever come to see them when I heard them spoken of. They are dogs with large heads and great long ears; the hair is like sheep's wool, and they have great claws; they are suited to assist people. It seemed as if they could swallow me without chewing; I was very much afraid, but one was not very big, it was about the size of the dogs of black people, when it barks, it says so with a great voice. Also, I saw sheep rather unlike others, in the tail here it was very large, the head was small, and the body was large and fat.

I have forgotten to mention something which I ought to have said before; when I came out of the ship and walked on land the earth seemed to move, and when I entered a house, it seemed to imitate the sailing of a ship, and when I lay down it seemed to move.

I saw an ox-wagon here, but I had not imagined that I should see a wagon.

We go to a very large beautiful Church; I don't forget the people who sing, the English; the prayers are said with thin voices as if it were singing; but the chief thing done is singing frequently, all the while there is continually singing, and then sitting. There is a Kafir school here; I went one day, they were reading; they can read well; there are also carpenters &c.

There is another place besides that which I said is like the bush, and in that place there are trees and flowers, and two fountains; a thing is stuck in, and the water comes out above. I saw the date-tree when it is young; it is one leaf, yet when it is grown, it is a very large tree. In that place there are wild birds, doves are there, and those birds which the English call canaries, and a very beautiful bird, its tail is long, its bill is red.

Yesterday the soldiers had sports, the music-band played, and when they finished playing they fired. They were many, and they fired together. And as we were walking, they fired; I was very much startled and afraid. And to-day they are playing the music. It seems to-day it exceeds in sweetness, I mean its sound.

There came a person here who is a Kafir. I rejoiced very much when I heard that he too was one. He asked me what I had come to do here; I said "I am only travelling." He asked whether I was a prisoner, and I said "No." He said he was very glad, he had thought I was a prisoner. I told him that I was going away again, and he said "May you go in peace, the Lord preserve you well till you arrive whence you came." I never saw a person like him of such kindness; he said he had come here to learn, he came from where I did; but I should not have known him to be a Kafir, and he did not know that I was one.

There are creatures which are eaten; they come from the sea, their name is called crawfish, they are frightful in appearance, yet their flesh is very fine and white.

The person of this house is a dyer of clothes, the white he makes red, and the red green, and the brown he makes black. I saw the wood with which they dye. Soap is cut in pieces, and put in water, and heated and boiled well, and continually stirred. This thing—dyeing clothes, is a great work. Water is even in the house; I don't know where it comes from, a person turns a thing, and fresh water comes out as if it were of a river.

There are also carts for selling meat, and for selling bread. I saw the fire-wagon, I did nothing but wonder. I did not know that it was such a big thing. It is long, with many wheels, they are not so large as those of an ox-wagon; people sit in places inside. The wheels run on metal; I say I could do nothing but wonder very much. I had not thought that it was such a great thing. And when it is about to proceed it says "Sh!" I don't know whether it is the boiling of the water; it hastens exceedingly, a person would be unable to notice it well, yet now some people say that this is a small one which I have seen. If it treads on anything, it must smash it, it is a very great thing. I shall never forget it. Where I saw it, the place was fenced on both sides, and I beheld it from the outside. I entered it another week after I had seen it; we went to Somerset West and slept one night. In the morning we returned by it: when I was inside, the earth seemed to move; it is pleasant to ride inside. I end now although this is not all the news about it. When I was in it, I saw a sugar plant; it is not a large plant, it is short with red flowers. I saw other trees at Somerset West which I had never seen before.

One day I saw people going to a burial, the carriages were black, but that people should wear black clothes is done also among the natives where a person has died; there were stuck up black feathers, and on the graves were placed stones with writing; the name of the person was written, and the years of his age, and the year in which he died.

I have seen to-day another thing which I did not know of, that thing which is said to be always done by white people in this month of May. They make themselves black people, they smear themselves with something black, with red patches on the cheeks; a thing is made with evergreens, and a man is put inside, and two people carry it, and another man carries a pan, and goes begging for money.

Another thing which I saw during the past month, was people going to the Governor's house—little chiefs, and chiefs of the soldiers, some had hats with red and white feathers, and silver coats, and gold swords, and the bishop went too. I heard it said that they were going to hear the things which were about to be spoken by people who had come from Graham's Town, King William's Town, Beaufort, and other places; it was said that these people were going to speak of the state of those towns and the doings of the people who live there. I do not say that those coats were really of gold, I say there was gold on some parts of them, on the arms and the back.

Also I have seen the fruit of the tree which the English call the chestnut; I did not see what the tree is like, the fruit is nice, the outside of it is hard; when you eat it it is sweet and edible like the potato, you can roast it or boil it. There is another fruit called Banana in English, it also is a nice fruit; it is not boiled or roasted, it is eaten like other fruits. There is a great white sweet potato, it is called Sweet Potato; those potatoes are very large, I had never seen them before, they are nearly all long: I do not know whether they are the potatoes named "Medicine" by the Fingoes.

I am puzzled to know how to begin to relate what was done yesterday, but I will try. Yesterday was said to be the wedding-day of the Great Son of Victoria, but it was not really the day of his marriage, for he has been married some time. The thing first done was arranging the children of the schools and I was there too. All walked in threes, going from one street to another. When we left the school-house we took up our station on an open piece of ground, other people climbed on the houses, and others looked on from below. On one house where we were standing there was the figure of a man like a king, a red cloth was put as if it were held by him, it is called in English a flag. Amongst all of us there were flags of different beautiful kinds; we stood there a great while, till we saw a multitude of soldiers and their officers and little chiefs and different sorts of people: one set wore clothes all alike, another had different clothes and ancient hats which were worn by the people of that time. All these now went in front, a very long line, then followed the ranks of another school, and we came after them. When we had finished going through many streets, we went to stand in another open spot of ground. All the time we were walking we were singing the song of Victoria. And there we saw the Governor and his wife; we all saluted. Although it seems that I have written a great deal I have not yet wondered at the things done at night, but let me finish those of the day. We were given food. We saw boats going along with people inside and boys wearing red clothes; there followed one with an old man, his hairs were long and white. There was a woman at his side wearing short clothes. Other boats followed with people in them, all the time they were appearing the drum and trumpets were sounded. I don't know how I shall make myself understood. I never saw such a beautiful thing; some of the men wore short dresses and short coats, and others wore short trousers like those of the French. All these things were red. When we had finished walking we went to stand in an open piece of ground, then we all went home. I do not know if any other things were done.

We went out again in the evening to see the fireworks. First we went into the gardens, where there were what I shall call candles; but nevertheless they are not called so in English. They were lights put inside little red and green glasses—When I was at a distance I thought they were little round things, all these were hung up and fastened in the trees,—there were some large ones and there were others not put in glasses.

We walked and went to a great crowd of people, we could not tell what we should do to see that which we came to see. There we saw a tall man with a high hat, I did not understand how it was made, and another man wearing women's clothes continually playing with that tall man. All these things have their names in English, some were called *Punch & Judy*, *Spectre*, *Father of the Doomed Arm-chair*, or the *Maid, the Murderer and the Midnight Avenger*,[1] and many other plays besides these. We passed on from that woman and man and went to see white people smeared with soot, they went into a house made of a tent where there were stools, and two came out and spoke to the people saying, "Ladies and gentlemen, come in and see what we have got here inside." Some went in and others did not, afterwards they opened that the people might see; there were black people sitting on chairs and singing. So we left; at the entrance of the garden there was written in letters of fire, "GOD bless Albert and Alexandra." In another place there were other things of fire, that place is called in English the Parade, where there was a thing like a light-house, on all sides there were candles. Some people sent up fire from Table Mountain, others from Green Point, others sent up fire in the midst of the town, it went up and came down again.

Besides these things there was another thing done, an ox was baked whole, the legs were not removed, only the inside and the hoofs. Many tables were set underneath the trees; that ox was intended for the poor people.

I am going to end now; I am very glad that I was brought here to see things which I never thought I should see.

There is another thing which has lately taken place, the birthday of Queen Victoria. Two balloons were made, no one went in them, there were only lights. That sort is called fire-balloons. The first was sent up; it rose very high till it was like a star: I did not see it again where it went. The other reappeared, it did not rise high like the first, it burnt, and fire came down like two stars.

I saw where newspapers are printed; four people were at work. I do not know what I shall say to tell about it. There is a thing which folds the papers and another thing which continually receives them. It made us sleepy.

E.M.

Translator unknown

[1] *Spectre ... Avenger* Popular plays of the period.

The Early Twentieth Century: From 1900 to Mid-Century

The first half of the twentieth century saw a fracturing of almost every aspect of British life. At the beginning of the century, Queen Victoria, monarch for 63 years, still reigned over a nation that had become the world's greatest economic and political power. Over the course of the nineteenth century, the industrial revolution had transformed the economy and Great Britain had become "factory to the world." Despite a high level of religious anxiety among the educated classes of the late Victorian period, the established church retained its authority over a God-fearing society. The working class was not always contented with its lot—and with reason—but the class hierarchy remained extraordinarily stable. So, too, did gender roles; a small minority of women was pressing to be given the vote, but they were regarded as extremists by the vast majority of the population. Expressions of sexuality were tightly circumscribed, and the possibility of anything other than heterosexuality was in much of society unmentioned (except for occasional veiled references to difficulties or scandals "of the Oscar Wilde sort"). And the British Empire had reached its zenith. The vast dominions of Canada and Australia had become semi-autonomous (in 1867 and 1901 respectively), but overwhelmingly their people were proud to call themselves British subjects. Despite a lively debate in the latter half of the nineteenth century as to whether Britain's imperial ambitions were truly benefiting either the colonizers or the colonized, the majority of English people were not "little Englanders" looking to reduce Britain's overseas dominance; they were pleased that British rule extended over all of India, a very large part of Africa, and a considerable amount of the rest of the world. England was seen by the English, in the words of the popular poet W.E. Henley, as the "Chosen daughter of the Lord." Britain had certainly not been immune to change in the second half the nineteenth century—indeed, many of the lines along which twentieth-century society would fracture were in place in the late Victorian era. Political and ideological strains that would shake class structure were already forming; categories of gender and sexuality were already becoming markedly different from what they had been a decade or two earlier; and the "Aesthetes" had begun in the 1890s to break free of characteristically Victorian patterns of anxiety over the religious, the moral, and the aesthetic. But for most people of the United Kingdom the world in 1900 seemed recognizably the same world as that of 1850, and Britain held a central place within it.

By 1950 that world had been distinctly altered. The four years of World War I had resulted in the deaths of millions and had had a catastrophic effect on the nation's spirit; the great economic depression of the 1930s had bred poverty and despair; the seven years of World War II had threatened Britain's survival and left the nation exhausted, even in victory; and immediately in its wake, with Britain still physically and emotionally devastated, had begun a new war, a "Cold War" against the Soviet Union. Exhausted by these struggles, Britain in 1950 had lost its place as the world's leading power to the United States. Daily life had been radically altered by the radio, the telephone, and the automobile. Church-going was in decline, and the nation was well on its way to becoming a secular society. Though Britain remained more class-conscious than North America or Australia, the class structure itself had seen great change; only the wealthy had servants, and all social classes partook of the same culture to an unprecedented extent. The Labour Party government of Clement Attlee, elected in 1945 in a clean break from Winston Churchill and the glorious but conservative path that he represented, had for five years been building a welfare state; this was Britain's first avowedly socialist government. "Votes for women"—to most minds a far-fetched notion in 1900—had in 1950 been a reality for over 20 years; women had done "men's work" during two long world wars, and were starting to wonder if winning the vote might represent the beginning rather than the end of the struggle for gender equality. Much of Britain was as repressed sexually as it had been in 1900—but more and more people were starting to see the awkwardness that surrounded sexual matters as an obstacle to be overcome rather than as the expression of a necessary and appropriate sense of modesty. And the sun was rapidly setting on the British Empire. The dominions were now fully independent and beginning to drift away from Britain culturally; India had been partitioned in 1947 into two independent nations; and in Britain's African and Caribbean possessions the stirrings of unrest that would lead to independence had already begun. In literature Britain had in the years between 1900 and 1950 undergone the Modernist revolution.[1] The sometimes fractured, sometimes free-flowing approaches to form that the poetry of T.S. Eliot, the plays of Samuel Beckett, and the prose fiction of James Joyce and Virginia Woolf represented had not been taken up by the majority of writers. Yet many serious writers in 1950 were aware of the expanded possibilities of literary form that modernism had revealed—and many wrote with a sense that the world was not the ordered and coherent whole that it had been widely assumed to be at the dawn of the twentieth century.

[1] "Modernist" and "Modernism" are commonly used as umbrella terms to describe a wide range of inter-connected intellectual and aesthetic developments of the first half of the twentieth century that occurred in France, Italy, the United States and other areas as well as in Britain. A connecting thread is that expressions of Modernism tend to shun the linear, the decorative, and the sentimental. They tend too towards the presentation of reality fractured into its component pieces—and conversely, towards a rejection of aesthetic traditions through which reality is represented through the construction of conventionally unified wholes, through a single point of view, or through a single, unbroken narrative. Modernism is discussed more fully later in this introduction.

THE EDWARDIAN PERIOD

King Edward VII.

If it is true to say that the first half of the twentieth century may be characterized as a period in which the old Britain and the old world broke apart, it is also true that much of that fracturing did not begin to be readily visible until the years after 1910. 1910 was marked by the death of Edward VII, but more significantly this was the time of the first explosions of Modernism—Cubism in painting, Imagism in poetry, in music such ground-breaking works as Stravinsky's *The Rite of Spring* (1913). With these began the fracturing of form that would become a dominant theme in the cultural history of much of the rest of the century. With 1914 came the outbreak of World War I, and with 1915 and 1916—the years of the gruesomely drawn-out battles of Ypres and of the Somme—came a more visceral sense of fracturing as the full horror of the war's unprecedented carnage began to sink home.

The deaths of Victoria in 1901 and of her son Edward nine years later have often been seen as defining moments in the change from the Victorian to the modern world. Edwardian Britain liked to see itself as highly distinct from its Victorian predecessor. And certainly there were some changes; architectural style became rather less ornate, for example, and social style

The streets of London decorated for the Coronation of Edward VII, 1902.

A sternwheel steamer and trading canoes at Okopedi on the Eyong River, Nigeria, 1909. Nigeria was among the last British possessions to be governed through a trading company; in 1900, control was transferred from the Royal Niger Company to a government run by the British, and the territory became the Protectorate of Southern Nigeria. The Niger Company continued as the leading trading entity in the region.

rather less formal. But at its core the Edwardian era was as much a continuation from the Victorian one as a break with it. Established religion, a hierarchy of social class, a largely inflexible set of attitudes towards gender roles, a complacent confidence in Britain's dominant position in the world—all these remained largely unchanged.

In the literary world Victorian traditions were being carried forward by novelists such as George Moore and Arnold Bennett, dramatists such as Arthur Wing Pinero and Cicely Hamilton, and poets such as Robert Bridges, Katharine Tynan, and W.E. Henley, the immensely popular author of "Invictus" and "Pro Rege Nostro" ("England, My England"). And even much of the literature that we now think of as recognizably modern may as readily be seen as connecting with that of the late Victorian era as anticipating the later literature of the century. The prose fiction of Joseph Conrad, for example, with its laying bare of the dark corners of the human soul (and of the dark realities of colonialism), touches the nerves of the reader in ways that we think of as distinctively modern. Indeed, the cry "that was no more than a breath" of the dying ivory agent Kurtz in Conrad's *Heart of Darkness* (1899, 1902)—"The horror!

In some respects a "Victorian" sense of Empire carried on into the 1920s and 1930s. This advertisement for the 1924 British Empire Exhibition was one of several highlighting displays that were promoted as particularly "exotic." Though some complained that the Exhibition's strongly patriotic flavor was excessively self-congratulatory, it was highly popular with most Londoners. The Gold Coast remained a British Colony until 1957, when it became Ghana and gained independence.

The horror!"—is often regarded as a defining expression of the anguish that came to be felt as characteristic of the twentieth century. And some of Conrad's narrative techniques break ground that would become heavily tilled in the twentieth century; through layering of viewpoints (stories within stories, multiple narrators) Conrad found ways to create a narrative density that at once intensifies and destabilizes the reader's experience of the events being recounted. But Conrad was an extraordinary innovator, not a revolutionary; however original, the threads of most of his fiction are still woven through a storytelling art that draws on the conventions of fiction writing that held sway through the nineteenth century—conventions of realism through which implausible coincidences or exotic adventures could be made believable to the reader. As a *New York Times* reviewer put it in 1903, "the adventures he describes are little short of miraculous and are laid among scenes wholly alien to commonplace life, [but] they are wrought into a tissue of truth so firm and so tough as to resist the keenest scepticism. … Not even his Kurtz, the man of impenetrable darkness of soul, is either a bloodless or an incredible figure."

The novelist E.M. Forster is recognizably an author of the twentieth century in his treatment not only of the sexual (see below for a discussion of his novel *Maurice*) but also of the spiritual; his approach to the spiritual realities that transcend everyday life connects to the work of later twentieth-century writers such as Elizabeth Bowen, Graham Greene, and Kazuo Ishiguro. And in some stylistic respects (notably, the shifting, ironic narrative voice of *A Passage to India* [1924]), his fiction has affinities with modernism. But the texture of his work—most notably of the novels *A Room With a View* (1908) and *Howard's End* (1910)—is woven of nuances of social interaction and of subtle modulations of feeling, and relates at least as strongly to the conventions of Victorian realism as it does to those of Modernism. Forster is above all a social novelist, whose work recognizably connects with the traditions of his nineteenth-century predecessors.

Much of H.G. Wells's fiction was forward-looking in a more precise sense. Beginning in 1895 with the publication of *The Time Machine*, and continuing with *The Island of Dr. Moreau* (1896), *The Invisible Man* (1897), and *The War of the Worlds* (1898), Wells played a major role in the development of science fiction. He continued in this vein in the new century with such works as *The First Men in the Moon* (1901) and *The War in the Air* (1908). But in the style of his fiction Wells, too, was a traditional storyteller. And, though he is remembered today primarily for his science fiction, he wrote in a vein of social comedy with at least as much frequency, and with even greater success in his own lifetime. *Love and Mr. Lewisham* (1900), *Kipps: The*

Members of a slum-dwelling family in London, c. 1913. Though Britain was the world's wealthiest nation, the poor often lived in appalling conditions of hardship.

Story of a Simple Soul (1905), and *The History of Mr. Polly* (1910) are comic novels that paint an entertaining but strongly critical picture of the English social class system.

Like many writers of the time—playwright Bernard Shaw perhaps most prominent among them—Wells became a committed socialist in the early years of the twentieth century. The chief vehicle of socialist response in Britain at the time was the Fabian society, founded in 1884 to promote *evolutionary* socialism (thus disavowing violent class struggle). The Fabian Society, led by Shaw, Sidney Webb, and Beatrice Potter Webb, was instrumental in forming the Labour Representation Committee in 1900; that committee, with substantial input as well from the Trades Union Congress, transformed itself into a political party in 1906, and over the course of the next generation the Labour Party managed to displace the Liberal Party as the main political alternative to Britain's Conservative Party. *Mrs Warren's Profession* is among the earliest of a long series of plays that give dramatic life to Shaw's progressive views; among its most memorable successors are *Major Barbara* (1905) and *Pygmalion* (1913). Shaw continued to write for the stage well into the 1920s (and lived until 1950), but he too expressed a powerful sense of change more in the content of his work than in its form.

Women writers of the period also put forward innovative, even revolutionary, ideas within texts that were structured in fairly traditional ways. Writer and activist Sarah Grand's work, for example, portrayed feminist women committed to radical change and critiqued the institution of marriage. She contributed to the burgeoning genre of "New Woman" literature, which helped to define new possibilities of social and political action for educated, feminist, and independent women around the turn of the century. Ella Hepworth Dixon was another prominent writer whose works helped define the New Woman; in her *One Doubtful Hour and Other Side-Lights on the Feminine Temperament* (1904), for instance, she tackled the problem of sexual double standards for men and women. Cicely Hamilton, a prominent suffragist, wrote plays that were intended as propaganda for the cause, including *How the Vote Was Won* (1909) and *A Pageant of Great Women* (1909). These writers were instrumental in creating change, not only as political activists, but also as artists whose works imagined how women might live according to principles of greater gender equality.

Workers share a paper to read the news during the General Strike of 1926. The condition of the working class had improved somewhat by the 1920s, but in some sectors— notably coal mining—efforts were being made to roll back improvements in wages and working conditions. The 1926 General Strike in support of the coal miners lasted nine days.

David Lloyd George, 1906. Lloyd George was a leading advocate of the interests of the working class in the early years of the century. As Chancellor of the Exchequer, he introduced the "Peoples' Budget" of 1909, calling for new taxes on the better-off to pay for measures to improve the lot of the poor, including an old age pension. The Old Age Pensions Act was resisted so strongly by the House of Lords that the Liberal Government acted to reduce the power of the House; both that Act and the Parliament Act, which established the supremacy of the House of Commons, became law in 1911. Lloyd George was also responsible for the National Insurance Act (1911), which provided some protection for workers who lost earnings through illness or unemployment.

THE WORLD WARS

As Lord Earl Grey, the British Foreign Secretary, watched the streetlights being lit from his office window one evening just before the outbreak of war in August 1914, he is famously reported to have remarked to a friend, "The lamps are going out all over Europe; we shall not see them lit again in our lifetime." At the time such thinking went against the grain; at the outset of the "Great War," many in England firmly expected their soldiers to be home before Christmas. But over the next thirty years many came to believe that the moment at which the First World War broke out had heralded nothing less than the collapse of civilization as it had long been known. At the outset of the Second World War in 1940, George Orwell adopted this vein of apocalyptic pessimism in his long essay "Inside the Whale":

> The war of 1914–1918 was only a heightened moment in an almost continuous crisis. At this date it hardly needs a war to bring home to us the disintegration of our society and the increasing helplessness of all decent people. ... While I have been writing this book another European war has broken out. It will either last several years and tear western civilization to pieces, or it will end inconclusively and prepare the way for yet another war that will do the job once and for all.

Western civilization proved to be rather more resilient than Orwell had feared, but his view of the period beginning in 1914 as "an almost continuous crisis" is now widely shared by historians; increasingly the two world wars of the twentieth century are being seen as part of a continuum. From more than one angle this makes sense. In both wars, Britain and its Empire/Commonwealth allies, joined belatedly by the United States, were fighting against a militaristic and aggressive Germany. In both wars much of the rest of the world was drawn into the conflict, though there was no parallel in World War I to the crucial importance of the Pacific theater and the struggle between the Allies and Japan in World War II.

The Western Front in World War I, 1915.

The two wars are also linked through a chain of causation. Though all authorities agree that both wars had multiple causes, it is also universally agreed that one vitally important cause of the Second World War was the decision by the allies after World War I to demand reparations—a decision that had the effect in the short term of crippling Germany economically—and that had the even more pernicious effect over the longer term of so embittering the German people as to make a majority highly receptive to Hitler's appeals to nationalism, expansionism, anti-Semitism, and hate. The British economist John Maynard Keynes had been among those prescient enough to foresee the problem early on. In his chapter on "Europe After the Treaty" in *The Economic Consequences of the Peace* (1919), he summarized the matter with blunt eloquence:

> This chapter must be one of pessimism. The treaty includes no provisions for the economic rehabilitation of Europe—nothing to make the defeated ... into good neighbours, nothing to stabilise the new states of Europe; ... Nor does it promote in any way a compact of economic solidarity amongst the Allies themselves[.] ... It is an extraordinary fact that the fundamental

economic problem of a Europe starving and disintegrating before their eyes, was the one question in which it was impossible to arouse the interest of the Four [powers that imposed the peace treaty].

Hitler's eventual rise to power, then, was partly fueled by the hardships imposed on the Germans by the Allies at the conclusion of World War I.

Londoners sleeping in the Elephant and Castle underground station during the bombing raids of 1940. These raids, popularly referred to as "the Blitz," were intended by the Nazis to "soften up" the English in preparation for a German invasion. Though much of London (and of other cities) was destroyed, the efforts of the British Air Force against superior numbers in what came to be known as the "Battle of Britain" were highly successful, and Hitler eventually decided against attempting an invasion of the British Isles; only the two Channel Islands fell to the Nazi forces. The Battle of Britain during the Blitz subsequently became a defining event in the British national consciousness.

If there are similarities and connections between the two world wars, there are also important differences. There are differences in the way the wars were fought, to start with—the trench warfare, stagnation, and machine gun carnage of World War I contrasts with the tanks, submarines, airplanes, and bombs of World War II. There is usually also agreed to be a substantial difference in the moral context in which the two wars were fought. Many have suggested that ethically there was little to choose between the two sides in World War I—that the essential nature of the conflict was simply a power struggle between Britain and Germany as co-aggressors. And it has often (and rightly) been suggested that the tangle of old world alliances that existed prior to the First World War did much to facilitate the sort of stumbling into war that occurred in the wake of the assassination of Archduke Franz Ferdinand of Austria on 28 June 1914. In fact there probably was to some degree a legitimate moral case to be made on the side of Britain at the outset of World War I—much as the jingoism of the time on all sides may now strike us as repulsive. There is no question, though, that the moral imperative that lay behind the Allies' decision to go to war with Germany in 1939 was far stronger than it was at any time during World War I. Nazi atrocities against the Jews had in 1939 not yet reached their full extent, but already Hitler had shown that he was a dictator willing to persecute minorities ruthlessly and to invade neighboring countries on the flimsiest of pretexts.

World War II, then, was driven far more persuasively than was World War I by a moral imperative, and there was thus much less of a disconnect than there had been in World War I between idealistic calls for sacrifice and the reality as it was sensed by the ordinary soldier; few looked at Nazi Germany in the autumn of 1939 with the detached tone that the poet W.H. Auden famously adopted in "September 1, 1939" in seeking to explain the phenomenon of Hitler, the "psychopathic god": "Those to whom evil is done / Do evil in return." To most it seemed clear that both in the case of Hitler as an individual and in the case of the people of Nazi Germany as a whole, the evil that was being done was far disproportionate to whatever evil had been committed against them. (Even today, many who admire Auden's poem as an affirmation of the humane in the face of the more basely human and in the face of war as a general proposition find the feelings the poem expresses odd or inappropriate in the moral context of World War II.)

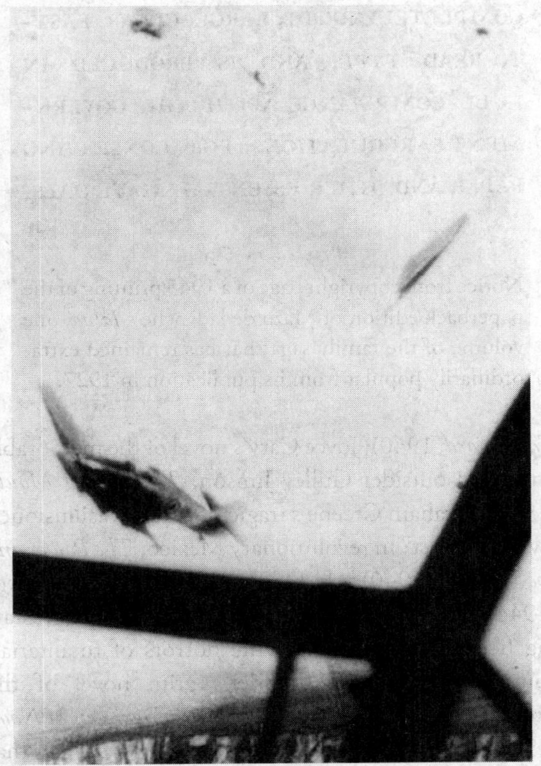

This image of the 1940 Battle of Britain was taken from the cockpit of a German fighter plane. It shows a British Hurricane fighter with its left wing torn off; the wing is visible in the top right of the photo, and the pilot, parachuting to safety, is seen in the top left.

A crucial difference between the experience of World War I and II was that in World War II the horrors of war had less shock value. Paul Fussell, whose *The Great War and Modern Memory* is a landmark study of the connections between wartime experience and literature, was a soldier himself in World War II; by the time of World War II, as he put it, "we didn't need to be told by people like Remarqué [author of *All Quiet on the Western Front*] and Siegfried Sassoon how nasty war was. We knew that already, and we just had to pursue it in a sort of controlled despair. It didn't have the ironic shock value of the Great War." It should perhaps not surprise us, then, that the body of serious literature that arose *directly* from the experience of World War II turned out to be slighter than the body of such literature that emerged during and after World War I. Certainly works such as Robert Graves's *Goodbye to All That*, Siegfried Sassoon's *Memoirs of an Infantry Officer*, David Jones's *In Parenthesis*, and the poetry of Wilfred Owen, Isaac Rosenberg, and others all seem to have secured a place in the canon of British literature, whereas few if any works emerging directly out of the combat experience of World War II have staked such a claim. Indeed, Auden's "September 1, 1939" and Virginia Woolf's *Between the Acts* are among the few works still widely read from that time on themes that relate to the experience of the war even tangentially.

Two aspects of the 1939–45 conflict have come to be seen as defining elements of twentieth-century experience. The first of these was the planned extermination of an entire people—the event that resulted in the murder of approximately six million Jews (as well as significant numbers of other groups deemed "undesirables" by the Nazis, notably LGBT people and Roma), and that has come to be known as "The Holocaust." The second is the use of the atomic bomb against Japan by the United States in 1945—and the consequent dawning among the world's population of an awareness that humans now had the capacity to destroy the entire human race. From those most horrific aspects of World War II has emerged a literature that will surely be lasting (including the works of Primo Levi, the diaries of Anne Frank, John Hersey's *Hiroshima*)—but few if any of its most important works are by British writers.

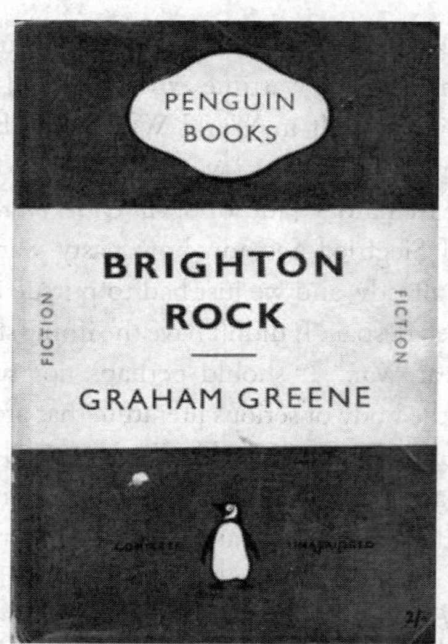

Brighton Rock (1938), Graham Greene's "entertainment" about the lives of young British gangsters, was first issued in a Penguin paperback in 1943. The price of 2 shillings is equivalent to a little over £4 in UK 2017 currency.

THIS IS A WARTIME BOOK

THIS POCKET BOOK INCLUDES EVERY WORD CONTAINED IN THE ORIGINAL, HIGHER-PRICED EDITION. IT IS PRINTED FROM BRAND-NEW PLATES MADE FROM COMPLETELY RESET, LARGE, CLEAR, EASY-TO-READ TYPE, AND IS PRODUCED IN FULL COMPLIANCE WITH THE GOVERNMENT'S REGULATIONS FOR CONSERVING PAPER AND OTHER ESSENTIAL MATERIALS.

F-I

Printed in Canada

Notice from copyright page of a 1945 printing of the paperback edition of Mazo de la Roche's *Jalna*, one volume of the family saga that has remained extraordinarily popular from its publication in 1927.

During both World Wars, however, there was a rich body of literary work produced in Britain that was not directly *about* the war. Works of this sort in the years 1914–18 include T.S. Eliot's *Prufrock and Other Observations* (1917), James Joyce's *Portrait of the Artist as a Young Man* (1916), and many of Katherine Mansfield's most important short stories. In the years 1939–45, the list of such works is both long and remarkably diverse, and includes the exuberant verse of Dylan Thomas's *The Map of Love* (1939); Eliot's *Four Quartets* (which he regarded as his finest work); many of Auden's finest lyrics, including "Lay Your Sleeping Head, My Love," "Musee des Beaux Arts," and "Song (As I Walked Out One Evening)" (all first published in 1940); the bubbling hilarity of Noel Coward's play about the afterlife, *Blithe Spirit* (1942); the memorably self-deprecating and socially observant light comedy of Monica Dickens's memoir *One Pair of Hands* (1939); now-classic memoirs by Vera Brittain (*Testament of Friendship*, 1940) and Flora Thompson (*Lark Rise to Candleford*, 1940); Joyce Cary's novel of the memorable artist and outsider Gulley Jimson, *The Horse's Mouth* (1944); Graham Greene's tragic novel of a disillusioned "whisky priest" in revolutionary Mexico, *The Power and the Glory* (1940); H.D.'s modernist epic *Trilogy* (1944–46); and two very different but equally devastating fictional treatments of the horrors of totalitarian communism, Arthur Koestler's grim novel of the suffering endured by a "deviationist," *Darkness at Noon* (1940), and Orwell's fable of a collectivist society that comes to be based on the principle that "all animals are equal, but some are more equal than others," *Animal Farm* (1945). In writing the following comments in 1940 about the literature of World War I, Orwell clearly also had World War II in mind:

> In 1917 there was nothing a thinking and sensitive person could do, except remain human, if possible. … By simply staying aloof and keeping in touch with pre-war emotions, Eliot [in publishing *Prufrock* in 1917] was carrying on the human heritage.… So different from bayonet drill! After the bombs and the food queues and the recruiting posters, a human voice! What a relief!

Much as the writing of World War II and especially World War I has secured an enduring place in British literature, the most lasting literary work relating to the World Wars of the twentieth century may well be a pacifist work of non-fiction written between the wars—Virginia Woolf's *Three Guineas*. Part personal reflection, part literary history, and part political analysis, the book frames its discussions of war and peace in the context of patriarchical oppression in ways that struck entirely new chords—chords which continue to resonate powerfully in the hearts and minds of twenty-first century readers.

MARX, EINSTEIN, FREUD, AND MODERNISM

Several towering figures in the intellectual and cultural life of the twentieth century played a key part in shaping the world view according to which human life was subject to forces over which, individually, humans could have little control, and of which they would often be entirely unaware. The first of these figures—Karl Marx—died 17 years before the end of the nineteenth century. But his vision of economic forces and class struggles saturated with historical inevitability continued to shape political and social attitudes (as well as a good many literary ones) throughout the twentieth century. An intellectual underpinning derived from Marx is, to a large extent, what differentiates the attitudes of social realist writers such as Shaw, Wells, and George Gissing from those of predecessors such as Charles Dickens and Elizabeth Gaskell. Much as Dickens and Gaskell had deplored the conditions of inequality that beset Victorian Britain, they believed that the actions and the goodwill of individual human beings could ameliorate social problems. The approach of 1890s and early twentieth-century socially progressive writers, in contrast, derived largely from the Marxist view that individuals are typically caught in a web of large social and economic forces over which they have no control; that class oppression is a systemic matter; and that mass struggle and political action (rather than appeals to the higher natures of the ruling classes) are the appropriate means of bringing about a better world. Thus for Shaw, for example, the "fundamental condition of the existence" of prostitution was that "a large class of women are more highly paid and better treated as prostitutes than they would be as respectable women." The activist writer and publisher Nancy Cunard was equally alert to the interactions of class, gender, money—and race. Author of a number of important essays on colonialism (and publisher of such key modernist works as Samuel Beckett's *Whoroscope* and Pound's *Cantos*), Cunard spoke of the British Empire in unvarnished terms of class and race as few had before: when writing in *Negro* of the system of British rule in Jamaica, for example, she understood it clearly as having been purposefully structured as "white at the top, mulatto in the centre and black at the bottom of the economic and social scale" so as to reinforce the small numbers of white colonizers with a class of privileged and educated people—"mulattoes"—who were set apart as privileged, and thus would not join in any political action against the colonizers. Black Jamaicans, at the bottom of this social scale, received the most menial jobs. Cunard saw that this system was subtler than the racism operating in American society but that it was equally racist and oppressive to the black population.

If the socially progressive literature of the early twentieth century had intellectual underpinnings derived largely from Marx, the intellectual underpinnings of twentieth-century modernist literature are intimately connected with the ideas of physicist Albert Einstein, of philosophers of language such as Bertrand Russell, and of the psychoanalyst Sigmund Freud. Einstein's paper, "The Electrodynamics of Moving Bodies" (1905), later to become known as his Special Theory of Relativity, posited that both time and motion are not absolute but rather relative to the observer. In the same year, he completed his thesis on "A New Determination of Molecular Dimension," a major step forward in the development of quantum theory in which he postulated (among other things) that light was both waves and tiny particles of light quanta, or photons. Much as they may have been imperfectly understood, the broad outlines of Einstein's theories became widely disseminated in subsequent years, and clearly contributed to a growing sense of a world that was far less stable than had been previously thought.

New language-based trends in analytic philosophy were also undermining certainties. The ideas developed by Gottlob Frege, Bertrand Russell, and Ludwig Wittgenstein in the late nineteenth and early twentieth century had the effect of destabilizing what had been thought of as largely fixed relationships between words and meanings. The focus of these philosophers was on analyzing the content of what we mean when we make statements, whether they be statements referring to objects in the "real" world or statements involving claims of a more abstract sort. They endeavored to design symbolic systems that could convey meaning more reliably than words, for their work suggested that relationships between a word and a presumed referent were exceedingly complex and inherently unstable; Wittgenstein's work, in particular, suggested that it was in the nature of language for words to float largely free of fixed referents in any world of "objective truth." Indeed, Wittgenstein suggested in his groundbreaking 1921 work *Tractatus Logico-Philosophicus* that "Language disguises thought. So much so, that from the outward form of the clothing it is impossible to infer the form of the thought beneath it, because the outward form of the clothing is not designed to reveal the form of the body, but for entirely different purposes."

The perceived unreliability and instability of language and of meaning affected the realm of ethics as much as it did those of metaphysics and epistemology, and from about 1910 onward, moral relativism was a subject of lively debate. (G.E. Moore's *Ethics*, an influential attempt to hold such relativism at bay, was published in 1912; T.S. Eliot read a paper on "The Relativity of the Moral Judgement" in the Cambridge rooms of his friend Bertrand Russell in 1915.) Russell became famous as a result of his pacifism (for which he was jailed in 1918), his efforts to undermine the authority of Christianity over Western society, and his challenge to societal constrictions on sexual behavior. But the changes that he helped to bring about to the foundations of analytic philosophy may have been even more revolutionary—and more influential in the literary realm—than his shocking views on social issues.

The intellectual life of the twentieth century was also dramatically changed by several explorers of the human psyche. Of these, pride of place is traditionally accorded to Sigmund Freud, an Austrian psychiatrist who advanced revolutionary notions of the importance and complexity of sexuality in the human psyche, and of the importance of the unconscious in human thought and behavior. Both notions had an enormous effect on twentieth-century intellectuals and artists, and on imaginative literature in particular, as writers sought ways to represent sexuality as a much more central element of human experience than had been the habit of the Victorians, and sought ways in which to represent the richness of the human unconscious.[1]

Another key pioneer in the study of the human mind was the American William James (brother of novelist Henry James). Among James's most important contributions was his conceptualization of the fluidity of consciousness. James entitled a chapter in his *Principles of Psychology* (1892) "The Stream of Consciousness," beginning by observing that "within each personal consciousness states are always changing" and that "each personal consciousness is sensibly continuous." The connections between the ideas of James and twentieth-century literary developments are not difficult to discern. Most obviously, the "stream of consciousness" technique of prose fiction that features so prominently in core Modernist texts such as Virginia Woolf's *Mrs. Dalloway* (1925) and James Joyce's *Ulysses* (1922) represents a new form of realism that is psychological rather than social in character. These writers aim at an increased awareness of the ways in which the mind

[1] Though Freud's important work began in the 1890s, he began to become well known in the English-speaking world only after 1910, with the publication of a series of lectures he had given at Clark University in the United States on *The Origin and Development of Psychoanalysis*. Of his most important works, *The Interpretation of Dreams* (1900) was translated in 1913, *The Psychopathology of Everyday Life* (1901) in 1914; soon after, his work came to the attention of the Bloomsbury Group in England, and both Leonard Woolf and Lytton Strachey wrote reviews of or commentaries on Freud's work. (In the 1920s the Woolfs' Hogarth Press became for a time the leading publisher of English translations of Freud's work.)

associates freely, in which "irrelevant" thoughts may connect with repressed impulses or emotions that are central to the psyche, and in which unpredictable but meaningful details are constantly jostling together with the quotidian.

It is too often forgotten that Woolf and Joyce were not the first to write fiction in a "stream of consciousness" style. That distinction belongs to Dorothy Richardson, whose *Painted Roofs* appeared in 1915 as the first of what became the thirteen volumes (referred to by Richardson as "chapters") of *Pilgrimage*, a work chronicling the life of Miriam Henderson, a "New Woman" rejecting Victorian ideals of femininity and domesticity. If *Pilgrimage* is important for the ways it captures the interior psychological life of its protagonist, it is also important for the ways in which it chronicles the exterior world of Henderson's everyday existence. Rejecting the realist styles of then-admired novelists such as Honoré de Balzac and Arnold Bennett, Richardson explicitly linked style and gender, declaring in her foreword to *Pilgrimage* her intention to "create a feminine equivalent of the current masculine realism."

In a famous 1918 review of the first three volumes novels of *Pilgrimage* that deserves to be quoted at length, May Sinclair shed a good deal of light on Richardson's method:

> [The characters in the book] are presented to us in the same vivid but fragmentary way in which they appeared to Miriam, the fragmentary way in which people appear to most of us. Miss Richardson has only imposed on herself the conditions that life imposes on us all. …
>
> In this series [of novels] there is no drama, no situation, no set scene. Nothing happens. It is just life going on and on. It is Miriam Henderson's stream of consciousness going on and on. And in neither is there any grossly discernible beginning or middle or end.
>
> In identifying herself with this life, which is Miriam's stream of consciousness, Miss Richardson produces her effect of being the first, of getting closer to reality than any of our novelists who are trying so desperately to get close.

Sinclair herself, it should be added, was an important novelist who straddles the ground between traditional realism and Modernism. Her first novel, *The Tysons* (1898), is recognizably of its time; her autobiographical *Mary Olivier: A Life* (1919) is clearly influenced by Richardson's innovations in the presentation of a psychological interior; her *The Life and Death of Harriett Frean*, a novel concerning a woman contemplating suicide that partakes of both traditional and Modernist strands, is widely regarded as a masterpiece.

If the disconnectedness and apparent lack of shape of the human "stream of consciousness" became in the teens and twenties a vitally important subject of literary fiction, it became a feature as well of Modernist poetry—most obviously in the disjunctions that characterize the work of poets such as T.S. Eliot, Ezra Pound, and H.D. To be sure, many have argued persuasively that a unity both of thought and of feeling emerges from the extended allusive density of poems such as *The Waste Land*. But it is abundantly clear that any such unity is very different in character from the unity that emerges, say, from a defining long poem of the Victorian period such as Tennyson's *In Memoriam*, just as whatever unity emerges from Joyce's *Ulysses* is very different in character from that of the classic realism of Victorian novels such as George Eliot's *Middlemarch*.

Less frequently discussed is the modernity of Eliot's later poetry—most notably, *Four Quartets* (1935–43), an extended poetic expression of the search for meaning and truth in a context of instability. Much as the poem is infused with the Anglo-Catholicism to which Eliot had converted in 1927, it is also deeply colored by the sorts of destabilizing awareness that were so central to the habits of thought that came to the fore in the first half of the twentieth century. The poet continually struggles to conceptualize the movements of time, but finds that

> Words strain,
> Crack, and sometimes break, under the burden,
> Under the tension, slip, slide, perish,
> Decay with imprecision, will not stay in place,
> Will not stay still.

Samuel Beckett, one of the first to appreciate that most disconnected of all Joyce's works, *Finnegans Wake* (1939), became a central figure in the later period of Modernist literature. It was Beckett, above all, who pioneered the expression in action of the psychological insights of Modernism and the despair that so often accompanied them. It is perhaps the case that "action" should here be put in quotation marks, however, for Beckett's plays—perhaps most notably *Waiting for Godot* (1952), *Krapp's Last Tape* (1958), and *Endgame* (1957)—are informed by an unprecedented awareness of the degree to which a *lack* of action may be as expressive as action, just as silences may be as expressive as words. Beckett extended the Modernist project in his prose fiction as well as in his plays—and in French as well as in English through to the 1970s.

A common tendency is to assume that what is aesthetically revolutionary will substantially overlap with what is politically revolutionary (or at least with what is progressive). In fact there is no necessary connection between the two—and, indeed, a striking feature of twentieth-century Modernism is that many of its key figures were politically conservative or even reactionary.[1] During his lifetime, T.S. Eliot was probably almost as influential for his political, religious, and cultural conservatism as he was for his revolutionary aesthetic. Writer and artist Wyndham Lewis, whose concept of Vorticism was for a time central to the intellectual currents of Modernism, embraced political views that could fairly be characterized as reactionary rather than conservative. Ezra Pound, for his part, who was even more revolutionary than Eliot in his Modernist aesthetic, wound up even further to the right politically—notoriously lending his support to the fascist cause, and calling for the extermination of Jews during World War II. Eliot and Pound were also far from progressive in their attitudes on gender and sex; many have suggested that a dark sense of sexuality is a fundamental aspect of Eliot's world view—and almost as many have suggested that a disturbing element of misogyny lurks not far below the surface of much of his writing (his early writing in particular).

Leading modernist women writers, by contrast, more often combined the freedom of modernist forms with progressive, unconventional, or even revolutionary political and social views. The futurist poet Mina Loy, for example, was a strong feminist and decidedly left of center politically; Nancy Cunard was a pioneer of left-of-center class analysis as well as of modernist publishing; and Virginia Woolf, though she rarely shared the unqualified sense of political conviction that came to motivate her husband Leonard (who ran for Parliament as a Labour Party candidate in 1920), was herself not only a powerful voice for feminism but also a Labour Party member and a supporter of a variety of socialist and progressive causes.

It was Woolf who famously assigned a specific point in time to the great change that Modernism represented: "on or about December 1910," she commented in a 1924 essay, "human character changed." She was, of course, exaggerating for effect; few in her era were more acutely aware of how erratically change may occur, and of the ways in which the characteristics of one era may extend into the next. In that connection it is worth reminding ourselves that, much as the Modernism of Eliot, Joyce, and Woolf has come to take on the character of the defining spirit of British literature in the 1910s and 1920s, its centrality was far from obvious at the time. For every admirer of the Cubist paintings of Picasso and Braque, there were many who reacted with contempt or ridicule. For every gallery-goer who was stirred by the modernist sculptures of Jacob Epstein (such as the young colonial P.K. Page, as recounted in her poem "Ecce Homo"), there were many chuckling over the way in which such sculpture was lampooned in the pages of the satirical magazine *Punch*. And for every dedicated reader of *The Waste Land* or *To the Lighthouse* there were dozens of readers of the ballads of Robert Service, and of the traditionally structured novels of Arnold Bennett and John Galsworthy. Not until 1948 and 1969 respectively were T.S. Eliot and Samuel Beckett awarded the Nobel Prize for literature; the only

[1] The roots of this conservatism are in part to be found in various nineteenth-century political and ideological developments—especially a strain of ultra-conservatism in France that developed in the second half of the century and that connects both with Pound and the Symbolists and with twentieth-century fascisms.

British writers to receive the award before 1940 were Rudyard Kipling (1907), W.B. Yeats (1923), George Bernard Shaw (1925), and Galsworthy (1932).

"Peter Pan Playing Pipes," illustration by Mabel Lucie Attwell, from *Peter Pan and Wendy* (1921). The early decades of the twentieth century are remembered for the dawn of Modernism, but they were also something of a golden age for children's literature; in addition to Sir J.M. Barrie's *Peter Pan* (1906) and its sequels, E. Nesbit's *The Railway Children* (1906), Kenneth Grahame's *The Wind in the Willows* (1908), Lucy Maud Montgomery's *Anne of Green Gables* (1908), and A.A. Milne's *Winnie the Pooh* (1926) and *The House at Pooh Corner* (1928) all remain popular classics.

THE STRUGGLE FOR WOMEN'S EQUALITY

As well as being a central figure of Modernism in the British literary tradition, Woolf is central to what is arguably the most important historical development of the twentieth century, the attempt to free women from the dense network of social, economic, and legal restrictions that had always ensured male dominance and control. If *To the Lighthouse* (1927) and *Mrs. Dalloway* (1925), with their psychological realism, are key documents of Modernism, *A Room of One's Own* (1929) is a key document of the struggle by women in the twentieth century for full equality. Woolf's call for change, and also her evocation of personal experience in a male-dominated social and literary milieu, continue to resonate with readers in the present century.

Illustration accompanying the article "Presentation Day at London University," by "A Lady Graduate" in *The Girl's Own Paper*, July 1898. The University of London had begun to admit women as full degree students at the undergraduate level in 1878.

As the twentieth century opened, women were still second-class citizens in almost every respect—unable to vote, subject to a variety of employment limitations, restricted for the most part from higher education, and restricted too in myriad intangible ways by social nuance and convention. Oppression in the workplace in the context of the industrial revolution has long been widely acknowledged; at least as pervasive in the late nineteenth and early twentieth centuries was the exploitation of retail workers, as the Report of the Royal Commission on Labour detailed:

> The maximum salary in addition to board and lodging ever paid to women in the shop working 70 3/4 hours was stated at 35 to 40 shillings [equivalent to roughly £200 in 2015]; in the other shops 30 shillings was stated as the maximum salary ever given. The girls declared that they had nothing to complain of, except the long hours of work and the short time allowed for meals, which had seriously affected their health. No one closed earlier than 11:00 p.m. on Saturdays, 9:30 on Fridays, and 9:00 on Mondays, Tuesdays, and Wednesdays, beginning in each case at 8:30 a.m.

For decades, those in the suffrage movement and other women's groups struggled to bring change. In 1903, Emmeline Pankhurst, together with others frustrated with the pace of change and with the "ladylike" tone of the protests by other women's groups, formed The Women's Social and Political Union, taking as their motto "Deeds Not Words." As Pankhurst recalled in 1914,

> From the very first, in those early London days, when … we were few in numbers and very poor in purse, we made the public aware of the woman suffrage movement as it had never been before. We adopted Salvation Army methods and went out into the highways and byways after converts.

Real change finally began to take effect just before the end of the war in 1918, with the Representation of the People Act granting the vote to all men over the age of 21 and to women over the age of 30 who also met one or more of several restrictive criteria regarding marital status and property. (Not until 1928 were all such restrictions lifted and all women over 21 granted the franchise.) The London *Times* provided a (doubtless oversimplified) summary of the effect of the war on the suffrage movement in an article on the occasion of the 1930 commemoration by Prime Minister Stanley Baldwin of a statue of Pankhurst:

> The World War came. In the twinkling of an eye … the militant suffragettes laid aside their banners. They put on their overalls and went into the factory and into the field; they were nursing, they made munitions, and they endured sacrifices with the men, and the effective opposition to the movement melted in the furnace of the War.

The success of the suffrage movement and the change in the role women played in the workplace were the most dramatic gender-related changes during this period, but there were many other important developments; the era was also characterized by changing notions regarding gender and education, contraception and reproductive technology, and the nature of masculinity.

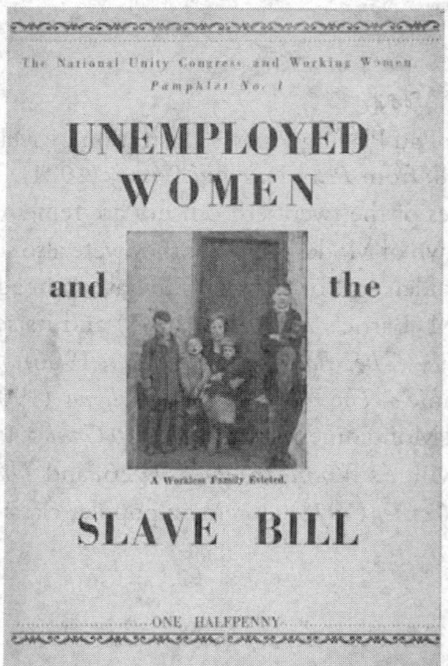

Pamphlet issued for the 1934 Congress of Action against the government's treatment of the unemployed. Under the provisions of early 1930s legislation in Britain (the Unemployment Act and the Anomalies Act), part-time workers, casual workers, and various classes of women workers were labeled "anomalies" and excluded from insurance coverage—were not eligible, in other words, to receive assistance if they were thrown out of work.

Sylvia Pankhurst (daughter of suffragette leader Emmeline Pankhurst) painting the slogan "Votes for Women" on the front of the Women's Social Defence League offices in London, 1912.

Avant-Garde and Mass Culture

The concept of the avant-garde, of a tiny minority far in advance of the popular taste in culture (or of the majority view politically) came into its own in the twentieth century. No doubt it may have resonated with particular force simply because of the degree to which cultural activity was being extended to "the masses"; with primary education having been made compulsory in Britain through the Education Act of 1870, the twentieth century was the first in which the vast majority of British people were fully literate. The expansion of libraries had helped to spread the habit of reading through the nineteenth century, and with the publishing industry's shift in the 1890s away from "triple deckers" intended for purchase by libraries and toward one-volume novels of modest length aimed at individual buyers, the habit of book-buying began to spread at a comparable rate. In the early years of the century, publishers introduced series of relatively affordable hardcover editions of literary classics, aimed at a broad popular market (chief among them the Everyman's Library series from Dent and the World's Classics series from Oxford University Press).

The arrest of Emmeline Parkhurst during a suffragette demonstration near Buckingham Palace, 1914.

THE PUBLISHERS OF *EVERYMAN'S LIBRARY* WILL BE PLEASED TO SEND FREELY TO ALL APPLICANTS A LIST OF THE PUBLISHED AND PROJECTED VOLUMES TO BE COMPRISED UNDER THE FOLLOWING THIRTEEN HEADINGS:

TRAVEL ❖ SCIENCE ❖ FICTION
THEOLOGY & PHILOSOPHY
HISTORY ❖ CLASSICAL
FOR YOUNG PEOPLE
ESSAYS ❖ ORATORY
POETRY & DRAMA
BIOGRAPHY
REFERENCE
ROMANCE

IN FOUR STYLES OF BINDING: CLOTH, FLAT BACK, COLOURED TOP; LEATHER, ROUND CORNERS, GILT TOP; LIBRARY BINDING IN CLOTH, & QUARTER PIGSKIN

London: J. M. DENT & SONS, Ltd.
New York: E. P. DUTTON & CO.

Preliminary advertising page from *Captain Cook's Voyages of Discovery*, one of the Everyman's Library volumes published in 1906, the year the series was founded. Eventually its list grew to include over 1,000 titles.

The British film industry was competitive with that of the United States in the 1920s and early 1930s. In this 1920s photograph a scene from the (now lost) film *The Thrill* is being shot on a beach near Brighton.

An even more revolutionary step came in 1936, with the introduction of Penguin Books' series of affordable paperback editions. "The Penguin books are splendid value for sixpence," wrote George Orwell in reviewing Penguin's third batch of ten titles, "so splendid that if the other publishers had any sense they could combine against them and suppress them. [If instead] the other publishers follow suit, the result may be a flood of cheap reprints which will cripple the lending libraries ... and check the output of new novels." Within a few years the paperback novel had indeed become ubiquitous in British society, but with none of the disastrous effects Orwell had feared; the size of the market for books had been expanded sufficiently by the arrival of the paperback to more than compensate authors and publishers for the lower revenue per copy sold.

Along with the spread of a mass literary culture—and the spread as well of the cinema and of radio—came huge social and cultural changes. If Modernism was a cultural movement concentrated in a small elite, modernity swept through every corner of society in the 1920s and 1930s. The social and cultural attitudes of the late Victorian age may have persisted through to the end of the Edwardian era, but within 10 years "Victorian" had become a synonym for "stuffy and old fashioned." The book that set the tone more than any other was Lytton Strachey's *Eminent Victorians* (1918), a series of biographical essays on four leading members of Victorian society (Henry Edward Cardinal Manning, Florence Nightingale, Matthew Arnold, and General Charles George Gordon). Strachey's work is often characterized as "satirical," but "irreverent" is perhaps a better adjective. He writes in a breezy, brilliant, style, but he is interested in the depths of human emotion as well as the surfaces. He pokes fun at his subjects, to be sure, but he is more interested in exploring the workings of what he sees as pretension, hypocrisy, ambition, and self-deception than he is in ridiculing them. Here is how Strachey begins his essay on Florence Nightingale:

> Everyone knows the popular conception of Florence Nightingale. The saintly, self-sacrificing woman, the delicate maiden of high degree who threw aside the pleasures of a life of ease to succour the afflicted, the Lady with the Lamp, gliding through the horrors of the hospital at Scutari, and consecrating with the radiance of her goodness the dying soldier's couch—the vision is familiar to all. But the truth was different. The Miss Nightingale of fact was not as facile fancy painted her. She worked in another fashion, and towards another end; she moved under the stress of an impetus which finds no place in the popular imagination. A Demon possessed her. Now demons, whatever else they may be, are full of interest. And so it happens that in the real Miss Nightingale there was more that was interesting than in the legendary one; there was also less that was agreeable.

The deft touch of Strachey's satire became simplified and coarsened in the ridicule popularly directed at Victorian styles—and, in particular, at Victorian attitudes towards sexuality—as an emerging mass society sought to define itself against the backdrop of supposed Victorian narrowness and prudery. The reaction may have been overdone, and certainly the characterization of the Victorians was simplistic, but there could be no doubt that the short skirts, jazz music, and sexual

World War I and the years that followed brought huge changes in women's fashion, with shorter skirts and dresses and more freedom of movement. This photograph, from the 1920s, shows two London models.

Ottoline Morrell, photograph of Virginia Woolf with fellow Bloomsbury member Lytton Strachey, 1923.

Bill Brandt, *The Lambeth Walk*, 1936. This photo, originally published in the illustrated weekly magazine *Picture Post*, was taken in the Bethnal Green area of London. The girl performs a dance popular at the time.

attitudes of the 1920s and 1930s were as far removed from those of only fifteen or twenty years before as those of 1905 or 1910 had been from the attitudes and styles of a full century earlier. Virginia Woolf's recollections of a Bloomsbury scene from the 1920s in which Woolf, her sister Vanessa Bell, and Vanessa's husband Clive Bell are together in the drawing room at 46 Gordon Square give something of the flavor of the time:

> Suddenly the door opened and the long and sinister figure of Mr. Lytton Strachey stood on the threshold. He pointed a finger at a stain on Vanessa's white dress.
>
> "Semen?" he said.
>
> Can one really say it? I thought, and we burst out laughing. With that one word all barriers of reticence and reserve went down.... So there was now nothing that one could not say, nothing that one could not do, at 46 Gordon Square.

Few places in Britain in the 1920s and 1930s had left Victorian conventions of respectability so firmly behind as had 46 Gordon Square; few others had traveled so far in the same direction, or so fast, as had the "bohemians" of the Bloomsbury Group.

Two women, outside a London bookshop, holding copies of the newly-published paperback edition of *Lady Chatterley's Lover* (1960).

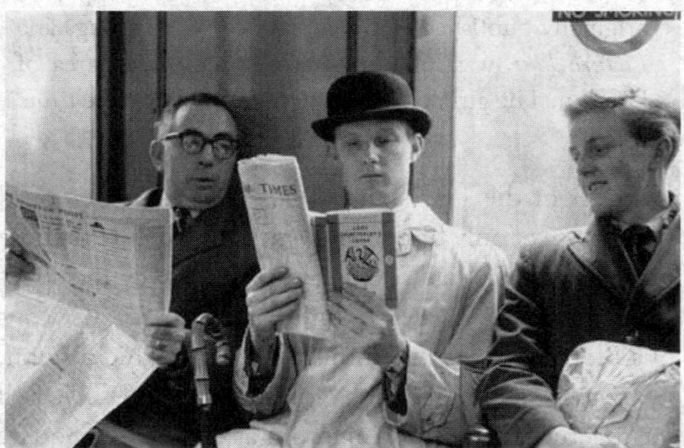

A commuter chooses *Lady Chatterley's Lover* over *The Times*, London, 1960.

Indeed, the literary portrayal even of heterosexual love (let alone of same-sex love) remained largely off limits through to the 1960s. A litmus test was D.H. Lawrence's *Lady Chatterley's Lover*, which was published in 1928, but with certain passages, which were considered objectionable on account of their sexual content, removed. Not until 1960, after a high profile court case, was the unexpurgated text of the novel (by today's standards still far from explicit in its portrayal of sexuality) finally published. Despite such strictures, however, change was occurring throughout society, and "Victorian" attitudes seemed to many to be part of the distant past.

SEXUAL ORIENTATION

The number of leading writers in the first half of the twentieth century who acknowledged a same-sex sexual orientation, at least among their circle of friends, was probably greater than it had been in any previous era of British history—certainly greater than at any time since the early years of the seventeenth century. The list of writers and intellectuals who are now known to have been gay, lesbian, or bisexual includes not only W.H. Auden and Virginia Woolf, but also Christopher Isherwood, Katherine Mansfield, Wilfred Owen, A.E. Housman, Nancy Cunard, E.M. Forster, Radclyffe Hall, John Maynard Keynes, Lytton Strachey, Sylvia Townsend-Warner, and a number of others.

It should be emphasized here that sexual identities are far from being stable, trans-historical categories; notions of and attitudes towards same-sex orientation were in flux throughout the late nineteenth and early twentieth centuries. Until well into the second half of the twentieth century, however (interestingly, at about the time that the word gay began to be more commonly used to identify those with a same-sex sexual orientation), there was little or no tolerance of same-sex sexuality in most sectors of society. As Auden and his friend and sometime literary collaborator Isherwood tacitly recognized when they moved to the United States, Britain in the 1920s and 1930s was even less ready than was America to openly acknowledge the legitimacy of same-sex relationships. Famously, the novelist and playwright Oscar Wilde had been tried and imprisoned in 1895 for "acts of gross indecency," and same-sex sexuality continued to be widely regarded (in a somewhat contradictory fashion) both as a sin and as a disease throughout the first half of the century. It also remained criminal for men, thousands of whom were imprisoned for "gross indecency" before the law was changed in 1967. E.M. Forster's novel on the theme of love between men, *Maurice*, which was not published until after his death in 1971, but which he had completed in 1914, gives a strong sense of the reality. When Maurice, having realized that "he loved men and had always loved them," confesses to his doctor that he is "an unspeakable of the Oscar Wilde sort," he is met with disgust and denial:

> "Rubbish, rubbish! … Now listen to me, Maurice, never let that evil hallucination, that temptation from the devil, occur to you again."
>
> The voice impressed him; was not science speaking?
>
> "Who put that lie into your head? You whom I see and know to be a decent fellow! We'll never mention it again. No—I'll not discuss. I'll not discuss. The worst thing I could do for you is to discuss it."

Maurice eventually does accept his sexual identity, but not before a further consultation, this one with a Mr. Lasker-Jones, who claims a fifty-per cent rate of "cure" by means of hypnotism for what he terms "congenital homosexuality."

If sexuality between men remained "unspeakable" through much of this period, sexuality between women remained for many unimaginable. In 1921 the British Parliament debated adding "acts of gross indecency between women" to the list of acts prohibited in the criminal statutes, but elected not to do so for fear of advertising lesbianism to "innocent" women. A few years later Hall's novel *The Well of Loneliness* was the occasion for the greatest literary storm of the era, over its alleged "obscenity." The novel recounts the story of a young woman named Stephen (whose parents had hoped for and expected a boy, and gone forward with the planned name regardless when the baby turned out to be a girl), and the romantic relationships she forms with other women. That the book could have been deemed obscene is astonishing to many readers today. In many ways the book is striking for the sense of normalcy it evokes as to the quotidian aspects of love:

> And now for the first time the old house was home. Mary went quickly from room to room humming a little tune as she did so, feeling that she saw with a new understanding the intimate objects that filled those rooms—were they not Stephen's? Every now and again she must pause to touch them because they were Stephen's.

Even when the novel's prose becomes effusive over the physical and spiritual aspects of the union, the most specific suggestions of the expression of sexual love between two women are passages such as the following: "Stephen bent down and kissed Mary's hands very humbly, for now she could find no words any more … and that night they were not divided."

Radclyffe Hall, c. 1920.

Such effusive attestations of the rapturous purity of unions at once physical and spiritual as one finds in *Maurice* and *The Well of Loneliness* may seem unexceptionable today, and even at the time many people were supportive; *The Well of Loneliness* was published to a generally favorable reception in the press. In the view of *The Sunday Times*, Hall's novel was written "with distinction, with a lively sense of characterization, and with a feeling for the background of her subject which makes her work delightful reading. And, first and last, she has courage and honesty." *The Daily Herald* asserted that there was "nothing pornographic" in the book:

> The evil minded will seek in vain in these pages for any stimulant to sexual excitement. The lustful [figures] of popular fiction may continue their sadistic course unchecked in those pornographic novels which are sold by the million, but Miss Radclyffe Hall has entirely ignored these crude and violent figures of sexual melodrama. She has given to English literature a profound and moving study of a profound and moving problem.

The Daily Express was the lone dissenter; a 19 August 1928 article headed "A Book That Must Be Suppressed" accused the novel of "devastating young souls" with its story of "sexual inversion and perversion." It seems probable that the *Express* represented popular feeling at the time more accurately than did the *Sunday Times* or the *Daily Herald*; soon after the *Express* article appeared, the Home Office advised the publishers to discontinue publication, and the police then charged the publishers under the 1857 Obscene Publications Act. Despite the support of dozens of high-profile authors and intellectuals, the magistrate Sir Charles Biron ruled against *The Well of Loneliness*:

> Unfortunately these women exist, and the book asks that their existence and vices should be recognised and tolerated, and not treated with condemnation, as they are at present by all decent people. This being the tenor of the book I have no hesitation in saying it is an … offence against public decency, and an obscene libel, and I shall order it to be destroyed.

The inevitable focus of history on landmark cases such as those of Oscar Wilde and *The Well of Loneliness* has to a considerable degree sensationalized and darkened our sense of late nineteenth- and early twentieth-century life outside the heterosexual mainstream. That it could be a dark and difficult existence there can be no doubt—the pessimism that Forster expressed even as late as 1960 ("police prosecutions will continue …") is surely understandable. But, as documents such as the letters exchanged between Strachey and Keynes attest, it could also be one of self-assured candor, zestful comedy, and a wholehearted enjoyment of life. "Our time will come," declared Strachey, speaking confidently in an 8 April 1906 letter to Keynes of the situation of gay people in Britain, "about a hundred years hence."

Ireland

If a remarkable amount of memorable literature emerged in Britain from the years of turmoil between the two World Wars in the first half of the twentieth century, the same statement could be made of Ireland, as the Irish endured a state of turmoil that remained constant throughout the first half of the century. The fiction of James Joyce and the plays of Samuel Beckett have already been mentioned as central to the evolution of Modernist literature. The other important Irish literary work of the period includes J.M. Synge's vivid portrayals of the elemental life of the Aran Islanders on the coast of western Ireland in plays such as *Riders of the Sea* (1904) and *The Playboy of the Western World* (1907); the plays of Lady Augusta Gregory; the sweeping expressiveness of Sean O'Casey's great dramas *Juno and the Paycock* (1924) and *The Plough and the Stars* (1926); and the extraordinary range of the poetry of William Butler Yeats from the 1890s through the 1930s—lyrical, Romantic, Symbolist, mystical, political, Existential, and perhaps above all, passionate.

To this list should be added the plays of Bernard Shaw, who was born in Dublin and lived there for the first twenty years of his life. Shaw has often been called the most important dramatist in English after Shakespeare; he was a socially committed writer who understood, as he puts it in the "Preface" to his 1905 play *Major Barbara*, that "it is difficult to make people realise that an evil is an evil." Shaw *was* able to make people realize such things, not only through effective polemic but also (and more memorably) through the sparkling wit of his plays. Shaw's important work extends from brilliantly biting works of the 1890s and early 1900s such as *Mrs Warren's Profession*, *Arms and the Man*, and *Major*

Barbara (on the topics of prostitution, militaristic attitudes, and religion and social reform, respectively); to *Pygmalion* (1912), a satire of attitudes toward social class and its expression through language, on which the 1950s musical *My Fair Lady* was based; to the epic historical drama *Saint Joan* (1923).

Cover, *Major Barbara: A Screen Version*, Penguin, 1945. This early "film tie-in" publication (number 500 in the Penguin series) was still in the standard early Penguin format; not until the 1960s did it become common for book publishers to employ a different cover design in such situations.

If the Irish Shaw is arguably the greatest "British" dramatist of the twentieth century, one of the greatest "British" writers of the 1890s, Oscar Wilde, had also been born and raised in Ireland before moving to London. Indeed, many have judged the literary outpouring from Irish writers during the period 1890–1960 to amount to a more important body of work than the entire literature of England, Scotland, and Wales over the same period—despite the fact that the combined population of England, Scotland, and Wales, at almost 50 million, was more than ten times that of Ireland.

But how are Britain and Ireland to be defined? Here matters become tangled, for during this period Ireland, for centuries a predominantly Catholic (and mostly unwilling) component of the United Kingdom, finally achieved the status of an independent republic. In the process, however, it became geographically split, with several largely Protestant counties of Northern Ireland remaining a political unit of the United Kingdom.

The Irish had been treated as second-class citizens throughout the centuries of English rule over Ireland. But the hardships they endured in the nineteenth century were particularly severe; the potato famine of 1845–51 alone is estimated to have killed almost a million Irish—almost 10 per cent of the population. By the 1880s and 1890s political pressure in Ireland for radical change had become extremely powerful. And there was pressure for cultural change too; the Celtic Revival (also known as the Irish Literary revival), begun in 1896 by Irish intellectuals such as Yeats and Lady Augusta Gregory, was remarkably successful both in increasing appreciation for the traditions of Irish culture and in encouraging the creation of new works in those traditions.

In the late nineteenth century, too, many in England became more sympathetic to Irish aspirations. In an effort to end the long history of oppression and resistance in British-controlled Ireland, Liberal governments twice introduced bills providing for one form or another of "Home Rule" (the term used to refer to limited Irish self-government) in the British House of Commons. The second of these was passed by the House of Commons but defeated in the Conservative-dominated House of Lords. In 1912, another Home Rule Bill was passed, and again the House of Lords rejected it. But now the rules had been changed; as a result of the previous year's Parliament Act, a veto by the House of Lords retained force for only three years. As the date in 1914 approached when the veto was due to expire and Home Rule would thus come into effect, tension rose to such a pitch that many felt civil war to be a real possibility. Substantial areas of the north of Ireland that had been forcibly settled by the English in earlier eras were now staunchly Protestant and vowed resistance to any government order to allow an Ireland dominated by "Papists" to become independent of Britain. And since Protestants from Ulster, in the north of Ireland, were heavily represented in the British army's contingent of troops stationed in Ireland, the military could not be relied on to carry out orders. With the onset of World War I, however, the implementation of the Home Rule Bill was postponed until after the war—and in a fateful move, Prime Minister Herbert Asquith promised that the British government would never force Ulster Protestants to accept Home Rule involuntarily.

Given the long history of vetoes and postponements—and given that the promised self-government in any case was to bring only a limited independence from Britain—it is unsurprising that Irish nationalists were impatient. On Easter Monday, 1916, rebels stormed public buildings in Dublin and proclaimed a republic. In the struggle, as Yeats famously wrote in "Easter, 1916," the Irish were "transformed utterly" and "a terrible beauty" was born. The uprising was brutally suppressed, but the nationalist Sinn Fein continued to wage a guerrilla opposition to British rule. Yet another Home Rule Bill was passed in 1920, providing for six counties of Ulster to be partitioned at independence, and the remainder of the island to remain a part of the British Empire but to be granted Dominion status (parallel to that of Canada, Australia, New Zealand, and South Africa) as the Irish Free State. That limited form of independence came into effect in 1922, but many Irish Republicans refused to accept any form of subservience to the British Crown, and the Irish Republican Army continued a clandestine struggle. In 1937 a new constitution changed the status of the country to that of a sovereign state within the British Commonwealth—a status sufficiently independent of Britain that Ireland was able to remain neutral in World War II—and in 1949 an Irish Republic was finally proclaimed, with the nation withdrawing from the Commonwealth. But the long struggle was still not fully over; tensions within Northern Ireland would continue to haunt Britain into the twenty-first century.

A young boy sings nationalist songs to a crowd outside Mountjoy Prison, Dublin, where an Irish Republican Army prisoner is about to be executed (1921).

An understanding of the politics and religion of Ireland is essential background for an understanding of Irish history—and Irish literary history—during this period. But it gives little sense of the daily reality of Catholics and Protestants who lived largely in isolation from each other, Catholics overwhelmingly the majority in Ireland, Protestants forming the majority in Northern Ireland. The novelist Elizabeth Bowen, who was raised mainly in Dublin in an Irish Protestant family (she "was taught to say 'Church of Ireland,' not 'Protestant'") later described her experiences in *Seven Winters: Memories of a Dublin Childhood* (1943):

> It was not until the end of those seven winters that I understood that we Protestants were a minority, and that the unquestioned rules of our being came, in fact, from the closeness of a minority world.… I took the existence of Roman Catholics for granted but met few and was not interested in them. They were, simply, "the others," whose world lay alongside ours but never touched. As to the difference

between the two religions, I was too discreet to ask questions—if I wanted to know. This appeared to share a delicate, awkward aura with those two other differences—of sex, of class. So quickly in a child's mind does prudery seed itself and make growth that I remember, even, an almost sexual shyness on the subject of Roman Catholics. I walked with hurried steps and averted cheek past porticos of churches that were "not ours," uncomfortably registering in my nostrils the pungent, unlikely smell [of incense] that came round curtains, through swinging doors.

Ideology and Economics in the 1930s and 1940s

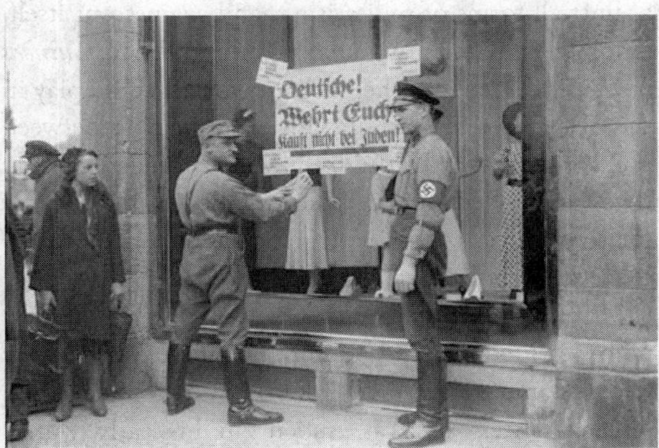

Nazi authorities affix a poster to a shop as part of their campaign of persecution, 1935. The sign reads "Buy nothing from Jews!"

How do ideologies differ from ideas? In part they are simply sets of ideas, but the question goes beyond that: an ideology is a systematic set of beliefs that is shared widely, and that prescribes a program of political action in association with those beliefs. In the twentieth century, such ideologies as communism, socialism, fascism, and liberalism all exerted enormous power. The central concepts of liberal democracy took shape in the nineteenth century, and by the end of the twentieth century had spread to much of the world. But for much of the twentieth century they were powerfully challenged by those of other ideologies: socialism (and its relative, communism) and fascism.

Fascism is identified as an ideology of the far right and it has indeed often co-existed with capitalist economic structures. But the strength of its appeal is—like that of communism—collectivist in nature. As the official name of the Nazi party in Germany (the National Socialist Party) suggests, fascism is "socialist" in its appeal to the egalitarian instincts of the populace. But whereas socialism and communism are (in theory at least) internationalist, appealing to the fellow-feeling of humans *as humans*, fascism appeals strongly to nationalist feeling—to the instinct of the population to pull together *as a nation*. More broadly, the egalitarian ideals of fascist societies are never inclusive; the nation defines itself not only against other nations, but typically also against a backdrop of a perceived "other" within its midst. Whether the "other" be immigrants, those of a different skin color, those of a different religion, or a group such as the Jews that is defined by race, culture, and religion, the otherness is typically used as a focal point for defining the nation's identity, and for lending intensity to the ideological allegiance of the fascist core.

If fascism weirdly approaches socialism from one direction, communism departs from socialist ideals in another. Socialist ideals are above all those of fairness and equality in a society in which government is prepared to intervene consistently on behalf of the greater good—to control capitalism, in socialism's weaker version (social democracy), or to replace it with a system of government ownership of the means of production on behalf of the entire population, in the full-fledged socialist model. Such ideals are built on foundations very similar to those of communist ideology, but the differences turn out in practice to be crucial. Perhaps the most important difference is that communist ideology—especially as it attained full force in the twentieth century—embodied the paradoxical notion that an elite could act as the "vanguard" for the masses, and that a "dictatorship of the proletariat" could reasonably act on behalf of all the people, without the people in practice having a direct say in who was to govern, or how. With the benefit of hindsight, it seems obvious that such an ideology was likely to result in a degree of oppression and cruelty similar to that of fascism. But in a Russia that had been laboring under the inequalities of a semi-feudal system, or indeed in Depression-era North America or Great Britain, when the engines of capitalism seemed to be merciless and unrestrained by government, to many communism seemed the only realistic path toward a society that would be both more free and more fair for all citizens.

The greatest ideological struggles of the first half of the century were unquestionably those that unfolded in Russia in 1917 and in Germany and Italy in the 1930s, but an ideologically charged climate was a worldwide reality. In some ways, the twentieth-century ideological tapestry may be seen in sharpest focus in the context of the Spanish Civil War (1936–39). Under the banner of those fighting for the Republican cause were liberals, socialists, communists, and anarchists—all ranged against the fascist forces of Generalissimo Françisco Franco. As George Orwell details in his account of the ideological and physical battles of the war, *Homage to Catalonia* (1938), the Spanish Civil War became a battleground not only between democracy and fascism, but also between the various factions on the Republican side, with idealism all too often being trumped by self-interest or by the dictates of outside governments lending support. In the end, the Communist government of the Soviet Union was as reluctant as were the capitalist governments of Britain or the United States to stand in the way of the anticipated "stable" government that the fascist General Franco represented.

The Spanish Civil War is often regarded as central to 1930s intellectual currents, and certainly the degree to which intellectuals from Britain (and indeed, from throughout the western world) rallied to the Republican side was remarkable. Sylvia Townsend Warner was among the leading British writers in Spain during the war; as she reported in a 1937 magazine article, the conflict was extraordinary not least of all for the bond that grew up between intellectuals and common citizens: "It is unusual for writers to hear words such as 'Here come the Intellectuals' spoken by working-class people and common soldiers in tones of kindliness and enthusiasm."

A young woman takes aim during target practice, Spain, 1936.

Others spoke out not only against fascism but against all forms of militarism—and against war itself. Notably, Virginia Woolf's polemic *Three Guineas* (1938) inquired into the role that women could play in the prevention of war, drawing a connection between the world of the powerful from which women had been thus far excluded—a "procession of the sons of educated men" overinvested in profit and prestige—and the forces that lead to political violence.

Even before the Spanish Civil War became a focal point for literature and politics, literature in the 1930s had become more highly political than that of the 1920s. Writers such as Auden (in his early work), Christopher Isherwood, C. Day Lewis, Louis MacNeice, Stephen Spender, and Edward Upward were all, in the view of MacNeice in his *Modern Poetry* (1932), "unlike Yeats and Eliot … emotionally partisan":

> Yeats [in the 1930s] proposed to turn his back on desire and hatred; Eliot sat back and watched other people's emotions with ennui and ironical self-pity. … The whole poetry, on the other hand, of Auden, Spender, and Day Lewis implies that they have desires and hatreds of their own and, further, that they think some things *ought* to be desired and others hated.

Many of these writers joined or were sympathetic to the Communist Party through much of the 1930s. In the later twentieth century it would have been unimaginable for most of the important writers of a generation to be sympathetic to "the Party," as it came to be called, but in the early 1930s the brutality of Soviet communism under Stalin was not yet public knowledge—and the mainstream parties in Britain (Labour as well as the Conservatives) were dealing timorously and ineffectively with an economic downturn of unprecedented severity.

The Great Depression that began late in 1929 and lasted until the outbreak of war ten years later was a worldwide phenomenon—and one exacerbated in Britain (as in North America) by the determination of governments not to go into debt in order to provide support for the unemployed and otherwise impoverished, or to invest in getting the economy moving. Individuals, too, reacted with fear, and strove to increase their savings, thereby contributing to what British economist John Maynard Keynes termed "the paradox of thrift": when people saved rather than spending what little they had, they further reduced the demand for goods, which in turn led to further reductions in production, more unemployment, lower wages for those still working—and so the cycle continued. By the end of 1930, some 20% of the British workforce was unemployed, and by the mid-1930s it was estimated that a quarter of the population had been reduced to a subsistence diet.

Keynes—an important figure in the Bloomsbury Group, and something of a cultural icon as well as one of the most important twentieth-century economists—broke new ground with his arguments for government intervention in the economy—recommending both that governments intervene to control inflation and that they act to "even out" the imbalances of the economic cycle by spending more during downturns. Conservatives argued that such imbalances would right themselves in the long run in any case, and should not be tampered with; Keynes's response was that "the long run is a misleading guide to current affairs. In the long run we are all dead." It was not until after World War II, though, that governments in Britain and elsewhere adopted Keynes's prescriptions for smoothing out the business cycle; although economic conditions improved somewhat in the south of Britain in the late 1930s, it was not until the war that economic growth resumed throughout the country.

Given the severity of the Great Depression, it is perhaps unsurprising that writers and intellectuals moved further to the left politically during the 1930s than at any other time during the century. But why did they embrace, in such large numbers, the relatively rigid doctrines of the Communist Party? As Orwell looked back in 1940, he took the view that the ideological coloring of the intellectual life of the 1930s had been as broadly connected to cultural as it had been to economic trends:

> By 1930 … the debunking of western civilization had reached its climax. … How many of the values by which our grandfathers lived could now be taken seriously? Patriotism, religion, the Empire, the family, the sanctity of marriage, the Old School Tie, birth, breeding, honour, discipline—anyone of ordinary education could turn the whole lot of them inside out in three minutes. But what do you achieve, after all, by getting rid of such primal things as patriotism and religion? You have not necessarily gotten rid of the need for something to believe in. … It is significant that [those intellectuals who did embrace religion in these years] went almost invariably to the Roman Church. … They went, that is, to the church with a world-wide organization, the one with a rigid discipline, the one with power and prestige behind it. … I do not think one need look farther than this for the reason the young writers of the thirties flocked into or towards the Communist Party. It was simply something to believe in. Here was a church, an army, an orthodoxy, a discipline.

With World War II, however, another form of discipline inevitably took hold; even though Britain and the United States became allies, the ties between the British and American intellectual communities and the Soviet Communist Party steadily loosened. With the beginning of the "Cold War" between the West and the USSR immediately following the end of World War II (and a new sense of purpose in the Labour Party under Clement Attlee), the link between British intellectuals and the

Communist Party had for the most part come to an end.

The Literature of the 1930s and 1940s

George Orwell may be seen as one of the writers who most fully expresses the ideological conflicts over socialism, communism, fascism, and liberal democracy that were at the heart of so much of twentieth-century life. His earlier works detail the appalling toll that capitalism was exacting on the working class. In *Down and Out in Paris and London* (1933), he recounts from personal experience the reality of the life of a vagrant, and of the life of the lowest of workers in the Paris hotel and restaurant industry. In *The Road to Wigan Pier* (1937), Orwell details the hardships of miners in the north of England, and of the working-class population throughout the country. Orwell was an avowed socialist; ironically enough, however, the two works for which he remains best known have often been portrayed as attacks on socialism; they are both novels in which he attacks the corruption of socialist ideals under Soviet-style communism. *Animal Farm* is a fable that shows the ways in which power may readily be seized by the unprincipled in a "collectivist" system; *1984* is a futurist view of a society in which "Big Brother" controls people's minds as much as their actions.

Another writer of central importance to twentieth-century literature who was initially defined against a backdrop of ideology is the poet W.H. Auden. Auden first became famous as a political poet, particularly with his memorable call to arms against fascism in "Spain 1937." Auden quickly became disenchanted with political polemic, however, not least of all his own. He became disillusioned with the Republican side in the Spanish Civil War after witnessing the persecution of Catholic priests by members of the Republican army, and after traveling through China in the wake of the 1937–38 Nanking Massacre he became convinced that violence is a disease that lurks within every human heart. "The act of taking sides," he became convinced, "spelled out the death of free culture and the triumph … of its enemies." Auden's poetic response to the

Like Orwell's *1984*, Aldous Huxley's *Brave New World* (1932) is a dystopia in which the State effectively controls the minds of its citizens, who are convinced that they are expressing human potential to its fullest.

outbreak of World War II, "September 1, 1939," was famously equivocal, the emphasis being placed on the expiration of the 1930s—dubbed by Auden "a low, dishonest decade"—rather than on the imminence of the fascist threat to freedom.

"Spain 1937" and "September 1, 1939" were among those poems that Auden refused to allow to be printed in later volumes of his poetry. Even in the 1930s, his work was extraordinarily diverse, and more and more as the years went by his name became paired with that of T.S. Eliot; after the death of Yeats in 1939, Eliot and Auden were almost universally regarded as the leading poets of the day. But the two may in more than one respect be seen as polar opposites. Whereas Eliot had moved permanently from the United States to England as a young man, Auden moved permanently from Britain to New York to 1939. Eliot's first marriage had failed in the face of the mental illness of his wife, Vivienne; she was eventually confined in a mental institution, and

Eliot embraced the stiff collar traditions of the Church and of respectable society with ever-greater conviction. Auden's marriage to novelist Thomas Mann's daughter Erica also ended, but it could hardly have been said to have "failed," since it had been entered into only to protect Erica from persecution at the hands of the Nazis. Auden made no secret of his same-sex sexual orientation (at a time when it took considerable courage to do so), and felt stifled by the society of which Eliot was a pillar; he moved in 1939 to New York, where he soon entered into a lifelong relationship with the poet Chester Kallman, and where his rumpled figure became a quiet fixture on the literary scene. If Eliot was a central figure of Modernism, Auden's connections to the forms of Modernism were more tenuous. His skill with poetic forms was extraordinarily wide ranging, but unlike Eliot he kept returning to accentual-syllabic meters, and to the use of rhyme.

The explosive sexuality of D.H. Lawrence's fiction has been touched on above. If sexual love was one of the great themes of his work, the other was surely the corrosive effect that the British class system exerted on human relationships. In the 1930s that became a theme more and more widely taken up by novelists, in works such as Henry Green's *Living* (1929), Walter Greenwood's *Love on the Dole* (1933), and J.B. Priestley's *Angel Pavement* (1930). With the notable exception of the novels and stories of Edward Upward, however, expressions of outrage against the capitalist order of things tended to be fewer in number and milder in tone in the prose fiction of the time than they were in its poetry.

At least as numerous and at least as popular in Britain during this era were fiction writers of a more conservative political stripe, including Somerset Maugham, with his tightly crafted novels and short stories; Evelyn Waugh, with his bitingly satirical novels; and P.G. Wodehouse, with his more light-hearted brand of satirical fiction. Many have seen an inherent conservatism, too, in what was then a new genre of popular fiction, the detective novel. The genre saw few if any worthy successors to Sir Arthur Conan Doyle's nineteenth-century creation, Sherlock Holmes, until Agatha Christie introduced her detective Hercule Poirot and the equally astute Jane Marple to readers in the late 1920s and 1930s. Together with the Father Brown novels of the Catholic conservative G.K. Chesterton, Christie's works founded an enduring tradition of English mystery novels.

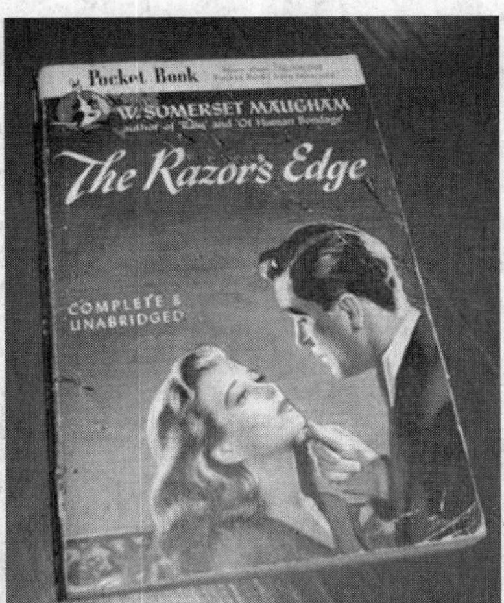

W. Somerset Maugham's *The Razor's Edge* (1944), a novel of romance and spirituality, became one of the twentieth century's bestselling novels both in Britain and in North America. It was issued in paperback editions on both sides of the Atlantic in 1946. Pocket Books, which had followed Penguin's lead and introduced mass market paperbacks into the United States in 1941, published the American paperback edition (shown here).

Many of the writers who contributed to the establishment of Modernism in the 1910s and 1920s extended their experimentation into the following decades. Virginia Woolf's *The Waves* (1931), for example, is arguably her most unconventional novel, approaching poetry in its lyricism and in its near-abandonment of traditional understandings of character and plot. David Jones's World War I epic *In Parenthesis* (1937), written partly in prose, partly in free verse, also blurs genre boundaries and bears the unmistakable stamp of Modernism. Throughout the 30s and 40s Dorothy Richardson continued to publish instalments of her novel-

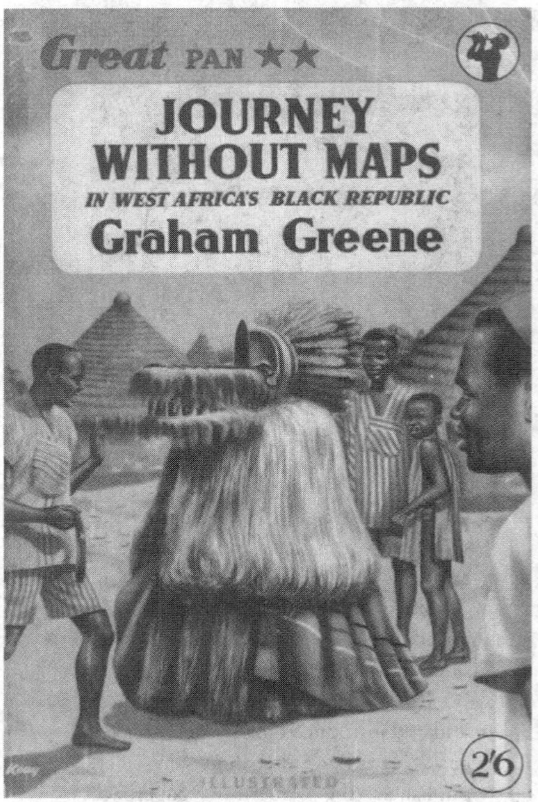

Greene's *Journey Without Maps*, an account of the author's travels in Liberia, was first published in 1936; this cover appeared with the 1948 Pan paperback edition.

sequence *Pilgrimage*, with the last appearing posthumously in 1967. Some of the founders of Imagism produced their most ambitious work after the 1920s; H.D.'s major epic *Trilogy* (1944–46) takes up psychoanalytic theory, mythology, and the occult in its response to the events of World War II, while Pound continued to work on and publish portions of his *Cantos*, with some of his most important work on the project appearing in print in 1948. T.S. Eliot, however, seemed to be backing away from Modernism with his ritualized play *Murder in the Cathedral* (1935)— and, following World War II, with a series of drawing room comedies. In general, most writers of the 30s and 40s did not take up Modernism's formal innovations, and during this period realism was a much stronger current in British literature than was Modernism.

From the late 1930s well into the 1970s one of the leading figures of British literature was unquestionably Graham Greene. Greene exploded onto the literary scene in 1938 with the publication of *Brighton Rock*, a tautly written exploration of the seediness and cruelty that lurked not far below the surface of much of British life. In subsequent novels, perhaps most notable among them *The Power and the Glory* (1940) and *The Heart of the Matter* (1948), Greene went on to explore the same qualities in human life generally. The setting of Greene's novels might be colonial Africa, rural Mexico, or war-torn London, but it is always recognizably "Greeneland"; always in the background is a sense of anguished Catholicism tinged with a bleak sense of despair.

Literature and Empire

No matter how widely Greene's geographical imagination ranged, the human souls he was interested in exploring were mostly those of white males from the Western world. Other British writers of the time, however, were beginning to reach for an understanding of the world that would take fuller account of the lives and the souls of those who lived under British rule in Africa, India, and much of the rest of the world. The essays of Nancy Cunard, along with those of Orwell, expressed a wide-ranging understanding of the mechanisms of Imperial rule, and of the reality of life for many who suffered under it. In fiction, the novelist Joyce Cary broke new ground with his *Mr. Johnson* (1939), a comic novel with a Nigerian clerk as its protagonist. The novel represents the Nigerian in ways that are bound to make today's reader wince. Yet it also gives expression to a specifically Nigerian sense of humor, and conveys a genuinely sympathetic understanding of the situation both of Johnson and of Nigerians generally under British rule. *Mr. Johnson* is a long way from the literature of the last few decades of the twentieth century in its approach to colonial and multicultural realities (let alone the debates of the late twentieth century over "appropriation of voice"). Yet in a very real sense it marks a step forward for British literature in the possibilities it demonstrates for the British imagination of connecting with the rest of the world. In a very direct sense there is also a connection between *Mr. Johnson* and the explosion of African literature later in the century (in the first half of the century exceedingly few African writers were published). As Chinua Achebe later recalled, reading the Cary novel was one of the things that led him to become a writer; "in spite of [Cary's] ability, in spite of his sympathy and understanding, he could not get under the skin of his African. They just did not communicate. And I felt if a good [white English] writer could make this mess perhaps we ought to try our hand."

The twentieth century had begun for Britain with a war in South Africa that had ended with a Pyrrhic victory. In a struggle against white colonists of Dutch background (Afrikaaners, or "Boers") that came to involve the Zulus and other native populations, the superior firepower of the British prevailed—but not without the adoption of a variety of brutally oppressive measures as the British struggled to control a guerrilla campaign by the Afrikaaners. At the time, the war seemed an extension of the British struggle against the Afrikaaners that had been continuing on and off for more than fifty years—and, as with previous conflicts, this one resulted in an expansion of the size of the British Empire. The war aroused objections to the Imperial project to an unprecedented degree, however; more than a century later, it is difficult not to see in it a foreshadowing of the loss of Empire. The brutalities in which the British engaged as they struggled to assert control seem a foretaste of the struggles against the Independence Movement in India in the 1930s and 1940s that would end with the independence of India in 1947, and of the struggles in Kenya and elsewhere in Africa in the 1950s that could be resolved only through the independence of those colonies. In one of his most famous speeches during the dark days of the Battle of Britain in 1940, Prime Minister Winston Churchill alluded to the possibility of the British Empire lasting for "a thousand years." Even then its foundations had crumbled, and within another 20 years the edifice of Empire would be almost entirely dismantled.

The English Language in the Early Twentieth Century

Many trends in the development of the English language that had begun in the nineteenth century or earlier continued through the first half of the twentieth. Punctuation became simpler: whereas, for example, it remained common in Britain through to the end of the nineteenth century and into the twentieth to precede a dash with a comma, by mid-century the norm was always to use one or the other, never both. Long periodic sentences had been on the decline through most of the nineteenth century, and this trend continued into the twentieth; on both sides of the Atlantic, sentences became shorter. Paragraphs also became shorter. To these generalizations, however, there were significant exceptions. With the growth of universities and the expansion of business, government, and political bureaucracies came an increase in academic, administrative, and political jargon of the sort of which Orwell complained in his famous essay "Politics and the English Language" (1946). While the majority of people (including most writers of fiction) were using shorter sentences, in other quarters writers were, in Orwell's words, "gumming together long strips of words which have already been set in order by someone else, and making the results presentable by sheer humbug."

In the twentieth century spelling was largely stable on both sides of the Atlantic; though shortened forms of some of the more archaic spellings in standard English became common in down-market forms of advertising, particularly in the United States (*thru*, *donut*), even there few of these came close to displacing the longer traditional forms. Conventions for marking direct speech also stabilized on both sides of the Atlantic, with the British using single quotation marks and the Canadians adopting the American convention of using double quotation marks.

Vocabulary, of course, continued to expand, with many new coinages entering the language as the result of new developments in science and technology. Interestingly, Britain and the United States developed largely separate terminologies regarding that most influential of twentieth-century developments in technology, the automobile; in Britain cars run on *petrol*, the engine is under the *bonnet*, the luggage goes in the *boot*, and you drive on the *motorway*—without much noise unless there is a hole in your *silencer*. In numerous other areas in which new coinages were necessary, British usage developed as quite distinct from that in the United States—from television *presenters* (hosts); to *breeze block* construction (concrete block), to battery-powered *torches* (flashlights), to *Wellingtons* (rubber boots), to *hire purchase plans* (installment plans), British English remained distinct from American English. (Former British possessions such as Canada and Australia partook of both in forming their own national patterns.)

Perhaps the greatest structural shift in English in the first half of the twentieth century was the simplification or elimination of forms marking the subjunctive mood. In constructions such as "If I were to travel through time I would ...," for example, the old subjunctive form came to be largely replaced by the simple past form of the verb ("If I traveled through time I would ...").

Throughout the nineteenth century, the spread of literacy and of mass transportation led to a steady decrease in the distinctiveness of the various dialects of English spoken in Britain, and in the distinctiveness of regional accents. That movement toward standardization continued in the twentieth century, with radio and television as its new vehicles. In 1922, the government set up the BBC (at first the initials stood for British Broadcasting Company, but the name was soon changed to British Broadcasting Corporation), and it remained the dominant force in British radio—and, from the 1950s on, British television—for most of the century. In 1926, John Reith, the BBC's managing director, created an Advisory Committee on Spoken English, chaired by Robert Bridges, then the Poet Laureate, with the task of making recommendations to facilitate a standard of pronunciation over the air. Reith specifically asked that the committee seek a "style or quality of English that would not be laughed at in any part of the country." In practice, the standardized pronunciations recommended by the committee—which remained largely mandatory for announcers until 1989—were broadly similar to the pronunciations taught in the nation's elite "public" schools (see the glossary at the back of this volume for a discussion of this term) in southern England. Indeed, the three terms "public school pronunciation," "BBC pronunciation," and "Received Standard Pronunciation" (a term introduced by Henry Cecil Wyld in the early twentieth century to denote "the form which ... is heard with practically no variation among speakers of the better class all over the country") are all roughly synonymous. Despite the ongoing trend towards standardization of speech in the twentieth century, however, the varieties of British English remained extraordinarily diverse throughout the century—so much so that someone from London could at century's end still have great difficulty understanding the accent of a Glaswegian or a "Geordie" (a native of the Newcastle area).

History of the Language and of Print Culture

In an effort to provide for readers a direct sense of the development of the language and of print culture, examples of texts in their original form, of illustrations, and of other materials related to book culture have been provided in each volume. A list of these within the portion of the present volume addressing the twentieth and twenty-first centuries, arranged chronologically, appears below. An overview of developments in the history of language during the first half of the century appears on pages 1307 to 1308; material on developments in the history of language since World War II appears on pages 1629–30, 1638–40, and 1644–46.

Joseph Conrad
1857 – 1924

The critic Edward Said wrote of Joseph Conrad that "the moment one enters his writing the aura of dislocation, instability and strangeness is unmistakable. No one could represent the fate of lostness and disorientation better than he did, and no one was more ironic about the effort of trying to replace that condition with new arrangements and accommodations—which invariably lured one into further traps." In his efforts to capture this condition of inescapable "lostness and disorientation," Conrad was at the forefront of the development of Modernism. His stories and novels, which use fragmented chronologies and multiple, layered points of view, throw into question many past sureties, including the concepts of self, of Empire, and of capitalism—and the ideal of social and political cohesion. Conrad's themes of alienation, adventure, and exile; his critique of power; and his continual return to the conflict between the individual and the unknowable all reflect his own experience as an outsider, beginning with his childhood as a Polish exile and including decades spent in world travel.

Conrad was born Jozef Teodor Konrad Nalecz Korzeniowski on 3 December 1857, in Poland (then under Russian rule). His parents, Apollo and Evalina, were members of the educated, landed gentry who opposed Czarist Russian control. Apollo was arrested for revolutionary conspiracy, and, in 1862, the family was exiled to Vologda in northern Russia, where they were forced to endure years of hardship and illness. Conrad's mother died in 1865 and his father in 1868. Following the death of his parents, Conrad came under the guardianship of his maternal uncle in Kraków, Poland. He spent much of the next few years reading translations of Shakespeare, Dickens, and Victor Hugo. At age fifteen, bored by schoolwork, he first expressed his desire to go to sea, and he spent the next two years pressing his family for permission. His pleas were eventually heard, and in 1874, nearing his seventeenth birthday, Conrad traveled to Marseilles and joined the French merchant navy.

From 1874 to 1877, Conrad made a number of voyages to Martinique and the West Indies aboard French ships. During these years he engaged in illicit gunrunning on behalf of the Carlist Royalists in Spain. In 1878, burdened by massive smuggling and gambling debts, Conrad shot himself in the chest. He later claimed that this injury was the result of a duel, rather than what seems to have been a suicide attempt; whatever the case, Conrad recovered from his injury and escaped his creditors by joining the British merchant navy. Knowing just a few words in English, he began to learn the language during voyages aboard a coal schooner between the ports of Lowescroft and Newcastle.

Over the next sixteen years, Conrad traveled to Australia, South America, India, Borneo, and the South Pacific in the service of the British merchant navy. In 1886, he became a British citizen and changed his name to Joseph Conrad. In 1888, Conrad was given his first and only sea command as captain of the *Otago*, and he spent the next 15 months journeying from Bangkok to Singapore, around the Malay Archipelago, and to Australia and Mauritius. Conrad would later use his experiences aboard the *Otago* as inspiration for his 1912 short story "The Secret Sharer." In 1890 he took a steamboat up the Congo River to take command of a Belgian steamer—an expedition that would provide the background for his best-known work, *Heart of Darkness*. While in the Congo, Conrad contracted malaria, the effects of which would plague him for years. In ill health and with his interest in writing increasing steadily, Conrad retired from seafaring and settled permanently in England in 1894. He would dedicate the rest of his life to literary pursuits, writing prolifically until his death of a heart attack, near Canterbury, in 1924.

Conrad wrote 13 novels, two volumes of memoirs, and 28 short stories. Because his experiences at sea form the background for many of his stories, he frequently depicts the regions and peoples held forcibly under the sway of the British Empire and other European imperial interests. As writer Ngũgĩ's Wa Thiong'o puts it, Conrad "share[s] the same world" as the colonized peoples of Africa, Asia, and the Americas, with whom he came into constant contact during his naval voyages. Naval life would play a central role in nearly all of his works of fiction. In *The Nigger of the "Narcissus"* (1897), he shows the plight of a dying black mariner affecting the morale of an entire ship's crew. In *Lord Jim* (1900) he explores the concept of personal honor by presenting a sailor whose life is spent in atonement for a youthful act of cowardice. In *Heart of Darkness* (1902), Conrad revisits his own journey to the Congo, and he attempts to convey the avarice, cruelty, disorder, and abuse that characterized colonial rule in the area.

Conrad's representation of colonized people and places has been the subject of fierce critical debate. In 1975, for example, Chinua Achebe argued that his portrayal of the Congo in *Heart of Darkness* was inherently racist, that the narrative silenced the African characters, divested them of agency, and diminished their humanity: "Conrad saw and condemned the evil of imperial exploitation but was strangely unaware of the racism on which it sharpened its iron tooth." Achebe claimed that the novella's racism was sufficiently egregious to make the book unworthy of consideration as a work of art. Other critics, such as Edward Said, agreed that Conrad seemed to view imperialism as inevitable, but argued that Conrad's own position as outsider gave his works an ironic distance from the colonial project: "Conrad's way of demonstrating this discrepancy between the orthodox and his own views of empire is to keep drawing attention to how ideas and values are constructed (and deconstructed) through dislocations in the narrator's language." Every reader encountering Conrad's works—many of which touch on themes similar to those in *Heart of Darkness*—must do so within these important post-colonial critical contexts.

In three of his later works, Conrad shifts attention away from the sea to consider the issue of revolutionary violence and its relationship to capitalism. In *Nostromo* (1904), which Conrad described as his "most ambitious performance," he portrays a fictional colonized country in South America where a revolution and civil war expose the greed that undermines political and social progress and that poisons even the most idealistic and honorable lives. *The Secret Agent* (1906) also focuses on political violence, with a narrative that revolves around an anarchist bomb plot in London, and *Under Western Eyes* (1911) presents a story of betrayal and redemption amidst antigovernment upheaval in Czarist Russia. These three novels were less highly regarded in Conrad's lifetime, but they have since come to command a great deal of critical attention and appreciation.

Conrad's work, while it continues to be appreciated in aesthetic terms and interpreted as pivotal to the Modernist movement, is also of critical interest for what it suggests about imperialism and race, about the effects of capitalism, and, more generally, about the individual's relation to history and the powers that shape it. Conrad's writing begins on the borders of the ineffable and ventures in, seeking new forms and new language to express what is found there. As he writes in *Lord Jim*, "A man that is born falls into a dream like a man who falls into the sea. If he tries to climb out into the air as inexperienced people endeavor to do, he drowns."

⌘⌘⌘

The Preface to *The Nigger of the "Narcissus"*[1]
[The Task of the Artist]

A work that aspires, however humbly, to the condition of art should carry its justification in every line. And art itself may be defined as a single-minded attempt to render the highest kind of justice to the visible universe, by bringing to light the truth, manifold and one, underlying its every aspect. It is an attempt to find in its forms, in its colours, in its light, in its shadows, in the aspects of matter and in the facts of life, what of each is fundamental, what is enduring and essential—their one illuminating and convincing quality—the very truth of their existence. The artist, then, like the thinker or the scientist, seeks the truth and makes his appeal. Impressed by the aspect of the world the thinker plunges into ideas, the scientist into facts—whence, presently, emerging they make their appeal to those qualities of our being that fit us best for the hazardous enterprise of living. They speak authoritatively to our common-sense, to our intelligence, to our desire of peace or to our desire of unrest; not seldom to our prejudices, sometimes to our fears, often to our egoism—but always to our credulity. And their words are heard with reverence, for their concern is with weighty matters: with the cultivation of our minds and the proper care of our bodies; with the attainment of our ambitions; with the perfection of the means and the glorification of our precious aims.

It is otherwise with the artist.

Confronted by the same enigmatical spectacle the artist descends within himself, and in that lonely region of stress and strife, if he be deserving and fortunate, he finds the terms of his appeal. His appeal is made to our less obvious capacities: to that part of our nature which, because of the warlike conditions of existence, is necessarily kept out of sight within the more resisting and hard qualities—like the vulnerable body within the steel armour. His appeal is less loud, more profound, less distinct, more stirring—and sooner forgotten. Yet its effect endures for ever. The changing wisdom of successive generations discards ideas, questions facts, demolishes theories. But the artist appeals to that part of our being which is not dependent on wisdom: to that in us which is a gift and not an acquisition—and, therefore, more permanently enduring. He speaks to our capacity for delight and wonder, to the sense of mystery surrounding our lives; to our sense of pity, and beauty, and pain; to the latent feeling of fellowship with all creation—and to the subtle but invincible, conviction of solidarity that knits together the loneliness of innumerable hearts: to the solidarity in dreams, in joy, in sorrow, in aspirations, in illusions, in hope, in fear, which binds men to each other, which binds together all humanity—the dead to the living and the living to the unborn.

It is only some such train of thought, or rather of feeling, that can in a measure explain the aim of the attempt, made in the tale which follows, to present an unrestful episode in the obscure lives of a few individuals out of all the disregarded multitude of the bewildered, the simple and the voiceless. For, if there is

[1] *Preface … Narcissus* Conrad's novella *The Nigger of the "Narcissus"* was first published in *The New Review* in 1897. Conrad added the preface when it came out in book form in 1898. The novella deals with the death of a black sailor aboard a merchant ship called the *Narcissus*. Conrad had served as first mate on a ship bearing that name in 1883. The pejorative term "nigger" was not used in the American edition, which at the suggestion of the publisher was entitled *Children of the Sea*. The reason given for the change, however, was not that the term was inherently offensive but rather that a book perceived to be about a black man would not interest many readers. Surprisingly, the term "nigger" continued for decades to appear in book titles in Britain; the Agatha Christie mystery novel now known by its original American title, *And Then There Were None*, first appeared in the UK in 1939 as *Ten Little Niggers*.

any part of truth in the belief confessed above, it becomes evident that there is not a place of splendour or a dark corner of the earth that does not deserve, if only a passing glance of wonder and pity. The motive, then, may be held to justify the matter of the work; but this preface, which is simply an avowal of endeavour, cannot end here—for the avowal is not yet complete.

Fiction—if it at all aspires to be art—appeals to temperament. And in truth it must be, like painting, like music, like all art, the appeal of one temperament to all the other innumerable temperaments whose subtle and resistless power endows passing events with their true meaning, and creates the moral, the emotional atmosphere of the place and time. Such an appeal, to be effective, must be an impression conveyed through the senses; and, in fact, it cannot be made in any other way, because temperament, whether individual or collective, is not amenable to persuasion. All art, therefore, appeals primarily to the senses, and the artistic aim when expressing itself in written words must also make its appeal through the senses, if its high desire is to reach the secret spring of responsive emotions. It must strenuously aspire to the plasticity of sculpture, to the colour of painting, and to the magic suggestiveness of music—which is the art of arts. And it is only through complete, unswerving devotion to the perfect blending of form and substance; it is only through an unremitting, never-discouraged care for the shape and ring of sentences that an approach can be made to plasticity, to colour; and the light of magic suggestiveness may be brought to play for an evanescent instant over the commonplace surface of words: of the old, old words, worn thin, defaced by ages of careless usage.

The sincere endeavour to accomplish that creative task, to go as far on that road as his strength will carry him, to go undeterred by faltering, weariness or reproach, is the only valid justification for the worker in prose. And if his conscience is clear, his answer to those who, in the fulness of a wisdom which looks for immediate profit, demand specifically to be edified, consoled, amused; who demand to be promptly improved, or encouraged, or frightened, or shocked, or charmed, must run thus:—My task which I am trying to achieve is, by the power of the written word, to make you hear, to make you feel—it is, before all, to make you *see*. That—and no more, and it is everything. If I succeed, you shall find there according to your deserts: encouragement, consolation, fear, charm—all you demand; and, perhaps, also that glimpse of truth for which you have forgotten to ask.

To snatch in a moment of courage, from the remorseless rush of time, a sapping phase of life is only the beginning of the task. The task approached in tenderness and faith is to hold up unquestioningly, without choice and without fear, the rescued fragment before all eyes and in the light of a sincere mood. It is to show its vibration, its colour, its form; and through its movement, its form, and its colour, reveal the substance of its truth—disclose its inspiring secret: the stress and passion within the core of each convincing moment. In a single-minded attempt of that kind, if one be deserving and fortunate, one may perchance attain to such clearness of sincerity that at last the presented vision of regret or pity, of terror or mirth, shall awaken in the hearts of the beholders that feeling of unavoidable solidarity; of the solidarity in mysterious origin, in toil, in joy, in hope, in uncertain fate, which binds men to each other and all mankind to the visible world.

It is evident that he who, rightly or wrongly, holds by the convictions expressed above cannot be faithful to any one of the temporary formulas of his craft. The enduring part of them—the truth which each only imperfectly veils—should abide with him as the most precious of his possessions, but they all: Realism, Romanticism, Naturalism, even the unofficial sentimentalism (which, like the poor, is exceedingly difficult to get rid of[1]); all these gods must, after a short period of fellowship, abandon him—even on the very threshold of the temple—to the stammerings of his conscience and to the outspoken consciousness of the difficulties of his work. In that uneasy solitude the supreme cry of Art for Art, even, loses the exciting ring of its apparent immorality. It sounds far off. It has ceased to be a cry, and is

[1] *like the poor ... get rid of* The reference is to John 12.8: "for the poor always you have with you."

heard only as a whisper, often incomprehensible, but at times, and faintly, encouraging.

Sometimes, stretched at ease in the shade of a roadside tree, we watch the motions of a labourer in a distant field, and after a time, begin to wonder languidly as to what the fellow may be at. We watch the movements of his body, the waving of his arms, we see him bend down, stand up, hesitate, begin again. It may add to the charm of an idle hour to be told the purpose of his exertions. If we know he is trying to lift a stone, to dig a ditch, to uproot a stump, we look with a more real interest at his efforts; we are disposed to condone the jar of his agitation upon the restfulness of the landscape; and even, if in a brotherly frame of mind, we may bring ourselves to forgive his failure. We understood his object, and, after all, the fellow has tried, and perhaps he had not the strength, and perhaps he had not the knowledge. We forgive, go on our way—and forget.

And so it is with the workman of art. Art is long and life is short,[1] and success is very far off. And thus, doubtful of strength to travel so far, we talk a little about the aim—the aim of art, which, like life itself, is inspiring, difficult—obscured by mists. It is not in the clear logic of a triumphant conclusion; it is not in the unveiling of one of those heartless secrets which are called the Laws of Nature. It is not less great, but only more difficult.

To arrest, for the space of a breath, the hands busy about the work of the earth, and compel men entranced by the sight of distant goals to glance for a moment at the surrounding vision of form and colour, of sunshine and shadows; to make them pause for a look, for a sigh, for a smile—such is the aim, difficult and evanescent, and reserved only for a very few to achieve. But sometimes, by the deserving and the fortunate, even that task is accomplished. And when it is accomplished—behold!—all the truth of life is there: a moment of vision, a sigh, a smile—and the return to an eternal rest.

—1898

[1] *Art is long and life is short* The Latin proverb *ars longa, vita brevis* derives from a saying of the Greek physician Hippocrates.

The Secret Sharer

I

On my right hand there were lines of fishing stakes resembling a mysterious system of half-submerged bamboo fences, incomprehensible in its division of the domain of tropical fishes, and crazy of aspect as if abandoned forever by some nomad tribe of fishermen now gone to the other end of the ocean; for there was no sign of human habitation as far as the eye could reach. To the left a group of barren islets, suggesting ruins of stone walls, towers, and blockhouses, had its foundations set in a blue sea that itself looked solid, so still and stable did it lie below my feet; even the track of light from the westering sun shone smoothly, without that animated glitter which tells of an imperceptible ripple. And when I turned my head to take a parting glance at the tug which had just left us anchored outside the bar, I saw the straight line of the flat shore joined to the stable sea, edge to edge, with a perfect and unmarked closeness, in one leveled floor half brown, half blue under the enormous dome of the sky. Corresponding in their insignificance to the islets of the sea, two small clumps of trees, one on each side of the only fault in the impeccable joint, marked the mouth of the river Meinam[2] we had just left on the first preparatory stage of our homeward journey; and, far back on the inland level, a larger and loftier mass, the grove surrounding the great Paknam pagoda,[3] was the only thing on which the eye could rest from the vain task of exploring the monotonous sweep of the horizon. Here and there gleams as of a few scattered pieces of silver marked the windings of the great river; and on the nearest of them, just within the bar, the tug steaming right into the land became lost to my sight, hull and funnel and masts, as though the impassive earth had swallowed her up without an effort, without a tremor. My eye followed

[2] *the river Meinam* Conrad may have been referring to the Chao Phraya river in the city of Samut Prakan, Thailand. Located just south of Bangkok, Samut Prakan is a port city on the Gulf of Thailand.

[3] *Paknam pagoda* Located in Samut Prakan, the Phra Samut Chedi pagoda was originally built in the middle of the river. Today it adjoins the west bank due to silt accumulation.

the light cloud of her smoke, now here, now there, above the plain, according to the devious curves of the stream, but always fainter and farther away, till I lost it at last behind the miter-shaded hill of the great pagoda. And then I was left alone with my ship, anchored at the head of the Gulf of Siam.[1]

She floated at the starting point of a long journey, very still in an immense stillness, the shadows of her spars[2] flung far to the eastward by the setting sun. At that moment I was alone on her decks. There was not a sound in her—and around us nothing moved, nothing lived, not a canoe on the water, not a bird in the air, not a cloud in the sky. In this breathless pause at the threshold of a long passage we seemed to be measuring our fitness for a long and arduous enterprise, the appointed task of both our existences to be carried out, far from all human eyes, with only sky and sea for spectators and for judges.

There must have been some glare in the air to interfere with one's sight, because it was only just before the sun left us that my roaming eyes made out beyond the highest ridges of the principal islet of the group something which did away with the solemnity of perfect solitude. The tide of darkness flowed on swiftly; and with tropical suddenness a swarm of stars came out above the shadowy earth, while I lingered yet, my hand resting lightly on my ship's rail as if on the shoulder of a trusted friend. But, with all that multitude of celestial bodies staring down at one, the comfort of quiet communion with her was gone for good. And there were also disturbing sounds by this time—voices, footsteps forward; the steward flitted along the main-deck, a busily ministering spirit; a hand bell tinkled urgently under the poop deck[3] …

I found my two officers waiting for me near the supper table, in the lighted cuddy.[4] We sat down at once, and as I helped the chief mate, I said:

"Are you aware that there is a ship anchored inside the islands? I saw her mastheads above the ridge as the sun went down."

He raised sharply his simple face, overcharged by a terrible growth of whisker, and emitted his usual ejaculations: "Bless my soul, sir! You don't say so!"

My second mate was a round-cheeked, silent young man, grave beyond his years, I thought; but as our eyes happened to meet I detected a slight quiver on his lips. I looked down at once. It was not my part to encourage sneering on board my ship. It must be said, too, that I knew very little of my officers. In consequence of certain events of no particular significance, except to myself, I had been appointed to the command only a fortnight before. Neither did I know much of the hands forward. All these people had been together for eighteen months or so, and my position was that of the only stranger on board. I mention this because it has some bearing on what is to follow. But what I felt most was my being a stranger to the ship; and if all the truth must be told, I was somewhat of a stranger to myself. The youngest man on board (barring the second mate), and untried as yet by a position of the fullest responsibility, I was willing to take the adequacy of the others for granted. They had simply to be equal to their tasks; but I wondered how far I should turn out faithful to that ideal conception of one's own personality every man sets up for himself secretly.

Meantime the chief mate, with an almost visible effect of collaboration on the part of his round eyes and frightful whiskers, was trying to evolve a theory of the anchored ship. His dominant trait was to take all things into earnest consideration. He was of a painstaking turn of mind. As he used to say, he "liked to account to himself" for practically everything that came in his way, down to a miserable scorpion he had found in his cabin a week before. The why and the wherefore of that scorpion—how it got on board and came to select his room rather than the pantry (which was a dark place and more what a scorpion would be partial to), and how on earth it managed to drown itself in the inkwell of his writing desk—had exercised him infinitely. The ship

---

[1] *Siam* Thailand.

[2] *spars* Mast attachments securing the sail; also called booms or gaffs.

[3] *poop deck* Highest and hindmost deck on a ship.

[4] *cuddy* Small ship-board cabin.

within the islands was much more easily accounted for; and just as we were about to rise from table he made his pronouncement. She was, he doubted not, a ship from home lately arrived. Probably she drew too much water to cross the bar except at the top of spring tides. Therefore she went into that natural harbour to wait for a few days in preference to remaining in an open roadstead.

"That's so," confirmed the second mate, suddenly, in his slightly hoarse voice. "She draws over twenty feet. She's the Liverpool ship *Sephora* with a cargo of coal. Hundred and twenty-three days from Cardiff."

We looked at him in surprise.

"The tugboat skipper told me when he came on board for your letters, sir," explained the young man. "He expects to take her up the river the day after tomorrow."

After thus overwhelming us with the extent of his information he slipped out of the cabin. The mate observed regretfully that he "could not account for that young fellow's whims." What prevented him telling us all about it at once, he wanted to know.

I detained him as he was making a move. For the last two days the crew had had plenty of hard work, and the night before they had very little sleep. I felt painfully that I—a stranger—was doing something unusual when I directed him to let all hands turn in without setting an anchor watch. I proposed to keep on deck myself till one o'clock or thereabouts. I would get the second mate to relieve me at that hour.

"He will turn out the cook and the steward at four," I concluded, "and then give you a call. Of course at the slightest sign of any sort of wind we'll have the hands up and make a start at once."

He concealed his astonishment. "Very well, sir." Outside the cuddy he put his head in the second mate's door to inform him of my unheard-of caprice to take a five hours' anchor watch on myself. I heard the other raise his voice incredulously—"What? The Captain himself?" Then a few more murmurs, a door closed, then another. A few moments later I went on deck.

My strangeness, which had made me sleepless, had prompted that unconventional arrangement, as if I had expected in those solitary hours of the night to get on terms with the ship of which I knew nothing, manned by men of whom I knew very little more. Fast alongside a wharf, littered like any ship in port with a tangle of unrelated things, invaded by unrelated shore people, I had hardly seen her yet properly. Now, as she lay cleared for sea, the stretch of her main-deck seemed to me very fine under the stars. Very fine, very roomy for her size, and very inviting. I descended the poop and paced the waist, my mind picturing to myself the coming passage through the Malay Archipelago, down the Indian Ocean, and up the Atlantic. All its phases were familiar enough to me, every characteristic, all the alternatives which were likely to face me on the high seas—everything! … except the novel responsibility of command. But I took heart from the reasonable thought that the ship was like other ships, the men like other men, and that the sea was not likely to keep any special surprises expressly for my discomfiture.

Arrived at that comforting conclusion, I bethought myself of a cigar and went below to get it. All was still down there. Everybody at the after end of the ship was sleeping profoundly. I came out again on the quarter-deck, agreeably at ease in my sleeping suit on that warm breathless night, barefooted, a glowing cigar in my teeth, and, going forward, I was met by the profound silence of the fore end of the ship. Only as I passed the door of the forecastle, I heard a deep, quiet, trustful sigh of some sleeper inside. And suddenly I rejoiced in the great security of the sea as compared with the unrest of the land, in my choice of that untempted life presenting no disquieting problems, invested with an elementary moral beauty by the absolute straightforwardness of its appeal and by the singleness of its purpose.

The riding light in the forerigging burned with a clear, untroubled, as if symbolic, flame, confident and bright in the mysterious shades of the night. Passing on my way aft along the other side of the ship, I observed that the rope side ladder, put over, no doubt, for the master of the tug when he came to fetch away our letters, had not been hauled in as it should have been. I became annoyed at this, for exactitude in some small matters is the very soul of discipline. Then I reflected that I had myself peremptorily dismissed my officers from duty, and by my own act had prevented the anchor watch being formally set and things properly attended to. I asked myself whether it was wise ever to interfere with the established routine of duties even from the kindest of motives. My action might have made me appear eccentric. Goodness only knew how that absurdly whiskered mate would "account" for my conduct, and what the whole ship thought of that informality of their new captain. I was vexed with myself.

Not from compunction certainly, but, as it were mechanically, I proceeded to get the ladder in myself. Now a side ladder of that sort is a light affair and comes in easily, yet my vigorous tug, which should have brought it flying on board, merely recoiled upon my body in a totally unexpected jerk. What the devil!... I was so astounded by the immovableness of that ladder that I remained stockstill, trying to account for it to myself like that imbecile mate of mine. In the end, of course, I put my head over the rail.

The side of the ship made an opaque belt of shadow on the darkling glassy shimmer of the sea. But I saw at once something elongated and pale floating very close to the ladder. Before I could form a guess a faint flash of phosphorescent light, which seemed to issue suddenly from the naked body of a man, flickered in the sleeping water with the elusive, silent play of summer lightning in a night sky. With a gasp I saw revealed to my stare a pair of feet, the long legs, a broad livid back immersed right up to the neck in a greenish cadaverous glow. One hand, awash, clutched the bottom rung of the ladder. He was complete but for the head. A headless corpse! The cigar dropped out of my gaping mouth with a tiny plop and a short hiss quite audible in the absolute stillness of all things under heaven. At that I suppose he raised up his face, a dimly pale oval in the shadow of the ship's side. But even then I could only barely make out down there the shape of his black-haired head. However, it was enough for the horrid, frost-bound sensation which had gripped me about the chest to pass off. The moment of vain exclamations was past, too. I only climbed on the spare spar and leaned over the rail as far as I could, to bring my eyes nearer to that mystery floating alongside.

As he hung by the ladder, like a resting swimmer, the sea lightning played about his limbs at every stir; and he appeared in it ghastly, silvery, fishlike. He remained as mute as a fish, too. He made no motion to get out of the water, either. It was inconceivable that he should not attempt to come on board, and strangely troubling to suspect that perhaps he did not want to. And my first words were prompted by just that troubled incertitude.

"What's the matter?" I asked in my ordinary tone, speaking down to the face upturned exactly under mine.

"Cramp," it answered, no louder. Then slightly anxious, "I say, no need to call anyone."

"I was not going to," I said.

"Are you alone on deck?"

"Yes."

I had somehow the impression that he was on the point of letting go the ladder to swim away beyond my ken—mysterious as he came. But, for the moment, this being appearing as if he had risen from the bottom of the sea (it was certainly the nearest land to the ship) wanted only to know the time. I told him. And he, down there, tentatively:

"I suppose your captain's turned in?"

"I am sure he isn't," I said.

He seemed to struggle with himself, for I heard something like the low, bitter murmur of doubt. "What's the good?" His next words came out with a hesitating effort.

"Look here, my man. Could you call him out quietly?"

I thought the time had come to declare myself.

"I am the captain."

I heard a "By Jove!" whispered at the level of the water. The phosphorescence flashed in the swirl of the water all about his limbs, his other hand seized the ladder.

"My name's Leggatt."

The voice was calm and resolute. A good voice. The self-possession of that man had somehow induced a corresponding state in myself. It was very quietly that I remarked:

"You must be a good swimmer."

"Yes. I've been in the water practically since nine o'clock. The question for me now is whether I am to let go this ladder and go on swimming till I sink from exhaustion, or—to come on board here."

I felt this was no mere formula of desperate speech, but a real alternative in the view of a strong soul. I should have gathered from this that he was young; indeed, it is only the young who are ever confronted by such clear issues. But at the time it was pure intuition on my part. A mysterious communication was established already between us two—in the face of that silent, darkened tropical sea. I was young, too; young enough to make no comment. The man in the water began suddenly to climb up the ladder, and I hastened away from the rail to fetch some clothes.

Before entering the cabin I stood still, listening in the lobby at the foot of the stairs. A faint snore came through the closed door of the chief mate's room. The second mate's door was on the hook, but the darkness in there was absolutely soundless. He, too, was young and could sleep like a stone. Remained the steward, but he was not likely to wake up before he was called. I got a sleeping suit out of my room and, coming back on deck, saw the naked man from the sea sitting on the main hatch, glimmering white in the darkness, his elbows on his knees and his head in his hands. In a moment he had concealed his damp body in a sleeping suit of the same gray-stripe pattern as the one I was wearing and followed me like my double on the poop. Together we moved right aft, barefooted, silent.

"What is it?" I asked in a deadened voice, taking the lighted lamp out of the binnacle,[1] and raising it to his face.

"An ugly business."

He had rather regular features; a good mouth; light eyes under somewhat heavy, dark eyebrows; a smooth, square forehead; no growth on his cheeks; a small, brown mustache, and a well-shaped, round chin. His expression was concentrated, meditative, under the inspecting light of the lamp I held up to his face; such as a man thinking hard in solitude might wear. My sleeping suit was just right for his size. A well-knit young fellow of twenty-five at most. He caught his lower lip with the edge of white, even teeth.

"Yes," I said, replacing the lamp in the binnacle. The warm, heavy tropical night closed upon his head again.

"There's a ship over there," he murmured.

"Yes, I know. The *Sephora*. Did you know of us?"

"Hadn't the slightest idea. I am the mate of her—" He paused and corrected himself. "I should say I *WAS*."

"Aha! Something wrong?"

"Yes. Very wrong indeed. I've killed a man."

"What do you mean? Just now?"

"No, on the passage. Weeks ago. Thirty-nine south. When I say a man—"

"Fit of temper," I suggested, confidently.

The shadowy, dark head, like mine, seemed to nod imperceptibly above the ghostly gray of my sleeping suit. It was, in the night, as though I had been faced by my own reflection in the depths of a somber and immense mirror.

"A pretty thing to have to own up to for a Conway boy," murmured my double, distinctly.

"You're a Conway boy?"

"I am," he said, as if startled. Then, slowly… "Perhaps you too—"

It was so; but being a couple of years older I had left before he joined. After a quick interchange of dates a silence fell; and I thought suddenly of my absurd mate with his terrific whiskers and the "Bless my soul—you don't say so" type of intellect. My double gave me an inkling of his thoughts by saying: "My father's a parson in Norfolk. Do you see me before a judge and jury on that charge? For myself I can't see the necessity. There are fellows that an angel from heaven—And I am not that. He was one of those creatures that are just simmering all the time with a silly sort of wickedness. Miserable devils that have no business to live at all. He wouldn't do his duty and wouldn't let anybody else do theirs. But what's the good of talking! You know well enough the sort of ill-conditioned snarling cur—"

He appealed to me as if our experiences had been as identical as our clothes. And I knew well enough the pestiferous danger of such a character where there are no

[1] *binnacle* Box, or stand, containing a compass and lantern.

means of legal repression. And I knew well enough also that my double there was no homicidal ruffian. I did not think of asking him for details, and he told me the story roughly in brusque, disconnected sentences. I needed no more. I saw it all going on as though I were myself inside that other sleeping suit.

"It happened while we were setting a reefed foresail,[1] at dusk. Reefed foresail! You understand the sort of weather. The only sail we had left to keep the ship running; so you may guess what it had been like for days. Anxious sort of job, that. He gave me some of his cursed insolence at the sheet. I tell you I was overdone with this terrific weather that seemed to have no end to it. Terrific, I tell you—and a deep ship. I believe the fellow himself was half crazed with funk. It was no time for gentlemanly reproof, so I turned round and felled him like an ox. He up and at me. We closed just as an awful sea made for the ship. All hands saw it coming and took to the rigging, but I had him by the throat, and went on shaking him like a rat, the men above us yelling, 'Look out! look out!' Then a crash as if the sky had fallen on my head. They say that for over ten minutes hardly anything was to be seen of the ship—just the three masts and a bit of the forecastle head and of the poop all awash driving along in a smother of foam. It was a miracle that they found us, jammed together behind the forebitts. It's clear that I meant business, because I was holding him by the throat still when they picked us up. He was black in the face. It was too much for them. It seems they rushed us aft together, gripped as we were, screaming 'Murder!' like a lot of lunatics, and broke into the cuddy. And the ship running for her life, touch and go all the time, any minute her last in a sea fit to turn your hair gray only a-looking at it. I understand that the skipper, too, started raving like the rest of them. The man had been deprived of sleep for more than a week, and to have this sprung on him at the height of a furious gale nearly drove him out of his mind. I wonder they didn't fling me overboard after getting the carcass of their precious shipmate out of my fingers. They had rather a job to separate us, I've been told. A sufficiently fierce story to make an old judge and a respectable jury sit up a bit. The first thing I heard when I came to myself was the maddening howling of that endless gale, and on that the voice of the old man. He was hanging on to my bunk, staring into my face out of his sou'wester.[2]

"'Mr. Leggatt, you have killed a man. You can act no longer as chief mate of this ship.'"

His care to subdue his voice made it sound monotonous. He rested a hand on the end of the skylight to steady himself with, and all that time did not stir a limb, so far as I could see. "Nice little tale for a quiet tea party," he concluded in the same tone.

One of my hands, too, rested on the end of the skylight; neither did I stir a limb, so far as I knew. We stood less than a foot from each other. It occurred to me that if old "Bless my soul—you don't say so" were to put his head up the companion and catch sight of us, he would think he was seeing double, or imagine himself come upon a scene of weird witchcraft; the strange captain having a quiet confabulation by the wheel with his own gray ghost. I became very much concerned to prevent anything of the sort. I heard the other's soothing undertone.

"My father's a parson in Norfolk," it said. Evidently he had forgotten he had told me this important fact before. Truly a nice little tale.

"You had better slip down into my stateroom now," I said, moving off stealthily. My double followed my movements; our bare feet made no sound; I let him in, closed the door with care, and, after giving a call to the second mate, returned on deck for my relief.

"Not much sign of any wind yet," I remarked when he approached.

"No, sir. Not much," he assented, sleepily, in his hoarse voice, with just enough deference, no more, and barely suppressing a yawn.

"Well, that's all you have to look out for. You have got your orders."

"Yes, sir."

[1] *reefed foresail* The sail set furthest forward; also known as the jib. A reefed sail has been tied back to reduce the sail area.

[2] *sou'wester* Waterproof, often oilskin, hat with a wide slanting brim that is longer in back than in front.

I paced a turn or two on the poop and saw him take up his position face forward with his elbow in the ratlines of the mizzen[1] rigging before I went below. The mate's faint snoring was still going on peacefully. The cuddy lamp was burning over the table on which stood a vase with flowers, a polite attention from the ship's provision merchant—the last flowers we should see for the next three months at the very least. Two bunches of bananas hung from the beam symmetrically, one on each side of the rudder casing. Everything was as before in the ship—except that two of her captain's sleeping suits were simultaneously in use, one motionless in the cuddy, the other keeping very still in the captain's stateroom.

It must be explained here that my cabin had the form of the capital letter L, the door being within the angle and opening into the short part of the letter. A couch was to the left, the bed place to the right; my writing desk and the chronometers' table faced the door. But anyone opening it, unless he stepped right inside, had no view of what I call the long (or vertical) part of the letter. It contained some lockers surmounted by a bookcase; and a few clothes, a thick jacket or two, caps, oilskin coat, and such like, hung on hooks. There was at the bottom of that part a door opening into my bathroom, which could be entered also directly from the saloon. But that way was never used.

The mysterious arrival had discovered the advantage of this particular shape. Entering my room, lighted strongly by a big bulkhead lamp swung on gimbals above my writing desk, I did not see him anywhere till he stepped out quietly from behind the coats hung in the recessed part.

"I heard somebody moving about, and went in there at once," he whispered.

I, too, spoke under my breath.

"Nobody is likely to come in here without knocking and getting permission."

He nodded. His face was thin and the sunburn faded, as though he had been ill. And no wonder. He had been, I heard presently, kept under arrest in his cabin for nearly seven weeks. But there was nothing sickly in his eyes or in his expression. He was not a bit like me, really; yet, as we stood leaning over my bed place, whispering side by side, with our dark heads together and our backs to the door, anybody bold enough to open it stealthily would have been treated to the uncanny sight of a double captain busy talking in whispers with his other self.

"But all this doesn't tell me how you came to hang on to our side ladder," I inquired, in the hardly audible murmurs we used, after he had told me something more of the proceedings on board the *Sephora* once the bad weather was over.

"When we sighted Java Head I had had time to think all those matters out several times over. I had six weeks of doing nothing else, and with only an hour or so every evening for a tramp on the quarter-deck."

He whispered, his arms folded on the side of my bed place, staring through the open port. And I could imagine perfectly the manner of this thinking out—a stubborn if not a steadfast operation; something of which I should have been perfectly incapable.

"I reckoned it would be dark before we closed with the land," he continued, so low that I had to strain my hearing near as we were to each other, shoulder touching shoulder almost. "So I asked to speak to the old man. He always seemed very sick when he came to see me—as if he could not look me in the face. You know, that foresail saved the ship. She was too deep to have run long under bare poles. And it was I that managed to set it for him. Anyway, he came. When I had him in my cabin—he stood by the door looking at me as if I had the halter round my neck already—I asked him right away to leave my cabin door unlocked at night while the ship was going through Sunda Straits.[2] There would be the Java coast within two or three miles, off Angier Point. I wanted nothing more. I've had a prize for swimming my second year in the Conway."

"I can believe it," I breathed out.

"God only knows why they locked me in every night. To see some of their faces you'd have thought

[1] *mizzen* The shorter mast behind the main mast aboard a ketch or yawl.

[2] *Sunda Straits* Located between the islands of Sumatra and Java in Indonesia.

they were afraid I'd go about at night strangling people. Am I a murdering brute? Do I look it? By Jove! If I had been he wouldn't have trusted himself like that into my room. You'll say I might have chucked him aside and bolted out, there and then—it was dark already. Well, no. And for the same reason I wouldn't think of trying to smash the door. There would have been a rush to stop me at the noise, and I did not mean to get into a confounded scrimmage. Somebody else might have got killed—for I would not have broken out only to get chucked back, and I did not want any more of that work. He refused, looking more sick than ever. He was afraid of the men, and also of that old second mate of his who had been sailing with him for years—a gray-headed old humbug; and his steward, too, had been with him devil knows how long—seventeen years or more—a dogmatic sort of loafer who hated me like poison, just because I was the chief mate. No chief mate ever made more than one voyage in the *Sephora*, you know. Those two old chaps ran the ship. Devil only knows what the skipper wasn't afraid of (all his nerve went to pieces altogether in that hellish spell of bad weather we had)—of what the law would do to him—of his wife, perhaps. Oh, yes! she's on board. Though I don't think she would have meddled. She would have been only too glad to have me out of the ship in any way. The 'brand of Cain' business, don't you see. That's all right. I was ready enough to go off wandering on the face of the earth—and that was price enough to pay for an Abel of that sort. Anyhow, he wouldn't listen to me. 'This thing must take its course. I represent the law here.' He was shaking like a leaf. 'So you won't?' 'No!' 'Then I hope you will be able to sleep on that,' I said, and turned my back on him. 'I wonder that *you* can,' cries he, and locks the door.

"Well after that, I couldn't. Not very well. That was three weeks ago. We have had a slow passage through the Java Sea; drifted about Carimata for ten days. When we anchored here they thought, I suppose, it was all right. The nearest land (and that's five miles) is the ship's destination; the consul would soon set about catching me; and there would have been no object in holding to these islets there. I don't suppose there's a drop of water on them. I don't know how it was, but tonight that steward, after bringing me my supper, went out to let me eat it, and left the door unlocked. And I ate it—all there was, too. After I had finished I strolled out on the quarter-deck. I don't know that I meant to do anything. A breath of fresh air was all I wanted, I believe. Then a sudden temptation came over me. I kicked off my slippers and was in the water before I had made up my mind fairly. Somebody heard the splash and they raised an awful hullabaloo. 'He's gone! Lower the boats! He's committed suicide! No, he's swimming.' Certainly I was swimming. It's not so easy for a swimmer like me to commit suicide by drowning. I landed on the nearest islet before the boat left the ship's side. I heard them pulling about in the dark, hailing, and so on, but after a bit they gave up. Everything quieted down and the anchorage became still as death. I sat down on a stone and began to think. I felt certain they would start searching for me at daylight. There was no place to hide on those stony things—and if there had been, what would have been the good? But now I was clear of that ship, I was not going back. So after a while I took off all my clothes, tied them up in a bundle with a stone inside, and dropped them in the deep water on the outer side of that islet. That was suicide enough for me. Let them think what they liked, but I didn't mean to drown myself. I meant to swim till I sank—but that's not the same thing. I struck out for another of these little islands, and it was from that one that I first saw your riding light. Something to swim for. I went on easily, and on the way I came upon a flat rock a foot or two above water. In the daytime, I dare say, you might make it out with a glass from your poop. I scrambled up on it and rested myself for a bit. Then I made another start. That last spell must have been over a mile."

His whisper was getting fainter and fainter, and all the time he stared straight out through the porthole, in which there was not even a star to be seen. I had not interrupted him. There was something that made comment impossible in his narrative, or perhaps in himself; a sort of feeling, a quality, which I can't find a name for. And when he ceased, all I found was a futile whisper: "So you swam for our light?"

"Yes—straight for it. It was something to swim for. I couldn't see any stars low down because the coast was in the way, and I couldn't see the land, either. The water was like glass. One might have been swimming in a confounded thousand-feet deep cistern with no place for scrambling out anywhere; but what I didn't like was the notion of swimming round and round like a crazed bullock before I gave out; and as I didn't mean to go back … No. Do you see me being hauled back, stark naked, off one of these little islands by the scruff of the neck and fighting like a wild beast? Somebody would have got killed for certain, and I did not want any of that. So I went on. Then your ladder—"

"Why didn't you hail the ship?" I asked, a little louder.

He touched my shoulder lightly. Lazy footsteps came right over our heads and stopped. The second mate had crossed from the other side of the poop and might have been hanging over the rail for all we knew.

"He couldn't hear us talking—could he?" My double breathed into my very ear, anxiously.

His anxiety was in answer, a sufficient answer, to the question I had put to him. An answer containing all the difficulty of that situation. I closed the porthole quietly, to make sure. A louder word might have been overheard.

"Who's that?" he whispered then.

"My second mate. But I don't know much more of the fellow than you do."

And I told him a little about myself. I had been appointed to take charge while I least expected anything of the sort, not quite a fortnight ago. I didn't know either the ship or the people. Hadn't had the time in port to look about me or size anybody up. And as to the crew, all they knew was that I was appointed to take the ship home. For the rest, I was almost as much of a stranger on board as himself, I said. And at the moment I felt it most acutely. I felt that it would take very little to make me a suspect person in the eyes of the ship's company.

He had turned about meantime; and we, the two strangers in the ship, faced each other in identical attitudes.

"Your ladder—" he murmured, after a silence. "Who'd have thought of finding a ladder hanging over at night in a ship anchored out here! I felt just then a very unpleasant faintness. After the life I've been leading for nine weeks, anybody would have got out of condition. I wasn't capable of swimming round as far as your rudder chains. And, lo and behold! there was a ladder to get hold of. After I gripped it I said to myself, 'What's the good?' When I saw a man's head looking over I thought I would swim away presently and leave him shouting—in whatever language it was. I didn't mind being looked at. I—I liked it. And then you speaking to me so quietly—as if you had expected me—made me hold on a little longer. It had been a confounded lonely time—I don't mean while swimming. I was glad to talk a little to somebody that didn't belong to the *Sephora*. As to asking for the captain, that was a mere impulse. It could have been no use, with all the ship knowing about me and the other people pretty certain to be round here in the morning. I don't know—I wanted to be seen, to talk with somebody, before I went on. I don't know what I would have said. … 'Fine night, isn't it?' or something of the sort."

"Do you think they will be round here presently?" I asked with some incredulity.

"Quite likely," he said, faintly.

He looked extremely haggard all of a sudden. His head rolled on his shoulders.

"H'm. We shall see then. Meantime get into that bed," I whispered. "Want help? There."

It was a rather high bed place with a set of drawers underneath. This amazing swimmer really needed the lift I gave him by seizing his leg. He tumbled in, rolled over on his back, and flung one arm across his eyes. And then, with his face nearly hidden, he must have looked exactly as I used to look in that bed. I gazed upon my other self for a while before drawing across carefully the two green serge curtains which ran on a brass rod. I thought for a moment of pinning them together for greater safety, but I sat down on the couch, and once there I felt unwilling to rise and hunt for a pin. I would do it in a moment. I was extremely tired, in a peculiarly intimate way, by the strain of stealthiness, by the effort of whispering and the general secrecy of this excitement. It was three o'clock by now and I had been on my feet since nine, but I was not sleepy; I could not have gone to sleep. I sat there, fagged out, looking at the curtains, trying to clear my mind of the confused sensation of being in two places at once, and greatly bothered by an exasperating knocking in my head. It was a relief to discover suddenly that it was not in my head at all, but on the outside of the door. Before I could collect myself the words "Come in" were out of my mouth, and the steward entered with a tray, bringing in my morning coffee. I had slept, after all, and I was so frightened that I shouted, "This way! I am here, steward," as though he had been miles away. He put down the tray on the table next the couch and only then said, very quietly, "I can see you are here, sir." I felt him give me a keen look, but I dared not meet his eyes just then. He must have wondered why I had drawn the curtains of my bed before going to sleep on the couch. He went out, hooking the door open as usual.

I heard the crew washing decks above me. I knew I would have been told at once if there had been any wind. Calm, I thought, and I was doubly vexed. Indeed, I felt dual more than ever. The steward reappeared suddenly in the doorway. I jumped up from the couch so quickly that he gave a start.

"What do you want here?"

"Close your port, sir—they are washing decks."

"It is closed," I said, reddening.

"Very well, sir." But he did not move from the doorway and returned my stare in an extraordinary, equivocal manner for a time. Then his eyes wavered, all his expression changed, and in a voice unusually gentle, almost coaxingly:

"May I come in to take the empty cup away, sir?"

"Of course!" I turned my back on him while he popped in and out. Then I unhooked and closed the door and even pushed the bolt. This sort of thing could not go on very long. The cabin was as hot as an oven, too. I took a peep at my double, and discovered that he had not moved, his arm was still over his eyes; but his chest heaved; his hair was wet; his chin glistened with perspiration. I reached over him and opened the port.

"I must show myself on deck," I reflected.

Of course, theoretically, I could do what I liked, with no one to say nay to me within the whole circle of the horizon; but to lock my cabin door and take the key away I did not dare. Directly I put my head out of the companion I saw the group of my two officers, the second mate barefooted, the chief mate in long India-rubber boots, near the break of the poop, and the steward halfway down the poop ladder talking to them eagerly. He happened to catch sight of me and dived, the second ran down on the main-deck shouting some order or other, and the chief mate came to meet me, touching his cap.

There was a sort of curiosity in his eye that I did not like. I don't know whether the steward had told them that I was "queer" only, or downright drunk, but I know the man meant to have a good look at me. I watched him coming with a smile which, as he got into point-blank range, took effect and froze his very whiskers. I did not give him time to open his lips.

"Square the yards by lifts and braces before the hands go to breakfast."

It was the first particular order I had given on board that ship; and I stayed on deck to see it executed, too. I had felt the need of asserting myself without loss of time. That sneering young cub got taken down a peg or two on that occasion, and I also seized the opportunity of having a good look at the face of every foremast man as they filed past me to go to the after braces. At breakfast time, eating nothing myself, I presided with such frigid dignity that the two mates were only too glad to escape from the cabin as soon as decency permitted; and all the time the dual working of my mind distracted me almost to the point of insanity. I was constantly watching myself, my secret self, as dependent on my actions as my own personality, sleeping in that bed, behind that door which faced me as I sat at the head of the table. It was very much like being mad, only it was worse because one was aware of it.

I had to shake him for a solid minute, but when at last he opened his eyes it was in the full possession of his senses, with an inquiring look.

"All's well so far," I whispered. "Now you must vanish into the bathroom."

He did so, as noiseless as a ghost, and then I rang for the steward, and facing him boldly, directed him to tidy up my stateroom while I was having my bath—"and be quick about it." As my tone admitted of no excuses, he said, "Yes, sir," and ran off to fetch his dustpan and brushes. I took a bath and did most of my dressing, splashing, and whistling softly for the steward's edification, while the secret sharer of my life stood drawn up bolt upright in that little space, his face looking very sunken in daylight, his eyelids lowered under the stern, dark line of his eyebrows drawn together by a slight frown.

When I left him there to go back to my room the steward was finishing dusting. I sent for the mate and engaged him in some insignificant conversation. It was, as it were, trifling with the terrific character of his whiskers; but my object was to give him an opportunity for a good look at my cabin. And then I could at last shut, with a clear conscience, the door of my stateroom and get my double back into the recessed part. There was nothing else for it. He had to sit still on a small folding stool, half smothered by the heavy coats hanging there. We listened to the steward going into the bathroom out of the saloon, filling the water bottles there, scrubbing the bath, setting things to rights, whisk, bang, clatter—out again into the saloon—turn the key—click. Such was my scheme for keeping my second self invisible. Nothing better could be contrived under the circumstances. And there we sat; I at my writing desk ready to appear busy with some papers, he behind me out of sight of the door. It would not have been prudent to talk in daytime; and I could not have stood the excitement of that queer sense of whispering to myself. Now and then, glancing over my shoulder, I saw him far back there, sitting rigidly on the low stool, his bare feet close together, his arms folded, his head hanging on his breast—and perfectly still. Anybody would have taken him for me.

I was fascinated by it myself. Every moment I had to glance over my shoulder. I was looking at him when a voice outside the door said:

"Beg pardon, sir."

"Well!" … I kept my eyes on him, and so when the voice outside the door announced, "There's a ship's boat coming our way, sir," I saw him give a start—the first movement he had made for hours. But he did not raise his bowed head.

"All right. Get the ladder over."

I hesitated. Should I whisper something to him? But what? His immobility seemed to have been never disturbed. What could I tell him he did not know already?… Finally I went on deck.

2

The skipper of the *Sephora* had a thin red whisker all round his face, and the sort of complexion that goes with hair of that colour; also the particular, rather smeary shade of blue in the eyes. He was not exactly a showy figure; his shoulders were high, his stature but middling—one leg slightly more bandy than the other. He shook hands, looking vaguely around. A spiritless tenacity was his main characteristic, I judged. I behaved with a politeness which seemed to disconcert him. Perhaps he was shy. He mumbled to me as if he were ashamed of what he was saying; gave his name (it was something like Archbold—but at this distance of years I hardly am sure), his ship's name, and a few other particulars of that sort, in the manner of a criminal making a reluctant and doleful confession. He had had terrible weather on the passage out—terrible—terrible—wife aboard, too.

By this time we were seated in the cabin and the steward brought in a tray with a bottle and glasses. "Thanks! No." Never took liquor. Would have some water, though. He drank two tumblerfuls. Terrible thirsty work. Ever since daylight had been exploring the islands round his ship.

"What was that for—fun?" I asked, with an appearance of polite interest.

"No!" He sighed. "Painful duty."

As he persisted in his mumbling and I wanted my double to hear every word, I hit upon the notion of informing him that I regretted to say I was hard of hearing.

"Such a young man, too!" he nodded, keeping his smeary blue, unintelligent eyes fastened upon me. "What was the cause of it—some disease?" he inquired, without the least sympathy and as if he thought that, if so, I'd got no more than I deserved.

"Yes; disease," I admitted in a cheerful tone which seemed to shock him. But my point was gained, because he had to raise his voice to give me his tale. It is not worth while to record his version. It was just over two months since all this had happened, and he had thought so much about it that he seemed completely muddled as to its bearings, but still immensely impressed.

"What would you think of such a thing happening on board your own ship? I've had the *Sephora* for these fifteen years. I am a well-known shipmaster."

He was densely distressed—and perhaps I should have sympathized with him if I had been able to detach my mental vision from the unsuspected sharer of my cabin as though he were my second self. There he was on the other side of the bulkhead, four or five feet from us, no more, as we sat in the saloon. I looked politely at Captain Archbold (if that was his name), but it was the other I saw, in a gray sleeping suit, seated on a low stool, his bare feet close together, his arms folded, and every word said between us falling into the ears of his dark head bowed on his chest.

"I have been at sea now, man and boy, for seven-and-thirty years, and I've never heard of such a thing happening in an English ship. And that it should be my ship. Wife on board, too."

I was hardly listening to him.

"Don't you think," I said, "that the heavy sea which, you told me, came aboard just then might have killed the man? I have seen the sheer weight of a sea kill a man very neatly, by simply breaking his neck."

"Good God!" he uttered, impressively, fixing his smeary blue eyes on me. "The sea! No man killed by the sea ever looked like that." He seemed positively scandalized at my suggestion. And as I gazed at him certainly not prepared for anything original on his part, he advanced his head close to mine and thrust his tongue out at me so suddenly that I couldn't help starting back.

After scoring over my calmness in this graphic way he nodded wisely. If I had seen the sight, he assured me, I would never forget it as long as I lived. The weather was too bad to give the corpse a proper sea burial. So next day at dawn they took it up on the poop, covering its face with a bit of bunting; he read a short prayer, and then, just as it was, in its oilskins and long boots, they launched it amongst those mountainous seas that seemed ready every moment to swallow up the ship herself and the terrified lives on board of her.

"That reefed foresail saved you," I threw in.

"Under God—it did," he exclaimed fervently. "It was by a special mercy, I firmly believe, that it stood some of those hurricane squalls."

"It was the setting of that sail which—" I began.

"God's own hand in it," he interrupted me. "Nothing less could have done it. I don't mind telling you that I hardly dared give the order. It seemed impossible that we could touch anything without losing it, and then our last hope would have been gone."

The terror of that gale was on him yet. I let him go on for a bit, then said, casually—as if returning to a minor subject:

"You were very anxious to give up your mate to the shore people, I believe?"

He was. To the law. His obscure tenacity on that point had in it something incomprehensible and a little awful; something, as it were, mystical, quite apart from his anxiety that he should not be suspected of "countenancing any doings of that sort." Seven-and-thirty virtuous years at sea, of which over twenty of immaculate command, and the last fifteen in the *Sephora*, seemed to have laid him under some pitiless obligation.

"And you know," he went on, groping shamefacedly amongst his feelings, "I did not engage that young fellow. His people had some interest with my owners. I was in a way forced to take him on. He looked very smart, very gentlemanly, and all that. But do you know—I never liked him, somehow. I am a plain man. You see, he wasn't exactly the sort for the chief mate of a ship like the *Sephora*."

I had become so connected in thoughts and impressions with the secret sharer of my cabin that I felt as if I, personally, were being given to understand that I, too, was not the sort that would have done for the chief mate of a ship like the *Sephora*. I had no doubt of it in my mind.

"Not at all the style of man. You understand," he insisted, superfluously, looking hard at me.

I smiled urbanely. He seemed at a loss for a while.

"I suppose I must report a suicide."

"Beg pardon?"

"Suicide! That's what I'll have to write to my owners directly I get in."

"Unless you manage to recover him before tomorrow," I assented, dispassionately… "I mean, alive."

He mumbled something which I really did not catch, and I turned my ear to him in a puzzled manner. He fairly bawled:

"The land—I say, the mainland is at least seven miles off my anchorage."

"About that."

My lack of excitement, of curiosity, of surprise, of any sort of pronounced interest, began to arouse his distrust. But except for the felicitous pretense of deafness I had not tried to pretend anything. I had felt utterly incapable of playing the part of ignorance properly, and therefore was afraid to try. It is also certain that he had brought some ready-made suspicions with him, and that he viewed my politeness as a strange and unnatural phenomenon. And yet how else could I have received him? Not heartily! That was impossible for psychological reasons, which I need not state here. My only object was to keep off his inquiries. Surlily? Yes, but surliness might have provoked a point-blank question. From its novelty to him and from its nature, punctilious courtesy was the manner best calculated to restrain the man. But there was the danger of his breaking through my defense bluntly. I could not, I think, have met him by a direct lie, also for psychological (not moral) reasons. If he had only known how afraid I was of his putting my feeling of identity with the other to the test! But, strangely enough—(I thought of it only afterwards)—I believe that he was not a little disconcerted by the reverse side of that weird situation, by something in me that reminded him of the man he was seeking—suggested a mysterious similitude to the young fellow he had distrusted and disliked from the first.

However that might have been, the silence was not very prolonged. He took another oblique step.

"I reckon I had no more than a two-mile pull to your ship. Not a bit more."

"And quite enough, too, in this awful heat," I said.

Another pause full of mistrust followed. Necessity, they say, is mother of invention, but fear, too, is not barren of ingenious suggestions. And I was afraid he would ask me point-blank for news of my other self.

"Nice little saloon, isn't it?" I remarked, as if noticing for the first time the way his eyes roamed from one closed door to the other. "And very well fitted out, too. Here, for instance," I continued, reaching over the back of my seat negligently and flinging the door open, "is my bathroom."

He made an eager movement, but hardly gave it a glance. I got up, shut the door of the bathroom, and invited him to have a look round, as if I were very proud of my accommodation. He had to rise and be shown round, but he went through the business without any raptures whatever.

"And now we'll have a look at my stateroom," I declared, in a voice as loud as I dared to make it, crossing the cabin to the starboard side with purposely heavy steps.

He followed me in and gazed around. My intelligent double had vanished. I played my part.

"Very convenient—isn't it?"

"Very nice. Very comf … " He didn't finish and went out brusquely as if to escape from some unrighteous wiles of mine. But it was not to be. I had been too frightened not to feel vengeful; I felt I had him on the run, and I meant to keep him on the run. My polite insistence must have had something menacing in it, because he gave in suddenly. And I did not let him off a single item; mate's room, pantry, storerooms, the very sail locker which was also under the poop—he had to look into them all. When at last I showed him out on the quarter-deck he drew a long, spiritless sigh, and mumbled dismally that he must really be going back to his ship now. I desired my mate, who had joined us, to see to the captain's boat.

The man of whiskers gave a blast on the whistle which he used to wear hanging round his neck, and yelled, "*Sephora*'s away!" My double down there in my cabin must have heard, and certainly could not feel more relieved than I. Four fellows came running out from somewhere forward and went over the side, while my own men, appearing on deck too, lined the rail. I escorted my visitor to the gangway ceremoniously, and nearly overdid it. He was a tenacious beast. On the very ladder he lingered, and in that unique, guiltily conscientious manner of sticking to the point:

"I say … you … you don't think that—"

I covered his voice loudly:

"Certainly not … I am delighted. Good-by."

I had an idea of what he meant to say, and just saved myself by the privilege of defective hearing. He was too shaken generally to insist, but my mate, close witness of that parting, looked mystified and his face took on a thoughtful cast. As I did not want to appear as if I wished to avoid all communication with my officers, he had the opportunity to address me.

"Seems a very nice man. His boat's crew told our chaps a very extraordinary story, if what I am told by the steward is true. I suppose you had it from the captain, sir?"

"Yes. I had a story from the captain."

"A very horrible affair—isn't it, sir?"

"It is."

"Beats all these tales we hear about murders in Yankee ships."

"I don't think it beats them. I don't think it resembles them in the least."

"Bless my soul—you don't say so! But of course I've no acquaintance whatever with American ships, not I so I couldn't go against your knowledge. It's horrible enough for me…. But the queerest part is that those fellows seemed to have some idea the man was hidden aboard here. They had really. Did you ever hear of such a thing?"

"Preposterous—isn't it?"

We were walking to and fro athwart the quarter-deck. No one of the crew forward could be seen (the day was Sunday), and the mate pursued:

"There was some little dispute about it. Our chaps took offense. 'As if we would harbour a thing like that,' they said. 'Wouldn't you like to look for him in our coal-hole?' Quite a tiff. But they made it up in the end. I suppose he did drown himself. Don't you, sir?"

"I don't suppose anything."

"You have no doubt in the matter, sir?"

"None whatever."

I left him suddenly. I felt I was producing a bad impression, but with my double down there it was most trying to be on deck. And it was almost as trying to be below. Altogether a nerve-trying situation. But on the whole I felt less torn in two when I was with him. There was no one in the whole ship whom I dared take into my confidence. Since the hands had got to know his story, it would have been impossible to pass him off for anyone else, and an accidental discovery was to be dreaded now more than ever….

The steward being engaged in laying the table for dinner, we could talk only with our eyes when I first went down. Later in the afternoon we had a cautious try at whispering. The Sunday quietness of the ship was against us; the stillness of air and water around her was against us; the elements, the men were against us—everything was against us in our secret partnership; time itself—for this could not go on forever. The very trust in Providence was, I suppose, denied to his guilt. Shall I confess that this thought cast me down very much? And as to the chapter of accidents which counts for so much in the book of success, I could only hope that it was closed. For what favourable accident could be expected?

"Did you hear everything?" were my first words as soon as we took up our position side by side, leaning over my bed place.

He had. And the proof of it was his earnest whisper, "The man told you he hardly dared to give the order."

I understood the reference to be to that saving foresail.

"Yes. He was afraid of it being lost in the setting."

"I assure you he never gave the order. He may think he did, but he never gave it. He stood there with me on the break of the poop after the main topsail blew away, and whimpered about our last hope—positively whimpered about it and nothing else—and the night coming on! To hear one's skipper go on like that in such weather was enough to drive any fellow out of his mind. It worked me up into a sort of desperation. I just took it into my own hands and went away from him, boiling, and—But what's the use telling you? YOU know! … Do you think that if I had not been pretty fierce with them I should have got the men to do anything? Not it! The bo's'n[1] perhaps? Perhaps! It wasn't a heavy sea—it was a sea gone mad! I suppose the end of the world will be something like that; and a man may have the heart to see it coming once and be done with it—but to have to face it day after day—I don't blame anybody. I was precious little better than the rest. Only—I was an officer of that old coal wagon, anyhow—"

"I quite understand," I conveyed that sincere assurance into his ear. He was out of breath with whispering; I could hear him pant slightly. It was all very simple. The same strung-up force which had given twenty-four men a chance, at least, for their lives, had, in a sort of recoil, crushed an unworthy mutinous existence.

But I had no leisure to weigh the merits of the matter—footsteps in the saloon, a heavy knock. "There's enough wind to get under way with, sir." Here was the call of a new claim upon my thoughts and even upon my feelings.

"Turn the hands up," I cried through the door. "I'll be on deck directly."

I was going out to make the acquaintance of my ship. Before I left the cabin our eyes met—the eyes of the only two strangers on board. I pointed to the recessed part where the little campstool awaited him and laid my finger on my lips. He made a gesture—somewhat vague—a little mysterious, accompanied by a faint smile, as if of regret.

This is not the place to enlarge upon the sensations of a man who feels for the first time a ship move under his feet to his own independent word. In my case they were not unalloyed. I was not wholly alone with my command; for there was that stranger in my cabin. Or rather, I was not completely and wholly with her. Part of me was absent. That mental feeling of being in two places at once affected me physically as if the mood of secrecy had penetrated my very soul. Before an hour had elapsed since the ship had begun to move, having occasion to ask the mate (he stood by my side) to take a compass bearing of the pagoda, I caught myself reaching up to his ear in whispers. I say I caught myself, but enough had escaped to startle the man. I can't describe it otherwise than by saying that he shied. A grave, preoccupied manner, as though he were in possession of some perplexing intelligence, did not leave him henceforth. A little later I moved away from the rail to look at the compass with such a stealthy gait that the helmsman noticed it—and I could not help noticing the unusual roundness of his eyes. These are trifling instances, though it's to no commander's advantage to be suspected of ludicrous eccentricities. But I was also more seriously affected. There are to a seaman certain words, gestures, that should in given conditions come as naturally, as instinctively as the winking of a menaced eye. A certain order should spring on to his lips without thinking; a certain sign should get itself made, so to speak, without reflection. But all unconscious alertness had abandoned me. I had to make an effort of will to recall myself back (from the cabin) to the conditions of the moment. I felt that I was appearing an irresolute commander to those people who were watching me more or less critically.

And, besides, there were the scares. On the second day out, for instance, coming off the deck in the afternoon (I had straw slippers on my bare feet) I stopped at the open pantry door and spoke to the steward. He was doing something there with his back to me. At the sound of my voice he nearly jumped out of his skin, as the saying is, and incidentally broke a cup.

"What on earth's the matter with you?" I asked, astonished.

[1] *bo's'n* Boatswain (petty officer in charge of ship's rigging, sails, anchors, and deck crew).

He was extremely confused. "Beg your pardon, sir. I made sure you were in your cabin."

"You see I wasn't."

"No, sir. I could have sworn I had heard you moving in there not a moment ago. It's most extraordinary ... very sorry, sir."

I passed on with an inward shudder. I was so identified with my secret double that I did not even mention the fact in those scanty, fearful whispers we exchanged. I suppose he had made some slight noise of some kind or other. It would have been miraculous if he hadn't at one time or another. And yet, haggard as he appeared, he looked always perfectly self-controlled, more than calm—almost invulnerable. On my suggestion he remained almost entirely in the bathroom, which, upon the whole, was the safest place. There could be really no shadow of an excuse for anyone ever wanting to go in there, once the steward had done with it. It was a very tiny place. Sometimes he reclined on the floor, his legs bent, his head sustained on one elbow. At others I would find him on the campstool, sitting in his gray sleeping suit and with his cropped dark hair like a patient, unmoved convict. At night I would smuggle him into my bed place, and we would whisper together, with the regular footfalls of the officer of the watch passing and repassing over our heads. It was an infinitely miserable time. It was lucky that some tins of fine preserves were stowed in a locker in my stateroom; hard bread I could always get hold of; and so he lived on stewed chicken, *paté de foie gras*, asparagus, cooked oysters, sardines—on all sorts of abominable sham delicacies out of tins. My early-morning coffee he always drank; and it was all I dared do for him in that respect.

Every day there was the horrible maneuvering to go through so that my room and then the bathroom should be done in the usual way. I came to hate the sight of the steward, to abhor the voice of that harmless man. I felt that it was he who would bring on the disaster of discovery. It hung like a sword over our heads.

The fourth day out, I think (we were then working down the east side of the Gulf of Siam, tack for tack, in light winds and smooth water)—the fourth day, I say, of this miserable juggling with the unavoidable, as we sat at our evening meal, that man, whose slightest movement I dreaded, after putting down the dishes ran up on deck busily. This could not be dangerous. Presently he came down again; and then it appeared that he had remembered a coat of mine which I had thrown over a rail to dry after having been wetted in a shower which had passed over the ship in the afternoon. Sitting stolidly at the head of the table I became terrified at the sight of the garment on his arm. Of course he made for my door. There was no time to lose.

"Steward," I thundered. My nerves were so shaken that I could not govern my voice and conceal my agitation. This was the sort of thing that made my terrifically whiskered mate tap his forehead with his forefinger. I had detected him using that gesture while talking on deck with a confidential air to the carpenter. It was too far to hear a word, but I had no doubt that this pantomime could only refer to the strange new captain.

"Yes, sir," the pale-faced steward turned resignedly to me. It was this maddening course of being shouted at, checked without rhyme or reason, arbitrarily chased out of my cabin, suddenly called into it, sent flying out of his pantry on incomprehensible errands, that accounted for the growing wretchedness of his expression.

"Where are you going with that coat?"

"To your room, sir."

"Is there another shower coming?"

"I'm sure I don't know, sir. Shall I go up again and see, sir?"

"No! never mind."

My object was attained, as of course my other self in there would have heard everything that passed. During this interlude my two officers never raised their eyes off their respective plates; but the lip of that confounded cub, the second mate, quivered visibly.

I expected the steward to hook my coat on and come out at once. He was very slow about it; but I dominated my nervousness sufficiently not to shout after him. Suddenly I became aware (it could be heard plainly enough) that the fellow for some reason or other was opening the door of the bathroom. It was the end. The place was literally not big enough to swing a cat in. My voice died in my throat and I went stony all over. I expected to hear a yell of surprise and terror, and made a movement, but had not the strength to get on my legs. Everything remained still. Had my second self taken the poor wretch by the throat? I don't know what I could have done next moment if I had not seen the steward come out of my room, close the door, and then stand quietly by the sideboard.

"Saved," I thought. "But, no! Lost! Gone! He was gone!"

I laid my knife and fork down and leaned back in my chair. My head swam. After a while, when sufficiently recovered to speak in a steady voice, I instructed my mate to put the ship round at eight o'clock himself.

"I won't come on deck," I went on. "I think I'll turn in, and unless the wind shifts I don't want to be disturbed before midnight. I feel a bit seedy."

"You did look middling bad a little while ago," the chief mate remarked without showing any great concern.

They both went out, and I stared at the steward clearing the table. There was nothing to be read on that wretched man's face. But why did he avoid my eyes, I asked myself. Then I thought I should like to hear the sound of his voice.

"Steward!"

"Sir!" Startled as usual.

"Where did you hang up that coat?"

"In the bathroom, sir." The usual anxious tone. "It's not quite dry yet, sir."

For some time longer I sat in the cuddy. Had my double vanished as he had come? But of his coming there was an explanation, whereas his disappearance would be inexplicable … I went slowly into my dark room, shut the door, lighted the lamp, and for a time dared not turn round. When at last I did I saw him standing bolt-upright in the narrow recessed part. It would not be true to say I had a shock, but an irresistible doubt of his bodily existence flitted through my mind. Can it be, I asked myself, that he is not visible to other eyes than mine? It was like being haunted. Motionless, with a grave face, he raised his hands slightly at me in a gesture which meant clearly, "Heavens! what a narrow escape!" Narrow indeed. I think I had come creeping quietly as near insanity as any man who has not actually gone over the border. That gesture restrained me, so to speak.

The mate with the terrific whiskers was now putting the ship on the other tack. In the moment of profound silence which follows upon the hands going to their stations I heard on the poop his raised voice: "Hard alee!"[1] and the distant shout of the order repeated on the main-deck. The sails, in that light breeze, made but a faint fluttering noise. It ceased. The ship was coming round slowly: I held my breath in the renewed stillness of expectation; one wouldn't have thought that there was a single living soul on her decks. A sudden brisk shout, "Mainsail haul!" broke the spell, and in the noisy cries and rush overhead of the men running away with the main brace we two, down in my cabin, came together in our usual position by the bed place.

He did not wait for my question. "I heard him fumbling here and just managed to squat myself down in the bath," he whispered to me. "The fellow only opened the door and put his arm in to hang the coat up. All the same—"

"I never thought of that," I whispered back, even more appalled than before at the closeness of the shave, and marveling at that something unyielding in his character which was carrying him through so finely. There was no agitation in his whisper. Whoever was being driven distracted, it was not he. He was sane. And the proof of his sanity was continued when he took up the whispering again.

"It would never do for me to come to life again."

It was something that a ghost might have said. But what he was alluding to was his old captain's reluctant admission of the theory of suicide. It would obviously serve his turn—if I had understood at all the view which seemed to govern the unalterable purpose of his action.

"You must maroon me as soon as ever you can get amongst these islands off the Cambodge[2] shore," he went on.

[1] *Hard alee* "Hard a lee" (meaning "hard towards the leeward side") is the command given when a ship comes about.

[2] *Cambodge* Cambodia.

"Maroon you! We are not living in a boy's adventure tale," I protested. His scornful whispering took me up.

"We aren't indeed! There's nothing of a boy's tale in this. But there's nothing else for it. I want no more. You don't suppose I am afraid of what can be done to me? Prison or gallows or whatever they may please. But you don't see me coming back to explain such things to an old fellow in a wig and twelve respectable tradesmen, do you? What can they know whether I am guilty or not—or of *what* I am guilty, either? That's my affair. What does the Bible say? 'Driven off the face of the earth.' Very well, I am off the face of the earth now. As I came at night so I shall go."

"Impossible!" I murmured. "You can't."

"Can't? ... Not naked like a soul on the Day of Judgment. I shall freeze on to this sleeping suit. The Last Day is not yet—and ... you have understood thoroughly. Didn't you?"

I felt suddenly ashamed of myself. I may say truly that I understood—and my hesitation in letting that man swim away from my ship's side had been a mere sham sentiment, a sort of cowardice.

"It can't be done now till next night," I breathed out. "The ship is on the off-shore tack and the wind may fail us."

"As long as I know that you understand," he whispered. "But of course you do. It's a great satisfaction to have got somebody to understand. You seem to have been there on purpose." And in the same whisper, as if we two whenever we talked had to say things to each other which were not fit for the world to hear, he added, "It's very wonderful."

We remained side by side talking in our secret way—but sometimes silent or just exchanging a whispered word or two at long intervals. And as usual he stared through the port. A breath of wind came now and again into our faces. The ship might have been moored in dock, so gently and on an even keel she slipped through the water, that did not murmur even at our passage, shadowy and silent like a phantom sea.

At midnight I went on deck, and to my mate's great surprise put the ship round on the other tack. His terrible whiskers flitted round me in silent criticism. I certainly should not have done it if it had been only a question of getting out of that sleepy gulf as quickly as possible. I believe he told the second mate, who relieved him, that it was a great want of judgment. The other only yawned. That intolerable cub shuffled about so sleepily and lolled against the rails in such a slack, improper fashion that I came down on him sharply.

"Aren't you properly awake yet?"

"Yes, sir! I am awake."

"Well, then, be good enough to hold yourself as if you were. And keep a lookout. If there's any current we'll be closing with some islands before daylight."

The east side of the gulf is fringed with islands, some solitary, others in groups. On the blue background of the high coast they seem to float on silvery patches of calm water, arid and gray, or dark green and rounded like clumps of evergreen bushes, with the larger ones, a mile or two long, showing the outlines of ridges, ribs of gray rock under the dark mantle of matted leafage. Unknown to trade, to travel, almost to geography, the manner of life they harbour is an unsolved secret. There must be villages—settlements of fishermen at least—on the largest of them, and some communication with the world is probably kept up by native craft. But all that forenoon, as we headed for them, fanned along by the faintest of breezes, I saw no sign of man or canoe in the field of the telescope I kept on pointing at the scattered group.

At noon I gave no orders for a change of course, and the mate's whiskers became much concerned and seemed to be offering themselves unduly to my notice. At last I said:

"I am going to stand right in. Quite in—as far as I can take her."

The stare of extreme surprise imparted an air of ferocity also to his eyes, and he looked truly terrific for a moment.

"We're not doing well in the middle of the gulf," I continued, casually. "I am going to look for the land breezes tonight."

"Bless my soul! Do you mean, sir, in the dark amongst the lot of all them islands and reefs and shoals?"

"Well—if there are any regular land breezes at all on this coast one must get close inshore to find them, mustn't one?"

"Bless my soul!" he exclaimed again under his breath. All that afternoon he wore a dreamy, contemplative appearance which in him was a mark of perplexity. After dinner I went into my stateroom as if I meant to take some rest. There we two bent our dark heads over a half-unrolled chart lying on my bed.

"There," I said. "It's got to be Koh-ring. I've been looking at it ever since sunrise. It has got two hills and a low point. It must be inhabited. And on the coast opposite there is what looks like the mouth of a biggish river—with some towns, no doubt, not far up. It's the best chance for you that I can see."

"Anything. Koh-ring let it be."

He looked thoughtfully at the chart as if surveying chances and distances from a lofty height—and following with his eyes his own figure wandering on the blank land of Cochin-China, and then passing off that piece of paper clean out of sight into uncharted regions. And it was as if the ship had two captains to plan her course for her. I had been so worried and restless running up and down that I had not had the patience to dress that day. I had remained in my sleeping suit, with straw slippers and a soft floppy hat. The closeness of the heat in the gulf had been most oppressive, and the crew were used to seeing me wandering in that airy attire.

"She will clear the south point as she heads now," I whispered into his ear. "Goodness only knows when, though, but certainly after dark. I'll edge her in to half a mile, as far as I may be able to judge in the dark—"

"Be careful," he murmured, warningly—and I realized suddenly that all my future, the only future for which I was fit, would perhaps go irretrievably to pieces in any mishap to my first command.

I could not stop a moment longer in the room. I motioned him to get out of sight and made my way on the poop. That unplayful cub had the watch. I walked up and down for a while thinking things out, then beckoned him over.

"Send a couple of hands to open the two quarter-deck ports," I said, mildly.

He actually had the impudence, or else so forgot himself in his wonder at such an incomprehensible order, as to repeat:

"Open the quarter-deck ports! What for, sir?"

"The only reason you need concern yourself about is because I tell you to do so. Have them open wide and fastened properly."

He reddened and went off, but I believe made some jeering remark to the carpenter as to the sensible practice of ventilating a ship's quarter-deck. I know he popped into the mate's cabin to impart the fact to him because the whiskers came on deck, as it were by chance, and stole glances at me from below—for signs of lunacy or drunkenness, I suppose.

A little before supper, feeling more restless than ever, I rejoined, for a moment, my second self. And to find him sitting so quietly was surprising, like something against nature, inhuman.

I developed my plan in a hurried whisper.

"I shall stand in as close as I dare and then put her round. I will presently find means to smuggle you out of here into the sail locker, which communicates with the lobby. But there is an opening, a sort of square for hauling the sails out, which gives straight on the quarter-deck and which is never closed in fine weather, so as to give air to the sails. When the ship's way is deadened in stays and all the hands are aft at the main braces you will have a clear road to slip out and get overboard through the open quarter-deck port. I've had them both fastened up. Use a rope's end to lower yourself into the water so as to avoid a splash—you know. It could be heard and cause some beastly complication."

He kept silent for a while, then whispered, "I understand."

"I won't be there to see you go," I began with an effort. "The rest ... I only hope I have understood, too."

"You have. From first to last"—and for the first time there seemed to be a faltering, something strained in his whisper. He caught hold of my arm, but the ringing of the supper bell made me start. He didn't though; he only released his grip.

After supper I didn't come below again till well past eight o'clock. The faint, steady breeze was loaded with dew; and the wet, darkened sails held all there was of propelling power in it. The night, clear and starry, sparkled darkly, and the opaque, lightless patches shifting slowly against the low stars were the drifting islets. On the port bow there was a big one more distant and shadowily imposing by the great space of sky it eclipsed.

On opening the door I had a back view of my very own self looking at a chart. He had come out of the recess and was standing near the table.

"Quite dark enough," I whispered.

He stepped back and leaned against my bed with a level, quiet glance. I sat on the couch. We had nothing to say to each other. Over our heads the officer of the watch moved here and there. Then I heard him move quickly. I knew what that meant. He was making for the companion; and presently his voice was outside my door.

"We are drawing in pretty fast, sir. Land looks rather close."

"Very well," I answered. "I am coming on deck directly."

I waited till he was gone out of the cuddy, then rose. My double moved too. The time had come to exchange our last whispers, for neither of us was ever to hear each other's natural voice.

"Look here!" I opened a drawer and took out three sovereigns.[1] "Take this anyhow. I've got six and I'd give you the lot, only I must keep a little money to buy some fruit and vegetables for the crew from native boats as we go through Sunda Straits."

He shook his head.

"Take it," I urged him, whispering desperately. "No one can tell what—"

He smiled and slapped meaningly the only pocket of the sleeping jacket. It was not safe, certainly. But I produced a large old silk handkerchief of mine, and tying the three pieces of gold in a corner, pressed it on him. He was touched, I supposed, because he took it at last and tied it quickly round his waist under the jacket, on his bare skin.

Our eyes met; several seconds elapsed, till, our glances still mingled, I extended my hand and turned the lamp out. Then I passed through the cuddy, leaving the door of my room wide open..."Steward!"

He was still lingering in the pantry in the greatness of his zeal, giving a rub-up to a plated cruet stand the last thing before going to bed. Being careful not to wake up the mate, whose room was opposite, I spoke in an undertone.

He looked round anxiously. "Sir!"

"Can you get me a little hot water from the galley?"

"I am afraid, sir, the galley fire's been out for some time now."

"Go and see."

He flew up the stairs.

"Now," I whispered, loudly, into the saloon—too loudly, perhaps, but I was afraid I couldn't make a sound. He was by my side in an instant—the double captain slipped past the stairs—through a tiny dark passage ... a sliding door. We were in the sail locker, scrambling on our knees over the sails. A sudden thought struck me. I saw myself wandering barefooted, bareheaded, the sun beating on my dark poll. I snatched off my floppy hat and tried hurriedly in the dark to ram it on my other self. He dodged and fended off silently. I wonder what he thought had come to me before he understood and suddenly desisted. Our hands met gropingly, lingered united in a steady, motionless clasp for a second ... No word was breathed by either of us when they separated.

I was standing quietly by the pantry door when the steward returned.

"Sorry, sir. Kettle barely warm. Shall I light the spirit lamp?"

"Never mind."

I came out on deck slowly. It was now a matter of conscience to shave the land as close as possible—for now he must go overboard whenever the ship was put in stays. Must! There could be no going back for him. After a moment I walked over to leeward and my heart flew into my mouth at the nearness of the land on the bow. Under any other circumstances I would not have held on a minute longer. The second mate had followed me anxiously.

I looked on till I felt I could command my voice.

[1] *sovereigns* Gold coins worth one British pound each.

"She will weather," I said then in a quiet tone.

"Are you going to try that, sir?" he stammered out incredulously.

I took no notice of him and raised my tone just enough to be heard by the helmsman.

"Keep her good full."

"Good full, sir."

The wind fanned my cheek, the sails slept, the world was silent. The strain of watching the dark loom of the land grow bigger and denser was too much for me. I had shut my eyes—because the ship must go closer. She must! The stillness was intolerable. Were we standing still?

When I opened my eyes the second view started my heart with a thump. The black southern hill of Koh-ring seemed to hang right over the ship like a towering fragment of everlasting night. On that enormous mass of blackness there was not a gleam to be seen, not a sound to be heard. It was gliding irresistibly towards us and yet seemed already within reach of the hand. I saw the vague figures of the watch grouped in the waist, gazing in awed silence.

"Are you going on, sir?" inquired an unsteady voice at my elbow.

I ignored it. I had to go on.

"Keep her full. Don't check her way. That won't do now," I said warningly.

"I can't see the sails very well," the helmsman answered me, in strange, quavering tones.

Was she close enough? Already she was, I won't say in the shadow of the land, but in the very blackness of it, already swallowed up as it were, gone too close to be recalled, gone from me altogether.

"Give the mate a call," I said to the young man who stood at my elbow as still as death. "And turn all hands up."

My tone had a borrowed loudness reverberated from the height of the land. Several voices cried out together: "We are all on deck, sir."

Then stillness again, with the great shadow gliding closer, towering higher, without a light, without a sound. Such a hush had fallen on the ship that she might have been a bark of the dead floating in slowly under the very gate of Erebus.[1]

"My God! Where are we?"

It was the mate moaning at my elbow. He was thunderstruck, and as it were deprived of the moral support of his whiskers. He clapped his hands and absolutely cried out, "Lost!"

"Be quiet," I said, sternly.

He lowered his tone, but I saw the shadowy gesture of his despair. "What are we doing here?"

"Looking for the land wind."

He made as if to tear his hair, and addressed me recklessly.

"She will never get out. You have done it, sir. I knew it'd end in something like this. She will never weather, and you are too close now to stay. She'll drift ashore before she's round. O my God!"

I caught his arm as he was raising it to batter his poor devoted head, and shook it violently.

"She's ashore already," he wailed, trying to tear himself away.

"Is she? … Keep good full there!"

"Good full, sir," cried the helmsman in a frightened, thin, childlike voice.

I hadn't let go the mate's arm and went on shaking it. "Ready about, do you hear? You go forward"—shake—"and stop there"—shake—"and hold your noise"—shake—"and see these head-sheets properly overhauled"—shake, shake—shake.

And all the time I dared not look towards the land lest my heart should fail me. I released my grip at last and he ran forward as if fleeing for dear life.

I wondered what my double there in the sail locker thought of this commotion. He was able to hear everything—and perhaps he was able to understand why, on my conscience, it had to be thus close—no less. My first order "Hard alee!" re-echoed ominously under the towering shadow of Koh-ring as if I had shouted in a mountain gorge. And then I watched the land intently. In that smooth water and light wind it was impossible to feel the ship coming-to. No! I could not

[1] *Erebus* In classical myth, a place of darkness between earth and Hades, the underworld.

feel her. And my second self was making now ready to ship out and lower himself overboard. Perhaps he was gone already…?

The great black mass brooding over our very mastheads began to pivot away from the ship's side silently. And now I forgot the secret stranger ready to depart, and remembered only that I was a total stranger to the ship. I did not know her. Would she do it? How was she to be handled?

I swung the mainyard and waited helplessly. She was perhaps stopped, and her very fate hung in the balance, with the black mass of Koh-ring like the gate of the everlasting night towering over her taffrail.[1] What would she do now? Had she way on her yet? I stepped to the side swiftly, and on the shadowy water I could see nothing except a faint phosphorescent flash revealing the glassy smoothness of the sleeping surface. It was impossible to tell—and I had not learned yet the feel of my ship. Was she moving? What I needed was something easily seen, a piece of paper, which I could throw overboard and watch. I had nothing on me. To run down for it I didn't dare. There was no time. All at once my strained, yearning stare distinguished a white object floating within a yard of the ship's side. White on the black water. A phosphorescent flash passed under it. What was that thing? … I recognized my own floppy hat. It must have fallen off his head … and he didn't bother. Now I had what I wanted—the saving mark for my eyes. But I hardly thought of my other self, now gone from the ship, to be hidden forever from all friendly faces, to be a fugitive and a vagabond on the earth, with no brand of the curse on his sane forehead to stay a slaying hand … too proud to explain.

And I watched the hat—the expression of my sudden pity for his mere flesh. It had been meant to save his homeless head from the dangers of the sun. And now—behold—it was saving the ship, by serving me for a mark to help out the ignorance of my strangeness. Ha! It was drifting forward, warning me just in time that the ship had gathered sternaway.

"Shift the helm," I said in a low voice to the seaman standing still like a statue.

The man's eyes glistened wildly in the binnacle light as he jumped round to the other side and spun round the wheel.

I walked to the break of the poop. On the overshadowed deck all hands stood by the forebraces waiting for my order. The stars ahead seemed to be gliding from right to left. And all was so still in the world that I heard the quiet remark, "She's round," passed in a tone of intense relief between two seamen.

"Let go and haul."

The foreyards ran round with a great noise, amidst cheery cries. And now the frightful whiskers made themselves heard giving various orders. Already the ship was drawing ahead. And I was alone with her. Nothing! no one in the world should stand now between us, throwing a shadow on the way of silent knowledge and mute affection, the perfect communion of a seaman with his first command.

Walking to the taffrail, I was in time to make out, on the very edge of a darkness thrown by a towering black mass like the very gateway of Erebus—yes, I was in time to catch an evanescent glimpse of my white hat left behind to mark the spot where the secret sharer of my cabin and of my thoughts, as though he were my second self, had lowered himself into the water to take his punishment: a free man, a proud swimmer striking out for a new destiny.

—1912

[1] *taffrail* Stern rail.

Siegfried Sassoon

1886 – 1967

Siegfried Sassoon gained his reputation during and after World War I as a poet who stridently protested the war. Shocked by the realities of the front, he transformed his horror and disgust into accusatory, didactic verse meant to confront those at home with the atrocities he had witnessed.

The Sassoons were an extremely wealthy merchant family, and Siegfried had a privileged upbringing in Kent, though his father had been disinherited for marrying outside the Jewish faith. Sassoon's hobbies included horseback riding, fox hunting, and cricket. He attended but did not graduate from Cambridge, and in the years leading up to 1914, he had his first volumes of poetry privately published without success. At the time of the war's outbreak, he was an enthusiastic supporter and enlisted even before war was officially declared.

When Sassoon was first commissioned into the Royal Welch Fusiliers, his poetry was neither satirical nor disillusioned; like many young poets of the day, he gave voice to patriotic sentiments. His perception changed dramatically after surviving the Battle of the Somme on 1 July 1916—a day on which 19,000 British men were killed and 38,000 wounded. Sassoon distinguished himself with his fierce courage in this battle—earning himself a Military Cross (which he later threw away) and the nickname "Mad Jack"—but the experience purged him of any romantic notions as to the glory of battle.

In a new, starkly realistic voice, Sassoon attacked commanding officers, Church, and State, and all those back home who were ignorant of or indifferent to the conditions of the war. His compressed, intense verses use graphic descriptions, colloquial language, and explosive direct speech to convey the brutality of what he and other soldiers experienced. They often also rely on simple oppositions—such as between innocent and guilty, home and front, men and women—to achieve ironic effect.

In April 1917, Sassoon was sent home to recover from a sniper wound. There he drafted his famous public protest, published in *The Times* on 31 July 1917, in which he declared that the war had become a mere matter of "aggression and conquest" and that it was being deliberately prolonged. Sassoon was saved from prison only by the intervention of his friend Robert Graves, a fellow poet and Welch Fusilier, who testified that Sassoon was shell-shocked. Eager to avoid making a martyr of Sassoon, a medical board sent him to Edinburgh's Craiglockhart War Hospital instead.

While at Craiglockhart (where he met Wilfred Owen, another poet), Sassoon began to experiment with longer, dramatic-narrative poems that evoked the physical details of the trench. He was declared fit for active duty in 1918, but was on the front lines only a month before he received a shot in the head that sent him back to England for good. His war poems were published in *The Old Huntsman* (1917) and *Counter-Attack and Other Poems* (1918). Though the ruthless honesty of these volumes was met with far more outrage than critical acclaim in Britain, it made Sassoon's poetry very popular on the front. After the war, Sassoon continued to launch vociferous poetic salvos, now directed against the Allies' vindictive treatment of Germany and the British government's neglect of returned soldiers.

Over the next few decades, Sassoon continued to take up the war in his work, but he shifted his focus from poetry to prose autobiography. The first three volumes, *Memoirs of a Fox-Hunting Man* (1928), *Memoirs of an Infantry Officer* (1930), and *Sherston's Progress* (1936), revisit the past under the guise of a fictional persona, George Sherston, while the second three, *The Old Century and Seven More Years* (1938), *The Weald of Youth* (1942), and *Siegfried's Journey: 1916–1920* (1945) are autobiography in the conventional sense. These works—especially *Memoirs of a Fox-Hunting Man* and *Memoirs of an Infantry Officer*—were well-received by critics. They draw on Sassoon's youth and war experiences, but reveal little about the personal suffering he experienced beyond the war. Sassoon's posthumously published diaries make clear exactly how much he had omitted, including the turbulent events surrounding his marriage in 1933, the birth of his son George in 1936, the dissolution of his marriage in 1941, and a long period of anguish over his sexuality (he was either gay or bisexual).

Sassoon continued to write, but he published most of his later poetry collections privately. He felt his work was frequently misunderstood, particularly as his religious faith increased and he became a self-proclaimed "religious poet" in the years preceding his conversion to Roman Catholicism in 1957. After this point Sassoon wrote very little poetry, and he spent the remainder of his life in relative seclusion at his home in Wiltshire, where he died in 1967.

⌘⌘⌘

They

The Bishop tells us: "When the boys come back
They will not be the same; for they'll have fought
In a just cause: they lead the last attack
On Anti-Christ; their comrades' blood has bought
New right to breed an honourable race,
They have challenged Death and dared him face to face."
"We're none of us the same!" the boys reply.
"For George lost both his legs; and Bill's stone blind;
Poor Jim's shot through the lungs and like to die;
And Bert's gone syphilitic: you'll not find
A chap who's served that hasn't found *some* change."
And the Bishop said: "The ways of God are strange!"
—1917 (written 31 October 1916)

Glory of Women

You love us when we're heroes, home on leave,
Or wounded in a mentionable place.
You worship decorations; you believe
That chivalry redeems the war's disgrace.
You make us shells. You listen with delight,
By tales of dirt and danger fondly thrilled.
You crown our distant ardours while we fight,
And mourn our laurelled memories when we're killed.
You can't believe that British troops "retire"
When hell's last horror breaks them, and they run,
Trampling the terrible corpses—blind with blood.
O German mother dreaming by the fire,
While you are knitting socks to send your son
His face is trodden deeper in the mud.
—1918 (written 1917)

Everyone Sang

Everyone suddenly burst out singing;
And I was filled with such delight
As prisoned birds must find in freedom,
Winging wildly across the white
Orchards and dark-green fields; on—on—and out of sight.

Everyone's voice was suddenly lifted;
And beauty came like the setting sun:
My heart was shaken with tears; and horror
Drifted away … O, but Everyone
Was a bird; and the song was wordless; the singing will never be done.
—1919

from *Memoirs of an Infantry Officer*[1]

On July the first, the weather, after an early morning mist, was of the kind commonly called heavenly. Down in our frowsty[2] cellar we breakfasted at six, unwashed and apprehensive. Our table, appropriately enough, was an empty ammunition box. At six-forty-five the final bombardment began, and there was nothing for us to do except sit round our candle until the tornado ended. For more than forty minutes the air vibrated and the earth rocked and shuddered. Through the sustained uproar the tap and rattle of machine-guns could be identified; but except for the whistle of bullets no retaliation came our way until a few 5.9 shells[3] shook the roof of our dugout. Barton and I sat speechless, deafened and stupefied by the seismic state of affairs, and when he lit a cigarette the match flame staggered crazily. Afterwards I asked him what he had been thinking about. His reply was "Carpet slippers and Kettle-holders." My own mind had been working in much the same style, for during that cannonading cataclysm the following refrain was running in my head:

> They come as a boon and a blessing to men,
> The Something, the Owl, and the Waverley Pen.[4]

For the life of me I couldn't remember what the first one was called. Was it the Shakespeare? Was it the Dickens? Anyhow it was an advertisement which I'd often seen in smoky railway stations. Then the bombardment lifted and lessened, our vertigo abated, and we looked at one another in dazed relief. Two brigades of our division were now going over the top on our right. Our brigade was to attack "when the main assault had reached its final objective." In our fortunate role of privileged spectators Barton and I went up the stairs to see what we could from Kingston Road Trench. We left Jenkins crouching in a corner, where he remained most of the day. His haggard blinking face haunts my memory. He was an example of the paralysing effect which such an experience could produce on a nervous system sensitive to noise, for he was a good officer both before and afterwards. I felt no sympathy for him at the time, but I do now. From the support-trench, which Barton called "our opera box," I observed as much of the battle as the formation of the country allowed, the rising ground on the right making it impossible to see anything of the attack towards Mametz. A small shiny black notebook contains my pencilled particulars, and nothing will be gained by embroidering them with afterthoughts. I cannot turn my field-glasses on to the past.

* * *

7.45.
The barrage is now working to the right of Fricourt and beyond. I can see the 21st Division advancing about three-quarters of a mile away on the left and a few Germans coming to meet them, apparently surrendering. Our men in small parties (not extended in line) go

[1] *from … Officer* The following excerpt, which describes the beginning of the Battle of the Somme in 1916, is taken from Section 4, Chapter 2, entitled "Battle."

[2] *frowsty* Musty; stale or unpleasant smelling.

[3] *5.9 shells* 5.9-caliber shells.

[4] *They come … Pen* This then-popular slogan of MacNiven and Cameron, Ltd. (a producer of pen nibs) advertised three types of nibs: the Pickwick (the missing term), the Owl, and the Waverley.

steadily on to the German front-line. Brilliant sunshine and a haze of smoke drifting along the landscape. Some Yorkshires[1] a little way below on the left, watching the show and cheering as if at a football match. The noise almost as bad as ever.

9.30. Came back to dug-out and had a shave. 21st Division still going across the open, apparently without casualties. The sunlight flashes on bayonets as the tiny figures move quietly forward and disappear beyond mounds of trench debris. A few runners come back and ammunition parties go across. Trench-mortars[2] are knocking hell out of Sunken Road Trench and the ground where the Manchesters will attack soon. Noise not so bad now and very little retaliation.

9.50. Fricourt half-hidden by clouds of drifting smoke, blue, pinkish and grey. Shrapnel bursting in small bluish-white puffs with tiny flashes. The birds seem bewildered; a lark begins to go up and then flies feebly along, thinking better of it. Others flutter above the trench with querulous cries, weak on the wing. I can see seven of our balloons,[3] on the right. On the left our men still filing across in twenties and thirties. Another huge explosion in Fricourt and a cloud of brown-pink smoke. Some bursts are yellowish.

10.50. I can see the Manchesters down in New Trench, getting ready to go over. Figures filing down the trench. Two of them have gone out to look at our wire gaps![4] Have just eaten my last orange.... I am staring at a sunlit picture of Hell, and still the breeze shakes the yellow weeds, and the poppies glow under Crawley Ridge where some shells fell a few minutes ago. Manchesters are sending forward some scouts. A bayonet glitters. A runner comes back across the open to their Battalion Headquarters, close here on the right. 21st Division still trotting along the sky line toward La Boisselle. Barrage going strong to the right of Contalmaison Ridge. Heavy shelling toward Mametz.

12.15. Quieter the last two hours. Manchesters still waiting. Germans putting over a few shrapnel shells. Silly if I got hit! Weather cloudless and hot. A lark singing confidently overhead.

1.30. Manchesters attack at 2.30. Mametz and Montauban reported taken. Mametz consolidated.

2.30. Manchesters left New Trench and apparently took Sunken Road Trench, bearing rather to the right. Could see about 400. Many walked casually across with sloped arms. There were about forty casualties on the left (from machine-gun in Fricourt). Through my glasses I could see one man moving his left arm up and down as he lay on his side; his face was a crimson patch. Others lay still in the sunlight while the swarm of figures disappeared over the hill. Fricourt was a cloud of pinkish smoke. Lively machine-gun fire on the far side of the hill. At 2.50 no one to be seen in No Man's Land except the casualties (about half-way across). Our dug-out shelled again since 2.30.

5.0. I saw about thirty of our A Company crawl across to Sunken Road from New Trench. Germans put a few big shells on the cemetery and traversed Kingston Road with machine-gun. Manchester wounded still out there. Remainder of A Company went across—about 100 altogether. Manchesters reported held up in Bois Français Support. Their Colonel went across and was killed.

8.0. Staff Captain of our brigade has been along. Told Barton that Seventh Division has reached its objectives with some difficulty, except on this brigade front. Manchesters are in trouble, and Fricourt attack has failed. Several hundred prisoners brought in on our sector.

9.30. Our A Company holds Rectangle and Sunken Road. Jenkins gone off in charge of a carrying-party.[5] Seemed all right again. C Company now reduced to six runners, two stretcher-bearers, Company-Sergeant-Major, signallers, and Barton's servant. Flook away on

[1] *Yorkshires* I.e., men belonging to one of the battalions of the Yorkshire Regiment that fought at the Battle of the Somme.

[2] *Trench-mortars* Small mortars used to propel bombs into enemy trenches.

[3] *balloons* As a defense against hostile aircraft, troops set up a series of connected balloons attached to long wire cables.

[4] *wire gaps* Holes made in the protective barbed wire by enemy shells.

[5] *carrying-party* Party sent to deliver supplies.

carrying-party. Sky cloudy westward. Red sunset. Heavy gunfire on the left.

2.30. (Next afternoon.) Adjutant[1] has just been up here, excited, optimistic, and unshaven. He went across last night to ginger up A Company who did very well, thanks to the bombers. About 40 casualties; only 4 killed. Fricourt and Rose Trench occupied this morning without resistance. I am now lying out in front of our trench in the long grass, basking in sunshine where yesterday there were bullets. Our new front-line on the hill is being shelled. Fricourt is full of troops wandering about in search of souvenirs. The village was a ruin and is now a dust heap. A gunner (Forward Observation Officer) has just been along here with a German helmet in his hand. Said Fricourt is full of dead; he saw one officer lying across a smashed machine-gun with his head bashed in—"a fine looking chap," he said, with some emotion, which rather surprised me.

8.15. Queer feeling, seeing people moving about freely between here and Fricourt. Dumps being made. Shacks and shelters being put up under skeleton trees and all sorts of transport arriving at Cemetery Cross Roads. We stay here till to-morrow morning. Feel a bit of a fraud.

—1930 (WRITTEN 1916)

[1] *Adjutant* Military officer whose role is to communicate the orders of superior officers.

Isaac Rosenberg

1890 – 1918

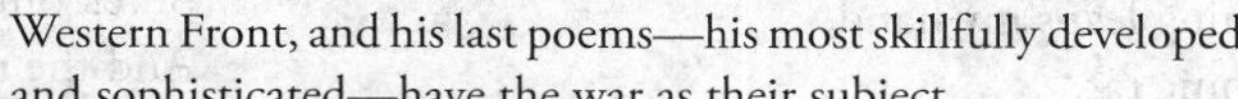

Ironically, Isaac Rosenberg's reputation as a poet rests on a handful of poems he considered marginal to his *oeuvre*. Known primarily as a "war poet" and frequently discussed alongside Wilfred Owen, Rupert Brooke, Siegfried Sassoon, and Robert Graves, he is a prominent figure in any examination of World War I poetry. However, Rosenberg neither supported the war nor sought it as a primary topic for his writing. Upon enlisting, he declared, "I am determined that this war, with all its powers for devastation, shall not master my poeting." Unfortunately, he was killed on the Western Front, and his last poems—his most skillfully developed and sophisticated—have the war as their subject.

Born in Bristol on 25 November 1890, Rosenberg was the son of Jewish refugees from Russia. Rosenberg's family struggled to make a living in England, and when he was seven they moved to London's East End in the hopes of improving their circumstances. At fourteen, Rosenberg apprenticed as an engraver, taking night classes in art and writing poetry in his spare time. Eventually he was able to study art full time at the Slade School of Art, but his passion for poetry soon eclipsed his earlier love of painting.

He devoted himself to achieving success as a poet with remarkable determination, distributing his works in pamphlets published at his own expense. The first, *Night and Day*, was published in 1912, followed in 1915 by *Youth* and then by the verse play *Moses* in 1916. These pamphlets remained his only publications until "Marching Song" and "Break of Day in the Trenches" were published in *Poetry* in 1916, and "Koelue" appeared in the anthology *Georgian Poetry* in 1917. Rosenberg received some encouragement and financial support from Edward Marsh, the editor of *Georgian Poetry*, but his background distanced him from Marsh and the anthology's other contributors, all of whom were from the upper classes and had been educated at Cambridge or Oxford. Rosenberg's poems were founded in a knowledge of Yiddish, of the Old Testament, and of Jewish myth and history that his contemporaries at *Poetry* lacked; though he drew to some extent on the innovations of Imagism, his work was also unlike that of other English poets in their form, imagery, and rhythm.

After the war broke out, Rosenberg found it increasingly difficult to find the work necessary to supplement his family's income. After months of deliberation, he decided in late 1915 to enlist, despite "the immorality of joining with no patriotic convictions," in order to provide his mother with a military allowance. Once on the Western Front, he remained on or near the line until he was killed in a German offensive on 1 April 1918.

Rosenberg's war poems are frequently described as "raw." Their direct, simple language, their sense of immediacy and involvement (many of the poems' speakers participate directly in the war), and their strongly visual descriptions of the horrors of battle all convey an elemental sense of war. Yet at the time of Rosenberg's death and for some time afterward, his poetry had little impact. His work was rediscovered by the poets of World War II, whose conceptions of war often approximated his own, and since then the originality of his voice has been increasingly appreciated.

⌘⌘⌘

Break of Day in the Trenches

The darkness crumbles away.
It is the same old druid[1] Time as ever,
Only a live thing leaps my hand,
A queer sardonic rat,
As I pull the parapet's[2] poppy
To stick behind my ear.
Droll rat, they would shoot you if they knew
Your cosmopolitan sympathies.
Now you have touched this English hand
You will do the same to a German
Soon, no doubt, if it be your pleasure
To cross the sleeping green between.
It seems you inwardly grin as you pass
Strong eyes, fine limbs, haughty athletes,
Less chanced than you for life,
Bonds to the whims of murder,
Sprawled in the bowels of the earth,
The torn fields of France.
What do you see in our eyes
At the shrieking iron and flame
Hurled through still heavens?
What quaver—what heart aghast?
Poppies whose roots are in man's veins
Drop, and are ever dropping;
But mine in my ear is safe—
Just a little white with the dust.
—1916

[1] *druid* Member of an ancient Celtic order in Gaul and Britain. Druids often figure in Irish and Welsh legend as magicians, sorcerers, and soothsayers.

[2] *parapet* Defence of earth in front of a military trench.

Dead Man's Dump

The plunging limbers[3] over the shattered track
Racketed with their rusty freight,
Stuck out like many crowns of thorns,
And the rusty stakes like sceptres old
To stay the flood of brutish men
Upon our brothers dear.

The wheels lurched over sprawled dead
But pained them not, though their bones crunched,
Their shut mouths made no moan.
They lie there huddled, friend and foeman,
Man born of man, and born of woman,
And shells go crying over them
From night till night and now.

Earth has waited for them,
All the time of their growth
Fretting for their decay:
Now she has them at last!
In the strength of their strength
Suspended—stopped and held.

What fierce imaginings their dark souls lit?
Earth! have they gone into you?
Somewhere they must have gone,
And flung on your hard back
Is their soul's sack,
Emptied of God-ancestralled essences.
Who hurled them out? Who hurled?

[3] *limbers* Two-wheeled carriages that hold guns or ammunition chests.

None saw their spirits' shadow shake the grass,
Or stood aside for the half-used life to pass
Out of those doomed nostrils and the doomed mouth,
When the swift iron burning bee
Drained the wild honey of their youth.

What of us who, flung on the shrieking pyre,
Walk, our usual thoughts untouched,
Our lucky limbs as on ichor[1] fed,
Immortal seeming ever?
Perhaps when the flames beat loud on us,
A fear may choke in our veins
And the startled blood may stop.

The air is loud with death,
The dark air spurts with fire,
The explosions ceaseless are.
Timelessly now, some minutes past,
These dead strode time with vigorous life,
Till the shrapnel called "An end!"
But not to all. In bleeding pangs
Some borne on stretchers dreamed of home,
Dear things, war-blotted from their hearts.

Maniac Earth! howling and flying, your bowel
Seared by the jagged fire, the iron love,
The impetuous storm of savage love.
Dark Earth! dark Heavens! swinging in chemic smoke,
What dead are born when you kiss each soundless soul
With lightning and thunder from your mined heart,
Which man's self dug, and his blind fingers loosed?[2]

A man's brains splattered on
A stretcher-bearer's face;
His shook shoulders slipped their load,
But when they bent to look again
The drowning soul was sunk too deep
For human tenderness.

They left this dead with the older dead,
Stretched at the crossroads.

Burnt black by strange decay
Their sinister faces lie;
The lid over each eye,
The grass and coloured clay
More motion have than they,
Joined to the great sunk silences.

Here is one not long dead;
His dark hearing caught our far wheels,
And the choked soul stretched weak hands
To reach the living word the far wheels said,
The blood-dazed intelligence beating for light,
Crying through the suspense of the far torturing wheels
Swift for the end to break,
Or the wheels to break,
Cried as the tide of the world broke over his sight.

Will they come? Will they ever come?
Even as the mixed hoofs of the mules,
The quivering-bellied mules,
And the rushing wheels all mixed
With his tortured upturned sight.
So we crashed round the bend,
We heard his weak scream,
We heard his very last sound,
And our wheels grazed his dead face.
—1922

Louse Hunting

Nudes—stark and glistening,
Yelling in lurid glee. Grinning faces
And raging limbs
Whirl over the floor one fire.
For a shirt verminously busy
Yon soldier tore from his throat, with oaths
Godhead might shrink at, but not the lice.
And soon the shirt was aflare
Over the candle he'd lit while we lay.

[1] *ichor* Ethereal fluid that, according to Greek mythology, flowed in the veins of the immortal gods.

[2] *Maniac Earth … fingers loosed* This stanza is omitted in some versions of the poem.

Then we all sprang up and stript
To hunt the verminous brood.
Soon like a demons' pantomime
The place was raging.
See the silhouettes agape,
See the gibbering shadows
Mixed with the battled arms on the wall.
See gargantuan hooked fingers
Pluck in supreme flesh
To smutch supreme littleness.
See the merry limbs in hot Highland fling[1]
Because some wizard vermin
Charmed from the quiet this revel
When our ears were half lulled
By the dark music
Blown from Sleep's trumpet.
—1922

[1] *Highland fling* Scottish dance in which the legs are moved vigorously.

Returning, We Hear the Larks

Sombre the night is.
And though we have our lives, we know
What sinister threat lurks there.

Dragging these anguished limbs, we only know
This poison-blasted track opens on our camp—
On a little safe sleep.

But hark! joy—joy—strange joy.
Lo! heights of night ringing with unseen larks.
Music showering on our upturned list'ning faces.

Death could drop from the dark
As easily as song—
But song only dropped,
Like a blind man's dreams on the sand

By dangerous tides,
Like a girl's dark hair for she dreams no ruin lies there,
Or her kisses where a serpent hides.
—1922

Wilfred Owen

1893 – 1918

Wilfred Owen's humane responses to World War I, his compassionate depictions of the suffering that war engendered, and his critique of nationalism challenged the imperialist rhetoric of honor, glory, and patriotic duty, prompting Dylan Thomas later to declare him "a poet of all times, all places, and all wars."

Owen was the first-born son of Thomas Owen and Susan Shaw of Shropshire, and the favorite of his mother, who hoped to see him become a member of the clergy. When Owen left school in 1911 he took a post as lay assistant to the Vicar of Dunsden, who would help him prepare for his university entrance exam in exchange for parish work. Owen, however, became increasingly critical of the Church's response to the suffering of the poor, and found his passion for poetry eclipsed his religious faith. He left the vicarage and, having failed to win a university scholarship, departed for France to work as a private tutor.

Though Owen had little intention of joining up when war broke out, pressure to do so increased as the fighting continued. In 1915 he returned to England, enlisted in the Artists' Rifles, and was commissioned lieutenant in the Manchester Regiment. Owen crossed the channel in December of 1916 to join his platoon on the Somme, where he immediately began recording his impressions in letters and poems. His use of a pastoral mode owed much to the influence of Keats, but his powerful descriptions of death, wounded bodies, and the weapons of war, which coupled startling images and shifting angles of vision, subverted the traditional pastoral. Owen also developed his own approach to rhyme, in which half rhymes (pararhymes) and assonance featured prominently. This gave his poetry a discordant, mournful quality that echoed his pessimistic warnings of further suffering to come, and helped create haunting elegies for the generation he shows being slaughtered like cattle in "Anthem for Doomed Youth" (1920).

Owen had been at the front only four months when a shell exploded a few feet from his head, resulting in his nearly being buried alive. A few weeks later he was removed to Craiglockhart War Hospital, outside Edinburgh, and treated for shell shock. There he met Siegfried Sassoon, another war poet whose stridently satirical poetry Owen greatly admired. It was during this time, while recovering from his trauma, that Owen wrote most of his poems. The influence of Sassoon is especially evident in his more didactic work, such as "Dulce et Decorum Est" (1920), which uses graphic descriptions of the battlefield and powerful direct speech to attack the classic dictum that it is sweet and fitting to die for one's country.

Owen's personal attitude toward war was more complex than his famous poem may suggest. Though he opposed the violence in principle, he was glad to be able to return to the front in August 1918 and to resume leading his platoon in battle. About two months after his return to the front, he wrote to Sassoon of the psychological toll his command was taking: "I shall feel anger again as soon as I dare, but now I must not. I don't take the cigarette out of my mouth when I write Deceased over their letters. But one day I will write Deceased over many books." Owen was killed two weeks later—only a week before the war's end—while leading an offensive on the banks of the Sambre Canal.

At the time of Owen's death, hardly any of his poetry had been published, but Sassoon saw to the publication of *Poems* (1920), which established Owen's reputation as a war poet; a further collection, *The Poems of Wilfred Owen* (1931) was even more well-received, and his formal and stylistic innovations became influential among British poets of the 1930s. Unfortunately, Owen's mother and brother intervened strenuously in the management of his image so as to soften his expressions of religious doubt and to conceal the fact that he was gay; much of his personal writing, as well as some of his poetry, has been lost as a result.

⌘⌘⌘

A Terre

(Being the philosophy of many Soldiers.)

Sit on the bed, I'm blind, and three parts shell,
Be careful; can't shake hands now; never shall.
Both arms have mutinied against me—brutes.
My fingers fidget like ten idle brats.

I tried to peg out° soldierly—no use! *die*
One dies of war like any old disease.
This bandage feels like pennies on my eyes.[1]
I have my medals?—Discs to make eyes close,
My glorious ribbons?—Ripped from my own back
In scarlet shreds. (That's for your poetry book.)

A short life and a merry one, my brick!° *reliable chum*
We used to say we'd hate to live dead old—
Yet now … I'd willingly be puffy, bald,
And patriotic. Buffers[2] catch from boys
At least the jokes hurled at them. I suppose
Little I'd ever teach a son, but hitting,
Shooting, war, hunting, all the arts of hurting.
Well, that's what I learnt—that, and making money.

Your fifty years ahead seem none too many?
Tell me how long I've got? God! For one year
To help myself to nothing more than air!
One Spring! Is one too good to spare, too long?
Spring wind would work its own way to my lung,
And grow me legs as quick as lilac-shoots.

My servant's lamed, but listen how he shouts!
When I'm lugged out, he'll still be good for that.
Here in this mummy-case, you know, I've thought
How well I might have swept his floors for ever,
I'd ask no night off when the bustle's over,
Enjoying so the dirt. Who's prejudiced
Against a grimed hand when his own's quite dust,
Less live than specks that in the sun-shafts turn,
Less warm than dust that mixes with arms' tan?
I'd love to be a sweep,[3] now, black as Town,
Yes, or a muckman. Must I be his load?

O Life, Life, let me breathe—a dug-out rat!
Not worse than ours the existences rats lead—
Nosing along at night down some safe vat,
They find a shell-proof home before they rot.
Dead men may envy living mites in cheese,
Or good germs even. Microbes have their joys,
And subdivide, and never come to death,
Certainly flowers have the easiest time on earth.

[1] *pennies on my eyes* Reference to the ancient practice of placing coins on the eyes of the dead.

[2] *Buffers* Old men who are out of touch with present times.

[3] *sweep* Chimney sweep.

"I shall be one with nature, herb, and stone,"
Shelley[1] would tell me. Shelley would be stunned;
The dullest Tommy° hugs that fancy now. *British soldier*
"Pushing up daisies," is their creed you know.
To grain, then, go my fat, to buds my sap,
For all the usefulness there is in soap.
D'you think the Boche° will ever stew man-soup? *Germans*
Some day, no doubt, if …
Friend, be very sure
I shall be better off with plants that share
More peaceably the meadow and the shower.
Soft rains will touch me—as they could touch once,
And nothing but the sun shall make me ware.° *aware*
Your guns may crash around me. I'll not hear;
Or, if I wince, I shall not know I wince.
Don't take my soul's poor comfort for your jest.
Soldiers may grow a soul when turned to fronds,
But here the thing's best left at home with friends.

My soul's a little grief, grappling your chest,
To climb your throat on sobs; easily chased
On other sighs and wiped by fresher winds.

Carry my crying spirit till it's weaned
To do without what blood remained these wounds.
—1919

The Sentry

We'd found an old Boche° dug-out, and he knew, *German*
And gave us hell, for shell on frantic shell
Hammered on top, but never quite burst through.
Rain, guttering down in waterfalls of slime
Kept slush waist high, that rising hour by hour,
Choked up the steps too thick with clay to climb.
What murk of air remained stank old, and sour
With fumes of whizz-bangs,[2] and the smell of men
Who'd lived there years, and left their curse in the den,
If not their corpses …
There we herded from the blast
Of whizz-bangs, but one found our door at last.
Buffeting eyes and breath, snuffing the candles.
And thud! flump! thud! down the steep steps came thumping
And splashing in the flood, deluging muck—
The sentry's body; then his rifle, handles
Of old Boche bombs, and mud in ruck on ruck.
We dredged him up, for killed, until he whined
"O sir, my eyes—I'm blind—I'm blind, I'm blind!"
Coaxing, I held a flame against his lids
And said if he could see the least blurred light
He was not blind; in time he'd get all right.
"I can't," he sobbed. Eyeballs, huge-bulged like squids
Watch my dreams still; but I forgot him there
In posting next for duty, and sending a scout
To beg a stretcher somewhere, and floundering about
To other posts under the shrieking air.

* * *

Those other wretches, how they bled and spewed,
And one who would have drowned himself for good—
I try not to remember these things now.
Let dread hark back for one word only: how
Half-listening to that sentry's moans and jumps,
And the wild chattering of his broken teeth,
Renewed most horribly whenever crumps[3]
Pummelled the roof and slogged the air beneath—
Through the dense din, I say, we heard him shout
"I see your lights!" But ours had long died out.
—1919

Disabled

He sat in a wheeled chair, waiting for dark,
And shivered in his ghastly suit of grey,
Legless, sewn short at elbow. Through the park
Voices of boys rang saddening like a hymn,
Voices of play and pleasure after day,
Till gathering sleep had mothered them from him.

[1] *Shelley* Romantic poet Percy Shelley; the above line is paraphrased from his *Adonais: An Elegy on the Death of John Keats* (1821).

[2] *whizz-bangs* Shells fired by small-caliber, high-velocity guns.

[3] *crumps* Sounds of exploding shells.

About this time Town used to swing so gay
When glow-lamps budded in the light-blue trees
And girls glanced lovelier as the air grew dim,
—In the old times, before he threw away his knees.
Now he will never feel again how slim
Girls' waists are, or how warm their subtle hands,
All of them touch him like some queer disease.

There was an artist silly for his face,
For it was younger than his youth, last year.
Now he is old; his back will never brace;
He's lost his colour very far from here,
Poured it down shell-holes till the veins ran dry,
And half his life-time lapsed in the hot race,
And leap of purple spurted from his thigh.
One time he liked a bloodsmear down his leg,
After the matches carried shoulder-high.
It was after football, when he'd drunk a peg,[1]
He thought he'd better join. He wonders why. …
Someone had said he'd look a god in kilts.[2]

That's why; and maybe, too, to please his Meg,
Aye, that was it, to please the giddy jilts[3]
He asked to join. He didn't have to beg;
Smiling they wrote his lie; aged nineteen years.
Germans he scarcely thought of; all their guilt
And Austria's,[4] did not move him. And no fears
Of Fear came yet. He thought of jewelled hilts
For daggers in plaid socks; of smart salutes;
And care of arms; and leave; and pay arrears;
Esprit de corps;[5] and hints for young recruits.
And soon, he was drafted out with drums and cheers.

Some cheered him home, but not as crowds cheer Goal.
Only a solemn man who brought him fruits
Thanked him; and then enquired about his soul.

Now, he will spend a few sick years in institutes,
And do what things the rules consider wise,
And take whatever pity they may dole.
To-night he noticed how the women's eyes
Passed from him to the strong men that were whole.
How cold and late it is! Why don't they come
And put him into bed? Why don't they come?
—1919

Strange Meeting

It seemed that out of battle I escaped
Down some profound dull tunnel, long since scooped
Through granites which titanic wars had groined.
Yet also there encumbered sleepers groaned,
Too fast in thought or death to be bestirred.
Then, as I probed them, one sprang up, and stared
With piteous recognition in fixed eyes,
Lifting distressful hands as if to bless.
And by his smile, I knew that sullen hall,
By his dead smile I knew we stood in Hell.
With a thousand pains that vision's face was grained;
Yet no blood reached there from the upper ground,
And no guns thumped, or down the flues made moan.
"Strange friend," I said, "here is no cause to mourn."
"None," said the other, "save the undone years,
The hopelessness. Whatever hope is yours,
Was my life also; I went hunting wild
After the wildest beauty in the world,
Which lies not calm in eyes, or braided hair,
But mocks the steady running of the hour,
And if it grieves, grieves richlier than here.
For of my glee might many men have laughed,
And of my weeping something had been left,
Which must die now. I mean the truth untold,
The pity of war, the pity war distilled.
Now men will go content with what we spoiled.
Or, discontent, boil bloody, and be spilled.
They will be swift with swiftness of the tigress,

[1] *peg* Quantity of alcohol.

[2] *kilts* Part of the uniform for Scottish soldiers during World War I.

[3] *giddy jilts* Scottish slang: flirtatious young women.

[4] *Austria* Ally of Germany during World War I.

[5] *Esprit de corps* Fellowship within a group.

None will break ranks, though nations trek from progress.
Courage was mine, and I had mystery,
Wisdom was mine, and I had mastery;
To miss the march of this retreating world
Into vain citadels that are not walled.
Then, when much blood had clogged their chariot-
wheels,
I would go up and wash them from sweet wells,
Even with truths that lie too deep for taint.
I would have poured my spirit without stint
But not through wounds; not on the cess° of war. *bog*
Foreheads of men have bled where no wounds were.
I am the enemy you killed, my friend.
I knew you in this dark; for so you frowned
Yesterday through me as you jabbed and killed.
I parried; but my hands were loath and cold.
Let us sleep now. ..."
—1920

Parable of the Old Man and the Young

So Abram rose, and clave the wood, and went,
And took the fire with him, and a knife.[1]
And as they sojourned both of them together,
Isaac the first-born spake and said, My Father,
Behold the preparations, fire and iron,
But where the lamb for this burnt-offering?
Then Abram bound the youth with belts and straps,
And builded parapets[2] and trenches there,
And stretchèd forth the knife to slay his son.
When lo! an angel called him out of heaven,
Saying, Lay not thy hand upon the lad,
Neither do anything to him. Behold,
A ram caught in a thicket by its horns;
Offer the Ram of Pride instead of him.
But the old man would not so, but slew his son,
And half the seed of Europe, one by one.[3]
—1920

[1] *So Abram ... a knife* Cf. Genesis 22. In the biblical story, God instructs Abraham to sacrifice his son Isaac as a burnt offering. Abraham is about to kill his son when the angel of the Lord appears to stop him; Abraham finds a ram and sacrifices it in Isaac's stead.

[2] *parapets* Defenses of earth built in front of military trenches.

[3] *And half ... by one* This line is absent from some published versions of the poem.

Arms and the Boy

Let the boy try along this bayonet-blade
How cold steel is, and keen with hunger of blood;
Blue with all malice, like a madman's flash;
And thinly drawn with famishing for flesh.

Lend him to stroke these blind, blunt bullet-heads
Which long to nuzzle in the hearts of lads,
Or give him cartridges of fine zinc teeth,
Sharp with the sharpness of grief and death.

For his teeth seem for laughing round an apple.
There lurk no claws behind his fingers supple;
And God will grow no talons at his heels,
Nor antlers through the thickness of his curls.
—1920

Anthem for Doomed Youth

What passing-bells for these who die as cattle?
Only the monstrous anger of the guns.
Only the stuttering rifles' rapid rattle
Can patter out their hasty orisons.° *prayers*
No mockeries for them from prayers or bells,
Nor any voice of mourning save the choirs,—
The shrill, demented choirs of wailing shells;
And bugles calling for them from sad shires.

What candles may be held to speed them all?
Not in the hands of boys, but in their eyes
Shall shine the holy glimmers of good-byes.
The pallor of girls' brows shall be their pall;[4]

[4] *pall* Cloth spread over a coffin, hearse, or tomb.

Their flowers the tenderness of silent minds,
And each slow dusk a drawing-down of blinds.
—1920

The Send-Off

Down the close, darkening lanes they sang their way
To the siding-shed,
And lined the train with faces grimly gay.

Their breasts were stuck all white with wreath and spray
As men's are, dead.

Dull porters watched them, and a casual tramp
Stood staring hard,
Sorry to miss them from the upland camp.

Then, unmoved, signals nodded, and a lamp
Winked to the guard.

So secretly, like wrongs hushed-up, they went.
They were not ours:
We never heard to which front these were sent.

Nor there if they yet mock what women meant
Who gave them flowers.

Shall they return to beatings of great bells
In wild trainloads?
A few, a few, too few for drums and yells,

May creep back, silent, to still village wells
Up half-known roads.
—1920

Dulce et Decorum Est[1]

Bent double, like old beggars under sacks,
Knock-kneed, coughing like hags, we cursed through sludge,
Till on the haunting flares we turned our backs,
And towards our distant rest began to trudge.
Men marched asleep. Many had lost their boots,
But limped on, blood-shod. All went lame, all blind;
Drunk with fatigue; deaf even to the hoots
Of gas-shells dropping softly behind.

Gas! GAS! Quick, boys!—An ecstasy of fumbling,
Fitting the clumsy helmets just in time,
But someone still was yelling out and stumbling
And flound'ring like a man in fire or lime—
Dim, through the misty panes[2] and thick green light,
As under a green sea, I saw him drowning.

In all my dreams before my helpless sight
He plunges at me, guttering, choking, drowning.

If in some smothering dreams, you too could pace
Behind the wagon that we flung him in,
And watch the white eyes writhing in his face,
His hanging face, like a devil's sick of sin;
If you could hear, at every jolt, the blood
Come gargling from the froth-corrupted lungs,
Bitter as the cud
Of vile, incurable sores on innocent tongues,—
My friend, you would not tell with such high zest
To children ardent for some desperate glory,
The old Lie: Dulce et decorum est
Pro patria mori.
—1920

[1] *Dulce et Decorum Est* Owen's poem takes its title from a famous line from the Roman poet Horace's *Odes* (3.2): "Dulce et decorum est pro patria mori" (Latin: "Sweet and fitting it is to die for one's country").

[2] *panes* Visors of the gas masks.

Futility

Move him into the sun—
Gently its touch awoke him once,
At home, whispering of fields half-sown.
Always it woke him, even in France,
Until this morning and this snow.
If anything might rouse him now
The kind old sun will know.

Think how it wakes the seeds—
Woke once the clays of a cold star.
Are limbs, so dear achieved, are sides
Full-nerved, still warm, too hard to stir?
Was it for this the clay grew tall?
—O what made fatuous sunbeams toil
To break earth's sleep at all?
—1920

THE GREAT WAR

CONTEXTS

Britain declared war on Germany on 4 August 1914, and nearly every family in England had lost someone before the Armistice on 11 November 1918. Roughly one million British soldiers died (and roughly ten million soldiers overall)—nearly one in every eight who enlisted. More than twice as many were wounded. While soldiers and civilians alike began the war filled with idealism, there was little room for glory in the trench warfare that became the dominant mode of conflict during the war. The battle line on the Western Front remained virtually unmoved for three years, with both sides making attempted advancements at great loss of life. The British landing at Gallipoli (1915), the German use of poison gas at the second battle of Ypres (1915), and the British introduction of tanks at the Somme (1916) were all undertaken in the hope they would lead to a victorious break-through—and all had horrific results. Indeed, the "Great War," as it was called at the time, was characterized from first to last by extreme disillusionment, from the misplaced hope at its outset that the fighting would end by Christmas 1914, to the confidence voiced by Woodrow Wilson (the American President who brought the United States into the war in 1917) that the conflict would lead nations to come together in a new League of Nations that would make this "a war to end all wars." After the war the British people would never again recapture the idealism and firm faith in technology, progress, and traditional values that had been prevalent earlier in the century. In stark contrast to Wilson's optimism, many were persuaded by the war's end that technological progress and failed humanity were driving civilization towards a perpetual state of war. Subsequent years were filled with unrest as the British people struggled to make sense of the sweeping changes war had brought.

The war was certainly unprecedented in its technology—airplanes as well as tanks were used for the first time in warfare, and machine guns facilitated new levels of mass slaughter. And the industrial nature of the war meant that civilians were relied upon nearly as much as soldiers for military success. Morale was thus important almost as much at home as on the front, and artists, photographers, poets, actors, and performers became important participants in the manufacture of patriotism. This section opens with a testament to the importance of patriotic poetry during wartime, and a sampling of popular poems and songs. There was little that was heroic or romantic about the daily life of soldiers in the trenches, but through songs such as "I Learned to Wash in Shell-holes" and "Oh, It's a Lovely War" soldiers might keep up morale by viewing their deplorable living conditions with humor. ("Oh, It's a Lovely War," by J.P. Long and Maurice Scott, became once again widely known after the 1960s stage production *Oh, What a Lovely War!* and the film that took its title from the play's.)

The war was remarkable too in its geographic scope; the fighting extended into Africa and the Middle East as well as across Europe and into Asia. The British Empire fought as one, with troops from all areas serving under imperial command. Canadian troops were particularly influential at Vimy Ridge, where in April 1917 they forced German troops to retreat from their dominant position on the northern part of the Western front. Soldiers from Australia and New Zealand were vitally important in offensives at the Somme and Gallipoli, where they sustained heavy losses.

War transformed everyday life and affected every aspect of society. Everyone was at risk, and everyone had a part to play in the war effort. While Victorian society had been characterized by rigid boundaries—between public and private space, between masculine and feminine realms and duties, and between classes—the war forced a sudden breakdown of these categories. After the war they were partially restored, but society was forever transformed. In her essay "The Cordite Makers," Rebecca West (the pen name of Cicily Fairfield) highlights the parallels between the daily lives of soldiers on the home front and that of many women working in the arms industry—particularly in terms of the personal sacrifices that they made and the dangers that they faced.

Ivor Gurney's poem "To His Love" and Vance Palmer's "The Farmer Remembers the Somme," both of which appear below, provide a grim sense of how firm a grip the memory of horror and of loss had upon those who had experienced the fighting at first hand. Less focused on the horror of battle is the excerpt below from poet Robert Graves's *Good-Bye to All That*. Graves's description of his war years as an officer in the Royal Welch Fusiliers is among the most vivid and detailed prose accounts of life on the front. The passage excerpted here gives among other things a clear sense of the stark differences between civilians' and soldiers' perceptions of the war.

⌘⌘⌘

from Anonymous, Introduction to *Songs and Sonnets for England in War Time* (1914)

The *Songs and Sonnets for England in War Time* anthology was the first of a genre that became common in World War I, the popular anthology of war poetry. The introduction provides a straightforward statement of the rationale for such volumes.

In the stress of a nation's peril, the poet at last comes into his own again, and with clarion call he rouses the sleeping soul of the Empire. Prophet he is, champion and consoler.

If in these later times the poet has been neglected, now in our infinite need, in our pride and our sorrow, he is here to strengthen, comfort and inspire. The poet is vindicated.

What can so nobly uplift the hearts of a people facing war with its unspeakable agony as music and poetry? The sound of martial music steels men's hearts before battle. The sound of martial words inspires human souls to do and to endure. God, His poetry, and His music are the Holy Trinity of war.

… The greatest songs [have not always been those] that have sent men on to victory. Sometimes it has been a modest verse that has found refuge in the heart of the soldier ready for the ultimate sacrifice, cheered on his way by the lilt of a humble song. Who else, indeed, can take the place of a poet?

Recruitment poster for South Australia, 1914.

Recruitment poster for Canada, 1914.

"In Flanders Fields": The Poem and Some Responses

Canadian physician John McCrae's "In Flanders Fields," scribbled in twenty minutes while he was sitting on the back of an ambulance just north of the field of Ypres, remains the most widely recited poem of the war. McCrae, not satisfied with the poem, would have thrown it away, but a fellow officer sent it to London, where it was published by *Punch* (after being rejected by *The Spectator*). The responses to the poem reproduced below are only three of many—a testimony to the strength of emotion the poem evoked in readers. Elizabeth Daryush's more personal description of loss provides a sharp contrast to the two more patriotic poems by Mitchell and Armstrong.

John McCrae, "In Flanders Fields" (1915)

In Flanders Fields the poppies blow
Between the crosses, row on row,
That mark our place; and in the sky
The larks, still bravely singing, fly
Scarce heard amid the guns below.

We are the Dead. Short days ago
We lived, felt dawn, saw sunset glow,
Loved and were loved, and now we lie
In Flanders Fields.

Take up our quarrel with the foe:
To you from failing hands we throw

In Flanders Fields

—

In Flanders fields the poppies grow
Between the crosses, row on row
That mark our place: and in the sky
The larks still bravely singing, fly
Scarce heard amid the guns below.

We are the Dead. Short days ago
We lived, felt dawn, saw sunset glow,
Loved, and were loved, and now we lie
In Flanders fields.

Take up our quarrel with the foe:
To you from failing hands we throw
The Torch: be yours to hold it high!
If ye break faith with us who die
We shall not sleep, though poppies grow
In Flanders fields.

John McCrae

An autograph copy of McCrae's famous poem.
Note that in this version he has replaced "blow" with "grow" in the first line.

The torch; be yours to hold it high.
If ye break faith with us who die
We shall not sleep, though poppies grow
In Flanders Fields.

John Mitchell, "Reply to 'In Flanders Fields'" (1916)

Oh! sleep in peace where poppies grow;
The torch your falling hands let go
Was caught by us, again held high,
A beacon light in Flanders sky
That dims the stars to those below.
You are our dead, you held the foe,
And ere the poppies cease to blow,
We'll prove our faith in you who lie
In Flanders Fields.

Oh! rest in peace, we quickly go
To you who bravely died, and know
In other fields was heard the cry,
For freedom's cause, of you who lie,
So still asleep where poppies grow,
In Flanders Fields.

As in rumbling sound, to and fro,
The lightning flashes, sky aglow,
The mighty hosts appear, and high
Above the din of battle cry,
Scarce heard amidst the guns below,
Are fearless hearts who fight the foe,
And guard the place where poppies grow.
Oh! sleep in peace, all you who lie
In Flanders Fields.

And still the poppies gently blow,
Between the crosses, row on row.
The larks, still bravely soaring high,
Are singing now their lullaby
To you who sleep where poppies grow
In Flanders Fields.

German troops in a trench on the Western Front, 1918.

J.A. Armstrong, "Another Reply to 'In Flanders Fields'" (1916)

In Flanders Fields the cannons boom,
And fitful flashes light the gloom;
While up above, like eagles, fly
The fierce destroyers of the sky;
With stains the earth wherein you lie
Is redder than the poppy bloom,
In Flanders Fields.
Sleep on, ye brave! The shrieking shell,
The quaking trench, the startling yell,
The fury of the battle hell
Shall wake you not, for all is well;
Sleep peacefully, for all is well.
Your flaming torch aloft we bear,
With burning heart and oath we swear
To keep the faith, to fight it through,
To crush the foe, or sleep with you,
In Flanders Fields.

Elizabeth Daryush, "Flanders Fields" (1916)

Here the scented daisy glows
Glorious as the carmined° rose; *reddened*
Here the hill-top's verdure mean
Fair is with unfading green;
Here, where sorrow still must tread,
All her graves are garlanded.

And still, O glad passer-by
Of the fields of agony,
Lower laughter's voice, and bare
Thy head in the valley where
Poppies bright and rustling wheat
Are a desert to love's feet.

Anonymous, "I Learned to Wash in Shell-Holes"

I learned to wash in shell-holes and to shave myself in tea,
While the fragments of a mirror did a balance on my knee;
I learned to dodge the whizzbangs[1] and the flying lumps of lead,
And to keep a foot of earth between the snipers and my head.

I learned to keep my haversack[2] well filled with buckshee[3] food,
To take my army issue and to pinch what else I could;
I learned to cook Maconochie[4] with candle ends and string,
With four-by-two[5] and sardine oil and any old darn thing.

I learned to use my bayonet according, as you please,
For a bread-knife or a chopper or a prong for toasting cheese;

[1] *whizzbangs* Shells fired by small-caliber, high-velocity German guns.

[2] *haversack* Stout canvas bag for carrying daily rations.

[3] *buckshee* Extra, spare.

[4] *Maconochie* Tinned vegetable stew (named after its inventor).

[5] *four-by-two* Rag for cleaning the barrel of a rifle.

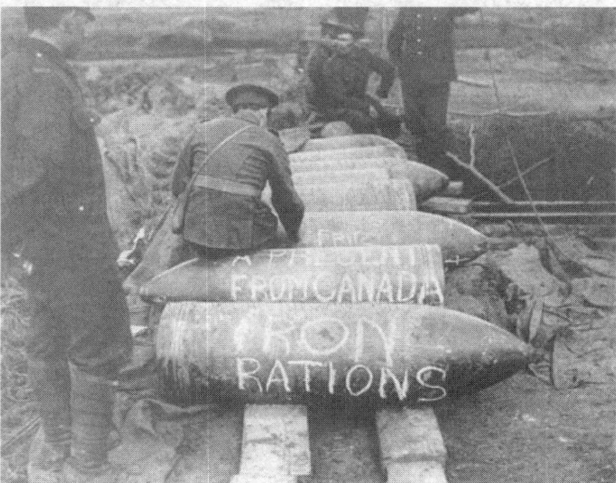

Shells inscribed by soldiers. (Imperial War Museum, London.)

I learned to gather souvenirs that home I hoped to send,
And hump them round for months and months and dump them in the end.

I never used to grumble after breakfast in the line
That the eggs were cooked too lightly or the bacon cut too fine;
I never told the sergeant just exactly what I thought;
I never did a pack-drill[6] for I never quite got caught.
I never stopped a whizzbang though I've stopped a lot of mud,
But the one that Fritz[7] sent over with my name on was a dud.

J.P. Long and Maurice Scott, "Oh! It's a Lovely War" (1917)

Up to your waist in water, up to your eyes in slush,
Using the kind of language that makes the sergeant blush,
Who wouldn't join the army? That's what we all enquire.
Don't we pity the poor civilians sitting beside the fire.

[6] *pack-drill* Form of drill used as punishment, in which soldiers had to march in full uniform while carrying a heavy pack.

[7] *Fritz* Nickname for a German soldier.

(*Chorus*)
Oh, oh, oh it's a lovely war.
Who wouldn't be a soldier, eh? Oh it's a shame to take the pay.
As soon as reveille[1] *has gone we feel just as heavy as lead,*
But we never get up till the sergeant brings our breakfast up to bed.
Oh, oh, oh it's a lovely war.
What do we want with eggs and ham when we've got plum and apple jam?
Form fours. Right turn. How shall we spend the money we earn?
Oh, oh, oh it's a lovely war.

When does a soldier grumble? When does he make a fuss?
No one is more contented in all the world than us.
Oh it's a cushy life, boys, really we love it so:
Once a fellow was sent on leave and simply refused to go.

Come to the cookhouse door, boys, sniff at the lovely stew.
Who is it says the colonel gets better grub than you?
Any complaints this morning? Do we complain? Not we.
What's the matter with lumps of onion floating around the tea?

A ship full of Australian and New Zealand troops on their way to the Turkish peninsula of Gallipoli in the summer of 1915. The Gallipoli offensive was disastrous. Winston Churchill (then First Lord of the Admiralty) had hoped Gallipoli would provide an alternative to the trench warfare of the sort endured in Flanders, but the offensive was doomed by poor planning, insufficient knowledge of the terrain, and an underestimation of the enemy's strength.

from Rebecca West, "The Cordite Makers" (1916)

The world was polished to brightness by an east wind when I visited the cordite[2] factory, and shone with hard colours like a German toy-landscape. The marshes were very green and the scattered waters very blue, and little white clouds roamed one by one across the sky like grazing sheep on a meadow. On the hills around stood elms, and grey churches and red farms and yellow ricks,[3] painted bright by the sharp sunshine. And very distinct on the marshes there lay the village which is always full of people, and yet is the home of nothing except death.

In the glare it showed that like so many institutions of the war it has the disordered and fantastic quality of a dream. It consists of a number of huts, some like the government-built cottages for Irish labourers, and some like the open-air shelters in a sanatorium, scattered over five hundred acres; they are connected by raised wooden gangways and interspersed with green mounds and rush ponds. It is of such vital importance to the State that it is ringed with barbed-wire entanglements and patrolled by sentries, and its products must have sent tens of thousands of our enemies to their death. And it is inhabited chiefly by pretty young girls clad in a Red-Riding-Hood fancy dress of khaki and scarlet.

Every morning at six, when the night mist still hangs over the marshes, 250 of these girls are fetched by a light railway from their barracks on a hill two miles away. When I visited the works they had already been at work

[1] *reveille* Morning drum beat or bugle call to wake the soldiers.
[2] *cordite* Type of smokeless explosive.
[3] *ricks* Haystacks.

for nine hours, and would work for three more. This twelve-hour shift is longer than one would wish, but it is not possible to introduce three shifts, since the girls would find an eight-hour day too light and would complain of being debarred from the opportunity of making more money; and it is not so bad as it sounds, for in these airy and isolated huts there is neither the orchestra of rattling machines nor the sense of a confined area crowded with tired people which make the ordinary factory such a fatiguing place. Indeed, these girls, working in teams of six or seven in those clean and tidy rooms, look as if they were practising a neat domestic craft rather than a deadly domestic process.…

But how deceptive this semblance of normal life is; what extraordinary work this is for women and how extraordinarily they are doing it, is made manifest in a certain row of huts where the cordite is being pressed through wire mesh. This, in all the world, must be the place where war and grace are closest linked. Without, a strip of garden runs beside the huts, gay with shrubs and formal with a sundial. Within there is a group of girls that composes into so beautiful a picture that one remembers that the most glorious painting in the world, Velasquez's[1] *The Weavers,* shows women working just like this.

One girl stands high on a platform against the wall, filling the cordite paste into one of the two great iron presses, and when she has finished with that she swings round the other one on a swivel with a fine free gesture. The other girls stand round the table laying out the golden cords in graduated sizes from the thickness of rope to the thinness of macaroni, the clear khaki and scarlet of their dresses shining back from the wet floor in a perpetually changing pattern as they move quickly about their work. They look very young in their pretty, childish dresses, and one thinks them good children for working so diligently. And it occurs to one as something incredible that they are now doing the last three hours of a twelve-hour shift.

If one asks the manager whether this zeal can possibly be normal, whether it is not perhaps the result of his presence, one is confronted by the awful phenomenon, beside which a waterspout or a volcano in eruption would be a little thing, of a manager talking about his employees with reverence. It seems that the girls work all day with a fury which mounts to a climax in the last three hours before the other 250 girls step into their places for the twelve-hour night shift. In these hours spies are sent out to walk along the verandah to see how the teams in the other huts are getting on, and their reports set the girls on to an orgy of competitive industry. Here again it was said that for attention, enthusiasm and discipline, there could not be better workmen than these girls.

There is matter connected with these huts, too, that showed the khaki and scarlet hoods to be no fancy dress, but a military uniform. They are a sign, for they have been dipped in a solution that makes them fireproof, that the girls are ready to face an emergency, which had arisen in those huts only a few days ago. There had been one of those incalculable happenings of which high explosives are so liable, an inflammatory mixture of air with acetone, and the cordite was ignited. Two huts were instantly gutted, and the girls had to walk out through the flame. In spite of the uniform one girl lost a hand. These, of course, are the everyday dangers of the high-explosives factory. There is very little to be feared by our enemies by land, and it is the sentries' grief and despair that their total bag for the eighteen months of their patrol of the marshes consists of one cow.

Surely, never before in modern history can women have lived a life so completely parallel to that of the regular Army. The girls who take up this work sacrifice almost as much as men who enlist; for although they make on an average 30*s*[2] a week they are working much harder than most of them, particularly the large number who were formerly domestic servants, would ever have dreamed of working in peacetime. And, although their colony of wooden huts has been well planned by their employers, and is pleasantly administered by the Young Women's Christian Association, it is, so far as severance of home-ties goes, barrack life. For although they are

[1] *Velasquez* Spanish painter Diego Velázquez (1599–1660).

[2] *s* Shillings.

allowed to go home for Sunday, travelling is difficult from this remote village, and the girls are so tired that most of them spend the day in bed.

And there are two things about the cordite village which the State ought never to forget, and which ought to be impressed upon the public mind by the bestowal of military rank upon the girls. First of all there is the cold fact that they face more danger every day than any soldier on home defence has seen since the beginning of the war. And secondly, there is the fact—and one wishes it could be expressed in terms of the saving of English and the losing of German life—that it is because of this army of cheerful and disciplined workers that this cordite factory has been able to increase its output since the beginning of the war by something over 1,500 per cent. It was all very well for the Army to demand high explosives, and for Mr. Lloyd George[1] to transmit the demand to industry; in the last resort the matter lay in the hands of the girls in the khaki and scarlet hoods, and the State owes them a very great debt for the way in which they have handled it.

Female workers at a Birmingham airplane factory in September 1918.

from Francis Marion Beynon, *Aleta Day* (1919)

The following excerpt is from Francis Marion Beynon's autobiographical novel *Aleta Day*, which recounts the heroine's childhood in a small town in Manitoba, Canada, and her subsequent love for a man who enlists when World War I begins. Beynon herself was a journalist known for her feminist views and her pacifism—a stance that lost her her job in 1917. This excerpt, however, expresses the idealism that permeated the nation in the months after the declaration of war, before the realities of trench warfare were realized.

from CHAPTER 24: WAR

Then the war came. It burst like a cloud upon our holidaying world, and set us all a-tremble and a-thrill.

Germany had broken the peace of the world and plunged us into night. Very well, we would collect a few Canadians and send them over and they would settle the matter in a few months and come home, and we would give them a banquet, and allow them to die in the poorhouse, as had been done to the heroes of other wars.

What days those were! An extra[2] every half-hour! War maps in every hand! A half mile towards Paris—gloom for two days! A great ship sunk—gloom for a week! Our hearts were sensitive to suffering then and the death of a hundred thousand men meant something to us. The blood reeked in our nostrils.

Yet for all that we [were] women, old men and cripples, how we did shout our patriotism from the housetops, so that nobody should miss our voice in the great songs.

What days those were!

The even tramp of troops along the streets! The morning call of the bugle! The thrill of an hourly

[1] *Mr. Lloyd George* David Lloyd George (1863–1945), British Prime Minister.

[2] *extra* Additional issue of a newspaper.

excitement! The awful torment of soul as one read of rivers full of dead bodies. Human bodies! It broke our hearts to read of men with their legs and arms blown off; with their faces shattered to pieces; men who would go on living under the most horrible physical limitations. That was early in the war before we had grown callous to the pain of other human beings.

And yet, mixed with our horror, there was a thrill, a feeling that something had really happened in our time.

What days those were!

Ivor Gurney, "To His Love" (1919)

Ivor Gurney (1890–1937) fought on the Western front from May 1916 to October 1917 (when he was poisoned by gas). He published two collections of war poems, as well as composing numerous songs and poetry on other subjects. He was increasingly affected by severe mental illness for which he spent the last fifteen years of his life hospitalized, but he continued to write prolifically until his death.

He's gone, and all our plans
Are useless indeed.
We'll walk no more on Cotswold[1]
Where the sheep feed
Quietly and take no heed.

His body that was so quick
Is not as you
Knew it, on Severn River
Under the blue
Driving our small boat through.

You would not know him now....
But still he died
Nobly, so cover him over
With violets of pride
Purple from Severn side.

Cover him, cover him soon!
And with thick-set
Masses of memoried flowers
Hide that red wet
Thing I must somehow forget.

Vance Palmer, "The Farmer Remembers the Somme" (1920)

Both Vance Palmer (1885–1959), who was better known as a writer of fiction than as a poet, and his wife, Nettie Palmer, a leading critic as well as a poet, played central roles in Australian cultural life from the 1920s through to the 1950s. Vance Palmer joined the Australian Army in 1918, but never saw active service.

Will they never fade or pass!
The mud, and the misty figures
endlessly coming
In file through the foul morass,° *marsh*
And the grey flood-water lipping the reeds and grass,
And the steel wings drumming.

The hills are bright in the sun:
There's nothing changed or marred in the well-known places;
When work for the day is done
There's talk, and quiet laughter, and gleams of fun
On the old folks' faces.

I have returned to these:
The farm, and the kindly Bush, and the young calves lowing;
But all that my mind sees
Is a quaking bog in a mist—stark, snapped trees,
and the dark Somme flowing.

[1] *Cotswold* Range of hills in western England.

11th Month NOVEMBER 1917	1917 NOVEMBER 30 Days
4 Sun—22nd after Trinity 5 Mon	8 Th
6 Tues—(Last Quarter, 3.2 p.m.	9 Fri
7 Wed	10 Sat—s. r. 7.10, s. s. 4.18

NEWLY-DUG TRENCHES. Apart from uniforms, there are times when soldiers have no chance of disguising their whereabouts from an enemy. A hastily-prepared trench may indicate your position more clearly than the brightest accoutrements.

Suppose, as in the sketch on opposite page, you have only just had time to throw up an entrenchment, the newly-turned earth, AA, will stand up in the shape of a very distinct wall against a green background, and so your enemy will quickly "spot" you.

A page from the *Soldier's Own Diary*, copies of which were widely distributed to troops during the war.

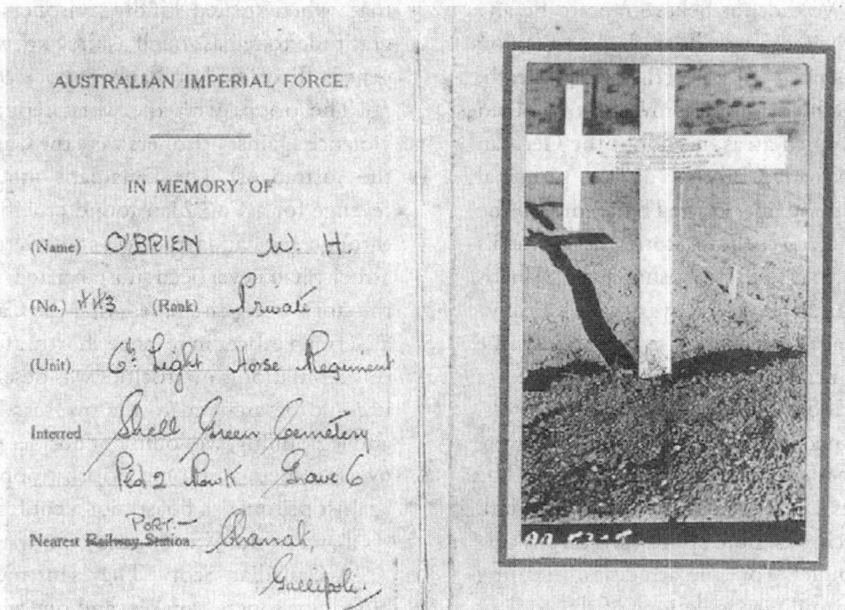

AUSTRALIAN IMPERIAL FORCE.

IN MEMORY OF

(Name) O'BRIEN W. H.

(No.) 443 (Rank) Private

(Unit) 6th Light Horse Regiment

Interred Shell Green Cemetery Plot 2 Row K Grave 6

Nearest ~~Railway Station~~ Port — Chanak, Gallipoli.

Memorial card for an Australian soldier killed and buried at Gallipoli. After the war, when the process of gathering the remains of soldiers and of constructing cemeteries began, Gallipoli became the final resting place for many New Zealand and Australian soldiers. Because most families could not arrange a visit to their loved one's grave, pictures were supplied to these families upon request.

from Robert Graves, *Good-Bye to All That* (1929, revised 1957)

from CHAPTER 17

We[1] once discussed which were the cleanest troops in trenches, taken by nationalities. We agreed on a descending-order list like this: English and German Protestants; Northern Irish, Welsh and Canadians; Irish and German Catholics; Scots, with certain higher-ranking exceptions; Mohammedan Indians; Algerians; Portuguese; Belgians; French. We put the Belgians and French there for spite; they could not have been dirtier than the Algerians and the Portuguese.

Propaganda reports of atrocities were, it was agreed, ridiculous. We remembered that while the Germans *could* commit atrocities against enemy civilians, Germany itself, except for an early Russian cavalry raid, had never had the enemy on her soil. We no longer believed the highly-coloured accounts of German atrocities in Belgium; knowing the Belgians now at first-hand. By atrocities we meant, specifically, rape, mutilation and torture—not summary shootings of suspected spies, harbourers of spies, *francs-tireurs*,[2] or disobedient local officials. If the atrocity-list had to include the accidental-on-purpose bombing or machine-gunning of civilians from the air, the Allies were now committing as many atrocities as the Germans. French and Belgian civilians had often tried to win our sympathy by exhibiting mutilations of children—stumps of hands and feet, for instance—representing them as deliberate, fiendish atrocities when, as likely as not, they were merely the

[1] *We* Graves, who was an officer in the Royal Welch Fusiliers, is here recounting his discussions with other British officers.

[2] *francs-tireurs* French: irregular soldiers.

result of shell-fire. We did not believe rape to be any more common on the German side of the line than on the Allied side. And since a bully-beef diet, fear of death, and absence of wives made ample provision of women necessary in the occupied areas, no doubt the German Army authorities provided brothels in the principal French towns behind the line, as the French did on the Allied side. We did not believe stories of women's forcible enlistment in these establishments. "What's wrong with the voluntary system?" we asked cynically.

As for atrocities against soldiers—where should one draw the line? The British soldier, at first, regarded as atrocious the use of bowie-knives[1] by German patrols. After a time, he learned to use them himself; they were cleaner killing weapons than revolvers or bombs. The Germans regarded as equally atrocious the British Mark VII rifle-bullet, which was more apt to turn on striking than the German bullet. For true atrocities, meaning personal rather than military violations of the code of war, few opportunities occurred—except in the interval between the surrender of prisoners and their arrival (or non-arrival) at Headquarters. Advantage was only too often taken of this opportunity. Nearly every instructor in the Mess could quote specific instances of prisoners having been murdered on the way back. The commonest motives were, it seems, revenge for the death of friends or relatives, jealousy of the prisoner's trip to a comfortable prison camp in England, military enthusiasm, fear of being suddenly overpowered by the prisoners or, more simply, impatience with the escorting job. In any of these cases the conductors would report on arrival at Headquarters that a German shell had killed the prisoners; and no questions would be asked. We had every reason to believe that the same thing happened on the German side, where prisoners, as useless mouths to feed in a country already short of rations, would be even less welcome. None of us had heard of German prisoners being more than threatened at Headquarters to get military information from them. The sort that they could give was not of sufficient importance to make torture worth while; and anyhow, it had been found that, when treated kindly, prisoners were anxious in gratitude to tell as much as they knew. German intelligence officers had probably discovered that too.

The troops with the worst reputation for acts of violence against prisoners were the Canadians (and later the Australians). The Canadians' motive was said to be revenge for a Canadian found crucified with bayonets through his hands and feet in a German trench. This atrocity had never been substantiated; nor did we believe the story, freely circulated, that the Canadians crucified a German officer in revenge shortly afterwards. How far this reputation for atrocities was deserved, and how far it could be ascribed to the overseas habit of bragging and leg-pulling, we could not decide. At all events, most overseas men, and some British troops, made atrocities against prisoners a boast, not a confession.

Later in the War, I heard two first-hand accounts.

A Canadian-Scot: "They sent me back with three bloody prisoners, you see, and one started limping and groaning, so I had to keep on kicking the sod down the trench. He was an officer. It was getting dark and I felt fed up, so I thought: 'I'll have a bit of a game.' I had them covered with the officer's revolver and made 'em open their pockets without turning round. Then I dropped a Mills bomb[2] in each, with the pin out, and ducked behind a traverse. Bang, bang, bang! No more bloody prisoners. No good Fritzes[3] but dead 'uns."

An Australian: "Well, the biggest lark I had was at Morlancourt, when we took it the first time. There were a lot of Jerries[4] in a cellar, and I said to 'em: 'Come out, you Camarades!' So out they came, a dozen of 'em, with their hands up. 'Turn out your pockets,' I told 'em. They turned 'em out. Watches, and gold and stuff, all dinkum.[5] Then I said: 'Now back to your cellar, you sons of bitches!' For I couldn't be bothered with 'em. When they were all safely down I threw half a dozen Mills bombs in after 'em. I'd got the stuff all right, and we weren't taking prisoners that day."

[1] *bowie-knives* Curved, double-edged knives of about 15 inches in length.

[2] *Mills bomb* Type of hand grenade made to form shrapnel on explosion.

[3] *Fritzes* Nickname for German soldiers.

[4] *Jerries* Nickname for German soldiers.

[5] *dinkum* Australian slang: genuine, authentic.

An old woman at Cardonette on the Somme gave me my first-hand account of large-scale atrocities. I was billeted with her in July 1916. Close to her home, a battalion of French Turcos[1] overtook the rear-guard of a German division retreating from the Marne in September 1914. The Turcos surprised the dead-weary Germans while still marching in column. The old woman went, with gestures, through the pantomime of slaughter, and ended: "*Et enfin, ces animaux leur ont arraché les oreilles et les ont mis à la poche!*"[2] …

We discussed the continuity of regimental morale. A captain in a Line battalion of a Surrey regiment said: "Our battalion has never recovered from the first Battle of Ypres. What's wrong is that we have a rotten depot. The drafts are bad, and so we get a constant re-infection." He told me one night in our sleeping hut: "In both the last two shows I had to shoot a man of my company to get the rest out of the trench. It was so bloody awful, I couldn't stand it. That's why I applied to be sent down here." This was the truth, not the usual loose talk that one heard at the base. I felt sorrier for him than for any other man I met in France. He deserved a better regiment.

The boast of every good battalion was that it had never lost a trench; both our Line battalions made it—meaning, that they had never been forced out of a trench without recapturing it before the action ended. Capturing a German trench and being unable to hold it for lack of reinforcements did not count; nor did retirement by order from Headquarters, or when the battalion next door had broken and left a flank in the air. And, towards the end of the War, trenches could be honourably abandoned as being wholly obliterated by bombardment, or because not really trenches at all, but a line of selected shell-craters.

We all agreed on the value of arms-drill as a factor in morale. "Arms-drill as it should be done," someone said, "is beautiful, especially when the company feels itself as a single being, and each movement is not a synchronized movement of every man together, but the single movement of one large creature." I used to get big bunches of Canadians to drill: four or five hundred at a time. Spokesmen stepped forward once and asked what sense there was in sloping and ordering arms, and fixing and unfixing bayonets. They said they had come across to fight, and not to guard Buckingham Palace. I told them that in every division of the four in which I had served—the First, Second, Seventh and Eighth—there had been three different kinds of troops. Those that had guts but were no good at drill; those that were good at drill but had no guts; and those that had guts and were good at drill. These last, for some reason or other, fought by far the best when it came to a show—I didn't know why, and I didn't care. I told them that when they were better at fighting than the Guards they could perhaps afford to neglect their arms-drill.

We often theorized in the Mess about drill. I held that the best drill never resulted from being bawled at by a sergeant-major: that there must be perfect respect between the man who gives the order and the men who carry it out. The test of drill came, I said, when the officer gave an incorrect word of command. If his company could, without hesitation, carry out the order intended or, if the order happened to be impossible, could stand absolutely still, or continue marching, without confusion in the ranks, that was good drill. Some instructors regarded the corporate spirit that resulted from drilling together as leading to loss of initiative in the men drilled.

Others argued that it acted just the other way round: "Suppose a section of men with rifles get isolated from the rest of the company, without an N.C.O.[3] in charge, and meet a machine-gun. Under the stress of danger this section will have that all-one-body feeling of drill, and obey an imaginary word of command. There may be no communication between its members, but there will be a drill movement, with two men naturally opening fire on the machine-gun while the remainder work round, part on the left flank and part on the right; and the final rush will be simultaneous. Leadership is supposed to be the perfection for which drill has been instituted. That's

[1] *French Turcos* Algerians serving in the French infantry.

[2] *Et enfin … poche* French: And finally, these animals tore off their ears [i.e., the ears of their prisoners] and put them in their pockets.

[3] *N.C.O.* Non-commissioned officer.

wrong. Leadership is only the first stage. Perfection of drill is communal action. Though drill may seem to be antiquated parade-ground stuff, it's the foundation of tactics and musketry. Parade-ground musketry won all the battles in our regimental histories; this War, which is unlikely to open out, and must end with the collapse, by 'attrition,' of one side or the other, will be won by parade-ground tactics—by the simple drill tactics of small units fighting in limited spaces, and in noise and confusion so great that leadership is quite impossible." Despite variance on this point we all agreed that regimental pride remained the strongest moral force that kept a battalion going as an effective fighting unit; contrasting it particularly with patriotism and religion.

Patriotism, in the trenches, was too remote a sentiment, and at once rejected as fit only for civilians, or prisoners. A new arrival who talked patriotism would soon be told to cut it out. As "Blighty,"[1] a geographical concept, Great Britain was a quiet, easy place for getting back to out of the present foreign misery; but as a nation it included not only the trench-soldiers themselves and those who had gone home wounded, but the staff, Army Service Corps, lines-of-communication troops, base units, home-service units, and all civilians down to the detested grades of journalists, profiteers, "starred" men exempted from enlistment, conscientious objectors, and members of the Government. The trench-soldier, with this carefully graded caste-system of honour, never considered that the Germans opposite might have built up exactly the same system themselves. He thought of Germany as a nation in arms, a unified nation inspired with the sort of patriotism that he himself despised. He believed most newspaper reports on conditions and sentiments in Germany, though believing little or nothing of what he read about similar conditions and sentiments in England. Yet he never under-rated the German as a soldier. Newspaper libels on Fritz's courage and efficiency were resented by all trench-soldiers of experience.

Women celebrating on Armistice Day, London, 1918.

Hardly one soldier in a hundred was inspired by religious feeling of even the crudest kind. It would have been difficult to remain religious in the trenches even if one had survived the irreligion of the training battalion at home. A regular sergeant at Montagne, a Second Battalion man, had recently told me that he did not hold with religion in time of war. He said that the "niggers" (meaning the Indians) were right in officially relaxing their religious rules while fighting. "And all this damn nonsense, Sir—excuse me, Sir—that we read in the papers, Sir, about how miraculous it is that the wayside crucifixes are always getting shot at, but the figure of our Lord Jesus somehow don't get hurt, it fairly makes me sick, Sir." This was his explanation why, when giving practice fire-orders from the hill-top, he had shouted, unaware that I stood behind him: "Seven hundred, half left, bloke on cross, five rounds, concentrate, FIRE!" And why, for "concentrate," he had humorously substituted "consecrate." His platoon, including the two unusual "Bible-wallahs" whose letters home always began in the same formal way: "Dear Sister in Christ," or "Dear Brother in Christ," blazed away.

[1] *Blighty* England; home.

William Butler Yeats

1865 – 1939

In *On Poetry and Poets* (1957), fellow poet and contemporary T.S. Eliot wrote of William Butler Yeats: "Born into a world in which the doctrine of 'Art for Art's Sake' was generally accepted, and living on into one in which art has been asked to be instrumental to social purposes, he held firmly to the right view which is between these, though not in any way a compromise between them, and showed that an artist, by serving his art with entire integrity, is at the same time rendering the greatest service he can to his own nation and to the whole world." In truth, few poets of the twentieth century have contributed as much to the cultural, political, and social framework of Ireland—or to British literature in general. An analysis of Yeats's poetry, however, is impossible without understanding the deeply personal and biographical nature of his writing, and Yeats's own endeavor to shape his entire canon of work into a unified body of art.

William Butler Yeats was born in the Dublin suburb of Sandymount on 13 June 1865. His father, John Butler Yeats, had given up law to take up portrait painting, a decision that, though artistically and intellectually stimulating, led to many years of uprooted existence and strained finances for his family. When William was two, the family moved to London, yet much of his childhood was spent moving between schooling in London and retreats to the family home of his mother, Susan Pollexfen, in County Sligo, Ireland. In County Sligo, Yeats would find inspiration in the beauty of the countryside, the local folklore, and Irish tradition. In 1880, the family returned permanently to Ireland and settled in Howth, close to Dublin. In 1883, having completed high school, Yeats decided to become an artist and enrolled in the Metropolitan School of Art, but he soon left to pursue his true passion, poetry. His first published poems appeared in the *Dublin University Review* in 1885; three years later he wrote "The Lake Isle of Innisfree" (first published in 1890), which established his reputation as a poet of powerful emotions deeply rooted in Irish tradition and in the Irish landscape.

Also at an early age, influenced by his father's religious skepticism, Yeats developed a strong interest in occultism, folklore, and theosophism, a system of philosophical thought based on the direct and immediate experience of the divine. In 1885 he joined with friends to form the Dublin Hermetic Society, a group devoted to discussion of occult sciences and pseudo-sciences of the day. This group was predominantly influenced by a more famous mystical society, The Theosophical Society, founded in New York by Madame Helena Blavatsky. In 1887, Yeats met with Madame Blavatsky and later joined the Esoteric section of the London chapter of The Theosophical Society. In 1890, Yeats left the Society to join the Hermetic Order of the Golden Dawn, an occult society that drew upon astrology, tarot, kabbala, and Eastern mysticism for its teachings. Throughout his life and career, Yeats would turn to mythology and the occult as tools for developing his own vision of history and imagination. In much of his poetry, this vision is evident in an elaborate system of images and symbols that Yeats would continually investigate and refine.

In 1889 Yeats's first collection, *The Wanderings of Oisin and Other Poems*, was published. The collection was well received, but the attention of one reader in particular would lead to what Yeats would term "the troubling of my life." The beautiful actor and Irish nationalist Maud Gonne was introduced to Yeats by a mutual friend, John O'Leary, shortly after the collection was published. The meeting marked a fateful moment in the life of Yeats, as Gonne would become his obsession for the next quarter-century, and his poetry would resonate with his love and despair for her in poems such as "No Second Troy" (1910) and "A Prayer for My Daughter" (1921). She also helped to inspire him in two new cultural endeavors: the establishment of an Irish national theater and the development of a public voice for the Irish nationalist movement for independence.

Through the 1890s Yeats continued to gain literary prominence with further collections of poetry—among them *The Rose* (1893) and *Poems* (1895)—as well as anthologies, works of prose fiction, and studies of Irish folklore and fairy tales. The vivid lushness that characterizes much of Yeats's early poetry reaches a high point with poems such as "The Secret Rose" in the 1899 collection *The Wind Among the Reeds*.

In 1896 Yeats met Lady Augusta Gregory, a fellow writer and promoter of Irish literature, who invited him to stay in her country house at Coole Park. Her influence also contributed to Yeats's involvement in the founding of the Irish National Theatre in 1899. In writing for the theater, Yeats found a new voice for his interest in mythology, mysticism, and Irish nationalism. In 1904, the Irish National Theatre's permanent home, The Abbey Theatre, opened with Yeats's play *On Baile's Strand*. As the Abbey's director and dramatist, Yeats helped develop it into one of the world's leading theaters and, perhaps more importantly to him, into the center of the Irish literary renaissance.

The publication of *The Green Helmet and Other Poems* in 1910 marks Yeats's transition into the second phase of his poetic career. Where his early poems often offered romantic melancholy and idyllic meditations on pagan themes, the poetry of this second phase became more direct in its analysis of the events and attitudes of the period. As Yeats became embittered by the small-minded nationalism of The Abbey's middle-class audiences, and as he watched with horror the growing violence in the struggle for Irish independence, he began to write poems such as "Easter 1916" and "Nineteen Hundred and Nineteen," reflecting his distrust of popular judgment and concern for the future of his country.

At the same time, Yeats continued to develop his complex system of symbolism and esoteric theories regarding the movement of history and human intellect. In 1917, having exhausted his proposals to Maud Gonne and also having made an unsuccessful proposal to Gonne's daughter Iseult, Yeats married Georgie Hyde-Lees, whom he had met in 1911. On their honeymoon, Hyde-Lees delighted Yeats with her gift for automatic writing (believed by Yeats to be dictated by spirits), and for several years her writings inspired Yeats to refine his symbolic system, as described in his book *A Vision* (1925). Although Yeats's later poetry is by no means unintelligible without an understanding of *A Vision*, many of his poems refer directly to the patterns and imagery examined within its pages. According to Yeats, the progress of art and thought is directly interwoven through the spirals, or gyres, of human history, represented in *A Vision* by two interpenetrating cones that make up antithetical cycles of 2000 years. These ideas became increasingly evident in his poetic works, particularly later poems such as "Byzantium" and "Sailing to Byzantium."

In 1922 Yeats was elected Senator of the Irish Free State; a year later, he was awarded the Nobel Prize for Literature, becoming the first Irish writer to receive the award. Yeats continued to produce major poetry well into his later years. As his health began to decline, his poetry took on a defiant tone, reflecting an awareness of his own mortality. Poems of this period, such as "Lapis Lazuli" and "The Circus Animals' Desertion," rage against old age while reflecting on his life and body of work. Poems published in *The Tower* (1928), *The Winding Stair* (1933), and *Last Poems* (1939) are thought by many critics to be among his finest.

Following a long period of heart trouble, Yeats died on 28 January 1939; he was buried in Roquebrune, France, where he had been spending the winter. In 1948, his remains were reinterred, as he had wished, in Drumcliff, County Sligo. Also according to his wishes, his epitaph is taken from "Under Ben Bulben": "Cast a cold eye / On life, on death. / Horseman, pass by!"

⌘⌘⌘

The Lake Isle of Innisfree[1]

I will arise and go now, and go to Innisfree,
And a small cabin build there, of clay and wattles[2] made;
Nine bean-rows will I have there, a hive for the honey bee,
And live alone in the bee-loud glade.

And I shall have some peace there, for peace comes dropping slow,
Dropping from the veils of the morning to where the cricket sings;
There midnight's all a glimmer, and noon a purple glow,
And evening full of the linnet's° wings. *small songbird's*

I will arise and go now, for always night and day
I hear lake water lapping with low sounds by the shore;
While I stand on the roadway, or on the pavements grey,
I hear it in the deep heart's core.
—1890

[1] *Lake Isle of Innisfree* A small island in Lough Gill, County Sligo; Innisfree (*Inis Fraoigh* in Gaelic) means "Heather Island."

[2] *wattles* Poles and reeds interwoven to create a thatched wall or roof.

When You Are Old[3]

When you are old and gray and full of sleep,
And nodding by the fire, take down this book,
And slowly read, and dream of the soft look
Your eyes had once, and of their shadows deep;

How many loved your moments of glad grace,
And loved your beauty with love false or true,
But one man loved the pilgrim soul in you,
And loved the sorrows of your changing face;

And bending down beside the glowing bars,
Murmur, a little sadly, how Love fled
And paced upon the mountains overhead
And hid his face amid a crowd of stars.
—1892

The Secret Rose[4]

Far-off, most secret, and inviolate Rose,
Enfold me in my hour of hours; where those
Who sought thee in the Holy Sepulchre,[5]
Or in the wine vat, dwell beyond the stir

[3] *When You Are Old* Based on one of Pierre de Ronsard's (1524–85) *Sonnets pour Hélène*, "*Quand vous serez bien vieille, au soir, à la chandelle,*" which translates to: "When you are very old, sitting by the candlelight at night."

[4] *The Secret Rose* First published under the title "O'Sullivan Rua to the Secret Rose."

[5] *Holy Sepulchre* Cave in which Jesus Christ's body was placed before his resurrection.

And tumult of defeated dreams; and deep
Among pale eyelids, heavy with the sleep
Men have named beauty. Thy great leaves enfold
The ancient beards, the helms of ruby and gold
Of the crowned Magi;[1] and the king whose eyes
Saw the Pierced Hands and Rood° of elder rise *cross*
In druid vapour and make the torches dim;
Till vain frenzy awoke and he died;[2] and him
Who met Fand walking among flaming dew
By a grey shore where the wind never blew,
And lost the world and Emer for a kiss;[3]
And him who drove the gods out of their liss,[4]
And till a hundred morns had flowered red,
Feasted, and wept the barrows° of his dead; *grave mounds*
And the proud dreaming king who flung the crown
And sorrow away, and calling bard and clown
Dwelt among wine-stained wanderers in deep woods:[5]
And him who sold tillage,° and house, *farmland*
and goods,
And sought through lands and islands numberless years,
Until he found with laughter and with tears,
A woman, of so shining loveliness
That men threshed corn at midnight by a tress,° *lock of hair*
A little stolen tress.[6] I, too, await
The hour of thy great wind of love and hate.
When shall the stars be blown about the sky,
Like the sparks blown out of a smithy,° *blacksmith's forge*
and die?
Surely thine hour has come, thy great wind blows,
Far-off, most secret, and inviolate Rose?
—1896

No Second Troy[7]

Why should I blame her[8] that she filled my days
With misery, or that she would of late[9]
Have taught to ignorant men most violent ways,
Or hurled the little streets upon the great,
Had they but courage equal to desire?
What could have made her peaceful with a mind
That nobleness made simple as a fire,
With beauty like a tightened bow, a kind
That is not natural in an age like this,
Being high and solitary and most stern?
Why, what could she have done being what she is?
Was there another Troy for her to burn?
—1910

[1] *Magi* Three wise men who came from the East to bring gifts to the baby Jesus.

[2] *the king … he died* King Conchobar, who was said to have the same birth date and death date as Jesus Christ. Conchobar had an object embedded in his head, an injury from a past battle; when he was told of Christ's execution, he grew so angry that the object burst out of his skull and he died. Here, Yeats imagines Conchobar witnessing the crucifixion in a vision brought by Druids, priests of Celtic religion. Yeats identifies this and the poem's other references to Irish myth and folktale in an extensive note accompanying some editions of the poem.

[3] *and him … a kiss* In Irish myth, the great hero Cúchulainn became a lover to the goddess Fand and accompanied her to the otherworld, leaving his wife Emer.

[4] *And him … their liss* Caoilte, a hero of Irish legend. Seized by rage after almost all of his friends were killed in a battle, he drove the nearby gods out of their home; *liss* Circular fort common in iron-age Ireland.

[5] *And the proud … deep woods* Legendary Irish king Fergus. According to Yeats, he fell so deeply in love with a woman that he was motivated to give up his throne to her son Conchobar, and he spent the rest of his days feasting and hunting in the forest.

[6] *And him who sold … stolen tress* Reference to an Irish folktale in which a working man, while traveling on the road in the dark, discovers a box containing a brightly glowing lock of hair. He uses it as a lamp to work at night until the king learns of the hair and sends him to find the woman to whom it belongs.

[7] *Troy* During the Trojan War, the Greeks besieged and destroyed the city of Troy in an effort to retrieve Helen, who had been abducted by the Trojan, Paris, from her husband, the Greek Menelaus.

[8] *her* Maud Gonne.

[9] *of late* Gonne ceased her political work in 1905.

Easter 1916 [1]

I have met them at close of day
Coming with vivid faces
From counter or desk among grey
Eighteenth-century houses.
I have passed with a nod of the head
Or polite meaningless words,
Or have lingered awhile and said
Polite meaningless words,
And thought before I had done
Of a mocking tale or a gibe
To please a companion
Around the fire at the club,
Being certain that they and I
But lived where motley° is worn: *jester's costume*
All changed, changed utterly:
A terrible beauty is born.

That woman's days were spent
In ignorant good-will,
Her nights in argument
Until her voice grew shrill.[2]
What voice more sweet than hers
When, young and beautiful,
She rode to harriers?
This man had kept a school
And rode our wingèd horse;[3]
This other his helper and friend[4]
Was coming into his force;
He might have won fame in the end,
So sensitive his nature seemed,
So daring and sweet his thought.
This other man I had dreamed
A drunken, vainglorious lout.[5]
He had done most bitter wrong
To some who are near my heart,
Yet I number him in the song;
He, too, has resigned his part
In the casual comedy;
He, too, has been changed in his turn,
Transformed utterly:
A terrible beauty is born.

Hearts with one purpose alone
Through summer and winter seem
Enchanted to a stone
To trouble the living stream.
The horse that comes from the road,
The rider, the birds that range
From cloud to tumbling cloud,
Minute by minute they change;
A shadow of cloud on the stream
Changes minute by minute;
A horse-hoof slides on the brim,
And a horse plashes within it;
The long-legged moor-hens dive,
And hens to moor-cocks call;
Minute by minute they live:
The stone's in the midst of all.

Too long a sacrifice
Can make a stone of the heart.
O when may it suffice?
That is Heaven's part, our part
To murmur name upon name,

[1] *Easter 1916* On Easter Monday, 24 April 1916, Irish nationalists instigated an unsuccessful rebellion against the British government (which was then at war with Germany); the Easter rebellion lasted until 29 April. Many of the Irish nationalist leaders were executed that May.

[2] *That woman's … shrill* Countess Markiewicz, née Constance Gore-Booth (1868–1927), played a central role in the Easter Rebellion; she was arrested and sentenced to death (though the death sentence was later commuted). Yeats later wrote a poem about her and her Irish-nationalist sister, "In Memory of Eva Gore-Booth and Con Markiewicz" (1929).

[3] *This man … wingèd horse* Pádraic Pearse (1879–1916) founded St. Enda's School near Dublin. He was a leader in the effort to revive the Gaelic language, and wrote both Irish and English poetry; the "wingèd horse" refers to Pegasus, the horse of the Muses.

[4] *This other his helper and friend* Thomas MacDonagh (1878–1916), an Irish poet and playwright who also taught school.

[5] *vainglorious lout* Major John MacBride (1865–1916), estranged husband of Irish nationalist Maud Gonne; their separation just two years after marriage was due in part to his drinking bouts.

As a mother names her child
When sleep at last has come
On limbs that had run wild.
What is it but nightfall?
No, no, not night but death;
Was it needless death after all?
For England may keep faith
For all that is done and said.[1]
We know their dream; enough
To know they dreamed and are dead;
And what if excess of love
Bewildered them till they died?
I write it out in a verse—
MacDonagh and MacBride
And Connolly[2] and Pearse[3]
Now and in time to be,
Wherever green is worn,
Are changed, changed utterly:
A terrible beauty is born.
—1916

The Wild Swans at Coole[4]

The trees are in their autumn beauty,
The woodland paths are dry,
Under the October twilight the water
Mirrors a still sky;
Upon the brimming water among the stones
Are nine-and-fifty swans.

The nineteenth autumn[5] has come upon me
Since I first made my count;
I saw, before I had well finished,
All suddenly mount
And scatter wheeling in great broken rings
Upon their clamorous wings.

I have looked upon those brilliant creatures,
And now my heart is sore.
All's changed since I, hearing at twilight,
The first time on this shore,
The bell-beat of their wings above my head,
Trod with a lighter tread.

Unwearied still, lover by lover,
They paddle in the cold
Companionable streams or climb the air;
Their hearts have not grown old;
Passion or conquest, wander where they will,
Attend upon them still.

But now they drift on the still water,
Mysterious, beautiful;
Among what rushes will they build,
By what lake's edge or pool
Delight men's eyes, when I awake some day
To find they have flown away?
—1917

In Memory of Major Robert Gregory[6]

I

Now that we're almost settled in our house[7]
I'll name the friends that cannot sup with us
Beside a fire of turf[8] in th' ancient tower,
And having talked to some late hour
Climb up the narrow winding stair to bed:

[1] *For England … said* England had originally granted Ireland Home Rule in 1913, but then postponed it due to World War I, promising to institute it after the war.

[2] *Connolly* James Connolly (1868–1916), Irish Socialist.

[3] *MacDonagh … Pearse* All four men were executed for their involvement in the Easter Uprising of 1916.

[4] *Coole* Coole Park, County Galway estate of Lady Gregory, friend and patron of Yeats.

[5] *nineteenth autumn* Yeats first visited Coole Park in 1897, nineteen years before he wrote this poem.

[6] [Yeats's note] Major Robert Gregory [Lady Gregory's only son (1881–1918)], R.F.C. [Royal Flying Corps], M.C. [Military Cross], Legion of Honour, was killed in action on the Italian Front, January 23, 1918.

[7] *our house* Yeats had bought a section of Lady Gregory's estate at Coole Park; Thoor Ballylee, an ancient Norman tower situated there, became his home.

[8] *turf* Dried peat used for fuel.

Discoverers of forgotten truth
Or mere companions of my youth,
All, all are in my thoughts tonight being dead.

2

Always we'd have the new friend meet the old
And we are hurt if either friend seem cold,
And there is salt to lengthen out the smart
In the affections of our heart,
And quarrels are blown up upon that head;
But not a friend that I would bring
This night can set us quarrelling,
For all that come into my mind are dead.

3

Lionel Johnson[1] comes the first to mind,
That loved his learning better than mankind,
Though courteous to the worst; much falling he
Brooded upon sanctity
Till all his Greek and Latin learning seemed
A long blast upon the horn that brought
A little nearer to his thought
A measureless consummation that he dreamed.

4

And that enquiring man John Synge[2] comes next,
That dying chose the living world for text
And never could have rested in the tomb
But that, for long travelling, he had come
Towards nightfall upon certain set apart
In a most desolate stony place,[3]
Towards nightfall upon a race
Passionate and simple like his heart.

5

And then I think of old George Pollexfen,[4]
In muscular youth well known to Mayo[5] men
For horsemanship at meets or at racecourses,
That could have shown how pure-bred horses
And solid men, for all their passion, live
But as the outrageous stars incline
By opposition, square and trine;[6]
Having grown sluggish and contemplative.

6

They were my close companions many a year,
A portion of my mind and life, as it were,
And now their breathless faces seem to look
Out of some old picture-book;
I am accustomed to their lack of breath,
But not that my dear friend's dear son,
Our Sidney[7] and our perfect man,
Could share in that discourtesy of death.

7

For all things the delighted eye now sees
Were loved by him; the old storm-broken trees
That cast their shadows upon road and bridge;
The tower set on the stream's edge;
The ford where drinking cattle make a stir
Nightly, and startled by that sound
The water-hen must change her ground;
He might have been your heartiest welcomer.

8

When with the Galway foxhounds he would ride
From Castle Taylor to the Roxborough side
Or Esserkelly plain, few kept his pace;
At Mooneen[8] he had leaped a place
So perilous that half the astonished meet
Had shut their eyes; and where was it
He rode a race without a bit?
And yet his mind outran the horses' feet.

[1] *Lionel Johnson* English poet and scholar (1867–1902).

[2] *John Synge* Irish playwright (1871–1909), co-director, along with Yeats and Lady Gregory, of the Abbey Theatre.

[3] *set apart … place* Synge had set some of his plays in the Aran Islands, off the west coast of Ireland.

[4] *George Pollexfen* Yeats's maternal uncle, an astrologer.

[5] *Mayo* County north of Galway.

[6] *opposition, square and trine* Astrological terms used to describe angles between heavenly bodies.

[7] *Sidney* Elizabethan poet Sir Philip Sidney (1554–86), who, like Robert Gregory, was an artist and scholar who died young in battle.

[8] *Castle … Mooneen* Country manors in the County of Galway: Roxborough was Lady Gregory's childhood home; Moneen is beside Esserkelly, which is near Ardrahan in County Galway.

9

We dreamed that a great painter had been born
To cold Clare[1] rock and Galway rock and thorn,
To that stern colour and that delicate line
That are our secret discipline
Wherein the gazing heart doubles her might.
Soldier, scholar, horseman, he,
And yet he had the intensity
To have published all to be a world's delight.

10

What other could so well have counselled us
In all lovely intricacies of a house
As he that practised or that understood
All work in metal or in wood,
In moulded plaster or in carven stone?
Soldier, scholar, horseman, he,
And all he did done perfectly
As though he had but that one trade alone.

11

Some burn faggots,° others may consume *bundles of twigs*
The entire combustible world in one small room
As though dried straw, and if we turn about
The bare chimney is gone black out
Because the work had finished in that flare.
Soldier, scholar, horseman, he,
As 'twere all life's epitome,
What made us dream that he could comb grey hair?

12

I had thought, seeing how bitter is that wind
That shakes the shutter, to have brought to mind
All those that manhood tried, or childhood loved
Or boyish intellect approved,
With some appropriate commentary on each;
Until imagination brought
A fitter welcome; but a thought
Of that late death took all my heart for speech.
—1918

[1] *Clare* County to the south of Galway.

Nineteen Hundred and Nineteen[2]

I

Many ingenious lovely things are gone
That seemed sheer miracle to the multitude,
Protected from the circle of the moon
That pitches common things about. There stood
Amid the ornamental bronze and stone
An ancient image made of olive wood[3]—
And gone are Phidias' famous ivories[4]
And all the golden grasshoppers and bees.[5]

We too had many pretty toys when young;
A law indifferent to blame or praise,
To bribe or threat; habits that made old wrong
Melt down, as it were wax in the sun's rays;
Public opinion ripening for so long
We thought it would outlive all future days.
O what fine thought we had because we thought
That the worst rogues and rascals had died out.

All teeth were drawn, all ancient tricks unlearned,
And a great army but a showy thing;
What matter that no cannon had been turned
Into a ploughshare?[6] Parliament and king
Thought that unless a little powder burned
The trumpeters might burst with trumpeting
And yet it lack all glory; and perchance
The guardsmen's drowsy chargers would not prance.

[2] *Nineteen Hundred and Nineteen* 1919 was a year of increasing armed confrontation between the Irish Republican Army and the Irish government, which was controlled by Britain.

[3] *ancient … wood* Statue of Athena, patron goddess of Athens, was carved out of the wood of the sacred olive tree and stood on the Acropolis; the statue was later destroyed in a fire.

[4] *Phidias' famous ivories* Phidias (sometimes spelled "Pheidias" or "Phideas," c. 500–c. 432 BCE) was a celebrated Greek sculptor who created an ivory- and gold-encrusted statue of Athena (since destroyed) in the Parthenon.

[5] *golden grasshoppers and bees* Offerings to the gods in the form of golden trinkets; Thucydides wrote of the Athenian custom of tying up a lock of hair with a golden grasshopper.

[6] *no cannon … ploughshare* Cf. Isaiah 2.4: "They shall beat their swords into plowshares … nation shall not lift up sword against nation, neither shall they learn war anymore."

Now days are dragon-ridden, the nightmare
Rides upon sleep: a drunken soldiery
Can leave the mother, murdered at her door,
To crawl in her own blood, and go scot-free;
The night can sweat with terror as before
We pieced our thoughts into philosophy,
And planned to bring the world under a rule,
Who are but weasels fighting in a hole.

He who can read the signs nor sink unmanned
Into the half-deceit of some intoxicant
From shallow wits; who knows no work can stand,
Whether health, wealth or peace of mind were spent
On master-work of intellect or hand,
No honour leave its mighty monument,
Has but one comfort left: all triumph would
But break upon his ghostly solitude.

But is there any comfort to be found?
Man is in love and loves what vanishes,
What more is there to say? That country round
None dared admit, if such a thought were his,
Incendiary or bigot could be found
To burn that stump on the Acropolis,
Or break in bits the famous ivories
Or traffic in the grasshoppers or bees.

2

When Loie Fuller's[1] Chinese dancers enwound
A shining web, a floating ribbon of cloth,
It seemed that a dragon of air
Had fallen among dancers, had whirled them round
Or hurried them off on its own furious path;
So the Platonic Year[2]
Whirls out new right and wrong,
Whirls in the old instead;
All men are dancers and their tread
Goes to the barbarous clangour of a gong.

3

Some moralist or mythological poet
Compares the solitary soul to a swan;
I am satisfied with that,
Satisfied if a troubled mirror show it,
Before that brief gleam of its life be gone,
An image of its state;
The wings half spread for flight,
The breast thrust out in pride
Whether to play, or to ride
Those winds that clamour of approaching night.

A man in his own secret meditation
Is lost amid the labyrinth that he has made
In art or politics;
Some Platonist affirms that in the station
Where we should cast off body and trade
The ancient habit sticks,
And that if our works could
But vanish with our breath
That were a lucky death,
For triumph can but mar our solitude.

The swan has leaped into the desolate heaven:
That image can bring wildness, bring a rage
To end all things, to end
What my laborious life imagined, even
The half-imagined, the half-written page;
O but we dreamed to mend
Whatever mischief seemed
To afflict mankind, but now
That winds of winter blow
Learn that we were crack-pated when we dreamed.

4

We, who seven years ago
Talked of honour and of truth,
Shriek with pleasure if we show
The weasel's twist, the weasel's tooth.

5

Come let us mock at the great
That had such burdens on the mind

[1] *Loie Fuller* An American dancer and choreographer (1862–1928); her dancers were Japanese, not Chinese.

[2] *Platonic Year* Full revolution of the constellations in relation to the equinoxes, approximately 26,000 years.

And toiled so hard and late
To leave some monument behind,
Nor thought of the levelling wind.

Come let us mock at the wise;
With all those calendars whereon
They fixed old aching eyes,
They never saw how seasons run,
And now but gape at the sun.

Come let us mock at the good
That fancied goodness might be gay,
And sick of solitude
Might proclaim a holiday:
Wind shrieked—and where are they?

Mock mockers after that
That would not lift a hand maybe
To help good, wise or great
To bar that foul storm out, for we
Traffic in mockery.

6

Violence upon the roads: violence of horses;
Some few have handsome riders, are garlanded
On delicate sensitive ear or tossing mane,
But wearied running round and round in their courses
All break and vanish, and evil gathers head:
Herodias' daughters have returned again,[1]
A sudden blast of dusty wind and after
Thunder of feet, tumult of images,
Their purpose in the labyrinth of the wind;
And should some crazy hand dare touch a daughter
All turn with amorous cries, or angry cries,
According to the wind, for all are blind.
But now wind drops, dust settles; thereupon
There lurches past, his great eyes without thought
Under the shadow of stupid straw-pale locks,
That insolent fiend Robert Artisson[2]
To whom the love-lorn Lady Kyteler brought
Bronzed peacock feathers, red combs of her cocks.[3]
—1919

A Prayer for My Daughter[4]

Once more the storm is howling, and half hid
Under this cradle-hood and coverlid
My child sleeps on. There is no obstacle
But Gregory's wood[5] and one bare hill
Whereby the haystack- and roof-levelling wind,
Bred on the Atlantic, can be stayed;
And for an hour I have walked and prayed
Because of the great gloom that is in my mind.

I have walked and prayed for this young child an hour
And heard the sea-wind scream upon the tower,[6]
And under the arches of the bridge, and scream
In the elms above the flooded stream;
Imagining in excited reverie
That the future years had come,
Dancing to a frenzied drum,
Out of the murderous innocence of the sea.

May she be granted beauty and yet not
Beauty to make a stranger's eye distraught,
Or hers before a looking-glass, for such,
Being made beautiful overmuch,
Consider beauty a sufficient end,
Lose natural kindness and maybe

---

[1] *Herodias' ... again* The reference here is not to the Biblical character (whose daughter was Salomé) but rather to the eponymous witch-goddess of Germanic mythology. Her daughters are associated with violently whirling winds.

[2] [Yeats's note] My last symbol, Robert Artisson, was an evil spirit much run after in Kilkenny at the start of the fourteenth century.

[3] *To whom ... cocks* It was said that Artisson seduced Lady Kyteler, who supposedly sacrificed cocks and peacocks to him and was accused of poisoning her husbands; *combs* Pronounced ridges on cocks' crowns.

[4] *My Daughter* Anne Butler Yeats, born 26 February 1919.

[5] *Gregory's wood* Lady Gregory's wood at Coole Park, her estate in western Ireland.

[6] *tower* Thoor Ballylee, the ancient Norman tower on the land Yeats bought from Lady Gregory in June 1917.

The heart-revealing intimacy
That chooses right, and never find a friend.

Helen[1] being chosen found life flat and dull
And later had much trouble from a fool,
While that great Queen, that rose out of the spray,[2]
Being fatherless could have her way
Yet chose a bandy-leggèd smith[3] for man.
It's certain that fine women eat
A crazy salad with their meat
Whereby the Horn of Plenty is undone.

In courtesy I'd have her chiefly learned;
Hearts are not had as a gift but hearts are earned
By those that are not entirely beautiful;
Yet many, that have played the fool
For beauty's very self, has charm made wise,
And many a poor man that has roved,
Loved and thought himself beloved,
From a glad kindness cannot take his eyes.

May she become a flourishing hidden tree
That all her thoughts may like the linnet be,
And have no business but dispensing round
Their magnanimities of sound,
Nor but in merriment begin a chase,
Nor but in merriment a quarrel.
O may she live like some green laurel
Rooted in one dear perpetual place.

My mind, because the minds that I have loved,
The sort of beauty that I have approved,
Prosper but little, has dried up of late,
Yet knows that to be choked with hate
May well be of all evil chances chief.
If there's no hatred in a mind
Assault and battery of the wind
Can never tear the linnet from the leaf.

An intellectual hatred is the worst,
So let her think opinions are accursed.
Have I not seen the loveliest woman[4] born
Out of the mouth of Plenty's horn,
Because of her opinionated mind
Barter that horn and every good
By quiet natures understood
For an old bellows full of angry wind?

Considering that, all hatred driven hence,
The soul recovers radical innocence
And learns at last that it is self-delighting,
Self-appeasing, self-affrighting,
And that its own sweet will is Heaven's will;
She can, though every face should scowl
And every windy quarter howl
Or every bellows burst, be happy still.

And may her bridegroom bring her to a house
Where all's accustomed, ceremonious;
For arrogance and hatred are the wares
Peddled in the thoroughfares.
How but in custom and in ceremony
Are innocence and beauty born?
Ceremony's a name for the rich horn,
And custom for the spreading laurel tree.

—1919

An Irish Airman Foresees His Death

I know that I shall meet my fate
Somewhere among the clouds above;
Those that I fight I do not hate
Those that I guard I do not love;
My country is Kiltartan Cross,[5]

[1] *Helen* Wife of Menelaus. She was abducted by Paris, the son of the king of Troy; the Greeks besieged the city for ten years to save her, finally bringing her back to her husband.

[2] *that great Queen … spray* Aphrodite, the Greek goddess of love, beauty, and fecundity, rose out of the sea at birth.

[3] *bandy-leggèd smith* Hephaestus, god of fire and husband of Aphrodite, was born lame.

[4] *loveliest woman* Maud Gonne, whom Yeats had loved, was an important Irish liberation activist; she married Major John MacBride in 1903.

[5] *Kiltartan Cross* In County Galway, Ireland.

My countrymen Kiltartan's poor,
No likely end could bring them loss
Or leave them happier than before.
Nor law, nor duty bade me fight,
Nor public man, nor cheering crowds,
A lonely impulse of delight
Drove to this tumult in the clouds;
I balanced all, brought all to mind,
The years to come seemed waste of breath,
A waste of breath the years behind
In balance with this life, this death.
—1919

The Second Coming[1]

Turning and turning in the widening gyre[2]
The falcon cannot hear the falconer;
Things fall apart; the centre cannot hold;
Mere anarchy is loosed upon the world,
The blood-dimmed tide is loosed, and everywhere
The ceremony of innocence is drowned;
The best lack all conviction, while the worst
Are full of passionate intensity.

Surely some revelation is at hand;
Surely the Second Coming is at hand.
The Second Coming! Hardly are those words out
When a vast image out of *Spiritus Mundi* [3]
Troubles my sight: somewhere in sands of the desert
A shape with lion body and the head of a man,[4]
A gaze blank and pitiless as the sun,
Is moving its slow thighs, while all about it
Reel shadows of the indignant desert birds.
The darkness drops again; but now I know
That twenty centuries of stony sleep
Were vexed to nightmare by a rocking cradle,[5]
And what rough beast, its hour come round at last,
Slouches towards Bethlehem to be born?
—1920

Leda and the Swan[6]

A sudden blow: the great wings beating still
Above the staggering girl, her thighs caressed
By the dark webs, her nape caught in his bill,
He holds her helpless breast upon his breast.

How can those terrified vague fingers push
The feathered glory from her loosening thighs?
And how can body, laid in that white rush,
But feel the strange heart beating where it lies?

A shudder in the loins engenders there
The broken wall, the burning roof and tower
And Agamemnon dead.[7]
Being so caught up,
So mastered by the brute blood of the air,
Did she put on his knowledge with his power
Before the indifferent beak could let her drop?
—1924

Among School Children

I

I walk through the long schoolroom questioning;
A kind old nun in a white hood replies;
The children learn to cipher and to sing,
To study reading-books and history,
To cut and sew, be neat in everything

[1] *The Second Coming* The return of Christ, as predicted in the New Testament. See Revelation 1.7: "Behold, he cometh with clouds; and every eye shall see him."

[2] *gyre* Spiral formed from concentric circles.

[3] *Spiritus Mundi* Universal spirit that houses the images of civilization's past memories and provides divine inspiration for the poet; the human race is a connected whole in the *spiritus mundi*.

[4] *shape … man* The Egyptian Sphinx.

[5] *rocking cradle* Cradle of the Christ Child.

[6] *Leda and the Swan* Zeus came to Leda in the form of a swan and raped her; she then gave birth to Helen of Troy (whose abduction from her husband, King Menelaus, by Paris, initiated the Trojan War) and the twins, Castor and Pollux.

[7] *broken wall … Agamemnon dead* Events of the Trojan War.

In the best modern way—the children's eyes
In momentary wonder stare upon
A sixty-year-old smiling public man.

2

I dream of a Ledaean[1] body, bent
Above a sinking fire, a tale that she
Told of a harsh reproof, or trivial event
That changed some childish day to tragedy—
Told, and it seemed that our two natures blent
Into a sphere from youthful sympathy,
Or else, to alter Plato's parable,
Into the yolk and white of the one shell.[2]

3

And thinking of that fit of grief or rage
I look upon one child or t'other there
And wonder if she stood so at that age—
For even daughters of the swan[3] can share
Something of every paddler's heritage—
And had that colour upon cheek or hair,
And thereupon my heart is driven wild:
She stands before me as a living child.

4

Her present image floats into the mind—
Did Quattrocento finger[4] fashion it
Hollow of cheek as though it drank the wind
And took a mess of shadows for its meat?
And I though never of Ledaean kind
Had pretty plumage once—enough of that,
Better to smile on all that smile, and show
There is a comfortable kind of old scarecrow.

5

What youthful mother, a shape upon her lap
Honey of generation[5] had betrayed,
And that must sleep, shriek, struggle to escape
As recollection or the drug decide,
Would think her son, did she but see that shape
With sixty or more winters on its head,
A compensation for the pang of his birth,
Or the uncertainty of his setting forth?

6

Plato thought nature but a spume that plays
Upon a ghostly paradigm of things;[6]
Solider Aristotle played the taws
Upon the bottom of a king of kings;[7]
World-famous golden-thighed Pythagoras
Fingered upon a fiddle-stick or strings[8]
What a star sang and careless Muses heard:
Old clothes upon old sticks to scare a bird.

7

Both nuns and mothers worship images,
But those the candles light are not as those
That animate a mother's reveries,
But keep a marble or a bronze repose.
And yet they too break hearts—O Presences
That passion, piety or affection knows,

[1] *Ledaean* Like that of Leda (see note on Leda below).

[2] *Plato's parable … shell* A speaker in Plato's *Symposium* claims that the original form of human beings was that of two bodies fused together; as a punishment, Zeus split them in half "as you might divide an egg with a hair." Love, the speaker explains, is motivated by the desire to reunite with one's missing half.

[3] *daughters of the swan* Leda, raped by Zeus in the form of a swan, gave birth to Helen of Troy.

[4] *Quattrocento finger* Skillful hand of a fifteenth-century Italian artist.

[5] [Yeats's note] I have taken the "honey of generation" from Porphyry's essay on "The Cave of the Nymphs," but find no warrant in Porphyry for considering it the "drug" that destroys the "recollection" of prenatal freedom. [The Neoplatonic philosopher Porphyry (233–c. 304) stated that the pleasure of sexual intercourse, like the sweetness of honey, drugs infants, thereby causing them to forget prenatal bliss before being born into this mortal world.]

[6] *Plato … things* Plato argued that the appearance of nature was merely an imitation of the real world; therefore, nature itself was unreal, but provided a "ghostly" image of the real "paradigm of things."

[7] *Solider … kings* Unlike Plato, Aristotle believed that reality took form in the image of nature; therefore, nature was reality itself. Aristotle tutored Alexander the Great, the son of King Philip of Macedonia; *taws* Leather whip.

[8] *golden-thighed … strings* Pythagoras, a Greek philosopher of the sixth century BCE, developed a theory of the mathematical regularity of the universe and the mathematical origins of musical harmony. He was said to have a golden thigh.

And that all heavenly glory symbolise—
O self-born mockers of man's enterprise;

8

Labour is blossoming or dancing where
The body is not bruised to pleasure soul,
Nor beauty born out of its own despair,
Nor blear-eyed wisdom out of midnight oil.
O chestnut tree, great-rooted blossomer,
Are you the leaf, the blossom, or the bole?° *trunk*
O body swayed to music, O brightening glance,
How can we know the dancer from the dance?
—1927

Sailing to Byzantium[1]

1

That is no country for old men. The young
In one another's arms, birds in the trees
—Those dying generations—at their song,
The salmon-falls, the mackerel-crowded seas,
Fish, flesh, or fowl, commend all summer long
Whatever is begotten, born, and dies.
Caught in that sensual music all neglect
Monuments of unageing intellect.

2

An aged man is but a paltry thing,
A tattered coat upon a stick, unless
Soul clap its hands and sing, and louder sing
For every tatter in its mortal dress,
Nor is there singing school but studying
Monuments of its own magnificence;
And therefore I have sailed the seas and come
To the holy city of Byzantium.

3

O sages standing in God's holy fire
As in the gold mosaic of a wall,
Come from the holy fire, perne in a gyre,[2]
And be the singing-masters of my soul.
Consume my heart away; sick with desire
And fastened to a dying animal
It knows not what it is; and gather me
Into the artifice of eternity.

4

Once out of nature I shall never take
My bodily form from any natural thing,
But such a form as Grecian goldsmiths make
Of hammered gold and gold enamelling
To keep a drowsy Emperor awake;
Or set upon a golden bough to sing[3]
To lords and ladies of Byzantium
Of what is past, or passing, or to come.
—1927

Byzantium[4]

The unpurged images of day recede;
The Emperor's drunken soldiery are abed;
Night resonance recedes, night walkers'[5] song
After great cathedral[6] gong;
A starlit or a moonlit dome disdains
All that man is,

---

[1] *Byzantium* Ancient city eventually renamed Constantinople (now Istanbul), capital of the Eastern Roman Empire. In *A Vision*, Yeats envisioned Byzantium as a center for artists: "The painter, the mosaic worker, the worker in gold and silver, the illuminator of sacred books were almost impersonal, almost perhaps without the consciousness of individual design, absorbed in their subject matter and that the vision of a whole people."

[2] *perne in a gyre* Rotate in a spiral; the literal definition of "perne" is bobbin.

[3] [Yeats's note] I have read somewhere that in the Emperor's palace at Byzantium was a tree made of gold and silver, and artificial birds that sang.

[4] *Byzantium* Constantinople (today, Istanbul); Yeats recorded "the subject for a poem" in his diary of 1930: "Describe Byzantium as it is in the system towards the end of the first Christian millennium… Flames at the street corners where the soul is purified, birds of hammered gold singing in the golden trees, in the harbour [dolphins] offering their backs to the wailing dead that they may carry them to Paradise."

[5] *night walkers* Prostitutes.

[6] *great cathedral* Church of St. Sophia, built in Byzantium by the emperor Justinian I in 532–37.

All mere complexities,
The fury and the mire of human veins.

Before me floats an image, man or shade,
Shade more than man, more image than a shade;
For Hades'[1] bobbin° bound in mummy-cloth *spool*
May unwind the winding path;
A mouth that has no moisture and no breath
Breathless mouths may summon;
I hail the superhuman;
I call it death-in-life and life-in-death.[2]

Miracle, bird or golden handiwork,
More miracle than bird or handiwork,
Planted on the star-lit golden bough,
Can like the cocks of Hades crow,[3]
Or, by the moon embittered, scorn aloud
In glory of changeless metal
Common bird or petal
And all complexities of mire or blood.

At midnight on the Emperor's pavement flit
Flames that no faggot feeds, nor steel has lit,
Nor storm disturbs, flames begotten of flame,
Where blood-begotten spirits come
And all complexities of fury leave,
Dying into a dance,
An agony of trance,
An agony of flame that cannot singe a sleeve.

Astraddle on the dolphin's mire and blood,[4]
Spirit after spirit! The smithies break the flood,
The golden smithies of the Emperor!
Marbles of the dancing floor
Break bitter furies of complexity,
Those images that yet
Fresh images beget,
That dolphin-torn, that gong-tormented sea.
—1930

Crazy Jane Talks with the Bishop

I met the Bishop on the road
And much said he and I.
"Those breasts are flat and fallen now,
Those veins must soon be dry;
Live in a heavenly mansion,
Not in some foul sty."

"Fair and foul are near of kin,
And fair needs foul," I cried.
"My friends are gone, but that's a truth
Nor grave nor bed denied,
Learned in bodily lowliness
And in the heart's pride.

"A woman can be proud and stiff
When on love intent;
But Love has pitched his mansion in
The place of excrement;
For nothing can be sole or whole
That has not been rent."
—1933

[1] *Hades* Greek god of the underworld.

[2] *death-in-life and life-in-death* Cf. Tennyson's "Tears, Idle Tears," 20: "O Death in Life" and Coleridge's *The Rime of the Ancient Mariner* 3.193: "The Nightmare LIFE-IN-DEATH was she."

[3] *the cocks of Hades crow* Because cocks symbolized rebirth and resurrection, they appeared on Roman tombstones as a sign of the continuation of human life.

[4] *Astraddle … blood* According to Neoplatonism, dolphins symbolize the soul in transition, as they transport the recently departed to the Islands of the Blest.

Lapis Lazuli [1]

(*For Harry Clifton*)[2]

I have heard that hysterical women say
They are sick of the palette and fiddle-bow,
Of poets that are always gay,
For everybody knows or else should know
That if nothing drastic is done
Aeroplane and Zeppelin[3] will come out,
Pitch like King Billy bomb-balls[4] in
Until the town lie beaten flat.

All perform their tragic play,
There struts Hamlet, there is Lear,
That's Ophelia, that Cordelia;[5]
Yet they, should the last scene be there,
The great stage curtain about to drop,
If worthy their prominent part in the play,
Do not break up their lines to weep.
They know that Hamlet and Lear are gay;
Gaiety transfiguring all that dread.
All men have aimed at, found and lost;
Black out; Heaven blazing into the head:
Tragedy wrought to its uttermost.
Though Hamlet rambles and Lear rages,
And all the drop-scenes drop at once
Upon a hundred thousand stages,
It cannot grow by an inch or an ounce.

On their own feet they came, or on shipboard,
Camel-back, horse-back, ass-back, mule-back,
Old civilisations put to the sword.
Then they and their wisdom went to rack:
No handiwork of Callimachus,[6]
Who handled marble as if it were bronze,
Made draperies that seemed to rise
When sea-wind swept the corner, stands;
His long lamp-chimney shaped like the stem
Of a slender palm, stood but a day;
All things fall and are built again,
And those that build them again are gay.

Two Chinamen, behind them a third,
Are carved in lapis lazuli,
Over them flies a long-legged bird,
A symbol of longevity;
The third, doubtless a serving-man,
Carries a musical instrument.

Every discoloration of the stone,
Every accidental crack or dent,
Seems a water-course or an avalanche,
Or lofty slope where it still snows
Though doubtless plum or cherry-branch
Sweetens the little half-way house
Those Chinamen climb towards, and I
Delight to imagine them seated there;
There, on the mountain and the sky,
On all the tragic scene they stare.
One asks for mournful melodies;
Accomplished fingers begin to play.
Their eyes mid many wrinkles, their eyes,
Their ancient, glittering eyes, are gay.
—1938

---

[1] *Lapis Lazuli* Yeats received a carving made of lapis lazuli (semiprecious blue stone) on his birthday, 13 June 1935. Yeats described the stone in a letter to Dorothy Wellesley (English poet and friend): "Ascetic, pupil, hard stone, eternal theme of the sensual east. The heroic cry in the midst of despair. But no, I am wrong, the east has its solutions always and therefore knows nothing of tragedy. It is we, not the east, that must raise the heroic cry."

[2] *Harry Clifton* Yeats's apprentice, who gave the elder poet a gift made of lapis lazuli for his seventieth birthday.

[3] *Zeppelin* German airship used to bomb London during World War I; in 1938 another war with Germany seemed imminent.

[4] *King Billy bomb-balls* King William III (William of Orange) overcame the soldiers of the deposed king James II at the Battle of the Boyne in Ireland, 1690. An anonymous ballad describes the fight: "King William he threw his bomb-balls in, / And set them on fire." Also a nickname for Kaiser Wilhelm II, German emperor and king of Prussia during World War I.

[5] *There struts … Cordelia* References to tragedies by Shakespeare: *Hamlet* tells the story of the death of Ophelia, beloved of Prince Hamlet, and then of Hamlet himself; *King Lear* tells of the death first of Lear's daughter Cordelia, then of Lear himself.

[6] *Callimachus* Greek sculptor of the fifth century BCE.

The Circus Animals' Desertion

I

I sought a theme and sought for it in vain,
I sought it daily for six weeks or so.
Maybe at last, being but a broken man,
I must be satisfied with my heart, although
Winter and summer till old age began
My circus animals were all on show,
Those stilted boys, that burnished chariot,[1]
Lion and woman and the Lord knows what.

2

What can I but enumerate old themes?
First that sea-rider Oisín[2] led by the nose
Through three enchanted islands, allegorical dreams,
Vain gaiety, vain battle, vain repose,
Themes of the embittered heart, or so it seems,
That might adorn old songs or courtly shows;
But what cared I that set him on to ride,
I, starved for the bosom of his faery bride?

And then a counter-truth filled out its play,
The Countess Cathleen[3] was the name I gave it;
She, pity-crazed, had given her soul away,
But masterful Heaven had intervened to save it.
I thought my dear must her own soul destroy,
So did fanaticism and hate enslave it,
And this brought forth a dream and soon enough
This dream itself had all my thought and love.

And when the Fool and Blind Man stole the bread
Cuchulain fought the ungovernable sea;[4]
Heart-mysteries there, and yet when all is said
It was the dream itself enchanted me:
Character isolated by a deed
To engross the present and dominate memory.
Players and painted stage took all my love,
And not those things that they were emblems of.

3

Those masterful images because complete
Grew in pure mind, but out of what began?
A mound of refuse or the sweepings of a street,
Old kettles, old bottles, and a broken can,
Old iron, old bones, old rags, that raving slut[5]
Who keeps the till. Now that my ladder's gone,
I must lie down where all the ladders start,
In the foul rag-and-bone shop of the heart.
—1939

[1] *Those stilted … chariot* Yeats may be alluding to the ancient Irish heroes of his first works; the chariot may refer to the carriage built on the stage of his play, *The Unicorn from the Stars* (1908).

[2] *Oisín* Irish warrior of Yeats's *The Wanderings of Oisín* (1889); Oisín is led by the fairy, Niamh, to three islands—called Delight, Many Fears, Forgetfulness—purported to be paradisiacal. When he returns to Ireland 150 years later he finds his friends dead and his country converted to Christianity.

[3] *The Countess Cathleen* Play written by Yeats in 1892; an Irish countess, modeled on the Irish activist Maud Gonne, sells her soul to the devil to save the starving peasantry, but in the end is saved by God for her magnanimous motives.

[4] *And when … sea* In Yeats's play *On Baile's Strand* (1904), Cuchulain goes mad after he discovers that he has killed his own son. He runs out to the sea to fight the waves; meanwhile, the fool and the blind man steal bread from the ovens of the townspeople watching Cuchulain's sea-battle.

[5] *slut* Foul or unkempt woman. (Here the word has no connotation of sexual looseness.)

Virginia Woolf
1882 – 1941

A towering figure in the history of twentieth-century feminist thought, Virginia Woolf also occupies a central place in the development of the twentieth-century novel. Woolf, along with contemporaries such as James Joyce and Dorothy Richardson, rejected the traditional conventions of fiction, which included narrative coherence, omniscient narration, and emphasis on external settings and events. Instead, she explored the everyday, internal lives of her characters in a style—often called stream-of-consciousness—that mimics the flow of her characters' thoughts. In her fiction and essays alike, she examined the ways in which social roles and values are constructed and the effects these have on the lives and interactions of individuals.

Virginia Woolf was born Adeline Virginia Stephen, the third child of an illustrious, upper-middle-class London family. Her father, Leslie Stephen, a philosopher and literary critic, was primarily known as editor of the *Dictionary of National Biography* and President of the London Library. Her mother, born Julia Jackson, had been married into the Duckworth publishing family, and then married Stephen some time after the death of her first husband. Deeply connected to Victorian literary circles, the Stephen family included among its friends Henry James, Matthew Arnold, and George Eliot. From childhood, Woolf was drawn to a literary career, and her father in particular encouraged her, as she says, "to read what one liked because one liked it, never to pretend to admire what one did not.… To write in the fewest possible words, as clearly as possible, exactly what one meant."

Surrounded by her father's impressive library, Woolf immersed herself in the study of languages and literary classics. While her brothers Thoby and Adrian went to public schools and eventually to university at Cambridge, Woolf and her sister Vanessa were educated at home by their father and private tutors. The lack of formal education for women would become a pervasive issue in Woolf's novels and later essays such as *A Room of One's Own* (1929) and *Three Guineas* (1938). A frequent exploration into the emotional effects of death in her later writing would also stem from Woolf's youthful experience. In 1895, her mother died of influenza; a few months later, at the age of thirteen, Woolf suffered a mental breakdown, symptoms of which included hearing voices, avoiding food, and experiencing extreme anxiety. Her mother's death was followed by that of her beloved half-sister and maternal substitute, Stella Duckworth, in childbirth, and then by that of her father, from cancer, in 1904. A second breakdown resulted. These breakdowns were harbingers of Woolf's lifelong struggle with manic and depressive episodes, which were generally brought about by stress—such as the emotional and mental anxiety that accompanied the completion of a book.

Despite Woolf's emotional turmoil in the year following her father's death, the event freed her from her family's inhibiting influence and facilitated her emergence amongst London's intelligentsia. With an unsigned review, she obtained her first publication in *The Guardian*, and against her extended family's attempts to introduce her into polite society, Woolf and her siblings moved to the Bloomsbury area of London. There they began associating with her brother Thoby's Cambridge friends, and what began as a social gathering of casual friends for drinks and conversation eventually came to be known as the Bloomsbury Group, a cultural circle bound together by an intense interest in current literary, philosophical, artistic, sexual, and political issues. Its members included novelist E.M. Forster, biographer and essayist Lytton Strachey, painter Duncan Grant, art critics Roger Fry and Clive Bell (the future husband of Woolf's sister Vanessa), economist John Maynard Keynes, and political theorist Leonard Woolf. Although Thoby Stephen died of typhoid in 1906, the group continued to meet throughout Woolf's lifetime. It attracted a certain amount of controversy as a result of the new ideas (particularly concerning sexuality) and frank artistic expression it fostered, and also because of the class snobbery it was perceived to exhibit (to the extent that the word *Bloomsbury* later became widely used to connote an insular and patronizing aestheticism).

In 1912, Virginia Stephen married Leonard Woolf, who throughout her life provided her with the time, encouragement, and emotional support necessary for her to continue writing as she alternated between periods of stability and intense productivity and episodes of immobilizing emotional collapse. In 1915, *The Voyage Out*, Woolf's first major novel, was published, introducing her readers for the first time to the character of Clarissa Dalloway, whom Woolf would make central to her later novel *Mrs. Dalloway* (1925). *The Voyage Out* and its successor, *Night and Day* (1919), are Woolf's most conventional works.

In 1917, Woolf and her husband bought a hand press and established Hogarth Press at their London home, intending to publish their own works and those of their friends. The Hogarth Press soon became a highly successful enterprise, publishing the early works of authors such as E.M. Forster, Katherine Mansfield, and T.S. Eliot, as well as English translations of the works of Sigmund Freud.

Woolf's 1922 novel *Jacob's Room*, based on the life and death of Woolf's brother Thoby, represented a stylistic breakthrough for her. In this novel, she tried an entirely different approach, ignoring much of the framework of external events and descriptions present in her earlier work. In this novel, she said, there was "no scaffolding; scarcely a brick to be seen; all crepuscular." By 1925, Woolf had completed *Mrs. Dalloway*, the culmination of many years' experimentation with narrative technique. Originally titled *The House*, *Mrs. Dalloway* takes place over a twenty-four hour period in London, and explores the subjectivities of characters who never meet, but whose observations, experiences, and memories reveal a curious kinship between them. Describing her new method of characterization, Woolf said, "I dig out beautiful caves behind my characters. … The idea is that the caves shall connect and each come to daylight at the present moment."

In her next novel, *To the Lighthouse* (1927), Woolf further developed her stream-of-consciousness style, relying heavily on imagery and rich symbolism to convey meaning. Divided into three distinct parts that take place against the backdrop of ordinary domestic events, the novel experiments with the passage of time through the consciousness of its various characters. By alternating between various viewpoints, Woolf demonstrates how rare, tenuous, and fleeting the moments of real connection between people are.

In 1929, Woolf's best-known work of non-fiction was published. Originally constructed as lecture notes for talks to be given at Newnham and Girton Colleges at Cambridge, the work was expanded and published as *A Room of One's Own*. The essay, which has become a foundational text of literary feminism, explores the traditional barriers and prejudices faced by women writers. At the core of Woolf's argument is her conclusion that a woman must have financial independence and privacy (a room of her own) if she is to write fiction successfully. In presenting the concept of the androgynous mind, Woolf also provides insight into her own literary process. As defined by Woolf, successful authors of whatever sex must possess the ability to draw creative forces from all facets of their emotional and intellectual beings—regardless of whether these facets are traditionally classified as "masculine" or "feminine." To do so, authors must move beyond any awareness of their own gender roles as dictated by social customs; as Woolf says, "It is fatal for anyone who writes to think of their sex." In her novel of the previous year, *Orlando*, Woolf had celebrated what she saw as the androgynous creative mind of her friend and lover Vita Sackville-West. Subtitled *A Biography*, *Orlando* plays overtly with the form of the genre as Woolf follows her main character—who is able to change sex as the times and his or her desires demand—across several hundred years of British history.

For the next twelve years, Woolf continued to pursue more radical experiments with form while developing her ideas about writing, genre, and gender roles in numerous essays (most of which are collected in two volumes of *The Common Reader*). Woolf's next novel, *The Waves* (1931), is a poem-novel written "to a rhythm and not to a plot" that focuses on the mutability of life. In 1938, Woolf extended the feminist critique of male privilege begun in *A Room of One's Own* with *Three Guineas*, which implicitly links the values of patriarchal society with those of fascism. Less popular at the time than its predecessor, *Three Guineas*, and the pacifism it advocates, have found a more receptive audience in the later twentieth and early twenty-first centuries.

Just as *The Waves* sought to combine poetry and the novel, Woolf described her 1937 work *The Years* as an "essay-novel," and her final novel, *Between the Acts* (1941), is something of a drama-novel, focusing on the audience reception of an amateur pageant that takes place as the threat of war is imminent. Woolf herself, discouraged by the progress of World War II and its implications for herself and her Jewish husband, and dreading the critical reception this work would receive, faced another emotional breakdown. Before she could complete the revisions of *Between the Acts*, she began to feel mental illness engulf her. She composed a note to her husband explaining that she felt that this time she would not recover, filled her pockets with stones, and drowned herself in the River Ouse near her home.

Throughout her lifetime, Woolf was offered numerous honors, all of which she refused because of her avowed contempt for patriarchal society. After declining an honorary degree from Manchester University, she wrote in her diary, "It is an utterly corrupt society …, and I will take nothing that it can give me." She did not want to be condescended to or used as a "token woman." Nevertheless, the honors continued to be offered, and, after her death, the loss of her unique vision and style were greatly mourned. She has since been hailed as a pioneer of the modernist novel, a central figure in the development of feminist theory, and a central figure in the twentieth-century world of letters. Her personal diaries and letters, published posthumously in several volumes, provide unique insight into her aims as an artist and her intellectual development in a remarkable literary and artistic milieu.

⌘⌘⌘

The Mark on the Wall

Perhaps it was the middle of January in the present year that I first looked up and saw the mark on the wall. In order to fix a date it is necessary to remember what one saw. So now I think of the fire; the steady film of yellow light upon the page of my book; the three chrysanthemums in the round glass bowl on the mantelpiece. Yes, it must have been the winter time, and we had just finished our tea, for I remember that I was smoking a cigarette when I looked up and saw the mark on the wall for the first time. I looked up through the smoke of my cigarette and my eye lodged for a moment upon the burning coals, and that old fancy of the crimson flag flapping from the castle tower came into my mind, and I thought of the cavalcade of red knights riding up the side of the black rock. Rather to my relief the sight of the mark interrupted the fancy, for it is an old fancy, an automatic fancy, made as a child perhaps. The mark was a small round mark, black upon the white wall, about six or seven inches above the mantelpiece.

How readily our thoughts swarm upon a new object, lifting it a little way, as ants carry a blade of straw so feverishly, and then leave it. … If that mark was made by a nail, it can't have been for a picture, it must have been for a miniature—the miniature of a lady with white powdered curls, powder-dusted cheeks, and lips like red carnations. A fraud of course, for the people who had this house before us would have chosen pictures in that way—an old picture for an old room. That is the sort of people they were—very interesting people, and I think of them so often, in such queer places, because one will never see them again, never know what happened next. They wanted to leave this house because they wanted to change their style of furniture, so he said, and he was in process of saying that in his opinion art should have ideas behind it when we were torn asunder, as one is torn from the old lady about to pour out tea and the young man about to hit the tennis ball in the back garden of the suburban villa as one rushes past in the train.

But as for that mark, I'm not sure about it; I don't believe it was made by a nail after all; it's too big, too round, for that. I might get up, but if I got up and looked at it, ten to one I shouldn't be able to say for certain; because once a thing's done, no one ever knows how it happened. Oh! dear me, the mystery of life! The inaccuracy of thought! The ignorance of humanity! To show how very little control of our possessions we have—what an accidental affair this living is after all our civilization—let me just count over a few of the things lost in our lifetime, beginning, for that seems always the most mysterious of losses—what cat would gnaw, what rat would nibble—three pale blue canisters of book-binding tools? Then there were the bird cages, the iron hoops, the steel skates, the Queen Anne coal-scuttle, the bagatelle board,[1] the hand organ—all gone, and jewels too. Opals and emeralds, they lie about the roots of turnips. What a scraping paring affair it is to be sure! The wonder is that I've any clothes on my back, that I sit surrounded by solid furniture at this moment. Why, if one wants to compare life to anything, one must liken it to being blown through the Tube[2] at fifty miles an hour—landing at the other end without a single hairpin in one's hair! Shot out at the feet of God entirely naked! Tumbling head over heels in the asphodel[3] meadows like brown paper parcels pitched down a shoot in the post office! With one's hair flying back like the tail of a racehorse. Yes, that seems to express the rapidity of life, the perpetual waste and repair; all so casual, all so haphazard. …

But after life. The slow pulling down of thick green stalks so that the cup of the flower, as it turns over, deluges one with purple and red light. Why, after all, should one not be born there as one is born here, helpless, speechless, unable to focus one's eyesight, groping at the roots of the grass, at the toes of the Giants? As for saying which are trees, and which are men and women, or whether there are such things, that one won't be in a condition to do for fifty years or so. There will be nothing but spaces of light and dark, intersected by thick stalks, and rather higher up perhaps, rose-shaped blots of an indistinct colour—dim pinks and blues—which will, as time goes on, become more definite, become—I don't know what. …

And yet the mark on the wall is not a hole at all. It may even be caused by some round black substance, such as a small rose leaf, left over from the summer, and I, not being a very vigilant housekeeper—look at the dust on the mantelpiece, for example, the dust which, so

[1] *bagatelle board* Playing surface for a game similar to billiards.

[2] *Tube* Nickname for the London Underground, the system of subway lines that underlies the city of London.

[3] *asphodel* Genus of liliaceous flowers; said to cover the Elysian fields, the paradise where (according to Greek mythology) the blessed would reside after death.

they say, buried Troy three times over, only fragments of pots utterly refusing annihilation, as one can believe.

The tree outside the window taps very gently on the pane ... I want to think quietly, calmly, spaciously, never to be interrupted, never to have to rise from my chair, to slip easily from one thing to another, without any sense of hostility, or obstacle. I want to sink deeper and deeper, away from the surface, with its hard separate facts. To steady myself, let me catch hold of the first idea that passes ... Shakespeare ... Well, he will do as well as another. A man who sat himself solidly in an arm-chair, and looked into the fire, so—A shower of ideas fell perpetually from some very high Heaven down through his mind. He leant his forehead on his hand, and people, looking in through the open door—for this scene is supposed to take place on a summer's evening—But how dull this is, this historical fiction! It doesn't interest me at all. I wish I could hit upon a pleasant track of thought, a track indirectly reflecting credit upon myself, for those are the pleasantest thoughts, and very frequent even in the minds of modest mouse-coloured people, who believe genuinely that they dislike to hear their own praises. They are not thoughts directly praising oneself; that is the beauty of them; they are thoughts like this:

"And then I came into the room. They were discussing botany. I said how I'd seen a flower growing on a dust heap on the site of an old house in Kingsway. The seed, I said, must have been sown in the reign of Charles the First. What flowers grew in the reign of Charles the First?" I asked—(but I don't remember the answer). Tall flowers with purple tassels to them perhaps. And so it goes on. All the time I'm dressing up the figure of myself in my own mind, lovingly, stealthily, not openly adoring it, for if I did that, I should catch myself out, and stretch my hand at once for a book in self-protection. Indeed, it is curious how instinctively one protects the image of oneself from idolatry or any other handling that could make it ridiculous, or too unlike the original to be believed in any longer. Or is it not so very curious after all? It is a matter of great importance. Suppose the looking-glass smashes, the image disappears, and the romantic figure with the green of forest depths all about it is there no longer, but only that shell of a person which is seen by other people—what an airless, shallow, bald, prominent world it becomes! A world not to be lived in. As we face each other in omnibuses and underground railways we are looking into the mirror; that accounts for the vagueness, the gleam of glassiness, in our eyes. And the novelists in future will realise more and more the importance of these reflections, for of course there is not one reflection but an almost infinite number; those are the depths they will explore, those the phantoms they will pursue, leaving the description of reality more and more out of their stories, taking a knowledge of it for granted, as the Greeks did and Shakespeare perhaps—but these generalisations are very worthless. The military sound of the word is enough. It recalls leading articles, cabinet ministers—a whole class of things indeed which as a child one thought the thing itself, the standard thing, the real thing, from which one could not depart save at the risk of nameless damnation. Generalisations bring back somehow Sunday in London, Sunday afternoon walks, Sunday luncheons, and also ways of speaking of the dead, clothes, and habits—like the habit of sitting all together in one room until a certain hour, although nobody liked it. There was a rule for everything. The rule for tablecloths at that particular period was that they should be made of tapestry with little yellow compartments marked upon them, such as you may see in photographs of the carpets in the corridors of the royal palaces. Tablecloths of a different kind were not real tablecloths. How shocking, and yet how wonderful it was to discover that these real things, Sunday luncheons, Sunday walks, country houses, and tablecloths were not entirely real, were indeed half phantoms, and the damnation which visited the disbeliever in them was only a sense of illegitimate freedom. What now takes the place of those things I wonder, those real standard things? Men perhaps, should you be a woman; the masculine point of view which governs our lives, which sets the standard, which establishes Whitaker's Table of Precedency,[1] which has become, I suppose, since the war half a phantom to many men and women, which soon, one may hope, will

[1] *Table of Precedency* Table in *Whitaker's Almanac* that illustrates the hierarchy of the various ranks of the British social order.

be laughed into the dustbin where the phantoms go, the mahogany sideboards and the Landseer prints,[1] Gods and Devils, Hell and so forth, leaving us all with an intoxicating sense of illegitimate freedom—if freedom exists. …

In certain lights that mark on the wall seems actually to project from the wall. Nor is it entirely circular. I cannot be sure, but it seems to cast a perceptible shadow, suggesting that if I ran my finger down that strip of the wall it would, at a certain point, mount and descend a small tumulus, a smooth tumulus like those barrows on the South Downs[2] which are, they say, either tombs or camps. Of the two I should prefer them to be tombs, desiring melancholy like most English people, and finding it natural at the end of a walk to think of the bones stretched beneath the turf … There must be some book about it. Some antiquary[3] must have dug up those bones and given them a name … What sort of a man is an antiquary, I wonder? Retired Colonels for the most part, I daresay, leading parties of aged labourers to the top here, examining clods of earth and stone, and getting into correspondence with the neighbouring clergy, which, being opened at breakfast time, gives them a feeling of importance, and the comparison of arrowheads necessitates cross-country journeys to the country towns, an agreeable necessity both to them and to their elderly wives, who wish to make plum jam or to clean out the study, and have every reason for keeping that great question of the camp or the tomb in perpetual suspension, while the Colonel himself feels agreeably philosophic in accumulating evidence on both sides of the question. It is true that he does finally incline to believe in the camp; and, being opposed, indites a pamphlet which he is about to read at the quarterly meeting of the local society when a stroke lays him low, and his last conscious thoughts are not of wife or child, but of the camp and that arrowhead there, which is now in the case at the local museum, together with the foot of a Chinese murderess, a handful of Elizabethan nails, a great many Tudor clay pipes, a piece of Roman pottery, and the wine-glass that Nelson drank out of—proving I really don't know what.

No, no, nothing is proved, nothing is known. And if I were to get up at this very moment and ascertain that the mark on the wall is really—what shall I say?—the head of a gigantic old nail, driven in two hundred years ago, which has now, owing to the patient attrition of many generations of housemaids, revealed its head above the coat of paint, and is taking its first view of modern life in the sight of a white-walled fire-lit room, what should I gain? Knowledge? Matter for further speculation? I can think sitting still as well as standing up. And what is knowledge? What are our learned men save the descendants of witches and hermits who crouched in caves and in woods brewing herbs, interrogating shrew-mice and writing down the language of the stars? And the less we honour them as our superstitions dwindle and our respect for beauty and health of mind increases … Yes, one could imagine a very pleasant world. A quiet spacious world, with the flowers so red and blue in the open fields. A world without professors or specialists or house-keepers with the profiles of policemen, a world which one could slice with one's thought as a fish slices the water with his fin, grazing the stems of the water-lilies, hanging suspended over nests of white sea eggs. … How peaceful it is down here, rooted in the centre of the world and gazing up through the grey waters, with their sudden gleams of light, and their reflections—if it were not for Whitaker's Almanack—if it were not for the Table of Precedency!

I must jump up and see for myself what that mark on the wall really is—a nail, a rose-leaf, a crack in the wood?

Here is Nature once more at her old game of self-preservation. This train of thought, she perceives, is threatening mere waste of energy, even some collision with reality, for who will ever be able to lift a finger against Whitaker's Table of Precedency? The Archbishop of Canterbury is followed by the Lord High Chancellor; the Lord High Chancellor is followed by the Archbishop of York. Everybody follows somebody,

[1] *Landseer prints* Sir Edwin Henry Landseer (1802–73) produced paintings and engravings of animals.

[2] *South Downs* Range of chalk hills in southeastern England; *barrows* Mounds of earth or stone.

[3] *antiquary* Collector of antiquities, usually a non-professional.

such is the philosophy of Whitaker; and the great thing is to know who follows whom. Whitaker knows, and let that, so Nature counsels, comfort you, instead of enraging you; and if you can't be comforted, if you must shatter this hour of peace, think of the mark on the wall.

I understand Nature's game—her prompting to take action as a way of ending any thought that threatens to excite or to pain. Hence, I suppose, comes our slight contempt for men of action—men, we assume, who don't think. Still, there's no harm in putting a full stop to one's disagreeable thoughts by looking at a mark on the wall.

Indeed, now that I have fixed my eyes upon it, I feel that I have grasped a plank in the sea; I feel a satisfying sense of reality which at once turns the two Archbishops and the Lord High Chancellor to the shadows of shades. Here is something definite, something real. Thus, waking from a midnight dream of horror, one hastily turns on the light and lies quiescent, worshipping the chest of drawers, worshipping solidity, worshipping reality, worshipping the impersonal world which is proof of some existence other than ours. That is what one wants to be sure of. … Wood is a pleasant thing to think about. It comes from a tree; and trees grow, and we don't know how they grow. For years and years they grow, without paying any attention to us, in meadows, in forests, and by the side of rivers—all things one likes to think about. The cows swish their tails beneath them on hot afternoons; they paint rivers so green that when a moorhen dives one expects to see its feathers all green when it comes up again. I like to think of the fish balanced against the stream like flags blown out; and of water-beetles slowly raising domes of mud upon the bed of the river. I like to think of the tree itself: first the close dry sensation of being wood; then the grinding of the storm; then the slow, delicious ooze of sap. I like to think of it, too, on winter's nights standing in the empty field with all leaves close-furled, nothing tender exposed to the iron bullets of the moon, a naked mast upon an earth that goes tumbling, tumbling all night long. The song of birds must sound very loud and strange in June; and how cold the feet of insects must feel upon it, as they make laborious progresses up the creases of the bark, or sun themselves upon the thin green awning of the leaves, and look straight in front of them with diamond-cut red eyes. … One by one the fibres snap beneath the immense cold pressure of the earth, then the last storm comes and, falling, the highest branches drive deep into the ground again. Even so, life isn't done with; there are a million patient, watchful lives still for a tree, all over the world, in bedrooms, in ships, on the pavement, lining rooms, where men and women sit after tea, smoking cigarettes. It is full of peaceful thoughts, happy thoughts, this tree. I should like to take each one separately—but something is getting in the way. … Where was I? What has it all been about? A tree? A river? The Downs? Whitaker's Almanack? The fields of asphodel? I can't remember a thing. Everything's moving, falling, slipping, vanishing. … There is a vast upheaval of matter. Someone is standing over me and saying—

"I'm going out to buy a newspaper."

"Yes?"

"Though it's no good buying newspapers. … Nothing ever happens. Curse this war; God damn this war! … All the same, I don't see why we should have a snail on our wall."

Ah, the mark on the wall! It was a snail.

—1921

Blue & Green

GREEN

The pointed fingers of glass hang downwards. The light slides down the glass, and drops a pool of green. All day long the ten fingers of the lustre drop green upon the marble. The feathers of parakeets—their harsh cries—sharp blades of palm trees—green, too; green needles glittering in the sun. But the hard glass drips on to the marble; the pools hover above the desert sand; the camels lurch through them; the pools settle on the marble; rushes edge them; weeds clog them; here and there a white blossom; the frog flops over; at night the stars are set there unbroken. Evening comes, and the shadow sweeps the green over the mantelpiece; the ruffled surface of ocean. No ships come; the aimless waves sway beneath the empty sky. It's night; the needles drip blots of blue. The green's out.

BLUE
The snub-nosed monster rises to the surface and spouts through his blunt nostrils two columns of water, which, fiery-white in the centre, spray off into a fringe of blue beads. Strokes of blue line the black tarpaulin of his hide. Slushing the water through mouth and nostrils he sinks, heavy with water, and the blue closes over him dowsing the polished pebbles of his eyes. Thrown upon the beach he lies, blunt, obtuse, shedding dry blue scales. Their metallic blue stains the rusty iron on the beach. Blue are the ribs of the wrecked rowing boat. A wave rolls beneath the blue bells. But the cathedral's different, cold, incense laden, faint blue with the veils of madonnas.

—1921

Kew Gardens

From the oval-shaped flower-bed there rose perhaps a hundred stalks spreading into heart-shaped or tongue-shaped leaves half way up and unfurling at the tip red or blue or yellow petals marked with spots of colour raised upon the surface; and from the red, blue or yellow gloom of the throat emerged a straight bar, rough with gold dust and slightly clubbed at the end. The petals were voluminous enough to be stirred by the summer breeze, and when they moved, the red, blue, and yellow lights passed one over the other, staining an inch of the brown earth beneath with a spot of the most intricate colour. The light fell either upon the smooth grey back of a pebble, or the shell of a snail with its brown circular veins, or, falling into a raindrop, it expanded with such intensity of red, blue, and yellow the thin walls of water that one expected them to burst and disappear. Instead, the drop was left in a second silver grey once more, and the light now settled upon the flesh of a leaf, revealing the branching thread of fibre beneath the surface, and again it moved on and spread its illumination in the vast green spaces beneath the dome of the heart-shaped and tongue-shaped leaves. Then the breeze stirred rather more briskly overhead and the colour was flashed into the air above, into the eyes of the men and women who walk in Kew Gardens in July.

The figures of these men and women straggled past the flower-bed with a curiously irregular movement not unlike that of the white and blue butterflies who crossed the turf in zig-zag flights from bed to bed. The man was about six inches in front of the woman, strolling carelessly, while she bore on with greater purpose, only turning her head now and then to see that the children were not too far behind. The man kept this distance in front of the woman purposely, though perhaps unconsciously, for he wanted to go on with his thoughts.

"Fifteen years ago I came here with Lily," he thought. "We sat somewhere over there by a lake, and I begged her to marry me all through the hot afternoon. How the dragon-fly kept circling round us: how clearly I see the dragon-fly and her shoe with the square silver buckle at the toe. All the time I spoke I saw her shoe and when it moved impatiently I knew without looking up what she was going to say: the whole of her seemed to be in her shoe. And my love, my desire, were in the dragon-fly; for some reason I thought that if it settled there, on that leaf, the broad one with the red flower in the middle of it, if the dragonfly settled on the leaf she would say 'Yes' at once. But the dragon-fly went round and round: it never settled anywhere—of course not, happily not, or I shouldn't be walking here with Eleanor and the children—Tell me, Eleanor, d'you ever think of the past?"

"Why do you ask, Simon?"

"Because I've been thinking of the past. I've been thinking of Lily, the woman I might have married … Well, why are you silent? Do you mind my thinking of the past?"

"Why should I mind, Simon? Doesn't one always think of the past, in a garden with men and women lying under the trees? Aren't they one's past, all that remains of it, those men and women, those ghosts lying under the trees … one's happiness, one's reality?"

"For me, a square silver shoe-buckle and a dragon-fly—"

"For me, a kiss. Imagine six little girls sitting before their easels twenty years ago, down by the side of a lake, painting the water-lilies, the first red water-lilies I'd ever seen. And suddenly a kiss, there on the back of my neck. And my hand shook all the afternoon so that I couldn't paint. I took out my watch and marked the hour when I would allow myself to think of the kiss for five minutes only—it was so precious—the kiss of an old grey-haired woman with a wart on her nose, the mother of all my kisses all my life. Come Caroline, come Hubert."

They walked on past the flower-bed, now walking four abreast, and soon diminished in size among the trees and looked half transparent as the sunlight and shade swam over their backs in large trembling irregular patches.

In the oval flower-bed the snail, whose shell had been stained red, blue and yellow for the space of two minutes or so, now appeared to be moving very slightly in its shell, and next began to labour over the crumbs of loose earth which broke away and rolled down as it passed over them. It appeared to have a definite goal in front of it, differing in this respect from the singular high-stepping angular green insect who attempted to cross in front of it, and waited for a second with its antennae trembling as if in deliberation, and then stepped off as rapidly and strangely in the opposite direction. Brown cliffs with deep green lakes in the hollows, flat blade-like trees that waved from root to tip, round boulders of grey stone, vast crumpled surfaces of a thin crackling texture—all these objects lay across the snail's progress between one stalk and another to his goal. Before he had decided whether to circumvent the arched tent of a dead leaf or to breast it there came past the bed the feet of other human beings.

This time they were both men. The younger of the two wore an expression of perhaps unnatural calm; he raised his eyes and fixed them very steadily in front of him while his companion spoke, and directly his companion had done speaking he looked on the ground again and sometimes opened his lips only after a long pause and sometimes did not open them at all. The elder man had a curiously uneven and shaky method of walking, jerking his hand forward and throwing up his head abruptly, rather in the manner of an impatient carriage horse tired of waiting outside a house; but in the man these gestures were irresolute and pointless. He talked almost incessantly; he smiled to himself and again began to talk, as if the smile had been an answer. He was talking about spirits—the spirits of the dead, who, according to him, were even now telling him all sorts of odd things about their experiences in Heaven.

"Heaven was known to the ancients as Thessaly, William, and now, with this war, the spirit matter is rolling between the hills like thunder." He paused, seemed to listen, smiled, jerked his head and continued:—

"You have a small electric battery and a piece of rubber to insulate the wire—isolate?—insulate?—well, we'll skip the details, no good going into details that wouldn't be understood—and in short the little machine stands in any convenient position by the head of the bed, we will say, on a neat mahogany stand. All arrangements being properly fixed by workmen under my direction, the widow applies her ear and summons the spirit by sign as agreed. Women! Widows! Women in black—"

Here he seemed to have caught sight of a woman's dress in the distance, which in the shade looked a purple black. He took off his hat, placed his hand upon his heart, and hurried towards her muttering and gesticulating feverishly. But William caught him by the sleeve and touched a flower with the tip of his walking-stick in order to divert the old man's attention. After looking at it for a moment in some confusion the old man bent his ear to it and seemed to answer a voice speaking from it, for he began talking about the forests of Uruguay which he had visited hundreds of years ago in company with the most beautiful young woman in Europe. He could be heard murmuring about forests of Uruguay blanketed with the wax petals of tropical roses, nightingales, sea beaches, mermaids and women drowned at sea, as he suffered himself to be moved on by William, upon whose face the look of stoical patience grew slowly deeper and deeper.

Following his steps so closely as to be slightly puzzled by his gestures came two elderly women of the lower middle class, one stout and ponderous, the other rosy-cheeked and nimble. Like most people of their station[1] they were frankly fascinated by any signs of eccentricity betokening a disordered brain, especially in the well-to-do; but they were too far off to be certain whether the gestures were merely eccentric or genuinely mad. After they had scrutinised the old man's back in silence for a moment and given each other a queer, sly look, they went on energetically piecing together their very complicated dialogue:

"Nell, Bert, Lot, Cess, Phil, Pa, he says, I says, she says, I says, I says, I says—"

"My Bert, Sis, Bill, Grandad, the old man, sugar,
Sugar, flour, kippers, greens
Sugar, sugar, sugar."

The ponderous woman looked through the pattern of falling words at the flowers standing cool, firm and upright in the earth, with a curious expression. She saw them as a sleeper waking from a heavy sleep sees a brass candlestick reflecting the light in an unfamiliar way, and closes his eyes and opens them, and seeing the brass candlestick again, finally starts broad awake and stares at the candlestick with all his powers. So the heavy woman came to a standstill opposite the oval-shaped flower-bed, and ceased even to pretend to listen to what the other woman was saying. She stood there letting the words fall over her, swaying the top part of her body slowly backwards and forwards, looking at the flowers. Then she suggested that they should find a seat and have their tea.

The snail had now considered every possible method of reaching his goal without going round the dead leaf or climbing over it. Let alone the effort needed for climbing a leaf, he was doubtful whether the thin texture which vibrated with such an alarming crackle when touched even by the tip of his horns would bear his weight; and this determined him finally to creep beneath it, for there was a point where the leaf curved high enough from the ground to admit him. He had just inserted his head in the opening and was taking stock of the high brown roof and was getting used to the cool brown light when two other people came past outside on the turf. This time they were both young, a young man and a young woman. They were both in the prime of youth, or even in that season which precedes the prime of youth, the season before the smooth pink folds of the flower have burst their gummy case, when the wings of the butterfly, though fully grown, are motionless in the sun.

"Lucky it isn't Friday," he observed.

"Why? D'you believe in luck?"

"They make you pay sixpence on Friday."

"What's sixpence anyway? Isn't it worth sixpence?"

"What's 'it'—what do you mean by 'it'?"

"O anything—I mean—you know what I mean."

Long pauses came between each of these remarks: they were uttered in toneless and monotonous voices. The couple stood still on the edge of the flower-bed, and together pressed the end of her parasol deep down into the soft earth. The action and the fact that his hand rested on the top of hers expressed their feelings in a strange way, as these short insignificant words also expressed something, words with short wings for their heavy body of meaning, inadequate to carry them far and thus alighting awkwardly upon the very common objects that surrounded them and were to their inexperienced touch so massive: but who knows (so they thought as they pressed the parasol into the earth) what precipices aren't concealed in them, or what slopes of ice don't shine in the sun on the other side? Who knows? Who has ever seen this before? Even when she wondered what sort of tea they gave you at Kew, he felt that something loomed up behind her words, and stood vast and solid behind them; and the mist very slowly rose and uncovered—O Heavens,—what were those shapes?—little white tables, and waitresses who looked first at her and then at him; and there was a bill that he would pay with a real two shilling piece, and it was real, all real, he assured himself, fingering the coin in his pocket, real to everyone except to him and to her; even to him it began to seem real; and then—but it was too exciting to stand and think any longer, and he pulled

[1] *their station* I.e., their position in English society.

the parasol out of the earth with a jerk and was impatient to find the place where one had tea with other people, like other people.

"Come along, Trissie; it's time we had our tea."

"Wherever does one have one's tea?" she asked with the oddest thrill of excitement in her voice, looking vaguely round and letting herself be drawn on down the grass path, trailing her parasol, turning her head this way and that way, forgetting her tea, wishing to go down there and then down there, remembering orchids and cranes among wild flowers, a Chinese pagoda and a crimson-crested bird; but he bore her on.

Thus one couple after another with much the same irregular and aimless movement passed the flower-bed and were enveloped in layer after layer of green-blue vapour, in which at first their bodies had substance and a dash of colour, but later both substance and colour dissolved in the green-blue atmosphere. How hot it was! So hot that even the thrush chose to hop, like a mechanical bird, in the shadow of the flowers, with long pauses between one movement and the next; instead of rambling vaguely the white butterflies danced one above another, making with their white shifting flakes the outline of a shattered marble column above the tallest flowers; the glass roofs of the palm house shone as if a whole market full of shiny green umbrellas had opened in the sun; and in the drone of the aeroplane the voice of the summer sky murmured its fierce soul. Yellow and black, pink and snow white, shapes of all these colours, men, women, and children, were spotted for a second upon the horizon, and then, seeing the breadth of yellow that lay upon the grass, they wavered and sought shade beneath the trees, dissolving like drops of water in the yellow and green atmosphere, staining it faintly with red and blue. It seemed as if all gross and heavy bodies had sunk down in the heat motionless and lay huddled upon the ground, but their voices went wavering from them as if they were flames lolling from the thick waxen bodies of candles. Voices, yes, voices, wordless voices, breaking the silence suddenly with such depth of contentment, such passion of desire, or, in the voices of children, such freshness of surprise; breaking the silence? But there was no silence; all the time the motor omnibuses were turning their wheels and changing their gear; like a vast nest of Chinese boxes all of wrought steel turning ceaselessly one within another the city murmured; on the top of which the voices cried aloud and the petals of myriads of flowers flashed their colours into the air.

—1921

Mrs. Dalloway in Bond Street

Mrs. Dalloway said she would buy the gloves herself. Big Ben was striking as she stepped out into the street. It was eleven o'clock and the unused hour was fresh as if issued to children on a beach. But there was something solemn in the deliberate swing of the repeated strokes; something stirring in the murmur of wheels and the shuffle of footsteps.

No doubt they were not all bound on errands of happiness. There is much more to be said about us than that we walk the streets of Westminster. Big Ben too is nothing but steel rods consumed by rust were it not for the care of H.M.'s Office of Works. Only for Mrs. Dalloway the moment was complete; for Mrs. Dalloway June was fresh. A happy childhood—and it was not to his daughters only that Justin Parry had seemed a fine fellow (weak of course on the Bench); flowers at evening, smoke rising; the caw of rooks falling from ever so high, down down through the October air—there is nothing to take the place of childhood. A leaf of mint brings it back: or a cup with a blue ring.

Poor little wretches, she sighed, and pressed forward. Oh, right under the horses' noses, you little demon! and there she was left on the kerb stretching her hand out, while Jimmy Dawes grinned on the further side.

A charming woman, poised, eager, strangely white-haired for her pink cheeks, so Scope Purvis, C.B.,[1] saw her as he hurried to his office. She stiffened a little, waiting for Durtnall's van to pass. Big Ben struck the tenth; struck the eleventh stroke. The leaden circles dissolved in the air. Pride held her erect, inheriting,

[1] *C.B.* Companion of the Bath. The Order of the Bath is an order of chivalry conferred by the sovereign of England.

handing on, acquainted with discipline and with suffering. How people suffered, how they suffered, she thought, thinking of Mrs. Foxcroft at the Embassy last night decked with jewels, eating her heart out, because that nice boy was dead, and now the old Manor House (Durtnall's van passed) must go to a cousin.

"Good morning to you!" said Hugh Whitbread raising his hat rather extravagantly by the china shop, for they had known each other as children. "Where are you off to?"

"I love walking in London," said Mrs. Dalloway. "Really it's better than walking in the country!"

"We've just come up," said Hugh Whitbread. "Unfortunately to see doctors."

"Milly?" said Mrs. Dalloway, instantly compassionate.

"Out of sorts," said Hugh Whitbread. "That sort of thing. Dick all right?"

"First rate!" said Clarissa.

Of course, she thought, walking on, Milly is about my age—fifty—fifty-two. So it is probably that, Hugh's manner had said so, said it perfectly—dear old Hugh, thought Mrs. Dalloway, remembering with amusement, with gratitude, with emotion, how shy, like a brother—one would rather die than speak to one's brother—Hugh had always been, when he was at Oxford, and came over, and perhaps one of them (drat the thing!) couldn't ride. How then could women sit in Parliament? How could they do things with men? For there is this extraordinarily deep instinct, something inside one; you can't get over it; it's no use trying; and men like Hugh respect it without our saying it, which is what one loves, thought Clarissa, in dear old Hugh.

She had passed through the Admiralty Arch and saw at the end of the empty road with its thin trees Victoria's white mound,[1] Victoria's billowing motherliness, amplitude and homeliness, always ridiculous, yet how sublime, thought Mrs. Dalloway, remembering Kensington Gardens and the old lady in horn spectacles and being told by Nanny to stop dead still and bow to the Queen. The flag flew above the Palace. The King and Queen were back then. Dick had met her at lunch the other day—a thoroughly nice woman. It matters so much to the poor, thought Clarissa, and to the soldiers. A man in bronze stood heroically on a pedestal with a gun on her left hand side—the South African war. It matters, thought Mrs. Dalloway walking towards Buckingham Palace. There it stood four-square, in the broad sunshine, uncompromising, plain. But it was character, she thought; something inborn in the race; what Indians respected. The Queen went to hospitals, opened bazaars—the Queen of England, thought Clarissa, looking at the Palace. Already at this hour a motor car passed out at the gates; soldiers saluted; the gates were shut. And Clarissa, crossing the road, entered the Park,[2] holding herself upright.

June had drawn out every leaf on the trees. The mothers of Westminster with mottled breasts gave suck to their young. Quite respectable girls lay stretched on the grass. An elderly man, stooping very stiffly, picked up a crumpled paper, spread it out flat and flung it away. How horrible! Last night at the Embassy Sir Dighton had said, "If I want a fellow to hold my horse, I have only to put up my hand." But the religious question is far more serious than the economic, Sir Dighton had said, which she thought extraordinarily interesting, from a man like Sir Dighton. "Oh, the country will never know what it has lost," he had said, talking of his own accord, about dear Jack Stewart.

She mounted the little hill lightly. The air stirred with energy. Messages were passing from the Fleet to the Admiralty. Piccadilly and Arlington Street and the Mall[3] seemed to chafe the very air in the Park and lift its leaves hotly, brilliantly, upon waves of that divine vitality which Clarissa loved. To ride; to dance; she had adored all that. Or going long walks in the country, talking, about books, what to do with one's life, for young people were amazingly priggish—oh, the things one had said! But one had conviction. Middle age is the devil. People like Jack'll never know that, she thought; for he never once thought of death, never, they said, knew he

[1] *Victoria's white mound* Monument to Queen Victoria at the entrance to Buckingham Palace.

[2] *the Park* St. James's Park, London.

[3] *the Mall* Walk bordered by trees in St. James's Park.

was dying. And now can never mourn—how did it go?—a head grown grey ... From the contagion of the world's slow stain[1] ... have drunk their cup a round or two before.[2] ... From the contagion of the world's slow stain! She held herself upright.

But how Jack would have shouted! Quoting Shelley, in Piccadilly! "You want a pin," he would have said. He hated frumps. "My God Clarissa! My God Clarissa!"—she could hear him now at the Devonshire House[3] party, about poor Sylvia Hunt in her amber necklace and that dowdy old silk. Clarissa held herself upright for she had spoken aloud and now she was in Piccadilly, passing the house with the slender green columns, and the balconies; passing club windows full of newspapers; passing old Lady Burdett-Coutts's house where the glazed white parrot used to hang; and Devonshire House, without its gilt leopards; and Claridge's,[4] where she must remember Dick wanted her to leave a card on Mrs. Jepson or she would be gone. Rich Americans can be very charming. There was St. James's Palace; like a child's game with bricks; and now—she had passed Bond Street—she was by Hatchard's book shop. The stream was endless—endless—endless. Lords, Ascot, Hurlingham—what was it? What a duck, she thought, looking at the frontispiece of some book of memoirs spread wide in the bow window, Sir Joshua perhaps or Romney;[5] arch, bright, demure; the sort of girl—like her own Elizabeth—the only real sort of girl. And there was that absurd book, Soapy Sponge,[6] which Jim used to quote by the yard; and Shakespeare's Sonnets. She knew them by heart. Phil and she had argued all day about the Dark Lady, and Dick had said straight out at dinner that night that he had never heard of her. Really, she had married him for that! He had never read Shakespeare! There must be some little cheap book she could buy for Milly—*Cranford*[7] of course! Was there ever anything so enchanting as the cow in petticoats? If only people had that sort of humour, that sort of self-respect now, thought Clarissa, for she remembered the broad pages; the sentences ending; the characters—how one talked about them as if they were real. For all the great things one must go to the past, she thought. From the contagion of the world's slow stain ... Fear no more the heat o' the sun.[8]... And now can never mourn, can never mourn, she repeated, her eyes straying over the window; for it ran in her head; the test of great poetry; the moderns had never written anything one wanted to read about death, she thought; and turned.

Omnibuses joined motor cars; motor cars vans; vans taxicabs, taxicabs motor cars—here was an open motor car with a girl, alone. Up till four, her feet tingling, I know, thought Clarissa, for the girl looked washed out, half asleep, in the corner of the car after the dance. And another car came; and another. No! No! No! Clarissa smiled good-naturedly. The fat lady had taken every sort of trouble, but diamonds! orchids! at this hour of the morning! No! No! No! The excellent policeman would, when the time came, hold up his hand. Another motor car passed. How utterly unattractive! Why should a girl of that age paint black round her eyes? And a young man, with a girl, at this hour, when the country—The admirable policeman raised his hand and Clarissa acknowledging his sway, taking her time, crossed, walked towards Bond Street; saw the narrow crooked street, the yellow banners; the thick notched telegraph wires stretched across the sky.

[1] *how did it ... stain* See Percy Shelley's *Adonais* (1821): "From the contagion of the world's slow stain / He is secure, and now can never mourn. / A heart grown cold, a head grown grey in vain" (lines 356–58).

[2] *have drunk ... before* See Edward Fitzgerald's *The Rubâiyát of Omar Khayyám* (1859): "Lo! some we loved, the loveliest and best / That Time and Fate of all their Vintage prest / Have drunk their Cup a Round or two before / And one by one crept silently to Rest."

[3] *Devonshire House* London home of the Duke of Devonshire.

[4] *Claridge's* Claridge's Hotel.

[5] *Sir Joshua ... Romney* Sir Joshua Reynolds (1723–92) and George Romney (1734–1802), English painters.

[6] *Soapy Sponge* The nickname of the protagonist of R.S. Surtees's novel *Mr. Sponge's Sporting Tour* (1853).

[7] *Cranford* Novel by Elizabeth Gaskell (1853). In the book, Miss Betsy Barker dresses her cow in grey flannel after a fall into a lime pit removes all its hair.

[8] *Fear ... sun* From Shakespeare's *Cymbeline*, 4.2: "Fear no more the heat o' the sun / Nor the furious winter's rages / Thou thy worldly task hast done / Home art gone, and ta'en thy wages / Golden lads and girls all must / As chimney-sweepers, come to dust."

A hundred years ago her great-great-grandfather, Seymour Parry, who ran away with Conway's daughter, had walked down Bond Street. Down Bond Street the Parrys had walked for a hundred years, and might have met the Dalloways (Leighs on the mother's side) going up. Her father got his clothes from Hill's. There was a roll of cloth in the window, and here just one jar on a black table, incredibly expensive; like the thick pink salmon on the ice block at the fishmonger's. The jewels were exquisite—pink and orange stars, paste, Spanish, she thought, and chains of old gold; starry buckles, little brooches which had been worn on sea-green satin by ladies with high head-dresses. But no good looking! One must economise. She must go on past the picture dealer's where one of the odd French pictures hung, as if people had thrown confetti—pink and blue—for a joke. If you had lived with pictures (and it's the same with books and music) thought Clarissa, passing the Aeolian Hall, you can't be taken in by a joke.

The river of Bond Street was clogged. There, like a Queen at a tournament, raised, regal, was Lady Bexborough. She sat in her carriage, upright, alone, looking through her glasses. The white glove was loose at her wrist. She was in black, quite shabby, yet, thought Clarissa, how extraordinarily it tells, breeding, self-respect, never saying a word too much or letting people gossip; an astonishing friend; no one can pick a hole in her after all these years, and now, there she is, thought Clarissa, passing the Countess who waited powdered, perfectly still, and Clarissa would have given anything to be like that, the mistress of Clarefield, talking politics, like a man. But she never goes anywhere, thought Clarissa, and it's quite useless to ask her, and the carriage went on and Lady Bexborough was borne past like a Queen at a tournament, though she had nothing to live for and the old man is failing and they say she is sick of it all, thought Clarissa and the tears actually rose to her eyes as she entered the shop.

"Good morning," said Clarissa in her charming voice. "Gloves," she said with her exquisite friendliness and putting her bag on the counter began, very slowly, to undo the buttons. "White gloves," she said. "Above the elbow," and she looked straight into the shop-woman's face—but this was not the girl she remembered? She looked quite old. "These really don't fit," said Clarissa. The shop-girl looked at them. "Madame wears bracelets?" Clarissa spread out her fingers. "Perhaps it's my rings." And the girl took the grey gloves with her to the end of the counter.

Yes, thought Clarissa, if it's the girl I remember, she's twenty years older. … There was only one other customer, sitting sideways at the counter, her elbow poised, her bare hand drooping, vacant; like a figure on a Japanese fan, thought Clarissa, too vacant perhaps, yet some men would adore her. The lady shook her head sadly. Again the gloves were too large. She turned round the glass. "Above the wrist," she reproached the grey-headed woman; who looked and agreed.

They waited; a clock ticked; Bond Street hummed, dulled, distant; the woman went away holding gloves. "Above the wrist," said the lady, mournfully, raising her voice. And she would have to order chairs, ices, flowers, and cloak-room tickets, thought Clarissa. The people she didn't want would come; the others wouldn't. She would stand by the door. They sold stockings—silk stockings. A lady is known by her gloves and her shoes, old Uncle William used to say. And through the hanging silk stockings quivering silver she looked at the lady, sloping shouldered, her hand drooping, her bag slipping, her eyes vacantly on the floor. It would be intolerable if dowdy women came to her party! Would one have liked Keats[1] if he had worn red socks? Oh, at last—she drew into the counter and it flashed into her mind:

"Do you remember before the war you had gloves with pearl buttons?"

"French gloves, Madame?"

"Yes, they were French," said Clarissa. The other lady rose very sadly and took her bag, and looked at the gloves on the counter. But they were all too large—always too large at the wrist.

"With pearl buttons," said the shop-girl, who looked ever so much older. She split the lengths of tissue paper

[1] *Keats* John Keats (1795–1821), English Romantic poet.

apart on the counter. With pearl buttons, thought Clarissa, perfectly simple—how French!

"Madame's hands are so slender," said the shop-girl, drawing the glove firmly, smoothly, down over her rings. And Clarissa looked at her arm in the looking-glass. The glove hardly came to the elbow. Were there others half an inch longer? Still it seemed tiresome to bother her—perhaps the one day in the month, thought Clarissa, when it's an agony to stand. "Oh, don't bother," she said. But the gloves were brought.

"Don't you get fearfully tired," she said in her charming voice, "standing? When d'you get your holiday?"

"In September, Madame, when we're not so busy."

When we're in the country thought Clarissa. Or shooting. She has a fortnight at Brighton. In some stuffy lodging. The landlady takes the sugar. Nothing would be easier than to send her to Mrs. Lumley's right in the country (and it was on the tip of her tongue). But then she remembered how on their honeymoon Dick had shown her the folly of giving impulsively. It was much more important, he said, to get trade with China. Of course he was right. And she could feel the girl wouldn't like to be given things. There she was in her place. So was Dick. Selling gloves was her job. She had her own sorrows quite separate, "and now can never mourn, can never mourn," the words ran in her head. "From the contagion of the world's slow stain," thought Clarissa holding her arm stiff, for there are moments when it seems utterly futile (the glove was drawn off leaving her arm flecked with powder)—simply one doesn't believe, thought Clarissa, any more in God.

The traffic suddenly roared; the silk stockings brightened. A customer came in.

"White gloves," she said, with some ring in her voice that Clarissa remembered.

It used, thought Clarissa, to be so simple. Down down through the air came the caw of the rooks. When Sylvia died, hundreds of years ago, the yew hedges looked so lovely with the diamond webs in the mist before early church. But if Dick were to die tomorrow, as for believing in God—no, she would let the children choose, but for herself, like Lady Bexborough, who opened the bazaar, they say, with the telegram in her hand—Roden, her favourite, killed—she would go on. But why, if one doesn't believe? For the sake of others, she thought, taking the glove in her hand. The girl would be much more unhappy if she didn't believe.

"Thirty shillings," said the shop-woman. "No, pardon me Madame, thirty-five. The French gloves are more."

For one doesn't live for oneself, thought Clarissa.

And then the other customer took a glove, tugged it, and it split.

"There!" she exclaimed.

"A fault of the skin," said the grey-headed woman hurriedly. "Sometimes a drop of acid in tanning. Try this pair, Madame."

"But it's an awful swindle to ask two pound ten!"

Clarissa looked at the lady; the lady looked at Clarissa.

"Gloves have never been quite so reliable since the war," said the shop-girl, apologising, to Clarissa.

But where had she seen the other lady?—elderly, with a frill under her chin; wearing a black ribbon for gold eyeglasses; sensual, clever, like a Sargent[1] drawing. How one can tell from a voice when people are in the habit, thought Clarissa, of making other people—"It's a shade too tight," she said—obey. The shop-woman went off again. Clarissa was left waiting. Fear no more she repeated, playing her finger on the counter. Fear no more the heat o' the sun. Fear no more she repeated. There were little brown spots on her arm. And the girl crawled like a snail. Thou thy worldly task hast done. Thousands of young men had died that things might go on. At last! Half an inch above the elbow; pearl buttons; five and a quarter. My dear slow coach, thought Clarissa, do you think I can sit here the whole morning? Now you'll take twenty-five minutes to bring me my change!

There was a violent explosion in the street outside. The shop-women cowered behind the counters. But Clarissa, sitting very upright, smiled at the other lady. "Miss Anstruther!" she exclaimed.

—1923

[1] *Sargent* John Singer Sargent (1856–1925), the celebrated American artist, was (and is) known for his portraits of women of fashion.

Modern Fiction

In making any survey, even the freest and loosest, of modern fiction, it is difficult not to take it for granted that the modern practice of the art is somehow an improvement upon the old. With their simple tools and primitive materials, it might be said, Fielding did well and Jane Austen even better,[1] but compare their opportunities with ours! Their masterpieces certainly have a strange air of simplicity. And yet the analogy between literature and the process, to choose an example, of making motor cars scarcely holds good beyond the first glance. It is doubtful whether in the course of the centuries, though we have learnt much about making machines, we have learnt anything about making literature. We do not come to write better; all that we can be said to do is to keep moving, now a little in this direction, now in that, but with a circular tendency should the whole course of the track be viewed from a sufficiently lofty pinnacle. It need scarcely be said that we make no claim to stand, even momentarily, upon that vantage ground. On the flat, in the crowd, half blind with dust, we look back with envy to those happier warriors, whose battle is won and whose achievements wear so serene an air of accomplishment that we can scarcely refrain from whispering that the fight was not so fierce for them as for us. It is for the historian of literature to decide; for him to say if we are now beginning or ending or standing in the middle of a great period of prose fiction, for down in the plain little is visible. We only know that certain gratitudes and hostilities inspire us; that certain paths seem to lead to fertile land, others to the dust and the desert; and of this perhaps it may be worth while to attempt some account.

Our quarrel, then, is not with the classics, and if we speak of quarrelling with Mr. Wells, Mr. Bennett, and Mr. Galsworthy,[2] it is partly that by the mere fact of their existence in the flesh their work has a living, breathing, everyday imperfection which bids us take what liberties with it we choose. But it is also true that, while we thank them for a thousand gifts, we reserve our unconditional gratitude for Mr. Hardy, for Mr. Conrad, and in a much lesser degree for the Mr. Hudson of *The Purple Land, Green Mansions,* and *Far Away and Long Ago*.[3] Mr. Wells, Mr. Bennett, and Mr. Galsworthy have excited so many hopes and disappointed them so persistently that our gratitude largely takes the form of thanking them for having shown us what they might have done but have not done; what we certainly could not do, but as certainly, perhaps, do not wish to do. No single phrase will sum up the charge or grievance which we have to bring against a mass of work so large in its volume and embodying so many qualities, both admirable and the reverse. If we tried to formulate our meaning in one word we should say that these three writers are materialists. It is because they are concerned not with the spirit but with the body that they have disappointed us, and left us with the feeling that the sooner English fiction turns its back upon them, as politely as may be, and marches, if only into the desert, the better for its soul. Naturally, no single word reaches the centre of three separate targets. In the case of Mr. Wells it falls notably wide of the mark. And yet even with him it indicates to our thinking the fatal alloy in his genius, the great clod of clay that has got itself mixed up with the purity of his inspiration. But Mr. Bennett is perhaps the worst culprit of the three, inasmuch as he is by far the best workman. He can make a book so well constructed and solid in its craftsmanship that it is difficult for the most exacting of critics to see through what chink or crevice decay can creep in. There is not so much as a draught between the frames of the windows, or a crack in the boards. And yet—if life should refuse to live there? That is a risk which the creator of *The Old Wives'*

[1] *Fielding … better* Henry Fielding (1707–54) and Jane Austen (1775–1817), British novelists.

[2] *Mr. Wells … Galsworthy* H.G. Wells (1866–1946), Arnold Bennett (1867–1931), and John Galsworthy (1867–1933), three popular novelists at the time.

[3] *Mr. Hardy … Ago* Thomas Hardy (1840–1928), author of *Tess of the d'Urbervilles* and *Jude the Obscure*; Joseph Conrad (1857–1924), author of *Heart of Darkness*; William Henry Hudson (1841–1922), Argentinean author and naturalist who lived in London. *The Purple Land* and *Green Mansions* are romances set in Argentina, and *Far Away and Long Ago* is an account of Hudson's early life in Argentina.

Tale, George Cannon, Edwin Clayhanger,[1] and hosts of other figures, may well claim to have surmounted. His characters live abundantly, even unexpectedly, but it remains to ask how do they live, and what do they live for? More and more they seem to us, deserting even the well-built villa in the Five Towns,[2] to spend their time in some softly padded first-class railway carriage, pressing bells and buttons innumerable; and the destiny to which they travel so luxuriously becomes more and more unquestionably an eternity of bliss spent in the very best hotel in Brighton. It can scarcely be said of Mr. Wells that he is a materialist in the sense that he takes too much delight in the solidity of his fabric. His mind is too generous in its sympathies to allow him to spend much time in making things shipshape and substantial. He is a materialist from sheer goodness of heart, taking upon his shoulders the work that ought to have been discharged by Government officials, and in the plethora of his ideas and facts scarcely having leisure to realise, or forgetting to think important, the crudity and coarseness of his human beings. Yet what more damaging criticism can there be both of his earth and of his Heaven than that they are to be inhabited here and hereafter by his Joans and his Peters? Does not the inferiority of their natures tarnish whatever institutions and ideals may be provided for them by the generosity of their creator? Nor, profoundly though we respect the integrity and humanity of Mr. Galsworthy, shall we find what we seek in his pages.

If we fasten, then, one label on all these books, on which is one word materialists, we mean by it that they write of unimportant things; that they spend immense skill and immense industry making the trivial and the transitory appear the true and the enduring.

We have to admit that we are exacting, and, further, that we find it difficult to justify our discontent by explaining what it is that we exact. We frame our question differently at different times. But it reappears most persistently as we drop the finished novel on the crest of a sigh—Is it worth while? What is the point of it all? Can it be that, owing to one of those little deviations which the human spirit seems to make from time to time, Mr. Bennett has come down with his magnificent apparatus for catching life just an inch or two on the wrong side? Life escapes; and perhaps without life nothing else is worth while. It is a confession of vagueness to have to make use of such a figure as this, but we scarcely better the matter by speaking, as critics are prone to do, of reality. Admitting the vagueness which afflicts all criticism of novels, let us hazard the opinion that for us at this moment the form of fiction most in vogue more often misses than secures the thing we seek. Whether we call it life or spirit, truth or reality, this, the essential thing, has moved off, or on, and refuses to be contained any longer in such ill-fitting vestments as we provide. Nevertheless, we go on perseveringly, conscientiously, constructing our two and thirty chapters after a design which more and more ceases to resemble the vision in our minds. So much of the enormous labour of proving the solidity, the likeness to life, of the story is not merely labour thrown away but labour misplaced to the extent of obscuring and blotting out the light of the conception. The writer seems constrained, not by his own free will but by some powerful and unscrupulous tyrant who has him in thrall, to provide a plot, to provide comedy, tragedy, love interest, and an air of probability embalming the whole so impeccable that if all his figures were to come to life they would find themselves dressed down to the last button of their coats in the fashion of the hour. The tyrant is obeyed; the novel is done to a turn. But sometimes, more and more often as time goes by, we suspect a momentary doubt, a spasm of rebellion, as the pages fill themselves in the customary way. Is life like this? Must novels be like this?

Look within and life, it seems, is very far from being "like this." Examine for a moment an ordinary mind on an ordinary day. The mind receives a myriad impressions—trivial, fantastic, evanescent, or engraved with the sharpness of steel. From all sides they come, an incessant shower of innumerable atoms; and as they fall, as they shape themselves into the life of Monday or

---

[1] *George … Clayhanger* Characters from Bennett's novels *The Roll-Call* and *Clayhanger*.

[2] *the Five Towns* Five towns in Staffordshire that comprise the center of England's pottery industry and that provide the setting for many of Bennett's novels.

Tuesday, the accent falls differently from of old; the moment of importance came not here but there; so that, if a writer were a free man and not a slave, if he could write what he chose, not what he must, if he could base his work upon his own feeling and not upon convention, there would be no plot, no comedy, no tragedy, no love interest or catastrophe in the accepted style, and perhaps not a single button sewn on as the Bond Street tailors would have it. Life is not a series of gig lamps symmetrically arranged; life is a luminous halo, a semi-transparent envelope surrounding us from the beginning of consciousness to the end. Is it not the task of the novelist to convey this varying, this unknown and uncircumscribed spirit, whatever aberration or complexity it may display, with as little mixture of the alien and external as possible? We are not pleading merely for courage and sincerity; we are suggesting that the proper stuff of fiction is a little other than custom would have us believe it.

It is, at any rate, in some such fashion as this that we seek to define the quality which distinguishes the work of several young writers, among whom Mr. James Joyce[1] is the most notable, from that of their predecessors. They attempt to come closer to life, and to preserve more sincerely and exactly what interests and moves them, even if to do so they must discard most of the conventions which are commonly observed by the novelist. Let us record the atoms as they fall upon the mind in the order in which they fall, let us trace the pattern, however disconnected and incoherent in appearance, which each sight or incident scores upon the consciousness. Let us not take it for granted that life exists more fully in what is commonly thought big than in what is commonly thought small. Any one who has read *The Portrait of the Artist as a Young Man* or, what promises to be a far more interesting work, *Ulysses*,[2] now appearing in the *Little Review*, will have hazarded some theory of this nature as to Mr. Joyce's intention. On our part, with such a fragment before us, it is hazarded rather than affirmed; but whatever the intention of the whole, there can be no question but that it is of the utmost sincerity and that the result, difficult or unpleasant as we may judge it, is undeniably important. In contrast with those whom we have called materialists, Mr. Joyce is spiritual; he is concerned at all costs to reveal the flickerings of that innermost flame which flashes its messages through the brain, and in order to preserve it he disregards with complete courage whatever seems to him adventitious, whether it be probability, or coherence, or any other of these signposts which for generations have served to support the imagination of a reader when called upon to imagine what he can neither touch nor see. The scene in the cemetery,[3] for instance, with its brilliancy, its sordidity, its incoherence, its sudden lightning flashes of significance, does undoubtedly come so close to the quick of the mind that, on a first reading at any rate, it is difficult not to acclaim a masterpiece. If we want life itself, here surely we have it. Indeed, we find ourselves fumbling rather awkwardly if we try to say what else we wish, and for what reason a work of such originality yet fails to compare, for we must take high examples, with *Youth* or *The Mayor of Casterbridge*.[4] It fails because of the comparative poverty of the writer's mind, we might say simply and have done with it. But it is possible to press a little further and wonder whether we may not refer our sense of being in a bright yet narrow room, confined and shut in, rather than enlarged and set free, to some limitation imposed by the method as well as by the mind. Is it the method that inhibits the creative power? Is it due to the method that we feel neither jovial nor magnanimous, but centred in a self which, in spite of its tremor of susceptibility, never embraces or creates what is outside itself and beyond? Does the emphasis laid, perhaps didactically, upon indecency, contribute to the effect of something angular and isolated? Or is it merely that in any effort of such originality it is much easier, for contemporaries especially, to feel what it lacks than to name what it gives? In any case it is a mistake to stand outside examining "methods." Any method is right, every

[1] *Mr. James Joyce* James Joyce (1882–1941), Irish novelist.

[2] [Woolf's note] Written in April, 1919.

[3] *The scene ... cemetery* In the "Hades" section of *Ulysses*.

[4] *Youth ... Casterbridge* By Joseph Conrad and Thomas Hardy, respectively.

method is right, that expresses what we wish to express, if we are writers; that brings us closer to the novelist's intention if we are readers. This method has the merit of bringing us closer to what we were prepared to call life itself; did not the reading of *Ulysses* suggest how much of life is excluded or ignored, and did it not come with a shock to open *Tristram Shandy* or even *Pendennis*[1] and be by them convinced that there are not only other aspects of life, but more important ones into the bargain.

However this may be, the problem before the novelist at present, as we suppose it to have been in the past, is to contrive means of being free to set down what he chooses. He has to have the courage to say that what interests him is no longer "this" but "that": out of "that" alone must he construct his work. For the moderns "that," the point of interest, lies very likely in the dark places of psychology. At once, therefore, the accent falls a little differently; the emphasis is upon something hitherto ignored; at once a different outline of form becomes necessary, difficult for us to grasp, incomprehensible to our predecessors. No one but a modern, no one perhaps but a Russian, would have felt the interest of the situation which Tchekov[2] has made into the short story which he calls "Gusev."[3] Some Russian soldiers lie ill on board a ship which is taking them back to Russia. We are given a few scraps of their talk and some of their thoughts; then one of them dies and is carried away; the talk goes on among the others for a time, until Gusev himself dies, and looking "like a carrot or a radish" is thrown overboard. The emphasis is laid upon such unexpected places that at first it seems as if there were no emphasis at all; and then, as the eyes accustom themselves to twilight and discern the shapes of things in a room we see how complete the story is, how profound, and how truly in obedience to his vision Tchekov has chosen this, that, and the other, and placed them together to compose something new. But it is impossible to say "this is comic," or "that is tragic," nor are we certain, since short stories, we have been taught, should be brief and conclusive, whether this, which is vague and inconclusive, should be called a short story at all.

The most elementary remarks upon modern English fiction can hardly avoid some mention of the Russian influence, and if the Russians are mentioned one runs the risk of feeling that to write of any fiction save theirs is waste of time. If we want understanding of the soul and heart where else shall we find it of comparable profundity? If we are sick of our own materialism the least considerable of their novelists has by right of birth a natural reverence for the human spirit. "Learn to make yourself akin to people. ... But let this sympathy be not with the mind—for it is easy with the mind—but with the heart, with love towards them." In every great Russian writer we seem to discern the features of a saint, if sympathy for the sufferings of others, love towards them, endeavour to reach some goal worthy of the most exacting demands of the spirit constitute saintliness. It is the saint in them which confounds us with a feeling of our own irreligious triviality, and turns so many of our famous novels to tinsel and trickery. The conclusions of the Russian mind, thus comprehensive and compassionate, are inevitably, perhaps, of the utmost sadness. More accurately indeed we might speak of the inconclusiveness of the Russian mind. It is the sense that there is no answer, that if honestly examined life presents question after question which must be left to sound on and on after the story is over in hopeless interrogation that fills us with a deep, and finally it may be with a resentful, despair. They are right perhaps; unquestionably they see further than we do and without our gross impediments of vision. But perhaps we see something that escapes them, or why should this voice of protest mix itself with our gloom? The voice of protest is the voice of another and an ancient civilisation which seems to have bred in us the instinct to enjoy and fight rather than to suffer and understand. English fiction from Sterne to Meredith[4] bears witness to our natural delight in humour and comedy, in the beauty of earth, in the

[1] *Tristram ... Pendennis* Novels by Laurence Sterne (1713–68) and William Makepeace Thackeray (1811–68), respectively.

[2] *Tchekov* Russian playwright and short story writer Anton Chekhov (1860–1904).

[3] *Gusev* Published in 1890.

[4] *Meredith* George Meredith, novelist and poet (1828–1909).

activities of the intellect, and in the splendour of the body. But any deductions that we may draw from the comparison of two fictions so immeasurably far apart are futile save indeed as they flood us with a view of the infinite possibilities of the art and remind us that there is no limit to the horizon, and that nothing—no "method," no experiment, even of the wildest—is forbidden, but only falsity and pretence. "The proper stuff of fiction" does not exist; everything is the proper stuff of fiction, every feeling, every thought; every quality of brain and spirit is drawn upon; no perception comes amiss. And if we can imagine the art of fiction come alive and standing in our midst, she would undoubtedly bid us break her and bully her, as well as honour and love her, for so her youth is renewed and her sovereignty assured.

—1925

from *A Room of One's Own*[1]

Chapter 1

But, you may say, we asked you to speak about women and fiction—what has that got to do with a room of one's own? I will try to explain. When you asked me to speak about women and fiction I sat down on the banks of a river and began to wonder what the words meant. They might mean simply a few remarks about Fanny Burney; a few more about Jane Austen; a tribute to the Brontës and a sketch of Haworth Parsonage under snow; some witticisms if possible about Miss Mitford; a respectful allusion to George Eliot; a reference to Mrs. Gaskell[2] and one would have done. But at second sight the words seemed not so simple. The title women and fiction might mean, and you may have meant it to mean, women and what they are like; or it might mean women and the fiction that they write; or it might mean women and the fiction that is written about them; or it might mean that somehow all three are inextricably mixed together and you want me to consider them in that light. But when I began to consider the subject in this last way, which seemed the most interesting, I soon saw that it had one fatal drawback. I should never be able to come to a conclusion. I should never be able to fulfil what is, I understand, the first duty of a lecturer—to hand you after an hour's discourse a nugget of pure truth to wrap up between the pages of your notebooks and keep on the mantel-piece for ever. All I could do was to offer you an opinion upon one minor point—a woman must have money and a room of her own if she is to write fiction; and that, as you will see, leaves the great problem of the true nature of woman and the true nature of fiction unsolved. I have shirked the duty of coming to a conclusion upon these two questions—women and fiction remain, so far as I am concerned, unsolved problems. But in order to make some amends I am going to do what I can to show you how I arrived at this opinion about the room and the money. I am going to develop in your presence as fully and freely as I can the train of thought which led me to think this. Perhaps if I lay bare the ideas, the prejudices, that lie behind this statement you will find that they have some bearing upon women and some upon fiction. At any rate, when a subject is highly controversial—and any question about sex is that—one cannot hope to tell the truth. One can only show how one came to hold whatever opinion one does hold. One can only give one's audience the chance of drawing their own conclusions as they observe the limitations, the prejudices, the idiosyncrasies of the speaker. Fiction here is likely to contain more truth than fact. Therefore I propose, making use of all the liberties and licences of a novelist, to tell you the story of the two

[1] [Woolf's note] This essay is based upon two papers read to the Arts Society at Newnham and the Odtaa at Girton in October 1928. The papers were too long to be read in full, and have since been altered and expanded. [Newnham and Girton are women's colleges at Cambridge University, and Odtaa (an acronym for "One Damn Thing After Another") was a literary society whose name was taken from John Masefield's 1926 novel of that title.]

[2] *Fanny Burney* (1752–1840) Novelist, diarist, and dramatist; *Haworth Parsonage* The family home of novelists Charlotte (1816–55), Emily (1818–48), and Anne (1820–49) Brontë; *Miss Mitford* Mary Russell Mitford (1787–1855), poet; *George Eliot* Pseudonym of Mary Anne Evans (1819–80), author of many novels, including *The Mill on the Floss* (1860) and *Adam Bede* (1859); *Mrs. Gaskell* Elizabeth Gaskell (1810–65), author of *Cranford* and *Mary Barton*.

days that preceded my coming here—how, bowed down by the weight of the subject which you have laid upon my shoulders, I pondered it, and made it work in and out of my daily life. I need not say that what I am about to describe has no existence; Oxbridge is an invention; so is Fernham;[1] "I" is only a convenient term for somebody who has no real being. Lies will flow from my lips, but there may perhaps be some truth mixed up with them; it is for you to seek out this truth and to decide whether any part of it is worth keeping. If not, you will of course throw the whole of it into the wastepaper basket and forget all about it.

Here then was I (call me Mary Beton, Mary Seton, Mary Carmichael[2] or by any name you please—it is not a matter of any importance) sitting on the banks of a river a week or two ago in fine October weather, lost in thought. That collar I have spoken of, women and fiction, the need of coming to some conclusion on a subject that raises all sorts of prejudices and passions, bowed my head to the ground. To the right and left bushes of some sort, golden and crimson, glowed with the colour, even it seemed burnt with the heat, of fire. On the further bank the willows wept in perpetual lamentation, their hair about their shoulders. The river reflected whatever it chose of sky and bridge and burning tree, and when the undergraduate had oared his boat through the reflections they closed again, completely, as if he had never been. There one might have sat the clock round lost in thought. Thought—to call it by a prouder name than it deserved—had let its line down into the stream. It swayed, minute after minute, hither and thither among the reflections and the weeds, letting the water lift it and sink it, until—you know the little tug—the sudden conglomeration of an idea at the end of one's line: and then the cautious hauling of it in, and the careful laying of it out? Alas, laid on the grass how small, how insignificant this thought of mine looked; the sort of fish that a good fisherman puts back into the water so that it may grow fatter and be one day worth cooking and eating. I will not trouble you with that thought now, though if you look carefully you may find it for yourselves in the course of what I am going to say.

But however small it was, it had, nevertheless, the mysterious property of its kind—put back into the mind, it became at once very exciting, and important; and as it darted and sank, and flashed hither and thither, set up such a wash and tumult of ideas that it was impossible to sit still. It was thus that I found myself walking with extreme rapidity across a grass plot. Instantly a man's figure rose to intercept me. Nor did I at first understand that the gesticulations of a curious-looking object, in a cut-away coat and evening shirt, were aimed at me. His face expressed horror and indignation. Instinct rather than reason came to my help; he was a Beadle;[3] I was a woman. This was the turf; there was the path. Only the Fellows and Scholars are allowed here; the gravel is the place for me. Such thoughts were the work of a moment. As I regained the path the arms of the Beadle sank, his face assumed its usual repose, and though turf is better walking than gravel, no very great harm was done. The only charge I could bring against the Fellows and Scholars of whatever the college might happen to be was that in protection of their turf, which has been rolled for 300 years in succession, they had sent my little fish into hiding.

What idea it had been that had sent me so audaciously trespassing I could not now remember. The spirit of peace descended like a cloud from heaven, for if the spirit of peace dwells anywhere, it is in the courts and quadrangles of Oxbridge on a fine October morning. Strolling through those colleges past those ancient halls the roughness of the present seemed smoothed away; the body seemed contained in a miraculous glass cabinet through which no sound could penetrate, and the mind, freed from any contact with facts (unless one trespassed on the turf again), was at liberty to settle down upon whatever meditation was in harmony with the moment. As chance would have it, some stray

[1] *Oxbridge* Amalgamation of the names of the Universities of Oxford and Cambridge, a term used to describe the two collectively; *Fernham* Woolf combines characteristics of Newnham and Girton in her description of this fictional college.

[2] *Mary Beton … Carmichael* See the "Ballad of Mary Hamilton," in which the companions of Mary, Queen of Scots were "Mary Beton and Mary Seton, / Mary Carmichael and me."

[3] *Beadle* Minor church or college official.

memory of some old essay about revisiting Oxbridge in the long vacation brought Charles Lamb[1] to mind—Saint Charles, said Thackeray,[2] putting a letter of Lamb's to his forehead. Indeed, among all the dead (I give you my thoughts as they came to me), Lamb is one of the most congenial; one to whom one would have liked to say, Tell me then how you wrote your essays? For his essays are superior even to Max Beerbohm's,[3] I thought, with all their perfection, because of that wild flash of imagination, that lightning crack of genius in the middle of them which leaves them flawed and imperfect, but starred with poetry. Lamb then came to Oxbridge perhaps a hundred years ago. Certainly he wrote an essay—the name escapes me—about the manuscript of one of Milton's poems which he saw here. It was *Lycidas* perhaps, and Lamb wrote how it shocked him to think it possible that any word in *Lycidas* could have been different from what it is. To think of Milton changing the words in that poem seemed to him a sort of sacrilege. This led me to remember what I could of *Lycidas* and to amuse myself with guessing which word it could have been that Milton had altered, and why. It then occurred to me that the very manuscript itself which Lamb had looked at was only a few hundred yards away, so that one could follow Lamb's footsteps across the quadrangle to that famous library[4] where the treasure is kept. Moreover, I recollected, as I put this plan into execution, it is in this famous library that the manuscript of Thackeray's *Esmond* is also preserved. The critics often say that *Esmond* is Thackeray's most perfect novel. But the affectation of the style, with its imitation of the eighteenth century, hampers one, so far as I remember; unless indeed the eighteenth-century style was natural to Thackeray—a fact that one might prove by looking at the manuscript and seeing whether the alterations were for the benefit of the style or of the sense. But then one would have to decide what is style and what is meaning, a question which—but here I was actually at the door which leads into the library itself. I must have opened it, for instantly there issued, like a guardian angel barring the way with a flutter of black gown instead of white wings, a deprecating, silvery, kindly gentleman, who regretted in a low voice as he waved me back that ladies are only admitted to the library if accompanied by a Fellow of the College or furnished with a letter of introduction.

That a famous library has been cursed by a woman is a matter of complete indifference to a famous library. Venerable and calm, with all its treasures safe locked within its breast, it sleeps complacently and will, so far as I am concerned, so sleep for ever. Never will I wake those echoes, never will I ask for that hospitality again, I vowed as I descended the steps in anger. Still an hour remained before luncheon, and what was one to do? Stroll on the meadows? Sit by the river? Certainly it was a lovely autumn morning; the leaves were fluttering red to the ground; there was no great hardship in doing either. But the sound of music reached my ear. Some service or celebration was going forward. The organ complained magnificently as I passed the chapel door. Even the sorrow of Christianity sounded in that serene air more like the recollection of sorrow than sorrow itself; even the groanings of the ancient organ seemed lapped in peace. I had no wish to enter had I the right, and this time the verger[5] might have stopped me, demanding perhaps my baptismal certificate, or a letter of introduction from the Dean. But the outside of these magnificent buildings is often as beautiful as the inside. Moreover, it was amusing enough to watch the congregation assembling, coming in and going out again, busying themselves at the door of the chapel like bees at the mouth of a hive. Many were in cap and gown; some had tufts of fur on their shoulders; others were wheeled in bath-chairs;[6] others, though not past middle age,

---

[1] *Charles Lamb* English essayist (1775–1834). The essay referred to later in this paragraph is "Oxford in the Vacation" (1820).

[2] *Thackeray* William Makepeace Thackeray, English novelist (1811–63).

[3] *Max Beerbohm* English parodist, essayist, and cartoonist (1872–1956).

[4] *that famous library* The manuscript of Milton's *Lycidas* held by the library of Trinity College, Cambridge.

[5] *verger* Church attendant.

[6] *bath-chairs* Large chairs on wheels for invalids, so named for Bath, an English spa city, and retreat for ill and elderly people.

seemed creased and crushed into shapes so singular that one was reminded of those giant crabs and crayfish who heave with difficulty across the sand of an aquarium. As I leant against the wall the University indeed seemed a sanctuary in which are preserved rare types which would soon be obsolete if left to fight for existence on the pavement of the Strand.[1] Old stories of old deans and old dons came back to mind, but before I had summoned up courage to whistle—it used to be said that at the sound of a whistle old Professor —— instantly broke into a gallop—the venerable congregation had gone inside. The outside of the chapel remained. As you know, its high domes and pinnacles can be seen, like a sailing-ship always voyaging never arriving, lit up at night and visible for miles, far away across the hills.[2] Once, presumably, this quadrangle with its smooth lawns, its massive buildings, and the chapel itself was marsh too, where the grasses waved and the swine rootled.[3] Teams of horses and oxen, I thought, must have hauled the stone in wagons from far countries, and then with infinite labour the grey blocks in whose shade I was now standing were poised in order one on top of another, and then the painters brought their glass for the windows, and the masons were busy for centuries up on that roof with putty and cement, spade and trowel. Every Saturday somebody must have poured gold and silver out of a leathern purse into their ancient fists, for they had their beer and skittles[4] presumably of an evening. An unending stream of gold and silver, I thought, must have flowed into this court perpetually to keep the stones coming and the masons working; to level, to ditch, to dig and to drain. But it was then the age of faith, and money was poured liberally to set these stones on a deep foundation, and when the stones were raised, still more money was poured in from the coffers of kings and queens and great nobles to ensure that hymns should be sung here and scholars taught. Lands were granted; tithes were paid. And when the age of faith was over and the age of reason had come, still the same flow of gold and silver went on; fellowships were founded; lectureships endowed; only the gold and silver flowed now, not from the coffers of the king, but from the chests of merchants and manufacturers, from the purses of men who had made, say, a fortune from industry, and returned, in their wills, a bounteous share of it to endow more chairs, more lectureships, more fellowships in the university where they had learnt their craft. Hence the libraries and laboratories; the observatories; the splendid equipment of costly and delicate instruments which now stands on glass shelves, where centuries ago the grasses waved and the swine rootled. Certainly, as I strolled round the court, the foundation of gold and silver seemed deep enough; the pavement laid solidly over the wild grasses. Men with trays on their heads went busily from staircase to staircase. Gaudy blossoms flowered in window-boxes. The strains of the gramophone blared out from the rooms within. It was impossible not to reflect—the reflection whatever it may have been was cut short. The clock struck. It was time to find one's way to luncheon.

It is a curious fact that novelists have a way of making us believe that luncheon parties are invariably memorable for something very witty that was said, or for something very wise that was done. But they seldom spare a word for what was eaten. It is part of the novelist's convention not to mention soup and salmon and ducklings, as if soup and salmon and ducklings were of no importance whatsoever, as if nobody ever smoked a cigar or drank a glass of wine. Here, however, I shall take the liberty to defy that convention and to tell you that the lunch on this occasion began with soles, sunk in a deep dish, over which the college cook had spread a counterpane of the whitest cream, save that it was branded here and there with brown spots like the spots on the flanks of a doe. After that came the partridges, but if this suggests a couple of bald, brown birds on a plate you are mistaken. The partridges, many and various, came with all their retinue of sauces and salads, the sharp and the sweet, each in its order; their potatoes,

[1] *the Strand* Busy street in London that runs parallel to the northern bank of the Thames.

[2] *As you … hills* Description of the chapel of King's College, Cambridge, which was built from 1446 to 1547.

[3] *rootled* Rooted about.

[4] *skittles* Game resembling bowling. The expression "all beer and skittles" denotes pure enjoyment.

thin as coins but not so hard; their sprouts, foliated as rosebuds but more succulent. And no sooner had the roast and its retinue been done with than the silent serving-man, the Beadle himself perhaps in a milder manifestation, set before us, wreathed in napkins, a confection which rose all sugar from the waves. To call it pudding and so relate it to rice and tapioca would be an insult. Meanwhile the wineglasses had flushed yellow and flushed crimson; had been emptied; had been filled. And thus by degrees was lit, halfway down the spine, which is the seat of the soul, not that hard little electric light which we call brilliance, as it pops in and out upon our lips, but the more profound, subtle and subterranean glow, which is the rich yellow flame of rational intercourse. No need to hurry. No need to sparkle. No need to be anybody but oneself. We are all going to heaven and Vandyck is of the company[1]—in other words, how good life seemed, how sweet its rewards, how trivial this grudge or that grievance, how admirable friendship and the society of one's kind, as, lighting a good cigarette, one sunk among the cushions in the window-seat.

If by good luck there had been an ashtray handy, if one had not knocked the ash out of the window in default, if things had been a little different from what they were, one would not have seen, presumably, a cat without a tail. The sight of that abrupt and truncated animal padding softly across the quadrangle changed by some fluke of the subconscious intelligence the emotional light for me. It was as if some one had let fall a shade. Perhaps the excellent hock[2] was relinquishing its hold. Certainly, as I watched the Manx cat pause in the middle of the lawn as if it too questioned the universe, something seemed lacking, something seemed different. But what was lacking, what was different, I asked myself, listening to the talk. And to answer that question I had to think myself out of the room, back into the past, before the war indeed, and to set before my eyes the model of another luncheon party held in rooms not very far distant from these; but different. Everything was different. Meanwhile the talk went on among the guests, who were many and young, some of this sex, some of that; it went on swimmingly, it went on agreeably, freely, amusingly. And as it went on I set it against the background of that other talk, and as I matched the two together I had no doubt that one was the descendant, the legitimate heir of the other. Nothing was changed; nothing was different save only—here I listened with all my ears not entirely to what was being said, but to the murmur or current behind it. Yes, that was it—the change was there. Before the war at a luncheon party like this people would have said precisely the same things but they would have sounded different, because in those days they were accompanied by a sort of humming noise, not articulate, but musical, exciting, which changed the value of the words themselves. Could one set that humming noise to words? Perhaps with the help of the poets one could. A book lay beside me and, opening it, I turned casually enough to Tennyson. And here I found Tennyson was singing:

There has fallen a splendid tear
From the passion-flower at the gate.
She is coming, my dove, my dear;
She is coming, my life, my fate;
The red rose cries, "She is near, she is near;"
And the white rose weeps, "She is late;"
The larkspur listens, "I hear, I hear;"
And the lily whispers, "I wait."[3]

Was that what men hummed at luncheon parties before the war? And the women?

My heart is like a singing bird
Whose nest is in a water'd shoot;
My heart is like an apple tree
Whose boughs are bent with thick-set fruit;
My heart is like a rainbow shell
That paddles in a halcyon sea;

[1] *We are all … company* These were said to be the last words of English portrait and landscape painter Thomas Gainsborough (1727–88); *Vandyck* Sir Anthony Van Dyck (1599–1641), portrait artist.

[2] *hock* I.e., Hochheimer, a German white wine.

[3] *There has … wait* From Alfred, Lord Tennyson's *Maud* (1855), 1.22.10.

My heart is gladder than all these
Because my love is come to me.[1]

Was that what women hummed at luncheon parties before the war?

There was something so ludicrous in thinking of people humming such things even under their breath at luncheon parties before the war that I burst out laughing, and had to explain my laughter by pointing at the Manx cat, who did look a little absurd, poor beast, without a tail, in the middle of the lawn. Was he really born so, or had he lost his tail in an accident? The tailless cat, though some are said to exist in the Isle of Man, is rarer than one thinks. It is a queer animal, quaint rather than beautiful. It is strange what a difference a tail makes—you know the sort of things one says as a lunch party breaks up and people are finding their coats and hats.

This one, thanks to the hospitality of the host, had lasted far into the afternoon. The beautiful October day was fading and the leaves were falling from the trees in the avenue as I walked through it. Gate after gate seemed to close with gentle finality behind me. Innumerable beadles were fitting innumerable keys into well-oiled locks; the treasure-house was being made secure for another night. After the avenue one comes out upon a road—I forget its name—which leads you, if you take the right turning, along to Fernham. But there was plenty of time. Dinner was not till half-past seven. One could almost do without dinner after such a luncheon. It is strange how a scrap of poetry works in the mind and makes the legs move in time to it along the road. Those words—

There has fallen a splendid tear
From the passion-flower at the gate.
She is coming, my dove, my dear—

sang in my blood as I stepped quickly along towards Headingley. And then, switching off into the other measure, I sang, where the waters are churned up by the weir:

My heart is like a singing bird
Whose nest is in a water'd shoot;
My heart is like an apple tree ....

What poets, I cried aloud, as one does in the dusk, what poets they were!

In a sort of jealousy, I suppose, for our own age, silly and absurd though these comparisons are, I went on to wonder if honestly one could name two living poets now as great as Tennyson and Christina Rossetti were then. Obviously it is impossible, I thought, looking into those foaming waters, to compare them. The very reason why the poetry excites one to such abandonment, such rapture, is that it celebrates some feeling that one used to have (at luncheon parties before the war perhaps), so that one responds easily, familiarly, without troubling to check the feeling, or to compare it with any that one has now. But the living poets express a feeling that is actually being made and torn out of us at the moment. One does not recognize it in the first place; often for some reason one fears it; one watches it with keenness and compares it jealously and suspiciously with the old feeling that one knew. Hence the difficulty of modern poetry; and it is because of this difficulty that one cannot remember more than two consecutive lines of any good modern poet. For this reason—that my memory failed me—the argument flagged for want of material. But why, I continued, moving on towards Headingley, have we stopped humming under our breath at luncheon parties? Why has Alfred ceased to sing

She is coming, my dove, my dear?

Why has Christina ceased to respond

My heart is gladder than all these
Because my love is come to me?

Shall we lay the blame on the war? When the guns fired in August 1914, did the faces of men and women show so plain in each other's eyes that romance was killed? Certainly it was a shock (to women in particular with their illusions about education, and so on) to see the faces of our rulers in the light of the shell-fire. So ugly

[1] *My heart ... me* The opening stanza of Christina Rossetti's "A Birthday" (1861).

they looked—German, English, French—so stupid. But lay the blame where one will, on whom one will, the illusion which inspired Tennyson and Christina Rossetti to sing so passionately about the coming of their loves is far rarer now than then. One has only to read, to look, to listen, to remember. But why say "blame"? Why, if it was an illusion, not praise the catastrophe, whatever it was, that destroyed illusion and put truth in its place? For truth ... those dots mark the spot where, in search of truth, I missed the turning up to Fernham. Yes indeed, which was truth and which was illusion, I asked myself. What was the truth about these houses, for example, dim and festive now with their red windows in the dusk, but raw and red and squalid, with their sweets and their boot-laces, at nine o'clock in the morning? And the willows and the river and the gardens that run down to the river, vague now with the mist stealing over them, but gold and red in the sunlight—which was the truth, which was the illusion about them? I spare you the twists and turns of my cogitations, for no conclusion was found on the road to Headingley, and I ask you to suppose that I soon found out my mistake about the turning and retraced my steps to Fernham.

As I have said already that it was an October day, I dare not forfeit your respect and imperil the fair name of fiction by changing the season and describing lilacs hanging over garden walls, crocuses, tulips and other flowers of spring. Fiction must stick to facts, and the truer the facts the better the fiction—so we are told. Therefore it was still autumn and the leaves were still yellow and falling, if anything, a little faster than before, because it was now evening (seven twenty-three to be precise) and a breeze (from the southwest to be exact) had risen. But for all that there was something odd at work:

My heart is like a singing bird
Whose nest is in a water'd shoot;
My heart is like an apple tree
Whose boughs are bent with thick-set fruit—

perhaps the words of Christina Rossetti were partly responsible for the folly of the fancy—it was nothing of course but a fancy—that the lilac was shaking its flowers over the garden walls, and the brimstone butterflies were scudding hither and thither, and the dust of the pollen was in the air. A wind blew, from what quarter I know not, but it lifted the half-grown leaves so that there was a flash of silver grey in the air. It was the time between the lights when colours undergo their intensification and purples and golds burn in window-panes like the beat of an excitable heart; when for some reason the beauty of the world revealed and yet soon to perish (here I pushed into the garden, for, unwisely, the door was left open and no beadles seemed about), the beauty of the world which is so soon to perish, has two edges, one of laughter, one of anguish, cutting the heart asunder. The gardens of Fernham lay before me in the spring twilight, wild and open, and in the long grass, sprinkled and carelessly flung, were daffodils and bluebells, not orderly perhaps at the best of times, and now wind-blown and waving as they tugged at their roots. The windows of the building, curved like ships' windows among generous waves of red brick, changed from lemon to silver under the flight of the quick spring clouds. Somebody was in a hammock, somebody, but in this light they were phantoms only, half guessed, half seen, raced across the grass—would no one stop her?—and then on the terrace, as if popping out to breathe the air, to glance at the garden, came a bent figure, formidable yet humble, with her great forehead and her shabby dress—could it be the famous scholar, could it be J—— H——[1] herself? All was dim, yet intense too, as if the scarf which the dusk had flung over the garden were torn asunder by star or sword—the flash of some terrible reality leaping, as its way is, out of the heart of the spring. For youth—

Here was my soup. Dinner was being served in the great dining-hall. Far from being spring it was in fact an evening in October. Everybody was assembled in the big dining-room. Dinner was ready. Here was the soup. It was a plain gravy soup. There was nothing to stir the fancy in that. One could have seen through the transparent liquid any pattern that there might have been on the plate itself. But there was no pattern. The plate was

[1] *J—— H——* Jane Harrison (1850–1928), cultural anthropologist and archaeologist who was a Fellow at Newnham College.

plain. Next came beef with its attendant greens and potatoes—a homely trinity, suggesting the rumps of cattle in a muddy market, and sprouts curled and yellowed at the edge, and bargaining and cheapening, and women with string bags on Monday morning. There was no reason to complain of human nature's daily food, seeing that the supply was sufficient and coal-miners doubtless were sitting down to less. Prunes and custard followed. And if any one complains that prunes, even when mitigated by custard, are an uncharitable vegetable (fruit they are not), stringy as a miser's heart and exuding a fluid such as might run in misers' veins who have denied themselves wine and warmth for eighty years and yet not given to the poor, he should reflect that there are people whose charity embraces even the prune. Biscuits and cheese came next, and here the water-jug was liberally passed round, for it is the nature of biscuits to be dry, and these were biscuits to the core. That was all. The meal was over. Everybody scraped their chairs back; the swing-doors swung violently to and fro; soon the hall was emptied of every sign of food and made ready no doubt for breakfast next morning. Down corridors and up staircases the youth of England went banging and singing. And was it for a guest, a stranger (for I had no more right here in Fernham than in Trinity or Somerville or Girton or Newnham or Christchurch[1]), to say, "The dinner was not good," or to say (we were now, Mary Seton and I, in her sitting-room), "Could we not have dined up here alone?" for if I had said anything of the kind I should have been prying and searching into the secret economies of a house which to the stranger wears so fine a front of gaiety and courage. No, one could say nothing of the sort. Indeed, conversation for a moment flagged. The human frame being what it is, heart, body and brain all mixed together, and not contained in separate compartments as they will be no doubt in another million years, a good dinner is of great importance to good talk. One cannot think well, love well, sleep well, if one has not dined well. The lamp in the spine does not light on beef and prunes. We are all *probably* going to heaven, and Vandyck is, we *hope*, to meet us round the next corner—that is the dubious and qualifying state of mind that beef and prunes at the end of the day's work breed between them. Happily my friend, who taught science, had a cupboard where there was a squat bottle and little glasses—(but there should have been sole and partridge to begin with)—so that we were able to draw up to the fire and repair some of the damages of the day's living. In a minute or so we were slipping freely in and out among all those objects of curiosity and interest which form in the mind in the absence of a particular person, and are naturally to be discussed on coming together again—how somebody has married, another has not; one thinks this, another that; one has improved out of all knowledge, the other most amazingly gone to the bad—with all those speculations upon human nature and the character of the amazing world we live in which spring naturally from such beginnings. While these things were being said, however, I became shamefacedly aware of a current setting in of its own accord and carrying everything forward to an end of its own. One might be talking of Spain or Portugal, or book or racehorse, but the real interest of whatever was said was none of those things, but a scene of masons on a high roof some five centuries ago. Kings and nobles brought treasure in huge sacks and poured it under the earth. This scene was for ever coming alive in my mind and placing itself by another of lean cows and a muddy market and withered greens and the stringy hearts of old men—these two pictures, disjointed and disconnected and nonsensical as they were, were for ever coming together and combating each other and had me entirely at their mercy. The best course, unless the whole talk was to be distorted, was to expose what was in my mind to the air, when with good luck it would fade and crumble like the head of the dead king when they opened the coffin at Windsor. Briefly, then, I told Miss Seton about the masons who had been all those years on the roof of the chapel, and about the kings and queens and nobles bearing sacks of gold and silver on their shoulders, which they shovelled into the earth; and then how the great financial magnates of our own time came

[1] *Trinity ... Christchurch* Somerville and Christchurch are colleges at Oxford, while Trinity, Girton, and Newnham are Cambridge colleges.

and laid cheques and bonds, I suppose, where the others had laid ingots and rough lumps of gold. All that lies beneath the colleges down there, I said; but this college, where we are now sitting, what lies beneath its gallant red brick and the wild unkempt grasses of the garden? What force is behind the plain china off which we dined, and (here it popped out of my mouth before I could stop it) the beef, the custard and the prunes?

Well, said Mary Seton, about the year 1860—Oh, but you know the story, she said, bored, I suppose, by the recital. And she told me—rooms were hired. Committees met. Envelopes were addressed. Circulars were drawn up. Meetings were held; letters were read out; so-and-so has promised so much; on the contrary, Mr. —— won't give a penny. The *Saturday Review* has been very rude. How can we raise a fund to pay for offices? Shall we hold a bazaar? Can't we find a pretty girl to sit in the front row? Let us look up what John Stuart Mill[1] said on the subject. Can any one persuade the editor of the —— to print a letter? Can we get Lady —— to sign it? Lady —— is out of town. That was the way it was done, presumably, sixty years ago, and it was a prodigious effort, and a great deal of time was spent on it. And it was only after a long struggle and with the utmost difficulty that they got thirty thousand pounds together.[2] So obviously we cannot have wine and partridges and servants carrying tin dishes on their heads, she said. We cannot have sofas and separate rooms. "The amenities," she said, quoting from some book or other, "will have to wait."[3]

At the thought of all those women working year after year and finding it hard to get two thousand pounds together, and as much as they could do to get thirty thousand pounds, we burst out in scorn at the reprehensible poverty of our sex. What had our mothers been doing then that they had no wealth to leave us? Powdering their noses? Looking in at shop windows? Flaunting in the sun at Monte Carlo? There were some photographs on the mantel-piece. Mary's mother—if that was her picture—may have been a wastrel[4] in her spare time (she had thirteen children by a minister of the church), but if so her gay and dissipated life had left too few traces of its pleasures on her face. She was a homely body; an old lady in a plaid shawl which was fastened by a large cameo; and she sat in a basket-chair, encouraging a spaniel to look at the camera, with the amused, yet strained expression of one who is sure that the dog will move directly the bulb is pressed. Now if she had gone into business; had become a manufacturer of artificial silk or a magnate on the Stock Exchange; if she had left two or three hundred thousand pounds to Fernham, we could have been sitting at our ease tonight and the subject of our talk might have been archaeology, botany, anthropology, physics, the nature of the atom, mathematics, astronomy, relativity, geography. If only Mrs. Seton and her mother and her mother before her had learnt the great art of making money and had left their money, like their fathers and their grandfathers before them, to found fellowships and lectureships and prizes and scholarships appropriated to the use of their own sex, we might have dined very tolerably up here alone off a bird and a bottle of wine; we might have looked forward without undue confidence to a pleasant and honourable lifetime spent in the shelter of one of the liberally endowed professions. We might have been exploring or writing; mooning about the venerable places of the earth; sitting contemplative on the steps of the Parthenon, or going at ten to an office and coming home comfortably at half-past four to write a little poetry. Only, if Mrs. Seton and her like had gone into business at the age of fifteen, there would have been—that was the snag in the argument—no Mary. What, I asked, did Mary think of that? There between the

[1] *John Stuart Mill* English philosopher and economist (1806–73) who was interested in the status and treatment of women; author of *The Subjection of Women*.

[2] [Woolf's note] "We are told that we ought to ask for 30,000 at least.... It is not a large sum, considering that there is to be but one college of this sort for Great Britain, Ireland, and the Colonies, and considering how easy it is to raise immense sums for boys' schools. But considering how few people really wish women to be educated, it is a good deal."—Lady Stephen, *Life of Miss Emily Davies*.

[3] [Woolf's note] "Every penny which could be scraped together was set aside for building, and the amenities had to be postponed." —R. Strachey, *The Cause*.

[4] *wastrel* Spendthrift.

curtains was the October night, calm and lovely, with a star or two caught in the yellowing trees. Was she ready to resign her share of it and her memories (for they had been a happy family, though a large one) of games and quarrels up in Scotland, which she is never tired of praising for the fineness of its air and the quality of its cakes, in order that Fernham might have been endowed with fifty thousand pounds or so by a stroke of the pen? For, to endow a college would necessitate the suppression of families altogether. Making a fortune and bearing thirteen children—no human being could stand it. Consider the facts, we said. First there are nine months before the baby is born. Then the baby is born. Then there are three or four months spent in feeding the baby. After the baby is fed there are certainly five years spent in playing with the baby. You cannot, it seems, let children run about the streets. People who have seen them running wild in Russia say that the sight is not a pleasant one. People say, too, that human nature takes its shape in the years between one and five. If Mrs. Seton, I said, had been making money, what sort of memories would you have had of games and quarrels? What would you have known of Scotland, and its fine air and cakes and all the rest of it? But it is useless to ask these questions, because you would never have come into existence at all. Moreover, it is equally useless to ask what might have happened if Mrs. Seton and her mother and her mother before her had amassed great wealth and laid it under the foundations of college and library, because, in the first place, to earn money was impossible for them, and in the second, had it been possible, the law denied them the right to possess what money they earned. It is only for the last forty-eight years that Mrs. Seton has had a penny of her own.[1] For all the centuries before that it would have been her husband's property—a thought which, perhaps, may have had its share in keeping Mrs. Seton and her mothers off the Stock Exchange. Every penny I earn, they may have said, will be taken from me and disposed of according to my husband's wisdom—perhaps to found a scholarship or to endow a fellowship in Balliol or Kings,[2] so that to earn money, even if I could earn money, is not a matter that interests me very greatly. I had better leave it to my husband.

At any rate, whether or not the blame rested on the old lady who was looking at the spaniel, there could be no doubt that for some reason or other our mothers had mismanaged their affairs very gravely. Not a penny could be spared for "amenities"; for partridges and wine, beadles and turf, books and cigars, libraries and leisure. To raise bare walls out of the bare earth was the utmost they could do.

So we talked standing at the window and looking, as so many thousands look every night, down on the domes and towers of the famous city beneath us. It was very beautiful, very mysterious in the autumn moonlight. The old stone looked very white and venerable. One thought of all the books that were assembled down there; of the pictures of old prelates and worthies hanging in the panelled rooms; of the painted windows that would be throwing strange globes and crescents on the pavement; of the tablets and memorials and inscriptions; of the fountains and the grass; of the quiet rooms looking across the quiet quadrangles. And (pardon me the thought) I thought, too, of the admirable smoke and drink and the deep armchairs and the pleasant carpets: of the urbanity, the geniality, the dignity which are the offspring of luxury and privacy and space. Certainly our mothers had not provided us with anything comparable to all this—our mothers who found it difficult to scrape together thirty thousand pounds, our mothers who bore thirteen children to ministers of religion at St. Andrews.

So I went back to my inn, and as I walked through the dark streets I pondered this and that, as one does at the end of the day's work. I pondered why it was that Mrs. Seton had no money to leave us; and what effect poverty has on the mind; and what effect wealth has on the mind; and I thought of the queer old gentlemen I had seen that morning with tufts of fur upon their shoulders; and I remembered how if one whistled one of them ran; and I thought of the organ booming in the

[1] *It is … own* Reference to the Married Women's Property Acts of 1870 and 1882, which allowed married women the same rights to their property that single women enjoyed.

[2] *Balliol or Kings* Two colleges, the first at Oxford and the second at Cambridge.

chapel and of the shut doors of the library; and I thought how unpleasant it is to be locked out; and I thought how it is worse perhaps to be locked in; and, thinking of the safety and prosperity of the one sex and of the poverty and insecurity of the other and of the effect of tradition and of the lack of tradition upon the mind of a writer, I thought at last that it was time to roll up the crumpled skin of the day, with its arguments and its impressions and its anger and its laughter, and cast it into the hedge. A thousand stars were flashing across the blue wastes of the sky. One seemed alone with an inscrutable society. All human beings were laid asleep—prone, horizontal, dumb. Nobody seemed stirring in the streets of Oxbridge. Even the door of the hotel sprang open at the touch of an invisible hand—not a boots[1] was sitting up to light me to bed, it was so late.

Chapter 2

The scene, if I may ask you to follow me, was now changed. The leaves were still falling, but in London now, not Oxbridge; and I must ask you to imagine a room, like many thousands, with a window looking across people's hats and vans and motor-cars to other windows, and on the table inside the room a blank sheet of paper on which was written in large letters Women and Fiction, but no more. The inevitable sequel to lunching and dining at Oxbridge seemed, unfortunately, to be a visit to the British Museum. One must strain off what was personal and accidental in all these impressions and so reach the pure fluid, the essential oil of truth. For that visit to Oxbridge and the luncheon and the dinner had started a swarm of questions. Why did men drink wine and women water? Why was one sex so prosperous and the other so poor? What effect has poverty on fiction? What conditions are necessary for the creation of works of art?—a thousand questions at once suggested themselves. But one needed answers, not questions; and an answer was only to be had by consulting the learned and the unprejudiced, who have removed themselves above the strife of tongue and the confusion of body and issued the result of their reasoning and research in books which are to be found in the British Museum. If truth is not to be found on the shelves of the British Museum, where, I asked myself, picking up a notebook and a pencil, is truth?

Thus provided, thus confident and enquiring, I set out in the pursuit of truth. The day, though not actually wet, was dismal, and the streets in the neighbourhood of the Museum were full of open coal-holes, down which sacks were showering; four-wheeled cabs were drawing up and depositing on the pavement corded boxes containing, presumably, the entire wardrobe of some Swiss or Italian family seeking fortune or refuge or some other desirable commodity which is to be found in the boarding-houses of Bloomsbury[2] in the winter. The usual hoarse-voiced men paraded the streets with plants on barrows. Some shouted; others sang. London was like a workshop. London was like a machine. We were all being shot backwards and forwards on this plain foundation to make some pattern. The British Museum was another department of the factory. The swing-doors swung open; and there one stood under the vast dome, as if one were a thought in the huge bald forehead which is so splendidly encircled by a band of famous names. One went to the counter; one took a slip of paper; one opened a volume of the catalogue, and ..... the five dots here indicate five separate minutes of stupefaction, wonder, and bewilderment. Have you any notion of how many books are written about women in the course of one year? Have you any notion how many are written by men? Are you aware that you are, perhaps, the most discussed animal in the universe? Here had I come with a notebook and pencil proposing to spend a morning reading, supposing that at the end of the morning I should have transferred the truth to my notebook. But I should need to be a herd of elephants, I thought, and a wilderness of spiders, desperately referring to the animals that are reputed longest lived and most multitudinously eyed, to cope with all this. I should need claws of steel and beak of brass even to

[1] *boots* I.e., hotel servant, because one of a servant's chores was to clean the guests' boots.

[2] *Bloomsbury* Area of London in which the British Museum is located and in which many of Woolf's circle (known collectively as "The Bloomsbury Group") lived.

penetrate the husk. How shall I ever find the grains of truth embedded in all this mass of paper, I asked myself, and in despair began running my eye up and down the long list of titles. Even the names of the books gave me food for thought. Sex and its nature might well attract doctors and biologists; but what was surprising and difficult of explanation was the fact that sex—woman, that is to say—also attracts agreeable essayists, light-fingered novelists, young men who have taken the M.A. degree; men who have taken no degree; men who have no apparent qualification save that they are not women. Some of these books were, on the face of it, frivolous and facetious; but many, on the other hand, were serious and prophetic, moral and hortatory. Merely to read the titles suggested innumerable schoolmasters, innumerable clergymen mounting their platforms and pulpits and holding forth with a loquacity which far exceeded the hour usually allotted to such discourse on this one subject. It was a most strange phenomenon; and apparently—here I consulted the letter M—one confined to male sex. Women do not write books about men—a fact that I could not help welcoming with relief, for if I had first to read all that men have written about women, then all that women have written about men, the aloe that flowers once in a hundred years would flower twice before I could set pen to paper. So, making a perfectly arbitrary choice of a dozen volumes or so, I sent my slips of paper to lie in the wire tray, and waited in my stall, among the other seekers for the essential oil of truth.

What could be the reason, then, of this curious disparity, I wondered, drawing cart-wheels on the slips of paper provided by the British taxpayer for other purposes. Why are women, judging from this catalogue, so much more interesting to men than men are to women? A very curious fact it seemed, and my mind wandered to picture the lives of men who spend their time in writing books about women; whether they were old or young, married or unmarried, red-nosed or humpbacked—anyhow, it was flattering, vaguely, to feel oneself the object of such attention, provided that it was not entirely bestowed by the crippled and the infirm—so I pondered until all such frivolous thoughts were ended by an avalanche of books sliding down on to the desk in front of me. Now the trouble began. The student who has been trained in research at Oxbridge has no doubt some method of shepherding his question past all distractions till it runs into its answer as a sheep runs into its pen. The student by my side, for instance, who was copying assiduously from a scientific manual was, I felt sure, extracting pure nuggets of the essential ore every ten minutes or so. His little grunts of satisfaction indicated so much. But if, unfortunately, one has had no training in a university, the question far from being shepherded into its pen flies like a frightened flock hither and thither, helter-skelter, pursued by a whole pack of hounds. Professors, schoolmasters, sociologists, clergymen, novelists, essayists, journalists, men who had no qualification save that they were not women, chased my simple and single question—Why are women poor?—until it became fifty questions; until the fifty questions leapt frantically into mid-stream and were carried away. Every page in my notebook was scribbled over with notes. To show the state of mind I was in, I will read you a few of them, explaining that the page was headed quite simply, WOMEN AND POVERTY, in block letters; but what followed was something like this:

Condition in Middle Ages of,
Habits in the Fiji Islands of,
Worshipped as goddesses by,
Weaker in moral sense than,
Idealism of,
Greater conscientiousness of,
South Sea Islanders, age of puberty among,
Attractiveness of,
Offered as sacrifice to,
Small size of brain of,
Profounder sub-consciousness of,
Less hair on the body of,
Mental, moral and physical inferiority of,
Love of children of,
Greater length of life of,
Weaker muscles of,
Strength of affections of,
Vanity of,
Higher education of,
Shakespeare's opinion of,

Lord Birkenhead's[1] *opinion of,*
Dean Inge's[2] *opinion of,*
La Bruyère's[3] *opinion of,*
Dr. Johnson's[4] *opinion of,*
Mr. Oscar Browning's[5] *opinion of, ...*

Here I drew breath and added, indeed, in the margin, Why does Samuel Butler[6] say, "Wise men never say what they think of women?" Wise men never say anything else apparently. But, I continued, leaning back in my chair and looking at the vast dome in which I was a single but by now somewhat harassed thought, what is so unfortunate is that wise men never think the same thing about women. Here is Pope:

> *Most women have no character at all.*[7]

And here is La Bruyère:

> *Les femmes sont extrêmes; elles sont meilleures ou pires que les hommes*[8]—

a direct contradiction by keen observers who were contemporary. Are they capable of education or incapable? Napoleon thought them incapable. Dr. Johnson thought the opposite.[9] Have they souls or have they not souls? Some savages say they have none. Others, on the contrary, maintain that women are half divine and worship them on that account.[10] Some sages hold that they are shallower in the brain; others that they are deeper in the consciousness. Goethe[11] honoured them; Mussolini[12] despises them. Wherever one looked men thought about women and thought differently. It was impossible to make head or tail of it all, I decided, glancing with envy at the reader next door who was making the neatest abstracts, headed often with an A or a B or a C, while my own notebook rioted with the wildest scribble of contradictory jottings. It was distressing, it was bewildering, it was humiliating. Truth had run through my fingers. Every drop had escaped.

I could not possibly go home, I reflected, and add as a serious contribution to the study of women and fiction that women have less hair on their bodies than men, or that the age of puberty among the South Sea Islanders is nine—or is it ninety?—even the handwriting had become in its distraction indecipherable. It was disgraceful to have nothing more weighty or respectable to show after a whole morning's work. And if I could not grasp the truth about W. (as for brevity's sake I had come to call her) in the past, why bother about W. in the future? It seemed pure waste of time to consult all those gentlemen who specialise in woman and her effect on whatever it may be—politics, children, wages, morality—numerous and learned as they are. One might as well leave their books unopened.

But while I pondered I had unconsciously, in my listlessness, in my desperation, been drawing a picture where I should, like my neighbour, have been writing a conclusion. I had been drawing a face, a figure. It was the face and the figure of Professor von X. engaged in

---

[1] *Lord Birkenhead* Frederick Edwin Smith, Earl of Birkenhead, who was Lord Chancellor from 1919 to 1922 and an opponent of women's suffrage.

[2] *Dean Inge* William Ralph Inge, Dean of St. Paul's Cathedral from 1911 to 1934.

[3] *La Bruyère* Jean de La Bruyère, French essayist and moralist (1645–96).

[4] *Dr. Johnson* Samuel Johnson (1709–84), British lexicographer, critic, poet, and essayist.

[5] *Mr. Oscar Browning* History lecturer at King's College, Cambridge (1837–1923).

[6] *Samuel Butler* Nineteenth-century English author (1835–1902).

[7] *Most ... all* From the opening of English poet and satirist Alexander Pope's Epistle 2, "To a Lady" from his *Moral Essays*: "Nothing so true as what you once let fall, / 'Most women have no character at all.'"

[8] *Les ... hommes* "Women are extreme: they are better or worse than men." From La Bruyère's *Les Caractères* (1688).

[9] [Woolf's note] "'Men know that women are an overmatch for them, and therefore they choose the weakest or the most ignorant. If they did not think so, they never would be afraid of women knowing as much as themselves.' ... In justice to the sex, I think it but candid to acknowledge that, in a subsequent conversation, he told me that he was serious in what he said."—Boswell, *The Journal of a Tour to the Hebrides*.

[10] [Woolf's note] "The ancient Germans believed that there was something holy in women, and accordingly consulted them as oracles."—Frazer, *Golden Bough*.

[11] *Goethe* German writer Johann Wolfgang von Goethe (1749–1832).

[12] *Mussolini* Benito Mussolini (1883–1945), Italian Fascist dictator.

writing his monumental work entitled *The Mental, Moral, and Physical Inferiority of the Female Sex.* He was not in my picture a man attractive to women. He was heavily built; he had a great jowl; to balance that he had very small eyes; he was very red in the face. His expression suggested that he was labouring under some emotion that made him jab his pen on the paper as if he were killing some noxious insect as he wrote, but even when he had killed it that did not satisfy him; he must go on killing it; and even so, some cause for anger and irritation remained. Could it be his wife, I asked, looking at my picture. Was she in love with a cavalry officer? Was the cavalry officer slim and elegant and dressed in astrachan?[1] Had he been laughed at, to adopt the Freudian theory, in his cradle by a pretty girl? For even in his cradle the professor, I thought, could not have been an attractive child. Whatever the reason, the professor was made to look very angry and very ugly in my sketch, as he wrote his great book upon the mental, moral and physical inferiority of women. Drawing pictures was an idle way of finishing an unprofitable morning's work. Yet it is in our idleness, in our dreams, that the submerged truth sometimes comes to the top. A very elementary exercise in psychology, not to be dignified by the name of psycho-analysis, showed me, on looking at my notebook, that the sketch of the angry professor had been made in anger. Anger had snatched my pencil while I dreamt. But what was anger doing there? Interest, confusion, amusement, boredom—all these emotions I could trace and name as they succeeded each other throughout the morning. Had anger, the black snake, been lurking among them? Yes, said the sketch, anger had. It referred me unmistakably to the one book, to the one phrase, which had roused the demon; it was the professor's statement about the mental, moral and physical inferiority of women. My heart had leapt. My cheeks had burnt. I had flushed with anger. There was nothing specially remarkable, however foolish, in that. One does not like to be told that one is naturally the inferior of a little man—I looked at the student next me—who breathes hard, wears a ready-made tie, and has not shaved this fortnight. One has certain foolish vanities. It is only human nature, I reflected, and began drawing cart-wheels and circles over the angry professor's face till he looked like a burning bush or a flaming comet—anyhow, an apparition without human semblance or significance. The professor was nothing now but a faggot[2] burning on the top of Hampstead Heath.[3] Soon my own anger was explained and done with; but curiosity remained. How explain the anger of the professors? Why were they angry? For when it came to analysing the impression left by these books there was always an element of heat. This heat took many forms; it showed itself in satire, in sentiment, in curiosity, in reprobation. But there was another element which was often present and could not immediately be identified. Anger, I called it. But it was anger that had gone underground and mixed itself with all kinds of other emotions. To judge from its odd effects, it was anger disguised and complex, not anger simple and open.

Whatever the reason, all these books, I thought, surveying the pile on the desk, are worthless for my purposes. They were worthless scientifically, that is to say, though humanly they were full of instruction, interest, boredom, and very queer facts about the habits of the Fiji Islanders. They had been written in the red light of emotion and not in the white light of truth. Therefore they must be returned to the central desk and restored each to his own cell in the enormous honeycomb. All that I had retrieved from that morning's work had been the one fact of anger. The professors—I lumped them together thus—were angry. But why, I asked myself, having returned the books, why, I repeated, standing under the colonnade among the pigeons and the prehistoric canoes, why are they angry? And, asking myself this question, I strolled off to find a place for luncheon. What is the real nature of what I call for the moment their anger? I asked. Here was a puzzle that would last all the time that it takes to be served with food in a small restaurant somewhere near the

[1] *astrachan* I.e., astrakhan, wool of very young lambs.

[2] *faggot* Bundle of sticks for fuel.

[3] *Hampstead Heath* Grassy area in north London and the highest point in the city.

British Museum. Some previous luncher had left the lunch edition of the evening paper on a chair, and, waiting to be served, I began idly reading the headlines. A ribbon of very large letters ran across the page. Somebody had made a big score in South Africa. Lesser ribbons announced that Sir Austen Chamberlain was at Geneva.[1] A meat axe with human hair on it had been found in a cellar. Mr. Justice —— commented in the Divorce Courts upon the Shamelessness of Women. Sprinkled about the paper were other pieces of news. A film actress had been lowered from a peak in California and hung suspended in mid-air. The weather was going to be foggy. The most transient visitor to this planet, I thought, who picked up this paper could not fail to be aware, even from this scattered testimony, that England is under the rule of a patriarchy. Nobody in their senses could fail to detect the dominance of the professor. His was the power and the money and the influence. He was the proprietor of the paper and its editor and sub-editor. He was the Foreign Secretary and the Judge. He was the cricketer; he owned the race-horses and the yachts. He was the director of the company that pays two hundred per cent to its shareholders. He left millions to charities and colleges that were ruled by himself. He suspended the film actress in mid-air. He will decide if the hair on the meat axe is human; he it is who will acquit or convict the murderer, and hang him, or let him go free. With the exception of the fog he seemed to control everything. Yet he was angry. I knew that he was angry by this token. When I read what he wrote about women I thought, not of what he was saying, but of himself. When an arguer argues dispassionately he thinks only of the argument; and the reader cannot help thinking of the argument too. If he had written dispassionately about women, had used indisputable proofs to establish his argument and had shown no trace of wishing that the result should be one thing rather than another, one would not have been angry either. One would have accepted the fact, as one accepts the fact that a pea is green or a canary yellow. So be it, I should have said. But I had been angry because he was angry. Yet it seemed absurd, I thought, turning over the evening paper, that a man with all this power should be angry. Or is anger, I wondered, somehow, the familiar, the attendant sprite on power? Rich people, for example, are often angry because they suspect that the poor want to seize their wealth. The professors, or patriarchs, as it might be more accurate to call them, might be angry for that reason partly, but partly for one that lies a little less obviously on the surface. Possibly they were not "angry" at all; often, indeed, they were admiring, devoted, exemplary in the relations of private life. Possibly when the professor insisted a little too emphatically upon the inferiority of women, he was concerned not with their inferiority, but with his own superiority. That was what he was protecting rather hot-headedly and with too much emphasis, because it was a jewel to him of the rarest price. Life for both sexes—and I looked at them, shouldering their way along the pavement—is arduous, difficult, a perpetual struggle. It calls for gigantic courage and strength. More than anything, perhaps, creatures of illusion as we are, it calls for confidence in oneself. Without self-confidence we are as babes in the cradle. And how can we generate this imponderable quality, which is yet so invaluable, most quickly? By thinking that other people are inferior to oneself. By feeling that one has some innate superiority—it may be wealth, or rank, a straight nose, or the portrait of a grandfather by Romney[2]—for there is no end to the pathetic devices of the human imagination—over other people. Hence the enormous importance to a patriarch who has to conquer, who has to rule, of feeling that great numbers of people, half the human race indeed, are by nature inferior to himself. It must indeed be one of the chief sources of his power. But let me turn the light of this observation on to real life, I thought. Does it help to explain some of those psychological puzzles that one notes in the margin of daily life? Does it explain my astonishment the other day when Z, most humane, most modest of men, taking up some book by

[1] *Sir Austen Chamberlain* Member of the British House of Commons and Secretary of State of Foreign Affairs from 1924 to 1929; *Geneva* Location of the League of Nations headquarters.

[2] *Romney* George Romney, eighteenth-century British painter and portraitist.

Rebecca West[1] and reading a passage in it, exclaimed, "The arrant feminist! She says that men are snobs!" The exclamation, to me so surprising—for why was Miss West an arrant feminist for making a possibly true if uncomplimentary statement about the other sex?—was not merely the cry of wounded vanity; it was a protest against some infringement of his power to believe in himself. Women have served all these centuries as looking-glasses possessing the magic and delicious power of reflecting the figure of man at twice its natural size. Without that power probably the earth would still be swamp and jungle. The glories of all our wars would be unknown. We should still be scratching the outlines of deer on the remains of mutton bones and bartering flints for sheepskins or whatever simple ornament took our unsophisticated taste. Supermen and Fingers of Destiny would never have existed. The Czar and the Kaiser would never have worn their crowns or lost them. Whatever may be their use in civilised societies, mirrors are essential to all violent and heroic action. That is why Napoleon and Mussolini both insist so emphatically upon the inferiority of women, for if they were not inferior, they would cease to enlarge. That serves to explain in part the necessity that women so often are to men. And it serves to explain how restless they are under her criticism; how impossible it is for her to say to them this book is bad, this picture is feeble, or whatever it may be, without giving far more pain and rousing far more anger than a man would do who gave the same criticism. For if she begins to tell the truth, the figure in the looking-glass shrinks; his fitness for life is diminished. How is he to go on giving judgement, civilising natives, making laws, writing books, dressing up and speechifying at banquets, unless he can see himself at breakfast and at dinner at least twice the size he really is? So I reflected, crumbling my bread and stirring my coffee and now and again looking at the people in the street. The looking-glass vision is of supreme importance because it charges the vitality; it stimulates the nervous system. Take it away and man may die, like the drug fiend deprived of his cocaine. Under the spell of that illusion, I thought, looking out of the window, half the people on the pavement are striding to work. They put on their hats and coats in the morning under its agreeable rays. They start the day confident, braced, believing themselves desired at Miss Smith's tea party; they say to themselves as they go into the room, I am the superior of half the people here, and it is thus that they speak with that self-confidence, that self-assurance, which have had such profound consequences in public life and lead to such curious notes in the margin of the private mind.

But these contributions to the dangerous and fascinating subject of the psychology of the other sex—it is one, I hope, that you will investigate when you have five hundred a year of your own—were interrupted by the necessity of paying the bill. It came to five shillings and ninepence. I gave the waiter a ten-shilling note and he went to bring me change. There was another ten-shilling note in my purse; I noticed it, because it is a fact that still takes my breath away—the power of my purse to breed ten-shilling notes automatically. I open it and there they are. Society gives me chicken and coffee, bed and lodging, in return for a certain number of pieces of paper which were left me by an aunt, for no other reason than that I share her name.

My aunt, Mary Beton, I must tell you, died by a fall from her horse when she was riding out to take the air in Bombay. The news of my legacy reached me one night about the same time that the act was passed that gave votes to women. A solicitor's letter fell into the post-box and when I opened it I found that she had left me five hundred pounds a year for ever. Of the two—the vote and the money—the money, I own, seemed infinitely the more important. Before that I had made my living by cadging odd jobs from newspapers, by reporting a donkey show here or a wedding there; I had earned a few pounds by addressing envelopes, reading to old ladies, making artificial flowers, teaching the alphabet to small children in a kindergarten. Such were the chief occupations that were open to women before 1918. I need not, I am afraid, describe in any detail the hardness of the work, for you know perhaps women who have done it; nor the difficulty of living on

[1] *Rebecca West* Assumed name of Cicily Fairfield (1892–1983), English novelist, critic, and journalist.

the money when it was earned, for you may have tried. But what still remains with me as a worse infliction than either was the poison of fear and bitterness which those days bred in me. To begin with, always to be doing work that one did not wish to do, and to do it like a slave, flattering and fawning, not always necessarily perhaps, but it seemed necessary and the stakes were too great to run risks; and then the thought of that one gift which it was death to hide—a small one but dear to the possessor—perishing and with it myself, my soul—all this became like a rust eating away the bloom of the spring, destroying the tree at its heart. However, as I say, my aunt died; and whenever I change a ten-shilling note a little of that rust and corrosion is rubbed off; fear and bitterness go. Indeed, I thought, slipping the silver into my purse, it is remarkable, remembering the bitterness of those days, what a change of temper a fixed income will bring about. No force in the world can take from me my five hundred pounds. Food, house, and clothing are mine for ever. Therefore not merely do effort and labour cease, but also hatred and bitterness. I need not hate any man; he cannot hurt me. I need not flatter any man; he has nothing to give me. So imperceptibly I found myself adopting a new attitude towards the other half of the human race. It was absurd to blame any class or any sex, as a whole. Great bodies of people are never responsible for what they do. They are driven by instincts which are not within their control. They too, the patriarchs, the professors, had endless difficulties, terrible drawbacks to contend with. Their education had been in some ways as faulty as my own. It had bred in them defects as great. True, they had money and power, but only at the cost of harbouring in their breasts an eagle, a vulture, for ever tearing the liver out and plucking at the lungs—the instinct for possession, the rage for acquisition which drives them to desire other people's fields and goods perpetually; to make frontiers and flags; battleships and poison gas; to offer up their own lives and their children's lives. Walk through the Admiralty Arch[1] (I had reached that monument), or any other avenue given up to trophies and cannon, and reflect upon the kind of glory celebrated there. Or watch in the spring sunshine the stockbroker and the great barrister going indoors to make money and more money and more money when it is a fact that five hundred pounds a year will keep one alive in the sunshine. These are unpleasant instincts to harbour, I reflected. They are bred of the conditions of life; of the lack of civilisation, I thought, looking at the statue of the Duke of Cambridge, and in particular at the feathers in his cocked hat, with a fixity that they have scarcely ever received before. And, as I realised these drawbacks, by degrees fear and bitterness modified themselves into pity and toleration; and then in a year or two, pity and toleration went, and the greatest release of all came, which is freedom to think of things in themselves. That building, for example, do I like it or not? Is that picture beautiful or not? Is that in my opinion a good book or a bad? Indeed my aunt's legacy unveiled the sky to me, and substituted for the large and imposing figure of a gentleman, which Milton recommended for my perpetual adoration,[2] a view of the open sky.

So thinking, so speculating, I found my way back to my house by the river. Lamps were being lit and an indescribable change had come over London since the morning hour. It was as if the great machine after labouring all day had made with our help a few yards of something very exciting and beautiful—a fiery fabric flashing with red eyes, a tawny monster roaring with hot breath. Even the wind seemed flung like a flag as it lashed the houses and rattled the hoardings.

In my little street, however, domesticity prevailed. The house painter was descending his ladder; the nursemaid was wheeling the perambulator carefully in and out back to nursery tea; the coal-heaver was folding his empty sacks on top of each other; the woman who keeps the green-grocer's shop was adding up the day's takings with her hands in red mittens. But so engrossed was I with the problem you have laid upon my shoulders that I could not see even these usual sights without

[1] *Admiralty Arch* Triple arch leading from Trafalgar Square into the Mall in London, forming part of the ceremonial approach to Buckingham Palace.

[2] *gentleman … adoration* In *Paradise Lost* (1667), Milton suggests that man (Adam) was formed "for God only" and woman (Eve) "for God in him" (4.299).

referring them to one centre. I thought how much harder it is now than it must have been even a century ago to say which of these employments is the higher, the more necessary. Is it better to be a coal-heaver or a nursemaid; is the charwoman[1] who has brought up eight children of less value to the world than the barrister who has made a hundred thousand pounds? It is useless to ask such questions; for nobody can answer them. Not only do the comparative values of charwomen and lawyers rise and fall from decade to decade, but we have no rods with which to measure them even as they are at the moment. I had been foolish to ask my professor to furnish me with "indisputable proofs" of this or that in his argument about women. Even if one could state the value of any one gift at the moment, those values will change; in a century's time very possibly they will have changed completely. Moreover, in a hundred years, I thought, reaching my own doorstep, women will have ceased to be the protected sex. Logically they will take part in all the activities and exertions that were once denied them. The nursemaid will heave coal. The shopwoman will drive an engine. All assumptions founded on the facts observed when women were the protected sex will have disappeared—as, for example (here a squad of soldiers marched down the street), that women and clergymen and gardeners live longer than other people. Remove that protection, expose them to the same exertions and activities, make them soldiers and sailors and engine-drivers and dock labourers, and will not women die off so much younger, so much quicker, than men that one will say, "I saw a woman today," as one used to say, "I saw an aeroplane." Anything may happen when womanhood has ceased to be a protected occupation, I thought, opening the door. But what bearing has all this upon the subject of my paper, Women and Fiction? I asked, going indoors.

Chapter 3

It was disappointing not to have brought back in the evening some important statement, some authentic fact. Women are poorer than men because—this or that. Perhaps now it would be better to give up seeking for the truth, and receiving on one's head an avalanche of opinion hot as lava, discoloured as dish-water. It would be better to draw the curtains; to shut out distractions; to light the lamp; to narrow the enquiry and to ask the historian, who records not opinions but facts, to describe under what conditions women lived, not throughout the ages, but in England, say in the time of Elizabeth.

For it is a perennial puzzle why no woman wrote a word of that extraordinary literature when every other man, it seemed, was capable of song or sonnet. What were the conditions in which women lived, I asked myself; for fiction, imaginative work that is, is not dropped like a pebble upon the ground, as science may be; fiction is like a spider's web, attached ever so lightly perhaps, but still attached to life at all four corners. Often the attachment is scarcely perceptible; Shakespeare's plays, for instance, seem to hang there complete by themselves. But when the web is pulled askew, hooked up at the edge, torn in the middle, one remembers that these webs are not spun in mid-air by incorporeal creatures, but are the work of suffering human beings, and are attached to grossly material things, like health and money and the houses we live in.

I went, therefore, to the shelf where the histories stand and took down one of the latest, Professor Trevelyan's *History of England*.[2] Once more I looked up Women, found "position of," and turned to the pages indicated. "Wife-beating," I read, "was a recognised right of man, and was practised without shame by high as well as low. … Similarly," the historian goes on, "the daughter who refused to marry the gentleman of her parents' choice was liable to be locked up, beaten and flung about the room, without any shock being inflicted on public opinion. Marriage was not an affair of personal affection, but of family avarice, particularly in the 'chivalrous' upper classes. … Betrothal often took place while one or both of the parties was in the cradle, and marriage when they were scarcely out of the nurses' charge." That was about 1470, soon after Chaucer's time. The next reference to the position of women is

[1] *charwoman* Cleaner.

[2] *Professor … England* George Macaulay Trevelyan's *History of England* (1929).

some two hundred years later, in the time of the Stuarts. "It was still the exception for women of the upper and middle class to choose their own husbands, and when the husband had been assigned, he was lord and master, so far at least as law and custom could make him. Yet even so," Professor Trevelyan concludes, "neither Shakespeare's women nor those of authentic seventeenth-century memoirs, like the Verneys and the Hutchinsons,[1] seem wanting in personality and character." Certainly, if we consider it, Cleopatra must have had a way with her; Lady Macbeth, one would suppose, had a will of her own; Rosalind, one might conclude, was an attractive girl.[2] Professor Trevelyan is speaking no more than the truth when he remarks that Shakespeare's women do not seem wanting in personality and character. Not being a historian, one might go even further and say that women have burnt like beacons in all the works of all the poets from the beginning of time—Clytemnestra, Antigone, Cleopatra, Lady Macbeth, Phedre, Cressida, Rosalind, Desdemona, the Duchess of Malfi, among the dramatists;[3] then among the prose writers: Millamant, Clarissa, Becky Sharp, Anna Karenina, Emma Bovary, Madame de Guermantes[4]—the names flock to mind, nor do they recall women "lacking in personality and character." Indeed, if woman had no existence save in the fiction written by men, one would imagine her a person of the utmost importance; very various; heroic and mean; splendid and sordid; infinitely beautiful and hideous in the extreme; as great as a man, some think even greater.[5] But this is woman in fiction. In fact, as Professor Trevelyan points out, she was locked up, beaten and flung about the room.

A very queer, composite being thus emerges. Imaginatively she is of the highest importance; practically she is completely insignificant. She pervades poetry from cover to cover; she is all but absent from history. She dominates the lives of kings and conquerors in fiction; in fact she was the slave of any boy whose parents forced a ring upon her finger. Some of the most inspired words, some of the most profound thoughts in literature fall from her lips; in real life she could hardly read, could scarcely spell, and was the property of her husband.

It was certainly an odd monster that one made up by reading the historians first and the poets afterwards—a worm winged like an eagle; the spirit of life and beauty in a kitchen chopping up suet. But these monsters, however amusing to the imagination, have no existence in fact. What one must do to bring her to life was to think poetically and prosaically at one and the same moment, thus keeping in touch with fact—that she is Mrs. Martin, aged thirty-six, dressed in blue, wearing a black hat and brown shoes; but not losing sight of fiction either—that she is a vessel in which all sorts of spirits and forces are coursing and flashing perpetually.

---

[1] *Verneys* The *Memoirs of the Verney Family* (published 1892) is a family history that records, as one of its authors boasted, "an ordinary gentleman's family of the higher class" consisting of "good average specimens of hundreds of men or women of their age"; *Hutchinsons* Lucy Hutchinson's *Memoirs of the Life of Colonel Hutchinson* (published 1806) detailed the life of her husband, John Hutchinson, and his experiences in the civil war.

[2] *Cleopatra ... girl* Cleopatra, Lady Macbeth, and Rosalind are the heroines of Shakespeare's *Antony and Cleopatra*, *Macbeth*, and *As You Like It*, respectively.

[3] *Clytemnestra ... dramatists* Heroines from Aeschylus's *Agamemnon*; Sophocles's *Antigone*; Shakespeare's *Antony and Cleopatra* and *Macbeth*; Racine's *Phèdre*; Shakespeare's *Troilus and Cressida*, *As You Like It*, and *Othello*; and Webster's *The Duchess of Malfi*.

[4] *then ... Guermantes* Characters from, respectively, Congreve's *Way of the World*; Richardson's *Clarissa*; Thackeray's *Vanity Fair*; Tolstoy's *Anna Karenina*; Flaubert's *Madame Bovary*; and Proust's *À la recherche du temps perdu*.

[5] [Woolf's note] "It remains a strange and almost inexplicable fact that in Athena's city, where women were kept in almost Oriental suppression as odalisques or drudges, the stage should yet have produced figures like Clytemnestra and Cassandra, Atossa and Antigone, Phèdre and Medea, and all the other heroines who dominate play after play of the 'misogynist' Euripides. But the paradox of this world where in real life a respectable woman could hardly show her face alone in the street, and yet on the stage woman equals or surpasses man, has never been satisfactorily explained. In modern tragedy the same predominance exists. At all events, a very cursory survey of Shakespeare's work (similarly with Webster, though not with Marlowe or Jonson) suffices to reveal how this dominance, this initiative of women, persists from Rosalind to Lady Macbeth. So too in Racine; six of his tragedies bear their heroines' names; and what male characters of his shall we set against Hermione and Andromaque, Bérénice and Roxane, Phèdre and Athalie? So again with Ibsen; what men shall we match with Solveig and Nora, Hedda and Hilda Wangel and Rebecca West?"—F.L. Lucas, *Tragedy*, pp. 114–15.

The moment, however, that one tries this method with the Elizabethan woman, one branch of illumination fails; one is held up by the scarcity of facts. One knows nothing detailed, nothing perfectly true and substantial about her. History scarcely mentions her. And I turned to Professor Trevelyan again to see what history meant to him. I found by looking at his chapter headings that it meant—"The Manor Court and the Methods of Open-field Agriculture … The Cistercians and Sheep-farming … The Crusades … The University … The House of Commons … The Hundred Years' War … The War of the Roses … The Renaissance Scholars … The Dissolution of the Monasteries … Agrarian and Religious Strife … The Origin of English Sea-power … The Armada … " and so on. Occasionally an individual woman is mentioned, an Elizabeth, or a Mary; a queen or a great lady. But by no possible means could middle-class women with nothing but brains and character at their command have taken part in any one of the great movements which, brought together, constitute the historian's view of the past. Nor shall we find her in any collection of anecdotes. Aubrey[1] hardly mentions her. She never writes her own life and scarcely keeps a diary; there are only a handful of her letters in existence. She left no plays or poems by which we can judge her. What one wants, I thought—and why does not some brilliant student at Newnham or Girton supply it?—is a mass of information; at what age did she marry; how many children had she as a rule; what was her house like; had she a room to herself; did she do the cooking; would she be likely to have a servant? All these facts lie somewhere, presumably, in parish registers and account books; the life of the average Elizabethan woman must be scattered about somewhere, could one collect it and make a book of it. It would be ambitious beyond my daring, I thought, looking about the shelves for books that were not there, to suggest to the students of those famous colleges that they should re-write history, though I own that it often seems a little queer as it is, unreal, lop-sided; but why should they not add a supplement to history? calling it, of course, by some inconspicuous name so that women might figure there without impropriety? For one often catches a glimpse of them in the lives of the great, whisking away into the background, concealing, I sometimes think, a wink, a laugh, perhaps a tear. And, after all, we have lives enough of Jane Austen; it scarcely seems necessary to consider again the influence of the tragedies of Joanna Baillie[2] upon the poetry of Edgar Allen Poe; as for myself, I should not mind if the homes and haunts of Mary Russell Mitford[3] were closed to the public for a century at least. But what I find deplorable, I continued, looking about the bookshelves again, is that nothing is known about women before the eighteenth century. I have no model in my mind to turn about this way and that. Here I am asking why women did not write poetry in the Elizabethan age, and I am not sure how they were educated; whether they were taught to write; whether they had sitting-rooms to themselves; how many women had children before they were twenty-one; what, in short, they did from eight in the morning till eight at night. They had no money evidently; according to Professor Trevelyan they were married whether they liked it or not before they were out of the nursery, at fifteen or sixteen very likely. It would have been extremely odd, even upon this showing, had one of them suddenly written the plays of Shakespeare, I concluded, and I thought of that old gentleman, who is dead now, but was a bishop, I think, who declared that it was impossible for any woman, past, present, or to come, to have the genius of Shakespeare. He wrote to the papers about it. He also told a lady who applied to him for information that cats do not as a matter of fact go to heaven, though they have, he added, souls of a sort. How much thinking those old gentlemen used to save one! How the borders of ignorance shrank back at their approach! Cats do not go to heaven. Women cannot write the plays of Shakespeare.

---

[1] *Aubrey* John Aubrey (1626–97), writer and antiquary known for his *Brief Lives*, a collection of short, informal biographies.

[2] *Joanna Baillie* Romantic Scottish poet and dramatist (1762–1851).

[3] *Mary Russell Mitford* Poet, novelist, and playwright whose correspondence with notable authors, including Elizabeth Barrett Browning, Charles Lamb, and Harriet Martineau, provides insight into the literary world of the early nineteenth century.

Be that as it may, I could not help thinking, as I looked at the works of Shakespeare on the shelf, that the bishop was right at least in this; it would have been impossible, completely and entirely, for any woman to have written the plays of Shakespeare in the age of Shakespeare. Let me imagine, since facts are so hard to come by, what would have happened had Shakespeare had a wonderfully gifted sister, called Judith, let us say. Shakespeare himself went, very probably—his mother was an heiress—to the grammar school, where he may have learnt Latin—Ovid, Virgil, and Horace—and the elements of grammar and logic. He was, it is well known, a wild boy who poached rabbits, perhaps shot a deer, and had, rather sooner than he should have done, to marry a woman in the neighbourhood, who bore him a child rather quicker than was right. That escapade sent him to seek his fortune in London. He had, it seemed, a taste for the theatre; he began by holding horses at the stage door. Very soon he got work in the theatre, became a successful actor, and lived at the hub of the universe, meeting everybody, knowing everybody, practising his art on the boards, exercising his wits in the streets, and even getting access to the palace of the queen. Meanwhile his extraordinarily gifted sister, let us suppose, remained at home. She was as adventurous, as imaginative, as agog to see the world as he was. But she was not sent to school. She had no chance of learning grammar and logic, let alone of reading Horace and Virgil. She picked up a book now and then, one of her brother's perhaps, and read a few pages. But then her parents came in and told her to mend the stockings or mind the stew and not moon about with books and papers. They would have spoken sharply but kindly, for they were substantial people who knew the conditions of life for a woman and loved their daughter—indeed, more likely than not she was the apple of her father's eye. Perhaps she scribbled some pages up in an apple loft on the sly, but was careful to hide them or set fire to them. Soon, however, before she was out of her teens, she was to be betrothed to the son of a neighbouring wool-stapler.[1] She cried out that marriage was hateful to her, and for that she was severely beaten by her father. Then he ceased to scold her. He begged her instead not to hurt him, not to shame him in this matter of her marriage. He would give her a chain of beads or a fine petticoat, he said; and there were tears in his eyes. How could she disobey him? How could she break his heart? The force of her own gift alone drove her to it. She made up a small parcel of her belongings, let herself down by a rope one summer's night and took the road to London. She was not seventeen. The birds that sang in the hedge were not more musical than she was. She had the quickest fancy, a gift like her brother's, for the tune of words. Like him, she had a taste for the theatre. She stood at the stage door; she wanted to act, she said. Men laughed in her face. The manager—a fat, loose-lipped man—guffawed. He bellowed something about poodles dancing and women acting[2]—no woman, he said, could possibly be an actress. He hinted—you can imagine what. She could get no training in her craft. Could she even seek her dinner in a tavern or roam the streets at midnight? Yet her genius was for fiction and lusted to feed abundantly upon the lives of men and women and the study of their ways. At last—for she was very young, oddly like Shakespeare the poet in her face, with the same grey eyes and rounded brows—at last Nick Greene the actor-manager took pity on her; she found herself with child by that gentleman and so—who shall measure the heat and violence of the poet's heart when caught and tangled in a woman's body?—killed herself one winter's night and lies buried at some cross-roads where the omnibuses now stop outside the Elephant and Castle.[3]

That, more or less, is how the story would run, I think, if a woman in Shakespeare's day had had Shakespeare's genius. But for my part, I agree with the deceased bishop, if such he was—it is unthinkable that any woman in Shakespeare's day should have had Shake-

[1] *wool-stapler* Dealer in wool.

[2] *He … acting* Reference to Samuel Johnson's infamous statement, recorded by Boswell, that "a woman's preaching is like a dog's walking on its hinder legs. It is not done well; but you are surprised to find it done at all" (James Boswell, *Life of Samuel Johnson*, 31 July 1763).

[3] *lies buried … Castle* It was common practice to bury victims of suicide at crossroads. The Elephant and Castle was a pub located south of the Thames.

speare's genius. For genius like Shakespeare's is not born among labouring, uneducated, servile people. It was not born in England among the Saxons and the Britons. It is not born today among the working classes. How, then, could it have been born among women whose work began, according to Professor Trevelyan, almost before they were out of the nursery, who were forced to it by their parents and held to it by all the power of law and custom? Yet genius of a sort must have existed among women as it must have existed among the working classes. Now and again an Emily Brontë or a Robert Burns blazes out and proves its presence. But certainly it never got itself on to paper. When, however, one reads of a witch being ducked, of a woman possessed by devils, of a wise woman selling herbs, or even of a very remarkable man who had a mother, then I think we are on the track of a lost novelist, a suppressed poet, of some mute and inglorious Jane Austen,[1] some Emily Brontë who dashed her brains out on the moor or mopped and mowed about the highways crazed with the torture that her gift had put her to. Indeed, I would venture to guess that Anon, who wrote so many poems without signing them, was often a woman. It was a woman Edward Fitzgerald,[2] I think, suggested who made the ballads and the folk-songs, crooning them to her children, beguiling her spinning with them, or the length of the winter's night.

This may be true or it may be false—who can say?—but what is true in it, so it seemed to me, reviewing the story of Shakespeare's sister as I had made it, is that any woman born with a great gift in the sixteenth century would certainly have gone crazed, shot herself, or ended her days in some lonely cottage outside the village, half witch, half wizard, feared and mocked at. For it needs little skill in psychology to be sure that a highly gifted girl who had tried to use her gift for poetry would have been so thwarted and hindered by other people, so tortured and pulled asunder by her own contrary instincts, that she must have lost her health and sanity to a certainty. No girl could have walked to London and stood at a stage door and forced her way into the presence of actor-managers without doing herself a violence and suffering an anguish which may have been irrational—for chastity may be a fetish invented by certain societies for unknown reasons—but were none the less inevitable. Chastity had then, it has even now, a religious importance in a woman's life, and has so wrapped itself round with nerves and instincts that to cut it free and bring it to the light of day demands courage of the rarest. To have lived a free life in London in the sixteenth century would have meant for a woman who was poet and playwright a nervous stress and dilemma which might well have killed her. Had she survived, whatever she had written would have been twisted and deformed, issuing from a strained and morbid imagination. And undoubtedly, I thought, looking at the shelf where there are no plays by women, her work would have gone unsigned. That refuge she would have sought certainly. It was the relic of the sense of chastity that dictated anonymity to women even so late as the nineteenth century. Currer Bell, George Eliot, George Sand,[3] all the victims of inner strife as their writings prove, sought ineffectively to veil themselves by using the name of a man. Thus they did homage to the convention, which if not implanted by the other sex was liberally encouraged by them (the chief glory of a woman is not to be talked of, said Pericles,[4] himself a much-talked-of man), that publicity in women is detestable. Anonymity runs in their blood. The desire to be veiled still possesses them. They are not even now as concerned about the health of their fame as men are, and, speaking generally, will pass a tombstone or a signpost without feeling an irresistible desire to cut their names on it, as Alf, Bert, or Chas. must do in obedience to their instinct, which murmurs if it sees a fine woman go by, or even a dog, Ce chien est à moi.[5] And, of course, it may not be a dog, I thought, remembering

[1] *some … Austen* See Thomas Gray, "Elegy Written in a Country Church-Yard" (1751): "Some mute and inglorious Milton here may rest" (line 59).

[2] *Edward Fitzgerald* Author of *The Rubáiyát of Omar Khayyám* (1859).

[3] *Currer … Sand* Male pseudonyms under which female authors Charlotte Brontë, Mary Anne Evans, and Amandine Dupin published.

[4] *Pericles* Athenian political leader (d. 429 BCE).

[5] *Ce … moi* French: This dog is mine.

Parliament Square, the Sièges Allée[1] and other avenues; it may be a piece of land or a man with curly black hair. It is one of the great advantages of being a woman that one can pass even a very fine negress without wishing to make an Englishwoman of her.

That woman, then, who was born with a gift of poetry in the sixteenth century, was an unhappy woman, a woman at strife against herself. All the conditions of her life, all her own instincts, were hostile to the state of mind which is needed to set free whatever is in the brain. But what is the state of mind that is most propitious to the act of creation, I asked. Can one come by any notion of the state that furthers and makes possible that strange activity? Here I opened the volume containing the Tragedies of Shakespeare. What was Shakespeare's state of mind, for instance, when he wrote *Lear* and *Antony and Cleopatra?* It was certainly the state of mind most favourable to poetry that there has ever existed. But Shakespeare himself said nothing about it. We only know casually and by chance that he "never blotted a line."[2] Nothing indeed was ever said by the artist himself about his state of mind until the eighteenth century perhaps. Rousseau[3] perhaps began it. At any rate, by the nineteenth century self-consciousness had developed so far that it was the habit for men of letters to describe their minds in confessions and autobiographies. Their lives also were written, and their letters were printed after their deaths. Thus, though we do not know what Shakespeare went through when he wrote *Lear*, we do know what Carlyle went through when he wrote the *French Revolution*; what Flaubert went through when he wrote *Madame Bovary*; what Keats was going through when he tried to write poetry against the coming of death and the indifference of the world.[4]

And one gathers from this enormous modern literature of confession and self-analysis that to write a work of genius is almost always a feat of prodigious difficulty. Everything is against the likelihood that it will come from the writer's mind whole and entire. Generally material circumstances are against it. Dogs will bark; people will interrupt; money must be made; health will break down. Further, accentuating all these difficulties and making them harder to bear is the world's notorious indifference. It does not ask people to write poems and novels and histories; it does not need them. It does not care whether Flaubert finds the right word or whether Carlyle scrupulously verifies this or that fact. Naturally, it will not pay for what it does not want. And so the writer, Keats, Flaubert, Carlyle, suffers, especially in the creative years of youth, every form of distraction and discouragement. A curse, a cry of agony, rises from those books of analysis and confession. "Mighty poets in their misery dead"[5]—that is the burden of their song. If anything comes through in spite of all this, it is a miracle, and probably no book is born entire and uncrippled as it was conceived.

But for women, I thought, looking at the empty shelves, these difficulties were infinitely more formidable. In the first place, to have a room of her own, let alone a quiet room or a sound-proof room, was out of the question, unless her parents were exceptionally rich or very noble, even up to the beginning of the nineteenth century. Since her pin money, which depended on the good will of her father, was only enough to keep her clothed, she was debarred from such alleviations as came even to Keats or Tennyson or Carlyle, all poor men, from a walking tour, a little journey to France, from the separate lodging which, even if it were miserable enough, sheltered them from the claims and tyrannies of their families. Such material difficulties were formidable; but much worse were the immaterial. The indifference of the world which Keats and Flaubert and other men of genius have found so hard to bear was in her case not indifference but hostility. The world did not say to her as it said to them, Write if you choose; it makes no difference to

[1] *Sièges Allée* Victory Avenue, in Berlin.

[2] *never … line* Ben Jonson, *Timber*: "I remember, the players have often mentioned it as an honour to Shakespeare that in his writing (whatsoever he penned) he never blotted out a line."

[3] *Rousseau* French philosopher Jean-Jacques Rousseau (1712–87).

[4] *we do … world* Philosopher Thomas Carlyle provided this autobiographical information in his *Reminiscences* (1881), while French novelist Gustave Flaubert and English Romantic poet John Keats wrote extensively about their writing experiences in their letters.

[5] *Mighty … dead* William Wordsworth, *Resolution and Independence* (1807).

me. The world said with a guffaw, Write? What's the good of your writing? Here the psychologists of Newnham and Girton might come to our help, I thought, looking again at the blank spaces on the shelves. For surely it is time that the effect of discouragement upon the mind of the artist should be measured, as I have seen a dairy company measure the effect of ordinary milk and Grade A milk upon the body of the rat. They set two rats in cages side by side, and of the two one was furtive, timid, and small, and the other was glossy, bold, and big. Now what food do we feed women as artists upon? I asked, remembering, I suppose, that dinner of prunes and custard. To answer that question I had only to open the evening paper and to read that Lord Birkenhead[1] is of opinion—but really I am not going to trouble to copy out Lord Birkenhead's opinion upon the writing of women. What Dean Inge[2] says I will leave in peace. The Harley Street[3] specialist may be allowed to rouse the echoes of Harley Street with his vociferations without raising a hair on my head. I will quote, however, Mr. Oscar Browning, because Mr. Oscar Browning was a great figure in Cambridge at one time, and used to examine the students at Girton and Newnham. Mr. Oscar Browning was wont to declare "that the impression left on his mind, after looking over any set of examination papers, was that, irrespective of the marks he might give, the best woman was intellectually the inferior of the worst man." After saying that Mr. Browning went back to his rooms—and it is this sequel that endears him and makes him a human figure of some bulk and majesty—he went back to his rooms and found a stable-boy lying on the sofa—"a mere skeleton, his cheeks were cavernous and sallow, his teeth were black, and he did not appear to have the full use of his limbs. … 'That's Arthur' [said Mr. Browning]. 'He's a dear boy really and most high-minded.'"[4] The two pictures always seem to me to complete each other. And happily in this age of biography the two pictures often do complete each other, so that we are able to interpret the opinions of great men not only by what they say, but by what they do.

But though this is possible now, such opinions coming from the lips of important people must have been formidable enough even fifty years ago. Let us suppose that a father from the highest motives did not wish his daughter to leave home and become writer, painter or scholar. "See what Mr. Oscar Browning says," he would say; and there was not only Mr. Oscar Browning; there was the *Saturday Review*; there was Mr. Greg—the "essentials of a woman's being," said Mr. Greg[5] emphatically, "are that *they are supported by, and they minister to, men*"—there was an enormous body of masculine opinion to the effect that nothing could be expected of women intellectually. Even if her father did not read out loud these opinions, any girl could read them for herself; and the reading, even in the nineteenth century, must have lowered her vitality, and told profoundly upon her work. There would always have been that assertion—you cannot do this, you are incapable of doing that—to protest against, to overcome. Probably for a novelist this germ is no longer of much effect; for there have been women novelists of merit. But for painters it must still have some sting in it; and for musicians, I imagine, is even now active and poisonous in the extreme. The woman composer stands where the actress stood in the time of Shakespeare. Nick Greene, I thought, remembering the story I had made about Shakespeare's sister, said that a woman acting put him in mind of a dog dancing. Johnson repeated the phrase two hundred years later of women preaching. And here, I said, opening a book about music, we have the very words used again in this year of grace, 1928, of women who try to write music. "Of Mlle. Germaine Tailleferre one can only repeat Dr. Johnson's dictum concerning a woman preacher, transposed into terms of music. 'Sir, a woman's composing is like a dog's walking on his hind legs. It is not done well, but you are surprised to find it done at all.'"[6] So accurately does history repeat itself.

[1] *Lord Birkenhead* Lord Chancellor from 1919 to 1922.

[2] *Dean Inge* Dean of St. Paul's Cathedral, London.

[3] *Harley Street* Street upon which many of the most highly regarded or fashionable medical practices were located.

[4] *Mr. Oscar Browning … high-minded* Oscar Browning (1837–1923), history lecturer at King's College, Cambridge.

[5] *Mr. Greg* Probably W.H. Greg, a well-known journalist of the era.

[6] [Woolf's note] *A Survey of Contemporary Music*, Cecil Gray, p.246.

Thus, I concluded, shutting Mr. Oscar Browning's life and pushing away the rest, it is fairly evident that even in the nineteenth century a woman was not encouraged to be an artist. On the contrary, she was snubbed, slapped, lectured, and exhorted. Her mind must have been strained and her vitality lowered by the need of opposing this, of disproving that. For here again we come within range of that very interesting and obscure masculine complex which has had so much influence upon the woman's movement; that the deep-seated desire, not so much that *she* shall be inferior as that *he* shall be superior, which plants him wherever one looks, not only in front of the arts, but barring the way to politics too, even when the risk to himself seems infinitesimal and the suppliant humble and devoted. Even Lady Bessborough,[1] I remembered, with all her passion for politics, must humbly bow herself and write to Lord Granville Leveson-Gower: " … notwithstanding all my violence in politics and talking so much on that subject, I perfectly agree with you that no woman has any business to meddle with that or any other serious business, farther than giving her opinion (if she is ask'd)." And so she goes on to spend her enthusiasm where it meets with no obstacle whatsoever upon that immensely important subject, Lord Granville's maiden speech in the House of Commons. The spectacle is certainly a strange one, I thought. The history of men's opposition to women's emancipation is more interesting perhaps than the story of that emancipation itself. An amusing book might be made of it if some young student at Girton or Newnham would collect examples and deduce a theory—but she would need thick gloves on her hands, and bars to protect her of solid gold.

But what is amusing now, I recollected, shutting Lady Bessborough, had to be taken in desperate earnest once. Opinions that one now pastes in a book labelled cock-a-doodle-dum and keeps for reading to select audiences on summer nights once drew tears, I can assure you. Among your grandmothers and great-grandmothers there were many that wept their eyes out. Florence Nightingale shrieked aloud in her agony.[2] Moreover, it is all very well for you, who have got yourselves to college and enjoy sitting-rooms—or is it only bed-sitting-rooms?—of your own to say that genius should disregard such opinions; that genius should be above caring what is said of it. Unfortunately, it is precisely the men or women of genius who mind most what is said of them. Remember Keats. Remember the words he had cut on his tombstone.[3] Think of Tennyson; think—but I need hardly multiply instances of the undeniable, if very unfortunate, fact that it is the nature of the artist to mind excessively what is said about him. Literature is strewn with the wreckage of men who have minded beyond reason the opinions of others.

And this susceptibility of theirs is doubly unfortunate, I thought, returning again to my original enquiry into what state of mind is most propitious for creative work, because the mind of an artist, in order to achieve the prodigious effort of freeing whole and entire the work that is in him, must be incandescent, like Shakespeare's mind, I conjectured, looking at the book which lay open at *Antony and Cleopatra*. There must be no obstacle in it, no foreign matter unconsumed.

For though we say that we know nothing about Shakespeare's state of mind, even as we say that, we are saying something about Shakespeare's state of mind. The reason perhaps why we know so little of Shakespeare—compared with Donne or Ben Jonson or Milton—is that his grudges and spites and antipathies are hidden from us. We are not held up by some "revelation" which reminds us of the writer. All desire to protest, to preach, to proclaim an injury, to pay off a score, to make the world the witness of some hardship or grievance was fired out of him and consumed. Therefore his poetry flows from him free and unimpeded. If ever a human being got his work expressed completely, it was Shakespeare. If ever a mind was incandescent, unimpeded, I thought, turning again to the bookcase, it was Shakespeare's mind.

—1929

[1] *Lady Bessborough* Henrietta Elizabeth, daughter of the first Earl Spencer, later Lady Bessborough (1761–1821). Lady Bessborough had an affair with Lord Granville.

[2] [Woolf's note] *See Cassandra*, by Florence Nightingale, printed in *The Cause*, by R. Strachey.

[3] *Remember … tombstone* "Here lies one whose name was writ in water."

In Context

Woolf and Bloomsbury[1]

Virginia Woolf was a central figure in a group of talented and influential friends that came to be known as the "Bloomsbury Group" after the part of London in which many of them lived. In addition to Woolf and her husband Leonard, the group included Woolf's sister Vanessa Bell, historian and intellectual Lytton Strachey, economist John Maynard Keynes, artist Duncan Grant, art critic Roger Fry, and novelist E.M. Forster. On the fringes of the group were such other leading figures as T.S. Eliot; since many of the group's central figures were widely connected, the social circle that revolved around Bloomsbury was a large one. As Eliot put it after she died, Woolf "was the center not merely of an esoteric group, but of the literary life of London. …With the death of Virginia Woolf, a whole pattern of culture is broken."[2]

Vanessa Bell, *Virginia Woolf*, 1912.

[1] *Woolf and Bloomsbury* Unless otherwise specified, all quotations are from *Recollections of Virginia Woolf*, edited by Joan Russell Noble (1972).

[2] *was the … broken* From T.S. Eliot's obituary of Woolf in *Horizon*, May 1941.

The Woolfs were publishers as well as writers; small though it was, Hogarth Press published several of the most important books of the era, including Eliot's *Poems*, Katherine Mansfield's *Prelude*, and the first English edition of several of Sigmund Freud's works, as well as Woolf's own fiction. One of their friends, John Lehman, has given a good sense of the press's physical operations:

> The Hogarth Press was named after Hogarth house in Richmond where [the Woolfs] were living when they began printing and publishing. In 1924 they moved to No. 52 Tavistock Square in Bloomsbury. Leonard and Virginia lived upstairs, and the activities of the Press were concentrated in the basement—a rather ramshackle basement, as was the case with any of the old Bloomsbury houses. The front room, looking on to the square, was the general office, in which there were as a rule not more than two or three girls at work, whose business it was to deal with the order, make out the invoices, pack up the books and handle the general correspondence. Leading out of the basement front room was a longish, dark corridor, piled with binders' packets of recently published books. On one side was the former scullery, in which Leonard had installed the treadle[1] printing press, still used for occasional small and special books.

Of Woolf herself, many have left vivid recollections—many of them touching on the strong sense of *joie de vivre* that she often radiated. In the context of the frequent depression that she experienced this may seem surprising, but the accounts are too numerous to be doubted. For Clive Bell, a sense of fun is the most lasting impression left by Woolf:[2]

> Writing was her passion and her joy and her poison. Yet, I repeat, hers was a happy nature. … My children, from the time they were old enough to enjoy anything beyond their animal satisfactions, enjoyed beyond anything a visit from Virginia: "Virginia's coming, what fun we shall have." That is what they said and felt when they were children and went on saying and feeling to the end. And so said all of us. So said everyone who knew her. … She might be divinely witty or outrageously fanciful; she might retail village gossip or tell stories of her London friends; always she was indescribably entertaining.

Bell also speaks of how Woolf sometimes "grew angry and lashed out" when she suspected she was being condescended to. She often felt resentful of "the way in which men, as she thought, patronized women, especially women who were attempting to create works of art or succeed in what were once considered manly professions. Assuredly Virginia did not wish to be a man, or to be treated as a man: she wished to be treated as an equal—just possibly as a superior."

Others describe a similar mixture in Woolf's personality. According to the novelist Elizabeth Bowen, Woolf could be "awfully naughty," even "fiendish." "She could say things about people, all in a flash, which remained with one. Fleetingly malicious, rather than outright cruel." Bowen also recalled a streak of superciliousness: "I was reminded sometimes of 'The Lord thy God is a jealous God: Thou shalt have no other God but me.' There was a touch of that about her." But, like Bell, Bowen recalls more strongly her exuberant and joyful spirit: "I was aware, one could not but be aware, of an undertow often of sadness, of melancholy, of great fear. But the main impression was of a

---

[1] *treadle* Lever worked by the foot.

[2] *Clive Bell … Woolf* All Clive Bell's recollections are from his *Old Friends: Personal Recollections* (1956).

creature of laughter and movement. … And her laughter was entrancing, it was outrageous laughter, almost like a child's laughter." Bowen has also likened Woolf's inquisitiveness to that of a child:

> She wanted to know all the details of people's lives. … She would say to anybody, to me, or anyone to whom she was talking, "Now what did you do, *exactly* what did you do? … You say you went to a party, where was it, who was there, what were they wearing?" Or, "You walked down the street, now *why* did you walk down the street? Who were you with? What did you see? Did you see a cat, did you see a dog?" It was that sort of inquisitiveness—almost childish. I never knew her to probe *deeply* into anything, and I don't know whether she really took much interest in people's affairs of the heart or not.… Past a point, her own imagination took over.

Bowen is one of many to have remarked on Woolf's intensity as a writer; another is E.M. Forster. As he put it when comparing her to many of her contemporaries, "she liked writing with an intensity which few writers have attained or desired":

> Most of them write with half an eye on their royalties, half an eye on their critics, and a third half eye on improving the world, which leaves them with only half an eye for the task on which she concentrated her entire vision. She would not look elsewhere, and her circumstances combined with her temperament to focus her. Money she had not to consider, because she possessed a private income, and though financial independence is not always a safeguard against commercialism, it was in her case.

Even those who were not always sympathetic to Woolf or to Bloomsbury recognized that her approach both to those around her and to the craft of writing was in many respects extraordinary. The poet Stephen Spender was among those who sniped at Bloomsbury, calling it a "clique" rather than a group, and suggesting that Woolf "moved in a very limited social world." Yet even he felt obliged to remark on the "undiluted purity of one of those uncorrupted natures which seem set aside from the world for a special task by a strange conjunction of fortune and misfortune."[1] With Woolf, he ventured, "style, form, and material are indivisible."

[1] *undiluted … misfortune* This and the following quotation are from Stephen Spender's obituary of Woolf in the *Listener*, 10 April 1941.

Lady Ottoline Morrell, *Virginia Woolf and T.S. Eliot*, 1924.

James Joyce
1882 – 1941

Irish novelist James Joyce's prose style and subject matter were so innovative and influential that fellow writer T.S. Eliot was prompted to declare that Joyce had helped to make "the modern world possible for art" by discovering "a way of controlling, or ordering, of giving a shape and a significance to the panorama of futility and anarchy which is contemporary history." Joyce's works as a whole redefined realism as they sought to access reality as perceived by the mind—whether awake or dreaming. Although throughout his life Joyce battled publishers, critics, and readers who objected to his frank treatment of the more "vulgar" aspects of his characters' thoughts and actions, Joyce became a literary figure of the first magnitude during his lifetime, and has remained one since.

James Augustus Aloysius Joyce was born in the middle-class Dublin suburb of Rathgar and was the first surviving son in a family of twelve siblings. Joyce's family situation would eventually devolve into poverty as John Joyce's increasing dependence on alcohol created strains both on the family's finances and on its morale. On the other hand, Joyce's mother, Mary Jane Joyce, exposed the young Joyce to the arts and to religion, as she was both accomplished in music and devout in her Catholicism. The former he would embrace with as much fervor as he rejected the latter.

At the age of 6, Joyce started his studies under the tutorship of the Jesuits. During the course of his schooling, however, he became increasingly cynical about the Church. His intellectual and spiritual rebelliousness grew so that by the time he entered university he had begun to believe that religion, family, and nation were all traps of conventionality that the true artist must avoid.

While at University College, Joyce attempted to write poetry and enjoyed writing articles parodying various literary styles. A penchant for experimentation with form would stay with him, from the economy of voice exhibited in *Dubliners*, to the variety of narrative expressions created for *A Portrait of the Artist as a Young Man* and *Ulysses*, to the radical linguistic experimentation of *Finnegans Wake*. In political matters, he rejected the single-minded nationalism of his peers and wrote outspoken articles that were published privately after the school advisory board barred publication in the school newspaper. Meanwhile, he was very successful in his chosen field of study—modern languages.

Joyce originally moved to Paris in 1902 to study medicine, but it was not until about 1904 that he took up his artistic mission in earnest and decided to leave Ireland. Apart from some brief periods, Joyce remained an exile from the country he would spend his life writing about. For Joyce, exile was a prerequisite for artistic objectivity and freedom; he believed that his self-imposed exile allowed him to see the truth of Ireland and Irishness with clarity, precision, and detachment.

In June 1904, Joyce was invited by the paper *The Irish Homestead* to submit a short story. In the end he wrote a series of fifteen stories that were published in 1914 under the title *Dubliners.* Along the way Joyce had a series of arguments with publishers similar to those that would also dog and delay the publication of *A Portrait of the Artist as a Young Man,* as editors objected to what they saw as the inappropriate subject matter and language of his work. In 1909, he wrote to London publisher Grant Richards, with whom he was in negotiations for *Dubliners,* "I seriously believe that you will retard the course of civilization in Ireland by preventing the Irish people from having one good look at themselves in my nicely polished looking-glass." Richards, however, was in no financial position to advance the course of Irish civilization, and the book was rejected, not to be published until 1914.

Joyce described *Dubliners* as "a chapter of the moral history of my country." The book is divided—according to a letter Joyce wrote to his publisher—into four sections, representing childhood, adolescence, maturity, and public life. The fifteenth story, "The Dead," was not part of Joyce's original manuscript. This story, the longest in the collection, became the showpiece of the book upon its publication. Thematically, each of the stories in *Dubliners* deals with the lives of ordinary people, many of whom suffer from a sort of emotional paralysis—as a result of internal or external forces or moral decay—that makes them unable to move forward. Many of these stories have as their focus a moment of self-recognition on the part of a character, a moment Joyce referred to as an "epiphany." The triggers to an epiphany are often accidental, "little errors and gestures—mere straws in the wind," as Joyce described them in a letter to his brother Stanislaus. The sharp focus allowed by a sudden flash of clarity is fleeting but allows characters a moment in which to see above their particular circumstances.

In 1904 Joyce also met the woman who would be his lifelong partner. As legend has it, it was on 16 June, or "Bloomsday" (the day on which the events in *Ulysses* take place), that James Joyce first went out walking with Nora Barnacle, a chambermaid from Galway. Uninterested in literature, but with a fresh charm and wit and, like Joyce, an interest in music, she followed Joyce to the city of Pola, in the Austro-Hungarian Empire, four months after their meeting. They lived there a short time, without the sanction of marriage, and later moved to Trieste, Italy, where Joyce continued to write and eked out a meager living teaching English. The couple had two children, Lucia and Georgio, and ultimately married, in 1931.

During their time in Trieste, in the fall of 1907, Joyce commenced editing, cutting, and reshaping the almost 1,000 pages of *Stephen Hero*, a novel he had begun in 1904. The result would be *A Portrait of the Artist as a Young Man*, which Joyce continued to work on intermittently for the next nine years. The novel-in-progress began to be published serially in *The Egoist* in 1914. It was not published as a volume until 1916, by the New York publisher B.W. Huebsch. It had been rejected by every London publisher to whom Joyce had sent it, despite the support of some major literary figures of the day, including W.B. Yeats, H.G. Wells, and Ezra Pound.

The hero of *Portrait*, Stephen Dedalus, bears a striking similarity to Joyce himself. The novel details the artistic growth of a writer, from childhood to the age of twenty, and outlines Joyce's artistic mission: to "record … with extreme care" epiphanic moments of sublime self-awareness; it also extends Joyce's experiments with style. The voice of the implied narrator changes and develops in correspondence with the development of the central character, from the first awakenings of consciousness of the small child, to the complex ethical and aesthetic meditations of the young man.

Ulysses details a day in Dublin life. Events in the novel follow the comings and goings of Stephen Dedalus, continuing the artistic journey on which Joyce set him in *A Portrait of the Artist as a Young Man*, and Leo Bloom, the Jewish-Irish Everyman who is the hero of the novel. *Ulysses* takes as its model Homer's *Odyssey*; an everyday journey through the neighborhoods of Dublin becomes highly symbolic as Leo Bloom follows a path that parallels that of Homer's hero. Meanwhile, Stephen Dedalus plays the role of Homer's Telemachus; Joyce imagines him an artist and visionary cut off from society. Joyce believed that Odysseus was perhaps the most well-rounded character in Western literature, embodying the best and the worst in human behavior: he was both brave and cowardly, a liar and an intellectual. Joyce's endeavors to portray these traits in his hero make Leo Bloom one of the most warmly compelling characters in all of twentieth-century literature.

In form, each chapter is an ironic rewriting of a chapter from Homer's *Odyssey*, and is written in a broadly different literary style from the one that precedes it. The novel adopts a stream-of-consciousness approach that makes little or no distinction between what is happening externally and what takes place in a character's mind. Perspectives move fluidly from internal to external dialogue, from character to character, and from event to event, with little to indicate the change. The novel's central themes are those that recur in Joyce's work: the inner life of Dublin in all its beauty and hollowness, and the outsider status of Leo Bloom (because of his Jewishness) and Stephen Dedalus (because of his artistic mission). This shared experience of Leo and Stephen, and Stephen's figurative search for an absent father, link the two thematically throughout the story.

Ulysses began to be published serially in the *Little Review* beginning in 1918, but in 1920 publication ceased in the face of obscenity charges. Not until 1922 was *Ulysses* published, and even then it was printed in Paris, not Britain. An American edition was published in 1934, after a landmark court case decided the book was not pornography. The weary judge at the time acquiesced to the view that the book was a work of art, even if many readers would not understand it. A British edition of *Ulysses* finally appeared in 1937.

It was not until about 1920 that the Joyce family began to attain a modest level of financial security, largely the result of the support and patronage of a number of people who had as much faith in Joyce's genius as he himself did. The family moved from Trieste to Zurich in 1914, then to Paris in 1920, then back to Zurich in 1940, where Joyce died of a perforated ulcer, just after seeing the publication of his final—and perhaps least understood—novel, *Finnegans Wake* (1939). In stylistic terms, the novel goes beyond the playful, self-conscious mode of *Ulysses* and enters a far more obscure territory. The title refers to a common folk song in which a laborer, Finnegan, falls and hits his head. His friends assume he is dead and hold a wake for him; he finally awakens after having whiskey spilled on him. *Finnegans Wake* is ostensibly the dream of Finnegan's successor, a Dublin Everyman with the initials H.C.E. (which stand for a variety of names, including Humphrey Chimpden Earwicker and Here Comes Everybody), and also features H.C.E.'s wife, A.L.P. (Anna Livia Plurabelle, Amnis Limina Permanent) and their twin sons, Shem and Shaun. Everything that occurs, and all the characters present, belong at least partially to the realm of dream. The novel's form relies on the cyclical view of history set out by Italian philosopher Giambattista Vico. The narrative is largely composed of multi-leveled puns that are fraught with symbolic meaning. Joyce used elements of English and seven other languages to create the texture of the novel, reinventing not just the form of the novel but the structure of language itself in order to escape the stifling traditions in which he felt conventional language was steeped.

During his lifetime Joyce promised his writing would "keep the professors busy," and in this he has succeeded, and continues to succeed, to an extent that even he might not have expected. For many years scholars were occupied with historical, cultural, and anthropological research into the background of Joyce's Dublin. While this research continues, developments in critical theory (such as postcolonialism) have also opened up many new ways to interpret Joyce's texts. During his lifetime much of his work was, as one of Joyce's friends said, "outside of literature"; "literature" has since shifted to accommodate Joyce.

⌘⌘⌘

Araby[1]

North Richmond Street, being blind,[2] was a quiet street except at the hour when the Christian Brothers' School set the boys free. An uninhabited house of two storeys stood at the blind end, detached from its neighbours in a square ground. The other houses of the street, conscious of decent lives within them, gazed at one another with brown imperturbable faces.

The former tenant of our house, a priest, had died in the back drawingroom. Air, musty from having been long enclosed, hung in all the rooms and the waste room behind the kitchen was littered with old useless papers. Among these I found a few papercovered books, the pages of which were curled and damp: *The Abbot* by Walter Scott, *The Devout Communicant* and *The Memoirs of Vidocq*.[3] I liked the last best because its leaves were yellow. The wild garden behind the house contained a central apple tree and a few straggling bushes under one of which I found the late tenant's rusty bicycle pump. He had been a very charitable priest; in his will he had left all his money to institutions and the furniture of his house to his sister.

When the short days of winter came dusk fell before we had well eaten our dinners. When we met in the street the houses had grown sombre. The space of sky above us was the colour of everchanging violet and towards it the lamps of the street lifted their feeble lanterns. The cold air stung us and we played till our bodies glowed. Our shouts echoed in the silent street. The career of our play brought us through the dark muddy lanes behind the houses where we ran the gantlet of the rough tribes from the cottages, to the back doors of the dark dripping gardens where odours arose from the ashpits, to the dark odorous stables where a coachman smoothed and combed the horse or shook music from the buckled harness. When we returned to the street light from the kitchen windows had filled the areas.[4] If my uncle was seen turning the corner we hid in the shadow until we had seen him safely housed. Or if Mangan's sister came out on the doorstep to call her brother in to his tea we watched her from our shadow peer up and down the street. We waited to see whether she would remain or go in and if she remained we left our shadow and walked up to Mangan's steps resignedly. She was waiting for us, her figure defined by the light from the half-opened door. Her brother always teased her before he obeyed and I stood by the railings looking at her. Her dress swung as she moved her body and the soft rope of her hair tossed from side to side.

Every morning I lay on the floor in the front parlour watching her door. The blind was pulled down to within an inch of the sash so that I could not be seen. When she came out on the doorstep my heart leaped. I ran to the hall, seized my books and followed her. I kept her brown figure always in my eye and when we came near the point at which our ways diverged I quickened my pace and passed her. This happened morning after morning. I had never spoken to her except for a few casual words and yet her name was like a summons to all my foolish blood.

Her image accompanied me even in places the most hostile to romance. On Saturday evenings when my aunt went marketing I had to go to carry some of the parcels. We walked through the flaring streets, jostled by drunken men and bargaining women, amid the curses of labourers, the shrill litanies of shop boys who stood on guard by the barrels of pigs' cheeks, the nasal chanting of street singers who sang a *come-all-you* about O'Donovan Rossa[5] or a ballad about the troubles in our native land. These noises converged in a single sensation of life for me: I imagined that I bore my chalice safely through a throng of foes. Her name sprang to my lips at

---

[1] *Araby* Charity bazaar held in Dublin in 1894.

[2] *blind* A dead end.

[3] *The Devout Communicant* Catholic religious manual published in 1831; *The Memoirs of Vidocq* Written by François-Eugène Vidocq (1775–1857), a career criminal who was appointed chief of a French detective force.

[4] *areas* Spaces between the railings and the fronts of houses, below street level.

[5] *come-all-you* Ballad (so called because many ballads started with this phrase); *O'Donovan Rossa* Jeremiah Donovan, Irish nationalist who was sentenced to a lifetime of penal servitude but was granted amnesty and departed for America.

moments in strange prayers and praises which I myself did not understand. My eyes were often full of tears (I could not tell why) and at times a flood from my heart seemed to pour itself out into my bosom. I thought little of the future. I did not know whether I would ever speak to her or not or, if I spoke to her, how I could tell her of my confused adoration. But my body was like a harp and her words and gestures were like fingers running upon the wires.

One evening I went into the back drawingroom in which the priest had died. It was a dark rainy evening and there was no sound in the house. Through one of the broken panes I heard the rain impinge upon the earth, the fine incessant needles of water playing in the sodden beds. Some distant lamp or lighted window gleamed below me. I was thankful that I could see so little. All my senses seemed to desire to veil themselves and, feeling that I was about to slip from them, I pressed the palms of my hands together until they trembled, murmuring: *O love! O love!* many times.

At last she spoke to me. When she addressed the first words to me I was so confused that I did not know what to answer. She asked me was I going to *Araby*. I forget whether I answered yes or no. It would be a splendid bazaar, she said; she would love to go.

—And why can't you? I asked.

While she spoke she turned a silver bracelet round and round her wrist. She could not go, she said, because there would be a retreat that week in her convent.[1] Her brother and two other boys were fighting for their caps and I was alone at the railings. She held one of the spikes, bowing her head towards me. The light from the lamp opposite our door caught the white curve of her neck, lit up the hair that rested there and, falling, lit up the hand upon the railing. It fell over one side of her dress and caught the white border of a petticoat, just visible as she stood at ease.

—It's well for you, she said.

—If I go, I said, I will bring you something.

What innumerable follies laid waste my waking and sleeping thoughts after that evening! I wished to annihilate the tedious intervening days. I chafed against the work of school. At night in my bedroom and by day in the classroom her image came between me and the page I strove to read. The syllables of the word *Araby* were called to me through the silence in which my soul luxuriated and cast an eastern enchantment over me. I asked for leave to go to the bazaar on Saturday night. My aunt was surprised and hoped it was not some freemason affair.[2] I answered few questions in class. I watched my master's face pass from amiability to sternness; he hoped I was not beginning to idle. I could not call my wandering thoughts together. I had hardly any patience with the serious work of life which, now that it stood between me and my desire, seemed to me child's play, ugly monotonous child's play.

On Saturday morning I reminded my uncle that I wished to go to the bazaar in the evening. He was fussing at the hallstand, looking for the hatbrush, and answered me curtly:

—Yes, boy, I know.

As he was in the hall I could not go into the front parlour and lie at the window. I left the house in bad humour and walked slowly towards the school. The air was pitilessly raw and already my heart misgave me.

When I came home to dinner my uncle had not yet been home. Still it was early. I sat staring at the clock for some time and when its ticking began to irritate me I left the room. I mounted the staircase and gained the upper part of the house. The high cold empty gloomy rooms liberated me and I went from room to room singing. From the front window I saw my companions playing below in the street. Their cries reached me weakened and indistinct and, leaning my forehead against the cool glass, I looked over at the dark house where she lived. I may have stood there for an hour seeing nothing but the brownclad figure cast by my imagination, touched discreetly by the lamplight at the curved neck, at the hand upon the railings and at the border below the dress.

1 *convent* I.e., convent school.

2 *freemason affair* Affiliated with the Freemasons, a secret society originally made up of skilled stone-workers. The society was said to be anti-Catholic, and the Archbishop of Dublin had decreed that any Catholics caught at a freemason bazaar could be excommunicated.

When I came downstairs again I found Mrs. Mercer sitting at the fire. She was an old garrulous woman, a pawnbroker's widow who collected used stamps for some pious purpose. I had to endure the gossip of the teatable. The meal was prolonged beyond an hour and still my uncle did not come. Mrs. Mercer stood up to go: she was sorry she couldn't wait any longer but it was after eight o'clock and she did not like to be out late as the night air was bad for her. When she had gone I began to walk up and down the room, clenching my fists. My aunt said:

—I'm afraid you may put off your bazaar for this night of Our Lord.

At nine o'clock I heard my uncle's latchkey in the halldoor. I heard him talking to himself and heard the hallstand rocking when it had received the weight of his overcoat. I could interpret these signs. When he was midway through his dinner I asked him to give me the money to go to the bazaar. He had forgotten.

—The people are in bed and after their first sleep now, he said.

I did not smile. My aunt said to him energetically:

—Can't you give him the money and let him go? You've kept him late enough as it is.

My uncle said he was very sorry he had forgotten. He said he believed in the old saying: *All work and no play makes Jack a dull boy*. He asked me where I was going and when I had told him a second time he asked me did I know *The Arab's Farewell to his Steed*.[1] When I left the kitchen he was about to recite the opening lines of the piece to my aunt.

I held a florin[2] tightly in my hand as I strode down Buckingham Street towards the station. The sight of the streets thronged with buyers and glaring with gas recalled to me the purpose of my journey. I took my seat in a third class carriage of a deserted train. After an intolerable delay the train moved out of the station slowly. It crept onward among ruinous houses and over the twinkling river. At Westland Row Station a crowd of people pressed at the carriage doors; but the porters moved them back, saying that it was a special train for the bazaar. I remained alone in the bare carriage. In a few minutes the train drew up beside an improvised wooden platform. I passed out on to the road and saw by the lighted dial of a clock that it was ten minutes to ten. In front of me was a large building which displayed the magical name.

I could not find any sixpenny entrance and, fearing that the bazaar would be closed, I passed in quickly through a turnstile, handing a shilling to a wearylooking man. I found myself in a big hall girdled at half its height by a gallery. Nearly all the stalls were closed and the greater part of the hall was in darkness. I recognised a silence like that which pervades a church after a service. I walked into the centre of the bazaar timidly. A few people were gathered about the stalls which were still open. Before a curtain over which the words *Café Chantant*[3] were written in coloured lamps two men were counting money on a salver. I listened to the fall of the coins.

Remembering with difficulty why I had come I went over to one of the stalls and examined porcelain vases and flowered teasets. At the door of the stall a young lady was talking and laughing with two young gentlemen. I remarked their English accents and listened vaguely to their conversation.

—O, I never said such a thing!

—O, but you did!

—O, but I didn't!

—Didn't she say that?

—She did. I heard her.

—O, there's a … fib!

Observing me the young lady came over and asked me did I wish to buy anything. The tone of her voice was not encouraging: she seemed to have spoken to me out of a sense of duty. I looked humbly at the great jars that stood like eastern guards at either side of the dark entrance to her stall and murmured:

—No, thank you.

The young lady changed the position of one of the vases and went back to the two young men. They began to talk of the same subject. Once or twice the young lady glanced at me over her shoulder.

[1] *The Arab's … Steed* Popular romantic poem by Caroline Norton (1808–77).

[2] *florin* Coin worth two shillings.

[3] *Café Chantant* Café that provides musical entertainment.

I lingered before her stall, though I knew my stay was useless, to make my interest in her wares seem the more real. Then I turned away slowly and walked down the middle of the bazaar. I allowed the two pennies to fall against the sixpence in my pocket. I heard a voice call from one end of the gallery that the light was out. The upper part of the hall was now completely dark.

Gazing up into the darkness I saw myself as a creature driven and derided by vanity: and my eyes burned with anguish and anger.

—1914

Eveline

She sat at the window watching the evening invade the avenue. Her head was leaned against the window curtains and in her nostrils was the odour of dusty cretonne.[1] She was tired.

Few people passed. The man out of the last house passed on his way home; she heard his footsteps clacking along the concrete pavement and afterwards crunching on the cinder path before the new red houses. One time there used to be a field there in which they used to play every evening with other people's children. Then a man from Belfast bought the field and built houses in it—not like their little brown houses but bright brick houses with shining roofs. The children of the avenue used to play together in that field—the Devines, the Waters, the Dunns, little Keogh the cripple, she and her brothers and sisters. Ernest, however, never played: he was too grown up. Her father used often to hunt them in out of the field with his blackthorn stick but usually little Keogh used to keep nix[2] and call out when he saw her father coming. Still they seemed to have been rather happy then. Her father was not so bad then, and besides her mother was alive. That was a long time ago; she and her brothers and sisters were all grown up; her mother was dead. Tizzie Dunn was dead, too, and the Waters had gone back to England. Everything changes. Now she was going to go away like the others, to leave her home.

Home! She looked round the room reviewing all its familiar objects which she had dusted once a week for so many years, wondering where on earth all the dust came from. Perhaps she would never see again those familiar objects from which she had never dreamed of being divided. And yet during all those years she had never found out the name of the priest whose yellowing photograph hung on the wall above the broken harmonium[3] beside the coloured print of the promises made to Blessed Margaret Mary Alacoque.[4] He had been a school friend of her father's. Whenever he showed the photograph to a visitor her father used to pass it with a casual word:

—He is in Melbourne now.

She had consented to go away, to leave her home. Was that wise? She tried to weigh each side of the question. In her home anyway she had shelter and food; she had those whom she had known all her life about her. Of course she had to work hard both in the house and at business. What would they say of her in the stores when they found out that she had run away with a fellow? Say she was a fool, perhaps; and her place would be filled up by advertisement. Miss Gavan would be glad. She had always had an edge on her, especially whenever there were people listening.

—Miss Hill, don't you see these ladies are waiting?

—Look lively, Miss Hill, please.

She would not cry many tears at leaving the stores.

But in her new home, in a distant unknown country, it would not be like that. Then she would be married—she, Eveline. People would treat her with respect then. She would not be treated as her mother had been. Even now, though she was over nineteen, she sometimes felt herself in danger of her father's violence. She knew it was that that had given her the palpitations. When they were growing up he had never gone for her,

[1] *cretonne* Thick, unglazed, cotton fabric often used for chair covers and curtains.

[2] *keep nix* Keep watch.

[3] *harmonium* Type of reed organ.

[4] *Blessed Margaret Mary Alacoque* Seventeenth-century French nun whose devotion led her to perform extreme acts of penance, such as drinking water in which laundry had been washed and carving the name of Jesus into her chest.

like he used to go for Harry and Ernest, because she was a girl; but latterly he had begun to threaten her and say what he would do to her only for her dead mother's sake. And now she had nobody to protect her. Ernest was dead and Harry, who was in the church decorating business, was nearly always down somewhere in the country. Besides, the invariable squabble for money on Saturday nights had begun to weary her unspeakably. She always gave her entire wages—seven shillings—and Harry always sent up what he could but the trouble was to get any money from her father. He said she used to squander the money, that she had no head, that he wasn't going to give her his hard earned money to throw about the streets and much more for he was usually fairly bad of a Saturday night. In the end he would give her the money and ask her had she any intention of buying Sunday's dinner. Then she had to rush out as quickly as she could and do her marketing, holding her black leather purse tightly in her hand as she elbowed her way through the crowds and returning home late under her load of provisions. She had hard work to keep the house together and to see that the two young children who had been left to her charge went to school regularly and got their meals regularly. It was hard work—a hard life—but now that she was about to leave it she did not find it a wholly undesirable life.

She was about to explore another life with Frank. Frank was very kind, manly, openhearted. She was to go away with him by the night boat to be his wife and to live with him in Buenos Ayres where he had a home waiting for her. How well she remembered the first time she had seen him; he was lodging in a house on the main road where she used to visit. It seemed a few weeks ago. He was standing at the gate, his peaked cap pushed back on his head and his hair tumbled forward over a face of bronze. Then they had come to know each other. He used to meet her outside the stores every evening and see her home. He took her to see the *Bohemian Girl*[1] and she felt elated as she sat in an unaccustomed part of the theatre with him. He was awfully fond of music and sang a little. People knew that they were courting and when he sang about the lass that loves a sailor she always felt pleasantly confused. He used to call her Poppens out of fun. First of all it had been an excitement for her to have a fellow and then she had begun to like him. He had tales of distant countries. He had started as a deck boy at a pound a month on a ship of the Allan line[2] going out to Canada. He told her the names of the ships he had been on and the names of the different services. He had sailed through the Straits of Magellan and he told her stories of the terrible Patagonians.[3] He had fallen on his feet in Buenos Ayres, he said, and had come over to the old country just for a holiday. Of course, her father had found out the affair and had forbidden her to have anything to say to him:

—I know these sailor chaps, he said.

One day he had quarrelled with Frank and after that she had to meet her lover secretly.

The evening deepened in the avenue. The white of two letters in her lap grew indistinct. One was to Harry, the other was to her father. Ernest had been her favourite but she liked Harry too. Her father was becoming old lately, she noticed; he would miss her. Sometimes he could be very nice. Not long before, when she had been laid up for a day, he had read her out a ghost story and made toast for her at the fire. Another day, when their mother was alive, they had all gone for a picnic to the Hill of Howth.[4] She remembered her father putting on her mother's bonnet to make the children laugh.

Her time was running out but she continued to sit by the window, leaning her head against the window curtain, inhaling the odour of dusty cretonne. Down far in the avenue she could hear a street organ playing. She knew the air. Strange that it should come that very night to remind her of the promise to her mother, her promise

[1] *Bohemian Girl* 1843 opera by Dubliner Michael William Balfe (1808–70).

[2] *the Allan line* The Allan Steamship Company, founded in 1852 by Sir Hugh Allan, made weekly departures from Liverpool to the Western coast of Canada (with stops along the way, including at Cape Horn and Buenos Aires).

[3] *the terrible Patagonians* Refers either to the strong, unpredictable Patagonian winds in the Strait of Magellan, or to a group of South American natives that early explorers had claimed were giants. By the beginning of the nineteenth century, this rumor was discredited.

[4] *Hill of Howth* Located northeast of Dublin, on the Howth peninsula.

to keep the home together as long as she could. She remembered the last night of her mother's illness; she was again in the close dark room at the other side of the hall and outside she heard a melancholy air of Italy. The organ player had been ordered to go away and given sixpence. She remembered her father strutting back into the sickroom saying:

—Damned Italians! coming over here!

As she mused the pitiful vision of her mother's life laid its spell on the very quick of her being—that life of commonplace sacrifices closing in final craziness. She trembled as she heard again her mother's voice saying constantly with foolish insistence:

—Derevaun Seraun! Derevaun Seraun![1]

She stood up in a sudden impulse of terror. Escape! She must escape! Frank would save her. He would give her life, perhaps love too. But she wanted to live. Why should she be unhappy? She had a right to happiness. Frank would take her in his arms, fold her in his arms. He would save her.

She stood among the swaying crowd in the station at the North Wall. He held her hand and she knew that he was speaking to her, saying something about the passage over and over again. The station was full of soldiers with brown baggages. Through the wide doors of the sheds she caught a glimpse of the black mass of the boat lying in beside the quay wall, with illumined portholes. She answered nothing. She felt her cheek pale and cold and out of a maze of distress she prayed to God to direct her, to show her what was her duty. The boat blew a long mournful whistle into the mist. If she went, tomorrow she would be on the sea with Frank, steaming towards Buenos Ayres. Their passage had been booked. Could she still draw back after all he had done for her? Her distress awoke a nausea in her body and she kept moving her lips in silent fervent prayer.

A bell clanged upon her heart. She felt him seize her hand:

—Come!

All the seas of the world tumbled about her heart. He was drawing her into them: he would drown her. She gripped with both hands at the iron railing.

—Come!

No! No! No! It was impossible. Her hands clutched the iron in frenzy. Amid the seas she sent a cry of anguish.

—Eveline! Evvy!

He rushed beyond the barrier and called to her to follow. He was shouted at to go on but he still called to her. She set her white face to him, passive, like a helpless animal. Her eyes gave him no sign of love or farewell or recognition.

—1914

The Dead

Lily, the caretaker's daughter, was literally run off her feet. Hardly had she brought one gentleman into the little pantry behind the office on the ground floor and helped him off with his overcoat when the wheezy hall-door bell clanged again and she had to scamper along the bare hallway to let in another guest. It was well for her she had not to attend to the ladies also. But Miss Kate and Miss Julia had thought of that and had converted the bathroom upstairs into a ladies' dressing-room. Miss Kate and Miss Julia were there, gossiping and laughing and fussing, walking after each other to the head of the stairs, peering down over the banisters and calling down to Lily to ask her who had come.

It was always a great affair, the Misses Morkan's annual dance. Everybody who knew them came to it, members of the family, old friends of the family, the members of Julia's choir, any of Kate's pupils that were grown up enough and even some of Mary Jane's pupils too. Never once had it fallen flat. For years and years it had gone off in splendid style as long as anyone could remember, ever since Kate and Julia, after the death of their brother Pat, had left the house in Stony Batter and taken Mary Jane, their only niece, to live with them in the dark gaunt house on Usher's Island, the upper part of which they had rented from Mr. Fullam, the corn

[1] *Derevaun Seraun* The meaning of this phrase, if there is one, is uncertain. While some scholars believe it to be garbled Irish, others assert it is gibberish.

factor[1] on the ground floor. That was a good thirty years ago if it was a day. Mary Jane, who was then a little girl in short clothes, was now the main prop of the household for she had the organ in Haddington Road. She had been through the academy[2] and gave a pupils' concert every year in the upper room of the Antient Concert Rooms. Many of her pupils belonged to better class families on the Kingstown and Dalkey line. Old as they were, her aunts also did their share. Julia, though she was quite grey, was still the leading soprano in Adam and Eve's[3] and Kate, being too feeble to go about much, gave music lessons to beginners on the old square piano in the back room. Lily, the caretaker's daughter, did housemaid work for them. Though their life was modest they believed in eating well, the best of everything: diamond bone sirloins, three shilling tea and the best bottled stout. But Lily seldom made a mistake in the orders so that she got on well with her three mistresses. They were fussy, that was all. But the only thing they would not stand was back answers.[4]

Of course they had good reason to be fussy on such a night. And then it was long after ten o'clock and yet there was no sign of Gabriel and his wife. Besides they were dreadfully afraid that Freddy Malins might turn up screwed.[5] They would not wish for worlds that any of Mary Jane's pupils should see him under the influence: and when he was like that it was sometimes very hard to manage him. Freddy Malins always came late but they wondered what could be keeping Gabriel: and that was what brought them every two minutes to the banisters to ask Lily had Gabriel or Freddy come.

—O, Mr. Conroy, said Lily to Gabriel when she opened the door for him, Miss Kate and Miss Julia thought you were never coming. Good night, Mrs. Conroy.

—I'll engage they did, said Gabriel, but they forget that my wife here takes three mortal hours to dress herself.

He stood on the mat, scraping the snow from his goloshes, while Lily led his wife to the foot of the stairs and called out:

—Miss Kate, here's Mrs. Conroy.

Kate and Julia came toddling down the dark stairs at once. Both of them kissed Gabriel's wife, said she must be perished alive and asked was Gabriel with her.

—Here I am as right as the mail, Aunt Kate! Go on up. I'll follow, called out Gabriel from the dark.

He continued scraping his feet vigorously while the three women went upstairs, laughing, to the ladies' dressingroom. A light fringe of snow lay like a cape on the shoulders of his overcoat and like toecaps on the toes of his goloshes; and, as the buttons of his overcoat slipped with a squeaking noise through the snow-stiffened frieze,[6] a cold fragrant air from out of doors escaped from crevices and folds.

—Is it snowing again, Mr. Conroy? asked Lily.

She had preceded him into the pantry to help him off with his overcoat. Gabriel smiled at the three syllables she had given his surname and glanced at her. She was a slim growing girl, pale in complexion and with haycoloured hair. The gas in the pantry made her look still paler. Gabriel had known her when she was a child and used to sit on the lowest step nursing[7] a rag doll.

—Yes, Lily, he answered, and I think we're in for a night of it. He looked up at the pantry ceiling which was shaking with the stamping and shuffling of feet on the floor above, listened for a moment to the piano and then glanced at the girl who was folding his overcoat carefully at the end of a shelf.

—Tell me, Lily, he said in a friendly tone, do you still go to school?

—O no, sir, she answered, I'm done schooling this year and more.

—O then, said Gabriel gaily, I suppose we'll be going to your wedding one of these fine days with your young man—eh?

The girl glanced back at him over her shoulder and said with great bitterness:

---

1 *corn factor* Grain merchant.

2 *the academy* Royal Irish Academy of Music.

3 *Adam and Eve's* Roman Catholic church in Dublin.

4 *back answers* Rudeness; back-talk.

5 *screwed* Drunk.

6 *frieze* Coarse woolen cloth.

7 *nursing* Here, taking care of.

—The men that is now is only all palaver[1] and what they can get out of you.

Gabriel coloured as if he felt he had made a mistake and, without looking at her, kicked off his goloshes and flicked actively with his muffler at his patent leather shoes.

He was a stout tallish young man. The high colour of his cheeks pushed upwards even to his forehead where it scattered itself in a few formless patches of pale red; and on his hairless face there scintillated restlessly the polished lenses and bright gilt rims of the glasses which screened his delicate and restless eyes. His glossy black hair was parted in the middle and brushed in a long curve behind his ears where it curled slightly beneath the groove left by his hat.

When he had flicked lustre into his shoes he stood up and pulled his waistcoat down more tightly on his plump body. Then he took a coin rapidly from his pocket.

—O Lily, he said, thrusting it into her hand, it's Christmas time, isn't it? Just … here's a little …

He walked rapidly towards the door.

—O no, sir! cried the girl, following him. Really, sir, I wouldn't take it.

—Christmas time! Christmas time! said Gabriel, almost trotting to the stairs and waving his hand to her in deprecation.

The girl, seeing that he had gained the stairs, called out after him:

—Well, thank you, sir.

He waited outside the drawingroom door until the waltz should finish, listening to the skirts that swept against it and to the shuffling of feet. He was still discomposed by the girl's bitter and sudden retort. It had cast a gloom over him which he tried to dispel by arranging his cuffs and the bows of his tie. Then he took from his waistcoat pocket a little paper and glanced at the headings he had made for his speech. He was undecided about the lines from Robert Browning[2] for he feared they would be above the heads of his hearers. Some quotation that they could recognise from Shakespeare or from the Melodies[3] would be better. The indelicate clacking of the men's heels and the shuffling of their soles reminded him that their grade of culture differed from his. He would only make himself ridiculous by quoting poetry to them which they could not understand. They would think that he was airing his superior education. He would fail with them just as he had failed with the girl in the pantry. He had taken up a wrong tone. His whole speech was a mistake from first to last, an utter failure.

Just then his aunts and his wife came out of the ladies' dressingroom. His aunts were two small plainly dressed old women. Aunt Julia was an inch or so the taller. Her hair, drawn low over the tops of her ears, was grey; and grey also, with darker shadows, was her large flaccid face. Though she was stout in build and stood erect her slow eyes and parted lips gave her the appearance of a woman who did not know where she was or where she was going. Aunt Kate was more vivacious. Her face, healthier than her sister's, was all puckers and creases like a shrivelled red apple and her hair, braided in the same oldfashioned way, had not lost its ripe nut colour.

They both kissed Gabriel frankly. He was their favourite nephew, the son of their dead elder sister Ellen who had married T.J. Conroy of the Port and Docks.[4]

—Gretta tells me you're not going to take a cab back to Monkstown tonight, Gabriel, said Aunt Kate.

—No, said Gabriel, turning to his wife, we had quite enough of that last year, hadn't we? Don't you remember, Aunt Kate, what a cold Gretta got out of it? Cab windows rattling all the way and the east wind blowing in after we passed Merrion. Very jolly it was. Gretta caught a dreadful cold.

Aunt Kate frowned severely and nodded her head at every word.

—Quite right, Gabriel, quite right, she said. You can't be too careful.

---

[1] *palaver* Flattering talk.

[2] *Robert Browning* English poet (1812–89).

[3] *Melodies* Thomas Moore's collection of poetry and songs, *Irish Melodies*.

[4] *Port and Docks* Dublin Port and Docks Board, an essential part of Dublin's commercial life.

—But as for Gretta there, said Gabriel, she'd walk home in the snow if she were let.

Mrs. Conroy laughed.

—Don't mind him, Aunt Kate, she said. He's really an awful bother, what with green shades for Tom's eyes at night and making him do the dumbbells and forcing Lottie to eat the stirabout.[1] The poor child! And she simply hates the sight of it! … O, but you'll never guess what he makes me wear now!

She broke out into a peal of laughter and glanced at her husband whose admiring and happy eyes had been wandering from her dress to her face and hair. The two aunts laughed heartily too for Gabriel's solicitude was a standing joke with them.

—Goloshes! said Mrs. Conroy. That's the latest. Whenever it's wet underfoot I must put on my goloshes. Tonight even he wanted me to put them on but I wouldn't. The next thing he'll buy me will be a diving suit.

Gabriel laughed nervously and patted his tie reassuringly while Aunt Kate nearly doubled herself so heartily did she enjoy the joke. The smile soon faded from Aunt Julia's face and her mirthless eyes were directed towards her nephew's face. After a pause she asked:

—And what are goloshes, Gabriel?

—Goloshes, Julia! exclaimed her sister. Goodness me, don't you know what goloshes are? You wear them over your … over your boots, Gretta, isn't it?

—Yes, said Mrs. Conroy. Guttapercha[2] things. We both have a pair now. Gabriel says everyone wears them on the continent.[3]

—O, on the continent, murmured Aunt Julia, nodding her head slowly.

Gabriel knitted his brows and said, as if he were slightly angered:

—It's nothing very wonderful but Gretta thinks it very funny because she says the word reminds her of christy minstrels.[4]

—But tell me, Gabriel, said Aunt Kate with brisk tact. Of course you've seen about the room. Gretta was saying …

—O, the room is all right, replied Gabriel. I've taken one in the Gresham.[5]

—To be sure, said Aunt Kate, by far the best thing to do. And the children, Gretta, you're not anxious about them?

—O, for one night, said Mrs. Conroy. Besides Bessie will look after them.

—To be sure, said Aunt Kate again. What a comfort it is to have a girl like that, one you can depend on! There's that Lily, I'm sure I don't know what has come over her lately. She's not the girl she was at all.

Gabriel was about to ask his aunt some questions on this point but she broke off suddenly to gaze after her sister who had wandered down the stairs and was craning her neck over the banisters.

—Now, I ask you, she said almost testily, where is Julia going. Julia! Julia! Where are you going?

Julia who had gone half way down one flight came back and announced blandly:

—Here's Freddy!

At the same moment a clapping of hands and a final flourish of the pianist told that the waltz had ended. The drawingroom door was opened from within and some couples came out. Aunt Kate drew Gabriel aside hurriedly and whispered into his ear:

—Slip down, Gabriel, like a good fellow and see if he's all right and don't let him up if he's screwed. I'm sure he's screwed. I'm sure he is.

Gabriel went to the stairs and listened over the banisters. He could hear two persons talking in the pantry. Then he recognised Freddy Malins' laugh. He went down the stairs noisily.

—It's such a relief, said Aunt Kate to Mrs. Conroy, that Gabriel is here. I always feel easier in my mind when he's here …

—Julia, there's Miss Daly and Miss Power will take some refreshment. Thanks for your beautiful waltz, Miss Daly. It made lovely time.

---

[1] *stirabout* Porridge.

[2] *Guttapercha* Substance similar to rubber and used for waterproofing.

[3] *continent* I.e., Europe.

[4] *christy minstrels* Minstrel show. From the nineteenth-century minstrel show founded by George Christy.

[5] *Gresham* One of Dublin's top hotels.

A tall wizenfaced man with a stiff grizzled moustache and swarthy skin who was passing out with his partner said:

—And may we have some refreshment too, Miss Morkan?

—Julia, said Aunt Kate summarily, and here's Mr. Browne and Miss Furlong. Take them in, Julia, with Miss Daly and Miss Power.

—I'm the man for the ladies, said Mr. Browne, pursing his lips until his moustache bristled and smiling in all his wrinkles. You know, Miss Morkan, the reason they are so fond of me is …

He did not finish his sentence but, seeing that Aunt Kate was out of earshot, at once led the three young ladies into the back room. The middle of the room was occupied by two square tables placed end to end and on these Aunt Julia and the caretaker were straightening and smoothing a large cloth. On the sideboard were arrayed dishes and plates and glasses and bundles of knives and forks and spoons. The top of the closed square piano served also as a sideboard for viands and sweets. At a smaller sideboard in one corner two young men were standing, drinking hop bitters.[1]

Mr. Browne led his charges thither and invited them all, in jest, to some ladies' punch, hot, strong and sweet. As they said they never took anything strong he opened three bottles of lemonade for them. Then he asked one of the young men to move aside and, taking hold of the decanter, filled out for himself a goodly measure of whisky. The young men eyed him respectfully while he took a trial sip.

—God help me, he said smiling, it's the doctor's orders.

His wizened face broke into a broader smile and the three young ladies laughed in musical echo to his pleasantry, swaying their bodies to and fro, with nervous jerks of their shoulders. The boldest said:

—O, now, Mr. Browne, I'm sure the doctor never ordered anything of the kind.

Mr. Browne took another sip of his whisky and said, with sidling mimicry:

—Well, you see, I'm like the famous Mrs. Cassidy who is reported to have said: *Now, Mary Grimes, if I don't take it make me take it for I feel I want it.*

His hot face had leaned forward a little too confidentially and he had assumed a very low Dublin accent so that the young ladies, with one instinct, received his speech in silence. Miss Furlong, who was one of Mary Jane's pupils, asked Miss Daly what was the name of the pretty waltz she had played; and Mr. Browne, seeing that he was ignored, turned promptly to the two young men who were more appreciative.

A redfaced young woman, dressed in pansy, came into the room, excitedly clapping her hands and crying:

—Quadrilles![2] Quadrilles!

Close on her heels came Aunt Kate, crying:

—Two gentlemen and three ladies, Mary Jane!

—O, here's Mr. Bergin and Mr. Kerrigan, said Mary Jane. Mr. Kerrigan, will you take Miss Power. Miss Furlong, may I get you a partner, Mr. Bergin. O, that'll just do now.

—Three ladies, Mary Jane, said Aunt Kate.

The two young gentlemen asked the ladies if they might have the pleasure and Mary Jane turned to Miss Daly.

—O, Miss Daly, you're really awfully good after playing for the last two dances but really we're so short of ladies tonight.

—I don't mind in the least, Miss Morkan.

—But I've a nice partner for you, Mr. Bartell D'Arcy, the tenor. I'll get him to sing later on. All Dublin is raving about him.

—Lovely voice, lovely voice! said Aunt Kate.

As the piano had twice begun the prelude to the first figure Mary Jane led her recruits quickly from the room. They had hardly gone when Aunt Julia wandered slowly into the room, looking behind her at something.

—What is the matter, Julia? asked Aunt Kate anxiously. Who is it?

Julia, who was carrying in a column of table-napkins, turned to her sister and said simply, as if the question had surprised her:

[1] *hop bitters* Unfermented liquor flavored with hops.

[2] *Quadrilles* Type of square dance.

—It's only Freddy, Kate, and Gabriel with him.

In fact right behind her Gabriel could be seen piloting Freddy Malins across the landing. The latter, a young man of about forty, was of Gabriel's size and build with very round shoulders. His face was fleshy and pallid, touched with colour only at the thick hanging lobes of his ears and at the wide wings of his nose. He had coarse features, a blunt nose, a convex and receding brow, tumid and protruded lips. His heavylidded eyes and the disorder of his scanty hair made him look sleepy. He was laughing heartily in a high key at a story which he had been telling Gabriel on the stairs and at the same time rubbing the knuckles of his left fist backwards and forwards into his left eye.

—Good evening, Freddy, said Aunt Julia.

Freddy Malins bade the Misses Morkan good evening in what seemed an offhand fashion by reason of the habitual catch in his voice and then, seeing that Mr. Browne was grinning at him from the sideboard, crossed the room on rather shaky legs and began to repeat in an undertone the story he had just told to Gabriel.

—He's not so bad, is he? said Aunt Kate to Gabriel.

Gabriel's brows were dark but he raised them quickly and answered:

—O no, hardly noticeable.

—Now, isn't he a terrible fellow! she said. And his poor mother made him take the pledge[1] on New Year's Eve. But come on, Gabriel, into the drawingroom.

Before leaving the room with Gabriel she signalled to Mr. Browne by frowning and shaking her forefinger in warning to and fro. Mr. Browne nodded in answer and, when she had gone, said to Freddy Malins:

—Now then, Teddy, I'm going to fill you out a good glass of lemonade just to buck you up.

Freddy Malins, who was nearing the climax of his story, waved the offer aside impatiently but Mr. Browne, having first called Freddy Malins' attention to a disarray in his dress, filled out and handed him a full glass of lemonade. Freddy Malins' left hand accepted the glass mechanically, his right hand being engaged in the mechanical readjustment of his dress. Mr. Browne, whose face was once more wrinkling with mirth, poured out for himself a glass of whisky while Freddy Malins exploded, before he had well reached the climax of his story, in a kink of highpitched bronchitic laughter and, setting down his untasted and overflowing glass, began to rub the knuckles of his left fist backwards and forwards into his left eye, repeating words of his last phrase as well as his fit of laughter would allow him.

Gabriel could not listen while Mary Jane was playing her academy piece, full of runs and difficult passages, to the hushed drawingroom. He liked music but the piece she was playing had no melody for him and he doubted whether it had any melody for the other listeners though they had begged Mary Jane to play something. Four young men, who had come from the refreshment room to stand in the doorway at the sound of the piano, had gone away quietly in couples after a few minutes. The only persons who seemed to follow the music were Mary Jane herself, her hands racing along the keyboard or lifted from it at the pauses like those of a priestess in momentary imprecation, and Aunt Kate standing at her elbow to turn the page.

Gabriel's eyes, irritated by the floor which glittered with beeswax under the heavy chandelier, wandered to the wall above the piano. A picture of the balcony scene in *Romeo and Juliet* hung there and beside it was a picture of the two murdered princes in the tower[2] which Aunt Julia had worked[3] in red, blue and brown wools when she was a girl. Probably in the school they had gone to as girls that kind of work had been taught, for one year his mother had worked for him as a birthday present a waistcoat of purple tabinet[4] with little foxes' heads upon it, lined with brown satin and having round mulberry buttons. It was strange that his mother had had no musical talent though Aunt Kate used to call her the brainscarrier of the Morkan family. Both she and Julia had always seemed a little proud of their serious

[1] *take the pledge* I.e., pledge to abstain from alcoholic beverages.

[2] *the two … tower* Edward IV's two sons were murdered in the Tower of London in about 1483–84, allegedly at the instigation of their uncle, the future Richard III.

[3] *worked* I.e., wrought; made.

[4] *tabinet* Fabric made of silk and wool, similar to poplin.

and matronly sister. Her photograph stood before the pierglass.[1] She held an open book on her knees and was pointing out something in it to Constantine who, dressed in a man-o'-war suit,[2] lay at her feet. It was she who had chosen the names for her sons for she was very sensible of the dignity of family life. Thanks to her, Constantine was now senior curate in Balbriggan and, thanks to her, Gabriel himself had taken his degree in the Royal University. A shadow passed over his face as he remembered her sullen opposition to his marriage. Some slighting phrases she had used still rankled in his memory. She had once spoken of Gretta as being country cute and that was not true of Gretta at all. It was Gretta who had nursed her all during her last long illness in their house at Monkstown.

He knew that Mary Jane must be near the end of her piece for she was playing again the opening melody with runs of scales after every bar and while he waited for the end the resentment died down in his heart. The piece ended with a trill of octaves in the treble and a final deep octave in the bass. Great applause greeted Mary Jane as, blushing and rolling up her music nervously, she escaped from the room. The most vigorous clapping came from the four young men in the doorway who had gone away to the refreshment room at the beginning of the piece but had come back when the piano had stopped.

Lancers[3] were arranged. Gabriel found himself partnered with Miss Ivors. She was a frankmannered talkative young lady with a freckled face and prominent brown eyes. She did not wear a lowcut bodice and the large brooch which was fixed in the front of her collar bore on it an Irish device.

When they had taken their places she said abruptly:

—I have a crow to pluck with you.

—With me? said Gabriel.

She nodded her head gravely.

—What is it? asked Gabriel, smiling at her solemn manner.

—Who is G.C.? answered Miss Ivors turning her eyes upon him.

Gabriel coloured and was about to knit his brows as if he did not understand when she said bluntly:

—O, innocent Amy! I have found out that you write for the *Daily Express*. Now aren't you ashamed of yourself?

—Why should I be ashamed of myself? asked Gabriel blinking his eyes and trying to smile.

—Well, I'm ashamed of you, said Miss Ivors frankly. To say you'd write for a rag like that. I didn't think you were a west Briton.[4]

A look of perplexity appeared on Gabriel's face. It was true that he wrote a literary column every Wednesday in the *Daily Express* for which he was paid fifteen shillings. But that did not make him a west Briton surely. The books he received for review were almost more welcome than the paltry cheque. He loved to feel the covers and turn over the pages of newly printed books. Nearly every day when his teaching in the college was ended he used to wander down the quays to the secondhand booksellers, to Hickey's on Bachelor's Walk, to Webb's or Massey's on Aston's Quay or to Clohissey's in the bystreet. He did not know how to meet her charge. He wanted to say that literature was above politics. But they were friends of many years' standing and their careers had been parallel, first at the university and then as teachers: he could not risk a grandiose phrase with her. He continued blinking his eyes and trying to smile and murmured lamely that he saw nothing political in writing reviews of books.

When their turn to cross had come he was still perplexed and inattentive. Miss Ivors promptly took his hand in a warm grasp and said in a soft friendly tone:

—Of course, I was only joking. Come, we cross now. When they were together again she spoke of the university question[5] and Gabriel felt more at ease. A

[1] *pierglass* Tall mirror.

[2] *man-o'-war suit* Sailor suit, frequently worn by children.

[3] *Lancers* Type of quadrille.

[4] *west Briton* Colloquial term for an Irish person who sees Ireland as the western part of Great Britain, rather than as a separate nation.

[5] *university question* Concerning the establishment of an Irish national university, the representation of "Irish" values in universities, and the provision of equal access to education for Catholics (Trinity College was open only to Protestants).

friend of hers had shown her his review of Browning's poems. That was how she had found out the secret: but she liked the review immensely. Then she said suddenly:

—O, Mr. Conroy, will you come for an excursion to the Aran Isles[1] this summer? We're going to stay there a whole month. It will be splendid out in the Atlantic. You ought to come. Mr. Clancy is coming and Mr. Kilkelly and Kathleen Kearney. It would be splendid for Gretta too if she'd come. She's from Connacht,[2] isn't she?

—Her people are, said Gabriel shortly.

—But you will come, won't you? said Miss Ivors, laying her warm hand eagerly on his arm.

—The fact is, said Gabriel, I have already arranged to go …

—Go where? asked Miss Ivors.

—Well, you know, every year I go for a cycling tour with some fellows and so …

—But where? asked Miss Ivors.

—Well, we usually go to France or Belgium or perhaps Germany, said Gabriel awkwardly.

—And why do you go to France and Belgium, said Miss Ivors, instead of visiting your own land?

—Well, said Gabriel, it's partly to keep in touch with the languages and partly for a change.

—And haven't you your own language to keep in touch with, Irish? asked Miss Ivors.

—Well, said Gabriel, if it comes to that, you know, Irish is not my language.

Their neighbours had turned to listen to the cross-examination. Gabriel glanced right and left nervously and tried to keep his good humour under the ordeal which was making a blush invade his forehead.

—And haven't you your own land to visit, continued Miss Ivors, that you know nothing of, your own people and your own country?

—O, to tell you the truth, retorted Gabriel suddenly, I'm sick of my own country, sick of it!

—Why? asked Miss Ivors.

Gabriel did not answer for his retort had heated him.

[1] *Aran Isles* Three islands off the coast of County Galway, on Ireland's west coast.

[2] *Connacht* Connaught, in west Ireland.

—Why? repeated Miss Ivors.

They had to go visiting[3] together and, as he had not answered her, Miss Ivors said warmly:

—Of course, you've no answer.

Gabriel tried to cover his agitation by taking part in the dance with great energy. He avoided her eyes for he had seen a sour expression on her face. But when they met in the long chain he was surprised to feel his hand firmly pressed. She looked at him from under her brows for a moment quizzically until he smiled. Then, just as the chain was about to start again, she stood on tiptoe and whispered into his ear:

—West Briton!

When the lancers were over Gabriel went away to a remote corner of the room where Freddy Malins' mother was sitting. She was a stout feeble old woman with white hair. Her voice had a catch in it like her son's and she stuttered slightly. She had been told that Freddy had come and that he was nearly all right. Gabriel asked her whether she had had a good crossing. She lived with her married daughter in Glasgow and came to Dublin on a visit once a year. She answered placidly that she had had a beautiful crossing and that the captain had been most attentive to her. She spoke also of the beautiful house her daughter kept in Glasgow and of the nice friends they had there. While her tongue rambled on Gabriel tried to banish from his mind all memory of the unpleasant incident with Miss Ivors. Of course the girl or woman or whatever she was was an enthusiast but there was a time for all things. Perhaps he ought not to have answered her like that. But she had no right to call him a west Briton before people, even in joke. She had tried to make him ridiculous before people, heckling him and staring at him with her rabbit's eyes.

He saw his wife making her way towards him through the waltzing couples. When she reached him she said into his ear:

—Gabriel, Aunt Kate wants to know won't you carve the goose as usual. Miss Daly will carve the ham and I'll do the pudding.

—All right, said Gabriel.

[3] *go visiting* Reference to the part of the dance in which the partners cross the floor together and meet another couple.

—She's sending in the younger ones first as soon as this waltz is over so that we'll have the table to ourselves.

—Were you dancing? asked Gabriel.

—Of course I was. Didn't you see me? What words had you with Molly Ivors?

—No words. Why! Did she say so?

—Something like that. I'm trying to get that Mr. D'Arcy to sing. He's full of conceit, I think.

—There were no words, said Gabriel moodily, only she wanted me to go for a trip to the west of Ireland and I said I wouldn't.

His wife clasped her hands excitedly and gave a little jump.

—O, do go, Gabriel, she cried. I'd love to see Galway again.

—You can go if you like, said Gabriel coldly.

She looked at him for a moment, then turned to Mrs. Malins and said:

—There's a nice husband for you, Mrs. Malins.

While she was threading her way back across the room Mrs. Malins, without adverting to the interruption, went on to tell Gabriel what beautiful places there were in Scotland and beautiful scenery. Her son-in-law brought them every year to the lakes and they used to go fishing. Her son-in-law was a splendid fisher. One day he caught a fish, a beautiful big big fish: and the man in the hotel boiled it for their dinner.

Gabriel hardly heard what she said. Now that supper was coming near he began to think again about his speech and about the quotation. When he saw Freddy Malins coming across the room to visit his mother Gabriel left the chair free for him and retired into the embrasure of the window. The room had already cleared and from the back room came the clatter of plates and knives. Those who still remained in the drawingroom seemed tired of dancing and were conversing quietly in little groups. Gabriel's warm trembling fingers tapped the cold pane of the window. How cool it must be outside! How pleasant it would be to walk out alone, first along by the river and then through the park! The snow would be lying on the branches of the trees and forming a bright cap on the top of the Wellington monument.[1] How much more pleasant it would be there than at the supper table!

He ran over the headings of his speech: Irish hospitality, sad memories, the Three Graces, Paris,[2] the quotation from Browning. He repeated to himself a phrase he had written in his review: *One feels that one is listening to a thought-tormented music.* Miss Ivors had praised the review. Was she sincere? Had she really any life of her own behind all her propagandism? There had never been any ill feeling between them until that night. It unnerved him to think that she would be at the supper table, looking up at him while he spoke with her critical quizzing eyes. Perhaps she would not be sorry to see him fail in his speech. An idea came into his mind and gave him courage. He would say, alluding to Aunt Kate and Aunt Julia: *Ladies and gentlemen, the generation which is now on the wane among us may have had its faults but for my part I think it had certain qualities of hospitality, of humour, of humanity, which the new and very serious and hypereducated generation that is growing up around us seems to me to lack.* Very good: that was one for Miss Ivors. What did he care that his aunts were only two ignorant old women?

A murmur in the room attracted his attention. Mr. Browne was advancing from the door, gallantly escorting Aunt Julia who leaned upon his arm, smiling and hanging her head. An irregular musketry of applause escorted her also as far as the piano and then, as Mary Jane seated herself on the stool and Aunt Julia, no longer smiling, half turned so as to pitch her voice fairly into the room, gradually ceased. Gabriel recognised the prelude. It was that of an old song of Aunt Julia's,

---

[1] *Wellington monument* Monument to the Duke of Wellington, an English military hero born in Ireland.

[2] *Three Graces* In Greek mythology, the three daughters of Zeus and Eurynome who embodied the qualities of beauty and charm; *Paris* In Greek mythology, Paris was asked by the gods to judge a beauty contest between Hera, Athena, and Aphrodite. All three goddesses offered Paris a bribe. When he chose Aphrodite, she rewarded him by granting him the most beautiful woman in the world, who was Helen of Troy. Paris's abduction of Helen from her husband, Menelaus, is the putative cause of the Trojan War.

Arrayed for the Bridal.[1] Her voice strong and clear in tone attacked with great spirit the runs which embellish the air and, though she sang very rapidly, she did not miss even the smallest of the grace notes. To follow the voice, without looking at the singer's face, was to feel and share the excitement of swift and secure flight. Gabriel applauded loudly with all the others at the close of the song and loud applause was borne in from the invisible supper table. It sounded so genuine that a little colour struggled into Aunt Julia's face as she bent to replace in the music stand the old leatherbound songbook that had her initials on the cover. Freddy Malins, who had listened with his head perched sideways to hear the better, was still applauding when everyone else had ceased and talking animatedly to his mother who nodded her head gravely and slowly in acquiescence. At last, when he could clap no more, he stood up suddenly and hurried across the room to Aunt Julia, whose hand he seized and held in both his hands, shaking it when words failed him or the catch in his voice proved too much for him.

—I was just telling my mother, he said, I never heard you sing so well, never. No, I never heard your voice so good as it is tonight. Now! Would you believe that now? That's the truth. Upon my word and honour that's the truth. I never heard your voice sound so fresh and so ... so clear and fresh, never.

Aunt Julia smiled broadly and murmured something about compliments as she released her hand from his grasp. Mr. Browne extended his open hand towards her and said to those who were near him in the manner of a showman introducing a prodigy to an audience:

—Miss Julia Morkan, my latest discovery!

He was laughing very heartily at this himself when Freddy Malins turned to him and said:

—Well, Browne, if you're serious you might make a worse discovery. All I can say is I never heard her sing half so well as long as I am coming here. And that's the honest truth.

—Neither did I, said Mr. Browne. I think her voice has greatly improved.

Aunt Julia shrugged her shoulders and said with meek pride:

—Thirty years ago I hadn't a bad voice as voices go.

—I often told Julia, said Aunt Kate emphatically, that she was simply thrown away in that choir. But she never would be said by[2] me.

She turned as if to appeal to the good sense of the others against a refractory child while Aunt Julia gazed in front of her, a vague smile of reminiscence playing on her face.

—No, continued Aunt Kate, she wouldn't be said or led by anyone, slaving there in that choir night and day, night and day. Six o'clock on Christmas morning! And all for what?

—Well, isn't it for the honour of God, Aunt Kate? asked Mary Jane twisting round on the piano stool and smiling.

Aunt Kate turned fiercely on her niece and said:

—I know all about the honour of God, Mary Jane, but I think it's not at all honourable for the pope to turn out the women out of the choirs that have slaved there all their lives and put little whippersnappers of boys over their heads. I suppose it is for the good of the church if the pope does it. But it's not just, Mary Jane, and it's not right.[3]

She had worked herself into a passion and would have continued in defence of her sister for it was a sore subject with her but Mary Jane, seeing that all the dancers had come back, intervened pacifically:

—Now, Aunt Kate, you're giving scandal to Mr. Browne who is of the other persuasion.[4]

Aunt Kate turned to Mr. Browne, who was grinning at this allusion to his religion, and said hastily:

---

[1] *Arrayed ... Bridal* Popular and challenging song from Bellini's opera *I Puritani* (1835) that begins with the words "Arrayed for the bridal, in beauty behold her."

[2] *be said by* Be ruled by; submit to.

[3] *I know ... right* On 22 November 1903, Pope Pius X issued a papal bull, in which he announced that the singing of Church music constituted a liturgical function for which women were ineligible and that, henceforth, soprano and alto voices would be produced by young boys.

[4] *of the other persuasion* I.e., a Protestant.

—O, I don't question the pope's being right. I'm only a stupid old woman and I wouldn't presume to do such a thing. But there's such a thing as common everyday politeness and gratitude. And if I were in Julia's place I'd tell that Father Healy straight up to his face …

—And besides, Aunt Kate, said Mary Jane, we really are all hungry and when we are hungry we are all very quarrelsome.

—And when we are thirsty we are also quarrelsome, added Mr. Browne.

—So that we had better go to supper, said Mary Jane, and finish the discussion afterwards.

On the landing outside the drawingroom Gabriel found his wife and Mary Jane trying to persuade Miss Ivors to stay for supper. But Miss Ivors, who had put on her hat and was buttoning her cloak, would not stay. She did not feel in the least hungry and she had already overstayed her time.

—But only for ten minutes, Molly, said Mrs. Conroy. That won't delay you.

—To take a pick itself,[1] said Mary Jane, after all your dancing.

—I really couldn't, said Miss Ivors.

—I am afraid you didn't enjoy yourself at all, said Mary Jane hopelessly.

—Ever so much, I assure you, said Miss Ivors, but you really must let me run off now.

—But how can you get home? asked Mrs. Conroy.

—O, it's only two steps up the quay. Gabriel hesitated a moment and said:

—If you will allow me, Miss Ivors, I'll see you home if you really are obliged to go.

But Miss Ivors broke away from them.

—I won't hear of it, she cried. For goodness' sake go in to your suppers and don't mind me. I'm quite well able to take care of myself.

—Well, you're the comical girl, Molly, said Mrs. Conroy frankly.

—*Beannacht libh*,[2] cried Miss Ivors with a laugh as she ran down the staircase.

[1] *a pick itself* I.e., a little bit.

[2] *Beannacht libh* An Irish farewell; literally, "my blessings go with you."

Mary Jane gazed after her, a moody puzzled expression on her face, while Mrs. Conroy leaned over the banisters to listen for the hall door. Gabriel asked himself was he the cause of her abrupt departure. But she did not seem to be in ill humour: she had gone away laughing. He stared blankly down the staircase.

At that moment Aunt Kate came toddling out of the supper room, almost wringing her hands in despair.

—Where is Gabriel? she cried. Where on earth is Gabriel? There's everyone waiting in there, stage to let, and nobody to carve the goose!

—Here I am, Aunt Kate! cried Gabriel with sudden animation, ready to carve a flock of geese, if necessary.

A fat brown goose lay at one end of the table and at the other end, on a bed of creased paper strewn with sprigs of parsley, lay a great ham, stripped of its outer skin and peppered over with crust crumbs, a neat paper frill round its shin, and beside this was a round of spiced beef. Between these rival ends ran parallel lines of side dishes: two little minsters of jelly, red and yellow, a shallow dish full of blocks of blancmange[3] and red jam, a large green leafshaped dish with a stalkshaped handle on which lay bunches of purple raisins and peeled almonds, a companion dish on which lay a solid rectangle of Smyrna figs, a dish of custard topped with grated nutmeg, a small bowl full of chocolates and sweets wrapped in gold and silver papers and a glass vase in which stood some tall celery stalks. In the centre of the table there stood, as sentries to a fruit stand which upheld a pyramid of oranges and American apples, two squat oldfashioned decanters of cut glass, one containing port and the other dark sherry. On the closed square piano a pudding in a huge yellow dish lay in waiting and behind it were three squads of bottles of stout and ale and minerals drawn up according to the colours of their uniforms, the first two black with brown and red labels, the third and smallest squad white, with transverse green sashes.

Gabriel took his seat boldly at the head of the table and, having looked to the edge of the carver, plunged his fork firmly into the goose. He felt quite at ease now

[3] *blancmange* Milk jelly.

for he was an expert carver and liked nothing better than to find himself at the head of a well laden table.

—Miss Furlong, what shall I send you? he asked. A wing or a slice of the breast?

—Just a small slice of the breast.

—Miss Higgins, what for you?

—O, anything at all, Mr. Conroy.

While Gabriel and Miss Daly exchanged plates of goose and plates of ham and spiced beef Lily went from guest to guest with a dish of hot floury potatoes wrapped in a white napkin. This was Mary Jane's idea and she had also suggested apple sauce for the goose but Aunt Kate had said that plain roast goose without any apple sauce had always been good enough for her and she hoped she might never eat worse. Mary Jane waited on her pupils and saw that they got the best slices and Aunt Kate and Aunt Julia opened and carried across from the piano bottles of stout and ale for the gentlemen and bottles of minerals for the ladies. There was a great deal of confusion and laughter and noise, the noise of orders and counterorders, of knives and forks, of corks and glass stoppers. Gabriel began to carve second helpings as soon as he had finished the first round without serving himself. Everyone protested loudly so that he compromised by taking a long draught of stout for he had found the carving hot work. Mary Jane settled down quietly to her supper but Aunt Kate and Aunt Julia were still toddling round the table, walking on each other's heels, getting in each other's way and giving each other unheeded orders. Mr. Browne begged of them to sit down and eat their supper and so did Gabriel but they said there was time enough so that, at last, Freddy Malins stood up and, capturing Aunt Kate, plumped her down on her chair amid general laughter.

When everyone had been well served Gabriel said smiling:

—Now if anyone wants a little more of what vulgar people call stuffing let him or her speak.

A chorus of voices invited him to begin his own supper and Lily came forward with three potatoes which she had reserved for him.

—Very well, said Gabriel amiably as he took another preparatory draught, kindly forget my existence, ladies and gentlemen, for a few minutes.

He set to his supper and took no part in the conversation with which the table covered Lily's removal of the plates. The subject of talk was the opera company which was then at the Theatre Royal. Mr. Bartell D'Arcy, the tenor, a dark-complexioned young man with a smart moustache, praised very highly the leading contralto of the company but Miss Furlong thought she had a rather vulgar style of production. Freddy Malins said there was a negro chieftain singing in the second part of the Gaiety pantomime who had one of the finest tenor voices he had ever heard.

—Have you heard him? he asked Mr. Bartell D'Arcy across the table.

—No, answered Mr. Bartell D'Arcy carelessly.

—Because, Freddy Malins explained, now I'd be curious to hear your opinion of him. I think he has a grand voice.

—It takes Teddy to find out the really good things, said Mr. Browne familiarly to the table.

—And why couldn't he have a voice too? asked Freddy Malins sharply. Is it because he's only a black?

Nobody answered this question and Mary Jane led the table back to the legitimate opera. One of her pupils had given her a pass for *Mignon*.[1] Of course, it was very fine, she said, but it made her think of poor Georgina Burns.[2] Mr. Browne could go back farther still to the old Italian companies that used to come to Dublin, Tietjens, Trebelli, Ilma de Murzka, Campanini, the great Giuglini, Ravelli, Aramburo. Those were the days, he said, when there was something like singing to be heard in Dublin. He told too of how the top gallery of the old Royal used to be packed night after night, of how one night an Italian tenor had sung five encores to *Let Me Like a Soldier Fall*, introducing a high C every time, and of how the gallery boys would sometimes in their enthusiasm unyoke the horses from the carriage of some great *prima donna* and pull her themselves through the streets to her hotel. Why did they never play the grand old operas now, he asked. *Dinorah*, *Lucrezia*

[1] *Mignon* 1866 opera by Ambroise Thomas.

[2] *Georgina Burns* Famous soprano who made her Dublin début in 1878.

Borgia?[1] Because they could not get the voices to sing them: that was why.

—O, well, said Mr. Bartell D'Arcy, I presume there are as good singers today as there were then.

—Where are they? asked Mr. Browne defiantly.

—In London, Paris, Milan, said Mr. Bartell D'Arcy warmly. I suppose Caruso,[2] for example, is quite as good, if not better than any of the men you have mentioned.

—Maybe so, said Mr. Browne. But I may tell you I doubt it strongly.

—O, I'd give anything to hear Caruso sing, said Mary Jane.

—For me, said Aunt Kate, who had been picking a bone, there was only one tenor. To please me, I mean. But I suppose none of you ever heard of him.

—Who was he, Miss Morkan? asked Mr. Bartell D'Arcy politely.

—His name, said Aunt Kate, was Parkinson. I heard him when he was in his prime and I think he had then the purest tenor voice that was ever put into a man's throat.

—Strange, said Mr. Bartell D'Arcy. I never even heard of him.

—Yes, yes, Miss Morkan is right, said Mr. Browne. I remember hearing of old Parkinson but he's too far back for me.

—A beautiful pure sweet mellow English tenor, said Aunt Kate with enthusiasm.

Gabriel having finished, the huge pudding was transferred to the table. The clatter of forks and spoons began again. Gabriel's wife served out spoonfuls of the pudding and passed the plates down the table. Midway down they were held up by Mary Jane who replenished them with raspberry or orange jelly or with blancmange and jam. The pudding was of Aunt Julia's making and she received praises for it from all quarters. She herself said that it was not quite brown enough.

—Well, I hope, Miss Morkan, said Mr. Browne, that I'm brown enough for you because, you know, I'm all brown.

All the gentlemen, except Gabriel, ate some of the pudding out of compliment to Aunt Julia. As Gabriel never ate sweets the celery had been left for him. Freddy Malins also took a stalk of celery and ate it with his pudding. He had been told that celery was a capital thing for the blood and he was just then under doctor's care. Mrs. Malins, who had been silent all through the supper, said that her son was going down to Mount Melleray[3] in a week or so. The table then spoke of Mount Melleray, how bracing the air was down there, how hospitable the monks were and how they never asked for a penny-piece from their guests.

—And do you mean to say, asked Mr. Browne incredulously, that a chap can go down there and put up there as if it were a hotel and live on the fat of the land and then come away without paying a farthing?

—O, most people give some donation to the monastery when they leave, said Mary Jane.

—I wish we had an institution like that in our church, said Mr. Browne candidly.

He was astonished to hear that the monks never spoke, got up at two in the morning and slept in their coffins.[4] He asked what they did it for.

—That's the rule of the order, said Aunt Kate firmly.

—Yes, but why? asked Mr. Browne.

Aunt Kate repeated that it was the rule, that was all. Mr. Browne still seemed not to understand. Freddy Malins explained to him, as best he could, that the monks were trying to make up for the sins committed by all the sinners in the outside world. The explanation was not very clear for Mr. Browne grinned and said:

—I like that idea very much but wouldn't a comfortable spring bed do them as well as a coffin?

—The coffin, said Mary Jane, is to remind them of their last end.

As the subject had grown lugubrious it was buried in a silence of the table during which Mrs. Malins could be

[1] *Dinorah* 1859 comic opera by Giacomo Meyerbeer; *Lucrezia Borgia* 1833 opera by Gaetano Donizetti.

[2] *Caruso* Tenor Enrico Caruso (1874–1921).

[3] *Mount Melleray* Site of the Abbey of St. Bernard de Trappe, founded in 1831 by the Cistercian monks.

[4] *slept in their coffins* Though commonly believed, this is not a real custom of the Cistercians.

heard saying to her neighbour in an indistinct undertone:

—They are very good men, the monks, very pious men.

The raisins and almonds and figs and apples and oranges and chocolates and sweets were now passed about the table and Aunt Julia invited all the guests to have either port or sherry. At first Mr. Bartell D'Arcy refused to take either but one of his neighbours nudged him and whispered something to him upon which he allowed his glass to be filled. Gradually as the last glasses were being filled the conversation ceased. A pause followed, broken only by the noise of the wine and by unsettlings of chairs. The Misses Morkan, all three, looked down at the tablecloth. Someone coughed once or twice and then a few gentlemen patted the table gently as a signal for silence. The silence came and Gabriel pushed back his chair and stood up.

The patting at once grew louder in encouragement and then ceased altogether. Gabriel leaned his ten trembling fingers on the tablecloth and smiled nervously at the company. Meeting a row of upturned faces he raised his eyes to the chandelier. The piano was playing a waltz tune and he could hear the skirts sweeping against the drawingroom door. People perhaps were standing in the snow on the quay outside, gazing up at the lighted windows and listening to the waltz music. The air was pure there. In the distance lay the park where the trees were weighted with snow. The Wellington monument wore a gleaming cap of snow that flashed westward over the white field of Fifteen Acres.

He began:

—Ladies and gentlemen.

—It has fallen to my lot this evening as in years past to perform a very pleasing task, but a task for which I am afraid my poor powers as a speaker are all too inadequate.

—No, no, said Mr. Browne.

—But, however that may be, I can only ask you tonight to take the will for the deed and to lend me your attention for a few moments while I endeavour to express to you in words what my feelings are on this occasion.

—Ladies and gentlemen. It is not the first time that we have gathered together under this hospitable roof, around this hospitable board. It is not the first time that we have been the recipients—or, perhaps I had better say, the victims—of the hospitality of certain good ladies.

He made a circle in the air with his arm and paused. Everyone laughed or smiled at Aunt Kate and Aunt Julia and Mary Jane who all turned crimson with pleasure. Gabriel went on more boldly:

—I feel more strongly with every recurring year that our country has no tradition which does it so much honour and which it should guard so jealously as that of its hospitality. It is a tradition that is unique so far as my experience goes (and I have visited not a few places abroad) among the modern nations. Some would say, perhaps, that with us it is rather a failing than anything to be boasted of. But granted even that, it is, to my mind, a princely failing and one that I trust will long be cultivated among us. Of one thing, at least, I am sure. As long as this one roof shelters the good ladies aforesaid—and I wish from my heart it may do so for many and many a long year to come—the tradition of genuine warmhearted courteous Irish hospitality, which our forefathers have handed down to us and which we in turn must hand down to our descendants, is still alive among us.

A hearty murmur of assent ran round the table. It shot through Gabriel's mind that Miss Ivors was not there and that she had gone away discourteously: and he said with confidence in himself:

—Ladies and gentlemen.

—A new generation is growing up in our midst, a generation actuated by new ideas and new principles. It is serious and enthusiastic for these new ideas and its enthusiasm, even when it is misdirected, is, I believe, in the main sincere. But we are living in a sceptical and, if I may use the phrase, a thought-tormented age: and sometimes I fear that this new generation, educated or hypereducated as it is, will lack those qualities of humanity, of hospitality, of kindly humour which belonged to an older day. Listening tonight to the names of all those great singers of the past it seemed to me, I must confess, that we were living in a less spacious age. Those days might without exaggeration be called spacious days: and if they are gone beyond recall let us hope, at least, that in gatherings such as this we shall still speak of them with pride and affection, still cherish in our hearts the memory of those dead and gone great ones whose fame the world will not willingly let die.

—Hear! hear! said Mr. Browne loudly.

—But yet, continued Gabriel, his voice falling into a softer inflection, there are always in gatherings such as this sadder thoughts that will recur to our minds: thoughts of the past, of youth, of changes, of absent faces that we miss here tonight. Our path through life is strewn with many such sad memories: and were we to brood upon them always we could not find the heart to go on bravely with our work among the living. We have all of us living duties and living affections which claim, and rightly claim, our strenuous endeavours.

—Therefore I will not linger on the past. I will not let any gloomy moralising intrude upon us here tonight. Here we are gathered together for a brief moment from the bustle and rush of our everyday routine. We are met here as friends, in the spirit of good fellowship, as colleagues also, to a certain extent, in the true spirit of camaraderie, and as the guests of—what shall I call them?—the three Graces of the Dublin musical world.

The table burst into applause and laughter at this sally. Aunt Julia vainly asked each of her neighbours in turn to tell her what Gabriel had said.

—He says we are the three Graces, Aunt Julia, said Mary Jane. Aunt Julia did not understand but she looked up, smiling, at Gabriel who continued in the same vein:

—Ladies and gentlemen.

—I will not attempt to play tonight the part that Paris played on another occasion. I will not attempt to choose between them. The task would be an invidious one and one beyond my poor powers. For when I view them in turn, whether it be our chief hostess herself, whose good heart, whose too good heart, has become a byword with all who know her, or her sister, who seems to be gifted with perennial youth and whose singing must have been a surprise and a revelation to us all tonight, or, last but not least, when I consider our youngest hostess, talented, cheerful, hard-working and the best of nieces, I confess, ladies and gentlemen, that I do not know to which of them I should award the prize.

Gabriel glanced down at his aunts and, seeing the large smile on Aunt Julia's face and the tears which had risen to Aunt Kate's eyes, hastened to his close. He raised his glass of port gallantly while every member of the company fingered a glass expectantly and said loudly:

—Let us toast them all three together. Let us drink to their health, wealth, long life, happiness and prosperity and may they long continue to hold the proud and self-won position which they hold in their profession and the position of honour and affection which they hold in our hearts.

All the guests stood up, glass in hand and, turning towards the three seated ladies, sang in unison with Mr. Browne as leader:

—For they are jolly gay fellows,
For they are jolly gay fellows,
For they are jolly gay fellows
Which nobody can deny.

Aunt Kate was making frank use of her handkerchief and even Aunt Julia seemed moved. Freddy Malins beat time with his pudding fork and the singers turned towards one another as if in melodious conference, while they sang with emphasis:

—Unless he tells a lie,
Unless he tells a lie.

Then turning once more towards their hostesses they sang:

—For they are jolly gay fellows,
For they are jolly gay fellows,
For they are jolly gay fellows
Which nobody can deny.

The acclamation which followed was taken up beyond the door of the supper room by many of the other guests and renewed time after time, Freddy Malins acting as officer with his fork on high.

The piercing morning air came into the hall where they were standing so that Aunt Kate said:

—Close the door, somebody. Mrs. Malins will get her death of cold.

—Browne is out there, Aunt Kate, said Mary Jane.

—Browne is everywhere, said Aunt Kate lowering her voice.

Mary Jane laughed at her tone.

—Really, she said archly, he is very attentive.

—He has been laid on here like the gas, said Aunt Kate in the same tone, all during the Christmas.

She laughed herself this time good-humouredly and then added quickly:

—But tell him to come in, Mary Jane, and close the door. I hope to goodness he didn't hear me.

At that moment the hall door was opened and Mr. Browne came in from the doorstep, laughing as if his heart would break. He was dressed in a long green overcoat with mock astrakhan[1] cuffs and collar and wore on his head an oval fur cap. He pointed down the snowcovered quay whence the sound of shrill prolonged whistling was borne in.

—Teddy will have all the cabs in Dublin out, he said. Gabriel advanced from the little pantry behind the office, struggling into his overcoat and, looking round the hall, said:

—Gretta not down yet?

—She's getting on her things, Gabriel, said Aunt Kate.

—Who's playing up there? asked Gabriel.

—Nobody. They're all gone.

—O no, Aunt Kate, said Mary Jane. Bartell D'Arcy and Miss O'Callaghan aren't gone yet.

—Someone is strumming at the piano, anyhow, said Gabriel. Mary Jane glanced at Gabriel and Mr. Browne and said with a shiver:

—It makes me feel cold to look at you two gentlemen muffled up like that. I wouldn't like to face your journey home at this hour.

—I'd like nothing better this minute, said Mr. Browne stoutly, than a rattling fine walk in the country or a fast drive with a good spanking goer between the shafts.

—We used to have a very good horse and trap[2] at home, said Aunt Julia sadly.

—The never-to-be-forgotten Johnny, said Mary Jane laughing. Aunt Kate and Gabriel laughed too.

—Why, what was wonderful about Johnny? asked Mr. Browne.

—The late lamented Patrick Morkan, our grandfather that is, explained Gabriel, commonly known in his later years as the old gentleman, was a glue boiler.

—O now, Gabriel, said aunt Kate laughing, he had a starch mill.

—Well, glue or starch, said Gabriel, the old gentleman had a horse by the name of Johnny. And Johnny used to work in the old gentleman's mill walking round and round in order to drive the mill. That was all very well; but now comes the tragic part about Johnny. One fine day the old gentleman thought he'd like to drive out with the quality to a military review in the park.

—The Lord have mercy on his soul, said Aunt Kate compassionately.

—Amen, said Gabriel. So the old gentleman, as I said, harnessed Johnny and put on his very best tall hat and his very best stock collar and drove out in grand style from his ancestral mansion somewhere near Back Lane, I think.

Everyone laughed, even Mrs. Malins, at Gabriel's manner and Aunt Kate said:

—O now, Gabriel, he didn't live in Back Lane really. Only the mill was there.

—Out from the mansion of his forefathers, continued Gabriel, he drove with Johnny. And everything went on beautifully until Johnny came in sight of King Billy's[3] statue: and whether he fell in love with the horse

[1] *astrakhan* Lambskin.

[2] *trap* Small, two-wheeled carriage on springs.

[3] *King Billy* King William III (William of Orange), who took the British throne in the Glorious Revolution of 1688.

King Billy sits on or whether he thought he was back again in the mill, anyhow he began to walk round the statue.

Gabriel paced in a circle round the hall in his goloshes amid the laughter of the others.

—Round and round he went, said Gabriel, and the old gentleman, who was a very pompous old gentleman, was highly indignant. *Go on, sir! What do you mean, sir? Johnny! Johnny! Most extraordinary conduct! Can't understand the horse!*

The peals of laughter which followed Gabriel's imitation of the incident were interrupted by a resounding knock at the hall door. Mary Jane ran to open it and let in Freddy Malins. Freddy Malins, with his hat well back on his head and his shoulders humped with cold, was puffing and steaming after his exertions.

—I could only get one cab, he said.

—O, we'll find another along the quay, said Gabriel.

—Yes, said Aunt Kate. Better not keep Mrs. Malins standing in the draught.

Mrs. Malins was helped down the front steps by her son and Mr. Browne and, after many manoeuvres, hoisted into the cab. Freddy Malins clambered in after her and spent a long time settling her on the seat, Mr. Browne helping him with advice. At last she was settled comfortably and Freddy Malins invited Mr. Browne into the cab. There was a good deal of confused talk, then Mr. Browne got into the cab. The cabman settled his rug over his knees and bent down for the address. The confusion grew greater and the cabman was directed differently by Freddy Malins and Mr. Browne, each of whom had his head out through a window of the cab. The difficulty was to know where to drop Mr. Browne along the route and Aunt Kate, Aunt Julia and Mary Jane helped the discussion from the doorstep with cross-directions and contradictions and abundance of laughter. As for Freddy Malins he was speechless with laughter. He popped his head in and out of the window every moment, to the great danger of his hat, and told his mother how the discussion was progressing till at last Mr. Browne shouted to the bewildered cabman above the din of everybody's laughter:

—Do you know Trinity College?

—Yes, sir, said the cabman.

—Well, drive bang up against Trinity College gates, said Mr. Browne, and then we'll tell you where to go. You understand now?

—Yes, sir, said the cabman.

—Make like a bird for Trinity College.

—Right, sir, cried the cabman.

The horse was whipped up and the cab rattled off along the quay amid a chorus of laughter and adieus.

Gabriel had not gone to the door with the others. He was in a dark part of the hall gazing up the staircase. A woman was standing near the top of the first flight in the shadow also. He could not see her face but he could see the terracotta and salmonpink panels of her skirt which the shadow made appear black and white. It was his wife. She was leaning on the banisters listening to something. Gabriel was surprised at her stillness and strained his ear to listen also. But he could hear little save the noise of laughter and dispute on the front steps, a few chords struck on the piano and a few notes of a man's voice singing.

He stood still in the gloom of the hall, trying to catch the air that the voice was singing and gazing up at his wife. There was grace and mystery in her attitude as if she were a symbol of something. He asked himself what is a woman standing on the stairs in the shadow, listening to distant music, a symbol of. If he were a painter he would paint her in that attitude. Her blue felt hat would show off the bronze of her hair against the darkness and the dark panels of her skirt would show off the light ones. *Distant Music* he would call the picture if he were a painter.

The hall door was closed and Aunt Kate, Aunt Julia and Mary Jane came down the hall, still laughing.

—Well, isn't Freddy terrible? said Mary Jane. He's really terrible.

Gabriel said nothing but pointed up the stairs towards where his wife was standing. Now that the hall door was closed the voice and the piano could be heard more clearly. Gabriel held up his hand for them to be silent. The song seemed to be in the old Irish tonality and the singer seemed uncertain both of his words and of his voice. The voice made plaintive by the distance and by the singer's hoarseness faintly illuminated the cadence of the air with words expressing grief:

—O, the rain falls on my heavy locks
And the dew wets my shin,
My babe lies cold …

—O, exclaimed Mary Jane. It's Bartell D'Arcy singing and he wouldn't sing all the night. O, I'll get him to sing a song before he goes.

—O do, Mary Jane, said Aunt Kate.

Mary Jane brushed past the others and ran to the staircase but before she reached it the singing stopped and the piano was closed abruptly.

—O, what a pity! she cried. Is he coming down, Gretta? Gabriel heard his wife answer yes and saw her come down towards them. A few steps behind her were Mr. Bartell D'Arcy and Miss O'Callaghan.

—O, Mr. D'Arcy, cried Mary Jane, it's downright mean of you to break off like that when we were all in raptures listening to you.

—I have been at him all the evening, said Miss O'Callaghan, and Mrs. Conroy too, and he told us he had a dreadful cold and couldn't sing.

—O, Mr. D'Arcy, said Aunt Kate, now that was a great fib to tell.

—Can't you see that I'm as hoarse as a crow? said Mr. D'Arcy roughly.

He went into the pantry hastily and put on his overcoat. The others, taken aback by his rude speech, could find nothing to say. Aunt Kate wrinkled her brows and made signs to the others to drop the subject. Mr. D'Arcy stood swathing his neck carefully and frowning.

—It's the weather, said Aunt Julia after a pause.

—Yes, everybody has colds, said Aunt Kate readily, everybody.

—They say, said Mary Jane, we haven't had snow like it for thirty years: and I read this morning in the newspaper that the snow is general all over Ireland.

—I love the look of snow, said Aunt Julia sadly.

—So do I, said Miss O'Callaghan. I think Christmas is never really Christmas unless we have the snow on the ground.

—But poor Mr. D'Arcy doesn't like the snow, said Aunt Kate smiling.

Mr. D'Arcy came from the pantry, fully swathed and buttoned, and in a repentant tone told them the history of his cold. Everyone gave him advice and said it was a great pity and urged him to be very careful of his throat in the night air. Gabriel watched his wife who did not join in the conversation. She was standing right under the dusty fanlight and the flame of the gas lit up the rich bronze of her hair which he had seen her drying at the fire a few days before. She was in the same attitude and seemed unaware of the talk about her. At last she turned towards them and Gabriel saw that there was colour on her cheeks and that her eyes were shining. A sudden tide of joy went leaping out of his heart.

—Mr. D'Arcy, she said, what is the name of that song you were singing?

—It's called *The Lass of Aughrim*,[1] said Mr. D'Arcy, but I couldn't remember it properly. Why? Do you know it?

—*The Lass of Aughrim*, she repeated. I couldn't think of the name.

—It's a very nice air, said Mary Jane. I'm sorry you were not in voice tonight.

—Now, Mary Jane, said Aunt Kate, don't annoy Mr. D'Arcy. I won't have him annoyed.

Seeing that all were ready to start she shepherded them to the door where goodnight was said:

—Well, goodnight Aunt Kate, and thanks for the pleasant evening.

—Goodnight, Gabriel. Goodnight, Gretta!

—Goodnight, Aunt Kate, and thanks ever so much. Goodnight, Aunt Julia.

—O, goodnight, Gretta, I didn't see you.

—Goodnight, Mr. D'Arcy. Goodnight, Miss O'Callaghan.

—Goodnight, Miss Morkan.

—Goodnight again.

—Goodnight all. Safe home.

[1] *The Lass of Aughrim* Irish ballad about a peasant girl who commits suicide when her noble seducer refuses to recognize her when she arrives at his door pregnant with his child.

—Goodnight. Goodnight.

The morning was still dark. A dull yellow light brooded over the houses and the river and the sky seemed to be descending. It was slushy underfoot and only streaks and patches of snow lay on the roofs, on the parapets of the quay and on the area railings. The lamps were still burning redly in the murky air and, across the river, the palace of the Four Courts[1] stood out menacingly against the heavy sky.

She was walking on before him with Mr. Bartell D'Arcy, her shoes in a brown parcel tucked under one arm and her hands holding her skirt up from the slush. She had no longer any grace of attitude but Gabriel's eyes were still bright with happiness. The blood went bounding along his veins and the thoughts went rioting through his brain, proud, joyful, tender, valorous.

She was walking on before him so lightly and so erect that he longed to run after her noiselessly, catch her by the shoulders and say something foolish and affectionate into her ear. She seemed to him so frail that he longed to defend her against something and then to be alone with her. Moments of their secret life together burst like stars upon his memory. A heliotrope envelope was lying beside his breakfast cup and he was caressing it with his hand. Birds were twittering in the ivy and the sunny web of the curtain was shimmering along the floor: he could not eat for happiness. They were standing on the crowded platform and he was placing a ticket inside the warm palm of her glove. He was standing with her in the cold, looking in through a grated window at a man making bottles in a roaring furnace. It was very cold. Her face, fragrant in the cold air, was quite close to his and suddenly she called out to the man at the furnace:

—Is the fire hot, sir?

But the man could not hear her with the noise of the furnace. It was just as well. He might have answered rudely.

A wave of yet more tender joy escaped from his heart and went coursing in warm flood along his arteries. Like the tender fire of stars moments of their life together, that no one knew of or would ever know of, broke upon and illumined his memory. He longed to recall to her those moments, to make her forget the years of their dull existence together and remember only their moments of ecstasy. For the years, he felt, had not quenched his soul or hers. Their children, his writing, her household cares had not quenched all their souls' tender fire. In one letter that he had written to her then he had said: *Why is it that words like these seem to me so dull and cold? Is it because there is no word tender enough to be your name?*

Like distant music these words that he had written years before were borne towards him from the past. He longed to be alone with her. When the others had gone away, when he and she were in their room in the hotel, then they would be alone together. He would call her softly:

—Gretta!

Perhaps she would not hear at once: she would be undressing. Then something in his voice would strike her. She would turn and look at him …

At the corner of Winetavern Street they met a cab. He was glad of its rattling noise as it saved him from conversation. She was looking out of the window and seemed tired. The others spoke only a few words, pointing out some building or street. The horse galloped along wearily under the murky morning sky, dragging his old rattling box after his heels, and Gabriel was again in a cab with her galloping to catch the boat, galloping to their honeymoon.

As the cab drove across O'Connell bridge Miss O'Callaghan said:

—They say you never cross O'Connell bridge without seeing a white horse.

—I see a white man this time, said Gabriel.

—Where? asked Mr. Bartell D'Arcy.

Gabriel pointed to the statue[2] on which lay patches of snow. Then he nodded familiarly to it and waved his hand.

—Goodnight, Dan, he said gaily.

[1] *palace … Courts* Judicial building; home of the four traditional divisions of the judicial system in Ireland.

[2] *the statue* The O'Connell Memorial, commemorating Irish nationalist Daniel O'Connell (1775–1847).

When the cab drew up before the hotel Gabriel jumped out and, in spite of Mr. Bartell D'Arcy's protest, paid the driver. He gave the man a shilling over his fare. The man saluted and said:

—A prosperous new year to you, sir.

—The same to you, said Gabriel cordially.

She leaned for a moment on his arm in getting out of the cab and while standing at the kerbstone bidding the others goodnight. She leaned lightly on his arm, as lightly as when she had danced with him a few hours before. He had felt proud and happy then, happy that she was his, proud of her grace and wifely carriage. But now after the kindling again of so many memories, the first touch of her body, musical and strange and perfumed, sent through him a keen pang of lust. Under cover of her silence he pressed her arm closely to his side: and, as they stood at the hotel door, he felt that they had escaped from their lives and duties, escaped from home and friends and run away together with wild and radiant hearts to a new adventure.

An old man was dozing in a great hooded chair in the hall. He lit a candle in the office and went before them to the stairs. They followed him in silence, their feet falling in soft thuds on the thickly carpeted stairs. She mounted the stairs behind the porter, her head bowed in the ascent, her frail shoulders curved as with a burden, her skirt girt tightly about her. He could have flung his arms about her hips and held her still for his arms were trembling with desire to seize her and only the stress of his nails against the palms of his hands held the wild impulse of his body in check. The porter halted on the stairs to settle his guttering candle. They halted too on the steps below him. In the silence Gabriel could hear the falling of the molten wax into the tray and the thumping of his own heart against his ribs.

The porter led them along a corridor and opened a door. Then he set his unstable candle down on a toilet table and asked at what hour they were to be called in the morning.

—Eight, said Gabriel.

The porter pointed to the tap of the electric light and began a muttered apology but Gabriel cut him short.

—We don't want any light. We have light enough from the street. And, I say, he added pointing to the candle, you might remove that handsome article, like a good man.

The porter took up his candle again, but slowly, for he was surprised by such a novel idea. Then he mumbled goodnight and went out. Gabriel shot the lock to.

A ghostly light from the street lamp lay in a long shaft from one window to the door. Gabriel threw his overcoat and hat on a couch and crossed the room towards the window. He looked down into the street in order that his emotion might calm a little. Then he turned and leaned against a chest of drawers with his back to the light. She had taken off her hat and cloak and was standing before a large swinging mirror, unhooking her waist. Gabriel paused for a few moments, watching her, and then said:

—Gretta!

She turned away from the mirror slowly and walked along the shaft of light towards him. Her face looked so serious and weary that the words would not pass Gabriel's lips. No, it was not the moment yet.

—You look tired, he said.

—I am a little, she answered.

—You don't feel ill or weak?

—No, tired: that's all.

She went on to the window and stood there, looking out. Gabriel waited again and then, fearing that diffidence was about to conquer him, he said abruptly:

—By the way, Gretta!

—What is it?

—You know that poor fellow Malins? he said quickly.

—Yes, what about him?

—Well, poor fellow, he's a decent sort of chap after all, continued Gabriel in a false voice. He gave me back that sovereign I lent him and I didn't expect it really. It's a pity he wouldn't keep away from that Browne because he's not a bad fellow at heart.

He was trembling now with annoyance. Why did she seem so abstracted? He did not know how he could begin. Was she annoyed too about something? If she would only turn to him or come to him of her own accord! To take her as she was would be brutal. No, he must see some ardour in her eyes first. He longed to be master of her strange mood.

—When did you lend him the pound? she asked after a pause. Gabriel strove to restrain himself from breaking out into brutal language about the sottish Malins and his pound. He longed to cry to her from his soul, to crush her body against his, to overmaster her. But he said:

—O, at Christmas, when he opened that little Christmas card shop in Henry Street.

He was in such a fever of rage and desire that he did not hear her come from the window. She stood before him for an instant looking at him strangely. Then, suddenly raising herself on tiptoe and resting her hands lightly on his shoulders, she kissed him.

—You are a very generous person, Gabriel, she said.

Gabriel, trembling with delight at her sudden kiss and at the quaintness of her phrase, put his hands on her hair and began smoothing it back, scarcely touching it with his fingers. The washing had made it fine and brilliant. His heart was brimming over with happiness. Just when he was wishing for it she had come to him of her own accord. Perhaps her thoughts had been running with his. Perhaps she had felt the impetuous desire that was in him and then the yielding mood had come upon her. Now that she had fallen to him so easily he wondered why he had been so diffident.

He stood, holding her head between his hands. Then, slipping one arm swiftly about her body and drawing her towards him, he said softly:

—Gretta dear, what are you thinking about?

She did not answer nor yield wholly to his arm. He said again softly:

—Tell me what it is, Gretta. I think I know what is the matter. Do I know?

She did not answer at once. Then she said in an outburst of tears:

—O, I am thinking about that song, *The Lass of Aughrim*.

She broke loose from him and ran to the bed and, throwing her arms across the bedrail, hid her face. Gabriel stood stockstill for a moment in astonishment and then followed her. As he passed in the way of the cheval glass he caught sight of himself in full length, his broad, wellfilled shirtfront, the face whose expression always puzzled him when he saw it in a mirror and his glimmering gilt-rimmed eyeglasses. He halted a few paces from her and said:

—What about the song? Why does that make you cry?

She raised her head from her arms and dried her eyes with the back of her hand like a child. A kinder note than he had intended went into his voice.

—Why, Gretta? he asked.

—I am thinking about a person long ago who used to sing that song.

—And who was the person long ago? asked Gabriel smiling.

—It was a person I used to know in Galway when I was living with my grandmother, she said.

The smile passed away from Gabriel's face. A dull anger began to gather again at the back of his mind and the dull fires of his lust began to glow angrily in his veins.

—Someone you were in love with? he asked ironically.

—It was a young boy I used to know, she answered, named Michael Furey. He used to sing that song, *The Lass of Aughrim*. He was very delicate.

Gabriel was silent. He did not wish her to think that he was interested in this delicate boy.

—I can see him so plainly, she said after a moment. Such eyes as he had, big dark eyes! And such an expression in them—an expression! …

—O, then you were in love with him? said Gabriel.

—I used to go out walking with him, she said, when I was in Galway.

A thought flew across Gabriel's mind.

—Perhaps that was why you wanted to go to Galway with that Ivors girl? he said coldly.

She looked at him and asked in surprise:

—What for?

Her eyes made Gabriel feel awkward. He shrugged his shoulders and said:

—How do I know? To see him, perhaps.

She looked away from him along the shaft of light towards the window in silence.

—He is dead, she said at length. He died when he was only seventeen. Isn't it a terrible thing to die so young as that?

—What was he? asked Gabriel, still ironically.

—He was in the gasworks, she said.

Gabriel felt humiliated by the failure of his irony and by the evocation of this figure from the dead, a boy in the gasworks. The irony of his mood soured into sarcasm. While he had been full of memories of their secret life together, full of tenderness and joy and desire, she had been comparing him in her mind with another. A shameful consciousness of his own person assailed him. He saw himself as a ludicrous figure, acting as a pennyboy for his aunts, a nervous wellmeaning sentimentalist, orating to vulgarians and idealising his own clownish lusts, the pitiable fatuous fellow he had caught a glimpse of in the mirror. Instinctively he turned his back more to the light lest she might see the shame that burned upon his forehead.

He tried to keep up his tone of cold interrogation but his voice when he spoke was humble and indifferent.

—I suppose you were in love with this Michael Furey, Gretta, he said.

—I was great with him at that time, she said.

Her voice was veiled and sad. Gabriel, feeling now how vain it would be to try to lead her whither he had purposed, caressed one of her hands and said also sadly:

—And what did he die of so young, Gretta? Consumption, was it?

—I think he died for me, she answered.

A vague terror seized Gabriel at this answer as if, at that hour when he had hoped to triumph, some impalpable and vindictive being was coming against him, gathering forces against him in its vague world. But he shook himself free of it with an effort of reason and continued to caress her hand. He did not question her again for he felt that she would tell him of herself. Her hand was warm and moist: it did not respond to his touch but he continued to caress it just as he had caressed her first letter to him that spring morning.

—It was in the winter, she said, about the beginning of the winter when I was going to leave my grandmother's and come up here to the convent. And he was ill at the time in his lodgings in Galway and wouldn't be let out and his people in Oughterard were written to. He was in decline, they said, or something like that. I never knew rightly.

She paused for a moment and sighed.

—Poor fellow, she said, he was very fond of me and he was such a gentle boy. We used to go out together walking, you know, Gabriel, like the way they do in the country. He was going to study singing only for his health. He had a very good voice, poor Michael Furey.

—Well, and then? asked Gabriel.

—And then when it came to the time for me to leave Galway and come up to the convent he was much worse and I wouldn't be let see him so I wrote him a letter saying I was going up to Dublin and would be back in the summer and hoping he would be better then.

She paused for a moment to get her voice under control and then went on:

—Then the night before I left I was in my grandmother's house in Nun's Island, packing up, and I heard gravel thrown up against the window. The window was so wet I couldn't see so I ran downstairs as I was and slipped out the back into the garden and there was the poor fellow at the end of the garden shivering.

—And did you not tell him to go back? asked Gabriel.

—I implored of him to go home at once and told him he would get his death in the rain. But he said he did not want to live. I can see his eyes as well as well![1] He was standing at the end of the wall where there was a tree.

—And did he go home? asked Gabriel.

—Yes, he went home. And when I was only a week in the convent he died and he was buried in Oughterard where his people came from. O, the day I heard that, that he was dead! …

[1] *as well as well* I.e., as well as well can be.

She stopped, choking with sobs and, overcome by emotion, flung herself face downward on the bed, sobbing in the quilt. Gabriel held her hand for a moment longer, irresolutely, and then, shy of intruding on her grief, let it fall gently and walked quietly to the window. She was fast asleep.

Gabriel, leaning on his elbow, looked for a few moments unresentfully at her tangled hair and half open mouth, listening to her deep drawn breath. So she had had that romance in her life: a man had died for her sake. It hardly pained him now to think how poor a part he, her husband, had played in her life. He watched her while she slept as though he and she had never lived together as man and wife. His curious eyes rested long upon her face and on her hair: and as he thought of what she must have been then, in that time of her first girlish beauty, a strange friendly pity for her entered his soul. He did not like to say even to himself that her face was no longer beautiful but he knew that it was no longer the face for which Michael Furey had braved death.

Perhaps she had not told him all the story. His eyes moved to the chair over which she had thrown some of her clothes. A petticoat string dangled to the floor. One boot stood upright, its limp upper fallen down: the fellow of it lay upon its side. He wondered at his riot of emotions of an hour before. From what had it proceeded? From his aunts' supper, from his own foolish speech, from the wine and dancing, the merrymaking when saying goodnight in the hall, the pleasure of the walk along the river in the snow. Poor Aunt Julia! She too would soon be a shade[1] with the shade of Patrick Morkan and his horse. He had caught that haggard look upon her face for a moment when she was singing *Arrayed for the Bridal*. Soon perhaps he would be sitting in that same drawingroom, dressed in black, his silk hat on his knees. The blinds would be drawn down and Aunt Kate would be sitting beside him, crying and blowing her nose and telling him how Julia had died. He would cast about in his mind for some words that might console her and would find only lame and useless ones. Yes, yes: that would happen very soon.

The air of the room chilled his shoulders. He stretched himself cautiously along under the sheets and lay down beside his wife. One by one they were all becoming shades. Better pass boldly into that other world, in the full glory of some passion, than fade and wither dismally with age. He thought of how she who lay beside him had locked in her heart for so many years that image of her lover's eyes when he had told her that he did not wish to live.

Generous tears filled Gabriel's eyes. He had never felt like that himself towards any woman but he knew that such a feeling must be love. The tears gathered more thickly in his eyes and in the partial darkness he imagined he saw the form of a young man standing under a dripping tree. Other forms were near. His soul had approached that region where dwell the vast hosts of the dead. He was conscious of, but could not apprehend, their wayward and flickering existence. His own identity was fading out into a grey impalpable world: the solid world itself which these dead had one time reared and lived in was dissolving and dwindling.

A few light taps upon the pane made him turn to the window. It had begun to snow again. He watched sleepily the flakes, silver and dark, falling obliquely against the lamplight. The time had come for him to set out on his journey westward. Yes, the newspapers were right: snow was general all over Ireland. It was falling on every part of the dark central plain, on the treeless hills, falling softly upon the Bog of Allen and, farther westward, softly falling into the dark mutinous Shannon waves. It was falling, too, upon every part of the lonely churchyard on the hill where Michael Furey lay buried. It lay thickly drifted on the crooked crosses and headstones, on the spears of the little gate, on the barren thorns. His soul swooned slowly as he heard the snow falling faintly through the universe and faintly falling, like the descent of their last end, upon all the living and the dead.

—1914

[1] *shade* Ghost.

Ulysses

The chapter of *Ulysses* reprinted here follows Book 5 of Homer's *Odyssey*, in which Odysseus is beached on the land of the Phaeacians, where he hides in a thicket to sleep. He is awakened by Princess Nausicaa and her ladies-in-waiting, who have come to do their washing on the beach and are playing a ball game. He reveals himself and begs for their help in returning home to his wife, Penelope. In Joyce's version, Leopold Bloom is loitering on the beach, avoiding returning home to his unfaithful Penelope, Molly Bloom. In this episode it is not Bloom but Gerty (the Nausicaa figure) who reveals herself.

from *Ulysses*

Chapter 13 [Nausicaa]

The summer evening had begun to fold the world in its mysterious embrace. Far away in the west the sun was setting and the last glow of all too fleeting day lingered lovingly on sea and strand,[1] on the proud promontory of dear old Howth[2] guarding as ever the waters of the bay, on the weedgrown rocks along Sandymount shore and, last but not least, on the quiet church whence there streamed forth at times upon the stillness the voice of prayer to her who is in her pure radiance a beacon ever to the stormtossed heart of man, Mary, star of the sea.[3]

The three girl friends were seated on the rocks, enjoying the evening scene and the air which was fresh but not too chilly. Many a time and oft were they wont to come there to that favourite nook to have a cosy chat beside the sparkling waves and discuss matters feminine, Cissy Caffrey and Edy Boardman with the baby in the push-car and Tommy and Jacky Caffrey, two little curlyheaded boys, dressed in sailor suits with caps to match and the name H.M.S. Belleisle printed on both. For Tommy and Jacky Caffrey were twins, scarce four years old and very noisy and spoiled twins sometimes but for all that darling little fellows with bright merry faces and endearing ways about them. They were dabbling in the sand with their spades and buckets, building castles as children do, or playing with their big coloured ball, happy as the day was long. And Edy Boardman was rocking the chubby baby to and fro in the pushcar while that young gentleman fairly chuckled with delight. He was but eleven months and nine days old and, though still a tiny toddler, was just beginning to lisp his first babyish words. Cissy Caffrey bent over him to tease his fat little plucks[4] and the dainty dimple in his chin.

—Now, baby, Cissy Caffrey said. Say out big, big. I want a drink of water.

And baby prattled after her:

—A jink a jink a jawbo.

Cissy Caffrey cuddled the wee chap for she was awfully fond of children, so patient with little sufferers and Tommy Caffrey could never be got to take his castor oil unless it was Cissy Caffrey that held his nose and promised him the scatty[5] heel of the loaf or brown bread with golden syrup on. What a persuasive power that girl had! But to be sure baby was as good as gold, a perfect little dote in his new fancy bib. None of your spoilt beauties, Flora Mac Flimsy[6] sort, was Cissy Caffrey. A truerhearted lass never drew the breath of life, always with a laugh in her gipsylike eyes and a frolicsome word on her cherryripe red lips, a girl lovable in the extreme. And Edy Boardman laughed too at the quaint language of little brother.

But just then there was a slight altercation between Master Tommy and Master Jacky. Boys will be boys and our two twins were no exception to this golden rule.

[1] *strand* Shore.

[2] *Howth* Fishing port on the northeast headland of Dublin Bay. Howth Head overlooks Sandymount, on the shore of Dublin Bay.

[3] *Mary … sea* The Roman Catholic Church of Mary, Star of the Sea, is located near Sandymount beach. *Stella Maris* is an attribute of the Virgin Mary.

[4] *plucks* Cheeks.

[5] *scatty* Crumbled.

[6] *Flora Mac Flimsey* Miss Flora MacFlimsey of Madison Square, a character in American poet William Allen Butler's "Nothing to Wear" (1857) who is mocked for her obsession with fashionable clothing.

The apple of discord[1] was a certain castle of sand which Master Jacky had built and Master Tommy would have it right go wrong that it was to be architecturally improved by a frontdoor like the Martello tower[2] had. But if Master Tommy was headstrong Master Jacky was selfwilled too and, true to the maxim that every little Irishman's house is his castle, he fell upon his hated rival and to such purpose that the wouldbe assailant came to grief and (alas to relate!) the coveted castle too. Needless to say the cries of discomfited Master Tommy drew the attention of the girl friends.

—Come here, Tommy, his sister called imperatively, at once! And you, Jacky, for shame to throw poor Tommy in the dirty sand. Wait till I catch you for that.

His eyes misty with unshed tears Master Tommy came at her call for their big sister's word was law with the twins. And in a sad plight he was after his misadventure. His little man-o'-war[3] top and unmentionables[4] were full of sand but Cissy was a past mistress in the art of smoothing over life's tiny troubles and very quickly not one speck of sand was to be seen on his smart little suit. Still the blue eyes were glistening with hot tears that would well up so she kissed away the hurtness and shook her hand at Master Jacky the culprit and said if she was near him she wouldn't be far from him, her eyes dancing in admonition.

—Nasty bold Jacky! she cried.

She put an arm round the little mariner and coaxed winningly:

—What's your name? Butter and cream?[5]

—Tell us who is your sweetheart, spoke Edy Boardman. Is Cissy your sweetheart?

—Nao, tearful Tommy said.

—Is Edy Boardman your sweetheart? Cissy queried.

—Nao, Tommy said.

—I know, Edy Boardman said none too amiably with an arch glance from her shortsighted eyes. I know who is Tommy's sweetheart, Gerty is Tommy's sweetheart.

—Nao, Tommy said on the verge of tears.

Cissy's quick motherwit guessed what was amiss and she whispered to Edy Boardman to take him there behind the pushcar where the gentlemen couldn't see and to mind he didn't wet his new tan shoes.

But who was Gerty?

Gerty MacDowell who was seated near her companions, lost in thought, gazing far away into the distance was in very truth as fair a specimen of winsome Irish girlhood as one could wish to see. She was pronounced beautiful by all who knew her though, as folks often said, she was more a Giltrap than a MacDowell. Her figure was slight and graceful, inclining even to fragility but those iron jelloids[6] she had been taking of late had done her a world of good much better than the Widow Welch's female pills[7] and she was much better of those discharges she used to get and that tired feeling. The waxen pallor of her face was almost spiritual in its ivorylike purity though her rosebud mouth was a genuine Cupid's bow, Greekly perfect. Her hands were of finely veined alabaster with tapering fingers and as white as lemon juice and queen of ointments could make them though it was not true that she used to wear kid gloves in bed or take a milk footbath either. Bertha Supple told that once to Edy Boardman, a deliberate lie, when she was black out at daggers drawn with Gerty (the girl chums had of course their little tiffs from time to time like the rest of mortals) and she told her to not let on whatever she did that it was her that told her or she'd never speak to her again. No. Honour where

[1] *apple of discord* Reference to the Greek myth in which Eris (goddess of discord) threw a golden apple into the midst of a wedding banquet and said that it belonged to the fairest goddess present. The subsequent argument between Athena, Aphrodite, and Hera as to its rightful owner and the resolution of the argument is the putative cause of the Trojan War.

[2] *Martello tower* Round, fortified tower near Sandymount, one of a series of such structures built by the British in the nineteenth century to deter a sea invasion.

[3] *man-o'-war* Sailor suit, frequently worn by children.

[4] *unmentionables* Underwear.

[5] *What's your ... cream* From a popular rhyme: "What's your name? / Butter an' crame / All the way from / Dirty Lane."

[6] *iron jelloids* Gelatine lozenges containing iron and sold as a cure for anemia.

[7] *Widow ... pills* Brand of medicine advertised as a remedy for gynecological problems.

honour is due. There was an innate refinement, a languid queenly *hauteur*[1] about Gerty which was unmistakably evidenced in her delicate hands and higharched instep. Had kind fate but willed her to be born a gentlewoman of high degree in her own right and had she only received the benefit of a good education Gerty MacDowell might easily have held her own beside any lady in the land and have seen herself exquisitely gowned with jewels on her brow and patrician suitors at her feet vying with one another to pay their devoirs[2] to her. Mayhap it was this, the love that might have been, that lent to her softlyfeatured face at whiles a look, tense with suppressed meaning, that imparted a strange yearning tendency to the beautiful eyes, a charm few could resist. Why have women such eyes of witchery? Gerty's were of the bluest Irish blue, set off by lustrous lashes and dark expressive brows. Time was when those brows were not so silkily seductive. It was Madame Vera Verity, directress of the Woman Beautiful page of the Princess novelette,[3] who had first advised her to try eyebrowleine which gave that haunting expression to the eyes, so becoming in leaders of fashion, and she had never regretted it. Then there was blushing scientifically cured and how to be tall increase your height and you have a beautiful face but your nose? That would suit Mrs. Dignam because she had a button one. But Gerty's crowning glory was her wealth of wonderful hair. It was dark brown with a natural wave in it. She had cut it that very morning on account of the new moon[4] and it nestled about her pretty head in a profusion of luxuriant clusters and pared her nails too, Thursday for wealth.[5] And just now at Edy's words as a telltale flush, delicate as the faintest rosebloom, crept into her cheeks she looked so lovely in her sweet girlish shyness that of a surety God's fair land of Ireland did not hold her equal.

For an instant she was silent with rather sad downcast eyes. She was about to retort but something checked the words on her tongue. Inclination prompted her to speak out: dignity told her to be silent. The pretty lips pouted a while but then she glanced up and broke out into a joyous little laugh which had in it all the freshness of a young May morning. She knew right well, no-one better, what made squinty Edy say that because of him cooling in his attentions when it was simply a lover's quarrel. As per usual somebody's nose was out of joint about the boy that had the bicycle always riding up and down in front of her window. Only now his father kept him in the evenings studying hard to get an exhibition in the intermediate[6] that was on and he was going to Trinity college to study for a doctor when he left the high school like his brother W.E. Wylie who was racing in the bicycle races in Trinity college university. Little recked[7] he perhaps for what she felt, that dull aching void in her heart sometimes, piercing to the core. Yet he was young and perchance he might learn to love her in time. They were protestants in his family and of course Gerty knew Who came first and after Him the blessed Virgin and then Saint Joseph.[8] But he was undeniably handsome with an exquisite nose and he was what he looked, every inch a gentleman, the shape of his head too at the back without his cap on that she would know anywhere something off the common and the way he turned the bicycle at the lamp with his hands off the bars and also the nice perfume of those good cigarettes and besides they were both of a size and that was why Edy Boardman thought she was so frightfully clever because he didn't go and ride up and down in front of her bit of a garden.

Gerty was dressed simply but with the instinctive taste of a votary of Dame Fashion for she felt that there was just a might that he might be out. A neat blouse of

[1] *hauteur* Haughtiness, elevation of manner.

[2] *devoirs* Dues; respects.

[3] *Princess novelette* Weekly London magazine *The Princess Novelettes*.

[4] *She had ... moon* According to popular superstition, it was best to cut one's hair during a new moon.

[5] *Thursday for wealth* According to astrologists, Thursday (the day sacred to Jupiter) is a good day on which to transact business and to be courageous.

[6] *exhibition in the intermediate* Exams given at the end of the school year to determine the winners of various cash prizes.

[7] *recked* Cared or knew.

[8] *Who came ... Joseph* More polite version of the oath "Jesus, Mary and Joseph."

electric blue, selftinted by dolly dyes[1] (because it was expected in the *Lady's Pictorial* that electric blue would be worn), with a smart vee opening down to the division and kerchief pocket (in which she always kept a piece of cottonwool scented with her favourite perfume because the handkerchief spoiled the sit) and a navy threequarter skirt cut to the stride showed off her slim graceful figure to perfection. She wore a coquettish little love of a hat of wideleaved nigger straw contrast trimmed with an underbrim of eggblue chenille and at the side a butterfly bow to tone. All Tuesday week[2] afternoon she was hunting to match that chenille but at last she found what she wanted at Clery's[3] summer sales, the very it, slightly shopsoiled but you would never notice, seven fingers two and a penny. She did it up all by herself and what joy was hers when she tried it on then, smiling at the lovely reflection which the mirror gave back to her! And when she put it on the waterjug to keep the shape she knew that that would take the shine out of some people she knew. Her shoes were the newest thing in footwear (Edy Boardman prided herself that she was very *petite* but she never had a foot like Gerty MacDowell, a five, and never would ash, oak or elm[4]) with patent toecaps and just one smart buckle at her higharched instep. Her well-turned ankle displayed its perfect proportions beneath her skirt and just the proper amount and no more of her shapely limbs encased in finespun hose with highspliced heels and wide garter tops. As for undies they were Gerty's chief care and who that knows the fluttering hopes and fears of sweet seventeen (though Gerty would never see seventeen again) can find it in his heart to blame her? She had four dinky sets, with awfully pretty stitchery, three garments and nighties extra, and each set slotted with different coloured ribbons, rosepink, pale blue, mauve and peagreen and she aired them herself and blued[5] them when they came home from the wash and ironed them and she had a brickbat[6] to keep the iron on because she wouldn't trust those washerwomen as far as she'd see them scorching the things. She was wearing the blue for luck, hoping against hope, her own colour and the lucky colour too for a bride to have a bit of blue somewhere on her because the green she wore that day week brought grief because his father brought him in to study for the intermediate exhibition and because she thought perhaps he might be out because when she was dressing that morning she nearly slipped up the old pair on her inside out and that was for luck and lovers' meetings if you put those things on inside out so long as it wasn't of a Friday.

And yet and yet! That strained look on her face! A gnawing sorrow is there all the time. Her very soul is in her eyes and she would give worlds to be in the privacy of her own familiar chamber where, giving way to tears, she could have a good cry and relieve her pentup feelings. Though not too much because she knew how to cry nicely before the mirror. You are lovely, Gerty, it said. The paly light of evening falls upon a face infinitely sad and wistful. Gerty MacDowell yearns in vain. Yes, she had known from the first that her daydream of a marriage has been arranged and the weddingbells ringing for Mrs. Reggy Wylie T.C.D.[7] (because the one who married the elder brother would be Mrs. Wylie) and in the fashionable intelligence[8] Mrs. Gertrude Wylie was wearing a sumptuous confection of grey trimmed with expensive blue fox was not to be. He was too young to understand. He would not believe in love, a woman's birthright. The night of the party long ago in Stoers' (he was still in short trousers) when they were alone and he stole an arm round her waist she went white to the very lips. He called her little one in a strangely husky voice and snatched a half kiss (the first!) but it was only the end of her nose and then he hastened from the room with a remark about refreshments. Impetuous fellow! Strength of character had never been Reggy Wylie's strong point and he who would woo and

[1] *dolly dyes* Brand of dye.

[2] *Tuesday week* I.e., a week ago last Tuesday.

[3] *Clery's* Major Dublin department store.

[4] *ash, oak or elm* I.e., for the rest of time.

[5] *blued* Treated with bluing, a cleaning agent that helps keep colors bright.

[6] *brickbat* Piece of brick.

[7] *T.C.D.* Trinity College, Dublin.

[8] *fashionable intelligence* I.e., society columns.

win Gerty MacDowell must be a man among men. But waiting, always waiting to be asked and it was leap year[1] too and would soon be over. No prince charming is her beau ideal to lay a rare and wondrous love at her feet but rather a manly man with a strong quiet face who had not found his ideal, perhaps his hair slightly flecked with grey, and who would understand, take her in his sheltering arms, strain her to him in all the strength of his deep passionate nature and comfort her with a long long kiss. It would be like heaven. For such a one she yearns this balmy summer eve. With all the heart of her she longs to be his only, his affianced bride for riches for poor, in sickness in health, till death us two part, from this to this day forward.

And while Edy Boardman was with little Tommy behind the pushcar she was just thinking would the day ever come when she could call herself his little wife to be. Then they could talk about her till they went blue in the face, Bertha Supple too, and Edy, the spitfire, because she would be twenty-two in November. She would care for him with creature comforts too for Gerty was womanly wise and knew that a mere man liked that feeling of hominess. Her griddlecakes done to a golden-brown hue and queen Ann's pudding of delightful creaminess had won golden opinions from all because she had a lucky hand also for lighting a fire, dredge in the fine selfraising flour and always stir in the same direction then cream the milk and sugar and whisk well the white of eggs though she didn't like the eating part when there were any people that made her shy and often she wondered why you couldn't eat something poetical like violets or roses and they would have a beautifully appointed drawingroom with pictures and engravings and the photograph of grandpapa Giltrap's lovely dog Garryowen that almost talked, it was so human, and chintz covers for the chairs and that silver toastrack in Clery's summer jumble sales like they have in rich houses. He would be tall with broad shoulders (she had always admired tall men for a husband) with glistening white teeth under his carefully trimmed sweeping moustache and they would go on the continent[2] for their honeymoon (three wonderful weeks!) and then, when they settled down in a nice snug and cosy little homely house, every morning they would both have brekky,[3] simple but perfectly served, for their own two selves and before he went out to business he would give his dear little wifey a good hearty hug and gaze for a moment deep down into her eyes.

Edy Boardman asked Tommy Caffrey was he done and he said yes, so then she buttoned up his little knickerbockers for him and told him to run off and play with Jacky and to be good now and not to fight. But Tommy said he wanted the ball and Edy told him no that baby was playing with the ball and if he took it there'd be wigs on the green[4] but Tommy said it was his ball and he wanted his ball and he pranced on the ground, if you please. The temper of him! O, he was a man already was little Tommy Caffrey since he was out of pinnies.[5] Edy told him no, no and to be off now with him and she told Cissy Caffrey not to give in to him.

—You're not my sister, naughty Tommy said. It's my ball.

But Cissy Caffrey told baby Boardman to look up, look up high at her finger and she snatched the ball quickly and threw it along the sand and Tommy after it in full career, having won the day.

—Anything for a quiet life, laughed Ciss.

And she tickled tiny tot's two cheeks to make him forget and played here's the lord mayor, here's his two horses, here's his gingerbread carriage and here he walks in, chinchopper, chinchopper, chinchopper chin. But Edy got as cross as two sticks about him getting his own way like that from everyone always petting him.

—I'd like to give him something, she said, so I would, where I won't say.

—On the beeoteetom, laughed Cissy merrily.

Gerty MacDowell bent down her head and crimsoned at the idea of Cissy saying an unladylike thing like

---

[1] *leap year* The only time, according to traditional belief, when it was permissible for a woman to propose to a man.

[2] *continent* I.e., Europe.

[3] *brekky* Breakfast.

[4] *wigs on the green* I.e., a brawl (Irish slang).

[5] *pinnies* Pinafores (babies' clothing).

that out loud she'd be ashamed of her life to say, flushing a deep rosy red, and Edy Boardman said she was sure the gentleman opposite heard what she said. But not a pin cared Ciss.

—Let him! she said with a pert toss of her head and a piquant tilt of her nose. Give it to him too on the same place as quick as I'd look at him.

Madcap Ciss with her golliwog[1] curls. You had to laugh at her sometimes. For instance when she asked you would you have some more Chinese tea and jaspberry ram and when she drew the jugs too and the men's faces on her nails with red ink make you split your sides or when she wanted to go where you know she said she wanted to run and pay a visit to the Miss White. That was just like Cissycums. O, and will you ever forget the evening she dressed up in her father's suit and hat and the burned cork moustache and walked down Tritonville road, smoking a cigarette. There was none to come up to her for fun. But she was sincerity itself, one of the bravest and truest hearts heaven ever made, not one of your twofaced things, too sweet to be wholesome.

And then there came out upon the air the sound of voices and the pealing anthem of the organ. It was the men's temperance retreat conducted by the missioner, the reverend John Hughes S.J.[2] rosary, sermon and benediction of the Most Blessed Sacrament. They were there gathered together without distinction of social class (and a most edifying spectacle it was to see) in that simple fane[3] beside the waves, after the storms of this weary world, kneeling before the feet of the immaculate, reciting the litany of Our Lady of Loreto, beseeching her to intercede for them, the old familiar words, holy Mary, holy virgin of virgins. How sad to poor Gerty's ears! Had her father only avoided the clutches of the demon drink, by taking the pledge or those powders the drink habit cured in Pearson's Weekly, she might now be rolling in her carriage, second to none. Over and over had she told herself that as she mused by the dying embers in a brown study[4] without the lamp because she hated two lights or oftentimes gazing out of the window dreamily by the hour at the rain falling on the rusty bucket, thinking. But that vile decoction which has ruined so many hearths and homes had cast its shadow over her childhood days. Nay, she had even witnessed in the home circle deeds of violence caused by intemperance and had seen her own father, a prey to the fumes of intoxication, forget himself completely for if there was one thing of all things that Gerty knew it was the man who lifts his hand to a woman save in the way of kindness deserves to be branded as the lowest of the low.

And still the voices sang in supplication to the Virgin most powerful, Virgin most merciful. And Gerty, rapt in thought, scarce saw or heard her companions or the twins at their boyish gambols[5] or the gentleman off Sandymount green that Cissy Caffrey called the man that was so like himself passing along the strand taking a short walk. You never saw him anyway screwed[6] but still and for all that she would not like him for a father because he was too old or something or on account of his face (it was a palpable case of doctor Fell[7]) or his carbuncly nose with the pimples on it and his sandy moustache a bit white under his nose. Poor father! With all his faults she loved him still when he sang *Tell me, Mary, how to woo thee* or *My love and cottage near Rochelle* and they had stewed cockles and lettuce with Lazenby's salad dressing for supper and when he sang *The moon hath raised* with Mr. Dignam that died suddenly and was buried, God have mercy on him, from a stroke. Her mother's birthday that was and Charley was home on his holidays and Tom and Mr. Dignam and Mrs. and Patsy and Freddy Dignam and they were to have had a group[8] taken. No-one would have thought

[1] *golliwog* Black-faced male doll with frizzy hair.

[2] *S.J.* Society of Jesus (the Jesuits).

[3] *fane* Temple.

[4] *in a brown study* Expression meaning lost in thought.

[5] *gambols* Merrymaking.

[6] *screwed* Drunk.

[7] *doctor Fell* John Fell was Dean of Christ Church, Oxford. When he supposedly threatened satirist Thomas Brown with expulsion from the college, Brown is said to have responded poetically: "I do not love thee, Dr. Fell / The reason why I cannot tell; / But this alone I know full well, / I do not love thee, Dr. Fell."

[8] *group* I.e., group photo.

the end was so near. Now he was laid to rest. And her mother said to him to let that be a warning to him for the rest of his days and he couldn't even go to the funeral on account of the gout and she had to go into town to bring him the letters and samples from his office about Catesby's cork lino,[1] artistic standard designs, fit for a palace, gives tiptop wear and always bright and cheery in the home.

A sterling good daughter was Gerty just like a second mother in the house, a ministering angel too with a little heart worth its weight in gold. And when her mother had those raging splitting headaches who was it rubbed on the menthol cone[2] on her forehead but Gerty though she didn't like her mother taking pinches of snuff and that was the only single thing they ever had words about, taking snuff. Everyone thought the world of her for her gentle ways. It was Gerty who turned off the gas at the main every night and it was Gerty who tacked up on the wall of that place where she never forgot every fortnight the chlorate of lime[3] Mr. Tunney the grocer's christmas almanac the picture of halcyon days where a young gentleman in the costume they used to wear then with a threecornered hat was offering a bunch of flowers to his ladylove with oldtime chivalry through her lattice window. You could see there was a story behind it. The colours were done something lovely. She was in a soft clinging white in a studied attitude and the gentleman was in chocolate and he looked a thorough aristocrat. She often looked at them dreamily when she went there for a certain purpose and felt her own arms that were white and soft just like hers with the sleeves back and thought about those times because she had found out in Walker's pronouncing dictionary that belonged to grandpapa Giltrap about the halcyon days[4] what they meant.

The twins were now playing in the most approved brotherly fashion, till at last Master Jacky who was really as bold as brass there was no getting behind that deliberately kicked the ball as hard as ever he could down towards the seaweedy rocks. Needless to say poor Tommy was not slow to voice his dismay but luckily the gentleman in black who was sitting there by himself came gallantly to the rescue and intercepted the ball. Our two champions claimed their plaything with lusty cries and to avoid trouble Cissy Caffrey called to the gentleman to throw it to her please. The gentleman aimed the ball once or twice and then threw it up the strand towards Cissy Caffrey but it rolled down the slope and stopped right under Gerty's skirt near the little pool by the rock. The twins clamoured again for it and Cissy told her to kick it away and let them fight for it so Gerty drew back her foot but she wished their stupid ball hadn't come rolling down to her and she gave a kick but she missed and Edy and Cissy laughed.

—If you fail try again, Edy Boardman said.

Gerty smiled assent and bit her lip. A delicate pink crept into her pretty cheek but she was determined to let them see so she just lifted her skirt a little but just enough and took good aim and gave the ball a jolly good kick and it went ever so far and the two twins after it down towards the shingle.[5] Pure jealousy of course it was nothing else to draw attention on account of the gentleman opposite looking. She felt the warm flush, a danger signal always with Gerty MacDowell, surging and flaming into her cheeks. Till then they had only exchanged glances of the most casual but now under the brim of her new hat she ventured a look at him and the face that met her gaze there in the twilight, wan and strangely drawn, seemed to her the saddest she had ever seen.

Through the open window of the church the fragrant incense was wafted and with it the fragrant names of her who was conceived without stain of original sin, spiritual vessel, pray for us, honourable vessel, pray for us, vessel of singular devotion, pray for us, mystical rose. And careworn hearts were there and toilers for their daily bread and many who had erred and wandered, their eyes wet with contrition but for all that bright with hope for the reverend father Hughes had told them

[1] *lino* Linoleum.

[2] *menthol cone* Menthol, with its cooling effects, was a common home remedy for headaches.

[3] *chlorate of lime* Used to disinfect and deodorize outdoor toilets.

[4] *halcyon days* Calm, peaceful days.

[5] *shingle* Pebbly beach.

what the great saint Bernard said in his famous prayer of Mary,[1] the most pious Virgin's intercessory power that it was not recorded in any age that those who implored her powerful protection were ever abandoned by her.

The twins were now playing again right merrily for the troubles of childhood are but as fleeting summer showers. Cissy played with baby Boardman till he crowed with glee, clapping baby hands in air. Peep she cried behind the hood of the pushcar and Edy asked where was Cissy gone and then Cissy popped up her head and cried ah! and, my word, didn't the little chap enjoy that! And then she told him to say papa.

—Say papa, baby. Say pa pa pa pa pa pa pa.

And baby did his level best to say it for he was very intelligent for eleven months everyone said and big for his age and the picture of health, a perfect little bunch of love, and he would certainly turn out to be something great, they said.

—Haja ja ja haja.

Cissy wiped his little mouth with the dribbling bib and wanted him to sit up properly and say pa pa pa but when she undid the strap she cried out, holy saint Denis, that he was possing wet and to double the half blanket the other way under him. Of course his infant majesty was most obstreperous at such toilet formalities and he let everyone know it:

—Habaa baaaahabaaa baaaa.

And two great big lovely big tears coursing down his cheeks. It was all no use soothering him with no, nono, baby, no and telling him about the geegee and where was the puffpuff but Ciss, always, readywitted, gave him in his mouth the teat of the suckingbottle and the young heathen was quickly appeased.

Gerty wished to goodness they would take their squalling baby home out of that and not get on her nerves no hour to be out and the little brats of twins. She gazed out towards the distant sea. It was like the paintings that man used to do on the pavement with all the coloured chalks and such a pity too leaving them there to be all blotted out, the evening and the clouds coming out and the Bailey light on Howth[2] and to hear the music like that and the perfume of those incense they burned in the church like a kind of waft. And while she gazed her heart went pitapat. Yes, it was her he was looking at and there was meaning in his look. His eyes burned into her as though they would search her through and through, read her very soul. Wonderful eyes they were, superbly expressive, but could you trust them? People were so queer. She could see at once by his dark eyes and his pale intellectual face that he was a foreigner the image of the photo she had of Martin Harvey, the matinee idol, only for the moustache which she preferred because she wasn't stagestruck like Winny Rippingham that wanted they two to always dress the same on account of a play but she could not see whether he had an aquiline nose or a slightly *retroussé*[3] from where he was sitting. He was in deep mourning,[4] she could see that, and the story of a haunting sorrow was written on his face. She would have given worlds to know what it was. He was looking up so intently, so still and he saw her kick the ball and perhaps he could see the bright steel buckles of her shoes if she swung them like that thoughtfully with the toes down. She was glad that something told her to put on the transparent stockings thinking Reggy Wylie might be out but that was far away. Here was that of which she had so often dreamed. It was he who mattered and there was joy on her face because she wanted him because she felt instinctively that he was like no-one else. The very heart of the girlwoman went out to him, her dreamhusband, because she knew on the instant it was him. If he had suffered, more sinned against than sinning, or even, even, if he had been himself a sinner, a wicked man, she cared not. Even if he was a protestant or methodist she could convert him easily if he truly loved her. There were wounds that wanted healing with heartbalm. She was a womanly woman not like other flighty girls, unfeminine, he had known, those cyclists showing off what they hadn't got and she just yearned to know all, to

[1] *his famous … Mary* Reference to the "Memorare," a prayer frequently used by Saint Bernard of Clairvaux but not actually composed by him.

[2] *Bailey … Howth* Lighthouse on Howth Head.

[3] *retroussé* Turned up.

[4] *in deep mourning* I.e., dressed in black, out of respect for a recently deceased friend or family member.

forgive all if she could make him fall in love with her, make him forget the memory of the past. Then mayhap he would embrace her gently, like a real man, crushing her soft body to him, and love her, his ownest girlie, for herself alone.

Refuge of sinners. Comfortress of the afflicted. *Ora pro nobis*.[1] Well has it been said that whosoever prays to her with faith and constancy can never be lost or cast away: and fitly is she too a haven of refuge for the afflicted because of the seven dolours which transpierced her own heart. Gerty could picture the whole scene in the church, the stained glass windows lighted up, the candles, the flowers and the blue banners of the blessed Virgin's sodality[2] and Father Conroy was helping Canon O'Hanlon at the altar, carrying things in and out with his eyes cast down. He looked almost a saint and his confessionbox was so quiet and clean and dark and his hands were just like white wax and if ever she became a Dominican nun in their white habit perhaps he might come to the convent for the novena of Saint Dominic. He told her that time when she told him about that in confession crimsoning up to the roots of her hair for fear he could see, not to be troubled because that was only the voice of nature and we were all subject to nature's laws, he said, in this life and that that was no sin because that came from the nature of woman instituted by God, he said, and that Our Blessed Lady herself said to the archangel Gabriel be it done unto me according to Thy Word. He was so kind and holy and often and often she thought and thought could she work a ruched teacosy with embroidered floral design for him as a present or a clock but they had a clock she noticed on the mantelpiece white and gold with a canary bird that came out of a little house to tell the time the day she went there about the flowers for the forty hours' adoration[3] because it was hard to know what sort of a present to give or perhaps an album of illuminated views of Dublin or some place.

The exasperating little brats of twins began to quarrel again and Jacky threw the ball out towards the sea and they both ran after it. Little monkeys common as ditch-water. Someone ought to take them and give them a good hiding for themselves to keep them in their places, the both of them. And Cissy and Edy shouted after them to come back because they were afraid the tide might come in on them and be drowned.

—Jacky! Tommy!

Not they! What a great notion they had! So Cissy said it was the very last time she'd ever bring them out. She jumped up and called them and she ran down the slope past him, tossing her hair behind her which had a good enough colour if there had been more of it but with all the thingamerry she was always rubbing into it she couldn't get it to grow long because it wasn't natural so she could just go and throw her hat at it.[4] She ran with long gandery strides it was a wonder she didn't rip up her skirt at the side that was too tight on her because there was a lot of the tomboy about Cissy Caffrey and she was a forward piece[5] whenever she thought she had a good opportunity to show off and just because she was a good runner she ran like that so that he could see all the end of her petticoat running and her skinny shanks up as far as possible. It would have served her just right if she had tripped up over something accidentally on purpose with her high crooked French heels on her to make her look tall and got a fine tumble. *Tableau!*[6] That would have been a very charming exposé for a gentleman like that to witness.

Queen of angels, queen of patriarchs, queen of prophets, of all saints, they prayed, queen of the most holy rosary and then Father Conroy handed the thurible[7] to Canon O' Hanlon and he put in the incense and censed the Blessed Sacrament and Cissy Caffrey

---

[1] *Ora pro nobis* Latin: Pray for us.

[2] *sodality* Religious guild or society.

[3] *forty hours' adoration* Forty hours' prayer in memory of the time during which Jesus lay in his tomb before the Resurrection.

[4] *throw her … it* When a woman could not attract a man's attention any other way (i.e., by her appearance), it was said that she might as well "throw her hat at him."

[5] *piece* Slang: attractive woman.

[6] *Tableau* French: Picture. Name of a popular parlor game in which participants would strike poses to convey a particular scene, announcing "tableau!" to indicate their pose was ready to be interpreted.

[7] *thurible* Vessel for burning and disseminating incense.

caught the two twins and she was itching to give them a ringing good clip on the ear but she didn't because she thought he might be watching but she never made a bigger mistake in all her life because Gerty could see without looking that he never took his eyes off of her and then Canon O'Hanlon handed the thurible back to Father Conroy and knelt down looking up at the Blessed Sacrament and the choir began to sing *Tantum ergo*[1] and she just swung her foot in and out in time as the music rose and fell to the *Tantumer gosa cramen turn.* Three and eleven she paid for those stockings in Sparrow's of George's street on the Tuesday, no the Monday before Easter and there wasn't a brack[2] on them and that was what he was looking at, transparent, and not at her insignificant ones that had neither shape nor form (the cheek of her!) because he had eyes in his head to see the difference for himself.

Cissy came up along the strand with the two twins and their ball with her hat anyhow on her to one side after her run and she did look a streel[3] tugging the two kids along with the flimsy blouse she bought only a fortnight before like a rag on her back and a bit of her petticoat hanging like a caricature. Gerty just took off her hat for a moment to settle her hair and a prettier, a daintier head of nutbrown tresses was never seen on a girl's shoulders, a radiant little vision, in sooth, almost maddening in its sweetness. You would have to travel many a long mile before you found a head of hair the like of that. She could almost see the swift answering flush of admiration in his eyes that set her tingling in every nerve. She put on her hat so that she could see from underneath the brim and swung her buckled shoe faster for her breath caught as she caught the expression in his eyes. He was eyeing her as a snake eyes its prey. Her woman's instinct told her that she had raised the devil in him and at the thought a burning scarlet swept from throat to brow till the lovely colour of her face became a glorious rose.

Edy Boardman was noticing it too because she was squinting at Gerty, half smiling, with her specs, like an old maid, pretending to nurse the baby. Irritable little gnat she was and always would be and that was why noone could get on with her, poking her nose into what was no concern of hers. And she said to Gerty:

—A penny for your thoughts.

—What? replied Gerty with a smile reinforced by the whitest of teeth. I was only wondering was it late.

Because she wished to goodness they'd take the snottynosed twins and their baby home to the mischief out of that so that was why she just gave a gentle hint about its being late. And when Cissy came up Edy asked her the time and Miss Cissy, as glib as you like, said it was half past kissing time, time to kiss again. But Edy wanted to know because they were told to be in early.

—Wait, said Cissy, I'll ask my uncle Peter over there what's the time by his conundrum.

So over she went and when he saw her coming she could see him take his hand out of his pocket, getting nervous, and beginning to play with his watchchain, looking at the church. Passionate nature though he was Gerty could see that he had enormous control over himself. One moment he had been there, fascinated by a loveliness that made him gaze and the next moment it was the quiet gravefaced gentleman, selfcontrol expressed in every line of his distinguishedlooking figure.

Cissy said to excuse her would he mind telling her what was the right time and Gerty could see him taking out his watch, listening to it and looking up and clearing his throat and he said he was very sorry his watch was stopped but he thought it must be after eight because the sun was set. His voice had a cultured ring in it and though he spoke in measured accents there was a suspicion of a quiver in the mellow tones. Cissy said thanks and came back with her tongue out and said uncle said his waterworks were out of order.

Then they sang the second verse of the *Tantum ergo* and Canon O'Hanlon got up again and censed the Blessed Sacrament and knelt down and he told Father Conroy that one of the candles was just going to set fire to the flowers and Father Conroy got up and settled it all right and she could see the gentleman winding his

[1] *Tantum ergo* Hymn beginning *Tantum ergo Sacramentum* (Latin: So great a sacrament).

[2] *brack* Flaw.

[3] *streel* Disreputable woman.

watch and listening to the works and she swung her leg more in and out in time. It was getting darker but he could see and he was looking all the time that he was winding the watch or whatever he was doing to it and then he put it back and put his hands back into his pockets. She felt a kind of a sensation rushing all over her and she knew by the feel of her scalp and that irritation against her stays that that thing must be coming on because the last time too was when she clipped her hair on account of the moon. His dark eyes fixed themselves on her again drinking in her every contour, literally worshipping at her shrine. If ever there was undisguised admiration in a man's passionate gaze it was there plain to be seen on that man's face. It is for you, Gertrude MacDowell, and you know it.

Edy began to get ready to go and it was high time for her and Gerty noticed that that little hint she gave had the desired effect because it was a long way along the strand to where there was the place to push up the pushcar and Cissy took off the twins' caps and tidied their hair to make herself attractive of course and Canon O'Hanlon stood up with his cope[1] poking up at his neck and Father Conroy handed him the card to read off and he read out *Panem de coelo praestitisti eis*[2] and Edy and Cissy were talking about the time all the time and asking her but Gerty could pay them back in their own coin and she just answered with scathing politeness when Edy asked her was she heartbroken about her best boy throwing her over. Gerty winced sharply. A brief cold blaze shone from her eyes that spoke volumes of scorn immeasurable. It hurt. O yes, it cut deep because Edy had her own quiet way of saying things like that she knew would wound like the confounded little cat she was. Gerty's lips parted swiftly to frame the word but she fought back the sob that rose to her throat, so slim, so flawless, so beautifully moulded it seemed one an artist might have dreamed of. She had loved him better than he knew. Lighthearted deceiver and fickle like all his sex he would never understand what he had meant to her and for an instant there was in the blue eyes a quick stinging of tears. Their eyes were probing her mercilessly but with a brave effort she sparkled back in sympathy as she glanced at her new conquest for them to see.

—O, responded Gerty, quick as lightning, laughing, and the proud head flashed up. I can throw my cap at who I like because it's leap year.

Her words rang out crystalclear, more musical than the cooing of the ringdove but they cut the silence icily. There was that in her young voice that told that she was not a one to be lightly trifled with. As for Mr. Reggy with his swank and his bit of money she could just chuck him aside as if he was so much filth and never again would she cast as much as a second thought on him and tear his silly postcard into a dozen pieces. And if ever after he dared to presume she could give him one look of measured scorn that would make him shrivel up on the spot. Miss puny little Edy's countenance fell to no slight extent and Gerty could see by her looking as black as thunder that she was simply in a towering rage though she hid it, the little kinnatt,[3] because that shaft had struck home for her petty jealousy and they both knew that she was something aloof, apart in another sphere, that she was not of them and there was somebody else too that knew it and saw it so they could put that in their pipe and smoke it.

Edy straightened up baby Boardman to get ready to go and Cissy tucked in the ball and the spades and buckets and it was high time too because the sandman was on his way for Master Boardman junior and Cissy told him too that Billy Winks was coming and that baby was to go deedaw and baby looked just too ducky, laughing up out of his gleeful eyes, and Cissy poked him like that out of fun in his wee fat tummy and baby, without as much as by your leave, sent up his compliments on to his brand-new dribbling bib.

—O my! Puddeny pie! protested Ciss. He has his bib destroyed.

The slight *contretemps*[4] claimed her attention but in two twos she set that little matter to rights.

[1] *cope* Cloak-like ecclesiastical vestment.

[2] *Panem … eis* Latin: You have given them bread from Heaven.

[3] *kinnatt* Impudent puppy.

[4] *contretemps* Mishap.

Gerty stifled a smothered exclamation and gave a nervous cough and Edy asked what and she was just going to tell her to catch it while it was flying but she was ever ladylike in her deportment so she simply passed it off with consummate tact by saying that that was the benediction because just then the bell rang out from the steeple over the quiet seashore because Canon O'Hanlon was up on the altar with the veil that Father Conroy put round him round his shoulders giving the benediction with the Blessed Sacrament in his hands.

How moving the scene there in the gathering twilight, the last glimpse of Erin,[1] the touching chime of those evening bells and at the same time a bat flew forth from the ivied belfry through the dusk, hither, thither, with a tiny lost cry. And she could see far away the lights of the lighthouses so picturesque she would have loved to do with a box of paints because it was easier than to make a man and soon the lamplighter would be going his rounds past the presbyterian church grounds and along by shady Tritonville avenue where the couples walked and lighting the lamp near her window where Reggy Wylie used to turn his freewheel like she read in that book *The Lamplighter*[2] by Miss Cummins, author of *Mabel Vaughan* and other tales. For Gerty had her dreams that no-one knew of. She loved to read poetry and when she got a keepsake from Bertha Supple of that lovely confession album with the coralpink cover to write her thoughts in she laid it in the drawer of her toilettable which, though it did not err on the side of luxury, was scrupulously neat and clean. It was there she kept her girlish treasures trove, the tortoiseshell combs, her child of Mary badge, the whiterose scent, the eyebrowleine, her alabaster pouncetbox and the ribbons to change when her things came home from the wash and there were some beautiful thoughts written in it in violet ink that she bought in Hely's of Dame Street for she felt that she too could write poetry if she could only express herself like that poem that appealed to her so deeply that she had copied out of the newspaper she found one evening round the potherbs. *Art thou real, my ideal?* it was called by Louis J. Walsh, Magherafelt,[3] and after there was something about twilight, *wilt thou ever?* and ofttimes the beauty of poetry, so sad in its transient loveliness, had misted her eyes with silent tears that the years were slipping by for her, one by one, and but for that one shortcoming she knew she need fear no competition and that was an accident coming down Dalkey hill and she always tried to conceal it. But it must end, she felt. If she saw that magic lure in his eyes there would be no holding back for her. Love laughs at locksmiths.[4] She would make the great sacrifice. Her every effort would be to share his thoughts. Dearer than the whole world would she be to him and gild his days with happiness. There was the allimportant question and she was dying to know was he a married man or a widower who had lost his wife or some tragedy like the nobleman with the foreign name from the land of song had to have her put into a madhouse, cruel only to be kind. But even if—what then? Would it make a very great difference? From everything in the least indelicate her finebred nature instinctively recoiled. She loathed that sort of person, the fallen women off the accommodation walk beside the Dodder[5] that went with the soldiers and coarse men, with no respect for a girl's honour, degrading the sex and being taken up to the police station. No, no: not that. They would be just good friends like a big brother and sister without all that other in spite of the conventions of Society with a big ess. Perhaps it was an old flame he was in mourning for from the days beyond recall. She thought she understood. She would try to understand him because men were so different. The old love was waiting, waiting with little white hands stretched out, with blue appealing eyes. Heart of mine! She would follow her dream of love, the dictates of her heart that told her he was her all in all, the only man in all the world for her for love was the master guide. Nothing else mattered. Come what might she would be wild, untrammelled, free.

[1] *Erin* Ireland.

[2] *The Lamplighter* Title of 1854 novel by American novelist Maria Cummins. Gerty is also the name of Cummins's protagonist.

[3] *Louis J. Walsh* Orator and versifier (1880–1942); *Magherafelt* Parish in northeastern Ireland.

[4] *Love ... locksmiths* Title of an 1803 play by George Colman that then became a proverbial phrase.

[5] *Dodder* River in Ireland.

Canon O'Hanlon put the Blessed Sacrament back into the tabernacle[1] and the choir sang *Laudate Dominum omnes gentes*[2] and then he locked the tabernacle door because the benediction was over and Father Conroy handed him his hat to put on and crosscat Edy asked wasn't she coming but Jacky Caffrey called out:

—O, look, Cissy!

And they all looked was it sheet lightning but Tommy saw it too over the trees beside the church, blue and then green and purple.

—It's fireworks, Cissy Caffrey said.

And they all ran down the strand to see over the houses and the church, helterskelter, Edy with the pushcar with baby Boardman in it and Cissy holding Tommy and Jacky by the hand so they wouldn't fall running.

—Come on, Gerty, Cissy called. It's the bazaar fireworks.

But Gerty was adamant. She had no intention of being at their beck and call. If they could run like rossies[3] she could sit so she said she could see from where she was. The eyes that were fastened upon her set her pulses tingling. She looked at him a moment, meeting his glance, and a light broke in upon her. Whitehot passion was in that face, passion silent as the grave and it had made her his. At last they were left alone without the others to pry and pass remarks and she knew he could be trusted to the death, steadfast, a sterling man, a man of inflexible honour to his fingertips. His hands and face were working and a tremor went over her. She leaned back far to look up where the fireworks were and she caught her knee in her hands so as not to fall back looking up and there was no-one to see only him and her when she revealed all her graceful beautifully shaped legs like that, supply soft and delicately rounded, and she seemed to hear the panting of his heart, his hoarse breathing, because she knew about the passion of men like that, hotblooded, because Bertha Supple told her once in dead secret and made her swear she'd never about the gentleman lodger that was staying with them out of the Congested Districts Board[4] that had pictures cut out of papers of those skirtdancers and highkickers and she said he used to do something not very nice that you could imagine sometimes in the bed. But this was altogether different from a thing like that because there was all the difference because she could almost feel him draw her face to his and the first quick hot touch of his handsome lips. Besides there was absolution so long as you didn't do the other thing before being married and there ought to be women priests that would understand without your telling out and Cissy Caffrey too sometimes had that dreamy kind of dreamy look in her eyes so that she too, my dear, and Winny Rippingham so mad about actors' photographs and besides it was on account of that other thing coming on the way it did.

And Jacky Caffrey shouted to look, there was another and she leaned back and the garters were blue to match on account of the transparent and they all saw it and shouted to look, look there it was and she leaned back ever so far to see the fireworks and something queer was flying about through the air, a soft thing to and fro, dark. And she saw a long Roman candle going up over the trees up, up, and, in the tense hush, they were all breathless with excitement as it went higher and higher and she had to lean back more and more to look up after it, high, high, almost out of sight, and her face was suffused with a divine, an entrancing blush from straining back and he could see her other things too, nainsook knickers, the fabric that caresses the skin, better than those other pettiwidth,[5] the green, four and eleven, on account of being white and she let him and she saw that he saw and then it went so high it went out of sight a moment and she was trembling in every limb from being bent so far back that he had a full view high up above her knee where no-one ever not even on the swing or wading and she wasn't ashamed and he wasn't either to look in that immodest way like that because he couldn't resist the sight of the wondrous revealment half

[1] *tabernacle* Receptacle for the consecrated Host.

[2] *Laudate … gentes* Latin: Give praise to the Lord, O ye nations.

[3] *rossies* Unchaste women.

[4] *Congested Districts Board* Established in 1891 to deal with the perceived problems of overpopulation in poor rural areas.

[5] *pettiwidth* Name of a brand of underwear.

offered like those skirtdancers behaving so immodest before gentlemen looking and he kept on looking, looking. She would fain have cried to him chokingly, held out her snowy slender arms to him to come, to feel his lips laid on her white brow, the cry of a young girl's love, a little strangled cry, wrung from her, that cry that has rung through the ages. And then a rocket sprang and bang shot blind blank and O! then the Roman candle burst and it was like a sigh of O! and everyone cried O! O! in raptures and it gushed out of it a stream of rain gold hair threads and they shed and ah! they were all greeny dewy stars falling with golden, O so lovely! O so soft, sweet, soft!

Then all melted away dewily in the grey air: all was silent. Ah! She glanced at him as she bent forward quickly, a pathetic little glance of piteous protest, of shy reproach under which he coloured like a girl. He was leaning back against the rock behind. Leopold Bloom (for it is he) stands silent, with bowed head before those young guileless eyes. What a brute he had been! At it again? A fair unsullied soul had called to him and, wretch that he was, how had he answered? An utter cad he had been. He of all men! But there was an infinite store of mercy in those eyes, for him too a word of pardon even though he had erred and sinned and wandered. Should a girl tell? No, a thousand times no. That was their secret, only theirs, alone in the hiding twilight and there was none to know or tell save the little bat that flew so softly through the evening to and fro and little bats don't tell.

Cissy Caffrey whistled, imitating the boys in the football field to show what a great person she was: and then she cried:

—Gerty! Gerty! We're going. Come on. We can see from farther up.

Gerty had an idea, one of love's little ruses. She slipped a hand into her kerchief pocket and took out the wadding and waved in reply of course without letting him and then slipped it back. Wonder if he's too far to. She rose. Was it goodbye? No. She had to go but they would meet again, there, and she would dream of that till then, tomorrow, of her dream of yester eve. She drew herself up to her full height. Their souls met in a last lingering glance and the eyes that reached her heart, full of a strange shining, hung enraptured on her sweet flowerlike face. She half smiled at him wanly, a sweet forgiving smile, a smile that verged on tears, and then they parted.

Slowly without looking back she went down the uneven strand to Cissy, to Edy, to Jacky and Tommy Caffrey, to little baby Boardman. It was darker now and there were stones and bits of wood on the strand and slippy seaweed. She walked with a certain quiet dignity characteristic of her but with care and very slowly because, because Gerty MacDowell was …

Tight boots? No. She's lame! O!

Mr. Bloom watched her as she limped away. Poor girl! That's why she's left on the shelf and the others did a sprint. Thought something was wrong by the cut of her jib.[1] Jilted beauty. A defect is ten times worse in a woman. But makes them polite. Glad I didn't know it when she was on show. Hot little devil all the same. Wouldn't mind. Curiosity like a nun or a negress or a girl with glasses. That squinty one is delicate. Near her monthlies, I expect, makes them feel ticklish. I have such a bad headache today.[2] Where did I put the letter? Yes, all right. All kinds of crazy longings. Licking pennies. Girl in Tranquilla convent that nun told me liked to smell rock oil. Virgins go mad in the end I suppose. Sister? How many women in Dublin have it today? Martha, she. Something in the air. That's the moon. But then why don't all women menstruate at the same time with same moon, I mean? Depends on the time they were born, I suppose. Or all start scratch then get out of step. Sometimes Molly and Milly[3] together. Anyhow I got the best of that. Damned glad I didn't do it in the bath this morning over her silly I will punish you letter. Made up for that tramdriver this morning. That gouger M'Coy stopping me to say nothing. And

[1] *cut of her jib* Originally a nautical term, referring to the configuration of a boat's sails. It was also commonly used to refer to a person's look or style.

[2] *I have … today* This sentence is from a letter Bloom received from his secret correspondent, Martha Clifford, earlier that morning.

[3] *Molly and Milly* Bloom's wife (Molly is short for Marion) and daughter.

his wife engagement in the country valise, voice like a pickaxe. Thankful for small mercies. Cheap too. Yours for the asking. Because they want it themselves. Their natural craving. Shoals of them every evening poured out of offices. Reserve better. Don't want it they throw it at you. Catch em alive, O. Pity they can't see themselves. A dream of wellfilled hose. Where was that? Ah, yes. Mutoscope[1] pictures in Capel street: for men only. Peeping Tom. Willy's hat and what the girls did with it. Do they snapshot those girls or is it all a fake. *Lingerie* does it. Felt for the curves inside her *deshabillé*.[2] Excites them also when they're. I'm all clean come and dirty me. And they like dressing one another for the sacrifice. Milly delighted with Molly's new blouse. At first. Put them all on to take them all off. Molly. Why I bought her the violet garters. Us too: the tie he[3] wore, his lovely socks and turnedup trousers. He wore a pair of gaiters the night that first we met. His lovely shirt was shining beneath his what? of jet. Say a woman loses a charm with every pin she takes out. Pinned together. O Mairy lost the pin of her. Dressed up to the nines for somebody. Fashion part of their charm. Just changes when you're on the track of the secret. Except the east: Mary, Martha:[4] now as then. No reasonable offer refused. She wasn't in a hurry either. Always off to a fellow when they are. They never forget an appointment. Out on spec probably. They believe in chance because like themselves. And the others inclined to give her an odd dig. Girl friends at school, arms round each other's necks or with ten fingers locked, kissing and whispering secrets about nothing in the convent garden. Nuns with whitewashed faces, cool coif and their rosaries going up and down, vindictive too for what they can't get. Barbed wire.[5] Be sure now and write to me. And I'll write to you. Now won't you? Molly and Josie Powell. Till Mr. Right comes along, then meet once in a blue moon. *Tableau!* O, look who it is for the love of God! How are you at all? What have you been doing with yourself? Kiss and delighted to, kiss, to see you. Picking holes in each other's appearance. You're looking splendid. Sister souls showing their teeth at one another. How many have you left? Wouldn't lend each other a pinch of salt.

Ah!

Devils they are when that's coming on them. Dark devilish appearance. Molly often told me feel things a ton weight. Scratch the sole of my foot. O that way! O, that's exquisite! Feel it myself too. Good to rest once in a way. Wonder if it's bad to go with them then. Safe in one way. Turns milk, makes fiddlestrings snap. Something about withering plants I read in a garden. Besides they say if the flower withers she wears she's a flirt. All are. Daresay she felt I. When you feel like that you often meet what you feel. Liked me or what? Dress they look at. Always know a fellow courting: collars and cuffs. Well cocks and lions do the same and stags. Same time might prefer a tie undone or something. Trousers? Suppose I when I was? No. Gently does it. Dislike rough and tumble. Kiss in the dark and never tell. Saw something in me. Wonder what. Sooner have me as I am than some poet chap with bearsgrease plastery hair, lovelock over his dexter optic.[6] To aid gentleman in literary. Ought to attend to my appearance my age. Didn't let her see me in profile. Still, you never know. Pretty girls and ugly men marrying. Beauty and the beast. Besides I can't be so if Molly. Took off her hat to show her hair. Wide brim bought to hide her face, meeting someone might know her, bend down or carry a bunch of flowers to smell. Hair strong in rut.[7] Ten bob I got for Molly's combings when we were on the rocks in Holies street. Why not? Suppose he gave her

[1] *Mutoscope* Device for viewing, in quick succession, a series of pictures of objects in motion.

[2] *deshabillé* Revealing undergarment. Here Bloom is remembering phrases from the pornographic book, *Sweets of Sin*, that he bought earlier that day.

[3] *he* Dublin singer Hugh "Blazes" Boylan, with whom Molly Bloom is having an affair.

[4] *Mary, Martha* Biblical sisters of Lazarus. See Luke 10.38–42.

[5] *Barbed wire* Reference to the fictitious belief that barbed wire was invented by nuns.

[6] *lovelock* Curl of particular shape or style; *dexter optic* Latin: right eye.

[7] *Hair … rut* During mating season, the odor of an animal's skin changes. Here Bloom imagines similar changes occurring in women.

money. Why not? All a prejudice. She's worth ten, fifteen, more a pound. What? I think so. All that for nothing. Bold hand. Mrs. Marion.[1] Did I forget to write address on that letter like the postcard I sent to Flynn. And the day I went to Drimmie's[2] without a necktie. Wrangle with Molly it was put me off. No, I remember. Richie Goulding. He's another. Weighs on his mind. Funny my watch stopped at half past four. Dust. Shark liver oil[3] they use to clean could do it myself. Save. Was that just when he, she?

O, he did. Into her. She did. Done.

Ah!

Mr. Bloom with careful hand recomposed his wet shirt. O Lord, that little limping devil. Begins to feel cold and clammy. After effect not pleasant. Still you have to get rid of it someway. They don't care. Complimented perhaps. Go home to nicey bread and milky and say night prayers with the kiddies. Well, aren't they. See her as she is spoil all. Must have the stage setting, the rouge, costume, position, music. The name too. *Amours*[4] of actresses. Nell Gwynn, Mrs. Bracegirdle, Maud Branscombe.[5] Curtain up. Moonlight silver effulgence. Maiden discovered with pensive bosom. Little sweetheart come and kiss me. Still I feel. The strength it gives a man. That's the secret of it. Good job I let off there behind coming out of Dignam's. Cider that was. Otherwise I couldn't have. Makes you want to sing after. *Lacaus esant taratara.*[6] Suppose I spoke to her. What about? Bad plan however if you don't know how to end the conversation. Ask them a question they ask you another. Good idea if you're in a cart. Wonderful of course if you say: good evening, and you see she's on for it: good evening. O but the dark evening in the Appian way[7] I nearly spoke to Mrs. Clinch O thinking she was. Whew! Girl in Meath street that night. All the dirty things I made her say all wrong of course. My arks she called it. It's so hard to find one who. Aho! If you don't answer when they solicit must be horrible for them till they harden. And kissed my hand when I gave her the extra two shillings. Parrots. Press the button and the bird will squeak. Wish she hadn't called me sir. O, her mouth in the dark! And you a married man with a single girl! That's what they enjoy. Taking a man from another woman. Or even hear of it. Different with me. Glad to get away from other chap's wife. Eating off his cold plate. Chap in the Burton today spitting back gum-chewed gristle. French letter[8] still in my pocketbook. Cause of half the trouble. But might happen sometime, I don't think. Come in. All is prepared. I dreamt. What? Worst is beginning. How they change the venue when it's not what they like. Ask you do you like mushrooms because she once knew a gentleman who. Or ask you what someone was going to say when he changed his mind and stopped. Yet if I went the whole hog, say: I want to, something like that. Because I did. She too. Offend her. Then make it up. Pretend to want something awfully, then cry off for her sake. Flatters them. She must have been thinking of someone else all the time. What harm? Must since she came to the use of reason, he, he and he. First kiss does the trick. The propitious moment. Something inside them goes pop. Mushy like, tell by their eye, on the sly. First thoughts are best. Remember that till their dying day. Molly, lieutenant Mulvey that kissed her under the Moorish wall[9] beside the gardens. Fifteen she told me. But her breasts were developed. Fell asleep then. After Glencree dinner that was when we drove home the featherbed mountain. Gnashing her teeth in sleep. Lord mayor had his eye on her too. Val Dillon. Apoplectic.

There she is with them down there for the fireworks. My fireworks. Up like a rocket, down like a stick. And

[1] *Mrs. Marion* Reference to the letter Blazes Boylan wrote to Marion Bloom.

[2] *Drimmie's* David Drimmie and Sons, the law office where Bloom used to work.

[3] *Shark liver oil* Used to lubricate machinery.

[4] *Amours* Love affairs.

[5] *Nell … Branscombe* Famous English actresses of the seventeenth, eighteenth, and nineteenth centuries, respectively.

[6] *Lacaus esant taratara* Bloom's rendition of a quote from Giacomo Meyerbeer's opera *Les Huguenots* (1836): *La causa è santa* (Italian: The cause is sacred).

[7] *Appian way* Street on the southern edge of Dublin.

[8] *French letter* Slang: Condom.

[9] *Moorish wall* In Gibraltar, where Molly was raised.

the children, twins they must be, waiting for something to happen. Want to be grownups. Dressing in mother's clothes. Time enough, understand all the ways of the world. And the dark one with the mop head and the nigger mouth. I knew she could whistle. Mouth made for that. Like Molly. Why that high class whore in Jammet's wore her veil only to her nose. Would you mind, please, telling me the right time? I'll tell you the right time up a dark lane. Say prunes and prisms forty times every morning, cure for fat lips.[1] Caressing the little boy too. Onlookers see most of the game. Of course they understand birds, animals, babies. In their line.

Didn't look back when she was going down the strand. Wouldn't give that satisfaction. Those girls, those girls, those lovely seaside girls. Fine eyes she had, clear. It's the white of the eye brings that out not so much the pupil. Did she know what I? Course. Like a cat sitting beyond a dog's jump. Women never meet one like that Wilkins in the high school drawing a picture of Venus with all his belongings on show. Call that innocence? Poor idiot! His wife has her work cut out for her. Never see them sit on a bench marked *Wet Paint*. Eyes all over them. Look under the bed for what's not there. Longing to get the fright of their lives. Sharp as needles they are. When I said to Molly the man at the corner of Cuffe street was goodlooking, thought she might like, twigged at once he had a false arm. Had too. Where do they get that? Typist going up Roger Greene's stairs two at a time to show her understandings. Handed down from father to mother to daughter, I mean. Bred in the bone. Milly for example drying her handkerchief on the mirror to save the ironing. Best place for an ad to catch a woman's eye on a mirror.[2] And when I sent her for Molly's Paisley shawl to Presscott's, by the way that ad I must, carrying home the change in her stocking. Clever little minx! I never told her. Neat way she carries parcels too. Attract men, small thing like that. Holding up her hand, shaking it, to let the blood flow back when it was red. Who did you learn that from? Nobody. Something the nurse taught me. O, don't they know? Three years old she was in front of Molly's dressingtable just before we left Lombard street west. Me have a nice pace. Mullingar. Who knows? Ways of the world. Young student. Straight on her pins anyway not like the other. Still she was game. Lord, I am wet. Devil you are. Swell of her calf. Transparent stockings, stretched to breaking point. Not like that frump today. A.E.[3] Rumpled stockings. Or the one in Grafton street. White. Wow! Beef to the heel.[4]

A monkey puzzle rocket burst, spluttering in darting crackles. Zrads and zrads, zrads, zrads. And Cissy and Tommy ran out to see and Edy after with the pushcar and then Gerty beyond the curve of the rocks. Will she? Watch! Watch! See! Looked round. She smelt an onion.[5] Darling, I saw your. I saw all.

Lord!

Did me good all the same. Off colour after Kiernan's, Dignam's. For this relief much thanks. In *Hamlet*,[6] that is. Lord! It was all things combined. Excitement. When she leaned back felt an ache at the butt of my tongue. Your head it simply swirls. He's right. Might have made a worse fool of myself however. Instead of talking about nothing. Then I will tell you all. Still it was a kind of language between us. It couldn't be? No, Gerty they called her. Might be false name however like my and the address Dolphin's barn a blind.

Her maiden name was Jemima Brown
And she lived with her mother in Irishtown.[7]

---

[1] *Say prunes ... lips* See Dickens's *Little Dorrit* (1857): "Papa, potatoes, poultry, prunes, and prism are all very good words for the lips: especially prunes and prism."

[2] *Best place ... mirror* Bloom is in the advertising industry; he sells ad space in newspapers.

[3] *A.E.* Pen name of Irish writer and artist George Russell (1865–1935).

[4] *Beef to the heel* Said of women whose legs are very thick, right down to their feet.

[5] *smelt an onion* Reference to a popular joke in which a man eats a raw onion whenever he will be around a woman so that she will not tempt him to become entangled in an affair. His plan is foiled when he meets a woman who finds the onion smell attractive.

[6] *In Hamlet* See *Hamlet* 1.1.8, in which one of the guards thanks another for relieving him.

[7] *Her maiden ... Irishtown* From an Irish street ballad.

Place made me think of that I suppose. All tarred with the same brush. Wiping pens in their stockings. But the ball rolled down to her as if it understood. Every bullet has its billet.[1] Course I never could throw anything straight at school. Crooked as a ram's horn. Sad however because it lasts only a few years till they settle down to pot-walloping and papa's pants will soon fit Willy and fullers' earth[2] for the baby when they hold him out to do ah ah. No soft job. Saves them. Keeps them out of harm's way. Nature. Washing child, washing corpse.[3] Dignam. Children's hands always round them. Cocoanut skulls, monkeys, not even closed at first, sour milk in their swaddles and tainted curds. Oughtn't to have given that child an empty teat to suck. Fill it up with wind. Mrs. Beaufoy, Purefoy. Must call to the hospital.[4] Wonder is nurse Callan there still. She used to look over some nights when Molly was in the Coffee Palace. That young doctor O'Hare I noticed her brushing his coat. And Mrs. Breen and Mrs. Dignam once like that too, marriageable. Worst of all at night Mrs. Duggan told me in the City Arms. Husband rolling in drunk, stink of pub off him like a polecat. Have that in your nose in the dark, whiff of stale boose. Then ask in the morning: was I drunk last night? Bad policy however to fault the husband. Chickens come home to roost. They stick by one another like glue. Maybe the women's fault also. That's where Molly can knock spots off them.[5] It is the blood of the south. Moorish. Also the form, the figure. Hands felt for the opulent. Just compare for instance those others. Wife locked up at home, skeleton in the cupboard. Allow me to introduce my. Then they trot you out some kind of a nondescript, wouldn't know what to call her. Always see a fellow's weak point in his wife. Still there's destiny in it, falling in love. Have their own secrets between them. Chaps that would go to the dogs if some woman didn't take them in hand. Then little chits of girls, height of a shilling in coppers,[6] with little hubbies. As God made them He matched them. Sometimes children turn out well enough. Twice nought makes one. Or old rich chap of seventy and blushing bride. Marry in May and repent in December. This wet is very unpleasant. Stuck. Well the foreskin is not back. Better detach.

Ow!

Other hand a sixfooter with a wifey up to his watch-pocket. Long and the short of it. Big he and little she. Very strange about my watch. Wristwatches are always going wrong. Wonder is there any magnetic influence between the person because that was about the time he. Yes, I suppose at once. Cat's away the mice will play. I remember looking in Pill lane. Also that now is magnetism. Back of everything magnetism. Earth for instance pulling this and being pulled. That causes movement. And time? Well that's the time the movement takes. Then if one thing stopped the whole ghesabo[7] would stop bit by bit. Because it's all arranged. Magnetic needle tells you what's going on in the sun, the stars. Little piece of steel iron. When you hold out the fork. Come. Come. Tip. Woman and man that is. Fork and steel. Molly, he. Dress up and look and suggest and let you see and see more and defy you if you're a man to see that and, like a sneeze coming, legs, look, look and if you have any guts in you. Tip. Have to let fly.

Wonder how is she feeling in that region. Shame all put on before third person. More put out about a hole in her stocking. Molly, her underjaw stuck out, head back, about the farmer in the ridingboots and spurs at the horse show. And when the painters were in Lombard street west. Fine voice that fellow had. How Giuglini[8] began. Smell that I did, like flowers. It was too. Violets. Came from the turpentine probably in the paint. Make their own use of everything. Same time doing it scraped her slipper on the floor so they wouldn't hear. But lots of them can't kick the beam,[9] I think.

---

[1] *Every bullet … billet* Expression meaning everything has its place.

[2] *fullers' earth* Used for cleaning grease from clothing.

[3] *washing corpse* It was traditionally the women's job to prepare a body for burial.

[4] *Must call … hospital* The Blooms's family friend, Mina Purefoy, is in labor.

[5] *knock spots off them* Beat them; be much better than they are.

[6] *shilling … coppers* Equal to twelve pennies ("coppers").

[7] *whole ghesabo* I.e., whole show.

[8] *Giuglini* Italian tenor Antonio Giuglini (1827–65).

[9] *kick the beam* Experience orgasm.

Keep that thing up for hours. Kind of a general all round over me and half down my back.

Wait. Hm. Hm. Yes. That's her perfume. Why she waved her hand. I leave you this to think of me when I'm far away on the pillow. What is it? Heliotrope? No, Hyacinth? Hm. Roses, I think. She'd like scent of that kind. Sweet and cheap: soon sour. Why Molly likes opoponax. Suits her with a little jessamine mixed. Her high notes and her low notes. At the dance night she met him, dance of the hours.[1] Heat brought it out. She was wearing her black and it had the perfume of the time before. Good conductor, is it? Or bad? Light too. Suppose there's some connection. For instance if you go into a cellar where it's dark. Mysterious thing too. Why did I smell it only now? Took its time in coming like herself, slow but sure. Suppose it's ever so many millions of tiny grains blown across. Yes, it is. Because those spice islands, Cinghalese this morning, smell them leagues off. Tell you what it is. It's like a fine fine veil or web they have all over the skin, fine like what do you call it gossamer and they're always spinning it out of them, fine as anything, rainbow colours without knowing it. Clings to everything she takes off. Vamp of her stockings. Warm shoe. Stays. Drawers: little kick, taking them off. Byby till next time. Also the cat likes to sniff in her shift on the bed. Know her smell in a thousand. Bathwater too. Reminds me of strawberries and cream. Wonder where it is really. There or the armpits or under the neck. Because you get it out of all holes and corners. Hyacinth perfume made of oil or ether or something. Muskrat. Bag under their tails one grain pour off odour for years. Dogs at each other behind. Good evening. Evening, How do you sniff? Hm. Hm. Very well, thank you. Animals go by that. Yes now, look at it that way. We're the same. Some women for instance warn you off when they have their period. Come near. Then get a hogo[2] you could hang your hat on. Like what? Potted herrings gone stale or. Boof! Please keep off the grass.

Perhaps they get a man smell off us. What though? Cigary gloves Long John had on his desk the other. Breath? What you eat and drink gives that. No. Mansmell, I mean. Must be connected with that because priests, that are supposed to be are different. Women buzz round it like flies round treacle. Railed off the altar get on to it at any cost. The tree of forbidden priest. O father, will you? Let me be the first to. That diffuses itself all through the body, permeates. Source of life and it's extremely curious the smell. Celery sauce. Let me.

Mr. Bloom inserted his nose. Hm. Into the. Hm. Opening of his waistcoat. Almonds or. No. Lemons it is. Ah no, that's the soap.[3]

O by the by that lotion. I knew there was something on my mind. Never went back and the soap not paid. Dislike carrying bottles like that hag this morning. Hynes might have paid me that three shillings. I could mention Meagher's[4] just to remind him. Still if he works that paragraph. Two and nine. Bad opinion of me he'll have. Call tomorrow. How much do I owe you? Three and nine? Two and nine, sir. Ah. Might stop him giving credit another time. Lose your customers that way. Pubs do. Fellows run up a bill on the slate and then slinking around the back streets into somewhere else.

Here's this nobleman passed before. Blown in from the bay. Just went as far as turn back. Always at home at dinnertime. Looks mangled out: had a good tuck in.[5] Enjoying nature now. Grace after meals. After supper walk a mile. Sure he has a small bank balance somewhere, government sit.[6] Walk after him now make him awkward like those newsboys me today. Still you learn something. See ourselves as others see us. So long as women don't mock what matter? That's the way to find out. Ask yourself who is he now. *The Mystery Man on the Beach,* prize titbit story by Mr. Leopold Bloom. Payment at the rate of one guinea per column. And that fellow today at the graveside in the brown macintosh. Corns on his kismet[7] however. Healthy perhaps absorb

---

[1] *dance of the hours* Ballet from Amilcare Ponchielli's *La Gioconda.*

[2] *hogo* Scent.

[3] *the soap* Bloom bought lemon soap earlier, and is carrying it in his pocket. He has also ordered the hand lotion that he mentions in the following paragraph.

[4] *Meagher's* A pub.

[5] *tuck in* Meal.

[6] *sit* Position.

[7] *Corns on his kismet* I.e., he is having bad luck.

all the. Whistle brings rain they say. Must be some somewhere. Salt in the Ormond damp. The body feels the atmosphere. Old Betty's joints are on the rack. Mother Shipton's prophecy that is about ships around they fly in the twinkling.[1] No. Signs of rain it is. The royal reader.[2] And distant hills seem coming nigh.

Howth. Bailey light. Two, four, six, eight, nine. See. Has to change or they might think it a house. Wreckers. Grace darling.[3] People afraid of the dark. Also glowworms, cyclists: lightingup time. Jewels diamonds flash better. Light is a kind of reassuring. Not going to hurt you. Better now of course than long ago. Country roads. Run you through the small guts for nothing. Still two types there are you bob against. Scowl or smile. Pardon! Not at all. Best time to spray plants too in the shade after the sun. Some light still. Red rays are longest. Roygbiv Vance taught us: red, orange, yellow, green, blue, indigo, violet. A star I see. Venus? Can't tell yet. Two, when three it's night. Were those nightclouds there all the time? Looks like a phantom ship. No. Wait. Trees are they? An optical illusion. Mirage. Land of the setting sun this. Homerule sun setting in the southeast. My native land, goodnight.

Dew falling. Bad for you, dear, to sit on that stone. Brings on white fluxions. Never have little baby then less he was big strong fight his way up through. Might get piles myself. Sticks too like a summer cold, sore on the mouth. Cut with grass or paper worst. Friction of the position. Like to be that rock she sat on. O sweet little, you don't know how nice you looked. I begin to like them at that age. Green apples. Grab at all that offer. Suppose it's the only time we cross legs, seated. Also the library today: those girl graduates. Happy chairs under them. But it's the evening influence. They feel all that. Open like flowers, know their hours, sunflowers, Jerusalem artichokes, in ballrooms, chandeliers, avenues under the lamps. Nightstock in Mat Dillon's garden where I kissed her shoulder. Wish I had a full length oilpainting of her then. June that was too I wooed. The year returns. History repeats itself. Ye crags and peaks I'm with you once again. Life, love, voyage round your own little world. And now? Sad about her lame of course but must be on your guard not to feel too much pity. They take advantage.

All quiet on Howth now. The distant hills seem. Where we.[4] The rhododendrons. I am a fool perhaps. He gets the plums and I the plumstones. Where I come in. All that old hill has seen. Names change: that's all. Lovers: yum yum.

Tired I feel now. Will I get up? O wait. Drained all the manhood out of me, little wretch. She kissed me. My youth. Never again. Only once it comes. Or hers. Take the train there tomorrow. No. Returning not the same. Like kids your second visit to a house. The new I want. Nothing new under the sun. Care of P.O. Dolphin's barn. Are you not happy in your? Naughty darling. At Dolphin's barn charades in Luke Doyle's house. Mat Dillon and his bevy of daughters: Tiny, Atty, Floey, Maimy, Louy, Hetty. Molly too. Eightyseven that was. Year before we. And the old major partial to his drop of spirits. Curious she an only child, I an only child. So it returns. Think you're escaping and run into yourself. Longest way round is the shortest way home. And just when he and she. Circus horse walking in a ring. Rip van Winkle we played. Rip: tear in Henny Doyle's overcoat. Van: breadvan delivering. Winkle: cockles and periwinkles. Then I did Rip van Winkle coming back. She leaned on the sideboard watching. Moorish eyes. Twenty years asleep in Sleepy Hollow. All changed. Forgotten. The young are old. His gun rusty from the dew.

Ba. What is that flying about? Swallow? Bat probably. Thinks I'm a tree, so blind. Have birds no smell?

---

[1] *Mother Shipton's … twinkling* Mother Shipton was a famous prophetess of Tudor England. Here Bloom confuses two quotations from Charles Hindley's 1862 fictional work *The Wonderful History and Surprising Prophecies of Mother Shipton*. The first is a prediction of the telegraph ("Around the world thoughts shall fly / In the twinkling of an eye"), and the second is a prediction of steam locomotion ("Water shall yet more wonders do, / Now strange, yet shall be true").

[2] *royal reader* School textbook.

[3] *Grace darling* Grace Darling and her father, William, were lighthouse keepers who became national heroes after they braved dangerous waters to rescue the victims of a shipwreck in 1838.

[4] *Where we* Where Leopold courted Molly.

Metempsychosis.[1] They believed you could be changed into a tree from grief. Weeping willow. Ba. There he goes. Funny little beggar. Wonder where he lives. Belfry up there. Very likely. Hanging by his heels in the odour of sanctity. Bell scared him out, I suppose. Mass seems to be over. Could hear them all at it. Pray for us. And pray for us. And pray for us. Good idea the repetition. Same thing with ads. Buy from us. And buy from us. Yes, there's the light in the priest's house. Their frugal meal. Remember about the mistake in the valuation when I was in Thom's. Twentyeight it is.[2] Two houses they have. Gabriel Conroy's brother is curate. Ba. Again. Wonder why they come out at night like mice. They're a mixed breed. Birds are like hopping mice. What frightens them, light or noise? Better sit still. All instinct like the bird in drouth got water out of the end of a jar by throwing in pebbles.[3] Like a little man in a cloak he is with tiny hands. Weeny bones. Almost see them shimmering, kind of a bluey white. Colours depend on the light you see. Stare the sun for example like the eagle[4] then look at a shoe see a blotch blob yellowish. Wants to stamp his trademark on everything. Instance, that cat this morning on the staircase. Colour of brown turf. Say you never see them with three colours. Not true. That half tabbywhite tortoiseshell in the *City Arms* with the letter em on her forehead. Body fifty different colours. Howth a while ago amethyst. Glass flashing. That's how that wise man what's his name with the burning glass.[5] Then the heather goes on fire. It can't be tourists' matches. What? Perhaps the sticks dry rub together in the wind and light. Or broken bottles in the furze act as a burning glass in the sun. Archimedes. I have it! My memory's not so bad.

Ba. Who knows what they're always flying for. Insects? That bee last week got into the room playing with his shadow on the ceiling. Might be the one bit me, come back to see. Birds too never find out what they say. Like our small talk. And says she and says he. Nerve they have to fly over the ocean and back. Lots must be killed in storms, telegraph wires. Dreadful life sailors have too. Big brutes of oceangoing steamers floundering along in the dark, lowing out like seacows. *Faugh a ballagh.*[6] Out of that, bloody curse to you. Others in vessels, bit of a handkerchief sail, pitched about like snuff at a wake when the stormy winds do blow. Married too. Sometimes away for years at the ends of the earth somewhere. No ends really because it's round. Wife in every port they say. She has a good job if she minds it till Johnny comes marching home again. If ever he does. Smelling the tail end of ports. How can they like the sea? Yet they do. The anchor's weighed. Off he sails with a scapular or a medal on him for luck. Well? And the tephilim[7] no what's this they call it poor papa's father had on his door to touch. That brought us out of the land of Egypt and into the house of bondage. Something in all those superstitions because when you go out never know what dangers. Hanging on to a plank or astride of a beam for grim life, lifebelt round him, gulping salt water, and that's the last of his nibs till the sharks catch hold of him. Do fish ever get seasick?

Then you have a beautiful calm without a cloud, smooth sea, placid, crew and cargo in smithereens, Davy Jones' locker.[8] Moon looking down. Not my fault, old cockalorum.[9]

A lost long candle wandered up the sky from Mirus bazaar in search of funds for Mercer's hospital and broke, drooping, and shed a cluster of violet but one white stars. They floated, fell: they faded. The shepherd's hour: the hour of folding: hour of tryst. From

[1] *Metempsychosis* Belief that after death the soul moves into another body.

[2] *Remember about … it is* Bloom seems to be referring to a mistake that was made while he was working for Thom's, in which the priest's house was evaluated at 28 pounds.

[3] *like the … pebbles* One of Aesop's Fables.

[4] *like the eagle* According to myth, eagles could stare at the sun, and by flying up toward the sun would rejuvenate their eyes.

[5] *wise man … glass* Greek mathematician Archimedes was said to have set the Roman fleet on fire by concentrating the sun's rays with mirrors.

[6] *Faugh a ballagh* Irish battle cry: Clear the way.

[7] *tephilim* Jewish phylactery. The word Bloom is thinking of is the Hebrew word "mezuzah," a piece of parchment containing biblical passages that is placed in a case on the doorpost.

[8] *Davy Jones' locker* According to sailors' folklore, this locker at the bottom of the ocean was where all things lost at sea were stored.

[9] *cockalorum* Self-important person.

house to house, giving his everwelcome double knock, went the nine o'clock postman, the glowworm's lamp at his belt gleaming here and there through the laurel hedges. And among the five young trees a hoisted lintstock[1] lit the lamp at Leahy's terrace. By screens of lighted windows, by equal gardens a shrill voice went crying, wailing: *Evening Telegraph, stop press edition! Result of the Gold Cup races!* and from the door of Dignam's house a boy ran out and called. Twittering the bat flew here, flew there. Far out over the sands the coming surf crept, grey. Howth settled for slumber tired of long days, of yumyum rhododendrons (he was old) and felt gladly the night breeze lift, ruffle his fell of ferns. He lay but opened a red eye unsleeping, deep and slowly breathing, slumberous but awake. And far on Kish bank the anchored lightship twinkled, winked at Mr. Bloom.

Life those chaps out there must have, stuck in the same spot. Irish Lights board.[2] Penance for their sins. Coastguards too. Rocket and breeches buoy and lifeboat. Day we went out for the pleasure cruise in the Erin's King,[3] throwing them the sack of old papers. Bears in the zoo. Filthy trip. Drunkards out to shake up their livers. Puking overboard to feed the herrings. Nausea. And the women, fear of God in their faces. Milly, no sign of funk. Her blue scarf loose, laughing. Don't know what death is at that age. And then their stomachs clean. But being lost they fear. When we hid behind the tree at Crumlin. I didn't want to. Mamma! Mamma! Babes in the wood. Frightening them with masks too. Throwing them up in the air to catch them. I'll murder you. Is it only half fun? Or children playing battle. Whole earnest. How can people aim guns at each other. Sometimes they go off. Poor kids. Only troubles wildfire and nettlerash. Calomel purge[4] I got her for that. After getting better asleep with Molly. Very same teeth she has. What do they love? Another themselves? But the morning she chased her with the umbrella. Perhaps so as not to hurt. I felt her pulse. Ticking. Little hand it was: now big. Dearest Papli.[5] All that the hand says when you touch. Loved to count my waistcoat buttons. Her first stays I remember. Made me laugh to see. Little paps to begin with. Left one is more sensitive, I think.[6] Mine too. Nearer the heart. Padding themselves out if fat is in fashion. Her growing pains at night, calling, wakening me. Frightened she was when her nature came on her first. Poor child! Strange moment for the mother too. Brings back her girlhood. Gibraltar. Looking from Buena Vista. O'Hara's tower. The seabirds screaming. Old Barbary ape that gobbled all his family. Sundown, gunfire for the men to cross the lines. Looking out over the sea she told me. Evening like this, but clear, no clouds. I always thought I'd marry a lord or a gentleman with a private yacht. *Buenas noches, señorita. El hombre ama la muchaha hermosa.*[7] Why me? Because you were so foreign from the others.

Better not stick here all night like a limpet. This weather makes you dull. Must be getting on for nine by the light. Go home. Too late for *Leah, Lily of Killarney*.[8] No. Might be still up. Call to the hospital to see. Hope she's over. Long day I've had. Martha, the bath, funeral, house of keys, museum with those goddesses, Dedalus' song. Then that bawler in Barney Kiernan's. Got my own back there. Drunken ranters. What I said about his God made him wince. Mistake to hit back. Or? No. Ought to go home and laugh at themselves. Always want to be swilling in company. Afraid to be alone like a child of two. Suppose he hit me. Look at it other way round. Not so bad then. Perhaps not to hurt he meant. Three cheers for Israel. Three cheers for the sister-in-law he hawked about, three fangs in her mouth. Same style of beauty. Particularly nice old party for a cup of tea. The sister of the wife of the wild man of Borneo has just

[1] *lintstock* Long staff with a forked head to hold a match.

[2] *Irish Lights board* Board that maintained lighthouses and lightships.

[3] *Erin's King* Ship that took tourists around Dublin Bay.

[4] *Calomel purge* Calomel is used to relieve skin irritations.

[5] *Dearest Papli* The opening of Milly's letter to her father, which he received that morning.

[6] *paps* Breasts; *Left one … think* A common belief, because the left breast is nearer to the heart.

[7] *Buenas … hermosa* Spanish: Good evening, Miss. The man loves the beautiful young girl.

[8] *Leah* C.M.S. McLellan's popular play *Leah Kleschna* (1904); *Lily of Killarney* Julius Benedict's opera *The Lily of Killarney* (1862).

come to town. Imagine that in the early morning at close range. Everyone to his taste as Morris said when he kissed the cow. But Dignam's put the boots on it.[1] Houses of mourning so depressing because you never know. Anyhow she wants the money. Must call to those Scottish Widows[2] as I promised. Strange name. Takes it for granted we're going to pop off first. That widow on Monday was it outside Cramer's that looked at me. Buried the poor husband but progressing favourably on the premium. Her widow's mite. Well? What do you expect her to do? Must wheedle her way along. Widower I hate to see. Looks so forlorn. Poor man O'Connor wife and five children poisoned by mussels here. The sewage. Hopeless. Some good matronly woman in a porkpie hat to mother him. Take him in tow, platter face and a large apron. Ladies' grey flanelette bloomers, three shillings a pair, astonishing bargain. Plain and loved, loved for ever, they say. Ugly: no woman thinks she is. Love, lie and be handsome for tomorrow we die. See him sometimes walking about trying to find out who played the trick. U. p.: up. Fate that is. He, not me. Also a shop often noticed. Curse seems to dog it. Dreamt last night? Wait. Something confused. She had red slippers on. Turkish. Wore the breeches. Suppose she does. Would I like her in pyjamas? Damned hard to answer. Nannetti's gone. Mailboat. Near Holyhead by now. Must nail that ad of Keyes's. Work Hynes and Crawford. Petticoats for Molly. She has something to put in them. What's that? Might be money.

Mr. Bloom stooped and turned over a piece of paper on the strand. He brought it near his eyes and peered. Letter? No. Can't read. Better go. Better. I'm tired to move. Page of an old copybook. All those holes and pebbles. Who could count them? Never know what you find. Bottle with story of a treasure in it thrown from a wreck. Parcels post. Children always want to throw things in the sea. Trust? Bread cast on the waters.[3] What's this? Bit of stick.

[1] *put the … it* I.e., brought things to a head.

[2] *Scottish Widows* Name of a life insurance company.

[3] *Bread … waters* See Ecclesiastes 11.1: "Cast thy bread upon the waters: for thou shalt find it after many days."

O! Exhausted that female has me. Not so young now. Will she come here tomorrow? Wait for her somewhere for ever. Must come back. Murderers do.[4] Will I?

Mr. Bloom with his stick gently vexed the thick sand at his foot. Write a message for her. Might remain. What?

I.

Some flatfoot tramp on it in the morning. Useless. Washed away. Tide comes here a pool near her foot. Bend, see my face there, dark mirror, breathe on it, stirs. All these rocks with lines and scars and letters. O, those transparent! Besides they don't know. What is the meaning of that other world. I called you naughty boy because I do not like.[5]

AM. A.

No room. Let it go.

Mr. Bloom effaced the letters with his slow boot. Hopeless thing sand. Nothing grows in it. All fades. No fear of big vessels coming up here. Except Guinness's barges. Round the Kish[6] in eighty days. Done half by design.

He flung his wooden pen away. The stick fell in silted sand, stuck. Now if you were trying to do that for a week on end you couldn't. Chance. We'll never meet again. But it was lovely. Goodbye, dear. Thanks. Made me feel so young.

Short snooze now if I had. Must be near nine. Liverpool boat long gone. Not even the smoke. And she can do the other. Did too. And Belfast.[7] I won't go. Race there, race back to Ennis.[8] Let him. Just close my eyes a moment. Won't sleep though. Half dream. It never comes the same. Bat again. No harm in him. Just a few.

O sweety all your little girlwhite up I saw dirty bracegirdle made me do love sticky we two naughty Grace darling she him half past the bed met him pike hoses frillies for Raoul to perfume your wife black hair

[4] *Must come … do* Reference to the old adage that murderers always return to the scene of the crime.

[5] *What is … like* From Martha Clifford's letter.

[6] *Kish* Southeast of Dublin Bay.

[7] *Belfast* Bloom is thinking of the concert tour on which Molly will be embarking with Blazes Boylan.

[8] *Ennis* Where Bloom's father committed suicide, and where Bloom will be returning for the anniversary of his father's death—June 27.

heave under embon *señorita* young eyes Mulvey plump years dreams return tail end Agendath swoony lovey showed me her next year in drawers return next in her next her next.

A bat flew. Here. There. Here. Far in the grey a bell chimed. Mr. Bloom with open mouth, his left boot sanded sideways, leaned, breathed. Just for a few

Cuckoo
Cuckoo
Cuckoo.

The clock on the mantelpiece in the priest's house cooed where Canon O'Hanlon and Father Conroy and the reverend John Hughes S.J. were taking tea and sodabread and butter and fried mutton chops with catsup and talking about

Cuckoo
Cuckoo
Cuckoo.

Because it was a little canarybird bird that came out of its little house to tell the time that Gerty MacDowell noticed the time she was there because she was as quick as anything about a thing like that, was Gerty MacDowell, and she noticed at once that that foreign gentleman that was sitting on the rocks looking was

Cuckoo
Cuckoo
Cuckoo.

—1922

In Context

Joyce's Dublin

The Custom House and the River Liffey, 1885.

Above: View from the O'Connell Bridge along what is now O'Connell Street (then Sackville Street), c. 1905. Daniel O'Connell (1775–1847), known as the Great Liberator, was a nationalist leader to whom Joyce claimed a family connection. The statue of O'Connell referred to in "The Dead" stands in front of Nelson's Pillar (in the background in this photograph).

Right: View of O'Connell Bridge and the Liffey, c. 1895.

D.H. Lawrence

1885 – 1930

D.H. Lawrence declared that "one sheds one's sicknesses in books." That claim suggests not only the sufferings of a man whose fierce desire to live was helplessly incarcerated in a body wasting away from tuberculosis, but also the broader afflictions associated with British modernization: the rise of machine culture, the devastating loss of life in World War I, and the out-moded moral values governing relations between the sexes and the classes. A prolific writer, Lawrence "shed" a staggering array of novels, short stories, essays, and poems that relentlessly—and usually scandalously—broke cultural prohibitions to pioneer a new language of sexual and social possibility.

Some critics claim that Lawrence's only lasting allegiance was to his mother, an omnipresent figure who haunted his thoughts long after her death from cancer when he was twenty-five. David Herbert Lawrence, the fourth of five children born in the English mining town of Eastwood, Nottinghamshire, was his mother's favorite. Lawrence's parents were miserably mismatched. Lydia Lawrence felt she had married beneath herself, and struggled to cultivate more than working-class sensibilities in her children. Arthur Lawrence, the miner father, felt belittled by his own family. Marital tensions remembered from childhood percolate through Lawrence's works. If at first he villainized his father in the guise of various literary characters, Lawrence slowly gained sympathy for his father's awkward role in the family and for his earthy vitality. Scenes of an educated woman being sexually liberated through a liaison with a virile working-class man—most controversially explicit in *Lady Chatterley's Lover* (1928)—are seen throughout the works of Lawrence. His early novel *Sons and Lovers* (1913), while often interpreted as an Oedipal tale of mother-love, has also been read as a story of matricide. Feminist critics have noted how his texts encode both adoration and dread of the primal power Lawrence imagined that the female held over the male.

Lawrence worked as a clerk and an elementary-school teacher to pay for his studies at Nottingham University College, and obtained his teacher's certificate in 1908. He secured a good teaching position at the Davidson Road School in Croydon, one of England's spacious new turn-of-the-century state schools. But two severe attacks of pneumonia, at ages sixteen and twenty-six, nearly killed Lawrence and led him to give up his teaching career. His close encounters with death left him, in the words of one critic, "with a heightened awareness of the physical world and a messianic tendency to preach." A suspected if not yet confirmed consumptive, Lawrence broke off an uninspired engagement to Louie Burrows on the grounds that his doctor advised against marriage.

Ford Madox Ford, editor of *The English Review* when the prestigious journal published Lawrence's first poems in 1909, introduced Lawrence to literati who were fascinated by the idea of meeting a young working-class genius in the flesh. A "primitivism" that at the time was prompting writers and artists to seek a remedy for European modernity in non-European cultures also supported fantasies about the curative raw talent of the working class. (Lawrence, romanticized for his class background, would himself exoticize Mexican culture in his 1926 novel *The Plumed Serpent*.)

Though Lawrence castigated same-sex male desire throughout his life (most sharply in his introduction to Maurice Magnus's steamy *Memoirs of the Foreign Legion*, 1924), a homoerotic element in his work makes its appearance in the first of his novels, *The White Peacock* (1910). The figure of "Cyril" in the novel, based upon his childhood friend Alan Chambers, may have represented one of the loves of Lawrence's life. Soon after his second illness, however, Lawrence was to have a fateful encounter with Frieda von Richthofen at the home of her husband Ernest Weekley, one of Lawrence's favorite professors from college. Lawrence was by now rebelling against the universe of Christian guilt and glorifying an animal instinct in its place; he quickly came to worship the sensuality of Weekley's wife, a German baroness (and cousin of the World War I German flying ace Manfred von Richthofen, the "Red Baron"). Though Frieda left her husband and three children to be with Lawrence, she had little intention of re-marrying; it was Lawrence who pressured Frieda into marriage and cut her off from her young children, fearful that he could not compete with the force of maternal love which he himself knew so well.

Before meeting Lawrence, Frieda had been the lover of Otto Gross, a Freudian disciple who believed in sexually revolutionizing society to a degree never endorsed by Freud, and the indomitable Frieda continued to have countless lovers after marrying Lawrence. Lawrence's commitment to monogamy was in conflict with his goal of transcending sexual possessiveness. The Lawrences' many arguments were recorded by many visitors, yet the two remained together until Lawrence's death. To an acquaintance who asked what his ultimate message was, Lawrence wrote, "You shall love your wife completely and implicitly and in entire nakedness of body and spirit." Yet as one biographer dryly noted, "Lawrence's complete love included throttling her and covering her with bruises."

Lawrence's second major work of fiction, *The Rainbow*, was published in 1915, but its descriptions of sex and its coarse language led not only to its suppression, but also to legal difficulties for Lawrence. Persecuted, as well, during the war years, on account of his German wife and his provocative views, Lawrence felt exiled. Leading an itinerant lifestyle with Frieda, Lawrence set up house successively in Italy, Australia, the United States, Mexico, and France. World War I bred in Lawrence a fierce desire to form a community of the like-minded in tune with archetypal life forces, and the Lawrences' nomadic lifestyle was largely fueled by his restless utopian desires. During this period Lawrence composed most of the material that would appear in *Birds, Beasts, and Flowers* (1923), a collection that includes many of his best-known poems.

If Lawrence's sexual frankness created controversy, his radical dissolution of conventional narrative voice also disturbed many contemporaries. By the time he published *Women in Love* (1921), a story of two sisters who leave the countryside in pursuit of modern careers and sexual freedom, Lawrence no longer put any stock in individual subjectivity. His fiction strove to capture poetically the impersonal forces of nature that work through individuals but are in themselves vast and impersonal.

The publication of *Lady Chatterley's Lover* (1928) further scandalized the British public. The novel graphically depicts the primal sexuality awakened in Constance Chatterley by her working-class lover, Mellors. An anonymous critic who reviewed the novel in *John Bull* famously called it "a cesspool, the most obscene book in the English language." The publication of the book provoked censorship debates in the British Parliament in 1929, and the novel's label of "obscene" was not officially lifted until 1960, when the unexpurgated version became a popular sensation. Lawrence's last poetry collection, *Pansies* (1929), was also interfered with by censors.

Both Lawrence and his wife refused to admit that he was dying of tuberculosis until the disease was too advanced to deny. He died in 1930 at the age of 45 in the south of France.

⌘⌘⌘

Snake

A Snake came to my water-trough
On a hot, hot day, and I in pyjamas for the heat,
To drink there.

In the deep, strange-scented shade of the great dark carob-tree
I came down the steps with my pitcher
And must wait, must stand and wait, for there he was at the trough before me.

He reached down from a fissure in the earth-wall in the gloom
And trailed his yellow-brown slackness soft-bellied down, over the edge of the stone trough
And rested his throat upon the stone bottom,
And where the water had dripped from the tap, in a small clearness,
He sipped with his straight mouth,
Softly drank through his straight gums, into his slack long body,
Silently.

Someone was before me at my water-trough,
And I, like a second comer, waiting.

He lifted his head from his drinking, as cattle do,
And looked at me vaguely, as drinking cattle do,
And flickered his two-forked tongue from his lips, and mused a moment,
And stooped and drank a little more,
Being earth-brown, earth-golden from the burning bowels of the earth
On the day of Sicilian July, with Etna[1] smoking.

The voice of my education said to me
He must be killed,
For in Sicily the black, black snakes are innocent, the gold are venomous.

And voices in me said, If you were a man
You would take a stick and break him now, and finish him off.

But must I confess how I liked him,
How glad I was he had come like a guest in quiet, to drink at my water-trough
And depart peaceful, pacified, and thankless,
Into the burning bowels of this earth?

Was it cowardice, that I dared not kill him?
Was it perversity, that I longed to talk to him?
Was it humility, to feel so honoured?
I felt so honoured.

And yet those voices:
If you were not afraid, you would kill him!

And truly I was afraid, I was most afraid,
But even so, honoured still more
That he should seek my hospitality
From out the dark door of the secret earth.

---

[1] *Etna* Volcano in Sicily.

He drank enough
And lifted his head, dreamily, as one who has
drunken,
And flickered his tongue like a forked night on the
air, so black,
Seeming to lick his lips,
And looked around like a god, unseeing, into the air,
And slowly turned his head,
And slowly, very slowly, as if thrice adream,
Proceeded to draw his slow length curving round
And climb again the broken bank of my wall-face.

And as he put his head into that dreadful hole,
And as he slowly drew up, snake-easing his shoulders,
and entered farther,
A sort of horror, a sort of protest against his
withdrawing into that horrid black hole,
Deliberately going into the blackness, and slowly
drawing himself after,
Overcame me now his back was turned.

I looked round, I put down my pitcher,
I picked up a clumsy log
And threw it at the water-trough with a clatter.

I think it did not hit him,
But suddenly that part of him that was left behind
convulsed in undignified haste,
Writhed like lightning, and was gone
Into the black hole, the earth-lipped fissure in the
wall-front,
At which, in the intense still noon, I stared with
fascination.

And immediately I regretted it.
I thought how paltry, how vulgar, what a mean act!
I despised myself and the voices of my accursed
human education.

And I thought of the albatross,[1]
And I wished he would come back, my snake.

For he seemed to me again like a king,
Like a king in exile, uncrowned in the underworld,
Now due to be crowned again.

And so, I missed my chance with one of the lords
Of life.
And I have something to expiate;
A pettiness.
—1923

Odour of Chrysanthemums

I

The small locomotive engine, Number 4, came clanking, stumbling down from Selston with seven full wagons. It appeared round the corner with loud threats of speed, but the colt that it startled from among the gorse,[2] which still flickered indistinctly in the raw afternoon, out-distanced it at a canter. A woman, walking up the railway line to Underwood, drew back into the hedge, held her basket aside, and watched the footplate of the engine advancing. The trucks thumped heavily past, one by one, with slow inevitable movement, as she stood insignificantly trapped between the jolting black wagons and the hedge; then they curved away towards the coppice[3] where the withered oak leaves dropped noiselessly, while the birds, pulling at the scarlet hips[4] beside the track, made off into the dusk that had already crept into the spinney.[5] In the open, the smoke from the engine sank and cleaved to the rough grass. The fields were dreary and forsaken, and in

[1] *albatross* Reference to Samuel Taylor Coleridge's *Rime of the Ancient Mariner* (1798), in which a sailor needlessly and thoughtlessly kills an albatross.

[2] *gorse* Prickly shrub.

[3] *coppice* Thicket of small trees.

[4] *hips* Fruits (of wild roses).

[5] *spinney* Small copse.

the marshy strip that led to the whimsey,[1] a reedy pit-pond, the fowls had already abandoned their run among the alders, to roost in the tarred fowl-house. The pit-bank loomed up beyond the pond, flames like red sores licking its ashy sides, in the afternoon's stagnant light. Just beyond rose the tapering chimneys and the clumsy black headstocks of Brinsley Colliery.[2] The two wheels were spinning fast up against the sky, and the winding engine rapped out its little spasms. The miners were being turned up.

The engine whistled as it came into the wide bay of railway lines beside the colliery, where rows of trucks stood in harbour.

Miners, single, trailing and in groups, passed like shadows diverging home. At the edge of the ribbed level of sidings squat a low cottage, three steps down from the cinder track. A large bony vine clutched at the house, as if to claw down the tiled roof. Round the bricked yard grew a few wintry primroses. Beyond, the long garden sloped down to a bush-covered brook course. There were some twiggy apple trees, winter-crack trees, and ragged cabbages. Beside the path hung dishevelled pink chrysanthemums, like pink cloths hung on bushes. A woman came stooping out of the felt-covered fowl-house, halfway down the garden. She closed and padlocked the door, then drew herself erect, having brushed some bits from her white apron.

She was a tall woman of imperious mien,[3] handsome, with definite black eyebrows. Her smooth black hair was parted exactly. For a few moments she stood steadily watching the miners as they passed along the railway: then she turned towards the brook course. Her face was calm and set, her mouth was closed with disillusionment. After a moment she called:

"John!" There was no answer. She waited, and then said distinctly:

"Where are you?"

[1] *whimsey* Machine used to raise water or ore from a mine.

[2] *headstocks* Supports of revolving machine parts; *Colliery* Coal mine.

[3] *mien* Bearing.

"Here!" replied a child's sulky voice from among the bushes. The woman looked piercingly through the dusk.

"Are you at that brook?" she asked sternly.

For answer the child showed himself before the raspberry-canes that rose like whips. He was a small, sturdy boy of five. He stood quite still, defiantly.

"Oh!" said the mother, conciliated. "I thought you were down at that wet brook—and you remember what I told you—"

The boy did not move or answer.

"Come, come on in," she said more gently, "it's getting dark. There's your grandfather's engine coming down the line!"

The lad advanced slowly, with resentful, taciturn movement. He was dressed in trousers and waistcoat of cloth that was too thick and hard for the size of the garments. They were evidently cut down from a man's clothes.

As they went slowly towards the house he tore at the ragged wisps of chrysanthemums and dropped the petals in handfuls among the path.

"Don't do that—it does look nasty," said his mother. He refrained, and she, suddenly pitiful, broke off a twig with three or four wan flowers and held them against her face. When mother and son reached the yard her hand hesitated, and instead of laying the flower aside, she pushed it in her apron-band. The mother and son stood at the foot of the three steps looking across the bay of lines at the passing home of the miners. The trundle of the small train was imminent. Suddenly the engine loomed past the house and came to a stop opposite the gate.

The engine-driver, a short man with round grey beard, leaned out of the cab high above the woman.

"Have you got a cup of tea?" he said in a cheery, hearty fashion.

It was her father. She went in, saying she would mash.[4] Directly, she returned.

"I didn't come to see you on Sunday," began the little grey-bearded man.

[4] *mash* Brew tea.

"I didn't expect you," said his daughter.

The engine-driver winced; then, reassuming his cheery, airy manner, he said:

"Oh, have you heard then? Well, and what do you think—?"

"I think it is soon enough," she replied.

At her brief censure the little man made an impatient gesture, and said coaxingly, yet with dangerous coldness:

"Well, what's a man to do? It's no sort of life for a man of my years, to sit at my own hearth like a stranger. And if I'm going to marry again it may as well be soon as late—what does it matter to anybody?"

The woman did not reply, but turned and went into the house. The man in the engine-cab stood assertive, till she returned with a cup of tea and a piece of bread and butter on a plate. She went up the steps and stood near the footplate of the hissing engine.

"You needn't 'a' brought me bread an' butter," said her father. "But a cup of tea"—he sipped appreciatively—"it's very nice." He sipped for a moment or two, then: "I hear as Walter's got another bout[1] on," he said.

"When hasn't he?" said the woman bitterly.

"I heerd tell of him in the 'Lord Nelson'[2] braggin' as he was going to spend that b—— afore he went: half a sovereign[3] that was."

"When?" asked the woman.

"A' Sat'day night—I know that's true."

"Very likely," she laughed bitterly. "He gives me twenty-three shillings."

"Aye, it's a nice thing, when a man can do nothing with his money but make a beast of himself!" said the grey-whiskered man. The woman turned her head away. Her father swallowed the last of his tea and handed her the cup.

"Aye," he sighed, wiping his mouth. "It's a settler,[4] it is—"

He put his hand on the lever. The little engine strained and groaned, and the train rumbled towards the crossing. The woman again looked across the metals. Darkness was settling over the spaces of the railway and trucks: the miners, in grey sombre groups, were still passing home. The winding engine pulsed hurriedly, with brief pauses. Elizabeth Bates looked at the dreary flow of men, then she went indoors. Her husband did not come.

The kitchen was small and full of firelight; red coals piled glowing up the chimney mouth. All the life of the room seemed in the white, warm hearth and the steel fender reflecting the red fire. The cloth was laid for tea; cups glinted in the shadows. At the back, where the lowest stairs protruded into the room, the boy sat struggling with a knife and a piece of white wood. He was almost hidden in the shadow. It was half-past four. They had but to await the father's coming to begin tea. As the mother watched her son's sullen little struggle with the wood, she saw herself in his silence and pertinacity; she saw the father in her child's indifference to all but himself. She seemed to be occupied by her husband. He had probably gone past his home, slunk past his own door, to drink before he came in, while his dinner spoiled and wasted in waiting. She glanced at the clock, then took the potatoes to strain them in the yard. The garden and fields beyond the brook were closed in uncertain darkness. When she rose with the saucepan, leaving the drain steaming into the night behind her, she saw the yellow lamps were lit along the high road that went up the hill away beyond the space of the railway lines and the field.

Then again she watched the men trooping home, fewer now and fewer.

Indoors the fire was sinking and the room was dark red. The woman put her saucepan on the hob, and set a batter-pudding near the mouth of the oven. Then she stood unmoving. Directly, gratefully, came quick young steps to the door. Someone hung on the latch a moment, then a little girl entered and began pulling off her outdoor things, dragging a mass of curls, just ripening from gold to brown, over her eyes with her hat.

---

[1] *bout* I.e., of drinking.

[2] *'Lord Nelson'* I.e., the pub.

[3] *sovereign* Coin worth twenty shillings.

[4] *settler* Finishing or deciding blow.

Her mother chid her for coming late from school, and said she would have to keep her at home the dark winter days.

"Why, mother, it's hardly a bit dark yet. The lamp's not lighted, and my father's not home."

"No, he isn't. But it's a quarter to five! Did you see anything of him?"

The child became serious. She looked at her mother with large, wistful blue eyes.

"No, mother, I've never seen him. Why? Has he come up an' gone past, to Old Brinsley? He hasn't, mother, 'cos I never saw him."

"He'd watch that," said the mother bitterly, "he'd take care as you didn't see him. But you may depend upon it, he's seated in the 'Prince o' Wales.' He wouldn't be this late."

The girl looked at her mother piteously.

"Let's have our teas, mother, should we?" said she.

The mother called John to table. She opened the door once more and looked out across the darkness of the lines. All was deserted: she could not hear the winding-engines.

"Perhaps," she said to herself, "he's stopped to get some ripping[1] done."

They sat down to tea. John, at the end of the table near the door, was almost lost in the darkness. Their faces were hidden from each other. The girl crouched against the fender slowly moving a thick piece of bread before the fire. The lad, his face a dusky mark on the shadow, sat watching her who was transfigured in the red glow.

"I do think it's beautiful to look in the fire," said the child.

"Do you?" said her mother. "Why?"

"It's so red, and full of little caves—and it feels so nice, and you can fair smell it."

"It'll want mending directly," replied her mother, "and then if your father comes he'll carry on and say there never is a fire when a man comes home sweating from the pit. A public-house is always warm enough."

There was silence till the boy said complainingly: "Make haste, our Annie."

"Well, I am doing! I can't make the fire do it no faster, can I?"

"She keeps wafflin' it about so's to make 'er slow," grumbled the boy.

"Don't have such an evil imagination, child," replied the mother.

Soon the room was busy in the darkness with the crisp sound of crunching. The mother ate very little. She drank her tea determinedly, and sat thinking. When she rose her anger was evident in the stern unbending of her head. She looked at the pudding in the fender, and broke out:

"It is a scandalous thing as a man can't even come home to his dinner! If it's crozzled[2] up to a cinder I don't see why I should care. Past his very door he goes to get to a public-house, and here I sit with his dinner waiting for him—"

She went out. As she dropped piece after piece of coal on the red fire, the shadows fell on the walls, till the room was almost in total darkness.

"I canna see," grumbled the invisible John. In spite of herself, the mother laughed.

"You know the way to your mouth," she said. She set the dust-pan outside the door. When she came again like a shadow on the hearth, the lad repeated, complaining sulkily:

"I canna see."

"Good gracious!" cried the mother irritably, "you're as bad as your father if it's a bit dusk!"

Nevertheless, she took a paper spill[3] from a sheaf on the mantelpiece and proceeded to light the lamp that hung from the ceiling in the middle of the room. As she reached up, her figure displayed itself just rounding with maternity.

"Oh, mother—!" exclaimed the girl.

"What?" said the woman, suspended in the act of putting the lamp-glass over the flame. The copper

1 *ripping* Cutting away coal.

2 *crozzled* Curled; burnt.

3 *paper spill* Folded or twisted paper used for lighting candle, fire, lamp, etc.

reflector shone handsomely on her, as she stood with uplifted arm, turning to face her daughter.

"You've got a flower in your apron!" said the child, in a little rapture at this unusual event.

"Goodness me!" exclaimed the woman, relieved. "One would think the house was afire." She replaced the glass and waited a moment before turning up the wick. A pale shadow was seen floating vaguely on the floor.

"Let me smell!" said the child, still rapturously, coming forward and putting her face to her mother's waist.

"Go along, silly!" said the mother, turning up the lamp. The light revealed their suspense so that the woman felt it almost unbearable. Annie was still bending at her waist. Irritably, the mother took the flowers out from her apron-band.

"Oh, mother—don't take them out!" Annie cried, catching her hand and trying to replace the sprig.

"Such nonsense!" said the mother, turning away. The child put the pale chrysanthemums to her lips, murmuring:

"Don't they smell beautiful!"

Her mother gave a short laugh.

"No," she said, "not to me. It was chrysanthemums when I married him, and chrysanthemums when you were born, and the first time they ever brought him home drunk, he'd got brown chrysanthemums in his button-hole."

She looked at the children. Their eyes and their parted lips were wondering. The mother sat rocking in silence for some time. Then she looked at the clock.

"Twenty minutes to six!" In a tone of fine bitter carelessness she continued: "Eh, he'll not come now till they bring him. There he'll stick! But he needn't come rolling in here in his pit-dirt, for *I* won't wash him. He can lie on the floor—Eh, what a fool I've been, what a fool! And this is what I came here for, to this dirty hole, rats and all, for him to slink past his very door. Twice last week—he's begun now—"

She silenced herself, and rose to clear the table. While for an hour or more the children played, subduedly intent, fertile of imagination, united in fear of the mother's wrath, and in dread of their father's home-coming, Mrs. Bates sat in her rocking-chair making a "singlet"[1] of thick cream-coloured flannel, which gave a dull wounded sound as she tore off the grey edge. She worked at her sewing with energy, listening to the children, and her anger wearied itself, lay down to rest, opening its eyes from time to time and steadily watching, its ears raised to listen. Sometimes even her anger quailed and shrank, and the mother suspended her sewing, tracing the footsteps that thudded along the sleepers outside; she would lift her head sharply to bid the children "hush," but she recovered herself in time, and the footsteps went past the gate, and the children were not flung out of their play-world.

But at last Annie sighed, and gave in. She glanced at her wagon of slippers, and loathed the game. She turned plaintively to her mother.

"Mother!"—but she was inarticulate.

John crept out like a frog from under the sofa. His mother glanced up.

"Yes," she said, "just look at those shirt-sleeves!"

The boy held them out to survey them, saying nothing. Then somebody called in a hoarse voice away down the line, and suspense bristled in the room, till two people had gone by outside, talking.

"It is time for bed," said the mother.

"My father hasn't come," wailed Annie plaintively. But her mother was primed with courage.

"Never mind. They'll bring him when he does come—like a log." She meant there would be no scene. "And he may sleep on the floor till he wakes himself. I know he'll not go to work tomorrow after this!"

The children had their hands and faces wiped with a flannel. They were very quiet. When they had put on their nightdresses, they said their prayers, the boy mumbling. The mother looked down at them, at the brown silken bush of intertwining curls in the nape of the girl's neck, at the little black head of the lad, and her heart burst with anger at their father, who caused all three such distress. The children hid their faces in her skirts for comfort.

[1] *singlet* Undershirt.

When Mrs. Bates came down, the room was strangely empty, with a tension of expectancy. She took up her sewing and stitched for some time without raising her head. Meantime her anger was tinged with fear.

2

The clock struck eight and she rose suddenly, dropping her sewing on her chair. She went to the stair-foot door, opened it, listening. Then she went out, locking the door behind her.

Something scuffled in the yard, and she started, though she knew it was only the rats with which the place was over-run. The night was very dark. In the great bay of railway lines, bulked with trucks, there was no trace of light, only away back she could see a few yellow lamps at the pit-top, and the red smear of the burning pit-bank on the night. She hurried along the edge of the track, then, crossing the converging lines, came to the stile by the white gates, whence she emerged on the road. Then the fear which had led her shrank. People were walking up to New Brinsley; she saw the lights in the houses; twenty yards farther on were the broad windows of the "Prince of Wales," very warm and bright, and the loud voices of men could be heard distinctly. What a fool she had been to imagine that anything had happened to him! He was merely drinking over there at the "Prince of Wales." She faltered. She had never yet been to fetch him, and she never would go. So she continued her walk towards the long straggling line of houses, standing back on the highway. She entered a passage between the dwellings.

"Mr. Rigley?—Yes! Did you want him? No, he's not in at this minute."

The raw-boned woman leaned forward from her dark scullery and peered at the other, upon whom fell a dim light through the blind of the kitchen window.

"Is it Mrs. Bates?" she asked in a tone tinged with respect.

"Yes. I wondered if your Master was at home. Mine hasn't come yet."

"'Asn't 'e! Oh, Jack's been 'ome an' 'ad 'is dinner an' gone out. 'E's just gone for 'alf an hour afore bed-time. Did you call at the 'Prince of Wales'?"

"No—"

"No, you didn't like—! It's not very nice." The other woman was indulgent. There was an awkward pause. "Jack never said nothink about—about your Master," she said.

"No!—I expect he's stuck in there!"

Elizabeth Bates said this bitterly, and with recklessness. She knew that the woman across the yard was standing at her door listening, but she did not care. As she turned:

"Stop a minute! I'll just go an' ask Jack if 'e knows anythink," said Mrs. Rigley.

"Oh no—I wouldn't like to put——!"

"Yes, I will, if you'll just step inside an' see as th' childer doesn't come downstairs and set theirselves afire."

Elizabeth Bates, murmuring a remonstrance, stepped inside. The other woman apologised for the state of the room.

The kitchen needed apology. There were little frocks and trousers and childish undergarments on the squab[1] and on the floor, and a litter of playthings everywhere. On the black American cloth[2] of the table were pieces of bread and cake, crusts, slops, and a teapot with cold tea.

"Eh, ours is just as bad," said Elizabeth Bates, looking at the woman, not at the house. Mrs. Rigley put a shawl over her head and hurried out, saying:

"I shanna be a minute."

The other sat, noting with faint disapproval the general untidiness of the room. Then she fell to counting the shoes of various sizes scattered over the floor. There were twelve. She sighed and said to herself: "No wonder!"—glancing at the litter. There came the scratching of two pairs of feet on the yard, and the Rigleys entered. Elizabeth Bates rose. Rigley was a big man, with very large bones. His head looked particularly bony. Across his temple was a blue scar, caused by a wound got in the pit, a wound in which the coal-dust remained blue like tattooing.

[1] *squab* Sofa.

[2] *American cloth* Flexible enameled cloth used for covering furniture.

"'Asna 'e come whoam yit?" asked the man, without any form of greeting, but with deference and sympathy. "I couldna say wheer he is—'e's non ower theer!"—he jerked his head to signify the "Prince of Wales."

"'E's 'appen gone up to th' 'Yew,'" said Mrs. Rigley. There was another pause. Rigley had evidently something to get off his mind:

"Ah left 'im finishin' a stint," he began. "Loose-all[1] 'ad bin gone about ten minutes when we com'n away, an' I shouted: 'Are ter comin', Walt?' an' 'e said: 'Go on, Ah shanna be but a'ef a minnit,' so we com'n ter th' bottom, me an' Bowers, thinkin' as 'e wor just behint, an' 'ud come up i' th' next bantle[2]—"

He stood perplexed, as if answering a charge of deserting his mate. Elizabeth Bates, now again certain of disaster, hastened to reassure him:

"I expect 'e's gone up to th' 'Yew Tree,' as you say. It's not the first time. I've fretted myself into a fever before now. He'll come home when they carry him."

"Ay, isn't it too bad!" deplored the other woman.

"I'll just step up to Dick's an' see if 'e *is* theer," offered the man, afraid of appearing alarmed, afraid of taking liberties.

"Oh, I wouldn't think of bothering you that far," said Elizabeth Bates, with emphasis, but he knew she was glad of his offer.

As they stumbled up the entry, Elizabeth Bates heard Rigley's wife run across the yard and open her neighbour's door. At this, suddenly all the blood in her body seemed to switch away from her heart.

"Mind!" warned Rigley. "Ah've said many a time as Ah'd fill up them ruts in this entry, sumb'dy 'll be breakin' their legs yit."

She recovered herself and walked quickly along with the miner.

"I don't like leaving the children in bed, and nobody in the house," she said.

"No, you dunna!" he replied courteously. They were soon at the gate of the cottage.

"Well, I shanna be many minnits. Dunna you be frettin' now, 'e'll be all right," said the butty.[3]

"Thank you very much, Mr. Rigley," she replied.

"You're welcome!" he stammered, moving away. "I shanna be many minnits."

The house was quiet. Elizabeth Bates took off her hat and shawl, and rolled back the rug. When she had finished, she sat down. It was a few minutes past nine. She was startled by the rapid chuff of the winding-engine at the pit, and the sharp whirr of the brakes on the rope as it descended. Again she felt the painful sweep of her blood, and she put her hand to her side, saying aloud: "Good gracious!—it's only the nine o'clock deputy going down," rebuking herself.

She sat still, listening. Half an hour of this, and she was wearied out.

"What am I working myself up like this for?" she said pitiably to herself, "I s'll only be doing myself some damage."

She took out her sewing again.

At a quarter to ten there were footsteps. One person! She watched for the door to open. It was an elderly woman, in a black bonnet and a black woollen shawl—his mother. She was about sixty years old, pale, with blue eyes, and her face all wrinkled and lamentable. She shut the door and turned to her daughter-in-law peevishly.

"Eh, Lizzie, whatever shall we do, whatever shall we do!" she cried.

Elizabeth drew back a little, sharply.

"What is it, mother?" she said.

The elder woman seated herself on the sofa.

"I don't know, child, I can't tell you!"—she shook her head slowly. Elizabeth sat watching her, anxious and vexed.

"I don't know," replied the grandmother, sighing very deeply. "There's no end to my troubles, there isn't. The things I've gone through, I'm sure it's enough—!" She wept without wiping her eyes, the tears running.

"But, mother," interrupted Elizabeth, "what do you mean? What is it?"

[1] *Loose-all* Signal to finish working in the pits.

[2] *bantle* Group.

[3] *butty* Buddy; workmate.

The grandmother slowly wiped her eyes. The fountains of her tears were stopped by Elizabeth's directness. She wiped her eyes slowly.

"Poor child! Eh, you poor thing!" she moaned. "I don't know what we're going to do, I don't—and you as you are—it's a thing, it is indeed!"

Elizabeth waited.

"Is he dead?" she asked, and at the words her heart swung violently, though she felt a slight flush of shame at the ultimate extravagance of the question. Her words sufficiently frightened the old lady, almost brought her to herself.

"Don't say so, Elizabeth! We'll hope it's not as bad as that; no, may the Lord spare us that, Elizabeth. Jack Rigley came just as I was sittin' down to a glass afore going to bed, an' 'e said: ''Appen you'll go down th' line, Mrs. Bates. Walt's had an accident. 'Appen you'll go an' sit wi' 'er till we can get him home.' I hadn't time to ask him a word afore he was gone. An' I put my bonnet on an' come straight down, Lizzie. I thought to myself: 'Eh, that poor blessed child, if anybody should come an' tell her of a sudden, there's no knowin' what'll 'appen to 'er.' You mustn't let it upset you, Lizzie—or you know what to expect. How long is it, six months—or is it five, Lizzie? Ay!"—the old woman shook her head—"time slips on, it slips on! Ay!"

Elizabeth's thoughts were busy elsewhere. If he was killed—would she be able to manage on the little pension and what she could earn?—she counted up rapidly. If he was hurt—they wouldn't take him to the hospital—how tiresome he would be to nurse!—but perhaps she'd be able to get him away from the drink and his hateful ways. She would—while he was ill. The tears offered to come to her eyes at the picture. But what sentimental luxury was this she was beginning? She turned to consider the children. At any rate she was absolutely necessary for them. They were her business.

"Ay!" repeated the old woman, "it seems but a week or two since he brought me his first wages. Ay—he was a good lad, Elizabeth, he was, in his way. I don't know why he got to be such a trouble, I don't. He was a happy lad at home, only full of spirits. But there's no mistake he's been a handful of trouble, he has! I hope the Lord'll spare him to mend his ways. I hope so, I hope so. You've had a sight o' trouble with him, Elizabeth, you have indeed. But he was a jolly enough lad wi' me, he was, I can assure you. I don't know how it is. ..."

The old woman continued to muse aloud, a monotonous irritating sound, while Elizabeth thought concentratedly, startled once, when she heard the winding-engine chuff quickly, and the brakes skirr with a shriek. Then she heard the engine more slowly, and the brakes made no sound. The old woman did not notice. Elizabeth waited in suspense. The mother-in-law talked, with lapses into silence.

"But he wasn't your son, Lizzie, an' it makes a difference. Whatever he was, I remember him when he was little, an' I learned to understand him and to make allowances. You've got to make allowances for them—"

It was half-past ten, and the old woman was saying: "But it's trouble from beginning to end; you're never too old for trouble, never too old for that—" when the gate banged back, and there were heavy feet on the steps.

"I'll go, Lizzie, let me go," cried the old woman, rising. But Elizabeth was at the door. It was a man in pit-clothes.

"They're bringin' 'im, Missis," he said. Elizabeth's heart halted a moment. Then it surged on again, almost suffocating her.

"Is he—is it bad?" she asked.

The man turned away, looking at the darkness:

"The doctor says 'e'd been dead hours. 'E saw 'im i' th' lamp-cabin."

The old woman, who stood just behind Elizabeth, dropped into a chair, and folded her hands, crying: "Oh, my boy, my boy!"

"Hush!" said Elizabeth, with a sharp twitch of a frown. "Be still, mother, don't waken th' children: I wouldn't have them down for anything!"

The old woman moaned softly, rocking herself. The man was drawing away. Elizabeth took a step forward.

"How was it?" she asked.

"Well, I couldn't say for sure," the man replied, very ill at ease. "'E wor finishin' a stint an' th' butties 'ad gone, an' a lot o' stuff come down atop 'n 'im."

"And crushed him?" cried the widow, with a shudder.

"No," said the man, "it fell at th' back of 'im. 'E wor under th' face, an' it niver touched 'im. It shut 'im in. It seems 'e wor smothered."

Elizabeth shrank back. She heard the old woman behind her cry:

"What?—what did 'e say it was?"

The man replied, more loudly: "'E wor smothered!"

Then the old woman wailed aloud, and this relieved Elizabeth.

"Oh, mother," she said, putting her hand on the old woman, "don't waken th' children, don't waken th' children."

She wept a little, unknowing, while the old mother rocked herself and moaned. Elizabeth remembered that they were bringing him home, and she must be ready. "They'll lay him in the parlour," she said to herself, standing a moment pale and perplexed.

Then she lighted a candle and went into the tiny room. The air was cold and damp, but she could not make a fire, there was no fireplace. She set down the candle and looked round. The candlelight glittered on the lustre-glasses, on the two vases that held some of the pink chrysanthemums, and on the dark mahogany. There was a cold, deathly smell of chrysanthemums in the room. Elizabeth stood looking at the flowers. She turned away, and calculated whether there would be room to lay him on the floor, between the couch and the chiffonier. She pushed the chairs aside. There would be room to lay him down and to step round him. Then she fetched the old red tablecloth, and another old cloth, spreading them down to save her bit of carpet. She shivered on leaving the parlour; so, from the dresser drawer she took a clean shirt and put it at the fire to air. All the time her mother-in-law was rocking herself in the chair and moaning.

"You'll have to move from there, mother," said Elizabeth. "They'll be bringing him in. Come in the rocker."

The old mother rose mechanically, and seated herself by the fire, continuing to lament. Elizabeth went into the pantry for another candle, and there, in the little pent-house[1] under the naked tiles, she heard them coming. She stood still in the pantry doorway, listening. She heard them pass the end of the house, and come awkwardly down the three steps, a jumble of shuffling footsteps and muttering voices. The old woman was silent. The men were in the yard.

Then Elizabeth heard Matthews, the manager of the pit, say: "You go in first, Jim. Mind!"

The door came open, and the two women saw a collier[2] backing into the room, holding one end of a stretcher, on which they could see the nailed pit-boots of the dead man. The two carriers halted, the man at the head stooping to the lintel[3] of the door.

"Wheer will you have him?" asked the manager, a short, white-bearded man.

Elizabeth roused herself and came from the pantry carrying the unlighted candle.

"In the parlour," she said.

"In there, Jim!" pointed the manager, and the carriers backed round into the tiny room. The coat with which they had covered the body fell off as they awkwardly turned through the two doorways, and the women saw their man, naked to the waist, lying stripped for work. The old woman began to moan in a low voice of horror.

"Lay th' stretcher at th' side," snapped the manager, "an' put 'im on th' cloths. Mind now, mind! Look you now—!"

One of the men had knocked off a vase of chrysanthemums. He stared awkwardly, then they set down the stretcher. Elizabeth did not look at her husband. As soon as she could get in the room, she went and picked up the broken vase and the flowers.

"Wait a minute!" she said.

---

[1] *pent-house* Subsidiary structure with a sloping roof, attached to the wall of the main building.

[2] *collier* Coal miner.

[3] *lintel* Horizontal support beam.

The three men waited in silence while she mopped up the water with a duster.

"Eh, what a job, what a job, to be sure!" the manager was saying, rubbing his brow with trouble and perplexity. "Never knew such a thing in my life, never! He'd no business to ha' been left. I never knew such a thing in my life! Fell over him clean as a whistle, an' shut him in. Not four foot of space, there wasn't—yet it scarce bruised him."

He looked down at the dead man, lying prone, half naked, all grimed with coal-dust.

"'Sphyxiated,' the doctor said. It *is* the most terrible job I've ever known. Seems as if it was done o' purpose. Clean over him, an' shut 'im in, like a mouse-trap"—he made a sharp, descending gesture with his hand.

The colliers standing by jerked aside their heads in hopeless comment.

The horror of the thing bristled upon them all.

Then they heard the girl's voice upstairs calling shrilly:

"Mother, mother—who is it? Mother, who is it?"

Elizabeth hurried to the foot of the stairs and opened the door:

"Go to sleep!" she commanded sharply. "What are you shouting about? Go to sleep at once—there's nothing—"

Then she began to mount the stairs. They could hear her on the boards, and on the plaster floor of the little bedroom. They could hear her distinctly:

"What's the matter now?—what's the matter with you, silly thing?"—her voice was much agitated, with an unreal gentleness.

"I thought it was some men come," said the plaintive voice of the child. "Has he come?"

"Yes, they've brought him. There's nothing to make a fuss about. Go to sleep now, like a good child."

They could hear her voice in the bedroom, they waited whilst she covered the children under the bedclothes.

"Is he drunk?" asked the girl, timidly, faintly.

"No! No—he's not! He—he's asleep."

"Is he asleep downstairs?"

"Yes—and don't make a noise."

There was silence for a moment, then the men heard the frightened child again:

"What's that noise?"

"It's nothing, I tell you, what are you bothering for?"

The noise was the grandmother moaning. She was oblivious of everything, sitting on her chair rocking and moaning. The manager put his hand on her arm and bade her "Sh—sh!!"

The old woman opened her eyes and looked at him. She was shocked by this interruption, and seemed to wonder.

"What time is it?" the plaintive thin voice of the child, sinking back unhappily into sleep, asked this last question.

"Ten o'clock," answered the mother more softly. Then she must have bent down and kissed the children.

Matthews beckoned to the men to come away. They put on their caps and took up the stretcher. Stepping over the body, they tiptoed out of the house. None of them spoke till they were far from the wakeful children.

When Elizabeth came down she found her mother alone on the parlour floor, leaning over the dead man, the tears dropping on him.

"We must lay him out," the wife said. She put on the kettle, then returning knelt at the feet, and began to unfasten the knotted leather laces. The room was clammy and dim with only one candle, so that she had to bend her face almost to the floor. At last she got off the heavy boots and put them away.

"You must help me now," she whispered to the old woman. Together they stripped the man.

When they arose, saw him lying in the naïve dignity of death, the woman stood arrested in fear and respect. For a few moments they remained still, looking down, the old mother whimpering. Elizabeth felt countermanded. She saw him, how utterly inviolable he lay in himself. She had nothing to do with him. She could not accept it. Stooping, she laid her hand on him, in claim. He was still warm, for the mine was hot where he had died. His mother had his face between her hands, and was murmuring incoherently. The old tears fell in succession as drops from wet leaves; the mother was not weeping, merely her tears flowed. Elizabeth embraced the body of her husband, with cheek and lips. She seemed to be listening, inquiring, trying to get some connection. But she could not. She was driven away. He was impregnable.

She rose, went into the kitchen, where she poured warm water into a bowl, brought soap and flannel and a soft towel.

"I must wash him," she said.

Then the old mother rose stiffly, and watched Elizabeth as she carefully washed his face, carefully brushing the big blond moustache from his mouth with the flannel. She was afraid with a bottomless fear, so she ministered to him. The old woman, jealous, said:

"Let me wipe him!"—and she kneeled on the other side drying slowly as Elizabeth washed, her big black bonnet sometimes brushing the dark head of her daughter-in-law. They worked thus in silence for a long time. They never forgot it was death, and the touch of the man's dead body gave them strange emotions, different in each of the women; a great dread possessed them both, the mother felt the lie was given to her womb, she was denied; the wife felt the utter isolation of the human soul, the child within her was a weight apart from her.

At last it was finished. He was a man of handsome body, and his face showed no traces of drink. He was blond, full-fleshed, with fine limbs. But he was dead.

"Bless him," whispered his mother, looking always at his face, and speaking out of sheer terror. "Dear lad—bless him!" She spoke in a faint, sibilant ecstasy of fear and mother love.

Elizabeth sank down again to the floor, and put her face against his neck, and trembled and shuddered. But she had to draw away again. He was dead, and her living flesh had no place against his. A great dread and weariness held her: she was so unavailing. Her life was gone like this.

"White as milk he is, clear as a twelve-month baby, bless him, the darling!" the old mother murmured to herself. "Not a mark on him, clear and clean and white, beautiful as ever a child was made," she murmured with pride. Elizabeth kept her face hidden.

"He went peaceful, Lizzie—peaceful as sleep. Isn't he beautiful, the lamb? Ay—he must ha' made his peace, Lizzie. 'Appen he made it all right, Lizzie, shut in there. He'd have time. He wouldn't look like this if he hadn't made his peace. The lamb, the dear lamb. Eh, but he had a hearty laugh. I loved to hear it. He had the heartiest laugh, Lizzie, as a lad—"

Elizabeth looked up. The man's mouth was fallen back, slightly open under the cover of the moustache. The eyes, half shut, did not show glazed in the obscurity. Life with its smoky burning gone from him, had left him apart and utterly alien to her. And she knew what a stranger he was to her. In her womb was ice of fear, because of this separate stranger with whom she had been living as one flesh. Was this what it all meant—utter, intact separateness, obscured by heat of living? In dread she turned her face away. The fact was too deadly. There had been nothing between them, and yet they had come together, exchanging their nakedness repeatedly. Each time he had taken her, they had been two isolated beings, far apart as now. He was no more responsible than she. The child was like ice in her womb. For as she looked at the dead man, her mind, cold and detached, said clearly: "Who am I? What have I been doing? I have been fighting a husband who did not exist. *He* existed all the time. What wrong have I done? What was that I have been living with? There lies the reality, this man." And her soul died in her for fear: she knew she had never seen him, he had never seen her, they had met in the dark and had fought in the dark, not knowing whom they met nor whom they fought. And now she saw, and turned silent in seeing. For she had been wrong. She had said he was something he was not; she had felt familiar with him. Whereas he was apart all the while, living as she never lived, feeling as she never felt.

In fear and shame she looked at his naked body, that she had known falsely. And he was the father of her children. Her soul was torn from her body and stood apart. She looked at his naked body and was ashamed, as if she had denied it. After all, it was itself. It seemed awful to her. She looked at his face, and she turned her own face to the wall. For his look was other than hers, his way was not her way. She had denied him what he was—she saw it now. She had refused him as himself. And this had been her life, and his life. She was grateful to death, which restored the truth. And she knew she was not dead.

And all the while her heart was bursting with grief and pity for him. What had he suffered? What stretch of horror for this helpless man! She was rigid with agony. She had not been able to help him. He had been cruelly injured, this naked man, this other being, and she could make no reparation. There were the children—but the children belonged to life. This dead man had nothing to do with them. He and she were only channels through which life had flowed to issue in the children. She was a mother—but how awful she knew it now to have been a wife. And he, dead now, how awful he must have felt it to be a husband. She felt that in the next world he would be a stranger to her. If they met there, in the beyond, they would only be ashamed of what had been before. The children had come, for some mysterious reason, out of both of them. But the children did not unite them. Now he was dead, she knew how eternally he was apart from her, how eternally he had nothing more to do with her. She saw this episode of her life closed. They had denied each other in life. Now he had withdrawn. An anguish came over her. It was finished then: it had become hopeless between them long before he died. Yet he had been her husband. But how little!

"Have you got his shirt, 'Lizabeth?"

Elizabeth turned without answering, though she strove to weep and behave as her mother-in-law expected. But she could not, she was silenced. She went into the kitchen and returned with the garment.

"It is aired," she said, grasping the cotton shirt here and there to try. She was almost ashamed to handle him; what right had she or anyone to lay hands on him; but her touch was humble on his body. It was hard work to clothe him. He was so heavy and inert. A terrible dread gripped her all the while: that he could be so heavy and utterly inert, unresponsive, apart. The horror of the distance between them was almost too much for her—it was so infinite a gap she must look across.

At last it was finished. They covered him with a sheet and left him lying, with his face bound. And she fastened the door of the little parlour, lest the children should see what was lying there. Then, with peace sunk heavy on her heart, she went about making tidy the kitchen. She knew she submitted to life, which was her immediate master. But from death, her ultimate master, she winced with fear and shame.

—1914

Katherine Mansfield

1888 – 1923

Famously described by Virginia Woolf as "the only writing I have ever been jealous of," Katherine Mansfield's work played a vital role in the development of Modernist short fiction. Her work is important for its experimentation with style and atmosphere, for its unconventional plot structures made up of loosely linked moments, and for its precise evocation of the details of human life and gradations of human psychology. Among Mansfield's favorite devices are internal monologues, daydreams, the flexible manipulation of time, the employment of different language and syntax to reflect changes in viewpoint, and the use of rhythm and sound to convey mood and meaning. Mansfield's contribution is such that, though she only lived to be 35, she was already established as a major figure in the literary world by the time of her death.

Kathleen Mansfield Beauchamp was born in Wellington, New Zealand, the third of six children of Harold Beauchamp and Annie Burnell Dyer Beauchamp. Her father was of working-class origins, but became a successful industrialist and later chairman of the Bank of New Zealand; his rise in the financial and commercial world was rewarded with a knighthood in the year of Mansfield's death. Dyer Beauchamp was a genteel woman of delicate persuasion, for whom the regimens of household management and child rearing seemed both too taxing and beneath her social ambitions. As a result, Mansfield's memories of her mother were more frequently detached than affectionate. Mansfield would have troubled relationships with her parents throughout her life, not least because they refused to accept her interest in what she once called "the whole octave of the sex" and were alarmed by her relationships with both men and women.

Mansfield's school years were divided between the country village of Karori and the capital, Wellington, where the family moved to a mansion at Tinakori Road (the setting for "The Garden Party"). In 1903, she and her sisters entered Queen's College in London, where she immersed herself in French and German while contemplating a career as a cellist. Mansfield also advanced her literary career as she became a contributor to and editor of the College's magazine. It was at Queen's College that she developed a close relationship with Ida Baker (whom she referred to as Leslie Moore)—a relationship Mansfield would depend upon for the rest of her life. By this time, the young author and musician Kathleen Beauchamp had decided to adopt the professional name of "Katherine Mansfield."

At the conclusion of her studies in London, Mansfield returned unwillingly to Wellington. Having flourished artistically in the cosmopolitan environment of London, she despised the provincial lifestyle of her home, and for nearly two years she exhausted her parents with constant pleas to return to England. In 1908, with the support of Baker, she was given leave to return to London and never saw New Zealand again.

Within weeks of returning, Mansfield fell in love with a fellow musician, Garnett Trowell. When their relationship collapsed within a few months, she impulsively married G.C. Bowden, a singing teacher whose name she bore for the next nine years, despite having left him on their wedding night. She returned to Trowell and traveled with his opera company until she became pregnant and was sent by her mother to an unfashionable Bavarian spa for the duration of her pregnancy, which ended in miscarriage. During her stay in Germany, she wrote a series of satirical sketches of German characters that were published individually in *The New Age*; they were later collected and published as *In a German Pension* (1911). On her return to London Mansfield was diagnosed with rheumatic fever; it was later discovered to be gonorrhea, a condition that contributed to her failing health for the rest of her life.

By late 1911, Mansfield had begun contributing to *Rhythm*, an avant-garde quarterly edited by John Middleton Murry. A year later she became *Rhythm*'s editor and began a lifelong, tumultuous love affair with Murry. The "Two Tigers," as they were known, cultivated several close relationships within literary circles, most notably with D.H. Lawrence (a friendship that would end bitterly in 1920), Virginia Woolf (with whom she shared an important mutual influence), and Aldous Huxley. Murry, Mansfield, and Lawrence shared a deep interest in Russian literature, with Murry particularly enamored with Dostoevsky and Mansfield drawing inspiration from the work of Chekhov. In 1913, *Rhythm* became *The Blue Review* after the publisher absconded, leaving Mansfield and Murry with considerable debts. *The Blue Review* folded after only three months, despite an impressive list of contributors including Lawrence, H.G. Wells, Hugh Walpole, and T.S. Eliot.

In 1915, Mansfield's youngest brother Leslie was killed in France. Her profound grief sent her into self-imposed exile in that country, where in an effort to console herself she began writing stories about her childhood in New Zealand; thus began her most productive and successful period as a writer. That same year Mansfield finally divorced G.C. Bowden and married John Murry. Later in the year she was diagnosed with tuberculosis; for the remaining years of her life she traveled between London, Switzerland, and the French Riviera in search of modern treatments and salubrious climates.

In 1919 Mansfield began reviewing novels for the *Athenaeum*, the editor of which was Murry, and a year later she published *Bliss, and Other Stories*. In the next two years she wrote many of her most notable works, several of which are included in *The Garden Party and Other Stories* (1922). In October of that year she entered the Gurdjieff Institute in France for controversial therapy under the guidance of mystic George Ivanovich Gurdjieff. In early 1923, Mansfield suffered a severe lung hemorrhage upon rapidly climbing the steps to her room; she died later that evening. Although Mansfield had requested in her will that Murry publish as little of her work as possible, two further collections of her stories were published, as well as a collection of poetry and other works.

The relatively small body of work that Mansfield left behind addresses grand themes such as the evolution of the self, the terrors of childhood, the solitude of the outsider, and the reality of death. Malcolm Cowley, a contemporary of Mansfield, wrote that her stories "have a thesis: namely, that life is a very wonderful spectacle, but disagreeable for the actors."

⌘⌘⌘

The Garden Party

And after all the weather was ideal. They could not have had a more perfect day for a garden party if they had ordered it. Windless, warm, the sky without a cloud. Only the blue was veiled with a haze of light gold, as it is sometimes in early summer. The gardener had been up since dawn, mowing the lawns and sweeping them, until the grass and the dark flat rosettes where the daisy plants had been seemed to shine. As for the roses, you could not help feeling they understood that roses are the only flowers that impress people at garden parties, the only flowers that everybody is certain of knowing. Hundreds, yes, literally hundreds, had come out in a single night; the green bushes bowed down as though they had been visited by archangels.

Breakfast was not yet over before the men came to put up the marquee.

"Where do you want the marquee put, mother?"

"My dear child, it's no use asking me. I'm determined to leave everything to you children this year. Forget I am your mother. Treat me as an honoured guest."

But Meg could not possibly go and supervise the men. She had washed her hair before breakfast, and she sat drinking her coffee in a green turban, with a dark wet curl stamped on each cheek. Jose, the butterfly, always came down in a silk petticoat and a kimono jacket.

"You'll have to go, Laura; you're the artistic one."

Away Laura flew, still holding her piece of bread and butter. It's so delicious to have an excuse for eating out of doors and, besides, she loved having to arrange things; she always felt she could do it so much better than anybody else.

Four men in their shirt sleeves stood grouped together on the garden path. They carried staves[1] covered with rolls of canvas and they had big toolbags slung on their backs. They looked impressive. Laura wished now that she was not holding that piece of bread and butter, but there was nowhere to put it and she couldn't possibly throw it away. She blushed and tried to look severe and even a little bit shortsighted as she came up to them.

"Good morning," she said, copying her mother's voice. But that sounded so fearfully affected that she was ashamed, and stammered like a little girl, "Oh—er—have you come—is it about the marquee?"

"That's right, miss," said the tallest of the men, a lanky, freckled fellow, and he shifted his tool bag, knocked back his straw hat and smiled down at her. "That's about it."

His smile was so easy, so friendly, that Laura recovered. What nice eyes he had, small, but such a dark blue! And now she looked at the others, they were smiling too. "Cheer up, we won't bite," their smile seemed to say. How very nice workmen were! And what a beautiful morning! She mustn't mention the morning; she must be businesslike. The marquee.

"Well, what about the lily lawn? Would that do?"

And she pointed to the lily lawn with the hand that didn't hold the bread and butter. They turned, they stared in the direction. A little fat chap thrust out his underlip and the tall fellow frowned.

"I don't fancy it," said he. "Not conspicuous enough. You see, with a thing like a marquee"—and he turned to Laura in his easy way—"you want to put it somewhere where it'll give you a bang slap in the eye, if you follow me."

Laura's upbringing made her wonder for a moment whether it was quite respectful of a workman to talk to her of bangs slap in the eye. But she did quite follow him.

"A corner of the tennis court," she suggested. "But the band's going to be in one corner."

"H'm, going to have a band, are you?" said another of the workmen. He was pale. He had a haggard look as his dark eyes scanned the tennis court. What was he thinking?

"Only a very small band," said Laura gently. Perhaps he wouldn't mind so much if the band was quite small. But the tall fellow interrupted.

"Look here, miss, that's the place. Against those trees. Over there. That'll do fine."

[1] *staves* Rods.

Against the karakas. Then the karaka trees would be hidden. And they were so lovely, with their broad, gleaming leaves, and their clusters of yellow fruit. They were like trees you imagined growing on a desert island, proud, solitary, lifting their leaves and fruits to the sun in a kind of silent splendour. Must they be hidden by a marquee?

They must. Already the men had shouldered their staves and were making for the place. Only the tall fellow was left. He bent down, pinched a sprig of lavender, put his thumb and forefinger to his nose and snuffed up the smell. When Laura saw that gesture she forgot all about the karakas in her wonder at him caring for things like that—caring for the smell of lavender. How many men that she knew would have done such a thing? Oh, how extraordinarily nice workmen were, she thought. Why couldn't she have workmen for friends rather than the silly boys she danced with and who came to Sunday night supper? She would get on much better with men like these.

It's all the fault, she decided, as the tall fellow drew something on the back of an envelope, something that was to be looped up or left to hang, of these absurd class distinctions. Well, for her part, she didn't feel them. Not a bit, not an atom.... And now there came the chock-chock of wooden hammers. Someone whistled, someone sang out, "Are you right there, matey?" "Matey!" The friendliness of it, the—the—Just to prove how happy she was, just to show the tall fellow how at home she felt, and how she despised stupid conventions, Laura took a big bite of her bread and butter as she stared at the little drawing. She felt just like a work girl.

"Laura, Laura, where are you? Telephone, Laura!" a voice cried from the house.

"Coming!" Away she skimmed, over the lawn, up the path, up the steps, across the veranda and into the porch. In the hall her father and Laurie were brushing their hats ready to go to the office.

"I say, Laura," said Laurie very fast, "you might just give a squiz[1] at my coat before this afternoon. See if it wants pressing."

"I will," said she. Suddenly she couldn't stop herself. She ran at Laurie and gave him a small, quick squeeze. "Oh, I do love parties, don't you?" gasped Laura.

"Ra–ther," said Laurie's warm, boyish voice, and he squeezed his sister too and gave her a gentle push. "Dash off to the telephone, old girl."

The telephone. "Yes, yes; oh yes. Kitty? Good morning, dear. Come to lunch? Do, dear. Delighted, of course. It will only be a very scratch[2] meal—just the sandwich crusts and broken meringue shells and what's left over. Yes, isn't it a perfect morning? Your white? Oh, I certainly should. One moment—hold the line. Mother's calling." And Laura sat back. "What, mother? Can't hear."

Mrs. Sheridan's voice floated down the stairs. "Tell her to wear that sweet hat she had on last Sunday."

"Mother says you're to wear that sweet hat you had on last Sunday. Good. One o'clock. Bye-bye."

Laura put back the receiver, flung her arms over her head, took a deep breath, stretched and let them fall. "Huh," she sighed, and the moment after the sigh she sat up quickly. She was still, listening. All the doors in the house seemed to be open. The house was alive with soft, quick steps and running voices. The green baize door[3] that led to the kitchen regions swung open and shut with a muffled thud. And now there came a long, chuckling absurd sound. It was the heavy piano being moved on its stiff castors. But the air! If you stopped to notice, was the air always like this? Little faint winds were playing chase in at the tops of the windows, out at the doors. And there were two tiny spots of sun, one on the inkpot, one on a silver photograph frame, playing too. Darling little spots. Especially the one on the inkpot lid. It was quite warm. A warm little silver star. She could have kissed it.

The front door bell pealed and there sounded the rustle of Sadie's print skirt on the stairs. A man's voice murmured; Sadie answered, careless, "I'm sure I don't know. Wait. I'll ask Mrs. Sheridan."

"What is it, Sadie?" Laura came into the hall.

[1] *squiz* Glance.

[2] *scratch* Quickly thrown together.

[3] *baize door* Door, covered with a green felt-like material, that separates the kitchen from the rest of the house in large English homes.

"It's the florist, Miss Laura."

It was, indeed. There, just inside the door, stood a wide, shallow tray full of pots of pink lilies. No other kind. Nothing but lilies—canna lilies, big pink flowers, wide open, radiant, almost frighteningly alive on bright crimson stems.

"O–oh, Sadie!" said Laura, and the sound was like a little moan. She crouched down as if to warm herself at that blaze of lilies; she felt they were in her fingers, on her lips, growing in her breast.

"It's some mistake," she said faintly. "Nobody ever ordered so many. Sadie, go and find mother."

But at that moment Mrs. Sheridan joined them.

"It's quite right," she said calmly. "Yes, I ordered them. Aren't they lovely?" She pressed Laura's arm. "I was passing the shop yesterday, and I saw them in the window. And I suddenly thought for once in my life I shall have enough canna lilies. The garden party will be a good excuse."

"But I thought you said you didn't mean to interfere," said Laura. Sadie had gone. The florist's man was still outside at his van. She put her arm round her mother's neck and gently, very gently, she bit her mother's ear.

"My darling child, you wouldn't like a logical mother, would you? Don't do that. Here's the man."

He carried more lilies still, another whole tray.

"Bank them up, just inside the door, on both sides of the porch, please," said Mrs. Sheridan. "Don't you agree, Laura?"

"Oh, I *do*, mother."

In the drawing room Meg, Jose and good little Hans had at last succeeded in moving the piano.

"Now, if we put this chesterfield against the wall and move everything out of the room except the chairs, don't you think?"

"Quite."

"Hans, move these tables into the smoking room, and bring a sweeper to take these marks off the carpet and—one moment, Hans—" Jose loved giving orders to the servants and they loved obeying her. She always made them feel they were taking part in some drama. "Tell mother and Miss Laura to come here at once."

"Very good, Miss Jose."

She turned to Meg. "I want to hear what the piano sounds like, just in case I'm asked to sing this afternoon. Let's try over 'This Life is Weary.'"

Pom! Ta-ta-ta *Tee*-ta! The piano burst out so passionately that Jose's face changed. She clasped her hands. She looked mournfully and enigmatically at her mother and Laura as they came in.

> This Life is *Wee*-ary,
> A Tear—a Sigh.
> A Love that *Chan*-ges,
> This Life is *Wee*-ary,
> A Tear—a Sigh.
> A Love that *Chan*-ges,
> And then … Goodbye!

But at the word "Goodbye," and although the piano sounded more desperate than ever, her face broke into a brilliant, dreadfully unsympathetic smile.

"Aren't I in good voice, mummy?" she beamed.

> This Life is *Wee*-ary,
> Hope comes to Die.
> A Dream—a *Wa*-kening.

But now Sadie interrupted them. "What is it, Sadie?"

"If you please, m'm, cook says have you got the flags for the sandwiches?"

"The flags for the sandwiches, Sadie?" echoed Mrs. Sheridan dreamily. And the children knew by her face that she hadn't got them. "Let me see." And she said to Sadie firmly, "Tell cook I'll let her have them in ten minutes."

Sadie went.

"Now, Laura," said her mother quickly, "come with me into the smoking room. I've got the names somewhere on the back of an envelope. You'll have to write them out for me. Meg, go upstairs this minute and take that wet thing off your head. Jose, run and finish dressing this instant. Do you hear me, children, or shall I have to tell your father when he comes home tonight? And—and, Jose, pacify cook if you do go into the kitchen, will you? I'm terrified of her this morning."

The envelope was found at last behind the dining room clock, though how it had got there Mrs. Sheridan could not imagine.

"One of you children must have stolen it out of my bag, because I remember vividly—cream cheese and lemon curd. Have you done that?"

"Yes."

"Egg and—" Mrs. Sheridan held the envelope away from her. "It looks like mice. It can't be mice, can it?"

"Olive, pet," said Laura, looking over her shoulder.

"Yes, of course, olive. What a horrible combination it sounds. Egg and olive."

They were finished at last, and Laura took them off to the kitchen. She found Jose there pacifying the cook, who did not look at all terrifying.

"I have never seen such exquisite sandwiches," said Jose's rapturous voice. "How many kinds did you say there were, cook? Fifteen?"

"Fifteen, Miss Jose."

"Well, cook, I congratulate you."

Cook swept up crusts with the long sandwich knife, and smiled broadly.

"Godber's has come," announced Sadie, issuing out of the pantry. She had seen the man pass the window.

That meant the cream puffs had come. Godber's were famous for their cream puffs. Nobody ever thought of making them at home.

"Bring them in and put them on the table, my girl," ordered cook.

Sadie brought them in and went back to the door. Of course Laura and Jose were far too grown up to really care about such things. All the same, they couldn't help agreeing that the puffs looked very attractive. Very. Cook began arranging them, shaking off the extra icing sugar.

"Don't they carry one back to all one's parties?" said Laura.

"I suppose they do," said practical Jose, who never liked to be carried back. "They look beautifully light and feathery, I must say."

"Have one each, my dears," said cook in her comfortable voice. "Yer ma won't know."

Oh, impossible. Fancy cream puffs so soon after breakfast. The very idea made one shudder. All the same, two minutes later Jose and Laura were licking their fingers with that absorbed inward look that only comes from whipped cream.

"Let's go into the garden, out by the back way," suggested Laura. "I want to see how the men are getting on with the marquee. They're such awfully nice men."

But the back door was blocked by cook, Sadie, Godber's man and Hans.

Something had happened.

"Tuk-tuk-tuk," clucked cook like an agitated hen. Sadie had her hand clapped to her cheek as though she had toothache. Han's face was screwed up in the effort to understand. Only Godber's man seemed to be enjoying himself; it was his story.

"What's the matter? What's happened?"

"There's been a horrible accident," said cook. "A man killed."

"A man killed! Where? How? When?"

But Godber's man wasn't going to have his story snatched from under his very nose.

"Know those little cottages just below here, miss?" Know them? Of course she knew them. "Well, there's a young chap living there, name of Scott, a carter. His horse shied at a traction engine, corner of Hawke Street this morning, and he was thrown out on the back of his head. Killed."

"Dead!" Laura stared at Godber's man.

"Dead when they picked him up," said Godber's man with relish. "They were taking the body home as I come up here." And he said to the cook, "He's left a wife and five little ones."

"Jose, come here." Laura caught hold of her sister's sleeve and dragged her through the kitchen to the other side of the green baize door. There she paused and leaned against it. "Jose!" she said, horrified, "however are we going to stop everything?"

"Stop everything, Laura!" cried Jose in astonishment. "What do you mean?"

"Stop the garden party, of course." Why did Jose pretend?

But Jose was still more amazed. "Stop the garden party? My dear Laura, don't be so absurd. Of course we can't do anything of the kind. Nobody expects us to. Don't be so extravagant."

"But we can't possibly have a garden party with a man dead just outside the front gate."

That really was extravagant, for the little cottages were in a lane to themselves at the very bottom of a steep rise that led up to the house. A broad road ran between. True, they were far too near. They were the greatest possible eyesore and they had no right to be in that neighbourhood at all. They were little mean dwellings painted a chocolate brown. In the garden patches there was nothing but cabbage stalks, sick hens and tomato cans. The very smoke coming out of their chimneys was poverty stricken. Little rags and shreds of smoke, so unlike the great silvery plumes that uncurled from the Sheridans' chimneys. Washerwomen lived in the lane and sweeps and a cobbler and a man whose house front was studded all over with minute birdcages. Children swarmed. When the Sheridans were little they were forbidden to set foot there because of the revolting language and of what they might catch. But since they were grown up Laura and Laurie on their prowls sometimes walked through. It was disgusting and sordid. They came out with a shudder. But still one must go everywhere; one must see everything. So through they went.

"And just think of what the band would sound like to that poor woman," said Laura.

"Oh, Laura!" Jose began to be seriously annoyed. "If you're going to stop a band playing every time someone has an accident, you'll lead a very strenuous life. I'm every bit as sorry about it as you. I feel just as sympathetic." Her eyes hardened. She looked at her sister just as she used to when they were little and fighting together. "You won't bring a drunken workman back to life by being sentimental," she said softly.

"Drunk! Who said he was drunk?" Laura turned furiously on Jose. She said just as they had used to say on those occasions, "I'm going straight up to tell mother."

"Do, dear," cooed Jose.

"Mother, can I come into your room?" Laura turned the big glass doorknob.

"Of course, child. Why, what's the matter? What's given you such a colour?" And Mrs. Sheridan turned round from her dressing table. She was trying on a new hat.

"Mother, a man's been killed," began Laura.

"*Not* in the garden?" interrupted her mother.

"No, no!"

"Oh, what a fright you gave me!" Mrs. Sheridan sighed with relief and took off the big hat and held it on her knees.

"But listen, mother," said Laura. Breathless, half choking, she told the dreadful story. "Of course, we can't have our party, can we?" she pleaded. "The band and everybody arriving. They'd hear us, mother; they're nearly neighbours!"

To Laura's astonishment her mother behaved just like Jose; it was harder to bear because she seemed amused. She refused to take Laura seriously.

"But, my dear child, use your common sense. It's only by accident we've heard of it. If someone had died there normally—and I can't understand how they keep alive in those poky little holes—we should still be having our party, shouldn't we?"

Laura had to say "yes" to that, but she felt it was all wrong. She sat down on her mother's sofa and pinched the cushion frill.

"Mother, isn't it really terribly heartless of us?" she asked.

"Darling!" Mrs. Sheridan got up and came over to her, carrying the hat. Before Laura could stop her she had popped it on. "My child!" said her mother, "the hat is yours. It's made for you. It's much too young for me. I have never seen you look such a picture. Look at yourself!" And she held up her hand-mirror.

"But, mother," Laura began again. She couldn't look at herself; she turned aside.

This time Mrs. Sheridan lost patience just as Jose had done.

"You are being very absurd, Laura," she said coldly. "People like that don't expect sacrifices from us. And it's not very sympathetic to spoil everybody's enjoyment as you're doing now."

"I don't understand," said Laura, and she walked quickly out of the room into her own bedroom. There, quite by chance, the first thing she saw was this charming girl in the mirror, in her black hat trimmed with gold daisies and a long black velvet ribbon. Never had she imagined she could look like that. Is mother right? she thought. And now she hoped her mother was right. Am I being extravagant? Perhaps it was extravagant. Just for a moment she had another glimpse of that poor woman and those little children and the body being carried into the house. But it all seemed blurred, unreal, like a picture in the newspaper. I'll remember it again after the party's over, she decided. And somehow that seemed quite the best plan. …

Lunch was over by half-past one. By half-past two they were all ready for the fray. The green-coated band had arrived and was established in a corner of the tennis court.

"My dear!" trilled Kitty Maitland, "aren't they too like frogs for words? You ought to have arranged them round the pond with the conductor in the middle on a leaf."

Laurie arrived and hailed them on his way to dress. At the sight of him Laura remembered the accident again. She wanted to tell him. If Laurie agreed with the others, then it was bound to be all right. And she followed him into the hall.

"Laurie!"

"Hallo!" He was halfway upstairs, but when he turned round and saw Laura he suddenly puffed out his cheeks and goggled his eyes at her. "My word, Laura! You do look stunning," said Laurie. "What an absolutely topping hat!"

Laura said faintly "Is it?" and smiled up at Laurie and didn't tell him after all.

Soon after that people began coming in streams. The band struck up; the hired waiters ran from the house to the marquee. Wherever you looked there were couples strolling, bending to the flowers, greeting, moving on over the lawn. They were like bright birds that had alighted in the Sheridans' garden for this one afternoon, on their way to—where? Ah, what happiness it is to be with people who all are happy, to press hands, press cheeks, smile into eyes.

"Darling Laura, how well you look!"

"What a becoming hat, child!"

"Laura, you look quite Spanish. I've never seen you look so striking."

And Laura, glowing, answered softly, "Have you had tea? Won't you have an ice? The passion fruit ices really are rather special." She ran to her father and begged him: "Daddy darling, can't the band have something to drink?"

And the perfect afternoon slowly ripened, slowly faded, slowly its petals closed.

"Never a more delightful garden party …" "The greatest success …" "Quite the most …"

Laura helped her mother with the goodbyes. They stood side by side in the porch till it was all over.

"All over, all over, thank heaven," said Mrs. Sheridan. "Round up the others, Laura. Let's go and have some fresh coffee. I'm exhausted. Yes, it's been very successful. But oh, these parties, these parties! Why will you children insist on giving parties!" And they all of them sat down in the deserted marquee.

"Have a sandwich, daddy dear. I wrote the flag."

"Thanks." Mr. Sheridan took a bite and the sandwich was gone. He took another. "I suppose you didn't hear of a beastly accident that happened today?" he said.

"My dear," said Mrs. Sheridan, holding up her hand, "we did. It nearly ruined the party. Laura insisted we should put it off."

"Oh, mother!" Laura didn't want to be teased about it.

"It was a horrible affair all the same," said Mr. Sheridan. "The chap was married too. Lived just below in the lane, and leaves a wife and half a dozen kiddies, so they say."

An awkward little silence fell. Mrs. Sheridan fidgeted with her cup. Really, it was very tactless of father…

Suddenly she looked up. There on the table were all those sandwiches, cakes, puffs, all uneaten, all going to be wasted. She had one of her brilliant ideas.

"I know," she said. "Let's make up a basket. Let's send that poor creature some of this perfectly good food. At any rate, it will be the greatest treat for the children. Don't you agree? And she's sure to have neighbours calling in and so on. What a point to have it all ready prepared. Laura!" She jumped up. "Get me the big basket out of the stairs cupboard."

"But, mother, do you really think it's a good idea?" said Laura.

Again, how curious, she seemed to be different from them all. To take scraps from their party. Would the poor woman really like that?

"Of course! What's the matter with you today? An hour or two ago you were insisting on us being sympathetic."

Oh well! Laura ran for the basket. It was filled, it was now heaped by her mother.

"Take it yourself, darling," said she. "Run down just as you are. No, wait, take the arum lilies too. People of that class are so impressed by arum lilies."

"The stems will ruin her lace frock," said practical Jose.

So they would. Just in time. "Only the basket, then. And, Laura!"—her mother followed her out of the marquee—"don't on any account—"

"What, mother?"

No, better not put such ideas into the child's head! "Nothing! Run along."

It was just growing dusky as Laura shut their garden gates. A big dog ran by like a shadow. The road gleamed white, and down below in the hollow the little cottages were in deep shade. How quiet it seemed after the afternoon. Here she was going down the hill to somewhere where a man lay dead, and she couldn't realise it. Why couldn't she? She stopped a minute. And it seemed to her that kisses, voices, tinkling spoons, laughter, the smell of crushed grass were somehow inside her. She had no room for anything else. How strange! She looked up at the pale sky, and all she thought was, "Yes, it was the most successful party."

Now the broad road was crossed. The lane began, smoky and dark. Women in shawls and men's tweed caps hurried by. Men hung over the palings; the children played in the doorways. A low hum came from the mean little cottages. In some of them there was a flicker of light, and a shadow, crab-like, moved across the window. Laura bent her head and hurried on. She wished now she had put on a coat. How her frock shone! And the big hat with the velvet streamer—if only it was another hat! Were the people looking at her? They must be. It was a mistake to have come; she knew all along it was a mistake. Should she go back even now?

No, too late. This was the house. It must be. A dark knot of people stood outside. Beside the gate an old, old woman with a crutch sat in a chair, watching. She had her feet on a newspaper. The voices stopped as Laura drew near. The group parted. It was as though she was expected, as though they had known she was coming here.

Laura was terribly nervous. Tossing the velvet ribbon over her shoulder, she said to a woman standing by, "Is this Mrs. Scott's house?" and the woman, smiling queerly, said, "It is, my lass."

Oh, to be away from this! She actually said, "Help me, God," as she walked up the tiny path and knocked. To be away from those staring eyes, or to be covered up in anything, one of those women's shawls even. I'll just leave the basket and go, she decided. I shan't even wait for it to be emptied.

Then the door opened. A little woman in black showed in the gloom.

Laura said, "Are you Mrs. Scott?" But to her horror the woman answered, "Walk in, please, miss," and she was shut in the passage.

"No," said Laura, "I don't want to come in. I only want to leave this basket. Mother sent—"

The little woman in the gloomy passage seemed not to have heard her. "Step this way, please, miss," she said in an oily voice, and Laura followed her.

She found herself in a wretched little low kitchen, lighted by a smoky lamp. There was a woman sitting before the fire.

"Em," said the little creature who had let her in. "Em! It's a young lady." She turned to Laura. She said meaningly, "I'm 'er sister, miss. You'll excuse 'er, won't you?"

"Oh, but of course!" said Laura. "Please, please don't disturb her. I—I only want to leave—"

But at that moment the woman at the fire turned round. Her face, puffed up, red, with swollen eyes and swollen lips, looked terrible. She seemed as though she couldn't understand why Laura was there. What did it mean? Why was this stranger standing in the kitchen with a basket? What was it all about? And the poor face puckered up again.

"All right, my dear," said the other. "I'll thenk the young lady."

And again she began, "You'll excuse her, miss, I'm sure," and her face, swollen too, tried an oily smile.

Laura only wanted to get out, to get away. She was back in the passage. The door opened. She walked straight through into the bedroom, where the dead man was lying.

"You'd like a look at 'im, wouldn't you?" said Em's sister, and she brushed past Laura over to the bed. "Don't be afraid, my lass"—and now her voice sounded fond and sly, and fondly she drew down the sheet—"'e looks a picture. There's nothing to show. Come along, my dear."

Laura came.

There lay a young man, fast asleep—sleeping so soundly, so deeply, that he was far, far away from them both. Oh, so remote, so peaceful. He was dreaming. Never wake him up again. His head was sunk in the pillow, his eyes were closed; they were blind under the closed eyelids. He was given up to his dream. What did garden parties and baskets and lace frocks matter to him? He was far from all those things. He was wonderful, beautiful. While they were laughing and while the band was playing, this marvel had come to the lane. Happy … happy.… All is well, said that sleeping face. This is just as it should be. I am content.

But all the same you had to cry, and she couldn't go out of the room without saying something to him. Laura gave a loud childish sob.

"Forgive my hat," she said.

And this time she didn't wait for Em's sister. She found her way out of the door, down the path past all those dark people. At the corner of the lane she met Laurie.

He stepped out of the shadow. "Is that you, Laura?"

"Yes."

"Mother was getting anxious. Was it all right?"

"Yes, quite, Oh, Laurie!" She took his arm, she pressed up against him.

"I say, you're not crying, are you?" asked her brother.

Laura shook her head. She was.

Laurie put his arm round her shoulder. "Don't cry," he said in his warm, loving voice. "Was it awful?"

"No," sobbed Laura. "It was simply marvellous. But, Laurie—" She stopped, she looked at her brother. "Isn't life," she stammered, "isn't life—" But what life was she couldn't explain. No matter. He quite understood.

"*Isn't* it, darling?" said Laurie.

—1922

T.S. Eliot

1888 – 1965

The poetry and prose of T.S. Eliot played a key role in the transformation of English writing that occurred in the first decades of the twentieth century. His Modernist poems of the 1910s and 1920s (*The Waste Land* chief among them) were revolutionary both in their form and in their content—yet Eliot himself, the most unlikely of revolutionaries, became an icon of the literary establishment. He voiced in unique fashion the bleakness and despair that was characteristically felt by many in the early twentieth century—yet he became a leading voice of traditional Christianity. He embraced difficulty as the literary strategy most consonant with the character of his era—yet he also wrote a succession of highly accessible plays for the popular stage. He strove for Christian virtue, but has been strongly criticized for expressions of hostility towards women and towards Jews. In short, he is a central figure of the twentieth century not only because his works are central documents of its literature, but also because they embody many of the paradoxes of the age.

Thomas Stearns Eliot was born in St. Louis, Missouri, in 1888, the youngest son in a distinguished New England family that traced its roots back to the first Puritan settlers of Massachusetts. Eliot followed his older brother to Harvard in 1906, where he joined the board of Harvard's literary magazine and started a lifelong friendship with Conrad Aiken, a fellow board member. In 1909, the year before he completed his MA, Eliot began drafting the poems that would become "The Love Song of J. Alfred Prufrock," "Preludes," "Portrait of a Lady," and "Rhapsody on a Windy Night." He spent a postgraduate year at the Sorbonne in Paris and then began doctoral studies in philosophy at Harvard. His dissertation was on the ideas of the then-influential French philosopher Henri Bergson, whose emphasis on the intuitive and subjective aspects of reality and on the importance of change may have influenced Eliot's poetic explorations of the human psyche. Certainly a strong awareness of the subjectivity of perception, of the importance of the unconscious, and of alienation and social claustrophobia in an unpredictably changing world are all powerful elements in Eliot's early poetry.

While both Eliot and Aiken were in London in 1914, Aiken showed the manuscript of "Prufrock" to American poet and critic Ezra Pound (then living abroad), who immediately recognized it as extraordinary work. The alliance of Pound and Eliot marked the beginning not only of Eliot's career as a poet (Pound and his wife financed the 1917 publication of *Prufrock and Other Observations*), but of a literary collaboration that profoundly influenced the development of modern literature.

"The Love Song of J. Alfred Prufrock," as critic James F. Knapp said, changed "our conception of what kind of shape a poem might take." With little connecting or transitional material, the poem juxtaposes disparate thoughts and scenes and combines classical literary references with images of urban, industrial twentieth-century life. Eliot was heavily influenced by French Symbolist poets Charles Baudelaire and Jules Laforgue. Their powerful, disconnected imagery, their ironic, detached tones, and their themes of alienation helped Eliot discover his own poetic voice. With strong rhythms that blend formal and informal speech and striking metaphors, Eliot creates an ironic love song in the frustrated inner voice of "Prufrock"'s central figure, who, in the face of his bleak physical and spiritual life, is unable to act on his love.

Inspired by what he referred to as "the mind of Europe," and with some persuasion by Pound, Eliot chose England as his permanent home. His decision was solidified by an impulsive decision in 1915 to marry Vivienne Haigh-Wood, an Englishwoman whom he had met that spring. In England, Eliot balanced writing and editorial work for the avant-garde magazine *The Egoist* with more reliable employment as a schoolteacher and then as a bank clerk at Lloyd's Bank in London.

Eliot's first book of criticism, *The Sacred Wood* (1920), established him as a discerning and erudite literary critic and introduced a new set of critical precepts that would become highly influential. Eliot placed a high value on "impersonality" in poetry, and on the idea of an "objective correlative" as a means of expressing emotion through a set of objects, circumstances, or chain of events. Eliot's introduction of these ideas to the literary world helped pave the way for the critical approach known as "New Criticism." In the writings of I.A. Richards and others of this school, the focus was on the work itself as an artefact independent of authorial intention. Eliot's essays also examined his sense of the necessary difficulty of modern writing, which he believed had the nearly impossible task of synthesizing the seemingly unrelated, chaotic experiences of modern citizens.

By 1921, affected by the strain of overwork and the increasing pressure of his wife's failing physical and mental health, Eliot had a nervous breakdown. During a three-month-long rest cure, he was finally able to complete *The Waste Land*, a project he had begun in 1914. Originally composed as a series of narrative poems, *The Waste Land* was considerably longer in its original version; Pound helped Eliot pare down and fuse the diverse materials into the poem's final form. Published in 1922, *The Waste Land* deviated far more decisively than had "Prufrock" from accepted notions of what constituted poetry. Written in fragmented form, this poem of complex imagery, multiple voices, jazz rhythms, and dense literary and mythological allusions jumps between perspectives and scenes without connective or transitional passages. With its radical break from established conventions in structure, theme, and expression, and its blending of western and of non-western ideologies, *The Waste Land* can be disorienting for readers—so much so, in fact, that when the poem first appeared some writers and critics wondered if the poem was a hoax orchestrated by Eliot and his literary friends.

Much as *The Waste Land* was derided in some quarters, in others it established Eliot as a groundbreaking writer. Meanwhile, his critical writing in the international literary journal *The Criterion* (which Eliot founded in 1922) helped to round out his reputation as one of London's leading literary figures. In 1925, Eliot was recruited by the publishing firm Faber and Gwyer (later Faber and Faber) as a literary editor and board member. The position, which he held for many years, further extended Eliot's influence, as he was able to cultivate young writers—such as W.H. Auden—whose work he found promising.

Eliot's next major poem, "The Hollow Men" (1925), in some ways extends *The Waste Land*'s articulation of alienation and despair, but it also deals with more transcendent themes of what Eliot called "the salvation of the soul." Eliot's Christian faith continued to strengthen, and in 1927, the same year he was naturalized as a British citizen, Eliot was baptized into the Church of England. Religion thereafter became central to his life, and in 1933 he moved to Glenville Place presbytery, where he served as a church warden for seven years. He wrote a series of poetic meditations on religious themes and scenarios, including "Journey of the Magi" (1927) and "Marina" (1930). Steeped in Eliot's studies of Shakespeare and Dante, these works meditate on spiritual growth while experimenting with more traditional dramatic forms. The dramatic monologue form in which "Journey of the Magi" is constructed, for example, is reminiscent of Robert Browning's work.

Much of Eliot's later career focused on dramatic writing. For many years he worked on *Sweeney Agonistes*, an unfinished experimental play of modern life, written in rhythmic prose accented by drum beats. He then published two ecclesiastical dramas, one of which was *Murder in the Cathedral* (1935), a ritual drama based on the murder of Thomas à Becket, before turning to clever West End social dramas such as *The Cocktail Party* (1950). Though innovative in their attempts to reconcile classical drama with modern themes, these plays have not been successfully revived in recent decades. Ironically, however, a book of playful children's verse that Eliot wrote for his godchildren, *Old Possum's Book of Practical Cats* (1939), has been much more successful on the stage than any of Eliot's plays; it was adapted by British composer Andrew Lloyd Webber into the hit musical *Cats* (1980).

Vivienne's mental illness intensified until, in 1933, Eliot felt compelled to separate from her; she was unable to accept this decision, and continued to seek him out, believing he had been kidnapped, until her institutionalization in 1938. Despite this emotional turbulence and a busy lecturing schedule, Eliot produced four long poems in the late 1930s and early 1940s that together, published as *Four Quartets* (1943), he considered his crowning achievement. Comprising "Burnt Norton," "The Dry Salvages," "East Coker," and "Little Gidding," *Four Quartets* was in part inspired by the later string quartets of Beethoven. With its powerfully suggestive imagery and elaborate patterns of sound, it is among Eliot's most complex and technically masterful works. It also gives voice to Eliot's conviction that, in a world otherwise devoid of meaning, submission to God is essential.

The late years of Eliot's life were filled with personal happiness and public recognition of his contribution to modern literature. He was awarded eighteen honorary degrees, and in 1948 he was awarded both a Nobel Prize for Literature and the British Order of Merit. Vivienne having died in 1947, in 1957 Eliot married Valerie Fletcher and enjoyed what he described as the only happy period of his life since childhood. He died in London in 1965 and was buried, according to his wishes, in his ancestors' parish church at East Coker. The plaque on the church wall bears his chosen epitaph, from *Four Quartets*: "In my beginning is my end, in my end is my beginning."

Near the end of his life Eliot commented, with sly irony, that he would "perhaps have a certain historical place in the literary history of our period." And indeed, he was lauded on his death as a unique literary figure; his obituary in *Life* magazine declared that "our age beyond any doubt has been, and will continue to be, the Age of Eliot." In subsequent decades the praise has been less effusive, and in two respects Eliot's work has been sharply criticized: most critics now acknowledge elements of misogyny and of anti-Semitism in his writing. But the impact of his poetic innovation is lasting, and a sense of the centrality of Eliot's work to the literary history of the twentieth century has remained constant. As Northrop Frye observed, "Whether he is liked or disliked is of no importance, but he must be read."

⌘⌘⌘

The Love Song of J. Alfred Prufrock [1]

S'io credesse che mia risposta fosse
A persona che mai tornasse al mondo,
Questa fiamma staria senza piu scosse.
Ma perciocche giammai di questo fondo
Non torno viva alcun, s'i'odo il vero,
Senza tema d'infamia ti rispondo. [2]

Let us go then, you and I,
When the evening is spread out against the sky
Like a patient etherized upon a table;
Let us go, through certain half-deserted streets,
The muttering retreats
Of restless nights in one-night cheap hotels
And sawdust restaurants with oyster-shells:
Streets that follow like a tedious argument
Of insidious intent
To lead you to an overwhelming question …
Oh, do not ask, "What is it?"
Let us go and make our visit.

In the room the women come and go
Talking of Michelangelo.

The yellow fog that rubs its back upon the window-panes,
The yellow smoke that rubs its muzzle on the
window-panes
Licked its tongue into the corners of the evening,
Lingered upon the pools that stand in drains,
Let fall upon its back the soot that falls from chimneys,
Slipped by the terrace, made a sudden leap,
And seeing that it was a soft October night,
Curled once about the house, and fell asleep.

And indeed there will be time
For the yellow smoke that slides along the street,
Rubbing its back upon the window panes;
There will be time, there will be time[3]
To prepare a face to meet the faces that you meet
There will be time to murder and create,
And time for all the works and days[4] of hands
That lift and drop a question on your plate;
Time for you and time for me,
And time yet for a hundred indecisions,
And for a hundred visions and revisions,
Before the taking of a toast and tea.

In the room the women come and go
Talking of Michelangelo.

And indeed there will be time
To wonder, "Do I dare?" and, "Do I dare?"
Time to turn back and descend the stair,
With a bald spot in the middle of my hair—
(They will say: "How his hair is growing thin!")
My morning coat,[5] my collar mounting firmly to the chin,
My necktie rich and modest, but asserted by a simple
pin—
(They will say: "But how his arms and legs are thin!")
Do I dare
Disturb the universe?
In a minute there is time
For decisions and revisions which a minute will reverse.

For I have known them all already, known them all—
Have known the evenings, mornings, afternoons,
I have measured out my life with coffee spoons;
I know the voices dying with a dying fall[6]
Beneath the music from a farther room.
So how should I presume?

---

[1] *J. Alfred Prufrock* The name is likely taken from the The Prufrock-Littau Company, a furniture dealer located in St. Louis, Eliot's birthplace.

[2] *S'io credesse … ti rispondo* Italian: "If I thought that my reply were given to anyone who might return to the world, this flame would stand forever still; but since never from this deep place has anyone ever returned alive, if what I hear is true, without fear of infamy I answer thee," Dante's *Inferno* 27.61–66; Guido da Montefeltro's speech as he burns in Hell.

[3] *there will be time* See Ecclesiastes 3.1–8: "To everything there is a season, and a time to every purpose under heaven: A time to be born, and a time to die; a time to plant, and a time to pluck up that which is planted; a time to kill, and a time to heal …"

[4] *works and days* Title of a poem by eighth-century BCE Greek poet Hesiod.

[5] *morning coat* A formal coat with tails.

[6] *with a dying fall* In Shakespeare's *Twelfth Night* 1.1.1–15, Duke Orsino commands, "That strain again, it had a dying fall."

And I have known the eyes already, known them all—
The eyes that fix you in a formulated phrase,
And when I am formulated, sprawling on a pin,
When I am pinned and wriggling on the wall,
Then how should I begin
To spit out all the butt-ends of my days and ways?
    And how should I presume?

And I have known the arms already, known them all—
Arms that are braceleted and white and bare
(But in the lamplight, downed with light brown hair!)
Is it perfume from a dress
That makes me so digress?
Arms that lie along a table, or wrap about a shawl.
    And should I then presume?
    And how should I begin?

* * *

Shall I say, I have gone at dusk through narrow streets
And watched the smoke that rises from the pipes
Of lonely men in shirt-sleeves, leaning out of
    windows? ...[1]
    I should have been a pair of ragged claws
Scuttling across the floors of silent seas.[2]

* * *

And the afternoon, the evening, sleeps so peacefully!
Smoothed by long fingers,
Asleep ... tired ... or it malingers,
Stretched on the floor, here beside you and me.
Should I, after tea and cakes and ices,
Have the strength to force the moment to its crisis?
But though I have wept and fasted, wept and prayed,
Though I have seen my head (grown slightly bald)
    brought in upon a platter,[3]
I am no prophet[4]—and here's no great matter;
I have seen the moment of my greatness flicker,
And I have seen the eternal Footman hold my coat,
    and snicker,
And in short, I was afraid.

And would it have been worth it, after all,
After the cups, the marmalade, the tea,
Among the porcelain, among some talk of you and me,
Would it have been worth while,
To have bitten off the matter with a smile,
To have squeezed the universe into a ball[5]
To roll it toward some overwhelming question,
To say: "I am Lazarus,[6] come from the dead,
Come back to tell you all, I shall tell you all"—
If one, settling a pillow by her head,
    Should say: "That is not what I meant at all;
    That is not it, at all."

And would it have been worth it, after all,
Would it have been worth while,
After the sunsets and the dooryards and the sprinkled
    streets,[7]
After the novels, after the teacups, after the skirts that
    trail along the floor—
And this, and so much more?—
It is impossible to say just what I mean!
But as if a magic lantern[8] threw the nerves in patterns
    on a screen:

---

[1] ... The ellipsis here makes note of a 38 line insertion written by Eliot, entitled *Prufrock's Pervigilium*. The subtitle and 33 of the lines were later removed.

[2] *I should ... seas* See Shakespeare's *Hamlet* 2.2, in which Hamlet tells Polonius, "for you yourself, sir, should be old as I am, if like a crab you could go backwards."

[3] *brought in upon a platter* Reference to Matthew 14.1–12, in which the prophet John the Baptist is beheaded at the command of Herod, and his head presented to Salomé upon a platter.

[4] *I am no prophet* See Amos 7.14. When commanded by King Amiziah not to prophesy, the Judean Amos answered: "I was no prophet, neither was I a prophet's son; but I was a herdsman, and a farmer of sycamore fruit."

[5] *squeezed ... ball* See Andrew Marvell's "To His Coy Mistress" 41–42: "Let us roll our strength and all / Our sweetness up into one ball."

[6] *Lazarus* Raised from the dead by Jesus in John 11.1–44.

[7] *sprinkled streets* Streets sprayed with water to keep dust down.

[8] *magic lantern* In Victorian times, a device used to project images painted on glass onto a blank screen or wall.

Would it have been worth while
If one, settling a pillow or throwing off a shawl,
And turning toward the window, should say:
 "That is not it at all,
 That is not what I meant, at all."

* * *

No! I am not Prince Hamlet, nor was meant to be;
Am an attendant lord, one that will do
To swell a progress,[1] start a scene or two,
Advise the prince; no doubt, an easy tool,
Deferential, glad to be of use,
Politic, cautious, and meticulous;
Full of high sentence,[2] but a bit obtuse;
At times, indeed, almost ridiculous—
Almost, at times, the Fool.

I grow old … I grow old …
I shall wear the bottoms of my trousers rolled.

Shall I part my hair behind? Do I dare to eat a peach?
I shall wear white flannel trousers, and walk upon the beach.
I have heard the mermaids singing,[3] each to each.

I do not think that they will sing to me.

I have seen them riding seaward on the waves
Combing the white hair of the waves blown back
When the wind blows the water white and black.

We have lingered in the chambers of the sea
By sea-girls wreathed with seaweed red and brown
Till human voices wake us, and we drown.
—1915, 1917[4]

[1] *progress* Journey made by royalty through the country.

[2] *high sentence* Serious, elevated sentiments or opinions.

[3] *I have … singing* See John Donne's "Song": "Teach me to hear the mermaids singing."

[4] *1915, 1917* The poem was first published in the Chicago magazine *Poetry* in 1915. Lines 15–34 were added when it appeared in *Prufrock and Other Observations* in 1917.

Preludes[5]

1

The winter evening settles down
With smell of steaks in passageways.
Six o'clock.
The burnt-out ends of smoky days.
And now a gusty shower wraps
The grimy scraps
Of withered leaves about your feet
And newspapers from vacant lots;
The showers beat
On broken blinds and chimney-pots,
And at the corner of the street
A lonely cab-horse steams and stamps.
And then the lighting of the lamps.

2

The morning comes to consciousness
Of faint stale smells of beer
From the sawdust-trampled[6] street
With all its muddy feet that press
To early coffee-stands.
With the other masquerades
That time resumes,
One thinks of all the hands
That are raising dingy shades
In a thousand furnished rooms.

3

You tossed a blanket from the bed,
You lay upon your back, and waited;
You dozed, and watched the night revealing
The thousand sordid images
Of which your soul was constituted;
They flickered against the ceiling.
And when all the world came back
And the light crept up between the shutters,
And you heard the sparrows in the gutters,

[5] *Preludes* In Parts 3 and 4 of this poem, many of the images and details of setting are taken from Charles-Louis Philippe's novel *Bubu-de-Montparnasse* (1898).

[6] *sawdust-trampled* Sawdust was placed on the floors of bars and restaurants to absorb dirt.

You had such a vision of the street
As the street hardly understands;
Sitting along the bed's edge, where
You curled the papers from your hair,[1]
Or clasped the yellow soles of feet
In the palms of both soiled hands.

4

His soul stretched tight across the skies
That fade behind a city block,
Or trampled by insistent feet
At four and five and six o'clock;
And short square fingers stuffing pipes,
And evening newspapers, and eyes
Assured of certain certainties,
The conscience of a blackened street
Impatient to assume the world.

I am moved by fancies that are curled
Around these images, and cling:
The notion of some infinitely gentle
Infinitely suffering thing.

Wipe your hand across your mouth, and laugh;
The worlds revolve like ancient women
Gathering fuel in vacant lots.
—1915

Burbank with a Baedeker: Bleistein[2] with a Cigar

Tra-la- la- la- la- la-laire—nil nisi divinum stabile est; caetera fumus[3]—the gondola stopped, the old palace was there, how charming its grey and pink[4]—goats and monkeys, with such hair too![5]—so the countess passed on until she came through the little park, where Niobe presented her with a cabinet, and so departed.[6]

Burbank crossed a little bridge
Descending at a small hotel;
Princess Volupine arrived,
They were together, and he fell.[7]

Defunctive° music under sea *dying*
Passed seaward with the passing bell
Slowly: the God Hercules
Had left him, that had loved him well.[8]

The horses, under the axletree
Beat up the dawn from Istria[9]
With even feet. Her shuttered barge
Burned on the water all the day.

But this or such was Bleistein's way:
A saggy bending of the knees
And elbows, with the palms turned out,
Chicago Semite Viennese.

A lustreless protrusive eye
Stares from the protozoic slime
At a perspective of Canaletto.[10]
The smoky candle end of time

[1] *papers … hair* I.e., "curl papers," used to curl hair.

[2] *Baedeker* Popular line of guide-books; *Bleistein* Jewish-German name literally meaning "Leadstone."

[3] *nil … fumus* Latin: nothing but the divine endures; all the rest is smoke.

[4] *the gondola … pink* From Henry James's *Aspern Papers* (1888), Chapter 1. The passage is narrated by an American woman living in Venice who is giving her visiting friend a tour of the city: "The gondola stopped, the old palace was there. … 'How charming! It's grey and pink!' my companion exclaimed."

[5] *goats and monkeys* An exclamation made by Othello in Shakespeare's *Othello* 4.1 (set in Venice) when he becomes convinced his wife is having an affair; *with such hair too* From Robert Browning's "A Toccata of Galuppi's," about the eighteenth-century Venetian composer Baldassare Galuppi (1706–85).

[6] *so the … departed* From the stage directions of *Entertainment of Alice, Dowager Countess of Derby* by John Marston (c.1575–1634); *Niobe* Mother in Greek myth who boasted that she had more children than Zeus.

[7] *They were … fell* From Alfred Tennyson's "The Sisters" (Eliot has changed the pronoun from "she" to "he").

[8] *Defunctive music … well* See Shakespeare's *Antony and Cleopatra* 4.3, in which Cleopatra's soldiers hear music just before they are defeated by Caesar's army. "'Tis the god Hercules, whom Antony lov'd, / Now leaves him," one soldier says.

[9] *horses … dawn* In classical myth, the sun is a chariot pulled across the sky; *Istria* Peninsula that juts into the northeast Adriatic.

[10] *Canaletto* Italian painter Giovanni Antonio Canal (1697–1768), famous for his paintings of Venice and London.

Declines. On the Rialto[1] once.
    The rats are underneath the piles.
The jew is underneath the lot.[2]
    Money in furs.[3] The boatman smiles,

Princess Volupine extends
    A meagre, blue-nailed, phthisic° hand *consumptive*
To climb the waterstair. Lights, lights,
    She entertains Sir Ferdinand

Klein. Who clipped the lion's wings[4]
    And flea'd his rump and pared his claws?
Thought Burbank, meditating on
    Time's ruins, and the seven laws.[5]
—1919

Gerontion[6]

Thou hast nor youth nor age
But as it were an after dinner sleep
Dreaming of both.[7]

Here I am, an old man in a dry month,
Being read to by a boy, waiting for rain.[8]
I was neither at the hot gates[9]
Nor fought in the warm rain
Nor knee deep in the salt marsh, heaving a cutlass,
Bitten by flies, fought.
My house is a decayed house,
And the jew squats on the window sill, the owner,
Spawned in some estaminet[10] of Antwerp,
Blistered in Brussels, patched and peeled in London.[11]
The goat coughs at night in the field overhead;
Rocks, moss, stonecrop,[12] iron, merds.° *feces*
The woman keeps the kitchen, makes tea,
Sneezes at evening, poking the peevish gutter.[13]
                I an old man,
A dull head among windy spaces.

Signs are taken for wonders. "We would see a sign!"
The word within a word, unable to speak a word,
Swaddled with darkness.[14] In the juvescence° *youth*
    of the year
Came Christ the tiger

[1] *Rialto* Island in Venice, containing the old mercantile quarter of the medieval city.

[2] *The jew … lot* For a discussion of the controversy over Eliot's attitudes towards Jewish people, see the "In Context" section on "T.S. Eliot and Anti-Semitism" later in this volume.

[3] *Money in furs* Venice was a center for fur trade from the Black Sea.

[4] *lion's wings* The winged lion was a symbol of the Venetian Republic.

[5] *seven laws* Either the seven laws of architecture that John Ruskin outlined in his *Seven Lamps of Architecture* (1849), which describes Venice's Gothic style as the ideal, or the Noachian Laws, the Seven Commandments of the Sons of Noah from the Jewish Talmud.

[6] *Gerontion* Greek: Little old man. Eliot originally planned to print this poem as a prelude to *The Waste Land*, but when Ezra Pound advised against this he published it separately.

[7] *Thou hast … both* From Shakespeare's *Measure for Measure* 3.1.32–34.

[8] *Here I … rain* These two lines are based on a sentence in A.C. Benson's biography *Edward Fitzgerald* (1905), in which the poet is described as sitting "in a dry month, old and blind, being read to by a country boy, longing for rain."

[9] *hot gates* Literal translation of the Greek *Thermopylae*, a pass between northern and central Greece and the location of several historical battles, including that between the Greeks and the Persians in 480 BCE.

[10] *estaminet* French: café.

[11] *the jew … London* The association of Jews with images of squalor, decay, and disgusting physicality was one of the many ways in which anti-Semitism was expressed in British literary tradition. For more on the controversy over such elements as they appear in Eliot's verse see the "In Context" section below.

[12] *stonecrop* Herb with yellow flowers that grows on rocks or old walls.

[13] *gutter* Sputtering fire.

[14] *Signs are … darkness* Reference to two biblical passages. The first is Matthew 12.39: "An evil and adulterous generation seeketh after a sign; and there shall no sign be given to it, but the sign of the prophet Jonas," and the second is John 1.1: "In the beginning was the Word, and the Word was with God, and the Word was God." Both of these passages were sources for a Christmas sermon given by Anglican preacher Lancelot Andrewes in 1618.

In depraved May, dogwood and chestnut,
flowering judas,[1]
To be eaten, to be divided, to be drunk
Among whispers; by Mr. Silvero
With caressing hands, at Limoges[2]
Who walked all night in the next room;

By Hakagawa, bowing among the Titians;[3]
By Madame de Tornquist, in the dark room
Shifting the candles; Fraulein von Kulp
Who turned in the hall, one hand on the door.
Vacant shuttles
Weave the wind. I have no ghosts,
An old man in a draughty house
Under a windy knob.[4]

After such knowledge, what forgiveness? Think now
History has many cunning passages, contrived
corridors
And issues, deceives with whispering ambitions,
Guides us by vanities. Think now
She gives when our attention is distracted
And what she gives, gives with such supple confusions
That the giving famishes the craving. Gives too late
What's not believed in, or if still believed,
In memory only, reconsidered passion. Gives too soon
Into weak hands,[5] what's thought can be dispensed with
Till the refusal propagates a fear. Think
Neither fear nor courage saves us. Unnatural vices
Are fathered by our heroism. Virtues
Are forced upon us by our impudent crimes.
These tears are shaken from the wrath-bearing tree.

The tiger springs in the new year. Us he devours.
Think at last
We have not reached conclusion, when I
Stiffen in a rented house. Think at last
I have not made this show purposelessly
And it is not by any concitation° *stirring up*
Of the backward devils.[6]
I would meet you upon this honestly.
I that was near your heart was removed therefrom
To lose beauty in terror, terror in inquisition.
I have lost my passion: why should I need to keep it
Since what is kept must be adulterated?
I have lost my sight, smell, hearing, taste and touch:
How should I use them for your closer contact?

These with a thousand small deliberations
Protract the profit of their chilled delirium,
Excite the membrane, when the sense has cooled,
With pungent sauces, multiply variety
In a wilderness of mirrors. What will the spider do,
Suspend its operations, will the weevil
Delay? De Bailhache, Fresca, Mrs. Cammel, whirled
Beyond the circuit of the shuddering Bear[7]
In fractured atoms. Gull against the wind, in the
windy straits
Of Belle Isle, or running on the Horn,[8]
White feathers in the snow, the Gulf[9] claims,
And an old man driven by the Trades[10]
To a sleepy corner.

Tenants of the house,
Thoughts of a dry brain in a dry season.
—1920

---

[1] *judas* Purple-flowered tree of southern Europe named after Judas, who was said to have hanged himself from a tree of this type after betraying Jesus.

[2] *Limoges* French town known for its china of the same name.

[3] *Titians* Paintings by Venetian painter Titian (1485–1576).

[4] *Vacant shuttles … knob* See Job 7.6–7: "My days are swifter than a weaver's shuttle, and are spent without hope. O remember that my life is wind: mine eye shall no more see good"; *knob* Knoll.

[5] *too soon … hands* See Percy Shelley's *Adonais* (1821), in which he describes Keats's death: "Too soon, and with weak hands."

[6] *backward devils* In Dante's *Inferno*, tellers of the future were punished by being forced to walk backwards.

[7] *Bear* Constellation Ursa Major (the Great Bear).

[8] *Belle Isle* Channel between Labrador and Newfoundland at the entrance to the Gulf of St. Lawrence; *the Horn* Cape Horn, the southernmost tip of South America.

[9] *Gulf* Gulf stream, a warm ocean current in the North Atlantic.

[10] *Trades* Trade winds, which blow, almost constantly, towards the equator.

The Waste Land

The title and plan of Eliot's groundbreaking poem *The Waste Land* were substantially influenced by Jessie Weston's *From Ritual to Romance* (1920), which details the various legends of the Holy Grail and explores the influence of pre-Christian religions on these legends. According to most accounts of the Grail, the sacred vessel lies in the heart of a (formerly fertile) Waste Land that is now stricken with drought and presided over by a Fisher King who is cursed with impotence. The land and its king can be saved only from permanent sterility by a knight who is able to pass several tests and attain the Grail, thus bringing about regeneration. Overlaying this myth with a modern setting and numerous cultural references, Eliot shows that a similar sterility plagues a contemporary society characterized by casual sexuality, blatant materialism, and industrial exploitation of nature.

With its disparate images, ever-shifting narrative events, and seemingly random structure, *The Waste Land* embraces the fragmented present while looking back to a more coherent past. Allusions to seventeenth-century poets, to Chaucer, to Shakespeare, to Dante, to pre-Socratic philosophers, and to works of history and anthropology, such as James Frazer's twelve-volume anthropological study *The Golden Bough* (1890–1915), gesture towards the presence of a recurring order beneath contemporary history and indicate the possibility of regeneration. The poem's disconnected and highly allusive character (which gives it a sense of difficulty more often heightened than alleviated by Eliot's copious notes) provoked charges of intentional obscurity upon the poem's publication, but Eliot maintained that any poetry developed out of such a complex and various society must itself be various and complex.

By its very nature, *The Waste Land* seems to resist order and any cohesive account of meaning; its complexity and ambiguity make possible a variety of interpretations. Even the identity of its narrator is unclear: are all the disparate voices filtered through any single voice? And, if so, is the voice that of the blind prophet Tiresias, or some other nameless narrator, or is the speaker Eliot himself? This very complexity may in large part be responsible for the continued vitality of the poem, however. Eliot's friend Conrad Aiken maintained that the poem was important primarily for its private "emotional value," and that readers should rely as much on their first responses to the diverse elements of the poem as on the copious and ever-expanding body of scholarship surrounding it. As much as *The Waste Land* has taken its place as a central document of the modernist movement, it retains as well the ability to speak directly to readers.

The Waste Land[1]

"Nam Sibyllam quidem Cumis ego ipse oculis meis vidi in ampulla pendere, et cum illi pueri dicerent: Σίβυλλα τί θέλεις; respondebat illa: ἀποθανεῖν θέλω."[2]

For Ezra Pound
il miglior fabbro.[3]

[1] [Eliot's note] Not only the title, but the plan and a good deal of the incidental symbolism of the poem were suggested by Miss Jessie L. Weston's book on the Grail legend: *From Ritual to Romance* (Cambridge). Indeed, so deeply am I indebted, Miss Weston's book will elucidate the difficulties of the poem much better than my notes can do; and I recommend it (apart from the great interest of the book itself) to any who think such elucidation of the poem worth the trouble. To another work of anthropology I am indebted in general, one which has influenced our generation profoundly; I mean [Sir James Frazer's 1890 to 1915 twelve-volume] *The Golden Bough*; I have used especially the two volumes *Adonis, Attis, Osiris.* Anyone who is acquainted with these works will immediately recognise in the poem certain references to vegetation ceremonies.

[2] *Nam … θέλω* Latin and Greek: "For once I saw with my own eyes the Sybil at Cumae hanging in a cage, and when the boys asked her, 'Sybil, what do you want?' she responded, 'I want to die.'" From the *Satyricon* of Petronius Arbiter (first-century CE Roman writer). The most famous of the prophetic Sibyls of Greek mythology, the Cumaean Sibyl received immortality from the god Apollo, but neglected to ask him for eternal youth.

[3] *il miglior fabbro* Italian: the better craftsman. This compliment was originally paid by Dante, in his *Purgatorio* (26.117), to the Provençal poet, Arnaut Daniel. Eliot adopts it for his dedication to fellow expatriate and Modernist American poet, Ezra Pound (1885–1972), who played a key editorial role in the poem's production.

I. The Burial of the Dead[1]

April is the cruellest month, breeding
Lilacs out of the dead land, mixing
Memory and desire, stirring
Dull roots with spring rain.
Winter kept us warm, covering
Earth in forgetful snow, feeding
A little life with dried tubers.
Summer surprised us, coming over the Starnbergersee[2]
With a shower of rain; we stopped in the colonnade,
And went on in sunlight, into the Hofgarten,[3]
And drank coffee, and talked for an hour.
Bin gar keine Russin, stamm' aus Litauen, echt
deutsch.[4]
And when we were children, staying at the archduke's,
My cousin's, he took me out on a sled,
And I was frightened. He said, Marie,
Marie, hold on tight. And down we went.
In the mountains, there you feel free.
I read, much of the night, and go south in the winter.

What are the roots that clutch, what branches grow
Out of this stony rubbish? Son of man,[5]
You cannot say, or guess, for you know only
A heap of broken images, where the sun beats,
And the dead tree gives no shelter, the cricket no
relief,[6]
And the dry stone no sound of water. Only
There is shadow under this red rock,[7]
(Come in under the shadow of this red rock),
And I will show you something different from either
Your shadow at morning striding behind you
Or your shadow at evening rising to meet you;
I will show you fear in a handful of dust.
Frisch weht der Wind
Der Heimat zu
Mein Irisch Kind,
Wo weilest du?[8]
"You gave me hyacinths first a year ago;
They called me the hyacinth girl."
—Yet when we came back, late, from the Hyacinth
garden,
Your arms full, and your hair wet, I could not
Speak, and my eyes failed, I was neither
Living nor dead, and I knew nothing,
Looking into the heart of light, the silence.
Oed' und leer das Meer.[9]

Madame Sosostris,[10] famous clairvoyante,
Had a bad cold, nevertheless
Is known to be the wisest woman in Europe,
With a wicked pack of cards.[11] Here, said she,

---

[1] *The Burial of the Dead* Reference to the Anglican Order for the Burial of the Dead.

[2] *Starnbergersee* Lake near Munich, Germany.

[3] *Hofgarten* Public park in Munich.

[4] *Bin … deutsch* German: I'm not Russian at all, I come from Lithuania, a pure German.

[5] *Son of man* Eliot's note cites Ezekiel 2.1, in which God addresses Ezekiel, whose mission will be to preach the coming of the Messiah to unbelievers, saying, "Son of man, stand upon thy feet, and I will speak unto thee."

[6] *cricket no relief* Eliot's note cites Ecclesiastes 12.5, in which the preacher speaks of the fearful deprivations of old age: "Also *when* they shall be afraid of *that which is* high, and fears *shall be* in the way, and the almond tree shall flourish, and the grasshopper shall be a burden, and desire shall fail: because man goeth to his long home, and the mourners go about the streets …"

[7] *There is shadow … rock* See Isaiah 32.2, in which the blessings of Christ's kingdom are described: "And a man shall be as an hiding place from the wind, and a covert from the tempest; as rivers of water in a dry place, as the shadow of a great rock in a weary land."

[8] *Frisch … du?* German: "Fresh blows the wind to the homeland—my Irish child, where do you tarry?" From Richard Wagner's opera *Tristan und Isolde* (1865), 1.5–8, this is a sailor's lament for the girl he has left behind in Ireland.

[9] *Oed' … Meer* German: "Desolate and empty is the sea." Eliot's note cites *Tristan und Isolde* 3.24, in which Tristan lies dying, waiting for his beloved, Isolde, to come to him, but there is no sign of her ship on the sea.

[10] *Madame Sosostris* This name is often thought to have been "unconsciously" borrowed by Eliot from the name of the fortune-teller Madame Sesostris in Aldous Huxley's novel *Crome Yellow* (1921). It may more plausibly have derived from the Greek word for savior, *soteros*.

[11] [Eliot's note] I am not familiar with the exact constitution of the Tarot pack of cards, from which I have obviously departed to suit my own convenience. The Hanged Man, a member of the traditional pack, fits my purpose in two ways: because he is associated in my mind with the Hanged God of Frazer, and because I [continued …]

Is your card, the drowned Phoenician Sailor,
(Those are pearls that were his eyes.[1] Look!)
Here is Belladonna, the Lady of the Rocks,[2]
The lady of situations.
Here is the man with three staves, and here the Wheel,[3]
And here is the one-eyed merchant, and this card,
Which is blank, is something he carries on his back,
Which I am forbidden to see. I do not find
The Hanged Man.[4] Fear death by water.
I see crowds of people, walking round in a ring.
Thank you. If you see dear Mrs. Equitone,
Tell her I bring the horoscope myself:
One must be so careful these days.

Unreal City,[5]
Under the brown fog of a winter dawn,
A crowd flowed over London Bridge, so many,
I had not thought death had undone so many.[6]
Sighs, short and infrequent, were exhaled,
And each man fixed his eyes before his feet.
Flowed up the hill and down King William Street,
To where Saint Mary Woolnoth[7] kept the hours
With a dead sound on the final stroke of nine.[8]
There I saw one I knew, and stopped him, crying
"Stetson![9]
You who were with me in the ships at Mylae![10]
That corpse you planted last year in your garden,
Has it begun to sprout? Will it bloom this year?
Or has the sudden frost disturbed its bed?
Oh keep the Dog far hence, that's friend to men,
Or with his nails he'll dig it up again! [11]
You! hypocrite lecteur!—mon semblable,—mon frère!"[12]

---

associate him with the hooded figure in the passage of the disciples to Emmaus in Part V. The Phoenician Sailor and the Merchant appear later; also the "crowds of people," and Death by Water is executed in Part IV. The Man with Three Staves (an authentic member of the Tarot pack) I associate, quite arbitrarily, with the Fisher King himself. [The Tarot pack, generally used for fortune-telling, consists of 78 cards in four suits—cups, wands, swords, and pentangles. It originated in France and Italy in the fourteenth century.]

[1] *Those are … eyes* From Ariel's song in Shakespeare's *The Tempest* 1.2.397–403: "Full fathom five thy father lies; / Of his bones are coral made; / Those are pearls that were his eyes; / Nothing of him that doth fade / But doth suffer a sea-change / Into something rich and strange: / Sea nymphs hourly ring his knell: / *Burden*. Ding-dong. / Hark! Now I hear them—ding-dong bell."

[2] *Belladonna* Italian: Beautiful woman. Also another name for the poisonous plant deadly nightshade, once used for cosmetic purposes by Italian women; *Lady of the Rocks* Possible ironic reference to Leonardo da Vinci's painting *Madonna of the Rocks*.

[3] *Wheel* Wheel of Fortune.

[4] *Hanged Man* This man's self-sacrifice in the role of fertility god is necessary for the annual rejuvenation of the land.

[5] *Unreal City* Eliot's note cites the following lines from the 1859 poem "Les sept vieillards" by poet Charles Baudelaire: "Fourmillante cité, cité pleine de rêves, / Où le spectre en plein jour raccroche le passant!" (French: "Swarming city, city full of dreams, / Where the daylight specter intercepts the passerby.") "The City" is the name for London's financial district, located north of London Bridge.

[6] *so many … so many* Eliot's note cites Dante's *Inferno* 3.55–57: "such a long stream / of people, that I would not have thought / that death had undone so many." This is spoken by Dante soon after he has entered the Gates of Hell in the company of Virgil, his guide through the underworld.

[7] *Saint Mary Woolnoth* Church in King William Street. Eliot joined a campaign to have this church, and others like it that were slated for demolition, preserved.

[8] [Eliot's note] A phenomenon which I have often noticed.

[9] *Stetson* Eliot, when questioned, maintained this was a reference to the average City clerk, and not, as some had suggested, to Ezra Pound, whose nickname was "Buffalo Bill."

[10] *Mylae* The Battle of Mylae (260 BCE) took place in the trade-based First Punic War between the Romans and the Carthaginians.

[11] *Oh keep … again* Eliot's note cites the dirge in John Webster's play *The White Devil* (1612) 5.4: "But keep the wolf far thence, that's foe to men, / For with his nails he'll dig them up again." Sirius, the Dog Star, heralded the annual flooding of the Nile in Egyptian mythology.

[12] *hypocrite … mon frère* French: hypocrite reader—my double—my brother! Eliot's note cites the preface of Baudelaire's *Fleurs du Mal*.

2. A GAME OF CHESS[1]

The Chair she sat in, like a burnished throne,[2]
Glowed on the marble, where the glass
Sustained by standards wrought with fruited vines
From which a golden Cupidon peeped out
(Another hid his eyes behind his wing)
Doubled the flames of sevenbranched candelabra
Reflecting light upon the table as
The glitter of her jewels rose to meet it,
From satin cases poured in rich profusion;
In vials of ivory and coloured glass
Unstoppered, lurked her strange synthetic perfumes,
Unguent, powdered, or liquid—troubled, confused
And drowned the sense in odours; stirred by the air
That freshened from the window, these ascended
In fattening the prolonged candle-flames,
Flung their smoke into the laquearia,[3]
Stirring the pattern on the coffered ceiling.
Huge sea-wood fed with copper
Burned green and orange, framed by the coloured
    stone,
In which sad light a carved dolphin swam.
Above the antique mantel was displayed
As though a window gave upon the sylvan scene[4]
The change of Philomel, by the barbarous king
So rudely forced;[5] yet there the nightingale
Filled all the desert with inviolable voice
And still she cried, and still the world pursues,
"Jug Jug"[6] to dirty ears.
And other withered stumps of time
Were told upon the walls; staring forms
Leaned out, leaning, hushing the room enclosed.
Footsteps shuffled on the stair.
Under the firelight, under the brush, her hair
Spread out in fiery points
Glowed into words, then would be savagely still.

"My nerves are bad to-night. Yes, bad. Stay with me.
Speak to me. Why do you never speak? Speak.
    What are you thinking of? What thinking? What?
I never know what you are thinking. Think."

I think we are in rats' alley[7]
Where the dead men lost their bones.

    "What is that noise?"
                The wind under the door.[8]
"What is that noise now? What is the wind doing?"
            Nothing again nothing.
                        "Do
You know nothing? Do you see nothing? Do you
    remember
Nothing?"

I remember
Those are pearls that were his eyes.
"Are you alive, or not? Is there nothing in your head?"
                        But

[1] *A GAME OF CHESS* Title of Thomas Middleton's 1624 satirical political drama. In Middleton's play *Women Beware Women*, a game of chess distracts a mother-in-law, preventing her from noticing that her daughter-in-law is being seduced upstairs. Each move in the chess game mirrors a move in the seduction.

[2] [Eliot's note] Cf. Antony and Cleopatra, 2.2.190. [This is the beginning of Enorbarbus's description of the first meeting of Antony and Cleopatra: "The barge she sat in, like a burnished throne, / Burned on the water."]

[3] *laquearia* Latin: paneled ceiling. Eliot's note cites Virgil's *Aeneid* 1.726, describing a banquet given by Queen Dido of Carthage for her soon-to-be lover, Aeneas: "Burning lamps hang from the gold-paneled ceiling, and torches dispel the night with their flames."

[4] *sylvan scene* Eliot's note cites Milton's *Paradise Lost* 4.140, which describes the Garden of Eden seen through Satan's eyes.

[5] *The change … forced* Eliot's notes for this passage cite Greek poet Ovid's *Metamorphoses* 6, which tells the Greek myth of Philomela, who was raped by King Tereus of Thrace (her sister's husband) and had her tongue cut out before being changed into a nightingale.

[6] *Jug Jug* In Elizabethan poetry, a conventional representation of a nightingale's song. Also, a crude reference to sexual intercourse.

[7] [Eliot's note] Cf. part 3, line 195 [of *Metamorphoses* 6].

[8] *The wind … door* Eliot's note cites a line from John Webster's *The Devil's Law Case* (3.2.162). A patient who is believed to have been stabbed to death groans in pain, prompting the surgeon to ask, "Is the wind in that door still?"

O O O O that Shakespeherian Rag[1]—
It's so elegant
So intelligent
"What shall I do now? What shall I do?
I shall rush out as I am, and walk the street
With my hair down, so. What shall we do to-morrow?
What shall we ever do?"
                    The hot water at ten.
And if it rains, a closed car at four.
And we shall play a game of chess,
Pressing lidless eyes and waiting for a knock upon the
    door.[2]

When Lil's husband got demobbed,[3] I said—
I didn't mince my words, I said to her myself,
HURRY UP PLEASE ITS TIME[4]
Now Albert's coming back, make yourself a bit smart.
He'll want to know what you done with that money he
    gave you
To get yourself some teeth. He did, I was there.
You have them all out, Lil, and get a nice set,
He said, I swear, I can't bear to look at you.
And no more can't I, I said, and think of poor Albert,
He's been in the army four years, he wants a good time,
And if you don't give it him, there's others will, I said.
Oh is there, she said. Something o' that, I said.
Then I'll know who to thank, she said, and give me a
    straight look.
HURRY UP PLEASE ITS TIME
If you don't like it you can get on with it, I said.
Others can pick and choose if you can't.
But if Albert makes off, it won't be for lack of telling.
You ought to be ashamed, I said, to look so antique.
(And her only thirty-one.)
I can't help it, she said, pulling a long face,
It's them pills I took, to bring it off, she said.
(She's had five already, and nearly died of young
    George.)
The chemist° said it would be alright, *pharmacist*
    but I've never been the same.
You are a proper fool, I said.
Well, if Albert won't leave you alone, there it is, I said,
What you get married for if you don't want children?
HURRY UP PLEASE ITS TIME
Well, that Sunday Albert was home, they had a hot
    gammon,° *smoked ham*
And they asked me in to dinner, to get the beauty of it
    hot—
HURRY UP PLEASE ITS TIME
HURRY UP PLEASE ITS TIME
Goonight Bill. Goonight Lou. Goonight May.
    Goonight.
Ta ta. Goonight. Goonight.
Good night, ladies, good night, sweet ladies, good
    night, good night.[5]

3. THE FIRE SERMON[6]

The river's tent is broken: the last fingers of leaf
Clutch and sink into the wet bank. The wind
Crosses the brown land, unheard. The nymphs are
    departed.
Sweet Thames, run softly, till I end my song.[7]
The river bears no empty bottles, sandwich papers,
Silk handkerchiefs, cardboard boxes, cigarette ends
Or other testimony of summer nights. The nymphs
    are departed.
And their friends, the loitering heirs of city directors;
Departed, have left no addresses.

---

[1] *O … Rag* Reference to a popular American ragtime song performed in Ziegfeld's Follies in 1912.

[2] [Eliot's note] Cf. the game of chess in Middleton's *Women Beware Women*.

[3] *demobbed* Demobilized; released from military service.

[4] *HURRY … TIME* Expression used by bartenders in Britain to announce closing time.

[5] *Good night … night* Ophelia's last words in Shakespeare's *Hamlet* (4.5.72–73) before she drowns herself. These words are taken by her father as evidence that she had been driven insane by Hamlet's seeming indifference to her.

[6] *THE FIRE SERMON* Sermon preached by the Buddha against passions (such as lust, anger, and envy) that consume people and prevent their escaping regeneration.

[7] *Sweet Thames … song* Eliot's note cites the refrain of Edmund Spenser's *Prothalamion* (1596), a poem that celebrates the ideals of marriage, written to commemorate the joint marriages of the two daughters of the Earl of Worcester.

By the waters of Leman I sat down and wept ...[1]
Sweet Thames, run softly till I end my song,
Sweet Thames, run softly, for I speak not loud or long.
But at my back in a cold blast I hear
The rattle of the bones, and chuckle spread from ear
 to ear.[2]

A rat crept softly through the vegetation
Dragging its slimy belly on the bank
While I was fishing in the dull canal
On a winter evening round behind the gashouse
Musing upon the king my brother's wreck
And on the king my father's death before him.[3]
White bodies naked on the low damp ground
And bones cast in a little low dry garret,
Rattled by the rat's foot only, year to year.
But at my back from time to time I hear
The sound of horns and motors, which shall bring[4]
Sweeney[5] to Mrs. Porter in the spring.
O the moon shone bright on Mrs. Porter
And on her daughter
They wash their feet in soda water[6]
Et O ces voix d'enfants, chantant dans la coupole![7]

Twit twit twit
Jug jug jug jug jug jug
So rudely forc'd.
Tereu[8]

Unreal City
Under the brown fog of a winter noon
Mr. Eugenides, the Smyrna[9] merchant
Unshaven, with a pocket full of currants
C.i.f. London: documents at sight,[10]
Asked me in demotic[11] French
To luncheon at the Cannon Street Hotel[12]
Followed by a weekend at the Metropole.[13]

At the violet hour, when the eyes and back
Turn upward from the desk, when the human engine
 waits
Like a taxi throbbing waiting,

---

[1] *By the ... wept* Reference to Psalm 137, in which the Hebrews lament their exile in Babylon and their lost homeland: "By the rivers of Babylon, there sat we down, yea, we wept, when we remembered Zion." For Babylon Eliot substitutes "Leman," the French name for Lake Geneva. "Leman" is also a medieval word meaning sweetheart.

[2] *But at ... ear* Eliot's note cites Andrew Marvell's "To His Coy Mistress": "But at my back I always hear / Time's wingèd chariot hurrying near" (lines 21–22).

[3] *And on ... him* Eliot's note cites Shakespeare's *The Tempest* 1.2.388–93, in which Ferdinand, shipwrecked on the shore, is prompted by Ariel's music to ponder the supposed drowning of his father, King Alonso: "Sitting on a bank, / Weeping again the king my father's wrack / This music crept by me upon the waters, / Allaying both their fury and my passion / With its sweet air." Eliot also quotes from this passage on line 257.

[4] [Eliot's note] Cf. [John] Day, *Parliament of Bees*: "When of the sudden, listening, you shall hear, / A noise of horns and hunting, which shall bring / Actaeon to Diana in the spring, / Where all shall see her naked skin ..." [According to classical myth, when the hunter Actaeon saw Diana, goddess of chastity and the hunt, bathing naked with her nymphs, she changed him into a stag and set his dogs upon him.]

[5] *Sweeney* Character in two earlier poems by Eliot, "Sweeney Erect" and "Sweeney Among the Nightingales."

[6] [Eliot's note] I do not know the origin of the ballad from which these are taken: it was reported to me from Sydney, Australia. [One version of this ballad, which was sung by Australian soldiers in World War I, is as follows: "O the moon shone bright on Mrs. Porter / And on the daughter / Of Mrs. Porter / They wash their feet in soda water / And so they oughter / To keep them clean."

[7] *Et O ... coupole* French: "And O those children's voices singing under the cupola." Eliot's note indicates that this is the last line of French poet Paul Verlaine's sonnet "Parsifal" (1886). Verlaine refers to the opera *Parsifal* (1882) by Richard Wagner, in which a choir of children sings while the innocent knight Parsifal has his feet washed before entering the Castle of the Grail.

[8] *Tereu* Latin vocative form of Tereus, who raped Philomela.

[9] *Smyrna* Port city in western Turkey.

[10] *C.i.f. ... sight* Eliot's note explains that "C.i.f." means that the price includes "cost, insurance, freight to London," and that "documents on sight" indicates that "the Bill of Lading, etc., were to be handed to the buyer upon payment of the sight draft."

[11] *demotic* Popular; vulgar.

[12] *Cannon Street Hotel* Hotel near the Cannon Street train station, a terminus for travelers to and from the continent.

[13] *Metropole* Large hotel on the seashore at Brighton.

I Tiresias,[1] though blind, throbbing between two lives,
Old man with wrinkled female breasts, can see
At the violet hour, the evening hour that strives
Homeward, and brings the sailor home from sea,[2]
The typist home at teatime, clears her breakfast, lights
Her stove, and lays out food in tins.
Out of the window perilously spread
Her drying combinations[3] touched by the sun's last rays,
On the divan are piled (at night her bed)
Stockings, slippers, camisoles, and stays.° *corset*
I Tiresias, old man with wrinkled dugs° *breasts*
Perceived the scene, and foretold the rest—
I too awaited the expected guest.
He, the young man carbuncular,° arrives, *pimply*
A small house agent's clerk, with one bold stare,
One of the low on whom assurance sits
As a silk hat on a Bradford[4] millionaire.
The time is now propitious, as he guesses,
The meal is ended, she is bored and tired,
Endeavours to engage her in caresses
Which still are unreproved, if undesired.
Flushed and decided, he assaults at once;
Exploring hands encounter no defence;
His vanity requires no response,
And makes a welcome of indifference.
(And I Tiresias have foresuffered all
Enacted on this same divan or bed;
I who have sat by Thebes below the wall
And walked among the lowest of the dead.[5])
Bestows one final patronising kiss,
And gropes his way, finding the stairs unlit …

She turns and looks a moment in the glass,
Hardly aware of her departed lover;
Her brain allows one half-formed thought to pass:
"Well now that's done: and I'm glad it's over."
When lovely woman stoops to folly and[6]
Paces about her room again, alone,
She smoothes her hair with automatic hand,
And puts a record on the gramophone.

"This music crept by me upon the waters"[7]
And along the Strand, up Queen Victoria Street.

---

[1] [Eliot's note] Tiresias, although a mere spectator and not indeed a "character," is yet the most important personage in the poem, uniting all the rest. Just as the one-eyed merchant, seller of currants, melts into the Phoenician Sailor, and the latter is not wholly distinct from Ferdinand Prince of Naples, so all the women are one woman, and the two sexes meet in Tiresias. What Tiresias sees, in fact, is the substance of the poem. The whole passage from Ovid is of great anthropological interest. [Eliot then quotes in Latin the passage from *Metamorphoses* that describes Tiresias's sex change. Jove, who had drunk a great deal, "jested with Juno. He said, 'Your pleasure in love is really greater than that enjoyed by men.' She denied it; so they decided to seek the opinion of the wise Tiresias, for he knew both aspects of love. For once, with a blow of his staff, he had committed violence on two huge snakes as they copulated in the green forest; and—wonderful to tell—was turned into a woman and thus spent seven years. In the eighth year he saw the same snakes again and said: 'If a blow struck at you is so powerful that it changes the sex of the giver, I will now strike at you again.' With these words she struck the snakes, and again became a man. So he was appointed arbiter in the playful quarrel, and supported Jove's statement. It is said that Saturnia [Juno] was quite disproportionately upset, and condemned the arbiter to perpetual blindness. But the almighty father (for no god may undo what has been done by another god), in return for the sight that was taken away, gave him the power to know the future and so lightened the penalty paid by the honor."]

[2] [Eliot's note] This may not appear as exact as Sappho's lines but I had in mind the "longshore" or "dory" fisherman, who returns at nightfall. [Eliot refers to seventh-century BCE Greek poet Sappho's poem, known as Fragment 149, in which Hesperus, the evening star, brings home "all things the bright dawn disperses," including "the sheep, the goat, the child to its mother."]

[3] *combinations* Undergarments that cover the wearer from shoulders to thighs.

[4] *Bradford* Textile center in industrial Yorkshire, many of whose residents became extremely wealthy during the textile boom that accompanied World War I.

[5] *I who … dead* In *Oedipus Rex*, by fifth-century BCE Greek dramatist Sophocles, Tiresias perceives that the curse of infertility that plagues the people and land of Thebes has been brought upon them by the unwitting marriage of Oedipus to his mother, Queen Jocasta. In book 9 of Homer's *Odyssey*, Odysseus journeys to the underworld, where he consults Tiresias.

[6] *When … and* Eliot's note cites Oliver Goldsmith's novel *The Vicar of Wakefield* (1762), in which Olivia, returning to the place where she was seduced, sings: "When lovely woman stoops to folly / And finds too late that men betray / What charm can soothe her melancholy, / What art can wash her guilt away? / The only art her guilt to cover, / To hide her shame from every eye, / To give repentance to her lover, / And wring his bosom—is to die."

[7] [Eliot's note] V. [I.e., "see," from the Latin *vide.*] *The Tempest*, as above.

O City city, I can sometimes hear
Beside a public bar in Lower Thames Street,
The pleasant whining of a mandoline
And a clatter and a chatter from within
Where fishmen lounge at noon: where the walls
Of Magnus Martyr[1] hold
Inexplicable splendour of Ionian white and gold.[2]

The river sweats[3]
Oil and tar
The barges drift
With the turning tide
Red sails
Wide
To leeward, swing on the heavy spar.
The barges wash
Drifting logs
Down Greenwich reach
Past the Isle of Dogs.[4]
Weialala leia
Wallala leialala[5]

Elizabeth and Leicester[6]
Beating oars
The stern was formed
A gilded shell
Red and gold
The brisk swell
Rippled both shores
Southwest wind
Carried down stream
The peal of bells
White towers
Weialala leia
Wallala leialala

"Trams and dusty trees.
Highbury bore me. Richmond and Kew
Undid me. By Richmond I raised my knees
Supine on the floor of a narrow canoe."[7]

"My feet are at Moorgate,[8] and my heart
Under my feet. After the event
He wept. He promised 'a new start.'
I made no comment. What should I resent?"

"On Margate Sands.[9]
I can connect
Nothing with nothing.
The broken fingernails of dirty hands.
My people humble people who expect
Nothing."
la la

---

[1] [Eliot's note] The interior of St. Magnus Martyr is to my mind one of the finest among [Sir Christopher] Wren's interiors. See *The Proposed Demolition of Nineteen City Churches* (P.S. King & Son, Ltd.).

[2] *Inexplicable … gold* Reference to the slender Ionic columns inside the church.

[3] [Eliot's note] The Song of the (three) Thames-daughters begins here. From line 292 to 306 inclusive they speak in turn. V. *Gotterdammerung*, 3.1: the Rhine-daughters. [Eliot refers to Wagner's opera *The Twilight of the Gods*, in which the Rhine maidens lament the theft of the Rhine's gold, which has also robbed the river of its beauty.]

[4] *Isle of Dogs* Peninsula formed by a bend in the river Thames. Opposite this peninsula, on the south side of the Thames, lies the London borough of Greenwich.

[5] *Weialala … leialala* In Wagner's opera, this is the ecstatic cry repeated by the maidens as they guard the lump of gold in the river.

[6] [Eliot's note] V. Froude, *Elizabeth,* Vol. 1, ch. 4, letter of De Quadra to Philip of Spain: "In the afternoon we were in a barge, watching the games on the river. (The queen) was alone with Lord Robert and myself on the poop, when they began to talk nonsense, and went so far that Lord Robert at last said, as I was on the spot there was no reason why they should not be married if the queen pleased." [Eliot refers to *History of England from the Fall of Wolsey to the Death of Elizabeth* (1856–70), by James Anthony Froude. Froude quotes from a letter by Alvarez de Quadra, Bishop of Aquila and Spanish Ambassador to Queen Elizabeth's court. De Quadra believed the young queen would marry Lord Dudley.]

[7] *Trams and … canoe* Eliot's note cites the lines from Dante's *Purgatorio* (5.130–36) that he parodies: "Remember me, who am La Pia [Piety]; / Sienna made me and the Maremma undid me"; *Highbury* Middle-class suburb in north London; *Richmond and Kew* Areas of London located on the Thames in southwest London. Between them lies Kew Gardens.

[8] *Moorgate* Area in the east of the City.

[9] *Margate Sands* Primary beach in the Kent seaside resort of Margate.

To Carthage then I came[1]

Burning burning burning burning[2]
O Lord Thou pluckest me out[3]
O Lord Thou pluckest

burning

4. Death by Water

Phlebas the Phoenician, a fortnight dead,
Forgot the cry of gulls, and the deep sea swell
And the profit and loss.
A current under sea
Picked his bones in whispers. As he rose and fell
He passed the stages of his age and youth
Entering the whirlpool.
Gentile or Jew
O you who turn the wheel and look to windward,
Consider Phlebas, who was once handsome and tall as you.

[1] *To Carthage ... came* Eliot's note cites the opening of Book 3 of *The Confessions of Saint Augustine*: "To Carthage then I came, where a cauldron of unholy loves sang all about mine ears."

[2] [Eliot's note] The complete text of the Buddha's Fire Sermon (which corresponds in importance to the Sermon on the Mount) from which these words are taken, will be found translated in the late Henry Clarke Warren's *Buddhism in Translation* (Harvard Oriental Series). Mr. Warren was one of the great pioneers of Buddhist studies in the Occident.

[3] [Eliot's note] From St. Augustine's *Confessions* again. The collocation of these two representatives of eastern and western asceticism, as the culmination of this part of the poem, is not an accident. [Eliot refers to 10.237–38 of the Confessions: "I entangle my steps with these outward beauties, but thou pluckest me out, O Lord, thou pluckest me out."]

5. What the Thunder Said[4]

After the torchlight red on sweaty faces
After the frosty silence in the gardens
After the agony in stony places
The shouting and the crying
Prison and palace and reverberation
Of thunder of spring over distant mountains
He who was living is now dead[5]
We who were living are now dying
With a little patience

Here is no water but only rock
Rock and no water and the sandy road
The road winding above among the mountains
Which are mountains of rock without water
If there were water we should stop and drink
Amongst the rock one cannot stop or think
Sweat is dry and feet are in the sand
If there were only water amongst the rock
Dead mountain mouth of carious[6] teeth that cannot spit
Here one can neither stand nor lie nor sit
There is not even silence in the mountains
But dry sterile thunder without rain
There is not even solitude in the mountains
But red sullen faces sneer and snarl
From doors of mudcracked houses
If there were water

And no rock
If there were rock
And also water
And water
A spring
A pool among the rock

[4] [Eliot's note] In the first part of Part 5 three themes are employed: the journey to Emmaus, the approach to the Chapel Perilous (see Miss Weston's book), and the present decay of eastern Europe. [*journey to Emmaus* See Luke 24.13–31, in which Jesus, after being resurrected, joins two of his disciples on the road to Emmaus, but they do not recognize him; *Chapel Perilous* The final stage of the Grail quest.]

[5] *After the torchlight ... dead* References to the events from the betrayal of Christ to his death.

[6] *carious* Decayed.

If there were the sound of water only
Not the cicada[1]
And dry grass singing
But sound of water over a rock
Where the hermit-thrush sings in the pine trees[2]
Drip drop drip drop drop drop drop
But there is no water

Who is the third who walks always beside you?[3]
When I count, there are only you and I together
But when I look ahead up the white road
There is always another one walking beside you
Gliding wrapt in a brown mantle, hooded
I do not know whether a man or a woman
—But who is that on the other side of you?

What is that sound high in the air
Murmur of maternal lamentation
Who are those hooded hordes swarming
Over endless plains, stumbling in cracked earth
Ringed by the flat horizon only
What is the city over the mountains
Cracks and reforms and bursts in the violet air
Falling towers
Jerusalem Athens Alexandria
Vienna London
Unreal[4]

A woman drew her long black hair out tight
And fiddled whisper music on those strings
And bats with baby faces in the violet light
Whistled, and beat their wings
And crawled head downward down a blackened wall
And upside down in air were towers
Tolling reminiscent bells, that kept the hours
And voices singing out of empty cisterns and exhausted wells.

In this decayed hole among the mountains
In the faint moonlight, the grass is singing
Over the tumbled graves, about the chapel
There is the empty chapel, only the wind's home.[5]
It has no windows, and the door swings,
Dry bones can harm no one.
Only a cock stood on the rooftree
Co co rico co co rico[6]
In a flash of lightning. Then a damp gust
Bringing rain

Ganga[7] was sunken, and the limp leaves
Waited for rain, while the black clouds

---

[1] *cicada* Grasshopper. See Ecclesiastes 12.4: "Also when they shall be afraid of that which is high, and fears shall be in the way, and the almond tree shall flourish, and the grasshopper shall be a burden, and desire shall fail: because man goeth to his long home, and the mourners go about the streets."

[2] [Eliot's note] This is *Turdus aonalaschkae pallasii*, the hermit-thrush which I have heard in Quebec Province. Chapman says (*Handbook of Birds of Eastern North America*) "it is most at home in secluded woodland and thickety retreats.… Its notes are not remarkable for variety or volume, but in purity and sweetness of tone and exquisite modulation they are unequalled." Its "water-dripping song" is justly celebrated.

[3] [Eliot's note] The following lines were stimulated by the account of one of the Antarctic expeditions (I forget which, but I think one of Shackleton's): it was related that the party of explorers, at the extremity of their strength, had the constant delusion that there was *one more member* than could actually be counted. [Eliot refers to Sir Ernest Shackleton's third journey to the Antarctic (1914–17), during which he and his men attempted to cross the Antarctic ice cap on foot. See *South: The Story of Shackleton's Last Expedition, 1914-1917* (1919).]

[4] *What is that … Unreal* Eliot's note for these lines quotes in German Herman Hesse, *Blick ins Chaos: Drei Aufsätze* (*A Glimpse into Chaos: Three Essays*). "Already half of Europe, already at least half of Eastern Europe, on the way to chaos, drives drunk in sacred infatuation along the edge of the precipice, singing drunkenly, as though singing hymns, as Dmitri Karamazov sang. The offended bourgeois laughs at the songs; the saint and the seer hear them with tears." Dmitri Karamazov is a character in Fyodor Dostoevsky's *The Brothers Karamazov* (1879–80).

[5] *There is … home* The Chapel Perilous appeared to be surrounded by death and decay; these nightmare visions were meant to induce despair in the questing knight. Once inside the Chapel, the knight's courage would be tested with further horrors.

[6] *Only a … rico* The crowing of the cock signals the coming of the morning and the departure of ghosts and evil spirits, as in *Hamlet* 1.1, when Hamlet's father's ghost disappears with its call. Also, in the Gospels Peter repents his repudiation of Christ after the cock crows.

[7] *Ganga* The Ganges, a sacred river in India.

Gathered far distant, over Himavant.[1]
The jungle crouched, humped in silence.
Then spoke the thunder
DA[2]
Datta: what have we given?
My friend, blood shaking my heart
The awful daring of a moment's surrender
Which an age of prudence can never retract
By this, and this only, we have existed
Which is not to be found in our obituaries
Or in memories draped by the beneficent spider[3]
Or under seals broken by the lean solicitor
In our empty rooms
DA
Dayadhvam: I have heard the key[4]
Turn in the door once and turn once only
We think of the key, each in his prison
Thinking of the key, each confirms a prison
Only at nightfall, aetherial rumours

[1] *Himavant* Sanskrit: Snowy. Adjective used to describe the Himalayas.

[2] [Eliot's note] "Datta, dayadhvam, damyata" (Give, sympathise, control). The fable of the meaning of the Thunder is found in the *Brihadaranyaka—Upanishad*, 5, 1. A translation is found in Deussen's *Sechzig Upanishads des Veda*, p. 489. [Eliot refers to the Hindu fable in which gods, men, and demons, each in turn ask the Lord of Creation, Prajapati, "Please instruct us, Sir." To each he utters the syllable "Da," and each group interprets the answer differently: "Damyata," practice self-control; "Datta," give alms; "Dayadhvam," have compassion. According to the fable, "This very thing is repeated even today by the heavenly voice, in the form of thunder, as 'Da,' 'Da,' 'Da,' which means: 'Control yourselves,' 'Give,' and 'Have compassion.'"]

[3] [Eliot's note] Cf. [John] Webster, *The White Devil*, 5, 6: "… they'll remarry / Ere the worm pierce your winding-sheet, ere the spider / Make a thin curtain for your epitaphs." [In this excerpt from the play, the villain Flamineo urges men never to trust their wives.]

[4] *I have … key* Eliot's note cites the passage in Dante's *Inferno* 33.46, in which Ugolino della Gherardesca remembers being locked up with his children in the tower, where they all starved to death. Eliot also quotes philosopher Francis Herbert Bradley's *Appearance and Reality: A Metaphysical Essay* (1893), p. 346: "My external sensations are no less private to myself than are my thoughts or my feelings. In either case my experience falls within my own circle, a circle closed on the outside; and, with all its elements alike, every sphere is opaque to the others which surround it.… In brief, regarded as an existence which appears in a soul, the whole world for each is peculiar and private to that soul."

Revive for a moment a broken Coriolanus[5]
DA
Damyata: The boat responded
Gaily, to the hand expert with sail and oar
The sea was calm, your heart would have responded
Gaily, when invited, beating obedient
To controlling hands

I sat upon the shore
Fishing, with the arid plain behind me[6]
Shall I at least set my lands in order?[7]
London Bridge is falling down falling down falling
down
Poi s'ascose nel foco che gli affina[8]
Quando fiam ceu chelidon[9]—O swallow swallow
Le Prince d'Aquitaine à la tour abolie[10]
These fragments I have shored against my ruins

[5] *Coriolanus* Roman general of Shakespeare's play of that name. A character who is motivated by pride rather than duty, Coriolanus leads the enemy against Rome, the city from which he has been exiled.

[6] *Fishing … me* Eliot's note refers readers to Weston's *From Ritual to Romance*, chapter 9, "The Fisher King." In this chapter, Weston comments upon the Fisher King's intimate relation with his people and his land, "a relation mainly dependent upon the identification of the King with the Divine principle of Life and Fertility." Weston also argues that "the Fish is a Life symbol of immemorial antiquity, and that the title of Fisher has, from the earliest ages, been associated with Deities who were held to be specially connected with the origin and preservation of life."

[7] *Shall I … order* See Isaiah 38.1, in which the prophet Isaiah counsels the sickly King Hezekiah, whose kingdom has been destroyed by the conquering Assyrians, "Thus saith the Lord, Set thine house in order: for thou shalt die, and not live."

[8] *Poi … affina* Italian: "Then he vanished into the fire that refines them" (Dante's *Purgatorio* 26.148). Eliot's note quotes, in Italian, the three lines of the *Purgatorio* immediately preceding, in which the poet Arnaut Daniel, who is in Purgatory for lust, says to Dante "Now I pray you, by the goodness that guides you to the top of the staircase [of purgatory], be mindful in time of my suffering."

[9] *Quando … chelidon* Latin: "When shall I be as the swallow?" Eliot's note cites an anonymous Latin poem about Venus and the spring, "The Vigil of Venus," as well as the story of Philomela, whose sister Procne (the wife of Tereus) was turned into a swallow. "The Vigil of Venus" refers to Philomela and Procne in its closing lines.

[10] *Le Prince … abolie* French: "The Prince of Aquitaine in the ruined tower." Eliot's note cites French poet Gerard de Nerval's sonnet "El Desdichado" (1853). One of the Tarot cards shows a tower struck by lightning.

Why then Ile fit you. Hieronymo's mad againe.[1]
Datta. Dayadhvam. Damyata.
Shantih shantih shantih[2]
—1922

Journey of the Magi[3]

"A cold coming we had of it,
Just the worst time of the year
For a journey, and such a long journey:
The ways deep and the weather sharp,
The very dead of winter."[4]
And the camels galled, sore-footed, refractory,
Lying down in the melting snow.
There were times we regretted
The summer palaces on slopes, the terraces,
And the silken girls bringing sherbet.
Then the camel men cursing and grumbling
And running away, and wanting their liquor and women,
And the night-fires going out, and the lack of shelters,
And the cities hostile and the towns unfriendly
And the villages dirty and charging high prices:
A hard time we had of it.
At the end we preferred to travel all night,
Sleeping in snatches,
With the voices singing in our ears, saying
That this was all folly.

Then at dawn we came down to a temperate valley,
Wet, below the snow line, smelling of vegetation;
With a running stream and a water-mill beating the darkness,
And three trees[5] on the low sky,
And an old white horse[6] galloped away in the meadow.
Then we came to a tavern with vine-leaves over the lintel,[7]
Six hands at an open door dicing for pieces of silver,[8]
And feet kicking the empty wine-skins.
But there was no information, and so we continued
And arrived at evening, not a moment too soon
Finding the place; it was (you may say) satisfactory.

All this was a long time ago, I remember,
And I would do it again, but set down
This set down
This: were we led all that way for
Birth or Death? There was a Birth, certainly,
We had evidence and no doubt. I had seen birth and death,
But had thought they were different; this Birth was
Hard and bitter agony for us, like Death, our death.
We returned to our places, these Kingdoms,
But no longer at ease here, in the old dispensation,
With an alien people clutching their gods.
I should be glad of another death.
—1927

[1] *Why then … againe* Eliot's note cites Thomas Kyd's *The Spanish Tragedy: Hieronymo Is Mad Againe* (1592). In the play, Hieronymo, whose son has been murdered, is asked to write a play for the court. He responds "Why then Ile fit you (i.e., "I'll accommodate you," or "I'll give you your due"). He writes the play and persuades the murderers to act in it. During the course of the play, his son's murder is avenged.

[2] [Eliot's note] Shantih. Repeated as here, a formal ending to an Upanishad. "The Peace which passeth understanding" is our equivalent to this word. [The Upanishads are poetic dialogues that comment on the Vedas, the ancient Hindu Scriptures. Eliot's phrasing derives from Paul's letter to the early Christians in Philippians 4.7: "And the peace of God, which passeth all understanding, shall keep your hearts and minds through Jesus Christ."]

[3] *Magi* Three wise men who journeyed to Bethlehem to honor Jesus at his birth (see Matthew 2.1–12).

[4] *A cold … winter* Adapted from a sermon given by Anglican bishop Lancelot Andrewes on Christmas Day, 1622.

[5] *three trees* Suggests the three crosses on Calvary, on which Christ and two criminals were crucified (see Luke 23.32–43).

[6] *white horse* Ridden by Christ in Revelation 6.2 and 19.11–14.

[7] *lintel* Doorframe.

[8] *dicing … silver* Allusion to Judas' betrayal of Jesus for thirty pieces of silver, and to the soldiers who throw dice for the robes of Christ at his crucifixion (Matthew 26.14 and 27.35).

Burnt Norton

τοῦ λόλου δ' ἐόντος ξυνοῦ ζώουσιν οἱ πολλοί ὡς ἰδίαν ἔχοντες φρόνησιν.

I. p. 77. Fr. 2

ὁδὸς ἄνω κάτω μία καὶ ὡυτή.

I. p. 89. Fr. 60

Diels: *Die Fragmente der Vorsokratiker* (*Herakleitos*).[1]

I

Time present and time past
Are both perhaps present in time future,
And time future contained in time past.
If all time is eternally present
All time is unredeemable.
What might have been is an abstraction
Remaining a perpetual possibility
Only in a world of speculation.
What might have been and what has been
Point to one end, which is always present.
Footfalls echo in the memory
Down the passage which we did not take
Towards the door we never opened
Into the rose-garden. My words echo
Thus, in your mind.
But to what purpose
Disturbing the dust on a bowl of rose-leaves
I do not know.
Other echoes
Inhabit the garden. Shall we follow?
Quick, said the bird, find them, find them,
Round the corner. Through the first gate,
Into our first world, shall we follow
The deception of the thrush? Into our first world.
There they were, dignified, invisible,
Moving without pressure, over the dead leaves,
In the autumn heat, through the vibrant air,
And the bird called, in response to
The unheard music hidden in the shrubbery,
And the unseen eyebeam crossed, for the roses
Had the look of flowers that are looked at.
There they were as our guests, accepted and accepting.
So we moved, and they, in a formal pattern,
Along the empty alley, into the box circle,
To look down into the drained pool.
Dry the pool, dry concrete, brown edged,
And the pool was filled with water out of sunlight,
And the lotos[2] rose, quietly, quietly,
The surface glittered out of heart of light,
And they were behind us, reflected in the pool.
Then a cloud passed, and the pool was empty.
Go, said the bird, for the leaves were full of children,
Hidden excitedly, containing laughter.
Go, go, go, said the bird: human kind
Cannot bear very much reality.
Time past and time future
What might have been and what has been
Point to one end, which is always present.

2

Garlic and sapphires in the mud
Clot the bedded axle-tree.
The trilling wire in the blood
Sings below inveterate scars
And reconciles forgotten wars.
The dance along the artery
The circulation of the lymph
Are figured in the drift of stars
Ascend to summer in the tree
We move above the moving tree
In light upon the figured leaf

---

[1] *Burnt Norton … (Herakleitos)* Name of a large country house in Gloucestershire, England, that was built on the site of an earlier home that had burned down in the seventeenth century. Eliot visited the home in 1934. This poem was first published in 1935, and then republished in 1943 as one of the *Four Quartets*. Eliot modeled the structure of this long poem on one of Beethoven's final quartets, particularly the A Minor Quartet (Beethoven's last), which Eliot found "quite inexhaustible to study. There is some sort of heavenly or at least more than human gaiety about some of his later things which one imagines must come to oneself as the fruit of reconciliation and relief after immense suffering; I should like to get something of that into verse before I die." The epigraphs are from the writings of sixth-century BCE philosopher Heraclitus; *τοῦ … φρόνησιν* Greek: Although the Word governs all things, most people live as though they had wisdom of their own; *ὁδὸς … ὡυτή* Greek: The way up and the way down are the same.

[2] *lotos* Plant whose flowers, according to Greek myth, produced dreamy forgetfulness in those who ate them.

And hear upon the sodden floor
Below, the boarhound and the boar
Pursue their pattern as before
But reconciled among the stars.

At the still point of the turning world. Neither flesh nor fleshless;
Neither from nor towards; at the still point, there the dance is,
But neither arrest nor movement. And do not call it fixity,
Where past and future are gathered. Neither movement from nor towards,
Neither ascent nor decline. Except for the point, the still point,
There would be no dance, and there is only the dance.
I can only say, *there* we have been: but I cannot say where.
And I cannot say, how long, for that is to place it in time.

The inner freedom from the practical desire,
The release from action and suffering, release from the inner
And the outer compulsion, yet surrounded
By a grace of sense, a white light still and moving,
Erhebung[1] without motion, concentration
Without elimination, both a new world
And the old made explicit, understood
In the completion of its partial ecstasy,
The resolution of its partial horror.
Yet the enchainment of past and future
Woven in the weakness of the changing body,
Protects mankind from heaven and damnation
Which flesh cannot endure.
Time past and time future
Allow but a little consciousness.
To be conscious is not to be in time
But only in time can the moment in the rose-garden,
The moment in the arbour where the rain beat,
The moment in the draughty church at smokefall
Be remembered; involved with past and future.
Only through time time is conquered.

3

Here is a place of disaffection
Time before and time after
In a dim light: neither daylight
Investing form with lucid stillness
Turning shadow into transient beauty
With slow rotation suggesting permanence
Nor darkness to purify the soul
Emptying the sensual with deprivation
Cleansing affection from the temporal.
Neither plenitude nor vacancy. Only a flicker
Over the strained time-ridden faces
Distracted from distraction by distraction
Filled with fancies and empty of meaning
Tumid apathy with no concentration
Men and bits of paper, whirled by the cold wind
That blows before and after time,
Wind in and out of unwholesome lungs
Time before and time after.
Eructation° of unhealthy souls *belching*
Into the faded air, the torpid
Driven on the wind that sweeps the gloomy hills of London,
Hampstead and Clerkenwell, Campden and Putney,
Highgate, Primrose and Ludgate. Not here
Not here the darkness, in this twittering world.

Descend lower, descend only
Into the world of perpetual solitude,
World not world, but that which is not world,
Internal darkness, deprivation
And destitution of all property,
Desiccation of the world of sense,
Evacuation of the world of fancy,
Inoperancy of the world of spirit;
This is the one way, and the other
Is the same, not in movement
But abstention from movement; while the world moves

[1] *Erhebung* German: Lifting up. Term used by the German philosopher Georg Wilhelm Friedrich Hegel (1770–1831) to denote a new level of understanding.

In appetency,[1] on its metalled ways
Of time past and time future.

4

Time and the bell have buried the day,
The black cloud carries the sun away.
Will the sunflower turn to us, will the clematis[2]
Stray down, bend to us; tendril and spray
Clutch and cling?
Chill
Fingers of yew be curled
Down on us? After the kingfisher's wing
Has answered light to light, and is silent, the light is still
At the still point of the turning world.

5

Words move, music moves
Only in time; but that which is only living
Can only die. Words, after speech, reach
Into the silence. Only by the form, the pattern,
Can words or music reach
The stillness, as a Chinese jar still
Moves perpetually in its stillness.
Not the stillness of the violin, while the note lasts,
Not that only, but the co-existence,
Or say that the end precedes the beginning,
And the end and the beginning were always there
Before the beginning and after the end.
And all is always now. Words strain,
Crack and sometimes break, under the burden,
Under the tension, slip, slide, perish,
Decay with imprecision, will not stay in place,
Will not stay still. Shrieking voices
Scolding, mocking, or merely chattering,
Always assail them. The Word in the desert
Is most attacked by voices of temptation,
The crying shadow in the funeral dance,
The loud lament of the disconsolate chimera.[3]

The detail of the pattern is movement,
As in the figure of the ten stairs.[4]
Desire itself is movement
Not in itself desirable;
Love is itself unmoving,
Only the cause and end of movement,
Timeless, and undesiring
Except in the aspect of time
Caught in the form of limitation
Between un-being and being.
Sudden in a shaft of sunlight
Even while the dust moves
There rises the hidden laughter
Of children in the foliage
Quick now, here, now, always—
Ridiculous the waste sad time
Stretching before and after.

—1935, 1943

Tradition and the Individual Talent

I

In English writing we seldom speak of tradition, though we occasionally apply its name in deploring its absence. We cannot refer to "the tradition" or to "a tradition"; at most, we employ the adjective in saying that the poetry of So-and-so is "traditional" or even "too traditional." Seldom, perhaps, does the word appear except in a phrase of censure. If otherwise, it is vaguely approbative, with the implication, as to the work approved, of some pleasing archaeological reconstruction. You can hardly make the word agreeable to English ears without this comfortable reference to the reassuring science of archaeology.

Certainly the word is not likely to appear in our appreciations of living or dead writers. Every nation, every race, has not only its own creative, but its own critical turn of mind; and is even more oblivious of the shortcomings and limitations of its critical habits than

---

1 *appetency* Instinctive inclination.

2 *clematis* Type of twining shrub.

3 *chimera* Fire-breathing monster of Greek mythology that was usually represented as part goat, part lion, and part serpent. Hence, any fantastic monster of disparate parts or fanciful illusion.

4 *ten stairs* According to Spanish poet and mystic St. John of the Cross (1542–91), there are ten steps on the mystical ladder of divine love.

of those of its creative genius. We know, or think we know, from the enormous mass of critical writing that has appeared in the French language, the critical method or habit of the French; we only conclude (we are such unconscious people) that the French are "more critical than we," and sometimes even plume ourselves a little with the fact, as if the French were the less spontaneous. Perhaps they are; but we might remind ourselves that criticism is as inevitable as breathing, and that we should be none the worse for articulating what passes in our minds when we read a book and feel an emotion about it, for criticizing our own minds in their work of criticism. One of the facts that might come to light in this process is our tendency to insist, when we praise a poet, upon those aspects of his work in which he least resembles anyone else. In these aspects or parts of his work we pretend to find what is individual, what is the peculiar essence of the man. We dwell with satisfaction upon the poet's difference from his predecessors, especially his immediate predecessors; we endeavour to find something that can be isolated in order to be enjoyed. Whereas if we approach a poet without this prejudice we shall often find that not only the best, but the most individual parts of his work may be those in which the dead poets, his ancestors, assert their immortality most vigorously. And I do not mean the impressionable period of adolescence, but the period of full maturity.

Yet if the only form of tradition, of handing down, consisted in following the ways of the immediate generation before us in a blind or timid adherence to its successes, "tradition" should positively be discouraged. We have seen many such simple currents soon lost in the sand; and novelty is better than repetition. Tradition is a matter of much wider significance. It cannot be inherited, and if you want it you must obtain it by great labour. It involves, in the first place, the historical sense, which we may call nearly indispensable to anyone who would continue to be a poet beyond his twenty-fifth year; and the historical sense involves a perception, not only of the pastness of the past, but of its presence; the historical sense compels a man to write not merely with his own generation in his bones, but with a feeling that the whole of the literature of Europe from Homer[1] and within it the whole of the literature of his own country has a simultaneous existence and composes a simultaneous order. This historical sense, which is a sense of the timeless as well as of the temporal and of the timeless and of the temporal together, is what makes a writer traditional. And it is at the same time what makes a writer most acutely conscious of his place in time, of his own contemporaneity.

No poet, no artist of any art, has his complete meaning alone. His significance, his appreciation is the appreciation of his relation to the dead poets and artists. You cannot value him alone; you must set him, for contrast and comparison, among the dead. I mean this as a principle of aesthetic, not merely historical, criticism. The necessity that he shall conform, that he shall cohere, is not one-sided; what happens when a new work of art is created is something that happens simultaneously to all the works of art which preceded it. The existing monuments form an ideal order among themselves, which is modified by the introduction of the new (the really new) work of art among them. The existing order is complete before the new work arrives; for order to persist after the supervention of novelty, the *whole* existing order must be, if ever so slightly, altered; and so the relations, proportions, values of each work of art toward the whole are readjusted; and this is conformity between the old and the new. Whoever has approved this idea of order, of the form of European, of English literature will not find it preposterous that the past should be altered by the present as much as the present is directed by the past. And the poet who is aware of this will be aware of great difficulties and responsibilities.

In a peculiar sense he will be aware also that he must inevitably be judged by the standards of the past. I say judged, not amputated, by them; not judged to be as good as, or worse or better than, the dead; and certainly not judged by the canons of dead critics. It is a judgement, a comparison, in which two things are measured by each other. To conform merely would be for the new work not really to conform at all; it would not be new,

[1] *Homer* Greek poet (c. 700 BCE), author of the *Iliad* and the *Odyssey*.

and would therefore not be a work of art. And we do not quite say that the new is more valuable because it fits in; but its fitting in is a test of its value—a test, it is true, which can only be slowly and cautiously applied, for we are none of us infallible judges of conformity. We say: it appears to conform, and is perhaps individual, or it appears individual, and may conform; but we are hardly likely to find that it is one and not the other.

To proceed to a more intelligible exposition of the relation of the poet to the past: he can neither take the past as a lump, an indiscriminate bolus,[1] nor can he form himself wholly on one or two private admirations, nor can he form himself wholly upon one preferred period. The first course is inadmissible, the second is an important experience of youth, and the third is a pleasant and highly desirable supplement. The poet must be very conscious of the main current, which does not at all flow invariably through the most distinguished reputations. He must be quite aware of the obvious fact that art never improves, but that the material of art is never quite the same. He must be aware that the mind of Europe—the mind of his own country—a mind which he learns in time to be much more important than his own private mind—is a mind which changes, and that this change is a development which abandons nothing *en route*, which does not superannuate either Shakespeare, or Homer, or the rock drawing of the Magdalenian draughtsmen.[2] That this development, refinement perhaps, complication certainly, is not, from the point of view of the artist, any improvement. Perhaps not even an improvement from the point of view of the psychologist or not to the extent which we imagine; perhaps only in the end based upon a complication in economics and machinery. But the difference between the present and the past is that the conscious present is an awareness of the past in a way and to an extent which the past's awareness of itself cannot show.

Someone said: "The dead writers are remote from us because we *know* so much more than they did." Precisely, and they are that which we know.

I am alive to a usual objection to what is clearly part of my programme for the *métier* of poetry. The objection is that the doctrine requires a ridiculous amount of erudition (pedantry), a claim which can be rejected by appeal to the lives of poets in any pantheon. It will even be affirmed that much learning deadens or perverts poetic sensibility. While, however, we persist in believing that a poet ought to know as much as will not encroach upon his necessary receptivity and necessary laziness, it is not desirable to confine knowledge to whatever can be put into a useful shape for examinations, drawing rooms, or the still more pretentious modes of publicity. Some can absorb knowledge, the more tardy must sweat for it. Shakespeare acquired more essential history from Plutarch[3] than most men could from the whole British Museum. What is to be insisted upon is that the poet must develop or procure the consciousness of the past and that he should continue to develop this consciousness throughout his career.

What happens is a continual surrender of himself as he is at the moment to something which is more valuable. The progress of an artist is a continual self-sacrifice, a continual extinction of personality.

There remains to define this process of depersonalization and its relation to the sense of tradition. It is in this depersonalization that art may be said to approach the condition of science. I therefore invite you to consider, as a suggestive analogy, the action which takes place when a bit of finely filiated[4] platinum is introduced into a chamber containing oxygen and sulphur dioxide.

2

Honest criticism and sensitive appreciation is directed not upon the poet but upon the poetry. If we attend to the confused cries of the newspaper critics and the susurrus[5] of popular repetition that follows, we shall

---

[1] *bolus* Round mass.

[2] *Magdalenian draughtsmen* Magdalenian cave paintings of the Paleolithic period are among the first known works of art.

[3] *Plutarch* Greek biographer of the first century CE who had a strong influence on English literature; Shakespeare drew some of his characters in plays such as *Coriolanus*, *Antony and Cleopatra*, and *Julius Caesar* from Plutarch's biographies.

[4] *filiated* Made into filament, or fine thread.

[5] *susurrus* Whispering or muttering.

hear the names of poets in great numbers; if we seek not Blue-book[1] knowledge but the enjoyment of poetry, and ask for a poem, we shall seldom find it. I have tried to point out the importance of the relation of the poem to other poems by other authors, and suggested the conception of poetry as a living whole of all the poetry that has ever been written. The other aspect of this Impersonal theory of poetry is the relation of the poem to its author. And I hinted, by an analogy, that the mind of the mature poet differs from that of the immature one not precisely in any valuation of "personality," not being necessarily more interesting, or having "more to say," but rather by being a more finely perfected medium in which special, or very varied, feelings are at liberty to enter into new combinations.

The analogy was that of the catalyst. When the two gases previously mentioned are mixed in the presence of a filament of platinum, they form sulphurous acid. This combination takes place only if the platinum is present; nevertheless, the newly formed acid contains no trace of platinum, and the platinum itself is apparently unaffected: has remained inert, neutral, and unchanged. The mind of the poet is the shred of platinum. It may partly or exclusively operate upon the experience of the man himself; but, the more perfect the artist, the more completely separate in him will be the man who suffers and the mind which creates; the more perfectly will the mind digest and transmute the passions which are its material.

The experience, you will notice, the elements which enter the presence of the transforming catalyst, are of two kinds: emotions and feelings. The effect of a work of art upon the person who enjoys it is an experience different in kind from any experience not of art. It may be formed out of one emotion, or may be a combination of several; and various feelings, inhering for the writer in particular words or phrases or images, may be added to compose the final result. Or great poetry may be made without the direct use of any emotion whatever: composed out of feelings solely. Canto XV of the *Inferno*[2] (Brunetto Latini) is a working up of the emotion evident in the situation; but the effect, though single as that of any work of art, is obtained by considerable complexity of detail. The last quatrain gives an image, a feeling attaching to an image, which "came," which did not develop simply out of what precedes, but which was probably in suspension in the poet's mind until the proper combination arrived for it to add itself to. The poet's mind is in fact a receptacle for seizing and storing up numberless feelings, phrases, images, which remain there until all the particles which can unite to form a new compound are present together.

If you compare several representative passages of the greatest poetry you see how great is the variety of types of combination, and also how completely any semi-ethical criterion of "sublimity" misses the mark. For it is not the "greatness," the intensity, of the emotions, the components, but the intensity of the artistic process, the pressure, so to speak, under which the fusion takes place, that counts. The episode of Paolo and Francesca[3] employs a definite emotion, but the intensity of the poetry is something quite different from whatever intensity in the supposed experience it may give the impression of. It is no more intense, furthermore, than Canto XXVI, the voyage of Ulysses, which has not the direct dependence upon an emotion. Great variety is possible in the process of transmutation of emotion: the murder of Agamemnon,[4] or the agony of Othello,[5] gives an artistic effect apparently closer to a possible original than the scenes from Dante. In the *Agamemnon,* the artistic emotion approximates to the emotion of an actual spectator; in *Othello* to the emotion of the protagonist himself. But the difference between art and the event is always absolute; the combination which is the murder of Agamemnon is probably as complex as that which is the voyage of Ulysses. In either case there has

[1] *Blue-book* Official reports of the British Government.

[2] *Canto XV of the Inferno* In this canto, Dante meets an old acquaintance, Brunetto Latini, who is in Hell for being a Sodomite.

[3] *episode of Paolo and Francesca* Two illicit lovers (Paolo is Francesca's husband's brother).

[4] *murder of Agamemnon* In Aeschylus's play, Clytemnestra kills her husband Agamemnon after he sacrifices their daughter to the god Artemis.

[5] *agony of Othello* In the play by Shakespeare, Othello mistakenly thinks that his wife is unfaithful, kills her, and then, upon learning the truth, commits suicide.

been a fusion of elements. The ode of Keats contains a number of feelings which have nothing particular to do with the nightingale, but which the nightingale, partly perhaps because of its attractive name, and partly because of its reputation, served to bring together.

The point of view which I am struggling to attack is perhaps related to the metaphysical theory of the substantial unity of the soul: for my meaning is, that the poet has, not a "personality" to express, but a particular medium, which is only a medium and not a personality, in which impressions and experiences combine in peculiar and unexpected ways. Impressions and experiences which are important for the man may take no place in the poetry, and those which become important in the poetry may play quite a negligible part in the man, the personality.

I will quote a passage which is unfamiliar enough to be regarded with fresh attention in the light—or darkness—of these observations:

And now methinks I could e'en chide myself
For doting on her beauty, though her death
Shall be revenged after no common action.
Does the silkworm expend her yellow labours
For thee? For thee does she undo herself?
Are lordships sold to maintain ladyships
For the poor benefit of a bewildering minute?
Why does yon fellow falsify highways,
And put his life between the judge's lips,
To refine such a thing—keeps horse and men
To beat their valours for her?[1] ...

In this passage (as is evident if it is taken in its context) there is a combination of positive and negative emotions: an intensely strong attraction toward beauty and an equally intense fascination by the ugliness which is contrasted with it and which destroys it. This balance of contrasted emotion is in the dramatic situation to which the speech is pertinent, but that situation alone is inadequate to it. This is, so to speak, the structural emotion, provided by the drama. But the whole effect, the dominant tone, is due to the fact that a number of floating feelings, having an affinity to this emotion by no means superficially evident, have combined with it to give us a new art emotion.

It is not in his personal emotions, the emotions provoked by particular events in his life, that the poet is in anyway remarkable or interesting. His particular emotions may be simple, or crude, or flat. The emotion in his poetry will be a very complex thing, but not with the complexity of the emotions of people who have very complex or unusual emotions in life. One error, in fact, of eccentricity in poetry is to seek for new human emotions to express; and in this search for novelty in the wrong place it discovers the perverse. The business of the poet is not to find new emotions, but to use the ordinary ones and, in working them up into poetry, to express feelings which are not in actual emotions at all. And emotions which he has never experienced will serve his turn as well as those familiar to him. Consequently, we must believe that "emotion recollected in tranquillity"[2] is an inexact formula. For it is neither emotion, nor recollection, nor, without distortion of meaning, tranquillity. It is a concentration, and a new thing resulting from the concentration, of a very great number of experiences which to the practical and active person would not seem to be experiences at all; it is a concentration which does not happen consciously or of deliberation. These experiences are not "recollected," and they finally unite in an atmosphere which is "tranquil" only in that it is a passive attending upon the event. Of course this is not quite the whole story. There is a great deal, in the writing of poetry, which must be conscious and deliberate. In fact, the bad poet is usually unconscious where he ought to be conscious, and conscious where he ought to be unconscious. Both errors tend to make him "personal." Poetry is not a turning loose of emotion, but an escape from emotion; it is not the expression of personality, but an escape from personality. But, of

[1] *And now ... for her* From *The Revenger's Tragedy* (1607), a play variously ascribed to Cyril Tourneur and to Thomas Middleton.

[2] *"emotion ... tranquillity"* From William Wordsworth's Preface to *Lyrical Ballads* (1800): "Poetry is the spontaneous overflow of powerful feelings: it takes its origin from emotion recollected in tranquillity: the emotion is contemplated till by a species of reaction the tranquillity gradually disappears, and an emotion, kindred to that which was before the subject of contemplation, is gradually produced, and does itself actually exist in the mind."

course, only those who have personality and emotions know what it means to want to escape from these things.

3

ὁ δὲ νοῦς ἴσως θειότερόν τι καὶ ἀπαθές ἐστιν[1]

This essay proposes to halt at the frontier of metaphysics or mysticism, and confine itself to such practical conclusions as can be applied by the responsible person interested in poetry. To divert interest from the poet to the poetry is a laudable aim: for it would conduce to a juster estimation of actual poetry, good and bad. There are many people who appreciate the expression of sincere emotion in verse, and there is a smaller number of people who can appreciate technical excellence. But very few know when there is an expression of *significant* emotion, emotion which has its life in the poem and not in the history of the poet. The emotion of art is impersonal. And the poet cannot reach this impersonality without surrendering himself wholly to the work to be done. And he is not likely to know what is to be done unless he lives in what is not merely the present, but the present moment of the past, unless he is conscious, not of what is dead, but of what is already living.

—1919

The Metaphysical Poets [2]

By collecting these poems from the work of a generation more often named than read, and more often read than profitably studied, Professor Grierson has rendered a service of some importance. Certainly the reader will meet with many poems already preserved in other anthologies, at the same time that he discovers poems such as those of Aurelian Townshend or Lord Herbert of Cherbury here included. But the function of such an anthology as this is neither that of Professor Saintsbury's admirable edition of Caroline poets nor that of *The Oxford Book of English Verse*. Mr. Grierson's book is in itself a piece of criticism, and a provocation of criticism; and we think that he was right in including so many poems of Donne, elsewhere (though not in many editions) accessible, as documents in the case of "metaphysical poetry." The phrase has long done duty as a term of abuse, or as the label of a quaint and pleasant taste. The question is to what extent the so-called metaphysicals formed a school (in our own time we should say a "movement"), and how far this so-called school or movement is a digression from the main current.

Not only is it extremely difficult to define metaphysical poetry, but difficult to decide what poets practise it and in which of their verses. The poetry of Donne (to whom Marvell and Bishop King are sometimes nearer than any of the other authors) is late Elizabethan, its feeling often very close to that of Chapman. The "courtly" poetry is derivative from Jonson, who borrowed liberally from the Latin; it expires in the next century with the sentiment and witticism of Prior. There is finally the devotional verse of Herbert, Vaughan, and Crashaw (echoed long after by Christina Rossetti and Francis Thompson); Crashaw, sometimes more profound and less sectarian than the others, has a quality which returns through the Elizabethan period to the early Italians. It is difficult to find any precise use of metaphor, simile, or other conceit, which is common to all the poets and at the same time important enough as an element of style to isolate these poets as a group. Donne, and often Cowley, employ a device which is sometimes considered characteristically "metaphysical"; the elaboration (contrasted with the condensation) of a figure of speech to the furthest stage to which ingenuity can carry it. Thus Cowley develops the commonplace comparison of the world to a chess-board through long stanzas ("To Destiny"[3]), and Donne, with more grace, in "A Valediction,"[4] the comparison of two lovers to a

[1] *ὁ δὲ … ἐστιν* Greek: "The mind is doubtless something more divine and unaffected." From Aristotle's *De Anima* (Latin: On the Soul) 1.4.

[2] *The Metaphysical Poets* Originally published in the *Times Literary Supplement* as a review of the Clarendon Press volume *Metaphysical Lyrics and Poems of the Seventeenth Century: Donne to Butler* (1921), edited by Herbert J.C. Grierson.

[3] *"To Destiny"* Abraham Cowley's "Destiny" (1656).

[4] *"A Valediction"* Donne's poem "A Valediction: Forbidding Mourning" (1633).

pair of compasses. But elsewhere we find, instead of the mere explication of the content of a comparison, a development by rapid association of thought which requires considerable agility on the part of the reader.

On a round ball
A workeman that hath copies by, can lay
An Europe, Afrique, and an Asia,
And quickly make that, which was nothing, All,
So doth each teare,
Which thee doth weare,
A globe, yea world by that impression grow,
Till thy tears mixt with mine doe overflow
This world, by waters sent from thee, my heaven dissolved so.[1]

Here we find at least two connexions which are not implicit in the first figure, but are forced upon it by the poet: from the geographer's globe to the tear, and the tear to the deluge. On the other hand, some of Donne's most successful and characteristic effects are secured by brief words and sudden contrasts:

A bracelet of bright hair about the bone,[2]

where the most powerful effect is produced by the sudden contrast of associations of "bright hair" and of "bone." This telescoping of images and multiplied associations is characteristic of the phrase of some of the dramatists of the period which Donne knew: not to mention Shakespeare, it is frequent in Middleton, Webster, and Tourneur, and is one of the sources of the vitality of their language.

Johnson, who employed the term "metaphysical poets," apparently having Donne, Cleveland, and Cowley chiefly in mind, remarks of them that "the most heterogeneous ideas are yoked by violence together."[3] The force of this impeachment lies in the failure of the conjunction, the fact that often the ideas are yoked but not united; and if we are to judge of styles of poetry by their abuse, enough examples may be found in Cleveland to justify Johnson's condemnation. But a degree of heterogeneity of material compelled into unity by the operation of the poet's mind is omnipresent in poetry. We need not select for illustration such a line as

Notre ame est un trois-mats cherchant son Icarie;[4]

we may find it in some of the best lines of Johnson himself (*The Vanity of Human Wishes*):

His fate was destined to a barren strand,
A petty fortress, and a dubious hand;
He left a name at which the world grew pale,
To point a moral, or adorn a tale—

where the effect is due to a contrast of ideas, different in degree but the same in principle, as that which Johnson mildly reprehended. And in one of the finest poems of the age (a poem which could not have been written in any other age), the *Exequy* of Bishop King, the extended comparison is used with perfect success: the idea and the simile become one, in the passage in which the Bishop illustrates his impatience to see his dead wife, under the figure of a journey:

Stay for me there; I will not faile
To meet thee in that hollow Vale.
And think not much of my delay;
I am already on the way,
And follow thee with all the speed
Desire can make, or sorrows breed.
Each minute is a short degree,
And ev'ry houre a step towards thee.
At night when I betake to rest,
Next morn I rise nearer my West
Of life, almost by eight houres sail,
Than when sleep breath'd his drowsy gale....
But heark! My Pulse, like a soft Drum
Beats my approach, tells Thee *I come;*
And slow howere my marches be,
I shall at last sit down by Thee.

[1] *On a round ... dissolved so* From Donne's "A Valediction: Of Weeping," 10–18.

[2] *A bracelet ... bone* From "The Relic" (1633), 6.

[3] *"the most ... together"* Samuel Johnson in his "Life of Cowley" (1779).

[4] *Notre ... Icarie* French: "Our soul is a three-masted ship seeking its Icarie." From Charles Baudelaire's *Le Voyage*.

(In the last few lines there is that effect of terror which is several times attained by one of Bishop King's admirers, Edgar Poe.) Again, we may justly take these quatrains from Lord Herbert's "Ode,"[1] stanzas which would, we think, be immediately pronounced to be of the metaphysical school:

So when from hence we shall be gone,
And be no more, nor you, nor I,
As one another's mystery,
Each shall be both, yet both but one.

This said, in her up-lifted face,
Her eyes, which did that beauty crown,
Were like two starrs, that having faln down,
Look up again to find their place:

While such a moveless silent peace
Did seize on their becalmed sense,
One would have thought some influence
Their ravished spirits did possess.

There is nothing in these lines (with the possible exception of the stars, a simile not at once grasped, but lovely and justified) which fits Johnson's general observations on the metaphysical poets in his essay on Cowley. A good deal resides in the richness of association which is at the same time borrowed from and given to the word "becalmed"; but the meaning is clear, the language simple and elegant. It is to be observed that the language of these poets is as a rule simple and pure; in the verse of George Herbert this simplicity is carried as far as it can go—a simplicity emulated without success by numerous modern poets. The *structure* of the sentences, on the other hand, is sometimes far from simple, but this is not a vice; it is a fidelity to thought and feeling. The effect, at its best, is far less artificial than that of an ode by Gray. And as this fidelity induces variety of thought and feeling, so it induces variety of music. We doubt whether, in the eighteenth century, could be found two poems in nominally the same metre, so dissimilar as Marvell's "Coy Mistress" and Crashaw's "Saint Teresa"; the one producing an effect of great speed by the use of short syllables, and the other an ecclesiastical solemnity by the use of long ones:

Love, thou art absolute sole lord
Of life and death.

If so shrewd and sensitive (though so limited) a critic as Johnson failed to define metaphysical poetry by its faults, it is worthwhile to inquire whether we may not have more success by adopting the opposite method: by assuming that the poets of the seventeenth century (up to the Revolution[2]) were the direct and normal development of the precedent age; and, without prejudicing their case by the adjective "metaphysical," consider whether their virtue was not something permanently valuable, which subsequently disappeared, but ought not to have disappeared. Johnson has hit, perhaps by accident, on one of their peculiarities, when he observes that "their attempts were always analytic"; he would not agree that, after the dissociation, they put the material together again in a new unity.

It is certain that the dramatic verse of the later Elizabethan and early Jacobean poets expresses a degree of development of sensibility which is not found in any of the prose, good as it often is. If we except Marlowe, a man of prodigious intelligence, these dramatists were directly or indirectly (it is at least a tenable theory) affected by Montaigne. Even if we except also Jonson and Chapman, these two were notably erudite, and were notably men who incorporated their erudition into their sensibility: their mode of feeling was directly and freshly altered by their reading and thought. In Chapman especially there is a direct sensuous apprehension of thought, or a re-creation of thought into feeling, which is exactly what we find in Donne:

in this one thing, all the discipline
Of manners and of manhood is contained;
A man to join himself with th' Universe
In his main sway, and make in all things fit

[1] *Lord Herbert's "Ode"* Edward Herbert, Lord Cherbury's "An Ode upon a Question Moved, Whether Love Should Continue Forever?" (1664).

[2] *Revolution* I.e., the English Revolution, 1640–60.

One with that All, and go on, round as it;
Not plucking from the whole his wretched part,
And into straits, or into nought revert,
Wishing the complete Universe might be
Subject to such a rag of it as he;
But to consider great Necessity.[1]

We compare this with some modern passage:

No, when the fight begins within himself,
A man's worth something. God stoops o'er his head
Satan looks up between his feet—both tug—
He's left, himself, i' the middle; the soul wakes
And grows. Prolong that battle through his life![2]

It is perhaps somewhat less fair, though very tempting (as both poets are concerned with the perpetuation of love by offspring), to compare with the stanzas already quoted from Lord Herbert's "Ode" the following from Tennyson:

One walked between his wife and child,
With measured footfall firm and mild,
And now and then he gravely smiled.

The prudent partner of his blood
Leaned on him, faithful, gentle,
Wearing the rose of womanhood.

And in their double love secure,
The little maiden walked demure,
Pacing with downward eyelids pure.

These three made unity so sweet,
My frozen heart began to beat,
Remembering its ancient beat.[3]

The difference is not a simple difference of degree between poets. It is something which had happened to the mind of England between the time of Donne or Lord Herbert of Cherbury and the time of Tennyson and Browning; it is the difference between the intellectual poet and the reflective poet. Tennyson and Browning are poets, and they think; but they do not feel their thought as immediately as the odour of a rose. A thought to Donne was an experience; it modified his sensibility. When a poet's mind is perfectly equipped for its work, it is constantly amalgamating disparate experience; the ordinary man's experience is chaotic, irregular, fragmentary. The latter falls in love, or reads Spinoza, and these two experiences have nothing to do with each other, or with the noise of the typewriter or the smell of cooking; in the mind of the poet these experiences are always forming new wholes.

We may express the difference by the following theory: The poets of the seventeenth century, the successors of the dramatists of the sixteenth, possessed a mechanism of sensibility which could devour any kind of experience. They are simple, artificial, difficult, or fantastic, as their predecessors were; no less nor more than Dante, Guido Cavalcanti, Guinicelli, or Cino. In the seventeenth century a dissociation of sensibility set in, from which we have never recovered; and this dissociation, as is natural, was aggravated by the influence of the two most powerful poets of the century, Milton and Dryden. Each of these men performed certain poetic functions so magnificently well that the magnitude of the effect concealed the absence of others. The language went on and in some respects improved; the best verse of Collins, Gray, Johnson, and even Goldsmith satisfies some of our fastidious demands better than that of Donne or Marvell or King. But while the language became more refined, the feeling became more crude. The feeling, the sensibility, expressed in the "Country Churchyard"[4] (to say nothing of Tennyson and Browning) is cruder than that in the "Coy Mistress."[5]

The second effect of the influence of Milton and Dryden followed from the first, and was therefore slow

---

[1] *in this one ... Necessity* From *The Revenge of Bussy d'Ambois* (1613), 4.1.

[2] *No ... life* From Robert Browning's "Bishop Blougram's Apology" (1855), 693–97.

[3] *One walked ... beat* From "The Two Voices" (1833), 412–23.

[4] *"Country Churchyard"* "Elegy Written in a Country Church-Yard," by Thomas Gray (1716–71).

[5] *"Coy Mistress"* "To His Coy Mistress," by Andrew Marvell (1621–78).

in manifestation. The sentimental age began early in the eighteenth century, and continued. The poets revolted against the ratiocinative, the descriptive; they thought and felt by fits, unbalanced; they reflected. In one or two passages of Shelley's "Triumph of Life," in the second *Hyperion*,[1] there are traces of a struggle toward unification of sensibility. But Keats and Shelley died, and Tennyson and Browning ruminated.

After this brief exposition of a theory—too brief, perhaps, to carry conviction—we may ask, what would have been the fate of the "metaphysical" had the current of poetry descended in a direct line from them, as it descended in a direct line to them? They would not, certainly, be classified as metaphysical. The possible interests of a poet are unlimited; the more intelligent he is the better; the more intelligent he is the more likely that he will have interests: our only condition is that he turn them into poetry, and not merely meditate on them poetically. A philosophical theory which has entered into poetry is established, for its truth or falsity in one sense ceases to matter, and its truth in another sense is proved. The poets in question have, like other poets, various faults. But they were, at best, engaged in the task of trying to find the verbal equivalent for states of mind and feeling. And this means both that they are more mature, and that they wear better, than later poets of certainly not less literary ability.

It is not a permanent necessity that poets should be interested in philosophy, or in any other subject. We can only say that it appears likely that poets in our civilization, as it exists at present, must be *difficult*. Our civilization comprehends great variety and complexity, and this variety and complexity, playing upon a refined sensibility, must produce various and complex results. The poet must become more and more comprehensive, more allusive, more indirect, in order to force, to dislocate if necessary, language into his meaning. (A brilliant and extreme statement of this view, with which it is not requisite to associate oneself, is that of M. Jean Epstein,[2] *La Poésie d'aujourd-hui*.) Hence we get something which looks very much like the conceit—we get, in fact, a method curiously similar to that of the "metaphysical poets," similar also in its use of obscure words and of simple phrasing.

O géraniums diaphanes, guerroyeurs sortilèges,
Sacrilèges monomanes!
Emballages, dévergondages, douches! O pressoirs
Des vendanges des grands soirs!
Layettes aux abois,
Thyrses au fond des bois!
Transfusions, représailles,
Relevailles, compresses et l'éternel potion,
Angélus! n'en pouvoir plus
De débâcles nuptiales! de débâcles nuptiales![3]

The same poet could write also simply:

Elle est bien loin, elle pleure,
Le grand vent se lamente aussi[4] …

Jules Laforgue, and Tristan Corbière in many of his poems, are nearer to the "school of Donne" than any modern English poet. But poets more classical than they have the same essential quality of transmuting ideas into sensations, of transforming an observation into a state of mind.

Pour l'enfant, amoureux de cartes et d'estampes,
L'univers est égal à son vaste appétit.
Ah, que le monde est grand à la clarté des lampes!
Aux yeux du souvenir que le monde est petit![5]

---

[1] *Hyperion* John Keats began his epic fragment in 1818; in 1819 he revised the poem and wrote *The Fall of Hyperion, A Dream*.

[2] *M. Jean Epstein* French intellectual (1897–1953).

[3] *O géraniums … nuptiales* French: "O diaphanous geraniums, warrior magic spells, / Monomaniacal sacrileges! / Packing materials, licentiousness, showers! O presses / Of the great evening grape harvests! / Pressed baby clothes, / Thyrsis deep in the woods! / Transfusions, reprisals, / Reawakenings, compresses, and the eternal potion, / Angelus! No longer able / Marriage debacles! Marriage debacles!" From Jules Laforgue's *Derniers vers* (1890).

[4] *Elle est bien … aussi* French: "She is far away, she cries, / The high wind also laments." From *Derniers vers*.

[5] *Pour l'enfant … est petit* French: "For the child, loving maps and stamps, / The universe is his vast appetite. / Ah, how large the world is by the clear light of the lamps! / To eyes remembering that the world is small." From Baudelaire's *Le Voyage*.

In French literature the great master of the seventeenth century—Racine—and the great master of the nineteenth—Baudelaire—are in some ways more like each other than they are like anyone else. The greatest two masters of diction are also the greatest two psychologists, the most curious explorers of the soul. It is interesting to speculate whether it is not a misfortune that two of the greatest masters of diction in our language, Milton and Dryden, triumph with a dazzling disregard of the soul. If we continued to produce Miltons and Drydens it might not so much matter, but as things are it is a pity that English poetry has remained so incomplete. Those who object to the "artificiality" of Milton or Dryden sometimes tell us to "look into our hearts and write." But that is not looking deep enough; Racine or Donne looked into a good deal more than the heart. One must look into the cerebral cortex, the nervous system, and the digestive tracts.

May we not conclude, then, that Donne, Crashaw, Vaughan, Herbert and Lord Herbert, Marvell, King, Cowley at his best, are in the direct current of English poetry, and that their faults should be reprimanded by this standard rather than coddled by antiquarian affection? They have been enough praised in terms which are implicit limitations because they are "metaphysical" or "witty," "quaint" or "obscure," though at their best they have not these attributes more than other serious poets. On the other hand, we must not reject the criticism of Johnson (a dangerous person to disagree with) without having mastered it, without having assimilated the Johnsonian canons of taste. In reading the celebrated passage in his essay on Cowley we must remember that by wit he clearly means something more serious than we usually mean today; in his criticism of their versification we must remember in what a narrow discipline he was trained, but also how well trained; we must remember that Johnson tortures chiefly the chief offenders, Cowley and Cleveland. It would be a fruitful work, and one requiring a substantial book, to break up the classification of Johnson and exhibit these poets in all their difference of kind and of degree, from the massive music of Donne to the faint, pleasing tinkle of Aurelian Townshend.

—1921

In Context

T.S. Eliot and Anti-Semitism

Considerable controversy occurred in the latter years of the twentieth century over the issue of T.S. Eliot and anti-Semitism. The issue had been raised here and there during Eliot's lifetime: J.V. Healy raised the matter in correspondence with Eliot in 1940; a letter of George Orwell's in 1948 reveals that some were then suggesting in conversation that Eliot was anti-Semitic, and so on. Orwell no doubt gave voice to a then-common view in dismissing the suggestion:

> It is nonsense what Fyvel said about Eliot being anti-Semitic. Of course you can find what would now be called antisemitic remarks in his early work, but who didn't say such things at that time? (Letter to Julian Symons, 29 October 1948)

That anti-Semitism was widespread in the 1910s and 1920s in both the USA and Britain is certain, and to some extent Eliot's views on the question were no doubt those of the majority at the time. But few published literary works displayed the consistency of association that one finds in Eliot's early poetry between what is Jewish and what is squalid and distasteful. Still, leading critics and scholars did not begin to air the matter publicly until 1971, when the issue of anti-Semitism in Eliot's works was raised by a leading critic, George Steiner, in a letter to *The Listener*:

> The obstinate puzzle is Eliot's uglier touches tend to occur at the heart of very good poetry (which is *not* the case with Pound). One thinks of the notorious "the Jew squats on the window-sill … Spawned in some estaminet of Antwerp" in "Gerontion"; of
>
> The rats are underneath the piles.
> The Jew is underneath the lot.
>
> In "Burbank with a Baedeker: Bleistein with a Cigar"; of
>
> Rachel nee Rabinovich
> tears at the grapes with murderous paws
>
> in "Sweeney among the Nightingales." (*The Listener*, 29 April 1971)

The question Steiner raised as to how the uglier touches in Eliot's work connected with the aesthetic quality of the whole is one that has continued to interest scholars and critics. In an important 1988 book, another leading scholar, Christopher Ricks, put forward an extended analysis of the ways in which various forms of prejudice may have animated both Eliot's work itself and responses to it. Ricks begins his study with a look at prejudice against women; he notes how the critics had picked up on the latent element of misogyny in two famous lines from "The Love Song of J. Alfred Prufrock," "In the room the women come and go / Talking of Michelangelo":

> John Crowe Ransom [puts a] rhetorical question: "How could they ['the women'] have had any inkling of that glory which Michaelangelo had put into his marbles and his paintings?"
>
> Helen Gardner does not as a woman have any different sense of the women: "The absurdity of discussing his giant art, in high-pitched feminine voices, drifting through a drawing room, adds merely extra irony to the underlying sense of the lines." …
>
> What none of the critics will own is how much their sense of the lines is incited by prejudice. … Grover Smith [writes that] "the women meanwhile are talking, no doubt tediously and ignorantly, of Michaelangelo." For all we know, as against suspect (perhaps justifiably, but still), the women could be talking as invaluably as [renowned art historian] Kenneth Clark (*T.S. Eliot and Prejudice*, 10–11).

Ricks analyzes at length and with considerable subtlety the "uglier touches" in Eliot's poetry, noting how these are associative rather than unequivocally prejudicial or inciteful. A line such as "The Jew is underneath the lot," he comments, does not "come clean, since the effect of the article 'The Jew' is to disparage all Jews … while nevertheless leaving open a bolt-hole for the disingenuous reply that a particular Jew only is meant" (35).

As Ricks points out, some of Eliot's other writings are at least as disturbing as the published poems. Particularly troubling are an unpublished poem, "Dirge," that was part of an early draft of *The Waste Land*, and a passage from *After Strange Gods*, a series of lectures given by Eliot in Virginia in 1933, and published in book form a year later. (Eliot never allowed the book to be reprinted.) In the passage Eliot is describing what he feels is to be striven for in a society that properly values tradition:

> The population should be homogenous.… What is still more important is unity of religious background; and reasons of race and religion combine to make any large number of free-thinking Jews undesirable. There must be a proper balance between urban and rural, industrial and agricultural development. And a spirit of excessive tolerance is to be deprecated (*After Strange Gods*, 20).

If Ricks's focus was primarily a literary one, that of Anthony Julius in his *T.S. Eliot, Anti-Semitism, and Literary Form* (1995) was more broadly social—and more clearly provocative. With his searing indictment both of the anti-Semitism of Eliot's age and its memorable expressions in Eliot's verse, Julius touched a raw nerve. Whereas Ricks's criticisms are often elliptical, and his tone generally reserved, Julius is direct and unrelenting:

> "Women," "jews," and "negroes" are not interchangeable "aliens" in Eliot's work. They are, respectively, intimidating, sightless, and transparent; their deaths are respectively longed for, delighted in, and noted without emotion.…
>
> … However, this does not amount to an argument for suppression. I censure; I do not wish to censor.… Eliot's anti-Semitic poems are integral to his oeuvre, an oeuvre which is to be valued and preserved.… One can teach anti-Semitism from such texts; one can also teach poetry. One reads them, appalled, and impressed.

Like Steiner a generation earlier, Julius concludes that Eliot is "able to place his anti-Semitism at the service of his art." A storm of controversy followed the publication of Julius's book, with many defending Julius but many others continuing to argue either that Eliot was not anti-Semitic or that anti-Semitism was irrelevant to his work. A further camp held that anti-Semitism was in fact a significant presence, but that the poetry succeeds despite such "uglier touches" rather than in any way because of them. Today there remains no consensus on these issues, but there can be no doubt that the controversy has left a mark; it is unlikely that extended discussion of Eliot's poetry will again be able to take place without any reference to this troubling issue.

Modernism and Modernity

CONTEXTS

According to Virginia Woolf's oft-quoted formulation, "on or about December 1910 human character changed." Woolf saw that date as marking the moment at which writers began smashing literary conventions in an effort to represent the complexity of human experience through "the spasmodic, the obscure, the fragmentary." At the same moment, painting and sculpture were breaking visual reality into fragments to express the reality of individual human experience—or indeed to express the reality of what increasingly seemed a fragmented world. Such is now a conventional account of the birth of Modernism.

There was, of course, a mock-precision in Woolf's dating, but many others have linked the birth of Modernism to developments that occurred at *about* this time: in painting, the development of Cubism by Pablo Picasso and Georges Braque; in music, the development of strikingly discordant styles such as that of Igor Stravinsky's *The Rite of Spring*; in poetry, the development of Imagism and its offshoots by Ezra Pound, H.D. and, a few years later, T.S. Eliot; in fiction, the development by Dorothy Richardson, James Joyce, Virginia Woolf, and others, of "stream of consciousness" techniques of narration; and, in the world of art as well as of ideas, the development of Futurism by F.T. Marinetti and others. The worldviews underlying these movements were inevitably affected by the developments in the sciences and related fields that characterized the Modern era. In physics, Albert Einstein's special theory of relativity, first published in German in 1905,[1] destabilized the fundamental concepts of time and space by showing that time is not absolute but varies depending on one's frame of reference (meaning, for example, that two events could be, say, ten seconds apart when timed from one point of observation, but ten minutes apart if observed from a different point). Another influential figure was Sigmund Freud, whose foundational work in the discipline of psychoanalysis first began to appear in English in the early 1910s. Freud's vision of individuals as motivated by unconscious forces—including sexual and other impulses far beyond the scope of the socially acceptable—helped to destabilize Victorian notions of morality and of the self.

Arguably, though, the birth of Modernism can be traced to developments that occurred in France considerably earlier—developments such as Arthur Rimbaud's wholesale rejection in 1871 of the conventions of Western poetry. In the 1880s and 90s the Symbolist aesthetic of poets Jules Laforgue and Stephane Mallarmé foreshadowed the coming of Modernism even more directly than had that of Rimbaud. In the 1891 interview excerpted below, Mallarmé asserted that "when a society is without stability, without unity, it cannot create a stable and definitive art," and suggested that we must not try to elude the intellectual work that is entailed in coming to terms with the appropriate obscurity of poetry. A generation later, T.S. Eliot declared (in his essay "The Metaphysical Poets") that "poets in our civilization must be *difficult*. Our civilization comprehends great variety and complexity, and this variety and complexity ... must produce various and complex results. The poet must become ... more allusive, more indirect, in order to force, to dislocate if necessary, language into his meaning."

[1] Einstein's presentation of his theory of special relativity did not appear in English until the early 1920s, but his ideas nonetheless penetrated English-speaking culture earlier than this.

The vortex of Modernism includes within it a wide variety of narrower "isms"—including not only post-Impressionism, Symbolism, Imagism, and Futurism, but also Vorticism, Absurdism, Dadaism, and a number of others. All shun the linear, the decorative, and the sentimental. All tend towards the presentation of reality fractured into its component pieces—and conversely, towards a rejection of all traditions within which reality is represented through the construction of conventionally unified wholes. Often, however, it was suggested that the fractured forms might represent the world as humans *perceive* it more realistically than other, seemingly more "realistic" forms of representation. Such was the case with stream of consciousness narration in fiction, for example, and also with Cubism; Picasso is famously reported to have said of his Cubist work, "I paint objects as I think them, not as I see them."

In the revolutionary ferment of the late eighteenth and early nineteenth centuries, there was a close correlation between literary or artistic positions and political ones; those who held radical political views tended also to hold radical aesthetic ones. In the revolutionary ferment of Modernism a century later, however, the lines of association between the aesthetic and the political are much more tangled; certainly it would be difficult to argue that Modernism was particularly friendly towards the political left. While Woolf and most of the Bloomsbury circle held progressive political views, Pound and many of the Futurists gravitated towards fascism, Eliot towards conservative High Anglicanism. Modernism's strong desire to recognize the force of often anarchic psychological impulse eventually found its most venomous expression in the racism and anti-Semitism of Pound ("Let us be done with Jews … / Let us spit on those who fawn on the Jews for their money"). Nor was Modernism on the whole friendly towards feminism—or, more generally, towards women. H.D., Richardson, and Woolf must be numbered among the major figures of Modernism—and in the long run, their writing on issues relating to gender has counted more than the less progressive pronouncements of some other Modernist figures. But in their own time, the virulent misogyny of such figures as Marinetti and Pound (and the much milder variety of Eliot) had a wide-ranging impact, on literature as in other contexts. The "modern woman" that had been so central to the cultural world at the turn of the century was of little interest to the major male figures of Modernism. Paradoxically, though, the climate that Modernism helped to create may not, finally, have been hostile to women or to progressive causes, if only because Modernism promoted the belief that nothing is stable—and thus implicitly that change can occur in surprising directions, and with surprising speed.

⌘⌘⌘

from Jules Huret, "Interview with Stephane Mallarmé," *L'Echo de Paris* (1891)

... "We are taking part, at this moment," he told me, "in an extraordinary spectacle, unique in all the history of poetry. ... Until now, poets had to have as accompaniment the grand organ notes of regular meter. Well, they have been played too much, and one gets tired of it. ... When he was dying I'm sure the great [Victor] Hugo convinced himself that he had buried poetry for a century—yet even then, Paul Verlaine had already written 'Sagesse'; [Hugo] failed above all to realise that in a society without stability, without unity, it is not possible to create art that is stable, that is definitive. ..."

"So much for the form," I said to Mr. Mallarmé. "And the content?"

"I believe," he answered me, "that the young are closer to the poetic ideal than the old Parnassians,[1] who ... try to present their subjects plainly and directly. I believe that it is necessary to have nothing but allusion. The contemplation of objects, images flying dreamlike from the eyes—these are the song. The Parnassians take the thing as a whole and look at it, but they rob it of its mystery. ... To name a thing is to take away three quarters of the enjoyment of a poem, which is to be found in divining little by little. ..."

"We come now," I said to him, "to a great objection that I am obliged to raise with you—the issue of *obscurity*."

"This is equally dangerous," he replied to me, "if the obscurity comes from the insufficiencies of the reader, or those of the poet—but it is deceitful to try to get away from this work [of unravelling the poem]. ... There ought always to be an enigma in poetry, and it is the purpose of literature—there is no other—to *evoke* objects."

... "Is it you, sir," I now demanded of him, "who has created the new movement?"

"I abhor schools," he said, "and all that they represent: ... literature, to the contrary, is entirely an individual matter. For me, the case of the poet in this society that does not allow one to live, resembles the situation of a man confined in isolation. ..."

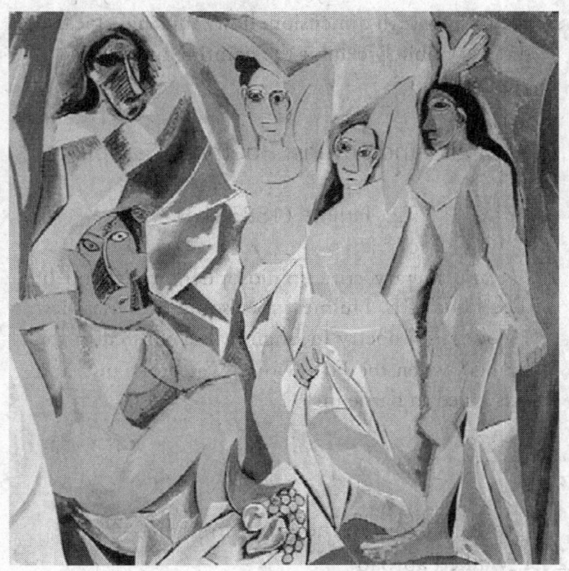

Pablo Picasso, *Les Demoiselles d'Avignon*, 1907. The style of painting known as Cubism was developed by the Spanish painter Pablo Picasso and French painter Georges Braque in 1907. Braque had been much influenced by the landscapes of the French Impressionist Paul Cézanne, in which land, sea, and sky are loosely broken up into soft blocks of color; by 1907 he was developing a style that fragmented landscape much more radically than had Cézanne. Meanwhile Picasso, influenced by traditions of African portraiture through mask, was developing a similarly radical approach to the depiction of the human body. When Braque visited Picasso's studio in the spring of 1907, Picasso showed his groundbreaking painting *Les Demoiselles d'Avignon*, which depicts five women from a brothel in dramatically fragmented fashion. For the next few years, Braque and Picasso followed similar lines of development in their painting.

Though *Les Demoiselles d'Avignon* is now regarded as a landmark in the development of Cubism

---

[1] *Parnassians* School of French poetry whose members (which included Paul Verlaine, Catulle Mendes, and Pierre Louÿs) reacted against Romanticism, preferring instead the formal structure and emotional detachment of classicist poetry.

—and of Modernism generally—it was not well received initially. The leading Post-Impressionist painter Henri Matisse thought the painting represented an attack on "the modern movement," while Picasso's friend and patron Leo Stein is reported to have said sarcastically, "You have been trying to paint the fourth dimension; how amusing!" Picasso did not publicly exhibit the painting until 1925.

Imagist and Futurist Poetry: A Sampling

T.E. Hulme (1883–1917)

Art and literary critic, philosopher, and friend of T.S. Eliot, T.E. Hulme wrote some of the earliest "Modernist" poetry in English. He enlisted in the artillery when the First World War broke out, and was killed in battle in 1917.

"Autumn" (1912)

A touch of cold in the Autumn night—
Walked abroad,
And saw the ruddy moon lean over a hedge
Like a red-faced farmer.
I did not stop to speak, but nodded,
And round about were the wistful stars
With white faces like town children.

Ezra Pound (1885–1972)

Ezra Pound was an expatriate American in London when he became a leading force behind the poetic movement known as "Imagism" and subsequently behind the intellectual and artistic movement known as "Vorticism." He exerted a prolonged influence on the poetry of T.S. Eliot, and is himself reckoned among the most important of Modernist poets. Unlike Eliot, however, Pound did not develop a lifelong attachment to Britain; he spent years in Italy (where, notoriously, he broadcast propaganda for Mussolini's Fascist government during World War II), and after the war he returned to the United States. The critic Hugh Kenner, who wrote extensively on Pound and his work, said that when he met the poet "I knew that I was in the presence of the center of Modernism."

"In a Station of the Metro" (1916, written c. 1911)

The apparition   of these faces   in the crowd;
Petals   on a wet, black   bough.

"Alba" (1916)

As cool as the pale wet leaves
    of lily-of-the-valley
She lay beside me in the dawn.

"L'Art, 1910" (1916)

Green arsenic smeared on an egg-white cloth,
Crushed strawberries! Come, let us feast our eyes.

H.D. (1886–1961)

Like T.S. Eliot and Ezra Pound (to whom she was twice engaged), H.D. was an American expatriate whose work was central to Modernism. Born and educated in Pennsylvania as Hilda Doolittle, she left for Europe in 1911, and soon became known as an Imagist poet. She lived thereafter in England and later in Switzerland, identifying herself as "H.D." beginning in 1913. A writer of fiction as well as of poetry, she wrote the pioneering novel *HERmione*, exploring the tension between a woman's lesbian and heterosexual feelings, in 1927. Her long poem *Trilogy* (1944–46) is regarded by many as her most important work.

"Oread" (1914)

Whirl up, sea—
whirl your pointed pines,

splash your great pines
on our rocks,
hurl your green over us,
cover us with your pools of fir.

"The Pool" (1915)

Are you alive?
I touch you.
You quiver like a sea-fish.
I cover you with my net.
What are you—banded one?

Mina Loy (1882–1966)

Loy is often categorized as a Futurist poet, though she had a stormy relationship with many of the Futurists. She is also often discussed as an American poet, although she was 34 and had already composed most of the work for which she is now best remembered when she left Europe for America. She moved to the United States in 1916 and soon became a part of the New York avant-garde. Born and raised in England, Loy had by then also spent several years amidst the literary and artistic community in Paris, devoting considerable time to painting before turning to poetry in the 1910s. When her "Love Songs" was published in the debut issue of a New York magazine called *Others* in 1915, both the poem and its author immediately became notorious. In 1921, Ezra Pound (then living outside America) suggested that Loy, Marianne Moore, and William Carlos Williams were the only three writers then in the United States "who can write anything of interest in verse."

Recently, Loy has again become notorious, this time for the *Feminist Manifesto* that she wrote in 1914, which includes such incendiary lines as "Men and women are enemies, with the enmity of the exploited for the parasite, the parasite for the exploited. … The only point at which the interests of the sexes merge—is the sexual embrace." Loy drafted the manifesto as an angry response to the misogynist manifestos of the Italian Futurists and (earlier that same year) the BLAST manifesto of Pound, Wyndham Lewis, and others; Loy considered it merely a rough draft, however, and chose not to publish it; the manifesto did not appear in print until 1982.

There are numerous versions of many of Loy's poems; notably, a longer and more explicitly erotic version of "Love Songs" appeared in 1917 under the title "Love Songs to Joannes."

from "Three Moments in Paris" (1915, written 1914)

1. ONE O'CLOCK AT NIGHT

Though you have never possessed me
I have belonged to you since the beginning of time
And sleepily I sit on your chair beside you
Leaning against your shoulder
And your careless arm across my back gesticulates
As your indisputable male voice roars
Through my brain and my body
Arguing "Dynamic Decomposition"
Of which I understand nothing
Sleepily
And the only less male voice of your brother
pugilist of the intellect
Booms as it seems to me so sleepy
Across an interval of a thousand miles
An interim of a thousand years
But you who make more noise than any man
in the world when you clear your throat
Deafening wake me
And I catch the thread of the argument
Immediately assuming my personal mental attitude
And cease to be a woman

Beautiful halfhour of being a mere woman
The animal woman
Understanding nothing of man
But mastery and the security of imparted
physical heat
Indifferent to cerebral gymnastics
Or regarding them as the self-indulgent play of children

Or the thunder of alien gods
But you wake me up
Anyhow   who am I that I should criticize
    your theories of "Plastic Velocity"

"Let us go home   she is tired   and wants to go to
    bed."

from "Love Songs" (1915)

I

Spawn of Fantasies
    Sitting[1] the appraisable
Pig Cupid[2]   his rosy snout
Rooting erotic garbage
"Once upon a time"
Pulls a weed   white star-topped
Among wild oats sown in mucous-membrane
I would an eye in a Bengal light
Eternity in a sky-rocket
Constellations in an ocean
Whose rivers run no fresher
Than a trickle of saliver[3]

These are suspect places
I must live in my lantern
Trimming subliminal flicker
Virginal   to the bellows
Of Experience
        Coloured glass

[1] *Sitting* The handwritten original may read "silting."

[2] *Pig Cupid* The poem as a whole is often referred to as "Pig Cupid."

[3] *saliver* In most published versions this spelling is corrected to "saliva," but the handwritten original reads "-er," and it seems plausible that a connection with the "-er" ending of "fresher" is intended.

Imagism and Vorticism

The first two of the following selections appeared together in a 1913 issue of *Poetry* magazine: a short article by civil servant, poet, and translator F.S. Flint on Imagism was followed by a longer discussion of Imagism by Ezra Pound. In an article on Vorticism three years later Pound made further efforts to define Imagism and Vorticism—as well as to define and comment on Impressionism and Post-Impressionism, Symbolism, and various other of the component movements of Modernism.

from F.S. Flint, "Imagisme,"[4] *Poetry* (March 1913)

Some curiosity has been aroused concerning *Imagisme*, and as I was unable to find anything definite about it in print, I sought out an *Imagiste*, with intent to discover whether the group itself knew anything about the "movement." I gleaned these facts.

The *Imagists* admitted that they were contemporaries of the Post Impressionists and the Futurists; but they had nothing in common with these schools. They had not published a manifesto. … They had a few rules, drawn up for their own satisfaction only, and they had not published them. They were:

1. Direct treatment of the "thing," whether subjective or objective.
2. To use absolutely no word that does not contribute to the presentation.
3. As regarding rhythm: to compose in sequence of the musical phrase, not in sequence of the metronome. By these standards they judged all poetry and found most of it wanting. …

I found among them an earnestness that is amazing to one accustomed to the usual London air of poetic

[4] [1913 note from the *Editors of Poetry* magazine] In response to many requests for information regarding Imagism and the Imagistes, we publish this note by Mr. Flint, supplementing it with further exemplification by Mr. Pound. It will be seen from these that Imagism is not necessarily associated with Hellenic subjects, or with *vers libre* as a prescribed form.

dilettantism. They consider that Art is all science, all religion, philosophy and metaphysic. It is true that *snobisme* may be urged against them; but it is at least *snobisme* in its most dynamic form, with a great deal of sound sense and energy behind it; and they are stricter with themselves than with any outsider.

from Ezra Pound, "A Few Don'ts by an Imagiste," *Poetry* (March 1913)

An "Image" is that which presents an intellectual and emotional complex in an instant of time. I use the term "complex" rather in the technical sense employed by the newer psychologists, such as Hart,[1] though we might not agree absolutely in our application.

It is the presentation of such a "complex" instantaneously which gives that sense of sudden liberation; that sense of freedom from time limits and space limits; that sense of sudden growth, which we experience in the presence of the greatest works of art.

It is better to present one Image in a lifetime than to produce voluminous works. …

Language

Use no superfluous word, no adjective, which does not reveal something.

Don't use such an expression as "dim lands of *peace*." It dulls the image. It mixes an abstraction with the concrete. It comes from the writer's not realizing that the natural object is always the *adequate* symbol.

Go in fear of abstractions. Don't retell in mediocre verse what has already been done in good prose. Don't think any intelligent person is going to be deceived when you try to shirk all the difficulties of the unspeakably difficult art of good prose by chopping your composition into line lengths. What the expert is tired of today the public will be tired of tomorrow.

Don't imagine that the art of poetry is any simpler than the art of music, or that you can please the expert before you have spent at least as much effort on the art of verse as the average piano teacher spends on the art of music. …

Rhythm and Rhyme

Let the candidate fill his mind with the finest cadences he can discover, preferably in a foreign language so that the meaning of the words may be less likely to divert his attention from the movement. …

It is not necessary that a poem should rely on its music, but if it does rely on its music that music must be such as will delight the expert.

Let the neophyte know assonance and alliteration, rhyme immediate and delayed, simple and polyphonic, as a musician would expect to know harmony and counterpoint and all the minutiae of his craft. No time is too great to give to these matters or to any one of them, even if the artists seldom have need of them. …

Don't chop your stuff into separate *iambs.* Don't make each line stop dead at the end, and then begin every next line with a heave. Let the beginning of the next line catch the rise of the rhythm wave, unless you want a definite longish pause.

In short, behave as a musician, a good musician, when dealing with that phase of your art which has exact parallels in music. The same laws govern, and you are bound by no others.

Naturally, your rhythmic structure should not destroy the shape of your words, or their natural sound, or their meaning. It is improbable that, at the start, you will be able to get a rhythm-structure strong enough to affect them very much, though you may fall a victim to all sorts of false stopping due to line ends and caesurae.

The musician can rely on pitch and the volume of the orchestra. You can not. The term harmony is misapplied to poetry; it refers to simultaneous sounds of different pitch. There is, however, in the best verse a sort of residue of sound which remains in the ear of the

[1] *Hart* Bernard Hart (1880–1960), British psychologist who played a central role in promulgating and expanding on the ideas of Sigmund Freud and Carl Jung concerning the unconscious. As the concept was used by Jung, a "complex" was a set of mental patterns in the unconscious which might predispose an individual towards pathological patterns of thought and action. Hart broadened the notion to include any "emotionally toned system of ideas" that might predispose certain patterns of conscious behavior, including patterns that might shape, for example, political biases, but also benign patterns such as those involved in following a hobby.

hearer and acts more or less as an organ-base. A rhyme must have in it some slight element of surprise if it is to give pleasure; it need not be bizarre or curious, but it must be well used if used at all. …

The first three simple proscriptions will throw out nine-tenths of all the bad poetry now accepted as standard and classic; and will prevent you from many a crime of production. …

from Ezra Pound, "Vorticism," *Gaudier-Brzeska* (1916)

"It is no more ridiculous that a person should receive or convey an emotion by means of an arrangement of shapes, or planes, or colours, than that they should receive or convey such emotion by an arrangement of musical notes."

I suppose this proposition is self-evident. Whistler[1] said as much, some years ago, and Pater[2] proclaimed that "All arts approach the condition of music."

Whenever I say this I am greeted with a storm of "Yes, but"s. "But why isn't this art futurism?" "Why isn't?" "Why don't?" and above all: "What, in Heaven's name, has it got to do with your Imagiste poetry?"

Let me explain at leisure, and in nice, orderly, old-fashioned prose. …

"Futurism," when it gets into art, is, for the most part, a descendant of impressionism. It is a sort of accelerated impressionism.

There is another artistic descent *via* Picasso and Kandinsky;[3] *via* Cubism and Expressionism. One does not complain of neo-Impressionism or of accelerated Impressionism and "simultaneity," but one is not wholly satisfied by them. One has perhaps other needs.

… Vorticism has been announced as including such and such painting and sculpture and "Imagisme" in verse. I shall explain "Imagisme," and then proceed to show its inner relation to certain modern paintings and sculpture.

Imagisme, in so far as it has been known at all, has been known chiefly as a stylistic movement, as a movement of criticism rather than of creation. This is natural, for, despite all possible celerity of publication, the public is always, and of necessity, some years behind the artists' actual thought. …

Imagisme is not Symbolism. The Symbolists dealt in "association," that is, in a sort of allusion, almost of allegory. They degraded the symbol to the status of a word. They made it a form of metonomy. One can be grossly "symbolic," for example, by using the term "cross" to mean "trial." The Symbolist's *symbols* have a fixed value, like numbers in arithmetic, like 1, 2, and 7. The Imagiste's images have a variable significance, like the signs *a, b,* and *x* in algebra.

Moreover, one does not want to be called a Symbolist, because Symbolism has usually been associated with mushy technique.

On the other hand, Imagisme is not Impressionism, though one borrows, or could borrow, much from the impressionist method of presentation. But this is only negative definition. …

The image is the poet's pigment.[4] The painter should use his colour because he sees it or feels it. I don't much care whether he is representative or non-representative. He should *depend,* of course, on the creative, not upon the mimetic or representational part in his work. It is the same in writing poems, the author must use his *image* because he sees it or feels it, *not* because he thinks he can use it to back up some creed or some system of ethics or economics.

An *image,* in our sense, is real because we know it directly. …

Any mind that is worth calling a mind must have needs beyond the existing categories of language, just as a painter must have pigments or shades more numerous than the existing names of the colours.

Perhaps this is enough to explain the words in my "Vortex":—

[1] *Whistler* American painter James Abbott McNeill Whistler (1834–1903).

[2] *Pater* English critic Walter Pater (1839–94).

[3] *Kandinsky* Russian abstract painter Wassily Kandinsky (1866–1944).

[4] [Pound's note] The image has been defined as "that which presents an intellectual and emotional complex in an instant of time."

"Every concept, every emotion, presents itself to the vivid consciousness in some primary form. It belongs to the art of this form. ..."

What I have said of one vorticist art can be transposed for another vorticist art. But let me go on then with my own branch of vorticism, about which I can probably speak with greater clarity. All poetic language is the language of exploration. Since the beginning of bad writing, writers have used images as ornaments. The point of Imagisme is that it does not use images *as ornaments.* The image is itself the speech. The image is the word beyond formulated language.

I once saw a small child go to an electric light switch and say, "Mamma, can I *open* the light?" She was using the age-old language of exploration, the language of art. It was a sort of metaphor, but she was not using it as ornamentation.

One is tired of ornamentations, they are all a trick, and any sharp person can learn them.

The Japanese have had the sense of exploration. They have understood the beauty of this sort of knowing. A Chinaman said long ago that if a man can't say what he has to say in twelve lines he had better keep quiet. The Japanese have evolved the still shorter form of the *hokku.*[1]

The fallen blossom flies back to its branch:
A butterfly.

That is the substance of a very well-known *hokku.* Victor Plarr[2] tells me that once, when he was walking over snow with a Japanese naval officer, they came to a place where a cat had crossed the path, and the officer said, "Stop, I am making a poem." Which poem was, roughly, as follows:—

The footsteps of the cat upon the snow:
(are like) plum-blossoms.

The words "are like" would not occur in the original, but I add them for clarity.

[1] *hokku* I.e., haiku.

[2] *Victor Plarr* English poet (1863–1929).

The "one image poem" is a form of super-position, that is to say, it is one idea set on top of another. I found it useful in getting out of the impasse in which I had been left by my metro emotion. I wrote a thirty-line poem, and destroyed it because it was what we call work "of second intensity." Six months later I made a poem half that length; a year later I made the following *hokku*-like sentence:—

The apparition of these faces in the crowd:
Petals on a wet, black bough.

I dare say it is meaningless unless one has drifted into a certain vein of thought.[3] In a poem of this sort one is trying to record the precise instant when a thing outward and objective transforms itself, or darts into a thing inward and subjective.

... I see no reason why I, and various men who agree with me, should be expected to call ourselves Futurists. We do not desire to evade comparison with the past. We prefer that the comparison be made by some intelligent person whose idea of "the tradition" is not limited by the conventional taste of four or five centuries and one continent.

Vorticism is an intensive art. I mean by this, that one is concerned with the relative intensity, or relative significance of different sorts of expression. One desires the most intense, for certain forms of expression *are* "more intense" than others. They are more dynamic. ...

The image is not an idea. It is a radiant node or cluster; it is what I can, and must perforce, call a VORTEX, from which, and through which, and into which, ideas are constantly rushing. In decency one can only call it a VORTEX. And from this necessity came the name "Vorticism."

[3] [Pound's note] Mr. Flint and Mr. Rodker have made longer poems depending on a similar presentation of matter. So also have Richard Aldington, in his *In Via Sestina*, and "H.D." in her *Oread*, which latter poems express much stronger emotions than that in my lines here given. Mr. Hueffer gives an interesting account of a similar adventure of his own in his review of the Imagiste anthology.

Cover of the second (and last) issue of *BLAST*, July 1915; the cover illustration is a Vorticist woodcut by Wyndham Lewis. The first issue (in 1914) included the famous Vorticist manifesto signed by Lewis, Pound, and others.

Dorothy Richardson and Stream of Consciousness

Dorothy Richardson's *Pointed Roofs* is generally considered the first stream-of-consciousness novel in English. It is also the first volume of *Pilgrimage* (1915–67), a novel sequence Richardson worked on throughout her career as she continued to develop the techniques of what she referred to as "interior monologue," the full representation in writing of a character's thoughts and perceptions. The first usage of the phrase "stream of consciousness" to describe this literary technique appears in critic and novelist May Sinclair's review (excerpted below) of the first three volumes of *Pilgrimage*. Also included below is a selection from the novel sequence's 1938 foreword, in which Richardson reflects upon her stylistic innovation and its historical context.

from May Sinclair, "The Novels of Dorothy Richardson," *The Little Review* (April 1918)

I have been asked to write—for this magazine which makes no compromise with the public taste—a criticism of the novels of Dorothy Richardson. The editors of the *Little Review* are committed to Dorothy Richardson by their declared intentions; for her works make no sort of compromise with the public taste. If they are not announced with the same proud challenge it is because the pride of the editors of the *Little Review* is no mate for the pride of Miss Richardson which ignores the very existence of the public and its taste.

I do not know whether this article is or is not going to be a criticism, for so soon as I begin to think what I shall say I find myself criticizing criticism, wondering what is the matter with it and what, if anything, can be done to make it better, to make it alive. Only a live criticism can deal appropriately with a live art. And it seems to me that the first step towards life is to throw off the philosophic cant of the XIXth Century. I don't mean that there is no philosophy of Art, or that if there has been there is to be no more of it; I mean that it is absurd to go on talking about realism and idealism, or objective and subjective art, as if the philosophies were sticking where they stood in the eighties.

In those days the distinction between idealism and realism, between subjective and objective was important and precise. And so long as the ideas they stand for had importance and precision those words were lamps to the feet and lanterns to the path of the critic. Even after they had begun to lose precision and importance they still served him as useful labels for the bewildering phenomena of the arts.

But now they are beginning to give trouble; they obscure the issues. Mr. J.B. [sic] Beresford in his admirable introduction to *Pointed Roofs* confesses to having felt this trouble. When he read it in manuscript he decided that it "was realism, was objective." When he read it in typescript he thought: "this ... is the most subjective thing I have ever read" (p. 256). It is evident that, when first faced with the startling "newness" of Miss Richardson's method and her form, the issues did seem a bit obscure to Mr. Beresford. It was as if up to one illuminating moment he had been obliged to think of methods and forms as definitely objective or definitely subjective. His illuminating moment came with the third reading when *Pointed Roofs* was a printed book. The book itself gave him the clue to his own trouble, which is my trouble, the first hint that criticism up till now has been content to think in clichés, missing the new trend of the philosophies of the XXth Century. All that we know of reality at first hand is given to us through contacts in which those interesting distinctions are lost. Reality is thick and deep, too thick and too deep and at the same time too fluid to be cut with any convenient carving knife. The novelist who would be close to reality must confine himself to this knowledge at first hand. He must, as Mr. Beresford says, simply "plunge in." Mr. Beresford also says that Miss Richardson is the first novelist who has plunged in. She has plunged so neatly and quietly that even admirers of her performance might remain unaware of what it is precisely that she has done. She has disappeared while they are still waiting for the splash. So that Mr. Beresford's introduction was needed.

When first I read *Pointed Roofs* and *Backwater* and *Honeycomb* I too thought, like Mr. Beresford, that Miss Richardson had been the first to plunge. But it seems to me rather that she has followed, independently, perhaps unconsciously, a growing tendency to plunge. As far back as the eighties the de Goncourts plunged completely, finally, in *Soeur Philomène*, *Germinie Lacerteux* and *Les Frères Zemganno*. Marguerite Audoux plunged in the best passages of *Marie Claire*. The best of every good novelist's best work is a more or less sustained immersion. The more modern the novelist the longer his capacity to stay under. Miss Richardson has not plunged deeper than Mr. James Joyce in his *Portrait of the Artist as a Young Man*.

By imposing very strict limitations on herself she has brought her art, her method, to a high pitch of perfection, so that her form seems to be newer than it perhaps is. She herself is unaware of the perfection of her method. She would probably deny that she has written with any deliberate method at all. She would say: "I only know there are certain things I mustn't do if I was to do what I wanted." Obviously, she must not interfere; she must not analyse or comment or explain. Rather less obviously, she must not tell a story, or handle a situation or set a scene; she must avoid drama as she avoids narration. And there are some things she must not be. She must not be the wise, all-knowing author. She must be Miriam Henderson. She must not know or divine anything that Miriam does not know or divine; she must not see anything that Miriam does not see. She has taken Miriam's nature upon her. She is not concerned, in the way that other novelists are concerned, with character. Of the persons who move through Miriam's world you know nothing but what Miriam knows. If Miriam is mistaken, well, she and not Miss Richardson is mistaken. Miriam is an acute observer, but she is very far from seeing the whole of these people. They are presented to us in the same vivid but fragmentary way in which they appeared to Miriam, the fragmentary way in which people appear to most of us. Miss Richardson has only imposed on herself the conditions that life imposes on all of us. And if you are going to quarrel with those conditions you will not find her novels satisfactory. But your satisfaction is not her concern.

And I find it impossible to reduce to intelligible terms this satisfaction that I feel. To me these three novels show an art and method and form carried to punctilious perfection. Yet I have heard other novelists say that they have no art and no method and no form, and that it is this formlessness that annoys them. They say that they have no beginning and no middle and no end, and that to have form a novel must have an end and a beginning and a middle. We have come to words that in more primitive times would have been blows on this subject. There is a certain plausibility in what they say, but it depends on what constitutes a beginning and a middle and an end. In this series there is no drama, no situation, no set scene. Nothing happens. It is just life going on and on. It is Miriam Henderson's stream of consciousness going on and on. And in neither is there any grossly discernible beginning or middle or end.

from Dorothy Richardson, "Foreword" to *Pilgrimage* (1938)

… [F]or a while when in the English literary world it began its career as a useful label, realism was synonymous with Arnold Bennett.[1]

But whereas both Balzac[2] and Bennett, while representing, the one in regard to a relatively concrete and coherent social system, the other in regard to a society already showing signs of disintegration, the turning of the human spirit upon itself, may be called realists by nature and unawares, their immediate successors possess an articulate creed.[3] They believe themselves to be substituting, for the telescopes of the writers of romance whose lenses they condemn as both rose-coloured and distorting, mirrors of plains glass. …

Since all these novelists happened to be men, the present writer, proposing at this moment to write a novel and looking round for a contemporary pattern, was faced with the choice between following one of her regiments and attempting to produce a feminine equivalent of the current masculine realism. Choosing the latter alternative, she presently set aside, at the bidding of a dissatisfaction that revealed its nature without supplying any suggestion as to the removal of its cause, a considerable mass of manuscript. Aware as she wrote, of the gradual falling away of the preoccupations that for a while had dictated the briskly moving scripts, and of the substitution, for these inspiring preoccupations, of a stranger in the form of contemplated reality having for the first time in her experience its own say and apparently justifying those who acclaim writing as the surest means of discovering the truth about one's own thoughts and beliefs, she had been at the same time increasingly tormented, not only by the failure, of this now so independently assertive reality, adequately to appear within the text, but by its revelation, whencesoever focused, of a hundred faces, any one of which, the moment it was entrapped within the close of mesh of direct statement, summoned its fellows to disqualify it.

In 1913, the opening pages of the attempted chronicle became the first chapter of "Pilgrimage," written to the accompaniment of a sense of being upon a fresh pathway, an adventure so searching and, sometimes, so joyous as to produce a longing for participation, not quite the same as a longing for publication, whose possibility, indeed, as the book grew, receded to vanishing point.

To a publisher, nevertheless, at the bidding of Mr. J.D. Beresford, the book was ultimately sent. By the time it returned, the second chapter was partly written and the condemned volume, put away and forgotten, would have remained in seclusion but for the persistence of the same kind friend, who acquired and sent it to Edward Garnett, then reading the Messrs Duckworth. In 1915, the covering title being at the moment in use elsewhere, it was published as "Pointed Roofs."

The lonely track, meanwhile, had turned out to be a populous highway. Amongst those who had simultaneously entered it, two figures[4] stood out. One a woman mounted upon a magnificently caparisoned charger, the other a man walking, with eyes devoutly closed, weaving as he went a rich garment of new words wherewith to clothe the antique dark material of his engrossment.

News came from France of one Marcel Proust, said to be producing an unprecedently profound and opulent reconstruction of experience focused from within the mind of a single individual, and, since Proust's first volume had been published and several others written by 1913, the France of Balzac now appeared to have produced the earliest adventurer. …

[1] *Arnold Bennett* English novelist (1897–1931).

[2] *Balzac* Honoré de Balzac, French journalist and novelist (1799–1850) whose great masterpiece, *La Comédie humaine*, comprises over 90 novels and short stories and includes over 2,000 characters from nearly all classes and professions of society.

[3] *their immediate … creed* Richardson probably had in mind, among others, W. Somerset Maugham (1874–1965), John Galsworthy (1867–1933), and H.G. Wells (1866–1946) as successors to Bennett and Balzac.

[4] *two figures* Virginia Woolf (1882–1941) and James Joyce (1882–1941).

Wyndham Lewis, *Workshop*, c. 1915. The Canadian-born writer and artist Wyndham Lewis (1882–1957) lived largely in England from 1908 onwards. In the period 1912–15 he was a leader among those painters variously described as Futurist, Cubist, and "Vorticist"—the last of these a term that Lewis himself coined. Though his writing—like that of Pound and others in their circle—is tainted by anti-Semitism, misogyny, and, in Lewis's case, venomous portrayals of gay and lesbian people, Lewis is unquestionably a figure central to British Modernism. *Workshop* is one of the works that extend furthest his vision of harsh lines and fragmented shapes conveying a sense of the modern city, and of modernity itself.

World War I recruiting poster used in Ireland, c. 1915.

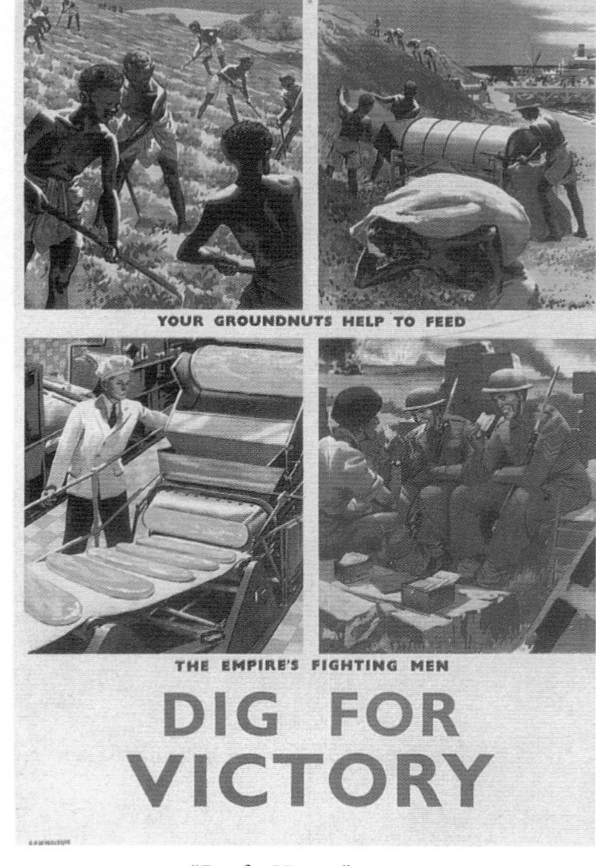

"Dig for Victory" poster,
distributed in Britain's West African colonies, 1940.

A bombed street in London, 1940. The photographer is unknown.

Francis Bacon, *Study after Velázquez's Portrait of Pope Innocent X*, 1953. For over ten years, between 1949 and the early 1960s, English artist Francis Bacon produced a series of paintings that reinterpret the influential Spanish court painter Diego Velázquez's masterpiece *Portrait of Pope Innocent X* (c. 1650). Bacon deeply admired Velázquez's portrait, which he deemed "miraculous," but for most of his life he refused to see it in person, working instead from black and white reproductions pinned to his studio wall. Also pinned to the wall was a photographic still of a screaming wounded nanny from a famous massacre scene in Russian director Sergei Eisenstein's film *Battleship Potemkin* (1925). This screaming mouth is a dominant image in Bacon's work; critic Gilles Deleuze said of it that "Bacon's scream is the operation through which the entire body escapes through the mouth." *Study after Velázquez's Portrait of Pope Innocent X*, along with the dozens of other paintings in the "screaming popes" series, established Bacon's reputation as a major painter.

Poster, The Beatles London Palladium Royal Command Performance, 1963. The Royal Variety Performance (also known as the Royal Command Performance) is a gala variety show held every year, the proceeds of which go to charity. When The Beatles performed at the show on 4 November 1963, the audience included the Queen Mother, Princess Margaret, and Lord Snowdon, but not the Queen. As the group was about to play their hit song "Twist and Shout," John Lennon made a request: "Will the people in the cheaper seats clap their hands? And the rest of you, if you'll just rattle your jewelry."

Tim Smith, Peel Square, Bradford, c. 1995. From the 1950s onwards many immigrants from Asia have settled in Bradford.

Notting Hill Carnival, Notting Hill, London, 1979. The Carnival was started in 1964 to celebrate Caribbean culture within Britain.

David Hockney, *Garrowby Hill*, 1998. Painter, printmaker, and photographer David Hockney (b. 1937) has long maintained his reputation as one of Britain's leading visual artists. He established his career during the Pop Art movement of the 1960s and continued in the following decades to experiment with color and perspective. Hockney, who is gay, painted portraits celebrating love between men even before such relationships were legal; his portrait subjects also include friends and family as well as, in many cases, himself. He is especially well-known for his series of paintings of California swimming pools (he has lived part of his life in Britain and part in the United States) and for his photocollages that depict the same image from multiple perspectives. In the 1990s and early 2000s, Hockney painted numerous landscapes of his native Yorkshire; the painting reproduced here is among the works from this period.

Chris Ofili, *No Woman, No Cry*, 1998. One of the best-known works by prominent Nigerian British artist Chris Ofili (b. 1968), *No Woman, No Cry* shares a title with Bob Marley's 1974 reggae song, in which the speaker urges a woman not to cry because "everything's gonna be alright." The painting also alludes to the death of Stephen Lawrence, a black English teenager whose murder was motivated by racial hatred; later investigation found that police response to his case had also been characterized by racism. Like many of Ofili's works from this period, the painting layers a number of materials and textures, including phosphorescent paint, photo collage, resin, and elephant dung. Dung forms the pendant worn by the woman in the painting, as well as providing the blocks the painting rests on. "RIP Stephen Lawrence 1974–1993" is written on the painting in phosphorescent paint, and images of Lawrence appear in the woman's tears, implying that she is Lawrence's mother.

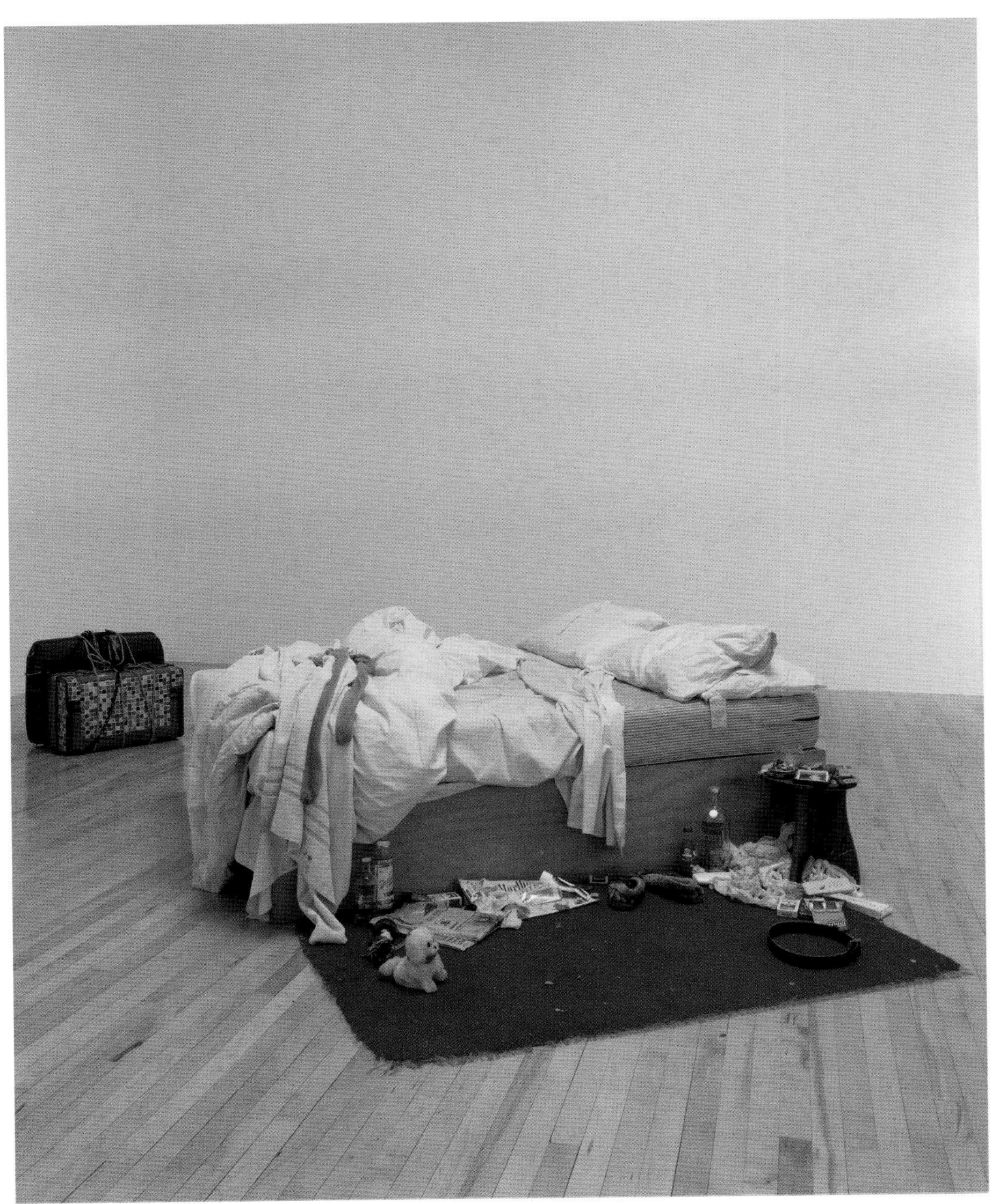

Tracey Emin, *My Bed*, 1998. In this landmark installation piece, English artist Tracey Emin (b. 1963) displays her actual bed surrounded by the objects accumulated after she spent several days in the bed binging on alcohol during a period of extreme depression. Some were shocked by the work's confessional content (items surrounding the bed include condoms, stained underwear, and empty alcohol bottles), and its selection as a finalist for the prestigious Turner Prize in 1999 was a subject of intense controversy.

Rebecca Belmore, *Mixed Blessing*, 2011. Canadian Anishinaabekwe artist Rebecca Belmore (b. 1960) is internationally respected for her work in a vast range of media including performance, sculpture, sound sculpture, and installation pieces. Belmore, who is a member of Lac Seul First Nation in northwestern Ontario, Canada, often takes up colonization and its impact as a theme in her art. The hoodie worn by the figure in the sculpture pictured here (photographed by Toni Hafkenscheid) reads horizontally "FUCKIN INDIAN"; vertically, it reads "FUCKIN ARTIST."

Jenny Saville, *Vis and Ramin I*, 2018. Renowned for her bravura technique—or virtuosic ability to use brushstrokes to make a bold, expressive statement—Jenny Saville is best known for her often distorted depictions of the female body. The title *Vis and Ramin* refers to an epic romance by the eleventh-century Persian poet Fakr al-Din As'ad Gorgāni. In Gorgāni's tale, Vis, the daughter of a Persian queen, is promised in marriage to Mo'bad, the ruler of a rival Parthian royal house. While en route to her betrothed, Vis falls in love with Mo'bad's brother Rāmin. She asks her nurse to make a talisman that renders Mo'bad unable to consummate their marriage, and Vis and Rāmin conduct a tumultuous and passionate affair despite the suspicions of her husband. Eventually Mo'bad is killed in a hunt, leaving Vis free to marry Rāmin; the two enjoy a long reign together as king and queen. Jenny Saville, *Vis and Ramin I*, 2018.

Banksy, street art on Coney Island Avenue, 2018.

Banksy, street art in Dover, England, 2017. The identity of England-based celebrity artist Banksy is unknown. Banksy is best known for politically provocative graffiti but also produces film, installation art, and controversial stunts (such as, perhaps most famously, selling a painting that shredded itself after being purchased). This mural, which depicts a star being chiseled from the flag of the European Union, was painted in the year following Britain's vote to leave the EU.

[Richardson briefly discusses two other writers—Henry James and Goethe—who, in their different ways, anticipated the principles of modernist fiction that follows the thoughts of the characters, she then turns to the ways in which twentieth-century critics had begun to categorize such fiction.]

Phrases began to appear, formulae devised to meet the exigencies of literary criticism. "The Stream of Consciousness" lyrically led the way, to be gladly welcomed by all who could persuade themselves of the possibility of comparing consciousness to a stream. Its transatlantic successors, "Interior Monologue" and "Slow-motion Photography," may each be granted a certain technical applicability leaving them, to this extent, unhampered by the defects of their qualities.

Lives in plenty have been devoted to the critic's exacting art and a lifetime might be spent in engrossed contemplation of the movements of its continuous ballet. When the dancers tread living boards, the boards will sometimes be heard to groan. The present writer groans, gently and resignedly, beneath the reiterated tap-tap accusing her of feminism, of failure to perceive the value of the distinctively masculine intelligence of pre-War sentimentality, of post-War Freudianity. But when her work is danced upon for being unpunctuated and therefore unreadable, she is moved to cry aloud. For here is truth. …

Modernity and the Sciences

Austrian Sigmund Freud (1856–1939) is considered the founder of psychoanalysis, a branch of psychiatry in which a doctor (the psychoanalyst) attempts to treat a patient's psychological symptoms by determining the symptoms' unconscious causes. Freud first used the word "psychoanalysis" in *The Interpretation of Dreams*, an early work in which he puts forward many of his key ideas about the role of the unconscious, of sexuality, and of childhood development in the formation of individual personalities. Dreams, he argues, can be interpreted as keys to unconscious desires—though these desires, as they find expression in dreams, become distorted by psychic forces of self-censorship; in the passage excerpted below, Freud outlines the processes that, in his view, create this distortion. *The Interpretation of Dreams* was not an immediate popular success, but over time its reputation and influence increased dramatically, and Freud published numerous revised editions in the course of his lifetime. Both in Freud's own time and in the years since, the scientific legitimacy of his theories has been called into question; though modern psychiatry does preserve some of his insights, psychoanalysis as Freud himself practiced it is now marginalized within the medical community. It is within the broader world that Freud's continuing influence is most profound. His ideas have continued to powerfully influence twentieth- and twenty-first-century popular understandings of the human psyche—as well as twentieth- and twenty-first-century art and literature.

As Freud led the way in shaping Modern understandings of the self, German theoretical physicist Albert Einstein (1879–1955) was at the forefront of a group of thinkers whose work shaped Modern understandings of the universe. With his 1905 paper "On the Electrodynamics of Moving Bodies," Einstein exposed the falsity of commonsensical notions of time and space by showing that the passage of time is not absolute but varied according to the frame of reference from which one measures it. The theory Einstein put forward in this paper would come to be known as "special relativity" after the 1915 publication of his far more complex general theory of relativity; the latter shows that gravity is a result of the bending of space and time by large objects. The selections that appear below are from *Relativity: The Special and General Theory*, a book in which Einstein attempts to make the fundamentals of relativity accessible to non-specialist readers.

from Sigmund Freud, *The Interpretation of Dreams*[1] (1899, 1911)

from CHAPTER 6
THE DREAM-WORK

All previous attempts to solve the problems of the dream have been based directly upon the manifest dream content as it is retained in the memory, and have undertaken to obtain an interpretation of the dream from this content, or, if interpretation was dispensed with, to base a judgment of the dream upon the evidence furnished by this content. We alone are in possession of new data; for us a new psychic material intervenes between the dream content and the results of our investigations: and this is the *latent* dream content or the dream thoughts which are obtained by our method. We develop a solution of the dream from this latter, and not from the manifest dream content. We are also confronted for the first time with a problem which has not before existed, that of examining and tracing the relations between the latent dream thoughts and the manifest dream content, and the processes through which the former have grown into the latter.

We regard the dream thoughts and the dream content as two representations of the same meaning in two different languages; or to express it better, the dream content appears to us as a translation of the dream thoughts into another form of expression, whose signs and laws of composition we are to learn by comparing the original with the translation. The dream thoughts are at once intelligible to us as soon as we have ascertained them. The dream content is, as it were, presented in a picture-writing, whose signs are to be translated one by one into the language of the dream thoughts. It would of course be incorrect to try to read these signs according to their values as pictures instead of according to their significance as signs. For instance, I have before me a picture-puzzle (rebus[2]): a house, upon whose roof there is a boat; then a running figure whose head has been apostrophised away,[3] and the like. I might now be tempted as a critic to consider this composition and its elements nonsensical. A boat does not belong on the roof of a house and a person without a head cannot run; the person, too, is larger than the house, and if the whole thing is to represent a landscape, the single letters of the alphabet do not fit into it, for of course they do not occur in pure nature. A correct judgment of the picture-puzzle results only if I make no such objections to the whole and its parts, but if, on the contrary, I take pains to replace each picture by the syllable or word which it is capable of representing by means of any sort of reference, the words which are thus brought together are no longer meaningless, but may constitute a most beautiful and sensible expression. Now the dream is a picture-puzzle of this sort, and our predecessors in the field of dream interpretation have made the mistake of judging the rebus as an artistic composition. As such it appears nonsensical and worthless.

from (A) THE CONDENSATION WORK

The first thing which becomes clear to the investigator in the comparison of the dream content with the dream thoughts is that a tremendous work of condensation has taken place. The dream is reserved, paltry, and laconic when compared with the range and copiousness of the dream thoughts. The dream when written down fills half a page; the analysis, in which the dream thoughts are contained, requires six, eight, twelve times as much space. The ratio varies with different dreams; it never changes its essential meaning, as far as I have been able to observe. As a rule the extent of the compression which has taken place is underestimated, owing to the fact that the dream thoughts which are brought to light are considered the complete material, while continued work of interpretation may reveal new thoughts which are concealed behind the dream. We have already mentioned that one is really never sure of having interpreted a dream completely; even if the solution seems

[1] *The Interpretation of Dreams* Translation by A.A. Brill, 1913.

[2] *rebus* Puzzle made up of images and letters that, taken together, represent a word or phrase.

[3] *apostrophized away* Omitted (and replaced with an apostrophe, as in a truncated word).

satisfying and flawless, it still always remains possible that there is a further meaning which is manifested by the same dream. …

… Every element of the dream content turns out to be *over-determined*—that is, it enjoys a manifold representation in the dream thoughts.

… Not only do the elements of the dream have a manifold determination in the dream thoughts, but the individual dream thoughts are represented in the dream by many elements. Starting from an element of the dream the path of associations leads to a number of dream thoughts; and from a dream thought to several elements of the dream. The formation of the dream does not, therefore, take place in such fashion that a single one of the dream thoughts or a group of them furnishes the dream content with an abridgment as its representative therein, and that then another dream thought furnishes another abridgment as its representative—somewhat as popular representatives are elected from among the people—but the whole mass of the dream thoughts is subjected to a certain elaboration, in the course of which those elements that receive the greatest and completest support stand out in relief, analogous, perhaps, to election by *scrutins des listes*.[1] Whatever dream I may subject to such dismemberment, I always find the same fundamental principle confirmed—that the dream elements are constructed from the entire mass of the dream thoughts and that every one of them appears in relation to the dream thoughts to have a multiple determination. …

… I shall cite the partial analysis of another dream for which I am indebted to an elderly lady who is being psychoanalytically treated. In harmony with the condition of severe anxiety from which the patient suffered, her dreams contained a great abundance of sexual thought material, the discovery of which astonished as well as frightened her. Since I cannot carry the interpretation of the dream to completion, the material seems to fall apart into several groups without apparent connection.

III. Content of the dream: *She remembers that she has two June bugs in a box, which she must set at liberty, for otherwise they will suffocate. She opens the box, and the bugs are quite exhausted; one of them flies out of the window, but the other is crushed on the casement while she is shutting the window, as some one or other requests her to do (expressions of disgust).*

Analysis: Her husband is away travelling, and her fourteen-year-old daughter is sleeping in the bed next to her. In the evening the little one calls her attention to the fact that a moth has fallen into her glass of water; but she neglects to take it out, and feels sorry for the poor little creature in the morning. A story which she had read in the evening told of boys throwing a cat into boiling water, and the twitchings of the animal were described. These are the occasions for the dream, both of which are indifferent in themselves. She is further occupied with the subject of *cruelty to animals*. Years before, while they were spending the summer at a certain place, her daughter was very cruel to animals. She started a butterfly collection, and asked her for arsenic with which to kill the butterflies. Once it happened that a moth flew about the room for a long time with a needle through its body; on another occasion she found that some moths which had been kept for metamorphosis had died of starvation. The same child while still at a tender age was in the habit of pulling out the wings of beetles and butterflies; now she would shrink in horror from these cruel actions, for she has grown very kind.

Her mind is occupied with this contrast. It recalls another contrast, the one between appearance and disposition, as it is described in *Adam Bede* by George Eliot. There a beautiful but vain and quite stupid girl is placed side by side with an ugly but high-minded one. The aristocrat who seduces the little goose, is opposed to the working man who feels *aristocratic*, and behaves accordingly. It is impossible to tell character from people's *looks*. Who could tell from her looks that she is tormented by sensual desires?

In the same year in which the little girl started her butterfly collection, the region in which they were staying suffered much from a pest of June bugs. The

[1] *scrutins des listes* Voting method whereby each party proposes a full list of candidates, and voters select the list they prefer.

children made havoc among the bugs, and *crushed* them cruelly. At that time she saw a person who tore the wings off the June bugs and ate them. She herself had been born in June and also married in June. Three days after the wedding she wrote a letter home, telling how happy she was. But she was by no means happy.

During the evening before the dream she had rummaged among her old letters and had read various ones, comical and serious, to her family—an extremely ridiculous letter from a piano-teacher who had paid her attention when she was a girl, as well as one from an aristocratic admirer.[1]

She blames herself because a bad book by de Maupassant[2] had fallen into the hands of one of her daughters.[3] The arsenic which her little girl asks for recalls the arsenic pills which restored the power of youth to the Duc de Mora in *Nabab*.[4]

"Set at liberty" recalls to her a passage from the *Magic Flute*:[5]

I cannot compel you to love,
But I will not give you your liberty.

"June bugs" suggests the speech of Katie:[6]

I love you like a little beetle.

Meanwhile the speech from *Tannhauser*:[7] "For you are wrought with evil passion."

She is living in fear and anxiety about her absent husband. The dread that something may happen to him on the journey is expressed in numerous fancies of the day. A little while before, during the analysis, she had come upon a complaint about his "senility" in her unconscious thoughts. The wish thought which this dream conceals may perhaps best be conjectured if I say that several days before the dream she was suddenly astounded by a command which she directed to her husband in the midst of her work: "*Go hang yourself.*" It was found that a few hours before she had read somewhere that a vigorous erection is induced when a person is hanged. It was for the erection which freed itself from repression in this terror-inspiring veiled form. "Go hang yourself" is as much as to say: "Get up an erection, at any cost." Dr. Jenkin's arsenic pills in *Nabab* belong in this connection; for it was known to the patient that the strongest aphrodisiac, cantharides, is prepared by *crushing bugs* (so-called Spanish flies). The most important part of the dream content has a significance to this effect.

Opening and shutting the *window* is the subject of a standing quarrel with her husband. She herself likes to sleep with plenty of air, and her husband does not. *Exhaustion* is the chief ailment of which she complains these days. …

from (B) THE WORK OF DISPLACEMENT

Another sort of relation, which is no less significant, must have come to our notice while we were collecting examples of dream condensation. We have seen that those elements which obtrude themselves in the dream content as its essential components play a part in the dream thoughts which is by no means the same. As a correlative to this the converse of this thesis is also true.

---

[1] [Freud's note] This is the real inciter of the dream.

[2] *de Maupassant* Guy de Maupassant (1850–93), French novelist and short story writer whose work aimed at the unflinching portrayal of real life; it thus touched on sexuality and other morally contentious subjects.

[3] [Freud's note] By way of supplement. Such books are poison to a young girl. She herself in youth had drawn much information from forbidden books.

[4] *Nabab* 1877 novel by Alphonse Daudet set in Parisian high society.

[5] *Magic Flute* 1791 opera by Wolfgang Amadeus Mozart with a libretto by Emanuel Schikaneder. The quoted lines are spoken by the demon Sarastro to the princess Pamina, whom he has kidnapped.

[6] [Freud's note] A further train of thought leads to *Penthesileia* by the same author: cruelty towards her lover. [Both references are to works by German playwright Heinrich von Kleist. In *Das Käthchen von Heilbronn* (1810), Katie is an emperor's illegitimate daughter who tries to run away with a count; the count is incorrectly accused of attempting to abduct her with the aid of magic. In *Penthesileia* (1808), the Amazon queen of the same name captures the heroic warrior Achilles and falls in love with him; she eventually kills him and then herself.]

[7] *Tannhauser* 1845 opera by Richard Wagner in which the musician-poet Tannhäuser abandons his beloved Elisabeth to pursue sexual pleasure in the realm of the goddess Venus.

That which is clearly the essential thing in the dream thoughts need not be represented in the dream at all. The dream, as it were, is *eccentric*;[1] its contents are grouped about other elements than the dream thoughts as a central point. … [I]n the dream about June bugs, whose subject is the relation of sexuality to cruelty, the factor of cruelty has indeed reappeared but in a different connection and without the mention of the sexual, that is to say, it has been torn from its context and transformed into something strange. …

The assumption is not now far distant that a psychic force is expressed in dream activity which on the one hand strips elements of high psychic value of their intensity, and which on the other hand creates new values, *by way of over-determination*, from elements of small value, these new values subsequently getting into the dream content. If this is the method of procedure, there has taken place in the formation of the dream a transference and displacement of the psychic intensities of the individual elements, of which the textual difference between the dream and the thought content appears as a result. The process which we assume here is nothing less than the essential part of the dream activity; it merits the designation of *dream displacement*. *Dream displacement* and *dream condensation* are the two craftsmen to whom we may chiefly attribute the moulding of the dream. …

from Albert Einstein, *Relativity: The Special and General Theory*[2] (1919)

from PART 1
THE SPECIAL THEORY OF RELATIVITY

from SECTION 3
SPACE AND TIME IN CLASSICAL MECHANICS

The purpose of mechanics is to describe how bodies change their position in space with "time." I should load my conscience with grave sins against the sacred spirit of lucidity were I to formulate the aims of mechanics in this way, without serious reflection and detailed explanations. Let us proceed to disclose these sins.

It is not clear what is to be understood here by "position" and "space." I stand at the window of a railway carriage which is travelling uniformly, and drop a stone on the embankment, without throwing it. Then, disregarding the influence of the air resistance, I see the stone descend in a straight line. A pedestrian who observes the misdeed from the footpath notices that the stone falls to earth in a parabolic curve. I now ask: do the "positions" traversed by the stone lie "in reality" on a straight line or on a parabola? Moreover, what is meant here by motion "in space"? … In the first place we entirely shun the vague word "space," of which, we must honestly acknowledge, we cannot form the slightest conception, and we replace it by "motion relative to a practically rigid body of reference." … If instead of "body of reference" we insert "system of co-ordinates," which is a useful idea for mathematical description, we are in a position to say: The stone traverses a straight line relative to a system of co-ordinates rigidly attached to the carriage, but relative to a system of co-ordinates rigidly attached to the ground (embankment) it describes a parabola. With the aid of this example it is clearly seen that there is no such thing as an independently existing trajectory (lit. "path-curve"[3]), but only a trajectory relative to a particular body of reference.

In order to have a *complete* description of the motion, we must specify how the body alters its position *with time*; *i.e.* for every point on the trajectory it must be stated at what time the body is situated there. These data must be supplemented by such a definition of time that, in virtue of this definition, these time-values can be regarded essentially as magnitudes (results of measurements) capable of observation. If we take our stand on the ground of classical mechanics, we can satisfy this requirement for our illustration in the following manner. We imagine two clocks of identical construction;

[1] *eccentric* I.e., not grouped around a shared central axis.

[2] *Relativity: The Special and General Theory* Translation by Robert W. Lawson, 1920.

[3] [Einstein's note] That is, a curve along which a body moves.

the man at the railway-carriage window is holding one of them, and the man on the footpath the other. Each of the observers determines the position on his own reference-body occupied by the stone at each tick of the clock he is holding in his hand. In this connection we have not taken account of the inaccuracy involved by the finiteness of the velocity of propagation[1] of light. With this and with a second difficulty prevailing here we shall have to deal in detail later. …

from SECTION 5
THE PRINCIPLE OF RELATIVITY (IN THE RESTRICTED SENSE)

[In the text omitted here, Einstein states the "principle of relativity" as it existed before the publication of this work; roughly, the principle states that the laws of physics apply in exactly the same way in any system (so long as that system as a whole is moving at a constant speed and direction and is not rotating).]

… As long as one was convinced that all natural phenomena were capable of representation with the help of classical mechanics, there was no need to doubt the validity of this principle of relativity. But in view of the more recent development of electrodynamics and optics it became more and more evident that classical mechanics affords an insufficient foundation for the physical description of all natural phenomena. At this juncture the question of the validity of the principle of relativity became ripe for discussion, and it did not appear impossible that the answer to this question might be in the negative. …

SECTION 6
THE THEOREM OF THE ADDITION OF VELOCITIES EMPLOYED IN CLASSICAL MECHANICS

Let us suppose our old friend the railway carriage to be travelling along the rails with a constant velocity v, and that a man traverses the length of the carriage in the direction of travel with a velocity w. How quickly or, in other words, with what velocity W does the man advance relative to the embankment during the process? The only possible answer seems to result from the following consideration: If the man were to stand still for a second, he would advance relative to the embankment through a distance v equal numerically to the velocity of the carriage. As a consequence of his walking, however, he traverses an additional distance w relative to the carriage, and hence also relative to the embankment, in this second, the distance w being numerically equal to the velocity with which he is walking. Thus in total he covers the distance $W = v + w$ relative to the embankment in the second considered. We shall see later that this result, which expresses the theorem of the addition of velocities employed in classical mechanics, cannot be maintained; in other words, the law that we have just written down does not hold in reality. For the time being, however, we shall assume its correctness.

from SECTION 7
THE APPARENT INCOMPATIBILITY OF THE LAW OF PROPAGATION OF LIGHT WITH THE PRINCIPLE OF RELATIVITY

There is hardly a simpler law in physics than that according to which light is propagated in empty space. Every child at school knows, or believes he knows, that this propagation takes place in straight lines with a velocity c = 300,000 km./sec. …

… Who would imagine that this simple law has plunged the conscientiously thoughtful physicist into the greatest intellectual difficulties? Let us consider how these difficulties arise.

Of course we must refer the process of the propagation of light (and indeed every other process) to a rigid reference-body (co-ordinate system). As such a system let us again choose our embankment. We shall imagine the air above it to have been removed. If a ray of light be sent along the embankment, we see from the above that the tip of the ray will be transmitted with the velocity c relative to the embankment. Now let us suppose that our railway carriage is again travelling along the railway lines with the velocity v, and that its direction is the

[1] *propagation* Extension through space.

same as that of the ray of light, but its velocity of course much less. Let us inquire about the velocity of propagation of the ray of light relative to the carriage. It is obvious that we can here apply the consideration of the previous section, since the ray of light plays the part of the man walking along relatively to the carriage. The velocity W of the man relative to the embankment is here replaced by the velocity of light relative to the embankment. w is the required velocity of light with respect to the carriage, and we have

$$w = c - v$$

The velocity of propagation of a ray of light relative to the carriage thus comes out smaller than c.

But this result comes into conflict with the principle of relativity set forth in Section 5. For, like every other general law of nature, the law of the transmission of light *in vacuo*[1] must, according to the principle of relativity, be the same for the railway carriage as reference-body as when the rails are the body of reference. But, from our above consideration, this would appear to be impossible. If every ray of light is propagated relative to the embankment with the velocity c, then for this reason it would appear that another law of propagation of light must necessarily hold with respect to the carriage—a result contradictory to the principle of relativity. …

At this juncture the theory of relativity[2] entered the arena. As a result of an analysis of the physical conceptions of time and space, it became evident that *in reality there is not the least incompatibility between the principle of relativity and the law of propagation of light*, and that by systematically holding fast to both these laws a logically rigid theory could be arrived at. This theory has been called the *special theory of relativity* to distinguish it from the extended theory, with which we shall deal later. In the following pages we shall present the fundamental ideas of the special theory of relativity. …

[1] *in vacuo* Latin: in a vacuum.

[2] *theory of relativity* I.e., Einstein's special theory of relativity (as opposed to the "principle of relativity" discussed before this point).

Jean Rhys

1890 – 1979

West-Indian-born novelist and short fiction writer Jean Rhys is widely respected for her technical skill: her prose is controlled, intense, and elegant, exploring themes of failed connection, isolation, and alienation, as well as giving voice, at a time when few did, to the female colonized. When Ford Madox Ford first read her work, he was struck by her "singular instinct for form" and her "terrific … passion for stating the case of the underdog." Rhys's work has been praised by critics for its exposure of the mechanisms of power—of colonial power, of the sexual and economic power wielded by men over women, and of the ways these intersect.

Rhys was born Ella Gwendolyn Rees Williams in 1890 in Roseau, Dominica, in the West Indies. Her father was a Welsh doctor, and her mother a Dominican Creole of Scottish lineage. She began her education in Roseau, in a convent school. As a white Creole in a predominantly black area, she often felt socially isolated, despite identifying with the black community from an early age. At sixteen she traveled to England, attending the prestigious Perse Preparatory girls' school in Cambridge. While there, Rhys excelled academically, taking first prize in Roman literature in the exams for Cambridge and Oxford. She attended one term at the Royal Academy of Dramatic Art in London in 1909, though she never made it to university; her father died in 1910, leaving Rhys in severely reduced circumstances. Alone and destitute in England, Rhys lived a drifter's life, taking on a variety of jobs: chorus girl (under the stage name Vivian Gray), actress, volunteer cook during World War I, secretary, and ghostwriter of a book about furniture.

In 1919 Rhys married the first of her three husbands, Jean Langlet. They had two children—a son, who died as an infant, and a daughter—and lived a largely itinerant existence, residing sporadically in Vienna, Budapest, and Paris. During this period Rhys acquainted herself with works of modern art and literature, and began to suffer from the alcoholism that would plague her for the rest of her life. In Paris in 1922, she met Modernist novelist Ford Madox Ford (1873–1939), who became her patron. She published her first short story, "Vienne," in Ford's magazine *The Transatlantic Review* in 1924, and followed this with her first collection, *The Left Bank and Other Stories*, in 1927. She continued to publish steadily during the 1930s. Her first novel, *Postures* (1928; *Quartet*, 1929, in the United States), further developed the typical Rhys heroine: sexually alluring, sensitive, and dependent. Rhys followed this with a trio of critically acclaimed semi-autobiographical novels, *After Leaving Mr. Mackenzie* (1930), *Voyage in the Dark* (1934), and *Good Morning, Midnight* (1939). For some time these publications allowed her to enjoy moderate literary recognition and financial security, but the late 1940s and 50s were marked for Rhys by near-poverty, continuing alcoholism, and trouble with the authorities. Her second husband, Leslie Tilden Smith, was jailed in the 1950s for financial misdoing, and she herself spent time in London's Holloway Prison in 1949 after an altercation with neighbors. Rhys brings this period to vivid life in "Let Them Call It Jazz," her story of the displaced black drifter Selina.

Rhys fell into relative obscurity during the 1940s and 50s, but interest in her work revived with the radio production of *Good Morning, Midnight* in 1958. She followed this with her 1966 masterpiece, *Wide Sargasso Sea*, which she had begun to write over twenty years earlier. This book, published when Rhys was in her seventies, won the prestigious W.H. Smith Literary Award and became one of the most widely read novels of the late twentieth century. The novel is a "prequel" to Charlotte Brontë's *Jane Eyre* (1847) in which Rhys gives a voice to Rochester's insane and confined Jamaican-born wife, Bertha Mason. Rhys made no secret of her motive for writing the book; as she remarked in an interview, "I was convinced Charlotte Brontë must have had something against the West Indies, and I was angry about it." She was thus led to explore the conflict of cultures between colonizer and colonized as she cast in a different light the central motif of *Jane Eyre*—that of a helpless female outsider, powerless and victimized, who relies on older European men for protection. In doing so, Rhys anticipated by a decade or more many of the insights of postcolonialism.

Rhys is quoted as saying that the fame and recognition that *Wide Sargasso Sea* brought came "too late," and that "if I could choose I would rather be happy than write." The rest of her career was devoted to her memoir, *Smile Please* (published posthumously in 1979), and to her short story collections *Tigers Are Better-Looking* (1968) and *Sleep It Off, Lady* (1976). Rhys died in Devonshire, England, at the age of 88.

⌘⌘⌘

Let Them Call It Jazz

One bright Sunday morning in July I have trouble with my Notting Hill[1] landlord because he ask for a month's rent in advance. He tell me this after I live there since winter, settling up[2] every week without fail. I have no job at the time, and if I give the money he want there's not much left. So I refuse. The man drunk already at that early hour, and he abuse me—all talk, he can't frighten me. But his wife is a bad one—now she walk in my room and say she must have cash. When I tell her no, she give my suitcase one kick and it burst open. My best dress fall out, then she laugh and give another kick. She say month in advance is usual, and if I can't pay find somewhere else.

Don't talk to me about London. Plenty people there have heart like stone. Any complaint—the answer is "prove it." But if nobody see and bear witness for me, how to prove anything? So I pack up and leave, I think better not have dealings with that woman. She too cunning, and Satan don't lie worse.

I walk about till a place nearby is open where I can have coffee and a sandwich. There I start talking to a man at my table. He talk to me already, I know him, but I don't know his name. After a while he ask, "What's the matter? Anything wrong?" and when I tell him my trouble he say I can use an empty flat[3] he own till I have time to look around.

This man is not at all like most English people. He see very quick, and he decide very quick. English people take long time to decide—you three-quarter dead before they make up their mind about you. Too besides, he speak very matter of fact, as if it's nothing. He speak as if he realize well what it is to live like I do—that's why I accept and go.

He tell me somebody occupy the flat till last week, so I find everything all right, and he tell me how to get

[1] *Notting Hill* At this time, an unfashionable and relatively cheap district in London.

[2] *settling up* Paying.

[3] *flat* Apartment.

there—three-quarters of an hour from Victoria Station,[1] up a steep hill, turn left, and I can't mistake the house. He give me the keys and an envelope with a telephone number on the back. Underneath is written "After 6 p.m. ask for Mr. Sims."

In the train that evening I think myself lucky, for to walk about London on a Sunday with nowhere to go—that take the heart out of you.

I find the place and the bedroom of the downstairs flat is nicely furnished—two looking glass, wardrobe, chest of drawers, sheets, everything. It smell of jasmine scent, but it smell strong of damp too.

I open the door opposite and there's a table, a couple chairs, a gas stove and a cupboard, but this room so big it look empty. When I pull the blind up I notice the paper peeling off and mushrooms growing on the walls—you never see such a thing.

The bathroom the same, all the taps rusty. I leave the two other rooms and make up the bed. Then I listen, but I can't hear one sound. Nobody come in, nobody go out of that house. I lie awake for a long time, then I decide not to stay and in the morning I start to get ready quickly before I change my mind. I want to wear my best dress, but it's a funny thing—when I take up that dress and remember how my landlady kick it I cry. I cry and I can't stop. When I stop I feel tired to my bones, tired like old woman. I don't want to move again—I have to force myself. But in the end I get out in the passage and there's a postcard for me. "Stay as long as you like. I'll be seeing you soon—Friday probably. Not to worry." It isn't signed, but I don't feel so sad and I think, "All right, I wait here till he come. Perhaps he know of a job for me."

Nobody else live in the house but a couple on the top floor—quiet people and they don't trouble me. I have no word to say against them.

First time I meet the lady she's opening the front door and she give me a very inquisitive look. But next time she smile a bit and I smile back—once she talk to me. She tell me the house very old, hundred and fifty year old, and she and her husband live there since long time. "Valuable property," she says, "it could have been saved, but nothing done of course." Then she tells me that as to the present owner—if he is the owner—well he have to deal with local authorities and she believe they make difficulties. "These people are determined to pull down all the lovely old houses—it's shameful."

So I agree that many things shameful. But what to do? What to do? I say it have an elegant shape, it make the other houses in the street look cheap trash, and she seem pleased. That's true too. The house sad and out of place, especially at night. But it have style. The second floor shut up, and as for my flat, I go in the two empty rooms once, but never again.

Underneath was the cellar, full of old boards and broken-up furniture—I see a big rat there one day. It was no place to be alone in I tell you, and I get the habit of buying a bottle of wine most evenings, for I don't like whisky and the rum here no good. It don't even *taste* like rum. You wonder what they do to it.

After I drink a glass or two I can sing and when I sing all the misery goes from my heart. Sometimes I make up songs but next morning I forget them, so other times I sing the old ones like *Tantalizin'* or *Don't Trouble Me Now.*

I think I go but I don't go. Instead I wait for the evening and the wine and that's all. Everywhere else I live—well, it doesn't matter to me, but this house is different—empty and no noise and full of shadows, so that sometimes you ask yourself what make all those shadows in an empty room.

I eat in the kitchen, then I clean up everything nice and have a bath for coolness. Afterwards I lean my elbows on the windowsill and look at the garden. Red and blue flowers mix up with the weeds and there are five-six apple trees. But the fruit drop and lie in the grass, so sour nobody want it. At the back, near the wall, is a bigger tree—this garden certainly take up a lot of room, perhaps that's why they want to pull the place down.

Not much rain all the summer, but not much sunshine either. More of a glare. The grass get brown and dry, the weeds grow tall, the leaves on the trees hang

[1] *Victoria Station* Major railway station in London.

down. Only the red flowers—the poppies—stand up to that light, everything else look weary.

I don't trouble about money, but what with wine and shillings for the slot-meters,[1] it go quickly; so I don't waste much on food. In the evening I walk outside—not by the apple trees but near the street—it's not so lonely.

There's no wall here and I can see the woman next door looking at me over the hedge. At first I say good evening, but she turn away her head, so afterwards I don't speak. A man is often with her, he wear a straw hat with a black ribbon and goldrim spectacles. His suit hang on him like it's too big. He's the husband it seems and he stare at me worse than his wife—he stare as if I'm wild animal let loose. Once I laugh in his face because why these people have to be like that? I don't bother them. In the end I get that I don't even give them one single glance. I have plenty other things to worry about.

To show you how I felt. I don't remember exactly. But I believe it's the second Saturday after I come that when I'm at the window just before I go for my wine I feel somebody's hand on my shoulder and it's Mr. Sims. He must walk very quiet because I don't know a thing till he touch me.

He says hullo, then he tells me I've got terrible thin, do I ever eat. I say of course I eat but he goes on that it doesn't suit me at all to be so thin and he'll buy some food in the village. (That's the way he talk. There's no village here. You don't get away from London so quick.)

It don't seem to me he look very well himself, but I just say bring a drink instead, as I am not hungry.

He come back with three bottles—vermouth, gin and red wine. Then he ask if the little devil who was here last smash all the glasses and I tell him she smash some, I find the pieces. But not all. "You fight with her, eh?"

He laugh, and he don't answer. He pour out the drinks then he says, "Now, you eat up those sandwiches."

Some men when they are there you don't worry so much. These sort of men you do all they tell you blindfold because they can take the trouble from your heart and make you think you're safe. It's nothing they say or do. It's a feeling they can give you. So I don't talk with him seriously—I don't want to spoil that evening. But I ask about the house and why it's so empty and he says:

"Has the old trout upstairs been gossiping?"

I tell him, "She suppose they make difficulties for you."

"It was a damn bad buy," he says and talks about selling the lease or something. I don't listen much.

We were standing by the window then and the sun low. No more glare. He puts his hand over my eyes. "Too big—much too big for your face," he says and kisses me like you kiss a baby. When he takes his hand away I see he's looking out at the garden and he says this—"It gets you. My God it does."

I know very well it's not me he means, so I ask him, "Why sell it then? If you like it, keep it."

"Sell what?" he says. "I'm not talking about this damned house."

I ask what he's talking about. "Money," he says. "Money. That's what I'm talking about. Ways of making it."

"I don't think so much of money. It don't like me and what do I care?" I was joking, but he turns around, his face quite pale and he tells me I'm a fool. He tells me I'll get push around all my life and die like a dog, only worse because they'd finish off a dog, but they'll let me live till I'm a caricature of myself. That's what he say, "Caricature of yourself." He say I'll curse the day I was born and everything and everybody in this bloody world before I'm done.

I tell him, "No I'll never feel like that," and he smiles, if you can call it a smile, and says he's glad I'm content with my lot. "I'm disappointed in you, Selina. I thought you had more spirit."

"If I contented that's all right," I answer him, "I don't see very many looking contented over here." We're standing staring at each other when the door bell rings. "That's a friend of mine," he says. "I'll let him in."

[1] *shillings* Coins used in the United Kingdom prior to 1971, each worth 1/20th of a pound; *slot-meters* Meters, here for hot water, operated by inserting a coin into a slot, often used to provide gas heating.

As to the friend, he's all dressed up in stripe pants and a black jacket and he's carrying a brief-case. Very ordinary looking but with a soft kind of voice.

"Maurice, this is Selina Davis," says Mr. Sims, and Maurice smiles very kind but it don't mean much, then he looks at his watch and says they ought to be getting along.

At the door Mr. Sims tells me he'll see me next week and I answer straight out, "I won't be here next week because I want a job and I won't get one in this place."

"Just what I'm going to talk about. Give it a week longer, Selina."

I say, "Perhaps I stay a few more days. Then I go. Perhaps I go before."

"Oh no you won't go," he says.

They walk to the gates quickly and drive off in a yellow car. Then I feel eyes on me and it's the woman and her husband in the next door garden watching. The man make some remark and she look at me so hateful, so hating I shut the front door quick.

I don't want more wine. I want to go to bed early because I must think. I must think about money. It's true I don't care for it. Even when somebody steal my savings—this happen soon after I get to the Notting Hill house—I forget it soon. About thirty pounds they steal. I keep it roll up in a pair of stockings, but I go to the drawer one day, and no money. In the end I have to tell the police. They ask me exact sum and I say I don't count it lately, about thirty pounds. "You don't know how much?" they say. "When did you count it last? Do you remember? Was it before you move or after?"

I get confuse, and I keep saying, "I don't remember," though I remember well I see it two days before. They don't believe me and when a policeman come to the house I hear the landlady tell him, "She certainly had no money when she came here. She wasn't able to pay a month's rent in advance for her room though it's a rule in this house." "These people terrible liars," she say and I think "it's you a terrible liar, because when I come you tell me weekly or monthly as you like." It's from that time she don't speak to me and perhaps it's she take it. All I know is I never see one penny of my savings again, all I know is they pretend I never have any, but as it's gone, no use to cry about it. Then my mind goes to my father, for my father is a white man and I think a lot about him. If I could see him only once, for I too small to remember when he was there. My mother is fair coloured woman, fairer than I am they say, and she don't stay long with me either. She have a chance to go to Venezuela when I three-four year old and she never come back. She send money instead. It's my grandmother take care of me. She's quite dark and what we call "country-cookie" but she's the best I know.

She save up all the money my mother send, she don't keep one penny for herself—that's how I get to England. I was a bit late in going to school regular, getting on for twelve years, but I can sew very beautiful, excellent—so I think I get a good job—in London perhaps.

However here they tell me all this fine handsewing take too long. Waste of time—too slow. They want somebody to work quick and to hell with the small stitches. Altogether it don't look so good for me, I must say, and I wish I could see my father. I have his name—Davis. But my grandmother tell me, "Every word that come out of that man's mouth a damn lie. He is certainly first class liar, though no class otherwise." So perhaps I have not even his real name.

Last thing I see before I put the light out is the postcard on the dressing table. "Not to worry."

Not to worry! Next day is Sunday, and it's on the Monday the people next door complain about me to the police. That evening the woman is by the hedge, and when I pass her she says in very sweet quiet voice, "*Must* you stay? *Can't* you go?" I don't answer. I walk out in the street to get rid of her. But she run inside her house to the window, she can still see me. Then I start to sing, so she can understand I'm not afraid of her. The husband call out: "If you don't stop that noise I'll send for the police." I answer them quite short. I say, "You go to hell and take your wife with you." And I sing louder.

The police come pretty quick—two of them. Maybe they just round the corner. All I can say about police, and how they behave is I think it all depend who they dealing with. Of my own free will I don't want to mix up with police. No.

One man says, you can't cause this disturbance here. But the other asks a lot of questions. What is my name? Am I tenant of a flat in No. 17? How long have I lived there? Last address and so on. I get vexed the way he speak and I tell him, "I come here because somebody steal my savings. Why you don't look for my money instead of bawling at me? I work hard for my money. All-you don't do one single thing to find it."

"What's she talking about?" the first one says, and the other one tells me, "You can't make that noise here. Get along home. You've been drinking."

I see that woman looking at me and smiling, and other people at their windows, and I'm so angry I bawl at them too. I say, "I have absolute and perfect right to be in the street same as anybody else, and I have absolute and perfect right to ask the police why they don't even look for my money when it disappear. It's because a dam' English thief take it you don't look," I say. The end of all this is that I have to go before a magistrate, and he fine me five pounds for drunk and disorderly, and he give me two weeks to pay.

When I get back from the court I walk up and down the kitchen, up and down, waiting for six o'clock because I have no five pounds left, and I don't know what to do. I telephone at six and a woman answers me very short and sharp, then Mr. Sims comes along and he don't sound too pleased either when I tell him what happen. "Oh Lord!" he says, and I say I'm sorry. "Well don't panic," he says, "I'll pay the fine. But look, I don't think … " Then he breaks off and talk to some other person in the room. He goes on, "Perhaps better not stay at No. 17. I think I can arrange something else. I'll call for you Wednesday—Saturday latest. Now behave till then." And he hang up before I can answer that I don't want to wait till Wednesday, much less Saturday. I want to get out of that house double quick and with no delay. First I think I ring back, then I think better not as he sound so vex.

I get ready, but Wednesday he don't come, and Saturday he don't come. All the week I stay in the flat. Only once I go out and arrange for bread, milk and eggs to be left at the door, and seems to me I meet up with a lot of policemen. They don't look at me, but they see me all right. I don't want to drink—I'm all the time listening, listening and thinking, how can I leave before I know if my fine is paid? I tell myself the police let me know, that's certain. But I don't trust them. What they care? The answer is Nothing. Nobody care. One afternoon I knock at the old lady's flat upstairs, because I get the idea she give me good advice. I can hear her moving about and talking, but she don't answer and I never try again.

Nearly two weeks pass like that, then I telephone. It's the woman speaking and she say, "Mr. Sims is not in London at present." I ask, "When will he be back—it's urgent," and she hang up. I'm not surprised. Not at all. I knew that would happen. All the same I feel heavy like lead. Near the phone box is a chemist's shop, so I ask him for something to make me sleep, the day is bad enough, but to lie awake all night—Ah no! He gives me a little bottle marked "*One or two tablets only*" and I take three when I go to bed because more and more I think that sleeping is better than no matter what else. However, I lie there, eyes wide open as usual, so I take three more. Next thing I know the room is full of sunlight, so it must be late afternoon, but the lamp is still on. My head turn around and I can't think well at all. At first I ask myself how I get to the place. Then it comes to me, but in pictures—like the landlady kicking my dress, and when I take my ticket at Victoria Station, and Mr. Sims telling me to eat the sandwiches, but I can't remember everything clear, and I feel very giddy and sick. I take in the milk and eggs at the door, go in the kitchen, and try to eat but the food hard to swallow.

It's when I'm putting the things away that I see the bottles—pushed back on the lowest shelf in the cupboard.

There's a lot of drink left, and I'm glad I tell you. Because I can't bear the way I feel. Not any more. I mix a gin and vermouth and I drink it quick, then I mix another and drink it slow by the window. The garden looks different, like I never see it before. I know quite well what I must do, but it's late now—tomorrow. I have one more drink, of wine this time, and then a song come in my head, I sing it and I dance it, and more I sing, more I am sure this is the best tune that has ever come to me in all my life.

The sunset light from the window is gold colour. My shoes sound loud on the boards. So I take them off, my stockings too and go on dancing but the room feel shut in, I can't breathe, and I go outside still singing. Maybe I dance a bit too. I forget all about that woman till I hear her saying, "Henry, look at this." I turn around and I see her at the window. "Oh yes, I wanted to speak with you," I say, "Why bring the police and get me in bad trouble? Tell me that."

"And you tell *me* what you're doing here at all," she says. "This is a respectable neighbourhood."

Then the man come along. "Now young woman, take yourself off. You ought to be ashamed of this behaviour."

"It's disgraceful," he says, talking to his wife, but loud so I can hear, and she speaks loud too—for once. "At least the other tarts[1] that crook installed here were *white* girls," she says.

"You a dam' fouti[2] liar," I say. "Plenty of those girls in your country already. Numberless as the sands on the shore. You don't need me for that."

"You're not a howling success at it certainly." Her voice sweet sugar again. "And you won't be seeing much more of your friend Mr. Sims. He's in trouble too. Try somewhere else. Find somebody else. If you can, of course." When she say that my arm moves of itself. I pick up a stone and bam! through the window. Not the one they are standing at but the next, which is of coloured glass, green and purple and yellow.

I never see a woman look so surprise. Her mouth fall open she so full of surprise. I start to laugh, louder and louder—I laugh like my grandmother, with my hands on my hips and my head back. (When she laugh like that you can hear her to the end of our street.) At last I say, "Well, I'm sorry. An accident. I get it fixed tomorrow early." "That glass is irreplaceable," the man says. "Irreplaceable." "Good thing," I say, "those colours look like they sea-sick to me. I buy you a better window-glass."

He shake his fist at me. "You won't be let off with a fine this time," he says. Then they draw the curtains. I call out at them. "You run away. Always you run away. Ever since I come here you hunt me down because I don't answer back. It's you shameless." I try to sing "Don't trouble me now."

> *Don't trouble me now*
> *You without honour.*
> *Don't walk in my footstep*
> *You without shame.*

But my voice don't sound right, so I get back indoors and drink one more glass of wine—still wanting to laugh, and still thinking of my grandmother for that is one of her songs.

It's about a man whose doudou[3] give him the go-by when she find somebody rich and he sail away to Panama. Plenty people die there of fever when they make that Panama canal so long ago. But he don't die. He come back with dollars and the girl meet him on the jetty, all dressed up and smiling. Then he sing to her, "You without honour, you without shame." It sound good in Martinique patois[4] too: "Sans honte."

Afterwards I ask myself, "Why I do that? It's not like me. But if they treat you wrong over and over again the hour strike when you burst out that's what."

Too besides, Mr. Sims can't tell me now I have no spirit. I don't care, I sleep quickly and I'm glad I break the woman's ugly window. But as to my own song it go *right* away and it never come back. A pity.

Next morning the doorbell ringing wake me up. The people upstairs don't come down, and the bell keeps on like fury self. So I go to look, and there is a policeman and a policewoman outside. As soon as I open the door the woman put her foot in it. She wear sandals and thick stockings and I never see a foot so big or so bad. It look like it want to mash up the whole world. Then she come in after the foot, and her face not so pretty either. The policeman tell me my fine is not paid and people

---

[1] *tarts* Women considered sexually promiscuous.

[2] *fouti* Crazy.

[3] *doudou* Sweetheart.

[4] *Martinique* West Indian island colonized by the French; *patois* Regional dialect, in this case the Creole dialect of Martinique.

make serious complaints about me, so they're taking me back to the magistrate. He show me a paper and I look at it, but I don't read it. The woman push me in the bedroom, and tell me to get dress quickly, but I just stare at her, because I think perhaps I wake up soon. Then I ask her what I must wear. She say she suppose I had some clothes on yesterday. Or not? "What's it matter, wear anything," she says. But I find clean underclothes and stockings and my shoes with high heels and I comb my hair. I start to file my nails, because I think they too long for magistrate's court but she get angry. "Are you coming quietly or aren't you?" she says. So I go with them and we get in a car outside.

I wait for a long time in a room full of policemen. They come in, they go out, they telephone, they talk in low voices. Then it's my turn, and first thing I notice in the court room is a man with frowning black eyebrows. He sit below the magistrate, he dressed in black and he so handsome I can't take my eyes off him. When he see that he frown worse than before.

First comes a policeman to testify I cause disturbance, and then comes the old gentleman from next door. He repeat that bit about nothing but the truth so help me God. Then he says I make dreadful noise at night and use abominable language, and dance in obscene fashion. He says when they try to shut the curtains because his wife so terrify of me, I throw stones and break a valuable stain-glass window. He say his wife get serious injury if she'd been hit, and as it is she in terrible nervous condition and the doctor is with her. I think, "Believe me, if I aim at your wife I hit your wife—that's certain." "There was no provocation," he says. "None at all." Then another lady from across the street says this is true. She heard no provocation whatsoever, and she swear that they shut the curtains but I go on insulting them and using filthy language and she saw all this and heard it.

The magistrate is a little gentleman with a quiet voice, but I'm very suspicious of these quiet voices now. He ask me why I don't pay my fine, and I say because I haven't the money. I get the idea they want to find out all about Mr. Sims—they listen so very attentive. But they'll find out nothing from me. He ask how long I have the flat and I say I don't remember. I know they want to trip me up like they trip me up about my savings so I won't answer. At last he ask if I have anything to say as I can't be allowed to go on being a nuisance. I think, "I'm nuisance to you because I have no money that's all." I want to speak up and tell him how they steal all my savings, so when my landlord asks for month's rent I haven't got it to give. I want to tell him the woman next door provoke me since long time and call me bad names but she have a soft sugar voice and nobody hear—that's why I broke her window, but I'm ready to buy another after all. I want to say all I do is sing in that old garden, and I want to say this in decent quiet voice. But I hear myself talking loud and I see my hands wave in the air. Too besides it's no use, they won't believe me, so I don't finish. I stop, and I feel the tears on my face. "Prove it." That's all they will say. They whisper, they whisper. They nod, they nod.

Next thing I'm in a car again with a different policewoman, dressed very smart. Not in uniform. I ask her where she's taking me and she says "Holloway"[1] just that "Holloway."

I catch hold of her hand because I'm afraid. But she takes it away. Cold and smooth her hand slide away and her face is china face—smooth like a doll and I think, "This is the last time I ask anything from anybody. So help me God."

The car come up to a black castle and little mean streets are all round it. A lorry[2] was blocking up the castle gates. When it get by we pass through and I am in jail. First I stand in a line with others who are waiting to give up handbags and all belongings to a woman behind bars like in a post office. The girl in front bring out a nice compact, look like gold to me, lipstick to match and a wallet full of notes. The woman keep the money, but she give back the powder and lipstick and she half-smile. I have two pounds seven shillings and sixpence in pennies. She take my purse, then she throw me my compact (which is cheap) my comb and my handkerchief like everything in my bag is dirty. So I think,

[1] *Holloway* Notorious women's prison in London.

[2] *lorry* Truck.

"Here too, here too." But I tell myself, "Girl, what you expect, eh? They all like that. All."

Some of what happen afterwards I forget, or perhaps better not remember. Seems to me they start by trying to frighten you. But they don't succeed with me for I don't care for nothing now, it's as if my heart hard like a rock and I can't feel.

Then I'm standing at the top of a staircase with a lot of women and girls. As we are going down I notice the railing very low on one side, very easy to jump, and a long way below there's the grey stone passage like it's waiting for you.

As I'm thinking this a uniform woman step up alongside quick and grab my arm. She say, "Oh no you don't."

I was just noticing the railing very low that's all—but what's the use of saying so.

Another long line waits for the doctor. It move forward slowly and my legs terrible tired. The girl in front is very young and she cry and cry. "I'm scared," she keeps saying. She's lucky in a way—as for me I never will cry again. It all dry up and hard in me now. That, and a lot besides. In the end I tell her to stop, because she doing just what these people want her to do.

She stop crying and start a long story, but while she is speaking her voice get very far away, and I find I can't see her face clear at all.

Then I'm in a chair, and one of those uniform women is pushing my head down between my knees, but let her push—everything go away from me just the same.

They put me in the hospital because the doctor say I'm sick. I have cell by myself and it's all right except I don't sleep. The things they say you mind I don't mind.

When they clang the door on me I think, "You shut me in, but you shut all those other dam' devils *out.* They can't reach me now."

At first it bothers me when they keep on looking at me all through the night. They open a little window in the doorway to do this. But I get used to it and get used to the night chemise[1] they give me. It very thick, and to my mind it not very clean either—but what's that matter to me? Only the food I can't swallow—especially the porridge. The woman ask me sarcastic, "Hunger striking?" But afterwards I can leave most of it, and she don't say nothing.

One day a nice girl comes around with books and she give me two, but I don't want to read so much. Beside one is about a murder, and the other is about a ghost and I don't think it's at all like those books tell you.

There is nothing I want now. It's no use. If they leave me in peace and quiet that's all I ask. The window is barred but not small, so I can see a little thin tree through the bars, and I like watching it.

After a week they tell me I'm better and I can go out with the others for exercise. We walk round and round one of the yards in that castle—it is fine weather and the sky is a kind of pale blue, but the yard is a terrible sad place. The sunlight fall down and die there. I get tired walking in high heels and I'm glad when that's over.

We can talk, and one day an old woman come up and ask me for dog-ends. I don't understand, and she start muttering at me like she very vexed. Another woman tell me she mean cigarette ends, so I say I don't smoke. But the old woman still look angry, and when we're going in she give me one push and I nearly fall down. I'm glad to get away from these people, and hear the door clang and take my shoes off.

Sometimes I think, "I'm here because I wanted to sing" and I have to laugh. But there's a small looking glass in my cell and I see myself and I'm like somebody else. Like some strange new person. Mr. Sims tell me I too thin, but what he say now to this person in the looking glass? So I don't laugh again.

Usually I don't think at all. Everything and everybody seem small and far away, that is the only trouble.

Twice the doctor come to see me. He don't say much and I don't say anything, because a uniform woman is always there. She look like she thinking, "Now the lies start." So I prefer not to speak. Then I'm sure they can't trip me up. Perhaps I there still, or in a worse place. But one day this happen.

[1] *night chemise* Nightgown.

We were walking round and round in the yard and I hear a woman singing—the voice come from high up, from one of the small barred windows. At first I don't believe it. Why should anybody sing here? Nobody want to sing in jail, nobody want to do anything. There's no reason, and you have no hope. I think I must be asleep, dreaming, but I'm awake all right and I see all the others are listening too. A nurse is with us that afternoon, not a policewoman. She stop and look up at the window.

It's a smoky kind of voice, and a bit rough sometimes, as if those old dark walls theyselves are complaining, because they see too much misery—too much. But it don't fall down and die in the courtyard; seems to me it could jump the gates of the jail easy and travel far, and nobody could stop it. I don't hear the words—only the music. She sing one verse and she begin another, then she break off sudden. Everybody starts walking again, and nobody says one word. But as we go in I ask the woman in front who was singing. "That's the Holloway song," she says. "Don't you know it yet? She was singing from the punishment cells, and she tell the girls cheerio and never say die." Then I have to go one way to the hospital block and she goes another so we don't speak again.

When I'm back in my cell I can't just wait for bed. I walk up and down and I think. "One day I hear that song on trumpets and these walls will fall and rest."[1] I want to get out so bad I could hammer on the door, for I know now that anything can happen, and I don't want to stay lock up here and miss it.

Then I'm hungry. I eat everything they bring and in the morning I'm still so hungry I eat the porridge. Next time the doctor come he tells me I seem much better. Then I say a little of what really happen in that house. Not much. Very careful.

He look at me hard and kind of surprised. At the door he shake his finger and says, "Now don't let me see you here again."

That evening the woman tells me I'm going, but she's so upset about it I don't ask questions. Very early, before it's light she bangs the door open and shouts at me to hurry up. As we're going along the passages I see the girl who gave me the books. She's in a row with others doing exercises. Up Down, Up Down, Up. We pass quite close and I notice she's looking very pale and tired. It's crazy, it's all crazy. This up down business and everything else too. When they give me my money I remember I leave my compact in the cell, so I ask if I can go back for it. You should see that policewoman's face as she shoo me on.

There's no car, there's a van and you can't see through the windows. The third time it stop I get out with one other, a young girl, and it's the same magistrates' court as before.

The two of us wait in a small room, nobody else there, and after a while the girl say, "What the hell are they doing? I don't want to spend all day here." She go to the bell and she keep her finger press on it. When I look at her she say, "Well, what are they *for*?" That girl's face is hard like a board—she could change faces with many and you wouldn't know the difference. But she get results certainly. A policeman come in, all smiling, and we go in the court. The same magistrate, the same frowning man sits below, and when I hear my fine is paid I want to ask who paid it, but he yells at me. "Silence."

I think I will never understand the half of what happen, but they tell me I can go, and I understand that. The magistrate ask if I'm leaving the neighbourhood and I say yes, then I'm out in the streets again, and it's the same fine weather, same feeling I'm dreaming.

When I get to the house I see two men talking in the garden. The front door and the door of the flat are both open. I go in, and the bedroom is empty, nothing but the glare streaming inside because they take the Venetian blinds away. As I'm wondering where my suitcase is, and the clothes I leave in the wardrobe, there's a knock and it's the old lady from upstairs carrying my case packed, and my coat is over her arm. She says she sees me come in. "I kept your things for you." I start to thank her but she turn her back and walk away. They like that here, and better not expect too much. Too besides, I bet they tell her I'm terrible person.

[1] *One day ... rest* Cf. Joshua 6, in which the sound of trumpets brings down the walls of Jericho.

I go in the kitchen, but when I see they are cutting down the big tree at the back I don't stay to watch.

At the station I'm waiting for the train and a woman asks if I feel well. "You look so tired," she says. "Have you come a long way?" I want to answer, "I come so far I lose myself on that journey." But I tell her, "Yes, I am quite well. But I can't stand the heat." She says she can't stand it either, and we talk about the weather till the train come in.

I'm not frightened of them any more—after all what else can they do? I know what to say and everything go like a clock works.

I get a room near Victoria where the landlady accept one pound in advance, and next day I find a job in the kitchen of a private hotel close by. But I don't stay there long. I hear of another job going in a big store—altering ladies' dresses and I get that. I lie and tell them I work in very expensive New York shop. I speak bold and smooth faced, and they never check up on me. I make a friend there—Clarice—very light coloured, very smart, she have a lot to do with the customers and she laugh at some of them behind their backs. But I say it's not their fault if the dress don't fit. Special dress for one person only—that's very expensive in London. So it's take in, or let out all the time. Clarice have two rooms not far from the store. She furnish them herself gradual and she gives parties sometimes Saturday nights. It's there I start whistling the Holloway Song. A man comes up to me and says, "Let's hear that again." So I whistle it again (I never sing now) and he tells me "Not bad." Clarice have an old piano somebody give her to store and he plays the tune, jazzing it up. I say, "No, not like that," but everybody else say the way he do it is first class. Well I think no more of this till I get a letter from him telling me he has sold the song and as I was quite a help he encloses five pounds with thanks.

I read the letter and I could cry. For after all, that song was all I had. I don't belong nowhere really, and I haven't money to buy my way to belonging. I don't want to either.

But when that girl sing, she sing to me, and she sing for me. I was there because I was *meant* to be there. It was *meant* I should hear it—this I *know.*

Now I've let them play it wrong, and it will go from me like all the other songs—like everything. Nothing left for me at all.

But then I tell myself all this is foolishness. Even if they played it on trumpets, even if they played it just right, like I wanted—no walls would fall so soon. "So let them call it jazz," I think, and let them play it wrong. That won't make no difference to the song I heard.

I buy myself a dusty pink dress with the money.

—1962

Stevie Smith

1902 – 1971

The poetry Stevie Smith produced in the years surrounding World War II has been considered some of the most original of its time. Sharing elements with the work of such diverse poets as William Blake, Robert Browning, Edward Lear, and Ogden Nash, Smith's poetry fits into no established genres and follows few known conventions. So unusual is her work, with its weighty themes explored in deceptively simple tones, that for many years her critical reputation remained ambiguous—she was for the most part not regarded as a "serious" poet. Smith experienced immense popularity during her lifetime, but her writing has only recently received substantial critical attention.

Stevie Smith was born in Hull on 20 September 1902. (Christened Florence Margaret, Smith was many years later nicknamed Stevie—after the then-famous jockey Steve Donaghue—when horseback riding with friends one day.) Shortly after her birth, her father abandoned the family, and her mother took Smith and her sister to live with their aunt in Palmer's Green, a London suburb. After Smith's mother died in 1919 she was raised by her aunt, whom she affectionately called "The Lion Aunt of Hull." Smith and her aunt lived together in the house in Palmer's Green until the Lion Aunt's death in 1968, after which point Smith remained in the house alone.

After completing school, Smith pursued a secretarial course and acquired a position in 1922 as private secretary to Sir Neville Pearson, chair of the leading publishing firm of Pearson, Newness; she would retain this position until her retirement in 1953. Smith had begun writing poetry in her twenties, and in 1935 she approached the publisher Chatto and Windus with a collection of several pieces. The firm's editor turned down the poems, advising her to write a novel instead. The result, completed six weeks later, was *Novel on Yellow Paper* (1936), thus named because Smith had typed it while at work, on Pearson's yellow carbon-copy paper.

Novel on Yellow Paper was widely and favorably reviewed. Readers were astonished by the deft insights and frantic pace of its chatty-voiced narrator, who tells her story in a stream-of-consciousness style which many have compared to that of Virginia Woolf. Although Smith wrote two sequels to her first novel, *Over the Frontier* (1938) and *The Holiday* (1949), she preferred writing poetry to prose. With the commercial success of *Novel on Yellow Paper*, Smith was able to ensure the publication of her first volume of poems, *A Good Time Was Had by All* (1937). This was soon followed by the collections *Tender Only to One* (1938) and *Mother, What Is Man?* (1942).

Readers appreciated the unique sense of humor that characterized Smith's neat, economical poems. The simple language, often-ridiculous rhymes, odd syntax, and repetitive, singsong rhythms conveyed the sense of a child-like sensibility—a sense that was accentuated by the bizarre doodles she published alongside the poems. When she began holding her own poetry readings after the war, Smith emphasized the nursery-rhyme quality of her poems; she would arrive in her customary schoolgirl's frocks and pageboy haircut and proceed to sing her poems in a loud, off-key voice to the tunes of well-known hymns or children's songs.

Underneath the apparent frivolity of Smith's poems, however, lie powerful themes. She frequently rewrote common myths and legends and satirized accepted ideas or conventions. In "The Blue from Heaven" (1957), for example, she isolates and dissects one image from the myth of King Arthur, while in "The New Age" (1957) she mocks the often-heard lament over the decline of culture and civilization. Though she called herself an agnostic, Smith had a lifelong attachment to the Church of England, and many of her poems deal with Christian themes; she once described the main business of her life as "death, loneliness, God, and the devil." Her fascination with death—a subject of many of her poems—has been much commented upon. She claimed to find comfort in the knowledge that death was always an option, and in poems such as "Thoughts about the Person from Porlock" (1962) and "Is It Wise?" (1937) she contemplates the release that death would bring. But Smith's poetry also celebrates life, even at its most bizarre and unpleasant. She possessed a remarkable ability to see the comic in tragic events, as is evident in the black humor of "Not Waving but Drowning"(1957).

By the 1960s Stevie Smith had published numerous collections of poetry and was something of a cult figure, idolized by her younger peers for her indifference to established conventions, her cynicism, and her fierce honesty. When she died in 1971 she was at the height of her popularity, having recently been honored with the Cholmondeley Award for Poetry (1966) and the Queen's Medal for Poetry (1969). Smith herself did not necessarily believe that poets should occupy a privileged position in society. On the contrary, she said a poet should "be just made to get on with his writing: put in a room with pencils and pen or a typewriter; and then if his poems are no good, then he must just be thrown out."

⌘⌘⌘

Mother, Among the Dustbins

Mother, among the dustbins and the manure
I feel the measure of my humanity, an allure
As of the presence of God. I am sure

In the dustbins, in the manure, in the cat at play,
Is the presence of God, in a sure way
He moves there. Mother, what do you say?

I too have felt the presence of God in the broom
I hold, in the cobwebs in the room,
But most of all in the silence of the tomb.

Ah! but that thought that informs the hope of our kind
Is but an empty thing, what lies behind?—
Naught but the vanity of a protesting mind

That would not die. This is the thought that bounces
Within a conceited head and trounces
Inquiry. Man is most frivolous when he pronounces.

Well Mother, I shall continue to feel as I do,
And I think you would be wise to do so too,
Can you question the folly of man in the creation of God?
Who are you?

—1938

The River God

I may be smelly, and I may be old,
Rough in my pebbles, reedy in my pools,
But where my fish float by I bless their swimming
And I like the people to bathe in me, especially women.
But I can drown the fools

Who bathe too close to the weir,[1] contrary to rules.
And they take a long time drowning
As I throw them up now and then in a spirit of clowning.
Hi yih, yippity-yap, merrily I flow,
O I may be an old foul river but I have plenty of go.
Once there was a lady who was too bold
She bathed in me by the tall black cliff where the
water runs cold,
So I brought her down here
To be my beautiful dear.
Oh will she stay with me will she stay
This beautiful lady, or will she go away?
She lies in my beautiful deep river bed with many a weed
To hold her, and many a waving reed.
Oh who would guess what a beautiful white face lies there
Waiting for me to smooth and wash away the fear
She looks at me with. Hi yih, do not let her
Go. There is no one on earth who does not forget her
Now. They say I am a foolish old smelly river
But they do not know of my wide original bed
Where the lady waits, with her golden sleepy head.
If she wishes to go I will not forgive her.
—1950

Not Waving but Drowning

Nobody heard him, the dead man,
But still he lay moaning:
I was much further out than you thought
And not waving but drowning.

Poor chap, he always loved larking
And now he's dead
It must have been too cold for him his heart gave way,
They said.

Oh, no no no, it was too cold always
(Still the dead one lay moaning)
I was much too far out all my life
And not waving but drowning.
—1957

[1] *weir* Barrier or dam to hold back water.

The Blue from Heaven

A legend of King Arthur of Britain.

King Arthur rode in another world
And his twelve knights rode behind him
And Guinevere was there
Crying: Arthur, where are you dear?

Why is the King so blue
Why is he this blue colour?
It is because the sun is shining
And he rides under the blue cornflowers.

High wave the cornflowers
That shed the pale blue light
And under the tall cornflowers
Rides King Arthur and his twelve knights.

And Guinevere is there
Crying: Arthur, where are you dear?

First there were twelve knights riding
And then there was only one
And King Arthur said to the one knight,
Be gone.

All I wish for now, said Arthur,
Is the beautiful colour blue
And to ride in the blue sunshine
And Guinevere I do not wish for you.

Oh Lord, said Guinevere
I do not see the colour blue
And I wish to ride where our knights rode,
After you.

Go back, go back, Guinevere,
Go back to the palace, said the King.
So she went back to the palace
And her grief did not seem to her a small thing.

The Queen has returned to the palace
Crying: Arthur, where are you dear?
And every day she speaks of Arthur's grandeur
To the knights who are there.

That Arthur has fallen from the grandeur
Of his powers all agree
And the falling off of Arthur
Becomes their theme presently.

As if it were only temporarily
And it was not for ever
They speak, but the Queen knows
He will come back never.

Yes, Arthur has passed away
Gladly he has laid down his reigning powers
He has gone to ride in the blue light
Of the peculiar towering cornflowers.
—1957

Thoughts about the Person from Porlock[1]

Coleridge received the Person from Porlock
And ever after called him a curse,
Then why did he hurry to let him in?
He could have hid in the house.

It was not right of Coleridge in fact it was wrong
(But often we all do wrong)
As the truth is I think he was already stuck
With Kubla Khan.

He was weeping and wailing: I am finished, finished,
I shall never write another word of it,
When along comes the Person from Porlock
And takes the blame for it.

It was not right, it was wrong,
But often we all do wrong.

* * *

May we inquire the name of the Person from Porlock?
Why, Porson, didn't you know?
He lived at the bottom of Porlock Hill
So had a long way to go,

He wasn't much in the social sense
Though his grandmother was a Warlock,
One of the Rutlandshire[2] ones I fancy
And nothing to do with Porlock,

And he lived at the bottom of the hill as I said
And had a cat named Flo,
And had a cat named Flo.

I long for the Person from Porlock
To bring my thoughts to an end,
I am becoming impatient to see him
I think of him as a friend,

Often I look out of the window
Often I run to the gate
I think, He will come this evening,
I think it is rather late.

I am hungry to be interrupted
Forever and ever amen
O Person from Porlock come quickly
And bring my thoughts to an end.

[1] *Person from Porlock* In a note written in 1816, Samuel Taylor Coleridge gives an account of the composition of his fragmentary poem "Kubla Khan" (1797–98). According to this account, after taking opium, falling asleep, and dreaming several hundred lines of poetry, he woke up, recalled the dream visions perfectly, and immediately set down the surviving lines of "Kubla Khan." Unfortunately, before Coleridge could complete the work, he writes that "a person on business from Porlock" came to the door and "detained [Coleridge] above an hour" and that, after the visit had ended, he "found, to his no small surprise and mortification" that the remaining lines "had passed away like the images on the surface of a stream into which a stone had been cast, but, alas! without the after restoration of the latter[.] …"; *Porlock* Village on the coast of Somerset, England.

[2] *Rutlandshire* Small county in the east Midlands of England.

* * *

I felicitate the people who have a Person from Porlock
To break up everything and throw it away
Because then there will be nothing to keep them
And they need not stay.

* * *

Why do they grumble so much?
He comes like a benison° *blessing*
They should be glad he has not forgotten them
They might have had to go on.

* * *

These thoughts are depressing I know. They are depressing,
I wish I was more cheerful, it is more pleasant,
Also it is a duty, we should smile as well as submitting
To the purpose of One Above who is experimenting
With various mixtures of human character which goes best,
All is interesting for him it is exciting, but not for us.
There I go again. Smile, smile, and get some work to do
Then you will be practically unconscious without positively having to go.
—1962

Pretty

Why is the word pretty so underrated?
In November the leaf is pretty when it falls
The stream grows deep in the woods after rain
And in the pretty pool the pike stalks

He stalks his prey, and this is pretty too,
The prey escapes with an underwater flash
But not for long, the great fish has him now
The pike is a fish who always has his prey

And this is pretty. The water rat is pretty
His paws are not webbed, he cannot shut his nostrils
As the otter can and the beaver, he is torn between
The land and water. Not "torn," he does not mind.

The owl hunts in the evening and it is pretty
The lake water below him rustles with ice
There is frost coming from the ground, in the air mist
All this is pretty, it could not be prettier.

Yes, it could always be prettier, the eye abashes
It is becoming an eye that cannot see enough,
Out of the wood the eye climbs. This is prettier
A field in the evening, tilting up.

The field tilts to the sky. Though it is late
The sky is lighter than the hill field
All this looks easy but really it is extraordinary
Well, it is extraordinary to be so pretty.

And it is careless, and that is always pretty
This field, this owl, this pike, this pool are careless,
As Nature is always careless and indifferent
Who sees, who steps, means nothing, and this is pretty.

So a person can come along like a thief—pretty!—
Stealing a look, pinching the sound and feel,
Lick the icicle broken from the bank
And still say nothing at all, only cry pretty.

Cry pretty, pretty, pretty and you'll be able
Very soon not even to cry pretty
And so be delivered entirely from humanity
This is prettiest of all, it is very pretty.
—1962

George Orwell

1903 – 1950

George Orwell struggled throughout his life to live his convictions as well as to write from them. His most famous novels, *Animal Farm* (1945) and *1984* (1949), have been translated into more than sixty languages and have sold over forty million copies. While his writerly craft and strongly articulated views on the importance of linguistic integrity (most directly expressed in his 1946 essay "Politics and the English Language") are admired and respected, he is recognized even more widely for his moral integrity, independence of mind, and scope of vision.

Born Eric Arthur Blair in Motihari, India, on 25 June 1903, Orwell came from a family with strong colonial ties on both sides. His father, Richard Blair, worked as an opium agent for the British Imperial government; his mother, Ida Limouzin, grew up in Burma surrounded by a large staff of native servants, taking work as a governess in India when her father lost his wealth. Although the baby Eric returned to England with his mother and older sister in 1904, his sense of identity was molded by the colonial experience. He was also strongly marked by his experiences as an economically poor but culturally middle-class student in English boarding schools, first at St. Cyprian's School (an experience later immortalized in his 1953 *Such, Such Were the Joys*) and then as a scholarship student at Eton.

Despite his evident abilities as a scholar, Eric did not apply himself while at Eton and was ultimately discouraged from pursuing university-level studies; in fact, he was himself more interested in returning to his colonial roots and pursuing a more adventurous career. After sitting eight days of qualifying examinations, he was selected to travel to Burma to join the Imperial Police. He served there from 1922 to 1927 in an array of posts around the country before deciding that the work was not suited to his character or his ideals; it had also taken its toll physically. His experiences left him feeling profoundly ambivalent about the colonial presence of the British, and about the nature of imperialist authority in general. He resigned his assignment upon his return to England, filled with a profound sense of guilt.

Although he was at this point determined to become a writer, he had not written much of anything while in Burma, nor published any adult work. Nevertheless, he decided that living in poverty, first in the East End of London, then in Paris, taking various low-paying jobs here and there, would help provide him with suitable material and would also condition his mind for the task of writing. He spent the years 1928–29 in Paris, taking menial jobs in restaurants and hotels and contracting pneumonia in the process, and then returned to England where he spent some time living as a tramp. His first book, *Down and Out in Paris and London*, appeared in 1933 under the pseudonym of George Orwell, chosen to protect his family and to distance himself from them and from his own earlier life.

Orwell spent nine months in 1934 living with his parents while he finished his second book, the novel *A Clergyman's Daughter* (1935). He then moved out, took work in a bookshop, and continued to write; his *Burmese Days*, which drew on his experiences in Burma and expressed his strong views regarding imperialism, appeared in 1934. *A Clergyman's Daughter* was published the following year; in it Orwell attempted to use his tramping experiences as material for fiction, but was himself dissatisfied with the results. In later years he did his best to keep this and his next autobiographical novel, *Keep the Aspidistra Flying* (1936), out of view, preventing their reissues; the latter did not appear in the United States until 1956.

In 1936, emboldened by an advance for his next, nonfictional project, Orwell married Eileen O'Shaughnessy. Eileen abandoned her graduate studies in Educational Psychology at University College in London to move with Orwell into a tiny, isolated, and primitive cottage in Wallington, Hertfordshire, where they kept a garden, goats, and chickens, and managed a small shop, and where Orwell continued to write. His study of the dismal lives of the poor and unemployed in the industrial towns of the north of England took him tramping once again; *The Road to Wigan Pier* (1937) gave voice to his socialist views and established his reputation as a political writer.

Orwell's political idealism was severely tested when he fought for the Republicans in the Spanish Civil War. He witnessed first-hand the intense in-fighting amongst the various factions of the Left, and he became profoundly critical of all political orthodoxies as a result. His next book, *Homage to Catalonia*, combined personal recollection with biting political analysis; it was as critical of the Soviet-influenced Communist faction in Spain as it was of Franco's Fascists. It received a mixed reception when it appeared in 1938. Today, however, it is recognized as an eloquent illustration of Orwell's passionate intellectual and political independence of mind.

World War II broke out three months after the publication of Orwell's next novel, *Coming Up for Air* (1939); unable to join the army due to his poor health, Orwell worked for two years for the BBC's Eastern Service, in addition to writing various essays and reviews. In 1944, Orwell and his wife adopted a son, Richard Horatio Blair, to whom they were both deeply devoted. But in 1945, Orwell's life changed: Eileen died (and her death devastated Orwell), and *Animal Farm* was published and brought overnight literary and financial success. This short novel is a fable that satirizes the corruption of socialist ideals that had by then occurred in the Soviet Union under Joseph Stalin; everyone was supposedly equal but "some animals are more equal than others," in Orwell's famous phrase.

Orwell spent most of the last years of his life in an isolated cottage on the island of Jura, off the coast of Scotland, with Richard, a nanny, and his sister Avril for company. As he gradually succumbed to tuberculosis, he wrote *1984*, widely considered his most ambitious and important work. This dark novel, published in 1949, imagines a totalitarian future in which absolute conformity is rigidly enforced; "Big Brother is watching you" is the catchword of a society in which privacy and individual freedom have all but disappeared. His health still weakening, Orwell was admitted to University College Hospital in London, where, in his hospital room, he married Sonia Brownell in the fall of 1949. He died several months later, on 21 January 1950.

⌘⌘⌘

Politics and the English Language

Most people who bother with the matter at all would admit that the English language is in a bad way, but it is generally assumed that we cannot by conscious action do anything about it. Our civilization is decadent and our language—so the argument runs—must inevitably share in the general collapse. It follows that any struggle against the abuse of language is a sentimental archaism, like preferring candles to electric light or hansom cabs to aeroplanes. Underneath this lies the half-conscious belief that language is a natural growth and not an instrument which we shape for our own purposes.

Now, it is clear that the decline of a language must ultimately have political and economic causes: it is not due simply to the bad influence of this or that individual writer. But an effect can become a cause, reinforcing the original cause and producing the same effect in an intensified form, and so on indefinitely. A man may take to drink because he feels himself to be a failure, and then fail all the more completely because he drinks. It is rather the same thing that is happening to the English language. It becomes ugly and inaccurate because our thoughts are foolish, but the slovenliness of our language makes it easier for us to have foolish thoughts. The point is that the process is reversible. Modern English, especially written English, is full of bad habits which spread by imitation and which can be avoided if one is willing to take the necessary trouble. If one gets rid of these habits one can think more clearly, and to think clearly is a necessary first step towards political regeneration: so that the fight against bad English is not frivolous and is not the exclusive concern of professional writers. I will come back to this presently, and I hope that by that time the meaning of what I have said here will have become clearer. Meanwhile, here are five specimens of the English language as it is now habitually written.

These five passages have not been picked out because they are especially bad—I could have quoted far worse if I had chosen—but because they illustrate various of the mental vices from which we now suffer. They are a little below the average, but are fairly representative samples. I number them so that I can refer back to them when necessary:

> 1. I am not, indeed, sure whether it is not true to say that the Milton who once seemed not unlike a seventeenth-century Shelley had not become, out of an experience ever more bitter in each year, more alien (*sic*) to the founder of that Jesuit sect which nothing could induce him to tolerate.
>
> Professor Harold Laski
>
> (Essay in *Freedom of Expression*).

> 2. Above all, we cannot play ducks and drakes with a native battery of idioms which prescribes such egregious collocations of vocables as the Basic *put up with* for *tolerate* or *put at a loss* for *bewilder.*
>
> Professor Lancelot Hogben (*Interglossa*).

> 3. On the one side we have the free personality: by definition it is not neurotic, for it has neither conflict nor dream. Its desires, such as they are, are transparent, for they are just what institutional approval keeps in the forefront of consciousness; another institutional pattern would alter their number and intensity; there is little in them that is natural, irreducible, or culturally dangerous. But *on the other side*, the social bond itself is nothing but the mutual reflection of these self-secure integrities. Recall the definition of love. Is not this the very picture of a small academic? Where is there a place in this hall of mirrors for either personality or fraternity?
>
> Essay on psychology in *Politics* (New York).

> 4. All the "best people" from the gentlemen's clubs, and all the frantic Fascist captains, united in common hatred of Socialism and bestial horror of the rising tide of the mass revolutionary movement, have turned to acts of provocation, to foul incendiarism, to medieval legends of poisoned wells, to legalise their own destruction to proletarian organisations, and rouse the agitated petty-bourgeoisie to chauvinistic fervour on behalf of the fight against the revolutionary way out of the crisis.
>
> Communist pamphlet.

> 5. If a new spirit *is* to be infused into this old country, there is one thorny and contentious reform which must be tackled, and that is the humanisation and galvanisation of the BBC.[1] Timidity here will bespeak canker and atrophy of the soul. The heart of Britain may be sound and of strong beat, for instance, but the British lion's roar at present is like that of Bottom in Shakespeare's *Midsummer Night's Dream*—as gentle as any sucking dove. A virile new Britain cannot continue indefinitely to be traduced in the eyes, or rather ears, of the world by the effete languors of Langham Place,[2] brazenly masquerading as "standard English." When the Voice of Britain is heard at nine o'clock, better far and infinitely less ludicrous to hear aitches honestly dropped than the present priggish, inflated, inhibited, school-ma'amish arch braying of blameless bashful mewing maidens!
>
> Letter in *Tribune*.

Each of these passages has faults of its own, but, quite apart from avoidable ugliness, two qualities are common to all of them. The first is staleness of imagery: the other is lack of precision. The writer either has a meaning and cannot express it, or he inadvertently says something else, or he is almost indifferent as to whether his words mean anything or not. This mixture of vagueness and sheer incompetence is the most marked characteristic of modern English prose, and especially of any kind of political writing. As soon as certain topics are raised, the concrete melts into the abstract and no one seems able to think of turns of speech that are not hackneyed: prose consists less and less of *words* chosen for the sake of their meaning, and more of *phrases* tacked together like the sections of a prefabricated hen-house. I list below, with notes and examples, various of the tricks by means of which the work of prose construction is habitually dodged:

Dying metaphors. A newly invented metaphor assists thought by evoking a visual image, while on the other hand a metaphor which is technically "dead" (e.g., *iron resolution*) has in effect reverted to being an ordinary word and can generally be used without loss of vividness. But in between these two classes there is a huge dump of worn-out metaphors which have lost all evocative power and are merely used because they save people the trouble of inventing phrases for themselves. Examples are: *Ring the changes on, take up the cudgels for, toe the line, ride roughshod over, stand shoulder to shoulder with, play into the hands of, no axe to grind, grist to the mill, fishing in troubled waters, rift within the lute, on the order of the day, Achilles' heel, swan song, hotbed.* Many of these are used without knowledge of their meaning (What is a "rift," for instance?), and incompatible metaphors are frequently mixed, a sure sign that the writer is not interested in what he is saying. Some metaphors now current have been twisted out of their original meaning without those who use them even being aware of the fact. For example, *toe the line* is sometimes written *tow the line*. Another example is *the hammer and the anvil*, now always used with the implication that the anvil gets the worst of it. In real life it is always the anvil that breaks the hammer, never the other way about: a writer who stopped to think what he was saying would be aware of this, and would avoid perverting the original phrase.

Operators, or *verbal false limbs*. These save the trouble of picking out appropriate verbs and nouns, and at the same time pad each sentence with extra syllables which give it an appearance of symmetry. Characteristic phrases are: *render inoperative, militate against, prove unacceptable, make contact with, be subjected to, give rise to, give grounds for, have the effect of, play a leading part* (*role*) *in, make itself felt, take effect, exhibit a tendency to, serve the purpose of*, etc., etc. The keynote is the elimination of simple verbs. Instead of being a single word, such as *break, stop, spoil, mend, kill*, a verb becomes a *phrase*, made up of a noun or adjective tacked on to some general-purposes verb such as *prove, serve, form, play, render.* In addition, the passive voice is wherever possible used in preference to the active, and noun constructions are used instead of gerunds (*by examination of* instead of *by examining*). The range of verbs is further cut down by means of the *-ise* and *de-* formations, and banal state-

[1] *BBC* British Broadcasting Corporation.

[2] *Langham Place* Location of the main office of the BBC.

ments are given an appearance of profundity by means of the *not un-* formation. Simple conjunctions and prepositions are replaced by such phrases as *with respect to, having regard to, the fact that, by dint of, in view of, in the interests of, on the hypothesis that;* and the ends of sentences are saved from anticlimax by such resounding commonplaces as *greatly to be desired, cannot be left out of account, a development to be expected in the near future, deserving of serious consideration, brought to a satisfactory conclusion*, and so on and so forth.

Pretentious diction. Words like *phenomenon, element, individual* (as noun), *objective, categorical, effective, virtual, basic, primary, promote, constitute, exhibit, exploit, utilise, eliminate, liquidate*, are used to dress up simple statements and give an air of scientific impartiality to biassed judgements. Adjectives like *epoch-making, epic, historic, unforgettable, triumphant, age-old, inevitable, inexorable, veritable*, are used to dignify the sordid processes of international politics, while writing that aims at glorifying war usually takes on an archaic colour, its characteristic words being: *realm, throne, chariot, mailed fist, trident, sword, shield, buckler, banner, jack-boot, clarion.* Foreign words and expressions such as *cul de sac, ancien régime, deus ex machina, mutatis mutandis, status quo, Gleichschaltung, Weltanschauung*,[1] are used to give an air of culture and elegance. Except for the useful abbreviations *i.e., e.g.*, and *etc.*, there is no real need for any of the hundreds of foreign phrases now current in English. Bad writers, and especially scientific, political, and sociological writers, are nearly always haunted by the notion that Latin or Greek words are grander than Saxon ones, and unnecessary words like *expedite, ameliorate, predict, extraneous, deracinated, clandestine, subaqueous* and hundreds of others constantly gain ground from their Anglo-Saxon opposite numbers.[2] The jargon peculiar to Marxist writing (*hyena, hangman, cannibal, petty bourgeois, these gentry, lacquey, flunkey, mad dog, White Guard*, etc.) consists largely of words and phrases translated from Russian, German, or French; but the normal way of coining a new word is to use a Latin or Greek root with the appropriate affix and, where necessary, the *-ise* formation. It is often easier to make up words of this kind (*deregionalise, impermissible, extramarital, non-fragmentatory* and so forth) than to think up the English words that will cover one's meaning. The result, in general, is an increase in slovenliness and vagueness.

Meaningless words. In certain kinds of writing, particularly in art criticism and literary criticism, it is normal to come across long passages which are almost completely lacking in meaning.[3] Words like *romantic, plastic, values, human, dead, sentimental, natural, vitality*, as used in art criticism, are strictly meaningless, in the sense that they not only do not point to any discoverable object, but are hardly even expected to do so by the reader.

When one critic writes, "The outstanding features of Mr. X's work is its living quality," while another writes, "The immediately striking thing about Mr. X's work is its peculiar deadness," the reader accepts this as a simple difference of opinion. If words like *black* and *white* were involved, instead of the jargon words *dead* and *living*, he would see at once that language was being used in an improper way. Many political words are similarly abused. The word *Fascism* has now no meaning except in so far as it signifies "something not desirable." The words *democracy, socialism, freedom, patriotic, realistic, justice*, have each of them several different meanings which cannot be reconciled with one another. In the

[1] *ancien ... Weltanschauung* Phrases meaning, respectively, old system of government (French), god from the machine (Latin), the necessary changes being made (Latin), the state of things (Latin), enforced political conformity (German), philosophy of life (German).

[2] [Orwell's note] An interesting illustration of this is the way in which the English flower names which were in use till very recently are being ousted by Greek ones, *snapdragon* becoming *atirrhinum, forget-me-not* becoming *myosotis*, etc. It is hard to see any practical reason for this change in fashion: it is probably due to an instinctive turning-away from the more homely word and a vague feeling that the Greek word is scientific.

[3] [Orwell's note] Example: "Comfort's catholicity of perception and image, strangely Whitmanesque in range, continues to evoke that trembling atmospheric accumulative hinting at a cruel, an inexorably serene timelessness ... Wrey Gardiner scores by aiming at simple bullseyes with precision. Only they are not so simple, and through this contented sadness runs more than the surface bitter-sweet of resignation" (*Poetry Quarterly*).

case of a word like *democracy*, not only is there no agreed definition, but the attempt to make one is resisted from all sides. It is almost universally felt that when we call a country democratic we are praising it: consequently the defenders of every kind of regime claim that it is a democracy, and fear that they might have to stop using the word if it were tied down to any one meaning. Words of this kind are often used in a consciously dishonest way. That is, the person who uses them has his own private definition, but allows his hearer to think he means something quite different. Statements like *Marshal Pétain*[1] *was a true patriot*, *The Soviet press is the freest in the world*, *The Catholic Church is opposed to persecution*, are almost always made with intent to deceive. Other words used in variable meanings, in most cases more or less dishonestly, are: *class*, *totalitarian*, *science*, *progressive*, *reactionary*, *bourgeois*, *equality*.

Now that I have made this catalogue of swindles and perversions, let me give another example of the kind of writing that they lead to. This time it must of its nature be an imaginary one. I am going to translate a passage of good English into modern English of the worst sort. Here is a well-known verse from *Ecclesiastes*:

> I returned and saw under the sun, that the race is not to the swift, nor the battle to the strong, neither yet bread to the wise, nor yet riches to men of understanding, nor yet favour to men of skill; but time and chance happeneth to them all.

Here it is in modern English:

> Objective considerations of contemporary phenomena compels the conclusion that success or failure in competitive activities exhibits no tendency to be commensurate with innate capacity, but that a considerable element of the unpredictable must invariably be taken into account.

This is a parody, but not a very gross one. Exhibit 3, above, for instance, contains several patches of the same kind in English. It will be seen that I have not made a full translation. The beginning and ending of the sentence follow the original meaning fairly closely, but in the middle the concrete illustrations—race, battle, bread—dissolve into the vague phrase "success or failure in competitive activities." This had to be so, because no modern writer of the kind I am discussing—no one capable of using phrases like "objective consideration of contemporary phenomena"—would ever tabulate his thoughts in that precise and detailed way. The whole tendency of modern prose is away from concreteness. Now analyse these two sentences a little more closely. The first contains forty-nine words but only sixty syllables, and all its words are those of everyday life. The second contains thirty-eight words of ninety syllables: eighteen of its words are from Latin roots, and one from Greek. The first sentence contains six vivid images, and only one phrase ("time and chance") that could be called vague. The second contains not a single fresh, arresting phrase, and in spite of its ninety syllables it gives only a shortened version of the meaning contained in the first. Yet without a doubt it is the second kind of sentence that is gaining ground in modern English. I do not want to exaggerate. This kind of writing is not yet universal, and outcrops of simplicity will occur here and there in the worst-written page. Still, if you or I were told to write a few lines on the uncertainty of human fortunes, we should probably come much nearer to my imaginary sentence than to the one from *Ecclesiastes*.

As I have tried to show, modern writing at its worst does not consist in picking out words for the sake of their meaning and inventing images in order to make the meaning clearer. It consists in gumming together long strips of words which have already been set in order by someone else, and making the results presentable by sheer humbug. The attraction of this way of writing is that it is easy. It is easier—even quicker, once you have the habit—to say *In my opinion it is a not unjustifiable assumption that* than to say *I think*. If you use ready-made phrases, you not only don't have to hunt about for words; you also don't have to bother with the rhythms of your sentences, since these phrases are generally so arranged as to be more or less euphonious. When you

[1] *Marshal Pétain* French general (1856–1951) who was appointed head of the Vichy government, which ruled Occupied France during World War II in collaboration with the Nazis.

are composing in a hurry—when you are dictating to a stenographer, for instance, or making a public speech—it is natural to fall into a pretentious, Latinized style. Tags like *a consideration which we should do well to bear in mind* or *a conclusion to which all of us would readily assent* will save many a sentence from coming down with a bump. By using stale metaphors, similes, and idioms, you save much mental effort, at the cost of leaving your meaning vague, not only for your reader but for yourself. This is the significance of mixed metaphors. The sole aim of a metaphor is to call up a visual image. When these images clash—as in *The Fascist octopus has sung its swan song, the jackboot is thrown into the melting pot*—it can be taken as certain that the writer is not seeing a mental image of the objects he is naming; in other words he is not really thinking.

Look again at the examples I gave at the beginning of this essay. Professor Laski (1) uses five negatives in 53 words. One of these is superfluous, making nonsense of the whole passage, and in addition there is the slip *alien* for akin, making further nonsense, and several avoidable pieces of clumsiness which increase the general vagueness. Professor Hogben (2) plays ducks and drakes with a battery which is able to write prescriptions, and, while disapproving of the everyday phrase *put up with*, is unwilling to look *egregious* up in the dictionary and see what it means. (3), if one takes an uncharitable attitude towards it, is simply meaningless: probably one could work out its intended meaning by reading the whole of the article in which it occurs. In (4) the writer knows more or less what he wants to say, but an accumulation of stale phrases chokes him like tea-leaves blocking a sink. In (5) words and meaning have almost parted company. People who write in this manner usually have a general emotional meaning—they dislike one thing and want to express solidarity with another—but they are not interested in the detail of what they are saying. A scrupulous writer, in every sentence that he writes, will ask himself at least four questions, thus: What am I trying to say? What words will express it? What image or idiom will make it clearer? Is this image fresh enough to have an effect? And he will probably ask himself two more: Could I put it more shortly? Have I said anything that is avoidably ugly? But you are not obliged to go to all this trouble. You can shirk it by simply throwing your mind open and letting the ready-made phrases come crowding in. They will construct your sentences for you—even think your thoughts for you, to a certain extent—and at need they will perform the important service of partially concealing your meaning even from yourself. It is at this point that the special connection between politics and the debasement of language becomes clear.

In our time it is broadly true that political writing is bad writing. Where it is not true, it will generally be found that the writer is some kind of rebel, expressing his private opinions, and not a "party line." Orthodoxy, of whatever colour, seems to demand a lifeless, imitative style. The political dialects to be found in pamphlets, leading articles, manifestos, White Papers,[1] and the speeches of Under-Secretaries do, of course, vary from party to party, but they are all alike in that one almost never finds in them a fresh, vivid, homemade turn of speech. When one watches some tired hack on the platform mechanically repeating the familiar phrases—*bestial atrocities, iron heel, blood-stained tyranny, free peoples of the world, stand shoulder to shoulder*—one often has a curious feeling that one is not watching a live human being but some kind of dummy: a feeling which suddenly becomes stronger at moments when the light catches the speaker's spectacles and turns them into blank discs which seem to have no eyes behind them. And this is not altogether fanciful. A speaker who uses that kind of phraseology has gone some distance towards turning himself into a machine. The appropriate noises are coming out of his larynx, but his brain is not involved as it would be if he were choosing his words for himself. If the speech he is making is one that he is accustomed to make over and over again, he may be almost unconscious of what he is saying, as one is when one utters the responses in church. And this reduced state of consciousness, if not indispensable, is at any rate favourable to political conformity.

[1] *White Papers* Parliamentary documents.

In our time, political speech and writing are largely the defence of the indefensible. Things like the continuance of British rule in India, the Russian purges and deportations, the dropping of the atom bombs on Japan, can indeed be defended, but only by arguments which are too brutal for most people to face, and which do not square with the professed aims of political parties. Thus political language has to consist largely of euphemism, question-begging and sheer cloudy vagueness. Defenceless villages are bombarded from the air, the inhabitants driven out into the countryside, the cattle machine-gunned, the huts set on fire with incendiary bullets: this is called *pacification*. Millions of peasants are robbed of their farms and sent trudging along the roads with no more than they can carry: this is called *transfer of population* or *rectification of frontiers*. People are imprisoned for years without trial, or shot in the back of the neck, or sent to die of scurvy in Arctic lumber camps: this is called *elimination of unreliable elements*. Such phraseology is needed if one wants to name things without calling up mental pictures of them. Consider for instance some comfortable English professor defending Russian totalitarianism. He cannot say outright, "I believe in killing off your opponents when you can get good results by doing so." Probably, therefore, he will say something like this:

> While freely conceding that the Soviet regime exhibits certain features which the humanitarian may be inclined to deplore, we must, I think, agree that a certain curtailment of the right to political opposition is an unavoidable concomitant of transitional periods, and that the rigours which the Russian people have been called upon to undergo have been amply justified in the sphere of concrete achievement.

The inflated style is itself a kind of euphemism. A mass of Latin words falls upon the facts like soft snow, blurring the outlines and covering up all the details. The great enemy of clear language is insincerity. When there is a gap between one's real and one's declared aims, one turns as it were instinctively to long words and exhausted idioms, like a cuttlefish[1] squirting out ink. In our age there is no such thing as "keeping out of politics." All issues are political issues, and politics itself is a mass of lies, evasions, folly, hatred and schizophrenia. When the general atmosphere is bad, language must suffer. I should expect to find—this is a guess which I have not sufficient knowledge to verify—that the German, Russian, and Italian languages have all deteriorated in the last ten or fifteen years, as a result of dictatorship.

But if thought corrupts language, language can also corrupt thought. A bad usage can spread by tradition and imitation, even among people who should and do know better. The debased language that I have been discussing is in some ways very convenient. Phrases like *a not unjustifiable assumption*, *leaves much to be desired*, *would serve no good purpose*, *a consideration which we should do well to bear in mind*, are a continuous temptation, a packet of aspirins always at one's elbow. Look back through this essay, and for certain you will find that I have again and again committed the very faults I am protesting against. By this morning's post I have received a pamphlet dealing with conditions in Germany. The author tells me that he "felt impelled" to write it. I open it at random, and here is almost the first sentence that I see: "(The Allies) have an opportunity not only of achieving a radical transformation of Germany's social and political structure in such a way as to avoid a nationalistic reaction in Germany itself, but at the same time of laying the foundations of a co-operative and unified Europe." You see, he "feels impelled" to write—feels, presumably, that he has something new to say—and yet his words, like cavalry horses answering the bugle, group themselves automatically into the familiar dreary pattern. This invasion of one's mind by ready-made phrases (*lay the foundations*, *achieve a radical transformation*) can only be prevented if one is constantly on guard against them, and every such phrase anaesthetises a portion of one's brain.

I said earlier that the decadence of our language is probably curable. Those who deny this would argue, if

---

[1] *cuttlefish* Octopus.

they produced an argument at all, that language merely reflects existing social conditions, and that we cannot influence its development by any direct tinkering with words and constructions. So far as the general tone or spirit of a language goes, this may be true, but it is not true in detail. Silly words and expressions have often disappeared, not through any evolutionary process but owing to the conscious action of a minority. Two recent examples were *explore every avenue* and *leave no stone unturned*, which were killed by the jeers of a few journalists. There is a long list of flyblown metaphors which could similarly be got rid of if enough people would interest themselves in the job; and it should also be possible to laugh the *not un-* formation out of existence,[1] to reduce the amount of Latin and Greek in the average sentence, to drive out foreign phrases and strayed scientific words, and, in general, to make pretentiousness unfashionable. But all these are minor points. The defence of the English language implies more than this, and perhaps it is best to start by saying what it does *not* imply.

To begin with it has nothing to do with archaism, with the salvaging of obsolete words and turns of speech, or with the setting up of a "standard English" which must never be departed from. On the contrary, it is especially concerned with the scrapping of every word or idiom which has outworn its usefulness. It has nothing to do with correct grammar and syntax, which are of no importance so long as one makes one's meaning clear, or with the avoidance of Americanisms, or with having what is called a "good prose style." On the other hand it is not concerned with fake simplicity and the attempt to make written English colloquial. Nor does it even imply in every case preferring the Saxon word to the Latin one, though it does imply using the fewest and shortest words that will cover one's meaning. What is above all needed is to let the meaning choose the word, and not the other way about. In prose, the worst thing one can do with words is to surrender to them. When you think of a concrete object, you think wordlessly, and then, if you want to describe the thing you have been visualizing you probably hunt about till you find the exact words that seem to fit it. When you think of something abstract you are more inclined to use words from the start, and unless you make a conscious effort to prevent it, the existing dialect will come rushing in and do the job for you, at the expense of blurring or even changing your meaning. Probably it is better to put off using words as long as possible and get one's meaning as clear as one can through pictures or sensations. Afterwards one can choose—not simply accept—the phrases that will best cover the meaning, and then switch round and decide what impression one's words are likely to make on another person. This last effort of the mind cuts out all stale or mixed images, all prefabricated phrases, needless repetitions, and humbug and vagueness generally. But one can often be in doubt about the effect of a word or a phrase, and one needs rules that one can rely on when instinct fails. I think the following rules will cover most cases:

(i) Never use a metaphor, simile, or other figure of speech which you are used to seeing in print.

(ii) Never use a long word where a short one will do.

(iii) If it is possible to cut a word out, always cut it out.

(iv) Never use the passive where you can use the active.

(v) Never use a foreign phrase, a scientific word, or a jargon word if you can think of an everyday English equivalent.

(vi) Break any of these rules sooner than say anything outright barbarous.

These rules sound elementary, and so they are, but they demand a deep change of attitude in anyone who has grown used to writing in the style now fashionable. One could keep all of them and still write bad English, but one could not write the kind of stuff that I quoted in those five specimens at the beginning of this article.

I have not here been considering the literary use of language, but merely language as an instrument for expressing and not for concealing or preventing

[1] [Orwell's note] One can cure oneself of the *not un-* formation by memorizing this sentence: *A not unblack dog was chasing a not unsmall rabbit across a not ungreen field.*

thought. Stuart Chase and others have come near to claiming that all abstract words are meaningless, and have used this as a pretext for advocating a kind of political quietism. Since you don't know what Fascism is, how can you struggle against Fascism? One need not swallow such absurdities as this, but one ought to recognise that the present political chaos is connected with the decay of language, and that one can probably bring about some improvement by starting at the verbal end. If you simplify your English, you are freed from the worst follies of orthodoxy. You cannot speak any of the necessary dialects, and when you make a stupid remark its stupidity will be obvious, even to yourself. Political language—and with variations this is true of all political parties, from Conservatives to Anarchists—is designed to make lies sound truthful and murder respectable, and to give an appearance of solidity to pure wind. One cannot change this all in a moment, but one can at least change one's own habits, and from time to time one can even, if one jeers loudly enough, send some worn-out and useless phrase—some *jackboot*, *Achilles' heel*, *hotbed*, *melting pot*, *acid test*, *veritable inferno* or other lump of verbal refuse—into the dustbin where it belongs.

—1946

Shooting an Elephant

In Moulmein, in Lower Burma, I was hated by large numbers of people—the only time in my life that I have been important enough for this to happen to me. I was sub-divisional police officer of the town, and in an aimless, petty kind of way anti-European feeling was very bitter. No one had the guts to raise a riot, but if a European woman went through the bazaars alone somebody would probably spit betel juice over her dress. As a police officer I was an obvious target and was baited whenever it seemed safe to do so. When a nimble Burman tripped me up on the football field and the referee (another Burman) looked the other way, the crowd yelled with hideous laughter. This happened more than once. In the end the sneering yellow faces of young men that met me everywhere, the insults hooted after me when I was at a safe distance, got badly on my nerves. The young Buddhist priests were the worst of all. There were several thousands of them in the town and none of them seemed to have anything to do except stand on street corners and jeer at Europeans.

All this was perplexing and upsetting. For at that time I had already made up my mind that imperialism was an evil thing and the sooner I chucked up my job and got out of it the better. Theoretically—and secretly, of course—I was all for the Burmese and all against their oppressors, the British. As for the job I was doing, I hated it more bitterly than I can perhaps make clear. In a job like that you see the dirty work of Empire at close quarters. The wretched prisoners huddling in the stinking cages of the lock-ups, the grey, cowed faces of the long-term convicts, the scarred buttocks of the men who had been flogged with bamboos—all these oppressed me with an intolerable sense of guilt. But I could get nothing into perspective. I was young and ill-educated and I had had to think out my problems in the utter silence that is imposed on every Englishman in the East. I did not even know that the British Empire is dying, still less did I know that it is a great deal better than the younger empires that are going to supplant it. All I knew was that I was stuck between my hatred of the empire I served and my rage against the evil-spirited little beasts who tried to make my job impossible. With one part of my mind I thought of the British Raj as an unbreakable tyranny, as something clamped down, *in saecula saeculorum*,[1] upon the will of prostrate peoples; with another part I thought that the greatest joy in the world would be to drive a bayonet into a Buddhist priest's guts. Feelings like these are the normal by-products of imperialism; ask any Anglo-Indian official, if you can catch him off duty.

One day something happened which in a roundabout way was enlightening. It was a tiny incident in itself, but it gave me a better glimpse than I had had before of the real nature of imperialism—the real motives for which despotic governments act. Early one morning the sub-inspector at a police station the other end of the town rang me up on the 'phone and said that

[1] *in saecula saeculorum* Latin: for centuries upon centuries; forever.

an elephant was ravaging the bazaar. Would I please come and do something about it? I did not know what I could do, but I wanted to see what was happening and I got on to a pony and started out. I took my rifle, an old .44 Winchester and much too small to kill an elephant, but I thought the noise might be useful *in terrorem*.[1] Various Burmans stopped me on the way and told me about the elephant's doings. It was not, of course, a wild elephant, but a tame one which had gone "must."[2] It had been chained up, as tame elephants always are when their attack of "must" is due, but on the previous night it had broken its chain and escaped. Its mahout,[3] the only person who could manage it when it was in that state, had set out in pursuit, but had taken the wrong direction and was now twelve hours' journey away, and in the morning the elephant had suddenly reappeared in the town. The Burmese population had no weapons and were quite helpless against it. It had already destroyed somebody's bamboo hut, killed a cow, and raided some fruit-stalls and devoured the stock; also it had met the municipal rubbish van, and, when the driver jumped out and took to his heels, had turned the van over and inflicted violences upon it.

The Burmese sub-inspector and some Indian constables were waiting for me in the quarter where the elephant had been seen. It was a very poor quarter, a labyrinth of squalid bamboo huts, thatched with palm-leaf, winding all over a steep hillside. I remember that it was a cloudy, stuffy morning at the beginning of the rains. We began questioning the people as to where the elephant had gone, and, as usual, failed to get any definite information. That is invariably the case in the East; a story always sounds clear enough at a distance, but the nearer you get to the scene of events the vaguer it becomes. Some of the people said that the elephant had gone in one direction, some said that he had gone in another, some professed not even to have heard of any elephant. I had almost made up my mind that the whole story was a pack of lies, when we heard yells a little distance away. There was a loud, scandalized cry of "Go away, child! Go away this instant!" and an old woman with a switch in her hand came round the corner of a hut, violently shooing away a crowd of naked children. Some more women followed, clicking their tongues and exclaiming; evidently there was something that the children ought not to have seen. I rounded the hut and saw a man's dead body sprawling in the mud. He was an Indian, a black Dravidian coolie, almost naked, and he could not have been dead many minutes. The people said that the elephant had come suddenly upon him round the corner of the hut, caught him with its trunk, put its foot on his back and ground him into the earth. This was the rainy season and the ground was soft, and his face had scored a trench a foot deep and a couple of yards long. He was lying on his belly with arms crucified and head sharply twisted to one side. His face was coated with mud, the eyes wide open, the teeth bared and grinning with an expression of unendurable agony. (Never tell me, by the way, that the dead look peaceful. Most of the corpses I have seen looked devilish.) The friction of the great beast's foot had stripped the skin from his back as neatly as one skins a rabbit. As soon as I saw the dead man I sent an orderly to a friend's house nearby to borrow an elephant rifle. I had already sent back the pony, not wanting it to go mad with fright and throw me if it smelt the elephant.

The orderly came back in a few minutes with a rifle and five cartridges, and meanwhile some Burmans had arrived and told us that the elephant was in the paddy fields below, only a few hundred yards away. As I started forward practically the whole population of the quarter flocked out of the houses and followed me. They had seen the rifle and were all shouting excitedly that I was going to shoot the elephant. They had not shown much interest in the elephant when he was merely ravaging their homes, but it was different now that he was going to be shot. It was a bit of fun to them, as it would be to an English crowd; besides they wanted the meat. It made me vaguely uneasy. I had no intention of shooting the elephant—I had merely sent for the rifle to defend myself if necessary—and it is always unnerving to have a crowd following you. I marched down the hill, look-

---

[1] *in terrorem* Latin: in fright, terror, or alarm.

[2] *must* I.e., condition characterized by aggressive behavior brought on by a surge in testosterone.

[3] *mahout* Elephant trainer or keeper.

ing and feeling a fool, with the rifle over my shoulder and an ever-growing army of people jostling at my heels. At the bottom, when you got away from the huts, there was a metalled road and beyond that a miry waste of paddy fields a thousand yards across, not yet ploughed but soggy from the first rains and dotted with coarse grass. The elephant was standing eight yards from the road, his left side towards us. He took not the slightest notice of the crowd's approach. He was tearing up bunches of grass, beating them against his knees to clean them and stuffing them into his mouth.

I had halted on the road. As soon as I saw the elephant I knew with perfect certainty that I ought not to shoot him. It is a serious matter to shoot a working elephant—it is comparable to destroying a huge and costly piece of machinery—and obviously one ought not to do it if it can possibly be avoided. And at that distance, peacefully eating, the elephant looked no more dangerous than a cow. I thought then and I think now that his attack of "must" was already passing off; in which case he would merely wander harmlessly about until the mahout came back and caught him. Moreover, I did not in the least want to shoot him. I decided that I would watch him for a little while to make sure that he did not turn savage again, and then go home.

But at that moment I glanced round at the crowd that had followed me. It was an immense crowd, two thousand at the least and growing every minute. It blocked the road for a long distance on either side. I looked at the sea of yellow faces above the garish clothes—faces all happy and excited over this bit of fun, all certain that the elephant was going to be shot. They were watching me as they would watch a conjurer about to perform a trick. They did not like me, but with the magical rifle in my hands I was momentarily worth watching. And suddenly I realized that I should have to shoot the elephant after all. The people expected it of me and I had got to do it; I could feel their two thousand wills pressing me forward, irresistibly. And it was at this moment, as I stood there with the rifle in my hands, that I first grasped the hollowness, the futility of the white man's dominion in the East. Here was I, the white man with his gun, standing in front of the unarmed native crowd—seemingly the leading actor of the piece; but in reality I was only an absurd puppet pushed to and fro by the will of those yellow faces behind. I perceived in this moment that when the white man turns tyrant it is his own freedom that he destroys. He becomes a sort of hollow, posing dummy, the conventionalized figure of a sahib. For it is the condition of his rule that he shall spend his life in trying to impress the "natives," and so in every crisis he has got to do what the "natives" expect of him. He wears a mask, and his face grows to fit it. I had got to shoot the elephant. I had committed myself to doing it when I sent for the rifle. A sahib has got to act like a sahib; he has got to appear resolute, to know his own mind and do definite things. To come all that way, rifle in hand, with two thousand people marching at my heels, and then to trail feebly away, having done nothing—no, that was impossible. The crowd would laugh at me. And my whole life, every white man's life in the East, was one long struggle not to be laughed at.

But I did not want to shoot the elephant. I watched him beating his bunch of grass against his knees, with that preoccupied grandmotherly air that elephants have. It seemed to me that it would be murder to shoot him. At that age I was not squeamish about killing animals, but I had never shot an elephant and never wanted to. (Somehow it always seems worse to kill a *large* animal.) Besides, there was the beast's owner to be considered. Alive, the elephant was worth at least a hundred pounds; dead, he would only be worth the value of his tusks, five pounds, possibly. But I had got to act quickly. I turned to some experienced-looking Burmans who had been there when we arrived, and asked them how the elephant had been behaving. They all said the same thing: he took no notice of you if you left him alone, but he might charge if you went too close to him.

It was perfectly clear to me what I ought to do. I ought to walk up to within, say, twenty-five yards of the elephant and test his behaviour. If he charged I could shoot, if he took no notice of me it would be safe to leave him until the mahout came back. But also I knew that I was going to do no such thing. I was a poor shot with a rifle and the ground was soft mud into which one would sink at every step. If the elephant charged and I missed him, I should have about as much chance as a toad under a steam-roller. But even then I was not thinking particularly of my own skin, only of the watchful yellow faces behind. For at that moment, with the crowd watching me, I was not afraid in the ordinary sense, as I would have been if I had been alone. A white man mustn't be frightened in front of "natives"; and so, in general, he isn't frightened. The sole thought in my mind was that if anything went wrong those two thousand Burmans would see me pursued, caught, trampled on and reduced to a grinning corpse like that Indian up the hill. And if that happened it was quite probable that some of them would laugh. That would never do. There was only one alternative. I shoved the cartridges into the magazine and lay down on the road to get a better aim.

The crowd grew very still, and a deep, low, happy sigh, as of people who see the theatre curtain go up at last, breathed from innumerable throats. They were going to have their bit of fun after all. The rifle was a beautiful German thing with cross-hair sights. I did not then know that in shooting an elephant one would shoot to cut an imaginary bar running from ear-hole to ear-hole. I ought, therefore, as the elephant was sideways on, to have aimed straight at his ear-hole; actually I aimed several inches in front of this, thinking the brain would be further forward.

When I pulled the trigger I did not hear the bang or feel the kick—one never does when a shot goes home—but I heard the devilish roar of glee that went up from the crowd. In that instant, in too short a time, one would have thought, even for the bullet to get there, a mysterious, terrible change had come over the elephant. He neither stirred nor fell, but every line of his body had altered. He looked suddenly stricken, shrunken, immensely old, as though the frightful impact of the bullet had paralysed him without knocking him down. At last, after what seemed a long time—it might have been five seconds, I dare say—he sagged flabbily to his knees. His mouth slobbered. An enormous senility seemed to have settled upon him. One could have imagined him thousands of years old. I fired again into the same spot. At the second shot he did not collapse but climbed with desperate slowness to his feet and stood weakly upright, with legs sagging and head drooping. I fired a third time. That was the shot that did for him. You could see the agony of it jolt his whole body and knock the last remnant of strength from his legs. But in falling he seemed for a moment to rise, for as his hind legs collapsed beneath him he seemed to tower upwards like a huge rock toppling, his trunk reaching skywards like a tree. He trumpeted, for the first and only time. And then down he came, his belly towards me, with a crash that seemed to shake the ground even where I lay.

I got up. The Burmans were already racing past me across the mud. It was obvious that the elephant would never rise again, but he was not dead. He was breathing very rhythmically with long rattling gasps, his great mound of a side painfully rising and falling. His mouth was wide open—I could see far down into caverns of pale pink throat. I waited a long time for him to die, but his breathing did not weaken. Finally I fired my two remaining shots into the spot where I thought his heart must be. The thick blood welled out of him like red velvet, but still he did not die. His body did not even jerk when the shots hit him, the tortured breathing continued without a pause. He was dying, very slowly and in great agony, but in some world remote from me where not even a bullet could damage him further. I felt that I had got to put an end to that dreadful noise. It seemed dreadful to see the great beast lying there, powerless to move and yet powerless to die, and not even to be able to finish him. I sent back for my small rifle and poured shot after shot into his heart and down his throat. They seemed to make no impression. The tortured gasps continued as steadily as the ticking of a clock.

In the end I could not stand it any longer and went away. I heard later that it took him half an hour to die. Burmans were bringing dahs[1] and baskets even before I left, and I was told they had stripped his body almost to the bones by the afternoon.

Afterwards, of course, there were endless discussions about the shooting of the elephant. The owner was

[1] *dahs* Short swords or knives.

furious, but he was only an Indian and could do nothing. Besides, legally I had done the right thing, for a mad elephant has to be killed, like a mad dog, if its owner fails to control it. Among the Europeans opinion was divided. The older men said I was right, the younger men said it was a damn shame to shoot an elephant for killing a coolie, because an elephant was worth more than any damn Coringhee coolie. And afterwards I was very glad that the coolie had been killed; it put me legally in the right and it gave me a sufficient pretext for shooting the elephant. I often wondered whether any of the others grasped that I had done it solely to avoid looking a fool.

—1950

In Context

Elephants in Asia

There are two types of elephant: the African elephant is by definition a wild animal, but the smaller Asian (or Indian) elephant may be tamed. The latter has long been employed as a beast of burden in many parts of Asia, used for transport, logging, and various other tasks—including hunting, as in the photograph below, of a royal expedition to India in 1912, illustrates.

W.H. Auden

1907 – 1973

In essays written in the 1930s, W.H. Auden described art as something that "shall teach man to unlearn hatred and learn love," to expand "our knowledge of good and evil, perhaps making the necessity for action more urgent and its nature more clear." A poet with an impeccable ear for language and meter who mastered an immense variety of forms and registers, Auden wrote some of the most iconic love poems and elegies of the twentieth century, as well as some of the century's most incisive political poetry. His work grapples with the philosophical concerns that shaped his time, including Marxism and the psychology of Freud, and he understood and wrote about the perils of fascism earlier than most others. For many people, his work epitomized both the anxiety and potential of the modern age. "Auden was an epoch-making poet on public themes," Seamus Heaney said, "the register of a new sensibility."

Born in York, England, in 1907, Wystan Hugh Auden was the youngest of three sons. His chief childhood interests were scientific: he was fascinated by engineering, mineralogy, and geology, and won a scholarship to study natural science at Oxford. A developing passion for poetry, however, led him to transfer to English, although his interest in science—and his experiences growing up in industrial England (he spent his childhood in Birmingham)—remain evident in the themes that permeate his poetry. He became a central member of a group of writers known as the "Oxford Group," which included Cecil Day Lewis, Stephen Spender, and Louis MacNeice. Auden published numerous poems in undergraduate magazines, and when he had assembled a first volume, he sent it to T.S. Eliot at the publishing house of Faber and Gwyer (later Faber and Faber). The volume was rejected, and Auden had it printed privately on Spender's handpress. Eliot had expressed interest in Auden's work, however, and in 1930 he published Auden's *Poems*. Heavily colored by a sense of political commitment, *Poems* addresses concrete social problems, such as poverty in depressed areas of industrial England. Many poems are experiments with tone and form—for example, Auden melded Anglo-Saxon sound patterns with modern subject matter.

After graduating from Oxford, Auden spent a year in Germany with a university friend, Christopher Isherwood, and was influenced by German music, literature, and theater—particularly the leftist political theater of Bertolt Brecht and Kurt Weill. When he returned to England, Auden worked variously as a schoolmaster, a university lecturer, a writer of experimental drama, and a verse commentator on documentary films. In this last position he worked with composer Benjamin Britten, who became a close friend and artistic collaborator. Collaborative work appealed to Auden, who went on to co-write three plays with Isherwood: *The Dog Beneath the Skin* (1935), *The Ascent of F6* (1936), and *On the Frontier* (1938). A trip to Iceland with MacNeice, funded by Auden's publishers, resulted in the collaborative travel book *Letters from Iceland* (1937), an unconventional collection of essays, poems, letters, and notes on everything from touring the country to contemporary politics.

Although Auden was openly gay, he agreed in 1935 to marry German novelist Thomas Mann's daughter Erika, whose passport was about to be revoked by the Nazis. When the Spanish Civil War began a year later, he volunteered for the Spanish Republic as a medical worker, but the authorities instead gave him work in the censor's office, writing government propaganda. He was disturbed by the extent to which Stalin's government controlled the Republic and also by the fact that the government had forced the churches to close. Although Auden had abandoned his religious beliefs after childhood, his Civil War experience caused him to reconsider the importance of spirituality.

Auden later traveled with Isherwood to China and Japan to observe the Sino-Japanese war. There they wrote *Journey to a War* (1939), largely about the complexity of political writing. In his poems of this period Auden developed his characteristically sparse, terse, and often fragmented style, relying on concrete images and colloquial language to create a sense of immediacy and intensity. His explicitly political poems of this period, such as "Spain 1937," helped to establish his reputation as a poet, but in 1939, the year he moved to New York, he decided he would never again write anything that resembled propaganda, regardless of cause. In fact, in later years he often rewrote and even suppressed his earlier poems.

In New York, where Auden settled for most of his later life, he devoted himself to his poetry with renewed energy. He became involved in a serious relationship with Chester Kallman, a nineteen-year-old student who would become his lifelong partner and an important literary collaborator. The 1940 volume *Another Time* signals his desire to move on to explore new subjects and modes of expression. *Another Time* meticulously measures the social pulse of the thirties—which Auden characterized as "the age of anxiety"—and includes some of his best-known works, including "Musée des Beaux Arts," "September 1, 1939" (his response to the declaration of war), and elegies to poets Matthew Arnold, A.E. Housman, and W.B. Yeats, all of whom had been significant influences on his poetic development.

From then on, Auden's poetry began to take on more intimate and subjective overtones, often with religious themes. In 1941 he began attending the Anglican church regularly and experienced a renewal of religious faith. While his earlier poetry examined concrete social ills, his later poetry developed a more complex worldview, often focusing on spiritual aspects of society and casting social problems in terms of personal responsibility. His next major collection, *For the Time Being* (1944), includes the Christmas Oratorio "For the Time Being" and "The Sea and the Mirror," a poetic commentary on Shakespeare's *The Tempest* that explored Auden's ideas of poetry in the light of Christianity. With *The Collected Poetry* (1945), Auden began revising and retitling his earlier work, a task he would continue, almost compulsively, throughout his life.

In 1948, Auden was awarded the Pulitzer Prize for *The Age of Anxiety* (1947), a verse dialogue between four people in a New York bar. *The Shield of Achilles* (1955), which won the National Book Award, displays the influence of Anglo-Catholic theology and rituals, which Auden increasingly explored in verse. During these years he also wrote a considerable body of criticism and taught at various universities. In 1956 he became a Professor of Poetry at Oxford, where he gave three lectures per year for five years. These lectures, together with numerous reviews and essays, were collected in *The Dyer's Hand* (1962).

In his later years, with volumes such as *About the House* (1965) and *City Without Walls* (1969), Auden cemented his reputation as one of the leading poets of his day. After awarding him the National Medal for Literature in 1967, the National Book Committee declared that Auden's poetry "has illuminated our lives and times with grace, wit, and vitality. His work, branded by the moral and ideological fires of our age, breathes with eloquence, perception, and intellectual power." In 1972, seeking to return to a small community in which he could live peacefully as a writer, Auden accepted an honorary studentship at Christ Church, Oxford, his alma mater. He died there the following year. A final volume of poetry, *Thank You, Fog*, was published posthumously in 1974. Auden's careful attention to poetic form and meter, his sensitivity to language and to the music of words, and his concern with eternal questions of spirituality, love, and humanity's place in the world have all served to secure his current standing as one of the twentieth century's most significant poetic voices.

⌘⌘⌘

[*At last the secret is out*]

At last the secret is out, as it always must come in
the end,
The delicious story is ripe to tell to the intimate friend;
Over the tea-cups and into the square the tongue has
its desire;
Still waters run deep, my dear, there's never smoke
without fire.

Behind the corpse in the reservoir, behind the ghost
on the links,[1]
Behind the lady who dances and the man who madly
drinks,
Under the look of fatigue the attack of migraine and
the sigh
There is always another story, there is more than
meets the eye.

For the clear voice suddenly singing, high up in the
convent wall,
The scent of the elder bushes, the sporting prints in
the hall,
The croquet matches in summer, the handshake, the
cough, the kiss,
There is always a wicked secret, a private reason for this.
—1936

[1] *links* Undulating, sandy ground near a shore.

[*Funeral Blues*][2]

Stop all the clocks, cut off the telephone,
Prevent the dog from barking with a juicy bone,
Silence the pianos and with muffled drum
Bring out the coffin, let the mourners come.

Let aeroplanes circle moaning overhead
Scribbling on the sky the message He Is Dead,
Put crêpe bows[3] round the white necks of the public
doves,
Let the traffic policemen wear black cotton gloves.

He was my North, my South, my East and West,
My working week and my Sunday rest,
My noon, my midnight, my talk, my song;
I thought that love would last for ever: I was wrong.

The stars are not wanted now: put out every one;
Pack up the moon and dismantle the sun;
Pour away the ocean and sweep up the wood;
For nothing now can ever come to any good.
—1936, 1940

[2] [*Funeral Blues*] This poem first appeared in *The Ascent of F6*, a play co-written by Auden and Christopher Isherwood. It then appeared, in a revised version and with this present title, in Auden's 1940 collection *Another Time*.

[3] *crêpe bows* Black crepe, a woven fabric with a wrinkled surface, is the traditional fabric of mourning clothes.

[*Lullaby*]

Lay your sleeping head, my love,
Human on my faithless arm;
Time and fevers burn away
Individual beauty from
Thoughtful children, and the grave
Proves the child ephemeral:
But in my arms till break of day
Let the living creature lie,
Mortal, guilty, but to me
The entirely beautiful.

Soul and body have no bounds:
To lovers as they lie upon
Her tolerant enchanted slope
In their ordinary swoon,
Grave the vision Venus[1] sends
Of supernatural sympathy,
Universal love and hope;
While an abstract insight wakes
Among the glaciers and the rocks
The hermit's carnal ecstasy.

Certainty, fidelity
On the stroke of midnight pass
Like vibrations of a bell,
And fashionable madmen raise
Their pedantic boring cry:
Every farthing of the cost,
All the dreaded cards foretell,
Shall be paid, but from this night
Not a whisper, not a thought,
Not a kiss nor look be lost.

Beauty, midnight, vision dies:
Let the winds of dawn that blow
Softly round your dreaming head
Such a day of sweetness show
Eye and knocking heart may bless,
Find the mortal world enough;
Noons of dryness see you fed
By the involuntary powers,
Nights of insult let you pass
Watched by every human love.
—1937

[1] *Venus* Roman goddess of beauty and love, mother of Cupid.

Musée des Beaux Arts[2]

About suffering they were never wrong,
The Old Masters: how well they understood
Its human position; how it takes place
While someone else is eating or opening a window or
just walking dully along;
How, when the aged are reverently, passionately waiting
For the miraculous birth, there always must be
Children who did not specially want it to happen,
skating
On a pond at the edge of the wood:
They never forgot
That even the dreadful martyrdom must run its course
Anyhow in a corner, some untidy spot
Where the dogs go on with their doggy life and the
torturer's horse
Scratches its innocent behind on a tree.

In Brueghel's *Icarus*, for instance: how everything
turns away
Quite leisurely from the disaster;[3] the ploughman may
Have heard the splash, the forsaken cry,
But for him it was not an important failure; the sun
shone

[2] *Musée des Beaux Arts* The Royal Museum of Fine Arts in Brussels owns several paintings by Flemish painter Pieter Brueghel (1525–69), including *Landscape with the Fall of Icarus*. According to Greek myth, Icarus and his father, Daedalus, escaped from the island of Crete, where they were imprisoned, by constructing wings with feathers and wax. Icarus flew too close to the sun, however, and the wax of his wings melted, causing him to plummet into the sea.

[3] *how everything … disaster* In Brueghel's painting, a shepherd, a farmer, and a fisher carry on with their respective jobs, ignoring Icarus's legs disappearing into the water in the picture's lower right corner.

As it had to on the white legs disappearing into the green
Water; and the expensive delicate ship that must have seen
Something amazing, a boy falling out of the sky,
Had somewhere to get to and sailed calmly on.
—1939, 1940

In Memory of W.B. Yeats[1]

(d. Jan. 1939)

I

He disappeared in the dead of winter:
The brooks were frozen, the airports almost deserted,
And snow disfigured the public statues;
The mercury sank in the mouth of the dying day.
O all the instruments agree[2]
The day of his death was a dark cold day.

Far from his illness
The wolves ran on through the evergreen forests,
The peasant river was untempted by the fashionable quays;
By mourning tongues
The death of the poet was kept from his poems.

But for him it was his last afternoon as himself,
An afternoon of nurses and rumours;
The provinces of his body revolted,
The squares of his mind were empty,
Silence invaded the suburbs,
The current of his feeling failed: he became his admirers.

Now he is scattered among a hundred cities
And wholly given over to unfamiliar affections;
To find his happiness in another kind of wood
And be punished under a foreign code of conscience.
The words of a dead man
Are modified in the guts of the living.

But in the importance and noise of to-morrow
When the brokers are roaring like beasts on the floor of the Bourse,[3]
And the poor have the sufferings to which they are fairly accustomed,
And each in the cell of himself is almost convinced of his freedom;
A few thousand will think of this day
As one thinks of a day when one did something slightly unusual.

O all the instruments agree
The day of his death was a dark cold day.

2

You were silly like us: your gift survived it all;
The parish of rich women, physical decay,
Yourself. Mad Ireland hurt you into poetry.
Now Ireland has her madness and her weather still,
For poetry makes nothing happen: it survives
In the valley of its saying where executives
Would never want to tamper, flows on south
From ranches of isolation and the busy griefs,
Raw towns that we believe and die in; it survives,
A way of happening, a mouth.

3

Earth, receive an honoured guest;
William Yeats is laid to rest:
Let the Irish vessel lie
Emptied of its poetry.

Time that is intolerant
Of the brave and innocent,
And indifferent in a week
To a beautiful physique,

Worships language and forgives
Everyone by whom it lives;

[1] *W.B. Yeats* Irish poet William Butler Yeats (1865–1939).

[2] *O all … agree* Auden later changed this line to read "What instruments we have agree."

[3] *Bourse* Paris Stock Exchange.

Pardons cowardice, conceit,
Lays its honours at their feet.

Time that with this strange excuse
Pardoned Kipling and his views,[1]
And will pardon Paul Claudel,[2]
Pardons him for writing well.

In the nightmare of the dark
All the dogs of Europe bark,
And the living nations wait,
Each sequestered in its hate;

Intellectual disgrace
Stares from every human face,
And the seas of pity lie
Locked and frozen in each eye.

Follow, poet, follow right
To the bottom of the night,
With your unconstraining voice
Still persuade us to rejoice;

With the farming of a verse
Make a vineyard of the curse,
Sing of human unsuccess
In a rapture of distress;

In the deserts of the heart
Let the healing fountain start,
In the prison of his days
Teach the free man how to praise.

—1939

[1] *Kipling … views* Rudyard Kipling (1865–1936) was an Indian-born English writer whose work often celebrated imperialism.

[2] *Paul Claudel* French-Catholic poet, playwright, and diplomat (1868–1955) who was widely criticized for supporting Franco's fascist insurgency in the Spanish Civil War.

September 1, 1939[3]

I sit in one of the dives
On Fifty-Second Street
Uncertain and afraid
As the clever hopes expire
Of a low dishonest decade:
Waves of anger and fear
Circulate over the bright
And darkened lands of the earth,
Obsessing our private lives;
The unmentionable odour of death
Offends the September night.

Accurate scholarship can
Unearth the whole offence
From Luther[4] until now
That has driven a culture mad,
Find what occurred at Linz,[5]
What huge imago[6] made
A psychopathic god:
I and the public know
What all schoolchildren learn,
Those to whom evil is done
Do evil in return.

[3] *September 1, 1939* Date of Hitler's invasion of Poland; Britain and France declared war on Germany two days later. Auden had moved to New York in January 1939.

[4] *Luther* Martin Luther (1483–1546), German monk whose attempts to reform the Catholic Church were instrumental in bringing about the Protestant Reformation. Luther's writings grew markedly more anti-Semitic as he aged; in *Mein Kampf,* Hitler ranks Martin Luther as one of three great German cultural heroes, along with Frederick the Great and Richard Wagner.

[5] *Linz* Town in Austria in which Hitler grew up; he returned in 1938 to announce Germany's annexation of Austria.

[6] *imago* According to psychiatrist and founder of analytical psychology C.G. Jung (1875–1961), an idealized image of a person formed in childhood.

Exiled Thucydides[1] knew
All that a speech can say
About Democracy,
And what dictators do,
The elderly rubbish they talk
To an apathetic grave;
Analysed all in his book,
The enlightenment driven away,
The habit-forming pain,
Mismanagement and grief:
We must suffer them all again.

Into this neutral air
Where blind skyscrapers use
Their full height to proclaim
The strength of Collective Man,
Each language pours its vain
Competitive excuse:
But who can live for long
In an euphoric dream;
Out of the mirror they stare,
Imperialism's face
And the international wrong.

Faces along the bar
Cling to their average day:
The lights must never go out,
The music must always play,
All the conventions conspire
To make this fort assume
The furniture of home;
Lest we should see where we are,
Lost in a haunted wood,
Children afraid of the night
Who have never been happy or good.

The windiest militant trash
Important Persons shout
Is not so crude as our wish:
What mad Nijinsky wrote
About Diaghilev[2]
Is true of the normal heart;
For the error bred in the bone
Of each woman and each man
Craves what it cannot have,
Not universal love
But to be loved alone.

From the conservative dark
Into the ethical life
The dense commuters come,
Repeating their morning vow,
"I *will* be true to the wife,
I'll concentrate more on my work,"
And helpless governors wake
To resume their compulsory game:
Who can release them now,
Who can reach the deaf,
Who can speak for the dumb?

All I have is a voice
To undo the folded lie,
The romantic lie in the brain
Of the sensual man-in-the-street
And the lie of Authority
Whose buildings grope the sky:
There is no such thing as the State
And no one exists alone;
Hunger allows no choice
To the citizen of the police;
We must love one another or die.[3]

[1] *Thucydides* Greek historian and general (c. 460–c. 400 BCE) and author of *The History of the Peloponnesian War* who was exiled at the war's end for failing to prevent the surrender of Amphipolis to the Spartans. One of the speeches in Thucydides's *History*, Pericles's funeral oration for the dead Athenian soldiers, outlines the dangers and benefits of democracy. Elected 16 times to the position of general, Pericles instituted many democratic reforms while retaining a significant degree of personal power.

[2] *Nijinsky … Diaghilev* Vaslav Nijinsky (1890–1950), Russian ballet dancer and choreographer who was diagnosed with schizophrenia in 1919. In 1936, Nijinsky's wife published a heavily edited version of her husband's 1919 diary, in which he said of his former lover, founder of the Ballets Russes Sergei Pavlovich Diaghilev, "Some politicians are hypocrites like Diaghilev, who does not want universal love, but to be loved alone."

[3] *All I have … die* In a revised edition of this poem, printed in *The Collected Poetry of W.H. Auden* (1945), this stanza is removed.

Defenceless under the night
Our world in stupor lies;
Yet, dotted everywhere,
Ironic points of light
Flash out wherever the Just
Exchange their messages:
May I, composed like them
Of Eros[1] and of dust,
Beleaguered by the same
Negation and despair,
Show an affirming flame.
—1939

from *The Sea and the Mirror*

[Song of the Master and Boatswain][2]

At Dirty Dick's and Sloppy Joe's
We drank our liquor straight,
Some went upstairs with Margery,
And some, alas, with Kate;
And two by two like cat and mouse
The homeless played at keeping house.

There Wealthy Meg, the Sailor's Friend,
And Marion, cow-eyed,
Opened their arms to me but I
Refused to step inside;
I was not looking for a cage
In which to mope in my old age.

The nightingales[3] are sobbing in
The orchards of our mothers,
And hearts that we broke long ago
Have long been breaking others;
Tears are round, the sea is deep:
Roll them overboard and sleep.
—1944

[1] *Eros* In contrast to The New Testament *agape*, or Christian love, *eros* represents earthly, or sexual love. In Greek myth, the winged Eros, son of Aphrodite, is the god of love.

[2] *Song … Boatswain* Auden's *The Sea and the Mirror* is a poetic response to Shakespeare's *The Tempest*. "The Master and Boatswain" refers to the prostitutes mentioned by a drunken Stephano in 2.2.46–54:

The master, the swabber, the boatswain, and I,
The gunner and his mate,
Loved Mall, Meg, and Marian, and Margery,
But none of us cared for Kate;
For she had a tongue with a tang,
Would cry to a sailor, "Go hang!"
She loved not the savour of tar nor of pitch,
Yet a tailor might scratch her where e'er she did itch.
Then to sea, boys, and let her go hang!

[3] *nightingales* In Greek myth, Philomela, the daughter of the king of Athens, was transformed into a nightingale after being raped by her brother-in-law, Tereus, King of Thrace, who had cut out her tongue to prevent her from talking. A "nightingale" is also a slang term for a prostitute.

World War II

CONTEXTS

World War II officially began with Hitler's invasion of Poland on 1 September 1939 (the origins of which can be traced back to the peace treaties of World War I). After Poland, Hitler took Denmark, Luxemborg, Norway, the Netherlands, and Belgium. With the fall of these last two nations, British troops were surrounded on land by German forces and were forced to flee by sea from Dunkirk. Then, in June 1940, France surrendered, making a separate peace with Germany. With England as his next goal, Hitler deployed the German Luftwaffe (Air Force) in force. The Blitz, during which the Royal Air Force battled the German bombers nightly over the skies of England, began in August 1940.

While World War I had been largely defined by trench warfare and by grueling casualties with little movement on either side, World War II was a war of the bomb. This meant unprecedented civilian casualties on both sides (the July 1943 Allied bombing of Hamburg alone killed more than 40,000 people); it also meant that, as had not been the case in World War I, the arena of warfare extended to the British Isles themselves. The Blitz, eight months of nearly nightly bombings of the United Kingdom's metropolitan centers, caused great destruction: 30,000 civilians were killed between 7 September and 2 November 1940, with half of those being inhabitants of London, and half a million people were left homeless. In London, landmarks such as Buckingham Palace and the House of Commons were destroyed or severely damaged. Amidst this assault, England's citizens were tested to the limits of their courage and patience. While most faced their daily tribulations with courage, the possibility of a potentially successful invasion could never be far from their minds. Some had plans to commit suicide rather than submit to Hitler, should such an invasion occur; writer Vita Sackville-West and her husband, diplomat Harold Nicholson, discuss their plans to take a lethal pill in the excerpts from their letters below. Virginia Woolf, whose diary is also excerpted here, made it clear in her correspondence that the sound of the bombs falling on London was a contributing factor in the despair that caused her to take her own life in March 1941. (Woolf and her husband, who was Jewish, had also decided to take their own lives should Hitler invade.)

It was largely through the efforts of Prime Minister Winston Churchill that the nation remained unified and optimistic even in the dark months before Germany gave up its attempt to conquer Britain from the air, in May 1941, and the United States entered the war, in December 1941, allowing the Allies to eventually mount a major offensive on the European mainland. Churchill was a powerful orator, as well as an experienced journalist and essayist, and his speeches (some of the most famous of which are excerpted here) gave his people hope and pride and reminded them of their common cause. For the duration of the war, party politics were largely laid aside, and many found that the war provided them with an exhilarating sense of strength and purpose.

There is little naive idealism in the literature of the war, however; World War II has no Rupert Brooke or John McCrae. Most of the nation had lived through the previous war and the subsequent economic depression of the '30s, and many writers had documented the struggle against fascism in the Spanish Civil War (1936–39). World War II writers documented the grim realities of war as they appeared. But their devotion to realism did not preclude patriotic sentiment. The work of writers such as Keith Douglas, for example, whose poem "Vergissmeinnicht" appears below, manages to celebrate the gallantry and heroism of soldiers while simultaneously acknowledging the folly that is an inevitable part of war. Poets such as Douglas and Henry Reed (whose work is also represented below) were often influenced by the more realistic war poets of the previous generation, such as Wilfred Owen and Edward Thomas. And, as the two poems by Douglas LePan, published in 1987, demonstrate, the war remained alive in the minds of those who participated in it for decades after its official end.

In nearly all the works excerpted here, one senses clearly that the fate of Europe and of most of the rest of the world was felt to be hanging in the balance during the war. Many of these writers felt that, regardless of the outcome of the war, their lives and homes would never be the same. In this battle of democracy versus fascism, the war also prompted many writers to examine their views on fascism (and anti-Semitism) and to stand up for their beliefs. Examinations of war crimes and fascism continued long after the war, particularly during the Nuremberg Trials, on which Rebecca West (the pen name of Cicily Fairfield) reported in "Greenhouse with Cyclamens," excerpted below.

⌘⌘⌘

Advertisement issued by the British Ministry of Fuel and Power.

Posters erected by the British Ministry of Information.

Winston Churchill, Speeches to the House of Commons

from "Blood, Toil, Tears, and Sweat" (13 May 1940)

At the beginning of May 1940, after the failure of the British operations in Norway, Neville Chamberlain resigned as Prime Minister, and the subsequent debate in the Commons resulted in a drastic reduction in the Government's majority. Churchill, who was then First Lord of the Admiralty (a position he had also held during World War I), replaced him as Prime Minister. In this, his first speech in the new position, Churchill introduces the House to the new administration he has formed to lead the nation through the war.

... To form an Administration of this scale and complexity is a serious undertaking in itself, but it must be remembered that we are in the preliminary stage of one of the greatest battles in history, that we are in action at many other points in Norway and in Holland, that we have to be prepared in the Mediterranean, that the air battle is continuous and that many preparations, such as have been indicated by my Honorable Friend below the Gangway,[1] have to be made here at home. In this crisis I hope I may be pardoned if I do not address the House at any length today. I hope that any of my friends and colleagues, or former colleagues, who are affected by the political reconstruction, will make allowance, all allowance, for any lack of ceremony with which it has been necessary to act. I would say to the House, as I said to those who have joined this government: "I have nothing to offer but blood, toil, tears and sweat."

We have before us an ordeal of the most grievous kind. We have before us many, many long months of struggle and of suffering. You ask, what is our policy? I can say: It is to wage war, by sea, land and air, with all our might and with all the strength that God can give us; to wage war against a monstrous tyranny, never surpassed in the dark, lamentable catalogue of human crime. That is our policy. You ask, what is our aim? I can answer in one word: It is victory, victory at all costs, victory in spite of all terror, victory, however long and hard the road may be; for without victory, there is no survival. Let that be realised; no survival for the British Empire, no survival for all that the British Empire has stood for, no survival for the urge and impulse of the ages, that mankind will move forward towards its goal. But I take up my task with buoyancy and hope. I feel sure that our cause will not be suffered to fail among men. At this time I feel entitled to claim the aid of all, and I say, "Come then, let us go forward together with our united strength."

from "We Shall Fight on the Beaches" (4 June 1940)

This rallying speech was delivered shortly after the demoralizing defeat of the French and British armies in April and May of 1940. However, through the heroism of the Royal Air Force, who protected the Dunkirk evacuees from attacks by air, over 330,000 Allied troops had been successfully evacuated. In the midst of this national effort, Churchill here warns that Britain might soon be forced to fight alone, and on her own soil.

... We have found it necessary to take measures of increasing stringency, not only against enemy aliens and suspicious characters of other nationalities, but also against British subjects who may become a danger or a nuisance should the war be transported to the United Kingdom. I know there are a great many people affected by the orders which we have made who are the passionate enemies of Nazi Germany. I am very sorry for them, but we cannot, at the present time and under the present stress, draw all the distinctions which we should like to do. If parachute landings were attempted and fierce fighting attendant upon them followed, these unfortunate people would be far better out of the way, for their own sakes as well as for ours. There is, however, another class, for which I feel not the slightest sympathy. Parliament has given us the powers to put down

[1] *Gangway* In the House of Commons, the cross-passage about halfway down, located in front of the rear benches.

Fifth Column[1] activities with a strong hand, and we shall use those powers subject to the supervision and correction of the House, without the slightest hesitation until we are satisfied, and more than satisfied, that this malignancy in our midst has been effectively stamped out.

Winston Churchill relaxing in a shelter during an RAF-Luftwaffe battle over Dover.

Turning once again, and this time more generally, to the question of invasion, I would observe that there has never been a period in all these long centuries of which we boast when an absolute guarantee against invasion, still less against serious raids, could have been given to our people. In the days of Napoleon the same wind which would have carried his transports across the Channel might have driven away the blockading fleet. There was always the chance, and it is that chance which has excited and befooled the imaginations of many Continental tyrants. Many are the tales that are told. We are assured that novel methods will be adopted, and when we see the originality of malice, the ingenuity of aggression, which our enemy displays, we may certainly prepare ourselves for every kind of novel stratagem and every kind of brutal and treacherous manoeuvre. I think that no idea is so outlandish that it should not be considered and viewed with a searching, but at the same time, I hope, with a steady eye. We must never forget the solid assurances of sea power and those which belong to air power if it can be locally exercised.

I have, myself, full confidence that if all do their duty, if nothing is neglected, and if the best arrangements are made, as they are being made, we shall prove ourselves once again able to defend our Island home, to ride out the storm of war, and to outlive the menace of tyranny, if necessary for years, if necessary alone. At any rate, that is what we are going to try to do. That is the resolve of His Majesty's Government—every man of them. That is the will of Parliament and the nation. The British Empire and the French Republic, linked together in their cause and in their need, will defend to the death their native soil, aiding each other like good comrades to the utmost of their strength. Even though large tracts of Europe and many old and famous States have fallen or may fall into the grip of the Gestapo[2] and all the odious apparatus of Nazi rule, we shall not flag or fail. We shall go on to the end, we shall fight in France, we shall fight on the seas and oceans, we shall fight with growing confidence and growing strength in the air, we shall defend our Island, whatever the cost may be, we shall fight on the beaches, we shall fight on the landing grounds, we shall fight in the fields and in the streets, we shall fight in the hills; we shall never surrender, and even if, which I do not for a moment believe, this island or a large part of it were subjugated and starving, then our Empire beyond the seas, armed and guarded by the British Fleet, would carry on the struggle, until, in God's good time, the New World, with all its power and might, steps forth to the rescue and the liberation of the old.

[1] *Fifth Column* I.e., treasonous. The term originated in the Spanish Civil War, when a fascist general led four columns of troops in an attack against Madrid, and later claimed he was helped by a "fifth column" of secret supporters inside the city.

[2] *Gestapo* Secret police of Nazi Germany.

from "Their Finest Hour" (18 June 1940)

With French resistance crumbling, the French government fled Paris on 10 June 1940, and although Churchill made two visits to Paris to try to persuade the nation not to surrender, six days later Marshal Henri Philippe Pétain formed a new government, which then sued for peace. In this speech Churchill discusses these recent events and reaffirms the nation's resolve to continue fighting alone.

... During the first four years of the last war the Allies experienced nothing but disaster and disappointment. That was our constant fear: one blow after another, terrible losses, frightful dangers. Everything miscarried. And yet at the end of those four years the morale of the Allies was higher than that of the Germans, who had moved from one aggressive triumph to another, and who stood everywhere triumphant invaders of the lands into which they had broken. During that war we repeatedly asked ourselves the question: How are we going to win? and no one was able ever to answer it with much precision, until at the end, quite suddenly, quite unexpectedly, our terrible foe collapsed before us, and we were so glutted with victory that in our folly we threw it away.

We do not yet know what will happen in France or whether the French resistance will be prolonged, both in France and in the French Empire overseas. The French Government will be throwing away great opportunities and casting adrift their future if they do not continue the war in accordance with their Treaty obligations, from which we have not felt able to release them. The House will have read the historic declaration in which, at the desire of many Frenchmen—and of our own hearts—we have proclaimed our willingness at the darkest hour in French history to conclude a union of common citizenship in this struggle. However matters may go in France or with the French Government, or other French Governments, we in this Island and in the British Empire will never lose our sense of comradeship with the French people. If we are now called upon to endure what they have been suffering, we shall emulate their courage, and if final victory rewards our toils they shall share the gains, aye, and freedom shall be restored to all. We abate nothing of our just demands; not one jot or tittle[1] do we recede. Czechs, Poles, Norwegians, Dutch, Belgians have joined their causes to our own. All these shall be restored.

Winston Churchill inspects the damage done to the Debating Chamber of the House of Commons.

What General Weygand[2] called the Battle of France is over. I expect that the Battle of Britain is about to begin. Upon this battle depends the survival of Christian civilization. Upon it depends our own British life, and the long continuity of our institutions and our Empire. The whole fury and might of the enemy must very soon be turned on us. Hitler knows that he will have to break us in this Island or lose the war. If we can stand up to him, all Europe may be free and the life of the world may move forward into broad, sunlit uplands. But if we fail, then the whole world, including the United States, including all that we have known and cared for, will sink into the abyss of a new Dark Age made more sinister, and perhaps more protracted, by the lights of perverted science. Let us therefore brace our-

[1] *jot or tittle* Minute amount.

[2] *General Weygand* Maxime Weygand, French general (1867–1965), who served as Supreme Allied Commander until the fall of France.

selves to our duties, and so bear ourselves that, if the British Empire and its Commonwealth last for a thousand years, men will still say, "This was their finest hour."

from Harold Nicholson, *The War Years: 1939–1945* (Volume 2 of *The Diaries and Letters of Harold Nicholson*, 1972)

Harold Nicholson was a Member of Parliament throughout the war, and served briefly in Churchill's government as Parliamentary Secretary to the Ministry of Information, from May 1940 until July 1941. As a result of his position, he was frequently forced to be in London, away from his home and his wife, Vita Sackville-West. Their letters to one another demonstrate their concern for one another's safety, as well as their conviction that their world could never be the same after the war. They were serious in their determination to commit suicide by ingesting a lethal dose of drugs (referred to in their correspondence as "the bare bodkin," or unsheathed dagger) should Hitler invade and should it appear that either of them might be taken by the Germans. While Sackville-West's letters give a sense of the war experienced by those left helplessly watching from home, Nicholson's letters, and particularly his diary entries, often give a sense of the exhilarating patriotism that motivated others.

H.N. to V.S-W.

27 May 1940
Ministry of Information

I am afraid that the news this afternoon is very bad indeed, and that we must expect the Germans to surround a large proportion of our Army and to occupy the whole area of Belgium and Northern France. We must also face the possibility that the French may make a separate peace, especially if Italy joins in the conflict. I warn you of this so that you will prepare your mind for the bad news when it comes and be ready to summon all the courage that is in you. I think you had better keep this to yourself for the moment.

V.S-W. to H.N.

28 May 1940
Sissinghurst

God help us, I have just heard about the Belgians! Well, we must wait. In the meantime, how deeply I agree with you about love and also about the bodkin. I promise you never to do anything rash or impetuous with the latter, but I should like to have it by me. So see Pierre Lansel[1] as soon as you can, for both our sakes, and get it for yourself and also post me a little parcel. There must be something quick and painless and portable. Oh my dear, my dearest, that we should come to this! Anyhow, we have had our lives, or at any rate more than half of them, so let us never repine. I won't write more. I know you are busy, and it is not necessary for me to say more than that I have loved you more than anyone or anything in all my life.

V.S-W. to H.N.

5 June 1940
Sissinghurst

I wish I had heard Winston making that magnificent speech![2] Even repeated by the announcer it sent shivers (not of fear) down my spine. I think that one of the reasons why one is stirred by his Elizabethan phrases is that one feels the whole massive backing of power and resolve behind them, like a great fortress: they are never words for words' sake.

How strange it is to have no knowledge of what is about to befall us. In ordinary times one seldom thinks how odd it is to have no knowledge of what may happen even within the next hour, but now the consciousness of this ignorance becomes acute. I see the future only in terms of colour: scarlet and black. But as you say, courage and hope. And there is always the bare bodkin.

---

[1] *Pierre Lansel* Nicholson's doctor.

[2] *that magnificent speech* The "We Shall Fight on the Beaches" speech of 4 June.

H.N. to V.S-W.

19 June 1940
4 King's Bench Walk, E.C.4

I think it practically certain that the Americans will enter the war in November, and if we can last till then, all is well. Anyhow, as a precaution, I have got the bare bodkin. I shall bring down your half on Sunday. It all looks very simple.

How I wish Winston would not talk on the wireless[1] unless he is feeling in good form. He hates the microphone, and when we bullied him into speaking last night, he just sulked and read his House of Commons speech[2] over again. Now, as delivered in the House of Commons, that speech was magnificent, especially the concluding sentences. But it sounded ghastly on the wireless. All the great vigour he put into it seemed to evaporate. …

Harold Nicholson, *Diary*

12 July 1940

… The national problem is this. When bombing begins on a large scale, people will ask, "What are we fighting for? Would we not be better off with peace plus Hitler?" In order to combat the first, we must have Free Trade and pooled resources. In order to combat the second we must have Socialism. I suggest that I should draft in leaflet form a manifesto promising the world free trade and our own country equality of opportunity. They agree. But it will be difficult to get Duff[3] to put it to the War Cabinet. Will it not be felt that we had better leave this sleeping tiger to sleep in its own way?

[1] *wireless* Radio.

[2] *his House … speech* The "Their Finest Hour" speech that he had delivered to the House the previous day (18 June).

[3] *Duff* Politician (Alfred) Duff Cooper (1890–1954), who was then serving as Minister of Information. Nicholson served on Cooper's Committee on German Refugees.

King George VI and Queen Elizabeth walk through the wreckage of the north side of Buckingham Palace, which was hit by a bomb on 10 September 1940.

Harold Nicholson, *Diary*

20 July 1940

I think that Hitler will probably invade us within the next few days. He has 6,000 aeroplanes ready for the job. How strange it all is! We know that we are faced with a terrific invasion. We half-know that the odds are heavily against us. Yet there is a sort of exhilaration in the air. If Hitler were to postpone invasion and fiddle about in Africa and the Mediterranean, our morale might weaken. But we are really proud to be the people who will not give way. The reaction to Hitler's speech yesterday[4] is a good reaction. Yet I know well that we shall be exposed to horrible punishment. It is so strange

[4] *Hitler's speech yesterday* Hitler's speech to the Reichstag, the parliament of Germany until 1945, in which he implied that he might be willing to discuss peace terms with the British.

that in this moment of anxiety there is no hatred of Hitler or the Germans. Opinion slides off into oblique animosities such as criticism of the Old Gang and rage that the L.D.V.[1] are not better equipped. All this is dangerous, since it is in essence a form of escapism and appeasement. We are really frightened of Hitler, and avoid the dynamic resistance to him which is uniform hatred. 130 years ago all this hatred was concentrated against [Napoleon] Bonaparte. We flinch today from central enmity. If we are invaded we may become angry.

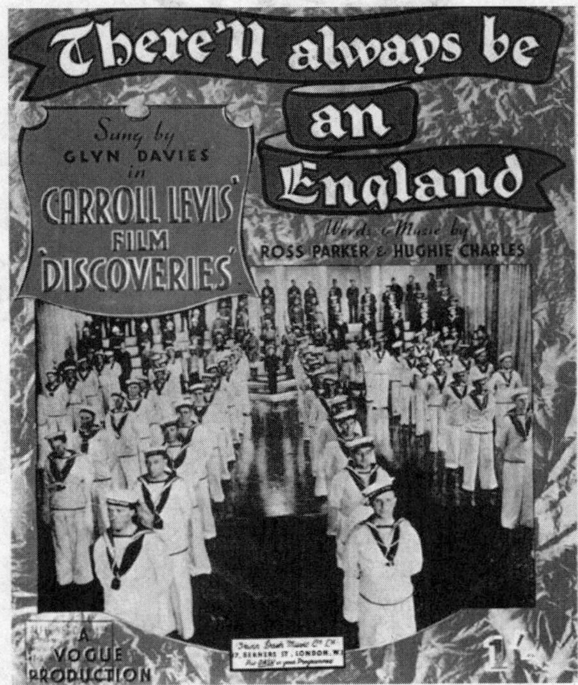

During the Blitz came an outpouring of patriotic and defiant songs—such as this song, "There'll Always Be an England"—that were played on the radio and in pubs and music halls.

Nose art on a heavy bomber from RCAF Squadron 420, Tholthorpe, England, c. 1944. Adding nose art to planes was a common World War II practice. In this case, "City of London" refers to London, Ontario, in recognition of the support of the London Ontario Air Force Wives Association for the squadron. A stuffed snowy owl was the squadron's mascot. The illustration beside the message "Donald's Delivery" shows Donald Duck forcefully directing a bomb downwards with his foot. The cartoon character was featured in several short propaganda films during World War II and became something of an icon for the war effort. (Photo by Max Davidson; provided courtesy of Jennifer McCue.)

Nat Burton and Walter Kent, "The White Cliffs of Dover" (1941)

This song was among those made famous by Vera Lynn, whose lively voice and upbeat persona made her extraordinarily popular during World War II.

I'll never forget the people I met
Braving those angry skies;
I remember well as the shadows fell,
The light of hope in their eyes.
And tho' I'm far away,
I still can hear them say "Thumbs up!"
For when the dawn comes up:

[1] *L.D.V.* Local Defence Volunteers.

There'll be bluebirds over the white cliffs of Dover
Tomorrow, just you wait and see.
There'll be love and laughter and peace ever after,
Tomorrow, when the world is free.

The shepherd will tend his sheep,
The valley will bloom again,
And Jimmy will go to sleep,
In his own little room again.

There'll be bluebirds over the white cliffs of Dover
Tomorrow, just you wait and see.
There'll be love and laughter and peace ever after,
Tomorrow, when the world is free.

When night shadows fall I always recall,
Out there across the sea,
Twilight falling down a little town—
It's fresh in my memory.
I hear a mother pray,
And to her baby say "Don't Cry";
This is her lullaby:

There'll be bluebirds over the white cliffs of Dover
Tomorrow, just you wait and see.
There'll be love and laughter and peace ever after,
Tomorrow, when the world is free.

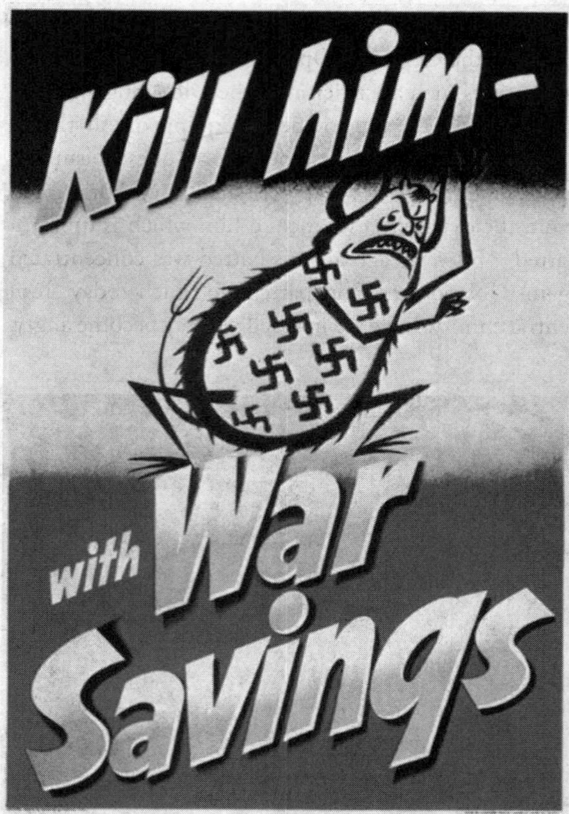

War savings poster.

Keith Douglas, "Vergissmeinnicht"[1] (1944)

A student at Oxford when war broke out, Keith Douglas enlisted in a cavalry regiment (which was soon outfitted with tanks instead of horses) and was sent to the Egyptian desert in 1942. He was later killed in the assault on the Normandy beaches in 1944.

Three weeks gone and the combatants gone
returning over the nightmare ground
we found the place again, and found
the soldier sprawling in the sun.

The frowning barrel of his gun
overshadowing. As we came on
that day, he hit my tank with one
like the entry of a demon.

Look. Here in the gunpit spoil
the dishonoured picture of his girl
who has put: *Steffi. Vergissmeinnicht*
in a copybook gothic script.

We see him almost with content,
abased, and seeming to have paid
and mocked at by his own equipment
that's hard and good when he's decayed.

[1] *Vergissmeinnicht* German: Forget me not.

But she would weep to see today
how on his skin the swart° flies move; *black*
the dust upon the paper eye
and the burst stomach like a cave.

For here the lover and killer are mingled
who had one body and one heart.
And death who had the soldier singled
has done the lover mortal hurt.

from Henry Reed, *Lessons of War* (1945)

During World War II, Henry Reed was conscripted into the Royal Army Ordnance Corps. In *Lessons of War* (from which "Naming of Parts" is the best known individual poem) Reed plays upon the rhythms he noticed in the speech of his weapons instructor, the lulling patterns of which contrast sharply with the military-manual vocabulary.

Vixi duellis nuper idoneus
Et militavi non sine gloria[1]

1. Naming of Parts

Today we have naming of parts. Yesterday,
We had daily cleaning. And tomorrow morning,
We shall have what to do after firing. But today,
Today we have naming of parts. Japonica[2]
Glistens like coral in all of the neighbouring gardens,
And today we have naming of parts.

This is the lower sling swivel. And this
Is the upper sling swivel, whose use you will see,
When you are given your slings. And this is the piling swivel,
Which in your case you have not got. The branches
Hold in the gardens their silent, eloquent gestures,
Which in our case we have not got.

This is the safety-catch, which is always released
With an easy flick of the thumb. And please do not let me
See anyone using his finger. You can do it quite easy
If you have any strength in your thumb. The blossoms
Are fragile and motionless, never letting anyone see
Any of them using their finger.

And this you can see is the bolt. The purpose of this
Is to open the breech, as you see. We can slide it
Rapidly backwards and forwards: we call this
Easing the spring. And rapidly backwards and forwards
The early bees are assaulting and fumbling the flowers:
They call it easing the Spring.

They call it easing the Spring: it is perfectly easy
If you have any strength in your thumb; like the bolt,
And the breech, and the cocking-piece, and the point of balance,
Which in our case we have not got; and the almond-blossom
Silent in all of the gardens and the bees going backwards and forwards,
For today we have naming of parts.

Douglas LePan

In World War II Douglas LePan (1914–98) served in the Canadian army during the Italian campaign in 1943. His poetry about the war includes work published in the 1940s and 1950s (notably in *The Net and the Sword*, winner of the Governor General's Award for poetry) as well as poems such as those below, written some forty years after LePan's battlefield experiences.

[1] *Vixi ... gloria* Latin: Lately I have lived in the midst of battles, credibly enough, / And have soldiered, not without glory. (An adaptation of Horace, *Odes* 3.261–62, with the word *puellis* ("girls") changed to *duellis* ("battles").

[2] *Japonica* Spring-flowering plant.

"Below Monte Cassino" (1987)

Having had too much sex the night before for a man
over sixty, he feels a dull ache in the small of his back
about the size of a pie-plate, and suddenly remembers
(as he urinates into the toilet-bowl) dead
American boys in a field below Monte Cassino
and how surprised he had been as he picked his way
forward (avoiding the bodies as best as he could,
scared shitless of trip-mines and shoe-mines and glass-mines)
by one dead boy lying face down in the mud
with his arms and his legs flung wide and one big wound
in the small of his back about the size of a pie-plate,
having been caught there by a fragment of mortar-fire—
surprised then, and still surprised now, that what was
oozing from the wide wound was, not blood, but shit.

"The Haystack" (1987)

It doesn't take a Hiroshima[1] to burn a man to a crisp.
A haystack will do. And what could be more bucolic
than that? And you get tired of sleeping in cellars or slit-trenches,
so why not behind a haystack that has simmered all day
in the warmth of an Italian September sun? But at night
the jackals are ready to spring, the German eighty-eights,
with their high muzzle-velocities and their low trajectories,

St. Paul's Cathedral, London, during the Blitz.

so that the haystack ignites like a torch and a gunner is burnt
to a crisp. How far back was that? thirty years? forty years?
He doesn't remember. He only remembers the stench
of fear, his own fear, and a grey army blanket, and a young
sunburned back alive on the banks of the Volturno,[2]
then burning, burning. By dire subtleties such as these
he was being prepared for the carbonization of cities.

Life at Home

During the war, the Ministry of Information recorded and reported on the attitudes and actions of British residents, and particularly Londoners, in the face of the threat of invasion. From most reports, people coped with the war and the Blitz with stoicism, courage, and patience. During the heaviest raids, the government was on the look-out for signs of panic, but incidents were rare and isolated. Confronted with the nightly danger of bombings, the loss of belongings, and the privations of wartime restrictions, the English people responded with resignation or even cheerful acceptance. Virginia Woolf understood such loss and privation at first

[1] *Hiroshima* Japanese city that was the first city to ever be a target of a nuclear weapon. The United States dropped an atomic bomb on Hiroshima on 6 August 1945, killing approximately 130,000 people and leveling 90 per cent of the city.

[2] *Volturno* River in south-central Italy, the bank of which formed the Volturno line, a German defensive position in World War II.

hand; the Woolfs retreated to the relative safety of their country home in Sussex after their Bloomsbury home, where they had kept their press, was bombed in September 1940. In a diary entry dated 19 December 1940, Virginia Woolf stepped back and examined the daily privations endured by people in even the most comfortable situations:

It would be interesting if I could take today, Thursday, and say exactly how the war changes it. It changes it when I order dinner. Our ration of margarine is so small that I can't think of any pudding save milk pudding. We have no sugar to make sugar puddings: no pastry, unless I buy it ready made. The shops don't fill till midday. Things are bought fast. In the afternoon they are often gone. Meat ration diminishes this week. Milk is so cut that we have to consider even the cat's saucer. I spent an hour making butter from our skim of cream—a week's takings provides about ½ lb. Petrol changes the day too. Nessa[1] can only come here when she goes to Lewes[2] shopping. All prices rise steadily. The screw is much increased since the summer. We buy no clothes but make do with the old. These are inconveniences rather than hardships. We don't go hungry or cold. But luxury is nipped off, & hospitality. It takes thought & trouble to feed one extra. … The pinch is said to be worse than last war. If it increases much we shall be hungry, I suppose. … Then the black out—that's half an hour daily drudgery. We can't use the dining room after dark. …

In a December 1940 letter to her friend, American editor Irita Van Doren, journalist and writer Rebecca West described some of the emotional and physical difficulties of the war:

This is a beastly war—like the stage of seasickness when you are not sure you are seasick but realise that everything but seasickness has ceased to exist. … We are all working like dogs, indeed, because in an odd way the connective tissue of life has gone. Everybody is living miles away from where they usually do and has shut up their house and if anybody gets ill the relevant doctors and surgeons aren't to be found, so if you have stayed in London life goes in endless odd jobs. If it weren't for the sailors being drowned one could stand it, and of course it's a disappointment about the Finns. It did seem that once we had declared war we wouldn't have this awful business of being comparatively safe and seeing the smaller peoples being butchered.

Many people left London for safety, as the Woolfs did, and those who stayed sought shelter during air raids in the safest places they could. For many, the best shelter was London's Underground, or subway system. Here they could sleep without fear of bombing. In another diary entry, dated 20 October 1940, and written on a visit to London, Virginia Woolf described the long lines of people waiting to take shelter in the Underground:

The most—what?—impressive, no, that's not it—sight in London on Friday was the queue, mostly children with suitcases, outside Warren Street tube.[3] This was about 11.30. We thought they were evacuees waiting for a bus. But there they were, in a much longer line, with women, men, more bags, blankets, sitting still at 3. Lining up for the shelter in the night's raid—which came of course. Thus, if they left the tube at 6 (a bad raid on Thursday) they were back again at 11.

Despite the courage exhibited across the nation, the stress of the nightly air raids did take its toll. Sleep was constantly interrupted, and people lived under the threat of death. It was impossible not to contemplate the worst, as Woolf did in this diary entry from 2 October 1940:

Should I think of death? Last night a great heavy plunge of bomb under the window. So near we both started. A plane had passed dropping this fruit. … I said to L.[4]: I don't want to die yet. The chances are against

[1] *Nessa* Woolf's sister, Vanessa Bell.

[2] *Lewes* Large market town in East Sussex.

[3] *tube* I.e., Underground station.

[4] *L.* Leonard Woolf, Virginia's husband.

Women workers make aircraft components in a disused section of the London Underground. Many such tunnels were pressed into service for the war industry.

it. But they're aiming at the railway and the power works. They get closer every time. Caburn[1] was crowned with what looked like a settled moth, wings extended—a Messerschmitt[2] it was, shot down on Sunday. … Oh I try to imagine how one's killed by a bomb. I've got it fairly vivid—the sensation: but can't see anything but suffocating nonentity following after. I shall think—oh I wanted another 10 years—not this—and shan't, for once, be able to describe it. It—I mean death; no, the scrunching and scrambling, the crushing of my bone shade in on my very active eye and brain: the process of putting out the light—painful? Yes. Terrifying. I suppose so. Then a swoon; a drain; two or three gulps attempting consciousness—and then dot dot dot.

During the Blitz the citizens of London proved that it was not only soldiers who could become accustomed to death and destruction, and learn to remain calm in the face of danger. Women, children, and ordinary shopkeepers and workers were equally capable of this courage. A woman in her thirties who had just returned from Scotland, where she had fled when the war began, described her feelings around the air raids:

Sweated with fear at the mere idea of being woken in the night by sirens, let alone at that of bombs and shells; was constantly imagining car and other noises were sirens or guns. Convinced of being most utter and complete coward—very ashamed. Sure I was bound to panic and lose control if things got hot. … Now I find myself almost completely proof against fear and jumpiness … am the most fearless among my own circle of friends. …

As this woman's testimony demonstrates, bombings could often be an exhilarating experience when citizens realized they had reserves of courage of which they had never been aware. There was a sense

[1] *Caburn* Mount Caburn, an isolated peak that is East Sussex's highest landmark.

[2] *Messerschmitt* German aircraft.

British women jitterbug with American GIs at the American Red Cross Club, 1945.

of excitement associated with the air raids in that they gave civilians a sense of life on the "front line," as part of the action. They were no longer idle observers, helplessly hearing about the war from the safety of their homes. Their daily struggles, and their determination to cope with them, became essential to the success of the war effort. Here a young woman describes a narrow escape she had during a bombing in Hampstead:

"Are you all right?" … people kept asking; and it was only then—silly though it sounds—that it occurred to me that I might have been hurt! That I had been in actual danger, really! Somehow, right up to that minute I had taken everything for granted, in a queer, brainless way, as if it was all perfectly ordinary. I never even thought about injury or death, for any of us. …

I lay there feeling indescribably happy and triumphant. "I've been bombed!" I kept on saying to myself, over and over again—trying the phrase on, like a new dress, to see how it fitted. "I've been bombed!" … "I've been bombed—me!"

It seems a terrible thing to say, when many people were killed and injured last night; but never in my whole life have I ever experienced such pure and flawless happiness.

Richard Titmuss, a historian and advisor to the Ministry of Economic Warfare at the time, attempted to explain this exhilaration:

What this period of the war meant to a great many people was less social disparagement. There was nothing to be ashamed of in being "bombed out" by the enemy. Public sympathy with, and approval of, families who suffered in the raids was in sharp contrast to the low social evaluation accorded to those who lost in material standards through being unemployed during the nineteen-thirties. The civilian war of 1939–45, with its many opportunities for service in civil defence and other schemes, also helped to satisfy an often inarticulate need; the need to be a wanted member of society. Circumstances were thus favourable to fuller self-expression, for there was plenty of scope for relieving a sense of inferiority and failure.

The war effort gave civilians a sense of purpose in other ways as well, and allowed them to lead lives very different from those they would have led in peacetime. Many women who would have moved directly from their parents's homes to those of their husbands left the house to find work in munitions factories or as nurses or civil servants. Whether driven by loneliness while their husbands were away, by economic need, or by patriotism, many of these women reveled in their new-found independence. For many women, this was the first time that they had had money of their own—even if they were generally receiving just over half of the remuneration made to men for the same work.

One other result of the war, however, was that teenaged girls tended not to be very strictly supervised—particularly if their fathers were at war and their mothers were working—and there was widespread concern that morals were becoming looser. A particular concern was the rise in teenaged prostitution. A patrolling officer of the Public Morality Council expressed anxiety concerning the moral climate:

I must again refer to the very large proportion of girls of about 16 to 18 years of age, always looking for a good time at somebody else's expense. These girls, a large number of whom travel from the East End and usually in couples, throng the amusement and sports arcades, often undoubtedly for the warmth and light offered, but principally to get off with the American troops who seem to use these places for a like purpose. There is no solicitation, but they easily get into conversation whilst playing with the various machines, and then they are on a very slippery slope, which in many instances ends in disaster.

Anti-Semitism and World War II

In hindsight, the Holocaust—the systematic murder by the Nazi regime of about 6,000,000 Jewish people[1]—is for many the central event of the war; this was the horror that other nations were fighting to overthrow. At the time, however, the persecution of Jewish people was for most people of much less central importance.

It was widely known by the mid-1930s that German Jews were subject to severe and escalating levels of oppression, but the decision to attempt the systematic murder of all Jewish people was not taken until some time in 1941; the outbreak of war in 1939 had been sparked primarily by Hitler's taking over the territory of other nations. By the end of 1942, enough evidence of the Holocaust had emerged to make it clear that mass murder was occurring, and the Allies issued a widely publicized condemnation of "this bestial policy" in December of that year. That, however, was the only such declaration made prior to 1944, and the Allies did not back up their words with concrete action; they did not bomb the gas chambers or the train tracks leading to them (even when they were already bombing nearby factories); they did not lift restrictions on Jewish immigration.

To be sure, details of the operation of the camps and of the gas chambers were not available until the spring of 1944, and the full import of the Nazi atrocities did not begin to sink fully into the consciousness of the world until photographic depictions of the liberation of the camps and of the condition of the survivors were published early in 1945. (To some extent it may be said that the full impact did not sink home even until years after that.) Yet it would be difficult to argue that the lack of information was all that

[1] Many other groups—among them Slavs, Romani people, and people with disabilities—were also targeted by the Nazis; the total death toll of the Holocaust and these related systematic mass murders is approximately 17 million.

prevented the Allies from making a stronger response to the horror of the Holocaust. The inescapable fact is that, even towards the end of World War II, many in Britain, the United States, Canada, Australia, and elsewhere who were not otherwise Nazi sympathizers shared a strong anti-Semitic prejudice. The case of Ezra Pound is one of the best-known and most extreme cases—the pioneering poet of Modernism had always displayed an anti-Semitic streak, and during the war the streak widened. He moved to Italy and began broadcasting hate propaganda on behalf of the fascist government. (Below is an excerpt from one of Pound's speeches.)

There can be no doubt that most Britons and North Americans in the 1940s were repelled by the help that Pound was giving to the Axis cause. But nor can there be any doubt that a remarkably high level of anti-Semitism remained prevalent throughout these years. The excerpt reprinted below from a 1945 essay by George Orwell is a striking reminder of the extent to which ordinary citizens remained in the habit of "blaming the victim."

from Ezra Pound, "Speech to the English" (Broadcast on Radio Rome, 15 March 1942)

… Your enemy is not Germany, your enemy is money on loan. And it would be better for you to be infected with typhus, and dysentery, and Bright's disease,[1] than to be infected with this blindness which prevents you from understanding HOW you are undermined, how you are ruined.

The big Jew is so bound up with this Leihkapital[2] that no one is able to unscramble that omelet. It would be better for you to retire to Derbyshire and defy New Jerusalem, better for you to retire to Gloucester and find one spot that is England than to go on fighting for Jewry and ignoring the process.

It is an outrage that any clean lad from the country—I suppose there are STILL a few ENGLISH lads from the country—it is an outrage that any nice young man from the suburbs should be expected to die for Victor Sassoon, it is an outrage that any drunken footman's byblow[3] should be asked to die for Sassoon.

As to your Empire, it was not all of it won by clean fighting. But however you got it, you did for a time more or less justify keeping it, on the ground that you exported good government or better government than the natives would have had without England.

You let in the Jew and the Jew rotted your Empire. … And the big Jew has rotted EVERY nation he has wormed into. A millstone. Well, an exceptionally good swimmer MIGHT conceivably be cast into the sea with a stone tied round his neck. He might perhaps untie it. …

WHAT is their system? Unvarying, cheap goods, sweated out of cheap labor, dung dust hurled on the world, the WORLD conceived as sweat shop, to hell with the eight-hour day, down with abundance. DUMPING sweated goods, dumped against any and every nation that pays a just price for labor. That is your ALLY. …

Is there a RACE left in England? Has it ANY will left to survive? You can carry slaughter to Ireland. Will that save you? I doubt it. Nothing can save you, save a purge. Nothing can save you, save an affirmation that you are English. …

In the year 1942 Anno Domini, there is only one start you can make. And that is a start toward being England. A refusal to be a province of Israel, or an outpost of Yankee-Judaea.

---

[1] *Bright's disease* Generic term for kidney disease.

[2] *Leihkapital* Pound's term for what he calls "Loan Capital."

[3] *byblow* I.e., illegitimate child.

Floodlights illuminate London on VE Day (8 May 1945), lighting London for the first time in years.

from George Orwell, "Anti-Semitism in Britain" (1945)

… It is generally admitted that anti-Semitism is on the increase, that it has been greatly exacerbated by the war, and that humane and enlightened people are not immune to it. … Here are some samples of anti-Semitic remarks that have been made to me during the past year or two:

> Middle-aged office employee: "I generally come to work by bus. It takes longer, but I don't care about using the Underground from Golders Green[1] nowadays. There's too many of the Chosen Race travelling on that line."

> Young intellectual, Communist or near-Communist: "No, I do *not* like Jews. I've never made any secret of that. I can't stick them. Mind you, I'm not anti-Semitic, of course."

> Middle-class woman: "Well, no one could call me anti-Semitic, but I do think the way these Jews behave is too absolutely stinking. The way they push their way to the head of queues, and so on. They're so abominably selfish. I think they're responsible for a lot of what happens to them."

> Milk roundsman: "A Jew don't do no work, not the same as what an Englishman does. 'E's too clever. We work with this 'ere" (flexes his biceps). "They work with that there" (taps his forehead).

> Chartered accountant, intelligent, left-wing in an undirected way: "These bloody Yids are all pro-German. They'd change sides tomorrow if the Nazis got here. I see a lot of them in my business. They admire Hitler at the bottom of their hearts. They'll always suck up to anyone who kicks them."

> Intelligent woman, on being offered a book dealing with anti-Semitism and German atrocities: "Don't show it me, *please* don't show it to me. It'll only make me hate the Jews more than ever."

[1] *Golders Green* Suburban area in northeast London that has been the site of a thriving Jewish community since the early 1900s.

I could fill pages with similar remarks, but these will do to go on with. Two facts emerge from them. One—which is very important and which I must return to in a moment—is that above a certain intellectual level people are ashamed of being anti-Semitic and are careful to draw a distinction between "anti-Semitism" and "disliking Jews." The other is that anti-Semitism is an irrational thing. The Jews are accused of specific offences (for instance, bad behaviour in food queues) which the person speaking feels strongly about, but it is obvious that these accusations merely rationalize some deep-rooted prejudice. To attempt to counter them with facts and statistics is useless, and may sometimes be worse than useless. As the last of the above-quoted remarks shows, people can remain anti-Semitic, or at least anti-Jewish, while being fully aware that their outlook is indefensible. If you dislike somebody, you dislike him and there is an end of it: your feelings are not made any better by a recital of his virtues.

It so happens that the war has encouraged the growth of anti-Semitism and even, in the eyes of many ordinary people, given some justification for it. To begin with, the Jews are one people of whom it can be said with complete certainty that they will benefit by an Allied victory. Consequently the theory that "this is a Jewish war" has a certain plausibility, all the more so because the Jewish war effort seldom gets its fair share of recognition. The British Empire is a huge heterogeneous organization held together largely by mutual consent, and it is often necessary to flatter the less reliable elements at the expense of the more loyal ones. To publicize the exploits of Jewish soldiers, or even to admit the existence of a considerable Jewish army in the Middle East, rouses hostility in South Africa, the Arab countries and elsewhere: it is easier to ignore the whole subject and allow the man in the street to go on thinking that Jews are exceptionally clever at dodging military service. …

from Rebecca West, "Greenhouse with Cyclamens" (1946)

Writer and journalist Rebecca West and her husband, Henry Andrews, provided shelter for wartime refugees, particularly Jewish people and former residents of Yugoslavia (where West had traveled extensively before the war in order to report on the threat Germany posed to that nation). Immediately after the war, West wrote extensively on the psychology of espionage and treason, and gained a reputation as a reporter on the Nuremberg Trials, the topic of the article excerpted here. These trials lasted from 1945 until 1949.

The Bavarian city of Nuremberg was made a national shrine by the Nazis when Hitler came to power. It was the center of anti-Semitic propaganda throughout the war, and in 1935 it was the site of the party congress that set out the so-called Nuremberg Laws, which stripped German Jews of their civic rights. Nearly half of all airplane, tank, and submarine engines produced during the war were made in Nuremberg. After the war, Nuremberg's Palace of Justice was the site of the international tribunal for war crimes.

In the excerpt below, West notes the very ordinary appearance of the defendants—a fact that surprised many spectators of the trials. Of the 21 defendants, West mentions below Hermann Göring, commander of the Luftwaffe, who was sentenced to death (but committed suicide the night before his execution); Hjalmar Schacht, the pre-war president of the Reichsbank, who was acquitted; Albert Speer, Reichminister of Armaments and Munitions and friend of Hitler's, who expressed repentance and was sentenced to twenty years in prison; and Rudolf Hess, Nazi Party leader, who was sentenced to life in prison.

… It seemed ridiculous for the defendants to make any effort to stave off the end, for they admitted by their appearance that nothing was to go well with them again on this earth. These Nazi leaders, self-dedicated to the breaking of all rules, broke last of all the rule that the verdict of a court must not be foretold. Their appearance announced what they believed. The Russians had asked for the death penalty for all of them, and it was plain that the defendants thought that wish would be granted. Believing that they were to lose everything, they forgot what possession had been. Not the slightest trace of their power and their glory remained; none of them looked as if he could ever have exercised any valid authority. Göring still used imperial gestures, but they were so vulgar that they did not suggest that he had really filled any great position; it merely seemed probable that in certain bars the frequenters had called him by some such nick-name as "The Emperor." These people were also surrendering physical characteristics which might have been thought inalienable during life, such as the colour and texture of their skins and the moulding of their features. Most of them, except Schacht, who was white-haired, and Speer, who was black like a monkey, were neither dark nor fair any more; and there was amongst them no leanness that did not sag and no plumpness that seemed more than inflation by some thin gas. So diminished were their personalities that it was hard to keep in mind which was which, even after one had sat and looked at them for days; and those who stood out defined themselves by oddity rather than character.

Hess was noticeable because he was so plainly mad: so plainly mad that it seemed shameful that he should be tried. His skin was ashen, and he had that odd faculty, peculiar to lunatics, of falling into strained positions which no normal person could maintain for more than a few minutes, and staying fixed in contortion for hours. He had the classless air characteristic of asylum inmates; evidently his distracted personality had torn up all clue to his past. He looked as if his mind had no surface, as if every part of it had been blasted away except the depth where the nightmares live. …

As these men gave up the effort to be themselves, they joined to make a common pattern which simply reiterated the plea of not guilty. All the time they made quite unidiosyncratic gestures expressive of innocence and outraged common sense, and in the intervals they stood up and chatted among themselves, forming little protesting groups, each one of which, painted as a mural, would be instantly recognized as a holy band that had tried to save the world but had been frustrated by mistaken men. But this performance they rendered more weakly every day. They were visibly receding from the field of existence and were, perhaps, no longer conscious of the recession. It is possible that they never thought directly of death or even of imprisonment, and there was nothing positive in them at all except their desire to hold time still. They were all praying with their sharp-set nerves: "Let this trial never finish, let it go on for ever and ever, without end." The nerves of all others present in the Palace of Justice were sending out a counter-prayer: the eight judges on the bench, who were plainly dragging the proceedings over the threshold of their consciousness by sheer force of will; the lawyers and the secretaries who sat sagged in their seats at the tables in the well of the court; the interpreters twittering unhappily in their glass box like cage-birds kept awake by a bright light, feeding the microphones with French and Russian and English versions of the proceedings for the spectators' earphones; the guards who stood with their arms gripping their white truncheons behind their backs, all still and hard as metal save their childish faces, which were puffy with boredom. All these people wanted to leave Nuremberg as urgently as a dental patient enduring the drill wants to up and leave the chair. …

[Sir Hartley Shawcross's] words were full of a living pity, which gave the men in the box their worst hour. … And when Sir Hartley quoted the deposition of a witness who had described a Jewish father who, standing with his little son in front of a firing squad, "pointed to the sky, stroked his head, and seemed to explain something to the boy," all the defendants wriggled on their seats, like children rated by a schoolmaster, while their faces grew old.

There was a mystery there: that [they] should have committed such a huge, cold crime. … Somebody had been collecting tattooed human skin, and it is hard to think where such a connoisseur could find his pieces unless he had power over a concentration camp. Some of these pelts were infinitely pathetic, because of their obscenity. Through the years came the memory of the inconveniently high-pitched voice of an English child among a crowd of tourists watching a tournament of water-jousting in a French port: "Mummy, come and look, there's a sailor who's got no shirt on, and he has the funniest picture on his back—there's a lady with no clothes on upside down on a St. Andrew's Cross, and there's a snake crawling all over her and somebody with a whip." There had been men who had thought they could make a pet of cruelty, and the grown beast had flayed them.

But it was astonishing that there had been so much sadism. The French doctor in charge of these exhibits pondered, turning in his hand a lampshade made of tattooed human skin. "These people where I live send me in my breakfast tray strewn with pansies, beautiful pansies. I have never seen more beautiful pansies, arranged with exquisite taste. I have to remind myself that they belong to the same race that supplied me with my exhibits, the same race that tortured me month after month, year after year, at Mauthausen."[1] And, indeed, flowers were the visible sign of that mystery, flowers that were not only lovely but beloved. In the windowboxes of the high-gabled houses the pink and purple petunias were bright like lamps. In the gardens of the cottages bordering a road which was no longer there, which was a torn trench, the phloxes shone white and clear pink and mauve, as under harsh heat they will not do, unless they are well watered. It is tedious work, training clematis over low posts, so that its beauty does not stravaig[2] up the walls but lies open under the eye; but on the edge of the town many gardeners grew it thus. The countryside beyond continued this protestation of innocence. A path might mount the hillside, through the lacework of light and shadow the pine trees cast over the soft reddish bed of the pine needles, to the upland farm where the wedding party poured out of the door, riotous with honest laughter, but freezing before a camera into honest solemnity; it might fall to the valley and follow the trout stream, where the dragonflies drew iridescent patterns just above the cloudy green water, to the edge of the millpond, where the miller's flax-haired little son played with the grey kittens among the meadow-sweet; it would not lead to any place where it seemed other than plain that Germany was a beautiful country, inhabited by a people who loved all pleasant things and meant no harm.

---

1 *Mauthausen* Concentration camp near Linz, Austria.

2 *stravaig* Wander aimlessly.

The Late Twentieth and Twenty-First Centuries: From 1945 Onward

The End of the War and the Coming of the Welfare State

Winston Churchill had inspired the nation—many said saved the nation—in the dark days of 1940, and remained over the following five years, by all accounts, one of the greatest war leaders in British history. Yet in 1945, the electorate unceremoniously dumped him and the Conservative Party from office, and installed the Labour Party under Clement Attlee in its place. Much as people were grateful to Churchill for his leadership in the war effort, he was seen very much as a war leader and a figure of the past at a time when people felt strongly that they had fought not so much to preserve the world of the past as for their right to make a better world.[1] All too clearly, voters had seen that Churchill's fondest wish at the end of the war was to return to the peacetime Britain of earlier days—a Britain with a vast Empire abroad and a rigid class system at home. Unlike the Prime Minister, at war's end the British people were increasingly seeing Imperial possessions as a drain on the nation's scarce resources, and the class system as an impediment to prosperity and an affront to notions of equality. With remarkably little fanfare, the old British world of masters and servants had already largely disappeared, but its husk still gave shape to many social attitudes; it remained almost impossibly difficult to "get ahead" if one came from a working-class background and had the "wrong accent," one could never be fully accepted in many social milieus if one's background was "in trade," and so on.

[1] Churchill might still have been elected had it not been for his veer to the extreme ideological right during the course of the campaign. Apparently strongly influenced by having read F.A. Hayek's polemic against socialism, in his speech on 4 June 1945 Churchill likened Britain's Labour Party to Hitler's secret police, suggesting that no Labour government "could afford to allow free expression of public discontent. … They would have to fall back on some sort of Gestapo."

Quite aside from the issue of increasingly anachronistic social attitudes, the working class and the lower middle class continued to face great obstacles simply in their daily physical existence. For many, conditions at the end of World War II were little better than they had been at the end of World War I; with its calls to redistribute wealth and to engage the forces of government throughout the economy on behalf of the general good, Labour represented a real change. And unquestionably, the various measures enacted by the Attlee government (many of them following on the recommendations of the 1942 and 1944 Reports to Parliament of William Beveridge) made Britain a much fairer society than it had been at any time previously in its history. The new initiatives included the establishment of the National Health Service and the National Insurance Act, which provided a measure of protection against poverty resulting from unemployment—or indeed from any other source.

If British life became more egalitarian during the Attlee years, however, much of what was being shared was still hardship. In a fifty-years-on retrospective, Doug Saunders memorably summarized the situation in postwar Britain:

> Food rationing during the war was bad. After the war it was terrible. Posters were put up reading "Eat Less Bread: Eat Potatoes Instead." Then, in the spring of 1946, those posters went down: there was no bread at all.… Coal supplies were cut back to almost nil, so that in the winter of 1947, the coldest in British history, people were ordered not to heat their homes.… If the economies and buildings and cities were fractured, even worse damage was done to families. About four million children had been shipped away from their parents to unknown locations and with almost no contact, for years. Chil-

dren and parents alike returned from the war to find things utterly different.... Susan Goodman, who was ten years old at the end of the war, had lived in the countryside, with her mother in London and her father in the armed forces. She recalls the moment when "this man got off the train—he was very tall and very yellow. He came up and said, 'Hello Sue, I'm Daddy,' and I put out my hand and said 'How do you do.' It was not auspicious."

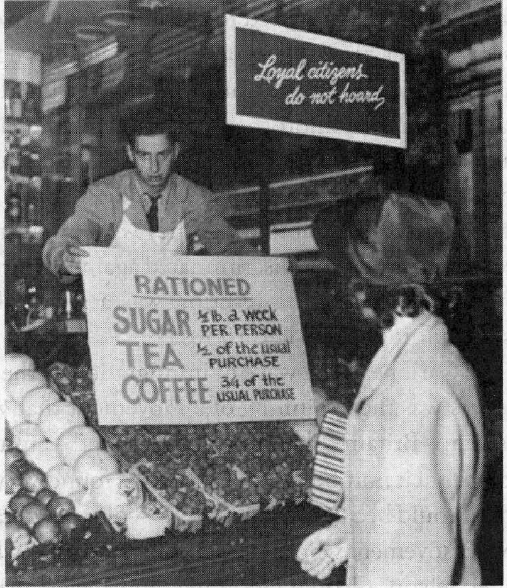

Wartime rationing in Montreal, 1942. Unlike in Britain, hardships on the home front ended soon after the war in countries such as Canada and Australia.

Even into the 1950s, food and fuel shortages persisted—and as the hardships continued, people grew as tired of Attlee and Labour as they had been of Churchill and the Conservatives in 1945. With the 1950 election Churchill was returned to office, and he presided over a period of relative calm from 1950 to 1955. In terms of the ideological direction of the nation, however, it was the election of 1945 that had represented the great turning point. From the late 1940s through to the late 1970s, periods of Labour rule (first under Attlee, later under Prime Ministers Harold Wilson and James Callaghan) alternated with periods of Conservative rule (first under Churchill again, later under Prime Ministers Harold Macmillan and Edward Heath). Under Labour, the growth of what came to be known as the "welfare state" was fostered, while under the Conservatives, the social activism of Labour was eschewed—but even while the Conservatives were in power, little attempt was made to dismantle the structures through which Labour was attempting to reshape British society. For thirty years the domestic agenda for Britain remained one of building a more egalitarian society.

The "London fog" for which the city became famous in the nineteenth and twentieth centuries was primarily created by air pollution. From December 1953 to March 1954, conditions became worse than ever, and there were more than 12,000 smog-related deaths. After the 1950s air (and water) quality in London improved dramatically as a result of anti-pollution measures.

If the political shape of the 1950s, 1960s, and 1970s in Britain has something of a unity to it, the same cannot be said for the shape of its economic and cultural life over that period. Britain recovered far more slowly economically after World War II than did North America and many other parts of the world. The 1950s in North America are thought of as years of robust economic growth. Not so in Britain, and, for many, through much of that decade British life remained dreary and unsatisfying. A major literary movement of the era—the writings of the so-called "angry young men"—represented a reaction against the dreariness and lack of opportunity that characterized so much of British life. John Osborne's play *Look Back in Anger* (1956), which depicted the struggles of the rebellious Jimmy Porter, became the touchstone in discussions of the movement, but works of prose fiction such as John Braine's *Room at the Top* (1957) and Alan Sillitoe's *Saturday Night and Sunday Morning* (1958) and *The Loneliness of the Long Distance Runner* (1959), which also dealt with the conflicts and resentments of young working-class or lower middle-class men struggling to get on in society, had almost as great an impact.

Two other writers—Kingsley Amis and Philip Larkin—were initially often mentioned in the same breath as Osborne and Sillitoe, but even in the 1950s these two were on quite different literary paths, and, in the 1960s and 1970s, their work diverged even further both from that of angry young men and from each other's (though the two remained lifelong friends). With *Lucky Jim* (1954), a social satire about class distinctions, romantic bungling, and university life, Amis achieved literary celebrity at an early age. His subsequent novels were written in a similar vein—social satire bordering on farce—but as the years went on, the humor was tinged more with bitterness than with insight, and was discolored by misogyny. Larkin, too, tried his hand early on in his career with social satire—*A Girl in Winter* (1947) being the more notable of his two novels—but with Larkin, the satire was more gentle, and did not sit entirely at ease with his evident aim of achieving a high degree of psychological realism. It was as a poet that Larkin made a lasting mark; poetry turned out to be the perfect medium for his unique variety of psychological understanding, his sometimes wry biting wit, and his bleak honesty about old age and death. Like Amis, Larkin had his share of bitter and misogynist feelings (as his posthumously published letters revealed), but these are far less obtrusive in his work than they are in that of Amis, and where Amis's work became more coarse and superficial over the years, Larkin's became more varied, more resonant, and more memorable. In its subject matter but also in its form, Larkin's poetry was quite out of step with the vast majority of British poetry published in the second half of the twentieth century; almost all his poems are built on a foundation of accentual syllabic meter, and most have a regular rhyme scheme. Yet they found a remarkably large audience; his final book, *High Windows*, made some British best seller lists in 1974.

Another quite different group of writers might with equal appropriateness be described as "angry young men": those who emigrated to Britain from its overseas possessions. Particularly prominent were immigrants from the Caribbean; large numbers were recruited from Jamaica, Trinidad, and other Caribbean islands in the decade following World War II to help rebuild Britain's bombed-out cities. Though they made an important contribution to that rebuilding, they were often treated as second-class citizens, discriminated against in virtually every public sphere; the reaction was a series of race riots, beginning in the late 1950s.

The Caribbean-led wave of immigration in the post-war years was the beginning of a movement that would transform Britain demographically and culturally. Amongst their number were many of the founding voices of what would become known as post-colonial literature, a global movement whose key Caribbean voices included Samuel Selvon, George Lamming, and Derek Walcott. From the beginning, they wrote largely in opposition to (rather than within) British literary traditions; this was the beginning of the literary movement that Salman Rushdie memorably characterized a few decades later with the phrase "The Empire writes back."

The important women writers from this period were arguably less angry in their work than their male counterparts—though doubtless they had at least as much cause to be. The novels of Iris Murdoch, of Muriel Spark, and of Doris Lessing work with vastly different settings and story materials, ranging from the story of the life of a school mistress at a girls' boarding school in Spark's *The Prime of Miss Jean Brodie* (1961) to a philosophically tinged exploration of faith and moral imagination in Iris Murdoch's *The Bell* (1958) to an evocation of the gritty edges of colonial existence in Southern Rhodesia in Lessing's *The Grass Is Singing*

(1950). Almost all are written in the vein of social or psychological realism—and most have something of an ethos of stoicism in the face of adversity. As a character in Murdoch's *Under the Net* (1954) puts it, "one must just blunder on. Truth lies in blundering on."

THE END OF EMPIRE

If in the generation following World War II, the Conservatives came to accept many of the egalitarian social principles in which Labour believed, they also came to accept that the old approach to Empire was no longer workable. Britain's stature as a world power suffered serious damage during the Suez crisis of 1956, when it attempted unsuccessfully to block the nationalization by Egypt of the Suez Canal, and it suffered as well in the face of increasing resistance to Imperial rule in British colonies. (Perhaps most notably, the Mau Mau rebellion in East Africa of 1952–56 showed to what extent a relatively small uprising could destabilize colonial rule, inspiring brutal reprisals and widespread fear.) By the early 1960s the die was cast; Harold Macmillan's 1960 "Wind of Change" speech signaled Britain's intention to grant independence to virtually all of its remaining colonies, in Asia and the Caribbean as well as in Africa. Independence in a significant number of these nations also meant majority rule by blacks, which was anathema to many white settlers. In some new nations, independence was followed by an exodus of whites, while in Rhodesia, the government of Ian Smith unilaterally declared independence from Britain in order to maintain the white minority's privileged position and prevent majority rule. Most nations joined Britain in refusing to recognize Smith's regime and imposing sanctions against it, but it was not until 1980, after a ten-year guerrilla war, that the people of Rhodesia—renamed Zimbabwe—established a state based on the principles of majority rule. By 1980, then, all of Britain's former colonial possessions in Africa were independent, as were most in Asia and the Caribbean; the only remnants of the British Empire were a scattering of small territories such as Hong Kong, Gibraltar, the Falkland Islands off the coast of Argentina, and several Caribbean islands. It is important to note, however, that these changes did not necessarily mean an end to hardship in Britain's former colonies; in many ways, the patterns of economic and cultural exploitation established by colonialism were altered but not erased in the post-colonial era.

The HMS *Antelope* under attack during the Falklands War, 1982. One case in which the British forcibly resisted efforts to wrest a colonial possession from their control was that of the Falkland Islands off the coast of Argentina, to which Argentina also laid claim. When the Argentinian Armed Forces invaded in April 1982, Margaret Thatcher's government declared war. By early June, the British had retaken the Islands, and on June 14, Argentina surrendered. Before the war Thatcher had been deeply unpopular; in its wake her popularity soared, and in 1983 she was re-elected in a landslide.

Doris Lessing was one of many post-war writers to focus in their fiction on the failings of colonialism. A few years before her novels and stories of southern Africa began to appear, Alan Paton's *Cry the Beloved Country* (1948), an emotionally powerful tale of the hardships suffered by black South Africans under white rule, had achieved enormous success. At first such hardships were recounted for a wide audience only in novels by white writers. In the 1960s and 1970s, however, a new generation of writers of color emerged, and rapidly achieved a place in the first rank of writing in English. Among the most important of these are V.S. Naipaul, whose major works include novels set in India (*A House for Mr. Biswas*, 1962), in Africa (*A Bend in the River*, 1979), and in his native Trinidad (*Miguel Street*, 1959); the Nigerian playwright Wole Soyinka, awarded the Nobel Prize for Literature in 1986; the Nigerian novelist Chinua Achebe, whose novels of struggle, corruption, and loss in the post-colonial era (*Things Fall Apart* [1958] most notable among them) have taken on iconic status; the Trinidadian poet Derek Walcott; and the Kenyan novelist Ngũgĩ wa Thiong'o.

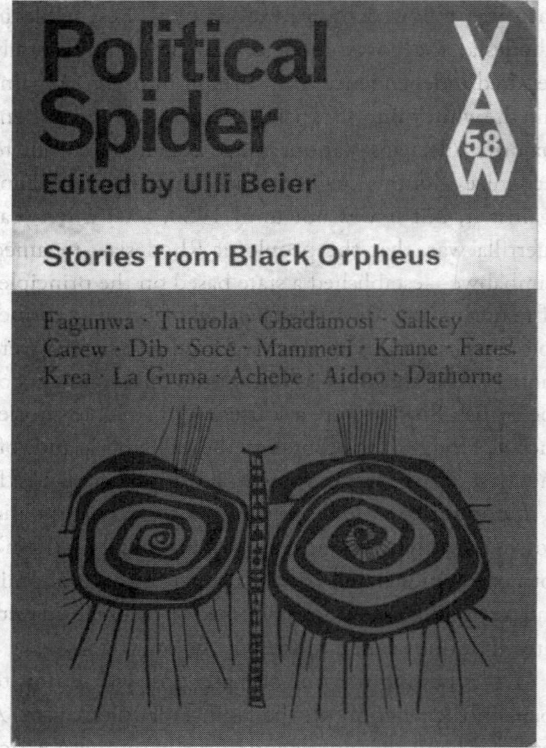

One of the most important vehicles with which African writing was brought to the attention of the rest of the world was the African Writers Series, launched by the UK publisher Heinemann in 1962 at the instigation of Alan Hill and initially under the general editorship of Chinua Achebe. By the end of 1969, the year that *Political Spider: Stories from Black Orpheus* was published, the series had grown to 82 titles, including Achebe's *Things Fall Apart* and *Arrow of God*; *Weep Not Child* and *A Grain of Wheat* by "James Ngugi" (Ngũgĩ wa Thiong'o); and Wole Soyinka's *The Interpreters.*

All of these authors deal pointedly with issues of colonialism and post-colonialism in their work. It is Ngũgĩ, however, who has raised most pointedly the issue of the ways in which politics and literature connect also with language. Ngũgĩ's early novels—including *A River Between* (1965), a novel about young people grappling with the conventions of tribal life in a world in which almost no one speaks English—were written in English, and Ngũgĩ established a worldwide reputation as an English novelist. In midlife, he decided for both personal and political reasons to write instead in his first language, Gikuyu; he argues persuasively in *Decolonizing the Mind* (1986) that English is inherently tainted by the culture of the colonizer: "language has a dual character; it is both a means of communication and a carrier of culture." The debate over this issue involved many of the leading writers in Britain's former colonies; Achebe and Soyinka were among those who decided to write some works in English, others in their first language. Even those who chose to write in English, however, no longer felt obliged to adopt the "correct" English of the English themselves; whether through the use of idioms, of non-standard syntax, or of local dialects and rhythms of speech, such writers have extended the linguistic range of literature in English.

While the 1960s and '70s saw an explosion of literature in English in nations newly independent from Britain, these decades also ushered in a new vibrancy and maturity in the literatures of Canada and Australia, which had long been formally independent from Britain but had retained into the 1950s a pervasive sense of Great Britain as "the mother country." By the '60s and '70s both nations were beginning to define themselves as much in terms of their relationship with the United States (and, in the case of Australia, with Asian countries) as they did in connection with their old relationship towards Britain. Here and there the work of important Canadian and Australian authors such as Margaret Atwood, P.K. Page, and Judith Wright illuminated the old connections with Britain, but just as often the work of these writers—like that of other major Australian and Canadian authors such as Patrick White (winner of the Nobel Prize in 1973), Les Murray, Peter Carey, Alice Munro, Carol Shields, and Michael Ondaatje—bears few traces of a British connection. Increasingly, indeed, literature in English had started to become more broadly international. Ondaatje, for example, has shown himself to be as comfortable writing about Italy and North Africa in World War II (in his Booker Prize-winning novel *The English Patient*) as he has writing about his native Sri Lanka and Canada. Rohinton Mistry has lived in Canada since he was 23, but he continues to set his major works—most notably his novel *A Fine Balance* (1996)—in his native India.

In a controversial award, the Beatles were appointed MBEs (Members of the British Empire) in 1965; the above image shows fans and police outside Buckingham Palace on the day.

From the 1960s to Century's End

Within Britain, the 1960s and '70s were also a time of cultural explosion—though here literature may be said to have shared the stage with other forms of cultural expression, most notably popular music. The music of The Beatles and The Rolling Stones played a central part in defining "the swinging '60s," but these groups were part of a much broader movement as a large generation of young people sought—through long hair, the lively clothing styles of Carnaby Street, and a new-found sexual freedom—to reject the values of their parents' generation.

Ironically, the most lasting literary reflections of this memorable cultural moment may not be in any literary expression of exuberance from the 1960s, but in detached and faintly critical after-the-fact poems on the subject by Larkin, such as "Annus Mirabilis":

> Sexual intercourse began
> In nineteen sixty-three
> (which was rather late for me)—
> Between the end of the *Chatterley* ban
> And the Beatles' first LP.

The comic novels of Amis and of David Lodge (notably *Changing Places*, 1975) also give some sense of the cultural moment. But several of the most important figures of British literature of these years maintained a considerable distance between their own work and the cultural ferment of the times. Lawrence Durrell completed the last of his series of evocative novels of the Anglo-Egyptian world, *The Alexandria Quartet*, in 1960; Anthony Powell continued to publish novels in his unique sequence *A Dance to the Music of Time*; and William Golding, who had burst onto the literary scene in 1954 with *Lord of the Flies*, a horrific depiction of young boys forced to create a society for themselves, continued to publish novelistic explorations of the psyche and of ethical questions.

One of the most important poetic voices to emerge in Britain in the 1960s and '70s also maintained a certain distance from the cultural mainstream; the focus of Ted Hughes's work remained largely on the natural world, and on the ways in which humans might connect to that world on a primal level. Doris Lessing, however, with the publication of her novel *The Golden Notebook* (1962), most certainly did connect with the mainstream of social and cultural change. Along with the non-fiction work *The Female Eunuch* by the Australian Germaine Greer, *The Golden Notebook* became a touchstone for women as they realized the extent to which they had been suppressed by the patriarchal structures and attitudes of society.

Lord of the Flies has sold exceptionally well ever since its publication in 1954—including to high schools. This still from Peter Brook's 1963 film version of *Lord of the Flies* was also used as a cover image for the "educational edition" of the book the same year.

Sirkka-Liisa Konttinen, *Kendal Street*, 1969. A member of the Amber collective, between 1969 and 1983 Finnish-born Konttinen documented the life and eventual demolition of Byker, a terraced community in Newcastle upon Tyne in northern England. In 2003 she and Amber returned to document the Byker Wall Estate that replaced it.

Committed as politicians had been to egalitarianism from the 1940s through to the 1970s, they had been largely unable to loosen the control that the British upper class and upper middle class continued to exert over key elements of British society. Perhaps the most egregious expression of this control was the connection that continued to exist between the best jobs and the old established universities. In almost all professions, preference continued to be given to graduates of Oxford and Cambridge. Though the Education Act of 1944 had put forward measures to increase the number of working-class students at British universities, many of the old attitudes persisted.

Ironically, it may have been a Conservative rather than a Labour government that challenged the old ethos most successfully. Margaret Thatcher (Prime Minister from 1979 to 1990), represented a very different brand of Conservatism from that of Winston Churchill and earlier Conservatives, much as she admired him and shared some of the old notions of Britain as a power in world affairs. A grocer's daughter, she stood in her own way as firmly against the restrictions of a hierarchical class structure as did her political opponents. But whereas Labour had sought to achieve equity by creating a welfare state, Thatcher aimed to do so by bringing the universities to heel, creating a sense of empowerment among the working class and lower middle class—and dismantling much of the welfare state in order to lower taxes. Thatcher succeeded in changing a great many British attitudes over the eleven years she held power, but in the course of doing so she fiercely divided the nation.

The 18 years of Conservative party government in Britain from 1979 to 1997—for the most part under Thatcher as Prime Minister—was a period in which government support for culture was cut back. In a series of moves that paralleled developments in the United States under Ronald Reagan, Thatcher attacked the foundations of the welfare state and conveyed a sense that Britain's cultural identity was to be expressed through fiercely defending the last remnants of Empire (she led a war against Argentina over the Falkland Islands in 1982) and in resisting integration with continental Europe rather than in fostering cultural expression through literature, music, and the visual arts. Ironically, this period saw perhaps the greatest flowering of British literature since the first decades of the twentieth century. Novelists were especially prominent, with Margaret Drabble, A.S. Byatt, Ian McEwan, Martin Amis, Graham Swift, and Jeanette Winterson all creating impressive bodies of work. Ironically, too, literature in Britain experienced a cultural broadening that stands in direct contrast to the narrowness of Thatcher's cultural focus. Britain itself was increasingly becoming a multi-cultural society with the continuing influx of immigrants from former British possessions; more and more, that diversity began to shape the British literary scene. Among the major figures of British literature during this period are Salman Rushdie, a novelist with a Pakistani family background whose works—from *Midnight's Children* (1980) and *Shame* (1983) to *Shalimar's Clown* (2005)—explore the cultures of India and Pakistan as much as they do that of Britain; Vikram Seth, another novelist whose major works (most notable among them *A Suitable Boy*, 1993) are set in India; Zadie Smith, who burst onto the literary scene in 2000 with a wide-ranging novel of post-colonial communities in England, *White Teeth*, and whose 2012 novel *NW* (after the postal code of north-west London) offered further insight into the ways in which race and class interact in modern Britain; and Nagasaki-born Kazuo Ishiguro, whose Japanese heritage informs much of his work but who has lived in Britain since the age of six.

Ishiguro's best known work, *The Remains of the Day* (1989), recounts the story of a British butler in a country house where collaborators with the Nazi regime are holding secret meetings; the novel has been widely acclaimed as a fully rounded fictional expression of life under the old British class system, and of the stifling of human feeling under the sense of reserve that formed an integral part of that system. Much of Ishiguro's other work is set in the world of post-war Japan (*A Pale View of Hills*, 1982) and/or in dreamlike worlds that resist identification with fixed geographical or temporal locations (*The Unconsoled*, 1995). In his acclaimed novel *Never Let Me Go* (2005), young people are prepared for a mysterious fate at a boarding school in an English countryside where the precise geographical setting remains vague, and the temporal setting in an unspecified future even more so.

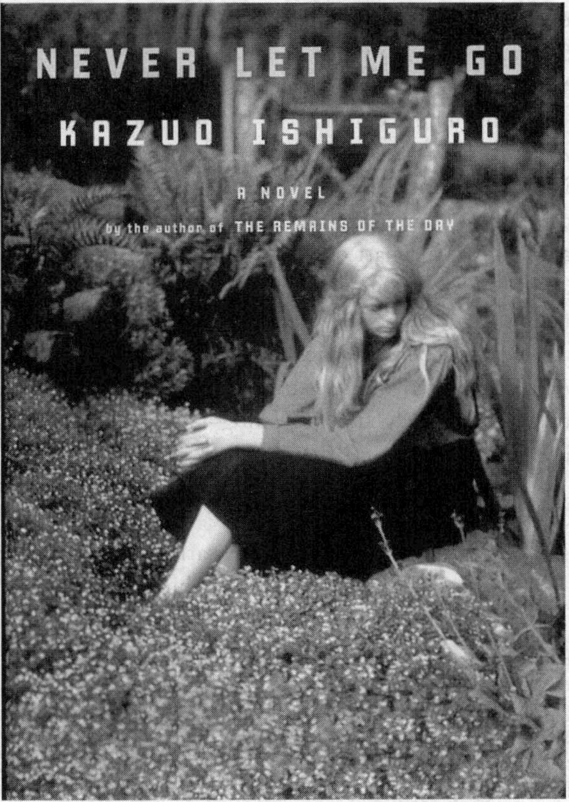

The image on this cover of Ishiguro's *Never Let Me Go* is "Christina," from a famous 1912–13 series of photographs by Lieutenant-Colonel Mervyn O'Gorman of his daughters.

Like the literatures of Canada and Australia, that of Britain in the late twentieth and early twenty-first centuries was often more difficult to place. The diversity of British writing also came to be expressed during this period through an increased openness regarding sexual orientation. Sex between men, punishable by imprisonment in the earlier part of the century, was largely decriminalized in England and Wales in 1967, and in Scotland and Northern Ireland in the early 1980s. Whereas leading writers such as W.H. Auden in the 1930s and Thom Gunn in the 1950s had left Britain for America in large part because American cities such as New York and San Francisco were then far more accepting of same-sex orientation than was London (let alone any other part of the British Isles), in the 1980s and 1990s gay and lesbian writers such as Hanif Kureishi and Jeanette Winterson remained in Britain and became central figures of London's literary culture. And in the twenty-first century, Carol Ann Duffy came to be acknowledged as a leading—arguably, *the* leading—poetic voice in Britain.

Diversity of form and style also became increasingly characteristic of British literature in the 1980s and 1990s. Poets such as Geoffrey Hill carried on something akin to the Modernist tradition, while poets such as Tony Harrison infused their work with powerful political content; poets such as Alice Oswald revived and extended traditions of English nature poetry; and poets such as Grace Nichols, Moniza Alvi, and Linton Kwesi Johnson gave full expression to the new Britain. Women poets came to the fore as never before, in Ireland as well as in Britain, with Eavan Boland and Medbh McGuckian particularly highly regarded.

The 1980s and 1990s may in some respects be characterized as the era of postmodernism in British literary culture; *postmodern* is a notoriously slippery term, however, and one worth pausing over. The most fruitful avenue of approach may be to look at Modernism and postmodernism side by side. In some ways postmodernism represents a reaction to Modernism, in others an extension of it—and in many ways the history of the one parallels that of the other. As Modernism had been the leading artistic and intellectual movement of the second and third decades of the twentieth century, so was postmodernism during the century's final two decades—at least in literature and the visual arts. Both Modernism and postmodernism may be said to have begun in France—Modernism with poets such as Arthur Rimbaud and Stephane Mallarmé and the Post-Impressionist and Cubist painters, postmodernism with philosophers such as Jacques Derrida and Michel Foucault. Modernism had at its core a rejection of traditional artistic forms and a tendency towards fragmentation of meaning as well as of form. The breaking down of the image in poetry and in painting was accompanied by extensive theorizing—by Mallarmé and the French

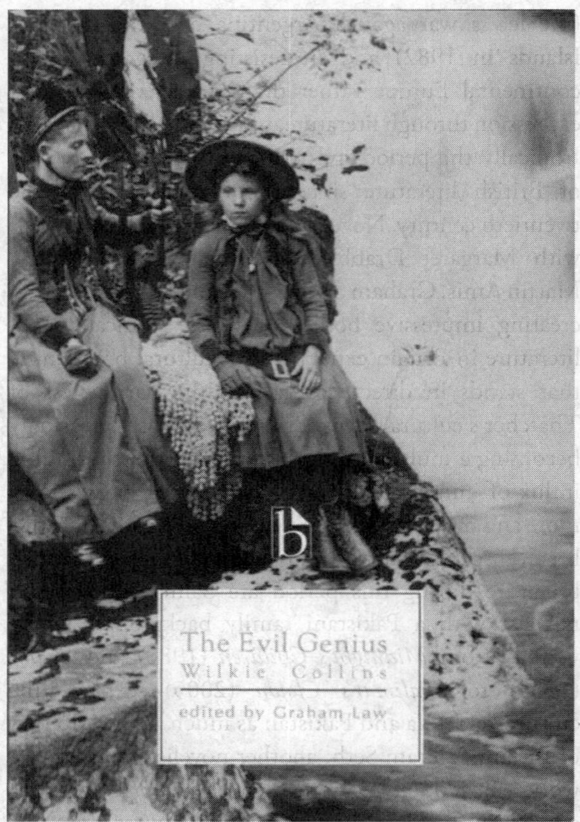

Graham Law's edition of Wilkie Collins's *The Evil Genius*, one of the series-launching batch of four Broadview Literary Texts published in 1994. Even as English Studies focused to an unprecedented degree in the 1980s and '90s on literary theory, the discipline was also becoming increasingly aware of the importance of historicizing literary works—understanding them first of all in the cultural context out of which they emerged. An important related publishing venture was the launch of the Broadview series (later renamed Broadview Editions), which includes within each volume appendices of relevant historical and cultural documents.

Symbolists, by Ezra Pound and the Imagists, by the Italian Futurists, and by various others. Postmodernism was even more deeply colored by theory; indeed, it may be said to have begun at the "meta" level of theorizing rather than at the level of practice. It is notoriously resistant to definition—indeed, resistance to fixed definitions is itself a characteristic of postmodernism. Like Modernism, postmodernism embraces difficulty and distrusts the simple and straightforward. More broadly, postmodernism is characterized by a rejection of absolute truth or value, of closed systems, of grand unified narratives. As the French social philosopher Jean Baudrillard put it in 1987, "truth is what we should rid ourselves of as fast as possible and pass it on to somebody else. As with illnesses, it's the only way to be cured of it. He who hangs on to truth has lost."

As a style of discourse rather than a philosophical system, postmodernist theory dominated the academic study of literature in British and North American universities through much of the 1980s and 1990s. Postmodernism never came to dominate literature itself during that period to anything like the same degree, but the 1980s and 1990s fictions of Rushdie, Byatt, Ishiguro, Winterson, and Will Self, among others, often played with reality and illusion in ways that could be broadly characterized as postmodern. Works such as Byatt's novel *Possession* (1990) and Winterson's *Written on the Body* (1992), for example, display a willingness to combine different styles or forms in a single work—just as in architecture the postmodernist spirit embodies a willingness to borrow from seemingly disparate styles in designing a single structure.

One of the main thrusts of Modernism had been to apprehend consciousness directly in its often-chaotic progression. The main thrust of postmodernism, by contrast, was one of analysis more than of direct apprehension; the characteristic spirit of postmodernism is one of *self*-consciousness, of a highly attuned awareness to the problematized state of the writer, artist, or theorist as observer. Often that awareness encompasses a playfulness with regard to time—as famously expressed, for example, in the opening lines of Rushdie's Booker Prize-winning novel *Midnight's Children* (1980): "I was born in the city of Bombay ... once upon a time. No, that won't do, there's no getting away from the date."

British drama, which was influenced both by Modernism and by postmodernism, experienced great success throughout most of the second half of the twentieth century, and the beginning of the twenty-first. Major figures such as Harold Pinter and Tom Stoppard followed on from the work of Samuel Beckett in the attention that they paid to life's absurdity. In his most important plays, Pinter's focus was on personal and family relationships, whereas Stoppard's was on surprising conjunctions of circumstance and large ideas. In the groundbreaking *Rosencrantz and Guildenstern Are Dead* (1967), for example, he rewrote Shakespeare's *Hamlet* from the point of view of two of its most minor characters; in *Arcadia* (1993), which takes place both in the present and in the early years of the nineteenth century, he brought together ideas about eighteenth-century formal gardens, the science of Isaac Newton, and the life of Byron. Other leading dramatists of the period extended the frontiers of British drama in a variety of other directions. David Hare combined elements of realism with an often larger-than-life framework in plays such as *Plenty* (1978); Caryl Churchill experimented broadly with form in plays such as *Cloud Nine* (1979) and *Top Girls* (1982)—the latter informed both by an ear for dialogue closely attuned to the realities of contemporary Britain and by Churchill's strong feminist convictions; Alan Ayckbourn displayed a talent for farce in the extraordinary tour-de-force *The Norman Conquests*, and a deep sense, as well, of the ways in which the apparently meaningless surface details of life relate to its sad undertones; and Michael Frayn created works ranging from farce as broad as that of Ayckbourn (as in *Noises Off*, 1982) to large scale dramas of ideas (such as *Copenhagen*, 1998) as ambitious as those of Stoppard.

As British literature underwent these changes in the last few decades of the twentieth century, so too did it expand to embrace a range of new modes of expression. In the 1940s and 1950s, Graham Greene had been a rarity among major British writers in his willingness to write screenplays for films based on his works. By the end of the century, however, "crossover" writing of this sort had become common with Harold Pinter, Tom Stoppard, Hanif Kureishi, Neil Jordan, and Irvine Welsh among those who had written screenplays based on their novels or plays. Many also wrote for television; indeed, some of the finest drama of the era was written for the BBC. Some regularly scheduled British television programs may also lay claim to being among the more important works of the second half of the twentieth century. The comedy sketches of *Monty Python's Flying Circus* invented a new form of absurdist comedy in the early 1970s; the twelve episodes of *Fawlty Towers* (1975) set what some argued to be entirely new standards of farce; and the many episodes of *Yes, Minister* and its sequel *Yes, Prime Minister* introduced a new brand of cynical and yet warmly human comedy about the workings of British politics. Arguably, later television programs such as *The Office* (2001–02) and *Extras* (2005–07) have reached an equally high standard of comedy.

A gaping hole in front of the Grand Hotel in Brighton, site of the Conservative Party's conference in October 1980, was the result of an IRA bomb. Five were killed and many others injured; Prime Minister Thatcher was in her suite at the hotel when the explosion occurred, but was unharmed. An IRA statement acknowledged that Thatcher had been a target; "Today we were unlucky, but remember—we only have to be lucky once: you will have to be lucky always."

IRELAND, SCOTLAND, WALES

The establishment of the Republic of Ireland in 1949 did not bring enduring peace to the island. With the six Ulster counties of Northern Ireland remaining a part of the United Kingdom of Great Britain and Northern Ireland, there was ongoing tension and, beginning in the late 1960s, almost recurrent violence over the status of Northern Ireland. The conflict came to be referred to as "The Troubles." A cycle of violence and repression continued, into the 1990s, as the Irish Republican Army (IRA) launched attacks on targets in England as well as in Northern Ireland, and the police and the British army launched repeated crackdowns, often involving considerable brutality. Staunchly Protestant Northern Irish politicians (the Reverend Ian Paisley most prominent among them) vowed "no surrender" to those who sought a compromise solution with Ireland and the Catholic minority in Northern Ireland.

In the late 1970s and early 1980s, a series of hunger strikes by IRA prisoners under British internment heightened tensions still further, and even after an Anglo-Irish agreement in 1985, periodic ceasefires brought only temporary cessations of conflict. In 1997, however, the IRA was persuaded to declare a ceasefire that showed promise of holding, and its political arm, Sinn Fein, joined in the multilateral Stormont talks aimed at finding a lasting solution. On 10 April 1998, an agreement was finally signed by the British and Irish governments. The Belfast Agreement (or "Good Friday Agreement") was endorsed by the major political parties of Ireland and of Northern Ireland, and in separate referendums by the electorates of both Ireland and Northern Ireland. Among the key provisions of the agreement were a commitment by all involved to an exclusively peaceful and democratic approach to change;

abandonment by the Republic of its territorial claim to Northern Ireland; acceptance of the principle that the citizens of Northern Ireland had the right to determine by majority vote their constitutional future (in other words, partition was formally accepted, but so was the possibility that the Northern Irish could one day vote to join the Republic); and provision for a Northern Ireland Assembly to which additional power would devolve from the British government (still leaving Northern Ireland as part of the United Kingdom). Troubles of one sort or another remained in both Ireland and Northern Ireland, but "The Troubles" ended with the 1998 agreement; leaders on both sides were awarded the Nobel Peace Prize for their efforts.

Murals in Belfast, 2011. There is a long tradition in cities such as Belfast and Derry of decorating fences and walls with murals—many of them highly political in nature. The content of murals was often inflammatory and militaristic during the long period of the Troubles in the twentieth century, when fighting between Catholic and Protestant—and the stark division of cities into Catholic and Protestant neighborhoods—found expression in murals with starkly different messages. Newer murals are more likely to confront squarely the history of British colonialism in Ireland than to take issue between Protestant and Catholic—and many newer murals convey messages of peace rather than of antagonism. Older murals documenting the sectarian strife have not disappeared, though; many have been preserved and restored, as reminders of an earlier time few wish to return to.

Perhaps as important to the evolution of late twentieth- and early twenty-first-century Ireland as the coming of peace have been a precipitous decline of religious authority over Irish life and an extraordinary economic boom that has transformed the economy, particularly of the Irish Republic. Ireland was slower than other Roman-Catholic-dominated societies of Europe (such as France, Italy, and Spain) to distance itself from the more socially conservative pronouncements of the papacy. Not until 1995, for example, was divorce permitted under Irish law. But over the past generation, Ireland was steadily becoming a more secular society—and the process began to accelerate in the second decade of the new century. In 2015 same-sex marriage was legalized when 62% expressed their approval in a referendum, and the same year brought recognition of the right of transgender people to legally change gender without medical intervention. The year 2017 saw the election of *Taoiseach* (or Prime Minister) Leo Varadkar, which many interpreted as a symbol of the continuing liberalization of Irish values: Varadkar is Ireland's first openly gay Taoiseach, as well as the first Taoiseach of immigrant background (his father having been born in India). In 2018, following another referendum, the government began moving to legalize abortion.

Over the course of a remarkably brief period in the 1980s and 1990s, Ireland also went from being one of the poorest countries in Europe to one of the wealthiest and most dynamic. Changed attitudes, a highly educated workforce, and programs to encourage particular sectors of high-tech industry wrought an extraordinary economic transformation (albeit one that was followed by a devastating recession in 2008–13).

Perhaps not surprisingly, given these circumstances, one of the most engaging literary treatments in all of English literature of the transformative effects of capitalism on the human psyche emerged from this period of economic and cultural change in Ireland. Dublin novelist Roddy Doyle's *The Van* (1991) deals with a variety of business start-up—a fish-and-chip van—that is at the opposite end of the economic spectrum from the high-tech businesses that were the well-publicized stars of Ireland's economic transformation. But in the tragicomic microcosm that Doyle creates, he captures with deep understanding the ways in which energy, imagination, and heartlessness fuse together in the heated environment in which businesses grow. (Doyle's distinguished body of work includes two trilogies, among them the Barrytown trilogy of which *The Van* forms a part, as well as his 1993 Booker Prize-winning novel of childhood, *Paddy Clarke Ha Ha Ha*.)

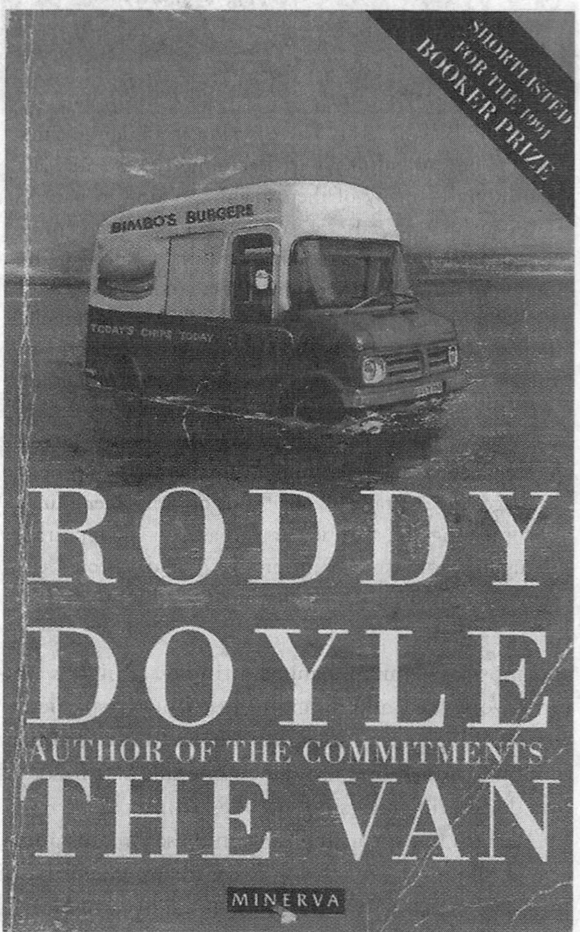

Cover of Doyle's *The Van*, Secker & Warburg, 1991.

The Irish contribution to the literature of the English-speaking world was scarcely less in the late twentieth century than it had been in the extraordinary period 1890–1960—the period of Oscar Wilde, George Bernard Shaw, J.M. Synge, W.B. Yeats, James Joyce, and Samuel Beckett. Interestingly, a disproportionate number of the important Irish writers of the late twentieth and early twenty-first centuries are poets of Northern Irish background—among them Seamus Heaney, Derek Mahon, Medbh McGuckian, Paul Muldoon, and Tom Paulin. (It is important to note here that Heaney self-identified as Irish, as do some others on this list, rather than Northern Irish.) The list of important Irish writers in this period, however, includes writers in all genres and regions, from the short story writer William Trevor, whose work often engages with the Catholic-Protestant tensions he witnessed during his early years in a Protestant family in County Cork; to the acclaimed poet and Dubliner Eavan Boland, groundbreaking in her exploration of women's experiences and history at a time when Irish poetry was heavily male-dominated; to the fiction-writer and film-maker Neil Jordan, a native of County Sligo in the northwest of Ireland, whose *The Crying Game* (1992) remains among the most memorable depictions of "The Troubles"; to the novelist Edna O'Brien, whose reaction against her childhood in what she later described as the "enclosed, fervid, and bigoted" atmosphere of the 1930s in a small village in County Clare colored much of her later fiction; to the novelist and Belfast native (in later life, Canadian citizen) Brian Moore; to the novelist, journalist, and Wexford native John Banville, whose *The Sea* (2005) was awarded the Booker Prize; to Dublin dramatist and film-maker Conor McPherson, whose plays *The Weir* (1997) and *Shining City* (2004) explore the worlds of the living and the dead, and the ways in which Ireland continues to be possessed by its past; and to Colm Tóibín, among whose most acclaimed works are fictionalized treatments of the lives of Henry James (*The Master*, 2004) and of Mary, mother of Jesus (*The Testament of Mary*, 2012). Writers who choose to write in Irish have also gained prominence—perhaps most notable among them the poet Nuala Ní Dhomhnaill, whose collections have often appeared with facing page English translations.

Discontent with the dominant role played by England within Great Britain was a constant throughout the twentieth century in both Wales and Scotland, though in neither case was there a history of violence. In 1997 Tony Blair's Labour Party included in its election platform a commitment to devolution—a granting of power by the central government to proposed regional governments in Scotland and Wales. (Unlike the allocation of powers in a federal system, the granting of power under a system of devolution may be reversed; ultimate authority continues to reside with the central government.) Labour was elected with a solid majority, and devolution was approved in Scottish and Welsh referendums in the autumn of 1997; elections for the new Scottish Parliament and Welsh National assembly were held in May 1999, and since then the two regional governments have assumed a variety of responsibilities in such areas as health, housing, education, and culture.

In the twenty-first century, however, an increasing percentage in Scotland came to desire not merely a greater devolution of powers, but outright independence. The Scottish National Party, which favors independence, first came to power in the Scottish Parliament with a minority government in 2007. They won the largest number of seats in the Scottish elections of 2011 and 2016 as well, and in 2014 the SNP held a referendum on the issue of whether or not Scotland should become independent. Though the "No" side won, the vote (55% to 45%) was close enough to sustain hope in the SNP that they would indeed be able to attain independence in the not too distant future.

The UK election of 2015 and the referendum on EU membership in 2016 provided further evidence that Scotland was moving in a different direction than was England. In 2015 (under new leader Nicola Sturgeon) the SNP won 56 of 59 Scottish seats in the UK general election, essentially replacing the Labour Party as the left-of-center alternative to the Conservatives for Scottish voters. And in the referendum on EU membership, a decisive majority of Scottish voters voted to remain in the EU, with only 38% voting "Leave."

Important Scottish and Welsh writers of the second half of the twentieth century include the Scottish novelist Muriel Spark, the Scottish fiction writer James Kelman, the Scottish poet Edwin Muir, the Welsh poets Dylan Thomas and Gillian Clarke, and the Welsh fiction writers Rhys Davies and Raymond Williams (the latter better-known outside Wales as a literary and cultural critic). Moving into the twenty-first century, important twenty-first century Welsh writers include the multi-genre writer Owen Sheers, the Welsh-language novelist Angharad Price, and the poet Gwyneth Lewis, who writes both in English and in Welsh. In 2005 Lewis was named Wales's first Poet Laureate. Significant Scottish writers include the poet John Burnside and the novelist and short-story writer Ali Smith. Smith's novels—such as *Hotel World* (2001), *There but for the* (2011), *Autumn* (2016), and *Winter* (2017)—are notable for their experimental narrative style and structure. Much of her work is also distinguished by its remarkable immediacy in commenting on current political events in Britain (*Autumn* has frequently been described as an important post-Brexit novel).

Concern over the preservation of local language has been a constant both in Scotland and in Wales. The language known as Gaelic in Scotland, where it is the traditional language of the Highlands, is closely related to the language known in Ireland simply as Irish. On either side of the Irish Sea these languages were long under pressure from the English, but both were substantially revived in Scotland and Ireland over the course of the twentieth century. In Ireland, both Irish and English are official languages, and at the time of the 2011 census more than 1,770,000 were able to speak at least some Irish; in Scotland, there were in the late twentieth century approximately 80,000 able to speak Gaelic—though this number had declined to 57,000 by 2011. Lowland Scots, on the other hand, is a variant of English—a very substantially different dialect from that spoken by most in England, but still a related tongue. It, too, was considered to be threatened by "Standard English," but determined efforts were made in the twentieth century to maintain its vitality. In the early twentieth century, the poet and political activist Hugh MacDiarmid (1892–1978) played a leading role in such efforts. A founder in 1928 of the National Party of Scotland, MacDiarmid worked to revive many of the words he found in John Jamieson's 1808 *Etymological*

Dictionary of the Scottish Language, and enjoyed considerable success in reviving Scots as a language of poetry. And in the late twentieth and early twenty-first centuries, Lowland Scots has remained very much alive, in literature as well as in speech. Such is the case, for example, with the Edinburgh dialect that is reproduced by the novelist and film-maker Irvine Welsh in *Trainspotting* (novel 1993; film screenplay 1996): "Johnny wis a junky as well as a dealer. Ye hud tae go a wee bit further up the ladder before ye found a dealer whae didnae use."

Like Gaelic/Irish, Welsh is a language quite distinct from English. From the time of Henry VIII until the second half of the twentieth century, the Welsh language had been in more or less steady decline. Henry VIII had united England and Wales and forbidden the use of Welsh for official purposes with the 1536 Statute of Wales and the 1542 Acts of Union. In 1962, however, as a central element in the budding Welsh nationalist movement, a Welsh Language Society (Cymdeithas yr Iaith Gymraeg) was formed, and in 1967 its protests prompted the British Government to pass the Welsh Language Act, assigning equal status within Wales to Welsh and English—and declaring Wales to be no longer an official part of England. Since then the teaching of Welsh has been made an integral part of the educational system, and public agencies are obliged to offer bilingual service. It is now estimated that over 560,000 people in Wales are bilingual in Welsh and English.

The New Millennium

Through the era of Conservative government under Thatcher and John Major, Britain remained deeply divided politically—over cultural politics and issues such as immigration policy; the extent to which Britain should be a free market economy or a social democratic one; and over foreign affairs. With the coming to power of Tony Blair and "New Labour," as the Labour Party began to style itself in 1994, a new era dawned in British politics. Blair had blunted the power of the unions within his own party, and the party now blended its long-standing commitment to social justice with a commitment to economic enterprise and to modernity that many felt had been sorely lacking in the Labour Party for the previous generation or more. At century's end, long-divisive issues such as the racial composition of Britain and the conflict in Northern Ireland seemed far less divisive than they had been in the preceding decades. Constitutional reforms had included not only the devolution of considerable power to new assemblies in Scotland and Wales but also a phasing-out of the hereditary peerage; no longer would one be able to inherit a seat in the House of Lords. Class divisions had receded, and Britons expressed a fresh confidence and a fresh sense of unity. The British seemed to have finally come to terms with their place in the world—a position of far less importance than that which they had held a century earlier, but one that no longer forced them to carry the economic and moral baggage associated with the maintenance of the British Empire. It was also a position of surprising strength economically—particularly in the south of England, with London consolidating its position as one of the financial centers of the world. Britain seemed to be in the forefront culturally, too. In the visual arts and in fashion, London held a central place, with publicity generating an annual furor over the awarding of the Turner Prize for best work by a British artist under the age of 50, and with brashly controversial artists such as Damien Hirst, Chris Ofili, and Gillian Wearing and celebrity collectors such as advertising mogul Charles Saatchi driving a culture of "Sensation" (to echo the name of the highly controversial 1997 and 2000 exhibitions from the Saatchi Collection in London and Brooklyn, respectively). London also could arguably claim to be the literary center of the world. "Rule, Britannia" had been Britain's defining song at its Imperial zenith; "Cool Britannia" was the term now coined to define Britain. During the millennium celebrations of 2000, Britain was as confident, as united, and as prosperous as it had been at any time since the great celebrations over the Diamond Jubilee of Queen Victoria, 100 years before Tony Blair, New Labour, and "Cool Britannia."

The sky over Britain at the millennium was far from cloudless, however, and in the early years of the twenty-first century many perceived Britain's problems as standing out in bolder relief than her triumphs. In the first few years of the twentieth century the British people—the *English* people, especially—were stereotypically thought of as a people of civility and self-restraint, adhering to religion and religious propriety, and possessing a modesty that verged on prudery. In the first few years of the twenty-first century the stereotype of the British—again, the *English*, especially—included the behavior of the "lager louts" that went on nightly rampages in city centers; the lowest rates of church attendance in Europe; drunken hooliganism among soccer fans, displayed since the 1970s at matches across Europe as well as at home; and poverty-stricken and largely racially defined ghettos in post-industrial towns such as Leeds—areas which, as the suicide bombings on the London transport system in 2005 made painfully clear, could become breeding grounds for terrorism. According to social critics such as Theodore Dalrymple in works such as *Life at the Bottom* (2002), the lack of civility commonly associated with an alienated underclass was becoming more and more pervasive throughout all Britain, fueled by a "radical egotism" that had taken root in the new cultural freedom of the 1960s and that had become more and more strongly tainted during the late 1970s and the Thatcher years by materialism and uncaring individualism.

Grafted onto concern over these domestic issues was a broad concern over the place of a new Britain in a changed world. Was Britain's appropriate role that of aggressive ally to an increasingly bellicose United States? Could intervention in other nations' affairs, on either humanitarian or strategic grounds, be readily justified in a world in which concerns about terrorism, about human rights, and about the potential for a world-wide clash of cultures were coming to the fore? Britain's participation in the early twenty-first century wars in Afghanistan and Iraq provided powerful fuel for these debates.

These troubled aspects of British life are memorably represented in the literature of the late twentieth and early twenty-first centuries. The hooliganism that began to plague England in the late 1960s and 1970s was foreshadowed in Anthony Burgess's novel *A Clockwork Orange* (1962), in which the protagonist, fifteen-year-old Alex DeLarge, leads a gang that commits a variety of violent crimes purely for the "kick" it gives them. The early fiction of Ian McEwan—perhaps most notably his first novel, *The Cement Garden* (1978)—depicts the grim plight of young people fending for themselves in the bleakness of a post-industrial landscape. The occasion for Tony Harrison's wide-ranging long poem *v* (1985) was the graffiti left on gravestones by Leeds United soccer hooligans; in a cemetery above the ground where "Leeds United play but disappoint their fans week after week," the fans "spray words on tombstones, pissed on beer":

Subsidence makes the obelisks all list.
One leaning left's marked FUCK, one right's
  marked SHIT
sprayed by some peeved supporter who was pissed....

In some cases the graffiti is football-related as well as foul-mouthed:

Or, more expansively, there's LEEDS v.
the opponent of last week, this week, or next,
and a repertoire of blunt four-letter curses
on the team or race that makes the sprayer vexed.

And, Harrison suggests, there is a wider resonance to these oppositions:

These Vs are all the versuses of life
From LEEDS v. DERBY, Black/White
and (as I've known to my cost) man v. wife,
Communist v. Fascist, Left v. Right,

Class v. class as bitter as before,
the unending violence of US and THEM ...

Hanif Kureishi's *My Son the Fanatic* (both a short story and a screenplay for a film, 1997) depicts the violent radicalization in Britain of Islamic youth as a reaction to what they see as the hypocrisy and decadence of their fathers' assimilated Britishness. Caryl Churchill's work—notably her short apocalyptic play *Far Away* (2000)—

presents a world in which individuals abandon responsibility for one another, and in which the possibility of wider and wider conflict (not only nations or civilizations at war with one another, but also the human at war with the non-human environment) is beginning to seem increasingly real. And Ian McEwan's celebrated novel *Saturday* (2005) expresses an ambivalence towards violence that at the time was coming to seem a part of British life—violence both on the streets of Britain and overseas. That novel, which concerns a surgeon who becomes terrorized by violent criminals and is provoked to violent response, is set against a backdrop of looming military conflict in Iraq. Asked if he is "for the war," the beleaguered surgeon Henry Perowne replies, "I'm not for any war. But this one could be the lesser evil. In five years' time we'll know." Five years on and more, it was still being argued whether the war in Iraq (or that in Afghanistan) could be considered a "lesser evil": most Britons thought not.

In the space of a few hours in 2005 Britain experienced the extremes of jubilation and anguish as four coordinated terrorist attacks by suicide bombers (three of them British born) shook the London Transport system less than 24 hours after London had been announced as the surprise winner in the competition to host the 2012 Summer Olympics. Those experiences pointed in dramatically different directions. Would the lively spirit that animated Britain culturally and economically at the turn of the millennium continue to flourish and expand, with the 2012 Olympics taking its place as a symbol of a renewed nation? Or would the shadows that had been cast across modern Britain lengthen—and darken?

Gordon Brown, Blair's successor as Prime Minister, struggled in the face of scandals, the worldwide recession of 2008–09, and a widespread perception that "New Labour" had gone stale. Meanwhile Britain's Conservative Party, after years of indirection, began under David Cameron to find its way as a more modern and moderate party. The election of May 2010 gave the Conservatives the most seats—though as a minority looking for support to Britain's third party, Nick Clegg's Liberal Democrats. Many saw the rise of Cameron—like Clegg, an energetic and forward-looking young leader whose policies often cut across ideological lines—as signaling a return to the spirit not of the previous Conservative era dominated by Margaret Thatcher, but rather to that of the early days of Tony Blair and New Labour in the 1990s. But Cameron found it difficult to maintain the delicate balance required for a successful coalition government. Much of his Conservative base was made unhappy by his attempt to reform the House of Lords (abandoned in 2012 in the face of stiff opposition), by his support of same-sex marriage, and by his reluctance to turn Britain away from the European Union. Yet his efforts to weave back and forth in search of a middle ground often left his Liberal Democratic partners unhappy too. And the country as a whole was left unhappy by the performance of Britain's economy; in late 2011 and early 2012 the country endured another economic downturn.

Cameron made what many feel was his worst mistake during the election campaign of 2015, when, largely in order to quell anti-EU feelings within his own party, he promised a renegotiation of the terms of Britain's membership in the EU, and a referendum on the fundamental question of whether Britain should or should not remain in the European Union. He managed to unify the Conservative Party and win the election with a majority, but the limited concessions he was able to extract from the rest of the union on the terms of Britain's membership left many unconvinced that the advantages of EU membership outweighed the disadvantages. To the astonishment of pollsters, 52% of voters in the June 2016 referendum chose "Brexit," with only 48% voting to remain in the EU.

The referendum results revealed huge fissures in British society. Those who had completed university degrees voted "Remain" by a margin of 68% to 32%, and many highly educated Britons (both right-of-center and left-of-center politically) were dismayed by the referendum results. It had long been taken for granted in these circles that Britain was a European nation, with unbreakable ties to continental Europe that were cultural as well as economic in nature. Young middle-class Britons welcomed their freedom to travel and to find employment anywhere on the continent (71% of 18–24-

year olds voted "Remain"), and felt that the welcome Britain extended in the other direction to Europeans made the country richer in every way—in terms of cultural diversity as much as economic strength. Much of that strength had been built on the success of the city of London as a European financial and cultural center, but EU membership had brought significant benefits to much of the populous south-east of the country as well. It was much less clear that the north of the country—the old industrial heartland—or in more heavily rural areas (such as Devon and Somerset in the southwest, and Norfolk and Lincolnshire in the East Midlands) had benefited economically from being part of the EU, and certainly many in these areas were less comfortable with the greater diversity that had accompanied EU membership. (Outside the London-Brighton, London-Oxford, and London-Cambridge corridors, virtually all areas of England voted "Leave"—as did 52.5% of voters in Wales.) The UK Independence Party (led by Nigel Farange) was especially active in stoking the fires of resentment with their campaign against multiculturalism and alleged "Islamification," but many in the Conservative Party (61% of whose members voted "Leave") expressed similarly xenophobic views in less inflammatory language.

In the wake of the referendum debacle, David Cameron stepped down as Prime Minister, to be replaced (rather unexpectedly) by the previous Home Secretary, Theresa May. Though she had supported the "Remain" side in the referendum, May promised to follow the wishes of the electorate as expressed in that vote and negotiate a smooth withdrawal from the Union. As she discovered, doing so was anything but easy, particularly since Brexit had been vehemently opposed by a majority in Northern Ireland. How could one withdraw from the EU and yet retain (as everyone wished to retain) an open border between Ireland and Northern Ireland?

As Britain's close cultural ties to Europe have seemed in danger of fraying, its cultural ties to America have arguably grown stronger than ever. On television, a longstanding tradition of successful British exports has continued; crime dramas such as *Broadchurch*, *Sherlock*, and *Luther* have attracted large audiences in North America (just as *Prime Suspect*, *Cracker*, and *Inspector Morse* did a generation earlier), and a tradition of successful historical drama has continued too—notably with the American-British co-productions such as *Victoria* and *The Crown*. In film, *Skyfall* (2012) and *Spectre* (2015) have been among the most successful of the half-century-old series of James Bond films, and stand-alone films as diverse as Ken Loach's tale of an unemployed laborer, *I, Daniel Blake* (2016), and Christopher Nolan's sweeping war drama *Dunkirk* (2017) and have won both critical and popular acclaim. On the stage, British productions retain a prominent place on both sides of the Atlantic—from Andrew Lloyd Webber musical productions (such as the endlessly successful *Phantom of the Opera*) to Jez Butterworth's ambitious play about the Troubles in Northern Ireland, *The Ferryman* (2017). In literature, the world's most prestigious English-language literary prize, Britain's Man Booker, which had been restricted since its inception to works of fiction by British or Commonwealth writers, was opened to Americans in 2014. Perhaps no event symbolized the cultural convergence of Britain and America more clearly than the 2018 wedding of Prince Harry to Meghan Markle. In an earlier generation Markle would have been effectively disqualified in multiple ways from marrying someone in line to the throne—as an actor, as an American, and as a woman of color. But in 2018 the match was broadly celebrated, with the ceremony including music by a Gospel choir and an address by an American bishop.

No account of the cultural history of the new century would be complete without some mention of J.K. Rowling's series of fantasy novels that began with the 1997 publication of *Harry Potter and the Philosopher's Stone*. The series became a phenomenon in popular culture; more than 500 million copies of the seven novels were sold, the film adaptations were massively successful—and the series was credited with engendering a love for reading in many young people in an era when many were predicting the demise of the book. The Harry Potter phenomenon was given new life with the Broadway premiere in 2016 of *Harry Potter and the Cursed Child*, a two-part play by Jack Thorne (based on a story that he co-wrote with Rowling), and, in the same year, with the premier of the first instalment in the "Fantastic Beasts" film series, written by Rowling as a prequel to the Harry Potter story.

But popular fantasy has been only one of many directions that British literature has taken in recent years. Very much in vogue have been historical novels, ranging from McEwan's acclaimed 2007 short novel *On Chesil Beach*, set in the pre-Beatles 1960s, to Hilary Mantel's two Booker Prize-winning novels, *Wolf Hall* (2009) and *Bring Up the Bodies* (2012), both set in the time of Henry VIII, Thomas Cromwell, and Sir Thomas More. Rhyme has become a more and more frequent presence in serious poetry, with young poets as diverse as Patience Agbabi and Sophie Hannah joining Duffy, Oswald, and others in using rhyme extensively; few in today's Britain associate a habit of rhyming in verse with stuffy attitudes or with political conservatism. Leading poets have also tried their hand at variations on heroic narrative models, with considerable success. Seamus Heaney's *Beowulf* (2000) and Simon Armitage's *Sir Gawain and the Green Knight* (2007) were both praised as translations that deserve to be read as important poetic works in their own right, while Alice Oswald's acclaimed *Memorial: An Excavation of The Iliad* (2011) broke new ground in its poetic commemoration of characters from Homeric epic.

Literary currents in the world of "British" literature seem to become more and more international with each passing year. Zadie Smith and Peter Carey are among the best-known of the many British writers now living in New York, where the acclaimed novelist Colum McCann is among the many Irish writers resident—as is his compatriot Colm Tóibín for half the year. Another famous native Irish writer, Emma Donohue, has lived in Canada since 1998. Chimamanda Ngozi Adichie divides her time between her native Nigeria and the suburbs of Baltimore. Aravond Adinga, author of *The White Tiger*, the 2008 Booker Prize-winning novel of poverty, corruption, and religious conflict in India, was born and raised in India, and lives there again now, but has also lived for years at a time in Australia, New York, and Oxford. Kiran Desai, whose 2006 novel *The Inheritance of Loss* also won the Booker, is a citizen of India—but one who lived for some time in Britain after leaving India at the age of 14, and who is now a long-time resident of the United States. Even Hilary Mantel, who in 2009 became the first British citizen in five years to win the Booker Prize, spent more than a decade living in Botswana and in Saudi Arabia. If it has always been difficult to circumscribe "British literature," it is surely even more so today—as difficult, perhaps, as it is to draw any firm conclusions as to the future of Britain or of its place in the world. But there can be little doubt of the continuing vitality of its literary traditions as we move further into the twenty-first century.

The History of the English Language

Perhaps the most extraordinary feature of English language in the late twentieth and early twenty-first centuries has been the pace of its growth—growth in its size and communicative capacity, but also in the extent to which it is spoken around the world. The two phenomena are now closely linked. Linguist Paul Payack of Global Language Monitor has estimated that English likely passed the one million word mark in 2006. (By comparison, the number of words in Old English was less than 60,000.) As in the first half of the twentieth century, much of that growth comes from new scientific coinages. But much of it is now also coming from Chinese-English, Hindi-English, and other dual-language coinages. "Torunbusiness," for example, draws both on English and on the Mandarin word meaning *operating*; it means *open*, with reference to a business during opening hours.

In the twenty-year period 1947–67, almost all of Britain's former colonies became independent. Recognising the importance of English as a world-wide means of communication, most retained some official status for the English language. When India became independent in 1947, Hindi was declared the official language, English an "associate official language." In many new nations, English was accorded equal status with one or more other languages; thus in Malawi English and Chichewa are the official languages, in Swaziland,

English and Swazi. In former colonies such as Nigeria and Zambia, where many local languages are spoken in different areas of the country, English was declared the *only* official language.

The speaking of English acquired a different coloring as it became the world's lingua franca, not only in the proliferation of accents but also in the timing of speech, and in the use of pitch rather than stress to mark "strong" syllables. English as it is spoken in Britain, the United States, Canada, Australia, and New Zealand remains a strongly inflected, stress-timed language; in other words, speakers typically stress certain syllables much more strongly than others, and vary the speed of speech in order to make the elapsed time between stresses more nearly equal. In other regions, however, where most people's first language is syllable- rather than stress-timed, and where pitch rather than stress marks "accented" syllables, those habits tend to be carried over into local habits of English pronunciation.

Inevitably, very substantial differences have arisen as well in the conventions of grammar and usage in different areas of the world. In some cases—as in Jamaica and several other Caribbean nations—pidgin and Creole forms of English that have become independent languages are more widely spoken than English itself. Elsewhere, conventions of spoken and of written English very different from those of "Standard English" have come to be broadly received as acceptable variants. In India "He is working here, isn't it?" or "I am not very much pleased" are generally regarded as entirely acceptable local usage. Indian Prime Minister Manmohan Singh put the matter clearly in a 2005 speech at Oxford University:

> Of course, people here may not recognise the language we speak, but let me assure you that it *is* English! In indigenising English, as so many people have done in so many nations across the world, we have made the language our own. Our choice of prepositions may not always be the Queen's English; we might occasionally split the infinitive; and we may drop an article here and add an extra one there. I am sure everyone will agree, however, that English has been enriched by Indian creativity. …

Some of the most important changes in the English language in the second half of the twentieth century stemmed from the growing realization that the language had a systemic bias towards the male. In a landmark case referred to Britain by the Canadian courts, the Privy Council ruled in 1929 that the word *person* could not legally be taken to refer only to men. But could the word *man* be taken in an unbiased fashion to mean *human being*? To many, such usages seemed unproblematic—until they started to be brought up short by usages such as "the gestation period of the elephant is eleven months; that of man is nine months." From the 1970s onward it came to be more and more widely understood that *man* and *mankind* would always carry with them a whiff of malenesss, and thus could never fully and fairly represent all of humanity. Similarly the use of *he* to stand for both males and females has come to be widely criticized—and widely replaced, whether by "he or she" or simply by the use of plural constructions ("students … they" rather than "a student … he"); gender-specific nouns have largely been superceded by gender-neutral alternatives (*police officer* for *policeman*, *server* for *waitress*); and patronizing gender terms ("the girls in the office") have largely fallen into disuse. Such change did not occur without a struggle, however. For many decades, those who ventured to suggest gender-neutral alternatives to the general practice were subjected to the sort of ridicule that H.W. Fowler and F.G. Fowler (authors of *Modern English Usage* and for most of the twentieth century considered the leading arbiters of proper English usage) aimed at one S. Ferrier in *The King's English* (1906, 1931; issued without further revision in paperback, 1962). Existing habit or convention was in such cases often the only "argument" advanced against principles of fairness:

> *He, his, him* may generally be allowed to stand for the common gender; the particular aversion to them shown by Miss Ferrier … may be referred to her sex; and, ungallant as it may seem, we shall probably persist in refusing women their due here as stubbornly as Englishmen continue to offend the Scots by saying *England* instead of *Britain*.

One of the visible manifestations of changes in attitudes in the late twentieth century was the radical shift in the meaning of certain words and expressions relating to sexual behavior and sexual orientation. At mid-century *queer* was both an adjective meaning strange and a "descriptive" term with derogatory implications, used casually and openly by heterosexuals to denote gay and lesbian people; in the 1970s it had come to be acknowledged as an offensive word that should be avoided; in the 1980s and 1990s it was claimed by the gay, lesbian, and bisexual community, many of whom began to self-identify as queer. In the academic community queer theory grew up as a sub-discipline of literary theory and criticism. *Gay*, which until mid-century had in most circles meant *merry* or *given to merriment*, began in the 1970s to replace *queer* as a colloquial designator—but one that carried positive rather than negative connotations. (Towards the end of the century, however, those positive associations began to be eroded somewhat, as heterosexual youth began to use *gay* in a derogatory fashion.)

Terms relating to heterosexual relationships were often also unstable. A noteworthy example is *making love*, which until the 1950s referred to the process of courting, emphatically not including the act of sexual intercourse. In the early 1960s, the meaning of the phrase quickly shifted, so that by the 1970s, the *only* commonly used denotation of *to make love* was *to have sex*. That was one of many examples of an increasingly overt sexualization of the language. In the case of a number of words that in the early twentieth century could carry either a sexual or a non-sexual meaning (e.g., *intercourse, ejaculate*), the sexual meaning had completely crowded out the non-sexual one by the end of the 1960s.

The twentieth century also saw a great change in the use of obscenities. In 1914, the utterance on stage of the phrase "not bloody likely" caused an uproar during the first English performance of Bernard Shaw's *Pygmalion*. Over the first half of the century, other swear words gradually made their way into print ("d— it all," for example, eventually gave way to "damn it all"). As the Christian religion held less and less sway over Britain in the second half of the century, so the sharp shock of swear words with religious referents was rubbed smooth, and stronger and stronger sexual terms came to replace them. In the world of literary publishing the publication of Philip Larkin's "This Be the Verse" in 1974 ("They fuck you up, your mum and dad") was something of a watershed. For some time after that, most reputable newspapers and magazines resisted the appearance of "the f-word" in their pages, but in the last few years of the twentieth century and the early twenty-first that, too, has changed. In 2006, even the eminently respectable British newsmagazine *The Economist* found it acceptable to use such language in the course of quoting others; here is how their report in their 25–31 March 2006 issue on the state of Iraq three years after the 2003 invasion by American and British troops concluded: "On a toilet-wall in an American airbase in Western Iraq an American soldier has scrawled his own summary analysis: 'We came, we wasted a year of our lives. At least we got the fuckers to vote.'" In 1903—even in 1953 or 1963—such language in a respectable publication would have been entirely unimaginable.

Until very late in the twentieth century height and sightline restrictions kept tall buildings from the London skyline. Several skyscrapers were constructed as part of the late twentieth-century development of the Canary Wharf financial district, however, and in the twenty-first century skyscrapers have risen in other parts of London. Notable among them are the 41-storey Norman Foster-designed 2004 tower known as "The Gherkin," and the 72-storey tower known as "The Shard," which opened in 2013.

London's Millennium Bridge (above). The Bridge, the first new river crossing since the Tower Bridge opened in 1894, was designed jointly by Foster and Partners and Sir Anthony Caro. It opened on 10 June 2000 but had to be closed three days later due to unexpectedly strong swaying. Since its re-opening on 22 February 2002 it has proved enormously popular. To the north is St. Paul's Cathedral, to the south the Tate Modern gallery. The Tate Modern opened on 12 May 2000 in a building that had previously served as the Battersea Power Station. It now houses the Tate's collection of international twentieth- and twenty-first century art; the original Tate Gallery in Chelsea, now renamed Tate Britain, houses the gallery's British collection.

Samuel Beckett
1906 – 1989

Though Samuel Beckett was a prolific writer of poetry, prose fiction, and criticism, he remains best known for two of his plays, *Waiting for Godot* and *Endgame*, which are credited with having revolutionized theater, and which continue to be performed worldwide today. Fragmented, filled with absences and silences, and sparing of plot, characterization, and setting, Beckett's work is broadly innovative; it attempts to dispense with elements previously thought to be essential to dramatic productions. By paring down his writing to the bare necessities, Beckett created new possibilities of form and produced works whose brevity and lack of structure leaves them open to a variety of critical interpretations.

Beckett was born on 13 April 1906 in Foxrock, an upper-class, Protestant suburb of Dublin. He attended a boarding school in Northern Ireland and from there continued on (in 1923) to Trinity College, Dublin, where he studied French and Italian. Upon graduation, having excelled academically, Beckett was offered a two-year position as an exchange lecturer in Paris, and it was there that his writing career began. Within months of arriving in Paris he had been introduced to fellow Dublin writer James Joyce, whose writing Beckett greatly admired. Beckett established himself as part of Joyce's circle of literary friends in Paris, and in 1928 was commissioned to write an essay on Joyce's *Finnegans Wake*, which was still a work in progress at the time; that essay and a short story of Beckett's were published simultaneously in the Paris literary magazine *transition*. Shortly thereafter his first poem, *Whoroscope* (1930), was published by Nancy Cunard's Hours Press. Beckett had been encouraged by a friend to submit a poem to Cunard's competition for the best short poem on the subject of time. Using existing notes, he composed the prize-winning poem about French philosopher René Descartes in one night.

After living in Paris for two years, Beckett was loath to return to Ireland. He found the atmosphere and literary community in Paris far more conducive to his writing, but largely as a result of financial pressures, he spent the following seven years (1930–37) in Ireland, moving between Foxrock, where his family home was located, and Dublin, where he taught at Trinity College for two years immediately following his departure from Paris. Beckett also spent some time in London undergoing therapy for recurring panic attacks and bouts of depression. During these seven years he worked on several projects, including his first novel, *Dream of Fair to Middling Women*; the series of short stories *More Pricks than Kicks* (1934); the novel *Murphy*; and a small collection of poems. This early work was not well received: his collection of poetry barely sold, *Dream* (1992) was not published during his lifetime, *More Pricks* received mixed reviews, and *Murphy* was rejected dozens of times before finally being accepted in 1938, two years after its completion.

In October 1937 Beckett returned to Paris, intending to settle there permanently and devote himself to his writing. This writer's life, however, was not without incident. Walking home late one night in January 1938, Beckett was stabbed in the chest and spent months recovering in hospital.

There he was visited by Suzanne Deschevaux-Dumesnil, the woman who eventually became his wife. (Though the two were living together less than a year later, they did not marry until 1961.) Beckett and Deschevaux-Dumesnil were forced to leave Paris twice during World War II. The first time, in 1940, they escaped the city days before it fell to German forces. Upon returning to Paris a few months later, Beckett began working for the French Resistance (for which service he was decorated by the French government after the war). In 1942 the two had to flee Paris again when Beckett's Resistance cell was betrayed. They escaped their apartment only hours before the Gestapo arrived, and Beckett spent the rest of the war in Roussillon, in southeastern France, where he continued to assist the Resistance.

Though Beckett was able to do some writing while in hiding in the south of France, his most prolific period occurred after his return to his Paris flat in 1945. Between 1946 and 1950 he underwent what he referred to as "the siege in the room," composing four novellas, two plays, and four novels. Three of these novels—*Molloy* (1951), *Malone Dies* (*Malone meurt*, 1951), and *The Unnamable* (*L'innommable*, 1953)—comprise a trilogy and are perhaps his most highly regarded prose works. All the prose from this period departs from his earlier work in several ways. First, Beckett had decided to write entirely in French, translating his work back into English once it was completed. This helped him to avoid lyricism and enhanced the distinctive sparseness of his writing style. He also abandoned the omniscient narration of his earlier novels in favor of a first-person point of view. Frequently, as in *Texts for Nothing* (*Textes pour rien*, 1955) these narratives are more like fragmented meditations or monologues than stories. In fact, Beckett's prose, like his plays, tended towards monologue as his writing career progressed, to the point where the distinction between the two sometimes becomes blurred; many of his later works of short prose, such as *Imagination Dead Imagine* (*Imagination morte imaginez*, 1965), have been given stage performances.

To take a break from his trilogy, Beckett began working on *Waiting for Godot* (*En attendant Godot*, 1952), the two-act play in which, as Irish critic Vivian Mercier famously said, "Nothing happens, twice." The lack of progression in this play about two men waiting for someone called Godot (who never arrives) is characteristic of the majority of Beckett's drama. Set on practically bare stages, lacking significant character development, and consisting of plots with neither climax nor resolution, Beckett's plays have been referred to as more "anti-theater" than theater. The spareness of the setting of *Godot* ("A country road. A tree.") is exceeded by that of the setting of *Endgame* (*Fin de partie*, 1957)—a nearly empty room. In *Endgame*, which Beckett called "more inhuman than *Godot*," the characters are also waiting, though for nothing in particular, except the inevitable end. The frequently nonsensical dialogue of this play, like that of Beckett's others, often doubles back on itself and is interrupted by long silences.

Beckett's characters are largely of a piece. They tend to be aging, homeless, in mental and physical pain, and isolated from those around them yet desperately trying to maintain a sense of connection. Their bodies are sources of anguish, and they are constantly plagued by some difficulty or other. Their sense of disconnection from the outside world and from one another is a source of anxiety, as is the seemingly tenuous nature of their sterile existence. They attempt to alleviate this anxiety and give meaning to their existence through action, but to little avail. The dialogue, movements, and choices of these characters are rarely shown to have logic or consequence, and the result is by turns painful and funny to watch. Beckett's plays, like those of Eugène Ionesco and Jean Genet, are central texts to any discussion of absurdist theater—they present the absurdity and futility of the human condition as a given. Though often bleak, absurdist drama can also be highly comic; as Nell says in *Endgame*, "Nothing is funnier than unhappiness."

At no point in his career did Beckett demonstrate any concern for audience expectations, or feel the need to write in any currently popular style. Perhaps as a result, his work pushed the limits of what was thought possible. His willingness to experiment with new ideas, new media, and new technology resulted in a remarkably rich and diverse body of work. In 1958, shortly after reel-to-reel tape recorders were invented, Beckett incorporated one into a ground-breaking short play, *Krapp's Last Tape* (*La dernière bande*, 1958), in which a man conducts a "conversation" with a recording of his own voice from years before. In 1964 Beckett forayed into the world of film, writing a script for a film (titled simply *Film*) and traveling to New York to assist in making it.

As he aged, Beckett increasingly despaired of the ability of language to express anything meaningful about the nature of human existence. His 1969 play *Breath* is the most extreme manifestation of such feelings; it lasts less than one minute and includes sounds but no articulated words.

The extraordinary importance of Beckett's work was acknowledged in 1969 when he was awarded the Nobel Prize for Literature. He continued to direct many of his plays and to assist in their production for television up until only a few years before his death in 1989.

⌘⌘⌘

Endgame

A Play in One Act

THE CHARACTERS:

Nagg
Nell
Hamm
Clov

Bare interior.
Grey light.
Left and right back, high up, two small windows, curtains drawn.
Front right, a door. Hanging near door, its face to wall, a picture.
Front left, touching each other, covered with an old sheet, two ashbins.
Centre, in an armchair on castors, covered with an old sheet, Hamm.
Motionless by the door, his eyes fixed on Hamm, Clov. Very red face.
Brief tableau.

Clov goes and stands under window left. Stiff, staggering walk. He looks up at window left. He turns and looks at window right. He goes and stands under window right. He looks up at window right. He turns and looks at window left. He goes out, comes back immediately with a small step-ladder, carries it over and sets it down under window left, gets up on it, draws back curtain. He gets down, takes six steps (for example) towards window right, goes back for ladder, carries it over and sets it down under window right, gets up on it, draws back curtain. He gets down, takes three steps towards window left, goes back for ladder, carries it over and sets it down under window left, gets up on it, looks out of window. Brief laugh. He gets down, takes one step towards window right, goes back for ladder, carries it over and sets it down under window right, gets up on it, looks out of window. Brief laugh. He gets down, goes with ladder towards ashbins, halts, turns, carries back ladder and sets it down under window right, goes to ashbins, removes sheet covering them, folds it over his arm. He raises one lid, stoops and looks into bin. Brief laugh. He closes lid. Same with other bin. He goes to Hamm, removes sheet covering him, folds it over his arm. In a dressing-gown, a stiff toque on his head, a large blood-stained handkerchief over his face, a whistle hanging from his neck, a rug over his knees, thick socks on his feet, Hamm seems to be asleep. Clov looks him over. Brief laugh. He goes to door, halts, turns towards auditorium.

CLOV. (*Fixed gaze, tonelessly.*) Finished, it's finished, nearly finished, it must be nearly finished. (*Pause.*) Grain upon grain, one by one, and one day, suddenly, there's a heap, a little heap, the impossible heap. (*Pause.*) I can't be punished any more. (*Pause.*) I'll go now to my kitchen, ten feet by ten feet by ten feet, and wait for him to whistle me. (*Pause.*) Nice dimensions, nice proportions, I'll lean on the table, and look at the wall, and wait for him to whistle me.

(*He remains a moment motionless, then goes out. He comes back immediately, goes to window right, takes up the ladder and carries it out. Pause. Hamm stirs. He yawns under the handkerchief. He removes the handkerchief from his face. Very red face. Glasses with black lenses.*)

HAMM. Me—(*he yawns*)—to play. (*He holds the handkerchief spread out before him.*) Old stancher! (*He takes off his glasses, wipes his eyes, his face, the glasses, puts them on again, folds the handkerchief and puts it back neatly in the breast pocket of his dressing gown. He clears his throat, joins the tips of his fingers.*) Can there be misery—(*he yawns*)—loftier than mine? No doubt. Formerly. But now? (*Pause.*) My father? (*Pause.*) My mother? (*Pause.*) My … dog? (*Pause.*) Oh I am willing to believe they suffer as much as such creatures can suffer. But does that mean their sufferings equal mine? No doubt. (*Pause.*) No, all is a—(*he yawns*)—bsolute, (*proudly*) the bigger a man is the fuller he is. (*Pause. Gloomily.*) And the emptier. (*He sniffs.*) Clov! (*Pause.*) No, alone. (*Pause.*) What dreams! Those forests! (*Pause.*) Enough, it's time it ended, in the shelter, too. (*Pause.*) And yet I hesitate, I hesitate to … to end. Yes, there it is, it's time it ended and yet I hesitate to—(*he yawns*)—to end. (*Yawns.*) God, I'm tired, I'd be better off in bed.

(*He whistles. Enter Clov immediately. He halts beside the chair.*)

You pollute the air! (*Pause.*) Get me ready, I'm going to bed.

CLOV. I've just got you up.

HAMM. And what of it?

CLOV. I can't be getting you up and putting you to bed every five minutes, I have things to do. (*Pause.*)

HAMM. Did you ever see my eyes?

CLOV. No.

HAMM. Did you never have the curiosity, while I was sleeping, to take off my glasses and look at my eyes?

CLOV. Pulling back the lids? (*Pause.*) No.

HAMM. One of these days I'll show them to you. (*Pause.*) It seems they've gone all white. (*Pause.*) What time is it?

CLOV. The same as usual.

HAMM. (*Gesture towards window right.*) Have you looked?

CLOV. Yes.

HAMM. Well?

CLOV. Zero.

HAMM. It'd need to rain.

CLOV. It won't rain. (*Pause.*)

HAMM. Apart from that, how do you feel?

CLOV. I don't complain.

HAMM. You feel normal?

CLOV. (*Irritably.*) I tell you I don't complain.

HAMM. I feel a little queer. (*Pause.*) Clov!

CLOV. Yes.

HAMM. Have you not had enough?

CLOV. Yes! (*Pause.*) Of what?

HAMM. Of this … this … thing.

CLOV. I always had. (*Pause.*) Not you?

HAMM. (*Gloomily.*) Then there's no reason for it to change.

CLOV. It may end. (*Pause.*) All life long the same questions, the same answers.

HAMM. Get me ready.

(*Clov does not move.*)

Go and get the sheet.

(*Clov does not move.*)

Clov!

CLOV. Yes.

HAMM. I'll give you nothing more to eat.

CLOV. Then we'll die.

HAMM. I'll give you just enough to keep you from dying. You'll be hungry all the time.

CLOV. Then we won't die. (*Pause.*) I'll go and get the sheet. (*He goes towards the door.*)

HAMM. No!

(*Clov halts.*)

I'll give you one biscuit per day. (*Pause.*) One and a half. (*Pause.*) Why do you stay with me?

CLOV. Why do you keep me?

HAMM. There's no one else.

CLOV. There's nowhere else. (*Pause.*)

HAMM. You're leaving me all the same.

CLOV. I'm trying.

HAMM. You don't love me.

CLOV. No.

HAMM. You loved me once.

CLOV. Once!

HAMM. I've made you suffer too much. (*Pause.*) Haven't I?

CLOV. It's not that.

HAMM. (*Shocked.*) I haven't made you suffer too much?

CLOV. Yes!

HAMM. (*Relieved.*) Ah, you gave me a fright! (*Pause. Coldly.*) Forgive me. (*Pause. Louder.*) I said, Forgive me.

CLOV. I heard you. (*Pause.*) Have you bled?

HAMM. Less. (*Pause.*) Is it not time for my pain-killer?

CLOV. No. (*Pause.*)

HAMM. How are your eyes?

CLOV. Bad.

HAMM. How are your legs?

CLOV. Bad.

HAMM. But you can move.

CLOV. Yes.

HAMM. (*Violently.*) Then move!

(*Clov goes to back wall, leans against it with his forehead and hands.*)

Where are you?

CLOV. Here.

HAMM. Come back!

(*Clov returns to his place beside the chair.*)

Where are you?

CLOV. Here.

HAMM. Why don't you kill me?

CLOV. I don't know the combination of the cupboard. (*Pause.*)

HAMM. Go and get two bicycle-wheels.

CLOV. There are no more bicycle-wheels.

HAMM. What have you done with your bicycle?

CLOV. I never had a bicycle.

HAMM. The thing is impossible.

CLOV. When there were still bicycles I wept to have one. I crawled at your feet. You told me to go to hell. Now there are none.

HAMM. And your rounds? When you inspected my paupers. Always on foot?

CLOV. Sometimes on horse.

(*The lid of one of the bins lifts and the hands of Nagg appear, gripping the rim. Then his head emerges. Nightcap. Very white face. Nagg yawns, then listens.*)

I'll leave you, I have things to do.

HAMM. In your kitchen?

CLOV. Yes.

HAMM. Outside of here it's death. (*Pause.*) All right, be off.

(*Exit Clov. Pause.*)

We're getting on.

NAGG. Me pap!

HAMM. Accursed progenitor!

NAGG. Me pap!

HAMM. The old folks at home! No decency left! Guzzle, guzzle, that's all they think of.

(*He whistles. Enter Clov. He halts beside the chair.*)

Well! I thought you were leaving me.

CLOV. Oh not just yet, not just yet.

NAGG. Me pap!

HAMM. Give him his pap.

CLOV. There's no more pap.

HAMM. (*To Nagg.*) Do you hear that? There's no more pap. You'll never get any more pap.

NAGG. I want me pap!

HAMM. Give him a biscuit.

(*Exit Clov.*)

Accursed fornicator! How are your stumps?

NAGG. Never mind me stumps.

(*Enter Clov with biscuit.*)

CLOV. I'm back again, with the biscuit.

(*He gives biscuit to Nagg who fingers it, sniffs it.*)

NAGG. (*Plaintively.*) What is it?

CLOV. Spratt's[1] medium.

NAGG. (*As before.*): It's hard! I can't!

HAMM. Bottle him!

(*Clov pushes Nagg back into the bin, closes the lid.*)

CLOV. (*Returning to his place beside the chair.*) If age but knew!

HAMM. Sit on him!

CLOV. I can't sit.

HAMM. True. And I can't stand.

CLOV. So it is.

HAMM. Every man his specialty. (*Pause.*) No phone calls? (*Pause.*) Don't we laugh?

CLOV. (*After reflection.*) I don't feel like it.

HAMM. (*After reflection.*) Nor I. (*Pause.*) Clov!

CLOV. Yes.

HAMM. Nature has forgotten us.

CLOV. There's no more nature.

[1] *Spratt's* Dog-biscuit manufacturer.

HAMM. No more nature! You exaggerate.

CLOV. In the vicinity.

HAMM. But we breathe, we change! We lose our hair, our teeth! Our bloom! Our ideals!

CLOV. Then she hasn't forgotten us.

HAMM. But you say there is none.

CLOV. (*Sadly.*) No one that ever lived ever thought so crooked as we.

HAMM. We do what we can.

CLOV. We shouldn't. (*Pause.*)

HAMM. You're a bit of all right, aren't you?

CLOV. A smithereen. (*Pause.*)

HAMM. This is slow work. (*Pause.*) Is it not time for my pain-killer?

CLOV. No. (*Pause.*) I'll leave you, I have things to do.

HAMM. In your kitchen?

CLOV. Yes.

HAMM. What, I'd like to know.

CLOV. I look at the wall.

HAMM. The wall! And what do you see on your wall? Mene, mene?[2] Naked bodies?

CLOV. I see my light dying.

HAMM. Your light dying! Listen to that! Well, it can die just as well here, *your* light. Take a look at me and then come back and tell me what you think of your light. (*Pause.*)

CLOV. You shouldn't speak to me like that. (*Pause.*)

HAMM. (*Coldly.*) Forgive me. (*Pause. Louder.*) I said, Forgive me.

CLOV. I heard you.

(*The lid of Nagg's bin lifts. His hands appear, gripping the rim. Then his head emerges. In his mouth the biscuit. He listens.*)

HAMM. Did your seeds come up?

CLOV. No.

HAMM. Did you scratch round them to see if they had sprouted?

[2] *And what … mene* In Daniel 5, cryptic writing appears on the wall during a feast held by the Babylonian king Belshazzar. Daniel reads the words—"Mene, Mene, Tekel, Upharsin"—and translates "mene" as "God hath numbered thy kingdom, and finished it."

CLOV. They haven't sprouted.

HAMM. Perhaps it's still too early.

CLOV. If they were going to sprout they would have sprouted. (*Violently.*) They'll never sprout!

(*Pause. Nagg takes biscuit in his hand.*)

HAMM. This is not much fun. (*Pause.*) But that's always the way at the end of the day, isn't it, Clov?

CLOV. Always.

HAMM. It's the end of the day like any other day, isn't it, Clov?

CLOV. Looks like it. (*Pause.*)

HAMM. (*Anguished.*) What's happening, what's happening?

CLOV. Something is taking its course. (*Pause.*)

HAMM. All right, be off.

(*He leans back in his chair, remains motionless. Clov does not move, heaves a great groaning sigh. Hamm sits up.*)

I thought I told you to be off.

CLOV. I'm trying. (*He goes to the door, halts.*) Ever since I was whelped. (*Exit Clov.*)

HAMM. We're getting on.

(*He leans back in his chair, remains motionless. Nagg knocks on the lid of the other bin. Pause. He knocks harder. The lid lifts and the hands of Nell appear, gripping the rim. Then her head emerges. Lace cap. Very white face.*)

NELL. What is it, my pet? (*Pause.*) Time for love?

NAGG. Were you asleep?

NELL. Oh no!

NAGG. Kiss me.

NELL. We can't.

NAGG. Try.

(*Their heads strain towards each other, fail to meet, fall apart again.*)

NELL. Why this farce, day after day? (*Pause.*)

NAGG. I've lost me tooth.

NELL. When?

NAGG. I had it yesterday.

NELL. (*Elegiac.*) Ah yesterday.

(*They turn painfully towards each other.*)

NAGG. Can you see me?

NELL. Hardly. And you?

NAGG. What?

NELL. Can you see me?

NAGG. Hardly.

NELL. So much the better, so much the better.

NAGG. Don't say that. (*Pause.*) Our sight has failed.

NELL. Yes.

(*Pause. They turn away from each other.*)

NAGG. Can you hear me?

NELL. Yes. And you?

NAGG. Yes. (*Pause.*) Our hearing hasn't failed.

NELL. Our what?

NAGG. Our hearing.

NELL. No. (*Pause.*) Have you anything else to say to me?

NAGG. Do you remember—

NELL. No.

NAGG. When we crashed on our tandem and lost our shanks.

(*They laugh heartily.*)

NELL. It was in the Ardennes.[1]

(*They laugh less heartily.*)

NAGG. On the road to Sedan.[2]

(*They laugh still less heartily.*)

Are you cold?

NELL. Yes, perished. And you?

---

[1] *Ardennes* Mountainous region spanning portions of France, Belgium, and other nearby countries.

[2] *Sedan* French town in the Ardennes near the Belgian border.

NAGG. (*Pause.*) I'm freezing. (*Pause.*) Do you want to go in?

NELL. Yes.

NAGG. Then go in. (*Nell does not move.*) Why don't you go in?

NELL. I don't know. (*Pause.*)

NAGG. Has he changed your sawdust?

NELL. It isn't sawdust. (*Pause. Warily.*) Can you not be a little accurate, Nagg?

NAGG. Your sand then. It's not important.

NELL. It is important. (*Pause.*)

NAGG. It was sawdust once.

NELL. Once!

NAGG. And now it's sand. (*Pause.*) From the shore. (*Pause. Impatiently.*) Now it's sand he fetches from the shore.

NELL. Now it's sand.

NAGG. Has he changed yours?

NELL. No.

NAGG. Nor mine. (*Pause.*) I won't have it! (*Pause. Holding up the biscuit.*) Do you want a bit?

NELL. No. (*Pause.*) Of what?

NAGG. Biscuit. I've kept you half. (*He looks at the biscuit. Proudly.*) Three quarters. For you. Here. (*He proffers the biscuit.*) No? (*Pause.*) Do you not feel well?

HAMM. (*Wearily.*) Quiet, quiet, you're keeping me awake. (*Pause.*) Talk softer. (*Pause.*) If I could sleep I might make love. I'd go into the woods. My eyes would see ... the sky, the earth. I'd run, run, they wouldn't catch me. (*Pause.*) Nature! (*Pause.*) There's something dripping in my head. (*Pause.*) A heart, a heart in my head. (*Pause.*)

NAGG. (*Soft.*) Do you hear him? A heart in his head! (*He chuckles cautiously.*)

NELL. One mustn't laugh at those things, Nagg. Why must you always laugh at them?

NAGG. Not so loud!

NELL. (*Without lowering her voice.*) Nothing is funnier than unhappiness, I grant you that. But—

NAGG. (*Shocked.*) Oh!

NELL. Yes, yes, it's the most comical thing in the world. And we laugh, we laugh, with a will, in the beginning. But it's always the same thing. Yes, it's like the funny story we have heard too often, we still find it funny, but we don't laugh any more. (*Pause.*) Have you anything else to say to me?

NAGG. No.

NELL. Are you quite sure? (*Pause.*) Then I'll leave you.

NAGG. Do you not want your biscuit? (*Pause.*) I'll keep it for you. (*Pause.*) I thought you were going to leave me.

NELL. I am going to leave you.

NAGG. Could you give me a scratch before you go?

NELL. No. (*Pause.*) Where?

NAGG. In the back.

NELL. No. (*Pause.*) Rub yourself against the rim.

NAGG. It's lower down. In the hollow.

NELL. What hollow?

NAGG. The hollow! (*Pause.*) Could you not? (*Pause.*) Yesterday you scratched me there.

NELL. (*Elegiac.*) Ah yesterday!

NAGG. Could you not? (*Pause.*) Would you like me to scratch you? (*Pause.*) Are you crying again?

NELL. I was trying. (*Pause.*)

HAMM. Perhaps it's a little vein. (*Pause.*)

NAGG. What was that he said?

NELL. Perhaps it's a little vein.

NAGG. What does that mean? (*Pause.*) That means nothing. (*Pause.*) Shall I tell you the story of the tailor?

NELL. No. (*Pause.*) What for?

NAGG. To cheer you up.

NELL. It's not funny.

NAGG. It always made you laugh. (*Pause.*) The first time I thought you'd die.

NELL. It was on Lake Como.[1] (*Pause.*) One April afternoon. (*Pause.*) Can you believe it?

NAGG. What?

NELL. That we once went out rowing on Lake Como. (*Pause.*) One April afternoon.

NAGG. We had got engaged the day before.

NELL. Engaged!

NAGG. You were in such fits that we capsized. By rights we should have been drowned.

NELL. It was because I felt happy.

[1] *Lake Como* Lake in Northern Italy.

NAGG. (*Indignant.*) It was not, it was not, it was my story and nothing else. Happy! Don't you laugh at it still? Every time I tell it. Happy!

NELL. It was deep, deep. And you could see down to the bottom. So white. So clean.

NAGG. Let me tell it again. (*Raconteur's voice.*) An Englishman, needing a pair of striped trousers in a hurry for the New Year festivities, goes to his tailor who takes his measurements. (*Tailor's voice.*) "That's the lot, come back in four days, I'll have it ready." Good. Four days later. (*Tailor's voice.*) "So sorry, come back in a week, I've made a mess of the seat." Good, that's all right, a neat seat can be very ticklish. A week later. (*Tailor's voice.*) "Frightfully sorry, come back in ten days, I've made a hash of the crotch." Good, can't be helped, a snug crotch is always a teaser. Ten days later. (*Tailor's voice.*) "Dreadfully sorry, come back in a fortnight, I've made a balls of the fly." Good, at a pinch, a smart fly is a stiff proposition. (*Pause. Normal voice.*) I never told it worse. (*Pause. Gloomy.*) I tell this story worse and worse. (*Pause. Raconteur's voice.*) Well, to make it short, the bluebells are blowing and he ballockses the buttonholes. (*Customer's voice.*) "God damn you to hell, Sir, no, it's indecent, there are limits! In six days, do you hear me, six days, God made the world. Yes Sir, no less Sir, the WORLD! And you are not bloody well capable of making me a pair of trousers in three months!" (*Tailor's voice, scandalized.*) "But my dear Sir, my dear Sir, look—(*disdainful gesture, disgustedly*)—at the world—(*pause*) and look—(*loving gesture, proudly*)—at my TROUSERS!"

(*Pause. He looks at Nell who has remained impassive, her eyes unseeing. He breaks into a high forced laugh, cuts it short, pokes his head towards Nell, launches his laugh again.*)

HAMM. Silence!

(*Nagg starts, cuts short his laugh.*)

NELL. You could see down to the bottom.

HAMM. (*Exasperated.*) Have you not finished? Will you never finish? (*With sudden fury.*) Will this never finish?

(*Nagg disappears into his bin, closes the lid behind him. Nell does not move. Frenziedly.*)

My kingdom for a nightman![1]

(*He whistles. Enter Clov.*)

Clear away this muck! Chuck it in the sea!

(*Clov goes to bins, halts.*)

NELL. So white.

HAMM. What? What's she blathering about?

(*Clov stoops, takes Nell's hand, feels her pulse.*)

NELL. (*To Clov.*) Desert!

(*Clov lets go her hand, pushes her back in the bin, closes the lid.*)

CLOV. (*Returning to his place beside the chair.*) She has no pulse.

HAMM. What was she drivelling about?

CLOV. She told me to go away, into the desert.

HAMM. Damn busybody! Is that all?

CLOV. No.

HAMM. What else?

CLOV. I didn't understand.

HAMM. Have you bottled her?

CLOV. Yes.

HAMM. Are they both bottled?

CLOV. Yes.

HAMM. Screw down the lids.

(*Clov goes towards door.*)

---

[1] *My kingdom for a nightman* See Shakespeare's *Richard III* 5.4, in which Richard III declares, "My kingdom for a horse!"; *nightman* Person whose job is to empty cesspools of human waste.

Time enough.

(*Clov halts.*)

My anger subsides, I'd like to pee.

CLOV. (*With alacrity.*) I'll go get the catheter. (*He goes towards door.*)

HAMM. Time enough.

(*Clov halts.*)

Give me my pain-killer.

CLOV. It's too soon. (*Pause.*) It's too soon on top of your tonic, it wouldn't act.

HAMM. In the morning they brace you up and in the evening they calm you down. Unless it's the other way round. (*Pause.*) That old doctor, he's dead naturally?

CLOV. He wasn't old.

HAMM. But he's dead?

CLOV. Naturally. (*Pause.*) You ask *me* that? (*Pause.*)

HAMM. Take me for a little turn.

(*Clov goes behind the chair and pushes it forward.*)

Not too fast!

(*Clov pushes chair.*)

Right round the world!

(*Clov pushes chair.*)

Hug the walls, then back to the centre again.

(*Clov pushes chair.*)

I was right in the centre, wasn't I?

CLOV. (*Pushing.*) Yes.

HAMM. We'd need a proper wheel-chair. With big wheels. Bicycle wheels! (*Pause.*) Are you hugging?

CLOV. (*Pushing.*) Yes.

HAMM. (*Groping for wall.*) It's a lie! Why do you lie to me?

CLOV. (*Bearing closer to wall.*) There! There!

HAMM. Stop!

(*Clov stops chair close to back wall. Hamm lays his hand against wall.*)

Old wall! (*Pause.*) Beyond is the ... other hell. (*Pause. Violently.*) Closer! Closer! Up against!

CLOV. Take away your hand.

(*Hamm withdraws his hand. Clov rams chair against wall.*)

There!

(*Hamm leans towards wall, applies his ear to it.*)

HAMM. Do you hear? (*He strikes the wall with his knuckles.*) Do you hear? Hollow bricks! (*He strikes again.*) All that's hollow! (*Pause. He straightens up. Violently.*) That's enough. Back!

CLOV. We haven't done the round.

HAMM. Back to my place!

(*Clov pushes chair back to centre.*)

Is that my place?

CLOV. Yes, that's your place.

HAMM. Am I right in the centre?

CLOV. I'll measure it.

HAMM. More or less! More or less!

CLOV. (*Moving chair slightly.*) There!

HAMM. I'm more or less in the centre?

CLOV. I'd say so.

HAMM. You'd say so! Put me right in the centre!

CLOV. I'll go and get the tape.

HAMM. Roughly! Roughly!

(*Clov moves chair slightly.*)

Bang in the centre!

CLOV. There! (*Pause.*)

HAMM. I feel a little too far to the left.

(*Clov moves chair slightly.*)

Now I feel a little too far to the right.

(*Clov moves chair slightly.*)

I feel a little too far forward.

(*Clov moves chair slightly.*)

Now I feel a little too far back.

(*Clov moves chair slightly.*)

Don't stay there, (*i.e. behind the chair*) you give me the shivers.

(*Clov returns to his place beside the chair.*)

CLOV. If I could kill him I'd die happy. (*Pause.*)
HAMM. What's the weather like?
CLOV. As usual.
HAMM. Look at the earth.
CLOV. I've looked.
HAMM. With the glass?
CLOV. No need of the glass.
HAMM. Look at it with the glass.
CLOV. I'll go and get the glass. (*Exit Clov.*)
HAMM. No need of the glass!

(*Enter Clov with telescope.*)

CLOV. I'm back again, with the glass. (*He goes to window right, looks up at it.*) I need the steps.
HAMM. Why? Have you shrunk?

(*Exit Clov with telescope.*)

I don't like that, I don't like that.

(*Enter Clov with ladder, but without telescope.*)

CLOV. I'm back again, with the steps. (*He sets down ladder under window right, gets up on it, realizes he has not the telescope, gets down.*) I need the glass. (*He goes towards door.*)
HAMM. (*Violently.*) But you have the glass!
CLOV. (*Halting, violently.*) No, I haven't the glass! (*Exit Clov.*)
HAMM. This is deadly.

(*Enter Clov with the telescope. He goes towards ladder.*)

CLOV. Things are livening up. (*He gets up on ladder, raises the telescope, lets it fall.*) I did it on purpose. (*He gets down, picks up the telescope, turns it on auditorium.*) I see … a multitude … in transports … of joy. (*Pause.*) That's what I call a magnifier. (*He lowers the telescope, turns toward Hamm.*) Well? Don't we laugh?
HAMM. (*After reflection.*) I don't.
CLOV. (*After reflection.*) Nor I. (*He gets up on ladder, turns the telescope on the without.*) Let's see. (*He looks, moving the telescope.*) Zero … (*he looks*) … zero … (*he looks*) … and zero.
HAMM. Nothing stirs. All is—
CLOV. Zer—
HAMM. (*Violently.*) Wait till you're spoken to! (*Normal voice.*) All is … all is … all is what? (*Violently.*) All is what?
CLOV. What all is? In a word? Is that what you want to know? Just a moment. (*He turns the telescope on the without, looks, lowers the telescope, turns towards Hamm.*) Corpsed. (*Pause.*) Well? Content?
HAMM. Look at the sea.
CLOV. It's the same.
HAMM. Look at the ocean!

(*Clov gets down, takes a few steps towards window left, goes back for ladder, carries it over and sets it down under window left, gets up on it, turns the telescope on the without, looks at length. He starts, lowers the telescope, examines it, turns it again on the without.*)

CLOV. Never seen anything like that!

HAMM. (*Anxious.*) What? A sail? A fin? Smoke?

CLOV. (*Looking.*) The light is sunk.

HAMM. (*Relieved.*) Pah! We all knew that.

CLOV. (*Looking.*) There was a bit left.

HAMM. The base.

CLOV. (*Looking.*) Yes.

HAMM. And now?

CLOV. (*Looking.*) All gone.

HAMM. No gulls?

CLOV. (*Looking.*) Gulls!

HAMM. And the horizon? Nothing on the horizon?

CLOV. (*Lowering the telescope, turning towards Hamm, exasperated.*) What in God's name could there be on the horizon? (*Pause.*)

HAMM. The waves, how are the waves?

CLOV. The waves? (*He turns the telescope on the waves.*) Lead.

HAMM. And the sun?

CLOV. (*Looking.*) Zero.

HAMM. But it should be sinking. Look again.

CLOV. (*Looking.*) Damn the sun.

HAMM. Is it night already then?

CLOV. (*Looking.*) No.

HAMM. Then what is it?

CLOV. (*Looking.*) Gray. (*Lowering the telescope, turning towards Hamm, louder.*) Gray! (*Pause. Still louder.*) GRRAY! (*Pause. He gets down, approaches Hamm from behind, whispers in his ear.*)

HAMM. (*Starting.*) Gray! Did I hear you say gray?

CLOV. Light black. From pole to pole.

HAMM. You exaggerate. (*Pause.*) Don't stay there, you give me the shivers.

(*Clov returns to his place beside the chair.*)

CLOV. Why this farce, day after day?

HAMM. Routine. One never knows. (*Pause.*) Last night I saw inside my breast. There was a big sore.

CLOV. Pah! You saw your heart.

HAMM. No, it was living. (*Pause. Anguished.*) Clov!

CLOV. Yes.

HAMM. What's happening?

CLOV. Something is taking its course. (*Pause.*)

HAMM. Clov!

CLOV. (*Impatiently.*) What is it?

HAMM. We're not beginning to … to … mean something?

CLOV. Mean something! You and I, mean something! (*Brief laugh.*) Ah that's a good one!

HAMM. I wonder. (*Pause.*) Imagine if a rational being came back to earth, wouldn't he be liable to get ideas into his head if he observed us long enough. (*Voice of rational being.*) Ah, good, now I see what it is, yes, now I understand what they're at!

(*Clov starts, drops the telescope and begins to scratch his belly with both hands. Normal voice.*)

And without going so far as that, we ourselves … (*with emotion*) … we ourselves … at certain moments … (*Vehemently.*) To think perhaps it won't all have been for nothing!

CLOV. (*Anguished, scratching himself.*) I have a flea!

HAMM. A flea! Are there still fleas?

CLOV. On me there's one. (*Scratching.*) Unless it's a crablouse.

HAMM. (*Very perturbed.*) But humanity might start from there all over again! Catch him, for the love of God!

CLOV. I'll go and get the powder. (*Exit Clov.*)

HAMM. A flea! This is awful! What a day!

(*Enter Clov with a sprinkling-tin.*)

CLOV. I'm back again, with the insecticide.

HAMM. Let him have it!

(*Clov loosens the top of his trousers, pulls it forward and shakes powder into the aperture. He stoops, looks, waits, starts, frenziedly shakes more powder, stoops, looks, waits.*)

CLOV. The bastard!

HAMM. Did you get him?

CLOV. Looks like it. (*He drops the tin and adjusts his trousers.*) Unless he's laying doggo.

HAMM. Laying! Lying, you mean. Unless he's *lying* doggo.

CLOV. Ah? One says lying? One doesn't say laying?

HAMM. Use your head, can't you. If he was laying we'd be bitched.

CLOV. Ah. (*Pause.*) What about that pee?

HAMM. I'm having it.

CLOV. Ah that's the spirit, that's the spirit! (*Pause.*)

HAMM. (*With ardour.*) Let's go from here, the two of us! South! You can make a raft and the currents will carry us away, far away, to other … mammals!

CLOV. God forbid!

HAMM. Alone, I'll embark alone! Get working on that raft immediately. Tomorrow I'll be gone forever.

CLOV. (*Hastening towards door.*) I'll start straight away.

HAMM. Wait!

(*Clov halts.*)

Will there be sharks, do you think?

CLOV. Sharks? I don't know. If there are there will be. (*He goes towards door.*)

HAMM. Wait!

(*Clov halts.*)

Is it not yet time for my pain-killer?

CLOV. (*Violently.*) No! (*He goes towards door.*)

HAMM. Wait!

(*Clov halts.*)

How are your eyes?

CLOV. Bad.

HAMM. But you can see.

CLOV. All I want.

HAMM. How are your legs?

CLOV. Bad.

HAMM. But you can walk.

CLOV. I come … and go.

HAMM. In my house. (*Pause. With prophetic relish.*) One day you'll be blind like me. You'll be sitting here, a speck in the void, in the dark, for ever, like me. (*Pause.*) One day you'll say to yourself, I'm tired, I'll sit down, and you'll go and sit down. Then you'll say, I'm hungry, I'll get up and get something to eat. But you won't get up. You'll say, I shouldn't have sat down, but since I have I'll sit on a little longer, then I'll get up and get something to eat. But you won't get up and you won't get anything to eat. (*Pause.*) You'll look at the wall a while, then you'll say, I'll close my eyes, perhaps have a little sleep, after that I'll feel better, and you'll close them. And when you open them again there'll be no wall any more. (*Pause.*) Infinite emptiness will be all around you, all the resurrected dead of all the ages wouldn't fill it, and there you'll be like a little bit of grit in the middle of the steppe. (*Pause.*) Yes, one day you'll know what it is, you'll be like me, except that you won't have anyone with you, because you won't have had pity on anyone and because there won't be anyone left to have pity on. (*Pause.*)

CLOV. It's not certain. (*Pause.*) And there's one thing you forgot.

HAMM. Ah?

CLOV. I can't sit down.

HAMM. (*Impatiently.*) Well you'll lie down then, what the hell! Or you'll come to a standstill, simply stop and stand still, the way you are now. One day you'll say, I'm tired, I'll stop. What does the attitude matter? (*Pause.*)

CLOV. So you all want me to leave you.

HAMM. Naturally.

CLOV. Then I'll leave you.

HAMM. You can't leave us.

CLOV. Then I won't leave you. (*Pause.*)

HAMM. Why don't you finish us? (*Pause.*) I'll tell you the combination of the cupboard if you promise to finish me.

CLOV. I couldn't finish you.

HAMM. Then you won't finish me. (*Pause.*)

CLOV. I'll leave you, I have things to do.

HAMM. Do you remember when you came here?

CLOV. No. Too small, you told me.

HAMM. Do you remember your father?

CLOV. (*Wearily.*) Same answer. (*Pause.*) You've asked me these questions millions of times.

HAMM. I love the old questions. (*With fervour.*) Ah the old questions, the old answers, there's nothing like them! (*Pause.*) It was I was a father to you.

CLOV. Yes. (*He looks at Hamm fixedly.*) You were that to me.

HAMM. My house a home for you.

CLOV. Yes. (*He looks about him.*) This was that for me.

HAMM. (*Proudly.*) But for me, (*gesture towards himself*) no father. But for Hamm, (*gesture towards surroundings*) no home. (*Pause.*)

CLOV. I'll leave you.

HAMM. Did you ever think of one thing?

CLOV. Never.

HAMM. That here we're down in a hole. (*Pause.*) But beyond the hills? Eh? Perhaps it's still green. Eh? (*Pause.*) Flora! Pomona! (*Ecstatically.*) Ceres![1] (*Pause.*) Perhaps you won't need to go very far.

CLOV. I can't go very far. (*Pause.*) I'll leave you.

HAMM. Is my dog ready?

CLOV. He lacks a leg.

HAMM. Is he silky?

CLOV. He's a kind of Pomeranian.

HAMM. Go and get him.

CLOV. He lacks a leg.

HAMM. Go and get him!

(*Exit Clov.*)

We're getting on.

(*Enter Clov holding by one of its three legs a black toy dog.*)

CLOV. Your dogs are here. (*He hands the dog to Hamm who feels it, fondles it.*)

HAMM. He's white, isn't he?

CLOV. Nearly.

HAMM. What do you mean, nearly? Is he white or isn't he?

CLOV. He isn't. (*Pause.*)

HAMM. You've forgotten the sex.

CLOV. (*Vexed.*) But he isn't finished. The sex goes on at the end. (*Pause.*)

HAMM. You haven't put on his ribbon.

CLOV. (*Angrily.*) But he isn't finished, I tell you! First you finish your dog and then you put on his ribbon! (*Pause.*)

HAMM. Can he stand?

CLOV. I don't know.

HAMM. Try.

(*He hands the dog to Clov who places it on the ground.*)

Well?

CLOV. Wait! (*He squats down and tries to get the dog to stand on its three legs, fails, lets it go. The dog falls on its side.*)

HAMM. (*Impatiently.*) Well?

CLOV. He's standing.

HAMM. (*Groping for the dog.*) Where? Where is he?

(*Clov holds up the dog in a standing position.*)

CLOV. There.

(*He takes Hamm's hand and guides it towards the dog's head.*)

HAMM. (*His hand on the dog's head.*) Is he gazing at me?

CLOV. Yes.

HAMM. (*Proudly.*) As if he were asking me to take him for a walk?

CLOV. If you like.

HAMM. (*As before.*) Or as if he were begging me for a bone. (*He withdraws his hand.*) Leave him like that, standing there imploring me.

(*Clov straightens up. The dog falls on its side.*)

CLOV. I'll leave you.

HAMM. Have you had your visions?

CLOV. Less.

HAMM. Is Mother Pegg's light on?

CLOV. Light! How could anyone's light be on?

---

[1] *Flora ... Ceres* Flora, Pomona, and Ceres are ancient Roman goddesses associated with spring and flowers, with fruit, and with grain and agriculture, respectively.

HAMM. Extinguished!

CLOV. Naturally it's extinguished. If it's not on it's extinguished.

HAMM. No, I mean Mother Pegg.

CLOV. But naturally she's extinguished! (*Pause.*) What's the matter with you today?

HAMM. I'm taking my course. (*Pause.*) Is she buried?

CLOV. Buried! Who would have buried her?

HAMM. You.

CLOV. Me! Haven't I enough to do without burying people?

HAMM. But you'll bury me.

CLOV. No I won't bury you. (*Pause.*)

HAMM. She was bonny once, like a flower of the field. (*With reminiscent leer.*) And a great one for the men!

CLOV. We too were bonny—once. It's a rare thing not to have been bonny—once. (*Pause.*)

HAMM. Go and get the gaff.

(*Clov goes to the door, halts.*)

CLOV. Do this, do that, and I do it. I never refuse. Why?

HAMM. You're not able to.

CLOV. Soon I won't do it any more.

HAMM. You won't be able to any more.

(*Exit Clov.*)

Ah the creatures, the creatures, everything has to be explained to them.

(*Enter Clov with gaff.*)

CLOV. Here's your gaff. Stick it up.

(*He gives the gaff to Hamm who, wielding it like a puntpole, tries to move his chair.*)

HAMM. Did I move?

CLOV. No.

(*Hamm throws down the gaff.*)

HAMM. Go and get the oilcan.

CLOV. What for?

HAMM. To oil the castors.

CLOV. I oiled them yesterday.

HAMM. Yesterday! What does that mean? Yesterday!

CLOV. (*Violently.*) That means that bloody awful day, long ago, before this bloody awful day. I use the words you taught me. If they don't mean anything any more, teach me others. Or let me be silent. (*Pause.*)

HAMM. I once knew a madman who thought the end of the world had come. He was a painter—and engraver. I had a great fondness for him. I used to go and see him, in the asylum. I'd take him by the hand and drag him to the window. Look! There! All that rising corn! And there! Look! The sails of the herring fleet! All that loveliness! (*Pause.*) He'd snatch away his hand and go back into his corner. Appalled. All he had seen was ashes. (*Pause.*) He alone had been spared. (*Pause.*) Forgotten. (*Pause.*) It appears the case is … was not so … so unusual.

CLOV. A madman? When was that?

HAMM. Oh way back, way back, you weren't in the land of the living.

CLOV. God be with those days!

(*Pause. Hamm raises his toque.*)

HAMM. I had a great fondness for him. (*Pause. He puts on his toque again.*) He was a painter—and engraver.

CLOV. There are so many terrible things.

HAMM. No, no, there are not so many now. (*Pause.*) Clov!

CLOV. Yes.

HAMM. Do you not think this has gone on long enough?

CLOV. Yes! (*Pause.*) What?

HAMM. This … this … thing.

CLOV. I've always thought so. (*Pause.*) You not?

HAMM. (*Gloomily.*) Then it's a day like any other day.

CLOV. As long as it lasts. (*Pause.*) All life long the same inanities.

HAMM. I can't leave you.

CLOV. I know. And you can't follow me. (*Pause.*)

HAMM. If you leave me how shall I know?

CLOV. (*Briskly.*) Well you simply whistle me and if I don't come running it means I've left you. (*Pause.*)

HAMM. You won't come and kiss me goodbye?

CLOV. Oh I shouldn't think so. (*Pause.*)

HAMM. But you might be merely dead in your kitchen.

CLOV. The result would be the same.

HAMM. Yes, but how would I know, if you were merely dead in your kitchen?

CLOV. Well ... sooner or later I'd start to stink.

HAMM. You stink already. The whole place stinks of corpses.

CLOV. The whole universe.

HAMM. (*Angrily.*) To hell with the universe. (*Pause.*) Think of something.

CLOV. What?

HAMM. An idea, have an idea. (*Angrily.*) A bright idea!

CLOV. Ah good. (*He starts pacing to and fro, his eyes fixed on the ground, his hands behind his back. He halts.*) The pains in my legs! It's unbelievable! Soon I won't be able to think any more.

HAMM. You won't be able to leave me.

(*Clov resumes his pacing.*)

What are you doing?

CLOV. Having an idea. (*He paces.*) Ah! (*He halts.*)

HAMM. What a brain! (*Pause.*) Well?

CLOV. Wait! (*He meditates. Not very convinced.*) Yes ...(*Pause. More convinced.*) Yes! (*He raises his head.*) I have it! I set the alarm. (*Pause.*)

HAMM. This is perhaps not one of my bright days, but frankly—

CLOV. You whistle me. I don't come. The alarm rings. I'm gone. It doesn't ring. I'm dead. (*Pause.*)

HAMM. Is it working? (*Pause. Impatiently.*) The alarm, is it working?

CLOV. Why wouldn't it be working?

HAMM. Because it's worked too much.

CLOV. But it's hardly worked at all.

HAMM. (*Angrily.*) Then because it's worked too little!

CLOV. I'll go and see.

(*Exit Clov. Brief ring of alarm off. Enter Clov with alarm-clock. He holds it against Hamm's ear and releases alarm. They listen to it ringing to the end. Pause.*)

Fit to wake the dead! Did you hear it?

HAMM. Vaguely.

CLOV. The end is terrific!

HAMM. I prefer the middle. (*Pause.*) Is it not time for my pain-killer?

CLOV. No! (*He goes to door, turns.*) I'll leave you.

HAMM. It's time for my story. Do you want to listen to my story?

CLOV. No.

HAMM. Ask my father if he wants to listen to my story.

(*Clov goes to bins, raises the lid of Nagg's, stoops, looks into it. Pause. He straightens up.*)

CLOV. He's asleep.

HAMM. Wake him.

(*Clov stoops, wakes Nagg with the alarm. Unintelligible words. Clov straightens up.*)

CLOV. He doesn't want to listen to your story.

HAMM. I'll give him a bon-bon.

(*Clov stoops. As before.*)

CLOV. He wants a sugar-plum.

HAMM. He'll get a sugar-plum.

(*Clov stoops. As before.*)

CLOV. It's a deal.

(*He goes towards door. Nagg's hands appear, gripping the rim. Then the head emerges. Clov reaches door, turns.*)

Do you believe in the life to come?

HAMM. Mine was always that.

(*Exit Clov.*)

Got him that time!

NAGG. I'm listening.

HAMM. Scoundrel! Why did you engender me?

NAGG. I didn't know.

HAMM. What? What didn't you know?

NAGG. That it'd be you. (*Pause.*) You'll give me a sugar-plum?

HAMM. After the audition.

NAGG. You swear?

HAMM. Yes.

NAGG. On what?

HAMM. My honour.

(*Pause. They laugh heartily.*)

NAGG. Two.

HAMM. One.

NAGG. One for me and one for—

HAMM. One! Silence! (*Pause.*) Where was I? (*Pause. Gloomily.*) It's finished, we're finished. (*Pause.*) Nearly finished. (*Pause.*) There'll be no more speech. (*Pause.*) Something dripping in my head, ever since the fontanelles.

(*Stifled hilarity of Nagg.*)

Splash, splash, always on the same spot. (*Pause.*) Perhaps it's a little vein. (*Pause.*) A little artery. (*Pause. More animated.*) Enough of that, it's story time, where was I? (*Pause. Narrative tone.*) The man came crawling towards me, on his belly. Pale, wonderfully pale and thin, he seemed on the point of—(*Pause. Normal tone.*) No, I've done that bit. (*Pause. Narrative tone.*) I calmly filled my pipe—the meerschaum, lit it with … let us say a vesta,[1] drew a few puffs. Aah! (*Pause.*) Well, what is it *you* want? (*Pause.*) It was an extra-ordinarily bitter day, I remember, zero by the thermometer. But considering it was Christmas Eve there was nothing … extra-ordinary about that. Seasonable weather, for once in a way. (*Pause.*) Well, what ill wind blows you my way? He raised his face to me, black with mingled dirt and tears. (*Pause. Normal tone.*) That should do it. (*Narrative tone.*) No no, don't look at me, don't look at me. He dropped his eyes and mumbled something, apologies I presume. (*Pause.*) I'm a busy man, you know, the final touches, before the festivities, you know what it is. (*Pause. Forcibly.*) Come on now, what is the object of this invasion? (*Pause.*) It was a glorious bright day, I remember, fifty by the heliometer,[2] but already the sun was sinking down into the … down among the dead. (*Normal tone.*) Nicely put, that. (*Narrative tone.*) Come on now, come on, present your petition and let me resume my labors. (*Pause. Normal tone.*) There's English for you. Ah well … (*Narrative tone.*) It was then he took the plunge. It's my little one, he said. Tsstss, a little one, that's bad. My little boy, he said, as if the sex mattered. Where did he come from? He named the hole. A good half-day, on horse. What are you insinuating? That the place is still inhabited? No no, not a soul, except himself and the child—assuming he existed. Good. I enquired about the situation at Kov,[3] beyond the gulf. Not a sinner. Good. And you expect me to believe you have left your little one back there, all alone, and alive into the bargain? Come now! (*Pause.*) It was a howling wild day, I remember, a hundred by the anemometer.[4] The wind was tearing up the dead pines and sweeping them … away. (*Pause. Normal tone.*) A feeble bit, that. (*Narrative tone.*) Come on, man, speak up, what is it you want from me, I have to put up my holly. (*Pause.*) Well to make it short it finally transpired that what he wanted from me was … bread for his brat? Bread? But I have no bread, it doesn't agree with me. Good. Then perhaps a little corn? (*Pause. Normal tone.*) That should do it. (*Narrative tone.*) Corn, yes, I have corn, it's true, in my granaries. But use your head. I give you some corn, a pound, a pound and a half, you bring it back to your child and you make him—if he's still alive—a nice pot of porridge,

[1] *meerschaum* Pipe carved from a mineral that is also called meerschaum; *vesta* Match.

[2] *heliometer* Instrument first developed to measure the diameter of the sun.

[3] *Kov* Though there is no place by this name, some critics have argued that the sound suggests the Irish port town of Cobh (pronounced "cove").

[4] *anemometer* Instrument used to measure the speed of wind.

(*Nagg reacts*)

a nice pot and a half of porridge, full of nourishment. Good. The colours come back into his little cheeks—perhaps. And then? (*Pause.*) I lost patience. (*Violently.*) Use your head, can't you, use your head. You're on earth, there's no cure for that! (*Pause.*) It was an exceedingly dry day, I remember, zero by the hygrometer.[1] Ideal weather, for my lumbago. (*Pause. Violently.*) But what in God's name do you imagine? That the earth will awake in the spring? That the rivers and seas will run with fish again? That there's manna in heaven still for imbeciles like you? (*Pause.*) Gradually I cooled down, sufficiently at least to ask him how long he had taken on the way. Three whole days. Good. In what condition he had left the child. Deep in sleep. (*Forcibly.*) But deep in what sleep, deep in what sleep already? (*Pause.*) Well to make it short I finally offered to take him into my service. He had touched a chord. And then I imagined already that I wasn't much longer for this world. (*He laughs. Pause.*) Well? (*Pause.*) Well? Here if you were careful you might die a nice natural death, in peace and comfort. (*Pause.*) Well? (*Pause.*) In the end he asked me would I consent to take in the child as well—if he were still alive. (*Pause.*) It was the moment I was waiting for. (*Pause.*) Would I consent to take in the child … (*Pause.*) I can see him still, down on his knees, his hands flat on the ground, glaring at me with his mad eyes, in defiance of my wishes. (*Pause. Normal tone.*) I'll soon have finished with this story. (*Pause.*) Unless I bring in other characters. (*Pause.*) But where would I find them? (*Pause.*) Where would I look for them?

(*Pause. He whistles. Enter Clov.*)

Let us pray to God.

NAGG. Me sugar-plum!

CLOV. There's a rat in the kitchen!

HAMM. A rat! Are there still rats?

CLOV. In the kitchen there's one.

HAMM. And you haven't exterminated him?

CLOV. Half. You disturbed us.

HAMM. He can't get away?

CLOV. No.

HAMM. You'll finish him later. Let us pray to God.

CLOV. Again!

NAGG. Me sugar-plum!

HAMM. God first! (*Pause.*) Are you right?

CLOV. (*Resigned.*) Off we go.

HAMM. (*To Nagg.*) And you?

NAGG. (*Clasping his hands, closing his eyes, in a gabble.*) Our Father which art[2]—

HAMM. Silence! In silence! Where are your manners? (*Pause.*) Off we go. (*Attitudes of prayer. Silence. Abandoning his attitude, discouraged.*) Well?

CLOV. (*Abandoning his attitude.*) What a hope! And you?

HAMM. Sweet damn all! (*To Nagg.*) And you?

NAGG. Wait! (*Pause. Abandoning his attitude.*) Nothing doing!

HAMM. The bastard! He doesn't exist!

CLOV. Not yet.

NAGG. Me sugar-plum!

HAMM. There are no more sugar-plums! (*Pause.*)

NAGG. It's natural. After all I'm your father. It's true if it hadn't been me it would have been someone else. But that's no excuse. (*Pause.*) Turkish Delight, for example, which no longer exists, we all know that, there is nothing in the world I love more. And one day I'll ask you for some, in return for a kindness, and you'll promise it to me. One must live with the times. (*Pause.*) Whom did you call when you were a tiny boy, and were frightened, in the dark? Your mother? No. Me. We let you cry. Then we moved you out of earshot, so that we might sleep in peace. (*Pause.*) I was asleep, as happy as a king, and you woke me up to have me listen to you. It wasn't indispensable, you didn't really need to have me listen to you. (*Pause.*) I hope the day will come when you'll really need to have me listen to you, and need to hear my voice, any voice. (*Pause.*) Yes, I hope I'll live till then, to hear you calling me like when you were a tiny

[1] *hygrometer* Instrument used to measure humidity.

[2] *Our Father which art* First words of the Lord's Prayer, which is included in the New Testament (see Matthew 6.9–13) and used in most Christian churches.

boy, and were frightened, in the dark, and I was your only hope. (*Pause. Nagg knocks on lid of Nell's bin. Pause.*) Nell! (*Pause. He knocks louder. Pause. Louder.*) Nell! (*Pause. Nagg sinks back into his bin, closes the lid behind him. Pause.*)

HAMM. Our revels now are ended.[1] (*He gropes for the dog.*) The dog's gone.

CLOV. He's not a real dog, he can't go.

HAMM. (*Groping.*) He's not there.

CLOV. He's lain down.

HAMM. Give him up to me.

(*Clov picks up the dog and gives it to Hamm. Hamm holds it in his arms. Pause. Hamm throws away the dog.*)

Dirty brute!

(*Clov begins to pick up the objects lying on the ground.*)

What are you doing?

CLOV. Putting things in order. (*He straightens up. Fervently.*) I'm going to clear everything away! (*He starts picking up again.*)

HAMM. Order!

CLOV. (*Straightening up.*) I love order. It's my dream. A world where all would be silent and still and each thing in its last place, under the last dust. (*He starts picking up again.*)

HAMM. (*Exasperated.*) What in God's name do you think you're doing?

CLOV. (*Straightening up.*) I'm doing my best to create a little order.

HAMM. Drop it!

(*Clov drops the objects he has picked up.*)

CLOV. After all, there or elsewhere. (*He goes towards door.*)

HAMM. (*Irritably.*) What's wrong with your feet?

CLOV. My feet?

HAMM. Tramp! Tramp!

[1] *Our revels … ended* This line is spoken by the exiled duke Prospero in Shakespeare's *The Tempest* 4.1.

CLOV. I must have put on my boots.

HAMM. Your slippers were hurting you? (*Pause.*)

CLOV. I'll leave you.

HAMM. No!

CLOV. What is there to keep me here?

HAMM. The dialogue. (*Pause.*) I've got on with my story. (*Pause.*) I've got on with it well. (*Pause. Irritably.*) Ask me where I've got to.

CLOV. Oh, by the way, your story?

HAMM. (*Surprised.*) What story?

CLOV. The one you've been telling yourself all your days.

HAMM. Ah you mean my chronicle?

CLOV. That's the one. (*Pause.*)

HAMM. (*Angrily.*) Keep going, can't you, keep going!

CLOV. You've got on with it, I hope.

HAMM. (*Modestly.*) Oh not very far, not very far. (*He sighs.*) There are days like that, one isn't inspired. (*Pause.*) Nothing you can do about it, just wait for it to come. (*Pause.*) No forcing, no forcing, it's fatal. (*Pause.*) I've got on with it a little all the same. (*Pause.*) Technique, you know. (*Pause. Irritably.*) I say I've got on with it a little all the same.

CLOV. (*Admiringly.*) Well I never! In spite of everything you were able to get on with it!

HAMM. (*Modestly.*) Oh not very far, you know, not very far, but nevertheless, better than nothing.

CLOV. Better than nothing! Is it possible?

HAMM. I'll tell you how it goes. He comes crawling on his belly—

CLOV. Who?

HAMM. What?

CLOV. Who do you mean, he?

HAMM. Who do I mean! Yet another.

CLOV. Ah him. I wasn't sure.

HAMM. Crawling on his belly, whining for bread for his brat. He's offered a job as gardener. Before—

(*Clov bursts out laughing.*)

What is there so funny about that?

CLOV. A job as gardener!

HAMM. Is that what tickles you?

CLOV. It must be that.

HAMM. It wouldn't be the bread?

CLOV. Or the brat. (*Pause.*)

HAMM. The whole thing is comical, I grant you that. What about having a good guffaw the two of us together?

CLOV. (*After reflection.*) I couldn't guffaw again today.

HAMM. (*After reflection.*) Nor I. (*Pause.*) I continue then. Before accepting with gratitude he asks if he may have his little boy with him.

CLOV. What age?

HAMM. Oh tiny.

CLOV. He would have climbed the trees.

HAMM. All the little odd jobs.

CLOV. And then he would have grown up.

HAMM. Very likely. (*Pause.*)

CLOV. Keep going, can't you, keep going!

HAMM. That's all. I stopped there. (*Pause.*)

CLOV. Do you see how it goes on?

HAMM. More or less.

CLOV. Will it not soon be the end?

HAMM. I'm afraid it will.

CLOV. Pah! You'll make up another.

HAMM. I don't know. (*Pause.*) I feel rather drained. (*Pause.*) The prolonged creative effort. (*Pause.*) If I could drag myself down to the sea! I'd make a pillow of sand for my head and the tide would come.

CLOV. There's no more tide. (*Pause.*)

HAMM. Go and see is she dead.

(*Clov goes to bins, raises the lid of Nell's, stoops, looks into it. Pause.*)

CLOV. Looks like it.

(*He closes the lid, straightens up. Hamm raises his toque. Pause. He puts it on again.*)

HAMM. (*With his hand to his toque.*) And Nagg?

(*Clov raises lid of Nagg's bin, stoops, looks into it. Pause.*)

CLOV. Doesn't look like it. (*He closes the lid, straightens up.*)

HAMM. (*Letting go his toque.*) What's he doing?

(*Clov raises lid of Nagg's bin, stoops, looks into it. Pause.*)

CLOV. He's crying. (*He closes lid, straightens up.*)

HAMM. Then he's living. (*Pause.*) Did you ever have an instant of happiness?

CLOV. Not to my knowledge. (*Pause.*)

HAMM. Bring me under the window.

(*Clov goes towards chair.*)

I want to feel the light on my face.

(*Clov pushes chair.*)

Do you remember, in the beginning, when you took me for a turn? You used to hold the chair too high. At every step you nearly tipped me out. (*With senile quaver.*) Ah great fun, we had, the two of us, great fun. (*Gloomily.*) And then we got into the way of it.

(*Clov stops the chair under window right.*)

There already? (*Pause. He tilts back his head.*) Is it light?

CLOV. It isn't dark.

HAMM. (*Angrily.*) I'm asking you is it light?

CLOV. Yes. (*Pause.*)

HAMM. The curtain isn't closed?

CLOV. No.

HAMM. What window is it?

CLOV. The earth.

HAMM. I knew it! (*Angrily.*) But there's no light there! The other!

(*Clov pushes chair towards window left.*)

The earth!

(*Clov stops the chair under window left. Hamm tilts back his head.*)

That's what I call light! (*Pause.*) Feels like a ray of sunshine. (*Pause.*) No?

Clov. No.

Hamm. It isn't a ray of sunshine I feel on my face?

Clov. No. (*Pause.*)

Hamm. Am I very white? (*Pause. Angrily.*) I'm asking you am I very white?

Clov. Not more so than usual. (*Pause.*)

Hamm. Open the window.

Clov. What for?

Hamm. I want to hear the sea.

Clov. You wouldn't hear it.

Hamm. Even if you opened the window?

Clov. No.

Hamm. Then it's not worth while opening it?

Clov. No.

Hamm. (*Violently.*) Then open it!

(*Clov gets up on the ladder, opens the window. Pause.*)

Have you opened it?

Clov. Yes. (*Pause.*)

Hamm. You swear you've opened it?

Clov. Yes. (*Pause.*)

Hamm. Well ...! (*Pause.*) It must be very calm. (*Pause. Violently.*) I'm asking you is it very calm!

Clov. Yes.

Hamm. It's because there are no more navigators. (*Pause.*) You haven't much conversation all of a sudden. Do you not feel well?

Clov. I'm cold.

Hamm. What month are we? (*Pause.*) Close the window, we're going back.

(*Clov closes the window, gets down, pushes the chair back to its place, remains standing behind it, head bowed.*)

Don't stand there, you give me the shivers!

(*Clov returns to his place beside the chair.*)

Father! (*Pause. Louder.*) Father! (*Pause.*) Go and see did he hear me.

(*Clov goes to Nagg's bin, raises the lid, stoops. Unintelligible words. Clov straightens up.*)

Clov. Yes.

Hamm. Both times?

(*Clov stoops. As before.*)

Clov. Once only.

Hamm. The first time or the second?

(*Clov stoops. As before.*)

Clov. He doesn't know.

Hamm. It must have been the second.

Clov. We'll never know. (*He closes lid.*)

Hamm. Is he still crying?

Clov. No.

Hamm. The dead go fast. (*Pause.*) What's he doing?

Clov. Sucking his biscuit.

Hamm. Life goes on.

(*Clov returns to his place beside the chair.*)

Give me the rug, I'm freezing.

Clov. There are no more rugs. (*Pause.*)

Hamm. Kiss me. (*Pause.*) Will you not kiss me?

Clov. No.

Hamm. On the forehead.

Clov. I won't kiss you anywhere. (*Pause.*)

Hamm. (*Holding out his hand.*) Give me your hand at least. (*Pause.*) Will you not give me your hand?

Clov. I won't touch you. (*Pause.*)

Hamm. Give me the dog.

(*Clov looks round for the dog.*)

No!

Clov. Do you not want your dog?

Hamm. No.

Clov. Then I'll leave you.

Hamm. (*Head bowed, absently.*) That's right.

(*Clov goes to door, turns.*)

CLOV. If I don't kill that rat he'll die.
HAMM. (*As before.*) That's right.

(*Exit Clov. Pause.*)

Me to play. (*He takes out his handkerchief, unfolds it, holds it spread out before him.*) We're getting on. (*Pause.*) You weep, and weep, for nothing, so as not to laugh, and little by little … you begin to grieve. (*He folds the handkerchief, puts it back in his pocket, raises his head.*) All those I might have helped. (*Pause.*) Helped! (*Pause.*) Saved. (*Pause.*) Saved! (*Pause.*) The place was crawling with them! (*Pause. Violently.*) Use your head, can't you, use your head, you're on earth, there's no cure for that! (*Pause.*) Get out of here and love one another! Lick your neighbour as yourself! (*Pause. Calmer.*) When it wasn't bread they wanted it was crumpets. (*Pause. Violently.*) Out of my sight and back to your petting parties! (*Pause.*) All that, all that! (*Pause.*) Not even a real dog! (*Calmer.*) The end is in the beginning and yet you go on. (*Pause.*) Perhaps I could go on with my story, end it and begin another. (*Pause.*) Perhaps I could throw myself out on the floor. (*He pushes himself painfully off his seat, falls back again.*) Dig my nails into the cracks and drag myself forward with my fingers. (*Pause.*) It will be the end and there I'll be, wondering what can have brought it on and wondering what can have … (*he hesitates*) … why it was so long coming. (*Pause.*) There I'll be, in the old shelter, alone against the silence and … (*he hesitates*) … the stillness. If I can hold my peace, and sit quiet, it will be all over with sound, and motion, all over and done with. (*Pause.*) I'll have called my father and I'll have called my … (*he hesitates*) … my son. And even twice, or three times, in case they shouldn't have heard me, the first time, or the second. (*Pause.*) I'll say to myself, He'll come back. (*Pause.*) And then? (*Pause.*) And then? (*Pause.*) He couldn't, he has gone too far. (*Pause.*) And then? (*Pause. Very agitated.*) All kinds of fantasies! That I'm being watched! A rat! Steps! Breath held and then … (*He breathes out.*) Then babble, babble, words, like the solitary child who turns himself into children, two, three, so as to be together, and whisper together, in the dark. (*Pause.*) Moment upon moment, pattering down, like the millet grains of … (*he hesitates*) … that old Greek,[1] and all life long you wait for that to mount up to a life. (*Pause. He opens his mouth to continue, renounces.*) Ah let's get it over!

(*He whistles. Enter Clov with alarm-clock. He halts beside the chair.*)

What? Neither gone nor dead?
CLOV. In spirit only.
HAMM. Which?
CLOV. Both.
HAMM. Gone from me you'd be dead.
CLOV. And vice versa.
HAMM. Outside of here it's death! (*Pause.*) And the rat?
CLOV. He's got away.
HAMM. He can't go far. (*Pause. Anxious.*) Eh?
CLOV. He doesn't need to go far. (*Pause.*)
HAMM. Is it not time for my pain-killer?
CLOV. Yes.
HAMM. Ah! At last! Give it to me! Quick! (*Pause.*)
CLOV. There's no more pain-killer. (*Pause.*)
HAMM. (*Appalled.*) Good …! (*Pause.*) No more pain-killer!
CLOV. No more pain-killer. You'll never get any more pain-killer. (*Pause.*)
HAMM. But the little round box. It was full!
CLOV. Yes. But now it's empty.

(*Pause. Clov starts to move about the room. He is looking for a place to put down the alarm-clock.*)

HAMM. (*Soft.*) What'll I do? (*Pause. In a scream.*) What'll I do?

---

[1] *that old Greek* The ancient Greek philosopher Zeno (fifth century BCE) is best known for a series of paradoxes; one asks how it is that a single grain of millet falling makes no sound, while a large quantity of millet makes a sound if it falls all at once. Eubulides of Miletus (fourth century BCE), a follower of Zeno, articulated a paradox involving heaps: if a single grain of sand is not a heap, and we cannot turn a collection of grains of sand into a heap by adding one more grain of sand, how is it possible for a heap of sand to ever form?

(*Clov sees the picture, takes it down, stands it on the floor with its face to the wall, hangs up the alarm-clock in its place.*)

What are you doing?

CLOV. Winding up.

HAMM. Look at the earth.

CLOV. Again!

HAMM. Since it's calling to you.

CLOV. Is your throat sore? (*Pause.*) Would you like a lozenge? (*Pause.*) No. (*Pause.*) Pity. (*Clov goes, humming, towards window right, halts before it, looks up at it.*)

HAMM. Don't sing.

CLOV. (*Turning towards Hamm.*) One hasn't the right to sing any more?

HAMM. No.

CLOV. Then how can it end?

HAMM. You want it to end?

CLOV. I want to sing.

HAMM. I can't prevent you.

(*Pause. Clov turns towards window right.*)

CLOV. What did I do with that steps? (*He looks around for ladder.*) You didn't see that steps? (*He sees it.*) Ah, about time. (*He goes towards window left.*) Sometimes I wonder if I'm in my right mind. Then it passes over and I'm as lucid as before. (*He gets up on ladder, looks out of window.*) Christ, she's under water! (*He looks.*) How can that be? (*He pokes forward his head, his hand above his eyes.*) It hasn't rained. (*He wipes the pane, looks. Pause.*) Ah what a fool I am! I'm on the wrong side! (*He gets down, takes a few steps towards window right.*) Under water! (*He goes back for ladder.*) What a fool I am! (*He carries ladder towards window right.*) Sometimes I wonder if I'm in my right senses. Then it passes off and I'm as intelligent as ever. (*He sets down ladder under window right, gets up on it, looks out of window. He turns towards Hamm.*) Any particular sector you fancy? Or merely the whole thing?

HAMM. Whole thing.

CLOV. The general effect? Just a moment. (*He looks out of window. Pause.*)

HAMM. Clov.

CLOV. (*Absorbed.*) Mmm.

HAMM. Do you know what it is?

CLOV. (*As before.*) Mmm.

HAMM. I was never there. (*Pause.*) Clov!

CLOV. (*Turning towards Hamm, exasperated.*) What is it?

HAMM. I was never there.

CLOV. Lucky for you. (*He looks out of window.*)

HAMM. Absent, always. It all happened without me. I don't know what's happened. (*Pause.*) Do you know what's happened? (*Pause.*) Clov!

CLOV. (*Turning towards Hamm, exasperated.*) Do you want me to look at this muckheap, yes or no?

HAMM. Answer me first.

CLOV. What?

HAMM. Do you know what's happened?

CLOV. When? Where?

HAMM. (*Violently.*) When! What's happened? Use your head, can't you! What has happened?

CLOV. What for Christ's sake does it matter? (*He looks out of window.*)

HAMM. I don't know.

(*Pause. Clov turns towards Hamm.*)

CLOV. (*Harshly.*) When old Mother Pegg asked you for oil for her lamp and you told her to get out to hell, you knew what was happening then, no? (*Pause.*) You know what she died of, Mother Pegg? Of darkness.

HAMM. (*Feebly.*) I hadn't any.

CLOV. (*As before.*) Yes, you had. (*Pause.*)

HAMM. Have you the glass?

CLOV. No, it's clear enough as it is.

HAMM. Go and get it.

(*Pause. Clov casts up his eyes, brandishes his fists. He loses balance, clutches on to the ladder. He starts to get down, halts.*)

CLOV. There's one thing I'll never understand. (*He gets down.*) Why I always obey you. Can you explain that to me?

HAMM. No. … Perhaps it's compassion. (*Pause.*) A kind of great compassion. (*Pause.*) Oh you won't find it easy, you won't find it easy.

(*Pause. Clov begins to move about the room in search of the telescope.*)

CLOV. I'm tired of our goings on, very tired. (*He searches.*) You're not sitting on it? (*He moves the chair, looks at the place where it stood, resumes his search.*)

HAMM. (*Anguished.*) Don't leave me there!

(*Angrily Clov restores the chair to its place.*)

Am I right in the centre?

CLOV. You'd need a microscope to find this—(*He sees the telescope.*) Ah, about time. (*He picks up the telescope, gets up on the ladder, turns the telescope on the without.*)

HAMM. Give me the dog.

CLOV. (*Looking.*) Quiet!

HAMM. (*Angrily.*) Give me the dog!

(*Clov drops the telescope, clasps his hands to his head. Pause. He gets down precipitately, looks for the dog, sees it, picks it up, hastens towards Hamm and strikes him violently on the head with the dog.*)

CLOV. There's your dog for you. (*The dog falls to the ground. Pause.*)

HAMM. He hit me!

CLOV. You drive me mad, I'm mad!

HAMM. If you must hit me, hit me with the axe. (*Pause.*) Or with the gaff, hit me with the gaff. Not with the dog. With the gaff. Or with the axe.

(*Clov picks up the dog and gives it to Hamm who takes it in his arms.*)

CLOV. (*Impatiently.*) Let's stop playing!

HAMM. Never! (*Pause.*) Put me in my coffin.

CLOV. There are no more coffins.

HAMM. Then let it end!

(*Clov goes towards ladder.*)

With a bang!

(*Clov gets up on ladder, gets down again, looks for telescope, sees it, picks it up, gets up on ladder, raises telescope.*)

Of darkness! And me? Did anyone ever have pity on me?

CLOV. (*Lowering the telescope, turning towards Hamm.*) What? (*Pause.*) Is it me you're referring to?

HAMM. (*Angrily.*) An aside, ape! Did you never hear an aside before? (*Pause.*) I'm warming up for my last soliloquy.

CLOV. I warn you. I'm going to look at this filth since it's an order. But it's the last time. (*He turns the telescope on the without.*) Let's see. (*He moves the telescope.*) Nothing … nothing … good … good … nothing … goo— (*He starts, lowers the telescope, examines it, turns it again on the without. Pause.*) Bad luck to it!

HAMM. More complications!

(*Clov gets down.*)

Not an underplot, I trust.

(*Clov moves ladder nearer window, gets up on it, turns telescope on the without.*)

CLOV. (*Dismayed.*) Looks like a small boy!

HAMM. (*Sarcastic.*) A small … boy!

CLOV. I'll go and see. (*He gets down, drops the telescope, goes towards door, turns.*) I'll take the gaff. (*He looks for the gaff, sees it, picks it up, hastens towards door.*)

HAMM. No!

(*Clov halts.*)

CLOV. No? A potential procreator?

HAMM. If he exists he'll die there or he'll come here. And if he doesn't … (*Pause.*)

CLOV. You don't believe me? You think I'm inventing? (*Pause.*)

HAMM. It's the end, Clov, we've come to the end. I don't need you any more. (*Pause.*)

CLOV. Lucky for you. (*He goes towards door.*)

HAMM. Leave me the gaff. (*Clov gives him the gaff, goes towards door, halts, looks at alarm-clock, takes it down, looks round for a better place to put it, goes to bins, puts it on lid of Nagg's bin. Pause.*)

CLOV. I'll leave you. (*He goes towards door.*)

HAMM. Before you go …

(*Clov halts near door.*)

… say something.

CLOV. There is nothing to say.

HAMM. A few words … to ponder … in my heart.

CLOV. Your heart!

HAMM. Yes. (*Pause. Forcibly.*) Yes! (*Pause.*) With the rest, in the end, the shadows, the murmurs, all the trouble, to end up with. (*Pause.*) Clov … He never spoke to me. Then, in the end, before he went, without my having asked him, he spoke to me. He said …

CLOV. (*Despairingly.*) Ah …!

HAMM. Something … from your heart.

CLOV. My heart!

HAMM. A few words … from your heart. (*Pause.*)

CLOV. (*Fixed gaze, tonelessly, towards auditorium.*) They said to me, That's love, yes, yes, not a doubt, now you see how—

HAMM. Articulate!

CLOV. (*As before.*) How easy it is. They said to me, That's friendship, yes, yes, no question, you've found it. They said to me, Here's the place, stop, raise your head and look at all that beauty. That order! They said to me, Come now, you're not a brute beast, think upon these things and you'll see how all becomes clear. And simple! They said to me, What skilled attention they get, all these dying of their wounds.

HAMM. Enough!

CLOV. (*As before.*) I say to myself—sometimes, Clov, you must learn to suffer better than that if you want them to weary of punishing you—one day. I say to myself—sometimes, Clov, you must be better than that if you want them to let you go—one day. But I feel too old, and too far, to form new habits. Good, it'll never end, I'll never go. (*Pause.*) Then one day, suddenly, it ends, it changes, I don't understand, it dies, or it's me, I don't understand that either. I ask the words that remain—sleeping, waking, morning, evening. They have nothing to say. (*Pause.*) I open the door of the cell and go. I am so bowed I only see my feet, if I open my eyes, and between my legs a little trail of black dust. I say to myself that the earth is extinguished, though I never saw it lit. (*Pause.*) It's easy going. (*Pause.*) When I fall I'll weep for happiness. (*Pause. He goes towards door.*)

HAMM. Clov!

(*Clov halts, without turning.*)

Nothing.

(*Clov moves on.*)

Clov!

(*Clov halts, without turning.*)

CLOV. This is what we call making an exit.

HAMM. I'm obliged to you, Clov. For your services.

CLOV. (*Turning sharply.*) Ah pardon, it's I am obliged to you.

HAMM. It's we are obliged to each other.

(*Pause. Clov goes towards door.*)

One thing more.

(*Clov halts.*)

A last favor.

(*Exit Clov.*)

Cover me with the sheet. (*Long pause.*) No? Good. (*Pause.*) Me to play. (*Pause. Wearily.*) Old endgame lost of old, play and lose and have done with losing. (*Pause. More animated.*) Let me see. (*Pause.*) Ah yes!

(*He tries to move the chair, using the gaff as before. Enter Clov, dressed for the road. Panama hat, tweed coat, raincoat over his arm, umbrella, bag. He halts by the door and stands there, impassive and motionless, his eyes fixed on Hamm, till the end. Hamm gives up.*)

Good. (*Pause.*) Discard. (*He throws away the gaff, makes to throw away the dog, thinks better of it.*) Take it easy. (*Pause.*) And now? (*Pause.*) Raise hat. (*He raises his toque.*) Peace to our … arses. (*Pause.*) And put on again. (*He puts on his toque.*) Deuce. (*Pause. He takes off his glasses.*) Wipe. (*He takes out his handkerchief and, without unfolding it, wipes his glasses.*) And put on again. (*He puts on his glasses, puts back the handkerchief in his pocket.*) We're coming. A few more squirms like that and I'll call. (*Pause.*) A little poetry. (*Pause.*) You prayed—(*Pause. He corrects himself.*) You CRIED for night; it comes—(*Pause. He corrects himself.*) It FALLS: now cry in darkness. (*He repeats, chanting.*) You cried for night; it falls: now cry in darkness. (*Pause.*) Nicely put, that. (*Pause.*) And now? (*Pause.*) Moments for nothing, now as always, time was never and time is over, reckoning closed and story ended. (*Pause. Narrative tone.*) If he could have his child with him … (*Pause.*) It was the moment I was waiting for. (*Pause.*) You don't want to abandon him? You want him to bloom while you are withering? Be there to solace your last million last moments? (*Pause.*) He doesn't realize, all he knows is hunger, and cold, and death to crown it all. But you! You ought to know what the earth is like, nowadays. Oh I put him before his responsibilities! (*Pause. Normal tone.*) Well, there we are, there I am, that's enough. (*He raises the whistle to his lips, hesitates, drops it. Pause.*) Yes, truly! (*He whistles. Pause. Louder. Pause.*) Good. (*Pause.*) Father! (*Pause. Louder.*) Father! (*Pause.*) Good. (*Pause.*) We're coming. (*Pause.*) And to end up with? (*Pause.*) Discard. (*He throws away the dog. He tears the whistle from his neck.*) With my compliments. (*He throws the whistle towards the auditorium. Pause. He sniffs. Soft.*) Clov! (*Long pause.*) No? Good. (*He takes out the handkerchief.*) Since that's the way we're playing it … (*he unfolds handkerchief*) … let's play it that way … (*he unfolds*) … and speak no more about it … (*he finishes unfolding*) … speak no more. (*He holds handkerchief spread out before him.*) Old stancher! (*Pause.*) You … remain. (*Pause. He covers his face with handkerchief, lowers his arms to armrests, remains motionless.*)

(*Brief tableau.*)

CURTAIN

—1957

Dylan Thomas

1914 – 1953

The fiery career of Dylan Thomas left a burning after-image on the poetic retina of the English-speaking world in the mid-twentieth century. Thomas was a rollicking, even raucous, fixture in the taverns of London's Soho-Fitzrovia district, but he also haunted the rural hills and seashores of Wales, where he sought to articulate, through the tumbling power of his words, his sense that life and death were rolled together in nature's driving "green fuse."

Born in Swansea, Wales, Dylan Thomas grew up speaking English; his mother, Florence Hannah Williams, and his father, D.J. Thomas, chose the Anglicized urban world of Swansea over their Welsh roots. Thomas's father was a schoolteacher at Swansea Grammar School, which Dylan Thomas attended and where he proved to be far from a prize pupil. However, from an early age Dylan Thomas was writing poems whose images, rhythms, and rhymes would soon be romanticized as "dark-rooted" and "atavistic" by critics who located his passionate verse in Celtic tradition. Yet if Thomas tapped into Welsh imagery, by the age of 15 he was more consciously modeling himself after the French symbolist poet Arthur Rimbaud, even calling himself "the Rimbaud of Cwmdonkin Drive." What attracted Thomas to poets such as Rimbaud and Keats was not only their iconoclasm, but also the fact that they had died young. Thomas regularly cut classes to pore over his own poetry, and launched into a habit of boisterous drinking that was destined to make his career as tragically brief as those of his idols.

In 1933, when Thomas was only 18 years old, the *New English Weekly* published an astonishing poem, his "And Death Shall Have No Dominion." When Thomas's *18 Poems* was published the following year, the strange and disturbing power of his verse woke up London's literary establishment. The cool, controlled style of T.S. Eliot, which conditioned poetic attitudes well into the 1950s, appeared subdued next to the chaotic heat generated by what one critic calls Thomas's "belligerent syntax." For a time, Thomas was labeled a Surrealist and a Dadaist, labels that framed his poetry as a jumble of random signs and erotic images startled out of a Freudian unconscious. Thomas initially exploited the cultural mileage that these early associations gave him, but when his reputation grew sturdier he was careful to distinguish his work from the Surrealists', and to avow that Freud had never been a direct influence. *18 Poems* won Thomas many admirers, including Edith Sitwell, a tireless champion of the curly-haired, Anglo-Welsh "cherub" who churned out formidable verse. "And Death Shall Have No Dominion" was included in his next volume, *25 Poems* (1936), which was also well received. *The Map of Love* (1939) failed to excite much critical acclaim, but with the postwar publication of *Deaths and Entrances* (1946) Thomas won over both the literati and the general public with the lilting rhythms and fresh imagery of poems such as "Fern Hill."

By this time, Thomas had become notorious as an indefatigable carouser, constantly appealing to friends for money and adored by women who wanted to "save" him from his excesses. In 1937, he met Caitlin Macnamara and entered into a stormy marriage that somehow survived an endless stream of creditors, mad bouts of drinking, and mutual infidelities. The couple had three children.

During the Second World War, Thomas avoided military service on the grounds of poor health, instead finding employment writing film and radio scripts for Strand Films and the BBC. While Thomas remains best known for his early poetry, some critics contend that he was a better playwright and prose writer than poet. The autobiographical stories compiled in *Portrait of the Artist as a Young Dog* (1940) and the posthumously published *Adventures in the Skin Trade* (1955) feature prose that is by turns humorous, raw, and risqué. In his 1945 BBC broadcast "Quite Early One Morning," Thomas's love of place, his fine ear for dialogue, his comic wit and his unforgettable voice fused in a narrative of everyday life in New Quay which endeared him to radio audiences. Around the same time in America, Thomas's poetry was inspiring an almost devotional following with the publications of *The World I Breathe* (1939), *New Poems* (1943), and *Selected Writings* (1946).

For Thomas, the meaning of a word was by no means fixed. As with "Wales," which he savoured as if it were a "gobstopper of magical properties, ringing the word like a bell, making it rise and fall, whisper and thunder like the Welsh sea," Thomas was fascinated by the earthy taste, cadence, and physical horseplay inspired by language. He held that poetry was quintessentially the spoken word, and was meant to be read out loud. In a booming voice that detonated the energy stored in language, Thomas performed radio broadcasts and poetry readings throughout the 1940s and the early 50s—performances that were hugely popular both in Europe and in North America. In 1950 he traveled to New York, where the poet John Malcolm Brinnin had arranged a taxing, but lucrative, schedule of public readings and talks. (The lucre, as usual, quickly evaporated.) Whether reciting his own poetry or favorite poems by Auden, Hardy, and Sitwell, Thomas retained the ability to enthrall a crowd with his magnetic voice and his wildboy antics. His reputation preceded him across the American midwest, and on to San Francisco and Vancouver.

Some critics hold that in the last years of his life Thomas was running on empty, producing only strained works that tried to simulate the tremendous effect captured in his earliest poetry. Others see his writing mature in later works such as "Poem in October" (1945) and the radio drama *Under Milk Wood* (1954). Only a few years before Thomas's final, fatal trip to the United States, he and his family moved into The Boat House in Laugharne, Wales. His stay at The Boat House was to prove the last time Thomas would immerse himself in the landscape of the Welsh shoreline, where he had so often glimpsed the cycle that seemed to him to turn living and dying into almost indistinguishable forces. The respite was short-lived: on a third trip to New York in 1953, Thomas fell into a coma as a result of pneumonia worsened by his doctor's incompetence and Thomas's own continued drinking. A few days later he died, as he had always imagined he would, before reaching the age of 40.

⌘⌘⌘

The Force That Through the Green Fuse Drives the Flower

The force that through the green fuse drives the flower
Drives my green age; that blasts the roots of trees
Is my destroyer.
And I am dumb to tell the crooked rose
My youth is bent by the same wintry fever.

The force that drives the water through the rocks
Drives my red blood; that dries the mouthing streams
Turns mine to wax.
And I am dumb to mouth unto my veins
How at the mountain spring the same mouth sucks.

The hand that whirls the water in the pool[1]
Stirs the quicksand; that ropes the blowing wind
Hauls my shroud sail.
And I am dumb to tell the hanging man
How of my clay is made the hangman's lime.[2]

The lips of time leech to the fountain head;
Love drips and gathers, but the fallen blood
Shall calm her sores.
And I am dumb to tell a weather's wind
How time has ticked a heaven round the stars.

And I am dumb to tell the lover's tomb
How at my sheet goes the same crooked worm.
—1933

Fern Hill

Now as I was young and easy under the apple boughs
About the lilting house and happy as the grass was green,
The night above the dingle[3] starry,
Time let me hail and climb
Golden in the heydays of his eyes,
And honoured among wagons I was prince of the apple towns
And once below a time I lordly had the trees and leaves
Trail with daisies and barley
Down the rivers of the windfall light.

And as I was green and carefree, famous among the barns
About the happy yard and singing as the farm was home,
In the sun that is young once only,
Time let me play and be
Golden in the mercy of his means,
And green and golden I was huntsman and herdsman, the calves
Sang to my horn, the foxes on the hills barked clear and cold,
And the sabbath rang slowly
In the pebbles of the holy streams.

All the sun long it was running, it was lovely, the hay
Fields high as the house, the tunes from the chimneys, it was air
And playing, lovely and watery
And fire green as grass.
And nightly under the simple stars
As I rode to sleep the owls were bearing the farm away,
All the moon long I heard, blessed among stables, the nightjars[4]
Flying with the ricks,° and the horses *haystacks*
Flashing into the dark.

And then to awake, and the farm, like a wanderer white
With the dew, come back, the cock on his shoulder: it was all
Shining, it was Adam and maiden,
The sky gathered again
And the sun grew round that very day.
So it must have been after the birth of the simple light
In the first, spinning place, the spellbound horses walking warm

[1] *hand … pool* See John 5.4.

[2] *lime* Mineral used to speed up decomposition.

[3] *dingle* Wooded dell.

[4] *nightjars* Nocturnal birds.

Out of the whinnying green stable
On to the fields of praise.

And honoured among foxes and pheasants by the gay house
Under the new made clouds and happy as the heart was long,
In the sun born over and over,
I ran my heedless ways,
My wishes raced through the house high hay
And nothing I cared, at my sky blue trades,[1] that time allows
In all his tuneful turning so few and such morning songs
Before the children green and golden
Follow him out of grace,

Nothing I cared, in the lamb white days, that time would take me
Up to the swallow thronged loft by the shadow of my hand,
In the moon that is always rising,
Nor that riding to sleep
I should hear him fly with the high fields
And wake to the farm forever fled from the childless land.
Oh as I was young and easy in the mercy of his means,
Time held me green and dying
Though I sang in my chains like the sea.
—1946

Do Not Go Gentle into That Good Night

Do not go gentle into that good night,
Old age should burn and rave at close of day;
Rage, rage against the dying of the light.

Though wise men at their end know dark is right,
Because their words had forked no lightning they
Do not go gentle into that good night.

Good men, the last wave by, crying how bright
Their frail deeds might have danced in a green bay,
Rage, rage against the dying of the light.

Wild men who caught and sang the sun in flight,
And learn, too late, they grieved it on its way,
Do not go gentle into that good night.

Grave men, near death, who see with blinding sight
Blind eyes could blaze like meteors and be gay,
Rage, rage against the dying of the light.

And you, my father, there on the sad height,
Curse, bless, me now with your fierce tears, I pray.
Do not go gentle into that good night.
Rage, rage against the dying of the light.
—1951

A Refusal to Mourn the Death, by Fire, of a Child in London

Never until the mankind making
Bird beast and flower
Fathering and all humbling darkness
Tells with silence the last light breaking
And the still hour
Is come of the sea tumbling in harness

And I must enter again the round
Zion[2] of the water bead
And the synagogue of the ear of corn
Shall I let pray the shadow of a sound
Or sow my salt seed
In the least valley of sackcloth to mourn

The majesty and burning of the child's death.
I shall not murder
The mankind of her going with a grave truth
Nor blaspheme down the stations of the breath

[1] *trades* Occupations.

[2] *Zion* Hill in Jerusalem, previous center of Jewish worship; by extension, the house of God.

With any further
Elegy of innocence and youth.

Deep with the first dead lies London's daughter,
Robed in the long friends,
The grains beyond age, the dark veins of her mother,
Secret by the unmourning water
Of the riding Thames.[1]
After the first death, there is no other.
—1946

[1] *Thames* River in London.

Philip Larkin

1922 – 1985

Although Philip Larkin published two novels in his lifetime as well as several other nonfiction works, his reputation as a major figure in twentieth-century British literature rests on his poetry. His accessible style and straightforward language; the commentary he provided on Britain's changing post-war status; and above all the extraordinary skill with which he crafted poetic expressions of emotions widely shared (if not always expressed) made him one of the most popular poets of his time. Though often described as anti-social, Larkin was a witty conversationalist, and a loyal friend who maintained several key relationships that spanned most of his adult life. His work is often (and rightly) described as bleakly pessimistic, and frequently touches on themes of solitude and mortality. Yet his poems are also often funny—Larkin is equally capable of dry wit and broad humor.

Larkin was born in Coventry in the West Midlands of England in 1922 to Sydney and Eva Larkin. He was their second child and only son. Although he would later describe his childhood as "dull, pot-bound, and slightly mad," he appears to have had a comfortable upbringing. His father was the city treasurer and the family led a typical middle-class existence. Larkin described his parents as "awkward" and "shy"; it seems likely that the sterility of their relationship influenced his own views towards marriage. The family home may have been emotionless, but his father kept a well-stocked library, where Larkin was first introduced to the classics. Between 1930 and 1940 Larkin attended King Henry VIII School, where he described himself as having been unhappy, an "unsuccessful schoolboy." His unhappiness may have been caused by his stammer, a condition he continued to experience until he was well into his thirties. Whether despite or because of his unhappiness, Larkin did begin writing during this period; his first poem was published in the school paper, *The Coventrian*, in 1934, when he was 12.

In 1940, Larkin sent one of his poems to the literary magazine *The Listener*, which accepted and published "Ultimatum" in November of that year. In the same year he entered Oxford to study English, and the experience of university turned out to be a great stimulus for him in terms both of writing and of personal friendships. It was while he was at Oxford that he met Kingsley Amis, some years later to become famous as a novelist; the two remained fast friends for life. (Although they often showed each other their work in its early stages, it was a love of jazz above all that first drew them together.) Larkin developed in these years a distrust of the Modernist notion that twentieth-century literature should express the difficulties of twentieth-century life, and gained an appreciation for a plainer style of writing. He greatly admired W.H. Auden and W.B. Yeats, and tried for years to mimic Yeats's writing in particular.

Larkin graduated in 1943 and returned to his parents' house in Coventry that year, his poor eyesight making him ineligible to fight in World War II. After failing the civil service exam twice,

Larkin answered an advertisement in the paper for a librarian in Wellington, Shropshire. He remained in the profession for the rest of his life, stating that "librarianship suits me." The solitude of the work as well as the regular hours gave him sufficient time to pursue his writing; during this period he produced his first volume of poetry, *The North Ship*, published at his own expense in 1945. It went largely unnoticed. The following two years produced Larkin's only novels, *Jill* in 1946 and *A Girl in Winter* in 1947. Larkin later described the novels as "over-sized poems"; their lack of success encouraged him to give up the form, and from that point onwards he concentrated on poetry. While in Shropshire Larkin also qualified professionally as a librarian; from 1955 until his death he worked as a librarian at the University of Hull.

In the 1950s Larkin began to be associated with a literary group known simply as "The Movement." Its members included Amis as well as Bruce Montgomery, Thom Gunn, and Donald Davie. They were all representatives of a new style of British writing that was anti-romantic, sardonic, and concerned with everyday British life. In Larkin's case, it was *The Less Deceived* (1955), and the poem "Church Going" in particular, that solidified his poetic reputation as an anti-romantic poet. With this volume Larkin moved beyond the imitation of Yeats and established his own style and voice. Spare in their imagery, and typically with a strong but unobtrusive framework of rhythm and rhyme, the poems often chronicle the place of choice or fate in a person's life. Loneliness, misunderstanding, and deception are central themes in Larkin's work, and the aesthetic act often seemed his only bulwark against despair. "People say I'm very negative and I suppose I am," he admitted, "but the impulse for producing a poem is never negative; the most negative poem in the world is a very positive thing to have done." Larkin's negative outlook has often been considered a reason why, despite having a number of romantic relationships, he never married (he once said that "two can live as stupidly as one"). However, the publication in 1992 of Larkin's *Selected Letters*, which contains derogatory language about women, as well as slurs against socialists and various racial groups, led many to attribute Larkin's views on marriage as much to his tendency towards misogyny as to his innate pessimism with regard to the human condition.

The Less Deceived was followed by *The Whitsun Weddings* and *High Windows* in 1964 and 1974 respectively; the poems in these later collections are largely in the same vein as Larkin's earlier work but are less frequently ironic, more often directly revealing of emotion. Larkin also occasionally adopted a different voice in which the presence of rhyme is more obtrusive, the thoughts bluntly pointed, and the tone loudly sardonic. Two of the poems from *High Windows* written in this tone —"This Be the Verse" and "Annus Mirabilis"—caused something of a sensation on the book's publication, and have remained among the most often quoted of Larkin's poems.

In addition to his poetry, Larkin was engaged with other literary pursuits. From 1961 to 1971 he published a regular jazz column in *The Daily Telegraph*. Some of these columns were later reproduced in *All What Jazz*, published in 1970. He was editor of the *Oxford Book of Twentieth-Century Verse* (1973), and his nonfiction writing was collected in *Required Writing* (1983). Larkin won the Queen's Gold Medal for Poetry in 1965, was appointed a Companion of the British Empire in 1975, and received seven honorary doctorates. He was offered the position of British Poet Laureate in 1984, but turned it down because he did not want the media attention with which it was associated. Larkin's poetic output was much reduced in the 1980s; his last major poem, "Aubade," was published in the *Times Literary Supplement* in 1977. Larkin was admitted to hospital in 1985, suffering from cancer, and had his esophagus removed. He died later that year.

⌘⌘⌘

Days

What are days for?
Days are where we live.
They come, they wake us
Time and time over.
They are to be happy in:
Where can we live but days?

Ah, solving that question
Brings the priest and the doctor
In their long coats
Running over the fields.
—1953

Church Going

Once I am sure there's nothing going on
I step inside, letting the door thud shut.
Another church: matting, seats, and stone,
And little books; sprawlings of flowers, cut
For Sunday, brownish now; some brass and stuff
Up at the holy end; the small neat organ;
And a tense, musty, unignorable silence,
Brewed God knows how long. Hatless, I take off
My cycle-clips in awkward reverence,

Move forward, run my hand around the font.[1]
From where I stand, the roof looks almost new—
Cleaned, or restored? Someone would know: I don't.
Mounting the lectern, I peruse a few
Hectoring large-scale verses, and pronounce
"Here endeth" much more loudly than I'd meant.
The echoes snigger briefly. Back at the door
I sign the book, donate an Irish sixpence,
Reflect the place was not worth stopping for.

Yet stop I did: in fact I often do,
And always end much at a loss like this,
Wondering what to look for; wondering, too,
When churches fall completely out of use
What we shall turn them into, if we shall keep
A few cathedrals chronically on show,
Their parchment, plate and pyx[2] in locked cases,
And let the rest rent-free to rain and sheep.
Shall we avoid them as unlucky places?

Or, after dark, will dubious women come
To make their children touch a particular stone;
Pick simples° for a cancer; or on some *medicinal herbs*
Advised night see walking a dead one?
Power of some sort or other will go on
In games, in riddles, seemingly at random;
But superstition, like belief, must die,
And what remains when disbelief has gone?
Grass, weedy pavement, brambles, buttress, sky,

A shape less recognisable each week,
A purpose more obscure. I wonder who
Will be the last, the very last, to seek
This place for what it was; one of the crew
That tap and jot and know what rood-
lofts° were? *church galleries*
Some ruin-bibber, randy for antique,
Or Christmas-addict, counting on a whiff
Of gown-and-bands and organ-pipes and myrrh?
Or will he be my representative,

Bored, uninformed, knowing the ghostly silt
Dispersed, yet tending to this cross of ground
Through suburb scrub because it held unspilt
So long and equably what since is found
Only in separation—marriage, and birth,
And death, and thoughts of these—for which was built
This special shell? For, though I've no idea
What this accoutred frowsty° barn is worth, *stuffy*
It pleases me to stand in silence here;

A serious house on serious earth it is,
In whose blent air all our compulsions meet,
Are recognised, and robed as destinies.

[1] *font* Baptismal receptacle.

[2] *pyx* Vessel in which the bread of the Eucharist is kept.

And that much never can be obsolete,
Since someone will forever be surprising
A hunger in himself to be more serious,
And gravitating with it to this ground,
Which, he once heard, was proper to grow wise in,
If only that so many dead lie round.
—1954

Talking in Bed

Talking in bed ought to be easiest,
Lying together there goes back so far,
An emblem of two people being honest.

Yet more and more time passes silently.
Outside, the wind's incomplete unrest
Builds and disperses clouds about the sky,

And dark towns heap up on the horizon.
None of this cares for us. Nothing shows why
At this unique distance from isolation

It becomes still more difficult to find
Words at once true and kind,
Or not untrue and not unkind.
—1960

Annus Mirabilis[1]

Sexual intercourse began
In nineteen sixty-three
(Which was rather late for me)—
Between the end of the *Chatterley* ban[2]
And the Beatles' first L.P.

Up till then there'd only been
A sort of bargaining,
A wrangle for a ring,
A shame that started at sixteen
And spread to everything.

Then all at once the quarrel sank:
Everyone felt the same,
And every life became
A brilliant breaking of the bank,
A quite unlosable game.

So life was never better than
In nineteen sixty-three (Though just too late for me)—
Between the end of the *Chatterley* ban
And the Beatles' first L.P.
—1967

High Windows

When I see a couple of kids
And guess he's fucking her and she's
Taking pills or wearing a diaphragm,
I know this is paradise

Everyone old has dreamed of all their lives—
Bonds and gestures pushed to one side
Like an outdated combine harvester,
And everyone young going down the long slide

To happiness, endlessly. I wonder if
Anyone looked at me, forty years back,
And thought, *That'll be the life;*
No God any more, or sweating in the dark

About hell and that, or having to hide
What you think of the priest. He
And his lot will all go down the long slide
Like free bloody birds. And immediately

Rather than words comes the thought of high windows:
The sun-comprehending glass,

[1] *Annus Mirabilis* Latin: Wondrous Year.

[2] *the Chatterley ban* D.H. Lawrence's novel *Lady Chatterley's Lover* was banned in both the UK and US on the grounds of obscenity; it contained four-letter words and descriptions of sexual activity that were, for the time, quite explicit. On 2 November 1960, Penguin Books won an obscenity trial over the issue, and the ban was lifted in the UK.

And beyond it, the deep blue air, that shows
Nothing, and is nowhere, and is endless.
—1967

This Be the Verse

They fuck you up, your mum and dad.
    They may not mean to, but they do.
They fill you with the faults they had
    And add some extra, just for you.

But they were fucked up in their turn
    By fools in old-style hats and coats,
Who half the time were soppy-stern
    And half at one another's throats.

Man hands on misery to man.
    It deepens like a coastal shelf.
Get out as early as you can,
    And don't have any kids yourself.
—1971

The Old Fools

What do they think has happened, the old fools,
    To make them like this? Do they somehow suppose
It's more grown-up when your mouth hangs
    open and drools
And you keep on pissing yourself, and can't remember
Who called this morning? Or that, if they only chose,
They could alter things back to when they danced all night,
Or went to their wedding, or sloped arms some September?
Or do they fancy there's really been no change,
And they've always behaved as if they were crippled or
    tight,
Or sat through days of thin continuous dreaming
Watching light move? If they don't (and they can't),
    it's strange;
            Why aren't they screaming?

At death, you break up: the bits that were you
Start speeding away from each other for ever
With no one to see. It's only oblivion, true:
We had it before, but then it was going to end,
And was all the time merging with a unique endeavour
To bring to bloom the million-petalled flower
Of being here. Next time you can't pretend
There'll be anything else. And these are the first signs:
Not knowing how, not hearing who, the power
Of choosing gone. Their looks show that they're for it:
Ash hair, toad hands, prune face dried into lines—
            How can they ignore it?

Perhaps being old is having lighted rooms
Inside your head, and people in them, acting.
People you know, yet can't quite name; each looms
Like a deep loss restored, from known doors turning,
Setting down a lamp, smiling from a stair, extracting
A known book from the shelves; or sometimes only
The rooms themselves, chairs and a fire burning,
The blown bush at the window, or the sun's
Faint friendliness on the wall some lonely
Rain-ceased midsummer evening. That is where they
    live:
Not here and now, but where all happened once.
            This is why they give

An air of baffled absence, trying to be there
Yet being here. For the rooms grow farther, leaving
Incompetent cold, the constant wear and tear
Of taken breath, and them crouching below
Extinction's alp, the old fools, never perceiving
How near it is. This must be what keeps them quiet:
The peak that stays in view wherever we go
For them is rising ground. Can they never tell
What is dragging them back, and how it will end?
Not at night? Not when the strangers come? Never,
    throughout
The whole hideous inverted childhood? Well,
            We shall find out.
—1973

Aubade[1]

I work all day, and get half-drunk at night.
Waking at four to soundless dark, I stare.
In time the curtain-edges will grow light.
Till then I see what's really always there:
Unresting death, a whole day nearer now,
Making all thought impossible but how
And where and when I shall myself die.
Arid interrogation: yet the dread
Of dying, and being dead,
Flashes afresh to hold and horrify.

The mind blanks at the glare. Not in remorse
—The good not done, the love not given, time
Torn off unused—nor wretchedly because
An only life can take so long to climb
Clear of its wrong beginnings, and may never;
But at the total emptiness for ever,
The sure extinction that we travel to
And shall be lost in always. Not to be here,
Not to be anywhere,
And soon; nothing more terrible, nothing more true.

This is a special way of being afraid
No trick dispels. Religion used to try,
That vast moth-eaten musical brocade
Created to pretend we never die,
And specious° stuff that says *No rational being* misleading
Can fear a thing it will not feel, not seeing
That this is what we fear—no sight, no sound,
No touch or taste or smell, nothing to think with,
Nothing to love or link with,
The anaesthetic from which none come round.

And so it stays just on the edge of vision,
A small unfocused blur, a standing chill
That slows each impulse down to indecision.
Most things may never happen: this one will,
And realisation of it rages out
In furnace-fear when we are caught without
People or drink. Courage is no good:
It means not scaring others. Being brave
Lets no one off the grave.
Death is no different whined at than withstood.

Slowly light strengthens, and the room takes shape.
It stands plain as a wardrobe, what we know,
Have always known, know that we can't escape,
Yet can't accept. One side will have to go.
Meanwhile telephones crouch, getting ready to ring
In locked-up offices, and all the uncaring
Intricate rented world begins to rouse.
The sky is white as clay, with no sun.
Work has to be done.
Postmen like doctors go from house to house.
—1977

[1] *Aubade* From the Old French "alba," an early morning song or poem, the motif of which is usually a call for lovers to wake before parting.

Ted Hughes

1930 – 1998

When Ted Hughes was chosen to succeed Sir John Betjeman as England's Poet Laureate in 1984, a reporter in *The Times* described the selection as "a bit like appointing a grim young cow to replace a cuddly old teddy bear." Coming on the British literary scene in the 1950s, Hughes startled readers with his poetic voice. With bold metaphors and forceful rhythms, his poems paint grim, often violent, visions of human existence. At the same time, he celebrates the power of nature and attempts to reunite humanity with the natural world, using myth and folklore to explore alternative possibilities of spirituality.

Edward James Hughes was born in Mytholmroyd, a county in West Yorkshire, the landscape of which—with its valleys, cliffs, and surrounding moors—pervades much of his poetry. Hughes studied English literature for two years at Cambridge before switching to archaeology and anthropology in his final year of study—seeking to escape what he called "the terrible, suffocating, maternal octopus" of the English poetic tradition. In 1956 after graduating, Hughes met and married Sylvia Plath, an American student studying at Cambridge on a Fulbright Fellowship. The following year, having published some individual poems, Hughes released his first collection, *The Hawk in the Rain* (1957). The poems of this début—including "The Thought-Fox" and "Pike"—depict animals participating in a natural world from which humans are isolated by their intellect.

After teaching briefly in the United States, Hughes and Plath returned to England, where their two children were born and where Hughes published his second collection, *Lupercal* (1960). Hughes also began writing children's books and radio plays during this period. After Plath committed suicide in 1963, following the couple's separation, Hughes put his own poetry on hold to focus on editing and publishing his wife's poems and journals. He oversaw the publication of the work that would establish her importance as a major poet, but was vehemently criticized for some of his interventions, including the destruction of the journals she kept in the months leading up to her suicide.

Hughes's return to poetry, *Wodwo* (1967), signaled a change in direction from his earlier work. An interest in anthropology began to color his work, as did a marked interest in occult, mythic, and folktale sources. The volume following, *Crow: From the Life and Songs of the Crow* (1970), created in collaboration with artist Leonard Baskin, presents a series of poems informed by Hughes's own mythology. These poems, which follow a crow from the genesis of the world until nuclear apocalypse, lay bare the brutality in nature, though with more humor than was present in his earlier work. Hughes said his goal in the Crow poems was to achieve a certain style consisting of "a super-simple and a super-ugly language which would in a way shed everything except just what he [Crow] wanted to say." Perhaps not surprisingly, this carrion-eating, graceless, self-serving protagonist (who became the main character of several subsequent works) brought charges of misanthropy and crudeness upon Hughes.

With *Crow* Hughes discovered his penchant for collaborative ventures, and more followed, including *Cave Birds* (1978), also with Leonard Baskin; *Remains of Elmet* (1979), in which he explores, with photographer Fay Godwin, the history of his native region from ancient to industrial times; and *River* (1983), which, accompanied by photographs by Peter Keen, provides a composite view of a river over the course of a year. Another of his later collections, *Moortown* (1979), documents his experiences dairy farming with Jack Orchard, the father of his second wife, Carol.

Though Hughes continued to publish volumes of new and collected poems, in his later years he devoted himself increasingly to judging competitions and performing readings—particularly for children—and became an active supporter of environmental and ecological causes. Hughes also turned to writing prose and to translating, publishing *Tales from Ovid* (1997), a collection of essays entitled *Winter Pollen* (1994), and his critical work on Shakespeare, *Shakespeare and the Goddess of Complete Being* (1992), which united his interest in the author with his passion for mythology.

In 1998 Hughes broke his thirty-year silence concerning his marriage with Plath and published *Birthday Letters*, a series of poems addressed to his dead wife. During the years following her death, Hughes had frequently been accused by some of Plath's admirers of "murdering" the female poet, and his surname was repeatedly defaced on her gravestone. Hughes's deeply personal examination of his relationship with Plath made his last collection important not only as an answer to these accusations but also as a complex and affecting work of poetry.

Hughes was diagnosed with colon cancer in 1997 and died in 1998, two weeks after receiving the Order of Merit from Queen Elizabeth II. Hughes's unique vision of the natural world—and of humanity's place in it—has endured after his death, and his poetry remains widely read and studied. Of his continued popularity, British poet and critic Dick Davis explains, "He brings back to our suburban, centrally-heated and, above all, *safe* lives reports from an authentic frontier of reality and the imagination. His poems speak to us of a world that is constantly true in a way that we know our temporary comforts cannot be."

⌘⌘⌘

The Thought-Fox

I imagine this midnight moment's forest:
Something else is alive
Beside the clock's loneliness
And this blank page where my fingers move.

Through the window I see no star:
Something more near
Though deeper within darkness
Is entering the loneliness:

Cold, delicately as the dark snow
A fox's nose touches twig, leaf;
Two eyes serve a movement, that now
And again now, and now, and now

Sets neat prints into the snow
Between trees, and warily a lame
Shadow lags by stump and in hollow
Of a body that is bold to come

Across clearings, an eye,
A widening deepening greenness,
Brilliantly, concentratedly,
Coming about its own business

Till, with a sudden sharp hot stink of fox,
It enters the dark hole of the head.
The window is starless still; the clock ticks,
The page is printed.
—1957

Pike

Pike, three inches long, perfect
Pike in all parts, green tigering the gold.
Killers from the egg: the malevolent aged grin.
They dance on the surface among the flies.

Or move, stunned by their own grandeur,
Over a bed of emerald, silhouette
Of submarine delicacy and horror.
A hundred feet long in their world.

In ponds, under the heat-struck lily pads—
Gloom of their stillness:
Logged on last year's black leaves, watching upwards.
Or hung in an amber cavern of weeds

The jaws' hooked clamp and fangs
Not to be changed at this date;
A life subdued to its instrument;
The gills kneading quietly, and the pectorals.

Three we kept behind glass,
Jungled in weed: three inches, four,
And four and a half: fed fry to them—
Suddenly there were two. Finally one.

With a sag belly and the grin it was born with.
And indeed they spare nobody.
Two, six pounds each, over two feet long,
High and dry and dead in the willow-herb—

One jammed past its gills down the other's gullet:
The outside eye stared: as a vice locks—
The same iron in this eye
Though its film shrank in death.

A pond I fished, fifty yards across,
Whose lilies and muscular tench[1]
Had outlasted every visible stone
Of the monastery that planted them—

Stilled legendary depth:
It was as deep as England. It held
Pike too immense to stir, so immense and old
That past nightfall I dared not cast

But silently cast and fished
With the hair frozen on my head
For what might move, for what eye might move.
The still splashes on the dark pond,

Owls hushing the floating woods
Frail on my ear against the dream
Darkness beneath night's darkness had freed,
That rose slowly towards me, watching.
—1959

[1] *tench* Fish, like a carp.

Heptonstall Old Church[2]

A great bird landed here.

Its song drew men out of rock,
Living men out of bog and heather.

Its song put a light in the valleys
And harness on the long moors.

Its song brought a crystal from space
And set it in men's heads.

Then the bird died.

Its giant bones
Blackened and became a mystery.

The crystal in men's heads
Blackened and fell to pieces.

The valleys went out.
The moorland broke loose.
—1979

[2] *Heptonstall Old Church* The town of Heptonstall was three miles from Hughes's childhood home of Mytholmroyd, in West Yorkshire. The ruins of the "old church" (dating from the thirteenth century) stand beside the present church, constructed in 1854. The bodies of Sylvia Plath and of Hughes's parents are buried in its churchyard.

Fay Godwin, *Heptonstall backlit, Yorkshire,* 1971.

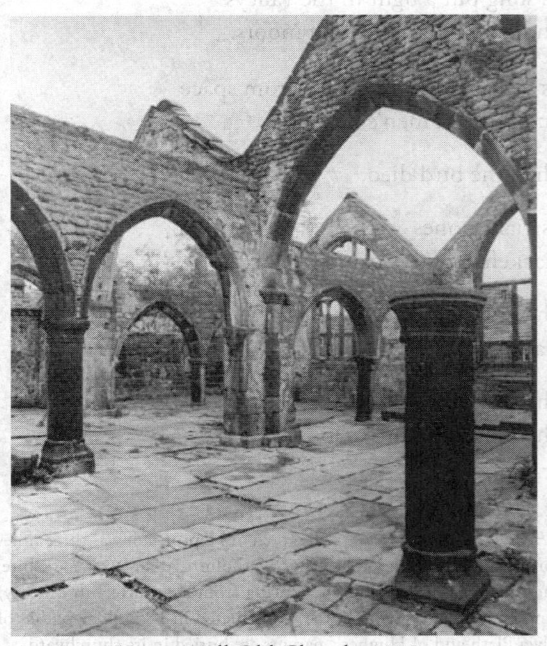

Heptonstall Old Church, 1970s.

Daffodils

Remember how we[1] picked the daffodils?
Nobody else remembers, but I remember.
Your daughter came with her armfuls, eager and happy,
Helping the harvest. She has forgotten.
She cannot even remember you. And we sold them.
It sounds like sacrilege, but we sold them.
Were we so poor? Old Stoneman, the grocer,
Boss-eyed, his blood-pressure purpling to beetroot
(It was his last chance,
He would die in the same great freeze as you),
He persuaded us. Every Spring
He always bought them, sevenpence a dozen,
"A custom of the house."

[1] *we* I.e., Hughes and Sylvia Plath.

Besides, we still weren't sure we wanted to own
Anything. Mainly we were hungry
To convert everything to profit.
Still nomads—still strangers
To our whole possession. The daffodils
Were incidental gilding of the deeds,
Treasure trove. They simply came,
And they kept on coming.
As if not from the sod but falling from heaven.
Our lives were still a raid on our own good luck.
We knew we'd live for ever. We had not learned
What a fleeting glance of the everlasting
Daffodils are. Never identified
The nuptial flight of the rarest ephemera—
Our own days!
We thought they were a windfall.
Never guessed they were a last blessing.
So we sold them. We worked at selling them
As if employed on somebody else's
Flower-farm. You bent at it
In the rain of that April—your last April.
We bent there together, among the soft shrieks
Of their jostled stems, the wet shocks shaken
Of their girlish dance-frocks—
Fresh-opened dragonflies, wet and flimsy,
Opened too early.

We piled their frailty lights on a carpenter's bench,
Distributed leaves among the dozens—
Buckling blade-leaves, limber, groping for air, zinc-silvered—
Propped their raw butts in bucket water,
Their oval, meaty butts,
And sold them, sevenpence a bunch—

Wind-wounds, spasms from the dark earth,
With their odourless metals,
A flamy purification of the deep grave's stony cold
As if ice had a breath—

We sold them, to wither.
The crop thickened faster than we could thin it.
Finally, we were overwhelmed
And we lost our wedding-present scissors.

Every March since they have lifted again
Out of the same bulbs, the same
Baby-cries from the thaw,
Ballerinas too early for music, shiverers
In the draughty wings of the year.
On that same groundswell of memory, fluttering
They return to forget you stooping there
Behind the rainy curtains of a dark April,
Snipping their stems.

But somewhere your scissors remember.
Wherever they are.
Here somewhere, blades wide open,
April by April
Sinking deeper
Through the sod—an anchor, a cross of rust.
—1998

Chinua Achebe

1930 – 2013

Chinua Achebe gained international attention with the publication of his first novel, *Things Fall Apart* (1958); it has since attained the status of a modern classic, and has sold over ten million copies. *Things Fall Apart*, together with Achebe's subsequent novels, follows the course of Nigerian history from just before colonial rule until immediately after independence. Focused on the perspective of colonized Nigerians, these works record the trauma that resulted from Africa's experience with European rule and—without idealizing Nigerians—demonstrate the value, dignity, and beauty of a culture that was all but lost during colonial rule. Though Achebe's writing, whether short story, novel, or political essay, often focuses explicitly on his native country, he argued against a narrowly nationalistic approach, seeking what he called "universal communication across racial and cultural boundaries as a means of fostering respect for all people."

Achebe was born Albert Chinualumoga Achebe in 1930 in eastern Nigeria. Both of Achebe's parents were Christian converts, and his father was employed as a catechist for the Church Missionary Society. Achebe attended the prestigious Government College at Umuahia before enrolling in University College, Ibadan, a newly constituent college of the University of London. There Achebe decided to study literature, following a curriculum that mirrored that of the College's British parent school—with the sole addition of some writers thought relevant to African students, such as Joseph Conrad, H. Rider Haggard, and colonial administrators such as Joyce Cary (whose novel *Mister Johnson* had a profound influence on Achebe). The work of these writers, which frequently features stereotypical and racist depictions of African people, helped to persuade Achebe to write, and also determined his choice to write in English. Unlike many other African writers (such as Kenyan writer Ngũgĩ wa Thiong'o) who choose to use their native language rather than that of their colonizers, Achebe felt that by writing in English he could more directly take issue with these colonial writers by replacing their portraits of Africans with his own.

While in university, Achebe contributed several stories to the *University Herald*. These works, published much later in *Girls at War and Other Stories* (1972), foreground the ways in which conflicts between modern and traditional values have been exacerbated by colonial contact. The traditional balance between material and spiritual aspects of society, and between a concern for self and for community, is typically disrupted, robbing subjects of a strong culture on which to rely. Achebe, himself educated in a system that favored all elements of the new, colonial order—whether cultural, religious, or academic—over those of traditional Igbo society, had to learn for himself much of the history of his people.

After graduating from university, Achebe married, started a family, and embarked on a twelve-year career as a producer for the Nigerian Broadcasting Corporation. Encouraged by literary critic Gilbert Phelps, one of his teachers at the BBC staff school, Achebe published *Things Fall Apart* in 1958. Readers of this novel were struck not least of all by Achebe's ability to adapt the English language to his own goals in writing about Nigeria. He makes heavy use of Igbo proverbs—which often highlight the themes of his work or help further characterization—and vernacular speech patterns, as well as of native imagery and folklore. In this way his English manages to convey the flavor of Nigerian experience, belief, and culture. In Achebe's view, "the price a world language must be prepared to pay is submission to many different kinds of use. The African writer should aim to use English in a way that brings out his message best.... He should aim at fashioning out an English which is at once universal and able to carry his peculiar experience." *Things Fall Apart* became the first book in London publisher Heinemann's influential African Writers Series, of which Achebe was the first series editor; through his editorship as well as through his own writing, Achebe helped to foster the creation of an internationally recognized canon of African literature.

No Longer at Ease (1960), *Arrow of God* (1964), *A Man of the People* (1966), and *Anthills of the Savannah* (1987), Achebe's other novels, are also highly acclaimed. Achebe's prescience was often noted in his examinations of Nigeria's political situation. *A Man of the People*, for example, expressed Achebe's concern over what he identified as Nigeria's lack of strong leadership—a lack that led to Nigeria's first military coup in January 1966, the month of the novel's publication.

During the civil war that followed, Achebe traveled and spoke extensively on behalf of his people, who briefly formed the independent state of Biafra in 1967. Following the conclusion of civil war in 1970, Achebe continued his political activities while accepting various teaching posts at American schools. The poetry and essays written during this period are more overtly political than his earlier work. *Morning Yet on Creation Day* (1974) contains both literary and political essays; many of these were reprinted in the collection *Hopes and Impediments* (1988), which opens with Achebe's controversial essay on Joseph Conrad's *Heart of Darkness*.

Achebe returned to work at the University of Nigeria in 1976, but after a serious car accident in 1990 he moved to the United States to recuperate, accepting a post at Bard College, New York. There he published the essay and poetry collection *Another Africa* (1997), then the autobiographical essay collections *Home and Exile* (2000) and *The Education of a British-Protected Child* (2009). In 2012, the year before his death, he released *There Was a Country: A Personal History of Biafra*, a non-fiction work combining historical analysis with his personal recollections of the Nigerian Civil War

Throughout his career Achebe insisted that his political actions and his literary pursuits were not two separate activities, but two ways of attempting to achieve the same end. He firmly believed that storytelling, far from being an idle pursuit, is a socially relevant form of political engagement. "Literature, whether handed down by word of mouth or in print, gives us a second handle on reality; enabling us to encounter in the safe manageable dimensions of make-believe the very same threats to integrity that may assail the psyche in real life; and at the same time providing through the self-discovery which it imparts, a veritable weapon for coping with these threats."

⌘⌘⌘

Dead Men's Path

Michael Obi's hopes were fulfilled much earlier than he had expected. He was appointed headmaster of Ndume Central School in January 1949. It had always been an unprogressive school, so the Mission authorities[1] decided to send a young and energetic man to run it. Obi accepted this responsibility with enthusiasm. He had many wonderful ideas and this was an opportunity to put them into practice. He had had sound secondary school education which designated him a "pivotal teacher" in the official records and set him apart from the other headmasters in the mission field. He was outspoken in his condemnation of the narrow views of these older and often less-educated ones.

"We shall make a good job of it, shan't we?" he asked his young wife when they first heard the joyful news of his promotion.

"We shall do our best," she replied. "We shall have such beautiful gardens and everything will be just *modern* and delightful...." In their two years of married life she had become completely infected by his passion for "modern methods" and his denigration of "these old and superannuated people in the teaching field who would be better employed as traders in the Onitsha[2] market." She began to see herself already as the admired wife of the young headmaster, the queen of the school.

The wives of the other teachers would envy her position. She would set the fashion in everything.... Then, suddenly, it occurred to her that there might not be other wives. Wavering between hope and fear, she asked her husband, looking anxiously at him.

"All our colleagues are young and unmarried," he said with enthusiasm which for once she did not share. "Which is a good thing," he continued.

"Why?"

"Why? They will give all their time and energy to the school."

Nancy was downcast. For a few minutes she became skeptical about the new school; but it was only for a few minutes. Her little personal misfortune could not blind her to her husband's happy prospects. She looked at him as he sat folded up in a chair. He was stoop-shouldered and looked frail. But he sometimes surprised people with sudden bursts of physical energy. In his present posture, however, all his bodily strength seemed to have retired behind his deep-set eyes, giving them an extraordinary power of penetration. He was only twenty-six, but looked thirty or more. On the whole, he was not unhandsome.

"A penny for your thoughts, Mike," said Nancy after a while, imitating the woman's magazine she read.

"I was thinking what a grand opportunity we've got at last to show these people how a school should be run."

Ndume School was backward in every sense of the word. Mr. Obi put his whole life into the work, and his wife hers too. He had two aims. A high standard of teaching was insisted upon, and the school compound was to be turned into a place of beauty. Nancy's dream-gardens came to life with the coming of the rains, and blossomed. Beautiful hibiscus and allamanda hedges in brilliant red and yellow marked out the carefully tended school compound from the rank neighborhood bushes.

One evening as Obi was admiring his work he was scandalized to see an old woman from the village hobble right across the compound, through a marigold flower-bed and the hedges. On going up there he found faint signs of an almost disused path from the village across the school compound to the bush on the other side.

"It amazes me," said Obi to one of his teachers who had been three years in the school, "that you people allowed the villagers to make use of this footpath. It is simply incredible." He shook his head.

"The path," said the teacher apologetically, "appears to be very important to them. Although it is hardly used, it connects the village shrine with their place of burial."

"And what has that got to do with the school?" asked the headmaster.

---

[1] *Mission authorities* Many schools in African countries formerly colonized by the British were run by Christian missionary organizations.

[2] *Onitsha* City in southeastern Nigeria; the Onitsha market is one of the largest in West Africa.

"Well, I don't know," replied the other with a shrug of the shoulders. "But I remember there was a big row some time ago when we attempted to close it."

"That was some time ago. But it will not be used now," said Obi as he walked away. "What will the Government Education Officer think of this when he comes to inspect the school next week? The villagers might, for all I know, decide to use the schoolroom for a pagan ritual during the inspection."

Heavy sticks were planted closely across the path at the two places where it entered and left the school premises. These were further strengthened with barbed wire.

Three days later the village priest of *Ani*[1] called on the headmaster. He was an old man and walked with a slight stoop. He carried a stout walking-stick which he usually tapped on the floor, by way of emphasis, each time he made a new point in his argument.

"I have heard," he said after the usual exchange of cordialities, "that our ancestral footpath has recently been closed...."

"Yes," replied Mr. Obi. "We cannot allow people to make a highway of our school compound."

"Look here, my son," said the priest bringing down his walking-stick, "this path was here before you were born and before your father was born. The whole life of this village depends on it. Our dead relatives depart by it and our ancestors visit us by it. But most important, it is the path of children coming in to be born...."

Mr. Obi listened with a satisfied smile on his face.

"The whole purpose of our school," he said finally, "is to eradicate just such beliefs as that. Dead men do not require footpaths. The whole idea is just fantastic. Our duty is to teach your children to laugh at such ideas."

"What you say may be true," replied the priest, "but we follow the practices of our fathers. If you reopen the path we shall have nothing to quarrel about. What I always say is: let the hawk perch and let the eagle perch." He rose to go.

"I am sorry," said the young headmaster. "But the school compound cannot be a thoroughfare. It is against our regulations. I would suggest your constructing another path, skirting our premises. We can even get our boys to help in building it. I don't suppose the ancestors will find the little detour too burdensome."

"I have no more words to say," said the old priest, already outside.

Two days later a young woman in the village died in childbed. A diviner was immediately consulted and he prescribed heavy sacrifices to propitiate ancestors insulted by the fence.

Obi woke up next morning among the ruins of his work. The beautiful hedges were torn up not just near the path but right round the school, the flowers trampled to death and one of the school buildings pulled down ... That day, the white Supervisor came to inspect the school and wrote a nasty report on the state of the premises but more seriously about the "tribal-war situation developing between the school and the village, arising in part from the misguided zeal of the new headmaster."

—1953

from *An Image of Africa: Racism in Conrad's* Heart of Darkness

In the fall of 1974 I was walking one day from the English Department at the University of Massachusetts to a parking lot. It was a fine autumn morning such as encouraged friendliness to passing strangers. Brisk youngsters were hurrying in all directions, many of them obviously freshmen in their first flush of enthusiasm. An older man going the same way as I turned and remarked to me how very young they came these days. I agreed. Then he asked me if I was a student too. I said no, I was a teacher. What did I teach? African literature. Now that was funny, he said, because he knew a fellow who taught the same thing, or perhaps it was African history, in a certain community college not far from here. It always surprised him, he went on to say, because he never had thought of Africa as having

[1] *Ani* Traditional belief system, often called Odinani, of the Igbo people of Nigeria.

that kind of stuff, you know. By this time I was walking much faster. "Oh well," I heard him say finally, behind me: "I guess I have to take your course to find out."

A few weeks later, I received two very touching letters from high school children in Yonkers, New York, who—bless their teacher—had just read *Things Fall Apart*. One of them was particularly happy to learn about the customs and superstitions of an African tribe.

I propose to draw from these rather trivial encounters rather heavy conclusions which at first sight might seem somewhat out of proportion to them. But only, I hope, at first sight.

The young fellow from Yonkers, perhaps partly on account of his age, but I believe also for much deeper and more serious reasons, is obviously unaware that the life of his own tribesmen in Yonkers, New York, is full of odd customs and superstitions and, like everybody else in his culture, imagines that he needs a trip to Africa to encounter those things.

The other person being fully my own age could not be excused on the grounds of his years. Ignorance might be a more likely reason; but here again I believe that something more willful than a mere lack of information was at work. For did not that erudite British historian and Regius Professor at Oxford, Hugh Trevor-Roper,[1] also pronounce that African history did not exist?

If there is something in these utterances more than youthful inexperience, more than a lack of factual knowledge, what is it? Quite simply it is the desire—one might indeed say the need—in Western psychology to set Africa up as a foil to Europe, as a place of negations at once remote and vaguely familiar, in comparison with which Europe's own state of spiritual grace will be manifest.

This need is not new; which should relieve us all of considerable responsibility and perhaps make us even willing to look at this phenomenon dispassionately. I have neither the wish nor the competence to embark on the exercise with the tools of the social and biological sciences but do so more simply in the manner of a novelist responding to one famous book of European fiction: Joseph Conrad's *Heart of Darkness*, which better than any other work that I know displays that Western desire and need which I have just referred to. Of course there are whole libraries of books devoted to the same purpose, but most of them are so obvious and so crude that few people worry about them today. Conrad, on the other hand, is undoubtedly one of the great stylists of modern fiction and a good storyteller into the bargain. His contribution therefore falls automatically into a different class—permanent literature—read and taught and constantly evaluated by serious academics. *Heart of Darkness* is indeed so secure today that a leading Conrad scholar has numbered it "among the half-dozen greatest short novels in the English language."[2] I will return to this critical opinion in due course, because it may seriously modify my earlier suppositions about who may or may not be guilty in some of the matters I will now raise.

Heart of Darkness projects the image of Africa as "the other world," the antithesis of Europe and therefore of civilization, a place where man's vaunted intelligence and refinement are finally mocked by triumphant bestiality. The book opens on the River Thames, tranquil, resting peacefully "at the decline of day after ages of good service done to the race that peopled its banks." But the actual story will take place on the River Congo, the very antithesis of the Thames. The River Congo is quite decidedly not a River Emeritus. It has rendered no service and enjoys no old-age pension. We are told that "going up that river was like travelling back to the earliest beginning of the world."

Is Conrad saying then that these two rivers are very different, one good, the other bad? Yes, but that is not the real point. It is not the differentness that worries Conrad but the lurking hint of kinship, of common ancestry. For the Thames too "has been one of the dark places of the earth." It conquered its darkness, of course, and is now in daylight and at peace. But if it were to visit its primordial relative, the Congo, it would run the

[1] *British ... Trevor-Roper* In 1963, Trevor-Roper made the comment, "Perhaps in the future there will be some African history to teach. But at the present there is none; there is only the history of Europeans in Africa. The rest is darkness, and darkness is not the subject of history."

[2] *among the ... language* From Albert J. Guerard's introduction to *Heart of Darkness*, 1950.

terrible risk of hearing grotesque echoes of its own forgotten darkness, and falling victim to an avenging recrudescence of the mindless frenzy of the first beginnings. These suggestive echoes comprise Conrad's famed evocation of the African atmosphere in *Heart of Darkness*. In the final consideration his method amounts to no more than a steady, ponderous, fake-ritualistic repetition of two antithetical sentences, one about silence and the other about frenzy. We can inspect samples of this on pages 103 and 105 of the New American Library edition:[1] (a) "It was the stillness of an implacable force brooding over an inscrutable intention" and (b) "The steamer toiled along slowly on the edge of a black and incomprehensible frenzy." Of course there is a judicious change of adjective from time to time, so that instead of "inscrutable," for example, you might have "unspeakable," even plain "mysterious," etc., etc.

The eagle-eyed English critic F.R. Leavis drew attention long ago to Conrad's "adjectival insistence upon inexpressible and incomprehensible mystery."[2] That insistence must not be dismissed lightly, as many Conrad critics have tended to do, as a mere stylistic flaw; for it raises serious questions of artistic good faith. When a writer while pretending to record scenes, incidents, and their impact is in reality engaged in inducing hypnotic stupor in his readers through a bombardment of emotive words and other forms of trickery, much more has to be at stake than stylistic felicity. Generally normal readers are well armed to detect and resist such underhand activity. But Conrad chose his subject well—one which was guaranteed not to put him in conflict with the psychological predisposition of his readers or raise the need for him to contend with their resistance. He chose the role of purveyor of comforting myths.

The most interesting and revealing passages in *Heart of Darkness* are, however, about people. I must crave the indulgence of my reader to quote almost a whole page from about the middle of the story when representatives of Europe in a steamer going down the Congo encounter the denizens of Africa:

> We were wanderers on a prehistoric earth, on an earth that wore the aspect of an unknown planet. We could have fancied ourselves the first of men taking possession of an accursed inheritance, to be subdued at the cost of profound anguish and of excessive toil. But suddenly, as we struggled round a bend, there would be a glimpse of rush walls, of peaked grass-roofs, a burst of yells, a whirl of black limbs, a mass of hands clapping, of feet stamping, of bodies swaying, of eyes rolling, under the droop of heavy and motionless foliage. The steamer toiled along slowly on the edge of the black and incomprehensible frenzy. The prehistoric man was cursing us, praying to us, welcoming us—who could tell? We were cut off from the comprehension of our surroundings; we glided past like phantoms, wondering and secretly appalled, as sane men would be before an enthusiastic outbreak in a madhouse. We could not understand because we were too far and could not remember because we were travelling in the night of first ages, of those ages that are gone, leaving hardly a sign—and no memories.
>
> The earth seemed unearthly. We are accustomed to look upon the shackled form of a conquered monster, but there—there you could look at a thing monstrous and free. It was unearthly, and the men were—No, they were not inhuman. Well, you know, that was the worst of it—this suspicion of their not being inhuman. It would come slowly to one. They howled and leaped, and spun, and made horrid faces; but what thrilled you was just the thought of their humanity—like yours—the thought of your remote kinship with this wild and passionate uproar. Ugly. Yes, it was ugly enough; but if you were man enough you would admit to yourself that there was in you just the faintest trace of a response to the terrible frankness of that noise, a dim suspicion of there being a meaning in it which you—you so remote from the night of first ages—could comprehend. [107–08]

[1] *pages ... edition* Pages 105 and 107 of the Broadview edition (D.C.R.A. Goonetilleke, ed., 2nd edition, 1999). From this point on, all page numbers, provided in square brackets, are those of the Broadview edition.

[2] *adjectival ... mystery* From F.R. Leavis, *The Great Tradition* (1950).

Herein lies the meaning of *Heart of Darkness* and the fascination it holds over the Western mind: "What thrilled you was just the thought of their humanity—like yours ... Ugly."

Having shown us Africa in the mass, Conrad then zeros in, half a page later, on a specific example, giving us one of his rare descriptions of an African who is not just limbs or rolling eyes:

> And between whiles I had to look after the savage who was fireman. He was an improved specimen; he could fire up a vertical boiler. He was there below me, and, upon my word, to look at him was as edifying as seeing a dog in a parody of breeches and a feather hat, walking on his hind legs. A few months of training had done for that really fine chap. He squinted at the steam gauge and at the water gauge with an evident effort of intrepidity—and he had filed his teeth, too, the poor devil, and the wool of his pate shaved into queer patterns, and three ornamental scars on each of his cheeks. He ought to have been clapping his hands and stamping his feet on the bank, instead of which he was hard at work, a thrall to strange witchcraft, full of improving knowledge. [108]

As everybody knows, Conrad is a romantic on the side. He might not exactly admire savages clapping their hands and stamping their feet but they have at least the merit of being in their place, unlike this dog in a parody of breeches. For Conrad things being in their place is of the utmost importance. "Fine fellows—cannibals—in their place," he tells us pointedly. Tragedy begins when things leave their accustomed place, like Europe leaving its safe stronghold between the policeman and the baker to take a peep into the heart of darkness.

Before the story takes us into the Congo basin proper we are given this nice little vignette as an example of things in their place:

> Now and then a boat from the shore gave one a momentary contact with reality. It was paddled by black fellows. You could see from afar the white of their eyeballs glistening. They shouted, sang; their bodies streamed with perspiration; they had faces like grotesque masks—these chaps; but they had bone, muscle, a wild vitality, an intense energy of movement, that was as natural and true as the surf along their coast. They wanted no excuse for being there. They were a great comfort to look at. [80]

Towards the end of the story Conrad lavishes a whole page quite unexpectedly on an African woman who has obviously been some kind of mistress to Mr. Kurtz and now presides (if I may be permitted a little liberty) like a formidable mystery over the inexorable imminence of his departure:

> She was savage and superb, wild-eyed and magnificent ... She stood looking at us without a stir and like the wilderness itself, with an air of brooding over an inscrutable purpose. [137–38]

This Amazon is drawn in considerable detail, albeit of a predictable nature, for two reasons. First, she is in her place and so can win Conrad's special brand of approval; and second, she fulfils a structural requirement of the story: a savage counterpart to the refined, European woman who will step forth to end the story:

> She came forward, all in black with a pale head, floating toward me in the dusk. She was in mourning ... She took both my hands in hers and murmured, "I had heard you were coming" ... She had a mature capacity for fidelity, for belief, for suffering. [154]

The difference in the attitude of the novelist to these two women is conveyed in too many direct and subtle ways to need elaboration. But perhaps the most significant difference is the one implied in the author's bestowal of human expression to the one and the withholding of it from the other. It is clearly not part of Conrad's purpose to confer language on the "rudimentary souls" of Africa. In place of speech they made "a violent babble of uncouth sounds." They "exchanged short grunting phrases" even among themselves. But most of the time they were too busy with their frenzy. There are two occasions in the book, however, when

Conrad departs somewhat from his practice and confers speech, even English speech, on the savages. The first occurs when cannibalism gets the better of them:

> "Catch 'im," he snapped, with a bloodshot widening of his eyes and a flash of sharp white teeth—"catch 'im. Give 'im to us." "To you, eh?" I asked; "what would you do with them?" "Eat 'im!" he said curtly. [113]

The other occasion was the famous announcement:

> "Mistah Kurtz—he dead." [148]

At first sight these instances might be mistaken for unexpected acts of generosity from Conrad. In reality they constitute some of his best assaults. In the case of the cannibals the incomprehensible grunts that had thus far served them for speech suddenly proved inadequate for Conrad's purpose of letting the European glimpse the unspeakable craving in their hearts. Weighing the necessity for consistency in the portrayal of the dumb brutes against the sensational advantages of securing their conviction by clear, unambiguous evidence issuing out of their own mouths, Conrad chose the latter. As for the announcement of Mr. Kurtz's death by the "insolent black head in the doorway," what better or more appropriate *finis* could be written to the horror story of that wayward child of civilization who wilfully had given his soul to the powers of darkness and "taken a high seat amongst the devils of the land" than the proclamation of his physical death by the forces he had joined?

It might be contended, of course, that the attitude to the African in *Heart of Darkness* is not Conrad's but that of his fictional narrator, Marlow, and that far from endorsing it Conrad might indeed be holding it up to irony and criticism. Certainly, Conrad appears to go to considerable pains to set up layers of insulation between himself and the moral universe of his story. He has, for example, a narrator behind a narrator. The primary narrator is Marlow, but his account is given to us through the filter of a second, shadowy person. But if Conrad's intention is to draw a *cordon sanitaire*[1] between himself and the moral and psychological *malaise* of his narrator, his care seems to me totally wasted because he neglects to hint, clearly and adequately, at an alternative frame of reference by which we may judge the actions and opinions of his characters. It would not have been beyond Conrad's power to make that provision if he had thought it necessary. Conrad seems to me to approve of Marlow, with only minor reservations—a fact reinforced by the similarities between their two careers.

Marlow comes through to us not only as a witness of truth, but one holding those advanced and humane views appropriate to the English liberal tradition which required all Englishmen of decency to be deeply shocked by atrocities in Bulgaria or the Congo of King Leopold of the Belgians or wherever.

Thus Marlow is able to toss out such bleeding-heart sentiments as these:

> They were all dying slowly—it was very clear. They were not enemies, they were not criminals, they were nothing earthly now—nothing but black shadows of disease and starvation, lying confusedly in the greenish gloom. Brought from all the recesses of the coast in all the legality of time contracts, lost in uncongenial surroundings, fed on unfamiliar food, they sickened, became inefficient, and were then allowed to crawl away and rest. [84]

The kind of liberalism espoused here by Marlow/Conrad touched all the best minds of the age in England, Europe, and America. It took different forms in the minds of different people but almost always managed to sidestep the ultimate question of equality between white people and black people. That extraordinary missionary Albert Schweitzer,[2] who sacrificed brilliant careers in music and theology in Europe for a life of service to Africans in much the same area as Conrad writes about, epitomizes the ambivalence. In a comment which has often been quoted Schweitzer says:

---

[1] *cordon sanitaire* French: quarantine line.

[2] *Albert Schweitzer* M.D., humanitarian, and winner of the Nobel Peace Prize (1875–1965).

"The African is indeed my brother but my junior brother." And so he proceeded to build a hospital appropriate to the needs of junior brothers with standards of hygiene reminiscent of medical practice in the days before the germ theory of disease came into being. Naturally he became a sensation in Europe and America. Pilgrims flocked, and I believe still flock even after he has passed on, to witness the prodigious miracle in Lambéréné,[1] on the edge of the primeval forest.

Conrad's liberalism would not take him quite as far as Schweitzer's, though. He would not use the word "brother" however qualified; the farthest he would go was "kinship." When Marlow's African helmsman falls down with a spear in his heart he gives his white master one final disquieting look:

> And the intimate profundity of that look he gave me when he received his hurt remains to this day in my memory—like a claim of distant kinship affirmed in a supreme moment. [125–26]

It is important to note that Conrad, careful as ever with his words, is concerned not so much about "distant kinship" as about someone *laying a claim* on it. The black man lays a claim on the white man which is well-nigh intolerable. It is the laying of this claim which frightens and at the same time fascinates Conrad, "the thought of their humanity—like yours … Ugly."

The point of my observations should be quite clear by now, namely that Joseph Conrad was a thoroughgoing racist. That this simple truth is glossed over in criticisms of his work is due to the fact that white racism against Africa is such a normal way of thinking that its manifestations go completely unremarked. Students of *Heart of Darkness* will often tell you that Conrad is concerned not so much with Africa as with the deterioration of one European mind caused by solitude and sickness. They will point out to you that Conrad is, if anything, less charitable to the Europeans in the story than he is to the natives, that the point of the story is to ridicule Europe's civilizing mission in Africa. A Conrad student informed me in Scotland that Africa is merely a setting for the disintegration of the mind of Mr. Kurtz.

Which is partly the point. Africa as setting and backdrop which eliminates the African as human factor. Africa as a metaphysical battlefield devoid of all recognizable humanity, into which the wandering European enters at his peril. Can nobody see the preposterous and perverse arrogance in thus reducing Africa to the role of props for the break-up of one petty European mind? But that is not even the point. The real question is the dehumanization of Africa and Africans which this age-long attitude has fostered and continues to foster in the world. And the question is whether a novel which celebrates this dehumanization, which depersonalizes a portion of the human race, can be called a great work of art. My answer is: No, it cannot.

—1977

---

[1] *miracle in Lambéréné* Hospital built in 1913 by Schweitzer and his wife, Helene Bresslau, in what is now Gabon.

Derek Walcott

1930 – 2017

Unlike many Caribbean writers who felt they had to move abroad in order to achieve recognition and be published, Derek Walcott remained rooted in the Caribbean. Although he taught part of the year at Boston University, his home was always either Trinidad or St. Lucia. His love of the region and his "multicultural commitment" were noted by the Nobel committee when they awarded him the prize for literature in 1992; he became the first Caribbean writer to receive this honor. Throughout his career Walcott grappled with the central issues of twentieth-century Caribbean writing: the use of the English language versus that of Creole; the effects of a history of slavery and colonization on the region; and the deep-seated ambivalence towards English culture that had been passed down to the colonies.

Walcott was born into a Methodist, English-speaking family in the predominantly Roman Catholic, French Creole-speaking island of St. Lucia. Instead of feeling isolated, he embraced the diverse aspects of his island, learning to love both the English language and Creole culture. His mother, a schoolteacher in the local Methodist school, instilled in Walcott a love of literature and a disciplined work ethic. After his father died when he was a year old, his mother took in sewing to support Walcott, his twin brother, and their elder sister. Walcott's passion for the arts became evident early, and he knew he wanted to be either a painter or a poet. When he was a child, his mother would give him a poem to copy and imitate before going to bed each evening. This early training instilled in him a strong sense of the importance of meter, rhyme, and metaphor.

After graduating from high school, Walcott became a junior teacher at the school he had once attended. By 1948, he was starting to be known in St. Lucia as an emerging poet; in that year he self-published his first volume of poetry, *25 Poems*. Walcott also began to write plays during this period (an interest he shared with his brother), and these plays began to be produced locally. His plays often reflect his interest in local culture (*Ti-Jean and His Brothers; Dream on Monkey Mountain*) and regional history (*Henri-Christophe*).

In the late 1940s and early 1950s many of Walcott's contemporaries left the Caribbean to study in Britain or North America, a path seen by many as the only way to "better oneself." Walcott's high-school marks had not been high enough to allow him to take this route, but he eventually obtained a scholarship to attend the University of the West Indies in Jamaica. There Walcott was an indifferent student, more interested in painting and doing independent reading than in his courses. By this time he was writing regularly, usually rising at 5 a.m. and writing until noon. Some of his more popular poems, including "Ruins of a Great House" and "A Far Cry from Africa," date from this period, during which Walcott also married and became a father.

"Ruins of a Great House" illustrates much of the cultural ambivalence Walcott was beginning to feel. A descendant both of Europeans and of former slaves, he felt torn between the two sides of his heritage. (He refers in another one of his works to "the ancestor who sold me ... and the ancestor who bought me.") His call for compassion in dealing with the effects of history has sometimes been criticized in the Caribbean as inadequate; some have felt that stronger measures needed to be taken—an unequivocal return to African traditions, or a turning away from the English language in favor of Creole. In response to criticism of his commitment to the English language, he has responded that the New World use of English is "Adamic," and that English has been shaped by and continues to be shaped by those who use it.

In 1959 Walcott moved to Trinidad after spending a year studying theater in New York on a Rockefeller Fellowship. His first marriage had dissolved, he felt he needed a change from St. Lucia, and he was attracted to the diversity of Trinidad. He continued to write poetry and plays, and established The Trinidad Theatre Workshop, which produced many of his early plays. Walcott's time with the Workshop was key to developing an indigenous theater tradition in the region. He remarried and had two daughters. In 1962 he published his breakthrough volume of poetry, *In a Green Night*. He was beginning to be known internationally, and some of his poems began appearing in *The New Statesman* and *The New Yorker*. He also began writing *Another Life*, his long autobiographical poem. Completed in 1973, this volume would win several awards, including *The New Statesman* Jock Campbell Award, and garner him international acclaim. The next two decades would cement Walcott's growing international status. He toured widely and continued to publish both poems and plays, including *The Star-Apple Kingdom, The Fortunate Traveller, Midsummer*, and *The Arkansas Testament*.

Walcott published his magnum opus in 1990. *Omeros* was the culmination of his development as a writer: 325 pages written in terza rima, re-casting as a Caribbean story the legend of Achilles, Hector, and Helen, with the story of the island of St. Lucia woven into it. The long poem touches on aspects of Walcott's own history, as he grapples with the region's historical ties to the British and the Caribbean's ties to Africa. The Nobel Committee awarded him the prize in 1992 "for a poetic *oeuvre* of great luminosity, sustained by a historical vision, the outcome of multicultural commitment." In his Nobel acceptance speech Walcott expressed his wish that the people of the Caribbean would move beyond the pain that history has caused in the region; in his words, "[we] make too much of that long groan which underlines the past." He proffered instead a vision of the Caribbean as the synthesis of the past and beginning of a new history: "Antillean art is this restoration of our shattered histories."

Walcott continued to write until his death in 2017, publishing *The Bounty* in 1997, *Tiepolo's Hound* in 2000, *The Prodigal* in 2004, and *White Egrets* in 2010, for which he was awarded the prestigious T.S. Eliot prize. In 2016, he collaborated with painter Peter Doig to create *Morning, Paramin*, a book of poems paired with paintings. When he died he was mourned as a major figure in the literature of the Caribbean and of the world. "It is hard to overstate the importance of Derek Walcott," read his obituary in *The Journal of Commonwealth Literature*. "His was a vast scope of feeling. With a single strophe Walcott could evoke a nation or the intricate and intimate gestures of its people."

⌘⌘⌘

A Far Cry from Africa

A wind is ruffling the tawny pelt
Of Africa. Kikuyu,[1] quick as flies,
Batten upon the bloodstreams of the veldt.[2]
Corpses are scattered through a paradise.
Only the worm, colonel of carrion, cries:
"Waste no compassion on these separate dead!"
Statistics justify and scholars seize
The salients of colonial policy.
What is that to the white child hacked in bed?
To savages, expendable as Jews?

Threshed out by beaters, the long rushes break
In a white dust of ibises[3] whose cries
Have wheeled since civilization's dawn
From the parched river or beast-teeming plain.
The violence of beast on beast is read
As natural law, but upright man
Seeks his divinity by inflicting pain.
Delirious as these worried beasts, his wars
Dance to the tightened carcass of a drum,
While he calls courage still that native dread
Of the white peace contracted by the dead.

Again brutish necessity wipes its hands
Upon the napkin of a dirty cause, again
A waste of our compassion, as with Spain,[4]
The gorilla wrestles with the superman.
I who am poisoned with the blood of both,
Where shall I turn, divided to the vein?
I who have cursed
The drunken officer of British rule, how choose
Between this Africa and the English tongue I love?
Betray them both, or give back what they give?
How can I face such slaughter and be cool?
How can I turn from Africa and live?
—1962

[1] *Kikuyu* Bantu-speaking people of Kenya who fought against British colonial settlers as part of the eight-year Mau Mau uprising.

[2] *Batten upon* Thrive on; revel in; *veldt* Open country.

[3] *ibises* Long-legged, stork-like birds that inhabit lakes and swamps.

[4] *Spain* I.e., the Spanish Civil War (1936–39).

Ruins of a Great House

though our longest sun sets at right declensions
and makes but winter arches, it cannot be long before we
lie down in darkness, and have our light in ashes …
—BROWNE, *Urn Burial*

Stones only, the disjecta membra[5] of this Great House,
Whose moth-like girls are mixed with candledust,
Remain to file the lizard's dragonish claws.
The mouths of those gate cherubs shriek with stain;
Axle and coach wheel silted under the muck
Of cattle droppings.
Three crows flap for the trees
And settle, creaking the eucalyptus boughs.
A smell of dead limes quickens in the nose
The leprosy of empire.
"Farewell, green fields,
Farewell, ye happy groves!"
Marble like Greece, like Faulkner's South[6] in stone,
Deciduous beauty prospered and is gone,
But where the lawn breaks in a rash of trees
A spade below dead leaves will ring the bone
Of some dead animal or human thing
Fallen from evil days, from evil times.

It seems that the original crops were limes
Grown in the silt that clogs the river's skirt;
The imperious rakes[7] are gone, their bright girls gone,
The river flows, obliterating hurt.
I climbed a wall with the grille ironwork

[5] *disjecta membra* Latin: scattered remains.

[6] *Faulkner's South* The American South as depicted in the novels of William Faulkner (1897–1962).

[7] *rakes* Wild young noblemen.

Of exiled craftsmen protecting that great house
From guilt, perhaps, but not from the worm's rent
Nor from the padded cavalry of the mouse.
And when a wind shook in the limes I heard
What Kipling[1] heard, the death of a great empire, the
    abuse
Of ignorance by Bible and by sword.

A green lawn, broken by low walls of stone,
Dipped to the rivulet, and pacing, I thought next
Of men like Hawkins, Walter Raleigh, Drake,[2]
Ancestral murderers and poets, more perplexed
In memory now by every ulcerous crime.
The world's green age then was a rotting lime
Whose stench became the charnel° galleon's text. *mortuary*
The rot remains with us, the men are gone.
But, as dead ash is lifted in a wind
That fans the blackening ember of the mind,
My eyes burned from the ashen prose of Donne.[3]

Ablaze with rage I thought,
Some slave is rotting in this manorial lake,
But still the coal of my compassion fought
That Albion[4] too was once
A colony like ours, "part of the continent, piece of the
    main,"[5]
Nook-shotten, rook o'erblown, deranged
By foaming channels and the vain expense
Of bitter faction.

All in compassion ends
So differently from what the heart arranged:
"as well as if a manor of thy friend's ..."
—1962

[1] *Kipling* Rudyard Kipling (1865–1936), English novelist and short-story writer whose works often interrogated British imperialism.

[2] *Hawkins* John Hawkins, sixteenth-century British slave trader who brought slaves from Africa to West Indian plantations; *Walter Raleigh* English explorer and poet (1552–1618); *Drake* Sir Francis Drake (1543–96), British explorer and military commander who became the first English person to sail around the world.

[3] *Donne* English poet John Donne (1572–1631).

[4] *Albion* England.

[5] *part of ... main* From John Donne's *Devotions upon Emergent Occasions*, Meditation 17 (1624): "No man is an island, entire of itself; every man is a piece of the continent, a part of the main. If a clod be washed away by the sea, Europe is the less, as well as if a promontory were, as well as if a manor of thy friend's or of thine own were: any man's death diminishes me, because I am involved in mankind, and therefore never send to know for whom the bells tolls; it tolls for thee."

from *Omeros*[6]

from Book 1

from Chapter 2

3

"Omeros," she[7] laughed. "That's what we call
    him in Greek,"
stroking the small bust with its boxer's broken nose,
and I thought of Seven Seas[8] sitting near the reek

of drying fishnets, listening to the shallows' noise.
I said: "Homer and Virg[9] are New England farmers,
and the winged horse[10] guards their gas-station,
    you're right."

[6] *Omeros* Modern Greek: Homer. "Homer" is traditionally considered the author of the *Iliad* and the *Odyssey*, Greek epics written in the late seventh or early eighth centuries BCE. Classicists are not sure if the epics were composed by one artist or if they are cultural products composed by many hands. Walcott's poem, which includes a character named Omeros, also alludes to the *Iliad* and *Odyssey* extensively, though it does not parallel or overlay those epics.

The poem is divided into seven books and sixty-four chapters, with various threads of narrative woven together in a circling pattern.

[7] *she* The narrator is speaking with a Greek girl named Antigone; in Greek mythology, Antigone is the daughter born to Oedipus by his own mother, Jocasta. Antigone is the subject of an eponymous tragedy by Sophocles (c. 497–406 BCE).

[8] *Seven Seas* An old, wise, blind poet-prophet with shamanistic powers; at times, Seven Seas and Omeros blend into one figure, and Seven Seas can be understood as a contemporary embodiment of the ancient poet.

[9] *Virg* Virgil, a Roman poet best known for *The Aeneid* (c. 29–19 BCE), an epic poem that also makes extensive reference to Homer's works; he also authored *The Georgics* (c. 29 BCE), a poem on the subject of farming.

[10] *winged horse* Pegasus. In Greek mythology, Pegasus is a winged stallion symbolic of poetic imagination. A Pegasus is the symbol of the Mobil Oil company.

I felt the foam head watching as I stroked an arm, as
cold as its marble, then the shoulders in winter light
in the studio attic. I said, "Omeros,"

and *O* was the conch-shell's invocation, *mer* was
both mother and sea in our Antillean patois,[1]
os,[2] a grey bone, and the white surf as it crashes

and spreads its sibilant collar on a lace shore.
Omeros was the crunch of dry leaves, and the washes
that echoed from a cave-mouth when the tide has ebbed.

The name stayed in my mouth. …

from Chapter 3

3

"*Mais qui ça qui rivait- ous, Philoctete?*"[3]
"*Moin blessé.*"[4]
"But what is wrong wif you, Philoctete?"
"I am blest

wif this wound, Ma Kilman,[5] qui *pas ka guérir pièce.*
Which will never heal."

"Well, you must take it easy.
Go home and lie down, give the foot a
lickle° rest." *little*
Philoctete, his trouser-legs rolled, stares out to sea

from the worn rumshop window. The itch in the sore
tingles like the tendrils of the anemone,
and the puffed blister of Portuguese man-o'-war.[6]

He believed the swelling came from the chained ankles
of his grandfathers. Or else why was there no cure?
That the cross he carried was not only the anchor's

but that of his race, for a village black and poor
as the pigs that rooted in its burning garbage,
then were hooked on the anchors of the
abattoir.° *slaughterhouse*

Ma Kilman was sewing. She looked up and saw his face
squinting from the white of the street. He was waiting
to pass out on the table. This went on for days.

The ice turned to warm water near the self-hating
gesture of clenching his head tight in both hands. She
heard the boys in blue uniforms, going to school,

screaming at his elbow: "Pheeloh! Pheelosophee!"
A mummy embalmed in Vaseline and alcohol.
In the Egyptian silence she muttered softly:

"It have a flower somewhere, a medicine, and ways
my grandmother would boil it. I used to watch ants
climbing her white flower-pot. But, God, in which place?"

Where was this root? What senna, what tepid tisanes,[7]
could clean the branched river of his corrupted blood,
whose sap was a wounded cedar's? What did it mean,

this name that felt like a fever? Well, one good heft
of his garden-cutlass would slice the damned name
clean
from its rotting yam. He said, "*Merci.*"[8] Then he
left. …

[1] *Antillean patois* Nation language of the West Indies, combining African languages with the colonial languages that were imposed upon the people.

[2] *os* Latin and French: bone.

[3] *Philoctete* Character who shares a name with Philoctetes, a famed Greek archer in the *Iliad*. On the journey to Troy, a wound in Philoctetes' foot festers, and the smell is overwhelming; his shipmates abandon him on the island of Lemnos. Ten years later a prophecy sends a group of Greeks to recover Philoctetes' bow and arrows, which are necessary for victory against the Trojans; finding Philoctetes alive, they bring him back to the war. Fully healed, he fights bravely for the Greek side.

[4] *blessé* French patois for "wounded," though it is translated below as "blessed."

[5] *Ma Kilman* Kilman is introduced earlier in the poem as owner of the No Pain Café. Over the course of the poem, she rediscovers her identity as an Obeah woman, a West Indian prophetess and healer.

[6] *Portuguese man-o'-war* Jellyfish-like organism with a powerful sting; it is so named because it is shaped like a ship with its sails unfurled.

[7] *senna* Tropical shrub with healing properties; *tisanes* Infusions of medicinal herbs.

[8] *Merci* French: Thank you.

from CHAPTER 4

from 3

… That was when I turned with him[1] towards the village,
and saw, through the caging wires of the noon sky,
a beach with its padding panther; now the mirage

dissolved to a woman with a madras head-tie,[2]
but the head proud, although it was looking for work.
I felt like standing in homage to a beauty

that left, like a ship, widening eyes in its wake.[3]
"Who the hell is that?" a tourist near my table
asked a waitress. The waitress said, "She? She too proud!"

As the carved lids of the unimaginable
ebony mask unwrapped from its cotton-wool cloud,
the waitress sneered, "Helen."[4] And all the rest followed. …

from CHAPTER 13

2

"Walk me down to the wharf."[5]
At the corner of Bridge
Street, we saw the liner° as white as a mirage, *cruise ship*
Its hull bright as paper, preening with privilege.

"Measure the days you have left. Do just that labour
which marries your heart to your right hand: simplify
your life to one emblem, a sail leaving harbour

and a sail coming in. All corruption will cry
to be taken aboard. Fame is that white liner
at the end of your street, a city to itself,

taller than the Fire Station, and much finer,
with its brass-ringed portholes, mounting shelf after shelf,
than anything Castries[6] could ever hope to build."

The immaculate hull insulted the tin roofs
beneath it, its pursers° were milk, even the bilge *stewards*
bubbling from its stern in quietly muttering troughs

and its humming engines spewed expensive garbage
where boys balanced on logs or, riding old tires,
shouted up past the hull to tourists on the rails

to throw down coins, as cameras caught their black cries,
then jackknife or swan-dive—their somersaulting tails
like fishes flipped backwards—as the coins grew in size

in the wobbling depth; then, when they surfaced, fights
for possession, their heads butting like porpoises,
till, like a city leaving a city, the lights

blazed in its moving rooms, and the liner would glide
over its own phosphorus, and wash hit the wharves
long after stewards had set the service inside

the swaying chandeliered salons, and the black waves
settle down to their level. The stars would renew
their studded diagrams over Achille's[7] canoe.

From here, in his boyhood, he had seen women climb
like ants up a white flower-pot, baskets of coal

---

[1] *him* A waiter. The narrator is sitting in a restaurant at the beach, watching a waiter serve drinks to tourists.

[2] *madras head-tie* Traditional, colorful head-wrap made of madras (Indian) cotton.

[3] *beauty that left … wake* See Christopher Marlowe's *The Tragical History of Dr. Faustus* (1604). Upon seeing a shade of Helen of Troy, summoned by Mephistopheles, Faustus says, "Was this the face that launched a thousand ships / And burnt the topless towers of Illium?" (5.1.90–91).

[4] *Helen* In Greek mythology, Helen is the most beautiful woman in the world, married to King Menelaus of Sparta. When she is carried off by Paris, a prince of Troy, Menelaus and his brother Agamemnon lead the Greeks in an attempt to recover her, resulting in the ten-year-long Trojan War. The *Iliad* records the events of several pivotal weeks during the war.

[5] *Walk me … wharf* The narrator is walking and conversing with his father, who speaks this sentence.

[6] *Castries* Capital city of St. Lucia.

[7] *Achille* Character in the poem who shares a name with the Greek warrior Achilles, the hero of the *Iliad*.

balanced on their torchoned[1] heads, without touching
them,

up the black pyramids, each spine straight as a pole,
and with a strength that never altered its rhythm.
He spoke for those Helens from an earlier time:

"Hell was built on those hills. In that country of coal
without fire, that inferno the same colour
as their skins and shadows, every labouring soul

climbed with her hundredweight basket, every load for
one copper penny, balanced erect on their necks
that were tight as the liner's hawsers[2] from the weight.

The carriers were women, not the fair, gentler sex.
Instead, they were darker and stronger, and their gait
was made beautiful by balance, in their ascending

the narrow wooden ramp built steeply to the hull
of a liner tall as a cloud, the unending
line crossing like ants without touching for the whole

day. That was one section of the wharf, opposite
your grandmother's house where I watched the
silhouettes
of these women, while every hundredweight basket

was ticked by two tally clerks in their white pith-helmets,[3]
and the endless repetition as they climbed the
infernal anthracite° hills showed *high-quality coal*
you hell, early."

3

"Along this coal-blackened wharf, what Time decided
to do with my treacherous body after this,"
he said, watching the women, "will stay in your head

as long as a question you have no right to ask,
only to doubt, not hate our infuriating
silence. I am only the shadow of that task

as much as their work, your pose of a question waiting,
as you crouch with a writing lamp over a desk,
remains in the darkness after the light has gone,

and whether night is palpable between dawn and dusk
is not for the living; so you mind your business,
which is life and work, like theirs, but I will say this:

O Thou, my Zero, is an impossible prayer,
utter extinction is still a doubtful conceit.
Though we pray to nothing, nothing cannot be there.

Kneel to your load, then balance your staggering feet
and walk up that coal ladder as they do in time,
one bare foot after the next in ancestral rhyme.

Because Rhyme remains the parentheses of palms
shielding a candle's tongue, it is the language's
desire to enclose the loved world in its arms;

or heft a coal-basket; only by its stages
like those groaning women will you achieve that height
whose wooden planks in couplets lift your pages

higher than those hills of infernal anthracite.
There, like ants or angels, they see their native town,
unknown, raw, insignificant. They walk, you write;

keep to that narrow causeway without looking down,
climbing in their footsteps, that slow, ancestral beat
of those used to climbing roads; your own work owes
them

because the couplet of those multiplying feet
made your first rhymes. Look, they climb, and no one
knows them;
they take their copper pittances, and your duty

[1] *torchoned* Wrapped (in madras, or other cloth).

[2] *hawsers* Ropes used for mooring a ship.

[3] *pith-helmets* Also known as "sun helmets" or "safari helmets," pith helmets were worn by Europeans in hot climates during the nineteenth and into the mid-twentieth century. These helmets became symbols of colonial rule.

from the time you watched them from your
grandmother's house
as a child wounded by their power and beauty
is the chance you now have, to give those feet a voice."

from Book 3
from Chapter 28

1

Now he heard the griot[1] muttering his prophetic song
of sorrow that would be the past. It was a note,
long-drawn
and endless in its winding like the brown river's tongue:

"We were the colour of shadows when we came down
with tinkling leg-irons to join the chains of the sea,
for the silver coins multiplying on the sold horizon,

and these shadows are reprinted now on the white sand
of antipodal coasts, your ashen ancestors
from the Bight of Benin, from the margin of Guinea.[2]

There were seeds in our stomachs, in the cracking pods
of our skulls on the scorching decks, the tubers
withered in no time. We watched as the river-gods

changed from snakes into currents. When inspected,
our eyes showed dried fronds in their brown irises,
and from our curved spines, the rib-cages radiated

like fronds from a palm-branch. Then, when the dead
palms were heaved overside, the ribbed corpses
floated, riding, to the white sand they remembered,

to the Bight of Benin, to the margin of Guinea.
So, when you see burnt branches riding the swell,
trying to reclaim the surf through crooked fingers,

after a night of rough wind by some stone-white hotel,
past the bright triangular passage of the windsurfers,
remember us to the black waiter bringing the bill."

But they crossed, they survived. There is the epical
splendour.
Multiply the rain's lances, multiply their ruin,
the grace born from subtraction as the hold's iron door

rolled over their eyes like pots left out in the rain,
and the bolt rammed home its echo, the way that
thunderclaps
perpetuate their reverberation.

So there went the Ashanti one way, the Mandingo
another,
the Ibo another, the Guinea.[3] Now each man was a nation
in himself, without mother, father, brother.

2

The worst crime is to leave a man's hands empty.
Men are born makers, with that primal simplicity
in every maker since Adam. This is pre-history,

that itching instinct in the criss-crossed net
of their palms, its wickerwork. They could not
stay idle too long. The chained wrists couldn't forget

the carver for whom antelopes leapt, or
the bow-maker the shaft, or the armourer
his nail-studs, the shield held up to Hector[4]

that was the hammerer's art. So the wet air
revolved in the potter's palms, in the painter's eye
the arcs of a frantic springbok° bucked *gazelle*
soundlessly,

[1] *he* Achille; *griot* West African name for an oral storyteller, folk historian, or poet.

[2] *Bight of Benin … Guinea* The Bight of Benin is a curve along the coastline of West Africa. Modern-day Ghana, Togo, Benin, Nigeria, Cameroon and Equatorial Guinea border its waters.

[3] *Ashanti … Guinea* West African tribes; it was from these tribes on the coast that slave traders took people across the Atlantic to imperial colonies such as those in the Caribbean.

[4] *shield … Hector* In Book 18 of the *Iliad*, the god of fire, Hephaestus, forges a shield of unparalleled beauty and artistry for Achilles to take into his battle with Hector, the prince of Troy. In *Omeros*, characters named Achille and Hector also fight for the love of Helen.

baboons kept signing their mimetic alphabet
in case men forgot it, so out of habit
their fingers grew leaves in the foetid ground of the boat.

So now they were coals, firewood, dismembered
branches, not men. They had left their remembered
shadows to the firelight. Scratching a board

they made the signs for their fading names on the wood,
and their former shapes returned absently; each carried
the nameless freight of himself to the other world. …

from BOOK 6
from CHAPTER 49

1

She bathed him in the brew of the root.[1] The basin
was one of those cauldrons from the old sugar-mill,
with its charred pillars, rock pasture, and one grazing

horse, looking like helmets that have tumbled downhill
from an infantry charge. Children rang them with stones.
Wildflowers sprung in them when the dirt found a seam.

She had one in her back yard, close to the crotons,[2]
agape in its crusted, agonized O: the scream
of centuries. She scraped its rusted scabs, she scoured

the mouth of the cauldron, then fed a crackling pyre
with palms and banana-trash. In the scream she poured
tin after kerosene tin, its base black from fire,

of seawater and sulphur. Into this she then fed
the bubbling root and leaves. She led Philoctete
to the gurgling lava. Trembling, he entered

his bath like a boy. The lime leaves leeched to his wet
knuckled spine like islands that cling to the basin
of the rusted Caribbean. An icy sweat

glazed his scalp, but he could feel the putrescent shin
drain in the seethe like sucked marrow, he felt it drag
the slime from his shame. She rammed him back to his place

as he tried climbing out with: "*Not yet!*" With a rag
sogged in a basin of ice she rubbed his squeezed face
the way boys enjoy their mother's ritual rage,

and as he surrendered to her, the foul flower
on his shin whitened and puckered, the corolla
closed its thorns like the sea-egg.° What else did it cure? *sea urchin*

2

The bow leapt back to the palm of the warrior.
The yoke of the wrong name lifted from his shoulders.
His muscles loosened like those of a brown river

that was dammed with silt, and then silkens its boulders
with refreshing strength. His ribs thudded like a horse
cantering on a beach that bursts into full gallop

while a boy yanks at its rein with terrified "Whoas!"
The white foam unlocked his coffles, his ribbed shallop[3]
broke from its anchor, and the water, which he swirled

like a child, steered his brow into the right current,
as calm as *In God We Troust*[4] to that other world,
and his flexed palm enclosed an oar with the ident-

ical closure of a mouth around its own name,
the way a sea-anemone closes slyly
into a secrecy many mistake for shame.

---

[1] *She bathed … root* Ma Kilman is treating Philoctete's wound in an herbal bath.

[2] *crotons* Tropical plants with healing properties.

[3] *coffles* Line of slaves chained together; used here metonymically to refer to the shackles or chains themselves; *shallop* Large boat, a sloop.

[4] *In God We Troust* Earlier in the poem (1.1.2) Achille cuts these words into his canoe as a motto.

Centuries weigh down the head of the swamp-lily,
its tribal burden arches the sea-almond's[1] spine,
in barracoon[2] back yards the soul-smoke still passes,

but the wound has found her own cure. The soft
days spin
the spittle of the spider in webbed glasses,
as she drenches the burning trash to its last flame,

and the embers steam and hiss to the schoolboys' cries
when he'd weep in the window for their tribal shame.
A shame for the loss of words, and a language tired

of accepting that loss, and then all accepted.
That was why the sea stank from the frothing urine
of surf, and fish-guts reeked from the government shed,

and why God pissed on the village for months of rain.
But now, quite clearly the tears trickled down his face
like rainwater down a cracked carafe from Choiseul,[3]

as he stood like a boy in his bath with the first clay's
innocent prick! So she threw Adam a towel.
And the yard was Eden. And its light the first day's. …

from BOOK 7

from CHAPTER 56

3

"I saw you in London," I said, "sunning on the steps
of St. Martin-in-the-Fields,[4] your dog-eared manuscript
clutched to your heaving chest. The queues at the
bus-stops

smiled at your seaman's shuffle, and a curate kicked
you until you waddled down to the summery Thames."
"That's because I'm a heathen. They don't know my age.

Even the nightingales[5] have forgotten their names.
The goat[6] declines, head down, with these rocks for a
stage
bare of tragedy. The Aegean's chimera[7]

is a camera, you get my drift, a drifter
is the hero of my book."
"I never read it,"
I said. "Not all the way through." The lift of the

arching eyebrows paralyzed me like Medusa's
shield,[8] and I turned cold the moment I had said it.
"Those gods with hyphens, like Hollywood producers,"

I heard my mouth babbling as ice glazed over my chest.
"The gods and the demi-gods aren't much use to us."
"Forget the gods," Omeros growled, "and read the rest."

Then there was the silence any injured author
knows, broken by the outcry of a frigate-bird,
as we both stared at the blue dividing water,

and in that gulf, I muttered, "I have always heard
your voice in that sea, master, it was the same song
of the desert shaman, and when I was a boy

[1] *sea-almond* Large tropical shade tree whose leaves have medicinal properties.

[2] *barracoon* Sheds or rough barracks used for housing slaves.

[3] *Choiseul* City in southwestern St. Lucia.

[4] *St. Martin-in-the-Fields* Anglican church in Trafalgar Square, London.

[5] *nightingales* European birds associated with poetry because of their beautiful, mournful singing. See the *Odyssey* 19.512–25 and Ovid's *Metamorphoses* 6.438–674.

[6] *goat* The word "tragedy" is derived from a Greek word meaning "goat-song," though the reasons for this are not precisely known. It is possible that goats were awarded to the winners of Athenian play competitions or that goats were sacrificed at festivals where plays were performed.

[7] *Aegean* Sea between the Greek and Turkish mainlands, where the archipelago of Greek islands is located; *chimera* In Greek mythology, a fire-breathing monster with a goat's body, a lion's head, and a serpent's tail. In modern use, the term often signifies a flight of fancy, an illusory imagining.

[8] *Medusa's shield* In Greek mythology, Medusa was a monster who turned anyone who looked at her to stone. Perseus killed her with the aid of a mirrored shield given to him by the goddess Athena. Afterwards, he gave the head, which retained its powers to petrify, to Athena, who placed it on her own shield.

your name was as wide as a bay, as I walked along
the curled brow of the surf; the word 'Homer' meant joy,
joy in battle, in work, in death, then the numbered peace

of the surf's benedictions, it rose in the cedars,
in the laurier-cannelles,[1] pages of rustling trees.
Master, I was the freshest of all your readers." …

from Book 7
from Chapter 57
from I[2]

… The wharf was rowing
farther away from me till the white liner stuck

to the green harbour was no bigger than a toy,
as Seven Seas watched me with each receding stroke.
And my cheeks were salt with tears, but those of a boy,

and he saw how deeply I had loved the island.
Perhaps the oarsman knew this, but I didn't know.
Then I saw the ebony of his lifted hand.

And Omeros nodded: "We will both praise it now."
But I could not before him. My tongue was a stone
at the bottom of the sea, my mouth a parted conch

from which nothing sounded, and then I heard his own
Greek calypso[3] coming from the marble trunk,
widening the sea with a blind man's anger:

"*In the mist of the sea there is a horned island*[4]
with deep green harbours where the Greek ships anchor"
and the waves were swaying to the stroke of his hand,

as I heard my own thin voice riding on his praise
the way a swift follows a crest, leaving its shore:
"*It was a place of light with luminous valleys*

under thunderous clouds. A Genoan wanderer[5]
saying the beads of the Antilles[6] *named the place*
for a blinded saint.[7] *Later, others would name her*

for a wild wife.[8] *Her mountains tinkle with springs*
among moss-bearded forests, and the screeching of birds
stitches its tapestry.[9] *The white egret makes rings*

stalking its pools. African fishermen make boards
from trees as tall as their gods with their echoing
axes, and a volcano, stinking with sulphur,

has made it a healing place." My voice was going
under the strength of his voice, which carried so far
that a black frigate heard it, steadying its wing. …
—1990

[1] *laurier-cannelles* Plant native to St. Lucia. The name combines two French names for aromatic spices, bay and cinnamon.

[2] *I* At the beginning of this section, the narrator and Seven Seas (whose identity at this point in the poem is blended with that of Omeros) board a "black canoe" piloted by a mysterious "oarsman." There are intimations that they are traveling to the land of the dead: the passengers have no weight and people on the shore cannot see them. The oarsman recalls Charon, who, in Greek mythology, transports dead souls across the river Styx (in some versions, the river Acheron) to Hades.

[3] *calypso* Musical form that originated in Trinidad and Tobago and is rooted in the West African Kaiso. Calypso songs are highly rhythmic and often carry political subtexts.

[4] *horned island* Another name for St. Lucia, with its two mountainous "horns": the peaks Gros Piton and Petit Piton, located on either side of Jalousie Bay. In the *Odyssey* 12, Odysseus visits Thrinacia, an island whose name is sometimes translated as "three horned."

[5] *Genoan wanderer* Christopher Columbus (1451–1506), born in Genoa, was traditionally credited with captaining the first European ship to reach St. Lucia; he is now thought to have sailed past the island.

[6] *saying the beads* Praying with a rosary; *Antilles* Archipelago of islands that lie between the Caribbean Sea, the Gulf of Mexico, and the Atlantic. The reference here is to the Lesser Antilles, of which St. Lucia is one: a chain of smaller volcanic islands that are located southeast of the Greater Antilles (Cuba, Hispaniola, Puerto Rico, and Jamaica).

[7] *blinded saint* According to Christian tradition, St. Lucia's eyes were gouged out as part of her martyrdom.

[8] *wild wife* I.e., Helen of Troy. Because St. Lucia switched many times between British and French colonial control, the island was known as "the Helen of the West Indies."

[9] *stitches its tapestry* Reference to *Iliad* 3.125–28, where Helen stitches a tapestry depicting the events of the Trojan War.

Love after Love

The time will come
when, with elation,
you will greet yourself arriving
at your own door, in your own mirror,
and each will smile at the other's welcome,

and say sit here. Eat.
You will love again the stranger who was your self,
Give wine. Give bread. Give back your heart
to itself, to the stranger who has loved you
all your life, whom you ignored
for another, who knows you by heart.
Take down the love letters from the bookshelf

the photographs, the desperate notes,
peel your own image from the mirror.
Sit. Feast on your life.
—1976

Seamus Heaney

1939 – 2013

The American poet Robert Lowell once referred to Seamus Heaney as "the best Irish poet since Yeats." Awarded the Nobel Prize for literature in 1995, he was among the most popular as well as the most acclaimed English-language poets of his era. Often praised for its lyricism, Heaney's work reflects his rural upbringing, with a focus on the soil, the past, and lost friends. Many of his poems also deal with the troubles in his native Northern Ireland, and some commentators have criticized him for an alleged ambivalence about the political conflict.

Heaney grew up in a Roman Catholic household in the predominantly Protestant north. The eldest of nine children, he was not marked in childhood by the strife that would later affect the region. Instead, he experienced a community that lived in harmony, regardless of religious affiliation. Heaney's parents were farmers in County Derry, just outside Belfast. He grew up with an appreciation for country life, for those who work the land, and for the importance of close-knit community. Heaney frequently drew on these roots for poetic inspiration, and many of his poems recall his childhood or use the details of rural life—such as digging potatoes or churning milk—to comment on universal issues.

Heaney's career as a published poet began while he was completing a teacher's certificate at St. Joseph's College in Belfast. Writing under the pseudonym "Incertus," he had just finished his Bachelor of Arts in English Language and Literature at Queen's University when he joined a poetry workshop. Known as "The Belfast Group," this forum allowed new poets to showcase their work and have it critiqued by their peers. The Group introduced him to other young poets, including his future wife, and was also a forum for the discussion of the political issues of the day. Many of Heaney's early poems were first read and discussed at Group meetings.

The publication in 1966 of Heaney's first book of poems, *Death of a Naturalist*, began what would be a career filled with awards and accolades. This volume won the Somerset Maugham Award, among others. While establishing his career as a poet, Heaney was working as a lecturer in English at various colleges in Ireland and the United States to support his growing family, which would eventually include two sons and a daughter. His move south to the Republic of Ireland in 1972 was in many respects a positive one, but moving away from the political controversies of Northern Ireland to the relative stability of the south was seen by some as a betrayal. Establishing a home just outside Dublin did not, however, lead Heaney to forget the political turmoil of his birthplace. It was during this time that he wrote some of his most political works: *North* (1975) and *Field Work* (1979). He did not want to be seen solely as a political poet, though, and felt he needed distance from the conflicts of the north to provide scope for objectivity.

Heaney's rising international fame led to his appointment as Boylston Professor of Rhetoric and Oratory at Harvard in 1984. This position allowed him to teach one semester at Harvard in the spring and spend the remaining eight months of the year at his home in Dublin. The death of Heaney's mother, also in 1984, was the occasion for some of his most touching poetry, published in

The Haw Lantern (1987). When questioned about his memorializing of lost friends and family, Heaney responded: "The elegiac Heaney? There's nothing else." Often, Heaney's work evokes the past in order to comment indirectly on the present; for example, in one of his "bog poems," "Punishment," he compares a first-century BCE girl who was drowned as punishment for adultery to women in late twentieth-century Northern Ireland.

In 1995 Heaney was awarded the Nobel Prize for literature. In making the award, the committee cited his "works of lyrical beauty and ethical depth, which exalt everyday miracles and the living past." In his Nobel acceptance speech he wrote that the "form of the poem … is crucial to poetry's power to do the thing which always is and always will be to poetry's credit: the power to persuade that vulnerable part of our consciousness of its rightness in spite of the evidence of wrongness all around it."

In 1999 Heaney published a translation of *Beowulf*, which won the Whitbread Book of the Year Award. His T.S. Eliot Prize-winning collection *District and Circle* was published in 2006; a few months later, he suffered a minor stroke, leading him to spend a year away from public life. His experience of the stroke inspired many of the poems in *Human Chain* (2010), the last major collection he would complete before his death. The volume is characteristic of Heaney in that, as Colm Tóibín observed, the poems offer "consolation or transformation only because they contain tones and phrases that are perfectly tuned; they are true to memory and loss, and thus somehow, at times miraculously, they offer a vision of what is beyond them or above them."

⌘⌘⌘

Digging

Between my finger and my thumb
The squat pen rests; snug as a gun.

Under my window, a clean rasping sound
When the spade sinks into gravelly ground:
My father, digging. I look down

Till his straining rump among the flowerbeds
Bends low, comes up twenty years away
Stooping in rhythm through potato drills[1]
Where he was digging.

The coarse boot nestled on the lug, the shaft
Against the inside knee was levered firmly.
He rooted out tall tops, buried the bright edge deep
To scatter new potatoes that we picked
Loving their cool hardness in our hands.

By God, the old man could handle a spade.
Just like his old man.

My grandfather cut more turf[2] in a day
Than any other man on Toner's bog.
Once I carried him milk in a bottle
Corked sloppily with paper. He straightened up
To drink it, then fell to right away
Nicking and slicing neatly, heaving sods
Over his shoulder, going down and down
For the good turf. Digging.

The cold smell of potato mould, the squelch and slap
Of soggy peat, the curt cuts of an edge
Through living roots awaken in my head.
But I've no spade to follow men like them.

Between my finger and my thumb
The squat pen rests.
I'll dig with it.

—1966

[1] *potato drills* Row of sown potatoes.

[2] *turf* Slabs of peat.

Thatcher

Bespoke for weeks, he turned up some morning
Unexpectedly, his bicycle slung
With a light ladder and a bag of knives.
He eyed the old rigging, poked at the eaves,

Opened and handled sheaves of lashed wheat-straw.
Next, the bundled rods: hazel and willow
Were flicked for weight, twisted in case they'd snap.
It seemed he spent the morning warming up:

Then fixed the ladder, laid out well-honed blades
And snipped at straw and sharpened ends of rods
That, bent in two, made a white-pronged staple
For pinning down his world, handful by handful.

Couchant° for days on sods above the rafters, *lying*
He shaved and flushed the butts,[1] stitched all together
Into a sloped honeycomb, a stubble patch,
And left them gaping at his Midas touch.[2]
—1969

The Wife's Tale

When I had spread it all on linen cloth
Under the hedge, I called them over.
The hum and gulp of the thresher ran down
And the big belt slewed to a standstill, straw
Hanging undelivered in the jaws.
There was such quiet that I heard their boots
Crunching the stubble twenty yards away.

He lay down and said, "Give these fellows theirs,
I'm in no hurry," plucking grass in handfuls
And tossing it in the air. "That looks well."
(He nodded at my white cloth on the grass.)
"I declare a woman could lay out a field
Though boys like us have little call for cloths."
He winked, then watched me as I poured a cup
And buttered the thick slices that he likes.
"It's threshing better than I thought, and mind
It's good clean seed. Away over there and look."
Always this inspection has to be made
Even when I don't know what to look for.

But I ran my hand in the half-filled bags
Hooked to the slots. It was hard as shot,
Innumerable and cool. The bags gaped
Where the chutes ran back to the stilled drum
And forks were stuck at angles in the ground
As javelins might mark lost battlefields.
I moved between them back across the stubble.

They lay in the ring of their own crusts and dregs,
Smoking and saying nothing. "There's good yield,
Isn't there?"—as proud as if he were the land itself—
"Enough for crushing and for sowing both."
And that was it. I'd come and he had shown me,
So I belonged no further to the work.
I gathered cups and folded up the cloth
And went. But they still kept their ease,
Spread out, unbuttoned, grateful, under the trees.
—1969

The Grauballe Man[3]

As if he had been poured
in tar, he lies
on a pillow of turf
and seems to weep

the black river of himself
The grain of his wrists
is like bog oak,[4]
the ball of his heel

[1] *butts* Branch tips.

[2] *Midas touch* Reference to the Greek myth of King Midas, whose touch turned everything to gold.

[3] *Grauballe Man* Man from the third century BCE whose preserved remains were found in 1952, in a peat bog near the village of Grauballe, Denmark.

[4] *bog oak* Wood of an oak tree preserved in peat-bog.

like a basalt egg.
His instep has shrunk
cold as a swan's foot
or a wet swamp root.

His hips are the ridge
and purse of a mussel,
his spine an eel arrested
under a glisten of mud.

The head lifts,
the chin is a visor
raised above the vent
of his slashed throat

that has tanned and toughened.
The cured wound
opens inwards to a dark
elderberry place.

Who will say "corpse"
to his vivid cast?
Who will say "body"
to his opaque repose?

And his rusted hair,
a mat unlikely
as a foetus's.
I first saw his twisted face

in a photograph,
a head and shoulder
out of the peat,
bruised like a forceps baby,

but now he lies
perfected in my memory,
down to the red horn
of his nails,

hung in the scales
with beauty and atrocity:
with the Dying Gaul
too strictly compassed

on his shield,
with the actual weight
of each hooded victim,
slashed and dumped.
—1975

Punishment[1]

I can feel the tug
of the halter at the nape
of her neck, the wind
on her naked front.

It blows her nipples
to amber beads,
it shakes the frail rigging
of her ribs.

I can see her drowned
body in the bog,
the weighing stone,
the floating rods and boughs.

Under which at first
she was a barked sapling
that is dug up
oak-bone, brain-firkin:[2]

her shaved head
like a stubble of black corn,
her blindfold a soiled bandage,
her noose a ring

[1] *Punishment* In 1951 the body of a fourteen-year-old girl from the first century BCE was discovered in a German bog. The left side of her head had been shaved, her eyes bandaged shut, and a collar tied around her neck. Her body had been weighed down with tree branches and a stone. Germanic people often punished adulterous women by shaving their hair and either killing them or expelling them from the village. After the girl's body was found, the brain was removed and examined.

[2] *firkin* Small cask or barrel.

to store
the memories of love.
Little adulteress,
before they punished you

you were flaxen-haired,
undernourished, and your
tar-black face was beautiful.
My poor scapegoat,

I almost love you
but would have cast, I know,
the stones of silence.
I am the artful voyeur

of your brain's exposed
and darkened combs,
your muscles' webbing
and all your numbered bones:

I who have stood dumb
when your betraying sisters,
cauled° in tar, *capped*
wept by the railings,[1]

who would connive
in civilized outrage
yet understand the exact
and tribal, intimate revenge.
—1975

Casualty

I

He would drink by himself
And raise a weathered thumb
Towards the high shelf,
Calling another rum
And blackcurrant, without
Having to raise his voice,
Or order a quick stout
By a lifting of the eyes
And a discreet dumb-show
Of pulling off the top;
At closing time would go
In waders and peaked cap
Into the showery dark,
A dole-kept breadwinner
But a natural for work.
I loved his whole manner,
Sure-footed but too sly,
His deadpan sidling tact,
His fisherman's quick eye
And turned observant back.

Incomprehensible
To him, my other life.
Sometimes, on his high stool,
Too busy with his knife
At a tobacco plug
And not meeting my eye,
In the pause after a slug
He mentioned poetry.
We would be on our own
And, always politic
And shy of condescension,
I would manage by some trick
To switch the talk to eels
Or lore of the horse and cart
Or the Provisionals.[2]

But my tentative art
His turned back watches too:
He was blown to bits
Out drinking in a curfew
Others obeyed, three nights
After they shot dead
The thirteen men in Derry.
PARAS THIRTEEN, the walls said,
BOGSIDE NIL.[3] That Wednesday

[1] *your betraying … railings* In Belfast, women who kept company with British soldiers were sometimes shaved, stripped, tarred, and handcuffed to railings by the IRA as punishment.

[2] *Provisionals* Members of the Provisional Branch of the IRA.

[3] *PARAS … NIL* I.e., the British Army's Parachute Regiment had killed thirteen people, while the Roman Catholic people of the Bogside district, in Londonderry, had killed none.

Everybody held
His breath and trembled.

2

It was a day of cold
Raw silence, wind-blown
Surplice and soutane:[1]
Rained-on, flower-laden
Coffin after coffin
Seemed to float from the door
Of the packed cathedral
Like blossoms on slow water.
The common funeral
Unrolled its swaddling band,
Lapping, tightening
Till we were braced and bound
Like brothers in a ring.

But he would not be held
At home by his own crowd
Whatever threats were phoned,
Whatever black flags waved.
I see him as he turned
In that bombed offending place,
Remorse fused with terror
In his still knowable face,
His cornered outfaced stare
Blinding in the flash.

He had gone miles away
For he drank like a fish
Nightly, naturally
Swimming towards the lure
Of warm lit-up places,
The blurred mesh and murmur
Drifting among glasses
In the gregarious smoke.
How culpable was he
That last night when he broke
Our tribe's complicity?
"Now you're supposed to be
An educated man,"
I hear him say. "Puzzle me
The right answer to that one."

3

I missed his funeral,
Those quiet walkers
And sideways talkers
Shoaling out of his lane
To the respectable
Purring of the hearse …
They move in equal pace
With the habitual
Slow consolation
Of a dawdling engine,
The line lifted, hand
Over fist, cold sunshine
On the water, the land
Banked under fog: that morning
I was taken in his boat,
The screw° purling, turning *propeller*
Indolent fathoms white,
I tasted freedom with him.
To get out early, haul
Steadily off the bottom,
Dispraise the catch, and smile
As you find a rhythm
Working you, slow mile by mile,
Into your proper haunt
Somewhere, well out, beyond …

Dawn-sniffing revenant,[2]
Plodder through midnight rain,
Question me again.
—1979

[1] *Surplice and soutane* Vestments worn by the Roman Catholic clergy.

[2] *revenant* One who returns to life from the dead.

Anything Can Happen[1]

after Horace,[2] Odes, I, 34

Anything can happen. You know how Jupiter[3]
Will mostly wait for clouds to gather head
Before he hurls the lightning? Well, just now
He galloped his thunder cart and his horses

Across a clear blue sky. It shook the earth
And the clogged underearth, the River Styx,[4]
The winding streams, the Atlantic shore itself.
Anything can happen, the tallest towers

Be overturned, those in high places daunted,
Those overlooked regarded. Stropped-beak Fortune
Swoops, making the air gasp, tearing the crest off one,
Setting it down bleeding on the next.

Ground gives. The heaven's weight
Lifts up off Atlas[5] like a kettle-lid.
Capstones shift, nothing resettles right.
Telluric[6] ash and fire-spores boil away.
—2001

[1] *Anything Can Happen* First published under the title "Horace and the Thunder" (2001) before being reprinted under the present title (2004).

[2] *Horace* Roman poet (65 BCE–8 BCE).

[3] *Jupiter* King of the Roman gods, who was capable of throwing thunderbolts.

[4] *River Styx* In Greek mythology, a river that the souls of the dead must cross to reach the underworld.

[5] *Atlas* In Greek mythology, a Titan who, as punishment for leading a war against the gods, was condemned to hold up the sky for thousands of years.

[6] *Telluric* Of the earth, of soil (from *tellus*, a Latin word meaning "earth").

Uncoupled

1

Who is this coming to the ash pit
Walking tall, as if in a procession,
Bearing in front of her a slender pan

Withdrawn just now from underneath
The firebox, weighty, full to the brim
With whitish dust and flakes still sparking hot

That the wind is blowing into her apron bib,
Into her mouth and eyes while she proceeds
Unwavering, keeping her burden horizontal still,

Hands in a tight, sore grip round the metal knob,
Proceeds until we have lost sight of her
Where the worn path turns behind the henhouse.

2

Who is this, not much higher than the cattle,
Working his way towards me through the pen,
His ashplant° in one hand *walking stick*

Lifted and pointing, a stick of keel[7]
In the other, calling to where I'm perched
On top of a shaky gate,

Waving and calling something I cannot hear
With all the lowing and roaring, lorries revving
At the far end of the yard, the dealers

Shouting among themselves, and now to him
So that his eyes leave mine and I know
The pain of loss before I know the term.
—2010

[7] *keel* Pigment used to mark livestock.

[*The door was open and the house was dark*]

in memory of David Hammond

The door was open and the house was dark
Wherefore I called his name, although I knew
The answer this time would be silence

That kept me standing listening while it grew
Backwards and down and out into the street
Where as I'd entered (I remember now)

The streetlamps too were out.
I felt, for the first time there and then, a stranger,
Intruder almost, wanting to take flight

Yet well aware that here there was no danger,
Only withdrawal, a not unwelcoming
Emptiness, as in a midnight hangar

On an overgrown airfield in late summer.
—2010

Ngũgĩ wa Thiong'o

b. 1938

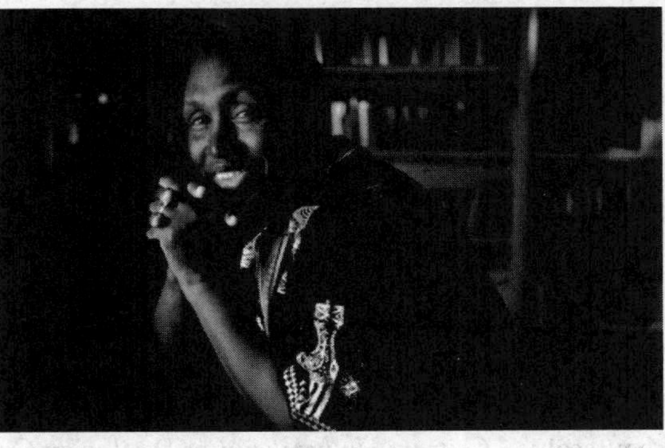

A novelist, playwright, essayist, and lecturer, Kenyan author Ngũgĩ (pronounced "Nn-goog-y") wa Thiong'o is one of East Africa's most important voices. Most of Ngũgĩ's fiction and non-fiction deals with African history and human rights issues; two acclaimed early novels, *Weep Not, Child* (1964) and *A Grain of Wheat* (1967), are sympathetic accounts of the Mau Mau uprisings of the 1950s that determined Kenya's future. These works have been followed by numerous novels, stories, essays, and plays that deal with colonialism and neo-colonialism—that state of oppression, according to Ngũgĩ, that is "nurtured in the womb of colonialism," leaving economic and spiritual control in the hands of the colonists long after they have departed. Ngũgĩ has written extensively and passionately about the need to preserve African cultures and languages. He dedicated *Decolonising the Mind* (1986) "to all those who write in African languages, and to all those who over the years have maintained the dignity of the literature, culture, philosophy, and other treasures carried by African languages." For the past three decades he has written all of his creative work in Gĩkũyũ, his native tongue.

Ngũgĩ was born to Thiong'o wa Nducu and Wanjika wa Ngũgĩ, in Kamiriithu, Kenya, in 1938. His was a large peasant family composed of his father, his mother, his father's three other wives, and twenty-eight children. His childhood was scarred by violent struggles between the Mau Mau rebels, who were primarily from the Gĩkũyũ tribe, and the British colonial forces; Ngũgĩ's brother was killed, his mother tortured, and his entire village obliterated. He attended Christian schools as a youth and for a time became a devout Christian himself, but he renounced the religion in 1976 and ceased using his Christian name, James Ngugi. After acquiring a BA from Makerere University in Uganda, Ngũgĩ worked as a journalist for the Nairobi *Daily Nation* and was editor of the literary journal *Zuka*—"Emerge" in Swahili—from 1967 to 1970. He eventually did graduate work at Leeds University in England, obtaining his MA and PhD. He married Nyambura, a Kenyan woman, in 1961, and they had six children.

Ngũgĩ's own literary career began in 1963 (coincidentally, the year in which Kenya achieved independence from Britain) with the successful production of his first play, *The Black Hermit*. His first novel, *The River Between* (1965), is still widely regarded as a classic of African and English literature. It is a finely observed and deeply compassionate novel of the tension between the traditional ways of rural Kenya and those of Christianity in the era of colonization (including such highly charged issues as those surrounding the practice of female circumcision). *The River Between* was written in English, as were *A Grain of Wheat* (1967) and *Weep Not, Child* (1964). The popularity of Ngũgĩ's 1977 play *Ngaahika Ndeenda* (*I Will Marry When I Want*), co-written with Ngugi wa Mirii, led to his exile from Kenya. Working class people and farmers were so enamored of the play and its themes of empowerment and land rights that the government feared an uprising and banned the production. Soon afterward Ngũgĩ was imprisoned for political dissent, an experience he recounts in 1981's *Detained: A Writer's Prison Diary*. He was not reinstated in his post at the University of Nairobi after his detainment, and he left the country in 1982; since then he has lived in the United States. In 1987 he wrote another political novel, *Matigari Ma Njiruungi*, based on a Gĩkũyũ fable about a freedom fighter; the Kenyan government issued another warrant for his arrest.

The 1977 novel *Petals of Blood* marked Ngũgĩ's "farewell to the English language as a vehicle of my writing of plays, novels and short stories," and *Decolonising the Mind* was his farewell to non-fiction writing in English. "From now on," he said, "it is Gĩkũyũ and Kiswahili all the way." By going back to his original language, especially after having succeeded in eliminating the University of Nairobi's English Department while he was Chair, he worked to end "the domination of the mental universe of the colonised." *Petals of Blood* also marked a change in the focus of his work, from themes of colonialism to those of neo-colonialism. For Ngũgĩ, the problems in Africa did not begin, nor did they end, with the slave trade. According to him, in order to control the native people of Africa, colonizers set out to obliterate African independence both by destroying African culture and by superimposing their own culture and languages. Ngũgĩ has said that neo-colonialism continues long after the colonizers have departed, with more economically powerful countries and corporations exploiting African goods and services, keeping the economy "still in the hands of the imperialist bourgeoisie." *Caitaani Mutharabaini*, or *Devil on the Cross* (1982), was written soon after *Petals of Blood* (while he was in a Nairobi prison) and, according to the author, is one of his most important novels.

In a 2004 interview Ngũgĩ said, "In a spiritual sense I have never left Kenya. Kenya and Africa are always in my mind. But I look forward to a physical reunion with Kenya, my beloved country." Soon after giving this interview, he made his long-awaited return. Crowds of people celebrated his homecoming, but tragedy followed in the form of an assault upon Ngũgĩ and Njeeri, his second wife (whom he married after Nyambura's death). The couple and their two children fled the country the following day.

Ngũgĩ has taught at universities in New Zealand and Germany, as well as at New York University, Yale, and Smith in the United States. Much of his writing since the early 1990s has focused on cultural theory, such as the 1993 volume *Moving the Centre: The Struggle for Cultural Freedom*, but in 2004 he published his first novel in two decades, *Mũrogi wa Kagogo* (*Wizard of the Crow*). In addition to further critical writing, he has also released several volumes of autobiography detailing his early life and the political and cultural context in which he came of age. Ngũgĩ is a Distinguished Professor at the University of California, Irvine, where for several years he was Director of the International Center for Writing and Translation.

⌘⌘⌘

from *Decolonising the Mind*

Chapter 3

I was born into a large peasant family: father, four wives and about twenty-eight children. I also belonged, as we all did in those days, to a wider extended family and to the community as a whole.

We spoke Gĩkũyũ as we worked in the fields. We spoke Gĩkũyũ in and outside the home. I can vividly recall those evenings of storytelling around the fireside. It was mostly the grown-ups telling the children but everybody was interested and involved. We children would re-tell the stories the following day to other children who worked in the fields picking the pyrethrum flowers, tea-leaves or coffee beans of our European and African landlords.

The stories, with mostly animals as the main characters, were all told in Gĩkũyũ. Hare, being small, weak but full of innovative wit and cunning, was our hero. We identified with him as he struggled against the brutes of prey like lion, leopard, hyena. His victories were our victories and we learnt that the apparently weak can outwit the strong. We followed the animals in their struggle against hostile nature—drought, rain, sun, wind—a confrontation often forcing them to search for forms of co-operation. But we were also interested in their struggles amongst themselves, and particularly between the beasts and the victims of prey. These twin struggles, against nature and other animals, reflected real-life struggles in the human world.

Not that we neglected stories with human beings as the main characters. There were two types of characters in such human-centred narratives: the species of truly human beings with qualities of courage, kindness, mercy, hatred of evil, concern for others; and a man-eat-man two-mouthed species with qualities of greed, selfishness, individualism and hatred of what was good for the larger co-operative community. Co-operation as the ultimate good in a community was a constant theme. It could unite human beings with animals against ogres and beasts of prey, as in the story of how dove, after being fed with castor-oil seeds, was sent to fetch a smith working far away from home and whose pregnant wife was being threatened by these man-eating two-mouthed ogres.

There were good and bad story-tellers. A good one could tell the same story over and over again, and it would always be fresh to us, the listeners. He or she could tell a story told by someone else and make it more alive and dramatic. The differences really were in the use of words and images and the inflexion of voices to effect different tones.

We therefore learnt to value words for their meaning and nuances. Language was not a mere string of words. It had a suggestive power well beyond the immediate and lexical meaning. Our appreciation of the suggestive magical power of language was reinforced by the games we played with words through riddles, proverbs, transpositions of syllables, or through nonsensical but musically arranged words. So we learnt the music of our language on top of the content. The language, through images and symbols, gave us a view of the world, but it had a beauty of its own. The home and the field were then our pre-primary school but what is important, for this discussion, is that the language of our evening teach-ins, and the language of our immediate and wider community, and the language of our work in the fields were one.

And then I went to school, a colonial school, and this harmony was broken. The language of my education was no longer the language of my culture. I first went to Kamaandura, missionary run, and then to another called Maanguuũ run by nationalists grouped around the Gĩkũyũ Independent and Karinga Schools[1] Association. Our language of education was still Gĩkũyũ. The very first time I was ever given an ovation for my writing was over a composition in Gĩkũyũ. So for my first four years there was still harmony between the language of my formal education and that of the Limuru[2] peasant community.

It was after the declaration of a state of emergency over Kenya in 1952 that all the schools run by patriotic nationalists were taken over by the colonial regime and were placed under District Education Boards chaired by Englishmen. English became the language of my formal education. In Kenya, English became more than a language: it was *the* language, and all the others had to bow before it in deference.

Thus one of the most humiliating experiences was to be caught speaking Gĩkũyũ in the vicinity of the school. The culprit was given corporal punishment—three to five strokes of the cane on bare buttocks—or was made to carry a metal plate around the neck with inscriptions such as I AM STUPID or I AM A DONKEY. Sometimes the culprits were fined money they could hardly afford. And how did the teachers catch the culprits? A button was initially given to one pupil who was supposed to hand it over to whoever was caught speaking his mother tongue. Whoever had the button at the end of the day

[1] *Karinga Schools* Run by the Orthodox and Pentecostal churches.

[2] *Limuru* Located in the Nairobi region.

would sing who had given it to him and the ensuing process would bring out all the culprits of the day. Thus children were turned into witch-hunters and in the process were being taught the lucrative value of being a traitor to one's immediate community.

The attitude to English was the exact opposite: any achievement in spoken or written English was highly rewarded; prizes, prestige, applause; the ticket to higher realms. English became the measure of intelligence and ability in the arts, the sciences, and all the other branches of learning. English became *the* main determinant of a child's progress up the ladder of formal education.

As you may know, the colonial system of education in addition to its apartheid racial demarcation had the structure of a pyramid: a broad primary base, a narrowing secondary middle, and an even narrower university apex. Selections from primary into secondary were through an examination, in my time called Kenya African Preliminary Examination, in which one had to pass six subjects ranging from Maths to Nature Study and Kiswahili.[1] All the papers were written in English. Nobody could pass the exam who failed the English language paper no matter how brilliantly he had done in the other subjects. I remember one boy in my class of 1954 who had distinctions in all subjects except English, which he had failed. He was made to fail the entire exam. He went on to become a turn boy in a bus company. I who had only passes but a credit in English got a place at the Alliance High School, one of the most elitist institutions for Africans in colonial Kenya. The requirements for a place at the University, Makerere University College, were broadly the same: nobody could go on to wear the undergraduate red gown, no matter how brilliantly they had performed in all the other subjects unless they had a credit—not even a simple pass!—in English. Thus the most coveted place in the pyramid and in the system was only available to the holder of an English language credit card. English was the official vehicle and the magic formula to colonial elitedom.

Literary education was now determined by the dominant language while also reinforcing that dominance. Orature (oral literature) in Kenyan languages stopped. In primary school I now read simplified Dickens and Stevenson alongside Rider Haggard. Jim Hawkins, Oliver Twist, Tom Brown[2]—not Hare, Leopard and Lion—were now my daily companions in the world of imagination. In secondary school, Scott and G.B. Shaw vied with more Rider Haggard, John Buchan, Alan Paton, Captain W.E. Johns. At Makerere I read English: from Chaucer to T.S. Eliot with a touch of Grahame Greene.

Thus language and literature were taking us further and further from ourselves to other selves, from our world to other worlds.

What was the colonial system doing to us Kenyan children? What were the consequences of, on the one hand, this systematic suppression of our languages and the literature they carried, and on the other the elevation of English and the literature it carried? To answer those questions, let me first examine the relationship of language to human experience, human culture, and the human perception of reality.

CHAPTER 4

Language, any language, has a dual character: it is both a means of communication and a carrier of culture. Take English. It is spoken in Britain and in Sweden and Denmark. But for Swedish and Danish people English is only a means of communication with non-Scandinavians. It is not a carrier of their culture. For the British, and particularly the English, it is additionally, and inseparably from its use as a tool of communication, a carrier of their culture and history. Or take Swahili in East and Central Africa. It is widely used as a means of communication across many nationalities. But it is not the carrier of a culture and history of many of those nationalities. However in parts of Kenya and Tanzania, and particularly in Zanzibar, Swahili is inseparably both a means of communication and a carrier of the culture of those people to whom it is a mother-tongue.

Language as communication has three aspects or

[1] *Kiswahili* Swahili language.

[2] *Jim Hawkins … Tom Brown* Characters in Robert Louis Stevenson's *Treasure Island*, Charles Dickens's *Oliver Twist*, and Thomas Hughes's *Tom Brown's Schooldays* respectively.

elements. There is first what Karl Marx once called the language of real life, the element basic to the whole notion of language, its origins and development: that is, the relations people enter into with one another in the labour process, the links they necessarily establish among themselves in the act of a people, a community of human beings, producing wealth or means of life like food, clothing, houses. A human community really starts its historical being as a community of co-operation in production through the division of labour; the simplest is between man, woman and child within a household; the more complex divisions are between branches of production such as those who are sole hunters, sole gatherers of fruits or sole workers in metal. Then there are the most complex divisions such as those in modern factories where a single product, say a shirt or a shoe, is the result of many hands and minds. Production is co-operation, is communication, is language, is expression of a relation between human beings and it is specifically human.

The second aspect of language as communication is speech and it imitates the language of real life, that is communication in production. The verbal signposts both reflect and aid communication or the relation established between human beings in the production of their means of life. Language as a system of verbal signposts makes that production possible. The spoken word is to relations between human beings what the hand is to the relations between human beings and nature. The hand through tools mediates between human beings and nature and forms the language of real life: spoken words mediate between human beings and form the language of speech.

The third aspect is the written signs. The written word imitates the spoken. Where the first two aspects of language as communication through the hand and the spoken word historically evolved more or less simultaneously, the written aspect is a much later historical development. Writing is representation of sounds with visual symbols, from the simplest knot among shepherds to tell the number in a herd or the hieroglyphics among the Agĩkũyũ gicaandi singers and poets of Kenya, to the most complicated and different letter and picture writing systems of the world today.

In most societies the written and the spoken languages are the same, in that they represent each other: what is on paper can be read to another person and be received as that language, which the recipient has grown up speaking. In such a society there is broad harmony for a child between the three aspects of language as communication. His interaction with nature and with other men is expressed in written and spoken symbols or signs which are both a result of that double interaction and a reflection of it. The association of the child's sensibility is with the language of his experience of life.

But there is more to it: communication between human beings is also the basis and process of evolving culture. In doing similar kinds of things and actions over and over again under similar circumstances, similar even in their mutability, certain patterns, moves, rhythms, habits, attitudes, experiences and knowledge emerge. Those experiences are handed over to the next generation and become the inherited basis for their further actions on nature and on themselves. There is a gradual accumulation of values which in time become almost self-evident truths governing their conception of what is right and wrong, good and bad, beautiful and ugly, courageous and cowardly, generous and mean in their internal and external relations. Over a time this becomes a way of life distinguishable from other ways of life. They develop a distinctive culture and history. Culture embodies those moral, ethical and aesthetic values, the set of spiritual eyeglasses, through which they come to view themselves and their place in the universe. Values are the basis of a people's identity, their sense of particularity as members of the human race. All this is carried by language. Language as culture is the collective memory bank of a people's experience in history. Culture is almost indistinguishable from the language that makes possible its genesis, growth, banking, articulation and indeed its transmission from one generation to the next.

Language as culture also has three important aspects. Culture is a product of the history which it in turn reflects. Culture in other words is a product and a reflection of human beings communicating with one another in the very struggle to create wealth and to control it. But culture does not merely reflect that history, or rather it does so by actually forming images or pictures of the world of nature and nurture. Thus the second aspect of language as culture is as an image-forming agent in the mind of a child. Our whole conception of ourselves as a people, individually and collectively, is based on those pictures and images which may or may not correctly correspond to the actual reality of the struggles with nature and nurture which produced them in the first place. But our capacity to confront the world creatively is dependent on how those images correspond or not to that reality, how they distort or clarify the reality of our struggles. Language as culture is thus mediating between me and my own self; between my own self and other selves; between me and nature. Language is mediating in my very being. And this brings us to the third aspect of language as culture. Culture transmits or imparts those images of the world and reality through the spoken and the written language, that is through a specific language. In other words, the capacity to speak, the capacity to order sounds in a manner that makes for mutual comprehension between human beings is universal. This is the universality of language, a quality specific to human beings. It corresponds to the universality of the struggle against nature and that between human beings. But the particularity of the sounds, the words, the word order into phrases and sentences, and the specific manner, or laws, of their ordering is what distinguishes one language from another. Thus a specific culture is not transmitted through language in its universality but in its particularity as the language of a specific community with a specific history. Written literature and orature are the main means by which a particular language transmits the images of the world contained in the culture it carries.

Language as communication and as culture are then products of each other. Communication creates culture: culture is a means of communication. Language carries culture, and culture carries, particularly through orature and literature, the entire body of values by which we come to perceive ourselves and our place in the world. How people perceive themselves affects how they look at their culture, at their politics and at the social production of wealth, at their entire relationship to nature and to other beings. Language is thus inseparable from ourselves as a community of human beings with a specific form and character, a specific history, a specific relationship to the world.

Chapter 5

So what was the colonialist imposition of a foreign language doing to us children?

The real aim of colonialism was to control the people's wealth: what they produced, how they produced it, and how it was distributed; to control, in other words, the entire realm of the language of real life. Colonialism imposed its control of the social production of wealth through military conquest and subsequent political dictatorship. But its most important area of domination was the mental universe of the colonised, the control, through culture, of how people perceived themselves and their relationship to the world. Economic and political control can never be complete or effective without mental control. To control a people's culture is to control their tools of self-definition in relationship to others.

For colonialism this involved two aspects of the same process: the destruction or the deliberate undervaluing of a people's culture, their art, dances, religions, history, geography, education, orature and literature, and the conscious elevation of the language of the coloniser. The domination of a people's language by the languages of the colonising nations was crucial to the domination of the mental universe of the colonised.

Take language as communication. Imposing a foreign language, and suppressing the native languages as spoken and written, were already breaking the harmony previously existing between the African child and the three aspects of language. Since the new language as a means of communication was a product of and was reflecting the "real language of life" elsewhere, it could never as spoken or written properly reflect or imitate the real life of that community. This may in part explain why technology always appears to us as slightly external, *their* product and not *ours*. The word "missile" used to hold an alien far-away sound until I recently learnt its equivalent in Gĩkũyũ, *ngurukuhĩ* and it made me apprehend it differently. Learning, for a colonial child, became a cerebral activity and not an emotionally felt experience.

But since the new, imposed languages could never completely break the native languages as spoken, their most effective area of domination was the third aspect of language as communication, the written. The language of an African child's formal education was foreign. The language of the books he read was foreign. The language of his conceptualisation was foreign. Thought, in him, took the visible form of a foreign language. So the written language of a child's upbringing in the school (even his spoken language within the school compound) became divorced from his spoken language at home. There was often not the slightest relationship between the child's written world, which was also the language of his schooling, and the world of his immediate environment in the family and the community. For a colonial child, the harmony existing between the three aspects of language as communication was irrevocably broken. This resulted in the disassociation of the sensibility of that child from his natural and social environment, what we might call colonial alienation. The alienation became reinforced in the teaching of history, geography, music, where bourgeois Europe was always the centre of the universe.

This disassociation, divorce, or alienation from the immediate environment becomes clearer when you look at colonial language as a carrier of culture.

Since culture is a product of the history of a people which it in turn reflects, the child was now being exposed exclusively to a culture that was a product of a world external to himself. He was being made to stand outside himself to look at himself. *Catching Them Young* is the title of a book on racism, class, sex, and politics in children's literature by Bob Dixon. "Catching them young" as an aim was even more true of a colonial child. The images of his world and his place in it implanted in a child take years to eradicate, if they ever can be.

Since culture does not just reflect the world in images but actually, through those images, conditions a child to see that world a certain way, the colonial child was made to see the world and where he stands in it as seen and defined by or reflected in the culture of the language of imposition.

And since those images are mostly passed on through orature and literature it meant the child would now only see the world as seen in the literature of his language of adoption. From the point of view of alienation, that is of seeing oneself from outside oneself as if one was another self, it does not matter that the imported literature carried the great humanist tradition of the best Shakespeare, Goethe, Balzac, Tolstoy, Gorky, Brecht, Sholokhov, Dickens. The location of this great mirror of imagination was necessarily Europe and its history and culture and the rest of the universe was seen from that centre.

But obviously it was worse when the colonial child was exposed to images of his world as mirrored in the written languages of his coloniser. Where his own native languages were associated in his impressionable mind with low status, humiliation, corporal punishment, slow-footed intelligence and ability or downright stupidity, non-intelligibility and barbarism, this was reinforced by the world he met in the works of such geniuses of racism as a Rider Haggard or a Nicholas Monsarrat; not to mention the pronouncement of some of the giants of western intellectual and political establishment, such as Hume ("... The negro is naturally inferior to the whites ..."), Thomas Jefferson ("... The blacks ... are inferior to the whites on the endowments of both body and mind ..."), or Hegel with his Africa comparable to a land of childhood still enveloped in the dark mantle of the night as far as the development of self-conscious history was concerned. Hegel's statement that there was nothing harmonious with humanity to be found in the African character is representative of the racist images of Africans and Africa such a colonial child was bound to encounter in the literature of the colonial languages. The results could be disastrous.

—1986

Margaret Atwood

b. 1939

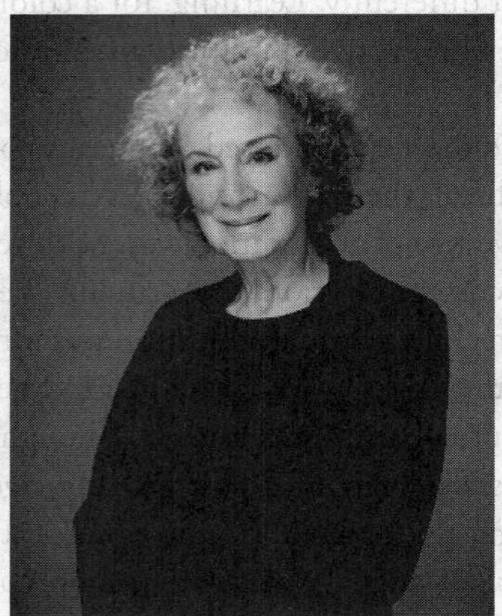

When she was coming of age in the 1960s and 1970s, Margaret Atwood's work helped define and bring attention to Canadian literature; more recently she has been an international figure quite as much as a Canadian one. Always prolific, she has written more than 40 books that have been translated into more than 30 languages. Her creative work—poetry, fiction, and children's literature—often uses a fantastic or speculative framework to address contentious issues. She has also been a leader in highlighting feminist concerns such as reproductive rights, sexual violence, and gender stereotypes. Atwood has received numerous awards over the years, including the Booker Prize in 2000 and the Governor General's Award, Canada's national literary award, in 1966 and 1985.

The "bush," or wilderness, is important to Atwood and often appears as a thematic element in her fiction. As a child, Atwood would regularly spend the spring, summer, and fall months in isolated areas of northern Ontario with her entomologist father and her mother, a former teacher. Living for long periods surrounded by the bush left Atwood with a powerful appreciation of the natural world. She also developed a love of reading as a response to the many hours of solitude provided by living in a log cabin with no other source of entertainment.

Born in Ottawa, Atwood moved with her family to Toronto in 1946 so that her father could take up a teaching position at the University of Toronto. Her advanced reading level allowed her to move ahead a grade in high school, where she decided that she wanted to be a writer. She was, however, forced to contend with 1950s gender stereotypes; according to the social code of the time, women who wished to work should be educated as nurses, teachers, or secretaries—and be prepared to resign their careers when they married. Atwood also had to contend with the many obstacles facing aspiring writers, whether male or female, in Canada's still largely undeveloped literary culture. The graduation message printed in her yearbook turned out to be quite prophetic: "Peggy's not-so-secret ambition is to write THE Canadian novel—and with those English marks, who doubts that she will?"

Atwood moved on to Victoria College at the University of Toronto in 1957, where she studied under the scholar and critic Northrop Frye. It was while she was at university that she first started publishing her poems in university magazines and small journals. At the time, she was publishing under the non-gendered name M.E. Atwood in an attempt to evade gender discrimination.

When Atwood completed her BA, Frye encouraged her to go to graduate school. She arrived in Boston in 1961 to pursue a Master's degree at Harvard University. Being at Harvard allowed her the distance to consider what it meant to be Canadian. Atwood came to believe that the physical and cultural landscape was central to any conception of Canadian literature; the writer must consider what it is to write in or of the Canadian space. Atwood explored these ideas as she continued writing poetry. She completed her Master's degree in 1962 and started a doctorate the following year, but financial constraints eventually forced her to put her studies on hold. She also felt that she needed more time to devote to her creative work.

Atwood accepted a lecturer's position at the University of British Columbia in Vancouver in 1964. Vancouver turned out to be a place where she could do both creative and critical work; while there she wrote her first published book and first professionally published volume of poetry, as well as making a significant start on several other books. *The Circle Game* (poetry) was published in 1966, and resulted in her first Governor General's Award. At the time she was, at 27, the youngest writer ever to have won the award. While at UBC, Atwood also wrote *The Edible Woman*, which would be published in 1969. The novel depicts a woman with an eating disorder and examines the role of consumerism in western culture; in both its feminist and anti-consumerist themes the book captured the mood of the times, and became a considerable international success. At this point, Atwood had returned to Boston to try to complete her doctorate, but she continued to produce poetry and publish while working on her studies. Although she wrote more than two-thirds of it, she never would complete her doctoral dissertation.

In 1970 Atwood published a collection of poems, *The Journals of Susanna Moodie*, in which she adopted the point of view of a nineteenth-century immigrant newly arrived in Canada. Atwood felt that Moodie's doubleness, as British and Canadian, exemplified a characteristically Canadian ambivalence. Atwood also continued her interest in the relationships between men and women in her influential poetry collection *Power Politics* (1971). The following year, she published a critical text on Canadian literature, *Survival: A Thematic Guide to Canadian Literature*, in which she argued that Canadian literature must confront and survive Canadian nature in order to thrive. The book was a major success and prompted reassessments of Canadian literature in many quarters. While working on *Survival* Atwood began a relationship with another writer, Graeme Gibson; the two remain together, and have one child.

Atwood has continued to write prolifically across multiple genres, including poetry, short fiction, and non-fiction. Her major novels include *Surfacing* (1973); *Lady Oracle* (1977); *Bodily Harm* (1982); *The Handmaid's Tale* (1986), for which she won her second Governor General's Award; *Cat's Eye* (1988); *The Robber Bride* (1993); *Alias Grace* (1996); *The Blind Assassin* (2000), for which she won the Booker Prize; *The Penelopiad* (2005); and the linked novels *Oryx and Crake* (2003), *The Year of the Flood* (2009), and *MaddAddam* (2013). Through these works, Atwood has developed a broad range as a writer; her major novels have ventured into the genres of fantastical satire (*The Robber Bride*), historical fiction and murder mystery (*Alias Grace*), layered fiction (*Alias Grace*), retold classical myth (*The Penelopiad*), and dystopic fantasy with powerful political implications for the present-day world (*The Handmaid's Tale*, *Oryx and Crake*). In 2016, she became the author of a graphic novel series, *Angel Catbird*. She has also continued her critical work with such publications as *Negotiating the Dead: A Writer on Writing* (2002) and *In Other Worlds: SF and the Human Imagination* (2012). Atwood's international stature has also been enhanced by numerous adaptations of her work, including the acclaimed Hulu television series *The Handmaid's Tale*, which premiered in 2017.

Atwood has long been involved in various human rights organizations, including Amnesty International and PEN Canada. She was also a founding member of the Writers' Union of Canada. Her work continues to draw attention to a variety of issues, including the oppression of women and the exploitation of nature. To Atwood, neither nature nor myth are to be separated from our everyday lives; instead, they are a "valued and necessary part of the human mentality."

⌘⌘⌘

Death of a Young Son by Drowning

He, who navigated with success
the dangerous river of his own birth
once more set forth

on a voyage of discovery
into the land I floated on
but could not touch to claim.

His feet slid on the bank,
the currents took him;
he swirled with ice and trees in the swollen water

and plunged into distant regions,
his head a bathysphere;[1]
through his eyes' thin glass bubbles

he looked out, reckless adventurer
on a landscape stranger than Uranus
we have all been to and some remember.

There was an accident; the air locked,
he was hung in the river like a heart.
They retrieved the swamped body,

cairn° of my plans and future charts, *stone memorial*
with poles and hooks
from among the nudging logs.

It was spring, the sun kept shining, the new grass
leapt to solidity;
my hands glistened with details.

After the long trip I was tired of waves.
My foot hit rock. The dreamed sails
collapsed, ragged.

I planted him in this country
like a flag.

—1970

[1] *bathysphere* Spherical chamber used for deep-sea observation.

The Immigrants

They are allowed to inherit
the sidewalks involved as palmlines, bricks
exhausted and soft, the deep
lawnsmells, orchards whorled
to the land's contours, the inflected weather

only to be told they are too poor
to keep it up, or someone
has noticed and wants to kill them; or the towns
pass laws which declare them obsolete.

I see them coming
up from the hold smelling of vomit,
infested, emaciated, their skins grey
with travel; as they step on shore

the old countries recede, become
perfect, thumbnail castles preserved
like gallstones in a glass bottle, the
towns dwindle upon the hillsides
in a light paperweight-clear.

They carry their carpetbags and trunks
with clothes, dishes, the family pictures;
they think they will make an order
like the old one, sow miniature orchards,
carve children and flocks out of wood

but always they are too poor, the sky
is flat, the green fruit shrivels
in the prairie sun, wood is for burning;
and if they go back, the towns

in time have crumbled, their tongues
stumble among awkward teeth, their ears
are filled with the sound of breaking glass.
I wish I could forget them
and so forget myself:

my mind is a wide pink map
across which move year after year
arrows and dotted lines, further and further,
people in railway cars

their heads stuck out of the windows
at stations, drinking milk or singing,
their features hidden with beards or shawls
day and night riding across an ocean of unknown
land to an unknown land.
—1970

[*you fit into me*]

You fit into me
like a hook into an eye

a fish hook
an open eye
—1971

The Door

The door swings open,
you look in.
It's dark in there,
most likely spiders:
nothing you want.
You feel scared.
The door swings closed.

The full moon shines,
it's full of delicious juice;
you buy a purse,
the dance is nice.
The door opens
and swings closed so quickly
you don't notice.

The sun comes out,
you have swift breakfasts
with your husband, who is still thin;
you wash the dishes,
you love your children,
you read a book,
you go to the movies.
It rains moderately.

The door swings open,
you look in:
why does this keep happening now?
Is there a secret?
The door swings closed.

The snow falls,
you clear the walk while breathing heavily;
it's not as easy as once.
Your children telephone sometimes.
The roof needs fixing.
You keep yourself busy.
The spring arrives.

The door swings open:
it's dark in there,
with many steps going down.
But what is that shining?
Is it water?
The door swings closed.

The dog has died.
This happened before.
You got another;
not this time though.
Where is your husband?
You gave up the garden.
It became too much.
At night there are blankets;
nonetheless you are wakeful.

The door swings open:
O god of hinges,
god of long voyages,
you have kept faith.
It's dark in there.
You confide yourself to the darkness.
You step in.
The door swings closed.
—2007

Angela Carter

1940 – 1992

Fiction writer Angela Carter spent much of her life in defiance of dominant literary trends, creating works that both fascinated and baffled her readers. Carter (whom Margaret Atwood described as "born subversive") liked to disrupt conventions and deny expectations. Her writing inhabits a gray area between the fantastic and the real, and makes innovative use of numerous familiar genres—most of which (Gothic, fantasy, science fiction, magic realism) were somewhat outside the literary mainstream in the twentieth century. Her unusually dense, allusive texts revel in linguistic play as they combine material from a myriad of sources, including folklore, tabloid headlines, French surrealism, Hollywood movies, and eighteenth-century allegorical fiction. Since her death, appreciation for her inventiveness and for the originality of her artistic vision has continued to grow; she is one of the most widely taught British writers of fiction.

Carter was born Angela Olive Stalker in Sussex in 1940. Much of her early childhood was spent with her grandmother in industrial Yorkshire, to which she and her brother had been evacuated to escape war-time bombings. After she finished high school, Carter's father, a journalist, got her a job as a reporter for a south London paper. Over the following decades, she would continue to use journalism as a source of income as she established her career in fiction. She soon married, at the age of nineteen—a decision that afforded escape from her conservative and oppressively protective parents—and in 1961 she left London to follow her husband, Paul Carter, to Bristol. There she entered Bristol University, where she studied medieval literature.

Her first published novel, *Shadow Dance* (1966), marked the beginning of a fertile creative period; two more novels, *The Magic Toyshop* (1967) and *Several Perceptions* (1968) quickly followed. Though many of her early works are set in the Bristol of her youth, they are permeated with elements of the Gothic fairy tale and an underlying threat of violence, while distinctions between reality and daydream are often blurred.

Several Perceptions won the prestigious Somerset Maugham award; the £500 prize enabled Carter to depart for Japan, where she lived for two years, leaving her faltering marriage behind. In Japan, Carter began what she referred to as an "apprenticeship in the language of signs." She had gone seeking a culture that had never been Judeo-Christian, and in attempting to interpret such an utterly foreign culture—with no knowledge of the language—she was forced to rely on a heightened awareness of visual social cues, observing how roles (particularly those of gender) and customs were created and maintained. After her return to Britain in 1972, the new, radical self-awareness that resulted from her life in Japan led her to examine her own social and cultural heritage from her newly gained viewpoint of an outsider.

Much of Carter's fiction relies heavily on allegory, and also makes use of many elements of science fiction and magic realism. *The Infernal Desire Machine of Doctor Hoffman* (1972), in particular, is often classified as science fiction, though it also draws on the picaresque. This novel has remained one of her most controversial, frequently criticized for an alleged male chauvinistic viewpoint that seems to celebrate the pornographic. With Carter's use of multiple voices and ever-shifting narrative positions, however, it is sometimes difficult to tell whether she is embracing or parodying the gender roles she sets out.

The Sadeian Woman (1979), Carter's first book of nonfiction and another highly controversial work, attacks the prestige she sees as often being accorded to the suffering of women, and criticizes portrayals of women as blameless victims. These strategies, she believes, only valorize the role of the powerless outsider. From a perspective informed by feminist and psychoanalytic theory, the book interprets the pornographic works of the Marquis de Sade (the eighteenth-century writer for whom sadism was named). She finds liberatory possibilities for women in his examinations of sexuality and power—a reading that many feminists of the period found outrageous. In the book's opening, Carter also articulates her position on the purpose of narrative, which she claims should be a means of exploring ideas that are relevant to real lived experience: "Fine art, that exists for itself alone, is art in a final state of impotence. If nobody, including the artist, acknowledges art as a means of *knowing* the world, then art is relegated to a kind of rumpus room of the mind."

Published in the same year as *The Sadeian Woman*, *The Bloody Chamber* is Carter's best-known work. In this collection of short stories, she reshapes material from classic fairy tales such as "Red Riding Hood," "Beauty and the Beast," and "Bluebeard." Many of these tales had been collected in prose for the first time by the seventeenth-century French author Charles Perrault, whose writing Carter was translating at the same time as she drafted her own stories. In *The Bloody Chamber*, she brings a gothic sensibility to the fairy tale, exploiting its potential as a vehicle for the exploration of gender, sexuality, and the unconscious. "My intention," she wrote "was not to do 'versions' or, as the American edition of the book said, horribly, 'adult' fairy tales, but to extract the latent content from the traditional stories and to use it as the beginnings of new stories." Carter also co-wrote a screenplay based on a story from the collection, "The Company of Wolves," which became a successful 1984 film of the same title.

The publication of *The Bloody Chamber* marked a turning point in Carter's career. As her work began to be more favorably reviewed, she took on a demanding lecturing and teaching schedule that saw her traveling around the world. In 1983 she also began a family, giving birth to a son, Alexander, with Mark Pearce, whom she married in 1991. Despite her busy schedule, Carter produced her longest novel, *Nights at the Circus*, in 1984. This story about a Cockney trapeze artist with wings has often been compared to Gabriel Garcia Marquez's *One Hundred Years of Solitude* (1967)—a comparison that brought Carter more into the mainstream than she had perhaps ever been. This and her final novel, *Wise Children* (1991), were both very well received, and when Carter died of lung cancer in 1992, she was mourned as a central literary figure of her day.

Many observed that her obituary notices spoke of her work more generously than most of her reviews had. But critical acceptance had never been a goal of Carter's; she was always suspicious of critical consensus of any kind. Indeed, her writing seeks to provoke those whose opinions are widely accepted, and, in doing so, to produce fruitful critical debate. As one of her critics said, "I'll please no one, least of all her, by trying to say she's not offensive."

⌘⌘⌘

The Werewolf

It is a northern country; they have cold weather, they have cold hearts.

Cold; tempest; wild beasts in the forest. It is a hard life. Their houses are built of logs, dark and smoky within. There will be a crude icon of the virgin behind a guttering candle, the leg of a pig hung up to cure, a string of drying mushrooms. A bed, a stool, a table. Harsh, brief, poor lives.

To these upland woodsmen, the Devil is as real as you or I. More so; they have not seen us nor even know that we exist, but the Devil they glimpse often in the graveyards, those bleak and touching townships of the dead where the graves are marked with portraits of the deceased in the naïf style[1] and there are no flowers to put in front of them, no flowers grow there, so they put out small, votive offerings, little loaves, sometimes a cake that the bears come lumbering from the margins of the forests to snatch away. At midnight, especially on Walpurgisnacht,[2] the Devil holds picnics in the graveyards and invites the witches; then they dig up fresh corpses, and eat them. Anyone will tell you that.

Wreaths of garlic on the doors keep out the vampires. A blue-eyed child born feet first on the night of St. John's Eve[3] will have second sight. When they discover a witch—some old woman whose cheeses ripen when her neighbour's do not, another old woman whose black cat, oh, sinister! *follows her about all the time*, they strip the crone, search for her marks, for the supernumerary nipple her familiar sucks. They soon find it. Then they stone her to death.

Winter and cold weather.

Go and visit grandmother, who has been sick. Take her the oatcakes I've baked for her on the hearthstone and a little pot of butter.

The good child does as her mother bids—five miles' trudge through the forest; do not leave the path because of the bears, the wild boar, the starving wolves. Here, take your father's hunting knife; you know how to use it.

The child had a scabby coat of sheepskin to keep out the cold, she knew the forest too well to fear it but she must always be on her guard. When she heard that freezing howl of a wolf, she dropped her gifts, seized her knife and turned on the beast.

It was a huge one, with red eyes and running, grizzled chops; any but a mountaineer's child would have died of fright at the sight of it. It went for her throat, as wolves do, but she made a great swipe at it with her father's knife and slashed off its right forepaw.

The wolf let out a gulp, almost a sob, when she saw what had happened to it; wolves are less brave than they seem. It went lolloping off disconsolately between the trees as well as it could on three legs, leaving a trail of blood behind it. The child wiped the blade of her knife clean on her apron, wrapped up the wolf's paw in the cloth in which her mother had packed the oatcakes and went on towards her grandmother's house. Soon it came on to snow so thickly that the path and any footsteps, track, or spoor that might have been upon it were obscured.

She found her grandmother was so sick she had taken to her bed and fallen into a fretful sleep, moaning and shaking so that the child guessed she had a fever. She felt the forehead, it burned. She shook out the cloth from her basket, to use it to make the old woman a cold compress, and the wolf's paw fell to the floor.

But it was no longer a wolf's paw. It was a hand, chopped off at the wrist, a hand toughened with work and freckled with old age. There was a wedding ring on the third finger and a wart on the index finger. By the wart, she knew it for her grandmother's hand.

She pulled back the sheet but the old woman woke up, at that, and began to struggle, squawking and shrieking like a thing possessed. But the child was strong, and armed with her father's hunting knife; she managed to hold her grandmother down long enough to see the cause of her fever. There was a bloody stump

---

[1] *naïf style* Artistic style not shaped by formal training.

[2] *Walpurgisnacht* In European folklore, the night of an annual witches' gathering with the devil. It is the night before the pagan festival of May Day and the Christian feast of St. Walpurga, a saint associated with protection from witchcraft.

[3] *St. John's Eve* Night before the Christian feast of St. John. It takes place on or near the summer solstice.

where her right hand should have been, festering already.

The child crossed herself and cried out so loud the neighbours heard her and came rushing in. They knew the wart on the hand at once for a witch's nipple; they drove the old woman, in her shift as she was, out into the snow with sticks, beating her old carcass as far as the edge of the forest, and pelted her with stones until she fell down dead.

Now the child lived in her grandmother's house; she prospered.

—1977, REVISED 1979

The Snow Child

Midwinter—invincible, immaculate. The Count and his wife go riding, he on a grey mare and she on a black one, she wrapped in the glittering pelts of black foxes; and she wore high, black, shining boots with scarlet heels, and spurs. Fresh snow fell on snow already fallen; when it ceased, the whole world was white. "I wish I had a girl as white as snow," says the Count. They ride on. They come to a hole in the snow; this hole is filled with blood. He says: "I wish I had a girl as red as blood." So they ride on again; here is a raven, perched on a bare bough. "I wish I had a girl as black as that bird's feathers."

As soon as he completed her description, there she stood, beside the road, white skin, red mouth, black hair and stark naked; she was the child of his desire and the Countess hated her. The Count lifted her up and sat her in front of him on his saddle but the Countess had only one thought: how shall I be rid of her?

The Countess dropped her glove in the snow and told the girl to get down to look for it; she meant to gallop off and leave her there but the Count said: "I'll buy you new gloves." At that, the furs sprang off the Countess's shoulders and twined round the naked girl. Then the Countess threw her diamond brooch through the ice of a frozen pond: "Dive in and fetch it for me," she said; she thought the girl would drown. But the Count said: "Is she a fish to swim in such cold weather?" Then her boots leapt off the Countess's feet and on to the girl's legs. Now the Countess was bare as a bone and the girl furred and booted; the Count felt sorry for his wife. They came to a bush of roses, all in flower. "Pick me one," said the Countess to the girl. "I can't deny you that," said the Count.

So the girl picks a rose; pricks her finger on the thorn; bleeds; screams; falls.

Weeping, the Count got off his horse, unfastened his breeches and thrust his virile member into the dead girl. The Countess reined in her stamping mare and watched him narrowly; he was soon finished.

Then the girl began to melt. Soon there was nothing left of her but a feather a bird might have dropped; a blood stain, like the trace of a fox's kill on the snow; and the rose she had pulled off the bush. Now the Countess had all her clothes on again. With her long hand, she stroked her furs. The Count picked up the rose, bowed and handed it to his wife; when she touched it, she dropped it.

"It bites!" she said.

—1979

John Cleese and Graham Chapman

b. 1939, and 1941 – 1989

Graham Chapman and John Cleese were the founders of the influential British comedy troupe Monty Python's Flying Circus. Their work with fellow Pythons Michael Palin (1943–), Eric Idle (1943–), Terry Jones (1942–), and Terry Gilliam (1940–) attracted huge followings not just in Britain but also throughout the English-speaking world. In 2000, the British Film Institute named their television series, *Monty Python's Flying Circus*, number five in their listing of the top 100 greatest British television programs.

John Cleese was born on 27 October 1939 in Weston-Super-Mare, Somerset, England. He studied at Clifton College, Bristol, and then at Cambridge University's Downing College, where he completed a degree in law. He began working in comedy as part of the Cambridge Footlights Revue, an amateur theatrical club run by students. It was here that he met Graham Chapman.

Chapman was born in Leicester on 8 January 1941. As a schoolboy, he participated in school productions, including plays by Shakespeare and Gilbert and Sullivan, and revue shows. In 1959, he was admitted to Emmanuel College at Cambridge University, where he studied medicine. He eventually qualified as a doctor at St. Bartholomew's Hospital Medical College, London.

Like Cleese, Chapman joined the Cambridge Footlights Revue and toured to New Zealand and New York. Upon returning in 1965, Cleese and Chapman wrote and performed in various British radio and television comedy series, including *The Dick Emery Show* (1965–84), *Doctor in the House* (1969–70), *At Last the 1948 Show* (1967), and *I'm Sorry, I'll Read That Again* (1964–72). When the two were hired to write for *The Frost Report* (1966–67), a BBC comedy/variety series, they were introduced to Eric Idle, Terry Jones, and Michael Palin. It was here that the future colleagues developed their trademark comedy style.

In 1969, Chapman and Cleese were offered their own television series. Their partnership was not an easy one; Chapman had developed a drinking problem, and Cleese found himself bearing most of the burden of the show. As a result, Cleese invited Palin, Idle, Jones, and Terry Gilliam (an American animator he had met while in New York) to work on the show, and the Monty Python troupe was born. Their television show, *Monty Python's Flying Circus*, ran between 1969 and 1974. The show's humor was quirky and irreverent, featuring cartoonish authority figures, strange satirical takes on the idiosyncrasies of British life, and frequent references to philosophers, literary figures, and famous works of art.

The troupe produced 45 episodes of *Monty Python's Flying Circus*, in four series. They also made five films: *And Now for Something Completely Different* (1971), a collection of re-filmed sketches from the television show; *Monty Python and the Holy Grail* (1974), a spoof of the Arthurian legends; *Monty Python's Life of Brian* (1979), a controversial send-up of organized religion and epic Bible movies;

Monty Python Live at the Hollywood Bowl (1982), a live film of a public performance; and *Monty Python's The Meaning of Life* (1983), a darkly comic philosophical meditation.

Cleese left the show after its third series, unhappy with the strain of working with Chapman, whose alcoholism continued to interfere with their collaboration (Cleese would, however, return to work on the troupe's major films). He went on to co-write and star as Basil Fawlty in the very popular television series *Fawlty Towers* and to continue making films, most notably *A Fish Called Wanda* (1988), one of the most financially successful British films in history. Graham Chapman's career faltered after Monty Python. He gave up drinking in 1977, but his only solo film project, *Yellowbeard* (1983), suffered both critically and commercially. In late 1988, Chapman was diagnosed with throat cancer, which quickly spread to his spine. He died on 4 October 1989.

⌘⌘⌘

from *Monty Python's Flying Circus*

DEAD PARROT SKETCH[1]

THE CAST:

PRALINE: John Cleese
SHOPKEEPER: Michael Palin
PORTER: Terry Jones

PRALINE. Hello, I wish to register a complaint. … Hello? Miss?

SHOPKEEPER. What do you mean, miss?

PRALINE. Oh, I'm sorry, I have a cold. I wish to make a complaint.

SHOPKEEPER. Sorry, we're closing for lunch.

PRALINE. Never mind that my lad, I wish to complain about a parrot what I purchased not half an hour ago from this very boutique.

SHOPKEEPER. Oh yes, the Norwegian Blue. What's wrong with it?

PRALINE. I'll tell you what's wrong with it. It's dead, that's what's wrong with it.

SHOPKEEPER. No, no it's resting look!

PRALINE. Look my lad, I know a dead parrot when I see one and I'm looking at one right now.

SHOPKEEPER. No, no sir, it's not dead. It's resting.

PRALINE. Resting?

SHOPKEEPER. Yeah, remarkable bird the Norwegian Blue, beautiful plumage, innit?[2]

PRALINE. The plumage don't enter into it—it's stone dead.

SHOPKEEPER. No, no—it's just resting.

PRALINE. All right then, if it's resting I'll wake it up. (*Shouts into cage.*) Hello Polly! I've got a nice cuttlefish for you when you wake up, Polly Parrot!

SHOPKEEPER. (*Jogging cage.*) There it moved.

PRALINE. No he didn't. That was you pushing the cage.

SHOPKEEPER. I did not.

PRALINE. Yes, you did. (*Takes parrot out of cage, shouts.*) Hello Polly, Polly. (*Bangs it against the counter.*) Polly Parrot, wake up. Polly. (*Throws it in the air and it lands on the floor.*) Now that's what I call a dead parrot.

SHOPKEEPER. No, no it's stunned.

PRALINE. Look my lad, I've had just about enough of this. That parrot is definitely deceased. And when I bought it not half an hour ago, you assured me that its lack of movement was due to it being tired and shagged out after a long squawk.

SHOPKEEPER. It's probably pining for the fjords.

PRALINE. Pining for the fjords, what kind of talk is that? Look, why did it fall flat on its back the moment I got it home?

SHOPKEEPER. The Norwegian Blue prefers kipping[3] on its back. Beautiful bird, lovely plumage.

PRALINE. Look, I took the liberty of examining the parrot, and I discovered that the only reason that it had

[1] *DEAD PARROT SKETCH* From *Monty Python's Flying Circus*, Episode 9.

[2] *innit* I.e., isn't it.

[3] *kipping* Sleeping.

been sitting on its perch in the first place was that it had been nailed there.

SHOPKEEPER. Well of course it was nailed there. Otherwise it would muscle up to those bars and voom.

PRALINE. Look matey (*Picks up parrot.*) this parrot wouldn't go voom if I put four thousand volts through it. It's bleeding demised.

SHOPKEEPER. It's not. It's pining.

PRALINE. It's not pining, it's passed on. This parrot is no more. It has ceased to be. It's expired and gone to meet its maker. This is a late parrot. It's a stiff. Bereft of life, it rests in peace. If you hadn't nailed it to the perch, it would be pushing up the daisies. It's rung down the curtain and joined the choir invisible. This is an ex-parrot.

SHOPKEEPER. Well I'd better replace it then.

PRALINE. (*To camera.*) If you want to get anything done in this country you've got to complain till you're blue in the mouth.

SHOPKEEPER. Sorry guv, we're right outa parrots.

PRALINE. I see. I see. I get the picture.

SHOPKEEPER. I've got a slug.

PRALINE. Does it talk?

SHOPKEEPER. Not really, no.

PRALINE. Well, it's scarcely a replacement, then is it?

SHOPKEEPER. Listen, I'll tell you what, (*Handing over a card.*) tell you what, if you go to my brother's pet shop in Bolton[1] he'll replace your parrot for you.

PRALINE. Bolton eh?

SHOPKEEPER. Yeah.

PRALINE. All right.

(*He leaves, holding the parrot.*
Caption: "A similar pet shop in Bolton, Lancs"[2]
Close-up of sign on door reading: "Similar Pet Shops Ltd." Pull back from sign to see same pet shop. Shopkeeper now has a moustache. Praline walks into the shop. He looks around with interest, noticing the empty parrot cage on the floor.)

PRALINE. Er, excuse me. This is Bolton, is it?

SHOPKEEPER. No, no it's, er, Ipswich.[3]

PRALINE. (*To camera.*) That's Inter-City Rail for you. (*Leaves.*)

(*Man in porter's outfit standing at complaints desk for railways. Praline approaches.*)

PRALINE. I wish to make a complaint.

PORTER. I don't have to do this, you know.

PRALINE. I beg your pardon?

PORTER. I'm a qualified brain surgeon. I only do this because I like being my own boss.

PRALINE. Er, excuse me, this is irrelevant, isn't it?

PORTER. Oh yeah, it's not easy to pad these out to thirty minutes.

PRALINE. Well I wish to make a complaint. I got on to the Bolton train and found myself deposited here in Ipswich.

PORTER. No, this is Bolton.

PRALINE. (*To camera.*) The pet shop owner's brother was lying.

PORTER. Well you can't blame British Rail for that.

PRALINE. If this is Bolton, I shall return to the pet shop.

(*Caption: "A Little Later Ltd."*
Praline walks into the shop again.)

PRALINE. I understand this *is* Bolton.

SHOPKEEPER. Yes.

PRALINE. Well, you told me it was Ipswich.

SHOPKEEPER. It was a pun.

PRALINE. A pun?

SHOPKEEPER. No, no, not a pun, no. What's the other thing which reads the same backwards as forwards?

PRALINE. A palindrome?

SHOPKEEPER. Yes, yes.

PRALINE. It's not a palindrome. The palindrome of Bolton would be Notlob. It don't work.

SHOPKEEPER. Look, what do you want?

PRALINE. No, I'm sorry, I'm not prepared to pursue my line of enquiry any further as I think this is getting too silly.

—1969

[1] *Bolton* Town near Manchester in northern England.

[2] *Lancs* Lancashire, a county in the north of England.

[3] *Ipswich* County town in East Anglia, in the east of England, 390 kilometers (243 miles) from Bolton.

PET CONVERSION[1]

THE CAST:

MAN: John Cleese
SHOPKEEPER: Michael Palin
HARRY: Graham Chapman

(*Superimposed caption: A Pet Shop Somewhere Near Melton Mowbray.*[2])

MAN. Good morning, I'd like to buy a cat.

SHOPKEEPER. Certainly sir. I've got a lovely terrier. (*Indicates a box on the counter.*)

MAN. (*Glancing in box.*) No, I want a cat really.

SHOPKEEPER. (*Taking box off counter and then putting it back on counter as if it is a different box.*) Oh yeah, how about that?

MAN. (*Looking in box.*) No, that's the terrier.

SHOPKEEPER. Well, it's as near as dammit.

MAN. Well what do you mean? I want a cat.

SHOPKEEPER. Listen, tell you what. I'll file its legs down a bit, take its snout out, stick a few wires through its cheeks. There you are, a lovely pussy cat.

MAN. It's not a proper cat.

SHOPKEEPER. What do you mean?

MAN. Well it wouldn't miaow.

SHOPKEEPER. Well it would howl a bit.

MAN. No, no, no, no. Er, have you got a parrot?

SHOPKEEPER. No, I'm afraid not, actually guv, we're fresh out of parrots. I'll tell you what though … I'll lop its back legs off, make good, strip the fur, stick a couple of wings on and staple on a beak of your own choice. (*Taking small box and rattling it.*) No problem. Lovely parrot.

MAN. And how long would that take?

SHOPKEEPER. Oh, let me see … er, stripping the fur off, no legs … (*Calling.*) Harry … can you do a parrot job on this terrier straight away?

HARRY. (*Off screen.*) No, I'm still putting a tuck in the Airedale, and then I got the frogs to let out.

SHOPKEEPER. Friday?

MAN. No I need it for tomorrow. It's a present.

SHOPKEEPER. Oh dear, it's a long job. You see parrot conversion … Tell you what though, for free, terriers make lovely fish. I mean I could do that for you straight away. Legs off, fins on, stick a little pipe through the back of its neck so it can breathe, bit of gold paint, make good …

MAN. You'd need a very big tank.

SHOPKEEPER. It's a great conversation piece.

MAN. Yes, all right, all right … but, er, only if I can watch.

—1969

[1] *PET CONVERSION* Featured in *Monty Python's Flying Circus*, Episode 10.

[2] *Melton Mowbray* Town in county Leicestershire.

DIRTY HUNGARIAN PHRASEBOOK[3]

THE CAST:

HUNGARIAN: John Cleese
TOBACCONIST: Terry Jones
POLICEMAN: Graham Chapman

(*Set: A tobacconist's shop.*)

(*Roller caption: In 1970, the British Empire lay in ruins, and foreign nationalists frequented the streets—many of them Hungarians [not the streets—the foreign nationals]. Anyway, many of these Hungarians went into tobacconists' shops to buy cigarettes …*)

(*Enter Hungarian gentleman with phrase book. He is looking for the right phrase.*)

HUNGARIAN. I will not buy this record. It is scratched.

TOBACCONIST. Sorry?

HUNGARIAN. I will not buy this record. It is scratched.

TOBACCONIST. No, no, no. This … tobacconist's.

HUNGARIAN. Ah! I will not buy this tobacconist's. It is scratched.

TOBACCONIST. No, no, no … tobacco … er, cigarettes?

HUNGARIAN. Yes, cigarettes. My hovercraft is full of eels.

TOBACCONIST. What?

HUNGARIAN. (*Miming matches.*) My hovercraft is full of eels.

[3] *DIRTY HUNGARIAN PHRASEBOOK* Featured in *Monty Python's Flying Circus*, Episode 25.

TOBACCONIST. Matches, matches?

HUNGARIAN. Yah, yah. (*He takes cigarettes and matches and pulls out loose change; he consults his book.*) Er, do you want … do you want to come back to my place, bouncy bouncy?

TOBACCONIST. I don't think you're using that thing right.

HUNGARIAN. You great pouf.[1]

TOBACCONIST. That'll be six and six,[2] please.

HUNGARIAN. If I said you had a beautiful body, would you hold it against me? I am no longer infected.

TOBACCONIST. (*Miming that he wants to see the book; he takes the book.*) It costs six and six … (*Mumbling as he searches*) Costs six and six … Here we are … Yandelvayasna grldenwi stravenka.

(*Hungarian hits him between the eyes. Policeman walking along street suddenly stops and puts his hand to his ear. He starts running down the street, round corner and down another street, round yet another corner and down another street into the shop.*)

POLICEMAN. What's going on here then?

HUNGARIAN. (*Opening book and pointing at Tobacconist.*) You have beautiful thighs.

POLICEMAN. What?

TOBACCONIST. He hit me.

HUNGARIAN. Drop your panties, Sir William, I cannot wait till lunchtime.

POLICEMAN. Right! (*Grabs him and drags him out.*)

HUNGARIAN. My nipples explode with delight.

(*Cut to a courtroom.*)

THE CAST:

JUDGE: Terry Jones
CLERK: Eric Idle
LAWYER: John Cleese
POLICEMAN: Graham Chapman (still)
YAHLT: Michael Palin

CLERK. Call Alexander Yahlt!

VOICES. Call Alexander Yahlt. Call Alexander Yahlt. Call Alexander Yahlt.

(*They do this three times, finishing with harmony.*)

MAGISTRATE. Oh, shut up.

(*Alexander Yahlt enters. He is not Hungarian but an ordinary man in a mac.*[3])

CLERK. (*To publisher.*) You are Alexander Yahlt?

YAHLT. (*Derek Nimmo's*[4] *voice dubbed on.*) Oh, I am.

CLERK. Skip the impersonations. You are Alexander Yahlt?

YAHLT. (*Normal voice.*) I am.

CLERK. You are hereby charged that on the 28th day of May 1970 you did wilfully, unlawfully, and with malice aforethought publish an alleged English–Hungarian phrase book with intent to cause a breach of the peace. How do you plead?

YAHLT. Not guilty.

CLERK. You live at 46, Horton Terrace?

YAHLT. I do live at 46, Horton Terrace.

CLERK. You are the director of a publishing company?

YAHLT. I am the director of a publishing company.

CLERK. Your company publishes phrasebooks?

YAHLT. My company does publish phrasebooks.

CLERK. You did say 46, Horton Terrace did you?

YAHLT. Yes.

(*He claps his hand to his mouth; gong sounds—general applause.*)

CLERK. Ha, ha, ha, I got him.

MAGISTRATE. Get on with it! Get on with it!

CLERK. Yes, m'lud,[5] on the 28th of May you published this phrasebook.

YAHLT. I did.

CLERK. I quote one example. The Hungarian phrase meaning "Can you direct me to the station?" is

[1] *pouf* Derogatory British slang for gay man.

[2] *six and six* Six shillings and sixpence.

[3] *mac* I.e., mackintosh, a raincoat.

[4] *Derek Nimmo* British comedic actor and BBC Radio game show panelist who had a distinctive, aristocratic voice.

[5] *m'lud* I.e., my lord.

translated by the English phrase, "please fondle my bum."

YAHLT. I wish to plead incompetence.

(*The Policeman stands up.*)

POLICEMAN. Please may I ask for an adjournment, m'lud?

MAGISTRATE. An adjournment? Certainly not.

(*The Policeman sits down; there is a loud raspberry;*[1] *the policeman goes bright red.*)

Why on earth didn't you say *why* you wanted an adjournment?

POLICEMAN. I didn't know an acceptable legal phrase, m'lud.

(*Cut to stock film of Women's Institute*[2] *applauding. Cut back to the magistrate.*)

MAGISTRATE. If there's any more stock film of women applauding I shall clear the court.

—1970

SPAM[3]

THE CAST:

MR. BUN: Eric Idle
MRS. BUN: Graham Chapman
WAITRESS: Terry Jones
HUNGARIAN: John Cleese
HISTORIAN: Michael Palin

(*Scene: A cafe. All the customers are Vikings. Mr. and Mrs. Bun enter—downwards, on wires.*)

MR. BUN. Morning.

WAITRESS. Morning.

MR. BUN. What have you got, then?

WAITRESS. Well there's egg and bacon; egg sausage and bacon; egg and spam; egg, bacon and spam; egg, bacon, sausage and spam; spam, bacon, sausage and spam; spam, egg, spam, spam, bacon and spam; spam, spam, spam, egg and spam; spam, spam, spam, spam, spam, spam, baked beans, spam, spam, spam, and spam; or lobster thermidor aux crevettes with a mornay sauce garnished with truffle pâté, brandy and a fried egg on top and spam.

MRS. BUN. Have you got anything without spam in it?

WAITRESS. Well, there's spam, egg, sausage and spam. That's not got *much* spam in it.

MRS. BUN. I don't want *any* spam.

MR. BUN. Why can't she have egg, bacon, spam and sausage?

MRS. BUN. That's got spam in it!

MR. BUN. Not as much as spam, egg, sausage and spam.

MRS. BUN. Look, could I have egg, bacon, spam and sausage without the spam.

WAITRESS. Uuuuuuggggh!

MRS. BUN. What do you mean uuuggggh! I don't like spam.

VIKINGS. (*Singing.*) Spam, spam, spam, spam, spam … spam, spam, spam, spam … lovely spam, wonderful spam …

(*Brief stock shot of a Viking ship.*)

WAITRESS. Shut up! Shut up! Shut up! You can't have egg, bacon, spam and sausage without the spam.

MRS. BUN. (*Shrieks.*) I don't like spam!

MR. BUN. Don't make a fuss, dear. I'll have your spam. I love it. I'm having spam, spam, spam, spam, spam …

VIKINGS. (*Singing.*) Spam, spam, spam, spam …

MR. BUN. … baked beans, spam, spam and spam.

WAITRESS. Baked beans are off.

MR. BUN. Well can I have spam instead?

WAITRESS. You mean spam, spam, spam, spam, spam, spam, spam, spam, spam, spam?

VIKINGS. (*Still singing.*) Spam, spam, spam, spam … (*etc.*)

MR. BUN. Yes.

WAITRESS. Arrggh!

VIKINGS. … lovely spam, wonderful, spam.

WAITRESS. Shut up! Shut up!

(*The Vikings shut up momentarily. Enter the Hungarian.*)

---

[1] *raspberry* Rude sound, generally made with the lips and tongue. Here, denotes flatulence.

[2] *Women's Institute* Organization for women in England and Wales.

[3] *SPAM* Featured in *Monty Python's Flying Circus*, Episode 25.

Hungarian. Great boobies, honeybun, my lower intestine is full of spam, egg, spam, bacon, spam, tomato, spam …

Vikings. (*Starting up again.*) Spam, spam, spam, spam …

Waitress. Shut up.

(*A policeman rushes in and bundles the Hungarian out.*)

Hungarian. My nipples explode …

(*Cut to a historian. Superimposed caption: "A HISTORIAN."*)

Historian. Another great Viking victory was at the Green Midget café at Bromley. Once again the Viking strategy was the same. They sailed from these fjords here (*indicating map with arrows on it*), assembled at Trondheim and waited for the strong north-easterly winds to blow their oaken galleys to England whence they sailed on May 23rd. Once in Bromley they assembled at the Green Midget café and spam selecting a spam particular spam item from the spam menu would spam, spam, spam, spam, spam …

(*The backdrop behind him rises to reveal the café again. The Vikings start singing again and the historian conducts them.*)

Vikings. (*Singing.*) Spam, spam, spam, spam, spam, lovely spam, wonderful spam. Lovely spam, wonderful spam …

(*Mr. and Mrs. Bun rise slowly in the air.*)

—1970

Eavan Boland

b. 1944

In a time and place where being a woman and being a poet were considered two divergent pursuits, Eavan Boland established herself as one of the most important Irish writers of her time. Leading largely through personal example rather than political activism, she has proudly accepted the mantle of "woman poet," stating in recent years that this dual designation shows "that poetry is more of an open city now than it once was." The recipient of many awards, she has been a member of the Irish Academy of Letters and served on the board of the Irish Arts Council, and she has been a writer in residence at Trinity College and University College Dublin, as well as a poet in residence at the National Maternity Hospital.

Boland was born in Dublin, Ireland, to parents Frederick Boland and Frances Kelly, a diplomat and a painter. Her father's work took the family out of Ireland when Boland was six years old, and they lived in London and New York before returning to Ireland during Boland's teenage years. As a seventeen-year-old working in Dublin the summer before beginning studies at Trinity College, Boland embarked on her own study of poetry, spending many evenings reading the works of Yeats, Joyce, and the nineteenth-century poets that would shape her understanding of the evolution of the poetic form. She was also beginning to write her own poems, though she experienced difficulty fully realizing an identity as a poet; she would later recall feeling that she "was looking for that solid land-bridge between writing poems and being a poet." While attending Trinity College, Boland continued to write, and in 1962 she published her first collection, *23 Poems*.

After graduating with a BA, Boland wrote poetry reviews for the *Irish Times* and immersed herself in Dublin's literary scene. With her marriage to writer Kevin Casey and the birth of their two daughters, she experienced a radical shift. In the culture of mid-twentieth-century Ireland, where suburban ideals of womanhood seemed to relegate women to the domestic sphere, Boland faced a sudden professional isolation. The domestic reality of her new life, however, enabled her to access a vibrant daily experience from which she drew unprecedented inspiration: "Finally, I had joined together my life as a woman and a poet. On the best days I lived as a poet, the language at the end of my day—when the children were asleep and the curtains drawn—was the language all through my day: it had waited for me." Boland's unsentimental, evocative depictions of ordinary and personal scenes soon caught the attention of readers in her own country and beyond. Her poems, published in collections such as *In Her Own Image* (1980), *Night Feed* (1982), *The Journey* (1983), and *In a Time of Violence* (1994), wove scenes of the daily domestic together with re-imagined mythological figures and motifs, finding the personal and everyday a powerful site that could be captured and re-experienced poetically by both writers and readers.

Boland has credited American poets such as Adrienne Rich and Denise Levertov as influences on her work, though she has also acknowledged the continuing influence of the Irish and Scottish poets she had first encountered as a student. As she studied the poets of the Irish lyric tradition and carved out her own place in this lineage, she found spaces for subversion within the English language, a medium bestowed by colonizers but, Boland has argued, one that has enabled her to write of her nation's loss. In 1989, Boland published *A Kind of Scar*, a scholarly discussion of Irish female poets. In that book she argues that the margin space that Irish female poets must occupy provides a unique perspective from which writers can tell the stories found in the silences of the past; she distinguishes these from history, "itself a constructed narrative." From that space she has produced over twenty collections of poems, including *Against Love Poetry* (2001), *Domestic Violence* (2007), and *A Woman Without a Country* (2014).

Though she does not claim affiliation with a specific literary movement, Boland's writing and teaching activities have linked her with a wide community of writers, readers, and scholars; she is a co-founder of Arlen House, a feminist press that publishes the work of Irish writers. Among her prose works is the reflective memoir *Object Lessons: The Life of the Woman and the Poet in Our Time* (1995), in which she discusses her development as an artist both from a personal perspective and in a wider social and literary context. In her 1997 "Letter to a Young Woman Poet," she addresses an imagined audience of poets following in her footsteps, telling them that the "very past in poetry which simplified us as women and excluded us as poets now needs us to change it." Her guidance of young writers has also extended to the classroom; she has taught at Trinity College, Dublin's University College, Bowdoin College, Washington University, and the University of Utah. In 1997 she became the director of Stanford University's prestigious creative writing program.

⌘⌘⌘

Night Feed

This is dawn.
Believe me
This is your season, little daughter.
The moment daisies open,
The hour mercurial rainwater
Makes a mirror for sparrows.
It's time we drowned our sorrows.

I tiptoe in.
I lift you up
Wriggling
In your rosy, zipped sleeper.
Yes, this is the hour
For the early bird and me
When finder is keeper.

I crook the bottle.
How you suckle!
This is the best I can be,
Housewife
To this nursery
Where you hold on,
Dear life.

A slit of milk.
The last suck.
And now your eyes are open,
Birth-coloured and offended.
Earth wakes.
You go back to sleep.
The feed is ended.

Worms turn.
Stars go in.
Even the moon is losing face.
Poplars stilt for dawn
And we begin
The long fall from grace.
I tuck you in.

—1982

The Lost Land

I have two daughters.

They are all I ever wanted from the earth.

Or almost all.

I also wanted one piece of ground.

One city trapped by hills. One urban river.
An island in its element.

So I could say *mine. My own.*
And mean it.

Now they are grown up and far away

and memory itself
has become an emigrant,
wandering in a place
where love dissembles itself as landscape.

Where the hills
are the colours of a child's eyes,
where my children are distances, horizons.

At night,
on the edge of sleep,
I can see the shore of Dublin Bay,
its rocky sweep and its granite pier.

Is this, I say
how they must have seen it,
backing out on the mailboat at twilight,

shadows falling
on everything they had to leave?
And would love forever?
And then

I imagine myself
at the landward rail of that boat
searching for the last sight of a hand.

I see myself
on the underworld side of that water,
the darkness coming in fast, saying
all the names I know for a lost land.

Ireland. Absence. Daughter.

—1998

Salman Rushdie

b. 1947

Salman Rushdie, who was born and raised in India but educated in England, is a writer whose novels reflect the hybridity of his own experience, blending Indian and English cultures, and exploring the experiences of the colonized as well as those of migrants in the diaspora. His novels are often described as magical realist, a genre that interweaves realist elements with the mythic and fantastical. Rushdie is widely recognized as a key figure of postmodernist fiction and postcolonial writing who has helped shape a generation of Indian writing in English, and whose influence extends across the globe. But his achievements were for many years overshadowed by the furor created by the violent opposition of Islamic fundamentalists to his novel *The Satanic Verses* (1988); this opposition became one of the major artistic and religious controversies of the twentieth century. Forced to live in hiding for over ten years, Rushdie has become a symbolic leader of those who oppose censorship and religious violence.

Born Ahmed Salman Rushdie to "happily irreligious" Muslim parents in Bombay (now Mumbai), India, Rushdie was first educated at the Cathedral School in Bombay. He moved to England at age 14, where he attended Rugby School, one of England's most prestigious boarding schools. His time there was not entirely pleasant: Rushdie later recounted how he was the object of racially motivated attacks by white students. After graduating, he moved back to Bombay but soon returned to England to attend Cambridge University's King's College, where he studied history. After earning his BA in 1968, Rushdie worked in television in Pakistan for several years, then returned to England to become a copywriter for an advertising agency.

In his first novel, *Grimus* (1975), Rushdie began to develop the magic realist approach that would become characteristic of his later work. An adaptation of an old Sufi poem, *Grimus* met with little success. But Rushdie's next novel, *Midnight's Children* (1981), catapulted him to the top of the English-language literary world. *Midnight's Children* presents the life of pickle-factory worker Saleem Sinai, who was born (like Rushdie) at the time of India's independence from Britain, as an allegory for the history of postcolonial India. The novel's defining blend of mythology and historical specificity is suggested by its famous opening: "I was born in the city of Bombay ... once upon a time. No, that won't do, there's no getting away from the date: I was born in Doctor Narlikar's Nursing Home on August 15th, 1947." Released at the dawn of literary postmodernism—and at a time when literary critics were just beginning to regard works on postcolonial themes as central to the literature of the English-speaking world—Rushdie's work struct a chord. In 1981 the novel won the prestigious Booker Prize for Fiction, and in 1993 it won the Booker of Bookers Prize for the novel deemed to be the best of all those granted the award in its first twenty-five years. Rushdie's next work was a short novel, *Shame* (1983), which examined the lives of Pakistan's rulers, particularly former Prime Minister

Zulfikar Ali Bhutto and General Muhammad Zia-ul-Haq, and which meditated upon the connection between shame and violence.

In 1988 Rushdie published a novel that was to change the course of his life: *The Satanic Verses*. Like *Midnight's Children* and *Shame*, *The Satanic Verses* was critically acclaimed and distinguished by a unique blend of realism and fantasy. But to some, the events described in the text were altogether too real. The novel was condemned by a number of prominent Muslim leaders on the grounds that its unflattering portrayal of the prophet Muhammed was blasphemous; banned in eleven countries, *The Satanic Verses* was the subject of violent protests. The controversy over the book escalated on 14 February 1989, when Iran's spiritual and political leader, the Ayatollah Ruhollah Khomeini, issued a fatwa (or legal pronouncement) calling for Rushdie's death. Ten days later, Khomeini placed a $3 million (US) bounty on Rushdie's head. Rushdie went into hiding, under the protection of British authorities. The Japanese translator of the book was murdered in Tokyo in 1991. Other translators were attacked and harassed. In 1998 the Iranian government made a public pledge not to carry out the death sentence against Rushdie. Nevertheless, the fatwa still stands, and was in fact renewed in 2016.

While in hiding, Rushdie published a children's book, *Haroun and the Sea of Stories* (1990), an allegorical exploration of India and Pakistan's dispute over the State of Kashmir that also advances harsh criticisms of literary censorship. In 1991, he released a book of essays, *Imaginary Homelands: Essays and Criticism 1981–1991*, from which the essay below is taken. Much of Rushdie's later work examines the intersection of Indian and Western cultures. In *The Moor's Last Sigh* (1995), he considers the connections between the descendants of Portuguese settlers and their Indian neighbors. *The Ground Beneath Her Feet* (1999), a variation on the Greek Orpheus myth, deals with the influence of American rock and roll music in India.

In 2000, Rushdie moved to New York, a city he described as "a Western rewrite of Bombay," from which he has served as an outspoken critic of the "horrible mangling" of religious narratives by fanatics. In 2006, after violent demonstrations followed the publication of cartoons depicting Muhammad in a Danish newspaper, Rushdie—along with twelve other authors—signed a letter that called for the championing of "secular values and freedom." Rushdie's deeply held commitment to personal liberty and secularism continues to put his life in jeopardy. When he was knighted in 2007, terrorist leader Ayman al-Zawahiri promised that "catastrophes" would follow. In 2010, Rushdie was listed by Al-Qaeda as "Wanted: Dead or Alive."

Despite living under constant threat of violence, Rushdie remains dedicated to producing literature and acting as an adviser to new authors. He earned another Booker prize for his 2008 work *The Enchantress of Florence*, which describes an exchange of people and ideas between Renaissance Florence and Sikri, the capital of the Mughal Empire. In 2012, he released a third-person autobiography recounting the years he spent in hiding; the book's title, *Joseph Anton*, is the alias he used. From 2007 to 2012, Rushdie taught in the English Department of Emory University, and in 2015, he became a Distinguished Writer in Residence at New York University. New York served as the primary setting for his next novels, *Two Years Eight Months and Twenty-Eight Nights* (2015) and *The Golden House* (2017). *Two Years Eight Months* retains Rushdie's usual magic realism, while *The Golden House* is a more traditionally realist novel—but both adopt his singular mode of political satire. Regarding his own writing as a form of resistance against those who seek to "purify" reality, Rushdie avows his commitment to a "rhetoric of not cleansing, of allowing things to be what they really are in life, which is all mixed up together and muddied."

⌘⌘⌘

Is Nothing Sacred?[1]

I grew up kissing books and bread. In our house, whenever anyone dropped a book or let fall a chapati or a "slice," which was our word for a triangle of buttered leavened bread, the fallen object was required not only to be picked up but also kissed, by way of apology for the act of clumsy disrespect. I was as careless and butter-fingered as any child and, accordingly, during my childhood years, I kissed a large number of "slices" and also my fair share of books.

Devout households in India often contained, and still contain, persons in the habit of kissing holy books. But we kissed everything. We kissed dictionaries and atlases. We kissed Enid Blyton[2] novels and Superman comics. If I'd ever dropped the telephone directory I'd probably have kissed that, too.

All this happened before I had ever kissed a girl. In fact it would almost be true, true enough for a fiction writer, anyhow, to say that once I started kissing girls, my activities with regard to bread and books lost some of their special excitement. But one never forgets one's first loves.

Bread and books: food for the body and food for the soul—what could be more worthy of our respect, and even love?

It has always been a shock to me to meet people for whom books simply do not matter, and people who are scornful of the act of reading, let alone writing. It is perhaps always astonishing to learn that your beloved is not as attractive to others as she is to you. My most beloved books have been fictions, and in the last twelve months I have been obliged to accept that for many millions of human beings, these books are entirely without attraction or value. We have been witnessing an attack upon a particular work of fiction that is also an attack upon the very ideas of the novel form, an attack of such bewildering ferocity that it has become necessary to restate what is most precious about the art of literature—to answer the attack, not by an attack, but by a declaration of love.

Love can lead to devotion, but the devotion of the lover is unlike that of the True Believer in that it is not militant. I may be surprised—even shocked—to find that you do not feel as I do about a given book or work of art or even person; I may very well attempt to change your mind; but I will finally accept that your tastes, your loves, are your business and not mine. The True Believer knows no such restraints. The True Believer knows that he is simply right, and you are wrong. He will seek to convert you, even by force, and if he cannot he will, at the very least, despise you for your unbelief.

Love need not be blind. Faith must, ultimately, be a leap in the dark.

The title of this lecture is a question usually asked, in tones of horror, when some personage or idea or value or place held dear by the questioner is treated to a dose of iconoclasm. White cricket balls for night cricket? Female priests? A Japanese takeover of Rolls-Royce cars? *Is nothing sacred?*

Until recently, however, it was a question to which I thought I knew the answer. The answer was No.

No, nothing is sacred in and of itself, I would have said. Ideas, texts, even people can be made sacred—the word is from the Latin *sacrare,* "to set apart as holy"—but even though such entities, once their sacredness is established, seek to proclaim and to preserve their own absoluteness, their inviolability, the act of making sacred is in truth an event in history. It is the product of the many and complex pressures of the time in which the act occurs. And events in history must always be subject to questioning, deconstruction, even to declarations of their obsolescence. To respect the sacred is to be paralysed by it. The idea of the sacred is quite simply one of the most conservative notions in any culture, because it seeks to turn other ideas—Uncertainty, Progress, Change—into crimes.

---

[1] *Is Nothing Sacred?* This essay was the Herbert Read Memorial Lecture for 1990, delivered at the Institute of Contemporary Arts in London on 6 February 1990. It was read by playwright Harold Pinter. Rushdie himself was for many years prevented from making public appearances by the widely publicized call for his death issued by Iran's Ayatollah Khomeini.

[2] *Enid Blyton* Prolific English author of children's books (1897–1968).

To take only one such declaration of obsolescence: I would have described myself as living in the aftermath of the death of God. On the subject of the death of God, the American novelist and critic William H. Gass had this to say, as recently as 1984:

> The death of god represents not only the realization that gods have never existed, but the contention that such a belief is no longer even irrationally possible: that neither reason nor the taste and temper of the times condone it. The belief lingers on, of course, but it does so like astrology or a faith in a flat earth.

I have some difficulty with the uncompromising bluntness of this obituary notice. It has always been clear to me that God is unlike human beings in that it can die, so to speak, in parts. In other parts, for example India, God continues to flourish, in literally thousands of forms. So that if I speak of living after this death, I am speaking in a limited, personal sense—my sense of God ceased to exist long ago, and as a result I was drawn towards the great creative possibilities offered by surrealism, modernism and their successors, those philosophies and aesthetics born of the realization that, as Karl Marx said, "all that is solid melts into air."

It did not seem to me, however, that my ungodliness, or rather my post-godliness, need necessarily bring me into conflict with belief. Indeed, one reason for my attempt to develop a form of fiction in which the miraculous might coexist with the mundane was precisely my acceptance that notions of the sacred and the profane both needed to be explored, as far as possible without pre-judgement, in any honest literary portrait of the way we are.

That is to say: the most secular of authors ought to be capable of presenting a sympathetic portrait of a devout believer. Or, to put it another way: I had never felt the need to totemize my lack of belief, and so make it something to go to war about.

Now, however, I find my entire world-picture under fire. And as I find myself obliged to defend the assumptions and processes of literature, which I had believed that all free men and women could take for granted, and for which all unfree men and women continue every day to struggle, so I am obliged to ask myself questions I admit to finding somewhat unnerving.

Do I, perhaps, find something sacred after all? Am I prepared to set aside as holy the idea of the absolute freedom of the imagination and alongside it my own notions of the World, the Text and the Good? Does this add up to what the apologists of religion have started calling "secular fundamentalism"? And if so, must I accept that this "secular fundamentalism" is as likely to lead to excesses, abuses and oppressions as the canons of religious faith?

A lecture in memory of Herbert Read is a highly appropriate occasion for such an exploration, and I am honoured to have been asked to deliver it. Herbert Read, one of the leading British advocates of the modernist and surrealist movements, was a distinguished representative of the cultural values closest to my heart. "Art is never transfixed," Read wrote. "Change is the condition of art remaining art." This principle is also mine. Art, too, is an event in history, subject to the historical process. But it is also *about* that process, and must constantly strive to find new forms to mirror an endlessly renewed world. No aesthetic can be a constant, except an aesthetic based on the idea of inconstancy, metamorphosis, or, to borrow a term from politics, "perpetual revolution."

The struggle between such ideas and the eternal, revealed truths of religion is dramatized this evening, as I hope I may be excused for pointing out, by my absence. I must apologize for this. I did, in fact, ask my admirable protectors how they would feel if I were to deliver my text in person. The answer was, more or less, "What have we done to deserve this?" With regret, I took the point.

It is an agony and a frustration not to be able to re-enter my old life, not even for such a moment. However, I should like to thank Harold Pinter, through his own mouth, for standing in my place. Perhaps this event could be thought of as a form of secular revelation: a man receives a text by mysterious processes from

Elsewhere—above? below? New Scotland Yard?[1]—and brings it out before the people, and recites …

More than twenty years ago, I stood packed in at the back of this theatre, listening to a lecture by Arthur Koestler.[2] He propounded the thesis that language, not territory, was the prime cause of aggression, because once language reached the level of sophistication at which it could express abstract concepts, it acquired the power of totemization; and once peoples had erected totems, they would go to war to defend them. (I ask pardon of Koestler's ghost. I am relying on an old memory, and that's an untrustworthy shoulder to lean on.)

In support of his theory, he told us about two tribes of monkeys living on, I think, one of the northern islands of Japan. The two tribes lived in close proximity in the woods near a certain stream, and subsisted, not unusually, on a diet of bananas. One of the tribes, however, had developed the curious habit of washing its bananas in the stream before eating them, while the other tribe continued to be non-banana-washers. And yet, said Koestler, the two tribes continued to live contentedly as neighbours, without quarrelling. And why was this? It was because their language was too primitive to permit them to totemize either the act of banana-washing or that of eating bananas unwashed. With a more sophisticated language at their disposal, both wet and dry bananas could have become the sacred objects at the heart of a religion, and then, look out!—Holy war.

A young man rose from the audience to ask Koestler a question. Perhaps the real reason why the two tribes did not fight, he suggested, was that there were enough bananas to go round. Koestler became extremely angry. He refused to answer such a piece of Marxist claptrap. And, in a way, he was right. Koestler and his questioner were speaking different languages, and their languages were in conflict. Their disagreement could even be seen as the proof of Koestler's point. If he, Koestler, were to be considered the banana-washer and his questioner the dry-banana man, then their command of a language more complex than the Japanese monkeys' had indeed resulted in totemizations. Now each of them had a totem to defend: the primacy of language versus the primacy of economics: and dialogue therefore became impossible. They were at war.

Between religion and literature, as between politics and literature, there is a linguistically based dispute. But it is not a dispute of simple opposites. Because whereas religion seeks to privilege one language above all others, one set of values above all others, one text above all others, the novel has always been *about* the way in which different languages, values and narratives quarrel, and about the shifting relations between them, which are relations of power. The novel does not seek to establish a privileged language, but it insists upon the freedom to portray and analyse the struggle between the different contestants for such privileges.

Carlos Fuentes has called the novel "a privileged *arena*." By this he does not mean that it is the kind of holy space which one must put off one's shoes to enter; it is not an arena to revere; it claims no special rights *except the right to be the stage upon which the great debates of society can be conducted.* "The novel," Fuentes writes, "is born from the very fact that we do not understand one another, because unitary, orthodox language has broken down. Quixote and Sancho, the Shandy brothers, Mr. and Mrs. Karenin:[3] their novels are the comedy (or the drama) of their misunderstandings. Impose a unitary language: you kill the novel, but you also kill the society."

He then poses the question I have been asking myself throughout my life as a writer: *Can the religious mentality survive outside of religious dogma and hierarchy?* Which is to say: Can art be the third principle that mediates between the material and spiritual worlds; might it, by "swallowing" both worlds, offer us some-

[1] *New Scotland Yard* Headquarters for the metropolitan police force of Greater London.

[2] *Arthur Koestler* Hungarian-born novelist (1905–83), political activist, and social philosopher, whose most famous work, *Darkness at Noon* (1940), depicts extremes of censorship and oppression under a Soviet-style Marxist dictatorship.

[3] *Quixote … Karenin* Characters from Cervantes's *Don Quixote*, Laurence Sterne's *Tristram Shandy*, and Tolstoy's *Anna Karenina*, respectively.

thing new—something that might even be called a secular definition of transcendence?

I believe it can. I believe it must. And I believe that, at its best, it does.

What I mean by transcendence is that flight of the human spirit outside the confines of its material, physical existence which all of us, secular or religious, experience on at least a few occasions. Birth is a moment of transcendence which we spend our lives trying to understand. The exaltation of the act of love, the experience of joy and very possibly the moment of death are other such moments. The soaring quality of transcendence, the sense of being more than oneself, of being in some way joined to the whole of life, is by its nature short-lived. Not even the visionary or mystical experience ever lasts very long. It is for art to capture that experience, to offer it to, in the case of literature, its readers; to be, for a secular, materialist culture, some sort of replacement for what the love of god offers in the world of faith.

It is important that we understand how profoundly we all feel the needs that religion, down the ages, has satisfied. I would suggest that these needs are of three types: firstly, the need to be given an articulation of our half-glimpsed knowledge of exaltation, of awe, of wonder; life is an awesome experience, and religion helps us understand why life so often makes us feel small, by telling us what we are *smaller than*; and, contrariwise, because we also have a sense of being special, of being *chosen,* religion helps us by telling us what we have been chosen by, and what for. Secondly, we need answers to the unanswerable: How did we get here? How did "here" get here in the first place? Is this, this brief life, all there is? How can it be? What would be the point of that? And, thirdly, we need codes to live by, "rules for every damn thing." The idea of god is at once a repository for our awestruck wonderment at life and an answer to the great questions of existence, and a rule book, too. The soul needs all these explanations—not simply rational explanations, but explanations of the heart.

It is also important to understand how often the language of secular, rationalist materialism has failed to answer these needs. As we witness the death of communism in Central Europe, we cannot fail to observe the deep religious spirit with which so many of the makers of these revolutions are imbued, and we must concede that it is not only a particular political ideology that has failed, but the idea that men and women could ever define themselves in terms that exclude their spiritual needs.

It seems obvious, but relevant, to point out that in all the countries now moving towards freedom, art was repressed as viciously as was religion. That the Czech revolution began in the theatres and is led by a writer[1] is proof that people's spiritual needs, more than their material needs, have driven the commissars from power. What appears plain is that it will be a very long time before the peoples of Europe will accept any ideology that claims to have a complete, totalized explanation of the world. Religious faith, profound as it is, must surely remain a private matter. This rejection of totalized explanations is the modern condition. And this is where the novel, the form created to discuss the fragmentation of truth, comes in. The film director Luis Buñuel used to say: "I would give my life for a man who is looking for the truth. But I would gladly kill a man who thinks he has found the truth." (This is what we used to call a joke, before killing people for their ideas returned to the agenda.) The elevation of the quest for the Grail over the Grail itself, the acceptance that all that is solid has melted into air, that reality and morality are not givens but imperfect human constructs, is the point from which fiction begins. This is what J.-F. Lyotard called, in 1979, *La Condition Postmoderne.* The challenge of literature is to start from this point, and still find a way of fulfilling our unaltered spiritual requirements.

---

[1] *the Czech revolution ... by a writer* Czech playwright and intellectual Václav Havel (1936–2011) was a leading anti-communist revolutionary. He later served as President of Czechoslovakia, then of the Czech Republic.

Moby Dick meets that challenge by offering us a dark, almost Manichean vision[1] of a universe (the *Pequod*[2]) in the grip of one demon, Ahab, and heading inexorably towards another; namely the Whale. The ocean always was our Other, manifesting itself to us in the form of beasts—the worm Ouroboros, Kraken, Leviathan.[3] Herman Melville delves into these dark waters in order to offer us a very modern parable: Ahab, gripped by his possession, perishes; Ishmael, a man without strong feeling or powerful affiliations, survives. The self-interested modern man is the sole survivor; those who worship the Whale—for pursuit is a form of worship—perish by the Whale.

Joyce's wanderers, Beckett's tramps, Gogol's tricksters, Bulgakov's devils, Bellow's[4] high-energy meditations on the stifling of the soul by the triumphs of materialism; these, and many more, are what we have instead of prophets and suffering saints. But while the novel answers our need for wonderment and understanding, it brings us harsh and unpalatable news as well.

It tells us there are no rules. It hands down no commandments. We have to make up our own rules as best we can, make them up as we go along.

And it tells us there are no answers; or, rather, it tells us that answers are easier to come by, and less reliable, than questions. If religion is an answer, if political ideology is an answer, then literature is an inquiry; great literature, by asking extraordinary questions, opens new doors in our minds.

Richard Rorty, in *Philosophy and the Mirror of Nature,* insists on the importance of historicity, of giving up the illusions of being in contact with Eternity. For him, the great error is what he calls "foundationalism," which the theologian Don Cupitt, commenting on Rorty, calls "the attempt, as old as (and even much older than) Plato, to give permanence and authority to our knowledge and values by purporting to found them in some unchanging cosmic realm, natural or noumenal, outside the flux of our human conversation." It is better, Cupitt concludes, "to be an adaptable pragmatist, a nomad."

Michel Foucault, also a confirmed historicist, discusses the role of the author in challenging sacralized absolutes in his essay, "What Is an Author?" This essay argues, in part, that "texts, books and discourses really began to have authors ... to the extent that authors became subject to punishment, that is, to the extent that discourses could be transgressive." This is an extraordinary, provocative idea, even if it is stated with Foucault's characteristic airiness and a complete absence of supporting evidence: *that authors were named only when it was necessary to find somebody to blame.* Foucault continues:

> In our culture (and doubtless in many others), discourse was not originally a product, a thing, a kind of goods; it was essentially an act—an act placed in the bipolar field of the sacred and the profane, the licit and the illicit, the religious and the blasphemous. Historically it was a gesture fraught with risks ...

In our beginnings we find our essences. To understand a religion, look at its earliest moments. (It is regrettable that Islam, of all religions the easiest to study in this way, because of its birth during the age of recorded history, has set its face so resolutely against the idea that it, like all ideas, is an event inside history.) And to understand an artistic form, too, Foucault suggests, look at its origins. If he is right about the novel, then literature is, of all the arts, the one best suited to challenging absolutes of all kinds; and, because it is in its origin the schismatic Other of the sacred (and authorless) text, so it is also the art mostly likely to fill our god-shaped holes.

---

[1] *Manichean vision* Form of dualism, in which the world is seen to be determined by the tension between the forces of good and evil.

[2] *the Pequod* Captain Ahab's ship (in Herman Melville's novel *Moby-Dick* [1851]).

[3] *Ouroboros ... Leviathan* Ouroboros is an ancient symbol from many cultures that depicts a snake or a dragon devouring itself. The Kraken is an enormous sea monster said to be living in the ocean between Norway and Iceland. Leviathan is a sea monster referred to in various places in the Bible.

[4] *Joyce ... Bellow* Authors James Joyce (1882–1941), Samuel Beckett (1906–89), Nikolai Gogol (1809–52), Mikhail Bulgakov (1891–1940), and Saul Bellow (1915–2005).

There are other reasons, too, for proposing the novel as the crucial art form of what I can no longer avoid calling the post-modern age. For one thing, literature is the art least subject to external control, because it is made in private. The act of making it requires only one person, one pen, one room, some paper. (Even the room is not absolutely essential.) Literature is the most low-technology of the art forms. It requires neither a stage nor a screen. It calls for no interpreters, no actors, producers, camera crews, costumers, musicians. It does not even require the traditional apparatus of publishing, as the long-running success of samizdat literature[1] demonstrates. The Foucault essay suggests that literature is as much at risk from the enveloping, smothering forces of the market economy, which reduces books to mere products. This danger is real, and I do not want to seem to be minimizing it. But the truth is that of all the forms, literature can still be the most free. The more money a piece of work costs, the easier it is to control it. Film, the most expensive of art forms, is also the least subversive. This is why, although Carlos Fuentes cites the work of film-makers like Buñuel, Bergman and Fellini as instances of successful secular revolts into the territory of the sacred, I continue to believe in the greater possibilities of the novel. Its singularity is its best protection.

Among the childhood books I devoured and kissed were large numbers of cheap comics of a most unliterary nature. The heroes of these comic books were, or so it seemed, almost always mutants or hybrids or freaks: as well as the Batman and the Spiderman there was Aquaman, who was half-fish, and of course Superman, who could easily be mistaken for a bird or a plane. In those days, the middle 1950s, the super-heroes were all, in their various ways, hawkish law-and-order conservatives, leaping to work in response to the Police Commissioner's Bat-Signal, banding together to form the Justice League of America, defending what Superman called "truth, justice and the American way." But in spite of this extreme emphasis on crime-busting, the lesson they taught children—or this child, at any rate—was the perhaps unintentionally radical truth that exceptionality was the greatest and most heroic of values; that those who were unlike the crowd were to be treasured the most lovingly; and that this exceptionality was a treasure so great and so easily misunderstood that it had to be concealed, in ordinary life, beneath what the comic books called a "secret identity." Superman could not have survived without "mild-mannered" Clark Kent; "millionaire socialite" Bruce Wayne made possible the nocturnal activities of the Batman.

Now it is obviously true that those other freakish, hybrid, mutant, exceptional beings—novelists—those creators of the most freakish, hybrid and metamorphic of forms, the novel, have frequently been obliged to hide behind secret identities, whether for reasons of gender or terror. But the most wonderful of the many wonderful truths about the novel form is that the greater the writer, the greater his or her exceptionality. The geniuses of the novel are those whose voices are fully and undisguisably their own, who, to borrow William Gass's[2] image, *sign every word they write*. What draws us to an author is his or her "unlikeness," even if the apparatus of literary criticism then sets to work to demonstrate that he or she is really no more than an accumulation of influences. Unlikeness, the thing that makes it impossible for a writer to stand in any regimented line, is a quality novelists share with the Caped Crusaders of the comics, though they are only rarely capable of leaping tall buildings in a single stride.

What is more, the writer is there, in his work, in the reader's hands, utterly exposed, utterly defenceless, entirely without the benefit of an alter ego to hide behind. What is forged, in the secret act of reading, is a different kind of identity, as the reader and writer merge, through the medium of the text, to become a collective being that both writes as it reads and reads as it writes, and creates, jointly, that unique work, "their" novel. This "secret identity" of writer and reader is the novel form's greatest and most subversive gift.

And this, finally, is why I elevate the novel above other forms, why it has always been, and remains, my

[1] *samizdat literature* Underground, self-published literature, originally created in the Soviet Union to undermine the system of state censorship.

[2] *William Gass* American novelist, essayist, and critic.

first love: not only is it the art involving least compromises, but it is also the only one that takes the "privileged arena" of conflicting discourses *right inside our heads.* The interior space of our imagination is a theatre that can never be closed down; the images created there make up a movie that can never be destroyed.

In this last decade of the millennium, as the forces of religion are renewed in strength and as the all-pervasive power of materialism wraps its own weighty chains around the human spirit, where should the novel be looking? It seems clear that the renewal of the old, bipolar field of discourse, between the sacred and the profane, which Michel Foucault proposes, will be of central importance. It seems probable, too, that we may be heading towards a world in which there will be no real alternative to the liberal-capitalist social model (except, perhaps, the theocratic, foundationalist model of Islam). In this situation, liberal capitalism or democracy or the free world will require novelists' most rigorous attention, will require reimagining and questioning and doubting as never before. "Our antagonist is our helper," said Edmund Burke, and if democracy no longer has communism to help it clarify, by opposition, its own ideas, then perhaps it will have to have literature as an adversary instead.

I have made a large number of sweeping claims for literature during the course of this piece, and I am aware of a slightly messianic tone in much of what I've written. The reverencing of books and writers, by writers, is nothing particularly new, of course. "Since the early 19th century," writes Cupitt, "imaginative writers have claimed—have indeed enjoyed—a guiding and representative role in our culture. Our preachers are novelists, poets, dramatists, film-makers and the like, purveyors of fiction, ambiguous people, deceivers. Yet we continue to think of ourselves as rational."

But now I find myself backing away from the idea of sacralizing literature with which I flirted at the beginning of this text; I cannot bear the idea of the writer as secular prophet; I am remembering that one of the very greatest writers of the century, Samuel Beckett, believed that all art must inevitably end in failure. This is, clearly, no reason for surrender. "Ever tried. Ever failed. Never mind. Try again. Fail better."

Literature is an interim report from the consciousness of the artist, and so it can never be "finished" or "perfect." Literature is made at the frontier between the self and the world, and in the act of creation that frontier softens, becomes permeable, allows the world to flow into the artist and the artist to flow into the world. Nothing so inexact, so easily and frequently misconceived, deserves the protection of being declared sacrosanct. We shall just have to get along without the shield of sacralization, and a good thing, too. We must not become what we oppose.

The only privilege literature deserves—and this privilege it requires in order to exist—is the privilege of being the arena of discourse, the place where the struggle of languages can be acted out.

Imagine this. You wake up one morning and find yourself in a large, rambling house. As you wander through it you realize it is so enormous that you will never know it all. In the house are people you know, family members, friends, lovers, colleagues; also many strangers. The house is full of activity: conflicts and seductions, celebrations and wakes. At some point you understand that there is no way out. You find that you can accept this. The house is not what you'd have chosen, it's in fairly bad condition, the corridors are often full of bullies, but it will have to do. Then one day you enter an unimportant-looking little room. The room is empty, but there are voices in it, voices that seem to be whispering just to you. You recognize some of the voices, others are completely unknown to you. The voices are talking about the house, about everyone in it, about everything that is happening and has happened and should happen. Some of them speak exclusively in obscenities. Some are bitchy. Some are loving. Some are funny. Some are sad. The most interesting voices are all these things at once. You begin to go to the room more and more often. Slowly you learn that most of the people in the house use such rooms sometimes. Yet the rooms are all discreetly positioned and unimportant-looking.

Now imagine that you wake up one morning and you are still in the large house, but all the voice-rooms have disappeared. It is as if they have been wiped out. Now there is nowhere in the whole house where you can go to hear voices talking about everything in every possible way. There is nowhere to go for the voices that can be funny one minute and sad the next, that can sound raucous and melodic in the course of the same sentence. Now you remember: there is no way out of this house. Now this fact begins to seem unbearable. You look into the eyes of the people in the corridors—family, lovers, friends, colleagues, strangers, bullies, priests. You see the same thing in everybody's eyes. *How do we get out of here?* It becomes clear that the house is a prison. People begin to scream, and pound the walls. Men arrive with guns. The house begins to shake. You do not wake up. You are already awake.

Literature is the one place in any society where, within the secrecy of our own heads, we can hear *voices talking about everything in every possible way.* The reason for ensuring that that privileged arena is preserved is not that writers want the absolute freedom to say and do whatever they please. It is that we, all of us, readers and writers and citizens and generals and godmen, need that little, unimportant-looking room. We do not need to call it sacred, but we do need to remember that it is necessary.

"Everybody knows," wrote Saul Bellow in *The Adventures of Augie March,* "there is no fineness or accuracy of suppression. If you hold down one thing, you hold down the adjoining."

Wherever in the world the little room of literature has been closed, sooner or later the walls have come tumbling down.

—1990

TOMSON HIGHWAY

b. 1951

Tomson Highway is a Canadian playwright, novelist, and composer, and a member of the Barren Lands First Nation. Infusing English with the humor, sensibility, and speed of his first language, Cree, Highway's plays and fiction are innovative and influential in their blending of Indigenous and Western artistic traditions. His work has played a central part in the growth of an internationally recognized Indigenous Canadian literature—an accomplishment for which, in 1994, Highway became the first Aboriginal writer to receive the Order of Canada.

The eleventh child of bead-worker and quilt-maker Pelagie Highway, and famed dogsled racer and caribou hunter Joe Highway, Tomson Highway was born in a remote Aboriginal community near Brochet, in Northern Manitoba. As a child, he grew up speaking two languages, Cree and Dene, and exploring the region's beautiful, sub-Arctic expanses. "My beginnings were magical beyond belief," Highway recalls; "I grew up in a garden of Eden, a northern paradise that was pure and magic." At age six, Highway was taken to Guy Hill Indian Residential School, where he and his brother René were not just deprived of the freedom they enjoyed at home, but also subjected to physical and sexual abuse. While at the school, Highway began an education in classical music, and he graduated with ambitions to become a concert pianist.[1] He studied music and literature at the Universities of Manitoba and Western Ontario, where he was one of very few Indigenous students on campus; Highway reports being the first person from his parents' community to attend university. After obtaining his degree, he spent the next seven years engaged in social work with Indigenous people on reserves, in urban centers, and in prisons, an experience he credits with deepening his work's portrayal of Indigenous Canadian lives. In the 1980s, Highway also began to hone his playwriting skills, and he began a relationship with Raymond Lalonde, who became his long-term partner.

Highway himself has said that as late as the 1970s "there was no such thing as native literature in this country. You could count the number of native writers [and] native books published on the fingers of two hands. I counted 19 books published before 1980. And then around 1980 it just exploded." With a breakthrough year in 1986, Highway became a central figure in this "explosion." That year saw the premiere of his sixth play, *The Rez Sisters*—his first major critical and commercial success—as well as his appointment as the first full-time artistic director of the theater company Native Earth Performing Arts, which, under his direction from 1986 to 1992, became a major institution of Indigenous theater in Canada. In 1989, Highway staged a companion piece to *Rez Sisters*, *Dry Lips Oughta Move to Kapuskasing*, which, like *Rez Sisters*, was extremely well-received.

---

[1] Highway's own discussion of his residential school experience has shifted over the years; in earlier decades he was quite outspoken regarding the damage caused by the schools, but in interviews given later in life he has been more inclined to speak positively of the education he obtained there.

Highway's plays often incorporate Cree language, dance, philosophy, and mythological elements such as the figure of the Trickster, a two-spirit[1] shape-shifter who appears under different names in many Indigenous cultures but is often referred to in Highway's work as Nanabush. As Highway puts it in *Kiss of the Fur Queen*, the Trickster is "the clown who bridges humanity and God—a God who laughs, a God who's here, not for guilt, not for suffering, but for a good time." In its incorporation of mythology on a human scale, and in its structure, Highway's dramatic work also draws upon ancient Greek drama; among more recent playwrights, he has cited Québécois dramatist Michel Tremblay as a major influence (*Rez Sisters*, for example, parallels Tremblay's 1968 *Les Belles-soeurs* in its focus on women characters and its use of bingo as a key motif).

In 1990, Highway's brother and long-time collaborator René, a dancer and choreographer, died of complications from AIDS. His final words were "Don't mourn me, be joyful." Driven to memorialize his brother—whose death he blamed upon the residential schools and the predators who ran them—and increasingly frustrated by the logistical challenges of producing plays, Highway began working on a new project: telling the story of his and his brother's survival. In 1998, he released *Kiss of the Fur Queen*, an intensely personal novel about two brothers forced to attend a residential school and their lives before and after that experience. Highway's novel is frequently studied as a testament to the horror of the residential schools and as a witty takedown of the hypocrisy of Catholic involvement in the schools. It is also a significant postmodern achievement, using Highway's own brand of magic realism as a means of integrating Cree myth and story with narration of the ordinary lives of its twentieth-century characters. Here, as in Highway's greatest plays, Nanabush figures prominently, this time as the titular "Fur Queen" whose presence emerges at key points in the narrative.

Though the novel incorporates Cree phrases, Highway wrote *Kiss of the Fur Queen* in English—or, as he later recounted, "I wrote the book in Cree, really, and translated it as I went along. … The humour, the workings of the spirit world, the fact that Cree has no gender, the concept of god as two-spirited—everything is so difficult to explain in English." The importance of Cree language in his work has, if anything, become more prominent in the twenty-first century; Highway followed his first novel with three bilingual children's books, *Caribou Song* (2001), *Dragonfly Kites* (2002), and *Fox on the Ice* (2003), as well as the libretto for *Pimooteewin* (*The Journey*, 2005), the first opera in Cree. In 2010, he published Cree editions of *Rez Sisters* and *Dry Lips* in what he referred to as their "original versions"—*Iskooniguni Iskweewuk* and *Paasteewitoon Kaapooskaysing Tageespichit*.

As his contribution to opera suggests, music plays an important role in Highway's theatrical work. Several of his plays—such as *The Sage, The Dancer, and The Fool* (1989), a collaboration with René; *Rose* (1999), which shares characters with *Rez Sisters* and *Dry Lips*; and *The (Post) Mistress* (2013), a one-woman show about a postal clerk—are musicals. In 2015, he premiered a cabaret entitled *Songs in the Key of Cree*, which he has performed all over the world. In this cabaret, Highway addresses often challenging subject matter with his

[1] "Two spirit" is an umbrella term used by some Indigenous people of nonbinary gender and/or same-sex sexual orientation; many Indigenous cultures have specific two-spirit cultural roles and spiritual traditions that can differ significantly from Western LGBTQ traditions.

characteristic wit and fierce joy. As critic Shelagh Rogers has put it, "Throughout his work, Tomson hasn't shied away from the issues. He's tackled abuse in residential schools, poverty on reserves, as well as misogyny and homophobia in the Aboriginal community. But there's no heavy-handedness to his writing because he tells rough truths beautifully, lacing his stories with mythological magic and exuberant humor."

⌘⌘⌘

Hearts and Flowers

Daniel Daylight sits inside Mr. Tipper's travelling car. It is cold—not cold, though, like outside; of this fact Daniel Daylight is quite certain. He looks out through the window on his right and, as always, sees white forest rushing by; maybe rabbits will bound past on that snowbank in the trees, he sits thinking. He has seen them, after all, on past Thursdays just like this one. It is dark, too. Not pitch-black, though, for that half moon hangs unhidden, making snow—on the road, on the roadside, rocks, ground, trees (mostly spruce though some birch and some poplar)—glow, as with dust made of silver, Daniel Daylight sits there thinking. Daniel Daylight, at age eight, is on his way to his piano lesson in Prince William, Manitoba.

Twenty miles lie between the Watson Lake Indian Residential School,[1] where resides Daniel Daylight, and Prince William, where he takes his weekly lesson. The Watson Lake Indian Residential School, after all, has no one to teach him how to play the piano, while Prince William has elderly and kind Mrs. Hay. So his teacher in Grade Three at the Watson Lake Indian Residential School, Mr. Tipper, drives him every Thursday, 6:00 p.m. on the nose, to his piano teacher's house, Mrs. Hay's, in Prince William.

Orange brick and cement from the top to the bottom, held in by a steel mesh fence, then by forest (mostly spruce though some birch and some poplar), the Watson Lake Indian Residential School stands like a fort on the south shore of a lake called Watson Lake, 550 miles north of Winnipeg, Mr. Tipper's place of birth. Prince William, quite by contrast, is a town that stands on the south bank of a river called the Moostoos River, just across from which sprawls a village called Waskeechoos (though "settlement" is a noun more accurate, Mr. Tipper has explained on previous Thursdays, for no "village" can be seen, only houses peeking out of the forest here and there). Waskeechoos, on the north bank of the muddy Moostoos River, is an Indian reserve, Mr. Tipper has informed Daniel Daylight, not unlike the one from which hails Daniel Daylight: Minstik Lake, Manitoba, 350 miles north of Waskeechoos, Prince William, and the Watson Lake Indian Residential School. It takes half an hour for Daniel Daylight to make the journey every week, in Mr. Tipper's travelling car, from the Watson Lake Indian Residential School south through the heart of Waskeechoos and across the Moostoos River to Prince William, so he has time on his hands for reflection (so, at least, Mr. Tipper calls such thinking).

Daniel Daylight likes these trips. For one thing, he gets to practice what he knows of the language they call English with elderly and kind Mrs. Hay, with the waiters at the Nip House or at Wong's (where he sometimes goes for snacks with Mr. Tipper once he's finished with his lesson), and with friends of Mr. Tipper whom he meets at the Nip House or at Wong's. He

---

[1] *Watson Lake Indian Residential School* Indian residential schools were boarding schools for Indigenous students that were funded by the Canadian government and run by Christian churches. The aim of these schools was to assimilate Canada's First Nations peoples into Euro-Canadian society, and eradicate Indigenous culture and language. Children were often forcibly taken from their parents to live in these schools, in which mortality rates were high, and sexual and physical abuse was common. Watson Lake Indian Residential School is a fictional institution, but hundreds of such schools existed in Canada between 1828 and 1997.

enjoys speaking English just as he enjoys speaking Cree with the students at the residential school (though, of course, mother tongues need no practice, not like English with its *v*'s that make one's teeth come right out and bite one's lower lip). Daniel Daylight, for another thing, likes to ride in "travelling cars" (as he calls them for the *v* in "travel"). Standing at the northern tip of a lake called Minstik Lake, the Minstik Lake Indian Reserve, after all, has no cars and no trucks, just dog-sleds in the winter, canoes in the summer. A third reason why Daniel Daylight likes these trips is that he enjoys being dazzled by lights of a city like Prince William (for to him, the railway depot is a city of one million, not a town of five thousand) with its streets, its cafés, hotels, stores, and huge churches with tall steeples, whereas Minstik Lake, with its six hundred people, has no streets, no cafés, no hotels, just dirt paths, one small store, and one church. Daniel Daylight, for a fourth thing, likes these trips because Mr. Tipper's travelling car has a radio that plays songs that he can learn in his head. When it stops playing music, furthermore, it plays *spoken* English words, which, of course, he can practise understanding. Tonight, for example, people living in the east of the country (Mr. Tipper has explained) are discussing voting patterns of the nation (Mr. Tipper has explained), even though Daniel Daylight knows the word "vote" for one reason: it begins with the sound that forces one to sink one's teeth deep into one's lower lip and then growl. Sound, that is to say, thrills Daniel Daylight. Which is why, best of all, Daniel Daylight likes these trips: because he gets to play the piano. He gets to play, for elderly and kind Mrs. Hay, "Sonatina"[1] by Clementi, which he now knows well enough to play page 1 from the top to the bottom without stopping. He gets to play, for the third time this winter, "Pirates of the Pacific," with the bass that sounds like a drum-beat. He gets to play, this week, for the first time, *with* Jenny Dean, the duet—for four hands—called "Hearts and Flowers."

"Jenny Dean is a white girl," he has overhead someone say at the Nip House, just a few days before Christmas, in fact, when he was there having fries and Coca-Cola with Mr. Tipper. "Daniel Daylight is an *Indian*. A Cree Indian. Indian boys do *not* play the piano with white girls," he has overheard one white girl whisper *loudly* to another over Coca-Cola in a bottle, "not here in our Prince William, not anywhere on earth or in heaven." Daniel Daylight let it pass. He, after all, was eight years old, not thirty-one like Mr. Tipper; what could he have done to the girl who had made such a statement? Bop her on the head with her bottle? Shove a french fry up her nose? Scratch her face? Besides, neither Jenny Dean's parents, Mrs. Hay, nor Mr. Tipper seemed to mind the notion of Jenny Dean making music with a boy whose father was a *Cree* caribou hunter and a celebrated dogsled racer.

"There it is," says Mr. Tipper. And so it is, for the travelling car has rounded the bend in the road from which the lights of Prince William and the Indian reserve on this side of the river from the town can be seen for the first time. This first view of both town and reserve, to Daniel Daylight, always looks like a spaceship landed on Plant Earth, not unlike the spaceship in the comic book that his older brother, John-Peter Daylight, gave him as a Christmas present twenty-one days ago and that Daniel Daylight keeps hidden under his pillow in the dormitory at the residential school. Daniel Daylight likes, in fact, to imagine all those lights in the distance as exactly that: a spaceship come to take him to a place where exist not Indian people, not white people, just good people and good music. In fact, he can hear in his mind already "Sonatina" by Clementi, key of G, allegro moderato.[2] He can hear "Pirates of the Pacific" with that drumbeat in the bass that goes *boom*. He can hear "Hearts and Flowers." He has practiced all three pieces to the point of exhaustion, after all, in the one room at the residential school that has a piano, what the nuns and the priests call the "library" but, in fact, is a storage room for pencils and erasers, papers, rulers, chalk, and some old spelling books. Feeling on the tips of his fingers all the keys of Mrs. Hay's brown piano, Daniel Daylight sees the sign on the roadside that

[1] *Sonatina* Short musical piece, often used to teach students piano.

[2] *allegro moderato* Musical term meaning "moderately fast."

announces, "Waskeechoos Welcomes You." Mr. Tipper's travelling car speeds past the sign, thus bringing Daniel Daylight onto land that belongs "to the Indians," Mr. Tipper, for some reason, likes proclaiming, as on a radio. "Speed Limit 30 MPH," Daniel Daylight reads on the sign that then follows. The road now mud, dried, cracked, and frozen, pot-holed and iced, the travelling car first slows down to a crawl, then bumps, rattles, slides.

"Indian people are not human," says Mr. Tipper, dodging first this small patch of ice then that small patch of ice, "at least not according to the government. They cannot vote."[1] Daniel Daylight sits unsurprised—Mr. Tipper's use of English, white as a sheet and from Winnipeg as he may be, is not always perfect, Daniel Daylight has simply come to accept. The young Cree piano player, in any case, does not feel confident enough, in either his grasp of English *or* his age, to say much in rebuttal. His father, after all, speaks maybe ten words of English, his mother just two or three; of his eight living siblings, older all than him, only John-Peter Daylight, who is three grades ahead of Daniel Daylight at the Watson Lake Indian Residential School (and perhaps Florence, who once studied there, too, but quit at just Grade Four), speaks English. No one on the Minstik Lake Indian Reserve where Daniel Daylight was born, for that matter, speaks the language, not even Chief Samba Cheese Weetigo *or* his wife, Salad. Like people right here in Waskeechoos (as Mr. Tipper has informed Daniel Daylight in the past), they speak Cree and Cree only. So how, indeed, *can* they be human, Daniel Daylight asks himself, *if* they don't even know what the word means or looks like on a page?

At the bridge that spans like a giant spider's web the muddy, winding Moostoos River, a bottleneck is fast taking shape. Built mainly for trains, the bridge makes room for car and truck traffic only by means of a one-way lane off to one side. The traffic light glowing red like a charcoal on this side of the crossing, four cars sit at its base humming and putt-putt-putting; the travellers from Watson, as happened last Thursday, will just have to sit there for four or five minutes, much too long for Daniel Daylight, who can't wait to play the piano with Jenny Dean. Preparing, in a sense, for conversing with elderly and kind Mrs. Hay when he gets to her house (for Mrs. Hay's Cree, of course, is like Mr. Tipper's—it does not exist), Daniel Daylight makes a decision: he will practise his English. On Mr. Tipper.

"Human, what it mean, Mr. Tip—" But Mr. Tipper does not let him finish.

"If a man, or a woman, aged twenty-one or older cannot vote," says Mr. Tipper—who, from the side, resembles Elmer Fudd, Bugs Bunny's worst enemy in the comics, thinks Daniel Daylight—"then how on earth can he be human, hmmm, Daniel Daylight?"

"'Vote'?" Daniel Daylight feels himself bite his thick lower lip with both sets of teeth, so unlike Cree which has no such sound or letter, he sits there regretting.

"'Vote' is when a person helps choose the leaders that will make the laws for his country," replies Mr. Tipper. He snorts once and then continues. "Every four years, in Winnipeg where I come from, for instance, the person who has the right to vote will go to a church or a school or some such building that has a hall, step inside a little ... room—the *voting* booth, this room is called—take a small piece of paper on which are written the names of the four, five, or six people from that region or that neighbourhood who want to go to Ottawa to speak for the people of that region or that neighbourhood." Daniel Daylight is having trouble keeping up with the torrent of words pouring out of Mr. Tipper's mouth. Still, he manages to catch what he thinks Mr. Tipper, in the past, has referred to as "the drift." "The person then votes—that is to say, chooses—by checking off the name of the person on that list who he thinks will best speak for him and his needs, and the person on that list whose name ends up being checked off by the greatest number of people in that region or that neighbourhood is voted, in this way, into power, and that person goes to Ottawa to help our prime minister run our country, is what the word 'vote' means,

[1] *They cannot vote* After Confederation in 1867, Indigenous peoples in Canada, with very few exceptions, were considered wards of the federal government and prohibited from participating in elections. Inuit peoples did not obtain suffrage until 1950, and status Indians were not able to vote until 1960.

Daniel Daylight," says Mr. Tipper. "You 'vote' for your leader. *You* decide how *you* want *your* life to be in *your* country. That's what makes you a human. Otherwise, you're not."

The traffic light changes first to yellow, then to green. Daniel Daylight has always taken pleasure in looking at what, to him, is an act of magic. *Thump, thump*, goes the travelling car as it crosses the bridge built for trains. The *thump, thump* stops. And now they're in Prince William (or in land that is human, as Mr. Tipper calls it, where people can "vote," just like in Winnipeg)—paved streets, lights so bright Daniel Daylight has to squint, lights so bright it looks like mid-afternoon. On Mr. Tipper's car radio, the music is back; some sad, lonely man is howling away about being "cheated" by someone, maybe his wife. To Daniel Daylight, it sounds, for some reason, like the Indians are being cheated.

In Mrs. Hay's living room, Daniel Daylight sits straight-backed at her upright Baldwin piano.[1] Sitting in a chair right beside him, her hairdo white, short, and fluffy, her face as wrinkled as prunes, the elderly and kind human woman smiles at her one Cree student through glasses so thick they could be ashtrays, Daniel Daylight sits there thinking. Scales first, chords next, then arpeggios, key of E. Major. Right hand only, two octaves up: E, G-sharp, B, E, G-sharp, B, E. And two octaves down: E, G-sharp, B, E, G-sharp, B, E. Back up, back down, Mrs. Hay humming softly along, in her cracked, quavery voice, with the tune such as it is. Daniel Daylight cannot help but wonder as he plays his arpeggio in E major if playing the piano will or will not make him human. Left hand next, same arpeggio, only two octaves lower, first up: E, G-sharp, B, E, G-sharp, B, E. And two octaves down: E, G-sharp, B, E, G-sharp, B, E. He is dying to stop right there at the E with the brown stain and confront Mrs. Hay with the question, for Mr. Tipper, as always, has left him with her, alone, at her house for the hour.

"Very good, Danny," says Mrs. Hay, giving him no chance to ask any questions. Only she, of all the people he knows in the world, calls or has called him Danny. Not his five older brothers, not his six older sisters, not his one hundred friends, not even his parents call him "Danny Daylight." Daniel Daylight is not sure he likes it. But he says nothing. In any case, it's too late now; she has called him "Danny" ever since he first walked into her house that fine, sunny day in September almost three years ago. They move on. First "Sonatina" by Clementi, key of G, allegro moderato, a Grade Six piece; of this fact, Daniel Daylight is very proud if only because he has been taking piano lessons for only two and a half years and should, by rights, still be in Grade Three, not Grade Six already.

"It's the 14th of January," says Mrs. Hay as she peers over her glasses at the calendar that hangs on the wall with the picture, right above the calendar's big, black "1960," of her husband, Mr. Hay, driving a train and smiling and waving. "The festival starts on the 29th of March." Daniel Daylight thus has ten weeks to practise and memorize "Sonatina," for that is his solo entry at the festival and he plans nothing less than to win first prize. As he plays "Sonatina," a piece energetic and happy because it, after all, is written in the key of G, major, allegro moderato (meaning, in Italian, "fast, but not too fast," as in "moderate"), Daniel Daylight, in his mind, sees his father, Cheechup Daylight, and his mother, Adelaide, standing in a line at the little wooden church in the village of Minstik Lake, a worn yellow pencil in each hand. They are lining up to vote. At this point in their lives, they are not human, for a sign on their backs says as much: "Non-human." The melody line for Clementi's "Sonatina" soars like a swallow flying up to the clouds, tugging at the heart of Daniel Daylight as with a rope. If he plays it well enough, his parents will surely turn, allegro moderato, into humans, Daniel Daylight prays as he plays. He comes to the end: dominant chord (his right thumb adding the minor seventh) followed, *seemak* (right away), by the tonic. *Thump. Thump.* In the pianist's mind, Cheechup Daylight and his wife, Adelaide, are turned away from the little voting

[1] *Baldwin piano* Baldwin Piano Company was, for almost a century, the biggest producer of pianos in North America.

booth by the missionary priest, Father Roy. They are not human. They cannot vote.

"Very good, Danny," says Mrs. Hay. "Jenny should be here in just five minutes," she adds, smiling. "But ..." And this is where Mrs. Hay, kind as a *koogoom* (grandmother) as she may be, criticizes him and his playing, sometimes in a manner that takes him quite by surprise. He is tensing up at his right temple as he plays, says Mrs. Hay. If he is tensing up, at his right temple, meaning to say that a vein pops up in that region, as she calls it, every time he reaches for a high note, then his right arm is tensing up and if his right arm is tensing up then his right hand is tensing up. Which is why the melody, from measure 17 to measure 21, in particular, sounds not very happy, forced, not quite "there," explains Mrs. Hay. He must try it again. He does, Mrs. Hay, this time, holding her bone-thin, liver-spotted, white right hand, gentle as a puff of absorbent cotton, on Daniel Daylight's thin right wrist, guiding him, as it were, from phrase to phrase to phrase. Better this time, he can feel it: his right arm is not tensing up, not as much anyway. Again, however, as "Sonatina" comes to an end, his parents are turned away from the little cardboard booth at the church that stands on the hill overlooking the northern extremity of Minstik Lake. *Still*, they are not human. *Ding*, goes Mrs. Hay's electric doorbell. And into the vestibule of her back entrance blow a flurry of snow *and* Jenny Dean. Taking off her bulky winter outerwear—mitts, coat, hat, scarf, boots—her cheeks glow pink from the cold of a mid-January evening in far north Manitoba and her hazel cat-like eyes sparkle as does her blond, curly hair—yes, decides Daniel Daylight, Jenny Dean looks, indeed, like a human.

Now Jenny Dean is sitting on the brown wooden bench right there beside Daniel Daylight. She smells so nice, thinks Daniel Daylight, like snow just fallen on a green spruce bough. The sheet music for the duet Mrs. Hay has chosen as their entry at the festival sits open on the piano's music stand before them. He can feel his red-flannel-sleeved right arm pressing up against the girl's yellow-pullovered left arm. His is the lower part, the part with the bass line and chord structure, hers the higher part, the part with the melody but the with occasional *part* of a chord, meaning that the Cree Indian, non-human, pianist, the "Heart," Daniel Daylight, and the white girl human pianist, the "Flower," Jenny Dean, will be sharing chords, in public, from a piece of music called "Hearts and Flowers" written in the key of C, major, andante cantabile—meaning, in Italian, "at a walking pace *and* singing"—by a human woman named Joan C. McCumber.

Water-like, limpid, and calm, the chords start playing, they float, placed with care on the keyboard by Daniel Daylight. The bass sneaks in, the melody begins. Playing octaves, Jenny Dean's hands begin at the two Cs above middle C, arc up to the G in a curve graceful and smooth, then waft back down to the F, move on down to the E, and thence to the D, skip down to the B and swerve back up to the C whence they had started. The melody pauses, Daniel Daylight's series of major chords billow out to fill the silence, the melody resumes with another arcing phrase, filled with sunlight. For Daniel Daylight, two things happen. First, from where he sits, he sees four hands, two brown (non-human), two white (human), playing the piano. He is sure, somehow, that once he and Jenny Dean have mastered the piece and won first prize in the duet section of the music festival, he—and his parents—will be human. They will have the vote. Father Roy will *not* be able to turn Cheechup Daylight and his wife, Adelaide, away from the little voting booth at the little wooden church that overlooks the northern extremity of beautiful, extraordinary Minstik Lake with its ten thousand islands.

One month later, Daniel Daylight sits at a table in a booth at the Nip House on Prince William's main thoroughfare, looking with amazement at the valentine just given him, at Mrs. Hay's, by the human piano player Jenny Dean. Standing upright on the table one foot before him, the card is covered with hearts and flowers. High above it looms the very white face of Mr. Tipper with his Elmer-Fudd-like, round, pudgy nose, and behind Mr. Tipper, a wall made of one giant mirror. On the radio that sits on the counter five tables, and therefore five booths, behind Daniel Daylight, Kitty

Wells is singing, "Three Ways to Love You, It's True," his sister, Florence Daylight's, favourite song, the one she sings with her boyfriend, Alec Cook, as they sit there on the shores of Minstik Lake strumming and strumming their two old guitars. Now it is mid-February, the Kiwanis Music Festival looms even closer—just six weeks, Mrs. Hay has informed Daniel Daylight *and* Jenny Dean, so Daniel Daylight is excited to the point where he can't stop slurping, through a straw and as loudly as he can, at his glass half-filled with black Coca-Cola. They are sitting in the "Indians Only" section of the restaurant, Mr. Tipper, for some reason, chooses this moment to explain to Daniel Daylight, his blue eyes peering at the restaurant spread out behind and over Daniel Daylight's shoulder. Daniel Daylight stops his slurping and peers past the rim of the tall thin glass at the wall behind Mr. Tipper, the wall which, of course, is one giant mirror. Darting his eyeballs about like tiny searchlights, he looks for a sign that will, indeed, say "Indians Only."

"There is no sign that says 'Indians only,'" says Mr. Tipper, knowing, as almost always, what is going on inside the mind of Daniel Daylight.

"Indians only ..." Kitty Wells has stopped singing, Daniel Daylight suddenly observes, and a man's speaking voice has taken over on the radio. Daniel Daylight locks his eyes with Mr. Tipper's—what on earth will the man say next about ...?

"Hamburger deluxe, gravy on the side!" yells the big, fat waitress who always scowls at Daniel Daylight, drowning out the voice of the man on the radio, at least temporarily.

"... cannot vote," the man on the radio ends his speech.

"You see?" says Mr. Tipper, sipping at his coffee with his thick purplish lips. "They're not human, not according to the radio, not according to the government. It is the law."

"Who made the law?" Daniel Daylight feels emboldened to ask Mr. Tipper.

"No one," says Mr. Tipper. "They are unwritten. It's the same thing at the movie house right here in Prince William, the taverns, the bingo hall, even the churches, Baptist, Anglican, *and* Catholic—Indians on one side, whites on the other."

Suddenly ignoring his half-finished plate of french fries with gravy, his Coke, and his valentine, Daniel Daylight twists his back around to look at the rest of the restaurant—looking in the mirror will *not* do: 1) the Nip House has room for at least sixty customers; 2) the fire-engine-red-vinyl-covered booths are not high enough to hide anyone from anyone; 3) true to Mr. Tipper's unwanted observation, white people sit on one side of the restaurant, Indian people on the other. He turns back to the mirror and to Mr. Tipper, who, of course, is the one exception, being as he is a white man sitting with the brown-skinned, black-haired, non-human, Cree Indian pianist Daniel Daylight on the "Indians Only" side of the restaurant. Mr. Tipper must be brave, Daniel Daylight thinks rather sadly, lets go his Coke, and slips his valentine into a pocket of his black woollen parka. Suddenly, he is no longer hungry.

Six weeks later, Daniel Daylight sits inside Mr. Tipper's travelling car with the radio playing, again, country music, a song that Daniel Daylight does not know. He is about to ask when Mr. Tipper asks him, "What they will think when they see you and Jenny Dean playing together at the festival?" Daniel Daylight has no answer, not at the moment anyway, for "They will love our music" sounds somehow hypocritical, facetious, not quite truthful. Again they are going down the winding gravel road, with snow-covered forest rushing by as always, a rabbit bounding past on the snowbank just to the right. Daniel Daylight is on his way, this time, to the Kiwanis Music Festival[1] in Prince William. He is going there to compete in the solo/Grade Six section with his "Sonatina" by Clementi, key of G, allegro moderato, which he now has down note-perfect *and* memorized. More important, however—at least so says Mr. Tipper, and with this notion Daniel Daylight is inclined to agree—he is going there to compete in the

[1] *Kiwanis Music Festival* Kiwanis is a worldwide, volunteer-led service club. Since 1908, Kiwanis clubs have hosted musical festivals, at which musicians can compete for prizes in cities across Canada.

duet section of the annual event with the white girl/human, Jenny Dean, in a piece with the title "Hearts and Flowers," written by the human composer Joan C. McCumber.

They come to the Indian reserve called Waskeechoos, the sign that says so just going by and the next one saying "Speed Limit 30 MPH." The travelling car slows down. It bumps, rocks, and rattles. One pot-hole here, two there. Ice. The travelling car slides once, for six inches, then stops. A non-human man walks past, from the town and back to his home in Waskeechoos.

"People can't vote?" asks Daniel Daylight, his English, and his confidence, having bloomed rather nicely in the last two months for, of course, it is now the 31st of March, 1960, the last day of the three-day-long Kiwanis Music Festival, and northern Manitoba is still gripped hard by winter.

"Soon they might," says Mr. Tipper. "I heard on the radio the other day ..." But the traffic light at the railway bridge has just turned green and Daniel Daylight, in any case, has drifted off already to his own reserve 350 miles north, where his father and his mother are standing in line at the church on the hill that overlooks beautiful, extraordinary Minstik Lake, a worn yellow pencil each in hand. They are getting ready to select a man they can send to Ottawa to speak for Minstik Lake and all its people, perhaps even Chief Samba Cheese Weetigo. Into the line behind and in front of them are crushed all six hundred people of Minstik Lake, even babies. And they are roaring; they want to vote. "Apparently the law is changing," says Mr. Tipper, "soon. Or so I heard on the radio." Good, thinks Daniel Daylight, all these people back there in Waskeechoos, like those people where I come from, will soon be human, he sits there thinking. He doesn't even notice that they are now on "human territory," as Mr. Tipper calls it, for already he can see himself on stage at the Kiwanis Auditorium in downtown Prince William, sitting at the piano beside Jenny Dean, playing music with all his might so his parents, and therefore he, can change from non-human to human. He is glad that Sister St. Alphonse, the principal seamstress at the Watson Lake Indian Residential School, has found him a suit for the evening: black, white shirt, red necktie, black shoes, all, for the moment, under his black woollen parka. His hands, meanwhile, are wrapped in woollen mittens so thick they do *not* stand a chance of getting cold, stiff, or claw-like, he has decided, not when he has to use them, tonight, to make *a point*.

At the Kiwanis Auditorium in downtown Prince William, Daniel Daylight sits in the audience with his back tall and straight, like all good pianists, Mrs. Hay has always insisted. From where he sits, in the middle and on the room's right side, he can see—now that he is two months wiser, courtesy of Mr. Tipper—that the room is, indeed, divided: white people on one side, Indian people on the other, the latter a little on the sparse side. Just like at the Nip House and at Wong's, Daniel Daylight sits there and thinks, *and* at the movies, the bingo hall, the taverns, and the churches—according, anyway, to Mr. Tipper, who has been to all these places. As he sits there waiting for his turn on stage, he can, on the left side of the hall, see Jenny Dean and her parents, with Mrs. Hay, waving at him and waving at him, beckoning him to come to their side. Shyly, he shakes his head. Jenny Dean, with her parents, belongs on the human side, he, with his parents (who are not only non-human but absent) on the other. Only Mr. Tipper sits beside him, and he is not even supposed to be there. On stage, some dreadful music is playing: two human boys at the piano, aged ten years or so (guesses Daniel Daylight), wearing green V-neck sweaters, white shirts, and bowties, their hair yellow as hay, skin white as cake mix. According to the program, they are playing a duet called "Squadrons of the Air" but Daniel Daylight can't really tell; whatever the word "squadrons" means, it sounds like they are dropping bombs from the air on some poor hapless village. Next come two human girls, plump as bran muffins, red-haired, freckled, dressed in Virgin-Mary-blue smocks with long-sleeved white blouses, again aged ten years or so. They haven't even sat down on the bench when they charge like tanks into a duet called "Swaying Daffodils." For Daniel Daylight, the daffodils try desperately to sway first this way and then that but can't quite do it; to him, first they bang around, then leap about, then bang around some more, until they just droop from exhaustion, stems halfbent over, heads hanging down, sad daffodils, unlucky plants. They are next, he, Daniel Daylight, and, she, Jenny Dean.

Daniel Daylight marches down the aisle that separates the Indian section of the huge auditorium from the white section. Jenny Dean joins him from the other side. Two hundred and fifty human people look at them as with the eyes of alligators, Daniel Daylight thinks, for he can feel them on his back, cold and wet and gooey. He shudders, then climbs the steps that lead to the stage and the upright piano, following the eight-year-old white girl Jenny Dean in her fluffy pink cotton dress with white lace collar and shoulders that puff out like popcorn. They reach the piano. They sit down. From where he sits, Daniel Daylight can see Mr. Tipper looking up at him with eyes, he is sure of it, that say, "Go on, you can do it." Only twenty-five or so Indian people, mostly women, sit scattered around him, also looking up at him but with dark eyes that say nothing. On the room's other side, he can see the eyes that, to him, are screaming, "No, you can't; you can't do it. You can't do it at all." Feeling Jenny Dean's naked left arm pressing up against his own black-suited, white-shirted arm, he takes his right hand off his lap, raises it above the keyboard of the Heintzman upright.[1] He can hear a gasp from the audience. Then he is sure he can hear the white side whispering to one another, "What's he doing there, little Indian boy, brown-skinned boy? His people cannot vote; therefore they are not human. Non-human boys do *not* play the piano, not in public, and not with human girls." Daniel Daylight, however, will have none of it. Instead, gentle as snow on spruce boughs at night, he lets fall his right hand right on the C-major chord.

Water-like, limpid, calm as silence, the chords for "Hearts and Flowers" begin their journey. Placed with care, every note of them, on the keyboard by Daniel Daylight, they float, float like mist. The bass sneaks in, the melody begins. Playing octaves, Jenny Dean's hands begin at the two Cs above middle C, arc up to the G in a curve smooth and graceful, then waft back down to the F, move on down to the E, and thence to the D, skip down to the B and thus swerve back, up to the C whence they had started. The melody pauses, Daniel Daylight's series of major chords billow out to fill the silence, Jenny Dean's elegant melody resumes its journey. In love with the god sound, Daniel Daylight sends his/her[2] waves, as prayer from the depths of his heart, the depths of his being, right across the vast auditorium, right through the flesh and bone and blood of some three hundred people, through the walls of the room, beyond them, north across the Moostoos River, through Waskeechoos, north to the Watson Lake Indian Residential School and thus through the lives of the two hundred Indian children who live there, then northward and northward and northward until the sound waves wash up on the shores, and the islands, of vast Minstik Lake. And there, deep inside the blood of Daniel Daylight, where lives Minstik Lake and all her people, Daniel Daylight sees his parents, Cheechup Daylight and his wife, Adelaide, walking up the hill to the little voting booth at the little wooden church that overlooks the northern extremity of beautiful, extraordinary Minstik Lake with its ten thousand islands. And Daniel Daylight, with the magic that he weaves like a tiny little master, *wills* his parents to walk right past Father Roy in his great black cassock and into the booth with their worn yellow pencils. And there they vote. Frozen into place by the prayer of Daniel Daylight *and* his "flower," Jenny Dean, Father Roy can do nothing, least of all stop

[1] *Heintzman upright* Heintzman & Co. is a Canadian piano maker well-known for producing high-quality instruments.

[2] [Highway's note] Like all North American Aboriginal languages (that I know of anyway, and there are a lot, fifty-two in Canada alone!), the Cree language has no gender. According to its structure, therefore, we are all, in a sense, he/shes, as is all of nature (trees, vegetation, even rocks), as is God, one would think. That is why I, for one have so much trouble just thinking in the English language—because it is a language that is, first and foremost, "motored," as it were, by a theology/mythology that is "monotheistic" in structure, a structure where there is only one God and that god is male and male only. Other world systems are either "polytheistic" or "pantheistic" in structure, having, for instance (now or in the past, as in ancient Greece), room for gods who are female or even male/female, systems where all of nature, including sound, just for instance, simply "bristles," as it were, with divinity.

Cheechup Daylight and his wife, Adelaide, from becoming human.

Receiving, on stage, his trophy beside Jenny Dean from a human man in black suit, shirt, and tie—Mayor Bill Hicks of Prince William, has explained Mr. Tipper—Daniel Daylight beams at the crowd that fills, for the most part, the Kiwanis Auditorium in downtown Prince William, Manitoba. Both sides are standing, the Indian side with its two dozen people, the white side with its 250. And they are clapping. And clapping and clapping. Some of them, in fact, are crying, white and Indian, human and … well, they don't look non-human any more, not from where stands exulting—and weeping—the Cree Indian, *human* pianist Daniel Daylight.

Daniel Daylight sits inside Mr. Tipper's travelling car. It is cold—not cold, though, like outside, of this fact Daniel Daylight is quite certain. He looks out through the window on his right and, as always, sees white forest rushing by; maybe rabbits will bound past on that snowbank in the trees, he sits thinking. Snow falling gently, it looks, to Daniel Daylight, like he is being hurtled through the heart of a giant snowflake. In his back-trousered lap, meanwhile, rests his trophy, a ten-inch-tall golden angel with wings outspread and arms wide open, beaming up at her winner through the glow of the travelling car's dashboard lights. On the radio, the music has stopped and people living in the east of the country, explains Mr. Tipper, are discussing a matter that takes Daniel Daylight completely by surprise: the Indian people of Canada, it seems, were given that day, the 31st of March, 1960, the right to vote in federal elections, in their own country.

"You see?" Daniel Daylight says to Mr. Tipper, his English, and his confidence, having grown quite nicely in just two months. "We are human. I knew it. And you know why I knew it, Mr. Tipper?"

"Why, Daniel Daylight?"

"Because I played it."

—2004

Kazuo Ishiguro

b. 1954

Kazuo Ishiguro is best known for his Booker Prize-winning *The Remains of the Day* (1989) and the dystopian *Never Let Me Go* (2005), but his other novels have also received significant international acclaim. A 2017 Nobel-Prize winner who was knighted in 2018, he has been hailed—along with writers such as Salman Rushdie, Michael Ondaatje, Vikram Seth, and Timothy Mo—as part of a new movement of "world fiction." Like these writers, he writes in English but is of non-Anglo-Saxon ancestry, and often depicts characters and settings that differ from those traditionally found in English literature. With influences that include Japanese pop culture of the 1940s and 1950s, nineteenth-century American writers, and Russian authors Dostoevsky and Chekhov, Ishiguro often produces work that challenges his readers' expectations.

Ishiguro was born in Nagasaki, Japan, in 1954. When he was five his father accepted a one-year research position at the National Institute of Oceanography in Britain, and the family left for England. Ishiguro's parents educated him in the expectation that the family would return to Japan—providing him with Japanese magazines, books, and movies—but their return continued to be postponed, and eventually they became permanent British residents. Ishiguro studied English and philosophy at the University of Kent at Canterbury, where he received his BA. He went on to a Master's degree in Creative Writing at the University of East Anglia in Norwich, where he was a member of a postgraduate class directed by Malcolm Bradbury.

Ishiguro, who for several years had attempted unsuccessfully to establish himself as a singer/songwriter, enjoyed almost immediate success as a writer of fiction. His first two novels, *A Pale View of Hills* (1982) and *An Artist of the Floating World* (1986), won prestigious literary awards in England and established him as an important new novelist. Both these early novels are set in Japan, although Ishiguro would not make his first return to Japan until 1989. Ishiguro has said that the Japan of these novels is one of his own imagination, constructed on a foundation of childhood memories.

Throughout his life, Ishiguro has retained something of an outsider's perspective. When he began writing, he realized he "wasn't a very English Englishman, and [he] wasn't a very Japanese Japanese either." This unique perspective enables him to dissect cultural norms and stereotypes, and to fulfill what he considers one of an artist's most important jobs: to "tackle and rework myths." Lurking behind the faintly comic resolution of *An Artist of the Floating World* is Ishiguro's knowledge that many Western readers—familiar only with stereotypes of Japanese society—would expect the novel to end with the cultural cliché of the protagonist's ritual suicide by seppuku.

The Remains of the Day is widely regarded as a major work of twentieth-century fiction. Its story concerns Stevens, an aging butler who looks back in the summer of 1956 on the events of the mid-1930s, when his employer, Lord Darlington, organized clandestine support in Britain for Germany's Nazi government, and an unacknowledged love blossomed between Stevens and the housekeeper at Darlington Hall. The story is told in Stevens's voice, and between the lines of the butler's spare and emotionally reserved narrative, the reader is left to piece together a tale of misplaced loyalty, lost opportunity, and almost unbearable sadness.

Although Ishiguro's novels often center on characters who attempt to cope with traumatic events of history, he has little interest in investigating the historic events themselves. *The Remains of the Day* looks back from the 1950s to the impending Nazi threat of the 1930s with barely a glance at its culmination during World War II. Similarly, although *A Pale View of Hills* is set in Nagasaki in the late 1940s, no mention is made of the atomic bomb, even though its effects permeate every aspect of the protagonist's existence. As Ishiguro says, this is because he is "more interested in what people tell themselves happened … than what actually happened." Often recounted in the first person by unreliable narrators who are haunted by their past, Ishiguro's narratives frequently center on distortions of perception or of memory. His writing style mimics the workings of memory, moving fluidly across time and through tangentially connected episodes.

Ishiguro's settings tend to be loosely defined, as in "A Village after Dark" (2001) or in *The Unconsoled* (1995), which could be set in any European city. Whether they take place in Japan, England, or Shanghai—the setting of *When We Were Orphans* (2002)—there is often a somewhat unsettling universality to the experiences described; the locations are important only in that they provide backdrops for, and insights into, Ishiguro's characters. As a result, Ishiguro's fiction—which has been printed in over thirty languages—is well suited for translation.

Never Let Me Go (2005) was widely praised as Ishiguro's most accomplished work since *The Remains of the Day*. Set largely in a boarding school where the atmosphere is at once warmly familiar and deeply disturbing, the novel explores, against a futuristic background, the roots of social exclusion, the sometimes-frightening consequences of medical science and human notions of progress, the nature of love, and the shadow cast by death on human existence.

Throughout his career, Ishiguro has flouted the conventional wisdom that authors should limit their subject matter to the compass of their own life experience. "Write about what you know is the most stupid thing I've heard," he explains. His 2015 novel, *The Buried Giant*, which is set in a mythical rendering of early medieval England, is a testament to his unending desire to use fiction to explore unfamiliar settings, situations, and voices.

⌘⌘⌘

A Village after Dark

There was a time when I could travel England for weeks on end and remain at my sharpest—when, if anything, the travelling gave me an edge. But now that I am older I become disoriented more easily. So it was that on arriving at the village just after dark I failed to find my bearings at all. I could hardly believe I was in the same village in which not so long ago I had lived and come to exercise such influence.

There was nothing I recognized, and I found myself walking forever around twisting, badly lit streets hemmed in on both sides by the little stone cottages characteristic of the area. The streets often became so narrow I could make no progress without my bag or my elbow scraping one rough wall or another. I persevered nevertheless, stumbling around in the darkness in the hope of coming upon the village square—where I could at least orient myself—or else of encountering one of the villagers. When after a while I had done neither, a weariness came over me, and I decided my best course was just to choose a cottage at random, knock on the door, and hope it would be opened by someone who remembered me.

I stopped by a particularly rickety-looking door, whose upper beam was so low that I could see I would have to crouch right down to enter. A dim light was leaking out around the door's edges, and I could hear voices and laughter. I knocked loudly to insure that the occupants would hear me over their talk. But just then someone behind me said, "Hello."

I turned to find a young woman of around twenty, dressed in raggedy jeans and a torn jumper, standing in the darkness a little way away.

"You walked straight past me earlier," she said, "even though I called to you."

"Did I really? Well, I'm sorry. I didn't mean to be rude."

"You're Fletcher, aren't you?"

"Yes," I said, somewhat flattered.

"Wendy thought it was you when you went by our cottage. We all got very excited. You were one of that lot, weren't you? With David Maggis and all of them."

"Yes," I said, "but Maggis was hardly the most important one. I'm surprised you pick him out like that. There were other, far more important figures." I reeled off a series of names and was interested to see the girl nodding at each one in recognition. "But this must have all been before your time," I said. "I'm surprised you know about such things."

"It was before our time, but we're all experts on your lot. We know more about all that than most of the older ones who were here then. Wendy recognized you instantly just from your photos."

"I had no idea you young people had taken such an interest in us. I'm sorry I walked past you earlier. But you see, now that I'm older, I get a little disoriented when I travel."

I could hear some boisterous talk coming from behind the door. I banged on it again, this time rather impatiently, though I was not so eager to bring the encounter with the girl to a close.

She looked at me for a moment, then said, "All of you from those days are like that. David Maggis came here a few years ago. In '93, or maybe it was '94. He was like that. A bit vague. It must get to you after a while, travelling all the time."

"So Maggis was here. How interesting. You know, he wasn't one of the really important figures. You mustn't get carried away with such an idea. Incidentally, perhaps you could tell me who lives in this cottage." I thumped the door again.

"The Petersons," the girl said. "They're an old house. They'll probably remember you."

"The Petersons," I repeated, but the name meant nothing to me.

"Why don't you come to our cottage? Wendy was really excited. So were the rest of us. It's a real chance for us, actually talking to someone from those days."

"I'd very much like to do that. But first of all I'd better get myself settled in. The Petersons, you say."

I thumped the door again, this time quite ferociously. At last it opened, throwing warmth and light out into the street. An old man was standing in the doorway. He looked at me carefully, then asked, "It's not Fletcher, is it?"

"Yes, and I've just got into the village. I've been travelling for several days."

He thought about this for a moment, then said, "Well, you'd better come in."

I found myself in a cramped, untidy room full of rough wood and broken furniture. A log burning in the fireplace was the only source of light, by which I could make out a number of hunched figures sitting around the room. The old man led me to a chair beside the fire with a grudgingness that suggested it was the very one he had just vacated. Once I sat down, I found I could not easily turn my head to see my surroundings or the others in the room. But the warmth of the fire was very welcome, and for a moment I just stared into its flames, a pleasant grogginess drifting over me. Voices came from behind me, inquiring if I was well, if I had come far, if I was hungry, and I replied as best I could, though I was aware that my answers were barely adequate. Eventually, the questions ceased, and it occurred to me that my presence was creating a heavy awkwardness, but I was so grateful for the warmth and the chance to rest that I hardly cared.

Nonetheless, when the silence behind me had gone unbroken for several minutes, I resolved to address my hosts with a little more civility, and I turned in my chair. It was then, as I did so, that I was suddenly seized by an intense sense of recognition. I had chosen the cottage quite at random, but now I could see that it was none other than the very one in which I had spent my years in this village. My gaze moved immediately to the far corner—at this moment shrouded in darkness—to the spot that had been *my* corner, where once my mattress had been and where I had spent many tranquil hours browsing through books or conversing with whoever happened to drift in. On summer days, the windows, and often the door, were left open to allow a refreshing breeze to blow right through. Those were the days when the cottage was surrounded by open fields and there would come from outside the voices of my friends, lazing in the long grass, arguing over poetry or philosophy. These precious fragments of the past came back to me so powerfully that it was all I could do not to make straight for my old corner then and there.

Someone was speaking to me again, perhaps asking another question, but I hardly listened. Rising, I peered through the shadows into my corner, and could now make out a narrow bed, covered by an old curtain, occupying more or less the exact space where my mattress had been. The bed looked extremely inviting, and I found myself cutting into something the old man was saying.

"Look," I said, "I know this is a bit blunt. But, you see, I've come such a long way today. I really need to lie down, close my eyes, even if it's just for a few minutes. After that, I'm happy to talk all you like."

I could see the figures around the room shifting uneasily. Then a new voice said, rather sullenly, "Go ahead then. Have a nap. Don't mind us."

But I was already picking my way through the clutter toward my corner. The bed felt damp, and the springs creaked under my weight, but no sooner had I curled up with my back to the room than my many hours of travelling began to catch up with me. As I was drifting off, I heard the old man saying, "It's Fletcher, all right. God, he's aged."

A woman's voice said, "Should we let him go to sleep like that? He might wake in a few hours and then we'll have to stay up with him."

"Let him sleep for an hour or so," someone else said. "If he's still asleep after an hour, we'll wake him."

At this point, sheer exhaustion overtook me.

It was not a continuous or comfortable sleep. I drifted between sleep and waking, always conscious of voices behind me in the room. At some point, I was aware of a woman saying, "I don't know how I was ever under his spell. He looks such a ragamuffin now."

In my state of near-sleep, I debated with myself whether these words applied to me or, perhaps, to David Maggis, but before long sleep engulfed me once more.

When I next awoke, the room appeared to have grown both darker and colder. Voices were continuing behind me in lowered tones, but I could make no sense of the conversation. I now felt embarrassed at having gone to sleep in the way I had, and for a few further moments remained motionless with my face to the wall. But something about me must have revealed that I was awake, for a woman's voice, breaking off from the general conversation, said, "Oh, look, look." Some whispers were exchanged, then I heard the sound of someone coming toward my corner. I felt a hand placed gently on my shoulder, and looked up to find a woman kneeling over me. I did not turn my body sufficiently to see the room, but I got the impression that it was lit by dying embers, and the woman's face was visible only in shadow.

"Now, Fletcher," she said. "It's time we had a talk. I've waited a long time for you to come back. I've thought about you often."

I strained to see her more clearly. She was somewhere in her forties, and even in the gloom I noticed a sleepy sadness in her eyes. But her face failed to stir in me even the faintest of memories.

"I'm sorry," I said. "I have no recollection of you. But please forgive me if we met some time ago. I do get very disoriented these days."

"Fletcher," she said, "when we used to know one another, I was young and beautiful. I idolized you, and everything you said seemed like an answer. Now here you are, back again. I've wanted to tell you for many years that you ruined my life."

"You're being unfair. All right, I was mistaken about a lot of things. But I never claimed to have any answers. All I said in those days was that it was our duty, all of us, to contribute to the debate. We knew so much more about the issues than the ordinary people here. If people like us procrastinated, claiming we didn't yet know enough, then who was there to act? But I never claimed I had the answers. No, you're being unfair."

"Fletcher," she said, and her voice was oddly gentle, "you used to make love to me, more or less every time I wandered in here to your room. In this corner, we did all kinds of beautifully dirty things. It's odd to think how I could have once been so physically excited by you. And here you're just a foul-smelling bundle of rags now. But look at me—I'm still attractive. My face has got a bit lined, but when I walk in the village streets I wear dresses I've made specially to show off my figure. A lot of men want me still. But you, no woman would look at you now. A bundle of stinking rags and flesh."

"I don't remember you," I said. "And I've no time for sex these days. I've other things to worry about. More serious things. Very well, I was mistaken about a lot in those days. But I've done more than most to try and make amends. You see, even now I'm travelling. I've never stopped. I've travelled and travelled trying to undo what damage I may once have caused. That's more than can be said of some others from those days. I bet Maggis, for instance, hasn't worked nearly as hard to try and put things right."

The woman was stroking my hair.

"Look at you. I used to do this, run my fingers through your hair. Look at this filthy mess. I'm sure you're contaminated with all sorts of parasites." But she continued slowly to run her fingers through the dirty knots. I failed to feel anything erotic from this, as perhaps she wished me to do. Rather, her caresses felt maternal. Indeed, for a moment it was as though I had finally reached some cocoon of protectiveness, and I began once more to feel sleepy. But suddenly she stopped and slapped me hard on the forehead.

"Why don't you join the rest of us now? You've had your sleep. You've got a lot of explaining to do." With that she got up and left.

For the first time, I turned my body sufficiently to survey the room. I saw the woman making her way past the clutter on the floor, then sitting down in a rocking chair by the fireplace. I could see three other figures hunched around the dying fire. One I recognized to be the old man who had opened the door. The two others—sitting together on what looked like a wooden trunk—seemed to be women of around the same age as the one who had spoken to me.

The old man noticed that I had turned, and he indicated to the others that I was watching. The four of them proceeded to sit stiffly, not speaking. From the way they did this, it was clear that they had been discussing me thoroughly while I was asleep. In fact, as I watched them I could more or less guess the whole shape their conversation had taken. I could see, for instance, that they had spent some time expressing concern for the young girl I had met outside, and about the effect I might have on her peers.

"They're all so impressionable," the old man would have said. "And I heard her inviting him to visit them."

To which, no doubt, one of the women on the trunk would have said, "But he can't do much harm now. In our time, we were all taken in because all his kind—they were young and glamorous. But these days the odd one passing through from time to time, looking all decrepit and burned out like that—if anything, it goes to demystify all that talk about the old days. In any case, people like him have changed their position so much these days. They don't know themselves what they believe."

The old man would have shaken his head. "I saw the way that young girl was looking at him. All right, he looks a pitiful mess over there just now. But once his ego's fed a little, once he has the flattery of the young people, sees how they want to hear his ideas, then there'll be no stopping him. It'll be just like before. He'll have them all working for his causes. Young girls like that, there's so little for them to believe in now. Even a stinking tramp like this could give them a purpose."

Their conversation, all the time I slept, would have gone something very much like that. But now, as I observed them from my corner, they continued to sit in guilty silence, staring at the last of their fire. After a while, I rose to my feet. Absurdly, the four of them kept their gazes averted from me. I waited a few moments to see if any of them would say anything. Finally, I said, "All right, I was asleep earlier, but I've guessed what you were saying. Well, you'll be interested to know I'm going to do the very thing you feared. I'm going this moment to the young people's cottage. I'm going to tell them what to do with all their energy, all their dreams, their urge to achieve something of lasting good in this world. Look at you, what a pathetic bunch. Crouching in your cottage, afraid to do anything, afraid of me, of Maggis, of anyone else from those times. Afraid to do anything in the world out there, just because once we made a few mistakes. Well, those young people haven't yet sunk so low, despite all the lethargy you've been preaching at them down the years. I'll talk to them. I'll undo in half an hour all of your sorry efforts."

"You see," the old man said to the others. "I knew it would be this way. We ought to stop him, but what can we do?"

I crashed my way across the room, picked up my bag, and went out into the night.

The girl was still standing outside when I emerged. She seemed to be expecting me and with a nod began to lead the way.

The night was drizzly and dark. We twisted and turned along the narrow paths that ran between the cottages. Some of the cottages we passed looked so decayed and crumbling that I felt I could destroy one of them simply by running at it with all my weight.

The girl kept a few paces ahead, occasionally glancing back at me over her shoulder. Once she said, "Wendy's going to be so pleased. She was sure it was you when you went past earlier. By now, she'll have guessed she was right, because I've been away this long, and she'll have brought the whole crowd together. They'll all be waiting."

"Did you give David Maggis this sort of reception, too?"

"Oh, yes. We were really excited when he came."

"I'm sure he found that very gratifying. He always had an exaggerated sense of his own importance."

"Wendy says Maggis was one of the interesting ones, but that you were, well, important. She thinks you were really important."

I thought about this for a moment.

"You know," I said, "I've changed my mind on very many things. If Wendy's expecting me to say all the things I used to all those years ago, well, she's going to be in for a disappointment."

The girl did not seem to hear this, but continued to lead me purposefully through the clusters of cottages.

After a little while, I became aware of footsteps following a dozen or so paces behind us. At first, I assumed this was just some villager out walking and refrained from turning round. But then the girl halted under a street lamp and looked behind us. I was thus obliged also to stop and turn. A middle-aged man in a dark overcoat was coming toward us. As he approached, he held out his hand and shook mine, though without smiling.

"So," he said, "you're here."

I then realized I knew the man. We had not seen each other since we were ten years old. His name was Roger Button, and he had been in my class at the school I had attended for two years in Canada before my family returned to England. Roger Button and I had not been especially close, but, because he had been a timid boy, and because he, too, was from England, he had for a while followed me about. I had neither seen nor heard from him since that time. Now, as I studied his appearance under the street lamp, I saw the years had not been kind to him. He was bald, his face was pocked and lined, and there was a weary sag to his whole posture. For all that, there was no mistaking my old classmate.

"Roger," I said, "I'm just on my way to visit this young lady's friends. They've gathered together to receive me. Otherwise I'd have come and looked you up straightaway. As it was, I had it in my mind as the next thing to do, even before getting any sleep tonight. I was just thinking to myself, However late things finish at the young people's cottage, I'll go and knock on Roger's door afterward."

"Don't worry," said Roger Button as we all started to walk again. "I know how busy you are. But we ought to talk. Chew over old times. When you last saw me—at school, I mean—I suppose I was a rather feeble specimen. But, you know, that all changed when I got to fourteen, fifteen. I really toughened up. Became quite a leader type. But you'd long since left Canada. I always wondered what would have happened if we'd come across each other at fifteen. Things would have been rather different between us, I assure you."

As he said this, memories came flooding back. In those days, Roger Button had idolized me, and in return I had bullied him incessantly. However, there had existed between us a curious understanding that my bullying him was all for his own good; that when, without warning, I suddenly punched him in the stomach on the playground, or when, passing him in the corridor, I impulsively wrenched his arm up his back until he started to cry, I was doing so in order to help him toughen up. Accordingly, the principal effect such attacks had on our relationship was to keep him in awe of me. This all came back to me as I listened to the weary-looking man walking beside me.

"Of course," Roger Button went on, perhaps guessing my train of thought, "it might well be that if you hadn't treated me the way you did I'd never have become what I did at fifteen. In any case, I've often wondered how it would have been if we'd met just a few years later. I really was something to be reckoned with by then."

We were once again walking along the narrow twisted passages between cottages. The girl was still leading the way, but she was now walking much faster. Often we would only just manage to catch a glimpse of her turning some corner ahead of us, and it struck me that we would have to keep alert if we were not to lose her.

"Today, of course," Roger Button was saying, "I've let myself go a bit. But I have to say, old fellow, you seem to be in much worse shape. Compared with you, I'm an athlete. Not to put too fine a point on it, you're just a filthy old tramp now, really, aren't you? But, you know, for a long time after you left I continued to idolize you. Would Fletcher do this? What would Fletcher think if he saw me doing that? Oh, yes. It was only when I got to fifteen or so that I looked back on it all and saw through you. Then I was very angry, of course. Even now, I still think about it sometimes. I look back and think, Well, he was just a thoroughly nasty so-and-so. He had a little more weight and muscle at that age than I did, a little more confidence, and he took full advantage. Yes, it's very clear, looking back, what a nasty little person you were. Of course, I'm not implying you still are today. We all change. That much I'm willing to accept."

"Have you been living here long?" I asked, wishing to change the subject.

"Oh, seven years or so. Of course, they talk about you a lot around here. I sometimes tell them about our early association. 'But he won't remember me,' I always tell them. 'Why would he remember a skinny little boy he used to bully and have at his beck and call?' Anyway, the young people here, they talk about you more and more these days. Certainly, the ones who've never seen you tend to idealize you the most. I suppose you've come back to capitalize on all that. Still, I shouldn't blame you. You're entitled to try and salvage a little self-respect."

We suddenly found ourselves facing an open field, and we both halted. Glancing back, I saw that we had walked our way out of the village; the last of the cottages were some distance behind us. Just as I had feared, we had lost the young woman; in fact, I realized we had not been following her for some time.

At that moment, the moon emerged, and I saw we were standing at the edge of a vast grassy field—extending, I supposed, far beyond what I could see by the moon.

Roger Button turned to me. His face in the moonlight seemed gentle, almost affectionate.

"Still," he said, "it's time to forgive. You shouldn't keep worrying so much. As you see, certain things from the past will come back to you in the end. But then we can't be held accountable for what we did when we were very young."

"No doubt you're right," I said. Then I turned and looked around in the darkness. "But now I'm not sure where to go. You see, there were some young people waiting for me in their cottage. By now they'd have a warm fire ready for me and some hot tea. And some home-baked cakes, perhaps even a good stew. And the moment I entered, ushered in by that young lady we were following just now, they'd all have burst into applause. There'd be smiling, adoring faces all around me. That's what's waiting for me somewhere. Except I'm not sure where I should go."

Roger Button shrugged. "Don't worry, you'll get there easily enough. Except, you know, that girl was being a little misleading if she implied you could walk to Wendy's cottage. It's much too far. You'd really need to catch a bus. Even then, it's quite a long journey. About two hours, I'd say. But don't worry, I'll show you where you can pick up your bus."

With that, he began to walk back toward the cottages. As I followed, I could sense that the hour had got very late and my companion was anxious to get some sleep. We spent several minutes walking around the cottages again, and then he brought us out into the village square. In fact, it was so small and shabby it hardly merited being called a square; it was little more than a patch of green beside a solitary street lamp. Just visible beyond the pool of light cast by the lamp were a few shops, all shut up for the night. There was complete silence and nothing was stirring. A light mist was hovering over the ground.

Roger Button stopped before we had reached the green and pointed.

"There," he said. "If you stand there, a bus will come along. As I say, it's not a short journey. About two hours. But don't worry, I'm sure your young people will wait. They've so little else to believe in these days, you see."

"It's very late," I said. "Are you sure a bus will come?"

"Oh, yes. Of course, you may have to wait. But eventually a bus will come." Then he touched me reassuringly on the shoulder. "I can see it might get a little lonely standing out here. But once the bus arrives your spirits will rise, believe me. Oh, yes. That bus is always a joy. It'll be brightly lit up, and it's always full of cheerful people, laughing and joking and pointing out the window. Once you board it, you'll feel warm and comfortable, and the other passengers will chat with you, perhaps offer you things to eat or drink. There may even be singing—that depends on the driver. Some drivers encourage it, others don't. Well, Fletcher, it was good to see you."

We shook hands, then he turned and walked away. I watched him disappear into the darkness between two cottages.

I walked up to the green and put my bag down at the foot of the lamppost. I listened for the sound of a vehicle in the distance, but the night was utterly still. Nevertheless, I had been cheered by Roger Button's description of the bus. Moreover, I thought of the reception awaiting me at my journey's end—of the adoring faces of the young people—and felt the stirrings of optimism somewhere deep within me.

—2001

Carol Ann Duffy

b. 1955

As the British newspaper *The Guardian* has put it, "in the world of British poetry, Carol Ann Duffy is a superstar." Lauded by reviewers and by academic critics, her work has also been enormously popular with the general public. This widespread appeal led to her appointment as Poet Laureate of the United Kingdom in 2009—making her the first woman poet, first openly gay poet, and first Scottish poet to occupy the role. Duffy first made her mark in the 1980s as a writer of dramatic monologues, many of them poems of controlled edginess (such as "Stealing") that give voice to tough, working class personae. She has since become equally well known for tightly crafted lyrics of concentrated emotional force, especially on the themes of love and loss.

The eldest child of five, Duffy was born in Glasgow to an Irish mother and Scottish father, and raised largely in the north Midlands town of Stafford, where her father became a member of the local council and was a Labour Party candidate for Parliament. She attended St. Joseph's Convent School and Stafford Girls High School before studying philosophy at Liverpool University. She then worked for some years in London, where she was editor of the poetry magazine *Ambit*. In 1996 Duffy moved to Manchester, and since then she has taught at Manchester Metropolitan University, where in 2005 she was appointed Creative Director of the Writing School.

With her early collections—most notably her first book, *Standing Female Nude* (1985)—Duffy established a reputation as a powerful feminist voice, as a poet of considerable versatility, and as an entertainer equally capable of writing in comic, dramatic, and lyric modes. In *Mean Time* (1993), the emotional as well as technical range of her work broadened. Her 1999 book *The World's Wife* is a striking *tour de force* in which each poem is written in the persona of a wife, sister, or lover of a famous man from history or mythology, from "Mrs. Faust" and "Anne Hathaway" to "Mrs. Lazarus." Her 2005 collection *Rapture* is also a unified work, though of a very different sort; here she presents a chronologically ordered series of poems that trace the emotional trajectory of a relationship of love. *Rapture* is confessedly autobiographical, but in the only interview on the collection that Duffy consented to give, she declined to discuss any specifics: "I could not feel more deeply than I have in these poems," she said, "but these are not journals or diaries or letters, they are works of art. A transformation takes place—it has to, if the feeling is to be revealed to others." Duffy's next major volume, *The Bees* (2011), epitomizes her intellectual and emotional breadth, incorporating poems on war and climate change alongside lyrics on the death of the poet's mother.

Though Duffy's poetry often bristles with contemporaneity in its tone and subject matter, it also exhibits a remarkable range of formal accomplishment; many of her poems follow accentual-syllabic metrical patterns, and many use rhyme extensively. It is perhaps more a reflection on reading habits that took root in the second half of the twentieth century than it is on Duffy's work itself that as formal patterns of rhythm and rhyme began to play a larger and larger role in her work, some began to wonder, in Jeanette Winterson's words, "whether Duffy had lost her balance. Had she stopped writing poetry and slopped into verse?" Unlike many poets who are inclined toward formal complexity, Duffy eschews unusual diction: as she has put it, "I'm not interested, as a poet, in words like 'plash'—Seamus Heaney words, interesting words. I like to use simple words but in a complicated way."

As a lesbian writer, Duffy rejects any exceptionalist status. "I'm not a lesbian poet, whatever that is. If I am a lesbian icon and a role model, that's great, but if it is a word that is used to reduce me, then you have to ask why. … I define myself as a poet and a mother—that's all." Duffy's daughter Ella was born in 1995.

Duffy has written or edited over thirty books, including several plays, collections of poetry for children, and a variety of edited volumes. Among the many awards she has received are the Forward Poetry Prize (in 1993 for *Mean Time*), the Whitbread (now Costa) Poetry Award (in 1993 for *Mean Time* and in 2011 for *The Bees*), and the T.S. Eliot Prize (in 2005 for *Rapture*). She was appointed an Officer of the British Empire in 1993 and a Dame Commander of the British Empire in 2015.

⌘⌘⌘

The Good Teachers

You run round the back to be in it again.
No bigger than your thumbs, those virtuous women
size you up from the front row. Soon now,
Miss Ross will take you for double History.
You breathe on the glass, making a ghost of her, say
South Sea Bubble Defenestration of Prague.[1]

You love Miss Pirie. So much, you are top
of her class. So much, you need two of you
to stare out from the year, serious, passionate.
The River's Tale by Rudyard Kipling[2] by heart.
Her kind intelligent green eye. Her cruel blue one.
You are making a poem up for her in your head.

But not Miss Sheridan. Comment vous appelez.[3]
But not Miss Appleby. Equal to the square
of the other two sides. Never Miss Webb.
Dar es Salaam. Kilimanjaro.[4] Look. The good teachers
swish down the corridor in long, brown skirts,
snobbish and proud and clean and qualified.

And they've got your number. You roll the waistband
of your skirt over and over, all leg, all
dumb insolence, smoke-rings. You won't pass.
You could do better. But there's the wall you climb
into dancing, lovebites, marriage, the Cheltenham
and Gloucester,[5] today. The day you'll be sorry one day.

—1993

[1] *South Sea … Prague* Two unconnected historical incidents.

[2] *Rudyard Kipling* English novelist, poet, and short-story writer who was born in Bombay (1865–1936).

[3] *Comment vous appelez* French: What do you call.

[4] *Dar es Salaam. Kilimanjaro* The largest city and the tallest mountain, respectively, in Tanzania.

[5] *Cheltenham and Gloucester* The name of a commercial bank in the United Kingdom.

Drunk

Suddenly the rain is hilarious.
The moon wobbles in the dusk.

What a laugh. Unseen frogs
belch in the damp grass.

The strange perfumes of darkening trees.
Cheap red wine

and the whole world a mouth.
Give me a double, a kiss.
—1993

Mrs. Lazarus[1]

I had grieved. I had wept for a night and a day
over my loss, ripped the cloth I was married in
from my breasts, howled, shrieked, clawed
at the burial stones till my hands bled, retched
his name over and over again, dead, dead.

Gone home. Gutted the place. Slept in a single cot,
widow, one empty glove, white femur
in the dust, half. Stuffed dark suits
into black bags, shuffled in a dead man's shoes,
noosed the double knot of a tie round my bare neck,

gaunt nun in the mirror, touching herself. I learnt
the Stations of Bereavement, the icon of my face
in each bleak frame; but all those months
he was going away from me, dwindling
to the shrunk size of a snapshot, going,

going. Till his name was no longer a certain spell
for his face. The last hair on his head
floated out from a book. His scent went from the
house.
The will was read. See, he was vanishing
to the small zero held by the gold of my ring.

Then he was gone. Then he was legend, language;
my arm on the arm of the schoolteacher—the shock
of a man's strength under the sleeve of his coat—
along the hedgerows. But I was faithful
for as long as it took. Until he was memory.

So I could stand that evening in the field
in a shawl of fine air, healed, able
to watch the edge of the moon occur to the sky
and a hare thump from a hedge; then notice
the village men running towards me, shouting,

behind them the women and children, barking dogs,
and I knew. I knew by the sly light
on the blacksmith's face, the shrill eyes
of the barmaid, the sudden hands bearing me
into the hot tang of the crowd parting before me.

He lived. I saw the horror on his face.
I heard his mother's crazy song. I breathed
his stench; my bridegroom in his rotting shroud,
moist and dishevelled from the grave's slack chew,
croaking his cuckold name, disinherited, out of his
time.
—1999

[1] *Mrs. Lazarus* In the story recounted in John 11.41–44, "a man named Lazarus" is sick; his sisters Martha and Mary send for Jesus asking for help. Jesus sends a reply asserting that "the sickness will not end in death," but does not come at once to help. When he does arrive a few days later Lazarus is dead and has been entombed for four days, but when Jesus has the stone covering the entrance to the tomb rolled back, Lazarus emerges in his grave-cloths. There is no mention of Lazarus's wife in the biblical account.

Rapture

Thought of by you all day, I think of you.
The birds sing in the shelter of a tree.
Above the prayer of rain, unacred blue,
not paradise, goes nowhere endlessly.
How does it happen that our lives can drift
far from our selves, while we stay trapped in time,
queuing for death? It seems nothing will shift
the pattern of our days, alter the rhyme
we make with loss to assonance with bliss.
Then love comes, like a sudden flight of birds
from earth to heaven after rain. Your kiss,
recalled, unstrings, like pearls, this chain of words.
Huge skies connect us, joining here to there.
Desire and passion on the thinking air.
—2005

John Barleycorn[1]

Although I knew they'd laid him low,
thrashed him, hung him out to dry,
had tortured him with water and with fire,
then dashed his brains out on a stone,
I saw him in the Seven Stars
and in the Plough.[2]
I saw him in the Crescent Moon
and in the Beehive and the Barley Mow,
my green man,[3] newly-born, alive, John Barleycorn.
I saw him seasonally, at harvest time
in the Wheatsheaf and the Load of Hay.
I saw him, heard his laughter,
in the Star and Garter, in the Fountain, in the Bell,
the Corn Dolly,[4] the Woolpack° and the Flowing Spring. *bale of wool*
I saw him in the Rising Sun,
the Moon and Sixpence and the Evening Star.
I saw him in the Rose and Crown,
my green man, ancient, barely born, John Barleycorn.

He moved through Britain, bright and dark
like ale in glass. I saw him run across the fields
towards the Gamekeeper, the Poacher and the Blacksmith's Arms.
He knew the Ram, the Lamb, the Lion and the Swan,
White Hart, Blue Boar, Red Dragon, Fox and Hounds.
I saw him in the Three Goats' Heads,
the Black Bull and Dun Cow,
Shoulder of Mutton, Griffin, Unicorn,
green man, beer borne, good health, long life,
John Barleycorn.

I saw him festively, when people sang
for victory, or love, or New Year's Eve,
in the Raven and the Bird in Hand,
the Golden Eagle, the Kingfisher, the Dove.
I saw him grieve, or mourn, a shadow at the bar
in the Falcon, the Marsh Harrier, the Sparrow Hawk,
the Barn Owl, Cuckoo, Heron, Nightingale;
a pint of bitter in the Jenny Wren
for my green man, alone, forlorn, John Barleycorn.

Britain's soul, as the crow flies so flew he.
I saw him in the Hollybush, the Yew Tree,
the Royal Oak, the Ivy Bush, the Linden.
I saw him in the Forester, the Woodman.

---

[1] *John Barleycorn* Personification of barley, and of beer and whisky made from barley. In the comic British folk song of the same name, he undergoes a series of tortures (thrashing, drowning, burning, etc.) as he is cultivated and transformed into alcohol.

[2] *the Seven Stars … the Plough* The many proper nouns listed in the poem are all names commonly used for British pubs.

[3] *green man* Man dressed in greenery, an English folk figure associated with spring fertility. Green man faces, which combine human features with foliage, often appear in English church decorations but are probably pagan in origin.

[4] *Corn Dolly* Pub named for a figurine traditionally made from the last stalks of grain gathered during the year's harvest.

He history, I saw him in the Wellington, the Nelson,[1]
Greyfriars Bobby,[2] Wicked Lady, Bishop's Finger.
I saw him in the Ship, the Golden Fleece,[3] the Flask,
the Railway Inn, the Robin Hood and Little John,
my green man, legend strong, re-born, John
Barleycorn.

Scythed down, he crawled, knelt, stood.
I saw him in the Crow, Newt, Stag, all weathers,
noon or night. I saw him in the Feathers, Salutation,
Navigation, Knot, the Bricklayer's Arms, Hop Inn,
the Maypole and the Regiment, the Horse and Groom,
the Dog and Duck, the Flag. And where he supped,
the past lived still; and where he sipped, the glass
brimmed full.
He was in the King's Head and Queen's Arms, I saw
him there,
green man, well-born, spellbound, charming one,
John Barleycorn.
—2011

Water

Your last word was *water*,
which I poured in a hospice plastic cup, held
to your lips—your small sip, half-smile, sigh—
then, in the chair beside you,
fell asleep.
Fell asleep for three lost hours,
only to waken, thirsty, hear then see
a magpie warn in a bush outside—
dawn so soon—and swallow from your still-full cup.

Water. The times I'd call as a child
for a drink, till you'd come, sit on the edge
of the bed in the dark, holding my hand,
just as we held hands now and you died.

A good last word.
Nights since I've cried, but gone
to my own child's side with a drink, watched
her gulp it down then sleep. *Water*.
What a mother brings
through darkness still
to her parched daughter.
—2011

[1] *the Wellington* Pub named for Arthur Wellesley, 1st Duke of Wellington (1768–1852), British Prime Minister and military Commander-in-Chief; *the Nelson* Pub named for Viscount Horatio Nelson (1758–1805), British admiral and war hero.

[2] *Greyfriars Bobby* Pub named for a famous nineteenth-century dog said to have guarded his dead master's grave for more than a decade.

[3] *Golden Fleece* Pub named for the mythological fleece of a flying ram, an object of quests in Greek stories.

Jeanette Winterson

b. 1959

Described by one literary journal as having "a reputation as a holy terror, a lesbian desperado and a literary genius," Jeanette Winterson is as complex as her often outlandish and magical characters. Blatantly and often outrageously self-promoting and outspoken, she tells numerous (sometimes conflicting) stories about her own past. Best known for her numerous novels, Winterson has also written many short stories, a collection of essays on art and culture, a television screenplay on aviation, regular columns in newspapers, a radio drama, a theatrical play, and children's books. In her fiction, Winterson continues to experiment in language, form, and subject matter, bringing surreal elements down to earth and "marginal" characters to the fore.

Winterson was born in Manchester in 1959 and raised by adoptive Evangelical parents in a small town in Lancashire, where her father, John Winterson, worked in a factory. Her mother, Constance Brownrigg Winterson, was very religious and raised her daughter to be a preacher and missionary. There were few books in the house other than religious texts; Winterson's mother was said to have read *Jane Eyre* to her, but in doing so to have changed the ending so that Jane marries St. John Rivers, a missionary, rather than the "immoral" Rochester. In her sixteenth year Winterson admitted to having an affair with a young woman whom she had converted to the Pentecostal church, and both her mother and others in the church denounced her and attempted to exorcise her "demon." This incident led to Winterson's leaving her family home that year and working at odd jobs—driving an ice-cream truck, putting makeup on cadavers at a funeral home, working as an orderly in a hospital for the mentally ill—in order to put herself through school.

Eventually Winterson studied at Oxford, earning a degree in English in 1982. A few years later, during an interview with Pandora House (where she succeeded in obtaining a job as an editor), she related some aspects of her life to her interviewer. Philippa Brewster found the details fascinating, but she was also impressed with the eloquent and creative way in which Winterson told her stories. Thus encouraged to put her thoughts into print, Winterson created her first novel, *Oranges Are Not the Only Fruit* (1985), in which a fictional character named Jeanette is manipulated by a fundamentalist religious mother, Mrs. Winterson. When Jeanette enters into a romantic relationship with a girl, her mother denounces her and attempts, with the help of the church, to exorcise her "demons." Although Winterson does admit that she was "trying to make sense of a bizarre childhood and an unusual personal history," she insists that her story is fictional, with its embedded fairy tales and a narrator who at times speaks directly to the reader. Described as a "daring, unconventionally comic novel" by the *Chicago Tribune*, *Oranges* won England's Whitbread First Novel Award and earned substantial public and critical acclaim.

Winterson's second novel, *Boating for Beginners*, followed *Oranges* in the same year. Her third novel, *The Passion* (1987), solidified Winterson's reputation in the literary world. Based partly on historical events, *The Passion* uses magic realism to tell the story of Henri—an androgynous military cook who works to feed Napoleon and his army—and Villanelle, the Venetian gondolier's daughter who, beautiful and web-footed, incites passion in both men and women.

Sexing the Cherry (1989) and *Written on the Body* (1992) confirmed Winterson's reputation as a major novelist and delve even further into issues of gender and sexuality. Like much of Winterson's work, *Sexing the Cherry* is highly allusive, deconstructing earlier stories—in this case fairy tales—while constructing new versions of them; for example, in one narrative a princess does not seek marriage, but escapes from it "like a bird from a snare." *Written on the Body* recounts a love affair between a woman and a narrator whose gender is never identified. This novel was also groundbreaking in its conflation of genres: the narrator, who at times directly addresses the reader and at times does not, also offers meditations, essayistic writing on various topics, and aphorisms, creating a narrative in which the epistemological reality of the story itself is rendered unstable. Winterson continued to take a postmodern approach to storytelling in works such as the science-fiction novel *The Stone Gods* (2007), a self-referential examination of environmental apocalypse in which characters and events recur throughout history.

In 2011, Winterson returned to the childhood experiences underlying her first novel, this time in a direct autobiography, the critically acclaimed *Why Be Happy When You Could Be Normal?* Her next work returned to the pattern of a historical novel with a fantastical element—this time a gothic one. In *The Daylight Gate* (2012), set during the seventeenth-century witchcraft trials in Pendle, England, magic is real but, as a *Guardian* reviewer observes, "true horror lies" not in witchcraft but in the violence associated with the subjugation of women, children, and others. With works such as these, Winterson continues to expand the boundaries of traditional genres, blending satire and magical realism to create experimental narratives that ask us to rethink what we think we know and understand. As Winterson wrote in her book *Art and Lies* (1994), "The rebellion of art is a daily rebellion against the state of living death routinely called real life." In 2018, she was made a Commander of the Order of the British Empire (CBE) for her contributions to literature.

⌘⌘⌘

from *Oranges Are Not the Only Fruit*

from GENESIS

Like most people I lived for a long time with my mother and father. My father liked to watch the wrestling, my mother liked to wrestle; it didn't matter what. She was in the white corner and that was that.

She hung out the largest sheets on the windiest days. She *wanted* the Mormons to knock on the door. At election time in a Labour mill town she put a picture of the Conservative candidate in the window.

She had never heard of mixed feelings. There were friends and there were enemies.

Enemies were:	The Devil (in his many forms)
	Next Door
	Sex (in its many forms)
	Slugs
Friends were:	God
	Our dog
	Auntie Madge
	The Novels of Charlotte Brontë[1]
	Slug pellets

and me, at first, I had been brought in to join her in a tag match against the Rest of the World. She had a mysterious attitude towards the begetting of children; it

[1] *Charlotte Brontë* English writer best known for her novel *Jane Eyre* (1847).

wasn't that she couldn't do it, more that she didn't want to do it. She was very bitter about the Virgin Mary getting there first. So she did the next best thing and arranged for a foundling. That was me.

I cannot recall a time when I did not know that I was special. We had no Wise Men[1] because she didn't believe there were any wise men, but we had sheep. One of my earliest memories is me sitting on a sheep at Easter while she told me the story of the Sacrificial Lamb.[2] We had it on Sundays with potato.

Sunday was the Lord's day, the most vigorous day of the whole week; we had a radiogram[3] at home with an imposing mahogany front and a fat Bakelite knob to twiddle for the stations. Usually we listened to the Light Programme, but on Sundays always the World Service,[4] so that my mother could record the progress of our missionaries. Our Missionary Map was very fine. On the front were all the countries and on the back a number chart that told you about Tribes and their Peculiarities. My favourite was Number 16, *The Buzule of Carpathian*. They believed that if a mouse found your hair clippings and built a nest with them you got a headache. If the nest was big enough, you might go mad. As far as I knew no missionary had yet visited them.

My mother got up early on Sundays and allowed no one into the parlour until ten o'clock. It was her place of prayer and meditation. She always prayed standing up, because of her knees, just as Bonaparte always gave orders from his horse, because of his size.[5] I do think that the relationship my mother enjoyed with God had a lot to do with positioning. She was Old Testament through and through. Not for her the meek and paschal[6] Lamb, she was out there, up front with the prophets, and much given to sulking under trees when the appropriate destruction didn't materialise. Quite often it did, her will or the Lord's I can't say.

She always prayed in exactly the same way. First of all she thanked God that she had lived to see another day, and then she thanked God for sparing the world another day. Then she spoke of her enemies, which was the nearest thing she had to a catechism.

As soon as "Vengeance is mine saith the Lord" boomed through the wall into the kitchen, I put the kettle on. The time it took to boil the water and brew the tea was just about the length of her final item, the sick list. She was very regular. I put the milk in, in she came, and taking a great gulp of tea said one of three things.

"The Lord is good" (steely-eyed into the back yard).

"What sort of tea is this?" (steely-eyed at me).

"Who was the oldest man in the Bible?"

No. 3 of course, had a number of variations, but it was always a Bible quiz question. We had a lot of Bible quizzes at church and my mother liked me to win. If I knew the answer she asked me another, if I didn't she got cross, but luckily not for long, because we had to listen to the World Service. It was always the same; we sat down on either side of the radiogram, she with her tea, me with a pad and pencil; in front of us, the Missionary Map. The faraway voice in the middle of the set gave news of activities, converts and problems. At the end there was an appeal for YOUR PRAYERS. I had to write it all down so that my mother could deliver her church report that night. She was the Missionary Secretary. The Missionary Report was a great trial to me because our mid-day meal depended upon it. If it went well, no deaths and lots of converts, my mother cooked a joint.[7] If the Godless had proved not only stubborn, but murderous, my mother spent the rest of the morning listening to the Jim Reeves Devotional Selection,

---

[1] *Wise Men* In Matthew 2.1–12, three wise men bring gifts to the infant Jesus: frankincense, gold, and myrrh.

[2] *Sacrificial Lamb* In John 1.29, Jesus is described by John the Baptist as the "Lamb of God," an innocent sacrifice who will "taketh away the sin of the world."

[3] *radiogram* Piece of furniture that houses both a radio and a record player or gramophone.

[4] *Light Programme* BBC (British Broadcasting Corporation) entertainment radio station that ran from 1945 to 67; *World Service* BBC radio network founded in 1932.

[5] *Bonaparte … size* French emperor and general Napoleon Bonaparte (1769–1821) was 5 feet 2 inches tall.

[6] *paschal* Related to Easter, the Christian celebration of the resurrection of Christ.

[7] *joint* Portion of meat, usually a leg or shoulder.

and we had to have boiled eggs and toast soldiers.[1] Her husband was an easy-going man, but I knew it depressed him. He would have cooked it himself but for my mother's complete conviction that she was the only person in our house who would tell a saucepan from a piano. She was wrong, as far as we were concerned, but right as far as she was concerned, and really, that's what mattered.

Somehow we got through those mornings, and in the afternoon she and I took the dog for a walk, while my father cleaned all the shoes. "You can tell someone by their shoes," my mother said. "Look at Next Door."

"Drink," said my mother grimly as we stepped out past their house. "That's why they buy everything from Maxi Ball's Catalogue Seconds. The Devil himself is a drunk" (sometimes my mother invented theology).

Maxi Ball owned a warehouse, his clothes were cheap but they didn't last, and they smelt of industrial glue. The desperate, the careless, the poorest, vied with one another on a Saturday morning to pick up what they could, and haggle over the price. My mother would rather not eat than be seen at Maxi Ball's. She had filled me with a horror of the place. Since so many people we knew went there, it was hardly fair of her but she never was particularly fair; she loved and she hated, and she hated Maxi Ball. Once, in winter, she had been forced to go there to buy a corset and in the middle of communion, that very Sunday, a piece of whalebone[2] slipped out and stabbed her right in the stomach. There was nothing she could do for an hour. When we got home she tore up the corset and used the whalebone as supports for our geraniums, except for one piece that she gave to me. I still have it, and whenever I'm tempted to cut corners I think about that whalebone and I know better.

My mother and I walked on towards the hill that stood at the top of our street. We lived in a town stolen from the valleys, a huddled place full of chimneys and little shops and back-to-back houses with no gardens. The hills surrounded us, and our own swept out into the Pennines,[3] broken now and again with a farm or a relic from the war. There used to be a lot of old tanks but the council took them away. The town was a fat blot and the streets spread back from it into the green, steadily upwards. Our house was almost at the top of a long, stretchy street. A flagged[4] street with a cobbly road. When you climb to the top of the hill and look down you can see everything, just like Jesus on the pinnacle except it's not very tempting.[5] Over to the right was the viaduct and behind the viaduct Ellison's tenement, where we had the fair once a year. I was allowed to go there on condition I brought back a tub of black peas for my mother. Black peas look like rabbit droppings and they come in a thin gravy made of stock and gypsy mush. They taste wonderful. The gypsies made a mess and stayed up all night and my mother called them fornicators but on the whole we got on very well. They turned a blind eye to toffee apples going missing, and sometimes, if it was quiet and you didn't have enough money, they still let you have a ride on the dodgems.[6] We used to have fights round the caravans, the ones like me, from the street, against the posh ones from the Avenue. The posh ones went to Brownies and didn't stay for school dinners.

Once, when I was collecting the black peas, about to go home, the old woman got hold of my hand. I thought she was going to bite me. She looked at my palm and laughed a bit. "You'll never marry," she said, "not you, and you'll never be still." She didn't take any money for the peas, and she told me to run home fast. I ran and ran, trying to understand what she meant. I hadn't thought about getting married anyway. There were two women I knew who didn't have any husbands at all; they were old though, as old as my mother. They

[1] *Jim Reeves Devotional Selection* Gospel songs by country music singer Jim Reeves (1923–64); *toast soldiers* Toast cut into thin strips for dipping into a soft-boiled egg.

[2] *whalebone* Baleen, often called whalebone, was used to structure corsets.

[3] *Pennines* Range of mountains separating North West and North East England.

[4] *flagged* Paved with flagstones.

[5] *Jesus … tempting* In Luke 4.9, the devil tempts Christ by setting him on the pinnacle of the temple in Jerusalem, saying that if he really were the Son of God he could cast himself off without injury.

[6] *dodgems* Bumper cars.

ran the paper shop and sometimes, on a Wednesday, they gave me a banana bar with my comic. I liked them a lot, and talked about them a lot to my mother. One day they asked me if I'd like to go to the seaside with them. I ran home, gabbled it out, and was busy emptying my money box to buy a new spade, when my mother said firmly and forever, no. I couldn't understand why not, and she wouldn't explain. She didn't even let me go back to say I couldn't. Then she cancelled my comic and told me to collect it from another shop, further away. I was sorry about that. I never got a banana bar from Grimsby's. A couple of weeks later I heard her telling Mrs White about it. She said they dealt in unnatural passions. I thought she meant they put chemicals in their sweets.

My mother and I climbed until the town fell away and we reached the memorial stone at the very top. The wind was always strong so that my mother had to wear extra hat pins. Usually she wore a headscarf, but not on Sunday. We sat on the stone's base and she thanked the Lord we had managed the ascent. Then she extemporised on the nature of the world, the folly of its peoples, and the wrath of God inevitable. After that she told me a story about a brave person who had despised the fruits of the flesh and worked for the Lord instead. …

There was the story of the "converted sweep," a filthy degenerate, given to drunkenness and vice, who suddenly found the Lord whilst scraping the insides of a flue. He remained in the flue in a state of rapture for so long that his friends thought he was unconscious. After a great deal of difficulty they persuaded him to come out; his face, they declared, though hardly visible for the grime, shone like an angel's. He started to lead the Sunday School and died some time later, bound for glory. There were many more; I particularly like the "Hallelujah Giant," a freak of nature, eight feet tall shrunk to six foot three through the prayers of the faithful.

Now and again my mother liked to tell me her own conversion story; it was very romantic. I sometimes think that if Mills and Boon[1] were at all revivalist in their policy my mother would be a star.

One night, by mistake, she had walked into Pastor Spratt's Glory Crusade. It was in a tent on some spare land, and every evening Pastor Spratt spoke of the fate of the damned, and performed healing miracles. He was very impressive. My mother said he looked like Errol Flynn,[2] but holy. A lot of women found the Lord that week. Part of Pastor Spratt's charisma stemmed from his time spent as an advertising manager for Rathbone's Wrought Iron. He knew about bait. "There is nothing wrong with bait," he said, when the *Chronicle* somewhat cynically asked him why he gave pot plants to the newly converted. "We are commanded to be Fishers of Men."[3] When my mother heard the call, she was presented with a copy of the Psalms and asked to make her choice between a Christmas Cactus (non-flowering) and a lily of the valley. She had opted for the lily of the valley. When my father went the next night, she told him to be sure and go for the cactus, but by the time he got to the front they had all gone. "He's not one to push himself," she often said, and after a little pause, "Bless him."

Pastor Spratt came to stay with them for the rest of his time with the Glory Crusade, and it was then that my mother discovered her abiding interest in missionary work. The pastor himself spent most of his time out in the jungle and other hot places converting the Heathen. We have a picture of him surrounded by black men with spears. My mother keeps it by her bed. My mother is very like William Blake; she has visions and dreams and she cannot always distinguish a flea's head from a king.[4] Luckily she can't paint.

She walked out one night and thought of her life and thought of what was possible. She thought of the

[1] *Mills and Boon* Imprint of British romance publisher Harlequin Inc.

[2] *Errol Flynn* Australian-American film actor (1909–59), famous for his roles as a romantic lead.

[3] *Fishers of Men* In Matthew 4.18–20, Christ walks by the Sea of Galilee and meets two fishers, the brothers Peter and Andrew. Christ says "Follow me, and I will make you fishers of men." The two put down their nets and become apostles.

[4] *William Blake* English poet, artist, and visionary (1757–1827). Blake claimed that his work was inspired by—and even dictated by—archangels and other spirits of whom he had visions; *flea's head from a king* In 1819–20, Blake drew a series of portraits of his visions of historical figures and other beings, known now as *The Visionary Heads*; one of these is entitled "The Visionary Head of the Ghost of a Flea" (c. 1819).

things she couldn't be. Her uncle had been an actor. "A very fine Hamlet," said the *Chronicle*.

But the rags and the ribbons turn to years and then the years are gone. Uncle Will had died a pauper, she was not so young these days and people were not kind. She liked to speak French and to play the piano, but what do these things mean?

Once upon a time there was a brilliant and beautiful princess, so sensitive that the death of a moth could distress her for weeks on end. Her family knew of no solution. Advisers wrung their hands, sages shook their heads, brave kinds left unsatisfied. So it happened for many years, until one day, out walking in the forest, the princess came to the hut of an old hunchback who knew the secrets of magic. This ancient creature perceived in the princess a woman of great energy and resourcefulness.

"My dear," she said, "you are in danger of being burned by your own flame."

The hunchback told the princess that she was old, and wished to die, but could not because of her many responsibilities. She had in her charge a small village of homely people, to whom she was advisor and friend. Perhaps the princess would like to take over? Her duties would be:

(1) To milk the goats
(2) To educate the people
(3) To compose songs for their festival

To assist her she would have a three-legged stool and all the books belonging to the hunchback. Best of all, the old woman's harmonium, an instrument of great antiquity and four octaves. The princess agreed to stay and forgot all about the palace and the moths. The old woman thanked her, and died at once.

My mother, out walking that night, dreamed a dream and sustained it in daylight. She would get a child, train it, build it, dedicate it to the Lord:

a missionary child,
a servant of God,
a blessing

And so it was that on a particular day, some time later, she followed a star until it came to settle above an orphanage, and in that place was a crib, and in that crib, a child. A child with too much hair.

She said, "This child is mine from the Lord."

She took the child away and for seven days and seven nights the child cried out, for fear and not knowing. The mother sang to the child, and stabbed the demons. She understood how jealous the Spirit is of flesh.

Such warm tender flesh.

Her flesh now, sprung from her head.[1]

Her vision.

Not the jolt beneath the hip bone, but water and the word.

She had a way out now, for years and years to come.

We stood on the hill and my mother said, "This world is full of sin."

We stood on the hill and my mother said, "You can change the world." …

—1985

[1] *sprung from her head* In Greek mythology, Athena, the goddess of wisdom, is born from the head of the god-king Zeus.

Zadie Smith

b. 1975

By age twenty-five, Zadie Smith had become a literary super star. Her first novel, *White Teeth*, was published in 2000 to widespread acclaim, prompting critics to declare her the most important British writer to appear since Salman Rushdie. In the years since her debut, Smith has lived up to her initial promise and matured into a highly respected author, educator, and social commentator. Smith's essays are valued for their emotional depth and intellectual vibrancy; as a novelist she is renowned for her compelling evocation of multicultural London, her psychologically astute portrayal of an extraordinarily wide range of characters, and her continually evolving narrative style.

Born Sadie Smith in a working-class North London borough to a black Jamaican mother and a white English father, Smith changed her first name to Zadie at the age of 14. In 1998 she earned a BA in English Literature from King's College, Cambridge, where she published short stories in the Oxford/Cambridge Mays Anthologies of student writing. After working on the draft of *White Teeth* over her last year at Cambridge, Smith sent an incomplete manuscript to the high-profile literary agent Andrew Wylie. A competition for the right to publish the text ensued, which concluded when the publishing house Hamish Hamilton offered Smith a rumored £250,000 advance—an extraordinary amount for a previously unknown author. *White Teeth* proved to be a major success and was one of the bestselling books of 2001.

White Teeth was celebrated for its textured depiction of the multicultural society that Britain had become at the turn of the twenty-first century. As the novel's narrator reflects, "This has been the century of strangers, brown, yellow, and white. This has been the century of the great immigrant experiment." Over the course of *White Teeth*'s complicated plot, races, religions, cultures, customs, and personalities all clash in the polyglot melting pot of North London. The novel's acute social observation encompasses both psychologically realist characters and satirically absurd caricatures (a group of violent Islamic extremists, for example, operates under the acronym KEVIN). Despite its overwhelmingly positive reception, *White Teeth* was not without critics. Most notably, James Wood lamented the squandering of Smith's talent on a genre he called "hysterical realism"—a cartoonish representation of existence, rather than a "picture of life"—positioning her book as typical of a movement in which he also included David Foster Wallace and Thomas Pynchon. Another scathing review denounced the novel as "the literary equivalent of a hyperactive, ginger-haired, tap-dancing 10-year-old"; this review turned out to have been composed by Smith herself.

The BBC released a miniseries based on *White Teeth* in 2002, and the same year saw the publication of Smith's second novel, *The Autograph Man*, about a Londoner of Chinese and Jewish descent who makes his living buying and selling autographs. Smith's third novel, *On Beauty* (2005), focuses on a rivalry between two university professors: the white, English, liberal atheist Howard Belsey and the black, Trinidadian, conservative Christian Monty Kipps. In these, as in all of her works of fiction, Smith imagines the lived experiences of wildly different people. "I am explicitly a voyeur," she explains. "That's why I started writing: because I wanted to know what it's like to be a Jewish Chinese guy or an old black woman or white professor or whatever. That is my absolute intention to get under the skin."

Prior to the publication of her fourth novel, *NW* (2012), Smith released a work of nonfiction, *Changing My Mind: Occasional Essays* (2009), served as a reviewer for *Harper's Magazine*, and contributed numerous essays and opinion pieces to such publications as *The Guardian* and *The New York Review of Books*. Smith's articles touch on music and popular culture—she famously interviewed rapper Jay-Z, whom she compared to Chaucer—as well as technology and politics. Despite her interest in contemporary social justice issues, Smith refuses to identify too closely with any particular political figure. "Any artist who aligns themselves with a politician is making a category error," she claims. "[W]hat politicians do is not on a human scale, it is on a geopolitical scale." Smith published a second collection of essays, *Feel Free*, in 2018.

NW's title references the postcode of the working-class London neighborhood that provides the novel's background, and its story concerns the efforts of four characters to navigate adulthood. Written in a free indirect style, the novel leaps between first- and third-person perspectives. *NW* was taken by many critics to exemplify the approach Smith had championed in her 2008 essay "Two Paths for the Novel," in which she argued against the dominance of a certain "breed of lyrical Realism" in the literary world, claiming that experimentation in form, language, and character are necessary if the novel is really to convey human experience instead of merely indulging "the fears and weaknesses of its readers." In *Swing Time* (2016), Smith limits herself to first-person narration, describing the lives and sexual explorations of two biracial girls who meet at tap-dancing class in 1982. "The whole book to me is about power relations—between people, countries, races," Smith has remarked. "I was interested in the people on the edges."

In addition to her work as an author of fiction and nonfiction, Smith has also dedicated significant time to teaching creative writing. After posts at Harvard and Columbia, she was appointed Professor of Creative Writing at New York University in 2010. Smith regards her contact with students as an invaluable means to stay in touch with emerging literary trends and changing social attitudes. "Having [a] conversation every Monday and Tuesday with 12 19- and 20-year-olds has been extremely useful for me," she observes. "I hope it's been useful for them." Smith is married to fellow writer Nick Laird, with whom she has two children.

Smith continues to examine in much of her work the complexity and hybridity of contemporary British life, particularly issues of race and class. She also remains fearlessly experimental in her narrative technique. In her essay "Fail Better" she says, "When I write I am trying to express my way of being[.] … This is primarily a process of elimination: once you have removed all the dead language, the second-hand dogma, the truths that are not your own but other people's, the mottos, the slogans, the out-and-out lies of your nation, the myths of your historical moment—once you have removed all that warps experience into a shape you do not recognize and do not believe in—what you are left with is something approximating the truth of your own conception."

⌘⌘⌘

The Waiter's Wife[1]

In the spring of 1975, Samad and Alsana Iqbal left Bangladesh and came to live in Whitechapel,[2] London, the other side of town from Archie and Clara Jones. Samad and Archie had a friendship dating back to the Second World War, back to the hot and claustrophobic Churchill tank[3] in which they sat side by side for three months, close enough to smell each other and to recognize those scents thirty years later when Samad emerged from Gate 12, Heathrow, with a young wife and a paisley patterned luggage set in tow. "Long time no see," Archie had said, reaching out to grasp his old friend's palm, but Samad converted the handshake into a hug almost immediately, "*Archibald Jones*. Long time no bloody *smell*."

They fell back into easy conversation, two old boys slipping swiftly into an acquaintance as comfortable as slippers while their wives stood either side of the bags noting they had this thing in common and no more: that they were young, much younger than the men they stood awkwardly beside. They looked an unlikely pair. Alsana was small and rotund, moon-faced and with thick fingers she hid in the folds of her cardigan. Clara was tall, striking, a black girl with a winning smile, wearing red shorts of a shortness that Alsana had never imagined possible, even in this country.

"Hot pants," said Clara, shyly, in response to Alsana's wide eyes, "I made dem myself."

"I sew also," Alsana replied, and they had a pleasant enough chat about seams and bobbins, materials and prices per yard, in a motorway service station over an indigestible lunch. "The wives get on like a house on fire," Archie had said merrily, giving Samad a nudge in the ribs. But this made them nervous, the two young wives, and after the ice-cream sundaes they sat in silence.

So some black people *are* friendly, thought Alsana after that first meeting was over. It was her habit to single one shining exception out of every minority she disliked; certain dentists, certain singers, certain film stars had been granted specialist treatment in the past and now Clara Jones was to be given Alsana's golden reprieve. Their relations were hesitant in the beginning—a few lunch dates here and there, the occasional coffee; neither wished to admit how much time they had on their hands though newly wed, or that Archie and Samad were always together. It wasn't until the Iqbals moved north, two minutes from Archie and his favourite watering hole, that the women truly resigned themselves to their husbands' mutual appreciation society and started something of a rearguard action. Picnics, the movies, museums, swimming pools—just the two of them. But even when they became fairly close, it was impossible to forget what a peculiar couple they made on the bus, in the park.

It took the Iqbals a year to get to Willesden High Road: a year of mercilessly hard graft[4] to make the momentous move from the wrong side of Whitechapel to the wrong side of Willesden.[5] A year's worth of Alsana banging away at the old Singer machine that sat in the kitchen, sewing together pieces of black plastic for a shop called Domination in Soho (many were the nights Alsana would hold up a piece of clothing she had just made—following the plans she was given—and wonder what on earth it was). A year's worth of Samad softly inclining his head at exactly the correct deferential angle, pencil in his right hand, notepad in his left, listening to the appalling pronunciation of the British, Spanish, American, French, Australian:

Go Bye Ello Sag,[6] Please.

Chicken Jail Fret See[7] Wiv Chips, Fanks.

From six in the evening until four in the morning was work and the rest was sleep, sleep without pause, until daylight was as rare as a decent tip. For what is the

---

[1] *The Waiter's Wife* This short story, published in *Granta* in 1999, was drawn from the manuscript of Smith's novel *White Teeth*; the completed novel would be published the following year.

[2] *Whitechapel* East London district where a large proportion of residents are of Bangladeshi background.

[3] *Churchill tank* Tank used by British forces during World War II.

[4] *graft* British slang: work.

[5] *Willesden* Ethnically diverse district in Northwest London.

[6] *Go Bye Ello Sag* I.e., Gobi Aloo Saag, a South Asian dish made with cauliflower, potato, and spinach.

[7] *Chicken Jail Fret See* I.e., Chicken Jalfrezi, a spicy curry dish.

point, Samad would think, pushing aside two mints and a receipt to find fifteen pence, what is the point of tipping a man the same amount you would throw in a fountain to chase a wish? But before the illegal thought of folding the fifteen pence discreetly in his napkin hand had a chance to give itself form, Mukhul, Ardashir Mukhul, who ran The Palace and whose wiry frame paced the restaurant, one benevolent eye on the customers, one ever-watchful eye on the staff—Ardashir Mukhul was upon him.

"Saaamaad," he said in his cloying, oleaginous[1] way, "did you kiss the necessary backside this evening, Cousin?"

Samad and Ardashir were distant cousins, Samad the elder by six years. With what joy (pure bliss!) had Ardashir opened the letter last January, to find his older, cleverer, handsomer cousin could get no work as a food inspector in England and could he possibly…

"Fifteen pence, Cousin," said Samad lifting his palm.

"Well, every little helps, every little helps," said Ardashir, his dead-fish lips stretching into a stringy smile. "Into the Piss-Pot with it."

The Piss-Pot was a black cooking pot that sat on a plinth outside the staff toilets into which all tips were pooled and then split at the end of the night. For the younger, good-looking waiters like Shiva this was a great injustice. Shiva was the only Hindu on the staff, a tribute to his waitering skills that had triumphed over religious difference. He could make fifteen pounds in tips in an evening if the blubberous white divorcee in the corner was lonely enough, and he batted his long lashes at her effectively. He also made money from the polo-necked directors and producers (The Palace sat in the centre of London's Theatreland) who flattered the boy, watched his ass wiggle provocatively to the bar and back, and swore that the next time someone put *A Passage to India*[2] on the stage, the casting couch would be his. For Shiva then, the Piss-Pot system was simply daylight robbery. But for men like Samad, in his forties, and for the even older, like the white-haired Mohammed (Ardashir's great-uncle), who was eighty if he was a day, who had deep pathways dug into the sides of his mouth where he had smiled when he was young—for men like this the Piss-Pot could not be complained about. It was a boon if anything, and it made more sense to join the collective than pocket fifteen pence and risk being caught (and docked a week's tips).

"You're all on my back!" Shiva would snarl, when he had to relinquish five pounds at the end of the night and drop it into the pot. "You all live off my back! Somebody get these losers off my back! That was my fiver and now it's going to be split sixty-five-fucking-million ways as a hand out to these losers! What is this, communism?"

And the rest would avoid his glare, and busy themselves quietly with other things until one evening, one fifteen-pence evening, Samad said, "Shut up, boy," quietly, almost underneath his breath.

"You!" Shiva swung round to where Samad stood crushing a great tub of lentils for tomorrow's dhal.[3] "You're the worst of them! You're the worst fucking waiter I've ever seen! You couldn't get a tip if you mugged the bastards! I hear you trying to talk to the customer about biology this, politics that—just serve the food, you idiot—you're a waiter, for fuck's sake, you're not Michael Parkinson.[4] *Did I hear you say Delhi—*" Shiva put his apron over his arm and began posturing around the kitchen (he was a pitiful mimic) "*—I was there myself, you know, Delhi University, it was most fascinating, yes—and I fought in the war, for England, yes—yes, yes, charming, charming—*" round and round the kitchen he went, bending his head and rubbing his hands over and over like Uriah Heep,[5] bowing and genuflecting to the head cook, to the old man arranging great hunks of meat in the walk-in freezer, to the young boy scrubbing the inside of the oven. "Samad, *Samad*

[1] *oleaginous* Oily, insincere.

[2] *A Passage to India* Santha Rama Rau's theatrical adaptation (1960) of E.M. Forster's 1924 novel set in India during British colonial rule.

[3] *dhal* Spicy South Asian dish made with lentils, tomatoes, onions, and various seasonings.

[4] *Michael Parkinson* British television personality whose popular talk show *Parkinson* ran on the BBC network from 1971–82.

[5] *Uriah Heep* Insincerely humble character from Charles Dickens's *David Copperfield* (1849–50).

…" he said with what seemed infinite pity, then stopped abruptly, pulled the apron off and wrapped it round his waist, "you're a sad bastard."

Mohammed looked up from his pot-scrubbing and shook his head again and again. To no one in particular he said, "These young people—what kind of talk? What happened to respect? What kind of talk is this?"

"And you, you can fuck off too—" said Shiva, brandishing a ladle in his direction, "—You old fool! You're not my father."

"Second cousin of your mother's uncle," a voice muttered from the back.

"Bollocks," said Shiva. "Bollocks to that."

He grabbed the mop and was heading off for the toilets, when he stopped by Samad and placed the broom inches from Samad's mouth.

"Kiss it," he sneered: and then impersonating Ardashir's sluggish drawl, "Who knows, Cousin, you might get a raise!"

And that's what it was like most nights; abuse from Shiva and others; condescension from Ardashir; never seeing Alsana; never seeing the sun; clutching fifteen pence and then releasing it; wanting desperately to be wearing a sign, a large white placard that said:

I AM NOT A WAITER. THAT IS, I AM A WAITER, BUT NOT JUST A WAITER. I HAVE BEEN A STUDENT, A SCIENTIST, A SOLDIER. MY WIFE IS CALLED ALSANA. WE LIVE IN EAST LONDON BUT WE WOULD LIKE TO MOVE NORTH. I AM A MUSLIM BUT ALLAH HAS FORSAKEN ME OR I HAVE FORSAKEN ALLAH. I'M NOT SURE. I HAVE AN ENGLISH FRIEND—ARCHIE—AND OTHERS. I AM FORTY-NINE BUT WOMEN STILL TURN IN THE STREET. SOMETIMES.

But no such placard existing, he had instead the urge, the need, to speak to every man, and like the Ancient Mariner[1] to explain, always to explain, to reassert something, anything. Wasn't that important? But then the heartbreaking disappointment—to find out that the inclining of one's head, poising of one's pen, these were important, so important. It was important to be a good waiter, to listen when someone said:

Lamb Dawn Sock[2] and Rice. Please. With Chips. Thank you.

And fifteen pence clinked on china. Thank you Sir. Thank you so very much.

One evening, shortly after he had put the down payment on the Willesden flat, Samad had waited till everyone left and then climbed the loudly carpeted stairs to Ardashir's office, for he had something to ask him.

"Cousin!" said Ardashir with a friendly grimace at the sight of Samad's body curling cautiously round the door. He knew that Samad had come to enquire about a pay increase, and he wanted his cousin to feel that he had at least considered the case in all his friendly judiciousness before he declined.

"Cousin, come in!"

"Good evening, Ardashir Mukhul," said Samad, stepping fully into the room.

"Sit down, sit down," said Ardashir warmly. "No point standing on ceremony now, is there?"

Samad was glad this was so. He said as much. He took a moment to look with the necessary admiration around the room with its relentless flashes of gold, its thick pile carpet, its furnishings in various shades of yellow and green. One had to admire Ardashir's business sense. He had taken the simple idea of an Indian restaurant (small room, pink tablecloth, loud music, atrocious wallpaper, meals) and just made it bigger. He hadn't improved anything; it was the same old crap but bigger in a bigger building in the biggest tourist trap in London. Leicester Square.[3] You had to admire it and admire the man, who now sat like a benign locust, his slender insectile body swamped in a black leather chair,

[1] *Ancient Mariner* Title character of Samuel Taylor Coleridge's poem *The Rime of the Ancient Mariner* (1798), who is compelled to wander the land and recount the events that followed his killing of an albatross, an act that doomed the rest of his crew to death at sea.

[2] *Lamb Dawn Sock* I.e., Lamb Dhansak, a curry dish made with lamb, squash, and lentils.

[3] *Leicester Square* Entertainment and tourism hub in London's West End.

leaning over the desk, all smiles, a parasite disguised as a philanthropist.

"Cousin, what can I do for you?"

Samad took a deep breath. The matter was … what was the matter? The house was the matter. Samad was moving out of East London (where one couldn't bring up children, indeed, one couldn't, not if one didn't wish them to come to bodily harm), from East London, with its National Front[1] gangs, to North London, north-west in fact, where things were more … more … liberal. Ardashir's eyes glazed over a little as Samad explained his situation. His skinny legs twitched beneath the desk, and in his fingers he manipulated a paperclip until it looked reasonably like an *A*. *A* for Ardashir.

"I need only a small wage increase to help me finance the move. To make things a little easier as we settle in. And Alsana, well, she is pregnant."

Pregnant. Difficult. Ardashir realized the case called for extreme diplomacy.

"Don't mistake me, Samad, we are both intelligent, frank men and I think I can speak frankly … I know you're not a *fucking* waiter—" he whispered the expletive and smiled indulgently after it, as if it were a naughty, private thing that brought them closer together, "I see your position … of course I do … but you must understand mine … If I made allowances for every relative I employ I'd be walking around like bloody Mr. Gandhi.[2] Without a pot to piss in. Spinning my thread by the light of the moon. An example: at this very moment that wastrel Fat Elvis brother-in-law of mine, Hussein Ishmael—"

"The butcher?"

"The butcher, demands that I should raise the price I pay for his stinking meat! 'But Ardashir, we are brothers-in-law!' he is saying to me. And I am saying to him, but Mohammed, this is *retail* …"

It was Samad's turn to glaze over. He thought of his wife, Alsana, who was not as meek as he had assumed when they married, to whom he must deliver the bad news: Alsana, who was prone to moments, even fits—yes, fits was not too strong a word—of rage. Cousins, aunts, brothers thought it a bad sign. They wondered if there wasn't some "funny mental history" in Alsana's family, they sympathized with him the way you sympathize with a man who has bought a stolen car with more mileage on it than first thought. In his naivety Samad had simply assumed a woman so young would be … easy. But Alsana was not … no, she was not easy. It was, he supposed, the way with young women these days.

Ardashir came to the end of what he felt was his perfectly worded speech, sat back satisfied, and laid the *M* for Mukhul he had moulded next to the *A* for Ardashir that sat on his lap.

"Thank you, Sir," said Samad. "Thank you so very much."

That evening there was an awful row. Alsana slung the sewing machine, with the black studded hot pants she was working on, to the floor.

"Useless! Tell me, Samad Miah, what is the point of moving here—nice house, yes very nice, very nice—but where is the food?"

"It is a nice area, we have friends here…"

"Who are they?" she slammed her little fist on to the kitchen table, sending the salt and pepper flying to collide spectacularly with each other in the air. "I don't know them! You fight in an old, forgotten war with some Englishman … married to a black! Whose friends are they? These are the people my child will grow up around? Their children—half blacky-white? But tell me," she shouted, returning to her favoured topic, "where is our food?"

Theatrically, she threw open every cupboard in the kitchen, "Where is it? Can we eat china?"

Two plates smashed to the floor. She patted her stomach to indicate her unborn child and pointed to the pieces, "Hungry?"

Samad, who had an equally melodramatic nature when prompted, yanked open the freezer and pulled out a mountain of meat which he piled in the middle of the room. His mother worked through the night preparing

[1] *National Front* Extreme right-wing British political party often associated with racist views.

[2] *Mr. Gandhi* Mohandas Gandhi (1869–1948), Indian activist known for practicing asceticism and nonviolence.

meals for her family, he said. His mother did not, he said, spend the household money, as Alsana did, on prepared meals, yogurts and tinned spaghetti. Alsana punched him full square in the stomach.

"Samad Iqbal the traditionalist! Why don't I just squat in the street over a bucket and wash clothes? Eh? In fact, what about my clothes? Edible?"

As Samad clutched his winded belly, there in the kitchen she ripped to shreds every stitch she had on and added them to the pile of frozen lamb, spare cuts from the restaurant. She stood naked before him for a moment, the as yet small mound of her pregnancy in full view, then put on a long, brown coat and left the house.

But all the same, she reflected, slamming the door behind her, it was a nice area; she couldn't deny it as she stormed towards the high street, avoiding pavement trees where previously, in Whitechapel, she had avoided flung-out mattresses and the homeless. It would be good for the child. Alsana had a deep-seated belief that living near green spaces was morally beneficial to the young and there to her right was Gladstone Park, a sweeping horizon of green named after the Liberal prime minister (Alsana was from a respected old Bengal family and had read her English History), and in the Liberal tradition it was a park without fences, unlike the more affluent Queen's Park (Victoria's) with its pointed metal railings. Willesden was not as pretty as Queen's Park but it was a nice area. No denying it. No NF kids breaking the basement windows with their steel-capped boots like in Whitechapel. Now she was pregnant she needed a little bit of peace and quiet. Though it was the same here in a way; they all looked at her strangely, this tiny Indian woman stalking the high street in a mackintosh,[1] her plentiful hair flying every which way. *Mali's Kebabs, Mr. Cheungs, Raj's, Malkovich Bakeries*—she read the new, unfamiliar signs as she passed. She was shrewd. She saw what this was. "Liberal? Hosh-kosh nonsense!" No one was more liberal than anyone else anywhere anyway. It was only that here, in Willesden, there wasn't enough of any one thing to gang up against any other thing and send it running to the cellars while windows were smashed.

"Survival is what it is about!" she concluded out loud (she spoke to her baby: she liked to give it one sensible thought a day), making the bell above Crazy Shoes tinkle as she opened the door. Her niece Neena worked here. It was an old-fashioned cobbler's. Neena fixed heels back on to stilettos.

"Alsana, you look like dog shit," Neena called over in Bengali. "What is that horrible coat?"

"It's none of your business is what it is," replied Alsana in English. "I came to collect my husband's shoes not to chit-chat with Niece-Of-Shame."

Neena was used to this, and now Alsana had moved to Willesden there would only be more of it. It used to come in longer sentences (such as, "Niece, you have brought nothing but shame ..."), but now because Alsana no longer had the time or energy to summon up the necessary shock each time, it had become abridged to Niece-Of-Shame, an all-purpose tag that summed up the general feeling.

"See these soles?" said Neena, taking Samad's shoes off the shelf and handing Alsana the little blue ticket. "They were so worn through, Aunty Alsi, I had to reconstruct them from the very base. From the base! What does he do in them? Run marathons?"

"He works," replied Alsana tersely. "And prays," she added, for she liked to make a point of her respectability, and besides she was really very traditional, very religious, lacking nothing except the faith.

"And don't call me Aunty, I am only two years older than you."

Alsana swept the shoes into a plastic carrier bag and turned to leave.

"I thought that praying was done on people's knees," said Neena, laughing lightly.

"Both, both, asleep, waking, walking," snapped Alsana, as she passed under the tinkly bell once more. "We are never out of sight of the Creator."

"How's the new house, then?" Neena called after her.

But she had gone. Neena shook her head and sighed as she watched her young aunt disappear down the road

[1] *mackintosh* Raincoat.

like a little brown bullet. Alsana. She was young and old at the same time, Neena reflected. She acted so sensible, so straight-down-the-line in her long sensible coat, but you got the feeling—

"Oi! Miss! There's shoes back here that need your attention!" came a voice from the storeroom.

"Keep your tits on," said Neena.

At the corner of the road, Alsana popped behind the post office and removed her pinchy sandals in favour of Samad's shoes. (It was an oddity about Alsana. She was small but her feet were enormous, as if she had more growing to do.) In seconds she whipped her hair into an efficient bun, and wrapped her coat tighter around her to keep out the wind. Then she set off, past the library and up a long green road she had never walked along before. "Survival is all, Little Iqbal," she said to her bump once more. "Survival."

Clara was also pregnant. When their bumps became too large and cinema seats no longer accommodated them, the two women began to meet up for lunch in Kilburn Park, often with the Niece-Of-Shame, the three of them squeezed on to a generous bench, Alsana pressing a thermos of PG Tips[1] into Clara's hand, without milk, with lemon. Unwrapping several layers of cling film to reveal today's peculiar delight: savoury dough-like balls, crumbly Indian sweets shot through with the colours of the kaleidoscope, thin pastry with spiced beef inside, salad with onion, she says to Clara: "Eat up! Stuff yourself silly! They're in there, wallowing around in your belly, waiting for the menu. Woman, don't torture them! You want to starve the bumps?" for, despite appearances, there are six people on that bench (three living, three coming); one girl for Clara, two boys for Alsana.

Alsana says: "Nobody's complaining, let's get that straight. A boy is good and two boys is bloody good. But I tell you, when I turned my head and saw the ultra-business thingummybob—"

"Ultrasound," corrects Clara, through a mouthful of rice.

"—Yes, I almost had the heart attack to finish me off! Two! Feeding one is enough!"

Clara laughs and says she can imagine Samad's face when he saw it.

"No dearie,"—Alsana is reproving, tucking her large feet underneath the folds of her sari, "he didn't see anything. He wasn't there. I am not letting him see things like that. A woman has to have the private things—a husband needn't be involved in body-business, in a lady's … *parts*."

Niece-Of-Shame, who is sat between them, sucks her teeth.

"Bloody Hell, Alsi, he must have been involved in your parts sometime, or is this the immaculate bloody conception?"[2]

"So rude," says Alsana to Clara in a snooty, English way. "Too old to be so rude and too young to know any better." And then Clara and Alsana, with the accidental mirroring that happens when two people are sharing the same experience, both lay their hands on their bulges.

Neena, to redeem herself: "Yeah, well how are you doing on names? Any ideas?"

Alsana is decisive. "*Magid* and *Millat*. Ems are good. Ems are strong. Mahatma, Mohammed, that funny Mr Morecambe, from Morecambe and Wise[3]—letter you can trust."

But Clara is more cautious, because naming seems to her a fearful responsibility, a godlike task for a mere mortal: "I tink I like *Irie*. It patois.[4] Means everyting OK, cool, peaceful, you know?"

Alsana is mock-horrified before the sentence is finished, "'OK'? This is a name for a child? You might as well call her 'Wouldsirlike-anypopadumswiththat?'[5] or 'Niceweatherwearehaving'—"

[1] *PG Tips* Popular British brand of bagged tea.

[2] *immaculate … conception* Phrase that has come to be commonly associated with the virgin conception of Jesus, though in traditional Christian doctrine it refers to the conception of Jesus' mother, Mary.

[3] *Mahatma* Epithet applied to a sage or person whose wisdom is deeply admired, such as Mohandas Gandhi; *Mohammed* Prophet and founder of Islam (570–632); *Morecambe and Wise* Eric Morecambe (1926–84) and Ernie Wise (1925–99), a popular British comedy duo.

[4] *patois* I.e., Jamaican Patois, a language blending English and several African languages.

[5] *popadums* Cracker-like Indian flatbreads.

"… and Archie likes *Sarah*. Well, dere not much you can argue wid Sarah, but dere's not much to get happy bout either. I suppose if it was good enough for the wife of Abraham[1] …"

"Ibrahim," Alsana corrects, out of instinct more than Koranic pedantry. "Popping out babies when she was a hundred years old, by the grace of Allah."

And then Neena, groaning at the turn the conversation is taking: "Well I *like* Irie. It's funky. It's different."

Alsana loves this: "For pity's sake, what does Archibald know about *funky* and *different*? If I were you, dearie," she says patting Clara's knee, "I'd choose Sarah and let that be an end to it. Sometimes you have to let these men have it their way. Anything for a little—how do you say it in the English? For a little—" she puts her finger over tightly pursed lips, like a guard at the gate, "—*shush*."

But in response Niece-Of-Shame bats her voluminous eyelashes, wraps her college scarf round her head like purdah,[2] and says, "Oh yes, Auntie, yes, the little submissive Indian woman. You don't talk to him, he talks at you. You scream and shout at each other, but there's no communication. And in the end he wins anyway because he does whatever he likes when he likes. You don't even know where he is, what he does, what he *feels*, half the time. It's 1975, Alsi. You can't conduct relationships like that any more. It's not like back home. There has to be communication between men and women in the West, they've got to listen to each other, otherwise …" Neena mimes a small mushroom cloud going off in her hand.

"What a load of the codswallop," says Alsana sonorously, closing her eyes, shaking her head. "It is you who do not listen. By Allah, I will always give as good as I get. But you presume I *care* what he does. You presume I want to *know*. The truth is, for a marriage to survive you don't need all this talk, talk, talk; all this 'I am this' and 'I am really like this' like on the television, all this *revelation*—especially when your husband is old, when he is wrinkly and falling apart—you do not *want* to know what is slimy underneath the bed and rattling in the wardrobe."

Neena frowns. Clara cannot raise a serious objection, and the rice is handed around once more.

"Moreover," says Alsana after a pause, folding her dimpled arms underneath her breasts, pleased to be holding forth on a subject close to this formidable bosom, "when you are from families such as ours you should have learned that *silence*, what is *not* said, is the very *best* recipe for family life."

"So let me get this straight," says Neena, derisively. "You're saying that a good dose of repression keeps a marriage healthy?"

And as if someone had pressed a button, Alsana is outraged: "Repression! Nonsense silly-billy word! I'm just talking about common sense. What is my husband? What is yours?" she says pointing to Clara. "Twenty-five years they live before we are even born. What are they? What are they capable of? What blood do they have on their hands? What is sticky and smelly in their private areas? Who knows?" She throws her hands up, releasing the questions into the unhealthy Kilburn air, sending a troupe of sparrows up with them.

"What you don't understand, my Niece-Of-Shame, what none of your generation understand—"

"But Auntie," begs Neena, raising her voice, because this is what she really wants to argue about—the largest sticking point between the two of them—Alsana's arranged marriage, "how could you bear to marry someone you didn't know from Adam?"

In response, an infuriating wink. Alsana always likes to appear jovial at the very moment that her interlocutor becomes hot under the collar. "Because, *Miss Smarty-pants*, it is by far the easier option. It was exactly because Eve did not know Adam from Adam that they got on so A-OK. Let me explain. Yes, I was married to Samad Iqbal the same evening of the very day I met him. Yes, I didn't know him from Adam. But I liked him well enough. We met in the breakfast room on a steaming Dhaka[3] day and he fanned me with *The Times*. I thought he had a good face, a sweet voice, and his

[1] *Abraham* Biblical figure who is mentioned frequently in the Koran by the name of Ibrahim.

[2] *purdah* Practice of concealing women from public view through the use of a veil or through seclusion.

[3] *Dhaka* Capital city of Bangladesh.

backside was high and well formed for a man of his age. Very good. Now every time I learn something more about him *I like him less*. So you see, we were better off the way we were."

Neena stamps her foot in exasperation at the skewed logic.

"—Besides, I will never know him well. Getting anything out of my husband is like trying to squeeze water out when you're stoned."

Neena laughs despite herself, "Water out of a stone."

"Yes, yes. You think I'm so stupid. But I am wise about things like men. I tell you," Alsana prepares to deliver her summation as she has seen it done many years previously by the young Dhaka lawyers with their slick side-partings, "men are the last mystery. God is easy compared with men. Now, enough of the philosophy. Samosa?"

She peels the lid off the plastic tub and sits fat, pretty and satisfied on her conclusion.

"Shame that you're having them," says Neena to her aunt, lighting a fag. "Boys, I mean. Shame that you're going to have boys."

"What do you mean?"

This is Clara, who has secretly subscribed (a secret from Alsana and Archie) to a lending library of Neena's through which she has read, in a few short months, *The Female Eunuch* by Greer, *Sex, Race and Class* by Selma James and Jong's *Fear of Flying*, all in a clandestine attempt, on Neena's part, to rid Clara of her "false consciousness."[1]

"I mean, I just think men have caused enough chaos this century. There's enough bloody men in the world. If I knew I was going to have a boy ..." she pauses to prepare her two falsely conscious friends for this new concept, "I'd have to seriously consider abortion."

Alsana screams, claps her hands over one of her own ears and one of Clara's, and then almost chokes on a piece of aubergine[2] with the physical exertion. For some reason the remark simultaneously strikes Clara as funny: hysterically, desperately funny, miserably funny; and the Niece-Of-Shame sits between them, nonplussed, while the two egg-shaped women bend over themselves, one in laughter, the other in horror and near asphyxiation.

"Are you all right, ladies?" It is Sol Jozefowicz, the park keeper, standing in front of them, ready as always to be of aid.

"We are all going to burn in hell, Mr. Jozefowicz, if you call that being all right ..." explains Alsana, pulling herself together.

Niece-Of-Shame rolls her eyes: "Speak for yourself."

But Alsana is faster than any sniper when it comes to firing back: "I do, I do—thankfully Allah has arranged it that way."

"Good afternoon, Neena, good afternoon, Mrs. Jones," says Sol, offering a neat bow to each. "Are you sure you are all right? Mrs. Jones?"

Clara cannot stop the tears from squeezing out of the corners of her eyes. She cannot work out, at this moment, whether she is crying or laughing; the two states suddenly seem only a stone's throw from each other.

"I'm fine, fine. Sorry to have worried you, Mr. Jozefowicz. Really, I'm fine."

"I do not see what so very funny-funny," mutters Alsana. "The murder of innocents—is this funny?"

"Not in my experience, Mrs. Iqbal, no," says Sol Jozefowicz in the collected manner in which he says everything, passing his handkerchief to Clara. It strikes all three women—the way history will: embarrassingly, without warning, like a blush—what the park keeper's experience might have been. They fall silent.

"Well, as long as you ladies are fine, I'll be getting on," says Sol, motioning that Clara can keep the handkerchief and replacing the hat he had removed in the old fashion. He bows his neat little bow once more, and sets off slowly anticlockwise round the park.

Once Sol is out of earshot Neena says: "OK, Aunty Alsi. I apologize. I apologize ... What more do you want?"

---

[1] *The Female Eunuch* Influential feminist text by Germaine Greer, published in 1970; *Sex, Race and Class* 1973 article by Selma James championing the cause of women, especially those working without wages; *Fear of Flying* 1973 novel by Erica Jong depicting the sexual liberation of protagonist Isadora Wing; *false consciousness* Marxist term for a worldview or set of beliefs that impedes a person's ability to accurately comprehend his or her own circumstances.

[2] *aubergine* Eggplant.

"Oh, every-bloody-thing," says Alsana, her voice losing the fight, becoming vulnerable. "The whole bloody universe made clear—in a little nutshell. I cannot understand a thing any more, and I am just beginning. You understand?"

She sighs, not waiting for an answer, not looking at Neena, but across the way at the hunched, disappearing figure of Sol winding in and out of the yew trees. "You may be right about Samad … about many things … maybe there are no good men, not even the two in this belly … and maybe I do not talk enough with mine, maybe I have married a stranger … you might see the truth better than I … what do I know, a barefoot country girl who never went to the universities …"

"Oh, Alsi," Neena keeps saying, weaving her regret in and out of Alsana's words like tapestry, feeling bad, "you know I didn't mean it like that."

"But I cannot be worrying-worrying all the time about the truth. I have to worry about the truth that can be lived with. And that is the difference between losing your marbles drinking the salty sea, or swallowing the stuff from the streams. My Niece-Of-Shame believes in the talking cure,[1] eh?" says Alsana, with something of a grin. "Talk, talk, talk and it will be better. Be honest, slice open your heart and spread the red stuff around. But the past is made of more than words, dearie. We married old men, you see? These bumps," Alsana pats them both, "they will always have Daddy-long-legs for fathers. One leg in the present, one in the past. No talking will change this. Their roots will always be tangled."

Just as he reaches the far gate, Sol Jozefowicz turns round to wave, and the three women wave back. And Clara feels a little theatrical, flying the park keeper's cream handkerchief above her head. As if she is seeing someone off on a train journey which crosses the border of two countries.

—1999

[1] *talking cure* Therapy method that requires a patient to talk about traumas and other psychological obstacles.

Chimamanda Ngozi Adichie

b. 1977

In Chimamanda Adichie's 2009 TED talk "The Danger of a Single Story," she speaks about her belief in the redemptive possibilities of fiction: "Stories have been used to dispossess and to malign. But stories can also be used to empower, and to humanize." In her own fiction, Adichie creates windows into the worlds of others, tracing the psychological and emotional experiences of her characters while simultaneously portraying the larger movements of history in which their lives are entangled. In prose that is at once clear, straightforward, and lyrical, Adichie invites readers to immerse themselves in, for example, the Nigerian Civil War in *Half of a Yellow Sun*, or in the ordeal of a young woman's immigration from Nigeria to America in *Americanah*. Widely considered to be among the most important writing of her generation, Adichie's work has been translated into thirty languages and become a staple in the curricula of schools across the world. Her widely viewed lectures and TED talks have made her one of the most prominent intellectuals and feminist icons in the world today.

Adichie was born in 1977 in Enugu, Nigeria, but grew up in Nsukka, a town in the southeast, where the University of Nigeria is located. Adichie and her five brothers and sisters were raised there by Igbo parents, both of whom worked at the University: her father as a professor of statistics, her mother as an administrator. The family were all practicing Catholics. Adichie has said of her young life that it was "a very happy childhood, full of laughter and love, in a very close-knit family." Both of her grandfathers, however, had been killed in the Nigerian Civil War (1967–70), and the consequences of that conflict, in which the Igbo struggle to create an independent Biafran state was brutally suppressed, continued to affect the community long after the war ended. Repressive military governments also made life periodically difficult for Adichie's family, with food shortages and with her parents' salaries at times left unpaid. Adichie was popular in school and successful academically. She studied medicine at the University of Nigeria but decided after a year to change her program and pursue further education in America.

Adichie studied Communications at Drexel University in Philadelphia and then transferred to Eastern Connecticut State University. She completed her BA in 2001 and followed it with a year-long Master's program in Creative Writing at Johns Hopkins University. During her time at Johns Hopkins she finished a book she had begun the previous year: *Purple Hibiscus* (2003), a coming-of-age novel about a young girl growing up in an intolerant and abusive household in late twentieth-century Nigeria. *Purple Hibiscus* received the Commonwealth Writers' Prize for Best First Book, was shortlisted for the Orange Prize, and was longlisted for the Booker Prize. Hilary Mantel, in her review of the novel in the *Times Literary Supplement*, said that "the secret of Adichie's style is simplicity, rhythm and balance. She writes a poet's sentences … the final impression of the novel is gentleness, gravity and grace."

In 2005, as she began a fellowship at Princeton University, Adichie also undertook work on a novel set during the Nigerian Civil War. The novel, published the following year as *Half of a Yellow Sun*, cemented Adichie's reputation and earned her significant commercial success. Set in the late nineteen-sixties, *Half of a Yellow Sun* tells the story of an extended family living through a war that inflicted genocide and starvation upon the Igbo population. With compassion, sympathy, and fierce intelligence, the novel reaches into the potential of the human heart to love, but also to hate. Upon reading *Half of a Yellow Sun*, Chinua Achebe said of Adichie that she "is a new writer endowed with the gift of ancient storytellers. … She is fearless, or she would not have taken on the intimidating horror of Nigeria's civil war." *Half of a Yellow Sun* won the Orange Prize, among other honors. In 2008, Adichie was awarded a MacArthur Fellowship, or "Genius Grant," and in the same year she completed an MA in African Studies at Yale University.

In 2009, she published a collection of twelve short stories, *The Thing around Your Neck*, which explores the lives and experiences of characters living in Africa and the United States. Moving deftly between the personal and the political, Adichie's short fiction continues to embody the careful attention to craft and detail that brings her work such intense emotional and intellectual appeal. That year she also gave a TED talk, "The Danger of a Single Story," in which she extols the importance of stories that counter the stereotypical and reductive narratives imposed by the powerful. When we engage a multiplicity of stories, she argues, sharing them across cultures, we not only expand our own humanity but challenge oppressive power structures.

In 2012, Adichie gave another TED talk, "We Should All Be Feminists," which popularizes feminist ideas regarding the damage caused by oppressive gender roles and the ways gender oppression can be combated. By changing how we raise our sons and daughters, Adichie suggests, we can make progress towards a fairer world. The talk was a great success, and it was released as a book in 2014. It also brought Adichie celebrity status—Beyoncé included a passage from it in her song "Flawless" (2013), and Boots, a UK beauty retailer, chose Adichie as the face for their makeup line. After Adichie gave birth to a daughter in 2016, she expanded further on some of the ideas in "We Should All Be Feminists" in the pamphlet *Dear Ijeawele, or a Feminist Manifesto in Fifteen Suggestions* (2017). She outlines in this manifesto her ideas for raising children outside restrictive gender paradigms.

Adichie's next novel, *Americanah*, was published in 2013. It is the story of a young woman and a young man who leave Nigeria for school in the West, and who face complex issues of identity and race like those Adichie encountered when she first moved to the United States. As she writes in her essay "The Color of an Awkward Conversation," when she first moved to America the racism she experienced came as a shock, because being black in Nigeria and black in America were two quite different things: "I had recently arrived from Nigeria, a country where, thanks to the mosquitoes that kept British colonizers from settling, my skin color did not determine my identity, did not limit my dreams or my confidence." *Americanah* became a bestseller and won the National Book Critics Circle Award. In this novel, as in most of her work, Adichie writes in the realist mode, though she does employ some post-modern techniques, such as interspersing the narrative with the protagonist's blog posts.

Realism is an approach to storytelling that Adichie defends in "To Instruct and Delight: A Case for Realist Literature," her Commonwealth Lecture from 2012: "When we read human stories, we become alive in bodies not our own. … It seems to me that we live in a world where it has become increasingly important to try and live in bodies not our own, to embrace empathy, to constantly be reminded that we share, with everybody in every part of the world, a common and equal humanity. … This is part of realist literature's magic: that we are able to thrill to the magnificent diversity of the world."

⌘⌘⌘

A Private Experience

Chika climbs in through the store window first and then holds the shutter as the woman climbs in after her. The store looks as if it was deserted long before the riots started; the empty rows of wooden shelves are covered in yellow dust, as are the metal containers stacked in a corner. The store is small, smaller than Chika's walk-in closet back home. The woman climbs in and the window shutters squeak as Chika lets go of them. Chika's hands are trembling, her calves burning after the unsteady run from the market in her high-heeled sandals. She wants to thank the woman, for stopping her as she dashed past, for saying "No run that way!" and for leading her, instead, to this empty store where they could hide. But before she can say thank you, the woman says, reaching out to touch her bare neck, "My necklace lost when I'm running."

"I dropped everything," Chika says. "I was buying oranges and I dropped the oranges and my handbag." She does not add that the handbag was a Burberry,[1] an original one that her mother had bought on a recent trip to London.

The woman sighs and Chika imagines that she is thinking of her necklace, probably plastic beads threaded on a piece of string. Even without the woman's strong Hausa[2] accent, Chika can tell she is a Northerner, from the narrowness of her face, the unfamiliar rise of her cheekbones; and that she is Muslim, because of the scarf. It hangs around the woman's neck now, but it was probably wound loosely round her face before, covering her ears. A long, flimsy pink and black scarf, with the garish prettiness of cheap things. Chika wonders if the woman is looking at her as well, if the woman can tell, from her light complexion and the silver finger rosary her mother insists she wear, that she is Igbo and Christian. Later, Chika will learn that, as she and the woman are speaking, Hausa Muslims are hacking down Igbo Christians with machetes, clubbing them with stones. But now she says, "Thank you for calling me. Everything happened so fast and everybody ran and I was suddenly alone and I didn't know what I was doing. Thank you."

"This place safe," the woman says, in a voice that is so soft it sounds like a whisper. "Them not going to small-small shop, only big-big shop and market."

"Yes," Chika says. But she has no reason to agree or disagree, she knows nothing about riots: the closest she has come is the prodemocracy rally at the university a few weeks ago, where she had held a bright-green branch and joined in chanting "The military must go! Abacha[3] must go! Democracy now!" Besides, she would not even have participated in that rally if her sister Nnedi had not been one of the organizers who had gone from hostel to hostel to hand out fliers and talk to students about the importance of "having our voices heard."

Chika's hands are still trembling. Just half an hour ago, she was in the market with Nnedi. She was buying oranges and Nnedi had walked farther down to buy groundnuts[4] and then there was shouting in English, in

---

[1] *Burberry* Luxury British fashion brand.

[2] *Hausa* African ethnic group living in various communities in West Africa, including the northern part of Nigeria. When Britain created the state of Nigeria in 1914, it merged the Southern Nigeria Protectorate with the Northern Nigeria Protectorate. The Muslim Hausa population lived mainly in the north, the Christian Igbo population in the east, and the Yoruba peoples in the west. Igbo people living in the north were persecuted and then massacred in 1966, leading to the Nigerian Civil War (1967–70), during which the eastern region separated from Nigeria and formed the Republic of Biafra. The 30-month civil war ended in the defeat of Biafra, and the loss of between 1 and 3 million lives, many from starvation caused by a siege inflicted on the Biafran state. The end of the war was succeeded by thirty years of control by juntas, during which successive military governments sought to profit from Nigeria's oil revenues while doing little to provide a good standard of living for the people; ethnic conflict also continued, with periodic riots and massacres. Since democracy was instated in 1999, the federal Nigerian governments have been largely Christian, while the northern Muslim states have embraced strict Sharia law. Ethnic violence has escalated since, with riots killing thousands of people on both sides, and with the extremist organization Boko Haram fighting a war against the Nigerian government, killing and capturing thousands of Christians and others deemed opponents of Islam.

[3] *Abacha* In 1993 General Sani Abacha (1943–98) overwhelmed the previous Nigerian regime with a military coup, suppressing civilian protest and taking dictatorial power. Abacha's regime ended in 1998.

[4] *groundnuts* Peanuts or similar legumes.

pidgin, in Hausa, in Igbo. "Riot! Trouble is coming, oh! They have killed a man!" Then people around her were running, pushing against one another, overturning wheelbarrows full of yams, leaving behind bruised vegetables they had just bargained hard for. Chika smelled the sweat and fear and she ran, too, across wide streets, into this narrow one, which she feared—felt—was dangerous, until she saw the woman.

She and the woman stand silently in the store for a while, looking out of the window they have just climbed through, its squeaky wooden shutters swinging in the air. The street is quiet at first, and then they hear the sound of running feet. They both move away from the window, instinctively, although Chika can still see a man and a woman walking past, the woman holding her wrapper up above her knees, a baby tied to her back. The man is speaking swiftly in Igbo and all Chika hears is "She may have run to Uncle's house."

"Close window," the woman says.

Chika shuts the windows and without the air from the street flowing in, the dust in the room is suddenly so thick she can see it, billowing above her. The room is stuffy and smells nothing like the streets outside, which smell like the kind of sky-coloured smoke that wafts around during Christmas when people throw goat carcasses into fires to burn the hair off the skin. The streets where she ran blindly, not sure in which direction Nnedi had run, not sure if the man running beside her was a friend or an enemy, not sure if she should stop and pick up one of the bewildered-looking children separated from their mothers in the rush, not even sure who was who or who was killing whom.

Later she will see the hulks of burned cars, jagged holes in place of their windows and windshields, and she will imagine the burning cars dotting the city like picnic bonfires, silent witnesses to so much. She will find out it had all started at the motor park, when a man drove over a copy of the Holy Koran that had been dropped on the roadside, a man who happened to be Igbo and Christian. The men nearby, men who sat around all day playing draughts, men who happened to be Muslim, pulled him out of his pickup truck, cut his head off with one flash of a machete, and carried it to the market, asking others to join in; the infidel had desecrated the Holy Book. Chika will imagine the man's head, his skin ashen in death, and she will throw up and retch until her stomach is sore. But now, she asks the woman, "Can you still smell the smoke?"

"Yes," the woman says. She unties her green wrapper and spreads it on the dusty floor. She has on only a blouse and a shimmery black slip torn at the seams. "Come and sit."

Chika looks at the threadbare wrapper on the floor; it is probably one of the two the woman owns. She looks down at her own denim skirt and red T-shirt embossed with a picture of the Statue of Liberty, both of which she bought when she and Nnedi spent a few summer weeks with relatives in New York. "No, your wrapper will get dirty," she says.

"Sit," the woman says. "We are waiting here long time."

"Do you have an idea how long ...?"

"This night or tomorrow morning."

Chika raises her hand to her forehead, as though checking for a malaria fever. The touch of her cool palm usually calms her, but this time her palm is moist and sweaty. "I left my sister buying groundnuts. I don't know where she is."

"She is going safe place."

"Nnedi."

"Eh?"

"My sister. Her name is Nnedi."

"Nnedi," the woman repeats, and her Hausa accent sheaths the Igbo name in a feathery gentleness.

Later, Chika will comb the hospital mortuaries looking for Nnedi; she will go to newspaper offices clutching the photo of herself and Nnedi taken at a wedding just the week before, the one where she has a stupid half smile on her face because Nnedi pinched her just before the photo was taken, the two of them wearing matching off-the-shoulder Ankara gowns.[1] She will tape photocopies of the photo on the walls of the market and the nearby stores. She will not find Nnedi.

[1] *Ankara gowns* Formal dresses made from Ankara fabric, a brightly colored and patterned cotton.

She will never find Nnedi. But now she says to the woman, "Nnedi and I came up here last week to visit our auntie. We are on vacation from school."

"Where you go school?" the woman asks.

"We are at the University of Lagos.[1] I am reading medicine. Nnedi is in political science." Chika wonders if the woman even knows what going to university means. And she wonders, too, if she mentioned school only to feed herself the reality she needs now—that Nnedi is not lost in a riot, that Nnedi is safe somewhere, probably laughing in her easy, mouth-all-open way, probably making one of her political arguments. Like how the government of General Abacha was using its foreign policy to legitimise itself in the eyes of other African countries. Or how the huge popularity in blond hair attachments was a direct result of British colonialism.

"We have only spent a week here with our auntie, we have never even been to Kano[2] before," Chika says, and she realises that what she feels is this: she and her sister should not be affected by the riot. Riots like this were what she read about in newspapers. Riots like this were what happened to other people.

"Your auntie is in market?" the woman asks.

"No, she's at work. She is the director at the secretariat."[3] Chika raises her hand to her forehead again. She lowers herself and sits, much closer to the woman than she ordinarily would have, so as to rest her body entirely on the wrapper. She smells something on the woman, something harsh and clean like the bar soap their housegirl uses to wash the bed linen.

"Your auntie is going safe place."

"Yes," Chika says. The conversation seems surreal; she feels as if she is watching herself. "I still can't believe this is happening, this riot."

The woman is staring straight ahead. Everything about her is long and slender, her legs stretched out in front of her, her fingers with henna-stained nails, her feet. "It is work of evil," she says finally.

Chika wonders if that is all the woman thinks of the riots, if that is all she sees them as—evil. She wishes Nnedi were here. She imagines the cocoa brown of Nnedi's eyes lighting up, her lips moving quickly, explaining that riots do not happen in a vacuum, that religion and ethnicity are often politicised because the ruler is safe if the hungry ruled are killing one another. Then Chika feels a prick of guilt for wondering if this woman's mind is large enough to grasp any of that.

"In school you are seeing sick people now?" the woman asks.

Chika averts her gaze quickly so that the woman will not see the surprise. "My clinicals? Yes, we started last year. We see patients at the Teaching Hospital." She does not add that she often feels attacks of uncertainty, that she slouches at the back of the group of six or seven students, avoiding the senior registrar's eyes, hoping she will not be asked to examine a patient and give her differential diagnosis.

"I am trader," the woman says. "I'm selling onions."

Chika listens for sarcasm or reproach in the tone, but there is none. The voice is as steady and as low, a woman simply telling what she does.

"I hope they will not destroy market stalls," Chika replies; she does not know what else to say.

"Every time when they are rioting, they break market," the woman says.

Chika wants to ask the woman how many riots she has witnessed but she does not. She has read about the others in the past: Hausa Muslim zealots attacking Igbo Christians, and sometimes Igbo Christians going on murderous missions of revenge. She does not want a conversation of naming names.

"My nipple is burning like pepper," the woman says.

"What?

"My nipple is burning like pepper."

Before Chika can swallow the bubble of surprise in her throat and say anything, the woman pulls up her blouse and unhooks the front clasp of a threadbare black

[1] *University of Lagos* Government-run research university in Lagos, the largest city in Nigeria, located in the southwest.

[2] *Kano* City in northern Nigeria. The population is predominantly Hausa.

[3] *secretariat* Administrative body of government.

bra. She brings out the money, ten- and twenty-naira[1] notes, folded inside her bra, before freeing her full breasts.

"Burning-burning like pepper," she says, cupping her breasts and leaning toward Chika, as though in an offering. Chika shifts. She remembers the pediatrics rotation only a week ago: the senior registrar, Dr. Olunloyo, wanted all the students to feel the stage 4 heart murmur of a little boy, who was watching them with curious eyes. The doctor asked her to go first and she became sweaty, her mind blank, no longer sure where the heart was. She had finally placed a shaky hand on the left side of the boy's nipple, and the *brrr-brrr-brrr* vibration of swishing blood going the wrong way, pulsing against her fingers, made her stutter and say "Sorry, sorry" to the boy, even though he was smiling at her.

The woman's nipples are nothing like that boy's. They are cracked, taut and dark brown, the areolas lighter-toned. Chika looks carefully at them, reaches out and feels them. "Do you have a baby?" she asks.

"Yes. One year."

"Your nipples are dry, but they don't look infected. After you feed the baby, you have to use some lotion. And while you are feeding, you have to make sure the nipple and also this other part, the areola, fit inside the baby's mouth."

The woman gives Chika a long look. "First time of this. I'm having five children."

"It was the same with my mother. Her nipples cracked when the sixth child came, and she didn't know what caused it, until a friend told her that she had to moisturize," Chika says. She hardly ever lies, but the few times she does, there is always a purpose behind the lie. She wonders what purpose this lie serves, this need to draw on a fictional past similar to the woman's; she and Nnedi are her mother's only children. Besides, her mother always had Dr. Igbokwe, with his British training and affectation, a phone call away.

[1] *naira* Nigerian currency. About 360 naira is equivalent to 1 U.S. dollar.

"What is your mother rubbing on her nipple?" the woman asks.

"Cocoa butter. The cracks healed fast."

"Eh?" The woman watches Chika for a while, as if this disclosure has created a bond. "All right, I get it and use." She plays with her scarf for a moment and then says, "I am looking for my daughter. We go market together this morning. She is selling groundnut near bus stop, because there are many customers. Then riot begin and I am looking up and down market for her."

"The baby?" Chika asks, knowing how stupid she sounds even as she asks.

The woman shakes her head and there is a flash of impatience, even anger, in her eyes. "You have ear problem? You don't hear what I am saying?"

"Sorry," Chika says.

"Baby is at home! This one is first daughter. Halima." The woman starts to cry. She cries quietly, her shoulders heaving up and down, not the kind of loud sobbing that the women Chika knows do, the kind that screams *Hold me and comfort me because I cannot deal with this alone.* The woman's crying is private, as though she is carrying out a necessary ritual that involves no one else.

Later, when Chika will wish that she and Nnedi had not decided to take a taxi to the market just to see a little of the ancient city of Kano outside their aunt's neighborhood, she will wish also that the woman's daughter, Halima, had been sick or tired or lazy that morning, so that she would not have sold groundnuts that day.

The woman wipes her eyes with one end of her blouse. "Allah keep your sister and Halima in safe place," she says. And because Chika is not sure what Muslims say to show agreement—it cannot be "amen"—she simply nods.

The woman has discovered a rusted tap in a corner of the store, near the metal containers. Perhaps where the trader washed his or her hands, she says, telling Chika that the stores on this street were abandoned months ago, after the government declared them illegal structures to be demolished. The woman turns on the tap and they both watch—surprised—as water trickles out.

Brownish, and so metallic Chika can smell it already. Still, it runs.

"I wash and pray," the woman says, her voice louder now, and she smiles for the first time to show even-sized teeth, the front ones stained brown. Her dimples sink into her cheeks, deep enough to swallow half a finger, and unusual in a face so lean. The woman clumsily washes her hands and face at the tap, then removes her scarf from her neck and places it down on the floor. Chika looks away. She knows the woman is on her knees, facing Mecca, but she does not look. It is like the woman's tears, a private experience, and she wishes that she could leave the store. Or that she, too, could pray, could believe in a god, see an omniscient presence in the stale air of the store. She cannot remember when her idea of God has not been cloudy, like the reflection from a steamy bathroom mirror, and she cannot remember ever trying to clean the mirror.

She touches the finger rosary that she still wears, sometimes on her pinky or her forefinger, to please her mother. Nnedi no longer wears hers, once saying with that throaty laugh, "Rosaries are really magical potions, and I don't need those, thank you."

Later, the family will offer Masses over and over for Nnedi to be found safe, though never for the repose of Nnedi's soul. And Chika will think about this woman, praying with her head to the dustfloor, and she will change her mind about telling her mother that offering Masses is a waste of money, that it is just fundraising for the church.

When the woman rises, Chika feels strangely energized. More than three hours have passed and she imagines that the riot is quieted, the rioters drifted away. She has to leave, she has to make her way home and make sure Nnedi and her auntie are fine.

"I must go," Chika says.

Again the look of impatience on the woman's face. "Outside is danger."

"I think they have gone. I can't even smell any more smoke."

The woman says nothing, seats herself back down on the wrapper. Chika watches her for a while, disappointed without knowing why. Maybe she wants a blessing from the woman, something. "How far away is your house?" she asks.

"Far. I'm taking two buses."

"Then I will come back with my auntie's driver and take you home," Chika says.

The woman looks away. Chika walks slowly to the window and opens it. She expects to hear the woman ask her to stop, to come back, not to be rash. But the woman says nothing and Chika feels the quiet eyes on her back as she climbs out of the window.

The streets are silent. The sun is falling, and in the evening dimness, Chika looks around, unsure which way to go. She prays that a taxi will appear, by magic, by luck, by God's hand. Then she prays that Nnedi will be inside the taxi, asking her where the hell she has been, they have been so worried about her. Chika has not reached the end of the second street, toward the market, when she sees the body. She almost doesn't see it, walks so close to it that she feels its heat. The body must have been very recently burned. The smell is sickening, of roasted flesh, unlike that of any she has ever smelled.

Later, when Chika and her aunt go searching throughout Kano, a policeman in the front seat of her aunt's air-conditioned car, she will see other bodies, many burned, lying lengthwise along the sides of the street, as though someone carefully pushed them there, straightening them. She will look at only one of the corpses, naked, stiff, facedown, and it will strike her that she cannot tell if the partially burned man is Igbo or Hausa, Christian or Muslim, from looking at that charred flesh. She will listen to BBC[1] radio and hear the accounts of the deaths and the riots—"religious with undertones of ethnic tension" the voice will say. And she will fling the radio to the wall and a fierce red rage will run through her at how it has all been packaged and sanitized and made to fit into so few words, all those bodies. But now, the heat from the burned body is so close to her, so present and warm that she turns and dashes back toward the store. She feels a sharp pain along her lower leg as she runs. She gets to the store and

[1] *BBC* British Broadcasting Corporation.

raps on the window, and she keeps rapping until the woman opens it.

Chika sits on the floor and looks closely, in the failing light, at the line of blood crawling down her leg. Her eyes swim restlessly in her head. It looks alien, the blood, as though someone had squirted tomato paste on her.

"Your leg. There is blood," the woman says, a little wearily. She wets one end of her scarf at the tap and cleans the cut on Chika's leg, then ties the wet scarf around it, knotting it at the calf.

"Thank you," Chika says.

"You want toilet?"

"Toilet? No."

"The containers there, we are using for toilet," the woman says. She takes one of the containers to the back of the store, and soon the smell fills Chika's nose, mixes with the smells of dust and metallic water, makes her feel light-headed and queasy. She closes her eyes.

"Sorry, oh! My stomach is bad. Everything happening today," the woman says from behind her. Afterwards, the woman opens the window and places the container outside, then washes her hands at the tap. She comes back and she and Chika sit side by side in silence; after a while they hear raucous chanting in the distance, words Chika cannot make out. The store is almost completely dark when the woman stretches out on the floor, her upper body on the wrapper and the rest of her not.

Later, Chika will read in *The Guardian*[1] that "the reactionary Hausa-speaking Muslims in the North have a history of violence against non-Muslims," and in the middle of her grief, she will stop to remember that she examined the nipples and experienced the gentleness of a woman who is Hausa and Muslim.

Chika hardly sleeps all night. The window is shut tight; the air is stuffy, and the dust, thick and gritty, crawls up her nose. She keeps seeing the blackened corpse floating in a halo by the window, pointing accusingly at her. Finally she hears the woman get up and open the window, letting in the dull blue of early dawn. The woman stands there for a while before climbing out. Chika can hear footsteps, people walking past. She hears the woman call out, voice raised in recognition, followed by rapid Hausa that Chika does not understand.

The woman climbs back into the store. "Danger is finished. It is Abu. He is selling provisions. He is going to see his store. Everywhere policeman with tear gas. Soldier-man is coming. I go now before soldier-man will begin to harass somebody."

Chika stands slowly and stretches; her joints ache. She will walk all the way back to her auntie's home in the gated estate, because there are no taxis on the street, there are only army Jeeps and battered police station wagons. She will find her auntie, wandering from one room to the next with a glass of water in her hand, muttering in Igbo, over and over, "Why did I ask you and Nnedi to visit? Why did my chi[2] deceive me like this?" And Chika will grasp her auntie's shoulders tightly and lead her to a sofa.

Now, Chika unties the scarf from her leg, shakes it as though to shake the bloodstains out, and hands it to the woman.

"Thank you."

"Wash your leg well-well. Greet your sister, greet your people," the woman says, tightening her wrapper around her waist.

"Greet your people also. Greet your baby and Halima," Chika says. Later, as she walks home, she will pick up a stone stained the copper of dried blood and hold the ghoulish souvenir to her chest. And she will suspect right then, in a strange flash while clutching the stone, that she will never find Nnedi, that her sister is gone. But now, she turns to the woman and adds, "May I keep your scarf? The bleeding might start again."

The woman looks for a moment as if she does not understand; then she nods. There is perhaps the beginning of future grief on her face, but she smiles a slight, distracted smile before she hands the scarf back to Chika and turns to climb out of the window.

—2009

[1] *The Guardian* Prominent British newspaper.

[2] *chi* "Chi" is a complex concept in Igbo theology but can be described as the spiritual complement of a person's earthly identity; the term is often translated as "spirit" or "guardian angel."

Literature, Politics, and Cultural Identity in the Late Twentieth and Twenty-First Centuries

In recent generations, literature in Britain—and the public discussion of this literature—has often been infused with strongly political content. The politics of postcolonialism and of race are here important strands, but the politics of gender, of class, of the environment, and of aesthetics have often been just as hotly debated. Writers such as Tony Harrison have powerfully addressed issues relating to social class; Paul Muldoon and others have spoken out provocatively on issues in British and Irish politics; artists such as the poet and dramatist Liz Lochhead and the poet Kim Moore have questioned the power dynamics between men and women; and so on.

The past few decades have seen women writers and gay, lesbian, and bisexual writers achieve greater prominence within mainstream British literature—a change that is perhaps most strikingly evident in the realm of poetry. As late as the 1980s, almost any list of acknowledged major living poets in England, Scotland, Wales, and Ireland would have been composed overwhelmingly of men; although there were of course women poets writing in large numbers, most of these were not acknowledged by a male-dominated literary establishment. This is no longer the case; the past generation is perhaps the first in the history of British poetry in which significant women poets have been recognized in numbers at least as great as those of their male counterparts.

There has been a shift of attitude with regard to sexual orientation, too, such that it is no longer an object of controversy within much of the literary community, or within much of the rest of British society. The twentieth century saw the coming into prominence of the first openly gay poets, among them W.H. Auden and, later, Thom Gunn and Edwin Morgan, then of openly lesbian poets such as Jackie Kay. In 2009 Carol Ann Duffy became both the first woman and the first openly gay writer to be appointed Poet Laureate of the United Kingdom—a sign of significant change in Britain's literary landscape as well as of the importance of Duffy's work. This is not, however, to suggest that discrimination on the basis of gender or sexual orientation is no longer a matter of concern; on the contrary, struggles for equality in these areas continue to impact British politics and culture. The issue of sexual violence and harassment, for example, came to the forefront of public consciousness with the global #MeToo movement, with particular attention in Britain paid to sexual misconduct in government and in government-adjacent organizations such as the charity Oxfam.

Another shift has been towards increasing identification of writers with national groups. The late 1990s saw the establishment of separate government assemblies in Wales and in Northern Ireland, and a separate parliament in Scotland—changes that both reflected and reinforced the importance of separate national cultures within Britain. Scotland in particular has a strong independence movement, and in 2014 held a referendum to become an independent country, though voters chose to remain a part of the United Kingdom. Among those writers strongly identified with Scotland are Sorley Maclean, a major figure in Scottish Gaelic poetry; Liz Lochhead, who often employs Scots dialect in her drama and in poems such as "Kidspoem/Bairnsang"; and Edwin Morgan, who envisions the full sweep of Scottish history—including an imagined independent future—in his *Sonnets from Scotland*. There has also been an extraordinary outpouring of work from poets born and raised in

Northern Ireland, including Paul Muldoon and Medbh McGuckian. (It is essential here to note, however, that many poets from this area have self-identified as Irish rather than as Northern Irish.) In Welsh literature, Gwyneth Lewis has led the way in forging a fresh tradition as a bilingual poet in Welsh and English, finding immense poetic resources in the sounds as well as the meanings of the two languages.

Meanwhile, many English writers draw on specifically English culture; much of Tony Harrison's work, for example, asserts the poetic value of contemporary working-class Yorkshire dialect. (Simon Armitage, too, often refers to northern English language and everyday life in his work, although he cautions critics that he is "a professional poet, not a professional Yorkshireman.") In their different ways, the work of Scottish, English, Welsh, and Irish writers has placed much greater emphasis on national (and sometimes regional) identity than on any sense of overarching "Britishness"—and some Scottish, Welsh, and Irish writers explicitly reject the label of "British" altogether. As Bill Buford, editor of the UK-based international literary magazine *Granta*, observed in 2003, "I still don't know anyone who is British. I know people who are English or Scottish or Northern Irish (not to mention born-in-Nigeria-but-living-here or born-in-London-of-Pakistani-parents-and-living-here)." The negotiation of British identity was complicated by the Brexit referendum in 2016, as the citizens of Britain voted to leave the European Union (notably, a majority of Northern Irish and of Scottish voters would have preferred to remain a part of the EU). The decision, which rendered Britain's economic and cultural future uncertain, was largely condemned by the literary community.

As nations within the UK continue to develop specific traditions, so do writers whose work links to a heritage from outside the British Isles—and to the heritage of British colonialism. Immigration to Britain, especially from its former colonies, began to increase in the 1950s; as Zadie Smith has argued, it is now "impossible to write about England without mentioning the fact that … there are a huge amount of people from the Indian subcontinent in England, there are a huge amount of Caribbeans, those people are English." The role of immigration in British culture, always controversial, became more so during the 2010s, as large numbers of people displaced by the Syrian Civil War and other crises sought asylum in the EU; in the end Britain accepted fewer refugees, as a percentage of its population, than almost any other Western European nation. Writers such as Louise Bennett, Grace Nichols, Moniza Alvi, Jackie Kay, and Warsan Shire focus strongly in their work on issues of race, culture, and global politics, drawing from their personal and cultural backgrounds a range of styles and concerns that have broadened the scope of British literature immeasurably. One important example of this sort of development is the work of dub poets such as Linton Kwesi Johnson and Jean Binta Breeze, which blends poetry and reggae music to create hybrid expressions of the traditions of the Caribbean and the realities of present-day Britain. Writers living in nations that were once British colonies have also been forced to negotiate the effects of colonial history—and of present-day global inequality—in building independent national literatures. Barbadian poet Kamau Brathwaite, for example, has written about the inadequacy of English to the demands of Caribbean culture and landscape, and in his own poetry has envisioned ways of addressing those demands.[1]

Although nature has long been an important subject in British literature—and especially British poetry—writing about nature has taken on a more overtly political dimension in recent decades, as fears about environmental destruction and global climate change have become increasingly prominent in public consciousness. Poems by Alice Oswald, Gillian Clarke, Jean Binta Breeze, and Jackie Kay here address humans' relationship to nature in a politically charged fashion. In this, as in many other

[1] See also, represented elsewhere in this anthology, Nigerian novelist, critic, and editor Chinua Achebe; Kenyan novelist, critic, and activist Ngũgĩ wa Thiong'o; Saint Lucian poet Derek Walcott; Canadian Cree novelist and playwright Tomson Highway; and Nigerian novelist and essayist Chimamanda Ngozi Adichie.

respects, literature of the twenty-first century has reflected anxiety in the population at large over the many ways our global socioeconomic order has been changing.

⌘⌘⌘

Sorley MacLean (1911–1996)

A native Scottish Gaelic speaker born on the Island of Raasay on Scotland's northeastern coast, Sorley MacLean is known for bringing a modern sensibility to Scottish Gaelic poetry—thus reinvigorating a genre that had long been heavily dominated by tradition. His books include *17 Poems for 6d* (1940), *Dàin do Eimhir agus Dàin Eile* (1943, translated as *Poems to Eimhir* in 1971), and *O Choille gu Bearradh / From Wood to Ridge: Collected Poems in Gaelic and English* (1989).

All of MacLean's major work was composed in Scottish Gaelic, though he also offered his own English translations; his poem "Hallaig" below appears in the original Gaelic, MacLean's own translation, and a later translation by Irish poet Seamus Heaney.

Ban-Ghàidheal

Am faca Tu i, Iùdhaich mhóir,
ri 'n abrar Aon Mhac Dhé?
Am fac' thu 'coltas air Do thriall
ri strì an fhìon-lios chéin?

An cuallach mhiosan air a druim,
fallus searbh air mala is gruaidh;
's a' mhias chreadha trom air cùl
a cinn chrùibte bhochd thruaigh.

Chan fhaca Tu i, Mhic an t-saoir,
ri 'n abrar Rìgh na Glòir,
a miosg nan cladach carrach siar,
fo fhallus cliabh a lòin.

An t-earrach seo agus seo chaidh
's gach fichead earrach bho 'n an tùs,
tharraing ise 'n fheamainn fhuar
chum biadh a cloinne 's duais an tùir.

A Highland Woman[1]

Hast Thou seen her, great Jew,
who art called the One Son of God?
Hast Thou seen on Thy way the like of her
labouring in the distant vineyard?

The load of fruits on her back,
a bitter sweat on brow and cheek,
and the clay basin heavy on the back
of her bent poor wretched head.

Thou hast not seen her, Son of the carpenter,
who art called the King of Glory,
among the rugged western shores
in the sweat of her food's creel.[2]

This Spring and last Spring
and every twenty Springs from the beginning,
she has carried the cold seaweed
for her children's food and the castle's reward.

---

[1] *A Highland Woman* Translated from Scottish Gaelic by Sorley MacLean.

[2] *creel* Gathering into a creel, a type of wicker basket.

'S gach fichead foghar tha air triall
chaill i samhradh buidh nam blàth;
is threabh an dubh-chosnadh an clais
tarsuinn mìnead ghil a clàir.

Agus labhair T' eaglais chaomh
mu staid chaillte a h-anama thruaigh;
agus leag an cosnadh dian
a corp gu sàmhchair dhuibh an uaigh.

Is thriall a tìm mar shnighe dubh
a' drùdhadh tughaidh fàrdaich bochd;
mheal ise an dubh-chosnadh cruaidh;
is glas a cadal suain an nochd.
—1938

And every twenty Autumns gone
she has lost the golden summer of her bloom,
and the Black Labour[1] has ploughed the furrow
across the white smoothness of her forehead.

And Thy gentle church has spoken
about the lost state of her miserable soul,
and the unremitting toil has lowered
her body to a black peace in a grave.

And her time has gone like a black sludge
seeping through the thatch of a poor dwelling:
the hard Black Labour was her inheritance;
grey is her sleep tonight.
—1977

Hallaig

"Tha tìm, am fiadh, an coille Hallaig"

Tha bùird is tàirnean air an uinneig
troimh 'm faca mi an Aird an Iar
's tha mo ghaol aig Allt Hallaig
'na craoibh bheithe, 's bha i riamh

eadar an t-Inbhir 's Poll a' Bhainne,
thall 's a bhos mu Bhaile-Chùirn:
tha i 'na beithe, 'na calltuinn,
'na caorann dhìreach sheang ùir.

Hallaig[2]

"Time, the deer, is in the wood of Hallaig"

The window is nailed and boarded
through which I saw the West
and my love is at the Burn of Hallaig,
a birch tree, and she has always been

between Inver and Milk Hollow,
here and there about Baile-Chuirn:[3]
she is a birch, a hazel,
a straight, slender young rowan.

---

[1] *Black Labour* Originally, this term referred specifically to work done for a landlord in return for reduced rent; it came to refer more broadly to any physically punishing labor.

[2] *Hallaig* Ruined settlement on the southeastern coast of the Island of Raasay, part of the Inner Hebrides on Scotland's northwestern coast. During the Highland Clearances of the eighteenth and nineteenth centuries, landlords evicted whole communities of tenants in order to transform the land into pasture for sheep. Hallaig's population was forced out by one such clearance in the mid-eighteenth century; most of its inhabitants were sent to Australia.

This translation from Scottish Gaelic is by Sorley MacLean; a translation by Seamus Heaney follows this.

[3] *Baile-Chuirn* Coastal community on the west side of Raasay; Inver and Milk Hollow (Poll a' Bhainne) are nearby.

Ann an Screapadal mo chinnidh,
far robh Tarmad 's Eachann Mór,
tha 'n nigheanan 's am mic 'nan coille
a' gabhail suas ri taobh an lóin.

Uaibhreach a nochd na coilich ghiuthais
a' gairm air mullach Cnoc an Rà,
dìreach an druim ris a' ghealaich—
chan iadsan coille mo ghràidh.

Fuirichidh mi ris a' bheithe
gus an tig i mach an Càrn,
gus am bi am bearradh uile
o Bheinn na Lice f' a sgàil.

Mura tig 's ann theàrnas mi a Hallaig
a dh'ionnsaigh sàbaid nam marbh,
far a bheil an sluagh a' tathaich,
gach aon ghinealach a dh'fhalbh.

Tha iad fhathast ann a Hallaig,
Clann Ghill-Eain's Clann MhicLeòid,
na bh' ann ri linn Mhic Ghille Chaluim:
chunnacas na mairbh beò.

Na fir 'nan laighe air an lianaig
aig ceann gach taighe a bh' ann,
na h-igheanan 'nan coille bheithe,
dìreach an druim, crom an ceann.

In Screapadal[1] of my people
where Norman and Big Hector[2] were,
their daughters and their sons are a wood
going up beside the stream.

Proud tonight the pine cocks
crowing on the top of Cnoc an Ra,[3]
straight their backs in the moonlight—
they are not the wood I love.

I will wait for the birch wood
until it comes up by the cairn,
until the whole ridge from Beinn na Lice[4]
will be under its shade.

If it does not, I will go down to Hallaig,
to the Sabbath of the dead,
where the people are frequenting,
every single generation gone.

They are still in Hallaig,
MacLeans and MacLeods,
all who were there in the time of Mac Gille Chaluim:[5]
the dead have been seen alive.

The men lying on the green
at the end of every house that was,
the girls a wood of birches,
straight their backs, bent their heads.

---

[1] *Screapadal* Raasay community north of Hallaig that was also emptied during the Highland Clearances.

[2] *Norman* Given name of numerous chiefs of clan MacLeod; *Big Hector* Title of the 12th (1497–1568) and 16th (d. 1626) chiefs of clan MacLean. The MacLeod and MacLean clans both have links to the Inner Hebrides.

[3] *Cnoc an Ra* Hill on the southwestern side of Raasay.

[4] *Beinn na Lice* Limestone ridge south of Hallaig.

[5] *Mac Gille Chaluim* Designation used by the chief of the MacLeods of Raasay.

Eadar an Leac is na Feàrnaibh
tha 'n rathad mór fo chóinnich chiùin,
's na h-igheanan 'nam badan sàmhach
a' dol a Chlachan mar o thùs.

Agus a' tilleadh as a' Chlachan,
á Suidhisnis 's á tir nam beò;
a chuile té òg uallach
gun bhristeadh cridhe an sgeòil.

O Allt na Feàrnaibh gus an fhaoilinn
tha soilleir an dìomhaireachd nam beann
chan eil ach coimthional nan nighean
a' cumail na coiseachd gun cheann.

A' tilleadh a Hallaig anns an fheasgar,
anns a' chamhanaich bhalbh bheò,
a' lìonadh nan leathadan casa,
an gàireachdaich 'nam chluais 'na ceò,

's am bòidhche 'na sgleò air mo chridhe
mun tig an ciaradh air na caoil,
's nuair theàrnas grian air cùl Dhùn Cana
thig peileir dian á gunna Ghaoil;

's buailear am fiadh a tha 'na thuaineal
a' snòtach nan làraichean feòir;
thig reothadh air a shùil 's a' choille:
chan fhaighear lorg air fhuil ri m' bheò.
—1954

Between the Leac and Fearns[1]
the road is under mild moss
and the girls in silent bands
go to Clachan[2] as in the beginning,

and return from Clachan,
from Suisnish[3] and the land of the living;
each one young and light-stepping,
without the heartbreak of the tale.

From the Burn° of Fearns to the raised beach *stream*
that is clear in the mystery of the hills,
there is only the congregation of the girls
keeping up the endless walk,

coming back to Hallaig in the evening,
in the dumb living twilight,
filling the steep slopes,
their laughter a mist in my ears,

and their beauty a film on my heart
before the dimness comes on the kyles,[4]
and when the sun goes down behind Dun Cana[5]
a vehement bullet will come from the gun of Love;

and will strike the deer that goes dizzily,
sniffing at the grass-grown ruined homes;
his eye will freeze in the wood,
his blood will not be traced while I live.
—1977

[1] *the Leac and Fearns* Settlements on the east coast of Raasay that have been empty since the Clearances; both are south of Hallaig.

[2] *Clachan* Harbor village across the island from Fearns.

[3] *Suisnish* Ruined settlement south of Clachan that was also cleared in the mid-eighteenth century.

[4] *kyles* Channels.

[5] *Dun Cana* Raasay's highest hill, northwest of Hallaig.

Hallaig[1]

Time, the deer, is in Hallaig Wood

There's a board nailed across the window
I looked through to see the west
And my love is a birch forever
By Hallaig Stream, at her tryst

Between Inver and Milk Hollow,
somewhere around Baile-chuirn,
A flickering birch, a hazel,
A trim, straight sapling rowan.

In Screapadal, where my people
Hail from, the seed and breed
Of Hector Mor and Norman
By the banks of the stream are a wood.

To-night the pine-cocks crowing
On Cnoc an Ra, there above,
And the trees standing tall in moonlight—
They are not the wood I love.

I will wait for the birches to move,
The wood to come up past the cairn
Until it has veiled the mountain
Down from Beinn na Lice in shade.

If it doesn't, I'll go to Hallaig,
To the sabbath of the dead,
Down to where each departed
Generation has gathered.

Hallaig is where they survive,
All the MacLeans and MacLeads
Who were there in the time of Mac Gille Chaluim:
The dead have been seen alive,

The men at their length on the grass
At the gable of every house,
The girls a wood of birch trees
Standing tall, with their heads bowed.

Between The Leac and Fearns
The road is plush with moss
And the girls in a noiseless procession
Going to Clachan as always

And coming back from Clachan
And Suisnish, their land of the living,
Still lightsome and unheartbroken,
Their stories only beginning.

From Fearns Burn° to the raised beach *stream*
Showing clear in the shrouded hills
There are only girls congregating,
Endlessly walking along

Back through the gloaming to Hallaig
Through the vivid speechless air,
Pouring down the steep slopes,
Their laughter misting my ear

And their beauty a glaze on my heart.
Then as the kyles go dim
And the sun sets behind Dun Cana
Love's loaded gun will take aim.

It will bring down the lightheaded deer
As he sniffs the grass round the wallsteads[2]
And his eye will freeze: while I live,
His blood won't be traced in the woods.
—2002

[1] *Hallaig* Translation by Seamus Heaney, 2002.

[2] *wallsteads* Ruins of stone buildings.

LOUISE BENNETT (1919–2006)

Jamaican writer Louise Bennett, known as "Miss Lou," was awarded the Order of Jamaica and designated a cultural ambassador for her promotion of Jamaican language and folklore in her home country and around the world. A dynamic performer, teacher, broadcaster, and writer, Bennett was the author of such celebrated books as *Dialect Verses* (1942), *Jamaica Labrish* (1966), *Anancy and Miss Lou* (1979), and *Aunty Roachy Seh* (1993).

Colonization in Reverse

Wat a joyful news, Miss Mattie,
I feel like me heart gwine burs
Jamaica people colonizin
Englan in reverse.

By de hundred, by de tousan
From country and from town,
By de ship load, by de plane-load
Jamaica is Englan boun.

Dem a pour out o Jamaica,
Everybody future plan
Is fe get a big-time job
An settle in de mother lan.

What a islan! What a people!
Man an woman, old an young
Jus a pack dem bag an baggage
An tun history upside dung!

Some people doan like travel,
But fe show dem loyalty
Dem all a open up cheap-fare-
To-England agency.

An week by week dem shippin off
Dem countryman like fire,
Fe immigrate an populate
De seat o de Empire.

Oonoo see how life is funny,
Oonoo see de tunabout,
Jamaica live fe box bread
Outa English people mout.

For wen dem catch a Englan,
An start play dem different role,
Some will settle down to work
An some will settle fe de dole.

Jane say de dole is not too bad
Bacause dey payin she
Two pounds a week fe seek a job
Dat suit her dignity.

Me say Jane will never find work
At the rate how she dah-look,
For all day she stay pon Aunt Fan couch
An read love-story book.

Wat a devilment a Englan!
Dem face war an brave de worse,
But me wonderin how dem gwine stan
Colonizin in reverse.
—1966

EDWIN MORGAN (1920–2010)

Edwin Morgan was known for his use of inventive language, facility with traditional and experimental forms, and exploration of a wide range of subject matter. Morgan taught for three decades at the University of Glasgow, and in 2004 he became the first Scots Makar, the national poet of Scotland. His books include *The Vision of Cathkin Braes* (1952), *The Second Life* (1968), *From Glasgow to Saturn* (1973), *Love and a Life* (2003), and *Poems and Other Nightmares* (2010).

The Coin[1]

We brushed the dirt off, held it to the light.
The obverse showed us *Scotland*, and the head
of a red deer; the antler-glint had fled
but the fine cut could still be felt. All right:
we turned it over, read easily *One Pound*,
but then the shock of Latin, like a gloss,
Respublica Scotorum,[2] sent across
such ages as we guessed but never found
at the worn edge where once the date had been
and where as many fingers had gripped hard
as hopes their silent race had lost or gained.
The marshy scurf[3] crept up to our machine,
sucked at our boots. Yet nothing seemed
ill-starred.° *unlucky, doomed*
And least of all the realm the coin contained.
—1984

KAMAU BRATHWAITE (B. 1930)

Acclaimed Barbadian poet and critic Kamau Brathwaite is a major literary voice from the West Indies. As a poet and cultural historian, Brathwaite has sought to reclaim and understand the complex valences of Caribbean identity, particularly how that identity is manifested by the poetic voice. Among Brathwaite's best-known poetry volumes are *The Arrivants* (1973), *Black + Blues* (1997), *Born to Slow Horses* (2005), *Elegguas* (2010), and *Strange Fruit, Peepal Tree* (2015). His non-fiction publications include *Barbados Poetry: A Checklist: Slavery to the Present* (1979) and *History of the Voice: The Development of Nation Language in Anglophone Caribbean Poetry* (1984).

[1] *The Coin* This poem is part of the 51-sonnet sequence *Sonnets from Scotland*, which Morgan conceived of as a response to the failed 1979 referendum that, had it succeeded, would have granted a greater degree of political independence to Scotland. The sequence, focused on Scottish politics and culture, embraces an enormous temporal span, from prehistory to an imagined future.

[2] *Respublica Scotorum* Latin: Scottish Republic. No pound coin bears this imprint, as Scotland has never been a republic.

[3] *scurf* Encrustation of organic or mineral deposits.

from *History of the Voice: The Development of Nation Language in Anglophone Caribbean Poetry*[4]

What I am going to talk about this morning is language from the Caribbean, the process of using English in a different way from the "norm." English in a new sense as I prefer to call it. English in an ancient sense. English in a very traditional sense. And sometimes not English at all, but *language*. …

We in the Caribbean have a similar kind of plurality [of languages as that of South Africa]:[5] we have English, which is the imposed language on much of the archipelago. English is an imperial language, as are French, Dutch, and Spanish. We have what we call creole English, which is a mixture of English and an adaptation that English took in the new environment of the Caribbean when it became mixed with the other imported languages. We have also what is called *nation language*, which is the kind of English spoken by the people who were brought to the Caribbean, not the official English now, but the language of slaves and labourers, the servants who were brought in by the conquistadors.[6] Finally, we have the remnants of ancestral languages still persisting in the Caribbean. There is Amerindian, which is active in certain parts of Central America but not in the Caribbean because the Amerindians are a destroyed people, and their languages were practically destroyed. We have Hindi, spoken by some of the more traditional East Indians who live in the Caribbean, and there are also varieties of Chinese.[7] And, miraculously, there are

[4] *History of … Poetry* Brathwaite's *History of the Voice* began as a lecture given at CARIFESTA II (1976) in Jamaica and at Harvard in 1979; it was published in book form in 1984. A version of the lecture with additional revisions was included in Brathwaite's 1986 essay collection *Roots*.

[5] *South Africa* South Africa had been discussed in a presentation given at Carifesta the day before by South African poet Dennis Brutus.

[6] *conquistadors* Term used to refer to Spanish and Portuguese explorers and soldiers that colonized large territories of the world. Brathwaite applies the term more widely to all colonizers.

[7] [Brathwaite's note] No one, as far as I know, has yet made a study of the impact of Asiatic language structures on the contemporary languages of the Caribbean, and even study of the [continued …]

survivals of African languages still persisting in the Caribbean. So we have that spectrum—that prism—of languages similar to the kind of structure that Dennis described for South Africa. Now, I have to give you some kind of background to the development of these languages, the historical development of this plurality, because I can't take it for granted that you know and understand the history of the Caribbean.

The Caribbean is a set of islands stretching out from Florida in a mighty curve. You must know of the Caribbean at least from television, at least now with hurricane David[1] coming right into it. The islands stretch out on an arc of some two thousand miles from Florida through the Atlantic to the South American coast, and they were originally inhabited by Amerindian people, Taino, Siboney, Carib, Arawak. In 1492, Columbus "discovered" (as it is said) the Caribbean, and with that discovery came the intrusion of European culture and peoples and a fragmentation of the original Amerindian culture. We had Europe "nationalizing" itself into Spanish, French, English, and Dutch so that people had to start speaking (and *thinking*) in four metropolitan languages rather than possibly a single native language. Then, with the destruction of the Amerindians, which took place within 30 years of Columbus' discovery (one million dead a year), it was necessary for the Europeans to import new labour bodies into the Caribbean. And the most convenient form of labour was the labour on the very edge of the trade winds—the labour on the edge of the *slave* trade winds, the labour on the edge of the hurricane, the labour on the edge of West Africa. And so the peoples of Ashanti, Congo, Nigeria, from all that mighty coast of western Africa were imported into the Caribbean. And we had the arrival in that area of a new language structure. It consisted of many languages, but basically they had a common semantic and stylistic form.[2] What these languages had to do, however, was to submerge themselves, because officially the conquering peoples—the Spaniards, the English, the French, and the Dutch did not wish to hear people speaking Ashanti or any of the Congolese languages. So there was a submergence of this imported language. Its status became one of inferiority. Similarly, its speakers were slaves. They were conceived of as inferiors—nonhuman, in fact. But this very submergence served an interesting intercultural purpose, because although people continued to speak English as it was spoken in Elizabethan times and on through the Romantic and Victorian ages, that English was nonetheless, still being influenced by the underground language, the submerged language that the slaves had brought. And that underground language was itself constantly transforming itself into new forms. It was moving from a purely African form to a form that was African, but which was adapting to the new environment and to the cultural imperatives of the European languages. And it was influencing the way in which the French, Dutch, and Spanish spoke their own languages. So there was a very complex process taking place which is now beginning to surface in our literature.

In the Caribbean, as in South Africa (and in any area of cultural imperialism for that matter), the educational system did not recognize the presence of these various languages. What our educational system did was to recognize and maintain the language of the conquistador—the language of the planter, the language of the official, the language of the Anglican preacher. It insisted that not only would English be spoken in the anglophone Caribbean, but that the educational system would carry the contours of an English heritage. Hence, as Dennis said, Shakespeare, George Eliot, Jane Austen—British literature and literary forms, the models that were intimate to Great Britain, that had very little

African impact is still in its infancy. For development of Anglophone Caribbean culture, see Edward Kamau Brathwaite, *Contradictory Omens: Cultural Diversity and Integration in the Caribbean* (Mona, Jamaica: Savacou Publishers, 1974).

[1] *hurricane David* Category 5 hurricane that made landfall on the coast of the Dominican Republic in 1979.

[2] [Brathwaite's note] See Alan Lomax, "Africanisms in New World Negro Music: A Cantrometric Analysis," in *Research and Resources of Haiti*, Richard P. Schaedel (New York: Research Institute for the Study of Man, 1969) and in *The Haitian Potential,* Vera Rubin and Richard P. Schaedel (New York: Teachers College Press, 1975); Mervyn C. Alleyne, "The Linguistic Continuity of Africa in the Caribbean," *Black Academy Review* 1, no. 4, Winter 1970, 3–16.

to do, really with the environment and the reality of the Caribbean—were dominant in the Caribbean educational system. People were forced to learn things that had no relevance to themselves. Paradoxically, in the Caribbean (as in many other "cultural disaster" areas), the people educated in this system came to know more, even today, about English kings and queens than they do about our own national heroes, our own slave rebels—the people who helped to build and to destroy our society. We are more excited by English literary models, by the concept of, say, Sherwood Forest and Robin Hood, than we are by Nanny of the Maroons, a name some of us didn't even know until a few years ago.[1] And in terms of what we write, our perceptual models, we are more conscious (in terms of sensibility) of the falling of snow for instance—the models are all there for the falling of the snow—than of the force of the hurricanes that take place every year. In other words, we haven't got the syllables, the syllabic intelligence, to describe the hurricane, which is our own experience;[2] whereas we can describe the imported alien experience of the snowfall. It is that kind of situation that we are in.

Now the creole adaptation to all this is the child who, instead of writing in an essay "The snow was falling on the fields of Shropshire" (which is what our children literally were writing until a few years ago, below drawings they made of white snow fields and the corn-haired people who inhabited such a landscape), wrote "The snow was falling on the cane fields."[3] The child had not yet reached the obvious statement that it wasn't snow at all, but rain that was probably falling on the cane fields. She was trying to have both cultures at the same time. But that is creolization.

What is even more important, as we develop this business of emergent language in the Caribbean, is the actual rhythm and the syllables, the very body work, in a way, of the language. What English has given us as a model for poetry, and to a lesser extent, prose (but poetry is the basic tool here), is the pentameter: "The curfew tolls the knell of parting day."[4] There have, of course, been attempts to break it. And there were other dominant forms like, for example, *Beowulf* (c. 750), *The Seafarer*,[5] and what Langland (1322?–1400) had produced:

For trewthe telleth that love. is triacle of hevene;
May no synne be on him sene. that useth that spise,
And alle his werkes he wrougte. with love as him liste.[6]

Or, from *Piers the Plowman* (which does not make it into *Palgrave's Golden Treasury*,[7] but which we all had to "do" at school) the haunting prologue:

In a somer seson. whan soft was the sonne
I shope me into shroudes. as I a shepe were

Which has recently inspired our own Derek Walcott[8] to his first major nation language effort:

---

[1] [Brathwaite's note] The Maroons were Africans and escaped slaves who, after running away or participating in successful rebellions, set up autonomous societies throughout plantation America in marginal and certainly inaccessible areas outside European influence. See Richard Price, ed., *Maroon Societies: Rebel Slave Communities in the Americas* (Garden City, New York: Anchor Books, 1973). Nanny of the Maroons, an ex-Ashanti (?) Queen Mother, is regarded as one of the greatest of the Jamaica freedom fighters. See Edward Kamau Brathwaite, *Wars of Respect: Nanny, Sam Sharpe, and the Struggle for People's Liberation* (Kingston, Jamaica: Agency for Public Information, 1977).

[2] [Brathwaite's note] But see Anthony Hinkson's Barbados hurricane poem, "Janet," in his unpublished collection "Slavation" (Bridgetown, Barbados: unpublished, c. 1976).

[3] [Brathwaite's note] I am indebted to Ann Walmsley, editor of the anthology *The Sun's Eye: West Indian Writing for Young Readers* (London: Longmans, Green & Co., Ltd., 1968), for this example. For experiences of teachers trying to cope with West Indian English in Britain, see Chris Searle, *The Forsaken Lover: White Words and Black People* (London: Routledge & Kegan Paul, 1972) and *Okike* 15 (August 1979).

[4] *The curfew tolls ... day* First line of English poet Thomas Gray's "Elegy Written in a Country Churchyard" (1751); the line is often used as an example of iambic pentameter.

[5] *Beowulf ... Seafarer* Both *Beowulf* and *The Seafarer* are Old English poems written in alliterative verse, a verse form that uses the repetition of consonant sounds to structure the poetic line.

[6] *For trewthe ... liste* These lines are from William Langland's Middle English poem *Piers Plowman* (c. 1370).

[7] *Palgrave's Golden Treasury* Popular and influential anthology of English poetry that has been in print since 1861.

[8] *Derek Walcott* Saint Lucian poet (1930–2017).

In idle August, while the sea soft,
and leaves of brown islands stick to the rim
of this Caribbean, I blow out the light
by the dreamless face of Maria Concepcion
to ship as a seaman on the schooner Flight.[1]

But by the time we reach Chaucer (1345–1400), the pentameter prevails. Over in the New World, the Americans—Walt Whitman[2]—tried to bridge or to break the pentameter through a cosmic movement, a large movement of sound. Cummings[3] tried to fragment it. And Marianne Moore attacked it with syllabics.[4] But basically the pentameter remained, and it carries with it a certain kind of experience, which is not the experience of a hurricane. The hurricane does not roar in pentameter. And that's the problem: how do you get a rhythm that approximates the natural experience, the environmental experience. We have been trying to break out of the entire pentametric model in the Caribbean and to move into a system that more closely and intimately approaches our own experience. So that is what we are talking about now.

It is nation language in the Caribbean that, in fact, largely ignores the pentameter. Nation language is the language that is influenced very strongly by the African model, the African aspect of our New World/Caribbean heritage. English it may be in terms of its lexicon, but it is not English in terms of its syntax. And English it certainly is not in terms of its rhythm and timbre, its own sound explosion. In its contours, it is not English, even though the words, as you hear them, would be English to a greater or lesser degree. And this brings us back to the question that some of you raised yesterday: can English be a revolutionary language? And the lovely answer that came back was: it is not English that is the agent. It is not language, but people, who make revolutions.

I think, however, that language does really have a role to play here, certainly in the Caribbean. But it is an English that is not the standard, imported, educated English, but that of the submerged, surrealist experience and sensibility, which has always been there and which is now increasingly coming to the surface and influencing the perception of contemporary Caribbean people. It is what I call, as I say, *nation language*. I use the term in contrast to *dialect*. The word dialect has been bandied about for a long time, and it carries very pejorative overtones. Dialect is thought of as "bad" English. Dialect is "inferior" English. Dialect is the language when you want to make fun of someone. Caricature speaks in dialect. Dialect has a long history coming from the plantation where people's dignity was distorted through their languages and the descriptions that the dialect gave to them. Nation language, on the other hand, is the submerged area of that dialect that is much more closely allied to the African aspect of experience in the Caribbean. It may be in English, but often it is in an English which is like a howl, or a shout, or a machine-gun, or the wind, or a wave. It is also like the blues. And sometimes it is English and African at the same time....

Now I'd like to describe for you some of the characteristics of our nation language. First of all it is from as I've said, an oral tradition. The poetry, the culture itself, exists not in a dictionary but in the tradition of the spoken word. It is based as much on sound as it is on song. That is to say, the noise that it makes is part of the meaning, and if you ignore the noise (or what you would think of as noise, shall I say), then you lose part of the meaning. When it is written, you lose the sound or the noise, and therefore you lose part of the meaning. Which is, again, why I have to have a tape recorder for this presentation. I want you to get the sound of it, rather than the sight of it.

Now in order to break down the pentameter, we discovered an ancient form which was always there, the

---

[1] [Brathwaite's note] Derek Walcott, "The Schooner *Flight*," in *The Star-Apple Kingdom* (New York: Farrar, Straus, and Giroux, 1979), p. 3. William Langland's prelude to *Piers the Plowman* is often softened into "In somer season, whan soft was the sonne / I shope me in shroudes as I shepe were," which places it closer to Walcott—and to the pentameter.

[2] *Walt Whitman* American poet (1819–92) whose long lines of free verse departed from the conventional rhythm and rhyme patterns used by his contemporaries.

[3] *Cummings* American poet E.E. Cummings (1894–1962).

[4] *Marianne Moore* American poet (1887–1962); *syllabics* In syllabic verse, the form is governed by the number of syllables, rather than the stresses, in a line.

calypso.[1] This is a form that I think everyone knows about. It does not employ the iambic pentameter. It employs dactyls.[2] It therefore mandates the use of the tongue in a certain way, the use of sound in a certain way. It is a model that we are moving naturally toward now.

(Iambic Pentameter)
To be or not to be, that is the question

(Kaiso) The stone had skidded arc'd and
bloomed into islands
Cuba San Domingo
Jamaica Puerto Rico[3]

Not only is there a difference in syllabic or stress pattern, there is an important difference in shape of intonation. In the Shakespeare (above), the voice travels in a single forward plane toward the horizon of its end. In the kaiso, after the skimming movement of the first line, we have a distinct variation. The voice dips and deepens to describe an intervallic pattern. …

The other thing about nation language is that it is part of what may be called *total expression*, a notion that is not unfamiliar to you because you are coming back to that kind of thing now. Reading is an isolated, individualistic expression. The oral tradition, on the other hand, makes demands not only on the poet but also on the audience to complete the community: the noise and sounds that the poet makes are responded to by the audience and are returned to him. Hence we have the creation of a continuum where the meaning truly resides. And this total expression comes about because people live in the open air, because people live in conditions of poverty, because people come from a historical experience where they had to rely on their own breath patterns rather than on paraphernalia like books and museums. They had to depend on *immanence*, the power within themselves, rather than the technology outside themselves. …

Today we have a very confident movement of nation language. In fact, it is inconceivable that any Caribbean poet writing today is not going to be influenced by this submerged culture, which is, in fact, an emerging culture. And it is obvious now to most Caribbean writers, I would say, except perhaps some of the exiled,[4] that one has to communicate with the audience. No one is going to assert that a poet cannot live in his ivory tower, or that a poet cannot be an individual—all that we have been through already. But the point is that for the needs of the kind of emerging society that I am defending—for the people who have had to recite "The boy/stood on/the burn/ing deck"[5] for so long, who are unable to express the power of the hurricane in the way that they write their words—at last our poets today are recognizing that it is essential that they use the resources

[1] [Brathwaite's note] The calypso (kaiso) is well treated in historical and musicological perspective by J.D. Elder, *Evolution of the Traditional Calypso of Trinidad and Tobago: a Socio-Cultural Analysis of Song-change* (Ann Arbor, Mich: University Microfilms, 1967), and by Errol Hill, *The Trinidad Carnival* (Austin: University of Texas Press, 1972). But it is Gordon Rohlehr, a critic and Reader in English at the University of the West Indies, who, apart from a few comments by C.L.R. James and Derek Walcott, is almost the only major Caribbean writer to have dealt with the literary aspects of kaiso, and with the relationship between kaiso (and reggae) and literature. Among Rohlehr's articles are: "Sparrow and the Language of the Calypso," *CAM Newsletter* 2 (1967), and *Savacou* 2 (1970); "Calypso and morality," *Moko* (17 June 1969); "The calypso as rebellion," *S.A.G.* 3 (1970); "Sounds and pressure: Jamaican blues," *Cipriani Labour College Review* (Jan. 1970); "Calypso and politics," *Moko* (29 Oct. 1971); "Forty years of calypso," *Tapia* (3 and 17 Sept. 1972 and 8 Oct. 1972); "Samuel Selvon and the language of the people," in Edward Baugh, ed., *Critics on Caribbean Literature* (London: George Allen & Unwin, 1978), pp. 153–161; and "The folk in Caribbean literature," *Tapia* (17 Dec. 1972).

[2] *dactyls* Metrical feet that are composed of one stressed syllable followed by two unstressed syllables.

[3] *To be … question* Shakespeare's *Hamlet* 3.1.57; *The stone … Puerto Rico* Opening lines from Brathwaite's poem "Calypso" (1967).

[4] [Brathwaite's note] Exile is the first significant feature of Anglophone Caribbean writing: it is the need—or the imagined need—to emigrate to metropolitan centres in order to exist as writers. Our native literature begins with McKay the exile (see his *Home to Harlem* (New York: Harper & Brothers, 1928)); and it is ending its first phase with Lamming, *Pleasures of Exile* and V.S. Naipaul (see *Newsweek*, 18 August 1980).

[5] *The boy … ing deck* Opening words of English poet Felicia Hemans's *Casabianca* (1826), a poem often memorized and recited by schoolchildren in England and its colonies from the Victorian era into the twentieth century.

that have always been there, but which have been denied to them—which they have sometimes themselves denied.

—1976 (REVISED 1984, 1986)

Calypso[1]

1

The stone had skidded arc'd and bloomed into islands:
Cuba and San Domingo
Jamaica and Puerto Rico
Granada Guadeloupe Bonaire[2]

curved stone hissed into reef
wave teeth fanged into clay
white splash flashed into spray
Bathsheba Montego Bay[3]

bloom of the arcing summers …

2

The islands roared into green plantations
ruled by silver sugar cane
sweat and profit
cutlass profit
islands ruled by sugar cane

And of course it was a wonderful time
a profitable hospitable well-worth-your-time
when captains carried receipts for rices
letters spices wigs
opera glasses swaggering asses
debtors vices pigs

O it was a wonderful time
an elegant benevolent redolent time—
and young Mrs. P.'s quick irrelevant crime
at four o'clock in the morning …

3

But what of black Sam
with the big splayed toes
and the shoe black shiny skin?

He carries bucketfulls of water
'cause his Ma's just had another daughter.

And what of John with the European name
who went to school and dreamt of fame
his boss one day called him a fool
and the boss hadn't even been to school …

4

Steel drum steel drum
hit the hot calypso dancing
hot rum hot rum
who goin' stop this bacchanalling?[4]

For we glance the banjo
dance the limbo
grow our crops by maljo[5]

have loose morals
gather corals
father our neighbour's quarrels

perhaps when they come
with their cameras and straw
hats: sacred pink tourists from the frozen Nawth

we should get down to those
white beaches
where if we don't wear breeches

---

[1] *Calypso* Musical form that originated in Trinidad and Tobago and is rooted in the West African Kaiso. Calypso songs are highly rhythmic and often carry political subtexts.

[2] *Cuba … Bonaire* Islands in the Caribbean.

[3] *Bathsheba* Village on the east coast of Barbados; *Montego Bay* City in Jamaica.

[4] *bacchanalling* Partying; a bacchanal is a festival in honor of the Greek god of wine, Bacchus, and is associated with drunken revelry. "Bacchanal" can also refer to a song sung in honor of the god.

[5] *maljo* Trinidadian term for "evil eye."

it becomes an island dance
Some people doin' well
while others are catchin' hell

o the boss gave our Johnny the sack
though we beg him please
please to take 'im back

so the boy now nigratin' overseas …
—1967

GEOFFREY HILL (1932–2016)

Geoffrey Hill, often referred to as a "late modernist" poet, began publishing important work in the 1950s. Hill grew up in a small town in Worcestershire, and the history and geography of the West Midlands are a continuing presence in his writing, perhaps most notably in *Mercian Hymns* (1971); more broadly, his poetry often explores connections with history and poetic tradition. His numerous books include *For the Unfallen* (1959), *Tenebrae* (1978), *The Orchards of Syon* (2002), *Without Title* (2006), and *Clavics* (2011). He was knighted in 2012.

A Short History of British India (2)

Suppose they sweltered here three thousand years
patient for our destruction. There is a greeting
beyond the act. Destiny is the great thing,
true lord of annexation and arrears.

Our law-books overrule the emperors.
The mango is the bride-bed of light. Spring
jostles the flame-tree. But new mandates bring
new images of faith, good subahdars![1]

The flittering candles of the wayside shrines
melt into dawn. The sun surmounts the dust.
Krishna from Radha[2] lovingly untwines.

Lugging the earth, the oxen bow their heads.
The alien conscience of our days is lost
among the ruins and on endless roads.
—1978

[1] *subahdars* Nobles.

[2] *Krishna from Radha* In Hinduism the relationship between Krishna and Radha is expressive of the utmost passion and devotion, and of the harmony of souls.

GILLIAN CLARKE (B. 1937)

Poet, translator, and playwright Gillian Clarke's work is distinctive in its precise musicality, its historical and emotional depth, and its grounding in the Welsh landscape. Clarke served as the National Poet of Wales from 2008 to 2016 and is the author of numerous poetry collections including *Snow on the Mountain* (1971), *Letter from a Far Country* (1982), *A Recipe for Water* (2009), *Ice* (2012), and *Zoology* (2017).

Polar

Snowlight and sunlight, the lake glacial.
Too bright to open my eyes
in the dazzle and doze
of a distant January afternoon.

It's long ago and the house naps in the plush silence
of a house asleep, like absence,
I'm dreaming on the white bear's shoulder,
paddling the slow hours, my fingers in his fur.

His eyes are glass, each hair a needle of light.
He's pegged by his claws to the floor like a shirt on
the line.
He is a soul. He is what death is. He is transparency,
a loosening floe on the sea.

But I want him alive.
I want him fierce

with belly and breath and growl and beating heart,
I want him dangerous,

I want to follow him over the snows
between the immaculate earth and now,
between the silence and the shot that rang
over the ice at the top of the globe,

when the map of the earth was something we knew by heart,
and they had not shot the bear,
had not loosed the ice,
had not, had not …
—2011

TONY HARRISON (B. 1937)

The northern English writer Tony Harrison is among the most versatile and prolific of British poets. His many books of poetry include *The Loiners* (1970), the long poem *V* (1985), *The Gaze of the Gorgon* (1992), *The Shadow of Hiroshima* (1995), and *Under the Clock* (2005); he is also the author of numerous translations and adaptations of poetic drama. Much of Harrison's poetry is infused with political content, particularly on subjects such as class and modern warfare.

Them & [uz]

for Professors Richard Hoggart & Leon Cortez[1]

I

αἰαῖ, ay, ay! … stutterer Demosthenes[2]
gob full of pebbles outshouting seas—

4 words only of *mi' art*[3] *aches* and … "Mine's broken,
you barbarian, T.W.!" *He* was nicely spoken.
"Can't have our glorious heritage done to death!"

I played the Drunken Porter in *Macbeth*.[4]

"Poetry's the speech of kings. You're one of those
Shakespeare gives the comic bits to: prose!
All poetry (even Cockney Keats?)[5] you see
's been dubbed by [ËS] into RP,
Received Pronunciation, please believe [ËS]
your speech is in the hands of the Receivers."

"We say [ËS] not [uz] T.W.!" That shut my trap.
I doffed my flat a's (as in "flat cap")
my mouth all stuffed with glottals, great
lumps to hawk up and spit out … *E-nun-ci-ate!*

2

So right, yer buggers, then! We'll occupy
your lousy leasehold Poetry.

I chewed up Littererchewer and spat the bones
into the lap of dozing Daniel Jones,
dropped the initials I'd been harried as
and used my *name* and own voice: [uz] [uz] [uz],
ended sentences with by, with, from,[6]
and spoke the language that I spoke at home.
R.I.P. RP. R.I.P. T.W.
I'm *Tony* Harrison no longer you!

[1] *Richard Hoggart* British sociologist and cultural commentator (1918–2014); *Leon Cortez* British film, radio, and television actor (1898–1970).

[2] *Demosthenes* Greatest of all orators in ancient Greece, Demosthenes (384–322 BCE) is said to have placed rocks in his mouth in an effort to improve his enunciation.

[3] *'art* Heart. The dropped "h" has often been regarded in Britain as a sign of "lower class" pronunciation. "My heart aches" are the first words of John Keats's "Ode to a Nightingale."

[4] *Drunken Porter … Macbeth* Servant with a small, comic role in Shakespeare's play.

[5] *Cockney Keats* The Romantic poet John Keats (1795–1821) came from a Cockney (i.e., east London) background and was attacked for allegedly representing a "Cockney School of Poetry."

[6] *by, with, from* Three examples of prepositions; strict grammarians assert that a sentence must not end with a preposition.

You can tell the Receivers where to go
(and not aspirate[1] it) once you know
Wordsworth's *matter/water* are full rhymes,
[uz] can be loving as well as funny.

My first mention in the *Times*
automatically made Tony Anthony!
—1981

Liz Lochhead (b. 1947)

A celebrated playwright as well as a poet, Liz Lochhead has become known for engaging with feminist concerns and issues of national identity without confining herself to one voice or perspective. Lochhead served as Scots Makar from 2011 to 2016. Her collections of poetry include *Memo for Spring* (1972), *Dreaming Frankenstein* (1984), *The Colour of Black and White: Poems 1984–2003* (2003), and *Choosing: The Selected Poetry of Liz Lochhead* (2011).

Men Talk

(*Rap*)

Women
Rabbit rabbit rabbit women
Tattle and titter
Women prattle
Women waffle and witter

Men Talk. Men Talk.

Woman into Girl Talk
About Women's trouble
Trivia 'n' Small Talk
They yap and they babble

Men Talk. Men Talk.

Women yatter
Women chatter
Women chew the fat, women spill the beans
Women aint been takin'
The oh-so Good Advice in them
Women's Magazines.

A Man likes A Good Listener.

Oh yeah
I like A Woman
Who likes me enough
Not to nitpick
Not to nag and
Not to interrupt 'cause I call that treason
A woman with the Good Grace
To be struck dumb
By me Sweet Reason. Yes—

A Man likes a Good Listener

A Real
Man
Likes a Real Good Listener

Women yap yap yap
Verbal Diarrhoea is a Female Disease
Woman she spread she rumours round she
Like Philadelphia Cream Cheese.

Oh
Bossy Women Gossip
Girlish Women Giggle
Women natter, women nag
Women niggle niggle niggle

Men Talk.

Men
Think First, Speak Later
Men Talk.
—1985

[1] *aspirate* Pronounce the "h" when it appears at the beginning of a word (as opposed to dropping it).

Kidspoem/Bairnsang

it wis January
and a gey dreich day
the first day Ah went to the school
so my Mum happed me up in ma
good navy-blue napp coat wi the rid tartan hood
birled a scarf aroon ma neck
pu'ed oan ma pixie an' my pawkies
it wis that bitter
said *noo ye'll no starve*
gie'd me a wee kiss and a kid-oan skelp oan the bum
and sent me aff across the playground
tae the place Ah'd learn to say
it was January
and a really dismal day
the first day I went to school
so my mother wrapped me up in my
best navy-blue top coat with the red tartan hood,
twirled a scarf around my neck,
pulled on my bobble-hat and mittens
it was so bitterly cold
said *now you won't freeze to death*
gave me a little kiss and a pretend slap on the bottom
to the place I'd learn to forget to say
it wis January
and a gey dreich day
the first day Ah went to the school
so my Mum happed me up in ma
good navy-blue napp coat wi the rid tartan hood,
birled a scarf aroon ma neck,
pu'ed oan ma pixie an' ma pawkies
it wis that bitter.

Oh saying it was one thing
but when it came to writing it
in black and white
the way it had to be said
was as if you were posh, grown-up, male, English and dead.

—1995

GRACE NICHOLS (B. 1950)

A native of Guyana, Grace Nichols moved to England in 1977 and began to make a mark as a poet in the 1980s with work of challenging and exuberant directness, often written with a view as much to performance as to the printed page. Her books include *I is a long-memoried woman* (1983), *The Fat Black Woman's Poems* (1984), *Everybody Got a Gift* (2005), *Picasso, I Want My Face Back* (2009), and *The Insomnia Poems* (2017).

Skanking[1] *Englishman Between Trains*

Met him at Birmingham Station[2]
small yellow hair Englishman
hi fi stereo swinging in one hand
walking in rhythm to reggae sound/Man

he was alive
he was full-o-jive
said he had a lovely
Jamaican wife

Said he couldn't remember
the taste of English food
I like mih drops[3]
me johnny cakes[4]
me peas and rice
me soup/Man

he was alive
he was full-o-jive
said he had a lovely
Jamaican wife

Said, showing me her photo
whenever we have a little quarrel

[1] *Skanking* Dancing; swaggering.

[2] *Birmingham Station* Located in the British Midlands, the city of Birmingham's railway station is a hub where many train lines meet.

[3] *drops* Drop-shaped cakes; also, sugar plums or candies.

[4] *johnny cakes* In the West Indies, a term for dumplings or scones.

you know/to sweeten her up
I surprise her with a nice mango/Man

he was alive
he was full-o-jive
said he had a lovely Jamaican wife
—1984

Epilogue

I have crossed an ocean
I have lost my tongue
from the root of the old one
a new one has sprung
—1984

White

Never mind how or why—
this slow delight
of waking to a room
that comes out of the
memory of night,
A dusky dawning—
paintings, wardrobe,
hangings …

Then walking, a sleepwalker,
holding on to walls of vanilla,
great solid slabs
you could sink your mouth into.
The memories of ancestors,
all that blackness
against whiteness.
The starched religiousness of it.

O I could hold
the globe like a face,
Januslike[1] spinning
from the depths of my dreaming
I could face-up
to the stark white page
already seeded
with the best invisible poem.
—1996

Medbh McGuckian (b. 1950)

Medbh McGuckian came into prominence as a writer in the 1980s and 1990s. McGuckian's work, known for its difficulty and elusiveness, is often focused on women and women's creativity; early collections such as *The Flower Master* (1982) hint at her experiences as a poet with postpartum depression. Some of her later work is more direct in its attention to history and politics, as in *Blaris Moor* (2016), which examines instances of political violence in Ireland.

Slips

The studied poverty of a moon roof
The earthenware of dairies cooled by apple trees,
The apple tree that makes the whitest wash …

But I forget names, remembering them wrongly
Where they touch upon another name,
A town in France like a woman's Christian name.

My childhood is preserved as a nation's history,
My favourite fairytales the shells
Leased by the hermit crab.

I see my grandmother's death as a piece of ice,
My mother's slimness restored to her,
My own key slotted in your door—

[1] *Januslike* I.e., having two faces; referring to Janus, the Roman god of doorways and of beginnings and endings, who was depicted with two faces, each looking in the opposite direction.

Tricks you might guess from this unfastened button,
A pen mislaid, a word misread,
My hair coming down in the middle of a conversation.
—1982

The Dream-Language of Fergus

1

Your tongue has spent the night
in its dim sack as the shape of your foot
in its cave. Not the rudiment
of half a vanquished sound,
the excommunicated shadow of a name,
has rumpled the sheets of your mouth.

2

So Latin sleeps, they say, in Russian speech,
so one river inserted into another
becomes a leaping, glistening, splashed
and scattered alphabet
jutting out from the voice,
till what began as a dog's bark
ends with bronze, what began
with honey ends with ice;
as if an aeroplane in full flight
launched a second plane,
the sky is stabbed by their exits
and the mistaken meaning of each.

3

Conversation is as necessary
among these familiar campus trees
as the apartness of torches;
and if I am a threader
of double-stranded words, whose
Quando[1] has grown into now,
no text can return the honey
in its path of light from a jar,
only a seed-fund, a pendulum,
pressing out the diasporic snow.
—1991

---

[1] *Quando* Latin: When.

PAUL MULDOON (B. 1951)

Paul Muldoon first began publishing poetry in the 1970s; he has since worked as a producer for the BBC Network in Belfast, taught at Princeton University, and served as poetry editor for *The New Yorker*. His collections include *New Weather* (1973), *Quoof* (1983), *Hay* (1998), *Moy Sand and Gravel* (2002), *Maggot* (2010), and *One Thousand Things Worth Knowing* (2015). Known for his inventive use of traditional forms, Muldoon uses his trademark wit and wordplay to bring to life both personal and universal images.

Milkweed and Monarch

As he knelt by the grave of his mother and father
the taste of dill, or tarragon—
he could barely tell one from the other—

filled his mouth. It seemed as if he might smother.
Why should he be stricken
with grief, not for his mother and father,

but a woman slinking from the fur of a sea-otter
in Portland, Maine, or, yes, Portland, Oregon—
he could barely tell one from the other—

and why should he now savour
the tang of her, her little pickled gherkin,
as he knelt by the grave of his mother and father?

He looked about. He remembered her palaver
on how both earth and sky would darken—
"You could barely tell one from the other"—

while the Monarch butterflies passed over
in their milkweed-hunger: "A wing-beat, some reckon,
may trigger off the mother and father

of all storms, striking your Irish Cliffs of Moher
with the force of a hurricane."

Then: "Milkweed and Monarch 'invented' each
other."

———

He looked about. Cow's-parsley in a samovar.[1]
He'd mistaken his mother's name, "Regan," for
"Anger":
as he knelt by the grave of his mother and father
he could barely tell one from the other.
—1994

At Tuam[2]

Among the hundreds of children who stare up at
us from their septic tank
is James Muldoon, who died in 1927
at the age of four months. At least he would never be
forced to thank
the Lord for mercies large or small. That cry to high
heaven
must come from Brendan Muldoon, who died in 1943
at a mere five weeks. A teenage nun bows before an
unleavened
host held up by a priest like a moon held up by an
ash tree.
In 1947 the eleven month old Bridget Muldoon,
a namesake of the mother
who would shortly give birth to me,
has already distinguished herself as being a bit of a
bother
while Dermott Muldoon, three months old in 1950,
is about to join the ranks
of my foster-sisters and foster-brothers
in that unthinkable world where a wasp may recognize
another wasp's face[3]
and an elephant grieve for an elephant down at the
watering place.
—2017

[1] *samovar* Russian tea urn.

[2] *Tuam* Town in County Galway, Ireland. Tuam was the site of the Bon Secours Mother and Baby Home, an institution operated by Catholic nuns as a site for unmarried mothers to give birth and as a foster home for the children who were born there. Mothers were in some cases separated from their children without their consent, and hundreds of children were sent to the United States for illegal adoptions. The home, which operated from 1925 to 1961, had had a remarkably high infant death rate, and in the 2010s it was discovered that the remains of a large number of children had been buried in an unmarked grave, in what appeared to be a sewage tank. A list of the names and ages of the children who died at the home was also published; "At Tuam" mentions all of the children with the last name Muldoon who appeared on the list.

[3] *wasp … wasp's face* In the early 2000s, it was demonstrated that members of some species of paper wasp can recognize the facial markings of other individuals of the species.

Linton Kwesi Johnson (b. 1952)

Born in Jamaica, Linton Kwesi Johnson has lived for most of his life in south London. The first and best-known practitioner of "dub poetry" (a term coined by Johnson to describe a blend of poetry and reggae music), he has worked as a journalist and broadcaster as well as a poet and musician. His books include *Dread, Beat, an' Blood* (1975), *Tings an' Times* (1991), and *Mi Revalueshanary Fren* (2002).

Inglan Is a Bitch

W'en mi jus' come to Landan toun
mi use to work pan di andahgroun[4]
but workin' pan di andahgroun
y'u don't get fi know your way aroun'

Inglan is a bitch
dere's no escapin' it
Inglan is a bitch
dere's no runnin' whey fram it

mi get a lickle jab in a big 'otell
an' awftah a while, mi woz doin' quite well
dem staat mi aaf as a dish-washah
but w'en mi tek a stack, mi noh tun clack-watchah!

[4] *andahgroun* Underground (i.e., subway).

Inglan is a bitch
dere's no escapin' it
Inglan is a bitch
noh baddah try fi hide fram it

w'en dem gi' yu di lickle wage packit
fus dem rab it wid dem big tax racket
y'u haffi struggle fi mek en's meet
an' w'en y'u goh a y'u bed y'u jus' cant sleep

Inglan is a bitch
dere's no escapin' it
Inglan is a bitch fi true
a noh lie mi a tell, a true

mi use to work dig ditch w'en it cowl noh bitch
mi did strang like a mule, but, bwoy, mi did fool
den awftah a while mi jus' stap dhu ovahtime
den awftah a while mi jus' phu dung mi tool

Inglan is a bitch
dere's no escapin' it
Inglan is a bitch
y'u haffi know how fi suvvive in it

well mi dhu day wok an' mi dhu nite wok
mi dhu clean wok an' mi dhu dutty wok
dem seh dat black man is very lazy
but if y'u si how mi wok y'u woulda seh mi crazy

Inglan is a bitch
dere's no escapin' it
Inglan is a bitch
y'u bettah face up to it

dem have a lickle facktri up inna Brackly[1]
inna disya facktri all dem dhu is pack crackry
fi di laas fifteen years dem get mi laybah
now awftah fifteen years mi fall out a fayvah

Inglan is a bitch
dere's no escapin' it

[1] *Brackly* Industrial area of London.

Inglan is a bitch
dere's no runnin' whey fram it

mi know dem have work, work in abundant
yet still, dem mek mi redundant[2]
now, at fifty-five mi gettin' quite ol'
yet still, dem sen' mi fi goh draw dole

Inglan is a bitch
dere's no escapin' it
Inglan is a bitch fi true
is whey wi a goh dhu 'bout it?
—1980

[2] *mek mi redundant* Make me redundant (i.e., lay me off).

Moniza Alvi (b. 1954)

An important voice in the generation of British poets who came to prominence in the 1990s, Moniza Alvi has been a school teacher and college tutor as well as a poet. Born in Pakistan, she has lived in England since infancy; much of her poetry concerns issues of identity. Alvi's books include *The Country at My Shoulder* (1993), *A Bowl of Warm Air* (1996), *How the Stone Found Its Voice* (2005), *At the Time of Partition* (2013), and *Blackbird, Bye Bye* (2018).

And If

If you could choose a country
to belong to—
perhaps you had one
snatched away,
once offered to you
like a legend
in a basket covered with a cloth—

and if the sun were a simple flare,
the streets beating out
the streets, and your breath
lost on the road

with the Yadavs,[1] herding cattle,
then you could rest, absorb
it all in the cool of the hills,

but still you might peel back one face
to retrieve another
and another, down to the face that is
unbearable, so clear
so complex, hinting at nations,
castes and sub-castes
and you would touch it once—

and if this Eastern track were
a gusty English lane
where rain makes mirrors
in the holes,
a rat lies lifeless, sodden
as an old floorcloth,
you'd be untouchable[2]—as one

defined by someone else—
one who cleans the toilets,
burns the dead.
—1996

How the World Split in Two

Was it widthways or lengthways?
a quarrel with the equator?
Did the rawness of the inside sparkle?

Only this is true:
there was an arm on one side
and a hand on the other,
a thought on one side
and a hush on the other.

And a luminous tear
carried on the back of a beetle
went backwards and forwards
from one side to the other.
—2005

[1] *Yadavs* One of the most ancient Aryan groups of Bharata, the Yadavs live in parts of India, Nepal, and Bangladesh, and most follow the Hindu religion.

[2] *untouchable* In the caste system of Hindu societies, the lowest caste is that of the untouchables, who are traditionally restricted from any jobs other than menial ones (such as cleaning toilets and cremating bodies).

Jean Binta Breeze (b. 1957)

One of Britain's leading "dub" poets (and a female pioneer in that male-dominated genre), Jean Binta Breeze spent her early years in Jamaica; she has lived primarily in London since the late 1970s. Her work deals extensively with political themes, with a frequent focus on the cultural connections between Britain and the Caribbean. Her books include *Ryddim Ravings* (1988), *The Arrival of Brighteye and Other Poems* (2000), *The Fifth Figure* (2006), *Third World Girl: Selected Poems* (2011), and *The Verandah Poems* (2016).

earth cries

She doesn't cry for water
she runs rivers deep
she doesn't cry for food
she has suckled trees
she doesn't cry for clothing
she weaves all that she wears
she doesn't cry for shelter
she grows thatch everywhere
she doesn't cry for children
she's got more than she can bear
she doesn't cry for heaven
she knows it's everywhere
you don't know why she's crying
when she's got everything
how could you know she's crying
for just one humane being
—2000

GWYNETH LEWIS (B. 1959)

A leading poet in both Welsh and English, Gwyneth Lewis has expressed through her work an abiding fascination with issues relating to culture and language. Among her books of poetry in English are *Parables and Faxes* (1995), *Zero Gravity* (1998), *Keeping Mum* (2003), and *Sparrow Tree* (2011). In 2005 she was appointed the first National Poet for Wales.

Mother Tongue

"I started to translate in seventy-three
in the schoolyard. For a bit of fun
to begin with—the occasional 'fuck'
for the bite of another language's smoke
at the back of my throat, its bitter chemicals.
Soon I was hooked on whole sentences
behind the shed, and lessons in Welsh
seemed very boring. I started on print,
Jeeves & Wooster, Dick Francis,[1] James Bond,
in Welsh covers. That worked for a while
until Mam discovered Jean Plaidy[2] inside
a Welsh concordance[3] one Sunday night.
There were ructions:[4] a language, she screamed,
should be for a lifetime. Too late for me.
Soon I was snorting Simenon
and Flaubert.[5] Had to read much more
for any effect. One night I OD'd
after reading far too much Proust.[6]
I came to, but it scared me. For a while
I went Welsh-only but it was bland
and my taste was changing. Before too long
I was back on translating, found that three
languages weren't enough. The 'ch'
in German was easy, Rilke[7] a buzz …
For a language fetishist like me
sex is part of the problem. Umlauts[8] make me sweat,
so I need a multilingual man
but they're rare in West Wales and tend to be
married already. If only I'd kept
myself much purer, with simpler tastes,
the Welsh might be living …
Detective, you speak
Russian, I hear, and Japanese.
Could you whisper some softly?
I'm begging you. Please …"
—2004

[1] *Jeeves & Wooster* Main characters in a series of popular English comic novels by P.G. Wodehouse (1881–1975); *Dick Francis* Former jockey and author of dozens of popular thrillers set against a backdrop of horseracing (1920–2010).

[2] *Jean Plaidy* Popular English author of romance novels (1910–83).

[3] *concordance* Alphabetical list of the main words contained in a book, with excerpts from the passages in which they occur.

[4] *ructions* Quarrels.

[5] *Simenon* Georges Simenon (1903–89), a Belgian novelist best known for his popular detective stories; *Flaubert* Gustave Flaubert (1821–80), a French novelist perhaps most celebrated for his novel *Madame Bovary* (1856).

[6] *Proust* Marcel Proust (1871–1922), a French novelist who was one of the most celebrated literary figures of the late nineteenth and early twentieth centuries; best known for his seven-volume work *À la recherche du temps perdu*.

[7] *Rilke* Renowned German poet Rainer Maria Rilke (1875–1926).

[8] *Umlauts* Diacritical signs (¨) placed over vowels to express a change in the sound of that vowel because of the influence of an adjacent vowel.

KENAN MALIK (B. 1960)

After studying neurobiology and the history and philosophy of science, Kenan Malik became a lecturer, broadcaster, and writer. His books include *The Meaning of Race* (1996), *Man, Beast and Zombie* (2000), *Strange Fruit* (2008), *From Fatwa to Jihad* (2009), and *The Quest for a Moral Compass* (2014). His writing explores a wide range of topics, including scientific, political, and social thought regarding multiculturalism, race, and human nature.

Multiculturalism and the Road to Terror

How could four ordinary men born and brought up in Britain turn into such savage killers? That is the question Britain has been asking itself in wake of the London tube bombings that killed 52 people on 7 July.[1] Three of the four men involved, Mohammed Sidique Khan, Shehzad Tanweer and Hasib Hussain came from Yorkshire in the North of England. The fourth, Jamaican-born Germaine Lindsay, lived in Luton about 30 miles north of London. None of them were considered extremists, all of them were seemingly well integrated into their communities.

The popular picture of Islamic terrorists is drawn from the caricatures of mad mullahs,[2] bearded fanatics and foreign zealots that people the press. Yet few recent terrorists have fitted this picture. Many have been Western born, Western educated, and seemingly ordinary. The most detailed study yet on Al-Qaeda[3] supporters, carried out by Marc Sageman of the University of Pennsylvania, shows that the majority are middle class with good jobs. Most are college educated, usually in the West. Fewer than one in 10 have been to religious school.

Shortly after the bombings the government set up an "extremism taskforce," composed mainly of Muslim leaders, to try to answer the question as to how men such as these could get gripped by a fanatic zeal for an irrational, murderous dogma, and be possessed with a hatred for such virtues as democracy and decency. And how could it be prevented from happening again? The taskforce has just published its first conclusions. The London bombings, it reported, were the work of young men alienated by Islamophobia. The best way to combat extremism, the taskforce suggested, is by recognising Muslim grievances and by establishing a more plural society in which moderate Muslim leaders are able to wield greater political power. Its recommendations included a "rapid rebuttal unit" to combat Islamophobia, a better reflection of Islam in the national educational curriculum, a national "roadshow" of Muslim scholars to tour Muslim communities and a training programme for imams.[4]

The taskforce hopes that these proposals will isolate extremists and build a better relationship between Muslims and the government. In fact the proposals will make matters worse. The real problem is not Islamophobia but the culture of grievance created by Britain's multicultural policies. Certainly Muslims face discrimination and harassment. But the extent of such discrimination has been greatly exaggerated by both government and Muslim leaders. There is, for instance, a widespread perception that Muslims are disproportionately stopped and searched by the police under Britain's anti-terror laws. Last year I interviewed Iqbal Sacranie, general secretary of the Muslim Council of Britain, for a documentary I was making for British TV. He claimed that "95 to 98 per cent" of those stopped under the terror laws were Muslim. In fact the vast majority are white. Just 15 per cent are Asians (Britain collects figures by race rather than by religion).

The more that the threat of Islamophobia is embellished in this fashion, the more that ordinary Muslims come to accept that theirs is a community under constant attack. It helps create a siege mentality, stoking up anger and resentment, and making Muslim community more inward looking and more open to religious extremism. What we need is not for exaggerated grievances to be nurtured but to be challenged.

Muslims have been in Britain in large numbers since the 1950s. Only recently has fanaticism taken hold. The first generation of immigrants faced greater hardships and more intense racism than do today's Muslims. Yet most thought of themselves as British and were proud to be here. While that first generation often put up with racism, the second generation (my generation) challenged it head on, often leading to fierce confrontations with the police and other authorities. But however fierce those confrontations, we recognised that to fight racism

[1] *London tube … 7 July* The series of four coordinated suicide bombings occurred on London's public transit system in 2005.

[2] *mullahs* Scholars of Islam.

[3] *Al-Qaeda* Islamic fundamentalist organization responsible for several major terrorist attacks, including the 11 September 2001 attacks on the World Trade Center and other American targets.

[4] *imams* Islamic religious leaders.

we needed to find a common set of values, hopes and aspirations that united whites and non-whites, Muslims and non-Muslims, not separate ourselves from the rest of society.

It has only been over the past decade that radical Islam has found a hearing in Britain. Today "radical" in an Islamic context means someone who espouses a fundamentalist theology. Twenty years ago it meant the opposite: a secularist who challenged the power of the mosques within Muslim communities. The expunging of that radical secularist tradition has played an important part in the rise of Islamic militancy in this country. To understand how this happened we need to look closely at what happened in the 80s and in particular at how the emergence of multicultural policies helped create a more fragmented nation with little sense of a common identity and created the space for the growth of Islamic militancy.

Thirty years ago, Britain was a very different place than it is now. When I was growing up in the 1970s and 1980s racism was vicious, visceral and often fatal. Stabbings were common, firebombings almost weekly events. I remember having to organise patrols on East London estates in the 1980s to protect Asian families from racist thugs. Police harassment was common. The so-called "sus" laws, which allowed the police to stop and search people on "suspicion" of committing an offence were used to persecute immigrant communities. Deaths in police custody were not uncommon; between 1969 and 1999 more than 1000 people died while in the hands of the police. Discrimination in housing, employment and the services was the norm. These issues shaped immigrant struggles. In the sixties and seventies four main issues dominated the struggle for racial equality: opposition to discriminatory immigration controls; the fight against racist attacks; the struggle for equality in the workplace; and, most explosively, the issue of police brutality.

These struggles politicised a new generation of activists and came to an explosive climax in the inner city riots of the late seventies and early eighties. Just as the extremism taskforce argues now, so the authorities argued then that unless black and Asian communities were given a political stake in the system, their frustration could threaten the stability of British cities. It was against this background that the policies of multiculturalism emerged. The Greater London Council, led by Ken Livingstone (who today is the mayor of London) pioneered a new strategy of making immigrant communities feel part of British society. It organised consultation with black and Asian communities, drew up equal opportunities policies, established race relations units and dispensed millions of pounds in grants to community organisations.

At the heart of the strategy was a redefinition of racism. Racism now meant not simply the denial of equal rights but the denial of the right to be different. Black and Asian people, many argued, should not be forced to accept British values, or to adopt a British identity. Rather different peoples should have the right to express their identities, explore their own histories, formulate their own values, pursue their own lifestyles. In this process, the very meaning of equality was transformed: from possessing the same rights as everyone else to possessing different rights, appropriate to different communities. Equality no longer meant treating everybody equally despite their racial, cultural, ethnic or religious differences but treating people differently because of them.

Many local authorities followed London's lead, including Bradford, the heart of Britain's Muslim community. By the early 80s Bradford too was facing militancy within Asian communities and unrest on the streets. In 1977 young Asians formed the Asian Youth Movement (AYM) to defend their civil rights. AYM activists did not distinguish themselves as Muslim, Hindu or Sikh; indeed many did not even see themselves as specifically Asian, preferring to call themselves "black" which they viewed as an all-inclusive term for non-white immigrants. They challenged not just racism but also many traditional values too, particularly within the Muslim community, helping establish an alternative leadership that confronted traditionalists on issues such as the role of women and the dominance of the mosque. In response, Bradford council drew up equal opportunity statements, established race relations units and began funding Asian organisations. A 12-point race relations plan declared that every section of the "multiracial, multicultural city" had "an equal right to maintain its own identity, culture, language, religion and customs."

Multiculturalism transformed the character of antiracism. By the mid-eighties the focus of antiracist protest in Bradford had shifted from political issues, such as policing and immigration, to religious and cultural issues: a demand for Muslim schools and for separate education for girls, a campaign for halal[1] meat to be served at school, and, most explosively, the confrontation over the publication of Salman Rushdie's *The Satanic Verses*.[2]

Political struggles unite across ethnic or cultural divisions; cultural struggles inevitably fragment. As different groups began asserting their particular identities ever more fiercely, so the shift from the political to the cultural arena helped create a more tribal city. At the same time, since every group was now defined by its culture, militancy came to be seen as the demand for greater cultural authenticity. Secular Muslims were regarded as betraying their culture while radical Islam became not just more acceptable but, to many, more authentic.

This process was strengthened by a new relationship between the local council and the local mosques. In 1981, the council helped set up and fund the Bradford Council of Mosques and looked to it as a voice of the community. This helped marginalise secular radicals—the Asian Youth Movement eventually broke up—and allowed religious leaders to reassert their power. As the secular tradition became squeezed out, so the only place offering shelter for disaffected youth was militant Islam.

In the wake of the London bombings much was said about the strength of Britain as a multicultural nation. What makes London great, mayor Ken Livingstone pointed out, was what the bombers most fear: a city full of people from across the globe free to pursue their own lives. I agree, and that's why I choose to live in this city. Multiculturalism as a lived experience enriches our lives. But multiculturalism as a political ideology has helped create a tribal Britain with no political or moral centre.

For an earlier generation of Muslims their religion was not so strong that it prevented them from identifying with Britain. Today many young British Muslims identify more with Islam than Britain primarily because there no longer seems much that is compelling about being British. Of course, there is little to romanticise in old-style Britishness with its often racist vision of belongingness. Back in the fifties policy makers feared that, in the words of a Colonial Office report, "a large coloured community would weaken … the concept of England or Britain."

That old racist notion of identity has thankfully crumbled. But nothing new has come to replace it. The very notion of creating common values has been abandoned except at a most minimal level. Britishness has come to be defined simply as a toleration of difference. The politics of ideology has given way to the politics of identity, creating a more fragmented Britain, and one where many groups assert their identity through a sense of victimhood and grievance, something that has been particularly true of Muslim communities.

Multiculturalism did not create militant Islam, but it helped create a space for it within British Muslim communities that had not existed before. It fostered a more tribal nation, created a grievance culture, strengthened the hand of conservative religious leaders, undermined progressive trends within the Muslim communities and created a vacuum into which radical Islam stepped, and all in the name of combating racism. The danger with the recommendations of the extremism taskforce is that history might be about to repeat itself.
—2006

[1] *halal* In conformity with Islamic law; the term is frequently applied to food that is prepared in the appropriate way.

[2] *confrontation over … Satanic Verses* *The Satanic Verses* (1988), a novel by Salman Rushdie, was condemned by many Muslim leaders for its portrayal of the prophet Muhammed, and there were violent protests in the United Kingdom and elsewhere against Rushdie. Iran's leader, Ayatollah Ruhollah Khomeini, issued a *fatwa* calling for Rushdie to be killed, and the author went into hiding for several years.

JACKIE KAY (B. 1961)

Born in Scotland to a Nigerian father and Scottish mother, Jackie Kay was brought up by adoptive parents; her first book of poetry, *The Adoption Papers* (1991), focuses on issues of personal and cultural identity. Among her widely praised subsequent works are the poetry collections *Other Lovers* (1993), *Life Mask* (2005), and *Fiere* (2011); the memoir *Red Dust Road* (2010); and the novel *Trumpet* (1998). Kay was appointed Scots Makar in 2016; in the announcement of her appointment she was praised for "her poignant and honest words" and for her "particular Scottish brand of gallus humour."[1]

In My Country

Walking by the waters
down where an honest river
shakes hands with the sea,
a woman passed round me
in a slow watchful circle,
as if I were a superstition;

or the worst dregs of her imagination,
so when she finally spoke
her words spliced into bars
of an old wheel. A segment of air.
"*Where do you come from?*"
"Here," I said. "Here. These parts."
—1991

Extinction

We closed the borders, folks, we nailed it.
No trees, no plants, no immigrants.
No foreign nurses, no Doctors; we smashed it.
We took control of our affairs. No fresh air.
No birds, no bees, no HIV, no Poles, no pollen.
No pandas, no polar bears, no ice, no dice.
No rainforests, no foraging, no France.
No frogs, no golden toads, no Harlequins.[2]
No Greens, no Brussels,[3] no vegetarians, no lesbians.
No carbon curbed emissions, no Co_2 questions.
No lions, no tigers, no bears. No BBC picked audience.
No loony lefties,[4] please. No politically correct classes.
No classes. No Guardian[5] readers. No readers.
No emus, no EUs, no Eco warriors, no Euros,
No rhinos, no zebras, no burnt bras, no elephants.
We shut it down! No immigrants, no immigrants.
No sniveling-recycling-global-warming nutters.
Little man, little woman, the world is a dangerous place.
Now, pour me a pint, dear. Get out of my fracking face.
—2015, REVISED 2016

SIMON ARMITAGE (B. 1963)

Simon Armitage is equally at home with subtle lyricism and with the poetry of politics and performance. A native of northern England, Armitage has written widely in many genres. His books of poetry include *Zoom!* (1989), *Kid* (1992), *The Universal Home Doctor* (2002), *Tyrannosaurus Rex Versus the Corduroy Kid* (2006), *Seeing Stars* (2010), and *The Unaccompanied* (2017).

The English

They are a gentleman farmer, living
on reduced means, a cricketer's widow
sowing a kitchen garden with sweet peas.
A lighthouse-keeper counting aeroplanes.

[1] *gallus humour* Gallows humor, a style of humor that incorporates irony and bleak or shocking subject matter.

[2] *golden toads* The golden toad was one of the first species to become extinct as world amphibian populations began to decline; many other amphibian species have become extinct since then, and hundreds are critically endangered; *Harlequins* Many types of harlequin toad are already extinct; others are endangered.

[3] *Greens* Members of the left-wing Scottish Green party; *Brussels* Headquarters of the European Union.

[4] *loony lefties* Term popularized by Conservative politicians and news organizations during Britain's 1987 general election.

[5] *Guardian* Prominent British newspaper whose readers tend toward the left of the political spectrum.

Old blackout curtains staunch the break of day.
Regard the way they dwell, the harking back:
how the women at home went soldiering on
with pillows for husbands, fingers for sons,

how man after man emerged at dawn
from his house, in his socks, then laced his boots
on the step, locked up, then steadied himself
to post a key back through the letterbox.

The afternoon naps, the quaint hours they keep.
But since you ask them, that is how they sleep.
—2002

Poundland[1]

Came we then to the place abovementioned,[2]
crossed its bristled threshold through robotic
glass doors,
entered its furry heat, its flesh-toned fluorescent light.
Thus with wire-wrought baskets we voyaged,
and some with trolleys, back wheels flipping like
trout tails,
cruised the narrow canyons twixt cascading shelves,
the prow of our journeying cleaving stale air.
Legion were the items that came tamely to hand:
five stainless steel teaspoons, ten corn-relief plasters,
the Busy Bear pedal-bin liners fragranced with
country lavender,
the Disney design calendar and diary set, three cans
of Vimto,[3]
cornucopia of potato-based snacks and balm for a
sweet tooth,
toys and games, goods of Orient made, and of
Cathay,° *China*
all under the clouded eye of CCTV,
beyond the hazard cone where serious chutney
spillage had occurred.
Then emerged souls: the duty manager with a face
like Doncaster,[4]
mumbling, "For so much, what shall we give in return?"[5]
The blood-stained employee of the month,
sobbing on a woolsack[6] of fun-fur rugs,
many uniformed servers, spectral, drifting between
aisles.
Then came Elpenor, our old friend Elpenor,[7]
slumped and shrunken by the Seasonal Products display.
In strangled words I managed,
"How art thou come to these shady channels,
into hell's ravine?"[8]
And he:
"To loan sharks I owe the bone and marrow of
my all."
Then Walt Whitman, enquiring politely of the
delivery boy.[9]
And from Special Occasions came forth Tiresias,
dead in life, alive in death, cider-scented and sockless,
Oxfam-clad,[10] shaving cuts to both cheeks.
And my own mother reaching out, slipping a tin
of stewing steak[11]

---

[1] *Poundland* British discount chain store.

[2] *Came we then … abovementioned* See Ezra Pound, Canto 1: "The ocean flowing backward, came we then to the place / Aforesaid by Circe." Pound's canto is itself a loose translation of a portion of Book 11 of the *Odyssey* in which Odysseus summons the souls of the dead so that he can ask the guidance of the dead prophet-king Tiresias.

[3] *Vimto* Brand of British soft drink.

[4] *Doncaster* Large town in Northern England.

[5] *For so … in return* Psalm 116.12.

[6] *woolsack* Name given to the seat of the Lord Chancellor in the House of Lords, which was made of a large sack of wool.

[7] *Then came … Elpenor* See Pound's Canto 1: "first Elpenor came, our friend Elpenor."

[8] *How art … hell's ravine* See Pound's Canto 1: "Elpenor, how art thou come to this dark coast?"

[9] *Walt Whitman … delivery boy* See Allen Ginsberg, "A Supermarket in California" (1956): "I saw you, Walt Whitman, childless, lonely old grubber, poking among the meats in the refrigerator and eyeing the grocery boys."

[10] *Oxfam-clad* Wearing clothes from second-hand stores operated by the large charity organization Oxfam.

[11] *my own mother* In the *Odyssey* Book 11, after he speaks with Tiresias Odysseus encounters the spirit of his mother and learns that she has died of longing to see him; *slipping a … stewing steak* See David Bowie's 1969 song "God Knows I'm Good": "a woman hot with worry slyly slipped a tin of stewing steak / Into the paper bag at her side."

to the skirt pocket of her wedding dress,
blessed with a magician's touch, practised in need.

But never until the valley widened at the gated brink
did we open our lips to fish out those corn-coloured
coins,
those minted obols,[1] hard-won tokens graced with
our monarch's head,
kept hidden beneath the tongue's eel, blood-tasting,
both ornament and safeguard, of armour made.
And paid forthwith, then broke surface
and breathed extraordinary daylight into starved lungs,
steered for home through precincts and parks scalded
by polar winds,
laden with whatnot, lightened of golden quids.
—2014

ALICE OSWALD (B. 1967)

Trained as a classicist and as a gardener, Alice Oswald has established herself as a leading British poet, known for her unsentimental nature lyrics and her contemporary and innovative reworkings of classical myth. Her books include *The Gap-Stone Stile* (1996), *Dart* (2002), *Woods etc.* (2005), *A Sleepwalk on the Severn* (2009), *Memorial* (2011), and *Falling Awake* (2016).

Dunt[2]

a poem for a nearly dried-up river

Very small and damaged and quite dry,
a Roman water nymph[3] made of bone
tries to summon a river out of limestone.

Very eroded faded,
her left arm missing and both legs from the knee down,
a Roman water nymph made of bone
tries to summon a river out of limestone.

Exhausted, utterly worn down,
a Roman water nymph made of bone,
being the last known speaker of her language,
she tries to summon a river out of limestone.

Little distant sound of dry grass. Try again.

A Roman water nymph made of bone,
very endangered now,
in a largely unintelligible monotone,
she tries to summon a river out of limestone.

Little distant sound as of dry grass. Try again.

Exquisite bone figurine with upturned urn,
in her passionate self-esteem, she smiles, looking
sideways.
She seemingly has no voice but a throat-clearing rustle
as of dry grass. Try again.

She tries leaning,
pouring pure outwardness from a grey urn.

Little slithering sounds as of a rabbit man in full night
gear.
Who lies so low in the rickety willow herb
that a fox trots out of the woods
and over his back and away. Try again.
Very small and damaged and quite dry,
a Roman water nymph made of bone,
she pleads, she pleads a river out of limestone.

Little hobbling tripping of a nearly dried-up river
not really moving through the fields,
having had the gleam taken out of it
to the point where it resembles twilight.
Little grumbling shivering last-ditch attempt at a river
more nettles than water. Try again.

---

[1] *obols* Ancient Greek coins. Classical custom required the placement of an obol in the mouths of deceased people so that they could pay the ferry fare to cross the River Styx (or, in some versions, the River Acheron) as they journeyed to the underworld.

[2] *Dunt* Stream in the Gloucestershire county area of England.

[3] *nymph* In classical mythology, a beautiful spirit associated with a natural setting.

Very speechless, very broken old woman,
her left arm missing and both legs from the knee down,
she tries to summon a river out of limestone.

Little stoved-in, sucked-thin
low-burning glint of stones,
rough-sleeping and trembling and clinging to its rights.
Victim of Swindon.[1]
Puddle midden.[2]
Slum of overgreened foot-churn and pats
whose crayfish are cheap toolkits
made of the mud stirred up when a stone's lifted.

It's a pitiable likeness of clear running,
struggling to keep up with what's already gone:
the boat the wheel the sluice gate,
the two otters larricking° along. Go on. *gallivanting*

And they say oh they say
in the days of better rainfall
it would flood through five valleys, there'd be cows
and milking stools
washed over the garden walls
and when it froze you could skate for five miles. Yes
go on.

Little loose-end shorthand unrepresented
beautiful disused route to the sea,
fish path with nearly no fish in.
—2006

Kim Moore (b. 1981)

Cumbria-based poet Kim Moore received the Faber Prize for her first full-length collection, *The Art of Falling* (2015), the centerpiece of which is a poem sequence focused on an abusive relationship. Moore is also a brass musician and music teacher, and in 2016 she began a PHD at Manchester Metropolitan University on the subject of poetry and everyday sexism.

[1] *Swindon* Town in Wiltshire, England.

[2] *midden* Garbage heap.

In That Year

And in that year my body was a pillar of smoke
and even his hands could not hold me.

And in that year my mind was an empty table
and he laid his thoughts down like dishes of plenty.

And in that year my heart was the old monument,
the folly, and no use could be found for it.

And in that year my tongue spoke the language
of insects and not even my father knew me.

And in that year I waited for the horses
but they only shifted their feet in the darkness.

And in that year I imagined a vain thing;
I believed that the world would come for me.

And in that year I gave up on all the things
I was promised and left myself to sadness.

And then that year lay down like a path
And I walked it, I walked it, I walk it.
—2014

I Have Been a Long Time Without Thinking

The mind as an empty and flooded field.
The mind as water that rises up through the
green.
The mind as the tree at the edge of the field.

I have been a long time without thinking.
White birds with no names.
They row away through the air.

I have been a long time without thoughts of my own.
They built a fence round the field.
They named the trees and the birds.

They built this train and the line that runs past.
They told me to walk up and down.
If I did it they cheered.

I am reading in the place that they built.
Adrienne Rich[1] said *read as if your life depended on it.*
A man asks me what I'm reading.

He tells me about his job and his wife and his children.
I put my book away. Repeat. Repeat. I put my book away.
He tells me about money and Brexit and immigration.

I have been putting my book away all my life.
I put away my hands and my mouth and my eyes.
I can sit here and listen and live without field or water or green.

Or go back and fold into myself.
Or enter the field and drink at the flooded place.
Or enter and prepare to be followed. Or not.

I am worried that they made the field.
Maybe they gave me the water.
I am worried about madness and the next sixty seconds.

I put away my heart and the stillness inside.
I smile and say so what do you do tell me again and
how many kids do you have remind me again of your wife
—2018

Warsan Shire (b. 1988)

Born in Kenya and raised in London by Somali parents, Warsan Shire is a British poet and political activist best known for her advocacy for refugees. Shire first became known through her evocative use of the social media platforms Tumblr and Twitter, and her prominence in popular culture is reflected in her work's appearance in Beyoncé's visual album *Lemonade* (2016). Her published poetry collections include *Teaching My Mother How to Give Birth* (2011), *Our Men Do Not Belong to Us* (2014), and *Her Blue Body* (2015).

from *Conversations about Home (at the Deportation Centre)*

Well, I think home spat me out, the blackouts and curfews like tongue against loose tooth. God, do you know how difficult it is, to talk about the day your own city dragged you by the hair, past the old prison, past the school gates, past the burning torsos erected on poles like flags? When I meet others like me I recognize the longing, the missing, the memory of ash on their faces. No one leaves home unless home is the mouth of a shark. I've been carrying the old anthem in my mouth for so long that there's no space for another song, another tongue or another language. I know a shame that shrouds, totally engulfs. I tore up and ate my own passport in an airport hotel. I'm bloated with language I can't afford to forget.

They ask me *how did you get here*? Can't you see it on my body? The Libyan desert red with immigrant bodies, the Gulf of Aden[2] bloated, the city of Rome with no jacket.[3] I hope the journey meant more than miles because all of my children are in the water. I thought the sea was safer than the land. I want to make love, but my hair smells of war and running and running. I want to lay down, but these countries are like uncles who touch you when you're young and asleep. Look at all these borders, foaming at the mouth with bodies broken and desperate. I'm the colour of hot sun on the face, my mother's remains were never buried. I spent days and nights in the stomach of the truck, I did not come out the same. Sometimes it feels like someone else is wearing my body. …
—2011

[1] *Adrienne Rich* American feminist poet and theorist (1929–2012).

[2] *Gulf of Aden* Body of water that separates Ethiopia and Somalia from Yemen. Thousands of Somali and Ethiopian refugees cross every year, with many dying on the voyage.

[3] *city of Rome with no jacket* Shire wrote this poem after meeting in 2009 with refugees living in the abandoned Somali Embassy in Rome.

Backwards

for Saaid Shire

The poem can start with him walking backwards into a room.
He takes off his jacket and sits down for the rest of his life;
that's how we bring Dad back.
I can make the blood run back up my nose, ants rushing into a hole.
We grow into smaller bodies, my breasts disappear,
your cheeks soften, teeth sink back into gums.
I can make us loved, just say the word.
Give them stumps for hands if even once they touched us without consent,
I can write the poem and make it disappear.
Step-Dad spits liquor back into glass,
Mum's body rolls back up the stairs, the bone pops back into place,
maybe she keeps the baby.
Maybe we're okay kid?
I'll rewrite this whole life and this time there'll be so much love,
you won't be able to see beyond it.

You won't be able to see beyond it,
I'll rewrite this whole life and this time there'll be so much love.
Maybe we're okay kid,
maybe she keeps the baby.
Mum's body rolls back up the stairs, the bone pops back into place,
Step-Dad spits liquor back into glass.
I can write the poem and make it disappear,
give them stumps for hands if even once they touched us without consent,
I can make us loved, just say the word.
Your cheeks soften, teeth sink back into gums
we grow into smaller bodies, my breasts disappear.
I can make the blood run back up my nose, ants rushing into a hole,
that's how we bring Dad back.
He takes off his jacket and sits down for the rest of his life.
The poem can start with him walking backwards into a room.

—2014

Reading Poetry

WHAT IS A POEM?

Most of us know what a poem is when we see one. Still, even poets find it difficult to define a poem, or poetry. In a lecture on "The Name and Nature of Poetry" (1933), the English poet A.E. Housman stated that he could "no more define poetry than a terrier can define a rat"; however, he added, "we both recognize the object by the symptoms which it provokes in us." Housman knew he was in the presence of poetry if he experienced a shiver down the spine, or "a constriction of the throat and a precipitation of water to the eyes." Implicit in Housman's response is a recognition that we have to go beyond mere formal characteristics—stanzas, rhymes, rhythms—if we want to know what poetry is, or why it differs from prose. Poetry both represents and *creates* emotions in a highly condensed way. Therefore, any definition of the genre needs to consider, as much as possible, the impact of poetry on us as readers or listeners.

Worth consideration too is the role of the listener or reader not only as passive recipient of a poem, but also as an active participant in its performance. Poetry is among other things the locus for a communicative exchange. A section below deals with the sub-genre of performance poetry, but in a very real sense all poetry is subject to performance. Poems are to be read aloud as well as on the page, and both in sensing meaning and in expressing sound the reader plays a vital role in bringing a poem to life, no matter how long dead its author may be; as W.H. Auden wrote memorably of his fellow poet W.B. Yeats, "the words of a dead man / Are modified in the guts of the living."

For some readers, poetry is, in William Wordsworth's phrase, "the breath and finer spirit of all knowledge" ("Preface" to the *Lyrical Ballads*). They look to poetry for insights into the nature of human experience, and expect elevated thought in carefully wrought language. In contrast, other readers distrust poetry that seems moralistic or didactic. "We hate poetry that has a palpable design upon us," wrote John Keats to his friend J.H. Reynolds; rather, poetry should be "great & unobtrusive, a thing which enters into one's soul, and does not startle it or amaze it with itself but with its subject." The American poet Archibald MacLeish took Keats's idea a step further: in his poem "Ars Poetica" he suggested that "A poem should not mean / But be." MacLeish was not suggesting that a poem should lack meaning, but rather that meaning should inhere in the poem's expressive and sensuous qualities, not in some explicit statement or versified idea.

Whatever we look for in a poem, the infinitude of forms, styles, and subjects that make up the body of literature we call "poetry" is, in the end, impossible to capture in a definition that would satisfy all readers. All we can do, perhaps, is to agree that a poem is a discourse that is characterized by a heightened attention to language, form, and rhythm, by an expressiveness that works through figurative rather than literal modes, and by a capacity to stimulate our imagination and arouse our feelings.

THE LANGUAGE OF POETRY

To speak of "the language of poetry" implies that poets make use of a vocabulary that is somehow different from the language of everyday life. In fact, all language has the capacity to be "poetic," if by poetry we understand a use of language to which some special importance is attached. The ritualistic utterances of religious ceremonies sometimes have this force; so do the skipping rhymes of children in the schoolyard. We can distinguish such uses of language from the kind of writing we find in, say, a computer user's manual: the author of the manual can describe a given function in a variety of ways, whereas the magic of the skipping rhyme can be invoked only by getting the right words in the right order. So with the poet: he or she chooses particular words in a particular order; the *way* the poet speaks is as important to our understanding as what is said. This doesn't mean that an instruction manual couldn't have poetic qualities—indeed, modern poets have created "found" poems from even less likely materials—but it does mean that in poetry there is an intimate relation amongst language, form, and meaning, and that the writer deliberately structures and manipulates language to achieve very particular ends.

THE BEST WORDS IN THE BEST ORDER

Wordsworth provides us with a useful example of the way that poetry can invest quite ordinary words with a high emotional charge:

> No motion has she now, no force,
> She neither hears nor sees;
> Rolled round in earth's diurnal course
> With rocks, and stones, and trees.

To paraphrase the content of this stanza from "A Slumber Did My Spirit Seal," "she" is dead and buried. But the language and structures used here give this prosaic idea great impact. For example, the regular iambic meter of the two last lines conveys something of the inexorable motion of the earth and of Lucy embedded in it; the monosyllabic last line is a grim reminder of her oneness with objects in nature; the repeated negatives in the first two lines drive home the irreparable destructiveness of death; the alliteration in the third and fourth lines gives a tangible suggestion of roundness, circularity, repetition in terms of the earth's shape and motion, suggesting a cycle in which death is perhaps followed by renewal. Even the unusual word "diurnal" (which would not have seemed so unusual to Wordsworth's readers) seems "right" in this context; it lends more weight to the notion of the earth's perpetual movement than its mundane synonym "daily" (which, besides, would not scan here). It is difficult to imagine a change of any kind to these lines; they exemplify another attempted definition of poetry, this time by Wordsworth's friend Samuel Taylor Coleridge: "the best words in the best order" (*Table Talk*, 1827).

POETIC DICTION AND THE ELEVATED STYLE

Wordsworth's diction in the "Lucy" poem cited above is a model of clarity; he has chosen language that, in its simplicity and bluntness, conveys the strength of the speaker's feelings far more strongly than an elaborate description of grief in more conventionally "poetic" language might have done. Wordsworth, disturbed by what he felt was a deadness and artificiality in the poetry of his day, sought to "choose incidents and situations from common life" and to describe them in "a selection of language really used by men" ("Preface" to *Lyrical Ballads*). His plan might seem an implicit reproach of the "raised" style, the elevated diction of epic poetry we associate with John Milton's *Paradise Lost*:

Anon out of the earth a fabric huge
Rose like an exhalation, with the sound
Of dulcet symphonies and voices sweet,
Built like a temple, where pilasters round
Were set, and Doric pillars overlaid
With golden architrave; nor did there want
Cornice or frieze, with bossy sculptures graven;
The roof was fretted gold.

(*Paradise Lost* I.710–17)

At first glance this passage, with its Latinate vocabulary and convoluted syntax, might seem guilty of inflated language and pretentiousness. However, Milton's description of the devils' palace in Hell deliberately seeks to distance us from its subject in order to emphasize the scale and sublimity of the spectacle, far removed from ordinary human experience. In other words, language and style in *Paradise Lost* are well adapted to suit a particular purpose, just as they are in "A Slumber Did My Spirit Seal," though on a wholly different scale. Wordsworth criticized the poetry of his day, not because of its elevation, but because the raised style was too often out of touch with its subject; in his view, the words did not bear any significant relation to the "truths" they were attempting to depict.

"PLAIN" LANGUAGE IN POETRY

Since Wordsworth's time, writers have been conscious of a need to narrow the apparent gap between "poetic" language and the language of everyday life. In much of the poetry of the past century, especially free verse, we can observe a growing approximation to speech—even to conversation—in the diction and rhythms of poetry. This may have something to do with the changed role of the poet, who today has discarded the mantle of teacher or prophet that was assumed by poets of earlier times, and who is ready to admit all fields of experience and endeavor as appropriate for poetry. The modern poet looks squarely at life, and can often find a provoking beauty in even the meanest of objects.

We should not assume, however, that a greater concern with the "ordinary," with simplicity, naturalness, and clarity, means a reduction in complexity or suggestiveness. A piece such as Stevie Smith's "Mother, Among the Dustbins," for all the casual and playful domesticity of some of its lines, skillfully evokes a range of emotions and sense impressions defying simple paraphrase.

IMAGERY, SYMBOLISM, AND FIGURES OF SPEECH

The language of poetry is grounded in the objects and phenomena that create sensory impressions. Sometimes the poet renders these impressions quite literally, in a series of *images* that seek to recreate a scene in the reader's mind:

Only a man harrowing clods
In a slow silent walk
With an old horse that stumbles and nods
Half asleep as they stalk.

Only thin smoke without flame
From the heaps of couch-grass;
Yet this will go onward the same
Though Dynasties pass.

Yonder a maid and her wight
Come whispering by:
War's annals will cloud into night
Ere their story die.

(Thomas Hardy, "In Time of 'The Breaking of Nations'")

Here, the objects of everyday life are re-created with sensory details designed to evoke in us the sensations or responses felt by the speaker viewing the scene. At the same time, the writer invests the objects with such significance that the poem's meaning extends beyond the literal to the symbolic: that is, the images come to stand for something much larger than the objects they represent. Hardy's poem moves from the presentation of stark images of rural life to a sense of their timelessness. By the last stanza we see the ploughman, the burning grass, and the maid and her companion as symbols of recurring human actions and motives that defy the struggles and conflicts of history.

IMAGISM

The juxtaposition of clear, forceful images is associated particularly with the Imagist movement that flourished at the beginning of the twentieth century. Its chief representatives (in their early work) were the American poets H.D. and Ezra Pound, who defined an image as "that which represents an intellectual and emotional complex in an instant of time." Pound's two-line poem "In a Station of the Metro" provides a good example of the Imagists' goal of representing emotions or impressions through the use of concentrated images:

The apparition of these faces in the crowd,
Petals on a wet, black bough.

As in a Japanese *haiku*, a form that strongly influenced the Imagists, the poem uses sharp, clear, concrete details to evoke both a sensory impression and the emotion or the atmosphere of the scene. Though the Imagist movement itself lasted only a short time (from about 1912 to 1917), it had a far-reaching influence on modern poets such as T.S. Eliot and William Carlos Williams.

FIGURES OF SPEECH

Imagery often works together with figurative expression to extend and deepen the meaning or impact of a poem. "Figurative" language means language that is metaphorical, not literal or referential. Through "figures of speech" such as metaphor and simile, metonymy, synecdoche, and personification, the writer may alter the ordinary, denotative meanings of words in order to convey greater force and vividness to ideas or impressions, often by showing likenesses between unlike things.

With *simile*, the poet makes an explicit comparison between the subject (called the *tenor*) and another object or idea (known as the *vehicle*), using "as" or "like":

> It is a beauteous evening, calm and free,
> The holy time is quiet as a Nun
> Breathless with adoration. …

In this opening to a sonnet, Wordsworth uses a visual image of a nun in devout prayer to convey in concrete terms the less tangible idea of evening as a "holy time." The comparison also introduces an emotional dimension, conveying something of the feeling that the scene induces in the poet. The simile can thus illuminate and expand meaning in a compact way. The poet may also extend the simile to elaborate at length on any points of likeness.

In *metaphor*, the comparison between tenor and vehicle is implied: connectives such as "like" are omitted, and a kind of identity is created between the subject and the term with which it is being compared. Thus in John Donne's "The Good-Morrow," a lover asserts the endless joy that he and his beloved find in each other:

> My face in thine eye, thine in mine appears,
> And true plain hearts do in the faces rest;
> Where can we find two better hemispheres,
> Without sharp north, without declining west?

Here the lovers are transformed into "hemispheres," each of them a half of the world not subject to the usual natural phenomena of wintry cold ("sharp north") or the coming of night ("declining west"). Thus, they form a perfect world in balance, in which the normal processes of decay or decline have been arrested. Donne renders the abstract idea of a love that defies change in pictorial and physical terms, making it more real and accessible to us. The images here are all the more arresting for the degree of concentration involved; it is not merely the absence of "like" or "as" that gives the metaphor such direct power, but the fusion of distinct images and emotions into a new idea.

Personification is the figure of speech in which the writer endows abstract ideas, inanimate objects, or animals with human characteristics. In other words, it is a type of implied metaphorical comparison in which aspects of a non-human subject are compared to the feelings, appearance, or actions of a human being. In the second stanza of his ode "To Autumn," Keats personifies the concept of autumnal harvesting in the form of a woman, "sitting careless on a granary floor, / Thy hair soft-lifted by the winnowing wind." Personification may also help to create a mood, as when Thomas Gray attributes human feelings to a hooting owl in "Elegy Written in a Country Churchyard"; using such words as "moping" and "complain," Gray invests the bird's cries with the quality of human melancholy:

> … from yonder ivy-mantled tow'r
> The moping owl does to the moon complain
> Of such, as wand'ring near her secret bow'r,
> Molest her ancient solitary reign.

In his book *Modern Painters* (1856), the English critic John Ruskin criticized such attribution of human feelings to objects in nature. Calling this device the "pathetic fallacy," he objected to what he saw as an irrational distortion of reality, producing "a falseness in all our impressions of external things." Modern criticism, with a distrust of any notions of an objective "reality," tends to use Ruskin's term as a neutral label simply to describe instances of extended personification of natural objects.

Apostrophe, which is closely related to personification, has the speaker directly addressing a non-human object or idea as if it were a sentient human listener. Blake's "The Sick Rose," Shelley's "Ode to the West Wind," and his ode "To a Sky-Lark" all employ apostrophe, personifying the object addressed. Keats's "Ode on a Grecian Urn" begins by apostrophizing the urn ("Thou still unravish'd bride of quietness"), then addresses it in a series of questions and reflections through which the speaker attempts to unravel the urn's mysteries.

Apostrophe also appeals to or addresses a person who is absent or dead. W.H. Auden's lament "In Memory of W.B. Yeats" apostrophizes both the earth in which Yeats is to be buried ("Earth, receive an honoured guest") and the dead poet himself ("Follow, poet, follow right / To the bottom of the night …"). Religious prayers offer an illustration of the usefulness of apostrophe, since they are direct appeals from an earth-bound supplicant to an invisible god. The suggestion of strong emotion associated with such appeals is a common feature of apostrophe in poetry also, especially poetry with a religious theme, like Donne's Holy Sonnets (e.g., "Batter My Heart, Three-Personed God").

Metonymy and *synecdoche* are two closely related figures of speech that further illustrate the power of metaphorical language to convey meaning more intensely and vividly than is possible with prosaic statement. *Metonymy* (from the Greek, meaning "change of name") involves referring to an object or concept by substituting the name of another object or concept with which it is usually associated: for example, we might speak of "the Crown" when we mean the monarch, or describe the US executive branch as "the White House." When the writer uses only part of something to signify the whole, or an individual to represent a class, we have an instance of *synecdoche*: T.S. Eliot provides an example in "The Love Song of J. Alfred Prufrock" when a crab is described as "a pair of ragged claws." Similarly, synecdoche is present in Milton's contemptous term "blind mouths" to describe the "corrupted clergy" he attacks in "Lycidas."

Dylan Thomas employs both metonymy and synecdoche in his poem "The Hand That Signed the Paper":

The hand that signed the paper felled a city;
Five sovereign fingers taxed the breath,
Doubled the globe of dead and halved a country;
These five kings did a king to death.

The mighty hand leads to a sloping shoulder,
The finger joints are cramped with chalk;
A goose's quill has put an end to murder
That put an end to talk.

The hand that signed the treaty bred a fever,
And famine grew, and locusts came;

Great is the hand that holds dominion over
Man by a scribbled name.

The five kings count the dead but do not soften
The crusted wound nor stroke the brow;
A hand rules pity as a hand rules heaven;
Hands have no tears to flow.

The "hand" of the poem is evidently a synecdoche for a great king who enters into treaties with friends and foes to wage wars, conquer kingdoms, and extend his personal power—all at the expense of his suffering subjects. The "goose quill" of the second stanza is a metonymy, standing for the pen used to sign the treaty or the death warrant that brings the war to an end.

Thomas's poem is an excellent example of the power of figurative language, which, by its vividness and concentrated force, can add layers of meaning to a poem, make abstract ideas concrete, and intensify the poem's emotional impact.

THE POEM AS PERFORMANCE: WRITER AND PERSON

Poetry is always dramatic. Sometimes the drama is explicit, as in Robert Browning's monologues, in which we hear the voice of a participant in a dialogue; in "My Last Duchess" we are present as the Duke reflects on the portrait of his late wife for the benefit of a visitor who has come to negotiate on behalf of the woman who is to become the Duke's next wife. Or we listen with amusement and pity as the dying Bishop addresses his venal and unsympathetic sons and tries to bargain with them for a fine burial ("The Bishop Orders His Tomb at St. Praxed's"). In such poems, the notion of a speaking voice is paramount: the speaker is a personage in a play, and the poem a means of conveying plot and character.

Sometimes the drama is less apparent, and takes the form of a plea, or a compliment, or an argument addressed to a silent listener. In Donne's "The Flea" we can infer from the poem the situation that has called it forth: a lover's advances are being rejected by his beloved, and his poem is an argument intended to overcome her reluctance by means of wit and logic. We can see a similar example in Marvell's "To His Coy Mistress": here the very shape of the poem, its three-paragraph structure, corresponds to the stages of the speaker's argument as he presents an apparently irrefutable line of reasoning. Much love poetry has this kind of background as its inspiration; the yearnings or lamentations of the lover are part of an imagined scene, not merely versified reflections about an abstraction called "love."

Meditative or reflective poetry can be dramatic too. Donne's Holy Sonnets are pleas from a tormented soul struggling to find its god; Tennyson's In Memoriam follows the agonized workings of a mind tracing a path from grief and anger to acceptance and renewed hope.

We should never assume that the speaker, the "I" of the poem, is simply a voice for the writer's own views. The speaker in W.H. Auden's "To an Unknown Citizen," presenting a summary of the dead citizen's life, appears to be an official spokesperson for the society which the citizen served ("Our report on his union"; "Our researchers …" etc.). The speaker's words are laudatory, yet we perceive immediately that Auden's own views of this society are anything but approving. The speaker seems satisfied with the highly regimented nature of his society, one in which every aspect of the individual's life is under scrutiny and subject to correction. The only things necessary to the happiness of the

"Modern Man," it seems, are "A phonograph, a radio, a car, and a frigidaire." The tone here is subtly ironic, an irony created by the gap between the imagined speaker's perception and the real feelings of the writer.

PERFORMANCE POETRY

Poetry began as an oral art, passed on in the form of chants, myths, ballads, and legends recited to an audience of listeners rather than readers. Even today, the dramatic qualities of a poem may extend beyond written text. "Performance poets" combine poetry and stagecraft in presenting their work to live audiences. Dramatic uses of voice, rhythm, body movement, music, and sometimes other visual effects make the "text" of the poem multi-dimensional. For example, Edith Sitwell's poem-sequence *Façade* (1922) was originally set to music: Sitwell read from behind a screen, while a live orchestra played. This performance was designed to enhance the verbal and rhythmic qualities of her poetry:

Beneath the flat and paper sky
The sun, a demon's eye
Glowed through the air, that mask of glass;
All wand'ring sounds that pass

Seemed out of tune, as if the light
Were fiddle-strings pulled tight.
The market-square with spire and bell
Clanged out the hour in Hell.

By performing their poetry, writers can also convey cultural values and traditions. The cultural aspect of performance is central to Black poetry, which originates in a highly oral tradition of folklore and storytelling. From its roots in Africa, this oral tradition has been manifested in the songs and stories of slaves, in spirituals, in the jazz rhythms of the Twenties and the Thirties and in the rebelliousness of reggae and of rap. Even when it remains "on the page," much Black poetry written in the oral tradition has a compelling rhythmic quality. The lines below from Linton Kwesi Johnson's "Mi Revalueshanary Fren," for example, blur the line between spoken poetry and song. Johnson often performs his "dub poetry" against reggae musical backings.

yes, people powa jus a showa evry howa
an evrybady claim dem democratic
but some a wolf an some a sheep
an dat is problematic

The chorus of Johnson's poems, with its constant repetitions, digs deeply into the roots of African song and chant. Its performance qualities become clearer when the poem is read aloud:

Husak
e ad to go
Honnicka
e ad to go

Chowcheskhu
e ad to go
Just like apartied
will av to go

To perform a poem is one way to see and hear poetry as multi-dimensional, cultural, historical, and often also political. Performance is also another way to discover how poetic "meaning" can be constructed in the dynamic relation between speaker and listener.

TONE: THE SPEAKER'S ATTITUDE

In understanding poetry, it is helpful to imagine a poem as having a "voice." The voice may be close to the poet's own, or that of an imagined character, a *persona* adopted by the poet. The tone of the voice will reveal the speaker's attitude to the subject, thus helping to shape our understanding and response. In speech we can indicate our feelings by raising or lowering our voices, and we can accompany words with physical actions. In writing, we must try to convey the tonal inflections of the speaking voice through devices of language and rhythm, through imagery and figures of speech, and through allusions and contrasts.

THE IRONIC TONE

Housman's poem "Terence, This Is Stupid Stuff" offers a useful example of ways in which manipulating tone can reinforce meaning. When Housman, presenting himself in the poem as "Terence," imagines himself to be criticized for writing gloomy poems, his response to his critics takes the form of an ironic alternative: perhaps they should stick to drinking ale:

Oh, many a peer of England brews
Livelier liquor than the Muse,
And malt does more than Milton can
To justify God's ways to man.

The tone here is one of heavy scorn. The speaker is impatient with those who refuse to look at the realities of life and death, and who prefer to take refuge in simple-minded pleasure. The ludicrous comparisons, first between the brewers who have been made peers of England and the classical Muse of poetry, then between malt and Milton, create a sense of disproportion and ironic tension; the explicit allusion to *Paradise Lost* ("To justify God's ways to man") helps to drive home the poet's bitter recognition that his auditors are part of that fallen world depicted by Milton, yet unable or unwilling to acknowledge their harsh condition. The three couplets that follow offer a series of contrasts: in each case, the first line sets up a pleasant expectation and the second dashes it with a blunt reminder of reality:

Ale, man, ale's the stuff to drink
For fellows whom it hurts to think:
Look into the pewter pot

To see the world as the world's not.
And faith, 'tis pleasant till 'tis past:
The mischief is that 'twill not last.

These are all jabs at the "sterling lads" who would prefer to lie in "lovely muck" and not think about the way the world is. Housman's sardonic advice is all the more pointed for its sharp and ironic tone.

POETIC FORMS

In poetry, language is intimately related to form, which is the structuring of words within identifiable patterns. In prose we speak of phrases, sentences, and paragraphs; in poetry, we identify structures by lines, stanzas, or complete forms such as the sonnet or the ode (though poetry in complete or blank verse has paragraphs of variable length, not formal stanzas: see below).

Rightly handled, the form enhances expression and meaning, just as a frame can define and enhance a painting or photograph. Unlike the photo frame, however, form in poetry is an integral part of the whole work. At one end of the scale, the term "form" may describe the *epic*, the lengthy narrative governed by such conventions as division into books, a lofty style, and the interplay between human and supernatural characters. At the other end lies the *epigram*, a witty and pointed saying whose distinguishing characteristic is its brevity, as in Alexander Pope's famous couplet,

I am his Highness' dog at Kew;
Pray tell me sir, whose dog are you?

Between the epic and the epigram lie many other poetic forms, such as the sonnet, the ballad, or the ode. "Form" may also describe stanzaic patterns like *couplets* and *quatrains.*

"FIXED FORM" POEMS

The best-known poetic form is probably the sonnet, the fourteen-line poem inherited from Italy (the word itself is from the Italian *sonetto*, little song or sound). Within those fourteen lines, whether the poet chooses the "Petrarchan" rhyme scheme or the "English" form (see below in the section on "Rhyme"), the challenge is to develop an idea or situation that must find its statement and its resolution within the strict confines of the sonnet frame. Typically, there is an initial idea, description, or statement of feeling, followed by a "turn" in the thought that takes the reader by surprise, or that casts the situation in an unexpected light. Thus in Sonnet 130, "My Mistress' Eyes Are Nothing Like the Sun," William Shakespeare spends the first three quatrains apparently disparaging his lover in a series of unfavorable comparisons—"If snow be white, why then her breasts are dun"—but in the closing couplet his point becomes clear:

And yet, by heaven, I think my love as rare
As any she belied with false compare.

In other words, the speaker's disparaging comparisons have really been parodies of sentimental clichés which falsify reality; his mistress has no need of the exaggerations or distortions of conventional love poetry.

Other foreign forms borrowed and adapted by English-language poets include the *ghazal* and the *pantoum*. The *ghazal*, strongly associated with classical Urdu literature, originated in Persia and Arabia and was brought to the Indian subcontinent in the twelfth century. It consists of a series of couplets held together by a refrain, a simple rhyme scheme (a/a, b/a, c/a, d/a…), and a common rhythm, but only loosely related in theme or subject. Some English-language practitioners of the form have captured the epigrammatic quality of the ghazal, but most do not adhere to the strict pattern of the classical form.

The *pantoum*, based on a Malaysian form, was imported into English poetry via the work of nineteenth-century French poets. Typically it presents a series of quatrains rhyming *abab*, linked by a pattern of repetition in which the second and fourth lines of a quatrain become the first and third lines of the stanza that follows. In the poem's final stanza, the pattern is reversed: the second line repeats the third line of the first stanza, and the last line repeats the poem's opening line, thus creating the effect of a loop.

Similar to the pantoum in the circularity of its structure is the *villanelle*, originally a French form, with five *tercets* and a concluding *quatrain* held together by only two rhymes (aba, aba, aba, aba, aba, abaa) and by a refrain that repeats the first line at lines 6, 12, and 18, while the third line of the first tercet reappears as lines 9, 15, and 19. With its interlocking rhymes and elaborate repetitions, the villanelle can create a variety of tonal effects, ranging from lighthearted parody to the sonorous and earnest exhortation of Dylan Thomas's "Do Not Go Gentle into That Good Night."

STANZAIC FORMS

Recurring formal groupings of lines within a poem are usually described as "stanzas." Both the recurring and the formal aspects of stanzaic forms are important; it is a common misconception to think that any group of lines in a poem, if it is set off by line spaces, constitutes a stanza. If such a group of lines is not patterned as one of a recurring group sharing similar formal characteristics, however, then it may be more appropriate to refer to such irregular groupings in the way we do for prose—as paragraphs. A ballad is typically divided into stanzas; a prose poem or a poem written in free verse, on the other hand, will rarely be divided into stanzas.

A stanza may be identified by the number of lines and the patterns of rhyme repeated in each grouping. One of the simpler traditional forms is the *ballad stanza*, with its alternating four and three-foot lines and its *abcb* rhyme scheme. Drawing on this form's association with medieval ballads and legends, Keats produces the eerie mystery of "La Belle Dame sans Merci":

I saw pale kings and princes too,
Pale warriors, death-pale were they all;
They cried—"La Belle Dame sans Merci
Hath thee in thrall!"

Such imitations are a form of literary allusion; Keats uses a traditional stanza form to remind us of poems like "Sir Patrick Spens" or "Barbara Allen" to dramatize the painful thralldom of love by placing it within a well-known tradition of ballad narratives with similar forms and themes.

The four-line stanza, or *quatrain*, may be used for a variety of effects: from the elegiac solemnity of Gray's "Elegy Written in a Country Churchyard" to the apparent lightness and simplicity of some of Emily Dickinson's poems. Tennyson used a rhyming quatrain to such good effect in *In Memoriam* that the form he employed (four lines of iambic tetrameter rhyming *abba*) is known as the "In Memoriam stanza."

Other commonly used forms of stanza include the *rhyming couplet*, *terza rima*, *ottava rima*, *rhyme royal*, and the *Spenserian stanza*. Each of these is a rhetorical unit within a longer whole, rather like a paragraph within an essay. The poet's choice among such forms is dictated, at least in part, by the effects that each may produce. Thus the *rhyming couplet* often expresses a complete statement within two lines, creating a sense of density of thought, of coherence and closure; it is particularly effective where the writer wishes to set up contrasts, or to achieve the witty compactness of epigram:

> Of all mad creatures, if the learn'd are right,
> It is the slaver kills, and not the bite.
> A fool quite angry is quite innocent:
> Alas! 'tis ten times worse when they repent.
>
> (from Pope, "Epistle to Dr. Arbuthnot")

Ottava rima, as its Italian name implies, is an eight-line stanza, with the rhyme scheme *abababcc*. Like the sonnet, it is long enough to allow the development of a single thought in some detail and complexity, with a concluding couplet that may extend the central idea or cast it in a wholly unexpected light. W.B. Yeats uses this stanza form in "Sailing to Byzantium" and "Among Schoolchildren." Though much used by Renaissance poets, it is particularly associated with George Gordon, Lord Byron's *Don Juan*, in which the poet exploits to the full its potential for devastating irony and bathos. It is long enough to allow the development of a single thought in some detail and complexity; the concluding couplet can then, sonnet-like, turn that thought upon its head, or cast it in a wholly unexpected light:

> Sagest of women, even of widows, she
> Resolved that Juan should be quite a paragon,
> And worthy of the noblest pedigree
> (His sire was of Castile, his dam from Aragon).
> Then for accomplishments of chivalry,
> In case our lord the king should go to war again,
> He learned the arts of riding, fencing, gunnery,
> And how to scale a fortress—or a nunnery.
>
> (*Don Juan* I.38)

FREE VERSE

Not all writers want the order and symmetry—some might say the restraints and limitations—of traditional forms, and many have turned to *free verse* as a means of liberating their thoughts and feelings. Deriving its name from the French "vers libre" made popular by the French Symbolistes at the end of the nineteenth century, free verse is characterized by irregularity of meter, line length, and rhyme. This does not mean that it is without pattern; rather, it tends to follow more closely than other forms the unforced rhythms and accents of natural speech, making calculated use of spacing, line breaks, and "cadences," the rhythmic units that govern phrasing in speech.

Free verse is not a modern invention. Milton was an early practitioner, as was Blake; however, it was the great modern writers of free verse—first Walt Whitman, then Pound, Eliot, and William Carlos Williams (interestingly, all Americans, at least originally)—who gave this form a fluidity and flexibility that could free the imagination to deal with any kind of feeling or experience. Perhaps because it depends so much more than traditional forms upon the individual intuitions of the poet, it is the form of poetic structure most commonly found today. The best practitioners recognize that free verse, like any other kind of poetry, demands clarity, precision, and a close connection between technique and meaning.

PROSE POETRY

At the furthest extreme from traditional forms lies poetry written in prose. Contradictory as this label may seem, the two have much in common. Prose has at its disposal all the figurative devices available to poetry, such as metaphor, personification, or apostrophe; it may use structuring devices such as verbal repetition or parallel syntactical structures; it can draw on the same tonal range, from pathos to irony. The difference is that prose poetry accomplishes its ends in sentences and paragraphs, rather than lines or stanzas. First given prominence by the French poet Charles Baudelaire (*Petits Poèmes en prose*, 1862), the form is much used to present fragments of heightened sensation, conveyed through vivid or impressionistic description. It draws upon such prosaic forms as journal entries, lists, even footnotes. Prose poetry should be distinguished from "poetic prose," which may be found in a variety of settings (from the King James Bible to the fiction of Jeanette Winterson); the distinction—which not all critics would accept—appears to lie in the writer's intention.

Christan Bök's *Eunoia* is an interesting example of the ways in which a writer of prose poetry may try to balance the demands of each medium. *Eunoia* is an avowedly experimental work in which each chapter is restricted to the use of a single vowel. The text is governed by a series of rules described by the author in an afterword; they include a requirement that all chapters "must allude to the art of writing. All sentences must accent internal rhyme through the use of syntactical parallelism. The text must exhaust the lexicon for each vowel, citing at least 98% of the available repertoire…." Having imposed such constraints upon the language and form of the work, Bök then sets himself the task of showing that "even under such improbable conditions of duress, language can still express an uncanny, if not sublime, thought." The result is a surrealistic narrative that blends poetic and linguistic devices to almost hypnotic effect.

THE POEM AS A MATERIAL OBJECT

Both free verse and prose poetry pay attention in different ways to the poem as a living thing on the printed page. But the way in which poetry is presented in material form is an important part of the existence of almost any form of poetry. In the six volumes of this anthology the material form of the poem is highlighted by the inclusion of a number of facsimile reproductions of poems of other eras in their earliest extant material form.

RHYTHM AND SCANSION

When we read poetry, we often become aware of a pattern of rhythm within a line or set of lines. The formal analysis of that rhythmic pattern, or "meter," is called *scansion*. The verb "to scan" may carry different meanings, depending upon the context: if the *critic* "scans" a line, he or she is attempting to determine the metrical pattern in which it is cast; if the *line* "scans," we are making the observation that the line conforms to particular metrical rules. Whatever the context, the process of scansion is based on the premise that a line of verse is built on a pattern of stresses, a recurring set of more or less regular beats established by the alternation of light and heavy accents in syllables and words. The rhythmic pattern so distinguished in a given poem is said to be the "meter" of that poem. If we find it impossible to identify any specific metrical pattern, the poem is probably an example of free verse.

QUANTITATIVE, SYLLABIC, AND ACCENTUAL-SYLLABIC VERSE

Although we owe much of our terminology for analyzing or describing poetry to the Greeks and Romans, the foundation of our metrical system is quite different from theirs. They measured a line of verse by the duration of sound ("quantity") in each syllable, and by the combination of short and long syllables. Such poetry is known as *quantitative* verse.

Unlike Greek or Latin, English is a heavily accented language. Thus poetry of the Anglo-Saxon period, such as *Beowulf*, was *accentual*: that is, the lines were based on a fixed number of accents, or stresses, regardless of the number of syllables in the line:

Oft Scyld Scefing   sceapena þreatum
monegum maegþum   meodosetla ofteah.

Few modern poets have written in the accentual tradition. A notable exception was Gerard Manley Hopkins, who based his line on a pattern of strong stresses that he called "sprung rhythm." Hopkins experimented with rhythms and stresses that approximate the accentual quality of natural speech; the result is a line that is emphatic, abrupt, even harsh in its forcefulness:

I caught this morning morning's minion, king-
dom of daylight's dauphin, dapple-dawn-drawn Falcon, in his riding
Of the rolling level underneath him steady air …
(from "The Windhover")

Under the influence of French poetry, following the Norman invasion of the eleventh century, English writers were introduced to *syllabic* prosody: that is, poetry in which the number of syllables is the determining factor in the length of any line, regardless of the number of stresses or their placement. A few modern writers have successfully produced syllabic poetry.

However, the accentual patterns of English, in speech as well as in poetry, were too strongly ingrained to disappear. Instead, the native accentual practice combined with the imported syllabic conventions to produce the *accentual-syllabic* line, in which the writer works with combinations of stressed and unstressed syllables in lines of equal syllabic length. Geoffrey Chaucer was the first great writer to employ the accentual-syllabic line in English poetry:

x / / x x / x /x / x
Ther was also a Nonne, a Prioresse,

x / x /x x / x x /
That of hir smiling was ful simple and coy.
x / x / x / x / x /
Hir gretteste ooth was but by saintè Loy,
x / x / x / x / x / x
And she was clepèd Madame Eglantine.
(from *The Canterbury Tales*)

The fundamental pattern here is the ten-syllable line (although the convention of sounding the final "e" at the end of a line in Middle English verse sometimes produces eleven syllables). Each line contains five stressed syllables, each of which alternates with one or two unstressed syllables. This was to become the predominant meter of poetry in English until the general adoption of free verse in the twentieth century.

IDENTIFYING POETIC METER

Conventionally, meter is established by dividing a line into roughly equal parts, based on the rise and fall of the rhythmic beats. Each of these divisions, conventionally marked by a bar, is known as a "foot," and within the foot there will be a combination of stressed and unstressed syllables, indicated by the prosodic symbols / (stressed) and x (unstressed).

x / x / x / x /
I know | that I | shall meet | my fate
/ x x / x / x /
Somewhere | among | the clouds | above …
(from Yeats, "An Irish Airman Foresees His Death")

To describe the meter used in a poem, we must first determine what kind of foot predominates, and then count the number of feet in each line. To describe the resultant meter we use terminology borrowed from classical prosody. In identifying the meter of English verse we commonly apply the following labels:

iambic (x /): a foot with one weak stress followed by one strong stress

x / x / x / x / x /
("Look home | ward, Ang | el, now, | and melt | with ruth")

trochaic (/ x): strong followed by weak

/ x / x / x /
("Ty-ger! | Ty-ger! | burning | bright")

anapaestic (x x /): two weak stresses, followed by a strong

x x / x x / x x /
("I have passed | with a nod | of the head")

dactylic (/ x x): strong stress followed by two weak

/ x x / x x /
("Hickory | dickory | dock")

spondaic (/ /): two strong stresses

/ / / x / x / x
("If hate | killed men,| Brother | Lawrence,
/ / / x / x /
God's blood,| would not | mine kill | you?")

We also use classical terms to describe the number of feet in a line. Thus, a line with one foot is *monometer*; with two feet, *dimeter*; three feet, *trimeter*; four feet, *tetrameter*; five feet, *pentameter*; and six feet, *hexameter*.

Scansion of the two lines from Yeats's "Irish Airman" quoted above shows that the predominant foot is iambic (x /), that there are four feet to each line, and that the poem is therefore written in *iambic tetrameters*. The first foot of the second line, however, may be read as a trochee ("Somewhere"); the variation upon the iambic norm here is an example of *substitution*, a means whereby the writer may avoid the monotony that would result from adhering too closely to a set rhythm. We very quickly build up an expectation about the dominant meter of a poem; the poet will sometimes disturb that expectation by changing the beat, and so through substitution create a pleasurable tension in our awareness.

The prevailing meter in English poetry is iambic, since the natural rhythm of spoken English is predominantly iambic. Nonetheless, poets may employ other rhythms where it suits their purpose. Thus W.H. Auden can create a solemn tone by the use of a trochaic meter (/ x):

/ x / x / x /
Earth, receive an honoured guest;
/ x / x / x /
William Yeats is laid to rest:
/ x / x / x /
Let the Irish vessel lie
/ x / x / x x
Emptied of its poetry.

The same meter may be much less funereal, as in Ben Jonson's song "*To Celia*":

/ x / x / x /
Come, my Celia, let us prove,
/ x / x / x /
While we may, the sports of love.
/ x / x / x / x
Time will not be ours forever;
/ x / x / x / x
He, at length, our good will sever.

The sense of greater pace in this last example derives in part from the more staccato phrasing, and also from the greater use of monosyllabic words. A more obviously lilting, dancing effect is obtained from anapaestic rhythm (x x /):

x / x x / x x / x x /
I sprang to the stirrup, and Joris, and he;
x / x x / x x / x x /
I galloped, Dirck galloped, we galloped all three.
/ / x x / x x / x x /
"Good speed!" cried the watch, as the gatebolts undrew;

/ / x x / x x / x x /
"Speed!" echoed the wall to us galloping through.
(from Browning, "How They Brought the Good News from Ghent to Aix")

Coleridge wittily captured the varying effects of different meters in "Metrical Feet: Lesson for a Boy," which the poet wrote for his sons, and in which he marked the stresses himself:

/ x / x / x /
Trochee trips from long to short;
x / x / x / x /
From long to long in solemn sort
/ / x / / / x / / x
Slow Spondee stalks; strong foot! yet ill able
/ x x / x x / x x / x x
Ever to come up with Dactyl trisyllable.
x / x / x / x /
Iambics march from short to long:—
x x / x x / x x / x x /
With a leap and a bound the swift Anapaests throng. …

A meter which often deals with serious themes is unrhymed iambic pentameter, also known as *blank verse*. This is the meter of Shakespeare's plays, notably his great tragedies; it is the meter, too, of Milton's *Paradise Lost*, to which it lends a desired sonority and magnificence; and of Wordsworth's "Lines Composed a Few Miles above Tintern Abbey," where the flexibility of the meter allows the writer to move by turns from description, to narration, to philosophical reflection.

RHYME, CONSONANCE, ASSONANCE, AND ALLITERATION

Perhaps the most obvious sign of poetic form is rhyme: that is, the repetition of syllables with the same or similar sounds. If the rhyme words are placed at the end of the line, they are known as *end-rhymes*. The opening stanza of Housman's "To an Athlete Dying Young" has two pairs of end-rhymes:

The time you won your town the *race*
We chaired you through the market-*place*;
Man and boy stood cheering *by*,
And home we brought you shoulder-*high*.

Words rhyming within a line are *internal rhymes*, as in the first and third lines of this stanza from Coleridge's "The Rime of the Ancient Mariner":

The fair breeze *blew*, the white foam *flew*
The furrow followed free;
We were the *first* that ever *burst*
Into that silent sea.

When, as is usually the case, the rhyme occurs in a stressed syllable, it is known as a *masculine rhyme*; if the rhyming word ends in an unstressed syllable, it is referred to as *feminine*. The difference is apparent in the opening stanzas of Alfred Tennyson's poem "The Lady of Shalott," where the first stanza establishes the basic iambic meter with strong stresses on the rhyming words:

On either side the river *lie*
Long fields of barley and of *rye*,
That clothe the wold and meet the *sky*;
And through the field the road runs *by*
To many-towered Camelot ...

In the second stanza Tennyson changes to trochaic lines, ending in unstressed syllables and feminine rhymes:

Willows whiten, aspens *quiver*,
Little breezes dusk and *shiver*
Through the wave that runs *forever*
By the island in the *river*
Flowing down to Camelot.

Not only does Tennyson avoid monotony here by his shift to feminine rhymes, he also darkens the mood by using words that imply a contrast with the bright warmth of day—"quiver," "dusk," "shiver"—in preparation for the introduction of the "silent isle" that embowers the Lady.

NEAR RHYMES

Most of the rhymes in "The Lady of Shalott" are exact, or "*perfect*" rhymes. However, in the second of the stanzas just quoted, it is evident that "forever" at the end of the third line is not a "perfect" rhyme; rather, it is an instance of "*near*" or "*slant*" rhyme. Such "*imperfect*" rhymes are quite deliberate; indeed, two stanzas later we find the rhyming sequence "early," "barley," "cheerly," and "clearly," followed by the rhymes "weary," "airy," and "fairy." As with the introduction of feminine rhymes, such divergences from one dominant pattern prevent monotony and avoid a too-mechanical sing-song effect.

More importantly, near-rhymes have an oddly unsettling effect, perhaps because they both raise and frustrate our expectation of a perfect rhyme. Their use certainly gives added emphasis to the words at the end of these chilling lines from Wilfred Owen's "*Strange Meeting*":

For by my glee might many men have laughed,
And of my weeping something had been left,
Which must die now. I mean the truth untold,
The pity of war, the pity war distilled.
Now men will go content with what we spoiled,
Or, discontent, boil bloody, and be spilled.

CONSONANCE AND ASSONANCE

In Owen's poem, the near-rhymes "laughed / left" and "spoiled / spilled" are good examples of *consonance*, which pairs words with similar consonants but different intervening vowels. Other examples from Owen's poem include "groined / groaned," "hall / Hell," "years / yours," and "mystery / mastery."

Related to consonance as a linking device is *assonance*, the echoing of similar vowel sounds in the stressed syllables of words with differing consonants (lane/hail, penitent/reticence). A device favored particularly by descriptive poets, it appears often in the work of the English Romantics, especially Shelley and Keats, and their great Victorian successor Tennyson, all of whom had a good ear for the musical quality of language. In the following passage, Tennyson makes effective use of repeated "o" and "ow" sounds to suggest the soft moaning of the wind as it spreads the seed of the lotos plant:

The Lotos blooms below the barren peak,
The Lotos blows by every winding creek;
All day the wind breathes low with mellower tone;
Through every hollow cave and alley lone
Round and round the spicy downs the yellow Lotos dust is blown.

(from "The Lotos-Eaters")

ALLITERATION

Alliteration connects words which have the same initial consonant. Like consonance and rhyme, alliteration adds emphasis, throwing individual words into strong relief, and lending force to rhythm. This is especially evident in the work of Gerard Manley Hopkins, where alliteration works in conjunction with the heavy stresses of *sprung rhythm*:

Brute beauty and valour and act, oh, air, pride, plume, here
Buckle! AND the fire that breaks from thee then, a billion
Times told lovelier, more dangerous, O my chevalier!

(from "The Windhover")

Like assonance, alliteration is useful in descriptive poetry, reinforcing an impression or mood through repeated sounds:

Thou on whose stream, 'mid the steep sky's commotion,
Loose clouds like Earth's decaying leaves are shed,
Shook from the tangled boughs of Heaven and Ocean ...

(from Percy Shelley, "Ode to the West Wind")

The repetition of "s" and "sh" sounds conveys the rushing sound of a wind that drives everything before it. This effect is also an example of *onomatopoeia*, a figure of speech in which the sound of the words seems to echo the sense.

RHYME AND POETIC STRUCTURE

Rhyme may play a central role in the structure of a poem. This is particularly apparent in the *sonnet* form, where the expression of the thought is heavily influenced by the poet's choice of rhyme-scheme. The "English" or "Shakespearean" sonnet has three quatrains rhyming *abab*, *cdcd*, *efef*, and concludes with a rhyming couplet, *gg*. This pattern lends itself well to the statement and restatement of an idea, as we find, for example, in Shakespeare's sonnet "That time of year thou mayst in me behold." Each of the quatrains presents an image of decline or decay—a tree in winter, the coming of night, a dying fire; the closing couplet then relates these images to the thought of an impending separation and attendant feelings of loss.

The organization of the "Italian" or "Petrarchan" sonnet, by contrast, hinges on a rhyme scheme that creates two parts, an eight-line section (the *octave*) typically rhyming *abbaabba*, and a concluding six-line section (the *sestet*) rhyming *cdecde* or some other variation. In the octave, the writer describes a thought or feeling; in the sestet, the writer may elaborate upon that thought, or may introduce a sudden "turn" or change of direction. A good example of the Italian form is Donne's "Batter My Heart, Three-Personed God."

The rhyming pattern established at the beginning of a poem is usually followed throughout; thus the opening sets up an expectation in the reader, which the poet may sometimes play on by means of an unexpected or surprising rhyme. This is especially evident in comic verse, where peculiar or unexpected rhymes can contribute a great deal to the comic effect:

I shoot the Hippopotamus
with bullets made of platinum,
Because if I use leaden ones
his hide is sure to flatten 'em.
(Hilaire Belloc, "The Hippopotamus")

Finally, one of the most obvious yet important aspects of rhyme is its sound. It acts as a kind of musical punctuation, lending verse an added resonance and beauty. And as anyone who has ever had to learn poetry by heart will testify, the sound of rhyme is a powerful aid to memorization and recall, from helping a child to learn numbers—

One, two,
Buckle my shoe,
Three, four,
Knock at the door—

—to selling toothpaste through an advertising jingle in which the use of rhyme drives home the identity of a product:

You'll wonder where the yellow went,
When you brush your teeth with Pepsodent.

OTHER FORMS WITH INTERLOCKING RHYMES

Other forms besides the sonnet depend upon rhyme for their structural integrity. These include the *rondeau*, a poem of thirteen lines in three stanzas, with two half lines acting as a refrain, and having only two rhymes. The linking effect of rhyme is also essential to the three-line stanza called *terza rima*, the form chosen by Shelley for his "Ode to the West Wind," where the rhyme scheme (*aba, bcb, cdc*, etc.) gives a strong sense of forward movement. But a poet need not be limited to particular forms to use interlocking rhyme schemes.

THE POET'S TASK

The poet's task, in Sir Philip Sidney's view, is to move us to virtue and well-doing by coming to us with

> words set in delightful proportion, either accompanied with, or prepared for, the well-enchanting skill of music; and with a tale forsooth he cometh unto you, with a tale which holdeth children from play, and old men from the chimney corner; and pretending no more, doth intend the winning of the mind from wickedness to virtue: even as the child is often brought to take most wholesome things by hiding them in such other as have a pleasant taste.
>
> (*The Defence of Poesy*, 1593)

Modern poets have been less preoccupied with the didactic or moral force of poetry, its capacity to win the mind to virtue; nonetheless, like their Renaissance counterparts, they view poetry as a means to understanding, a point of light in an otherwise dark universe. To Robert Frost, a poem "begins in delight and ends in wisdom":

> It begins in delight, it inclines to the impulse, it assumes direction with the first line laid down, it runs a course of lucky events, and ends in a clarification of life—not necessarily a great clarification, such as sects and cults are founded on, but in a momentary stay against confusion.
>
> ("The Figure a Poem Makes," *Collected Poems*, 1939)

Rhyme and meter are important tools at the poet's disposal, and can be valuable aids in developing thought as well as in creating rhythmic or musical effects. However, the technical skills needed to turn a good line or create metrical complexities should not be confused with the ability to write good poetry. Sidney wryly observes in his *Defence of Poesy* that "there have been many excellent poets that never versified, and now swarm many versifiers that need never answer to the name of poets. ... [I]t is not rhyming and versing that maketh a poet, no more than a long gown maketh an advocate." Technical virtuosity may arouse our admiration, but something else is needed to bring that "constriction of the throat and ... precipitation of water to the eyes" that A.E. Housman speaks about. What that "something" is will always elude definition, and is perhaps best left for readers and listeners to determine for themselves through their own encounters with poetry.

Maps

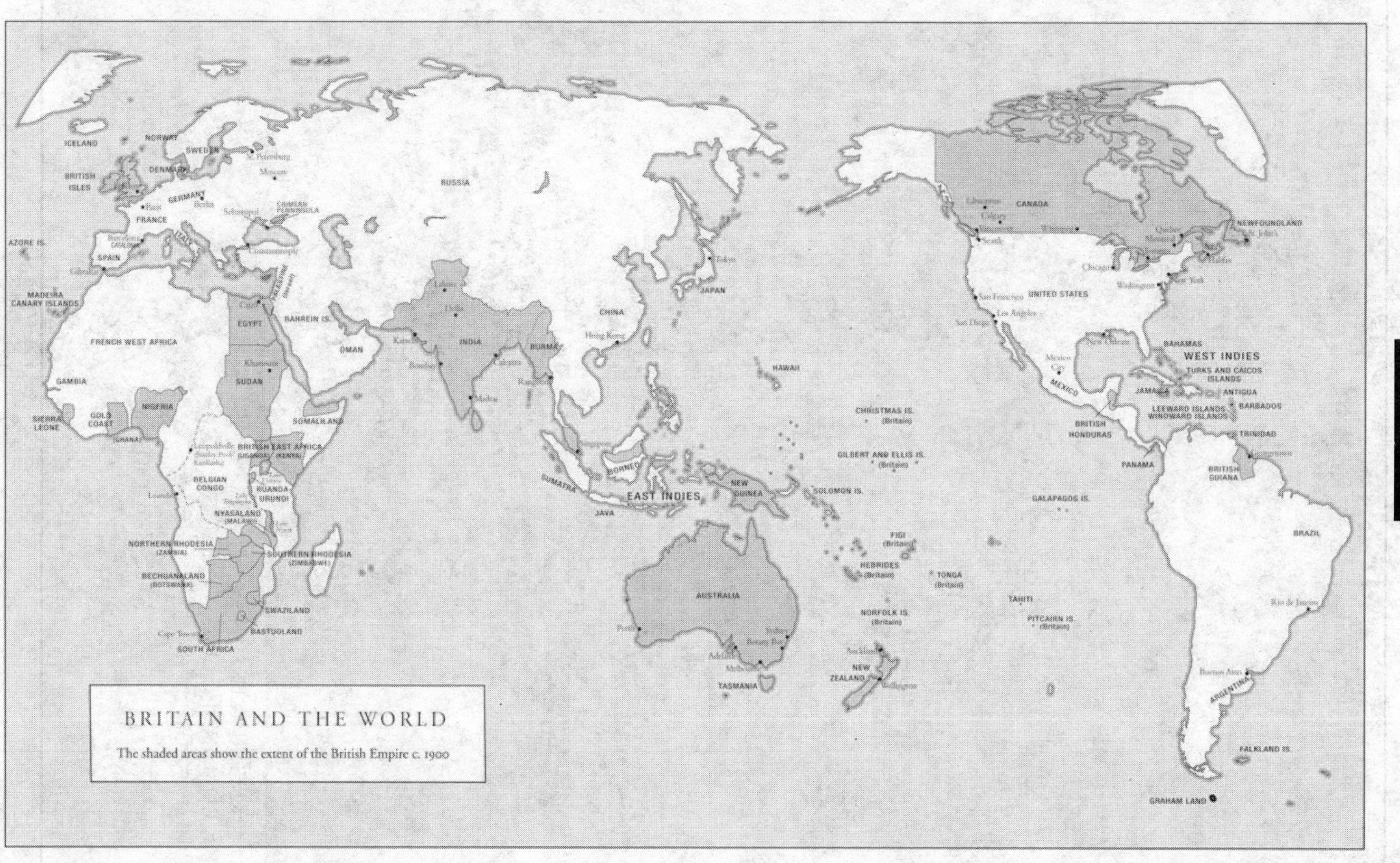

BRITAIN AND THE WORLD

The shaded areas show the extent of the British Empire c. 1900

THE BRITISH ISLES IN THE ROMANTIC ERA
ORKNEY ISLANDS
North Sea
HEBRIDES
ISLE OF SKYE
Elgin
Inverness
HIGHLANDS
Aberdeen
SCOTLAND
Dunkeld
Dundee
Perth
St. Andrews
Stirling
Loch Lomond
Dunfermline
Firth of Forth
Glasgow
Edinburgh
Clyde R.
Ayr
Urr
Tyne R.
Newcastle upon Tyne
THE LAKE DISTRICT
Grasmere
Durham
ISLE OF MAN
PENNINES
Leeds
York
Hull
Humber
Irish Sea
Wakefield
Liverpool
Manchester
THE PEAKS
Sheffield
Lincoln
Holyhead
Chester
Bangor
Wrexham
ENGLAND
Derby
Nottingham
The Wash
Harlech
Dee R.
Stoke-on-Trent
Leicester
Lynn
NORFOLK BROADS
Norwich
Birmingham
Coventry
Ely
Aberystwyth
Rugby
Cardigan
Warwick
Avon R.
Stratford-upon-Avon
Cambridge
WALES
Severn R.
Tintern Abbey
Gloucester
Oxford
St. Albans
Ipswich
Thames R.
Eton
London
Pembroke
Swansea
Reading
Greenwich
Milford Haven
Cardiff
Bristol
SALISBURY PLAIN
Windsor
Canterbury
Bath
Richmond
Royal Tunbridge Wells
Rochester
Dover
Salisbury
Ouse
Strait of Dover
Southampton
Winchester
THE WEALD
Winchelsea
Bournemouth
SOUTH DOWNS
Hastings
Exeter
DORSET DOWNS
Lewes
DARTMOOR
Lyme Regis
Chichester
Brighton
Portsmouth
ISLE OF WIGHT
Plymouth
St. Ives
LAND'S END
Penzance
English Channel
Cherbourg
GUERNSEY
CHANNEL ISLANDS
JERSEY
Le Havre
Rouen
Caen
NORMANDY
Paris
Brest
BRITTANY
Orléans
Calais
FLANDERS
Ghent
Oostende
Bruges
Antwerp
Amsterdam
The Hague
Londonderry
ULSTER
Donegal
Donegal Bay
BEN BULBEN
Belfast
Armagh
Sligo
Dundalk
Croagh Patrick
CONNAUGHT
Kells
Tara
ARAN ISLANDS
IRELAND
Dublin
Glendalough
Kilkenny
LEINSTER
Limerick
Monaincha
Tipperary
Waterford
Wexford
MUNSTER
Cork
Dungarvan
N
E
S
W

THE BRITISH ISLES IN THE VICTORIAN ERA

THE BRITISH ISLES IN THE
TWENTY-FIRST CENTURY
N
S
E
W
North Sea
Irish Sea
English Channel
ORKNEY ISLANDS
HEBRIDES
ISLE OF SKYE
HIGHLANDS
SCOTLAND
Elgin
Inverness
Aberdeen
Dunkeld
Dundee
Perth
St. Andrews
Stirling
Loch Lomond
Dunfermline
Firth of Forth
Glasgow
Edinburgh
Clyde R.
Ayr
Urr
Tyne R.
Newcastle upon Tyne
Sunderland
Durham
Middlesbrough
THE LAKE DISTRICT
ISLE OF MAN
MOORS
Scarborough
Bradford
York
Leeds
PENNINES
Blackpool
Hull
Heptonstall
Wigan
Liverpool
Manchester
Grimsby
THE PEAKS
Sheffield
Lincoln
Holyhead
Bangor
Wrexham
ENGLAND
Derby
Nottingham
The Wash
Harlech
Dee R.
Stoke-on-Trent
Leicester
Grantham
NORFOLK BROADS
Norwich
WALES
Birmingham
Coventry
Ely
Aberystwyth
Rugby
Avon R.
Stratford-upon-Avon
Cardigan
Cambridge
The Nortons
Milton Keynes
Ipswich
Gloucester
Oxford
St. Albans
Luton
Pembroke
Swansea
Cardiff
Thames R.
Reading
Eton
London
Greenwich
Southend-on-Sea
Milford Haven
Bristol
SALISBURY PLAIN
Windsor
Richmond
Rochester
Canterbury
Margate
Ramsgate
Bath
Weston-Super-Mare
Royal Tunbridge Wells
Basingstoke
Sissinghurst
Salisbury
Crawley
Rye
Dover
Southampton
Winchester
THE WEALD
Dorchester
Folkestone
DORSET
Bournemouth
Chichester
East Grinstead
Winchelsea
Exeter
Lyme Regis
Portsmouth
Lewes
Hastings
DARTMOOR
Weymouth
Brighton
Eastbourne
Plymouth
Torquay
ISLE OF WIGHT
St. Ives
LAND'S END
Penzance
Cherbourg
GUERNSEY
CHANNEL ISLANDS
JERSEY
Le Havre
Rouen
Caen
NORMANDY
Paris
Brest
BRITTANY
Orléans
Amsterdam
The Hague
Oostende
Bruges
Antwerp
Dunkirk
Calais
FLANDERS
Ghent
IRELAND
ULSTER
Londonderry
Donegal
Donegal Bay
BEN BULBEN
Sligo
Armagh
Belfast
Dundalk
Croagh Patrick
CONNAUGHT
Kells
Tara
Dublin
ARAN ISLANDS
Kilkenny
Glendalough
LEINSTER
Limerick
Monaincha
Tipperary
Waterford
Wexford
MUNSTER
Cork
Dungarvan

N
S
E
W
ORKNEY
ORKNEY ISLANDS
HEBRIDES
ISLE OF SKYE
WESTERN ISLES
HIGHLAND
GRAMPIAN
SCOTLAND
Atlantic Ocean
North Sea
TAYSIDE
FIFE
CENTRAL
Firth of Forth
Clyde
LOTHIAN
STRATHCLYDE
BORDERS
Tweed
ARRAN ISLAND
North Channel
NORTH-UMBERLAND
DUMFRIES AND GALLOWAY
Tyne
DONEGAL
DERRY
LONDONDERRY
ANTRIM
NORTHERN IRELAND
TYRONE
Donegal Bay
FERMANAGH
ULSTER
ARMAGH
DOWN
SLIGO
MONAGHAN
LEITRIM
MAYO
CAVAN
ROSCOMMON
LONGFORD
LOUTH
MEATH
WESTMEATH
GALWAY
OFFALY
KILDARE
DUBLIN
IRELAND
CLARE
LAOIGHIS
WICKLOW
TIPPERARY
CARLOW
LIMERICK
KILKENNY
WEXFORD
KERRY
CORK
WATERFORD
St. George's Channel
DURHAM
CLEVELAND
CUMBRIA
ISLE OF MAN
NORTH YORKSHIRE
Ouse
HUMBERSIDE
Irish Sea
Aire
WEST YORKSHIRE
LANCASHIRE
SOUTH YORKSHIRE
LINCOLNSHIRE
CHESHIRE
DERBYSHIRE
NOTTINGHAMSHIRE
CLWYD
The Wash
GWYNEDD
Trent
ENGLAND
SHROPSHIRE
LEICESTERSHIRE
NORFOLK
Great Ouse
POWYS
Severn
STAFFORDSHIRE
CAMBRIDGESHIRE
NORTHAMPTONSHIRE
SUFFOLK
WORCESTER
WARWICKSHIRE
WALES
HEREFORD
BEDFORDSHIRE
Wye
DYFED
BUCKINGHAMSHIRE
HERTFORDSHIRE
ESSEX
GLOUCESTERSHIRE
GWENT
OXFORDSHIRE
Thames
London
WEST GLAMORGAN
SOUTH GLAMORGAN
AVON
BERKSHIRE
WILTSHIRE
SURREY
KENT
SOMERSET
HAMPSHIRE
WEST SUSSEX
EAST SUSSEX
Strait of Dover
DEVON
DORSET
ISLE OF WIGHT
CORNWALL
English Channel
ISLES OF SCILLY
CHANNEL ISLANDS
COUNTIES OF BRITAIN AND IRELAND
FRANCE

GREATER LONDON
Tottenham
Finchley
Harrow
EPPING FOREST
Hampstead Heath
Wembley
Islington
Twyford Abbey
West Ham
London
Tower
Millenium Dome
Westminster
Fulham
Chelsea
Woolwich
Greenwich
Heathrow Airport
Richmond
Battersea
Deptford
Twickenham
Wandsworth
Dartford
Crystal Palace
Kingston
Wimbledon
Sydenham
Hampton Court
Merton
Bromley
Croydon

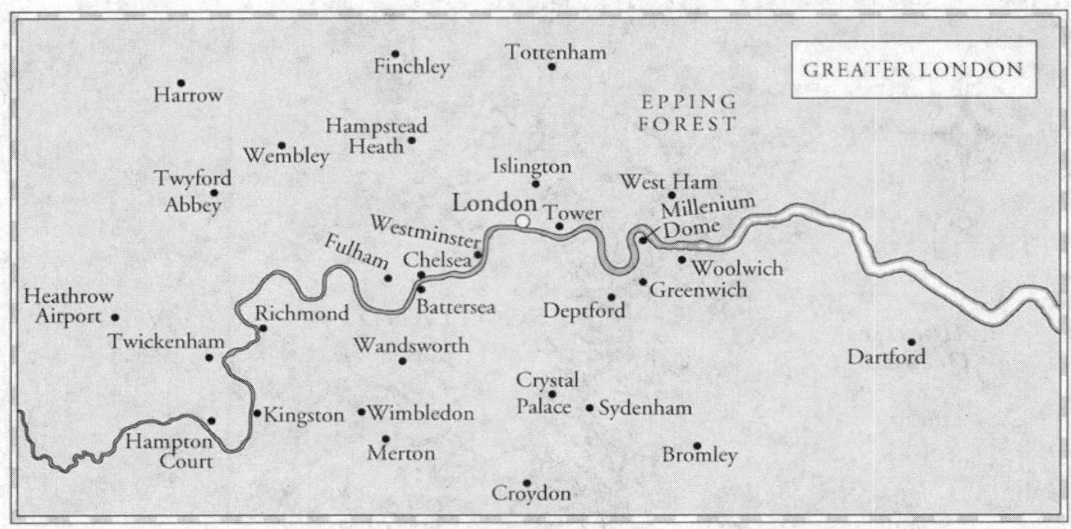

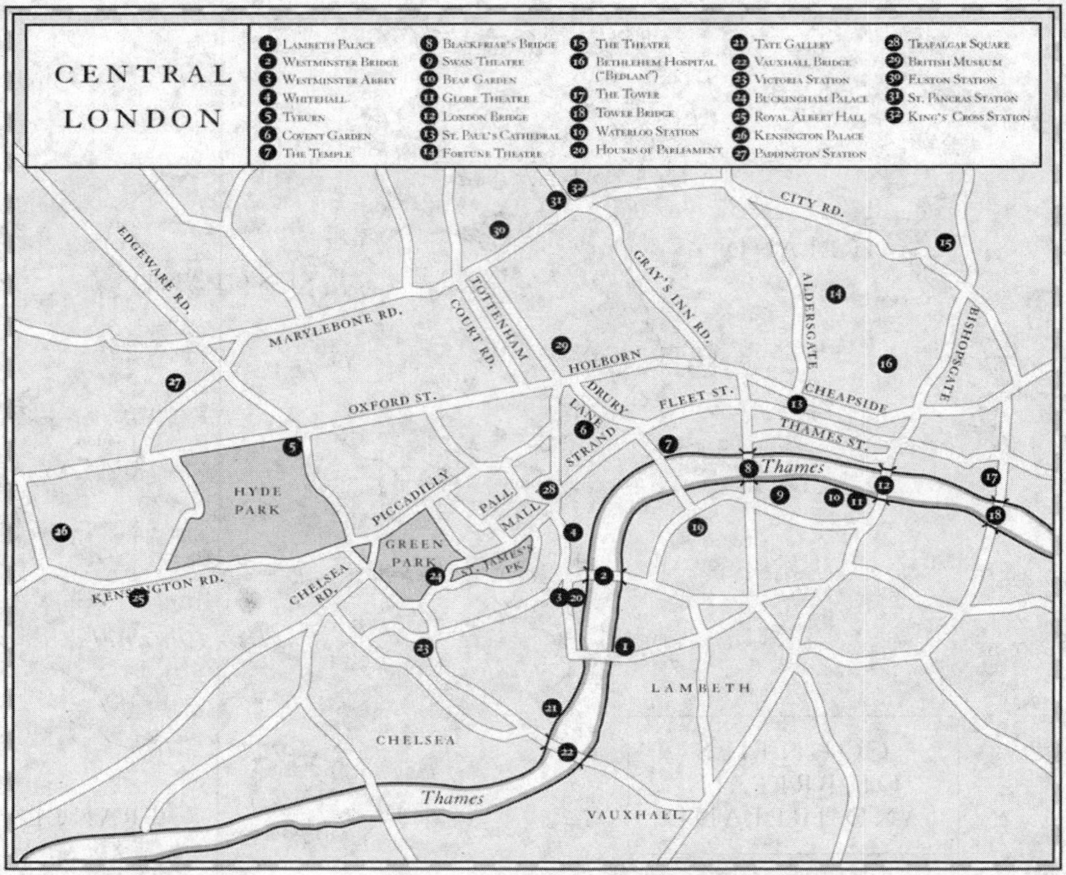

CENTRAL LONDON
1 Lambeth Palace
2 Westminster Bridge
3 Westminster Abbey
4 Whitehall
5 Tyburn
6 Covent Garden
7 The Temple
8 Blackfriar's Bridge
9 Swan Theatre
10 Bear Garden
11 Globe Theatre
12 London Bridge
13 St. Paul's Cathedral
14 Fortune Theatre
15 The Theatre
16 Bethlehem Hospital ("Bedlam")
17 The Tower
18 Tower Bridge
19 Waterloo Station
20 Houses of Parliament
21 Tate Gallery
22 Vauxhall Bridge
23 Victoria Station
24 Buckingham Palace
25 Royal Albert Hall
26 Kensington Palace
27 Paddington Station
28 Trafalgar Square
29 British Museum
30 Euston Station
31 St. Pancras Station
32 King's Cross Station
CITY RD.
EDGEWARE RD.
TOTTENHAM COURT RD.
GRAY'S INN RD.
ALDERSGATE
BISHOPSGATE
MARYLEBONE RD.
HOLBORN
DRURY LANE
FLEET ST.
CHEAPSIDE
OXFORD ST.
THAMES ST.
STRAND
Thames
HYDE PARK
PICCADILLY
PALL MALL
GREEN PARK
ST. JAMES'S PK
KENSINGTON RD.
CHELSEA RD.
LAMBETH
CHELSEA
Thames
VAUXHALL

Monarchs and Prime Ministers

MONARCHS

House of Wessex

Egbert (Ecgberht)	829–39
Æthelwulf	839–58
Æthelbald	858–60
Æthelbert	860–66
Æthelred I	866–71
Alfred the Great	871–99
Edward the Elder	899–924
Athelstan	924–40
Edmund I	940–46
Edred (Eadred)	946–55
Edwy (Eadwig)	955–59
Edgar	959–75
Edward the Martyr	975–78
Æthelred II (the Unready)	978–1016
Edmund II (Ironside)	1016

Danish Line

Canute (Cnut)	1016–35
Harold I (Harefoot)	1035–40
Harthacnut	1040–42

Wessex Line, Restored

Edward the Confessor	1042–66
Harold II (Godwinson)	1066

Norman Line

William I (the Conqueror)	1066–87
William II (Rufus)	1087–1100
Henry I (Beauclerc)	1100–35
Stephen	1135–54
Matilda	1141

Harold II

William I

MONARCHS

PLANTAGENET, ANGEVIN LINE

Henry II	1154–89
Richard I (Coeur de Lion)	1189–99
John (Lackland)	1199–1216
Henry III	1216–72
Edward I (Longshanks)	1272–1307
Edward II	1307–27
Edward III	1327–77
Richard II	1377–99

Henry VIII

PLANTAGENET, LANCASTRIAN LINE

Henry IV	1399–1413
Henry V	1413–22
Henry VI	1422–61; 1470–71

PLANTAGENET, YORKIST LINE

Edward IV	1461–70; 1471–83
Edward V	1483
Richard III	1483–85

Mary I

HOUSE OF TUDOR

Henry VII	1485–1509
Henry VIII	1509–47
Edward VI	1547–53
Jane	1553
Mary I	1553–58
Elizabeth I	1558–1603

HOUSE OF STUART

James I/VI	1603–25
Charles I	1625–49

(The Commonwealth)	1649–60
Oliver Cromwell	1649–58
Richard Cromwell	1658–59

MONARCHS		PRIME MINISTERS	
HOUSE OF STUART, RESTORED			
Charles II	1660–85		
James II	1685–89		
HOUSE OF ORANGE AND STUART			
William III and Mary II	1689–94		
William III	1694–1702		
HOUSE OF STUART			
Anne	1702–14		
HOUSE OF BRUNSWICK, HANOVER LINE			
George I	1714–27	Sir Robert Walpole (Whig)	1721–42
George II	1727–60	Earl of Wilmington (Whig)	1742–43
		Henry Pelham (Whig)	1743–54
		Duke of Newcastle (Whig)	1754–56
		Duke of Devonshire (Whig)	1756–57
George III	1760–1820	Duke of Newcastle (Whig)	1757–62
		Earl of Bute (Tory)	1762–63
		George Grenville (Whig)	1763–65
		Marquess of Rockingham (Whig)	1765–66
		William Pitt the Elder (Earl of Chatham) (Whig)	1766–68
		Duke of Grafton (Whig)	1768–70
		Frederick North (Lord North) (Tory)	1770–82
		Marquess of Rockingham (Whig)	1782
		Earl of Shelburne (Whig)	1782–83
		Duke of Portland (Whig)	1783
		William Pitt the Younger (Tory)	1783–1801
		Henry Addington (Tory)	1801–04
		William Pitt the Younger (Tory)	1804–06
		William Wyndham Grenville (Baron Grenville) (Whig)	1806–07

George III

George, Prince of Wales, Prince Regent

MONARCHS

George, Prince of Wales, Prince Regent	1811–20
George IV	1820–30
William IV	1830–37
Victoria	1837–1901

Victoria

HOUSE OF SAXE-COBURG-GOTHA

Edward VII	1901–10

HOUSE OF WINDSOR

George V	1910–36

PRIME MINISTERS

Duke of Portland (Tory)	1807–09
Spencer Perceval (Tory)	1809–12
Earl of Liverpool (Tory)	1812–27
George Canning (Tory)	1827
Viscount Goderich (Tory)	1827–28
Duke of Wellington (Tory)	1828–30
Earl Grey (Whig)	1830–34
Viscount Melbourne (Whig)	1834
Duke of Wellington (Tory)	1834
Sir Robert Peel (Tory)	1834–35
Viscount Melbourne (Whig)	1835–41
Sir Robert Peel (Tory)	1841–46
Lord John Russell (later Earl) (Whig)	1846–52
Earl of Derby (Con.)	1852
Earl of Aberdeen (Tory/Peelite)	1852–55
Viscount Palmerston (Lib.)	1855–58
Earl of Derby (Con.)	1858–59
Viscount Palmerston (Lib.)	1859–65
Earl Russell (Liberal)	1865–66
Earl of Derby (Con.)	1866–68
Benjamin Disraeli (Con.)	1868
William Gladstone (Lib.)	1868–74
Benjamin Disraeli (Con.)	1874–80
William Gladstone (Lib.)	1880–85
Marquess of Salisbury (Con.)	1885–86
William Gladstone (Lib.)	1886
Marquess of Salisbury (Con.)	1886–92
William Gladstone (Lib.)	1892–94
Earl of Rosebery (Lib.)	1894–95
Marquess of Salisbury (Con.)	1895–1902
Arthur Balfour (Con.)	1902–05
Sir Henry Campbell-Bannerman (Lib.)	1905–08
Herbert Asquith (Lib.)	1908–16

MONARCHS		PRIME MINISTERS	
		David Lloyd George (Lib.)	1916–22
		Bonar Law (Con.)	1922–23
		Stanley Baldwin (Con.)	1923–24
		Ramsay MacDonald (Labour)	1924
		Stanley Baldwin (Con.)	1924–29
		Ramsay MacDonald (Labour)	1929–35
Edward VIII	1936	Stanley Baldwin (Con.)	1935–37
George VI	1936–52	Neville Chamberlain (Con.)	1937–40
		Winston Churchill (Con.)	1940–45
		Clement Attlee (Labour)	1945–51
Elizabeth II	1952–	Sir Winston Churchill (Con.)	1951–55

Winston Churchill

Sir Anthony Eden (Con.)	1955–57
Harold Macmillan (Con.)	1957–63
Sir Alec Douglas-Home (Con.)	1963–64
Harold Wilson (Labour)	1964–70
Edward Heath (Con.)	1970–74
Harold Wilson (Labour)	1974–76
James Callaghan (Labour)	1976–79
Margaret Thatcher (Con.)	1979–90
John Major (Con.)	1990–97
Tony Blair (Labour)	1997–2007
Gordon Brown (Labour)	2007–10
David Cameron (Con.)	2010–16
Theresa May (Con.)	2016–

Glossary of Terms

Accent: the natural emphasis (stress) speakers place on a syllable.

Accentual Verse: poetry in which a line is measured only by the number of accents or stresses, not by the number of syllables.

Accentual-Syllabic Verse: the most common metrical system in traditional English verse, in which a line is measured by the number of syllables and by the pattern of accented (stressed) and unaccented (unstressed) syllables.

Aesthetes: members of a late nineteenth-century movement that valued "art for art's sake"—for its purely aesthetic qualities, as opposed to valuing art for the moral content it may convey, for the intellectual stimulation it may provide, or for a range of other qualities.

Alexandrine: a line of verse that is 12 syllables long. In English verse, the alexandrine is always an iambic hexameter: that is, it has six iambic feet. The most-often quoted example is the second line in a couplet from Alexander Pope's "Essay on Criticism" (1711): "A needless Alexandrine ends the song / That, like a wounded snake, drags its slow length along." See also *Spenserian stanza.*

Allegory: a narrative with both a literal meaning and secondary, often symbolic meaning or meanings. Allegory frequently employs personification to give concrete embodiment to abstract concepts or entities, such as feelings or personal qualities. It may also present one set of characters or events in the guise of another, using implied parallels for the purposes of satire or political comment, as in John Dryden's poem "Absalom and Achitophel."

Alliteration: the grouping of words with the same initial consonant (e.g., "break, blow, burn, and make me new"). The repetition of sound acts as a connector. See also *assonance* and *consonance.*

Alliterative Verse: poetry that employs alliteration of stressed syllables in each line as its chief structural principle.

Allusion: a reference, often indirect or unidentified, to a person, thing, or event. A reference in one literary work to another literary work, whether to its content or its form, also constitutes an allusion.

Ambiguity: an "opening" of language created by the writer to allow for multiple meanings or differing interpretations. In literature, ambiguity may be deliberately employed by the writer to enrich meaning; this differs from any unintentional, unwanted, ambiguity in non-literary prose.

Amphibrach: a metrical foot with three syllables, the second of which is stressed: x / x (e.g., sensation).

Analogy: a broad term that refers to our processes of noting similarities among things or events. Specific forms of analogy in poetry include *simile* and *metaphor* (see below).

Anapaest: a metrical foot containing two unstressed syllables followed by one stressed syllable: xx/ (e.g., underneath, intervene).

Anglican Church / Church of England: formed after Henry VIII's break with Rome in the 1530s, the Church of England had acquired a permanently Protestant cast by the 1570s. There has remained considerable variation within the Church, however, with distinctions often drawn among High Church, Broad Church, and Latitudinarian. At one extreme High Church Anglicans (some of whom prefer to be known as "Anglo-Catholics") prefer relatively elaborate church rituals not dissimilar in form to those of the Roman Catholic Church and place considerable emphasis on church hierarchy, while in the other direction Latitudinarians prefer relatively informal religious services and tend far more towards egalitarianism.

Antistrophe: from Greek drama, the chorus's countermovement or reply to an initial movement (strophe). See *ode* below.

Apostrophe: a figure of speech (a trope; see *figures of speech* below) in which a writer directly addresses an object—or a dead or absent person—as if the imagined audience were actually listening.

Archetype: in literature and mythology, a recurring idea, symbol, motif, character, or place. To some scholars and psychologists, an archetype represents universal human thought-patterns or experiences.

Assonance: the repetition of identical or similar vowel sounds in stressed syllables in which the surrounding consonants are different: for example, "shame" and "fate"; "gale" and "cage"; or the long "i" sounds in "Beside the pumice isle."

Aubade: a lyric poem that greets or laments the arrival of dawn.

Ballad: a folk song, or a poem originally recited to an audience, which tells a dramatic story based on legend or history.

Ballad Stanza: a quatrain with alternating four-stress and three-stress lines, rhyming *abcb*. A variant is "common measure," in which the alternating lines are strictly iambic, and rhyme *abab*.

Ballade: a fixed form most commonly characterized by only three rhymes, with an 8-line stanza rhyming *ababbcbc* and an envoy rhyming *bcbc*. Both Chaucer and Dante Gabriel Rossetti ("Ballad of the Dead Ladies") adopted this form.

Baroque: powerful and heavily ornamented in style. "Baroque" is a term from the history of visual art and of music that is sometimes also used to describe certain literary styles, such as that of Richard Crashaw.

Bathos: an anticlimactic effect brought about by a writer's descent from an elevated subject or tone to the ordinary or trivial.

Benedictine Rule: set of instructions for monastic communities, composed by Saint Benedict of Nursia (died c. 457).

Blank Verse: unrhymed lines written in iambic pentameter, a form introduced to English verse by Henry Howard, Earl of Surrey, in his translation of parts of Virgil's *Aeneid* in 1547.

Bombast: inappropriately inflated or grandiose language.

Broadside: individual sheet of paper printed on only one side. From the sixteenth through to the eighteenth centuries broadsides of a variety of different sorts (e.g., ballads, political tracts, short satires) were sold on the streets.

Broken Rhyme: in which a multi-syllable word is split at the end of a line and continued onto the next, to allow an end-rhyme with the split syllable.

Burlesque: satire of a particularly exaggerated sort, particularly that which ridicules its subject by emphasizing its vulgar or ridiculous aspects.

Caesura: a pause or break in a line of verse occurring where a phrase, clause, or sentence ends, and indicated in scansion by the mark II. If it occurs in the middle of the line, it is known as a "medial" caesura.

Canon: in literature, those works that are commonly accepted as possessing authority or importance. In practice, "canonical" texts or authors are those that are discussed most frequently by scholars and taught most frequently in university courses.

Canto: a sub-section of a long (usually epic) poem.

Canzone: a short song or poem, with stanzas of equal length and an envoy.

Carpe Diem: Latin (from Horace) meaning "seize the day." The idea of enjoying the moment is a common one in Renaissance love poetry. See, for example, Marvell's "To His Coy Mistress."

Catalexis: the omission of unstressed syllables from a line of verse (such a line is referred to as "catalectic"). In iambic verse it is usually the first syllable of the line that is omitted; in trochaic, the last. For example, in the first stanza of Housman's "To an Athlete Dying Young" the third line is catalectic: i.e., it has dropped the first, unstressed syllable called for by the poem's iambic tetrameter form: "The time you won your town the race / We chaired you through the market-place; / Man and boy stood cheering by, / And home we brought you shoulder-high."

Catharsis: the arousal through the performance of a dramatic tragedy of "emotions of pity and fear" to a point where "purgation" or "purification" occurs and the feelings are released or transformed.

The concept was developed by Aristotle in his *Poetics* from an ancient Greek medical concept, and adapted by him into an aesthetic principle.

Chiasmus: a figure of speech (a scheme) that reverses word order in successive parallel clauses. If the word order is A-B-C in the first clause, it becomes C-B-A in the second: for example, Donne's line "She is all states, and all princes, I" ("The Sun Rising") incorporates this reversal (though with an ellipsis).

Classical: originating in or relating to ancient Greek or Roman culture. As commonly conceived, *classical* implies a strong sense of formal order. The term *neoclassical* is often used with reference to literature of the Restoration and eighteenth century that was strongly influenced by ancient Greek and Roman models.

Closet Drama: a play (typically in verse) written for private performance. The term came into use in the first half of the nineteenth century.

Colored Narrative: alternative term for *free indirect discourse.*

Comedy: as a literary term, used originally to denote that class of ancient Greek drama in which the action ends happily. More broadly the term has been used to describe a wide variety of literary forms of a more or less light-hearted character.

***Commedia dell'arte*:** largely improvised comic performances conducted by masked performers and involving considerable physical activity. The genre of *commedia dell'arte* originated in Italy in the sixteenth century; it was influential throughout Europe for more than two centuries thereafter.

Commonwealth: from the fifteenth century, a term roughly equivalent to the modern "state," but tending to emphasize the commonality of interests among all citizens. In the seventeenth century Britain was named a commonwealth under Oliver Cromwell. In the twentieth century, the term came to be applied to associations of many nations; the British Commonwealth became the successor to the British Empire.

Conceit: an unusually elaborate metaphor or simile that extends beyond its original tenor and vehicle, sometimes becoming a "master" analogy for the entire poem (see, for example, Donne's "The Flea," and Robert Frost's sonnet "She is as in a field a silken tent"). Ingenious or fanciful images and comparisons were especially popular with the metaphysical poets of the seventeenth century, giving rise to the term "metaphysical conceit."

Concrete Poetry: an experimental form, most popular during the 1950s and 60s, in which the printed type itself forms a visual image of the poem's key words or ideas. See also *pattern poetry, assonance.*

Connotation: the implied, often unspoken meaning(s) of a given word, as distinct from its denotation, or literal meaning. Connotations may have highly emotional undertones and are usually culturally specific.

Conservative Party: See *Political Parties.*

Consonance: the pairing of words with similar initial and ending consonants, but with different vowel sounds (live/love, wander/wonder). See also *alliteration.*

Convention: aesthetic approach, technique, or practice accepted as characteristic and appropriate for a particular form. It is a convention of certain sorts of plays, for example, that the characters speak in blank verse, of other sorts of plays that characters speak in rhymed couplets, and of still other sorts of dramatic performances that characters frequently break into song to express their feelings.

Couplet: a pair of rhyming lines, usually in the same meter. If they form a complete unit of thought and are grammatically complete, the lines are known as a closed couplet. See also *heroic couplet* below.

Dactyl: a metrical foot containing one strong stress followed by two weak stresses: / xx (e.g., muttering, helplessly). A minor form known as "double dactyls" makes use of this meter for humorous purposes, e.g., "Jiggery pokery" or "Higgledy piggledy."

Denotation: See *connotation* above.

Devolution: process through which a degree of political power was transferred in the late twentieth and early twenty-first centuries from the British government to assemblies in Scotland and in Wales.

Dialogue: words spoken by characters to one another. (When a character is addressing him or her self or the audience directly, the words spoken are referred to as a *monologue.*)

Diction: word choice. Whether the diction of a literary work (or of a literary character) is colloquial, conversational, formal, or of some other type contributes significantly to the tone of the text as well as to characterization.

Didacticism: aesthetic approach emphasizing moral instruction.

Dimeter: a poetic line containing two metrical feet.

Dirge: a song or poem that mourns someone's death. See also *elegy* and *lament* below.

Disestablishmentarianism: movement opposing an official state-supported religion, in particular the Church of England in that role.

Dissonance: harsh, unmusical sounds or rhythms which poets may use deliberately to achieve certain effects.

Dramatic Irony: this form of irony occurs when the audience's reception of a speech by a character on the stage is affected by the possession by the audience of information not available to the character.

Dramatic Monologue: a lyric poem that takes the form of an utterance by a single person addressing a silent listener. The speaker may be an historical personage (as in some of Robert

Browning's dramatic monologues), a figure drawn from myth or legend (as in some of Tennyson's), or an entirely imagined figure, as in Webster's "A Castaway."

Dub Poetry: a form of protest poetry originating in Jamaica, with its roots in dance rhythms, especially reggae, and often accompanied in performance by drums and music. See also *rap*.

Duple Foot: a duple foot of poetry has two syllables. The possible duple forms are iamb (in which the stress is on the second of the two syllables), trochee (in which the stress is on the first of the two syllables), spondee (in which both are stressed equally), and pyrrhic (in which both syllables are unstressed).

Eclogue: now generally used simply as an alternative name for a pastoral poem. In classical times and in the early modern period, however, an *eclogue* (or *idyll*) was a specific type of pastoral poem—a dialogue or dramatic monologue involving rustic characters. (The other main sub-genre of the pastoral was the *georgic*.)

Elegiac Stanza: a quatrain of iambic pentameters rhyming *abab*, often used in poems meditating on death or sorrow. The best-known example is Thomas Gray's "Elegy Written in a Country Churchyard."

Elegy: a poem which formally mourns the death of a particular person (e.g., Tennyson's "In Memoriam") or in which the poet meditates on other serious subjects (e.g., Gray's "Elegy"). See also *dirge*.

Elision: omitting or suppressing a letter or an unstressed syllable at the beginning or end of a word, so that a line of verse may conform to a given metrical scheme. For example, the three syllables at the beginning of Shakespeare's sonnet 129 are reduced to two by the omission of the first vowel: "Th' expense of spirit in a waste of shame." See also *syncope*.

Ellipsis: the omission of a word or words necessary for the complete grammatical construction of a sentence, but not necessary for our understanding of the sentence.

End-Rhyme: See *rhyme*.

End-Stopped: a line of poetry is said to be end-stopped when the end of the line coincides with a natural pause in the syntax, such as the conclusion of a sentence; e.g., in this couplet from Pope's "Essay on Criticism," both lines are end-stopped: "A little learning is a dangerous thing; / Drink deep, or taste not the Pierian spring." Compare this with *enjambement*.

Enjambement: the "running-on" of the sense from one line of poetry to the next, with no pause created by punctuation or syntax. (The more commonly found alternative is referred to as an *end-stopped line*.)

Envoy (Envoi): a stanza or half-stanza that forms the conclusion of certain French poetic forms, such as the *sestina* or the *ballade*. It often sums up or comments upon what has gone before.

Epic: a lengthy narrative poem, often divided into books and sub-divided into cantos. It generally celebrates heroic deeds or events, and the style tends to be lofty and grand. Examples in English include Spenser's *The Faerie Queene* and Milton's *Paradise Lost.*

Epic Simile: an elaborate simile, developed at such length that the vehicle of the comparison momentarily displaces the primary subject with which it is being compared.

Epigram: a very short poem, sometimes in closed couplet form, characterized by pointed wit.

Epigraph: a quotation placed at the beginning of a discourse to indicate or foreshadow the theme.

Epiphany: a moment at which matters of significance are suddenly illuminated for a literary character (or for the reader), typically triggered by something small and seemingly of little import. The term first came into wide currency in connection with the fiction of James Joyce.

Episodic Plot: plot comprising a variety of episodes that are only loosely connected by threads of story material (as opposed to plots that present one or more continually unfolding narratives where successive episodes build one on another).

Epithalamion: a poem celebrating a wedding. The best-known example in English is probably Edmund Spenser's "Epithalamion" (1595).

Eulogy: text expressing praise, especially for a distinguished person recently deceased.

Euphemism: mode of expression through which aspects of reality considered to be vulgar, crudely physical, or unpleasant are referred to indirectly rather than named explicitly. A variety of euphemisms exist for the processes of urination and defecation; *passed away* is often used as a euphemism for *died.* (The word *euphemism* has the same root as *Euphuism* (see below), but has taken on a different meaning.)

Euphony: pleasant, musical sounds or rhythms—the opposite of dissonance.

Euphuism: In the late sixteenth century John Lyly published a prose romance, *Euphues*, which employed a style that featured long sentences filled with balanced phrases and clauses, many of them adding little to the content. This highly mannered style was popular in the court of Elizabeth I for a few years following the publication of Lyly's famous work, and the style became known as *Euphuism.*

European Union (EU): group of nations formed in 1993 as the successor to the European Economic Community (Common Market). Britain first applied for membership in the latter in 1961; at first its efforts to join were blocked by the French government, but in 1973 Prime Minister Edward Heath successfully negotiated Britain's entry into the group. Britain resisted some moves towards full integration with the European community, in particular retaining its own currency when other European nations adopted the Euro on 1 January 2002. In 2016, a referendum was held and the UK voted to leave the EU altogether.

Exchequer: in earlier eras, the central royal financial office, responsible for receiving and keeping track of crown revenues. In later eras, part of the bureaucracy equivalent to the Ministry of Finance in Canada or the Treasury in the United States (the modern post of Chancellor of the Exchequer is equivalent to the American post of Secretary of the Treasury, the Canadian post of Minister of Finance, or the Australian post of Treasurer).

Exposition: the setting out of material in an ordered form, either in speech or in writing. In a play those parts of the action that do not occur on stage but are rather recounted by the characters are frequently described as being presented in exposition. Similarly, when the background narrative is filled in near the beginning of a novel, such material is often described as having been presented in exposition. Somewhat confusingly, however, the term "expository prose" is usually used with reference not to fiction but to the setting forth of arguments or descriptions in the context of essays or other works of prose non-fiction.

Eye-Rhyme: See *rhyme* below.

Feminine Ending: the ending of a line of poetry on an "extra," and, especially, on an unstressed syllable. See, for example, the first line of Keat's "Ode on a Grecian Urn": "A thing of beauty is a joy forever," a line of iambic pentameter in which the final foot is an amphibrach rather than an iamb.

Feminine Rhyme: See *rhyme* below.

Figures of Speech: deliberate, highly concentrated uses of language to achieve particular purposes or effects on an audience. There are two kinds of figures: schemes and tropes. Schemes involve changes in word-sound and word-order, such as *alliteration* and *chiasmus*. Tropes play on our understandings of words to extend, alter, or transform meaning, as in *metaphor* and *personification*.

First-Person Narrative: narrative recounted using *I* and *me*. See also *narrative perspective*.

Fixed Forms: the term applied to a number of poetic forms and stanzaic patterns, many derived from French models, such as *ballade*, *rondeau*, *sestina*, *triolet*, and *villanelle*. Other "fixed forms" include the *sonnet*, *rhyme royal*, *haiku*, and *ottava rima*.

Folio: largest of several sizes of book page commonly used in the first few centuries after the introduction of the printing press. A folio size results from sheets of paper of at least 14 inches by 20 inches being folded in half (a folio page size will thus be at least 7 inches by 10 inches). When the same sheet is folded twice a quarto is produced, and when it is folded 3 times an octavo.

Foot: a unit of a line of verse which contains a particular combination of stressed and unstressed syllables. Dividing a line into metrical feet (*iambs*, *trochees*, etc.), then counting the number of feet per line, is part of *scansion*. See also *meter*.

Franklin: in the late medieval period, a landholder of free status, but ranking below the gentry.

Free Indirect Discourse: in prose fiction, commentary in which a seemingly objective and omniscient narrative voice assumes the point of view of one or more characters. When we hear through the third person narrative voice of Jane Austen's *Pride and Prejudice*, for example, that Mr. Darcy "was the proudest, most disagreeable man in the world, and every body hoped that he would never come there again," the narrative voice has assumed the point of view of "every body" in the community; we as readers are not meant to take it that Mr. Darcy is indeed the most disagreeable man in the world. Similarly, in the following passage from the same novel, we are likely to take it as being the view of the character Charlotte that marriage is "the only honourable provision for well-educated young women of small fortune," not to take it to be an objective statement of perceived truth on the part of the novel's third person narrative voice:

> [Charlotte's] reflections were in general satisfactory. Mr. Collins to be sure was neither sensible nor agreeable; his society was irksome, and his attachment to her must be imaginary. But still he would be her husband. Without thinking highly either of men or of matrimony, marriage had always been her object; it was the only honourable provision for well-educated young women of small fortune, and however uncertain of giving happiness, must be their pleasantest preservative from want.

The term free indirect discourse may also be applied to situations in which it may not be entirely clear if the thoughts expressed emanate from the character, the narrator, or some combination of the two. (In the above-quoted passage expressing Charlotte's thoughts, indeed, some might argue that the statement concerning marriage should be taken as the expression of a belief that the narrative voice shares, at least in part.)

Free Verse: poetry that does not follow any regular meter, line length, or rhyming scheme. In many respects, though, free verse follows the complex natural "rules" and rhythmic patterns (or cadences) of speech.

Gaelic: Celtic language, variants of which are spoken in Ireland and Scotland.

Genre: a particular literary form. The concept of genre may be used with different levels of generality. At the most general, poetry, drama, and prose fiction are distinguished as separate genres. At a lower level of generality various sub-genres are frequently distinguished, such as (within drama) comedy and tragedy, or, at a still lower level of generality, Elizabethan domestic tragedy, Edwardian drawing-room comedy, and so on.

Georgic: (from Virgil's *Georgics*) a poem that celebrates the natural wealth of the countryside and advises how to cultivate and live in harmony with it. Pope's *Windsor Forest* and James Thomson's *Seasons* are classed as georgics. They were often said to make up, with eclogues, the two alliterative forms of pastoral poetry.

Ghazal: derived from Persian and Indian precedents, the ghazal presents a series of thoughts in closed couplets joined by a simple rhyme-scheme: *aa ba ca da*, etc.

Gothic: in architecture and the visual arts, a term used to describe styles prevalent from the twelfth to the fourteenth centuries, but in literature a term used to describe work with a sinister or grotesque tone that seeks to evoke a sense of terror on the part of the reader or audience. Gothic literature originated as a genre in the eighteenth century with works such as Horace Walpole's *The Castle of*

Otranto. To some extent the notion of the medieval itself then carried with it associations of the dark and the grotesque, but from the beginning an element of intentional exaggeration (sometimes verging on self-parody) attached itself to the genre. The Gothic trend of youth culture that began in the late twentieth century is less clearly associated with the medieval, but shares with the various varieties of Gothic literature (from Walpole in the eighteenth century, to Bram Stoker in the early twentieth, to Stephen King and Anne Rice in the late twentieth) a fondness for the sensational and the grotesque, as well as a propensity to self-parody.

Guilds: non-clerical associations that arose in the late Anglo-Saxon period, devoted both to social purposes (such as the organization of feasts for the members) and to piety. In the later medieval period guilds developed strong associations with particular occupations.

Haiku: a Japanese form, using three unrhymed lines of five, seven, and five syllables. Conventionally, it uses precise, concentrated images to suggest states of feeling.

Heptameter: a line containing seven metrical feet.

Heroic Couplet: a pair of rhymed iambic pentameters, so called because the form was much used in seventeenth- and eighteenth-century poems and plays on heroic subjects.

Hexameter: a line containing six metrical feet.

Home Rule: movement dedicated to making Ireland politically independent from Britain.

Horatian Ode: inspired by the work of the Roman poet Horace, an ode that is usually calm and meditative in tone, and homostrophic (i.e., having regular stanzas) in form. Keats's odes are English examples.

House of Commons: elected legislative body, in Britain currently consisting of six hundred and fifty members of Parliament. See also *Parliament*.

House of Lords: the "Upper House" of the British Houses of Parliament. Since the nineteenth century the House of Lords has been far less powerful than the elected House of Commons. The House of Lords is currently made up of both hereditary peers (Lords whose title is passed on from generation to generation) and life peers. As a result of legislation enacted by the Labour government of Tony Blair, the role of hereditary peers in Parliament is being phased out.

Humors: The four humors were believed in until the sixteenth and seventeenth centuries to be elements in the makeup of all humans; a person's temperament was thought to be determined by the way in which the humors were combined. When the *choleric* humor was dominant, the person would tend towards anger; when the *sanguine* humor was dominant, towards pleasant affability; when the *phlegmatic* humor was dominant, towards a cool and calm attitude and/or a lack of feeling or enthusiasm; and when the *melancholic* humor was dominant, towards withdrawal and melancholy.

Hymn: a song whose theme is usually religious, in praise of divinity. Literary hymns may praise more secular subjects.

Hyperbole: a *figure of speech* (a trope) that deliberately exaggerates or inflates meaning to achieve particular effects, such as the irony in A.E. Housman's claim (from "Terence, This Is Stupid Stuff") that "malt does more than Milton can / To justify God's ways to man."

Iamb: the most common metrical foot in English verse, containing one unstressed syllable followed by a stressed syllable: x / (e.g., between, achieve).

Idyll: traditionally, a short pastoral poem that idealizes country life, conveying impressions of innocence and happiness.

Image: the recreation in words of objects perceived by the senses, sometimes thought of as "pictures," although other senses besides sight are involved. Besides this literal application, the term also refers more generally to the descriptive effects of figurative language, especially in *metaphor* and *simile.*

Imagism: a poetic movement that was popular mainly in the second decade of the twentieth century. The goal of Imagist poets (such as H.D. and Ezra Pound in their early work) was to represent emotions or impressions through highly concentrated imagery.

Incantation: a chant or recitation of words that are believed to have magical power. A poem can achieve an "incantatory" effect through a compelling rhyme scheme and other repetitive patterns.

In Memoriam Stanza: a four-line stanza in iambic tetrameter, rhyming *abba*: the type of stanza used by Tennyson in *In Memoriam.*

Interlocking Rhyme: See *rhyme.*

Internal Rhyme: See *rhyme.*

Irony: a subtle form of humor in which a statement is understood to convey a quite different (and often entirely opposite) meaning. A writer achieves this by carefully making sure that the statement occurs in a context which undermines or twists the statement's "literal" meaning. *Hyperbole* and *litotes* are often used for ironic effect. *Sarcasm* is a particularly strong or crude form of irony (usually spoken), in which the meaning is conveyed largely by the tone of voice adopted; something said sarcastically is meant clearly to imply its opposite.

Labour Party: See *Political Parties.*

Lament: a poem which expresses profound regret or grief either because of a death, or because of the loss of a former, happier state.

Language Poetry: a movement that defies the usual lyric and narrative conventions of poetry, and that challenges the structures and codes of everyday language. Often seen as both politically and aesthetically subversive, its roots lie in the works of modernist writers like Ezra Pound and Gertrude Stein.

Liberal Party: See *Political Parties.*

Litotes: a *figure of speech* (a trope) in which a writer deliberately uses understatement to highlight the importance of an argument, or to convey an ironic attitude.

Liturgical Drama: drama based on and/or incorporating text from the liturgy—the text recited during religious services.

Lollard: member of the group of radical Christians that took its inspiration from the ideas of John Wyclif (c. 1330–84). The Lollards, in many ways precursors of the Protestant Reformation, advocated making the Bible available to all, and dedication to the principles of evangelical poverty in imitation of Christ.

Luddites: protestors against the mechanization of industry on the grounds that it was leading to the loss of employment and to an increase in poverty. In the years 1811 to 1816 there were several Luddite protests in which machines were destroyed.

Lyric: a poem, usually short, expressing an individual speaker's feelings or private thoughts. Originally a song performed with accompaniment on a lyre, the lyric poem is often noted for musicality of rhyme and rhythm. The lyric genre includes a variety of forms, including the *sonnet*, the *ode*, the *elegy*, the *madrigal*, the *aubade*, the *dramatic monologue*, and the *hymn*.

Madrigal: a lyric poem, usually short and focusing on pastoral or romantic themes. A madrigal is often set to music.

Masculine Ending: a metrical line ending on a stressed syllable. *Masculine Rhyme*: see *rhyme.*

Masque: an entertainment typically combining music and dance, with a limited script, extravagant costumes and sets, and often incorporating spectacular special effects. Masques, which were performed before court audiences in the early seventeenth century, often focused on royal themes and frequently drew on classical mythology.

Mass: within Christianity, a church service that includes the sacrament of the Eucharist (Holy Communion), in which bread and wine are consumed which are believed by those of many Christian denominations to have been transubstantiated into the body and blood of Christ. Anglicans (Episcopalians) are more likely to believe the bread and wine merely symbolizes the body and blood.

Melodrama: originally a term used to describe nineteenth-century plays featuring sensational story lines and a crude separation of characters into moral categories, with the pure and virtuous pitted against evil villains. Early melodramas employed background music throughout the action of the play as a means of heightening the emotional response of the audience. By extension, certain sorts of prose fictions or poems are often described as having melodramatic elements.

Metaphor: a *figure of speech* (in this case, a trope) in which a comparison is made or identity is asserted between two unrelated things or actions without the use of "like" or "as." The primary subject is known as the *tenor*; to illuminate its nature, the writer links it to wholly different images, ideas, or actions referred to as the *vehicle*. Unlike a *simile*, which is a direct comparison of two things, a metaphor "fuses" the separate qualities of two things, creating a new idea. For example, Shakespeare's "Let slip the dogs of war" is a metaphorical statement. The tenor, or primary subject, is "war"; the vehicle of the metaphor is the image of hunting dogs released from their leash. The line fuses the idea of war with the qualities of ravening bloodlust associated with hunting dogs.

Metaphysical Poets: a group of seventeenth-century English poets, notably Donne, Cowley, Marvell, and Herbert, who employed unusual difficult imagery and *conceits* (see above) in order to develop intellectual and religious themes. The term was first applied to these writers to mark as far-fetched their use of philosophical and scientific ideas in a poetic context.

Meter: the pattern of stresses, syllables, and pauses that constitutes the regular rhythm of a line of verse. The meter of a poem written in the English accentual-syllabic tradition is determined by identifying the stressed and unstressed syllables in a line of verse, and grouping them into recurring units known as feet. See *accent*, *accentual-syllabic*, *caesura*, *elision*, and *scansion*. For some of the better known meters, see *iamb*, *trochee*, *dactyl*, *anapaest*, and *spondee*. See also *monometer*, *dimeter*, *trimeter*, *tetrameter*, *pentameter*, and *hexameter*.

Methodist: Protestant denomination formed in the eighteenth century as part of the religious movement led by John and Charles Wesley. Originally a movement within the Church of England, Methodism entailed enthusiastic evangelism, a strong emphasis on free will, and a strict regimen of Christian living.

Metonymy: a *figure of speech* (a trope), meaning "change of name," in which a writer refers to an object or idea by substituting the name of another object or idea closely associated with it: for example, the substitution of "crown" for monarchy, "the press" for journalism, or "the pen" for writing. *Synecdoche* (see below) is a kind of metonymy.

Mock-heroic: a style applying the elevated diction and vocabulary of epic poetry to low or ridiculous subjects. An example is Alexander Pope's "The Rape of the Lock."

Monologue: words spoken by a character to him or herself or to an audience directly.

Monometer: a line containing one metrical foot.

Mood: This can describe the writer's attitude, implied or expressed, towards the subject (see *tone* below); or it may refer to the atmosphere that a writer creates in a passage of description or narration.

Motif: an idea, image, action, or plot element that recurs throughout a literary work, creating new levels of meaning and strengthening structural coherence. The term is taken from music, where it describes recurring melodies or themes. See also *theme*.

Narrative Perspective: in fiction, the point of view from which the story is narrated. A first-person narrative is recounted using *I* and *me*, whereas a third person narrative is recounted using *he*, *she*, *they*, and so on. When a narrative is written in the third person and the narrative voice evidently "knows" all that is being done and thought, the story is typically described as being recounted by an "omniscient narrator."

Neoclassical: adapted from or substantially influenced by the cultures of ancient Greece and Rome. The term *neoclassical* is often used to describe the ideals of Restoration and eighteenth-century writers and artists who looked to ancient Greek and Roman civilization for models.

Nobility: privileged class, the members of which are distinguished by the holding of titles. Dukes, Marquesses, Earls, Viscounts, and Barons (in that order of precedence) are all holders of hereditary titles—that is to say, in the British patrilineal tradition, titles passed on from generation to generation to the eldest son. The title of Baronet, also hereditary, was added to this list by James I. Holders of non-hereditary titles include Knights and Dames.

Nonconformist: general term used to describe one who does not subscribe to the Church of England.

Nonsense Verse: light, humorous poetry which contradicts logic, plays with the absurd, and invents words for amusing effects. Lewis Carroll is one of the best-known practitioners of nonsense verse.

Octave: also known as "octet," the first eight lines in an Italian/Petrarchan sonnet, rhyming *abbaabba*. See also *sestet* and *sonnet*.

Octosyllabic: a line of poetry with eight syllables, as in iambic tetrameter.

Ode: originally a classical poetic form, used by the Greeks and Romans to convey serious themes. English poetry has evolved three main forms of ode: the Pindaric (imitative of the odes of the Greek poet Pindar); the Horatian (modeled on the work of the Roman writer Horace); and the irregular ode. The Pindaric ode was an irregular stanza in English, has a tripartite structure of "strophe," "antistrophe," and "epode" (meaning turn, counterturn, and stand), modeled on the songs and movements of the Chorus in Greek drama. The Horatian ode is more personal, reflective, and literary, and employs a pattern of repeated stanzas. The irregular ode, as its name implies, avoids a recurrent stanza pattern, and is sometimes irregular in line length also (see, for example, Wordsworth's "Ode: Intimations of Immortality").

Onomatopoeia: a *figure of speech* (a scheme) in which a word "imitates" a sound, or in which the sound of a word seems to reflect its meaning.

Ottava Rima: an eight-line stanza, usually in iambic pentameter, with the rhyme scheme *abababcc*. For an example, see Byron's *Don Juan*, or Yeats's "Sailing to Byzantium."

Oxymoron: a *figure of speech* (a trope) in which two words whose meanings seem contradictory are placed together, a paradox: for example, the phrase "darkness visible," from Milton's *Paradise Lost*.

Paean: a triumphant, celebratory song, often associated with a military victory.

Pale: in the medieval period, term for a protective zone around a fortress. As of the year 1500 three of these had been set up to guard frontiers of territory controlled by England—surrounding Calais in France, Berwick-upon-Tweed on the Scottish frontier, and Dublin in Ireland. The Dublin Pale was the largest of the three, and the term remained in use for a longer period there.

Pantoum: a poem in linked quatrains that rhyme *abab*. The second and fourth lines of one stanza are repeated as the first and third lines of the stanza that follows. In the final stanza the pattern is reversed: the second line repeats the third line of the first stanza, the fourth and final line repeats the first line of the first stanza.

Parliament: in Britain, the legislative body, comprising both the House of Commons and the House of Lords. Since the eighteenth century, the most powerful figure in the British government has been the Prime Minister rather than the monarch, the House of Commons has been the dominant body in Parliament, and members of the House of Commons have been organized in political parties. Since the mid-nineteenth century the effective executive in the British Parliamentary system has been the Cabinet, each member of which is typically in charge of a department of government. Unlike the American system, the British Parliamentary system (sometimes called the "Westminster system," after the location of the Houses of Parliament) brings together the executive and legislative functions of government, with the Prime Minister leading the government party in the House of Commons as well as directing the cabinet. By convention it is understood that the House of Lords will not contravene the wishes of the House of Commons in any fundamental way, though the "Upper House," as it is often referred to, may sometimes modify or reject legislation.

Parody: a close, usually mocking imitation of a particular literary work, or of the well-known style of a particular author, in order to expose or magnify weaknesses. Parody is a form of satire—that is, humor that may ridicule and scorn its object.

Pastiche: a discourse which borrows or imitates other writers' characters, forms, style, or ideas. Unlike a parody, a pastiche is usually intended as a compliment to the original writer.

Pastoral: in general, pertaining to country life; in prose, drama, and poetry, a stylized type of writing that idealizes the lives and innocence of country people, particularly shepherds and shepherdesses. Also see *eclogue, georgic, idyll,* above.

Pastoral Elegy: a poem in which the poet uses the pastoral style to lament the death of a friend, usually represented as a shepherd. Milton's "Lycidas" provides a good example of the form, including its use of such conventions as an invocation of the muse and a procession of mourners.

Pathetic Fallacy: a form of personification in which inanimate objects are given human emotions: for example, rain clouds "weeping." The word "fallacy" in this connection is intended to suggest the distortion of reality or the false emotion that may result from an exaggerated use of personification.

Pathos: the emotional quality of a discourse; or the ability of a discourse to appeal to our emotions. It is usually applied to the mood conveyed by images of pain, suffering, or loss that arouse feelings of pity or sorrow in the reader.

Pattern Poetry: a predecessor of modern concrete poetry, in which the shape of the poem on the page is intended to suggest or imitate an aspect of the poem's subject. George Herbert's "Easter Wings" is an example of pattern poetry.

Penny Dreadful: Victorian term for a cheap and poorly produced work of short fiction, usually of a sensational nature.

Pentameter: a line of verse containing five metrical feet.

Performance Poetry: poetry composed primarily for oral performance, often very theatrical in nature. See also *dub poetry* and *rap*.

Persona: the assumed identity or "speaking voice" that a writer projects in a discourse. The term "persona" literally means "mask." Even when a writer speaks in the first person, we should be aware that the attitudes or opinions we hear may not necessarily be those of the writer in real life.

Personification: a *figure of speech* (a trope), also known as "prosopopoeia," in which a writer refers to inanimate objects, ideas, or animals as if they were human, or creates a human figure to represent an abstract entity such as Philosophy or Peace.

Petrarchan Sonnet: the earliest form of the sonnet, also known as the Italian sonnet, with an 8-line octave and a six-line sestet. The Petrarchan sonnet traditionally focuses on love and descriptions of physical beauty.

Phoneme: a linguistic term denoting the smallest unit of sound that it is possible to distinguish. The words *fun* and *phone* each have three phonemes, though one has three letters and one has five. (Each makes up a single syllable.)

Pindaric: See *ode*.

Plot: the organization of story materials within a literary work. The order in which story material is presented (especially causes and consequences); the inclusion of elements that allow or encourage the reader or audience to form expectations as to what is likely to happen; the decision to present some story material through exposition rather than in more extended form as part of the main action of the narrative—all these are matters of plotting.

Political Parties: The party names "Whig" and "Tory" began to be used in the late seventeenth century; before that time members of the House of Commons acted individually or through shifting and very informal factions. At first the Whigs and Tories had little formal organization either, but by the mid-eighteenth century parties had acknowledged leaders, and the leader of the party with the largest number of members in the House of Commons had begun to be recognized as the Prime Minister. The Tories evolved into the modern Conservative Party, and the Whigs into the Liberal Party. In the late nineteenth century the Labour Party was formed in an effort to provide better representation in Parliament for the working class, and since the 1920s Labour and the Conservatives have alternated as the party of government, with the Liberals reduced to third-party status. (Since

1988, when the Liberals merged with a breakaway faction from Labour known as the Social Democrats, this third party has been named the Liberal Democrats.)

Pre-Raphaelites: originally a group of Victorian artists and writers, formed in 1848. Their goal was to revive what they considered the simpler, fresher, more natural art that existed before Raphael (1483–1520). The poet Dante Gabriel Rossetti was one of the founders of the group.

Presbyterian: term applied to a group of Protestants (primarily English and Scottish) who advocated replacing the traditional hierarchical church in which bishops and archbishops governed lower level members of the clergy with a system in which all presbyters (or ministers) would be equal. The Presbyterians, originally led by John Knox, were strongly influenced by the ideas of John Calvin.

Prose Poem: a poetic discourse that uses prose formats (e.g., it may use margins and paragraphs rather than line breaks or stanzas) yet is written with the kind of attention to language, rhythm, and cadence that characterizes verse.

Prosody: the study and analysis of meter, rhythm, rhyme, stanzaic pattern, and other devices of versification.

Protagonist: the central character in a literary work.

Prothalamion: a wedding song; a term coined by the poet Edmund Spenser, adapted from "epithalamion" (see above).

Public School: See *schools* below.

Pun: a play on words, in which a word with two or more distinct meanings, or two words with similar sounds, may create humorous ambiguities. Also known as *paranomasia*.

Puritan: term, originally applied only in a derogatory fashion but later widely accepted as descriptive, referring to those in England who favored religious reforms that went beyond those instituted as part of the Protestant Reformation, or, more generally, who were more forceful and uncompromising in pressing for religious purity both within the Church and in society as a whole.

Pyrrhic: a metrical foot containing two weak stresses: xx.

Quadrivium: group of four academic subjects (arithmetic, astronomy, geometry, and music) that made up part of the university coursework in the Middle Ages. There were studied after the more basic subjects of the *Trivium*.

Quantitative Meter: a metrical system used by Greek and Roman poets, in which a line of verse was measured by the "quantity," or length of sound of each syllable. A foot was measured in terms of syllables classed as long or short.

Quantity: duration of syllables in poetry. The line "There is a Garden in her face" (the first line from the poem of the same name by Thomas Campion) is characterized by the short quantities of the syllables. The last line of Thomas Hardy's "During Wind and Rain" has the same number of syllables as the line by Campion, but the quantities of the syllables are much longer—in other words, the line takes much longer to say: "Down their carved names the rain drop ploughs."

Quatrain: a four-line stanza, usually rhymed.

Quintet: a five-line stanza. Sometimes given as *quintain.*

Rap: originally coined to describe informal conversation, "rap" now usually describes a style of performance poetry in which a poet will chant rhymed verse, sometimes improvised and usually with musical accompaniment that has a heavy beat.

Realism: as a literary term, the presentation through literature of material closely resembling real life. As notions both of what constitutes "real life" and of how it may be most faithfully represented in literature have varied widely, "realism" has taken a variety of meanings. The term *naturalistic* has sometimes been used as a synonym for *realistic*; *naturalism* originated in the nineteenth century as a term denoting a form of realism focusing in particular on grim, unpleasant, or ugly aspects of the real.

Refrain: one or more words or lines repeated at regular points throughout a poem, often at the end of each stanza or group of stanzas. Sometimes a whole stanza may be repeated to create a refrain, like the chorus in a song.

Reggae: a style of heavily rhythmic music from the West Indies with lyrics that are colloquial in language and often anti-establishment in content and flavor. First popularized in the 1960s and 1970s, reggae has had a lasting influence on performance poetry and rap and is a progenitor of dub.

Rhetoric: in classical Greece and Rome, the art of persuasion and public speaking. From the Middle Ages onwards, the study of rhetoric gave greater attention to style, particularly figures of speech. Today in poetics, the term rhetoric may encompass not only figures of speech, but also the persuasive effects of forms, sounds, and word choices.

Rhyme: the repetition of identical or similar sounds, usually in pairs and generally at the ends of metrical lines.

End-Rhyme: a rhyming word or syllable at the end of a line.

Eye-Rhyme: rhyming that pairs words whose spellings are alike but whose pronunciations are different: for example, though/slough.

Feminine Rhyme: a two-syllable (also known as "double") rhyme. The first syllable is stressed and the second unstressed: for example, hasty/tasty. See also *triple rhyme* below.

Interlocking Rhyme: the repetition of rhymes from one stanza to the next, creating links that add to the poem's continuity and coherence. Examples may be found in Shelley's use of *terza rima* in "Ode to the West Wind" and in Dylan Thomas's villanelle "Do Not Go Gentle into That Good Night."

Internal Rhyme: the placement of rhyming words within lines so that at least two words in a line rhyme with each other.

Masculine Rhyme: a correspondence of sound between the final stressed syllables at the end of two or more lines, as in grieve/leave, arr-ive/sur-vive.

Slant Rhyme: an imperfect or partial rhyme (also known as "near" or "half" rhyme) in which the final consonants of stressed syllables match but the vowel sounds do not. E.g., spoiled/spilled, taint/stint.

Triple Rhyme: a three-syllable rhyme in which the first syllable of each rhyme-word is stressed and the other two unstressed (e.g., lottery/coterie).

True Rhyme: a rhyme in which everything but the initial consonant matches perfectly in sound and spelling.

Rhyme Royal: a stanza of seven iambic pentameters, with a rhyme-scheme of *ababbcc*. This is also known as the Chaucerian stanza, as Chaucer was the first English poet to use this form. See also *septet*.

Rhythm: in speech, the arrangement of stressed and unstressed syllables creates units of sound. In song or verse, these units usually form a regular rhythmic pattern, a kind of beat, described in prosody as *meter*.

Romanticism: a major social and cultural movement, originating in Europe, that shaped much of Western artistic thought in the late eighteenth and nineteenth centuries. Opposing the ideal of controlled, rational order of the Enlightenment, Romanticism emphasizes the importance of spontaneous self-expression, emotion, and personal experience in producing art. In Romanticism, the "natural" is privileged over the conventional or the artificial.

Rondeau: a fifteen-line poem, generally octosyllabic, with only two rhymes throughout its three stanzas, and an unrhymed refrain at the end of the ninth and fifteenth lines, repeating part of the opening line.

Sarcasm: See *irony*.

Satire: literary work designed to make fun of or seriously criticize its subject. According to many literary theories of the Renaissance and neoclassical periods, the ridicule through satire of a certain sort of behavior may function for the reader or audience as a corrective of such behavior.

Scansion: the formal analysis of patterns of rhythm and rhyme in poetry. Each line of verse will have a certain number of fairly regular "beats" consisting of alternating stressed and unstressed syllables. To "scan" a poem is to count the beats in each line, to mark stressed and unstressed syllables and indicate their combination into "feet," to note pauses, and to identify rhyme schemes with letters of the alphabet.

Scheme: See *figures of speech*.

Schools: In the sixteenth and seventeenth centuries the different forms of school in England included Cathedral schools (often founded with a view to the education of members of the choir); grammar schools (often founded by towns or by guilds, and teaching a much broader curriculum than the modern sense of "grammar" might suggest); private schools, operated by private individuals out of private residences; and public schools, which (like the private schools and the grammar schools) operated independent of any church authority, but unlike the grammar schools and private schools were organized as independent charities, and often offered free education. Over the centuries certain of these public schools, while remaining not-for-profit institutions, began to accept fee-paying students and to adopt standards that made them more and more exclusive. In the eighteenth and nineteenth century attendance at such prestigious public boarding schools as Eton, Westminster, and Winchester had become almost exclusively the preserve of the upper classes; by the nineteenth century such "public" schools were the equivalent of private schools in North America. A few girls attended some early grammar schools, but the greater part of this educational system was for boys only. Though a number of individuals of earlier periods were concerned to increase the number of private schools for girls, the movement to create a parallel girls' system of public schools and grammar schools dates from the later nineteenth century.

Septet: a stanza containing seven lines.

Serf: in the medieval period, a person of unfree status, typically engaged in working the land.

Sestet: a six-line stanza that forms the second grouping of lines in an Italian/Petrarchan sonnet, following the octave. See *sonnet* and *sestina.*

Sestina: an elaborate unrhymed poem with six six-line stanzas and a three-line envoy.

Shire: originally a multiple estate; since the late medieval period a larger territory forming an administrative unit—also referred to as a county.

Simile: a *figure of speech* (a trope) which makes an explicit comparison between a particular object and another object or idea that is similar in some (often unexpected) way. A simile always uses "like" or "as" to signal the connection. Compare with *metaphor* above.

Sonnet: a highly structured lyric poem, which normally has fourteen lines of iambic pentameter. We can distinguish four major variations of the sonnet.

Italian/Petrarchan: named for the fourteenth-century Italian poet Petrarch, has an octave rhyming *abbaabba*, and a sestet rhyming *cdecde*, or *cdcdcd* (other arrangements are possible here). Usually, a turn in argument takes place between octave and sestet.

Miltonic: developed by Milton and similar to the Petrarchan in rhyme scheme, but eliminating the turn after the octave, thus giving greater unity to the poem's structure of thought.

Shakespearean: often called the English sonnet, this form has three quatrains and a couplet. The quatrains rhyme internally but do not interlock: *abab cdcd efef gg*. The turn may occur after the second quatrain, but is usually revealed in the final couplet. Shakespeare's sonnets are the best-known examples of this form.

Spenserian: after Edmund Spenser, who developed the form in his sonnet cycle *Amoretti*. This sonnet form has three quatrains linked through interlocking rhyme, and a separately rhyming couplet: *abab bcbc cdcd ee*.

Speaker: in the late medieval period, a member of the Commons in Parliament who spoke on behalf of that entire group. (The Commons first elected a Speaker in 1376.) In later eras the role of Speaker became one of chairing debates in the House of Commons and arbitrating disputes over matters of procedure.

Spenserian Stanza: a nine-line stanza, with eight iambic pentameters and a concluding alexandrine, rhyming *ababbcbcc*.

Spondee: a metrical foot containing two strong stressed syllables: // (e.g., blind mouths).

Sprung Rhythm: a modern variation of accentual verse, created by the English poet Gerard Manley Hopkins, in which rhythms are determined largely by the number of strong stresses in a line, without regard to the number of unstressed syllables. Hopkins felt that sprung rhythm more closely approximated the natural rhythms of speech than did conventional poetry.

Stanza: any lines of verse that are grouped together in a poem and separated from other similarly structured groups by a space. In metrical poetry, stanzas share metrical and rhyming patterns; however, stanzas may also be formed on the basis of thought, as in irregular odes. Conventional stanza forms include the *tercet*, the *quatrain*, *rhyme royal*, the *Spenserian stanza*, the *ballad stanza*, and *ottava rima*.

Stream of Consciousness: narrative technique that attempts to convey in prose fiction a sense of the progression of the full range of thoughts and sensations occurring within a character's mind. Twentieth-century pioneers in the use of the stream of consciousness technique include Dorothy Richardson, Virginia Woolf, and James Joyce.

Stress: See *accent*.

Strophe: the first stanza in a Pindaric ode. This is followed by an *antistrophe* (see above), which presents the same metrical pattern and rhyme scheme, and finally by an *epode*, differing in meter from the preceding stanzas. Upon completion of this "triad," the entire sequence can recur. *Strophe* may also describe a stanza or other subdivision in other kinds of poem.

Sublime: a concept, most popular in eighteenth-century England, of the qualities of grandeur, power, and awe that may be inherent in or produced by undomesticated nature or great art. The sublime was thought of as higher and loftier than something that is merely beautiful.

Subplot: a line of story that is subordinate to the main storyline of a narrative. (Note that properly speaking a subplot is a category of story material, not of plot.)

Substitution: a deliberate change from the dominant pattern of stresses in a line of verse to create emphasis or variation. Thus the first line of Shakespeare's sonnet "'Shall I compare thee to a summer's day?'" is decidedly iambic in meter (x / x / x / x / x /), whereas the second line substitutes a trochee (/ x) in the opening foot: "Thou art more lovely and more temperate."

Subtext: implied or suggested meaning of a passage of text, or of an entire work.

Syllabic Verse: poetry in which the length of a line is measured solely by the number of syllables, regardless of accents or patterns of stress.

Syllable: vocal sound or group of sounds forming a unit of speech; a syllable may be formed with a single effort of articulation. Some syllables consist of a single phoneme (e.g., the word *I*, or the first syllable in the word *u*-ni-ty) but others may be made up of several phonemes (as with one-syllable words such as *lengths*, *splurged*, and *through*). By contrast, the much shorter words *ago*, *any*, and *open* each have two syllables.

Symbol: a word, image, or idea that represents something more, or other, than for what it at first appears to stand. Like metaphor, the symbol extends meaning; but while the tenor and vehicle of metaphor are bound in a specific relationship, a symbol may have a range of connotations. For example, the image of a rose may call forth associations of love, passion, transience, fragility, youth, and beauty, among others. Depending upon the context, such an image could be interpreted in a variety of ways, as in Blake's lyric, "The Sick Rose." Though this power of symbolic representation characterizes all language, poetry most particularly endows the concrete imagery evoked through language with a larger meaning. Such meaning is implied rather than explicitly stated; indeed, much of the power of symbolic language lies in the reader's ability to make meaningful sense of it.

Syncope: in poetry, the dropping of a letter or syllable from the middle of a word, as in "trav'ler." Such a contraction allows a line to stay within a metrical scheme. See also *catalexis* and *elision*.

Synecdoche: a kind of *metonymy* in which a writer substitutes the name of a part of something to signify the whole: for example, "sail" for ship or "hand" for a member of the ship's crew.

Tercet: a group, or stanza, of three lines, often linked by an interlocking rhyme scheme as in *terza rima*. See also *triplet*.

Terza Rima: an arrangement of tercets interlocked by a rhyme scheme of *aba bcb cdc ded*, etc., and ending with a couplet that rhymes with the second-last line of the final tercet (for example, *efe, ff*). See, for example, Percy Shelley's "Ode to the West Wind."

Tetrameter: a line of poetry containing four metrical feet.

Theme: the governing idea of a discourse, conveyed through the development of the subject, and through the recurrence of certain words, sounds, or metrical patterns. See also *motif*.

Third-Person Narrative: See *narrative perspective*.

Tone: the writer's attitude toward a given subject or audience, as expressed through an authorial persona or "voice." Tone can be projected through particular choices of wording, imagery, figures of speech, and rhythmic devices. Compare *mood.*

Tories: See *Political Parties*.

Tragedy: in the traditional definition originating in discussions of ancient Greek drama, a serious narrative recounting the downfall of the protagonist. More loosely, the term has been applied to a wide variety of literary forms in which the tone is predominantly a dark one and the narrative does not end happily.

Transcendentalism: a philosophical movement that influenced such Victorian writers as Thomas Carlyle and Robert Browning. Also a mode of Romantic thought, Transcendentalism places the supernatural and the natural within one great Unity and believes that each individual person embodies aspects of the divine.

Trimeter: a line of poetry containing three metrical feet.

Triolet: a French form in which the first line appears three times in a poem of only eight lines. The first line is repeated at lines 4 and 7; the second line is repeated in line 8. The triolet has only two rhymes: *abaaabab*.

Triple Foot: poetic foot of three syllables. The possible varieties of triple foot are the anapest (in which two unstressed syllables are followed by a stressed syllable), the dactyl (in which a stressed syllable is followed by two unstressed lines), and the mollossus (in which all three syllables are stressed equally). English poetry tends to use duple rhythms far more frequently than triple rhythms.

Triplet: a group of three lines with the same end-rhyme, much used by eighteenth-century poets to vary or punctuate the flow of couplets. See also *tercet*.

Trivium: group of three academic subjects (dialectic, grammar, and rhetoric) that were part of the university curriculum in the Middle Ages. Their study precedes that of the more advanced subjects of the *quadrivium*.

Trochee: a metrical foot containing one strong stress followed by one weak stress: / x (heaven, lover).

Trope: any figure of speech that plays on our understandings of words to extend, alter, or transform "literal" meaning. Common tropes include *metaphor*, *simile*, *personification*, *hyperbole*, *metonymy*, *oxymoron*, *synecdoche*, and *irony*. See also *figures of speech*, above.

Turn (Italian "volta"): the point in a *sonnet* where the mood or argument changes. The turn may occur between the octave and sestet, i.e., after the eighth line, or in the final couplet, depending on the kind of sonnet.

Unities: Many literary theorists of the late sixteenth through late eighteenth centuries held that a play should ideally be presented as representing a single place, and confining the action to a single day and a single dominant event. They disapproved of plots involving gaps or long periods of time, shifts in place, or subplots. These concepts, which came to be referred to as the unities of space, time, and action, were based on a misreading of classical authorities (principally of Aristotle).

***Vers de societé*:** literally, "verse about society." The term originated with poetry written by aristocrats and upper-middle-class poets that specifically disavows the ambition of creating "high art" while treating the concerns of their own group in verse forms that demonstrate a high degree of formal control (e.g., artful rhymes, surprising turns of diction).

***Vers libre*:** See *free verse* above.

Verse: a general term for works of poetry, usually referring to poems that incorporate some kind of metrical structure. The term may also describe a line of poetry, though more frequently it is applied to a stanza.

Villanelle: a poem usually consisting of 19 lines, with five 3-line stanzas (tercets) rhyming *aba*, and a concluding quatrain rhyming *abaa*. The first and third lines of the first tercet are repeated at fixed intervals throughout the rest of the poem. See, for example, Dylan Thomas's "Do Not Go Gentle into That Good Night."

Whigs: See *Political Parties*.

Workhouse: public institution in which the poor were provided with a minimal level of sustenance and with lodging in exchange for work performed. Early workhouses were typically administered by individual parishes. In 1834 a unified system covering all of England and Wales was put into effect.

Zeugma: a *figure of speech* (trope) in which one word links or "yokes" two others in the same sentence, often to comic or ironic effect. For example, a verb may govern two objects, as in Pope's line "Or stain her honour, or her new brocade."

Permissions Acknowledgments

Texts

Achebe, Chinua. "Dead Men's Path," from *Girls at War and Other Stories*. Copyright © 1972, 1973 by Chinua Achebe. Reprinted in the United States by permission of Doubleday, an imprint of the Knopf Doubleday Publishing Group, a division of Penguin Random House LLC. All rights reserved. Any third party use of this material, outside of this publication, is prohibited. Interested parties must apply directly to Penguin Random House LLC for permission. "An Image of Africa: Racism in Conrad's 'Heart of Darkness," from *Hopes and Impediments: Selected Essays*. Copyright © 1988 by Chinua Achebe. Reprinted in the United States with the permission of Doubleday, an imprint of the Knopf Doubleday Publishing Group, a division of Penguin Random House LLC. All rights reserved.

Adichie, Chimamanda Ngozi. "A Private Experience," from *The Thing Around Your Neck*. Copyright © 2009 by Chimamanda Adichie. Used by permission of The Wylie Agency LLC.

Alvi, Moniza. "And If" and "How the World Split in Two," from *Split World: Poems 1990-2005*. Northumberland: Bloodaxe Books, 2008. Reprinted with the permission of Bloodaxe Books.

Armitage, Simon. "The English," from *The Universal Home Doctor*, Faber and Faber, 2002. Copyright © Simon Armitage. Reprinted in Canada by permission of Faber and Faber Ltd. Reprinted in the United States by permission of David Godwin Associates. "Poundland," from *The Unaccompanied*, Faber and Faber, 2017. Copyright © Simon Armitage.

Atwood, Margaret. "The Door," from *The Door: Poems by Margaret Atwood*. Copyright © 2007 by O.W. Toad Ltd. Reprinted in the United States with the permission of Houghton Mifflin Harcourt Publishing Company. All rights reserved. Reprinted in Canada with the permission of McClelland & Stewart, a division of Penguin Random House Canada Limited. All rights reserved. Any third party use of this material, outside of this publication, is prohibited. Interested parties must apply directly to Penguin Random House Canada for permission. "Death of a Young Son by Drowning," "The Immigrants," and "You Fit Into Me," from *Selected Poems 1965-1975*. Copyright © 1976 by Margaret Atwood. Reprinted in the United States with the permission of Houghton Mifflin Harcourt Publishing Company. All rights reserved. Copyright © 1990, Oxford University Press Canada. Reprinted in Canada with the permission of Oxford University Press Canada. "The Handmaid's Tale and Oryx and Crake in Context." *PMLA* 119.3 (2004): 513-517.

Auden, W.H. "At last the secret is out (Twelve Songs: VIII)," copyright © 1936, 1937, and renewed 1964 by W.H. Auden and Christopher Isherwood. From *Collected Poems* by W.H. Auden. Used by permission of Random House, an imprint and division of Penguin Random House LLC. All rights reserved. Any third party use of this material, outside of this publication, is prohibited. Interested parties must apply directly to Penguin Random House LLC for permission. "Funeral Blues," "Lullaby," "In Memory of W. B. Yeats," "Musée des Beaux Arts," and "September 1, 1939," copyright © 1940 and renewed 1968 by W.H. Auden. From *Collected Poems* by W.H. Auden. Used by permission of Random House, an imprint and division of Penguin Random House LLC. All rights reserved. Any third party use of this material, outside of this publication, is prohibited. Interested parties must apply directly to Penguin Random House LLC for permission. "Song of the Master and Boatswain," from *The Sea and the Mirror*, copyright © 1944 and renewed 1972 by W.H. Auden. From *Collected Poems* by W.H. Auden. Used by permission of Random House, an imprint and division of Penguin Random House LLC. All rights reserved. Any third party use of this material, outside of this publication, is prohibited. Interested parties must apply directly to Penguin Random House LLC for permission.

Beckett, Samuel. "Endgame," from *Endgame and Act Without Words*. Copyright © 1958 by Grove Press, Inc. Reprinted with the permission of Grove/Atlantic, Inc. Any third party use of this material, outside of this publication, is prohibited.

Bennett, Louise. "Colonization in Reverse," from *Louise Bennett: Selected Poems*. Copyright © Louise Bennett Coverley. Reprinted with the permission of the executors of the Louise Bennett Coverley Estate, Judge Pamela Appelt, and Fabian Coverley; pappelt@cogeco.ca; fcoverley@gmail.com.

Boland, Eavan. "Night Feed," copyright © 1982 by Eavan Boland; "The Lost Land," copyright © 1998 by Eavan Boland; from *New Collected Poems*. Used by permission of W.W. Norton & Company, Inc.

Brathwaite, Kamau. Excerpt from "Nation Language," in *Roots*. Ann Arbor Paperbacks, University of Michigan Press, 1993; reprinted with permission. "Calypso," from *The Arrivants: A New World Trilogy*. London: Oxford University Press, 1981. Reprinted with the permission of Oxford University Press.

Breeze, Jean "Binta". "earth cries," from *Third World Girl: Selected Poems*. Northumberland: Bloodaxe Books, 2011. Reprinted with the permission of Bloodaxe Books, www.bloodaxebooks.com.

Carter, Angela. "The Snow Child," and "The Werewolf," from *The Bloody Chamber*. Published by Victor Gollancz, 1979. Copyright © Angela Carter. Reproduced by permission of the estate of the author c/o Rogers, Coleridge & White Ltd., 20 Powis Mews, London W11 1JN.

Chapman, Graham, et al. "Dead Parrot Sketch," and "Pet Conversion," from *Monty Python's Flying Circus: Just the Words, Volume One*. London: Methuen, 1999. "Dirty Hungarian Phrasebook," and "Spam," from *Monty Python's Flying Circus: Just the Words, Volume Two*. London: Methuen, 1999. Reprinted with the permission of Methuen Publishing Ltd.

Clarke, Gillian. "Polar," from *Ice*. Published by Carcanet Press, 2012. Copyright © Gillian Clarke. Reproduced by permission of the author c/o Rogers, Coleridge & White Ltd., 20 Powis Mews, London W11 1JN.

Douglas, Keith. "Vergissmeinnicht," from *The Complete Poems*, Third Edition. Copyright © 1998 The Estate of Keith Douglas. Reprinted with the permission of Farrar, Straus and Giroux.

Duffy, Carol Ann. "Rapture," from *Rapture*. Copyright © 2005 by Carol Ann Duffy. Reprinted in the United States with the permission of Farrar, Straus and Giroux. Reprinted in Canada with the permission of Picador. "Mrs. Lazarus," from *The World's Wife*. Copyright © 1999 by Carol Ann Duffy. Reprinted in the United States with the permission of Farrar, Straus and Giroux. Reprinted in Canada with the permission of Picador. "The Good Teachers," and "Drunk," from *Mean Time*. Published by Anvil Press Poetry, 1993. Copyright © Carol Ann Duffy. Reproduced by permission of the author c/o Rogers, Coleridge & White Ltd., 20 Powis Mews, London W11 1JN. "John Barleycorn," and "Water," from *The Bees*. Published by Picador, 2011. Reproduced in Canada by permission of the author c/o Rogers, Coleridge & White Ltd., 20 Powis Mews, London W11 1JN.

Eliot, T.S. "Journey of the Magi," from *Collected Poems 1909-1962*. Copyright © 1936 by Houghton Mifflin Harcourt Publishing Company. Copyright © renewed 1964 by Thomas Stearns Eliot. Reprinted in the United States with the permission of Houghton Mifflin Harcourt Publishing Company. All rights reserved. "Burnt Norton," from *Four Quartets*. Copyright © 1936 by Houghton Mifflin Harcourt Publishing Company; copyright © renewed 1964 by T.S. Eliot; copyright © renewed 1969, 1970 by Esme Valerie Eliot. Reprinted in the United States with the permission of Houghton Mifflin Harcourt Publishing Company. All rights reserved.

Galloway, Janice. "Jellyfish," Freight Books, 2015. Reproduced with the permission of Granta Books.

Gramich, Katie (translator). "The End of the Year," by Sarah Jane Rees; "A New Year Greeting," and "Song of the Worker's Wife," by Alice Gray Jones, from *Welsh Women's Poetry 1460-2001: An Anthology*, edited by Katie Gramich and Catherine Brennan. Honno Press, Aberystwyth, Wales, 2003. Reprinted with the permission of Katie Gramich.

Graves, Robert. Excerpts from Chapter 17 of *Good-Bye to All That*. Doubleday Anchor Books, Garden City, New York. Copyright © 1929, renewed 1957. Reprinted with the permission of Carcanet Press Ltd.

Harrison, Tony. "Them & [uz]" (1 & 2) from Selected Poems. London: Penguin, 1987. Reprinted with the permission of Faber and Faber Ltd.

Heaney, Seamus. "Digging," "Thatcher," "The Wife's Tale," "The Grauballe Man," "Punishment," and "Casualty," from *Opened Ground: Selected Poems 1966-1996*. Copyright © 1998 by Seamus Heaney. Reprinted in the United States with the permission of Farrar, Straus and Giroux. Reprinted in Canada with the permission of Faber and Faber Ltd. "Anything Can Happen," from *District and Circle*. Copyright © 2006 by Seamus Heaney. Reprinted in the United States with the permission of Farrar, Straus and Giroux. Reprinted in Canada with the permission of Faber and Faber Ltd. "Uncoupled," and "The door was open and the house was dark," from *Human Chain*. Copyright © 2010 by Seamus Heaney. Reprinted in the United States with the permission of Farrar, Straus and Giroux. Reprinted in Canada with the permission of Faber and Faber Ltd. Excerpts from "Englands of the Mind," from *Preoccupations: Selected Prose 1968-1978*. New York: Farrar, Straus & Giroux. Reproduced in Canada with the permission of Faber and Faber Ltd.

Highway, Tomson. "Hearts and Flowers," from *Our Story: Aboriginal Voices on Canada's Past.* Doubleday (Penguin Random House Canada), 2005. Reprinted with the permission of Tomson Highway.

Hill, Geoffrey. "A Short History of British India (II)," from *Selected Poems: Geoffrey Hill.* Penguin Books, 2006. Copyright © Geoffrey Hill 2006. Reproduced by permission of Penguin Books Ltd.

Hughes, Ted. "Daffodils," from *Birthday Letters.* Copyright © 1998 by Ted Hughes. Reprinted in the United States with the permission of Farrar, Straus and Giroux. Reprinted in Canada with the permission of Faber and Faber Ltd. "Heptonstall Old Church," from *Collected Poems.* Copyright © 2003 by The Estate of Ted Hughes. Reprinted in the United States with the permission of Farrar, Straus and Giroux. Reprinted in Canada with the permission of Faber and Faber Ltd. "The Thought-Fox," and "Pike," from *Selected Poems 1957-1994.* Copyright © 2002 by The Estate of Ted Hughes. Reprinted in the United States with the permission of Farrar, Straus and Giroux. Reprinted in Canada with the permission of Faber and Faber Ltd.

Ishiguro, Kazuo. "A Village After Dark," originally published in *The New Yorker*, May 21 2001. Reproduced by permission of the author c/o Rogers, Coleridge & White Ltd., 20 Powis Mews, London W11 1JN.

Johnson, Linton Kwesi. "Inglan Is a Bitch," from *Tings and Times.* Northumberland: Bloodaxe Books, 1991. Reprinted with the permission of Linton Kwesi Johnson.

Kay, Jackie. "In My Country," from *Darling: New & Selected Poems.* Northumberland: Bloodaxe Books, 2007. Reprinted with the permission of Bloodaxe Books, www.bloodaxebooks.com. "Extinction," copyright © 2015 by Jackie Kay. Used by permission of The Wylie Agency LLC.

Kent, Walter, and Nat Burton. "The White Cliffs of Dover," copyright © 1941, Nat Burton and Walter Kent; copyright © 1968 Dorothy Schwartz and Jerome B. Schwartz.

Larkin, Philip. "Church Going," "Talking in Bed," "This Be the Verse," "The Old Fools," "Days," "Annus Mirabilis," "High Windows," and "Aubade," from *The Complete Poems of Philip Larkin*, edited by Archie Burnett. Copyright © 2012 by The Estate of Philip Larkin. Reprinted in the United States with the permission of Farrar, Straus & Giroux. Reprinted in Canada with the permission of Faber and Faber Ltd.

Lawrence, D.H. "Snake," 1923, from *Birds, Beasts and Flowers: Poems by D.H. Lawrence.* New York: Haskell House Publishers Ltd., 1974. Reproduced by permission of Paper Lion Ltd and The Estate of Frieda Lawrence Ravagli and Cambridge University Press.

LePan, Douglas. "Below Monte Cassino" and "The Haystack," from *Weathering It: Complete Poems 1948-1987.* Toronto: McClelland and Stewart, 1987. Copyright © 1987 The Estate of Douglas LePan. Reprinted with the permission of Literary Executor Don LePan. "Personality of the Poet: Some Recollections of T.S. Eliot," from *Bright Glass of Memory.* Toronto: McGraw Hill, 1979. Copyright © 1979 The Estate of Douglas LePan. Reprinted with the permission of Literary Executor Don LePan.

Lewis, Gwyneth. "Mother Tongue," from *Chaotic Angels: Poems in English*. Northumberland: Bloodaxe Books, 2005. Reprinted with the permission of Bloodaxe Books, www.bloodaxebooks.com

Lochhead, Liz. "Men Talk," from *True Confessions & New Clichés*. Copyright © Liz Lochhead, 1985. Edinburgh: Birlinn Ltd. Reproduced with permission of the Licensor through PLSclear. "Kidspoem/Bairnsang," from *The Colour of Black & White: Poems 1984-2003*. Copyright © Liz Lochhead, 2003. Edinburgh: Birlinn Ltd. Reproduced with permission of the Licensor through PLSclear.

Maclean, Sorley. "A Highland Woman," [English and Gaelic] from *O Choille gu Bearradh/From Wood to Ridge*. Carcanet Press, 1999. "Hallaig," (Gaelic), and "Hallaig" (English translation) by Sorley Maclean. Published by The Sorley Maclean Trust, 2002. Reprinted with the permission of Carcanet Press Limited. "Hallaig," (English), translated by Seamus Heaney. Reprinted with the permission of Faber and Faber Ltd.

Malik, Kenan. "Multiculturalism and the Road to Terror," from *Handelsblatt*, January 3, 2006. Reprinted with the permission of Toby Mundy Associates.

McGuckian, Medbh. "Slips," from *The Flower Master and Other Poems*, 1993. Reprinted with the kind permission of the author and The Gallery Press, Loughcrew, Oldcastle, County Meath, Ireland. "The Dream-Language of Fergus," from *On Ballycastle Beach*. North Carolina: Wake Forest University Press, 1995. Reprinted with the permission of Wake Forest University Press.

Moore, Kim. "I Have Been a Long Time Without Thinking," and "In That Year," from *#MeToo - Rallying Against Sexual Assault and Harassment: A Women's Poetry Anthology*, edited by Deborah Alma. Fair Acre Press, 2018. Reprinted with the permission of Kim Moore, Fair Acre Press, and Seren Books. "In That Year" was originally published by Seren Books in *The Art of Falling*, 2015.

Morgan, Edwin. "The Coin," from *New Selected Poems*. Carcanet Press, 2000. Reprinted with the permission of Carcanet Press Ltd. "For the Opening of the Scottish Parliament, 9 October 2004." Reprinted under the Open Scottish Parliament Licence V.2: https://www.parliament.scot/Fol/OpenScottishParliamentLicence.pdf

Muldoon, Paul. "Milkweed and Monarch," from *Poems 1968-1998*. Copyright © 2001 by Paul Muldoon. Reprinted by permission of Farrar, Straus and Giroux. "At Tuam," from "Ireland Wanted to Forget. But the Dead Don't Always Stay Buried," in *The New York Times*, 28 Oct. 2017. Reprinted with the permission of Paul Muldoon.

Munro, Alice. "Silence," from *The New Yorker*, June 14, 2004.

Nichols, Grace. "Skanking Englishman Between Trains," and "Epilogue," from *The Fat Black Woman's Poems*, copyright © 1984, Grace Nichols. "White," from *Sunris*, copyright © 1996, Grace Nichols. All works reprinted with the permission of Curtis Brown Group Ltd., on behalf of Grace Nichols.

Nicolson, Harold. Excerpts from "The War Years: 1939-1945," Volume 2 of *The Diaries and Letters of Harold Nicolson*, 1972. Reprinted with the permission of Juliet Nicolson.

Orwell, George. "Politics and the English Language," and "Shooting an Elephant," from *A Collection of Essays*. Copyright © 1950 by Sonia Brownell Orwell. Copyright © renewed 1978 by Sonia Pitt-Rivers. Reprinted in the United States with the permission of Houghton Mifflin Harcourt Publishing Company. All rights reserved. Excerpts from "Anti-Semitism in Britain," in *Such, Such Were the Joys*. Copyright © 1953 by Sonia Brownell Orwell and renewed 1981 by Mrs. George K. Perutz, Mrs. Miriam Gross, and Dr. Michael Dickson, Executors of the Estate of Sonia Brownell. Reprinted with the permission of Houghton Mifflin Harcourt Publishing Company. All rights reserved.

Oswald, Alice. "Dunt," from *The 2008 Rhysling Anthology*, edited by Drew Morse. Science Fiction Poetry Association, 2008. Reprinted with the permission of United Agents LLP on behalf of Alice Oswald.

Pound, Ezra. Excerpt from "Ezra Pound Speaking: Radio Speeches of World War II," copyright © 1978 by the Trustees of the Ezra Pound Literary Property Trust. Reprinted with the permission of New Directions Publishing Corp. "In a Station of the Metro," "Alba," and "L'Art 1910," from *Personae*. Copyright © 1926 by Ezra Pound. Reprinted with the permission of New Directions Publishing Corp. Excerpts from "A Retrospect: A Few Don'ts," from *Literary Essays of Ezra Pound*. Copyright © 1935 by Ezra Pound. Reprinted with the permission of New Directions Publishing Corp. Excerpts from "Vorticism," from *Gaudier-Brzeska*. Copyright © 1980 by New Directions Publishing Corp. Reprinted with the permission of New Directions Publishing Corp.

Reed, Henry. "I: Naming of Parts," from *Collected Poems*, edited by Jon Stallworthy. Oxford University Press, 1991. Reprinted with the permission of Oxford University Press.

Rhys, Jean. "Let Them Call It Jazz," from *Tigers are Better-Looking: With A Selection From the Left Bank*. London: Penguin, 1972.

Richardson, Dorothy. "Foreword" to *Pilgrimage*. Virago, 1979. Reprinted with the permission of The Marsh Agency Ltd.

Rushdie, Salman. "Is Nothing Sacred?" copyright © 1990 by Salman Rushdie. From *Imaginary Homelands: Essays and Criticism 1981-1991*, by Salman Rushdie. Reprinted with the permission of Viking Books, an imprint of Penguin Publishing Group, a division of Penguin Random House LLC. All rights reserved. Any third party use of this material, outside of this publication, is prohibited. Interested parties must apply directly to Penguin Random House LLC for permission.

Sassoon, Siegfried. Excerpts from Part II of *Memoirs of an Infantry Officer*. Copyright © Siegfried Sassoon. Reprinted with the kind permission of the Estate of George Sassoon.

Shire, Warsan. "Backwards," copyright © 2014 by Warsan Shire. Reprinted with permission. "Conversations About Home (at the Deportation Centre)," from *Teaching My Mother How to Give Birth*. Mouthmark Series (No.10), flipped eye publishing, 2011. Reprinted with permission.

Smith, Stevie. "Mother, Among the Dustbins," Pretty," "The Blue From Heaven," "The River God," and "Thoughts about the Person from Porlock," from *Collected Poems of Stevie Smith*, copyright © 1972 by Stevie Smith. "Not Waving But Drowning," from *Collected Poems of Stevie Smith*, copyright © 1957 by Stevie Smith. Reprinted with the permission of New Directions Publishing Corp.

Smith, Zadie. "The Waiter's Wife," from *Granta 67: Women and Children First*. Autumn 1999. Copyright © Zadie Smith. Reproduced by permission of the author c/o Rogers, Coleridge & White Ltd., 20 Powis Mews, London W11 1JN.

Thomas, Dylan. "The Force That Through the Green Fuse Drives the Flower," from *The Poems of Dylan Thomas*, copyright © 1939 by New Directions Publishing Corp. "A Refusal to Mourn the Death, by Fire, of a Child in London," and "Fern Hill," from *The Poems of Dylan Thomas*, copyright © 1945 by The Trustees for the Copyrights of Dylan Thomas. "Do Not Go Gentle Into That Good Night," from *The Poems of Dylan Thomas*, copyright © 1952 by Dylan Thomas. All poems reprinted in the United States with the permission of New Directions Publishing Corp.

Thiong'o, Ngũgĩ wa. Sections 3, 4, and 5 from "The Language of African Literature" in *Decolonising the Mind: the Politics of Language in African Literature*. Heinemann, 1986. Reprinted by permission of Ngũgĩ wa Thiong'o and the Watkins/Loomis Agency.

Walcott, Derek. "A Far Cry from Africa," Ruins of a Great House," and "Love After Love," from *Collected Poems 1948-1984*. Copyright © 1986 by Derek Walcott. Reprinted by permission of Farrar, Straus and Giroux. Excerpt from *Omeros*. Copyright © 1990 by Derek Walcott. Reprinted by permission of Farrar, Straus and Giroux.

West, Rebecca. "Greenhouse with Cyclamens," from *A Train of Powder*. Reprinted by permission of Peters Fraser & Dunlop (www.petersfraserdunlop.com) on behalf of the Estate of Rebecca West.

Winterson, Jeanette. Excerpt from *Oranges are Not the Only Fruit*, copyright © 1985 by Jeanette Winterson. Used by permission of Grove/Atlantic, Inc. Any third party use of this material, outside of this publication, is prohibited.

Woolf, Virginia. Excerpt from "A Room of One's Own," copyright © 1929 by Houghton Mifflin Harcourt Publishing Company. Copyright © renewed 1957 by Leonard Woolf. Reprinted in the United States with the permission of Houghton Mifflin Harcourt Publishing Company. All rights reserved. "Mrs. Dalloway in Bond Street," from *The Complete Shorter Fiction of Virginia Woolf*. Copyright © 1985, 1989 by Quentin Bell and Angelica Garnett. Reprinted with the permission of Houghton Mifflin Harcourt Publishing Company. All rights reserved. "Modern Fiction," from *The Common Reader*. Copyright © 1925 by Houghton Mifflin Harcourt Publishing Company, renewed 1953 by Leonard Woolf. Reprinted with the permission of Houghton Mifflin Harcourt Publishing Company. All rights reserved. Excerpts from *The Diary of Virginia Woolf: Volume V, 1936-1941*. Diary copyright © 1984 by Quentin Bell and Angelica Garnett. Reprinted in the United States with the permission of Houghton Mifflin Harcourt Publishing Company. All rights reserved.

Yeats, William Butler. "Leda and the Swan," "Among School Children," and "Sailing to Byzantium," from *The Collected Works of W.B. Yeats, Volume I: The Poems, Revised*, edited by Richard

AUTHOR PORTRAITS

Color Insert Illustrations

A Stoppage to a Stride Over the Globe, published by Piercy Roberts. Copyright ©Trustees of the British Museum. Elizabeth Leveson-Gower, Duchess-Countess of Sutherland (1765–1839). Philippe Jacques de Loutherbourgh. "Coalbrookdale by Night," 1801. The Science Museum / Science and Society Picture Library. *Composition: Mountain Landscape*, 1765–1830. Photo © Tate, London 2017. *Dig for Victory*, Private Collection / The Stapleton Collection / Bridgeman Images. Francis Bacon. *Study after Velasquez's Portrait of Pope Innocent X*, 1953. Copyright © The Estate of Francis Bacon. All rights reserved. DACS / SOCAN (2018). Peel Square, Bradford, c. 1995. Photo by Tim Smith. Notting Hill Carnival August 1979. Reprinted with the permission of David Hoffman. David Hockney. *Garrowby Hill*, 1998. Oil on canvas, 60 x 76". Copyright © David Hockney. Photo Credit: Prudence Cuming Associates. Collection: Museum of Fine Arts, Boston. Chris Ofili. *No Woman, No Cry*, 1998. Reproduced with the permission of the artist and Victoria Miro Gallery, London. Tracey Emin (b. 1963). *My Bed*, 1998; © Tracey Emin. Photo © Tate, London 2018. *Mixed Blessing* by Rebecca Belmore, photographed by Toni Hafkenscheid. Reprinted with permission. Jenny Saville. *Vis and Ramin I*, 2018. Copyright © Jenny Saville / SOCAN (2018). Photo: Mike Bruce. Courtesy of the artist and Gagosian. [Banksy, street art on Coney Island Avenue.] Courtesy of Pest Control Office, Banksy, Coney Island, 2018. [Banksy, street art in Dover, England.] Courtesy of Pest Control Office, Banksy, Dover, 2017.

Other Illustrations

Page 6: Thomas Girtin. *Westminster and Lambeth, a drawing*. Copyright © The Trustees of the British Museum. Page 22: J.M.W. Turner (1775–1851). *Melrose Abbey*, 1822. Gift of the Manton Art Foundation in memory of Sir Edwin and Lady Manton, 2007. Image courtesy of the Clark Art Institute, Williamstown, Massachusetts, USA. Page 134: George Henry Harlow (1787-1819). *Mrs. Siddons as Lady Macbeth*, courtesy of The Garrick Club, UK. Page 733: Anonymous. *The New Poor Law*, poster ca. 1834; HO 44/27 pt 2. Copyright © National Archives. Reprinted with permission. Page 1282: Workers reading a newspaper, Hulton Archive. Photo by Fox Photos/Getty Images. Page 1284: Londoners sleeping in the Elephant and Castle underground station, 1940, by Bill Brandt. Copyright © Bill Brandt Archive Ltd. Page 1285: German plane over England's chalk cliffs caught a British pilot (upper center) and his opening parachute as he bailed out of his crippled Hurricane fighter, center, Nov. 21, 1940 in England. A wing, torn loose from the falling plane, is visible at right and above the plane. Chalk cliffs can be seen below. Copyright © AP/Wide World Photos. Page 1286: Cover image of *Brighton Rock* by Graham Greene. Penguin Books, 1943. Copyright © Penguin Books, 1943. Page 1295: East End girl dancing the Lambeth Walk, 1939, by Bill Brandt. Copyright © Bill Brandt Archive Ltd. Page 1296: Commuter reading *Lady Chatterley's Lover*. Fox Photos/Hulton Archive/Getty Images. Page 1296: Two women holding copies of *Lady Chatterley's Lover*, 1960. Hulton Archive. Photo by Keystone/Getty Images. Page 1299: Cover image of *Major Barbara* by George Bernard Shaw. Penguin Books, 1946. Copyright © Penguin Books, 1946. Page 1301: Nazi authorities affix a poster to a shop. Photo by Hulton Archive/Getty Images. Page 1302: A young woman takes aim during target practice, Spain, 1936. Bettman/Getty Images. Page 1304: Cover image of *Brave New World* by Aldous Huxley. Cover artist: Leslie Holland. Published by Chatto & Windus. Reprinted by permission of The Random House Group Limited, copyright © 1932. Page 1428: Vanessa Bell, *Virginia Woolf*, 1912. Copyright © National Portrait Gallery,

London. Page 1431: Photograph of Virginia Woolf and T.S. Eliot, by Lady Ottoline Morrell, 1924. Copyright © National Portrait Gallery, London. Reprinted with permission. Page 1627: November 1953: A couple walking in London wearing smog masks on a foggy day. Hulton Archive. Photo by Monty Fresco/Topical Press Agency/Getty Images. Page 1629: The HMS Antelope under attack during the Falklands War, 1982. Martin Cleaver/PA Archive/PA Images. Page 1631: Beatles Fans Storm Buckingham Palace. Photo by © Hulton-Deutsch Collection/CORBIS/Corbis via Getty Images. Page 1632: Kendal Street, 1969, copyright © Sirkka-Liisa Konttinen, courtesy Amber / L. Parker Stephenson Photographs. Page 1632: Still from *Lord of the Flies*, photograph by Thomas Hollyman. Reprinted with the permission of Burnes Hollyman. Page 1633: Cover image of *Never Let Me Go* by Kazuo Ishiguro. Used by permission of Alfred A. Knopf Canada, a division of Penguin Random House Canada Limited. Page 1636: A gaping hole in the front of the Grand Hotel in Brighton. Hulton Archive. Photo by Express/Express/Getty Images. Page 1638: Cover image of *The Van* by Roddy Doyle, published by Secker & Warburg. Reprinted by permission of The Random House Group Limited, copyright © 1991. Page 1688: Fay Godwin. "Heptonstall." British Library, London, UK. Copyright © the British Library Board. Bridgeman Images; all rights reserved. Page 1734: "A chainmail-clad John Cleese reads a newspaper while Graham Chapman smokes a quiet pipe on the set of 'Monty Python and the Holy Grail.'" 21st May 1974. Hulton Archive. Photo by John Downing/Express/Getty Images.

The publisher has endeavored to contact rights holders of all copyright material and would appreciate receiving any information as to errors or omissions.

Index of First Lines

Index of Authors and Titles

From the Publisher

A name never says it all, but the word "Broadview" expresses a good deal of the philosophy behind our company. We are open to a broad range of academic approaches and political viewpoints. We pay attention to the broad impact book publishing and book printing has in the wider world; for some years now we have used 100% recycled paper for most titles. Our publishing program is internationally oriented and broad-ranging. Our individual titles often appeal to a broad readership too; many are of interest as much to general readers as to academics and students.

Founded in 1985, Broadview remains a fully independent company owned by its shareholders—not an imprint or subsidiary of a larger multinational.

For the most accurate information on our books (including information on pricing, editions, and formats) please visit our website at www.broadviewpress.com. Our print books and ebooks are also available for sale on our site.

broadview press
www.broadviewpress.com